VIRGINIA RULES ANNOTATED

Including the Rules of the Courts and Commissions in Virginia, the Rules of the Federal Courts, and the Rules of the Supreme Court of the United States.

2014 EDITION

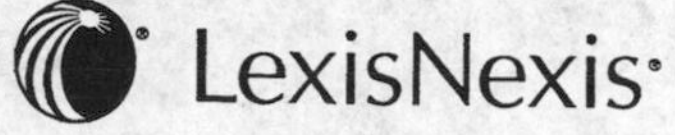

701 East Water Street, Charlottesville, VA 22902-5389

4922631

ISBN 978-1-6304-3042-9

www.lexis.com

Customer Service: 1-800-833-9844

(Pub.49226)

Preface

This volume has been prepared by the publisher in order to provide a much needed and useful collection of the rules of practice and procedure followed by the courts in Virginia. It contains rules and amendments thereto received by the publisher through September 25, 2013.

A separate index has been prepared for each set of rules in this volume. The indexes immediately follow each set of rules.

To better serve our customers, by making our annotations more current, LexisNexis has changed the sources that are read to create annotations for this publication. Rather than waiting for cases to appear in printed reporters, we now read court decisions as they are released by the courts. A consequence of this more current reading of cases, as they are posted online on LEXIS, is that the most recent cases annotated may not yet have print reporter citations. These will be provided, as they become available, through later publications.

This publication contains annotations taken from decisions from the Virginia Supreme Court, Virginia Court of Appeals, and selected federal decisions posted on LEXIS as of July 26, 2013. These cases will be printed in the following reports:

South Eastern Reporter, Second Series.
Supreme Court Reporter.
Federal Reporter, Third Series.
Federal Supplement, Second Series.
Federal Rules Decisions.
Bankruptcy Reporter.

Additionally, annotations have been taken from the following sources:

Virginia Law Review, Volume 98, through November 2012.
Washington and Lee Law Review, Volume 69, through Winter 2012.
William and Mary Law Review, Volume 54, through November 2012.
University of Richmond Law Review, Volume 46, through January 2012.
George Mason University Law Review, Volume 19, through Winter 2012.

Circuit Court Opinions, 1999 Va. Cir. LEXIS 727 (6/25/99) through 2013 Va. Cir. LEXIS 13 (3/25/13).
Opinions of the Attorney General through December 2012.

Unpublished Opinions of Court of Appeals

Some of the annotations contained in this publication are derived from unpublished opinions of the Court of Appeals of Virginia. These opinions will not appear in the Court of Appeals Reports or any other court reporter.

The Court of Appeals has placed the following footnote on all unpublished opinions: "Pursuant to Code § 17.1-413, recodifying § 17-116.010, this opinion is not designated for publication."

"Although an unpublished opinion of the Court has no precedential value, . . . a court or . . . commission does not err by considering the rationale and adopting it to the extent it is persuasive." Fairfax County School Board v. Rose, 29 Va. App. 32, 509 S.E.2d 525 (1999).

A copy of the full text of any unpublished opinion can be obtained by contacting: Court of Appeals of Virginia, Attention: Clerk's Assistant (Opinions), 109 North Eighth Street, Richmond, Virginia 23219. See also, **www.courts.state.va.us.**

The unpublished opinions may also be viewed at **www.lexisnexis.com.**

Suggestions, comments, or questions about this publication are welcome. You may call us toll free at (800) 833-9844, fax us at (518) 487-3584, email us at customer.support@lexisnexis.com, or write Code of Virginia Editor, LexisNexis, 701 East Water Street, Charlottesville, Virginia 22902-5389.

For an online bookstore, technical and customer service, and other company information, visit our website at **http://www.lexisnexis.com.**

LexisNexis

November 2013

Table of Contents

State Rules

PAGE

Rules of Supreme Court of Virginia 1
Part One. General Rules Applicable to All Proceedings 2
Appendix of Forms 53
Part One A. Foreign Attorneys 57
Appendix of Forms 75
Part Two. Virginia Rules of Evidence 79
Part Two A. Appeals Pursuant to the Administrative Process Act 101
Part Three. Practice and Procedure in Civil Actions 111
Part Three A. Criminal Practice and Procedure 147
Appendix of Forms 196
Part Three B. Traffic Infractions and Uniform Fine Schedule 211
Part Three C. Non-Traffic Prepayable Offenses and Uniform Fine Schedule . 239
Part Three D. [Repealed] 267
Part Four. Pretrial Procedures, Depositions and Production at Trial 269
Part Five. The Supreme Court 315
Appendix of Forms 379
Part Five A. The Court of Appeals 389
Appendix of Forms 484
Part Six. Integration of the State Bar 493
Section I. Unauthorized Practice Rules and Considerations 495
Section II. Virginia Rules of Professional Conduct 516
Section III. Canons of Judicial Conduct for the State of Virginia 612
Section IV. Organization and Government 632
Section V. [Deleted] 694
Section VI. [Deleted] 694
Section VII. Acts of the General Assembly (The Bar Act of 1938 and Appendix) 694
Part Seven A. General District Courts — In General 695
Part Seven B. General District Courts — Civil 701
Part Seven C. General District Courts — Criminal and Traffic 705
Part Eight. Juvenile and Domestic Relations District Courts 709
Index 719
Medical Malpractice Rules of Practice 763
Appendix of Forms 770
Index 771
Rules of the Judicial Inquiry and Review Commission 773
Index 781
Bylaws of the Virginia State Bar and Council 783
Index 791
Mandatory Continuing Legal Education Regulations 793
Appendix of Forms 804
Index 809
Clients' Protection Fund Rules 813
Index 821
Rules of the Virginia Workers' Compensation Commission 823
Index 871
Rules of Practice and Procedure of the State Corporation Commission 873
Index 885

Federal Rules

PAGE

Federal Rules of Civil Procedure 889
Appendix of Forms 1084
Supplemental Rules for Admiralty or Maritime Claims and Asset Forfeiture Actions 1120
Index 1131
Rules of Criminal Procedure for United States District Courts 1147
Index 1225
Rules Governing Section 2254 Cases in the United States District Courts 1233
Appendix of Forms 1237
Index 1253
Rules Governing Section 2255 Proceedings for the United States District Courts 1255
Appendix of Forms 1259
Index 1273
Rules of Procedure for the Trial of Misdemeanors Before United States Magistrates 1275
Rules of Evidence for United States Courts and Magistrate Judges 1277
Index 1331
Rules of the United States District Court for the Eastern District of Virginia .. 1339
Appendix A: Plan for Third Year Practice Rule 1381
Appendix B: Federal Rules of Disciplinary Enforcement 1383
Index 1389
Local Rules of Practice of the United States Bankruptcy Court for the Eastern District of Virginia 1393
Index 1465
United States District Court for the Western District of Virginia Local Rules .. 1473
Index 1487
Local Rules of Practice of the United States Bankruptcy Court for the Western District of Virginia 1491
Appendix of Forms 1515
Index 1533
Federal Rules of Appellate Procedure for United States Courts of Appeals, Local Rules and Internal Operating Procedures for the Fourth Circuit 1537
Appendix A: Plan of the United States Court of Appeals for the Fourth Circuit in Implementation of the Criminal Justice Act 1612
Appendix B: Death Penalty Representation in the Fourth Circuit 1619
Appendix C: Guidelines for Preparation of Appellate Trancripts in the Fourth Circuit 1622
Appendix D: Case Management/Electronic Case Filing System 1632
Appendix E: Plan for the Composition and Administration of the CJA Appellate and Capital Appellate Panels 1633
Appendix of Forms 1637
Index 1663
Rules of the Judicial Council of the Fourth Circuit Governing Complaints of Judicial Misconduct and Disability 1675
Form 1702
Index 1705
Rules of the United States Supreme Court 1709
Index 1737

RULES OF SUPREME COURT OF VIRGINIA

Parts One, One A, Two, Three, Four and Five of these Rules were adopted November 22, 1971, and generally made effective March 1, 1972. They constituted a revision of, and replaced all prior rules, except for the Rules of Criminal Practice and Procedure (Part Three A) and the Rules for the Integration of the Virginia State Bar (Part Six). Part Three A was adopted June 15, 1971, and made effective January 1, 1972. Part Two A was adopted May 19, 1977, effective July 1, 1977. Part Three B was adopted June 22, 1977, effective July 1, 1977. Part Three C was promulgated effective August 28, 1978. Part Three D was adopted February 17, 1982, effective July 1, 1982. Part Five A was adopted May 1, 1984, effective October 1, 1984, except for Rule 5A:11, which became effective November 1, 1984. The Medical Malpractice Rules of Practice were promulgated by the Chief Justice on November 1, 1976, and became immediately effective. Part Four was revised by amendment adopted July 22, 1977, effective October 1, 1977. Part Three A was revised by amendment adopted May 1, 1984, effective July 1, 1984. Part Five was revised by amendment adopted May 16, 1985, effective August 1, 1985. Parts Three B and Three C were revised by amendment adopted December 21, 1987, effective July 1, 1988. Part Three D was repealed effective July 1, 1989. Parts Seven A, Seven B and Seven C were adopted effective July 1, 1989. Part 8 was adopted effective July 1, 1992. Part Two was repealed and Part Three was revised by amendment, effective January 1, 2006. Parts 5 and 5A were rewritten by order effective July 1, 2010.

The Virginia Rules of Evidence were promulgated by the Supreme Court September 12, 2011, and became the new Part Two, effective July 1, 2012.

The statements of source and the comments that appear after some of the rules were prepared by the subcommittee that presented the rules to the Judicial Council. They are not part of the Rules as adopted by the Supreme Court, but are included for the useful information that they give the practitioner. The rules referred to in the statements of source, and the "present" or "existing" rules referred to in the comments, are the former Rules of the Supreme Court of Appeals, as amended.

Many of the cases cited in the annotations under the various rules were decided under similar earlier rules.

Part One

General Rules Applicable to All Proceedings .... Rules 1:1 through 1:15

Circuit Courts of Virginia — Times for the Commencement of the Regular Terms

General Rule Applicable to All Proceedings .... Rules 1:16 through 1:23

Appendix of Forms

Part One A

Foreign Attorneys .... Rules 1A:1 through 1A:7

Part Two

Virginia Rules of Evidence . . Rules 2:101 through 2:1101

Part Two A

Appeals Pursuant to the Administrative Process Act .... Rules 2A:1 through 2A:6

Part Three

Practice and Procedure in Civil Actions .... Rules 3:1 through 3:25

Part Three A

Criminal Practice and Procedure ...... Rules 3A:1 through 3A:25

Appendix of Forms

Part Three B

Traffic Infractions and Uniform Fine Schedule .... Rules 3B:1, 3B:2

Part Three C

Non-Traffic Prepayable Offenses and Uniform Fine Schedule .... Rules 3C:1, 3C:2

Part Three D

Civil Practice and Procedure in the General District Courts .... Repealed

Part Four

Pretrial Procedures, Depositions and Production at Trial .... Rules 4:0 through 4:15

Part Five

The Supreme Court .... Rules 5:1 through 5:43

Appendix of Forms

Part Five A

The Court of Appeals .... Rules 5A:1 through 5A:37

Appendix of Forms

Part Six

Integration of the State Bar .... Sections I through VII

Part Seven A

General District Courts — In General .... Rules 7A:1 through 7A:16

Part Seven B

General District Courts — Civil .... Rules 7B:1 through 7B:11

Part Seven C

General District Courts — Criminal and Traffic . . Rules 7C:1 through 7C:7

Part Eight

Juvenile and Domestic Relations District Courts .. Rules 8:1 through 8:22

Index.

Editor's note. — For website of the Virginia Supreme Court, including amendments to the rules of the court, see **www.courts.state.va.us.**

Research References. — For rules changes and related developments in Virginia practice and the federal courts, see Virginia Advance Court Rules and Practice Service (6 issues per year).

PART ONE
GENERAL RULES APPLICABLE TO ALL PROCEEDINGS

Rule

1:1. Finality of Judgments, Orders and Decrees.
1:1A. Recovery of Appellate Attorney's Fees in Circuit Court.
1:2. [Repealed.]
1:3. Reporters and Transcripts of Proceedings in Courts.
1:4. General Provisions as to Pleadings.
1:4A. Special Rule for Pleadings in General District Courts. (Repealed.)
1:5. Counsel.
1:6. Res Judicata Claim Preclusion.
1:7. Computation of Time.
1:8. Amendments.
1:9. Discretion of Court.
1:10. Verification.
1:11. Striking the Evidence.
1:12. Service of Papers after the Initial Process.
1:13. Endorsements.

Rule

1:14. Preservation of the Record.
1:15. Local Rules of Court.
Circuit Courts of Virginia — Times for the Commencement of the Regular Terms.
1:16. Filing Format and Procedure.
1:17. Electronic Filing and Service.
1:18. Pretrial Scheduling Order.
1:19. Pretrial Conferences.
1:20. Scheduling Civil Cases for Trial.
1:21. Preliminary Voir Dire Information.
1:22. Exercise of Challenges to Prospective Jurors.
1:23. Note Taking by Jurors.

Appendix of Forms.

1. Praecipe (Rule 1:15(b)).
2. Instructions (Rule 1:15(c)).
3. Uniform Pretrial Scheduling Order (Rule 1:18B).

Rule

Editor's note. — Part One became effective March 1, 1972. The statements of the source appearing after the several rules in this part, which were prepared by a subcommittee and presented to the Judicial Council, are not part of the Rules as adopted by the Supreme Court of Virginia.

Rule 1:1. Finality of Judgments, Orders and Decrees.

All final judgments, orders, and decrees, irrespective of terms of court, shall remain under the control of the trial court and subject to be modified, vacated, or suspended for twenty-one days after the date of entry, and no longer. But notwithstanding the finality of the judgment, in a criminal case the trial court may postpone execution of the sentence in order to give the accused an opportunity to apply for a writ of error and supersedeas; such postponement, however, shall not extend the time limits hereinafter prescribed for applying for a writ of error. The date of entry of any final judgment, order, or decree shall be the date it is signed by the judge either on paper or by electronic means in accord with Rule 1:17.

Cross references. — As to injunction against decree subject to bill of review and as to time for filing bill of review, see § 8.01-623.

Concerning the time periods for obtaining a new trial in district courts in civil and criminal cases, see §§ 16.1-97.1 and 16.1-133.1.

Source. — Rule 1:9.

Comment on the 1976 amendment. — The first sentence is changed to add authority for the trial court to suspend, by order entered within 21 days, a final judgment pending disposition of a motion for a new trial, a petition for rehearing, or a like pleading. The new material following the semicolon in the second sentence is intended to eliminate misunderstanding concerning the effect of postponement of execution of sentence in a criminal case.

The amendment, effective May 2, 2011, adopted March 1, 2011, in the last sentence, substituted "it" for "the judgment, order, or decree" preceding, and added "either on paper or by electronic means in accord with Rule 1:17" following, "is signed by the judge."

Law Review. — For article comparing Virginia Rules of Court with Federal Rules of Civil Procedure, see 47 Va. L. Rev. 906 (1961). For article reviewing recent developments and changes in legislation, case law, and Virginia Supreme Court Rules affecting civil litigation, see "Civil Practice and Procedure," 26 U. Rich. L. Rev. 679 (1992). For a review of civil practice and procedure in Virginia for year 1999, see 33 U. Rich. L. Rev. 801 (1999). For article reviewing recent developments and changes in legislation, case law, and Virginia Supreme Court Rules affecting civil litigation, see "Civil Practice and Procedure," see 40 U. Rich. L. Rev. 95 (2005). For annual survey of Virginia law article, "Civil Practice and Procedure," see 47 U. Rich. L. Rev. 113 (2012).

Research References. — Houts and Rogosheske, Art of Advocacy: Appeals (Matthew Bender).

Lawrence J. Smith, Art of Advocacy: Summation (Matthew Bender).

Michie's Jurisprudence. — For related discussion, see 1B M.J. Amendments, § 29; 1B M.J. Appeal and Error, §§ 125, 127, 131, 200; 4A M.J. Contempt, § 35; 5A M.J. Courts, §§ 4, 8, 13, 14, 16, 24; 5B M.J. Criminal Procedure, §§ 70, 75, 76, 85; 8A M.J. Executions, § 9; 8B M.J. Former Adjudication or Res Judicata, § 16; 11A M.J. Judgments and Decrees, §§ 7, 34, 118, 119, 124, 125, 128, 175, 199, 205; 13B M.J. New Trials, § 49.

CASE NOTES

I. General Consideration.
II. Final Judgment.
III. Postponement of Execution in Criminal Cases.

I. GENERAL CONSIDERATION.

Applicability of rule. — This rule is addressed to the matter of finality only for purposes of defining procedural rights after entry of a judgment. The rule has no application where the question is the conclusive effect which must be given to a judgment which is pending for review by the Virginia Supreme Court. Prudential Ins. Co. of Am. v. Tull, 524 F. Supp. 166 (E.D. Va. 1981).

Obtaining a judgment by confession pursuant to § 8.01-432 is an extraordinary remedy that permits a creditor to obtain an enforceable judgment against a debtor without the need to file suit or to establish any fact other than the existence of a valid instrument permitting the creditor to direct an attorney-in-fact to confess the judgment; when the creditor obtains a confessed judgment, that judgment is subject to the same rules governing all judgments, including the limitation imposed by Va. Sup. Ct. R. 1:1. Safrin v. Travaini Pumps USA, Inc., 269 Va. 412, 611 S.E.2d 352, 2005 Va. LEXIS 46 (2005).

As to appellant's motions to vacate his conviction for sexual battery filed ten months after entry of the conviction order, the language of § 16.1-272.1 was not susceptible to an interpretation that suggested it was intended to abrogate Va. Sup. Ct. R. 1:1 and other procedural requirements that had to be satisfied before asserting a claim of error, as appellant claimed. Locklear v. Commonwealth, 46 Va. App. 488, 618 S.E.2d 361, 2005 Va. App. LEXIS 361 (2005).

Because: (1) the circuit court lacked the authority to dismiss plaintiff's personal injury action under Norfolk, Va., Cir. Ct. R. 2(F)(3); (2) the local rule conflicted with the provisions governing the discontinuance of cases set forth in § 8.01-335; and (3) the local rule abridged plaintiff's right to take a nonsuit under § 8.01-380 and recommence the action, said dismissal was void ab initio, and not subject to the limitation period of Va. Sup. Ct. R. 1:1. Collins v. Shepherd, 274 Va. 390, 649 S.E.2d 672, 2007 Va. LEXIS 116 (2007).

Construction with other law. — Appeals court rejected a husband's six claims of error from a QDRO awarding a wife the gains earned on the portion of his retirement account distributed to her in the couple's divorce decree, as the husband failed to comply with Va. Sup. Ct. R. 5A:20(c) and (e), and despite his pro se status, he was required to comply with the rules of court. Blythe v. Blythe, 2006 Va. App. LEXIS 392 (Aug. 22, 2006).

Plain meaning of subsection B of § 8.01-335 is that any action in which there is no activity by the parties for three or more years may be removed from a court's docket, either by dismissal or discontinuance; thereafter a court may reinstate the case on motion but only within one year of the dismissal or discontinuance. Thus, the statute creates a rare exception to the rule that a circuit court loses jurisdiction over a case 21 days after entering a final order. Conger v. Barrett, 280 Va. 627, 702 S.E.2d 117, 2010 Va. LEXIS 261 (2010).

Section 19.2-303 operated as a statutory exception to Va. Sup. Ct. R. 1:1, and where the requirements of § 19.2-303 were satisfied, the trial court retained jurisdiction to modify defendant's sentences even after twenty-one days from entry of the final order because defendant had not yet been transferred to the Department of Corrections. Harris v. Commonwealth, 57 Va. App. 205, 700 S.E.2d 475, 2010 Va. App. LEXIS 422 (2010).

The provisions of Rule 1:1 are mandatory in order to assure the certainty and stability that the finality of judgments brings. Only an order within the 21-day time period that clearly and expressly modifies, vacates, or suspends the final judgment will interrupt or extend the running of that time period so as to permit the trial court to retain jurisdiction in the case. Super Fresh Food Mkts. of Va., Inc. v. Ruffin, 263 Va. 555, 561 S.E.2d 734, 2002 Va. LEXIS 60 (2002).

Neither court nor parties may extend 21-day period. — A trial court's order purporting to extend its jurisdiction over a case past the 21 days is ineffectual as is any agreement between the Commonwealth and the defendant to extend the time. Weese v. Commonwealth, 30 Va. App. 484, 517 S.E.2d 740 (1999).

Because neither party requested the trial court to retain jurisdiction over the distribution of their property, the husband failed to timely request an equitable distribution hearing during the 21-day period following entry of the decree during which the trial court retained jurisdiction over the case and, the trial court properly held that it lacked jurisdiction to reopen the divorce proceedings in order to equitably distribute the parties' marital property, the husband's appeal from the judgment of the trial court lacked merit. Miller v. Miller, 2007 Va. App. LEXIS 212 (May 22, 2007).

No threshold showing required to justify revision of order. — This rule allows a trial court to correct or change an order within the 21-day window whenever circumstances require and, in making such a change, there is no threshold showing that must be made as might be the case to justify modification of an order that had become final. Cloutier v. Queen, 35 Va. App. 413, 545 S.E.2d 574, 2001 Va. App. LEXIS 240 (2001).

The purpose of the 1976 amendment was to add authority for the trial court to suspend, by order entered within 21 days, a final judgment pending disposition of a motion for a new trial or a like pleading. The meaning of this rule is clear. Expression of a mere desire to consider a sentencing order further is not sufficient to comply with the rule. In re Commonwealth, Dep't of Cors., 222 Va. 454, 281 S.E.2d 857 (1981).

Prior to 1976 amendment a trial court had no power to extend the 21-day period and was without jurisdiction to enter any orders after its expiration. Godfrey v. Williams, 217 Va. 845, 234 S.E.2d 301 (1977).

The authority granted by § 20-109 to modify a spousal support award is not an exception to the requirements of Rule 1:1. Hamilton v. Hamilton, No. 0830-90-4 (Ct. of Appeals Apr. 23, 1991).

Clerical mistakes in judgments. — Clerical mistakes in judgments "arising from oversight or from an inadvertent omission may be corrected by the court at any time." The power conferred by § 8.01-428 B is not limited by this rule, but is confined to "the rare situation where the evidence clearly supports the conclusion that an error covered by § 8.01-428 B has been made." Dixon v. Pugh, No. 1647-90-2, 224 Va. 539, 423 S.E.2d 169 (Ct. of Appeals Aug. 13, 1991).

Trial court's authority to correct clerical errors not impaired. — This rule was not intended to limit, and in fact could not limit, the trial court's statutory authority to correct clerical errors in the judgment or errors therein arising from oversight or from an inadvertent omission at any time. Neither this rule nor Richardson v. Moore, 217 Va. 422, 229 S.E.2d 864 (1976), precludes a trial court, under § 8.01-428 B, from correcting, nunc pro tunc, a mutually unintended drafting error contained in a divorce decree. Dorn v. Dorn, 222 Va. 288, 279 S.E.2d 393 (1981).

Rule bars only further litigation of issues over which court had power to adjudicate. Hayes v. Hayes, 3 Va. App. 499, 351 S.E.2d 590 (1986).

Time limit not applicable to orders void ab initio. — The terms of this rule limiting the jurisdiction of a court to twenty-one days after the entry of the final order do not apply to an order which is void ab initio; such an order is a complete nullity and may be impeached directly or collaterally by all persons, anywhere, at any time, or in any manner. Singh v. Mooney, 261 Va. 48, 541 S.E.2d 549, 2001 Va. LEXIS 2 (2001).

"Void judgment." A void judgment is one that has been procured by extrinsic or collateral fraud, or entered by a court that did not have jurisdiction over the subject matter or the parties. Rook v. Rook, 233 Va. 92, 353 S.E.2d 756 (1987).

Void decree or order is a nullity and may on proper application be vacated at any time. Matthews v. Commonwealth, 216 Va. 358, 218 S.E.2d 538 (1975).

This rule is not a limitation on power and authority of court to vacate void order. Virginia Dep't of Cors. v. Crowley, 227 Va. 254, 316 S.E.2d 439 (1984).

Judgments that are void may be attacked in any court at any time, directly or collaterally, and thus are not encompassed by this rule. Rook v. Rook, 233 Va. 92, 353 S.E.2d 756 (1987).

Order not complying with notice and endorsement requirements not void. — An order that violates the notice and endorsement requirements of Rule 1:13 is not void ab initio but merely voidable, and therefore, a trial court has no authority to reconsider such an order after 21 days have passed. Singh v. Mooney, 261 Va. 48, 541 S.E.2d 549, 2001 Va. LEXIS 2 (2001).

After 21 days from its date of entry, a voidable judgment can be corrected only by writ of error to the Supreme Court for review, and proper steps must be taken to obtain the review within the time prescribed by statute. Smith v.

Commonwealth, 195 Va. 297, 77 S.E.2d 860 (1953); Hirschkop v. Commonwealth, 209 Va. 678, 166 S.E.2d 322, cert. denied, 396 U.S. 845, 90 S. Ct. 72, 24 L. Ed. 2d 94 (1969).

Oral ruling cannot nullify written final order. — Although a circuit court, after entering an order sustaining the defendants' demurrer, had agreed orally in a conference with all counsel to extend the time within which the plaintiff could file an amended motion for judgment, that oral ruling could not nullify the court's written final order; it was incumbent upon the plaintiff to submit timely a written order to the circuit court suspending, modifying, or vacating the order sustaining the demurrers and, having failed to do so, the court lost control over its order 21 days from the date the order was entered and could not thereafter grant the plaintiff a nonsuit. Berean Law Group, P.C. v. Cox, 259 Va. 622, 528 S.E.2d 108, 2000 Va. LEXIS 68 (2000).

Only order suspending or vacating final order can toll running of time. — Neither the filing of post-trial or post-judgment motions nor the court's taking such motions under consideration, nor the pendency of such motions on the 21st day after final judgment, was sufficient to toll or extend the running of the 21-day period prescribed by this rule or the 30-day period prescribed by Rule 5:9 since the running of time under those rules may be interrupted only by the entry, within the 21-day period after final judgment, of an order suspending or vacating the final order. School Bd. v. Caudill Rowlett Scott, Inc., 237 Va. 550, 379 S.E.2d 319 (1989); Vokes v. Vokes, 28 Va. App. 349, 504 S.E.2d 865 (1998).

Neither the filing of post-trial or post-judgment motions, nor the court's taking such motions under consideration, nor the pendency of such motions on the twenty-first day after final judgment, is sufficient to toll or extend the running of the 21-day period prescribed by this Rule or the 30-day period prescribed by Rule 5:9. The running of time under those rules may be interrupted only by the entry, within the 21-day period after final judgment, of an order suspending or vacating the final order. Triggs v. Triggs, No. 1922-90-4 (Ct. of Appeals Dec. 24, 1991).

The mere filing of a request for reconsideration of a decree does not toll the 21 day limitation contained in this Rule. Triggs v. Triggs, No. 1922-90-4 (Ct. of Appeals Dec. 24, 1991).

In order to toll the time limitations of this rule and Rule 5A:6(a), it is not sufficient for the trial judge merely to express a desire to consider action or take the issue under advisement; rather, the trial judge must issue an order modifying, vacating or suspending the sentence within 21 days of the entry of sentence. D'Alessandro v. Commonwealth, 15 Va. App. 163, 423 S.E.2d 199 (1992).

Neither the filing of post-trial or post-judgment motions, nor the court's taking such motions under consideration, nor the pendency of such motions on the twenty-first day after final judgment, is sufficient to toll or extend the running of the 21-day period prescribed by this rule; the running of time under this rule may be interrupted only by the entry, within the 21-day period after final judgment, of an order suspending or vacating the final order. Berean Law Group, P.C. v. Cox, 259 Va. 622, 528 S.E.2d 108, 2000 Va. LEXIS 68 (2000).

Acknowledgment of post-judgment motion is inadequate. — To interrupt the running of the twenty-one day time period of Rule 1:1, it is not sufficient that the trial court enter an order acknowledging the filing of a post-trial or post-judgment motion within 21 days following the entry of a final judgment. Rather, the rule requires that the trial court enter an order that expressly modifies, vacates, or suspends the judgment. Super Fresh Food Mkts. of Va., Inc. v. Ruffin, 263 Va. 555, 561 S.E.2d 734, 2002 Va. LEXIS 60 (2002).

Order entered more than twenty-one days after final decree held void. — Where, after expiration of 21 days, trial court lost jurisdiction over case and decree became final and conclusive, and where trial court during this 21-day period had vacated decree pertaining to life insurance policy in amount of $100,000, trial court retained jurisdiction over provision for securing $100,000 life insurance policy, retained no jurisdiction to modify final decree except as life insurance, and therefore, order pertaining to qualified domestic relations order and any other additions, subtractions, or modifications made contrary to original final decree were void. Williams v. Williams, No. 0384-88-2 (Ct. of Appeals Feb. 14, 1989).

The trial court did not have jurisdiction to enter an order of contempt where (1) the court entered a final order on May 1 which fully distributed the settlement proceeds of a wrongful death action, (2) on June 1, the court required the defendant to return funds to the court, and (3) on July 24, the court held the defendant in contempt for not doing so; the court lost jurisdiction over the defendant 21 days after the May 1 order and did not have jurisdiction at the time of the latter two orders. Stultz v. Albaugh, No. 0070-98-4 (Ct. of Appeals Nov. 24, 1998).

Although the trial court arguably erred in imposing a sentence for malicious wounding below the statutory minimum and in failing to impose a suspended sentence under subsection A of § 19.2-311, the errors only rendered the sentence voidable; however, because more than 21 days had passed since the entry of defendant's original sentencing order, the trial court no longer had jurisdiction to enter an amended order under Rule 1:1, and could not reacquire jurisdiction, even by entry of a nunc pro tunc order. Because a probation violation order attempted to revoke a sentence imposed by the amended sentencing order, it too was invalid. Gautier v. Commonwealth, 2007 Va. App. LEXIS 35 (Feb. 6, 2007).

Because defendant's motion to withdraw defendant's guilty plea was filed more than 21 days after entry of the final judgment, the trial court properly found that Va. Sup. Ct. R. 1:1 barred the motion. Draghia v. Commonwealth, 54 Va. App. 291, 678 S.E.2d 272, 2009 Va. App. LEXIS 290 (2009).

Motion to set aside verdict filed more than 21 days after entry of judgment was not timely raised. — Defendant's objections in motion to set aside verdict filed more than 21 days after entry of judgment were not timely raised. Mueller v. Commonwealth, 15 Va. App. 649, 426 S.E.2d 339 (1993).

Motion for new trial filed more than 21 days after entry of judgment was not timely. —

Where the trial court did not vacate or suspend execution of its judgment in order to retain jurisdiction prior to the expiration of the 21-day-period, nor was it requested to do so; the trial court lacked jurisdiction to vacate and reconsider the convictions. Lewis v. Commonwealth, 18 Va. App. 5, 441 S.E.2d 47 (1994).

Jurisdiction to award attorney's fees lost after 21 days. — Where a circuit court order disposed of the whole subject, granted all contemplated relief and did not reserve jurisdiction to award attorneys' fees at a later time, and where no order was entered modifying, vacating or suspending that final order within 21 days of its entry, the circuit court lacked jurisdiction to award attorneys' fees and costs to the plaintiffs for legal services rendered in the circuit court proceedings. Commonwealth v. Residents Involved in Saving Env't, No. 0769-99-2, 2000 Va. App. LEXIS 232 (Ct. of Appeals Mar. 28, 2000).

No jurisdiction to enter discovery sanctions after 21 days. — Trial court's order of discovery sanctions after the expiration of the statutory 21-day period were null and void, as the court no longer had jurisdiction to enter the same. James v. James, 263 Va. 474, 562 S.E.2d 133, 2002 Va. LEXIS 51 (2002).

Order that trial court had jurisdiction to enter could not be vacated more than 21 days after entry. — Under subsection B of § 8.01-380, a patient's failure to provide notice to a podiatrist of her second motion for nonsuit in her second malpractice suit against him had not deprived the trial court of jurisdiction to enter an order dismissing her case without prejudice, since there had been no showing of fraud. Therefore, under Va. Sup. Ct. R. 1:1, the trial court erred in vacating the second nonsuit order more than 21 days after its entry. Janvier v. Arminio, 272 Va. 353, 634 S.E.2d 754, 2006 Va. LEXIS 88 (2006).

Authority to consider sanctions after nonsuit granted. — Because an employer's § 8.01-271.1 motion for sanctions was pending when the employee moved for a first nonsuit, the trial court was empowered to consider the sanctions motion either before the entry of the nonsuit order or within 21 days after the entry of the nonsuit order under Va. Sup. Ct. R. 1:1. Williamsburg Peking Corp. v. Xianchin Kong, 270 Va. 350, 619 S.E.2d 100, 2005 Va. LEXIS 83 (2005).

Trial court did not lack jurisdiction to consider and impose sanctions because the court properly suspended a nonsuit order within the 21-day period provided for in Va. Sup. Ct. R. 1:1. The court retained jurisdiction over the suit until 21 days after the date upon which the trial court lifted the suspension of the nonsuit order and entered the final order in the case. N. Va. Real Estate, Inc. v. Martins, 283 Va. 86, 720 S.E.2d 121, 2012 Va. LEXIS 11 (2012).

Continuing jurisdiction under § 20-107.3. — Trial court did not lose jurisdiction over the husband and wife's divorce case even though it ordinarily would 21 days after entry of the final decree pursuant to Va. Sup. Ct. R. 1:1; the trial court had continuing jurisdiction under § 20-107.3 to enter additional orders necessary to effectuate the expressed intent of the original divorce decree, and, thus, it had the power to order the wife to repay a certain sum paid to her by the entity administering the husband's thrift savings plan in order to comply with the parties expressed intent of splitting his retirement savings evenly. Overcash v. Overcash, 2006 Va. App. LEXIS 36 (Jan. 24, 2006).

Court lacked jurisdiction. — Wife's appeal from the trial court's ruling granting the husband spousal support lacked merit; as the wife filed the objections 29 days after entry of the final decree, the trial court no longer had jurisdiction over the case. Gantt v. Gantt, No. 1973-02-3, 2003 Va. App. LEXIS 112 (Ct. of Appeals Mar. 4, 2003).

Although a trial court normally retained jurisdiction for a certain time period over certain judgments, orders, and decrees, it did not have jurisdiction over defendant's motion to reduce his sentence, as defendant's earlier concession that he had already been transferred to a Virginia Department of Corrections facility meant that the trial court was divested, at the time of the transfer, of its authority, pursuant to § 19.2-303, to retain jurisdiction over his case. Chilton v. Commonwealth, No. 0789-02-2, 2004 Va. App. LEXIS 38 (Ct. of Appeals Jan. 28, 2004).

Although wife timely presented her issues to the trial court for reconsideration in her motion to set aside the final decree, the filing of her motion did not stay or extend the trial court's time limit for ruling on that motion; hence, because the trial court did not rule on the motion to set aside the final decree until the 21-day period under Va. Sup. Ct. R. 1:1 had expired, the trial court lacked authority to enter an order setting the final decree aside, rendering it a nullity, and leaving the appellate court nothing to review. Crutchfield v. Crutchfield, 2005 Va. App. LEXIS 449 (Nov. 8, 2005).

Trial court correctly ruled that it no longer had jurisdiction to consider a mother's motions to reconsider a final order in a custody case because more than 21 days had passed since the entry of the final order, and the mother did not show that the exception to the bar of Va. Sup. Ct. R. 1:1 applied. Smith v. Novak, 2007 Va. App. LEXIS 139 (Apr. 3, 2007).

Letter filed by an employee's counsel allegedly raising some of the procedural issues asserted in the employee's appeal of a decision that upheld disciplinary action taken by her employer was not timely under Va. Sup. Ct. R. 1:1 as it was filed May 16, 2008, more than 21 days after the circuit court's decision on April 16; therefore, the circuit court did not have jurisdiction to modify, vacate, or suspend the judgment. Winfield v. Southside Va. Training Ctr., 2008 Va. App. LEXIS 484 (Oct. 28, 2008).

Circuit court erred when it issued a writ of mandamus to a judge that required the judge to change a previously entered order and convict and sentence a criminal defendant for driving under the influence rather than reckless driving, in part due to the fact that the judge's order had become final and therefore, the judge lacked jurisdiction to change the order. Kelley v. Stamos, 285 Va. 68, 737 S.E.2d 218, 2013 Va. LEXIS 10 (2013).

Court did not lack jurisdiction. — Court did not lack jurisdiction as the trial court was authorized to deny a landowner's motion to re-open the underlying case at a show-cause hearing, and thus, had jurisdiction to hear the separate issue of his contempt of its July 2005, order. Phelps v. Bd. of

County Supervisors, 2007 Va. App. LEXIS 262 (July 3, 2007).

Where a dock owner agreed to remove a boat dock pursuant to a wrongful death settlement agreement that was included in the court order approving the settlement, the dock owner was properly found in contempt because: (1) the dock owner used structures or objects on the property to moor or dock a boat; and (2) the trial court had subject matter jurisdiction to enforce the terms of the settlement since Va. Sup. Ct. R. 1:1 did not bar the petition for the issuance of a rule to show cause. Fisher v. Salute, 51 Va. App. 293, 657 S.E.2d 169, 2008 Va. App. LEXIS 99 (2008).

Circuit court retained jurisdiction to consider a motion for sanctions beyond 21 days after entry of a nonsuit order which stated that the court was retaining jurisdiction and that the order was not a final order for purposes of Va. Sup. Ct. R. 1:1. Johnson v. Woodard, 281 Va. 403, 707 S.E.2d 325, 2011 Va. LEXIS 48 (2011).

Active jurisdiction retained. — Trial court's phrasing, strike-out, and notation that the order did not preclude a hearing on any pending motion on sanctions showed that it did not merely intend to address issues in the future, but intended to retain active jurisdiction to address pending matters, and to forestall the commencement of the Va. Sup. Ct. R. 1:1 period. Gerensky-Greene v. Gerensky, 2012 Va. App. LEXIS 206 (June 19, 2012).

This rule concerns further proceedings within very suit in which final judgment has been entered. Niklason v. Ramsey, 233 Va. 161, 353 S.E.2d 783 (1987).

Effect of second suit with different parties and issues. — The fact that a second, separate lawsuit with different parties and issues directly impacted upon a previous suit does not mean that this rule is implicated. Niklason v. Ramsey, 233 Va. 161, 353 S.E.2d 783 (1987).

Period not extended by holding motion in abeyance pending transcription of record. — Filing of a motion for new trial with the clerk on the twenty-first day after final judgment, with the request that the motion be held in abeyance pending transcription of the record, did not have the effect of extending the time within which the judgment was subject to change. Smith v. Commonwealth, 207 Va. 459, 150 S.E.2d 545 (1966).

Limits of trial court's authority to suspend sentence. — Reading this rule and former § 53-272 (see now § 19.2-303) together, after the expiration of 21 days from the sentencing order if a defendant convicted of a felony has been committed and delivered to the penitentiary and no order has been entered within 21 days after final judgment suspending the sentence, the trial court has no further authority to suspend the sentence. In re Commonwealth, Dep't of Cors., 222 Va. 454, 281 S.E.2d 857 (1981).

Section 19.2-303 is one of the exceptions to Va. Sup. Ct. R. 1:1. This is so because § 19.2-303 permits a trial court, in cases where a defendant has been sentenced for a felony to the Virginia Department of Corrections but has not actually been transferred to the Department, to suspend or otherwise modify the unserved portion of the defendant's sentence after the 21-day limit specified in Va. Sup. Ct. R. 1:1. Baldwin v. Commonwealth, 43 Va. App. 415, 598 S.E.2d 754, 2004 Va. App. LEXIS 309 (2004).

Section 19.2-303 exception not applicable. — Trial court has no authority under § 19.2-303 to terminate the remaining portion of the suspension of sentence. Patterson v. Commonwealth, 39 Va. App. 610, 575 S.E.2d 583, 2003 Va. App. LEXIS 34 (2003).

Effect of taking motions to suspend sentences under advisement. — In view of this rule and former § 53-272 (see § 19.2-303), where the trial court took under advisement motions to set aside the verdicts and judgments and to suspend or modify all or part of the sentences of defendants convicted of drug-related offenses within 21 days of the entry of sentencing orders, the court did not "modify, vacate, or suspend" the judgments, and, therefore, the motions and the orders entered thereon did not affect the finality of the sentencing orders and the court lost jurisdiction to act on the motions to suspend at the end of the 21-day period and delivery of the defendants to the penitentiary. In re Commonwealth, Dep't of Cors., 222 Va. 454, 281 S.E.2d 857 (1981).

Modification or suspension of sentence. — Circuit court did not lose jurisdiction to consider defendant's motion to modify his sentence under § 19.2-303 because time limitations imposed by Va. Sup. Ct. R. 1:1 did not impact jurisdiction where defendant had not been transferred to the Virginia Department of Corrections but had been in a federal correctional institution for crimes committed while he was on supervised probation relating to a suspended two-year state sentence for possession of cocaine. Commonwealth v. Neely, 271 Va. 1, 624 S.E.2d 657, 2006 Va. LEXIS 8 (2006).

Sentencing order void ab initio. — Sentencing order was a final order under Va. Sup. Ct. R. 1:1 as it adjudicated guilt, imposed a sentence, remanded defendant to the sheriff's custody, and required that defendant register as a sex offender on his release; the sentencing order was void ab initio because § 19.2-303 did not authorize the trial court to reduce defendant's conviction from a felony to a misdemeanor after he had served the active portion of the sentence. The doctrine of invited error did not bar defendant's motion to vacate the sentencing order. Burrell v. Commonwealth, 283 Va. 474, 722 S.E.2d 272, 2012 Va. LEXIS 50 (2012).

Writ of prohibition to bar release or suspension of sentence. — The Department of Corrections had standing to seek a writ of prohibition barring the trial court from ordering the release from custody and suspension of sentences of prisoners convicted, and still held in custody, where the trial court had taken under advisement the motions of the prisoners within 21 days of the entry of sentencing orders, but had not ordered the judgments modified, vacated or suspended within the 21-day period. In re Commonwealth, Dep't of Cors., 222 Va. 454, 281 S.E.2d 857 (1981).

A writ of prohibition could not be used to revoke the releases of prisoners from custody and the suspension of their sentences, even if the orders of the trial court were improperly entered for failure of the court to act within 21 days of entry of sentencing orders and before delivery to the penitentiary, since the writ of prohibition is not available to correct errors already committed. In re

Commonwealth, Dep't of Cors., 222 Va. 454, 281 S.E.2d 857 (1981).

Probation. — Court could remove a good behavior requirement as a probation condition but lacked jurisdiction to alter good behavior and related provisions imposed as conditions of the suspension of a sentence more than 21 days after entry of a sentencing order. McFarland v. Commonwealth, 39 Va. App. 511, 574 S.E.2d 311, 2002 Va. App. LEXIS 770 (2002).

Use of other convictions as evidence before 21-day period expires. — The trial court did not err in admitting evidence at a penalty trial in a capital murder case of convictions of the defendant for other noncapital offenses prior to the expiration of the period during which the orders of conviction might be modified, vacated or suspended, and prior to the expiration of the time in which an appeal could be perfected, where the convictions were based on guilty pleas which were voluntarily and intelligently tendered, since, when a conviction is rendered upon such a plea and the punishment fixed by law is in fact imposed in a proceeding free of jurisdictional defect, no appeal will lie because there is nothing to appeal. Mason v. Commonwealth, 219 Va. 1091, 254 S.E.2d 116, cert. denied, 444 U.S. 919, 100 S. Ct. 239, 62 L. Ed. 2d 176 (1979).

Time for perfecting appeal runs from date motion disposed of. — Where the record showed that a motion to set aside or vacate a judgment of conviction had been made and taken under consideration by the trial court before the judgment had become final, the time for perfecting an appeal ran from the date on which such motion was disposed of. Lyle v. Ekleberry, 209 Va. 349, 164 S.E.2d 586 (1968).

Expiration of stay. — While the circuit court may have rendered its judgment on motion for remittitur at the conclusion of the hearing, it did not enter that judgment until almost two months later, at a time the court no longer had jurisdiction over the action because the 30-day stay of the final order had expired and the court had not entered another order extending the length of the stay. Thus, the order two months later was a nullity. Wagner v. Shird, 257 Va. 584, 514 S.E.2d 613 (1999).

Expiration of suspension period of suspended judgment. — Doctor's appeal from a final judgment in favor of a patient was untimely because it was not filed within 30 days of the expiration of a 14-day suspension period entered by the trial court pursuant to Va. Sup. Ct. R. 1:1, as required by Va. Sup. Ct. R. 5:9. The doctor's motion to set aside the verdict did not extend the period for filing the notice of appeal, pursuant to Va. Sup. Ct. R. 5:5. Hutchins v. Talbert, 278 Va. 650, 685 S.E.2d 658, 2009 Va. LEXIS 98 (2009).

Time limitations after a continuance. — Where a continuance did not dispose of the whole subject or give all the relief contemplated, the trial judge did not violate the time limits of Va. Sup. Ct. R. 1:1 by finding the ex-wife in contempt more than 21 days later. McDonald v. Minton, No. 2531-03-4, 2004 Va. App. LEXIS 118 (Ct. of Appeals Mar. 23, 2004).

Where orders releasing the appellees and suspending their sentences were entered after the 21-day limitation in this rule had expired and the appellees had been transferred to the penitentiary, those orders were void for lack of jurisdiction and the trial court erred in dismissing the motions to vacate. Virginia Dep't of Cors. v. Crowley, 227 Va. 254, 316 S.E.2d 439 (1984).

Refusal to amend charge to lesser offense. — A trial court did not err in refusing to consider a motion to amend the charge on which the defendant had been convicted to a lesser offense pursuant to the terms of a plea agreement which the court had memorialized in the final order where the motion was not made until more than 21 days after the final judgment and after the defendant had been committed to the Department of Juvenile Justice. Weese v. Commonwealth, 30 Va. App. 484, 517 S.E.2d 740 (1999).

Refusal to correct support order entered 10 years earlier not error. — The trial court did not err in not correcting the provision of an order for alimony and child support requiring the husband to support his 18-year-old daughter, although she may have been emancipated because of her age, where the unitary support award also provided support for the wife and two infant children. Their rights became vested as the payments accrued, and should not be defeated by an error which may have occurred in an order, entered 10 years prior to an action to recover delinquent payments, which the trial court was without power to modify or vacate. Johnson v. Johnson, 1 Va. App. 330, 338 S.E.2d 353 (1986).

Amendment of pleading and decree based on "record evidence" as to last place of marital cohabitation. — Where there was ample unrefuted "record evidence" that the last place of marital cohabitation, as properly defined in the context of the divorce venue statute, between parties who were divorced in 1966 was in the City of Alexandria, the trial court had the inherent power to allow an appropriate amendment to the bill of complaint to disregard the erroneous conclusion of law contained in the commissioner's report, stating that the parties last cohabited in Danville, and to amend its final decree of divorce nunc pro tunc, in order to make the record "speak the truth." Netzer v. Reynolds, 231 Va. 444, 345 S.E.2d 291 (1986).

Challenge to validity of separation agreement should have been raised within 21 days. — Challenge to the validity of separation agreement incorporated in divorce decree could and should have been raised before the divorce decree was entered or within 21 days thereafter. After the expiration of 21 days from the date the decree was entered, the trial court lost jurisdiction of the case, except for the limited purposes of revising child custody and support and exercising its enforcement powers and the trial court erred in modifying the divorce decree by declaring the incorporated property settlement agreement invalid. Rook v. Rook, 233 Va. 92, 353 S.E.2d 756 (1987).

Challenge to validity of separation agreement incorporated in divorce decree. — Contention of defendant husband in defense of contempt proceeding brought by ex-wife that property settlement agreement incorporated into divorce decree was void ab initio and unenforceable because it was against public policy was an attack on the decree and not merely the property settlement agreement. Rook v. Rook, 233 Va. 92, 353 S.E.2d 756 (1987).

Conforming divorce decree's pension provision to effectuate its intent not improper. — Divorce decree entitled a former wife to half of the net pension benefits paid by the former husband's employer when he started receiving them. As the company that employed the husband when he retired 16 years later was a successor in interest to his former employer, in awarding the wife a share of the pension benefits the husband received from that company, the trial court did not modify the decree in violation of Va. Sup. Ct. R. 1:1, but conformed its terms to effectuate the decree's expressed intent. Strausbaugh v. Strausbaugh, 2007 Va. App. LEXIS 198 (May 15, 2007).

Judgment final despite wife's fraud allegations. — The judgment of the trial court became final 21 days after entry of the final decree. Wife's fraud allegations were of an intrinsic nature and were raised in the trial court after that court lost jurisdiction over the case. Young v. Young, No. 2321-91-1 (Ct. of Appeals Oct. 20, 1992).

Michigan divorce decree not subject to modification. — Where Michigan decrees, once registered, were to be treated in the same manner as support orders issued by a court of this Commonwealth, and because more than 21 days had expired after their entry, the two Michigan decrees were final and not subject to modification; they were subject to being vacated only upon proof that they were based upon deficient jurisdiction or upon extrinsic fraud. Trevino v. Talmadge, 17 Va. App. 514, 438 S.E.2d 489 (1993).

Impermissible modification of sentencing order. — Trial judge may not modify a sentencing order after a convicted felon has been released by the Department of Corrections on parole and impose for the first time a requirement of probation. Russnak v. Commonwealth, 10 Va. App. 317, 392 S.E.2d 491 (1990).

Authority to modify condition of suspended sentence. — Payment allotted to defendant's wife from defendant's military retirement benefit was a condition of defendant's suspended sentences rather than a condition of probation; thus, the trial court correctly concluded it lacked authority under Va. Sup. Ct. R. 1:1 to modify the condition pursuant to § 19.2-304. Reinke v. Commonwealth, 51 Va. App. 357, 657 S.E.2d 805, 2008 Va. App. LEXIS 111 (2008).

Final decree impermissibly modified. — Where the decree entered by the trial court constituted a modification of a previous final order entered more than 21 days prior thereto, such decree was an impermissible modification of the final order. McDysan v. McDysan, No. 1085-86-4 (Ct. of Appeals Nov. 1, 1988).

Consent decree impermissibly modified. — As a consent decree was a final judgment and contained the parties' agreement that property owners would comply with a zoning ordinance within 60 days and refrain from any future use of a property as a "junk yard," or pay to a county a fine of $100 per day for every day that they were found to have been in violation of the terms, the court erred in amending the decree and reducing the fine as the terms were not subject to alteration under Va. Sup. Ct. R. 1:1. McLane v. Vereen, 278 Va. 65, 677 S.E.2d 294, 2009 Va. LEXIS 72 (2009).

Proposed order inconsistent with final equitable distribution order. — Wife's motion for entry of a Qualified Domestic Relations Order was properly denied as the wife did not challenge the final equitable distribution order, which awarded the husband 37 percent of the wife's military retirement benefits, and the wife's proposed order was inconsistent with the equitable distribution order, as it would have awarded 37 percent of the marital portion of the wife's military retirement benefits to the husband; no statute, including subdivision K 4 of § 20-107.3, authorized the trial court to modify the final decree, and Rule 1:1 prohibited the trial court from modifying the final decree in the manner requested by the wife. James-Dietrich v. Dietrich, No. 2893-03-2, 2004 Va. App. LEXIS 287 (Ct. of Appeals June 22, 2004).

Right to appeal held preserved. — Plaintiffs preserved their right to appeal where plaintiffs' counsel, during the hearing on the motion to dismiss, repeatedly made known to the court his position, and during the 21-day period under this rule within which the trial court retained jurisdiction over the final order, the plaintiffs filed a motion for rehearing and a nine-page memorandum contending that the plaintiffs' claims were not barred by the doctrine of waiver, and counsel for the plaintiffs endorsed the order denying the motion for reconsideration as "Seen: and all Exceptions noted." Weidman v. Babcock, 241 Va. 40, 400 S.E.2d 164 (1991).

Change of conviction and sentencing orders a nullity. — Trial court's power to correct clerical mistakes did not authorize it to enter post-appeal order changing conviction and sentencing orders entered five years before to reflect that defendant had been convicted under different section; those orders became final 21 days after their entry. The trial court's order being a nullity, it was not an order from which an appeal to challenge defendant's conviction could be brought anew. Myers v. Commonwealth, 26 Va. App. 544, 496 S.E.2d 80 (1998).

Purported extension of 21-day period ineffective. — The language of the trial court's September 12, 2000 order purporting to extend the period of the trial court's jurisdiction beyond the post-judgment 21 day time period of Rule 1:1, made for the purpose of permitting the trial court to take under advisement the motion for reconsideration filed after the entry of the final judgment, was ineffective where that order did not modify, vacate, or suspend the final judgment rendered by the August 23, 2000 order. Super Fresh Food Mkts. of Va., Inc. v. Ruffin, 263 Va. 555, 561 S.E.2d 734, 2002 Va. LEXIS 60 (2002).

Finding of contempt based on valid conviction. — Finding that defendant was in contempt of court was based on a valid conviction; contention that the district court had dismissed the underlying charge 129 days after conviction was without merit, as the district court no longer had jurisdiction to do so and could not dismiss defendant's conviction. Wilson v. Commonwealth, No. 1959-01-4, 2002 Va. App. LEXIS 465 (Ct. of Appeals Aug. 13, 2002).

Applied in Federal Realty & Dev. Corp. v. N. Litterio & Co., 213 Va. 3, 189 S.E.2d 314 (1972);

Smith v. Commonwealth, 217 Va. 329, 228 S.E.2d 557 (1976); Prohm v. Anderson, 220 Va. 74, 255 S.E.2d 491 (1979); Landcraft Co. v. Kincaid, 220 Va. 865, 263 S.E.2d 419 (1980); Via v. Superintendent, Powhatan Correctional Ctr., 643 F.2d 167 (4th Cir. 1981); Williams v. Fairfax County Redevelopment & Hous. Auth., 227 Va. 309, 315 S.E.2d 202 (1984); Parra v. Parra, 1 Va. App. 118, 336 S.E.2d 157 (1985); Clephas v. Clephas, 1 Va. App. 209, 336 S.E.2d 897 (1985); Crowley v. Landon, 780 F.2d 440 (4th Cir. 1985); M.E.D. v. J.P.M., 3 Va. App. 391, 350 S.E.2d 215 (1986); Dixon v. Pugh, 244 Va. 539, 423 S.E.2d 169 (1992); Kelley v. Kelley, 17 Va. App. 93, 435 S.E.2d 421 (1993); Smith v. Smith, 18 Va. App. 427, 444 S.E.2d 269 (1994); Concerned Taxpayers v. County of Brunswick, 249 Va. 320, 455 S.E.2d 712 (1995); Parrish v. Jessee, 250 Va. 514, 464 S.E.2d 141 (1995); Hoy v. Hoy, 29 Va. App. 115, 510 S.E.2d 253 (1999); Rogers v. Commonwealth, 29 Va. App. 580, 513 S.E.2d 876 (1999); Hastie v. Hastie, 29 Va. App. 776, 514 S.E.2d 800 (1999); Smith v. Commonwealth, 32 Va. App. 766, 531 S.E.2d 11, 2000 Va. App. LEXIS 499 (2000); King George County Serv. Auth. v. Presidential Serv. Co. Tier II, 267 Va. 448, 593 S.E.2d 241, 2004 Va. LEXIS 37 (2004); Rose v. Jaques, 268 Va. 137, 597 S.E.2d 64, 2004 Va. LEXIS 92 (2004); Estate of Hackler v. Hackler, 44 Va. App. 51, 602 S.E.2d 426, 2004 Va. App. LEXIS 454 (2004); Epps v. Commonwealth, 59 Va. App. 71, 717 S.E.2d 151, 2011 Va. App. LEXIS 351 (2011).

II. FINAL JUDGMENT.

"Final order" defined. — A final order is one which disposes of the whole subject, gives all the relief contemplated, provides with reasonable completeness for giving effect to the sentence, and leaves nothing to be done in the cause save to superintend ministerially the execution of the order. Daniels v. Truck & Equip. Corp., 205 Va. 579, 139 S.E.2d 31 (1964).

A judgment is not final for the purposes of res judicata or collateral estoppel when it is being appealed or when the time limits fixed for perfecting the appeal have not expired. Faison v. Hudson, 243 Va. 413, 417 S.E.2d 302 (1992).

Exception justified only when error clear, substantial, and material. — Although both this rule and Supreme Court Rule 5:25 provide exceptions to accommodate "good cause" and "obtain the ends of justice," this is justified only when the record reflects error which is clear, substantial, and material. Johnson v. Commonwealth, No. 0259-91-1 (Ct. of Appeals Nov. 10, 1992).

Handwritten order still a final judgment. — Where a judge directed the clerk, via a post-it note affixed to his handwritten order, not to record the order, indicating that a typewritten order would be substituted, the order still constituted a final order under Rule 1:1 because it disposed of the whole subject, (child custody), gave all the relief that was contemplated, provided with reasonable completeness for giving effect to the ruling, and left nothing to be done in the cause save to superintend ministerially the execution of the decree. Key v. Key, No. 1079-04-1, 2004 Va. App. LEXIS 608 (Ct. of Appeals Dec. 14, 2004).

Court speaks only through its written orders; and, orders speak as of the day they were entered. Wagner v. Shird, 257 Va. 584, 514 S.E.2d 613 (1999).

Decision announced from bench not "entered." All procedure relating to orders of the circuit court of Virginia relate to the date of "entry" of the final order appealed from and, therefore, there is nothing in the rules that would prohibit the judge who has announced a decision from the bench from modifying or otherwise changing such opinion so announced after due reflection since a final order had not been "entered." Costner's Furn., Inc. v. Cawthorn, 1 Bankr. 267 (Bankr. W.D. Va. 1979).

Procedure where sentencing order differs from oral pronouncement. — If the sentencing order specifies a sentence other than that which the trial court pronounced in open court, defendant has 21 days to note an objection and move that the order be modified. Absent timely objection and an appropriate motion, the order is presumed to contain an accurate statement of what transpired in the trial court. In re Brown, No. 0320-85 (Ct. of Appeals Nov. 22, 1985).

When judgment final. — A final judgment or sentence valid in a court of original entry is final and conclusive upon all courts (except on appeal) after the court pronouncing judgment has lost jurisdiction of the case. Smith v. Commonwealth, 207 Va. 459, 150 S.E.2d 545 (1966); Hirschkop v. Commonwealth, 209 Va. 678, 166 S.E.2d 322, cert. denied, 396 U.S. 845, 90 S. Ct. 72, 24 L. Ed. 2d 94 (1969); Prudential Ins. Co. of Am. v. Tull, 524 F. Supp. 166 (E.D. Va. 1981).

Within the purview of the Virginia statutes and rules, the finality of an adjudication is the order, decree or judgment "entered" of record and it is that order, decree or judgment which can be made the subject of an appeal, and therefore has binding effect as a final adjudication upon the merits. Costner's Furn., Inc. v. Cawthorn, 1 Bankr. 267 (Bankr. W.D. Va. 1979).

After the expiration of 21 days from the entry of a judgment, the court rendering the judgment loses jurisdiction of the case, and, absent a perfected appeal, the judgment is final and conclusive. Rook v. Rook, 233 Va. 92, 353 S.E.2d 756 (1987).

This rule is a mandatory rule, and states that all final judgments, orders, and decrees, irrespective of terms of court, shall remain under the control of the trial court and subject to be modified, vacated, or suspended for 21 days after the date of entry, and no longer; at the expiration of that 21-day period, the trial court loses jurisdiction to disturb a final judgment, order, or decree. Bogart v. Bogart, 21 Va. App. 280, 464 S.E.2d 157 (1995).

A judgment is not final for purposes of execution until the expiration of the 21-day period. Wick v. IRS (In re Bhatti), 126 Bankr. 229 (Bankr. W.D. Va. 1991).

In a domestic relations case where the judgment did not violate the husband's right to due process, the trial court did not err in concluding that this rule prevented it from setting aside the judgment. Eddine v. Eddine, 12 Va. App. 760, 406 S.E.2d 914 (1991).

Because the court had personal jurisdiction over defendant, it had the authority to determine when that jurisdiction attached and based upon that decision to determine and enter judgment for the support arrearage; that order became final 21 days after being entered, and because defendant failed to appeal that order, he could not attack the holding in the order through an appeal filed nearly six years later. Grimshaw v. Grimshaw, No. 2592-94-3 (Ct. of Appeals Mar. 19, 1996).

It is the firmly established law of this Commonwealth that a trial court speaks only through its written orders. Furthermore, "orders speak as of the day they were entered," and an order of the court becomes final 21 days after its entry unless vacated or suspended by the court during that time. Davis v. Mullins, 251 Va. 141, 466 S.E.2d 90 (1996).

At the expiration of the 21-day period established by this rule, the trial court loses jurisdiction to disturb a final judgment, order, or decree. Hickson v. Hickson, 34 Va. App. 246, 540 S.E.2d 508, 2001 Va. App. LEXIS 29 (2001).

Wife was not entitled to one-third of the loan amount her ex-husband owed to a securities account where the principle of res judicata prevented the trial court from disturbing the final divorce decree that divided the account as a marital asset; the trial court lost jurisdiction to revisit the issue 21 days after the decree was entered pursuant to Va. Sup. Ct. R. 1:1. Medure v. Medure, No. 1597-01-3, 2002 Va. App. LEXIS 111 (Ct. of Appeals Feb. 19, 2002).

Trial court did not err in modifying defendant's sentence, as it was entitled to do so because, among other things, the modification was not made more than 21 days after the entry of a final sentencing order. Hilleary v. Commonwealth, No. 0423-02-4, 2003 Va. App. LEXIS 144 (Ct. of Appeals Mar. 18, 2003).

Mere indication that the trial court intends to rule on pending motions is insufficient to negate the finality of an order rendering a final judgment on the merits of a case, and this is particularly true where the trial court's intention regarding the pending motions is not even expressed in the order rendering the final judgment. Carrithers v. Harrah, 60 Va. App. 69, 723 S.E.2d 638, 2012 Va. App. LEXIS 117 (2012).

Because a trial court's order contained no language retaining jurisdiction to address the parties' pending requests for attorneys' fees and costs, the order rendered a final judgment, and the trial court's letter, which directed the parties to file briefs regarding their motions for attorneys' fees and costs, did not affect the finality of the order entered that same day disposing of the merits of the case; even if an order granting a final judgment on the merits of a case contains express language indicating that the trial court intends to rule on a request for attorneys' fees at a future time, such language does not negate the fact that such an order is in fact a final judgment. Carrithers v. Harrah, 60 Va. App. 69, 723 S.E.2d 638, 2012 Va. App. LEXIS 117 (2012).

Since a father did not appeal a final decree, the order was final, and the father could not argue that a clause in the parties' property settlement agreement was void; the property settlement agreement was incorporated, but not merged, into the final decree of divorce, and the father did not appeal the final decree of divorce and its incorporation of the property settlement agreement. McPhail v. McPhail, 2012 Va. App. LEXIS 301 (Sept. 25, 2012).

Trial court's ruling on a mother's motion to reconsider was a nullity and review by the appellate court was barred on the issue flowing from the trial court's denial of the motion because the trial court lacked jurisdiction to consider the motion after the 21-day period in Va. Sup. Ct. R. 1:1 expired. Anderson v. Anderson, No. 2187-12-4, 2013 Va. App. LEXIS 79 (Ct. of Appeals Mar. 12, 2013).

In a dissolution matter, although a trial court's January 12, 2011, order included language to "monitor" a husband's payments and for entry of orders dividing a military pension, the order was an appealable final order, Va. Sup. Ct. R. 1:1, because the remaining actions were ministerial; thus, the husband's challenge to the division of the formal marital was not reviewed because the husband failed to file a timely notice of appeal from the January order. Gunning v. Gunning, No. 1140-12-1, 2013 Va. App. LEXIS 151 (Ct. of Appeals May 14, 2013).

Authority to modify sentence. — Trial court properly found that it had no authority under § 19.2-303 to modify defendant's sentence where he had already been transferred to the Virginia Department of Corrections because the legislature in § 19.2-303 had created an absolute event when a trial court could no longer modify a sentence and clearly limited the authority of the trial court to do so. The statute contained no exceptions. Stokes v. Commonwealth, 61 Va. App. 388, 736 S.E.2d 330, 2013 Va. App. LEXIS 17 (2013).

When read in conjunction with Va. Sup. Ct. R. 1:1, § 19.2-303 establishes an absolute event, i.e., a transfer to the Virginia Department of Corrections, when a trial court can no longer modify a sentence. Because § 19.2-303 clearly allows a court to modify an unserved portion of a sentence any time before a person is transferred to the Department of Corrections, the operative date in question is when the court makes its ruling, not when the motion is filed, and not when the matter initially comes before the court. Stokes v. Commonwealth, 61 Va. App. 388, 736 S.E.2d 330, 2013 Va. App. LEXIS 17 (2013).

Date judgment is final. — Debtor's former spouse was considered an insider when a trustee sought to set aside a transfer under 11 U.S.C.S. § 547 because at the time of the transfer of the property the spouse and the debtor were not legally divorced. The final divorce judgment had not been signed and entered by the court as required by § 8.01-2, and Va. Sup. Ct. R. 1:1. Prunty v. Terry (In re Paschall), 408 B.R. 79, 2009 U.S. Dist. LEXIS 45623 (E.D. Va. 2009), aff'd, 2010 U.S. App. LEXIS 14613 (4th Cir. Va. 2010).

A judgment which has been properly vacated or suspended under Rule 1:1 does not become a final judgment thereafter without a subsequent order confirming it as originally entered or as modified. Super Fresh Food Mkts. of Va., Inc. v. Ruffin, 263 Va. 555, 561 S.E.2d 734, 2002 Va. LEXIS 60 (2002).

Authority of trial court where judgment has not become final. — Where at the time of the last motion the judgments had not become final under this rule, the lower court had full power and authority to inquire into the sufficiency of the evidence to sustain the verdicts and the objections made during the trial to its rulings on the instructions. Gabbard v. Knight, 202 Va. 40, 116 S.E.2d 73 (1960).

Issues still pending. — This rule prohibited modification of custody order more than 21 days after its entry, but did not deny trial court jurisdiction over issues still pending and unaffected by that order. Summers v. Summers, No. 2759-98-4 (Ct. of Appeals June 15, 1999).

Although a trial court's order indicated that it was a final decree, it failed to make any reference to the former wife's appeal of a domestic relations court's denial of her motion to amend, which ruling had been consolidated with the former wife's action for injunctive and declaratory relief; thus, as the trial court did not dispose of the whole subject of the suit, its order was not a final, appealable order. Brown v. Josey, 2011 Va. App. LEXIS 137 (Apr. 26, 2011).

Show cause order, which reaffirmed the parties' separation agreement, was not a final order because it failed to dispose of the whole subject of the cause; accordingly, the trial court did not lose jurisdiction over the order after twenty-one days. Guirguis v. Salib, No. 0038-12-1, 2013 Va. App. LEXIS 12 (2013).

Final order not found. — Order sustaining seller's demurrer and dismissing buyer's action for breach of duty was not a final order because order also granted buyer leave to file an amended motion; therefore lower court maintained jurisdiction to enter order granting nonsuit in buyer's action for breach of duty until after expiration of time for buyer to amend motion. Norris v. Mitchell, 255 Va. 235, 495 S.E.2d 809 (1998).

In a divorce case, the trial court bifurcated the underlying hearing on the merits of the motion to vacate the order for future distribution of retirement pay and informed the parties that it would hear arguments relating to attorney's fees after reaching a ruling on the merits; because the order denying the motion to vacate did not dispose of the issue of attorney's fees — relief contemplated by both parties prior to issuance of the order — the order was not a final order. Because the order was not a final order, the trial court had jurisdiction to hear the wife's motion for attorney's fees even though 21 days had elapsed since entry of the order resolving the merits of the underlying motion to vacate; thus, the trial court improperly concluded that it lacked jurisdiction over the issue of attorney's fees, and the case was remanded to the trial court to determine the merits of the wife's motion for an award of attorney's fees and costs. Mina v. Mina, 45 Va. App. 215, 609 S.E.2d 622, 2005 Va. App. LEXIS 86 (2005).

Trial court did not err when it rescinded a portion of an order requiring a mother to cooperate with an attorney, who was representing her son in expulsion proceedings because the order was not a final order; the subsequent order from which a father appealed was the final order, and, therefore, the trial court had jurisdiction to amend the order. Christovich v. Christovich, 2009 Va. App. LEXIS 404 (Sept. 15, 2009).

Because a husband failed to preserve his arguments, his assignments of error were not addressed on appeal; the circuit court did not consider the merits of the husband's motion to reconsider because at the time of the hearing on the motion, the 21-day period prescribed by Va. Sup. Ct. R. 1:1 had elapsed, depriving the circuit court of further jurisdiction in the case, and thus, the court of appeals was barred from addressing those issues on appeal. Stevens v. Stevens, 59 Va. App. 274, 717 S.E.2d 854, 2011 Va. App. LEXIS 391 (2011).

Finality of judgment in child custody case. — See Shank v. Department of Social Servs., 217 Va. 506, 230 S.E.2d 454 (1976).

Order which merely ordered defendants to file their pleadings within 15 days was not a final judgment. Daniels v. Truck & Equip. Corp., 205 Va. 579, 139 S.E.2d 31 (1964).

Order sustaining demurrer with leave to file amended motion for judgment. — An order that sustains a demurrer and dismisses the case if the plaintiff fails to amend his motion for judgment within a specified time becomes a final order upon the plaintiff's failure to file an amended motion within the specified time. Berean Law Group, P.C. v. Cox, 259 Va. 622, 528 S.E.2d 108, 2000 Va. LEXIS 68 (2000).

Order overruling defendants' renewed motion for a new trial, entering judgment on the verdict of the jury, and distributing the proceeds was a final judgment. With the passing of 21 days thereafter this judgment was no longer under the control of the trial court and subject to be modified or vacated by it. Lyle v. Ekleberry, 209 Va. 349, 164 S.E.2d 586 (1968).

Order setting execution date was not a final order because it was not a disposition of the whole subject before the court in the case. Rather, it was a ministerial act that served only to "fix a day when the judgment already existing should be executed." Davidson v. Commonwealth, 246 Va. 168, 432 S.E.2d 178 (1993).

This rule does not preclude the entry of an order staying an execution date because such an order would not modify, vacate, or suspend a capital murder conviction and sentence of death. A stay order merely postpones the date when a final judgment will be executed; it does not alter the substantive provisions of that final judgment. Thus, a stay order is distinguishable from an order suspending a previously-imposed sentence. Davidson v. Commonwealth, 246 Va. 168, 432 S.E.2d 178 (1993).

Finality not affected where authority pursuant to § 20-107.3 (K) retained. — Trial judge did not err in finding that divorce decree was a final order. Although the trial judge retained authority pursuant to subsection K of § 20-107.3 to enter further orders to implement the sale of the marital residence, this authority did not affect the finality of the decree as to matters resolved in the decree and to which the parties preserved no objections. Galligan v. Galligan, No. 1406-97-4 (Ct. of Appeals Dec. 9, 1997).

Order not final where value of marital residence has not been established. — Order captioned "Final Decree of Divorce" was not a final order, as it did not dispose of the whole subject, give all the relief requested, and leave nothing to be done by the trial court; it did not establish the value of the husband's share of the marital residence and could hardly be final with such a significant omission. Thus, the trial court did not violate Va. Sup. Ct. R. 1:1 by subsequently entering orders establishing the husband's share of the marital home and offsetting this award against the wife's interest in retirement accounts. Andersen v. Andersen, 2008 Va. App. LEXIS 524 (Dec. 2, 2008).

Jurisdiction divests with entry of final order. — After the order became final, the trial court, pursuant to this rule, was divested of jurisdiction and every action of the court thereafter to alter or vacate that order, was a nullity unless one of the limited exceptions to the preclusive effect of this rule applies. Davis v. Mullins, 251 Va. 141, 466 S.E.2d 90 (1996); Vokes v. Vokes, 28 Va. App. 349, 504 S.E.2d 865 (1998).

The order in which the trial judge ruled that the husband was entitled to a credit was entered more than two years after entry of the final decree. In the absence of an exception to this rule, the trial judge lost jurisdiction over the case twenty-one days after the initial judgment, and he could not issue a valid modification order. Decker v. Decker, 22 Va. App. 486, 471 S.E.2d 775 (1996).

The trial judge could not act upon a substantive issue after entry of a final order. Decker v. Decker, 22 Va. App. 486, 471 S.E.2d 775 (1996).

Trial court did not err in refusing to revisit issues in divorce decree, where neither party appealed decree and it became final 21 days after its entry. Deane v. Deane, No. 2347-98-2 (Ct. of Appeals July 20, 1999).

Circuit court lacked jurisdiction to award attorneys' fees and costs more than 21 days after order which disposed of the whole subject of the litigation, and granted all contemplated relief, by affirming department's issuance of permit. Commonwealth v. Residents Involved in Saving Env't, Inc., No. 0769-99-2 (Ct. of Appeals Mar. 28, 2000).

Trial court lacked jurisdiction to consider defendant's motion for bond pending appeal where: (1) there was no order suspending or vacating the May 4, 2005, sentencing order within 21 days of its entry, so the trial court retained jurisdiction over defendant's sentence only until May 25, 2005, (2) defendant filed his notice of appeal on May 20, 2005, which divested the trial court of jurisdiction to postpone or suspend the execution of defendant's sentence for purposes of the bond motion, (3) § 19.2-319 required the sentence or the execution of the sentence to be suspended before the trial court could set bail, and (4) no exception to Va. Sup. Ct. R. 1:1 applied. Bowen v. Commonwealth, 2006 Va. App. LEXIS 119 (Mar. 28, 2006).

Because a mother did not comply with subsection A of § 16.1-296 and § 16.1-133.1 by appealing a dispositional order within 10 days of its entry or applying to reopen the case within 60 days, pursuant to Va. Sup. Ct. R. 1:1, the juvenile court lost jurisdiction of a charge and its dismissal of that charge had no force; therefore, since the juvenile court had authority under § 16.1-278.8 A.13.c. to maintain custody of the child with the social services department, the circuit court properly denied the mother's motion to dismiss proceedings and return custody of her son. Lee v. Frederick County Dep't of Soc. Servs., 2008 Va. App. LEXIS 370 (Aug. 5, 2008).

Circuit court erred in awarding heirs attorney fees on the ground that a city had taken a second nonsuit in its action seeking to sell a parcel of land in order to satisfy delinquent real estate tax liens on the property because the circuit court's order granted a first nonsuit as a matter of right to the city as to the heirs and was final under Va. Sup. Ct. R. 1:1, and, therefore, the circuit court had no jurisdiction to award attorney fees and costs twenty-one days after entry of that order, and the award was a nullity; because the action the city filed against the heirs was not the same cause of action it had previously filed against property owners, the nonsuit in the prior action did not operate to extinguish its right to take a first nonsuit, and the record did not support the heirs' assertion that they were parties to the prior suit as successors in title because assuming that the heirs could establish an ownership interest in the property, the city sought recovery for delinquent taxes for different tax years. City of Suffolk v. Lummis Gin Co., 278 Va. 270, 683 S.E.2d 549, 2009 Va. LEXIS 90 (2009).

Denial of a husband's motion to offset was proper as: (1) the only evidence before the trial court on the payment was that husband made the payment to the wife in error, in reliance upon and at the insistence of the wife's attorney; (2) the husband failed to timely correct the mistake under Va. Sup. Ct. 1:1, and the trial court lacked jurisdiction to correct the error; and (3) the trial court could not have corrected the mistake under subsection B of § 8.01-428 as the mistake was not clerical, but was a failure by the husband to present evidence. Wright v. Wright, 2012 Va. App. LEXIS 120 (Apr. 17, 2012).

Nolle prosequi. — Defendant was not entitled to dismissal based on the prosecutor's nolle prosequi of prior charges, which were identical to charges in the later proceeding, because under § 19.2-265.3, absent vindictive intent resulting in oppressive and unfair trial tactics, or other prosecutorial misconduct, courts deferred to the prosecutor in these circumstances; the presence or absence of good cause in the prior proceeding could not have been collaterally reviewed by the trial court in the later proceeding. It changed nothing that, in the earlier proceeding, an unsuccessful continuance motion preceded the motion for nolle prosequi. Duggins v. Commonwealth, 59 Va. App. 785, 722 S.E.2d 663, 2012 Va. App. LEXIS 80 (2012).

Husband failed to secure the entry of an order staying the execution of orders. — In a divorce action, although the husband timely filed the motions to reconsider the July 9, 2010, orders, he did not secure the entry of an order staying the execution of the July 9, 2010, orders and therefore, the trial court lost jurisdiction to consider the motions after 21 days. Harnois v. Riley-Harnois, 2011 Va. App. LEXIS 311 (Oct. 11, 2011).

Jurisdiction not lost. — Trial court did not lose its jurisdiction 21 days after the entry of a final divorce decree to modify an order intended to divide a husband's pension so as to conform its qualified domestic relations order to effectuate the intent of the original order to divide the husband's pension equally from the date of the decree. Irwin v. Irwin, 47 Va. App. 287, 623 S.E.2d 438, 2005 Va. App. LEXIS 529 (2005).

Trial court retained jurisdiction to reconsider its order when the trial court had to rule on the public authority's motion for satisfaction of judgment regarding the judgment awarded in what otherwise appeared to be the trial court's final order. The trial court could suspend its own order to consider whether the judgment had been satisfied. Upper

Occoquan Sewage Auth. v. Blake Constr. Co., 275 Va. 41, 655 S.E.2d 10, 2008 Va. LEXIS 17 (2008).

Trial court erred in denying defendant's motion to suspend or modify sentence under § 19.2-303 on the ground that it did not have jurisdiction to entertain the motion because the trial court had jurisdiction to entertain the motion when defendant had been convicted of a felony and not yet transferred to the Department; however, the error was harmless because defendant failed to present evidence that would have justified a modification or suspension of her sentence under § 19.2-303. Wilson v. Commonwealth, 54 Va. App. 631, 681 S.E.2d 74, 2009 Va. App. LEXIS 363 (2009).

Authority to modify at time of removal. — Language of 28 U.S.C.S. § 1442 does not distinguish cases that have proceeded to judgment from cases that have not; therefore, in an asbestos case, removal under § 144(a)(1) of a dismissed case was allowed because the state court still had jurisdiction to modify at the time of removal under Va. Sup. Ct. R. 1:1. Because the federal court assumed the case in that posture, it was allowed to correct the state's dismissal order to reflect the true intention of the parties. Holmes v. AC&S, Inc., 388 F. Supp. 2d 663, 2004 U.S. Dist. LEXIS 28566 (E.D. Va. 2004).

Submission to personal jurisdiction by making a personal appearance. — By moving the trial court to vacate its decree while it retained jurisdiction to modify, vacate, or suspend its judgment in a divorce proceeding and by arguing the merits of the case without raising the issue of personal jurisdiction, the husband made a general appearance, waived service of process, and submitted himself to the trial court's jurisdiction. Lee v. Lee, No. 2195-01-2, 2002 Va. App. LEXIS 516 (Ct. of Appeals Aug. 20, 2002).

Tolling of dismissal order. — Appellate court, after finding that the trial court should not have entered its judgment suppressing evidence against defendant, found that it did not need to address the trial court's subsequent dismissal of the three indictments against defendant. Pursuant to § 19.2-400 and Va. Sup. Ct. R. 1:1, the Commonwealth's appeal of the trial court's ruling on the suppression order suspended the dismissal of the indictments pending the Commonwealth's appeal and since the Commonwealth prevailed, the indictments were treated as not having been dismissed at all. Commonwealth v. DeBusk, 2008 Va. App. LEXIS 268 (June 3, 2008).

III. POSTPONEMENT OF EXECUTION IN CRIMINAL CASES.

Finality of judgment not affected. — All final judgments remain under the control of the trial court and are subject to be modified or vacated for 21 days after the date of entry and no longer. In a criminal case the trial court may postpone execution of the sentence in order to give an accused the opportunity to apply for a writ of error and supersedeas. However, this does not affect the finality of the judgment, and the trial court loses control over it after an elapse of 21 days from the date of its entry. Hirschkop v. Commonwealth, 209 Va. 678, 166 S.E.2d 322, cert. denied, 396 U.S. 845, 90 S. Ct. 72, 24 L. Ed. 2d 94 (1969).

Fact that execution of judgment was suspended did not affect the finality of the judgment. Hirschkop v. Commonwealth, 209 Va. 678, 166 S.E.2d 322, cert. denied, 396 U.S. 845, 90 S. Ct. 72, 24 L. Ed. 2d 94 (1969).

Motion for bail. — Construction of § 19.2-319 that allowed a trial court to consider suspending defendant's sentence after defendant had indicated defendant's intention to file a writ of error was not in conflict with Va. Sup. Ct. R. 1:1, but rather was consistent with that rule's express terms, and, thus, the trial court could consider defendant's motion for bail if it suspended defendant's sentence even where defendant had indicated an intent to file a writ of error. Askew v. Commonwealth, 49 Va. App. 127, 638 S.E.2d 118, 2006 Va. App. LEXIS 558 (2006).

CIRCUIT COURT OPINIONS

Pendente lite decree. — The trial court amended a pendente lite order in a divorce action by removing language requiring the husband to pay the wife's uninsured medical expenses as the parties had not agreed on that issue and the issue was never presented to and ruled on by the court; the order was not a final order over which the court no longer had jurisdiction and the removal of the subject language amounted to no more than the correction of a clerical error. Dalton-Reitz v. Reitz, 54 Va. Cir. 187, 2000 Va. Cir. LEXIS 570 (Loudoun 2000).

"Final order" defined. — Parties' divorce decree became final after 21 days and a father did not note a timely appeal; thus, the divorce decree, which imputed income to the father, was final and binding on the parties and a mistake in the imputation of income could not be used as a reason to modify the father's child support obligation. Cherpes v. Cherpes, 2004 Va. Cir. LEXIS 119 (Loudoun County July 7, 2004).

Where an order granted plaintiffs leave to amend within a prescribed time frame but did not explicitly dismiss the case if they failed to do so, dismissal was not warranted, because the order sustaining defendants' demurrer did not become final since the order was not accompanied by language expressly dismissing the case. Kalley v. Long & Foster Real Estate, Inc., 74 Va. Cir. 161, 2007 Va. Cir. LEXIS 176 (Fairfax County 2007).

Order entered more than 21 days after final decree held void. — Juvenile court's attempt to set appeal bonds more than 21 days after the orders were entered were a nullity. Commonwealth v. Neal, 58 Va. Cir. 205, 2002 Va. Cir. LEXIS 142 (Richmond 2002).

Although a group home administrator's second motion for reconsideration was still pending in an administrative appeal of a finding of physical neglect, where the circuit court did not purport to modify, vacate, or suspend its order within 21 days, the matters under consideration were no longer under the circuit court's control pursuant to Va. Sup. Ct. R. 1:1, and the circuit court's later order denying the second motion for reconsideration was a nullity. Wells v. Shenandoah Valley Dep't of Soc.

Servs., 56 Va. App. 208, 692 S.E.2d 286, 2010 Va. App. LEXIS 176 (2010).

Order could be modified for fraud. — While more than 21 days had passed since the entry of the orders finding a father in arrears of his child support obligation and in contempt, under subsection D of § 8.01-428 there was jurisdiction to set aside a judgment or decree for fraud at any time, notwithstanding Va. Sup. Ct. R. 1:1. Hazraty v. Hazraty, 2007 Va. Cir. LEXIS 146 (Fairfax County Aug. 22, 2007).

Jurisdiction directed after 21 days. — Since default judgment in favor of a magazine seller was a final judgment and, pursuant to Rule 1:1, remained within the court's control for 21 days, the court had no jurisdiction to hear purchasers' motion to reconsider which was filed outside of the 21-day period. Haas Publ'g Cos. v. Quantum Communications, Inc., 58 Va. Cir. 319, 2002 Va. Cir. LEXIS 56 (Fairfax County 2002).

Trial court lost power to consider resident's motion to reinstate the resident's case, and other motions, as the trial court's entry of a final judgment, and the fact that there was no challenge to the final order within 21 days after entry of the final order, meant the trial court lost authority over the action. Stearns v. Va. Marine Res. Comm'n, 60 Va. Cir. 296, 2002 Va. Cir. LEXIS 395 (Norfolk 2002).

Circuit court lost jurisdiction over a case because a motion for clarification was not filed until more than 21 days after a final order was entered. Brannon v. Brannon, 2006 Va. Cir. LEXIS 128 (Fairfax County July 17, 2006).

Because more than 21 days had lapsed since the entry of a final sentencing order, and because none of the exceptions in § 19.2-303 applied, the circuit court lacked jurisdiction to alter defendant's sentence under Va. Sup. Ct. R. 1:1. Commonwealth v. Flinchum, 79 Va. Cir. 549, 2009 Va. Cir. LEXIS 224 (Salem Nov. 30, 2009).

Va. Sup. Ct. R. 1:1 precluded a circuit court from entering a second default judgment order in favor of a home owners association because 21 days had passed since entry of the first default judgment order entered in its favor; the first default judgment order constituted a final order because it disposed of all the issues in the case and awarded a judgment against the owner, and that order did not retain any jurisdiction. Reston Home Owners Ass'n v. Ramirez, 2011 Va. Cir. LEXIS 28 (Fairfax County Mar. 15, 2011).

Final judgment. — While trial court had the authority to reserve jurisdiction after the entry of final divorce decree to later enter a qualified domestic relations order, once the order was entered the order became subject to the finality provisions of Rule 1:1 and its substantive provisions could not be changed; thus, the trial court did not have the power to change the order even though the retirement plan argued for such a change because the retirement plan at issue allegedly had declined in value since the divorce hearing. Lewis v. Lewis, 57 Va. Cir. 271, 2002 Va. Cir. LEXIS 205 (Warren County 2002).

When a property owner filed three actions against a property owner's association, two of which were dismissed, the association could not, in the third action, recover attorney's fees against the owner as the prevailing party in the first two cases under § 55-515 of the Virginia Property Owners' Association Act, § 55-508 et seq., because it did not seek such relief in those cases and, under Va. Sup. Ct. R. 1:1, the trial court lost jurisdiction to award it 21 days after entering a final order dismissing the cases, as it did not retain jurisdiction to award attorney's fees at a later time, so the property owner was entitled to summary judgment as to the association's request for fees in the prior cases. Rebarick v. Georgetown Woods Owners Ass'n, 62 Va. Cir. 155, 2003 Va. Cir. LEXIS 96 (Fairfax County 2003).

Where no appeal was taken from an order of expungement in a timely fashion and 21 days had passed from the entry of the order, that order was final. Moran v. Commonwealth, 73 Va. Cir. 241, 2007 Va. Cir. LEXIS 225 (Rockingham County Apr. 4, 2007).

Jurisdiction to award attorney's fees lost after 21 days. — Because an inmate's complaint for a declaratory judgment was untimely under Va. Sup. Ct. R. 1:1, and because the issues raised by the inmate in the complaint had already been considered in the inmate's various appeals and petitions for habeas relief, the circuit court no longer had jurisdiction to rule on the complaint. Lerch v. Commonwealth, 2012 Va. Cir. LEXIS 2 (Norfolk Jan. 11, 2012).

Grant of nonsuit not precluded where an earlier demurrer did not dismiss the action, as there was no final judgment. — Purchaser's motion for nonsuit pursuant to § 8.01-380 in an action alleging misuse of escrow funds was granted, as the grant of a demurrer to sellers was not a final order pursuant to Va. Sup. Ct. R. 1:1, considered in conjunction with Va. Sup. Ct. R. 1:8 and 1:9, even after the purchaser failed to amend the complaint in a timely fashion, and because the matter was not submitted to the court, the purchaser was entitled to a nonsuit as of right. Min Kyu Sue v. Sung Hoon Park, 70 Va. Cir. 113, 2005 Va. Cir. LEXIS 301 (Fairfax County 2005).

Continuance. — Although a General Assembly member made a motion within 21 days from time an order was signed, the order was not changed during the 21-day modification period and, as he was not a counsel of record during the case, statutory continuance was unavailable. Commonwealth v. Johnson, 56 Va. Cir. 476, 2001 Va. Cir. LEXIS 488 (Norfolk 2001).

Discontinuance. — Whereas a case extinguished by a judgment and effectuated by the 21-day rule, codified at § 8.01-428, is fully dispositive of all disputed issues and facts pertaining thereto, a case dismissed pursuant to § 8.01-335 is not dead but in a state of suspended animation. Consequently, the two-year statute affords those parties to dismissed proceedings the opportunity to be heard and have their disputes resolved by the legal system if requested within the statutorily mandated period of time in order to promote the principles of justice without clogging the dockets of Virginia's courts. Cook v. Wayland, 64 Va. Cir. 386, 2004 Va. Cir. LEXIS 60 (Waynesboro 2004).

Prisoner's request for a name change. — Prisoner's petition to have the court amend his sentencing order for the purpose of having the Department of Corrections recognize his name change was denied, because the court lacked the authority to make such a ruling under Va. Sup. Ct. R. 1:1 and subsection B of § 8.01-428. Anderson v. Ray, 63 Va. Cir. 550, 2004 Va. Cir. LEXIS 1 (Portsmouth 2004).

Approval of an accounting by Commission of Accounts not final order. — Approval of an accounting by the Commission of Accounts is not tantamount to a final order under Va. Sup. Ct. R. 1:1 because the Commissioner is a quasi-judicial officer who is not estopped from raising legitimate questions about the propriety of an accounting that have not been previously raised; this is especially true while the matter remains pending before the Commissioner. In re Estate of Clark, 85 Va. Cir. 143, 2012 Va. Cir. LEXIS 78 (Fairfax July 24, 2012).

Rule 1:1A. Recovery of Appellate Attorney's Fees in Circuit Court.

a) Notwithstanding any provision of Rule 1:1, in any civil action in which an appeal lies from the circuit court to the Supreme Court and a petition for appeal is denied by the Supreme Court (and, if a petition for rehearing has been filed pursuant to Rule 5:20, such petition has been denied), an appellee who has recovered attorneys' fees, costs or both in the circuit court pursuant to a contract, statute or other applicable law may make application in the circuit court in which judgment was entered for attorneys' fees, costs or both incurred on appeal. The application must be filed within thirty (30) days after denial of the petition for appeal or of any petition for rehearing, whichever is later, and may be made in the same case from which the appeal was taken, which case shall be reinstated on the circuit court docket upon the filing of the application. The appellee shall not be required to file a separate suit or action to recover the fees and costs incurred on appeal, and the circuit court shall have continuing jurisdiction of the case for the purpose of adjudicating the application. The circuit court's order granting or refusing the application, in whole or in part, shall be a final order for purposes of Rule 1:1.

b) Nothing in this Rule shall restrict or prohibit the exercise of any other right or remedy for the recovery of attorneys' fees or costs, by separate suit or action, or otherwise.

Effective date. — This rule, adopted December 22, 2004, became effective April 1, 2005.

Rule 1:2. Venue in Criminal Cases. (Repealed).

Cross references. — As to venue in criminal cases, see Rule 3A:2.1.

Editor's note. — Repealed by order of court December 20, 2006, effective March 1, 2007.

Rule 1:3. Reporters and Transcripts of Proceedings in Courts.

Reporters shall be first duly sworn to take down and transcribe the proceedings faithfully and accurately to the best of their ability, and shall be subject to the control and discipline of the judge.

When a reporter takes down any proceeding in a court, any person interested shall be entitled to obtain a transcript of the proceedings or any part thereof upon terms and conditions to be fixed in each case by the judge.

The proceedings may be taken down by means of any recording device approved by the judge.

Cross references. — As to criminal practice and procedure in the general district courts, see Rule 7C:4.

Source. — Rule 1:10.

Michie's Jurisprudence. — For related discussion, see 5A M.J. Costs, § 12; 5A M.J. Courts, §§ 26, 27.

CASE NOTES

Transcript denial not harmless error. — Denial of a preliminary hearing transcript for an indigent defendant was not harmless error because the ruling denied defendant equal protection since defendant established a need for the transcript to impeach prosecution witnesses, and at trial, the prosecution relied heavily upon witnesses who testified at the preliminary hearing. Asfaw v. Commonwealth, 56 Va. App. 158, 692 S.E.2d 261, 2010 Va. App. LEXIS 167 (2010).

Rule 1:4. General Provisions as to Pleadings.

(a) Counsel tendering a pleading gives his assurance as an officer of the court that it is filed in good faith and not for delay.

(b) A pleading that is sworn to is an affidavit for all purposes for which an affidavit is required or permitted.

(c) Counsel or an unrepresented party who files a pleading shall sign it and state his address.

(d) Every pleading shall state the facts on which the party relies in numbered paragraphs, and it shall be sufficient if it clearly informs the opposite party of the true nature of the claim or defense.

(e) An allegation of fact in a pleading that is not denied by the adverse party's pleading, when the adverse party is required by these Rules to file such pleading, is deemed to be admitted. An allegation in a pleading that the party does not know whether a fact exists shall be treated as a denial that the fact exists.

(f) Requirements of pleadings applicable to instruments not under seal shall apply to instruments under seal.

(g) Requirements of pleadings applicable to legal defenses shall apply to equitable defenses.

(h) The clerk shall note and attest the filing date on every pleading. In an Electronically Filed Case, the procedures of Rule 1:17 shall be applicable to the notation by the clerk of the date of filing.

(i) The mention in a pleading of an accompanying exhibit shall, of itself and without more, make such exhibit a part of the pleading. Filing of such exhibits shall be governed by Rule 3:4.

(j) Brevity is enjoined as the outstanding characteristic of good pleading. In any pleading a simple statement, in numbered paragraphs, of the essential facts is sufficient.

(k) A party asserting either a claim, counterclaim, cross-claim, or third-party claim or a defense may plead alternative facts and theories of recovery against alternative parties, provided that such claims, defenses, or demands for relief so joined arise out of the same transaction or occurrence. When two or more statements are made in the alternative and one of them if made independently would be sufficient, the pleading is not made insufficient by the insufficiency of one or more of the alternative statements. A party may also state as many separate claims or defenses as he has regardless of consistency and whether based on legal or equitable grounds.

(*l*) Every pleading, motion or other paper served or filed shall contain at the foot the Virginia State Bar number, office address and telephone number of the counsel of record submitting it, along with any electronic mail (E-mail) address and facsimile number regularly used for business purposes by such counsel of record.

Cross references. — As to practice and procedure in the general district courts, see Rule 7A:8.

As to signing of pleadings, motions, and other papers by attorney and effect of such signing of oral motion, see § 8.01-271.1.

Source. — Various rules in Parts Two and Three.

Comment on the 1977 amendment. — The Oct. 1, 1977 amendment added paragraph (k) to conform to § 8.01-281.

The amendment effective February 1, 1999, adopted November 23, 1998, added subdivision (*l*).

The amendment effective May 2, 2011, adopted March 1, 2011, added the last sentence of subdivisions (h) and (i).

The amendment effective January 1, 2013, adopted November 1, 2012, in subdivision (*l*), inserted "Virginia State Bar number," and "any electronic mail (E-mail) address and."

Law Review. — For note, "The Specificity of Pleading in Modern Civil Practice: Addressing Common Misconceptions," see 25 U. Rich. L. Rev. 135 (1990). For annual survey commentary, "The Merger of Common-Law and Equity Pleading in Virginia," see 41 U. Rich. L. Rev. 77 (2006). For annual survey of Virginia law article, "Civil Practice and Procedure," see 47 U. Rich. L. Rev. 113 (2012).

Michie's Jurisprudence. — For related discussion, see 1A M.J. Abatement, Survival and Revival, §§ 22, 23; 1A M.J. Actions, § 18; 1A M.J. Affidavits, § 5; 1B M.J. Appeal and Error, § 178; 3C M.J. Clerks of Court, § 5; 5C M.J. Customs and Usages, § 3; 5C M.J. Damages, §§ 75, 81; 5C M.J. Debt, Action of, §§ 17, 20; 7A M.J. Equity, §§ 53, 54, 94, 97; 7B M.J. Evidence, § 60; 13A M.J. Motions for Judgment, §§ 12, 14, 20; 14A M.J. Parties, § 17; 14B M.J. Pleading, §§ 3, 6, 7, 9, 13, 28, 31, 33, 37,

40, 69; 14B M.J. Profert and Oyer, § 1; 19 M.J. Trial, §§ 5, 12; 19 M.J. Venue, § 20; 20 M.J. Witnesses, § 77.

CASE NOTES

I. General Consideration.
II. Punitive Damages.
III. Defensive Pleadings.

I. GENERAL CONSIDERATION.

Relief not pleaded will not be granted. — Pleadings are as essential as proof, and no relief should be granted that does not substantially accord with the case as made in the pleading. Ted Lansing Supply Co. v. Royal Aluminum & Constr. Corp., 221 Va. 1139, 277 S.E.2d 228 (1981).

No court can base its judgment or decree upon facts not alleged or upon a right which has not been pleaded and claimed. Ted Lansing Supply Co. v. Royal Aluminum & Constr. Corp., 221 Va. 1139, 277 S.E.2d 228 (1981).

Alternative pleading is permitted where the pleader has no knowledge as to which of two sets of facts should be alleged and the opposite party would be equally liable under either. Manassas Park Dev. Co. v. Offutt, 203 Va. 382, 124 S.E.2d 29 (1962).

Because it was a suit in equity and there was no motion for an issue out of chancery, the chancellor correctly held that he must first determine whether the activities complained of constituted a nuisance. Packett v. Herbert, 237 Va. 422, 377 S.E.2d 438 (1989).

Because a stepmother essentially sought alternative theories of recovery, as prescribed by Va. Sup. Ct. R. 1:4(k), and §§ 64.1-77 and 64.1-88, the trial court properly denied the children's motion to dismiss her appeal of a clerk's order concerning a 1995 will based on allegations of approbation and reprobation on her part. Matthews v. Matthews, 277 Va. 522, 675 S.E.2d 157, 2009 Va. LEXIS 58 (2009).

Since Va. Sup. Ct. R. 1:4(k) permitted a party to state in a pleading as many claims as he had regardless of consistency, the fact that a laborer's first count alleged facts that might have framed a cause of action for promissory estoppel, if such had been available, was immaterial to the claim made in his second count for damages based on quantum meruit. Mongold v. Woods, 278 Va. 196, 677 S.E.2d 288, 2009 Va. LEXIS 68 (2009).

Signature on complaint. — Because of the strong public policy considerations underlying § 8.01-271.1, Va. Sup. Ct. R. 1:4 and 1A:4(2), the Supreme Court of Virginia construes them to require that a lawyer who files a pleading in a Virginia tribunal must append his personal, handwritten signature to a pleading; thus, a complaint signed on behalf of a licensed Virginia attorney by an attorney not licensed in Virginia was a nullity and as none of the relation back situations for amending pleadings applied, the defect could not be cured by providing the appropriate signature. Shipe v. Hunter, 280 Va. 480, 699 S.E.2d 519, 2010 Va. LEXIS 231 (2010).

Where a pro se plaintiff signed a motion for judgment an attorney who filed a cover letter to the clerk of the court requesting filing was not the attorney of record in the action. Walker v. Am. Ass'n of Prof'l Eye Care Specialists, P.C., 268 Va. 117, 597 S.E.2d 47, 2004 Va. LEXIS 91 (2004).

Filing of motion to determine marital property rights in divorce action. — Where wife filed within a week after filing her answer and cross-bill to husband's bill of complaint seeking final divorce, and still within the twenty-one day period allotted a separate document in the clerk's office entitled "Motion for Determination of Marital Property Rights," the court held that this instrument was in substantial compliance with the provisions of § 20-107.3, which only required that she "request" the court to apply the provisions of the equitable distribution statute to the case. Gologanoff v. Gologanoff, 6 Va. App. 340, 369 S.E.2d 446 (1988).

Cause of action sufficiently stated. — See Moore v. Jefferson Hosp., 208 Va. 438, 158 S.E.2d 124 (1967).

In a divorce action, a motion filed by a husband for the trial court to set forth the proper division of assets set forth in the parties' outline of settlement terms sufficiently informed the wife of his claim, given the previous proceedings and events in the case. Tobin v. Tobin, 2006 Va. App. LEXIS 231 (Apr. 18, 2006).

Pleadings sufficient. — Because a trustee's claim that an owner's subdivision violated Fauquier County, Va., Subdivision Ordinance § 2-39(3)(C)(3),(4) and (5) did not introduce a new claim, the circuit court erred in refusing to consider her arguments relating to those provisions; pursuant to Va. Sup. Ct. R. 1:4(d), the trustee's allegations were sufficient to put the owner on notice of the "true nature" of the claim because the amended complaint alleged the facts surrounding the execution of the restrictive covenant and the owner's subdivision. Fein v. Payandeh, 284 Va. 599, 734 S.E.2d 655, 2012 Va. LEXIS 196 (2012).

Applied in Stanardsville Volunteer Fire Co. v. Berry, 229 Va. 578, 331 S.E.2d 466 (1985); Lucas v. HCMF Corp., 238 Va. 446, 384 S.E.2d 92 (1989); Hoar v. Great E. Resort Mgt., 256 Va. 374, 506 S.E.2d 777 (1998); Perel v. Brannan, 267 Va. 691, 594 S.E.2d 899, 2004 Va. LEXIS 71 (2004); O'Rourke v. Vuturo, 49 Va. App. 139, 638 S.E.2d 124, 2006 Va. App. LEXIS 572 (2006); Ford Motor Co. v. Benitez, 273 Va. 242, 639 S.E.2d 203, 2007 Va. LEXIS 18 (2007); N. Va. Real Estate, Inc. v. Martins, 283 Va. 86, 720 S.E.2d 121, 2012 Va. LEXIS 11 (2012); Online Res. Corp. v. Lawlor, 285 Va. 40, 736 S.E.2d 886, 2013 Va. LEXIS 2 (2013).

II. PUNITIVE DAMAGES.

Plaintiff must make express claim for punitive damages. — Punitive damages may only be recovered where the plaintiff has made an express claim for them in the prayer for relief or ad damnum clause, sufficient to put the defendant on notice that an award of punitive damages is sought apart from, and in addition to, the compensatory damages claimed. Harrell v. Woodson, 233 Va. 117, 353 S.E.2d 770 (1987).

Failure to state claim for punitive damages. — A motion for judgment which fails to inform the defendant that he will be faced by a claim for punitive damages at trial lacks the fairness, candor, and clarity required by subsection (d) of this rule and former Rule 3:16(b) [see now Rule 3:18]. Harrell v. Woodson, 233 Va. 117, 353 S.E.2d 770 (1987).

III. DEFENSIVE PLEADINGS.

Purpose of a defensive pleading is to inform the opposite party, and to permit the court to determine, what is the true nature of the defense. Unless this purpose is achieved, such a pleading is not sufficient at law. Lumbermen's Mut. Cas. Co. v. Hodge, 205 Va. 36, 135 S.E.2d 187 (1964).

Defense held not to be put in issue. — Where, in an action on an insurance policy, defendant's response did not inform the plaintiff, nor permit the court to determine, that defendant was relying on lack of timely notice as a defense, it was not sufficient to put the question of notice in issue. Lumbermen's Mut. Cas. Co. v. Hodge, 205 Va. 36, 135 S.E.2d 187 (1964).

Statement in defendant's responsive pleading which is no more than an equivocal evasion of an allegation in plaintiff's motion for judgment does not constitute a denial of such allegation. Lumbermen's Mut. Cas. Co. v. Hodge, 205 Va. 36, 135 S.E.2d 187 (1964).

CIRCUIT COURT OPINIONS

Incorporation by reference permitted. — After co-appellant was dismissed from an appeal of an administrative decision, appellant was permitted to proceed on the appeal where he had incorporated by reference in his pleadings the dismissed co-appellant's pleadings and arguments. City of Norfolk Wetlands Bd. v. Va. Marine Resources Comm'n, 54 Va. Cir. 294, 2000 Va. Cir. LEXIS 599 (Norfolk 2000).

Alternative pleading permitted. — While negligence based on a breach of contract and legal malpractice appear to be essentially the same causes of action, §§ 8.01-272 and 8.01-281, and Va. Sup. Ct. R. 1:4 allow a party to plead as many matters, whether of law or fact, as he shall think necessary, as long as the claims arise out of the same transaction or occurrence. Lockney v. Vroom, 61 Va. Cir. 359, 2003 Va. Cir. LEXIS 263 (Norfolk 2003).

Although an administratrix is permitted to proceed both on a survivorship and a wrongful death claim, she can recover on only one theory pursuant to §§ 8.01-25 and 8.01-56. There is no reason to prohibit her from arguing contradictory theories of liability pursuant to § 8.01-281 and Va. Sup. Ct. R. 1:4(k). Williams v. Med. Facilities of Am., 75 Va. Cir. 416, 2005 Va. Cir. LEXIS 380 (Virginia Beach 2005).

Because the responses sought by a hospital from a decedent's survivor attempted to force the survivor to proceed solely under either § 8.01-50 or 8.01-25, which was contrary to § 8.01-281, and improperly forced the survivor to elect his remedies, his answers to two requests for admissions were deemed sufficient. Richard Montgomery Bros. v. Rockingham Mem. Hosp., 75 Va. Cir. 85, 2008 Va. Cir. LEXIS 29 (Rockingham County 2008).

Although creditors' unjust enrichment claim was subject to demurrer, since the complaint contained a factual allegation of the existence of an express contract with the debtors, pursuant to Va. Sup. Ct. R. 1:4(k), the creditors could file an amended complaint containing an alternative count to their breach of contract claim in order to properly assert their unjust enrichment claim. Lemon v. Hufford, 77 Va. Cir. 386, 2009 Va. Cir. LEXIS 95 (Roanoke County 2009).

Cause of action sufficiently stated. — Although a company's claim that it was a third-party beneficiary of a December 24, 2003 contract because the company was a party to a December 29, 2003 contract between itself and an excess insurer and an insurance group was rejected, the company stated a valid cause of action for breach of a third-party beneficiary contract under § 55-22 by adequately alleging under Va. Sup. Ct. R. 1:4(d) that when the excess insurers entered into the December 24, 2003 contract with a hospital, those parties intended to directly benefit the company by settling the hospital's claims for payment of company's employee's medical bills, which were covered by the company plan and the excess coverage. Old Dominion Freight Line, Inc. v. Std. Sec. Life Ins. Co., 73 Va. Cir. 441, 2007 Va. Cir. LEXIS 135 (Richmond 2007).

Complaint stated a claim for a Virginia Uniform Trade Secrets Act, § 59.1-336 et seq., violation under the notice pleading rules of Va. Sup. Ct. R. 1:4(d) as it alleged that: (1) an employee acquired a corporation's customer information that the corporation had employed reasonable efforts to keep secret; (2) the employee disseminated that information to a direct competitor; and (3) the employee knew that knowledge of the information was acquired under circumstances giving rise to a duty to maintain its secrecy or limit its use. Strategic Enter. Solutions, Inc. v. Ikuma, 77 Va. Cir. 179, 2008 Va. Cir. LEXIS 144 (Fairfax County 2008).

Father's demurrers to an attorney's complaint alleging that statements the father made in a letter were defamatory and defamatory per se were overruled because the attorney sufficiently stated causes of action; the statements contained in the father's letter imputed conduct tending to injure and prejudice the attorney in his profession, and the father made the statements knowing that they were false or with reckless disregard for their truth. Donner v. Rubin, 77 Va. Cir. 309, 2008 Va. Cir. LEXIS 238 (Chesapeake 2008).

Overruling of plaintiffs' exceptions in an action involving a prescriptive easement was proper, in part because the parties asserting the right to a prescriptive easement adequately pleaded their respective claims; while some of the language used was arguably misplaced or not as precise as it could have been, a full and fair reading of the various pleadings demonstrated that the prescriptive easement claims were sufficiently stated. Further, no motion was filed by plaintiffs concerning the sufficiency of the pleadings and no bill of particulars was requested. Frazier v. Bledsoe, 79 Va. Cir. 278, 2009 Va. Cir. LEXIS 233 (Orange County Sept. 14, 2009).

Property owner's demurrer was overruled on the basis of failure to state sufficient facts to support a landowner's claim of unjust enrichment because whether the property owner was unjustly enriched and whether it was possible for the property to be unjustly enriched were questions of fact to be determined at trial, not on demurrer. Narayanswarup, Inc. v. Doswell Hospitality, L.L.C., 80 Va. Cir. 650, 2010 Va. Cir. LEXIS 183 (Hanover County Aug. 26, 2010).

Property owner's demurrer, which contended that a landowner's complaint failed to allege any ground for punitive damages was overruled because the landowner stated facts sufficient to support its claim for punitive damages, and the landowner properly made an express claim for punitive damages in the ad damnum clause of the complaint; in the complaint, the landowner alleged the trespass of the property owner, a contractor, and a subcontractor was wanton, willful, and intentional and in calculated disregard of it rights, and the complaint further alleged the existence of an agency relationship between the property owner and the contractor and subcontractor and stated that it directed the acts that were the subject of the complaint. Narayanswarup, Inc. v. Doswell Hospitality, L.L.C., 80 Va. Cir. 650, 2010 Va. Cir. LEXIS 183 (Hanover County Aug. 26, 2010).

Property owner's demurrer was overruled on the basis of failure to state sufficient facts to support a landowner's claim that an agency relationship existed because the complaint set forth the essential facts of an agency relationship and informed the property owner of the true nature of the claim; in support of its claim that an agency relationship existed, the landowner alleged that the property directed a contractor to do the acts that were the subject of the complaint and that the contractor and a subcontractor were acting on behalf of and in furtherance of the property owner's business interest when the alleged trespass and conversion occurred. Narayanswarup, Inc. v. Doswell Hospitality, L.L.C., 80 Va. Cir. 650, 2010 Va. Cir. LEXIS 183 (Hanover County Aug. 26, 2010).

Claim alleging that defendants conspired with one another to injure a company in its reputation, trade, business and profession in violation of §§ 18.2-499 and 18.2-500 was sufficient under Va. Sup. Ct. R. 1:4(d) to survive a demurrer as the intracorporate immunity doctrine did not apply to a conspiracy claim against employees, officers or agents who combined to harm their corporation. Colgate v. Disthene Group, Inc., 2013 Va. Cir. LEXIS 9 (Buckingham County Feb. 4, 2013).

Breach of fiduciary duty claim was sufficient under Va. Sup. Ct. R. 1:4(d) to survive a demurrer where the claim alleged that defendants: (1) failed to exercise business judgment; (2) engaged in self-dealing transactions; (3) turned a blind eye to their family's self-dealing transactions; (4) facilitated others' alleged misdeeds; and (5) failed to take action for conversion of the company's assets. Colgate v. Disthene Group, Inc., 2013 Va. Cir. LEXIS 9 (Buckingham County Feb. 4, 2013).

Party was informed of true nature of claim. — Defendants' third-party motion for judgment was sufficient, because it clearly informed the opposing party of their claim of fraud, so the opposing party's demurrer as to their claim was not proper. Colinsky Consulting, Inc. v. Holloway, 57 Va. Cir. 403, 2002 Va. Cir. LEXIS 225 (Norfolk 2002).

As the employee's motion for judgment informed the railroad of the true nature of the employee's negligence claim, and under Rule 1:4(j), the facts were stated with sufficient clearness to prevent surprise and enable the court to proceed upon the merits of the cause, the railroad's demurrer was overruled. Worley v. Norfolk S. Ry. Co., 60 Va. Cir. 228, 2002 Va. Cir. LEXIS 262 (Roanoke 2002).

Failure to inform defendants of true nature of claim. — Demurrer was sustained as to a patient's allegation in a motion for judgment that two doctors and a medical association (physician defendants) were negligent in "such other ways" as might come to light during discovery, as this allegation stated no facts and failed to inform the physician defendants of the true nature of the claim. Elliott v. Cook, 60 Va. Cir. 1, 2002 Va. Cir. LEXIS 121 (Loudoun County 2002).

When plaintiffs' allegation that their claim was based upon "other instruments of writing" did not clearly inform the court of the true nature of plaintiffs' claim based on written documents other than a stock purchase agreement, the court in deciding defendants' demurrer motions would consider only the agreement and the other factual allegations in plaintiffs' bill. Booker v. Humphreys, 73 Va. Cir. 543, 2005 Va. Cir. LEXIS 375 (Lancaster County 2005).

Complaint did not state facts relied upon. — Executives' demurrers to a lender's complaint seeking to recover money it loaned to a corporation were sustained because the complaint stated a bare legal conclusion rather than facts on which the lender relied as required under Va. Sup. Ct. R. 1:4(e). Vogen v. Wener, 84 Va. Cir. 449, 2010 Va. Cir. LEXIS 322 (Roanoke Apr. 23, 2010).

Pleading fraud. — Fraud must be pleaded with specificity so that the defendant may have the opportunity of shaping a defense accordingly; actual fraud must be specifically pleaded with facts supporting the allegation. MDM Assocs. v. Johns Bros. Energy Techs., JFB, Inc., 59 Va. Cir. 295, 2002 Va. Cir. LEXIS 377 (Norfolk July 31, 2002).

Interrogatory answers were sufficient in light of insured's claims under alternative facts or theories. — Where an insured was defended by an insurer under a reservation of rights, and then sued the insurer following the settlement of the claims against the insured, the insured had the burden of proving that the settlement amount was paid in exchange for a covered claim as part of the insured's prima facie case; the insured was required to answer interrogatories, pursuant to Va. Sup. Ct. R. 4:1(b), as to the basis for the insured's claims against the insurer, but in the instant case the insured's answers were sufficient, as the insured was asserting alternative facts or theories of recovery, as permitted under Va. Sup. Ct. R. 1:4(k), and therefore the insurer's motion to compel discovery was denied. RML Corp. v. Assurance Co. of Am.,

60 Va. Cir. 269, 2002 Va. Cir. LEXIS 392 (Norfolk 2002).

Claims with differing procedural rights. — Assertion of different rights of action, with varying procedural rights, in the same proceeding is not authorized; and business that filed an action in equity waived its right to a jury trial on legal claims asserted in its complaint. Builders Floor Serv. v. Kirby, 60 Va. Cir. 171, 2002 Va. Cir. LEXIS 261 (Fairfax County 2002).

Underlying torts of conspiracy claim. — Plaintiff who alleges a conspiracy to commit a tort need not make a separate claim for the underlying tort, but may simply allege the elements of the underlying tort in the pleading; this is consistent with the generally liberal rules of pleading provided by Va. Sup. Ct. R. 1:4(k). Thus, when plaintiff alleged conspiracy to commit actual fraud and constructive fraud, it was not necessary that she also plead separate counts of fraud. Witcher v. Reid, 70 Va. Cir. 415, 2006 Va. Cir. LEXIS 164 (Norfolk 2006).

Negligence claim sufficiently stated. — Student's complaint against an athletic association sufficiently stated a negligence claim arising out of the student's assault at a school during a basketball game because the athletic association knew that assaults had occurred at the school and would continue to occur there, and that the school provided a known target for repeat criminal activity, and the student's claims that the athletic association scheduled the event, oversaw it, and coordinated security, sufficiently alleged that it owed the student a legal duty; the student's claims that the athletic association failed to have adequate security in place, failed to train, failed to warn, and failed to control sufficiently alleged that it breached its duty. The student also sufficiently alleged that the athletic association's breach was the proximate cause of her injuries from the assault. Lane v. St. Paul's College, 77 Va. Cir. 150, 2008 Va. Cir. LEXIS 133 (Brunswick County 2008).

Improper filing of counterclaim. — Retailer's counterclaim against a computer company alleging that the computer company damaged computers and other items, did not bear a file stamp of the court clerk's office as required by Va. Sup. Ct. R. 1:4(h). Cox v. Sounds Unlimited, Inc., 60 Va. Cir. 243, 2002 Va. Cir. LEXIS 416 (Danville 2002).

Election of remedies. — Car buyer, whom was sold what was represented to be a new car that was actually a used car, was awarded damages for both fraud and for a violation of the Virginia Consumer Protection Act; although the buyer properly pleaded alternative theories, the buyer had to elect between remedies, as both causes of action were based upon a single transaction. Wilkins v. Peninsula Motor Cars, Inc., 59 Va. Cir. 329, 2002 Va. Cir. LEXIS 247 (Newport News 2002).

Judicial estoppel. — Defendant was not judicially estopped from seeking relief after a default judgment was entered against him in a law case, based upon his initial pleading in an earlier chancery case he filed, in which he asserted that he had no potential avenue for relief outside of an equitable claim under subsection D of § 8.01-428, as there was no basis to conclude that defendant, or his counsel, had engaged in any improper or inequitable conduct. Cordova v. Alper, 64 Va. Cir. 87, 2004 Va. Cir. LEXIS 36 (Fairfax County 2004).

Attached exhibits. — Where covenants were attached as exhibits to the bill and referred to in the bill, they were a part of the pleading pursuant to Va. Sup. Ct. R. 1:4(i), and could be considered on demurrer. Mut. Funding, Inc. v. Collins, 62 Va. Cir. 34, 2003 Va. Cir. LEXIS 68 (Spotsylvania County 2003).

The court may consider the pleading and the exhibits and take as true "all fair inferences deducible therefrom," however, a demurrer does not admit the correctness of the pleader's conclusions of law, and a court considering a demurrer may ignore a party's factual allegations contradicted by the terms of authentic, unambiguous documents that are properly a part of the pleadings. Allaun v. Scott, 59 Va. Cir. 461, 2002 Va. Cir. LEXIS 360 (Norfolk Sept. 19, 2002).

In a tort action by a decedent's personal representative against twenty-one defendants, including security service companies, the court ignored an alleged copy of a security contract attached to the security service companies' demurrer to a third-party beneficiary claim for breach because neither party submitted the actual contract and review was limited to the sufficiency of the facts pleaded within the four corners of the complaint. Bosworth v. Vornado Realty L.P., 83 Va. Cir. 549, 2010 Va. Cir. LEXIS 206 (Roanoke Dec. 20, 2010).

Leave of court. — Wife's request, which was made in the final portion of a memorandum in opposition, for attorney's fees and costs incurred as a result of her husband's motion for reconsideration and the wife's motion for clarification was denied because the wife could not unilaterally expand the scope of the motion for reconsideration without leave of court, pursuant to Va. Sup. Ct. Rules 3:18(a), 1:4, and 4:15. Brannon v. Brannon, 2006 Va. Cir. LEXIS 128 (Fairfax County July 17, 2006).

Ministerial requirement. — While dismissal of a corporation's administrative appeal could be based on violations of Va. Sup. Ct. R. 1:4, Va. Sup. Ct. R. 2A:4, and Va. Sup. Ct. R. 2A:2, this latter failure to comply with a ministerial requirement was not prejudicial, and was not fatally defective or jurisdictional. Birchwood Motel, Inc. v. Va. Marine Res. Comm'n, 74 Va. Cir. 298, 2007 Va. Cir. LEXIS 188 (Accomack County 2007).

Page length of brief. — Thirty-five page complaint not allowed. In re Scott, 79 Va. Cir. 299, 2009 Va. Cir. LEXIS 83 (Norfolk Sept. 18, 2009).

Good faith basis requirement. — Plea in bar filed by an agent and the agent's assistant in buyers' fraud case was denied because, pursuant to § 8.01-249, the statute of limitations for fraud did not begin to run until the fraud reasonably should have been discovered, and the buyers could only have discovered the alleged fraud of the agent and the agent's assistant through discovery conducted in their original case against the sellers; at the time the buyers filed their first action against the sellers, they arguably lacked any good faith basis, required by Va. Sup. Ct. R. 1:4, to sue the agent and the agent's assistant for fraud. The buyers only knew and could only reasonably have known that the sellers had attempted to conceal alleged defects at the home. Rosenburgs v. Ohlsons, 2008 Va. Cir. LEXIS 71 (Fairfax County Apr. 1, 2008).

Demurrer sustained. — In an action for damages by injured workers, the complaint failed to state causes of action for strict liability, gross negligence, and assault and battery and the demurrer was sustained as to those claims. The use of propane was not an ultra-hazardous activity that allowed for strict liability, failing to properly follow safety precautions was not so extreme as to shock a fair minded person, and there were no facts alleged upon which a claim for assault and battery caused by recklessness could have been based. Foret v. Kellogg, Brown and Root Servs., 79 Va. Cir. 76, 2009 Va. Cir. LEXIS 262 (Chesapeake May 26, 2009).

Demurrers filed by a city and city officials were sustained because a property owner failed to state facts sufficient to allege a violation of the Fourth and Fourteenth Amendments or 42 U.S.C.S. § 1983; the owner did not identify a city policy statement, ordinance, regulation, or decision pursuant to which defendants had acted. Comfort v. City of Norfolk, 82 Va. Cir. 89, 2011 Va. Cir. LEXIS 153 (Norfolk Jan. 6, 2011).

Demurrers filed by a city and city officials were sustained in a property owner's action alleging violations of the Fifth Amendment because the Fifth Amendment protected against deprivations of property by the federal government, and there had been no allegation thereof. Comfort v. City of Norfolk, 82 Va. Cir. 89, 2011 Va. Cir. LEXIS 153 (Norfolk Jan. 6, 2011).

Demurrers filed by a city and city officials were sustained in a property owner's action alleging violations of § 36-105 and the city code because the remedies provided in the Virginia and city codes were exclusive since penal and regulatory statutes did not automatically create private rights of action; § 36-105 provides that the local building departments are responsible for enforcement of the Uniform State Building Code provisions, and the Norfolk, Virginia, City Code provides that the director of public health and certain law-enforcement officers are authorized to enforce its provisions. Comfort v. City of Norfolk, 82 Va. Cir. 89, 2011 Va. Cir. LEXIS 153 (Norfolk Jan. 6, 2011).

Demurrers filed by a city and city officials were sustained because a property owner failed to plead any of the elements necessary to establish a cause of action for negligence. Comfort v. City of Norfolk, 82 Va. Cir. 89, 2011 Va. Cir. LEXIS 153 (Norfolk Jan. 6, 2011).

Demurrer denied. — Although the client's allegations of legal malpractice based on a failure to move to set aside a property settlement agreement were insufficient, the alleged failures to respond to discovery requests, to properly defend against pretrial motions, and to assert valid claims for attorney's fees were sufficient to survive demurrer, and whether or not these alleged failures amounted to breach of duty, whether they caused damages, and if so, in what amount, were questions of fact; if the lawyer desired a more definite statement regarding the alleged failures, he may have moved for a bill of particulars. Because the client alleged facts that put the lawyer on notice as to the nature and character of the claims, the lawyer's demurrer was denied with respect to those alleged failures. McCarthy v. King, 2012 Va. Cir. LEXIS 61 (Fairfax County June 13, 2012).

Complaint considered. — Seller demurred to each of the claims of breach of contract, and in determining if a cause of action was stated for such, the court considered the specific complaint allegations and the language of the contract, which was a part of the pleadings. Langmaid v. Lee V, 2013 Va. Cir. LEXIS 1 (Northumberland County Jan. 9, 2013).

Rule 1:4A. Special Rule for Pleadings in General District Courts. (Repealed.)

Cross references. — As to civil practice and procedure in the general district courts, see Parts Seven A, Seven B.

For pleading requirements in the juvenile and domestic relations district courts, see Part Eight.

Rule 1:5. Counsel.

When used in these Rules, the word "counsel" includes a partnership, a professional corporation or an association of members of the Virginia State Bar practicing under a firm name.

When such firm name is signed to a pleading, notice or brief, the name of at least one individual member or associate of such firm must be signed to it. Papers filed electronically may be signed electronically or by inclusion of a digital image of the signature, as provided in Rule 1:17. Signatures to briefs and petitions for rehearing may be printed or typed and need not be in handwriting.

Service on one member or associate of such firm shall constitute service on the firm. Service is not required to be made on foreign attorneys.

"Counsel of record" includes a counsel or party who has signed a pleading in the case or who has notified the other parties and the clerk in writing that he appears in the case. Counsel of record shall not withdraw from a case except by leave of court after notice to the client of the time and place of a motion for leave to withdraw.

Cross references. — As to practice and procedure in the general district courts, see Rule 7A:3.

Source. — Rule 1:13.

The amendment, effective May 2, 2011, adopted March 1, 2011, added the second sentence of the second paragraph.

Michie's Jurisprudence. — For related discussion, see 2A M.J. Attorney and Client, §§ 10, 11, 16, 19, 25; 19 M.J. Venue, § 20.

CASE NOTES

Once attorney has appeared as counsel of record, service on him is proper until the court enters a withdrawal order. Francis v. Francis, 30 Va. App. 584, 518 S.E.2d 842 (1999).

Until counsel had effectively withdrawn pursuant to the provisions of this section, service upon him was proper. Therefore, wife's contention that she was denied due process was without merit. Francis v. Francis, 30 Va. App. 584, 518 S.E.2d 842 (1999).

Service upon counsel of record during midst of ongoing litigation is notice reasonably calculated to apprise interested parties of the course of the proceedings. Francis v. Francis, 30 Va. App. 584, 518 S.E.2d 842 (1999).

Service on attorney valid where he represented defendant in earlier stage of continuing proceeding. — In a proceeding on a motion to vacate, service of a copy of the motion on the attorney who had been defendant's counsel of record in a prohibition proceeding was not defective, since the two proceedings were continuing stages of a proceeding initiated by the defendant and counsel had never withdrawn by leave of court and notice to defendant, pursuant to this rule. Virginia Dep't of Cors. v. Crowley, 227 Va. 254, 316 S.E.2d 439 (1984).

Service on counsel of record prior to formal withdrawal. — Until a husband's counsel had effectively withdrawn, service upon her was proper and in compliance with this rule, despite the absence of endorsement and actual notice to both the court and opposing counsel that the husband was no longer represented by counsel of record. Hickson v. Hickson, 34 Va. App. 246, 540 S.E.2d 508, 2001 Va. App. LEXIS 29 (2001).

Mere presence not tantamount to written notice of appearance. — Wife's contention that her mere presence and comments at the depositions were tantamount to written notice of appearance in the case is without support in the Rules. Diamond v. Diamond, 20 Va. App. 481, 458 S.E.2d 303 (1995).

Interests were adequately represented where counsel was present throughout hearing. — Wife's interests were adequately represented where her counsel was present throughout a hearing, and the record showed that the trial court did not enter the order granting counsel's motion to withdraw until the conclusion of said hearing. Lwasa v. Lwasa, 2005 Va. App. LEXIS 450 (Nov. 8, 2005).

Pro se litigant held to rules of court. — Appeals court rejected a husband's six claims of error from a QDRO, awarding a wife the gains earned on the portion of his retirement account distributed to her in the couple's divorce decree, as the husband failed to comply with Va. Sup. Ct. R. 5A:20(c) and (e), and despite his pro se status, he was required to comply with the rules of court. Blythe v. Blythe, 2006 Va. App. LEXIS 392 (Aug. 22, 2006).

Invited error. — Defendant's claims that he violated Rules 1:5 and 1:12 by filing pro se motions to modify his sentence while he was represented by counsel, were rejected as defendant filed the pro se motions without the advice of counsel, and filed the motions ex parte, and defense counsel signed the trial court's order suspending his sentence under the designation "I ask for this"; defendant was barred from invoking the claims on appeal as defense counsel was aware that the pro se motions had been filed, yet neither defendant, nor defense counsel, acted to correct the deficiencies. Coe v. Commonwealth, No. 3293-02-2, 2004 Va. App. LEXIS 181 (Ct. of Appeals Mar. 2, 2004).

Where a pro se plaintiff signed a motion for judgment an attorney who filed a cover letter to the clerk of the court requesting filing was not the attorney of record in the action. Walker v. Am. Ass'n of Prof'l Eye Care Specialists, P.C., 268 Va. 117, 597 S.E.2d 47, 2004 Va. LEXIS 91 (2004).

Signature of licensed Virginia counsel required on pleadings. — Because of the strong public policy considerations underlying Va. Code Ann. § 8.01-271.1, Va. Sup. Ct. R. 1:4 and 1A:4(2), the Supreme Court of Virginia construes them to require that a lawyer who files a pleading in a Virginia tribunal must append his personal, handwritten signature to a pleading; thus, a complaint signed on behalf of a licensed Virginia attorney by an attorney not licensed in Virginia was a nullity and as none of the relation back situations for amending pleadings applied, the defect could not be cured by providing the appropriate signature. Shipe v. Hunter, 280 Va. 480, 699 S.E.2d 519, 2010 Va. LEXIS 231 (2010).

Applied in Davis v. Commonwealth, 215 Va. 816, 213 S.E.2d 785 (1975); Autry v. Bryan, 224 Va. 451, 297 S.E.2d 690 (1982).

CIRCUIT COURT OPINIONS

Counsel of record. — Defendant having filed no responsive pleadings, the fact that she appeared and argued before the court did not make her "counsel of record" under Va. Sup. Ct. R. 1:5; therefore, she was not entitled to notice of plaintiff's motion for entry of default judgment. Moreover, having been mailed a copy of the motion, she received sufficient notice under Va. Sup. Ct. R. 3:19(a). Brin v. A Home Come True, Inc., 74 Va. Cir. 45, 2007 Va. Cir. LEXIS 36 (Fairfax County 2007).

OPINIONS OF THE ATTORNEY GENERAL

Rules applicable to Commonwealth's attorney. — Where a Commonwealth's attorney has become "counsel of record" by making an appearance in a particular court, whether in civil or criminal proceedings, Va. Sup. Ct. R. 1.13 and this Rule apply. See opinion of Attorney General to The Honorable Charles E. Dorsey, Chief Judge Twenty-Third Judicial Circuit, 08-056 (10/21/08).

A Commonwealth's attorney is not required to seek leave from the circuit court to withdraw from an appeal of a misdemeanor conviction from general district court, if he has not yet made an appearance in that de novo proceeding. See opinion of Attorney General to The Honorable Charles E. Dorsey, Chief Judge Twenty-Third Judicial Circuit, 08-056 (10/21/08).

Rule 1:6. Res Judicata Claim Preclusion.

(a) *Definition of Cause of Action.* — A party whose claim for relief arising from identified conduct, a transaction, or an occurrence, is decided on the merits by a final judgment, shall be forever barred from prosecuting any second or subsequent civil action against the same opposing party or parties on any claim or cause of action that arises from that same conduct, transaction or occurrence, whether or not the legal theory or rights asserted in the second or subsequent action were raised in the prior lawsuit, and regardless of the legal elements or the evidence upon which any claims in the prior proceeding depended, or the particular remedies sought. A claim for relief pursuant to this rule includes those set forth in a complaint, counterclaim, cross-claim or third-party pleading.

(b) *Effective Date.* — This rule shall apply to all Virginia judgments entered in civil actions commenced after July 1, 2006.

(c) *Exceptions.* — The provisions of this Rule shall not bar a party or a party's insurer from prosecuting separate personal injury and property damage suits arising out of the same conduct, transaction or occurrence, and shall not bar a party who has pursued mechanic's lien remedies pursuant to Virginia Code § 43-1 et seq. from prosecuting a subsequent claim against the same or different defendants for relief not recovered in the prior mechanic's lien proceedings, to the extent heretofore permitted by law.

(d) *Privity.* — The law of privity as heretofore articulated in case law in the Commonwealth of Virginia is unaffected by this Rule and remains intact. For purposes of this Rule, party or parties shall include all named parties and those in privity.

Cross references. — The Rule formerly at this location (Service of Notice to Take Depositions) was rescinded and is now covered in Part Four.

Effective date. — This rule, adopted February 28, 2006, became effective July 1, 2006.

Law Review. — For annual survey commentary, "The Merger of Common-Law and Equity Pleading in Virginia," see 41 U. Rich. L. Rev. 77 (2006). For 2007 annual survey article, "Civil Practice and Procedure," see 42 U. Rich. L. Rev. 229 (2007). For annual survey essay, "Election of Remedies in the Twenty-First Century: Centra Health, Inc. v. Mullins," 44 U. Rich. L. Rev. 149 (2009).

CASE NOTES

Failure to raise matters at an earlier evidentiary hearing. — Judgment that barred the employee in a workers' compensation action from litigating injuries that he alleged in his initial claim but did not raise at his evidentiary hearing was appropriate under Va. Sup. Ct. R. 1:6(a) because the Workers' Compensation Commission applied settled principles of res judicata to bar him from litigating matters he neglected to raise at his earlier evidentiary hearing. Brock v. Voith Siemens Hydro Power Generation, 59 Va. App. 39, 716 S.E.2d 485, 2011 Va. App. LEXIS 325 (2011).

Employment discrimination action barred. — Because plaintiff elected to litigate his wrongful discharge claim in state court, and because he could have asserted his discrimination claims as part of his wrongful discharge action in that court, but failed to do so, plaintiff's Title VII claim was barred by Virginia's claim preclusion doctrine. Ibrahim Martin-Bangura v. Commonwealth Dep't of Mental Health, 640 F. Supp. 2d 729, 2009 U.S. Dist. LEXIS 67800 (E.D. Va. 2009).

Claim was barred. — Res judicata applied to all issues that could have been litigated between a condominium owners' association and a debtor in state court as to user fees assessed against certain storage units prior to 2009, including the set-offs that could have arisen from them and that were asserted by the debtor in its objection to the association's proof of claim. However, the debtor's claim that it was improperly charged an off-site owner fee as a non-resident unit owner arose from different conduct, transactions, and occurrences than those that were the subject of the state court case, and they were not barred. Gordon Props., LLC v. First Owners' Ass'n of Forty Six Hundred Condo. (In re Gordon Props., LLC), 2011 Bankr. LEXIS 2863 (Bankr. E.D. Va. July 21, 2011).

Debtor asserted a setoff for user fees it paid on storage spaces; the condominium association prevailed on this claim in the Circuit Court. Once having litigated this issue, debtor was precluded from litigating it a second time as a setoff. Gordon Props., LLC v. First Owners' Association of Forty Six Hundred Condominium, Inc. (In re Gordon Props., LLC), 2012 Bankr. LEXIS 3868 (Bankr. E.D. Va. Aug. 23, 2012).

Claim not barred. — Circuit court case was about the additional condominium assessments for 2003 through 2008 but the resolution was not on the merits; relief was denied to the association because it had not made the assessment that it sought to collect. Because the resolution was not on the merits, the association, having now made the assessment, was not barred by res judicata from attempting to collect it. Gordon Props., LLC v. First Owners' Association of Forty Six Hundred Condominium, Inc. (In re Gordon Props., LLC), 2012 Bankr. LEXIS 3868 (Bankr. E.D. Va. Aug. 23, 2012).

Off-site owners fees were not part of the prior litigation and were unrelated to the validity or amount of the condominium assessments in issue. They arose from a separate resolution of the board of directors; they were not barred by res judicata because they did not arise from the same transaction as the assessments. Gordon Props., LLC v. First Owners' Association of Forty Six Hundred Condominium, Inc. (In re Gordon Props., LLC), 2012 Bankr. LEXIS 3868 (Bankr. E.D. Va. Aug. 23, 2012).

CIRCUIT COURT OPINIONS

Applicability. — Daughter's plea in bar was overruled in a mother's action alleging fraud and breach of fiduciary duty because a prior order sustaining the daughter's demurrer on those counts in the mother's original complaint was a decision on the merits but was not a final judgment, and the counts of fraud and breach of fiduciary duty were still pending at the time of the mother's voluntary nonsuit in that case; the order granting the nonsuit constituted a final judgment with respect to the counts of fraud and breach of fiduciary duty but was not a decision on the merits, and absent a final judgment on the merits, res judicata and Va. Sup. Ct. R. 1:6 did not apply. Carter v. Brooks, 77 Va. Cir. 363, 2009 Va. Cir. LEXIS 112 (Greensville County 2009).

Transactional principle of Va. Sup. Ct. R. 1:6 did not apply to plaintiffs' case against defendants because plaintiffs' prior chancery action was commenced on November 18, 2005; because subsequent claims are barred on the basis of prior final judgments, the "judgments entered" to which the rule's effective date refers are the final judgments in the original actions, and thus, for a claim to be barred by res judicata under Rule 1:6, both the original action yielding final judgment and the subsequent action had to have been filed after July 1, 2006. Coleman v. Pascarella, 81 Va. Cir. 167, 2010 Va. Cir. LEXIS 300 (Chesapeake Sept. 9, 2010).

Nonsuit of prior claim. — Trial court found that the attorney and law firm's theories of res judicata, collateral estoppel, judicial estoppel, and accord and satisfaction advanced in their plea in bar did not bar the client's present action against them for professional negligence, breach of contract, and breach of fiduciary duty based on a consent decree entered in a prior action where the attorney and law firm collected unpaid legal fees the client owed to them and the client's counterclaim was nonsuited; the effect of the nonsuit was that no ruling was made on the merits of the counterclaim, which meant the trial court could consider the merits of the client's current claims. Russell v. Hartsoe, 2006 Va. Cir. LEXIS 219 (Fairfax County Nov. 9, 2006).

Privity. — All parties in a condominium unit owner's first and second suits were in privity under Va. Sup. Ct. R. 1:6(d) as the owner alleged that a developer's sole shareholder represented the same legal right as the developer, and the owner was derivatively requesting the developer's corporate veil be pierced so personal liability could be imposed on the shareholder; there was no distinction between the legal rights of the developer and the shareholder. Asterita v. Ghent Dev. Partners, 2009 Va. Cir. LEXIS 23 (Norfolk Jan. 6, 2009).

Law firm's suit to have a deed of trust declared void was barred by res judicata because it sought the same relief as a prior suit on behalf of a debtor against the same creditor, and the firm and the debtor were in privity since the debtor had assigned his deed of trust to the firm to secure payment of his legal fees. Law Office of Frank Driscoll, Jr., P.L.L.C. v. Plexus Lending, L.L.C., 78 Va. Cir. 411, 2009 Va. Cir. LEXIS 178 (Norfolk July 14, 2009).

Claim was barred. — Former employee's claim for a second arbitration relating to termination of the employee's employment and non-compete agreement was barred by the doctrine of res judicata, because the identities of parties and of the transaction were the same and the employee had asserted a counterclaim against the employer and could have and should have asserted all claims against the employer at the first arbitration. Winchester Neurological Consultants, Inc. v. Landrio, 74 Va. Cir. 480, 2008 Va. Cir. LEXIS 59 (Winchester 2008).

Claims were barred by res judicata under Va. Sup. Ct. R. 1:6 since a current suit arose from the same occurrence as a prior suit, with a unit owner claiming a different right to a remedy and a different remedy; the violations of the Virginia Condominium Act, § 55-79.39 et seq., and breach of warranty claims could have been brought in the prior suit, and each breach of warranty was listed in the first suit. Asterita v. Ghent Dev. Partners, 2009 Va. Cir. LEXIS 23 (Norfolk Jan. 6, 2009).

Employee's motion to dismiss administrators' actions with prejudice pursuant to Va. Sup. Ct. R. 1:6(a) on the ground that they were barred by the doctrine of res judicata was granted because the prior cases against the employee were dismissed on procedural grounds with prejudice; like dismissals based on a statute of limitations or sovereign immunity, the dismissal was with prejudice and extinguished the viability of the administrators' claims even though the dismissal was not based on an adjudication of the merits. Peterson v. Commonwealth, 84 Va. Cir. 239, 2012 Va. Cir. LEXIS 129 (Montgomery County Jan. 25, 2012).

Clients' legal malpractice action was barred by a prior judgment under the principles of res judicata pursuant to Va. Sup. Ct. R. 1:6 because the parties in a prior action and the current action were identical for purposes of res judicata, and both actions arose from the same conduct, transaction, or occurrence. Estate of Faustina Chiocca v. Spinella, 84 Va. Cir. 493, 2012 Va. Cir. LEXIS 122 (Richmond May 3, 2012).

Claim not barred. — Res judicata did not bar buyers' Virginia Consumer Protection Act claim regarding a $35,000 liquidated damages provision: the buyers could not have raised the claim in the prior seller's prior unlawful detainer action because the general district court did not have jurisdiction over claims exceeding $15,000, pursuant to § 8.01-195.4. Kearney v. Robinson Land Trust, 80 Va. Cir. 467, 2010 Va. Cir. LEXIS 162 (Charlottesville June 29, 2010).

Commonwealth's motion to dismiss administrators' actions with prejudice pursuant to Va. Sup. Ct. R. 1:6(a) on the ground that they were barred by the doctrine of res judicata was denied because although the claims against an employee had been barred, there had been no affirmative finding that he was not negligent. Peterson v. Commonwealth, 84 Va. Cir. 239, 2012 Va. Cir. LEXIS 129 (Montgomery County Jan. 25, 2012).

Rule 1:7. Computation of Time.

Whenever a party is required or permitted under these Rules, or by direction of the court, to do an act within a prescribed time after service of a paper upon counsel of record, three (3) days shall be added to the prescribed time when the paper is served by mail, or one (1) day shall be added to the prescribed time when the paper is served by facsimile, electronic mail or commercial delivery service. With respect to Parts Five and Five A of the Rules, this Rule applies only to the time for filing a brief in opposition.

Cross references. — As to practice and procedure in the general district courts, see Rule 7A:2.

Source. — New; cf. Rule 5:3, § 5.

Comment. — The provisions of former subsection (a) are covered by Code § 1-13.3:1. The addition of the second sentence of the retained paragraph merely explicates the current application of the three-day rule.

The amendment, effective February 1, 1999, adopted November 23, 1998, in the first sentence, substituted "counsel of record" for "him and the paper is served by mail," inserted "(3)" following "three," and substituted "time when the paper is served by mail, or one (1) day shall be added to the prescribed time when the paper is served by facsimile or commercial delivery service" for "period."

The amendment, effective October 15, 2003, adopted August 15, 2003, inserted "or by direction of the court" following "under these Rules" near the beginning, and "electronic mail" following "by facsimile" near the end, of the first sentence.

Law Review. — For survey of Virginia law on practice and pleading in the year 1971-1972, see 58 Va. L. Rev. 1309 (1972). For 2003/2004 survey of civil practice and procedure, see 39 U. Rich. L. Rev. 87 (2004).

Michie's Jurisprudence. — For related discussion, see 1A M.J. Abatement, Survival and Revival, § 21; 2A M.J. Assumpsit, § 55; 13A M.J. Motions for Judgment, § 18.

Rule 1:8. Amendments.

No amendments shall be made to any pleading after it is filed save by leave of court. Leave to amend shall be liberally granted in furtherance of the ends of justice. Unless otherwise provided by order of the court in a particular case, any written motion for leave to file an amended pleading shall be accompanied by a properly executed proposed amended pleading, in a form suitable for filing. If the motion is granted, the amended pleading accompanying the motion shall be deemed filed in the clerk's office as of the date of the court's order permitting such amendment. If the motion is granted in part, the court may provide for filing an amended pleading as the court may deem reasonable and proper. Where leave to amend is granted other than upon a written motion, whether on demurrer or oral motion or otherwise, the amended pleading shall be filed within 21 days after leave to amend is granted or in such time as the court may prescribe. In granting leave to amend, the court may make such provision for notice thereof and opportunity to make response as the court may deem reasonable and proper.

Cross references. — As to practice and procedure in the general district courts, see Rule 7A:9.

Source. — Rules 2:12, 3:13.

The amendment, effective May 2, 2011, adopted March 1, 2011, rewrote the Rule.

Michie's Jurisprudence. — For related discussion, see 1A M.J. Accounts and Accounting, § 13; 1B M.J. Amendments, §§ 2, 3, 6, 11, 12, 14, 17, 28, 29, 33, 34, 35, 38, 39; 1B M.J. Appeal and Error, § 189; 5A M.J. Costs, § 6; 5C M.J. Debt, Action of, § 26; 7A M.J. Equity, § 64; 12A M.J. Limitation of Actions, § 38; 13A M.J. Motions for Judgment, § 13; 16 M.J. Seduction, § 16.

CASE NOTES

Amendments to pleadings may only be made with leave of court under this rule. Griffin v. Rainer, 212 Va. 627, 186 S.E.2d 10 (1972).

The tendency of modern decisions is reflected in the rule which directs that "Leave to amend shall be liberally granted in furtherance of the ends of justice." Jacobson v. Southern Biscuit Co., 198 Va. 813, 97 S.E.2d 1 (1957); Goode v. Courtney, 200 Va. 804, 108 S.E.2d 396 (1959).

Discretion of court. — The right to file amended pleadings pursuant to this rule rests in the sound discretion of the court, but shall be liberally granted in furtherance of the ends of justice. Bentz v. Bentz, 2 Va. App. 486, 345 S.E.2d 773 (1986).

Whether to grant an amendment is a matter resting within the sound discretion of the trial court. Kole v. City of Chesapeake, 247 Va. 51, 439 S.E.2d 405 (1994).

Where nothing in the record suggested that the defendants would have been prejudiced by allowing an amended motion for judgment and plaintiff had not previously amended his motion, the trial court abused its discretion in failing to allow this motion. Mortarino v. Consultant Eng'g Servs., Inc., 251 Va. 289, 467 S.E.2d 778 (1996).

Court is expressly authorized to impose conditions to the granting of leave to amend pleadings. Haymore v. Brizendine, 210 Va. 578, 172 S.E.2d 774 (1970).

Action constituting substantial compliance with the trial court's decree permitting amendment was sufficient to prevent dismissal with prejudice. Pennsylvania-Little Creek Corp. v. Cobb, 215 Va. 44, 205 S.E.2d 661 (1974).

Failure to comply with conditions for amendment. — The trial court, in the exercise of its discretion, may permit a litigant to amend his motion for judgment, and impose such terms and conditions as may be reasonable and proper, and if the litigant fails to comply with the conditions within the time specified, he is barred from further prosecution of the same cause, against the same parties. Bibber v. McCreary, 194 Va. 394, 73 S.E.2d 382 (1952).

Effect of failure to amend on federal habeas corpus petition. — Inmate was properly denied habeas corpus relief on his claim that he could not be executed because he was mentally retarded because the claim was not fairly presented to the state supreme court, as the inmate could have, but chose not to, amend his state habeas petition to add his *Atkins* claim. The claim was procedurally defaulted because the inmate could not return to state court to file a new state habeas petition, as § 8.01-654.1 precluded consideration of the claim. Hedrick v. True, 443 F.3d 342, 2006 U.S. App. LEXIS 7904 (4th Cir. 2006), cert. denied, 548 U.S. 928, 127 S. Ct. 10, 165 L. Ed. 2d 992 (2006).

Amended motions without leave of court. — Plaintiff's amended motion was without legal efficacy because he failed to obtain leave of court to amend his original motion for judgment; thus, the court did not acquire jurisdiction to adjudicate any causes of action alleged in the amended motion. Mechtensimer v. Wilson, 246 Va. 121, 431 S.E.2d 301 (1993).

Because a wife failed to request permanent or temporary spousal support in any valid pleading, and because the wife failed to comply with subdivision (9)(a) of § 20-91 and Va. Sup. Ct. R. 1:8, it was error for the trial court to grant a reservation of spousal support to her pursuant to § 20-107.1. Harrell v. Harrell, 272 Va. 652, 636 S.E.2d 391, 2006 Va. LEXIS 105 (2006).

Allowing further pleadings where party fails to fully adhere to decree allowing amendments. — If plaintiff had not, in the opinion of the trial court, fully adhered to the language of its decree allowing amendment, that court should have granted plaintiff's motion, made both orally and in writing, for leave to permit the filing of further pleadings. Pennsylvania-Little Creek Corp. v. Cobb, 215 Va. 44, 205 S.E.2d 661 (1974).

Failing to allow amendment abuse of discretion. — Where nothing in the record suggested that city would have been prejudiced by allowance of the amended bill of complaint by landowners in challenge to the city's rezoning ordinance, trial court abused its discretion in failing to allow the filing of the amended bill. Kole v. City of Chesapeake, 247 Va. 51, 439 S.E.2d 405 (1994).

Because a wife's Va. Sup. Ct. R. 1:8 motion to amend her answer was not merely a way to avoid trial, and because the husband should have been prepared to litigate the equitable distribution of marital property under § 20-107.3 as there was no property settlement agreement, the wife's motion for leave to amend should have been granted. Costanzo v. Costanzo, 2009 Va. App. LEXIS 38 (Feb. 3, 2009).

Refusal to allow amendment necessitating new trial or reopening of case. — The trial court did not abuse its discretion in overruling the motion to amend after the taking of evidence had been completed and each side had rested, where to have granted the motion at that time would have necessitated either a new trial or a reopening of the case for the taking of evidence on an issue not previously raised at the trial. Griffin v. Rainer, 212 Va. 627, 186 S.E.2d 10 (1972).

Allowing defendant to amend and rely on statute of limitations. — The court did not abuse its discretion when it allowed defendants to amend and rely upon the statute of limitations. Herndon v. Wickham, 198 Va. 824, 97 S.E.2d 5 (1957).

Intervener's claim must be germane to subject matter of suit. — Even though under this rule leave to amend should be granted liberally by the trial court in furtherance of the ends of justice, under former Rule 2:15 [see now Rule 3:14] a new party may not intervene and assert a claim in a pending suit unless the claim is "germane to the subject matter of the suit." Layton v. Seawall Enters., Inc., 231 Va. 402, 344 S.E.2d 896 (1986).

May not substitute new plaintiff for one who lacked standing. — Rule that even an amendment substituting a new plaintiff or defendant for an original party may be granted if the substituted party bears a real relation of interest to the original party and no new cause of action is introduced has always been subject to the limitation that a new plaintiff may not be substituted for an original plaintiff who lacked standing to bring the suit. Chesapeake House on Bay, Inc. v. Virginia Nat'l Bank, 231 Va. 440, 344 S.E.2d 913 (1986).

Amendment of pleading and decree based on "record evidence" as to last place of marital cohabitation. — Where there was ample unrefuted "record evidence" that the last place of marital cohabitation, as properly defined in the context of the divorce venue statute, between parties who were discovered in 1966 was in the City of Alexandria, the trial court had the inherent power to allow an appropriate amendment to the bill of complaint to disregard the erroneous conclusion of law contained in the commissioner's report, stating that the parties last cohabited in Danville, and to amend its final decree of divorce nunc pro tunc, in order to make the record "speak the truth." Netzer v. Reynolds, 231 Va. 444, 345 S.E.2d 291 (1986).

Grounds for divorce. — A trial court is authorized by Rule 1:8 and Code § 8.01-377 to permit a party to amend pleadings to allege a different or dual grounds of divorce from that initially pleaded. Megill v. Megill, No. 1906-96-2 (Ct. of Appeals Apr. 29, 1997).

Post-verdict amendments to ad damnum not allowed. — In a case involving an unliquidated damage claim for personal injury, post-verdict amendments increasing the ad damnum may not be granted. This rule simply does not bear upon post-verdict amendments such as this. Powell v. Sears, Roebuck & Co., 231 Va. 464, 344 S.E.2d 916 (1986).

Effective date of amended complaint. — Administrator's amended complaint was properly dismissed on statute of limitations grounds because, while the administrator had moved to amend three days before the statute of limitations expired, Va. Sup. Ct. R. 1:8 required leave of court to amend a pleading, so the amended complaint was without legal efficacy until leave to amend was granted. Ahari v. Morrison, 275 Va. 92, 654 S.E.2d 891, 2008 Va. LEXIS 8 (2008).

Amendments allowed. — Property owners who failed to state a justiciable controversy for purposes of their declaratory judgment actions, such that a demurrer due to their lack of standing was sustained, were entitled to an opportunity to amend their complaints pursuant to Va. Sup. Ct. R. 1:8, as such amendment served the ends of justice. Barnes v. Orange County BOS, 78 Va. Cir. 392, 2009 Va. Cir. LEXIS 223 (June 22, 2009).

Circuit court did not err in allowing a father leave to amend a petition for review to conform with Va. Sup. Ct. R. 2A:4(b) becuase Va. Sup. Ct. R. 1:8 applied to agency appeals. Chabolla v. Va. Dep't of Soc. Servs., 55 Va. App. 531, 687 S.E.2d 85, 2010 Va. App. LEXIS 1 (Jan. 12, 2010).

Where the Commonwealth initially relied on an opinion of a psychologist who was not qualified in treatment under subsection B of § 37.2-904 of the Virginia Sexually Violent Predator Act, § 37.2-900 et seq., the trial court did not abuse its discretion by granting the Commonwealth motion to file an amended commitment petition which substituted a second psychologist's report for the initial report. Warrington v. Commonwealth, 280 Va. 365, 699 S.E.2d 233, 2010 Va. LEXIS 238 (2010).

Amendments properly denied. — Where complainant, seeking to enforce a mechanic's lien, stated that his original bill had inadvertently identified the wrong lien and proffered an amendment identifying a second lien, it was held that the amendment was properly denied on the ground that it introduced "a new or different demand," in that the two liens affected different parties; they came into existence at different times; their terminal dates were different; and, as against other lienholders, they created different priorities. On the date complainant made his motion to amend, it was too late to bring a new suit to enforce the second lien; the right and its remedy, both creatures of statute, had expired. The chancellor could not judicially create a new right and a new remedy to enforce it by granting motion and allowing the proffered amendment to "relate back" to the date suit was filed on the first lien. Neff v. Garrard, 216 Va. 496, 219 S.E.2d 878 (1975).

Where insureds expressly limited their claim against insurer under a fire insurance policy to the motel expenses they had incurred and did not include a claim for damages to the residence or personal property, the insurer requested that all issues be resolved by the court in one action, the insureds did not accept that request and delayed resolution of the additional living-expenses claim with motions, amendments, and a request for a continuance, the insureds did not seek to join their claims for dwelling and property damage with their claim for additional living expenses until 27 months after the loss and 22 months after the action was filed, and by the time the insureds moved to amend the warrant to include these two claims, discovery and preparation for trial on the single issue of additional living expenses was virtually complete, the trial court did not abuse its discretion by denying the insureds' motion to amend. Hetland v. Worcester Mut. Ins. Co., 231 Va. 44, 340 S.E.2d 574 (1986).

Because an administrator could only prosecute a wrongful death action on behalf of the beneficiaries identified in § 8.01-53, the administrator was not entitled to file the action pro se; therefore, in the absence of a valid motion for judgment, there were no pleadings that could be amended. Kone v. Wilson, 272 Va. 59, 630 S.E.2d 744, 2006 Va. LEXIS 70 (2006).

In a divorce action, denial of leave to amend to include a request for spousal support was proper because the request was an attempt to circumvent a ruling denying the former husband's motion to file a cross-complaint, and allowing such an amendment would have resulted in delay. Ritter v. Ritter, 2009 Va. App. LEXIS 529 (Dec. 1, 2009).

Amendment improperly denied. — Trial court erred in denying a husband's Va. Sup. Ct. R. 1:8 motion to amend the complaint to include a prayer for spousal support in a divorce action, as the wife knew early in the proceedings that the husband was going to request support, so the grant of leave to amend would not have prejudiced the wife. Dritselis v. Dritselis, 2005 Va. App. LEXIS 451 (Nov. 8, 2005).

Trial court abused its discretion in denying the surety's motion for leave to amend its pleading in order to assert that it had the right to recover under the takeover agreements that it had entered into with the state transportation department, as those agreements provided a possible basis for the surety to recover from the state transportation department. XL Specialty Ins. Co. v. Commonwealth, 47 Va. App. 424, 624 S.E.2d 658, 2006 Va. App. LEXIS 14 (2006).

Applied in Haymore v. Brizendine, 210 Va. 578, 172 S.E.2d 774 (1970); Griffin v. Rainer, 212 Va. 627, 186 S.E.2d 10 (1972); Niese v. Klos, 216 Va. 701, 222 S.E.2d 798 (1976); Roberts v. Roberts, 223 Va. 736, 292 S.E.2d 370 (1982); Bell v. Kirby, 226 Va. 641, 311 S.E.2d 799 (1984); Seidman v. Fishburne-Hudgins Educ. Found., Inc., 724 F.2d 413 (4th Cir. 1984); Mallory v. Smith, 27 F.3d 991 (4th Cir. 1994); Orbe v. True, 233 F. Supp. 2d 749, 2002 U.S. Dist. LEXIS 22958 (E.D. Va. 2002); Billups v. Carter, 268 Va. 701, 604 S.E.2d 414, 2004 Va. LEXIS 139 (2004); Ford Motor Co. v. Benitez, 273 Va. 242, 639 S.E.2d 203, 2007 Va. LEXIS 18 (2007); Addison v. Jurgelsky, 281 Va. 205, 704 S.E.2d 402, 2011 Va. LEXIS 16 (2011); Online Res. Corp. v. Lawlor, 285 Va. 40, 736 S.E.2d 886, 2013 Va. LEXIS 2 (2013).

CIRCUIT COURT OPINIONS

Lack of prejudice justifies amendment. — Where petitioners sought to amend their pleadings less than four months after they filed a declaratory judgment action, had not sought to amend before, had done nothing to delay or hinder the resolution of this case, and the amendment would not prejudice defendants, the amendment was allowed. Petitioners had no burden under the rules to show that the amendment would not be futile or to produce a copy of their proposed amendment. Booher v. Bd. of Supervisors, 65 Va. Cir. 53, 2004 Va. Cir. LEXIS 77 (Botetourt County 2004).

Time of filing of amended pleading. — Failure to comply with the rule divested the trial court of jurisdiction to adjudicate on the amended pleadings. Verdolotti v. Chung, 56 Va. Cir. 358, 2001 Va. Cir. LEXIS 126 (Portsmouth 2001).

Where a customer raised new slander claims for the first time in an amended motion for judgment and the statute of limitations had not been tolled, the new claims were barred by the statute of limitations; in addition, because the only alleged claim in the original motion that had not been barred by the statute of limitations was not alleged in the amended motion, there was nothing for the court to decide. Armstrong v. Bank of Am., 61 Va. Cir. 131, 2003 Va. Cir. LEXIS 57 (Fairfax County 2003).

Grant of nonsuit not precluded where an earlier demurrer did not dismiss the action, even where the pleadings were not amended in a timely fashion. — Purchaser's motion for nonsuit pursuant to § 8.01-380 in an action alleging misuse of escrow funds was granted, as the grant of a demurrer to sellers was not a final order pursuant to Va. Sup. Ct. R. 1:1, considered in conjunction with Va. Sup. Ct. R. 1:8 and 1:9, even after the purchaser failed to amend the complaint in a timely fashion, and because the matter was not submitted to the court, the purchaser was entitled to a nonsuit as of right. Min Kyu Sue v. Sung Hoon Park, 70 Va. Cir. 113, 2005 Va. Cir. LEXIS 301 (Fairfax County 2005).

Discretion of court. — Amendments to add or substitute a proper party lie within the discretion of the court under § 8.01-5; under Rule 1:8 no amendments shall be made to any pleading after it is filed save by leave of court. Gearing v. Every Citizen Has Opportunities, Inc., 59 Va. Cir. 41, 2002 Va. Cir. LEXIS 118 (Loudoun County 2002).

Where the debtor's demurrer in the lender's action alleging fraud and seeking punitive damages was granted, the lender was given leave to amend his motion for judgment pursuant to Va. Sup. Ct. R. 1:8. Amburgery v. Peters, 61 Va. Cir. 266, 2003 Va. Cir. LEXIS 34 (Roanoke 2003).

Congregations seeking a determination regarding the division of church property pursuant to subsection A of § 57-9, following the congregations' separation from the diocese, would be severely prejudiced if the trial court granted the diocese's motion for leave to amend to "clarify" answers that the diocese provided in the case. Even under Va. Sup. Ct. R. 1:8's liberal standard for allowing leave to amend pleadings, allowing leave to amend in the present case would be improper because the diocese had not previously raised the affirmative defense of waiver, the diocese had already long ago forced the congregations to defend against the claim that the statute had not been properly invoked and was not constitutional, and the diocese was trying to claim through its "clarification" that the statute did not apply at all. In re Multi-Circuit Episcopal Church Prop. Litig., 76 Va. Cir. 947, 2008 Va. Cir. LEXIS 104 (Fairfax County 2008).

Amended complaint dismissed. — Amended complaint was dismissed because, by filing the amended complaint past the date it was conditioned on, plaintiffs no longer had leave by the court to file it, and under Va. Sup. Ct. R. 1:8, the amended complaint lacked legal efficacy; to have entered an order nunc pro tunc with a later filing date would have improperly created a fiction that plaintiff had timely filed for a leave to extend the original filing date, and such an order would have been beyond the scope of the powers of the court. An extension in this case would have been outside the scope of when a discretionary extension should have been granted under Va. Sup. Ct. R. 1:9. Bates v. Merritt, 83 Va. Cir. 134, 2011 Va. Cir. LEXIS 239 (Loudoun County June 29, 2011).

Amending the ad damnum. — Where a default judgment was equivalent to a verdict, and the case involved unliquidated contractual damages, a general contractor could not amend a post-default judgment to increase an ad damnum. Callahan Constr., Inc. v. Hardy Plumbing Heating Corp., 61 Va. Cir. 714, 2002 Va. Cir. LEXIS 317 (Roanoke 2002).

Plaintiff's motion for leave to file an amended

complaint, to increase the amount of damages requested in the ad damnum clause, was granted because the plaintiff was entitled under § 16.1-114.1 and Va. Sup. Ct. R. 1:8 to seek an amendment following an appeal by a defendant in an attempt to procure full compensation for damages suffered. The court, in making its determination, noted that: (1) there was no showing that either the defendant or the codefendant would have been prejudiced by an amendment increasing the ad damnum clause; (2) the motion for leave to amend was the plaintiff's first request to amend the complaint; and (3) the parties had ample time to prepare based on the increased ad damnum clause because the trial was more than six months away. Khan v. Washington, 74 Va. Cir. 95, 2007 Va. Cir. LEXIS 255 (Alexandria 2007).

Efficacy of amended complaint. — Where plaintiffs attached an amended complaint to their opposition to defendants' demurrer, the amended complaint filed as an attachment to the demurrer opposition was without legal efficacy because the amended complaint was filed without leave of court. Kalley v. Long & Foster Real Estate, Inc., 74 Va. Cir. 161, 2007 Va. Cir. LEXIS 176 (Fairfax County 2007).

Former employee's motion to amend his complaint to add a "procuring cause" claim was denied, because procuring cause was neither a cause of action nor a remedy, but an element of proof in a cause of action to recover a commission for breach of an agency or brokerage agreement. Studer v. Hurley, 82 Va. Cir. 406, 2011 Va. Cir. LEXIS 146 (Norfolk Mar. 29, 2011).

Court denied a former employee's motion to amend his complaint to add a declaratory judgment claim, as an action for breach of contract was the proper procedure. Studer v. Hurley, 82 Va. Cir. 406, 2011 Va. Cir. LEXIS 146 (Norfolk Mar. 29, 2011).

Former employee's motion to amend his complaint to add a constructive trust claim was denied because the amended complaint did not allege fraud or unconscionable conduct by defendants. Studer v. Hurley, 82 Va. Cir. 406, 2011 Va. Cir. LEXIS 146 (Norfolk Mar. 29, 2011).

Former employee's motion to amend his complaint to add a quantum meruit claim was denied, as such a claim was inconsistent with his status as an at-will employee. Studer v. Hurley, 82 Va. Cir. 406, 2011 Va. Cir. LEXIS 146 (Norfolk Mar. 29, 2011).

Proposed amendment failed to state a claim. — Former employee's motion to amend his complaint to add a breach of contract claim was denied because, as an at-will employee, he was not entitled to post-termination profits, and an alleged "agreement in principle" to pay a severance package was unenforceable. Studer v. Hurley, 82 Va. Cir. 406, 2011 Va. Cir. LEXIS 146 (Norfolk Mar. 29, 2011).

Amendments allowed. — In a municipal employee grievance matter, the grievants were to be permitted to amend their grievances to conform their grievances to the evidence. Drewery v. City of Roanoke, 63 Va. Cir. 609, 2001 Va. Cir. LEXIS 512 (Roanoke 2001).

Although plaintiff selected only the "contract" box on warrant in debt, plaintiff was permitted to amend its pleadings to include damages not arising from contract because, in light of the trial occurring in the lower court, the tenant could not claim that she was not properly informed as to the true nature of the claims against her. Amendment was permitted under § 16.1-114.1 and Va. Sup. Ct. R. 1:8. PNG Invs., L.L.C. v. Gravely-Robinson, 71 Va. Cir. 140, 2006 Va. Cir. LEXIS 242 (Roanoke County 2006).

Leave to amend was proper under Va. Sup. Ct. R. 1:8 as a homeowners' association would not be prejudiced from granting such leave and no previous request for an amendment had been granted. Pedigo v. Flattop Mt. Landowners Ass'n, 73 Va. Cir. 26, 2007 Va. Cir. LEXIS 54 (Greene County 2007).

Because the amendments that proposes by plaintiff only augmented existing claims and did not add new ones, and in light of the court's ruling on defendants' demurrers, it was unlikely that defendants would find it necessary to file new dispositive motion, the court granted plaintiff's motion to amend her complaint. Guilliams v. Wray, 79 Va. Cir. 244, 2009 Va. Cir. LEXIS 86 (Roanoke Sept. 9, 2009).

Because the guarantor's liability was dependent upon a breach by the second corporation, and because the complaint failed to allege or imply any breach by that second corporation, the company's complaint failed to state a claim against the guarantor; however, the company was granted leave to amend the complaint because there had been no prior amendments and the parties would not experience any undue delay. Reese Merifalls, LLC v. Park's Rest. Enters., 2010 Va. Cir. LEXIS 29 (Fairfax County Mar. 1, 2010).

Amendments not allowed. — Because new discovery would be required, a bank would be substantially prejudiced if a company's amendments were allowed; therefore, the company's motion to amend its answer and grounds for defense was denied. Banc of Am. Leasing & Capital v. ePLUS Group, 70 Va. Cir. 380, 2006 Va. Cir. LEXIS 47 (Fairfax County 2006).

Defendants' motion to amend in order to file a third-party complaint and a counterclaim was denied, as allowing the amendment would not serve the ends of justice. The counterclaim was barred by res judicata, and allowing individual members of a condominium association to be joined as third-party defendants was improper under § 55-79.80:1, which required that tort and contract actions involving condominiums be brought against the association. Highridge Place Condo. Unit Owner's Ass'n v. Langley, 72 Va. Cir. 21, 2006 Va. Cir. LEXIS 187 (Nelson County 2006).

Diocese could not pursuant to Va. Sup. Ct. R. 1:8 amend its answers that it filed to the congregations' § 57-9 petitions seeking decisions about how church property would be divided. The diocese claimed that the petitions violated § 57-2.02, but any amendment the trial court could have granted would have been futile given that § 57-2.02, aimed at preserving religious freedom, did not apply to private parties, such as the diocese and congregation in the present case. In re Multi-Circuit Episcopal Church Prop. Litig., 76 Va. Cir. 873, 2008 Va. Cir. LEXIS 49 (Fairfax County 2008).

Former employee's motion to amend his complaint against his former employers to add a claim for an accounting under § 8.01-31 was denied; as an employer had no fiduciary duty to an employee and the parties were not joint tenants, tenants in common, or coparceners, § 8.01-31 was not applicable. Studer v. Hurley, 82 Va. Cir. 406, 2011 Va. Cir. LEXIS 146 (Norfolk Mar. 29, 2011).

Rule 1:9. Discretion of Court.

All steps and procedures in the clerk's office touching the filing of pleadings and the maturing of suits or actions may be reviewed and corrected by the court.

The time allowed for filing pleadings may be extended by the court in its discretion and such extension may be granted although the time fixed already has expired; but the time fixed for the filing of a motion challenging the venue shall in no case be extended except to the extent permitted by § 8.01-264.

Cross references. — As to practice and procedure in the general district courts, see Rule 7A:5.

Source. — Rules 2:23, 3:13.

Comment on the 1977 amendment. — Pleas in abatement have been abolished by § 8.01-276 and references to such pleas have been eliminated from the Rules by the amendments effective Oct. 1, 1977. Matters formerly raised by a plea in abatement should be raised by written motion. The principal purpose of a plea in abatement is to challenge venue; that is now to be done by motion within the time limits established by § 8.01-264.

Michie's Jurisprudence. — For related discussion, see 2A M.J. Assault and Battery, § 21; 2A M.J. Assumpsit, § 55; 7A M.J. Equity, § 70; 14B M.J. Pleading, §§ 5, 38, 39; 19 M.J. Trial, §§ 7, 8; 19 M.J. Venue, § 16.

CASE NOTES

Discretion depends upon circumstances of particular case. — By the express terms of this rule extension of the time for filing pleadings, including an answer, is left to the discretion of the trial court. Whether such discretion has been properly exercised will, of course, depend upon the circumstances of the particular case. Westfall v. Westfall, 196 Va. 97, 82 S.E.2d 487 (1954).

Denial of extension not abuse of discretion absent motion therefor. — There was no abuse of discretion by the trial court in failing to extend time where defendant never moved for such extension and where, furthermore, defendant offered no excuse for the delay. Levine v. Lacy, 204 Va. 297, 130 S.E.2d 443, cert. denied, 375 U.S. 932, 84 S. Ct. 330, 11 L. Ed. 2d 264 (1963), reh'g denied, 375 U.S. 982, 84 S. Ct. 479, 11 L. Ed. 2d 428 (1964).

Under the circumstances, there was no abuse of discretion in allowing defendant's answer to be filed on the day of trial. American Liberty Ins. Co. v. Breslerman, 201 Va. 822, 113 S.E.2d 862 (1960).

Filing of amended pleading. — The trial court may in its discretion permit the filing of an amended pleading even though the time previously fixed by the court for such filing has expired. Commercial & Sav. Bank v. Maher, 202 Va. 286, 117 S.E.2d 120 (1960).

Allowance of further time in which to file grounds of defense is in the sound discretion of the court. Williams v. Service, Inc., 199 Va. 326, 99 S.E.2d 648 (1957).

The lower court, in the exercise of its discretion, was fully justified in refusing to allow the defendant to file his grounds of defense after having been in default for more than six months. Cooper v. Davis, 199 Va. 472, 100 S.E.2d 691 (1957).

No authority to require posting bond as condition of time extension. — This rule does not say that trial courts are given discretion to decide questions of late filing as the courts may deem appropriate since this rule gives the trial courts discretion, but it is a circumscribed discretion, not a broad discretion. It is the discretion to grant or deny an extension of time; that is the extent of it and the trial court had no authority to require plaintiff to post a bond as a condition of being granted an extension of time in which to file pleadings. Lilienfield v. Baroff, 237 Va. 617, 378 S.E.2d 831 (1989).

Withdrawal of answer and interposition of a demurrer. — If the status of a cause be such that the rights of no one will be prejudiced by withdrawal of a guardian ad litem's answer and interposition of a demurrer, such procedure rests within the sound discretion of the chancellor and does not violate this rule of court. O'Neill v. Cole, 194 Va. 50, 72 S.E.2d 382 (1952).

Trial court had discretion under this rule to permit appellant to pay the writ tax and clerk's fees after service of the petition for appeal, even though Rule 2A:4 contemplates payment of the tax and fees before service. Sours v. Virginia Bd. for Architects, Professional Eng'rs, Land Surveyors & Landscape Architects, 30 Va. App. 313, 516 S.E.2d 712 (1999).

Acceptance of late filing not abuse of discretion. — Trial court did not abuse its discretion in accepting the Board of Dentistry's response one business day late, as the dentist presented no evidence to show that the dentist was prejudiced by the one day or that the filing one business day late caused a delay of any kind in the remainder of the proceedings. Lennon v. Va. Bd. of Dentistry, 2007 Va. App. LEXIS 475 (Dec. 27, 2007).

Proceedings before the Virginia Workers' Compensation Commission. — The Virginia Workers' Compensation Commission has the authority to permit filing of a late response under Rule 1:9 and a deputy commissioner properly allowed the Virginia Birth-Related Neurological Injury Compensation Program to file a response to a claim submitted under § 38.2-5000 et seq., after the time allowed by subsection D of § 38.2-5004. Kidder v. Va. Birth-Related Neurological Injury Comp. Program, 37 Va. App. 764, 560 S.E.2d 907, 2002 Va. App. LEXIS 174 (2002).

Applied in Conrad v. Carter, 224 Va. 485, 297 S.E.2d 706 (1982); Counts v. Stone Container Corp.,

239 Va. 152, 387 S.E.2d 481 (1990); State Farm Mut. Auto. Ins. Co. v. Remley, 270 Va. 209, 618 S.E.2d 316, 2005 Va. LEXIS 75 (2005).

CIRCUIT COURT OPINIONS

Extension of time in which to file response. — In a personal injury action against an out-of-state corporation that did not respond within the required time, where significant damages were being requested, and confusion had resulted from the corporation's communications with the injured party's counsel in two states, and had the mistaken belief, in good faith, that the injured party did not expect it to file responsive pleadings, due to ongoing settlement negotiations, it was appropriate for the trial court to deny the injured party's motion for default judgment and to exercise its discretion to deem the corporation's responsive pleadings to have been timely filed. Mack v. Starwood Hotels & Resorts Worldwide, Inc., 57 Va. Cir. 390, 2002 Va. Cir. LEXIS 222 (Norfolk 2002).

Although the Commonwealth failed to respond to a licensee's petition seeking judicial review of the revocation of his driver's license within 21 days, the court had discretion to permit a late filing and to consider the Commonwealth's opposition, pursuant to Va. Sup. Ct. R. 1:9; however, the fact that the licensee's petition was not filed within 60 days of having received notice of the revocation rendered it untimely, pursuant to § 46.2-410.1, and the court was without jurisdiction to consider the matter on the merits. Vasquez v. Commonwealth, 63 Va. Cir. 106, 2003 Va. Cir. LEXIS 179 (Fairfax County 2003).

Broad discretion is given to trial courts in determining whether to extend the time for filing pleadings under Va. Sup. Ct. R. 1:9 and an appellate court, in determining whether a trial court has abused its discretion by granting or denying leave to file a late pleading, should look to the existence or absence of good cause for the delay, together with other compelling circumstances. Jay-Ton Constr. Co. v. Bowen Constr. Servs., 62 Va. Cir. 414, 2003 Va. Cir. LEXIS 289 (Portsmouth 2003).

Trial court denied the claimant's motion for default or other relief, as even though the alleged wrongdoer's amended answer was filed three days beyond the time allotted for filing it, the trial court had the discretion to extend the time for filing, the late filing was not made for the purpose of gaining a tactical advantage or otherwise in bad faith, and the pleading sufficiently complied with the requirements of § 8.01-271.1, Va. Sup. Ct. R. 1:4(a), and the trial court's orders. Fletcher v. Inova Health Care Servs., 71 Va. Cir. 331, 2006 Va. Cir. LEXIS 142 (Fairfax County 2006).

Because an insurer's failure to timely file a responsive pleading was not due to dilatory tactics, because its motion for extension was filed less than a week after a responsive pleading was due, and because an extension would not prejudice the insured, the insurer was granted leave to file responsive pleadings within seven days pursuant to Va. Sup. Ct. R. 1:9. Brown's Buick, Inc. v. Granite State Ins. Co., 78 Va. Cir. 22, 2008 Va. Cir. LEXIS 193 (Alexandria 2008).

Passenger's motion for judgment by default was denied, and an airline's motion to file late responsive pleadings was granted because there was no intent to delay the proceedings or otherwise prejudice the rights of the passenger, the airline would be greatly prejudiced if the motion for a default judgment was granted, and the delay did not work a prejudice to the passenger's pursuit of her action for damages since the passenger showed no injury to her ability to pursue her claim, other than the expenditure of fees and costs in connection with the motions; within a week of being served, the airline's counsel contacted the owner's claims manager respecting a response to the claim, and because they had limited dealings with each other, that reasonably explained the subsequent confusion over who would be filing a timely response, and promptly upon the passenger's filing of the motion for default, the airline sought leave to file a late response. Sanders v. Shuttle Am., 75 Va. Cir. 378, 2008 Va. Cir. LEXIS 262 (Loudoun County Aug. 15, 2008).

Whether a secretary was working in the secretary's capacity as secretary to the city attorney or the city manager, the secretary was a person "in charge of the office," within the meaning of § 8.01-300; therefore, because a 13-day delay in filing an answer was not significant and would not prejudice the injured plaintiff, pursuant to Va. Sup. Ct. R. 1:9, the city was allowed to file a late answer. Tarpley v. City of Martinsville, 82 Va. Cir. 222, 2011 Va. Cir. LEXIS 164 (Martinsville Feb. 9, 2011).

Extension of time to file answer and defense was granted. — In an action for accounting by a decedent's widow against the executor of an estate of which the decedent was a beneficiary and against the executor's surety, the court granted the surety's motion for leave to extend the time to file its answer and grounds for its defense pursuant to Rule 1:9 after the surety belatedly filed both its response and defense pursuant to former Rule 3:5 [see now Rule 3:8], because although it was clear that responsibility for the delay in filing solely rested with the surety and not the neglect of its attorneys, the ends of justice would be further served by allowing the extension where no prejudice was demonstrated by the widow, no trial date had been set, and there was no indication in the file that the widow had propounded any discovery requests upon either of defendants or taken any action to further prosecute the matter. Furthermore, no evidence of bad faith of the surety was demonstrated, and the surety asserted that it had acted in good faith by submitting an answer and grounds of defense immediately after counsel was retained, and in conducting discussions with the widow as to the merits of the case and settlement negotiations. Brown v. Allen, 64 Va. Cir. 349, 2004 Va. Cir. LEXIS 70 (Fairfax County 2004).

Amended complaint dismissed. — Amended complaint was dismissed because, by filing the amended complaint past the date it was conditioned on, plaintiffs no longer had leave by the court to file it, and under Va. Sup. Ct. R. 1:8, the amended complaint lacked legal efficacy; to have entered an order nunc pro tunc with a later filing date would have improperly created a fiction that plaintiff had timely filed for a leave to extend the original filing date, and such an order would have been beyond the scope of the powers of the court. An extension in this case would have been outside the scope of when a discretionary extension should have been granted under Va. Sup. Ct. R. 1:9. Bates v. Merritt, 83 Va. Cir. 134, 2011 Va. Cir. LEXIS 239 (Loudoun County June 29, 2011).

Improper filing of counterclaim. — Retailer's counterclaim against a computer company alleging that the computer company damaged computers and other items was dismissed pursuant to Va. Sup. Ct. R. 1:9; the counterclaim was actually captioned "Responsive Pleadings," did not bear a file stamp of the court clerk's office as required by Va. Sup. Ct. R. 1:4(h), and the record also failed to show that the court clerk's filing fee for a counterclaim was paid by the retailer, as required by § 17.1-275. Cox v. Sounds Unlimited, Inc., 60 Va. Cir. 243, 2002 Va. Cir. LEXIS 416 (Danville 2002).

Failure to request leave to file late counterclaim. — Company's counterclaim in a worker's action alleging malicious prosecution and negligence was dismissed; the counterclaim was not filed within 21 days of the service of the motion for judgment, and the company did not obtain leave to file a late counterclaim. Ekizian v. Microstrategy, Inc., 71 Va. Cir. 425, 2005 Va. Cir. LEXIS 128 (Fairfax County 2005).

Grant of nonsuit not precluded where an earlier demurrer did not dismiss the action, even where the pleadings were not amended in a timely fashion. — Purchaser's motion for nonsuit pursuant to § 8.01-380 in an action alleging misuse of escrow funds was granted, as the grant of a demurrer to sellers was not a final order pursuant to Va. Sup. Ct. R. 1:1, considered in conjunction with Va. Sup. Ct. R. 1:8 and 1:9, even after the purchaser failed to amend the complaint in a timely fashion, and because the matter was not submitted to the court, the purchaser was entitled to a nonsuit as of right. Min Kyu Sue v. Sung Hoon Park, 70 Va. Cir. 113, 2005 Va. Cir. LEXIS 301 (Fairfax County 2005).

Rule 1:10. Verification.

If a statute requires a pleading to be sworn to, and it is not, or requires a pleading to be accompanied by an affidavit, and it is not, but contains all the allegations required, objection on either ground must be made within seven days after the pleading is filed by a motion to strike; otherwise the objection is waived. At any time before the court passes on the motion or within such time thereafter as the court may prescribe, the pleading may be sworn to or the affidavit filed. In an Electronically Filed Case, verification shall be subject to the provisions of Rule 1:17.

Cross references. — As to civil practice and procedure in the general district courts, see Rule 7B:6.

Source. — Rules 2:20.1, 3:14.

The amendment, effective May 2, 2011, adopted March 1, 2011, added the last sentence.

Michie's Jurisprudence. — For related discussion, see 1A M.J. Abatement, Survival and Revival, § 23; 1B M.J. Appeal and Error, § 112; 2A M.J. Assumpsit, § 46; 2B M.J. Automobiles, § 81; 5C M.J. Debt, Action of, § 16; 7A M.J. Equity, §§ 54, 68; 12B M.J. Mechanics' Liens, § 24; 13A M.J. Motions for Judgment, § 20; 14B M.J. Pleading, § 14.

CASE NOTES

Section 8.01-28 compared. — Section 8.01-28 relating to when a plaintiff is to be granted judgment in an action for payment of money in which the defendant fails to deny the plaintiff's claim under oath and this rule providing that the statutory benefit provided the plaintiff will be waived unless the plaintiff timely claims it, read together in light of their respective histories and prevailing case law, are fully compatible and complementary. The statute creates only an optional benefit; this rule simply defines one mode of waiver. Sheets v. Ragsdale, 220 Va. 322, 257 S.E.2d 858 (1979).

Filing of affidavit before ruling on demurrer. — The complainant's filing of the verifying affidavit required by § 43-22 after defendant filed a demurrer but before the court acted upon the demurrer served to overcome the objection. Herbert Bros. v. McCarthy Co., 220 Va. 907, 265 S.E.2d 685 (1980).

Failure to file the affidavit required by § 43-22 is typical of the situations for which this rule was designed to provide a remedy, viz., the avoidance of dismissals, for purely technical defects, of what otherwise might be meritorious claims. Herbert Bros. v. McCarthy Co., 220 Va. 907, 265 S.E.2d 685 (1980).

Motion to quash process need not be sworn to. Eure v. Morgan Jones & Co., 195 Va. 678, 79 S.E.2d 862 (1954).

Applied in Sheets v. Ragsdale, 220 Va. 322, 257 S.E.2d 858 (1979); Roberts v. Roberts, 223 Va. 736, 292 S.E.2d 370 (1982); Richman v. National Health Labs., Inc., 235 Va. 353, 367 S.E.2d 508 (1988).

CIRCUIT COURT OPINIONS

Objection to affidavit waived. — By not objecting to the lack of an affidavit within seven days after a complaint was filed, defendants waived their objection that plaintiffs had not filed the affidavit. Robinson v. Brugiere, 72 Va. Cir. 109, 2006 Va. Cir. LEXIS 191 (Amherst County 2006).

Rule 1:11. Striking the Evidence.

If the court sustains a motion to strike the evidence of either party in a civil case being tried before a jury, or the evidence of the Commonwealth in a criminal case being so tried, then the court shall enter summary judgment or partial summary judgment in conformity with its ruling on the motion to strike.

If the court overrules a motion to strike the evidence and there is a hung jury, the moving party may renew the motion immediately after the discharge of the jury, and, if the court is of opinion that it erred in denying the motion, it shall enter summary judgment or partial summary judgment in conformity with its ruling on the motion to strike.

Cross references. — As to entry of summary judgment or partial summary judgment in conformity with ruling on motion to strike, see § 8.01-378.

Source. — Rule 1:11.

Michie's Jurisprudence. — For related discussion, see 5B M.J. Criminal Procedure, §§ 62, 67, 68; 7B M.J. Evidence, § 291; 11B M.J. Jury, § 60.

CASE NOTES

Renewal of motions to strike adversary's evidence after hung jury. — See R.G. Pope Constr. Co. v. Guard Rail of Roanoke, Inc., 219 Va. 111, 244 S.E.2d 774 (1978).

Standard for renewed motions identical to that during trial. — When the trial court considers a renewed motion to strike after the jury has been unable to return a verdict, it should sustain the motion only if it "is of the opinion that it erred in denying the motion" made before the case was submitted to the jury; thus, the standard for granting a motion to strike in such cases is identical to that for granting such motions made during trial. Austin v. Shoney's, Inc., 254 Va. 134, 486 S.E.2d 285 (1997).

Motion to strike properly denied. — Defendant's motion to strike was properly denied as under the totality of the circumstances, evidence was not illegally seized under the Fourth Amendment as the police officer had a particularized and objective basis for suspecting that defendant was involved in criminal activity where: (1) defendant fled a consensual encounter with the officer; (2) the officer had a reasonable suspicion to detain defendant where he suspiciously, while in a high-crime area, leaned toward a car tire as the officer approached; (3) defendant could not provide an address in the housing area, which had been posted as a "no trespassing" area, without squinting at a building behind him and giving the officer that address; and (4) defendant's placement of his hands underneath him and his unusual movements after he fell suggested that he was attempting to remove something from his clothing. White v. Commonwealth, No. 2091-02-1, 2003 Va. App. LEXIS 367 (Ct. of Appeals June 24, 2003).

Trial court did not err in denying defendant's motion to strike the evidence of proof of defendant's probation violation, as the Commonwealth introduced sufficient circumstantial evidence at the probation revocation hearing to establish that defendant was the probationer, which is the only issue that defendant raised regarding the motion to strike. Moss v. Commonwealth, No. 1320-02-3, 2003 Va. App. LEXIS 241 (Ct. of Appeals Apr. 22, 2003).

Because a witness's criminal history was provided to defendant during trial and its contents were disclosed during cross-examination, defendant failed to establish actual prejudice or a *Brady* violation; consequently, the trial court did not err in denying defendant's motion to strike the witness's testimony. Harvey v. Commonwealth, 2005 Va. App. LEXIS 403 (Oct. 11, 2005).

Grant of motion to strike held proper. — In a wrongful death suit, where an officer fired frangible breaching rounds at a door, killing decedent, the trial court properly struck plaintiff's evidence as to her count alleging willful and wanton conduct and her request for punitive damages because there was no evidence the officer had actual or constructive knowledge that there were people in the room. Green v. Ingram, 269 Va. 281, 608 S.E.2d 917, 2005 Va. LEXIS 19 (2005).

Grant of motion to strike held improper. — See C & P Tel. Co. v. APAC/Virginia, Inc., 236 Va. 492, 373 S.E.2d 927 (1988).

Where reasonable minds could differ as to whether defendants, jointly or severally, were guilty of negligence that proximately caused plaintiff's injuries, jury issues were presented, and the trial court erred in striking plaintiff's evidence as to each defendant. Payne v. Gloeckl, 236 Va. 356, 374 S.E.2d 32 (1988).

In a wrongful death suit, evidence was sufficient to allow jury to conclude that an officer who fired frangible breaching rounds at door, killing decedent, acted with gross negligence; therefore, trial court erred in striking plaintiff's evidence as to this count. Green v. Ingram, 269 Va. 281, 608 S.E.2d 917, 2005 Va. LEXIS 19 (2005).

Applied in Hoffner v. Kreh, 227 Va. 48, 313 S.E.2d 656 (1984).

CIRCUIT COURT OPINIONS

Damages for diminished life expectancy recoverable. — Trial court denied the doctor's motion to strike alleging that Virginia law did not recognize diminished life expectancy as an element of damages which could be recovered in a personal injury medical malpractice lawsuit, as such damages, if properly proven, were recoverable. Straus v. McDonald, 67 Va. Cir. 116, 2005 Va. Cir. LEXIS 14 (Fairfax County 2005).

Rule 1:12. Service of Papers after the Initial Process.

All pleadings, motions and other papers not required to be served otherwise and requests for subpoenas duces tecum shall be served by delivering, dispatching by commercial delivery service, transmitting by facsimile, delivering by electronic mail when Rule 1:17 so provides or when consented to in writing signed by the person to be served, or by mailing, a copy to each counsel of record on or before the day of filing.

Subject to the provisions of Rule 1:17, service pursuant to this Rule shall be effective upon such delivery, dispatch, transmission or mailing, except that papers served by facsimile transmission completed after 5:00 p.m. shall be deemed served on the next day that is not a Saturday, Sunday, or legal holiday. Service by electronic mail under this Rule is not effective if the party making service learns that the attempted service did not reach the person to be served.

At the foot of such pleadings and requests shall be appended either acceptance of service or a certificate of counsel that copies were served as this Rule requires, showing the date of delivery and method of service, dispatching, transmitting, or mailing. When service is made by electronic mail, a certificate of counsel that the document was served by electronic mail shall be served by mail or transmitted by facsimile to each counsel of record on or before the day of service.

Cross references. — As to practice and procedure in the general district courts, see Rule 7A:10.

Source. — Rules 2:17, 3:15.

Comment on the 1976 amendment. — New language in this rule requires service of requests for subpoenas duces tecum upon each counsel of record.

The amendment, effective February 1, 1999, adopted November 23, 1998, substituted "Service of Papers after the Initial Process" for "Copies of Pleadings and Requests for Subpoenas Duces Tecum to Be Furnished" in the catchline; in the first paragraph, inserted "motions and other papers," deleted "on each counsel of record" following "shall be served," inserted "dispatching by commercial delivery service, transmitting by facsimile," and substituted "each counsel of record" for "him"; inserted the second paragraph; and inserted "dispatching, transmitting" in the present third paragraph.

The amendment, effective October 15, 2003, adopted August 15, 2003, inserted "otherwise" following "to be served" and "delivering by electronic mail when consented to in writing signed by the person to be served" following "by facsimile" in the first paragraph; added the second sentence of the second paragraph; and in the third paragraph, inserted "and method of service" following "date of delivery" in the first sentence, and added the second sentence.

The amendment, effective May 2, 2011, adopted March 1, 2011, inserted "when Rule 1:17 so provides or" near the middle of the first paragraph, and added "Subject to the provisions of Rule 1:17" at the beginning of the second paragraph.

Law Review. — For 2003/2004 survey of civil practice and procedure, see 39 U. Rich. L. Rev. 87 (2004).

Michie's Jurisprudence. — For related discussion, see 2A M.J. Attorney and Client, §§ 10, 11; 7A M.J. Equity, § 114; 19 M.J. Venue, § 20.

CASE NOTES

Invited error. — Defendant's claims that he violated Rules 1:5 and 1:12 by filing pro se motions to modify his sentence while he was represented by counsel were rejected as defendant filed the pro se motions without the advice of counsel and filed the motions ex parte, and defense counsel signed the trial court's order suspending his sentence under the designation "I ask for this"; defendant was barred from invoking the claims on appeal as defense counsel was aware that the pro se motions had been filed, yet neither defendant, nor defense counsel, acted to correct the deficiencies. Coe v. Commonwealth, No. 3293-02-2, 2004 Va. App. LEXIS 181 (Ct. of Appeals Mar. 2, 2004).

Party notified of appeal. — Trial court had jurisdiction to hear an appeal of the juvenile and domestic relations district court's ruling on the biological mother's petition to modify custody and visitation; the biological mother filed a proper civil appeal notice in the case, was not required to serve the husband with it in order for the trial court to have jurisdiction over the appeal, and, in any event, the husband did not contend that he never received notice that the biological mother filed an appeal.

Albert v. Ramirez, 45 Va. App. 799, 613 S.E.2d 865, 2005 Va. App. LEXIS 225 (2005).

Service. — Because the amendment to Va. Sup. Ct. R. 2A:4 changed the service requirement to conform to the general rules applicable "in a civil action," "service" can be accomplished pursuant to Va. Sup. Ct. R. 1:12 if the parties are already at issue by the time an appeal is made to the circuit court. Muse Constr. Group, Inc. v. Commonwealth Bd. for Contrs. & Warren & Beverly Wharton, 60 Va. App. 92, 724 S.E.2d 216, 2012 Va. App. LEXIS 133 (2012).

Circuit court erred in dismissing a contractor's appeal of a decision of the Commonwealth of Virginia Board for Contractors because the contractor's service by certified mail of the petition for appeal satisfied the requirements of Va. Sup. Ct. R. 2A:4; because Rule 2A:4 did not require that the petition for appeal be served by a process server, the contractor complied with Rule 2A:4 by serving a copy of the petition on the agency secretary pursuant to Va. Sup. Ct. R. 1:12 within the prescribed time period. Muse Constr. Group, Inc. v. Commonwealth Bd. for Contrs. & Warren & Beverly Wharton, 60 Va. App. 92, 724 S.E.2d 216, 2012 Va. App. LEXIS 133 (2012).

Applied in Iliff v. Richards, 221 Va. 644, 272 S.E.2d 645 (1980).

CIRCUIT COURT OPINIONS

Initial process. — Since a cross-claim was a new action under former Va. Sup. Ct. Rule 3:9 (see now Rule 3:10), service of the cross-claim was not "mesne process" and therefore could not be accomplished by mail under Va. Sup. Ct. Rule 1:12. Lesner Pointe Condo. Ass'n v. Harbour Point Bldg. Corp., 61 Va. Cir. 609, 2002 Va. Cir. LEXIS 424 (Virginia Beach 2002). See also, Bd. of Dirs. of the Lesner Pointe Condo. on the Chesapeake Bay Ass'n v. Harbour Point Bldg. Corp., 2002 Va. Cir. LEXIS 421 (Virginia Beach Oct. 25, 2002).

Rule 1:13. Endorsements.

Drafts of orders and decrees shall be endorsed by counsel of record, or reasonable notice of the time and place of presenting such drafts together with copies thereof shall be served pursuant to Rule 1:12 upon all counsel of record who have not endorsed them. Compliance with this Rule and with Rule 1:12 may be modified or dispensed with by the court in its discretion. In an Electronically Filed Case, endorsement and specification of any objections to the draft order shall be accomplished as provided in Rule 1:17.

Cross references. — As to procedure in the general district courts, see Rule 7A:11. Regarding procedure in the juvenile and domestic relations district courts, see Rule 8:19.

Source. — Rules 2:18, 3:16.

The amendment, effective February 1, 1999, adopted November 23, 1998, inserted "dispatching by commercial delivery service, transmitting by facsimile" in the first sentence.

The amendment, effective October 15, 2003, adopted August 15, 2003, substituted "pursuant to Rule 1:12 upon" for "by delivering, dispatching by commercial delivery service, transmitting by facsimile or mailing to" in the first sentence.

The amendment, effective May 2, 2011, adopted March 1, 2011, added the last sentence.

Law Review. — For 2003/2004 survey of civil practice and procedure, see 39 U. Rich. L. Rev. 87 (2004).

Michie's Jurisprudence. — For related discussion, see 2A M.J. Attorney and Client, § 10; 11A M.J. Judgments and Decrees, §§ 34, 119.

CASE NOTES

This rule is designed to protect parties without notice. State Hwy. State Hwy. Comm'r v. Easley, 215 Va. 197, 207 S.E.2d 870 (1974).

And failure to comply with the rule prejudices only the rights of such parties. State Hwy. Comm'r v. Easley, 215 Va. 197, 207 S.E.2d 870 (1974).

The failure to comply with this rule renders an order voidable, not void ab initio. Singh v. Mooney, 261 Va. 48, 541 S.E.2d 549, 2001 Va. LEXIS 2 (2001).

A decree or order entered in violation of this rule is merely voidable, not void ab initio, and is not subject to collateral attack, but must be challenged within 21 days of its entry pursuant to Rule 1:1, by a bill of review within the time prescribed by § 8.01-623, or by an independent action pursuant to § 8.01-428. Whiting v. Whiting, 262 Va. 3, 2001 Va. LEXIS 83 (2001).

A decree that fails to comply with this section is void. Francis v. Francis, 30 Va. App. 584, 518 S.E.2d 842 (1999). But see Napert v. Napert, 261 Va. 45, 540 S.E.2d 882, 2001 Va. LEXIS 13 (2001); Singh v. Mooney, 261 Va. 48, 541 S.E.2d 549, 2001 Va. LEXIS 2 (2001); Whiting v. Whiting, 262 Va. 3, 2001 Va. LEXIS 83 (2001).

However, where requirement of notice was complied with, and the notice included the time and place of presenting such drafts together with copies thereof, trial court did not err in waiving endorsement of wife's counsel of record and entering the decree. Francis v. Francis, 30 Va. App. 584, 518 S.E.2d 842 (1999).

A party whose counsel induced violation of this rule has no standing to assert that the order is void because of that violation, or that the trial court, in its discretion, could not properly have entered the order without requiring compliance with the rule. State Hwy. Comm'r v. Easley, 215 Va. 197, 207 S.E.2d 870 (1974).

Order should not be entered without endorsement or notice. — Draft order for appointment of a receiver to take charge of partnership assets should not have been entered, where endorsement of defendant's counsel was not obtained nor was counsel furnished with reasonable notice of the time and place of presenting the draft for entry. The fact that the attorneys were at odds on the form of the order made the requirement of notice and an opportunity for a hearing all the more important in this case. Rosillo v. Winters, 235 Va. 268, 367 S.E.2d 717 (1988).

Endorsement required absent order to the contrary. — A draft of an order or decree must be endorsed by counsel of record unless the endorsement is modified or dispensed with by the court. Whiting v. Whiting, 32 Va. App. 192, 526 S.E.2d 806, 2000 Va. App. LEXIS 279 (2000).

But requirements may be modified or dispensed with. — The mere fact that an order may have been entered without endorsement of or direct notice to counsel of record does not automatically render it void; this rule specifically provides that compliance with the rule may be modified or dispensed with by the court in its discretion Smith v. Commonwealth, 32 Va. App. 766, 531 S.E.2d 11, 2000 Va. App. LEXIS 499 (2000).

Trial court's order regarding an equitable distribution decision and the final divorce decree were not void even though they were not endorsed by counsel pursuant to Va. Sup. Ct. R. 1:13, as Rule 1:13 allowed the trial court to exercise its discretion to dispense with the requirements, and the trial court presumably exercised that discretion even though it did not expressly state that it was doing so in its orders. Taylor v. Caccia, No. 1733-02-2, 2003 Va. App. LEXIS 238 (Ct. of Appeals Apr. 22, 2003).

Under circumstances in which notice of the date to which the trial was continued was given when the mother was represented by counsel by means of a letter to her counsel, and, although she had notice, the mother failed to appear for the final hearing, the trial court did not abuse its discretion by dispensing with the mother's endorsement of the final order, which contained rulings the trial court made at the completion of the final hearing; the trial court had discretion to modify or dispense with compliance with Va. Sup. Ct. R. 1:13. Smith v. Novak, 2007 Va. App. LEXIS 139 (Apr. 3, 2007).

Express dispensation of compliance with rule not required. — Although a better practice would be for a trial court to include a statement reflecting its decision to exercise its discretion to dispense with compliance with this rule, in the absence of such a statement, the court on appeal will presume that the trial court exercised its discretion to dispense with the rule's requirements. Napert v. Napert, 261 Va. 45, 540 S.E.2d 882, 2001 Va. LEXIS 13 (2001). See also, Taylor v. Caccia, No. 1733-02-2, 2003 Va. App. LEXIS 238 (Ct. of Appeals Apr. 22, 2003).

Presumption that court exercised discretion in dispensing with endorsement or notice. — When dispensing with endorsement or notice pursuant to this rule, a better practice would be for trial court to include a statement reflecting its decision to exercise its discretion, but in the absence of such a statement, the court on appeal will presume that the trial court exercised its discretion. Edwards v. Commonwealth, No. 0469-00-1, 2001 Va. App. LEXIS 189 (Ct. of Appeals Apr. 10, 2001).

Courts are presumed to act in accordance with the law, so a claim that opposing counsel submitted the wrong last page of order, without any allegation of fraud, indicates that the court exercised it discretion in dispensing with endorsement of the decree. Gantt v. Gantt, No. 1973-02-3, 2003 Va. App. LEXIS 112 (Ct. of Appeals Mar. 4, 2003).

Divorce decree without endorsement or notice to party held void. — Where a final divorce decree was not endorsed by counsel of record for the husband and the record did not indicate that the trial court modified or dispensed with the requirement, the decree was void because the husband received no notice of the final decree and never endorsed it. Whiting v. Whiting, 32 Va. App. 192, 526 S.E.2d 806, 2000 Va. App. LEXIS 279 (2000).

Order dismissing appeal held void absent proper endorsement, notice, or waiver of rule's requirements. — Order dismissing appeal of an entrustment agreement decision by the juvenile court and remanding the case to the juvenile court was void ab initio and properly vacated where it was only endorsed by the attorney for social services and was not endorsed by, nor was notice given to, mother's guardian ad litem, infant's guardian ad litem, or the unknown father's guardian ad litem; was entered by the circuit court without notice of a hearing date to the opposing parties; and was clearly not in compliance with this rule, nothing in the order itself indicating that compliance with this rule was being waived by the parties or reflecting any decision by the court that compliance was being modified or dispensed with for good cause. Norfolk Div. of Social Servs. v. Unknown Father, 2 Va. App. 420, 345 S.E.2d 533 (1986).

Judge's order was void ab initio because no notice was given to either party of the entry of the order, no endorsements were obtained, and nothing new in the order indicated that compliance with the rule was waived or dispensed with for good cause. Smiley v. Erickson, 29 Va. App. 426, 512 S.E.2d 842 (1999).

Notice to or endorsement by counsel is unnecessary prior to entry of a final written order of dismissal where counsel were present in court when the ruling was made orally and were fully aware of the court's decision; preparation and entry of the order in standard form was all that remained to be done to end the case in the trial court. Smith v. Stanaway, 242 Va. 286, 410 S.E.2d 610 (1991).

This rule is designed to protect parties without notice. However, the mere fact that an order may have been entered without endorsement of counsel of record does not automatically render it void. The last sentence of this rule authorizes the trial court in its discretion to modify or dispense with the requirement of endorsement of counsel. Thus, the endorsement of counsel is unnecessary under circumstances where "counsel are present in court when the ruling is made orally and are fully aware of the court's decision; preparation and entry of an order in standard form is all that remains to be done to end the case in the trial court." Davis v. Mullins, 251 Va. 141, 466 S.E.2d 90 (1996).

Decree properly entered without endorsement. — The trial court did not abuse its discretion in dispensing with the requirement that the final decree be endorsed by all counsel of record where all counsel of record were present at trial, although defense counsel was not allowed to participate due to the defendant's refusal to appear, the court sent a facsimile and mailed a copy of the proposed findings to all counsel of record and entered the final decree that same day, and defense counsel did not request an opportunity to endorse the final decree. Fox v. Fox, No. 0721-97-4, 1998 Va. App. LEXIS 157 (Ct. of Appeals March 17, 1998).

The trial court did not abuse its discretion by waiving endorsement by wife's counsel and entering a final divorce decree where it was clear from the record as a whole that the wife had notice of the court's rulings because she was present in court with counsel when the court issued its decision. Venie v. Venie, No. 0342-98-4, 1998 Va. App. LEXIS 469 (Ct. of Appeals Sept. 1, 1998).

Husband had ability to note his objections to the trial court's rulings. — Husband's argument that the trial court erred by waiving the requirement to file objections and denying him the opportunity to file objections to the decrees was improper because, although the trial court dispensed with the requirement of the husband endorsing the July 9, 2010, orders, it was clear from the record that he had the ability to note his objections to the trial court's rulings by filing his objections with the court. Harnois v. Riley-Harnois, 2011 Va. App. LEXIS 311 (Oct. 11, 2011).

Mere presence not tantamount to written notice of appearance. — Wife's contention that her mere presence and comments at the depositions were tantamount to written notice of appearance in the case is without support in the Rules. Diamond v. Diamond, 20 Va. App. 481, 458 S.E.2d 303 (1995).

Where the final decree of divorce was not endorsed by counsel of record, and nothing in the record indicated that this requirement was modified or dispensed with by the court, the decree would be valid only if reasonable notice was given in accordance with the requirements of this rule. Westerberg v. Westerberg, 9 Va. App. 248, 386 S.E.2d 115 (1989).

A husband was not entitled to the vacatur of a final divorce decree on the basis that it was not endorsed by his counsel where (1) wife's counsel attempted to obtain such an endorsement, (2) the trial court did not enter the decree until 21 days after it sent the decree to wife's counsel, (3) both the court and wife's counsel served notice on husband's counsel at the address given in the court files, and (4) the court dispensed with an endorsement by husband's counsel after the notice was returned by the post office. Cronin v. Cronin, No. 0444-98-3 (Ct. of Appeals Oct. 27, 1998).

Failure to make timely challenge to voidable decree. — Where a husband received no notice of the final divorce decree and never endorsed it, the decree was voidable, not void, and, because the husband failed to properly challenge the decree within the time permitted, the decree remained in full force and effect. Whiting v. Whiting, 262 Va. 3, 2001 Va. LEXIS 83 (2001).

Notice must include copy of proposed decree. — Since the notice in a divorce case did not include a copy of the proposed decree, it did not comply with this rule and a decree that fails to comply with this rule is void. Westerberg v. Westerberg, 9 Va. App. 248, 386 S.E.2d 115 (1989).

Harmless error. — Order of the trial court was not vacated because any error was harmless, and thus, the trial court did not abuse its discretion in dispensing with compliance of Va. Sup. Ct. R. 1:13; the husband received notice of the time and place for the presentation of the draft order and received a copy of the order, he admitted he had time to request a continuance, and even if the rule were violated, no prejudice resulted from the failure to attach a copy of the proposed order to the notice. Klein v. Klein, No. 0211-03-4, 2003 Va. App. LEXIS 621 (Ct. of Appeals Dec. 2, 2003).

Applied in Iliff v. Richards, 221 Va. 644, 272 S.E.2d 645 (1980); Zedan v. Westheim, 60 Va. App. 556, 729 S.E.2d 785, 2012 Va. App. LEXIS 257 (2012).

OPINIONS OF THE ATTORNEY GENERAL

Rules applicable to Commonwealth's attorney. — Where a Commonwealth's attorney has become "counsel of record" by making an appearance in a particular court, whether in civil or criminal proceedings, Va. Sup. Ct. R. 1.5 and this Rule apply. See opinion of Attorney General to The Honorable Charles E. Dorsey, Chief Judge Twenty-Third Judicial Circuit, 08-056 (10/21/08).

Although this Rule applies to Commonwealth's attorneys regarding notice and endorsement of orders, courts have broad discretion to dispense with endorsements. See opinion of Attorney General to The Honorable Charles E. Dorsey, Chief Judge Twenty-Third Judicial Circuit, 08-056 (10/21/08).

Rule 1:14. Preservation of the Record.

A court may authorize the use of electronic or photographic means for the preservation of the record or parts thereof.

Cross references. — As to practice and procedure in the general district courts, see Rule 7A:6.

Michie's Jurisprudence. — For related discussion, see 5B M.J. Criminal Procedure, § 38; 19 M.J. Trial, § 3.

CASE NOTES

Constitutionality. — Neither § 19.2-266 nor this rule violates the equal protection clause of the Constitution of the United States. Diehl v. Commonwealth, 9 Va. App. 191, 385 S.E.2d 228 (1989).

Rule 1:15. Local Rules of Court.

(a) Whenever a local rule is prescribed by a circuit court it shall be spread upon the order book and a copy with the date of entry shall be forthwith posted in the clerk's office, filed with the Executive Secretary of the Supreme Court, and furnished to attorneys regularly practicing before that circuit court; and whenever an attorney becomes counsel of record in any proceedings in a circuit court in which he does not regularly practice, it shall be his responsibility to ascertain the rules of that court and abide thereby. The clerk shall, upon request, promptly furnish a copy of all rules then in force and effect.

(b) Whenever a local rule is prescribed by a circuit court providing for the orderly management of the civil docket by use of the praecipe system, the praecipe shall be substantially in the form appearing in the appendix of forms at the end of this Part One.

(c) Whenever a local rule is prescribed by a circuit court providing for the submission of instructions prior to trial, such local rule shall be substantially in the form appearing in the appendix of forms at the end of this Part One.

(d) The chief judges of the circuit and juvenile and domestic relations district courts shall, on or before December 31 of each year, furnish the Executive Secretary of the Supreme Court current general information relating to the management of the courts within each circuit and district. This information shall be assembled and published electronically by the Executive Secretary.

Cross references. — As to practice and procedure in the general district courts, see Rule 7A:15.

Comment on the 1976 amendment. — The only change in paragraph (a) from the present rule is to require the filing of local rules with the executive secretary of the Supreme Court rather than with the executive director of the State Bar.

Paragraphs (b) and (c) are recommended to provide suggested forms for those circuits using the praecipe system in calling the civil docket and/or those courts requiring that instructions be submitted prior to trial. There is no requirement that circuit courts adopt such rules; however, should they do so, the procedure will be uniform in circuits having such rules.

Paragraph (d) provides for the publication as an appendix to the Rules of the Supreme Court of current information on each circuit and district court to meet the present problems confronting attorneys and litigants in ascertaining general information and local procedures. This information would include the name, location, and telephone number of the court and clerk's office; names of judges and clerk; terms of court, including when grand juries are convened and docket call procedures in civil and criminal cases; procedures including pretrial conferences and furnishing of instructions prior to trial; motion days, etc.

Editor's note. — The appendix of current general information relating to the management of the courts, referred to in paragraph (d) of this rule, is on file with the clerks of the circuit and district courts throughout the State. The appendix lists the judges, clerks, addresses, telephone numbers, office hours, terms and other information for all of the circuit and district courts in the State.

The amendment effective July 1, 2009, adopted June 12, 2009, in subdivision (d), deleted "on forms provided by him" following "Supreme Court" in the first sentence and substituted "electronically by the executive Secretary" for "on or before July 1 of each year as an appendix to the Rules of the Supreme Court" at the end of the second sentence; and made stylistic and punctuation changes in subdivisions (a) and (d).

CASE NOTES

Applied in Bunton v. Commonwealth, 6 Va. App. 557, 370 S.E.2d 470 (1988).

CIRCUIT COURTS OF VIRGINIA
Times for the Commencement of the Regular Terms

CIRCUIT	COUNTY OR CITY	TERM
First	Chesapeake	Criminal terms: First Tuesday of each month, 2:00 p.m. except when election date or a holiday is Term Day, then Term Day will be held on Wednesday after the first Tuesday. Civil terms: First Tuesday of each month, 10:00 a.m. except when election date or a holiday is Term Day, then Term Day will be held on Wednesday after the first Tuesday.
Second	Virginia Beach	First Monday in each month unless holiday, then following day.
	Accomack	First Monday in February, April, June, August, October and December.
	Northampton	Second Monday in January, March, May, July, September and November.
Third	Portsmouth	First Thursday in each month.
Fourth	Norfolk	Terms begin the first day of the month.
Fifth	Isle of Wight	Second Monday in January, March, May, July, September and November.
	Southampton	Third Monday in January, March, May, July, September and November.
	Suffolk	Fourth Monday in January, March, May, July, September and November.
Sixth	Hopewell	Second Tuesday in February, April, June, August, October and December.
	Prince George	Third Tuesday in January, March, May, July, September and November.
	Surry	Fourth Tuesday in January, March, May, July, September and November.
	Sussex	Second Tuesday in January, March, July, September and November. May term usually begins at an alternate date.
	Greensville	First Tuesday in February, April, June, August, October and December.
	Brunswick	Fourth Tuesday in February, April, June, August, October and December.
Seventh	Newport News	Criminal terms: Second Monday in each month. Civil terms: Second Monday in January, March, May, July, September and November.
Eighth	Hampton	First Monday in February, April, June, August, October and December. Criminal Term Grand Juries: First Monday of each month at 9:00 a.m.
Ninth	James City County/ Williamsburg	Third Wednesday in January, March, May, July, September and November.
	York County/Poquoson	Third Tuesday in January, March, July, September and November. Term day for May 2012 will be May 22, 2012.
	Charles City	First Tuesday in January, March, May, July, September, and November 1.
	New Kent	Second Monday in January; third Monday in March, May, July, September and November.

CIRCUIT COURTS OF VIRGINIA
Times for the Commencement of the Regular Terms

CIRCUIT	COUNTY OR CITY	TERM
Ninth (cont'd)	Gloucester	First Monday in January, March, May, July, September and November. If Term Day falls on legal holiday, Term Day is the following day.
	Mathews	Third Monday in January, March, May, July, September and November. If Term Day falls on legal holiday, Term Day is the following day.
	Middlesex	Fourth Monday in January, March, May, July, September and November. If Term Day falls on legal holiday, Term Day is the following day.
	King William	First Monday in February, April, June, August, October and December. If Term Day falls on legal holiday, Term Day is the following day.
	King and Queen	Second Tuesday in February, April, June, August, October and December. If Term Day falls on legal holiday, Term Day is the following day.
Tenth	Halifax	Second Monday in January, March, May, July, September and November.
	Mecklenburg	Third Monday in January, February, March, April, May, June, July, August, September, October, November; and the second Monday in December. If Term Day falls on legal holiday, Term Day is the following day.
	Lunenburg	First Monday in February, April, June, August, October and December. If Term Day falls on legal holiday, Term Day is the following day.
	Charlotte	Wednesday after the first Monday in February, April, June, August, October and December.
	Prince Edward	Tuesday after the third Monday in January, April, June, September and November.
	Buckingham	Tuesday after the second Monday in January, April, June, September and November.
	Cumberland	Tuesday following the fourth Monday in January, April, June, September, and November.
	Appomattox	Tuesday after the first Monday in January, April, June, September and November. If Term Day falls on legal holiday, Term Day is the following day.
Eleventh	Powhatan	Second Tuesday in February, April, June, October and December, 10:00 a.m. Criminal Days: 2nd Friday and 4th Monday each month, 9:00 a.m.
	Dinwiddie	Term Days: Third Tuesday each month, 10:00 a.m. Criminal Days: 2nd Tuesday, January, March, May, July, September and November; 4th Tuesday, 3rd Thursday & 4th Friday each month.
	Nottoway	First Tuesday in January, March, May, July, September and November, 10:00 a.m.. Criminal Days: 2nd Monday & 4th Thursday each month, 9:00 a.m.

CIRCUIT COURTS OF VIRGINIA
Times for the Commencement of the Regular Terms

CIRCUIT	COUNTY OR CITY	TERM
Eleventh (cont'd)	Amelia	First Tuesday in February, April, June, August, October and December at 10:00 a.m. Criminal Days: 1st Thursday and 3rd Friday each month, 9:00 a.m.
	Petersburg	Criminal and Civil terms: Third Thursday in each month.
Twelfth	Chesterfield	Criminal and Civil terms: Tuesday following third Monday in January, and third Monday in March, May, July, September and November.
	Colonial Heights	First Tuesday in January, March, May, July, September and November.
Thirteenth	Richmond City	Criminal terms: First Monday in each month. Civil terms: Fourth Monday in January, April, July and October.
Fourteenth	Henrico	Criminal terms: Second Monday in January, March, May, July, September and November. Civil cases set second Monday in January, April (2:00 p.m.), July and October or may be set by telephone. Criminal cases set when appealed or at preliminary hearing.
Fifteenth	Caroline	First Wednesday at 10:00 a.m. in January, March, May, July, September and November.
	Essex	Fourth Wednesday in January, April, July and October.
	Fredericksburg	Fourth Monday in January, April, July and October.
	Hanover	Third Tuesday in January, March, May, July, September and November. Cout convenes 9:00 a.m.
	King George	Second Thursday in January, April, July and October at 10 a.m.
	Lancaster	Fourth Friday in January, April, July and October.
	Northumberland	Fourth Tuesday in January, April, July and October.
	Richmond County	Fourth Monday of January, April, July and October.
	Spotsylvania	Third Monday in January, April, July and October, at 9:00 a.m. Criminal Term/ Grand Jury: 3rd Monday each month. Misdemeanor appeals on 3rd Friday (4th Friday if 3rd Friday is a holiday).
	Stafford	Criminal Term: First Monday in each month at 9:00 a.m. Civil Terms: First Monday in January, April, July and October at 11:00 a.m. If any Monday is a State holiday, Term Day will be held the following day.
	Westmoreland	Fourth Thursday in January, April, July and October.
Sixteenth	Charlottesville	Third Monday in April, June, August, October and December; Tuesday following the third Monday in February.
	Madison	First Monday in January, March, May, July, September and November.

CIRCUIT COURTS OF VIRGINIA
Times for the Commencement of the Regular Terms

CIRCUIT	COUNTY OR CITY	TERM
Sixteenth (cont'd)	Louisa	Second Monday in January, March, July, September and November. May Term Day will be May 7, 2012.
	Greene	Second Monday in February, April, June, August, October and December. October Term: Tuesday after 2nd Monday as 2nd Monday is holiday.
	Orange	Fourth Monday in January, March, May, July, September and November.
	Albemarle	Criminal Terms: First Monday in February, April, June, August, October and December. Civil Terms: Last Thursday of each month except November and December (which is the third Thursday).
	Goochland	Second Tuesday in February, April, June, August, October and December.
	Culpeper	Third Monday in February, April, June, August, October and December.
	Fluvanna	Fourth Monday in February, April, June, August and October; and third Tuesday in December.
Seventeenth	Arlington	Third Monday (or Tuesday, if holiday falls on Monday) in February, April, June, August, October and December.
Eighteenth	Alexandria	Second Monday in January, March, May, July, September and November; at 9:00 a.m.; cases may also be set for trial by telephone (703-746-4123).
Nineteenth	Fairfax	Term begins: Third Monday January, March, May, July, September, November, except if it is a holiday, then 3rd Tuesday. Criminal terms: Tuesday following third Monday in January, March, May, July, September and November except when Monday is holiday, then Criminal Term is Wednesday after 3rd Tuesday. Misdemeanor Term Day: First Monday each month unless holiday, then second Monday. Civil terms: Fourth Monday in January, March, May, July, September and November, except when Monday is a holiday, then Civil Term begins on the Fourth Tuesday.
Twentieth	Fauquier	Terms: Fourth Monday in January, March, May, July, September and November.
	Loudoun	Second Monday in February, April, June, August and December; and Tuesday following second Monday in October.
	Rappahannock	Second Monday in January, March, May, July, September and November.
Twenty-First	Henry	Tuesday following Third Monday, 9:00 a.m., in July, Sept., Nov., March & May; 1st Tuesday after 3rd Monday, 9:00 a.m., in January.

CIRCUIT COURTS OF VIRGINIA
Times for the Commencement of the Regular Terms

CIRCUIT	COUNTY OR CITY	TERM
Twenty-First (cont'd)	Martinsville	Criminal terms: First Monday in November; 2nd Monday, Feb.; 1st Monday, May; 4th Monday, July. Civil cases set by Pretrial Scheduling Order.
	Patrick	First Monday in March, June, September and December.
Twenty-Second	Danville	Grand Juries and Terms: January 4, March 1, May 3, July 5, September 6, and November 8.
	Pittsylvania	Third Monday in February, April, June, August, October and December.
	Franklin	First Monday in February, April, June, August, October and December.
Twenty-Third	Roanoke County	Criminal terms: First Friday in February, April, June, October and December; and the second Friday in August. Civil terms: First Friday in January, February, April, June, October and December; and second Friday in August.
	Roanoke City	Civil terms: Tuesday after first Monday, monthly. Criminal terms: First Monday, monthly.
	Salem	Third Friday in February, May, July and September; and the second Friday in December.
Twenty-Fourth	Lynchburg	Criminal and Civil terms: First Monday, monthly.
	Amherst	Second Tuesday in February, April, June, October and December.
	Bedford	First Tuesday in January, March, May, July, September and November.
	Campbell	Second Monday in January, March, May, July, September and November.
	Nelson	Fourth Tuesday in January, March, May, September and November.
Twenty-Fifth	Buena Vista	Fourth Wednesday in January and July; the first Monday in April; and the fourth Monday in September.
	Staunton	Third Monday in January, April, July and October.
	Waynesboro	Second Monday in January, March, May, September and November.
	Alleghany	Second Monday in January, April and July, and the first Tuesday after second Monday in October.
	Augusta	Fourth Monday in January, April, July and October.
	Bath	Third Monday (or Tuesday if holiday falls on Monday) in January, June and September; and the first Monday in April.
	Botetourt	First Monday in March, June, August, October and December.
	Craig	Last Monday in February; and the second Monday in May, September and November.
	Highland	Third Tuesday in March, June, September and December.

CIRCUIT COURTS OF VIRGINIA
Times for the Commencement of the Regular Terms

CIRCUIT	COUNTY OR CITY	TERM
Twenty-Fifth (cont'd)	Rockbridge	First Monday in February, May and November; second Monday in July; and Tuesday following Labor Day in September.
Twenty-Sixth	Clarke	Third Monday in January, April, July and October.
	Frederick	Thursday after the first Monday in January, April, July and October.
	Page	Fourth Monday in January, April, July and October.
	Shenandoah	Wednesday after the second Monday in January, April, July and October.
	Warren	First Monday in January, April, July and October.
	Winchester	Third Monday in January, April, July and October.
	Rockingham	Civil terms: First Monday and Wednesday after third Monday each month except Wednesday after third Monday only in January and August. Criminal terms: Third Monday in January, April, July and October.
Twenty-Seventh	Bland	Criminal terms: Second Monday in March, June, September and December. Civil terms: Immediately following end of criminal term.
	Carroll	Third Monday in March, June and September; and the second Monday in December.
	Floyd	First day of March, June, September and December.
	Giles	Second Tuesday in January, April, July and October.
	Grayson	Fourth Friday in January, April, July and October.
	Montgomery	Second Tuesday of January, April, July and October.
	Pulaski	Third Monday in February and November; the fourth Monday in May; and the second Monday in September.
	Radford	Second Friday in March, June, September and December.
	Wythe	Third Monday in January, April, July and October.
Twenty-Eighth	Washington	Fourth Tuesday in January, April, July and October.
	Smyth	Fourth Tuesday in March, June and September; and second Tuesday in December.
	Bristol	Fourth Tuesday in August, November, February and May.
Twenty-Ninth	Buchanan	Terms begin second Monday in January, April, July and October. Criminal terms: Fourth Monday in January, April, July and October. Civil terms: Second Tuesday in January, April, July and October.

CIRCUIT COURTS OF VIRGINIA
Times for the Commencement of the Regular Terms

CIRCUIT	COUNTY OR CITY	TERM
Twenty-Ninth (cont'd)	Dickenson	Criminal terms: Second Monday in March, June and September; and the first Monday in December. Civil terms: Tuesday, following Grand Jury. Grand Juries: Second Monday in March, June and September; first Monday in December).
	Russell	Second Monday in February, May, August and November.
	Tazewell	Second Tuesday in January, March, May, July, September and November.
Thirtieth	Wise/Norton	First Tuesday after the third Monday in January; and the third Monday in April, July and October.
	Scott	First Monday in February, May, August and November.
	Lee	First Monday in March, June and December; and second Monday in September.
Thirty-First	Prince William	First Monday in February, April, June, August, October and December.

Rule 1:16. Filing Format and Procedure.

(a) Except as provided in Rules 1:17, 3:3, 3A:23, 7A:7(c), and 8:8(f) pertaining to Electronically Filed Cases,

(1) All pleadings, motions, briefs, depositions, requests for discovery and responses thereto, and all other documents filed in any clerk's office in any proceeding pursuant to these Rules shall be produced on pages 8 ½ by 11 inches in size and all typed material shall be double spaced except for quotations.

(2) Subdivision (a)(1) of this Rule shall not apply to tables, charts, plats, photographs, and other material that cannot be reasonably reproduced on paper of that size.

(b) No paper shall be refused for failure to comply with the provisions of this Rule, but the clerk may require that the paper be redone in compliance with this Rule and substituted for the paper initially filed. Counsel shall certify that the substituted paper is identical in content to the paper initially filed.

Cross references. — As to practice and procedure in the general district courts, see Rule 7A:7.

The amendment, effective May 2, 2011, adopted March 1, 2011, rewrote the Rule heading, added the introductory paragraph of subsection (a), redesignated former subsections (a) and (b) as subdivisions (1) and (2) of (a), added "Subdivision (a)(1) of" at the beginning of subdivision (a)(2), and redesignated former subsection (c) as subsection (b).

Rule 1:17. Electronic Filing and Service.

(a) *Scope of Electronic Filing Rules.* Pursuant to § 8.01-271.01 and Article 4.1 (§§ 17.1-258.2 et seq.) of Chapter 2 of Title 17.1 of the Code of Virginia, this Rule shall be applicable in any court that has established an electronic filing system under the standards and procedures set forth in subdivision (c) of this Rule, and applies in civil cases in circuit court as provided in Rule 3:3, in criminal cases in circuit court as provided in Rule 3A:23, in general district court proceedings as provided in Rule 7A:7(c), and in juvenile and domestic relations district court proceedings as provided in Rule 8:8(f).

(b) *Definitions.*

(1) *"Electronic Document"* means any defined set of textural matter, graphic content or other encoded information in an approved format, that can be read, printed, and stored or retained as electrical, magnetic or optically encoded signals in some medium and that can be transmitted by a data-link.

(2) *"Data-Link"* refers to any means of electronic transmission of a document in a coded form such that the document can be received, read, printed, and stored by the recipient.

(3) *"E-Filing Portal"* means the electronic web site maintained by the Supreme Court of Virginia designated as the facility for electronically filing documents, or an alternative which meets the standards set forth in this Rule and is made available by individual circuit courts.

(4) *"Electronic filing"* means the official filing of an electronic document on the court's docket and case files in electronic form by transmission over a data-link.

(5) *"Electronically Filed Case"* means a case in which pleadings, motions, notices and other filings are made electronically in accordance with these rules.

(6) *Hyperlink"* means an electronic connection or reference to another place in the document, such that when the hyperlink is selected the user is taken to the portion of the document to which the link refers. It is not in itself a part of the document.

(c) *System Operational Standards.* In addition to the obligations and procedures set forth in subdivision (d) of this Rule, electronic filing systems under this Rule shall meet these requirements:

(1) Electronic documents must be stored without loss of content or material alteration of appearance.

(2) Files capable of carrying viruses into court computers must be scanned for viruses prior to being written to disk in the clerk's office.

(3) The electronic filing system must be capable of securing the document upon receipt so that it is protected from alteration.

(4) The electronic filing system must be capable of establishing the identity of a sender of a document by means of a registered user identity and password, or by

digitally encrypted electronic signatures, or by any other means reasonably calculated to ensure identification to a high degree of certainty.

(5) Remote electronic access to documents submitted in an electronically filed case and stored electronically shall be limited to judges, court personnel, any persons assisting such persons in the administration of the electronic filing system, and to active members of the Virginia State Bar and their authorized agents, who have complied with the registration requirements to use the electronic filing system.

(6) If the court accepts payment of fees by credit card, debit card, debit account, or electronic funds transfer, registration for the user identity shall include submission of all information required to effect the payment of fees. Electronic submission of this information shall be deemed a signature by the cardholder sender, authorizing the payment of document filing fees. This information shall be kept confidential. There shall be an electronic confirmation from the clerk of any charge to or the debit from the user's account.

(7) No unauthorized person shall be permitted access to other court networks, data or applications unrelated to electronic filing. Administrative access to computer equipment and networks handling electronic filing will be restricted to designated court employees or authorized maintenance personnel.

(8) Electronic filing systems must reasonably protect filed documents against system and security failures and must provide, at a minimum, for daily backup, periodic off-site backup storage if feasible, and prudent disaster recovery mechanisms.

(d) *Electronic Service and Filing Practice and Procedures.*

(1) In an Electronically Filed Case, all pleadings, motions, notices and other material filed with the court shall be in the form of Electronic Documents except where otherwise expressly provided by statute or the Rules of Court, or where the court orders otherwise in an individual case for good cause shown.

(2) Each attorney admitted to practice in the Commonwealth shall be entitled to a registered User ID and password issued by the clerk, or access using any comparable identification system approved by the Supreme Court, for the electronic filing and retrieval of documents.

(3) The clerk shall provide a means, in the courthouse or other designated location, for the parties, counsel and the public to review and copy electronic records from the electronic file during normal business hours.

(4) The format for electronically filed material shall be the Portable Document Format (PDF). Notice will be provided if any other format is approved.

(5)(i) Subject to the provisions of subsections (d) (6) and (7) of this Rule, an electronic document shall be filed by following the procedures of the applicable E-Filing Portal, and shall be deemed filed on the date that it is received in the E-Filing Portal without regard to whether the filing occurred within or outside of standard business hours. If the electronic document is received in the E-Filing Portal on a Saturday, Sunday, legal holiday, or any day or part of a day on which the clerk's office is closed as authorized by an act of the General Assembly, then such document shall be deemed filed on the next day that is not a Saturday, Sunday, legal holiday, or day or part of a day on which the clerk's office is closed.

(ii) Upon electronic filing of a document, an electronic confirmation shall be transmitted to the filing party indicating that the document has been successfully filed through the E-Filing Portal. In addition, the court to which the document is directed shall promptly transmit an electronic acknowledgement of its receipt of the electronically filed document, specifying the identity of the receiving court, the date the document was received by the court, and a court-assigned document reference or docketing number.

(6) A person who files a document electronically shall have the same responsibility as a person filing a document in paper form to ensure that the document is properly filed, complete, and readable. However,

(i) if technical problems at the E-Filing Portal result in a failure to timely file the electronic document, counsel shall provide to the clerk of the court on the next business day all documentation which exists demonstrating the attempt to file the document through the E-Filing Portal, any delivery failure notice received in response to the attempt, and a copy of the document, and

(ii) in the event that the E-Filing Portal was not available due to technical problems during the last filing hours of a business day, the office of the clerk of the court to which the document is directed shall be deemed to have been closed on that day solely with respect to that attempted filing and the provisions of Virginia Code § 1-210(B) and (C) shall apply to that particular attempted filing for purposes of computing the last day for performing any act in a judicial proceeding or the filing of any legal action.

(7) Clerk's notice of defects in a filing; striking documents; court orders.

(i) Incorrect or missing fee. If the clerk of court determines that an electronically filed document is defective because of an incorrect or missing filing fee, and

(A) if the clerk has been provided by the filing party with a credit or payment account through which to obtain payment of fees, the clerk shall immediately process payment of the correct fee through such credit or payment account; or

(B) if processing by the clerk of the proper payment through a credit or payment account authorized by the filing party is not feasible, notice shall be sent by the clerk electronically to the filing party, and all other parties who have appeared in the case.

(ii) Document filed in the wrong case by counsel. If the clerk of court determines prior to acceptance that an electronic document has been filed by counsel under the wrong case or docket number, the clerk shall notify the filing party as soon as practicable, by notice through the E-Filing system, by telephone, or by other effective means.

(iii) A copy of all notices transmitted by the clerk under this subpart (d) (7) shall be retained in the permanent electronic case file maintained by the clerk. A copy of any document stricken shall be retained by the clerk with a designation clearly reflecting that it was stricken and the date of such striking, as a record of its content and disposition.

(8) The clerk's office must accommodate the submission of non-electronic documents in an Electronically Filed Case if filing in electronic form cannot, as a practical matter, be achieved. Such documents shall be imaged to facilitate the creation of a single electronic case file to the extent reasonably possible. An outsized document that is capable of being imaged shall be retained in the form submitted.

(9) When an order is entered, the electronic record will be updated to identify the judge who directed entry of the order and the date it was entered, and a notification shall be sent to counsel of record that the order has been entered, along with a copy of the order or an electronic link providing access to such order. If the entry of an order is done on a paper copy of the order, a digital image of such order shall be made a part of the electronic record, and the endorsed original paper shall be retained for the record.

(10) Hyperlinks between two portions of a filed document or between two or more documents filed in the same case, are permissible, but hyperlinks to other documents, or to external websites, are prohibited. A hyperlink is not itself a part of the official filed document and each hyperlink must contain a text reference to the target of the link.

(e) *Application of, and Compliance with, Other Rules.* In an Electronically Filed Case:

(1) Unless otherwise agreed by all parties, or ordered by the court in an individual case for good cause shown, all documents required to be served — after the initial service of process — shall be served by electronic transmission. Such service shall be effective as provided in Rule 1:12.

(2) Annotation by the clerk as provided in Rule 1:4(h) is not required to be made physically upon the face of the pleading and — if it is made by a separate document — it shall specify the pleading to which such annotation pertains.

(3) An e-mail address of the counsel of record shall be included in the electronic documents filed as required by Rule 1:4(l).

(4) The approved electronic identification accompanying the document when filed shall constitute that person's signature on the document for purposes of Rule 1:5 and Virginia Code § 8.01-271.1.

(5) The provisions of Article 4.1 (§§ 17.1-258.2 et seq.) of Chapter 2 of Title 17.1 of the Code of Virginia shall be applicable where a document is to be notarized, sworn, attested, verified, or otherwise certified, or if any sworn signatures, stamps, seals or other authentications relating to the document are required by any statute or Rule, and an electronic or digitally imaged document with such accompanying entries shall be filed in the clerk's office. Electronic notarization in compliance with the Virginia Notary Act (§§ 47.1-1 et seq.) may also be employed with the filing.

(6) An acceptance of service or a certificate of counsel that electronic copies were served as this Rule requires, showing the date of delivery, shall electronically accompany the served papers and shall satisfy Rule 1:12.

(7) In compliance with Rule 1:13, drafts of orders, decrees and notices shall be served on each counsel of record. Such service may be by electronic transmission and shall make provision for electronic endorsement by multiple parties where applicable. Objections or other notations by the parties shall be entered upon the drafts so circulated, or appended to such drafts by specific cross-reference or other unambiguous association. Endorsed drafts shall be submitted electronically whenever possible, and shall be accompanied by proof of service or acceptance of service when required by the rules of court. If there is no practical means of submitting an electronic or digitally imaged endorsed draft, the manually endorsed document shall be filed in the clerk's office. The clerk shall accommodate the imaging of the document into electronic form and shall retain the original endorsed document.

Effective date. — This rule, adopted November 22, 1999, became effective February 1, 2000.

The amendment effective October 1, 2001, adopted July 30, 2001, in subdivision (c)(3), substituted "Authorized submission of electronic files" for "The public, counsel and the parties must be permitted the legally authorized access to the electronic file" in the first sentence, inserted "in the courthouse or other designated location" in the second sentence, and added the third sentence.

The amendment effective May 2, 2011, adopted March 1, 2011, rewrote (a); in (b), deleted "representation of" preceding "encoded information" and substituted "that can be read, printed, and" for "able to be" and "that can be read, printed," for "able to be" in (1), substituted "is" for "refers to" and inserted "printed" in (2), added (3) and redesignated the following subdivisions accordingly, rewrote (4) and (5), and substituted "means an electronic" for "is an electronic"; rewrote (c) and (d); and added (e).

The amendment effective January 1, 2013, adopted November 1, 2012, in subdivision (c)(5), substituted "active members of the Virginia State Bar and their authorized agents" for "counsel of record, including parties appearing pro se"; in subdivision (d)(5)(i), added "without regard to whether the filing occurred within or outside of standard business hours" at the end of the first sentence and rewrote the second sentence; rewrote subdivision (d)(7); in subdivision (d)(9), substitued "When an order is entered, the electronic record will be updated to identify the judge who directed entry of the order and the date it was entered, and a notification shall be sent" for "When a judge enters an order, the judge or clerk will update the electronic record to indicate the identity of the judge entering the order and the date it was entered, and shall send a notification" at the beginning of the first sentence; and in subdivision (e)(1), substituted "shall be served" for "may be served" near the middle, and deleted ", or mailing, dispatching by commercial delivery service, transmitting by facsimile, or mailing a copy to each counsel of record on or before the day of filing" at the end, of the first sentence.

Rule 1:18. Pretrial Scheduling Order.

A. In any civil case the parties, by counsel of record, may agree and submit for approval and entry by the court a pretrial scheduling order. If the court determines that the submitted order is not consistent with the efficient and orderly administration of justice, then the court shall notify counsel and provide an opportunity to be heard.

B. In any civil case where a pretrial scheduling order is not entered pursuant to paragraph A of this Rule, the court may, upon request of counsel of record for any party, or in its own discretion, enter the pretrial scheduling order contained in Section 3 of the Appendix of Forms at the end of Part I of these Rules (Uniform Pretrial Scheduling Order). No court shall enter the Uniform Pretrial Scheduling Order unless notice has been provided to all counsel of record at least 14 days prior to entry of the order. Upon motion by any party objecting to entry of the Uniform Pretrial Scheduling Order, the court shall hold a hearing prior to entry of the order. With the exception of domestic relations cases, a court may not enter a scheduling order which deviates from the terms of the Uniform Pretrial Scheduling Order unless either (1) counsel of record for all parties agree to different provisions, or (2) the court, after providing an opportunity for counsel of record to be heard, makes a finding that the scheduling order contained in the Appendix is not consistent with the efficient and orderly administration of justice under the specific circumstances of that case.

Effective date. — This rule, adopted May 1, 2000, became effective July 1, 2000.

CASE NOTES

Applied in Rahnema v. Rahnema, 47 Va. App. 645, 626 S.E.2d 448, 2006 Va. App. LEXIS 57 (2006).

Rule 1:19. Pretrial Conferences.

In addition to the pretrial scheduling conferences provided for by Rule 4:13, each trial court may, upon request of counsel of record, or in its own discretion, schedule a final pretrial conference within an appropriate time before the commencement of trial. At the final pretrial conference, the court and counsel of record may consider any of the following:

(a) settlement;

(b) a determination of the issues remaining for trial and whether any amendments to the pleadings are necessary;

(c) the possibility of obtaining stipulations of fact, including, but not limited to, the admissibility of documents;

(d) a limitation of the number of expert and/or lay witnesses;

(e) any pending motions including motions *in limine*;

(f) issues relating to proposed jury instructions; and

(g) such other matters as may aid in the disposition of the action.

Effective date. — This rule, adopted May 1, 2000, became effective July 1, 2000.

CIRCUIT COURT OPINIONS

Scope of rule. — While Va. Sup. Ct. R. 1:19(c) granted a circuit court jurisdiction to establish the amount of unliquidated damages, the rule did not authorize a plaintiff to introduce additional facts of a defendant's liability. Riney v. Park Moving & Storage Co., 74 Va. Cir. 40, 2007 Va. Cir. LEXIS 68 (Fairfax County 2007).

Rule 1:20. Scheduling Civil Cases for Trial.

The circuit courts of the Commonwealth shall adopt one or a combination of the following procedures for scheduling civil cases for trial.

(a) Counsel of record may agree to a trial date and may secure approval of the court by telephone call or other electronic communication to the designated court official.

(b) Counsel of record may agree to a trial date as a part of a written plan prepared and submitted to the court for approval pursuant to Rule 1:18.

(c) The court may, at the request of counsel of record, or may in its own discretion, direct counsel of record to appear, in person or by telephone, for a conference to set a trial date and consider other matters set forth in Rule 1:19 or Rule 4:13.

(d) The court may set civil cases for trial at a docket call held on a day as provided by § 17.1-517.

(e) Following the submission of a praecipe, the court may set civil cases for trial at a docket call held on a day as provided by § 17.1-517.

The Executive Secretary shall make accessible these procedures on the Internet. The clerk of each district and circuit court shall make their respective procedures available in the office of the clerk of that court.

Effective date. — This rule, adopted May 1, 2000, became effective July 1, 2000.

The amendment effective July 1, 2009, adopted June 12, 2009, rewrote the concluding paragraph of the section.

Rule 1:21. Preliminary Voir Dire Information.

At the outset of jury selection in any civil or criminal case, the court shall deliver preliminary instructions that: (1) explain the purpose of the voir dire examination, (2) explain the difference between peremptory challenges and removals for cause, (3) summarize the nature of the case, (4) estimate how long the trial may last, and (5) indicate whether it is anticipated that the jury will be sequestered.

Effective date. — This rule, adopted October 24, 2001, became effective January 1, 2002.

Rule 1:22. Exercise of Challenges to Prospective Jurors.

Counsel shall be afforded the opportunity to challenge jurors for cause out of the presence of the panel.

Effective date. — This rule, adopted October 24, 2001, became effective January 1, 2002.

Rule 1:23. Note Taking by Jurors.

A. The court, in the exercise of its discretion, may permit jurors to take notes during the trial.

B. If notes are taken by any of the jurors, at the conclusion of each day of a trial, the court shall collect juror notes and provide for their security until the trial resumes. Upon conclusion of the trial, the court shall collect and destroy all juror notes.

Effective date. — This rule, adopted October 24, 2001, became effective January 1, 2002.

APPENDIX OF FORMS.

1. Praecipe (Rule 1:15(b)).

VIRGINIA: IN THE CIRCUIT COURT OF THE

................., Plaintiff
v.
................., Defendant

AT LAW NO. .....
or
IN CHANCERY NO. .....

PRAECIPE

I certify that the above styled cause is matured for trial on its merits and request the Clerk to place it on the docket to be called on ....
date of next docket call
to be set for trial *with* ( ) or *without* ( ) a jury.
Dated this .... day of ...., 20.....

....
Counsel for ....

CERTIFICATE OF SERVICE

I certify that on the .... day of ...., 20...., I mailed or delivered a true copy of the foregoing praecipe to all counsel of record herein pursuant to the provisions of Rule 1:12 of the Rules of the Supreme Court of Virginia, and served a true copy upon parties not represented by counsel, if any.

....
Counsel for ....

2. Instructions (Rule 1:15(c)).

Counsel for all parties, unless compliance is waived by the court, shall, two days before a civil jury trial date, submit to the court a copy of all instructions such counsel proposes to request — in electronic or paper form as directed by the court — and noting thereon the authority or authorities relied upon for such instructions. Counsel may be required to exchange copies of proposed instructions. This rule shall not preclude the offering of additional instructions at the trial.

The amendment, effective May 2, 2011, adopted March 1, 2011, in the last sentence, inserted "— in electronic or paper form as directed by the court — and" near the end of the first sentence.

3. Uniform Pretrial Scheduling Order (Rule 1:18B).

I. Trial

The trial date is ____________________ (with a jury) (without a jury).
The estimated length of trial is ____________________.

II. Discovery

The parties shall complete discovery, including depositions, by 30 days before trial; however, depositions taken in lieu of live testimony at trial will be permitted until 15 days before trial. "Complete" means that all interrogatories, requests for production, requests for admissions and other discovery must be served sufficiently in advance of trial to allow a timely response at least 30 days before trial. Depositions may be taken after the specified time period by agreement of counsel of record or for good cause shown, provided however, that the taking of a deposition after the deadline established herein shall not provide a basis for continuance of the trial date or the scheduling of motions inconsistent with the normal procedures of the court. The parties have a duty to seasonably supplement and amend discovery responses pursuant to Rule 4:1(e) of the Rules of Supreme Court of Virginia. Seasonably means as soon as practical. No provision of this Order supersedes the Rules of Supreme Court of Virginia governing discovery. Any discovery motion filed shall contain a certification that counsel has made a good faith effort to resolve the matters set forth in the motion with opposing counsel.

III. Designation of Experts

If requested in discovery, plaintiff's, counter-claimant's, third party plaintiff's, and cross-claimant's experts shall be identified on or before 90 days before trial. If requested in discovery, defendant's and all other opposing experts shall be identified on or before 60 days before trial. If requested in discovery, experts or opinions responsive to new matters raised in the opposing parties, identification of experts shall be designated no later than 45 days before trial. If requested, all information discoverable under Rule 4:1(b)(4)(A)(i) of the Rules of Supreme Court of Virginia shall be provided or the expert will not ordinarily be permitted to express any nondisclosed opinions at trial. The foregoing deadlines shall not relieve a party of the obligation to respond to discovery requests within the time periods set forth in the Rules of Supreme Court of Virginia, including, in particular, the duty to supplement or amend prior responses pursuant to Rule 4:1(e).

IV. Dispositive Motions

All dispositive motions shall be presented to the court for hearing as far in advance of the trial date as practical. All counsel of record are encouraged to bring on for hearing all demurrers, special pleas, motions for summary judgment or other dispositive motions not more than 60 days after being filed.

V. Exhibit and Witness List

Counsel of record shall exchange 15 days before trial a list specifically identifying each exhibit to be introduced at trial, copies of any exhibits not previously supplied in discovery, and a list of witnesses proposed to be introduced at trial. The lists of exhibits and witnesses shall be filed with the Clerk of the Court simultaneously therewith but the exhibits shall not then be filed. Any exhibit or witness not so identified and filed will not be received in evidence, except in rebuttal or for impeachment or unless the admission of such exhibit or testimony of the witness would cause no surprise or prejudice to the opposing party and the failure to list the exhibit or witness was through inadvertence. Any objections to exhibits or witnesses shall state the legal reasons therefor except on relevancy grounds, and shall be filed with the Clerk of the Court and a copy delivered to opposing counsel at least five days before trial or the objections will be deemed waived absent leave of court for good cause shown.

VI. Pretrial Conferences

Pursuant to Rule 4:13 of the Rules of Supreme Court of Virginia, when requested by any party or upon its own motion, the court may order a pretrial conference wherein motions in limine, settlement discussions or other pretrial motions which may aid in the disposition of this action can be heard.

VII. Motions in Limine

Absent leave of court, any motion in limine which requires argument exceeding five minutes shall be duly noticed and heard before the day of trial.

VIII. Witness Subpoenas

Early filing of a request for witness subpoenas is encouraged so that such subpoenas may be served at least 10 days before trial.

IX. Continuances

Continuances will only be granted by the court for good cause shown.

X. Jury Instructions

Counsel of record, unless compliance is waived by the court, shall, two business days before a civil jury trial date, exchange proposed jury instructions. At the commencement of trial, counsel of record shall tender the court the originals of all agreed upon instructions and copies of all contested instructions with appropriate citations. This requirement shall not preclude the offering of additional instructions at the trial.

XI. Deposition Transcripts to be Used at Trial

Counsel of record shall confer and attempt to identify and resolve all issues regarding the use of depositions at trial. It is the obligation of the proponent of any deposition of any non-party witness who will not appear at trial to advise opposing counsel of record of counsel's intent to use all or a portion of the deposition at trial at the earliest reasonable opportunity. Other than trial depositions taken after completion of discovery under Paragraph II, designations of portions of non-party depositions, other than for rebuttal or impeachment, shall be exchanged no later than 15 days before trial, except for good cause shown or by agreement of counsel. It becomes the obligation of the opponent of any such deposition to bring any objection or other unresolved issues to the court for hearing before the day of trial, and to counter-designate any additional portions of designated depositions at least 5 days before such hearing.

XII. Waiver or Modification of Terms of Order

Upon motion, the time limits and prohibitions contained in this order may be waived or modified by leave of court for good cause shown.

Editor's note. — At the direction of the clerk's office of the Supreme Court of Virginia, a cross reference in subsection III was changed to correct a typographical error. In the fourth sentence "Rule 4:1(b)(4)(A)(i)" was substituted for "Rule 4:1(b)(4)(A)(1)."

The amendment, effective May 3, 2010, adopted February 26, 2010, in Paragraph XI, inserted the third sentence and added ", and to counter-designate any additional portions of designated depositions at least 5 days before such hearing" at the end of the fourth sentence.

PART ONE A
FOREIGN ATTORNEYS

Rule
1A:1. Foreign Attorneys — When Admitted to Practice in This State Without Examination.
1A:2. Foreign Patent and Trademark Attorneys — When Admitted to Practice in the Courts of This State Limited to Patent and Trademark Law Without Examination.
1A:3. Revocation of Certificates Issued to Foreign Attorneys.
1A:4. Out-of-State Lawyers — When Allowed by Comity to Participate in a Case *Pro Hac Vice*.

Rule
1A:5. Virginia Corporate Counsel & Corporate Counsel Registrants.
1A:6. Foreign Attorneys — Registered Military Legal Assistance Attorneys.
1A:7. Certification of Foreign Legal Consultants.

Appendix of Forms.

1. Application to Appear *Pro Hac Vice* Before A Virginia Tribunal.
2. Motion and Oath for Admission as Corporate Counsel.

Editor's note. — Part One A became effective March 1, 1972. The statements of source, which were prepared by a subcommittee and presented to the Judicial Council, are not part of the Rules as adopted by the Supreme Court of Virginia.

Rule 1A:1. Foreign Attorneys — When Admitted to Practice in This State Without Examination.

Any person who has been admitted to practice law before the court of last resort of any state or territory of the United States or of the District of Columbia may file an application to be admitted to practice law in this Commonwealth without examination, if counsel licensed to practice here may be admitted to practice there without examination.

The applicant shall:

(1) File with the secretary of the Virginia Board of Bar Examiners an application, under oath, upon a form furnished by the Board.

(2) Furnish a certificate, signed by the presiding judge of the court of last resort of the jurisdiction in which the applicant is entitled to practice law, stating that the applicant has been so licensed for at least five years.

(3) Complete the Applicant's Character and Fitness Questionnaire and furnish a report of the National Conference of Bar Examiners, or such other report as the Board may prescribe, concerning the applicant's past practice and record, and pay the fee for such report.

(4) Pay such filing fee as may be fixed from time to time by the Board.

Thereafter, the Board will determine in accordance with guidelines approved by the Supreme Court whether the applicant has established by satisfactory evidence that he or she:

(a) Is a proper person to practice law.

(b) Has made such progress in the practice of law that it would be unreasonable to require the applicant to take an examination.

(c) Intends to practice full time as a member of the Virginia State Bar.

In the determination of these matters the Board may require the applicant to appear personally before the Board, the Character and Fitness Committee of the Board, or a member of either the Board or the Committee, and furnish such information as may be required.

If it is determined that the applicant has established that he or she meets all of the aforementioned requirements, the Board shall notify the applicant that some member of the Virginia State Bar who is qualified to practice before the Supreme Court may make an oral motion in open Court for the applicant's admission to practice law in this Commonwealth.

Upon such motion for admission, the applicant shall thereupon take and subscribe to the oaths required of attorneys at law, whereupon the Board shall issue to the applicant a certificate to practice law in the Commonwealth, and the applicant shall, upon payment of applicable dues, become an active member of the Virginia State Bar.

Source. — Rule 1:5.

Regulations Governing Applications for Admission to the Virginia Bar Pursuant to the Rules of the Supreme Court of Virginia — Rule 1A:1.

INTRODUCTION

Each person who has met the educational requirements and has proved that he or she satisfies the character and fitness requirements as established by the law of Virginia may seek admission to the Virginia Bar by taking the Virginia Bar Examination. A primary purpose of the Virginia Bar Examination is to determine whether an applicant is able to demonstrate his or her current minimum competency to engage in the general practice of law in Virginia.

In addition to admission to the Bar by examination, the Supreme Court of Virginia, in its discretion, has determined that a person currently engaged in the active practice of law, who has been so engaged for at least five years, may seek to demonstrate that he or she has made such progress in the practice of law that it would be unreasonable to require the person to take an examination to demonstrate current minimum competency. In other words, an applicant's experience in the practice of law may, at the discretion of the Court, be accepted as adequate evidence of current minimum competency in lieu of the bar examination.

The Supreme Court of Virginia has assigned to the Virginia Board of Bar Examiners (the "Board") the responsibility to assess the information furnished by an applicant for admission without examination and to determine, from the information so furnished, whether the applicant's experience in the practice of law is sufficient to demonstrate his or her current competence, good character, and fitness to practice law in Virginia.

In order to guide the Board in its determinations, the Court has adopted the following criteria to be applied by the Board in assessing applications for admission to the bar of Virginia without examination:

THRESHOLD REQUIREMENTS

1. Reciprocity. The purpose of the reciprocity requirement is to encourage other jurisdictions to grant the same privilege to Virginia lawyers. The Board shall consider applications for admission without examination only from a person who is admitted to practice before the court of last resort of a jurisdiction (*i.e.,* a state or territory of the United States, or the District of Columbia) that permits lawyers licensed in Virginia to be admitted to practice without examination in such jurisdiction (a "Reciprocal Jurisdiction"), and who has either:

(a) taken and passed the general bar examination of such Reciprocal Jurisdiction, is currently an active member in good standing of the bar of such Reciprocal Jurisdiction, and has held an unrestricted license to practice law therein for at least two years; or

(b) been admitted without examination (*i.e.,* on motion) to the bar of such Reciprocal Jurisdiction, is currently an active member in good standing of the bar of such Reciprocal Jurisdiction, holds an unrestricted license to practice law therein, and has been engaged in the full-time active practice of law within such Reciprocal Jurisdiction for at least five of the of the seven years immediately preceding the date the application is filed.

2. Minimum Period of Active Law Practice. The applicant must have been engaged in the active practice of law for at least five years.

3. Requirement of Current Active Practice. An applicant may apply for admission without examination only if the applicant has been engaged in the active practice of law (as defined in these Regulations) for at least five (5) of the last seven (7) years immediately preceding his or her application for admission to the Virginia Bar. The applicant must have been engaged in this practice on a full-time basis (as defined in these Regulations) in a jurisdiction other than Virginia. Only practice occurring subsequent to the applicant's having been issued an unrestricted license to practice law in such other jurisdiction shall qualify. Practice from an office located in a foreign country shall not be accepted as qualifying practice. Persons holding a Virginia Corporate Counsel Certificate under Part I of Rule 1A:5 may receive credit as provided in such Rule.

4. Active Practice. For purposes of admission without examination, "active practice of law" ordinarily shall mean (i) private practice as a sole practitioner or for a law firm, legal services office, legal clinic, or similar entity, provided such practice was subsequent to having been issued an unrestricted license to practice law in the jurisdiction in which that practice occurred; (ii) practice as an attorney for a corporation, partnership, trust, individual or other entity, provided such practice was subsequent to having been issued an unrestricted license to practice law in the jurisdiction in which the practice occurred, and involved the primary duties of furnishing legal counsel, drafting legal documents and pleadings, interpreting and giving advice regarding the law, and preparing, trying or presenting cases before courts or administrative agencies; (iii) practice as an attorney for the federal or a state or local government with the same primary duties as described above regarding attorneys for a corporation, provided such practice was subsequent to having been issued an unrestricted license to practice law in the jurisdiction in which that practice occurred; (iv) employment as a judge for the federal or a state government, provided that such position requires a valid unrestricted license to practice law in the jurisdiction in which such employment occurred; (v) service as a judicial law clerk for a state or federal court subsequent to having been issued an unrestricted license to practice law in the jurisdiction where the court is located; or (vi) service on active duty in a branch of the armed forces of the United States as a judge advocate or law specialist, as those terms are defined in the Uniform Code of Military Justice, 10 U.S.C. § 801, as amended, provided that such position requires a valid license to practice law and involves the same primary duties as described above regarding attorneys for a corporation. With the exception of the positions described in (iv) and (v) above, each qualifying position must have involved an attorney-client relationship. For purposes of determining whether an applicant's practice was in a jurisdiction subsequent to having been issued an unrestricted license to practice law therein, only the jurisdiction where the applicant's primary office was located shall be considered.

5. Legal Education. The applicant must have received a J.D. law degree from a law school that was approved by the American Bar Association at the time of such applicant's graduation.

6. Bar Examination History. The applicant must have failed no more than two bar examinations of any of the states or territories of the United States (including Virginia), or the District of Columbia, and must have failed no bar examination within the five years immediately preceding the application for admission to the Virginia Bar.

7. Intent to Practice Full Time in Virginia. An applicant must intend, promptly after being admitted to practice in Virginia without examination, to establish his or her office in Virginia and to practice full time from such Virginia office. Full time is defined as being engaged in the active practice of law (as defined above) as one's primary occupation for at least thirty-five (35) hours weekly and having an office where clients can be seen on the premises. The Board shall not approve an application unless the applicant has verifiable plans to practice in Virginia (*i.e.*, a job offer from a Virginia firm, a relocation to the Virginia office of the applicant's firm, an executed lease for office space in Virginia, etc.). Practice from one's residence shall not constitute satisfactory evidence of intent to practice law full time unless the applicant's residence is in a zoning classification which permits seeing clients on the premises and displaying an exterior sign identifying the law office. Virtual offices or shared occupancy arrangements shall not be acceptable. In addition, an applicant shall not divide his or her time between an office within Virginia and one in another jurisdiction. An applicant who is a member of or associated with a firm which has offices outside Virginia must be resident at such firm's Virginia office, shall not maintain an office at a location outside Virginia, and may work at one of his or her firm's other offices only on an occasional and not on a regular basis. The Court will monitor to determine whether an applicant maintains his or her Virginia office.

ASSESSMENT OF FITNESS AND PROGRESS

If an applicant provides satisfactory evidence that he or she meets all of the above threshold requirements, the Board shall thereafter determine from the evidence provided by the applicant and the results of any investigation conducted by the Board or its designee whether such applicant (i) is a person of honest demeanor and good moral character and possesses the requisite fitness to perform the obligations and responsibilities of a practicing attorney, and (ii) has made such progress in the practice of law that it would be unreasonable to require the applicant to take an examination to demonstrate current minimum competency.

The applicant has the burden to prove by clear and convincing evidence that he or she is a person of honest demeanor and good moral character and possesses the requisite fitness to perform the obligations and responsibilities of a practicing attorney and thus is a proper person to practice law in Virginia. If an applicant fails to answer any question on the Character and Fitness Questionnaire or which is otherwise propounded by the Board, or to supply any requested documentary material, the Board may find that the applicant has not met the burden of proving his or her good moral character.

The primary purposes of character and fitness screening before admission to the Virginia Bar are to assure the protection of the public and safeguard the system of justice. An attorney should be one whose record of conduct justifies the trust of clients, adversaries, courts, and others with respect to the professional duties owed to them. A record manifesting a significant deficiency in the honesty, trustworthiness, diligence, or reliability of an applicant may constitute a basis for denial of admission. The revelation or discovery of any of the following may be treated as cause for further inquiry before the Board decides whether the applicant possesses the character and fitness to practice law:

A. commission or conviction of a crime;

B. violation of the honor code of the applicant's college or university, law school, or other academic misconduct;

C. making of false statements or omissions, including failing to provide complete and accurate information concerning the applicant's past;

D. misconduct in employment;

E. other than an honorable discharge from any branch of the armed services;

F. acts involving dishonesty, fraud, deceit or misrepresentation;

G. abuse of legal process;

H. neglect of financial responsibilities;

I. neglect of professional obligations;

J. violation of an order of a court;

K. denial of admission to the bar in another jurisdiction on character and fitness grounds;

L. disciplinary action by a lawyer disciplinary agency or other professional disciplinary agency of any jurisdiction, including pending, unresolved disciplinary complaints against the applicant;

M. commission of an act constituting the unauthorized practice of law, or unresolved complaints involving allegations of the unauthorized practice of law;

N. any other conduct which reflects adversely upon the character or fitness of an applicant.

The Board shall determine whether the present character and fitness of an applicant qualifies the applicant for admission to the practice of law. In making this determination, the following factors will be considered in assigning weight and significance to the applicant's prior conduct:

i. age of the applicant at the time of the conduct;

ii. recency of the conduct;

iii. reliability of the information concerning the conduct;

iv. seriousness of the conduct;

v. factors underlying the conduct;

vi. cumulative effect of the conduct or information;

vii. evidence of rehabilitation;

viii. positive social contributions of the applicant since the conduct;

ix. candor of the applicant in the admissions process; and

x. materiality of any omissions or misrepresentations.

The Board's obligation to the public requires the Board to address recent mental health and chemical or psychological dependency matters, which may affect, or if untreated could affect, an applicant's ability to perform any of the obligations and responsibilities of a practicing lawyer in a competent and professional manner. Accordingly, the Board will inquire concerning

i. mental or emotional instability and

ii. existing and untreated drug or alcohol dependency.

The mere fact of treatment for mental health problems or chemical or psychological dependency is not, in itself, a basis on which an applicant is ordinarily denied admission in Virginia, and the Board of Bar Examiners regularly issues certificates to individuals who have demonstrated personal responsibility and maturity in dealing with mental health and chemical or psychological dependency issues. The Board encourages applicants who may benefit from treatment or counseling to seek it. A license or certificate may be denied or deferred when an applicant's ability to function is impaired in a manner relevant to the practice of law at the time the admission decision is made, or when an applicant demonstrates a lack of candor by his or her responses.

In addition, an application will not be approved unless the applicant is an active member in good standing of the reciprocal bar at the time the Board receives the character report and conducts its review of that report. If the applicant's license has ever been suspended or revoked in any jurisdiction, it must be fully reinstated and in good standing (no pending disciplinary charges).

In evaluating whether an applicant has demonstrated satisfactory progress in the practice of law for admission to the practice of law in Virginia without examination, the Board considers whether the following requirements are evident from the information supplied by the applicant and from the investigative report:

1. Knowledge of the fundamental principles of law and the ability to recall that knowledge, to reason, to analyze, and to apply one's knowledge to relevant facts;

2. The ability to communicate clearly, candidly and civilly with clients, attorneys, courts, and others;

3. The ability to exercise good judgment in conducting one's professional business;

4. The ability to conduct oneself with a high degree of honesty, integrity, and trustworthiness in all professional relationships and with respect to all legal obligations;

5. The ability to conduct oneself with respect for and in accordance with the law and the Rules of Professional Conduct;

6. The ability to avoid acts that exhibit disregard for the health, safety and welfare of others;

7. The ability to conduct oneself diligently and reliably in fulfilling all obligations to clients, attorneys, courts, and others;

8. The ability to use honesty and good judgment in financial dealings on behalf of oneself, clients, and others;

9. The ability to comply with deadlines and time constraints; and

10. The ability to conduct oneself professionally and in a manner that engenders respect for the law and the profession.

Editor's note. — The regulations above were adopted effective December 1, 2008.

The amendment effective July 6, 1998, adopted May 7, 1998, in subdivision (1), substituted "secretary of the Virginia Board of Bar Examiners" for "clerk of the Supreme Court at Richmond," and substituted "Board" for "clerk" at the end of the subdivision; in subdivision (3), inserted "Complete the Applicant's Character and Fitness Questionnaire and" at the beginning of the subdivision, inserted "or such other report as the Board may prescribe," following "Examiners," and inserted "and pay the fee for such report" at the end of the subdivision; in the seventh paragraph, substituted "Board" for "Supreme Court," inserted "in accordance with guidelines approved by the Supreme Court," and inserted "has established by satisfactory evidence that he or she"; in subdivision (c), inserted "State"; in the eleventh paragraph, substituted "Board may require" for "Supreme Court may call upon," and substituted "the Board, the Character and Fitness Committee of the Board, or a member of either the Board or the Committee," for "a member of the Court or its executive secretary"; in the twelfth paragraph, substituted "it is determined that the applicant has established that he or she meets all of the aforementioned requirements, the Board shall notify the applicant" for "all of the aforementioned matters are determined favorable for the applicant, he or she shall be notified" and inserted "State"; and in the last paragraph, substituted "such motion for" for "the applicant's," substituted "the applicant" for "he or she," and substituted "Board shall issue to the applicant a certificate to practice law in the Commonwealth, and the applicant shall, upon payment of the applicable dues" for "applicant shall."

The amendment effective and adopted March 21, 2001, in subdivision (4), substituted "such filing fee as may be fixed from time to time by the Board" for "a filing fee of five hundred dollars."

Law Review. — For note, "What Price the Bar? Examining the Constitutionality of the Virginia Bar Admission Requirements in Friedman v. Supreme Court of Virginia," see 45 Wash. & Lee L. Rev. 213 (1988). For note, "Invalidation of Residency Requirements for Admission to the Bar: Opportunities for General Reform," see 23 U. Rich. L. Rev. 231 (1989). For article, "Professional Responsibility," see 39 U. Rich. L. Rev. 315 (2004).

Michie's Jurisprudence. — For related discussion, see 2A M.J. Attorney and Client, §§ 5, 6.

CASE NOTES

I. General Consideration.
II. Constitutionality.
III. Intent to Practice Full Time.

I. GENERAL CONSIDERATION.

Words "practice law" do not include every instance involving a transaction tied to Virginia. Brown v. Supreme Court, 359 F. Supp. 549 (E.D. Va.), aff'd sub nom. Titus v. Supreme Court, 414 U.S. 1034, 94 S. Ct. 533, 534, 38 L. Ed. 2d 327 (1973).

Right to practice law in Virginia is governed by statute as supplemented by the Rules of the Supreme Court of Virginia. Brown v. Supreme Court, 359 F. Supp. 549 (E.D. Va.), aff'd sub nom. Titus v. Supreme Court, 414 U.S. 1034, 94 S. Ct. 533, 534, 38 L. Ed. 2d 327 (1973).

Virginia has created two classes of attorneys. — The first encompasses those attorneys licensed by examination, and the second includes those licensed without examination. In re Brown, 213 Va. 282, 191 S.E.2d 812 (1972).

Comity or reciprocity in admission to the bar is essentially a state discretionary function. Brown v. Supreme Court, 359 F. Supp. 549 (E.D. Va.), aff'd sub nom. Titus v. Supreme Court, 414 U.S. 1034, 94 S. Ct. 533, 534, 38 L. Ed. 2d 327 (1973).

There is no inherent right to practice law. — The right arises after qualification under the rules has been established. Brown v. Supreme Court, 359 F. Supp. 549 (E.D. Va.), aff'd sub nom. Titus v. Supreme Court, 414 U.S. 1034, 94 S. Ct. 533, 534, 38 L. Ed. 2d 327 (1973).

There is no "fundamental right" of a foreign attorney to practice law in every state merely because he is capable and of good moral character. Brown v. Supreme Court, 359 F. Supp. 549 (E.D. Va.), aff'd sub nom. Titus v. Supreme Court, 414 U.S. 1034, 94 S. Ct. 533, 534, 38 L. Ed. 2d 327 (1973).

Requirements in Virginia for admission without examination are not more stringent than in other states. Brown v. Supreme Court, 359 F. Supp. 549 (E.D. Va.), aff'd sub nom. Titus v. Supreme Court, 414 U.S. 1034, 94 S. Ct. 533, 534, 38 L. Ed. 2d 327 (1973).

Difficulties with enforcing the new rule do not support the right of any foreign attorney to be admitted to practice. Brown v. Supreme Court, 359 F. Supp. 549 (E.D. Va.), aff'd sub nom. Titus v. Supreme Court, 414 U.S. 1034, 94 S. Ct. 533, 534, 38 L. Ed. 2d 327 (1973).

II. CONSTITUTIONALITY.

Prevention of nonresidents from admission to bar on motion is unconstitutional. — This rule, which formerly permitted some Virginia residents, but prevented nonresidents, from gaining admission to the Virginia bar on motion without having to take the bar examination, violated the Privileges and Immunities Clause of Article IV, § 2 of the United States Constitution. Friedman v. Supreme Court, 822 F.2d 423 (4th Cir. 1987), aff'd, 487 U.S. 59, 108 S. Ct. 2260, 101 L. Ed. 2d 56 (1988).

Virginia's former residency requirement for admission to the state's bar without examination violated the Privileges and Immunities Clause. Supreme Court v. Friedman, 487 U.S. 59, 108 S. Ct. 2260, 101 L. Ed. 2d 56 (1988).

Separate classification of applicants is constitutional. — The Supreme Court has the constitutional right to separately classify applicants taking the bar examination and those foreign attorneys who seek admission by comity or reciprocity since there is a rational basis for making the separate classifications, as long as the classifications are not plainly arbitrary or discriminatory. Brown v. Supreme Court, 359 F. Supp. 549 (E.D. Va.), aff'd sub nom. Titus v. Supreme Court, 414 U.S. 1034, 94 S. Ct. 533, 534, 38 L. Ed. 2d 327 (1973).

Fact that this rule may result in "incidental individual inequality" does not make it offensive to the Fourteenth Amendment. Brown v. Supreme Court, 359 F. Supp. 549 (E.D. Va.), aff'd sub nom. Titus v. Supreme Court, 414 U.S. 1034, 94 S. Ct. 533, 534, 38 L. Ed. 2d 327 (1973).

Laxity in enforcement does not render rule unconstitutional. — Virginia State Bar may have been lax in its enforcement efforts under this rule, but this in no sense renders the rule unconstitutional. Brown v. Supreme Court, 359 F. Supp. 549 (E.D. Va.), aff'd sub nom. Titus v. Supreme Court, 414 U.S. 1034, 94 S. Ct. 533, 534, 38 L. Ed. 2d 327 (1973).

III. INTENT TO PRACTICE FULL TIME.

Subdivision (4)(c) affords due process and respects federal primacy in interstate commerce. Goldfarb v. Supreme Court, 766 F.2d 859 (4th Cir. 1985), cert. denied, 474 U.S. 1086, 106 S. Ct. 862, 88 L. Ed. 2d 901 (1986).

There is a rational connection of a full-time practice requirement for the admission to the bar with the qualification of capacity to practice law. In re Brown, 213 Va. 282, 191 S.E.2d 812 (1972).

Preadmission showing of intent to practice full time. — As to those Virginia attorneys licensed without examination, there is a requirement of a preadmission showing of intent to practice full time as a member of the Virginia bar. As to those Virginia attorneys licensed by examination, there is no requirement of a preadmission showing of intent to practice full time as a member of the Virginia bar. In re Brown, 213 Va. 282, 191 S.E.2d 812 (1972).

Rule 1A:2. Foreign Patent and Trademark Attorneys — When Admitted to Practice in the Courts of This State Limited to Patent and Trademark Law Without Examination.

No lawyer admitted to practice limited to patent and trademark law as defined in § 54.1-3901(A) prior to July 1, 2000, pursuant to this Rule 1A:2 prior to July 1, 2000, shall hold himself or herself out as authorized to practice law generally in this Commonwealth.

Source. — Rule 1:5.1.

Comment on the 1982 amendment. — The General Assembly in 1981 revised § 54-42.1 [now § 54.1-3901(A)] on which this rule is based. The revision conforms the rule to the amended statute.

The amendment effective July 6, 1998, adopted May 7, 1998, in subdivision (1), substituted "secretary of the Virginia Board of Bar Examiners" for "clerk of the Supreme Court at Richmond," and substituted "Board" for "clerk"; in subdivision (3), inserted "Complete the Applicant's Character and Fitness Questionnaire and" at the beginning of the subdivision, inserted "or such other report as the Board may prescribe," and inserted "and pay the fee for such report" at the end of the subdivision; in the seventh paragraph, substituted "Board" for "Supreme Court," inserted "in accordance with guidelines approved by the Supreme Court," and inserted "has established by satisfactory evidence that he or she"; in the eleventh paragraph, substituted "Board may require" for "Supreme Court may call upon," and substituted "the Board, the Character and Fitness Committee of the Board, or a member of either the Board or the Committee" for "a member of the Court or its executive secretary"; in the twelfth paragraph, substituted "it is" for "all of the aforementioned matters are," substituted "that the applicant has established that he or she meets all of the aforementioned requirements, the Board shall notify the applicant" for "favorable for the applicant, he or she shall be notified," inserted "State," and deleted "the courts of" following "trademark law in"; in the thirteenth paragraph, substituted "such motion for" for "the applicant's," substituted "the applicant" for "he or she," deleted "in open court" following "thereupon," inserted "the Board shall issue to the applicant a certificate to practice law in the Commonwealth limited to patent, trademark, copyright and unfair competition causes, and," and inserted "upon payment of the applicable dues."

The amendment, effective July 1, 2000, adopted June 16, 2000, rewrote the Rule by deleting all provisions except for the last paragraph. The remaining paragraph was amended by inserting "to practice limited to patent and trademark law as defined in § 54.1-3901(A) prior to July 1, 2000" and "1A:2 prior to July 1, 2000."

Michie's Jurisprudence. — For related discussion, see 2A M.J. Attorney and Client, § 6.

Rule 1A:3. Revocation of Certificates Issued to Foreign Attorneys.

Following receipt of evidence satisfactory to the Supreme Court that a person who has been admitted to practice pursuant to Rule 1A:1 no longer satisfies the requirement of clause (c) of that section or that a person who has been admitted to practice pursuant to Rule 1A:2 prior to July 1, 2000, no longer satisfies the requirement of clause (c) of that section, the Supreme Court may revoke the certificate issued to that person. Following receipt of evidence that a person who has been admitted to practice pursuant to Rule 1A:1 or Rule 1A:2 prior to July 1, 2000, has been disbarred pursuant to Part Six of the Rules, the Supreme Court will revoke the certificate issued to that person.

Source. — Rule 1:5.2.

The amendment, effective July 6, 1998, adopted May 7, 1998, substituted "certificate" for "license" in two places.

The amendment, effective July 1, 2000, adopted June 16, 2000, inserted "prior to July 1, 2000" in two places.

Law Review. — For note, "Invalidation of Residency Requirements for Admission to the Bar: Opportunities for General Reform," see 23 U. Rich. L. Rev. 231 (1989).

Michie's Jurisprudence. — For related discussion, see 2A M.J. Attorney and Client, § 6.

Rule 1A:4. Out-of-State Lawyers — When Allowed by Comity to Participate in a Case *Pro Hac Vice*.

1. *Introduction.* — A lawyer who is not a member of the Virginia State Bar, but is currently licensed and authorized to practice law in another state, territory, or possession of the United States of America (hereinafter called an "out-of-state lawyer") may apply to appear as counsel *pro hac vice* in a particular case before any court, board

or administrative agency (hereinafter called "tribunal") in the Commonwealth of Virginia upon compliance with this rule.

2. *Association of Local Counsel.* — No out-of-state lawyer may appear *pro hac vice* before any tribunal in Virginia unless the out-of-state lawyer has first associated in that case with a lawyer who is an active member in good standing of the Virginia State Bar (hereinafter called "local counsel"). The name of local counsel shall appear on all notices, orders, pleadings, and other documents filed in the case. Local counsel shall personally appear and participate in pretrial conferences, hearings, trials, or other proceedings actually conducted before the tribunal. Local counsel associating with an out-of-state lawyer in a particular case shall accept joint responsibility with the out-of-state lawyer to the client, other parties, witnesses, other counsel and to the tribunal in that particular case. Any pleading or other paper required to be served (whether relating to discovery or otherwise) shall be invalid unless it is signed by local counsel. The tribunal in which such case is pending shall have full authority to deal with local counsel exclusively in all matters connected with the pending case. If it becomes necessary to serve notice or process in the case, any notice or process served upon local counsel shall be deemed valid as if served on the out-of-state lawyer.

3. *Procedure for applying.* — Appearance *pro hac vice* in a case is subject to the discretion and approval of the tribunal where such case is pending. An out-of-state lawyer desiring to appear *pro hac vice* under this rule shall comply with the procedures set forth herein for each case in which *pro hac vice* status is requested. For good cause shown, a tribunal may permit an out-of-state lawyer to appear *pro hac vice* on a temporary basis prior to completion by the out-of-state lawyer of the application procedures set forth herein. At the time such temporary admission is granted, the tribunal shall specify a time limit within which the out-of-state lawyer must complete the application procedures, and any temporary *pro hac vice* admission shall be revoked in the event the out-of-state lawyer fails to complete the application procedure within the time limit.

(a) Notarized Application. In order to appear *pro hac vice* as counsel in any matter pending before a tribunal in the Commonwealth of Virginia, an out-of-state lawyer shall deliver to local counsel to file with the tribunal an original notarized application and a non-refundable application fee of $250.00 payable to the Clerk of the Supreme Court. *Pro hac vice* counsel must submit a notarized application with the non-refundable application fee of $250.00 for each separate case before a tribunal. The fee shall be paid to the Clerk of the Supreme Court of Virginia. The tribunal shall file a copy of the notarized application, as well as its order granting *pro hac vice* admission in the case and the $250.00 fee, with the Clerk of the Supreme Court of Virginia. Original, notarized applications and orders granting, denying or revoking applications to appear *pro hac vice* shall be retained in a separate file containing all applications. The clerk of the tribunal shall maintain the application for a period of three years after completion of the case and all appeals.

(b) Motion to associate counsel *pro hac vice*. Local counsel shall file a motion to associate the out-of-state lawyer as counsel *pro hac vice* with the tribunal where the case is pending, together with proof of service on all parties in accordance with the Rules of the Supreme Court of Virginia. The motion of local counsel shall be accompanied by: (1) the original, notarized application of the out-of-state lawyer; (2) a proposed order granting or denying the motion; and (3) the required application fee.

(c) Entry of Order. The order granting or denying the motion to associate counsel *pro hac vice* shall be entered by the tribunal promptly and a copy of the order shall be forwarded to the Clerk of the Supreme Court. An out-of-state lawyer shall make no appearance in a case until the tribunal where the case is pending enters the order granting the motion to associate counsel *pro hac vice* unless temporary admission has been approved pursuant to this rule. The order granting *pro hac vice* status shall be valid until the case is concluded in the courts of this Commonwealth or a court revokes the *pro hac vice* admission.

4. *Notarized Application.* — The notarized application required by this rule shall be on a form approved by the Supreme Court of Virginia and available at the office of the clerk of the tribunal where the case is pending.

5. *Discretion and Limitation on Number of Matters.* — The grant or denial of a motion pursuant to this rule by the tribunal is discretionary. The tribunal shall deny the motion if the out-of-state lawyer has been previously admitted *pro hac vice* before any tribunal or tribunals in Virginia in twelve (12) cases within the last twelve (12)

months preceding the date of the current application. In the enforcement of this limitation, the tribunal may consider whether the pending case is a related or consolidated matter for which the out-of-state lawyer has previously applied to appear *pro hac vice*. Before ruling on a *pro hac vice* motion, the tribunal shall verify with the Supreme Court of Virginia the number of cases during the preceding twelve (12) months in which the out-of-state lawyer was admitted in Virginia *pro hac vice*.

6. *Transfer of Venue and Appeal.* — The out-of-state lawyer's *pro hac vice* admission shall be deemed to continue in the event the venue in the case or proceeding is transferred to another tribunal or is appealed; provided, however, that the tribunal having jurisdiction over such transferred or appealed case shall have the discretion to revoke the authority of the out-of-state lawyer to appear *pro hac vice*.

7. *Duty to Report Status.* — An out-of-state lawyer admitted *pro hac vice* shall have a continuing obligation during the period of such admission to advise the tribunal promptly of any disposition made of pending disciplinary charges or the institution of any new disciplinary proceedings or investigations. The tribunal shall advise the Clerk of the Supreme Court of Virginia if the tribunal denies or revokes the out-of-state lawyer's permission to appear *pro hac vice*.

8. *Record-keeping.* — The Clerk of the Supreme Court of Virginia will maintain an electronic database necessary for the administration and enforcement of this rule.

9. *Disciplinary Jurisdiction of the Virginia State Bar.* — An out-of-state lawyer admitted *pro hac vice* pursuant to this rule shall be subject to the jurisdiction of all tribunals and agencies of the Commonwealth of Virginia, and the Virginia State Bar, with respect to the laws and rules of Virginia governing the conduct and discipline of out-of-state lawyers to the same extent as an active member of the Virginia State Bar. An applicant or out-of-state lawyer admitted *pro hac vice* may be disciplined in the same manner as a member of the Virginia State Bar.

10. *In-State Services Related to Out-of-State Proceedings.* — Subject to the requirements and limitations of Rule 5.5 of the Virginia Rules of Professional Conduct, an out-of-state lawyer may provide the following services without the entry of a *pro hac vice* order:

(a) In connection with a proceeding pending outside of Virginia, an out-of-state lawyer admitted to appear in that proceeding may render legal services in Virginia pertaining to or in aid of such proceeding.

(b) In connection with a case in which an out-of-state lawyer reasonably believes he is eligible for admission *pro hac vice* under this rule: (1) the out-of-state lawyer may consult in Virginia with a member of the Virginia State Bar concerning a pending or potential proceeding in Virginia; (2) the out-of-state lawyer may, at the request of a person in Virginia contemplating or involved in a proceeding in Virginia, consult with that person about that person's retention of the out-of-state lawyer in connection with that proceeding; and (3) on behalf of a client residing in Virginia or elsewhere, the out-of-state lawyer may render legal services in Virginia in preparation for a potential case to be filed in Virginia.

(c) An out-of-state lawyer may render legal services to prepare for and participate in an ADR process, regardless of where the ADR process or proceeding is expected to take place or actually takes place.

Source. — Rule 1:6.

The amendment, effective July 1, 2007, adopted November 28, 2006, rewrote the Rule. The amendment was originally effective February 1, 2007; however, by order adopted January 16, 2007, the effective date was changed to July 1, 2007.

Law Review. — For case comment discussing malpractice suits against local counsel or specialists in light of Ortiz v. Barrett, 222 Va. 118, 278 S.E.2d 833 (1981), see 68 Va. L. Rev. 571 (1982). For article, "Professional Responsibility," see 43 U. Rich. L. Rev. 255 (2008). For annual survey of Virginia law article, "Civil Practice and Procedure," see 47 U. Rich. L. Rev. 113 (2012).

Michie's Jurisprudence. — For related discussion, see 2A M.J. Attorney and Client, §§ 6, 24.

CASE NOTES

Revocation of *pro hac vice* admission. — When a circuit court acts within its discretion in imposing sanctions on attorneys for pleadings they have filed in violation of § 8.01-271.1, the circuit court does not abuse its discretion in revoking the *pro hac vice* admission of one of the attorneys who filed those pleadings; where sanctions were properly awarded against an out-of-state attorney under § 8.01-271.1, the circuit court did not abuse its discretion in revoking the *pro hac vice* admission of the attorney. Williams & Connolly, LLP v. People for the Ethical Treatment of Animals, Inc., 273 Va. 498, 643 S.E.2d 136, 2007 Va. LEXIS 45 (2007).

Requirements for practicing law based on compelling state interest. — The State has acted rationally and with a compelling state interest in insisting that any foreign attorney, seeking to practice law generally, as contrasted with his association with local counsel on a case-by-case basis, must express an intention to reside permanently in Virginia and devote his full time to the practice of law therein. Brown v. Supreme Court, 359 F. Supp. 549 (E.D. Va.), aff'd sub nom. Titus v. Supreme Court, 414 U.S. 1034, 94 S. Ct. 533, 534, 38 L. Ed. 2d 327 (1973), decided prior to 1988 amendments to Part 1A.

Alteration of contractual arrangement unnecessary. — Neither former § 54-24 nor this rule requires the alteration of the contractual arrangement between a foreign attorney and his client so that local counsel in Virginia will replace the foreign attorney as chief or lead counsel for the client. Ortiz v. Barrett, 222 Va. 118, 278 S.E.2d 833 (1981).

Liability of local attorney to client. — Where a foreign attorney hires a local attorney to perform services on an hourly basis, and where the foreign attorney remains lead counsel in the action and the local attorney has no direct contact with the client, the local attorney does not escape liability to the client for his negligence in the discharge of his assigned duties since he has an implied obligation to act with reasonable care. Ortiz v. Barrett, 222 Va. 118, 278 S.E.2d 833 (1981).

Pleading signed only by foreign attorney invalid. — Where a defendant did not sign her own responsive pleading, did not retain a member of the Virginia State Bar as counsel, and did not have her pleading signed by a member of the Virginia State Bar, the defendant's pleading was invalid, even though it was signed by an attorney admitted to practice in another jurisdiction. Nelson v. Gecelosky, No. 0242-00-4, 2000 Va. App. LEXIS 502 (Ct. of Appeals July 11, 2000).

Because of the strong public policy considerations underlying § 8.01-271.1, Va. Sup. Ct. R. 1:4 and 1A:4(2), the Supreme Court of Virginia construes them to require that a lawyer who files a pleading in a Virginia tribunal must append his personal, handwritten signature to a pleading; thus, a complaint signed on behalf of a licensed Virginia attorney by an attorney not licensed in Virginia was a nullity and as none of the relation back situations for amending pleadings applied, the defect could not be cured by providing the appropriate signature. Shipe v. Hunter, 280 Va. 480, 699 S.E.2d 519, 2010 Va. LEXIS 231 (2010).

Circuit court did not abuse its discretion in excluding a patient's expert witnesses on the ground that it disregarded Va. Sup. Ct. R. 4:1(g) because the rule was not violated since the supplemental designation was signed by at least one attorney of record; the problem was that the patients' out-of-state attorney was not admitted to practice law in Virginia, and therefore, Va. Sup. Ct. R. 1A:4(2) was implicated. Landrum v. Chippenham & Johnston-Willis Hosps., Inc., 282 Va. 346, 717 S.E.2d 134, 2011 Va. LEXIS 224 (2011).

Circuit court did not abuse its discretion in excluding a patient's expert witnesses because the patient failed to obey the circuit court's pretrial order to file a supplemental designation on or before January 28; the patient's supplemental designation had no legal effect because it was not signed by local counsel as required under Va. Sup. Ct. R. 1A:4(2), and the supplemental designation could not be amended to comply with that rule since it was an invalid instrument. Landrum v. Chippenham & Johnston-Willis Hosps., Inc., 282 Va. 346, 717 S.E.2d 134, 2011 Va. LEXIS 224 (2011).

Notice of appeal signed only by foreign counsel was invalid. — Notice of appeal by a coal company in a breach of contract case was invalid pursuant to Rule 1A:4 where it was signed only by the coal company's foreign counsel, and the defect in the signature was not curable as a clerical error pursuant to subsection B of § 8.01-428, as the failure of the coal company's Virginia counsel to append that counsel's own signature to the notice of appeal was not the kind of clerical error contemplated by § 8.01-428. Wellmore Coal Corp. v. Harman Mining Corp., 264 Va. 279, 568 S.E.2d 671, 2002 Va. LEXIS 103 (2002).

Expert witnesses excluded. — Circuit court did not abuse its discretion in excluding a patient's expert witnesses because it warned the patient multiple times that her failure to obey its pretrial orders would lead to sanctions, including the exclusion of the expert witnesses; the patient proved herself unable to comply with the rules, running afoul of not just Va. Sup. Ct. R. 1A:4(2) and 4:1(b)(4)(A)(i), but also Va. Sup. Ct. R. 1A:4(3), 4:1(e)(1)(B), and 4:15. Landrum v. Chippenham & Johnston-Willis Hosps., Inc., 282 Va. 346, 717 S.E.2d 134, 2011 Va. LEXIS 224 (2011).

Applied in In re Brown, 213 Va. 282, 191 S.E.2d 812 (1972); Whitt v. Commonwealth, No. 0885-11-3, 61 Va. App. 637, 739 S.E.2d 254, 2013 Va. App. LEXIS 100 (Mar. 26, 2013).

CIRCUIT COURT OPINIONS

"Signature" of attorney. — Because a Virginia attorney authorized a Maryland attorney to sign the Virginia attorney's name on a motion, the signature had the same legal effect under Va. Sup. Ct. R. 1A:4 as a physical signature by the Virginia attorney and, therefore, constituted a signing of the motion by Virginia attorney. Bernhard v. Washington, 69 Va. Cir. 195, 2005 Va. Cir. LEXIS 325 (Fauquier County 2005).

Business organization had to be represented by lawyer authorized to practice in Virginia. — Judgment debtor's motion to quash a garnishment summons pursuant to § 8.01-477 was denied because the time expired for it to file a responsive pleading, and papers signed by the debtor's chief financial officer and filed with the clerk of court had no legal effect; the papers were not a responsive pleading because the debtor, a business organization, could not file a pleading pro se since it had to be represented by a lawyer authorized to practice law in Virginia pursuant to Va. Sup. Ct. R. 1A:4. Modular Wood Sys., Inc. v. World Trade Group, L.L.P., 77 Va. Cir. 403, 2009 Va. Cir. LEXIS 103 (Henrico County 2009).

Rule 1A:5. Virginia Corporate Counsel & Corporate Counsel Registrants.

Introduction

Notwithstanding any rule of this Court to the contrary, after July 1, 2004, any person employed in Virginia as a lawyer exclusively for a for-profit or a non-profit corporation, association, or other business entity, including its subsidiaries and affiliates, that is not a government entity, and the business of which consists solely of lawful activities other than the practice of law or the provisions of legal services ("Employer"), for the primary purpose of providing legal services to such Employer, including one who holds himself or herself out as "in-house counsel," "corporate counsel," "general counsel," or other similar title indicating that he or she is serving as legal counsel to such Employer, shall either (i) be a regularly admitted active member of the Virginia State Bar; (ii) be issued a Corporate Counsel Certificate as provided in Part I of this rule and thereby become an active member of the Virginia State Bar with his or her practice limited as provided therein; or (iii) register with the Virginia State Bar as provided in Part II of this rule; provided, however, no person who is or has been a member of the Virginia State Bar, and whose Virginia License, at the time of application, is revoked or suspended, shall be issued a Corporate Counsel Certificate or permitted to register under this Rule.

Part I

Virginia Corporate Counsel

(a) A lawyer admitted to the practice of law in a state (other than Virginia), or territory of the United States, or the District of Columbia may apply to the Virginia State Bar for a certificate as a Registered Virginia Corporate Counsel ("Corporate Counsel Certificate") to practice law as in-house counsel in this state when he or she is employed by an Employer in Virginia.

(b) Each applicant for a Corporate Counsel Certificate shall:

(1) File with the Virginia State Bar an application, under oath, upon a form furnished by the Virginia State Bar.

(2) Furnish a certificate, signed by the presiding judge of the court of last resort of a jurisdiction in which the applicant is admitted to practice law, stating that the applicant is licensed to practice law and is an active member in good standing of the bar of such jurisdiction.

(3) File an affidavit, upon a form furnished by the Virginia State Bar, from an officer of the applicant's Employer attesting to the fact that the applicant is employed as legal counsel to provide legal services exclusively to the Employer, including its subsidiaries and affiliates; that the nature of the applicant's employment conforms to the requirements of Part I of this rule; and that the Employer shall notify the Virginia State Bar immediately upon the termination of the applicant's employment.

(4) Certify that the applicant has read and is familiar with the Virginia Rules of Professional Conduct.

(5) Pay an application fee of one-hundred and fifty dollars.

(c) During the period in which an application for a Corporate Counsel Certificate is pending with the Virginia State Bar until the applicant is notified that either (i) his or her application is rejected; or (ii) he or she is eligible to practice pursuant to Part I of this rule, the applicant may be employed in Virginia as Certified Corporate Counsel on a provisional basis by an Employer furnishing the affidavit required by Part I(b)(3) of this rule.

(d) Upon a finding by the Virginia State Bar that the applicant has complied with the requirements of Part I(b) of this rule, the Virginia State Bar shall notify the applicant that he or she is eligible to be issued a Corporate Counsel Certificate. After the applicant has taken and subscribed to the oath required of attorneys at law, the applicant shall be issued a Corporate Counsel Certificate, which shall permit the applicant to practice law in Virginia solely as provided in Part I(f) of this rule. The applicant may take the required oath by appearing before the Justices of the Supreme

Court of Virginia in Richmond at an appointed date and time or by appearing before a judge of a court of record in Virginia. The necessary motion and oath for an applicant who appears before a judge of a court of record can be found in the Appendix of Forms following Part One A of the Rules.

(e) A lawyer issued a Corporate Counsel Certificate shall immediately become an active member of the Virginia State Bar, with his or her practice limited as provided in Part I(f) of this rule, and shall pay to the Virginia State Bar the annual dues required of regularly admitted active members of the Virginia State Bar.

(f) The practice of a lawyer certified pursuant to Part I of this rule shall be limited to practice exclusively for the Employer furnishing the affidavit required by Part I(b)(3) of this rule, including its subsidiaries and affiliates, and may include appearing before a Virginia court or tribunal as counsel for the Employer. Except as specifically authorized under Part I (g) below, no lawyer certified pursuant to Part I of this rule shall (i) undertake to represent any person other than his or her Employer before a Virginia court or tribunal; (ii) offer or provide legal services to any person other than his or her Employer; (iii) undertake to provide legal services to any other person through his or her Employer; or (iv) hold himself or herself out to be authorized to provide legal services or advice to any person other than his or her Employer.

(g) Notwithstanding the restrictions set out in Part I(f) above on the scope of practice, a lawyer certified pursuant to Part I of this rule may, and is encouraged to, provide voluntary *pro bono publico* services in accordance with Rule 6.1 of the Virginia Rules of Professional Conduct.

(h) All legal services provided in Virginia by a lawyer certified pursuant to Part I of this rule shall be deemed the practice of law and shall subject the lawyer to all rules governing the practice of law in Virginia, including the Virginia Rules of Professional Conduct and Part 6, Section IV, Paragraph 13 of the Rules of the Supreme Court of Virginia. Jurisdiction of the Virginia State Bar shall continue whether or not the lawyer retains the Corporate Counsel Certificate and irrespective of the lawyer's presence in Virginia.

(i) A lawyer certified pursuant to Part I of this rule shall be subject to the same membership obligations as other active members of the Virginia State Bar, including Mandatory Continuing Legal Education requirements. A lawyer certified pursuant to Part I of this rule shall use as his or her address of record with the Virginia State Bar a business address in Virginia of the Employer furnishing the affidavit required by Part I(b)(3) of this rule.

(j) A lawyer certified pursuant to Part I of this rule shall promptly report to the Virginia State Bar any change in employment, any change in bar membership status in any state, territory of the United States or the District of Columbia in which the lawyer has been admitted to the practice of law, or the imposition of any disciplinary sanction in a state, territory of the United States or the District of Columbia or by any federal court or agency before which the lawyer has been admitted to practice.

(k) A lawyer's authority to practice law which may be permitted pursuant to Part I of this rule shall be automatically suspended when (i) employment by the Employer furnishing the affidavit required by Part I(b)(3) of this rule is terminated, (ii) the lawyer fails to comply with any provision of Part I of this rule, or (iii) when the lawyer is suspended or disbarred for disciplinary reasons in any state, territory of the United States or the District of Columbia or by any federal court or agency before which the lawyer has been admitted to practice. Any lawyer whose authority to practice is suspended pursuant to (i) above shall be reinstated upon evidence satisfactory to the Virginia State Bar that the lawyer is in full compliance with the requirements of Part I of this rule, which shall include an affidavit furnished by the lawyer's new Employer. Any lawyer whose authority to practice is suspended pursuant to (ii) above may be reinstated by compliance with applicable provisions of Part 6, Section IV, Paragraph 19 of the Rules of the Supreme Court of Virginia. Any lawyer whose authority to practice is suspended or terminated under (iii) above shall petition for reinstatement pursuant to Part 6, Section IV, Paragraph 13 I.7. of the Rules of the Supreme Court of Virginia.

(*l*) The period of time a lawyer practices law is permitted by a Corporate Counsel Certificate issued pursuant to Part I of this rule shall be considered in determining whether the lawyer has fulfilled the requirements for admission to practice law in Virginia without examination pursuant to Rule 1A:1 and any guidelines approved by the Supreme Court of Virginia for review of applications for admission without examination.

(m) The Virginia State Bar may adopt regulations as needed to implement the requirements of Part I of this rule.

Part II

Corporate Counsel Registrants

(a) Notwithstanding the requirements of Part I of this rule, any lawyer as defined in the Introduction and Part I(a) of this rule may register with the Virginia State Bar as a "Corporate Counsel Registrant." A person admitted to the practice of law only in a country other than the United States, and who is a member in good standing of a recognized legal profession in that country, the members of which are admitted to practice law as lawyers, counselors at law, or the equivalent, and are subject to effective regulation and discipline by a duly constituted professional body or public authority, may also register under Part II of this rule.

(b) A registrant shall:

(1) Register with the Virginia State Bar upon a form, under oath, furnished by the Virginia State Bar, which shall include affirmations that (i) he or she will at no time undertake to represent his or her Employer or any other person, organization or business entity before a Virginia court or tribunal except as permitted pursuant to Rule 1A:4 of this Court, (ii) his or her work is limited to business and legal services related to issues confronting his or her Employer at a regional, national or international level with no specific nexus to Virginia, and (iii) he or she will not provide legal advice or services to any person other than his or her Employer.

(2) Furnish a certificate, signed by the presiding judge of the court of last resort of a jurisdiction in which the registrant is admitted to practice law, stating that the registrant is licensed to practice law and is an active member in good standing of the bar of such jurisdiction.

(3) File an affidavit, upon a form furnished by the Virginia State Bar, from an officer of the registrant's Employer attesting to the fact that the registrant is employed as legal counsel to provide legal services exclusively to the Employer, including its subsidiaries and affiliates; that the nature of the registrant's employment conforms to the requirements of Part II of this rule; and that the Employer shall notify the Virginia State Bar immediately upon the termination of the registrant's employment.

(4) Certify that the registrant has read and is familiar with the Virginia Rules of Professional Conduct.

(5) Pay a registration fee of one hundred and fifty dollars.

(c) During the period in which a corporate counsel registration is pending with the Virginia State Bar until the registrant is notified that either (i) his or her registration is rejected; or (ii) he or she is eligible to practice pursuant to Part II of this rule, the registrant may be employed in Virginia as a Corporate Counsel Registrant on a provisional basis by the Employer furnishing the affidavit required by Part II(b)(3) of this rule.

(d) Upon completion of the requirements of Part II(b) of this rule, the registrant shall immediately be recorded by the Virginia State Bar as a Corporate Counsel Registrant. Each registrant shall pay to the Virginia State Bar the annual dues required of regularly admitted active members of the Virginia State Bar. No lawyer registered pursuant to Part II of this rule shall (i) undertake to represent his or her Employer or any other person or entity before a Virginia court or tribunal except as permitted for lawyers licensed and in good standing in another United States jurisdiction pursuant to Rule 1A:4 of this Court; (ii) offer or provide legal services to any person other than his or her Employer; (iii) undertake to provide legal services to another through his or her Employer; or (iv) hold himself or herself out to be authorized to provide legal services or advice to any person other than his or her Employer.

(e) The provision of legal services to his or her Employer by a lawyer registered pursuant to Part II of this rule shall be deemed the practice of law in Virginia only for purposes of subjecting the lawyer to the Virginia Rules of Professional Conduct; the jurisdiction of the disciplinary system of the Virginia State Bar; and Part 6, Section IV, Paragraph 13 of the Rules of the Supreme Court of Virginia. Jurisdiction of the Virginia State Bar shall continue whether or not the lawyer maintains the registration and irrespective of the lawyer's presence in Virginia.

(f) A lawyer registered pursuant to Part II of this rule shall use as his or her address of record with the Virginia State Bar a business address in Virginia of the Employer furnishing the affidavit required by Part II(b)(3) of this rule.

(g) A lawyer registered pursuant to Part II of this rule shall promptly report to the Virginia State Bar any change in employment, any change in bar membership status in any state, territory of the United States, the District of Columbia, or other country in which the lawyer has been admitted to the practice of law, or the imposition of any disciplinary sanction in a state, territory of the United States, the District of Columbia, or other country, or by any federal court or agency before which the lawyer has been admitted to practice.

(h) A lawyer's authority to provide legal services which may be permitted pursuant to Part II of this rule shall be automatically suspended when (i) employment by the Employer furnishing the affidavit required by Part II(b)(3) of this rule is terminated, (ii) the lawyer fails to comply with any provision of Part II of this rule, or (iii) the lawyer is suspended or disbarred for disciplinary reasons in any state, territory of the United States, the District of Columbia, other country, or by any federal court or agency before which the lawyer has been admitted to practice. Any lawyer whose authority to practice is suspended pursuant to (i) above shall be reinstated upon evidence satisfactory to the Virginia State Bar that the lawyer is in full compliance with the requirements of Part II of this rule, which shall include an affidavit furnished by the lawyer's new Employer. Any lawyer whose authority to practice is suspended pursuant to (ii) above may be reinstated by compliance with applicable provisions of Part 6, Section IV, Paragraph 19 of the Rules of the Supreme Court of Virginia. Any lawyer whose authority to practice is suspended or terminated pursuant to (iii) above, shall petition for reinstatement pursuant to Part 6, Section IV, Paragraph 13 I.7. of the Rules of the Supreme Court of Virginia.

(i) No time spent as Corporate Counsel Registrant shall be considered in determining eligibility for admission to the Virginia Bar without examination.

(j) The Virginia State Bar may adopt regulations as needed to implement the requirements of Part II of this rule.

The amendment effective January 1, 2004, adopted September 26, 2003, added "provided, however, no person who is or has been a member of the Virginia State Bar, and whose Virginia License, at the time of application, is revoked or suspended, shall be issued a Corporate Counsel Certificate or permitted to register under this Rule" at the end of the paragraph following the Introduction heading.

The amendment, effective March 4, 2005, adopted March 4, 2005, in Part I, substituted "Certified Corporate Counsel" for "legal counsel" in subdivision (c), and substituted "certified" for "certificated" in subdivisions (f), (g), (h), and (i); and in Part II, added the second sentence of subdivision (a), substituted "a Corporate Counsel Registrant" for "legal counsel" in subdivision (c), inserted "for lawyers licensed and in good standing in another United States jurisdiction" in clause (ii) of the third sentence of subdivision (d), substituted "United States, the District of Columbia, or other country" for "United States or the District of Columbia" twice in subdivision (g), and substituted "United States, the District of Columbia, other country, or" for "United States or the District of Columbia or" in subdivision (h).

The amendment, effective May 1, 2006, adopted February 28, 2006, in Part I, substituted "one-hundred and fifty dollars" for "fifty dollars" at the end of subdivision (b)(5), inserted "Except as specifically authorized under Part I(g) below," at the beginning of the second sentence of subdivision (f), added present subdivision (g), and redesignated former subdivisions (g) through (*l*) as present subdivisions (h) through (m); and in Part II, substituted "one hundred and fifty dollars" for "fifty dollars" at the end of subdivision (b)(5).

The amendment, effective April 15, 2011, adopted April 15, 2011, in Part I, rewrote subdivisions (g) and (h).

The amendment, effective June 10, 2011, adopted June 10, 2011, in Part I, added the third and fourth sentences in subdivision (d).

Effective date. — This rule, adopted June 4, 2003, became effective September 1, 2003.

Law Review. — For article, "Professional Responsibility," see 39 U. Rich. L. Rev. 315 (2004). For 2007 annual survey article, "Civil Practice and Procedure," see 42 U. Rich. L. Rev. 229 (2007).

Rule 1A:6. Foreign Attorneys — Registered Military Legal Assistance Attorneys.

(a) A lawyer admitted to the practice of law in a state or territory of the United States, other than Virginia, who is serving in or employed by the armed services and is authorized to provide legal assistance pursuant to 10 U.S. Code § 1044, may apply to the Board of Bar Examiners for a certificate as a Registered Military Legal Assistance Attorney in Virginia ("Military Legal Assistance Attorney Certificate") to represent clients eligible for legal assistance in the courts and tribunals of this Commonwealth while the lawyer is employed, stationed, or assigned within Virginia.

(b) Each applicant for a Military Legal Assistance Attorney Certificate shall:

(1) File with the secretary of the Virginia Board of Bar Examiners an application, under oath, upon a form furnished by the Board.

(2) Furnish a certificate, signed by the presiding judge of the court of last resort, or other appropriate official of the jurisdiction in which the applicant is admitted to practice law, stating that the applicant is licensed to practice law and is an active member in good standing of the bar of such jurisdiction.

(3) File an affidavit, upon a form furnished by the Board, from commanding officer, staff judge advocate or chief legal officer of the military base in Virginia where the applicant is employed, stationed, or assigned, attesting to the fact that the applicant is serving as a lawyer to provide legal services exclusively for the military, that the nature of the applicant's employment or service conforms to the requirements of this rule, and that the commanding officer, staff judge advocate or chief legal officer, or his or her successor, shall notify the Virginia State Bar immediately upon the termination of the applicant's employment or service at the military base.

(c) Upon a finding by the Board of Bar Examiners that the applicant has produced evidence sufficient to satisfy the Board that the applicant is a person of honest demeanor and good moral character who possesses the requisite fitness to perform the obligations and responsibilities of a practicing attorney at law and satisfies all other requirements of this rule, the Board shall notify the applicant that he or she is eligible to be issued a Military Legal Assistance Attorney Certificate. After the applicant has taken and subscribed to the oaths required of attorneys at law, the Board shall issue to the applicant a Military Legal Assistance Attorney Certificate, which shall entitle the applicant to represent clients eligible for legal assistance in the courts and tribunals of this Commonwealth solely as provided in this rule.

(d) Each lawyer issued a Military Legal Assistance Attorney Certificate shall immediately register as an active member of the Virginia State Bar, with his or her practice limited as provided in this rule, and pay to the Virginia State Bar the same dues required of regularly admitted active members. (The requirement to pay dues shall be waived for a lawyer during the first two years immediately following the initial issue of a Military Legal Assistance Attorney Certificate to that lawyer.)

(e) The practice of a lawyer registered under this rule shall be limited within this Commonwealth to practice exclusively pursuant to the laws, rules, and regulations governing the military services, and may include appearing before a court or tribunal of this Commonwealth as counsel for a client eligible for legal assistance on:

(1) Adoptions,

(2) Guardianships,

(3) Name changes,

(4) Divorces,

(5) Paternity,

(6) Child custody and visitation, and child and spousal support,

(7) Landlord-tenant disputes on behalf of tenants,

(8) Consumer advocacy cases involving alleged breaches of contracts or warranties, repossession, or fraud,

(9) Garnishment defense,

(10) Probate,

(11) Enforcement of rights under the Soldiers' and Sailors' Civil Relief Act of 1940 (50 U.S. Code App. §§ 501-548, 560-593),

(12) Enforcement of rights under the Uniformed Services Employment and Reemployment Rights Act of 1994 (38 U.S. Code §§ 4301-4333), and

(13) Such other cases within the discretion of the court or tribunal before which the matter is pending.

(f) Representation in proceedings before courts or tribunals of this Commonwealth shall be limited to low-income legal assistance clients for whom hiring a lawyer in private practice would entail a substantial financial hardship to themselves or their families. All pleadings filed by a legal assistance attorney will cite this rule, include the name, complete address, and telephone number of the military legal office representing the client and the name, rank or grade, and armed service of the lawyer registered under this rule providing representation.

(g) No lawyer registered under this rule shall (i) undertake to represent any person other than an eligible legal assistance client before a court or tribunal of this

Commonwealth, (ii) offer to provide legal services in this Commonwealth to any person other than as authorized by his or her military service, (iii) undertake to provide legal services in this Commonwealth to any person other than as authorized by his or her military service, or (iv) hold himself or herself out in this Commonwealth to be authorized to provide legal services to any person other than as authorized by his or her military service.

(h) Representing clients eligible for legal assistance in the courts or tribunals of this Commonwealth under this rule shall be deemed the practice of law and shall subject the lawyer to all rules governing the practice of law in Virginia, including the Virginia Rules of Professional Conduct and the Rules of Procedure for Disciplining Lawyers (Rules of Court, Pt. 6, Section IV, Paragraph 13). Jurisdiction of the Virginia State Bar shall continue whether or not the lawyer retains the Military Legal Assistance Attorney Certificate and irrespective of the lawyer's presence in Virginia.

(i) Each person registered with the Virginia State Bar as an active member on the basis of a Military Legal Assistance Attorney Certificate shall be subject to the same membership obligations as other active members, including completion of the required Professionalism Course and annual Mandatory Continuing Education requirements. A lawyer registered under this rule shall use as his or her address of record with the Virginia State Bar the military address in Virginia of the commanding officer, staff judge advocate or chief legal officer which filed the affidavit on the lawyer's behalf.

(j) Each person issued a Military Legal Assistance Attorney Certificate shall promptly report to the Virginia State Bar any change in employment or military service, any change in bar membership status in any state or territory of the United States, or the District of Columbia where the applicant has been admitted to the practice of law, or the imposition of any disciplinary sanction in a state or territory of the United States or the District of Columbia or by any federal court or agency where the applicant has been admitted to the practice of law.

(k) The limited authority to practice law which may be granted under this rule shall be automatically terminated when (i) the lawyer is no longer employed, stationed, or assigned at the military base in Virginia from which affidavit required by this rule was filed, (ii) the lawyer has been admitted to the practice of law in this state by examination or pursuant to any other provision of part 1A of these Rules, (iii) the lawyer fails to comply with any provision of this rule, (iv) the lawyer fails to maintain current good standing as an active member of a bar in at least one state or territory of the United States, other than Virginia, or the District of Columbia, or (v) when suspended or disbarred for disciplinary reasons in any state or territory of the United States or the District of Columbia or by any federal court or agency where the lawyer has been admitted to the practice of law. If a lawyer is no longer employed, stationed, or assigned at the military base in Virginia from which affidavit required by this rule was filed, but the lawyer, within six months after the last day of employment or service, is re-employed by, or militarily reassigned to, the same military base or by another military base in Virginia filing the affidavit required by this rule, the Military Legal Assistance Attorney Certificate shall be reinstated upon evidence satisfactory to the Board that the lawyer remains in full compliance with all requirements of this rule.

(*l*) The period of time a lawyer practices law full time on the basis of a Military Legal Assistance Attorney Certificate issued pursuant to this rule shall be considered in determining whether such lawyer has fulfilled the requirements for admission to practice law in this Commonwealth without examination under Rule 1A:1 and any guidelines approved by the Supreme Court of Virginia for review of applications for admission without examination.

Effective date. — This rule, adopted January 14, 2003, became effective January 14, 2003.

Law Review. — For article, "Professional Responsibility," see 39 U. Rich. L. Rev. 315 (2004).

Rule 1A:7. Certification of Foreign Legal Consultants.

(a) *General Requirements.* — A person admitted to practice law by the duly constituted and authorized professional body or governmental authority of any foreign nation may apply to the Virginia Board of Bar Examiners ("Board") for a certificate as a foreign legal consultant, provided the applicant:

(1) is a member in good standing of a recognized legal profession in a foreign nation, the members of which are admitted to practice as attorneys or counselors at law or the

equivalent and are subject to effective regulation and discipline by a duly constituted professional body or a governmental authority;

(2) for at least five of the seven years immediately preceding his or her application has been a member in good standing of such legal profession and has actually been engaged in the authorized practice of law, substantially involving or relating to the rendering of advice or the provision of legal services concerning the law of the said foreign nation;

(3) possesses the good moral character and general fitness requisite for a member of the bar of this Commonwealth;

(4) is at least twenty-six years of age; and

(5) intends to practice as a foreign legal consultant in this Commonwealth and maintain an office in this Commonwealth for that purpose.

(b) *Proof Required.* — An applicant under this rule shall file with the secretary of the Board:

(1) an application for a foreign legal consultant certificate, on a form furnished by the Board,

(2) a certificate, for each foreign nation in which the applicant is admitted to practice, from the professional body or governmental authority in such foreign country having final jurisdiction over professional discipline, certifying as to the applicant's admission to practice and the date thereof, and as to his or her good standing as an attorney or counselor at law or the equivalent;

(3) a letter of recommendation, for each foreign nation in which the applicant is admitted to practice, from one of the members of the executive body of such professional body or governmental authority or from one of the judges of the highest law court or court of original jurisdiction of such foreign country;

(4) a duly authenticated English translation of each certificate and letter if, in either case, it is not in English;

(5) a copy or summary of the law, regulations, and customs of the foreign country that describes the opportunity afforded to a member of the Virginia State Bar ("the Bar") to establish an office to provide legal services to clients in such foreign country, together with an authenticated English translation if it is not in English;

(6) the requisite documentation establishing the applicant's compliance with the immigration laws of the United States; and

(7) such other evidence as to the applicant's educational and professional qualifications, good moral character and general fitness, and compliance with the requirements of paragraph (a) of this rule as the Board may require.

(c) *Reciprocal Treatment of Members of the Bar of this Commonwealth.* — In considering whether to certify an applicant to practice as a foreign legal consultant, the Board may in its discretion take into account whether a member of the Bar would have a reasonable and practical opportunity to establish an office and give legal advice to clients in the applicant's country of admission. Any member of the Bar who is seeking or has sought to establish an office or give advice in that country may request the Board to consider the matter, or the Board may do so *sua sponte*.

(d) *Scope of Practice.* — A person certified to practice as foreign legal consultant under this Rule may render legal services in the Commonwealth only with regard to matters involving the law of foreign nation(s) in which the person is admitted to practice or international law. For purposes of this paragraph, the term "international law" means a body of laws, rules or legal principles that are based on custom, treaties or legislation and that control or affect (1) the rights and duties of nations in relation to other nations or their citizens, or (2) the rights and obligations pertaining to international transactions.

The practice permitted under this rule does not authorize the foreign legal consultant to appear in court.

(e) *Rights and Obligations.* — Subject to the scope of practice limitations set forth in paragraph (d) of this rule, a person certified as a foreign legal consultant under this rule shall be entitled and subject to:

(1) the rights and obligations contained in the Virginia Rules of Professional Conduct as set forth in Part 6, Section II of the Rules of the Supreme Court of Virginia; and the procedure for disciplining attorneys as set forth in Part 6, Section IV, Paragraph 13 of the Rules of the Supreme Court of Virginia

(2) the rights and obligations of a member of the Bar with respect to:

(i) affiliation in the same law firm with one or more members of the bar of this Commonwealth, including by:

(A) employing one or more members of the Bar;

(B) being employed by one or more members of the Bar or by any partnership or other limited liability entity authorized to practice law pursuant to Part 6, Section IV, Paragraph 14 of the Rules of the Supreme Court of Virginia, which such entity includes an active member of the Bar or which maintains an office in this Commonwealth;

(C) being a director, partner, member, manager or shareholder in any partnership or other professional limited liability entity authorized by Part 6, Section IV, Paragraph 14 to practice law in this Commonwealth which includes an active member of the Bar or which maintains an office in this Commonwealth;

(ii) employment as in-house counsel under Part II of Rule 1A:5; and

(iii) attorney-client privilege, work-product privilege and similar professional privileges.

(3) No time spent practicing as a foreign legal consultant shall be considered in determining eligibility for admission to the Virginia bar without examination.

(f) *Disciplinary Provisions.* — A person certified to practice as a foreign legal consultant under this Rule shall be subject to professional discipline in the same manner and to the same extent as any member of the Bar and to this end:

(1) Every person certified to practice as a foreign legal consultant under these Rules:

(i) shall be subject to regulation by the Bar and to admonition, reprimand, suspension, removal or revocation of his or her certificate to practice in accordance with the rules of procedure for disciplinary proceedings set forth in Part 6, Section IV, Paragraph 13 of the Rules of the Supreme Court of Virginia; and

(ii) shall execute and file with the Bar, in such form and manner as the Bar may prescribe:

(A) his or her commitment to observe the Virginia Rules of Professional Conduct and any other rules of court governing members of the bar to the extent they may be applicable to the legal services authorized under paragraph (d) of this Rule;

(B) a written undertaking to notify the Bar of any change in such person's good standing as a member of any foreign legal profession referred to in paragraph (a)(1) of this rule and of any final action of any professional body or governmental authority referred to in paragraph (b)(2) of this rule imposing any disciplinary censure, suspension, or other sanction upon such person; and

(C) a duly acknowledged instrument, in writing, setting forth his or her address in this Commonwealth which shall be both his or her address of record with the Bar and such person's actual place of business for rendering services authorized by this rule. Such address shall be one where process can be served and the foreign legal consultant shall have a duty to promptly notify the Membership Department of the Bar in writing of any changes in his or her address of record.

(g) *Application and Renewal Fees.* — An applicant for a certificate as a foreign legal consultant under this rule shall pay to the Virginia Board of Bar Examiners the application fee and costs as may be fixed from time to time by the Board. A person certified as a foreign legal consultant shall pay an annual fee to the Virginia State Bar which shall also be fixed by the Supreme Court of Virginia. A person certified as a foreign legal consultant who fails to complete and file the renewal form supplied by the Bar or pay the annual fee shall have his or her certificate as a foreign legal consultant administratively suspended in accordance with the procedures set out in Part 6, Section IV, Paragraph 19 of the Rules of the Supreme Court of Virginia.

(h) *Revocation of Certificate for Non-Compliance.* — In the event that the Bar determines that a person certified as a foreign legal consultant under this rule no longer meets the requirements under this rule, it shall revoke the certificate granted to such person hereunder.

(i) *Reinstatement.* — Any foreign legal consultant whose authority to practice is suspended shall be reinstated upon evidence satisfactory to the Bar that such person is in full compliance with this rule; however, a reinstatement of a foreign legal consultant's certificate following a suspension for non-compliance with paragraph (g) of this rule shall be governed by Part 6, Section IV, Paragraph 19 of the Rules of the Supreme Court of Virginia; and reinstatement of a foreign legal consultant's certificate following a disciplinary suspension or revocation shall be governed by Part Six, Section IV, Paragraph 13 of the Rules of the Supreme Court of Virginia.

(j) *Admission to Bar.* — In the event that a person certified as a foreign legal consultant under this rule is subsequently admitted as a member of the Bar under the provisions of the rules governing such admission, the certificate granted to such person hereunder shall be deemed superseded by the admission of such person to the Bar.

(k) *Regulations.* — The Bar and the Board may adopt regulations as needed to implement their respective responsibilities under this rule.

(*l*) *Effective Date.* — This rule shall become effective on January 1, 2009.

Effective date. — This rule, adopted October 31, 2008, became effective January 1, 2009.

The amendment effective January 1, 2009, adopted December 30, 2008, substituted "Bar" for "Board" in subdivision (h).

APPENDIX OF FORMS.

[Note: *the following form may be submitted electronically pursuant to Rule 1:17 and related provisions of Virginia law.*]

1. Application to Appear *Pro Hac Vice* Before A Virginia Tribunal.

I, ..., the

NAME OF APPLICANT

undersigned attorney, hereby apply to this tribunal of the Commonwealth of Virginia, ..., to appear as counsel

NAME OF TRIBUNAL

pro hac vice pursuant to Rule 1A:4 of the Rules of the Supreme Court of Virginia. I further state the following:

1. The case in which I seek to appear *pro hac vice* is styled ...., has docket number .... and is pending in ....
This case [ ] is [ ] is not a related or consolidated matter for which I have previously applied to appear *pro hac vice*.

2. ....

APPLICANT'S RESIDENCE ADDRESS

....

APPLICANT'S OFFICE ADDRESS

3. ....

NAME OF LOCAL COUNSEL VSB NUMBER

....

STREET ADDRESS

....
....

FAX NUMBER EMAIL ADDRESS TELEPHONE NUMBER

4. ....

NAME OF PARTY TO CASE

....

NAME AND ADDRESS OF COUNSEL FOR PARTY

....

NAME OF PARTY TO CASE

....

NAME AND ADDRESS OF COUNSEL FOR PARTY

....

NAME OF PARTY TO CASE

....

NAME AND ADDRESS OF COUNSEL FOR PARTY

[ ] Additional Sheet attached.

5. ....

COURT TO WHICH APPLICANT IS ADMITTED DATE OF ADMISSION

....

COURT TO WHICH APPLICANT IS ADMITTED DATE OF ADMISSION

[ ] Additional Sheet attached.

6. I am a member in good standing and authorized to appear in the courts identified in paragraph 5.
7. I am not currently disbarred or suspended in any state, territory, United States possession or tribunal.
8. I [ ] am not [ ] am subject to a pending disciplinary investigation or proceeding by any court, agency or organization authorized to discipline me as a lawyer. (If such an investigation or proceeding is pending, attach to this application and incorporate by reference a statement specifying the jurisdiction, the nature of the matter under investigation or being prosecuted, and the name and address of the disciplinary authority investigating or prosecuting the matter.)
9. Within the past three (3) years, I [ ] have not [ ] have been disciplined by any court, agency or organization authorized to discipline me as a lawyer. (If so, attach to this application and incorporate by reference a statement specifying the name of the court, agency or organization imposing discipline, the date(s) of such discipline, the nature of the complaint or charge on which discipline was imposed, and the sanction.)
10. Within the last twelve (12) months preceding this application, I [ ] have not [ ] have sought admission *pro hac vice* under this rule. (If so, attach to this application and incorporate by reference a copy of the order of the tribunal granting or denying your previous application. Such order(s) must include the name of the tribunal, the style of case and the docket number for the case(s) in which you filed an application and whether the application was granted or denied.)

    [ ] Order(s) attached and incorporated by reference.
11. I hereby consent to the jurisdiction of the courts and agencies of the Commonwealth of Virginia and of the Virginia State Bar and I further consent to service of process at any address(es) required by this Rule.
12. I agree to review and comply with appropriate rules of procedure as required in the case for which I am applying to appear *pro hac vice*.
13. I understand and I agree to comply with the rules and standards of professional conduct required of members of the Virginia State Bar.

....

DATE SIGNATURE OF APPLICANT

Commonwealth/State of ....
[ ] City [ ] County of ....
Subscribed and sworn to/affirmed before me on this date by the above-named person.

....

DATE NOTARY PUBLIC

My commission expires: ....

(Added February 1, 2007.)

2. Motion and Oath for Admission as Corporate Counsel.

ADMISSION ON MOTION
(CORPORATE COUNSEL)

MAY IT PLEASE THE COURT, I WISH TO PRESENT

____,
A MEMBER OF THE BAR OF THE STATE OF ______________________
(OR THE DISTRICT OF COLUMBIA), WHO HAS FILED AN APPLICATION TO BE ADMITTED TO PRACTICE LAW IN THE COMMONWEALTH OF VIRGINIA AS CORPORATE COUNSEL.

____ HAS BEEN NOTIFIED THAT HIS/HER APPLICATION HAS BEEN APPROVED, AND I NOW MOVE HIS/HER ADMISSION AS A CORPORATE COUNSEL TO THE BAR OF THE SUPREME COURT OF VIRGINIA.

____
Signature of Sponsor

______________________________ # ______________________________
Printed Name of Sponsor Virginia Bar Number

ATTORNEY OATH (CORPORATE COUNSEL)

I do solemnly swear or affirm that I will support the Constitution of the United States and the Constitution of the Commonwealth of Virginia, and that I will faithfully, honestly, professionally, and courteously demean myself in the practice of law and execute my office of attorney at law to the best of my ability, so help me God.

(Print Full Name) ______________________________
(Signature) ______________________________
(Phone and email) ______________________________

____
Signature of Judge Administering Oath

____
Printed Name of Judge Administering Oath

____
Name of Court

____
Date
(Added June 10, 2011.)

PART TWO
VIRGINIA RULES OF EVIDENCE

Article I. General Provisions.

Rule
2:101. Title.
2:102. Scope and Construction of These Rules.
2:103. Objections and Proffers.
2:104. Preliminary Determinations.
2:105. Proof Admitted for Limited Purposes.
2:106. Remainder of a Writing or Recorded Statement (Rule 2:106(b) derived from Code § 8.01-417.1).

Article II. Judicial Notice.

2:201. Judicial Notice of Adjudicative Facts.
2:202. Judicial Notice of Law (derived from Code §§ 8.01-386 and 19.2-265.2).
2:203. Judicial Notice of Official Publications (derived from Code § 8.01-388).

Article III. Presumptions.

2:301. Presumptions in General in Civil Actions and Proceedings.
2:302. Applicability of Federal Law in Civil Actions and Proceedings.

Article IV. Relevancy, Policy, and Character Trait Proof.

2:401. Definition of "Relevant Evidence."
2:402. Relevant Evidence Generally Admissible; Irrelevant Evidence Inadmissible.
2:403. Exclusion of Relevant Evidence on Grounds of Prejudice, Confusion, Misleading the Jury, or Needless Presentation of Cumulative Evidence.
2:404. Character Evidence Not Admissible to Prove Conduct; Exceptions; Other Crimes.
2:405. Methods of Proving Character Traits.
2:406. Habit and Routine Practice in Civil Cases (derived from Code § 8.01-397.1).
2:407. Subsequent Remedial Measures (derived from Code § 8.01-418.1).
2:408. Compromise and Offers to Compromise.
2:409. Evidence of Abuse Admissible in Certain Criminal Trials (derived from Code § 19.2-270.6).
2:410. Withdrawn Pleas, Offers to Plead, and Related Statements.
2:411. Insurance.
2:412. Admissibility of Complaining Witness' Prior Sexual Conduct; Criminal Sexual Assault Cases; Relevance of Past Behavior (derived from Code § 18.2-67.7).

Article V. Privileges.

2:501. Privileged Communications.
2:502. Attorney-Client Privilege.
2:503. Clergy and Communicant Privilege (derived from Code §§ 8.01-400 and 19.2-271.3).
2:504. Spousal Testimony and Marital Communications Privileges (Rule 2:504(a) derived

Rule
from Code § 8.01-398; and Rule 2:504(b) derived from Code § 19.2-271.2).
2:505. Healing Arts Practitioner and Patient Privilege (derived from Code § 8.01-399).
2:506. Mental Health Professional and Client Privilege (derived from Code § 8.01-400.2).
2:507. Privileged Communications Involving Interpreters (derived from Code §§ 8.01-400.1, 19.2-164, and 19.2-164.1).

Article VI. Witness Examination.

2:601. General Rule of Competency.
2:602. Lack of Personal Knowledge.
2:603. Oath or Affirmation.
2:604. Interpreters (derived from Code § 8.01-406).
2:605. Competency of Court Personnel as Witnesses (derived from Code § 19.2-271).
2:606. Competency of Juror as Witness.
2:607. Incompetency of Witnesses (Rule 2:607(b) derived from Code § 8.01-401(A); and Rule 2:607(c) derived from Code § 8.01-403).
2:608. Impeachment by Evidence of Reputation for Truthtelling and Conduct of Witness.
2:609. Impeachment by Evidence of Conviction of Crime (derived from Code § 19.2-269).
2:610. Bias or Prejudice of a Witness.
2:611. Mode and Order of Interrogation and Presentation (Rule 2:611(c) derived from Code § 8.01-401(A).
2:612. Writing or Object Used to Refresh Memory.
2:613. Prior Statements of Witness (Rule 2:613(a)(i) derived from Code § 8.01-403; Rule 2:613(b)(i) derived from Code §§ 8.01-404 and 19.2-268.1; and Rule 2:613(b)(ii) derived from Code § 8.01-404).
2:614. Calling and Interrogation of Witnesses by Court.
2:615. Exclusion of Witnesses (Rule 2:615(a) derived from Code §§ 8.01-375, 19.2-184, and 19.2-265.1; Rule 2:615(b) derived from Code § 8.01-375; and Rule 2:615(c) derived from Code § 19.2-265.1).

Article VII. Opinions and Expert Testimony.

2:701. Opinion Testimony by Lay Witnesses (derived from Code § 8.01-401.3(B)).
2:702. Testimony by Experts (Rule 2:702(a)(i) derived from Code § 8.01-401.3(A)).
2:703. Basis of Expert Testimony (Rule 2:703(a) derived from Code § 8.01-401.1).
2:704. Opinion on Ultimate Issue (Rule 2:704(a) derived from Code § 8.01-401.3(B) and (C)).
2:705. Facts or Data Used in Testimony (Rule 2:705(a) derived from Code § 8.01-401.1).
2:706. Use of Learned Treatises With Experts (Rule 2:706(a) derived from Code § 8.01-401.1).

Article VIII. Hearsay.

Rule
2:801. Definitions.
2:802. Hearsay Rule.
2:803. Hearsay Exceptions Applicable Regardless of Availability of the Declarant (Rule 2:803(10)(a) derived from Code § 8.01-390(B); Rule 2:803(10)(b) derived from Code § 19.2-188.3; Rule 2:803(17) derived from Code § 8.2-724; and Rule 2:803(23) is derived from Code § 19.2-268.2).
2:804. Hearsay Exceptions Applicable Where the Declarant Is Unavailable (Rule 2:804(b)(5) derived from Code § 8.01-397).
2:805. Hearsay Within Hearsay.
2:806. Attacking and Supporting Credibility of Hearsay Declarant.

Article IX. Authentication.

2:901. Requirement of Authentication or Identification.

Rule
2:902. Self-Authentication.
2:903. Subscribing Witness Testimony Not Necessary.

Article X. Best Evidence.

2:1001. Definitions.
2:1002. Requirement of Production of Original.
2:1003. Use of Substitute Checks (derived from Code § 8.01-391(A) and (B)).
2:1004. Admissibility of Other Evidence of Contents.
2:1005. Admissibility of Copies (derived from Code § 8.01-391).
2:1006. Summaries.
2:1007. Testimony or Written Admission of a Party.
2:1008. Functions of Court and Jury.

Article XI. Applicability.

2:1101. Applicability of Evidentiary Rules.

Editor's note. — Former Part Two, Equity Practice and Procedure, was repealed [and reserved for future use], effective January 1, 2006, by order adopted June 14, 2005.

Present Part Two, Virginia Rules of Evidence, was approved and promulgated by the Supreme Court of Virginia, September 12, 2011. The Virginia Rules of Evidence were submitted to and approved by the Virginia Code Commission.

Acts 2012, cc. 688 and 708, in cl. 3 provide: "That the Supreme Court of Virginia has prepared and adopted Rules of Evidence in accordance with its rulemaking authority under § 8.01-3 of the Code of Virginia."

Acts 2012, cc. 688 and 708, in cl. 4 provide: "That the Rules of Evidence prepared and adopted by the Supreme Court of Virginia have been submitted to and approved by the Virginia Code Commission as required by subsection E of § 8.01-3 of the Code of Virginia and by § 30-153 of the Code of Virginia."

Acts 2012, cc. 688 and 708, cl. 5, amended Rule 2:102 by adding the third sentence thereof.

Acts 2012, cc. 688 and 708, in cl. 7 provide: "That the provisions of this act shall become effective on July 1, 2012, and that the Rules of Evidence shall become effective on July 1, 2012."

Acts 2012, cc. 688 and 708, in cl. 8 provide: "That the Rules of Evidence shall be applicable in all proceedings held on or after the effective date of this act in any civil action or criminal case pending on that date or commenced thereafter."

Acts 2012, cc. 688 and 708, in cl. 9 provide: "That in the event of any conflict between any enactment of the General Assembly and any rule contained in the Rules of Evidence, the enactment of the General Assembly shall control."

ARTICLE I. GENERAL PROVISIONS.

Rule 2:101. Title.

These Rules shall be known as Virginia Rules of Evidence.

Law Review. — For annual survey of Virginia law article, "Civil Practice and Procedure," see 47 U. Rich. L. Rev. 113 (2012). For symposium, "The Restyled Federal Rules of Evidence," see 53 Wm. and Mary L. Rev. 1435 (2012).

Rule 2:102. Scope and Construction of These Rules.

These Rules state the law of evidence in Virginia. They are adopted to implement established principles under the common law and not to change any established case law rendered prior to the adoption of the Rules. Common law case authority, whether decided before or after the effective date of the Rules of Evidence, may be argued to the courts and considered in interpreting and applying the Rules of Evidence. As to matters not covered by these Rules, the existing law remains in effect. Where no rule is set out on a particular topic, adoption of the Rules shall have no effect on current law or practice on that topic. (As amended by Acts 2012, cc. 688, 708, cl. 5, effective July 1, 2012.)

The amendments by Acts 2012, cc. 688 and 708, cl. 5, effective July 1, 2012, are identical, and added the third sentence.

Law Review. — For annual survey of Virginia law article, "Civil Practice and Procedure," see 47 U. Rich. L. Rev. 113 (2012).

Rule 2:103. Objections and Proffers.

(a) *Admission or exclusion of evidence.* — Error may not be predicated upon admission or exclusion of evidence, unless:

(1) As to evidence admitted, a contemporaneous objection is stated with reasonable certainty as required in Rule 5:25 and 5A:18 or in any continuing objection on the record to a related series of questions, answers or exhibits if permitted by the trial court in order to avoid the necessity of repetitious objections; or

(2) As to evidence excluded, the substance of the evidence was made known to the court by proffer.

(b) *Hearing of jury.* — In jury cases, proceedings shall be conducted so as to prevent inadmissible evidence from being made known to the jury.

Rule 2:104. Preliminary Determinations.

(a) *Determinations made by the court.* — The qualification of a person to be a witness, the existence of a privilege, or the admissibility of evidence shall be decided by the court, subject to the provisions of subdivision (b).

(b) *Relevancy conditioned on proof of connecting facts.* — Whenever the relevancy of evidence depends upon proof of connecting facts, the court may admit the evidence upon or, in the court's discretion, subject to, the introduction of proof sufficient to support a finding of the connecting facts.

(c) *Hearing of jury.* — Hearings on the admissibility of confessions in all criminal cases shall be conducted out of the hearing of the jury. Hearings on other preliminary matters in all cases shall be so conducted whenever a statute, rule, case law or the interests of justice require, or when an accused is a witness and so requests.

(d) *Testimony by accused.* — The accused does not, by testifying upon a preliminary matter, become subject to cross-examination as to other issues in the case.

(e) *Evidence of weight or credibility.* — This rule does not limit the right of any party to introduce before the jury evidence relevant to weight or credibility.

Rule 2:105. Proof Admitted for Limited Purposes.

When evidence is admissible as to one party or for one purpose but not admissible as to another party or for another purpose, the court upon motion shall restrict such evidence to its proper scope and instruct the jury accordingly. The court may give such limiting instructions sua sponte, to which any party may object.

Rule 2:106. Remainder of a Writing or Recorded Statement (Rule 2:106(b) derived from Code § 8.01-417.1).

(a) *Related Portions of a Writing in Civil and Criminal Cases.* — When part of a writing or recorded statement is introduced by a party, upon motion by another party the court may require the offering party to introduce any other part of the writing or recorded statement which ought in fairness to be considered contemporaneously with it, unless such additional portions are inadmissible under the Rules of Evidence.

(b) *Lengthy Documents in Civil cases.* — To expedite trials in civil cases, upon timely motion, the court may permit the reading to the jury, or the introduction into evidence, of relevant portions of lengthy and complex documents without the necessity of having the jury hear or receive the entire document. The court, in its discretion, may permit the entire document to be received by the jury, or may order the parties to edit from any such document admitted into evidence information that is irrelevant to the proceedings.

ARTICLE II. JUDICIAL NOTICE.

Rule 2:201. Judicial Notice of Adjudicative Facts.

(a) *Notice.* — A court may take judicial notice of a factual matter not subject to reasonable dispute in that it is either (1) common knowledge or (2) capable of accurate and ready determination by resort to sources whose accuracy cannot reasonably be questioned.

(b) *Time of taking notice.* — Judicial notice may be taken at any stage of the proceeding.

(c) *Opportunity to be heard.* — A party is entitled upon timely motion to an opportunity to be heard as to the propriety of taking judicial notice.

Rule 2:202. Judicial Notice of Law (derived from Code §§ 8.01-386 and 19.2-265.2).

(a) *Notice To Be Taken.* — Whenever, in any civil or criminal case it becomes necessary to ascertain what the law, statutory, administrative, or otherwise, of this Commonwealth, of another state, of the United States, of another country, or of any political subdivision or agency of the same, or under an applicable treaty or international convention is, or was, at any time, the court shall take judicial notice thereof whether specially pleaded or not.

(b) *Sources of Information.* — The court, in taking such notice, shall consult any book, record, register, journal, or other official document or publication purporting to contain, state, or explain such law, and may consider any evidence or other information or argument that is offered on the subject.

Rule 2:203. Judicial Notice of Official Publications (derived from Code § 8.01-388).

The court shall take judicial notice of the contents of all official publications of the Commonwealth and its political subdivisions and agencies required to be published pursuant to the laws thereof, and of all such official publications of other states, of the United States, of other countries, and of the political subdivisions and agencies of each published within those jurisdictions pursuant to the laws thereof.

ARTICLE III. PRESUMPTIONS.

Rule 2:301. Presumptions in General in Civil Actions and Proceedings.

Unless otherwise provided by Virginia common law or statute, in a civil action a rebuttable presumption imposes on the party against whom it is directed the burden of going forward with evidence to rebut or meet the presumption, but does not shift to such party the burden of proof, which remains throughout the trial upon the party on whom it originally rested.

Rule 2:302. Applicability of Federal Law in Civil Actions and Proceedings.

The effect of a presumption is determined by federal law in any civil action or proceeding as to which federal law supplies the rule of decision.

ARTICLE IV. RELEVANCY, POLICY, AND CHARACTER TRAIT PROOF.

Rule 2:401. Definition of "Relevant Evidence."

"Relevant evidence" means evidence having any tendency to make the existence of any fact in issue more probable or less probable than it would be without the evidence.

Rule 2:402. Relevant Evidence Generally Admissible; Irrelevant Evidence Inadmissible.

(a) *General Principle.* — All relevant evidence is admissible, except as otherwise provided by the Constitution of the United States, the Constitution of Virginia, statute, Rules of the Supreme Court of Virginia, or other evidentiary principles. Evidence that is not relevant is not admissible.

(b) *Results of Polygraph Examinations.* — The results of polygraph examinations are not admissible.

Rule 2:403. Exclusion of Relevant Evidence on Grounds of Prejudice, Confusion, Misleading the Jury, or Needless Presentation of Cumulative Evidence.

Relevant evidence may be excluded if:

(a) the probative value of the evidence is substantially outweighed by (i) the danger of unfair prejudice, or (ii) its likelihood of confusing or misleading the trier of fact;

(b) the evidence is needlessly cumulative.

CIRCUIT COURT OPINIONS

Probative value outweighed risk of unfair prejudice. — Probative value of the evidence outweighed the risk of unfair prejudice because the defense was not powerless to rebut, or impeach the Commonwealth's evidence, and robberies in three counties were sufficiently idiosyncratic to permit an inference that defendant was probably the common perpetrator. Commonwealth v. Bagby, 2013 Va. Cir. LEXIS 27 (Hanover County Feb. 22, 2013).

Rule 2:404. Character Evidence Not Admissible to Prove Conduct; Exceptions; Other Crimes.

(a) *Character evidence generally.* — Evidence of a person's character or character trait is not admissible for the purpose of proving action in conformity therewith on a particular occasion, except:

(1) *Character trait of accused.* Evidence of a pertinent character trait of the accused offered by the accused, or by the prosecution to rebut the same;

(2) *Character trait of victim.* Except as provided in Rule 2:412, evidence of a pertinent character trait or acts of violence by the victim of the crime offered by an accused who has adduced evidence of self defense, or by the prosecution (i) to rebut defense evidence, or (ii) in a criminal case when relevant as circumstantial evidence to establish the death of the victim when other evidence is unavailable; or

(3) *Character trait of witness.* Evidence of the character trait of a witness, as provided in Rules 2:607, 2:608, and 2:609.

(b) *Other crimes, wrongs, or acts.* — Evidence of other crimes, wrongs, or acts is generally not admissible to prove the character trait of a person in order to show that the person acted in conformity therewith. However, if the legitimate probative value of such proof outweighs its incidental prejudice, such evidence is admissible if it tends to prove any relevant fact pertaining to the offense charged, such as where it is relevant to show motive, opportunity, intent, preparation, plan, knowledge, identity, absence of mistake, accident, or if they are part of a common scheme or plan.

CIRCUIT COURT OPINIONS

Other crimes. — Commonwealth was entitled to introduce evidence of other crimes pursuant to the identity exception of Va. Sup. Ct. R. 2:404(b), as incidents of Henrico and Richmond County robberies were sufficiently similar to those of a Hanover County robbery to permit an inference that defendant was probably the common perpetrator in all three; the offenses were each committed in the afternoon when defendant was not working and within a reasonable proximity to each other. Commonwealth v. Bagby, 2013 Va. Cir. LEXIS 27 (Hanover County Feb. 22, 2013).

Rule 2:405. Methods of Proving Character Traits.

(a) *Reputation proof.* — Where evidence of a person's character trait is admissible under these Rules, proof may be made by testimony as to reputation; but a witness may not give reputation testimony except upon personal knowledge of the reputation. On cross-examination, inquiry is allowable into relevant specific instances of conduct.

(b) *Specific instances of conduct.* — In cases in which a character trait of a person is an essential element of a charge, claim, or defense, proof may also be made of specific instances of conduct of such person on direct or cross-examination.

Rule 2:406. Habit and Routine Practice in Civil Cases (derived from Code § 8.01-397.1).

(a) *Admissibility.* — In a civil case, evidence of a person's habit or of an organization's routine practice, whether corroborated or not and regardless of the presence of eyewitnesses, is relevant to prove that the conduct of the person or organization on a particular occasion conformed with the habit or routine practice. Evidence of prior conduct may be relevant to rebut evidence of habit or routine practice.

(b) *Habit and routine practice defined.* — A "habit" is a person's regular response to repeated specific situations. A "routine practice" is a regular course of conduct of a group of persons or an organization in response to repeated specific situations.

Rule 2:407. Subsequent Remedial Measures (derived from Code § 8.01-418.1).

When, after the occurrence of an event, measures are taken which, if taken prior to the event, would have made the event less likely to occur, evidence of such subsequent measures is not admissible to prove negligence or culpable conduct as a cause of the occurrence of the event; provided that evidence of subsequent measures shall not be required to be excluded when offered for another purpose for which it may be admissible, including, but not limited to, proof of ownership, control, feasibility of precautionary measures if controverted, or for impeachment.

Rule 2:408. Compromise and Offers to Compromise.

Evidence of offers and responses concerning settlement or compromise of any claim which is disputed as to liability or amount is inadmissible regarding such issues. However, an express admission of liability, or an admission concerning an independent fact pertinent to a question in issue, is admissible even if made during settlement negotiations. Otherwise admissible evidence is not excludable merely because it was presented in the course of compromise negotiations. Nor is it required that evidence of settlement or compromise negotiations be excluded if the evidence is offered for another purpose, such as proving bias or prejudice of a witness or negating a contention of undue delay.

Rule 2:409. Evidence of Abuse Admissible in Certain Criminal Trials (derived from Code § 19.2-270.6).

In any criminal prosecution alleging personal injury or death, or the attempt to cause personal injury or death, relevant evidence of repeated physical and psychological abuse of the accused by the victim shall be admissible, subject to the general rules of evidence.

Rule 2:410. Withdrawn Pleas, Offers to Plead, and Related Statements.

Admission of evidence concerning withdrawn pleas in criminal cases, offers to plead, and related statements shall be governed by Rule 3A:8(c)(5) of the Rules of Supreme Court of Virginia and by applicable provisions of the Code of Virginia.

Rule 2:411. Insurance.

Evidence that a person was or was not insured is not admissible on the question whether the person acted negligently or otherwise wrongfully, and not admissible on the issue of damages. But exclusion of evidence of insurance is not required when offered for another purpose, such as proof of agency, ownership, or control, or bias or prejudice of a witness.

Rule 2:412. Admissibility of Complaining Witness' Prior Sexual Conduct; Criminal Sexual Assault Cases; Relevance of Past Behavior (derived from Code § 18.2-67.7).

(a) In prosecutions under Article 7, Chapter 4 of Title 18.2 of the Code of Virginia, under clause (iii) or (iv) of § 18.2-48, or under §§18.2-370, 18.2-370.01, or 18.2-370.1, general reputation or opinion evidence of the complaining witness' unchaste character or prior sexual conduct shall not be admitted. Unless the complaining witness voluntarily agrees otherwise, evidence of specific instances of his or her prior sexual conduct shall be admitted only if it is relevant and is:

1. Evidence offered to provide an alternative explanation for physical evidence of the offense charged which is introduced by the prosecution, limited to evidence designed to explain the presence of semen, pregnancy, disease, or physical injury to the complaining witness' intimate parts; or

2. Evidence of sexual conduct between the complaining witness and the accused offered to support a contention that the alleged offense was not accomplished by force, threat or intimidation or through the use of the complaining witness' mental incapacity or physical helplessness, provided that the sexual conduct occurred within a period of time reasonably proximate to the offense charged under the circumstances of this case; or

3. Evidence offered to rebut evidence of the complaining witness' prior sexual conduct introduced by the prosecution.

(b) Nothing contained in this Rule shall prohibit the accused from presenting evidence relevant to show that the complaining witness had a motive to fabricate the charge against the accused. If such evidence relates to the past sexual conduct of the complaining witness with a person other than the accused, it shall not be admitted and may not be referred to at any preliminary hearing or trial unless the party offering same files a written notice generally describing the evidence prior to the introduction of any evidence, or the opening statement of either counsel, whichever first occurs, at the preliminary hearing or trial at which the admission of the evidence may be sought.

(c) Evidence described in subdivisions (a) and (b) of this Rule shall not be admitted and may not be referred to at any preliminary hearing or trial until the court first determines the admissibility of that evidence at an evidentiary hearing to be held before the evidence is introduced at such preliminary hearing or trial. The court shall exclude from the evidentiary hearing all persons except the accused, the complaining witness, other necessary witnesses, and required court personnel. If the court determines that the evidence meets the requirements of subdivisions (a) and (b) of this Rule, it shall be admissible before the judge or jury trying the case in the ordinary course of the preliminary hearing or trial. If the court initially determines that the evidence is inadmissible, but new information is discovered during the course of the preliminary hearing or trial which may make such evidence admissible, the court shall determine in an evidentiary hearing whether such evidence is admissible.

ARTICLE V. PRIVILEGES.

Rule 2:501. Privileged Communications.

Except as otherwise required by the Constitutions of the United States or the Commonwealth of Virginia or provided by statute or these Rules, the privilege of a witness, person, government, State, or political subdivision thereof, shall be governed by the principles of common law as they may be interpreted by the courts of the Commonwealth in the light of reason and experience.

Rule 2:502. Attorney-Client Privilege.

Except as may be provided by statute, the existence and application of the attorney-client privilege in Virginia, and the exceptions thereto, shall be governed by the principles of common law as interpreted by the courts of the Commonwealth in the light of reason and experience.

Rule 2:503. Clergy and Communicant Privilege (derived from Code §§ 8.01-400 and 19.2-271.3).

A *clergy member* means any regular minister, priest, rabbi, or accredited practitioner over the age of 18 years, of any religious organization or denomination usually referred to as a church. A clergy member shall not be required:

(a) in any civil action, to give testimony as a witness or to disclose in discovery proceedings the contents of notes, records or any written documentation made by the clergy member, where such testimony or disclosure would reveal any information communicated in a confidential manner, properly entrusted to such clergy member in a professional capacity and necessary to enable discharge of the functions of office according to the usual course of the clergy member's practice or discipline, wherein the person so communicating such information about himself or herself, or another, was seeking spiritual counsel and advice relating to and growing out of the information so imparted; and

(b) in any criminal action, in giving testimony as a witness to disclose any information communicated by the accused in a confidential manner, properly entrusted to the clergy member in a professional capacity and necessary to enable discharge of the functions of office according to the usual course of the clergy member's practice or discipline, where the person so communicating such information about himself or herself, or another, was seeking spiritual counsel and advice relating to and growing out of the information so imparted.

Rule 2:504. Spousal Testimony and Marital Communications Privileges (Rule 2:504(a) derived from Code § 8.01-398; and Rule 2:504(b) derived from Code § 19.2-271.2).

(a) *Privileged Marital Communications in Civil Cases.*

1. Husband and wife shall be competent witnesses to testify for or against each other in all civil actions.

2. In any civil proceeding, a person has a privilege to refuse to disclose, and to prevent anyone else from disclosing, any confidential communication between such person and his or her spouse during their marriage, regardless of whether such person is married to that spouse at the time he or she objects to disclosure. This privilege may not be asserted in any proceeding in which the spouses are adverse parties, or in which either spouse is charged with a crime or tort against the person or property of the other or against the minor child of either spouse. For the purposes of this Rule, "confidential communication" means a communication made privately by a person to his or her spouse that is not intended for disclosure to any other person.

(b) *Testimony of Husband and Wife in Criminal Cases.*

1. In criminal cases husband and wife shall be allowed, and, subject to the Rules of Evidence governing other witnesses, may be compelled to testify in behalf of each other, but neither shall be compelled to be called as a witness against the other, except (i) in the case of a prosecution for an offense committed by one against the other, against a minor child of either, or against the property of either; (ii) in any case where either is charged with forgery of the name of the other or uttering or attempting to utter a writing bearing the allegedly forged signature of the other; or (iii) in any proceeding relating to a violation of the laws pertaining to criminal sexual assault (§§ 18.2-61 through 18.2-67.10), crimes against nature (§ 18.2-361) involving a minor as a victim and provided the defendant and the victim are not married to each other, incest (§ 18.2-366), or abuse of children (§§ 18.2-370 through 18.2-371). The failure of either husband or wife to testify, however, shall create no presumption against the accused, nor be the subject of any comment before the court or jury by any attorney.

2. Except in the prosecution for a criminal offense as set forth in subsections (b)(1)(i), (ii) and (iii) above, in any criminal proceeding, a person has a privilege to refuse to disclose, and to prevent anyone else from disclosing, any confidential communication between such person and his or her spouse during their marriage, regardless of whether the person is married to that spouse at the time the person objects to disclosure. For the purposes of this Rule, "confidential communication" means a communication made privately by a person to his or her spouse that is not intended for disclosure to any other person.

The amendment effective July 1, 2012, adopted June 18, 2012, substituted "subsections (b)(1)(i), (ii), and (iii)" for "subsections (B)(i), (ii), or (iii)" in subdivision (b)(2).

Rule 2:505. Healing Arts Practitioner and Patient Privilege (derived from Code § 8.01-399).

The scope and application of the privilege between a patient and a physician or practitioner of the healing arts in a civil case shall be as set forth in any specific statutory provisions, including Code § 8.01-399, as amended from time to time, which presently provides:

A. Except at the request or with the consent of the patient, or as provided in this section, no duly licensed practitioner of any branch of the healing arts shall be permitted to testify in any civil action, respecting any information that he may have acquired in attending, examining or treating the patient in a professional capacity.

B. If the physical or mental condition of the patient is at issue in a civil action, the diagnoses, signs and symptoms, observations, evaluations, histories, or treatment plan of the practitioner, obtained or formulated as contemporaneously documented during the course of the practitioner's treatment, together with the facts communicated to, or otherwise learned by, such practitioner in connection with such attendance, examination or treatment shall be disclosed but only in discovery pursuant to the Rules of Court or through testimony at the trial of the action. In addition, disclosure may be ordered when a court, in the exercise of sound discretion, deems it necessary to the proper administration of justice. However, no order shall be entered compelling a party to sign a release for medical records from a health care provider unless the health care provider is not located in the Commonwealth or is a federal facility. If an order is issued pursuant to this section, it shall be restricted to the medical records that relate to the physical or mental conditions at issue in the case. No disclosure of diagnosis or treatment plan facts communicated to, or otherwise learned by, such practitioner shall occur if the court determines, upon the request of the patient, that such facts are not relevant to the subject matter involved in the pending action or do not appear to be reasonably calculated to lead to the discovery of admissible evidence. Only diagnosis offered to a reasonable degree of medical probability shall be admissible at trial.

C. This section shall not (i) be construed to repeal or otherwise affect the provisions of § 65.2-607 relating to privileged communications between physicians and surgeons and employees under the Workers' Compensation Act; (ii) apply to information communicated to any such practitioner in an effort unlawfully to procure a narcotic drug, or unlawfully to procure the administration of any such drug; or (iii) prohibit a duly licensed practitioner of the healing arts, or his agents, from disclosing information as required by state or federal law.

D. Neither a lawyer nor anyone acting on the lawyer's behalf shall obtain, in connection with pending or threatened litigation, information concerning a patient from a practitioner of any branch of the healing arts without the consent of the patient, except through discovery pursuant to the Rules of Supreme Court as herein provided. However, the prohibition of this subsection shall not apply to:

1. Communication between a lawyer retained to represent a practitioner of the healing arts, or that lawyer's agent, and that practitioner's employers, partners, agents, servants, employees, co-employees or others for whom, at law, the practitioner is or may be liable or who, at law, are or may be liable for the practitioner's acts or omissions;

2. Information about a patient provided to a lawyer or his agent by a practitioner of the healing arts employed by that lawyer to examine or evaluate the patient in accordance with Rule 4:10 of the Rules of Supreme Court; or

3. Contact between a lawyer or his agent and a nonphysician employee or agent of a practitioner of healing arts for any of the following purposes: (i) scheduling appearances, (ii) requesting a written recitation by the practitioner of handwritten records obtained by the lawyer or his agent from the practitioner, provided the request is made in writing and, if litigation is pending, a copy of the request and the practitioner's response is provided simultaneously to the patient or his attorney, (iii) obtaining information necessary to obtain service upon the practitioner in pending litigation, (iv) determining when records summoned will be provided by the practitioner or his agent, (v) determining what patient records the practitioner possesses in order to summons records in pending litigation, (vi) explaining any summons that the lawyer or his agent caused to be issued and served on the practitioner, (vii) verifying dates the practitioner treated the patient, provided that if litigation is pending the information obtained by the lawyer or his agent is promptly given, in writing, to the patient or his attorney, (viii) determining charges by the practitioner for appearance at a deposition or to testify before any tribunal or administrative body, or (ix) providing to or obtaining from the practitioner directions to a place to which he is or will be summoned to give testimony.

E. A clinical psychologist duly licensed under the provisions of Chapter 36 (§ 54.1-3600 et seq.) of Title 54.1 shall be considered a practitioner of a branch of the healing arts within the meaning of this section.

F. Nothing herein shall prevent a duly licensed practitioner of the healing arts, or his agents, from disclosing any information that he may have acquired in attending, examining or treating a patient in a professional capacity where such disclosure is necessary in connection with the care of the patient, the protection or enforcement of a practitioner's legal rights including such rights with respect to medical malpractice actions, or the operations of a health care facility or health maintenance organization or in order to comply with state or federal law.

Rule 2:506. Mental Health Professional and Client Privilege (derived from Code § 8.01-400.2).

Except at the request of or with the consent of the client, no licensed professional counselor, as defined in Code § 54.1-3500; licensed clinical social worker, as defined in Code § 54.1-3700; licensed psychologist, as defined in Code § 54.1-3600; or licensed marriage and family therapist, as defined in Code § 54.1-3500, shall be required in giving testimony as a witness in any civil action to disclose any information communicated in a confidential manner, properly entrusted to such person in a professional capacity and necessary to enable discharge of professional or occupational services according to the usual course of his or her practice or discipline, wherein the person so communicating such information about himself or herself, or another, is seeking professional counseling or treatment and advice relating to and growing out of the information so imparted; provided, however, that when the physical or mental condition of the client is at issue in such action, or when a court, in the exercise of sound discretion, deems such disclosure necessary to the proper administration of justice, no fact communicated to, or otherwise learned by, such practitioner in connection with such counseling, treatment or advice shall be privileged, and disclosure may be required. The privileges conferred by this Rule shall not extend to testimony in matters relating to child abuse and neglect nor serve to relieve any person from the reporting requirements set forth in § 63.2-1509.

Rule 2:507. Privileged Communications Involving Interpreters (derived from Code §§ 8.01-400.1, 19.2-164, and 19.2-164.1).

Whenever a deaf or non-English-speaking person communicates through an interpreter to any person under such circumstances that the communication would be privileged, and such person could not be compelled to testify as to the communications, the privilege shall also apply to the interpreter.

ARTICLE VI. WITNESS EXAMINATION.

Rule 2:601. General Rule of Competency.

(a) *Generally* — Every person is competent to be a witness except as otherwise provided in other evidentiary principles, Rules of Court, Virginia statutes, or common law.

(b) *Rulings.* — A court may declare a person incompetent to testify if the court finds that the person does not have sufficient physical or mental capacity to testify truthfully, accurately, or understandably.

CASE NOTES

Victim competent. — Finding that the child victim, who was deaf and mute, was competent to testify was not erroneous, as the trial court also paid close attention to the victim's demeanor and emotive cues, finding them consistent with her efforts to testify truthfully and completely; any claim of undue influence by the victim's mother went to the weight of the testimony, not the competency of the victim. Bynum v. Commonwealth, No. 0854-12-1, 2013 Va. App. LEXIS 170 (Ct. of Appeals June 4, 2013).

Rule 2:602. Lack of Personal Knowledge.

A witness may not testify to a matter unless evidence is introduced sufficient to support a finding that the witness has personal knowledge of the matter. Evidence to prove personal knowledge may, but need not, consist of the testimony of the witness. This Rule does not bar testimony admissible under Rules 2:701, 2:702 and 2:703.

Rule 2:603. Oath or Affirmation.

Before testifying, every witness shall be required to declare that he or she will testify truthfully, by oath or affirmation administered in a form calculated to awaken the conscience and impress the mind of the witness with the duty to do so.

Rule 2:604. Interpreters (derived from Code § 8.01-406).

An interpreter shall be qualified as competent and shall be placed under oath or affirmation to make a true translation.

Rule 2:605. Competency of Court Personnel as Witnesses (derived from Code § 19.2-271).

(a) No judge shall be competent to testify in any criminal or civil proceeding as to any matter which came before the judge in the course of official duties.

(b) No clerk of any court, magistrate, or other person having the power to issue warrants, shall be competent to testify in any criminal or civil proceeding, except proceedings wherein the defendant is charged with perjury, as to any matter which came before him or her in the course of official duties. Such person shall be competent to testify in any criminal proceeding wherein the defendant is charged pursuant to the provisions of § 18.2-460 or in any proceeding authorized pursuant to § 19.2-353.3.

Notwithstanding any other provision of this section, any judge, clerk of any court, magistrate, or other person having the power to issue warrants, who is the victim of a crime, shall not be incompetent solely because of his or her office to testify in any criminal or civil proceeding arising out of the crime. Nothing in this subpart (b) shall preclude otherwise proper testimony by a clerk or deputy clerk concerning documents filed in the official records.

Rule 2:606. Competency of Juror as Witness.

Upon inquiry regarding the validity of a verdict or indictment, a juror is precluded from testifying as to any matter or statement occurring during the course of the jury's deliberations or to the effect of anything upon any juror's mind or emotions as influencing any juror to assent to or dissent from the verdict or indictment or concerning any juror's mental processes in connection therewith.

A juror may testify only as to questions regarding extraneous prejudicial information improperly brought to the jury's attention as a result of conduct outside the jury room, or whether any improper influence was brought to bear upon any juror from a source outside the jury room.

Rule 2:607. Incompetency of Witnesses (Rule 2:607(b) derived from Code § 8.01-401(A); and Rule 2:607(c) derived from Code § 8.01-403).

(a) *In general.* — Subject to the provisions of Rule 2:403, the credibility of a witness may be impeached by any party other than the one calling the witness, with any proof that is relevant to the witness's credibility. Impeachment may be undertaken, among other means, by:

(i) introduction of evidence of the witness's bad general reputation for the traits of truth and veracity, as provided in Rule 2:608(a) and (b);

(ii) evidence of prior conviction, as provided in Rule 2:609;

(iii) evidence of prior unadjudicated perjury, as provided in Rule 2:608(d);

(iv) evidence of prior false accusations of sexual misconduct, as provided in Rule 2:608(e);

(v) evidence of bias as provided in Rule 2:610;

(vi) prior inconsistent statements as provided in 2:613;

(vii) contradiction by other evidence; and

(viii) any other evidence which is probative on the issue of credibility because of a logical tendency to convince the trier of fact that the witness's perception, memory, or narration is defective or impaired, or that the sincerity or veracity of the witness is questionable.

Impeachment pursuant to subdivisions (a)(i) and (ii) of this Rule may not be undertaken by a party who has called an adverse witness.

(b) *Witness with adverse interest.* — A witness having an adverse interest may be examined with leading questions by the party calling the witness. After such an adverse direct examination, the witness is subject to cross-examination.

(c) *Witness proving adverse.*

(i) If a witness proves adverse, the party who called the witness may, subject to the discretion of the court, prove that the witness has made at other times a statement inconsistent with the present testimony as provided in Rule 2:613.

(ii) In a jury case, if impeachment has been conducted pursuant to this subdivision (c), the court, on motion by either party, shall instruct the jury to consider the evidence of such inconsistent statements solely for the purpose of contradicting the witness.

Rule 2:608. Impeachment by Evidence of Reputation for Truthtelling and Conduct of Witness.

(a) *Reputation evidence of the character trait for truthfulness or untruthfulness.* — The credibility of a witness may be attacked or supported by evidence in the form of reputation, subject to these limitations: (1) the evidence may relate only to character trait for truthfulness or untruthfulness; (2) evidence of truthful character is admissible only after the character trait of the witness for truthfulness has been attacked by reputation evidence or otherwise; and (3) evidence is introduced that the person testifying has sufficient familiarity with the reputation to make the testimony probative.

(b) *Specific instances of conduct; extrinsic proof.* — Except as otherwise provided in this Rule, by other principles of evidence, or by statute, (1) specific instances of the conduct of a witness may not be used to attack or support credibility; and (2) specific instances of the conduct of a witness may not be proved by extrinsic evidence.

(c) *Cross-examination of character witness.* — Specific instances of conduct may, if probative of truthfulness or untruthfulness, be inquired into on cross-examination of a character witness concerning the character trait for truthfulness or untruthfulness of another witness as to whose character trait the witness being cross-examined has testified.

(d) *Unadjudicated perjury.* — If the trial judge makes a threshold determination that a reasonable probability of falsity exists, any witness may be questioned about prior specific instances of unadjudicated perjury. Extrinsic proof of the unadjudicated perjury may not be shown.

(e) *Prior false accusations in sexual assault cases.* — Except as otherwise provided by other evidentiary principles, statutes or Rules of Court, a complaining witness in a sexual assault case may be cross-examined about prior false accusations of sexual misconduct.

Rule 2:609. Impeachment by Evidence of Conviction of Crime (derived from Code § 19.2-269).

Evidence that a witness has been convicted of a crime may be admitted to impeach the credibility of that witness subject to the following limitations:

(a) *Party in a civil case or criminal defendant.*

(i) The fact that a party in a civil case or an accused who testifies has previously been convicted of a felony, or a misdemeanor involving moral turpitude, and the number of such convictions may be elicited during examination of the party or accused.

(ii) If a conviction raised under subdivision (a)(i) is denied, it may proved by extrinsic evidence.

(iii) In any examination pursuant to this subdivision (a), the name or nature of any crime of which the party or accused was convicted, except for perjury, may not be shown, nor may the details of prior convictions be elicited, unless offered to rebut other evidence concerning prior convictions.

(b) *Other witnesses.* The fact that any other witness has previously been convicted of a felony, or a misdemeanor involving moral turpitude, the number, and the name and nature, but not the details, of such convictions may be elicited during examination of the witness or, if denied, proved by extrinsic evidence.

(c) *Juvenile adjudications.* Juvenile adjudications may not be used for impeachment of a witness on the subject of general credibility, but may be used to show bias of the witness if constitutionally required.

(d) *Adverse Witnesses.* A party who calls an adverse witness may not impeach that adverse witness with a prior conviction.

Rule 2:610. Bias or Prejudice of a Witness.

A witness may be impeached by a showing that the witness is biased for or prejudiced against a party. Extrinsic evidence of such bias or prejudice may be admitted.

Rule 2:611. Mode and Order of Interrogation and Presentation (Rule 2:611(c) derived from Code § 8.01-401(A).

(a) *Presentation of evidence.* — The mode and order of interrogating witnesses and presenting evidence may be determined by the court so as to (1) facilitate the ascertainment of the truth, (2) avoid needless consumption of time, and (3) protect witnesses from harassment or undue embarrassment.

(b) *Scope of cross-examination.*

(i) Cross-examination should be limited to the subject matter of the direct examination and matters affecting the credibility of the witness. The court may, in the exercise of discretion, permit inquiry into additional matters as if on direct examination.

(ii) In a criminal case, if a defendant testifies on his or her own behalf and denies guilt as to an offense charged, cross-examination of the defendant may be permitted in the discretion of the court into any matter relevant to the issue of guilt or innocence.

(c) *Leading questions.* — Leading questions should not be used on the direct examination of a witness except as may be permitted by the court in its discretion to allow a party to develop the testimony. Leading questions should be permitted on cross-examination. Whenever a party calls a hostile witness, an adverse party, a witness having an adverse interest, or a witness proving adverse, interrogation may be by leading questions.

CASE NOTES

Applied in Preferred Sys. Solutions, Inc. v. GP Consulting, LLC, 284 Va. 382, 732 S.E.2d 676, 2012 Va. LEXIS 160 (2012).

Rule 2:612. Writing or Object Used to Refresh Memory.

If while testifying, a witness uses a writing or object to refresh his memory, an adverse party is entitled to have the writing or object produced at the trial, hearing, or deposition in which the witness is testifying.

Rule 2:613. Prior Statements of Witness (Rule 2:613(a)(i) derived from Code § 8.01-403; Rule 2:613(b)(i) derived from Code §§ 8.01-404 and 19.2-268.1; and Rule 2:613(b)(ii) derived from Code § 8.01-404).

(a) *Examining witness concerning prior oral statement.*

(i) *Prior oral statements of witnesses.* — In examining a witness in any civil or criminal case concerning a prior oral statement, the circumstances of the supposed statement, sufficient to designate the particular occasion, must be mentioned to the witness, and the witness must be asked whether the statement was made.

(ii) *Extrinsic evidence of prior inconsistent oral statement of witness.* — Extrinsic evidence of a prior inconsistent oral statement by a witness is not admissible unless the witness is first given an opportunity to explain or deny the statement and the opposing party is given an opportunity to interrogate the witness thereon, or the interests of justice otherwise require. This provision does not apply to admissions of a party opponent.

Extrinsic evidence of a witness' prior inconsistent statement is not admissible unless the witness denies or does not remember the prior inconsistent statement. Extrinsic evidence of collateral statements is not admissible.

(b) *Contradiction by prior inconsistent writing.*

(i) *General rule.* — In any civil or criminal case, a witness may be cross-examined as to previous statements made by the witness in writing or reduced to writing, relating to the subject matter of the action, without such writing being shown to the witness; but if the intent is to contradict such witness by the writing, his or her attention must, before such contradictory proof can be given, be called to the particular occasion on which the writing is supposed to have been made; the witness may be asked whether he or she made a writing of the purport of the one to be offered, and if the witness denies making it, or does not admit its execution, it shall then be shown to the witness, and if the witness admits its genuineness, the witness shall be allowed to make an explanation of it; but the court may, at any time during the trial, require the production of the writing for its inspection, and the court may then make such use of it for the purpose of the trial as it may think best.

(ii) *Personal Injury or Wrongful Death Cases.* — Notwithstanding the general principles stated in this subpart (b), in an action to recover for personal injury or wrongful death, no ex parte affidavit or statement in writing other than a deposition, after due notice, of a witness and no extrajudicial recording made at any time other than simultaneously with the wrongful act or negligence at issue of the voice of such witness, or reproduction or transcript thereof, as to the facts or circumstances attending the wrongful act or neglect complained of, shall be used to contradict such witness in the case. Nothing in this subdivision shall be construed to prohibit the use of any such ex parte affidavit or statement in an action on an insurance policy based upon a judgment recovered in a personal injury or wrongful death case.

Rule 2:614. Calling and Interrogation of Witnesses by Court.

(a) *Calling by the court in civil cases.* — The court, on motion of a party or on its own motion, may call witnesses, and all parties are entitled to cross-examine. The calling of a witness by the court is a matter resting in the trial judge's sound discretion and should be exercised with great care.

(b) *Interrogation by the court.* — In a civil or criminal case, the court may question witnesses, whether called by itself or a party, subject to the applicable Rules of Evidence.

Rule 2:615. Exclusion of Witnesses (Rule 2:615(a) derived from Code §§ 8.01-375, 19.2-184, and 19.2-265.1; Rule 2:615(b) derived from Code § 8.01-375; and Rule 2:615(c) derived from Code § 19.2-265.1).

(a) The court, in a civil or criminal case, may on its own motion and shall on the motion of any party, require the exclusion of every witness including, but not limited to, police officers or other investigators. The court may also order that each excluded witness be kept separate from all other witnesses. But each named party who is an individual, one officer or agent of each party which is a corporation, limited liability entity or association, and an attorney alleged in a habeas corpus proceeding to have acted ineffectively shall be exempt from the exclusion as a matter of right.

(b) Where expert witnesses are to testify in the case, the court may, at the request of all parties, allow one expert witness for each party to remain in the courtroom; however, in cases pertaining to the distribution of marital property pursuant to § 20-107.3 or the determination of child or spousal support pursuant to § 20-108.1, the court may, upon motion of any party, allow one expert witness for each party to remain in the courtroom throughout the hearing.

(c) Any victim as defined in Code § 19.2-11.01 who is to be called as a witness may remain in the courtroom and shall not be excluded unless pursuant to Code § 19.2-265.01 the court determines, in its discretion, that the presence of the victim would impair the conduct of a fair trial.

ARTICLE VII. OPINIONS AND EXPERT TESTIMONY.

Rule 2:701. Opinion Testimony by Lay Witnesses (derived from Code § 8.01-401.3(B)).

Opinion testimony by a lay witness is admissible if it is reasonably based upon the personal experience or observations of the witness and will aid the trier of fact in understanding the witness' perceptions. Lay opinion may relate to any matter, such as — but not limited to — sanity, capacity, physical condition or disability, speed of a vehicle, the value of property, identity, causation, time, the meaning of words, similarity of objects, handwriting, visibility or the general physical situation at a particular location. However, lay witness testimony that amounts only to an opinion of law is inadmissible.

Rule 2:702. Testimony by Experts (Rule 2:702(a)(i) derived from Code § 8.01-401.3(A)).

(a) *Use of Expert Testimony.*

(i) In a civil proceeding, if scientific, technical, or other specialized knowledge will assist the trier of fact to understand the evidence or to determine a fact in issue, a witness qualified as an expert by knowledge, skill, experience, training, or education may testify thereto in the form of an opinion or otherwise.

(ii) In a criminal proceeding, expert testimony is admissible if the standards set forth in subdivision (a)(i) of this Rule are met and, in addition, the court finds that the subject matter is beyond the knowledge and experience of ordinary persons, such that the jury needs expert opinion in order to comprehend the subject matter, form an intelligent opinion, and draw its conclusions.

(b) *Form of opinion.* — Expert testimony may include opinions of the witness established with a reasonable degree of probability, or it may address empirical data from which such probability may be established in the mind of the finder of fact. Testimony that is speculative, or which opines on the credibility of another witness, is not admissible.

Rule 2:703. Basis of Expert Testimony (Rule 2:703(a) derived from Code § 8.01-401.1).

(a) *Civil cases.* — In a civil action an expert witness may give testimony and render an opinion or draw inferences from facts, circumstances, or data made known to or perceived by such witness at or before the hearing or trial during which the witness is called upon to testify. The facts, circumstances, or data relied upon by such witness in forming an opinion or drawing inferences, if of a type normally relied upon by others in the particular field of expertise in forming opinions and drawing inferences, need not be admissible in evidence.

(b) *Criminal cases.* — In criminal cases, the opinion of an expert is generally admissible if it is based upon facts personally known or observed by the expert, or based upon facts in evidence.

CASE NOTES

No reference to inadmissable evidence during direct testimony. — In a products liability case against an auto manufacturer following a minivan fire, where evidence of three previous minivan fires was inadmissible because the evidence did not sufficiently establish that the fires were cause by the same or similar defect or danger as the decedent's fire, the estate administrator's expert witnesses were not entitled to refer to those fires during their direct testimony. This ruling did not preclude the administrator's experts from relying upon information regarding the three fires in formulating their opinions provided such information was of a type normally relied upon by others in the particular field of expertise in forming opinions and drawing inferences. Funkhouser v. Ford Motor Co., 284 Va. 214, 726 S.E.2d 302, 2012 Va. LEXIS 132 (2012).

Rule 2:704. Opinion on Ultimate Issue (Rule 2:704(a) derived from Code § 8.01-401.3(B) and (C)).

(a) *Civil cases.* — In civil cases, no expert or lay witness shall be prohibited from expressing an otherwise admissible opinion or conclusion as to any matter of fact solely because that fact is the ultimate issue or critical to the resolution of the case. But in no event shall such witness be permitted to express any opinion which constitutes a conclusion of law. Any other exceptions to the "ultimate fact in issue" rule recognized in the Commonwealth remain in full force.

(b) *Criminal cases.* — In criminal proceedings, opinion testimony on the ultimate issues of fact is not admissible. This Rule does not require exclusion of otherwise proper expert testimony concerning a witness' or the defendant's mental disorder and the hypothetical effect of that disorder on a person in the witness' or the defendant's situation.

Rule 2:705. Facts or Data Used in Testimony (Rule 2:705(a) derived from Code § 8.01-401.1).

(a) *Civil cases.* — In civil cases, an expert may testify in terms of opinion or inference and give reasons therefor without prior disclosure of the underlying facts or data, unless the court requires otherwise. The expert may in any event be required to disclose the underlying facts or data on cross-examination.

(b) *Criminal cases.* — In criminal cases, the facts on which an expert may give an opinion shall be disclosed in the expert's testimony, or set forth in a hypothetical question.

CASE NOTES

No reference to inadmissable evidence during direct testimony. — In a products liability case against an auto manufacturer following a minivan fire, where evidence of three previous minivan fires was inadmissible because the evidence did not sufficiently establish that the fires were cause by the same or similar defect or danger as the decedent's fire, the estate administrator's expert witnesses were not entitled to refer to those fires during their direct testimony. This ruling did not preclude the administrator's experts from relying upon information regarding the three fires in formulating their opinions provided such information was of a type normally relied upon by others in the particular field of expertise in forming opinions and drawing inferences. Funkhouser v. Ford Motor Co., 284 Va. 214, 726 S.E.2d 302, 2012 Va. LEXIS 132 (2012).

Rule 2:706. Use of Learned Treatises With Experts (Rule 2:706(a) derived from Code § 8.01-401.1).

(a) *Civil cases.* — To the extent called to the attention of an expert witness upon cross-examination or relied upon by the expert witness in direct examination, statements contained in published treatises, periodicals or pamphlets on a subject of history, medicine or other science or art, established as a reliable authority by testimony or by stipulation shall not be excluded as hearsay. If admitted, the statements may be read into evidence but may not be received as exhibits. If the statements are to be introduced through an expert witness upon direct examination, copies of the specific statements shall be designated as literature to be introduced during direct examination and provided to opposing parties 30 days prior to trial unless otherwise ordered by the court. If a statement has been designated by a party in accordance with and satisfies the requirements of this rule, the expert witness called by that party need not have relied on the statement at the time of forming his opinion in order to read the statement into evidence during direct examination at trial.

(b) *Criminal cases.* — Where an expert witness acknowledges on cross-examination that a published work is a standard authority in the field, an opposing party may ask whether the witness agrees or disagrees with statements in the work acknowledged. Such proof shall be received solely for impeachment purposes with respect to the expert's credibility.

The 2013 amendment effective July 1, 2013, adopted June 21, 2013, in subdivision (a), inserted "specific" and "designated as literature to be introduced during direct examination and" and substituted "30" for "thirty" in the third sentence, and added the fourth sentence.

ARTICLE VIII. HEARSAY.

Rule 2:801. Definitions.

The following definitions apply under this article:

(a) *Statement.* A "statement" is (1) an oral or written assertion or (2) nonverbal conduct of a person, if it is intended as an assertion.

(b) *Declarant.* A "declarant" is a person who makes a statement.

(c) *Hearsay.* "Hearsay" is a statement, other than one made by the declarant while testifying at the trial or hearing, offered in evidence to prove the truth of the matter asserted.

CASE NOTES

Statement not excited utterance. — Statement made by defendant's mother-in-law to his mother, when the mother called to inform the mother-in-law that defendant killed her daughter, indicating that she heard that defendant had depression was not an excited utterance because it was not a statement about an event or condition, but about her opinion. Kenston v. Commonwealth, No. 2487-11-4, 2013 Va. App. LEXIS 35 (Jan. 29, 2013).

Rule 2:802. Hearsay Rule.

Hearsay is not admissible except as provided by these Rules, other Rules of the Supreme Court of Virginia, or by Virginia statutes or case law.

CASE NOTES

Statements offered by police detective did not constitute hearsay. — Hearsay statements offered by a police detective from monitored phone calls defendant and his co-defendants made from jail were not offered for the truth of the matters asserted but were offered to prove the state of the declarant's mind as it bore on consciousness of guilt, efforts to conceal participation in crime and a desire to avoid detection, and therefore, the statements fell outside of the hearsay rule or came within well recognized exceptions to the hearsay rule. Henderson v. Commonwealth, 285 Va. 318, 736 S.E.2d 901, 2013 Va. LEXIS 11 (2013).

Rule 2:803. Hearsay Exceptions Applicable Regardless of Availability of the Declarant (Rule 2:803(10)(a) derived from Code § 8.01-390(B); Rule 2:803(10)(b) derived from Code § 19.2-188.3; Rule 2:803(17) derived from Code § 8.2-724; and Rule 2:803(23) is derived from Code § 19.2-268.2).

The following are not excluded by the hearsay rule, even though the declarant is available as a witness:

(0) *Admission by party-opponent.* — A statement offered against a party that is (A) the party's own statement, in either an individual or a representative capacity, or (B) a statement of which the party has manifested adoption or belief in its truth, or (C) a statement by a person authorized by the party to make a statement concerning the subject, or (D) a statement by the party's agent or employee, made during the term of

the agency or employment, concerning a matter within the scope of such agency or employment, or (E) a statement by a co-conspirator of a party during the course and in furtherance of the conspiracy.

(1) *Present sense impression.* — A spontaneous statement describing or explaining an event or condition made contemporaneously with, or while, the declarant was perceiving the event or condition.

(2) *Excited utterance.* — A spontaneous or impulsive statement prompted by a startling event or condition and made by a declarant with firsthand knowledge at a time and under circumstances negating deliberation.

(3) *Then existing mental, emotional, or physical condition.* — A statement of the declarant's then existing state of mind, emotion, sensation, or physical condition (such as intent, plan, motive, design, mental feeling, pain, and bodily health), but not including a statement of memory or belief to prove the fact remembered or believed unless it relates to the execution, revocation, identification, or terms of the declarant's will.

(4) *Statements for purposes of medical treatment.* — Statements made for purposes of medical diagnosis or treatment and describing medical history, or past or present symptoms, pain, or sensations, or the inception or general character of the cause or external source thereof insofar as reasonably pertinent to diagnosis or treatment.

(5) *Recorded recollection.* — Except as provided by statute, a memorandum or record concerning a matter about which a witness once had firsthand knowledge made or adopted by the witness at or near the time of the event and while the witness had a clear and accurate memory of it, if the witness lacks a present recollection of the event, and the witness vouches for the accuracy of the written memorandum. If admitted, the memorandum or record may be read into evidence but may not itself be received as an exhibit unless offered by an adverse party.

(6) *Business records.* — A memorandum, report, record, or data compilation, in any form, of acts, events, calculations or conditions, made at or near the time by, or from information transmitted by, a person with knowledge in the course of a regularly conducted business activity, and if it was the regular practice of that business activity to make and keep the memorandum, report, record, or data compilation, all as shown by the testimony of the custodian or other qualified witness, unless the source of information or the method or circumstances of preparation indicate lack of trustworthiness. The term "business" as used in this paragraph includes business, organization, institution, association, profession, occupation, and calling of every kind, whether or not conducted for profit.

(7) Reserved.

(8) *Public records and reports.* — In addition to categories of government records made admissible by statute, records, reports, statements, or data compilations, in any form, prepared by public offices or agencies, setting forth (A) the activities of the office or agency, or (B) matters observed within the scope of the office or agency's duties, as to which the source of the recorded information could testify if called as a witness; generally excluding, however, in criminal cases matters observed by police officers and other law enforcement personnel when offered against a criminal defendant.

(9) *Records of vital statistics.* — Records or data compilations, in any form, of births, fetal deaths, deaths, or marriages, if the report was made to a public office pursuant to requirements of law.

(10) *Absence of entries in public records and reports.*

(a) *Civil Cases.* An affidavit signed by an officer, or the deputy thereof, deemed to have custody of records of this Commonwealth, of another state, of the United States, of another country, or of any political subdivision or agency of the same, other than those located in a clerk's office of a court, stating that after a diligent search, no record or entry of such record is found to exist among the records in such office is admissible as evidence that the office has no such record or entry.

(b) *Criminal Cases.* In any criminal hearing or trial, an affidavit signed by a government official who is competent to testify, deemed to have custody of an official record, or signed by such official's designee, stating that after a diligent search, no record or entry of such record is found to exist among the records in such official's custody, is admissible as evidence that the office has no such record or entry, provided that the procedures set forth in subsection G of § 18.2-472.1 for admission of an affidavit have been satisfied, mutatis mutandis, and the accused has not objected to the admission of the affidavit pursuant to the procedures set forth in subsection H of

§ 18.2-472.1, mutatis mutandis. Nothing in this subsection (b) shall be construed to affect the admissibility of affidavits in civil cases under subsection (a) of this Rule.

(11) *Records of religious organizations.* — Statements of births, marriages, divorces, deaths, legitimacy, ancestry, relationship by blood or marriage, or other similar facts of personal or family history, contained in a regularly kept record of a religious organization.

(12) *Marriage, baptismal, and similar certificates.* — Statements of fact contained in a certificate that the maker performed a marriage or other ceremony or administered a sacrament, made by a clergyman, public official, or other person authorized by the rules or practices of a religious organization or by law to perform the act certified, and purporting to have been issued at the time of the act or within a reasonable time thereafter.

(13) *Family records.* — Statements of fact concerning personal or family history contained in family bibles, genealogies, charts, engravings on rings, inscriptions on family portraits, engravings on urns, crypts, or tombstones, or the like.

(14) *Records of documents affecting an interest in property.* — The record of a document purporting to establish or affect an interest in property, as proof of the content of the original recorded document and its execution, and delivery by each person by whom it purports to have been executed, if the record is a record of a public office and an applicable statute authorizes the recording of documents of that kind in that office.

(15) *Statements in documents affecting an interest in property.* — A statement contained in a document purporting to establish or affect an interest in property if the matter stated was relevant to the purpose of the document, unless dealings with the property since the document was made have been inconsistent with the truth of the statement or the purport of the document.

(16) *Statements in ancient documents.* — Statements generally acted upon as true by persons having an interest in the matter, and contained in a document in existence 30 years or more, the authenticity of which is established.

(17) *Market quotations.* — Whenever the prevailing price or value of any goods regularly bought and sold in any established commodity market is in issue, reports in official publications or trade journals or in newspapers or periodicals of general circulation published as the reports of such market shall be admissible in evidence. The circumstances of the preparation of such a report may be shown.

(18) *Learned treatises.* — *See* Rule 2:706.

(19) *Reputation concerning boundaries.* — Reputation in a community, arising before the controversy, as to boundaries of lands in the community, where the reputation refers to monuments or other delineations on the ground and some evidence of title exists.

(20) *Reputation as to a character trait.* — Reputation of a person's character trait among his or her associates or in the community.

(21) *Judgment as to personal, family, or general history, or boundaries.* — Judgments as proof of matters of personal, family or general history, or boundaries, essential to the judgment, if the same would be provable by evidence of reputation.

(22) *Statement of identification by witness.* — The declarant testifies at the trial or hearing and is subject to cross-examination concerning the statement, and the statement is one of identification of a person.

(23) *Recent complaint of sexual assault.* — In any prosecution for criminal sexual assault under Article 7 (§ 18.2-61 et seq.) of Chapter 4 of Title 18.2, a violation of §§ 18.2-361, 18.2-366, 18.2-370 or § 18.2-370.1, the fact that the person injured made complaint of the offense recently after commission of the offense is admissible, not as independent evidence of the offense, but for the purpose of corroborating the testimony of the complaining witness.

(24) *Price of goods.* — In shoplifting cases, price tags regularly affixed to items of personalty offered for sale, or testimony concerning the amounts shown on such tags.

CASE NOTES

Excited utterance. — Hearsay testimony concerning statements the victim made at the scene of the shooting were properly admitted under the excited utterance exception to the hearsay rule, because they were made while the victim was incapacitated, distraught, and bleeding just after being shot. Hicks v. Commonwealth, 60 Va. App. 237, 725 S.E.2d 748, 2012 Va. App. LEXIS 176 (2012).

Rule 2:804. Hearsay Exceptions Applicable Where the Declarant Is Unavailable (Rule 2:804(b)(5) derived from Code § 8.01-397).

(a) *Applicability.* — The hearsay exceptions set forth in subpart (b) hereof are applicable where the declarant is dead or otherwise unavailable as a witness.

(b) *Hearsay exceptions.* — The following are not excluded by the hearsay rule:

(1) *Former testimony.* Testimony given under oath or otherwise subject to penalties for perjury at a prior hearing, or in a deposition, if it is offered in reasonably accurate form and, if given in a different proceeding, the party against whom the evidence is now offered, or in a civil case a privy, was a party in that proceeding who examined the witness by direct examination or had the opportunity to cross-examine the witness, and the issue on which the testimony is offered is substantially the same in the two cases.

(2) *Statement under belief of impending death.* In a prosecution for homicide, a statement made by a declarant who believed when the statement was made that death was imminent and who had given up all hope of survival, concerning the cause or circumstances of declarant's impending death.

(3) *Statement against interest.* (A) A statement which the declarant knew at the time of its making to be contrary to the declarant's pecuniary or proprietary interest, or to tend to subject the declarant to civil liability. (B) A statement which the declarant knew at the time of its making would tend to subject the declarant to criminal liability, if the statement is shown to be reliable.

(4) *Statement of personal or family history.* If no better evidence is available, a statement made before the existence of the controversy, concerning family relationships or pedigree of a person, made by a member of the family or relative.

(5) *Statement by party incapable of testifying.* Code § 8.01-397, entitled "Corroboration required and evidence receivable when one party incapable of testifying," presently provides:

In an action by or against a person who, from any cause, is incapable of testifying, or by or against the committee, trustee, executor, administrator, heir, or other representative of the person so incapable of testifying, no judgment or decree shall be rendered in favor of an adverse or interested party founded on his uncorroborated testimony. In any such action, whether such adverse party testifies or not, all entries, memoranda, and declarations by the party so incapable of testifying made while he was capable, relevant to the matter in issue, may be received as evidence in all proceedings including without limitation those to which a person under a disability is a party. The phrase "from any cause" as used in this section shall not include situations in which the party who is incapable of testifying has rendered himself unable to testify by an intentional self-inflicted injury.

For the purposes of this section, and in addition to corroboration by any other competent evidence, an entry authored by an adverse or interested party contained in a business record may be competent evidence for corroboration of the testimony of an adverse or interested party. If authentication of the business record is not admitted in a request for admission, such business record shall be authenticated by a person other than the author of the entry who is not an adverse or interested party whose conduct is at issue in the allegations of the complaint.

The amendment effective July 1, 2013, adopted June 21, 2013, added the concluding paragraph of subdivision (b).

Rule 2:805. Hearsay Within Hearsay.

Hearsay included within hearsay is not excluded under the hearsay rule if each part of the combined statements conforms with an exception to the hearsay rule.

Rule 2:806. Attacking and Supporting Credibility of Hearsay Declarant.

When a hearsay statement has been admitted in evidence, the credibility of the declarant may be attacked, and if attacked may be supported, by any evidence which would be admissible for those purposes if the declarant had testified as a witness.

ARTICLE IX. AUTHENTICATION.

Rule 2:901. Requirement of Authentication or Identification.

The requirement of authentication or identification as a condition precedent to admissibility is satisfied by evidence sufficient to support a finding that the thing in question is what its proponent claims.

Rule 2:902. Self-Authentication.

Additional proof of authenticity as a condition precedent to admissibility is not required with respect to the following:

(1) *Domestic public records offered in compliance with statute.* Public records authenticated or certified as provided under a statute of the Commonwealth.

(2) *Foreign public documents.* A document purporting to be executed or attested in his official capacity by a person authorized by the laws of a foreign country to make the execution or attestation, and accompanied by a final certification as to the genuineness of the signature and official position (a) of the executing or attesting person, or (b) of any foreign official whose certificate of genuineness of signature and official position relates to the execution or attestation or is in a chain of certification of genuineness of signature and official position relating to the execution or attestation. A final certification may be made by a secretary of embassy or legation, consul general, consul, vice consul, or consular agent of the United States, or a diplomatic or consular official of the foreign country assigned or accredited to the United States. If reasonable opportunity has been given to all parties to investigate the authenticity and accuracy of official documents, the court may for good cause shown order that they be treated as presumptively authentic without final certification or permit them to be evidenced by an attested summary with or without final certification.

(3) *Presumptions created by law.* Any signature, document, or other matter declared by any law of the United States or of this Commonwealth, to be presumptively or prima facie genuine or authentic.

(4) *Medical records and medical bills in particular actions.* Where authorized by statute, medical records and medical bills, offered upon the forms of authentication specified in the Code of Virginia.

(5) *Specific certificates of analysis and reports.* Certificates of analysis and official reports prepared by designated persons or facilities, when authenticated in accordance with applicable statute.

Rule 2:903. Subscribing Witness Testimony Not Necessary.

The testimony of a subscribing witness is not necessary to authenticate a writing unless required by the laws of the jurisdiction whose laws govern the validity of the writing.

ARTICLE X. BEST EVIDENCE.

Rule 2:1001. Definitions.

For purposes of this Article, the following definitions are applicable.

(1) *Writings.* "Writings" consist of letters, words, or numbers, or their equivalent, set down by handwriting, typewriting, printing, photostating, photographing, magnetic impulse, mechanical or electronic recording, or other form of data compilation or preservation.

(2) *Original.* An "original" of a writing is the writing itself or any other writing intended to have the same effect by a person executing or issuing it.

Rule 2:1002. Requirement of Production of Original.

To prove the content of a writing, the original writing is required, except as otherwise provided in these Rules, Rules of the Supreme Court of Virginia, or in a Virginia statute.

Rule 2:1003. Use of Substitute Checks (derived from Code § 8.01-391(A) and (B)).

(a) *Admissibility generally.* — A substitute check created pursuant to the federal Check Clearing for the 21st Century Evidence Act, 12 U.S.C. § 5001 et seq., shall be admissible in evidence in any Virginia legal proceeding, civil or criminal, to the same extent the original check would be.

(b) *Presumption from designation and legend.* — A document received from a banking institution that is designated as a "substitute check" and that bears the legend "This is a legal copy of your check. You can use it the same way you would use the original check" shall be presumed to be a substitute check created pursuant to the Act applicable under subdivision (a) of this Rule.

Rule 2:1004. Admissibility of Other Evidence of Contents.

The original is not required, and other evidence of the contents of a writing is admissible if:

(a) *Originals lost or destroyed.* All originals are lost or have been destroyed, unless the proponent lost or destroyed them in bad faith; or

(b) *Original not obtainable.* No original can be obtained by any available judicial process or procedure, unless the proponent acted in bad faith to render the original unavailable; or

(c) *Original in possession of opponent.* At a time when an original was under the control of the party against whom offered, that party was put on notice, by the pleadings or otherwise, that the contents would be a subject of proof at the hearing, and that party does not produce the original at the hearing; or

(d) *Collateral matters.* The writing is not closely related to a controlling issue.

Rule 2:1005. Admissibility of Copies (derived from Code § 8.01-391).

In addition to admissibility of copies of documents as provided in Rules 2:1002 and 2:1004, and by statute, copies may be used in lieu of original documents as follows:

(a) Whenever the original of any official publication or other record has been filed in an action or introduced as evidence, the court may order the original to be returned to its custodian, retaining in its stead a copy thereof. The court may make any order to prevent the improper use of the original.

(b) If any department, division, institution, agency, board, or commission of this Commonwealth, of another state or country, or of the United States, or of any political subdivision or agency of the same, acting pursuant to the law of the respective jurisdiction or other proper authority, has copied any record made in the performance of its official duties, such copy shall be as admissible into evidence as the original, whether the original is in existence or not, provided that such copy is authenticated as a true copy either by the custodian of said record or by the person to whom said custodian reports, if they are different, and is accompanied by a certificate that such person does in fact have the custody.

(c) If any court or clerk's office of a court of this Commonwealth, of another state or country, or of the United States, or of any political subdivision or agency of the same, has copied any record made in the performance of its official duties, such copy shall be admissible into evidence as the original, whether the original is in existence or not, provided that such copy is authenticated as a true copy by a clerk or deputy clerk of such court.

(d) If any business or member of a profession or calling in the regular course of business or activity has made any record or received or transmitted any document, and again in the regular course of business has caused any or all of such record or document to be copied, the copy shall be as admissible in evidence as the original, whether the original exists or not, provided that such copy is satisfactorily identified and authenticated as a true copy by a custodian of such record or by the person to whom said custodian reports, if they be different, and is accompanied by a certificate that said person does in fact have the custody. Copies in the regular course of business shall be deemed to include reproduction at a later time, if done in good faith and without intent to defraud. Copies in the regular course of business shall include items such as checks which are regularly copied before transmission to another person or bank, or records which are acted upon without receipt of the original when the original is retained by another party.

(e) The original of which a copy has been made may be destroyed unless its preservation is required by law, or its validity has been questioned.

(f) The introduction in an action of a copy under this Rule precludes neither the introduction or admission of the original nor the introduction of a copy or the original in another action.

(g) Copy, as used in these Rules, shall include photographs, microphotographs, photostats, microfilm, microcard, printouts or other reproductions of electronically stored data, or copies from optical disks, electronically transmitted facsimiles, or any other reproduction of an original from a process which forms a durable medium for its recording, storing, and reproducing.

The amendment effective July 1, 2012, adopted June 18, 2012, inserted the subsection (e) designation and redesignated former subsections (e) and (f) as subsections (f) and (g).

CASE NOTES

Admissibility of copy of certificate of analysis. — Trial court did not err in admitting into evidence a copy of the certificate of analysis, which identified the substance as cocaine, as it identified two other suspects by name, a check mark appeared next to defendant's name, it included a photocopied stamp signed by a deputy clerk of the circuit court, and it displayed an original "Copy Teste" stamp and signature, authenticating the document as a copy made from court's record. Carter v. Commonwealth, No. 1621-11-3, 2012 Va. App. LEXIS 417 (Dec. 18, 2012).

Rule 2:1006. Summaries.

The contents of voluminous writings that, although admissible, cannot conveniently be examined in court may be represented in the form of a chart, summary, or calculation. Reasonably in advance of the offer of such chart, summary, or calculation, the originals or duplicates shall be made available for examination or copying, or both, by other parties at a reasonable time and place. The court may order that they be produced in court.

Rule 2:1007. Testimony or Written Admission of a Party.

Contents of writings may be proved by the admission of the party against whom offered without accounting for the nonproduction of the original.

Rule 2:1008. Functions of Court and Jury.

Whenever the admissibility of other evidence of contents or writings under these provisions depends upon the fulfillment of a condition of fact, the question whether the condition has been fulfilled is ordinarily for the court to determine. However, when an issue is raised whether (1) the asserted writing ever existed, or (2) another writing produced at the trial is the original, or (3) other evidence of contents correctly reflects the contents, the issue is for the trier of fact to determine.

ARTICLE XI. APPLICABILITY.

Rule 2:1101. Applicability of Evidentiary Rules.

(a) *Proceedings to which applicable generally.* — Evidentiary rules apply generally to (1) all civil actions and (2) proceedings in a criminal case (including preliminary hearings in criminal cases), and to contempt proceedings (except contempt proceedings in which the court may act summarily), in the Supreme Court of Virginia, the Court of Appeals of Virginia, the State Corporation Commission (when acting as a court of record), the circuit courts, the general district courts (except when acting as a small claims court as provided by statute), and the juvenile and domestic relations district courts.

(b) *Law of privilege.* — The law with respect to privileges applies at all stages of all actions, cases, and proceedings.

(c) *Permissive application.* — Except as otherwise provided by statute or rule, adherence to the Rules of Evidence (other than with respect to privileges) is permissive, not mandatory, in the following situations:

(1) Criminal proceedings other than (i) trial, (ii) preliminary hearings, (iii) sentencing proceedings before a jury, and (iv) capital murder sentencing hearings.

(2) Administrative proceedings.

PART TWO A
APPEALS PURSUANT TO THE ADMINISTRATIVE PROCESS ACT

Rule
2A:1. Authorization; Definitions; Application.
2A:2. Notice of Appeal.
2A:3. Record on Appeal.
2A:4. Petition for Appeal.
2A:5. Further Proceedings.
2A:6. Small Business Challenges.

Editor's note. — Part Two A was adopted May 19, 1977, effective July 1, 1977.

Rule 2A:1. Authorization; Definitions; Application.

(a) These rules are promulgated pursuant to § 2.2-4026 of the Code of Virginia. They shall apply to the review of, by way of direct appeal from, the adoption of a regulation or the decision of a case by an agency.

(b) All terms used in this part that are defined in Chapter 40, Article 1 of Title 2.2 are used with the definitions therein contained. Every agency may designate some individual to perform the function of "agency secretary." If there is no designated "agency secretary," that term shall mean the executive officer of the agency.

(c) The term "party" means any person affected by and claiming the unlawfulness of a regulation, or a party aggrieved who asserts a case decision is unlawful or any other affected person or aggrieved person who appeared in person or by counsel at a hearing, as defined in § 2.2-4001, with respect to the regulation or case decision as well as the agency itself. Whenever a case decision disposes of an application for a license, permit or other benefit, the applicant, licensee or permittee shall be a necessary party to any proceeding under this part.

The amendment, effective December 22, 2004, adopted December 22, 2004, substituted "§ 2.2-4026" for "§ 9-6.14:16" in subdivision (a); and in subdivision (b), substituted "Chapter 40, Article 1 of Title 2.2" for "Chapter 1.1:1 of Title 9" and "§ 2.2-4001" for "§ 9-6.14:4 E."

The amendment, effective May 3, 2010, adopted February 26, 2010, added the second sentence of subdivision (a), and rewrote subdivisions (b) and (c).

Law Review. — For an article, "Agency Adjudication, the Importance of Facts, and the Limitation of Labels," see 57 Wash. & Lee L. Rev. 351 (2000).

For article reviewing recent developments and changes in legislation, case law, and Virginia Supreme Court Rules affecting civil litigation, see "Civil Practice and Procedure," 40 U. Rich. L. Rev. 95 (2005).

CASE NOTES

A de facto rule may be challenged by bringing a suit claiming the unlawfulness of a case decision, as defined by the Virginia Administrative Process Act. Virginia Bd. of Medicine v. Virginia Physical Therapy Ass'n, 13 Va. App. 458, 413 S.E.2d 59 (1991), aff'd, 245 Va. 125, 427 S.E.2d 183 (1993).

Part held inapplicable to case decisions of State Water Control Board. — Actions of the State Water Control Board which in effect required privately owned utilities to abandon the treatment of sewage and connect their lines to those of publicly owned utility by a certain date were "case decisions" as defined by § 9-6.14:4 [now § 2.2-4001], and the "basic law under which the agency acted" was the State Water Control Law, § 62.1-44.2 et seq., which contains a detailed procedural scheme for judicial review of board actions; thus its appeal procedures applied and those of Part 2A of the Rules of the Supreme Court did not. Commonwealth ex rel. State Water Control Bd. v. County Utils. Corp., 223 Va. 534, 290 S.E.2d 867 (1982).

The landfill permit holder was not a "party" as defined in this rule. The permit holder was also not a person affected by and claiming the unlawfulness of a regulation because, an agency decision, not an agency regulation was at issue in this case; and the permit holder did not assert that the Director's issuance of the permit was unlawful. As the company that benefited from the agency's granting of the landfill permit, the permit holder was also not a party aggrieved who asserted that a case decision was unlawful. Residents Involved in Saving Env't, Inc. v. Commonwealth, Dep't of Envtl. Quality, 22 Va. App. 532, 471 S.E.2d 796 (1996).

Because the permit holder was not a "party" as defined in this rule, and the permit holder was allowed to intervene in the case to protect its interests, the court did not err in refusing to dismiss the appeal. Residents Involved in Saving Env't, Inc. v. Commonwealth, Dep't of Envtl. Quality, 22 Va. App. 532, 471 S.E.2d 796 (1996).

Failure to name proper party on appeal to circuit court. — Both § 9-6.14:16 [now § 2.2-4026] and this rule require that the agency rendering a case decision be made a party to the judicial review proceeding and, where such agency is not named, the appellant's petition may be dismissed. Somers v. Accomack County Dep't of Soc. Servs., No. 2899-00-1, 2001 Va. App. LEXIS 291 (Ct. of Appeals May 29, 2001).

The Virginia Board of Medicine has consented to and may be sued only for its promulgation of a rule or its decision of a case, as both are defined in the Virginia Administrative Process Act (VAPA). Virginia Bd. of Medicine v. Virginia Physical Therapy Ass'n, 13 Va. App. 458, 413 S.E.2d 59 (1991), aff'd, 245 Va. 125, 427 S.E.2d 183 (1993).

The General Assembly has waived sovereign immunity only to allow a party to obtain judicial review of the Virginia Board of Medicine's adoption of rules of the Board's case decisions, as such are defined in the Virginia Administrative Process Act (VAPA), in the manner provided in the VAPA. Virginia Bd. of Medicine v. Virginia Physical Therapy Ass'n, 13 Va. App. 458, 413 S.E.2d 59 (1991), aff'd, 245 Va. 125, 427 S.E.2d 183 (1993).

State Water Control Board. — Section 2.2-4026 of the Virginia Administrative Process Act provides that an appeal of a decision by the Virginia State Water Control Board must be brought in the manner provided by the Rules of the Supreme Court of Virginia; under Va. Sup. Ct. R. 2A:1, appeals brought under the Act are governed by Part 2A of the Rules. State Water Control Bd. v. Crutchfield, 265 Va. 416, 578 S.E.2d 762, 2003 Va. LEXIS 42 (2003).

Service. — Plain meaning of Va. Sup. Ct. R. 2A:1, 2A:2, 2A:3 and 2A:4, read in concert with the Virginia Administrative Process Act, distinguishes a direct review of an agency's case decision from a new action, which would require service by a process server. Muse Constr. Group, Inc. v. Commonwealth Bd. for Contrs. & Warren & Beverly Wharton, 60 Va. App. 92, 724 S.E.2d 216, 2012 Va. App. LEXIS 133 (2012).

CIRCUIT COURT OPINIONS

Lack of standing. — Hospital center's action seeking review of the State Health Commissioner's decisions denying the center party status and granting a community hospital an extension of its certificate of public need was dismissed for lack of standing because the center was not a named party, aggrieved party, necessary party, or party identified by Va. Sup. Ct. R. 2A:1; the center failed to establish itself as a party genuinely aggrieved, and the facts upon which the certificate of public need was issued were not impacted by the request for an extension. Inova Loudoun Hosp. v. Remley, 77 Va. Cir. 411, 2009 Va. Cir. LEXIS 96 (Loudoun County 2009).

Head of agency proper party to suit. — Under § 2.2-4026 and Va. Sup. Ct. R. 2A:1, the Commissioner of the Virginia Department of Motor Vehicles was a proper party to petitioner's suit challenging the Department's revocation of his vanity license plates. Bujno v. Commonwealth, 2012 Va. Cir. LEXIS 143 (Chesapeake Nov. 2, 2012).

Rule 2A:2. Notice of Appeal.

(a) Any party appealing from a regulation or case decision shall file with the agency secretary, within 30 days after adoption of the regulation or after service of the final order in the case decision, a notice of appeal signed by the appealing party or that party's counsel. In the event that a case decision is required by § 2.2-4023 or by any other provision of law to be served by mail upon a party, 3 days shall be added to the 30-day period for that party. Service under this Rule shall be sufficient if sent by registered or certified mail to the party's last address known to the agency.

(b) The notice of appeal shall identify the regulation or case decision appealed from, shall state the names and addresses of the appellant and of all other parties and their counsel, if any, shall specify the circuit court to which the appeal is taken, and shall conclude with a certificate that a copy of the notice of appeal has been mailed to each of the parties. Any copy of a notice of appeal that is sent to a party's counsel or to a party's registered agent, if the party is a corporation, shall be deemed adequate and shall not be a cause for dismissal of the appeal; provided, however, sending a notice of appeal to an agency's counsel shall not satisfy the requirement that a notice of appeal be filed with the agency secretary. The omission of a party whose name and address cannot, after due diligence, be ascertained shall not be cause for dismissal of the appeal.

(c) Any final agency case decision as described in § 2.2-4023 shall advise the party of the time for filing a notice of appeal under this Rule.

The amendment, effective December 22, 2004, adopted December 22, 2004, substituted "§ 2.2-4023" for "§ 9-6.14:14" twice.

The amendment, effective May 3, 2010, adopted February 26, 2010, added the subdivision designations and rewrote subdivision (a).

Law Review. — For article on legislative changes to Virginia administrative rulemaking, see

19 U. Rich. L. Rev. 107 (1984). For annual survey of Virginia law article, "Administrative Law," see 47 U. Rich. L. Rev. 7 (2012). For annual survey of Virginia law article, "Civil Practice and Procedure," see 47 U. Rich. L. Rev. 113 (2012).

Michie's Jurisprudence. — For related discussion, see 1B M.J. Appeal and Error, § 20.

CASE NOTES

Requirements. — Notice of appeal must be filed within 30 days after the adoption of a regulation. Bender v. Va. Marine Res. Comm'n, No. 1479-01-1, 2001 Va. App. LEXIS 599 (Ct. of Appeals Oct. 30, 2001).

Physical delivery required. — Physical delivery, not posting in United States mail, is required to satisfy "filing" requirement under this rule. Carter v. Crabtree, No. 1437-98-3 (Ct. of Appeals Sept. 7, 1999).

Thirty-day period not adopted for Education for All Handicapped Children Act claims. — This rule and Rule 2A:4 are sufficiently analogous to a federal Education for All Handicapped Children Act (EAHCA) claim to warrant adoption of the Rules' limitation period for EAHCA claims. However, the policies underlying the EAHCA are inconsistent with the 30-day limitation period imposed by the Rules. Accordingly, the 30-day limitation period of the rules is not adopted for EAHCA claims. Kirchgessner ex rel. Kirchgessner v. Davis, 632 F. Supp. 616 (W.D. Va. 1986).

Limitation period under § 8.01-248 applicable to action under 20 U.S.C. § 1415. — For case applying the one-year [now two-year] statute of limitations of § 8.01-248 to parents' action in federal district court pursuant to 20 U.S.C. § 1415 challenging school system's refusal to find handicapped child's placement in a certain out-of-state residential school, rather than the shorter limitations of this rule and Supreme Court Rule 2A:4 applicable under § 22.1-214, see Schimmel ex rel. Schimmel v. Spillane, 819 F.2d 477 (4th Cir. 1987).

Notice of appeal from building code review board. — The 30-day period within which a county was required to file its notice of appeal from a decision of the State Building Code Technical Review Board began on the date the board's chairman signed the final order. Occoquan Land Dev. Corp. v. Cooper, 239 Va. 363, 389 S.E.2d 464 (1990) (decided prior to the 1991 amendment).

Failure to file timely notice of appeal. — Circuit court did not err in granting the motion filed by the Virginia Board of Agriculture and Consumer Services to dismiss a citizen's petition for appeal because the citizen failed to file notice within the 30-day period as required by Va. Sup. Ct. R. 2A:2, and thus, the circuit court never gained appellate jurisdiction to consider the merits of any assignments of error with respect to the Board. Russell v. Va. Bd. of Agric. & Consumer Servs., 59 Va. App. 86, 717 S.E.2d 413, 2011 Va. App. LEXIS 364 (2011).

Jurisdiction not divested for failure to serve necessary party. — Where the petitioners' notice of appeal and original petition for appeal are timely filed within the 30-day time periods specified in Va. Sup. Ct. Rules 2A:2 and 2A:4, the circuit court has jurisdiction over the subject of the appeal; a failure to have a copy of the petition served on a necessary party does not divest the court of jurisdiction. State Water Control Bd. v. Crutchfield, 265 Va. 416, 578 S.E.2d 762, 2003 Va. LEXIS 42 (2003).

Failure to name party in caption of notice of appeal not fatal. — Company's failure to list the Virginia Apprenticeship Council (VAC) in the caption of its notice of appeal was not jurisdictional, where the body of the company's petition for appeal, which was appended to, delivered with, and referenced by, the notice of appeal, made plain that the company was appealing the VAC's decision; the notice of appeal protected the VAC by informing it that its decision would be appealed, and thus, fulfilled the purpose behind Rule 2A:2. Williams Steel Erection Co. v. DOL & Indus., 42 Va. App. 814, 595 S.E.2d 45, 2004 Va. App. LEXIS 166 (2004).

Sufficient service of case decision. — Trial court properly held that a department's letter regarding the classification of business park's facility as a materials recovery facility was a case decision, because the mailing of the letter to the business park was sufficient service. Frederick County Bus. Park, LLC v. Va. Dep't of Envtl. Quality, 52 Va. App. 40, 660 S.E.2d 698, 2008 Va. App. LEXIS 244 (2008), aff'd, 278 Va. 207, 677 S.E.2d 42, 2009 Va. LEXIS 64 (2009).

Service. — Plain meaning of Va. Sup. Ct. R. 2A:1, 2A:2, 2A:3 and 2A:4, read in concert with the Virginia Administrative Process Act, distinguishes a direct review of an agency's case decision from a new action, which would require service by a process server. Muse Constr. Group, Inc. v. Commonwealth Bd. for Contrs. & Warren & Beverly Wharton, 60 Va. App. 92, 724 S.E.2d 216, 2012 Va. App. LEXIS 133 (2012).

Applied in Forbes v. Kenley, 227 Va. 55, 314 S.E.2d 49 (1984); Broomfield v. Jackson, 18 Va. App. 854, 447 S.E.2d 880 (1994); Watkins v. Fairfax County Dep't of Family Servs., 42 Va. App. 760, 595 S.E.2d 19, 2004 Va. App. LEXIS 164 (2004).

CIRCUIT COURT OPINIONS

Filing of initial appeal. — Although Va. Sup. Ct. R. 2A:2 and 2A:4 required any party appealing a case to file its notice of appeal within 30 days of service of a final agency order and to file a petition for appeal within 30 days of filing the notice of appeal, the time limits in those rules only applied to the initial filing of an appeal. Those time limits did not apply to the refiling of an appeal nonsuited pursuant to § 8.01-380, which was governed by subdivision E 3 of § 8.01-229, and, thus, neither Va. Sup. Ct. R. 2A:2 nor 2A:4 were in conflict with subdivision E 3 of § 8.01-229 regarding the time in which the limited liability companies had to appeal a refiled action in the trial court. Joy House Senior Homes, L.C. v. Jones, 75 Va. Cir. 140, 2008 Va. Cir. LEXIS 36 (Fairfax County 2008).

Final decision. — Property owner could not challenge any Virginia Marine Resources Commission (VMRC) decision on appeal other than its granting of an after-the-fact permit application where the applicant's previous permits dating from December 2004 and January 2005, several months prior to his November 2005 after-the-fact permit application, constituted final, unreviewable decisions. Harrison v. Va. Marine Res. Comm'n, 73 Va. Cir. 111, 2007 Va. Cir. LEXIS 222 (Norfolk 2007), rev'd, Boone v. Harrison, 52 Va. App. 53, 660 S.E.2d 704, 2008 Va. App. LEXIS 246 (2008).

Failure to comply not prejudicial. — While dismissal of a corporation's administrative appeal could be based on violations of Va. Sup. Ct. R. 1:4(d)(j), Va. Sup. Ct. R. 2A:4, and Va. Sup. Ct. R. 2A:2, this latter failure to comply with a ministerial requirement was not prejudicial, and was not fatally defective or jurisdictional. Birchwood Motel, Inc. v. Va. Marine Res. Comm'n, 74 Va. Cir. 298, 2007 Va. Cir. LEXIS 188 (Accomack County 2007).

Rule 2A:3. Record on Appeal.

(a) If a formal hearing was held before the agency, the appellant shall deliver to the agency secretary with his notice of appeal, or within 30 days thereafter, a transcript of the testimony if it was taken down in writing, or if it was not taken down in writing, a statement of the testimony in narrative form. If the agency secretary deems the statement inaccurate, he may append a further statement specifying the inaccuracies.

(b) The agency secretary shall prepare and certify the record as soon as possible after the notice of appeal and transcript or statement of testimony is filed and served. Once the court has entered an order overruling any motions, demurrers and other pleas filed by the agency, or if none have been filed within the time provided by Rule 3:8 for the filing of a response to the process served under Rule 2A:4, the agency secretary shall, as soon as practicable or within such time as the court may order, transmit the record to the clerk of the court named in the notice of appeal. In the event of multiple appeals in the same proceeding, only one record need be prepared and it shall be transmitted to the clerk of the court named in the first notice of appeal filed. If there are multiple appeals to different courts from the same regulation or case decision, all such appeals shall be transferred to and heard by the court having jurisdiction that is named in the notice of appeal that is the first to be filed. The agency secretary shall notify all parties in writing when the record is transmitted, naming the court to which it is transmitted. Papers filed in any other clerk's office shall be forwarded by such clerk to the proper clerk's office.

(c) The record on appeal from an agency proceeding shall consist of all notices of appeal, any application or petition, all orders or regulations promulgated in the proceeding by the agency, the opinions, the transcript or statement of the testimony filed by appellant, and all exhibits accepted or rejected, together with such other material as may be certified by the agency secretary to be a part of the record.

(d) Upon the adoption of standards for the preparation of electronic or digital records for use in appeals, records under this Rule shall comply with such standards.

(e) In the event the agency secretary determines that the record is so voluminous that its certification and filing pursuant to part (b) of this Rule would be unduly burdensome upon the agency or upon the clerk of the court, the agency may, prior to and in lieu of filing the entire record, move the court for leave to file an index to such record. A party shall have the opportunity to respond to the agency's motion within 10 days of filing the motion. Thereafter, if the court grants the agency's motion, the record, or such parts thereof as the parties may agree upon or as the court may determine, shall be filed in the form of a joint appendix or in such other form as the court may direct. The agency shall nevertheless retain the entire record and make it available to the parties on reasonable request during the pendency of the appeal.

The amendment, effective May 3, 2010, adopted February 26, 2010, rewrote subdivision (b) and added subdivision (d).

The amendment, effective May 2, 2011, adopted March 1, 2011, added subdivision (d) and renumbered former subdivision (d) as (e).

CASE NOTES

Practice and procedure. — Circuit court did not err in permitting agency to challenge court's jurisdiction before satisfying requirements of this rule. Bender v. Virginia Marine Resources Comm'n, No. 1145-99-1 (Ct. of Appeals Jan. 27, 2000).

Separate appeals. — When eight nursing facilities were entitled to recover their attorney's fees and costs under subsection A of § 2.2-4030, the statutory limit of $25,000 applied to each facility, rather than to all of the facilities as a group, because, in permitting "any person" in "any civil case" to recover fees up to the stated limit, the legislature intended, where each facility independently filed its own notice of appeal, which was then consolidated with the other facilities' appeals into a single proceeding, in accordance with Va. Sup. Ct. Rules 2A:3(b) and 2A:4(a), each notice represented the commencement of a separate civil case, presenting its own issues with regard to the jurisdiction and fiscal years involved and the timeliness of filings in each case. Dep't of Med. Assistance Servs. v. Beverly Healthcare, 41 Va. App. 468, 585 S.E.2d 858, 2003 Va. App. LEXIS 474 (2003), aff'd, remanded, 268 Va. 278, 601 S.E.2d 604 (2004).

CIRCUIT COURT OPINIONS

Supplementation of record on appeal. — Reviewing court denied a retirement benefit claimant's motion that the Virginia Retirement System's record be supplemented with additional evidence pertaining to the claimant's social security benefits proceeding in a federal court because: (1) the procedures and principles of law that were applied to the social security dispute were not related to those that controlled the analysis of the case that was before the circuit court; (2) the evidence in question was irrelevant because the record that was relied on in connection with the federal social security case was not identical to the one that was before the circuit court; and (3) the motion as it pertained to the social security evidence was untimely. Mooney v. Va. Ret. Sys., 2005 Va. Cir. LEXIS 256 (Greene County Dec. 20, 2005).

Rule 2A:4. Petition for Appeal.

(a) Within 30 days after the filing of the notice of appeal, the appellant shall file a petition for appeal with the clerk of the circuit court named in the first notice of appeal to be filed. Such filing shall include within such 30-day period both the payment of all fees and the taking of all steps provided in Rule 3:2, 3:3 and 3:4 to cause a copy of the petition for appeal to be served (as in a civil action) on the agency secretary and on every other party. The petition may be filed electronically as provided under Rule 1:17.

(b) The petition for appeal shall designate the regulation or case decision appealed from, specify the errors assigned, state the reasons why the regulation or case decision is deemed to be unlawful and conclude with a specific statement of the relief requested.

The amendment, effective January 1, 2006, adopted June 14, 2005, in subdivision (a), substituted "Rules 3:2, 3:3 and 3:4" for "Rules 2:2 and 2:3" and "(as in a civil action)" for "(as in the case of a bill of complaint in equity)."

The amendment, effective May 3, 2010, adopted February 26, 2010, in subdivision (a), substituted "a" for "his" preceding "petition for appeal" in the first sentence, and inserted "within such 30-day period both the payment of all fees and the taking of" and "for appeal" in the second sentence.

The amendment, effective May 2, 2011, adopted March 1, 2011, added the last sentence of subdivision (a).

Law Review. — For article on legislative changes to Virginia administrative rulemaking, see 19 U. Rich. L. Rev. 107 (1984).

CASE NOTES

Time limit in subdivision (a) is mandatory. Mayo v. Department of Commerce, 4 Va. App. 520, 358 S.E.2d 759 (1987).

Rule 2A:5 may not be used by circuit court to extend mandatory time limitation found in this rule, and there is no sufficient basis from which to infer that the circuit court has implied authority to extend the time limitation of this rule. Mayo v. Department of Commerce, 4 Va. App. 520, 358 S.E.2d 759 (1987).

Timely filing of petition for appeal of agency decision is jurisdictional. Sours v. Virginia Bd. for Architects, Professional Eng'rs, Land Surveyors & Landscape Architects, 30 Va. App. 313, 516 S.E.2d 712 (1999).

Payment of writ tax and clerk's fees is not jurisdictional as long as the petition is otherwise served in compliance with the rules. Sours v. Virginia Bd. for Architects, Professional Eng'rs, Land Surveyors & Landscape Architects, 30 Va. App. 313, 516 S.E.2d 712 (1999).

Party respondent must be properly identified within specified time. — Identifying the correct party respondent must be accomplished during the 30-day period prescribed in this rule and, if such party is not properly named, the court is without jurisdiction and the appeal must be dismissed. Somers v. Accomack County Dep't of Soc. Servs., No. 2899-00-1, 2001 Va. App. LEXIS 291 (Ct. of Appeals May 29, 2001).

Amendments to petition. — If appellants timely file a petition for appeal under Rule 2A:4(a), pursuant to Rule 1:8, the trial court has discretion to grant them leave to amend the petition to name another party; thus, a failure to name that party in the original petition is not a jurisdictional defect in the pleading. Crutchfield v. State Water Control Bd., No. 1095-01-2, 2002 Va. App. LEXIS 206 (Ct. of Appeals Apr. 2, 2002), aff'd, 265 Va. 416, 578 S.E.2d 762 (2003).

Trial court erred in dismissing a company's appeal on the ground that Rule 2A:4 presented a jurisdictional bar to considering the company's motion for leave to file an amended complaint in which the company sought to substitute the Virginia Apprenticeship Council as a party in the caption of the petition for appeal; the trial court had jurisdiction over the subject of the appeal and the trial court's decision was a matter subject to the trial court's discretionary authority as the company timely filed its petition within 25 days of the filing of its notice of appeal. Williams Steel Erection Co. v. DOL & Indus., 42 Va. App. 814, 595 S.E.2d 45, 2004 Va. App. LEXIS 166 (2004).

Circuit court did not err in allowing a father leave to amend a petition for review to conform with Va. Sup. Ct. R. 2A:4(b) becuase Va. Sup. Ct. R. 1:8 applied to agency appeals. Chabolla v. Va. Dep't of Soc. Servs., 55 Va. App. 531, 687 S.E.2d 85, 2010 Va. App. LEXIS 1 (Jan. 12, 2010).

Rule 2A:4(b) is not jurisdictional. — While Va. Sup. Ct. R. 2A:4(a) is jurisdictional, Rule 2A:4(b) is not. Chabolla v. Va. Dep't of Soc. Servs., 55 Va. App. 531, 687 S.E.2d 85, 2010 Va. App. LEXIS 1 (Jan. 12, 2010).

Virginia Department of Social Services properly named party. — Petition (1) identified the decision of the Virginia Department of Social Services (VDSS) hearing officer, a designee of the VDSS Commissioner, as the agency ruling being appealed; (2) requested in the caption of the case service on the VDSS Commissioner, a task only required to be done under Va. Sup. Ct. R. 2A:4(a) for parties; (3) used the same style as the VDSS administrative caption of the case; and (4) certified that it was being mailed to the Commissioner of the VDSS; under these circumstances a reasonable reader would understand either from the petition's text or context or both that the agency was being mentioned as the party against whom the appeal was being taken. Christian v. Va. Dep't of Soc. Servs., 45 Va. App. 310, 610 S.E.2d 870, 2005 Va. App. LEXIS 123 (2005).

Thirty-day period not adopted for Education for All Handicapped Children Act claims. — Rule 2A:2 and this rule are sufficiently analogous to a federal Education for All Handicapped Children Act (EAHCA) claim to warrant adoption of the Rules' limitation period for EAHCA claims. However, the policies underlying the EAHCA are inconsistent with the 30-day limitation period imposed by the Rules. Accordingly, the 30-day limitation period of the rules is not adopted for EAHCA claims. Kirchgessner ex rel. Kirchgessner v. Davis, 632 F. Supp. 616 (W.D. Va. 1986).

Limitation period under § 8.01-248 applicable to action under 20 U.S.C. § 1415. — For case applying the one-year [now two-year] statute of limitations of § 8.01-248 to parents' action in federal district court pursuant to 20 U.S.C. § 1415 challenging school system's refusal to find handicapped child's placement in a certain out-of-state residential school, rather than the shorter limitations of this rule and Supreme Court Rule 2A:2 applicable under § 22.1-214, see Schimmel ex rel. Schimmel v. Spillane, 819 F.2d 477 (4th Cir. 1987).

Standing to appeal decision of the Virginia Marine Resources Commission. — Residents' petition for appeal of a decision of the Virginia Marine Resources Commission approving a city's pipeline project was not insulated from consideration of the motion to dismiss filed by the Commission and the city simply because it satisfied the four elements set out in Va. Sup. Ct. R. 2A:4(b), and the court of appeals erred in resolving the matter solely by reference to the Rule; subsection F of § 28.2-1205 provides that only a "person aggrieved" by a decision of the Commission is entitled to judicial review of that decision, and thus, compliance with Va. Sup. Ct. R. 2A:4 does not insulate a petition from a dispositive motion based on the failure to include allegations to show that the petitioner had the requisite standing to pursue the appeal since the Rule cannont supersede or displace other statues relevant to the appeal, the Virginia Administrative Process Act. Va. Marine Res. Comm'n v. Clark, 281 Va. 679, 709 S.E.2d 150, 2011 Va. LEXIS 83 (2011).

Property owners had standing to appeal. — Property owners' petition for appeal complied with Va. Sup. Ct. R. 2A:4(b) and contained all of the elements required by the rule. The circuit court improperly expanded the requirements of the rule when it found the owners' petition for appeal insufficient to establish standing and the owners were entitled to an evidentiary hearing in circuit court on the issue of standing. Clark v. Va. Marine Res. Comm'n, 55 Va. App. 328, 685 S.E.2d 863, 2009 Va. App. LEXIS 537 (2009).

Separate appeals. — When eight nursing facilities were entitled to recover their attorney's fees and costs under subsection A of § 2.2-4030, the statutory limit of $25,000 applied to each facility, rather than to all of the facilities as a group, because, in permitting "any person" in "any civil case" to recover fees up to the stated limit, the legislature intended, where each facility independently filed its own notice of appeal, which was then consolidated with the other facilities' appeals into a single proceeding, in accordance with Va. Sup. Ct. Rules 2A:3(b) and 2A:4(a), each notice represented the commencement of a separate civil case, presenting its own issues with regard to the jurisdiction and fiscal years involved and the timeliness of filings in each case. Dep't of Med. Assistance Servs. v. Beverly Healthcare, 41 Va. App. 468, 585 S.E.2d 858, 2003 Va. App. LEXIS 474 (2003), aff'd, remanded, 268 Va. 278, 601 S.E.2d 604 (2004).

Trial court had discretion under Rule 1:9 to permit appellant to pay the writ tax and clerk's fees after service of the petition for appeal, even though this rule contemplates payment of the tax and fees before service. Sours v. Virginia Bd. for Architects, Professional Eng'rs, Land Surveyors & Landscape Architects, 30 Va. App. 313, 516 S.E.2d 712 (1999).

No abuse of discretion found. — Trial court did not abuse its discretion in granting landowners leave to amend their petition for appeal to add the county, a necessary party, as a party where the petition for appeal and notice of appeal had been timely filed; the failure to serve the county was not a jurisdictional defect in the appeal. State Water Control Bd. v. Crutchfield, 265 Va. 416, 578 S.E.2d 762, 2003 Va. LEXIS 42 (2003).

Although the plain language of Va. Sup. Ct. Rule 2A:4(a) requires the petitioners to serve a copy of their original petition on a necessary party, their failure to do so does not prevent the circuit court from permitting them to amend their petition at a later date to add the party. State Water Control Bd. v. Crutchfield, 265 Va. 416, 578 S.E.2d 762, 2003 Va. LEXIS 42 (2003).

Requirements. — Appellant failed in his petition to demonstrate that he was affected by the amendments and failed to state why the amendments were deemed to be unlawful; statements unsupported by argument, authority, or citations to the record do not merit appellate consideration. Bender v. Va. Marine Res. Comm'n, No. 1479-01-1, 2001 Va. App. LEXIS 599 (Ct. of Appeals Oct. 30, 2001).

Although the trial court held that the citizen's due process rights in objecting to the commission's granting of the owner's after-the-fact application for a permit were violated because the commission allegedly refused to consider the citizen's written exhibits, the citizen's petition for administrative appeal to the trial court raised no due process claim. As a result, the contention could not be reviewed on appeal to the appellate court because under Va. Sup. Ct. R. 2A:4(b), all petitions for administrative appeal filed in the trial court had to "specify the errors assigned" as well as the "specific" relief requested, which was not true of the citizen's petition. Boone v. Harrison, 52 Va. App. 53, 660 S.E.2d 704, 2008 Va. App. LEXIS 246 (2008).

In a case in which a Medicaid claimant appealed a trial court's dismissal of his petition seeking review of a decision by the Virginia Department of Medical Assistance Services, the claimant's indefinite allegations against the Alexandria Department of Human Services did not satisfy Va. Sup. Ct. R. 2A:4(b)'s requirements that the petition for appeal specify the errors alleged and state the reasons why the agency's case decision violated the law. Sudduth v. City of Alexandria Dep't of Human Servs., 2009 Va. App. LEXIS 466 (Oct. 20, 2009).

Because the supreme court is presumed to be aware of the decisions of the court of appeals that addressed Va. Sup. Ct. R. 2A:4 prior to its amendment and is presumed to have chosen with care the words it used, the supreme court specifically chose to amend Rule 2A:4 to require that "service" be as in a civil action; the supreme court plainly removed the requirement that an agency secretary be served by a process server on an appeal of an administrative agency's case decision. Muse Constr. Group, Inc. v. Commonwealth Bd. for Contrs. & Warren & Beverly Wharton, 60 Va. App. 92, 724 S.E.2d 216, 2012 Va. App. LEXIS 133 (2012).

Because the amendment to Va. Sup. Ct. R. 2A:4 changed the service requirement to conform to the general rules applicable "in a civil action," "service" can be accomplished pursuant to Va. Sup. Ct. R. 1:12 if the parties are already at issue by the time an appeal is made to the circuit court. Muse Constr. Group, Inc. v. Commonwealth Bd. for Contrs. & Warren & Beverly Wharton, 60 Va. App. 92, 724 S.E.2d 216, 2012 Va. App. LEXIS 133 (2012).

Service of process. — In appeals from agency action, Va. Sup. Ct. R. 2A:4(a) requires service of process in the same manner in which process is served to initiate a civil action. Muse Constr. Group, Inc. v. Commonwealth Bd. for Contrs., 61 Va. App. 125, 733 S.E.2d 690, 2012 Va. App. LEXIS 365 (2012).

Service on agency secretary. — Trial court did not err in denying state regulation challenger's motion for summary judgment, in dismissing the state regulation challenger's petition for appeal, and in awarding sanctions, including attorney fees, to the state commission, as the state regulation challenger did not serve his petition on the "agency secretary" and did not furnish the clerk of court, in writing, the name and address of each defendant even though he knew from previous, similar litigation that he was required to do so. Bender v. Va. Marine Res. Comm'n, No. 1783-02-1, 2003 Va. App. LEXIS 253 (Ct. of Appeals Apr. 29, 2003).

Plain meaning of Va. Sup. Ct. R. 2A:1, 2A:2, 2A:3 and 2A:4, read in concert with the Virginia Administrative Process Act, distinguishes a direct review of an agency's case decision from a new action, which would require service by a process server. Muse Constr. Group, Inc. v. Commonwealth Bd. for Contrs. & Warren & Beverly Wharton, 60 Va. App. 92, 724 S.E.2d 216, 2012 Va. App. LEXIS 133 (2012).

Circuit court erred in dismissing a contractor's appeal of a decision of the Commonwealth of Virginia Board for Contractors because the contractor's service by certified mail of the petition for appeal satisfied the requirements of Va. Sup. Ct. R. 2A:4; because Rule 2A:4 did not require that the petition for appeal be served by a process server, the contractor complied with Rule 2A:4 by serving a copy of the petition on the agency secretary pursuant to Va. Sup. Ct. R. 1:12 within the prescribed time period. Muse Constr. Group, Inc. v. Commonwealth Bd. for Contrs. & Warren & Beverly Wharton, 60 Va. App. 92, 724 S.E.2d 216, 2012 Va. App. LEXIS 133 (2012).

Appeal of Virginia Board for Contractors's revocation of appellant's license was properly dismissed, as his mailing of a "courtesy copy" of a petition for appeal to the Board's Secretary did not constitute service of process under Va. Sup. Ct. R. 2A:4(a), nor did it satisfy the relaxed requirements of the curative statute, § 8.01-288. Muse Constr. Group, Inc. v. Commonwealth Bd. for Contrs., 61 Va. App. 125, 733 S.E.2d 690, 2012 Va. App. LEXIS 365 (2012).

Applied in Watkins v. Fairfax County Dep't of Family Servs., 42 Va. App. 760, 595 S.E.2d 19, 2004 Va. App. LEXIS 164 (2004).

CIRCUIT COURT OPINIONS

Filing of initial appeal. — Although Va. Sup. Ct. R. 2A:2 and 2A:4 required any party appealing a case to file its notice of appeal within 30 days of service of a final agency order and to file a petition for appeal within 30 days of filing the notice of appeal, the time limits in those rules only applied to the initial filing of an appeal. Those time limits did not apply to the refiling of an appeal nonsuited pursuant to § 8.01-380, which was governed by subdivision E 3 of § 8.01-229, and, thus, neither Va. Sup. Ct. R. 2A:2 nor 2A:4 were in conflict with subdivision E 3 of § 8.01-229 regarding the time in which the limited liability companies had to appeal a refiled action in the trial court. Joy House Senior Homes, L.C. v. Jones, 75 Va. Cir. 140, 2008 Va. Cir. LEXIS 36 (Fairfax County 2008).

Dismissal granted as to some, but not all grounds alleged. — While dismissal of a corporation's administrative appeal could be based on violations of Va. Sup. Ct. R. 1:4(d)(j), Va. Sup. Ct. R. 2A:4, and Va. Sup. Ct. R. 2A:2, this latter failure to comply with a ministerial requirement was not prejudicial, and was not fatally defective or jurisdictional. Birchwood Motel, Inc. v. Va. Marine Res.

Comm'n, 74 Va. Cir. 298, 2007 Va. Cir. LEXIS 188 (Accomack County 2007).

Rule 2A:5. Further Proceedings.

Further proceedings in an appeal under this Part Two-A shall be governed by the rules contained in Part Three, where not in conflict with the Code of Virginia or this part, subject to the following:

(1) No appeal or issue under this Part Two-A shall be referred to a commissioner in chancery.

(2) Except for Rule 4:15 where applicable under this Rule, the provisions of Part Four shall not apply to appeals under this part and, unless ordered by the court, depositions shall not be taken.

(3) Once any motions, demurrers or other pleas filed by the agency have been overruled, or if none have been filed within the time provided by Rule 3:8 for the filing of a response to the process served under Rule 2A:4, the appeal shall be deemed submitted and no answer or further pleadings shall be required except as provided herein or by order of the court.

(4) When the case is submitted and the record has been filed as provided in Rule 2A:3, the court shall establish by order a schedule for briefing and argument of the issues raised in the petition for appeal.

(5) The court shall dispose of the appeal by an order consistent with its authority set forth in §§ 2.2-4029 and 2.2-4030 of the Code of Virginia.

The amendment, effective May 3, 2010, adopted February 26, 2010, rewrote the Rule.

CASE NOTES

"Further proceedings" defined. — The phrase "further proceedings," as used in this rule, encompasses only matters arising subsequent to the time an appeal is perfected by the timely filing of a petition for appeal. Mayo v. Department of Commerce, 4 Va. App. 520, 358 S.E.2d 759 (1987).

This rule may not be used by circuit court to extend mandatory time limitation found in Rule 2A:4, and there is no sufficient basis from which to infer that the circuit court has implied authority to extend the time limitation of Rule 2A:4. Mayo v. Department of Commerce, 4 Va. App. 520, 358 S.E.2d 759 (1987).

Discovery excluded. — This rule clearly excludes discovery for administrative appeals. Baumann v. Virginia Retirement Sys., No. 1194-99-4, 2000 Va. App. LEXIS 632 (Ct. of Appeals Aug. 29, 2000).

Trial court did not abuse its discretion under Va. Sup. Ct. R. 2A:5 in denying a hospital center's motion to augment the record by conducting depositions in the administrative appeal of a decision by the Virginia State Health Commissioner to award a certificate of public need to a community hospital instead of the hospital center. The trial court in reaching its decision was presented with unequivocal disavowals of taint by a hearing administrator and the Commissioner, and the hospital center proffered only speculation and surmise to counter those disavowals. Loudoun Hosp. Ctr. v. Stroube, 50 Va. App. 478, 650 S.E.2d 879, 2007 Va. App. LEXIS 371 (2007).

Applied in Sours v. Virginia Bd. for Architects, Professional Eng'rs, Land Surveyors & Landscape Architects, 30 Va. App. 313, 516 S.E.2d 712 (1999).

CIRCUIT COURT OPINIONS

Suit in equity. — Action of limited liability companies to challenge the agency's denial of its licensing application became a suit in equity pursuant to Va. Sup. Ct. R. 2A:5 once the trial court obtained jurisdiction over it, and, thus, was no longer an administrative proceeding. Because the trial court was acting in an appellate capacity in reviewing the denial, § 8.01-380 governing nonsuits did not apply, the original action could not have been nonsuited, and the action could not be revived pursuant to subdivision E 3 of § 8.01-229. Joy House Senior Homes, L.C. v. Jones, 75 Va. Cir. 140, 2008 Va. Cir. LEXIS 36 (Fairfax County 2008).

Rule 2A:6. Small Business Challenges.

(a) In addition to the other remedies established in this Part Two-A, as provided by § 2.2-4027 of the Code of Virginia, a "small business" as defined in § 2.2-4007.1(A) of the Code of Virginia that is adversely affected or aggrieved by final agency regulatory action as described therein may seek judicial review for the limited purpose of appealing the issue of compliance with the requirements of §§ 2.2-4007.04 and 2.2-4007.1. Such appeal shall be initiated by filing a notice of appeal as described in Rule 2A:2 within one year of the date of such final agency action.

(b) In all other respects, the provisions of this Part Two-A shall apply to such appeals.

Effective date. — This rule, adopted February 26, 2010, became effective May 3, 2010.

PART THREE
PRACTICE AND PROCEDURE IN CIVIL ACTIONS

Rule
3:1. Scope.
3:2. Commencement of Civil Actions.
3:3. Filing of Pleadings; Return of Certain Writs.
3:4. Copies of Complaint.
3:5. The Summons.
3:6. Proof of Service.
3:7. Bills of Particulars.
3:8. Answers, Pleas, Demurrers and Motions.
3:9. Counterclaims.
3:10. Cross-Claims.
3:11. Reply.
3:12. Joinder of Additional Parties.
3:13. Third-Party Practice.
3:14. Intervention.
3:15. Statutory Interpleader.

Rule
3:16. New Parties.
3:17. Substitution of Parties.
3:18. General Provisions as to Pleadings.
3:19. Default.
3:20. Summary Judgment.
3:21. Jury Trial of Right.
3:22. Trial by Jury or by the Court.
3:22A. Examination of Prospective Trial Jurors (Voir Dire).
3:23. Use of and Proceedings Before a Commissioner in Chancery.
3:24. Appeal of Orders of Quarantine or Isolation regarding Communicable Diseases of Public Health Threat.
3:25. Claims for Attorney's Fees.

Editor's note. — The order effective January 1, 2006, adopted June 14, 2005, repealed former Part Three and adopted a new Part Three.

Rule 3:1. Scope.

There shall be one form of civil case, known as a civil action. These Rules apply to all civil actions, in the circuit courts, whether the claims involved arise under legal or equitable causes of action, unless otherwise provided by law. These rules apply in cases appealed or removed to such courts from inferior courts whenever applicable to such cases. These Rules shall not apply in petitions for a writ of habeas corpus. In matters not covered by these Rules, the established practices and procedures are continued. Whenever in this Part Three the words "action" or "suit" appear they shall refer to a civil action, which may include legal and equitable claims.

Cross references. — As to civil practice and procedure in the general district courts, see Parts 7A and 7B.

Law Review. — For annual survey commentary, "The Merger of Common-Law and Equity Pleading in Virginia," see 41 U. Rich. L. Rev. 77 (2006). For 2007 annual survey article, "Civil Practice and Procedure," see 42 U. Rich. L. Rev. 229 (2007).

Michie's Jurisprudence. — For related discussion, see 1 Counties, §§ 45, 88; 1A M.J. Accounts and Accounting, § 9; 1A M.J. Actions, §§ 2, 13; 1A M.J. Agency, § 110; 2A M.J. Assumpsit, § 2; 2A M.J. Attachment and Garnishment, § 2; 3A M.J. Boundaries, § 32; 5A M.J. Covenant, Action of, §§ 1, 49; 5C M.J. Death by Wrongful Act, § 8; 5C M.J. Debt, Action of, § 1; 6A M.J. Detinue and Replevin, § 10; 6B M.J. Ejectment, § 2; 8B M.J. Forcible Entry and Detainer, §§ 3, 15; 10B M.J. Insurance, §§ 64, 65; 11A M.J. Judgments and Decrees, §§ 201, 217.1; 12A M.J. Limitation of Actions, § 37; 13A M.J. Motions for Judgment, §§ 2, 4; 14A M.J. Parties, § 25; 14B M.J. Pleading, § 6; 14B M.J. Process, § 7; 16 M.J. Seduction, § 4; 16 M.J. Setoff, Recoupment and Counterclaim, §§ 5, 15; 16 M.J. Sheriffs, § 41; 19 M.J. Trover and Conversion, § 2.

CASE NOTES

The Rules of Court do not apply to eminent domain proceedings. Williamson v. Hopewell Redevelopment & Hous. Auth., 203 Va. 653, 125 S.E.2d 849 (1962), appeal dismissed, 371 U.S. 234, 83 S. Ct. 315, 9 L. Ed. 2d 495 (1963); Hornback v. State Hwy. Comm'r, 205 Va. 50, 135 S.E.2d 136 (1964) (decided under prior law).

Law in regard to venue not changed. —

While the rules prescribe the practice and procedure for prosecuting actions, they do not change the law as it previously existed in regard to venue. Commonwealth ex rel. Duvall v. Hall, 194 Va. 914, 76 S.E.2d 208 (1953) (decided under prior law).

CIRCUIT COURT OPINIONS

Joinder of claims. — Children were permitted under Va. Sup. Ct. R. 3:1 et seq., to file a probate proceeding and a breach of contract action in the same complaint because the claims arose out of the same transaction or occurrence. Further, they were allowed to bring such separate actions in their amended complaint because those claims were filed in separate counts that were able to stand alone, as the claims could not be filed together in the same individual count. Page v. Baker, 74 Va. Cir. 66, 2007 Va. Cir. LEXIS 291 (Roanoke County 2007).

Rule 3:2. Commencement of Civil Actions.

(a) *Commencement.* — A civil action shall be commenced by filing a complaint in the clerk's office. When a statute or established practice requires, a proceeding may be commenced by a pleading styled "Petition." Upon filing of the pleading, the action is then instituted and pending as to all parties defendant thereto. The statutory writ tax and clerk's fees shall be paid before the summons is issued.

(b) *Caption.* — The complaint shall be captioned with the name of the court and the full style of the action, which shall include the names of all the parties. The requirements of Code § 8.01-290 may be met by giving the address or other data after the name of each defendant.

(c) *Form and Content of the Complaint.* — (i) It shall be sufficient for the complaint to ask for the specific relief sought. Without more it will be understood that all defendants mentioned in the caption are made parties defendant and required to answer the complaint; that proper process against them is requested; that answers under oath are waived, except when required by law, and that all relief authorized by law and demanded in the complaint may be granted. No formal conclusion is necessary.

(ii) Every complaint requesting an award of money damages shall contain an ad damnum clause stating the amount of damages sought. Leave to amend the ad damnum clause shall be available under Rule 1:8.

The amendment, effective March 1, 2007, adopted December 20, 2006, in subdivision (a), inserted the present second sentence, and added "Upon filing of the pleading" at the beginning of the present third sentence; and in subdivision (c), added the clause (i) designator and deleted "the" preceding "defendants" in the second sentence thereof, and added clause (ii).

Law Review. — For survey on civil procedure and practice in Virginia for 1989, see 23 U. Rich. L. Rev. 511 (1989). For 1991 survey of civil practice and procedure, see 25 U. Rich. L. Rev. 663 (1991). For a review of civil practice and procedure in Virginia for year 1999, see 33 U. Rich. L. Rev. 801 (1999).

Michie's Jurisprudence. — For related discussion, see 5A M.J. Courts, § 11; 8B M.J. Forcible Entry and Detainer, § 18; 14B M.J. Pleading, § 6.

CASE NOTES

This rule was enacted to determine whether a plaintiff has taken action which will toll a state's statute of limitations, not to decide whether removal is appropriate. Sheppard v. Wire Rope Corp., 777 F. Supp. 1285 (E.D. Va. 1991) (decided under prior law); Saunders v. Wire Rope Corp., 777 F. Supp. 1281 (E.D. Va. 1991) (decided under prior law).

Action is commenced upon filing of the motion. — This rule provides that the action is commenced upon filing of the motion for judgment, not by service upon the defendant. Sheppard v. Wire Rope Corp., 777 F. Supp. 1285 (E.D. Va. 1991) (decided under prior law); Saunders v. Wire Rope Corp., 777 F. Supp. 1281 (E.D. Va. 1991) (decided under prior law).

Action "commenced" on date the complaint is filed. — Date of "commencement" of plaintiff's product liability action was the date on which plaintiff filed the complaint with the circuit court. Culkin v. CNH Am., LLC, 598 F. Supp. 2d 758, 2009 U.S. Dist. LEXIS 4775 (E.D. Va. 2009).

Habeas corpus. — Express language of the subsection B of § 8.01-655 filing provision does not contain any terms open for interpretation, and to the extent that Va. Sup. Ct. R. 3:2, 3:3, 3A:25 and 5:5 could be construed as conflicting with § 8.01-655, the statute will prevail over them. Lahey v. Johnson, 283 Va. 225, 720 S.E.2d 534, 2012 Va. LEXIS 22 (2012).

Nonsuit not permitted. — Action is commenced by the filing of a motion for judgment; therefore, in airlines' lawsuit against an insurer regarding certain business interruption insurance, where the insurer was added as a party after the initial suit was filed, and where the case became removable only after two of the airlines merged, the insurer's removal petition was untimely because, although the removal petition was filed within one year of the date that the insurer was served with process, the insurer's removal petition was filed more than one year after the airlines' litigation was commenced under Va. Sup. Ct. Rule 3:3 (now Rule 3:2). US Airways, Inc. v. PMA Capital Ins. Co., 340 F. Supp. 2d 699, 2004 U.S. Dist. LEXIS 20053 (E.D. Va. 2004) (decided under prior law).

Request for service of process. — The language of former Rule 2.2 clearly provided that once the bill of complaint was filed, proper process is requested against the named defendants, and the party filing the complaint does not need to make a separate request for service of process. Kessler v. Smith, 31 Va. App. 139, 521 S.E.2d 774 (1999) (decided under former Rule 2:2).

Court may grant relief not specifically requested. — Even where no prayer for general relief is included in the bill of complaint, a court in equity may properly grant appropriate relief not specifically requested. Johnson v. Buzzard Island Shooting Club, Inc., 232 Va. 32, 348 S.E.2d 220 (1986) (decided under former Rule 2:2).

General relief limited only in that it not be inconsistent with case alleged. — The only limitation placed on a grant of general relief is that it not be inconsistent with the case alleged by the bill or the relief specifically sought. Johnson v. Buzzard Island Shooting Club, Inc., 232 Va. 32, 348 S.E.2d 220 (1986) (decided under former Rule 2:2).

Decision of an irrelevant, unnecessary, and moot issue is not proper even though the bill of complaint includes a prayer for general relief. Layton v. Seawall Enters., Inc., 231 Va. 402, 344 S.E.2d 896 (1986) (decided under former Rule 2:2).

Remedy may not be based on facts not alleged. — Total absence from pleadings of any claim that a limited partnership owned pond's waters and that landowners were trespassing precluded a chancellor from determining water ownership and imposing a remedy based on facts not alleged. Jenkins v. Bay House Assocs., L.P., 266 Va. 39, 581 S.E.2d 510, 2003 Va. LEXIS 66 (2003) (decided under former Rule 2:2).

Applied in Conger v. Barrett, 280 Va. 627, 702 S.E.2d 117, 2010 Va. LEXIS 261 (2010); Muse Constr. Group, Inc. v. Commonwealth Bd. for Contrs., 61 Va. App. 125, 733 S.E.2d 690, 2012 Va. App. LEXIS 365 (2012).

CIRCUIT COURT OPINIONS

Action is commenced upon filing of the motion. — Motion for judgment was filed when presented to a court clerk even though it lacked sufficient filing funds; failure to date-stamp the motion for judgment when it was initially received was not same as refusing to accept it. Layfield v. Indian Acres Club of Thornburg, Inc., 58 Va. Cir. 233, 2002 Va. Cir. LEXIS 39 (Spotsylvania County 2002) (decided under prior law).

Under Va. Sup. Ct. R. 3:2(a), a civil action is "instituted" by filing a complaint in the clerk's office. Letters to defendants and their insurers threatening suit and proposing a settlement did not suffice to give the notice of filing required by § 8.01-6 to allow an amendment to the pleadings that would relate back to the original filing. Hart v. Savage, 72 Va. Cir. 41, 2006 Va. Cir. LEXIS 319 (Norfolk 2006).

Rule 3:3. Filing of Pleadings; Return of Certain Writs.

(a) *Filing Generally.* — The clerk shall receive and file all pleadings when tendered, without order of the court. The clerk shall note and attest the date of filing thereon. In an Electronically Filed Case, the procedures of Rule 1:17 shall be applicable to the notation by the clerk of the date of filing. Any controversy over whether a party who has filed a pleading has a right to file it shall be decided by the court.

(b) *Electronic Filing.* — In any circuit court which has established an electronic filing system pursuant to Rule 1:17:

(1) Any civil action for which electronic filing is available in the circuit court may be designated as an Electronically Filed Case upon consent of all parties in the case. Such designation shall be made promptly, complying with all filing and procedural requirements for making such designations as may be prescribed by such circuit court.

(2) Except where service and/or filing of an original paper document is expressly required by these rules, all pleadings, motions, notices and other filings in an Electronically Filed Case shall be formatted, served and filed as specified in the requirements and procedures of Rule 1:17; provided, however, that when any document listed below is filed in the case, the filing party shall notify the clerk of court that the original document must be retained.

(i) Any pleading or affidavit required by statute or rule to be sworn, verified or certified as provided in Rule 1:17(d)(5).

(ii) Any last will and testament or other testamentary document, whether or not it is holographic.

(iii) Any contract or deed.

(iv) Any prenuptial agreement or written settlement agreement, including any property settlement agreement.

(v) Any check or other negotiable instrument.

(vi) Any handwritten statement, waiver, or consent by a defendant or witness in a criminal proceeding.

(vii) Any form signed by a defendant in a criminal proceeding, including any typed statements or a guilty plea form.

(viii) Any document that cannot be converted into an electronic document in such a way as to produce a clear and readable image.

(c) *Return of writs.* — No writ shall be returnable more than 90 days after its date unless a longer period is provided by statute.

The amendment effective May 2, 2011, adopted March 1, 2011, inserted the second sentence of subdivision (a), added present subdivision (b), and redesignated former subdivision (b) as (c).

The amendment effective January 1, 2013, adopted November 1, 2012, in subdivision (b), rewrote paragraph (1), and deleted "electronically" following "filed" in paragraph (2).

Law Review. — For 2007 annual survey article, "Civil Practice and Procedure," see 42 U. Rich. L. Rev. 229 (2007).

Michie's Jurisprudence. — For related discussion, see 1A M.J. Actions, § 18; 1B M.J. Amendments, § 2; 1B M.J. Appeal and Error, § 184, 185, 242; 2A M.J. Appearances, §§ 7, 12, 15; 5A M.J. Courts, § 11; 5C M.J. Damages, §§ 81, 93; 6A M.J. Demurrers, § 38; 7A M.J. Equitable Conversion, § 2; 7A M.J. Equity, § 2; 8B M.J. Forcible Entry and Detainer, § 18; 12B M.J. Merger, § 3; 14B M.J. Pleading, § 6; 19 M.J. Trial, § 7.

CASE NOTES

Date of filing with clerk's office. — By the plain language of Va. Sup. Ct. R. 3:3, an action is commenced, and thus the one-year limitation period of 28 U.S.C.S. § 1446(b) begins to run on the date a party files a motion for judgment in the clerk's office, not the date the defendant was served. O'Quinn v. CNH Am., Inc., 457 F. Supp. 2d 678, 2006 U.S. Dist. LEXIS 76469 (E.D. Va. 2006).

Habeas corpus. — Express language of the subsection B of § 8.01-655 filing provision does not contain any terms open for interpretation, and to the extent that Va. Sup. Ct. R. 3:2, 3:3, 3A:25 and 5:5 could be construed as conflicting with § 8.01-655, the statute will prevail over them. Lahey v. Johnson, 283 Va. 225, 720 S.E.2d 534, 2012 Va. LEXIS 22 (2012).

CIRCUIT COURT OPINIONS

Clerk must treat pleadings as filed when received without passing on their validity. — Court's mandamus ordered clerk to do ministerial act: to treat woman's personal injury pleadings as received, filed, and on docket as of day they were presented to clerk (statute of limitation's last day) even though caption named wrong court; the clerk had no authority to pass upon the validity of instruments presented for filing. Burkholder v. McGraw, 63 Va. Cir. 537, 2003 Va. Cir. LEXIS 360 (Roanoke County 2003) (decided under prior law).

Failure to inform. — Because a patient's failure to give notice to the doctors and to fully inform the tribunal before entry of a second nonsuit order in accordance with Va. Sup. Ct. R. pt. 6, § II, R. 3:3(C), the second nonsuit was void as it was not suffered as prescribed in § 8.01-380; therefore, the tolling provisions of § 8.01-229 E 3 were not triggered, and the third action was time barred. Humphreys v. Carey, 71 Va. Cir. 67, 2006 Va. Cir. LEXIS 79 (Lynchburg 2006).

Delay in service of process. — In a medical negligence suit against state employees, suit could not be dismissed under Va. Sup. Ct. R. 3:3 due to a delay in service of process on one defendant because less than one year had passed since the motion for judgment was filed. Marsh v. Medical College of Va. Hosps. Aux. of Va. Commonwealth Health Sys., 71 Va. Cir. 404, 2006 Va. Cir. LEXIS 225 (Richmond 2006).

Rule 3:4. Copies of Complaint.

(a) *Copies for Service.* — Except in cases where service is waived pursuant to Code § 8.01-286.1, the plaintiff shall furnish the clerk when the complaint is filed with as many paper copies thereof as there are defendants upon whom it is to be served. In an Electronically Filed Case, the plaintiff shall file the complaint electronically and furnish paper copies to the clerk as provided in this Rule.

(b) *Exhibits.* — It is not required that physical copies of exhibits filed with the complaint be furnished or served. Unless an individual case is exempted by order of the court for good cause shown, an electronic or digitally imaged copy of all exhibits that are incorporated by reference in the pleading shall be filed with the complaint. Upon the adoption of standards for the preparation of electronic or digital records for use in appeals, exhibits under this Rule shall comply with such standards.

(c) *Additional copies.* — A deficiency in the number of copies of the complaint shall not affect the pendency of the action.

(1) If the plaintiff fails to furnish the required number of copies, the clerk shall request that additional copies be furnished by the plaintiff as needed, and if the plaintiff fails to do so promptly, the clerk shall bring the fact to the attention of the

judge, who shall notify the plaintiff's counsel, or the plaintiff personally if no counsel has appeared for plaintiff, to furnish them by a specified date. If the required copies are not furnished on or before that date, the court may enter an order dismissing the suit.

(2) Additionally, in an Electronically Filed Case, if the clerk has been provided by the plaintiff with a credit or payment account through which to obtain payment of fees for duplication of required copies of filings, the clerk shall promptly prepare additional copies of the pleading as needed, and process payment through such credit or payment account; or, if processing by the clerk of the proper payment for duplication of additional copies of the pleading through a credit or payment account authorized by the filing party is not feasible, the clerk shall proceed as provided in subpart (c) (1) of this Rule.

The amendment effective May 1, 2006, adopted February 28, 2006, added "Except in cases where service is waived pursuant to Code § 8.01-286.1" at the beginning of subdivision (a).

The amendment effective May 2, 2011, adopted March 1, 2011, inserted "paper" preceding "copies" in subdivision (a), and in subdivision (b), inserted "physical" preceding "copies" in the first sentence, and added the second and third sentences.

The amendment effective January 1, 2013, adopted November 1, 2012, added the second sentence in subdivision (a); and rewrote subdivision (c).

Michie's Jurisprudence. — For related discussion, see 6A M.J. Dismissal, Discontinuance and Nonsuit, § 10; 7A M.J. Equity, § 50.

CASE NOTES

Applied in Muse Constr. Group, Inc. v. Commonwealth Bd. for Contrs., 61 Va. App. 125, 733 S.E.2d 690, 2012 Va. App. LEXIS 365 (2012).

Rule 3:5. The Summons.

(a) *Form of process.* — The process of the courts in civil actions shall be a summons in substantially this form:

Commonwealth of Virginia

In the .... Court of the .... of ....

SUMMONS

Civil Action No. . . .

The party upon whom this summons and the attached complaint are served is hereby notified that unless within 21 days after such service response is made by filing in the clerk's office of this court a pleading in writing, in proper legal form, the allegations and charges may be taken as admitted and the court may enter an order, judgment or decree against such party either by default or after hearing evidence.

Appearance in person is not required by this summons.

Done in the name of the Commonwealth of Virginia, this ..... day of .... 20.....

................................., Clerk.

(b) *Affixing summons for service; voluntary appearance.* — Upon the commencement of a civil action defendants may appear voluntarily and file responsive pleadings and may appear voluntarily and waive process, but in cases of divorce or annulment of marriage only in accordance with the provisions of the controlling statutes. With respect to defendants who do not appear voluntarily or file responsive pleadings or waive service of process, the clerk shall issue summonses and securely attach one to and upon the front of each copy of the complaint to be served. The copies of the complaint, with a summons so attached, shall be delivered by the clerk for service together as the plaintiff may direct.

(c) *Defendant under a disability.* — Except when sued for divorce or annulment of marriage, or a judgment in personam is sought, a summons need not be issued for or served upon a defendant who is a person under a disability (except as otherwise provided in § 8.01-297), the procedure described in Code § 8.01-9 constituting due process as to such defendants.

(d) *Additional summonses.* — The clerk shall on request issue additional summonses, dating them as of the day of issuance.

(e) *Service more than one year after commencement of the action.* — No order, judgment or decree shall be entered against a defendant who was served with process more than one year after the institution of the action against that defendant unless the court finds as a fact that the plaintiff exercised due diligence to have timely service on that defendant.

Cross references. — As to service of process in proceedings for divorce and annulment of marriage, see §§ 8.01-288, 8.01-320, 8.01-327, 8.01-328.1, 20-99, and 20-99.1:1.

See §§ 8.01-275.1 and 8.01-277.

Law Review. — For 2007 annual survey article, "Civil Practice and Procedure," see 42 U. Rich. L. Rev. 229 (2007).

Michie's Jurisprudence. — For related discussion, see 5C M.J. Damages, § 51; 6A M.J. Divorce and Alimony, § 37; 7A M.J. Equity, § 50; 14B M.J. Process, §§ 2, 7, 9, 12, 16, 57, 59.

CASE NOTES

Editor's note. — Many of the cases annotated below were decided under prior rules.

Failure to exercise due diligence to effect service of process. — Despite notification from clerk's office that subpoena had not been served and respondent's pleading advising petitioner that it would not submit to jurisdiction until it was properly served with process, petitioner took no further steps to have subpoena in chancery issued and served, and therefore circuit court did not err in granting respondent's motion to dismiss. Bender v. Virginia Marine Resources Comm'n, No. 1145-99-1 (Ct. of Appeals Jan. 27, 2000) (decided under former Rule 2:4).

Due diligence not shown even though clerk stated that service had been made. — In an appeal from a final decision of the Virginia Retirement System, the circuit court did not err in determining that an individual failed to perfect service and failed to exercise due diligence to have timely service on the parties, even though she was told by the clerk's office that service had been made, where the individual waited 11 months after filing her petition for appeal before she attempted service of process. Chambliss v. Va. Ret. Sys., No. 2171-02-2, 2003 Va. App. LEXIS 683 (Ct. of Appeals Dec. 23, 2003) (decided under former Rule 2:4).

No variance between rule and statute. — There is no variance between former Rule 3:3(c) [now Rule 3:5] and § 8.01-275.1. Both of these provisions seek to promote a policy of timely prosecution of law suits and to avoid abuse of the judicial system; the statute, but not the rule, defines timely service as one year, while the rule implies that timely service means service within one year. Both the rule and the statute allow a plaintiff to establish the exercise of due diligence to perfect service within the one year period. Waterman v. Halverson, 261 Va. 203, 540 S.E.2d 867, 2001 Va. LEXIS 18 (2001).

Rule permitting nonsuit prior to service not invalidated by statute. — There is no basis to conclude that the enactment of § 8.01-275.1 nullified or invalidated the cases construing this rule and holding that the failure to comply with the one-year service provision of the rule does not preclude a trial court from granting a plaintiff's motion for nonsuit and that the refiled action is entitled to the tolling provisions of § 8.01-229(E)(3). Waterman v. Halverson, 261 Va. 203, 540 S.E.2d 867, 2001 Va. LEXIS 18 (2001).

Dismissal with prejudice. — If dismissal under this rule were without prejudice, the tolling provisions of Code § 8.01-229(E)(1) could be invoked, allowing repeated filings which effectively nullify the statute of limitations and potentially allow harassment of the defendant; thus, if a plaintiff who has suffered a dismissal for failure to comply with this rule retains the right to refile the cause of action against the previously unserved defendant, both the purpose of this rule and the statute of limitations are undermined; therefore a dismissal under the rule is a dismissal with prejudice. Gilbreath v. Brewster, 250 Va. 436, 463 S.E.2d 836 (1995).

Dismissal of the patient's medical malpractice complaint was proper, because the patient failed to obtain service of process on the doctor within 12 months of filing the complaint due to a failure to satisfy the requirement of § 8.01-20.1; the patient was not without a procedural remedy but could have taken a nonsuit as a matter of right and refiled the complaint. Bowman v. Concepcion, 283 Va. 552, 722 S.E.2d 260, 2012 Va. LEXIS 38 (2012).

Rule contemplates prompt efforts to secure service. — The general thrust of former Rule 3.3(c) [see now Rules 3:5 and 3:6] appears to contemplate and encourage prompt, bona fide efforts to secure service on defendants once the action has been filed. Saunders v. Wire Rope Corp., 777 F. Supp. 1281 (E.D. Va. 1991); Sheppard v. Wire Rope Corp., 777 F. Supp. 1285 (E.D. Va. 1991).

This rule gives a court authority to dismiss an action because of delay in the service of process only if process is served more than one year after the motion for judgment is filed in the clerk's office. Nelson v. Vaughan, 210 Va. 1, 168 S.E.2d 126 (1969).

Time limit imposed by rule inapplicable where process never served. — The portion of this rule generally providing that no judgment shall be entered against a defendant who was served with process more than one year after the commencement of the action against him applies only where there has been service of process; it does not preclude the entry of judgment where the defendant made a voluntary general appearance without having been served with process. Gilpin v. Joyce, 257 Va. 579, 515 S.E.2d 124 (1999).

Action against an incarcerated convict, although an abortive proceeding, is nevertheless an action as defined by this rule. Scott v. Nance, 202 Va. 355, 117 S.E.2d 279 (1960).

Personal injury action was dismissed under this rule where it had been pending since 1987 and defendant had not been served with valid process. Dennis v. Jones, 240 Va. 12, 393 S.E.2d 390 (1990).

Due diligence of plaintiff not shown. — There could be no judgment against the defendant where the filing of the Certificate of Compliance by the Commissioner did not occur until four days beyond the time allowed for effecting valid service under the rule and the plaintiff failed to show due diligence to have timely service; the request for service was made on the Commissioner only two business days before the expiration of the time for effecting service and nothing in the record reflected that the plaintiff even informed the Commissioner of the proximity of the deadline. Morton v. Meagher, 171 F. Supp. 2d 611, 2001 U.S. Dist. LEXIS 17681 (E.D. Va. 2001).

Nonsuit permitted. — Despite the fact that service of process upon a debtor was not effected within one year of the commencement of a lender's action against her, the lender was entitled to a voluntary nonsuit. Berry v. F&S Fin. Mktg., 271 Va. 329, 626 S.E.2d 821, 2006 Va. LEXIS 24 (2006).

Nonsuit not permitted. — Where a driver had moved to dismiss a motorist's personal injury action based on insufficient service of process under § 8.01-326.1 and former Va. Sup. Ct. Rule 3:3 [see now Rule 3:5], the matter clearly had been submitted to the trial court for decision, and no further submissions were contemplated, the trial court erred in granting the motorist's § 8.01-380 A motion for a nonsuit. Atkins v. Rice, 266 Va. 328, 585 S.E.2d 550, 2003 Va. LEXIS 85 (2003).

Action is commenced by the filing of a motion for judgment; therefore, in airlines' lawsuit against an insurer regarding certain business interruption insurance, where the insurer was added as a party after the initial suit was filed, and where the case became removable only after two of the airlines merged, the insurer's removal petition was untimely because, although the removal petition was filed within one year of the date that the insurer was served with process, the insurer's removal petition was filed more than one year after the airlines' litigation was commenced under Va. Sup. Ct. Rule 3:3 [now Rule 3:2]. US Airways, Inc. v. PMA Capital Ins. Co., 340 F. Supp. 2d 699, 2004 U.S. Dist. LEXIS 20053 (E.D. Va. 2004).

Required process not served. — Trial court erred in denying an ambulance service's motion to vacate a default judgment pursuant to § 8.01-428 entered in favor of an injured party as the service was not served with the notice portion of the motion for judgment required to be served under former Rule 3:3 [now Rule 3:5], so it never received process, and trial court lacked jurisdiction to enter the default judgment. Lifestar Response of Md., Inc. v. Vegosen, 267 Va. 720, 594 S.E.2d 589, 2004 Va. LEXIS 64 (2004).

Applied in Janvier v. Arminio, 272 Va. 353, 634 S.E.2d 754, 2006 Va. LEXIS 88 (2006).

CIRCUIT COURT OPINIONS

Construction with other law. — Former Rules 2:4 and 2:5 (now see Rules 3:5 and 3:6) necessarily imply that a return of service filed outside the 72-hour time limit, set forth in both § 8.01-325 and Rule 2:4 (now Rule 3:5), will not invalidate either the service or a decree entered based on the in personam jurisdiction; such a return constitutes prima facie evidence that the party was served in accordance with the return. Small v. Small, 58 Va. Cir. 114, 2001 Va. Cir. LEXIS 361 (Fairfax County 2001) (decided under former Rule 2:4).

Guarantor's motion to set aside a default judgment and to quash a return of service was denied, as: (1) he failed to allege that the statute allowing constructive service by posting was not followed; (2) the saving language of § 8.01-294 prohibited the court from setting aside the judgment; and (3) he failed to show any prejudice by the late return of service, nor did he allege that he did not receive actual notice, that he did not understand service was meant for him, or that the notation of "et al" was prejudicial to his position. Edward Don & Co. v. Istriana, Inc., 71 Va. Cir. 109, 2006 Va. Cir. LEXIS 106 (Fairfax County 2006).

Service of process. — As the rule of service was administrative, the court did not dismiss a case given the injured's plaintiff's good faith acts in trying to serve the student where the student was hard to locate and showed no prejudice in defending this suit. Palum v. Quinn, 59 Va. Cir. 35, 2002 Va. Cir. LEXIS 119 (Loudoun County 2002) (decided under prior law).

Overruling of the motion in abatement and plea in bar of the statute of limitations filed by the executrix of the decedent's estate after plaintiff filed a complaint to enforce a promissory note made by the decedent was proper because plaintiff recommenced the action within the limitations period prescribed by subdivision E 3 of § 8.01-229, and the executrix received service of process within one year of the institution of the action as required under Va. Sup. Ct. R. 3:5. Plaintiff properly identified the executrix in her capacity as estate's executrix and clearly informed both the court and the opposing party of the claim being made and the proper party against whom such a claim was being sought. Wiebel v. Estate of Johnson, 79 Va. Cir. 509, 2009 Va. Cir. LEXIS 263 (Charlottesville Nov. 16, 2009).

Divorce complaint. — Wife's divorce complaint had no vitality because the husband was not allowed to waive service until he filed an answer; although the husband eventually filed an answer more than a year after suit was filed, no attempt had been made to serve the husband in that year, and, pursuant to Va. Sup. Ct. R. 3:5, therefore, no decree could have been properly entered. Rathburn v. Rathburn, 2007 Va. Cir. LEXIS 102 (Roanoke County July 12, 2007).

In determining whether due diligence was shown in an attempt to effect service of process on a defendant, who was not served within one year of the date an action was filed, due diligence was distinguished from good cause, and due diligence did not account for other events occurring in a party's life which would impact his or her ability to have service of process timely effected. Lawson v. Roth, 62 Va. Cir. 175, 2003 Va. Cir. LEXIS 90 (Roanoke 2003) (decided under prior law).

Due diligence not found. — Injured party did not use due diligence in attempting to serve a doctor where the doctor was not served until 14 months after the injured party's motion for judgment, the injured party did not call any local hospitals to determine if the doctor worked there, and the injured party did not contact the Virginia Board of Medicine to obtain the doctor's address; doctor's motion to dismiss was granted. Doulgerakis v. Cooper, 57 Va. Cir. 326, 2002 Va. Cir. LEXIS 211 (Newport News 2002) (decided under prior law).

Where the first defendant may have followed the correct procedures under § 8.01-329(C) and failure to effect service of its cross-claim on the second defendant may have been due to the errors of the Secretary of the Commonwealth, the cross-claim was nonetheless dismissed under Va. Sup. Ct. R. 3.3 [now Rule 3:5], as subsection C of § 8.01-329 did not abrogate the duty of due diligence under Va. Sup. Ct. R. 3:3 [now Rule 3:5]; mere compliance with the statute might not in all cases constitute due diligence. Bd. of Dirs. of the Lesner Pointe Condo. on the Chesapeake Bay Ass'n v. Harbour Point Bldg. Corp., 2002 Va. Cir. LEXIS 421 (Virginia Beach Oct. 25, 2002) (decided under prior law).

That a party complied with subsection C of § 8.01-329 by serving another defendant by serving the Secretary of the Commonwealth did not abrogate its duty of due diligence under Va. Sup. Ct. R. 3:3 [see now Rule 3:5], where the Secretary's office had no record that the party followed the correct procedures to effectuate service. Lesner Pointe Condo. Ass'n v. Harbour Point Bldg. Corp., 61 Va. Cir. 609, 2002 Va. Cir. LEXIS 424 (Virginia Beach 2002) (decided under prior law).

In a medical malpractice action, two defendants were not immediately served because the patient thought she might require their support in a related personal injury action, but the patient's counsel did not believe he could have them served with process absent his client's consent, so they were not served until the patient contacted her counsel after her whereabouts were unknown for a significant amount of time, and they were not served within one year after the action was filed, as required by Va. Sup. Ct. R. 3:3(c) [see now Rule 3:5], and the patient could not show she had exercised due diligence trying to effect service of process on them, so the matter was dismissed with prejudice as to those defendants. Lawson v. Roth, 62 Va. Cir. 175, 2003 Va. Cir. LEXIS 90 (Roanoke 2003) (decided under prior law).

Court granted defendant's motion to quash service of process and vacated the default judgment entered against defendant on the ground that plaintiff did not exercise due diligence prior to requesting service through the Secretary of the Commonwealth since no bona fide attempt at service was made before such service was requested, plaintiff never made a written request to the Department of Motor Vehicles for defendant's address, and a proper review of the court file would have shown that the summons that was returned finding no such address had sought service at the wrong address. Valois v. Parrish, 67 Va. Cir. 40, 2005 Va. Cir. LEXIS 28 (Fairfax County 2005) (decided under prior law).

Plaintiff was not entitled to a default judgment under Va. Sup. Ct. R. 3:19(a) and 3:8(a) as plaintiff had not exercised due diligence as required by § 8.01-275.1 and Va. Sup. Ct. R. 3:5(e) to allow service of process more than one year after the filing of the suit since: (1) plaintiff used an address that had been determined to be a vacant building in a prior suit to attempt service; (2) plaintiff did not attempt personal service of process at the address provided on the accident information exchange form and the accident report; and (3) plaintiff's first use of the address on the accident information exchange form and the accident report was when plaintiff sought service through the Secretary of the Commonwealth of Virginia under subsection B of § 8.01-329. Shears v. Slade, 73 Va. Cir. 20, 2006 Va. Cir. LEXIS 298 (Newport News 2006).

Where a due diligence requirement concerned effecting timely service on defendant, not dealing with defendant or her representative as to filing responsive pleadings, it was irrelevant that plaintiff had not requested a default judgment, that plaintiff might have located defendant, that defendant might have received a copy of a motion for judgment (as opposed to receiving process), that defendant's insurer sought an extension to file responsive pleadings, or that plaintiff agreed to it. Hernandez v. Awld, 73 Va. Cir. 497, 2007 Va. Cir. LEXIS 217 (Loudoun County Aug. 7, 2007).

In a motion for a second nonsuit, the circuit court did not exercise its discretion to allow an extension of a one-year period to effectuate service on a defendant where plaintiff did not use due diligence in attempting to effect timely service on defendant; one defective attempt at service was not the due diligence required, and dismissal was appropriate. Hernandez v. Awld, 73 Va. Cir. 497, 2007 Va. Cir. LEXIS 217 (Loudoun County Aug. 7, 2007).

Plaintiff did not achieve service upon defendant within 12 months as required by § 8.01-275.1 or Va. Sup. Ct. R. 3:5 because defendant's last known address was not the usual abode where posted service was effected, and plaintiff did not exercise due diligence to obtain service within one year; defendant testified that the defendant had moved from the defendant's last known address by the time plaintiff refiled the palintiff's suit, and plaintiff merely attempted to serve defendant at the same address when the case was refiled and made no further effort to locate defendant. Johnston v. Robinson, 75 Va. Cir. 137, 2008 Va. Cir. LEXIS 92 (Amherst County 2008).

Due diligence found. — Judge determined that an accident victim exercised due diligence in the service of process, and, therefore, granted the victim an extension of time pursuant to § 8.01-277. Goldstein v. Bourgad, 68 Va. Cir. 132, 2005 Va. Cir. LEXIS 122 (Fairfax County 2005) (decided under prior law).

Dismissal. — Even if there was no service of process on a non-resident, the court could grant a nonsuit as failure to obtain proper service was not deliberate or from inattention and the plaintiff did not need a basis for her nonsuit. Dixon v. Messer, 56 Va. Cir. 366, 2001 Va. Cir. LEXIS 472 (Norfolk 2001) (decided under prior law).

Insurer's motion to dismiss an injured party's personal injury suit against an insured, which was filed by special appearance on behalf of the insured, was granted under § 8.01-275.1 and former Va. Sup. Ct. R. 3:3 (now Rule 3:5), because: (1) the injured party was advised that she had to obtain service upon the insured at a scheduling conference; (2) at that scheduling conference an order was entered, endorsed by the injured party, continuing the scheduling conference to allow the injured party time to serve the insured; and (3) to date, the injured party still had not obtained service upon the insured and failed to exercise due diligence in affecting such service. Flagler v. Liberty Mut. Ins. Co., 73 Va. Cir. 61, 2007 Va. Cir. LEXIS 34 (Fairfax County 2007) (decided under former Rule 3:3).

Nonsuit not permitted. — Injured party was not entitled to nonsuit, an action under § 8.01-275.1, against defendant doctor, who filed a defense and cross-claim against cross-defendant doctor, because defendant doctor was served with process, and was entitled to raise the defect in service in a motion to dismiss under § 8.01-277. Doulgerakis v. Cooper, 57 Va. Cir. 326, 2002 Va. Cir. LEXIS 211 (Newport News 2002) (decided under prior law).

Court granted defendants' motion to dismiss under § 8.01-275.1 on grounds they had not been served within one year, because plaintiffs' motion for nonsuit under § 8.01-380 was barred, inasmuch as defendants' counterclaims were incapable of independent adjudication. Parsch v. Massey, 71 Va. Cir. 209, 2006 Va. Cir. LEXIS 249 (Charlottesville 2006).

General appearance found. — Neither Va. Sup. Ct. R. 3:3 [see now Rule 3:5] nor § 8.01-277 allowed an engineering firm to file a demurrer, a special plea of the statute of limitations, an objection of venue, a motion to drop, a motion for a bill of particulars, a motion craving oyer, and a removal petition, participation in depositions and provision of expert assistance to another defendant in the case, without making a general appearance and waiving any challenge to the personal jurisdiction of the trial court; § 8.01-277 was to be strictly construed and provided for challenges to defects in process. City of Portsmouth v. Buro Happold Consulting Eng'rs, 69 Va. Cir. 397, 2005 Va. Cir. LEXIS 255 (Portsmouth 2005) (decided under prior law).

Amended motion for judgment to correct a misnomer filed after statute of limitations. — In a medical negligence suit against state employees, in which a nurse's name was misspelled in an original motion for judgment in the style of the case, but not in the body of the motion, resulting in an amended motion for judgment being filed after the statute of limitations expired, a nurse's plea in bar asserting that the matter was barred by the statute of limitations was not sustained under Va. Sup. Ct. R. 3:5 or § 8.01-277 because the amended motion for judgment only corrected a misnomer and did not change or add a party. Marsh v. Medical College of Va. Hosps. Aux. of Va. Commonwealth Health Sys., 71 Va. Cir. 404, 2006 Va. Cir. LEXIS 225 (Richmond 2006).

Rule 3:6. Proof of Service.

Returns shall be made on a paper styled "Proof of Service" which shall be substantially in this form:

Virginia:

In the .... Court of the .... of .... :

....................)

v. (short style)) Proof of Service

....................)

Returns shall be made hereon, showing service of the summons issued ...., 20....., with copy of the complaint filed ...., 20....., attached.

The clerk shall prepare as many as may be needed and deliver them with the summons and copies of the complaint.

The summons with copy of the complaint attached shall constitute and be served as one paper.

It shall be the duty of all persons eligible to serve process to make service within five days after receipt, and make return as to those served within 72 hours after the earliest service upon any party shown on each Proof of Service; but failure to make timely service and return shall not prejudice the rights of any party except as provided in Rule 3:5.

Additional copies of the Proof of Service may be obtained from the clerk and returns thereon made in similar manner.

Michie's Jurisprudence. — For related discussion, see 14B M.J. Process, §§ 12, 16, 37, 41, 45, 57.

CASE NOTES

Rule contemplates prompt efforts to secure service. — The general thrust of former Rule 3.3(c) [see now Rules 3:5 and 3:6] appears to contemplate and encourage prompt, bona fide efforts to secure service on defendants once the action has been filed. Saunders v. Wire Rope Corp., 777 F. Supp. 1281 (E.D. Va. 1991) (decided under prior law); Sheppard v. Wire Rope Corp., 777 F. Supp. 1285 (E.D. Va. 1991) (decided under prior law).

Return within five days mandatory. — The provision with respect to returning the notice within five days was held mandatory. Brame v. Nolen, 139 Va. 413, 124 S.E. 299 (1924) (decided under former Rule 3:4).

Effect of amendment of return after five days. — Where the original return was within time, but afterwards was amended and returned after the expiration of the five days, the notice as amended was within time. Alsop Motor Corp. v. Barker, 138 Va. 598, 123 S.E. 350 (1924) (decided under former Rule 3:4).

CIRCUIT COURT OPINIONS

Construction with other law. — Former Rules 2:4 and 2:5 (now Rules 3:5 and 3:6) necessarily imply that a return of service filed outside the 72-hour time limit, set forth in both § 8.01-325 and Rule 2:4 (now Rule 3:5), will not invalidate either the service or a decree entered based on the in personam jurisdiction; such a return constitutes prima facie evidence that the party was served in accordance with the return. Small v. Small, 58 Va. Cir. 114, 2001 Va. Cir. LEXIS 361 (Fairfax County 2001) (decided under former Rule 2:5).

Failure to show prejudice by late return of service. — Guarantor's motion to set aside a default judgment and to quash a return of service was denied, as: (1) he failed to allege that the statute allowing constructive service by posting was not followed; (2) the saving language of § 8.01-294 prohibited the court from setting aside the judgment; and (3) he failed to show any prejudice by the late return of service, nor did he allege that he did not receive actual notice, that he did not understand service was meant for him, or that the notation of "et al" was prejudicial to his position. Edward Don & Co. v. Istriana, Inc., 71 Va. Cir. 109, 2006 Va. Cir. LEXIS 106 (Fairfax County 2006).

Rule 3:7. Bills of Particulars.

(a) *Timing and Grounds.* — On motion made promptly, a bill of particulars may be ordered to amplify any pleading that does not provide notice of a claim or defense adequate to permit the adversary a fair opportunity to respond or prepare the case.

(b) *Striking of Insufficient Bills of Particulars.* — A bill of particulars that fails to inform the opposing party fairly of the true nature of the claim or defense may, on motion made promptly, be stricken and an amended bill of particulars ordered. If the amended bill of particulars fails to inform the opposite party fairly of the true nature of the claim or defense, the pleading not so amplified and the bills of particulars may be stricken.

(c) *Date for Filing Bill of Particulars.* — An order requiring or permitting a bill of particulars or amended bill of particulars shall fix the time within which it must be filed.

(d) *Date for Responding to Amplified Pleading.* — If the bill of particulars amplifies a complaint, a defendant shall respond to the amplified pleading within 21 days after the filing thereof, unless the defendant relies on pleadings already filed. If the bill of particulars amplifies any other pleading, any required response shall be filed within 21 days after the filing of the bill of particulars, or within such shorter or longer time as the court may prescribe.

CASE NOTES

Failure to fix time for filing responsive pleadings. — Defendants did not elect not to plead to amended motion for judgment because, when preparing order sustaining their demurrer to prior motion and permitting plaintiff to amend, they failed to specify a date for filing responsive pleadings, as required by this rule. Plaintiff was not prejudiced by such failure, in light of his own action in suggesting that defendants have 15 days to plead, which indicated he did not believe that defendants had elected not to plead. Daniels v. Truck & Equip. Corp., 205 Va. 579, 139 S.E.2d 31 (1964) (decided under prior law).

If defendant desires more definite information, or a more specific statement of the grounds of the complaint, he should request the court to require plaintiff to file a bill of particulars. Alexander v. Kuykendall, 192 Va. 8, 63 S.E.2d 746 (1951) (decided under prior law).

Procedure where bill of particulars does not sufficiently amplify motion. — Where a bill of particulars does not sufficiently amplify a specific allegation of the motion for judgment, the proper procedure is under this rule, not by way of summary judgment. Marshall v. Dean, 201 Va. 699, 112 S.E.2d 895 (1960) (decided under prior law).

CIRCUIT COURT OPINIONS

No bill of particulars requested. — Overruling of plaintiffs' exceptions in an action involving a prescriptive easement was proper, in part because the parties asserting the right to a prescriptive easement adequately pleaded their respective claims; while some of the language used was arguably misplaced or not as precise as it could have been, a full and fair reading of the various pleadings demonstrated that the prescriptive easement claims were sufficiently stated. Further, no motion was filed by plaintiffs concerning the sufficiency of the pleadings and no bill of particulars was requested. Frazier v. Bledsoe, 79 Va. Cir. 278, 2009 Va. Cir. LEXIS 233 (Orange County Sept. 14, 2009).

Rule 3:8. Answers, Pleas, Demurrers and Motions.

(a) *Response Requirement.* — A defendant shall file pleadings in response within 21 days after service of the summons and complaint upon that defendant, or if service of the summons has been timely waived on request under Code § 8.01-286.1, within 60 days after the date when the request for waiver was sent, or within 90 days after that date if the defendant was addressed outside the Commonwealth. A demurrer, plea, motion to dismiss, and motion for a bill of particulars shall each be deemed a pleading in response for the count or counts addressed therein. If a defendant files no other pleading than the answer, it shall be filed within said time. An answer shall respond to the paragraphs of the complaint. A general denial of the entire complaint or plea of the general issue shall not be permitted.

(b) *Response After Demurrer, Plea or Motion.* — When the court has entered its order overruling all motions, demurrers and other pleas filed by a defendant, such defendant shall, unless the defendant has already done so, file an answer within 21 days after the entry of such order, or within such shorter or longer time as the court may prescribe.

Cross references. — As to civil practice and procedure in the general district courts, see Rule 7B:2.

The amendment, effective May 1, 2006, adopted February 28, 2006, added ", or if service of the summons has been timely waived on request under Code § 8.01-286.1, within 60 days after the date when the request for waiver was sent, or within 90 days after that date if the defendant was addressed outside the Commonwealth" at the end of the first sentence of subdivision (a).

Michie's Jurisprudence. — For related discussion, see 1A M.J. Accord and Satisfaction, § 10; 1B M.J. Appeal and Error, § 175; 2A M.J. Appearances, § 12; 2A M.J. Arbitration and Award, §§ 33, 41; 2A M.J. Assault and Battery, § 21; 2A M.J. Assumpsit, §§ 51, 55; 5A M.J. Covenant, Action of, §§ 4, 5; 5C M.J. Customs and Usages, § 3; 5C M.J. Damages, § 81; 5C M.J. Death by Wrongful Act, § 11; 5C M.J. Debt, Action of, § 16; 6A M.J. Demurrers, § 51; 6B M.J. Ejectment, §§ 24, 25; 7A M.J. Estoppel, § 38; 7A M.J. Equity, §§ 70, 116; 11A M.J. Judgments and Decrees, § 195; 11B M.J. Jurisdiction, § 35; 13A M.J. Motions for Judgment, §§ 21, 22; 14B M.J. Pleading, §§ 3, 38, 39, 46, 49; 19 M.J. Trial, § 12; 19 M.J. Trust, Guaranty and Surety Companies, § 8.

CASE NOTES

I. Decisions under Current Law.
II. Decisions under Prior Law.

I. DECISIONS UNDER CURRENT LAW.

Hearing not required on demurrer with sufficient evidentiary basis. — Trial court properly ruled without an evidentiary hearing on a county's demurrer to a challenge by developers to the reasonableness of increases in county water and sewer connection fees; reports incorporated into the developers' pleadings presented both sides of the issue and provided an adequate evidentiary basis for the trial court to sustain the demurrer. Eagle Harbor L.L.C. v. Isle of Wight County, 271 Va. 603, 628 S.E.2d 298, 2006 Va. LEXIS 42 (2006).

Acceptance of late filing not abuse of discretion. Assuming without deciding that Va. Sup. Ct. R. 3:8 applied, the appellate court concluded that the trial court did not abuse its discretion in accepting the Board of Dentistry's response one business day late, as the dentist presented no evidence to show that the dentist was prejudiced by the one day or that the filing one business day late caused a delay of any kind in the remainder of the proceedings. Lennon v. Va. Bd. of Dentistry, 2007 Va. App. LEXIS 475 (Dec. 27, 2007).

Applied in AME Fin. Corp. v. Kiritsis, 281 Va. 384, 707 S.E.2d 820, 2011 Va. LEXIS 49 (2011).

II. DECISIONS UNDER PRIOR LAW.

Purpose of rule. — Former Rule 2:12 was designed to expedite the cause by commanding a timely presentation of defenses and thus prevent a delay through dilatory tactics on the part of the defendant. Westfall v. Westfall, 196 Va. 97, 82 S.E.2d 487 (1954).

This rule contemplates and requires that a defendant file his responsive pleading within 21 days after service on him of the notice of motion for judgment. Herndon v. Wickham, 198 Va. 824, 97 S.E.2d 5 (1957); Cooper v. Davis, 199 Va. 472, 100 S.E.2d 691 (1957).

Or he is in default. — A fair interpretation of this rule requires a finding that a defendant is in default if, after service of the motion for judgment upon him, more than 21 days expire before he files his "pleadings in response." [Note that this opinion was decided prior to 1976 amendment of former Rule 3:5, making bill of particulars a pleading in response. See now Rule 3:7.] Williams v. Service, Inc., 199 Va. 326, 99 S.E.2d 648 (1957).

Default upheld on failure of defendant to respond. — A default judgment entered against a defendant was held not in error where although a notice of motion for judgment was personally served on defendant and the face of the notice stated that defendant had 21 days to respond, defendant nevertheless failed to respond. Jackson v. Jackson, 236 Va. 199, 372 S.E.2d 155 (1988).

Extension of time. — This rule must be read in connection with Rule 1:9 which provides: "The time allowed for filing pleadings may be extended by the court in its discretion and such extension may be granted although the time fixed already has expired. . . ." Herndon v. Wickham, 198 Va. 824, 97 S.E.2d 5 (1957).

Removal to federal court. — Where more than 21 days after service of the motion for judgment, defendant removed the case to a federal court and then filed his responsive pleading, and subsequently the federal court remanded the case to the state court, defendant was in default. Levine v. Lacy, 204 Va. 297, 130 S.E.2d 443, cert. denied, 375 U.S. 932, 84 S. Ct. 330, 11 L. Ed. 2d 264 (1963), reh'g denied, 375 U.S. 982, 84 S. Ct. 479, 11 L. Ed. 2d 428 (1964).

Notice of appeal not equivalent to notice of motion for judgment. — Notice that an appeal has been docketed is not, by name, nature, or form, equivalent or even similar to a notice of motion for judgment. A notice of motion for judgment is notice to the defendant of a new action brought against him. In prescribed form, the notice specifically calls upon him timely to respond or suffer the enunciated danger of default. Overnite Transp. Co. v. Barnett's, Inc., 217 Va. 222, 227 S.E.2d 695 (1976).

Plea distinguished from grounds of defense. — A plea, whether at law or in equity, is a discrete form of defensive pleading. Distinguished from an answer or grounds of defense, a plea does not address the merits of the issues raised by the bill of complaint or the motion for judgment; rather, it alleges a single state of facts or circumstances (usually not disclosed or disclosed only in part by the record) which, if proven, constitutes an absolute defense to the claim. Nelms v. Nelms, 236 Va. 281, 374 S.E.2d 4 (1988).

Rule inapplicable to notice of appeal from general district court. — When this rule speaks of default for failure to respond to a notice of motion for judgment, the rule by its terms is not applicable to a notice that an appeal from general district court has been docketed in circuit court. Neither is there an "established practice or procedure" which requires a response to a notice of the docketing of an appeal. Overnite Transp. Co. v. Barnett's, Inc., 217 Va. 222, 227 S.E.2d 695 (1976).

But the circuit court may require a defendant in an appealed case to file responsive pleadings and declare him in default for failure to respond as required. Overnite Transp. Co. v. Barnett's, Inc., 217 Va. 222, 227 S.E.2d 695 (1976).

Damages on unliquidated claim not conceded. — The effect of the failure of a defendant to plead within the time prescribed by this rule is that he cannot defend on the merits of the case and he admits that plaintiff is entitled to recover some damages, however small. However, he does not concede the amount of damages on an unliquidated claim. Funkhouser v. Million, 209 Va. 89, 161 S.E.2d 725 (1968).

Affidavit of substantial defense is not a pleading previously filed. — An affidavit of substantial defense is not a pleading. It is a statutorily mandated filing, the purpose of which is to insure that meritorious cases are not removed from the general district court to the circuit court solely to harass or delay. It is a mechanism which allows the courts to monitor frivolous defenses and to prevent abuse of the removal procedures, and is not a pleading previously filed for purposes of this rule. Jackson v. Jackson, 236 Va. 199, 372 S.E.2d 155 (1988).

Statute of frauds. — Where there was nothing of record to suggest that the statute of frauds would be involved until plaintiff introduced his evidence, defendant could rely on the statute although not specifically set out in its grounds of defense. Lawson v. States Constr. Co., 193 Va. 513, 69 S.E.2d 450 (1952).

CIRCUIT COURT OPINIONS

One sentence answer not responsive pleading. — Defendant's self-styled "answer" did not constitute a responsive pleading pursuant to Va. Sup. Ct. Rule 3:8 because the one sentence of the answer, which stated that defendant had received the summons, did not respond to anything in plaintiff's application for confirmation of an arbitration award. FIA Card Servs. v. Worku, 75 Va. Cir. 8, 2008 Va. Cir. LEXIS 8 (Fairfax County 2008).

Extension granted in the absence of excusable neglect. — Trial courts' discretion to extend time limits does not require a finding of excusable neglect. Kohl v. Amerigas Propane, Inc., 64 Va. Cir. 49, 2004 Va. Cir. LEXIS 44 (Madison County 2004).

Granting of motion for judgment. — City's responses to the injured party's motion for judgment, its demurrer and its special plea of governmental immunity, had to be granted as the injured party did not show that the city failed to exercise ordinary care in keeping the parking lot, where the injured party fell safe for its invitees, and the maintenance of the city's parking lot was a government function, which meant the city was not liable on claims related to its maintenance of the lot.

Gambrell v. City of Norfolk, 60 Va. Cir. 328, 2002 Va. Cir. LEXIS 399 (Norfolk 2002).

Failure to timely file response. — In an action for construction of the rights under a declaration of trust, a default judgment pursuant to Va. Sup. Ct. R. 3:19(a) was proper because defense counsel failed to timely file responsive pleadings pursuant to Va. Sup. Ct. R. 3:8. The beneficiaries were not entitled to relief from the default because service of process and actual notice of the claim were timely provided, the delay in filing the responsive pleadings was inexcusable, and, if relief were granted, the trustee would have suffered an unfair consequence of faithfully following procedural rules while the beneficiaries disregarded them. Wyczalkowski v. Carter, 78 Va. Cir. 300, 2009 Va. Cir. LEXIS 164 (Loudoun County May 5, 2009).

Medical clinic failed to file a responsive pleading in a medical malpractice action as required by Va. Sup. Ct. R. 3:8. Because the clinic was in default according to Va. Sup. Ct. R. 3:19, and the clinic had failed to request a late responsive filing, it was appropriate to enter default as to the clinic. Youngblood v. Fasano, 81 Va. Cir. 260, 2010 Va. Cir. LEXIS 117 (Fairfax Oct. 4, 2010).

Defendant's response untimely. — Default judgment entered in a contract dispute where a corporation did not file a response within the 21-day period, a church stated a breach of contract cause of action, venue was waived and jurisdiction and notice were proper. New Life Christian Church v. Dynabilt Tech. Int'l Corp., 59 Va. Cir. 399, 2002 Va. Cir. LEXIS 367 (Norfolk 2002).

Counterclaim untimely. — Under § 16.1-88.01, defendant, sued in general district court, could not file its counterclaim there because it sought damages in excess of that court's jurisdictional limit. But the granting of its motion to remove the case to circuit court triggered defendant's obligation to file its counterclaim within 21 days pursuant to Va. Sup. Ct. R. 3:8; as it failed to do so, its counterclaim was dismissed. Millermusmar, P.C. v. Diakon Logistics, Inc., 72 Va. Cir. 69, 2006 Va. Cir. LEXIS 173 (Fairfax County 2006).

Responsive pleading timely. — Doctor's plea in bar in a dental malpractice action was timely filed because Va. Sup. Ct. R. 3:8(a) could not be interpreted to suggest that a motion for a bill of particulars that was filed did not constitute a responsive pleading. Carter v. Mazin Alayssami, D.M.D., P.C., 82 Va. Cir. 148, 2011 Va. Cir. LEXIS 36 (Stafford County Jan. 28, 2011).

Extension allowed. — In an action for accounting by a decedent's widow against the executor of an estate of which the decedent was a beneficiary and against the executor's surety, the court granted the surety's motion for leave to extend the time to file its answer and grounds for its defense pursuant to Rule 1:9 after the surety belatedly filed both its response and defense pursuant to Rule 3:5 [now Rule 3:8] because although it was clear that responsibility for the delay in filing solely rested with the surety and not the neglect of its attorneys, the ends of justice would be further served by allowing the extension where no prejudice was demonstrated by the widow, no trial date had been set, and there was no indication in the file that the widow had propounded any discovery requests upon either of defendants or taken any action to further prosecute the matter. Furthermore, no evidence of bad faith of the surety was demonstrated, and the surety asserted that it had acted in good faith by submitting an answer and grounds of defense immediately after counsel was retained, and in conducting discussions with the widow as to the merits of the case and settlement negotiations. Brown v. Allen, 64 Va. Cir. 349, 2004 Va. Cir. LEXIS 70 (Fairfax County 2004).

Extension not allowed. — Motion filed by a limited liability company (LLC) for leave to submit its answer late was denied, and default judgment was entered in favor of plaintiff because the failure of the LLC's system for receiving and responding to service of process, without any showing of circumstances that were sufficiently compelling, did not constitute a reasonable or legal excuse for the LLC's failure to comply with the filing requirements; the LLC was aware of plaintiff's action, it failed to adjust its e-mail system to receive messages from its registered agent despite its knowledge of the pending action, and counsel could not establish that anyone monitored the action for service. Ellis v. Danville Reg'l Med. Ctr., 75 Va. Cir. 301, 2008 Va. Cir. LEXIS 217 (Danville July 1, 2008).

Breach of fiduciary duty. — Demurrer was overruled as to an insured's claim for breach of fiduciary duty based on the two-year statute of limitations as the insured alleged facts which, if proven, showed active concealment or fraud preventing any claim from being asserted and tolled the statute of limitations under subsection D of § 8.01-229; demurrer based on a question as to whether a sponsor could be liable vicariously for the fiduciary breaches alleged to have been committed by an insurance salesman was the proper subject for later proof. Nowland v. Tri Core, Inc., 60 Va. Cir. 469, 2000 Va. Cir. LEXIS 643 (Richmond 2000) (decided under prior law).

Plea in bar. — Mediation and arbitration clause within a retail buyers order between a car buyer and its seller was enforceable, and not precluded by the Magnuson/Moss Warranty Act, 15 U.S.C.S. §§ 2301 et seq., as the Act did not evince a congressional intent to bar arbitration of the buyer's warranty claims against the seller; hence, sellers plea in bar to compel mediation was sustained and the motion to stay the proceedings was granted. Aston v. Nissan N. Am., Inc., 71 Va. Cir. 430, 2005 Va. Cir. LEXIS 366 (Chesapeake 2005).

Demurrer overruled. — Property manager's demurrer against a patron's personal injury complaint was overruled, as the facts alleged therein were sufficient to create a duty owed to the patron, a business invitee, by the manager, as the property owner's agent, to maintain the premises in a reasonably safe condition. Milburn v. J.C. Penney Props., 2007 Va. Cir. LEXIS 42 (Fairfax County Mar. 30, 2007).

Rule 3:9. Counterclaims.

(a) *Scope.* — A defendant may, at that defendant's option, plead as a counterclaim any cause of action that the defendant has against the plaintiff or all plaintiffs jointly, whether or not it grows out of any transaction mentioned in the complaint, whether or not it is for liquidated damages, whether it is in tort or contract, and whether or not the amount demanded in the counterclaim is greater than the amount demanded in the complaint.

(b) *Time for initiation.* — (i) A counterclaim shall, subject to the provisions of Rule 1:9, be filed within 21 days after service of the summons and complaint upon the defendant asserting the counterclaim, or if service of the summons has been timely waived on request under Code §8.01-286.1, within 60 days after the date when the request for waiver was sent, or within 90 days after that date if the defendant was addressed outside the Commonwealth.

(ii) If a demurrer, plea, motion to dismiss, or motion for a bill of particulars is filed within the period provided in subsection (b)(i) of this Rule, the defendant may file any counterclaim at any time up to 21 days after the entry of the court's order ruling upon all such motions, demurrers and other pleas, or within such shorter or longer time as the court may prescribe.

(c) *Response to counterclaim.* — The plaintiff shall file pleadings in response to such counterclaim within 21 days after it is served.

(d) *Separate trials.* — The court in its discretion may order a separate trial of any cause of action asserted in a counterclaim.

Comment. — As a consequence of the creation of the "single cause of action" via statute and rule, in a suit for divorce or for annulling a marriage, a defendant's claim for affirmative relief against the plaintiff, formerly known as a "cross-bill" or a "cross-complaint," should be understood as a counterclaim.

The amendment, effective May 1, 2006, adopted February 28, 2006, added ", or if service of the summons has been timely waived on request under Code § 8.01-286.1, within 60 days after the date when the request for waiver was sent, or within 90 days after that date if the defendant was addressed outside the Commonwealth" at the end of subdivision (b).

The amendment effective July 1, 2008, adopted April 9, 2008, designated the existing provisions of subdivision (b) as sub-subdivision (i) and inserted sub-subdivision (ii).

Michie's Jurisprudence. — For related discussion, see 1A M.J. Accounts and Accounting, § 10; 1B M.J. Appeal and Error, § 297; 3C M.J. Commercial Law, § 33; 6A M.J. Divorce and Alimony, § 38; 7A M.J. Equity, §§ 77, 97, 103, 110, 114 - 117; 13A M.J. Motions for Judgment, § 22; 14B M.J. Process, § 5; 16 M.J. Removal of Causes, § 2; 16 M.J. Setoff, Recoupment and Counterclaim, §§ 1-4, 6, 8, 11, 17, 19, 21, 26, 45; 19 M.J. Trial, § 5.

CASE NOTES

I. DECISIONS UNDER PRIOR LAW.

Review of ruling on motion for separate trial. — When a trial judge has passed upon a motion for a separate trial, the Supreme Court will not disturb the ruling unless it plainly appears that the discretion, which the rule grants, has been abused. Leech v. Beasley, 203 Va. 955, 128 S.E.2d 293 (1962).

Separate trials not required for differing negligence claims. — The fact that one claim was based on ordinary negligence, while two others were based on gross negligence, was not sufficient to dictate separate trials. Leech v. Beasley, 203 Va. 955, 128 S.E.2d 293 (1962).

Inability to refute own testimony to defend against counterclaim not ground for separate trials. — There was no merit to plaintiff's contention that he was prejudiced by a joint trial because he could not refute, in defending the counterclaims, the testimony introduced by him and upon which he relied to prove his original claim. The general rule is that a party is forbidden to assume successive positions in the course of a suit, or series of suits, in reference to the same fact or state of facts, which are inconsistent with each other, or mutually contradictory. Leech v. Beasley, 203 Va. 955, 128 S.E.2d 293 (1962).

Whether identical question as counterclaim determined in prior county court proceeding was question of fact. — Whether the record and the extrinsic evidence of a prior county court proceeding showed that the identical question as a counterclaim now asserted was in issue and determined by the county court was a question of fact for the trial court in the second case to decide. Barkman v. Chevalier, 214 Va. 6, 196 S.E.2d 911 (1973).

Waiver of right to remove cause to federal court. — By filing a counterclaim, defendant became a plaintiff invoking the jurisdiction of the court and waived his right to remove the cause to federal district court. Sood v. Advanced Computer Techniques Corp., 308 F. Supp. 239 (E.D. Va. 1969).

Voluntary filing of a counterclaim or cross claim in Virginia is a waiver of the right to removal to federal district court. Bryant Elec. Co. v. Joe Rainero Tile Co., 84 F.R.D. 120 (W.D. Va. 1979).

Permissive counterclaim not basis for removal. — The federal district court could not look to the defendant's counterclaim to establish jurisdictional amount for purposes of removal of a case to federal court, since a counterclaim that is deemed "permissive" under state law may not be used to establish jurisdictional amount for such purposes, and since all counterclaims in Virginia are deemed to be permissive since they are at the option of the defendant. Bryant Elec. Co. v. Joe Rainero Tile Co., 84 F.R.D. 120 (W.D. Va. 1979).

There is no requirement in Virginia that a debt be liquidated in order to be raised as a set-off in a counterclaim. Piland Corp. v. League Constr. Co., 238 Va. 187, 380 S.E.2d 652 (1989).

The language of this rule explicitly allows a defendant to plead, as a counterclaim, any cause of action at law whether or not it is for liquidated damages and it would be patently illogical for the rules of court, as a matter of procedure, to encourage a defendant to plead unliquidated damages as a set-off, while not recognizing, as a matter of substance, his right to set off the unliquidated damages against the plaintiff's liquidated damages. Piland Corp. v. League Constr. Co., 238 Va. 187, 380 S.E.2d 652 (1989).

Decision not to bifurcate compensatory and punitive damages portion of case upheld. — There was no abuse of discretion in the trial court's decision not to bifurcate the compensatory and punitive damages portions of a case where plaintiffs alleged that a driver and owner were drunk at the time of a head-on collision; when considering a request for separate trials, the trial court had to consider any resulting unnecessary delay, expense, or use of judicial resources that would flow from separate trials of the claims at issue. Allstate Ins. Co. v. Wade, 265 Va. 383, 579 S.E.2d 180, 2003 Va. LEXIS 53 (2003).

This rule is merely procedural and provides the place, time, manner of filing and maturing a cross-bill against a plaintiff, but it does not state the substantive law applicable to a determination of the legality of such a bill when questioned under the varying circumstances of particular cases. Brewer v. Brewer, 199 Va. 626, 101 S.E.2d 516 (1958).

Rule must be complied with where answer treated as cross-bill. — Traditionally, in Virginia, where a defendant has set up a claim for affirmative relief in a defensive pleading, the court, in order to do complete justice between the parties and avoid a multiplicity of suits, may in its discretion treat an answer as a cross-bill by appropriate order. Shevel's, Inc.—Chesterfield v. Southeastern Assocs., 228 Va. 175, 320 S.E.2d 339 (1984).

Service of a cross-bill for divorce by mailing a copy to opposing counsel pursuant to this rule would be sufficient to satisfy the service requirement for a cross-bill, but was insufficient under § 20-99 and former Rule 2:9 to commence an action for divorce. Therefore, even if the cross-bill were treated as an initial pleading, it would still fail for lack of proper service. Bryant v. Bryant, No. 0073-84, (Ct. of Appeals Sept. 9, 1985).

Answer not treated as cross-bill. — See Feldman v. Rucker, 201 Va. 11, 109 S.E.2d 379 (1959).

CIRCUIT COURT OPINIONS

Filing deadlines after removal from general district court. — Defendant's removal of a suit from general district court to the circuit court supplies the requisite knowledge necessary to begin preparing a counterclaim. Because counterclaims are a response to the filing of a lawsuit, not necessarily a response to the specific allegations of the suit, the removal triggers the defendant's obligation to file its counterclaim within 21 days. Millermusmar, P.C. v. Diakon Logistics, Inc., 72 Va. Cir. 69, 2006 Va. Cir. LEXIS 173 (Fairfax County 2006).

Time limits for filing cross-bill in equity. — Va. Sup. Ct. R. 3:9 does not apply to cases filed before the merger of law and equity. In such cases, former Va. Sup. Ct. R. 2:13 applies and grants a defendant the right to file a cross-bill at any time when he would not be in default if he had not filed a pleading. Parsch v. Massey, 71 Va. Cir. 209, 2006 Va. Cir. LEXIS 249 (Charlottesville 2006).

Waiver of objection to timeliness of counterclaim. — Where plaintiffs sought a non-suit under § 8.01-380 against defendants who filed counterclaims, by answering the counterclaims without objecting to their legal sufficiency or untimeliness, plaintiffs waived their ability to do so. Parsch v. Massey, 71 Va. Cir. 209, 2006 Va. Cir. LEXIS 249 (Charlottesville 2006).

Rule 3:10. Cross-Claims.

(a) *Scope.* — A defendant may, at that defendant's option, plead as a cross-claim any cause of action that such defendant has or may have against one or more other defendants growing out of any matter pled in the complaint. Such cross-claim may include a claim that the party against whom it is asserted is or may be liable to the cross-claimant for all or part of a claim asserted in the action against the cross-claimant.

(b) *Time for initiation.* — A cross-claim shall, subject to the provisions of Rule 1:9, be filed within 21 days after service of the summons and complaint on the defendant asserting the cross-claim, or if service of the summons has been timely waived on request under Code § 8.01-286.1, within 60 days after the date when the request for waiver was sent, or within 90 days after that date if the defendant was addressed outside the Commonwealth.

(c) *Response to cross-claim.* — The cross-claim defendant shall file pleadings in response to such cross-claim within 21 days after it is served.

(d) *Separate trials.* — The court in its discretion may order a separate trial of any cause of action asserted in a cross-claim.

Cross references. — As to civil practice and procedure in the general district courts, see Rule 7B:3.

The amendment, effective May 1, 2006, adopted February 28, 2006, added "or if service of the summons has been timely waived on request under Code § 8.01-286.1, within 60 days after the date when the request for waiver was sent, or within 90 days after that date if the defendant was addressed outside the Commonwealth" at the end of subdivision (b).

Michie's Jurisprudence. — For related discussion, see 5A M.J. Creditors' Suits, § 32; 7A M.J. Equity, §§ 98, 110, 112, 114, 116, 117; 9B M.J. Indemnity, § 11; 13A M.J. Motions for Judgment, § 22; 19 M.J. Trial, § 5.

CASE NOTES

Former Rules 2:13 and 2:14 must be complied with where answer treated as cross-bill. — Traditionally, in Virginia, where a defendant has set up a claim for affirmative relief in a defensive pleading, the court, in order to do complete justice between the parties and avoid a multiplicity of suits, may in its discretion treat an answer as a cross-bill by appropriate order. In such a situation the parties must comply with former Rules 2:13 and 2:14 (now Rules 3:9 and 3:10). Shevel's, Inc. — Chesterfield v. Southeastern Assocs., 228 Va. 175, 320 S.E.2d 339 (1984) (decided under prior law).

CIRCUIT COURT OPINIONS

Construction. — The second defendant had not made a general appearance for purposes of the first defendant's cross-claim because it had not answered it or appeared in any way as defendants to the cross-claim; therefore, the first defendant's mailing a copy of the cross-claim to the second defendant's counsel was not proper service under Va. Sup. Ct. R. 1:12. Lesner Pointe Condo. Ass'n v. Harbour Point Bldg. Corp., 61 Va. Cir. 609, 2002 Va. Cir. LEXIS 424 (Virginia Beach 2002) (decided under prior law). See also, Bd. of Dirs. of the Lesner Pointe Condo. on the Chesapeake Bay Ass'n v. Harbour Point Bldg. Corp., 2002 Va. Cir. LEXIS 421 (Virginia Beach Oct. 25, 2002) (decided under former Rule 3:9).

Rule 3:11. Reply.

Responding to new matter. — If a pleading, motion or affirmative defense sets up new matter and contains words expressly requesting a reply, the adverse party shall within 21 days file a reply admitting or denying such new matter. If it does not contain such words, the allegation of new matter shall be taken as denied or avoided without further pleading. All allegations contained in a reply shall be taken as denied or avoided without further pleading.

Law Review. — For annual survey of Virginia law article, "Civil Practice and Procedure," see 47 U. Rich. L. Rev. 113 (2012).

Michie's Jurisprudence. — For related discussion, see 1B M.J. Amendments, § 80; 1B M.J. Appeal and Error, § 297; 2A M.J. Assault and Battery, § 21; 5C M.J. Debt, Action of, § 24; 12A M.J. Limitation of Actions, § 67; 13A M.J. Motions for Judgment, § 23; 14B M.J. Pleading, § 50.

CASE NOTES

Form of reply to responsive pleadings. — Where a plaintiff responded to defenses in memoranda and argument to the trial court, that party was not required to anticipate the defenses in his initial motion for declaratory judgment. Atkinson v. Penske Logistics, LLC, 268 Va. 129, 596 S.E.2d 518, 2004 Va. LEXIS 94 (2004) (decided under former Rule 3:12).

Applied in N. Va. Real Estate, Inc. v. Martins, 283 Va. 86, 720 S.E.2d 121, 2012 Va. LEXIS 11 (2012).

CIRCUIT COURT OPINIONS

New matter in affirmative defense requires timely reply. — The plain language of Va. Sup. Ct. R. 3:12 (now Rule 3:11) indicates that if the affirmative defense is "new" it is not something previously pleaded and if it is a new "matter," it contains substantial facts forming the basis of a claim or defense and facts that are material to the issue. A general contractor's affirmative defense that it did not pay the subcontractor because it was not paid on its prime contract and that provisions of the subcontract barred the subcontractor's claims in such a situation required a timely reply because that was a new matter that was not raised in previous pleadings. Jay-Ton Constr. Co. v. Bowen Constr. Servs., 62 Va. Cir. 414, 2003 Va. Cir. LEXIS 289 (Portsmouth 2003) (decided under prior law).

Rule 3:12. Joinder of Additional Parties.

(a) *Persons to Be Joined if Feasible.* — A person who is subject to service of process may be joined as a party in the action if (1) in the person's absence complete relief cannot be accorded among those already parties, or (2) the person claims an interest relating to the subject of the action and is so situated that the disposition of the action in the person's absence may (i) as a practical matter impair or impede the person's ability to protect that interest or (ii) leave any of the persons already parties subject to a substantial risk of incurring double, multiple, or otherwise inconsistent obligations by reason of the claimed interest of the person to be joined. If such a person should join as a plaintiff but refuses to do so, the person may be made a defendant, or, in a proper case, an involuntary plaintiff.

(b) *Method of Joinder.* — A motion to join an additional party shall, subject to the provisions of Rule 1:9, be filed with the clerk within 21 days after service of the complaint and shall be served on the party sought to be joined who shall thereafter be subject to all provisions of these Rules, except the provisions requiring payment of writ tax and clerk's fees.

(c) *Determination by Court Whenever Joinder Not Feasible.* — If a person as described in subdivision (a) hereof cannot be made a party, the court shall determine whether in equity and good conscience the action should proceed among the parties before it, or should be dismissed, the absent person being thus regarded as indispensable. The factors to be considered by the court include: first, to what extent a judgment rendered in the person's absence might be prejudicial to the absent person or those already parties; second, the extent to which, by protective provisions in the judgment, by the shaping of relief, or other measures, the prejudice can be lessened or avoided; third, whether a judgment rendered in the person's absence will be adequate; fourth, whether the plaintiff will have an adequate remedy if the action is dismissed for nonjoinder.

(d) *Pleading Reasons for Nonjoinder.* — A pleading asserting a claim for relief shall state the names, if known to the pleader, of any persons as described in subdivision (a) hereof who are not joined, and the reasons why they are not joined.

CASE NOTES

Joinder of potential beneficiaries not required. — The interests of potential beneficiaries are too remote to require the joinder of those potential beneficiaries as necessary parties. NationsBank v. Estate of Grandy, 248 Va. 557, 450 S.E.2d 140 (1994) (decided under prior law).

Making child party in paternity action. — By requiring that a child be made a party to the action to be bound by its results, the integrity of the fact-finding process is enhanced and the rights and interests of the child, which are paramount, are protected. The putative father, to ensure that he would not be subject to relitigation of the paternity issue, could have joined the child under this rule, and may now join the child as a necessary party under § 20-49.2. Commonwealth ex rel. Gray v. Johnson, 7 Va. App. 614, 376 S.E.2d 787 (1989) (decided under prior law).

A suit, time-barred as to any necessary party, must be dismissed because such necessary party is not subject to the court's jurisdiction. Mendenhall v. Douglas L. Cooper, Inc., 239 Va. 71, 387 S.E.2d 468 (1990) (decided under prior law).

Limited liability company is necessary party in derivative action. — Limited liability company was a necessary party in a derivative action brought by one of the members against the other members, pursuant to Va. Sup. Ct. R. 3:12. Siska Trust v. Milestone Dev., 282 Va. 169, 715 S.E.2d 21, 2011 Va. LEXIS 180 (2011).

CIRCUIT COURT OPINIONS

Indispensable party. — Metropolitan Washington Airports Authority (MWAA) was a necessary and indispensable party in a declaratory judgment suit seeking to invalidate the transfer of a toll road under Va. Sup. Ct. R. 3:12(c) since MWAA had sovereign immunity, and would be prejudiced by the outcome of case in invalidating the agreements for the transfer of a toll road to which it was a party; MWAA and the state entities did not have identical interests in the agreements, and MWAA's interests were not adequately protected by the state entities. Gray v. Va. Secy. of Transp., 77 Va. Cir. 224, 2008 Va. Cir. LEXIS 145 (Richmond 2008).

In a landowner's action against a city council, a

planning commission, and its director seeking an injunction and declaratory relief preventing the director from issuing a building permit to a church pursuant to a certificate of appropriateness issued to it under Norfolk City Zoning Ordinance § 9-0.4, the church constituted a proper, yet not a necessary party with respect to the claim for preliminary injunctive relief. However, it represented a necessary, indispensable party to a determination of the litigation on the merits. Owens v. City Council, 75 Va. Cir. 91, 2008 Va. Cir. LEXIS 223 (Norfolk Mar. 7, 2008).

Rule 3:13. Third-Party Practice.

(a) *When Defendant May Bring in Third Party.* — At any time after commencement of the action a defending party, as a third-party plaintiff, may file and serve a third-party complaint upon a person not a party to the action who is or may be liable to the third-party plaintiff for all or part of the plaintiff's claim against the third-party plaintiff. The third-party plaintiff need not obtain leave therefore if the third-party complaint is filed not later than 21 days after the third-party plaintiff serves an original pleading in response. Otherwise the third-party plaintiff must obtain leave therefore on motion after notice to all parties to the action. The person served with the third-party complaint, hereinafter called the third-party defendant, shall make defenses to the third-party plaintiff's claim as provided in Rules 3:7 and 3:8. The third-party defendant may plead counterclaims against the third-party plaintiff and cross-claims against other third-party defendants as provided in Rules 3:9 and 3:10. The third-party defendant may assert against the plaintiff any defenses that the third-party plaintiff has to the plaintiff's claim. The third-party defendant may also assert any claim against the plaintiff arising out of the transaction or occurrence that is the subject matter of the plaintiff's claim against the third-party plaintiff. The plaintiff may, at plaintiff's option, within 21 days after service of the third-party complaint upon the third-party defendant, assert any claim against the third-party defendant arising out of the transaction or occurrence that is the subject matter of the plaintiff's claim against the third-party plaintiff, and the third-party defendant thereupon shall assert defenses as provided in Rules 3:7 and 3:8 and any counterclaims and cross-claims, including claims against the plaintiff, as provided in Rules 3:9 and 3:10. Any party may move to strike the third-party complaint, or for its severance or separate trial. A third-party defendant may proceed under this rule against any person not a party to the action who is or may be liable to the third-party defendant for all or part of the claim made in the action against the third-party defendant.

(b) *When Plaintiff May Bring in Third Party.* — When a counterclaim is asserted against a plaintiff, the plaintiff may cause a third party to be brought in under circumstances that under this rule would entitle a defendant to do so.

Cross references. — As to civil practice and procedure in the general district courts, see Rule 7B:10.

Law Review. — For comment on the status of third-party practice in Virginia, see 13 U. Rich. L. Rev. 613 (1979). For note on third-party removal of an entire case: Who can remove, who cannot, see 41 Wash. & Lee L. Rev. 1533 (1984).

Michie's Jurisprudence. — For related discussion, see 1A M.J. Actions, § 18; 1B M.J. Appeal and Error, § 28; 3C M.J. Commercial Law, §§ 33, 90; 13A M.J. Motions for Judgment, § 7; 14A M.J. Parties, § 17; 21 M.J. Workers' Compensation, § 53.

CASE NOTES

I. DECISIONS UNDER PRIOR LAW.

This rule is the state counterpart of Rule 14 of the Federal Rules of Civil Procedure. Valley Landscape Co. v. Rolland, 218 Va. 257, 237 S.E.2d 120 (1977).

Procedure for filing a third-party motion for judgment. — Section 8.01-281 authorizes a party in a pending action to file a third-party motion for judgment (complaint) seeking indemnification or contribution. Subdivision (a) of this rule establishes the procedure for filing such a claim. When a claim for indemnity or contribution is filed as a separate cause of action, it does not accrue until the person seeking the relief has paid more than his or her share of the obligation. Virginia Int'l Terms., Inc. v. Ceres Marine Terms., Inc., 879 F. Supp. 31 (E.D. Va. 1995).

When claim may be asserted. — A third-party claim may be asserted under the rule only when the third party's liability is in some way dependent on the outcome of the main claim or when the third party is secondarily liable to defendant. The secondary or derivative liability notion is central and it is irrelevant whether the basis of the third-party claim is indemnity, subrogation, contribution, express or implied warranty, or some other theory. But impleader is proper only when a right to relief exists under the applicable substantive law. Valley Landscape Co. v. Rolland, 218 Va. 257, 237 S.E.2d 120 (1977).

Purpose for which defendant can bring in third party. — Under this rule a defendant can bring in a third-party defendant only for the purpose of passing through to the third-party defendant all or part of the liability which might be imposed on the defendant by the plaintiff as the result of the conduct of the third-party defendant. Valley Landscape Co. v. Rolland, 218 Va. 257, 237 S.E.2d 120 (1977).

Defendant not compelled to bring third party into litigation. — Under former Rule 3:10 (now Rule 3:13) of the Supreme Court of Virginia a defendant can bring in a third-party defendant only for the purpose of passing through to the third-party defendant all or part of the liability which might be imposed on the defendant by the plaintiff as the result of the conduct of the third-party defendant. Rule 3:10 is the state counterpart of Rule 14, Fed. R. Civ. P., which authorizes defendant to bring into a lawsuit any person "not a party to the action who is or may be liable to him for all or part of the plaintiff's claim against him." This language does not compel defendant to bring third parties into the litigation; rather, it simply permits the addition of anyone who meets the standard set forth in the rule. In many instances, tactical considerations will lead a party to pursue an independent action against a possible third-party defendant rather than resorting to impleader. Valley Landscape Co. v. Rolland, 218 Va. 257, 237 S.E.2d 120 (1977).

Mere procedural devices to promote judicial economy. — This rule and § 8.01-281 are mere procedural devices to promote judicial economy by having all claims, actual or potential, arising from the same transaction or occurrence determined in one proceeding. Virginia Int'l Terms., Inc. v. Ceres Marine Terms., Inc., 879 F. Supp. 31 (E.D. Va. 1995).

In the absence of § 8.01-281 and this rule, a party having a claim for indemnity or contribution against another would be prevented from pursuing the claim until it accrued. Virginia Int'l Terms., Inc. v. Ceres Marine Terms., Inc., 879 F. Supp. 31 (E.D. Va. 1995).

CIRCUIT COURT OPINIONS

Third party motion allowed. — Third-party plaintiff's motion for judgment was not subject to demurrer because, under former Rule 3:10 (now Rule 3:13), it properly joined an individual in an action filed by his corporation against the third-party plaintiffs, because they alleged the corporation was not a valid corporation at the time of the contract it was suing on, rendering the individual liable on their fraud claim, which established his breach of the same contract. Colinsky Consulting, Inc. v. Holloway, 57 Va. Cir. 403, 2002 Va. Cir. LEXIS 225 (Norfolk 2002) (decided under former Rule 3:10).

Rule 3:14. Intervention.

A new party may by leave of court file a pleading to intervene as a plaintiff or defendant to assert any claim or defense germane to the subject matter of the proceeding.

All provisions of these Rules applicable to civil cases, except those provisions requiring payment of writ tax and clerk's fees, shall apply to such pleadings. The parties on whom such pleadings are served shall respond thereto as provided in these Rules.

Michie's Jurisprudence. — For related discussion, see 5A M.J. Creditors' Suits, §§ 20, 21, 32; 7A M.J. Equity, § 95; 14A M.J. Parties, § 26.

CASE NOTES

Intervenor must assert right involved in suit. — In order for a stranger to become a party by intervention, he must assert some right involved in the suit. Layton v. Seawall Enters., Inc., 231 Va. 402, 344 S.E.2d 896 (1986) (decided under former Rule 2:15).

Intervenor must assert right germane to issues in suit. — Trial court erred in allowing workers' compensation carriers to intervene in a personal injury action, as the carriers' claim was limited to the protection of their right to reimbursement of amounts paid in workers' compensation benefits, and the carriers' lien attached automatically to amounts the injured worker might recover. Hudson v. Jarrett, 269 Va. 24, 606 S.E.2d 827, 2005 Va. LEXIS 2 (2005) (decided under former Rule 3:19).

Trial court properly denied an attorney's motion to intervene in an action he had filed while counsel for the guardian of an incompetent person in order to collect attorney's fees, as the attorney was not a party to the action, and the motion for attorney's fees was not germane, so former Va. Sup. Ct. R. 2:15 [now Rule 3:14], did not require the court to allow the attorney to intervene. Eads v. Clark, 272 Va. 192, 630 S.E.2d 502, 2006 Va. LEXIS 53 (2006).

Even though under Rule 1:8 leave to amend should be granted liberally by the trial court in furtherance of the ends of justice, under this rule a new party may not intervene and assert a claim in a pending suit unless the claim is "germane to the subject matter of the suit." Layton v. Seawall Enters., Inc., 231 Va. 402, 344 S.E.2d 896 (1986) (decided under former Rule 2:15).

Mechanic's lien suit. — Both the trustee and the named beneficiary of an antecedent deed of trust are necessary parties in a suit to enforce a mechanic's lien. Mendenhall v. Douglas L. Cooper, Inc., 239 Va. 71, 387 S.E.2d 468 (1990) (decided under former Rule 2:15).

Settlement mooted appeal of denial of motion to intervene. — In a case dealing with an application seeking permission to install a raw water intake on state-owned bottomlands, nothing in former Rule 2:15 (now this rule) or the Virginia Administrative Process Act, or the enabling statutes for the Virginia Marine Resources Commission (VMRC) gave the tribe the right to intervene; additionally, no settlement between the city and the VMRC could prejudice any rights the tribe had under its treaty. Thus, the settlement between the city and the VMRC, consummated by the entry of a consent dismissal order, mooted the tribe's appeal of the circuit court's decision to deny the tribe's motion to intervene. Mattaponi Indian Tribe v. Va. Marine Res. Comm'n, 45 Va. App. 208, 609 S.E.2d 619, 2005 Va. App. LEXIS 85 (2005) (decided under former Rule 2:15).

CIRCUIT COURT OPINIONS

Intervenor must assert right germane to issues in suit. — Where plaintiff employee alleged that he was injured as a result of defendant employee's negligence, intervenors, plaintiff's employer and its insurance carrier, were not entitled to enter as parties because they did not assert rights that were germane to the issues in plaintiff's action; instead, they were requesting to intervene on the mere prospect that judgment would be entered in plaintiff's favor. Stephen v. Dickens, 63 Va. Cir. 403, 2003 Va. Cir. LEXIS 348 (Norfolk 2003) (decided under former Rule 3:19).

Limit on claims. — Trustee's pleading on his own behalf exceeded the limits of the relief sought in the petition to intervene; the court did not grant the right to assert claims not arising out of a memorandum of understanding with the individual defendants. Roberts v. Touchstone Dev. Corp., 58 Va. Cir. 130, 2002 Va. Cir. LEXIS 135 (Loudoun County 2002) (decided under prior law).

Leave of court. — Because a trial court never granted a party leave to file a responsive pleading as required by Va. Sup. Ct. R. 3:14, dismissal of the pleading was appropriate as it was improperly before the court. Youngblood v. Fasano, 81 Va. Cir. 260, 2010 Va. Cir. LEXIS 117 (Fairfax Oct. 4, 2010).

Intervention allowed to assert defenses. — Because a business trust in effect, stated a cause of action against an alleged "dummy company," under the circumstances, the court would allow the "dummy company" to intervene so as to assert a defense to the business trust's allegations as its proposed defenses were germane to the subject matter raised. Lehner Family Bus. Trust v. United Leasing Corp., 71 Va. Cir. 150, 2006 Va. Cir. LEXIS 227 (Richmond 2006).

Intervention allowed to defend constitutionality of state statute. — Commonwealth could intervene in property dispute between private parties for limited purpose of defending the constitutionality of subsection A of § 57-9. Va. Sup. Ct. R. 3:14 did not address the issue, the attorney general had that right in federal cases under in 28 U.S.C.S. § 2403(b) and U.S. Sup. Ct. R. 29(4)(c), the attorney general had a unique interest in defending the constitutionality of state statutes, and no state case cited by the opponents of intervention had denied the attorney general intervenor status to defend a state statute's constitutionality. In re Multi-Circuit Episcopal Church Prop. Litig., 76 Va. Cir. 785, 2008 Va. Cir. LEXIS 76 (Fairfax County 2008).

Rule 3:15. Statutory Interpleader.

Proceedings brought pursuant to statutory provisions relating to interpleader shall, to the extent not inconsistent with the governing statutes, be conducted in accordance with the Rules contained in this Part Three.

Law Review. — For comment on interpleader in Virginia, see 13 U. Rich. L. Rev. 331 (1979). For article reviewing recent developments and changes in legislation, case law, and Virginia Supreme Court Rules affecting civil litigation, see "Civil Practice and Procedure," see 40 U. Rich. L. Rev. 95 (2005).

Rule 3:16. New Parties.

A new party may be added, on motion of the plaintiff, by order of the court at any stage of the case as the ends of justice may require. The motion, accompanied by a properly executed proposed amended complaint, shall be served on the existing parties as required by Rule 1:12. If the motion is granted, the amended pleading accompanying the motion shall be deemed filed in the clerk's office as of the date of the court's order permitting such amendment and all the provisions of Rule 3:4 shall apply as to the new parties, but no writ tax, clerk's fee, or deposit for costs is required. All defendants shall file pleadings in response thereto as required by these Rules unless otherwise ordered by the court.

The amendment, effective May 2, 2011, adopted March 1, 2011, substituted "a properly executed proposed amended" for "an amended" in the second sentence, substituted "pleading accompanying the motion" for "complaint," inserted "as of the date of the court's order permitting such amendment" and deleted "as" following "Rule 3:4 shall" in the third sentence, and added "unless otherwise ordered by the court" at the end of the fourth sentence.

Michie's Jurisprudence. — For related discussion, see 1B M.J. Amendments, §§ 65, 80; 6B M.J. Ejectment, §§ 19, 23; 14A M.J. Parties, § 25.

CIRCUIT COURT OPINIONS

Addition of new parties. — Where the trial court lacked subject matter jurisdiction to grant the motion for summary judgment due to the injured party's failure to join the necessary parties, the trial court was permitted under § 8.01-5 and Rule 3:14 (now Rule 3:16) to add the necessary parties rather than dismiss the case. Hester v. State Farm Mut. Auto. Ins. Co., 58 Va. Cir. 289, 2002 Va. Cir. LEXIS 148 (Chesterfield County 2002) (decided under prior law).

Because a final order had not been entered on the employee's motion for a declaratory judgment, the defect of missing parties could be cured through proper procedural remedies; therefore, the matter did not need to be dismissed. Hester v. State Farm Mut. Auto. Ins. Co., 58 Va. Cir. 289, 2002 Va. Cir. LEXIS 148 (Chesterfield County 2002) (decided under prior law).

Rule 3:17. Substitution of Parties.

(a) *Substitution of a successor.* — If a person becomes incapable of prosecuting or defending because of death, disability, conviction of felony, removal from office, or other cause, a successor in interest may be substituted as a party in such person's place.

(b) *Motion, Consent, Procedure.* — Substitution shall be made on motion of the successor or of any party to the suit. If the successor does not make or consent to the motion, the party making the motion shall file the motion and a proposed amended pleading effecting the substitution in the clerk's office and serve a copy of the motion and the proposed amended pleading upon the party to be substituted in the manner prescribed by the Code of Virginia for serving original process upon such party. Unless the movant and the party to be substituted agree otherwise, or the court orders a different schedule, the party sought to be substituted shall file a written response to the motion for substitution within 21 days after service of the motion and proposed amended pleading upon the party sought to be substituted.

Michie's Jurisprudence. — For related discussion, see 1A M.J. Abatement, Survival and Revival, §§ 7 - 9, 34, 35, 38, 39, 41, 43; 2A M.J. Assignments, § 37; 7A M.J. Equity, § 96; 14A M.J. Parties, § 23.

CASE NOTES

Convict's privilege to waive appointment of committee. — There are no statutes or rules to deny a convict, already within the civil jurisdiction of the court at the time of his felony conviction and incarceration, the privilege of waiving the appointment of a committee, and proceeding to trial and judgment in a law action in which he is represented by counsel of his own choosing. Dunn v. Terry, 216 Va. 234, 217 S.E.2d 849 (1975) (decided under former Rule 3:15).

Rule 3:18. General Provisions as to Pleadings.

(a) *Pleadings.* — All motions in writing, including a motion for a bill of particulars and a motion to dismiss, whether filed in paper document format or as electronic or digitally imaged filings, are pleadings.

(b) *Allegation of negligence.* — An allegation of negligence or contributory negligence is sufficient without specifying the particulars of the negligence.

(c) *Contributory negligence as a defense.* — Contributory negligence shall not constitute a defense unless pleaded or shown by the plaintiff's evidence.

(d) *Pleading the statute of limitations.* — An allegation that an action is barred by the statute of limitations is sufficient without specifying the particular statute relied on.

(e) *Separate or combined filings.* — Answers, counterclaims, cross-claims, pleas, demurrers, affirmative defenses and motions may all be included in the same filing if they are separately identified in both the caption and the body of the filing.

Cross references. — As to practice and procedure in the general district courts, see Rules 7B:2 and 7B:3.

The amendment, effective May 2, 2011, adopted March 1, 2011, inserted "whether filed in paper document format or as electronic or digitally imaged filings," in subdivision (a); and in subdivision (e), substituted "filings" for "paper" in the catchline, substituted "filing" for "paper" and added "in both the caption and the body of the filing."

Michie's Jurisprudence. — For related discussion, see 1A M.J. Abatement, Survival and Revival, § 21; 1B M.J. Animals, § 24; 1B M.J. Appeal and Error, § 175; 2A M.J. Attachment and Garnishment, § 28; 2B M.J. Automobiles, § 81; 3A M.J. Bill of Particulars, §§ 2 - 7, 9 - 11, 15; 3A M.J. Bonds, § 5; 5C M.J. Damages, § 79; 5C M.J. Death by Wrongful Act, § 9; 6A M.J. Demurrers, §§ 1, 7, 31; 11B M.J. Jurisdiction, § 33; 12A M.J. Limitation of Actions, §§ 66, 68; 13A M.J. Motions for Judgment, § 16; 13B M.J. Negligence, §§ 43, 45, 48, 51; 14B M.J. Pleading, § 40; 19 M.J. Venue, § 20.

CASE NOTES

I. Decisions under Prior Law.
A. General Consideration.
B. Pleading Negligence.

I. DECISIONS UNDER PRIOR LAW.

A. General Consideration.

Effect on common law. — The rules of practice and procedure in actions at law eliminate common-law declarations and require a plaintiff to state his case in a written motion for judgment. Prior to the adoption of the rules, neither bills of particulars nor grounds of defense were regarded as a part of the pleadings. Miller v. Grier S. Johnson, Inc., 191 Va. 768, 62 S.E.2d 870 (1951).

Motion to reject motion for summary judgment. — Appellant's written motion to reject appellee's motion for a summary judgment is a pleading. Blair, Inc. v. Norfolk Redevelopment & Hous. Auth., 200 Va. 815, 108 S.E.2d 259 (1959).

In Virginia practice, there is a distinct difference between an affirmative defense and a counterclaim. City of Hopewell v. Cogar, 237 Va. 264, 377 S.E.2d 385 (1989).

The trial court erred in refusing to grant plaintiff's motion for nonsuit where the pleadings were properly labelled an affirmative defense, treated by defendants as an affirmative defense and not identified as a counterclaim and under these circumstances, defendants could not be heard to say that what they identified as an affirmative defense actually was a counterclaim. City of Hopewell v. Cogar, 237 Va. 264, 377 S.E.2d 385 (1989).

B. Pleading Negligence.

Driving under the influence of intoxicants is a particular of negligence which is not required to be specified in the pleadings. Ragsdale v. Jones, 202 Va. 278, 117 S.E.2d 114 (1960).

Pleading contributory negligence in federal court. — The trial court's decision to permit a party to amend its complaint at trial to incorporate the defense theory of contributory negligence was a proper exercise of its discretion under Federal Rule of Civil Procedure 15(b). Subdivision (d) of this rule does not create substantive law which supersedes the liberal amendment provisions of Federal Rule of Civil Procedure 15(b). For the purpose of determining whether the Federal Rules of Civil Procedure apply, the Virginia rules are clearly procedural. A constitutionally valid federal rule must be given effect in district court, even if it would supply a different result than would state law. Seidman v. Fishburne-Hudgins Educ. Found., Inc., 724 F.2d 413 (4th Cir. 1984).

CIRCUIT COURT OPINIONS

Pleading negligence. — Rule permitted plaintiffs to generally allege negligence, without specifying all the facts giving rise to its negligence claim. Tanner v. Mobil Oil Corp., 54 Va. Cir. 90, 2000 Va. Cir. LEXIS 550 (Fairfax County 2000) (decided under former Rule 3:16).

Patient sufficiently alleged negligence against two doctors and a medical association (physician defendants) by alleging that they negligently prescribed medications that were, inter alia, unsuited to the patient's condition, and information regarding the medical condition, the types of medications, and which defendant prescribed which medication constituted particulars which did not have to be alleged. Elliott v. Cook, 60 Va. Cir. 1, 2002 Va. Cir. LEXIS 121 (Loudoun County 2002) (decided under former Rule 3:16).

Demurrer was sustained as to a patient's allegation in a motion for judgment that two doctors and a medical association (physician defendants) were negligent in "such other ways" as might come to light during discovery, as this allegation stated no facts and failed to inform the physician defendants of the true nature of the claim. Elliott v. Cook, 60 Va. Cir. 1, 2002 Va. Cir. LEXIS 121 (Loudoun County 2002) (decided under former Rule 3:16).

Amended complaint asserting a wrongful death claim against firefighters did not need to state all the details of the firefighters' alleged negligence; specifically, the administrator did not need to assert every single item of the firefighters' failure to follow their training manuals. Furthermore, the amended complaint did state that the firefighters deviated from their training procedures by failing to properly search for the decedent. Chiles v. Dunn, 2010 Va. Cir. LEXIS 239 (Fairfax County Dec. 29, 2010).

An allegation of negligence is sufficient without specifying the particulars of the negligence. — In an action stemming from an accident between a automobile and a tractor trailer, with respect to the objection that the passenger's complaint was insufficient as a matter of law in that it contained only vague and generic allegations, Va. Sup. Ct. R. 3:18(b) provided that an allegation of negligence was sufficient without specifying the particulars of the negligence. Dudley v. Cash, 82 Va. Cir. 1, 2010 Va. Cir. LEXIS 257 (Augusta County Mar. 25, 2010).

Administratrix did not have to allege the particulars of negligence under Va. Sup. Ct. R. 3:18(b) as she alleged sufficient facts to show that an electric cooperative had a duty as it knew, or should have known, of the danger created by an active overhead power line at a construction site, and that failure to perform the duty imposed on the cooperative was negligence; by alleging negligence, the administratrix alleged that the cooperative failed to perform that duty. Rodriguez v. N. Va. Elec. Coop., 79 Va. Cir. 266, 2009 Va. Cir. LEXIS 236 (Loudoun County Sept. 14, 2009).

Pleading gross negligence. — When an allegedly injured party claimed he slipped and fell due to an airport's gross negligence, Va. Sup. Ct. R. 3:18(b) did not require the party to plead gross negligence with greater particularity than simple negligence as Rule 3:18(b), under which an allegation of negligence was sufficient without specifying its particulars, did not differentiate between the varying degrees of negligence or the requirements to properly plead any of them, so, inferentially, gross negligence did not have to be pled differntly than any other degree of negligence, and, given the Rule's unambiguous language, had higher degrees of negligence required particularity when pled, the Rule would have so provided. Cunningham v. Roanoke Reg'l Airport Comm'n, 70 Va. Cir. 273, 2006 Va. Cir. LEXIS 25 (Roanoke 2006).

Partial summary judgment awarded on lessee's motion for summary judgment. — Because a lessee timely exercised her option to purchase under a lease contract, and hence, granted partial summary judgment on that issue, she was denied complete summary judgment on her specific performance claim, as contested factual matters remained related to her equitable burdens and regarding the specifics of the financing agreement, and such had to be resolved through further proceedings. Stevens v. Miller, 73 Va. Cir. 160, 2007 Va. Cir. LEXIS 28 (Portsmouth 2007).

Partial summary judgment granted. — Given a general contractor's admissions and concessions regarding its liability to its subcontractor on a specific invoice, the subcontractor was granted partial summary judgment as to said liability. But, because the general contractor's breach of contract and tortious interference claims raised a material fact issue, it was entitled to a trial on said claims, barring summary judgment. Gov't Telecomms., Inc. v. Verizon Fed. Inc., 74 Va. Cir. 373, 2007 Va. Cir. LEXIS 196 (Fairfax County 2007).

Summary judgment and sufficiency of pleading regarding tribe's rights. — Where an Indian tribe alleged that a proposed reservoir would infringe its water rights and rights under the 1677 Treaty at Middle Plantation, its treaty claims survived summary judgment because factual issues existed as to the ambiguous nature of the Treaty's language and the intent and meaning of its provisions; however, the tribe failed to sufficiently plead necessity as to its reserved water rights claim. Mattaponi Indian Tribe v. Commonwealth, 72 Va. Cir. 444, 2007 Va. Cir. LEXIS 155 (Newport News 2007).

Rule 3:19. Default.

(a) *Failure Timely to Respond.* — A defendant who fails timely to file a responsive pleading as prescribed in Rule 3:8 is in default. A defendant in default is not entitled to notice of any further proceedings in the case, including notice to take depositions, except that written notice of any further proceedings shall be given to counsel of record, if any. The defendant in default is deemed to have waived any right to trial of issues by jury.

(b) *Relief from Default.* — Prior to the entry of judgment, for good cause shown the court may grant leave to a defendant who is in default to file a late responsive pleading. Relief from default may be conditioned by the court upon such defendant reimbursing any extra costs and fees, including attorney's fees, incurred by the plaintiff solely as a result of the delay in the filing of a responsive pleading by the defendant.

(c) *Default Judgment and Damages.* — (1) Except in suits for divorce or annulling a marriage, the court shall, on motion of the plaintiff, enter judgment for the relief appearing to the court to be due. When service of process is effected by posting, no judgment by default shall be entered until the requirements of Code § 8.01-296(2)(b) have been satisfied.

(2) If the relief demanded is unliquidated damages, the court shall hear evidence and fix the amount thereof, unless the plaintiff demands trial by jury, in which event, a jury shall be impaneled to fix the amount of damages.

(3) If a defendant participates in the hearing to determine the amount of damages such defendant may not offer proof or argument on the issues of liability, but may (i) object to the plaintiff's evidence regarding damages, (ii) offer evidence regarding the quantum of damages, (iii) participate in jury selection if a jury will hear the damage

inquiry, (iv) submit proposed jury instructions regarding damages, and (v) make oral argument on the issues of damages.

(d) *Relief from Default Judgment.* —

(1) *Within 21 Days.* — During the period provided by Rule 1:1 for the modification, vacation or suspension of a judgment, the court may by written order relieve a defendant of a default judgment after consideration of the extent and causes of the defendant's delay in tendering a responsive pleading, whether service of process and actual notice of the claim were timely provided to the defendant, and the effect of the delay upon the plaintiff. Relief from default may be conditioned by the court upon the defendant reimbursing any extra costs and fees, including attorney's fees, incurred by the plaintiff solely as a result of the delay in the filing of a responsive pleading by the defendant.

(2) *After 21 Days.* — A final judgment no longer within the jurisdiction of the trial court under Rule 1:1 may not be vacated by that court except as provided in Virginia Code §§ 8.01-428 and 8.01-623.

Cross references. — As to civil practice and procedure in the general district courts, see Rule 7B:9. As to the validity of default judgments entered against defendants in military service, see 50 U.S.C.S. Appx. § 521.

Michie's Jurisprudence. — For related discussion, see 2A M.J. Appearances, §§ 6, 7; 5A M.J. Courts, § 10; 5C M.J. Damages, §§ 87, 93; 6A M.J. Divorce and Alimony, §§ 32, 44; 7A M.J. Equity, §§ 70, 97, 116, 117, 146; 11A M.J. Judgments and Decrees, § 199; 19 M.J. Trial, §§ 2, 3, 7.

Law Review. — For annual survey of Virginia law article, "Civil Practice and Procedure," see 47 U. Rich. L. Rev. 113 (2012).

CASE NOTES

I. Decisions under Current Law.
II. Decisions under Prior Law.
A. General Consideration.
B. Unliquidated Damages.

I. DECISIONS UNDER CURRENT LAW.

Default judgment upheld. — Because some of a corporation's claims on appeal from an order entering a default judgment against it, and refusing to set the same aside, were either not plead to the court below or were not supported by the record, which was incomplete on its face, the lower court's orders were affirmed. Prince Seating Corp. v. Rabideau, 275 Va. 468, 659 S.E.2d 305, 2008 Va. LEXIS 45 (2008).

Circuit court did not abuse its discretion in denying a corporate lender relief from default under Va. Sup. Ct. R. 3:19(b) because the lender had notice that an answer was to be filed by an attorney licensed to practice law in Virginia, but the lender's vice president signed the answer on behalf of the lender. Furthermore, in the following nearly one-month period, the lender failed to retain counsel, did not have any representative appear at a hearing on a motion to strike the lender's answer, and, despite numerous opportunities, the lender provided the circuit court no explanation for the lender's failure to appear at the hearing on the motion to strike its answer and for entry of default. AME Fin. Corp. v. Kiritsis, 281 Va. 384, 707 S.E.2d 820, 2011 Va. LEXIS 49 (2011).

A trial court is not required to find "actual notice" to a defendant or to articulate its consideration of and findings with regard to the factors listed in Va. Sup. Ct. R. 3:19(d)(1) when denying a motion for relief from a default judgment. Specialty Hosps. of Wash., LLC v. Rappahannock Goodwill Indus., 283 Va. 348, 722 S.E.2d 557, 2012 Va. LEXIS 39 (2012).

II. DECISIONS UNDER PRIOR LAW.

A. General Consideration.

Motion for judgment failing to state cause of action. — A default judgment may be invalidated when the motion for judgment fails to state a cause of action; under such circumstances, that failure is held to disable the court from entering a valid default judgment. Landcraft Co. v. Kincaid, 220 Va. 865, 263 S.E.2d 419 (1980).

When judgment valid. — As a general proposition, a default judgment is valid if the trial court had territorial jurisdiction, subject-matter jurisdiction and if adequate notice has been given to the defaulting party. Landcraft Co. v. Kincaid, 220 Va. 865, 263 S.E.2d 419 (1980).

Where defendant had been personally served and plaintiff had strictly complied with all the formalities of rules of pleading and the motion for judgment stated a cause of action, the trial court erred in vacating a default judgment, there being no errors on which an appellate court might reverse and no cognizable mistake. Landcraft Co. v. Kincaid, 220 Va. 865, 263 S.E.2d 419 (1980).

Default resulting from filing invalid pleading. — A defendant was in default for failing to file a timely responsive pleading where the pleading she had filed was invalid in that it was not signed by the defendant or a member of the Virginia State Bar but by an attorney who was licensed to practice in another state. Nelson v. Gecelosky, No. 0242-00-4, 2000 Va. App. LEXIS 502 (Ct. of Appeals July 11, 2000) (decided under former Rule 2:7).

Failure of defendant to plead responsively to the plaintiff's motion for judgment for

wrongful death was an admission that the plaintiff was entitled to recover some damages from him. Inherent in that admission was the acknowledgement by defendant of the negligence charged against him as proximately causing the collision and the concession that plaintiff's deceased was free of contributory negligence. Thus, under the circumstances of this case, the only issue before the trial court when it acted upon the plaintiff's motion for default was the amount of damages to be awarded for the death of the deceased; and it was the court's duty, sitting without a jury, to fix such damages. With defendant's failure to plead given its full effect, any evidence as to the manner in which the accident occurred was irrelevant and immaterial to the situation with which the court was ultimately confronted. Funkhouser v. Million, 209 Va. 89, 161 S.E.2d 725 (1968).

No default for not responding. — State commission was not in default for not responding to state regulation challenger's petition, as the state regulation challenger did not observe the proper procedural requirements in serving the state commission with process. Bender v. Va. Marine Res. Comm'n, No. 1783-02-1, 2003 Va. App. LEXIS 253 (Ct. of Appeals Apr. 29, 2003) (decided under former Rule 2:7).

Presentation of testimony by plaintiff at hearing does not waive right to default judgment. — In view of the plaintiff's continued insistence throughout the proceedings upon his right to a default judgment, his action in presenting testimony at the ex parte hearing did not constitute a waiver of such right. Nor should such testimony be given the effect of disproving the negligence of defendant and conclusively showing the contributory negligence of the deceased. Such testimony should not have been considered because it was irrelevant and immaterial to the sole issue of damages before the court at the time it ruled upon the motion for default judgment. Funkhouser v. Million, 209 Va. 89, 161 S.E.2d 725 (1968).

Pleadings of a codefendant, on file at the time of the ex parte hearing, did not inure to the benefit of the defendant against whom a default judgment was sought, where, at the time of decision, the codefendant had been nonsuited as a party, and its pleadings were no longer entitled to legal efficacy. It is the date of the ruling upon the motion for default judgment, and not the time of the ex parte hearing, which is controlling, and at that crucial point, defendant's default was just as complete and of the same effect under the rules as though the codefendant had never pleaded. Funkhouser v. Million, 209 Va. 89, 161 S.E.2d 725 (1968).

Confession is sufficient proof of all matters properly and specifically pleaded. — Where a bill is taken for confessed the confession is sufficient proof of all matters of fact properly and specifically pleaded in the bill. If these allegations of fact be sufficiently definite to base a final decree thereon, the plaintiff may have such a decree at once, without further grace to the defendant. Shocket v. Silberman, 209 Va. 490, 165 S.E.2d 414 (1969) (decided under prior law).

Jurisdiction. — Section 8.01-288 did not cure the defective process, as the statute cured only defects in the manner process was served, not defects in the process itself, and notwithstanding the service's actual notice of the proceedings, the trial court lacked jurisdiction to enter the default judgment; nothing in § 8.01-296 or Rule 3:17 (now Rule 3:19) purported to validate jurisdiction of a trial court when the trial court had not otherwise acquired jurisdiction over the defendant. Lifestar Response of Md., Inc. v. Vegosen, 267 Va. 720, 594 S.E.2d 589, 2004 Va. LEXIS 64 (2004).

Default judgment upheld. — A default judgment entered against a defendant was held not in error where although a notice of motion for judgment was personally served on defendant and the face of the notice stated that defendant had 21 days to respond, defendant nevertheless failed to respond. Jackson v. Jackson, 236 Va. 199, 372 S.E.2d 155 (1988).

Purpose of rule. — Former Rule 2:7 was designed to expedite the cause by commanding a timely presentation of defenses and thus prevent a delay through dilatory tactics on the part of defendant. Westfall v. Westfall, 196 Va. 97, 82 S.E.2d 487 (1954) (decided under prior law).

Former Rule 2:17 inapplicable to divorce suit. — Former Rule 2:17, dispensing with the notice of taking proofs "to any defendant as to whom a bill stands taken for confessed," is not applicable to a divorce suit, because such a bill is not taken for confessed. Hence, unless lack of notice or an irregularity in a notice to take depositions in a divorce suit is waived by appearance, there must be proof of service or acceptance of service of proper notice. Baker v. Baker, 194 Va. 284, 72 S.E.2d 632 (1952).

Unless defendant in divorce suit is proceeded against by publication. — When a respondent has been duly summoned by publication and has not appeared in person or by counsel within the period allowed, no notice of the taking of the depositions is required unless ordered by the court. Owens v. Owens, 197 Va. 681, 90 S.E.2d 776 (1956).

If a defendant in a divorce case is proceeded against by order of publication, or its equivalent, and fails to appear, notice of the taking of depositions is not necessary, unless ordered by the court. In all other divorce cases, such a notice is required. It is one of those procedural steps to which careful scrutiny must be afforded. Where such a notice is required, it should clearly appear, from the record, that proper notice was served, or was accepted by the opposite party, or was waived by him. Mackey v. Mackey, 203 Va. 526, 125 S.E.2d 194 (1962).

B. Unliquidated Damages.

Defaulting defendants may participate in a trial on the question of unliquidated damages to the same extent they would have been permitted if they were defending on the merits, except for the right to object to the admissibility of plaintiff's evidence, which is specifically prohibited. Chappell v. Smith, 208 Va. 272, 156 S.E.2d 572 (1967).

Since default is not concession of amount of unliquidated damages claim. — The effect of the failure of a defendant to plead within the time prescribed by Rule 3:5 (now Rule 3:8) is that he cannot defend on the merits of the case and he admits that plaintiff is entitled to recover some damages, however small. However, he does not concede the amount of damages on an unliquidated claim. This rule provides the procedure for ascertaining damages after defendant is in default. Where damages are unliquidated, this rule provides that the court or the jury shall hear evidence and fix the amount of damages. Funkhouser v. Million, 209 Va. 89, 161 S.E.2d 725 (1968).

CIRCUIT COURT OPINIONS

Federal court answer did not replace state court responsive pleadings. — After an insurer twice tried unsuccessfully to remove plaintiff's action to enforce a life insurance policy to federal court, plaintiff was entitled to a default judgment, the insurer was not entitled to an extension of time to respond, and its motion for reconsideration was denied; although removal suspended state court proceedings, the time to respond in state court elapsed before the second removal, an answer filed by the insurer in federal court did not replace state court responsive pleadings, plaintiff was prejudiced by the insurer's inordinate delay, and there was no reasonable basis for an extension. Wynn v. Allstate Life Ins. Co., 69 Va. Cir. 55, 2005 Va. Cir. LEXIS 347 (Richmond 2005).

Default is not concession of amount of damages. — Insurer's failure to respond to a suit by homeowners who alleged they breached the insurance contract, among other claims, by failing to pay them for the loss of their home due to fire, was a default and the trial court took the bill of complaint to be confessed. The only issue remaining to be decided was the amount of the homeowners' damages, and the insurer was allowed to present evidence and contest the amount of damages to be awarded. Le Morzellec v. Loudoun Mut. Ins. Co., 2004 Va. Cir. LEXIS 218 (Fairfax County July 26, 2004) (decided under prior law).

Not entitled to relief from default. — In an action for construction of the rights under a declaration of trust, a default judgment pursuant to Va. Sup. Ct. R. 3:19(a) was proper because defense counsel failed to timely file responsive pleadings pursuant to Va. Sup. Ct. R. 3:8. The beneficiaries were not entitled to relief from the default because service of process and actual notice of the claim were timely provided, the delay in filing the responsive pleadings was inexcusable, and, if relief were granted, the trustee would have suffered an unfair consequence of faithfully following procedural rules while the beneficiaries disregarded them. Wyczalkowski v. Carter, 78 Va. Cir. 300, 2009 Va. Cir. LEXIS 164 (Loudoun County May 5, 2009).

Notice of intent to seek default judgment not required. — Guarantor's motion to set aside a default judgment was denied, as constructive service of the motion under § 8.01-329 was properly effectuated, notice of an intent to seek default judgment was not required where such was made by praecipe, and any intrinsic fraud that did occur was insufficient to set the judgment aside under § 8.01-428; further, the guarantor's lack of diligence in checking his mail did not render the address incorrect for purposes of constructive service. Pallett Recycling, LLC v. Case, 70 Va. Cir. 125, 2006 Va. Cir. LEXIS 13 (Rockingham County 2006).

Defendant having filed no responsive pleadings, the fact that she appeared and argued before the court did not make her "counsel of record" under Va. Sup. Ct. R. 1:4(1); therefore, she was not entitled to notice of plaintiff's motion for entry of default judgment. Moreover, having been mailed a copy of the motion, she received sufficient notice under Va. Sup. Ct. R. 3:19(a). Brin v. A Home Come True, Inc., 74 Va. Cir. 45, 2007 Va. Cir. LEXIS 36 (Fairfax County 2007).

Default resulting from filing invalid pleading. — Motion filed by a limited liability company (LLC) for leave to submit its answer late was denied, and default judgment was entered in favor of plaintiff because the failure of the LLC's system for receiving and responding to service of process, without any showing of circumstances that were sufficiently compelling, did not constitute a reasonable or legal excuse for the LLC's failure to comply with the filing requirements; the LLC was aware of plaintiff's action, it failed to adjust its e-mail system to receive messages from its registered agent despite its knowledge of the pending action, and counsel could not establish that anyone monitored the action for service. Ellis v. Danville Reg'l Med. Ctr., 75 Va. Cir. 301, 2008 Va. Cir. LEXIS 217 (Danville July 1, 2008).

Entry of default judgment denied. — Although defendant was in default, pursuant to Va. Sup. Ct. R. 3:19(c)(1), the circuit court declined to grant plaintiff's motion for entry of a default judgment because plaintiff failed to show his entitlement to the requested relief: (1) plaintiff's claims arose from an alleged oral contract with defendant, pursuant to which defendant agreed to transfer his property to plaintiff if plaintiff cured defendant's mortgage default and thereafter made necessary payments for the property; (2) the Statute of Frauds applied to the contract; (3) the court could not impose a constructive trust on defendant's property because plaintiff did not present any corroborating evidence to support his claim that the oral contract existed, which evidence was necessary to overcome the Statute of Frauds and to support imposition of a constructive trust; and (4) although plaintiff might be able to recover damages based on a quantum meruit theory, he could only recover his net expenses, and he failed to present any evidence showing how much he had received in rent from the property or the precise net amount that he had expended on the property. Richardson v. Richardson, 72 Va. Cir. 316, 2006 Va. Cir. LEXIS 208 (Arlington County 2006).

Plaintiff was not entitled to a default judgment under Va. Sup. Ct. R. 3:19(a) and 3:8(a) as plaintiff had not exercised due diligence as required by § 8.01-275.1 and Va. Sup. Ct. R. 3:5(e) to allow service of process more than one year after the filing of the suit since: (1) plaintiff used an address that had been determined to be a vacant building in a prior suit to attempt service; (2) plaintiff did not attempt personal service of process at the address provided on the accident information exchange form and the accident report; and (3) plaintiff's first use of the address on the accident information exchange form and the accident report was when plaintiff sought service through the Secretary of the Commonwealth of Virginia under subsection B of

§ 8.01-329. Shears v. Slade, 73 Va. Cir. 20, 2006 Va. Cir. LEXIS 298 (Newport News 2006).

Entry of default judgment granted. — Medical clinic failed to file a responsive pleading in a medical malpractice action as required by Va. Sup. Ct. R. 3:8. Because the clinic was in default according to Va. Sup. Ct. R. 3:19, and the clinic had failed to request a late responsive filing, it was appropriate to enter default as to the clinic. Youngblood v. Fasano, 81 Va. Cir. 260, 2010 Va. Cir. LEXIS 117 (Fairfax Oct. 4, 2010).

Untimely filing. — Trial court denied the claimant's motion for default or other relief, as even though the alleged wrongdoer's amended answer was filed three days beyond the time allotted for filing it, the trial court had the discretion to extend the time for filing, the late filing was not made for the purpose of gaining a tactical advantage or otherwise in bad faith, and the pleading sufficiently complied with the requirements of § 8.01-271.1, Va. Sup. Ct. R. 1:4(a), and the trial court's orders. Fletcher v. Inova Health Care Servs., 71 Va. Cir. 331, 2006 Va. Cir. LEXIS 142 (Fairfax County 2006).

Extension of time in which to file response. — Trial court could exercise discretion in allowing defense counsel to file a late answer in a medical malpractice case, even though he was technically in default, where there was no showing of bad faith. Defense counsel promptly acted once he realized that he had inadvertently failed to file the answer, and the entry of a default judgment on liability would be an extremely harsh consequence for the blameless defendant parties. Nauman v. Samuels, 73 Va. Cir. 411, 2007 Va. Cir. LEXIS 227 (Charlottesville July 10, 2007).

Passenger's motion for judgment by default was denied, and an airline's motion to file late responsive pleadings was granted because there was no intent to delay the proceedings or otherwise prejudice the rights of the passenger, the airline would be greatly prejudiced if the motion for a default judgment was granted, and the delay did not work a prejudice to the passenger's pursuit of her action for damages since the passenger showed no injury to her ability to pursue her claim, other than the expenditure of fees and costs in connection with the motions; within a week of being served, the airline's counsel contacted the owner's claims manager respecting a response to the claim, and because they had limited dealings with each other, that reasonably explained the subsequent confusion over who would be filing a timely response, and promptly upon the passenger's filing of the motion for default, the airline sought leave to file a late response. Sanders v. Shuttle Am., 75 Va. Cir. 378, 2008 Va. Cir. LEXIS 262 (Loudoun County Aug. 15, 2008).

Rule 3:20. Summary Judgment.

Any party may make a motion for summary judgment at any time after the parties are at issue, except in an action for divorce or for annulment of marriage. If it appears from the pleadings, the orders, if any, made at a pretrial conference, the admissions, if any, in the proceedings, or, upon sustaining a motion to strike the evidence, that the moving party is entitled to judgment, the court shall enter judgment in that party's favor. Summary judgment, interlocutory in nature, may be entered as to the undisputed portion of a contested claim or on the issue of liability alone although there is a genuine issue as to the amount of damages. Summary judgment shall not be entered if any material fact is genuinely in dispute. No motion for summary judgment or to strike the evidence shall be sustained when based in whole or in part upon any discovery depositions under Rule 4:5, unless all parties to the action shall agree that such deposition may be so used, or unless the motion is brought in accordance with the provisions of subsection B of § 8.01-420.

Cross references. — See Rule 4:8(e).

The amendment effective July 1, 2013, adopted June 21, 2013, added "or unless the motion is brought in accordance with the provisions of subsection B of § 8.01-420" at the end of the fifth sentence.

Michie's Jurisprudence. — For related discussion, see 1B M.J. Appeal and Error, § 186; 6A M.J. Discovery, § 32; 7B M.J. Evidence, § 296; 11A M.J. Judgments and Decrees, §§ 217.1, 217.3, 217.4; 11B M.J. Jury, § 12; 13B M.J. Negligence, § 68; 19 M.J. Trial, § 5.

CASE NOTES

Editor's note. — Most of the cases annotated below were decided under former Rule 3:18.

Purpose of rule. — This rule was adopted to provide trial courts with authority to bring litigation to an end at an early stage, when it clearly appears that one of the parties is entitled to judgment within the framework of the case as made out. Its purpose is to expedite litigation with as few technicalities as possible and thus avoid common-law procedural tactics interposed for delay, but it does not substitute a new method of trial where an issue of fact exists. Carwile v. Richmond Newspapers, Inc., 196 Va. 1, 82 S.E.2d 588 (1954).

The purpose of this rule is to expedite litigation with as few technicalities as possible and thus avoid common-law procedural tactics interposed for delay. But this rule does not substitute a new method of trial where an issue of fact exists. Leslie v. Nitz, 212 Va. 480, 184 S.E.2d 755 (1971).

Rule applies only where no trial is necessary. — This rule provides for summary judgment in those cases that cannot be reached by demurrer in which the only dispute concerns a pure question of law. It applies only to cases in which no trial is necessary because no evidence could affect the result. Carwile v. Richmond Newspapers, Inc., 196 Va. 1, 82 S.E.2d 588 (1954); Kasco Mills, Inc. v. Ferebee, 197 Va. 589, 90 S.E.2d 866 (1956); William Schluderberg-T.J. Kurdle Co. v. Trice, 198 Va. 85, 92 S.E.2d 374 (1956); Goode v. Courtney, 200 Va. 804, 108 S.E.2d 396 (1959); General Accident Fire & Life Assurance Corp. v. Cohen, 203 Va. 810, 127 S.E.2d 399 (1962).

Motion for summary judgment was properly denied where facts were in issue. Day v. Abernathy, 204 Va. 723, 133 S.E.2d 299 (1963); Blair, Inc. v. Norfolk Redevelopment & Hous. Auth., 200 Va. 815, 108 S.E.2d 259 (1959); Goode v. Courtney, 200 Va. 804, 108 S.E.2d 396 (1959); Slone v. GMC, 249 Va. 520, 457 S.E.2d 51 (1995).

And summary judgment is error if issues of fact are in dispute. — The entry of summary judgment on the basis of facts appearing at the pretrial conference was error where issues of fact were in dispute which should have been settled by a jury. Kasco Mills, Inc. v. Ferebee, 197 Va. 589, 90 S.E.2d 866 (1956); Owens v. Redd, 215 Va. 13, 205 S.E.2d 669 (1974).

Dismissal erroneous where facts in dispute as to discovery of fraud. — The record showed that material facts were genuinely in dispute respecting when the plaintiff discovered, or by the exercise of due diligence should have discovered, the alleged fraud, and the trial court erred in summarily dismissing the fraud count. Gilmore v. Basic Indus., Inc., 233 Va. 485, 357 S.E.2d 514 (1987).

Motion should state grounds and otherwise meet requirements of rules. — When the motion for summary judgment is appropriate it should state the grounds upon which it is filed and otherwise meet the requirements of the rules with respect to pleadings. Carwile v. Richmond Newspapers, Inc., 196 Va. 1, 82 S.E.2d 588 (1954).

Effect of changing the language of this rule from "admissions, if any, in a deposition ..." to "admissions, if any, in the proceedings ..." was to broaden and extend what a trial court could consider in passing on motions for summary judgment. Leslie v. Nitz, 212 Va. 480, 184 S.E.2d 755 (1971).

Not substitute for demurrer or motion to strike. — Motion for summary judgment is not intended as a substitute for a demurrer, a demurrer to the evidence or a motion to strike. Carwile v. Richmond Newspapers, Inc., 196 Va. 1, 82 S.E.2d 588 (1954); Goode v. Courtney, 200 Va. 804, 108 S.E.2d 396 (1959).

A motion to strike is in effect a motion for summary judgment, which is not to be granted if any material fact is genuinely in dispute. Costner v. Lackey, 223 Va. 377, 290 S.E.2d 818 (1982).

And doubts resolved in favor of nonmoving party. — In considering a motion to strike the plaintiff's evidence, a trial court is required to resolve any reasonable doubt as to the sufficiency of the evidence in favor of the plaintiff. Costner v. Lackey, 223 Va. 377, 290 S.E.2d 818 (1982).

Standard for considering motion for summary judgment. — A court in considering a motion for summary judgment must adopt those inferences from the facts that are most favorable to the nonmoving party, unless the inferences are strained, forced, or contrary to reason. Carson ex rel. Meredith v. LeBlanc, 245 Va. 135, 427 S.E.2d 189 (1993).

Inferences must favor party whose evidence is to be stricken. — Although the inferences to be drawn from the evidence may differ in degree of probability, courts deciding upon motions for summary judgment must adopt those inferences most favorable to the party whose evidence it is sought to have struck, unless the inferences are strained, forced, or contrary to reason. Bloodworth v. Ellis, 221 Va. 18, 267 S.E.2d 96 (1980).

Cross-motions for summary judgment. — The filing of cross-motions for summary judgment does not, in itself, resolve the question whether material facts remain genuinely in dispute. Town of Ashland v. Ashland Inv. Co., 235 Va. 150, 366 S.E.2d 100 (1988).

Court's duty not obviated by cross motions. — A court's duty to ascertain whether facts remain in dispute or whether there are sufficient facts to decide the question presented is not obviated by cross motions for summary judgment. Central Nat'l Ins. Co. v. Virginia Farm Bureau Mut. Ins. Co., 222 Va. 353, 282 S.E.2d 4 (1981).

Summary judgment allows trial courts to bring litigation to an end at an early stage. — While summary judgment rules and discovery rules are not intended to substitute a new method for trial when an issue of fact exists, these rules were adopted to allow trial court to bring litigation to an end at an early stage when it clearly appeared that one of the parties was entitled to a judgment in the case as made out by the pleadings and the admissions of the parties. Carson ex rel. Meredith v. LeBlanc, 245 Va. 135, 427 S.E.2d 189 (1993).

Jury must resolve conflicts in evidence. — Where the evidence was in conflict on the question whether plaintiff breached a contract by failing to meet its completion schedule or whether defendant committed a breach by failing to comply with the payment schedule, it was for the jury, not the trial court, to resolve the conflict. Five Lakes, Inc. v. Randall, Inc., 214 Va. 4, 196 S.E.2d 906 (1973).

Where no motion for summary judgment had been served on a utility company, and the company was unaware that summary action was under consideration, it was a violation of due process for the State Corporation Commission to proceed sua sponte, reach its decision in camera, and in the process afford the utility company, an "interested person" entitled to "full and fair participation," no opportunity to be heard. VEPCO v. SCC, 226 Va. 541, 312 S.E.2d 25 (1984).

When existence of agency relationship is question of law. — Where a question of agency vel non rests upon written documents and the inferences deducible therefrom, the question is a question of law, for the construction of written documents is exclusively for the court. Thus, where the facts determinative of the question of actual agency were those contained in a license agreement, none of which was in dispute, the trial court did not exceed its authority in granting summary judgment. Murphy v. Holiday Inns, Inc., 216 Va. 490, 219 S.E.2d 874 (1975).

Failure to allow plaintiff to complete case in chief. — Although this rule allows a party to make a motion for summary judgment "at any time after the parties are at issue," trial court should have allowed plaintiff to complete his case in chief instead of preventing him from presenting all of his evidence during the trial by sustaining motions to strike the evidence and entering summary judgment after only plaintiff and a medical witness had testified. Any possible error was rendered harmless, however, because as the result of a stipulation the Virginia Supreme Court was able to consider all of the additional evidence which plaintiff would have offered had he been permitted to complete his case and such additional evidence was contained in discovery depositions which were a part of the record before the supreme court. Rouse v. Great Atl. & Pac. Tea Co., 216 Va. 293, 217 S.E.2d 891 (1975).

Authority of State Corporation Commission to enter summary judgment on prefiled evidence. — For purposes of due process, guidelines constraining authority to enter summary judgment on motion to strike the evidence and the principles upon which they rest apply with equal, if not greater, logic to the authority of the State Corporation Commission to enter summary judgment on prefiled evidence. In actions at law, all the issues are framed by adversary pleadings, discovery is conducted, and the plaintiff learns in advance what evidence will be necessary to survive a motion to strike. A public utility seeking a rate change is required to prefile its evidence without benefit of such forewarnings. VEPCO v. SCC, 226 Va. 541, 312 S.E.2d 25 (1984).

Conclusions of fact based on a summary judgment record had no binding effect whatsoever, in the context of appellate review, upon factual findings arising from a jury trial where the parties in the two cases were different, and where, unlike the summary judgment proceeding, the facts were fully developed. Commercial Bus. Sys. v. Halifax Corp., 253 Va. 292, 484 S.E.2d 892 (1997).

Plaintiff assigned as error the use of the depositions she introduced in the sovereign immunity hearing to decide the motion for summary judgment, absent her agreement. The ore tenus evidence cited above, however, supported the trial court's conclusions and there was nothing in the record to indicate the trial court used the depositions in deciding the summary judgment motion. Therefore, this assignment of error was without merit. Benjamin v. University Internal Medicine Found., 254 Va. 400, 492 S.E.2d 651 (1997).

Reliance on discovery depositions. — Trial court did not err in using the discovery deposition testimony from the patient's expert witness to sustain the surgeon's motion in limine that ultimately allowed for the granting of the surgeon's summary judgment motion. Although Va. Sup. Ct. R. 3:20 and § 8.01-420 normally kept parties from using discovery deposition testimony to support a summary judgment motion, the patient acquiesced by not objecting and the motion in limine was the functional equivalent of the summary judgment motion because granting the motion in limine allowed for the granting of the summary judgment motion. Lloyd v. Kime, 275 Va. 98, 654 S.E.2d 563, 2008 Va. LEXIS 13 (2008).

Inability to use depositions did not demonstrate that remand to state court would result in undue prejudice. — Personal injury action that a patron originally filed against a nightclub owner in state court to recover for injuries allegedly sustained in a barroom brawl was remanded to state court pursuant to 28 U.S.C.S. § 1447(e) because the patron's request to join nondiverse nightclub employees was not made to avoid federal jurisdiction, the patron's claims against the employees arose out of the same barroom brawl, the patron's delay in seeking joinder was not egregious, a denial of the patron's request for joinder would have resulted in significant injury to the patron, and the nightclub owner's inability to use two depositions in support of any summary judgment motion due to the operation of Va. Sup. Ct. R. 3:20 did not unduly prejudice the nightclub owner. Dobbs v. JBC of Norfolk, Va, Inc., 544 F. Supp. 2d 496, 2008 U.S. Dist. LEXIS 28614 (E.D. Va. 2008).

Motion to strike allowed. — Trial court did not err in granting a spouse's motion to strike the complaining spouse's complaint for divorce on the grounds of adultery and desertion because Va. Sup. Ct. R. 3:20 permitted the trial court to grant the spouse's motion to strike the evidence prior to the conclusion of the complaining spouse's case-in-chief. Jordan v. Jordan, 2012 Va. App. LEXIS 211 (June 26, 2012).

Entry of summary judgment held proper. — Trial court properly granted summary judgment to baseball clubs in a spectator's action to recover for injuries suffered when the spectator was hit with a foul ball; arguments advanced by the spectator, including the adequacy of warnings provided by the baseball clubs, and questions involving the lighting conditions and field dimensions at the stadium, did not present issues of fact that were material to the conclusion of law that was reached, because the spectator assumed the risk of being hit with a ball. Thurmond v. Prince William Prof'l Baseball Club, Inc., 265 Va. 59, 574 S.E.2d 246, 2003 Va. LEXIS 1 (2003).

Entry of summary judgment held error. — The trial judge, at the request of counsel, asked the jury foreman in the presence of all jurors if they had reached a unanimous opinion on the question of liability and the foreman replied that they had, but that the jury's difficulty was in arriving at a verdict with regard to the amount of damages the plaintiff should receive. In this case the jury had been instructed to return a general verdict. The exchange between the court and the jury foreman was not attended by the formalities normally associated with receiving a jury's verdict. There was no verdict in writing and the other jurors, while present, were not polled to ascertain if they agreed with this statement by the foreman. No verdict was rendered in the case and the trial court erred in entering summary judgment for the plaintiff and empaneling a jury to try only the issue of damages. Norfolk S. Ry. v. Fincham, 213 Va. 122, 189 S.E.2d 380 (1972).

Trial court erred in entering summary judgment for defendant automobile dealer after finding that the dealer was liable to the plaintiff bank and that the bank had been damaged by the dealer's breach of contract. United Va. Bank v. Dick Herriman Ford, Inc., 215 Va. 373, 210 S.E.2d 158 (1974).

It was error for the trial court to enter summary judgment, where plaintiffs' motion for judgment contained sufficient allegations of misconduct by defendant which, if supported by the proof, entitled the plaintiffs to an award of exemplary damages, and it was apparent that the exemplary damage claim was procedurally viable when the entry of summary judgment eliminated it. O'Brien v. Snow, 215 Va. 403, 210 S.E.2d 165 (1974).

Where considering the evidence as a whole and the alternative inferences it supported, reasonable men could have reached different conclusions as to whether the parties intended a blanket contract to cover a project such as the project in dispute, the trial court erred in sustaining the motion to strike and in entering summary judgment for the defendants. Richmond, F. & P.R.R. v. Sutton Co., 218 Va. 636, 238 S.E.2d 826 (1977).

Trial court erred in entering summary judgment under Va. Sup. Ct. R. 3:18 (now Rule 3:20) for a builder in the homeowners' suit for a violation of the Maryland Consumer Protection Act, Md. Code Ann., Commercial Law § 13-301 et seq.; the parties agreed that the discovery rule and § 8.01-248 were applicable, and reasonable minds could differ as to what notice a newspaper article gave to the homeowners. Hansen v. Stanley Martin Cos., 266 Va. 345, 585 S.E.2d 567, 2003 Va. LEXIS 80 (2003).

Where the chairperson of a school board sued a building inspector for malicious prosecution, summary judgment, under Va. Sup. Ct. R. 3:18 (now Rule 3:20), should not have been granted in favor of the building inspector, where the record did not show that the chairperson violated the law, and the chairperson's status as chairperson did not result in vicarious liability; the chairperson had been criminally charged with failure to obtain a building permit and concealing work prior to inspection, in violation of the Virginia Uniform Statewide Building Code, and the prosecutor decided to nolle prosequi the charges. Andrews v. Ring, 266 Va. 311, 585 S.E.2d 780, 2003 Va. LEXIS 86 (2003).

Appellants' suit to enforce a restrictive covenant was improperly dismissed on summary judgment, as the covenant did not, as appellee argued, authorize three-fourths of the subdivision's lot owners to grant the owner of appellee's lot a perpetual release of that lot from the covenant, but merely allowed an owner to make one-time re-subdivision of its lot with consent of three-fourths of the owners. Barris v. Keswick Homes, L.L.C., 268 Va. 67, 597 S.E.2d 54, 2004 Va. LEXIS 81 (2004).

Summary judgment was improperly granted to a physician's employer after a patient's claims against the physician were dismissed with prejudice because a review of the trial court's order mandated the conclusion that the dismissal of the physician "with prejudice" did not have any preclusive effect on the patient's ability to pursue her claims against the employer. The order plainly stated that the patient was entitled to proceed against the employer based on the pending allegations, and since the patient's entire case depended on her proof of the physician's negligent acts, the order's dismissal of the physician "with prejudice" did not equate to an adjudication on the merits so as to preclude the patient's ability to litigate matters relating to the physician's allegedly negligent conduct in pursuing her claims against the employer. Shutler v. Augusta Health Care for Women, P.L.C., 272 Va. 87, 630 S.E.2d 313, 2006 Va. LEXIS 65 (2006).

Applied in Smith v. Mountjoy, 280 Va. 46, 694 S.E.2d 598, 2010 Va. LEXIS 76 (2010).

CIRCUIT COURT OPINIONS

Editor's note. — Most of the cases below were decided under prior law.

Failure to respond. — Where a court had jurisdiction due to defendants' general appearance and where an owner did not respond to defendants' Va. Sup. Ct. R. 4:11 requests for admission, the matters were deemed admitted; therefore, the defendants were entitled to summary judgment. Martin v. Taylor, 61 Va. Cir. 582, 2001 Va. Cir. LEXIS 515 (Franklin County 2001).

Failure to state a sufficient cause of action. — Summary judgment was denied to an insurance agent where failure to state a sufficient cause of action was improperly under the summary judgment motion and facts were disputed. Rowland v. State Farm Fire & Cas. Co., 64 Va. Cir. 16, 2003 Va. Cir. LEXIS 201 (Fairfax County 2003).

Motion for summary judgment denied. — Summary judgment motion by real estate agency was denied where real estate agent was agent, not independent contractor, and issues of fact remained as to whether: (1) the real estate agent made representations to the buyers in his capacity as real estate agent or owner; (2) the agency could be held liable for the real estate agent's actions due to apparent authority; (3) the agency was liable for the real estate agent's actions as he was serving his personal interest; and (4) the real estate agent's actions should be imputed to the agency. Steffan v. Freemason Assocs., Inc., 60 Va. Cir. 216, 2002 Va. Cir. LEXIS 389 (Norfolk 2002). See also ; Stanley v. Storck, 63 Va. Cir. 628, 2002 Va. Cir. LEXIS 433 (Norfolk 2002); Lynchburg Communs. Sys. v. Ohio State Cellular Phone Co., 63 Va. Cir. 544, 2004 Va. Cir. LEXIS 2 (Roanoke 2004); Union Ins. Co. v. Coverage Inc., 2004 Va. Cir. LEXIS 23 (Fairfax County Feb. 9, 2004).

Summary judgment is error if issues of fact are in dispute. — Although plaintiff landlord asserted that defendant subtenant's negligent use of a stove in an apartment caused a fire, and defendant tenant opined in an interrogatory that the subtenant acted negligently, such opinions did not constitute facts or proof; since the subtenant's negligence was in dispute, the landlord was not entitled to summary judgment pursuant to Rule 3:18. Wallace v. Dramberger, 58 Va. Cir. 454, 2002 Va. Cir. LEXIS 162 (Roanoke 2002).

Whether or not a merger modified the employees' covenant not to compete was a question of fact; therefore, summary judgment was inappropriate. Johns Bros. Sec. v. Jennings, 61 Va. Cir. 373, 2003 Va. Cir. LEXIS 143 (Norfolk 2003).

Law firm's motion for summary judgment pursuant to Va. Sup. Ct. R. 3:18 in an attorney's breach of employment contract action was denied; genuine issues of material fact existed as to whether the attorney was hired for a portion of profits pursuant to an oral contract or as a salaried employee. Appleton v. Bondurant & Appleton, P.C., 67 Va. Cir. 95, 2005 Va. Cir. LEXIS 9 (Portsmouth 2005).

Summary judgment motion filed by an LLC in an action concerning a right of first refusal contained within its contract with a corporation involving certain parcels of property was denied, as construction of said provision was unclear, and after applying the plain meaning to the terms therein, a clear and unambiguous explanation could not be reached without a trial. High Country Assocs., LLC v. Wintergreen Partners, Inc., 68 Va. Cir. 302, 2005 Va. Cir. LEXIS 98 (Nelson County 2005).

Since the question of whether a party is entitled to summary judgment is a matter of procedure controlled by the law of the forum, and since summary judgment should not be granted in Virginia where there are issues of fact, and since it was obvious to the court based upon the assertions of the parties, and from the evidence at the hearing, that there was an issue of fact as to whether silicosis was a risk known and foreseeable to the railroad employee at the time he signed the release absolving the railroad from liability for any known or unknown claims under the Virginia summary judgment standard the issue had to be submitted to a jury. Aswad v. Norfolk S. Ry. Co., 2006 Va. Cir. LEXIS 43 (Portsmouth Apr. 18, 2006).

Because a lessee timely exercised her option to purchase under a lease contract, and hence, granted partial summary judgment on that issue, she was denied complete summary judgment on her specific performance claim, as contested factual matters remained related to her equitable burdens and regarding the specifics of the financing agreement, and such had to be resolved through further proceedings. Stevens v. Miller, 73 Va. Cir. 160, 2007 Va. Cir. LEXIS 28 (Portsmouth 2007).

Issues of material fact presented. — Second motion for a stay pending appeal from an order granting summary judgment was granted, where the court, in analyzing the four factors outlined in *Hilton v. Braunskill,* found that: (1) there was a strong likelihood that the movant would likely succeed on the merits of his appeal; (2) the order granting summary judgment was prematurely entered, given the lack of discovery conducted by the parties and issues of material fact presented; (3) the issue of whether respondent contractor waived the terms of the arbitration clause was to be resolved at trial; (4) the potential harm to the movant outweighed any prejudice to the contractor if arbitration was delayed; and (5) public policy favored arbitration. Navy League Bldg., L.L.C. v. James G. Davis Constr. Corp., 68 Va. Cir. 289, 2005 Va. Cir. LEXIS 192 (Arlington County July 28, 2005).

No factual question existed. — In an action seeking to establish that two residents of a subdivision were no longer required to pay 1/17th of their annual share of expenses collected for the estimated costs of road maintenance within the subdivision in which they resided, their homeowners' association was granted summary judgment, and was awarded any unpaid assessments at the 1/17th share, as an amendment to the restriction was impossible and the residents' action of vacating their lot line between the two lots to create one did not vitiate their obligation to pay the assessment as if both lots remained separate. Pond v. Bryant Mt. Prop. Owners Ass'n, 2005 Va. Cir. LEXIS 102 (Nelson County June 1, 2005).

No material fact genuinely in dispute in personal injury claim. — Court found that there was no material fact genuinely in dispute, and dismissed the automobile accident victim's personal injury claim because the victim testified that she accepted the driver's insurance agent's final offer for her bodily injury claim before any mention of the offer being contingent upon the check being cashed or the release signed. Lawrence v. Barnett, 63 Va. Cir. 436, 2003 Va. Cir. LEXIS 250 (Roanoke 2003).

Summary judgment granted as to one claim, but denied as to remaining claims. — Trial court granted the utility company summary judgment on the injured excavator's claim that the utility failed to mark a power line because the failure to mark the power line was not the proximate cause of the excavator's injuries; however, the court denied the utility company summary judgment on the excavator's negligent failure to deactivate and abandon a power line and incorrectly informing locating services claims because factual issues existed as to those claims. Fulcher v. Va. Elec. & Power Co., 60 Va. Cir. 199, 2002 Va. Cir. LEXIS 267 (Norfolk 2002). See also Parrish v. Erie Ins. Co., 63 Va. Cir. 470, 2003 Va. Cir. LEXIS 344 (Richmond 2003).

Where a serviceman received a promotion to lieutenant and received full back pay, which became effective on a date certain, he could not successfully argue that he could have or would have received the same earlier than that effective date; thus, summary judgment was entered on his interference with a prospective economic opportunity claim, but not his defamation claim. Morris v. Massingill, 64 Va. Cir. 202, 2004 Va. Cir. LEXIS 184 (Norfolk 2004).

Partial motion for summary judgment granted. — Injured party's motion for partial summary judgment under Va. Sup. Ct. R. 3:18 was granted as a cab company was vicariously liable for the acts of its drivers and its attempt to take advantage of its franchise, while avoiding liability from its business through leases with its drivers, violated public policy; the city ordinances provided that the cab company owned the cabs, notwithstanding the lease to the driver, and that the owners of cabs involved in accidents had to provide proof of insurance to the other drivers involved, presupposing that the cab company was financially responsible for the negligent acts of the driver. Belcher v. Dandridge, 61 Va. Cir. 684, 2002 Va. Cir. LEXIS 423 (Norfolk 2002).

Given a general contractor's admissions and concessions regarding its liability to its subcontractor on a specific invoice, the subcontractor was granted partial summary judgment as to said liability. But, because the general contractor's breach of contract and tortious interference claims raised a material fact issue, it was entitled to a trial on said claims, barring summary judgment. Gov't Telecomms., Inc. v. Verizon Fed. Inc., 74 Va. Cir. 373, 2007 Va. Cir. LEXIS 196 (Fairfax County 2007).

Cross-motion for summary judgment entered. — Contractor's cross-motion for summary judgment was entered, in its insurer's declaratory judgment action, holding that the insurer had a duty to defend the contractor's subcontractor in a liability suit filed against it, on grounds that the subcontractor's wrongful removal of a property owner's property amounted to an occurrence under the policy, and was thus accidental, and the insurer's liability was not otherwise vitiated either by an expected or intended injury exclusion, or a faulty work exclusion. Erie Ins. Exch. v. Sipos, 64 Va. Cir. 55, 2004 Va. Cir. LEXIS 21 (Fairfax County 2004).

Summary judgment entered in malicious prosecution action. — Summary judgment was granted dismissing plaintiff's claim for malicious prosecution because defendant confused the facts, in that the evidence showed that only two of eight crimes with which he was charged were nolle prossed, and even so, he failed to state a cause of action for malicious prosecution because he was ultimately convicted of six of the eight felonies, and thus, the matter terminated in a manner unfavorable to plaintiff. Moreover, the prosecutors were immune from liability because their actions were undertaken in the charging process. Crawford v. Tuong Pham, 66 Va. Cir. 192, 2004 Va. Cir. LEXIS 345 (Richmond Nov. 10, 2004).

Entry of summary judgment held proper. — Upon a review of the evidence, despite the running of the statute of limitations, a claimant's acceptance, through counsel, of an insurer's offer, which did not have a time limit attached to it, was valid and entitled to be enforced, as it would have been inequitable to rule that said acceptance was not effective; hence, the claimant was entitled to summary judgment and to the amount agreed to in said offer. Lester v. Nationwide Ins. Mut. Ins. Co., 71 Va. Cir. 26, 2006 Va. Cir. LEXIS 145 (Buchanan County 2006).

Rule 3:21. Jury Trial of Right.

(a) *Jury Trial Situations Unchanged.* — The right of trial by jury as declared by the Constitution of Virginia, or as given by an applicable statute or other authority, is unchanged by these rules, and shall be implemented as established law provides. Established practice for the trial and decision of equitable claims by the judge alone shall be continued.

(b) *Demand.* — Any party may demand a trial by jury of any issue triable of right by a jury in the complaint or by (1) serving upon other parties a demand therefore in writing at any time after the commencement of the action and not later than 10 days after the service of the last pleading directed to the issue, and (2) filing the demand with the trial court. Such demand may be endorsed upon a pleading of the party. In an Electronically Filed Case, endorsement of such demand may be made as provided in Rule 1:17. The court may set a final date for service of jury demands. Leave to file amended pleadings shall not extend the time for serving and filing a jury demand unless the order granting leave to amend expressly so states.

(c) *Specification of Issues.* — In the demand a party may specify the issues which the party wishes so tried; otherwise the party shall be deemed to have demanded trial by jury for all the issues so triable. If the party has demanded trial by jury for only some of the issues, any other party within 10 days after service of the demand or such lesser time as the court may order, may serve a demand for trial by jury of any other or all of the issues of fact in the action.

(d) *Waiver.* — Absent leave of court for good cause shown, the failure of a party to serve and file a demand as required by this rule constitutes a waiver by the party of trial by jury.

The amendment, effective March 1, 2007, adopted December 20, 2006, in subdivision (b), deleted "the" preceding "other parties" in clause (1) of the first sentence, and added the last sentence.

The amendment effective July 1, 2008, adopted April 9, 2008, added "Absent leave of court for good cause shown" at the beginning of subdivision (d).

The amendment, effective May 2, 2011, adopted March 1, 2011, added the present third sentence of subdivision (b).

Law Review. — For annual survey commentary, "The Merger of Common-Law and Equity Pleading in Virginia," see 41 U. Rich. L. Rev. 77 (2006).

Rule 3:22. Trial by Jury or by the Court.

(a) *By Jury.* — When trial by jury has been demanded as provided in Rule 3:21, the action shall be designated upon the docket as a jury action. The trial of all issues so demanded shall be by jury, unless (1) the parties or their attorneys of record, by written stipulation filed with the court or by an oral stipulation made in open court and entered in the record, consent to trial by the court sitting without a jury; or (2) the court upon motion or of its own initiative finds that a right of trial by jury on some or all of those issues does not exist under applicable law.

(b) *By the Court.* — Except as otherwise provided in this Rule, issues not demanded for trial by jury as provided in Rule 3:21, and issues as to which a right of trial by jury does not exist, shall be tried by the court.

(c) *Statutory Jury Rights in Certain Equitable Claims.* —

(1) In an equitable claim where no right to a jury trial otherwise exists, where impaneling of an advisory jury pursuant to Code § 8.01-336(E) to hear an issue will be helpful to the court concerning disputed fact issues, such a jury may be seated. Decision on such claims and issues shall be made by the judge.

(2) Where a jury trial on a defendant's plea in an equitable claim is authorized under Code § 8.01-336(D), trial of the issues presented by the plea shall be by a jury whose verdict on those issues has the same effect as if trial by jury had been a matter of right.

(d) *Party Consent to Jury.* — As to any claim not triable of right by a jury, the court, with the consent of the parties, may (i) order trial of any claim or issue with an advisory jury or, (ii) a trial with a jury whose verdict has the same effect as if trial by jury had been a matter of right.

(e) *Trial by Mixed Jury and Non-Jury Claims.* — In any case when there are both jury and non-jury issues to be tried, the court shall adopt trial procedures and a sequence of proceedings to assure that all issues properly heard by the jury are decided by it, and applicable factual determinations by the jury shall be used by the judge in resolving the non-jury issues in the case.

The amendment, effective March 1, 2007, adopted December 20, 2006, added subdivision (e).

Law Review. — For annual survey commentary, "The Merger of Common-Law and Equity Pleading in Virginia," see 41 U. Rich. L. Rev. 77 (2006).

CASE NOTES

Denial of jury trial proper. — Client was not entitled to a jury trial in his dispute over the payment of certain attorney's fees because the dispute arose within a circuit court's equity jurisdiction over the underlying action and neither subsection D or E of § 8.01-336, nor Va. Sup. Ct. R. 3:22(d) applied to provide the client with the right to a jury trial. Henderson v. Ayres & Hartnett, P.C., 285 Va. 556, 740 S.E.2d 518, 2013 Va. LEXIS 49 (2013).

Rule 3:22A. Examination of Prospective Trial Jurors (Voir Dire).

(a) *Examination.* — After the prospective jurors are sworn on the voir dire, the court shall question them individually or collectively to determine whether anyone:

(1) Is related by blood, adoption, or marriage to the accused or to the Plaintiff or Defendant;

(2) Is an officer, director, agent or employee of the Plaintiff or Defendant;

(3) Has any interest in the trial or the outcome of the case;

(4) Has acquired any information about the case or the parties from the news media or other sources and, if so, whether such information would affect the juror's impartiality in the case;

(5) Has expressed or formed any opinion about the case;

(6) Has a bias or prejudice against the Plaintiff or Defendant; or

(7) Has any reason to believe the juror might not give a fair and impartial trial to the Plaintiff and Defendant based solely on the law and the evidence.

Thereafter, the court, and counsel as of right, may examine on oath the venire, and any prospective juror, and ask questions relevant to the qualifications as an impartial juror. A party objecting to a juror may introduce competent evidence ln support of the objection.

(b) *Challenge for Cause.* — The court, on its own motion or following a challenge for cause, may excuse a prospective juror if it appears the juror is not qualified, and another shall be drawn or called and placed ln the juror's stead for the trial of that case.

Effective date. — This rule, adopted November 1, 2012, became effective January 1, 2013.

Rule 3:23. Use of and Proceedings Before a Commissioner in Chancery.

(a) Commissioners in chancery may be appointed in cases in circuit court, including uncontested divorce cases, only when (1) there is agreement by the parties with concurrence of the court or (2) upon motion of a party or the court on its own motion with a finding of good cause shown in each individual case.

(b) Upon entry of a decree by the court referring any matter to a commissioner in chancery, the clerk shall mail or deliver to the commissioner a copy of the decree of reference. Unless the decree prescribes otherwise, the commissioner shall promptly set a time and place for the first meeting of the parties or their attorneys, and shall notify the parties or their attorneys of the time and place so set. It shall be the duty of the commissioner to proceed with all reasonable diligence to execute the decree of reference.

(c) A commissioner may require the production of evidence upon all matters embraced in the decree of reference including the production of all books, papers, vouchers, documents and writings applicable thereto. The commissioner shall have the authority to call witnesses or the parties to the action to testify and may examine them upon oath. The commissioner may rule upon the admissibility of evidence unless otherwise directed by the decree of reference; but when a party so requests, the commissioner shall cause a record to be made of all proffered evidence which is excluded by the commissioner as inadmissible.

(d) The commissioner shall prepare a report stating his findings of fact and conclusions of law with respect to the matters submitted by the decree of reference. The commissioner shall file the report, together with all exhibits admitted in evidence and a transcript of the proceedings and of the testimony, with the clerk of the court. In an Electronically Filed Case, filing as required in this Rule shall be in accord with the requirements of Rule 1:17. The commissioner shall mail or deliver to counsel of record and to parties not represented by counsel, using the last address shown in the record, written notice of the filing of the report. Provided, however, that in divorce cases a copy of the report shall accompany the notice. Provided, further, that no such notice or copy shall be given parties who have not appeared in the proceeding.

The amendment, effective January 1, 2006, adopted August 29, 2005, added "Use of and" to the Rule heading; inserted present paragraph (a) and redesignated former paragraphs (a) through (c) as present paragraphs (b) through (d); deleted the former paragraph headings; deleted the former first sentence of present paragraph (b), which read: "To the extent permitted by law, a judge of the circuit court may enter a decree referring any matter arising in an equitable claim to a commissioner in chancery" and added "Upon entry of a decree by the court referring any matter to a commissioner in chancery," at the beginning of the present first sentence; and in present paragraph (d), inserted "his" in the first sentence and deleted "taken" following "testimony" in the second sentence.

The amendment, effective May 2, 2011, adopted March 1, 2011, inserted the third sentence in subdivision (d).

Law Review. — For 2007 annual survey article, "Civil Practice and Procedure," see 42 U. Rich. L. Rev. 229 (2007).

Michie's Jurisprudence. — For related discussion, see 16 M.J. Reference and Commissioners, §§ 12, 16, 18 - 21.

Rule 3:24. Appeal of Orders of Quarantine or Isolation regarding Communicable Diseases of Public Health Threat.

A. Where an order of quarantine has been issued relating to a communicable disease of public health threat pursuant to § 32.1-48.09, the provisions of § 32.1-48.010, and related sections of Article 3.02 of Title 32.1 of the Code of Virginia, shall govern any appeal of such order to the appropriate circuit court.

B. Where an order of isolation has been issued relating to a communicable disease of public health threat pursuant to § 32.1-48.012, the provisions of § 32.1-48.013 and related sections of Article 3.02 of Title 32.1 of the Code of Virginia shall govern any appeal of such order to the appropriate circuit court.

C. The circuit court shall hold hearings under this rule in a manner to protect the health and safety of individuals subject to any such order or quarantine or isolation, court personnel, counsel, witnesses, and the general public. To this end, the circuit court may take measures including, but not limited to, ordering the hearing to be held by telephone or video conference or ordering those present to take appropriate precautions, including wearing personal protective equipment.

Effective date. — This rule, adopted February 28, 2006, became effective May 1, 2006.

Law Review. — For 2007 annual survey article, "Civil Practice and Procedure," see 42 U. Rich. L. Rev. 229 (2007).

Rule 3:25. Claims for Attorney's Fees.

A. *Scope of Rule.* — This rule applies to claims for attorney's fees, excluding (i) attorney's fees under § 8.01-271.1 of the Code of Virginia, and (ii) attorney's fees in domestic relations cases.

B. *Demand.* — A party seeking to recover attorney's fees shall include a demand therefor in the complaint filed pursuant to Rule 3:2, in a counterclaim filed pursuant to Rule 3:9, in a cross-claim filed pursuant to Rule 3:10, in a third-party pleading filed pursuant to Rule 3:13, or in a responsive pleading filed pursuant to Rule 3:8. The demand must identify the basis upon which the party relies in requesting attorney's fees.

C. *Waiver.* — The failure of a party to file a demand as required by this rule constitutes a waiver by the party of the claim for attorney's fees, unless leave to file an amended pleading seeking attorney's fees is granted under Rule 1:8.

D. *Procedure.* — Upon the motion of any party, the court shall, or upon its own motion, the court may, in advance of trial, establish a procedure to adjudicate any claim for attorney's fees.

Effective date. — This rule, adopted February 27, 2009, became effective May 1, 2009.

Law Review. — For annual survey of Virginia law article, "Civil Practice and Procedure," see 47 U. Rich. L. Rev. 113 (2012).

CASE NOTES

Request for fees. — Because a corporation admitted that an amendment on the issue of attorney fees was unnecessary regarding claims for attorneys' fees under a severance agreement, and the court rejected a CEO's theory regarding expanded recovery of legal fees, the CEO's request for the severance agreement-related-fees was proper. Online Res. Corp. v. Lawlor, 285 Va. 40, 736 S.E.2d 886, 2013 Va. LEXIS 2 (2013).

[illegible] 2006 [illegible]

Rule 3:2[illegible]. [illegible] Attorney's Fees.

B. Demand. — A party seeking to recover attorney's fees shall include a demand therefor in the complaint filed pursuant to Rule 3:2, [illegible] filed pursuant to Rule 3:10 [illegible] The demand [illegible] the basis upon which the party relies in requesting [illegible]

D. [illegible] — [illegible] the court [illegible] a claim [illegible] attorney's fees [illegible]

[illegible]

[illegible]

PART THREE A
CRIMINAL PRACTICE AND PROCEDURE

Rule
3A:1. Scope.
3A:2. Purpose and Interpretation; Definitions.
3A:2.1. Venue in Criminal Cases.
3A:3. The Complaint.
3A:4. Arrest Warrant or Summons.
3A:5. The Grand Jury.
3A:6. The Indictment and the Information.
3A:7. Capias or Summons Upon Indictment or Information.
3A:8. Pleas.
3A:9. Pleadings and Motions for Trial; Defenses and Objections.
3A:10. Trial Together of More Than One Accused or More Than One Offense.
3A:11. Discovery and Inspection.
3A:12. Subpoena.
3A:13. Trial by Jury or by Court.
3A:14. Trial Jurors.
3A:14.1. Confidentiality of Juror Personal Information.
3A:15. Motion to Strike or to Set Aside Verdict; Judgment of Acquittal or New Trial.
3A:16. Instructions.
3A:17. Jury Verdicts.
3A:17.1. Proceedings in Bifurcated Jury Trials of Non-Capital Felonies and Class 1 Misdemeanors.
3A:18. Death Penalty.
3A:19. Appeals.
3A:20. Time.
3A:21. Service and Filing of Papers.
3A:22. Forms.
3A:23. Electronic Filing.
3A:24. Special Rule Applicable to Post-Conviction Proceedings: Circuit Court Orders Denying Petitions for Writs of Habeas Corpus.
3A:25. Special Rule Applicable to Post-Conviction Proceedings: Inmate Filings in the Trial Courts Under Code § 8.01-654.

Appendix of Forms.

Form
1. Criminal Complaint (Rule 3A:3).
2. Statement of Witness for Arrest Warrant (Rule 3A:3).
3. Summons (Rule 3A:4(b)).
4. Indictments (Rule 3A:6).
5. Capias (Rule 3A:7).
6. Suggested Questions to Be Put by the Court to an Accused Who Has Pleaded Guilty (Rule 3A:8).
7. Suggested Questions to Be Put by the Court to an Accused Who Has Pleaded Not Guilty (Rule 3A:8).
8. Subpoena (Rule 3A:12(a)).
9. Subpoena Duces Tecum (Rule 3A:12(b)).
10. Contents of Sentencing Orders.
11. Misdemeanor Proceedings in District and Circuit Courts (Rule 3A:8(b)(2); Rule 7C:6; and Rule 8:18).

Editor's note. — The order effective July 1, 1984, adopted May 1, 1984, repealed former Part Three A and adopted a new Part Three A and Appendix of Forms.

Rule 3A:1. Scope.

These Rules govern criminal proceedings in circuit courts and juvenile and domestic relations district courts (except proceedings concerning a child in a juvenile and domestic relations district court) and before the magistrates defined in Rule 3A:2 except for cases which have been returned to the general district court. Special statutes applicable to practices and procedures in juvenile and domestic relations district courts are incorporated herein by this reference and in such cases shall prevail over the general rule set forth in Part 3A.

Cross references. — As to the Supreme Court prescribing rules and the effective date thereof, see § 8.01-3, Code of Virginia. As to criminal practice and procedure in the general district courts, see Rule 7C:1.

Source. — Former Rule 3A:1.

Law Review. — For a review of criminal law in Virginia for year 1999, see 33 U. Rich. L. Rev. 857 (1999).

Research References. — Cipes, Bernstein, and Hall, Criminal Defense Techniques (Matthew Bender).

Criminal Law Advocacy Reporter (Matthew Bender).

Erickson, Neighbors, and George, United States Supreme Court Cases and Comments: Criminal Law and Procedure (Matthew Bender).

Kadish, Brofman, Criminal Law Advocacy (Matthew Bender).

McCloskey and Schoenberg, Criminal Law Deskbook (Matthew Bender).

Robert M. Cipes, Rules of Criminal Procedure (Matthew Bender).

Rudstein, Erlinder, and Thomas, Criminal Constitutional Law (Matthew Bender).

Michie's Jurisprudence. — For related discussion, see 1A M.J. Abatement, Survival and Revival, § 27; 5B M.J. Criminal Procedure, §§ 2, 9.

Rule 3A:2. Purpose and Interpretation; Definitions.

(a) *Purpose and Interpretation.* — These Rules are intended to provide for the just determination of criminal proceedings. They shall be interpreted so as to promote uniformity and simplicity in procedure, fairness in administration, and the elimination of unjustifiable expense and delay. Errors, defects, irregularities or variances that do not affect substantive rights shall not constitute reversible error.

(b) *Definitions.* — Except as otherwise expressly provided in this Part Three A or unless the context otherwise requires:

(1) "Clerk" includes deputy clerk.

(2) "Commonwealth's attorney" includes assistant or acting Commonwealth's attorney.

(3) "Continuance" includes adjournment or recess.

(4) "Indictment" includes presentment and information filed upon presentment.

(5) "Magistrate" means a judicial or quasi-judicial officer authorized to issue arrest and search warrants, commit arrested persons to jail or admit them to bail, or conduct preliminary hearings.

(6) "Recognizance" means an undertaking, with or without surety or other security, made before a magistrate to perform one or more acts — for example, to appear in court. A recognizance may be written or oral but, if oral, shall be evidenced by a memorandum signed by the magistrate.

(7) Writings or memoranda under these Rules, and any required signatures or sworn verifications, shall be valid in the form of electronic files or digital images as provided in Rule 1:17.

Source. — Former Rule 3A:2.

Comment. — With respect to former Rule 3A:2 the amendment deletes the second sentence of subdivision (b) (5).

The amendment, effective May 2, 2011, adopted March 1, 2011, added subdivision (b)(7).

Michie's Jurisprudence. — For related discussion, see 1B M.J. Appeal and Error, § 286; 2B M.J. Bail and Recognizance, § 2; 5B M.J. Criminal Procedure, §§ 14, 19.

CASE NOTES

Continuance. — Where a continuance did not dispose of the whole subject or give all the relief contemplated, the trial judge did not violate the time limits of Va. Sup. Ct. R. 1:1 by finding the ex-wife in contempt more than 21 days later. McDonald v. Minton, No. 2531-03-4, 2004 Va. App. LEXIS 118 (Ct. of Appeals Mar. 23, 2004).

Appellate review standard for request for continuance or recess. — The same standard of appellate review applies to the denial of a request for a recess during the trial as to a request for a continuance; the decision whether to grant a continuance is a matter within the sound discretion of the trial court, and abuse of discretion and prejudice to the complaining party are essential to reversal. Lowery v. Commonwealth, 9 Va. App. 304, 387 S.E.2d 508 (1990).

Applied in Crawford v. Commonwealth, 217 Va. 595, 231 S.E.2d 309 (1977); Yager v. Commonwealth, 220 Va. 608, 260 S.E.2d 251 (1979).

Rule 3A:2.1. Venue in Criminal Cases.

In criminal cases, questions of venue must be raised in the trial court and before the verdict in cases tried by a jury and before the finding of guilty in cases tried by a court.

Cross references. — As to criminal practice and procedure in the general district courts, see Rule 7C:2.

Effective date. — This rule, adopted December 20, 2006, became effective March 1, 2007.

CASE NOTES

Question of venue cannot be raised for the first time in the Supreme Court. Hicks v. Commonwealth, 157 Va. 939, 161 S.E. 919 (1932) (decided under prior law).

An objection that the venue was not properly laid, made for the first time in the appellate court, could not be sustained. Boyd v. Commonwealth, 156 Va. 934, 157 S.E. 546 (1931) (decided under prior law).

In a prosecution for the violation of a city ordinance by the sale of intoxicating liquors, it was claimed that there was no proof that the sale in question was made in the city or within three miles of its boundaries. The venue was not questioned in the trial court; therefore it could not be raised for the first time on appeal. Hodge v. City of Winchester, 153 Va. 904, 150 S.E. 392 (1929) (decided under prior law).

Rule 3A:3. The Complaint.

The complaint shall consist of sworn statements of a person or persons of facts relating to the commission of an alleged offense. The statements shall be made upon oath before a magistrate empowered to issue arrest warrants. The magistrate may require the sworn statements to be reduced to writing and signed if the complainant is a law-enforcement officer, but shall require the sworn statements to be reduced to writing if the complainant is not a law-enforcement officer.

Cross references. — As to criminal practice and procedure in the general district courts, see Rule 7C:3.

Source. — Former Rule 3A:3.

The amendment effective March 1, 2012, adopted December 22, 2011, added "if the complainant is a law-enforcement officer, but shall require the sworn statements to be reduced to writing if the complainant is not a law-enforcement officer" at the end of the third sentence.

Michie's Jurisprudence. — For related discussion, see 5B M.J. Criminal Procedure, § 12; 19 M.J. Warrants, § 2.

CASE NOTES

Defendant cannot be tried upon complaint. — In Virginia a complaint, as that word is defined in this rule, is not a document upon which a defendant may be tried. Locklear v. Commonwealth, 7 Va. App. 659, 376 S.E.2d 793 (1989).

Rule 3A:4. Arrest Warrant or Summons.

(a) *Issuance.* — More than one warrant or summons may issue on the same complaint. A warrant may be issued by a judicial officer if the accused fails to appear in response to a summons.

(b) *Form of Summons.* — A summons, whether issued by a magistrate or a law-enforcement officer, shall command the accused to appear at a stated time and place before a court of appropriate jurisdiction in the county, city or town in which the summons is issued. It shall (i) state the name of the accused or, if his name is unknown, set forth a description by which he can be identified with reasonable certainty, (ii) describe the offense charged and state whether the offense is a violation of state, county, city or town law, and (iii) be signed by the magistrate or the law-enforcement office, as the case may be.

(c) *Execution and Return.* — If a warrant has been issued but the officer does not have the warrant in his possession at the time of the arrest, he shall (i) inform the accused of the offense charged and that a warrant has been issued, and (ii) deliver a copy of the warrant to the accused as soon thereafter as practicable.

Cross references. — As to criminal practice and procedure in the general district courts, see Rule 7C:3.

Source. — Former Rule 3A:4.

Comment. — With respect to former Rule 3A:4, the amendment deletes the words "by a magistrate" from the title to subsection (a), deletes the first two sentences of subsection (a), deletes subsection (b), redesignates subsection (c) as subsection (b) and alters its title, deletes former subdivision (c) (1), deletes former subsection (d) in its entirety and adds a new subsection (c).

Michie's Jurisprudence. — For related discussion, see 2A M.J. Arrest, § 5; 5B M.J. Criminal Procedure, §§ 12, 17; 19 M.J. Warrants, §§ 2, 4.

CASE NOTES

Notice of nature and character of offense required. — Under this rule, an arrest warrant must describe the offense charged. This description must comply with Rule 3A:6(a), which deals with the description of the charge that must be contained in an indictment. Under Rule 3A:6(a) an indictment must give an accused notice of the nature and character of the offense. The same, therefore, is true of warrants. Greenwalt v. Commonwealth, 224 Va. 498, 297 S.E.2d 709 (1982).

A nonexistent code section on a summons is not fatal as long as the description of the charge was sufficient to give the accused notice of the nature and character of the offense for which he was charged. Lankford v. Commonwealth, No. 0883-92-4 (Ct. of Appeals Feb. 22, 1994).

Description of offense in traffic summons held sufficient. — In a case where the traffic summons stated that defendant was charged with "speed 59/45," this description was sufficient to give him notice of the nature and character of the offense for which he was charged, even though the warrant was erroneously amended to show the subsection as "46.1-193h(3)," a nonexistent subsection, and the error was not fatal to the conviction. Williams v. Commonwealth, 5 Va. App. 514, 365 S.E.2d 340 (1988).

Sufficient notification. — In describing the nature and character of an offense, it is not necessary to follow the exact words of the statute. Rules 3A:4 and 3A:6 may be satisfied by simply citing the statute at issue — the elements of the offense are deemed to be incorporated by reference. Watkins v. Commonwealth, No. 0975-96-3 (Ct. of Appeals May 6, 1997).

Arrest warrant sufficiently notified the defendant that he faced a Class 1 misdemeanor charge of intentional vandalism and did not prejudicially mislead him into believing he faced a Class 3 misdemeanor charge of unlawful vandalism; the defendant's failure to object to the active jail sentence, either at the district court or the circuit court level, confirmed that he understood the nature and character of the charge against him. Lamb v. Commonwealth, No. 1262-02-2, 2003 Va. App. LEXIS 252 (Ct. of Appeals Apr. 29, 2003).

Applied in Williams v. City of Petersburg, 216 Va. 297, 217 S.E.2d 893 (1975); Addison v. Commonwealth, 224 Va. 713, 299 S.E.2d 521 (1983).

OPINIONS OF THE ATTORNEY GENERAL

Execution of misdemeanor capias not in officer's possession. — A law-enforcement officer has the authority to execute a misdemeanor capias, not in his possession, based upon an official dispatch from another county, provided the officer informs the accused of the existence of, and the charges contained in, the capias and delivers the capias to the accused as soon thereafter as is practicable. See opinion of Attorney General to Mr. George S. Webb, III, Commonwealth's Attorney for Madison County, 05-017 (4/26/05).

Rule 3A:5. The Grand Jury.

(a) *Who May Be Present.* — Only the grand jurors and the witness under examination and, if directed by the court, an interpreter shall be present during the hearing of evidence by a grand jury. Only the grand jurors shall be present during their deliberations and voting.

(b) *Secrecy.* — No obligation of secrecy may be imposed upon any person except in accordance with law.

(c) *Finding and Return of Indictment.* — The indictment shall be endorsed "A True Bill" or "Not a True Bill" and signed by the foreman. The indictment shall be returned by the grand jury in open court.

(d) *Motion to Dismiss.* — A motion to dismiss the indictment may be based on constitutional objections to the array or on the lack of legal qualification of an individual juror.

Source. — Former Rule 3A:6.

Comment. — With respect to former Rule 3A:6, the amendment deletes subsection (a), deletes the second sentence of subsection (b), deletes the first sentence of subsection (c) and substitutes the word "law" for the words "this rule" at the end of the second sentence of subsection (c), deletes the second sentence of subsection (d), and deletes the second sentence of subsection (e).

Law Review. — For note, "Disclosure of Grand Jury Materials to Foreign Authorities Under Federal Rule of Criminal Procedure 6(e)," see 70 Va. L. Rev. 1623 (1984). For note, "Grand Jury Reform: A Proposal for Change in Virginia," see 23 U. Rich. L. Rev. 279 (1989).

Michie's Jurisprudence. — For related discussion, see 9A M.J. Grand Jury, §§ 2, 5 - 7, 19, 21, 22, 33, 37; 9B M.J. Indictments, Informations and Presentments, §§ 17, 51.

Rule 3A:6. The Indictment and the Information.

(a) *Contents.* — The indictment or information, in describing the offense charged, shall cite the statute or ordinance that defines the offense or, if there is no defining statute or ordinance, prescribes the punishment for the offense. Error in the citation of the statute or ordinance that defines the offense or prescribes the punishments therefor, or omission of the citation, shall not be grounds for dismissal of an indictment or information, or for reversal of a conviction, unless the court finds that the error or omission prejudiced the accused in preparing his defense.

(b) *Joinder of Offenses.* — Two or more offenses, any of which may be a felony or misdemeanor, may be charged in separate counts of an indictment or information if the offenses are based on the same act or transaction, or on two or more acts or transactions that are connected or constitute parts of a common scheme or plan.

(c) *Joinder of Defendants.* — Two or more accused may be charged with a count(s) of an indictment, if they are charged with participating in contemporaneous and related acts or occurrences or in a series of acts or occurrences constituting an offense or offenses.

(d) *Form.* — The indictment or information need not contain a formal commencement or conclusion. The return of an indictment shall be signed by the foreman of the grand jury, and the information shall be signed by the Commonwealth's attorney.

Cross references. — As to criminal practice and procedure in the general district courts regarding joinder of offenses, see Rule 7C:4.

Source. — Former Rule 3A:7.

Comment. — With respect to former Rule 3A:7, the 1984 revision deletes the first two sentences of subsection (a), and adds to subsection (a) the sentence beginning "The indictment or information, in describing the offense charged" and ending "prescribes the punishment for the offense."

Law Review. — For 1985 survey of Virginia criminal procedure, see 19 U. Rich. L. Rev. (1985). For survey of Virginia law on criminal law and procedure for the year 2007-2008, see 43 U. Rich. L. Rev. 149 (2008).

Michie's Jurisprudence. — For related discussion, see 1A M.J. Abatement, Survival and Revival, § 18; 4C Constitutional Law, § 78; 5B M.J. Criminal Procedure, §§ 12, 26; 6B M.J. Drugs and Druggists, § 5; 9A M.J. Grand Jury, §§ 32, 34; 9B M.J. Homicide, § 51; 9B M.J. Indictments, Informations and Presentments, § 51.

CASE NOTES

I. General Consideration.
II. Joinder.

I. GENERAL CONSIDERATION.

Indictment must give the accused notice of the nature and character of the offense charged so he can make his defense, although in charging a statutory offense it is not necessary to follow the identical words of the statute. Wilder v. Commonwealth, 217 Va. 145, 225 S.E.2d 411 (1976).

The indictment should "cite the statute or ordinance that defines the offense or, if there is no defining statute or ordinance, prescribes the punishment for the offense." Both the United States and Virginia Constitutions recognize that a criminal defendant enjoys the right to be advised of the cause and nature of the accusation lodged against him. The important concerns evident in these provisions are fully honored by Virginia Code §§ 19.2-220, 19.2-221. Rush v. Commonwealth, No. 2058-94-2 (Ct. of Appeals Mar. 26, 1996).

Notice requirements also applicable to warrants. — Under Rule 3A:4, an arrest warrant must describe the offense charged. This description must comply with this rule, which deals with the description of the charge that must be contained in an indictment. Under this rule an indictment must give an accused notice of the nature and character of the offense. The same, therefore, is true of warrants. Greenwalt v. Commonwealth, 224 Va. 498, 297 S.E.2d 709 (1982).

Defendant implicitly acknowledged fair notice that the indictment charged him with capital murder at the pre-trial hearings when he moved to quash the indictment, assigning only challenges to the facial constitutionality of the capital statutes. Boggs v. Commonwealth, 229 Va. 501, 331 S.E.2d 407 (1985), cert. denied, 475 U.S. 1031, 106 S. Ct. 1240, 89 L. Ed. 2d 347 (1986), 495 U.S. 940, 110 S. Ct. 2193, 109 L. Ed. 2d 521 (1990).

References at the foot of the charge to particular criminal statutes fail to save an indictment otherwise defective. Such references support, but do not replace, the "definite written statement," required in the body of an indictment. Wilder v. Commonwealth, 217 Va. 145, 225 S.E.2d 411 (1976).

The endorsement is not a substantive part of an indictment and is not determinative of the legal sufficiency of the accusation to charge the crime for which it is sought to hold the accused to answer; it neither strengthens nor weakens the legal force of the averments in the charging portion of the indictment. Wilder v. Commonwealth, 217 Va. 145, 225 S.E.2d 411 (1976).

Citation of statute. — In describing the nature and character of an offense, it is not necessary to follow the exact words of the statute. Rules 3A:4 and 3A:6 may be satisfied by simply citing the statute at issue — the elements of the offense are deemed to be incorporated by reference. Watkins v. Commonwealth, No. 0975-96-3 (Ct. of Appeals May 6, 1997).

Evidence was sufficient to convict defendant of breaking and entering under § 18.2-91 and there was not a fatal variance between the evidence offered at trial and the indictment, which charged defendant with breaking and entering with the intent to commit larceny, as: (1) § 18.2-91 was cited in the indictment in accordance with § 19.2-220 and Va. Sup. Ct. R. 3A:6(a); (2) the citation in the indictment to § 18.2-91 incorporated by reference the complete definition of the offense set forth in the statute and supplemented the charging language of the indictment; (3) as the statute's title reflected, the offense could be committed with the "intent to commit larceny, assault and battery or other felony"; (4) although the body of the charge omitted reference to the intent to commit assault and battery, that specific intent was alleged in the indictment; (5) in reciting an abbreviated title of the charged offense, the indictment specifically referenced the "intent to commit A and B," or assault and battery; and (6) the arrest warrant underlying the felony charge specifically accused defendant of breaking and entering in the nighttime the dwelling house of the victim with the intent to commit assault and battery. Barth v. Commonwealth, 2007 Va. App. LEXIS 56 (Feb. 20, 2007).

Amendment to an indictment was proper where the offense with which defendant was charged was plainly described in the body of the indictment as possession of cocaine while a prisoner and where the original reference to an erroneous statute did not prejudice defendant in the preparation of a defense. Mosby v. Commonwealth, No. 2990-08-3, 2010 Va. App. LEXIS 120 (Ct. of Appeals Mar. 30, 2010).

Subdivision (a) contemplates incorporation by reference. — Subdivision (a) of this rule, in relevant part, requires the indictment to "cite the statute or ordinance that defines the offense." These provisions clearly contemplate incorporation by reference of the statute or ordinance cited in the indictment. Trusty v. Commonwealth, No. 0278-93-1, (Ct. of Appeals Dec. 20, 1994).

Incorporation by reference of statute or ordinance. — Subdivision (a) of this rule requires the indictment to "cite the statute or ordinance that defines the offense." These provisions clearly contemplate incorporation by reference of the statute or ordinance cited in the indictment. Cantwell v. Commonwealth, 2 Va. App. 606, 347 S.E.2d 523 (1986).

The inference to be drawn from the provisions of § 19.2-220 and subdivision (a) of this rule is clearly that incorporation by such reference is contemplated by the rule. Reed v. Commonwealth, 3 Va. App. 665, 353 S.E.2d 166 (1987).

Pursuant to § 19.2-220 and Va. Sup. Ct. R. 3A:6(a), the citation to § 18.2-51.2 in the indictment incorporated by reference the complete definition of aggravated malicious wounding and supplemented the charging language of the indictment; therefore, the statutory citation, coupled with the facts alleged, was sufficient to set forth all relevant elements of the aggravated malicious wounding offense. Robinson v. Commonwealth, No. 1623-02-2, 2003 Va. App. LEXIS 327 (Ct. of Appeals June 3, 2003).

It is not necessary to include in the indictment an allegation of every fact in the chain of circumstances comprising the offense charged. Howard v. Commonwealth, 221 Va. 904, 275 S.E.2d 602 (1981).

An indictment need not be drafted in the exact words of the applicable statute so long as the accused is given notice of the nature and character of the offense charged. Black v. Commonwealth, 223 Va. 277, 288 S.E.2d 449 (1982).

This rule provides that an error in the citation of the statute which defines the offense or prescribes the punishment shall not be ground for dismissal of an indictment or for reversal of a conviction unless the court finds that the error or omission prejudiced the accused in preparing his defense. George v. Commonwealth, 242 Va. 264, 411 S.E.2d 12 (1991), cert. denied, 503 U.S. 973, 112 S. Ct. 1591, 118 L. Ed. 2d 308 (1992).

Additional unnecessary language included in the indictments which is surplusage does not invalidate the indictments. Black v. Commonwealth, 223 Va. 277, 288 S.E.2d 449 (1982).

By citation of § 53.1-203(2) in the indictment, appellant was informed of the essential elements of the case against him. He suffered no prejudice by the omission in the body of the indictment of the words "for the purpose of," and failure to use that phrase did not invalidate the indictment. Reed v. Commonwealth, 3 Va. App. 665, 353 S.E.2d 166 (1987).

Indictment held sufficient. — Indictment which informed defendant of the offense charged against defendant was sufficient where it incorporated by reference the statute defendant violated and the statute itself informed defendant that the Commonwealth could obtain a mandatory minimum sentence against defendant if it proved that he had previously been convicted of a violent offense, which the Commonwealth did prove. Thomas v. Commonwealth, 37 Va. App. 748, 561 S.E.2d 56, 2002 Va. App. LEXIS 176 (2002).

There was no need to reverse a defendant's grand larceny conviction where the indictment stated that he was indicted for grand larceny of a shotgun, without regard to its value; this was also true as to the petit larceny conviction. Winkler v. Commonwealth, No. 2998-01-2, 2003 Va. App. LEXIS 353 (Ct. of Appeals June 24, 2003).

No variance between indictment and proof at trial. — Trial court did not err in ruling that there was no fatal variance between the indictment and the proof at trial because defendant was informed of the nature and cause of accusation brought against her, obtaining property by false pretenses; the indictment did not describe, limit, or qualify the factual allegation to the exclusion of "money" from its scope because it utilized the word "property" in setting forth the nature and character of the offense charged. Polk v. Commonwealth, No.

1091-12-1, 2013 Va. App. LEXIS 200 (Ct. of Appeals July 16, 2013).

Manner in which Commonwealth may prove killing. — Under an indictment for murder in the form prescribed by this rule, Form 5 (see now Form 4) in the appendix of forms for these rules, the Commonwealth may prove a killing in any manner or in different manners. Thus, the Commonwealth was not required to elect whether it was proceeding against the defendant on the theory that the killing was willful, deliberate and premeditated or under the felony-murder doctrine that the killing occurred in the commission of abduction. Akers v. Commonwealth, 216 Va. 40, 216 S.E.2d 28 (1975).

Collateral attack on sufficiency. — As long as the indictment is not so defective so as to deprive the court of jurisdiction to render the judgment of conviction, a petitioner may not collaterally attack the sufficiency of the indictment by a petition for a writ of habeas corpus. Abney v. Warden, Mecklenburg Correctional Ctr., 1 Va. App. 26, 332 S.E.2d 802 (1985).

Applied in Washington v. Commonwealth, 216 Va. 185, 217 S.E.2d 815 (1975); Williams v. City of Petersburg, 216 Va. 297, 217 S.E.2d 893 (1975); Crawford v. Commonwealth, 217 Va. 595, 231 S.E.2d 309 (1977); Wall Distribs., Inc. v. City of Newport News, 228 Va. 358, 323 S.E.2d 75 (1984); KMA, Inc. v. City of Newport News, 228 Va. 365, 323 S.E.2d 78 (1984); Stamper v. Commonwealth, 228 Va. 707, 324 S.E.2d 682 (1985); Colclasure v. Commonwealth, 10 Va. App. 200, 390 S.E.2d 790 (1990); United States v. Breckenridge, 93 F.3d 132 (4th Cir. 1996); Satcher v. Netherland, 944 F. Supp. 1222 (E.D. Va. 1996); Yellardy v. Commonwealth, 38 Va. App. 19, 561 S.E.2d 739, 2002 Va. App. LEXIS 192 (2002); Raja v. Commonwealth, 40 Va. App. 710, 581 S.E.2d 237, 2003 Va. App. LEXIS 318 (2003).

II. JOINDER.

When joinder permitted. — Even if the requirements of paragraph (b) of this rule are met, joinder is not permitted unless "justice does not require separate trials." Cook v. Commonwealth, 7 Va. App. 225, 372 S.E.2d 780 (1988).

A court may direct that an accused be tried at one time for all offenses pending against him if (1) "justice does not require separate trials," and (2) "the offenses are based on the same act or transaction, or on two or more acts or transactions that are connected or constitute parts of a common scheme or plan." Whether different offenses should be tried separately is a matter that rests within the sound discretion of a trial court. Thus, a trial court's ruling on the matter will not be reversed absent a showing that the court abused its discretion. Cheng v. Commonwealth, 240 Va. 26, 393 S.E.2d 599 (1990).

In determining whether a joint trial would prejudice a defendant, the trial court should require the party moving for severance to establish that actual prejudice would result from a joint trial. Adkins v. Commonwealth, 24 Va. App. 159, 480 S.E.2d 777 (1997).

That three businesses, in close proximity, were burglarized within six days; that the same method of entry was used in each case; and that in each burglary, cash registers or parts of them were stolen, allowed the trial court to find that the crimes were connected or constituted parts of a common scheme or plan, Va. Sup. Ct. R. 3A:6(b), to such a degree that justice did not require that the charges be severed under Va. Sup. Ct. R. 3A:10(c). Kinnard v. Commonwealth, 2008 Va. App. LEXIS 340 (July 22, 2008).

Sales of cocaine did not meet requirement of "same act or transaction." Where sales of cocaine occurred as discreet events with a significant separation of time between each event, the sales did not meet the requirement of "the same act or transaction." Spence v. Commonwealth, 12 Va. App. 1040, 407 S.E.2d 916 (1991).

Four sales of cocaine did not arise out of transactions that were connected. — Four sales of cocaine did not arise out of acts or transactions that were connected since they occurred on different days and no evidence linked or connected one sale with the other. Spence v. Commonwealth, 12 Va. App. 1040, 407 S.E.2d 916 (1991).

"Common scheme" and "common plan" defined. — As used in Va. Sup. Ct. R. 3A:6(b), the term "common scheme" describes crimes that share features idiosyncratic in character, which permit an inference that each individual offense was committed by the same person or persons as part of a pattern of criminal activity involving certain identified crimes; in contrast, the term "common plan" describes crimes that are related to one another for the purpose of accomplishing a particular goal. The terms "common scheme" and "common plan," however, are not mutually exclusive; a series of crimes may exhibit both a "common scheme" and a "common plan." Scott v. Commonwealth, 274 Va. 636, 651 S.E.2d 630, 2007 Va. LEXIS 132 (2007).

Joinder proper where evidence showed common scheme. — Joinder of offenses was proper where the two offenses were "connected" in time, place, and manner, and were sufficiently idiosyncratic to permit an inference that the same person was involved in a "common scheme" of criminal activity; in each instance defendant and a companion knocked on a door to see if anyone was home, asking for someone who did not live there if anyone answered the door. Seis v. Commonwealth, 2007 Va. App. LEXIS 432 (Nov. 27, 2007).

Common scheme or plan not shown. — As the evidence showed only a general similarity of manner in which nine armed robberies were committed and failed to establish that the crimes shared idiosyncratic features permitting an inference of a pattern of criminal activity committed by the same person, and as there was no proof that the offenses were related to one another for the purpose of accomplishing a particular goal, the Commonwealth did not establish that there was a "common scheme or plan" within the meaning of Va. Sup. Ct. R. 3A:6(b). Therefore, joining the robberies in a single trial under Va. Sup. Ct. R. 3A:10(c) was error. Scott v. Commonwealth, 274 Va. 636, 651 S.E.2d 630, 2007 Va. LEXIS 132 (2007).

A common scheme or plan is present only if the relationship among offenses is dependent upon the existence of a plan that ties the offenses together and demonstrates that the objective of each offense was to contribute to the achievement of a goal not attainable by the commission of any of the individual offenses. Spence v. Commonwealth, 12 Va. App. 1040, 407 S.E.2d 916 (1991).

Failure to challenge. — In a prosecution on four charges of grand larceny and four charges of burglary, since defendant did not challenge the joinder of the offenses under Va. Sup. Ct. R. 3A:10(c) and 3A:6(b) at trial or on appeal and did not argue that the four burglaries were not part of a common scheme or plan, the trial court was entitled to consider the evidence of a common scheme or plan in evaluation of each offense in reaching its verdict. Wilkins v. Commonwealth, 2008 Va. App. LEXIS 483 (Oct. 28, 2008).

Two separate sales of a controlled substance by the same individual on different occasions do not constitute a common scheme or plan. Spence v. Commonwealth, 12 Va. App. 1040, 407 S.E.2d 916 (1991).

Misjoinder did not constitute reversible error where no substantive rights of a party were affected. Foster v. Commonwealth, 6 Va. App. 313, 369 S.E.2d 688 (1988).

Trial of misjoined counts together held not error. — Where counts of indictment were misjoined under subdivision (b), but the misjoinder did not affect defendant's substantive rights and the evidence of defendant's intent in any of the counts would have been admissible at the trial of any other counts, there was no error in trying all counts together. Foster v. Commonwealth, 6 Va. App. 313, 369 S.E.2d 688 (1988).

Any error in joinder harmless. — Any error in the joinder of the offenses arising out of two attacks was harmless, because the evidence of each offense would have been admissible at a trial for the other to prove that the attacks were part of a common plan and the evidence against defendant was so overwhelming that the outcome would not have changed absent the alleged improper evidence. Angel v. Commonwealth, 2009 Va. App. LEXIS 125 (Mar. 24, 2009).

Harmless error in failing to sever felony indictments from misdemeanor indictments. — Because: (1) evidence of defendant's separate misdemeanor offenses with two separate victims was not necessary to prove any relevant element of the felony offenses charged involving a third victim, or necessary to prove defendant's motive, intent or knowledge, and in a separate trial involving only the felony offenses; and (2) evidence of defendant's sexual offenses involving the two misdemeanor victims would do little more than show that defendant was a bad man likely to commit that sort of crime, the trial court abused its discretion by not granting defendant's motion to sever the felony indictments from the misdemeanor indictments for separate trials under Va. Sup. Ct. R. 3A:10(c); however, said error was harmless due to the overwhelming evidence of defendant's guilt. Smith v. Commonwealth, No. 1004-04-1, 2005 Va. App. LEXIS 140 (Ct. of Appeals Apr. 5, 2005).

Because justice required separate trials and the trial court erred in not granting defendant's motion to sever the indictments for separate trials, it was not necessary to decide whether the charged offenses satisfied the requirements of Va. Sup. Ct. R. 3A:6(b). Smith v. Commonwealth, No. 1004-04-1, 2005 Va. App. LEXIS 140 (Ct. of Appeals Apr. 5, 2005).

Justice often requires separate trials where highly prejudicial evidence of one of the crimes is not admissible in the trial of the other. Long v. Commonwealth, 20 Va. App. 223, 456 S.E.2d 138 (1995).

Denial of motion to sever held error where offenses not part of common plan. — The trial court erred when it denied the defendant's motion to sever the trial of two robbery and two use of a firearm offenses which, though factually similar, were not part of a common plan. A defendant should not be required to defend two criminal charges in same trial simply because they arose out of factually similar events. Godwin v. Commonwealth, 6 Va. App. 118, 367 S.E.2d 520 (1988).

Trial court's decision to try all of defendant's charged offenses together constituted an abuse of its discretion. Although uncontradicted evidence overwhelmingly proved defendant's guilt on all of the charges against him, because the jury had broad discretion in fixing the sentences on those charges, the appellate court could not say that trial court's error did not affect defendant's sentence. Long v. Commonwealth, 20 Va. App. 223, 456 S.E.2d 138 (1995).

Trying defendant on firearm/felony charge with the other charges would unduly prejudice him in the minds of the jury by letting them know that he had previously been convicted of a felony, which was irrelevant to the possession of heroin and firearm/heroin charges. Long v. Commonwealth, 20 Va. App. 223, 456 S.E.2d 138 (1995).

Separate trial unwarranted. — Trial court did not err in not ordering a separate trial on charges of involuntary manslaughter and unlawful distribution of a controlled substance, in violation of § 18.2-248, against a doctor, where the offenses were based on the same act or transactions, or on two or more acts or transactions that were connected or constitute parts of a common scheme or plan; moreover, defendant conceded that the evidence of the distribution was essential to the trial of the homicide charge. Jere v. Commonwealth, No. 2125-02-2, 2003 Va. App. LEXIS 465 (Ct. of Appeals Sept. 9, 2003).

Because defendant's arguments for severance of the charges under Va. Sup. Ct. R. 3A:6 and 3A:10(c) relied entirely upon the assumption that the testimony defendant would have given represented exculpatory evidence on the failure to appear charge, because the arguments were unpreserved under Va. Sup. Ct. R. 5A:18, and because defendant did not preserve a complete and proper record for review, the arguments were procedurally barred. Jackson v. Commonwealth, 2008 Va. App. LEXIS 80 (Feb. 19, 2008).

Denial of motion to sever upheld. — Where three offenses of concealment were committed within 30 minutes of each other at three separate 7-Eleven stores by the same defendant and accomplice, trial court's denial of a motion for severance did not cause undue prejudice, and justice did not require separate trials. Cook v. Commonwealth, 7 Va. App. 225, 372 S.E.2d 780 (1988).

Evidence and the reasonable inferences therefrom clearly supported a finding that the offenses for which defendant was indicted constituted parts of a common scheme to systematically bilk women drivers and were closely connected in the distinctive means of their commission; thus, pursuant to Va. Sup. Ct. R. 3A:6(b), a single trial for all of the offenses was proper. Traish v. Commonwealth, 36 Va. App. 114, 549 S.E.2d 5, 2001 Va. App. LEXIS 407 (2001).

Denial of motion to sever overruled. — Where the only similarity between the crimes was that they involved the use of a crowbar to break into several businesses which were located in the same part of the county and near major highways, but the crimes occurred over a period of almost six weeks; the businesses involved were several restaurants, an auto repair shop, a grocery store, and a church; the items taken were not similar; and the evidence failed to establish any connection among the offenses, the crimes were neither related transactions nor parts of a common scheme or plan, as required for joinder. Mills v. Commonwealth, No. 2305-92-3, (Ct. of Appeals Aug. 2, 1994).

Court did not abuse its discretion in ordering that indictments be consolidated. — The record disclosed that the trial court did not abuse its discretion in ordering that indictments be consolidated for trial; there was nothing indicated by the record that defendant's defense to either charge would have been altered in any respect if he had been granted separate trials; the offenses arose out of a series of related and connected events; most of the same evidence would have been submitted to the jury by both the Commonwealth and defense in separate trials; and furthermore, if severance had been ordered the Commonwealth would have been required on at least four different dates to secure the presence of an out-of-state witness. Ferrell v. Commonwealth, 11 Va. App. 380, 399 S.E.2d 614 (1990).

Election of offenses not required. — Defendant asked two people to kill his wife, formulated diagrams of his wife's house, explained when she would be at home, and paid two thousand dollars to the hit man. The evidence was sufficient to convict defendant of attempted capital murder for hire and solicitation of capital murder for hire; the Commonwealth did not err by failing to elect between the charges, because the solicitation and attempt were both parts of a common scheme or plan. Ashford v. Commonwealth, 47 Va. App. 676, 626 S.E.2d 464, 2006 Va. App. LEXIS 70 (2006).

Where defendant did not consent to the joinder of the charges for trial, joinder could be ordered only if the charges were part of a "common scheme" and justice did not require separate trials. Kirk v. Commonwealth, 21 Va. App. 291, 464 S.E.2d 162 (1995).

Linking courtroom attire to granting severance motion error. — Denying defendant the right to wear his navy uniform was not a valid consideration for granting of his severance motion. There is no basis to hold that a military uniform affords an unrealistic suggestion of good character any more than do neat and clean attire and good grooming. It is inappropriate for a trial court to deny a courtroom participant the right to present himself in his best posture. Johnson v. Commonwealth, 19 Va. App. 163, 449 S.E.2d 819 (1994).

CIRCUIT COURT OPINIONS

When joinder permitted. — Where defendant's acts all flowed from the same stream of events and the fact finder was sophisticated enough to be able to separate which evidence was applicable to which count, judicial economy required joinder of the charges pursuant to Va. Sup. Ct. R. 3A:6(b). Commonwealth v. Jimenez-Ventura, 61 Va. Cir. 717, 2002 Va. Cir. LEXIS 438 (Alexandria 2002).

The "connected" test of Rule 3A:6(b) is that the crimes should be so intimately connected and blended with the main facts adduced in evidence that they cannot be departed from with propriety. Defendant's motion for severance was granted to separate a count of driving under a suspended license and a count of operating a motor vehicle without paying fees from other counts that charged him with various criminal acts related to the deaths of two of his passengers in an automobile accident; those two counts had no relation to the manner in which defendant operated his vehicle and defendant was strictly liable for those counts regardless of the manner in which he drove, so defendant was entitled to severance of those two counts. Commonwealth v. Walsh, 62 Va. Cir. 511, 2003 Va. Cir. LEXIS 267 (Culpeper 2003).

Indictment held sufficient. — In a case in which defendant was convicted of violating former § 3.1-796.124 (now § 3.2-6571) and he filed a motion to set aside based on alleged deficiencies in the indictment, since he did not raise the issue of the validity of the indictment until 16 months after trial, defendant had waived his right to be more fully advised of the cause and nature of his accusation. Additionally, it was obvious that defendant, the Commonwealth, and the court all were fully aware of the cause and nature of the offense for which he was being tried and of which he was convicted. Commonwealth v. Taylor, 77 Va. Cir. 102, 2008 Va. Cir. LEXIS 228 (Chesapeake 2008).

In a case in which defendant had been charged with first-degree murder, use of a firearm in the commission of a felony, and grand larceny of a commercial dump truck, he unsuccessfully moved to sever his grand larceny charge from the charges of murder and use of a firearm on the ground that the latter two charges were in no way related to the grand larceny charge. Based on the proffered evidence, the charged offenses meet the requirements of Va. Sup. Ct. R. 3A:6(b) for a single trial in that the Commonwealth had sufficiently shown that the crimes were so intimately connected and blended with the main facts adduced in evidence that they cannot be departed from with propriety, and justice did require defendant to have separate trials. Commonwealth v. McMillian, 75 Va. Cir. 399, 2008 Va. Cir. LEXIS 266 (Chesapeake Aug. 28, 2008).

Rule 3A:7. Capias or Summons Upon Indictment or Information.

(a) *Form.* — (1) Capias. The form of the capias shall be the same as that provided for a warrant except that it shall be signed by the clerk and shall state that an indictment or information has been filed against the accused.

(2) Summons. The summons shall be in the same form as the capias except that it shall summons the accused to appear before the court at a stated time and place.

(b) *Execution and Return.* — (1) Execution. The capias shall be executed as provided in Rule 3A:4(c).

(2) Return. The officer executing a capias or summons shall endorse the date of execution thereon and make return thereof to the court that issued the capias or summons. At the request of the Commonwealth's attorney made at any time while the indictment or information is pending, a capias returned unexecuted and not cancelled or a summons returned unexecuted or a duplicate thereof may be delivered by the clerk to any authorized person for execution.

Source. — Former Rule 3A:9.

Comment. — With respect to former Rule 3A:9, the amendment deletes subsection (a) in its entirety, redesignates former subsection (b) as subsection (a), deletes the reference to Rule 3A:4(b) (1) in subdivision (b) (1), and deletes the last two sentences of former subdivision (c) (1), changes the reference to Rule 3A:4 (d) in former subdivision (c) (1) to Rule 3A:4 (c), and redesignates former subsection (c) as subsection (b).

Michie's Jurisprudence. — For related discussion, see 5B M.J. Criminal Procedure, § 12; 9B M.J. Indictments, Informations and Presentments, §§ 15, 26, 35, 42.

CASE NOTES

Description of charge. — Trial court's judgment of conviction was reversed and defendant's case was remanded to the trial court for resentencing in a case where defendant had been convicted of a third DWI within a 10-year period and had been sentenced in accordance with the enhanced punishment provisions of § 18.2-270; the Commonwealth did not prove that defendant had been previously convicted of a second offense of driving while intoxicated within a five-year period, as the evidence at most disclosed that defendant had been arraigned in the earlier proceeding and found guilty of "DWI, 2nd offense," and not the second offense of driving while intoxicated within a five-year period that would be needed to enhance the punishment in the current case. Stewart v. Commonwealth, 2007 Va. App. LEXIS 104 (Mar. 20, 2007).

Rule 3A:8. Pleas.

(a) *Pleas by a Corporation.* — A corporation, acting by counsel or through an agent, may enter the same pleas as an individual.

(b) *Determining Voluntariness of Pleas of Guilty or Nolo Contendere.* — (1) A circuit court shall not accept a plea of guilty or nolo contendere to a felony charge without first determining that the plea is made voluntarily with an understanding of the nature of the charge and the consequences of the plea.

(2) A circuit court shall not accept a plea of guilty or nolo contendere to a misdemeanor charge except in compliance with Rule 7C:6.

(c) *Plea Agreement Procedure.* — (1) The attorney for the Commonwealth and the attorney for the defendant or the defendant when acting pro se may engage in discussions with a view toward reaching an agreement that, upon entry by the defendant of a plea of guilty, or a plea of nolo contendere, to a charged offense, or to a lesser or related offense, the attorney for the Commonwealth will do any of the following:

(A) Move for nolle prosequi or dismissal of other charges;

(B) Make a recommendation, or agree not to oppose the defendant's request, for a particular sentence, with the understanding that such recommendation or request shall not be binding on the court;

(C) Agree that a specific sentence is the appropriate disposition of the case.

In any such discussions under this Rule, the court shall not participate.

(2) If a plea agreement has been reached by the parties, it shall, in every felony case, be reduced to writing, signed by the attorney for the Commonwealth, the defendant, and, in every case, his attorney, if any, and presented to the court. The court shall require the disclosure of the agreement in open court or, upon a showing of good cause, in camera, at the time the plea is offered. If the agreement is of the type specified in subdivision (c) (1) (A) or (C), the court may accept or reject the agreement, or may defer its decision as to the acceptance or rejection until there has been an opportunity to consider a presentence report. If the agreement is of the type specified in subdivision (c) (1) (B), the court shall advise the defendant that, if the court does not accept the recommendation or request, the defendant nevertheless has no right to withdraw his plea, unless the Commonwealth fails to perform its part of the agreement. In that event, the defendant shall have the right to withdraw his plea.

(3) If the court accepts the plea agreement, the court shall inform the defendant that it will embody in its judgment and sentence the disposition provided for in the agreement.

(4) If the agreement is of the type specified in subdivision (c) (1) (A) or (C) and if the court rejects the plea agreement, the court shall inform the parties of this fact, and advise the defendant personally in open court or, on a showing of good cause, in camera, that the court will not accept the plea agreement. Thereupon, neither party shall be bound by the plea agreement. The defendant shall have the right to withdraw his plea of guilty or plea of nolo contendere and the court shall advise the defendant that, if he does not withdraw his plea, the disposition of the case may be less favorable to him than that contemplated by the plea agreement; and the court shall further advise the defendant that, if he chooses to withdraw his plea of guilty or of nolo contendere, his case will be heard by another judge, unless the parties agree otherwise.

(5) Except as otherwise provided by law, evidence of a plea of guilty later withdrawn, or a plea of nolo contendere, or of an offer to plead guilty or nolo contendere to the crime charged, or any other crime, or of statements made in connection with and relevant to any of the foregoing pleas or offers, is not admissible in the case-in-chief in any civil or criminal proceeding against the person who made the plea or offer. But evidence of a statement made in connection with and relevant to a plea of guilty, later withdrawn, a plea of nolo contendere, or any offer to plead guilty or nolo contendere to the crime charged or to any other crime, is admissible in any criminal proceeding for perjury or false statement, if the statement was made by the defendant under oath and on the record. In the event that a plea of guilty or a plea of nolo contendere is withdrawn in accordance with this Rule, the judge having received the plea shall take no further part in the trial of the case, unless the parties agree otherwise.

Cross references. — As to criminal practice and procedure in the general district courts, see Rule 7C:6.

Source. — Former Rule 3A:11.

Comment. — With respect to former Rule 3A:11, the amendment deletes former subsections (a) and (b), adds a new subsection (a) regarding pleas by a corporation, redesignates former subsection (c) as subsection (b), and redesignates former subsection (d) as subsection (c) and changes the reference to a "court of record" in former subsection (c) to a "circuit court."

Comment on 1985 amendment. — § 19.2-153 was amended by Ch. 253 of the Acts of 1985.

The amendment, effective January 1, 2001, adopted November 2, 2000, deleted "in a misdemeanor case" following "a plea of guilty, or" in subdivision (c)(1).

The amendment, effective June 1, 2005, adopted March 1, 2005, in subdivision (b), added the designator (1), inserted "to a felony charge" near the middle of (1), and added (2).

Law Review. — For note, "Criminal Procedure and Criminal Law: Virginia Supreme Court Decisions During the 70's," see 15 U. Rich. L. Rev. 585 (1981). For note on competence to plead guilty and to stand trial when a criminal defendant waives counsel, see 68 Va. L. Rev. 1139 (1982). For a review of criminal law in Virginia for year 1999, see 33 U. Rich. L. Rev. 857 (1999). For survey of Virginia law on criminal law and procedure for the year 2007-2008, see 43 U. Rich. L. Rev. 149 (2008).

Michie's Jurisprudence. — For related discussion, see 4A M.J. Commonwealth's and State's Attorney, §§ 4, 7; 5B M.J. Criminal Procedure, §§ 30, 32, 33, 34; 9B M.J. Indictments, Informations and Presentments, §§ 7, 50.

CASE NOTES

Federal rule compared. — This rule is substantially equivalent to Fed. R. Crim. P. 11. Gardner v. Warden of Va. State Penitentiary, 222 Va. 491, 281 S.E.2d 876 (1981).

Guilty plea tendered in mid-trial irrelevant to right to enter plea. — The fact that a plea is tendered mid-trial is irrelevant to the analysis regarding a defendant's right to enter a plea of guilty; no limitations either under the Virginia Constitution, statutes or Rules of Court exist which provide a time by which a defendant must enter his plea of guilty. Graham v. Commonwealth, 11 Va. App. 133, 397 S.E.2d 270 (1990).

No "miscarriage of justice" where defendant's guilty plea tendered mid-trial was made knowingly, voluntarily and intelligently, despite that the trial court failed to inquire further of the defendant, or to make a written finding that the amended plea was voluntary and intelligent. Allen v. Commonwealth, 27 Va. App. 726, 501 S.E.2d 441 (1998).

Record must show that guilty plea was entered freely and intelligently. — There must be an affirmative showing in the record that a guilty plea is entered freely and intelligently. Stokes v. Slayton, 340 F. Supp. 190 (W.D. Va. 1972), aff'd, 473 F.2d 906 (4th Cir. 1973).

No particular ritual is required in order for the trial court to determine whether the plea is made voluntarily and with the understanding of its nature and consequences. Stokes v. Slayton, 340 F. Supp. 190 (W.D. Va. 1972), aff'd, 473 F.2d 906 (4th Cir. 1973).

Rejection of guilty plea to whole indictment only when plea constitutionally invalid. — Under the Virginia Constitution, the statutes and the Rules of the Supreme Court of Virginia, a trial court may reject a guilty plea to the whole of an indictment tendered without a plea agreement only when it determines that the plea is constitutionally invalid; further, this determination extends only to ensuring that a guilty plea is made voluntarily, intelligently and knowingly. Graham v. Commonwealth, 11 Va. App. 133, 397 S.E.2d 270 (1990).

Failure to inform defendant of possibility of trial without jury. — It is not fatal to the guilty plea that the defendant was not informed that he could be tried by the court without a jury with the consent of the court and the Commonwealth's attorney. Stokes v. Slayton, 340 F. Supp. 190 (W.D. Va. 1972), aff'd, 473 F.2d 906 (4th Cir. 1973).

Immigration consequences of guilty plea. — The trial court is not obliged to inform a defendant of any collateral consequences that may arise upon the entry of a guilty plea; the immigration implications of a guilty plea are a collateral consequence. Zigta v. Commonwealth, 38 Va. App. 149, 562 S.E.2d 347, 2002 Va. App. LEXIS 237 (2002).

Entry of plea on advice of counsel does not make it invalid. — That a guilty plea was entered upon the advice of counsel does not prevent it from being entered freely and voluntarily. Stokes v. Slayton, 340 F. Supp. 190 (W.D. Va. 1972), aff'd, 473 F.2d 906 (4th Cir. 1973).

Nor does phrasing of court's inquiry as to voluntariness as narrative statement. — That the court phrased its inquiry as to the voluntariness of the plea as a narrative statement is not sufficient to render a guilty plea invalid. Stokes v. Slayton, 340 F. Supp. 190 (W.D. Va. 1972), aff'd, 473 F.2d 906 (4th Cir. 1973).

Motion to withdraw plea should be granted if it appears from the surrounding circumstances that the plea of guilty was submitted in good faith under an honest mistake of material fact or facts, or if it was induced by fraud, coercion or undue influence and would not otherwise have been made. Jones v. Commonwealth, 29 Va. App. 503, 513 S.E.2d 431 (1999).

Determining whether court erred in declining to allow withdrawal of a guilty plea requires an examination of the circumstances confronting the accused immediately prior to and at the time he or she pleaded to the charge. Jones v. Commonwealth, 29 Va. App. 503, 513 S.E.2d 431 (1999).

Defense to charges not enought to set aside guilty plea. — Defense to the charges is not by itself sufficient to require a trial court to set aside a guilty plea because the guilty plea must also be entered inadvisedly; any number of circumstances might render a plea inadvised, including the fact that an attorney overlooked a viable defense or the defendant did not understand the nature of the charges. Pritchett v. Commonwealth, 61 Va. App. 777, 739 S.E.2d 922, 2013 Va. App. LEXIS 117 (2013).

Defendant is allowed to withdraw his or her guilty plea in situations where the defendant would not have pled guilty but for some external circumstance such as coercion, or poor or erroneous advice from counsel; a defendant who wishes to withdraw his or her guilty plea must do more than tender a defense. Pritchett v. Commonwealth, 61 Va. App. 777, 739 S.E.2d 922, 2013 Va. App. LEXIS 117 (2013).

Withdrawal of plea agreement improper where court accepted agreement. — As the trial court, by imposing terms of suspended incarceration and post-release supervision under § 18.2-10(g) and subsection A of § 19.2-295.2, which were not mentioned in the plea agreement but were required by law, did not implicitly reject the plea agreement, but, instead, sentenced defendant in accordance with its terms, defendant could not withdraw the agreement under Va. Sup. Ct. R 3A:8(c)(4). Wright v. Commonwealth, 275 Va. 77, 655 S.E.2d 7, 2008 Va. LEXIS 12 (2008).

Effect of failure to disclose plea bargain. — A guilty plea which was induced by a plea bargain was not constitutionally intelligent and voluntary where the bargain was not disclosed to the trial judge before the plea was accepted. Thus, even though subdivision (c)(2) of this rule was not in effect at the time the defendant was tried, the lower court erred in refusing to grant a writ of habeas corpus. Gardner v. Warden of Va. State Penitentiary, 222 Va. 491, 281 S.E.2d 876 (1981).

Inmate was not entitled to habeas relief based on his counsel's ineffectiveness in allegedly failing to communicate the prosecution's plea offer, as he offered no evidence that the offer was within the boundaries of acceptable plea agreements and sentences in the jurisdiction, or that the trial judge had ever accepted similar plea agreements and sentences in other cases involving similar facts and charges. Laster v. Russell, 286 Va. 17, 743 S.E.2d 272, 2013 Va. LEXIS 74 (2013).

Necessity of disclosure of charitable contribution as part of plea agreement. — When commonwealth's attorney, during presentation of plea agreement to judge for his acceptance, deliberately concealed the $25,000 charitable contributions to be made by defendant's father, and also asked defense counsel not to disclose it, the court rejected his contention that a prosecutor is not required to inform the sentencing court of any such condition. Morrissey v. Virginia State Bar, 248 Va. 334, 448 S.E.2d 615 (1994).

Appeal from conviction entered on plea of guilty. — An appeal does not lie from a conviction entered upon a valid plea of guilty, unless the trial court either lacked jurisdiction or imposed a sentence which exceeds that authorized by law. Stokes v. Slayton, 340 F. Supp. 190 (W.D. Va. 1972), aff'd, 473 F.2d 906 (4th Cir. 1973).

Entry of a knowing and voluntary, but nonconditional, plea waived appeal from denial of motion to suppress. — Because defendant did not enter a conditional guilty plea pursuant to § 19.2-254, to a charge of possession of Oxycodone, in violation of § 18.2-250, but he entered said plea voluntarily and intelligently, he waived his right to appeal from the judgment denying his motion to suppress the evidence seized against him. Hill v. Commonwealth, 47 Va. App. 667, 626 S.E.2d 459, 2006 Va. App. LEXIS 63 (2006).

Subdivision (c) confers only presentence right to withdraw guilty plea. — Subdivision (c) of this rule, which now provides that if a trial court decides to reject a plea agreement, it shall so advise the accused and shall give him an opportunity to withdraw his guilty plea, confers only a presentence right to withdraw a guilty plea. Where the defendant's motion for withdrawal is made after sentencing, judicial discretion is involved, and the applicable standard for exercising this discretion is enunciated in former Rule 3A:25(d). Lilly v. Commonwealth, 218 Va. 960, 243 S.E.2d 208 (1978); Holler v. Commonwealth, 220 Va. 961, 265 S.E.2d 715 (1980).

Defendant allowed to withdraw plea. — Because trial court rejected dispositional plea agreement, the trial court erred in refusing to permit defendant to withdraw his guilty pleas. Smith v. Commonwealth, 17 Va. App. 162, 435 S.E.2d 586 (1993).

Where defendant testified he pled guilty to malicious wounding because his counsel misinformed him that he faced a life sentence, and counsel denied this, defendant's motion to withdraw his guilty plea on grounds of mistake of fact was properly denied because the trial court was entitled to believe counsel. Johnson v. Commonwealth, No. 3206-03-2, 2005 Va. App. LEXIS 67 (Ct. of Appeals Feb. 15, 2005).

Defendant not entitled to withdraw guilty plea. — Denial of motion to withdraw guilty plea was supported by evidence that the trial court conducted a thorough and meaningful discussion with defendant regarding the significance and consequences associated with his decision to enter a guilty plea to the lesser charge of possession of cocaine, defendant twice affirmed that he was pleading guilty and was doing so freely after consultation with his attorney, the trial court explicitly told defendant that it had a range of sentences it could impose and defendant affirmed that he knew he was looking a penitentiary time, and, when the trial court asked defendant if he was satisfied with the services of his counsel, defendant unequivocally stated that he was. Fields v. Commonwealth, 2012 Va. App. LEXIS 157 (May 15, 2012).

Trial court did not err in denying defendant's motion to withdraw his guilty pleas because it followed the requirements of Va. Sup. Ct. R. 3A:8(c)(2); the trial court properly could consider the statements defendant made during the colloquy in assessing whether defendant's guilty pleas were entered into inadvisedly or based on a mistake concerning the trial court's ability to reject the recommendation of the prosecution. Pritchett v. Commonwealth, 61 Va. App. 777, 739 S.E.2d 922, 2013 Va. App. LEXIS 117 (2013).

Rejection of plea agreement. — Court rejected plea agreement when it failed to impose the sentence provided in the plea agreement. Smith v. Commonwealth, 17 Va. App. 162, 435 S.E.2d 586 (1993).

Refusal to consider plea agreement. — Trial judge's refusal to allow the parties an opportunity to put a proposed plea agreement in writing and his insistence that the case be tried before a plea agreement could be reduced to writing adversely affected defendant, particularly in light of the fact that, despite the reference in Va. Sup. Ct. R. 3A:8(c) to a written, signed plea agreement, creation of such an agreement does not depend on the agreement being in written form or on its specific terms being recited to the judge. Wilson v. Commonwealth, 272 Va. 19, 630 S.E.2d 326, 2006 Va. LEXIS 60 (2006).

Imposition of additional sentence. — Trial court did not err in imposing an additional sentence of three years supervision to defendant's life sentence after defendant pled guilty to first-degree murder in exchange for the life sentence; although the plea agreement was a contract, contract law included the law in force on the date the contract was formed, which included the suspended sentence and post-release supervision provisions of subdivision (g) of § 18.2-10 and 19.2-295.2. Wright v. Commonwealth, 49 Va. App. 58, 636 S.E.2d 489, 2006 Va. App. LEXIS 503 (2006).

Imposition of terms of suspended incarceration and post-release supervision proper though not mentioned in plea agreement. — Defendant entered into a plea agreement with the Commonwealth pursuant to Va. Sup. Ct. R. 3A:8(c)(1)(C). As contract principles applied to plea agreements, and the law in effect when the contract was made became part of the contract, the trial court, after accepting the plea agreement, properly imposed terms of suspended incarceration and post-release supervision under §§ 18.2-10(g) and 19.2-295.2(A), even though such terms were not mentioned in the plea agreement. Wright v. Commonwealth, 275 Va. 77, 655 S.E.2d 7, 2008 Va. LEXIS 12 (2008).

Rejection of the recommendation by imposition of a harsher sentence than recommended does not amount to a rejection of the plea agreement as contemplated under subdivision (c)(4) of this rule. Holler v. Commonwealth, 220 Va. 961, 265 S.E.2d 715 (1980).

Failure to reduce terms to writing or disclose to open court. — "Ends of justice" did not require review of the failure to reduce terms of the plea agreement to writing or disclose it in open court where the defendant's substantial rights were not implicated by the fact that the plea agreement was not in writing or disclosed in open court and the record showed that the terms of the plea agreement were fully presented to the trial court and that the defendant acknowledged that the oral presentation of the plea agreement was consistent with his understanding of the agreement. Hairston v. Commonwealth, 16 Va. App. 941, 434 S.E.2d 350 (1993).

Failure of Commonwealth's attorney to make sentencing recommendation. — The defendant waived his objection to the Commonwealth's attorney's noncompliance with plea agreement, which required the Commonwealth to recommend that he receive a suspended five-year sentence, where, at the sentencing hearing, defense counsel acknowledged that sentencing lay within the discretion of the trial court and did not complain about the Commonwealth's omission of a recommendation. Greene v. Commonwealth, No. 1137-97-3 (Ct. of Appeals April 28, 1998).

Failure of judge to reduce charge in accordance with sentencing recommendation. — Where the trial judge said that he accepted the sentencing recommendation and that he would suspend imposition of the sentence for one year, reduce the charge, and impose a fine if there were no further violations, by implication, he told the defendant that if he did not violate the law, the case would be disposed of after one year in accordance with the sentencing recommendation. Therefore, the judge failed to comply with the agreement where, upon appearance of the defendant for final disposition of the case, the trial judge first ascertained that there had been no known violations of the law by the defendant, and then proceeded to sentence the defendant to 12 months in jail, all suspended, but refused to reduce the felony conviction to the misdemeanor of disorderly conduct. Wolfe v. Commonwealth, 1 Va. App. 498, 339 S.E.2d 913 (1986).

Applied in Mason v. Commonwealth, 14 Va. App. 609, 419 S.E.2d 856 (1992); Jefferson v. Commonwealth, 27 Va. App. 477, 500 S.E.2d 219 (1998); Esparza v. Commonwealth, 29 Va. App. 600, 513 S.E.2d 885 (1999); Lampkins v. Commonwealth, 44 Va. App. 709, 607 S.E.2d 722, 2005 Va. App. LEXIS 22 (2005); Murphy v. Commonwealth, 51 Va. App. 535, 659 S.E.2d 538, 2008 Va. App. LEXIS 180 (2008).

CIRCUIT COURT OPINIONS

Circuit Court rejects the contention that it is solely the individual judge and not a court that is deemed to reject a plea agreement. — Circuit Court rejects any contention that it is solely the individual judge and not a court that is deemed to reject a plea agreement, otherwise, a defendant could seek to present a proposed agreed disposition to each individual judge in that circuit, and, if unsuccessful, to every other circuit court judge in the Commonwealth, hoping to find a judge who was willing to accept the agreed disposition rejected by all of his or her colleagues. Commonwealth v. Stepek, 2007 Va. Cir. LEXIS 183 (Fairfax County Aug. 23, 2007).

Use of statements made in connection with plea negotiations. — Under subdivision (c)(5), defendant's statement made during unsuccessful plea negotiations, at the Commonwealth's request, could be introduced as impeachment or rebuttal evidence at defendant's trial, if otherwise admissible. Commonwealth v. Evans, 55 Va. Cir. 237, 2001 Va. Cir. LEXIS 277 (Southampton County 2001).

Oral agreement not in nature of plea agreement. — Alleged agreement between defendant and the Commonwealth in which defendant alleged that the Commonwealth orally agreed to prosecute defendant in state court, rather than federal court, if she would cooperate with their investigation was not in the nature of a plea agreement because it did not provide for any of the three options set out in Va. Sup. Ct. R. 3A:8; it did not provide that upon a plea of guilty that the parties could agree to (1) move for nolle prosequi or dismissal of other charges, (2) make a recommendation, or agree not to oppose defendant's request for a particular sentence, or (3) agree that a specific sentence was appropriate. Commonwealth v. Stewart, 66 Va. Cir. 135, 2004 Va. Cir. LEXIS 325 (Portsmouth Oct. 22, 2004).

Guilty pleas. — Convicted killer's substantial rights were not implicated by the fact that his plea agreement was not in writing; accordingly, he did not show that the failure to obtain a written plea agreement affected either the voluntariness of his plea agreement or the adequacy of his counsel's representation, and the convicted killer presented no other ground that would support his request for relief pursuant to the habeas corpus petition he filed. Payne v. Wright, 57 Va. Cir. 207, 2001 Va. Cir. LEXIS 328 (Roanoke 2001).

Enforcement of plea following amendment of the indictment. — Defendant's motion to enforce an oral plea agreement was denied because he subsequently voluntarily agreed to amend the indictment, from distribution of imitation cocaine to distribution of cocaine, thus creating a new charge and thus invalidating and waiving the original plea agreement to distribution of imitation cocaine. Commonwealth v. Carter, 64 Va. Cir. 224, 2004 Va. Cir. LEXIS 183 (Norfolk 2004).

Despite plea agreement with Commonwealth, court had power to revoke bond. — Despite the Commonwealth's agreement not to move for revocation of the defendant's bond as part of its plea agreement, because the circuit court had an independent duty to assess whether the community's safety required the revocation of said bond, the court properly entered a revocation order, due to: (1) defendant's prior record, specifically, his two prior convictions of indecent exposure, designation as an habitual offender, and commission of the crimes of larceny and family assault; (2) the fact that the conduct that gave rise to the instant offense of a third charge of indecent exposure was especially egregious; and (3) his demonstrated unwillingness or inability to conform his conduct to the requirements of the law. Commonwealth v. Jordan, 2008 Va. Cir. LEXIS 33 (Fairfax County Mar. 24, 2008).

Rule 3A:9. Pleadings and Motions for Trial; Defenses and Objections.

(a) *Pleadings and Motions.* — Pleadings in a criminal proceeding shall be the indictment, information, warrant or summons on which the accused is to be tried and the plea of not guilty, guilty or nolo contendere. Defenses and objections made before trial that heretofore could have been made by other pleas or by demurrers and motions to quash shall be made only by motion to dismiss or to grant appropriate relief, as provided in these Rules.

(b) *The Motion Raising Defenses and Objections.* — (1) Defenses and Objections That Must Be Raised Before Trial. Defenses and objections based on defects in the institution of the prosecution or in the written charge upon which the accused is to be tried, other than that it fails to show jurisdiction in the court or to charge an offense, must be raised by motion made within the time prescribed by paragraph (c) of this

Rule. The motion shall include all such defenses and objections then available to the accused. Failure to present any such defense or objection as herein provided shall constitute a waiver thereof. Lack of jurisdiction or the failure of the written charge upon which the accused is to be tried to state an offense shall be noticed by the court at any time during the pendency of the proceeding.

(2) Defenses and Objections That May Be Raised Before Trial. In addition to the defenses and objections specified in subparagraph (b) (1) of this Rule, any defense or objection that is capable of determination without the trial of the general issue may be raised by motion before trial. Failure to present any such defense or objection before the jury returns a verdict or the court finds the defendant guilty shall constitute a waiver thereof.

(3) Form of Motion. Any motion made before trial shall be in writing if made in a circuit court, unless the court for good cause shown permits an oral motion. A motion shall state with particularity the grounds or grounds on which it is based.

(4) Hearing on Motion. A motion before trial raising defenses or objections shall be determined before the trial unless the court orders that it be deferred for determination at the trial of the general issue. An issue of fact shall be heard and determined by the court, unless a jury trial is required by constitution or statute.

(5) Effect of Determination. If a motion is determined adversely to the accused, his plea shall stand or he may plead over or, if the accused has not previously pleaded, he shall be permitted to plead. The motion need not be renewed if the accused properly saves the point for the purpose of appeal when the court first determines the motion.

(c) *Time of Filing Notice or Making Motion.* — A motion referred to in subparagraph (b) (1) shall be filed or made before a plea is entered and, in a circuit court, at least 7 days before the day fixed for trial, or, if the motion raises speedy trial or Double Jeopardy grounds as specified in Code § 19.2-266.2(A)(ii), at such time prior to trial as the grounds for the motion or objection shall arise, whichever occurs last. A copy of such motion shall, at the time of filing, be submitted to the judge of the circuit court who will hear the case, if known.

(d) *Relief From Waiver.* — For good cause shown the court may grant relief from any waiver provided for in this Rule.

Source. — Former Rule 3A:12.

Comment. — With respect to former Rule 3A:12, the amendment deletes the words "Notice of Insanity Defense" from the title of the Rule, deletes subsection (b), redesignates former subsections (c) and (d) and (e) as subsections (b) and (c) and (d), respectively, changes the references to a "court of record" in former subdivision (c) (3) and former subsection (d) to a "circuit court," and adds the language beginning "and a copy of such motion shall, at the time of filing" at the end of former subsection (d).

The amendment, effective August 29, 2005, adopted August 29, 2005, reenacted subdivision (b)(1) without change; and in paragraph (c), divided the former provisions into two sentences by substituting "trial, or, if the motion raises speedy trial or Double Jeopardy grounds as specified in Code §19.2-266.2(ii), at such time prior to trial as the grounds for the motion or objection shall arise, whichever occurs last. A copy" for "trial, a copy."

The amendment, effective October 31, 2006, adopted October 31, 2006, substituted "Code § 19,2-266.2 A (ii)" for "Code § 19.2-266.2(ii)" in subdivision (c).

The amendment, effective May 2, 2011, adopted March 1, 2011, in the subdivision (c), substituted "19.2-266.2(A)(ii)" for "19.2-266.2 A(ii)" and "be submitted" for "be mailed."

Michie's Jurisprudence. — For related discussion, see 1B M.J. Appeal and Error, §§ 106, 175; 2B M.J. Autrefois, Acquit and Convict, § 25; 5B M.J. Criminal Procedure, §§ 12, 20, 31, 37; 6A M.J. Demurrers, §§ 1, 5, 24; 9A M.J. Grand Jury, §§ 5, 7; 9B M.J. Indictments, Informations and Presentments, §§ 51 - 53, 55; 11B M.J. Jurisdiction, §§ 33 - 35; 19 M.J. Venue, §§ 14, 16, 20.

CASE NOTES

This rule does not apply to tentative, conditional or provisional rulings from the court. Harward v. Commonwealth, 5 Va. App. 468, 364 S.E.2d 511 (1988).

Evidentiary rulings not contemplated within this rule. — This rule recognizes a class of defenses and motions which must be raised before trial and a separate class which may be raised before trial. Evidentiary rulings or relevance and materiality issues usually can only be made at trial and are not contemplated within this rule. Harward v. Commonwealth, 5 Va. App. 468, 364 S.E.2d 511 (1988).

This rule is permissive and does not preclude counsel from raising defense and objections that can be determined without trial of the general issue any time before the jury returns a verdict or the court finds the defendant guilty. Simmons v. Commonwealth, 6 Va. App. 445, 371 S.E.2d 7 (1988), rev'd on other grounds, 238 Va. 200, 380 S.E.2d 656 (1989).

Timeliness of double jeopardy plea. — The trial court properly held that under the circumstances, the plea of double jeopardy should not be deemed waived where Grady v. Corbin, 495 U.S. 508, 110 S. Ct. 2084, 109 L. Ed. 2d 548 (1990), was decided on May 29, 1990, the appellant was tried on June 6, 1990 and to comply with Rule 3A:9, the appellant must have filed his motion by May 30, 1990, one day after the Grady decision. Freeman v. Commonwealth, 14 Va. App. 126, 414 S.E.2d 871 (1992).

To argue a violation of double jeopardy protections or of § 19.2-294, a defendant must present his plea in writing seven days prior to the trial date; if this rule is not followed, a defendant is deemed to have waived these concerns. Clay v. Commonwealth, No. 0619-99-2, 2000 Va. App. LEXIS 644 (Ct. of Appeals Sept. 5, 2000).

Test for double jeopardy. — The traditional test of double jeopardy is set forth in Blockburger v. United States, 284 U.S. 299, 52 S. Ct. 180, 76 L. Ed. 306 (1932), which states, "the test to be applied to determine whether there are two offenses or only one, is whether each provision requires proof of a fact which the other does not." However, Blockburger is not the only test for double jeopardy. In Grady v. Corbin, 495 U.S. 508, 110 S. Ct. 2084, 109 L. Ed. 2d 548 (1990), the Supreme Court set forth a further standard for determining whether successive prosecutions are barred: The Double Jeopardy Clause bars any subsequent prosecution in which the government, to establish an essential element of an offense charged in that prosecution, will prove conduct that constitutes an offense for which the defendant has already been prosecuted. Freeman v. Commonwealth, 14 Va. App. 126, 414 S.E.2d 871 (1992).

Trial court did not err in denying defendant's motion to dismiss the felony offenses of possession of materials with which explosive materials could be made with intent to manufacture such materials in violation of clause (i) of § 18.2-85 and possession of explosive materials in violation of clause (ii) of § 18.2-85 because his convictions did not violate the Double Jeopardy Clauses of the United States and Virginia Constitutions even though defendant had been convicted of violating Norfolk City, Va., Code §§ 17.1-43 and 17.1-44(25); each of the misdemeanor and felony offenses required an element of proof the other offenses did not. Saunders v. Commonwealth, No. 1195-10-1, 2011 Va. App. LEXIS 384 (Dec. 6, 2011).

Objection to indictment untimely. — Defendant's objection to the indictment, made after entry of a guilty plea, was untimely under Va. Sup. Ct. R. 3A:9(b)(1). Walker v. Commonwealth, 2007 Va. App. LEXIS 214 (May 22, 2007).

Defendant's argument that the circuit court erred in denying his motion to dismiss an indictment based upon prosecutorial misconduct involving the investigation of a special grand jury was barred by Va. Sup. Ct. R.3A:9(b)(1) because defendant failed to file his motion at least seven days before trial pursuant to Va. Sup. Ct. R. 3A:9(c); therefore, defendant waived any objection. Rambo v. Commonwealth, 51 Va. App. 418, 658 S.E.2d 688, 2008 Va. App. LEXIS 149 (2008).

Contemporaneous objection to admission of evidence. — Evidence admitted at trial that had been ruled provisionally admissible during pretrial motion in limine to suppress required defendant's contemporaneous objection or contention that the foundation for the evidence had not been established. Thus, even if this rule applies to rulings on the admissibility of evidence, it does not relieve the opponent of the evidence of the requirement of making a contemporaneous objection. Even if pretrial the trial court had ruled the evidence inadmissible counsel cannot sit in silence and permit evidence to be introduced contrary to the court's ruling. To do so invites error without affording the trial court the opportunity of knowing whether counsel continues to consider the evidence objectionable. Harward v. Commonwealth, 5 Va. App. 468, 364 S.E.2d 511 (1988).

Defendant's motions to suppress evidence found in an inventory of a car defendant was driving before the car was impounded and to strike were properly denied under the caretaker exception to the exclusionary rule where defendant could produce neither proof of ownership nor a valid driver's license when he was stopped in the early morning hours in a car with a broken window in an area that was not suitable for the car's safekeeping. Williams v. Commonwealth, 42 Va. App. 723, 594 S.E.2d 305, 2004 Va. App. LEXIS 156 (2004).

Failure to state issue with sufficient particularity. — Defendant's written motion failed to state the issue defendant wished to argue with the particularity required by Va. Sup. Ct. R. 3A:9. Therefore, the trial court was within its discretion to limit the scope of defendant's suppression hearing to only those issues raised by defendant in defendant's written motions. Clark v. Commonwealth, 2011 Va. App. LEXIS 219 (July 5, 2011).

Section 19.2-399 prevails over this rule when in conflict. — When conflicting provisions are found, the provisions of a rule are subordinate to those of a statute. Clarke v. Commonwealth, No. 2058-91-4, (Ct. of Appeals May 11, 1993).

Objection at time of examination of jury instructions timely. — Where the defendant could not have known that the Commonwealth would seek to use previous rape as a predicate for attempted capital murder charge until the proposed jury instructions were examined and at that time, he promptly objected, this issue was presented timely to the trial court. Curtis v. Commonwealth, 13 Va. App. 622, 414 S.E.2d 421 (1992).

Failure to timely raise a defense. — Because the defendant did not comply with the notice provisions of Rule 3A:9 and did not show good cause, the defendant waived any defense or objection based on defects in the institution of the prosecution or in the written charge upon which the defendant was to be tried. Harris v. Commonwealth, 39 Va. App. 670, 576 S.E.2d 228, 2003 Va. App. LEXIS 39 (2003).

The presentation of specific evidence in one trial does not forever prevent the introduction of that evidence in a subsequent proceeding. Curtis v. Commonwealth, 12 Va. App. 527, 405 S.E.2d 230 (1991).

Failure to raise objections before trial. — Trial court did not err in refusing to consider defendant's untimely motion to suppress, because defendant neither complied with pretrial filing requirements of § 19.2-266.2, nor made any showing as to what "good cause" existed for his not having motion timely heard pretrial, or why "in the interest of justice" it was necessary to hear his motion at trial. Graves v. Commonwealth, No. 1316-98-3 (Ct. of Appeals June 29, 1999).

"Good cause" shown for proceeding with motion orally. — No reversible error occurred where a motion to appoint a special prosecutor was not made in writing; because appellant had notice of entry of the order and an opportunity to object and make arguments, he received all of the process that was due. Moreover, judicial approval was not required to employ a special assistant prosecutor, and, even if a court order was required, good cause existed to excuse the Commonwealth's failure to submit a written motion. Tucker v. Commonwealth, No. 1527-12-2, 2013 Va. App. LEXIS 192 (Ct. of Appeals July 2, 2013).

Waiting until very start of trial to move for separate trial does not constitute waiver of the right to a severance, under this rule, since it does not apply to such a motion. Burgess v. Commonwealth, 224 Va. 368, 297 S.E.2d 654 (1982).

Waiver found. — Defendant's challenge to the grand jury's failure to vote on certain aggravating factors before indicting on capital murder charges was waived where defendant's challenge was not made until after a death sentence had been imposed. Wolfe v. Commonwealth, 265 Va. 193, 576 S.E.2d 471, 2003 Va. LEXIS 32, cert. denied, 540 U.S. 1019, 124 S. Ct. 566, 157 L. Ed. 2d 434 (2003).

Defendant waived his appellate claim that the allegations of an indictment were so vague that defendant was denied the opportunity to present a defense and that the jury was left to speculate on how many offenses defendant had committed because defendant failed to comply with Va. Sup. Ct. R. 3A:9 by raising the issue by a written motion at least seven days before the scheduled trial on 12 counts of forcible sodomy and 12 counts of custodial indecent liberties. Johnson v. Commonwealth, 2006 Va. App. LEXIS 450 (Oct. 10, 2006).

With regard to defendant's convictions on two capital murder counts and the imposition of two death sentences against him, the trial court did not err in denying his motion for grand jury information because he failed to show good cause why he should be excused under Va. Sup. Ct. R. 3A:9(d) from the waiver of his right to challenge the composition of the grand jury since he failed to raise his challenge to the composition of the grand jury before he entered a plea. Prieto v. Commonwealth, 283 Va. 149, 721 S.E.2d 484, 2012 Va. LEXIS 20 (2012).

Suppression motion properly denied. — Trial court properly denied defendant's suppression motion as a police officer had a reasonable, articulable suspicion that defendant might be armed and dangerous to justify a pat-down search, given: (1) defendant was in an area known for illegal drug activity, at night, (2) defendant attempted to hide something as the officer approached, (3) defendant was extremely nervous, his heart was beating fast, and he was out of breath, although he had not just engaged in any strenuous activity, and (4) the officer suspected that defendant possessed illegal narcotics. Walker v. Commonwealth, 42 Va. App. 782, 595 S.E.2d 30, 2004 Va. App. LEXIS 169 (2004).

Motion to suppress was properly denied because the evidence supported the finding that the police special agent advised defendant of his *Miranda* rights before taking his statement and, in light of defendant's previous experience with the criminal justice system, the agent's statement, that defendant's cooperation would surely be given favorable consideration, did not impair defendant's capacity to determine for himself whether to waive his rights to remain silent and have an attorney present. Washington v. Commonwealth, 43 Va. App. 291, 597 S.E.2d 256, 2004 Va. App. LEXIS 268 (2004).

Defendant's motion to suppress was properly denied as: (1) the fact that defendant was read his *Miranda* rights and informed of his Fifth Amendment right to counsel was a factor in determining whether defendant was subjected to a custodial interrogation, (2) defendant was never told he was under arrest, he agreed to accompany the officers to the police station, he rode in the front seat of the police cruiser, and he was not handcuffed, (3) he was offered a bathroom break and refreshments at the police station and he was interviewed by only one police officer, (4) defendant was not threatened or coerced during the interview, and (5) he was released after the interview. Holcomb v. Commonwealth, 2006 Va. App. LEXIS 269 (June 20, 2006).

Applied in Tharp v. Commonwealth, 221 Va. 487, 270 S.E.2d 752 (1980); Starks v. Commonwealth, 225 Va. 48, 301 S.E.2d 152 (1983); Evans v. Commonwealth, 226 Va. 292, 308 S.E.2d 126 (1983); Stamper v. Commonwealth, 228 Va. 707, 324 S.E.2d 682 (1985); Rider v. Commonwealth, 8 Va. App. 595, 383 S.E.2d 25 (1989); Waters v. Commonwealth, 29 Va. App. 133, 510 S.E.2d 262 (1999).

CIRCUIT COURT OPINIONS

Objection to indictment. — In a case in which defendant was convicted of violating former § 3.1-796.124 (now § 3.2-6571) and he filed a motion to set aside based on alleged deficiencies in the indictment, since he did not raise the issue of the validity of the indictment until 16 months after trial, defendant had waived his right to be more fully advised of the cause and nature of his accusation. Additionally, it was obvious that defendant, the Commonwealth, and the court all were fully aware of the cause and nature of the offense for which he was being tried and of which he was convicted. Commonwealth v. Taylor, 77 Va. Cir. 102, 2008 Va. Cir. LEXIS 228 (Chesapeake 2008).

Prosecutorial discretion. — Defendant's motion to dismiss an indictment charging him with false pretense was denied because the facts and circumstances did not rise to a level that would support the overriding of prosecutorial discretion in bringing the false pretense charge; the false pretense charge did not increase the risk to defendant, and it was a different charge than the forgery and uttering charges that were previously brought against defendant and were dismissed. Commonwealth v. Gomez, 75 Va. Cir. 151, 2008 Va. Cir. LEXIS 30 (Fairfax County 2008).

Test for double jeopardy. — Defendant's motion to dismiss an indictment charging him with false pretense was denied because res judicata did not bar prosecution; the false pretense charge was not identical to forgery and uttering charges that had previously been brought against defendant, and defendant failed to carry his burden of proving that the very same point or question was in issue and determined in the former cases. Commonwealth v. Gomez, 75 Va. Cir. 151, 2008 Va. Cir. LEXIS 30 (Fairfax County 2008).

Conviction in circuit court did not divest juvenile court of jurisdiction. — Despite the fact that defendant had already been tried and convicted on unrelated charges as an adult in the circuit court, the juvenile court retained jurisdiction to enforce its previous order revoking his probation and sentencing him to jail time, and the juvenile proceedings subsequent to his conviction were simply an exercise of the court's inherent authority to enforce its orders; hence, the Juvenile and Domestic Relations Court properly denied defendant's motion to dismiss a show cause summons regarding the same. Commonwealth v. Stewart, 71 Va. Cir. 313, 2006 Va. Cir. LEXIS 224 (Page County 2006).

"Good cause" shown for proceeding with motion orally. — Court permitted defendant to proceed with his motions to dismiss an indictment orally, because there was "good cause" to authorize defendant to proceed orally based upon representations of defense counsel that a computer virus prevented him from printing the written motions and briefs in support prior to the hearing and that he presented the court at oral argument with copies of cases in support of his arguments; further, the court took notice of the widely reported fact that, on the weekend prior to the hearing scheduled on defendant's motions, a computer virus infected and disabled many computer systems around the world. Commonwealth v. Simone, 63 Va. Cir. 216, 2003 Va. Cir. LEXIS 362 (Portsmouth 2003).

Rule 3A:10. Trial Together of More Than One Accused or More Than One Offense.

(a) *More Than One Accused — Joinder of Defendants.* — On motion of the Commonwealth, for good cause shown, the court shall order persons charged with participating in contemporaneous and related acts or occurrences or in a series of acts or occurrences constituting an offense or offenses to be tried jointly unless such joint trial would constitute prejudice to a defendant.

(b) *More Than One Accused — Severance of Defendants.* — If the court finds that a joint trial would constitute prejudice to a defendant, the court shall order severance as to that defendant or provide such other relief as justice requires.

(c) *An Accused Charged With More Than One Offense.* — The court may direct that an accused be tried at one time for all offenses then pending against him, if justice does not require separate trials and (i) the offenses meet the requirements of Rule 3A:6 (b) or (ii) the accused and the Commonwealth's attorney consent thereto.

Cross references. — As to criminal practice and procedure in the general district courts, see Rule 7C:4.

Source. — Former Rule 3A:13.

Comment. — With respect to former Rule 3A:13, the 1984 revision changes the reference to Rule 3A:7 (b) in subsection (a) to Rule 3A:6 (b), and changes the reference to Rule 3A:7 in subsection (b) to Rule 3A:6 (b).

The amendment, effective May 2, 2011, adopted March 1, 2011, substituted "shall" for ", in its discretion, may" in subdivision (a).

Law Review. — For article, "Criminal Law and Procedure," see 35 U. Rich. L. Rev. 537 (2001).

Michie's Jurisprudence. — For related discussion, see 5B M.J. Criminal Procedure, § 26; 19 M.J. Trial, § 5.

CASE NOTES

Rule not inconsistent with § 19.2-263 (see now § 19.2-262.1). — An apparent inconsistency exists between § 19.2-263 (see now § 19.2-262.1) and subdivision (a) of this rule. The statute speaks of the election of an accused to be tried separately, while the rule refers to the consent of two or more accuseds to be tried jointly. However, there is no real inconsistency between the statute and the rule, since election to be tried separately is a refusal of consent to be tried jointly; on the other hand, consent to be tried jointly is a waiver of the right to elect to be tried separately. Burgess v. Commonwealth, 224 Va. 368, 297 S.E.2d 654 (1982).

A motion for separate trials must be made before trial begins or it is deemed waived. Colclasure v. Commonwealth, 10 Va. App. 200, 390 S.E.2d 790 (1990).

When joinder permitted. — Even if the requirements of Rule 3A:6(b) are met, joinder is not permitted unless "justice does not require separate trials." Cook v. Commonwealth, 7 Va. App. 225, 372 S.E.2d 780 (1988).

A court may direct that an accused be tried at one time for all offenses pending against him if (1) "justice does not require separate trials," and (2) "the offenses are based on the same act or transaction, or on two or more acts or transactions that are connected or constitute parts of a common scheme or plan." Whether different offenses should be tried separately is a matter that rests within the sound discretion of a trial court. Thus, a trial court's ruling on the matter will not be reversed absent a showing that the court abused its discretion. Cheng v. Commonwealth, 240 Va. 26, 393 S.E.2d 599 (1990).

Where defendant did not consent to the joinder of the charges for trial, joinder could be ordered only if the charges were part of a "common scheme" and justice did not require separate trials. Kirk v. Commonwealth, 21 Va. App. 291, 464 S.E.2d 162 (1995).

In determining whether a joint trial would prejudice a defendant, the trial court should require the party moving for severance to establish that actual prejudice would result from a joint trial. Adkins v. Commonwealth, 24 Va. App. 159, 480 S.E.2d 777 (1997).

Joinder of cases by consent did not compel relatedness finding. — In a case where the issue was whether defendant's convictions were related for purposes of Sentencing Guidelines, and where joinder of the offenses in state court resulted from the consent of the accused by counsel and the Commonwealth attorney, and the state court, therefore, made no finding of a "common scheme or plan," the joinder by consent of the five cases did not compel a finding of relatedness as to those offenses. Breckenridge v. United States, 977 F. Supp. 766 (W.D. Va. 1997).

Right to separate trials held not waived by earlier consent to joint trial. — Where defendant granted his consent to a joint trial when he and his codefendant were represented by the same attorney, prior to the time the judge ruled that the attorney could not represent both defendants and that the two could not be tried together, the trial court should not have relied on prior consent in finding a waiver of the right to a separate trial. Burgess v. Commonwealth, 224 Va. 368, 297 S.E.2d 654 (1982).

Under this rule, a trial court has limited discretion to order that an accused be tried concurrently for multiple offenses. Goodson v. Commonwealth, 22 Va. App. 61, 467 S.E.2d 848 (1996).

Justice often requires separate trials where highly prejudicial evidence of one of the crimes is not admissible in the trial of the other. Long v. Commonwealth, 20 Va. App. 223, 456 S.E.2d 138 (1995).

Because: (1) evidence of defendant's separate misdemeanor offenses with two separate victims was not necessary to prove any relevant element of the felony offenses charged involving a third victim, or necessary to prove defendant's motive, intent or knowledge, and in a separate trial involving only the felony offenses; and (2) evidence of defendant's sexual offenses involving the two misdemeanor victims would do little more than show that defendant was a bad man likely to commit that sort of crime, the trial court abused its discretion by not granting defendant's motion to sever the felony indictments from the misdemeanor indictments for separate trials under Va. Sup. Ct. R. 3A:10(c); however, said error was harmless due to the overwhelming evidence of defendant's guilt. Smith v. Commonwealth, No. 1004-04-1, 2005 Va. App. LEXIS 140 (Ct. of Appeals Apr. 5, 2005).

Because the trial court erred in not granting defendant's motion to sever the indictments for separate trials, it was not necessary to decide whether the charged offenses satisfied the requirements of Va. Sup. Ct. R. 3A:6(b). Smith v. Commonwealth, No. 1004-04-1, 2005 Va. App. LEXIS 140 (Ct. of Appeals Apr. 5, 2005).

Evidence admissible for one charge but not for other. — It is well settled that justice requires separate trials under this rule where evidence of one crime is not admissible in the trial of the others; a harmless error analysis will not be applied to a trial court's clear error in refusing to sever a charge of possession of a firearm by a convicted felon from a related charge or charges since evidence of the defendant's prior convictions is admissible with respect to the firearms charge but is highly prejudicial and inadmissible with respect to the others. Hackney v. Commonwealth, 28 Va. App. 288, 504 S.E.2d 385 (1998).

Denial of motion to sever held error where offenses not part of common plan. — The trial court erred when it denied the defendant's motion to sever the trial of two robbery and two use of a firearm offenses which, though factually similar, were not part of a common plan. A defendant should not be required to defend two criminal charges in same trial simply because they arose out of factually similar events. Godwin v. Commonwealth, 6 Va. App. 118, 367 S.E.2d 520 (1988).

Trial court's decision to try all of defendant's charged offenses together constituted an abuse of its discretion. Although uncontradicted evidence overwhelmingly proved defendant's guilt on all of the charges against him, because the jury had broad discretion in fixing the sentences on those charges, the appellate court could not say that trial court's error did not affect defendant's sentence. Long v. Commonwealth, 20 Va. App. 223, 456 S.E.2d 138 (1995).

Trying defendant on firearm/felony charge with the other charges would unduly prejudice him in the minds of the jury by letting them know that he had previously been convicted of a felony, which was irrelevant to the possession of heroin and firearm/heroin charges. Long v. Commonwealth, 20 Va. App. 223, 456 S.E.2d 138 (1995).

Trial court erred when it denied appellant's motion to sever the possession of a firearm by a convicted felon charge from a murder charge. Appellant's prior felony was an element of the firearm possession charge, but not an element of the murder charge. The prior felony was not relevant to the murder charge, and the fact that appellant was a felon only served to prejudice the jury. Allison v. Commonwealth, No. 0792-94-4, (Ct. of Appeals Oct. 17, 1995).

Joinder proper where "common scheme" established. — Joinder of offenses was proper where the two offenses were "connected" in time, place, and manner, and were sufficiently idiosyncratic to permit an inference that the same person was involved in a "common scheme" of criminal activity; in each instance defendant and a companion knocked on a door to see if anyone was home, asking for someone who did not live there if anyone answered the door. Seis v. Commonwealth, 2007 Va. App. LEXIS 432 (Nov. 27, 2007).

That three businesses, in close proximity, were burglarized within six days; that the same method of entry was used in each case; and that in each burglary, cash registers or parts of them were stolen, allowed the trial court to find the that crimes were connected or constituted parts of a common scheme or plan, Va. Sup. Ct. R. 3A:6(b), to such a degree that justice did not require that the charges be severed under Va. Sup. Ct. R. 3A:10(c). Kinnard v. Commonwealth, 2008 Va. App. LEXIS 340 (July 22, 2008).

Joinder of offenses improper where common scheme not established. — As the evidence showed only a general similarity of manner in which nine armed robberies were committed and failed to establish that the crimes shared idiosyncratic features permitting an inference of a pattern of criminal activity committed by the same person, and as there was no proof that the offenses were related to one another for the purpose of accomplishing a particular goal, the Commonwealth did not establish that there was a "common scheme or plan" within the meaning of Va. Sup. Ct. R. 3A:6(b). Therefore, joining the robberies in a single trial under Va. Sup. Ct. R. 3A:10(c) was error. Scott v. Commonwealth, 274 Va. 636, 651 S.E.2d 630, 2007 Va. LEXIS 132 (2007).

Failure to challenge joinder. — In a prosecution on four charges of grand larceny and four charges of burglary, since defendant did not challenge the joinder of the offenses under Va. Sup. Ct. R. 3A:10(c) and 3A:6(b) at trial or on appeal and did not argue that the four burglaries were not part of a common scheme or plan, the trial court was entitled to consider the evidence of a common scheme or plan in evaluation of each offense in reaching its verdict. Wilkins v. Commonwealth, 2008 Va. App. LEXIS 483 (Oct. 28, 2008).

Any error in joinder harmless. — Any error in the joinder of the offenses arising out of two attacks was harmless, because the evidence of each offense would have been admissible at a trial for the other to prove that the attacks were part of a common plan and the evidence against defendant was so overwhelming that the outcome would not have changed absent the alleged improper evidence. Angel v. Commonwealth, 2009 Va. App. LEXIS 125 (Mar. 24, 2009).

Denial of motion to sever upheld. — Where three offenses of concealment were committed within 30 minutes of each other at three separate 7-Eleven stores by the same defendant and accomplice, the trial court's denial of a motion for severance caused no undue prejudice, and justice did not require separate trials. Cook v. Commonwealth, 7 Va. App. 225, 372 S.E.2d 780 (1988).

In a trial for robbery and felony murder, a trial court did not err in refusing to grant defendant's motion for separate trials, since the robbery and felony murder arose out of the same transaction and no prejudice would have resulted from trying the offenses together. Spain v. Commonwealth, 7 Va. App. 385, 373 S.E.2d 728 (1988).

In light of the distinctive method of operation that was employed in each of defendant's crimes and the fact that defendant claimed that he was not the person who committed the offenses, the probative value of the other offenses was obvious and a single trial was appropriate under subdivision (c) of this rule. Traish v. Commonwealth, 36 Va. App. 114, 549 S.E.2d 5, 2001 Va. App. LEXIS 407 (2001).

Trial court did not abuse its discretion by allowing the Commonwealth to try defendant for two robberies that occurred about an hour apart, because although the crimes were not part of same transaction, they were connected. Brown v. Commonwealth, 37 Va. App. 507, 559 S.E.2d 415, 2002 Va. App. LEXIS 88 (2002).

Where defendant was charged with six robberies, one of which involved the use of a firearm, the trial court did not abuse its discretion, under Rule 3A:10(c), by denying his motion to sever the robbery involving a firearm from the others on the ground that the jury could become confused and believe that a firearm was used in all the robberies. Valery v. Commonwealth, No. 2381-01-1, 2003 Va. App. LEXIS 133 (Ct. of Appeals Mar. 11, 2003).

Because defendant could point to no trial right that was compromised or any basis for concluding that the jury was prevented from making a reliable judgment about defendant's guilt or innocence, the trial court did not abuse its discretion by refusing defendant's request for a separate trial under § 19.2-262.1 and Va. Sup. Ct. R. 3A:10(a). Allen v. Commonwealth, 58 Va. App. 618, 712 S.E.2d 748, 2011 Va. App. LEXIS 258 (2011).

While defendant did not consent, the appellate court found that the evidence showed that the two drug offenses arose out of two or more acts or transactions that were connected based on "gradation," and thus, the trial court did not err in denying the motion to sever. Doss v. Commonwealth, 59 Va. App. 435, 719 S.E.2d 358, 2012 Va. App. LEXIS 5 (2012).

Separate trial unwarranted. — Trial court did not err in not ordering a separate trial on charges of involuntary manslaughter and unlawful distribution of a controlled substance, in violation of § 18.2-248, against a doctor, where the offenses were based on the same act or transactions, or on two or more acts or transactions that were connected or constitute parts of a common scheme or plan; moreover, defendant conceded that the evidence of the distribution was essential to the trial of the homicide charge. Jere v. Commonwealth, No. 2125-02-2, 2003 Va. App. LEXIS 465 (Ct. of Appeals Sept. 9, 2003).

Because defendant's arguments for severance of the charges under Va. Sup. Ct. R. 3A:6 and 3A:10(c) relied entirely upon the assumption that the testimony defendant would have given represented exculpatory evidence on the failure to appear charge, because the arguments were unpreserved under Va. Sup. Ct. R. 5A:18, and because defendant did not preserve a complete and proper record for review, the arguments were procedurally barred. Jackson v. Commonwealth, 2008 Va. App. LEXIS 80 (Feb. 19, 2008).

Denial of motion to sever overruled. — Where the only similarity between the crimes was that they involved the use of a crowbar to break into several businesses which were located in the same part of the county and near major highways, but the crimes occurred over a period of almost six weeks; the businesses involved were several restaurants, an auto repair shop, a grocery store, and a church; the items taken were not similar; and the evidence failed to establish any connection among the offenses, the crimes were neither related transactions nor parts of a common scheme or plan, as required for joinder. Mills v. Commonwealth, No. 2305-92-3, (Ct. of Appeals Aug. 2, 1994).

Testimony of each victim was inadmissible at the trial for the offenses allegedly committed against each of the other victims since a defendant's intent to commit the crime of rape was not the same issue as whether a victim consented to sexual intercourse; thus, the trial court abused its discretion in denying defendant's motion to sever the charges. Commonwealth v. Minor, 267 Va. 166, 591 S.E.2d 61, 2004 Va. LEXIS 24 (2004).

Linking courtroom attire to granting severance motion error. — Denying defendant the right to wear his navy uniform was not a valid consideration for granting of his severance motion. There is no basis to hold that a military uniform affords an unrealistic suggestion of good character any more than do neat and clean attire and good grooming. It is inappropriate for a trial court to deny a courtroom participant the right to present himself in his best posture. Johnson v. Commonwealth, 19 Va. App. 163, 449 S.E.2d 819 (1994).

Election of offenses not required. — Defendant asked two people to kill his wife, formulated diagrams of his wife's house, explained when she would be at home, and paid two thousand dollars to the hit man. The evidence was sufficient to convict defendant of attempted capital murder for hire and solicitation of capital murder for hire; the Commonwealth did not err by failing to elect between the charges, because the solicitation and attempt were both parts of a common scheme or plan. Ashford v. Commonwealth, 47 Va. App. 676, 626 S.E.2d 464, 2006 Va. App. LEXIS 70 (2006).

Applied in Brown v. Commonwealth, 223 Va. 601, 292 S.E.2d 319 (1982); Essex v. Commonwealth, 228 Va. 273, 322 S.E.2d 216 (1984); Ferrell v. Commonwealth, 11 Va. App. 380, 399 S.E.2d 614 (1990); Spence v. Commonwealth, 12 Va. App. 1040, 407 S.E.2d 916 (1991); Johnson v. Commonwealth, 20 Va. App. 49, 455 S.E.2d 261 (1995); United States v. Breckenridge, 93 F.3d 132 (4th Cir. 1996); Satcher v. Netherland, 944 F. Supp. 1222 (E.D. Va. 1996); Yellardy v. Commonwealth, 38 Va. App. 19, 561 S.E.2d 739, 2002 Va. App. LEXIS 192 (2002).

CIRCUIT COURT OPINIONS

When joinder permitted. — The "connected" test of Rule 3A:6(b) is that the crimes should be so intimately connected and blended with the main facts adduced in evidence that they cannot be departed from with propriety. Defendant's motion for severance was granted to separate a count of driving under a suspended license and a count of operating a motor vehicle without paying fees from other counts that charged him with various criminal acts related to the deaths of two of his passengers in an automobile accident; those two counts had no relation to the manner in which defendant operated his vehicle and defendant was strictly liable for those counts regardless of the manner in which he drove, so defendant was entitled to severance of those two counts. Commonwealth v. Walsh, 62 Va. Cir. 511, 2003 Va. Cir. LEXIS 267 (Culpeper 2003).

In a case in which defendant had been charged with first-degree murder, use of a firearm in the commission of a felony, and grand larceny of a commercial dump truck, he unsuccessfully moved to sever his grand larceny charge from the charges of murder and use of a firearm on the ground that the latter two charges were in no way related to the grand larceny charge. Based on the proffered evidence, the charged offenses meet the requirements of Va. Sup. Ct. R. 3A:6(b) for a single trial in that the Commonwealth had sufficiently shown that the crimes were so intimately connected and blended with the main facts adduced in evidence that they cannot be departed from with propriety, and justice did require defendant to have separate trials. Commonwealth v. McMillian, 75 Va. Cir. 399, 2008 Va. Cir. LEXIS 266 (Chesapeake Aug. 28, 2008).

Joinder of three defendants. — Joinder of three defendants' trials on home invasion charges was proper under § 19.2-262.1 and Va. Sup. Ct. R. 3A:10 because all defendants were charged with the same offenses, which allegedly arose out of the same events. Moreover, the joinder of defendants' trials would promote efficiency and judicial economy, and defendants' argument that they would be prejudiced because they would be unable to compel each other to testify under U.S. Const. amend. V was without merit. Commonwealth v. Rice, 81 Va. Cir. 215, 2010 Va. Cir. LEXIS 301 (Hanover County Sept. 23, 2010).

Rule 3A:11. Discovery and Inspection.

(a) *Application of Rule.* — This Rule applies to any prosecution for a felony in a circuit court and to any misdemeanor brought on direct indictment.

(b) *Discovery by the Accused.* — (1) Upon written motion of an accused a court shall order the Commonwealth's attorney to permit the accused to inspect and copy or photograph any relevant (i) written or recorded statements or confessions made by the accused, or copies thereof, or the substance of any oral statements or confessions made by the accused to any law enforcement officer, the existence of which is known to the attorney for the Commonwealth, and (ii) written reports of autopsies, ballistic tests, fingerprint analyses, handwriting analyses, blood, urine and breath tests, other scientific reports, and written reports of a physical or mental examination of the accused or the alleged victim made in connection with the particular case, or copies thereof, that are known by the Commonwealth's attorney to be within the possession, custody or control of the Commonwealth.

(2) Upon written motion of an accused a court shall order the Commonwealth's attorney to permit the accused to inspect and copy or photograph designated books, papers, documents, tangible objects, buildings or places, or copies or portions thereof, that are within the possession, custody, or control of the Commonwealth, upon a showing that the items sought may be material to the preparation of his defense and that the request is reasonable. This subparagraph does not authorize the discovery or inspection of statements made by Commonwealth witnesses or prospective Commonwealth witnesses to agents of the Commonwealth or of reports, memoranda or other internal Commonwealth documents made by agents in connection with the investigation or prosecution of the case, except as provided in clause (ii) of subparagraph (b)(1) of this Rule.

(c) *Discovery by the Commonwealth.* — If the court grants relief sought by the accused under clause (ii) of subparagraph (b) (1) or under subparagraph (b) (2) of this Rule, it shall, upon motion of the Commonwealth, condition its order by requiring that:

(1) The accused shall permit the Commonwealth within a reasonable time but not less than ten (10) days before trial or sentencing, as the case may be, to inspect, copy or photograph any written reports of autopsy examinations, ballistic tests, fingerprint, blood, urine and breath analyses, and other scientific tests that may be within the accused's possession, custody or control and which the defense intends to proffer or introduce into evidence at trial or sentencing.

(2) The accused disclose whether he intends to introduce evidence to establish an alibi and, if so, that the accused disclose the place at which he claims to have been at the time of the commission of the alleged offense.

(3) If the accused intends to rely upon the defense of insanity or feeblemindedness, the accused shall permit the Commonwealth to inspect, copy or photograph any written reports of physical or mental examination of the accused made in connection with the particular case, provided, however, that no statement made by the accused in the course of an examination provided for by this Rule shall be used by the Commonwealth in its case-in-chief, whether the examination shall be with or without the consent of the accused.

(d) *Time of Motion.* — A motion by the accused under this Rule must be made at least 10 days before the day fixed for trial. The motion shall include all relief sought under this Rule. A subsequent motion may be made only upon a showing of cause why such motion would be in the interest of justice.

(e) *Time, Place and Manner of Discovery and Inspection.* — An order granting relief under this Rule shall specify the time, place and manner of making the discovery and inspection permitted and may prescribe such terms and conditions as are just.

(f) *Protective Order.* — Upon a sufficient showing the court may at any time order that the discovery or inspection be denied, restricted or deferred, or make such other order as is appropriate. Upon motion by the Commonwealth the court may permit the Commonwealth to make such showing, in whole or in part, in the form of a written statement to be inspected by the court in camera. If the court denies discovery or inspection following a showing in camera, the entire text of the Commonwealth's statement shall be sealed and preserved in the records of the court to be made available to the appellate court in the event of an appeal by the accused.

(g) *Continuing Duty to Disclose; Failure to Comply.* — If, after disposition of a motion filed under this Rule, and before or during trial, counsel or a party discovers additional material previously requested or falling within the scope of an order previously entered, that is subject to discovery or inspection under this Rule, he shall promptly notify the other party or his counsel or the court of the existence of the additional material. If at any time during the course of the proceedings, it is brought to the attention of the court that a party has failed to comply with this Rule or with an order issued pursuant to this Rule, the court shall order such party to permit the discovery or inspection of materials not previously disclosed, and may grant such other relief as it may deem appropriate.

Cross references. — As to criminal practice and procedure in the general district courts, see Rule 7C:5. As to discovery required by attorney for the Commonwealth in misdemeanors in circuit courts, see Va. Code § 19.2-265.4 A.

Source. — Former Rule 3A:14.

Comment. — With respect to former Rule 3A:14, the amendment changes the reference to a "court of record" in subsection (a) to a "circuit court," and substantially rewrites subdivision (c) (1) to permit discovery by the Commonwealth of scientific reports that may be in the possession of the accused and which the defense intends to introduce into evidence at trial or at sentencing.

The amendment, effective April 1, 2004, adopted January 30, 2004, in subdivision (a), substituted "applies to any prosecution" for "applies only to prosecution"; and substituted "feeblemindedness" for "feeble-mindedness" near the beginning of subdivision (c)(3).

Law Review. — For comment on criminal discovery, see 15 U. Rich. L. Rev. 189 (1980). For note, "Criminal Procedure and Criminal Law: Virginia Supreme Court Decisions During the 70's," see 15 U. Rich. L. Rev. 585 (1981). For 1991 survey on criminal law and procedure, see 25 U. Rich. L. Rev. 731 (1991). For 2003/2004 survey of criminal law and procedure, see 39 U. Rich. L. Rev. 133 (2004).

Michie's Jurisprudence. — For related discussion, see 1A M.J. Abatement, Survival and Revival, §§ 18, 27; 5B M.J. Criminal Procedure, §§ 23, 31, 34; 6A M.J. Discovery, § 1.

CASE NOTES

I. General Consideration.
II. Discovery by Accused.
A. In General.
B. Statement and Confessions.
C. Written Scientific Reports.
III. Discovery by Commonwealth.
IV. Failure to Comply with Rule.

I. GENERAL CONSIDERATION.

There is no general constitutional right to discovery in a criminal case. Lowe v. Commonwealth, 218 Va. 670, 239 S.E.2d 112 (1977), cert. denied, 435 U.S. 930, 98 S. Ct. 1502, 55 L. Ed. 2d 526 (1978).

There exists no constitutional right to discovery in a criminal case in Virginia. However, this rule provides for limited pre-trial discovery by an accused in a felony case. Guba v. Commonwealth, 9 Va. App. 114, 383 S.E.2d 764 (1989).

There is no general constitutional right to discovery in a criminal case, even where a capital offense is charged. Strickler v. Commonwealth, 241 Va. 482, 404 S.E.2d 227, cert. denied, 502 U.S. 944, 112 S. Ct. 386, 116 L. Ed. 2d 337 (1991).

Section 19.2-268.1 was not intended to supplement discovery provisions of this rule. Rather, it was intended to be used as an evidentiary rule by the trial court to order the production, inspection and use of a written statement once a witness has been cross-examined about the existence or contents of a prior statement. Newton v. Commonwealth, 29 Va. App. 433, 512 S.E.2d 846, cert. denied, 528 U.S. 1025, 120 S. Ct. 540, 145 L. Ed. 2d 419 (1999).

Rule applies only to felony prosecutions in circuit court. — Defendant charged with misdemeanor offense of reckless driving was not entitled to pretrial discovery. Prezechowski v. Commonwealth, No. 0945-98-3 (Ct. of Appeals June 1, 1999).

Rule inapplicable to misdemeanors. — Because the defendant was charged with a misdemeanor, driving under the influence of alcohol, as a second offense within five years, this rule did not apply and the trial court did not err in refusing to issue a subpoena duces tecum. Moore v. Commonwealth, No. 0264-99-4, 2000 Va. App. LEXIS 538 (Ct. of Appeals July 25, 2000).

No right to discovery in misdemeanor cases. — There is no right to discovery when an accused is charged with a misdemeanor. Lewis v. Commonwealth, No. 2479-99-1, 2000 Va. App. LEXIS 560 (Ct. of Appeals Aug. 1, 2000).

A consent discovery order, rather than this rule, will govern discovery in a criminal case in when such an order is in place. Abunaaj v. Commonwealth, 28 Va. App. 47, 502 S.E.2d 135 (1998).

Where court failed to review statements and no motion made. — Where appellant contended that trial court erred in failing to review the alibi witness statements in camera, appellant did not move the trial court to review the witness statements, nor did he move that the documents be placed under seal for the record on appeal. The court of appeals did not need to rule upon the non-exercise of a judicial power that was not invoked. While the trial court could have reviewed the statements in camera sua sponte, it was not required to do so. Allen v. Commonwealth, No. 2737-96-2 (Ct. of Appeals Feb. 10, 1998).

Commonwealth's introduction of tape without protective order violated discovery order. — Where the trial court entered a written discovery order specifically requiring the Commonwealth to provide without restriction all written or recorded statements made by the defendant, where the police possessed the tape recording of defendant's statement and the prosecutor could have discovered its existence through the exercise of due diligence and where the Commonwealth did not seek a protective order, as authorized by subsection (f) of this rule, the Commonwealth's introduction of the tape into evidence without first making it available to defendant violated the discovery order. Conway v. Commonwealth, 11 Va. App. 103, 397 S.E.2d 263 (1990).

Trial court did not abuse its discretion. — Trial court did not abuse its discretion in denying defendant's motion to quash a subpoena duces tecum by which the Commonwealth sought the production of documents in the possession of a doctor who examined defendant; because the records were not protected by the attorney client privilege, as the doctor was not an agent of the defense attorney, the records were not in the attorney's possession, and there was a substantial basis for claiming that the records were material. Via v. Commonwealth, 42 Va. App. 164, 590 S.E.2d 583, 2004 Va. App. LEXIS 14 (2004).

Mere speculation not duty imposing. — Even pursuant to the broader discovery provisions afforded at trial, petitioner would not have had access to the materials under Virginia law, except as modified by *Brady*. Mere speculation that some exculpatory material may have been withheld is unlikely to establish good cause for a discovery request on collateral review. Nor, in the United States Supreme Court's opinion, should such suspicion suffice to impose a duty on counsel to advance a claim for which they have no evidentiary support. Proper respect for state procedures counsels against a requirement that all possible claims be raised in state collateral proceedings, even when no known facts support them. The presumption, well established by tradition and experience, that prosecutors have fully discharged their official duties, is inconsistent with the novel suggestion that conscientious defense counsel have a procedural obligation to assert constitutional error on the basis of mere suspicion that some prosecutorial misstep may have occurred. Strickler v. Greene, 527 U.S. 263, 119 S. Ct. 1936, 144 L. Ed. 2d 286 (1999).

Applied in Briley v. Commonwealth, 221 Va. 563, 273 S.E.2d 57 (1980); Bunch v. Commonwealth, 225 Va. 423, 304 S.E.2d 271 (1983); Mu'Min v. Commonwealth, 239 Va. 433, 389 S.E.2d 886 (1990); Williams v. Commonwealth, 30 Va. App. 378, 517 S.E.2d 246 (1999); Green v. Commonwealth, 266 Va. 81, 580 S.E.2d 834, 2003 Va. LEXIS 55 (2003).

II. DISCOVERY BY ACCUSED.

A. In General.

This rule provides for limited pretrial discovery by the accused in a felony case. Hackman v. Commonwealth, 220 Va. 710, 261 S.E.2d 555 (1980).

Subdivision (b)(2) of this rule provides for limited pretrial discovery and inspection by the defendant in felony cases and thereby liberalizes the rule laid down in the earlier cases. Bellfield v. Commonwealth, 215 Va. 303, 208 S.E.2d 771 (1974), cert. denied, 420 U.S. 965, 95 S. Ct. 1359, 43 L. Ed. 2d 444 (1975).

Subdivision (b)(2) provides for limited pretrial discovery by an accused in a felony case. Henshaw v. Commonwealth, 19 Va. App. 338, 451 S.E.2d 415 (1994).

Trial court was correct in denying defendant's request for "any contemporaneously made notes of statements attributed to defendant"; except for specifically designated items, Va. Sup. Ct. R. 3A:11(b) excluded the production of such notes. Muhammad v. Commonwealth, 269 Va. 451, 611 S.E.2d 537, 2005 Va. LEXIS 39 (2005), cert. denied, 547 U.S. 1136, 126 S. Ct. 2035, 164 L. Ed. 2d 794 (2006), and overruled in part on other grounds by Jay v. Commonwealth, 275 Va. 510, 659 S.E.2d 311, 2008 Va. LEXIS 53 (2008).

Preliminary hearing not to be used as discovery vehicle. — No statute or rule of court affords the accused a right to use the preliminary hearing as a discovery vehicle. Davis v. Commonwealth, 215 Va. 816, 213 S.E.2d 785 (1975).

When an accused is represented by counsel, the requirements of this rule are satisfied when defense counsel is afforded the opportunity to inspect the Commonwealth's evidence. Bell v. Commonwealth, 24 Va. App. 208, 481 S.E.2d 473 (1997).

Defendant may obtain exculpatory evidence known to the Commonwealth. Bellfield v. Commonwealth, 215 Va. 303, 208 S.E.2d 771 (1974), cert. denied, 420 U.S. 965, 95 S. Ct. 1359, 43 L. Ed. 2d 444 (1975).

Agents of the Commonwealth. — Employees of Commonwealth agencies do not automatically qualify as "agents of the Commonwealth" for purposes of this rule. However, where an agency is involved in the investigation or prosecution of a particular criminal case, agency employees become agents of the Commonwealth for purposes of this rule and must be considered a party to the action for purposes of Rule 3A:12. Ramirez v. Commonwealth, 20 Va. App. 292, 456 S.E.2d 531 (1995).

Information known to the police is information within the Commonwealth's knowledge and the prosecutor is obliged to disclose it regardless of the state of his actual knowledge. Lane v. Commonwealth, 20 Va. App. 592, 459 S.E.2d 525 (1995).

Policy directed against fishing expeditions into Commonwealth's files. — The policy of fundamental fairness in protecting the ability of the Commonwealth to prosecute is applicable to prevent a fishing expedition into the Commonwealth's files at trial. Bellfield v. Commonwealth, 215 Va. 303, 208 S.E.2d 771 (1974), cert. denied, 420 U.S. 965, 95 S. Ct. 1359, 43 L. Ed. 2d 444 (1975).

Examination of investigators. — Trial court did not abuse its discretion in denying defendant's motion to examine the Commonwealth of Virginia's investigators under oath, by which he sought to ensure that law enforcement officials had not concealed exculpatory evidence, because the motion sought material beyond the scope to which defendant was entitled under Va. Sup. Ct. R. 3A:11 or any other provision of law. Juniper v. Commonwealth, 271 Va. 362, 626 S.E.2d 383, 2006 Va. LEXIS 29 (2006).

Witness' written statements not discoverable after testimony given in court. — Written statements made by a prosecution witness to agents of the state are not discoverable for purposes of cross-examination and impeachment, after that witness has testified for the prosecution, upon grounds of public policy. Bellfield v. Commonwealth, 215 Va. 303, 208 S.E.2d 771 (1974), cert. denied, 420 U.S. 965, 95 S. Ct. 1359, 43 L. Ed. 2d 444 (1975).

Where there was no attempt to show that police notes were accurate verbatim transcripts of a prosecuting witness's initial report to police officers, to permit their use as evidence to cross-examine and impeach her would be manifestly unfair to the witness, who had neither seen their content nor approved them. Bellfield v. Commonwealth, 215 Va. 303, 208 S.E.2d 771 (1974), cert. denied, 420 U.S. 965, 95 S. Ct. 1359, 43 L. Ed. 2d 444 (1975).

Commonwealth not required to furnish names and addresses of eyewitnesses. — The Virginia rule of court providing for discovery in a criminal case contains no provision requiring the

Commonwealth to furnish the names and addresses of the eyewitnesses to a crime. Lowe v. Commonwealth, 218 Va. 670, 239 S.E.2d 112 (1977), cert. denied, 435 U.S. 930, 98 S. Ct. 1502, 55 L. Ed. 2d 526 (1978).

The prohibition against concealing exculpatory evidence does not create a constitutional requirement that the prosecution furnish the names of its witnesses before trial. Watkins v. Commonwealth, 229 Va. 469, 331 S.E.2d 422 (1985), cert. denied, 475 U.S. 1099, 106 S. Ct. 1503, 89 L. Ed. 2d 903 (1986).

But suppression of evidence favorable to accused may violate due process. — The suppression by the prosecution of evidence favorable to the accused upon request violates due process when the evidence is material either to guilt or to punishment, irrespective of the good faith or bad faith of the prosecution. At the core of this due process rule of fairness is that the evidence must be exculpatory, favorable to the accused. Lowe v. Commonwealth, 218 Va. 670, 239 S.E.2d 112 (1977), cert. denied, 435 U.S. 930, 98 S. Ct. 1502, 55 L. Ed. 2d 526 (1978).

The Commonwealth is required to deliver that evidence which is favorable to the accused and which, if suppressed, would deprive the accused of a fair trial. The nondisclosed evidence is considered material only if there is a reasonable probability that, had the evidence been disclosed to the defense, the result of the proceeding would have been different. Currie v. Commonwealth, 10 Va. App. 204, 391 S.E.2d 79 (1990).

When prosecution must respond to specific request. — Although there is no duty to provide defense counsel with unlimited discovery of everything known by the prosecutor, if the subject matter of a specific request is material, or indeed if a substantial basis for claiming materiality exists, it is reasonable to require the prosecutor to respond either by furnishing the information or by submitting the problem to the trial judge. When the prosecutor receives a specific and relevant request, the failure to make any response is seldom, if ever, excusable. Sennett v. Sheriff of Fairfax County, 608 F.2d 537 (4th Cir. 1979).

The refusal of the Commonwealth's attorney in a robbery prosecution, despite a specific request by the defendant's counsel, to identify two persons whose testimony could have discredited one of the Commonwealth's two key identification witnesses denied the defendant a fair trial. Sennett v. Sheriff of Fairfax County, 608 F.2d 537 (4th Cir. 1979).

Disclosure must afford accused time to assess evidence. — When a court orders discovery pursuant to this rule, the Commonwealth has a duty to disclose the materials in sufficient time to afford an accused an opportunity to assess and develop the evidence for trial. Lomax v. Commonwealth, 228 Va. 168, 319 S.E.2d 763 (1984).

Counsel for defendant were not afforded a reasonable time to investigate and prepare the trial of a serious, complex case, where they had only 15 days between the indictment and trial, the earliest that any reports on scientific evidence were available to them was less than a week before trial, some of this evidence was made known to defense counsel the day before trial, other material was produced for the first time at trial, and, moreover, some of the material specified in the discovery order was never submitted. Gilchrist v. Commonwealth, 227 Va. 540, 317 S.E.2d 784 (1984).

Where the defendant had been given an opportunity to interview prosecution's firearms expert prior to trial, and since the portion of the expert's testimony to which defendant objected was not part of his written report, expert's findings were not subject to disclosure under this rule. Clagett v. Commonwealth, 252 Va. 79, 472 S.E.2d 263 (1996), cert. denied, 519 U.S. 1122, 117 S. Ct. 972, 136 L. Ed. 2d 856 (1997).

Counsel should obtain order or stipulation specifying discoverable material. — Although the absence of a clarifying order on a defendant's motion for discovery under this rule in a prosecution for perjury did not prevent the determination on appeal of the issue of whether the Commonwealth failed to furnish statements to which the defendant was entitled, members of the trial bar are cautioned that it is generally advisable to have a court order or written stipulation specify precisely what is to be discoverable, thereby avoiding misunderstandings that may lead to fatal consequences on appeal. Hackman v. Commonwealth, 220 Va. 710, 261 S.E.2d 555 (1980).

Court erred in denying request for "mug shots." — Trial judge erred in denying defendant's pretrial request for production of "mug shots" of other women arrested in the same location for selling cocaine. The identity of women who were later arrested for selling drugs from that locale was material not because defendant alleged that they were eyewitnesses, but because it tended to support defendant's defense of misidentity. Davis v. Commonwealth, 25 Va. App. 588, 491 S.E.2d 288 (1997).

Prosecutor's delay in disclosing name of witness who changed his testimony in a way beneficial to defendant did not violate this rule. Read v. Virginia State Bar, 233 Va. 560, 357 S.E.2d 544 (1987).

Disclosure of information when received. — There was no violation of a discovery order where the Commonwealth disclosed information as soon as it was received, and no prejudice where the information was disclosed in time to be put to use. Bennett v. Commonwealth, 236 Va. 448, 374 S.E.2d 303 (1988), cert. denied, 490 U.S. 1028, 109 S. Ct. 1765, 104 L. Ed. 2d 200 (1989).

Subdivision (b)(2) does not afford the appellant a basis to inspect, photograph, or measure an individual's private residence which happened to be the crime scene. Henshaw v. Commonwealth, 19 Va. App. 338, 451 S.E.2d 415 (1994).

B. Statement and Confessions.

Scope of discovery by accused. — Subdivision (b)(1)(i), by its language, is not limited only to confessions or other post-arrest written or recorded statements. It places no limitation, except relevance, on the accused's right to discover written or recorded statements made by him. Naulty v. Commonwealth, 2 Va. App. 523, 346 S.E.2d 540 (1986).

Defendant entitled to substance of oral statement. — Defendant is entitled under subdivision (b)(1) to the substance of any oral statement that he made to an undercover police officer. Ulmer

v. Commonwealth, No. 0369-85 (Ct. of Appeals Aug. 26, 1986).

Under this rule, defendant may obtain copies of the substance of any oral arguments of the accused made to any law enforcement officer, the existence of which is known to the attorney for the Commonwealth. Knight v. Commonwealth, 18 Va. App. 207, 443 S.E.2d 165 (1994).

Since there was no verbatim account of defendant's statements in the possession of the police, the Commonwealth could not be expected to produce nonexistent items. McClain v. Commonwealth, 2005 Va. App. LEXIS 453 (Nov. 15, 2005).

Statement must be made by accused to be discoverable. — To be discoverable by an accused a statement must be given by the accused rather than by a witness who heard the accused speak. Hackman v. Commonwealth, 220 Va. 710, 261 S.E.2d 555 (1980).

Written statements made by prosecution witness not discoverable. — Statements sought by a defendant in a prosecution for perjury were not discoverable by the defendant under subdivision (1) of subsection (b) of this rule, since they were not written or recorded statements or confessions made by the defendant, but rather were statements made by prospective Commonwealth witnesses to agents of the Commonwealth in connection with the investigation or prosecution of the case; as such, they were expressly excluded from discovery by subdivision (2) of subsection (b) of this rule. Hackman v. Commonwealth, 220 Va. 710, 261 S.E.2d 555 (1980).

As a general rule the accused is not entitled to obtain statements made by prospective Commonwealth witnesses to police officers in connection with the investigation or prosecution of a criminal case. Currie v. Commonwealth, 10 Va. App. 204, 391 S.E.2d 79 (1990).

Statements must be reduced to writing. — While the potential difficulties in critically analyzing what amounts to a paraphrase of a statement made by a defendant may be recognized, this rule requires the Commonwealth to reduce the substance of oral statements to writing, so they can be properly inspected, copied or photographed by the accused, as provided for in the rule. Meadows v. Commonwealth, 35 Va. App. 298, 544 S.E.2d 876, 2001 Va. App. LEXIS 194 (2001).

Commonwealth's failure to disclose tape recording violated this rule; where one of the investigating officers of the bureau of police had possession of the tape, constructive knowledge of the existence of the tape was attributable to the attorney for the Commonwealth and disclosure was required under this rule. Conway v. Commonwealth, 11 Va. App. 103, 397 S.E.2d 263 (1990).

Where an investigating officer of city bureau of police had possession of tape recording of defendant's pre-arrest statements, constructive knowledge of the existence of the tape was attributable to the attorney for the Commonwealth and disclosure was required under this rule. Conway v. Commonwealth, 11 Va. App. 103, 397 S.E.2d 263 (1991).

Disclosure of recorded statements by rape defendant to accuser. — Under the terms of a consent discovery order, a tape recording of a conversation between a rape defendant and his accuser was a statement made by the defendant "to law enforcement officers" which the Commonwealth was required to disclose where the police had initiated the contact and had coached the accuser on what to say and the call had been made from the police station and recorded on police equipment in the presence of police officers; under these circumstances the police were involved to such a degree that the statements were effectively made to the police and the accuser's compliance with the police requests made her an agent of the police. Abunaaj v. Commonwealth, 28 Va. App. 47, 502 S.E.2d 135 (1998).

Videotape of defendant purchasing chemicals used to make PCP was a recorded statement made by defendant and discoverable under subdivision (b)(1)(i). Naulty v. Commonwealth, 2 Va. App. 523, 346 S.E.2d 540 (1986).

This rule did not require disclosure of defendant's statements to a fellow jail inmate that he and a buddy had sex with his wife since it was not exculpatory and was not a statement made to a law enforcement officer. Jeffries v. Commonwealth, 6 Va. App. 21, 365 S.E.2d 773 (1988).

Request denied. — Trial court was correct in denying defendant's request seeking "the specific questions, comments or statements of any person involved in the conversation with, or interrogation of defendant which brought about any response"; Va. Sup. Ct. R. 3A:11 required production of the substance of a defendant's statements but did not require production of the statements sought by defendant. Nonetheless, the trial court did order that if a video, audio, or otherwise transcribed interrogation existed, the entirety of such material would be provided to defendant. Muhammad v. Commonwealth, 269 Va. 451, 611 S.E.2d 537, 2005 Va. LEXIS 39 (2005), cert. denied, 547 U.S. 1136, 126 S. Ct. 2035, 164 L. Ed. 2d 794 (2006), and overruled in part on other grounds by Jay v. Commonwealth, 275 Va. 510, 659 S.E.2d 311, 2008 Va. LEXIS 53 (2008).

C. Written Scientific Reports.

Defendant was entitled to written scientific reports but not the work notes or memoranda that were the basis of the reports since this rule permits a defendant to discover written scientific reports, but the rule does not authorize the discovery of reports, memoranda or other internal Commonwealth documents made by agents in connection with the investigation or prosecution of the case. Spencer v. Commonwealth, 238 Va. 295, 384 S.E.2d 785 (1989), cert. denied, 493 U.S. 1093, 110 S. Ct. 1171, 107 L. Ed. 2d 1073 (1990).

As Child Protective Services (CPS) had investigated an allegation that defendant sexually abused a minor, it was an agent of the Commonwealth for purposes of Rule 3A:11(b)(2), and statements made to CPS and its reports, interview documentation, and internal documents were not discoverable by defendant. Spencer v. Commonwealth, No. 2207-01-2, 2002 Va. App. LEXIS 604 (Ct. of Appeals Oct. 8, 2002).

Accused is entitled to know if scientist used other authorities to reach conclusion in scientific paper. — The truth-finding process may not require that work papers or memoranda that assisted in the preparation of the scientific paper be revealed, but it does require that if the scientist used information contained in other authorities to reach his conclusion, the accused is entitled to know what they are so that the challenge anticipated by Code § 19.2-187.1 effectively can be made; this rule provides the vehicle to enable the accused to make an intelligent challenge. Ellis v. Commonwealth, 14 Va. App. 18, 414 S.E.2d 615 (1992).

Appellant entitled to subpoena writings used by chemist. — In trial for possession of cocaine with the intent to distribute, pursuant to this rule, appellant was entitled to subpoena all writings used by the chemist to conclude that the substance examined and tested by him was cocaine. Ellis v. Commonwealth, 14 Va. App. 18, 414 S.E.2d 615 (1992).

General log book and manuals. — Setting forth the operating procedures of correctional facility and the Department of Corrections were discoverable under subdivision (b)(2) of this rule. Rosser v. Commonwealth, 24 Va. App. 308, 482 S.E.2d 83 (1997).

Where defendant requested certificate of analysis under this rule, but did not comply with the terms of the discovery order, his claim that the trial judge erred in admitting the certificate of analysis because the Commonwealth failed to mail or deliver a copy of certificate as required by § 19.2-187, which pertains to admission into evidence of certain certificates of analysis, was without merit. By endorsing discovery order without objection, defendant was bound by terms of order for all matters of discovery, including request in defendant's discovery motion for any certificate of analysis. Coleman v. Commonwealth, 27 Va. App. 768, 501 S.E.2d 461 (1998).

Appellant's lack of technical or professional basis for challenge. — Although the Commonwealth asserted that appellant was required to have a technical or professional basis for challenging the state's test, at the time of his motion appellant could provide the trial judge with no more than his own assertions that seized substance was cookie or candy crumbs, not cocaine, in the absence of access to the substance itself. Under these circumstances, appellant's motion was reasonable, and this rule required that the trial judge grant it. Blackwell v. Commonwealth, No. 0124-94-3, (Ct. of Appeals July 25, 1995).

Diagram of crime scene not within scope of rule. — Evidence technician's diagram of crime scene was not a report or test included within the scope of Rule 3A:11 or defendant's discovery motion. To the contrary, the diagram was prepared by technician as he investigated the scene and was intended for use as a demonstrative exhibit only. It was not a written report of a ballistic test. Accordingly, the Commonwealth had no duty to disclose the diagram to defendant before trial. Because no discovery violation occurred, the trial judge did not err in refusing to exclude technician's testimony. Traynham v. Commonwealth, No. 0690-96-2 (Ct. of Appeals July 1, 1997).

Commonwealth had no duty to disclose evidence of officer's test firing of weapon to defendant in discovery, as such evidence was not a written report of a ballistics test embraced either by defendant's discovery motion or by Rule 3A:11; thus, the trial court properly permitted the officer to relate the officer's findings. Brown v. Commonwealth, No. 1574-01-4, 2002 Va. App. LEXIS 458 (Ct. of Appeals Aug. 6, 2002).

Where defendant's first and second attorneys were each provided with laboratory reports during discovery, nothing required the Commonwealth to once again disclose this same information to defendant's latest attorney. Bell v. Commonwealth, 24 Va. App. 208, 481 S.E.2d 473 (1997).

III. DISCOVERY BY COMMONWEALTH.

Extent state can enforce rules against defendant who fails to comply raises Sixth Amendment issues. — Whether and to what extent a state can enforce discovery rules against a defendant who fails to comply, by excluding relevant probative evidence, is a question raising Sixth Amendment issues. Boxley v. Commonwealth, No. 0029-91-4, (Ct. of Appeals Sept. 1, 1992).

Disclosure of information about defendant's experts in requesting payment of experts. — Where defendant was required to disclose information about his experts to support his request for the Commonwealth's payment of those experts because of defendant's indigency, the Commonwealth under this rule was not required to furnish the names of all its experts and the substance of their expected testimony. O'Dell v. Commonwealth, 234 Va. 672, 364 S.E.2d 491, cert. denied, 488 U.S. 871, 109 S. Ct. 186, 102 L. Ed. 2d 154 (1988).

Limitation on disavowal of alibi. — Where alibi notices were specifically related to pending criminal prosecution and filed in that cause by defendant's counsel pursuant to subsection (c) of this rule, permitting defendant to later disavow such declaration with impunity would at once visit an injustice upon the Commonwealth and countenance a subversion of the Rules governing discovery in criminal proceedings. Thomas v. Commonwealth, 24 Va. App. 614, 484 S.E.2d 607 (1997).

Use of alibi notices for impeachment upheld. — Where defendant was responsible for the content of his alibi notices, testified differently, and had the opportunity to explain on either cross or redirect examination the inconsistencies in his several statements, the trial court did not abuse its discretion in allowing the Commonwealth to use the notices for purposes of impeachment. Thomas v. Commonwealth, 24 Va. App. 614, 484 S.E.2d 607 (1997).

Jury instructions on alibi defense. — Virginia Sup. Ct. R. 3A:11(c)(2) has placed alibi on a different footing from other evidence in a case, and it should be left to a jury in an appropriate instruction on the subject, in addition to instructions on presumption of innocence and reasonable doubt. Cooper v. Commonwealth, 277 Va. 377, 673 S.E.2d 185, 2009 Va. LEXIS 36 (2009).

Defendant's proposed alibi instruction should have been given because defendant's alibi evidence sufficiently satisfied the test for the giving of an alibi instruction in that defendant and other witnesses testified that defendant was working at a construction site in another town when an alleged drug transaction occurred. Cooper v. Commonwealth, 277 Va. 377, 673 S.E.2d 185, 2009 Va. LEXIS 36 (2009).

IV. FAILURE TO COMPLY WITH RULE.

Sanction may not be arbitrary or disproportionate to purposes. — While there may be circumstances under which a criminal defendant ought to be precluded from presenting evidence because of his failure to comport with discovery rules, this sanction may not be arbitrary or disproportionate to the purposes it is designed to serve. Boxley v. Commonwealth, No. 0029-91-4, (Ct. of Appeals Sept. 1, 1992).

Deliberate attempt to introduce evidence not disclosed during discovery. — When it appears to a trial court that a party has deliberately attempted to introduce evidence which it knows is improper or inadmissible, either because it was not disclosed during discovery or because it otherwise is inadmissible under rules of evidence, it is the duty and responsibility of the court to deter such inappropriate tactics by taking such action, imposing such sanctions, or granting such relief as it deems appropriate. Stotler v. Commonwealth, 2 Va. App. 481, 346 S.E.2d 39 (1986).

Discretion of court. — The relief to be granted upon a violation of this rule is within the discretion of the trial court, giving due regard to the right of the accused to call for evidence in his favor and to investigate and evaluate the evidence in preparation for trial. Frye v. Commonwealth, 231 Va. 370, 345 S.E.2d 267 (1986).

Failure of Commonwealth to comply with discovery order. — When it is brought to the attention of a court that the Commonwealth has failed to comply with a discovery order, the court may prohibit the Commonwealth from introducing the evidence or enter such other order as it deems just under the circumstances. Certain circumstances may dictate a citation for contempt and/or require referral of the matter to the appropriate ethics committee of the bar. Stotler v. Commonwealth, 2 Va. App. 481, 346 S.E.2d 39 (1986).

Failure to disclose one of defendant's statements where defendant otherwise apprised of statements. — Where defendant was apprised of the substance of a substantial portion of his oral statements by means of the bill of particulars, and the only statement not disclosed to defendant was his remark about calling other persons he knew who might supply cocaine, admission of the statement did not constitute reversible error, since the undisclosed statement was not exculpatory and, thus, did not fall within the rule in *Brady v. Maryland,* 373 U.S. 83, 83 S. Ct. 1194, 10 L. Ed. 2d 215 (1963). Furthermore, defendant did not demonstrate that the failure to disclose the statement prejudiced his rights or would have altered the course of the trial. Ulmer v. Commonwealth, No. 0369-85, (Ct. of Appeals Aug. 26, 1986).

Error not reversible absent showing of prejudice. — A trial court's admission of relevant and material evidence at trial which was not disclosed as required by a discovery order is not reversible error in the absence of a showing of prejudice. Stotler v. Commonwealth, 2 Va. App. 481, 346 S.E.2d 39 (1986); Welshman v. Commonwealth, 28 Va. App. 20, 502 S.E.2d 122 (1998).

When a discovery violation does not prejudice the substantial rights of a defendant, a trial court does not err in admitting undisclosed evidence. Davis v. Commonwealth, 230 Va. 201, 335 S.E.2d 375 (1985); Naulty v. Commonwealth, 2 Va. App. 523, 346 S.E.2d 540 (1986).

Although the Commonwealth violated this rule by introducing testimony concerning an inculpatory oral statement made by the accused which had not been reduced to writing, this error was harmless where the accused had originally given a written statement, which had been provided to the accused in discovery and which was received into evidence without objection, in which he conceded the elements necessary to establish that he was a convicted felon in possession of a firearm. Meadows v. Commonwealth, 35 Va. App. 298, 544 S.E.2d 876, 2001 Va. App. LEXIS 194 (2001).

Commonwealth was required to turn over defendant's inculpatory letters but the late disclosure of the inculpatory evidence did not prejudice defendant's case and was not reversible error. Smoot v. Commonwealth, 37 Va. App. 495, 559 S.E.2d 409, 2002 Va. App. LEXIS 90 (2002).

Where the Commonwealth failed to provide an inculpatory recorded telephone conversation between defendant and his mother prior to seeking its admission at trial, as required by a discovery order, admission of the evidence was upheld because defendant failed to show prejudice by demonstrating how timely disclosure would have changed his trial strategy or affected the outcome of the trial. Romero-Diaz v. Commonwealth, No. 0489-09-4, 2010 Va. App. LEXIS 180 (Ct. of Appeals May 4, 2010).

Failure to comply with rule. — Trial court did not abuse its discretion in denying defendant's motion for a new trial as defendant's due process rights and the discovery rules were not violated by the Commonwealth's failure to disclose its witness's criminal record and her relationship with police department as: (1) the failure to disclose the misdemeanors was not material as they did not involve crimes of moral turpitude and could not be used to impeach the witness; (2) the felony convictions were in evidence at the trial; and (3) given that the witness admitted the felony convictions, her former drug use, and that she was a paid informant, there was no reasonable probability that disclosure of additional impeaching information would have led the trial court to a different conclusion. Johnson v. Commonwealth, 41 Va. App. 37, 581 S.E.2d 880, 2003 Va. App. LEXIS 399 (2003).

Waiver of right to assert error. — Although the Commonwealth conceded that it violated a discovery order requiring it to provide defendant with the opportunity to view a certain heroin capsule prior to trial, defendant's decision to move forward with the trial rather than accepting the trial court's offer of a continuance waived her objection to the trial court's decision to admit the heroin capsule into evidence. Wooden v. Commonwealth, 2006 Va. App. LEXIS 47 (Feb. 7, 2006).

Declaration of mistrial for failure to comply with discovery order held error. — The declaration of a mistrial by the trial judge in a prosecution for murder because of noncompliance by the Commonwealth with discovery orders was not supported by "manifest necessity," since the problem of nondisclosure could have been resolved without trial disruption, for example, by a continuance for disclosure. Therefore, the defendant's second trial constituted double jeopardy. Harris v. Young, 607 F.2d 1081 (4th Cir. 1979), cert. denied, 444 U.S.

1025, 100 S. Ct. 688, 62 L. Ed. 2d 659 (1980), decided under this rule as it stood prior to the amendment effective Jan. 15, 1978.

Where defendant declined to move for a remedy that would have permitted him to accommodate his defense to the discovered statement, he sought only suppression of the truth. Under those circumstances, the admission of the statement into evidence did not unjustly prejudice defendant's presentation of his defense. Lane v. Commonwealth, 20 Va. App. 592, 459 S.E.2d 525 (1995).

Prejudice shown. — The Commonwealth's violation of a discovery order by failing to disclose a tape recording of a telephone conversation between a defendant accused of rape and his accuser was prejudicial and rendered the tape inadmissible where the Commonwealth's case relied upon circumstantial evidence and the credibility of the witnesses and where the previously undisclosed recorded statements were used to contradict the defendant's trial testimony, clearly affecting his credibility before the jury, and the defendant was given no opportunity to explain his statements. Abunaaj v. Commonwealth, 28 Va. App. 47, 502 S.E.2d 135 (1998).

CIRCUIT COURT OPINIONS

Constitutionality. — Defendant's required pretrial notice of an alibi defense, pursuant to subdivision (c)(2), along with the required statement of his location at the time of the crime charged, did not violate his rights to due process, his privilege against self-incrimination, or his right to present evidence. Commonwealth v. Thasoonthorn, 55 Va. Cir. 28, 2001 Va. Cir. LEXIS 233 (Fairfax County 2001).

Right to "call for evidence." — Right to "call for evidence" under Va. Const., Art. I, § 8 is not the equivalent of unfettered discovery from the Commonwealth or its agents under Va. Sup. Ct. R. 3A:11, nor does the free exercise of the right demand the production of writings or things from third parties beyond the scope of Va. Sup. Ct. R. 3A:12(b). Commonwealth v. Hoard, 82 Va. Cir. 335, 2011 Va. Cir. LEXIS 40 (Augusta County Mar. 9, 2011).

Discovery of dispatcher transcripts is limited. — Defendant who was charged with three felony convictions could not obtain subpoenas duces tecum under Va. Sup. Ct. Rule 3A:12 to discover police dispatch records transmitted on the night of defendant's arrest, because the dispatcher, who was employed by the state, county and town police agencies, was acting as an agent of the state. Discovery of the transmissions was limited in scope to material that was discoverable under Va. Sup. Ct. Rule 3A:11 and *Brady*. Commonwealth v. Marsh, 65 Va. Cir. 229, 2004 Va. Cir. LEXIS 207 (Lancaster County 2004).

Discovery of tape-recorded message. — Prosecution was not entitled to obtain discovery from the Office of the Public Defender of a tape recorded message in the Office's possession that had been provided to the Office by a former client and that contained a message from a current client because the item did not meet the narrowly defined scope of discovery that was available to the prosecution as part of a criminal investigation. Commonwealth v. Peoples, 63 Va. Cir. 541, 2004 Va. Cir. LEXIS 90 (Norfolk 2004).

Videotapes of defendant. — Statements made by defendant on the videotaped drug transactions were recorded statements or confessions made by the accused and the commonwealth had to permit defense counsel to copy the videotape under Va. Sup. Ct. R. 3A:11(b). However, the court placed restrictions on the copying of the videotape. Commonwealth v. Murphy, 78 Va. Cir. 415, 2009 Va. Cir. LEXIS 192 (Sussex County July 15, 2009).

Commonwealth not required to disclose oral statements made by the defendant to parties other than law-enforcement officers. — Neither Rule 3A:11 nor the case law required the commonwealth to disclose oral statements made by the defendant to parties other than law-enforcement officers. Commonwealth v. Hernandez, 2004 Va. Cir. LEXIS 145 (Fairfax County June 17, 2004); Henderson v. Johnson, 75 Va. Cir. 479, 2007 Va. Cir. LEXIS 306 (Campbell County 2007).

Scope of discovery by accused. — Defendant could not subpoena a jail's inmate records because (1) Va. Sup. Ct. R. 3A:12(b) did not permit subpoenas directed to a party, (2) the county sheriff's department was responsible for both the jail's administrative operation and investigating defendant's case, (3) the sheriff's department's investigatory responsibility defined the department as a party to the case, and, (4) as parties, those who were responsible for operating the jail could not be subject to a subpoena, although discovery was potentially available pursuant to Va. Sup. Ct. R. 3A:11(b). Commonwealth v. Bowman, 85 Va. Cir. 199, 2012 Va. Cir. LEXIS 159 (Loudoun County Aug. 13, 2012).

Motion to quash subpoena duces tecum granted. — Commonwealth's motion to quash a subpoena duces tecum to be served on a jail was granted because defendant did not show that the information that she sought was material as required under Va. Sup. Ct. R. 3A:11(b)(2), and defendant's characterization of some of the information she sought was not supported by the evidence; because the jail was an agent of the Commonwealth for the purposes of Rule 3A:11(b)(2), and thus, not a third party under Va. Sup. Ct. R. 3A:12(b), even if some information was not addressed by the second sentence of Rule 3A:11(b)(2), which mandated an absolute limit on the circuit court's authority to grant the motion with respect to information developed in connection with the investigation or prosecution of the case, it was, nevertheless, covered by the first sentence, which authorized the circuit court to grant a motion on a showing that the information was material and that the request was reasonable. Commonwealth v. Hoard, 82 Va. Cir. 335, 2011 Va. Cir. LEXIS 40 (Augusta County Mar. 9, 2011).

Motion to dismiss denied. — Defendant's motion to dismiss under § 19.2-265.4 based on the Commonwealth's alleged discovery violation was denied. He had the opportunity to inspect evidence pursuant to the court's discovery order; he elicited testimony about certain evidence at issue; certain evidence discovered post-trial was inculpatory and not exculpatory, and the late discovery of inculpatory evidence neither changed the defense strategy nor denied him a fair trial. Commonwealth v. Javier-Paz, 2012 Va. Cir. LEXIS 19 (Fairfax County Feb. 9, 2012).

Rule 3A:12. Subpoena.

(a) *For Attendance of Witnesses.* — A subpoena for the attendance of a witness to testify before a court not of record shall be issued by the judge, clerk, magistrate, Commonwealth's Attorney or by the attorney for the defendant. A subpoena for the attendance of a witness to testify before a circuit court or a grand jury shall be issued by the clerk or Commonwealth's Attorney and, for the attendance of a witness to testify before a circuit court, by the attorney for the defendant as well. The subpoena shall (i) be directed to an appropriate officer or officers, (ii) name the witness to be summoned, (iii) state the name of the court and the title, if any, of the proceeding, (iv) command the officer to summon the witness to appear at the time and place specified in the subpoena for the purpose of giving testimony, and (v) state on whose application the subpoena was issued.

No subpoena or subpoena duces tecum shall be issued in any criminal case or proceeding, including any proceeding before any grand jury, which subpoena or subpoena duces tecum is (i) directed to a member of the bar of this Commonwealth or any other jurisdiction, and (ii) compels production or testimony concerning any present or former client of the member of the bar, unless the subpoena request has been approved in all specifics, in advance, by a judge of the circuit court wherein the subpoena is requested after reasonable notice to the attorney who is the subject of the proposed subpoena. The proceedings for approval may be conducted in camera, in the judge's discretion, and the judge may seal such proceedings. Such subpoena request shall be made by the Commonwealth's attorney for the jurisdiction involved, either on motion of the Commonwealth's attorney or upon request to the Commonwealth's attorney by the foreman of any grand jury.

(b) *For Production of Documentary Evidence and of Objects Before a Circuit Court.* — Upon notice to the adverse party and on affidavit by the party applying for the subpoena that the requested writings or objects are material to the proceedings and are in the possession of a person not a party to the action, the judge or the clerk may issue a subpoena duces tecum for the production of writings or objects described in the subpoena. Such subpoena shall command either (1) that the person to whom it is addressed shall appear with the items described either before the court or the clerk or (2) that such person shall deliver the items described to the clerk. The subpoena may direct that the writing or object be produced at a time before the trial or before the time when it is to be offered in evidence.

Any subpoenaed writings and objects, regardless by whom requested, shall be available for examination and review by all parties and counsel. Subpoenaed writings or objects shall be received by the clerk and shall not be open for examination and review except by the parties and counsel unless otherwise directed by the court. The clerk shall adopt procedures to ensure compliance with this paragraph.

Where subpoenaed writings and objects are of such nature or content that disclosure to other parties would be unduly prejudicial, the court, upon written motion and notice to all parties, may grant such relief as it deems appropriate, including limiting disclosure, removal and copying.

If a subpoena requires the production of information that is stored in an electronic format, the person to whom it is addressed shall produce a tangible copy of the information. If a tangible copy cannot be reasonably produced, the subpoenaed person shall permit the parties to review the information on a computer or by electronic means during normal business hours, provided that the information can be accessed and isolated. If a tangible copy cannot reasonably be produced and the information is commingled with information other than that requested in the subpoena and cannot reasonably be isolated, the person to whom the subpoena is addressed may file a motion for a protective order or motion to quash.

(c) *Service and Return.* — A subpoena may be executed anywhere in the State by an officer authorized by law to execute the subpoena in the place where it is executed. The officer executing a subpoena shall make return thereof to the court named in the subpoena.

(d) *Contempt.* — Failure by any person without adequate excuse to obey a subpoena served upon him may be deemed a contempt of the court to which the subpoena is returnable.

(e) *Recognizance of a Witness.* — If it appears that the testimony of a person is material in any criminal proceeding, a judicial officer may require him to give a recognizance for his appearance.

(f) *Photocopying of Subpoenaed Documents.* — Subject to the provisions of subsection (b), removal and photocopying of subpoenaed documents by any party or counsel shall be permitted. The court shall direct a procedure for removal, photocopying and return of such documents.

Source. — Former Rules 3A:15 and 3A:29 (d).

Comment. — With respect to former Rule 3A:15, the amendment adds the word "magistrate" after the word "clerk" and before the words "or Commonwealth's attorney" in subsection (a), and adds the words "Before a Circuit Court" to the title of subsection (b).

The addition to subsection (a) conforms the Rule to § 19.2-45 (4). The addition to subsection (b) is necessary because § 16.1-89 provides a different scheme for production of documentary evidence and of objects in general district court.

The amendment, effective July 1, 2000, adopted February 4, 2000, added the second and third paragraphs of subsection (b), and added subsection (f).

The amendment, effective January 1, 2003, adopted November 1, 2002, in subsection (b), in the first paragraph, substituted "person" for "individual" in clauses (1) and (2) of the second sentence, and deleted "in person and" following "shall appear" in the second sentence; and added the fourth paragraph.

The amendment effective July 1, 2008, adopted April 9, 2008, in the first paragraph of subdivision (a), added "by the attorney for the defendant" at the end of the first sentence and "and, for the attendance of a witness to testify before a circuit court, by the attorney for the defendant as well" at the end of the second sentence.

Law Review. — For survey of Virginia criminal law and procedure for the year 2004-2005, see 40 U. Rich. L. Rev. 197 (2005).

Michie's Jurisprudence. — For related discussion, see 1A M.J. Abatement, Survival and Revival, § 18, 27; 2B M.J. Bail and Recognizance, § 3; 4A M.J. Contempt, § 15; 5B M.J. Criminal Procedure, § 40; 8B M.J. Former Adjudication or Res Judicata, § 61; 10A M.J. Insane and Other Incompetent Persons, §§ 43, 46; 20 M.J. Witnesses, § 2.

CASE NOTES

The discovery process is not open to the press and public even though a recent amendment of subdivision (b) now requires that documents obtained through subpoenas be returnable to the court or clerk of court; the fact that a recent amendment makes discovery documents returnable to the clerk or court in no way demonstrates that there has been a history or tradition of openness in the discovery materials sought. Therefore, there is no constitutional right of access to documents under the First Amendment of the United States Constitution. In re Worrell Enters., Inc., 14 Va. App. 671, 419 S.E.2d 271 (1992).

Discovery in criminal trials historically has been a private matter between the parties; there is no tradition of openness to the "place or process" of discovery. In re Worrell Enters., Inc., 14 Va. App. 671, 419 S.E.2d 271 (1992).

Test of materiality. — When a defendant seeks disclosure of evidence, the standard to be applied in determining its materiality is whether a substantial basis for claiming materiality exists. Cox v. Commonwealth, 227 Va. 324, 315 S.E.2d 228 (1984).

Psychiatric records of a trial witness were not material to the proceedings where the only proceeding pending was to sentence the defendant because the witness's credibility was no longer at issue. Megel v. Commonwealth, 31 Va. App. 414, 524 S.E.2d 139 (2000).

The common law right of access to judicial records does not extend to pretrial discovery materials collected by the parties but not yet a part of the judicial record in the proceedings. In re Worrell Enters., Inc., 14 Va. App. 671, 419 S.E.2d 271 (1992).

Amendment did not change records from discovery material to "judicial records." Because this rule, prior to the 1990 amendment, was silent as to where materials should be delivered or where the person identified was to appear, the purpose of the amendment was to clarify these points; the amendment did not change the character of the records from discovery material to "judicial records." In re Worrell Enters., Inc., 14 Va. App. 671, 419 S.E.2d 271 (1992).

Not to be used for "fishing expedition." A subpoena duces tecum should not be used when it is not intended to produce evidentiary materials, but is intended as a "fishing expedition" in the hope of uncovering information material to the defendant's case. Farish v. Commonwealth, 2 Va. App. 627, 346 S.E.2d 736 (1986).

When the evidence sought is material or if a substantial basis for claiming materiality exists, it is reasonable to issue a subpoena requiring the production of the evidence. Farish v. Commonwealth, 2 Va. App. 627, 346 S.E.2d 736 (1986).

The trial court properly denied the defendant's request for access to the mental health records of the 13-year-old victim in a rape prosecution where the defendant asserted that the records were material because they would permit an attack on the victim's credibility, but acknowledged that he did not know what was in the records and was investigating and exploring possibilities, i.e., engaged in a "fishing expedition." Boyd v. Commonwealth, No. 2038-97-3 (Ct. of Appeals Dec. 8, 1998).

Writings or objects in possession of a party to the action. — A trial court properly refused to issue a subpoena in a criminal proceeding where the subpoena was to be directed to the chief of the county police; the materials in question were in the possession of the Commonwealth and thus were not in the possession of a person not a party to the action, as required by this rule. Moore v. Commonwealth, No. 0264-99-4, 2000 Va. App. LEXIS 538 (Ct. of Appeals July 25, 2000).

Agents of the Commonwealth. — Employees of Commonwealth agencies do not automatically qualify as "agents of the Commonwealth" for purposes of Rule 3A:11. However, where an agency is involved in the investigation or prosecution of a particular criminal case, agency employees become agents of the Commonwealth for purposes of Rule 3A:11 and must be considered a party to the action for purposes of this rule. Ramirez v. Commonwealth, 20 Va. App. 292, 456 S.E.2d 531 (1995).

Police department as extension of Commonwealth. — Information requested by defendant from the police department regarding drug dog's past individual case notes and percentages of times that an arrest was made based on the dog's effort was not discoverable pursuant Rule 3A:12, because the police department was an extension of the Commonwealth and thus, a party to the action. Everett v. Commonwealth, No. 3074-03-1, 2004 Va. App. LEXIS 558 (Ct. of Appeals Nov. 16, 2004).

Where materials in the hands of third parties could be used at trial, they are the proper subject of a subpoena duces tecum. Cox v. Commonwealth, 227 Va. 324, 315 S.E.2d 228 (1984).

Scope not limited to admissible objects. — The scope of a subpoena duces tecum is not limited to those objects or documents that may be used at trial. Gibbs v. Commonwealth, 16 Va. App. 697, 432 S.E.2d 514 (1993).

Prejudice must be shown. — Trial court's refusal to issue a subpoena duces tecum is not reversible error absent a showing of prejudice. Gibbs v. Commonwealth, 16 Va. App. 697, 432 S.E.2d 514 (1993).

Access to corporate records in embezzlement case. — In a prosecution for embezzlement, where defendant sought access to corporate records in order to prove that there was an informal agreement among the members of this closely held corporation that the members, including defendant, were entitled to use corporate accounts for personal purposes, it was error to restrict his access to those portions of the corporate minute book which specifically referred to defendant or to the general functions of the corporate officers. Patterson v. Commonwealth, 3 Va. App. 1, 348 S.E.2d 285 (1986).

Defendant did not show that victim's investigation was material to his defense. — Where before trial, defendant sought discovery of the corporation's records concerning the death of victim and where company had conducted an investigation of the incident because victim was hit by one of company's trains, the trial court correctly quashed the subpoena since defendant did not make a colorable showing that the railroad investigation of death was material to his defense for aggravated sexual battery. Kauffman v. Commonwealth, 8 Va. App. 400, 382 S.E.2d 279 (1989).

Medical records. — Even when a subpoena duces tecum complies with Va. Sup. Ct. R. 3A:12(b) and follows the form of the sample subpoena duces tecum included in the appendix to the rules of court, it will not be sufficient to request medical or counseling records in light of § 32.1-127.1:03. Hairston v. Commonwealth, 50 Va. App. 64, 646 S.E.2d 32, 2007 Va. App. LEXIS 241 (2007).

Victim's psychiatric records not discoverable where defendant's theory of case based on speculation. — Subpoena duces tecum sought by defendant, on trial for rape and forcible sodomy, directing the victim to produce records "of any psychiatrist or psychologist which she has visited for treatment and/or other services within the last five (5) years," was properly denied where defendant hoped that victim's psychiatric records would show that she had fantasies of being raped, thereby creating the inference that she consented to the sexual activity to punish her husband for arguing with her, but where defendant's theory of consent was based on nothing more than surmise and speculation. Farish v. Commonwealth, 2 Va. App. 627, 346 S.E.2d 736 (1986).

Victim's doctor's medical records were not material. — Defendant was not prejudiced by the trial court's refusal to provide him access to the victim's doctor's medical records because there was no reasonable probability that the result of the proceeding would have been different if the records were given to him; nothing in the documents would have provided defendant with material to impeach any witnesses or further avenues of investigation of which defendant was unaware. Nelson v. Commonwealth, 41 Va. App. 716, 589 S.E.2d 23, 2003 Va. App. LEXIS 615 (2003), aff'd, 268 Va. 665, 604 S.E.2d 76 (2004).

Evidence admissible. — Telephone records were not erroneously admitted into evidence to support a conviction for murder; the defendant had notice of the subpoena duces tecum as required by subsection (b) where he had been afforded the opportunity to cross-examine the witness with respect to such records but failed to move the court to continue or recess the proceedings to facilitate the preparation of such examination. Doss v. Commonwealth, No. 1319-00-1, 2001 Va. App. LEXIS 571 (Ct. of Appeals Oct. 16, 2001).

Subpoena quashed. — Order quashing defendant's subpoenas for victim's medical records was proper because there was basis to conclude that Commonwealth lacked authority to move to quash requests for the subpoenas, standing to move to quash the subpoenas was part of basic duties of the office of Commonwealth's attorney under § 15.2-1627; further, defendant failed to show the records he sought were material as defendant sought the records to enable him to show that the victim's mental status at the time of sentencing was not totally caused by his crime against her, but the evidence at sentencing did not address the victim's mental status but only her conduct and behavior as observed and recounted by her mother. The victim's mental condition never became an issue and was not a factor in fixing sentence and defendant made no showing of prejudice. Harmon v. Commonwealth, 2012 Va. App. LEXIS 107 (Apr. 10, 2012).

Applied in McDonnough v. Commonwealth, 25 Va. App. 120, 486 S.E.2d 570 (1997); Castelow v. Commonwealth, 29 Va. App. 305, 512 S.E.2d 137 (1999); Brooks v. Commonwealth, 49 Va. App. 155, 638 S.E.2d 131, 2006 Va. App. LEXIS 574 (2006).

CIRCUIT COURT OPINIONS

Subpoenas would not issue for police dispatch reports. — Defendant who was charged with three felony convictions could not obtain subpoenas duces tecum under Va. Sup. Ct. Rule 3A:12 to discover police dispatch records transmitted on the night of defendant's arrest, because the dispatcher, who was employed by the state, county and town police agencies, was acting as an agent of the state. Discovery of the transmissions was limited in scope to material that was discoverable under Va. Sup. Ct. Rule 3A:11 and *Brady*. Commonwealth v. Marsh, 65 Va. Cir. 229, 2004 Va. Cir. LEXIS 207 (Lancaster County 2004).

Victim's doctor's medical records were not material. — Trial court found that nothing in two sets of psychiatric records over which the trial court conducted in camera review following production of that material pursuant to subpoenas called into question the credibility of the complaining witness, and, thus, the psychiatric records were not material and would be sealed in a case where defendant was indicted by a grand jury for the aggravated battery and object sexual penetration of defendant's stepsister; while defendant had state and federal constitutional rights permitting defendant to call for the production of evidence in his favor and public policy concerns dictated that courts in criminal cases consider the impact on witnesses of releasing the records of healthcare providers who under civil law were protected by privileges from releasing such material, the trial court concluded after in camera review that the information in the records sought was not material because it did not call into question the alleged victim's assertion of abuse or the alleged victim's credibility. Commonwealth v. Arrington, 72 Va. Cir. 514, 2007 Va. Cir. LEXIS 8 (Portsmouth 2007).

Subpoena duces tecum for Department of Family Services records to mitigate punishment quashed. — When defendant had a subpoena duces tecum issued for records of the Department of Family Services regarding abuse or neglect of defendant or defendant's siblings as mitigating evidence should defendant be convicted of pending criminal charges, the subpoena was quashed because (1) the Department had a duty, under § 63.2-104, to keep the records confidential, and (2) defendant's request did not outweigh this duty, as the duty protected defendant's minor siblings, and defendant could not claim a legitimate interest in the records simply because the records might assist defendant in defendant's criminal case. Commonwealth v. Williams, 84 Va. Cir. 325, 2012 Va. Cir. LEXIS 20 (Fairfax County Feb. 22, 2012).

When defendant had a subpoena duces tecum issued for records of the Department of Family Services regarding abuse or neglect of defendant or defendant's siblings as mitigating evidence should defendant be convicted of pending criminal charges, the subpoena was quashed because (1) defendant improperly requested the subpoena's issuance to obtain Brady material under Va. Sup. Ct. R. 3A:12, and (2) DFS had a compelling interest in protecting the confidentiality of information concerning social services to or on behalf of individuals DFS served. Commonwealth v. Williams, 84 Va. Cir. 325, 2012 Va. Cir. LEXIS 20 (Fairfax County Feb. 22, 2012).

Agents of the Commonwealth. — Defendant could not subpoena a jail's inmate records because (1) Va. Sup. Ct. R. 3A:12(b) did not permit subpoenas directed to a party, (2) the county sheriff's department was responsible for both the jail's administrative operation and investigating defendant's case, (3) the sheriff's department's investigatory responsibility defined the department as a party to the case, and, (4) as parties, those who were responsible for operating the jail could not be subject to a subpoena, although discovery was potentially available pursuant to Va. Sup. Ct. R. 3A:11(b). Commonwealth v. Bowman, 85 Va. Cir. 199, 2012 Va. Cir. LEXIS 159 (Loudoun County Aug. 13, 2012).

Right to "call for evidence." — Right to "call for evidence" under Va. Const., Art. I, § 8 is not the equivalent of unfettered discovery from the Commonwealth or its agents under Va. Sup. Ct. R. 3A:11, nor does the free exercise of the right demand the production of writings or things from third parties beyond the scope of Va. Sup. Ct. R. 3A:12(b). Commonwealth v. Hoard, 82 Va. Cir. 335, 2011 Va. Cir. LEXIS 40 (Augusta County Mar. 9, 2011).

Not to be used for "fishing expedition." — While defendant had right to call for evidence under Va. Sup. Ct. R. 3A:12(a), defendant's wife's counsel was entitled to have subpoena duces tecum quashed, because defendant failed to show that the information he sought regarding his wife's communications with government entities regarding the pending criminal charges existed, let alone was material. Commonwealth v. Faulkner, 82 Va. Cir. 417, 2011 Va. Cir. LEXIS 147 (Augusta County Apr. 1, 2011).

Prosecution's subpoena quashed. — Subpoena duces tecum issued to the prosecution, which sought a tape-recorded message in the possession of the Office of the Public Defender was granted because the Office was not required to produce a document that had been given to it by a former client during the course of an investigation and that contained a message made by a current client. Commonwealth v. Peoples, 63 Va. Cir. 541, 2004 Va. Cir. LEXIS 90 (Norfolk 2004).

Subpoena quashed. — Although a business invitee could normally challenge a doctor chosen by a grocery store to conduct the examination at a hearing on the store's motion for a Rule 4:10(a) examination, a doctor did not have to appear pursuant to a witness subpoena at a hearing on the store's motion for a Rule 4:10(a) examination as the invitee failed to make a prima facie valid objection to the doctor conducting the examination at a hearing on the doctor's motion for a protective order. Young v. Food Lion Store No. 622, 70 Va. Cir. 313, 2006 Va. Cir. LEXIS 31 (Portsmouth 2006).

Commonwealth's motion to quash a subpoena

duces tecum to be served on a jail was granted because defendant did not show that the information that she sought was material as required under Va. Sup. Ct. R. 3A:11(b)(2), and defendant's characterization of some of the information she sought was not supported by the evidence; because the jail was an agent of the Commonwealth for the purposes of Rule 3A:11(b)(2), and thus, not a third party under Va. Sup. Ct. R. 3A:12(b), even if some information was not addressed by the second sentence of Rule 3A:11(b)(2), which mandated an absolute limit on the circuit court's authority to grant the motion with respect to information developed in connection with the investigation or prosecution of the case, it was, nevertheless, covered by the first sentence, which authorized the circuit court to grant a motion on a showing that the information was material and that the request was reasonable. Commonwealth v. Hoard, 82 Va. Cir. 335, 2011 Va. Cir. LEXIS 40 (Augusta County Mar. 9, 2011).

When defendant had a subpoena duces tecum issued for records of the Department of Family Services regarding abuse or neglect of defendant or defendant's siblings as mitigating evidence should defendant be convicted of pending criminal charges, the subpoena was quashed because the Department was not an agent of the Commonwealth of Virginia, for purposes of the subpoena, since the Department did not investigate the charges against defendant. Commonwealth v. Williams, 84 Va. Cir. 325, 2012 Va. Cir. LEXIS 20 (Fairfax County Feb. 22, 2012).

Rule 3A:13. Trial by Jury or by Court.

(a) *Right to Jury; Duty of Court in Nonjury Trial.* — The accused is entitled to a trial by jury only in a circuit court on a plea of not guilty.

(b) *Waiver of Jury in Circuit Court.* — If an accused who has pleaded not guilty in a circuit court consents to trial without a jury, the court may, with the concurrence of the Commonwealth's attorney, try the case without a jury. The court shall determine before trial that the accused's consent was voluntarily and intelligently given, and his consent and the concurrence of the court and the Commonwealth's attorney shall be entered of record.

Source. — Former Rule 3A:19.

Comment. — With respect to former Rule 3A:19, the amendment deletes the second sentence of subsection (a), deletes the third sentence of subsection (b) and deletes subsections (c) and (d), and changes the former Rule's references to a "court of record" to a "circuit court."

Michie's Jurisprudence. — For related discussion, see 11B M.J. Jury, § 14.

CASE NOTES

Circuit courts must assume that trial will be by jury. — Unless and until the accused knowingly and intelligently waives the right and the attorney for the Commonwealth and the trial court concur in the decision to forego a jury trial. Wright v. Commonwealth, 4 Va. App. 303, 357 S.E.2d 547 (1987).

A defendant's consent to waive trial by jury and consent of trial court and prosecutor must be entered into the record. Moffett v. Commonwealth, 24 Va. App. 387, 482 S.E.2d 846 (1997).

Procedure for waiver of jury. — In addition to requiring that the trial court determine whether an accused's consent is voluntarily and intelligently given, subdivision (b) provides that the trial court must enter of record the accused's consent, as well as the concurrence of the court and the prosecutor. Therefore, once the trial court determines that the accused's consent is voluntarily and intelligently given, it must then ascertain whether the prosecutor concurs in the accused's jury waiver and enter its findings of record. McCormick v. City of Va. Beach, 5 Va. App. 369, 363 S.E.2d 124 (1987).

The trial court was not required to memorialize by order its determination that the defendant's jury trial waiver was voluntary and intelligent; rather, once the court had made this determination, the court shall enter in the record the defendant's agreement to be tried without a jury. Commonwealth v. Williams, 262 Va. 661, 553 S.E.2d 760, 2001 Va. LEXIS 122 (2001).

Where trial court did not inquire whether defendant waived his right to jury trial it violated subdivision (b), which requires the trial court to determine before trial whether the accused voluntarily and intelligently consents to being tried without a jury. McCormick v. City of Va. Beach, 5 Va. App. 369, 363 S.E.2d 124 (1987).

Conviction set aside absent record of defendant's waiver. — The failure to include in the record the defendant's consent to waive his right to be tried by a jury or the concurrence by the Commonwealth's attorney and the court required that the conviction be set aside. Wright v. Commonwealth, 4 Va. App. 303, 357 S.E.2d 547 (1987).

Jury trial not waived absent any indication of waiver in record. — Where there was no indication that the trial court required the defendant at any time prior to the trial date to elect either trial by jury or trial by the bench, and nothing in the record showed that he knew of his right to trial by jury, the defendant did not waive his right to a jury trial. Wright v. Commonwealth, 4 Va. App. 303, 357 S.E.2d 547 (1987).

Trial court erred in refusing to grant defendant a jury trial because defendant was denied his right to a jury trial under Va. Const., Art. I, § 8, and he never waived his right to a jury trial under Va. Sup. Ct. R. 3A:13(b). Williams v. Commonwealth, 2011 Va. App. LEXIS 367 (Nov. 29, 2011).

Sufficiency of waiver. — Standing alone, a scheduling order merely setting a case down on the court's docket for a bench trial does not suffice as a waiver of jury trial because it does not show a deliberate action by the accused indicating an election to forego her right to a jury trial; such an order could suggest as little as the prediction of defense counsel that his client will accept his jury-waiver recommendation and, at the appropriate time, say as much when the trial court engages the defendant in the colloquy required by Va. Sup. Ct. R. 3A:13(b). Tokora-Mansary v. Commonwealth, 2009 Va. App. LEXIS 586 (Dec. 29, 2009).

Although over the course of a year, the trial date was scheduled, continued, and rescheduled five times and each of the judge's orders scheduled the matter for trial without a jury, none of the orders stated appellant expressly waived her right to a trial by jury; standing alone, a scheduling order merely setting a case down on the court's docket for a bench trial did not suffice as a waiver because it did not show a deliberate action by the accused indicating an election to forego her right to a jury trial. In addition, no transcript or statement of facts indicated appellant waived her right to a jury; the transcript of the trial court's remarks from the bench did not imply that on some prior occasion appellant expressly waived her right to a jury or, if she had, that the trial court satisfied itself that she did so knowingly, voluntarily, and intelligently. Tokora-Mansary v. Commonwealth, 2009 Va. App. LEXIS 586 (Dec. 29, 2009).

Weight given defense attorney's waiver of jury trial. — An attorney may not, without authorization, surrender an accused's right to a jury trial, and, thereby, permit the trial court to presume conclusively the effectuation of a valid waiver. The trial court may not rely on such waiver of an accused's right to a jury trial, by itself, as a de facto manifestation of voluntary and intelligent consent by the accused. Jones v. Commonwealth, 24 Va. App. 636, 484 S.E.2d 618 (1997).

Commonwealth must show defendant waived jury by some deliberate action. — Where the Commonwealth asserts that an accused elected a bench trial, there must be a showing of some deliberate action by the accused indicating an election to forego his right to a jury trial. Wright v. Commonwealth, 4 Va. App. 303, 357 S.E.2d 547 (1987).

"Voluntariness" of plea in discretion of trial court. — Determination of whether a defendant's waiver of a jury trial was voluntary, knowing and intelligent must be made by the trial court. Moffett v. Commonwealth, 24 Va. App. 387, 482 S.E.2d 846 (1997).

Voluntariness issue not preserved. — Where defendant did not ask for a jury trial and did not apprise the trial court of his argument that his prior jury waiver was not knowing, intelligent, and voluntary, defendant failed to make a timely objection in the trial court, and thus did not preserve this issue for appeal. Noel v. Commonwealth, No. 3248-02-2, 2004 Va. App. LEXIS 261 (Ct. of Appeals June 8, 2004).

Withdrawal of waiver untimely. — Where defendant voluntarily and knowingly waived his right to a jury trial prior to trial and his attempt to withdraw his waiver, made on the day of trial, was untimely, the trial court properly denied his request for a jury trial. Davis v. Commonwealth, No. 3318-02-3, 2003 Va. App. LEXIS 614 (Ct. of Appeals Dec. 2, 2003).

Part 3A applicable to guilty plea in capital case. — There is no provision in Article 4.1 of Chapter 15 of Title 19.2 concerning the entry by an accused of a plea of guilty in a capital murder case. There is no conflict, therefore, between Article 4.1 and subdivision (a) of this rule, and, hence, pursuant to Rule 3A:18, the provisions of Part 3A shall be applicable to the entry of a plea of guilty in a capital case. Pruett v. Commonwealth, 232 Va. 266, 351 S.E.2d 1 (1986), cert. denied, 482 U.S. 931, 107 S. Ct. 3220, 96 L. Ed. 2d 706 (1987).

Motion to plead guilty and submit question of punishment to jury properly denied. — In a prosecution for capital murder, after the trial court denied defendant's motion for two juries, the trial court correctly denied defendant's motion to permit him to plead guilty and submit to the jury the question of punishment alone. Subdivision (a) of this rule provides that "[t]he accused is entitled to a trial by jury only in a circuit court on a plea of not guilty." Pruett v. Commonwealth, 232 Va. 266, 351 S.E.2d 1 (1986), cert. denied, 482 U.S. 931, 107 S. Ct. 3220, 96 L. Ed. 2d 706 (1987).

Demand by prosecutor for retrial by jury. Where the defendant in a first-degree murder prosecution exercised his right to a jury trial at his first trial, prosecutorial vindictiveness did not exist where prosecutor demanded that the defendant's retrial also be by jury. Cooper v. Mitchell, 647 F.2d 437 (4th Cir.), cert. denied, 454 U.S. 849, 102 S. Ct. 171, 70 L. Ed. 2d 139 (1981).

Right to jury where charged with driving under influence and driving on revoked license. — Article I, § 8, of the Virginia Constitution and subdivision (a) of this rule guaranteed defendant a right to a jury in the trial court on both charges of driving under the influence and driving on a revoked operator's license. McCormick v. City of Va. Beach, 5 Va. App. 369, 363 S.E.2d 124 (1987).

Introduction of evidence in bench trials. — Defendant's claim the Commonwealth improperly failed to move defendant's physical appearance officially into evidence during its case-in-chief was rejected as the prosecutor did all the prosecutor needed to do to call defendant's physical appearance to the attention of the finder of fact by asking the victims whether defendant was in the courtroom and whether they could point defendant out; neither the prior evidence cases, Va. Sup. Ct. R. 3A:13, nor Va. Sup. Ct. R. 3A:15 seemed to specify any particular requirements for the introduction of evidence applicable only to bench trials and not to jury trials. Haley v. Commonwealth, 2007 Va. App. LEXIS 402 (Nov. 6, 2007).

Applied in Robinson v. Commonwealth, 36 Va. App. 1, 548 S.E.2d 227, 2001 Va. App. LEXIS 461 (2001).

Rule 3A:14. Trial Jurors.

(a) *Examination.* — After the prospective jurors are sworn on the voir dire, the court shall question them individually or collectively to determine whether anyone:

(1) Is related by blood, adoption, or marriage to the accused or to a person against whom the alleged offense was committed;

(2) Is an officer, director, agent or employee of the accused;
(3) Has any interest in the trial or the outcome of the case;
(4) Has acquired any information about the alleged offense or the accused from the news media or other sources and, if so, whether such information would affect the juror's impartiality in the case;
(5) Has expressed or formed any opinion as to the guilt or innocence of the accused;
(6) Has a bias or prejudice against the Commonwealth or the accused; or
(7) Has any reason to believe the juror might not give a fair and impartial trial to the Commonwealth and the accused based solely on the law and the evidence.

Thereafter, the court, and counsel as of right, may examine on oath any prospective juror and ask any questions relevant to the qualifications as an impartial juror. A party objecting to a juror may introduce competent evidence in support of the objection.

(b) *Challenge for Cause.* — The court, on its own motion or following a challenge for cause, may excuse a prospective juror if it appears the juror is not qualified, and another shall be drawn or called and placed in the juror's stead for the trial of that case.

Cross references. — As to the right of the court and counsel for either party to conduct voir dire examination of prospective jurors, see § 8.01-358.

Source. — Former Rule 3A:20.

Comment. — With respect to former Rule 3A:20, the amendment substitutes the word "and" for the word "or" between the words "court" and "counsel" in the second paragraph of subsection (a) (7), substitutes the words "as of right" for the words "with permission of the court," substitutes the word "and" for the words "may ask" in the same subsection, and deletes subsections (c), (d) and (e).

The amendment effective January 1, 2013, adopted December 14, 2012, inserted ", adoption," in (a)(1), substituted "the juror's" for "his" in (a)(4) and (b) and "the juror" for "he" in (a)(7) and (b); and in the last paragraph of (a), substituted "questions relevant to the qualifications" for "question relevant to his qualifications."

Michie's Jurisprudence. — For related discussion, see 1A M.J. Alibi, § 2; 11B M.J. Jury, §§ 32, 43, 44, 48, 145.1.

CASE NOTES

I. General Consideration.
II. Bias.
III. Capital Cases.

I. GENERAL CONSIDERATION.

Constitutional guarantee reinforced by legislative mandate and rules of court. — The constitutional guarantee of a trial by impartial jury is reinforced by legislative mandate and by the rules of court: Veniremen must "stand indifferent in the cause." Breeden v. Commonwealth, 217 Va. 297, 227 S.E.2d 734 (1976).

An accused is entitled to an impartial jury as a matter of constitutional guarantee, reinforced by legislative mandate and by the rules of court. Martin v. Commonwealth, 221 Va. 436, 271 S.E.2d 123 (1980).

The right to a trial by an impartial jury is guaranteed under both the United States and Virginia Constitutions and this guarantee is reinforced by legislative enactment and by the rules of court. Gosling v. Commonwealth, 7 Va. App. 642, 376 S.E.2d 541 (1989).

Impartial jury is a substantive right. — The constitutional and statutory guarantee of an impartial jury is no mere legal technicality, but a substantive right scrupulously to be observed in the day-to-day administration of justice. Martin v. Commonwealth, 221 Va. 436, 271 S.E.2d 123 (1980).

It is the duty of the trial court, to procure an impartial jury to try every case. Salina v. Commonwealth, 217 Va. 92, 225 S.E.2d 199 (1976).

Discretion of court in jury selection. — Generally, whether a prospective juror should be excluded for cause is a matter within the sound discretion of the trial court, and its action in refusing to exclude a particular venireman is entitled to great weight on appeal. Martin v. Commonwealth, 221 Va. 436, 271 S.E.2d 123 (1980).

Trial court's exercise of judicial discretion in deciding challenges for cause will not be disturbed on appeal, unless manifest error appears in the record. Stockton v. Commonwealth, 241 Va. 192, 402 S.E.2d 196, cert. denied, 502 U.S. 902, 112 S. Ct. 280, 116 L. Ed. 2d 231 (1991).

Trial court's decision whether to retain or exclude an individual venireman is given deference on appeal, since it is in a position to see and hear the juror. Caprio v. Commonwealth, No. 2225-98-1 (Ct. of Appeals Mar. 14, 2000).

Trial court did not abuse its discretion in refusing to strike a juror who worked with a sexual assault prevention team and with sexual assault victims in a trial where the defendant was accused of sexually assaulting a woman since the juror stated that he could be impartial and listen objectively to the evidence. Vance v. Commonwealth, No. 2450-00-4, 2002 Va. App. LEXIS 42 (Ct. of Appeals Jan. 29, 2002).

Trial court committed no error in excusing two

veniremen where the first was scheduled to be in criminal court for sentencing on the second day of the four-day trial and the other did not comprehend English well enough to even understand the questions being asked during voir dire. Shaikh v. Commonwealth, No. 2614-03-4, 2005 Va. App. LEXIS 29 (Ct. of Appeals Jan. 25, 2005).

Where there is a reasonable doubt whether a juror is qualified, that doubt must be resolved in favor of the accused. Salina v. Commonwealth, 217 Va. 92, 225 S.E.2d 199 (1976).

Any reasonable doubt whether a juror stands impartial is sufficient to ensure his exclusion because it is not only important that justice should be impartially administered, but it should also flow through channels as free from suspicion as possible. Mullis v. Commonwealth, 3 Va. App. 564, 351 S.E.2d 919 (1987).

Viewing the venire person's voir dire in its entirety, the record disclosed a series of tentative, equivocal responses to questioning intended to probe and ascertain the venire person's state of mind, leaving reasonable doubt of her partiality as a matter of law and requiring that she be removed for cause. Under such circumstances, it was reversible error to require defendant to exhaust a peremptory strike to remove the juror. Pennington v. Commonwealth, No. 1346-95-3 (Ct. of Appeals Feb. 4, 1997).

Reading of defendant's statement to prospective jurors not required. — The manner in which jury selection is conducted is within the discretion and control of the trial court, guided by § 8.01-358 and this rule, and there is no provision in Virginia law which requires a trial court to read to prospective jurors a statement offered by a defendant. Buchanan v. Commonwealth, 238 Va. 389, 384 S.E.2d 757 (1989), cert. denied, 493 U.S. 1063, 110 S. Ct. 880, 107 L. Ed. 2d 963 (1990).

Membership in a particular organization does not per se disqualify a prospective juror. Stockton v. Commonwealth, 241 Va. 192, 402 S.E.2d 196, cert. denied, 502 U.S. 902, 112 S. Ct. 280, 116 L. Ed. 2d 231 (1991).

Belief that accused must prove innocence. — The refusal to exclude for cause a venireman who believes an accused must prove his innocence is an abuse of discretion and a denial of a defendant's right to an impartial jury. Martin v. Commonwealth, 221 Va. 436, 271 S.E.2d 123 (1980).

Denial of a motion to permit each venireman to be questioned individually, out of the presence of all others, on voir dire was within the court's discretion. Fisher v. Commonwealth, 236 Va. 403, 374 S.E.2d 46 (1988), cert. denied, 490 U.S. 1028, 109 S. Ct. 1766, 104 L. Ed. 2d 201 (1989).

Failure to inquire as to opinion on defendant's burden of proof. — The trial court's failure to make inquiries, as required by § 8.01-358 and this rule, concerning opinion during the voir dire together with the court's refusal of a proposed voir dire question which would have resolved any doubt that the defendant did not have to prove his innocence, created a reasonable doubt as to the impartiality of the jury. Trent v. Commonwealth, No. 0896-85, (Ct. of Appeals Aug. 6, 1987).

Inquiry as to weight jurors would give to police officer's testimony. — In an appropriate case, counsel may inquire of prospective jurors whether they would give greater or less weight to the testimony of a police officer than to that of another witness simply because of his official status. When it is anticipated that a major part of the prosecution's case will hinge upon a credibility determination between prosecution witnesses who have an official status and other defense witnesses who do not, then not only is such an inquiry of whether jurors would give unqualified credence to those witnesses appropriate but it may be required. Mullis v. Commonwealth, 3 Va. App. 564, 351 S.E.2d 919 (1987).

Whether prospective juror should have been excluded for cause must be decided upon review of entire voir dire, rather than an isolated question and answer. Mullis v. Commonwealth, 3 Va. App. 564, 351 S.E.2d 919 (1987).

Removal of juror by peremptory challenge is irrelevant to decision on appeal if the court erred in refusing to strike him for cause. Scott v. Commonwealth, 1 Va. App. 447, 339 S.E.2d 899 (1986), aff'd, 233 Va. 5, 353 S.E.2d 460 (1987).

It is prejudicial error to force a defendant to use the peremptory strike to exclude a venireman who is not free from exception. Scott v. Commonwealth, 1 Va. App. 447, 339 S.E.2d 899 (1986), aff'd, 233 Va. 5, 353 S.E.2d 460 (1987).

No error in failure to dismiss. — Trial court did not abuse its discretion in denying defendant's motions to strike four potential jurors for cause as bias or prejudice on the part of the jurors was not shown by one juror's belief's regarding the death penalty and life imprisonment, one juror's concerns over children being the murder victims and pretrial media publicity, one juror's knowing the prosecutor, and one juror's hardship in being away from her employment. Juniper v. Commonwealth, 271 Va. 362, 626 S.E.2d 383, 2006 Va. LEXIS 29 (2006).

Applied in Martin v. Commonwealth, 221 Va. 436, 271 S.E.2d 123 (1980); Fitzgerald v. Commonwealth, 223 Va. 615, 292 S.E.2d 798 (1982); Educational Books, Inc. v. Commonwealth, 3 Va. App. 384, 349 S.E.2d 903 (1986); Mu'Min v. Commonwealth, 239 Va. 433, 389 S.E.2d 886 (1990); Moten v. Commonwealth, 14 Va. App. 956, 420 S.E.2d 250 (1992); Brown v. Commonwealth, 29 Va. App. 199, 510 S.E.2d 751 (1999).

II. BIAS.

Refusal to remove impartial juror not harmless even if peremptory strike used. — A trial court's refusal to remove a juror who is not impartial does not constitute harmless error even if counsel uses a peremptory strike to exclude the juror. David v. Commonwealth, 26 Va. App. 77, 493 S.E.2d 379 (1997).

Failure to raise issue of racial discrimination. — Where it did not appear that the petitioner raised the issue of systematic exclusion of blacks from the jury at his trial, and the Virginia rules of court and a Virginia statute in effect at the time of petitioner's trial required this as a prerequisite to a valid objection of racial discrimination in jury selection, these procedural requirements constituted an adequate and independent state ground for the refusal by the federal district court to hear the objection in petitioner's petition seeking federal habeas corpus relief. Shrader v. Riddle, 405 F. Supp.

752 (W.D. Va. 1975), aff'd, 551 F.2d 309 (4th Cir. 1977).

One related to the victim within the ninth degree by consanguinity or affinity is not competent to serve as a juror. Salina v. Commonwealth, 217 Va. 92, 225 S.E.2d 199 (1976).

Stockholders. — That a stockholder in a company which is a party to a lawsuit is incompetent to sit as a juror is well settled. Salina v. Commonwealth, 217 Va. 92, 225 S.E.2d 199 (1976).

A stockholder in a corporation is not only incompetent to act as a juror in a case where the corporation is a party, he is likewise incompetent to serve where the corporation has a direct pecuniary interest in the controversy. Salina v. Commonwealth, 217 Va. 92, 225 S.E.2d 199 (1976).

Where the criminal act suffered by the corporation has the direct effect of diminishing the assets of the corporation held for the benefit of its stockholders, a stockholder, regardless of the size of his holdings, could not be said to stand indifferent in the cause. Salina v. Commonwealth, 217 Va. 92, 225 S.E.2d 199 (1976).

The trial court committed reversible error when it refused to dismiss four members of the venire who owned stock in one or both of the banks from which defendant was charged with larceny by check. Salina v. Commonwealth, 217 Va. 92, 225 S.E.2d 199 (1976).

Prospective juror is not subject to automatic exclusion because of association with law-enforcement personnel, provided the juror has no knowledge of the facts of the case and demonstrates impartiality toward the parties. Clozza v. Commonwealth, 228 Va. 124, 321 S.E.2d 273 (1984), cert. denied, 469 U.S. 1230, 105 S. Ct. 1233, 84 L. Ed. 2d 370 (1985), 499 U.S. 913, 111 S. Ct. 1123, 113 L. Ed. 2d 231 (1991).

Trial court abused its discretion in not striking a prospective juror for cause. — Because of the prospective juror's long association with the sheriff's department, his conversation with members of that department concerning the specific case, and his initial concern about his impartiality, it was unlikely that the public would have confidence in the judicial process used in the case because of the failure to strike the prospective juror for cause. Patterson v. Commonwealth, 39 Va. App. 658, 576 S.E.2d 222, 2003 Va. App. LEXIS 38 (2003).

Juror who believes it improper to drive after drinking may be unable to evaluate fairly and impartially the evidence of one who drives after drinking but claims nevertheless not to have been intoxicated. Henshaw v. Commonwealth, 3 Va. App. 213, 348 S.E.2d 853 (1986).

In a prosecution for driving under the influence, it was improper for the court not to allow defendant's counsel to ask venire members "whether any of them thought it improper to drive after drinking alcoholic beverages." Any juror who thought it improper to drive after drinking might not have evaluated impartially his defense. Henshaw v. Commonwealth, 3 Va. App. 213, 348 S.E.2d 853 (1986).

Voir dire permitted regarding gangs. — Defendant's convictions for second-degree murder, use of a firearm during the commission of a felony, and possession of a firearm by a convicted felon were proper because at least some of defendant's proffered gang evidence was erroneously excluded and that evidence was to be admissible on retrial. The evidence of the victim's friend and the victim's gang membership was going to be squarely before the jury and on remand, defendant was entitled to voir dire the venire panel regarding that issue. Cousins v. Commonwealth, 56 Va. App. 257, 693 S.E.2d 283, 2010 Va. App. LEXIS 214 (2010).

Remarks by juror indicating lack of partiality. — Juror who, during luncheon recess, expressed to third parties a conviction that an individual who may be instrumental in obtaining the release of a person charged with a crime should "feel guilty" that the accused is "allowed to walk the streets," charged attorneys whose clients are released of having no remorse as long as the lawyers get paid, and opined that defendant either was not going to be "as fortunate" or was "not going to get off," was probably no longer impartial, even though he had promised the court that he could maintain an open mind on the issues until the remainder of the case was completed, and defendant's motion for mistrial should have been granted. Haddad v. Commonwealth, 229 Va. 325, 329 S.E.2d 17 (1985).

Family member victim of violent crime. — A prospective juror is not per se disqualified because a family member has been a victim of violent crime. Stockton v. Commonwealth, 241 Va. 192, 402 S.E.2d 196, cert. denied, 502 U.S. 902, 112 S. Ct. 280, 116 L. Ed. 2d 231 (1991).

Juror who has had association with law enforcement personnel. — Where prospective juror had served as a chief probation and parole officer for many years, but had retired long before this trial, the court correctly determined that juror would be impartial and there was nothing in the record supporting any challenge to that determination; if a prospective juror has no knowledge of the facts of the case and demonstrates impartiality, he is not subject to a challenge for cause merely because he has had an association with law enforcement personnel. Strickler v. Commonwealth, 241 Va. 482, 404 S.E.2d 227, cert. denied, 502 U.S. 944, 112 S. Ct. 386, 116 L. Ed. 2d 337 (1991).

Rehabilitative evidence based on assent to leading questions. — Where the record showed that after the juror declared her bias in favor of the prosecution, the evidence used to rehabilitate her did not come from her but was based on her mere assent to leading questions, this juror was not per se disqualified because of her declared bias; had her rehabilitative responses come from her in response to non-leading questions, the trial court would not have abused its discretion by refusing to strike her for cause. Because her rehabilitative responses consisted solely of her mere assent to the court's leading questions, she should have been stricken for cause. David v. Commonwealth, 26 Va. App. 77, 493 S.E.2d 379 (1997).

Defendant's claim that a question the trial court asked on voir dire was leading and inappropriately influenced the entire panel because it ultimately had the effect of other jurors not answering questions in an honest and forthright manner was rejected as: (1) the jurors requiring rehabilitation ultimately were struck for cause, (2) the trial court's question was asked only after both the trial court and defendant had multiple opportunities to query potential jurors on the issues of the burden of proof, the presumption of innocence, and the appropriateness of drawing adverse inferences from the failure of the accused to testify, and (3) based on the voir dire as a whole, no reasonable doubt existed as to the impartiality of the remaining jurors not struck for cause. Nelson v. Commonwealth, No. 3408-02-2, 2004 Va. App. LEXIS 224 (Ct. of Appeals May 18, 2004).

No error in failure to dismiss. — There was no manifest error in the court's refusal to dismiss juror for cause in state trooper murder trial. From a review of juror's entire voir dire, the trial court was justified in finding the juror—who told the court his wife's first cousin, a police officer, was murdered—could be impartial during the trial. Weeks v. Commonwealth, 248 Va. 460, 450 S.E.2d 379 (1994), cert. denied, 516 U.S. 829, 116 S. Ct. 100, 133 L. Ed. 2d 55 (1995).

In a case in which defendant appealed his conviction for rape, in violation of § 18.2-61, he argued unsuccessfully on appeal that the trial court erred in denying his motion to strike two prospective jurors, who indicated they were friends with police officers, based on their statements during voir dire. In light of the O'Dell decision, the two prospective jurors were not impermissibly biased in favor of police testimony, bias could not be presumed from the entirety of their statements during voir dire, and defendant had made claim during jury selection that any credibility determinations involving a police officer's testimony would be put to the jury. Weeks v. Commonwealth, 2009 Va. App. LEXIS 368 (Aug. 18, 2009).

Trial court did not err. — Trial court did not err in failing to strike juror one for cause under Va. Const., Art. 1, § 8, § 8.01-358, and Va. Sup. Ct. R. 3A:14 as: (1) although juror one indicated juror one would wonder why defendant did not testify, juror one immediately confirmed juror one's understanding of the legal principle affording defendant that right; (2) the trial court was justified in asking juror one a follow-up question to determine whether, like juror two, juror one thought juror one would be biased and unable to do juror one's duty as a juror, or whether serving as a juror and following the law, while difficult, was nevertheless within juror one's capabilities, and juror one responded that juror one thought juror one could sit and do it. Bufford v. Commonwealth, 2009 Va. App. LEXIS 335 (July 28, 2009).

Trial court did not err in denying defendant's motion to exclude several prospective jurors during voir dire because the isolated portion of voir dire defendant relied upon did not reveal that any of the prospective jurors were unable to decided the facts of the case fairly and impartially; the record did not establish that the prospective jurors whom defendant sought to exclude held firm opinions of such fixed character that repelled the presumption of innocence in a criminal case, and in whose mind the accused stood condemned already, and the prospective jurors indicated that they had no pre-existing opinions about defendant's guilt or innocence, that they had not obtained any information about the offenses charged against defendant, that they were not biased toward either defendant or the Commonwealth, and that they could give defendant a fair and impartial trial based on the applicable law and the facts of the case. Lovos-Rivas v. Commonwealth, 58 Va. App. 55, 707 S.E.2d 27, 2011 Va. App. LEXIS 106 (2011).

III. CAPITAL CASES.

Impartiality on both questions of guilt and punishment required. — Virginia Const., Art. I, § 8 and § 8.01-358 require jurors to be impartial not only upon the issue of guilt or innocence but also upon the question of punishment. Patterson v. Commonwealth, 222 Va. 653, 283 S.E.2d 212 (1981).

Elimination permitted for bias in favor of death penalty. — The process of selection of an impartial jury permits elimination for cause of those veniremen who are biased in favor of the death penalty under all circumstances as well as those who are biased against its imposition under all circumstances. Patterson v. Commonwealth, 222 Va. 653, 283 S.E.2d 212 (1981).

Exclusion of jurors who would not vote for death penalty under any circumstances. — Trial court correctly excluded three prospective jurors for cause where two stated that they would not convict a defendant of such a crime, despite what the evidence could show, and where another reiterated that he would not vote for the death penalty regardless of any instructions the court could give. Strickler v. Commonwealth, 241 Va. 482, 404 S.E.2d 227, cert. denied, 502 U.S. 944, 112 S. Ct. 386, 116 L. Ed. 2d 337 (1991).

Interracial crime. — A capital defendant accused of an interracial crime is entitled to have prospective jurors informed of the race of the victim and questioned on the issue of racial bias. Turner v. Murray, 476 U.S. 28, 106 S. Ct. 1683, 90 L. Ed. 2d 27 (1986).

By refusing to question prospective jurors on racial prejudice, trial judge failed to adequately protect petitioner's constitutional right to an impartial jury. Turner v. Murray, 476 U.S. 28, 106 S. Ct. 1683, 90 L. Ed. 2d 27 (1986).

Failure to question jury on bias invalidates death sentence. — In a prosecution for robbery and capital murder, the refusal by the trial judge to ask the jury whether, if the jury should happen to convict the defendant of capital murder, each juror would be able to consider voting for a sentence less than death, or to ask an equivalent question, was prejudicial error invalidating the sentence to death. Patterson v. Commonwealth, 222 Va. 653, 283 S.E.2d 212 (1981).

Exclusion of juror on trial court's motion. — Where the trial judge told a prospective juror he would hear evidence of one or more crimes committed by this defendant, "other than the capital murder for which he is convicted — I mean for which he's on trial," the fact that Va. Sup. Ct. R. 3A:14(b) authorized the trial court to excuse the juror for cause on its own motion did not relieve defendant from complying with Va. Sup. Ct. R. 5:25 and preserving his claim of error by a timely request to excuse this venire member. Green v. Commonwealth, 266 Va. 81, 580 S.E.2d 834, 2003 Va. LEXIS 55 (2003), cert. denied, 540 U.S. 1194, 124 S. Ct. 1448, 158 L. Ed. 2d 107 (2004).

Exclusion for cause upheld. — Where prospective juror made it clear that she would have to have "absolutely no doubt" that defendant was the right person before she could vote to impose the death sentence, the trial court was well within its discretion in excluding the juror for cause. Bennett v. Commonwealth, 236 Va. 448, 374 S.E.2d 303 (1988), cert. denied, 490 U.S. 1028, 109 S. Ct. 1765, 104 L. Ed. 2d 201 (1989).

CIRCUIT COURT OPINIONS

Intervention not allowed. Because a workers' compensation carrier sought to join an injured employee in asserting a single claim against the defendants, and because the carrier was subjected to the employee's rights under § 65.2-309, intervention was prohibited by Va. Sup. Ct. R. 3:14. Lusk v. Huynh, 72 Va. Cir. 142, 2006 Va. Cir. LEXIS 199 (Fairfax County 2006).

Rule 3A:14.1. Confidentiality of Juror Personal Information.

(a) *Motion for Order Regulating Disclosure of Jurors' Personal Information.* — As provided in Code § 19.2-263.3, on motion of any party or its own motion, and only upon a finding of good cause sufficient to warrant departure from the norm of open proceedings, the court may issue an order which may include provisions:

(1) regulating the disclosure of the personal information of jurors or prospective jurors in a criminal trial. The court may limit or preclude dissemination of such information to particular persons, but in no event shall such information be denied to counsel for either party; and/or

(2) requiring that during the course of the trial, counsel for the parties, and the jurors themselves, shall refer to jurors by number and not by name.

Under this Rule, a finding of "good cause" includes, but is not limited to, a determination by the court in a particular case that if personal information of jurors or prospective jurors is disclosed there is a reasonable possibility of bribery, tampering, physical injury, harassment, intimidation of a juror, or any other material interference with the proper discharge of the jury's functions, such as a reasonably perceived threat to the jury's safety, well-being, or capacity to properly focus upon and perform its trial and deliberative duties.

(b) *Modification of Order.* — An order under this Rule regulating the disclosure of personal information of the jurors in a criminal case may be modified by the court in the exercise of its discretion and for good cause shown, and such information may be disseminated to a person having a legitimate interest or need for the information, with such restrictions upon its use and further dissemination as may be deemed appropriate by the court.

(c) *Personal Information.* — For purposes of this Rule, "personal information" means any information collected by the court, clerk, or jury commissioner at any time, including but not limited to, a juror's name, age, occupation, home and business addresses, telephone numbers, email addresses, and any other identifying information that would assist another in locating or contacting the juror.

This rule, adopted March 1, 2011, became effective May 2, 2011.

Rule 3A:15. Motion to Strike or to Set Aside Verdict; Judgment of Acquittal or New Trial.

(a) *Motion to Strike Evidence.* — After the Commonwealth has rested its case or at the conclusion of all the evidence, the court on motion of the accused may strike the Commonwealth's evidence if the evidence is insufficient as a matter of law to sustain a conviction. If the court overrules a motion to strike the evidence and there is a hung jury, the accused may renew the motion within the time specified in Rule 1:11 and the court may take the action authorized by the Rule.

(b) *Motion to Set Aside Verdict.* — If the jury returns a verdict of guilty, the court may, on motion of the accused made not later than 21 days after entry of a final order, set aside the verdict for error committed during the trial or if the evidence is insufficient as a matter of law to sustain a conviction.

(c) *Judgment of Acquittal or New Trial.* — The court shall enter a judgment of acquittal if it strikes the evidence or sets aside the verdict because the evidence is insufficient as a matter of law to sustain a conviction. The court shall grant a new trial if it sets aside the verdict for any other reason.

Source. — Former Rule 3A:22.

Law Review. — For article, "Criminal Law and Procedure," see 35 U. Rich. L. Rev. 537 (2001).

Michie's Jurisprudence. — For related discussion, see 5A M.J. Courts, § 4; 5B M.J. Criminal Procedure, §§ 53, 62, 67, 68, 70, 75; 13B M.J. New Trials, §§ 31, 32, 38, 47, 49, 53.

CASE NOTES

When a defendant elects to present evidence on his behalf, he waives the right to stand on his motion to strike the evidence made at the conclusion of the Commonwealth's case. Anthony v. Commonwealth, No. 0986-02-3, 2003 Va. App. LEXIS 654 (Ct. of Appeals Dec. 16, 2003).

Sufficiency of evidence considered on appeal where raised in motion to set aside verdict. — Where the defendant's written motion to set aside the verdict articulated specific objections to the sufficiency of the evidence of possession and manufacturing of controlled substances, the sufficiency of the evidence could be considered on appeal, even though the defendant made no motion to strike the Commonwealth's evidence in the trial court. McGee v. Commonwealth, 4 Va. App. 317, 357 S.E.2d 738 (1987).

Motion to strike did not constitute a judgment of acquittal. — Defendant asserted that, in granting his motion to strike on the ground that the Commonwealth's evidence was insufficient to prove the charge of animate object sexual penetration under § 18.2-67.2, the trial court effectively acquitted him of that charge and dismissed the indictment, but the trial court concluded that, although the Commonwealth's evidence was insufficient to prove the element of force, threat, intimidation, or physical helplessness, the evidence was sufficient, as a matter of law, to sustain a conviction for carnal knowledge under § 18.2-63; thus, the trial court's granting of the motion to strike did not constitute a judgment of acquittal under Va. Sup. Ct. R. 3A:15. Therefore, the trial court's ruling on the motion to strike did not preclude the Commonwealth from proceeding on the amended charge of carnal knowledge; accordingly, his conviction was affirmed. Sandoval v. Commonwealth, 2006 Va. App. LEXIS 51 (Feb. 7, 2006).

Specificity required for motion to set aside a verdict. — Motion to set aside the verdict must state the question with sufficient particularity to submit the issue to the trial court. Anthony v. Commonwealth, No. 0986-02-3, 2003 Va. App. LEXIS 654 (Ct. of Appeals Dec. 16, 2003).

After 21-day period has elapsed, remedy is writ of habeas corpus. — While a claim of after-discovered evidence may support a timely motion for a new trial, after the 21-day period has elapsed, defendant's remedy is to petition for a writ of habeas corpus in either state or federal court. Woodfin v. Commonwealth, No. 1043-88-3, (Ct. of Appeals Apr. 2, 1991).

Authority of trial court to retry misdemeanor charge. — Trial court had authority under the Rules of the Supreme Court of Virginia to order a retrial only on misdemeanor charge of marijuana distribution after setting aside appellant's felony conviction based on insufficient evidence. Gorham v. Commonwealth, 15 Va. App. 673, 426 S.E.2d 493 (1993).

Newly discovered evidence. — Denial of defendant's motion for a new trial based on his discovery that the Commonwealth's witness had several show cause orders and a capias issued against her at the time that she worked with the drug task force was not an abuse of discretion as the proffered evidence was either irrelevant or would not have changed the outcome of the trial as: (1) the misdemeanor violations did not involve crimes of moral turpitude; (2) the witness's five felony convictions were in evidence at the trial; and (3) given that the witness admitted the felony convictions, her former drug use, and that she was a paid informant, there was no reasonable probability that disclosure of additional impeaching information would have led the trial court to a different conclusion. Johnson v. Commonwealth, 41 Va. App. 37, 581 S.E.2d 880, 2003 Va. App. LEXIS 399 (2003).

Because the trial court did not hear the Commonwealth's motion to introduce a certificate of analysis, pursuant to Va. Sup. Ct. R. 3A:15(a), the trial court properly verified its recollection of the motion by referring to the record of the proceedings and thereafter permitting the Commonwealth to reopen its case and introduce the certificate. Lewis v. Commonwealth, 2006 Va. App. LEXIS 145 (Apr. 11, 2006).

Defendant was not entitled to a new trial in his prosecution for murder because newly discovered eyewitness testimony would not result in a different outcome at trial because while the eyewitness stated that defendant was not the shooter, the eyewitness admitted that he could not see the face of the shooter based on the lighting; another witness, who had stood closer to the shooter, had testified at trial that the lighting conditions were adequate and had identified defendant as the shooter. Simmons v. Commonwealth, 2008 Va. App. LEXIS 86 (Feb. 19, 2008).

Trial court did not abuse its discretion when it denied defendant's motion for a new trial with regard to his conviction for assault and battery of a law-enforcement office as the proffered evidence of another witness who had observed the handshake between defendant and the victim officer was not considered newly discovered. Specifically, the witness, an attorney with whom defendant had previously dealt with, was known to defendant to have observed the handshake at issue and could have been secured for use at the trial in the exercise of reasonable diligence; the information contained in the proffer was very general, in that it reflected that there seemed to be nothing unusual about the handshake defendant gave the victim officer, which, in its entirety, was cumulative and corroborative of other witness testimony; and, likewise, the proffered testimony that the victim officer wiped off his hand before returning to work as though nothing had happened was regarded as mere corroboration of the testimony of the Commonwealth's witnesses since no witness testified that the victim officer did not continue his work after he cleaned his hand, and each account therefore seemed consistent with that portion of the proffer, or else collateral. Harman v. Commonwealth, 2009 Va. App. LEXIS 74 (Feb. 17, 2009).

New evidence that a victim's sense of smell had returned did not entitle defendant to a new aggravated malicious wounding trial under Va. Sup. Ct. R. 3A:15 because the evidence did not definitively prove that the results would have been different where metal plates in the victim's face showed that she was permanently and significantly injured. Lamm v. Commonwealth, 55 Va. App. 637, 688 S.E.2d 295, 2010 Va. App. LEXIS 48 (2010).

Nondisclosed evidence. — Nondisclosed evidence in defendant's case that the paid confidential informant had been giving the task force false accounts of his purchases of controlled substances, that the confidential informant had a criminal record and had been found with a smoking device but was not charged with possession of marijuana in exchange for his services to the task force, and that the confidential informant only paid if he made a buy and turned contraband over to the task force, could clearly have led to evidence admissible at trial for impeachment purposes; it was withheld by the Commonwealth and defendant was thereby prejudiced. The result was such as to impair confidence in the outcome of the trial; therefore, the court reversed the judgment appealed from and remanded the case to the court of appeals with instruction to further remand the same to the circuit court for a new trial consistent with the opinion if the Commonwealth be so advised. Bly v. Commonwealth, 280 Va. 656, 702 S.E.2d 120, 2010 Va. LEXIS 265 (2010).

Introduction of evidence in bench trials. — Defendant's claim the Commonwealth improperly failed to move defendant's physical appearance officially into evidence during its case-in-chief was rejected as the prosecutor did all the prosecutor needed to do to call defendant's physical appearance to the attention of the finder of fact by asking the victims whether defendant was in the courtroom and whether they could point defendant out; neither the prior evidence cases, Va. Sup. Ct. R. 3A:13, nor Va. Sup. Ct. R. 3A:15 seemed to specify any particular requirements for the introduction of evidence applicable only to bench trials and not to jury trials. Haley v. Commonwealth, 2007 Va. App. LEXIS 402 (Nov. 6, 2007).

Motion to strike certain evidence waived. — Because defendant waived the ability to stand on the first of two motions to strike by presenting evidence on his own behalf, and after a second motion, his own witness confirmed that the arrest occurred on date alleged in the indictment, the correct date of his arrest was properly received into evidence. Raikes v. Commonwealth, 2007 Va. App. LEXIS 386 (Oct. 23, 2007).

Motion denied. — Defendant's motion for a mistrial based on a juror's prior relationship with a detective assigned to the case was properly denied where there was no evidence subject juror could not have been stricken for cause as he was a fair and unbiased juror. Perez v. Commonwealth, 40 Va. App. 648, 580 S.E.2d 507, 2003 Va. App. LEXIS 299 (2003).

Although defendant claimed that an anxiety attack caused the erratic driving observed by a police officer, the trial court was not required to accept defendant's explanation, especially since there was credible evidence that defendant was intoxicated at the time; therefore, the trial court properly denied defendant's motion to strike the evidence. Cousins v. Commonwealth, No. 2140-02-2, 2003 Va. App. LEXIS 354 (Ct. of Appeals June 24, 2003).

Where an expert witness commented generally on the veracity of child abuse victims in a way that could have bolstered the child victim's credibility in the case in which the expert testified, the trial judge properly refused to set aside the verdict, pursuant to Rule 3A:15, that convicted defendant, as the trial judge in a bench trial was considered capable of separating the admissible from the inadmissible in a bench trial. Riffle v. Commonwealth, No. 0145-03-1, 2004 Va. App. LEXIS 446 (Ct. of Appeals Sept. 14, 2004).

Trial court did not err in denying defendant's motion to set aside the jury's verdict finding him guilty of involuntary manslaughter and reckless driving in a case where defendant, a Somalia native who had been in the United States for six years and who understood English, struck and fatally injured a pedestrian while defendant was driving a taxicab; defendant's due process rights were not violated because he was provided with adequate interpreter services and the evidence showed that he understood the trial process, which meant he was given a fair chance to defend himself against the State's accusations. Takow v. Commonwealth, 2006 Va. App. LEXIS 255 (June 6, 2006).

Evidence was sufficient to prove as a matter of law that defendant's abduction and detention of the victim was separate and distinct from the restraint inherent in the commission of the crimes of rape and forcible sodomy; accordingly, defendant's conviction for abduction with intent to defile was affirmed, and defendant's motion to set aside the abduction conviction was properly denied. Defendant clearly restricted the victim's liberty, with the intent to defile the victim, by the use of force far in excess of that inherent in the commission of rape and sodomy where defendant twice choked the victim to the point of unconsciousness; those acts substantially increased the risk of harm to the victim. Fields v. Commonwealth, 48 Va. App. 393, 632 S.E.2d 8, 2006 Va. App. LEXIS 312 (2006).

Because the prosecution did not have to prove that a weapon that was found in plain view during a warrantless search of defendant's residence was operable under § 18.2-308.2, the trial court properly denied defendant's motion to strike. Williams v. Commonwealth, 49 Va. App. 439, 642 S.E.2d 295, 2007 Va. App. LEXIS 113 (2007).

Motion for new trial properly denied. — Insurer was not entitled to a new trial, where its motion for a partial summary judgment was ultimately granted, due to the admission of testimony as to a witness's projections of future premiums the insurer might receive for an insurance product package put together by a corporation, which was based on incorrect assumptions; the jury was properly instructed that the testimony as to projections of future premiums could not be considered, and the jury was presumed to follow the instructions. Va. Fin. Assocs. v. ITT Hartford Group, Inc., 266 Va. 177, 585 S.E.2d 789, 2003 Va. LEXIS 82 (2003).

Because defendant failed to satisfy defendant's burden of reasonable diligence under Orndorff v. Commonwealth, 271 Va. 486, 501, 628 S.E.2d 344, 352 (2006), the trial court did not abuse its discretion in refusing to grant defendant's motion for reconsideration and in denying defendant's request for a new trial based on after-discovered evidence. To satisfy the reasonable diligence burden, defendant could have investigated the trial court's public records for robberies committed in a similar manner, in the same area, and during the same time frame. Shelton v. Commonwealth, 2008 Va. App. LEXIS 28 (Jan. 15, 2008).

There was no error in the denial of defendant's motion for a new trial based on newly-discovered evidence, as the victim's records could have been obtained by defendant prior to trial by an exercise of due diligence, and the circuit court observed that the records were merely "corroborative or collateral" to evidence of the business relationship between the victim and defendant. Garnett v. Commonwealth, 275 Va. 397, 657 S.E.2d 100, 2008 Va. LEXIS 24 (2008), cert. denied, 129 S. Ct. 116, 2008 U.S. LEXIS 7002, 172 L. Ed. 2d 90 (U.S. 2008).

Since defendant hired a private investigator prior to trial who uncovered the witness's convictions for disorderly conduct and for reckless driving, contrary to the witness's testimony at trial that she had no prior convictions, defendant did obtain that evidence prior to trial through the exercise of reasonable diligence. In addition, the convictions were not admissible to impeach the witness; thus, the trial court did not err in denying defendant's motion to reconsider based on the witness's and State's nondisclosure. Palmer v. Commonwealth, 2009 Va. App. LEXIS 337 (July 28, 2009).

Although the Commonwealth violated Brady by failing to disclose certain exculpatory evidence prior to trial where the defendant was convicted of eluding, leaving an accident scene, and assault and battery on a law-enforcement officer, the trial court properly denied defendant a new trial because defendant was not prejudiced by the nondisclosures, particularly as he was able to fully cross-examine the witnesses about this material, and the failure to disclose did not undermine confidence in the outcome of the trial. Coley v. Commonwealth, 55 Va. App. 624, 688 S.E.2d 288, 2010 Va. App. LEXIS 46 (Feb. 9, 2010).

Trial court did not abuse its discretion in denying defendant's motion for a new trial because the evidence supported a finding that he failed to prove the fourth prong of the after-discovered evidence test, that a letter of recantation from the Commonwealth's primary witness to the crime, defendant's girlfriend, was material and would produce opposite results on the merits at another trial; the trial court acted within its discretion in weighing all the evidence and concluding that the girlfriend's latest testimony at the hearing on the motion would not produce a different result in a new trial, and based on the totality of the circumstances, the trial could concluded by clear and convincing evidence that the girlfriend lied in her testimony at the motion hearing and not at the original trial. Schoening v. Commonwealth, 2010 Va. App. LEXIS 297 (July 27, 2010).

Motion to set aside verdict denied. — There was no error in the denial of defendant's motion to set aside the verdict for a *Brady* violation. The Commonwealth's summary of the victim's statements was an accurate summary of the exculpatory information contained in them, and there was not a failure to disclose by the Commonwealth in violation of *Brady*. Garnett v. Commonwealth, 275 Va. 397, 657 S.E.2d 100, 2008 Va. LEXIS 24 (2008), cert. denied, 129 S. Ct. 116, 2008 U.S. LEXIS 7002, 172 L. Ed. 2d 90 (U.S. 2008).

Trial court abused its discretion by failing either to declare a mistrial or to set aside the verdict finding defendant guilty of conspiracy to commit grand larceny of property worth $200 or more because without the slightest prompting, the jurors volunteered to the trial court that they "misread" and "obviously misunderstood" the conspiracy instruction and sought, without success, to reconsider their guilty verdict on the conspiracy charge, and it only made matters worse that the jurors were more confused than they even knew; despite the clarity of the conspiracy instruction and the trial court's efforts to reply to the jury's concerns, the jury persisted in the mistaken belief that it had convicted defendant of a conspiracy charge that required a finding that he committed grand larceny. Weeks v. Commonwealth, 55 Va. App. 157, 684 S.E.2d 829, 2009 Va. App. LEXIS 502 (2009).

Applied in DiPaola v. Riddle, 581 F.2d 1111 (4th Cir. 1978); Elliott v. Commonwealth, 267 Va. 396, 593 S.E.2d 270, 2004 Va. LEXIS 44 (2004); Walker v. Commonwealth, 42 Va. App. 782, 595 S.E.2d 30, 2004 Va. App. LEXIS 169 (2004).

CIRCUIT COURT OPINIONS

Apparently inconsistent verdicts. — Trial court had to deny defendant's motion to vacate verdict, even thought the verdicts against him for use of a firearm in commission of murder and voluntary manslaughter appeared to be inconsistent, as both verdicts would be upheld despite the apparent inconsistency since there was sufficient evidence to support both verdicts. Commonwealth v. Scott, 60 Va. Cir. 259, 2002 Va. Cir. LEXIS 390 (Norfolk 2002).

Motion to set aside verdict granted. — Trial court granted an injured party's motion to set aside a verdict in favor of a driver in a personal injury action pursuant to VA. Sup. Ct. R. 3A:15; the trial court erred in failing to strike a defense of contributory negligence by the driver, as the injured party's speed was not a proximate cause of the collision, because the driver pulled onto the road directly in front of the injured party without any excuse or justification. Campbell v. Reid, 61 Va. Cir. 321, 2003 Va. Cir. LEXIS 44 (Spotsylvania County 2003).

Motion to set aside verdict denied. — Although the amount of the jury verdict equaled the amount of an injured party's medical expenses through the date that the injured party stopped physical therapy, the jury's decision had a basis in the evidence and the instructions; therefore, the motion to vacate the verdict was denied because the jury reasonably could conclude that the injured party's later expenses were not necessary or proper. Mix v. Stallard, 64 Va. Cir. 73, 2004 Va. Cir. LEXIS 15 (Spotsylvania County 2004).

Motion to strike denied. — Even if defendants were originally at an apartment complex to fight a shooting culprit one-on-one, evidence that, once everyone arrived at the apartment, they agreed to move across the street to "handle it" indicated that the group, at that time, fell within the definition of a mob as contemplated by § 18.2-38 as the group had transformed into a collection of people who had the intention of committing an assault or battery upon any person or an act of violence. Moreover, the evidence showed that, during the altercation, the victim and the shooting culprit became focused on the common goal of fighting defendant; thus, defendant's motion to strike under Va. Sup. Ct. R. 3A:15 was denied. Commonwealth v. Puryear, 2009 Va. Cir. LEXIS 18 (Fairfax County Feb. 3, 2009).

Rule 3A:16. Instructions.

(a) *Giving of Instructions.* — In a felony case, the instructions shall be reduced to writing. In all cases the court shall instruct the jury before arguments of counsel to the jury.

(b) *Proposed Instructions.* — If directed by the court the parties shall submit proposed instructions to the court at such reasonable time before or during the trial as the court may specify and, whether or not proposed instructions have been submitted earlier, the parties may submit proposed instructions at the conclusion of all the evidence.

(c) *Objections.* — Before instructing the jury, the court shall advise counsel of the instructions to be given and shall give counsel the opportunity to make objections thereto. Objections shall be made out of the presence of the jury, and before the court instructs the jury unless the court grants leave to make objections at a later time.

(d) *Alternative Forms of Verdicts; Separate Verdicts.* — The court may submit alternate forms of verdicts to the jury. The jury shall be instructed to return a separate verdict on each count of an indictment or presentment.

Source. — Former Rule 3A:23.

Law Review. — For a casenote, "The Extension of the Bruton Rule at the Expense of Judicial Efficiency in Gray v. Maryland," see 33 U. Rich. L. Rev. 227 (1999).

Michie's Jurisprudence. — For related discussion, see 1B M.J. Appeal and Error, § 115; 5B M.J. Criminal Procedure, §§ 66, 67, 73; 10A M.J. Instructions, §§ 5, 6, 14, 37, 38, 50; 13B M.J. New Trials, § 49; 19 M.J. Verdict, §§ 13, 20.

CASE NOTES

Judge may not single out part of evidence to establish fact. — When a trial judge instructs the jury in the law, he or she may not single out for emphasis a part of the evidence tending to establish a particular fact; the danger of such emphasis is that it gives undue prominence by the trial judge to the highlighted evidence and may mislead the jury. Yeager v. Commonwealth, 16 Va. App. 761, 433 S.E.2d 248 (1993).

Contemporaneous objection to trial court's instructions required. — Where the defendant's attorney did not object to any of the trial court's instructions despite the fact that this rule requires that objections to instructions be made before the court instructs the jury, the failure of counsel to comply with this procedural rule precluded appellate review of the instructions, since Rule 5:25 provided that the Supreme Court of Virginia will not notice any objection requiring a ruling of the trial court unless the ground of objection was stated with reasonable certainty at the time of the ruling. These rules have been consistently interpreted together with their predecessors as requiring a contemporaneous objection to a trial court's instructions. Therefore, the failure of counsel to comply with the Virginia Rules bars him from habeas corpus relief. Frazier v. Weatherholtz, 572 F.2d 994 (4th Cir.), cert. denied, 439 U.S. 876, 99 S. Ct. 215, 58 L. Ed. 2d 191 (1978).

Where defense counsel did not object to the instructions given to jury even after it was made known to counsel and the trial court that a form involving a severed offense had been given to the jury, any objection on appeal was not timely made and defendant did not have a right to a new sentencing hearing. Irvine v. Commonwealth, 2006 Va. App. LEXIS 166 (May 2, 2006).

Because defendant did not object to a jury instruction, pursuant to Va. Sup. Ct. R. 3A:16 and Va. Sup. Ct. R. 5A:18, any previous objection by defendant was trumped by his acquiescence to jury Instruction Number 7, which allowed the jury to consider his prior statement. Younger v. Commonwealth, No. 1775-11-2, 2012 Va. App. LEXIS 328 (Oct. 16, 2012).

A statement made in the course of a judicial decision is not necessarily proper language for a jury instruction. Yeager v. Commonwealth, 16 Va. App. 761, 433 S.E.2d 248 (1993).

Trial court's granting of instruction defining reasonable doubt did not constitute re-

versible error. Cooper v. Commonwealth, 2 Va. App. 497, 345 S.E.2d 775 (1986).

Failure to inform counsel of proposed instruction. — The trial court violated this rule when, on its own motion, it informed the jurors that they could ignore two phrases of the instruction defining malice. The trial court should have informed both counsel of the content of its proposed instruction; failure to do so was error. Mason v. Commonwealth, 7 Va. App. 339, 373 S.E.2d 603 (1988).

Applied in Baker v. Muncy, 619 F.2d 327 (4th Cir. 1980); Tweety v. Mitchell, 682 F.2d 461 (4th Cir. 1982); McLean v. Commonwealth, 30 Va. App. 322, 516 S.E.2d 717 (1999).

Rule 3A:17. Jury Verdicts.

(a) *Return.* — In all criminal prosecutions, the verdict shall be unanimous, in writing and signed by the foreman, and returned by the jury in open court.

(b) *Several Accused.* — If there are two or more accused, the jury may return a verdict as to any of them as to whom it can agree.

(c) *Conviction of Lesser Offense.* — The accused may be found not guilty of an offense charged but guilty of any offense, or of an attempt to commit any offense, that is substantially charged or necessarily included in the charge against the accused. When the offense charged is a felony, the accused may be found not guilty thereof, but guilty of being an accessory after the fact to that felony.

(d) *Poll of Jury.* — When a verdict is returned, the jury shall be polled individually at the request of any party or upon the court's own motion. If upon the poll, all jurors do not agree, the jury may be directed to retire for further deliberations or may be discharged.

Source. — Former Rule 3A:24.

Michie's Jurisprudence. — For related discussion, see 1A M.J. Accomplices and Accessories, § 12; 2A M.J. Attempts and Solicitations, § 6; 5A M.J. Courts, § 7; 5B M.J. Criminal Procedure, §§ 11, 62, 67; 9B M.J. Indictments, Informations and Presentments, § 29; 19 M.J. Verdict, §§ 3, 14.

CASE NOTES

Discharged jury may not be reassembled to correct substantive defect. — Once a jury is discharged and leaves the presence of the court, it cannot be reassembled to correct a substantive defect in its verdict. LeMelle v. Commonwealth, 225 Va. 322, 302 S.E.2d 38 (1983).

Poll held not to cure defect in verdict. — Where it was impossible to determine from the transcript of trial proceedings whether the inquiry addressed to the jurors in polling them pertained to the verdict as written or the verdict as read by the clerk, the rule that a defect was cured by the poll of the jurors conducted before they were discharged, and hence, that the failure to send them back to their room to deliberate was not prejudicial error does not apply. LeMelle v. Commonwealth, 225 Va. 322, 302 S.E.2d 38 (1983).

Juror's belief contrary to verdict rendered. — When a juror, who fully understands the import of the question presented by the court in the polling of the jury, answers that his or her belief is contrary to the verdict rendered, the verdict is not unanimous and cannot be accepted. Carver v. Commonwealth, 17 Va. App. 7, 434 S.E.2d 916 (1993).

Where juror did not indicate expressly that the verdict was not her verdict but the facts of the case showed the coercive effect the court's comments to the jury as a whole had on juror's response to the jury poll, the trial court erred in concluding that the verdict was unanimous. Humbert v. Commonwealth, 29 Va. App. 783, 514 S.E.2d 804 (1999).

Accessory after the fact. — Before a defendant can be tried and convicted of being an accessory after the fact, he must be charged with that offense. Therefore, unless such a charge is specifically made, neither the state nor an accused is entitled to an accessory-after-the-fact instruction. Commonwealth v. Dalton, 259 Va. 249, 524 S.E.2d 860 (2000).

Accusation under § 46.2-605 neither substantially charged nor necessarily included a charge under § 46.2-613. — Because of the disparity of specified elements, namely the elements "uses" and "displays," an accusation under § 46.2-605 neither substantially charged nor necessarily included a charge under § 46.2-613. Smith v. Commonwealth, 17 Va. App. 37, 434 S.E.2d 914 (1993).

Conviction of lesser offense. — The last sentence of subsection (c) means that, even if the accused is acquitted of a felony, he may be found guilty of the separate misdemeanor crime of being an accessory after the fact. Commonwealth v. Dalton, 259 Va. 249, 524 S.E.2d 860 (2000).

The rule merely reiterates the proposition that the crime of being an accessory after the fact contains an element that the felony does not contain. Therefore, it is not a lesser-included offense, and an acquittal of the felony does not preclude a trial on the misdemeanor. Commonwealth v. Dalton, 259 Va. 249, 524 S.E.2d 860 (2000).

Refusal of accessory after the fact instruction appropriate. — Defendant's convictions for first-degree murder and use of a firearm in the commission of a felony were appropriate because her argument that the trial court erred in refusing to allow her to proceed on the theory that she was an accessory after the fact and refusing an instruction that would have permitted the jury to make that finding was without merit under § 19.2-286 and Va. Sup. Ct. R. 3A:17(c). Before a defendant could be tried and convicted of being an accessory after the fact, she must have been charged with that offense; unless such a charge was specifically made, neither the Commonwealth nor an accused was entitled to an accessory-after-the-fact instruction and accessory after the fact was not a lesser included offense of murder. Thomas v. Commonwealth, 279 Va. 131, 688 S.E.2d 220, 2010 Va. LEXIS 11, cert. denied, 131 S. Ct. 143, 178 L. Ed. 2d 8, 2010 U.S. LEXIS 6109 (U.S. 2010).

Applied in Evans v. Commonwealth, 228 Va. 468, 323 S.E.2d 114 (1984); Dalton v. Commonwealth, 27 Va. App. 381, 499 S.E.2d 22 (1998).

Rule 3A:17.1. Proceedings in Bifurcated Jury Trials of Non-Capital Felonies and Class 1 Misdemeanors.

(a) *Application.* — This Rule applies in cases of trial by jury upon a finding that the defendant is guilty of a non-capital felony or a Class 1 misdemeanor.

(b) *Bifurcated Proceedings.* — In any jury trial in which the jury returns a verdict of guilty to one or more non-capital felony offenses, or Class 1 misdemeanor a separate proceeding limited to the ascertainment of punishment shall be held as soon as practicable before the same jury.

(c) *Instruction at Guilt Phase.* — At the conclusion of all of the evidence in the guilt phase of the trial, the court shall instruct the jury as to punishment with respect to any Class 2, 3 or 4 misdemeanor being tried in the same proceeding or any lesser-included Class 2, 3 or 4 misdemeanor of any charged felony offense which may be properly considered by the jury. The jury shall not be instructed until the punishment phase with reference to the punishment for any charged or lesser-included felony offense or Class 1 misdemeanor.

(d) *Opening Statements at Penalty Phase.* — Both the Commonwealth and the defense shall be entitled if they choose, to make an opening statement prior to the presentation of any evidence to the jury relevant to the penalty to be imposed. The Commonwealth shall give its statement first.

(e) *Presentation of Evidence at Penalty Phase.* — If the jury convicts the defendant of one or more non-capital felony offenses, or a Class 1 misdemeanor the penalty phase shall proceed in the following order:

(1) The Commonwealth may present any victim impact testimony pursuant to § 19.2-295.3 and shall present the defendant's prior criminal history, including prior convictions and the punishments imposed, by certified, attested, or exemplified copies of the final order(s) as provided by law. As a prerequisite to the introduction of such evidence, the Commonwealth shall have advised the defense, in accord with the requirements of law, of its intention to introduce such evidence.

(2) The defense may introduce relevant admissible evidence related to punishment. The defense shall have the opportunity to present such evidence irrespective of whether or not the Commonwealth presents evidence of previous criminal history.

(3) The Commonwealth may introduce relevant admissible evidence related to punishment in rebuttal.

(4) The defense may introduce relevant, admissible evidence related to punishment in rebuttal.

(f) *Closing Arguments at Penalty Phase.* — Both the Commonwealth and defense shall be entitled to make a closing argument on the subject of punishment if they elect to do so. The Commonwealth shall be given the opportunity to argue first, followed by the defense. Rebuttal argument may be made by the Commonwealth.

(g) *Change of Plea.* — The accused may enter a plea of guilty to the whole of the indictment at any time until the jury returns a verdict on the issue of the defendant's guilt or innocence.

(h) *Non-Unanimous Jury at the Penalty Phase.* — Should the jury fail to reach unanimous agreement as to punishment on any charge for which it returned a verdict of guilty, the court shall impanel a different jury to ascertain punishment, unless the defendant, the attorney for the Commonwealth and the court agree that the court shall fix punishment in the manner provided in Section 19.2-257, for the offense upon which the jury unanimously returned a verdict of guilty.

The amendment effective January 1, 2003, adopted September 26, 2002, in subdivision (a), added "or a Class 1 misdemeanor" at the end thereof; in subdivision (b), inserted "or Class 1 misdemeanor" following "non-capital felony offenses"; in subdivision (c), inserted "Class 2, 3, or 4" preceding "misdemeanor" twice in the first sentence and added "or Class 1 misdemeanor" at the end of the second sentence; in subdivision (e), inserted "or a Class 1 misdemeanor" preceding "the penalty phase"; and in subdivision (h), substituted "lesser-included offense" for "lesser-included felony" twice in the second sentence.

The amendment effective July 1, 2008, adopted April 9, 2008, rewrote subdivision (e)(1).

The amendment effective November 1, 2012, adopted November 1, 2012, rewrote subdivision (h).

Effective date. — This rule, adopted December 15, 1997, became effective February 15, 1998.

CASE NOTES

Recidivism evidence proper in guilt phase of a jury trial. — Section 19.2-297.1 did not forbid recidivism evidence from being presented in the guilt phase of a jury trial, and neither the jury bifurcation statute, § 19.2-295.1, nor this rule, were inconsistent with this interpretation; recidivism evidence was properly admitted in a prosecution for malicious wounding "after having been twice convicted of a violent felony." Washington v. Commonwealth, 46 Va. App. 276, 616 S.E.2d 774, 2005 Va. App. LEXIS 320 (2005), aff'd, 272 Va. 449, 634 S.E.2d 310 (2006).

Rule 3A:18. Death Penalty.

The trial of capital cases shall proceed in accordance with the provisions of Article 4.1 of Chapter 15 of Title 19.2 and, except to the extent conflicting therewith, the provisions of this Part Three A shall be applicable thereto.

Except for good cause shown, the separate proceeding provided for in Section 19.2-264.3 C shall commence as if it were a continuation of the original trial and continue from day to day until concluded.

Source. — Former Rule 3A:25A.

CASE NOTES

Part 3A applicable to guilty plea in capital case. — There is no provision in Article 4.1 (§ 19.2-264.2 et seq.) of Chapter 15 of Title 19.2 concerning the entry by an accused of a plea of guilty in a capital murder case. There is no conflict, therefore, between Article 4.1 and Rule 3A:13(a), and, hence, pursuant to this rule, the provisions of Part 3A shall be applicable to the entry of a plea of guilty in a capital case. Pruett v. Commonwealth, 232 Va. 266, 351 S.E.2d 1 (1986), cert. denied, 482 U.S. 931, 107 S. Ct. 3220, 96 L. Ed. 2d 706 (1987).

Rule 3A:19. Appeals.

(a) *Appeal From Conviction in a Circuit Court.* — See Part Five of these Rules.

(b) *Appeal From Conviction in a Juvenile and Domestic Relations District Court.* — The accused or his counsel shall advise the judge or clerk of the juvenile and domestic relations district court, within 10 days after conviction, of his intention to appeal. The appeal shall be noted on the warrant or summons and, if the accused does not withdraw his appeal before the expiration of the 10-day period, the papers shall be filed with the circuit court at the end of such period. Paying a fine or beginning to serve a sentence does not impair the right to appeal.

Cross references. — As to practice and procedure in the general district courts, see Rule 7A:13.

Source. — Former Rule 3A:26.

Comment. — With respect to former Rule 3A:26, the amendment changes the reference to a "Court of Record" in the title of subsection (a) to a "Circuit Court," changes the references to a "Court Not of Record" in the title and in the first sentence of subsection (b) to a "District Court," deletes the portion of the first sentence of subdivision (b) (1) beginning "Upon conviction in a court not of record" and ending with "provided," adds the word "shall" before the word "advises" in former subdivision (b) (1), and deletes subdivisions (b) (2) and (b) (3).

Michie's Jurisprudence. — For related discussion, see 1B M.J. Appeal and Error, §§ 376 - 378; 11B M.J. Jury, § 60.

Rule 3A:20. Time.

(a) *Extension.* — When under this Part Three A an act is required or allowed to be done at or within a specified time, the court for cause shown may at any time in its discretion (1) with or without motion or notice, order the period extended if request therefor is made before the expiration of the period originally prescribed or as extended by a previous order, or (2) upon motion made after the expiration of the specified period, permit the act to be done if the failure to act was the result of excusable neglect; but the court may not extend the time for taking any action under Rules 3A:15 and 19; except to the extent and under the conditions stated in those Rules.

(b) *Unaffected by Expiration of Term.* — The period of time specified in this Part Three A for taking any action is not affected or limited by the expiration of a term of court.

Cross references. — As to practice and procedure in the general district courts, see Rule 7A:2.

Source. — Former Rule 3A:32.

Comment. — With respect to former Rule 3A:32, the amendment changes the references to Rules 3A:22 and 26 to Rules 3A:15 and 19 respectively.

Michie's Jurisprudence. — For related discussion, see 5B M.J. Criminal Procedure, §§ 27, 70, 75.

Rule 3A:21. Service and Filing of Papers.

(a) *Copies of Written Motions to Be Furnished.* — All written motions and notices not required to be served as process shall be served otherwise on each counsel of record by delivering or mailing a copy to him on or before the day of filing. In any case where electronic service and filing is permitted under Rule 1:17, delivery of an electronic copy or digital image of a document shall satisfy this requirement. At the foot of such motions and notices shall be appended either acceptance of service or a certificate of counsel that copies were served as this Rule requires, showing the date of delivery or mailing.

(b) *Filing.* — Motions, notices and other items required to be served shall be filed with the clerk.

Cross references. — As to practice and procedure in the general district courts, see Rule 7A:10.

Source. — Former Rule 3A:33.

The amendment, effective May 2, 2011, adopted March 1, 2011, inserted "as process" in the first sentence, and inserted the second sentence of subdivision (a), and substituted "Motions, notices and other items" for "Papers" at the beginning of subdivision (b).

Michie's Jurisprudence. — For related discussion, see 11A M.J. Judges, § 14.

Rule 3A:22. Forms.

Forms 1 through 9 and 11 in the Appendix of Forms are illustrative and not mandatory; however, Form 10 requires substantial compliance.

Source. — Former Rule 3A:35.

The amendment, effective February 28, 2006, adopted February 28, 2006, inserted "and 11."

Michie's Jurisprudence. — For related discussion, see 7B M.J. Evidence, § 291.

Rule 3A:23. Electronic Filing.

In any circuit court which has established an electronic filing system for criminal cases pursuant to Rule 1:17:

(a) Any criminal proceeding may be designated as an Electronically Filed Case upon consent of the Commonwealth and all defendants in the case.

(b) Except where service and/or filing of an original paper document is expressly required by these rules, all pleadings, motions, notices and other instruments in an Electronically Filed Case shall be formatted, served and filed as specified in the requirements and procedures of Rule 1:17; provided, however, that when any document listed below is filed in the case, the filing party shall notify the clerk of court that the original document must be retained.

(1) Any pleading or affidavit required by statute or rule to be sworn, verified or certified as provided in Rule 1:17(e)(5).

(2) Any check or other negotiable instrument.

(3) Any handwritten statement, waiver, or consent by a defendant or witness in a criminal proceeding.

(4) Any form signed by a defendant in a criminal proceeding, including any typed statements or a guilty plea form.

(5) Any document that cannot be converted into an electronic document in such a way as to produce a clear and readable image.

Source. — Former Rule 3A:36.

The amendment, effective May 2, 2011, adopted March 1, 2011, rewrote the Rule heading and text.

Rule 3A:24. Special Rule Applicable to Post-Conviction Proceedings: Circuit Court Orders Denying Petitions for Writs of Habeas Corpus.

Any Order of a circuit court denying a petition for a writ of habeas corpus shall include findings of fact and conclusions of law as required by Code § 8.01-654(B)(5). The order shall identify the substance of the claims asserted in the petition, and state the specific reason for the denial of each claim. Any such order may adopt a trial court's written opinion explaining its decision or a transcribed explanation of the court's ruling from the bench; however, an order shall not deny the petition without explanation, or rely upon incorporation by reference of a pleading filed in the case.

Effective date. — This rule, adopted March 25, 2003, became effective July 1, 2003.

Rule 3A:25. Special Rule Applicable to Post-Conviction Proceedings: Inmate Filings in the Trial Courts Under Code § 8.01-654.

In actions brought under Code § 8.01-654, filed by an inmate confined to an institution, a paper is timely filed if deposited in the institution's internal mail system, with first-class postage prepaid on or before the last day for filing. Timely filing of a paper by an inmate confined to an institution may be established by (1) an official stamp of the institution showing that the paper was deposited in the internal mail system on or before the last day for filing, (2) an official postmark dated on or before the last day for filing, or (3) a notarized statement signed by an official of the institution showing that the paper was deposited in the internal mail system on or before the last day for filing.

Effective date. — This rule, adopted June 25, 2004, became effective September 1, 2004.

CASE NOTES

Habeas corpus. — Express language of the subsection B of § 8.01-655 filing provision does not contain any terms open for interpretation, and to the extent that Va. Sup. Ct. R. 3:2, 3:3, 3A:25 and 5:5 could be construed as conflicting with § 8.01-655, the statute will prevail over them. Lahey v. Johnson, 283 Va. 225, 720 S.E.2d 534, 2012 Va. LEXIS 22 (2012).

APPENDIX OF FORMS.

Form 1. Criminal Complaint (Rule 3A:3).

CRIMINAL COMPLAINT

RULES 3A:3 and 7C:3

.... ☐ General District Court
☐ Juvenile and Domestic Relations District Court

I, The undersigned Complainant this day make oath that I have

reason to believe that the Accused, on or about ....
DATE

in the ☐ City ☐ County ☐ Town of ....

Committed an offense as follows:

....

....

I base my belief on the following facts:

....

....

....

....

....

....

The statements above are true and accurate to the best of my knowledge and belief.

In making this complaint, I have read and fully understand the following:

- By swearing to these facts, I also obligate myself to appear in court and testify on behalf of the Commonwealth of Virginia or the city, county or town whose laws allegedly have been violated if a warrant or summons is issued.
- The charge in this warrant cannot be dismissed except by the court, even at my request.

____
SIGNATURE OF COMPLAINANT

Subscribed and sworn to before me this day.

.... ______________________________
DATE AND TIME ☐ CLERK ☐ MAGISTRATE ☐ JUDGE

FORM DC-311 6/89 (114:9-015 7/91)

Case No.

CRIMINAL COMPLAINT

ACCUSED: Name, Description, Address / Location

....
LAST NAME, FIRST NAME, MIDDLE INITIAL

....

....

COMPLETE DATA BELOW IF KNOWN

RACE	SEX	BORN MO.	BORN DAY	BORN YR.	HT. FT.	HT. IN.	WGT.	EYES	HAIR
SSN									

other identification or location information

....

....

....

....

COMPLAINANT: Name, Address, Title (if any) and telephone number

....

....

....

....

....

Form 2. Statement of Witness for Arrest Warrant (Rule 3A:3).

Witness: (Name and address) ....

....

(County) (City) of ....

I, the undersigned witness, after being duly sworn, make oath that I have personal knowledge of the following facts: ....

....

....

....

....

____

(Signature of complainant and title, if any)

Subscribed and sworn to before me this day.

____________________ ______________________________

(Date and time) (Signature and title)

Form 3. Summons (Rule 3A:4(b)).

SUMMONS VA. CODE § 19.2-73 RULE 3A:4

CITY OR COUNTY

☐ General District Court

STREET ADDRESS OF COURT

☐ Juvenile and Domestic Relations District Court

STREET ADDRESS OF COURT

TO THE ACCUSED:
You are hereby commanded to appear before this Court on

DATE AND TIME OF HEARING ... to answer the charge that on or about ... DATE ... ,

within this ☐ Town of ... ☐ CITY ☐ COUNTY you did unlawfully

in violation of Section ..., ☐ Code of Virginia (OR)

☐ Ordinances of this City, County, or Town.

You must appear in court at the time and place shown above and to appear at all other times and places and before any court or judge to which this case may be rescheduled, continued, transferred or appealed.

WARNING TO THE ACCUSED: You may be tried and convicted in your absence if you fail to appear in response to this summons. Willful failure to appear is a separate offense.

I, the undersigned, have found probable cause to believe that the Accused committed the offense charged, based on the sworn statements of:

..., Complainant.

DATE AND TIME ISSUED ☐ CLERK ☐ MAGISTRATE ☐ JUDGE

CASE NO.

ACCUSED:

LAST NAME, FIRST NAME, MIDDLE NAME

ADDRESS/LOCATION

To be completed upon service
Mailing address ☐ Same as above

☐

COMPLETE DATA BELOW IF KNOWN

RACE	SEX	BORN MO.	BORN DAY	BORN YR.	HT FT.	HT IN.	WGT.	EYES	HAIR

SSN

☐ Commonwealth of Virginia
☐ CITY ☐ COUNTY ☐ TOWN of

SUMMONS
CLASS ——— MISDEMEANOR

☐ EXECUTED by delivering a true copy of this summons to the Accused in person today.
☐ For legal entities other than individuals, service pursuant to Va. Code § 19.2-76.
☐ The Accused certified to me the above mailing address.

DATE AND TIME OF SERVICE

, SERVING OFFICER

BADGE NO., AGENCY AND JURISDICTION

for SHERIFF

Attorney for the Accused:

HEARING DATE AND TIME

☐ Motion to Change Bond on: ....
☐ changed to $ ....
☐ no change

JUDGE

The Accused was this day:
☐ tried in absence
☐ present

Attorneys Present:

☐ PROSECUTING ATTORNEY (NAME)

☐ DEFENDANT'S ATTORNEY (NAME)

☐ NO ATTORNEY
☐ ATTORNEY WAIVED
☐ If convicted, no jail sentence will be imposed.

☐ Translator/Interpreter present:

NAME

The Accused PLEADED:
☐ not guilty
☐ nolo contendere
☐ guilty

☐ Plea Bargain ☐ Plea and Recommendation

And was TRIED and FOUND by me:
☐ not guilty
☐ guilty as charged
☐ guilty of. ....
☐ facts sufficient to find guilt but defer adjudication/ disposition and place accused on first time offender probation, §§ 18.2-57.3, 18.2-251 or 19.2-303.2.

And was FOUND by me to be:
☐ driving a commercial motor vehicle
☐ carrying hazardous materials

☐ I ORDER the charge dismissed
☐ I ORDER a nolle prosequi on prosecution's motion
☐ I ORDER the charge dismissed:
☐ conditioned upon payment of costs (accord and satisfaction) § 19.2-151
☐ conditioned upon payment of costs and successful completion of traffic school § 16.1-69.48:1

....
DATE

I impose the following Sentence:

☐ FINE of $ ....
with $ ....suspended;

☐ JAIL sentence of ....imposed
with ....suspended
conditioned upon being of good behavior and keeping the peace, and paying fines and costs. Pursuant to § 53.1-187, credit is granted from pre-trial detention.

☐ Serve jail sentence on weekends beginning ....
....

☐ Work release authorized if eligible
☐ Work release required
☐ Payment of $ .... to defray cost of incarceration
☐ on PROBATION for ....
☐ DRIVER'S LICENSE suspended ....
....

☐ Referred to VASAP
☐ Restricted Driver's License
☐ Travel to/from work ☐ Travel to/from VASAP
☐ Travel during work ☐ Travel to/from school
☐ Medically necessary travel ☐ Ignition Interlock
☐ Travel to/from day care/school/medical service facility for child

☐ Referred to community-based corrections program
☐ RESTITUTION of $ ....
due by ....
Payable to. ....
with interest thereon from. ....
as condition of suspended sentence.

☐ ....hours of community service to be performed for
....
....
☐ in addition to other sentence provisions
☐ to be credited against fines and costs
at $ ..../hr.

☐ Contact prohibited between defendant and victim/victim's spouse and children pursuant to Va. Code § 18.2-60.3.

☐ Other:
....
....

Bail on Appeal $ ....

☐ Remanded for CCRE Report

JUDGE

Case No.: ....

FINE

..........................$ ....
LOCALITY

COSTS

112 } 140 }	PROCESSING FEE	{ $.................. { ....
143		....
107 DOAF		....
113 WITNESS FEE		....
113 SENTENCE FEE		....
113 DRUG ANALYSIS FEE		....
113 NON-CONSEC. JAIL FEE		....
113		....
120 CT. APPT. ATTY.		....
125 WEIGHING FEE		....
132 CICF		....
133 BLOOD TEST FEE		....
137 TTP		....
223 LIQUIDATED DAMAGES		....
229 CHMF		....
OTHER (SPECIFY):		
....		$..................
TOTAL		$ ☐

Effective date. — This form was rewritten by order dated November 22, 1999, effective February 1, 2000.

Form 4. Indictments (Rule 3A:6).

Murder

COMMONWEALTH OF VIRGINIA

.... Court

.............................., 20.....

The Grand Jury charges that:

On or about ...., 20.... in the (County) (City) of .... the accused ....
(Name of accused)
feloniously did kill and murder .... *
(Name of victim)

Va. Code §§ 18.2-31, 18.2-32, 19.2-221.
A True Bill.

....
(Foreman)

Attempted Grand Larceny

On or about ...., 20..... in the (County) (City) of .... the accused ....
(Name of accused)
feloniously attempted to steal property, namely ....
(Describe property)
having a value of ($5 or more from the person of ....)
(Name of victim)
($200 or more belonging to ....).
(Name of victim)

(firearm of any value) belonging to ....
(Name of victim)

Va. Code §§ 18.2-95 and 18.2-26.

Burglary (Common Law)

On or about ...., 20..... in the (County) (City) of .... the accused ....
(Name of accused)
feloniously did break and enter in the nighttime
the dwelling house of ....
(Name of victim)
with intent to commit a (felony) (larceny) therein.
Va. Code § 18.2-89.

Statutory (Burglary, Murder, Rape, Robbery, Arson)
(Va. Code § 18.2-90)

On or about ...., 20..... in the (County) (City) of .... the accused ....
(Name of accused)
feloniously did (enter in the nighttime) (break and enter in the daytime) (enter and conceal himself in the daytime)
.... , with intent to
(Place described in Va. Code § 18.2-90)
commit (murder)(rape)(robbery)(arson).
Va. Code § 18.2-90.

* Language charging other offenses follows.

Statutory Burglary, Va. Code § 18.2-91

On or about ...., 20..... in the (County) (City) of ....
the accused ....
(Name of accused)
feloniously did (enter in the nighttime) (break and enter in the daytime) (enter and conceal himself in the daytime)
.... , with intent to
(Place described in Va. Code § 18.2-90)
commit (larceny) (...)
(Describe felony other than murder, rape, robbery or arson)
(assault and battery).
Va. Code § 18.2-91.

Driving While Intoxicated

On or about ...., 20..... in the (County) (City) of ....
the accused ....
(Name of accused)
(feloniously and) unlawfully did operate a motor vehicle while under the influence of alcohol, narcotic drug, or other self-administered intoxicant or drug of whatever nature.
Va. Code § 18.2-266.

Forgery—Check

On or about ...., 20..... in the (County) (City) of ....
the accused ....
(Name of accused)
feloniously forged with the intent to defraud a check of the following words and figures:

.... , 20.....
(Bank) (Date)
Pay to the order of .... $................ Dollars
(Endorsed ....).
Va. Code § 18.2-172.

Malicious or Unlawful Wounding

On or about ...., 20..... in the (County) (City) of ....
the accused ....
(Name of accused)
feloniously (maliciously) (unlawfully but not maliously) caused bodily injury
to ....
(Name of victim)
with intent to maim, disfigure, disable or kill.
Va. Code § 18.2-51.

Rape

On or about ...., 20..... in the (County) (City) of ....
the accused ....
(Name of accused)
feloniously did rape ....
(Name of victim)
Va. Code § 18.2-61.

Rape (Statutory, of Female of Age 13 or 14)

On or about ...., 20..... in the (County) (City) of ....
the accused ....
(Name of accused)
feloniously had (sexual intercourse with) (carnal knowledge of)
....
(Name of victim)
age ....
(Age of victim at time of offense)
Va. Code § 18.2-63.

Robbery

On or about ...., 20..... in the (County) (City) of ....

the accused ....
(Name of accused)
feloniously did rob ....
(Name of victim)
of ....
(Describe property)
Va. Code § 18.2-58.

Uttering—Check

On or about ...., 20..... in the (County) (City) of ....
the accused ....
(Name of accused)
feloniously uttered with the intent to defraud a forged check of the following words and figures:

...., 20.....
(Bank) (Date)
Pay to the order of .... $............... Dollars
(Endorsed ....).
Va. Code § 18.2-172.

Form 5. Capias (Rule 3A:7).

.... Court
Accused: (Name, description, address/location) ....
....
TO: .... or any other authorized officer
(Designation of officer)

You are hereby commanded in the name of the Commonwealth to forthwith arrest the accused and to bring him (her) before this Court to answer a charge that he (she) committed an offense in the (County) (City) of ...., on or about ...., ..., namely ....
(Describe offense)
....
.... as charged in an (indictment) (presentment) (information) dated ...., ...

....
(Date) (Clerk)

Form 6. Suggested Questions to Be Put by the Court to an Accused Who Has Pleaded Guilty (Rule 3A:8).

Before accepting your plea of guilty, I will ask you certain questions. If you do not understand any question, please ask me to explain it to you.

1. (a) What is your full name? ____________
   (b) What is your date of birth? ____________
   (c) What was the last grade in school which you completed? ____________
   (d) What other education have you received? ____________
2. Are you the person charged in the (indictment) (presentment) (information) (warrant) with commission of the offense(s) of ____________
3. Do you fully understand the charge(s) against you? ____________
   Have you discussed the charge(s) and (its) (their) elements with your lawyer and do you understand what the Commonwealth must prove before you may be found guilty of (this) (these) charge(s)? ____________
4. Have you had enough time to discuss with your lawyer any possible defenses which you may have to (this) (these) charge(s)? ____________
5. Have you discussed with your lawyer whether you should plead not guilty or guilty? ____________
6. After the discussion, did you decide for yourself that you should plead guilty? ____
7. Are you entering the plea of guilty freely and voluntarily? ____________
8. Are you entering the plea of guilty because you are, in fact, guilty of the crime(s) charged? ____________
   [If the defendant answers "No,"
   (a) Have the Commonwealth summarize the evidence on the record.

(b) Ask the defendant, "Are you pleading guilty because this is the Commonwealth's evidence, and you do not wish to take the risk that you will be found guilty beyond a reasonable doubt?"

(c) If the defendant answers "Yes," the court may, but need not, accept the plea; if the court accepts the plea, the court should note that there is substantial evidence against the defendant. Otherwise the court should not accept the plea. (See North Carolina v. Alford, 400 U.S. 25 (1970).]

9. Do you understand that, by pleading guilty, you are NOT entitled to a trial by jury? ________

10. Do you understand that, by pleading guilty, you waive your right not to incriminate yourself? ________

11. Do you understand that, by pleading guilty, you waive your right to confront and cross-examine your accusers? ________

12. Do you understand that, by pleading guilty, you waive your right to defend yourself? ________

13. [If the accused is in prison, on parole, or probation,]
Do you understand that conviction may (affect your right to parole) (cause revocation of your parole/probation?)

14. [If the crime involves possession/distribution of drugs,]
Have you discussed with your lawyer whether the defense of accommodation may apply in this case?

15. [If the accused may be sentenced under the habitual offender statute,]
Have you discussed with your lawyer the possibility that there may be mitigating circumstances that permit this court not to impose the mandatory sentence?

16. Has anyone connected with your arrest and prosecution, such as the police or the Commonwealth's attorney, or any other person, in any manner threatened you or forced you to enter this plea of guilty? Have they made any promises concerning your plea of guilty?

17. Do you understand that the maximum punishment for this crime is ________ years imprisonment and $________ fine plus all court costs? (If a guilty plea involves more than one offense, substitute the following: Do you understand that if you are sentenced consecutively, the maximum punishment for these crimes is ________ fine and $________ plus all court costs?) [If the crime has a mandatory punishment, also question accused on his understanding of the mandatory punishment.]

18. Are you entirely satisfied with the service (of the lawyer who was appointed to represent you) (of the lawyer representing you) in this matter? ________

19. Do you understand that, by pleading guilty, you may waive any right to appeal the decision of this court? [The judge may, but need not, inform the defendant that a guilty plea does not waive the right to appeal lack of jurisdiction or imposition of an impermissible sentence.]

20. [If a written guilty plea form is used,]
(a) Have you read the guilty plea form? ________
(b) Do you understand the guilty plea form? ________
(c) Are the statements in the guilty plea form true? ________

21. Have you entered into a plea agreement with the Commonwealth's attorney in this case? If the answer is in the affirmative, read or otherwise put the plea agreement into the record, then ask the following: Does it contain the full and complete agreement entered into among you, your lawyer, and the Commonwealth's attorney? Complete either (a) or (b), whichever is appropriate:

(a) [To be asked if the Commonwealth's attorney has agreed that a particular sentence is appropriate.] Do you understand that:

(1) The court may accept the agreement, reject the agreement, or may defer any decision to either accept or reject until there has been an opportunity to consider a presentence report? ________

(2) If the court accepts the agreement, the court will include in its judgment and sentence the sentence provided for in the agreement? ________

(3) If the court rejects the agreement, you will not be bound by the agreement and you will be given an opportunity to withdraw your plea of guilty, and if you do, your trial may be conducted by another judge of this court? ____

(4) If you still plead guilty after the court rejects the plea agreement, the sentence in the case may be more severe than the disposition contained in the plea agreement? ________

(b) [To be used if the Commonwealth's attorney merely recommends, or agrees not to oppose a request for, a specific sentence.] Do you understand that this agreement only provides for the Commonwealth's attorney (to make a recommendation) (to agree not to oppose a request for) a particular sentence, that this recommendation or request is not binding on the court, and if the court does not accept the recommendation or does not go along with the request, you have no right to withdraw your plea of guilty unless the Commonwealth fails to perform its part of the agreement? Do you also understand that the sentence the court imposes may be more severe than the sentence (recommended) (requested)?

22. [If the defendant was a juvenile at the time of the offense,]
Do you understand that if you were tried for this offense and found guilty, the court and not the jury would set the sentence? ____________
23. Do you understand all of these questions? ____________
24. Do you have any questions you wish to ask the court? ____________

Form 7. Suggested Questions to Be Put by the Court to an Accused Who Has Pleaded Not Guilty (Rule 3A:8).

Before accepting your plea of not guilty, I will ask you certain questions. If you do not understand any question, please ask me to explain it to you.

1. What is your full name and what is your age? ____________
2. Are you the person charged in the (indictment) (information) (warrant) with the commission of the offense(s)? ____________
3. Do you fully understand the charge(s) against you? ____________
4. Have you discussed the charge(s) with your lawyer? ____________
5. Have you had enough time to discuss with your lawyer any possible defense you may have to (this) (these) charge(s)? ____________
6. Have you given your lawyer the names of witnesses, and if so, are they present?
7. Are you entirely satisfied with the services of your lawyer? ____________
8. Are you entering this plea of not guilty freely and voluntarily? ____________
9. Are you ready for trial today? ____________
10. Do you understand that you are entitled to a trial by jury, but that you can consent to trial by the judge without a jury? ____________
Have you discussed with your lawyer the advisability of trial by a jury or by the judge without a jury? ____________
Do you wish to be tried by a jury or by the judge without a jury? ______
11. Do you understand all of the questions I have asked you? ____________

These questions were asked of the defendant in open court in the absence of a jury on ________, 20____

____
Signature of defendant

____
Signature of attorney representing defendant

Form 8. Subpoena (Rule 3A:12(a)).

.... Court

....
(Address of court)

TO: .... or any other authorized officer
(Designation of officer)

You are commanded to summon ....
(Name and address)

TO the person summoned:

You are commanded to appear in this Court on ...., 20.... at .... a.m., to testify in the case of Commonwealth v. ....

This subpoena is issued on application of the (Commonwealth) (City) (County) (Town) (Defendant) (Juvenile) in the case of the Commonwealth v.

....

....

(Date) (Judge) (Clerk) (Commonwealth's Attorney)

Form 9. Subpoena Duces Tecum (Rule 3A:12(b)).

.... Court

....

(Address of court)

TO: .... or any other authorized officer

(Designation of officer)

You are commanded to summon ....

(Name and address)

TO the person summoned:

[ ] You are commanded to appear in (this Court) (the Clerk's office of this Court) on ...., 20.... at .... a.m./p.m., and to bring with you the following:

....

....

....

....

OR

[ ] You are commanded to deliver to the Clerk's office of this Court on or before ...., 20.... at .... a.m./p.m. the following:

....

....

....

....

This subpoena is issued on application of the (Commonwealth) (City) (County) (Town) (Defendant) (Juvenile) in the case of the Commonwealth v. ....

....

(Date) (Judge) (Clerk)

Form 10. Contents of Sentencing Orders.

(Pursuant to the provisions of Code § 19.2-307, all orders wherein an accused is sentenced for a criminal conviction shall conform substantially to the following form. In cases where no prior criminal conviction order has been entered of record, state the defendant's plea, the verdict or findings, the adjudication, whether or not the case was tried by a jury, and, if not, whether the consent of the accused was concurred in by the court and the attorney for the Commonwealth.)

SENTENCING ORDER

VIRGINIA: IN THE CIRCUIT COURT OF ______________________________

FEDERAL INFORMATION PROCESSING STANDARDS CODE: ______

Hearing Date: ______________________________

Judge: ______________________________

COMMONWEALTH OF VIRGINIA

v.

______________________________, DEFENDANT

This case came before the Court for sentencing of the defendant, who appeared in person with his attorney, ______________________. The Commonwealth was represented by ______________________.

On ____________________ the defendant was found guilty of the following offenses:

CASE NUMBER	OFFENSE DESCRIPTION AND INDICATOR	OFFENSE DATE	VA. CODE SECTION	VIRGINIA CRIME CODE REFERENCE
________	____________________	________	________	________
________	____________________	________	________	________

The presentence report was considered and is ordered filed as a part of the record in this case in accordance with the provisions of Code § 19.2-299.

Pursuant to the provisions of Code § 19.2-298.01, the Court has considered and reviewed the applicable discretionary sentencing guidelines and the guidelines worksheets. The sentencing guidelines worksheets and the written explanation of any departure from the guidelines are ordered filed as a part of the record in this case.

Before pronouncing the sentence, the Court inquired if the defendant desired to make a statement and if the defendant desired to advance any reason why judgment should not be pronounced.

The Court **SENTENCES** the defendant to:

Incarceration with the Virginia Department of Corrections for the term of: ____________ for ____________, and ____________ for ____________. The total sentence imposed is ____________.

This sentence shall run (concurrently/consecutively) with ____________.

The Court **SUSPENDS** __________ of the __________ sentence and __________ of the __________ sentence, for a period of __________, for a total suspension of __________, upon the following condition(s):

Good behavior. The defendant shall be of good behavior for ______ from the defendant's release from confinement.

Supervised probation. ____________ of the sentence of incarceration is suspended. The defendant is placed on probation to commence ____________ under the supervision of a Probation Officer for ____________ or unless sooner released by the court or by the Probation Officer. The defendant shall comply with all the rules and requirements set by the Probation Officer. Probation shall include substance abuse counseling and/or testing as prescribed by the Probation Officer.

Community-based Corrections System Program pursuant to Virginia Code § 19.2-316.2 or 19.2-316.3. The defendant shall successfully complete the ____________ program. Successful program completion shall be followed by a period of intensive probation supervision of ____________ and followed by a period of supervised probation of (at least one year). (If applicable: The defendant shall remain in custody until program entry.)

Post-Incarceration supervision following felony conviction pursuant to Virginia Code § 18.2-10 and 19.2-295.2.

A. **Post-Incarceration Supervised Probation:** The court has imposed above a term of ____________ ____________ of incarceration and has suspended (at least 6 months) of the term of incarceration. The defendant is placed on supervised probation to commence upon release from incarceration for a period of (at least 6 months), unless released earlier by the court. The defendant shall comply with all the rules and requirements set by the Probation Officer.

OR

B. **Post-Incarceration Post-release Supervision:** In addition to the above sentence of incarceration, the court imposes an additional term of (not less than 6 months nor more than 3 years) of incarceration. This term is suspended and a period of post-release supervision of (not less than 6 months nor more than 3 years), which is to commence upon release from incarceration. The defendant shall comply with all the rules and requirements set by the Probation Officer.

Special Conditions. The defendant shall complete any substance abuse screening, assessment, testing and treatment as directed by the Probation Officer, as well as the following conditions: ____.

Costs. The defendant shall pay costs of ____________.

Fine. A fine of $______________ for ______________.

Restitution. The defendant shall make restitution as follows: ________ to ______________.

DNA and Fingerprints. The defendant shall provide a DNA sample and legible fingerprints as directed.

Credit for time served. The defendant shall be given credit for time spent in confinement while awaiting trial pursuant to Code § 53.1-187.

____
DATE

ENTER: ______________________
JUDGE

DEFENDANT IDENTIFICATION:
Name: ____
Alias: ______________________
SSN: ______________________________________ DOB: ____________ Sex: ____

SENTENCING SUMMARY:

TOTAL INCARCERATION SENTENCE IMPOSED: ____________________
TOTAL SENTENCE SUSPENDED: ____________________
TOTAL SUPERVISED PROBATION TERM: ____________________
TOTAL POSTRELEASE TERM IMPOSED and
SUSPENDED: ______________________________________

Effective date. — This form was added by order effective January 1, 1997, as adopted November 14, 1996; amended effective December 22, 2004, by order adopted December 22, 2004, and effective May 1, 2006, by order adopted February 28, 2006.

Form 11. Misdemeanor Proceedings in District and Circuit Courts (Rule 3A:8(b)(2); Rule 7C:6; and Rule 8:18).

Suggested Questions to Be Asked When Taking Pleas of Guilty or Nolo Contendere

A. Pleas of Guilty or Nolo Contendere with Plea Agreements Requiring Imposition of an Active or Suspended Sentence of Confinement in Jail

1. Do you understand the charge(s) against you?
2. When Defendant appears without counsel:
   a) Do you understand you have the right to be represented by a lawyer?
   b) Do you understand that if you do not have the financial ability to hire your own lawyer, and you want me to, I will have you interviewed to see if you qualify for court-appointed counsel and I will appoint an attorney to represent you if you qualify?
   c) Do you want to hire an attorney to represent you, or be interviewed for court-appointed counsel or do you want to proceed today without a lawyer?
3. In Circuit Court:
   a) Do you understand that you have the right to have your case heard by a jury?
   b) Do you want your case to be heard by a judge without a jury or do you want a jury trial?
4. a) I understand that you have agreed to plead guilty (no contest) with the understanding that you will be sentenced to ______________. Is that correct? or
   b) I understand that you have agreed to plead guilty (no contest) with the understanding that the prosecutor will recommend a sentence of ________________. Do you understand that I do not have to accept the

recommendation and that I can sentence you from ________________ to ________________?
(provide full sentence range allowed by law)

5. Have you been promised anything else to get you to plead guilty (no contest)?
6. Are you being forced or threatened into pleading guilty (no contest)?
7. Do you understand that by pleading guilty (no contest) you are giving up your right to a trial including the right to hear from and question the witnesses against you and the right to avoid being required to give evidence against yourself?
8. Do you have any questions before I accept your plea(s) of guilty (no contest)?

B. Pleas of Guilty or Nolo Contendere Without a Plea Agreement

1. Do you understand the charge(s) against you?
2. When Defendant appears without counsel:
   a) Do you understand you have the right to be represented by a lawyer?
   b) Do you understand that if you do not have the financial ability to hire your own lawyer, and you want me to, I will have you interviewed to see if you qualify for court-appointed counsel and I will appoint an attorney to represent you if you qualify?
   c) Do you want to hire an attorney to represent you, or be interviewed for court-appointed counsel or do you want to proceed today without a lawyer?
3. In Circuit Court:
   a) Do you understand that you have the right to have your case heard by a jury?
   b) Do you want your case to be heard by a judge without a jury or do you want a jury trial?
4. Do you understand that based upon your plea of guilty (no contest) the possible range of punishment is ________________ to ________________?
5. Have you been promised anything else to get you to plead guilty (no contest)?
6. Are you being forced or threatened into pleading guilty (no contest)?
7. Do you understand that by pleading guilty (no contest) you are giving up your right to a trial including the right to hear from and question the witnesses against you and the right to avoid being required to give evidence against yourself?
8. Do you have any questions before I accept your plea(s) of guilty (no contest)?

Suggested Plea of Guilty to Misdemeanor Plea Form with Plea Agreement Requiring Imposition of an Active or Suspended Sentence of Confinement in Jail

1. I understand the charge(s) against me.
2. a) I understand that I have the right to be represented by an attorney.
   b) I understand that if I do not have the financial ability to hire my own attorney, I could be interviewed to see if I qualify for court appointed counsel and if I did qualify the court would appoint an attorney to represent me.
   c) I do not want to be represented by an attorney and I do not want to be interviewed to see if I qualify for court appointed counsel. It is my desire to give up my right to counsel and to proceed today without an attorney.
3. In Circuit Court:
   a) I understand that I have the right to have my case heard by a jury.
   b) I do not want my case to be heard by a jury and wish to proceed to have my case heard today by a judge without a jury.
4. a) I am pleading guilty (no contest) today based upon my understanding that I will be sentenced to ________________.
   b) I am pleading guilty (no contest) today based upon my understanding that the prosecutor will recommend a sentence of ________________. I understand that the judge does not have to accept the recommendation and can sentence me from ________________ to ________________.
5. I have not been promised anything to get me to plead guilty (no contest).
6. I am not being forced or threatened to get me to plead guilty (no contest).
7. I understand that by pleading guilty (no contest) I am giving up my right to a trial including the right to hear from and question the witnesses against me and the right to avoid being required to give evidence against myself.
8. I do not have any questions to ask the court before the court decides whether to accept my plea of guilty (no contest).

____________________________ ____________________________

Counsel for Defendant Defendant

Suggested Plea of Guilty to Misdemeanor Plea Form without Plea Agreement

1. I understand the charge(s) against me.
2. a) I understand that I have the right to be represented by an attorney.
   b) I understand that if I do not have the financial ability to hire my own attorney, I could be interviewed to see if I qualify for court appointed counsel and if I did qualify the court would appoint an attorney to represent me.
   c) I do not want to be represented by an attorney and I do not want to be interviewed to see if I qualify for court appointed counsel. It is my desire to give up my right to counsel and to proceed today without an attorney.
3. In Circuit Court:
   a) I understand that I have the right to have my case heard by a jury.
   b) I do not want my case to be heard by a jury and wish to proceed to have my case heard today by a judge without a jury.
4. I am pleading guilty (no contest) today based upon my understanding that I could be sentenced from ________________ to ________________.
5. I have not been promised anything to get me to plead guilty (no contest).
6. I am not being forced or threatened to get me to plead guilty (no contest).
7. I understand that by pleading guilty (no contest) I am giving up my right to a trial including the right to hear from and question the witnesses against me and the right to avoid being required to give evidence against myself.
8. I do not have any questions to ask the court before the court decides to accept my plea of guilty (no contest).

____________________________ ____________________________

Counsel for Defendant Defendant

PART THREE B
TRAFFIC INFRACTIONS AND UNIFORM FINE SCHEDULE

Rule
3B:1. Purpose.
3B:2. Uniform Fine Schedule.

Editor's note. — Part Three B was revised, effective October 1, 1989, by order adopted September 28, 1989.

Rule 3B:1. Purpose.

These Rules are promulgated by the Supreme Court of Virginia pursuant to § 16.1-69.40:1 of the Code of Virginia to carry out the provisions of Chapter 585 of the Acts of Assembly of 1977 and Chapter 605 of the Acts of Assembly of 1978.

Michie's Jurisprudence. — For related discussion, see 5B M.J. Criminal Procedure, § 2.

Rule 3B:2. Uniform Fine Schedule.

For any offense listed below, whether prescribed by the specified State statute or by a parallel local ordinance adopted pursuant to the authority granted in Virginia Code § 46.2-1300, a driver may enter a written appearance, waiver of court hearing, plea of guilty, and pay fines and costs. For traffic offenses not listed below, a court hearing is required. Nothing in this Rule affects bonding procedures for those offenses not listed below. Likewise, nothing in this Rule shall be construed to alter the operation of or the penalties prescribed pursuant to §§ 46.2-1220 through 46.2-1230.

This schedule is applied uniformly throughout the Commonwealth, and a clerk or magistrate may not impose a fine different from the amounts shown here. Costs shall be paid in accordance with the provisions of the Code of Virginia or any rules or regulations promulgated thereunder. This schedule does not restrict the fine a judge may impose for an offense listed here in any case for which there is a court hearing.

Description of Offense*	Statute or Regulation	Fine	Processing Fee***	Total
1. Speed Violations				
Exceeding the speed limit	46.2-870 to 46.2-872, 46.2-873.1 to 46.2-876	$6 per mile over speed limit	$51	
Exceeding the speed limit in a school crossing	46.2-873	$7 per mile over speed limit	$51	

* The description of offense is for reference and is not a legal definition.
** Unless otherwise provided by statute.
*** See §§ 9.1-106 and 53.1-120 of the Code.

Description of Offense*	Statute or Regulation	Fine	Processing Fee***	Total
Exceeding the speed limits set by Transportation Commissioner	46.2-878	$6 per mile over speed limit	$51	
Exceeding the speed limit in a highway work zone	46.2-878.1	$7 per mile over speed limit	$51	
Exceeding the speed limit in a residence district	46.2-878.2	$200 plus $8 per mile over speed limit	$51	
Exceeding the speed limit in a 55 mph or 65 mph zone	46.2-870	$6 per mile over speed limit	$51	
Exceeding the speed limit on bridge	46.2-881	$6 per mile over speed limit	$51	
Impeding traffic by slow speed	46.2-877	$30	$51	$81
Failure to drive at approximate speed authorized for lane in which vehicle is moving, on highway where "slow moving traffic" lane is designated	46.2-804(1)	$30	$51	$81
2. Other Moving Offenses				
Moving violation committed in highway safety corridor	46.2-947	Double otherwise applicable fine	$51	
Failure to obey highway sign	46.2-830	$30	$51	$81
Coasting on downgrade with gears in neutral	46.2-811	$30	$51	$81
Driving more than 13 hours in a 24-hour period	46.2-812	$30	$51	$81

* The description of offense is for reference and is not a legal definition.

** Unless otherwise provided by statute.

*** See §§ 9.1-106 and 53.1-120 of the Code.

Description of Offense*	Statute or Regulation	Fine	Processing Fee***	Total
Causing or permitting vehicle to be driven more than 13 hours in a 24-hour period	46.2-812	$30	$51	$81
Improper failure to drive on right side of highway	46.2-802	$30	$51	$81
Failure to move in designated direction on one-way roadway	46.2-806	$30	$51	$81
Failure to drive to right of rotary traffic island	46.2-807	$30	$51	$81
Improper failure to keep right in crossing highway intersection	46.2-803	$30	$51	$81
Improper failure to keep right in crossing highway intersection by railroad right of way	46.2-803	$30	$51	$81
Improper failure to observe lanes marked for traffic:				
—failure of slow moving traffic to keep right	46.2-804(1)	$30	$51	$81
—improperly driving in center	46.2-804(2)	$30	$51	$81
—changing lane without first ascertaining safety of move	46.2-804(2)	$30	$51	$81
—improperly driving in center lane of 3-lane highway	46.2-804(3)	$30	$51	$81

* The description of offense is for reference and is not a legal definition.
** Unless otherwise provided by statute.
*** See §§ 9.1-106 and 53.1-120 of the Code.

Description of Offense*	Statute or Regulation	Fine	Processing Fee***	Total
—improperly crossing solid line driver's lane	46.2-804(5)	$30	$51	$81
—improperly crossing double solid line	46.2-804(6)	$30	$51	$81
Disregard of lane direction control signal	46.2-805	$30	$51	$81
Failure to obey traffic lights	46.2-833	$100	$51	$151
Evasion of a traffic control device	46.2-833.1	$50	$51	$101
Illegal right turn on red	46.2-835	$50	$51	$101
Illegal left turn on red	46.2-836	$50	$51	$101
Improper passing:				
—failure to remain on right side of highway when meeting vehicle proceeding in opposite direction	46.2-837	$30	$51	$81
—driving too close to vehicle being overtaken in same direction	46.2-838	$30	$51	$81
—returning to right side of highway before safely clear of overtaken vehicle	46.2-838	$30	$51	$81
—improperly passing to the right of a vehicle proceeding in same direction	46.2-841	$30	$51	$81

* The description of offense is for reference and is not a legal definition.

** Unless otherwise provided by statute.

*** See §§ 9.1-106 and 53.1-120 of the Code.

Description of Offense*	Statute or Regulation	Fine	Processing Fee***	Total
—failure to give way to the right to overtaking vehicle	46.2-842	$30	$51	$81
—improperly increasing speed when passed by overtaking vehicle	46.2-842	$30	$51	$81
—failure to give way to overtaking vehicle when driving abreast on divided highway	46.2-842.1	$30	$51	$81
—passing when left lane is not clearly visible	46.2-843	$30	$51	$81
—passing on left when oncoming traffic is too near to permit it in safety	46.2-843	$30	$51	$81
—truck or tractor and trailer impeding passage of following traffic by passing another truck or tractor and trailer on upgrade	46.2-843	$30	$51	$81
Following too closely:				
—motor vehicle following another more closely than is reasonable or prudent	46.2-816	$30	$51	$81
Improper U turn:				

* The description of offense is for reference and is not a legal definition.
** Unless otherwise provided by statute.
*** See §§ 9.1-106 and 53.1-120 of the Code.

Description of Offense*	Statute or Regulation	Fine	Processing Fee***	Total
—within business district, city or town, U turn other than at intersection	46.2-845	$30	$51	$81
—U turn on a curve or approaching crest of hill where not visible to vehicles approaching in any direction within 500 feet	46.2-845	$30	$51	$81
Improper position or method of turning at intersection:				
—unauthorized right turn from other than right hand curb or edge of roadway	46.2-846(A)(1)	$30	$51	$81
—on a two-way roadway, unauthorized left turn from other than lane nearest center line	46.2-846(A)(2)	$30	$51	$81
—on other than two-way roadway, unauthorized left turn from other than left-most available lane	46.2-846(A)(3)	$30	$51	$81
—failure to follow traffic control device of local authority	46.2-846(B)	$30	$51	$81

* The description of offense is for reference and is not a legal definition.
** Unless otherwise provided by statute.
*** See §§ 9.1-106 and 53.1-120 of the Code.

Description of Offense*	Statute or Regulation	Fine	Processing Fee***	Total
Starting, backing, stopping or turning without first seeing that such a move can be made in safety	46.2-848	$30	$51	$81
Starting, backing, stopping or turning without giving required signal	46.2-848	$30	$51	$81
Improper signals	46.2-849	$30	$51	$81
Improper change of course after giving signal	46.2-850	$30	$51	$81
Failure to signal prior to moving standing vehicle into traffic	46.2-851	$30	$51	$81
Failure to yield right of way or reduce speed on highway when approaching stopped vehicle with flashing blue, red or amber lights (not applicable to second and subsequent violations with vehicles flashing blue or red lights)	46.2-921.1	$100	$51	$151
Failure to yield right of way:				
—failure of driver on left to yield to driver on right entering intersection at same time	46.2-820	$30	$51	$81
—failure to obey "yield right of way" sign at intersection	46.2-821	$30	$51	$81

* The description of offense is for reference and is not a legal definition.
** Unless otherwise provided by statute.
*** See §§ 9.1-106 and 53.1-120 of the Code.

Description of Offense*	Statute or Regulation	Fine	Processing Fee***	Total
—failure of driver approaching or entering circular intersection to yield to driver already in the circle	46.2-822	$30	$51	$81
— failure to yield at uncontrolled "T" intersection	46.2-824	$30	$51	$81
—failure of driver turning left to yield to oncoming vehicle	46.2-825	$30	$51	$81
—failure to yield to left turning vehicle given right of way automatic signal device	46.2-825	$30	$51	$81
—failure to stop and yield when entering public highway or sidewalk from private road, etc.	46.2-826	$30	$51	$81
—failure to yield to U.S. Armed Services, National Guard, etc.	46.2-827	$30	$51	$81
—failure to yield to funeral procession under police escort	46.2-828	$30	$51	$81
—failure to yield right of way to emergency vehicle	46.2-829	$30	$51	$81
—following too near fire apparatus	46.2-921	$30	$51	$81

* The description of offense is for reference and is not a legal definition.
** Unless otherwise provided by statute.
*** See §§ 9.1-106 and 53.1-120 of the Code.

Description of Offense*	Statute or Regulation	Fine	Processing Fee***	Total
—driving over fire hose	46.2-922	$30	$51	$81
—failure to yield to pedestrian in clearly marked crosswalk or at intersection	46.2-924	$30	$51	$81
—failure to yield to pedestrian boarding or alighting from a bus	46.2-927	$30	$51	$81
—failure to stop and yield when approaching intersection of highway controlled by stop sign	46.2-821	$30	$51	$81
—failure to slow down or stop and yield when approaching intersection on highway controlled by "yield right of way" sign	46.2-821	$30	$51	$81
Driving through pedestrian safety zone	46.2-814	$30	$51	$81
Failure to obey railroad warning signal	46.2-884	$30	$51	$81
Proceeding improperly at railroad grade crossing:				
—generally	46.2-885	$30	$51	$81
—vehicles carrying passengers for hire, school bus or truck with flammable or explosive cargo	46.2-886	$30	$51	$81

* The description of offense is for reference and is not a legal definition.
** Unless otherwise provided by statute.
*** See §§ 9.1-106 and 53.1-120 of the Code.

Description of Offense*	Statute or Regulation	Fine	Processing Fee***	Total
—tractor, steam shovel, etc.	46.2-887	$30	$51	$81
Stopping bus or truck on highway to unload passengers or cargo	46.2-893	$30	$51	$81
Unlawful use of all-terrain vehicle	46.2-915.1	$30	$51	$81
Failure to yield right of way or reduce speed on highway when approaching stopped vehicle with flashing blue, red or amber lights (not applicable to second and subsequent violations with vehicles flashing blue or red lights)	46.2-921.1	$100	$51	$151
Failure to display headlights at night or during time of poor visibility	46.2-1030	$30	$51	$81
Driving with excessive lights for purpose of general illumination ahead of vehicle	46.2-1030	$30	$51	$81
Failure to display warning lights properly	46.2-1030	$30	$51	$81
Failure to dim headlights	46.2-1034	$30	$51	$81
Driving in violation of HOV Lane Restrictions	33.1-46.2	$100	$51	$151

* The description of offense is for reference and is not a legal definition.
** Unless otherwise provided by statute.
*** See §§ 9.1-106 and 53.1-120 of the Code.

Description of Offense*	Statute or Regulation	Fine	Processing Fee***	Total
Driving in violation of HOV Lane Restrictions, Planning District Eight (first offense)	33.1-46.2	$125	$51	$176
Driving in violation of HOV Lane Restrictions, Planning District Eight (second offense within five years from a first offense)	33.1-46.2	$250	$51	$301
Driving in violation of HOV Lane Restrictions, Planning District Eight (third offense within five years from a first offense)	33.1-46.2	$500	$51	$551
Driving in violation of HOV Lane Restrictions, Planning District Eight (fourth offense within five years from a first offense)	33.1-46.2	$1,000	$51	$1,051
Driving vehicle in violation of HOT lane vehicle classification restrictions (first offense)	33.1-56.3(D)	$125	$51	$176
Driving vehicle in violation of HOT lane vehicle classification restrictions (second offense within five years from a first offense)	33.1-56.3(D)	$250	$51	$301

* The description of offense is for reference and is not a legal definition.
** Unless otherwise provided by statute.
*** See §§ 9.1-106 and 53.1-120 of the Code.

Description of Offense*	Statute or Regulation	Fine	Processing Fee***	Total
Driving vehicle in violation of HOT lane vehicle classification restrictions (third offense within five years from a first offense)	33.1-56.3(D)	$500	$51	$551
Driving vehicle in violation of HOT lane vehicle classification restrictions (fourth and subsequent offense within five years from a first offense)	33.1-56.3(D)	$1000	$51	$1051
3. Equipment Violations				
Insufficient lighting equipment:	46.2-1010	$30	$51	$81
—less than two proper headlights on autos, trucks, busses, etc.	46.2-1011	$30	$51	$81
—motorcycle without proper headlight	46.2-1012	$30	$51	$81
—motorcycle with more than two headlights	46.2-1012	$30	$51	$81
—improper rear lights	46.2-1013	$30	$51	$81
—improper brake lights	46.2-1014	$30	$51	$81
—improper lighting equipment on all other mobile equipment	46.2-1016	$30	$51	$81

* The description of offense is for reference and is not a legal definition.
** Unless otherwise provided by statute.
*** See §§ 9.1-106 and 53.1-120 of the Code.

Description of Offense*	Statute or Regulation	Fine	Processing Fee***	Total
Failure of car to be equipped with supplemental high mount stop light	46.2-1014.1	$30	$51	$81
Improper dimension or marker lights:				
—generally	46.2-1017	$30	$51	$81
—vehicles or loads exceeding 35 feet	46.2-1018	$30	$51	$81
Spotlights or ditch-lights				
—more than two	46.2-1019	$30	$51	$81
—aimed left of highway center or more than 100 feet ahead of vehicle	46.2-1019	$30	$51	$81
—unapproved type	46.2-1019	$30	$51	$81
—use in conjunction with or in place of headlights, except in emergency	46.2-1019	$30	$51	$81
—improper use of auxiliary lamps on emergency vehicles	46.2-1028	$30	$51	$81
Headlights improperly aimed or of improper intensity:				
—single beam headlights	46.2-1031	$30	$51	$81
—multiple beam headlights	46.2-1032	$30	$51	$81

* The description of offense is for reference and is not a legal definition.

** Unless otherwise provided by statute.

*** See §§ 9.1-106 and 53.1-120 of the Code.

Description of Offense*	Statute or Regulation	Fine	Processing Fee***	Total
Failure of car to be equipped with windshield defroster or defogger	46.2-1055.1	$30	$51	$81
Inadequate brakes:				
—generally	46.2-1066	$30	$51	$81
—bicycles	46.2-1066	$15	$51	$66
—holding device	46.2-1068	$30	$51	$81
—motorcycles	46.2-1069	$30	$51	$81
—trailers or semitrailers	46.2-1070	$30	$51	$81
Improper alteration of suspension system	46.2-1063	$30	$51	$81
Inadequate steering gear	46.2-1065	$30	$51	$81
Inadequate horn	46.2-1059	$30	$51	$81
Illegal siren, whistle or horn	46.2-1060	$30	$51	$81
Use of speedometer not in good working order	46.2-1080	$30	$51	$81
Improper painting and lettering on school bus	46.2-1089	$30	$51	$81
Absence of or inadequate rear view mirrors:				
—generally	46.2-1082	$30	$51	$81
—vehicle registered for passenger vehicular transportation	46.2-1082	$30	$51	$81
Insufficient rear fenders, flags or guards on trucks	46.2-1083	$30	$51	$81

* The description of offense is for reference and is not a legal definition.

** Unless otherwise provided by statute.

*** See §§ 9.1-106 and 53.1-120 of the Code.

Description of Offense*	Statute or Regulation	Fine	Processing Fee***	Total
Improper signs on windshields, etc.	46.2-1052	$30	$51	$81
Driver's view obstructed because of suspended objects or altered vehicle	46.2-1054	$30	$51	$81
Inadequate windshield wipers	46.2-1055	$30	$51	$81
Absence of required safety glass	46.2-1056	$30	$51	$81
Absence of windshield	46.2-1057	$30	$51	$81
Improper replacement of glass in vehicle	46.2-1058	$30	$51	$81
Improper or inadequate tires:				
—violation of restrictions on solid rubber tires	46.2-1041	$30	$51	$81
—operation of vehicle with insufficient tire tread	46.2-1043	$30	$51	$81
—improper use of studded tires	46.2-1044	$30	$51	$81
Lack of or inadequate signal device	46.2-1038, 46.2-1039	$30	$51	$81
Failure to use flashing signals when stopped on highway	46.2-1040	$30	$51	$81
Inadequate exhaust system:				
—driver of vehicle	46.2-1049	$30	$51	$81

* The description of offense is for reference and is not a legal definition.
** Unless otherwise provided by statute.
*** See §§ 9.1-106 and 53.1-120 of the Code.

Description of Offense*	Statute or Regulation	Fine	Processing Fee***	Total
—owner permitting or allowing operation of vehicle	46.2-1049	$30	$51	$81
—vehicle without proper pollution control device	46.2-1048	$30	$51	$81
—muffler cutout, straight exhaust or gutted muffler	46.2-1047	$30	$51	$81
Operation of vehicle without securely affixed or properly located operator's seat	46.2-1084	$30	$51	$81
Improper motorcycle steering mechanism	46.2-1085	$30	$51	$81
Motorcycle without muffler	46.2-1050	$30	$51	$81
Improper cooling unit	46.2-1088	$30	$51	$81
Use of unapproved equipment	46.2-1002	$30	$51	$81
Use of defective or unsafe equipment	46.2-1003	$30	$51	$81
Operating vehicle not equipped with proper seat belts	46.2-1092	$30	$51	$81
Failure to have vehicle inspected	46.2-1158	$30	$51	$81
Failure to correct defects discovered by inspection	46.2-1158	$50	$51	$101
Driving after expiration of rejection inspection sticker	46.2-1158	$50	$51	$101

4. Parking or Stopping Violations

* The description of offense is for reference and is not a legal definition.

** Unless otherwise provided by statute.

*** See §§ 9.1-106 and 53.1-120 of the Code.

Description of Offense*	Statute or Regulation	Fine	Processing Fee***	Total
Parking too near fire apparatus	46.2-921	$20	$51	$71
Vehicle improperly stopped or parked on highway	46.2-888	$20	$51	$71
—parked or stopped at or near fire or accident so as to cause traffic hazard or interfere with emergency operations	46.2-890	$20	$51	$71
Failure to use proper warning device when vehicle disabled in highway:				
—bus, truck, trailer, house trailer, or mobile home	46.2-111	$20	$51	$71
—vehicle transporting inflammable liquids	46.2-111	$20	$51	$71
—failure to use red flags when vehicle disabled	46.2-111	$20	$51	$71
Parking in front of fire hydrant, or private driveway, near street corner, fire station, or rescue squad building and too close to intersection	46.2-1239	$20	$51	$71
Failure to dim headlights on parked vehicle	46.2-1035	$20	$51	$71

* The description of offense is for reference and is not a legal definition.

** Unless otherwise provided by statute.

*** See §§ 9.1-106 and 53.1-120 of the Code.

Description of Offense*	Statute or Regulation	Fine	Processing Fee***	Total
Vehicle parked or stopped on highway without lights at night or during low visibility	46.2-1037	$20	$51	$71
Failure to set hand-brake and turn wheels to curb on parked car	46.2-1071	$20	$51	$71
Improper use of parking space reserved for persons with disabilities	46.2-1242	$150	$51	$201
5. Trucks and Hauling or Towing Vehicles				
Absence of flag or light at end of load of four feet or more (excluding violation on a two-lane highway where passing is permitted)	46.2-1121	$30	$51	$81
Absence of flag or light at end of load of four feet or more on a two-lane highway where passing is permitted	46.2-1121	$250	$51	$301
Failure to prevent escape of vehicle contents	46.2-1156	$30	$51	$81
Failure to fasten load of logs, barrels, etc.	46.2-1155	$30	$51	$81
Load extending too far beyond front (excluding violation on a two-lane highway where passing is permitted)	46.2-1120	$30	$51	$81

* The description of offense is for reference and is not a legal definition.
** Unless otherwise provided by statute.
*** See §§ 9.1-106 and 53.1-120 of the Code.

Description of Offense*	Statute or Regulation	Fine	Processing Fee***	Total
Load extending too far beyond front on a two-lane highway where passing is permitted	46.2-1120	$30	$51	$81
Load extending too far beyond sides	46.2-1111	$250	$51	$301
Improper towing				
—improperly towing more than one trailer, etc. (excluding violation on a two-lane highway where passing is permitted)	46.2-1116	$30	$51	$81
—towing without draw bar not exceeding 15 feet and emergency chain (excluding violation on a two-lane highway where passing is permitted)	46.2-1118	$30	$51	$81
— improperly towing more than one trailer, etc., on a two-lane highway where passing is permitted	46.2-1116	$250	$51	$301
— towing without draw bar not exceeding 15 feet and emergency chain on a two-lane highway where passing is permitted	46.2-1118	$250	$51	$301
6. Pedestrian Violations				

* The description of offense is for reference and is not a legal definition.
** Unless otherwise provided by statute.
*** See §§ 9.1-106 and 53.1-120 of the Code.

Description of Offense*	Statute or Regulation	Fine	Processing Fee***	Total
Malicious or careless interference with vehicle passage	46.2-923	$15	$51	$66
Failure to observe pedestrian control signals	46.2-925	$15	$51	$66
Stepping into street where driver's vision obscured	46.2-926	$15	$51	$66
Soliciting rides	46.2-929	$15	$51	$66
Failure to walk on left edge of roadway where no sidewalk	46.2-928	$15	$51	$66
Unlawful loitering on bridge or highway right-of-way	46.2-930	$15	$51	$66
Playing on streets or highways	46.2-932	$15	$51	$66
7. Miscellaneous Offenses				
Unlawful riding of animal on highway at night	46.2-800.1	$30	$51	$81
Improper abandonment of motor vehicle	46.2-1209	$40	$51	$91
Failure to obtain registration	46.2-600	$25	$51	$76
Failure to carry license or registration	46.2-104	$10	$51	$61
Expiration of registration	46.2-613	$25	$51	$76
Operate vehicle which is unregistered, untitled, or without plates/decals or with expired registration/license/decals	46.2-613(1)	$25	$51	$76

* The description of offense is for reference and is not a legal definition.

** Unless otherwise provided by statute.

*** See §§ 9.1-106 and 53.1-120 of the Code.

Description of Offense*	Statute or Regulation	Fine	Processing Fee***	Total
Possess, lend or knowingly permit use of registration card, license plate, or decal by anyone not entitled to it	46.2-613(3)	$25	$51	$76
Expired registration	46.2-646	$25	$51	$76
Pedestrian, bicycle, animal, moped, prohibited vehicle on controlled access highway	46.2-808	$30	$51	$81
Operating motorcycle without headlight, horn or rear-view mirror at certain times	46.2-912	$30	$51	$81
Operating or riding a motorcycle without helmet; operating motorcycle without face shield, goggles or safety windshield	46.2-910(A)	$25	$51	$76
Occupation of trailer being towed on highways	46.2-813	$30	$51	$81
Unlawful use of radar detection device	46.2-1079	$40	$51	$91
Unlawful use of radar jamming device	46.2-1079	$40	$51	$91
Unlawful use of earphones while operating vehicle	46.2-1078	$25	$51	$76
Failure to display slow moving vehicle emblem	46.2-1081	$15	$51	$66
Failure to display license plate	46.2-711	$25	$51	$76
Improper display of license plate	46.2-715	$25	$51	$76

* The description of offense is for reference and is not a legal definition.
** Unless otherwise provided by statute.
*** See §§ 9.1-106 and 53.1-120 of the Code.

Description of Offense*	Statute or Regulation	Fine	Processing Fee***	Total
License plate improperly fastened or obscured	46.2-716	$25	$51	$76
Vehicle exceeding width limitations	46.2-1105	$250	$51	$301
Vehicle exceeding height limitations (excluding offenses of driving in violation of tunnel height restrictions and failure to report overhead bridge or structure collision)	46.2-1110	$250	$51	$301
Vehicle exceeding length requirement (excluding violation on a two-lane highway where passing is permitted)	46.2-1112	$250	$51	$301
Vehicle exceeding length regulations on a two-lane highway where passing is permitted	46.2-1112	$250	$51	$301
8. Bicycle Violations				
Riding bicycle improperly on roadway	46.2-905	$15	$51	$66
Carrying articles improperly on bicycle	46.2-906	$15	$51	$66
Bicycle without proper headlight	46.2-1015	$15	$51	$66
Bicycle without rear reflector or light	46.2-1015	$15	$51	$66
Bicycle on highway without adequate brake	46.2-1066	$15	$51	$66

* The description of offense is for reference and is not a legal definition.
** Unless otherwise provided by statute.
*** See §§ 9.1-106 and 53.1-120 of the Code.

Description of Offense*	Regulation[1]	Fine	Processing Fee***	Total
9. Motor Carrier Offenses[†]				
(a.) General Violations				
Marking of motor vehicle	49 C.F.R. § 390.21	$25	$51	$76
Railroad crossing/stopping	49 C.F.R. § 392.10	$100	$51	$151
(b.) Driver Violations				
No medical examiner's certificate	49 C.F.R. § 391.41	$50	$51	$101
Improper medical examiner's certificate	49 C.F.R. § 391.43	$50	$51	$101
Medical certificate invalid	49 C.F.R. § 391.43	$50	$51	$101
No medical waiver	49 C.F.R. § 391.49	$50	$51	$101
Ill/fatigued driver	49 C.F.R. § 392.3	$75	$51	$126
Possess alcoholic beverage	49 C.F.R. § 392.5	$100	$51	$151
Violate 10-hour rule, 15-hour rule	49 C.F.R. § 395.3	$100	$51	$151
Violate 60/70 hour rule	49 C.F.R. § 395.3	$100	$51	$151
Log book violation (general)	49 C.F.R. § 395.8	$100	$51	$151
No log book	49 C.F.R. § 395.8	$100	$51	$151
Log book not current	49 C.F.R. § 395.8	$100	$51	$151
Fail to retain previous seven days on log book	49 C.F.R. § 395.8	$100	$51	$151

[1] The category "regulation" refers to the section of the Code of Federal Regulations as incorporated by regulation at 19 VAC 30-20-80 of the Virginia Motor Carrier Safety Regulations. These regulations are included for identification and reference purposes only, since these violations are violations of Virginia regulations.

[†] These fines are imposed for violations of certain Virginia Motor Carrier Safety Regulations. The statutory authority to impose these fines is contained in § 52-8.4 of the code of Virginia and in 19 VAC 30-20-10, *et seq.*, of the Virginia Motor Carrier Safety Regulations, incorporating by reference 49 C.F.R. Parts 390-397.

* The description of offense is for reference and is not a legal definition.

** Unless otherwise provided by statute.

*** See §§ 9.1-106 and 53.1-120 of the Code.

Description of Offense*	Regulation[1]	Fine	Processing Fee***	Total
(c.) Equipment Violations				
Equipment — inspection/use	49 C.F.R. § 392.7	$50	$51	$101
Emergency equipment — inspection/use	49 C.F.R. § 392.8	$50	$51	$101
Safe loading (secured)	49 C.F.R. § 392.9	$100	$51	$151
Brakes — inoperative or missing	49 C.F.R. §§ 393.40 to 393.52	$100	$51	$151
Fuel tank securement	49 C.F.R. § 393.65	$50	$51	$101
Fuel leak/cap	49 C.F.R. § 393.67	$25	$51	$76
Coupling/towing devices	49 C.F.R. §§ 393.70, 393.71	$50	$51	$101
Defective tires/tire exceeds weight limit	49 C.F.R. § 393.75	$50	$51	$101
Bus violations	49 C.F.R. §§ 393.89 to 393.92	$50	$51	$101
Front end structure	49 C.F.R. § 393.106	$50	$51	$101
Frame — cracked, loose, sagging, broken	49 C.F.R. § 393.201	$100	$51	$151
Cab/body components — defective	49 C.F.R. § 393.203	$50	$51	$101
Wheels/rims defective	49 C.F.R. § 393.205	$50	$51	$101
Suspension — defective	49 C.F.R. § 393.207	$50	$51	$101
Steering system — defective	49 C.F.R. § 393.209	$100	$51	$151

[1] The category "regulation" refers to the section of the Code of Federal Regulations as incorporated by regulation at 19 VAC 30-20-80 of the Virginia Motor Carrier Safety Regulations. These regulations are included for identification and reference purposes only, since these violations are violations of Virginia regulations.

* The description of offense is for reference and is not a legal definition.

** Unless otherwise provided by statute.

*** See §§ 9.1-106 and 53.1-120 of the Code.

Description of Offense*	Regulation[1]	Fine	Processing Fee***	Total
Vehicle maintenance (general)	49 C.F.R. § 396.3	$100	$51	$151
No driver vehicle inspection report	49 C.F.R. § 396.11	$25	$51	$76
No periodic inspection	49 C.F.R. §§ 396.17 to 396.25	$25	$51	$76
(d.) Hazardous Materials — Driving and Parking				
Fail to attend Division 1.1, 1.2 or 1.3 material	49 C.F.R. § 397.5	$100	$51	$151
Fail to attend other hazardous materials class	49 C.F.R. § 397.5	$100	$51	$151
Improper parking Division 1.1, 1.2 or 1.3 material	49 C.F.R. § 397.7, § 397.11	$100	$51	$151
Improper parking other hazardous materials	49 C.F.R. § 397.7, § 397.11	$100	$51	$151
Fail to have route plan	49 C.F.R. § 397.67	$100	$51	$151
Smoking violations	49 C.F.R. § 397.13	$100	$51	$151
Instructions and document violations	49 C.F.R. § 397.19	$100	$51	$151

Cross references. — As to prepayment of fines for violations of speed limits, see § 46.2-878.3.

As to doubling of otherwise applicable fines set forth in Rule 3B:2 in the case of a waiver of appearance and plea of guilty under § 16.1-69.40:1 or § 19.2-254.2 for a violation of Chapter 8 (§ 46.2-800 et seq.) of Title 46.2 in a designated highway safety corridor, see § 46.2-947.

The amendment, effective August 15, 1997, adopted June 15, 1997, in the fine schedule, increased all processing fees by $1, deleted the entries beginning "failure to give prior warning,"; "chambered pipes"; "Crossing bridge or culvert"; "Vehicle exceeding weight limitations"; "Improper use of parking privilege"; "Unlawful riding or driving on sidewalk". Added entry beginning "failure to yield at" and added the entire subdivision 9.

The amendment, effective July 1, 1998, adopted April 23, 1998, in subdivision 4, inserted the entry beginning "Improper use of parking space

[1] The category "regulation" refers to the section of the Code of Federal Regulations as incorporated by regulation at 19 VAC 30-20-80 of the Virginia Motor Carrier Safety Regulations. These regulations are included for identification and reference purposes only, since these violations are violations of Virginia regulations.

* The description of offense is for reference and is not a legal definition.

** Unless otherwise provided by statute.

*** See §§ 9.1-106 and 53.1-120 of the Code.

reserved for persons with disabilities."

The amendment, effective October 21, 1998, adopted October 21, 1998, substituted "17.1-281" for 14.1-133.2" in footnote ***.

The amendment, effective February 1, 1999, adopted November 23, 1998, inserted the entry beginning "Unlawful use of radar jamming device" in subdivision 7.

The amendment, effective July 1, 2000, adopted May 1, 2000, in subdivision 2, Other Moving Violations, inserted the entries beginning "Evasion of a traffic control device," "Illegal right turn on red," and "Illegal left turn on red"; and in subdivision 7, Miscellaneous Offenses, inserted the entries beginning "Failure to carry license or registration," "Expired registration," "Pedestrian, bicycle, animal, moped, prohibited vehicle on controlled access highway," and "Operating or riding a motorcycle without helmet; operating motorcycle without face shield, goggles or safety windshield."

The amendment, effective January 1, 2001, adopted September 28, 2000, rewrote the first paragraph.

The amendment, effective July 1, 2001, adopted April 12, 2001, increased the fine for "Failure to obey traffic lights" from $50 to $100.

The amendment, effective April 1, 2002, adopted January 16, 2002, inserted the entry beginning "Use of speedometer not in good working order" in subdivision 3.

The amendment, effective May 1, 2002, adopted April 29, 2002, increased the processing fees from $28 to $40 for all offenses.

The amendment effective July 1, 2002, adopted April 29, 2002, substituted "46.2-871" for "46.2-870" in the entry beginning "Exceeding the speed limit"; "Exceeding the speed limit in a 55 mph or 65 mph zone 46.2-870 $5 per mile over speed limit $40" was substituted for "Exceeding speed limit set by Transportation Commissioner 46.2-878 $3 per mile over speed limit $40"; and an additional equipment violation, "Driving after expiration of rejection inspection sticker 46.2-1158 $50 $40 $90," was added following the entry beginning "Failure to correct defects discovered by inspection."

The amendment, effective December 23, 2002, adopted December 23, 2002, inserted the entry beginning "License plate improperly fastened or obscured" in subdivision 7.

The amendment, effective July 1, 2003, adopted June 4, 2003, substituted "46.2-870 to 46.2-872, 46.2-873.1 to 46.2-876" for "46.2-871 to 46.2-876" in the entry "Exceeding the speed limit"; increased the fine for "Exceeding the speed limit" and "Exceeding the speed limit on bridge" from "$3 per mile over speed limit" to "$5 per mile over speed limit"; inserted the entries beginning "Exceeding the speed limit in a school crossing," "Exceeding speed limits set by Transportation Commissioner," "Exceeding the speed limit in a highway work zone," "Exceeding the speed limit in a residence district," and "Moving violation committed in highway safety corridor"; increased the processing fees from $40 to $49 for all offenses; increased the fine for "Ill/fatigued driver" from $75 to $100; and substituted "§§ 9.1-106 and 53.1-120" for "§ 17.1-281" in footnote ***.

The amendment, effective July 22, 2003, adopted July 22, 2003, deleted the former entries beginning "Failure to submit vehicle to inspection" and "Failure to correct defects found by inspection" in subdivision 7.

The amendment, effective July 1, 2004, adopted August 9, 2004, increased the processing fees throughout the Rule; and in the entry beginning "Exceeding the speed limit in a residence district," inserted "$200 plus" at the beginning of the "Fine" column.

The amendment, effective January 1, 2006, in the entry beginning "Absence of flag or light" added "of four feet or more (excluding violation on a two-lane highway where passing is permitted)" and inserted the three entries immediately thereafter; in the entries beginning "— improperly towing more than one trailer, etc." and "towing without draw bar not exceeding 15 feet and emergency chain" added "(excluding violation on a two-lane highway where passing is permitted)" and inserted the two entries immediately following; and in the entry beginning "Vehicle exceeding length regulations" added "(excluding violation on a two-lane highway where passing is permitted)" and inserted the entry following.

The amendment, effective July 1, 2006, adopted June 7, 2006, in subdivision 2, increased the fine for "Driving in violation of HOV Lane Restrictions" and inserted the four entries beginning "Driving in violation of HOV Lane Restricts, Planning District Eight (first offense)" and ending with "Driving in violation of HOV Lane Restrictions, Planning District Eight (fourth offense within five years from a first offense); in subdivision 3, increased the fine for "Failure to correct defects discovered by inspection"; and in subdivision 7, inserted the entries beginning "Operate vehicle which is unregistered, untitled ..." and "Possess, lend of knowingly permit use...."

The amendment, effective January 1, 2007, adopted December 15, 2006, in subdivision 7, in the entry beginning "Vehicle exceeding height limitations," added the parenthetical language.

The amendment, effective July 1, 2008, adopted June 6, 2008, in subdivision 2, added the entries beginning "Driving vehicle in violation of HOT lane vehicle classification restrictions (first offense)"; and in subdivision 6, inserted "or highway right-of-way" following "Unlawful loitering on bridge."

The amendment, effective July 1, 2010, adopted June 1, 2010, in subdivision 1, increased the fines for speeding violations; and in subdivision 2, added the entry beginning "Failure to yield right of way or reduce speed on highway when approaching stopped vehicle with flashing blue, red or amber lights (not applicable to second and subsequent violations with vehicles flashing blue or red lights)."

The amendment, effective July 1, 2011, adopted June 10, 2011, effective July 1, 2011, in subdivision 3, substituted "46.2-1158" for "46.2-1157" in the entries for "Failure to have vehicle inspected" and "Failure to correct defects discovered by inspection."

The amendment effective March 1, 2012, adopted December 22, 2011, deleted "and §§ 46.2-1235 through 46.2-1237" at the end of the first paragraph; and in the second paragraph, deleted "and cost" following "a fine" in the first sentence, added the second sentence, and substituted "This" for "The" at the beginning of the third sentence.

The amendment effective July 1, 2012, adopted April 27, 2012, decreased the fine from $250 to $30 for the entry "Load extending too far beyond sides,"; increased the fine from $30 to $250 for the entry "Load extending too far beyond front on a two-lane highway where passing is permitted"; and increased the fine from $40 to $250 for the entries "Vehicle exceeding width limitations," "Vehicle exceeding height limitations (excluding offenses of driving in violation of tunnel height restrictions and failure to report overhead bridge or structure collision)" and "Vehicle exceeding length regulations (excluding violation on a two-lane highway where passing is permitted)."

The amendment effective July 1, 2013, adopted June 21, 2013, under description 2. Other Moving Offenses, deleted ": —entering or traveling in lane over which red signal is shown" following "Disregard of lane direction control signal," substituted "—failure to follow traffic control device of local authority" for "—failure to follow marker, button or sign of local authority," added the entry "Failure to yield right of way or reduce speed on highway when approaching stopped vehicle with flashing blue, red or amber lights (not applicable to second and subsequent violations with vehicles flashing blue or red lights) 46.2-921.1 $100 $51 $151," and substituted "—failure of driver approaching or entering circular intersection to yield to driver already in the circle" for "—failure of driver approaching or entering traffic circle to yield to driver already in traffic circle."

PART THREE C
NON-TRAFFIC PREPAYABLE OFFENSES AND UNIFORM FINE SCHEDULE

Rule
3C:1. Purpose and Effective Date.
3C:2. Uniform Fine Schedule.

Editor's note. — Part Three C was revised, effective July 1, 1988, by order adopted December 21, 1987.

Rule 3C:1. Purpose and Effective Date.

These rules are promulgated by the Supreme Court of Virginia pursuant to § 16.1-69.40:2 of the Code of Virginia to carry out the provisions of Chapter 605 of the Acts of Assembly of 1978 and Chapter 421 of the Acts of Assembly of 1989.

Michie's Jurisprudence. — For related discussion, see 5B M.J. Criminal Procedure, § 2.

Rule 3C:2. Uniform Fine Schedule.

Any person charged with any offense listed below may enter a written appearance, waiver of court hearing, plea of guilty, and pay fines and costs.

This schedule is applied uniformly throughout the Commonwealth, and a clerk or magistrate may not impose a fine different from the amounts shown here. Costs shall be paid in accordance with the provisions of the Code of Virginia or any rules or regulations promulgated thereunder. The schedule does not restrict the fine a judge may impose for an offense listed here in any case for which there is a court hearing.

Where injury to the person is involved, prepayment may not be made, even though the offense or violation appears on the list below. See Va. Code § 16.1-69.40:2(A).

A violation of a provision of Title 28.2 may be prepaid only if the person has not violated a provision of Title 28.2 within the past 12 months. See Va. Code § 28.2-903.

Description of Offense*	Statute or Regulation	Fine	Processing Fee***	Total
Drinking or tendering alcoholic beverage in public place	4.1-308	$25	$61	$86
Failing to assist forest warden in fighting fire	10.1-1139	$30	$61	$91
Unlawful burning of brush, leaves, etc.	10.1-1142(A) 10.1-1142(D)	$40	$61	$101
Unlawful burning during restricted period	10.1-1142(B) 10.1-1142(D)	$40	$61	$101

* The description of offense is for reference and is not a legal definition.

** Unless otherwise provided by statute.

*** See §§ 9.1-106 and 53.1-120 of the Code.

Description of Offense*	Statute or Regulation	Fine	Processing Fee*****	Total
Leaving certain fires unattended or failing to extinguish the same	10.1-1142(C) 10.1-1142(D)	$40	$61	$101
Hunting or trapping in state forests without special use permit	10.1-1151	$35	$61	$96
Hunting or trapping in state forests in violation of restrictions or conditions of special use permit	10.1-1153	$35	$61	$96
Failure to post signs regarding disposal of used motor oils	10.1-1422.6D	$25	$61	$86
Unlawful buying, selling or disposing of milk case or crate	18.2-102.2	$35	$61	$96
Unlawful refusal to return milk case or crate	18.2-102.2	$35	$61	$96
Unlawful defacing, cover up or removal of business identification on milk case or crate	18.2-102.2	$35	$61	$96
Bringing unleashed dog into Capitol Square	18.2-123	$10	$61	$71
Trespassing at night upon cemetery	18.2-125	$35	$61	$96
Trespassing at night upon church or school property	18.2-128(A)	$35	$61	$96
Trespassing upon lands to hunt, fish or trap without consent	18.2-132	$50	$61	$111
Computer invasion of privacy by intentionally examining personal information without authority	18.2-152.5	$50	$61	$111

* The description of offense is for reference and is not a legal definition.
** Unless otherwise provided by statute.
*** See §§ 9.1-106 and 53.1-120 of the Code.

Description of Offense*	Statute or Regulation	Fine	Processing Fee** ***	Total
Trespassing on railroad track	18.2-159	$35	$61	$96
Trespassing on railroad trains	18.2-160	$35	$61	$96
Boarding or riding train without lawful payment of fare	18.2-160.1(A) 18.2-160.1(B)	$100	$61	$161
Unlawfully intercepting or monitoring employee/customer telephone calls	18.2-167.1	$35	$61	$96
Failing to report removal, alteration of trademark or identification numbers on a business machine	18.2-214.1	$50	$61	$111
Using games, contests, lotteries to promote sale of products having both federal and state tax	18.2-242	$50	$61	$111
Expectorating in public	18.2-322	$15	$61	$76
Drinking alcoholic beverage while driving motor vehicle	18.2-323.1	$75	$61	$136
Gambling illegally	18.2-326	$35	$61	$96
Selling to, distributing to or purchasing for persons under age 18 tobacco products	18.2-371.2(A)	$75	—	$75
Purchasing or possessing tobacco products when under age 18	18.2-371.2(B)	$35	—	$35
Profanely cursing or swearing in public	18.2-388	$25	$61	$86
Being intoxicated in public	18.2-388	$25	$61	$86

* The description of offense is for reference and is not a legal definition.
** Unless otherwise provided by statute.
*** See §§ 9.1-106 and 53.1-120 of the Code.

Description of Offense*	Statute or Regulation	Fine	Processing Fee***	Total
Shooting pigeons for amusement or renting premises for such purpose	18.2-403.3(2) 3.2-6573	$35	$61	$96
Making false statement to secure a dog license	18.2-403.3(8) 3.2-6587(A)(1)	$35	$61	$96
Failing to pay dog license tax	18.2-403.3(9) 3.2-6530 3.2-6587(A)	$25	$61	$86
Concealing unlicensed dog	18.2-403.3(10) 3.2-6587(A)	$35	$61	$96
Unlawfully removing dog collar or tag	18.2-403.3(11) 3.2-6587(A)	$35	$61	$96
Using abusive language	18.2-416	$60	$61	$121
Using recorded telephone solicitation calls for initial sales contacts	18.2-425.1(A)	$50	$61	$111
Using recorded telephone solicitation calls which do not disengage when party called attempts to do so	18.2-425.1(B)	$50	$61	$111
Unlawfully communicating with prisoners by persons outside any jail	18.2-473.1	$75	$61	$136
Unlawfully possessing or duplicating keys to public buildings	18.2-503	$50	$61	$111
Unlawfully changing name	18.2-504.1	$60	$61	$121
Campaigning at election registration location	24.2-1003	$50	$61	$111
Failing to obey chief or other fire officer answering an alarm or operating at an emergency incident	27-15.1	$50	$61	$111

* The description of offense is for reference and is not a legal definition.
** Unless otherwise provided by statute.
*** See §§ 9.1-106 and 53.1-120 of the Code.

Description of Offense*	Statute or Regulation	Fine	Processing Fee***	Total
Unlawful setting of fishnets	28.2-309	$110	$61	$171
Taking fish or shellfish on or within 500 yards below Chickahominy Dam at Walker's on the Chickahominy River other than with rod and reel and hand line	28.2-311	$60	$61	$121
Having more than one-half gallon of shucked oysters on board a boat harvesting on the public rocks	28.2-514	$60	$61	$121
Buying, selling or possessing oysters under the prescribed size and undersized shells taken from the natural rocks, beds and shoals	28.2-510	$60	$61	$121
Having oysters or shells on culling board, deck, washboard or other receptacle above hold or in deckhouse when boat is oystering upon natural rocks, beds or shoals and not at anchor; when off the public rocks; when approaching a buy boat; or when approaching a landing	28.2-513	$110	$61	$171
Taking or catching oysters or shells for purpose of converting same into lime without permission from Commission	28.2-529	$110	$61	$171

* The description of offense is for reference and is not a legal definition.

** Unless otherwise provided by statute.

*** See §§ 9.1-106 and 53.1-120 of the Code.

Description of Offense*	Statute or Regulation	Fine	Processing Fee** ***	Total
Taking or catching crabs from statutorily prohibited area from June 1 to Sept. 15, for purpose of resale	28.2-709	$110	$61	$171
Placing or maintaining any crab, eel, or fish pot in navigable channel which has navigation aids installed or approved by any agency of U.S. government	28.2-710	$60	$61	$121
Placing, setting or leaving crab pots in tidal tributaries between Jan. 1 and Jan. 31 or other time period specified by Marine Res. Comm.	28.2-711	$35	$61	$96
Unlawful violation of regulations governing use of crab traps and pounds	28.2-701	$110	$61	$171
Unauthorized Transfer of License	PRFC Reg I 1a [1]		[2]	$250
Setting 1 to 5 More Crab Pots than Licensed	PRFC Reg I 2d(1) [1]		[2]	$150
Setting 6 to 10 More Crab Pots than Licensed	PRFC Reg I 2d(1) [1]		[2]	$250
Setting 11 to 15 More Crab Pots than Licensed	PRFC Reg I 2d(1) [1]		[2]	$350
Setting 16 to 20 More Crab Pots than Licensed	PRFC Reg I 2d(1) [1]		[2]	$450
Setting 21 or More Crab Pots than Licensed	PRFC Reg I 2d(1) [1]		[2]	$500

[1] This designation "PRF Reg" refers to the Potomac River Fisheries Commission Regulations. The cite provides the regulation number, the section number and the subsection number.

[2] Subtract fees from total and post balance to fine.

* The description of offense is for reference and is not a legal definition.

** Unless otherwise provided by statute.

*** See §§ 9.1-106 and 53.1-120 of the Code.

Description of Offense*	Statute or Regulation	Fine	Processing Fee***	Total
Improper Identification of Oyster Tong Vessel	PRFC Reg I 2 f (1) [1]			$125
Improper Identification of Hand Scrape Vessel	PRFC Reg I 2 f (3) [1]			$125
Gill Net Set in Water Depth More than 36′ MLW	PRFC Reg I 2 (i)(1) [1]		[2]	$250
Failure to Display Commercial Hook and Line Pennant	PRFC Reg I 2l(2) [1]		[2]	$125
More Unlicensed Commercial Hook and Line Crew Members than Allowed	PRFC Reg I 2 l (2) [1]		[2]	$300
Improper Identification of Eel, Fish, or Bait Pots or Vessel	PRFC Reg I 2 m(4) [1]		[2]	$125
Improper Identification of Pound, Gill or Fyke Net	PRFC Reg I 2 n(8) [1]		[2]	$125
Failing to Maintain 1 to 5 Stakes or Buoys	PRFC Reg I 2 n(9) [1]		[2]	$200
Failing to Maintain 6 to 10 Stakes or Buoys	PRFC Reg I 2 n(9) [1]		[2]	$250
Failing to Maintain 11 to 15 Stakes or Buoys	PRFC Reg I 2 n(9) [1]		[2]	$300
Failing to Maintain 16 to 20 Stakes or Buoys	PRFC Reg I 2 n(9) [1]		[2]	$350
Failing to Maintain 21 or more Stakes or Buoys	PRFC Reg I 2 n(9) [1]		[2]	$500
Improper Identification of Fish Trot Line or Vessel	PRFC Reg I 2q [1]		[2]	$125
Gill Net Set Out of Location	PRFC Reg I 2 s(1) [1]			$200

[1] This designation "PRF Reg" refers to the Potomac River Fisheries Commission Regulations. The cite provides the regulation number, the section number and the subsection number.

[2] Subtract fees from total and post balance to fine.

* The description of offense is for reference and is not a legal definition.

** Unless otherwise provided by statute.

*** See §§ 9.1-106 and 53.1-120 of the Code.

Description of Offense*	Statute or Regulation	Fine	Processing Fee***	Total
Failing to Remove 1 to 5 Stakes	PRFC Reg I 2 s (2)[1]		[2]	$200
Failing to Remove 6 to 10 Stakes	PRFC Reg I 2 s (2)[1]		[2]	$250
Failing to Remove 11 to 15 Stakes	PRFC Reg I 2 s (2)[1]		[2]	$300
Failing to Remove 16 to 20 Stakes	PRFC Reg I 2 s (2)[1]		[2]	$350
Failing to Remove 21 or more Stakes	PRFC Reg I 2 s (2)[1]		[2]	$500
No Reflective Material/ Flags on Gill, Fyke or Pound Net	PRFC Reg I 2 s (3)[1]		[2]	$125
Gill Net Set Out of Location	PRFC Reg I 2 s[1]		[2]	$75
Operating Charter Boat without Sport Decal	PRFC Reg I 2u[1]		[2]	$300
Commercial Fishing/ Crabbing/Oystering/ Clamming without License	PRFC Reg I 3b[1]		[2]	$300
Failure to Exhibit Commercial License	PRFC Reg I 3 b[1]		[2]	$125
Placing 1 to 10 Buoys, Gear or Pots in Marked Channel	PRFC Reg I 3 c[1]		[2]	$150
Placing 11 to 15 Buoys, Gear or Pots in Marked Channel	PRFC Reg I 3 c[1]		[2]	$200
Placing 16 or more Buoys, Gear or Pots in Marked Channel	PRFC Reg I 3 c[1]		[2]	$250
Altering/Modifying Striped Bass ID Tags per tab	PRFC Reg I 3e[1]		[2]	$250

[1] This designation "PRF Reg" refers to the Potomac River Fisheries Commission Regulations. The cite provides the regulation number, the section number and the subsection number.

[2] Subtract fees from total and post balance to fine.

* The description of offense is for reference and is not a legal definition.

** Unless otherwise provided by statute.

*** See §§ 9.1-106 and 53.1-120 of the Code.

Description of Offense*	Statute or Regulation	Fine	Processing Fee***	Total
Possessing Hand Scrape During Unlawful Time (note Order #)	PRFC Reg II 2 b[1]		[2]	$150
Oystering Before or After Closed Hours (note Order #)	PRFC Reg II 2 b[1]		[2]	$250
Oystering During Closed Season (note Order #)	PRFC Reg II 2 b[1]		[2]	$500
Possessing Patent Tong or Dredging Equipment without Permit	PRFC Reg II 2 e [1]		[2]	$125
Possessing 6 to 10% Unculled Oysters	PRFC Reg II 2 f (1) [1]		[2]	$200
Possessing 11 to 15% Unculled Oysters	PRFC Reg II 2 f (1)		[2]	$350
Possessing 16% or more Unculled Oysters	PRFC Reg II 2 f (1)[1]		[2]	$500
Not Culling on Oyster Bar	PRFC Reg II 2 f (2) [1]		[2]	$500
Possessing Oysters in Containers	PRFC Reg II 2 g [1]		[2]	$200
Possessing Oysters in Baskets without Permit	PRFC Reg II 2 g [1]		[2]	$125
Oystering in Closed Area (Sanctuaries)	PRFC Reg II 4 a [1]		[2]	$500
Exceeding Minimum or Maximum Mesh Size	PRFC Reg III 8 b[1]		[2]	$500
Violation of Haul Seine Regulations	PRFC Reg III 8 c(1-2) [1]		[2]	$200
Fishing During Closed Season (Commercial)	PRFC Reg III 9 a (1-7)[1]		[2]	$250
Possessing Fish During Closed Season (note Order #) *per fish*	PRFC Reg III 9 b[1]		[2]	$125

[1] This designation "PRF Reg" refers to the Potomac River Fisheries Commission Regulations. The cite provides the regulation number, the section number and the subsection number.

[2] Subtract fees from total and post balance to fine.

* The description of offense is for reference and is not a legal definition.

** Unless otherwise provided by statute.

*** See §§ 9.1-106 and 53.1-120 of the Code.

Description of Offense*	Statute or Regulation	Fine	Processing Fee***	Total
Exceeding Fish Catch/ Creel Limits (note Order #) *per fish*	PRFC Reg III 10 a[1]		[2]	$125
Possessing Striped Bass in Excess of Catch/ Creel Limits (note Order #) *per fish*	PRFC Reg III 10 a[1]		[2]	$150
Using Striped Bass ID Tags of Another	PRFC Reg III 10 b[1]		[2]	$250
Failure to Tag Commercially Caught Striped Bass *per fish*	PRFC Reg III 10 b[1]		[2]	$125
Unlawful Use of Striped Bass Tags (i.e. by gear type) (note Order #)	PRFC Reg III 10 b[1]		[2]	$500
Possessing Undersize Fish (note Order #) $125 first fish plus $10 each additional fish	PRFC Reg III 11 a[1]			$125
Possess Oversize Striped Bass (note Order #) *per fish*	PRFC Reg III 11 a[1]		[2]	$250
Improper Identification of Soft Clam Vessel	PRFC Reg V 1 a[1]		[2]	$125
Possessing 6% or more Undersized Clams	PRFC Reg V 3 a[1]		[2]	$150
Exceeding Clam Catch Limits *per bushel*	PRFC Reg V 4 a[1]		[2]	$250
Clamming in Closed Area	PRFC Reg V 6 d[1]		[2]	$500
Failure to Exhibit Sport Fishing License/Improper Display of License	PRFC Reg VI 2 c [1]			$125

[1] This designation "PRF Reg" refers to the Potomac River Fisheries Commission Regulations. The cite provides the regulation number, the section number and the subsection number.
[2] Subtract fees from total and post balance to fine.
* The description of offense is for reference and is not a legal definition.
** Unless otherwise provided by statute.
*** See §§ 9.1-106 and 53.1-120 of the Code.

Description of Offense*		Statute or Regulation	Fine	Processing Fee***	Total
Exceeding Unlicensed Recreational Crabbing Gear or Catch Limits		PRF CReg VI 4 a [1]		[2]	$150
Sport Crabbing without License		PRF Reg VI 4 b [1]		[2]	$150
Failure to Exhibit Sport Crabbing License		PRF Reg VI 4 b[1]		[2]	$125
Exceeding Licensed Sport Crabbing Gear Limits		PRF Reg VI 4 c[1]		[2]	$125
Improper Identification of Sport Crabbing Gear		PRF Reg VI 4 d[1]		[2]	$125
Exceeding Licensed Sport Crabbing Catch Limits		PRF Reg VI 4 e[1]		[2]	$125
Sport Fishing without License		PRF Reg VI 5 a[1]		[2]	$150
Fishing for Striped Bass During Closed Season without Barbless Hooks		PRF Reg VI 5 e[1]		[2]	$125
Failing to Remove Peeler Traps per trap		PRF Reg VII 1 d[1]		[2]	$200
Possessing Undersize Crabs					
#per Bushel	#per Barrel				
5 to 9	11 to 24	PRFC Reg VII 2 a [1]			$150
10 to 14	25 to 39	PRFC Reg VII 2 a [1]			$225
15 to 25	40 to 59	PRFC Reg VII 2 a [1]			$275
26 or more	60 or more	PRFC Reg VII 2 a [1]			$400

[1] This designation "PRF Reg" refers to the Potomac River Fisheries Commission Regulations. The cite provides the regulation number, the section number and the subsection number.
[2] Subtract fees from total and post balance to fine.
* The description of offense is for reference and is not a legal definition.
** Unless otherwise provided by statute.
*** See §§ 9.1-106 and 53.1-120 of the Code.

Description of Offense*	Statute or Regulation	Fine	Processing Fee***	Total
Improper Identification of Crab Pot Vessel	PRFC Reg VII 3 a [1]		[2]	$125
Improper Identification of Crabbing Gear	PRFC Reg VII 3 b [1]		[2]	$125
Crab Pots without Decal/Tag — 300 Pot License				
# pots without decal/tag				
1 to 15	PRFC Reg VII b 3 [1]		[2]	$250
16 to 30	PRFC Reg VII b 3 [1]		[2]	$500
Crab Pots without Decal/Tag — 400 Pot License				
# pots without decal/tag				
1 to 20	PRFC Reg VII 3 b [1]		[2]	$250
21 to 40	PRFC Reg VII 3 b [1]		[2]	$500
Crab Pots without Decal/Tag — 500 Pot License				
# pots without decal/tag				
1 to 25	PRFC Reg VII 3 b [1]		[2]	$250
26 - 50	PRFC Reg VII 3 b [1]		[2]	$500
Crabbing/Possession of Crabs During Closed Season	PRFC Reg VII 4 a [1]		[2]	$250
Crabbing at Night	PRFC Reg VII 5 b [1]			$200
No Culling Container on Board	PRFC Reg VII 6 a [1]			$200

[1] This designation "PRF Reg" refers to the Potomac River Fisheries Commission Regulations. The cite provides the regulation number, the section number and the subsection number.

[2] Subtract fees from total and post balance to fine.

* The description of offense is for reference and is not a legal definition.

** Unless otherwise provided by statute.

*** See §§ 9.1-106 and 53.1-120 of the Code.

Description of Offense*	Statute or Regulation	Fine	Processing Fee***	Total
Transporting Crabs not in Baskets or Barrels	PRFC Reg VII 6 a [1]			$200
No or Closed Cull Rings in 1 to 5 Pots	PRFC Reg VII 6 b [1]			$175
No or Closed Cull Rings in 6 to 10 Pots	PRFC Reg VII 6 b [1]			$275
No or Closed Cull Rings in 11 to 15 Pots	PRFC Reg VII 6 b [1]			$450
No or Closed Cull Rings in 16 to 20 Pots	PRFC Reg VII 6 b [1]			$500
Failure to Separate Crabs per container	PRFC Reg VII 6 c [1]		[2]	$150
Exceeding Crab Harvest Limit per bushel	PRFC Reg VII 7 a[1]		[2]	$150
Hunting, trapping, or fishing without license	29.1-335	$60 + fee equal to cost of License	$61	$121
Failing to carry hunting, trapping or fishing license	29.1-336	$35	$61	$96
Hunting bear or deer w/out special stamp	29.1-354	$35	$61	$96
Hunting, fishing or trapping in national forest w/out special permit	29.1-408	$35	$61	$96
Failing to obtain permit for taxidermy	29.1-415 29.1-412	$50	$61	$111
Failing to obtain permit for netting fish	29.1-416 29.1-412	$50	$61	$111
Failing to obtain permit for capturing, propagating and disposing of wildlife for authorized purposes	29.1-417 29.1-412	$50	$61	$111

[1] This designation "PRF Reg" refers to the Potomac River Fisheries Commission Regulations. The cite provides the regulation number, the section number and the subsection number.

[2] Subtract fees from total and post balance to fine.

* The description of offense is for reference and is not a legal definition.

** Unless otherwise provided by statute.

*** See §§ 9.1-106 and 53.1-120 of the Code.

Description of Offense*	Statute or Regulation	Fine	Processing Fee***	Total
Failing to obtain permit for collecting specimens	29.1-418 29.1-412	$50	$61	$111
Failing to obtain permit for taking, holding falcons, hawks and owls to use to hunt wild game	29.1-419 29.1-412	$50	$61	$111
Failing to secure permits required for field trials	29.1-422 18.2-403.3(6)	$50	$61	$111
Hunting with unauthorized weapons	29.1-519	$60	$61	$121
Violating hunting times	29.1-520	$60	$61	$121
Hunting on Sunday	29.1-521(A)(1)	$50	$61	$111
Hunting after obtaining daily or season limit	29.1-521(A)(3)	$50	$61	$111
Hunting over bait or occupying baited blind	29.1-521(A)(4)	$100	$61	$161
Providing no name or address on traps set on another's property	29.1-521(A)(7)	$25	$61	$86
Failing to visit traps daily and remove animals	29.1-521(A)(9)	$35	$61	$96
Unlawfully hunting, trapping, possessing, transporting animals or carcasses	29.1-521(A)(10)	$100	$61	$161
Violating blaze orange law	29.1-530.1	$25	$61	$86
Certain violations pertaining to sanctuaries, refuges, etc.	29.1-554	$60	$61	$121
Shooting, attempting to shoot, or taking game on preserve before complying with regulations	29.1-603	$35	$61	$96

* The description of offense is for reference and is not a legal definition.
** Unless otherwise provided by statute.
*** See §§ 9.1-106 and 53.1-120 of the Code.

Description of Offense*	Statute or Regulation	Fine	Processing Fee***	Total
Removing shot game from preserve without attaching seal	29.1-606	$35	$61	$96
Unregistered motorboat	29.1-702(A)	$75	$61	$136
No registration on board	29.1-702(B)	$25	$61	$86
Expired registration	29.1-703	$25	$61	$86
Failure to display registration	29.1-703	$25	$61	$86
Failure to display expiration decal	29.1-703	$25	$61	$86
Operating motorboat or manipulating skis in marked area	29.1-734	$35	$61	$96
Operation of vessel without proper safety equipment	29.1-735(C)	$35	$61	$96
Renting out a motorboat without safety equipment	29.1-736(A)	$35	$61	$96
Offering for rent other boats without sufficient life preservers	29.1-736(B)	$35	$61	$96
Violation of muffling device requirements for motorboats	29.1-737	$25	$61	$86
Absence of observer when towing water skier not wearing life preserver	29.1-742(A)	$35	$61	$96
Skiing before/after hours	29.1-742(B)	$75	$61	$136
Operating motorboat at excessive speed when within 50 feet of docks, piers, ramps, people in water	29.1-744.3	$50	$61	$111

* The description of offense is for reference and is not a legal definition.
** Unless otherwise provided by statute.
*** See §§ 9.1-106 and 53.1-120 of the Code.

Description of Offense*	Statute or Regulation	Fine	Processing Fee***	Total
Operating personal watercraft under age 14	29.1-748(A)(1)	$35	$61	$96
Operating personal watercraft without wearing personal flotation device	29.1-748(A)(3)	$35	$61	$96
Operating personal watercraft without a lanyard	29.1-748(A)(4)	$35	$61	$96
Operating personal watercraft between sunset and sunrise	29.1-748(A)(5)	$35	$61	$96
Exceeding capacity on personal watercraft	29.1-748(A)(6)	$35	$61	$96
Permitting operation of personal watercraft by person under age 14	29.1-749(A)	$75	$61	$136
Destruction of flowers, plants, minerals, etc. on a state park[3]	4 VAC 5-30-50[4]	$100	$61	$161
Destruction of buildings, signs, structures, etc. on a state park[3]	4 VAC 5-30-60[4]	$100	$61	$161
Disposal of refuse, garbage, etc. on a state park[3]	4 VAC 5-30-70[4]	$50	$61	$111
Pollution of waters on a state park[3]	4 VAC 5-30-80[4]	$100	$61	$161
Opening and closing hours of a state park[3]	4 VAC 5-30-120[4]	$50	$61	$111
Failure to pay fees in a fee area of a state park[3]	4 VAC 5-30-130[4]	$50	$61	$111
Picknicking in non-designated areas of a state park[3]	4 VAC 5-30-140[4]	$25	$61	$86

[3] "Park" is defined pursuant to § 4 VAC 5-30-10 as and is intended for the purposes of this rule to mean all designated parks, parkways, historical and natural areas, sites and other recreational areas under the jurisdiction of the Virginia Department of Conservation and Recreation.

[4] Established pursuant to §10.1-104 of the Code.

* The description of offense is for reference and is not a legal definition.

** Unless otherwise provided by statute.

*** See §§ 9.1-106 and 53.1-120 of the Code.

Description of Offense*	Statute or Regulation	Fine	Processing Fee***	Total
Camping in a state park[3] other than according to established rule	4 VAC 5-30-150[4]	$50	$61	$111
Swimming in unauthorized area or manner in a state park[3]	4 VAC 5-30-170[4]	$50	$61	$111
Boating in a state park[3] swimming area	4 VAC 5-30-190[4]	$50	$61	$111
Possession of firearms in a state park[3] by unauthorized persons	4 VAC 5-30-200[4]	$100	$61	$161
Fires in unauthorized areas of a state park[3]	4 VAC 5-30-220[4]	$100	$61	$161
Smoking in a prohibited area of a state park[3]	4 VAC 5-30-230[4]	$50	$61	$111
Unauthorized hunting in a state park[3]	4 VAC 5-30-240[4]	$100	$61	$161
Fishing in non-designated areas of a state park[3]	4 VAC 5-30-250[4]	$50	$61	$111
Allowing animals to run at large in a state park[3]	4 VAC 5-30-260[4]	$50	$61	$111
Games or athletic contests in non-designated areas of a state park[3]	4 VAC 5-30-270[4]	$50	$61	$111
Persons in non-designated areas of a state park[3] or failure to comply with a safety sign	4 VAC 5-30-274[4]	$50	$61	$111
Bicycle in non-designated areas of a state park[3] or failure to comply with a safety sign	4 VAC 5-30-276[4]	$50	$61	$111

[3] "Park" is defined pursuant to § 4 VAC 5-30-10 as and is intended for the purposes of this rule to mean all designated parks, parkways, historical and natural areas, sites and other recreational areas under the jurisdiction of the Virginia Department of Conservation and Recreation.

[4] Established pursuant to §10.1-104 of the Code.

* The description of offense is for reference and is not a legal definition.

** Unless otherwise provided by statute.

*** See §§ 9.1-106 and 53.1-120 of the Code.

Description of Offense*	Statute or Regulation	Fine	Processing Fee***	Total
Horses in non-designated areas of a state park[3]	4 VAC 5-30-280[4]	$50	$61	$111
Vehicles in a prohibited area of a state park[3]	4 VAC 5-30-290[4]	$50	$61	$111
Parking in an unauthorized area of a state park[3]	4 VAC 5-30-300[4]	$25	$61	$86
Obstructing traffic in a state park[3]	4 VAC 5-30-310[4]	$50	$61	$111
Operating an excessively loaded vehicle in a state park[3]	4 VAC 5-30-330[4]	$50	$61	$111
Engaging in commercial enterprise on a state park[3] without a permit	4 VAC 5-30-340[4]	$50	$61	$111
Operate a commercial vehicle on a state park[3] without a permit	4 VAC 5-30-360[4]	$50	$61	$111
Advertising within a state park[3] without a permit	4 VAC 5-30-370[4]	$50	$61	$111
Soliciting alms or contributions within a state park[3] without a permit	4 VAC 5-30-390[4]	$25	$61	$86
Landing an aircraft or parachute within a state park[3] without a permit	4 VAC 5-30-400[4]	$50	$61	$111
Importation of firewood into a state park[3] contrary to the limitations imposed by the DCR Director	4 VAC 5-30-410[4]	$100	$61	$161

[3] "Park" is defined pursuant to § 4 VAC 5-30-10 as and is intended for the purposes of this rule to mean all designated parks, parkways, historical and natural areas, sites and other recreational areas under the jurisdiction of the Virginia Department of Conservation and Recreation.

[4] Established pursuant to §10.1-104 of the Code.

* The description of offense is for reference and is not a legal definition.

** Unless otherwise provided by statute.

*** See §§ 9.1-106 and 53.1-120 of the Code.

Description of Offense*	Statute or Regulation	Fine	Processing Fee***	Total
Release of animals or wildlife captured or propagated elsewhere into a state park[3]	4 VAC 5-30-420[4]	$50	$61	$111
Feeding wildlife on a state park[3]	4 VAC 5-30-422[4]	$50	$61	$111
Constructing, maintaining or occupying unauthorized structures on department-owned lands or national forest lands	4 VAC 15-20-150[†]	$30	$61	$91
Using recorded or electronically amplified imitations of animal or bird calls or sounds to take wild animals and wild birds	4 VAC 15-40-30[†]	$50	$61	$111
Unlawfully possessing or using a bow or gun which is not unloaded and cased or dismantled on national forest lands statewide or on department-owned lands or on other department-managed lands west of the Blue Ridge Mountains during closed season	4 VAC 15-40-60(A)[†]	$75	$61	$136
Using a bow or firearm outside the established boundaries of an archery or shooting range or using a bow or firearm for other than target shooting at such archery or shooting range during closed season	4 VAC 15-40-60(D)[†]	$50	$61	$111

[3] "Park" is defined pursuant to § 4 VAC 5-30-10 as and is intended for the purposes of this rule to mean all designated parks, parkways, historical and natural areas, sites and other recreational areas under the jurisdiction of the Virginia Department of Conservation and Recreation.

[4] Established pursuant to §10.1-104 of the Code.

[†] These Regulations are promulgated pursuant to §§ 29.1-501 and 29.1-502 of the Code.

* The description of offense is for reference and is not a legal definition.

** Unless otherwise provided by statute.

*** See §§ 9.1-106 and 53.1-120 of the Code.

Description of Offense*	Statute or Regulation	Fine	Processing Fee***	Total
Chasing with a dog or training dogs on national forest lands or on department-owned lands outside authorized hunting, chasing or training seasons or during unauthorized raccoon hound field trials	4 VAC 15-40-60(E)†	$50	$61	$111
Failing to mark certain traps or snares with non-ferrous identity tags	4 VAC 15-40-170††	$25	$61	$86
Killing or crippling and knowingly allowing any nonmigratory game bird or game animal to be wasted without making a reasonable effort to retrieve and retain it	4 VAC 15-40-250†	$25	$61	$86
Unlawfully validate (notch) a bear license prior to killing a bear or after killing bear fail to validate a bear license tag before moving the carcass from the place of kill	4 VAC 15-50-81(A)†	$50	$61	$111
Failing to present bear carcass at an authorized checking station after having validated the appropriate bear license tag or failing to comply with procedure at such checking station	4 VAC 15-50-81(B)†	$50	$61	$111

† These Regulations are promulgated pursuant to §§ 29.1-701 and 29.1-802 of the Code.

†† The Regulations are promulgated pursuant to §§ 29.1-103, 29.1-501 and 29.1-502 of the Code.

* The description of offense is for reference and is not a legal definition.

** Unless otherwise provided by statute.

*** See §§ 9.1-106 and 53.1-120 of the Code.

Description of Offense*	Statute or Regulation	Fine	Processing Fee***	Total
Destroying the identity (sex) of bear before validating bear license tag and checking at an authorized checking station	4 VAC 15-50-81(C)†	$50	$61	$111
Unlawfully validate a deer license tag prior to killing a deer or after killing deer fail to validate a deer license tag before moving the carcass from the place of kill	4 VAC 15-90-231(A)†	$50	$61	$111
Failing to either present deer carcass at an authorized checking station after having validated the appropriate deer license tag or report the kill through automated reporting system	4 VAC 15-90-231(B)†	$50	$61	$111
Destroying the identity (sex) of deer before validating deer license tag and checking at an authorized checking station	4 VAC 15-90-231(C)†	$50	$61	$111
Unlawfully validate a turkey license tag prior to killing a turkey or after killing turkey failing to validate a turkey license tag before moving the carcass from the place of kill	4 VAC 15-240-81(A)†	$50	$61	$111

† These Regulations are promulgated pursuant to §§ 29.1-701 and 29.1-802 of the Code.
* The description of offense is for reference and is not a legal definition.
** Unless otherwise provided by statute.
*** See §§ 9.1-106 and 53.1-120 of the Code.

Description of Offense*	Statute or Regulation	Fine	Processing Fee***	Total
Failing to either present turkey carcass at an authorized checking station after having validated the appropriate turkey license tag or during the spring season only report the kill through automated reporting system	4 VAC 15-240-81(B)†	$50	$61	$111
Destroying the identity (sex) of turkey before validating turkey license tag and checking at an authorized checking system	4 VAC 15-240-81(C)†	$50	$61	$111
Failing to use nontoxic shot for waterfowl hunting	4 VAC 15-260-140†	$25	$61	$86
Using a rifle of a calibre less than 23 for hunting or killing of bear or deer	4 VAC 15-270-10†††	$100	$61	$161
Exceeding the creel limits for various species of fish on designated waters	4 VAC 15-320-25†	$60	$61	$121
Possessing illegal size game fish	4 VAC 15-320-25†	$25	$61	$86
Fishing in designated stocked trout waters or in water specified in the regulations listed (during the period from May 16 through September 30) after obtaining the daily creel limit of trout	4 VAC 15-330-80†	$50	$61	$111
Feeding or baiting trout in designated stocked trout waters	4 VAC 15-330-90†	$10	$61	$71

† These Regulations are promulgated pursuant to §§ 29.1-701 and 29.1-802 of the Code.
††† The Regulations are promulgated pursuant to § 29.1-501 of the Code.
* The description of offense is for reference and is not a legal definition.
** Unless otherwise provided by statute.
*** See §§ 9.1-106 and 53.1-120 of the Code.

Description of Offense*	Statute or Regulation	Fine	Processing Fee***	Total
Taking or attempting to take fish at any time by snagging, grabbing, snaring, gigging, with a striking iron, or with the use of SCUBA gear	4 VAC 15-350-10†	$50	$61	$111
Unlawfully using trotline, jugline or set pole	4 VAC 15-350-60†	$25	$61	$86
Failure to display light while drifting or at anchor	4 VAC 15-420-100††††	$25	$61	$86
Vessel failing to obey regulatory markers; placing in, on or near the water unauthorized regulatory markers	4 VAC 15-370-50†	$30	$61	$91
Failure to keep to starboard when meeting head and head	4 VAC 15-390-20††††	$30	$61	$91
Failure to yield right-of-way when crossing	4 VAC 15-390-30††††	$30	$61	$91
Failure to keep clear when overtaking another vessel	4 VAC 15-390-40(A)††††	$30	$61	$91
Failure of motorboat to yield right of way to sailing vessel	4 VAC 15-390-50††††	$35	$61	$96
Failure to slacken speed to avoid endangerment of persons or property by wake	4 VAC 15-390-80††††	$30	$61	$91
Failure of person at least age 18 occupying front seat of vehicle to use safety belt system	46.2-1094(A) 46.2-1094(C)	$25	—	$25

† These Regulations are promulgated pursuant to §§ 29.1-701 and 29.1-802 of the Code.

†††† The Regulations are promulgated pursuant to §§ 29.1-701 and 29.1- and 29.1-802 of the Code.

* The description of offense is for reference and is not a legal definition.

** Unless otherwise provided by statute.

*** See §§ 9.1-106 and 53.1-120 of the Code.

Description of Offense*	Statute or Regulation	Fine	Processing Fee***	Total
Failure of driver to ensure that child up to age 8 is properly secured in approved child restraint device (first violation only)	46.2-1095(A) 46.2-1098	$50	—	$50
Failure of driver to ensure that another person 8 through 17 years of age is properly secured by safety belt system (first violation only)	46.2-1095(B) 46.2-1098	$50	—	$50
Failure of driver to carry written statement exempting child from use of child restraint device	46.2-1096 46.2-1098	$20	—	$20
Refusing officer's order to drive vehicle to weighing station	46.2-1137	$35	$61	$96
Driving in violation of HOT Lane Restrictions (first offense)	33.1-56.3(C)	$50	$61	$111
Driving in violation of HOT Lane Restrictions (second offense)	33.1-56.3(C)	$250	$61	$311
Driving in violation of HOT Lane Restrictions (third offense within two years of second offense)	33.1-56.3(C)	$500	$61	$561
Driving in violation of HOT Lane Restrictions (fourth and subsequent offense within three years of second offense)	33.1-56.3(C)	$1000	$61	$1061

The amendment, effective August 15, 1997, adopted June 12, 1997, changed second column heading to "Statute or Regulation"; changed the fine schedule by increasing Processing fees by $1; added entries beginning "Boarding or riding VRE"; "Violating blaze"; "Unregistered motorboat"; "No registration"; "Failure to display registration"; "Failure to display expiration"; "Operation of vessel without proper safety equipment" through "Failure to keep to starboard in narrow channel". Changed "drunk" to "intoxicated" in one place; added "at least age 16" to entry beginning "Failure of person"; and

* The description of offense is for reference and is not a legal definition.

** Unless otherwise provided by statute.

*** See §§ 9.1-106 and 53.1-120 of the Code.

changed the statute entry from 46.2-1094(D) to 46.2-1094(C); rewrote entry beginning "Failure of driver", and changed the statute entry to 46.2-1095 in two places; changed "Failure of parent to assure..." to "Failure of driver to ensure...", and changed the statute entry 46.2-1095(i) to 46.2-1095(A); deleted entry beginning "Selling to, distributing" and "Purchasing or possessing"; deleted statute 28.2-903 and deleted entry beginning "Failure of driver other than parent" and deleted the last three entries.

The amendment, effective October 21, 1998, adopted October 21, 1998, substituted "17.1-281" for "14.1-133.2" in footnote ***.

The amendment, effective February 1, 1999, adopted November 23, 1998, inserted the entries beginning "Improper Identification of Crab Pots or Vessel" through "No or Closed Cull Rings in 16 to 20 pots."

The amendment, effective July 1, 2000, adopted May 1, 2000, deleted the entry beginning "Trespassing upon grass in Capitol Square" preceding the entry "Bringing unleashed dog into Capitol Square"; inserted the entries beginning "Trespassing upon lands to hunt, fish or trap without consent," "Computer invasion of privacy by intentionally examining personal information without authority, "Failing to report removal, alteration of trademark or identification numbers on a business machine," "Using games, contests, lotteries to promote sale of products having both federal and state tax"; deleted the entry beginning "Failing to secure or exhibit permits required for field trials" preceding "Making false statement to secure dog license"; inserted the entry beginning "Using recorded telephone solicitation calls for initial sales contacts" and the three entries immediately thereafter; inserted the entries beginning "Campaigning at election registration location" and "Failing to obey chief or other fire officer answering an alarm or operating at an emergency incident," the entry beginning "Unauthorized Transfer of license," the entries beginning "Failure to Display Commercial Hook and Line Pennant" and "More Unlicensed Commercial Hook and Line Crew Members than Allowed," the entry beginnning "Oystering in Closed Area (Sanctuaries)," and the entry beginning "Unlawful Use of Striped Bass Tags (note Order #)," substituted the word "Fishing" in the entry beginning "Failure to Exhibit Sport Fishing License," inserted the five entries immediately thereafter; deleted the entries beginning "Incomplete Striped Bass Permit Log Sheet" and "Fishing During Striped Bass Season without Permit" following "Sport Fishing without License"; inserted the entry "Failing to obtain permit for taxidermy" and the five entries immediately thereafter; inserted the entry beginning "Hunting on Sunday" and the five entries immediately thereafter; inserted the entry beginning "Operating motorboat at excessive speed when within 50 feet of docks, piers, ramps, people in water"; inserted the entry beginning "Constructing, maintaining or occupying unauthorized structures on department-owned lands or national forest lands" and the twenty-two entries immediately thereafter; and inserted the entry beginning "Vessel failure to obey regulatory markers; placing in, on or near the water unauthorized regulatory markers."

The amendment, effective July 1, 2001, adopted April 25, 2001, inserted the entry beginning "Failure to post signs regarding disposal of used motor oils" following the entry beginning "Leaving certain fires unattended or failing to extinguish the same."

The amendment, effective May 1, 2002, adopted April 29, 2002, increased the processing fee for all offenses from $28 to $40 and removed the removed the processing fees for the entries beginning: "Failure of driver to ensure that child under age 4 is properly secured in approved child restraint device." and "Failure of driver to carry written statement exempting child from use of child restraint device."

The amendment effective July 1, 2002, adopted April 29, 2002, substituted the offense "Failure of driver to ensure that child 6 through 15 years of age is properly secured by safety belt system 46.2-1095 (B) 46.2-1098 $50 — $50" for "Failure of driver to ensure that child 4 through 15 years of age is properly secured by safety belt system 46.2-1095(B) 46.2-1095(D) $25 — $25"; substituted "through age 5" for "under age 4" in the entry beginning "Failure of driver to ensure that child through age 5 is properly secured in approved child restraint device"; and deleted the entry beginning "Keeping certain reptiles or permitting same to run at large."

The amendment effective April 1, 2003, adopted January 14, 2003, inserted the entry beginning "Fishing 21 or More Crab Pots than Licensed PRF Reg I 2 d(1)[1] 2 $500"; and by increasing the total for the following entries, beginning "Exceeding Fish Catch Limits (note Order # per fish)" from $50 to $100, "Exceeding Unlicensed Recreational Crabbing Gear or Catch Limits" from $80 to $100, "Failure to Exhibit Sport Crabbing License" from $80 to $100, "Improper Identification of Sport Crabbing Gear" from $80 to $100, "Sport Fishing without License" from $75 to $85, "Fishing for Striped Bass During Closed Season without Barbless Hooks" from $50 to $100, "Possessing Unculled Crabs, 5 to 9" from $75 to $125, "Possessing Unculled Crabs, 10 to 14" from $150 to $200, "Possessing Unculled Crabs, 15 to 25" from $200 to $250, "Possessing Unculled Crabs, 26 or more" from $300 to $350, "Possessing Unculled Crabs — non commercial persons" from $75 to $125, "Crabbing at Night" from $150 to $200, "No Culling Container on Board" from $100 to $200, "Transporting Crabs not in Baskets or Barrels" from $100 to $200, "No or Closed Cull Rings in 1 to 5 Pots" from $100 to $150, "No or Closed Cull Rings in 6 to 10 Pots" from $200 to $250, "No or Closed Cull Rings in 11 to 15 Pots" from $300 to $400, and "No or Closed Cull Rings in 16 to 20 Pots" from $400 to $500."

The amendment effective July 1, 2003, adopted June 4, 2003, increased the processing fee for all offenses from $40 to $59; inserted the entry beginning "Keeping certain reptiles or permitting same"; inserted "checking" preceding "station" at the end of the entry beginning "Failing to present the tagged carcass of a bear"; deleted the former entries beginning "Detaching game tag from any license to hunt turkey" and "Failing to attach license/permit tag" following the entry beginning "Failing to present the tagged carcass of a deer"; substituted "Failure of driver to ensure that child 4 through 5 years of age is properly secured by safety belt system 46.2-1095(B) 46.2-1098 $50 — $50" for "Failure of driver to ensure that child 6 through 15 years of age is properly secured by safety belt system 46.2-1095(B) 46.2-1098 $50 — $50" and "Failure of driver to ensure that child under age 4 is properly secured in approved child restraint device 46.2-1095(A) 46.2-1098 $50 — $50" for "Failure of driver to ensure that child through age 5 is properly secured in approved child restraint device"; and substituted "§§ 9.1-106 and 53.1-120" for "§ 17.1-281" in footnote ***.

The amendment effective February 6, 2004, adopted February 6, 2004, inserted the entries beginning "Improper Identification of Sport Crabbing Gear," "Exceeding Licensed Sport Crabbing Catch Limits," "Detaching game tag from any license to hunt turkey prior to killing and tagging of a turkey," and "Failing to attach license/permit tag to the carcass of a turkey at the place of kill before removal"; and deleted the former entry beginning "Keeping certain reptiles or permitting same to run at large."

The amendment effective July 1, 2004, adopted August 9, 2004, increased the processing fee throughout; and made several minor stylistic changes.

The amendment effective December 27, 2004, adopted December 27, 2004, substituted the present nine entries beginning with "Unlawfully validate (notch) a bear license prior to killing a bear . . ." and ending with "Destroying the identity (sex) of turkey before validating . . ." for the former eight entries beginning with "Detaching game tag from any license to hunt bear . . ." and ending with "Failing to present the tagged carcass of a turkey . . . " and deleted the two entries beginning "Failure to operate at reduced speed when vision obscured . . ." and "Failure to keep to starboard in narrow channel . . .."

The amendment effective July 1, 2007, adopted April 13, 2007, increased the fees for the entries "Improper Identification of Crab Pots or Vessel [and accompanying descriptive entries]," "Improper Identification of Oyster Tong Vessel," "Improper Identification of Hand Scrape Vessel," "Failure to Display Commercial Hook and Line Pennant," "Improper Identification of Eel, Fish, or Bait Pots or Vessel [and accompanying descriptive entries]," "Improper Identification of Fish Trot Line [and accompanying descriptive entries]," Failure to Exhibit Commercial License [and accompanying descriptive entries]," "Possessing Patent Tong or Dredging Equipment without Permit [and accompanying descriptive entries]," "Not Culling on Oyster Bar," "Possessing Oysters in Containers," "Possessiong Oysters in Baskets without Permit," "Possessing Undersize Fish (note Order #) *per fish*," "Failure to Exhibit Sport Fishing License," "Exceeding Unlicensed Recreational Crabbing Gear or Catch Limits," "Possessing Unculled Crabs [and accompanying descriptive entries]," "Crabbing at Night," "Crab Potting During Closed Season," and "Transporting Crabs not in Baskets or Barrels [and accompanying descriptive entries]."

The amendment effective July 1, 2007, adopted June 11, 2007, increased the fees for the entries beginning "Drinking alcoholic beverage while driving motor vehicle" and "Refusing officer's order to drive vehicle to weighing station"; inserted the entries beginning with "Destruction of flowers, plants, minerals, etc. on a state park" and ending with "Landing an aircraft or parachute within a state park without a permit"; substituted "up to age 8" for "through age 5" in the entry beginning "Failure of driver to ensure that child ..."; and substituted "8" for "6" in the second entry beginning "Failure of driver to ensure that child ...."

The amendment adopted April 9, 2008, and effective immediately, deleted "(plus $900 civil remedial fee due in three payments: $300 due to court with fine and costs, $300 payment due to DMV within 14 months of conviction, and $300 payment due to DMV within 26 months of conviction. Civil remedial fee applicable to VA residents only.)" following the fine in entries for "Drinking alcoholic beverages while driving motor vehicle" and "Refusing officer's order to drive vehicle to weighing station," and lowered totals accordingly.

The amendment effective July 1, 2008, adopted June 6, 2008, in the two entries for "Failure of driver to ensure that child ..." added "(first violation only)" at the end of each; and added the four entries beginning "Driving in violation of HOT Lane Restrictions ..." at the end of the Rule.

The amendment effective July 13, 2009, adopted July 13, 2009, deleted the entry for "Boarding or riding VRE train without paying fare."

The amendment effective January 11, 2010, adopted January 11, 2010, substituted the correct Title 3.2 references for the former Title 3.1 references in five entries.

The amendment effective July 1, 2010, adopted June 1, 2010, added the entries beginning "Hunting or trapping in state forests without special use permit," "Hunting or trapping in state forests in violation of restrictions or conditions of special use permit," "Boarding or riding train without lawful payment of fare," "Unlawfully intercepting or monitoring employee/customer telephone calls," "Setting 1 to 5 More Crab Pots than Licensed," "Setting 6 to 10 More Crab Pots than Licensed," "Setting 11 to 15 More Crab Pots than Licensed," "Setting 16 to 20 More Crab Pots than Licensed," "Setting 21 or More Crab Pots than Licensed," "Sport Crabbing without License," "Improper Identification of Crab Pot Vessel," "Improper Identification of Crabbing Gear," "Failure to Separate Crabs per container," "Exceeding Crab Harvest Limit per bushel," "Persons in non-designated areas of a state park or failure to comply with a safety sign," "Bicycle in non-designated areas of a state park or failure to comply with a safety sign," "Importation of firewood into a state park contrary to the limitations imposed by the DCR Director," "Release of animals or wildlife captured or propagated elsewhere into a state park," and "Feeding wildlife on a state park,"; deleted entries for "Intoxicating liquors or beverage on a state park," and "Possession of any explosive substance on a state park (e.g. fireworks)"; increased fines in many entries throughout; and made amendments to the beginning text of various entries.

The amendment effective March 1, 2012, adopted December 22, 2011, deleted "and cost" following "a fine" in the first sentence, and added the second sentence, of the second paragraph; updated the Statute or Regulation cite for the entries beginning "Operating personal watercraft with wearing personal flotation device" and ending "Exceeding capacity on personal watercraft," "Unlawfully validate (notch) a bear ... of kill" and ending "Destroying the identitity (sex) of turkey ... checking system," "Exceeding the creel limits for various species of fish on designated waters," "Possessing illegal size game fish," and "Failure to display light while drifting or at anchor"; substituted "automated reporting system" for "telephone checking system" in the entry beginning "Failing to either present turkey carcass ..."; substituted "gigging, with a striking iron, or with the use of SCUBA gear" for "gigging and with a striking iron" in the entry beginning "Taking or attempting to take fish at any time ..."; in the 1 footnotes, substituted "PRF Reg" for "PRFC Reg"; and in the † footnotes, substituted "§§ 29.1-501 and 29.1-502" for "§§ 29.1-701 and 29.1-802."

The amendment effective January 1, 2013, adopted November 1, 2012, increased the fees for the entry beginning "Drinking alcoholic beverage while driving motor vehicle" and added the nine entries beginning "Crab Pots without Decal/Tag — 300 Pot License.'"

Michie's Jurisprudence. — For related discussion, see 5B M.J. Criminal Procedure, § 2.

PART THREE D
CIVIL PRACTICE AND PROCEDURE IN THE GENERAL DISTRICT COURTS

Rules 3D:1 through 3D:8. Repealed.

Editor's note. — Part Three D was repealed, effective July 1, 1989, by order adopted Nov. 21, 1988. For rules relating to the general district courts, see now Parts Seven A, Seven B and Seven C.

PART FOUR
PRETRIAL PROCEDURES, DEPOSITIONS AND PRODUCTION AT TRIAL

Rule
4:0. Application of Part Four.
4:1. General Provisions Governing Discovery.
4:2. Depositions Before Action or Pending Appeal.
4:3. Persons Before Whom Depositions May Be Taken.
4:4. Stipulations Regarding Discovery.
4:5. Depositions Upon Oral Examination.
4:6. Depositions Upon Written Questions.
4:6A. Number of Depositions.
4:7. Use of Depositions in Court Proceedings.
4:7A. Audio-Visual Depositions.
4:8. Interrogatories to Parties.
4:9. Production by Parties of Documents, Electronically Stored Information, and Things; Entry on Land for Inspection and Other Purposes; Production at Trial.
4:9A. Production from Non-Parties of Documents, Electronically Stored Information, and Things and Entry on Land for Inspection and Other Purposes; Production at Trial.
4:10. Physical and Mental Examination of Persons.
4:11. Requests for Admission.
4:12. Failure to Make Discovery; Sanctions.
4:13. Pretrial Procedure; Formulating Issues.
4:14. Disposition of Discovery Material.
4:15. Motions Practice.

Editor's note. — Part Four was revised, effective Oct. 1, 1977, by order adopted July 22, 1977.

Rule 4:0. Application of Part Four.

(a) The Rules in this Part Four shall apply in civil cases in the circuit courts. They also shall apply to proceedings for separate maintenance, divorce or annulment of marriage, for the exercise of the right of eminent domain, and for writs of habeas corpus or in the nature of coram nobis as provided in Rule 4:1(b)(5). Whenever in this Part Four the word "action" appears it shall mean a civil case, whether the claims arise at law or in equity.

(b) No provision of any of the Rules in this Part Four shall affect the practice of taking evidence at trial in any action; but such practice, including that of generally taking evidence ore tenus in actions upon claims arising at law and of generally taking evidence by deposition in equitable claims, shall continue unaffected hereby.

Comment. — The distinction between discovery depositions and depositions de bene esse in suits in equity has substantially disappeared in practice and no longer serves a useful purpose. Any deposition taken in a suit in equity may be used to the extent permitted by Rule 4:7(a).

The amendment, effective January 1, 2006, adopted June 14, 2005, in subdivision (a), deleted "in both actions at law and suits in equity" following "civil cases" in the first sentence and substituted "mean a civil case, whether the claims arise at law or" for "include a suit" in the third sentence; and in subdivision (b), inserted "upon claims arising" and substituted "equitable claims" for "equity suits."

Law Review. — For 2007 annual survey article, "Civil Practice and Procedure," see 42 U. Rich. L. Rev. 229 (2007).

Michie's Jurisprudence. — For related discussion, see 1B M.J. Appeal and Error, §§ 210, 212; 5A M.J. Courts, § 24; 5C M.J. Damages, § 51; 6A M.J. Discovery, § 2; 6A M.J. Divorce and Alimony, § 39; 6B M.J. Election of Remedies, § 7; 19 M.J. Trial, § 7.

Rule 4:1. General Provisions Governing Discovery.

(a) *Discovery Methods.* — Parties may obtain discovery by one or more of the following methods: depositions upon oral examination or written questions; written interrogatories; production of documents, electronically stored information, or things or permission to enter upon land or other property, for inspection and other purposes; physical and mental examinations; and requests for admission.

(b) *Scope of Discovery.* — Unless otherwise limited by order of the court in accordance with these Rules, the scope of discovery is as follows:

(1) In General. Parties may obtain discovery regarding any matter, not privileged, which is relevant to the subject matter involved in the pending action, whether it relates to the claim or defense of the party seeking discovery or to the claim or defense of any other party, including the existence, description, nature, custody, condition and location of any books, documents, or other tangible things and the identity and location of persons having knowledge of any discoverable matter. It is not ground for objection that the information sought will be inadmissible at the trial if the information sought appears reasonably calculated to lead to the discovery of admissible evidence. Subject to the provisions of Rule 4:8 (g), the frequency or extent of use of the discovery methods set forth in subdivision (a) shall be limited by the court if it determines that: (i) the discovery sought is unreasonably cumulative or duplicative, or is obtainable from some other source that is more convenient, less burdensome, or less expensive; (ii) the party seeking discovery has had ample opportunity by discovery in the action to obtain the information sought; or (iii) the discovery is unduly burdensome or expensive, taking into account the needs of the case, the amount in controversy, limitations on the parties' resources, and the importance of the issues at stake in the litigation. The court may act upon its own initiative after reasonable notice to counsel of record or pursuant to a motion under subdivision (c).

(2) Insurance Agreements. A party may obtain discovery of the existence and contents of any insurance agreement under which any person (which includes any individual, corporation, partnership or other association) carrying on an insurance business may be liable to satisfy part or all of a judgment which may be entered in the action or to indemnify or reimburse for payments made to satisfy the judgment. Information concerning the insurance agreement is not by reason of disclosure admissible in evidence at trial. For purposes of this paragraph, an application for insurance shall not be treated as part of an insurance agreement.

(3) Trial Preparation: Materials. Subject to the provisions of subdivision (b)(4) of this Rule, a party may obtain discovery of documents and tangible things otherwise discoverable under subdivision (b)(1) of this Rule and prepared in anticipation of litigation or for trial by or for another party or by or for that other party's representative (including his attorney, consultant, surety, indemnitor, insurer, or agent) only upon a showing that the party seeking discovery has substantial need of the materials in the preparation of his case and that he is unable without undue hardship to obtain the substantial equivalent of the materials by other means. In ordering discovery of such materials when the required showing has been made, the court shall protect against disclosure of the mental impressions, conclusions, opinions, or legal theories of an attorney or other representative of a party concerning the litigation.

A party may obtain without the required showing a statement concerning the action or its subject matter previously made by that party. Upon request, a person not a party may obtain without the required showing a statement concerning the action or its subject matter previously made by that person. If the request is refused, the person may move for a court order. The provisions of Rule 4:12(a)(4) apply to the award of expenses incurred in relation to the motion. For purposes of this paragraph, a statement previously made is (A) a written statement signed or otherwise adopted or approved by the person making it, or (B) a stenographic, mechanical, electrical, or other recording, or a transcription thereof, which is a substantially verbatim recital of an oral statement by the person making it and contemporaneously recorded.

(4) Trial Preparation: Experts; Costs — Special Provisions for Eminent Domain Proceedings. Discovery of facts known and opinions held by experts, otherwise discoverable under the provisions of subdivision (b)(1) of this Rule and acquired or developed in anticipation of litigation or for trial, may be obtained only as follows:

(A) (i) A party may through interrogatories require any other party to identify each person whom the other party expects to call as an expert witness at trial, to state the subject matter on which the expert is expected to testify, and to state the substance of the facts and opinions to which the expert is expected to testify and a summary of the grounds for each opinion. (ii) A party may depose any person who has been identified as an expert whose opinion may be presented at trial, subject to the provisions of subdivision (b)(4)(C) of this Rule concerning fees and expenses. (iii) Upon motion, the court may order further discovery by other means, subject to such restrictions as to scope and such provisions, pursuant to subdivision (b)(4)(C) of this Rule, concerning fees and expenses as the court may deem appropriate.

(B) A party may discover facts known or opinions held by an expert who has been retained or specially employed by another party in anticipation of litigation or preparation for trial and who is not expected to be called as a witness at trial, only upon a showing of exceptional circumstances under which it is impracticable for the party seeking discovery to obtain facts or opinions on the same subject by other means.

(C) Unless manifest injustice would result, (i) the court shall require that the party seeking discovery pay the expert a reasonable fee for time spent and expenses incurred in responding to discovery under subdivisions (b)(4)(A)(ii), (b)(4)(A)(iii), and (b)(4)(B) of this Rule; and (ii) with respect to discovery obtained under subdivision (b)(4)(A)(iii) of this Rule the court may require, and with respect to discovery obtained under subdivision (b)(4)(B) of this Rule the court shall require, the party seeking discovery to pay the other party a fair portion of the fees and expenses reasonably incurred by the latter party in obtaining facts and opinions from the expert.

(D) Notwithstanding the provisions of subdivision (b)(4)(C) of this Rule, the condemnor in eminent domain proceedings, when it initiates discovery, shall pay all costs thereof, including without limitation the cost and expense of those experts discoverable under subdivision (b) of this Rule. The condemnor shall be deemed to have initiated discovery if it uses, or gives notice of the use of, any discovery method before the condemnee does so, even though the condemnee subsequently engages in discovery.

(5) Limitations on Discovery in Certain Proceedings. In any proceeding (1) for separate maintenance, divorce, or annulment of marriage, (2) for the exercise of the right of eminent domain, or (3) for a writ of habeas corpus or in the nature of coram nobis; (a) the scope of discovery shall extend only to matters which are relevant to the issues in the proceeding and which are not privileged; and (b) no discovery shall be allowed in any proceeding for a writ of habeas corpus or in the nature of coram nobis without prior leave of the court, which may deny or limit discovery in any such proceeding. In any proceeding for divorce or annulment of marriage, a notice to take depositions must be served in the Commonwealth by an officer authorized to serve the same, except that, in cases where such suits have been commenced and an appearance has been made on behalf of the defendant by counsel, notices to take depositions may be served in accordance with Rule 1:12.

(6) Claims of Privilege or Protection of Trial Preparation Materials. (i) When a party withholds information otherwise discoverable under these rules by claiming that it is privileged or subject to protection as trial preparation material, the party shall make the claim expressly and shall describe the nature of the documents, communications, or things not produced or disclosed in a manner that, without revealing information itself privileged or protected, will enable other parties to assess the applicability of the privilege or protection.

(ii) If a party believes that a document or electronically stored information that has already been produced is privileged or its confidentiality is otherwise protected the producing party may notify any other party of such claim and the basis for the claimed privilege or protection. Upon receiving such notice, any party holding a copy of the designated material shall sequester or destroy its copies thereof, and shall not duplicate or disseminate such material pending disposition of the claim of privilege or protection by agreement, or upon motion by any party. If a receiving party has disclosed the information before being notified of the claim of privilege or other protection, that party must take reasonable steps to retrieve the designated material. The producing party must preserve the information until the claim of privilege or other protection is resolved.

(7) Electronically Stored Information. A party need not provide discovery of electronically stored information from sources that the party identifies as not reasonably accessible because of undue burden or cost. On motion to compel discovery or for a protective order, the party from whom discovery is sought must show that the information is not reasonably accessible because of undue burden or cost. If that showing is made, the court may nonetheless order discovery from such sources if the requesting party shows good cause, considering the limitations of Rule 4:1(b)(1). The court may specify conditions for the discovery, including allocation of the reasonable costs thereof.

(8) Pre-Motion Negotiation. A motion under this Rule must be accompanied by a certification that the movant has in good faith conferred or attempted to confer with other affected parties in an effort to resolve the dispute without court action.

(c) *Protective Orders.* — Upon motion by a party or by the person from whom discovery is sought, accompanied by a certification that the movant has in good faith conferred or attempted to confer with other affected parties in an effort to resolve the dispute without court action, and for good cause shown, the court in which the action is pending or alternatively, on matters relating to a deposition, the court in the county or city where the deposition is to be taken, may make any order which justice requires to protect a party or person from annoyance, embarrassment, oppression, or undue burden or expense, including one or more of the following: (1) that the discovery not be had; (2) that the discovery may be had only on specified terms and conditions, including a designation of the time or place; (3) that the discovery may be had only by a method of discovery other than that selected by the party seeking discovery; (4) that certain matters not be inquired into, or that the scope of the discovery be limited to certain matters; (5) that discovery be conducted with no one present except persons designated by the court; (6) that a deposition after being sealed be opened only by order of the court; (7) that a trade secret or other confidential research, development, or commercial information not be disclosed or be disclosed only in a designated way; (8) that the parties simultaneously file specified documents or information enclosed in sealed envelopes to be opened as directed by the court.

If the motion for a protective order is denied in whole or in part, the court may, on such terms and conditions as are just, order that any party or person provide or permit discovery. The provisions of Rule 4:12(a)(4) apply to the award of expenses incurred in relation to the motion.

(d) *Sequence and Timing of Discovery.* — (1) Unless the court upon motion, for the convenience of parties and witnesses and in the interests of justice, orders otherwise, methods of discovery may be used in any sequence and the fact that a party is conducting discovery, whether by deposition or otherwise, shall not operate to delay any other party's discovery.

(2) Discovery shall continue after a demurrer, plea or dispositive motion addressing one or more claims or counter-claims has been filed and while such motion is pending decision — unless the court in its discretion orders that discovery on some or all issues in the action should be suspended.

(e) *Supplementation of Responses.* — A party who has responded to a request for discovery is under a duty to supplement or correct the response to include information thereafter acquired in the following circumstances.

(1) A party is under a duty promptly to amend and/or supplement all responses to discovery requests directly addressed to (A) the identity and location of persons having knowledge of discoverable matters, and (B) the identity of each person expected to be called as an expert witness at trial, the subject matter on which the expert is expected to testify, and the substance of the expert's testimony, when additional or corrective information becomes available.

(2) A party is under a duty promptly to amend and/or supplement all other prior responses to interrogatories, requests for production, or requests for admission if the party learns that any such response is in some material respect incomplete or incorrect and if the additional or corrective information has not otherwise been made known to the other parties during the discovery process or in writing.

(3) A court may order, or the parties may agree to provide, supplementation in addition to that required in subsections (1) and (2) of this subpart (e).

(4) A party may supplement a prior discovery response by filing an updated response labelled "Supplemental" or "Amended", or by otherwise notifying all other parties of the updated information in writing, signed by counsel of record.

(f) *Service Under This Part.* — Except for the service of the notice required under Rule 4:2(a)(2), any notice or document required or permitted to be served under this Part Four shall be served as provided in Rule 1:12 except that any notice or document permitted to be served with the initial pleading shall be served (or accepted) in the same manner as such pleading.

(g) *Signing of Discovery Requests, Responses, and Objections.* — Every request for discovery or response or objection thereto made by a party represented by an attorney shall be signed by at least one attorney of record in the attorney's individual name, whose address shall be stated. A party who is not represented by an attorney shall sign the request, response, or objection, and state the party's address. The signature of the attorney or party constitutes a certification that the signer has read the request, response, or objection, and that to the best of the signer's knowledge, information, and belief formed after a reasonable inquiry it is: (1) consistent with these Rules and warranted by existing law or a good faith argument for extension, modification, or reversal of existing law; (2) not interposed for any improper purpose, such as to harass or to cause unnecessary delay or needless increase in the cost of litigation; and (3) not unreasonable or unduly burdensome or expensive, given the needs of the case, the discovery already had in the case, the amount in controversy and the importance of the issues at stake in the litigation. If a request, response, or objection is not signed, it shall be stricken unless it is signed promptly after the omission is called to the attention of the party making the request, response, or objection, and a party shall not be obligated to take any action with respect to it until it is signed.

If a certification is made in violation of the rule, the court, upon motion or upon its own initiative, shall impose upon the person who made the certification, the party on whose behalf the request, response, or objection is made, or both, an appropriate sanction, which may include an order to pay the amount of the reasonable expenses incurred because of the violation, including a reasonable attorney's fee.

Cross references. — As to limiting further disclosure of discoverable materials and information and protective orders, see § 8.01-420.01, Code of Virginia.

As to disclosure of a communication or information covered by attorney-client privilege or work product protection, see § 8.01-427.

Comment on the 1983 amendment. — The Rules are confusing as to filing. Depositions are filed (Rules 4:2(a)(5); 4:5(f); 4:6(b)). The requirement of filing is not clear as to answers to interrogatories and admissions. This amendment makes the filing requirement unmistakable.

Comment. — Although the encompassing reference to "other papers" § 8.01-271.1 literally includes discovery papers, the certification requirement in that context is governed by new Rule 4:1(g). Discovery motions, however, fall within the ambit of § 8.01-271.1.

The amendment, effective July 1, 1999, adopted January 25, 1999, added subdivision (b)(6).

The amendment, effective January 1, 2001, adopted September 28, 2000, rewrote subdivision (e).

The amendment, effective January 1, 2002, adopted October 1, 2001, in subdivision (b)(4), in subparagraph (A), renumbered former sub-subparagraph (ii) as (iii) and added present (ii); in subparagraph (C), in item (i), deleted "his" following "spent and," and in item (ii), inserted "(b)(4)(A)(iii)" following "(b)(4)(A)(ii)" and substituted "(b)(4)(A)(iii)" for "(b)(4)(A)(ii)."

The amendment, effective January 1, 2002, adopted November 2, 2001, in subdivision (e), deleted "Disclosures and" from the heading; in the introductory paragraph, deleted "with a disclosure or response" following "for discovery," and deleted "disclosure or" preceding "response to include"; rewrote paragraphs (1) and (2); and added paragraphs (3) and (4).

The amendment, effective January 1, 2003, adopted November 1, 2002, in subdivision (c), in the first paragraph, inserted "accompanied by a certification that the movant has in good faith conferred or attempted to confer with other affected parties in an effort to resolve the dispute without court action" following "discovery is sought" in the first sentence.

The amendment, effective January 1, 2009, adopted October 1, 2008, inserted "electronically stored information" near the middle of subdivision (a); in subdivision (b)(6), designated the existing provisions as clause (i), and added clause (ii) thereof; and added subdivisions (b)(7) and (b)(8).

The amendment, effective May 3, 2010, adopted February 26, 2010, in subdivision (d), added the (1) designator to the existing language, and added paragraph (2).

Law Review. — For article on corporate and institutional accident investigations as work product pursuant to Rule 4:1(b)(3), see 17 U. Rich. L. Rev. 285 (1983). For article, "The Newsman's Confidential Source Privilege in Virginia," see 22 U. Rich. L. Rev. 377 (1988). For survey on civil procedure and practice in Virginia for 1989, see 23 U. Rich. L. Rev. 511 (1989). For survey on medical malpractice in Virginia for 1989, see 23 U. Rich. L. Rev. 731 (1989). For article, "Rethinking Work Product," see 77 Va. L. Rev. 1515 (1991). For essay "Protective Orders in Products Liability Litigation: Striking the Proper Balance," see 48 Wash. & Lee L. Rev. 1503 (1991). For a note, "Allocating Discovery Costs in the Computer Age: Deciding Who Should Bear the Costs of Discovery of Electronically Stored Data," see 57 Wash. & Lee L. Rev. 257 (2000). For 2003/2004 survey of civil practice and procedure, see 39 U. Rich. L. Rev. 87 (2004). For 2007 annual survey article, "Electronic Data: A Commentary on the Law in Virginia in 2007," see 42 U. Rich. L. Rev. 355 (2007). For article on medical malpractice law for the year 2007-2008, see 43 U. Rich. L. Rev. 227 (2008). For annual survey of Virginia law article, "Civil Practice and Procedure," see 47 U. Rich. L. Rev. 113 (2012).

Research References. — Arthur Ian Miltz, Art of Advocacy: Discovery (Matthew Bender).

Michie's Jurisprudence. — For related discussion, see 6A M.J. Discovery, §§ 3 - 7, 23, 34; 10B M.J. Insurance, §§ 161, 222.

CASE NOTES

Granting or denying of a request for discovery is a matter within the trial court's discretion and will be reversed only if the action taken was improvident and affected substantial rights.

Rakes v. Fulcher, 210 Va. 542, 172 S.E.2d 751 (1970).

Abuse of discretion. — Trial court erred in denying the alleged debtor the opportunity to conduct discovery regarding the alleged debtor's defense of double recovery in a case where the alleged creditor settled another action involving the assignment of loans to a trust, including the alleged debtor's loan, with another entity and the alleged debtor sought to assert the defense in the current action of double recovery; the alleged debtor sought not to assert that the alleged debtor's loan, on which the alleged debtor was a guarantor, had been discharged, but instead raised the defense of double recovery, the statute involving discharge, § 8.3A-601, did not in any event displace the defense of double recovery, and the trial court affected the alleged debtor's substantial rights in not allowing discovery to determine if the double recovery defense could be established. Nizan v. Wells Fargo Bank Minn. N.A., 274 Va. 481, 650 S.E.2d 497, 2007 Va. LEXIS 117 (2007).

Discovery ordinarily should not supplant the taking of evidence at a trial. Slone v. GMC, 249 Va. 520, 457 S.E.2d 51 (1995).

Pretrial depositions and interrogatories are not public components of a civil trial. There is no authority, respecting either a pre-judgment or a post-judgment right of public access to discovery data at common law, and in Virginia, trial courts are expressly authorized by this rule "for good cause shown [to] make any order which justice requires to protect a party or person from annoyance, embarrassment, oppression, or undue burden or expense." Shenandoah Publishing House, Inc. v. Fanning, 235 Va. 253, 368 S.E.2d 253 (1988).

Discoverable records. — Section 2.2-3704, restricting access to information under Virginia's Freedom of Information Act to Virginia citizens did not abridge the ability of petitioner, an out-of-state searcher for his title company clients, to engage in a common calling in the sense the Privileges and Immunities Clause prohibited and a claim of constitutional violation by defendant state officials for denying the information sought failed; many records were available through other means, such as through discovery or subpoenas under Va. Sup. Ct. R. 4:1, 4:9, or the under the Government Data Collection and Dissemination Practices Act, subdivision A 3 of § 2.2-3806. McBurney v. Young, 133 S. Ct. 1709, 185 L. Ed. 2d 758, 2013 U.S. LEXIS 3317 (2013).

Expert's opinion based on unsupported factual assumptions. — Since plaintiffs did not disclose the nature of the expert's opinion and the facts upon which he was going to rely to reach that opinion, the defendants were not considered to have waived their § 8.01-401.1 objection to the expert's opinion testimony when the expert was permitted to testify and while the trial court reserved its decision as to admissibility under Va. Sup. Ct. R. 5:25. Vasquez v. Mabini, 269 Va. 155, 606 S.E.2d 809, 2005 Va. LEXIS 10 (2005).

Expert witness disclosure requirements. — Sued railroad company's error claim, arising from an injured conductor's failure to comply fully with the expert disclosure requirements set out in Va. Sup. Ct. R. 4:1, was rendered moot because the conductor's Federal Employers' Liability Act, 45 U.S.C.S. §§ 51-60, personal injury suit was being remanded back. The company was now fully aware of the substance of the testimony that the expert would present should the conductor's case be retried. Norfolk & Portsmouth Belt Line R.R. Co. v. Wilson, 276 Va. 739, 667 S.E.2d 735, 2008 Va. LEXIS 117 (Oct. 31, 2008).

Any error in the Department of Human Services's failure to disclose a doctor as an expert was harmless, because the guardian ad litem was not required to disclose experts where the mother failed to request such disclosure in an interrogatory and the guardian would have called doctor as an expert for the child had the doctor's testimony been otherwise excluded. Hey v. Arlington County Dep't of Human Servs., 2008 Va. App. LEXIS 572 (Dec. 30, 2008).

Where an expert designation was sufficient and complied with Va. Sup. Ct. R. 4:1(b)(4), the fact that it did not contain the precise amounts of penalties and interest did not make the designation deficient because the types of damages were clearly disclosed. Condo. Servs. v. First Owners' Ass'n of Forty Six Hundred Condo., Inc., 281 Va. 561, 709 S.E.2d 163, 2011 Va. LEXIS 94 (2011).

Circuit court did not abuse its discretion in excluding a patient's expert witnesses on the ground that it disregarded Va. Sup. Ct. R. 4:1(g) because the rule was not violated since the supplemental designation was signed by at least one attorney of record; the problem was that the patients' out-of-state attorney was not admitted to practice law in Virginia, and therefore, Va. Sup. Ct. R. 1A:4(2) was implicated. Landrum v. Chippenham & Johnston-Willis Hosps., Inc., 282 Va. 346, 717 S.E.2d 134, 2011 Va. LEXIS 224 (2011).

Circuit court did not abuse its discretion in excluding a patient's expert witnesses because it warned the patient multiple times that her failure to obey its pretrial orders would lead to sanctions, including the exclusion of the expert witnesses; the patient proved herself unable to comply with the rules, running afoul of not just Va. Sup. Ct. R. 1A:4(2) and 4:1(b)(4)(A)(i), but also Va. Sup. Ct. R. 1A:4(3), 4:1(e)(1)(B), and 4:15. Landrum v. Chippenham & Johnston-Willis Hosps., Inc., 282 Va. 346, 717 S.E.2d 134, 2011 Va. LEXIS 224 (2011).

In a termination of parental rights case, because the department did not fail to comply with an interrogatory requesting expert designations or pre-trial disclosure of expert opinions and father was aware of the information the expert was using to form her opinions, the trial court did not abuse its discretion in allowing the expert to qualify as an expert. Farrell v. Warren County Dep't of Soc. Servs., 59 Va. App. 375, 719 S.E.2d 329, 2012 Va. App. LEXIS 1 (2012).

When discovery should not be granted. — Where both parties have an equal opportunity to investigate, and where all the witnesses to the accident are known and available to both sides, discovery should not be granted. Rakes v. Fulcher, 210 Va. 542, 172 S.E.2d 751 (1970).

Due process not denied. — While substitute counsel may have encountered unexpected problems related to the condition of the case's files, the court's refusal to extend its discovery cut-off or to allow the use of supplementary documents did not deny father due process of law. Evans v. Evans, No. 2281-96-4 (Ct. of Appeals Apr. 1, 1997).

Construction with federal habeas order. — The fact that the federal district court entered a broad discovery order even before federal habeas counsel had advanced a *Brady* claim did not demonstrate that a state court also would have done so. Indeed, under Virginia law, petitioner would not have been entitled to such discovery in state habeas proceedings without a showing of good cause. Strickler v. Greene, 527 U.S. 263, 119 S. Ct. 1936, 144 L. Ed. 2d 286 (1999).

Discovery procedures were not intended to open an attorney's files to opposing counsel. Rakes v. Fulcher, 210 Va. 542, 172 S.E.2d 751 (1970).

Nor to have opposing counsel investigate case. — Discovery procedures were not intended to afford an attorney the luxury of having opposing counsel investigate his case for him. Rakes v. Fulcher, 210 Va. 542, 172 S.E.2d 751 (1970).

"Work product" doctrine, which protects an attorney from opening his files for inspection by an opposing attorney, does not offer absolute immunity, and discovery will be permitted where a showing of necessity greater than the normal requirement for good cause is made. Rakes v. Fulcher, 210 Va. 542, 172 S.E.2d 751 (1970).

Evidence of post-accident design change was properly discoverable because that evidence, although inadmissible, was reasonably likely to lead to the discovery of admissible evidence. Turner v. Manning, Maxwell & Moore, Inc., 216 Va. 245, 217 S.E.2d 863 (1975).

Tax returns were discoverable in legal malpractice claim because they were relevant to plaintiff's damage claim and are not privileged. Lyle, Siegel, Croshaw & Beale v. Tidewater Capital Corp., 249 Va. 426, 457 S.E.2d 28 (1995).

Sanctions improperly imposed for failing to produce autopsy report. — An attorney representing an estate in a medical malpractice case was not subject to sanctions for failing to produce an autopsy report prepared at the request of the decedent's family a number of months after the decedent's death to determine whether a malpractice claim might be warranted where, after reasonable inquiry, the attorney could have formed a reasonable belief that the report was not a medical report discoverable under Rule 4:9 but, instead, was an expert's report discoverable only in compliance with the provisions of subdivision (b)(4) of this rule and the circuit court's scheduling order. Flora v. Shulmister, 262 Va. 215, 546 S.E.2d 427, 2001 Va. LEXIS 69 (2001).

As a husband never asked for expert reports pursuant to Rule 4:1, never filed a motion to compel the reports, and never asked for sanctions, the trial court improperly "short circuited" the legal process by prematurely imposing sanctions and preventing the wife from presenting evidence through her expert witnesses. Cirrito v. Cirrito, 44 Va. App. 287, 605 S.E.2d 268, 2004 Va. App. LEXIS 574 (2004).

Wife's tax returns irrelevant in action for delinquent support. — Since the court was without authority to make any change as to past due installments of alimony and child support, the wife's tax returns for 10 years preceding an action for delinquent support payments were irrelevant. Johnson v. Johnson, 1 Va. App. 330, 338 S.E.2d 353 (1986).

Discoverable records in support modification proceeding. — While records probative of husband's financial status prior to the divorce were arguable irrelevant to the instant proceedings for modification of previously ordered support, records of husband's economic circumstances subsequent to the earlier order, including the financial particulars of his corporation, were proper subjects of inquiry which appeared reasonably calculated to lead to the discovery of admissible evidence. Mancini v. Mancini, No. 1420-96-1 (Ct. of Appeals Apr. 8, 1997).

Failure to supplement did not necessitate exclusion of evidence. — Trial court was not required to bar non-disclosed evidence of attorney fees from being admitted at trial because the husband was not prejudiced by the wife's failure to supplement the original disclosure; the husband could not realistically assume that the wife did not continue to incur legal fees in the months preceding trial and the husband did not contend that the husband needed more time to study the invoices to insure the reasonableness of the fees or the hours devoted to specific litigation tasks. Hardey v. Metzger, 2008 Va. App. LEXIS 409 (Aug. 26, 2008).

Applied in Yeatts v. Murray, 249 Va. 285, 455 S.E.2d 18 (1995); Lee Gardens Arlington Ltd. Partnership v. Arlington County Bd., 250 Va. 534, 463 S.E.2d 646 (1995); Ayala v. Aggressive Towing & Transp., Inc., 276 Va. 169, 661 S.E.2d 480, 2008 Va. LEXIS 79 (2008).

CIRCUIT COURT OPINIONS

Privilege logs insufficient. — Defendant's privilege logs failed to comply with Va. Sup. Ct. R. 4:1(b)(6) as they contained numerous discrete pieces of information, gathered by various individuals at various dates for various purposes, and no specific information was provided with regard to any of these discrete pieces of information. Eppard v. Kelly, 62 Va. Cir. 57, 2003 Va. Cir. LEXIS 313 (Charlottesville 2003).

Witness under subpoena may not be excused by opposing counsel. — No provision in the Virginia Supreme Court Rules allows opposing counsel to excuse a witness under subpoena from attending a properly noticed deposition. Estate of Smith, 65 Va. Cir. 267, 2004 Va. Cir. LEXIS 153 (Madison County 2004).

Insurance agreements discoverable, but not admissible. — Trial court granted the insurance company's motion to prohibit, during trial, any mention of the insurance company's involvement in the case or its compensation to the insured for the allegedly negligent act of the tenant in causing a fire that burned the insured apartment; not only did the insurance company have a statutory right to bring the case in the name of the insured to avoid unfair prejudice, but the Virginia Supreme Court Rules, while making insurance agreements discoverable, expressly states that they were not admissible in evidence at trial. LeChow v. Reese, 63 Va. Cir. 110, 2003 Va. Cir. LEXIS 167 (Arlington County 2003).

Expert witness. — Plaintiff's expert witness was precluded from giving his opinion at trial because (1) the plaintiff failed to file a supplemental interrogatory answer furnishing required expert witness information, pursuant to Rule 4:1; (2) the report of the expert witness did not adequately set forth a summary of the grounds for each opinion; and (3) much of the proposed expert opinion invaded the province of the jury and was based on inadequate foundation. Goodman v. Hensley, 66 Va. Cir. 65, 2004 Va. Cir. LEXIS 261 (Nelson County 2004).

Because an arborist's opinion did not appear to be based on conjecture, a weather expert was a well-qualified meteorologist, and an economist's testimony would assist the jury, their testimony would not be excluded in an individual's personal injury action; however, because the individual failed to timely furnish an orthopedist's designation, and a vocational/rehabilitation expert's testimony was based on the orthopedist's testimony, their testimonies had to be excluded. Belshe v. Pinecrest Cluster Ass'n, 68 Va. Cir. 89, 2005 Va. Cir. LEXIS 56 (Fairfax County 2005).

First alleged debtor and second alleged debtor's legal malpractice expert was not properly disclosed pursuant to Va. Sup. Ct. R. 4:1(b)(4)(A)(i) regarding their legal malpractice counterclaim against the law firm trying to collect alleged outstanding attorney fees from them. They did not state the substance of facts to which the expert was expected to testify and did not provide a summary of the grounds for each of the opinions the expert expressed, which meant that the expert's testimony was inadmissible and could not be presented. Cook, Heyward, Lee, Hopper & Feehan, P.C. v. D'Eramo, 2007 Va. Cir. LEXIS 267 (Newport News Oct. 15, 2007).

Expert witness designation requirements. — Fair reading of defendants' designations of two orthopedic surgeons compelled the circuit court to deny plaintiff's motions to partially strike the designations because the designations had to be read as a whole, and so long as the requirements of the Va. Sup. Ct. R. 4:1(b)(4)(i) were met, the designations could withstand scrutiny; however, the motions were denied without prejudice to plaintiff to raise specific objections to the surgeons' testimony at trial based upon the designations. Graham v. Cook, 75 Va. Cir. 359, 2008 Va. Cir. LEXIS 263 (Loudoun County July 18, 2008).

Corporation's motion to quash a limited liability company's subpoena duces tecum of its expert witnesses was granted because compliance with the subpoenas would suggest another means at obtaining expert discovery not permitted by the Rules of the Supreme Court of Virginia; the Rules of the Supreme Court of Virginia control discovery of the facts known and opinions held by experts, Va. Sup. Ct. R. 4:1(b)(4). Pac. Century Dev. & Realty, Inc. v. Wheatland Farms, LLC, 2007 Va. Cir. LEXIS 340 (Loudoun County Mar. 28, 2007).

Amendment of expert list. — Due to the differences in the victim's and a witness's accounts of their "date rapes," the witness could not testify at trial, and the victim's motion to reconsider was denied; nevertheless, although evidence of drugging was excluded, the non-physician experts could testify and the expert designations could be amended. Hylton v. Hamilton, 68 Va. Cir. 305, 2005 Va. Cir. LEXIS 197 (Charlottesville Aug. 3, 2005).

Expert witness disclosure requirements. — Certifying opinion of plaintiff's expert was not discoverable as under § 8.01-20.1, a certifying expert was to remain confidential even after the expert was designated to testify at trial under Va. Sup. Ct. R. 4:1; the expert's certifying opinions and the basis for those opinions were not discoverable under Va. Sup. Ct. R. 4:1 and remained confidential. Grimaldi v. Burgess, 78 Va. Cir. 104, 2009 Va. Cir. LEXIS 13 (Fairfax County 2009).

Seasonable supplementation. — Trial court granted the health care providers motion to strike the testimony of the claimant's treating physician and another one of the claimant's expert witnesses; the claimant's failure for 10 months after standard expert witness interrogatories were propounded upon the claimant to disclose the treating physician and the other expert as expert witnesses and disclosure of them a mere five days before the trial court's scheduling deadline was not the required seasonable supplementation of discovery that the claimant was obligated to provide. Oakey v. Warren, 2007 Va. Cir. LEXIS 129 (Norfolk July 23, 2007).

Business invitee failed to show doctor selected to conduct examination was inappropriate. — Although a business invitee could normally challenge a doctor chosen by a grocery store to conduct a Va. Sup. Ct. R. 4:10(a) examination at a hearing on the store's motion for a Rule 4:10(a) examination, a doctor did not have to appear pursuant to a witness subpoena at a hearing on the store's motion for a Rule 4:10(a) examination as the invitee failed to make a prima facie valid objection to the doctor conducting the examination at a hearing on the doctor's motion for a protective order. Young v. Food Lion Store No. 622, 70 Va. Cir. 313, 2006 Va. Cir. LEXIS 31 (Portsmouth 2006).

Discovery requests adequately defined and relevant or likely to lead to relevant evidence. — Court granted defendant surety's Va. Sup. Ct. R. 4:12(a) motion to compel a plaintiff contractor to answer interrogatories and to provide documents because the information that the surety sought was adequately defined and was either relevant to the defense or was likely to lead to the discovery of relevant evidence. Dustin Constr. v. Selby Constr., 67 Va. Cir. 229, 2005 Va. Cir. LEXIS 168 (Loudoun County Apr. 7, 2005).

Because a subpoena duces tecum issued by a manufacturer and a distributor met the threshold requirements in Va. Sup. Ct. R. 4:1(b)(1), because the discovery sought was relevant in that it might lead to the identity of a subcontractor, and because a retailer's trade secrets could be adequately protected by a protective order, a limited motion to compel compliance with the subpoena would issue to the retailer. Lacoste Alligator, S.A. v. Doe, 81 Va. Cir. 412, 2010 Va. Cir. LEXIS 268 (Arlington County Dec. 17, 2010).

Relevant to the issues in the proceeding. — Phrase "relevant to the issues in the proceeding" in Va. Sup. Ct. R. 4:1(b)(5)(a) means the discovery must be relevant to an issue raised in the petition, the motion to dismiss, or the opposition to the motion to dismiss, not that discovery is to be allowed to the petitioner in the hope he or she might discover a new issue. Juniper v. Warden of the Sussex I State Prison, 2010 Va. Cir. LEXIS 201 (Norfolk Dec. 20, 2010).

Request relevant but exceeded scope of authority. — Court agreed that the larger area the injured party sought to measure and examine would be helpful and relevant, as a jury would have to determine if the railroad company provided a safe workplace. The court further concluded, however, that the request exceeded the scope of the railroad company's authority because the railroad company only had limited access pursuant to an agreement with another company that controlled the subject track area. Wilson v. Norfolk & Portsmouth Belt Line R.R. Co., 70 Va. Cir. 383, 2006 Va. Cir. LEXIS 44 (Portsmouth 2006).

Overly broad requests. — Granting of the driver's motion to compel was proper, in part, because the passenger put his mental and physical state at issue by filing the present lawsuit and affirmatively chose to share potentially relevant information with others on the internet and thus, his privacy expectations were therefore misplaced. However, the requests were overly broad and thus, the court would set limits on the amount and manner of access. James v. Edwards, 85 Va. Cir. 139, 2012 Va. Cir. LEXIS 183 (Greensville County July 23, 2012).

Information sought was beyond the scope of discovery. — Information regarding the hiring and credentialing of a doctor from his practice's personnel file was beyond the scope of discovery under Va. Sup. Ct. R. 4:1(b)(1) in light of the dismissal of the negligent credentialing, negligent hiring, and fraudulent representation claims filed by the executrix. Clements v. MCV Associated Physicians, 61 Va. Cir. 673, 2002 Va. Cir. LEXIS 419 (Richmond 2002).

Request for depositions of individuals, involved in the hiring process and with information about the doctor's eligibility to take the board examinations, made by an executrix were beyond the scope of discovery under Va. Sup. Ct. R. 4:1 as the negligent credentialing, negligent hiring, and fraudulent representation claims had been dismissed. Clements v. MCV Associated Physicians, 61 Va. Cir. 673, 2002 Va. Cir. LEXIS 419 (Richmond 2002).

Reports prepared by a third party company at the request of defendant after defendant received notice of plaintiff's claim of injury were protected as work product prepared in anticipation of litigation and did not need to be produced absent a showing by plaintiff of substantial need and inability to obtain the information elsewhere. McDonald v. Sentara Med. Group, 64 Va. Cir. 30, 2004 Va. Cir. LEXIS 176 (Norfolk 2004).

Under Va. Sup. Ct. R. 4:1(b)(5), an inmate was not entitled, in a habeas proceeding, to discover information related to the indictment and conviction of a third party because: (1) the inmate was only entitled to discovery of matters relevant to issues in the habeas proceeding; (2) nothing showed the discovery the inmate sought was relevant to any of the issues the inmate raised in the inmate's habeas petition, including juror misconduct, the Commonwealth's concealment of material exculpatory evidence, ineffective assistance of counsel, and deprivation of a fair trial; and (3) the inmate's allegation that the circumstances described in the third party's indictment included numerous similarities to the inmate's case was false. Porter v. Warden of the Sussex I State Prison, 2010 Va. Cir. LEXIS 204 (Norfolk Dec. 20, 2010).

Attorney work product. — Because letters between a defendant's criminal attorney and an investigator, as well as descriptions of the events and an audiotape of conversations with a critical witness, were obviously prepared in anticipation of litigation, they were privileged work product under Va. Sup. Ct. R. 4:1(b)(3); thus, the executors' motion to compel was overruled. Jondahl v. Gasper, 73 Va. Cir. 42, 2007 Va. Cir. LEXIS 118 (Virginia Beach 2007).

Doctor's motion to quash a duces tecum a patient served upon the president of the medical practice that employed the doctor was granted on the ground that the work product doctrine applied because the relevant documents that were in the president's possession were electronic mails exchanged by and between him, defense counsel, and the doctor, and the patient had no interest in the opinion work-product of defense counsel; the patient wanted the communications by and between the doctor, defense counsel, and the president regarding the facts, and the doctor's recollections regarding her and the treatment he provided her. Campbell v. Dastoor, 79 Va. Cir. 569, 2009 Va. Cir. LEXIS 141 (Salem Dec. 9, 2009).

Certain documents prepared before an attorney became involved in a case were nonetheless protected from production by the work product doctrine because they were prepared in anticipation of litigation where it was reasonably foreseeable at the time of their preparation that litigation might have arisen. Cranley v. Benchmark Mgmt. Co., 78 Va. Cir. 353, 2009 Va. Cir. LEXIS 175 (Loudoun County May 28, 2009).

Communications between the board of directors of a homeowners' association and the association's attorney were protected from discovery by the attorney-client privilege and the work product privilege because the documents requested specifically requested legal advice. Batt v. Manchester Oaks Homeowners Ass'n, 80 Va. Cir. 502, 2010 Va. Cir. LEXIS 90 (Fairfax July 6, 2010).

In this Federal Employers Liability Act action, the employee's motion to compel was granted because everything in the three documents was discoverable; the documents did not contain mental impressions of the employer's agent or strategies of an attorney. Lowe v. Norfolk & Southern Ry., 81 Va. Cir. 221, 2010 Va. Cir. LEXIS 299 (Hopewell Sept. 24, 2010).

Trial preparation materials. — Court declined to apply the work product doctrine to all financial documents without weighing whether plaintiff has a substantial need for the documents, whether plaintiff is unable without undue hardship to obtain their substantial equivalent by other means, and whether the documents represent mental impressions, conclusions and opinions or legal theories of an attorney. Rush v. Sunrise Senior Living, Inc., 2008 Va. Cir. LEXIS 12 (Fairfax County Feb. 12, 2008).

Hospital's risk manager's investigation of a patient's death proceeded with guidance and direction from the hospital's counsel and in anticipation of litigation; therefore, her notes of the investigation were protected from discovery by the Va. Sup. Ct. R. 4:1(b)(3) work product doctrine and the attorney-client privilege. Planicka v. Am. Anesthesiology of Va., P.C., 83 Va. Cir. 482, 2011 Va. Cir. LEXIS 135 (Fairfax County Nov. 22, 2011).

Disclosure leading to the discovery of admissible evidence. — Although the materials sought by an administratrix were not privileged under § 8.01-581.17, they moved beyond any peer review purpose and represented personnel policies as well as procedures for the operation of a hospital's radiology department; since disclosure would lead to the discovery of admissible evidence, pursuant to Va. Sup. Ct. R. 4:1(b)(1), the administratrix's motion to compel was denied. Hubbard v. Pascual, 71 Va. Cir. 265, 2006 Va. Cir. LEXIS 121 (Portsmouth 2006).

Undue burden. — Where a plaintiff filed 110 requests for admission pursuant to Va. Sup. Ct. R. 4:11, the requests were unreasonably cumulative and duplicative, were obtainable from other sources, and were unduly burdensome; therefore, defendant's objection thereto under Va. Sup. Ct. R. 4:1(b)(1) was sustained. Giddens v. Nunez, 62 Va. Cir. 100, 2003 Va. Cir. LEXIS 299 (Norfolk 2003).

Trial court, pursuant to Va. Sup. Ct. R. 4:1(b)(1), narrowed discovery requests that were to be met in the disclosure of documents regarding two appraisers, who were not experts retained in anticipation of litigation, because the requests in two subpoenas duces tecum were overly burdensome and some would also have been unreasonably duplicative. Wagner v. Wagner, 71 Va. Cir. 334, 2006 Va. Cir. LEXIS 253 (Prince George County 2006).

Request for admissions was unduly burdensome and responding would have resulted in unnecessary expense; additionally, the court had already conducted a pendente lite hearing, and the evidence at the hearing revealed a substantial amount of information regarding the financial circumstances of each party. A motion to compel discovery was denied. Brendle v. Brendle, 73 Va. Cir. 390, 2007 Va. Cir. LEXIS 105 (Orange County 2007).

Surveillance tapes. — If surveillance tapes existed, railroad was to notify plaintiff's attorney of their existence 20 days before trial, and the railroad was required to provide copies 15 days before trial. Fender v. Norfolk S. Ry. Co., 55 Va. Cir. 344, 2001 Va. Cir. LEXIS 295 (Norfolk 2001).

Court granted plaintiff's motion to compel immediate disclosure of surveillance documents and tape relied on by a doctor in performing an independent medical examination of plaintiff because such tape was not protected by the work-product doctrine, and disclosure would further the purposes of the rules of discovery to prevent surprise and promote an orderly trial. Defendant had the right to depose plaintiff prior to disclosure but had to produce the video after the deposition and at least 90 days before trial. Fare v. Doe, 66 Va. Cir. 61, 2004 Va. Cir. LEXIS 332 (Chesterfield County Sept. 13, 2004).

Surveillance information is discoverable. — In an action stemming from an accident between a automobile and a tractor trailer, the surveillance information at issue was discoverable and the driver should respond to the interrogatory, Va. Sup. Ct. R. 4:1(b)(3). If the driver's statements were to be given the status of work product, it was incumbent on him to state a basis for it, not merely that it was because he says it was; moreover, even if it was work product, that was not to say that the driver's statement might not be discoverable on a showing of another proper basis for discovery. Dudley v. Cash, 82 Va. Cir. 1, 2010 Va. Cir. LEXIS 257 (Augusta County Mar. 25, 2010).

Prelitigation investigations by insurance company. — Plaintiff motorist's driving record and claims history, obtained by defendant's insurer prior to institution of litigation, were not discoverable, and plaintiff's motion to compel was denied, as the information was obtainable from other sources, without undue hardship; the application of the work product doctrine to documents prepared by insurance companies during claims investigations was difficult because the nature of the insurance business was such that an insurance company had to investigate a claim prior to determining whether to pay its insured, and thus pre-litigation investigating was the routine practice of insurance companies, and the issue of whether an insurance company's investigatory reports were discoverable was subject to a case-by-case analysis. Lopez v. Woolever, 62 Va. Cir. 198, 2003 Va. Cir. LEXIS 95 (Fairfax County 2003).

Statements made to insurance adjuster in anticipation of litigation. — Because the specific statement sought by an injured party to an insurance adjuster was obtained in anticipation of litigation, it was protected by the work product doctrine; consequently, the statement was not discoverable absent a showing of substantial need as provided by Va. R. Sup. Ct. 4:1. Veney v. Duke, 69 Va. Cir. 209, 2005 Va. Cir. LEXIS 208 (Fairfax County 2005).

Recorded statements given by insured to his insurer after an accident but before any suit had been filed were made in anticipation of litigation and were protected as work product, which were unavailable to plaintiff in discovery because plaintiff failed to show a substantial need for the material or that a substantial equivalent of the material could not be obtained elsewhere. Piland v. White, 85 Va. Cir. 45, 2012 Va. Cir. LEXIS 162 (Chesapeake Feb. 27, 2012).

Statements made to insurance adjuster in the ordinary course of the insurer's business. — In a personal injury action filed by a bicyclist against an insured driver, the circuit judge granted the former's motion to compel production of a taped statement given by the latter to his insurer's adjuster, as the adjuster was not charged with safety responsibilities, and nothing in the statement indicated the adjuster's investigation was different from the manner in which he would investigate other claims in the ordinary course of the insurer's business; moreover, the circuit judge did not believe that the policies the Virginia General Assembly enacted in §§ 8.01-404 and 8.01-417 had any effect on the application of Va. Sup. Ct. R. 4:1(b)(3) to the facts made known to the judge. McKinnon v. Doman, 72 Va. Cir. 547, 2007 Va. Cir. LEXIS 27 (Norfolk 2007).

Plaintiff's motion to compel the discovery of statements defendant made to her insurance adjuster because in the absence of a deliberate expansion of the work product doctrine, the routine taking of statements by an auto insurance adjuster was work in the ordinary course of business, which failed to qualify as work product under Va. Sup. Ct. R. 4:1(b)(3); Rule 4:1(b)(3) was not engaged without the finding that the material collected was encompassed within the work product of an attorney. Popina v. Rice-Steward, 2013 Va. Cir. LEXIS 12 (Virginia Beach Apr. 5, 2013).

Interviews by insurance company not protected by work product doctrine. — Written statements of interviews in the possession of defendant's insurance company that were prepared prior to notification that plaintiff had retained counsel in his personal injury suit were not protected by the work product doctrine under Va. Sup. Ct. R. 4:1(a)(3) because they were not prepared in anticipation of litigation. The statements were not prepared for an attorney and did not otherwise reflect the employment of an attorney's legal expertise. Massenburg v. Hawkins, 70 Va. Cir. 13, 2005 Va. Cir. LEXIS 295 (Greensville County 2005).

Insurance adjuster's log. — In determining whether an insurance adjuster's log is work product, a court should apply the "case-by-case" test, which considers the reasonable foreseeability that litigation could arise by considering (1) the severity of the plaintiff's injuries; (2) the awareness that an insured plaintiff may have been negligent in bringing about the accident; (3) notification of the defendant that a claim may be pursued; (4) retention of counsel or materials requested by counsel; (5) the routine of investigation of plaintiff's claim; and (6) other factors. Hawkins v. Norfolk S. Ry. Co., 71 Va. Cir. 285, 2006 Va. Cir. LEXIS 247 (Brunswick County 2006).

Where plaintiff sued a railroad for negligence over injuries he sustained in an auto-train collision, as the adjuster's log of plaintiff's insurer, having been prepared in anticipation of litigation, was work product under Va. Sup. Ct. R. 4:1(b)(3), the railroad could not obtain it in discovery since it did not show that it needed the log to complete its defense, or that the information in it would be crucial to its case or especially relevant to its defense. Hawkins v. Norfolk S. Ry. Co., 71 Va. Cir. 285, 2006 Va. Cir. LEXIS 247 (Brunswick County 2006).

Insurance adjuster's log as work product. — As plaintiff, injured in an auto-train collision, advised his insurer he would file a claim against a railroad and expected a claim to be filed against him, it was likely the insurance adjuster believed that litigation would arise from the claim; therefore, the adjuster's log was prepared in anticipation of litigation and was exempt from discovery as work product under Va. Sup. Ct. R. 4:1(b)(3). Hawkins v. Norfolk S. Ry. Co., 71 Va. Cir. 285, 2006 Va. Cir. LEXIS 247 (Brunswick County 2006).

Health facility's policies, procedures, and training materials. — In an executor's action against a corporation and several limited partnerships that operated a nursing home, the trial court found that the defendants' policies, procedures, protocols, guidelines, and training materials relating to the prevention, treatment, and documentation of pressure ulcers and infections were not privileged materials under § 8.01-581.17 and it granted the executor's motion to compel production of those documents. Day v. Med. Facilities of Am., Inc., 59 Va. Cir. 378, 2002 Va. Cir. LEXIS 372 (Salem Aug. 21, 2002).

Polices, procedures, directives, instructions, and written memoranda from a hospital were not privileged under § 8.01-581.17 as they were not of the same character as peer review committee minutes; the documents were discoverable, given the broad scope of Va. Sup. Ct. R. 4:1 (b), the potential uses of the documents alternative to establishing the standard of care, and the potential to lead to discovery of admissible evidence. Auer v. Baker, 63 Va. Cir. 596, 2004 Va. Cir. LEXIS 93 (Norfolk 2004).

Hospital's motion to quash a patient's subpoena duces tecum, which requested the production of protocols, policies, and/or procedure manuals, was denied because the requested documents were calculated to lead to the discovery of admissible evidence, and the policies, protocols, and procedures that were requested were related to the subject matter in the sense that they were germane to the subject of the patient's medical malpractice lawsuit; although the policies, protocols, and procedures at issue were likely inadmissible at trial, the hospital confused the concepts of admissibility and discovery. Gravely v. Perren, 77 Va. Cir. 370, 2009 Va. Cir. LEXIS 113 (Martinsville 2009).

Hospital's CT scan protocols were not privileged under § 8.01-581.17 because the phrase "all communications" in § 8.01-581.17 was limited to the enumerated "proceedings, minutes, records, and reports," and the protocols were relevant in a patient's proceeding to gather adequate information to obtain an expert to make a § 8.01-20.1 certification. Jones v. Perez (In re Jones), 81 Va. Cir. 52, 2010 Va. Cir. LEXIS 278 (Chesapeake Oct. 26, 2010).

Inanimate and tangible pathology materials. — In a set of asbestos-related cases, inanimate and tangible pathology materials were subject to discovery, therefore, without a showing by plaintiffs' counsel of exceptional circumstances, plaintiffs were not entitled to the identification of, or opinion of, any non-testifying expert with whom defendants chose to consult on said pathology. All Asbestos Cases, 64 Va. Cir. 190, 2004 Va. Cir. LEXIS 58 (Newport News 2004).

Hospital's letters and complaints were relevant. — Hospital's letters and/or complaints relating to contamination and/or preservation of the integrity of samples and specimens were discoverable under Va. Sup. Ct. R. 4:1 (b) as the request was based on deposition testimony as to the existence of previous problems and the documents were relevant; the documents could be redacted to protect the confidential health information of the two patients involved, as required by the Virginia Patient Health Records Privacy Act, § 32.1-127.1:03, and the federal Health Insurance Portability and Accountability Act, 45 C.F.R. pt. 160-164. Auer v. Baker, 63 Va. Cir. 596, 2004 Va. Cir. LEXIS 93 (Norfolk 2004).

Information from person who holds power of attorney. — Trial court denied the motion to compel filed by the movant to obtain an accounting of actions the sister, who had held a power of attorney for the sister and movant's mother, had taken; the legislature had defined under statutory law the circumstances under which a party could obtain information from a person who held a power of attorney and since the legislature had statutorily defined those circumstances, the trial court was not allowed to enlarge the circumstances through the use of the state supreme court rules. Carrubba v. Rose, 65 Va. Cir. 94, 2004 Va. Cir. LEXIS 101 (Fairfax County 2004).

Medical incident reports. — Trial court granted the expectant mother's motion to compel production of medical incident reports that the doctor made after the alleged medical malpractice, as the reports were not privileged under the work product exception to the discovery rules; the reports were taken by the doctor's insurer in the routine course of the insurer's business so that it could be informed of incidents, the doctor was not sufficiently concerned about the potential for litigation to retain counsel, and the reports were not prepared in anticipation of litigation. Brown v. Lab. Corp., 67 Va. Cir. 232, 2005 Va. Cir. LEXIS 36 (Rockingham County 2005).

Ex parte communications with former employees. — Protective order was denied insofar as it sought to bar ex parte contact with former "control group" employees of a corporation sued by an executor in a medical malpractice case, or former non control group employees no longer employed by the corporation; ex parte contact was prohibited with current "control group" and non "control group" employees who provided resident care, but the executor's counsel was permitted to have ex parte contact with those employees on certain matters. Pruett v. Va. Health Servs., 69 Va. Cir. 80, 2005 Va. Cir. LEXIS 151 (Lancaster County 2005).

Reenactment request. — In a personal injury action brought by a railroad worker against his employer, the railroad, and a manufacturer, the trial court denied the worker's request to inspect the accident site, which was a motion filed two years after the accident, because the burdens and dangers created by a requested inspection of the site to set up a partial reenactment of the accident outweighed the degree to which the proposed inspection would have aided in the search for the truth. Wilson v. Norfolk & Portsmouth Belt Line R.R. Co., 69 Va. Cir. 153, 2005 Va. Cir. LEXIS 267 (Portsmouth 2005).

Interrogatory responses were sufficient. — Where an insured was defended by an insurer under a reservation of rights, and then sued the insurer following the settlement of the claims against the insured, the insured had the burden of proving that the settlement amount was paid in exchange for a covered claim as part of the insured's prima facie case; the insured was required to answer interrogatories, pursuant to Va. Sup. Ct. R. 4:1(b), as to the basis for the insured's claims against the insurer, but in the instant case the insured's answers were sufficient, as the insured was asserting alternative facts or theories of recovery, and therefore the insurer's motion to compel discovery was denied. RML Corp. v. Assurance Co. of Am., 60 Va. Cir. 269, 2002 Va. Cir. LEXIS 392 (Norfolk 2002).

Insurer's reservation of rights information. — In a personal injury case, responses to four interrogatories regarding a reservation of rights filed by defendant driver's insurer to deny coverage were compelled because the information was relevant under Va. Sup. Ct. R. 4:1(b)(1) as plaintiff's course of action could be materially affected by the weight independently ascribed to the insurer's reservation claim. Wood v. Campbell, 71 Va. Cir. 402, 2006 Va. Cir. LEXIS 250 (Loudoun County Sept. 6, 2006).

Denial of discovery stay for matters related to pending motions. — The court allowed the motion to stay all discovery related to the upcoming hearing since the motions to be addressed at the hearing primarily involved legal issues; but, the court allowed certain enumerated items of discovery, in part, since those items, including Freedom of Information Act disclosures, related to the county's plea in bar. Orion Sporting Group, LLC v. Bd. of Supervisors, 66 Va. Cir. 16, 2004 Va. Cir. LEXIS 256 (Nelson County 2004).

Treating physician entitled to fees. — Treating physician was entitled to receive a reasonable fee for her time spent being deposed by the sister because the physician testified not only on opinions formed during treatment but also on opinions formed in development of the deposition. Villar-Gonsalvez v. Villar-Gosalvez, 65 Va. Cir. 96, 2004 Va. Cir. LEXIS 97 (Albemarle County 2004).

Educational records. — When plaintiff alleged lead poisoning, the court permitted defendants to subpoena the school records of his mother under Va. Sup. Ct. R. 4:9 so that an expert could use them in determining whether plaintiff's deficits were due to lead or other factors, such as the mother's education and intelligence. The records were not privileged under subsection A of § 22.1-287, and they were relevant and reasonably calculated to lead to the discovery of admissible evidence under Va. Sup. Ct. R. 4:1; however, non-medical records in the school records were to be kept under seal because of their sensitive nature and medical records in the school records excluded from production because they did not contain information about the mother's intelligence or educational level. Bunch v. Artz, 71 Va. Cir. 358, 2006 Va. Cir. LEXIS 252 (Portsmouth 2006).

Discovery allowed. — In a defamation case arising from an advocacy group's television advertisement, considering the advocacy group's discovery requests in light of Va. Sup. Ct. R. 4:1, discovery of incidents of water pollution resulting in civil fines, citations, or litigation that did not give rise to criminal convictions was relevant to plaintiffs' damages. Massey Energy Co. v. UMW, AFL-CIO, CLE, 72 Va. Cir. 54, 2006 Va. Cir. LEXIS 129 (Fairfax County 2006).

Motion to compel answers to executor's questions relating to hotel's safety policies and procedures to two hotel employees at a deposition in a negligence suit filed by the executor against a nursing home was granted under Va. Sup. Ct. R. 4:1(b)(1), even though the hotel was not a party, as the questions were reasonably calculated to lead to information about how and why the decedent became lost, wandered around the hotel unsupervised for a time, and fell down a flight of stairs; the executor was granted attorney's fees under Va. Sup. Ct. R. 4:12(a)(4). Stone v. Clifton Forge Health Care, L.L.C., 83 Va. Cir. 479, 2011 Va. Cir. LEXIS 264 (Alleghany County Nov. 21, 2011).

Because the defendants' interrogatories/requests for production were facially allowable as to a decedent's income, or the extent to which the decedent's husband shared in it, and because the requests were not overly broad, burdensome, or vague, and would not divulge privileged material, they were within the scope of Va. Sup. Ct. R. 4:1. Bosworth v. Vornado Realty L.P., 84 Va. Cir. 353, 2012 Va. Cir. LEXIS 34 (Fairfax County Feb. 28, 2012).

Nonprofit corporation failed to set forth the good cause necessary for a protective order under Va. Sup. Ct. R. 4:1(c) where: (1) the complaint enumerated 16 defamatory statements a social media user had purportedly made; (2) the discovery propounded clearly sought to obtain relevant and otherwise discoverable information; and (3) the only harm the nonprofit corporation referenced were amorphous threats and risks that could befall the nonprofit and its members if the social media user was permitted to publish discovery materials on a Website. World Mission Soc'y Church of God v. Colon, 85 Va. Cir. 134, 2012 Va. Cir. LEXIS 74 (Fairfax County July 20, 2012).

As a defense expert had previously generated a document indicating the services he provided and the fees he recovered in litigation, he was required to provide an updated version of the document to plaintiff in litigation arising out of an accident. Piland v. White, 85 Va. Cir. 45, 2012 Va. Cir. LEXIS 162 (Chesapeake Feb. 27, 2012).

Motion denied. — Habeas corpus petitioner's motion to take the deposition of the complaining witness was denied because the testimony had little to do with petitioner's claim of ineffective assistance of counsel, which revolved around trial counsel's failure to object to certain statements the circuit court made at the time petitioner was found guilty. Henderson v. Johnson, 75 Va. Cir. 479, 2007 Va. Cir. LEXIS 306 (Campbell County 2007).

Habeas corpus petitioner's motion for discovery pursuant to Va. Sup. Ct. R. 4:1(b)(5) was denied because petitioner's discovery requests were narrow, and the statement in petitioner's motion for discovery that the general circumstances described in the indictment were similar to the investigator's actions in his case and provided good cause for discovery were false; petitioner's claim that the prosecution's case relied mainly on a "jailhouse snitch" was false because petitioner's fingerprint was found on a bloody broken knife blade not far from the victim's body, and his DNA was on the knife handle, and petitioner alleged that a witness gave police inconsistent statements, but the Commonwealth did not call the witness at petitioner's trial, and the witness was not named at the investigator's trial. Juniper v. Warden of the Sussex I State Prison, 2010 Va. Cir. LEXIS 201 (Norfolk Dec. 20, 2010).

Subpoenas duces tecum for mental health records quashed. — Father's motion to quash subpoenas duces tecum for his mental health care records in a divorce and custody case was proper in part because the "good cause" provision of subsection D of § 32.1-127.1:03 yielded to the more specific privilege provisions of § 20-124.3:1, which created a privilege that prevented disclosure of the mental health care records; § 20-124.3:1, however, did not apply to the records of a health care provider who was not a licensed mental health care provider. Cage v. Cage, 73 Va. Cir. 190, 2007 Va. Cir. LEXIS 30 (Portsmouth 2007).

Discovery misconduct. — In the buyers' action alleging that the sellers failed to disclose defects in a home addition, the buyers were ordered to pay attorney's fees and costs associated with sellers' motion for sanctions, because the buyers violated Va. Sup. Ct. R. 4:1 and 4:12 by failing to disclose the existence of the buyers' contractor and the specifics of the contractor's knowledge in response to the sellers' discovery requests. Skibinski v. Lunger, 74 Va. Cir. 428, 2008 Va. Cir. LEXIS 1 (Arlington County 2008).

While a plaintiff failed to disclose prior medical treatment to the defendants, as the parties would have sufficient time to explore the preexisting condition issue if the action were refiled, and given the sanctions reimposed and those that the plaintiff would avoid by a nonsuit, pursuant to § 8.01-271.1 and Va. Sup. Ct. R. 4:1(g), the defendants were entitled to only an award of fees and expenses related to a review of the plaintiff's answers and the discovery of and response to his untruthfulness. Hall v. Va. Int'l Terminals, Inc., 82 Va. Cir. 330, 2011 Va. Cir. LEXIS 181 (Norfolk Mar. 28, 2011).

Attorney violated § 8.01-271.1, Va. Sup. Ct. R. 4:1(g), and Va. Sup. Ct. R. 4:12 by omitting an e-mail and by his failure to submit the subject e-mail to the Court for in camera inspection. The attorney conceded that his behavior also violated Va. Sup. Ct. R. pt. 6, § II, R. 3.3 and 3.4; thus, he was liable for attorney fees. Lester v. Allied Concrete Co., 38 Va. Cir. 308, 2011 Va. Cir. LEXIS 245 (Charlottesville Sept. 6, 2011).

Counsel, when he signed and served an answer to an interrogatory and responses to request for production of documents, violated Va. Sup. Ct. R. 4:1(g) by stating falsely that his client, the injured person, did not have a Facebook page on the date that the response was signed; the court imposed reasonable expenses, including a reasonable attorney's fee, incurred because of counsel's violation. Lester v. Allied Concrete Co., 38 Va. Cir. 308, 2011 Va. Cir. LEXIS 245 (Charlottesville Sept. 6, 2011).

Rule 4:2. Depositions Before Action or Pending Appeal.

(a) *Before Action.* — (1) Petition. A person who desires to perpetuate his own testimony or that of another person regarding any matter that may be cognizable in any court of this Commonwealth may file a verified petition in the circuit court in the county or city of the residence of any expected adverse party. The petition shall be entitled in the name of the petitioner and shall show: (A) that the petitioner expects to be a party to an action cognizable in a court of this Commonwealth but is presently unable to bring it or cause it to be brought; (B) the subject matter of the expected action and his interest therein; (C) the facts which he desires to establish by the proposed testimony and his reasons for desiring to perpetuate it; (D) the names or a description of the persons he expects will be adverse parties and their addresses so far as known;

and (E) the names and addresses of the persons to be examined and the substance of the testimony which he expects to elicit from each, and shall ask for an order authorizing the petitioner to take the depositions of the persons to be examined named in the petition, for the purpose of perpetuating their testimony.

(2) Notice and Service. The petitioner shall thereafter serve a notice upon each person named in the petition as an expected adverse party, together with a copy of the petition, stating that the petitioner will apply to the court, at a time and place named therein, for the order described in the petition. At least 21 days before the date of hearing the notice shall be served either within the Commonwealth in the manner provided for service of a complaint or without the Commonwealth in the manner provided by Code § 8.01-320; but if such service cannot with due diligence be made upon any expected adverse party named in the petition, the court may make such order as is just for service by publication or otherwise, and shall appoint, for persons not so served, an attorney who shall represent them, and, in case they are not otherwise represented, shall cross-examine the deponent. If any expected adverse party is a person under a disability, a guardian ad litem shall be appointed to attend on his behalf.

(3) Order and Examination. If the court is satisfied that the perpetuation of the testimony may prevent a failure or delay of justice, it shall make an order designating or describing the persons whose depositions may be taken and specifying the subject matter of the examination and whether the depositions shall be taken upon oral examination or written interrogatories. The depositions may then be taken in accordance with these Rules. The attendance of witnesses may be compelled by subpoena, and the court may make orders of the character provided for by Rules 4:9 and 4:10. For the purpose of applying these Rules to depositions for perpetuating testimony, each reference therein to the court in which the action is pending shall be deemed to refer to the court in which the petition for such deposition was filed.

(4) Cost. The cost of such depositions shall be paid by the petitioner, except that the other parties in interest who produce witnesses on their behalf or who make use of witnesses produced by others shall pay their proportionate part of the cost of the transcribed testimony and evidence taken or given on behalf of each of such parties.

(5) Filing. The depositions shall be certified as prescribed in Rule 4:5 and then returned to and filed by the clerk of the court which ordered its taking.

(6) Use of Deposition. If a deposition to perpetuate testimony is taken under these Rules or if, although not so taken, it would be admissible in evidence in the courts of the state in which it is taken, it may be used in any action involving the same subject matter subsequently brought in a court of this Commonwealth in accordance with the provisions of Rule 4:1.

(b) *Pending Appeal.* — If an appeal has been taken from a judgment of a court of record or before the taking of an appeal if the time therefor has not expired, the court in which the judgment was rendered may allow the taking of the depositions of witnesses to perpetuate their testimony for use in the event of further proceedings in that court. In such case the party who desires to perpetuate the testimony may make a motion in the court in which the judgment was rendered for leave to take the depositions, upon the same notice and service thereof as if the action was pending therein. The motion shall show (1) the names and addresses of persons to be examined and the substance of the testimony which he expects to elicit from each; and (2) the reasons for perpetuating their testimony. If the court finds that the perpetuation of the testimony is proper to avoid a failure or delay of justice, it may make orders of the character provided for by Rules 4:9 and 4:10, and thereupon the depositions may be taken and used in the same manner and under the same conditions as are prescribed in these Rules for depositions taken in pending actions.

(c) *Perpetuation of Testimony.* — This Rule provides the exclusive procedure to perpetuate testimony.

The amendment, effective February 28, 2006, adopted February 28, 2006, in the second sentence of subdivision (a)(2), substituted "in the manner provided for service of a complaint or without the Commonwealth in the manner provided by Code § 8.01-320" for "in the manner provided for service of a bill of complaint or motion for judgment or without the Commonwealth in the manner provided by Code Section 8.01-320."

Research References. — Jeffrey A. Jannuzzo, Preparing for a Deposition in a Business Case (Matthew Bender).

Michie's Jurisprudence. — For related discussion, see 6A M.J. Discovery, §§ 7, 13 - 15, 22.

CASE NOTES

Sanctions for violation of rule. — After judgment had entered in a visitation modification matter, the father noticed the deposition of an expert without obtaining leave of court as required by subsection (b); the mother filed objections to the deposition. Although the father withdrew the notice of deposition, the trial court did not abuse its discretion in awarding the mother the attorney's fees she had incurred before he did so. Overcash v. Albertella, No. 1595-04-4, 2005 Va. App. LEXIS 32 (Ct. of Appeals Feb. 1, 2005).

CIRCUIT COURT OPINIONS

This rule not available after suit is filed. — Patient who had filed suit against a hospital and radiological technologist was not entitled to take a supplemental deposition pursuant to Va. Sup. Ct. R. 4:2, which only governed perpetuation of testimony prior to filing suit, but could take a deposition pursuant to Va. Sup. Ct. R. 4:5(a). CT scan protocols were not privileged under the peer review privilege statute, § 8.01-581.17. Jones v. Perez (In re Jones), 81 Va. Cir. 52, 2010 Va. Cir. LEXIS 308 (Chesapeake Nov. 22, 2010).

Because a patient had filed a separate suit directly against a radiological technologist following a deposition of the technologist, any amendments or supplemental depositions were not available pursuant to Va. Sup. Ct. R. 4:2. Due to the commencement of the new suit, however, the patient could undertake depositions of knowledgeable representatives of the hospital defendant, pursuant to Va. Sup. Ct. R. 4:5(a), in accordance with her amended notice of deposition. Jones v. Perez (In re Jones), 81 Va. Cir. 52, 2010 Va. Cir. LEXIS 278 (Chesapeake Oct. 26, 2010).

Rule 4:3. Persons Before Whom Depositions May Be Taken.

(a) *Within this Commonwealth.* — Within this Commonwealth depositions may be taken before any person authorized by law to administer oaths, and if certified by his hand may be received without proof of the signature to such certificate.

(b) *Within the United States.* — In any other State of the United States or within any territory or insular possession subject to the dominion of the United States, depositions may be taken before any officer authorized to take depositions in the jurisdiction wherein the witness may be, or before any commissioner appointed by the Governor of this Commonwealth.

(c) *No Commission Necessary.* — No commission by the Governor of this Commonwealth shall be necessary to take a deposition whether within or without this Commonwealth.

(d) *In Foreign Countries.* — In a foreign state or country depositions shall be taken (1) before any American minister plenipotentiary, charge d'affaires, secretary of embassy or legation, consul general, consul, vice-consul, or commercial agent of the United States in a foreign country, or any other representative of the United States therein, including commissioned officers of the armed services of the United States, or (2) before the mayor, or other magistrate of any city, town or corporation in such country, or any notary therein.

(e) *Certificate When Deposition Taken Outside Commonwealth.* — Any person before whom a deposition is taken outside this Commonwealth shall certify the same with his official seal annexed; and, if he have none, the genuineness of his signature shall be authenticated by some officer of the same state or country, under his official seal, except that no seal shall be required of a commissioned officer of the armed services of the United States, but his signature shall be authenticated by the commanding officer of the military installation or ship to which he is assigned.

Michie's Jurisprudence. — For related discussion, see 6A M.J. Discovery, §§ 16 - 18.

Rule 4:4. Stipulations Regarding Discovery.

Unless the court orders otherwise, the parties may by written stipulation (1) provide that depositions may be taken before any person, at any time or place, upon any notice, and in any manner and when so taken may be used like other depositions and (2) modify the procedures provided by these Rules for other methods of discovery, including discovery of electronically stored information. Stipulations may include agreements with non-party witnesses, consistent with Code § 8.01-420.4. Such stipulations shall be filed with the deposition or other discovery completed pursuant thereto.

The amendment effective August 29, 2005, adopted August 29, 2005, inserted the present second sentence, and added "or other discovery completed pursuant thereto" at the end of the present third sentence.

The amendment effective January 1, 2009, adopted October 31, 2008, inserted "including discovery of electronically stored information" at the end of the first sentence.

Law Review. — For 2007 annual survey article, "Civil Practice and Procedure," see 42 U. Rich. L. Rev. 229 (2007).

Michie's Jurisprudence. — For related discussion, see 6A M.J. Discovery, § 21; 17 M.J. Stipulations, § 2.

Rule 4:5. Depositions Upon Oral Examination.

(a) *When Depositions May Be Taken.* — After commencement of the action, any party may take the testimony of any person, including a party, by deposition upon oral examination. Leave of court, granted with or without notice, must be obtained only if the plaintiff seeks to take a deposition before the expiration of the period within which a defendant may file a responsive pleading under Rule 3:8, except that leave is not required (1) if a defendant has served a notice of taking deposition, or (2) if special notice is given as provided in subdivision (b)(2) of this Rule. The attendance of witnesses may be compelled by subpoena. The deposition of a person confined in prison may be taken only by leave of court on such terms as the court prescribes.

(a1) *Taking of Depositions.*

(i) Party Depositions. A deposition of a party, or any witness designated under Rule 4:5(b)(6) to testify on behalf of a party, shall be taken in the county or city in which suit is pending, in an adjacent county or city, at a place upon which the parties agree, or at a place that the court in such suit may, for good cause, designate. Good cause may include the expense or inconvenience of a non-resident party defendant appearing in one of the locations specified in this subsection. The restrictions as to parties set forth in this subdivision (a1)(i) shall not apply where no responsive pleading has been filed or an appearance otherwise made.

(ii) Non-party Witness Depositions. Unless otherwise provided by the law of the jurisdiction where a non-party witness resides, a deposition of a non-party witness shall be taken in the county or city where the non-party witness resides, is employed, or has a principal place of business; at a place upon which the witness and the parties to the litigation agree; or at a place that the court may, for good cause, designate.

(iii) Taking Depositions Outside the State. Within another state, or within a territory or insular possession subject to the dominion of the United States, or in a foreign country, depositions may be taken (1) on notice before a person authorized to administer oaths in the place in which the examination is held, either by the law thereof or, where applicable, the law of the United States, or (2) before a person appointed or commissioned by the court in which the action is pending, and such a person shall have the power by virtue of such appointment or commission to administer any necessary oath and take testimony, or (3) pursuant to a letter rogatory. A commission or letter rogatory shall be issued upon application and notice and on terms that are just and appropriate. It is not requisite to the issuance of a commission or a letter rogatory that the taking of the deposition in any other manner is impracticable or inconvenient. A notice or commission may designate the person before whom the deposition is to be taken either by name or descriptive title. A commission or letter rogatory may be addressed "To the Appropriate Authority in (here name the state, territory, or country)." Witnesses may be compelled to appear and testify at depositions taken outside this state by process issued and served in accordance with the law of the jurisdiction where the deposition is taken or, where applicable, the law of the United States. Upon motion, the courts of this State shall issue a commission or letter rogatory requesting the assistance of the courts or authorities of the foreign jurisdiction.

(iv) Uniform Interstate Depositions and Discovery Act. Depositions and related documentary production sought in Virginia pursuant to a subpoena issued under the authority of a foreign jurisdiction shall be subject to the provisions of the Uniform Interstate Depositions and Discovery Act, Virginia Code §§ 8.01-412.8 through 8.01-412.15.

(b) *Notice of Examination: General Requirements; Special Notice; Production of Documents and Things; Deposition of Organization.* —

(1) A party desiring to take the deposition of any person upon oral examination shall give reasonable notice in writing to every other party to the action. The notice shall

state the time and place for taking the deposition and the name and address of each person to be examined, if known, and, if the name is not known, a general description sufficient to identify him or the particular class or group to which he belongs. If a subpoena duces tecum is to be served on the person to be examined, the designation of the materials to be produced as set forth in the subpoena shall be attached to or included in the notice.

(2) Leave of court is not required for the taking of a deposition by plaintiff if the notice (A) states that the person to be examined is about to go out of the Commonwealth, or is about to go out of the United States, or is bound on a voyage to sea, and will be unavailable for examination unless his deposition is taken before expiration of the period for filing a responsive pleading under Rule 3:8, and (B) sets forth facts to support the statement. The plaintiff's attorney shall sign the notice, and his signature constitutes a certification by him that to the best of his knowledge, information, and belief the statement and supporting facts are true.

If a party shows that when he was served with notice under this subdivision (b)(2) he was unable through the exercise of diligence to obtain counsel to represent him at the taking of the deposition, the deposition may not be used against him.

(3) The court may for cause shown enlarge or shorten the time for taking the deposition.

(4) [Deleted.]

(5) The notice to a party deponent may be accompanied by a request made in compliance with Rule 4:9 for the production of documents and tangible things at the taking of the deposition. The procedure of Rule 4:9 shall apply to the request.

(6) A party may in his notice name as the deponent a public or private corporation or a partnership or association or governmental agency and designate with reasonable particularity the matters on which examination is requested. The organization so named shall designate one or more officers, directors, or managing agents, or other persons who consent to testify on its behalf, and may set forth, for each person designated, the matters on which he will testify. The persons so designated shall testify as to matters known or reasonably available to the organization. This subdivision (b)(6) does not preclude taking a deposition by any other procedure authorized in these Rules.

(7) Unless the court orders otherwise, a deposition may be taken by telephone, video conferencing, or teleconferencing. A deposition taken by telephone, video conferencing, or teleconferencing shall be taken before an appropriate officer in the locality where the deponent is present to answer questions propounded to him.

(c) *Examination and Cross-Examination; Record of Examination; Oath; Objections.* — Examination and cross-examination of witnesses may proceed as permitted at the trial. The officer before whom the deposition is to be taken shall put the witness on oath and shall personally, or by someone acting under his direction and in his presence, record the testimony of the witness. If requested by one of the parties, the testimony shall be transcribed.

All objections made at time of the examination to the qualifications of the officer taking the deposition, or to the manner of taking it, or to the evidence presented, or to the conduct of any party, and any other objection to the proceedings, shall be noted by the officer upon the deposition. Any objection must be stated concisely in a nonargumentative and nonsuggestive manner. Evidence objected to shall be taken subject to the objections. In lieu of participating in the oral examination, parties may serve written questions in a sealed envelope on the party taking the deposition and he shall transmit them to the officer, who shall propound them to the witness and record the answers verbatim.

(d) *Motion to Terminate or Limit Examination.* — At any time during the taking of the deposition, on motion of a party or of the deponent and upon a showing that the examination is being conducted in bad faith or in such manner as unreasonably to annoy, embarrass, or oppress the deponent or party, the court in which the action is pending or the court in the county or city where the deposition is being taken may order the officer conducting the examination to cease forthwith from taking the deposition, or may limit the scope and manner of the taking of the deposition as provided in Rule 4:1(c). If the order made terminates the examination, it shall be resumed thereafter only upon the order of the court in which the action is pending. Upon demand of the objecting party or deponent, the taking of the deposition shall be suspended for the time necessary to make a motion for an order. The provisions of Rule 4:12(a)(4) apply to the award of expenses incurred in relation to the motion.

(e) *Submission to Witness; Changes; Signing.* — When the testimony is fully transcribed, the deposition shall be submitted to the witness for examination and shall be read to or by him, unless such examination and reading are waived by the witness and by the parties. Any changes in form or substance which the witness desires to make shall be entered upon the deposition by the officer with a statement of the reasons given by the witness for making them. The deposition shall then be signed by the witness, unless the parties by stipulation waive the signing or the witness is ill or cannot be found or refuses to sign. If the deposition is not signed by the witness within 21 days of its submission to him, the officer shall sign it and state on the record the fact of the waiver or of the illness or absence of the witness or the fact of the refusal to sign together with the reason, if any, given therefor; and the deposition may then be used as fully as though signed unless on a motion to suppress under Rule 4:7(d)(4) the court holds that the reasons given for the refusal to sign require rejection of the deposition in whole or in part.

(f) *Certification and Filing by Officer; Exhibits; Copies; Notice of Filing.*

(1) The officer shall prepare an electronic or digitally imaged copy of the deposition transcript, including signatures and any changes as provided in subsection (e) of this Rule, and shall certify on the deposition that the witness was duly sworn by him and that the deposition is a true record of the testimony given by the witness. In a divorce or annulment case, the officer shall then promptly file the electronic or digitally imaged deposition in the office of the clerk, notifying all other parties of such action. In all other cases, he shall then lodge the deposition with the attorney for the party who initiated the taking of the deposition, notifying the clerk and all parties of such action. Depositions taken pursuant to this Rule or Rule 4:6 (except depositions taken in divorce and annulment cases) shall not be filed with the clerk until the court so directs, either on its own initiative or upon the request of any party prior to or during the trial. Any such filing shall be made electronically unless otherwise ordered by the judge.

Documents and things produced for inspection during the examination of the witness, shall, upon the request of a party, be marked for identification and annexed to and returned with the deposition, and may be inspected and copied by any party, except that (A) the person producing the materials may substitute copies to be marked for identification, if he affords to all parties fair opportunity to verify the copies by comparison with the originals, and (B) if the person producing the materials requests their return, the officer shall mark them, give each party an opportunity to inspect and copy them, and return them to the person producing them, and the materials may then be used in the same manner as if annexed to and returned with the deposition. Any party may move for an order that the original be annexed to and returned with the deposition to the court, pending final disposition of the case.

(2) Upon payment of reasonable charges therefor, the officer shall furnish a copy of the deposition to any party or to the deponent.

(3) The party taking the deposition shall give prompt notice of its filing to all other parties.

(g) *Failure to Attend or to Serve Subpoena; Expenses.* —

(1) If the party giving the notice of the taking of a deposition fails to attend and proceed therewith and another party attends in person or by attorney pursuant to the notice, the court may order the party giving the notice to pay to such other party the reasonable expenses incurred by him and his attorney in attending, including reasonable attorney's fees.

(2) If the party giving the notice of the taking of a deposition of a witness fails to serve a subpoena upon him and the witness because of such failure does not attend, and if another party attends in person or by attorney because he expects the deposition of that witness to be taken, the court may order the party giving the notice to pay to such other party the reasonable expenses incurred by him and his attorney in attending, including reasonable attorney's fees.

Comment. — See § 8.01-420.4.

Comment on 1983 amendment. — This addition is derived from Federal Rule 30(b)(7) as amended effective Aug. 1, 1980.

Comment on 1984 amendment. — This change is designed to eliminate filing of discovery material in the clerk's office unless required for use at the trial. The burden of maintaining discovery material in clerk's offices has become quite substantial.

Comment on 1985 amendment. — Depositions should be filed with the clerk in all divorce and annulment cases since *ore tenus* hearings — at least in many areas — are rare in such cases.

The amendment effective January 1, 2001, adopted September 28, 2000, rewrote subdivision (b)(7).

The amendment effective August 29, 2005, adopted August 29, 2005, rewrote paragraph (a1), which formerly read: "Depositions shall be taken in the county or city in which suit is pending, in an adjacent county or city or in the county or city of the Commonwealth of Virginia where a nonparty witness resides, is employed, or has his principal place of business, except that depositions may be taken at a place upon which the parties agree or at a place that the court in such suit may, for good cause, designate. If a nonparty witness is not a resident of the Commonwealth, his deposition may be taken in the locality where he resides or is employed or at any other location agreed upon by the parties. Additionally, the restrictions as to parties within the Commonwealth set forth in this Rule shall not apply where no responsive pleading has been filed or an appearance otherwise made."

The amendment effective January 1, 2006, by order adopted June 14, 2005, substituted "Rule 3:8" for "Rule 2:7 or 3:5" in the first sentence of subdivision (a) and in the first sentence of subdivision (b)(2)(A).

The amendment effective July 1, 2008, adopted April 9. 2008, added subdivision (a1)(iii).

The amendment effective July 1, 2009, adopted June 1, 2009, added subdivision (a1)(iv).

The amendment effective May 2, 2011, adopted March 1, 2011, in subdivision (f)(1), inserted "shall prepare an electronic or digitally imaged copy of the deposition transcript, including signatures and any changes as provided in subsection (e) of this Rule, and" in the first sentence, substituted "the officer" for "he," inserted "electronic or digitally imaged" and substituted "the deposition" for "he" in the second sentence, and combined the former two paragraphs into one paragraph.

The amendment effective January 1, 2013, adopted November 1, 2012, added the second sentence in the second paragraph of (c).

Law Review. — For a review of corporate law in Virginia for year 1999, see 33 U. Rich. L. Rev. 841 (1999). For article reviewing recent developments and changes in legislation, case law, and Virginia Supreme Court Rules affecting civil litigation, see "Civil Practice and Procedure," see 40 U. Rich. L. Rev. 95 (2005). For 2007 annual survey article, "Civil Practice and Procedure," see 42 U. Rich. L. Rev. 229 (2007).

Michie's Jurisprudence. — For related discussion, see 5A M.J. Costs, §§ 2, 3; 6A M.J. Discovery, §§ 21 - 26, 30; 17 M.J. Stipulations, § 2.

CASE NOTES

The trial court did not err in suppressing an out-of-state deposition taken by telephone without the agreement of opposing counsel or approval of the court, in violation of the provisions of this rule. Gillespie v. Davis, 242 Va. 300, 410 S.E.2d 613 (1991).

CIRCUIT COURT OPINIONS

Deposition could be taken in medical case although process had not been served. — Patient who had filed suit against a hospital and radiological technologist was not entitled to take a supplemental deposition pursuant to Va. Sup. Ct. R. 4:2, which only governed perpetuation of testimony prior to filing suit, but could take a deposition pursuant to Va. Sup. Ct. R. 4:5(a). CT scan protocols were not privileged under the peer review privilege statute, § 8.01-581.17. Jones v. Perez (In re Jones), 81 Va. Cir. 52, 2010 Va. Cir. LEXIS 308 (Chesapeake Nov. 22, 2010).

Because a patient had filed a separate suit directly against a radiological technologist following a deposition of the technologist, any amendments or supplemental depositions were not available pursuant to Va. Sup. Ct. R. 4:2. Due to the commencement of the new suit, however, the patient could undertake depositions of knowledgeable representatives of the hospital defendant, pursuant to Va. Sup. Ct. R. 4:5(a), in accordance with her amended notice of deposition. Jones v. Perez (In re Jones), 81 Va. Cir. 52, 2010 Va. Cir. LEXIS 278 (Chesapeake Oct. 26, 2010).

Producing unprepared corporate designee at deposition a violation. — Corporate defendants violated their duty to designate a representative with knowledge of each subject noticed for deposition and to ensure that the designee was prepared to answer questions on each of the subjects noted, as its designee took no steps to investigate the deposition subjects. Martin v. Nordic Group of Cos., 61 Va. Cir. 13, 2003 Va. Cir. LEXIS 11 (Fairfax County 2003).

Instructing client not to answer deposition questions. — Trial court found that a doctor's attorney acted improperly when she instructed her client not to answer questions that were asked by a patient's attorney during a deposition, but it decided not to impose monetary sanctions against the attorney because it sustained the objections she raised and the patient did not raise or pursue the issue of sanctions. Cuesta v. Shapiro, 65 Va. Cir. 79, 2004 Va. Cir. LEXIS 104 (Fairfax County 2004).

Use of deposition at trial. — Because a defense witness was more than 100 miles from the place of trial and was out of the Commonwealth, pursuant to Va. Sup. Ct. R. 4:7, the witness's deposition could be used at trial; there was no basis for a protective order that would be in contravention of Va. Sup. Ct. R. 4:5. Willis v. Tenekjian, 68 Va. Cir. 203, 2005 Va. Cir. LEXIS 73 (Portsmouth 2005).

Adjournment for further research not permitted. — No principle of law or rule of evidence allows a witness to halt or adjourn his testimony in order to provide him with an opportunity to prepare or to formulate better responses to inquiries or to do further research on what he is being asked. Estate of Smith, 65 Va. Cir. 267, 2004 Va. Cir. LEXIS 153 (Madison County 2004).

Sanctions. — Where plaintiff's counsel was careless in handling a notice of deposition and created a misunderstanding of what was desired, an award of attorneys fees was ordered as a sanction pursuant to Va. Sup. Ct. R. 4:5(g). Adams v. Cambridge Research Assocs., 61 Va. Cir. 425, 2003 Va. Cir. LEXIS 55 (Fairfax County 2003).

Respondent was awarded reasonable expenses, including attorney's fees, for a deposition that was halted to allow the witness more time to prepare precise and accurate answers. Estate of Smith, 65 Va. Cir. 267, 2004 Va. Cir. LEXIS 153 (Madison County 2004).

OPINIONS OF THE ATTORNEY GENERAL

What constitutes a "proceeding." — When an attorney files a copy of a letter to opposing counsel with the clerk of court, such a filing does not constitute a 'proceeding,' but the filed letter may indicate that there are other ongoing proceedings pending in the action, thereby foreclosing the discontinuance of the action. See opinion of Attorney General to The Honorable Jack Kennedy, Clerk, Circuit Court of Wise County, 11-057, 2011 Va. AG LEXIS 49 (7/22/11).

Rule 4:6. Depositions Upon Written Questions.

(a) *Serving Questions; Notice.* — After commencement of the action, any party may take the testimony of any person, including a party, by deposition upon written questions. The attendance of witnesses may be compelled by the use of subpoena. The deposition of a person confined in prison may be taken only by leave of court on such terms as the court prescribes.

A party desiring to take the deposition upon written questions shall serve them upon every other party with a notice stating (1) the name and address of the person who is to answer them, if known, and if the name is not known, a general description sufficient to identify him or the particular class or group to which he belongs, and (2) the name or descriptive title and address of the officer before whom the deposition is to be taken. A deposition upon written questions may be taken of a public or private corporation or a partnership or association or governmental agency in accordance with the provisions of Rule 4:5(b)(6).

Within 21 days after the notice and written questions are served, a party may serve cross questions upon all other parties. Within 10 days after being served with cross questions, a party may serve redirect questions upon all other parties. Within 10 days after being served with redirect questions, a party may serve recross questions upon all other parties. The court may for cause shown enlarge or shorten the time.

(b) *Officer to Take Responses and Prepare Record.* — A copy of the notice and copies of all questions served shall be delivered by the party taking the deposition to the officer designated in the notice, who shall proceed promptly, in the manner provided by Rule 4:5(c), (e), and (f), to take the testimony of the witness in response to the questions and to prepare, certify, and file the electronic or digitally imaged deposition or lodge the deposition with the attorney for the party who initiated the taking of the deposition, attaching thereto the copy of the notice and the questions received.

(c) *Notice of Filing.* — When the deposition is filed, the party taking it shall promptly give notice thereof to all other parties.

The amendment, effective May 2, 2011, adopted March 1, 2011, substituted "the electronic or digitally imaged deposition or lodge the deposition with the attorney for the party who initiated the taking of" for "or mail" and deleted "by him" following "questions received" in subdivision (b).

Michie's Jurisprudence. — For related discussion, see 6A M.J. Discovery, §§ 27 - 30.

CASE NOTES

Answers to interrogatories did not constitute depositions. — In appeal from order amending divorce decree, trial court erred in determining that answers to interrogatories from husband's former attorney constituted depositions upon written questions and were, therefore, admissible into evidence. On appeal, both parties agreed that these answers to interrogatories did not constitute a deposition upon written questions, and since husband had no opportunity to cross-examine witness, the court of appeals agreed. Arrington v. Arrington, No. 1404-87-3 (Ct. of Appeals Feb. 21, 1989).

Rule 4:6A. Number of Depositions.

There shall be no limit on the number of witnesses whose depositions may be taken by a party except by order of the court for good cause shown.

Comment on adoption of rule. — This new rule, designed to limit discovery sharply, is taken from the rules of the United States District Court for the Eastern District of Virginia.

The amendment, effective October 1, 2001, adopted July 30, 2001, rewrote the Rule.

Rule 4:7. Use of Depositions in Court Proceedings.

(a) *Use of Depositions.* — At the trial or upon the hearing of a motion or an interlocutory proceeding, any part or all of a deposition, so far as admissible under the rules of evidence applied as though the witness were then present and testifying, may be used against any party who was present or represented at the taking of the deposition or who had reasonable notice thereof, in accordance with any of the following provisions:

(1) Any deposition taken in a civil action may be used for any purpose in supporting or opposing an equitable claim; provided, however, that such a deposition may be used on an issue heard by an advisory jury empaneled pursuant to Code § 8.01-336(E) or a hearing ore tenus only as provided by subdivision (a)(4) of this Rule.

(2) Any deposition may be used by any party for the purpose of contradicting or impeaching the testimony of deponent as a witness.

(3) The deposition of a party or of anyone who at the time of taking the deposition was an officer, director, or managing agent, or a person designated under Rule 4:5(b)(6) or 4:6(a) to testify on behalf of a public or private corporation, partnership or association or governmental agency which is a party may be used by an adverse party for any purpose.

(4) The deposition of a witness, whether or not a party, may be used by any party for any purpose in any action upon a claim arising at law, issue heard by an advisory jury empaneled pursuant to Code § 8.01-336(E), or hearing ore tenus upon an equitable claim if the court finds: (A) that the witness is dead; or (B) that the witness is at a greater distance than 100 miles from the place of trial or hearing, or is out of this Commonwealth, unless it appears that the absence of the witness was procured by the party offering the deposition; or (C) that the witness is unable to attend or testify because of age, illness, infirmity, or imprisonment; or (D) that the party offering the deposition has been unable to procure the attendance of the witness by subpoena; or (E) that the witness is a judge, or is a superintendent of a hospital for the insane more than 30 miles from the place of trial, or is a physician, surgeon, dentist, chiropractor, or registered nurse who, in the regular course of his profession, treated or examined any party to the proceeding, or is in any public office or service the duties of which prevent his attending court provided, however, that if the deponent is subject to the jurisdiction of the court, the court may, upon a showing of good cause or sua sponte, order him to attend and to testify ore tenus; or (F) upon application and notice, that such exceptional circumstances exist as to make it desirable, in the interest of justice and with due regard to the importance of presenting the testimony of witnesses orally in open court, to allow the deposition to be used.

(5) If only part of a deposition is offered in evidence by a party, an adverse party may require him to introduce any other part which ought in fairness to be considered with the part introduced, and any party may introduce any other parts.

(6) No deposition shall be read in any action against a person under a disability unless it be taken in the presence of the guardian ad litem appointed or attorney serving pursuant to § 8.01-9, or upon questions agreed on by the guardian or attorney before the taking.

(7) In any action, the fact that a deposition has not been offered in evidence prior to an interlocutory decree or order shall not prevent its thereafter being so offered except as to matters ruled upon in such interlocutory decree or order; provided, however, that such deposition may be read as to matters ruled upon in such an interlocutory decree or order if the principles applicable to after-discovered evidence would permit its introduction.

Substitution of parties does not affect the right to use depositions previously taken; and when there are pending in the same court several actions or suits between the same parties, depending upon the same facts, or involving the same matter of controversy, in whole or in part, a deposition taken in one of such actions or suits, upon notice to the same party or parties, may be read in all, so far as it is applicable and relevant to the issue; and, when an action in any court of the United States or of this or any other state has been dismissed and another action involving the same subject matter is afterward brought between the same parties or their representatives or successors in interest, all depositions lawfully taken and duly filed in the one action may be used in the other as if originally taken therefor.

(b) *Form of Presentation; Objections to Admissibility.* — A party may offer deposition testimony pursuant to this Rule in stenographic or nonstenographic form. Except as otherwise directed by the court, if all or part of a deposition is offered, the offering party shall provide the court with a transcript of the portions so offered in either form or in electronic or digitally imaged form. Except as provided in Rule 1:18 and subject to the provisions of subdivision (d) (3) of this Rule, objection may be made at the trial or hearing to receiving in evidence any deposition or part thereof for any reason which would require the exclusion of the evidence if the witness were then present and testifying.

(c) *Effect of Taking or Using Depositions.* — A party does not make a person his own witness for any purpose by taking his deposition. The introduction in evidence of the deposition or any part thereof for any purpose other than that of contradicting or impeaching the deponent makes the deponent the witness of the party introducing the deposition, but this shall not apply to the use by an adverse party of a deposition under subdivision (a)(3) of this Rule. At the trial or hearing any party may rebut any relevant evidence contained in a deposition whether introduced by him or by any other party.

(d) *Effect of Errors and Irregularities in Depositions.* — (1) As to Notice. — All errors and irregularities in the notice for taking a deposition are waived unless written objection is promptly served upon the party giving the notice.

(2) As to Disqualification of Officer. — Objection to taking a deposition because of disqualification of the officer before whom it is to be taken is waived unless made before the taking of the deposition begins or as soon thereafter as the disqualification becomes known or could be discovered with reasonable diligence.

(3) As to Taking of Deposition. — (A) Objections to the competency of a witness or to the competency, relevancy, or materiality of testimony are not waived by failure to make them before or during the taking of the deposition, unless the ground of the objection is one which might have been obviated or removed if presented at that time.

(B) Errors and irregularities occurring at the oral examination in the manner of taking the deposition, in the form of the questions or answers, in the oath or affirmation, or in the conduct of parties, and errors of any kind which might be obviated, removed, or cured if promptly presented, are waived unless seasonable objection thereto is made at the taking of the deposition.

(C) Objections to the form of written questions submitted under Rule 4:6 are waived unless served in writing upon the party propounding them within the time allowed for serving the succeeding cross or other questions and within 5 days after service of the last questions authorized.

(4) As to Completion and Return of Deposition. — Errors and irregularities in the manner in which the testimony is transcribed or the deposition is prepared, signed, certified, sealed, endorsed, transmitted, filed or otherwise dealt with by the officer under Rules 4:5 and 4:6 are waived unless a motion to suppress the deposition or some part thereof is made with reasonable promptness after such defect is, or with due diligence might have been, ascertained.

(e) *Limitation on Use of Depositions.* — No motion for summary judgment or to strike the evidence shall be sustained when based in whole or in part upon any depositions under Rule 4:5, unless such use of depositions is permitted by § 8.01-420.

(f) *Record.* — Depositions shall become a part of the record only to the extent that they are offered in evidence.

Cross references. — As to depositions as basis for motion for summary judgment or to strike evidence, see § 8.01-420.

Comment. — The Rules are not clear as to when discovery material becomes a part of the record. Only Rule 4:11(c) relating to requests for admission and responses thereto makes the matter clear as to those documents. The record should not be cluttered with material not offered in evidence.

The amendment, effective July 1, 2000, adopted May 1, 2000, added "Except as provided in Rule 1:18 and" at the beginning of subdivision (b).

The amendment, effective October 15, 2003, adopted August 15, 2003, deleted "the" following "his attending" in clause (e) of subdivision (a)(4); in subdivision (b), added "Form of Presentation" at the beginning of the subdivision catchline, and added the two sentences at the beginning of the paragraph.

The amendment, effective January 1, 2006, by order adopted June 14, 2005, in subdivision (a)(1), substituted "civil action" for "suit in equity," inserted "in supporting or opposing an equitable claim," and substituted "heard by an advisory jury empaneled pursuant to Code § 8.01-336(E)" for "out of chancery"; and in subdivision (a)(4), inserted "upon a claim arising," substituted "heard by an advisory jury empaneled pursuant to Code § 8.01-336(E)" for "out of chancery," and inserted "upon an equitable claim."

The amendment, effective May 2, 2011, adopted March 1, 2011, in subdivision (b), deleted "in nonstenographic form," following "deposition is offered" and added "in either printed form or in electronic or digitally imaged form" in the second sentence, and deleted the former third sentence, which read: "Except as provided in Rule 1:18 and subject to the provisions of subdivision (d)(3) of this Rule, objection may be made at the trial or hearing to receiving in evidence any deposition or part thereof for any reason which would require the exclusion of the evidence if the witness were then present and testifying."

The amendment effective July 1, 2013, adopted June 21, 2013, in subdivision (b), deleted "also" preceding "provide" and "printed" preceding "form" in the second sentence, and added the third sentence; and in subdivision (e), deleted "in any action at law" following "summary judgement" and substituted "use of depositions is permitted by § 8.01-420" for "depositions are received in evidence under Rule 4:7(a)(4) or all parties to the suit or action shall agree that such deposition may be so used."

Law Review. — For 2003/2004 survey of civil practice and procedure, see 39 U. Rich. L. Rev. 87 (2004). For 2006 survey article, "Medical Malpractice Law," see 41 U. Rich. L. Rev. 231 (2006). For 2007 annual survey article, "Civil Practice and Procedure," see 42 U. Rich. L. Rev. 229 (2007).

Michie's Jurisprudence. — For related discussion, see 6A M.J. Discovery, §§ 10 - 12, 24, 28, 30; 20 M.J. Witnesses, § 30.

CASE NOTES

Depositions not intended as substitute for personal appearance. — As salutary as is the rule which permits the use in evidence of discovery depositions under certain specified circumstances and conditions, such depositions were never intended to be substituted for the personal appearance of party litigants or witnesses. King v. International Harvester Co., 212 Va. 78, 181 S.E.2d 656 (1971).

Deposition of an adverse party, offered as substantive evidence, is distinguished from a deposition offered under subdivision (a)(2) of this rule for the purpose of contradicting or impeaching the deponent. The former may adduce proof tending to establish or controvert any fact in issue; the latter serves merely to affect the deponent's credibility as a witness. Horne v. Milgrim, 226 Va. 133, 306 S.E.2d 893 (1983).

Deposition of an adverse party that is received in evidence as substantive proof is oral testimony, not an exhibit. Unless the court for good cause otherwise directs, it should be read to the jury, not submitted in written form, so that it receives no more emphasis than other oral testimony. Horne v. Milgrim, 226 Va. 133, 306 S.E.2d 893 (1983).

Party offering an adverse party's discovery deposition may tender only that part of it he considers relevant. If fairness requires the admission of additional parts, a remedy is provided by subdivision (a)(5) of this rule. Horne v. Milgrim, 226 Va. 133, 306 S.E.2d 893 (1983).

A party may introduce an adverse party's discovery deposition whether the deponent is present or not. Horne v. Milgrim, 226 Va. 133, 306 S.E.2d 893 (1983).

Use of adverse party's deposition testimony. — Trial court erred in refusing a patient's proffered adverse witness instruction on the patient's use of the defendant podiatrist's deposition testimony in his case in chief; the instruction was an accurate statement of the law because Va. Sup. Ct. R. 4:7(a)(3) and (c), read together, clearly establish that a party seeking to introduce the deposition testimony of an adverse party will not suffer the consequences of making the deponent his own witness. Thornton v. Glazer, 271 Va. 566, 628 S.E.2d 327, 2006 Va. LEXIS 33 (2006).

In a child custody case, as the father's deposition transcript consisted mainly of his answers to questions about his son's extra-curricular activities, his relationship to his son and mother, and his participation in family therapy, all of which were relevant to the issue of custody, and he did not show any examples of hearsay or irrelevance, the trial court properly admitted the deposition into evidence. Russell v. Russell, 2006 Va. App. LEXIS 440 (Oct. 3, 2006).

Trial court did not abuse its discretion when it admitted a student's deposition, as statements contained therein were not hearsay where they were made while the student was testifying under oath; those statements were treated as live, in-person testimony under Va. Sup. Ct. R. 4:7. Burns v. Gagnon, 283 Va. 657, 727 S.E.2d 634, 2012 Va. LEXIS 93 (2012).

Use of deposition at trial. — Trial court did not abuse its discretion when it admitted a student's deposition at the plea in bar hearing or at trial on a personal injury action, arising from a fight between two students, as it was admissible under Va. Sup. Ct. R. 4:7 where all of the requirements were met, including the witness's unavailability. Burns v. Gagnon, 283 Va. 657, 727 S.E.2d 634, 2012 Va. LEXIS 93 (2012).

Meaning of "absence" of witness. — The "absence" of the witness as used in the second condition of subdivision (a)(4) means absence from the trial. King v. International Harvester Co., 212 Va. 78, 181 S.E.2d 656 (1971).

"Procured" absence. — The voluntary and unexplained absence of a party is a "procured" absence. King v. International Harvester Co., 212 Va. 78, 181 S.E.2d 656 (1971).

When the absence of a witness is due merely to a preference to use his deposition rather than to testify orally at the trial, the rule does not permit of its use. Absence under such conditions is in effect "procured" by any party offering the deposition. King v. International Harvester Co., 212 Va. 78, 181 S.E.2d 656 (1971).

Trial court properly admitted an absent witness's deposition testimony, where in addition to being a non-party, his absence was not procured by a party, and while plaintiff used a subpoena to attempt to secure his presence, the witness was unavailable. Greater Richmond Transit Co. v. Massey, 268 Va. 354, 601 S.E.2d 609, 2004 Va. LEXIS 131 (2004).

Where the plaintiff was not absent for any valid reason permitted by the rule, defendants were under no obligation to make a motion at the outset of the trial that the court require his attendance in person. King v. International Harvester Co., 212 Va. 78, 181 S.E.2d 656 (1971).

Party who is out of this state or is a greater distance than 100 miles from the place of trial may not use his own deposition as evidence at the trial unless it appears that he could not be present and the court finds the existence of any one of the enumerated conditions. King v. International Harvester Co., 212 Va. 78, 181 S.E.2d 656 (1971).

Use of treating physician's deposition. — Trial court erred in refusing a patient's motion to use his treating physician's deposition testimony in rebuttal in a medical malpractice trial on the ground that the physician had testified earlier in the trial and was therefore not unavailable; pursuant to Va. Sup. Ct. R. 4:7(a)(4)(E), a party is entitled to offer into evidence the deposition testimony of a treating physician for any purpose even if the physician is available, unless the trial court finds good cause to order attendance to testify ore tenus. Thornton v. Glazer, 271 Va. 566, 628 S.E.2d 327, 2006 Va. LEXIS 33 (2006).

Error not preserved. — In a medical malpractice lawsuit regarding hip reconstruction surgery, although a certain testimonial statement by a treating radiologist, that the patient had "Stage II avascular necrosis as his major problem" was diagnostic, and thus, should have been made within a reasonable degree of medical probability under subsection B of § 8.01-399, the patient waived review because he failed to timely challenge this testimony at deposition, as required by Va. Sup. Ct. R. 4:7(d)(3)(B). Graham v. Cook, 278 Va. 233, 682 S.E.2d 535, 2009 Va. LEXIS 93 (2009).

Applied in Smith v. Givens, 223 Va. 455, 290 S.E.2d 844 (1982); Armistead v. Armistead, 228 Va. 352, 322 S.E.2d 836 (1984); Pace v. Richmond, 231 Va. 216, 343 S.E.2d 59 (1986); Henning v. Thomas, 235 Va. 181, 366 S.E.2d 109 (1988); Lombard v. Rohrbaugh, 262 Va. 484, 551 S.E.2d 349, 2001 Va. LEXIS 113 (2001).

CIRCUIT COURT OPINIONS

Use of deposition for summary judgment not allowed. — Medical center's motion to compel the doctor to provide full responses to requests for admission was denied, because the medical center was, in effect, seeking summary judgment based upon the doctor's deposition, which was not permitted by Rule 4:7(e). Walker v. Bon Secours Health Sys., 56 Va. Cir. 532, 2001 Va. Cir. LEXIS 497 (Norfolk 2001).

Use of deposition at trial. — Because a defense witness was more than 100 miles from the place of trial and was out of the Commonwealth, the witness's deposition could be used at trial; there was no basis for a protective order that would be in contravention of Va. Sup. Ct. R. 4:5(a1). Willis v. Tenekjian, 68 Va. Cir. 203, 2005 Va. Cir. LEXIS 73 (Portsmouth 2005).

De bene esse deposition. — There is no statute or rule of court specifically authorizing a de bene esse deposition. Since all depositions are governed by the Rules of Court, any deposition of a physician may potentially be used at trial pursuant to Va. Sup. Ct. R. 4:7(a)(4)(E); therefore, it is potentially a de bene esse deposition as that term has evolved. Boyer v. Dabinett, 74 Va. Cir. 19, 2007 Va. Cir. LEXIS 268 (Winchester 2007).

Contradictory statements. — Plea in bar arguing that owners had taken inconsistent positions in an earlier suit and in the current suit was denied where the potentially contradictory statements were made during the discovery phase of the earlier suit, not at trial, and so the *Burch* estoppel rule did not apply. Post Apt. Homes, L.P. v. RTKL Assocs., 63 Va. Cir. 355, 2003 Va. Cir. LEXIS 325 (Arlington County 2003).

Rule 4:7A. Audio-Visual Depositions.

(a) *When Depositions May Be Taken by Audio-Visual Means.* — Any depositions permitted under these Rules may be taken by audio-visual means including, but not limited to, videoconferencing and teleconferencing, as authorized by and when taken in compliance with law.

(b) *Procedure.* — (1) The deposition must begin with an oral or written statement on camera which includes (i) each operator's name and business address or, if applicable, the identity of the video conferencing or teleconferencing proprietor and locations participating in the video conference or teleconference; (ii) the name and business address of the operator's employer; (iii) the date, time and place of the deposition; (iv) the caption of the case; (v) the name of the witness; (vi) the party on whose behalf the deposition is being taken; (vii) with respect to video conferencing or teleconferencing, the identities of persons present at the deposition and the location of each such person; and (viii) any stipulations by the parties; and

(2) In addition, all counsel present on behalf of any party or witness shall identify themselves on camera. The oath for witnesses shall be administered on camera. If the length of a deposition requires the use of more than one recording unit, the end of each unit and the beginning of each succeeding unit shall be announced on camera. At the conclusion of a deposition, a statement shall be made on camera that the deposition is concluded. A statement may be made on camera setting forth any stipulations made by

counsel concerning the custody of the audio-visual recording and exhibits or other pertinent matters; and

(3) All objections must be made as in the case of stenographic depositions.

(c) *Editing.* — No audio-visual deposition shall be edited except pursuant to a stipulation of the parties or pursuant to order of the court and only as and to the extent directed in such stipulation and/or order. In any case where the parties stipulate or the court orders the audio-visual recording to be edited prior to its use, the original recording shall not be altered and the editing shall be done on a copy or copies.

(d) *Recording and Transcription.* — (1) Any deposition may be recorded by audio-visual means without a stenographic record. The audio-visual recording is an official record of the deposition. A transcript prepared by a court reporter shall also be deemed an official record of the deposition. Any party may make, at its own expense, a simultaneous stenographic or audio record of the deposition. Upon request and at his own expense, any party is entitled to an audio or audio-visual copy of the audio-visual recording.

(2) If an appeal is taken in the case, the appellant must cause to be prepared and filed with the clerk a written transcript of that portion of an audio-visual deposition made a part of the record in the trial court to the extent germane to an issue on appeal. The appellee may designate additional portions to be so prepared by the appellant and filed.

(e) *Use.* — An audio-visual deposition may be used for any purpose and under any circumstances in which a stenographic deposition may be used.

(f) *Submission to the Witness; Changes; Signing.* — The provisions of Rule 4:5(e) shall not apply to an audio-visual deposition. The other provisions of Rule 4:5 shall be applicable to the extent practicable.

(g) *Filing.* — Unless otherwise stipulated by the parties or ordered by the court, the original audio-visual recording of a deposition, any copy edited pursuant to stipulation or an order of the court, and exhibits shall be filed only in accord with Rule 4:5(f)(1).

The amendment effective January 1, 2001, adopted September 28, 2000, inserted "including but not limited to video conferencing and teleconferencing" in subdivision (a).

The amendment effective January 1, 2001, adopted November 2, 2000, substituted "means including, but not limited to, videoconferencing" for "means, including but not limited to video conferencing" in subdivision (a); added subdivision (b); in subdivision (c), inserted "stipulation and/or" near the end of the first sentence, and added the second sentence; in subdivision (d), added paragraph (1), and designated the former provisions as paragraph (2); rewrote subdivision (e); changed the subdivision (f) heading; and added subdivision (g).

Michie's Jurisprudence. — For related discussion, see 6A M.J. Discovery, §§ 24, 28.

Rule 4:8. Interrogatories to Parties.

(a) *Availability; Procedures for Use.* — Any party may serve upon any other party written interrogatories to be answered by the party served or, if the party served is a public or private corporation or a partnership or association or governmental agency, by any officer or agent, who shall furnish such information as is available to the party. Interrogatories may, without leave of court, be served upon the plaintiff after commencement of the action and upon any other party with or after service of the complaint upon that party.

(b) *Form.* — The party answering the interrogatories shall restate each question, by photocopying it or otherwise, then insert the word "Answer" and immediately thereafter state the response to that question. The answering party shall attach the necessary oath and certificate of service to the answers.

(c) *Filing.* — (1) Interrogatories and answers or objections thereto shall not be filed unless the court directs such filing on its own initiative or upon the request of any party prior to or during the trial.

(2) When the propriety or sufficiency of any interrogatory, answer or objection, or the service thereof, is challenged, or any other issue concerning such discovery is presented to the court for decision, copies of the relevant items, including any applicable certificates of service, shall be made available to the court by counsel.

(3) In an Electronically Filed Case, submission of interrogatories, answers, objections and certificates of service as provided in subdivisions (c)(1) and (c)(2) of this Rule shall be made by filing an electronic or digitally imaged copy thereof, unless the court directs otherwise.

(d) *Answers.* — Each interrogatory shall be answered separately and fully in writing under oath, unless it is objected to, in which event the reasons for objection shall be stated in lieu of an answer. The answers are to be signed by the person making them, and the objections signed by the attorney making them. The party upon whom the interrogatories have been served shall serve a copy of the answers, and objections if any, within 21 days after the service of the interrogatories, except that a defendant may serve answers or objections within 28 days after service of the bill of complaint or motion for judgment upon that defendant. The court may allow a shorter or longer time. The party submitting the interrogatories may move for an order under Rule 4:12(a) with respect to any objection to or other failure to answer an interrogatory.

(e) *Scope; Use.* — Interrogatories may relate to any matters which can be inquired into under Rule 4:1(b), and the answers may be used to the extent permitted by the rules of evidence and for the purposes of Rule 3:20. Only such interrogatories and the answers thereto as are offered in evidence shall become a part of the record.

An interrogatory otherwise proper is not necessarily objectionable merely because an answer to the interrogatory involves an opinion or contention that relates to fact or the application of law to fact, but the court may order that such an interrogatory need not be answered until after designated discovery has been completed or until a pre-trial conference or other later time.

(f) *Option to Produce Business Records.* — Where the answer to an interrogatory may be derived or ascertained from the business records, including electronically stored information, of the party upon whom the interrogatory has been served or from an examination, audit or inspection of such business records, or from a compilation, abstract or summary based thereon, and the burden of deriving or ascertaining the answer is substantially the same for the party serving the interrogatory as for the party served, it is a sufficient answer to such interrogatory to specify the records from which the answer may be derived or ascertained and to afford to the party serving the interrogatory reasonable opportunity to examine, audit or inspect such records and to make copies, compilations, abstracts or summaries. A specification shall be in sufficient detail to permit the interrogating party to locate and to identify, as readily as can the party served, the records from which the answer may be ascertained. A specification of electronically stored information may be made under this Rule if the information will be made available in a reasonably usable form or forms.

(g) *Limitation on Interrogatories.* — No party shall serve upon any other party, at any one time or cumulatively, more than thirty written interrogatories, including all parts and sub-parts without leave of court for good cause shown.

Comment on the 1983 amendment. — Subsection (b) has been inserted (and the other paragraphs relettered) in order to facilitate responses to interrogatories, to avoid the necessity of reproducing them, and to produce a single cohesive document. The change to subsection (d), like the addition to Rule 4:5, is designed to clarify the contents of the record. The addition of subsection (f), like Rule 4:6A, is taken from the Rules of the United States District Court for the Eastern District of Virginia.

Comment on the 1984 amendment. — The establishment of new subsection (c) is intended to relieve the crowded condition of clerks' offices. The amendment to subsection (d) makes it clear that interrogatories and their answers may be used in connection with summary judgments in suits in equity.

Comment on the 1985 amendment. — The first change eliminates an unnecessary act; the second is clarifying.

The amendment effective July 1, 1999, adopted January 25, 1999, added the last sentence in subdivision (f).

The amendment effective January 1, 2001, adopted September 28, 2000, rewrote subdivision (b).

The amendment effective January 1, 2006, by order adopted June 14, 2005, substituted "Rule 3:20" for "Rules 2:21 and 3:18" in the first paragraph of subdivision (e).

The amendment effective February 28, 2006, adopted February 28, 2006, deleted "bill of" preceding, and "or motion for judgment" following, "complaint" at the end of subdivision (a).

The amendment effective January 1, 2009, adopted October 31, 2008, in subdivision (f), inserted "including electronically stored information" near the beginning of the first sentence, and added the third sentence.

The amendment, effective May 2, 2011, adopted March 1, 2011, rewrote subdivision (c).

Law Review. — For 2007 annual survey article, "Civil Practice and Procedure," see 42 U. Rich. L. Rev. 229 (2007).

Michie's Jurisprudence. — For related discussion, see 6A M.J. Discovery, §§ 31 - 33.

CIRCUIT COURT OPINIONS

Option to produce business records. — When a party exercised the option, under Rule 4:8(f), to produce business records in lieu of an answer to an interrogatory, the strict requirements of the rule had to be met, and the party had to specify the records from which an answer to the interrogatory could be derived. Dawson v. Bd. of Supervisors, 2002 Va. Cir. LEXIS 126 (Loudoun County Apr. 11, 2002).

Discretion of courts. — Court has discretion to overrule objections to interrogatories, and interrogatories are not objectionable merely because the answer might involve an opinion or contention that relates to facts or the application of law to fact; the court partially granted an objection to an interrogatory, which asked a county to provide extensive information regarding the development of the sewerage system, because the disclosure of all of the requested documents would be burdensome and would bear little relevancy to the case, but the county was ordered to provide more limited information with regard to the system, including a basic description of the construction plans, the contents of any contracts entered into by the county for the construction of the system, the start date or anticipated start date of construction, the estimated completion date, and the identity of the entity that will operate the system. Janney v. Westmoreland County, 65 Va. Cir. 533, 2002 Va. Cir. LEXIS 451 (Westmoreland County 2002).

Sanctions not appropriate for failure to answer under oath. — Where plaintiff failed to answer interrogatories under oath, as required by Rule 4:8, court declined to impose sanctions, but decided to proceed under Rule 4:12 and order an action deemed to be "just" because the interrogatories propounded by defendant were difficult, awkward, and obscure. Court determined that the most just solution was to require plaintiff to supplement and more fully respond to certain interrogatories. Whalen v. Nelson, 68 Va. Cir. 485, 2001 Va. Cir. LEXIS 538 (Nelson County 2001).

Motion to compel granted. — Where defendants had failed to respond to plaintiff's first set of interrogatories and first set of requests for production of documents within 21 days under Va. Sup. Ct. R. 4:8(d) and 4:9(b) and had not requested a longer time for discovery, they had forced plaintiff to file a motion to compel; thus, the trial court ordered defendants to respond to certain interrogatories and requests for production. Kawar v. Bouk, 71 Va. Cir. 295, 2006 Va. Cir. LEXIS 137 (Fairfax County 2006).

Limitation on interrogatories. — When the number of interrogatories propounded violates the number permitted by Va. Sup. Ct. R. 4:8(g), no response by the opposing party is required. Brendle v. Brendle, 73 Va. Cir. 390, 2007 Va. Cir. LEXIS 105 (Orange County 2007).

Rule 4:9. Production by Parties of Documents, Electronically Stored Information, and Things; Entry on Land for Inspection and Other Purposes; Production at Trial.

(a) *Scope.* — Any party may serve on any other party a request (1) to produce and permit the party making the request, or someone acting on his behalf, to inspect, copy, test, or sample any designated documents or electronically stored information (including writings, drawings, graphs, charts, photographs, and other data or data compilations stored in any medium from which information can be obtained, translated, if necessary, by the respondent into reasonably usable form), or to inspect, copy, test, or sample any designated tangible things which constitute or contain matters within the scope of Rule 4:1(b) and which are in the possession, custody, or control of the party upon whom the request is served; or (2) to produce any such documents or electronically stored information to the court in which the proceeding is pending at the time of trial; or (3) to permit entry upon designated land or other property in the possession or control of the party upon whom the request is served for the purpose of inspection and measuring, surveying, photographing, testing, or sampling the property or any designated object or operation thereon, within the scope of Rule 4:1(b).

(b) *Procedure.* — (i) Initiation of the Request. The request may, without leave of court, be served upon the plaintiff after commencement of the action and upon any other party with or after service of the complaint upon that party. The request shall set forth the items to be inspected either by individual item or by category, and describe each item and category with reasonable particularity. The request shall specify a reasonable time, place, period and manner of making the inspection and performing the related acts. The request may specify the form or forms in which electronically stored information is to be produced.

(ii) Response. The party upon whom the request is served shall serve a written response within 21 days after the service of the request, except that a defendant may serve a response within 28 days after service of the complaint upon that defendant. The court may allow a shorter or longer time. The response shall state, with respect to each item or category, that inspection and related activities will be permitted as requested, unless the request is objected to, including an objection to the requested form or forms for producing electronically stored information, stating the reasons for the objection. If objection is made to part of an item or category, the part shall be specified and production shall be permitted as to the remaining parts. If objection is made to the requested form or forms for producing electronically stored information — or if no form was specified in the request — the responding party must state the form or forms it intends to use. The party submitting the request may move for an order under Rule 4:12(a) with respect to any objection to or other failure to respond to the request or any part thereof, or any failure to permit inspection as requested. A motion under this Rule must be accompanied by a certification that the movant has in good faith conferred or attempted to confer with other affected parties in an effort to resolve the dispute without court action.

(iii) Organization, Reasonable Accessibility, and Forms of Production. Unless the parties otherwise agree, or the court otherwise orders:

(A) Production of Documents. A party who produces documents for inspection either shall produce them as they are kept in the usual course of business or shall organize and label them to correspond with the categories in the request.

(B) Electronically Stored Information.

(1) Responses to a request for production of electronically stored information shall be subject to the provisions of Rules 4:1(b)(7) and 4:1(b)(8).

(2) If a request does not specify the form or forms for producing electronically stored information, or if a responding party objects to the requested form or forms of production, a responding party must produce the information as it is ordinarily maintained if it is reasonably usable in such form or forms, or must produce the information in another form or forms in which it is reasonably usable. A party need not produce the same electronically stored information in more than one form.

(iv) Proceedings Under the Uniform Interstate Depositions and Discovery Act. Production of documents and electronic records sought in Virginia pursuant to a subpoena issued under the authority of a foreign jurisdiction shall be subject to the provisions of the Uniform Interstate Depositions and Discovery Act, Virginia Code §§ 8.01-412.8 through 8.01-412.15.

(c) *Proceedings on Failure or Refusal to Comply.* — If a party fails or refuses to obey an order made under section (b) of this Rule, the court may proceed as provided by Rule 4:12(b)(2).

(d) *Filing.* — Requests to a party pursuant to this Rule and responses or objections shall be filed as provided in Rule 4:8(c).

Comment on 1985 amendment. — The purpose of the amendment is to reduce the clutter in the clerk's office.

The amendment effective February 1, 1999, adopted November 23, 1998, inserted "dispatched by commercial delivery service, transmitted by facsimile" in subdivision (c).

The amendment effective July 1, 1999, adopted January 25, 1999, added the last paragraph in subdivision (b).

The amendment effective July 1, 2000, adopted June 16, 2000, in subdivision (c), added the paragraph (1) designation and heading and inserted "or" preceding "delivered" in that paragraph, and added paragraph (2).

The amendment effective October 15, 2003, adopted August 15, 2003, deleted "or" following "commercial delivery service" in the first sentence of subdivision (c)(1); substituted "has been served pursuant to Rule 1:12 upon counsel of record" for "has been mailed, dispatched by commercial delivery service, transmitted by facsimile, or delivered to counsel of record" in the fourth sentence of subdivision (c)(2); and added subdivision (c-2).

The amendment effective April 1, 2004, adopted January 30, 2004, in the first sentence of subdivision (c)(1), substituted "has been served pursuant to Rule 1:12 upon counsel" for "has been mailed, dispatched by commercial delivery service, transmitted by facsimile, or delivered to counsel."

The amendment effective January 1, 2005, adopted September 30, 2004, added the last paragraph of subdivision (b).

The amendment effective February 28, 2006, adopted February 28, 2006, substituted "after service of the complaint" for "after service of the bill of complaint or motion for judgment" in the first sentence of the first two paragraphs of subdivision (b).

The amendment effective January 1, 2009, adopted October 31, 2008, rewrote the Rule.

The amendment effective July 1, 2009, adopted June 1, 2009, added subdivision (b)(iv).

Law Review. — For a note, "Allocating Discovery Costs in the Computer Age: Deciding Who Should Bear the Costs of Discovery of Electronically Stored Data," see 57 Wash. & Lee L. Rev. 257 (2000). For 2003/2004 survey of civil practice and procedure, see 39 U. Rich. L. Rev. 87 (2004). For article reviewing recent developments and changes in legislation, case law, and Virginia Supreme

Court Rules affecting civil litigation, see "Civil Practice and Procedure," see 40 U. Rich. L. Rev. 95 (2005). For 2007 annual survey article, "Electronic Data: A Commentary on the Law in Virginia in 2007," see 42 U. Rich. L. Rev. 355 (2007).

Michie's Jurisprudence. — For related discussion, see 6A M.J. Discovery, §§ 34 - 36.

CASE NOTES

Statement of facts tendered to the chancellor is essentially a summary of data contained in papers included in the record on appeal under Rule 5:8, including admissions under Rule 4:11, exhibits requested under this rule, the chancellor's letter opinion and the final decree. City of Richmond v. Randall, 215 Va. 506, 211 S.E.2d 56 (1975).

Failure to comply with subpoena duces tecum. — The failure or refusal of a non-party to comply with a properly issued and served subpoena duces tecum under subsection (c) was subject to a contempt sanction under Va. Code Ann. § 18.2-456; this express provision for the statutory application excluded the conduct of the non-party from the scope of Va. Sup. Ct. R. 4:12. Tonti v. Akbari, 262 Va. 681, 553 S.E.2d 769, 2001 Va. LEXIS 137 (2001).

Imposition of sanctions short of ruling document inadmissible held proper. — Where the trial court found plaintiff's failure to produce a document on discovery was inadvertent, defendant's counsel was promptly notified when the document was located less than a week before trial, and a copy of the document was delivered to him on the morning of the first day of the trial, there was no abuse of the trial court's discretion in imposing sanctions designed to alleviate the surprise claimed by the defendant, short of ruling the document inadmissible. First Charter Land Corp. v. Middle Atl. Dredging, Inc., 218 Va. 304, 237 S.E.2d 145 (1977).

Sanctions improperly imposed for failing to produce autopsy report. — An attorney representing an estate in a medical malpractice case was not subject to sanctions for failing to produce an autopsy report prepared at the request of the decedent's family a number of months after the decedent's death to determine whether a malpractice claim might be warranted where, after reasonable inquiry, the attorney could have formed a reasonable belief that the report was not a medical report discoverable under this rule but, instead, was an expert's report discoverable only in compliance with the provisions of Rule 4:1(b)(4) and the circuit court's scheduling order. Flora v. Shulmister, 262 Va. 215, 546 S.E.2d 427, 2001 Va. LEXIS 69 (2001).

Discoverable records. — Section 2.2-3704, restricting access to information under Virginia's Freedom of Information Act to Virginia citizens did not abridge the ability of petitioner, an out-of-state searcher for his title company clients, to engage in a common calling in the sense the Privileges and Immunities Clause prohibited and a claim of constitutional violation by defendant state officials for denying the information sought failed; many records were available through other means, such as through discovery or subpoenas under Va. Sup. Ct. R. 4:1, 4:9, or the under the Government Data Collection and Dissemination Practices Act, subdivision A 3 of § 2.2-3806. McBurney v. Young, 133 S. Ct. 1709, 185 L. Ed. 2d 758, 2013 U.S. LEXIS 3317 (2013).

Discoverable records in support modification proceeding. — While records probative of husband's financial status prior to the divorce were arguable irrelevant to the instant proceedings for modification of previously ordered support, records of husband's economic circumstances subsequent to the earlier order, including the financial particulars of his corporation, were proper subjects of inquiry which appeared reasonably calculated to lead to the discovery of admissible evidence. Mancini v. Mancini, No. 1420-96-1 (Ct. of Appeals Apr. 8, 1997).

Discovery of opinions of experts not subject to this rule. — A litigant cannot use a request for production of documents under this rule to circumvent the exclusive method established in Rule 4:1(b)(4) for discovering expert opinions. Flora v. Shulmister, 262 Va. 215, 546 S.E.2d 427, 2001 Va. LEXIS 69 (2001).

Applied in First Charter Land Corp. v. Middle Atl. Dredging, Inc., 218 Va. 304, 237 S.E.2d 145 (1977).

CIRCUIT COURT OPINIONS

Objection to subpoena. — While the provisions of Va. Sup. Ct. R. 4:9(c)(2) could be clearer with respect to the remedies available to a party who wishes to object to an attorney-issued subpoena, the only logical contextual meaning of the Virginia rule requires that a court read it so as to incorporate the provisions of Rule 4:9(c)(1) permitting a party to promptly file a motion to quash or modify the requested production. A motion requesting one of the three Rule 4:9(c)(1) restrictions is the proper procedural remedy available to a party seeking to limit production pursuant to a subpoena duces tecum issued on a non-party. Bunch v. Artz, 71 Va. Cir. 358, 2006 Va. Cir. LEXIS 252 (Portsmouth 2006).

Educational records. — When plaintiff alleged lead poisoning, the court permitted defendants to subpoena the school records of his mother under Va. Sup. Ct. R. 4:9 so that an expert could use them in determining whether plaintiff's deficits were due to lead or other factors, such as the mother's education and intelligence. The records were not privileged under subsection A of § 22.1-287, and they were relevant and reasonably calculated to lead to the discovery of admissible evidence under Va. Sup. Ct. R. 4:1; however, non-medical records in the school records were to be kept under seal because of their sensitive nature and medical records in the school records excluded from production because they did not contain information about the mother's intelligence or educational level. Bunch v. Artz, 71 Va. Cir. 358, 2006 Va. Cir. LEXIS 252 (Portsmouth 2006).

Reenactment request. — In a personal injury action brought by a railroad worker against his employer, the railroad, and a manufacturer, the trial court denied the worker's request to inspect the accident site, which was a motion filed two years after the accident, because the burdens and dangers created by a requested inspection of the site to set up a partial reenactment of the accident outweighed the degree to which the proposed inspection would have aided in the search for the truth. Wilson v. Norfolk & Portsmouth Belt Line R.R. Co., 69 Va. Cir. 153, 2005 Va. Cir. LEXIS 267 (Portsmouth 2005).

Computer files. — Virginia circuit courts may, pursuant to the powers governing discovery, grant "authority" for parties to access information otherwise protected by § 18.2-152.5. However, Va. Sup. Ct. R. 4:9 limits inspection and copying to "designated" documents; it does not allow a party to access computer files carte blanche. Albertson v. Albertson, 73 Va. Cir. 94, 2007 Va. Cir. LEXIS 132 (Fairfax County 2007).

Self-incrimination. — In a divorce action, issuance of a court order under Va. Sup. Ct. R. 4:9 granting the wife and a computer company "authority" under § 18.2-152.5 to access the husband's password protected files to determine if he committed acts of sodomy did not require the husband to perform a testimonial act and thus was not barred by his assertion of a self-incrimination privilege under Va. Const., Art. 1, § 8. Albertson v. Albertson, 73 Va. Cir. 94, 2007 Va. Cir. LEXIS 132 (Fairfax County 2007).

Party had no authority to require non-party to permit inspection of real property. — Virginia Sup. Ct. R. 4:9(c) did not provide a party with authority to require a non-party to permit inspections of its real property. Wilson v. Norfolk & Portsmouth Belt Line R.R. Co., 70 Va. Cir. 383, 2006 Va. Cir. LEXIS 44 (Portsmouth 2006).

Payment for discovery. — Because the Va. Sup. Ct. R. 4:9 requirement would be unduly burdensome on the company considering the bulk of the materials and the many notations throughout them, under Va. Sup. Ct. R. 4:9(c) governing protective orders, the order proposed by the company, including the provision for payment of the copying expenses, was a condition that was just. Williams v. Branch Banking & Trust Corp., 71 Va. Cir. 43, 2006 Va. Cir. LEXIS 233 (Richmond 2006).

Motion to compel granted. — Where defendants had failed to respond to plaintiff's first set of interrogatories and first set of requests for production of documents within 21 days under Va. Sup. Ct. R. 4:8(d) and 4:9(b) and had not requested a longer time for discovery, they had forced plaintiff to file a motion to compel; thus, the trial court ordered defendants to respond to certain interrogatories and requests for production. Kawar v. Bouk, 71 Va. Cir. 295, 2006 Va. Cir. LEXIS 137 (Fairfax County 2006).

Subpoenas duces tecum for mental health records quashed. — Father's motion to quash subpoenas duces tecum for his mental health care records in a divorce and custody case was proper in part because the "good cause" provision of subsection D of § 32.1-127.1:03 yielded to the more specific privilege provisions of § 20-124.3:1, which created a privilege that prevented disclosure of the mental health care records; § 20-124.3:1, however, did not apply to the records of a health care provider who was not a licensed mental health care provider. Cage v. Cage, 73 Va. Cir. 190, 2007 Va. Cir. LEXIS 30 (Portsmouth 2007).

OPINIONS OF THE ATTORNEY GENERAL

What constitutes a "proceeding." — When an attorney files a copy of a letter to opposing counsel with the clerk of court, such a filing does not constitute a 'proceeding,' but the filed letter may indicate that there are other ongoing proceedings pending in the action, thereby foreclosing the discontinuance of the action. See opinion of Attorney General to The Honorable Jack Kennedy, Clerk, Circuit Court of Wise County, 11-057, 2011 Va. AG LEXIS 49 (7/22/11).

Rule 4:9A. Production from Non-Parties of Documents, Electronically Stored Information, and Things and Entry on Land for Inspection and Other Purposes; Production at Trial.

(a) *Issuance of a Subpoena Duces Tecum.* — Except as provided in paragraph (d) of this Rule, a subpoena duces tecum may be issued:

(1) By the clerk of court. Upon written request therefor filed with the clerk of the court in which the action or suit is pending by counsel of record for any party or by a party having no counsel in any pending case, with a certificate that a copy thereof has been served pursuant to Rule 1:12 upon counsel of record and to parties having no counsel, the clerk shall issue to a person not a party therein a subpoena duces tecum subject to this Rule.

(2) By an attorney. In a pending civil proceeding, a subpoena duces tecum may be issued by an attorney-at-law as an officer of the court if he or she is an active member of the Virginia State Bar at the time of issuance. An attorney may not issue a subpoena duces tecum in those civil proceedings excluded in Virginia Code § 8.01-407. An attorney-issued subpoena duces tecum must be signed as if a pleading and must contain the attorney's address, telephone number and Virginia State Bar identification number. A copy of any attorney-issued subpoena duces tecum must be mailed or delivered to the clerk's office of the court in which the case is pending on the day of

issuance with a certificate that a copy thereof has been served pursuant to Rule 1:12 upon counsel of record and to parties having no counsel. If time for compliance with an attorney-issued subpoena duces tecum is less than fourteen (14) days after service of the subpoena, the person to whom the subpoena is directed may serve on the party issuing the subpoena a written objection setting forth any grounds upon which such production, inspection, copying, sampling or testing should not be had. If an objection is made, the party issuing the subpoena shall not be entitled to the requested production, inspection, copying, sampling or testing, except pursuant to an order of the court in which the civil proceeding is pending. If an objection is made, the party issuing the subpoena may, upon notice to the person to whom the subpoena is directed, move for an order to compel the production, inspection, copying, sampling or testing. Upon a timely motion, the court may quash, modify or sustain the subpoena as provided above in subsection (c) of this Rule.

(b) *Content of Subpoena Duces Tecum; Objections.* — Subject to paragraph (d) of this Rule, a subpoena duces tecum shall command the person to whom it is directed, or someone acting on his behalf, to produce the documents, electronically stored information, or designated tangible things (including writings, drawings, graphs, charts, photographs, and other data or data compilations stored in any medium from which information can be obtained, translated, if necessary, by the respondent into reasonably usable form) designated and described in said request, and to permit the party filing such request, or someone acting in his behalf, to inspect and copy, test, or sample any designated tangible things which constitute or contain matters within the scope of Rule 4:1(b) which are in the possession, custody or control of such person to whom the subpoena is directed, at a time and place and for the period specified in the subpoena. A subpoena may specify the form or forms in which electronically stored information is to be produced.

(c) *Responding to a Subpoena; Objections; Production of Documents and Electronically Stored Information.* — (1) Production of Documents. A person responding to a subpoena to produce documents shall produce them as they are kept in the usual course of business or shall organize and label them to correspond with the categories in the demand.

(2) Electronically Stored Information. (A) A person responding to a subpoena need not provide discovery of electronically stored information from sources the responder identifies as not reasonably accessible because of undue burden or cost. On motion to compel production or to quash a subpoena, the person from whom production is sought under the subpoena must show that the information sought is not reasonably accessible because of undue burden or cost. If that showing is made, the court may nonetheless order production of responsive material from such sources if the subpoenaing party shows good cause, considering the limitations of Rule 4:1(b)(1). The court may specify conditions for the production of such information, including allocation of the reasonable costs thereof.

(B) If a subpoena does not specify the form or forms for producing electronically stored information, a person responding thereto must produce the information as it is ordinarily maintained if it is reasonably usable in such form or forms, or must produce the information in another form or forms in which it is reasonably usable. A person responding to a subpoena need not produce the same electronically stored information in more than one form.

(3) Objections and Procedures. The court, upon written motion promptly made by the person so required to produce, or by the party against whom such production is sought, may (1) quash or modify the subpoena, or the method or form for production of electronically stored information, if the subpoena would otherwise be unduly burdensome or expensive, (2) condition denial of the motion to quash or modify upon the advancement by the party in whose behalf the subpoena is issued of some or all of the reasonable cost of producing the documents, electronically stored information, and tangible things so designated and described or (3) direct that the documents and tangible things subpoenaed, including electronically stored information (unless another location for production is agreed upon by the requesting and producing parties), be returned only to the office of the clerk of the court through which such documents and tangible things are subpoenaed in which event, upon request of any party in interest, or his attorney, the clerk of such court shall permit the withdrawal of such documents and tangible things by such party or his attorney for such reasonable period of time as will permit his inspection, photographing, or copying thereof.

(4) Pre-Motion Negotiation. A motion under this Rule must be accompanied by a certification that the movant has in good faith conferred or attempted to confer with other affected parties in an effort to resolve the dispute without court action.

(d) *Certain Officials.* — No request to produce made pursuant to paragraph (b) above shall be served, and no subpoena provided for in paragraph (c) above shall issue, until prior order of the court is obtained when the party upon whom the request is to be served or the person to whom the subpoena is to be directed is the Governor, Lieutenant Governor, or Attorney General of this Commonwealth, or a judge of any court thereof; the President or Vice President of the United States; any member of the President's Cabinet; any Ambassador or Consul; or any Military Officer on active duty holding the rank of Admiral or General.

(e) *Certain Health Records.* — Patient health records protected by the privacy provisions of *Code Section 32.1-127.1:03* shall be disclosed only in accordance with the provisions and procedures prescribed by that statute.

(f) *Copies of Documents and Other Subpoenaed Information.* — (1) Documents. When one party to a civil proceeding subpoenas documents, the subpoenaing party, upon receipt of the subpoenaed documents, shall, if requested, provide true and full copies of the same to any party or to the attorney for any other party in accordance with Code § 8.01-417(B).

(2) Electronically stored information. When one party to a civil proceeding subpoenas and obtains electronically stored information, the subpoenaing party shall, if requested, provide true and full copies of the same to any party or that party's attorney, in the form the subpoenaing party received the information, upon reimbursement of the proportionate cost of obtaining such materials.

(g) *Proceedings on Failure or Refusal to Comply.* — If a non-party, after being served with a subpoena issued under the provisions of this Rule, fails or refuses to comply therewith, he may be proceeded against as for contempt of court as provided in § 18.2-456.

Effective date. — This rule, adopted October 31, 2008, became effective January 1, 2009.

Rule 4:10. Physical and Mental Examination of Persons.

(a) *Order for Examination.* — When the mental or physical condition (including the blood group) of a party, or of a person in the custody or under the legal control of a party, is in controversy, the court in which the action is pending, upon motion of an adverse party, may order the party to submit to a physical or mental examination by one or more health care providers, as defined in § 8.01-581.1, employed by the moving party or to produce for examination the person in the party's custody or legal control. The order may be made only on motion for good cause shown and upon notice to the person to be examined and to all parties, shall specify the time, place, manner, conditions, and scope of the examination and the person or persons by whom it is to be made, and shall fix the time for filing the report and furnishing the copies.

(b) *Out-of-State Examiners.* — Examiners named in such an order shall be licensed to practice in, and shall be residents of or have an office in, this Commonwealth. However, notwithstanding the reference to licensure by this Commonwealth in the definition of health care providers in § 8.01-581.1, the court may, in the exercise of its sound discretion and upon determining that the ends of justice will be served, order an examination by one who is not licensed to practice in, is not a resident of, and does not have an office in, this Commonwealth but who is duly licensed in his or her jurisdiction.

(c) *Report of Examiner.* — (1) A written report of the examination shall be made by the examiner to the court and filed with the clerk thereof before the trial and a copy furnished to each party. The report shall be detailed, setting out the findings of the examiner, including results of all tests made, diagnosis and conclusions, together with like reports of all earlier examinations of the same condition. In an Electronically Filed Case, the report of examination shall be filed in electronic or digital image form as provided in Rule 1:17.

(2) The written report of the examination so filed with the clerk may be read into evidence if offered by the party who submitted to the examination. A party examined who takes the deposition of any examiner who shall have conducted an examination ordered pursuant to this Rule, waives any privilege that might have been asserted in

that action or in any other involving the same controversy, regarding the testimony of every other person who has examined or may thereafter examine the party in respect of the same mental or physical condition.

(3) This subdivision applies to examination made by agreement of the parties, unless the agreement expressly provides otherwise. This subdivision does not preclude discovery of a report of a health care examiner or the taking of a deposition of such examiner in accordance with the provisions of any other Rule.

Comment. — Attention should also be given to § 8.01-413.

The amendment, effective January 1, 2001, adopted November 2, 2000, rewrote subdivision (b).

The amendment, effective May 2, 2011, adopted March 1, 2011, added the last sentence of subdivision (c)(1).

Law Review. — For 2006 survey article, "Medical Malpractice Law," see 41 U. Rich. L. Rev. 231 (2006).

Michie's Jurisprudence. — For related discussion, see 6A M.J. Discovery, §§ 37, 38.

CASE NOTES

Purpose of this rule was to secure or preserve to a defendant the right, in a proper case, to have the injured person examined. Virginia Linen Serv., Inc. v. Allen, 198 Va. 700, 96 S.E.2d 86 (1957).

Discretion of court. — Subdivision (a) of this rule says the court "may order" the examination. Whether it will do so is in the sound judicial discretion of the court on the showing made. Virginia Linen Serv., Inc. v. Allen, 198 Va. 700, 96 S.E.2d 86 (1957).

Selection and payment of physician. — The rule provides that the examination shall be made by the physician or physicians named in the order. It does not say how the court shall determine who shall be named. If the court wishes it may require counsel to make suggestions or furnish a list of qualified persons. The court may investigate their fitness and their availability, then make its selection and name its choice in its order. The rule says the person named in the order shall be employed by the moving party. That means he is to be paid by the moving party and it is the business of the court to arrange about that. Virginia Linen Serv., Inc. v. Allen, 198 Va. 700, 96 S.E.2d 86 (1957).

Defendant cannot complain that court named physician suggested by him. — Where plaintiff agreed to be examined by any physician or physicians selected by the defendant, it was not error of which the defendant can complain that the court named the physician whom the defendant suggested. Virginia Linen Serv., Inc. v. Allen, 198 Va. 700, 96 S.E.2d 86 (1957).

Physician may be examined and cross-examined as any other witness. — It is not the purpose of this rule to create a final arbiter of medical disputes nor to provide a new way of settling conflicts between medical witnesses. That must remain the function of the jury, or of the court if there is no jury. The person appointed to make the examination is necessarily the selection of the court but that is not to invest him with the quality of inerrancy. He may be called as a witness by either party and examined and cross-examined as any other witness. If his report is put in evidence by the party examined, the other party may then cross-examine him. Virginia Linen Serv., Inc. v. Allen, 198 Va. 700, 96 S.E.2d 86 (1957).

A limited physician-patient relationship exists. — The patient and clinical psychologist had a limited physician-patient relationship arising out of the fact that the patient had impliedly agreed to an independent medical examination pursuant to Va. Sup. Ct. R. 4:10, the patient alleged sufficient facts from which it could be determined that the clinical psychologist owed her a duty not to conduct himself during the examination in such a way as to harm her and she alleged that his conduct in suggesting that she was faking her injury, when he allegedly knew that she suffered from post traumatic stress disorder and a brain injury, proximately caused her injury. Harris v. Kreutzer, 271 Va. 188, 624 S.E.2d 24, 2006 Va. LEXIS 11 (2006).

Denial of request for examination supported by evidence. — While the grandparents' expert testified as an expert in attachment theory, described factors that would indicate that the severing of a relationship had a harmful effect on a child, and testified that the child was attached to the grandparents, the trial court considered the evidence and found that the grandparents failed to prove that the child had suffered or would suffer actual harm. The child had not seen the grandparents for over a year and such an examination would subject the child to a significant degree of psychological poking and prodding. Richter v. Manning, No. 1166-12-4, 2013 Va. App. LEXIS 143 (Ct. of Appeals May 7, 2013).

Medical reports. — The contents of medical reports are not privileged, as otherwise might be true in the physician-patient relationship. When plaintiff files his motion for judgment seeking damages for personal injuries, and the extent of such injuries is questioned by defendant, his physical condition is at issue in the action and he cannot then refuse to divulge the contents of the medical report on the ground of privilege. City of Portsmouth v. Cilumbrello, 204 Va. 11, 129 S.E.2d 31 (1963).

Applied in Lombard v. Rohrbaugh, 262 Va. 484, 551 S.E.2d 349, 2001 Va. LEXIS 113 (2001).

CIRCUIT COURT OPINIONS

Business invitee failed to show doctor selected to conduct examination was inappropriate. — Although a business invitee could normally challenge a doctor chosen by a grocery store to conduct an examination at a hearing on the store's motion for a Rule 4:10(a) examination, a doctor did not have to appear pursuant to a witness subpoena at a hearing on the store's motion for a Rule 4:10(a) examination as the invitee failed to make a prima facie valid objection to the doctor conducting the examination at a hearing on the doctor's motion for a protective order. Young v. Food Lion Store No. 622, 70 Va. Cir. 313, 2006 Va. Cir. LEXIS 31 (Portsmouth 2006).

Opposition to doctor selected by movant. — Assuming that a movant carries its initial burden at a Va. Sup. Ct. R. 4:10(a) hearing, no examination of the proposed physician is warranted at a Rule 4:10 hearing unless the examinee alleges a good faith factually supported prima facie "valid objection"; even then, it is in the sound discretion of the trial court, based upon the facts of each case, whether to hear such testimony. Young v. Food Lion Store No. 622, 70 Va. Cir. 313, 2006 Va. Cir. LEXIS 31 (Portsmouth 2006).

Doctor not entitled to attorney fees. — Doctor was not entitled to attorney fees where his motion to quash a subpoena was granted as there was no controlling caselaw addressing the question whether Va. Sup. Ct. R. 4:10 provided a legal basis for issuing a subpoena to a proposed examiner before he had been appointed by the trial court, performed his examination, and rendered his report. Young v. Food Lion Store No. 622, 70 Va. Cir. 313, 2006 Va. Cir. LEXIS 31 (Portsmouth 2006).

Electrodiagnostic studies. — Motion to compel a personal injury victim to submit to electrodiagnostic studies failed to state good cause for the examination and did not state time, place, manner, conditions, and scope of the examination. Seidel v. Walker, 65 Va. Cir. 199, 2004 Va. Cir. LEXIS 270 (Loudoun County 2004).

Appropriate testimony and record review. — Where a medical center's proposed experts were from the same "group" as the child's treating physicians, the proposed experts' testimony and record review was inappropriate in the child's medical malpractice action. McCaffrey v. Va. Women's Ctr., Inc., 59 Va. Cir. 266, 2002 Va. Cir. LEXIS 380 (Richmond July 17, 2002).

Not applicable to examination of inanimate and tangible pathology materials. — In a set of asbestos-related cases, inanimate and tangible pathology materials were subject to discovery under Rule 4:1, not this rule; therefore, without a showing by plaintiffs' counsel of exceptional circumstances, plaintiffs were not entitled to the identification of, or opinion of, any non-testifying expert with whom defendants chose to consult on said pathology. All Asbestos Cases, 64 Va. Cir. 190, 2004 Va. Cir. LEXIS 58 (Newport News 2004).

Rule 4:11. Requests for Admission.

(a) *Request for Admission.* — A party may serve upon any other party a written request for the admission, for purposes of the pending action only, of the truth of any matters within the scope of Rule 4:1(b) set forth in the request that relate to statements or opinions of fact or of the application of law to fact, including the genuineness of any documents described in the request. Copies of documents shall be served with the request unless they have been or are otherwise furnished or made available for inspection and copying. The request may, without leave of court, be served upon the plaintiff after commencement of the action and upon any other party with or after service of the complaint upon that party.

Each matter of which an admission is requested shall be separately set forth. The matter is admitted unless, within 21 days after service of the request, or within such shorter or longer time as the court may allow, the party to whom the request is directed serves upon the party requesting the admission a written answer or objection addressed to the matter, signed by the party or by his attorney, but, unless the court shortens the time, a defendant shall not be required to serve answers or objections before the expiration of 28 days after service of the complaint upon him. If objection is made, the reasons therefor shall be stated. The answer shall specifically deny the matter or set forth in detail the reasons why the answering party cannot truthfully admit or deny the matter. A denial shall fairly meet the substance of the requested admission, and when good faith requires that a party qualify his answer or deny only a part of the matter of which an admission is requested, he shall specify so much of it as is true and qualify or deny the remainder. An answering party may not give lack of information or knowledge as a reason for failure to admit or deny unless he states that he has made reasonable inquiry and that the information known or readily obtainable by him is insufficient to enable him to admit or deny. A party who considers that a matter of which an admission has been requested presents a genuine issue for trial may not, on that ground alone, object to the request; he may, subject to the provisions of Rule 4:12(c), deny the matter or set forth reasons why he cannot admit or deny it.

The party who has requested the admissions may move to determine the sufficiency of the answers or objections. Unless the court determines that an objection is justified, it shall order that an answer be served. If the court determines that an answer does not comply with the requirements of this Rule, it may order either that the matter is admitted or that an amended answer be served. The court may, in lieu of these orders, determine that final disposition of the request be made at a pretrial conference or at a designated time prior to trial. The provisions of Rule 4:12(a)(4) apply to the award of expenses incurred in relation to the motion.

(b) *Effect of Admission.* — Any matter admitted under this Rule is conclusively established unless the court on motion permits withdrawal or amendment of the admission. Subject to the provisions of Rule 4:13 governing amendment of a pretrial order, the court may permit withdrawal or amendment when the presentation of the merits of the action will be subserved thereby and the party who obtained the admission fails to satisfy the court that withdrawal or amendment will prejudice him in maintaining his action or defense on the merits. Any admission made by a party under this Rule is for the purpose of the pending action only and is not an admission by him for any other purpose nor may it be used against him in any other proceeding.

(c) *Filing.* — Except as provided in Rules 3:3 and 1:17, requests for admissions and answers or objections shall be served and filed as provided in Rule 4:8.

(d) *Part of Record.* — Only such requests for admissions and the answers thereto as are offered in evidence shall become a part of the record.

Comment on the 1984 amendment. — This change is intended to eliminate the clutter in clerks' offices.

Comment on the 1985 amendment. — The change is designed to avoid clutter of the record.

The amendment, effective February 28, 2006, adopted February 28, 2006, substituted "after service of the complaint" for "after service of the bill of complaint or motion for judgment" in the first sentence of the first two paragraphs of subdivision (a).

The amendment, effective May 2, 2011, adopted March 1, 2011, added "Except as provided in Rules 3:3 and 1:17," at the beginning of subdivision (c).

Law Review. — For 1995 survey of civil practice and procedure, see 29 U. Rich. L. Rev. 897 (1995). For 2003/2004 survey of civil practice and procedure, see 39 U. Rich. L. Rev. 87 (2004).

Michie's Jurisprudence. — For related discussion, see 6A M.J. Discovery, §§ 39, 40; 7B M.J. Evidence, § 244; 11A M.J. Judgments and Decrees, § 217.4; 19 M.J. Trial, § 8.

CASE NOTES

There is a reciprocal duty upon the party requesting admissions to phrase his requests with clarity and fairness, so that the other party can safely "specify so much of [a request] as is true" without conceding away a disputed point. Erie Ins. Exch. v. Jones, 236 Va. 10, 372 S.E.2d 126 (1988).

Answers not constituting admissions. — A request for admissions was filed asking that defendant "admit or deny the truth of his testimony" at a previous trial. The defendant, by answer, neither admitted nor denied the truth of his testimony at the earlier trial, but alleged that he was "totally deaf" and that he was "not sure that he understood all of the questions propounded to him at said trial." Such an answer was permitted by this rule and did not constitute an admission. Clifton v. Gregory, 212 Va. 859, 188 S.E.2d 203 (1972).

Interrogatories to which was attached a transcript of defendant's testimony at a previous trial were directed to the defendant asking him to enumerate the questions which he did not understand and to state in each instance "what the defendant thought the question to be." The defendant's answer both reiterated that he had great difficulty in communicating with others because of his deafness and set forth a list of four questions which were "particularly not clear to him." This answer did not constitute an admission. Clifton v. Gregory, 212 Va. 859, 188 S.E.2d 203 (1972).

Admissions made by written answer to a request under this rule, which are thereafter amended under subdivision (b) of this rule, may be introduced as substantive evidence in the trial of the pending action. Food Lion, Inc. v. Melton, 250 Va. 144, 458 S.E.2d 580 (1995).

Statement of facts tendered to the chancellor is essentially a summary of data contained in papers included in the record on appeal under Rule 5:10, including admissions under this rule, exhibits requested under Rule 4:9, the chancellor's letter opinion and the final decree. City of Richmond v. Randall, 215 Va. 506, 211 S.E.2d 56 (1975).

Collateral estoppel not found. — Where plaintiffs filed a motion for summary judgment alleging that all the factual statements requested to be admitted or denied were, pursuant to this rule, deemed admitted when no timely denial or objection was filed by the debtor and where the circuit court entered a final judgment order awarding the plaintiffs monetary damages on each of the grounds alleged including fraud, the court found that the fraud judgment did not collaterally estop the debtor from litigating the issues presented in the complaint objecting to dischargeability of debt. Kulesa v. Stankovich, 171 Bankr. 27 (Bankr. E.D. Va. 1994).

Discretion of trial court. — Decisions on whether testimony contradicts admissions are committed to the sound discretion of the trial court and will only be set aside on appeal if those decisions are shown to be an abuse of discretion. Lockheed Info. Mgt. Sys. v. Maximus Inc., 259 Va. 92, 524 S.E.2d 420 (2000).

Withdrawal of admissions. — Trial court's discretion to permit withdrawal or amendment of an admission entered under Va. Sup. Ct. R. 4:11(b) must be exercised within certain parameters: (1) when the presentation of the merits of the action will be subserved thereby; and (2) the party who obtained the admission fails to satisfy the court that withdrawal or amendment will prejudice him in maintaining his action or defense on the merits. Shaheen v. County of Mathews, 265 Va. 462, 579 S.E.2d 162, 2003 Va. LEXIS 41 (2003).

Trial court properly allowed plaintiffs to withdraw admissions entered by default, as by such admissions they "admitted away the case," allowing withdrawal aided in the ascertainment of the truth and the development of the merits, and defendants did not demonstrate that they would have difficulty in the presentation of their defense or that they were less able to obtain the evidence needed to prove the matters that had been admitted. Shaheen v. County of Mathews, 265 Va. 462, 579 S.E.2d 162, 2003 Va. LEXIS 41 (2003).

Amendment properly denied where prejudice was shown. — Trial court properly denied defendants' motion to amend its response to plaintiffs' request for admissions in a suit to enforce a restrictive covenant with regard to real property wherein defendants sought to amend their response from admitting they removed certain trees from a buffer area to denying such act just before trial; plaintiffs demonstrated that the amendment prejudiced them by coming just three days before trial and they did not have time to prepare for and prove the location of the trees for trial. Perel v. Brannan, 267 Va. 691, 594 S.E.2d 899, 2004 Va. LEXIS 71 (2004).

Attorney's fees. — It was an abuse of discretion to award attorney's fees under Va. Sup. Ct. R. 4:12(c)(4) to the dominant owners of an easement because the dominant owners' request for an admission as to the lack of defenses available to servient owner was not a proper discovery request under Va. Sup. Ct. R. 4:11. Piney Meeting House Invs., Inc. v. Hart, 284 Va. 187, 726 S.E.2d 319, 2012 Va. LEXIS 124 (2012).

Applied in Envirotech Corp. v. Halco Eng'g, Inc., 234 Va. 583, 364 S.E.2d 215 (1988); State Farm Mut. Auto. Ins. Co. v. Haines, 250 Va. 71, 458 S.E.2d 285 (1995).

CIRCUIT COURT OPINIONS

Lack of diligence. — Because a defrauder had several opportunities to comply with the rules governing discovery and, instead, created the situation in which he failed to respond to the request for admissions, and he offered no reasonable justification for his lack of diligence, the defrauder was deemed to have admitted the request for admissions. Wallace v. Patillo, 82 Va. Cir. 125, 2011 Va. Cir. LEXIS 152 (Norfolk Jan. 19, 2011).

Undue burden. — Where a plaintiff filed 110 requests for admission pursuant to Va. Sup. Ct. R. 4:11, the requests were unreasonably cumulative and duplicative, were obtainable from other sources, and were unduly burdensome; therefore, defendant's objection thereto under Va. Sup. Ct. R. 4:1(b)(1) was sustained. Giddens v. Nunez, 62 Va. Cir. 100, 2003 Va. Cir. LEXIS 299 (Norfolk 2003).

Request for admissions was unduly burdensome and responding would have resulted in unnecessary expense; additionally, the court had already conducted a pendente lite hearing, and the evidence at the hearing revealed a substantial amount of information regarding the financial circumstances of each party. A motion to compel discovery was denied. Brendle v. Brendle, 73 Va. Cir. 390, 2007 Va. Cir. LEXIS 105 (Orange County 2007).

Answers to requests for admissions in wrongful death/survivial action could not force plaintiff to elect between remedies. — Because the responses sought by a hospital from a decedent's survivor attempted to force the survivor to proceed solely under either § 8.01-50 or 8.01-25, which was contrary to § 8.01-281, and improperly forced the survivor to elect his remedies, his answers to two requests for admissions were deemed sufficient. Richard Montgomery Bros. v. Rockingham Mem. Hosp., 75 Va. Cir. 85, 2008 Va. Cir. LEXIS 29 (Rockingham County 2008).

Effect of failure to respond. — Partial summary judgment was granted in a bad check case where defendant's counsel failed to timely respond to the plaintiff's request for admissions regarding that count because the request had been received by another attorney in the counsel's firm who placed the document in the case file and then went on military leave; all members of the law firm were charged with knowledge of the contents of the firm's files. Agarwal v. Das, 54 Va. Cir. 207, 2000 Va. Cir. LEXIS 576 (Loudoun County 2000).

Where a court had jurisdiction due to defendants' general appearance and where an owner did not respond to defendants' Va. Sup. Ct. R. 4:11 requests for admission, the matters were deemed admitted; therefore, the defendants were entitled to summary judgment. Martin v. Taylor, 61 Va. Cir. 582, 2001 Va. Cir. LEXIS 515 (Franklin County 2001).

County could be asked to disclose factual and legal bases for denying requests for admission. — It was not a valid objection to an interrogatory that disclosing the reasons for its denials would call for legal conclusions that only a court could decide. Janney v. Westmoreland County, 65 Va. Cir. 533, 2002 Va. Cir. LEXIS 451 (Westmoreland County 2002).

Discretion of the trial court. — Plaintiff, as the party who requested admissions, could move to determine the sufficiency of the answers or objections, but, striking defendant's pleadings in the manner requested would have the effect of penalizing him for exercising a constitutional right, which was prohibited by § 8.01-223.1. Hicks v. Been, 57 Va. Cir. 151, 2001 Va. Cir. LEXIS 427 (Norfolk 2001).

Trial court granted the corporation's motion to amend its answers to two requests to admit, which had the effect of changing answers that its written claim regarding payment for work performed pursuant to a contract with the state transportation agency was untimely to denying that was the case, as the state transportation agency could not show the trial court that amendment would prejudice the state transportation agency. Cleco Corp. v. Va. DOT, 73 Va. Cir. 534, 2004 Va. Cir. LEXIS 384 (Richmond County 2004).

Rule 4:12. Failure to Make Discovery; Sanctions.

(a) *Motion for Order Compelling Discovery.* — A party, upon reasonable notice to other parties and all persons affected thereby, may apply for an order compelling discovery as follows:

(1) Appropriate Court. An application for an order to a party may be made to the court in which the action is pending, or, on matters relating to a deposition, to the court in the county or city where the deposition is to be taken. An application for an order to a deponent who is not a party shall be made to the court in the county or city where the deposition is being taken.

(2) Motion. If a deponent fails to answer a question propounded or submitted under Rule 4:5 or 4:6, or a corporation or other entity fails to make a designation under Rule 4:5(b)(6) or 4:6(a), or a party fails to answer an interrogatory submitted under Rule 4:8, or if a party, in response to a request for inspection submitted under Rule 4:9, fails to respond that inspection will be permitted as requested or fails to permit inspection as requested, the discovering party may move for an order compelling an answer, or a designation, or an order compelling inspection in accordance with the request. When taking a deposition on oral examination, the proponent of the question may complete or adjourn the examination before he applies for an order.

A motion under subdivision (a) of this Rule must be accompanied by a certification that the movant has in good faith conferred or attempted to confer with other affected parties in an effort to resolve the dispute without court action.

If the court denies the motion in whole or in part, it may make such protective order as it would have been empowered to make on a motion made pursuant to Rule 4:1(c).

(3) Evasive or Incomplete Answer. For purposes of this subdivision an evasive or incomplete answer is to be treated as a failure to answer.

(4) Award of Expenses of Motion. If the motion is granted, the court shall, after opportunity for hearing, require the party or deponent whose conduct necessitated the motion or the party or attorney advising such conduct or both of them to pay to the moving party the reasonable expenses incurred in obtaining the order, including attorney's fees, unless the court finds that the opposition to the motion was substantially justified or that other circumstances make an award of expenses unjust.

If the motion is denied, the court shall, after opportunity for hearing, require the moving party or the attorney advising the motion or both of them to pay to the party or deponent who opposed the motion the reasonable expenses incurred in opposing the motion, including attorney's fees, unless the court finds that the making of the motion was substantially justified or that other circumstances make an award of expenses unjust.

If the motion is granted in part and denied in part, the court may apportion the reasonable expenses incurred in relation to the motion among the parties and persons in a just manner.

(b) *Failure to Comply With Order.* — (1) Sanctions by Court in County or City Where Deposition Is Taken. If a deponent fails to be sworn or to answer a question after being directed to do so by the court in the county or city in which the deposition is being taken, the failure may be considered a contempt of that court.

(2) Sanctions by Court in Which Action Is Pending. If a party or an officer, director, or managing agent of a party or a person designated under Rule 4:5(b) (6) or 4:6(a) to testify on behalf of a party fails to obey an order to provide or permit discovery, including an order made under subdivision (a) of this Rule or Rule 4:10, the court in which the action is pending may make such orders in regard to the failure as are just, and among others the following:

(A) An order that the matters regarding which the order was made or any other designated facts shall be taken to be established for the purposes of the action in accordance with the claim of the party obtaining the order;

(B) An order refusing to allow the disobedient party to support or oppose designated claims or defenses, or prohibiting him from introducing designated matters in evidence;

(C) An order striking out pleadings or parts thereof, or staying further proceedings until the order is obeyed, or dismissing the action or proceeding or any part thereof, or rendering a judgment by default against the disobedient party;

(D) In lieu of any of the foregoing orders or in addition thereto, an order treating as a contempt of court the failure to obey any orders except an order to submit to a physical or mental examination;

(E) Where a party has failed to comply with an order under Rule 4:10(a) requiring him to produce another for examination, such orders as are listed in paragraphs (A), (B), and (C) of this subdivision, unless the party failing to comply shows that he is unable to produce such person for examination.

In lieu of any of the foregoing orders or in addition thereto, the court shall require the party failing to obey the order or the attorney advising him or both to pay the reasonable expenses, including attorney's fees, caused by the failure, unless the court finds that the failure was substantially justified or that other circumstances make an award of expenses unjust.

(c) *Expenses on Failure to Admit.* — If a party fails to admit the genuineness of any document or the truth of any matter as requested under Rule 4:11, and if the party requesting the admissions thereafter proves the genuineness of the document or the truth of the matter, he may apply to the court for an order requiring the other party to pay him the reasonable expenses incurred in making that proof, including reasonable attorney's fees. The court shall make the order unless it finds that (1) the request was held objectionable pursuant to Rule 4:11(a), or (2) the admission sought was of no substantial importance, or (3) the party failing to admit had reasonable ground to believe that he might prevail on the matter, or (4) there was other good reason for the failure to admit.

(d) *Failure of Party to Attend at Own Deposition or Serve Answers to Interrogatories or Respond to Request for Inspection.* — If a party or an officer, director, or managing agent of a party or a person designated under Rule 4:5(b) (6) or 4:6(a) to testify on behalf of a party fails (1) to appear before the officer who is to take his deposition, after being served with a proper notice, or (2) to serve answers or objections to interrogatories submitted under Rule 4:8, after proper service of the interrogatories, or (3) to serve a written response to a request for inspection submitted under Rule 4:9, after proper service of the request, the court in which the action is pending on motion may make such orders in regard to the failure as are just, and among others it may take any action authorized under paragraphs (A), (B), and (C) of subdivision (b)(2) of this Rule. In lieu of any order or in addition thereto, the court shall require the party failing to act or the attorney advising him or both to pay the reasonable expenses, including attorney's fees, caused by the failure, unless the court finds that the failure was substantially justified or that other circumstances make an award of expenses unjust.

The failure to act described in this subdivision may not be excused on the ground that the discovery sought is objectionable unless the party failing to act has applied for a protective order as provided by Rule 4:1(c).

Cross references. — As to sanctions for the failure to make discovery involving the insurance of motor vehicles, § 38.2-2204 C.

The amendment, effective January 1, 2003, adopted November 1, 2002, in subdivision (a), added a new paragraph immediately following paragraph (2).

Law Review. — "Spoliation: Civil Liability for Destruction of Evidence," see 20 U. Rich. L. Rev. 191 (1985). For 2003/2004 survey of civil practice and procedure, see 39 U. Rich. L. Rev. 87 (2004). For annual survey of Virginia law article, "Civil Practice and Procedure," see 47 U. Rich. L. Rev. 113 (2012).

Michie's Jurisprudence. — For related discussion, see 5A M.J. Costs, §§ 2, 3; 6A M.J. Discovery, § 8; 19 M.J. Trial, § 8.

CASE NOTES

Application. — The application of subdivision (a)(2) with respect to discovery requests submitted under Va. Sup. Ct. R. 4:9 is expressly limited to instances in which a party, in response to a request for inspection, failed to respond that inspection would be permitted as requested or failed to permit inspection as requested. Tonti v. Akbari, 262 Va. 681, 553 S.E.2d 769, 2001 Va. LEXIS 137 (2001).

Trial court vested with broad discretion in determining sanctions to be imposed. — See First Charter Land Corp. v. Middle Atl. Dredging, Inc., 218 Va. 304, 237 S.E.2d 145 (1977).

This rule gives the trial court broad discretion in determining what sanctions, if any, will be imposed upon a litigant who fails to respond timely to discovery. Woodbury v. Courtney, 239 Va. 651, 391 S.E.2d 293 (1990).

Deference to trial court. — Because a trial court generally exercises broad discretion in determining the appropriate sanction for failure to comply with an order relating to discovery, an appellate court accords deference to the decision of the trial court and will reverse only if the trial court abused its discretion. Walsh v. Bennett, 260 Va. 171, 530 S.E.2d 904, 2000 Va. LEXIS 91 (2000).

Trial court in the court's discretion could decline to award attorney fees as a sanction against a father after the mother filed several pretrial motions, including discovery motions regarding the father's belated provision to the mother of discovery right before trial in a child support proceeding. The mother did not argue the motions before trial and, thus, the trial court could decline to consider those motions at the end of trial and also could determine that imposing sanctions pursuant to Va. Sup. Ct. R. 4:12 was not warranted. Hamilton v. Hamilton, 2008 Va. App. LEXIS 448 (Oct. 7, 2008).

Lesser sanction would not have remedied misconduct. — Trial court did not abuse its discretion in ordering default against a subcontractor for discovery misconduct because it was doubtful that any lesser sanction would have remedied the problem posed by the subcontractor's failure to obey the circuit court's order compelling the appearance of its corporate designee at a deposition. Am. Safety Cas. Ins. Co. v. C.G. Mitchell Constr., 268 Va. 340, 601 S.E.2d 633, 2004 Va. LEXIS 129 (2004).

Rule held inapplicable. — Where the appellant was held in contempt for failure to appear at a pretrial conference and there was nothing in the record to indicate that she failed to comply with a discovery order, the court's contempt power did not flow from this rule and, instead, the fine was limited to $50 under § 18.2-457. Roberts v. Haiar, No. 2096-97-1 (Ct. of Appeals February 24, 1998).

When court may dismiss motion for judgment. — Subsection (d), when read with the other provisions in this rule, authorizes a circuit court to dismiss a motion for judgment only when the plaintiff fails to comply with a court's order to provide or permit discovery. Brown v. Black, 260 Va. 305, 534 S.E.2d 727, 2000 Va. LEXIS 117 (2000).

Denial of motion in support modification proceeding upheld. — Where record established that (1) wife responded to husband's discovery requests, albeit perhaps in a manner that husband regarded as insufficient; (2) husband had the opportunity to conduct and to access a substantial amount of discovery generated by the prior proceedings in the spousal support matter; and (3) trial court observed this in denying husband's motion, noting that "the reason I overrule your motion is because there had been a tremendous amount of discovery in this case. And [wife] was on the witness stand to testify, and I realize you might have had some greater advantage if you'd had this information, but I think you had an opportunity to get it out on cross-examination;" the trial court did not abuse its discretion in denying husband's Sup. Ct. R. 4:12 motion and in proceeding with an evidentiary hearing. Tanger v. Diaz de Tanger, No. 3168-96-3 (Ct. of Appeals July 8, 1997).

Belief that one might prevail. — Where the party failing to admit the truth of a matter clearly has reasonable grounds to believe that he might prevail on the matter, it is an abuse of discretion to impose the sanctions authorized by this rule. Erie Ins. Exch. v. Jones, 236 Va. 10, 372 S.E.2d 126 (1988).

Jurisdiction in contempt ends upon death of the party. — Trial judge does not have jurisdiction to dispose of contempt findings if based on the violation of pendente lite orders that become void upon abatement of divorce proceedings due to a party's death. Estate of Hackler v. Hackler, 44 Va. App. 51, 602 S.E.2d 426, 2004 Va. App. LEXIS 454 (2004).

Imposition of sanctions short of ruling document inadmissible held proper. — Where the trial court found plaintiff's failure to produce a document on discovery was inadvertent, defendant's counsel was promptly notified when the document was located less than a week before trial, and a copy of the document was delivered to him on the morning of the first day of the trial, there was no abuse of the trial court's discretion in imposing sanctions designed to alleviate the surprise claimed by the defendant, short of ruling the document inadmissible. First Charter Land Corp. v. Middle Atl. Dredging, Inc., 218 Va. 304, 237 S.E.2d 145 (1977).

Admission of evidence not timely disclosed within trial court's discretion. — Trial court's decision to admit evidence that is not timely disclosed, rather than impose the sanction of excluding it, will not be reversed unless the court's action amounts to an abuse of discretion. Hoffman v. Hoffman, Nos. 0103-03-4, 0136 03-4, 2004 Va. App. LEXIS 216 (Ct. of Appeals May 11, 2004).

Admission of expert witness not timely disclosed within trial court's discretion. — Though an expert witness was not listed by the wife in a discovery order, the circuit court properly exercised its discretion under Va. Sup. Ct. R. 4:12 to consider the expert's testimony on the valuation of the husband's law practice in an equitable distribution of marital estate decision because the husband knew the wife was going to call the expert, had unsuccessfully sought to exclude his testimony, and the expert was fully qualified to evaluate the value of the husband's law practice. Barrett v. Barrett, 2005 Va. App. LEXIS 168 (Apr. 26, 2005).

Applicability of sanctions. — This Rule's sanctions for violation of a discovery order do not apply until an order has been entered and violated. Travis v. Finley, 36 Va. App. 189, 548 S.E.2d 906, 2001 Va. App. LEXIS 422 (2001).

Sanction held abuse of discretion. — A trial court's action in striking a plaintiff's designation of his only expert witness on the grounds that the plaintiff had failed to make the expert available for deposition was an abuse of discretion, where the deadline for such deposition had not yet passed and the plaintiff had thus not yet disobeyed the court's discovery order. Walsh v. Bennett, 260 Va. 171, 530 S.E.2d 904, 2000 Va. LEXIS 91 (2000).

It was an abuse of discretion to award attorney's fees under Va. Sup. Ct. R. 4:12(c)(4) to the dominant owners of an easement because the dominant owners' request for an admission as to the lack of defenses available to servient owner was not a proper discovery request under Va. Sup. Ct. R. 4:11. Piney Meeting House Invs., Inc. v. Hart, 284 Va. 187, 726 S.E.2d 319, 2012 Va. LEXIS 124 (2012).

Where defendants repeatedly failed to respond to discovery requests, the trial court did abuse its discretion in precluding defendants from opposing plaintiff's claims or introducing any evidence in support of their defenses, but it was an abuse of discretion to prohibit cross-examination and introduction of evidence by defendants in the damages presentation to the jury. Nolte v. MT Tech. Enters., LLC, 284 Va. 80, 726 S.E.2d 339, 2012 Va. LEXIS 120 (2012).

Sanctions held proper. — A trial court in a divorce action properly issued an order as a discovery sanction that precluded a husband from introducing evidence to support his claims and from introducing evidence to oppose the wife's claims for property distribution and attorney fees, and the trial court did not abuse its discretion by ruling that the sanction precluded the husband from conducting discovery from the wife, where, after the trial court ordered the husband to give complete responses to discovery, did not fully answer the wife's interrogatories and did not attend his deposition, and where the trial court gave the husband ample opportunity to rectify his behavior. Nolting v. Nolting, No. 0174-04-4, 2004 Va. App. LEXIS 322 (Ct. of Appeals July 13, 2004).

In an action arising from the parties' divorce, the trial court did not err in awarding a husband $5,000 in attorney's fees as a sanction for her misrepresentations and discovery violations. The wife failed to respond or appear, not once, but five times, and her violations fell within the reach and intent of Rule 4:12. Burstein v. Morriss, 2007 Va. App. LEXIS 303 (Aug. 14, 2007).

Trial court did not abuse its discretion in sanctioning a mother by not allowing her to introduce into evidence certain exhibits due to her failure to disclose them in discovery because the mother failed to comply fully with the trial court's discovery order; during discovery, a father was provided with a copy of a letter, but the exhibits that were enclosed with the letter were not included. Anonymous C v. Anonymous B, No. 2232-09-2, 2011 Va. App. LEXIS 14 (Ct. of Appeals Jan. 11, 2011).

Circuit court did not abuse its discretion in excluding a patient's expert witnesses because it warned the patient multiple times that her failure to obey its pretrial orders would lead to sanctions, including the exclusion of the expert witnesses; the patient proved herself unable to comply with the rules, running afoul of not just Va. Sup. Ct. R. 1A:4(2) and 4:1(b)(4)(A)(i), but also Va. Sup. Ct. R. 1A:4(3), 4:1(e)(1)(B), and 4:15. Landrum v. Chippenham & Johnston-Willis Hosps., Inc., 282 Va. 346, 717 S.E.2d 134, 2011 Va. LEXIS 224 (2011).

Circuit court did not abuse its discretion in excluding a patient's expert witnesses because the patient failed to obey the circuit court's pretrial order to file a supplemental designation on or before January 28; the patient's supplemental designation had no legal effect because it was not signed by local counsel as required under Va. Sup. Ct. R. 1A:4(2), and the supplemental designation could not be amended to comply with that rule since it was an invalid instrument. Landrum v. Chippenham & Johnston-Willis Hosps., Inc., 282 Va. 346, 717 S.E.2d 134, 2011 Va. LEXIS 224 (2011).

Where one defendant failed to appear at a deposition, the trial court did not abuse its discretion in granting a default judgment as a sanction against that defendant. Nolte v. MT Tech. Enters., LLC, 284 Va. 80, 726 S.E.2d 339, 2012 Va. LEXIS 120 (2012).

Sanctions for failing to provide expert reports improperly imposed. — As a husband never asked for expert reports pursuant to Rule 4:1, never filed a motion to compel the reports, and never asked for sanctions under Rule 4:12, the trial court improperly "short circuited" the legal process by prematurely imposing sanctions and preventing the wife from presenting evidence through her expert witnesses. Cirrito v. Cirrito, 44 Va. App. 287, 605 S.E.2d 268, 2004 Va. App. LEXIS 574 (2004).

Sanctions for failing to attend deposition held improper. — Because no order compelling a former husband's attendance at a deposition was ever entered in the divorce case, the trial court erred in imposing sanctions under Va. Sup. Ct. R. 4:12(b) that precluded him from introducing any evidence at a hearing on support and equitable distribution. Kapur v. Kapur, 2009 Va. App. LEXIS 234 (May 19, 2009).

Sanctions inappropriate. — On appeal from the parties' divorce action, the wife's argument that the trial court erred in granting and refusing to lift or modify the sanctions order was without merit under Va. Sup. Ct. R. 4:12(d); when the parties' attempts at settlement failed, the husband had again sought discovery from the wife and she again failed to respond. The trial court had entered an order compelling her to respond to interrogatories, and she again failed to provide any response; it was not until nearly four years after the complaint for divorce was filed, that the trial court entered its sanctions order. Spreadbury v. Spreadbury, 2010 Va. App. LEXIS 151 (Apr. 20, 2010).

Attorney fees. — Where evidence supported the conclusion that wife needlessly defied various court orders and discovery requests, and husband had incurred over $70,000 in legal fees and a debt of $20,000, excluding costs for representation at hearings, the trial court did not abuse its discretion in entering a $20,000 judgment for husband to defray a portion of his attorney fees. Rourke v. Rourke, No. 0165-93-4, (Ct. of Appeals Jan. 18, 1994).

Exclusion of objections to attorney fees. — Trial court was entitled to exclude husband's objections to attorney fees as a sanction for his inadequate response to interrogatories. Wampouille v. Barnett, No. 1006-99-4 (Ct. of Appeals Mar. 7, 2000).

Scope of authority of Workers' Compensation Commission. — Workers' Compensation Commission has the same authority as a court to punish for noncompliance with its discovery orders, and it has the inherent authority to strike a party's defenses for failure to comply with a discovery order. Jeff Coal, Inc. v. Phillips, 16 Va. App. 271, 430 S.E.2d 712 (1993).

Workers' Compensation Commission finding upheld. — Record supported a finding by the Virginia Workers' Compensation Commission that a worker who filed a claim for workers' compensation benefits did not suffer prejudice because a company that hired him failed to answer interrogatories he submitted until a few days before a deputy commissioner heard his claim, and the appellate court held that the Commission did not abuse its discretion when it denied the worker's motion for sanctions. North Star Home Improvement, Inc. v. Heddings, No. 2350-03-4, 2004 Va. App. LEXIS 81 (Ct. of Appeals Feb. 17, 2004).

Applied in Via v. Via, 14 Va. App. 868, 419 S.E.2d 431 (1992); McNally v. Rey, 275 Va. 475, 659 S.E.2d 279, 2008 Va. LEXIS 44 (2008); Comcast of Chesterfield County, Inc. v. Bd. of Supervisors, 277 Va. 293, 672 S.E.2d 870, 2009 Va. LEXIS 40 (2009).

CIRCUIT COURT OPINIONS

Applicability. — Where defendants failed to produce a letter showing they had notice of fires possibly caused by gas tanks they manufactured, until two and one-half years after plaintiff filed his discovery requests, submitted a false sworn answer to an interrogatory indicating that there had not been earlier gas tank incidents, and their corporate designee to be deposed took no steps to investigate the deposition subjects, the court declined to enter a default as a sanction, but barred defendants from denying at trial they had knowledge of gas tank defects. Martin v. Nordic Group of Cos., 61 Va. Cir. 13, 2003 Va. Cir. LEXIS 11 (Fairfax County 2003).

Notice not given. — Payor's request for relief with regard to a request for admission was denied because, prior to trial, the payer never asked for any relief in the form of a discovery motion regarding the request for admissions. Second, while Va. Sup. Ct. R. 4:12(c) provided the court with the authority to consider an award of fees, the construction company was never given notice that the trial on the merits would include a request for sanctions because of its pretrial discovery responses. Cornerstone Constr. Servs., L.L.C. v. Davison, 81 Va. Cir. 328, 2010 Va. Cir. LEXIS 286 (Orange County Nov. 3, 2010).

Answers to requests for admissions in wrongful death/survivial action could not force plaintiff to elect between remedies. — Because the responses sought by a hospital from a decedent's survivor attempted to force the survivor to proceed solely under either § 8.01-50 or 8.01-25, which was contrary to § 8.01-281, and improperly forced the survivor to elect his remedies, his answers to two requests for admissions were deemed sufficient. Richard Montgomery Bros. v. Rockingham Mem. Hosp., 75 Va. Cir. 85, 2008 Va. Cir. LEXIS 29 (Rockingham County 2008).

Stipulation to comply with a Bankruptcy Court order. — As a husband filed a proposed stipulation in order to comply with a Bankruptcy Court order that the total sum owed the wife's unsecured creditors did not exceed $690,939.58 and that the wife would receive that amount as a guaranteed minimum distribution in the divorce proceeding before any evidence was presented to the court, the court stood by its sanctions order prohibiting the wife, who failed to comply with discovery orders, from submitting defenses. Spreadbury v. Spreadbury, 78 Va. Cir. 142, 2009 Va. Cir. LEXIS 8 (Fauquier County 2009).

Sanctions. — Where it was clear that the injured was not truthful in her discovery responses and her answers were a conscious attempt to conceal the truth, sanctions were awarded; if she won, the injured had to pay the corporation 25 percent of her verdict. Guertler v. Ukrop's Supermarkets, 61 Va. Cir. 59, 2003 Va. Cir. LEXIS 131 (Richmond 2003).

Trial court found that a doctor's attorney acted improperly when she instructed her client not to answer questions that were asked by a patient's attorney during a deposition, but it decided not to impose monetary sanctions against the attorney because it sustained the objections she raised and the patient did not raise or pursue the issue of sanctions. Cuesta v. Shapiro, 65 Va. Cir. 79, 2004 Va. Cir. LEXIS 104 (Fairfax County 2004).

Because a notice of a deposition complied with § 8.01-412.3 by clearly stating that the deposition was to be taken before a qualified court reporter and videographer, and because the plaintiff failed to justify the failure to attend the deposition, the defendant was entitled to its costs and fees under Va. Sup. Ct. R. 4:12(d). Politi v. United Air Lines, Inc., 72 Va. Cir. 476, 2007 Va. Cir. LEXIS 18 (Fairfax County 2007).

Order to pay attorney's fees and costs. — In the buyers' action alleging that the sellers failed to disclose defects in a home addition, the buyers were ordered to pay attorney's fees and costs associated with sellers' motion for sanctions, because the buyers violated Va. Sup. Ct. R. 4:1 and 4:12 by failing to disclose the existence of the buyers' contractor and the specifics of the contractor's knowledge in response to the sellers' discovery requests. Skibinski v. Lunger, 74 Va. Cir. 428, 2008 Va. Cir. LEXIS 1 (Arlington County 2008).

Fees and costs not awarded. — Although the county board of supervisors refused to repair or replace certain county court facilities that were insufficient, under § 15.2-1643, fees and costs were not awarded to the Commonwealth, as statutes that authorized the award of costs were found to be in derogation of the common law and had to be strictly construed, and not enlarged in operation by construction beyond the statutes' express terms; the court could not determine that the supervisors' specific responses to certain discovery items were in bad faith, and found that expenses and fees would not be awarded under Va. Sup. Ct. R. 4:12(c). Commonwealth v. Appomattox County Bd. of Supervisors, 59 Va. Cir. 341, 2002 Va. Cir. LEXIS 375 (Appomattox County Aug. 9, 2002).

Attorney fees granted. — Motion to compel answers to executor's questions relating to hotel's safety policies and procedures to two hotel employees at a deposition in a negligence suit filed by the executor against a nursing home was granted under Va. Sup. Ct. R. 4:1(b)(1), even though the hotel was not a party, as the questions were reasonably calculated to lead to information about how and why the decedent became lost, wandered around the hotel unsupervised for a time, and fell down a flight of stairs; the executor was granted attorney's fees under Va. Sup. Ct. R. 4:12(a)(4). Stone v. Clifton Forge Health Care, L.L.C., 83 Va. Cir. 479, 2011 Va. Cir. LEXIS 264 (Alleghany County Nov. 21, 2011).

Dismissal. — Because an employee failed to comply with a court order compelling discovery, the employee's potential employer defamation claim was dismissed with prejudice as a sanction pursuant to Va. Sup. Ct. R. 4:12(b)(2). Edwards v. Ukrop's Super Mkts., Inc., 66 Va. Cir. 32, 2004 Va. Cir. LEXIS 352 (Richmond 2004).

Applicability of sanctions. — Where plaintiff failed to answer interrogatories under oath, as required by Rule 4:8, court declined to impose sanctions, but decided to proceed under this rule and order an action deemed to be "just" because the interrogatories propounded by defendant were difficult, awkward, and obscure. Court determined that the most just solution was to require plaintiff to supplement and more fully respond to certain interrogatories. Whalen v. Nelson, 68 Va. Cir. 485, 2001 Va. Cir. LEXIS 538 (Nelson County 2001).

Although defendants had failed to respond to plaintiff's discovery requests, the trial court found that it could not award plaintiff sanctions under Va. Sup. Ct. R. 4:12(a) because no motion for sanctions was filed and there had been no previous order to provide or permit discovery. Kawar v. Bouk, 71 Va. Cir. 295, 2006 Va. Cir. LEXIS 137 (Fairfax County 2006).

Where defendant filed an answer despite not having been served with a complaint, plaintiff was subject to the court's jurisdiction, even though she had not requested service of process. Therefore, she was subject to sanctions under Va. Sup. Ct. R. 4:12 for failing to respond to defendant's discovery requests. Lents v. Vetter, 80 Va. Cir. 268, 2010 Va. Cir. LEXIS 51 (Fairfax County Apr. 2, 2010).

While the pendency of plaintiff's motion to reconsider a motion to compel discovery did not relieve her of her duty to obey that order, as this was her only discovery violation and a trial date had not been set, dismissal under Va. Sup. Ct. R. 4:12(b)(2) was too harsh a sanction, and award of attorney fees to defendant would not be just. Lents v. Vetter, 80 Va. Cir. 268, 2010 Va. Cir. LEXIS 51 (Fairfax County Apr. 2, 2010).

Attorney violated § 8.01-271.1, Va. Sup. Ct. R. 4:1(g), and Va. Sup. Ct. R. 4:12 by omitting an e-mail and by his failure to submit the subject e-mail to the court for in camera inspection. The attorney conceded that his behavior also violated Va. Sup. Ct. R. pt. 6, § II, R. 3.3 and 3.4; thus, he was liable for attorney fees. Lester v. Allied Concrete Co., 38 Va. Cir. 308, 2011 Va. Cir. LEXIS 245 (Charlottesville Sept. 6, 2011).

Reenactment request. — In a personal injury action brought by a railroad worker against his employer, the railroad, and a manufacturer, the trial court denied the worker's request to inspect the accident site, which was a motion filed two years after the accident, because the burdens and dangers created by a requested inspection of the site to set up a partial reenactment of the accident outweighed the degree to which the proposed inspection would have aided in the search for the truth. Wilson v. Norfolk & Portsmouth Belt Line R.R. Co., 69 Va. Cir. 153, 2005 Va. Cir. LEXIS 267 (Portsmouth 2005).

Motion granted. — Court granted plaintiff's motion to compel immediate disclosure of surveillance documents and tape relied on by a doctor in performing an independent medical examination of plaintiff because such tape was not protected by the work-product doctrine, and disclosure would further the purposes of the rules of discovery to prevent surprise and promote an orderly trial. Defendant had the right to depose plaintiff prior to disclosure but had to produce the video after the deposition and at least 90 days before trial. Fare v. Doe, 66 Va. Cir. 61, 2004 Va. Cir. LEXIS 332 (Chesterfield County Sept. 13, 2004).

Court granted defendant surety's Va. Sup. Ct. R. 4:12 motion to compel a plaintiff contractor to answer interrogatories and to provide documents because the information that the surety sought was adequately defined and was either relevant to the defense or was likely to lead to the discovery of relevant evidence. Dustin Constr. v. Selby Constr., 67 Va. Cir. 229, 2005 Va. Cir. LEXIS 168 (Loudoun County Apr. 7, 2005).

Rule 4:13. Pretrial Procedure; Formulating Issues.

The court may in its discretion direct the attorneys for the parties to appear before it for a conference to consider:

(1) A determination of the issues;

(2) A plan and schedule of discovery;

(3) Any limitations on the scope and methods of discovery;

(4) The necessity or desirability of amendments to the pleadings;

(5) The possibility of obtaining admissions of fact and admissions regarding documents and information obtained through electronic discovery;

(6) The limitation of the number of expert witnesses;

(7) The advisability of a preliminary reference of issues to a master for findings to be used as evidence when the trial is to be by jury;

(8) issues relating to the preservation of potentially discoverable information, including electronically stored information and information that may be located in sources that are believed not reasonably accessible because of undue burden or cost;

(9) provisions for disclosure or discovery of electronically stored information;

(10) any agreements the parties reach for asserting claims of privilege or of protection as trial-preparation material after production;

(11) any provisions that will aid in the use of electronically stored or digitally imaged documents in the trial of the action; and

(12) Such other matters as may aid in the disposition of the action.

The court shall make an order which recites the action taken at the conference, the amendments allowed to the pleadings, the agreements made by the parties as to any of the matters considered, and which limits the issues for trial to those not disposed of by admissions or agreements of counsel; and such order when entered controls the subsequent course of the action, unless modified at the trial to prevent manifest injustice.

Comment on 1983 amendment. — This change is designed to give the court greater powers to limit discovery if it desires to exercise them.

The amendment effective January 1, 2009, adopted October 1, 2008, rewrote the Rule.

The amendment, effective May 2, 2011, adopted March 1, 2011, added subdivision (11) and redesignated former subdivision (11) as (12).

Law Review. — For article, "Pretrial in Virginia," see 40 Va. L. Rev. 359 (1954). For article, "Pretrial Conference: An Endorsement from the Bench" and an article on "Pretrial Conference: A Dissent from the Bar," see 45 Va. L. Rev. 141, 147 (1958). For article comparing Virginia Rules of Court with Federal Rules of Civil Procedure, see 47 Va. L. Rev. 906 (1961).

Michie's Jurisprudence. — For related discussion, see 1B M.J. Amendments, § 2; 7A M.J. Equity, § 2; 19 M.J. Trial, § 7.

CASE NOTES

This rule is designed to allow the court to consider such matters as will aid it in the disposition of the case in subsequent proceedings. Kasco Mills, Inc. v. Ferebee, 197 Va. 589, 90 S.E.2d 866 (1956).

And it is not intended to substitute new method of trial of issues of fact. — This rule was adopted to allow trial courts to bring litigation to an end at an early stage when it clearly appeared that one of the parties was entitled to a judgment in the case as made out by the pleadings and the admissions of the parties. It was not intended to substitute a new method of trial when an issue of fact exists. Kasco Mills, Inc. v. Ferebee, 197 Va. 589, 90 S.E.2d 866 (1956); William Schluderberg-T.J. Kurdle Co. v. Trice, 198 Va. 85, 92 S.E.2d 374 (1956).

CIRCUIT COURT OPINIONS

Ruling on plea at bar. — Because a defendant properly pleaded a statute of limitations defense under § 8.01-235, and pursuant to § 8.01-281 and Va. Sup. Ct. R. 4:13(8) ruling on a plea at bar did not have to be deferred until the date of trial, the plaintiff's petition for declaratory judgment under § 8.01-191 was dismissed. Trivedi v. Pansuria, 72 Va. Cir. 220, 2006 Va. Cir. LEXIS 196 (Chesterfield County 2006).

Rule 4:14. Disposition of Discovery Material.

Any discovery material not admitted in evidence filed in a clerk's office may be destroyed by the clerk after one year after entry of the final judgment or decree. But if the action or suit is the subject of an appeal, such material shall not be destroyed until the lapse of one year after receipt of the mandate on appeal or the entry of any final judgment or decree thereafter.

Comment on adoption of rule. — This is designed to benefit clerks of court who complain that storage space is not available.

Michie's Jurisprudence. — For related discussion, see 5A M.J. Courts, § 3.

Rule 4:15. Motions Practice.

All civil case motions in circuit court shall be scheduled and heard using the following procedures:

(a) Scheduling — All civil case motions in circuit court shall be scheduled and heard using the following procedures:

1. Presenting the motion on a day the court designates for motions hearings, or

2. Contacting designated personnel in the office of the clerk of the court or the chambers of the judge or judges of the court.

(b) Notice — Reasonable notice of the presentation of a motion shall be served on all counsel of record. Absent leave of court, and except as provided in paragraph (c) of this Rule, reasonable notice shall be in writing and served at least seven days before the hearing. Counsel of record shall make a reasonable effort to confer before giving notice of a motion to resolve the subject of the motion and to determine a mutually agreeable hearing date and time. The notice shall be accompanied by a certification that the movant has in good faith conferred or attempted to confer with other affected parties in an effort to resolve the dispute without court action. In an Electronically Filed Case, the notice provisions of this paragraph and the filing and service requirements of paragraph (c) of this Rule shall be accomplished in accord with Rule 1:17.

(c) Filing and Service of Briefs — Counsel of record may elect or the court may require the parties to file briefs in support of or in opposition to a motion. Any such briefs should be filed with the court and served on all counsel of record sufficiently before the hearing to allow consideration of the issues involved. Absent leave of court, if a brief in support of a motion is five or fewer pages in length, the required notice and the brief shall be filed and served at least 14 days before the hearing and any brief in opposition to the motion shall be filed and served at least seven days before the hearing. If a brief will be more than five pages in length, an alternative hearing date, notice requirement, and briefing schedule may be determined by the court or its designee. Absent leave of court, the length of a brief shall not exceed 20 pages double spaced.

(d) Hearing — Except as otherwise provided in this subparagraph, upon request of counsel of record for any party, or at the court's request, the court shall hear oral argument on a motion. Oral argument on a motion for reconsideration or any motion in any case where a pro se incarcerated person is counsel of record shall be heard orally only at the request of the court. A court may place reasonable limits on the length of oral argument. No party shall be deprived of the opportunity to present its position on the merits of a motion solely because of the unfamiliarity of counsel of record with the motions procedures of that court. A court, however, at the request of counsel of record, or in the judge's discretion, may postpone the hearing of the motion, or require the filing of briefs to assure fairness to all parties and the ability of the court to review all such briefs in advance of the hearing.

(e) Definition of Served — For purposes of this Rule, a pleading shall be deemed served when it is actually received by, or in the office of, counsel of record through delivery, mailing, facsimile transmission or electronic mail as provided in Rule 1:12.

Effective date. — This rule, adopted May 1, 2000, became effective July 1, 2000.

The amendment effective January 1, 2003, adopted November 1, 2002, in the introductory paragraph, substituted "All civil case motions in circuit court shall be" for "All motions shall be" and deleted "by the courts" following "heard"; in paragraph (a), redesignated subparagraphs (1) and (2) as 1. and 2.; in paragraph (b), substituted "in paragraph (c) of this Rule; reasonable notice shall be in writing and served at least seven days" for "in paragraph (c); reasonable notice shall be at least 7 days" in the second sentence, and added a fourth sentence; in paragraph (c), substituted "all counsel" for "opposing counsel" in the second sentence, substituted "seven days" for "7 days" in the third sentence, and substituted "20 days" for "twenty days" in the fifth sentence; and in paragraph (d), substituted "Except as otherwise provided in this subparagraph" for "Except as otherwise provided herein" at the beginning of the first sentence.

The amendment effective November 1, 2005, adopted August 29, 2005, deleted "or" preceding, and added "or electronic mail as provided in Rule 1:12" following, "facsimile transmission" at the end of paragraph (e).

The amendment, effective May 2, 2011, adopted March 1, 2011, added the last sentence of paragraph (b).

Michie's Jurisprudence. — For related discussion, see 12B M.J. Merger, § 3.

CASE NOTES

Timeliness. — Appellant's argument that appellee's motion to reconsider was not properly noticed or docketed was without merit as appellee filed the motion to reconsider and certified that the appellee sent a copy to the appellant well in excess of the seven days before the hearing on the motion as required by Va. Sup. Ct. R. 4:15(b). Soliman v. Soliman, No. 0030-10-4, 2010 Va. App. LEXIS 277 (Ct. of Appeals July 20, 2010).

Expert witnesses excluded. — Circuit court did not abuse its discretion in excluding a patient's expert witnesses because it warned the patient multiple times that her failure to obey its pretrial orders would lead to sanctions, including the exclusion of the expert witnesses; the patient proved herself unable to comply with the rules, running afoul of not just Va. Sup. Ct. R. 1A:4(2) and 4:1(b)(4)(A)(i), but also Va. Sup. Ct. R. 1A:4(3), 4:1(e)(1)(B), and 4:15. Landrum v. Chippenham & Johnston-Willis Hosps., Inc., 282 Va. 346, 717 S.E.2d 134, 2011 Va. LEXIS 224 (2011).

Hearing. — Trial court did not err in denying both an attorney's motion for a suspending order and the attorney's renewed motion for a suspending order without a hearing because it did not appear that the attorney requested a hearing on either motion before the trial court denied those motions. Additionally, the attorney repeatedly stated that the attorney sought the suspension to file and argue a motion for reconsideration, for which Va. Sup. Ct. R. 4:15(d) provided oral argument only at the request of the court. N. Va. Real Estate, Inc. v. Martins, 283 Va. 86, 720 S.E.2d 121, 2012 Va. LEXIS 11 (2012).

CIRCUIT COURT OPINIONS

Leave of court. — Wife's request, which was made in the final portion of a memorandum in opposition, for attorney's fees and costs incurred as a result of her husband's motion for reconsideration and the wife's motion for clarification was denied because the wife could not unilaterally expand the scope of the motion for reconsideration without leave of court, pursuant to Va. Sup. Ct. R. 3:18(a), 1:4, and 4:15. Brannon v. Brannon, 2006 Va. Cir. LEXIS 128 (Fairfax County July 17, 2006).

No dilatory delay found. — The court determined that it was not the proper venue for the action pursuant to §§ 8.01-261 and 8.01-262, because none of the parties had their principal place of business in the city, no chief officer or president of any party resided in the city, and the alleged cause of action did not arise in the city, and plaintiff did not engage in dilatory delay, as plaintiff filed a notice of hearing within the seven-day time frame provided by Va. Sup. Ct. R. 4:15(b). Xspedius Communs. v. Cricket Techs., 71 Va. Cir. 310, 2006 Va. Cir. LEXIS 259 (Hopewell 2006).

Failure to confer with opposing counsel. — Although defendant violated Va. Sup. Ct. R. 4:15 when defense counsel made no effort to confer with plaintiff's counsel before giving notice of a motion to strike, and there was no certification in either the motion or the praecipe that counsel had in good faith conferred or attempted to confer with opposing counsel, plaintiff waived a claim for Rule 4:15 sanctions when plaintiff's counsel agreed to let the court hear defendant's motion to strike. Hutchison v. Hagadone, 78 Va. Cir. 185, 2009 Va. Cir. LEXIS 156 (Loudoun County Mar. 13, 2009).

Certification insufficient. — Reconsideration was proper because there was no evidence that a mother waived service under § 8.01-286.1, and the father's mere mailing of the pleadings and Va. Sup. Ct. R. 4:15(e) certification were insufficient to constitute proper service under § 8.01-296. Natal v. Natal, 2012 Va. Cir. LEXIS 35 (Fairfax County Feb. 28, 2012).

PART FIVE
THE SUPREME COURT

A. General.

Rule
5:1. Scope, Citation, Applicability, and General Provisions.
5:1A. Penalties for Non-compliance; Show Cause; Dismissal.
5:2. Sessions and Divisions.
5:3. Convening of Court — When En Banc — When in Division.
5:4. Motions and Responses; Orders.
5:5. Filing Deadlines; Post Trial Proceedings Below; Timely Filing by Mail; Mailing from an Institution; Extension of Time.
5:6. Forms of Briefs and Other Papers.

B. Original Jurisdiction.

5:7. Petitions for Writs of Habeas Corpus, Mandamus, and Prohibition.
5:7A. Petitions for Writs of Habeas Corpus in Cases in Which the Sentence of Death Has Been Imposed.
5:7B. Petition for a Writ of Actual Innocence.

C. Procedure for Filing an Appeal From a Trial Court.

5:8. Applicability.
5:8A. Appeal From Partial Final Judgment in Multi-Party Cases.
5:9. Notice of Appeal.
5:10. Record on Appeal: Contents.
5:11. Record on Appeal: Transcript or Written Statement.
5:12. Judge Authorized to Act.
5:13. Record on Appeal: Preparation and Transmission.

D. Procedure for Filing an Appeal From the Court of Appeals.

5:14. Notice of Appeal; Certification.
5:15. Record on Appeal From Court of Appeals or Certification for Review.
5:16. Disposition of Record.

E. Perfecting the Appeal.

5:17. Petition for Appeal.
5:17A. Petition for Review Pursuant to Code § 8.01-626; Injunctions.
5:18. Brief in Opposition.
5:19. Reply Brief.
5:20. Petition for Rehearing After Refusal of Petition for Appeal or Disposition of an Original Jurisdiction Petition.
5:20A. Denial of Appeal; Petition for Rehearing.

F. Special Rules.

5:21. Special Rules Applicable to Certain Appeals of Right.
5:22. Special Rule for Appeals in Death Penalty Cases.

G. Procedure Following Perfection of Appeal.

Rule
5:23. Perfection of Appeal; Docketing.
5:24. Security for Appeal.
5:25. Preservation of Issues for Appellate Review.
5:26. General Requirements for All Briefs.
5:27. Requirements for Opening Brief of Appellant.
5:28. Requirements for Brief of Appellee.
5:29. Requirements for Reply Brief.
5:30. Briefs Amicus Curiae.
5:31. Covers of Documents.
5:32. Appendix.
5:33. Oral Argument.

H. Decision, Costs, and Mandate.

5:34. Notice of Decision.
5:35. Attorney's Fees, Costs, and Notarized Bill of Costs.
5:36. Mandate.
5:37. Petition for Rehearing After Consideration by the Full Court.

I. Settlement or Withdrawal.

5:38. Settlement or Withdrawal of Pending Appeal.

J. Supreme Court of the United States.

5:39. Delay in Issuing Mandate Upon Appeal or Petition to Supreme Court of the United States.

K. Certification of Questions of Law.

5:40. Certification Procedures.

L. Appeals Relating to Quarantine or Isolation Orders.

5:41. Appeal of Orders Relating to Quarantine or Isolation of Persons.

Appendix of Forms.

Form
1. Bond for Costs Alone — Appeal of Right From Circuit Court to Court of Appeals (including further appeal to the Supreme Court).
2. Bond for Costs and Suspension — Appeal From Circuit Court to Appellate Court.
3. Bond for Costs Alone Required by Appellate Court on Appeal From Circuit Court.
4. Bond for Suspension Alone Required by Appellate Court on Appeal From Circuit Court.
5. Bond for Costs and Suspension Required by Appellate Court on Appeal From Circuit Court.
6. Additional Bond Required by Appellate Court on Appeal From Circuit Court.
7. Bond for Costs Alone — Appeal of Right From Virginia Workers' Compensation Commission to Court of Appeals (including further appeal to the Supreme Court).
8. Bond for Costs Alone — Required by Supreme

Form
Court on Appeal of Right From State Corporation Commission.
9. Bond for Costs and Suspension — Required by Supreme Court on Appeal of Right From State Corporation Commission.

Form
10. Form for Execution and Acknowledgment of All Bonds.
11. Irrevocable Letters of Credit.
12. Petition for a Writ of Actual Innocence.

Editor's note. — The order effective Aug. 1, 1985, adopted May 16, 1985, repealed former Part Five and adopted a new Part Five.

Part Five was rewritten in its entirety by order adopted April 30, 2010, and effective July 1, 2010.

A. GENERAL.

Rule 5:1. Scope, Citation, Applicability, and General Provisions.

(a) *Scope of Rules.* — Part Five governs all proceedings in the Supreme Court of Virginia.

(b) *Citation.* — These Rules may be cited generally as the "Rules of the Supreme Court of Virginia" and specifically as "Rule 5:__."

(c) *Definitions.* — (1) "clerk" means clerk of the court or commission from which an appeal is taken unless some other clerk is specified and, unless the context otherwise requires, includes a deputy clerk;

(2) "clerk of this Court" includes a deputy clerk.

(3) "counsel" has the definition given in Rule 1:5 and in this Part Five includes a party not represented by counsel;

(4) "counsel for the appellant" means one of the attorneys representing each appellant represented by an attorney and each appellant not represented by an attorney;

(5) "counsel for the appellee" means one of the attorneys representing each appellee represented by an attorney and each appellee not represented by an attorney. In an appeal from the State Corporation Commission, "counsel for the appellee" shall also include counsel for the Commission and, unless the Commonwealth is the appellant, the Attorney General;

(6) "Court of Appeals" means the Court of Appeals of Virginia;

(7) "opposing counsel" means, depending on the context, "counsel for the appellant" or "counsel for the appellee";

(8) "judge" means judge of the trial court, unless the context otherwise requires, or if the judge of the trial court is not available, any judge authorized to act under Rule 5:12;

(9) "judgment" includes an order or decree from which an appeal is taken;

(10) "trial court" means the circuit court from which an appeal is taken;

(11) the "date of entry" of any final judgment or other appealable order or decree shall be the date the judgment, order, or decree is signed by the judge.

(d) *Service.* — Unless service or notice is otherwise specified in a given Rule, any paper or object filed with this Court must have included within it or appended to it a certificate of service or acceptance of service showing that a copy has been transmitted to all counsel and showing the date and manner of transmittal. If a word count is used, the certificate must also state the number of words (headings, footnotes, and quotations count towards the word limitation; the cover page, table of contents, table of authorities, and certificate do not count towards the word count).

(e) *Notice of Change of Address and Other Contact Information.* — If an attorney has a change in mailing address, telephone number, facsimile number, or e-mail address any time after the filing of the notice of appeal, the attorney must immediately notify the clerk of this Court and all other counsel of record in writing. The notice must reference the style and record number of all cases pending before this Court.

(f) *Citing Unpublished Judicial Dispositions.* — The citation of judicial opinions, orders, judgments, or other written dispositions that are not officially reported, whether designated as "unpublished," "not for publication," "non precedential," or the like, is permitted as informative, but shall not be received as binding authority. If the cited disposition is not available in a publicly accessible electronic database, a copy of that disposition must be filed with the brief or other paper in which it is cited.

Source. — Rule 5:1, Cf. Rule 5A:1.

Law Review. — For 1985 survey of Virginia civil procedure and practice, see 19 U. Rich. L. Rev. 679 (1985). For 1991 survey of civil practice and procedure, see 25 U. Rich. L. Rev. 663 (1991). For a review of civil practice and procedure in Virginia for year 1999, see 33 U. Rich. L. Rev. 801 (1999).

Michie's Jurisprudence. — For related discussion, see 1B M.J. Appeal and Error, §§ 6, 124, 135, 140, 201, 202; 15 M.J. Prohibition, § 25.

CASE NOTES

When legal presence of parties on appeal absolute necessity. — Where a party's interests in the subject matter of the appeal are so bound up with that of the other parties, its legal presence as a party to the proceeding is an absolute necessity, without which the appellate court cannot proceed. Asch v. Friends of Community of Mt. Vernon Yacht Club, 251 Va. 89, 465 S.E.2d 817 (1996).

Rule 5:1A. Penalties for Non-compliance; Show Cause; Dismissal.

(a) *Penalties; Show Cause; Dismissal.* — This Court may dismiss an appeal or impose such other penalty as it deems appropriate for non-compliance with these Rules. Except as provided in Rule 5:17(c) regarding assignments of error, prior to the dismissal of an appeal for any defect in the filings related to formatting, curable failure to comply with other requirements, or the failure to meet non-mandatory filing deadlines, this Court may issue a show cause order to counsel or a party not represented by an attorney, prescribing a time in which to cure such defect or to otherwise show cause why the appeal should not be dismissed or other penalty imposed.

(b) *Report to Virginia State Bar.* — If an attorney's failure to comply with these Rules results in the dismissal of an appeal, this Court may report the attorney to the Virginia State Bar in accordance with Rule 8.3 of the Virginia Rules of Professional Conduct.

Rule 5:2. Sessions and Divisions.

Except as provided in Code § 17.1-304, sessions and divisions of this Court will be held at Richmond, or at such other locations as this Court may designate consistent with applicable law, and will continue for such length of time as this Court may determine.

Source. — Rule 5:2.

Rule 5:3. Convening of Court — When En Banc — When in Division.

(a) This Court will sit en banc or in divisions.

(b) Whenever four or more of the Justices are convened, this Court shall be deemed to be sitting en banc and vested with all of the powers of this Court. Whenever three of the Justices are convened, this Court shall be deemed to be sitting as a division, and vested with all of the powers of a division of this Court.

(c) If the Justices composing any division shall differ as to the judgment to be rendered in any case, or if, within ten days after the decision is rendered by the division any Justice of such division shall file in the office of the clerk of this Court a certificate that, in the opinion of the Justice, such decision is in conflict with a prior decision of this Court or of one of the divisions thereof, or if this Court shall so determine, the case shall be reheard and decided by this Court sitting en banc.

Source. — Rule 5:3.

Rule 5:4. Motions and Responses; Orders.

(a) *Motions and Responses.* — (1) Motions. All motions, except motions for the qualification of attorneys at law to practice in this Court, shall be in writing and filed with the clerk of this Court. All motions shall contain a statement by the movant that the other parties to the appeal have been informed of the intended filing of the motion. For all motions in cases in which all parties are represented by counsel — except motions to dismiss petitions for a writ of habeas corpus — the statement by the movant shall also indicate whether the other parties consent to the granting of the motion, or intend to file responses in opposition.

(2) Responses. Opposing counsel may have 10 days after such motion is filed to file with such clerk a response to such motion, but this Court may act before the 10 days expire, if necessary.

(3) Number of Copies. An original and three copies of all motions or responses must be filed.

(4) Oral Argument. No motion shall be argued orally except by leave of this Court.

(b) *Orders.* — Promptly after this Court has entered an order, the clerk of this Court shall send a copy of the order to all counsel.

Advisory Note. — This rule is not intended to limit the scope of motions that may be filed in the Supreme Court. Such motions may be filed in any pending or contemplated appeal, and may request from the Court any form of relief that is available to the movant. The practitioner should consult individual rules relating to the filing of motions in particular matters; for example, Rule 5:12 (trial judge authorized to act on matters pertaining to record); Rule 5:30(a)(3) (motion for leave to file brief amicus curiae). Rehearings are not within the scope of this rule, but are governed by Rules 5:20, 5:20A, and 5:37.

Source. — Rule 5:4. Cf. Rule 5A:2.

Michie's Jurisprudence. — For related discussion, see 1B M.J. Appeal and Error, §§ 201, 234, 236.1.

Rule 5:5. Filing Deadlines; Post Trial Proceedings Below; Timely Filing by Mail; Mailing from an Institution; Extension of Time.

(a) *Filing Deadlines.* — The times prescribed for filing the notice of appeal (Rules 5:9(a), 5:14(a) and 5:21(c)), a petition for appeal (Rules 5:17(a) and 5:21(g)), a petition for review pursuant to Code § 8.01-626 (Rule 5:17A) and a petition for rehearing (Rules 5:20 and 5:37), are mandatory. A single extension not to exceed thirty days may be granted if at least two Justices of the Supreme Court of Virginia concur in a finding that an extension for papers to be filed is warranted by a showing of good cause sufficient to excuse the delay.

(b) *Post-Trial Proceedings Below and Their Effect on the Notice of Appeal.* — The time period for filing the notice of appeal is not extended by the filing of a motion for a new trial, a petition for rehearing, or a like pleading unless the final judgment is modified, vacated, or suspended by the trial court pursuant to Rule 1:1 or a timely petition for rehearing is filed in the Court of Appeals. In any such case, the time for filing the notice of appeal shall be computed from the date of final judgment entered following such modification, vacation, or suspension, or from the date the Court of Appeals refuses a timely petition for rehearing or enters final judgment following the granting of such a petition.

(c) *How to File by Mail in a Timely Manner.* — Any document required to be filed with the clerk of this Court shall be deemed to be timely filed if (1) it is transmitted expense pre-paid to the clerk of this Court by priority, express, registered, or certified mail via the United States Postal Service, or by a third-party commercial carrier for next-day delivery, and (2) if the official receipt therefor be exhibited upon demand of the clerk of this Court or any party and it shows such transmission or mailing within the prescribed time limits. This rule does not apply to documents to be filed in the office of the clerk of the trial court or clerk of the Virginia Workers' Compensation Commission or clerk of the State Corporation Commission.

(d) *Inmate Filing.* — A paper filed by an individual confined in an institution, including a prison, jail, or the Virginia Center for Behavioral Rehabilitation, is timely filed if deposited in the institution's internal mail system with first-class postage prepaid on or before the last day for filing. Timely filing of a paper by an individual confined in such an institution may be established by (1) an official stamp of the institution showing that the paper was deposited in the internal mail system on or before the last day for filing, (2) an official postmark dated on or before the last day for filing, or (3) a notarized statement signed by an official of the institution showing that the paper was deposited in the internal mail system on or before the last day for filing.

(e) *Extensions Generally.* — Except as provided in paragraph (a) of this Rule, a motion for an extension of time is timely if filed either within the original filing deadline or within any extension period specified by the governing rule. Filing the motion within the original filing deadline or within the specified extension period does not toll the original filing deadline or further extend the period of extension.

Cross references. — As to computation of time, see Rule 1:7. As to the filing of a petition for appeal, see also Rule 5:17(e) for filing fee requirement.

Source. — Rules 5:1A and 5:7. Cf. Rule 5A:3.

Comment. — See also Rule 1:7 regarding computation of time.

The amendment, effective May 2, 2011, adopted March 1, 2011, inserted "a petition for review pursuant to Code § 8.01-626 (Rule 5:17A)" in the first sentence of subdivision (a).

The amendment effective January 1, 2013, adopted December 14, 2012, in (d), substituted "individual" for "inmate" and inserted ", including a prison, jail, or the Virginia Center for Behavioral Rehabilitation," in the first sentence, and in the second sentence, substituted "individual" for "inmate" and inserted "such."

Michie's Jurisprudence. — For related discussion, see 9A M.J. Habeas Corpus, §§ 18, 20; 13B M.J. New Trials, § 60; 15 M.J. Prohibition, §§ 19, 21.

CASE NOTES

Editor's note. — Some of the annotations below were decided under prior rules.

Thirty-day requirement mandatory; extension of time requirement. — Subdivision (a) declares that the 30-day requirement for filing a notice of appeal is "mandatory." The Virginia Supreme Court has reiterated the unwaivable nature of this requirement and will extend its time requirement only in those cases in which the petitioner has a constitutional right to have the appeal heard. Coleman v. Thompson, 501 U.S. 722, 111 S. Ct. 2546, 115 L. Ed. 2d 640 (1991).

Time limit not extended by filing a motion to set aside verdict. — Doctor's appeal from a final judgment in favor of a patient was untimely because it was not filed within 30 days of the expiration of a 14-day suspension period entered by the trial court pursuant to Va. Sup. Ct. R. 1:1, as required by Va. Sup. Ct. R. 5:9. The doctor's motion to set aside the verdict did not extend the period for filing the notice of appeal, pursuant to Va. Sup. Ct. R. 5:5. Hutchins v. Talbert, 278 Va. 650, 685 S.E.2d 658, 2009 Va. LEXIS 98 (2009).

A paper is "filed" when delivered to the clerk by the agent selected by counsel. Mears v. Mears, 206 Va. 444, 143 S.E.2d 889 (1965).

Mere notice of appeal insufficient to confer appellate jurisdiction. — The mere fact that an indispensable party who was a litigant in the trial court has notice that an appeal has been perfected against another litigant is not sufficient to confer an appellate court's jurisdiction over the indispensable party against whom no appeal has been properly perfected. Asch v. Friends of Community of Mt. Vernon Yacht Club, 251 Va. 89, 465 S.E.2d 817 (1996).

Purpose of mailing provision. — The mailing provision was not created to extend the time in which a party has to file a petition, but to circumvent the inconvenience of having to personally appear in the clerk's office to effect a filing, and to protect a party from those delays that often occur in the regular dispatch of mail and naturally are outside a party's control. Reese v. Wampler Foods, Inc., 222 Va. 249, 278 S.E.2d 870 (1981).

Filing by mail. — Counsel who mails a paper assumes the risk that the paper may be delayed in transit or may not be received. Mears v. Mears, 206 Va. 444, 143 S.E.2d 889 (1965).

Notice of appeal considered as filed when inmate complied with Rule 5:5. — Inmate's claim for ineffective assistance of trial counsel, asserted pursuant to 28 U.S.C.S. § 2254, was not considered to be procedurally defaulted even though the inmate had not filed a timely notice of appeal of his state collateral proceeding with the Virginia Supreme Court as required by Va. Sup. Ct. R. 5:9, because it was essentially undisputed that the inmate had complied with the inmate mailing rules set forth in Va. Sup. Ct. R. 5:5 in filing a notice of appeal. Smallwood v. Young, 425 F. Supp. 2d 717, 2006 U.S. Dist. LEXIS 14128 (E.D. Va. 2006), appeal dismissed, 2007 U.S. App. LEXIS 16439 (4th Cir. Va. 2007).

"Consideration" of all filed papers does not override grant of dismissal based on procedural grounds. — Virginia Supreme Court's "consideration" of all filed papers in dismissing an appeal could not be read as overriding the court's explicit grant of a dismissal motion based solely on procedural grounds which were independent of federal law. Coleman v. Thompson, 501 U.S. 722, 111 S. Ct. 2546, 115 L. Ed. 2d 640 (1991).

CIRCUIT COURT OPINIONS

Time limitations are mandatory. — Because the requirements of Va. Sup. Ct. R. 5:11 were mandatory and jurisdictional, the statement of facts, submitted more than 55 days after the final order, were not properly before the court. Ahmed v. Wesley, 71 Va. Cir. 393, 2006 Va. Cir. LEXIS 140 (Fairfax County 2006).

Purpose of mailing provision. — When an inmate sued a retailer for assault and battery, false imprisonment and defamation for causing his arrest, Va. Sup. Ct. R. 5:5(c) did not cause his motion for judgment to have been timely filed because he alleged it was delivered to jail authorities before the statute of limitations expired because Rule 5:5(c) only applied to inmates filing appeals with the Supreme Court of Virginia, and it did not apply to inmates filing civil actions. McEvily v. K-Mart Corp., 73 Va. Cir. 51, 2007 Va. Cir. LEXIS 48 (Fairfax County 2007).

Rule 5:6. Forms of Briefs and Other Papers.

(a) *Paper Size, Line Spacing, Font, and Margins.* — (1) General Rules. Briefs, appendices, motions, petitions, and other papers may be printed by any process that yields a clear black image on white paper and must be on 8-½ x 11 inch paper. Margins must be at least one inch on all four sides of each page.

(2) Specific Rules for Motions, Petitions, and Briefs. Except by leave of Court, all motions, petitions, and briefs, including footnotes, must be in at least 14-point font, must use either Courier, Arial, or Verdana font, and must be printed on only one side of the page. Text shall not be reduced and must be double spaced except for headings, assignments of error, quotations, and footnotes, which must be single spaced. Page numbers are required and may appear in either the top or bottom margin, but no text, including footnotes, is permitted in the one inch margins. Page or word limits for motions, petitions, and briefs do not include the cover page, table of contents, table of authorities, or certificate.

(3) Specific Rules for the Appendix. The appendix may be printed using both sides of the page. Any transcript, including a deposition transcript, that is made a part of the appendix shall be in 12-point type or larger. Any transcript contained in the appendix that fails to conform to the 12-point type requirement may be returned to counsel, and counsel shall be required to promptly comply with this requirement in accordance with the instruction of this Court. The use of condensed or multi-page transcripts is prohibited. Page numbers are required and may appear in either the top or bottom margin.

(b) *Binding and Cover.* — All briefs and appendices shall be bound on the left margin in such a manner as to produce a flat, smooth binding. Spiral binding, acco fasteners, and the like are not acceptable. The style of the case (with the name of the appellant stated first) and the record number of the case shall be stated on the front cover of all briefs and appendices and, in addition, the name, Virginia State Bar number, mailing address, telephone number (including any applicable extension), facsimile number (if any), and e-mail address (if any) of counsel submitting the brief shall be placed on the front cover of all briefs.

(c) *Effect of Non-compliance.* — No appeal shall be dismissed for failure to comply with the provisions of this Rule; the clerk of this Court may, however, require that a document be redone in compliance with this Rule.

Source. — Rule 5:33. Cf. Rule 5A:4.

Michie's Jurisprudence. — For related discussion, see 1B M.J. Appeal and Error, §§ 137, 201; 6A M.J. Divorce and Alimony, §§ 49, 77.

B. ORIGINAL JURISDICTION.

Rule 5:7. Petitions for Writs of Habeas Corpus, Mandamus, and Prohibition.

(a) *Petition for Writ of Habeas Corpus.* — An application to this Court for a writ of habeas corpus under its original jurisdiction shall be by petition filed in the office of the clerk of this Court.

(1) When Petition Must be Filed. The petition for a writ of habeas corpus challenging a criminal conviction or sentence, except as provided in Rule 5:7A for cases in which the death penalty has been imposed, shall be filed within two years from the date of the final judgment in the trial court or within one year from either final disposition of the direct appeal in state court or the time for filing such appeal has expired, whichever is later. All other petitions for a writ of habeas corpus must be filed within one year after the cause of action accrues.

(2) What the Petition Must Contain. The petition must be notarized and must state whether the petitioner believes that the taking of evidence is necessary for the proper disposition of the petition. A memorandum of law citing relevant authorities must accompany each petition. All petitions must comply with the requirements of Code § 8.01-655.

(3) Service of Petitions. Except as provided herein, service of process must be accomplished in accordance with Chapter 8 of Title 8.01.

(i) Non-Public Officials. A petition must be accompanied by a return of service executed by the appropriate officer evidencing service of a copy thereof on the respondent or by an acceptance of service signed by the respondent.

(ii) Public Officials. When habeas corpus is directed to a public official, service shall be made on the respondent and shall also be made on or accepted by the Attorney

General or an Assistant Attorney General. A petition must be accompanied by a return of service executed by the appropriate officer evidencing service of a copy thereof on the respondent or by an acceptance of service signed by the respondent.

(iii) Prisoners Pro Se. In cases brought by prisoners pro se, a copy of the petition shall be forwarded to the respondent by first class mail, and the application shall contain a certificate at the end stating as follows:

I hereby certify that on the ___ day of ______________, 20___, I mailed a copy of the foregoing application to the respondent(s), ______________________,
Petitioner
by first class mail.

(4) When to Respond to a Petition. No responsive pleading to a petition filed by a prisoner acting pro se shall be required except as ordered by this Court. For all other petitions, a responsive pleading must be filed with the clerk of this Court within forty days after service of the petition.

(5) Contents of the Response. In one responsive pleading, the respondent may move to dismiss on any appropriate ground, including the failure to state facts upon which relief should be granted, and, in the alternative, may set forth grounds of defense as in an action at law. The answer shall state whether, in the opinion of the respondent, the taking of evidence is necessary for the proper disposition of the petition. A memorandum of law citing the relevant authorities shall accompany each responsive pleading.

(6) Length. Except by permission of a Justice of this Court, no petition, including the accompanying memorandum of law, or a response thereto, including its accompanying memorandum of law, shall exceed the longer of 50 printed pages or 8,750 words. Page and word limits do not include appendices, exhibits, cover page, table of contents, table of authorities, and certificate.

(7) Number of Copies. Ten copies of the petition, responsive pleading, memoranda of law, and motions shall be filed in the office of the clerk of this Court. Prisoners filing pro se shall only be required to file three copies.

(8) Calling up the Record. If this Court determines that any portion of the underlying trial or appellate record is necessary for a proper determination of the merits of the petition, the clerk of this Court is authorized to request the record and the clerk of the trial court, commission, or the Court of Appeals, as appropriate shall transmit it forthwith upon request without the necessity of an order.

(b) *Petitions for Writs of Mandamus and Prohibition.* — An application for a writ of mandamus or a writ of prohibition under the original jurisdiction of this Court shall be by petition filed in the office of the clerk of this Court.

(1) What the Petition Must Contain. The petition must be notarized and must state whether the petitioner believes that the taking of evidence is necessary for the proper disposition of the petition. A memorandum of law citing relevant authorities must accompany each petition.

(2) Service of Petitions.

(i) Generally. A petition must be accompanied by a return of service executed by the appropriate officer evidencing service of a copy thereof on the respondent or by an acceptance of service signed by the respondent. Except in cases brought by prisoners acting pro se, service of process must be accomplished in accordance with Chapter 8 of Title 8.01.

(ii) Prisoners Pro Se. In cases brought by prisoners pro se, a copy of the petition shall be forwarded to the respondent by first class mail, and the application shall contain a certificate at the end stating as follows:

I hereby certify that on the ___ day of ______________, 20___, I mailed a copy of the foregoing application to the respondent(s), ______________________,
Petitioner
by first class mail.

(3) Limitations for Petitions for Mandamus. A petition for writ of mandamus filed by or on behalf of a person confined in a state correctional facility must be brought within one year after the cause of action accrues.

(4) Petitions for Mandamus or Prohibition Against a Judge. A petition for writ of mandamus or writ of prohibition against a judge shall not bear the name of the judge but shall be entitled, "In re , Petitioner." When the Attorney General determines, with the concurrence of the judge, that it is impracticable or unnecessary for the Attorney

General to represent the judge, the judge may be represented pro forma by counsel for the party opposing the relief, who shall appear in the name of the party and not that of the judge. Or, in the alternative, the Attorney General may provide for the appointment of special counsel to represent the judge, in accordance with the provisions of Code §§ 2.2-507 or 2.2-510.

(5) When to Respond to a Petition. No responsive pleading shall be required for a petition filed by a prisoner acting pro se except as ordered by this Court. For all other petitions, a responsive pleading must be filed with the clerk of this Court within 21 days after service of the petition or the filing thereof, whichever date is later.

(6) Contents of the Response. In one responsive pleading, the respondent may move to dismiss on any appropriate ground, including the failure to state facts upon which relief should be granted, and, in the alternative, may set forth an answer as in an action at law. The answer shall state whether, in the opinion of the respondent, the taking of evidence is necessary for the proper disposition of the petition. A memorandum of law citing the relevant authorities should accompany each responsive pleading.

(7) Length. Except by permission of a Justice of this Court, no petition, including the accompanying memorandum of law, or a response thereto, including its accompanying memorandum of law, shall exceed the longer of 50 printed pages or 8,750 words. This page or word limit does not include appendices, exhibits, cover page, table of contents, table of authorities, and certificate.

(8) Number of Copies. Ten copies of the petition, responsive pleading, memoranda of law, and motions shall be filed in the office of the clerk of this Court. Prisoners filing pro se shall only be required to file three copies.

(c) *When this Court May Act on a Petition.* — This Court may act on any petition for a writ of habeas corpus, mandamus, or prohibition before a responsive pleading is filed. This Court may by order shorten the period within which a responsive pleading must be filed.

(d) *Further Proceedings on Petitions.* — Further proceedings shall be in accordance with the orders of this Court or a Justice thereof to whom this Court may delegate authority to determine all procedural matters. If this Court or the designated Justice determines that evidence is desirable, depositions shall be taken according to a schedule agreed upon by counsel and filed in the office of the clerk of this Court or, in the absence of agreement, according to a schedule determined by this Court or the designated Justice.

(e) *Amendment of Petition.* — If the statute of limitations has not expired, a petitioner may move — at any time before a ruling is rendered on the merits of the petition as initially filed — for leave of this Court to substitute an amended petition. This amendment can include additional claims not presented in the petition as initially filed. Any such motion shall attach a copy of the proposed amended petition.

Source. — Rule 5:5 and Rule 5A:5.

The amendment, effective May 2, 2011, adopted March 1, 2011, inserted "the longer of" preceding "50 printed" in subdivisions (a)(6) and (b)(7), and added subdivision (e).

Law Review. — For comment, "Prohibition: The Elusive and Misunderstood Writ," see 16 U. Rich. L. Rev. 693 (1982). For annual survey article, "Civil Practice and Procedure," see 46 U. Rich. L. Rev. 9 (2011).

Michie's Jurisprudence. — For related discussion, see 8A M.J. Exceptions, Bill of, § 1; 9A M.J. Habeas Corpus, §§ 17, 18, 20, 22, 23; 12B M.J. Mandamus, §§ 27, 28, 31; 15 M.J. Prohibition, § 24.

CASE NOTES

Habeas corpus petitions. — The Supreme Court is given original, but not exclusive, jurisdiction over habeas corpus petitions. Creasy v. McConnell, 262 F. Supp. 697 (W.D. Va. 1966).

Mandamus petitions. — Because an owner's cause of action for injury to property accrued upon a town's enactment of an ordinance in 1985, the circuit court properly determined that the statute of limitations in subsection B of § 8.01-243 had run; therefore, based on clear judicial precedent, the owner's petition for a writ of mandamus was untimely. C. Givens Bros., L.L.C. v. Town of Blacksburg, 273 Va. 281, 641 S.E.2d 113, 2007 Va. LEXIS 41 (2007).

Applied in Taylor v. Murray, 855 F. Supp. 124 (E.D. Va. 1994).

CIRCUIT COURT OPINIONS

Mandamus petitions. — Because a police officer's counsel refused to accept a city's attempt to correct its noncompliance by offering to schedule a Step 4 grievance hearing, the police officer was not entitled to mandamus relief. Newman v. City of Alexandria, 78 Va. Cir. 7, 2008 Va. Cir. LEXIS 192 (Alexandria 2008).

Rule 5:7A. Petitions for Writs of Habeas Corpus in Cases in Which the Sentence of Death Has Been Imposed.

In cases in which the sentence of death has been imposed:

(a) *Petition for the Writ.* — A petition for a writ of habeas corpus shall be filed in the office of the clerk of this Court within 60 days after the earliest of: (i) the denial by the Supreme Court of the United States of a petition for a writ of certiorari to the judgment of this Court on direct appeal, (ii) an order of the Supreme Court of the United States affirming imposition of the sentence of death in a case in which that Court granted a writ of certiorari to review the judgment of this Court on direct appeal, or (iii) the expiration of the period for filing a petition for a writ of certiorari in the Supreme Court of the United States without such a petition being filed.

(b) *Contents of Petition for Writ.* — Each petition for a writ of habeas corpus shall be verified and shall include an enumerated list of the grounds asserted for relief together with all supporting facts upon which the petitioner relies. The petition shall contain citation to the relevant legal authorities and an enumeration of all previous petitions and their disposition. The petition shall state whether, in the opinion of the petitioner, the taking of evidence is necessary for the proper disposition of the petition. The petition shall be accompanied by a return of service executed by the appropriate officer evidencing service of a copy thereof upon the Attorney General of Virginia or by an acceptance of service signed by the Attorney General or an Assistant Attorney General.

(c) *Response.* — Within 30 days after service of the petition, the Attorney General shall file with the clerk of this Court a responsive pleading, which may include a motion to dismiss. The response shall include citation to the relevant legal authorities and shall state whether, in the opinion of the Attorney General, the taking of evidence is necessary for the proper disposition of the petition.

(d) *Reply.* — Within 20 days after the Attorney General's responsive pleading is filed pursuant to subparagraph (c), the petitioner may file a reply.

(e) *Copies to be Filed.* — Ten copies of the petition, the Attorney General's responsive pleading, and the petitioner's reply shall be filed in the office of the clerk of this Court.

(f) *Motions.* — Upon the filing of any motion other than a motion to dismiss included in a responsive pleading filed pursuant to subparagraph (c) of this Rule, or upon the filing of an objection pursuant to Code § 8.01-654(C)(3), the opposing party may file a response within ten days of the filing of the motion or objection, or within such time as this Court may order.

(g) *Length.* — Except by permission of a justice of this Court, no petition for a writ of habeas corpus or a response thereto shall exceed the longer of 100 pages or 17,500 words, and no reply to a response shall exceed the longer of 50 pages or 8,750 words. Page or word limits under this Rule do not include appendices, the cover page, table of contents, table of authorities, and certificate. All petitions, responses, replies, motions, and other papers filed pursuant to this Rule shall conform to the provisions of Rule 5:6(a). If counsel wishes to file a petition or response in excess of the page or word limit prescribed in this paragraph, a motion to exceed the page or word limit must be filed with the clerk of this Court at least 10 days before the due date for the petition or response. If the motion is denied, or if no timely motion to exceed the page or word limit is filed, any pages in the petition or response that exceed the page or word limit, except the signature and certificate of service, shall be stricken and not considered by this Court.

(h) *Further Proceedings by Order of this Court.* — Further proceedings shall be conducted in accordance with the orders of this Court. If it is determined that an evidentiary hearing is necessary for the proper disposition of the petition, this Court shall enter an order directing the circuit court that entered the judgment imposing the sentence of death to conduct such a hearing in accordance with the provisions of Code § 8.01-654(C)(1), (2), and (3).

(i) *Amendment of Petition.* — If the statute of limitations has not expired, a petitioner may move — at any time before a ruling is rendered on the merits of the petition as initially filed — for leave of this Court to substitute an amended petition. This amendment can include additional claims not presented in the petition as initially filed. Any such motion shall attach a copy of the proposed amended petition.

The amendment, effective May 2, 2011, adopted March 1, 2011, inserted "the longer of" twice in the first sentence of subdivision (g).

Michie's Jurisprudence. — For related discussion, see 9A M.J. Habeas Corpus, § 1.

CASE NOTES

Length of petition. — Although certain claims were included in petitioner's motions to amend his state habeas petition, those claims were never presented to the state supreme court in compliance with the page limit established by Rule 5:7A(g); barring special and important reasons to grant petitioner leave to amend his petition and circumvent the page limit rule, the state supreme court could not, and did not, reach the merits of those claims. Therefore, those claims were not fairly presented to the state court, and it followed, then, that the claims were procedurally defaulted because they were not presented to the state court on direct appeal or on habeas review. Orbe v. True, 233 F. Supp. 2d 749, 2002 U.S. Dist. LEXIS 22958 (E.D. Va. 2002).

Rule 5:7B. Petition for a Writ of Actual Innocence.

(a) *Who may File a Petition.* — A petition for a writ of actual innocence based upon previously unknown or untested human biological evidence may be filed by any person who has been convicted of a felony upon a plea of not guilty, or who was adjudicated delinquent upon a plea of not guilty by a circuit court of an offense that would be a felony if committed by an adult, or by any person, regardless of plea, who has been sentenced to death, or convicted or adjudicated delinquent of a class 1 felony, a class 2 felony or any felony for which the maximum penalty is imprisonment for life.

(b) *Time for Filing.* — A petition under this Rule shall be filed in the office of the Clerk of this Court within 60 days after the date upon which exculpatory test results are obtained by the petitioner or his counsel of record from the Department of Forensic Science for any tests conducted on human biological evidence pursuant to Code § 19.2-327.1.

(c) *Contents of the Petition.* — Each petition for a writ of actual innocence shall be filed on a form provided by this Court and shall be verified under oath. The petition must state categorically and with specificity: (i) the offense or offenses for which petitioner was convicted or adjudicated delinquent, including all previous records, applications, petitions, and appeals relating to these convictions or adjudications of delinquency, and their dispositions; (ii) that the petitioner is actually innocent of the crime or crimes for which he was convicted or adjudicated delinquent; (iii) an exact description of the human biological evidence and the scientific testing supporting the allegation of innocence, attaching a copy of the test results; (iv) that the human biological evidence was not known or available to the petitioner or his attorney at trial, or if it was known, why it was not subject to scientific testing; (v) the earliest date the test results described in the petition became known to the petitioner or any attorney of record; (vi) that the petitioner or his attorney has filed the petition within 60 days of obtaining the test results; (vii) an explanation of the reason or reasons the evidence will prove that no rational trier of fact would have found the petitioner guilty or delinquent beyond a reasonable doubt of the offense or offenses for which the petitioner was convicted or adjudicated delinquent; and (viii) if the conviction or adjudication of delinquency became final in the circuit court after June 30, 1996, that the evidence was not available for testing under Code § 9.1-1104.

(d) *Service of the Petition and Return of Service.* — Prior to filing a petition, the petitioner shall serve the petition, along with all attachments, on the Attorney General and on the Commonwealth's Attorney for the jurisdiction where the conviction or adjudication of delinquency occurred. The petitioner shall file with the petition either (i) a duly executed return of service in the form of a verification that a copy of the petition and all attachments have been served, or (ii) an acceptance of service signed by either or both of the parties to be served, or (iii) a combination of the two.

(e) *Filing Fee.* — The petition must be accompanied by either (i) a check or money order for the filing fee required by statute, or (ii) an in forma pauperis affidavit demonstrating that the petitioner cannot afford the filing fee.

(f) *Response.* — The Attorney General shall respond to the petition as follows:

(1) Within 30 days after service of the petition, the Attorney General shall file with the clerk of this Court a pleading in the form of a declaration stating, in the opinion of

the Attorney General, with an explanation of the reasons therefor, whether the record of any trial or appellate proceedings involving the conviction or convictions, or adjudication or adjudications of delinquency, or of any proceedings under Code § 19.2-327.1, is necessary for preparation of a response to the petition. If the Attorney General asserts that the record, or any part thereof, of any trial or appellate court proceedings is necessary, the Attorney General shall request the production of such record by this Court, and shall describe with specificity, including the court, docket number and date of judgment, each and every record or part thereof which is requested.

(2) If the Attorney General asserts in the declaration required by subparagraph (f)(1) of this Rule that no trial or appellate court record, or any part thereof, is necessary for the preparation of a responsive pleading to the petition, the Attorney General shall file with the clerk of this Court within 30 days thereafter a pleading in response to the petition. Any pleading in response filed by the Attorney General may include a motion to dismiss. The response shall include citation to any relevant legal authorities, and may contain a proffer of any evidence pertaining to the guilt of the petitioner that is not included in the record of the case, including any evidence that was suppressed at trial.

(3) If the Attorney General asserts in the declaration required by subparagraph (f)(1) of this Rule that a trial or appellate court record, or any part thereof, is necessary for the preparation of a response to the petition, the court shall issue the writ of certiorari described in Code § 19.2-327.3(D) to the clerk of the respective court below for the production of the record forthwith to the clerk of this Court. Upon receipt of the record by the clerk of this Court, the clerk shall immediately notify in writing the petitioner, any attorney for the petitioner, the Attorney General, and the attorney for the Commonwealth of the jurisdiction where the conviction or convictions or adjudication or adjudications of delinquency occurred, of the date of receipt of the record. Within 30 days after receipt of the record by the clerk of this Court, the Attorney General shall file the responsive pleading described in subparagraph (f)(2) of this Rule.

(g) *Reply.* — Within 20 days after the Attorney General's responsive pleading is filed pursuant to subparagraph (f) of this Rule, the petitioner may file a reply.

(h) *Copies to be Filed.* — Ten copies of the petition, and the Attorney General's responsive pleading, and the petitioner's reply, if any, shall be filed in the office of the clerk of this Court.

(i) *Further Proceedings by Order of this Court.* — Further proceedings shall be conducted in accordance with the orders of this Court. If this Court determines that an evidentiary hearing is necessary for the proper disposition of the petition, this Court may order that the circuit court conduct a hearing within 90 days after the order has been issued to certify findings of fact with respect to such issues as this Court shall direct. The record and certified findings of fact of the circuit court shall be filed with the clerk of this Court within 30 days after the hearing is concluded.

(j) *Appointment of Counsel.* — In any petition filed pursuant to and in compliance with this Rule, petitioner shall be entitled to the appointment of counsel subject to the provisions of Code § 19.2-157 et seq. Any request for counsel in this Court must be made on the form provided by this Court, entitled REQUEST FOR COUNSEL — PETITION FOR A WRIT OF ACTUAL INNOCENCE, and must include: (i) all the information required by the in forma pauperis affidavit attached to the request for appointment of counsel, and (ii) an attested copy of the order of the circuit court ordering that testing of human biological evidence on the petitioner's behalf be conducted by the Department of Forensic Science pursuant to Code § 19.2-327.1.

(k) *Duty of Counsel.* — Any attorney(s) appointed to represent a petitioner pursuant to Code § 19.2-327.1 shall be deemed to be counsel of record for petitioner for all purposes and proceedings under this Rule until a final order of this Court is issued pursuant to Code § 19.2-327.5, or until counsel is relieved or replaced by other counsel by leave of this Court.

The amendment, effective May 2, 2011, adopted March 1, 2011, substituted "§ 9.1-1104" for "§ 9.1-121" in subdivision (c).

The amendment effective July 1, 2013, adopted June 21, 2013, inserted "or who was adjudicated delinquent upon a plea of not guilty by a circuit court of an offense that would be a felony if committed by an adult," and "or adjudicated delinquent" in subdivision (a); in subdivision (c), inserted the phrases "or adjudicated delinquent" and "or adjudications of delinquentcy" in clause (i), "or delinquent" in clause (ii), substituted "would" for "could" and inserted "or delinquent" and "or adjudicated delinquent" in clause (vii), and inserted "or adjudication of delinquency" in clause (viii); in subdivision (d), inserted "or adjudication of delinquency" near the end of the first sentence, deleted "when represented by counsel," at the beginning of the second sentence, and deleted the former third sentence, which read: " When not represented by counsel, the petitioner shall file with the petition a certificate that a copy of the petition and all attachments have been sent, by certified mail, to the Attorney General and the Commonwealth's Attorney for the jurisdiction where the conviction occurred." and inserted "or adjudication or adjudications of delinquency" in the first sentence of subdivision (f)(1) and the second sentence of subdivision (f)(3).

C. PROCEDURE FOR FILING AN APPEAL FROM A TRIAL COURT.

Rule 5:8. Applicability.

This Section C applies only to cases where direct appeal to this Court from a trial court is authorized by law.

Source. — New.

Michie's Jurisprudence. — For related discussion, see 2B M.J. Automobiles, § 117; 5A M.J. Courts, §§ 23, 24; 21 M.J. Workers' Compensation, § 80.

Rule 5:8A. Appeal From Partial Final Judgment in Multi-Party Cases.

(a) *When Available.* — When claims for relief are presented in a civil action against multiple parties — whether in a complaint, counterclaim, cross-claim, or third-party claim — the trial court may enter final judgment as to one or more but fewer than all of the parties only by entering an order expressly labeled "Partial Final Judgment" which contains express findings that (i) the interests of such parties, and the grounds on which judgment is entered as to them, are separate and distinct from those raised by the issues in the claims against remaining parties, and (ii) the results of any appeal from the partial final judgment cannot affect decision of the claims against the remaining parties, and (iii) decision of the claims remaining in the trial court cannot affect the disposition of claims against the parties subject to the Partial Final Judgment if those parties are later restored to the case by reversal of the Partial Final Judgment on appeal.

(b) *Time to Appeal.* — Entry of an order of Partial Final Judgment as provided in subparagraph (a) of this Rule commences the period for filing a notice of appeal from such Partial Final Judgment under Rule 5:9 and a petition for appeal under Rule 5:17, subject to the provisions of Rule 1:1 and these Rules.

(c) *Refusal of Partial Final Judgment.* — No appeal shall lie from a refusal by the trial court to enter a Partial Final Judgment under this Rule.

(d) *Other Dispositions Adjudicating Claims Against Fewer than All Parties.* — In the absence of the entry of a Partial Final Judgment order as provided in subparagraph (a) of this Rule, any order which adjudicates fewer than all the claims or the rights and liabilities of fewer than all the parties in the action is not a final judgment.

Source. — New.

Michie's Jurisprudence. — For related discussion, see 2B M.J. Automobiles, § 117; 5A M.J. Courts, §§ 23, 24; 21 M.J. Workers' Compensation, § 80.

Rule 5:9. Notice of Appeal.

(a) *Filing Deadline; Where to File.* — No appeal shall be allowed unless, within 30 days after the entry of final judgment or other appealable order or decree, or within any specified extension thereof granted by this Court pursuant to Rule 5:5(a), counsel for the appellant files with the clerk of the trial court a notice of appeal and at the same time mails or delivers a copy of such notice to all opposing counsel. A notice of appeal filed after the court announces a decision or ruling — but before the entry of such judgment or order — is treated as filed on the date of and after the entry.

(b) *Content.* — The notice of appeal shall contain a statement whether any transcript or statement of facts, testimony and other incidents of the case will be filed. In the event a transcript is to be filed, the notice of appeal shall certify that a copy of the transcript has been ordered from the court reporter who reported the case.

(c) *Separate Cases.* — Whenever two or more cases were tried together in the trial court, one notice of appeal and one record may be used to bring all of such cases before this Court even though such cases were not consolidated by formal order.

(d) *Special Provision for Cases Involving a Guardian Ad Litem.* — No appeal shall be dismissed because the notice of appeal fails to identify a guardian ad litem or to provide notice to a guardian ad litem. Upon motion for good cause shown or by sua sponte order of this Court, the notice of appeal may be amended to identify the guardian ad litem and to provide notice to such guardian.

Cross references. — As to transcript or written statement, see Rule 5:11.

Source. — Rules 5:6 and 5:16. Cf. Rule 5A:6.

Law Review. — For article, "Appellate Justice: A Crisis in Virginia?", see 57 Va. L. Rev. 3 (1971).

Michie's Jurisprudence. — For related discussion, see 1B M.J. Appeal and Error, §§ 124, 139, 210, 226; 19 M.J. Trial, § 8.

CASE NOTES

I. General Consideration.
II. Decisions Under Prior Law.

I. GENERAL CONSIDERATION.

Constitutionality. — The mandatory nature of this rule does not make it unconstitutional and dismissal of an application for discretionary review because it is untimely does not deprive the applicant of due process of law even in a capital case. Coleman v. Thompson, 895 F.2d 139 (4th Cir. 1990), aff'd, 501 U.S. 722, 111 S. Ct. 2546, 115 L. Ed. 2d 640 (1991).

Timeliness and content requirements mandatory. — This rule, like its predecessor, former Rule 5:1, § 4, is mandatory. Vaughn v. Vaughn, 215 Va. 328, 210 S.E.2d 140 (1974). See McClung v. McClung, 206 Va. 782, 146 S.E.2d 195 (1966).

Former Rule 5:1, § 4, was mandatory and not merely directory. Hall v. Hall, 192 Va. 721, 66 S.E.2d 595 (1951); Skeens v. Commonwealth, 192 Va. 200, 64 S.E.2d 764 (1951); Harlow v. Commonwealth, 195 Va. 269, 77 S.E.2d 851 (1953); Andrews v. Cahoon, 196 Va. 790, 86 S.E.2d 173 (1955); Mears v. Mears, 206 Va. 444, 143 S.E.2d 889 (1965).

Notice of appeal considered as filed when inmate complied with Rule 5:5. — Inmate's claim for ineffective assistance of trial counsel, asserted pursuant to 28 U.S.C.S. § 2254, was not considered to be procedurally defaulted even though the inmate had not filed a timely notice of appeal of his state collateral proceeding with the Virginia Supreme Court as required by Va. Sup. Ct. R. 5:9, because it was essentially undisputed that the inmate had complied with the inmate mailing rules set forth in Va. Sup. Ct. R. 5:5 in filing a notice of appeal. Smallwood v. Young, 425 F. Supp. 2d 717, 2006 U.S. Dist. LEXIS 14128 (E.D. Va. 2006), appeal dismissed, 2007 U.S. App. LEXIS 16439 (4th Cir. Va. 2007).

Appellate filing rule is rigorously enforced. Wise v. Williams, 982 F.2d 142 (4th Cir. 1992), cert. denied, 508 U.S. 964, 113 S. Ct. 2940, 124 L. Ed. 2d 689 (1993).

Grant of extensions and mandatory time limit. — The Virginia Supreme Court's periodic grant of extensions on motion does not mean that the mandatory time limit for notice of appeal is not strictly and regularly enforced. Wise v. Williams, 982 F.2d 142 (4th Cir. 1992), cert. denied, 508 U.S. 964, 113 S. Ct. 2940, 124 L. Ed. 2d 689 (1993).

Notice must be filed with clerk within specified period. — The requirement of the rule is met only if counsel files with the clerk the notice of appeal within the specified period. Mears v. Mears, 206 Va. 444, 143 S.E.2d 889 (1965); Carneal v. Carneal, 211 Va. 162, 176 S.E.2d 305 (1970).

Counsel's failure to file notice of appeal. — The district court did not err by ruling that the failure by defendant's counsel to file a timely notice of appeal from the final order of the state habeas court constituted a procedural default barring federal review of the claims asserted only in the state habeas corpus proceeding. Coleman v. Thompson, 895 F.2d 139 (4th Cir. 1990), aff'd, 501 U.S. 722, 111 S. Ct. 2546, 115 L. Ed. 2d 640 (1991).

Purpose of the specific time limit is not to penalize the appellant but to protect the appellee. If the required papers are not filed within the time limit, the appellee is entitled to assume that the litigation is ended, and to act on that assumption. Litigation is a serious and harassing matter, and the right to know when it is ended is a valuable right. Avery v. County Sch. Bd., 192 Va. 329, 64 S.E.2d 767 (1951).

Time, for the purposes of appeal, begins to run from the date final judgment is entered. Peyton v. Ellyson, 207 Va. 423, 150 S.E.2d 104 (1966).

Or date on which motion was disposed of. — Where the record showed that a motion to set aside or vacate a judgment of conviction had been made and taken under consideration by the trial court before the judgment had become final, the time for perfecting an appeal ran from the date on which such motion was disposed of. Lyle v. Ekleberry, 209 Va. 349, 164 S.E.2d 586 (1968).

Only order suspending or vacating final order can toll running of time. — Neither the filing of post-trial or post-judgment motions nor the court's taking such motions under consideration, nor the pendency of such motions on the 21st day after final judgment, was sufficient to toll or extend the running of the 21-day period prescribed by Rule 1:1 or the 30-day period prescribed by this rule since the running of time under those rules may be interrupted only by the entry, within the 21-day period after final judgment, of an order suspending or vacating the final order. School Bd. v. Caudill Rowlett Scott, Inc., 237 Va. 550, 379 S.E.2d 319 (1989); Triggs v. Triggs, No. 1922-90-4, (Ct. of Appeals Dec. 24, 1991).

Doctor's appeal from a final judgment in favor of a patient was untimely because it was not filed within 30 days of the expiration of a 14-day suspension period entered by the trial court pursuant to Va. Sup. Ct. R. 1:1, as required by Va. Sup. Ct. R. 5:9. The doctor's motion to set aside the verdict did not extend the period for filing the notice of appeal, pursuant to Va. Sup. Ct. R. 5:5. Hutchins v. Talbert, 278 Va. 650, 685 S.E.2d 658, 2009 Va. LEXIS 98 (2009).

Attendance of counsel at special session of legislature. — Where notice of appeal was filed two days past the time prescribed by the rule, but one of appellant's counsel had been in attendance at a special session of the legislature, the time for filing was extended 30 days under § 30-5, and the court took jurisdiction to decide the case on its merits. Hartsock v. Powell, 199 Va. 320, 99 S.E.2d 581 (1957).

When legal presence of parties on appeal absolute necessity. — Where a party's interests in the subject matter of the appeal are so bound up with that of the other parties, its legal presence as a party to the proceeding is an absolute necessity, without which the appellate court cannot proceed. Asch v. Friends of Community of Mt. Vernon Yacht Club, 251 Va. 89, 465 S.E.2d 817 (1996).

Date of filing noted by clerk is conclusive. — Ordinarily, the date of filing noted by the clerk on papers filed in his office is conclusive. Mears v. Mears, 206 Va. 444, 143 S.E.2d 889 (1965).

Error of clerk in marking date of filing. — Where defendant's notice of appeal was marked by the deputy clerk as having been filed after the expiration of the time period, but affidavits of defendant's counsel, of the Commonwealth's attorney, and of the deputy clerk herself, established that the notice had in fact been filed within the time period, a motion to dismiss was overruled. Leigh v. Commonwealth, 192 Va. 583, 66 S.E.2d 586 (1951).

Mailing is insufficient. — Mailing of the notice of appeal to the clerk does not satisfy the requirement of the rule. Mears v. Mears, 206 Va. 444, 143 S.E.2d 889 (1965).

Order dismissing the action against one defendant was held not final for purposes of appeal before the disposition of the case against the remaining defendants. Wells v. Whitaker, 207 Va. 616, 151 S.E.2d 422 (1966).

Habeas corpus. — Petitioners in habeas corpus must follow the rules of court by filing a notice of appeal, as must all other parties who wish to appeal. Meade v. Cox, 310 F. Supp. 233 (W.D. Va. 1970), aff'd, 438 F.2d 323 (4th Cir.), cert. denied, 404 U.S. 910, 92 S. Ct. 234, 30 L. Ed. 2d 182 (1971).

Federal habeas corpus relief was procedurally barred. — Petitioner failed to show that the procedural default relied upon by the Virginia Supreme Court was not an adequate and independent state ground, that his attorneys' error constituted cause to excuse the default, or that federal review of his claims was necessary to prevent a fundamental miscarriage of justice; therefore petitioner's claims for federal habeas corpus relief were procedurally barred from consideration. Wise v. Williams, 982 F.2d 142 (4th Cir. 1992), cert. denied, 508 U.S. 964, 113 S. Ct. 2940, 124 L. Ed. 2d 689 (1993).

Notice of appeal timely. — Mother's appeal of a circuit court order awarding custody of her child to the father was timely because the notice of appeal was filed within thirty days of the circuit court's order awarding the father attorney's fees, which was rendered a month after the child custody order; the custody order was not final because the circuit court retained jurisdiction to address the father's request for attorney's fees. Alexander v. Flowers, 51 Va. App. 404, 658 S.E.2d 355, 2008 Va. App. LEXIS 139 (2008).

Notice of appeal was untimely. — Amended notice of appeal in a breach of contract case was untimely pursuant to Rule 5:9(a) where it was not filed more than 30 days after entry of the final judgment in the case. Wellmore Coal Corp. v. Harman Mining Corp., 264 Va. 279, 568 S.E.2d 671, 2002 Va. LEXIS 103 (2002).

Admissibility of noncapital conviction orders in capital penalty trial within period for appeal. — The trial court did not err in admitting evidence at a penalty trial in a capital murder case of convictions of the defendant for other noncapital offenses prior to the expiration of the period during which the orders of conviction might be modified, vacated or suspended, and prior to the expiration of the time in which an appeal could be perfected, where the convictions were based on guilty pleas that were voluntarily and intelligently tendered, since, when a conviction is rendered upon such a plea and the punishment fixed by law is in fact imposed in a proceeding free of jurisdictional defect, no appeal will lie because there is nothing to appeal. Mason v. Commonwealth, 219 Va. 1091, 254 S.E.2d 116, cert. denied, 444 U.S. 919, 100 S. Ct. 239, 62 L. Ed. 2d 176 (1979).

Court was without jurisdiction to enter sanction order a month after final order. — Where a trial court entered a final order dismissing a case and, over a month later, entered another order awarding sanctions in the case, the court was without jurisdiction to enter the order for sanctions. Smith v. Stanaway, 242 Va. 286, 410 S.E.2d 610 (1991).

Mere notice of appeal insufficient to confer appellate jurisdiction. — The mere fact that an indispensable party who was a litigant in the trial court has notice that an appeal has been perfected against another litigant is not sufficient to confer an appellate court's jurisdiction over the indispensable party against whom no appeal has been properly perfected. Asch v. Friends of Community of Mt. Vernon Yacht Club, 251 Va. 89, 465 S.E.2d 817 (1996).

Applied in Johnson v. Commonwealth, 1 Va. App. 510, 339 S.E.2d 919 (1986); Faizi-Balal Int'l Corp. v. Burka, 248 Va. 219, 445 S.E.2d 125 (1994); Watkins v. Fairfax County Dep't of Family Servs., 42 Va. App. 760, 595 S.E.2d 19, 2004 Va. App. LEXIS 164 (2004); Rose v. Jaques, 268 Va. 137, 597 S.E.2d 64, 2004 Va. LEXIS 92 (2004); Whitt v. Commonwealth, No. 0885-11-3, 61 Va. App. 637, 739 S.E.2d 254, 2013 Va. App. LEXIS 100 (Mar. 26, 2013).

II. DECISIONS UNDER PRIOR LAW.

Editor's note. — The cases cited below were decided under former § 8.01-675 and other corresponding provisions of former law. The term "this section," as used below, refers to former provisions.

Right of appeal not absolute. — There was no such practice as an absolute right of appeal in civil or criminal cases. But the law required a petition, accompanied by a transcript of the record, to be presented to the court, or one of its judges, whose duty it was to examine the errors assigned and to grant or refuse a writ, as may seem proper. It was as much the duty of the court, or judge, to deny the petition when of opinion that the decision complained of was plainly right as it was to grant it when any doubt exists as to the propriety of the decision. McCue v. Commonwealth, 103 Va. 870, 49 S.E. 623 (1905).

When rejection final. — Where a petition for a writ of error has been rejected by the Supreme Court on the ground that the judgment complained of was plainly right, and the order of rejection so states, no amended or other petition for a writ to such judgment can afterwards be entertained. Morgan v. Commonwealth, 115 Va. 943, 79 S.E. 388 (1913).

The granting of an appeal does not of itself operate as a supersedeas to stay the issuance of executions under the judgments. Seal v. Puckett, 159 Va. 297, 165 S.E. 496 (1932).

A supersedeas operates to stay all further proceedings on the judgment, or as to any matter embraced therein. Its effect was to prevent the enforcement of the judgment to any further extent than has been had at the time it becomes effective, and, thereby, to preserve the status quo at the time the supersedeas becomes effective. Aetna Cas. & Sur. Co. v. Board of Supvrs., 160 Va. 11, 168 S.E. 617 (1933).

But it does not vacate or annul, even conditionally, the judgment, or impair its validity and effect as a judgment; nor does it operate retrospectively to undo what has already been done thereby or thereunder, or to restore and maintain the status quo existing at the time the judgment appealed from was rendered. Hence, what has been done thereby or thereunder before the supersedeas takes effect was upheld by the authority of the judgment. But after the supersedeas becomes effective, and while it remains in effect, what was done under authority of the judgment or toward its further enforcement was invalid, because the prospective authority of the judgment has been, in effect, suspended by the supersedeas. Aetna Cas. & Sur. Co. v. Board of Supvrs., 160 Va. 11, 168 S.E. 617 (1933).

Effect of supersedeas on self-executing judgment. — Generally, where a judgment was self-executing, if its execution of itself has not been stayed or postponed by the court rendering it, a supersedeas thereof did not have the effect of suspending the operation of the judgment pending a decision by the Supreme Court. Aetna Cas. & Sur. Co. v. Board of Supvrs., 160 Va. 11, 168 S.E. 617 (1933).

Premature appeals remanded for further proceedings below. — The court held that the appeal had been premature and that the case should be remanded in accordance with this section with direction that a reference to a commissioner be had. Boatright v. Litz, 125 Va. 613, 100 S.E. 547 (1919).

In a suit by a wife against her husband to secure a permanent separate maintenance for herself and infant daughter, it was premature to allow an appeal from a decree overruling defendant's demurrer to the bill, and, without deciding any question in the cause, awarding the plaintiff a pendente lite, allowance for support, etc., and referring the cause to a commissioner to ascertain the value of the estate and income of the husband, and a reasonable allowance to the wife for the support of herself and her child, and for fees to her counsel. The cause should have proceeded further in the trial court, and the rights of the parties be there adjudicated, before an appeal was allowed. Beatty v. Beatty, 105 Va. 213, 53 S.E. 2 (1906).

Rule 5:10. Record on Appeal: Contents.

(a) *Contents.* — The following constitute the record on appeal from the trial court:

(1) the original papers and exhibits filed or lodged in the office of the clerk of the trial court, including any report of a commissioner in chancery and the accompanying depositions and other papers;

(2) each instruction marked "given" or "refused" and initialed by the judge;

(3) each exhibit offered in evidence, whether admitted or not, and initialed by the trial judge (or any photograph thereof as authorized by § 19.2-270.4 (A) and (C)). (All non-documentary exhibits shall be tagged or labeled in the trial court and the tag or label initialed by the judge.);

(4) the original draft or a copy of each order entered by the trial court;

(5) any opinion or memorandum decision rendered by the judge of the trial court;

(6) any deposition and any discovery material encompassed within Part Four offered in evidence (whether admitted or rejected) at any proceeding; and

(7) the transcript of any proceeding or a written statement of facts, testimony, and other incidents of the case when made a part of the record as provided in Rule 5:11, or the official videotape recording of any proceeding in those circuit courts authorized by this Court to use videotape recordings. This Court may require that any videotape proceedings be transcribed, in whole or in part, and made a part of the record as provided in Rule 5:11, except that the transcript shall be filed within 60 days after the entry of the order requiring such transcript; and

(8) the notice of appeal.

(b) *Disagreement on Contents.* — If disagreement arises as to the contents of any part of the record, the matter shall, in the first instance, be submitted to and decided by the trial court.

Source. — Rules 5:8 and 5:10 Cf. Rule 5A:7.

Michie's Jurisprudence. — For related discussion, see 1B M.J. Appeal and Error, §§ 170, 172 - 174, 176, 178, 180 - 184, 186, 191, 196, 200 - 204; 5A M.J. Courts, §§ 22 — 24, 27; 8A M.J. Exceptions, Bill of, § 1; 9A M.J. Habeas Corpus, § 23; 10A M.J. Instructions, §§ 10, 50; 19 M.J. Trial, § 8

CASE NOTES

Scope of term "judicial records." — Where the documents in question have not been offered in evidence, they are not "judicial records," as that term has been defined by the Virginia Supreme Court. In re Worrell Enters., Inc., 14 Va. App. 671, 419 S.E.2d 271 (1992).

Whether the documents are filed with or in the custody of the court is not dispositive as to whether they are "judicial records." In re Worrell Enters., Inc., 14 Va. App. 671, 419 S.E.2d 271 (1992).

The common-law right of access to "judicial records" does not extend to pretrial discovery materials collected by the parties but not yet a part of the judicial record in the proceedings. In re Worrell Enters., Inc., 14 Va. App. 671, 419 S.E.2d 271 (1992).

Trial court cannot enlarge record beyond rule. — While the trial court is empowered by subdivision (b) to decide disagreements among counsel or between counsel and the clerk, the trial court has no power by rule or statute to add to the contents of the record on appeal anything not designated in this rule. Old Dominion Iron & Steel Corp. v. VEPCO, 215 Va. 658, 212 S.E.2d 715 (1975).

Effect of certiorari on enlarging record. — When the record has been transmitted in compliance with Rule 5:13(c) and a writ of error or appeal has been granted, the record on appeal cannot be enlarged, except upon award of a writ of certiorari. Old Dominion Iron & Steel Corp. v. VEPCO, 215 Va. 658, 212 S.E.2d 715 (1975).

Supreme Court cannot consider instructions not made part of record. — Where the various instructions tendered and refused are not properly made a part of the record, the Supreme Court cannot inquire into the propriety of the lower court's rulings with respect to them. Paddock v. Mason, 187 Va. 809, 48 S.E.2d 199 (1948).

Exhibits not considered where oral testimony not made part of record. — Where no testimony was certified in the period allowed and hence could not be considered on appeal, exhibits received and initialed by the trial judge will not be considered, for the oral testimony not made a part of the record may have weakened or destroyed their evidential value. Larchmont Properties v. Cooperman, 195 Va. 784, 80 S.E.2d 733 (1954).

Statement of facts tendered to the chancellor is essentially a summary of data contained in papers included in the record on appeal under this rule, including admissions under Rule 4:11, exhibits requested under Rule 4:9, the chancellor's letter opinion and the final decree. City of Richmond v. Randall, 215 Va. 506, 211 S.E.2d 56 (1975).

Opinion letter of the trial judge is a part of the record on appeal, without any requirement that it be filed with the clerk. Washington v. Commonwealth, 216 Va. 185, 217 S.E.2d 815 (1975).

Letters addressed by the court to counsel pertaining to setting aside the verdict were properly included in the record. Simmons v. Boyd, 199 Va. 806, 102 S.E.2d 292 (1958).

Freedom of Information Act materials. — Trial court erred in refusing to require a university to produce reports sought under the Freedom of Information Act so they could be made part of the record under Va. Sup. Ct. R. 5:10(a)(3), as the refusal prevented review by the appellate court, and confidential personnel information under § 2.2-3705.1 could have been shielded by a protective order. Bland v. Va. State Univ., 272 Va. 198, 630 S.E.2d 525, 2006 Va. LEXIS 55 (2006).

Argument not considered where interrogatories and answers not made part of record. — Supreme court would not consider argument that witnesses should not have been permitted to give certain testimony because such testimony and the bases therefor were not disclosed, as required by pretrial interrogatories. The court cannot consider these issues because neither the interrogatories nor the answers were made a part of the record, as authorized by this rule. Greater Richmond Transit Co. v. Wilkerson, 242 Va. 65, 406 S.E.2d 28 (1991).

Where an original suit in equity was dismissed with prejudice and never appealed, and none of its pleadings, motions, memoranda, exhibits, transcripts or orders was introduced as exhibits in proceedings on a motion for judgment, none is part of the record on appeal as defined by this rule. Old Dominion Iron & Steel Corp. v. VEPCO, 215 Va. 658, 212 S.E.2d 715 (1975).

Refusal of court to sign or alter narrative statement. — Where trial judge was informed that court reporter would be present to record proceedings and consequently failed to take any notes during trial, the court did not err in refusing to sign plaintiff's narrative statement or in failing to make alterations in, and additions to, the statement in an attempt to render it accurate and then sign it. Woods v. R.D. Hunt & Son, 207 Va. 281, 148 S.E.2d 779 (1966).

Applied in Packett v. Herbert, 237 Va. 422, 377 S.E.2d 438 (1989); Hardy v. Board of Zoning Appeals, 257 Va. 232, 508 S.E.2d 886 (1999); Rose v. Jaques, 268 Va. 137, 597 S.E.2d 64, 2004 Va. LEXIS 92 (2004).

Rule 5:11. Record on Appeal: Transcript or Written Statement.

(a) *Effect of Non-compliance.* — (1) Obligation of the Petitioner/Appellant. It is the obligation of the petitioner/appellant to ensure that the record is sufficient to enable the Court to evaluate and resolve the assignments of error. When the appellant fails to ensure that the record contains transcripts or a written statement of facts necessary to permit resolution of appellate issues related to the assignments of error, any assignments of error affected by the omission shall not be considered.

(2) Obligation of the Respondent/Appellee. It is the obligation of the respondent/appellee to ensure that the record is sufficient to enable the Court to evaluate and resolve any assignments of cross-error. When the respondent/appellee who assigns cross-error fails to ensure that the record contains transcripts or a written statement of facts necessary to permit resolution of appellate issues related to the assignments of cross-error, any assignments of cross-error affected by the omission shall not be considered.

(b) *Transcript.* — The transcript of any proceeding in the case that is necessary for the appeal shall be filed in the office of the clerk of the trial court within 60 days after entry of judgment.

(c) *Notice of Filing Transcript.* — (1) Within 10 days after the transcript is filed or, if the transcript is filed prior to the filing of the notice of appeal, within 10 days after the notice of appeal is filed, counsel for appellant shall (i) give written notice to all other counsel of the date on which the transcript was filed, and (ii) file a copy of the notice with the clerk of the trial court. There shall be appended to the notice either a certificate of counsel for appellant that a copy of the notice has been mailed to all other counsel or an acceptance of service of such notice by all other counsel.

(2) When multiple transcripts are filed, the 10 day period for filing the notice required by this Rule shall be calculated from the date on which the last transcript is filed, or from the date on which the notice of appeal is filed, whichever is later. The notice of filing transcripts shall identify all transcripts filed and the date upon which the last transcript was filed. If the notice of appeal states that no additional transcripts will be filed and identifies the transcripts that have been filed, if any, then no additional written notice of filing of transcripts is required and the notice of appeal will serve as the notice of filing transcripts for purposes of this Rule.

(3) Any failure to file the notice required by this Rule that materially prejudices an appellee will result in the affected transcripts being stricken from the record on appeal. For purposes of this Rule, material prejudice includes preventing the appellee from raising legitimate objections to the contents of the transcript or misleading the appellee about the contents of the record. The appellee shall have the burden of establishing such prejudice in the brief in opposition or, if no brief in opposition is filed, in a written statement filed with the clerk of this Court within the time fixed by these Rules for the filing of a brief in opposition.

(d) *Supplementation, Correction, or Modification of Transcript.* — If anything material to any party is omitted from or misstated in the transcript, or if the transcript or any portion thereof is untimely filed, by omission, clerical error, or accident, the filing may be supplemented, corrected, or modified at any time within 70 days from the entry of judgment appealed from. Notice as provided in paragraph (c) of this Rule must be given for any such supplementation, correction, or modification. Thereafter, such supplementation, correction, or modification may be made, by order of this Court sua sponte or upon motion of any party, if at least two Justices of this Court concur in a finding that any such supplementation, correction, or modification is warranted by a showing of good cause sufficient to excuse the deficiency.

(e) *Written Statement in Lieu of Transcript.* — A written statement of facts, testimony, and other incidents of the case, which may include or consist of a portion of the transcript, becomes a part of the record when:

(1) within 55 days after entry of judgment a copy of such statement is filed in the office of the clerk of the trial court. A copy must be mailed or delivered to opposing counsel on the same day that it is filed in the office of the clerk of the trial court, accompanied by notice that such statement will be presented to the trial judge no earlier than 15 days nor later than 20 days after such filing; and

(2) the statement is signed by the trial judge and filed in the office of the clerk of the trial court. The judge may sign the statement forthwith upon its presentation to him if it is signed by counsel for all parties, but if objection is made to the accuracy or completeness of the statement, it shall be signed in accordance with paragraph (g) of this Rule.

(f) The term "other incidents of the case" in subsection (e) includes motions, proffers, objections, and rulings of the trial court regarding any issue that a party intends to assign as error or otherwise address on appeal.

(g) *Objections.* — Any party may object to a transcript or written statement on the ground that it is erroneous or incomplete. Notice of such objection specifying the errors alleged or deficiencies asserted shall be filed with the clerk of the trial court within 15 days after the date the notice of filing the transcript (paragraph (c) of this Rule) or within 15 days after the date the notice of filing the written statement (paragraph (e) of this Rule) is filed in the office of the clerk of the trial court or, if the transcript or written statement is filed before the notice of appeal is filed, within 10 days after the notice of appeal has been filed with the clerk of the trial court. Counsel for the objecting party shall give the trial judge prompt notice of the filing of such objections. Within 10 days after the notice of objection is filed with the clerk of the trial court, the trial judge shall:

(1) overrule the objections; or
(2) make any corrections that the trial judge deems necessary;
(3) include any accurate additions to make the record complete; or
(4) certify the manner in which the record is incomplete; and
(5) sign the transcript or written statement.

At any time while the record remains in the office of the clerk of the trial court, the trial judge may, after notice to counsel and hearing, correct the transcript or written statement.

The judge's signature on a transcript or written statement, without more, shall constitute certification that the procedural requirements of this Rule have been satisfied.

Cross references. — For meaning of "clerk," "opposing counsel" and "counsel for the appellant," see Rule 5:1.

Source. — Rules 5:9 and 5:11. Cf. Rule 5A:8.

Law Review. — For 1985 survey of Virginia civil procedure and practice, see 19 U. Rich. L. Rev. 679 (1985). For 1995 survey of civil practice and procedure, see 29 U. Rich. L. Rev. 897 (1995).

Michie's Jurisprudence. — For related discussion, see 1B M.J. Appeal and Error, §§ 170, 176, 183, 188, 200, 202, 203, 206, 226; 5A M.J. Courts, §§ 23, 24, 27; 5B M.J. Criminal Procedure, § 69; 8A M.J. Exceptions, Bill of, § 1; 19 M.J. Trial, § 8.

CASE NOTES

I. General Consideration.
II. Objections.

I. GENERAL CONSIDERATION.

Purpose of rule. — This rule was adopted as part of an overall revision of the rules, to provide a simplified method of making a transcript a part of the record. Towler v. Commonwealth, 216 Va. 533, 221 S.E.2d 119 (1976).

Rule mandatory. — The jurisdictional nature of this rule necessitates compliance with its mandatory requirements. Towler v. Commonwealth, 216 Va. 533, 221 S.E.2d 119 (1976).

Rule is jurisdictional. — The provisions of this rule are simple and easily understood, but they are jurisdictional, and failure to comply therewith will result in dismissal, either before or after appeal is awarded. Towler v. Commonwealth, 216 Va. 533, 221 S.E.2d 119 (1976).

Use of the word "shall" in subparagraph (d) [now subsection (g)] is merely directory in meaning, not mandatory. Any other interpretation of "shall" in subparagraph (d) would be unrealistic and would implicitly impose upon trial judges the burden to draft narrative statements. White v. Morano, 249 Va. 27, 452 S.E.2d 856 (1995).

Transcript of a hearing is not a part of record on appeal if it has not been made such under the requirements of this rule. Washington v. Commonwealth, 216 Va. 185, 217 S.E.2d 815 (1975).

Suspension of time requirements of rules to permit prosecution of an appeal. — See Newsom v. Commonwealth, 207 Va. 844, 153 S.E.2d 235, cert. denied, 388 U.S. 918, 87 S. Ct. 2136, 18 L. Ed. 2d 1361 (1967).

The record must contain all evidence necessary and material for the appellate court to determine the existence of errors in the trial court transcript. Wansley v. Commonwealth, 205 Va. 419, 137 S.E.2d 870 (1964), cert. denied, 380 U.S. 922, 85 S. Ct. 920, 13 L. Ed. 2d 806 (1965).

Case will be considered on record sent from lower court. — On appeal the case will be considered on the record which is sent from the lower court, and not upon counsel's recollection of what occurred there. Justis v. Young, 202 Va. 631, 119 S.E.2d 255 (1961).

Trial court's decision presumed correct absent evidence in record to contrary. — Where evidence is presented to the chancellor and a jury on an issue out of chancery, and the chancellor, in his decree, does not follow the findings of the jury, and where the evidence on which the decree is based has not been made a part of the record to be considered by the Supreme Court, it is impossible for the Supreme Court to pass on the point that the decree is contrary to the law and the evidence. The decision of the chancellor is presumed to be correct and is binding. Lawrence v. Nelson, 200 Va. 597, 106 S.E.2d 618 (1959).

Appellant has primary responsibility of presenting evidence to Supreme Court. — An appellant who seeks the reversal of a decree on the ground that it is contrary to the law and the evidence has the primary responsibility of presenting to the Supreme Court, as a part of the printed record, the evidence introduced in the lower court, or so much thereof as is necessary and sufficient for the Supreme Court to give full consideration to the assignment of error. Lawrence v. Nelson, 200 Va. 597, 106 S.E.2d 618 (1959).

Evidence may be stated in narrative form. — The use of a narrative statement is a proper method of furnishing a record of evidence and incidents of trial for appeal. Houghtaling v. Commonwealth, 209 Va. 309, 163 S.E.2d 560 (1968), cert. denied, 394 U.S. 1021, 89 S. Ct. 1642, 23 L. Ed. 2d 46 (1969).

Where appellant presented to and had certified by the trial court a "narrative of proceedings" instead of having the testimony transcribed, a motion to dismiss was denied. Collins v. Pulaski County, 201 Va. 164, 110 S.E.2d 184 (1959); Valentine v. County of Brunswick, 202 Va. 696, 119 S.E.2d 486 (1961).

Record devoid of evidence and factual findings. — In reviewing a decision of a circuit court requiring a county board of supervisors to take certain action with respect to a subdivision application, the Supreme Court of Virginia must examine the record to determine whether the evidence sustains the court's findings and those of the county but, where the record is devoid of any evidence and factual findings, the case must be remanded to the circuit court for an evidentiary hearing. Hanover County v. Bertozzi, 256 Va. 350, 504 S.E.2d 618 (1998).

Because some of a corporation's claims on appeal from an order entering a default judgment against it, and refusing to set the same aside, were either not plead to the court below or were not supported by the record, which was incomplete on its face, the lower court's orders were affirmed. Prince Seating Corp. v. Rabideau, 275 Va. 468, 659 S.E.2d 305, 2008 Va. LEXIS 45 (2008).

Refusal of court to sign or alter narrative statement. — Where trial judge was informed that court reporter would be present to record proceedings and consequently failed to take any notes during trial, the court did not err in refusing to sign plaintiff's narrative statement or in failing to make alterations in, and additions to, the statement in an attempt to render it accurate and then sign it. Woods v. R.D. Hunt & Son, 207 Va. 281, 148 S.E.2d 779 (1966).

Dismissal of suit for failure to obtain a court reporter was erroneous because the circuit court refused to correct a proposed statement of facts or state the manner in which the statement was incorrect, as required by Va. Sup. Ct. R. 5:11(d). Shapiro v. Younkin, 279 Va. 256, 688 S.E.2d 157, 2010 Va. LEXIS 3 (2010).

Remedies where judge refuses to certify evidence. — While mandamus will lie to compel a judge to certify the evidence when he shall so refuse, it is also error to so refuse, of which any party injured may complain to the Supreme Court, and for which that Court will reverse the judgment of the court below. Harris v. Woodby, Inc., 203 Va. 946, 128 S.E.2d 278 (1962).

Appeal not dismissed where record otherwise sufficient. — Motion to dismiss the appeal on the ground that defendant did not comply with subsection (c) of this rule in that the judge refused to certify the "Statement of Facts Pursuant to Rule 5:9" was denied where the record was sufficient for the adjudication of the issues presented. City of Richmond v. Randall, 215 Va. 506, 211 S.E.2d 56 (1975).

Applied in Barrett v. Barrett, 1 Va. App. 378, 339 S.E.2d 208 (1986); White Consol. Indus., Inc. v. Swiney, 237 Va. 23, 376 S.E.2d 283 (1989); Rose v. Jaques, 268 Va. 137, 597 S.E.2d 64, 2004 Va. LEXIS 92 (2004); Covel v. Town of Vienna, 280 Va. 151, 694 S.E.2d 609, 2010 Va. LEXIS 75 (2010); Galumbeck v. Lopez, 283 Va. 500, 722 S.E.2d 551, 2012 Va. LEXIS 44 (Mar. 2, 2012).

II. OBJECTIONS.

This rule does not provide the exclusive procedure for correcting errors. Lamb v. Commonwealth, 222 Va. 161, 279 S.E.2d 389 (1981).

But it provides the preferred procedure that should be used in all cases to correct transcripts. Lamb v. Commonwealth, 222 Va. 161, 279 S.E.2d 389 (1981).

Certification by a judge is a judicial act. — When counsel for the respective parties are unable to agree on evidence to be included in the proposed transcript or statement, it is the duty of the judge to settle the conflicting views. In so doing, he may make reasonable additions, deletions, or changes, in order that the record may contain a fair statement of the facts. New Bay Shore Corp. v. Lewis, 193 Va. 400, 69 S.E.2d 320 (1952).

Burden upon complaining party to show error. — The burden of showing that the evidence is incorrect or incomplete is upon the complaining party. New Bay Shore Corp. v. Lewis, 193 Va. 400, 69 S.E.2d 320 (1952).

And to institute proper proceedings for certification of correct record. — If the record before the Supreme Court is not the correct record, it is the duty of the complaining party to institute proper proceedings for certification of the correct record. The Supreme Court must accept the record as they find it. New Bay Shore Corp. v. Lewis, 193 Va. 400, 69 S.E.2d 320 (1952).

Remedy where judge unable to determine accuracy of transcript or statement. — If, because of the lapse of time or lack of memory, the judge is unable to determine the accuracy of the transcript or statement, and the case is still under his control, he should order a new trial, so that a proper transcript or statement can be prepared. Harris v. Woodby, Inc., 203 Va. 946, 128 S.E.2d 278 (1962).

Correction after docketing of appeal. — Where a criminal appeal was docketed before an error in the trial transcript was discovered, correction could be made only with leave of the Supreme Court. Lamb v. Commonwealth, 222 Va. 161, 279 S.E.2d 389 (1981).

CIRCUIT COURT OPINIONS

Statement of facts rejected as incomplete. — Because a proposed statement of facts filed by a plaintiff failed to include actual or summarized trial testimony or a transcript, contained argument, and incorrectly listed a lawyer and her firm as a defendant despite an order denying plaintiff's request to add them as parties, the statement of facts was rejected as incomplete under Va. Sup. Ct. R. 5:11(d)(4). Morris v. McGuire, 72 Va. Cir. 379, 2007 Va. Cir. LEXIS 141 (Fauquier County 2007).

Where statement of facts is not timely filed. — Because the requirements of Va. Sup. Ct. R. 5:11 were mandatory and jurisdictional, the statement of facts, submitted more than 55 days after the final order, were not properly before the court. Ahmed v. Wesley, 71 Va. Cir. 393, 2006 Va. Cir. LEXIS 140 (Fairfax County 2006).

Rule 5:12. Judge Authorized to Act.

The judge authorized to act in all matters relating to the record on appeal shall be any judge having authority to enter orders in the case or in the court in which the case was heard or, in a case heard by three judges, any one of them.

Source. — Rules 5A:9 and 5:12.

Michie's Jurisprudence. — For related discussion, see 5A M.J. Courts, § 27.

Rule 5:13. Record on Appeal: Preparation and Transmission.

(a) *Preparation.* — The clerk of the trial court, disciplinary board, or commission in which the proceeding originated shall prepare the record as soon as possible after notice of appeal is filed. In the event of multiple appeals in the same case, or in cases tried together, only one record need be prepared and transmitted.

(b) *Form of the Record.* — (1) The record shall be compiled in the following order:

(i) a front cover setting forth the name of the court and the short style of the case;

(ii) a table of contents listing each paper included in the record and the page on which it begins;

(iii) each paper constituting a part of the record in chronological order; and

(iv) the certificate of the clerk of the trial court that the foregoing constitutes the true and complete record, except omitted exhibits as hereinafter provided.

(2) Each page of the record shall be numbered at the bottom.

(3) Transcripts, depositions, and reports of commissioners may be included in separate volumes identified by the clerk of the trial court if referred to in the table of contents and at the appropriate place in the record.

(4) Exhibits, other than those filed with pleadings, may be included in a separate volume or envelope certified by the clerk of the trial court, except that any exhibit that cannot be conveniently placed in a volume or envelope shall be identified by a tag. Each such volume or envelope shall include, on its cover or inside, a descriptive list of exhibits contained therein. Reference shall be made to exhibits in the table of contents and at the appropriate place in the record referred to in paragraph (b)(1) of this Rule. The clerk of the trial court shall not transmit the following types of exhibits, unless requested to do so by the clerk of this Court: drugs, guns and other weapons, ammunition, blood vials and other bio-hazard type materials, money, jewelry, articles of clothing, and bulky items such as large graphs and maps. The omission of any such exhibit shall be noted on the descriptive list of exhibits. Upon motion by counsel, this Court may order the trial court to transmit any of these prohibited exhibits.

(5) Any transcript or statement of facts that the clerk of the trial court deems not a part of the record because of untimely filing shall be certified as such and transmitted with the record.

(c) *Transmission.* — The clerk of the trial court shall retain the record for 21 days after the notice of appeal has been filed with him pursuant to Rule 5:9. If the notice of appeal states that a transcript or statement will thereafter be filed, the clerk of the trial court shall retain the record for 21 days after the filing in his office of such transcript or statement or, if objection is made to the transcript or statement pursuant to Rule 5:11(g), the clerk of the trial court shall retain the record for 5 days after the objection is acted upon by the trial judge. The clerk of the trial court shall then forthwith transmit the record to the clerk of this Court; provided, however, that, notwithstanding that the foregoing periods of retention may not have expired, the clerk of the trial court shall transmit the record sooner if requested in writing by counsel for all parties to the appeal and shall, whether or not so requested, transmit the record in time for delivery to the clerk of this Court within three months after entry of the judgment appealed from. The failure of the clerk of the trial court to transmit the record as herein provided shall not be a ground for dismissal of the appeal by this Court.

(d) *Record Returned to Trial Court.* — When the mandate is issued by this Court, the clerk of this Court shall return the record to the clerk of the trial court, disciplinary board, or commission in which the proceeding originated. The record shall be returned by that clerk upon the request of the clerk of this Court.

Source. — Rules 5:13, 5:14, 5:15, 5:16, and 5:17. Cf. Rule 5A:10.

The amendment, effective May 2, 2011, adopted March 1, 2011, inserted ", disciplinary board, or commission in which the proceeding originated" in subdivision (a).

Michie's Jurisprudence. — For related discussion, see 1B M.J. Appeal and Error, §§ 132, 135, 201, 204, 206, 208.

CASE NOTES

Notice must be timely filed. — Unless the notice of appeal is filed within the time allowed, the clerk is under no duty and has no authority to make up the record. Avery v. County Sch. Bd., 192 Va. 329, 64 S.E.2d 767 (1951).

Record may be transmitted by any method the clerk selects. — This is his responsibility. He may use the mail or express, or a trustworthy individual, as he chooses. Avery v. County Sch. Bd., 192 Va. 329, 64 S.E.2d 767 (1951).

It will be presumed that the clerk has performed his official duty to transmit the record. Avery v. County Sch. Bd., 192 Va. 329, 64 S.E.2d 767 (1951).

Transmitting record before expiration of retention period. — Where one of appellee's authorized attorneys united in a request of appellant's counsel that the record be transmitted, it was proper that it be transmitted before the retention period had expired. Frye v. Alford, 203 Va. 461, 125 S.E.2d 177 (1962).

Effect of certiorari on enlarging record. — When the record has been transmitted in compliance with this rule and a writ of error or appeal has been granted, the record on appeal cannot be enlarged, except upon award of a writ of certiorari. Old Dominion Iron & Steel Corp. v. VEPCO, 215 Va. 658, 212 S.E.2d 715 (1975).

When the record on appeal has been transmitted in compliance with this rule by the clerk of the trial court to the clerk of the Supreme Court and an appeal has been awarded, the record on appeal cannot be enlarged except upon a grant by the Supreme Court of a writ of certiorari under Va. Code § 8.01-673. Town of Narrows v. Clear-View Cable TV, Inc., 227 Va. 272, 315 S.E.2d 835, appeal dismissed and cert. denied, 469 U.S. 925, 105 S. Ct. 315, 83 L. Ed. 2d 253 (1984); Godfrey v. Commonwealth, 227 Va. 460, 317 S.E.2d 781 (1984).

D. PROCEDURE FOR FILING AN APPEAL FROM THE COURT OF APPEALS.

Rule 5:14. Notice of Appeal; Certification.

(a) *Notice of Appeal.* — No appeal from a judgment of the Court of Appeals which is subject to appeal to this Court shall be allowed unless, within 30 days after entry of final judgment or order denying a timely petition for rehearing, a notice of appeal is filed with the clerk of the Court of Appeals. If a party is granted a delayed appeal from the Court of Appeals, and has previously filed a notice of appeal with the Court of Appeals, no new notice of appeal will be required.

(b) *Notice of Certification.* — Whenever this Court shall certify a case pending in the Court of Appeals for review by this Court, notice of certification shall be given by the clerk of this Court to all counsel and to the clerk of the Court of Appeals. A case certified for review by this Court shall proceed as if a petition for appeal had been granted by this Court on the date of the certification for review, except as otherwise ordered.

(c) *Bail Pending Appeal in Criminal Cases.* — In criminal cases, either party may appeal an order of the Court of Appeals affirming, reversing, or modifying a circuit court order regarding bail pending appeal as provided by this Rule, Rule 5:15 and Rule 5:17.

Cross references. — As to certification for review by the Supreme Court, see also Va. Code § 17.1-411.

Source. — Rule 5:6(b) and 5:32.1.

The amendment effective March 1, 2012, adopted December 22, 2011, in subdivision (a), substituted "a notice of appeal is filed with the clerk of the Court of Appeals" for "counsel file with the clerk of the Court of Appeals a notice of appeal" at the end of the first sentence, and added the second sentence.

CASE NOTES

Construction. — Virginia Sup. Ct. R. 5:14 did not apply to transfers of appeal under § 8.01-677.1, and nothing in that section required that a notice of appeal be filed with the Virginia Court of Appeals when that court transferred an appeal to the Virginia Supreme Court. XL Specialty Ins. Co. v. DOT, 269 Va. 362, 611 S.E.2d 356, 2005 Va. LEXIS 38 (2005).

Assignments of error. — Supreme Court of Virginia rules required assignments of error to address the findings or rulings in the trial court or other tribunal from which an appeal is taken, Va. Sup. Ct. R. 5:17(c)(1)(iii), because the purpose of assignments of error was to point out the errors on which an appellant intends to ask a reversal of the judgment, and to limit discussion to these points; but unlike Va. Sup. Ct. R. 5:17(c)(1)(iii), Va. Sup. Ct. R. 5:14(a) did not require an appellant to challenge the final judgment in a notice of appeal from the Court of Appeals of Virginia because the purpose of the notice of appeal is merely to place the opposing party on notice and to direct the clerk to prepare the record on appeal. LaCava v. Commonwealth, 283 Va. 465, 722 S.E.2d 838, 2012 Va. LEXIS 45 (2012).

Rule 5:15. Record on Appeal From Court of Appeals or Certification for Review.

(a) *Generally.* — In cases on appeal from the Court of Appeals and those certified for review, the record in this Court shall consist of the record as filed in the office of the clerk of the Court of Appeals and, in addition, all other papers relating to the case which have been filed in the office of the clerk of the Court of Appeals, including any opinion or memorandum decision in cases decided by the Court of Appeals. The clerk of the Court of Appeals shall transmit all such documents to the clerk of this Court within 10 days after the filing of the notice of appeal to this Court or the issuance of the certification for review. The clerk of the Court of Appeals shall certify that the papers so transmitted constitute the record in the Court of Appeals.

(b) *Bail Pending Appeal in Criminal Cases.* — In criminal cases on appeal from a Court of Appeals' order affirming a trial court's order setting or denying bail pending appeal, the record shall consist of: (1) the sentencing order entered by the trial court; (2) a pre-sentence report when available; (3) the trial court's order denying or setting bail; (4) the transcript of the bail hearing or a stipulation of facts between the parties regarding what evidence was introduced at the hearing and the reason(s) the trial judge gave for the bail decision; (5) appellant's motion for review in the Court of Appeals; and (6) the order of the Court of Appeals on the motion for review.

Cross references. — As to review by the Supreme Court of decisions of the Court of Appeals, see Va. Code § 17.1-411. As to contents of record on appeal to Court of Appeals, see Rule 5A:7.

Source. — Rule 5:16.1.

Michie's Jurisprudence. — For related discussion, see 1B M.J. Appeal and Error, §§ 135, 199; 3B M.J. Certiorari, § 19.

CASE NOTES

Assignments of error. — Supreme Court of Virginia rules required assignments of error to address the findings or rulings in the trial court or other tribunal from which an appeal is taken, Va. Sup. Ct. R. 5:17(c)(1)(iii), because the purpose of assignments of error was to point out the errors on which an appellant intends to ask a reversal of the judgment, and to limit discussion to these points; but unlike Va. Sup. Ct. R. 5:17(c)(1)(iii), Va. Sup. Ct. R. 5:14(a) did not require an appellant to challenge the final judgment in a notice of appeal from the Court of Appeals of Virginia because the purpose of the notice of appeal is merely to place the opposing party on notice and to direct the clerk to prepare the record on appeal. LaCava v. Commonwealth, 283 Va. 465, 722 S.E.2d 838, 2012 Va. LEXIS 45 (2012).

Rule 5:16. Disposition of Record.

When there can be no further proceedings in this Court, the clerk of this Court shall return the record to the clerk of the trial court or commission in which the case originated. The record shall be returned by that clerk upon the request of the clerk of this Court.

Source. — Rule 5:17.

CASE NOTES

Applied in Barrett v. Barrett, 1 Va. App. 378, 339 S.E.2d 208 (1986).

E. PERFECTING THE APPEAL.

Rule 5:17. Petition for Appeal.

(a) *When the Petition Must be Filed.* — Unless otherwise provided by rule or statute, in every case in which the appellate jurisdiction of this Court is invoked, a petition for appeal must be filed with the clerk of this Court within the following time periods:

(1) in the case of an appeal direct from a trial court, not more than three months after entry of the order appealed from; or

(2) in the case of an appeal from the Court of Appeals, within 30 days after entry of the judgment appealed from or a denial of a timely petition for rehearing.

(b) *Who Must Receive a Copy of the Petition.* — When the petition for appeal is filed with the clerk of this Court, a copy of the petition shall be served on opposing counsel.

(c) *What the Petition Must Contain.* — A petition for appeal must contain the following:

(1) Assignments of Error. Under a heading entitled "Assignments of Error," the petition shall list, clearly and concisely and without extraneous argument, the specific errors in the rulings below upon which the party intends to rely. An exact reference to the page(s) of the transcript, written statement of facts, or record where the alleged error has been preserved in the trial court or other tribunal from which the appeal is taken shall be included with each assignment of error.

(i) Effect of Failure to Assign Error or Use Separate Heading. Only assignments of error assigned in the petition for appeal will be noticed by this Court. If the petition for appeal does not contain assignments of error, or if the assignments of error are not set forth under a separate heading as provided in subparagraph (c)(1) of this Rule, the petition shall be dismissed.

(ii) Nature of Assignments of Error in Appeals from the Court of Appeals. When appeal is taken from a judgment of the Court of Appeals, only assignments of error relating to assignments of error presented in, and to actions taken by, the Court of Appeals may be included in the petition for appeal to this Court.

(iii) Insufficient Assignments of Error. An assignment of error that does not address the findings or rulings in the trial court or other tribunal from which an appeal is taken, or which merely states that the judgment or award is contrary to the law and the evidence, is not sufficient. If the assignments of error are insufficient, the petition for appeal shall be dismissed.

(2) Required Statements When the Appeal is from the Court of Appeals.

When appeal is taken from a judgment of the Court of Appeals in a case in which judgment is made final under Code § 17.1-410, the petition for appeal shall contain a statement setting forth in what respect the decision of the Court of Appeals involves the following:

(i) a substantial constitutional question as a determinative issue, or

(ii) matters of significant precedential value.

If the petition for appeal does not contain such a statement, the appeal will be dismissed.

(3) Table of Contents and Table of Authorities. A table of contents and table of authorities with cases alphabetically arranged. Citations of all authorities shall include the year thereof.

(4) Nature of the Case and Material Proceedings Below. A brief statement of the nature of the case and of the material proceedings in the trial court or commission in which the case originated. This statement shall omit references to any paper filed or action taken that does not relate to the assignments of error.

(5) Statement of Facts. A clear and concise statement of the facts that relate to the assignments of error, with references to the pages of the record, transcript, or written statement of facts. Any quotation from the record should be brief. When the facts are in dispute, the petition shall so state. The testimony of individual witnesses should not be summarized seriatim unless the facts are in dispute and such a summary is necessary to support the appellant's version of the facts.

(6) Authorities and Argument. With respect to each assignment of error, the standard of review and the argument — including principles of law and the authorities — shall be stated in one place and not scattered through the petition. At the option of counsel, the argument may be preceded by a short summary.

(7) Conclusion. A short conclusion stating the precise relief sought.

(d) *Filing Fee Required With the Petition.* — When it is filed, the petition for appeal must be accompanied by a check or money order payable to the "Clerk of the Supreme Court of Virginia" for the amount required by statute. The clerk of this Court may file a petition for appeal that is not accompanied by such fee if the fee is received by the clerk within 10 days of the date the petition for appeal is filed. If the fee is not received within such time, the petition for appeal shall be dismissed.

(e) *Number of Copies to File.* — Seven copies of the petition shall be filed with the clerk of this Court.

(f) *Length.* — Except by leave of a Justice of this Court, a petition shall not exceed the longer of 35 pages or 6,125 words. The page or word limit does not include the cover page, table of contents, table of authorities, and certificate.

(g) *Use of a Single Petition in Separate Cases.* — Whenever two or more cases were tried together in the court or commission below, one petition for appeal may be used to bring all such cases before this Court even though the cases were not consolidated below by formal order.

(h) *Procedure for an Anders appeal.* — If counsel for appellant finds appellant's appeal to be without merit, counsel must comply with the requirements of *Anders v. California,* 386 U.S. 738 (1967), and *Brown v. Warden of Virginia State Penitentiary,* 238 Va. 551, 385 S.E.2d 587 (1989). In compliance therewith, counsel is required to file (1) a petition for appeal which refers to anything in the record which might arguably support the appeal and which demonstrates to this Court counsel's conscientious examination of the merits of the appeal; (2) a motion for leave to withdraw as counsel; and (3) a motion for an extension of time to allow the appellant to file a supplemental petition for appeal. The petition for appeal and the motion for leave to withdraw as counsel should specifically cite to *Anders*. All three pleadings must be served on opposing counsel and upon the client and must contain a certificate providing evidence of such service. This Court will rule upon the motion for extension of time upon its receipt, but will not rule on the motion to withdraw until this Court considers the case in its entirety, including any supplemental petition for appeal that may be filed.

(i) *What the Certificate Must Contain.* — The appellant shall include within the petition for appeal a certificate stating:

(1) the names of all appellants and appellees, the name, Virginia State Bar number, mailing address, telephone number (including any applicable extension), facsimile number (if any), and e-mail address (if any) of counsel for each party, and the mailing address, telephone number (including any applicable extension), facsimile number (if any), and e-mail address (if any) of any party not represented by counsel;

(2) that a copy of the petition for appeal has been mailed or delivered on the date stated therein to all opposing counsel and all parties not represented by counsel;

(3) if a word count is used, the number of words (headings, footnotes, and quotations count towards the word limitation; the cover page, table of contents, table of authorities, and certificate do not count towards the word count);

(4) in a criminal case or habeas corpus appeal, a statement whether counsel for defendant has been appointed or privately retained; and

(5) whether the appellant desires to state orally to a panel of this Court the reasons why the petition for appeal should be granted, and, if so, whether in person or by conference telephone call.

(j) *Oral Argument.* — (1) Right to Oral Argument. The appellant shall be entitled to state orally, in person or by telephone conference call, to a panel of this Court the reasons why the petition for appeal should be granted. The appellee shall not be entitled to oral argument, whether in person or by telephone conference call. Any lawyer not licensed in Virginia who seeks to appear pro hac vice to present oral argument to the Court must comply with the requirements of Rule 1A:4.

(2) Waiver of Right to Oral Argument. The appellant may waive the right to oral argument on the petition for appeal before a panel by notifying the clerk of this Court and opposing counsel in writing, or by filing a reply brief.

(3) No Oral Argument on Pro Se Inmate's Petition. If an appellant is not represented by counsel and is incarcerated, the petition for appeal may be considered by this Court without oral argument.

(4) Notice of Oral Argument. If the appellant has requested oral argument, notice of the date and time of such argument shall be provided to counsel for the appellant or to any pro se appellant. If requested in writing, notice of the oral argument shall also be provided to counsel for the appellee or any pro se appellee.

Cross references. — For limitations on questions that Supreme Court will consider on appeal, see Rule 5:25. As to filing fee charged by clerk of Supreme Court, see § 17.1-328.

Source. — Rules 5:21, 5:22, 5:24 and 5:25. Cf. Rule 5A:12.

The amendment, effective May 2, 2011, adopted March 1, 2011, inserted "the longer of" in the first sentence of subdivision (f).

Law Review. — For 2003/2004 survey of civil practice and procedure, see 39 U. Rich. L. Rev. 87 (2004). For annual survey of Virginia law article, "Criminal Law and Procedure," see 47 U. Rich. L. Rev. 143 (2012).

Michie's Jurisprudence. — For related discussion, see 1B M.J. Appeal and Error, §§ 124, 135, 137, 139 - 142, 210, 213, 233, 250; 9A M.J. Grand Jury, § 15.

CASE NOTES

When legal presence of parties on appeal absolute necessity. — Where a party's interests in the subject matter of the appeal are so bound up with that of the other parties, its legal presence as a party to the proceeding is an absolute necessity, without which the appellate court cannot proceed. Asch v. Friends of Community of Mt. Vernon Yacht Club, 251 Va. 89, 465 S.E.2d 817 (1996).

Mere notice of appeal insufficient to confer appellate jurisdiction. — The mere fact that an indispensable party who was a litigant in the trial court has notice that an appeal has been perfected against another litigant is not sufficient to confer an appellate court's jurisdiction over the indispensable party against whom no appeal has been properly perfected. Asch v. Friends of Community of Mt. Vernon Yacht Club, 251 Va. 89, 465 S.E.2d 817 (1996).

Habeas corpus not to be used to circumvent trial and appeal. — A prisoner is not entitled to use habeas corpus to circumvent the trial and appellate processes for an inquiry into an alleged nonjurisdictional defect of a judgment of conviction. Epperly v. Booker, 235 Va. 35, 366 S.E.2d 62 (1988).

Federal appellate review. — The Virginia Supreme Court's conclusion that claims were defaulted pursuant to subsection (c) of this rule barred them from consideration by the Fourth Circuit Court of Appeals, absent cause and prejudice or a miscarriage of justice, so long as subsection (c) was an independent and adequate state grounds for decision. Mueller v. Angelone, 181 F.3d 557 (4th Cir.), cert. denied, 527 U.S. 1065, 120 S. Ct. 37, 144 L. Ed. 2d 839 (1999).

Form and contents. — Plain reading of Rule 5:17(c) required one to brief the specific errors in the rulings below; nothing in the rule limited the opening brief to issues addressed in a lower court's evidentiary hearing. Hedrick v. True, 2004 U.S. Dist. LEXIS 4600 (W.D. Va. Mar. 23, 2004), aff'd, 443 F.3d 342 (4th Cir. 2006).

In a capital murder case in which defendant presented 82 assignments of error but failed to brief or provide an argument for a number of those assignments of error, they were deemed waived by the appellate court. Prieto v. Commonwealth, 278 Va. 366, 682 S.E.2d 910, 2009 Va. LEXIS 94 (2009), cert. denied, 177 L. Ed. 2d 332, 2010 U.S. LEXIS 4926 (U.S. 2010).

In a case in which defendant was convicted for involuntary manslaughter and he did not assign error to the Court of Appeals of Virginia's holding that his driving conduct was criminally negligent, that holding was binding on appeal, and the Supreme Court of Virginia considered only the remaining issue of proximate causation. Brown v. Commonwealth, 278 Va. 523, 685 S.E.2d 43, 2009 Va. LEXIS 112 (2009).

Party's assignment of error was barred by Va. Sup. Ct. R. 5:17(c) because the assignment of error did not reflect the circuit court's ruling. Thus, the assignment of error lacked legal efficacy. Heinrich Schepers GmbH & Co., KG v. Whitaker, 280 Va. 507, 702 S.E.2d 573, 2010 Va. LEXIS 267 (2010).

Where a subcontractor's assignments of error referenced a contract between a housing authority and a demolition company, rather than the relevant contract between the demolition company and a developer, the assignments failed to accurately address the facts of the trial below, such that they were deemed insufficient under Va. Sup. Ct. R. 5:17(c)(1)(iii). Envtl. Staffing Acquisition Corp. v. B

& R Constr. Mgmt., 283 Va. 787, 725 S.E.2d 550, 2012 Va. LEXIS 89 (2012).

Because petitioner inmate's state court petition for appeal of the denial of relief had been dismissed for not containing the appropriate assignments of errors required by Va. Sup. Ct. R. 5:17(c), it had not been "properly filed" so as to toll the time to seek federal habeas relief under 28 U.S.C.S. § 2244(d)(1), and his claims were time-barred. Escalante v. Watson, 2012 U.S. App. LEXIS 14963 (4th Cir. July 18, 2012).

Not "properly filed" for federal habeas purposes. — Habeas petitioner could not exclude from the limitations period, under 28 U.S.C.S. § 2244(d), time during which his state habeas petition was before the state supreme court; the state petition was not properly filed for § 2244(d) purposes because it did not meet the requirements of Rule 5:17(c), as it lacked list of specific errors and a separate heading entitled "Assignments of Error." Christian v. Baskerville, 232 F. Supp. 2d 605, 2001 U.S. Dist. LEXIS 25097 (E.D. Va.), cert. denied, 537 U.S. 834, 123 S. Ct. 144, 154 L. Ed. 2d 52 (2002).

Inmate was properly denied habeas corpus relief on his claim that the Commonwealth failed to reveal two of his accomplice's statements in violation of *Brady,* because the claim was procedurally defaulted. The state supreme court deemed the claim procedurally defaulted because the inmate failed to address it in his opening brief even though he raised the claim in his habeas petition; the court could not review it because the state court relied on an independent and adequate state ground. Hedrick v. True, 443 F.3d 342, 2006 U.S. App. LEXIS 7904 (4th Cir. 2006), cert. denied, 548 U.S. 928, 127 S. Ct. 10, 165 L. Ed. 2d 992 (2006).

The time limitation is mandatory and cannot be waived. Condrey v. Childress, 203 Va. 755, 127 S.E.2d 150 (1962).

Within the purview of the Virginia statutes and rules, the finality of an adjudication is the order, decree or judgment "entered" of record and it is that order, decree or judgment which can be made the subject of an appeal, and therefore, has binding effect as a final adjudication upon the merits. Costner's Furn., Inc. v. Cawthorn, 1 Bankr. 267 (Bankr. W.D. Va. 1979).

Extension of time for filing. — The Supreme Court will extend the time for filing a petition only if it is found that to deny the extension would abridge a constitutional right. Tharp v. Commonwealth, 211 Va. 1, 175 S.E.2d 277 (1970).

The language of an assignment of error may not be changed, especially when the assignment is set forth in the order of the Supreme Court awarding the appeal. The only time when the wording of an assignment of error does not remain an integral part of the appeal is on the rare occasion when the Supreme Court in an order, posits the issue to be debated. Hamilton Dev. Co. v. Broad Rock Club, Inc., 248 Va. 40, 445 S.E.2d 140 (1994).

The purpose of assignments of error is to point out the errors with reasonable certainty in order to direct this court and opposing counsel to the points on which appellant intends to ask a reversal of the judgment, and to limit discussion to these points. Yeatts v. Murray, 249 Va. 285, 455 S.E.2d 18 (1995).

Supreme Court of Virginia rules required assignments of error to address the findings or rulings in the trial court or other tribunal from which an appeal is taken, Va. Sup. Ct. R. 5:17(c)(1)(iii), because the purpose of assignments of error was to point out the errors on which an appellant intends to ask a reversal of the judgment, and to limit discussion to these points; but unlike Va. Sup. Ct. R. 5:17(c)(1)(iii), Va. Sup. Ct. R. 5:14(a) did not require an appellant to challenge the final judgment in a notice of appeal from the Court of Appeals of Virginia because the purpose of the notice of appeal is merely to place the opposing party on notice and to direct the clerk to prepare the record on appeal. LaCava v. Commonwealth, 283 Va. 465, 722 S.E.2d 838, 2012 Va. LEXIS 45 (2012).

Where the defendant failed to assign error to the jury's finding of future dangerousness, he cannot challenge on appeal the admission of any evidence relevant to his dangerousness. Sheppard v. Commonwealth, 250 Va. 379, 464 S.E.2d 131 (1995), cert. denied, 517 U.S. 1110, 116 S. Ct. 1332, 134 L. Ed. 2d 483 (1996).

Failure to assign error. — Because landowners did not assign error to the circuit court's ruling that they lacked standing to bring an as-applied challenged to an historic district ordinance, their challenge was waived under Va. Sup. Ct. R. 5:17(c). Covel v. Town of Vienna, 280 Va. 151, 694 S.E.2d 609, 2010 Va. LEXIS 75 (2010).

Averment irrelevant to the appeal. — Although in its brief, a homeowners association averred that it would have provided additional evidence in the form of expert testimony, no assignment of error asserted that the circuit court erred in awarding summary judgment because material facts were in dispute or that the court improperly excluded admissible evidence; the averment therefore had no relevance to the appeal. Newberry Station Homeowners Ass'n v. Bd. of Supervisors, 285 Va. 604, 740 S.E.2d 548, 2013 Va. LEXIS 52 (2013).

Consideration of issue on appeal was proper. — Consideration of the issue of whether a circuit court erred in denying a mother's motion for a continuance of her termination of parental rights hearing once authorities at the prison where she was incarcerated required that she end her participation by telephone in the hearing was proper because the question presented in her petition to the Court of Appeals was sufficiently broad to encompass the issue of whether the circuit court erred by failing to grant her request for a continuance because she was entitled to participate by telephone in the hearing. Haugen v. Shenandoah Valley Dep't of Soc. Servs., 274 Va. 27, 645 S.E.2d 261, 2007 Va. LEXIS 71 (2007).

Court was without jurisdiction to enter sanction order a month after final order. — Where a trial court entered a final order dismissing a case and, over a month later, entered another order awarding sanctions in the case, the court was without jurisdiction to enter the order for sanctions. Smith v. Stanaway, 242 Va. 286, 410 S.E.2d 610 (1991).

Mandatory dismissal of petition. — With the amendment of Va. Sup. Ct. R. 5A:12(c) to mandate dismissal of a petition for appeal if the assignments of error fail to comply with the requirements of the Rule, Va. Sup. Ct. R. 5A:12(c)(1)(ii), coupled with the Virginia Supreme Court's recent interpretation and application of such mandatory dismissal language in Va. Sup. Ct. R. 5:17(c)(1)(iii), the Virginia Court of Appeals now must dismiss a petition for appeal containing assignments of error that fail to comply with the requirements of Va. Sup. Ct. R. 5A:12(c)(1). Chatman v. Commonwealth, 60 Va. App. 622, 731 S.E.2d 24, 2012 Va. App. LEXIS 263 (Aug. 14, 2012).

Applied in Bonavita v. Board of Trustees, 236 Va. 31, 372 S.E.2d 366 (1988); Fisher v. Commonwealth, 236 Va. 403, 374 S.E.2d 46 (1988); Young v. Young, 240 Va. 57, 393 S.E.2d 398 (1990); Kroger Co. v. APCO, 244 Va. 560, 422 S.E.2d 757 (1992); Spencer v. Murray, 5 F.3d 758 (4th Cir. 1993); City of Winchester v. American Woodmark Corp., 250 Va. 451, 464 S.E.2d 148 (1995); Rash v. Hilb, Rogal & Hamilton Co., 251 Va. 281, 467 S.E.2d 791 (1996); Angstadt v. Atlantic Mut. Ins. Co., 254 Va. 286, 492 S.E.2d 118 (1997); Swisher v. Commonwealth, 256 Va. 471, 506 S.E.2d 763 (1998); Bolling v. D'Amato, 259 Va. 299, 526 S.E.2d 257 (2000); Pizzarelle v. Dempsey, 259 Va. 521, 526 S.E.2d 260 (2000); Caine v. Freier, 264 Va. 251, 564 S.E.2d 122, 2002 Va. LEXIS 82 (2002); Pulte Home Corp. v. Parex, Inc., 265 Va. 518, 579 S.E.2d 188, 2003 Va. LEXIS 51 (2003); MicroStrategy Inc. v. Li, 268 Va. 249, 601 S.E.2d 580, 2004 Va. LEXIS 132 (2004); Bentley Funding Group, L.L.C. v. SK&R Group, L.L.C., 269 Va. 315, 609 S.E.2d 49, 2005 Va. LEXIS 27 (2005); Goulet v. Johnson, 2005 U.S. Dist. LEXIS 36887 (W.D. Va. Dec. 16, 2005); Gov't Micro Res., Inc. v. Jackson, 271 Va. 29, 624 S.E.2d 63, 2006 Va. LEXIS 1 (2006); Juniper v. Commonwealth, 271 Va. 362, 626 S.E.2d 383, 2006 Va. LEXIS 29 (2006); Today Homes, Inc. v. Williams, 272 Va. 462, 634 S.E.2d 737, 2006 Va. LEXIS 91 (2006); Smallwood v. Young, 425 F. Supp. 2d 717, 2006 U.S. Dist. LEXIS 14128 (E.D. Va. 2006); Conyers v. Martial Arts World of Richmond, Inc., 273 Va. 96, 639 S.E.2d 174, 2007 Va. LEXIS 13 (2007); Teleguz v. Commonwealth, 273 Va. 458, 643 S.E.2d 708, 2007 Va. LEXIS 64 (2007); Philip Morris USA, Inc. v. Chesapeake Bay Found., Inc., 273 Va. 564, 643 S.E.2d 219, 2007 Va. LEXIS 67 (2007); In re Moseley, 273 Va. 688, 643 S.E.2d 190, 2007 Va. LEXIS 65 (2007); Ace Temps., Inc. v. City Council, 274 Va. 461, 649 S.E.2d 688, 2007 Va. LEXIS 106 (2007); Marcus, Santoro & Kozak, P.C. v. Wu, 274 Va. 743, 652 S.E.2d 777, 2007 Va. LEXIS 135 (2007); Kitchen v. City of Newport News, 275 Va. 378, 657 S.E.2d 132, 2008 Va. LEXIS 38 (2008); Miller-Jenkins v. Miller-Jenkins, 276 Va. 19, 661 S.E.2d 822, 2008 Va. LEXIS 65 (2008); Maine v. Adams, 277 Va. 230, 672 S.E.2d 862, 2009 Va. LEXIS 41 (2009); Estate of Parfitt v. Parfitt, 277 Va. 333, 672 S.E.2d 827, 2009 Va. LEXIS 33 (2009); Andrews v. Commonwealth, 280 Va. 231, 699 S.E.2d 237, 2010 Va. LEXIS 239 (2010); Harkleroad v. Linkous, 281 Va. 12, 704 S.E.2d 381, 2011 Va. LEXIS 14 (2011); Riverside Healthcare Ass'n v. Forbes, 281 Va. 522, 709 S.E.2d 156, 2011 Va. LEXIS 90 (2011); City of Richmond v. Suntrust Bank, 283 Va. 439, 722 S.E.2d 268, 2012 Va. LEXIS 43 (2012).

Rule 5:17A. Petition for Review Pursuant to Code § 8.01-626; Injunctions.

(a) *Time for Filing.* — In every case in which the jurisdiction of this Court is invoked pursuant to Code § 8.01-626, a petition for review must be filed with the clerk of this Court within 15 days of the order sought to be reviewed.

(b) *Copy to Opposing Counsel.* — At the time the petition for review is filed, a copy of the petition shall be served on counsel for the respondent.

(c) *Length and What the Petition for Review Must Contain.* — Except by permission of a Justice of this Court, a petition for review shall not exceed the longer of 15 pages or 2,625 words. The petition for review must otherwise comply with the requirements for a petition for appeal in Rule 5:17(c).

(d) *Number of Copies to File.* — Four copies shall be filed.

(e) *Filing Fee.* — The petition must be accompanied by a check or money order payable to the clerk of this Court for the amount required by statute. The statutory fee shall be collected at the time such petition is presented and the clerk of this Court shall not file a petition that is not accompanied by such fee.

(f) *Scope.* — Final judgments within the meaning of Code § 8.01-670 are not reviewable by a Justice of this Court under Code § 8.01-626. See *Omega Corp. v. Cobb,* 222 Va. 875, 292 S.E.2d 44 (1981).

(g) *Rehearing.* — The provisions of Rules 5:20, 5:20A, and 5:37 do not apply to proceedings under Code § 8.01-626.

The amendment, effective May 2, 2011, adopted March 1, 2011, inserted "the longer of" in the first sentence of subdivision (c).

Law Review. — For annual survey article, "Civil Practice and Procedure," see 46 U. Rich. L. Rev. 9 (2011).

Rule 5:18. Brief in Opposition.

(a) *Filing Time.* — A brief in opposition to granting the appeal may be filed with the clerk of this Court by the appellee within 21 days after petition for appeal is served on counsel for the appellee. Within the same time the counsel for appellee shall mail or deliver a copy to counsel for appellant. Seven copies shall be filed.

(b) *Form and Content.* — The brief in opposition shall conform in all respects to the content requirements for the brief of appellee in Rule 5:28. However, the brief in opposition need not be bound or have a blue cover. Except by leave of a Justice of this Court, the brief shall not exceed the longer of 25 pages or 4,375 words. If the brief exceeds 10 pages or 1,750 words, it shall contain a table of contents and table of authorities with cases alphabetically arranged.

(c) *Assignments of cross-error.* — The brief in opposition may include assignments of cross-error. If the brief in opposition contains an assignment or assignments of cross-error, the cover of the brief must so indicate by being styled, "Brief in Opposition and Assignment of Cross-Error."

(1) A cross-error must be assigned in the brief in opposition in order to be noticed by this Court.

(2) The provisions of Rule 5:25 shall apply to limit the assignments of cross-error which will be heard on the appeal.

(3) A brief in opposition containing assignments of cross-error shall conform to the form, content, and maximum word requirements of paragraph (b) of this Rule.

(4) When an appellee assigns cross-error in the brief in opposition:

(i) this Court will not grant any assignment of cross-error unless it first decides to grant some or all of the assignments of error contained in the appellant's petition for appeal.

(ii) the appellee shall not be permitted to present oral argument to a writ panel.

(iii) if the appellant withdraws the petition for appeal, the appeal will be dismissed without consideration of the cross-error assigned by an appellee.

(d) *Expedited Review.* — When it clearly appears that an appeal ought to be granted without further delay, an appeal may be granted before the filing of the brief in opposition.

Cross references. — For meaning of "counsel for the appellee" and "counsel for the appellant," see Rule 5:1.

Source. — Rule 5:27. Cf. Rule 5A:13.

Comment. — No appeal is granted on the basis of an assignment of cross-error alone. Cross-error will not be considered unless the appellant's petition for appeal is granted. An appellee desiring to assert error notwithstanding refusal of the appellant's petition must file his own notice of appeal within the required time (Rule 5:9) and his separate petition for appeal meeting all time limits and other requirements applicable to petitions for appeal.

The amendment, effective May 2, 2011, adopted March 1, 2011, inserted "the longer of" in the first sentence of subdivision (b).

Michie's Jurisprudence. — For related discussion, see 1B M.J. Appeal and Error, §§ 135, 142, 212, 233, 250; 4B M.J. Corporations, § 32; 15 M.J. Public Service and State Corporation Commissions, § 32.

CASE NOTES

Editor's note. — The cases below were decided prior to the addition of subdivision (c) by 2010 amendments.

Cross-error must be assigned within time period for brief in opposition. — Unquestionably, the word "then" in the second sentence of subdivision (b) refers to the time period fixed in subdivision (a). And, while subdivision (a) is expressed in permissive terms (an appellee in a civil case may forego filing a brief in opposition), the second sentence of subdivision (b) is couched in jurisdictional language, demonstrating that cross-error, when assigned, must be included in a brief in opposition filed within the time period fixed in subdivision (a). DeChene v. Smallwood, 226 Va. 475, 311 S.E.2d 749, cert. denied, 469 U.S. 857, 105 S. Ct. 184, 83 L. Ed. 2d 118 (1984).

Supreme Court would not consider property owner's contention that alleged lessees had no interest in disputed property because they were mere licensees whose license was revoked upon death of grantors; property owners, who prevailed below in declaratory judgment action, had failed to assign cross-error to chancellor's failure to rule for them on that issue. Wells v. Shoosmith, 245 Va. 386, 428 S.E.2d 909 (1993).

Trial court erred in granting the tortfeasor's plea in bar based on its conclusion that the parents had impliedly waived their claim for medical expenses for injuries the tortfeasor inflicted on their minor son in a fight; however, the state supreme court could not consider other defenses that the tortfeasor asserted that he raised in his plea in bar and that the trial court did not rule on, as he did not assign cross-error to the trial court's failure to rule on those defenses within the time period he was given to file a brief in opposition, although he was entitled to reassert those defenses on remand. Baumann v. Capozio, 269 Va. 356, 611 S.E.2d 597, 2005 Va. LEXIS 43 (2005).

Court will not consider ruling unfavorable to appellee not assigned as cross-error. — See Virginia ABC Bd. v. 1713 Wilson, Inc., 217 Va. 632, 231 S.E.2d 327 (1977).

State employee was precluded from asking the supreme court to affirm an order of the court of appeals on the ground that a hearing officer's decision was contrary to the hearing officer's own factual findings because the employee failed to assign cross-error to the judgment of the court of appeals on that basis. Va. Polytechnic Inst. v. Quesenberry, 277 Va. 420, 674 S.E.2d 854, 2009 Va. LEXIS 48 (2009).

Applied in Hughes v. Cole, 251 Va. 3, 465 S.E.2d 820 (1996); Patrick v. Commonwealth, 27 Va. App. 655, 500 S.E.2d 839 (1998); Pizzarelle v. Dempsey, 259 Va. 521, 526 S.E.2d 260 (2000); Horner v. Dep't of Mental Health, Mental Retardation, & Substance Abuse Servs., 268 Va. 187, 597 S.E.2d 202, 2004 Va. LEXIS 83 (2004); Today Homes, Inc. v. Williams, 272 Va. 462, 634 S.E.2d 737, 2006 Va. LEXIS 91 (2006); Hicks v. Mellis, 275 Va. 213, 657 S.E.2d 142, 2008 Va. LEXIS 36 (2008); Kitchen v. City of Newport News, 275 Va. 378, 657 S.E.2d 132, 2008 Va. LEXIS 38 (2008); Keener v. Keener, 278 Va. 435, 682 S.E.2d 545, 2009 Va. LEXIS 87 (2009); Smith v. Mountjoy, 280 Va. 46, 694 S.E.2d 598, 2010 Va. LEXIS 76 (2010).

Rule 5:19. Reply Brief.

(a) When a brief in opposition to the petition for appeal has been filed, the appellant may, within 7 days thereafter, in lieu of oral argument, file with the clerk of this Court a reply brief not to exceed the longer of 15 pages or 2,625 words in length. Seven copies shall be filed.

(b) When cross-error is assigned in a brief in opposition, the appellant may, without waiving oral argument, file with the clerk of this Court within the said 7-day period a reply brief not in excess of 10 pages or 1,750 words which addresses only the cross-error. Seven copies shall be filed.

Source. — Rule 5:28. Cf. Rule 5A:14.

The amendment, effective May 2, 2011, adopted March 1, 2011, inserted "the longer of" in the first sentence of subdivision (a).

Law Review. — For 2003/2004 survey of civil practice and procedure, see 39 U. Rich. L. Rev. 87 (2004).

Michie's Jurisprudence. — For related discussion, see 1B M.J. Appeal and Error, §§ 135, 142, 234.

CASE NOTES

Petition for writ of habeas corpus not precluded. — Petitioner is not precluded by this rule from later returning to the Supreme Court to argue a petition for a writ of habeas corpus, which would be a completely different petition. Creasy v. McConnell, 262 F. Supp. 697 (W.D. Va. 1966).

Rule 5:20. Petition for Rehearing After Refusal of Petition for Appeal or Disposition of an Original Jurisdiction Petition.

(a) *Petition for Appeal.* — When a petition for appeal is either refused or dismissed, the clerk of this Court shall mail a copy of the order denying the appeal to counsel for the appellant and counsel for the appellee. Counsel for the appellant may, within 14 days after the date of this notice, file in the office of the clerk of this Court a petition for rehearing. Oral argument on the petition for rehearing will not be allowed. No responsive brief shall be filed unless requested by this Court. The clerk of this Court shall notify counsel for the appellant and counsel for the appellee of the action taken by this Court on the petition for rehearing.

(b) *Original Jurisdiction Petition.* — When a petition filed pursuant to this Court's original jurisdiction (habeas corpus, mandamus, prohibition, or actual innocence) is decided, the clerk of this Court shall mail a copy of the order to counsel for the petitioner and counsel for the respondent. Counsel for either party may, within 30 days after the date of this order, file in the office of the clerk of this Court a petition for rehearing. Oral argument on the petition for rehearing will not be allowed. No responsive brief shall be filed unless requested by this Court. The clerk of this Court shall notify counsel for the petitioner and counsel for the respondent of the action taken by this Court on the petition for rehearing.

(c) *When Electronic Filing is Required.* — Except for petitions for rehearing filed by pro se prisoners or with leave of this Court, a petition for rehearing shall be filed as an Adobe Acrobat Portable Document Format (PDF) document attached to an e-mail in compliance with Rule 5:20A. Petitions filed by pro se prisoners or with leave of this Court shall be filed in compliance with this Rule.

(d) *Length and Number of Copies.* — The petition for rehearing shall not exceed the longer of 15 pages or 2,625 words in length. The petition shall state that a copy has been mailed or delivered to counsel for the appellee. Ten copies shall be filed.

(e) *Attorney's Fees.* — Attorney's Fees. Upon denial of a petition for appeal and any petition for rehearing, any appellee who has received attorney's fees and costs in the circuit court may make application in the circuit court for additional fees and costs incurred on appeal pursuant to Rule 1:1A.

Cross references. — For meaning of "counsel for the appellant" and "counsel for the appellee," see Rule 5:1.

Source. — Rule 5:29. Cf. Rule 5A:15.

The amendment, effective May 2, 2011, adopted March 1, 2011, inserted "the longer of" in the first sentence of subdivision (d).

Law Review. — For article, "The Subject Matter Jurisdiction of Virginia Courts in Divorce and Equitable Distribution Proceedings," see 11 G.M.U. L. Rev. 73 (1989). For 1995 survey of civil practice and procedure, see 29 U. Rich. L. Rev. 897 (1995). For article reviewing recent developments and changes in legislation, case law, and Virginia Supreme Court Rules affecting civil litigation, see "Civil Practice and Procedure," 40 U. Rich. L. Rev. 95 (2005).

Michie's Jurisprudence. — For related discussion, see 1B M.J. Appeal and Error, §§ 141, 143.

CASE NOTES

Assignment of error required. — Appellate court, under Va. Sup. Ct. R. 5A:12(c)(1)(i) and Va. Sup. Ct. R. 5:20(c), will not consider claims of error for which there is no assignment of error. Zedan v. Westheim, 60 Va. App. 556, 729 S.E.2d 785, 2012 Va. App. LEXIS 257 (2012).

Rule 5:20A. Denial of Appeal; Petition for Rehearing.

(a) Except for petitions for rehearing filed by pro se prisoners, or with leave of this Court, the petition shall be filed as an Adobe Acrobat Portable Document Format (PDF) document attached to an e-mail addressed to scvpfr@courts.state.va.us and will be timely filed if received by the clerk's office on or before 11:59 p.m. on the date due.

(b) The petition must be formatted to print on a page 8 ½ x 11 inches, must be in 14-point font or larger, must be double-spaced, must comply with Rule 5:6, and must not exceed the longer of 10 pages or a word count of 1,750 words. The petition must include a certificate of service to counsel for the appellee and the certificate shall specify the manner of service and the date of service. The petition must also include a certificate of compliance with the word count limit. The petition will be considered filed on the date and time that it is received by scvpfr@courts.state.va.us. If the petition does not meet the requirements of this rule as to format, the clerk shall so notify counsel and provide a specific amount of time for a corrected copy of the petition to be filed. A person who files a document electronically shall have the same responsibility as a person filing a document in paper form for ensuring that the document is properly filed, complete, and readable. However, if technical problems at the Supreme Court result in a failure to timely receive the electronically filed petition for rehearing, counsel shall provide to the clerk of this Court on the next business day all documentation which exists demonstrating the attempt to file the petition by e-mail, any delivery failure notice received in response to the attempt, and a copy of the petition for rehearing.

(c) The e-mail message to which the petition is attached shall recite in the subject line the style of the case and the Supreme Court record number. The e-mail message shall contain a paragraph stating that a petition for rehearing is being filed, the style of the case, the Supreme Court record number, the name and Virginia State Bar number of counsel filing the petition, as well as the law firm name, mailing address, telephone number, facsimile number (if any), and e-mail address (if any) of counsel. The message shall also state whether a copy of the petition has been served by e-mail or another means on opposing counsel and the date of such service. If opposing counsel has an e-mail address, that address shall also be included. Upon receipt of the petition for rehearing in the e-mail box of the clerk's office, an acknowledgment will automatically be forwarded to counsel seeking the rehearing.

(d) The clerk of this Court shall notify counsel for both parties of the action taken by this Court on the petition for rehearing via e-mail, if e-mail addresses for both counsel have been provided, or via U.S. Mail to any counsel or party who has not provided an e-mail address.

The amendment, effective May 2, 2011, adopted March 1, 2011, inserted "the longer of" in the first sentence of subdivision (b).

Law Review. — For article reviewing recent developments and changes in legislation, case law, and Virginia Supreme Court Rules affecting civil litigation, see "Civil Practice and Procedure," 40 U. Rich. L. Rev. 95 (2005).

F. SPECIAL RULES.

Rule 5:21. Special Rules Applicable to Certain Appeals of Right.

(a) *Appeals from the State Corporation Commission. —*

(1) Applicability. Paragraph (a) of this Rule applies to all appeals from the State Corporation Commission and supersedes all other Rules except as otherwise specified herein.

(2) Party. For the purposes of this Rule, the Commission, the Attorney General, the applicant or petitioner, and every person who made an appearance in person in a capacity other than as a witness or by counsel at any hearing in any proceeding before the Commission shall be the parties to such proceeding. Upon the request of any party, the clerk of the Commission shall prepare and certify a list of all parties (including their addresses and the names and addresses of their counsel) to a proceeding before the Commission. Initially, the parties to an appeal from an order in a proceeding shall be the parties to that proceeding, but the number of parties to an appeal may thereafter be limited as hereinafter provided. Service upon a party represented by counsel shall be made upon his counsel.

(3) Notice of Appeal. No appeal from an order of the Commission shall be allowed unless, within 30 days after entry of the order appealed from, counsel files in the office of the clerk of the Commission a notice of appeal. A copy of the notice of appeal shall be mailed or delivered to each party to the appeal, including the Attorney General of Virginia, and an acceptance of such service or a certificate showing the date of delivery or mailing shall be appended thereto. All petitions for appeal from the same order shall be deemed to be a consolidated case for the purpose of oral argument in this Court unless this Court shall order a severance for convenience of hearing.

(4) Record. The clerk of the Commission shall prepare and certify the record as soon as possible after the notice of appeal is filed and shall, as soon as it has been certified by him, transmit it to the clerk of this Court within 4 months after entry of the order appealed from. In the event of multiple appeals in the same case or in cases tried together below, only one record need be prepared and transmitted.

(5) Contents of Record. The record on appeal from the Commission shall consist of all notices of appeal, any application or petition, all orders entered in the case by the Commission, the opinions, the transcript of any testimony received, and all exhibits accepted or rejected, together with such other material as may be certified by the clerk of the Commission to be a part of the record. The record shall conform as nearly as practicable to the requirements of Rule 5:10.

(6) Alignment of Parties. Within 21 days after the notice of appeal shall have been filed in the office of the clerk of the Commission, each party who has not filed a notice of appeal and who intends to participate in the appeal shall file in the office of the clerk of the Commission and shall mail to every other party a notice that he intends to participate as an appellant or as an appellee. Every party who seeks reversal or modification of the order appealed from shall be deemed an appellant, and every party who seeks affirmance of the order appealed from shall be deemed an appellee. Every party who does not file such a notice and every party who, having filed such a notice as an appellant, does not thereafter file a petition for appeal shall be deemed no longer to be a party to the appeal, and no further papers need be served on him. Notwithstanding the foregoing provisions, (i) a necessary party who does not file such a notice or petition for appeal shall be deemed an appellee, and (ii) the Commission need not file such a notice and shall be deemed an appellee.

(7) Petition for Appeal. The petition(s) for appeal, accompanied by the prescribed filing fee, shall be filed in the office of the clerk of this Court within 4 months after entry of the final order, judgment or finding by the Commission. Each party deemed to be an appellant shall file a petition for appeal, as limited hereafter, and shall, before the petition is filed, mail or deliver a copy to every other party to the appeal. Except as

provided herein, the provisions of Rule 5:17 do not apply to a petition filed pursuant to this paragraph. The petition for appeal need only identify the order appealed from, with its date, contain a prayer that the appeal be granted, and include the certificate required by Rule 5:17(i). Oral argument on the petition shall not be allowed nor will a brief in opposition be received. If the petition prays for a suspension of the effectiveness of the order appealed from, it shall contain such statements of the facts and argument as shall be necessary for an understanding of the assignments of error. In that event, a brief in opposition will be received and oral argument may be granted.

(8) Award of Appeal. When the notice of appeal, the record, and the petition(s) for appeal appear to have been filed in the manner provided herein and within the time provided herein and by law, the clerk of this Court shall forthwith enter an order docketing the appeal, requiring such bond as the clerk shall deem proper. The clerk's action shall be subject to review by this Court.

(9) Assignments of Error. Within 10 days after the issuance by the clerk of this Court of the certificate pursuant to Rule 5:23, each party appellant shall file assignments of error in the office of the clerk of this Court and mail a copy thereof to every other party to the appeal. Under a heading entitled "Assignments of Error" shall be listed, clearly and concisely and without extraneous argument, the specific errors in the rulings below upon which the party intends to rely. A clear and exact reference to the pages of the transcript, written statement of facts, or record where the alleged error has been preserved shall be included with each assignment of error. Only errors so assigned will be noticed by this Court and no error not so assigned will be considered as grounds for reversal of the decision below. No ruling by the Commission will be considered as a basis for reversal unless an objection was stated with reasonable certainty at the time of the ruling, except for good cause shown or to enable this Court to attain the ends of justice. An assignment of error which merely states that the judgment is contrary to the law and the evidence is not sufficient.

(10) Further Proceedings. Further proceedings in this Court shall conform to Rules 5:23 through 5:38 provided that (i) the time within which the appellee may file with the clerk of this Court a designation of the additional parts of the record that the appellee wishes included in the appendix (Rule 5:32(b)) shall be extended to 30 days after the date of the certificate of the clerk of this Court pursuant to Rule 5:23 an appeal has been awarded; and (ii) the time within which the opening brief of the appellant shall be filed in the office of the clerk of this Court shall be extended to 50 days after such date.

(11) Additional Brief. An appellant who seeks relief different from that sought by another appellant may file an answering brief at the time prescribed for filing the brief of appellee.

(b) *Appeals from the Virginia State Bar Disciplinary Board or a Three-Judge Circuit Court Determination.* —

(1) Applicability. Paragraph (b) of this Rule applies to appeals from the Virginia State Bar Disciplinary Board, pursuant to Part 6, § IV, Paragraph 13-26 of the Rules of the Supreme Court of Virginia, and to appeals from the decisions of a three-judge circuit court pursuant to Code § 54.1-3935. As used in this paragraph, "Respondent" is defined as the attorney who is appealing the decision of the disciplinary proceeding.

(2) Perfecting the Appeal.

(i) Provisions for Appeals from the Virginia State Bar Disciplinary Board. No appeal shall be allowed under this paragraph unless the Respondent files a notice of appeal and assignments of error with the clerk of the Disciplinary System within 30 days after the Memorandum Order is served on the attorney by certified mail, return receipt requested, at the attorney's last address on record for membership purposes with the Virginia State Bar. At the same time the Respondent files a notice of appeal and assignments of error, a copy of the notice of appeal and assignments of error must be sent to the counsel for the Bar and the Attorney General of Virginia. The Respondent is responsible for filing a transcript in compliance with Rule 5:11. The date of the Memorandum Order shall be the date from which the time limits contained in Rule 5:11 shall run. This action within the time prescribed is mandatory. Upon timely compliance with these rules, the Clerk of the Supreme Court shall docket the appeal as provided in Rule 5:23.

(ii) Provisions for Appeals from a Three-Judge Circuit Court. No appeal shall be allowed under this paragraph unless the Respondent files a notice of appeal and assignments of error with the clerk of the three-judge circuit court within 30 days after the entry of the final judgment and, at the same time, mails a copy of the notice of appeal and assignments of error to counsel for the Bar and the Attorney General of Virginia. The Respondent is responsible for filing a transcript in compliance with Rule 5:11. The date of the judgment shall be the date from which the time limits contained in Rule 5:11 shall run. This action within the time prescribed is mandatory. Upon timely compliance with these rules, the Clerk of the Supreme Court shall docket the appeal as provided in Rule 5:23.

(3) Record on Appeal. The clerk of the Disciplinary System or the clerk of the three-judge circuit court shall compile and transmit the record as set out in Rules 5:10, 5:11, and 5:13. The clerk shall immediately notify by certified mail the Respondent, and the Respondent's counsel, if any, and the Attorney General of the date the record is filed with the clerk of this Court. At the time the record is filed, the clerk shall also notify the clerk of this Court and the Respondent whether the Attorney General or Bar Counsel will represent the interests of the Commonwealth as appellee.

(4) Time for Filing Briefs and Appendix. The parties shall designate the contents of the appendix pursuant to the requirements of Rule 5:32 and the Respondent shall be responsible for filing the appendix pursuant to that Rule. The Respondent shall file the opening brief in the office of the clerk of this Court within 40 days after the date the record is filed. The opening brief shall contain assignments of error and references to the pages of the appendix, transcript, written statement, or record where each assignment of error was preserved. The brief of the appellee shall be filed in the office of the clerk of this Court within 25 days after the filing of the Respondent's opening brief. The Respondent may file a reply brief within 14 days after the filing of the appellee's brief. All briefs and the appendix shall conform to the provisions of Rules 5:26 through 5:32.

(5) Stay Pending Appeal. The Respondent may file a motion with the clerk of this Court requesting a stay pending appeal of an order suspending the Respondent's license. The Respondent must file four copies of the motion for stay along with a copy of the order imposing the suspension and a copy of the Respondent's notice of appeal, which must contain the date stamp of the clerk showing the date the notice of appeal was filed.

(6) Procedure on Appeal. Except as provided in this paragraph, further proceedings shall be as provided in this Court's procedure following the perfection of an appeal set out in Rules 5:23, 5:25, and Rules 5:33 through 5:38.

Cross references. — For meaning of "clerk," see Rule 5:1.

Source. — Rule 5:18.

The amendment effective January 1, 2013, adopted November 1, 2012, in subdivision (a)(9), inserted the second sentence and rewrote the fifth sentence.

Michie's Jurisprudence. — For related discussion, see 1B M.J. Appeal and Error, §§ 124, 129, 135, 137, 139, 141, 176, 206, 212, 233; 8A M.J. Exceptions, Bill of, § 1.

CASE NOTES

Appeal of right to Supreme Court. — The Commonwealth, or any party in interest aggrieved by any final order of the Commission, has an appeal of right to the Supreme Court. Howell v. SCC, 214 Va. 128, 198 S.E.2d 611 (1973).

But the method of taking and prosecuting such an appeal must be in the manner prescribed by law or by the Rules of the Supreme Court. Howell v. SCC, 214 Va. 128, 198 S.E.2d 611 (1973).

The Supreme Court of Virginia considers appeals from only final orders of the Commission. Virginia Citizens Consumer Council v. C & P Tel. Co., 247 Va. 333, 443 S.E.2d 157 (1994).

Rule outlines necessary steps. — A litigant desiring to prosecute an appeal from the Commission will find the necessary steps outlined in this single rule, without being required to look to a number of varying statutes dealing with the subject. Seaboard Air Line R.R. v. Board of Supvrs., 197 Va. 130, 87 S.E.2d 799 (1955).

All parties to controversy permitted to intervene and appeal. — Subdivision (b) [now subdivision (a)(2)] expressly makes the Commission, the Attorney General, the applicant or petitioner, every person who filed a notice of protest with the commissioner and every person who made an appearance in person or by counsel at any hearing in any proceeding before the commission, parties on appeal to such proceeding. It can be said that both the Rules of Supreme Court and of the Commission are liberally applied and construed to the end that all parties having an interest in any matter in controversy before the Commission be permitted to intervene and to appeal. Blue Cross v. Commonwealth, 218 Va. 589, 239 S.E.2d 94 (1977).

Standards of review. — Abuse of discretion

standard applied to the appeal filed by an electric power company pursuant to Va. Sup. Ct. R. 5:21(c) [now 5:21(a)(2)] after the State Corporation Commission partially denied its request for a rate adjustment under former clause (i) of subsection B of § 56-582 because the Commission was clearly exercising its legislative authority under Va. Const., Art. IX, § 2, in ruling on the company's rate adjustment application: (1) the company explicitly asked the Commission to exercise its authority to adjust its capped rates, which relief clearly involved the exercise of the Commission's legislative, rate-making authority; (2) the fact that the Commission had to interpret a previously issued memorandum of understanding to determine the allowable rate adjustment did not transform the issue before the Commission from a legislative matter to a question of law; (3) the Commission did not abuse its discretion in adopting its staff's interpretation of the memorandum, rather than the interpretation proffered by the company; and (4) the Commission did not abuse its discretion in determining that the company was entitled to recover approximately $9.48 million in purchased power costs, rather than the $37.2 million that it requested, because the memorandum allowed only for the recovery of purchased power costs with regard to the company's power needs above its default service load of up to 367 MW. Potomac Edison Co. v. State Corp. Comm'n, 276 Va. 577, 667 S.E.2d 772, 2008 Va. LEXIS 121 (2008).

Rule 5:22. Special Rule for Appeals in Death Penalty Cases.

(a) *Notice of Receipt of Record.* — Upon receipt of a record pursuant to § 17.1-313 B, the clerk of this Court shall notify in writing counsel for the accused in the circuit court (who shall be deemed to be counsel for the appellant), the Attorney General (who shall be deemed to be counsel for the appellee), and the Director of the Department of Corrections of the date of its receipt. The date of the receipt of the record is the Filing Date and the case shall thereupon stand matured as if an appeal had been awarded to review the conviction and the sentence of death.

(b) *Stay of Sentence of Death.* — Upon the Filing Date, the notice issued by the clerk of this Court shall be deemed to be the certificate of the clerk of this Court pursuant to Rule 5:23 that an appeal has been awarded, and the enforcement of the sentence of death shall thereby be stayed pending the final determination of the case by this Court.

(c) *Filing of Assignments of Error and of the Appendix.* — Within 30 days after the Filing Date, counsel for the appellant shall file with the clerk of this Court assignments of error upon which the appellant intends to rely for reversal of the conviction or review of the sentence of death. Counsel for the appellant shall accompany the assignments of error with a designation of the parts of the record relevant to the review and to the assignments of error. Not more than 10 days after such assignments of error and designation are filed, counsel for the appellee may file with the clerk of this Court a designation of the additional parts of the record that he wishes included as germane to the review or to any assignments of error. Counsel for the appellant shall include in the appendix the parts so designated. The provisions of Rules 5:31 and 5:32 (except Rule 5:32(b)(1) and (b)(3)) shall apply to the appendix.

(d) *Assigning Error to the Sentence of Death.* — With respect to the sentence of death, it shall be a sufficient assignment of error to state that the sentence was imposed under the influence of passion, prejudice, or other arbitrary factor or that the sentence is excessive or disproportionate to the penalty imposed in similar cases.

(e) *Requirements for Briefs.* — (1) Brief of Appellant. The appellant shall file the opening brief, which shall not exceed the longer of 100 pages or 17,500 words, in the office of the clerk of this Court within 60 days after the Filing Date.

(2) Brief of the Appellee. The appellee shall file its brief, which shall not exceed the longer of 100 pages or 17,500 words, in the office of the clerk of this Court within 120 days after the Filing Date.

(3) Reply Brief of the Appellant. The appellant shall file the reply brief, which shall not exceed the longer of 50 pages or 8,750 words, in the office of the clerk of this Court within 140 days after the Filing Date.

The page or word limits under this Rule do not include appendices, the cover page, table of contents, table of authorities, and certificate. There shall be no exception to these limits except by permission of this Court on motion for extension of the limits.

(f) *Compliance with Rules for Perfected Appeals.* — Except to the extent that a conflict with this Rule may arise, in which case this Rule shall then be controlling, further proceedings in the case shall conform to the Rules relating to cases in which an appeal has been perfected.

(g) *Varying Procedure to Attain the Ends of Justice.* — This Court may, on motion in a particular case, vary the procedure prescribed by this Rule in order to attain the ends of justice and the purpose of § 17.1-313.

Cross references. — For meaning of "counsel for the appellant" and "clerk of this Court" see Rule 5:1.

Source. — Rule 5:20.

The amendment, effective May 2, 2011, adopted March 1, 2011, inserted "the longer of" in subdivisions (e)(1) through (e)(3).

Michie's Jurisprudence. — For related discussion, see 1B M.J. Appeal and Error, § 145.

CASE NOTES

Where the defendant failed to assign error to the jury's finding of future dangerousness, he cannot challenge on appeal the admission of any evidence relevant to his dangerousness. Sheppard v. Commonwealth, 250 Va. 379, 464 S.E.2d 131 (1995), cert. denied, 517 U.S. 1110, 116 S. Ct. 1332, 134 L. Ed. 2d 483 (1996).

Applied in Rogers v. Commonwealth, 242 Va. 307, 410 S.E.2d 621 (1991); Atkins v. Commonwealth, 257 Va. 160, 510 S.E.2d 445 (1999).

G. PROCEDURE FOLLOWING PERFECTION OF APPEAL.

Rule 5:23. Perfection of Appeal; Docketing.

(a) *Grant of Petition for Appeal.* — Promptly after a petition for appeal has been granted, the clerk of this Court shall certify this action to counsel for the appellant, counsel for the appellee, and the tribunal from which the appeal is taken. The case shall be considered mature for purposes of further proceedings from the date of such certificate.

(b) *Docketing.* — Cases shall be placed on the docket when they mature. Precedence shall be given to the following cases:

(1) review of sentences of death;
(2) criminal cases;
(3) cases from the State Corporation Commission;
(4) cases of original jurisdiction;
(5) cases to be reheard; and
(6) any other cases required by statute to be given precedence.

This Court may, however, for good cause shown or for reasons appearing sufficient to the Court, give preference to other cases.

Cross references. — For meaning of "counsel for the appellant" and "counsel for the appellee," see Rule 5:1.

Source. — Rules 5:30 and 5:32. Cf. Rule 5A:16.

Michie's Jurisprudence. — For related discussion, see 1B M.J. Appeal and Error, §§ 144, 145, 146, 156, 235.

CASE NOTES

This rule relates to the "Court's Argument Docket" on which are listed the cases to be heard at the current session. Fitzgerald v. Holton, 199 Va. 368, 99 S.E.2d 615 (1957).

Rule 5:24. Security for Appeal.

(a) *Compliance With Forms.* — All security for appeal required under Code § 8.01-676.1 shall substantially conform to the forms set forth in the Appendix to this Part Five.

(b) *Procedure Concerning Defects.* — No appeal shall be dismissed because of a defect in any bond or irrevocable letter of credit unless an appellee, within 21 days after the issuance of the certificate pursuant to Rule 5:23, files with the clerk of this Court a statement in writing of the defects in the bond or irrevocable letter of credit, and unless the appellant fails to correct such defects, if any, within 21 days after such statement is filed. If the appellant fails to correct such defects within such period of 21 days, an appellee may move that the appeal be dismissed and it shall be dismissed unless the appellant satisfies this Court that the bond or irrevocable letter of credit, either as originally given or as amended, has been filed in the required form.

Cross references. — For meaning of "clerk of this Court," see Rule 5:1.

Source. — Rule 5:31. Cf. Rule 5A:17.

Michie's Jurisprudence. — For related discussion, see 1B M.J. Appeal and Error, §§ 135, 146, 147, 150.

CASE NOTES

Purpose of rule. — This rule was designed to give the appellant an opportunity to correct a defective bond. Smith v. Jewell Ridge Coal Corp., 203 Va. 499, 125 S.E.2d 175 (1962).

Requirement substantially same as for Court of Appeals. — The appeal bond required by statute and the rules applicable to their filing are substantially the same in the Court of Appeals and the Supreme Court. Duckett v. Duckett, 1 Va. App. 279, 337 S.E.2d 759 (1985).

Failure to file timely appeal bond is jurisdictional defect. — The failure to file an appeal bond within the 15-day period prescribed by Va. Code § 8.01-676.1 B is not such a defect as may be corrected under this rule but is a jurisdictional defect requiring dismissal of an appeal either upon the appellee's motion or the Court's own motion. E.B. Rudiger & Sons v. Hanckel-Smith Sales Co., 230 Va. 255, 335 S.E.2d 257 (1985).

Rule 5:25. Preservation of Issues for Appellate Review.

No ruling of the trial court, disciplinary board, or commission before which the case was initially heard will be considered as a basis for reversal unless an objection was stated with reasonable certainty at the time of the ruling, except for good cause shown or to enable this Court to attain the ends of justice. A mere statement that the judgment or award is contrary to the law and the evidence is not sufficient to preserve the issue for appellate review.

Cross references. — As to assignment of errors, see also Rule 5:17(c).

Source. — Rule 5:21 and Rule 5A:18.

Law Review. — For note on attorney error as "cause" under Wainwright v. Sykes, and on the case for a reasonableness standard after Washington v. Downes, see 67 Va. L. Rev. 415 (1981). For 1991 survey of civil practice and procedure, see 25 U. Rich. L. Rev. 663 (1991). For 1991 survey on criminal law and procedure, see 25 U. Rich. L. Rev. 731 (1991). For a review of civil practice and procedure in Virginia for year 1999, see 33 U. Rich. L. Rev. 801 (1999). For an article, "Final and Interlocutory Appeals in Virginia," see 8 Geo. Mason L. Rev. 337 (1999). For 2003/2004 survey of criminal law and procedure, see 39 U. Rich. L. Rev. 133 (2004). For article reviewing recent developments and changes in legislation, case law, and Virginia Supreme Court Rules affecting civil litigation, see "Civil Practice and Procedure," 40 U. Rich. L. Rev. 95 (2005). For annual survey of Virginia law article, "Civil Practice and Procedure," see 47 U. Rich. L. Rev. 113 (2012).

Michie's Jurisprudence. — For related discussion, see 1B M.J. Appeal and Error, §§ 103 - 106, 111, 113, 115, 116, 198, 210, 213; 2A M.J. Argument and Conduct of Counsel, § 21; 2B M.J. Automobiles, § 117; 5A M.J. Costs, §§ 2, 3; 8A M.J. Exceptions, Bill of, § 1; 10A M.J. Instructions, § 50; 19 M.J. Verdict, § 36.

CASE NOTES

I. General Consideration.
II. Assignments of Error.
III. Objections.
 A. In General.
 B. Exceptions to Requirement for Objection.
  1. Good Cause Shown.
  2. To Attain Ends of Justice.
 C. Admissibility of Evidence.
 D. Instructions.
 E. Improper Remarks and Argument.
 F. Jury Selection, etc.
 G. Other Objections.

I. GENERAL CONSIDERATION.

Purpose of rule. — This rule was adopted not to obstruct petitioners but to make more certain the attainment of the ends of justice. It was intended to put the record in such shape that the case may be heard in the appellate court upon the same record upon which it was heard in the trial court; and to that end to prevent attorneys from dealing unfairly with the trial courts by making objection to matters requiring a ruling of the trial court, without stating the ground of their objection, and, in some instances, when asked to give their reasons, politely informing the court that they prefer to give their reasons in the appellate court. Kercher's Adm'r v.

Richmond, F. & P.R.R., 150 Va. 108, 142 S.E. 393 (1928).

This rule was passed for the protection of the trial court and to expedite the administration of justice. Norfolk S.R.R. v. Lewis, 149 Va. 318, 141 S.E. 228 (1928).

This rule was adopted for the purpose of preventing the setting of traps for trial courts. Keeney v. Commonwealth, 147 Va. 678, 137 S.E. 478 (1927).

This rule was applied in order that the trial judge could rule intelligently and avoid unnecessary appeals, reversals and mistrials. Woodson v. Commonwealth, 211 Va. 285, 176 S.E.2d 818 (1970), cert. denied, 401 U.S. 959, 91 S. Ct. 990, 28 L. Ed. 2d 244 (1971); Reid v. Baumgardner, 217 Va. 769, 232 S.E.2d 778 (1977); Washington v. Downes, 475 F. Supp. 573 (E.D. Va. 1979), overruled on other grounds, Carrier v. Hutto, 724 F.2d 396 (4th Cir. 1983).

This rule exists to protect the trial court from appeals based upon undisclosed grounds, to prevent the setting of traps on appeal, to enable the trial judge to rule intelligently, and to avoid unnecessary reversals and mistrials. Fisher v. Commonwealth, 236 Va. 403, 374 S.E.2d 46 (1988), cert. denied, 490 U.S. 1028, 109 S. Ct. 1766, 104 L. Ed. 2d 201 (1989).

The laudatory purpose behind Rule 5A:18, and this rule, frequently referred to as the contemporaneous objection rules, is to require that objections be promptly brought to the attention of the trial court with sufficient specificity that the alleged error can be dealt with and timely addressed and corrected when necessary and the rules promote orderly and efficient justice and are to be strictly enforced except where the error has resulted in manifest injustice. Brown v. Commonwealth, 8 Va. App. 126, 380 S.E.2d 8 (1989).

This rule and Supreme Court Rule 5A:18 are virtually identical, and both are included as part of the Rules of Virginia Supreme Court; under such circumstances, decisions pertaining to the construction and application of one rule inextricably relate to the other. Johnson v. Commonwealth, No. 0259-91-1, (Ct. of Appeals Nov. 10, 1992).

Rule not limited to evidentiary rulings. — The application of this rule is not limited to evidentiary rulings and includes a party's failure to object to the methodology used by the trial court in assessing damages. Reid v. Boyle, 259 Va. 356, 527 S.E.2d 137 (2000).

If the defect is not jurisdictional, the Supreme Court will not consider it for the first time on appeal. Wackwitz v. Roy, 244 Va. 60, 418 S.E.2d 861 (1992).

Contemporaneous objection rule applied in capital cases. — Although Va. Code § 17-110.1 [see now § 17.1-313] requires that the Supreme Court review every case in which a sentence of death has been entered, mandatory review in the Supreme Court is limited to certain issues. The Court is required to review only whether the sentence of death was imposed under the influence of passion, prejudice or any other arbitrary factor and whether the sentence of death is excessive or disproportionate to the penalty imposed in similar cases, considering both the crime and the defendant. Briley v. Bass, 584 F. Supp. 807 (E.D. Va.), aff'd, 742 F.2d 155 (4th Cir.), cert. denied, 469 U.S. 893, 105 S. Ct. 270, 83 L. Ed. 2d 206 (1984).

Defendant who represents himself is no less bound by the rules of procedure and substantive law than a defendant represented by counsel. Church v. Commonwealth, 230 Va. 208, 335 S.E.2d 823 (1985).

Applied in Barbuto v. Southern Bank, 231 Va. 63, 340 S.E.2d 813 (1986); Lumpkin v. McClamroch, 232 Va. 412, 350 S.E.2d 647 (1986); Litchford v. Hancock, 232 Va. 496, 352 S.E.2d 335 (1987); Stith v. Virginia State Bar, 233 Va. 222, 355 S.E.2d 310 (1987); Payne v. Commonwealth, 233 Va. 460, 357 S.E.2d 500 (1987); Tucker v. Virginia State Bar, 233 Va. 526, 357 S.E.2d 525 (1987); Avocet Dev. Corp. v. McLean Bank, 234 Va. 658, 364 S.E.2d 757 (1988); City of Norfolk v. Ingram, 235 Va. 433, 367 S.E.2d 725 (1988); Smith v. Woodlawn Constr. Co., 235 Va. 424, 368 S.E.2d 699 (1988); Mitchell v. Reardon Smith Line, 236 Va. 212, 372 S.E.2d 395 (1988); Mackall v. Commonwealth, 236 Va. 240, 372 S.E.2d 759 (1988); Bell v. Commonwealth, 236 Va. 298, 374 S.E.2d 13 (1988); Fisher v. Commonwealth, 236 Va. 403, 374 S.E.2d 46 (1988); Ford Motor Co. v. Courtesy Motors, Inc., 237 Va. 187, 375 S.E.2d 362 (1989); Packett v. Herbert, 237 Va. 422, 377 S.E.2d 438 (1989); Edmonds v. Coldwell Banker Residential Real Estate Servs., Inc., 237 Va. 428, 377 S.E.2d 443 (1989); Hoke v. Commonwealth, 237 Va. 303, 377 S.E.2d 595 (1989); Crone v. Richmond Newspapers, Inc., 238 Va. 248, 384 S.E.2d 77 (1989); Mastin v. Theirjung, 238 Va. 434, 384 S.E.2d 86 (1989); Lucas v. HCMF Corp., 238 Va. 446, 384 S.E.2d 92 (1989); Morrison v. Bestler, 239 Va. 166, 387 S.E.2d 753 (1990); Cheng v. Commonwealth, 240 Va. 26, 393 S.E.2d 599 (1990); Spencer v. Commonwealth, 240 Va. 78, 393 S.E.2d 609 (1990); Harris-Teeter, Inc. v. Burroughs, 241 Va. 1, 399 S.E.2d 801 (1991); Stockton v. Commonwealth, 241 Va. 192, 402 S.E.2d 196 (1991); Scott v. Greater Richmond Transit Co., 241 Va. 300, 402 S.E.2d 214 (1991); Hack v. Nester, 241 Va. 499, 404 S.E.2d 42 (1990); Jimenez v. Commonwealth, 241 Va. 244, 402 S.E.2d 678 (1991); Medlar v. Mohan, 242 Va. 162, 409 S.E.2d 123 (1991); Richardson v. Richardson, 242 Va. 242, 409 S.E.2d 148 (1991); Yeatts v. Commonwealth, 242 Va. 121, 410 S.E.2d 254 (1991); George v. Commonwealth, 242 Va. 264, 411 S.E.2d 12 (1991); Wackwitz v. Roy, 244 Va. 60, 418 S.E.2d 861 (1992); Brown v. Brown, 244 Va. 319, 422 S.E.2d 375 (1992); Kroger Co. v. APCO, 244 Va. 560, 422 S.E.2d 757 (1992); International Union, UMW v. Covenant Coal Corp., 244 Va. 417, 423 S.E.2d 197 (1992); Swann v. Commonwealth, 247 Va. 222, 441 S.E.2d 195 (1994); Buck v. Commonwealth, 247 Va. 449, 443 S.E.2d 414 (1994); Rodriguez v. Commonwealth, 18 Va. App. 277, 443 S.E.2d 419 (1994); Hamilton Dev. Co. v. Broad Rock Club, Inc., 248 Va. 40, 445 S.E.2d 140 (1994); Breard v. Commonwealth, 248 Va. 68, 445 S.E.2d 670 (1994); Sheppard v. Commonwealth, 250 Va. 379, 464 S.E.2d 131 (1995); Hughes v. Cole, 251 Va. 3, 465 S.E.2d 820 (1996); Swiss Re Life Co. Am. v. Gross, 479 S.E.2d 857 (1997); Angstadt v. Atlantic Mut. Ins. Co., 254 Va. 286, 492 S.E.2d 118 (1997); Fairfax Hosp. v. Curtis, 254 Va. 437, 492 S.E.2d 642 (1997); Cardinal Dev. Co. v. Stanley Constr. Co., 255 Va. 300, 497 S.E.2d 847 (1998); Commonwealth v. Jenkins, 255 Va. 516, 499 S.E.2d 263 (1998); Lilly v. Commonwealth, 255 Va. 558, 499 S.E.2d 522 (1998); Kelly v. Carrico, 256 Va. 282, 504 S.E.2d 368 (1998); Martin

& Martin, Inc. v. Bradley Enters., Inc., 256 Va. 288, 504 S.E.2d 849 (1998); Buck v. Jordan, 256 Va. 535, 508 S.E.2d 880 (1998); Bramblett v. Commonwealth, 257 Va. 263, 513 S.E.2d 400 (1999); Cherrix v. Commonwealth, 257 Va. 292, 513 S.E.2d 642; Lansdowne Dev. Co., L.L.C. v. Xerox Realty Corp., 257 Va. 392, 514 S.E.2d 157 (1999); Nichols v. Kaiser Found. Health Plan of Mid-Atl. States, Inc., 257 Va. 491, 514 S.E.2d 608 (1999); Phillips v. Commonwealth, 257 Va. 548, 514 S.E.2d 340 (1999); Weeks v. Angelone, 176 F.3d 249 (4th Cir. 1999); Moore v. Commonwealth, 259 Va. 405, 527 S.E.2d 415 (2000); Emmett v. Commonwealth, 264 Va. 364, 569 S.E.2d 39, 2002 Va. LEXIS 102 (2002); Wolfe v. Commonwealth, 265 Va. 193, 576 S.E.2d 471, 2003 Va. LEXIS 32; Blake Constr. Co./Poole & Kent v. Upper Occoquan Sewage Auth., 266 Va. 564, 587 S.E.2d 711, 2003 Va. LEXIS 108 (2003); Williams v. Gloucester Sheriff's Dep't, 266 Va. 409, 587 S.E.2d 546, 2003 Va. LEXIS 109 (2003); Commonwealth v. Hudson, 265 Va. 505, 578 S.E.2d 781, 2003 Va. LEXIS 49 (2003); Pulte Home Corp. v. Parex, Inc., 265 Va. 518, 579 S.E.2d 188, 2003 Va. LEXIS 51 (2003); Blevins v. Commonwealth, 267 Va. 291, 590 S.E.2d 365, 2004 Va. LEXIS 23 (2004); Elliott v. Commonwealth, 267 Va. 464, 593 S.E.2d 263, 2004 Va. LEXIS 41 (2004); Jerman v. Dir., Dep't of Corr., 267 Va. 432, 593 S.E.2d 255, 2004 Va. LEXIS 43 (2004); Elliott v. Commonwealth, 267 Va. 396, 593 S.E.2d 270, 2004 Va. LEXIS 44 (2004); Lewis v. Commonwealth, 267 Va. 302, 593 S.E.2d 220, 2004 Va. LEXIS 47; Hix v. Commonwealth, 270 Va. 335, 619 S.E.2d 80, 2005 Va. LEXIS 84 (2005); Montgomery v. McDaniel, 271 Va. 465, 628 S.E.2d 529, 2006 Va. LEXIS 41 (2006); Gunn v. Commonwealth, 272 Va. 580, 637 S.E.2d 324, 2006 Va. LEXIS 116 (2006); Nusbaum v. Berlin, 273 Va. 385, 641 S.E.2d 494, 2007 Va. LEXIS 26 (2007); Teleguz v. Commonwealth, 273 Va. 458, 643 S.E.2d 708, 2007 Va. LEXIS 64 (2007); McDonald v. Commonwealth, 274 Va. 249, 645 S.E.2d 918, 2007 Va. LEXIS 87 (2007); Elliott v. Warden of the Sussex I State Prison, 274 Va. 598, 652 S.E.2d 465, 2007 Va. LEXIS 137 (2007); Marcus, Santoro & Kozak, P.C. v. Wu, 274 Va. 743, 652 S.E.2d 777, 2007 Va. LEXIS 135 (2007); Marshall v. N. Va. Transp. Auth., 275 Va. 419, 657 S.E.2d 71, 2008 Va. LEXIS 25 (2008); Ayala v. Aggressive Towing & Transp., Inc., 276 Va. 169, 661 S.E.2d 480, 2008 Va. LEXIS 79 (2008); Levisa Coal Co. v. Consolidation Coal Co., 276 Va. 44, 662 S.E.2d 44, 2008 Va. LEXIS 77 (2008); Hawthorne v. VanMarter, 279 Va. 566, 692 S.E.2d 226, 2010 Va. LEXIS 54 (2010); Andrews v. Commonwealth, 280 Va. 231, 699 S.E.2d 237, 2010 Va. LEXIS 239 (2010); Blanton v. Commonwealth, 280 Va. 447, 699 S.E.2d 279, 2010 Va. LEXIS 237 (2010); Falls Church v. Protestant Episcopal Church in the United States, 285 Va. 651, 740 S.E.2d 530, 2013 Va. LEXIS 48 (2013).

II. ASSIGNMENTS OF ERROR.

Purpose of assignments of error is to point out the errors with reasonable certainty in order to direct the court and opposing counsel to the points on which appellant intends to ask a reversal of the judgment, and to limit discussion of these points. Harlow v. Commonwealth, 195 Va. 269, 77 S.E.2d 851 (1953).

The purpose of assignments of error is to point out the specific error committed by the trial court. Counsel should be required to "lay his finger on the error." Omohundro v. County of Arlington, 194 Va. 773, 75 S.E.2d 496 (1953).

Purpose of this rule is that the trial judge may be informed of the precise points of objection in the minds of counsel, so that he may be advised and rule intelligently. It is a salutary requirement, and must be adhered to unless the exceptions engrafted upon it apply. Ross v. Schneider, 181 Va. 931, 27 S.E.2d 154 (1943); Rook v. Atlantic Coast Line R.R., 184 Va. 670, 36 S.E.2d 559 (1946); Harlow v. Commonwealth, 195 Va. 269, 77 S.E.2d 851 (1953).

Court can consider only such errors as are presented to it by appropriate assignments in error. Wash v. Holland, 166 Va. 45, 183 S.E. 236 (1936).

Unassigned error not considered even though clear from record. — Even though the record on appeal clearly disclosed all of the defects the prisoner alleged in respect to his conviction, the Supreme Court would not have considered unassigned errors in passing on the writ of error. Ferguson v. Cox, 464 F.2d 461 (4th Cir. 1972).

Assignments of error argued before the Supreme Court which were not properly saved under this rule will be ignored. West v. L. Bromm Baking Co., 166 Va. 530, 186 S.E. 291 (1936). See also Van Dyke v. Commonwealth, 196 Va. 1039, 86 S.E.2d 848 (1955).

"Other errors apparent upon the record" is insufficient assignment. — Assignment of error which read, "3. Other errors apparent upon the record," was indefinite and insufficient and did not comply with this rule and would not be considered. Carr v. Patram, 193 Va. 604, 70 S.E.2d 308 (1952).

Failure to invoke privilege in trial court. — Where the defendant assigned error to the court's admission of evidence in violation of the interspousal confidential communication privilege, but that privilege was not invoked in the trial court the Supreme Court did not consider it as a ground for reversal on appeal. Church v. Commonwealth, 230 Va. 208, 335 S.E.2d 823 (1985).

Witness immunity. — Defendant's argument that the trial court's decision to grant immunity to a witness undermined his ability to cross-examine the witness, was actually a claim under the Sixth Amendment Confrontation Clause. As such, defendant's general assertion of a due process violation in the trial court was insufficient to preserve the argument for appeal. Juniper v. Commonwealth, 271 Va. 362, 626 S.E.2d 383, 2006 Va. LEXIS 29 (2006).

Preservation for review. — Defendant's sole contention at trial for his motions for the Commonwealth of Virginia to produce its files from his prior criminal convictions and of unadjudicated bad acts that would be referenced in the penalty phase was that granting the motions would save the Commonwealth money. As this was not the argument that defendant made on appeal of the court's rulings on those motions, consideration of either assignment of error regarding the motions was barred. Juniper v. Commonwealth, 271 Va. 362, 626 S.E.2d 383, 2006 Va. LEXIS 29 (2006).

Insurer's claims that the statute of limitations was tolled for a minor or that a five-year statute of limitations governed the parents' claims was barred under Va. Sup. Ct. R. 5:25 as: (1) the insurer did not have greater rights than its insured; (2) in its motion for judgment and first amended motion for judgment the insurer did not allege that the child assigned the child's rights to the insurer; and (3) the insurer only assigned error to the ruling that the statute of limitations barred the insurer's claims as subrogee. Peerless Ins. Co. v. County of Fairfax, 274 Va. 236, 645 S.E.2d 478, 2007 Va. LEXIS 78 (2007).

Because some of a corporation's claims on appeal from an order entering a default judgment against it, and refusing to set the same aside, were either not plead to the court below or were not supported by the record, which was incomplete on its face, the lower court's orders were affirmed. Prince Seating Corp. v. Rabideau, 275 Va. 468, 659 S.E.2d 305, 2008 Va. LEXIS 45 (2008).

Nephews' argument that the remainder interests of a grantor's siblings vested at the grantor's death was not procedurally barred because the requirements of Va. Sup. Ct. R. 5:25 were satisfied when the circuit court was able to rule intelligently on the same substantive argument that the nephews advanced on appeal; in the answer filed in the circuit court, the nephews stated that the remainder interests of the grantor's surviving siblings vested upon the grantor's death, and although the nephews did not use the term "vest" in their trial memorandum later filed with the circuit court, they alleged that the trust language unambiguously provided that if a sibling survived the grantor, then that sibling's share would not lapse but would be paid to the sibling or to the sibling's heirs upon the death of the husband. Harbour v. Suntrust Bank, 278 Va. 514, 685 S.E.2d 838, 2009 Va. LEXIS 101 (2009).

Supreme court would not consider on appeal landowners' challenge to an historic district ordinance on the ground that it was unconstitutionally vague both facially and as applied because they did not collectively preserve any objection. Covel v. Town of Vienna, 280 Va. 151, 694 S.E.2d 609, 2010 Va. LEXIS 75 (2010).

Tenant's argument was waived because nothing in the record indicated that the trial court was made aware that the tenant's motion for reconsideration and memorandum in support thereof were filed, and thus, the statutory requirement of subsection A of § 8.01-384 was not met; because there was no evidence in the record that the trial court had the opportunity to rule upon the argument the tenant presented on appeal, the case could not be heard in the supreme court upon the same record upon which it was heard in the trial court and, therefore, the purpose of Va. Sup. Ct. R. 5:25 was defeated. Brandon v. Cox, 284 Va. 251, 726 S.E.2d 298, 2012 Va. LEXIS 123 (2012).

III. OBJECTIONS.

A. In General.

Purpose of the requirement that grounds for objections be stated with reasonable certainty is to give the trial court an opportunity to rule intelligently and avoid unnecessary appeals, reversals and mistrials. Reid v. Baumgardner, 217 Va. 769, 232 S.E.2d 778 (1977); Marshall v. Goughnour, 221 Va. 265, 269 S.E.2d 801 (1980).

The purpose of this rule was to protect the trial court and to that end to compel litigants to present to the appellate court the same objections urged upon the lower court. Shocket v. Silberman, 209 Va. 490, 165 S.E.2d 414 (1969).

The object of this salutary rule is to compel litigants to present to the Supreme Court the same objections urged upon the trial court. Kelly v. Schneller, 148 Va. 573, 139 S.E. 275 (1927); Kessler v. Friedman, 152 Va. 446, 147 S.E. 201 (1929).

The purpose of this rule is to avoid unnecessary appeals by affording the trial judge an opportunity to rule intelligently on objections. State Hwy. Comm'r v. Easley, 215 Va. 197, 207 S.E.2d 870 (1974).

It is due to the trial court that the grounds of objections to be specified, so that the opposing party may have an opportunity to meet the objection. Hilton v. Fayen, 196 Va. 860, 86 S.E.2d 40 (1955).

Rule must be adhered to unless stated exceptions apply. — The trial judge must be informed of the precise points of objection in the minds of counsel so that he may rule intelligently, thereby avoiding delay and the expense incident to appeals, reversals and new trials upon grounds of objection which might have been obviated or corrected in the trial court. Therefore the rule must be adhered to unless the exceptions therein stated apply. Gooch v. City of Lynchburg, 201 Va. 172, 110 S.E.2d 236 (1959); Reil v. Commonwealth, 210 Va. 369, 171 S.E.2d 162 (1969); Williamson v. Commonwealth, 211 Va. 57, 175 S.E.2d 285 (1970).

Supreme Court will not notice error which has been invited by the party seeking to take advantage thereof on appeal. Saunders v. Commonwealth, 211 Va. 399, 177 S.E.2d 637 (1970).

Supreme Court is not disposed to relax this rule requiring that objections to all matters requiring a ruling of the trial court shall state with reasonable certainty the objection. Keeney v. Commonwealth, 147 Va. 678, 137 S.E. 478 (1927).

Rule constitutes adequate and independent state ground upon which federal review may be precluded. Weeks v. Angelone, 4 F. Supp. 2d 497 (E.D. Va. 1998).

Where defendant elected to act as his own counsel, but trial court appointed standby counsel to aid in his defense and defendant actively represented himself in substantial portions of the pretrial proceedings and at trial, his argument that the court should not require compliance with the contemporaneous objection rule, was rejected. O'Dell v. Commonwealth, 234 Va. 672, 364 S.E.2d 491, cert. denied, 488 U.S. 871, 109 S. Ct. 186, 102 L. Ed. 2d 154 (1988).

Matters urged for the first time on appeal cannot be considered. Southern Ry. v. Cohen Weenen & Co., 156 Va. 313, 157 S.E. 563 (1931).

As with all nonjurisdictional issues, a search and seizure question cannot be raised for the first time on appeal. Bunch v. Commonwealth, 225 Va. 423, 304 S.E.2d 271 (1983), cert. denied, 464 U.S. 977, 104 S. Ct. 414, 78 L. Ed. 2d 352 (1984).

Requirement of timely objection would otherwise be meaningless. — The requirement of timely objection under this rule would be meaningless and rendered a nullity if objections could be raised and considered for the first time on appeal. Berger v. Commonwealth, 217 Va. 332, 228 S.E.2d 559 (1976).

Litigant cannot specify objection for first time in Supreme Court. — A litigant will not be permitted to make a general objection to the overruling of his general motion to strike evidence in the trial court and then to specify his objections for the first time in the Supreme Court. Varner v. White, 149 Va. 177, 140 S.E. 128 (1927).

Argument was procedurally barred from appellate review. — Where husband never objected that trial court's rulings, on issue of whether contract was to be construed under New York law, were not based upon a consideration of New York law, and since he failed to raise any objection either during the hearing or in the final order, his argument was procedurally barred from appellate review. Chattin v. Chattin, 245 Va. 302, 427 S.E.2d 347 (1993).

Defendant's claims that the medical examiner's trial testimony differed from his pretrial testimony and that this testimony invaded the province of the jury were procedurally defaulted where he failed to object at trial. Barnabei v. Commonwealth, 252 Va. 161, 477 S.E.2d 270 (1996), cert. denied, 520 U.S. 1224, 117 S. Ct. 1724, 137 L. Ed. 2d 845 (1997).

Since defendant's challenge to the use of lethal injection, contending that it is cruel and unusual punishment, was not made in the trial court, it would not be considered for the first time on appeal. Mickens v. Commonwealth, 252 Va. 315, 478 S.E.2d 302 (1996), cert. denied, 520 U.S. 1269, 117 S. Ct. 2442, 138 L. Ed. 2d 202 (1997).

In a medical malpractice lawsuit regarding hip reconstruction surgery, where the patient objected at trial that certain testimony from a treating radiologist did not comply with subsection B of § 8.01-399, pursuant to Va. Sup. Ct. R. 5:25, the patient was barred from arguing on appeal that this same testimony was inadmissible habit testimony since this argument raised a new challenge to the testimony that was not addressed by the trial court. Graham v. Cook, 278 Va. 233, 682 S.E.2d 535, 2009 Va. LEXIS 93 (2009).

In a capital case in which defendant argued that the circuit court erred in its response to a question from the jury made during the sentencing phase, but he had not raised the argument in trial, the assignment of error was procedurally defaulted, and the appellate court would not consider it. Prieto v. Commonwealth, 278 Va. 366, 682 S.E.2d 910, 2009 Va. LEXIS 94 (2009), cert. denied, 177 L. Ed. 2d 332, 2010 U.S. LEXIS 4926 (U.S. 2010).

Defendant could not invoke on appeal a United States Supreme Court ruling regarding searches incident to arrests because defendant did not object to the search of defendant's vehicle incident to defendant's arrest below. McGhee v. Commonwealth, 280 Va. 620, 701 S.E.2d 58, 2010 Va. LEXIS 260 (2010).

This rule is a contemporaneous objection rule for the purposes of applying Wainwright v. Sykes, 433 U.S. 72, 97 S. Ct. 2497, 53 L. Ed. 2d 594 (1977), which held that a failure to comply with a state contemporaneous objection rule will foreclose federal habeas review unless the petitioner can show "cause" and "prejudice" in connection with his failure to object. Washington v. Downes, 475 F. Supp. 573 (E.D. Va. 1979), overruled on other grounds, Carrier v. Hutto, 724 F.2d 396 (4th Cir. 1983).

Nature of and practice under a state's contemporaneous objection rule is one for the state courts to apply under state law. Graves v. Garraghty, 618 F. Supp. 1348 (E.D. Va. 1985).

Objections not in conformity with contemporaneous objection rule may not be raised on habeas corpus. — Petitioner was barred from raising a claim of violation of his Miranda rights through the vehicle of a federal habeas petition when he had not complied with the State's contemporaneous objection rule at trial to perfect that claim unless a failure to adjudicate the claim through the federal habeas corpus vehicle would result in a miscarriage of justice to the criminal defendant. Conquest v. Mitchell, 618 F.2d 1053 (4th Cir. 1980).

Where defendant objected to the introduction of his confession at trial on the grounds that it was not turned over prior to trial pursuant to his discovery motion, but on a habeas petition in federal court instead argues that his fifth amendment rights were violated by the introduction of the testimony, he did not substantially comply with Virginia's contemporaneous objection rule and his objection in no way could have given the trial court notice that a fifth amendment issue was being raised and defendant is precluded from raising the fifth amendment argument pursuant to this rule. Conquest v. Mitchell, 618 F.2d 1053 (4th Cir. 1980).

Where the defendant's attorney did not object to any of the trial court's instructions despite the fact that Rule 3A:16(c) requires that objections to instructions be made before the court instructs the jury, the failure of counsel to comply with this procedural rule precluded appellate review of the instructions since this rule provided that the Supreme Court of Virginia will not notice any objection requiring a ruling of the trial court unless the ground of objection was stated with reasonable certainty at the time of the ruling. These rules have been consistently interpreted together with their predecessors, as requiring a contemporaneous objection to a trial court's instructions. Therefore the failure of counsel to comply with the Virginia Rules bars him from habeas corpus relief. Frazier v. Weatherholtz, 572 F.2d 994 (4th Cir.), cert. denied, 439 U.S. 876, 99 S. Ct. 215, 58 L. Ed. 2d 191 (1978).

A federal habeas corpus petitioner's failure to comply with the contemporaneous objection requirement embodied in Rule 5:21 is a legitimate ground for the application of the procedural default doctrine to bar a federal court's consideration of the petition's constitutional claims. Whitley v. Bair, 802 F.2d 1487 (4th Cir. 1986), cert. denied, 480 U.S. 951, 107 S. Ct. 1618, 94 L. Ed. 2d 802 (1987).

But habeas corpus not automatically precluded. — Wainwright v. Sykes, 433 U.S. 72, 97 S. Ct. 2497, 53 L. Ed. 2d 714 (1977), does not automatically preclude consideration in federal habeas corpus of alleged constitutional error not objected to prior to jury deliberation and verdict. Baker v. Muncy, 619 F.2d 327 (4th Cir. 1980).

Habeas corpus not precluded where procedural bar not applied. — Where the Supreme Court of Virginia declined to apply their own procedural bar, in that it disregarded any failure contemporaneously to object at the trial level, the doctrine that such failure to object precluded federal habeas review of petitioner's claims was inapplicable. Graves v. Garraghty, 618 F. Supp. 1348 (E.D. Va. 1985).

Defendant's failure to appeal from the circuit court's ruling on procedural default deprived the Virginia Supreme Court of the opportunity to rule on the merits of his claims. Such failure constituted a violation of the requirements of this rule, which applies to appeals of all Virginia cases, civil or criminal, and constituted a procedural default sufficient to preclude federal court review of the merits of those claims on which the circuit court declared defendant to have defaulted. Whitley v. Bair, 802 F.2d 1487 (4th Cir. 1986), cert. denied, 480 U.S. 951, 107 S. Ct. 1618, 94 L. Ed. 2d 802 (1987).

Inadvertent failure of counsel to raise claim of error is not cause for procedural default. — A federal habeas petitioner cannot show cause for a procedural default by establishing that competent defense counsel inadvertently failed to raise the substantive claim of error rather than deliberately withholding it for tactical reasons. Murray v. Carrier, 477 U.S. 478, 106 S. Ct. 2639, 91 L. Ed. 2d 397 (1986).

Statute on dispute resolution not cited. — Although admission of the evidence challenged in the two assignments of error relying on § 8.01-576.10 was the subject of several objections by plaintiff's counsel during the hearing, not once did counsel cite to the trial judge or rely on § 8.01-576.10, or any other statute dealing with dispute resolution proceedings. Thus, the trial court was never afforded the opportunity to address and rule on the issues that the plaintiff now raises, and the state supreme court will not consider them for the first time on appeal. Snyder-Falkinham v. Stockburger, 249 Va. 376, 457 S.E.2d 36 (1995).

Objection to ruling of court made at time of argument on motion to set aside verdict rather than at time of ruling is too late for correction of error, thus not sufficient to preserve issue on appeal. Ryan v. Commonwealth, 219 Va. 439, 247 S.E.2d 698 (1978).

Rule should not be applied when character of objection is patent. — This is a salutary rule and requires that the ground of objection be stated with reasonable certainty in the trial court. There is no necessity to apply the rule where the character of the objection is perfectly patent. Solomon v. Atlantic Coast Line R.R., 187 Va. 240, 46 S.E.2d 369 (1948).

This rule, requiring that objections shall state with reasonable certainty the ground of such objections, should not be applied where the character of the objection is perfectly patent. Smith v. Commonwealth, 165 Va. 776, 182 S.E. 124 (1935).

Under this rule, it is not necessary that reason be assigned for every objection taken, if the necessary reason would be immediately apparent. Evans v. Commonwealth, 161 Va. 992, 170 S.E. 756 (1933).

The chief reason for the adoption of this rule was to compel litigants to make their objections before the trial courts, and to prevent the trial in the Supreme Court of a different case from that presented to the trial court, but it was not intended that a strict compliance with the letter of the rule should be necessary to enable a litigant to ask the consideration by the Supreme Court of an objection which was plainly and manifestly made in the trial court, and the grounds of which appear from the ruling thereon by the trial court. Levine v. Levine, 144 Va. 330, 132 S.E. 320 (1926).

Obviously the reason for the provision in this rule that the reasons for objection shall be stated with reasonable certainty is to acquaint the judge whose ruling is sought with the precise legal questions involved. Where the vices urged to an instruction are perfectly patent, and there can be no doubt of the meaning of the instruction as related to the evidence, it would appear to be needless to assign them in order to observe a meticulous adherence to the rule. Davis v. Commonwealth, 161 Va. 1037, 171 S.E. 598 (1933).

Notice of substance of objection sufficient. — Where an objection could have been more definite and complete, but it seemed to have been sufficiently broad to have given the trial court notice of the substance of the objection, there was a substantial compliance with this rule. Overton v. Slaughter, 190 Va. 172, 56 S.E.2d 358 (1949).

If an objection is raised in such a manner so as to give the trial court notice of its substance, the rule will be deemed complied with even though the objection could have been more definitively given. Conquest v. Mitchell, 618 F.2d 1053 (4th Cir. 1980).

This rule contains no requirement that formal exceptions, or the absence thereof, be stated in the final order. — Nor is such a requirement implicit in the purpose of this rule. State Hwy. Comm'r v. Easley, 215 Va. 197, 207 S.E.2d 870 (1974).

Contention made and abandoned in trial court. — In a prosecution for larceny, defendant moved to strike the evidence on the ground that the corpus delicti had not been proven. During his argument on this motion, counsel for defendant abandoned the contention and no action was taken by the trial court. Defendant assigned as error the action of the trial court in refusing to sustain the motion to strike on the ground that the Commonwealth had failed to prove the corpus delicti. Since the defendant failed to comply with the provisions of this rule, there was no merit in the assignment of error. Latham v. Commonwealth, 184 Va. 934, 37 S.E.2d 36 (1946).

Renewal of objection by counsel. — Objection was timely made but overruled. Counsel should have insisted upon stating at that time the ground for his objection. Although he failed to do so, he subsequently renewed the objection, specified the reason for it, and requested the trial court to direct the jury to disregard the improper argument. These acts, while coming late in the proceedings, came soon enough to permit corrective action to be taken by the court. If the court had failed to understand the basis for the original objection, the explication cleared up any misunderstanding and afforded an opportunity for reconsideration and reversal of its earlier ruling. Reid v. Baumgardner, 217 Va. 769, 232 S.E.2d 778 (1977).

General sufficiency objection held inadequate in multiple crimes cases. — Where a criminal case is prosecuted on a theory of multiple rather than single offenses, a general sufficiency objection does not, by itself raise the issue of whether the defendant was properly convicted of one crime only, or of multiple crimes. Floyd v. Commonwealth, 219 Va. 575, 249 S.E.2d 171 (1978).

Failure to comply with rule. — Where no reason was assigned for the original objection and no ruling thereon was made by the trial court, there was a failure to comply with the rule. Woodson v. Commonwealth, 211 Va. 285, 176 S.E.2d 818 (1970), cert. denied, 401 U.S. 959, 91 S. Ct. 990, 28 L. Ed. 2d 244 (1971).

Pursuant to the rule, the consistent application of the rule advanced its purpose of avoiding unnecessary reversals and retrials; defendant's failure to state a timely objection to the circuit court's instruction barred his challenge to that instruction on appeal. Commonwealth v. Jerman, 263 Va. 88, 556 S.E.2d 754, 2002 Va. LEXIS 17 (2002).

Defendant's assignment of error that the trial court erred in the response it gave to the jury concerning the possibility of parole for a second-degree murder conviction was waived, as defendant neither objected at trial nor proffered a correction. Hopkins v. Commonwealth, No. 0208-02-3, 2003 Va. App. LEXIS 230 (Ct. of Appeals Apr. 22, 2003).

Failure to preserve issues. — Trucking company and its driver failed to preserve their arguments for review because they failed to make proper objections or offers of proof during the trial. Rose v. Jaques, 268 Va. 137, 597 S.E.2d 64, 2004 Va. LEXIS 92 (2004).

Defendant's failure to raise his public confidence argument at trial regarding the seating of the jurors barred consideration of the same on appeal, pursuant to Va. Sup. Ct. R. 5A:18 and 5:25; moreover, it was fundamentally unfair to overturn the valid decision of a jury for reasons never given to the trial court and which do not go to the merits of the case or the actual bias of a juror. Townsend v. Commonwealth, 270 Va. 325, 619 S.E.2d 71, 2005 Va. LEXIS 81 (2005), cert. denied, 547 U.S. 1008, 126 S. Ct. 1477, 164 L. Ed. 2d 257, 2006 U.S. LEXIS 2118 (2006).

In an action to recover a security deposit, a tenant did not sufficiently preserve the tenant's argument for appeal because, while the tenant's motion for reconsideration raised the argument, nothing in the record showed the tenant sought or received a ruling, and merely filing the motion in the clerk's office was insufficient, since the record did not show the trial court had a chance to rule, as the tenant's written statement of facts did not mention the motion or a ruling thereon, so nothing showed the trial court knew of the motion, and subsection A of § 8.01-384's requirement to make known to the court a party's objections and the grounds therefor was not met, nor could it be said that the case could be heard on appeal on the same record as in the trial court, defeating Va. Sup. Ct. R. 5:25's purpose. Brandon v. Cox, 284 Va. 251, 736 S.E.2d 695, 2012 Va. LEXIS 179 (2012).

In an action to recover a security deposit, a tenant did not sufficiently preserve the tenant's argument for appeal because the tenant did not preserve the issue at trial since neither the tenant's written statement of facts nor the trial court's order stated what argument was made at trial or what ruling was made. Brandon v. Cox, 284 Va. 251, 736 S.E.2d 695, 2012 Va. LEXIS 179 (2012).

Petition filed after rulings made and record complete. — It is not a compliance with the rule for the petitioner, after the rulings are made and record completed, to file a petition setting forth the reasons for his objections to such rulings. The trial court must have a fair opportunity to pass upon the grounds of the objection. Kessler v. Friedman, 152 Va. 446, 147 S.E. 201 (1929).

Certification by trial court that objections not made at trial. — When the trial court certifies that the objections relied upon in the Supreme Court were not made during the course of the trial, this precludes a consideration of the matters objected to. Pflaster v. Commonwealth, 149 Va. 457, 141 S.E. 115 (1928).

Failure to put court on notice as to new objection. — Where the jury made subsequent recourse to the transcript as an exhibit, no error was preserved to the trial court's ruling with respect to procedure, and defense counsel's reference to his "earlier objection" and his expressed wish that it be "continuing" failed to put the trial court on fair notice that a new ground of objection was being raised. Fisher v. Commonwealth, 236 Va. 403, 374 S.E.2d 46 (1988), cert. denied, 490 U.S. 1028, 109 S. Ct. 1766, 104 L. Ed. 2d 201 (1989).

Waiver of objection. — Objection to the trial court's ruling must be made at the time the occasion arises; otherwise the point is waived. Russo v. Commonwealth, 207 Va. 251, 148 S.E.2d 820 (1966), cert. denied, 386 U.S. 909, 87 S. Ct. 855, 17 L. Ed. 2d 782 (1967); Callands v. Commonwealth, 208 Va. 340, 157 S.E.2d 198 (1967); Witt v. Merricks, 210 Va. 70, 168 S.E.2d 517 (1969).

Although defendant objected to the court's rulings during voir dire of prospective juror, he voiced no objection when the court seated juror on the jury panel, therefore, defendant waived the objections he made during the voir dire of this rule. Spencer v. Commonwealth, 238 Va. 295, 384 S.E.2d 785 (1989), cert. denied, 493 U.S. 1093, 110 S. Ct. 1171, 107 L. Ed. 2d 1073 (1990).

Although defendants complained that, because they never learned of the trial date, they had no opportunity to assert valid defenses to several items of damages that were ultimately awarded as part of the final judgment; on its face, the notice of appeal indicated that, at least by May 11, 1993, the defendants had knowledge of the trial court's order before it became final on May 12, 1993. Although the defendants could have brought their objections to the trial court's attention, they failed to do so. Faizi-Balal Int'l Corp. v. Burka, 248 Va. 219, 445 S.E.2d 125 (1994).

A motion for a mistrial must be made promptly; otherwise, the claim is deemed to have been waived. Breard v. Commonwealth, 248 Va. 68, 445 S.E.2d 670, cert. denied, 513 U.S. 971, 115 S. Ct. 442, 130 L. Ed. 2d 353 (1994).

Revocation of defendant's sentence was properly based on a nunc pro tunc sentencing order (which was signed at the revocation hearing because the trial court had forgotten to sign it when the defendant's sentence was first pronounced) since the defendant waived, and was procedurally barred under Rules 5:25 and 5A:18 from making his argument that the order was invalid, because he had admitted the validity of the original sentence pronouncement. Jefferson v. Commonwealth, 269 Va. 136, 607 S.E.2d 107, 2005 Va. LEXIS 15 (2005).

Defendant argued that his death sentences should have been reversed because Virginia's lethal injection process would expose him to unnecessary pain thereby violating his right against cruel and unusual punishment; however, defendant never raised the motion again at any point before, during, or after the trial. Thus, the circuit court never ruled on the motion concerning the constitutionality of execution by lethal injection, and defendant's failure to obtain a ruling by the circuit court on the matter meant that he has waived the issue on appeal. Morva v. Commonwealth, 278 Va. 329, 683 S.E.2d 553, 2009 Va. LEXIS 84 (2009), cert. denied, 131 S. Ct. 97, 178 L. Ed. 2d 61, 2010 U.S. LEXIS 5806 (U.S. 2010).

Where counsel endorsed final order as "seen." — Where party did not object to entry of the final order and counsel for party merely endorsed the order as "Seen," party had not preserved for appeal the issues he raised. Langley v. Meredith, 237 Va. 55, 376 S.E.2d 519 (1989).

B. Exceptions to Requirement for Objection.

1. Good Cause Shown.

Bar of prosecution under another statute, provided by § 19.2-294, cannot be raised for the first time on appeal in the absence of good cause shown. Owens v. Commonwealth, 147 Va. 624, 136 S.E. 765 (1927).

2. To Attain Ends of Justice.

Requirements of the rule are not inflexible, and may be relaxed to enable the Supreme Court to attain the ends of justice. Shocket v. Silberman, 209 Va. 490, 165 S.E.2d 414 (1969).

Exception applicable only when rule alone would prevent reaching error. — The exception which permits the Supreme Court to consider error, notwithstanding the lack of proper objection, in order "to attain the ends of justice" should be applied only where the requirements of the rule alone stand in the way of reaching the alleged error. If there is a substantive rule of law barring reversal in any event, the exception need not be invoked, since the ends of justice are attained by the application of such substantive rules in a given case. Saunders v. Commonwealth, 211 Va. 399, 177 S.E.2d 637 (1970).

Exception justified only when error is clear, substantial, and material. — Although both this section and Supreme Court Rule 5:25 provide exceptions to accommodate "good cause" and "obtain the ends of justice," this is justified only when the record reflects error which is clear, substantial, and material. Johnson v. Commonwealth, No. 0259-91-1, (Ct. of Appeals Nov. 10, 1992).

Assignment considered where court and opposing counsel knew grounds for objection though not stated. — On appeal from a conviction of driving an automobile while under the influence of intoxicants, defendant assigned error to the refusal of the court to strike the evidence of a physician who had testified that he made an analysis of a sample of blood allegedly taken from defendant. According to the record the grounds for the motion were not stated. But since it was apparent that the court and counsel for the city knew this ground to be that the sample was not properly identified, this assignment was considered to attain the ends of justice. Newton v. City of Richmond, 198 Va. 869, 96 S.E.2d 775 (1957).

Court does not notice incorrect statements of the applicable laws, except in those rare instances when it is necessary to enable the court to attain the ends of justice. Ball v. Commonwealth, 221 Va. 754, 273 S.E.2d 790 (1981).

Where the language of an instruction is hopelessly confusing and meaningless, the attainment of the ends of justice requires the Supreme Court to consider an objection to the instruction on appeal though no objection was made in the lower court. Glasgow v. Peatross, 201 Va. 43, 109 S.E.2d 135 (1959).

Objection to admission of confession in prosecution for rape, on ground not raised in trial court, was considered on appeal to attain the ends of justice in Cooper v. Commonwealth, 205 Va. 883, 140 S.E.2d 688 (1965). But while it is true that in Cooper v. Commonwealth, 205 Va. 883, 140 S.E.2d 688 (1965), the Supreme Court applied the exception to the rule and considered the admissibility of evidence to which proper objection had not been made in the trial court, the ruling was specifically restricted to the peculiar facts of that case. There, the defendant had been indicted and was represented by counsel when the inculpatory statement in question was taken without his counsel being present. Woodson v. Commonwealth, 211 Va. 285, 176 S.E.2d 818 (1970), cert. denied, 401 U.S. 959, 91 S. Ct. 990, 28 L. Ed. 2d 244 (1971).

Obvious injustice. — Where the defendant was sentenced for a crime other than that for which he was convicted, the error was clear, material and substantial and the error was so contrary to fundamental notions of justice that to permit it to pass uncorrected would seriously undermine the integrity of the judicial system, and the ends of justice exception permits redress in those limited instances of obvious injustice. Brown v. Commonwealth, 8 Va. App. 126, 380 S.E.2d 8 (1989).

A miscarriage of justice occurred when the trial court sentenced the defendant for a crime other than that for which he had been convicted. While strict enforcement of court rules and procedure is essential to the orderly administration of justice, the error in this case was so manifestly unjust that the court must overlook the failure to make a contemporaneous objection and exercise its authority to consider this issue on appeal in order to attain the ends of justice since the defendant was, in fact, sentenced for a crime other than that for which he was convicted and accordingly, the sentence was vacated. Brown v. Commonwealth, 8 Va. App. 126, 380 S.E.2d 8 (1989).

"Ends of justice" exception not applicable. — Given that the record on appeal adequately demonstrated that the sentencing judge correctly understood his discretion and sentenced defendant within the lawful scope of that discretion, the Court of Appeals of Virginia declined to apply the ends of justice exception to Va. Sup. Ct. R. 5A:18. Scalf v. Commonwealth, 2008 Va. App. LEXIS 230 (May 13, 2008).

Judgment of the Court of Appeals of Virginia affirming convictions for credit card theft in violation of § 18.2-192 was affirmed because consideration of the issue raised with regard to those convictions was not preserved for appeal, and throughout the course of his appeal, defendant had not challenged the sufficiency of the evidence supporting his convictions of credit card theft. On that record, it was fair to assume that in whatever venue those charges were prosecuted, the end result would be no different, and thus, the court did not find the circumstances of the case sufficient to invoke the provisions of Va. Sup. Ct. R. 5:25 excusing the requirement that error be properly preserved for consideration on appellate review. Gheorghiu v. Commonwealth, 280 Va. 678, 701 S.E.2d 407, 2010 Va. LEXIS 268 (2010).

Appellate court declined to consider defendant's argument that a requirement of sex-offender therapy making defendant admit guilt to the crime of rape was a breach of defendant's Alford plea agreement because defendant's statement of the questions presented did not contain the words "breach" or "plea agreement," and the court could not say that if the exception was not applied a grave injustice would have resulted. Carroll v. Commonwealth, 280 Va. 641, 701 S.E.2d 414, 2010 Va. LEXIS 277 (2010).

C. Admissibility of Evidence.

Grounds to be stated with reasonable certainty. — Under this rule it must appear that the objections urged in the trial court to the admissibility of evidence are substantially the same objections which are relied upon in the Supreme Court. This rule requires that all objections to the admissibility of evidence requiring a ruling of the trial court shall state with reasonable certainty the grounds of such objection. This language is explicit, and, unless good cause is shown why the objections were not made in the trial court, the Supreme Court will not consider the objections relied upon, unless the ends of justice in the particular case demand it. Boggs v. Commonwealth, 153 Va. 838, 149 S.E. 464 (1929).

Whether objection to admissibility of evidence was stated with reasonable certainty deemed irrelevant where admission was harmless error. Robinson v. Commonwealth, 219 Va. 520, 248 S.E.2d 786 (1978).

Failure to object to evidence on every occasion. — Only if the matter of evidence about and comment on defendant's post-arrest silence is treated as wholly unitary and a rule applied that once the erroneous material is in without objection it is for every purpose, including reiteration and emphasis over objection, is there any foundation for holding that the contemporaneous objection rule was not complied with where defendant's counsel failed to object on the first occasion that the prosecution made such a comment but did object on all subsequent occasions. Williams v. Zahradnick, 632 F.2d 353 (4th Cir. 1980).

Objection to the admission of evidence on one ground will not preserve objections on other unstated grounds. Washington v. Downes, 475 F. Supp. 573 (E.D. Va. 1979), overruled on other grounds, Carrier v. Hutto, 724 F.2d 396 (4th Cir. 1983).

Waiver of objection. — Where timely objection was not made in the trial court to the court's considering facts obtained from personal investigation, the objection was waived. Smith v. Board of Supvrs., 201 Va. 87, 109 S.E.2d 501 (1959).

Where an accused unsuccessfully objects to evidence which he considers improper and then on his own behalf introduces evidence of the same character, he thereby waives his objection, and the Supreme Court cannot reverse for the alleged error. Saunders v. Commonwealth, 211 Va. 399, 177 S.E.2d 637 (1970).

Defendants' challenges to the admission of statistical evidence consisting of information from bar graphs contained in a nursing journal article and information kept and compiled by the medical center regarding other patient falls were waived because, inter alia, defendants failed to afford the trial court an opportunity to rule on their objection to the statistical evidence about other patient falls in the sole context of the negligence issue once the estate nonsuited the claim for punitive damages, for which the evidence was originally admitted. Riverside Hosp., Inc. v. Johnson, 272 Va. 518, 636 S.E.2d 416, 2006 Va. LEXIS 102 (2006).

In a case brought by the Judicial Inquiry and Review Commission pursuant to Va. Const., Art. VI, § 10 and § 17.1-902, citing to § 17.1-913, the judge unsuccessfully argued that it was improper for the Commission to admit and consider evidence of her prior contacts with the Commission; she contended that neither § 17.1-913 nor VA. Jud. Inq. and Rev. R. 16 allowed for the removal of the confidentiality of records of complaints that were not deemed well founded and that her two prior contacts were not determined to be well founded. At the outset of the Commission hearing, counsel for the Commission stated that the exhibits were all in the red binder there on the witness desk and that both the sides were in agreement that there was no objection to the admission of any of the exhibits; pursuant to Va. Sup. Ct. R. 5:25, the judge's agreement to the Commission's admission of the exhibits was fatal to her argument that the Commission erred in admitting those same exhibits. Judicial Inquiry & Review Comm'n of Va. v. Taylor, 278 Va. 699, 685 S.E.2d 51, 2009 Va. LEXIS 114 (2009), cert. denied, 177 L. Ed. 2d 304, 130 S.Ct. 3396, 2010 U.S. LEXIS 4645 (2010).

Although business records contained hearsay opinions related to a motorist's pre-existing physical conditions, those constituted an independent ground for objection, which the motorist failed to assert at trial; accordingly, it was deemed waived pursuant to Va. Sup. Ct. R. 5:25. Arnold v. Wallace, 283 Va. 709, 725 S.E.2d 539, 2012 Va. LEXIS 80 (2012).

Expert's opinion based on unsupported factual assumptions. — Since defendants made no objection to a plaintiff's flawed expert testimony while the testimony was being given, but moved to strike at its conclusion, after the flaws had become apparent, the trial court had been given a proper opportunity to correct the error of admitting it. Vasquez v. Mabini, 269 Va. 155, 606 S.E.2d 809, 2005 Va. LEXIS 10 (2005).

Objections to admissibility of evidence held not to meet requirements of rule. — In an action for death by wrongful act, complaint was made that the lower court erred in permitting a witness for plaintiff to testify that members of the family of deceased were very poor people, but there was no objection to the admission of the evidence, and it clearly appeared from the record that without objection other evidence of the same character was offered by both plaintiff and defendant. The objection could not be made the basis of an assignment of error. Crawford v. Hite, 176 Va. 69, 10 S.E.2d 561 (1940).

In an action by an administratrix for the death by wrongful act of her husband in an automobile collision, error was assigned to the ruling of the court in excluding from the evidence a written statement by a witness for plaintiff in which he estimated that the truck in which plaintiff's decedent was riding was being driven at from 35 to 40 miles per hour and that defendants' truck was being driven at 30 to 35 miles per hour. On the stand the witness estimated the speed of decedent's truck at 25 to 30 miles per hour, but he stated that he could not estimate the speed of defendants' truck. The record failed to show that proper objection and grounds for the objection were preserved in accordance with this rule. The contention of defendants could not be sustained. Saunders v. Hall, 176 Va. 526, 11 S.E.2d 592 (1940).

In an action to recover for injuries received while riding in a truck which was struck by a train at a railroad crossing, it was held that under this rule the Supreme Court would not consider whether excluded evidence tended to prove that the engineer was habitually negligent in failing to give the statutory signals, since that ground of objection to the evidence was not made in the lower court. Jackson v. C & O Ry., 179 Va. 642, 20 S.E.2d 489 (1942).

Plaintiff in error assigned as error the action of the court in admitting improper evidence and in refusing to admit proper evidence. The grounds of plaintiff in error's objections to the admission or rejection of such evidence were not stated to the trial court. Under this rule the assignment could not be considered by the appellate court. Kercher's Adm'r v. Richmond, F. & P.R.R., 150 Va. 108, 142 S.E. 393 (1928).

Where no ground of objection to the admission of evidence was stated as required by this rule, the Supreme Court will not consider an objection relating thereto. Hawse v. Bryan, 148 Va. 194, 138 S.E. 721 (1927).

Timeliness of objection. Pursuant to a timely objection under the contemporaneous objection rule, defense counsel in a negligence case satisfied the rule by making a motion to strike evidence of the injuries that a dog sustained in an accident. By making the motion, defense counsel did not, therefore, waive any objections to the admission of the evidence. Kondaurov v. Kerdasha, 271 Va. 646, 629 S.E.2d 181, 2006 Va. LEXIS 71 (2006).

Breath test result. — Where the objection was made when the Commonwealth offered the result of a breath test in evidence and it was admitted subject to defense counsel's cross-examination of the trooper, it was held that the Fourth Amendment objection was timely made and that the Fourth Amendment issue was properly before the court. Simmons v. Commonwealth, 6 Va. App. 445, 371 S.E.2d 7 (1988), rev'd on other grounds, 238 Va. 200, 380 S.E.2d 656 (1989).

Failure to object to witness testimony. — Defendant's convictions for first-degree murder and use of a firearm in the commission of a felony were proper because defendant's argument that the trial court erred in allowing a major to testify about two statements made by defendant's boyfriend was without merit; defendant never objected at trial to the second "statement" and consequently waived her objection on appeal. Additionally, there was no statement made by the boyfriend that was introduced on that subject; there was simply the observation by the major that the two co-defendants' stories did not line-up. Thomas v. Commonwealth, 279 Va. 131, 688 S.E.2d 220, 2010 Va. LEXIS 11, cert. denied, 131 S. Ct. 143, 178 L. Ed. 2d 8, 2010 U.S. LEXIS 6109 (U.S. 2010).

Defendant's convictions for first-degree murder and use of a firearm in the commission of a felony were proper because defendant's argument that the trial court erred in allowing the Commonwealth to introduce evidence that defendant had previously assaulted the victim because the prejudicial value of such evidence outweighed the probative value was barred from consideration since defendant failed to object to the admission of the evidence at the trial court. Defendant failed to assign error to the appellate court's holding and the supreme court refused to consider it. Thomas v. Commonwealth, 279 Va. 131, 688 S.E.2d 220, 2010 Va. LEXIS 11, cert. denied, 131 S. Ct. 143, 178 L. Ed. 2d 8, 2010 U.S. LEXIS 6109 (U.S. 2010).

D. Instructions.

Objections to instructions must state grounds of objection. — Assignments of error to the action of the court in giving and refusing instructions cannot be considered, under this rule, where it does not appear from the record that the plaintiff in error stated to the trial court the grounds of his objection to the rulings of the court in these matters. Pauley v. Commonwealth, 151 Va. 510, 144 S.E. 361 (1928); Ames & Webb, Inc. v. Commercial Laundry Co., 204 Va. 616, 133 S.E.2d 547 (1963). See also Myers v. Bibee Grocery Co., 148 Va. 282, 138 S.E. 570 (1927); Gray v. Commonwealth, 150 Va. 571, 142 S.E. 397 (1928).

Assignments of error to the action of the court in refusing instructions cannot be considered on appeal because of this rule, where the objections are in general terms, and no grounds therefor appear in the record. Pauley v. Commonwealth, 151 Va. 510, 144 S.E. 361 (1928). See also Hardyman v. Commonwealth, 153 Va. 954, 151 S.E. 286 (1930); James v. Powell, 154 Va. 96, 152 S.E. 539 (1930); Barnes v. Bess, 171 Va. 1, 197 S.E. 403 (1938); G.L. Webster Co. v. Steelman, 172 Va. 342, 1 S.E.2d 305 (1939).

Grounds of objection to instructions which are not stated before the instructions are granted will not be considered by the Supreme Court, unless they come within the terms of the exception stated in the rule, or unless the trial judge himself waives the application of the rule. James v. Haymes, 160 Va. 253, 168 S.E. 333 (1933).

Where assignments of error do not specifically point out the errors relied on nor identify the instructions which appellant contends were erroneously given and refused, the assignments are insufficient to warrant consideration because not in compliance with this rule. Farrow v. Commonwealth, 197 Va. 353, 89 S.E.2d 312 (1955).

When nothing is certified beyond the objection to instructions given by the trial court, the Supreme Court cannot consider the scope and phraseology of the instruction but is confined to the general question whether the evidence justified the instruction. Universal Motor Co. v. Snow, 149 Va. 690, 140 S.E. 653 (1927).

This rule requires that objections to instructions be given with reasonable certainty. Marshall v. Goughnour, 221 Va. 265, 269 S.E.2d 801 (1980).

Generally, the reason for objecting to the grant or refusal of a jury instruction must be presented to the trial court before such objection will be considered on appeal. Morgen Indus., Inc. v. Vaughan, 252 Va. 60, 471 S.E.2d 489 (1996).

Failure to state grounds results in insufficient compliance with rule. — An objection to an instruction does not comply with this rule when the record only shows that one of defendants "objected." Kelly v. Schneller, 148 Va. 573, 139 S.E. 275 (1927).

Where the defendant objected to instructions given but the record merely showed as to them that "the defendant objected," it was held that such action, under this rule, was plainly insufficient. Vandergrift v. Summerall, 158 Va. 725, 164 S.E. 718 (1932).

To say that an instruction is misleading and inappropriate upon the evidence, and does not correctly state the law applicable thereto, is too general to be of any assistance to the trial court, and is a plain violation of the letter and spirit of this rule. Powell v. Young, 151 Va. 985, 144 S.E. 624, rev'd on other grounds, 151 Va. 988, 145 S.E. 731 (1928).

Objection to an instruction does not comply with this rule when it was stated only that, "it is too vague and indefinite as to the supposed negligence." Norfolk S.R.R. v. Lewis, 149 Va. 318, 141 S.E. 228 (1928).

Objections to an instruction must be made when the instruction is tendered. Smith v. Commonwealth, 165 Va. 776, 182 S.E. 124 (1935).

It was urged that there was no evidence in the record upon which to base instructions upon the theory that the homicide in question was the joint act of the several defendants, or that the accused was present aiding and abetting in its commission. This was urged in the petition for appeal, but it was not suggested when the instructions were given, and so could not, under this rule, be considered. Nelson v. Commonwealth, 153 Va. 909, 150 S.E. 407 (1929).

In an action to recover for personal injuries sustained when a wagon in which plaintiff was riding was struck by a truck, defendants objected to the giving of an instruction offered by plaintiff, and when the objection was overruled they seasonably objected to the ruling of the trial judge, giving their reason therefor, all of which was clearly shown by the record. It was held that defendant had sufficiently complied with this rule. Atlantic Co. v. Roberts, 179 Va. 669, 20 S.E.2d 520 (1942).

And objection not made to instruction in lower court should not be considered on appeal. Taylor v. Turner, 205 Va. 828, 140 S.E.2d 641 (1965).

Objections to the action of the trial court in granting and refusing instructions not raised in the court below cannot be raised in the Supreme Court. Bruce v. Elliott, 168 Va. 490, 191 S.E. 654 (1937).

Where no objection to an instruction was made by the defendant in the lower court, this rule precludes the appellate court from considering the action of the trial court in granting the instruction. Louisville & N.R.R. v. Saltzer, 151 Va. 165, 144 S.E. 456 (1928).

Objection to an erroneous instruction on proximate causation was not a basis for reversal where the objection was not made in the trial court. Whitley v. Patterson, 204 Va. 36, 129 S.E.2d 19 (1963).

In an action for injuries received by plaintiff in a collision between a motorcycle and an automobile, the brief of plaintiff characterized certain instructions as fatally defective in that they were finding instructions based upon a partial and inadequate view of the evidence, but no objections were made to the instructions in the lower court. Under this rule the defective character of the instructions could not be relied on before the Supreme Court. Hickerson v. Burner, 186 Va. 66, 41 S.E.2d 451 (1947).

In a prosecution for homicide, the petition questioned instructions granted for the Commonwealth, which told the jury, among other things, that self-defense, where relied upon by the accused, must be established "by a preponderance of the evidence." It was held that, under this rule, the failure to point out the defect in the instructions at the trial precluded the Supreme Court from considering it as reversible error. Hale v. Commonwealth, 165 Va. 808, 183 S.E. 180 (1936).

In a prosecution for seduction, the failure of the court to grant an instruction requested by accused was assigned as error, but the record failed to show that accused objected to the action of the court in not granting the instruction, or that any objection was taken to the court's action. The assignment of error could not be considered because there has been a failure to comply with this rule. Tyree v. Commonwealth, 185 Va. 628, 39 S.E.2d 627 (1946).

Objection to instruction may be preserved by propounding contrary theory. — Timely objection to instruction may be shown and preserved where, in a refused instruction, the objecting party propounds the contrary theory to one set forth in a granted instruction. Pilot Life Ins. Co. v. Karcher, 217 Va. 497, 229 S.E.2d 884 (1976).

Instructions not objected to become law of case. — Where no objection to instructions was tendered in the trial court, and no error with respect to them was assigned on appeal, the instructions became the law of the case, and were binding upon the Supreme Court, irrespective of their correctness. Babbitt v. Miller, 192 Va. 372, 64 S.E.2d 718 (1951); Shamblee v. Virginia Transit Co., 204 Va. 591, 132 S.E.2d 712 (1963).

Where no assignment of error was directed to the giving and refusing of instructions on trial, those given became the law of the case before the Supreme Court and binding, irrespective of their correctness. Babbitt v. Miller, 192 Va. 372, 64 S.E.2d 718 (1951).

Since neither plaintiff nor defendants challenged any instructions given or refused by assignments of error, those given thereby became the law of the case. Beasley v. Barnes, 201 Va. 593, 113 S.E.2d 62 (1960).

In an action to recover for the death of a passenger in an automobile in a collision between the automobile and a freight train at a railroad crossing, the court, without objection from plaintiff, gave an instruction which told the jury that the uncontradicted evidence showed that the driver of the automobile looked in both directions. In the Supreme Court, plaintiff contended that the trial court erred in giving the instruction, but in the trial court counsel for plaintiff had not only failed to object but had expressly stated that they had no objection. The plaintiff's failure to object to the instruction or to state any grounds of objection thereto under this rule made it the law of the case. Rook v. Atlantic Coast Line R.R., 184 Va. 670, 36 S.E.2d 559 (1946).

Before one can invoke the principle that an instruction given without objection becomes the law of the case, it must announce and apply a rule of law, and not a statement of fact alone. Tignor v. VEPCO, 166 Va. 284, 184 S.E. 234 (1936).

Motion to set aside verdict did not cure failure to object to instructions. — Where the defendant did make a motion to set aside the verdict, this does not save him from his failure to object to the instructions which submitted the issues of contributory negligence and proximate cause to the jury. Spitzli v. Minson, 231 Va. 12, 341 S.E.2d 170 (1986).

Waiver of objection. — When defendant failed to object to the instruction submitting the entire case to the jury, and failed to move the court to set aside the verdict and grant a new trial, she waived her right to assign error under this rule. Hilton v. Fayen, 196 Va. 860, 86 S.E.2d 40 (1955).

Rule cannot be waived by agreement of counsel. — In a prosecution under an indictment in two counts, the first for murder and the second under the "hit-and-run" statute, no instructions were tendered by counsel, but it was agreed that the court might instruct the jury orally, and to its instructions no objections were made. Accused moved to set aside the verdict because it failed to designate on which count in the indictment he was found guilty. There was a stipulation between counsel that all questions raised, all rulings thereon, all objections thereto and the grounds of such objections, and other incidents of the trial, might be relied upon by either or both parties in the Supreme Court without separate objections as to each point raised and objected to. It was held that to give the stipulation the construction urged by counsel for accused would be to do away with this rule, which was not to be desired. Meade v. Commonwealth, 177 Va. 811, 12 S.E.2d 796 (1941).

Without the consent of the court, it was agreed between counsel that any ground of objection to the instructions, whether raised at the time the judge ruled thereon or not, might be incorporated and made a part of the record. It was held that this was in conflict with the provisions of this rule. James v. Haymes, 160 Va. 253, 168 S.E. 333 (1933).

Objections to instructions held not to meet requirements of rule. — The plaintiff objected to an instruction on the ground that it did not go "far enough as to the question of liability and to the question here as to whether or not she could have avoided this accident if she had been looking." Whatever the language of plaintiff's brief might mean, it was not a statement "with reasonable certainty," required by this rule. Hickerson v. Burner, 186 Va. 66, 41 S.E.2d 451 (1947).

Plaintiff in error assigned as error the refusal to give certain instructions offered by it. Appended to each of these instructions was the following certificate signed by the judge: "The foregoing instruction requested by the defendant was denied, and the defendant excepted." Under this rule, the appellate court was precluded from passing upon the instructions. Indemnity Ins. Co. v. Davis' Adm'r, 150 Va. 778, 143 S.E. 328 (1928).

The giving of improper instructions at the instance of defendants in error, and the refusing of proper instructions offered by the plaintiff in error, were assigned as error. No specific objections to the granting or to the refusing of instructions appeared to have been presented to the trial judge, the certificate of the judge merely saying: "The foregoing instruction requested by the plaintiff was denied and the plaintiff excepted." Again: "The foregoing instruction was granted at the request of the defendant and the plaintiff excepted." Under this rule, the appellate court was precluded from considering the objections raised from the first time on appeal in the brief of the plaintiff in error. Coopersmith v. Mahoney, 150 Va. 685, 143 S.E. 313 (1928).

Plaintiff in error assigned as error the action of the trial court in modifying, giving and refusing instructions, but as not one of the assignments of error relating to the modifying, giving or refusing of instructions complied with this rule, this could not be considered on appeal. The grounds of objection were not only not stated with "reasonable certainty," as required by the rule, but were not stated at all, the record simply saying that plaintiff in error "objected" to the action of the court in giving or refusing instructions. Kercher's Adm'r v. Richmond, F. & P.R.R., 150 Va. 108, 142 S.E. 393 (1928).

Under this rule defendant failed to preserve properly his objections to the giving and refusing of instructions where he merely objected to the action of the trial court without informing the judge with reasonable certainty of the grounds of objection. Harlow v. Commonwealth, 195 Va. 269, 77 S.E.2d 851 (1953).

Assignments of error that trial court erred by giving "improper instructions" and refusing "proper instructions" were insufficient under this rule since they did not specifically point out the errors relied on or identify the instructions allegedly erroneously given and refused. Harlow v. Commonwealth, 195 Va. 269, 77 S.E.2d 851 (1953).

The assignments of error dealing with instructions stated that the court having fully heard argument upon the instructions gave instructions numbered 1 through 5 for the Commonwealth, to which instructions defendant objected, fully stating his reasons to the court, and the court gave instructions A, B and C offered by the defendant and refused to give instructions D and E, to which action of the court defendant objected, fully stating his reasons. Under this rule this assignment of error could not be considered, as the Supreme Court could not possibly know what reasons were assigned in the court below when these objections were taken. Trent v. Commonwealth, 155 Va. 1128, 156 S.E. 567 (1931).

Where no objection was made to instruction No. 3, and nothing more than a mere "objection" was taken to the refusal to give instructions A and B, this did not constitute compliance with the rule, and the assignments of error pertaining to the giving and refusal of instructions would not be considered. Newton v. City of Richmond, 198 Va. 869, 96 S.E.2d 775 (1957).

Plaintiff contended that the court erred in giving an instruction which appeared in the record and upon which he based a petition for appeal. The petition contained no ground of objection to the instruction. This was contrary to the requirement of this rule. Amos v. Franklin, 159 Va. 19, 165 S.E. 510 (1932).

In an action to recover for personal injuries, the sole reason given by the plaintiff in error for his objection to the instructions given by the court was that their vice was apparent upon their face. This general objection did not meet the requirement of this rule. Ross v. Schneider, 181 Va. 931, 27 S.E.2d 154 (1943).

In an action for injuries alleged to have been caused by the negligence of a municipal corporation in improperly constructing one of its streets and in knowingly permitting it to remain in an unsafe condition, defendant assigned as error the refusal of the trial court to give certain instructions, but the ground of objection simply stated that the instructions should have been granted because they were supported by the law and the facts of the case. The assignment of error did not comply with this rule, requiring a statement of the grounds of objection. City of Norfolk v. Hall, 175 Va. 545, 9 S.E.2d 356 (1940).

In an action by a shipper against a carrier of livestock for damages in carriage to a horse shipped by the shipper, there was a verdict for plaintiff and defendant appealed. The second assignment of error was in the language of the petition: "Bill of Exceptions No. Two, erroneous instructions given for plaintiff." The point was made by the defendant in error that neither the certificate of Exceptions No. 2, nor any part of the record, showed the ground of objection to any of the instructions given at the request of the plaintiff or that any objection was taken to the granting of any of plaintiff's instructions; and that under this rule this assignment of error could not be considered. This point was well made. C & O Ry. v. Osborne, 154 Va. 477, 153 S.E. 865 (1930).

In a will contest, contestants objected in the lower court that certain instructions granted at the request of the proponents contained "reiterations prejudicial to complainants." These prejudicial reiterations were not pointed out in the objections below "with reasonable certainty" as is required by this rule, nor were they mentioned in the assignments of error, although referred to as "obvious repetitions" in appellants' reply brief. The Supreme Court would not examine the instructions and seek out the "reiterations prejudicial to complainants" or the "obvious repetitions" which counsel had not pointed out. Hall v. Hall, 181 Va. 67, 23 S.E.2d 810 (1943).

In a will contest, the court instructed the jury that the proponents of the will must "prove that the testator executed the paper writing offered as the will in the presence of two subscribing witnesses." The grounds of objection to the instruction set out that it "is confusing to the jury and it does not fully state the law." The objection failed to set out the grounds with reasonable certainty, under this rule. Barnes v. Bess, 171 Va. 1, 197 S.E. 403 (1938).

In a prosecution for homicide, the court instructed the jury that involuntary manslaughter was the killing of one accidentally, in the commission of some unlawful act, not felonious, or in the unlawful performance of a lawful act. Accused objected to the instruction on the ground that it was an abstract statement or definition, which, applied to a specific case, was misleading and confusing. No attempt was made to tell the trial court wherein the instruction could have misled or confused the jury. The objection of accused was without standing, since it failed to tell the trial court wherein the instruction could have misled or confused. Albert v. Commonwealth, 181 Va. 894, 27 S.E.2d 177 (1943).

In a prosecution for homicide, objection was made to certain instructions in the following form: "The foregoing instructions Nos. A, B, C, D, E, F, and G were offered by the defendant and refused by the court, to which action of the court the defendant excepted." It was held that this assignment of error failed to comply with this rule, which requires that error when assigned "shall state with reasonable certainty the ground of such objection." Smith v. Commonwealth, 165 Va. 776, 182 S.E. 124 (1935).

In a prosecution for murder no instruction defining manslaughter was given the jury. Neither the Commonwealth nor the accused offered any such instruction. The objection offered by the accused to the instructions given was "that the same did not correctly state the law applicable to this case and were not supported by the evidence." This was not a compliance with this rule. Funk v. Commonwealth, 163 Va. 1014, 175 S.E. 861 (1934).

Objections to instruction held to be sufficient. — Because the circuit court was informed with reasonable certainty of defendant's concern about the proposed answer to a jury's inquiry, the court had the ability to evaluate the merits of the objection and to make an intelligent decision regarding the potential effect of the instruction on the jury's deliberation process; thus, the objection to the error was preserved. Booker v. Commonwealth, 276 Va. 37, 661 S.E.2d 461, 2008 Va. LEXIS 84 (2008).

Whether trial court properly refused proffered instruction. — In a first-degree murder prosecution, defendant's proffer of a correct instruction on self-defense was sufficient to preserve for appeal the question of whether the trial court erred in refusing that instruction. It was not necessary for her to expressly articulate each element necessary to her defense, because the trial court heard the evidence and could evaluate its application to the proffered instruction. Commonwealth v. Cary, 271 Va. 87, 623 S.E.2d 906, 2006 Va. LEXIS 22 (2006).

E. Improper Remarks and Argument.

Improper remark of court or opposing counsel. — In a prosecution for homicide, in ruling on the propriety of the cross-examination of a witness for the Commonwealth by the attorney for the Commonwealth, the trial court said, in the presence of the jury: "If this witness is perjuring herself I think she has a right to show it." It was contended on appeal that this was an improper indication to the jury by the court that it thought that the witness was not telling the truth, but counsel for accused made no objection to the court's remark on the ground that it reflected on the credibility of the witness and the point was not brought to the attention of the trial court in any manner or at any time. Under this rule accused was not entitled to raise the point for the first time on appeal. Dickerson v. Commonwealth, 186 Va. 951, 45 S.E.2d 243 (1947).

In a prosecution for attempted rape of an infant, accused assigned as error the action of the trial court in refusing to grant a new trial because the court had misled the jury as to their right to recommend that, on a verdict for life imprisonment, no pardon be granted. After the jury had retired, they returned and asked the court if they could put a clause in the verdict to the effect that no pardon be given. The court stated that it would not be a part of their verdict, but that they could make any recommendation they might desire after writing the verdict. No objection was taken to the action of the court. Under the provisions of this rule, the assignment of error would not be considered on appeal. McCann v. Commonwealth, 174 Va. 429, 4 S.E.2d 768 (1939).

Evidence was admitted as to the transfer of her property by one of the defendants a short time prior to the trial of the case. This was held to be error, but harmless error. This was practically admitted by counsel, but it was argued that the remarks of plaintiff's attorney and the court on the subject were highly prejudicial under the circumstances, for which the judgment should be reversed. While the Supreme Court would have felt inclined to agree with this argument and give the defendant the benefit of the objection, if counsel had complied with this rule by calling the attention of the court, at the time, to the grounds upon which the objection was based, the objection made by counsel was to admissibility of the evidence, and not to the comments made by the plaintiff's attorney and the court. If informed at the time that the defendant objected to these statements, the trial court would have had an opportunity to correct any erroneous and harmful impression which might have been made on the minds of the jury by what was said. Sutherland v. Receiver for Dickenson County Bank, 163 Va. 949, 178 S.E. 12 (1935).

Objection to improper argument must be timely. — Except under unusual circumstances, objection to improper argument must be timely so that the trial court may rule effectively, and if not made until after the case has been submitted to the jury, it is too late. Reid v. Baumgardner, 217 Va. 769, 232 S.E.2d 778 (1977).

Supreme court declined to consider any of defendant's arguments regarding the circuit court's comments during the penalty phase of his capital murder trial because defendant did not timely object to any of the alleged comments. Porter v. Commonwealth, 276 Va. 203, 661 S.E.2d 415, 2008 Va. LEXIS 78 (2008), cert. denied, 129 S. Ct. 1999, 173 L. Ed. 2d 1097, 2009 U.S. LEXIS 3047 (U.S. 2009).

The approved procedure for counsel to follow is to object to improper argument at the time, giving reasons for the objection, and to move for a mistrial or for a cautionary instruction to the jury to disregard the improper remarks. Reid v. Baumgardner, 217 Va. 769, 232 S.E.2d 778 (1977).

Failure to object to argument or curative admonition. — Where opposing counsel not only failed to make contemporaneous objection to closing argument but also deliberately refrained from objecting to the general admonition which the trial court gave the jury after objection to the argument was made, the objection was waived. Pullen v. Nickens, 226 Va. 342, 310 S.E.2d 452 (1983).

F. Jury Selection, etc.

Objection to "death qualifications" questions to prospective jurors based on denial of equal protection not preserved for appellate review. Waye v. Commonwealth, 219 Va. 683, 251 S.E.2d 202, cert. denied, 442 U.S. 924, 99 S. Ct. 2850, 61 L. Ed. 2d 292 (1979).

Failure to object to discharge of jury. — Where the record shows more than mere failure of a party to make contemporaneous objection to the discharge of the jury, it shows his affirmative agreement that there were no significant facts in dispute, the party will not be heard on appeal to complain that the court erred in discharging the jury. Burns v. Eby & Walker, Inc., 226 Va. 218, 308 S.E.2d 114 (1983).

Since the defendant did not ask the trial court to strike certain prospective jurors for cause, after they heard another prospective juror state a belief that the defendant was guilty, he waived this objection to the empanelment of those jurors. Roach v. Commonwealth, 251 Va. 324, 468 S.E.2d 98, cert. denied, 519 U.S. 951, 117 S. Ct. 365, 136 L. Ed. 2d 256 (1996), overruled in part on other grounds by Morrisette v. Warden of the Sussex I State Prison, 270 Va. 188, 613 S.E.2d 551 (2005).

Objections concerning jury selection. — Where defendant did not object to the circuit court's decision to take his motion for change of venue under advisement pending the outcome of voir dire, and he failed to renew the motion before the jury was empanelled and sworn, or even to remind the court that it was still pending, and implicitly consented to the seating of the jury, he was barred under Va. Sup. Ct. R. 5:25 from raising the denial of this motion on appeal. Green v. Commonwealth, 266 Va. 81, 580 S.E.2d 834, 2003 Va. LEXIS 55 (2003), cert. denied, 540 U.S. 1194, 124 S. Ct. 1448, 158 L. Ed. 2d 107 (2004).

Where defendant did not argue to the circuit court that the bifurcated procedure for felony trials prevented him from asking prospective jurors at the guilt phase about evidence of other crimes that the Commonwealth intended to use at the penalty phase to prove future dangerousness, the appellate court would not consider this issue on appeal. Green v. Commonwealth, 266 Va. 81, 580 S.E.2d 834, 2003 Va. LEXIS 55 (2003), cert. denied, 540 U.S. 1194, 124 S. Ct. 1448, 158 L. Ed. 2d 107 (2004).

Where a judge told a prospective juror he would hear evidence of one or more crimes committed by this defendant, "other than the capital murder for which he is convicted — I mean for which he's on trial," the fact that Va. Sup. Ct. R. 3A:14(b) authorized the trial court to excuse the juror for cause on its own motion did not relieve defendant from complying with Va. Sup. Ct. R. 5:25 and preserving his claim of error by a timely request to excuse this venire member. Green v. Commonwealth, 266 Va. 81, 580 S.E.2d 834, 2003 Va. LEXIS 55 (2003), cert.

denied, 540 U.S. 1194, 124 S. Ct. 1448, 158 L. Ed. 2d 107 (2004).

Because defense counsel not only did not object to the trial court's decision to alter the standard death penalty voir dire language, but acquiesced to it; defendant waived any right to appeal the issue. Juniper v. Commonwealth, 271 Va. 362, 626 S.E.2d 383, 2006 Va. LEXIS 29 (2006).

Failure to object to third-party jury contact. — Defendant's convictions for attempted capital murder, use of a firearm during the commission of a felony, possession of cocaine, and possession of a firearm while in possession of cocaine were appropriate because his argument that the trial court erred by denying his posttrial motion for a mistrial or, in the alternative, for a hearing on the effect of a third-party contact with jurors was waived. Defendant failed to timely object when the trial court informed him of the third-party contact with the jury. King v. Commonwealth, 2011 Va. App. LEXIS 103 (Mar. 22, 2011).

G. Other Objections.

Constitutional argument raised for first time on appeal. — The Supreme Court will not on an inadequate record entertain a constitutional argument raised for the first time on appeal. Newlon v. City of Alexandria, 213 Va. 336, 193 S.E.2d 6 (1972).

Search and seizure questions. — As with all nonjurisdictional issues, a search and seizure question cannot be raised for the first time on appeal. Bunch v. Commonwealth, 225 Va. 423, 304 S.E.2d 271 (1983), cert. denied, 464 U.S. 977, 104 S. Ct. 414, 78 L. Ed. 2d 352 (1984).

Constitutionality of search and seizure. — If a defendant wishes to preserve his right to challenge on appeal the constitutionality of a search and seizure through which certain evidence has been obtained, he must take timely steps in the lower court, either through a motion to suppress the evidence before trial or by sufficient objection to the use of the evidence when offered at trial. Manley v. Commonwealth, 211 Va. 146, 176 S.E.2d 309 (1970), cert. denied, 403 U.S. 936, 91 S. Ct. 2245, 29 L. Ed. 2d 716 (1971).

If a challenge to the constitutionality of a search and seizure is to be made on appeal, the challenge must be made first in a pretrial motion to suppress or by objection at trial. Girardi v. Commonwealth, 221 Va. 459, 270 S.E.2d 743 (1980), cert. denied, 451 U.S. 913, 101 S. Ct. 1986, 68 L. Ed. 2d 303 (1981).

Objection that search warrant was not supported by an affidavit as required by statute cannot be raised for the first time on appeal from a conviction. Manley v. Commonwealth, 211 Va. 146, 176 S.E.2d 309 (1970), cert. denied, 403 U.S. 936, 91 S. Ct. 2245, 29 L. Ed. 2d 716 (1971).

Sufficiency of indictment. — In a prosecution for breaking and entering and stealing certain money and property, error was assigned to the action of the trial court in overruling a motion to quash the indictment on the ground that the indictment did not express the kind and denomination of the currency stolen nor describe the nature and character of certain coupons alleged to have been taken. Counsel, in the oral argument before the Supreme Court, abandoned the contention made in the trial court and attacked the indictment on entirely new grounds, raised in the Supreme Court for the first time. The assignment was without merit, for the reason that the Supreme Court would not take cognizance of the new attack on the indictment, since it was contrary to this rule. Miller v. Commonwealth, 185 Va. 17, 37 S.E.2d 864 (1946).

In a prosecution for pandering, the indictment charged that the money received by the defendant was not for a consideration deemed "good and valuable in law," instead of charging that it was not for a consideration deemed "good or valuable in law," the language used in the statute which defined the crime. Defendant moved to quash the indictment, which motion was overruled. The only objection to the indictment at the time of the trial was that it stated conclusions instead of facts, and it was perfectly clear that the motion was not based on the variance between the indictment and the statute, because the attorney told the court that the indictment had the same words as the statute. It was held that the ground on which defendant relied in the Supreme Court was not stated "with reasonable certainty" as required by this rule, and defendant was not entitled to have the case reversed on a technical point not called to the attention of the trial court and from which he had suffered no possible harm. Saunders v. Commonwealth, 186 Va. 1000, 45 S.E.2d 307 (1947).

General demurrer to indictment. — In a prosecution for embezzlement and larceny, there was a general demurrer to the indictment and to each court thereof, which was overruled, but the specific grounds of the demurrer were not stated. The overruling of the demurrer was assigned as error. It was held that the Supreme Court might have refused to consider this assignment of error because the specific grounds of the demurrer were not stated under this rule. Boyd v. Commonwealth, 156 Va. 934, 157 S.E. 546 (1931).

Variance between charge in bill of particulars and conviction. — Accused was convicted of the unlawful possession of ardent spirits. The bill of particulars furnished by the Commonwealth limited the charge to selling, keeping, storing and exposing for sale ardent spirits. It was assigned as error that there was a fatal variance between the charge embraced in the bill of particulars and the offense of which the accused was found guilty. The record failed to show that the question was raised in the lower court, or that that court had its attention called to it. Therefore, it did not appear that the lower court had any opportunity to pass upon the point. It was held that the point raised under this assignment of error, not having been made in the trial court, would not, under this rule, be considered by the Supreme Court. Regensburg v. Commonwealth, 159 Va. 1024, 167 S.E. 247 (1933).

No objection made in lower court to decree. — In a suit to determine the disposition of the proceeds of insurance policies, the lower court held that defendant had acquired the policies by purchase and was entitled to the full proceeds therefrom, except for a sum paid by assured as premiums after the date of his insolvency. Defendant undertook to assign cross-error to the award of this sum to plaintiff, but made no objection in the lower court to the decree. Under this rule, defendant could not raise the objection for the first time in the Supreme

Court. Fidelity & Deposit Co. v. Moore, 177 Va. 341, 14 S.E.2d 307 (1941).

Failure to allege notice of claim for damages against city. — In an action against a city for damages sustained when plaintiff stepped into a hole in the sidewalk of one of the streets of the city, there was no allegation of notice of a claim for damages given to the city, as required by the city's charter and § 8.01-222, there was no proof that such notice was actually given, and the record showed no attempt at compliance with the mandatory provisions of the statute and the charter. The question of failure to give the notice was raised for the first time in the Supreme Court. Under this rule the question of failure to give notice came too late. City of S. Norfolk v. Dail, 187 Va. 495, 47 S.E.2d 405 (1948).

Reference to probation officer. — A defendant, having failed to object at the time the trial court referred his case to a probation officer under § 19.2-299, and having taken his chance on a favorable report, ought not to be heard to object if he considers the report unfavorable. McClain v. Commonwealth, 189 Va. 847, 55 S.E.2d 49 (1949).

Burden of proof. — Where the burden of proof issue was not raised, it will not be considered by the Supreme Court as a ground for reversal. Hughes v. Moore, 214 Va. 27, 197 S.E.2d 214 (1973).

Cross-examination. — Where the record failed to show an objection to the court's ruling refusing to permit certain questions on cross-examination, an assignment of error as to such ruling was not considered on appeal. Barner v. Whitehead, 204 Va. 634, 133 S.E.2d 283 (1963).

In an action for alienation of affections and criminal conversation, plaintiff's wife was, during her cross-examination by plaintiff's attorney, repeatedly contradicted by the use of a previous written statement made by her in the attorney's office. While this procedure is not to be condoned, defendant at no time during the trial made objection. Hence under this rule he could not raise such objection for the first time on appeal. Daniels v. Morris, 199 Va. 205, 98 S.E.2d 694 (1957).

Prior to trial the defendant made a motion that no evidence be admitted of "alleged drinking" on his part but the court denied the motion in view of the state of the record at that time. At trial the defendant was asked, without objection, whether he had been drinking on the day in question. The defendant failed to save this point by timely objection at a time when the court could intelligently rule upon it. Facchina v. Richardson, 213 Va. 440, 192 S.E.2d 791 (1972).

Directing issue out of chancery. — Where no objection was made in trial court to action of the court in directing an issue out of chancery on its own motion, objection for the first time in the appellate court came too late and would not be considered. Twohy v. Harris, 194 Va. 69, 72 S.E.2d 329 (1952).

Objection to the introduction of evidence before a special master cannot be made for the first time in the Supreme Court. American Nat'l Bank v. Ames, 169 Va. 711, 194 S.E. 784, cert. denied, 304 U.S. 577, 58 S. Ct. 1046, 82 L. Ed. 1540 (1938).

General objection to sufficiency of evidence must state with specificity grounds of objection. Floyd v. Commonwealth, 219 Va. 575, 249 S.E.2d 171 (1978).

Motion to strike evidence. — Where defendant made no objection when the court overruled his motion to strike plaintiff's evidence, his assignment of error to that ruling will not be considered on appeal. Richardson v. Lovvorn, 199 Va. 688, 101 S.E.2d 511 (1957).

Objection to evidence made after verdict. — In an action for breach of contract, defendant contended that there was no identification of plans and specifications for the erection of a house sufficient to make them a part of the contract. There was no objection made on this point until after the verdict. Since timely objection to the introduction of the evidence was not made as required by this rule, such objection would not be entertained on appeal. Horner v. Holt, 187 Va. 715, 47 S.E.2d 365 (1948).

Summary of testimony in support of objection to sufficiency of evidence. — In an action to recover for personal injuries, the trial court, on plaintiff's motion, set aside the verdict on the grounds of inadequacy and ordered that a jury be impaneled to pass on the question of damages. At a subsequent term and before a jury was impaneled defendant moved the court to vacate that portion of the order theretofore entered limiting the new trial to the assessment of damages and to enter an order granting a "new trial in toto," which motion was denied. At the time the motion was made, the evidence had not been made a part of the record, but it was later included and both court and counsel treated the evidence as already in the record. The ground of objection to the court's ruling was stated to be that the evidence was not sufficient for the court "to pass upon the merits of the case" without ordering a new trial upon all issues. It was held that full compliance with this rule required defendant to indicate by a brief statement or appropriate reference the particular point which, in his opinion, the evidence proved or failed to prove. However, the summary of the testimony was short and, in the opinion of the Supreme Court, fully sustained defendant's contention. Even if he had not complied strictly with the rule, his case came within the exception named therein. Kirn v. Bembury, 163 Va. 891, 178 S.E. 53 (1935).

Sufficiency of proof of age. — A defendant who failed to raise any question as to the sufficiency of the proof of his age in the trial court is not entitled to raise the question for the first time in the Supreme Court. Forester v. Commonwealth, 210 Va. 764, 173 S.E.2d 851 (1970).

Validity of ordinance. — Accused was found guilty of driving an automobile while under the influence of intoxicants, and it was assigned as error that the town ordinance under which the warrant was issued and upon which the prosecution was based was void. Counsel for the accused in his brief admitted that "this point was raised by appellant for the first time in his petition to this honorable court." Under this rule this assignment would not be considered, because the point was not raised in the trial court. Pflaster v. Town of Berryville, 157 Va. 859, 161 S.E. 58 (1931).

Failure to introduce in evidence ordinance under which accused was tried. — Where accused knew she was being tried under a city ordinance, the mere motion to set aside the verdict as contrary to the law and the evidence was insufficient to bring to the attention of the trial court the failure of the city to introduce the ordinance in evidence. Gooch v. City of Lynchburg, 201 Va. 172, 110 S.E.2d 236 (1959).

Question whether or not an individual could enter into a partnership with a corporation was not properly presented by the objections offered in the trial court, and under this rule of the Supreme Court as to stating objections in trial courts, the court declined to pass on it. Ruth v. Timberlake, 160 Va. 822, 169 S.E. 573 (1933).

Rule held not to preclude reliance on defense. — In an action to recover broker's commissions on the sale of land, the undertaking of the broker by contract with the owner was to sell the property within the listing period at a stipulated price and upon specified terms, and not merely to procure within that time a purchaser who was ready, willing and able to buy at that price and upon those terms. The evidence on behalf of the broker showed that he entered into a verbal contract with a prospective purchaser but that the purchaser executed no written offer or contract binding him to purchase the property and after the expiration of the listing period the owner agreed to sell the property to another party and declined to consummate the sale to the broker's prospect. The contention was made that the defendant, seller, was precluded by this rule from relying upon the defense that the broker procured from the prospective purchaser a mere verbal contract to buy the property, because the point was not made in the court below that such a contract was unenforceable under the statute of frauds. There was no merit in the contention, since the defendant was not raising the question of the statute of frauds in the Supreme Court but was relying upon the defense that the evidence of the plaintiff broker was fatally insufficient in that it failed to show that the broker had effected a sale of the property by procuring a written enforceable contract signed by the prospective purchaser. Snider v. New River Ins. & Realty Corp., 187 Va. 548, 47 S.E.2d 398 (1948).

Defendant railroad did not waive its defense of contributory negligence. — In suit involving dump truck and train as a result of collision, railroad did not waive defense of contributory negligence although the railroad did not object to truck driver's instruction on contributory negligence, for trial court was afforded the opportunity to rule intelligently on the issue of contributory negligence, and the driver of truck was given adequate opportunity to address that issue. Wright v. Norfolk & W.R.R., 245 Va. 160, 427 S.E.2d 724 (1993).

Verdict. — Where no objection was made to the reception of a verdict by the trial court, an assignment of error to the action of the court in refusing to set aside the verdict on the ground that it was defective and insufficient falls under the ban of this rule. Pflaster v. Commonwealth, 149 Va. 457, 141 S.E. 115 (1928).

When an action is brought jointly by two or more plaintiffs and the verdict if for "the plaintiff," in the singular, the objection to the verdict falls within the saving clause of this rule, providing that objections not made in the court below may be considered by the Supreme Court, "for good cause shown, or to enable this court to attain the ends of justice." McClure Grocery Co. v. Watson, 148 Va. 601, 139 S.E. 288 (1927).

Former jeopardy. — Where no plea of former jeopardy was filed and no question of former jeopardy was raised in the trial court as required by this rule, the question of former jeopardy cannot be considered on appeal. Zimmerman v. Commonwealth, 148 Va. 745, 138 S.E. 569 (1927).

Rule 5:26. General Requirements for All Briefs.

(a) *Applicability.* — This Rule, along with Rule 5:6, sets forth the general requirements for all briefs filed in this Court. Rule 5:22 sets forth the special rule for appeals in death penalty cases.

(b) *Length.* — Except by permission of a Justice of this Court, neither the opening brief of appellant, nor the brief of appellee, nor a brief amicus curiae shall exceed the longer of 50 pages or 8,750 words. No reply brief shall exceed the longer of 15 pages or 2,625 words. The page or word limits under this Rule do not include appendices, the cover page, table of contents, table of authorities, and certificate. There shall be no exception to these limits except by permission of this Court on motion for extension of the limits.

(c) *Filing Time.* — In cases in which a petition for appeal has been granted by this Court, briefs shall be filed subject to the provisions of Rule 5:1(d), as follows:

(1) The appellant shall file the opening brief in the office of the clerk of this Court within 40 days after the date of the certificate of appeal issued by the clerk of this Court pursuant to Rule 5:23.

(2) The brief of appellee shall be filed in the office of the clerk of this Court within 25 days after filing of the opening brief.

(3) The appellant may file a reply brief in the office of the clerk of this Court within 14 days after filing of the brief of appellee.

(d) *Extension of Time.* — Upon motion and with permission of a Justice of this Court, the time for filing any brief in this Court may be altered.

(e) *Copies for Filing.* — One electronic version, in Adobe Acrobat Portable Document Format (PDF) format, must be filed with the clerk of this Court and served on opposing counsel, unless excused by this Court for good cause shown. The electronic version may be filed on CD-ROM or emailed to scvbriefs@courts.state.va.us. In addition, fifteen printed copies of each brief (including a brief amicus curiae) shall be filed in the office of the clerk of this Court and three copies shall be mailed or delivered to opposing counsel on or before the day on which the brief is filed. Three copies of a brief amicus curiae shall be mailed or delivered to counsel for all parties and to any other counsel amicus curiae. All briefs shall contain a certificate evidencing such mailing or delivery and the method of transmission to the clerk for filing.

(f) *Reference to Parties.* — In their briefs, counsel should avoid reference to parties by such designations as "appellant" and "appellee." Clarity is promoted by the use of the names of the parties or descriptive terms such as "the employee," "the injured person," "the driver," "the wife," or the designations used in the lower court or commission.

(g) *Arguments Made by Reference.* — Attempts to incorporate arguments made below by reference to pleadings, motions, memorandum, or other filings are prohibited.

(h) *Signature and Certificate.* — All briefs shall contain the signature, which need not be in handwriting, of at least one counsel of record, counsel's Virginia State Bar number, address, telephone number, facsimile number (if any), and email address (if any), and a certificate that there has been compliance with this Rule. If a word count is used, the certificate must also state the number of words (headings, footnotes, and quotations count towards the word limitation; the cover page, table of contents, table of authorities, and certificate do not count towards the word count).

(i) *Failure to File Complying Brief.* — Any party who fails to file a brief in compliance with these Rules or otherwise fails to file a required brief will not be heard orally, except for good cause shown.

Cross references. — For meaning of "clerk of this Court" and "opposing counsel," see Rule 5:1.

Source. — Rules 5:47, 5:48 and 5:49. Cf. Rule 5A:19.

The amendment, effective May 2, 2011, adopted March 1, 2011, inserted "the longer of" twice in the first sentence of subdivision (b).

Michie's Jurisprudence. — For related discussion, see 1B M.J. Appeal and Error, §§ 124, 137, 140, 233.

CASE NOTES

Applied in Thrasher v. Burlage, 219 Va. 1007, 254 S.E.2d 64 (1979); Stockton v. Commonwealth, 241 Va. 192, 402 S.E.2d 196 (1991); Weeks v. Angelone, 176 F.3d 249 (4th Cir. 1999).

Rule 5:27. Requirements for Opening Brief of Appellant.

The opening brief of the appellant shall comply with the requirements of Rules 5:6 and 5:26, and must contain the following:

(a) A table of contents and table of authorities with cases alphabetically arranged. Citations of all authorities shall include the year thereof.

(b) A statement of the case containing the material proceedings below and the facts, with references to the appendix.

(c) The assignments of error, with a clear and exact reference to the pages of the appendix where the alleged error has been preserved.

(d) The standard of review, the argument, and the authorities relating to each assignment of error. With respect to each assignment of error, the standard of review and the argument — including principles of law and the authorities — shall be stated in one place and not scattered through the brief. At the option of counsel, the argument may be preceded by a short summary.

(e) A short conclusion stating the precise relief sought.

Source. — Rule 5:42. Cf. Rule 5A:20.

Comment. — In their briefs and oral argument, counsel should avoid references to parties by such designations as "appellant" and "appellee." Clarity is promoted by the use of the names of the parties, or descriptive terms such as "the employee," "the injured person," "the driver" or "the husband," or the designations used in the lower court or commission.

Michie's Jurisprudence. — For related discussion, see 1B M.J. Appeal and Error, § 138; 6A M.J. Divorce and Alimony, §§ 49, 77.

CASE NOTES

Petitioner must indicate alleged error. — Where there is no concise and fair statement of pertinent facts, nor any legal question succinctly stated, the court will not search the record for errors not thus indicated. The petitioner must put his finger upon alleged errors, for to require an appellate court to seek out the substance of all contentions made during the progress of a trial would be to impose upon it an improper burden. Law v. Commonwealth, 171 Va. 449, 199 S.E. 516 (1938).

So as to avoid burden on court and appellee. — To require the appellee or the Supreme Court to hunt through the record for every conceivable error that the court below may have committed, when none has been pointed out by the party complaining of the judgment, is unreasonable and oppressive on the party recovering judgment, and most burdensome on the Supreme Court, unnecessarily impeding the progress of its business. Nicholas v. Harnsberger, 180 Va. 203, 22 S.E.2d 23 (1942).

Failure to object on ground of noncompliance. — The rule, requiring a brief statement of the errors assigned and questions involved, should be followed, but where the Attorney General does not raise objection to a brief on the ground of noncompliance with the rule, the Supreme Court will confine its attention to the points raised and discussed in the brief. Carr v. Commonwealth, 175 Va. 608, 9 S.E.2d 287 (1940).

Form and contents. — An opening brief must conform in all respects to the requirements of the petition for appeal set forth in Rule 5:17(c), pursuant to Rule 5:27. Hedrick v. True, 2004 U.S. Dist. LEXIS 4600 (W.D. Va. Mar. 23, 2004), aff'd, 443 F.3d 342 (4th Cir. 2006).

In a capital murder case in which defendant presented 82 assignments of error but failed to brief or provide an argument for a number of those assignments of error, they were deemed waived by the appellate court. Prieto v. Commonwealth, 278 Va. 366, 682 S.E.2d 910, 2009 Va. LEXIS 94 (2009), cert. denied, 177 L. Ed. 2d 332, 2010 U.S. LEXIS 4926 (U.S. 2010).

Defendant did not present any argument on brief to support defendant's contention that the Court of Appeals of Virginia erred in its determination that a constitutional issue was not preserved for appeal. Accordingly, the Supreme court of Virginia, pursuant to Va. Sup. Ct. R. 5:27(d), did not have to address whether defendant preserved defendant's claims based on a constitutional violation. Howard v. Commonwealth, 281 Va. 455, 706 S.E.2d 885, 2011 Va. LEXIS 47 (2011).

Averment irrelevant to the appeal. — Although in its brief, a homeowners association averred that it would have provided additional evidence in the form of expert testimony, no assignment of error asserted that the circuit court erred in awarding summary judgment because material facts were in dispute or that the court improperly excluded admissible evidence; the averment therefore had no relevance to the appeal. Newberry Station Homeowners Ass'n v. Bd. of Supervisors, 285 Va. 604, 740 S.E.2d 548, 2013 Va. LEXIS 52 (2013).

Applied in Stockton v. Commonwealth, 241 Va. 192, 402 S.E.2d 196 (1991); G.S. Foods, Inc. v. VEC, 12 Va. App. 541, 404 S.E.2d 741 (1991); Yeatts v. Commonwealth, 242 Va. 121, 410 S.E.2d 254 (1991); Atkisson v. Wexford Assocs., 254 Va. 449, 493 S.E.2d 524 (1997); Mueller v. Angelone, 181 F.3d 557 (4th Cir.); Emmett v. Commonwealth, 264 Va. 364, 569 S.E.2d 39, 2002 Va. LEXIS 102 (2002); Today Homes, Inc. v. Williams, 272 Va. 462, 634 S.E.2d 737, 2006 Va. LEXIS 91 (2006); Kitchen v. City of Newport News, 275 Va. 378, 657 S.E.2d 132, 2008 Va. LEXIS 38 (2008); Estate of Parfitt v. Parfitt, 277 Va. 333, 672 S.E.2d 827, 2009 Va. LEXIS 33 (2009); Andrews v. Commonwealth, 280 Va. 231, 699 S.E.2d 237, 2010 Va. LEXIS 239 (2010); John Crane, Inc. v. Hardick, 283 Va. 358, 722 S.E.2d 610, 2012 Va. LEXIS 35 (2012); Lawlor v. Commonwealth, 285 Va. 187, 738 S.E.2d 847, 2013 Va. LEXIS 13 (2013); Henderson v. Ayres & Hartnett, P.C., 285 Va. 556, 740 S.E.2d 518, 2013 Va. LEXIS 49 (2013).

Rule 5:28. Requirements for Brief of Appellee.

The brief of appellee shall comply with Rules 5:6 and 5:26, and must contain the following:

(a) A table of contents and table of authorities with cases alphabetically arranged. Citations of all authorities shall include the year thereof.

(b) A statement of the case if the appellee disagrees with the statement presented by the appellant. In an appeal of right to this Court from an order disciplining, suspending, or disbarring an attorney-at-law, the Virginia State Bar may include assignments of cross-error. In such cases, no cross-error not then assigned will be noticed by this Court.

(c) A statement of the facts necessary to correct or amplify the statement in the brief of appellant with appropriate references to the pages of the appendix. Any quotation from the record should be brief. The testimony of individual witnesses should not be summarized seriatim unless the facts are in dispute and such a summary is necessary to support the appellee's version of the facts.

(d) The standard of review, the argument, and the authorities relating to each assignment of error. With respect to each assignment of error, the standard of review and the argument — including principles of law and the authorities — shall be stated in one place and not scattered through the brief. At the option of counsel, the argument may be preceded by a short summary.

(e) With respect to the assignments of cross-error, if any:

(1) A statement of the assignment of cross-error, with a clear and exact reference to the pages of the appendix where the alleged cross-error has been preserved.

(2) The standard of review, the argument, and the authorities relating to each assignment of cross-error. With respect to each such assignment of cross-error, the standard of review and the argument — including principles of law and the authorities — shall be stated in one place and not scattered through the brief.

(3) A statement of the precise relief sought.

Cross references. — As to signatures to printed briefs, see Rule 1:5.

Source. — Rule 5:43. Cf. Rule 5A:21.

Comment. — In their briefs and oral argument, counsel should avoid references to parties by such designations as "appellant" and "appellee." Clarity is promoted by the use of the names of the parties, or descriptive terms such as "the employee," "the injured person," "the driver" or "the husband," or the designations used in the lower court or commission.

CASE NOTES

Applied in O'Dell v. Commonwealth, 234 Va. 672, 364 S.E.2d 491 (1988).

Rule 5:29. Requirements for Reply Brief.

The reply brief, if any, shall comply with the requirements of Rules 5:6 and 5:26 and shall contain only argument in reply to contentions made in the brief of appellee. No reply brief is necessary if the contentions have been adequately answered in the opening brief of appellant.

Source. — Rule 5:44. Cf. Rule 5A:22.

Rule 5:30. Briefs Amicus Curiae.

(a) *Stage of appellate proceedings.* — Subject to the requirements outlined in this Rule, a brief amicus curiae may be filed during the petition, perfected appeal or rehearing stages of the appellate proceedings in this Court.

(b) *Who May File a Brief Amicus Curiae Without Leave of Court.* — (1) The United States or the Commonwealth of Virginia; and

(2) Any other person whose filing is accompanied by the written consent of all counsel; and

(3) Any person requested by the Court to file a brief amicus curiae pursuant to paragraph (f) of this Rule.

(c) *Who Needs Leave of Court to File a Brief Amicus Curiae.* — Any person or entity other than those described in paragraph (b) of this Rule.

(d) *When a Brief Amicus Curiae Must Be Filed.* — A brief amicus curiae will be accepted only if filed on or before the date on which the brief of the party supported is required to be filed. A brief amicus curiae may be filed at the time of filing of the reply brief of the appellant only if an opening brief amicus curiae has been filed.

(e) *What a Brief Amicus Curiae Must Contain.* — A brief amicus curiae shall comply with the rules applicable to the brief of the party supported.

(f) *This Court's Authority to Request a Brief Amicus Curiae.* — Notwithstanding the provisions of this Rule, this Court may request that a brief amicus curiae be filed at any time.

Source. — Rule 5:45. Cf. Rule 5A:23.

Michie's Jurisprudence. — For related discussion, see 1B M.J. Amicus Curiae, § 3; 1B M.J. Appeal and Error, § 33.

CASE NOTES

Applied in McDonald v. Commonwealth, 274 Va. 249, 645 S.E.2d 918, 2007 Va. LEXIS 87 (2007).

Rule 5:31. Covers of Documents.

(a) *What Covers Must Be Used on Papers Filed with this Court.* — To facilitate identification, documents shall bear covers colored as follows:

Document	*Color of Cover*
Appendix	Red
Brief of the Appellant	White
Brief of the Appellee	Blue
Reply Brief of the Appellant	Green
Brief Amicus Curiae	Gray
Petition for Rehearing	Yellow

(b) *Effect of failure to comply.* — No appeal shall be dismissed for failure to comply with the provisions of this Rule.

Source. — Rules 5:34 and 5A:24.

Michie's Jurisprudence. — For related discussion, see 1B M.J. Appeal and Error, § 233.

Rule 5:32. Appendix.

(a) *Responsibility of the Appellant.* — (1) Contents of the Appendix. The appellant must prepare and file an appendix. The appendix shall contain:

(i) the initial pleading (as finally amended), unless other versions are necessary to consider the assignments of error;

(ii) final judgments of all tribunals that have considered the case, including the judgment appealed from, and any opinion relating to such judgments;

(iii) testimony and other incidents of the case germane to the assignments of error;

(iv) exhibits necessary for an understanding of the case that can reasonably be reproduced;

(v) the granted assignments of error and cross-error;

(vi) other parts of the record to which the parties wish to direct this Court's attention; and

(vii) a table of contents as described in paragraph (d) below.

(2) Assumptions and Excluded Material. It will be assumed that the appendix contains everything germane to the granted assignments of error and, if any, assignments of cross-error. Memoranda of law in the trial court should not be included in the appendix unless they have independent relevance. Parts of the record may be relied on by this Court or the parties even though not included in the appendix.

(3) Time to File; Number of Copies.

(i) Generally. The appellant must file 15 copies of the appendix with the appellant's brief, and must serve two copies on counsel for each party separately represented. This Court may by order require the filing or service of a different number.

(ii) Special Rule for Electronic Filing of the Appendix. In lieu of the 15 tangible copies required by paragraph (a)(3)(i) of this Rule, the appellant may file 10 tangible copies of the appendix and 10 electronic copies of the appendix as an Adobe Acrobat Portable Document Format (PDF) document on CD-ROMs. If the appellant files 10 electronic copies with this Court, then it must also serve one electronic copy on counsel for each party separately represented in addition to the one tangible copy required by paragraph (a)(3)(i) of this Rule.

(b) *Responsibility of All Parties.* — (1) Determining the Contents of the Appendix. The parties are encouraged to agree on the contents of the appendix. Within 15 days after the date of the certificate of the clerk of this Court issued pursuant to Rule 5:23, counsel for appellant shall file in the office of the clerk of this Court a written statement signed by all counsel setting forth an agreed designation of the parts of the record on appeal to be included in the appendix. In the absence of an agreement, the appellant must, within 15 days after the date of the certificate of appeal issued by the clerk of this Court pursuant to Rule 5:23, file with the clerk of this Court and serve on the appellee a designation of the parts of the record the appellant intends to include in the appendix. The appellee may, within 15 days after receiving the designation, file with the clerk of this Court and serve on the appellant a designation of additional parts of the record the appellee deems germane. The appellant must include the parts designated by the appellee in the appendix, together with any additional parts the appellant considers germane. The parties must not engage in an unnecessary designation of parts of the record, because the entire record is available to the Court.

(2) Sealed Materials in the Appendix. Appendices filed with this Court are a matter of public record. If counsel concludes it is necessary to include sealed material in the appendix, then, in order to maintain the confidentiality of the materials, counsel must

designate the sealed material for inclusion in a supplemental appendix to be filed separately from the regular appendix, and must file a specific motion asking this Court to seal the supplemental appendix within the time stated for the designation of the appendix in paragraph (b)(1) of this Rule.

(3) Costs of Appendix. Unless the parties agree otherwise, the appellant must initially pay the cost of the appendix, but if the appellant in good faith considers that parts of the record designated by the appellee for inclusion are unnecessary for the determination of the assignments of error, the appellant initially preparing the appendix may so advise the clerk of this Court and the appellee, and the appellee who designated the challenged material shall advance the cost of including such parts. The cost of producing the appendix shall be taxed as costs in the case, but if any party shall cause unnecessary material to be included in the appendix this Court sua sponte or upon motion may impose the cost of including such parts upon that party.

(c) *Appeal on the Original Record Without an Appendix.* — This Court may, sua sponte or on motion, enter an order dispensing with the appendix and permitting an appeal to proceed on the original record with any copies of the record, or relevant parts, that the Court may order the parties to file. A motion may be made under this rule within 10 days of the issuance of a writ. The making of a motion under this paragraph does not excuse the filing of the proposed contents of an appendix under paragraph (b)(1).

(d) *Table of Contents and Form of Presentation.* — The appendix must begin with a table of contents identifying the page at which each part begins. When the testimony of witnesses is included, the name of each witness who is testifying must be in the table of contents with a page number at which each portion of the testimony begins (direct, cross, redirect, etc.). Parts of the record should be in the appendix in chronological order. Omissions in the text of papers or of the transcript must be indicated by asterisks. The index for exhibits should include a description of the exhibit sufficient to inform this Court of its nature rather than merely an exhibit number.

(e) *Effect of Non-Compliance with this Rule.* — An appeal will not be dismissed for failure to file an appendix in compliance with this Rule. If an appendix is not filed within the time prescribed, or on its face fails to comply with this Rule, this Court may direct the filing of a proper appendix within a specific time and may require a non-complying attorney or unrepresented party to advance all or part of the cost of printing the appendix. This Court may dismiss an appeal for non-compliance with an order entered under this paragraph.

Source. — Rules 5:35 through 5:41. Cf. Rule 5A:25.

Comment. — As to the time for designation of additional portions of the record on an appeal from the State Corporation Commission, see Rule 5:21(a).

The amendment, effective May 2, 2011, adopted March 1, 2011, inserted ", together with any additional parts the appellant considers germane" at the end of the next-to-last sentence of subdivision (b)(1).

Michie's Jurisprudence. — For related discussion, see 1B M.J. Appeal and Error, §§ 201, 202, 204, 209, 226, 230, 250; 5A M.J. Costs, § 12.

CASE NOTES

Purpose of rule. — The purpose of this rule was to have included all that is germane to the assignments of error. Jenkins v. Womack, 201 Va. 68, 109 S.E.2d 97 (1959).

The purpose of this rule was to incorporate in the printed record everything essential and germane to an intelligent determination of the errors assigned and to relieve the Supreme Court of the burden of looking to the manuscript record for this purpose. Carter v. Nelms, 204 Va. 338, 131 S.E.2d 401 (1963).

The purpose of the rule is to prohibit inclusion of matters not germane to the assignments of error. Hundley v. Commonwealth, 193 Va. 449, 69 S.E.2d 336 (1952).

This rule was designed not only to avoid unnecessary printing costs, but also to furnish to the justices a printed record containing only those matters they need consider in disposing of the issues presented. City of Roanoke v. Young, 208 Va. 618, 159 S.E.2d 661 (1968).

This rule encourages parties to agree as to the contents of the appendix. — In the absence of agreement, it requires an appellant to designate the parts of the record that he intends to include in the appendix as germane to his assignments of error. Vaughan v. Johnson, 215 Va. 323, 210 S.E.2d 139 (1974).

Requirements of this rule are mandatory and failure to comply therewith is fatal to appeal. Vaughan v. Johnson, 215 Va. 323, 210 S.E.2d 139 (1974).

The requirement for filing a designation of the parts of the record under this rule is mandatory and jurisdictional. Andrews v. Cahoon, 196 Va. 790, 86 S.E.2d 173 (1955).

The requirement that appellant designate the parts of the record cannot be construed as merely directory, because it is an essential feature of the present method of taking an appeal. Avery v. County Sch. Bd., 192 Va. 329, 64 S.E.2d 767 (1951).

Waiver of requirements by appellee. — Appellee can waive all or some of the 10 days [now 15 days] that are allowed for his benefit, but he cannot waive the requirement that appellant file his designation. Avery v. County Sch. Bd., 192 Va. 329, 64 S.E.2d 767 (1951).

What designations should embrace. — While an abbreviation of the printed record is highly desirable, this rule contemplates that for the information and convenience of the court the designations embrace so much of the proceedings below, including all material evidence, as is pertinent to a full consideration of the assignments of error. Bonich v. Waite, 194 Va. 374, 73 S.E.2d 389 (1952).

Everything germane to an error assigned on appeal should be included, so that the printed record will contain everything essential to determine whether error was committed. Hall v. Miles, 197 Va. 644, 90 S.E.2d 815 (1956).

All matters germane to errors assigned must be contained or they would not be considered. Gaumont v. State Hwy. Comm'r, 205 Va. 223, 135 S.E.2d 790 (1964).

This rule required that all matters germane to errors assigned must be contained or they would not be considered by the Supreme Court. Powell v. Nichols, 209 Va. 654, 166 S.E.2d 243 (1969).

Unfavorable as well as favorable evidence must be included. — The appellant who asks the Supreme Court to set aside a finding of the trial court on the ground that it is not sustained by the evidence has the primary responsibility of including all of the evidence which is necessary and material to a determination of that issue. He must include not only that which is favorable to him, but that which is favorable to his opponent, for obviously without access to all of the material evidence it is impossible for the Supreme Court to determine its sufficiency. DeMott v. DeMott, 198 Va. 22, 92 S.E.2d 342 (1956); Carter v. Nelms, 204 Va. 338, 131 S.E.2d 401 (1963).

The appellant must include not only that which is favorable to him, but that which is favorable to his opponent, for obviously without access to all of the material evidence it is impossible for the Supreme Court to determine its sufficiency. Johnson v. Town of Damascus, 205 Va. 893, 140 S.E.2d 638 (1965).

Or Supreme Court may refuse to consider sufficiency of evidence. — Where the designation by the appellant included some evidence favorable to the plaintiff appellee, but, omitted considerable other evidence favorable to that party, this violation of the rule would justify the Supreme Court in refusing to consider the assignments of error involving the sufficiency of the evidence. Carter v. Nelms, 204 Va. 338, 131 S.E.2d 401 (1963).

Where a party on appeal challenged the sufficiency of the evidence, this rule required that he include all the material evidence, not just that favorable to his position. His failure in this respect might result in the court's refusal to consider the assignment of error; but the assignment might be considered in the interests of justice. Johnson v. Town of Damascus, 205 Va. 893, 140 S.E.2d 638 (1965).

When the evidence is not made a part of the record on appeal, all findings of fact by the trial court are presumed to be correct and must be accepted as conclusive. Vaughan v. Johnson, 215 Va. 323, 210 S.E.2d 139 (1974).

Failure of appellant to designate certain material parts of the evidence favorable to appellee was not grounds for dismissing the appeal. — Appellee was at liberty to designate any omitted evidence which he thought material. Frye v. Alford, 203 Va. 461, 125 S.E.2d 177 (1962).

Although appellant failed to designate the parts of the record as required by this rule, a motion to dismiss the appeal was overruled, since appellee's counsel exercised his right under the rule to make additional designations and all the material evidence was before the court in the printed record. Jenkins v. Womack, 201 Va. 68, 109 S.E.2d 97 (1959).

Where it appeared that material portions of the evidence not designated by appellants had been designated at the direction of appellees, the appeal would not be dismissed because of appellants' failure to make proper designations. Taylor v. Wood, 201 Va. 615, 112 S.E.2d 907 (1960).

Under this rule, appellee was afforded the opportunity to designate those additional portions of the evidence which she considered to be material, but she failed to exercise this right. Hence, her motion to dismiss is overruled. Bond v. Joyner, 205 Va. 292, 136 S.E.2d 903 (1964).

Where appellee filed a motion to dismiss appeal on ground that appellant failed to designate sufficient parts of the record as required by this rule, and counsel for appellee did not file "a designation of the additional parts of the record that he wishes" but printed in an appendix to his brief the evidence which he said should have been printed in the record, under these circumstances appellee was not entitled to have the appeal dismissed and his motion to dismiss was accordingly overruled. Barnette v. Dickens, 205 Va. 12, 135 S.E.2d 109 (1964).

Since the entire proceedings conducted before the Industrial Commission were included in the appendix and the appellee was not prejudiced, the failure of the appellant to designate the parts of the record that he intended to include in the appendix within the time required by former Rule 5:36(a), was not jurisdictional; hence, the motion to dismiss was overruled. Leonard v. Arnold, 218 Va. 210, 237 S.E.2d 97 (1977).

The designation was filed late in violation of this rule, but the appealing party included in the appendix the entire proceeding conducted below. For this reason, and because the opposing party had not been prejudiced, the failure to file the designation in time was "not jurisdictional." Rhoten v. United Va. Bank, 221 Va. 222, 269 S.E.2d 781 (1980).

Failure to designate a transcript or agreed statement of evidence was fatal to the contention that the judgment of the trial court was contrary to the law and evidence. Luhring v. Finley, 202 Va. 260, 117 S.E.2d 126 (1960).

Failure to comply with this rule of this rule is not ground for dismissal if an appellant includes in his or her appendix everything germane to the disposition of the appeal and the appellee has not been prejudiced by the failure. Wilcox v. Lauterbach Elec. Co., 233 Va. 416, 357 S.E.2d 197 (1987).

No reimbursement for unnecessary inclusion. — Where appellant included portions of record not needed for review, unsuccessful appellee would be required to reimburse appellant for only part of printing record. City of Roanoke v. Young, 208 Va. 618, 159 S.E.2d 661 (1968).

Instructions not contained would not be considered. — Where appellant assigned as error the court's refusal to grant instructions, but the Instructions were not contained, they would not be considered. Stanpark Realty Corp. v. City of Norfolk, 199 Va. 716, 101 S.E.2d 527 (1958).

Where plaintiff did not include any instructions, the assignments of error relating to rulings on such instructions need not be considered on appeal. Thompson v. Mann, 201 Va. 528, 111 S.E.2d 792 (1960).

Except in the interest of justice. — Where instructions, although not included, had been furnished as addenda to the briefs, and where such instructions showed that the case had been submitted to the jury on improper principles of law, the instructions were considered on appeal in the interest of justice. Gabbard v. Knight, 202 Va. 40, 116 S.E.2d 73 (1960).

Omission of objections to granting of instructions. — The Supreme Court was not required to consider errors assigned relating to rulings on instructions where appellants had failed to include their objections, with the reasons therefor, to the court's action in granting the instructions. County Sch. Bd. v. Thomas, 201 Va. 608, 112 S.E.2d 877 (1960).

Cost of producing ingermane pages. — In 2,216 pages in the six-volume appendix, where appellees designated at least 1,723 pages that were not germane to any issue in the appeal, the appellees shall bear the cost of producing 77 percent of that appendix. Metrocall of Del., Inc. v. Continental Cellular Corp., 246 Va. 365, 437 S.E.2d 189 (1993).

Rule 5:33. Oral Argument.

(a) *Notice.* — Whenever an appeal lies as a matter of right or a petition for appeal has been granted, the clerk of this Court, except in extraordinary circumstances, shall give at least 15 days notice to counsel of the date, approximate time, and location for oral argument.

(b) *Length.* — Except as otherwise directed by this Court, argument for a party shall not exceed 15 minutes in length. Such time may be apportioned among counsel for the same side at their discretion.

(c) *Appearance Pro Hac Vice.* — Any lawyer not licensed in Virginia who seeks to appear *pro hac vice* to present oral argument to the Court must comply with the requirements of Rule 1A:4.

(d) *Amicus Curiae.* — No oral argument by amicus curiae is permitted except by leave of this Court. Leave may be granted upon the joint written request of amicus curiae and the party whose position amicus curiae supports. The request shall specify the amount of its allotted time the supported party is willing to yield to amicus curiae.

(e) *Waiver.* — During oral argument, it shall not be necessary for any party to expressly reserve any argument made on brief, and the failure to raise any such argument shall not constitute a waiver. Any party may, without waiving the arguments made on brief, waive oral argument.

Cross references. — As to oral argument in Court of Appeals, see Rule 5A:28.

Editor's note. — Formerly Rule 5:35.

H. DECISION, COSTS, AND MANDATE.

Rule 5:34. Notice of Decision.

Promptly after this Court has decided a case, the clerk of this Court shall send a copy of the decision to all counsel of record and to the court or commission from which the appeal proceeded.

Cross references. — As to notice of decision of Court of Appeals, see Rule 5A:29.

Editor's note. — Formerly Rule 5:36.

Rule 5:35. Attorney's Fees, Costs, and Notarized Bill of Costs.

(a) *To Whom Allowed.* — Except as otherwise provided by law, if an appeal is dismissed, costs shall be taxed against the appellant unless otherwise agreed by the parties or ordered by this Court; if a judgment is affirmed, costs shall be taxed against the appellant unless otherwise ordered; if a judgment is reversed, costs shall be taxed against the appellee unless otherwise ordered; if a judgment is affirmed in part or reversed in part, or is vacated, costs shall be allowed as ordered by this Court.

(b) *Attorney's Fees.* — Upon refusal or dismissal of a petition for appeal and any petition for rehearing, any appellee who has received attorney's fees and costs in the circuit court may make application in the circuit court for additional fees and costs incurred on appeal pursuant to Rule 1:1A.

(c) *Taxable Costs.* — Costs, including the filing fee and costs incurred in the printing or producing of necessary copies of briefs, appendices, and petitions for rehearing, shall be taxable in this Court. Costs incurred in the preparation of transcripts may be taxable in this Court. See, Code § 17.1-128.

(d) *Notarized Bill of Costs.* — Counsel for a party who desires costs to be taxed shall itemize them in a notarized bill of costs, which shall be filed with the clerk of this Court within 14 days after the date of the decision in the case. Objections to the bill of costs must be filed with the clerk of this Court within 10 days after the date of filing the bill of costs.

(e) *Award.* — The clerk of this Court shall prepare and certify an itemized statement of costs taxed in this Court for insertion in the mandate, but the issuance of the mandate shall not be delayed for taxation of costs. If the mandate has been issued before final determination of costs, the statement, or any amendment thereof, shall be added to the mandate on request by the clerk of this Court to the clerk of the tribunal in which the case originated.

Cross references. — As to mandate in rules of Court of Appeals, see Rule 5A:31.

Editor's note. — Formerly Rule 5:37. **The amendment effective January 1, 2013,** adopted December 14, 2012, added the last two sentences in (c).

Rule 5:36. Mandate.

(a) *Time.* — When there can be no further proceedings in this Court, the clerk of this Court shall forward its mandate promptly to the clerk of the circuit court or commission in which the case originated and to the clerk of the Court of Appeals if the case has been heard by that court.

(b) *Opinions.* — If the judgment or order is supported by an opinion, a certified copy of the opinion shall accompany the mandate.

Cross references. — As to mandate in rules of Court of Appeals, see Rule 5A:31.

Editor's note. — Formerly Rule 5:38.

Rule 5:37. Petition for Rehearing After Consideration by the Full Court.

(a) *Scope.* — This Rule does not apply to the refusal or dismissal of a petition for appeal, or the refusal or dismissal of an original jurisdiction petition. See Rules 5:20 and 5:20A.

(b) *Notice of Intent.* — A party intending to apply for a rehearing shall file written notice with the clerk of this Court within 10 days after the date of the order or opinion of this Court deciding the case. If such notice is given, the clerk of this Court shall withhold certification of the mandate until time for filing the petition for rehearing has expired and, if the petition is filed, until it is disposed of.

(c) *Requirements for Pro Se Prisoners or By Leave of Court.* — Unless the rehearing is abandoned, 20 copies of a petition for rehearing not to exceed the longer of 10 pages or 1,750 words in length shall be thereafter filed in the office of the clerk of this Court and 3 copies delivered or mailed to opposing counsel within 30 days after the date of the order of this Court deciding the case.

(d) *Requirements for All Others.* — (1) Except for petitions filed by pro se prisoners, or with leave of this Court, the petition for rehearing shall be filed as an Adobe Acrobat Portable Document Format (PDF) document attached to an e-mail addressed to scvpfr@courts.state.va.us and will be timely filed if received by the clerk's office on or before 11:59 p.m. within 30 days after the date of the order or opinion of this Court deciding the case. The petition must be formatted to print on a page 8 ½ x 11 inches, must be in 14-point font or larger, must be double-spaced, and must not exceed the longer of 10 pages or 1,750 words. The petition must include a certificate of service to opposing counsel and the certificate shall specify the manner of service and the date of service. The petition must also include a certificate of compliance with the word count limit. The petition will be considered filed on the date and time that it is received by scvpfr@courts.state.va.us. If the petition does not meet the requirements of this rule as to format, the clerk shall so notify counsel and provide a specific amount of time for a corrected copy of the petition to be filed. A person who files a document electronically shall have the same responsibility as a person filing a document in paper form for ensuring that the document is properly filed, complete, and readable. However, if technical problems at this Court result in a failure to timely receive the electronically filed petition for rehearing, counsel shall provide to the clerk of this Court on the next business day all documentation which exists demonstrating the attempt to email the petition, any delivery failure notice received in response to the attempt, and a copy of the petition for rehearing.

(2) The e-mail message to which the petition is attached shall recite in the subject line the style of the case and the Supreme Court record number. The e-mail message shall contain a paragraph stating that a petition for rehearing is being filed, the style of the case, the Supreme Court record number, the name and Virginia State Bar number of counsel filing the petition, as well as the law firm name, mailing address, telephone number, facsimile number (if any), and e-mail address (if any) of counsel. The message shall also state whether a copy of the petition has been served by e-mail or another means on opposing counsel and the date of such service. If the petition has been served on opposing counsel by e-mail, the e-mail address for opposing counsel shall also be included. Upon receipt of the petition for rehearing in the e-mail box of the clerk's office, an acknowledgment will automatically be sent to counsel seeking the rehearing.

(e) *Grounds for Granting.* — No petition for rehearing shall be granted unless one of the Justices who decided the case adversely to the applicant determines that there is good cause for such rehearing. The proceedings upon such rehearing shall be in accordance with Code § 8.01-675.2. No oral argument will be permitted on applications for rehearing.

(f) *When a Rehearing is Granted.* — When a rehearing is granted, the Court will determine whether any additional briefing or argument is necessary. Thereafter, the Court may direct the respondent to electronically file a brief, in compliance with paragraph (d) of this Rule, that shall not exceed the longer of 15 pages in length or 2,625 words. After review of the petition for rehearing and the respondent's brief, if any is filed, the Court may set oral argument on the petition for rehearing at the next available session of the Court. Otherwise, the Court will issue a ruling on the rehearing without further briefing or oral argument.

Editor's note. — Formerly Rules 5A:39 and 5:39A.

The amendment, effective May 2, 2011, adopted March 1, 2011, inserted "the longer of" in subdivision (c), the second sentence of subdivision (d)(1), and in the third sentence of subdivision (f).

The amendment effective June 13, 2012, adopted April 13, 2012, rewrote subdivision (f).

Michie's Jurisprudence. — For related discussion, see 2B M.J. Automobiles, § 117; 5A M.J. Costs, § 12.

I. SETTLEMENT OR WITHDRAWAL.

Rule 5:38. Settlement or Withdrawal of Pending Appeal.

When a case has been settled or the appeal withdrawn at any time after the notice of appeal has been filed, it shall be the duty of counsel to notify the clerk of this Court by filing a written notice that the case has been settled or the appeal withdrawn. If counsel certifies that the terms of the settlement or withdrawal require further proceedings in the trial court, a single Justice may approve entry of an order of remand.

Cross references. — As to settlement and withdrawal before the Court of Appeals, see Rule 5A:36.

Editor's note. — Formerly Rule 5:40.

J. SUPREME COURT OF THE UNITED STATES.

Rule 5:39. Delay in Issuing Mandate Upon Appeal or Petition to Supreme Court of the United States.

If a party intends to file an appeal with the Supreme Court of the United States or seek a writ of certiorari from that court, this Court may, upon motion filed within 15 days after the date of the order of this Court deciding the case, and upon compliance with such conditions as this Court may impose, defer the issuance of its mandate until proceedings in the Supreme Court of the United States have been terminated. Thereupon, the mandate shall issue forthwith.

Editor's note. — Formerly Rule 5:41.

K. CERTIFICATION OF QUESTIONS OF LAW.

Rule 5:40. Certification Procedures.

(a) *Power to Answer.* — This Court may in its discretion answer questions of law certified to it by the Supreme Court of the United States, a United States court of appeals for any circuit, a United States district court, or the highest appellate court of any state, territory, or the District of Columbia. Such answer may be furnished, when requested by the certifying court, if a question of Virginia law is determinative in any proceeding pending before the certifying court and it appears there is no controlling precedent on point in the decisions of this Court or the Court of Appeals of Virginia.

(b) *Method of Invoking.* — This Rule may be invoked only by an order of one of the courts referred to in paragraph (a) of this Rule. No party litigant in the foregoing courts may file a petition or motion for certification in this Court.

(c) *Contents of Certification Order.* — A certification order shall set forth:

(1) the nature of the controversy in which the question arises;

(2) the question of law to be answered;

(3) a statement of all facts relevant to the question certified;

(4) the names of each of the parties involved;

(5) the name, Virginia State Bar number, mailing address, telephone number (including any applicable extension), facsimile number (if any), and e-mail address (if any) of counsel for each of the parties involved;

(6) a brief statement explaining how the certified question of law is determinative of the proceeding in the certifying court; and

(7) a brief statement setting forth relevant decisions, if any, of this Court and the Court of Appeals of Virginia and the reasons why such decisions are not controlling.

(d) *Preparation of Certification Order.* — The certification order shall be prepared by the certifying court, signed by the presiding justice or judge, and forwarded to this Court by the clerk of the certifying court under its official seal. This Court may require the original or copies of all or of any portion of the record before the certifying court to be filed, if, in the opinion of this Court, the record or portion thereof may be necessary in answering the certified question. This Court may in its discretion restate any question of law certified or may request from the certifying court additional clarification with respect to any question certified or with respect to any facts.

(e) *Notification of Acceptance or Rejection.* — This Court, in its discretion, may decide whether to answer any certified question of law. This Court will notify the certifying court and counsel for the parties of its decision to accept or to reject any certified question of law. A notice accepting a question will include a briefing schedule and, if this Court permits oral argument, a tentative date and the length of time allowed for such argument.

(f) *Revocation of Acceptance.* — This Court, in its discretion, may revoke its decision to answer a certified question of law at any time. This Court will notify the certifying court and counsel for the parties of any such action.

(g) *Costs of Certification.* — Fees and costs shall be the same as in civil appeals docketed in this Court and shall be paid as ordered by the certifying court in its order of certification.

(h) *Briefs.* — The form, length, and time for submission of briefs shall comply with Rules 5:26 through 5:32 mutatis mutandis.

(i) *Opinion.* — A written opinion or order of this Court stating the law governing each question certified will be rendered as soon as practicable after the submission of briefs and after any oral argument. The opinion or order will be sent by the clerk under the seal of this Court to the certifying court and to counsel for the parties and shall, if this Court so directs, be published in the Virginia Reports.

Editor's note. — Formerly Rule 5:42.

The amendment effective February 24, 2012, adopted February 24, 2012, inserted "or order" following "opinion" twice in subdivision (i).

Michie's Jurisprudence. — For related discussion, see 1B M.J. Appeal and Error, § 257.

CASE NOTES

Question regarding homeowner's policy exclusions. — Because the answer to whether the Supreme Court of Virginia would conclude that each of four exclusions in a homeowner's insurance policy was unambiguous and reasonable in its form, scope, and application in light of the unusual nature of the losses involving Chinese drywall was sufficiently unsettled and dispositive, certification was warranted. Travco Ins. Co. v. Ward, 2012 U.S. App. LEXIS 4397 (4th Cir. Mar. 1, 2012).

Certified questions proper. — Certified questions from a federal district court to the Supreme Court of Virginia were proper under Va. Sup. Ct. R. 5:40(a) with respect to whether a claim for tortious interference with parental rights existed under Virginia law, as the questions were determinative in the proceedings. Wyatt v. McDermott, 283 Va. 685, 725 S.E.2d 555, 2012 Va. LEXIS 92 (2012).

Certified question accepted. — Certified question was determinative because whether the executrix's wrongful death action was time-barred turned on whether the action accrued at the time of decedent's asbestosis diagnosis or at the time of his mesothelioma diagnosis; accordingly, the court accepted the certified question of law. Kiser v. A.W. Chesterton Co., 285 Va. 12, 736 S.E.2d 910, 2013 Va. LEXIS 12 (2013).

Certified question restated. — Because the certified question as posed encompassed a larger body of employees than was essential to produce a determinative answer, the supreme court exercised its discretion under Va. Sup. Ct. R. 5:40(d) to restate the question. VanBuren v. Grubb, 284 Va. 584, 733 S.E.2d 919, 2012 Va. LEXIS 193 (Nov. 1, 2012).

L. APPEALS RELATING TO QUARANTINE OR ISOLATION ORDERS.

Rule 5:41. Appeal of Orders Relating to Quarantine or Isolation of Persons.

A. *Quarantine Related Code Provisions.* — In proceedings involving circuit court orders of quarantine of a person or persons pursuant to Article 3.02 of Chapter 2 of Title 32.1 of the Code of Virginia, the provisions of Code § 32.1-48.010 shall apply with respect to appealability of such orders, the effect of an appeal upon any order of quarantine, availability of expedited review, stay of quarantine orders, and representation by counsel.

B. *Isolation Order Code Provisions.* — In proceedings involving circuit court orders of isolation of a person or persons pursuant to Article 3.02 of Chapter 2 of Title 32.1 of the Code of Virginia, the provisions of Code § 32.1-48.013 shall apply with respect to appealability of such orders, the effect of an appeal upon any order of isolation, availability of expedited review, stay of isolation orders, and representation by counsel.

C. *Transmission of Record.* — In all appeals under this rule, the clerk of the court from which an appeal is taken shall transmit the record to the Clerk of the Supreme Court immediately upon the filing of the notice of appeal.

D. *Expedited Procedures.* — Unless otherwise ordered by the Supreme Court, after the filing of the petition for appeal under this Rule, 48 hours shall be allowed for the filing of the brief in opposition. However, the Supreme Court may employ the expedited review provision in Rule 5:18(c). The Supreme Court shall act upon the petition within 72 hours of its filing. Should the Supreme Court grant a writ, the Supreme Court may, in its discretion, permit oral argument within 48 hours of granting the writ. The Supreme Court will issue an order within 24 hours of the argument or of its review of the case without oral argument. The Supreme Court has the authority to alter these time frames in any case.

E. *Oral Argument.* — The Court shall hold any oral argument in appeals under this rule in a manner so as to protect the health and safety of individuals subject to any such order or quarantine or isolation, court personnel, counsel, and the general public. To this end, the Court may take measures including, but not limited to, ordering any oral argument to be held by telephone or video conference or ordering those present to take appropriate precautions, including wearing personal protective equipment. If necessary, the Court may dispense with oral argument.

Editor's note. — Formerly Rule 5:43.
The amendment, effective May 2, 2011, adopted March 1, 2011, inserted "of Chapter 2" in subdivisions A and B.

APPENDIX OF FORMS.

Form 1. Bond for Costs Alone — Appeal of Right From Circuit Court to Court of Appeals (including further appeal to the Supreme Court).

KNOW ALL MEN BY THESE PRESENTS, That we,
____________________________________, principal, and
____________________________________, surety, are held and firmly bound unto ________________________
appellee(s)
in the sum of ____________________________ to the payment of which we bind ourselves, our heirs, successors, personal representatives and assigns, jointly and severally, firmly by these presents.

The condition of this obligation is such that:

Whereas judgment was rendered by the Circuit Court of ______________ on the ____________ day of ________________, _____, in the case of ____________________________________
____;

And whereas it is the intention of ________________________
____________ to appeal said judgment to the Court of Appeals of Virginia;

Now, therefore, if ________________________________
appellant(s)
shall pay all damages, costs, and fees which may be awarded against (him) (her) (them) (it) in the Court of Appeals and Supreme Court if it takes cognizance of the claim, then this obligation shall be void, otherwise to remain in full force and virtue.

Form 2. Bond for Costs and Suspension — Appeal From Circuit Court to Appellate Court.

KNOW ALL MEN BY THESE PRESENTS, That we,
____________________________________, principal, and
____________________________________, surety, are held and firmly bound unto ________________________
appellee(s)
in the sum of ____________________________ to the payment of which we bind ourselves, our heirs, successors, personal representatives and assigns, jointly and severally, firmly by these presents.

The condition of this obligation is such that:

Whereas judgment was rendered by the Circuit Court of ______________ on the ____________ day of ________________, _____, in the case of ____________________________________
____;

And whereas it is the intention of ________________________ to appeal said judgment to the (Supreme Court) (Court of Appeals) of Virginia, and suspension of execution of the judgment is sought;

Now, therefore, if ________________________________
appellant(s)
shall perform and satisfy and said judgment or the part thereof proceedings on which are stayed, in case such judgment or such part be affirmed in whole or in part, or the appeal be dismissed, refused or not timely prosecuted, and shall pay all damages, costs, and fees which may be awarded against (him) (her) (them) (it) in the (Supreme Court) (Court of Appeals and Supreme Court if it takes cognizance of the claim) and all actual damages incurred in consequence of the suspension, then this obligation shall be void, otherwise to remain in full force and virtue.

Form 3. Bond for Costs Alone Required by Appellate Court on Appeal From Circuit Court.

KNOW ALL MEN BY THESE PRESENTS, That we,
____________________________________, principal, and
____________________________________, surety, are held

and firmly bound unto ____
appellee(s)
in the sum of ____ to the payment of which we bind ourselves, our heirs, successors, personal representatives and assigns, jointly and severally, firmly by these presents.

The condition of this obligation is such that:

Whereas the (Supreme Court of Virginia) (Court of Appeals of Virginia) on the ________ day of ______________, ______, awarded an appeal from a judgment rendered against ______________________________ by the Circuit Court of
appellant(s)
______________________________, on the ________ day of ______________, ______, upon ______________________________
______________________________, or someone for (him) (her) (them) (it),
appellant(s)
filing an appeal bond with sufficient security in the clerk's office of the Circuit Court of ______________________________, in the penalty of ______________________________ within fifteen (15) days of the date of the certificate of appeal, with condition as the law directs;

Now, therefore, if ______________________________
appellant(s)
shall pay all damages, costs, and fees which may be awarded against (him) (her) (them) (it) in the (Supreme Court) (Court of Appeals and Supreme Court if it takes cognizance of the claim), then this obligation shall be void, otherwise to remain in full force and virtue.

Form 4. Bond for Suspension Alone Required by Appellate Court on Appeal From Circuit Court.

KNOW ALL MEN BY THESE PRESENTS, That we,

______________________________, principal, and
______________________________, surety, are held and firmly bound unto ______________________________
appellee(s)
in the sum of ______________________________ to the payment of which we bind ourselves, our heirs, successors, personal representatives and assigns, jointly and severally, firmly by these presents.

The condition of this obligation is such that:

Whereas the (Supreme Court of Virginia) (Court of Appeals of Virginia) on the ________ day of ______________, ______, awarded an appeal from a judgment rendered against ______________________________ by the Circuit Court of
appellant(s)
______________________________, on the ________ day of ______________, ______, upon ______________________________
______________________________, or some one for (him) (her) (them) (it),
appellant(s)
filing an appeal bond with sufficient security in the clerk's office of the Circuit Court of ______________________________, in the penalty of ______________________________ within fifteen (15) days of the date of the certificate of appeal, with condition as the law directs;

Now, therefore, if ______________________________
appellant(s)
shall perform and satisfy said judgment or the part thereof proceedings on which are stayed, in case such judgment or such part be affirmed in whole or in part, and shall pay all actual damages incurred in consequence of the suspension, then this obligation shall be void, otherwise to remain in full force and virtue.

Form 5. Bond for Costs and Suspension Required by Appellate Court on Appeal From Circuit Court.

KNOW ALL MEN BY THESE PRESENTS, That we,
______________________________, principal, and
______________________________, surety, are held
and firmly bound unto ______________________________
appellee(s)
in the sum of ______________________________ to
the payment of which we bind ourselves, our heirs, successors, personal representatives and assigns, jointly and severally, firmly by these presents.

The condition of this obligation is such that:

Whereas the (Supreme Court of Virginia) (Court of Appeals of Virginia) on the ________ day of ______________, ______, awarded an appeal and (suspension of judgment) (supersedeas) from a judgment rendered against ______________________________ by the Circuit
appellant(s)
Court of ______________, on the __________, day of ______________, ______,
upon ______________________________, or some one for
appellant(s)
for (him) (her) (them) (it), filing an appeal bond with sufficient security in the clerk's office of the Circuit Court of ______________, in the penalty of __________ within fifteen (15) days of the date of the certificate of appeal, with condition as the law directs;

Now, therefore, if ______________________________
appellant(s)
shall perform and satisfy said judgment or the part thereof proceedings on which are stayed, in case such judgment or such part be affirmed in whole or in part, and shall pay all damages, costs, and fees which may be awarded against (him) (her) (them) (it) in the (Supreme Court) (Court of Appeals and Supreme Court if it takes cognizance of the claim) and all actual damages incurred in consequence of the suspension, then this obligation shall be void, otherwise to remain in full force and virtue.

Form 6. Additional Bond Required by Appellate Court on Appeal From Circuit Court.

KNOW ALL MEN BY THESE PRESENTS, That we,
______________________________, principal, and
______________________________, surety, are held
and firmly bound unto ______________________________
appellee(s)
in the sum of ______________________________
to the payment of which we bind ourselves, our heirs, successors, personal representatives and assigns, jointly and severally, firmly by these presents.

The condition of this obligation is such that:

Whereas the (Supreme Court of Virginia) (Court of Appeals of Virginia) on the ________ day of ______________, ______, required additional bond on this appeal from a judgment rendered against ______________________________ by the
appellant(s)
Circuit Court of ______________________________,
on the __________ day of __________, ______, such additional bond to be filed in the clerk's office of the Circuit Court of ______________________________
in the penalty of ______________________________, and with the following additional requirements: ______________________________
______________________________,
within fifteen (15) days of the date of the order requiring additional bond, with condition as the law directs;

Now, therefore, if ______________________________
appellant(s)
shall perform and satisfy said judgment or the part thereof proceedings on which are stayed, in case such judgment or such part be affirmed in whole or in part, and shall

pay all actual damages incurred in consequence of the suspension, then this obligation shall be void, otherwise to remain in full force and virtue.

Form 7. Bond for Costs Alone — Appeal of Right From Virginia Workers' Compensation Commission to Court of Appeals (including further appeal to the Supreme Court).

KNOW ALL MEN BY THESE PRESENTS, That we,

______________________________, principal, and
______________________________, surety, are held
and firmly bound unto ______________________________
appellee(s)
in the sum of ______________________________ to the payment of which we bind ourselves, our heirs, successors, personal representatives and assigns, jointly and severally, firmly by these presents.

The condition of this obligation is such that:

Whereas an award was entered by the Virginia Workers' Compensation Commission on the ________ day of ____________, ______, in the case of ______________________________;

And whereas it is the intention of ______________________________ to appeal said award to the Court of Appeals of Virginia;

Now, therefore, if ______________________________
appellant(s)
shall pay all damages, costs, and fees which may be awarded against (him) (her) (them) (it) in the Court of Appeals and Supreme Court if it takes cognizance of the claim, then this obligation shall be void, otherwise to remain in full force and virtue.

Form 8. Bond for Costs Alone — Required by Supreme Court on Appeal of Right From State Corporation Commission.

KNOW ALL MEN BY THESE PRESENTS, That we,

______________________________, principal, and
______________________________, surety, are held
and firmly bound unto ______________________________
appellee(s)
in the sum of ______________________________ to the payment of which we bind ourselves, our heirs, successors, personal representatives and assigns, jointly and severally, firmly by these presents.

The condition of this obligation is such that:

Whereas the Supreme Court of Virginia on the ____________ day of ____________, ______, awarded an appeal from a final order entered in Case No. ____________ under the style of ______________________________ by the State Corporation Commission of Virginia, on the ____________ day of ____________, ______, on the condition that ______________________________
appellant(s)
or someone for (him) (her) (them) (it), file an appeal bond with sufficient security in the clerk's office of the State Corporation Commission, in the penalty of ______________________________ within fifteen (15) days of the date of the certificate of appeal, with condition as the law directs;

Now, therefore, if ______________________________
appellant(s)
shall pay all damages, costs, and fees which may be awarded against (him) (her) (them) (it) in the Supreme Court, then this obligation shall be void, otherwise to remain in full force and virtue.

Form 9. Bond for Costs and Suspension — Required by Supreme Court on Appeal of Right From State Corporation Commission.

KNOW ALL MEN BY THESE PRESENTS, That we,

______________________________, principal, and
______________________________, surety, are held

and firmly bound unto ______________________________
appellee(s)
in the sum of ______________________________ to the payment of which we bind ourselves, our heirs, successors, personal representatives and assigns, jointly and severally, firmly by these presents.

The condition of this obligation is such that:

Whereas the Supreme Court of Virginia on the ____________ day of ____________, ______, awarded an appeal and suspension from a final order entered in Case No. ____________ under the style of ____________ by the State Corporation Commission of Virginia, on the ____________ day of ____________, ______, on the condition that ____________, or some one for (him) (her) (them) (it), file an
appellant(s)
appeal bond with sufficient security in the clerk's office of the State Corporation Commission, in the penalty of ____________ within fifteen (15) days of the date of the certificate of appeal, with condition as the law directs;

Now, therefore, if ______________________________
appellant(s)
shall perform and satisfy said order or the part thereof proceedings on which are stayed, in case such order or such part be affirmed in whole or in part, and shall pay all damages, costs, and fees which may be awarded against (him) (her) (them) (it) in the Supreme Court and all actual damages incurred in consequence of the suspension, then this obligation shall be void, otherwise to remain in full force and virtue.

Form 10. Form for Execution and Acknowledgment of All Bonds.

In witness whereof, the said ____________ ____________, principal, and ____________ ____________, surety, have hereunto set their hands and seals, this ______ day of ____________, ______.

____________________ (SEAL)
____________________ (SEAL)

State of Virginia
City/County of ____________

The foregoing instrument was acknowledged before me this ____________ day of ____________, ______, by ____________ ____________.

____
Notary Public

My commission expires: ____________________

Form 11. Irrevocable Letters of Credit.

(Name and Address of Bank)

____________, 20____

U.S. $____________

On all communications please refer to (No. of Letter of Credit)

(Name and address of appellee(s))

Dear ____________:

We hereby establish our Irrevocable Letter of Credit No. ____________ in your favor, for the account of (name and address of appellant(s)), and hereby undertake to honor your draft at sight on us, not exceeding in the aggregate U.S. $ (amount in words). A draft drawn under this letter of credit must be marked "Drawn under (Name of Bank) Letter of Credit No. ____________, dated

_______________, 20___." Funds under this letter of credit will be available to you in a single drawing by presentation of your sight draft drawn on us, accompanied by:

(For Costs Alone)

1. The original of this letter of credit.
2. Your verified statement that ______________________ (has)(have) failed to
appellant(s)
pay all damages, costs and fees assessed against (him)(her)(them)(it) in the Supreme Court of Virginia in the case of ______________________.
3. A certified copy of an order or itemized statement of costs from the Supreme Court assessing such damages, costs and fees against ______________________.
appellant(s)

(For Suspension Alone)

1. The original of this letter of credit.
2. Your verified statement that ______________________ (has)(have) failed to
appellant(s)
perform and satisfy the judgment rendered against (him)(her)(them)(it) on ______________ by the Circuit Court of ______________ in the case of ______________, and (has)(have) failed to pay all actual damages incurred in consequence of the suspension of judgment.
3. A copy of the trial court judgment order, attested by its clerk.
4. A copy of an order of the Supreme Court of Virginia, attested by its clerk, affirming said judgment or refusing, dismissing or allowing withdrawal of the appeal of said judgment, or certification by the clerk of the Supreme Court that the appeal of said judgment was not prosecuted timely.
5. A copy of an order, if any, of the Supreme Court or trial court, attested by the clerk, assessing actual damages in consequence of the suspension of judgment.

(For Costs and Suspension)

1. The original of this letter of credit.
2. Your verified statement that ______________________ (has)(have) failed to
appellant(s)
perform and satisfy the judgment rendered against (him)(her)(them)(it) on ______________ by the Circuit Court of ______________ in the case of ______________, and (has)(have) failed to pay all damages, costs and fees assessed against (him)(her)(them)(it) in the Supreme Court of Virginia, and all actual damages incurred in consequence of the suspension of judgment.
3. A copy of the trial court judgment order, attested by its clerk.
4. A copy of an order of the Supreme Court, attested by its clerk, affirming said judgment or refusing, dismissing or allowing withdrawal of the appeal of said judgment, or certification by the clerk of the Supreme Court that the appeal of said judgment was not prosecuted timely.
5. A copy of an order, if any, of the Supreme Court, attested by the clerk, assessing damages, costs and fees against ______________________.
appellant(s)
6. A copy of an order, if any, of the Supreme Court or trial court, attested by the clerk, assessing actual damages in consequence of the suspension of judgment.

This letter of credit is valid until ____ p.m. local time _______, 20____, and a draft drawn hereunder, if accompanied by documents as specified above, will be honored if presented to (Presentation Address of Bank) on or before that date. However, this letter of credit automatically will be renewed for successive one (1) year periods from the initial expiration date or any renewal period expiration date hereunder, unless at least sixty (60) days prior to any such expiration date (Name of Bank) notifies you that it has elected not to renew this letter of credit for such additional one (1) year period. The notice required hereunder will be deemed to have been given when received by you.

In the event that (Name of Bank) elects not to renew this letter of credit as required above, the full amount of this letter of credit shall be payable to the Clerk of the Circuit Court of ______________ upon presentation of your verified statement that:

1. A final order of the Supreme Court of Virginia has not been entered in the case of ______________________________ (or, where there has been suspension of judgment, a final order has not been entered by the Supreme Court or trial court assessing actual damages in consequence of the suspension).
2. Thirty (30) days have elapsed since notice of non-renewal was given and appellant(s) (has)(have) not filed acceptable substitute security.

In the event of non-renewal, within fifteen (15) days after payment to the clerk under the previous paragraph, the appellant(s) or someone for (him)(her)(them)(it) shall file with said clerk an appeal bond in substantial conformance with the appropriate form in the Appendix to Part Five of the Rules of the Supreme Court of Virginia. The bond shall be in the penalty of the amount paid to said clerk under this letter of credit, and said funds shall be in lieu of surety.

Except as otherwise expressly stated herein, this letter of credit is subject to the Uniform Customs and Practice for Documentary Credits as most recently published by the International Chamber of Commerce.

Very truly yours,

__________________________ Bank

By __________________________

Authorized Signature

Form 12. Petition for a Writ of Actual Innocence.

PETITION FOR A WRIT OF ACTUAL INNOCENCE

TO THE SUPREME COURT OF VIRGINIA

In re: ____________________ Record No. ____________________

(FULL NAME OF PETITIONER) (TO BE SUPPLIED BY THE CLERK OF THE SUPREME COURT)

Circuit Court

____________________________ Case No.(s) ________________________

PRISONER NO., IF APPLICABLE)

____________________________ ________________________________

(PETITIONER'S ADDRESS)

____________________________ ________________________________

____

Pursuant to the provisions of Chapter 19.2 of Title 19.2 of the Code of Virginia, I,

____

NAME OF PETITIONER

hereby petition this Court for a writ of actual innocence. In support of this petition, I state under oath that the following information is true:

1. On __________________, I was convicted or adjudicated delinquent in the
DATE

____________________________ Circuit Court of the following offense(s):
NAME OF COURT

Description of Offense	Virginia Code	Class of Felony	Plea
__________	__________	__________	__________
__________	__________	__________	__________
__________	__________	__________	__________

[ ] ATTACHED ADDITIONAL SHEET(S)

2. I am innocent of the offense(s) for which I was convicted or adjudicated delinquent.

3. My claim of innocence is based upon the following human biological evidence and scientific testing:

____

____

[ ] ATTACHED ADDITIONAL SHEET(S)

4. Check one:

[ ] This evidence was not known or available to either me or my attorney at the time the conviction or adjudication of delinquency became final in the circuit court.

[ ] This evidence was known at the time the conviction or adjudication of delinquency became final in the circuit court, but was not tested because ____

[ ] ATTACHED ADDITIONAL SHEET(S)

5. This evidence was tested pursuant to the provisions of Virginia Code § 19.2-327.1 and the results were obtained by me or my attorney on ______________ .

DATE

This petition is filed within sixty days of obtaining those results and those test results are filed with this petition. Attached is a copy of the notice of the test results from the Department of Forensic Science.

6. The scientific evidence described in paragraph number 4 above will prove that no rational trier of fact would have found me to be guilty or delinquent beyond a reasonable doubt of the charge described above because

____

____

[ ] ATTACHED ADDITIONAL SHEET(S)

7. Check box if applicable and provide any additional information.

[ ] My conviction or adjudication of delinquency became final after June 30, 1996, and the scientific evidence described in paragraph number 4 above was not available for testing under Virginia Code § 9.1-1104 because:

____

____

[ ] ATTACHED ADDITIONAL SHEET(S)

8. This petition contains all relevant allegations of fact known to me at this time and all previous records, applications, petitions, appeals, and dispositions relating to this matter are attached. In support of this petition, the following documents are attached:

____

____

[ ] ATTACHED ADDITIONAL SHEET(S)

9. I understand that this petition must contain all relevant allegations of fact that are known to me at this time. I understand that it must include all previous records, applications, petitions, appeals, and their dispositions related to this conviction, as well as a copy of any test results of the scientific evidence described above. I understand that if this petition is not complete, this Court may dismiss the petition or return the petition to me pending the completion of such form. I understand that I am responsible for all statements contained in this petition. I understand that any knowingly or willfully made false statement shall be a ground for prosecution and conviction of perjury as provided in Virginia Code § 18.2-434. I understand that this Court shall not accept this petition unless it is accompanied by a duly executed return of service verifying that a copy of this petition and all attachments have been served

on the attorney for the Commonwealth of the jurisdiction where the conviction occurred and on the Attorney General of Virginia.

10. Check box if claiming in forma pauperis status and seeking to file this petition without payment of fees.

[ ] I claim in forma pauperis status and I request that this Court accept this petition without the payment of filing fees. I affirm under oath that I am eligible for in forma pauperis status and I have attached the completed affidavit to this effect.

Based on the above, I petition this Court pursuant to the provisions of Chapter 19.2 of Title 19.2 of the Code of Virginia for a writ of actual innocence.

____________________ ____________________

DATE SIGNATURE OF PETITIONER

FOR NOTARY PUBLIC'S USE ONLY:

State of .... [ ] City [ ] County of ....

Acknowledged, subscribed and sworn to before me this ... day of ...., 20......

.... ____________________

NOTARY REGISTRATION NUMBER NOTARY PUBLIC

My commission expires: ....)

AFFIDAVIT IN FORMA PAUPERIS

The petitioner, ____________________, being duly sworn, says,

1. I am unable to pay for counsel to prosecute this action;
2. My assets amount to a total of $ ____________________

____________________ ____________________

DATE SIGNATURE OF PETITIONER

FOR NOTARY PUBLIC'S USE ONLY:

State of .... [ ] City [ ] County of ....

Acknowledged, subscribed and sworn to before me this ... day of ...., 20......

.... ____________________

NOTARY REGISTRATION NUMBER NOTARY PUBLIC

My commission expires: ....)

Effective date. — This form, adopted March 1, 2011, became effective May 2, 2011; and has been amended by order adopted June 21, 2013, effective July 1, 2013.

PART FIVE A
THE COURT OF APPEALS

A. General.

Rule
5A:1. Scope, Citation, Applicability and General Provisions.
5A:2. Motions and Responses; Orders.
5A:3. Filing Deadlines; Post Trial Proceedings Below; Timely Filing by Mail; Inmate Filing; Extension of Time.
5A:4. Forms of Briefs and Other Papers.

B. Original Jurisdiction.

5A:5. Original Proceedings.

C. Procedure for Filing an Appeal From the Trial Court.

5A:6. Notice of Appeal.
5A:7. Record on Appeal: Contents.
5A:8. Record on Appeal: Transcript or Written Statement.
5A:9. Judge Authorized to Act.
5A:10. Record on Appeal: Preparation and Transmission.

D. Procedure for Filing an Appeal From the Workers' Compensation Commission.

5A:11. Special Rule Applicable to Appeals From the Virginia Workers' Compensation Commission.

E. Procedure on Petition for Appeal in Criminal Cases and Traffic Infractions

5A:12. Petition for Appeal.
5A:13. Brief in Opposition.
5A:14. Reply Brief.
5A:15. Denial of Petition for Appeal; Petition for Rehearing.
5A:15A. Denial of Petition for Appeal; Petition for Rehearing Filed by Electronic Means.

F. Procedure Following Perfection of Appeal.

5A:16. Perfection of Appeal; Docketing.
5A:17. Security for Appeal.
5A:18. Preservation of Issues for Appellate Review.
5A:19. General Requirements for All Briefs.
5A:20. Requirements for Opening Brief of Appellant.
5A:21. Requirements for Brief of Appellee or Guardian Ad Litem.
5A:22. Requirements for Reply Brief.
5A:23. Briefs Amicus Curiae.
5A:24. Covers of Documents.
5A:25. Appendix.

Rule
5A:26. Effect of Noncompliance With Rules Regarding Briefs.
5A:27. Summary Disposition.
5A:28. Oral Argument.

G. Decision, Costs, and Mandate.

5A:29. Notice of Decision.
5A:30. Costs and Notarized Bill of Costs.
5A:31. Mandate.

H. Rehearing.

5A:32. Scope.
5A:33. Rehearing — On Motion of a Party After Final Disposition of a Case.
5A:34. Rehearing En Banc After Final Disposition of a Case.
5A:35. Procedure for Rehearing.

I. Settlement, Withdrawal, and Mediation.

5A:36. Settlement or Withdrawal of Pending Appeal.
5A:37. Appellate Settlement Conference in the Court of Appeals.

Appendix of Forms.

Form
1. Bond for Costs Alone — Appeal of Right From Circuit Court to Court of Appeals (including further appeal to the Supreme Court).
2. Bond for Costs and Suspension — Appeal From Circuit Court to Appellate Court.
3. Bond for Costs Alone Required by Appellate Court on Appeal From Circuit Court.
4. Bond for Suspension Alone Required by Appellate Court on Appeal From Circuit Court.
5. Bond for Costs and Suspension Required by Appellate Court on Appeal From Circuit Court.
6. Additional Bond Required by Appellate Court on Appeal From Circuit Court.
7. Bond for Costs Alone — Appeal of Right From Virginia Workers' Compensation Commission to Court of Appeals (including further appeal to the Supreme Court).
8. Bond for Costs Alone — Required by Supreme Court on Appeal of Right From State Corporation Commission.
9. Bond for Costs and Suspension — Required by Supreme Court on Appeal of Right From State Corporation Commission.
10. Form for Execution and Acknowledgment of All Bonds.
11. Irrevocable Letters of Credit.
12. Petition for a Writ of Actual Innocence Based on Nonbiological Evidence.

Editor's note. — Part Five A, adopted May 1, 1984, became effective Oct. 1, 1984, except for Rule 5A:11, which became effective Nov. 1, 1984.

Part Five A was rewritten in its entirety by order adopted April 30, 2010, and effective July 1, 2010.

A. GENERAL.

Rule 5A:1. Scope, Citation, Applicability and General Provisions.

(a) *Scope of Rules.* — Five A governs all proceedings in the Court of Appeals of Virginia.

(b) *Citation.* — These Rules may be cited generally as the "Rules of the Court of Appeals of Virginia" and specifically as "Rule 5A:__."

(c) *Definitions.* — (1) "clerk of the trial court" means clerk of the trial court from which an appeal is taken to the Court of Appeals, and shall include a deputy clerk and the clerk of the Virginia Workers' Compensation Commission when the context requires;

(2) "clerk of the Court of Appeals" includes a deputy clerk;

(3) "counsel" has the definition given in Rule 1:5 for Counsel of Record and in this Part Five A includes a party not represented by counsel and any attorney appointed as a guardian ad litem;

(4) "counsel for appellant" means one of the attorneys representing each appellant represented by an attorney, and each appellant not represented by an attorney;

(5) "counsel for appellee" means one of the attorneys representing each appellee represented by an attorney, and each appellee not represented by an attorney and shall include a guardian ad litem, unless the guardian ad litem is the appellant;

(6) "opposing counsel" means, depending on the context, "counsel for the appellant" or "counsel for the appellee";

(7) "judge" means judge of the trial court, unless the context otherwise requires, or if he be not available, any judge authorized to act under Rule 5A:9;

(8) "judgment" includes an order or decree from which an appeal is taken;

(9) "File with the clerk" or "files with the clerk" or "filed with the clerk" means deliver to the clerk specified a paper, a copy of which has been mailed or delivered to opposing counsel, and appended to which is either acceptance of service or a certificate showing the date of mailing or delivery. "File in the office of the clerk" or "files in the office of the clerk" or "filed in the office of the clerk" means, on the other hand, deliver a paper to the clerk specified;

(10) "trial court" means the circuit court from which an appeal is taken to the Court of Appeals;

(11) the "date of entry" of any final judgment or other appealable order or decree shall be the date the judgment, order, or decree is signed by the judge.

(d) *Service.* — Unless service or notice is otherwise specified in a given Rule, any paper or object filed with this Court must have included within it or appended to it a certificate of service or acceptance of service showing that a copy has been transmitted to all counsel and showing the date and manner of transmittal. If a word count limitation is required, the certificate must also state the number of words (headings, footnotes, and quotations count towards the word limitation; the cover page, table of contents, table of authorities, and certificate do not count towards the word count).

(e) *Notice of Change of Address and Other Contact Information.* — If an attorney has a change in mailing address, telephone number, facsimile number, or e-mail address any time after the filing of the notice of appeal, the attorney must immediately notify the clerk of this Court and all other counsel of record in writing. The notice must reference the style and record number of all cases pending before this Court.

(f) *Citing Unpublished Judicial Dispositions.* — The citation of judicial opinions, orders, judgments, or other written dispositions that are not officially reported, whether designated as "unpublished," "not for publication," "non precedential," or the like, is permitted as informative, but shall not be received as binding authority. If the cited disposition is not available in a publicly accessible electronic database, a copy of that disposition must be filed with the brief or other paper in which it is cited.

Cross references. — As to appeals to the Court of Appeals, see Va. Code § 8.01-675.3 et seq. As to appeals generally, see Va. Code § 8.01-676.1 et seq. As to creation, organization, jurisdiction, and procedures of Court of Appeals, see Va. Code § 17.1-400 et seq.

Law Review. — For 1985 survey of Virginia civil procedure and practice, see 19 U. Rich. L. Rev. 679 (1985). For 2003/2004 survey of family and juvenile law, see 39 U. Rich. L. Rev. 241 (2004).

CASE NOTES

Notice of appeal under Rule 5A:11(b). — Provision of paragraph (10) [see Rule 5A:6(d)(2)] that a copy of the notice of appeal be mailed or delivered to opposing counsel does not defeat the filing of notice of appeal with the clerk of the Industrial (now Workers' Compensation) Commission under Rule 5A:11(b); this provision is directory rather than mandatory, because appellee is put on notice of the appeal when the clerk of court sends notice that the record has been filed and because appellee has no reason to assume that an appeal will not follow a favorable decision by the Commission, since such appeals are a matter of right rather than by petition. Johnson v. City of Clifton Forge, 7 Va. App. 538, 375 S.E.2d 540 (1989).

Failure to name necessary party required dismissal. — Because a father's counsel of record was an indispensable party to an appeal by a county department of social services (DSS), and because counsel was neither named in DSS's notice of appeal of the denial of its termination of the father's parental rights nor mailed a copy of the notice, as required by Va. Sup. Ct. R. 5A:6 and 5A:1, the court lacked jurisdiction to entertain DSS's appeal. Greene County Dep't of Soc. Servs. v. Green, 2006 Va. App. LEXIS 452 (Oct. 10, 2006).

Applied in Watkins v. Fairfax County Dep't of Family Servs., 42 Va. App. 760, 595 S.E.2d 19, 2004 Va. App. LEXIS 164 (2004); Griffin v. Griffin, 2012 Va. App. LEXIS 179 (May 29, 2012).

Rule 5A:2. Motions and Responses; Orders.

(a) *Motions and Responses.* — (1) Motions. All motions shall be in writing and filed with the clerk of this Court. All motions shall contain a statement by the movant that the other parties to the appeal have been informed of the intended filing of the motion. For all motions in cases when all parties are represented by counsel — except motions to dismiss petitions for a writ of habeas corpus — the statement by the movant shall also indicate whether the other parties consent to the granting of the motion, or intend to file responses in opposition.

(2) Responses. Opposing counsel may have ten days after such motion is filed to file with such clerk a response to such motion, but this Court may act before the ten days expire, if necessary.

(3) Number of Copies. An original and three copies of all motions or responses must be filed.

(4) Oral Argument. No motion shall be argued orally except by leave of this Court.

(b) *Motion for Review of Pre-trial Bail Orders in Criminal Cases.* — When a circuit court has granted or denied pre-trial bail or set a bond or terms of recognizance or revoked bail, either party may move this Court to review the order. With the motion for review, the party seeking review shall submit copies of: (1) the warrant(s) or indictment(s) in the case; (2) the order granting, denying, or setting bond; and (3) a transcript of the bond hearing or a stipulation between counsel stating the evidence introduced at the bond hearing and the ruling of the circuit court. An order setting or denying bail or setting terms of a bond or recognizance shall be reviewable for abuse of discretion.

(c) *Motion for Review of Post-trial Bail Pending Appeal Orders in Criminal Cases.* — When a notice of appeal has been filed in a criminal case, an appellant other than the Commonwealth may move this Court to review the trial court's order denying bail pending appeal or setting an excessive bail pending appeal. With the motion for review, the appellant shall submit copies of: (1) the sentencing order entered by the trial court; (2) a pre-sentence report when available; (3) the trial court's decision setting or denying bail; and (4) a transcript of the bail hearing or a stipulation between counsel stating the evidence introduced at the bail hearing and the reason the trial court gave for the bail decision. An order setting or denying bail pending appeal in a criminal case shall be reviewable for abuse of discretion. If this Court overrules a trial court decision denying bail pending appeal, this Court shall set the amount of the bail pending appeal or remand the matter to the trial court with directions to set bail pending appeal.

(d) *Orders.* — Promptly after this Court has entered an order, the clerk of this Court shall send a copy of the order to all counsel.

Rule 5A:3. Filing Deadlines; Post Trial Proceedings Below; Timely Filing by Mail; Inmate Filing; Extension of Time.

(a) *Filing Deadlines and Extensions.* — The times prescribed for filing the notice of appeal (Rules 5A:6 and 5A:11), a petition for appeal (Rule 5A:12), and a petition for rehearing (Rule 5A:33) and a request for rehearing en banc (Rule 5A:34) are mandatory. Except for the petition for appeal which is addressed in Rule 5A:12(a) and Code § 17.1-408, a single extension not to exceed thirty days may be granted if at least three judges of the Court of Appeals concur in a finding that an extension for papers to be filed is warranted upon a showing of good cause sufficient to excuse the delay. The time period for filing the notice of appeal is not extended by the filing of a motion for a new trial, a petition for rehearing, or a like pleading unless the final judgment is modified, vacated, or suspended by the trial court pursuant to Rule 1:1, in which case the time for filing shall be computed from the date of the final judgment entered following such modification, vacation, or suspension.

(b) *Extensions Generally.* — Except as provided in paragraph (a) of this Rule, the times prescribed in these Rules for filing papers, except transcripts (Rule 5A:8(a)), may be extended by a judge of the court in which the papers are to be filed upon a showing of good cause sufficient to excuse the delay.

(c) *Motions for Extension.* — A motion for extension of time is timely if filed:

(1) within the original filing deadline; or

(2) within the specified extension period - see Rules 5A:3(a) and 5A:12(a); or

(3) within any specific deadline governing motions to extend - see Rules 5A:8(a), 5A:13(a), 5A:14, 5A:19(b), and 5A:19(c).

Filing a motion for extension does not toll the applicable deadline or further extend the period of extension.

(d) *How to File by Mail in a Timely Manner.* — Any document required to be filed with the clerk of this Court shall be deemed to be timely filed if (1) it is transmitted expense pre-paid to the clerk of this Court by priority, express, registered, or certified mail via the United States Postal Service, or by a third-party commercial carrier for next-day delivery, and (2) if the official receipt therefor be exhibited upon demand of the clerk or any party and it shows such transmission or mailing within the prescribed time limits. This Rule does not apply to documents to be filed in the office of the clerk of the trial court or clerk of the Virginia Workers' Compensation Commission.

(e) *Inmate Filing.* — A paper filed by an inmate confined in an institution is timely filed if deposited in the institution's internal mail system with first-class postage prepaid on or before the last day for filing. Timely filing of a paper by an inmate confined in an institution may be established by (1) an official stamp of the institution showing that the paper was deposited in the internal mail system on or before the last day for filing, (2) an official postmark dated on or before the last day for filing, or (3) a notarized statement signed by an official of the institution showing that the paper was deposited in the internal mail system on or before the last day for filing.

Comment. — See also Rule 1:7 regarding computation of time. See § 17.1-408, Code of Virginia, regarding extension of time to file petition for appeal.

The amendment, effective May 2, 2011, adopted March 1, 2011, deleted "by" following "(1) it is" in subdivision (d).

CASE NOTES

Editor's note. — The cases annotated below were decided under prior rule.

"Notice of appeal" refers to notice filed in trial court. — Rule 5A:6(a) provides that a notice of appeal shall be filed with the clerk of the trial court, and this original paper filed in the trial court is the notice of appeal referred to in subdivision (a) of this rule as mandatory. Johnson v. Commonwealth, 1 Va. App. 510, 339 S.E.2d 919 (1986).

It does not refer to notice filed with Court of Appeals. — The copies of the notice of appeal required to be mailed or delivered to the clerk of the Court of Appeals are not the "notice of appeal" specified in subdivision (a) of this rule. Johnson v. Commonwealth, 1 Va. App. 510, 339 S.E.2d 919 (1986).

Time to file appeal bond may not be extended under subdivision (b), as it allows for the extension of time limits prescribed "in these Rules" and the bond is required by a statute. Lipscomb v. Rosenthal Chevrolet, No. 0404-85, (Ct. of Appeals Dec. 10, 1985); O'Brien v. O'Brien, No. 0335-85, (Ct. of Appeals Dec. 23, 1985).

Subdivision (b) does not authorize an extension of time for filing the bond. It provides that "the times prescribed in these Rules for filing papers may be extended by a judge of the court in which the papers are to be filed on motion for good cause shown and to attain the ends of justice." The bond is required by statute — not by rules of court. Therefore, there is no authority for any court to extend the time for filing an appeal bond. Burns v. C.W. Wright Constr.

Co., 1 Va. App. 256, 336 S.E.2d 908 (1985).

Failure to file an appeal bond as required by § 8.01-676.1 requires that an appeal be dismissed and neither subdivision (b) of this rule nor Rule 5A:17(b) can be used to extend the time for filing of bonds when none has been given. Burns v. C.W. Wright Constr. Co., 1 Va. App. 256, 336 S.E.2d 908 (1985).

Time for filing of transcript is not mandatory. — Unlike Supreme Court Rule 5:5(a), subdivision (a) of this rule contains no language which makes the time for filing of the transcript mandatory. Likewise, Rule 5A:7 does not require that the transcript be made a part of the record on appeal. Rule 5A:7 states that the transcript will be included in the record on appeal if it is properly made a part of the record in accordance with the provisions of Rule 5A:8. There is nothing in the Rules which makes timely filing of the transcript mandatory; rather, the clear objective of these Rules is to ensure that an accurate record, complete to the degree necessary to adjudicate the appeal, is transmitted to the court. Turner v. Commonwealth, 2 Va. App. 96, 341 S.E.2d 400 (1986).

Only trial court can extend time for filing transcript. — There is no authority in the Rules for the Court of Appeals to extend the time for filing the transcript or written statement. Subdivision (b) of this rule gives that power exclusively to the trial judge. Barrett v. Barrett, 1 Va. App. 378, 339 S.E.2d 208 (1986).

Time cannot be extended absent extension from trial judge. — Unless the appellant has received an extension of time from the circuit court judge upon a showing of good cause, the transcript must be filed within 60 days of the final order of judgment in the case. There is no provision anywhere in the rules which allows the Court of Appeals to extend the time for filing the transcript. Turner v. Commonwealth, 2 Va. App. 96, 341 S.E.2d 400 (1986).

In the absence of an extension having been granted by the trial court, the time for filing the transcript or written statement is a requirement under Rule 5A:8(a) which Court of Appeals cannot extend. Barrett v. Barrett, 1 Va. App. 378, 339 S.E.2d 208 (1986).

Official receipt must be produced on demand. — Although Rule 5A:3(c) allowed the Commonwealth of Virginia to mail its petition appealing the trial court's judgment granting defendant's motion to suppress evidence to the court of appeals, it required the Commonwealth to obtain an official receipt showing that the petition was mailed on time and to produce that receipt on demand, and the appellate court held that because the Commonwealth could not produce a receipt showing that it mailed its petition on or before the date it was due, and could not otherwise show that its petition was filed on time, the court lacked jurisdiction to hear the Commonwealth's appeal. Commonwealth v. Green, No. 1845-03-2, 2004 Va. App. LEXIS 16 (Ct. of Appeals Jan. 13, 2004).

Petition mailed by first class mail held untimely. — Where petition was due on December 2, 1987, and was received in the clerk's office of the Court of Appeals on December 7, and where the petition was mailed by first class mail, not by registered or certified mail, the petition was not timely filed and would be dismissed, since this rule specifically lists appropriate mailing methods which are deemed timely filed without mentioning first class mail as an alternative. Long v. Commonwealth, 7 Va. App. 503, 375 S.E.2d 368 (1988).

A motion to extend the time to file an opening brief must, within forty days after the filing of the record, be delivered to the clerk of the Court of Appeals, or be mailed in accordance with this rule. Uninsured Employers' Fund v. Coyle, 22 Va. App. 157, 468 S.E.2d 145 (1996).

Untimely appeal. — Although the trial judge had authority under § 20-107.3 to enter additional orders as necessary to effectuate and enforce an equitable distribution, because the husband's objections to the decree did not toll the appeal period, pursuant to Va. Sup. Ct. Rules 5A:3(a) and 5A:6(a), the husband's untimely notice of appeal was dismissed for lack of jurisdiction. Price v. Price, 2007 Va. App. LEXIS 75 (Mar. 6, 2007).

Applied in Williams v. Landon, 1 Va. App. 206, 336 S.E.2d 907 (1985); Riner v. Commonwealth, 40 Va. App. 440, 579 S.E.2d 671, 2003 Va. App. LEXIS 287 (2003); Estate of Hackler v. Hackler, 44 Va. App. 51, 602 S.E.2d 426, 2004 Va. App. LEXIS 454 (2004); Jay v. Commonwealth, 275 Va. 510, 659 S.E.2d 311, 2008 Va. LEXIS 53 (2008).

Rule 5A:4. Forms of Briefs and Other Papers.

(a) *Paper Size, Line Spacing, Font, and Margins.* — Briefs, appendices, motions, petitions, and other papers may be printed by any process that yields a clear black image on white paper and must be on pages 8-½ x 11 inch paper. All printed matter for briefs, motions, petitions, and other papers must be in at least 12-point font; appendices must be in at least 12-point font. Text shall not be reduced, and must be double-spaced except for headings, assignments of error, quotations, and footnotes. Margins must be at least one inch on all four sides of each page. The use of condensed or multi-page transcripts is prohibited.

(b) *Binding and Cover.* — All briefs, appendices, petitions for rehearing, and petitions for rehearing en banc shall be bound on the left margin in such a manner as to produce a flat, smooth binding. Spiral binding, acco fasteners, and the like are not acceptable. The style of the case (with the name of the appellant stated first) and the record number of the case and the name, Virginia State Bar number, mailing address, telephone number (including any applicable extension), facsimile number (if any), and e-mail address (if any) of counsel submitting the paper shall be placed on the front cover.

(c) *Effect of Non-compliance.* — No appeal shall be dismissed for failure to comply with the provisions of this Rule; however, the clerk of this Court may require that a document be redone in compliance with this Rule.

(d) *Certificate of Compliance with Word Count Limitation.* — Any brief, motion, petition, or other paper that has a word count limitation in these Rules must include a certificate by the attorney, or unrepresented party, that the document complies with the applicable word count limitation. The person preparing the certificate may rely on the word count of the word-processing system used to prepare the document. The certificate must state the number of words the document contains, excluding those parts specifically exempted by these Rules.

Cross references. — As to forms of briefs and other papers before the Supreme Court, see Rule 5:6.

Law Review. — For article reviewing recent developments and changes in legislation, case law, and Virginia Supreme Court Rules affecting civil litigation, see "Civil Practice and Procedure," 40 U. Rich. L. Rev. 95 (2005).

CASE NOTES

Failure to comply. — While an employee received notice of the deficiencies in the employee's brief and appendix under Va. Sup. Ct. R. 5A:4, 5A:18, 5A:20, 5A:24, 5A:25, because the employee failed to correct any of the defects, which in totality were significant, and never actually challenged the ruling of the issue on appeal, the employee's appeal lacked merit. Adams v. Va. Empl. Comm'n, 2012 Va. App. LEXIS 67 (Mar. 6, 2012).

B. ORIGINAL JURISDICTION.

Rule 5A:5. Original Proceedings.

(a) *Original Jurisdiction Proceedings Other Than Actual Innocence Petitions.* — With the exception of petitions for the issuance of writs of actual innocence under paragraph (b) of this Rule, all proceedings before the Court of Appeals pursuant to its original jurisdiction shall be conducted in accordance with the procedure prescribed by Rule 5:7 of the Rules of the Supreme Court.

(b) *Petition for a Writ of Actual Innocence.* — (1) **Scope.** — Any person convicted of a felony upon a plea of not guilty or any person who was adjudicated delinquent, upon a plea of not guilty, by a circuit court of an offense that would be a felony if committed by an adult, may file in the Court of Appeals a petition under Code § 19.2-327.10 et seq. seeking a writ of actual innocence based on nonbiological evidence.

(2) **Form and Contents of Petition.** — The petition must be filed using Form 12 in the Appendix of Forms following Part 5A and must include all allegations and documents required by subsections A and B of Code § 19.2-327.11. Under Code § 19.2-327.11(B) "relevant documents" shall include, but not be limited to, any orders of conviction, adjudication of delinquency, and sentencing being challenged, any appellate dispositions on direct review or any habeas corpus orders (issued by any federal or state court), and any prior petitions filed under Code § 19.2-327.10 et seq. in the Court of Appeals or under Code § 19.2-327.2 et seq. in the Supreme Court.

(3) **Parties.** — All pleadings shall name as the petitioner the person convicted of a felony or adjudicated delinquent who is seeking relief. The pleadings shall identify the Commonwealth, represented by the Attorney General, as respondent.

(4) **Filing Fee.** — The petition must be accompanied by either (i) a $25.00 check or money order for the filing fee, or (ii) an *in forma pauperis* affidavit demonstrating that the petitioner cannot afford the filing fee. An affidavit seeking *in forma pauperis* status shall list all assets and liabilities of petitioner, including the current balance of any inmate account maintained by correctional facility.

(5) **Appointment of Counsel.** — If this Court does not summarily dismiss the petition, the Court shall appoint counsel for any indigent petitioner who requests the appointment of counsel and satisfies the indigency criteria of Code § 19.2-159. In the Court's discretion, counsel may be appointed at an earlier stage of the proceeding at the petitioner's request upon a showing of requisite indigency. All requests for the appointment of counsel shall be made on the form provided by the Court of Appeals.

(6) **Service of Petition and Return of Service.** — Prior to filing a petition, the petitioner shall serve the petition, along with all attachments, on the Attorney General and on the Commonwealth's Attorney for the jurisdiction where the conviction or adjudication of delinquency occurred. When represented by counsel, the petitioner shall file with the petition either (i) a duly executed return of service in the form of a verification that a copy of the petition and all attachments have been served, or (ii) an acceptance of service signed by either or both of the parties to be served, or (iii) a combination of the two. When unrepresented by counsel, the petitioner shall file with the petition a certificate that a copy of the petition and all attachments have been sent, by certified mail, to the Attorney General and the Commonwealth's Attorney for the jurisdiction where the conviction or adjudication of delinquency occurred.

(7) **Response.** — If the Court of Appeals does not summarily dismiss the petition, the court will provide written notice to all parties directing the Commonwealth, within 60 days after receipt of such notice, to file a response to the petition pursuant to Code § 19.2-327.11(C). For good cause shown, the 60-day deadline may be extended by the Court of Appeals. The Commonwealth's response may include any information pertinent to the petitioner's guilt, delinquency, or innocence, including proffers of evidence outside the trial court record and evidence previously suppressed at trial.

(8) **Reply.** — The petitioner may file a reply to the Commonwealth's response only if directed to do so by the Court of Appeals.

(9) **Copies.** — An original and four copies of the petition, the Commonwealth's response, and the petitioner's reply, if any, shall be filed with the Court of Appeals. Attachments shall be included with the original petition, response, or reply, but not with any copies of the same.

(10) **Evidentiary Hearing.** — The Court of Appeals may order the circuit court that entered the conviction or adjudication of delinquency to conduct an evidentiary hearing and to certify factual findings pursuant to Code § 19.2-327.12. Such findings, however, shall be limited to the specific questions addressed by the Court of Appeals in its certification order. In the circuit court, the petitioner and the Commonwealth shall be afforded an opportunity to present evidence and to examine witnesses on matters relevant to the certified questions.

(11) **Oral Argument.** — Unless otherwise directed by the Court of Appeals, oral argument shall only be allowed on the final decision whether to grant or deny the writ under Code § 19.2-327.13.

(12) **Appeal.** — The petitioner or the Commonwealth may petition for appeal to the Supreme Court from any adverse final decision issued by the Court of Appeals under Code § 19.2-327.13 to issue or deny a writ of actual innocence. Such an appeal shall be initiated by the filing of a notice of appeal pursuant to Rule 5:14.

The amendment, effective May 2, 2011, adopted March 1, 2011, substituted "§§ 19.2-327.10" for "§ 19.2-3217.10" twice near the end of subdivision (b)(2).

The amendment effective July 1, 2013, adopted June 21, 2013, rewrote subdivision (b)(1); substituted "any orders of conviction, adjudication of delinquency, and sentencing being" for "any felony conviction, and sentencing orders being" in the second sentence of subdivision (b)(2); added the heading "Parties" and inserted "or adjudicated delinquent" in the first sentence of subdivision (b)(3); substituted "$25.00" for "$50.00" and deleted "required by statute" following "the filing fee" in clause (i) of the first sentence of subdivision (b)(4); inserted "or adjudication of delinquency" in the first and third sentences of subdivision (b)(6) and in the first sentence of subdivision (b)(10); and in subdivisions (b)(7) through (b)(9), substituted "the court" for "this court" and "the Court of Appals" for "this Court."

Law Review. — For 1985 survey of Virginia civil procedure and practice, see 19 U. Rich. L. Rev. 679 (1985). For 2007 annual survey article, "Civil Practice and Procedure," see 42 U. Rich. L. Rev. 229 (2007).

C. PROCEDURE FOR FILING AN APPEAL FROM THE TRIAL COURT.

Rule 5A:6. Notice of Appeal.

(a) *Filing Deadline; Where to File.* — No appeal shall be allowed unless, within 30 days after entry of final judgment or other appealable order or decree, or within any specified extension thereof granted by this Court under Rule 5A:3(a), counsel files with the clerk of the trial court a notice of appeal, and at the same time mails or delivers a copy of such notice to all opposing counsel. A notice of appeal filed after the court announces a decision or ruling — but before the entry of such judgment or order — is treated as filed on the date of and after the entry. A party filing a notice of an appeal of right to the Court of Appeals shall simultaneously file in the trial court an appeal bond in compliance with Code § 8.01-676.1.

(b) *Content.* — The notice of appeal shall contain a statement whether any transcript or statement of facts, testimony, and other incidents of the case will be filed.

(c) *Filing Fee.* — A copy of the notice of appeal shall be filed in the office of the clerk of the Court of Appeals and, except as otherwise provided by law, must be accompanied by a check or money order in the amount of $50 payable to the "Clerk of the Court of Appeals" for the filing fee required by statute. The fee shall be due at the time the notice of appeal is presented. The clerk of the Court of Appeals may file any notice of appeal that is not accompanied by such fee if the fee is received by the clerk within ten days of the date the notice of appeal is filed. If the fee is not received within such time, the appeal shall be dismissed.

(d) *Certificate.* — The appellant shall include with the notice of appeal a certificate stating:

(1) the names and addresses of all appellants and appellees, the name, Virginia State Bar number, mailing address, telephone number (including any applicable extension), facsimile number (if any), and e-mail address (if any) of counsel for each party, and the mailing address, telephone number, facsimile number (if any), and e-mail address (if any) of any party not represented by counsel; and

(2) that a copy of the notice of appeal has been mailed or delivered to all opposing counsel; and

(3) in a criminal case, a statement whether counsel for defendant has been appointed or privately retained; and

(4) that in the event a transcript is to be filed a copy of the transcript has been ordered from the court reporter who reported the case.

(e) *Separate Cases.* — Whenever two or more cases were tried together in the trial court, one notice of appeal and one record may be used to bring all of such cases before this Court even though such cases were not consolidated by formal order.

(f) *Special Provision for Cases Involving a Guardian Ad Litem.* — No appeal shall be dismissed because the notice of appeal fails to identify a guardian ad litem or to provide notice to a guardian ad litem. Upon motion for good cause shown or by sua sponte order of this Court, the notice of appeal may be amended to identify the guardian ad litem and to provide notice to such guardian.

Cross references. — As to time for filing notice of appeal, see also Va. Code §§ 8.01-675.3 and 17.1-408. For applicability of this rule to appeals from the Virginia Workers' Compensation Commission, see Rule 5A:11.

Law Review. — For 1985 survey of Virginia civil procedure and practice, see 19 U. Rich. L. Rev. 679 (1985). For 1995 survey of civil practice and procedure, see 29 U. Rich. L. Rev. 897 (1995).

Michie's Jurisprudence. — For related discussion, see 5A M.J. Courts, § 136.1.

CASE NOTES

Additional timely notice of appeal filing unnecessary after delayed appeal award. — Where a timely notice of appeal has been filed on direct appeal but the appeal is dismissed for failure to perfect it, and a delayed appeal has been awarded, an appellant need not file another timely notice of appeal after the delayed appeal is awarded. Sanchez v. Commonwealth, 14 Va. App. 256, 416 S.E.2d 705 (1992).

Only order suspending or vacating sentence can toll running of time. — In order to toll the time limitations of Rule 1:1 and subdivision (a), it is not sufficient for the trial judge merely to express a desire to consider action or take the issue under advisement; rather, the trial judge must issue an order modifying, vacating or suspending the sentence within 21 days of the entry of sentence. D'Alessandro v. Commonwealth, 15 Va. App. 163, 423 S.E.2d 199 (1992); Vokes v. Vokes, 28 Va. App. 349, 504 S.E.2d 865 (1998).

The thirty-day period of this rule cannot be tolled by either the filing of a post-judgment motion to set aside or reconsider the judgment or the pendency of such a motion on the thirtieth day after final judgment where the trial court has not issued an order modifying, vacating or suspending the prior order. Vokes v. Vokes, 28 Va. App. 349, 504 S.E.2d 865 (1998).

Requirement that notice be delivered to clerk of Court of Appeals not jurisdictional. — The part of the rule requiring a copy of the notice of appeal to be mailed or delivered to the clerk of the Court of Appeals is not jurisdictional. Johnson v. Commonwealth, 1 Va. App. 510, 339 S.E.2d 919 (1986).

Motion for delayed appeal properly denied. — Trial court did not err in denying a mother's motion for filing of a delayed appeal from a judgment terminating her parental rights because the mother filed her motion well after the trial court's jurisdiction under both Va. Sup. Ct. R. 5A:6 and subsection C of § 8.01-428 had elapsed, and the mother presented no other statutory exception to extend that jurisdiction. Butler v. City of Roanoke Dep't of Soc. Servs., 2008 Va. App. LEXIS 233 (May 13, 2008).

Notice of appeal timely. — Wife's appeal of the trial court's denial of her motion for judgment alleging that the husband breached the parties' marital settlement agreement was dismissed, as the wife's failure to file a notice of appeal from that ruling within 30 days of the date the trial court entered it meant that appellate court did not have jurisdiction to consider an appeal of that ruling. Samuel v. Samuel, Nos. 2501-01-2, 1417-01-2, 2004 Va. App. LEXIS 41 (Ct. of Appeals Jan. 28, 2004).

Time for filing an estate's appeal began to run from the trial court's entry of its order marked "final for purposes of appeal" and not from any earlier order. Estate of Hackler v. Hackler, 44 Va. App. 51, 602 S.E.2d 426, 2004 Va. App. LEXIS 454 (2004).

Mother's notice of appeal from the trial court's order was timely, having been made within 30 days of the final order, prepared by the father's attorney and incorporating a letter opinion. Olson v. Olson, 2009 Va. App. LEXIS 6 (Jan. 13, 2009).

In a case in which a father argued that the mother's appeal was unperfected because, he asserted, that she appealed the suspending orders rather than the final order, that argument failed. In their briefs, both parties address the questions mother raised in regard to the final order; the purpose of Va. Sup. Ct. R. 5A:6(a) was met because the mother did in fact file a notice of appeal and the father was given notice of continuing litigation. Haring v. Hackmer, 2009 Va. App. LEXIS 402 (Sept. 8, 2009).

Notice of appeal not timely. — Wife's appeal of the trial court's order awarding the husband one of the dependency tax exemptions for the parties' two children was dismissed, as the wife failed to timely file a notice of appeal. Jordan v. Jordan, Nos. 2583-03-2, 2616-03-2, 2004 Va. App. LEXIS 285 (Ct. of Appeals June 22, 2004).

Although the trial judge had authority under § 20-107.3 to enter additional orders as necessary to effectuate and enforce an equitable distribution, because the husband's objections to the decree did not toll the appeal period, pursuant to Va. Sup. Ct. Rules 5A:3(a) and 5A:6(a), the husband's untimely notice of appeal was dismissed for lack of jurisdiction. Price v. Price, 2007 Va. App. LEXIS 75 (Mar. 6, 2007).

Group home administrator's notice of appeal of a final order affirming a finding of physical neglect was untimely because it was filed 79 days after entry of the final order. Although it was filed only eight days after the entry of an order denying the administrator's second motion for reconsideration, that order was a nullity because the circuit court did not purport to modify, vacate, or suspend its previous order within 21 days, as required under Va. Sup. Ct. R. 1:1. Wells v. Shenandoah Valley Dep't of Soc. Servs., 56 Va. App. 208, 692 S.E.2d 286, 2010 Va. App. LEXIS 176 (2010).

Mere indication that the trial court intends to rule on pending motions is insufficient to negate the finality of an order rendering a final judgment on the merits of a case, and this is particularly true where the trial court's intention regarding the pending motions is not even expressed in the order rendering the final judgment. Carrithers v. Harrah, 60 Va. App. 69, 723 S.E.2d 638, 2012 Va. App. LEXIS 117 (2012).

Because a trial court's order contained no language retaining jurisdiction to address the parties' pending requests for attorneys' fees and costs, the order rendered a final judgment, and the trial court's letter, which directed the parties to file briefs regarding their motions for attorneys' fees and costs, did not affect the finality of the order entered that same day disposing of the merits of the case; even if an order granting a final judgment on the merits of a case contains express language indicating that the trial court intends to rule on a request for attorneys' fees at a future time, such language does not negate the fact that such an order is in fact a final judgment. Carrithers v. Harrah, 60 Va. App. 69, 723 S.E.2d 638, 2012 Va. App. LEXIS 117 (2012).

Wife's motion to dismiss a husband's appeal for failure to timely file his notice of appeal as required by Va. Sup. Ct. R. 5A:6(a) was granted because the husband failed to file his notice of appeal within thirty days of the trial court's order; therefore, the court of appeals had no jurisdiction to review his arguments. Carrithers v. Harrah, 60 Va. App. 69, 723 S.E.2d 638, 2012 Va. App. LEXIS 117 (2012).

Custody order not "final order" that commenced running of appeal period. — Former husband did not waive his argument regarding custody by failing to file a notice of appeal within 30 days from entry of the custody order. While the order stated that it was "final as to child custody," as it also continued the case for determination of spousal support, child support, and equitable distribution, it did not dispose of the whole controversy and thus was not a final order that started the running of the appeal period. Kapur v. Kapur, 2009 Va. App. LEXIS 231 (May 19, 2009).

Premature filing of notice of appeal did not deprive court of jurisdiction. — Where appellant filed a notice of appeal following the trial court's oral pronouncement of sentence but prior to entry of the sentencing orders, and where no new notice of appeal was filed after the orders were entered, appellant's premature filing of the notice of appeal did not deprive the court of appeals of jurisdiction over his appeal; the premature notice of appeal filed after oral pronouncement of judgment became effective when the final order was written and entered by the court. Saunders v. Commonwealth, 12 Va. App. 154, 402 S.E.2d 708 (1991).

Appeal of denial of motion to intervene. — Rule 5A:6 provides that no appeal "shall be allowed" unless a notice of appeal has been filed within 30 days "after" the appealable order, and the timing requirement has never been suspended altogether to resurrect an otherwise unsuccessful interlocutory appeal; a trial court's order denying a motion to intervene in an administrative appeal fell outside the appellate court's interlocutory appellate jurisdiction since it was not final, and the fact that the underlying trial court action had been settled did not render moot the question regarding the appellate court's jurisdiction over the appeal. Alliance to Save the Mattaponi v. Va. Marine Res. Comm'n, 43 Va. App. 724, 601 S.E.2d 684, 2004 Va. App. LEXIS 409 (2004).

Effect of clear error in reference. — A notice of appeal that is timely filed and correctly styled, but potentially misleading due to a clear error of reference, does not automatically fail on procedural grounds. Carlton v. Paxton, 14 Va. App. 105, 415 S.E.2d 600, aff'd, 15 Va. App. 265, 422 S.E.2d 423 (1992).

Defendant's notice of appeal was insufficient under Va. Sup. Ct. R. 5A:6 to identify the conviction appealed, which was a substantive rather than a procedural defect requiring dismissal, because the notice identified the appealed conviction by reference to the case file number for defendant's conviction of failing to appear, and not defendant's conviction for perjury. Evans v. Commonwealth, 61 Va. App. 339, 735 S.E.2d 252, 2012 Va. App. LEXIS 419 (2012).

Content provisions were not jurisdictional. — In termination of parental rights case, a cover letter, signed by the mother's guardian ad litem, did, in fact, indicate that the children's guardian ad litem received a copy of the notice of appeal, even though the certificate attached to the notice did not so indicate, and thus, the mother complied with Va. Sup. Ct. R. 5A:6(a); the reviewing court found that it had never held that the failure to comply with Va. Sup. Ct. R. 5A:6(d)'s provisions regarding the contents of the accompanying certificate were jurisdictional. M. G. v. Albemarle County Dep't of Soc. Servs., 41 Va. App. 170, 583 S.E.2d 761, 2003 Va. App. LEXIS 406 (2003).

Court of Appeals of Virginia erred by dismissing a portion of petitions for appeal filed separately by two defendants, upon their failure to comply with the requirements of Va. Sup. Ct. R. 5A:20(e), as: (1) the rule did not impose jurisdictional requirements; and (2) the Court of Appeals could have explored other options, short of dismissal, and should have considered whether any failure to strictly adhere to the requirements of the rule was insignificant, thus allowing the court to address the merits of a question presented. Jay v. Commonwealth, 275 Va. 510, 659 S.E.2d 311, 2008 Va. LEXIS 53 (2008).

Failure to name necessary party required dismissal. — Because a father's counsel of record was an indispensable party to an appeal by a county department of social services (DSS), and because counsel was neither named in DSS's notice of appeal of the denial of its termination of the father's parental rights nor mailed a copy of the notice, as required by Va. Sup. Ct. R. 5A:6 and 5A:1, the court lacked jurisdiction to entertain DSS's appeal. Greene County Dep't of Soc. Servs. v. Green, 2006 Va. App. LEXIS 452 (Oct. 10, 2006).

Although defendant filed a notice of appeal within the 30-day time period under Va. Sup. Ct. R. 5A:6 and § 8.01-675.3, defendant's failure to join a county, which prosecuted defendant for driving under the influence under Amherst County, Va., Code § 9.1 and was an indispensable party, within that mandatory time period deprived the appellate court of jurisdiction. Woody v. Commonwealth, 53 Va. App. 188, 670 S.E.2d 39, 2008 Va. App. LEXIS 568 (2008), appeal dismissed, 2010 Va. App. LEXIS 286 (Va. Ct. App. 2010).

Dismissal of defendant's appeal of his conviction of driving under the influence under a local ordinance was affirmed because the conviction was based on a local ordinance thereby making the city an indispensable appellee and defendant's notice of appeal failed to name the city as the appellee in violation of Va. Sup. Ct. R. 5A:6. Roberson v. Commonwealth, 279 Va. 396, 689 S.E.2d 706, 2010 Va. LEXIS 38 (2010).

Defendant's appeal his conviction for driving under the influence of alcohol was dismissed because the court appeals did not have jurisdiction over the appeal of his conviction under Amherst County, Va., Code § 9.1, which was based upon an order correcting a sentencing order, since defendant failed to file a timely notice of appeal that named the proper prosecuting authority, and the sentencing order was the final appealable conviction order; the corrected order, which was entered pursuant to subsection B of § 8.01-428, merely fixed a clerical error and clarified that defendant was convicted under the Amherst County Code, and subsection B of § 8.01-428 was a prescriptive statutory provision simply providing a mechanism to correct non-substantive errors in the record and neither enhanced nor diminished the jurisdiction of the court of appeals. Woody v. County of Amherst, 2010 Va. App. LEXIS 286 (July 20, 2010).

Notice of appeal was sufficient. — Despite defect in defendant's notice of appeal under Va. Sup. Ct. R. 5A:6 in not naming the proper appellee, dismissal of defendant's appeal was reversed because the notice of appeal was sufficient on its face to identify the conviction under a local ordinance as the case being appealed and the locality responded to the notice. Ghameshlouy v. Commonwealth, 279 Va. 379, 689 S.E.2d 698, 2010 Va. LEXIS 23 (2010).

Ineffective assistance of counsel. — Although defendant pleaded guilty, trial counsel's failure to file an appeal, after having been instructed to do so by defendant in accordance with Va. Sup. Ct. R. 5A:6, constituted deficient performance; defendant was entitled to habeas corpus relief and a belated appeal. Miles v. Sheriff of the Va. Beach City Jail, 266 Va. 110, 581 S.E.2d 191, 2003 Va. LEXIS 64 (2003).

Applied in Williams v. Landon, 1 Va. App. 206, 336 S.E.2d 907 (1985); Turner v. Commonwealth, 2 Va. App. 96, 341 S.E.2d 400 (1986); Williams Steel Erection Co. v. DOL & Indus., 42 Va. App. 814, 595 S.E.2d 45, 2004 Va. App. LEXIS 166 (2004); McCray v. Commonwealth, 44 Va. App. 334, 605 S.E.2d 291, 2004 Va. App. LEXIS 579 (2004); Rodgers v. Johnson, 2005 U.S. Dist. LEXIS 25553 (W.D. Va. Oct. 18, 2005); Va. Dep't of Corr. v. Compton, 47 Va. App. 202, 623 S.E.2d 397, 2005 Va. App. LEXIS 517 (2005); Smith v. Commonwealth, 281 Va. 464, 706 S.E.2d 889, 2011 Va. LEXIS 59 (2011).

Form

NOTICE OF APPEAL FROM TRIAL COURT
(Rule 5A:6) —

VIRGINIA: IN THE CIRCUIT COURT OF ______________________

(The style of the case in the Circuit Court shall be used.)

NOTICE OF APPEAL

______________________, ______________________
(name(s) of party(ies)) (plaintiff, defendant or other ______________________ hereby appeals to the Court of Appeals of designation in trial court)
Virginia from the ______________________
(final judgment or other appealable order or decree)
of this Court entered on ______________.
(date)

[If applicable] A transcript or statement of facts, testimony, and other incidents of the case will be filed.

CERTIFICATE

The undersigned certifies as follows:

(1) The name(s) and address(es) of appellant(s) are:

(2) The name(s), address(es), and telephone number(s) of counsel for appellant(s) are:

(3) The name(s) and address(es) of appellee(s) are:

(4) The name(s), address(es), and telephone number(s) of counsel for appellee(s) are:

(5) [If applicable] Counsel for appellant has ordered from the court reporter who reported the case the transcript for filing as required by Rule 5A:8(a).

(6) [If applicable] ______________________, ______________________
(name of party) (appellant)
______________, is not represented by counsel. ______________
(appellee) (his) (her)
address and telephone number are:

(7) [In criminal cases only] Counsel for defendant has been ______________
______________________.
(appointed) (privately retained)

(8) A copy of this Notice of Appeal has been mailed or delivered to all opposing counsel [and/or to unrepresented parties, if applicable] and to the Clerk of the Court of Appeals this ______ day of ______________, 20____.

____
(Signature of counsel or unrepresented party)

Rule 5A:7. Record on Appeal: Contents.

(a) *Contents.* — The following constitute the record on appeal from the trial court:

(1) the original papers and exhibits filed or lodged in the office of the clerk of the trial court, including any report of a commissioner in chancery and the accompanying depositions and other papers;

(2) each instruction marked "given" or "refused" and initialed by the judge;

(3) each exhibit offered in evidence, whether admitted or not, and initialed by the trial judge (or any photograph thereof as authorized by § 19.2-270.4 (A) and (C)). (All non-documentary exhibits shall be tagged or labeled in the trial court and the tag or label initialed by the judge.);

(4) the original draft or a copy of each order entered by the trial court;

(5) any opinion or memorandum decision rendered by the judge of the trial court;

(6) any deposition and any discovery material encompassed within Part Four offered in evidence (whether admitted or rejected) at any proceeding; and

(7) the transcript of any proceeding or a written statement of facts, testimony, and other incidents of the case when made a part of the record as provided in Rule 5A:8, or the official videotape recording of any proceeding in those circuit courts authorized by the Supreme Court to use videotape recordings. This Court may require that any videotape proceedings be transcribed, in whole or in part, and made a part of the record as provided in Rule 5A:8, except that the transcript shall be filed within 60 days after the entry of the order requiring such transcript; and

(8) the notice of appeal.

(b) *Disagreement on Contents.* — If disagreement arises as to the contents of any part of the record, the matter shall, in the first instance, be submitted to and decided by the trial court.

Cross references. — For applicability of this rule to appeals from the Virginia Workers' Compensation Commission, see Rule 5A:11. As to inspection of record of former appeal where case has previously been in an appellate court, see Va. Code § 8.01-675.4. As to writ of certiorari to clerk of trial court for purpose of obtaining omitted part of record, see Va. Code § 8.01-675.4.

Law Review. — For an article relating to all published Virginia criminal law decisions between July 1, 1997, and July 1, 1998, see 32 U. Rich. L. Rev. 1091 (1998).

CASE NOTES

The Court of Appeals is not restricted by § 8.01-675.4 to ordering only those portions of the appellate record as defined by the Rules of Court. Watkins v. Commonwealth, 26 Va. App. 335, 494 S.E.2d 859 (1998).

Absence or late filing of transcript does nothing to diminish jurisdiction. — If the record on appeal is sufficient in the absence of the transcript to determine the merits of the appellant's allegations, the court is free to proceed to hear the case. Turner v. Commonwealth, 2 Va. App. 96, 341 S.E.2d 400 (1986).

Timely filing of transcript is not mandatory. — Unlike the Supreme Court Rule 5:5(a), Rule 5A:3(a) contains no language which makes the time for filing of the transcript mandatory. Likewise, this rule does not require that the transcript be made a part of the record on appeal. This rule states that the transcript will be included in the record on appeal if it is properly made a part of the record in accordance with the provisions of Rule 5A:8. There is nothing in the Rules which makes timely filing of the transcript mandatory; rather, the clear objective of these Rules is to ensure that an accurate record, complete to the degree necessary to adjudicate the appeal, is transmitted to the court. Turner v. Commonwealth, 2 Va. App. 96, 341 S.E.2d 400 (1986).

Requirements for including transcript in record must be strictly adhered to. — If the transcript is indispensable to the determination of the case, then the requirements for making the transcript a part of the record on appeal must be strictly adhered to. The Court of Appeals has no authority to make exceptions to the filing requirements set out in the Rules. Turner v. Commonwealth, 2 Va. App. 96, 341 S.E.2d 400 (1986).

This Rule did not contemplate inclusion of the transcripted depositions as part of the instant record on appeal; proofs and other exhibits were not properly offered and received into evidence. Skeen v. Skeen, No. 0801-00-3, 2001 Va. App. LEXIS 470 (Ct. of Appeals Aug. 7, 2001).

Jury questionnaires not part of record. — Trial court did not err in destroying jury questionnaires completed by the members of the venire who were not selected to sit on the jury or as alternates because appellate review of the jury selection process had not been affected by the exclusion of the questionnaires from the record, and the questionnaires were not part of the record on appeal; the questionnaires at issue were neither filed with nor lodged with the clerk to be maintained as a part of the record, but were handed over to the clerk for destruction, and thus, the matter was submitted to and decided by the trial court. Rogers v. Commonwealth, 2009 Va. App. LEXIS 384 (Sept. 1, 2009).

Trial judge's personal notes, which were not filed or lodged with the clerk but were contained in the trial judge's personal file maintained in his chambers, were not properly part of the record on appeal from the trial court. Yohay v. Justice, No. 0631-89-4, (Ct. of Appeals Oct. 2, 1990).

Medical evidence in the record. — Court of appeals considered on appeal a 2010 MRI as well as the 2011 MRI as both MRI interpretations were in the record. County of Henrico v. Henry, 2012 Va. App. LEXIS 31 (Feb. 7, 2012).

Applied in Cantwell v. Commonwealth, 2 Va. App. 606, 347 S.E.2d 523 (1986); Smith v. Commonwealth, 59 Va. App. 710, 722 S.E.2d 310, 2012 Va. App. LEXIS 56 (2012); Wooddell v. Lagerquist, No. 2121-11-3, 2012 Va. App. LEXIS 374 (Nov. 20, 2012).

Rule 5A:8. Record on Appeal: Transcript or Written Statement.

(a) *Transcript.* — The transcript of any proceeding is a part of the record when it is filed in the office of the clerk of the trial court within 60 days after entry of the final judgment. This deadline may be extended by a Judge of the Court of Appeals only upon a written motion filed within 90 days after the entry of final judgment. Timely motions will be granted only upon a showing of good cause to excuse the delay.

(b) *Notice of Filing Transcript.* — (1) Time for Filing. Within 10 days after the transcript is filed or, if the transcript is filed prior to the filing of the notice of appeal, within 10 days after the notice of appeal is filed, counsel for appellant shall:

(i) give written notice to all other counsel of the date on which the transcript was filed, and

(ii) file a copy of the notice with the clerk of the trial court.

There shall be appended to the notice either a certificate of counsel for appellant that a copy of the notice has been mailed to all other counsel or an acceptance of service of such notice by all other counsel.

(2) Multiple Transcripts. When multiple transcripts are filed, the 10-day period for filing the notice required by this Rule shall be calculated from the date on which the last transcript is filed or from the date on which the notice of appeal is filed, whichever is later. The notice of filing transcripts shall identify all transcripts filed and the date upon which the last transcript was filed.

(3) Notice of No Further Transcripts. If the notice of appeal states that no additional transcripts will be filed and identifies the transcripts that have been filed, if any, then no additional written notice of filing transcripts is required and the notice of appeal will serve as the notice of filing transcripts for purposes of Rule 5A:8(b).

(4) Effect of Non-compliance.

(i) Any failure to file the notice required by this Rule that materially prejudices an appellee will result in the affected transcripts being stricken from the record on appeal. For purposes of this Rule, material prejudice includes preventing the appellee from raising legitimate objections to the contents of the transcript or misleading the appellee about the contents of the record. The appellee shall have the burden of establishing such prejudice in the brief in opposition or, if no brief in opposition is filed, in a written statement filed with the clerk of this Court within twenty-one days after the record is received by the clerk.

(ii) When the appellant fails to ensure that the record contains transcripts or a written statement of facts necessary to permit resolution of appellate issues, any assignments of error affected by such omission shall not be considered.

(c) *Written Statement in Lieu of Transcript.* — A written statement of facts, testimony, and other incidents of the case becomes a part of the record when:

(1) within 55 days after entry of judgment a copy of such statement is filed in the office of the clerk of the trial court. A copy must be mailed or delivered to opposing counsel on the same day that it is filed in the office of the clerk of the trial court, accompanied by notice that such statement will be presented to the trial judge no earlier than 15 days nor later than 20 days after such filing; and

(2) the statement is signed by the trial judge and filed in the office of the clerk of the trial court. The judge may sign the statement forthwith upon its presentation to him if it is signed by counsel for all parties, but if objection is made to the accuracy or completeness of the statement, it shall be signed in accordance with paragraph (d) of this Rule.

The term "other incidents of the case" in this subsection includes motions, proffers, objections, and rulings of the trial court regarding any issue that a party intends to assign as error or otherwise address on appeal.

(d) *Objections.* — Any party may object to a transcript or written statement on the ground that it is erroneous or incomplete. Notice of such objection specifying the errors alleged or deficiencies asserted shall be filed with the clerk of the trial court within 15 days after the date the notice of filing the transcript (paragraph (b) of this Rule) or within 15 days after the date the notice of filing the written statement (paragraph (c) of this Rule) is filed in the office of the clerk of the trial court or, if the transcript or written statement is filed before the notice of appeal is filed, within 10 days after the notice of appeal has been filed with the clerk of the trial court. The clerk shall give prompt notice of the filing of such objections to the trial judge. Within 10 days after the notice of objection is filed with the clerk of the trial court, the judge shall:

(1) overrule the objection; or

(2) make any corrections that the trial judge deems necessary; or

(3) include any accurate additions to make the record complete; or

(4) certify the manner in which the record is incomplete; and

(5) sign the transcript or written statement.

At any time while the record remains in the office of the clerk of the trial court, the trial judge may, after notice to counsel and hearing, correct the transcript or written statement.

The judge's signature on a transcript or written statement, without more, shall constitute certification that the procedural requirements of this Rule have been satisfied.

Cross references. — For applicability of this rule to appeals from the Virginia Workers' Compensation Commission, see Rule 5A:11.

Law Review. — For an article relating to all published Virginia criminal law decisions between July 1, 1997, and July 1, 1998, see 32 U. Rich. L. Rev. 1091 (1998).

Michie's Jurisprudence. — For related discussion, see 1B M.J. Appeal and Error, §§ 170, 172, 188, 206; 8A M.J. Exceptions, Bill of, § 1.

CASE NOTES

I. In General.
II. Compliance.
A. Requirements.
B. Timeliness.

I. IN GENERAL.

Transcripts and statements of facts serve identical purpose on appeal. — Fairness and common sense dictate that policies regarding transcripts and statements of facts be reasonably analogous; transcripts and statements of facts serve the identical purpose on appeal — to provide a record of the incidents of the trial proceeding. Anderson v. Commonwealth, 13 Va. App. 506, 413 S.E.2d 75 (1992).

Presentence report not substitute for record. — While a presentence report is filed as a part of the record, its narrative of trial proceedings is not a substitute for properly designated portions of the transcript or a statement of facts or copies of the orders. Jones v. Commonwealth, No. 1128-98-4, 2000 Va. App. LEXIS 215 (Ct. of Appeals Mar. 21, 2000).

Inconsistencies in the record. — Appellate court found that it did not have to remand a case, pursuant to Va. Sup. Ct. R. 5A:8(c)(2), because the court could resolve defendant's appeal based upon defendant's concession at oral argument that the entire record was clear that defendant pleaded no contest. With this concession, the other inconsistencies between the statement of facts and the balance of the record became moot. Smith v. Commonwealth, 59 Va. App. 710, 722 S.E.2d 310, 2012 Va. App. LEXIS 56 (2012).

Court's inability to consider issues on appeal where transcripts incomplete. — Parties chose not to make a part of the record their closing arguments or any other communication with the court. Therefore, this record failed to establish that the issues appealed by appellant were raised in the trial court by an objection with a statement of the reasons therefor. The court could not assume that appellant's objection and reasons were proffered but not made a part of the record. This rule requires appellant to present a complete transcript for this court to consider his or her issues on appeal. Lee v. Lee, 12 Va. App. 512, 404 S.E.2d 736 (1991).

Defendant failed to provide a record sufficient to permit proper appellate review by including either a transcript of the trial court proceedings or a written statement of facts. Wyant v. Commonwealth, No. 1496-01-2, 2002 Va. App. LEXIS 336 (Ct. of Appeals June 11, 2002).

Although father's counsel endorsed final termination order "Have Seen and Objected to," the written statement filed as the record did not recite the father's arguments or any objections he made to the trial court's ruling terminating his parental rights, and, thus, the reviewing court had to conclude that the father did not properly preserve any specific objection to the trial court's termination of his parental rights. Rivera v. City of Hampton Dep't of Soc. Servs., No. 1857-03-1, 2004 Va. App. LEXIS 221 (Ct. of Appeals May 11, 2004).

Where the husband in a divorce action filed no transcript or statement of facts with regards to several issues raised on appeal, where his appendix contained none of the pleadings, orders, testimony, or incidents of trial for the divorce action, as required, where, in relation to the issues in question, the husband did not properly refer to the pages of the transcript, written statement, record, or appendix where each question was preserved in the trial court, all of those additional issues were procedurally defaulted. Grethen v. Grethen, No. 3244-03-1, 2005 Va. App. LEXIS 68 (Ct. of Appeals Feb. 15, 2005).

Wife argued that the trial court erred by not finding the husband in contempt, awarding the parties' home to the husband, and approving a sale price of $200,000 for the home; however, there was no transcript or written statement of facts from the hearing from which these orders were issued. A transcript or written statement of facts was indispensable to a determination of this assignment of error and the appellate court did not consider it. Tromza v. Vossburg, No. 1184-12-4, 2013 Va. App. LEXIS 125 (Ct. of Appeals Apr. 23, 2013).

Where amended statement of facts did not bear judge's signature, the written statement did not become a part of the record. Mayhood v. Mayhood, 4 Va. App. 365, 358 S.E.2d 182 (1987).

New trial required where judge cannot sign statement of facts. — Once a trial judge is presented with a statement in lieu of a transcript prepared by one of the parties in compliance with the requirements of this rule, he must either sign the statement, correct it and sign the corrected statement or, if the judge cannot in good faith recall or accurately reconstruct the relevant proceedings, order a new trial. Kyhl v. Kyhl, 32 Va. App. 53, 526 S.E.2d 292 (2000).

Statement of facts not indispensable. — Although husband in divorce proceeding failed to file his statement of facts within time allowed by subdivision (c) of this rule, statement of facts was not indispensable to adjudicating remaining issues raised by husband on appeal. Woodson v. Woodson, No. 1257-99-3 (Ct. of Appeals Nov. 16, 1999).

Absence of transcript of proceedings below precluded review of issues on appeal. — On appeal from an equitable distribution award after a judgment of divorce, because a husband failed to submit either a transcript or a statement of facts from the trial court's hearing in which it found that a memorandum between the parties was unenforceable, and a record of that hearing was indispensable for the appellate court to review that decision, the appeals court declined to address that assignment of error. Lazarchic v. Lazarchic, 2005 Va. App. LEXIS 291 (July 26, 2005).

Husband's appeal of orders releasing funds from escrow to the Department of Child Support Enforcement (DCSE) and allowing a DCSE non-attorney to overrule a payment plan for a child support arrearage was dismissed because the court of appeals could not determine the precise factual or legal basis for the trial court's ruling when the record contained no timely filed transcript or written statement of facts with respect to the hearing that resulted in the orders; a timely filed transcript or written statement of facts concerning the hearing was indispensable to determining whether the trial court committed reversible error. Smith v. Smith, 2008 Va. App. LEXIS 184 (Apr. 15, 2008).

Under Va. Sup. Ct. R. 5A:8(b), the court could not determine whether the trial court misapplied an offset in a divorce case. The husband had failed to timely file a transcript or a statement of facts addressing the evidentiary basis underlying the issue; his argument that the trial court lacked sufficient information to calculate the offset and should have considered the specific monetary impact of potential tax liability depended heavily on the nature and weight of the specific evidence presented to the trial court. Andersen v. Andersen, 2008 Va. App. LEXIS 524 (Dec. 2, 2008).

Trial court's order finding appellant in civil contempt of court was affirmed because the record on appeal contained no transcript or statement of facts complying with Va. Sup. Ct. R. 5A:8; although appellant appeared to assert that the contempt order violated due process and that the evidence in support of the trial court's contempt findings was insufficient, the record on appeal contained no transcript or written statement of facts, and a transcript or written statement of facts was indispensable to a determination of whether the trial court erred in making its findings. Bowser v. Guenard, 2009 Va. App. LEXIS 266 (June 16, 2009).

In an appeal from an order finding a husband in contempt of a final divorce decree and ordering the husband to pay the wife an arrearage, three issues were not preserved for appeal because the record on appeal did not contain a timely filed transcript or written statement of facts from the hearing and, therefore, the record was insufficient for the purposes of appeal under Va. Sup. Ct. R. 5A:8. Jackson v. Jackson, 2010 Va. App. LEXIS 221 (June 1, 2010).

Defect under Va. Sup. Ct. R. 5A:8 of not timely filing a transcript of the hearing in a trial court operated as a waiver of the appellant's arguments because a timely filed transcript or written statement of facts was necessary to permit resolution of the assigned errors in a case. Nelson v. Nelson, 2012 Va. App. LEXIS 210 (June 26, 2012).

Last paragraph of subdivision (d) applicable to procedural requirements of subdivision (d). — This paragraph (5A:8(d)) is contained in the subsection of the rule which specifies the means by which objections to a transcript or written statement are to be made and resolved by the trial judge; the last paragraph of subdivision (d) of this rule is applicable to the procedural requirements of subdivision (d) of this rule. Anderson v. Commonwealth, 13 Va. App. 506, 413 S.E.2d 75 (1992).

Correction of written statement by trial judge. — Where the appellant husband filed a proposed written statement of facts but did not provide notice of a timely date of presentation and the trial judge corrected the proposed statement, the husband would not be heard to complain that the trial judge erred by correcting and signing the proposed statement without providing notice and holding a hearing since, but for the trial judge's certification, the written statement would not have been included in the record and this rule authorizes the trial judge to make any corrections that he deems necessary in a proposed written statement of facts. Serrano v. Serrano, No. 0934-00-4, 2000 Va. App. LEXIS 537 (Ct. of Appeals July 25, 2000).

Husband's challenge to the written statement of facts in his divorce case, which was based in part on the trial court's failure to provide the husband with a list of proposed corrections to the statement of facts prior to a hearing regarding the corrections, failed because Va. Sup. Ct. R. 5A:8(d) did not require the trial court to provide such a list. Wright v. Hamilton-Wright, 2008 Va. App. LEXIS 197 (Apr. 22, 2008).

Court erred in adopting statement of facts verbatim without considering objections. — Where husband complied with the provisions of this rule, where thereafter, wife filed her objections to the statement of facts submitted by husband and sent her counter-statement of facts directly to the trial judge without giving husband prior notice, and where without permitting husband the opportunity to file his objection to wife's counter-statement of facts within the permitted 15 days, the trial court adopted verbatim her written statement of facts, the trial court erred when it acted without considering husband's objections, which were timely filed, and moreover, this error required a reversal. Jordan v. Jordan, 12 Va. App. 96, 402 S.E.2d 246 (1991).

Appellate court bound by statement of agreed facts. — Appellate court was "bound" by a

Va. Sup. Ct. R. 5A:8(c) written statement of agreed facts in its review of the record on appeal. Mayhew v. Mayhew, No. 2714-09-3, 2011 Va. App. LEXIS 4 (Ct. of Appeals Jan. 11, 2011).

The Court of Appeals is not restricted by § 8.01-675.4 to ordering only those portions of the appellate record as defined by the Rules of Court. Watkins v. Commonwealth, 26 Va. App. 335, 494 S.E.2d 859 (1998).

Child support. — Where the trial judge made corrections to father's proposed written statement of facts without providing notice to the parties and holding a hearing, the appellate court could not consider the issue on appeal, since the father failed to object to the corrected statement of facts to the trial judge. Washington v. Hagens, No. 0059-04-4, 2004 Va. App. LEXIS 301 (Ct. of Appeals June 29, 2004).

Where father's opening brief on appeal from a trial court's decision modifying child support failed to comply with Va. Sup. Ct. Rule 5A:20, in that it did not contain an exact reference to the page of the record where each question was preserved in the trial court and did not ensure that the record contained transcripts or a written statement of facts necessary to permit resolution of appellate issues, as required by Va. Sup. Ct. Rule 5A:8(b), the appellate court refused to consider the father's arguments and summarily affirmed the decision of the trial court. Hylton v. Hylton, 2005 Va. App. LEXIS 146 (Apr. 12, 2005).

Record inadequate. — Record did not include a transcript or a written statement for the November 15, 2002 hearing, as required under Rule 5A:8; because the basis for the November 15, 2002 incarceration of the husband could not be examined, it could not be determined whether the trial court erred by committing the husband to jail and keeping him there until December 23, 2002. Klein v. Klein, No. 0211-03-4, 2003 Va. App. LEXIS 621 (Ct. of Appeals Dec. 2, 2003).

Defendant's claim that he acted within the legal proceedings exception in a peace bond required review of the evidence presented at trial and could not be reviewed as defendant did not include a transcript or a written statement of facts from the hearing. Stallings v. Commonwealth, No. 1692-03-4, 2004 Va. App. LEXIS 343 (Ct. of Appeals July 13, 2004).

Husband's appeal of a trial court's final decree granting a divorce to his wife was dismissed, where the husband failed to provide an adequate record for the appellate court to determine the issues. Montakhabi v. Montakhabi, No. 1531-04-4, 2005 Va. App. LEXIS 25 (Ct. of Appeals Jan. 18, 2005).

Where a mother's counsel endorsed final dismissal orders as "seen and objected to" in lieu of a transcript, and did not recite her arguments or objections made to the trial court's rulings sufficient to preserve the same for appeal, absent any exceptions for good cause or to meet the ends of justice, her appeal lacked merit; thus, finding the issue raised before the appellate court was procedurally defaulted under Va. Sup. Ct. R. 5A:18, the appeals court affirmed the judgments of the trial court. Carcamo v. Louisa County Dep't of Soc. Servs., 2005 Va. App. LEXIS 127 (Ct. of Appeals Mar. 29, 2005).

Where crucial testimony relating to the duress defense was absent from the record because of a malfunctioning recording device and where defendant failed to provide the appellate court with a narrative statement of facts in lieu of the record, the appellate court could not review the trial court's finding on duress. Doggett v. Commonwealth, 2005 Va. App. LEXIS 405 (Oct. 11, 2005).

In a challenge to a finding of abuse and a protective order, the parties relied on a written statement of facts pursuant to Va. Sup. Ct. R. 5A:8. The record failed to show a wife made the specific arguments she raised on appeal or that the trial court ruled on such objections; thus the issue was not preserved for appeal. Bowen v. Smith, 2006 Va. App. LEXIS 553 (Dec. 12, 2006).

Husband's appeal of an order finding him in contempt and sentencing him to one day in jail was dismissed because the husband failed to timely file a transcript or written statement of facts regarding the hearing that led to the order; a transcript of that hearing, which would show the events that gave rise to the contempt finding and sentence, was indispensable to addressing the husband's argument that the trial court's contempt finding and sentence violated § 18.2-456 and constituted reversible error. Smith v. Smith, 2008 Va. App. LEXIS 184 (Apr. 15, 2008).

Former wife did not comply with Va. Sup. Ct. R. 5A:8 because she had the responsibility to provide an accurate statement of facts, testimony, and other incidents of the case, not a diatribe filled with commentary and irrelevant recitations, but she failed to provide such a document; however the written statement of facts and the trial court's orders were sufficient for the court of appeals to review the questions presented. Deluca v. Katchmeric, 2009 Va. App. LEXIS 267 (June 16, 2009).

Trial court did not abuse its discretion in declining to certify a husband's statement of facts regarding a divorce trial because a transcript of the trial was available and the trial court found that the husband's statement of facts was incomplete and failed to accurately represent the full trial record. Cahill v. Cahill, No. 0305-12-1, 2012 Va. App. LEXIS 409 (Dec. 18, 2012).

Record adequate. — Wife's motion to dismiss the appeal was denied despite her claim that the husband failed to ensure that the record contained the evidence necessary for the resolution of his claims; the appellate court did not need the transcript of the final hearing to resolve the claims, as the final decree and an exhibit were included in the record and were all that was necessary to resolve the issues. Neveln v. Neveln, 2006 Va. App. LEXIS 35 (Jan. 24, 2006).

Because the rulings from the bench, which were incorporated by order, provided sufficient facts to address the assignments of error, the appellate court did not dismiss an appeal, pursuant to Va. Sup. Ct. R. 5A:8(b)(4)(ii), for failure to ensure that the record contained transcripts necessary to permit resolution of appellate issues. Craven v. Williamson, 2012 Va. App. LEXIS 2 (Jan. 10, 2012).

Preservation for review. — Wife did not file objections or a motion to reconsider the trial court's order refusing to certify the written statement of facts as required by Va. Sup. Ct. R. 5A:18 and her claim of error was not preserved; as she did not provide a transcript of the hearing and the trial court was unable to certify the written statement of facts, her claims that the trial court included irrelevant, self-contradicting and defaming allegations in the final decree, that her evidence of her husband's desertion was improperly excluded, and that his improper testimony was admitted could not be considered since it could not be determined whether the claims were preserved under Va. Sup; Ct. R. 5A:8 and 5A:18. Wang v. Crumpacker, No. 0263-12-4, 2012 Va. App. LEXIS 401 (Dec. 11, 2012).

Subdivision (d) of this rule does not expressly require party filing objections to a previously submitted written statement of facts to notice a separate hearing. Summers v. Summers, No. 1968-98-4 (Ct. of Appeals Aug. 3, 1999).

Applied in Bunton v. Commonwealth, 6 Va. App. 557, 370 S.E.2d 470 (1988); Thomas v. Commonwealth, 379 S.E.2d 134 (1989); Reid v. Reid, 12 Va. App. 1218, 409 S.E.2d 155 (1991); Dickerson v. Commonwealth, 36 Va. App. 8, 548 S.E.2d 230, 2001 Va. App. LEXIS 398 (2001); Shreve v. Commonwealth, 44 Va. App. 541, 605 S.E.2d 780, 2004 Va. App. LEXIS 605 (2004); Peake v. Commonwealth, 46 Va. App. 35, 614 S.E.2d 672, 2005 Va. App. LEXIS 238 (2005); Shiembob v. Shiembob, 55 Va. App. 234, 685 S.E.2d 192, 2009 Va. App. LEXIS 520 (2009); Reid v. Commonwealth, 57 Va. App. 42, 698 S.E.2d 269, 2010 Va. App. LEXIS 349 (2010); Wooddell v. Lagerquist, No. 2121-11-3, 2012 Va. App. LEXIS 374 (Nov. 20, 2012).

II. COMPLIANCE.

A. Requirements.

Prima facie compliance. — Once an appellant has complied with the first two elements of subdivision (c), he or she has established prima facie compliance with the requirements of the rule. Proctor v. Town of Colonial Beach, 15 Va. App. 608, 425 S.E.2d 818 (1993).

All requirements of rule must be complied with. — A written statement of facts becomes a part of the record only if all of the requirements of this rule are complied with by the parties and the trial judge. Mayhood v. Mayhood, 4 Va. App. 365, 358 S.E.2d 182 (1987); Anderson v. Commonwealth, 13 Va. App. 506, 413 S.E.2d 75 (1992).

Because a father failed to comply with Va. Sup. Ct. R. 5A:8 and 5A:18 in order to adequately preserve the issues he raised on appeal from an order terminating his residual parental rights to his minor child pursuant to subdivisions C 1 and C 2 of § 16.1-283, and the trial court's ruling was not narrow enough to make obvious the basis of the father's objection, said order was affirmed on appeal. Stewart v. Hopewell Dep't of Soc. Servs., 2007 Va. App. LEXIS 320 (Aug. 28, 2007).

Appellate court could not grant the wife relief on the wife's appeal from the trial court's rulings in the wife's divorce case. In addition to the many issues that were not properly preserved for review because they were not supported by any authority, the wife did not supply an adequate record as to the issue about requiring the wife to pay a certain amount to the marital estate, in violation of Va. Sup. Ct. R. 5A:8(b). Rahnema v. Rahnema, 2008 Va. App. LEXIS 279 (June 10, 2008).

In a case in which a Medicaid claimant argued that the trial court in a reconsideration hearing failed to provide visual-aid equipment in the courtroom to accommodate his disability, the claimant failed to comply with Va. Sup. Ct. R. 5A:8(b) because he did not provide a transcript of the hearing or a statement of facts either corroborating or disproving his assertion. Additionally, no order addressed the claimant's request for an accommodation for his visual disability. Sudduth v. City of Alexandria Dep't of Human Servs., 2009 Va. App. LEXIS 466 (Oct. 20, 2009).

Because defendant did not provide a record of the trial court proceedings or a written statement of facts to supplement the transcript in accordance with Va. Sup. Ct. R. 5A:8, and because the missing portion of the transcript was indispensable to review of the issue, the record was insufficient to allow the appellate court to determine whether the trial court erred in the manner claimed. Friel v. Commonwealth, 2011 Va. App. LEXIS 217 (June 28, 2011).

Court will not dismiss appeal where prima facie compliance but will remand. — The Court of Appeals will not dismiss an appeal where an appellant has established prima facie compliance with subdivision (c)(1). Rather, in such situations, the case will be remanded to the trial judge for appropriate action as required by subdivisions (c)(2) or (d). Proctor v. Town of Colonial Beach, 15 Va. App. 608, 425 S.E.2d 818 (1993).

Requirements for including transcript in record must be strictly adhered to. — If the transcript is indispensable to the determination of the case, then the requirements for making the transcript a part of the record on appeal must be strictly adhered to. The Court of Appeals has no authority to make exceptions to the filing requirements set out in the Rules. Turner v. Commonwealth, 2 Va. App. 96, 341 S.E.2d 400 (1986).

If the court determines that the transcript is indispensable and is not a part of the record before it for review, it must dismiss the appeal on the ground that the record on appeal is insufficient to fairly and accurately determine the issues presented. Smith v. Commonwealth, 32 Va. App. 766, 531 S.E.2d 11, 2000 Va. App. LEXIS 499 (2000).

Appeal was dismissed because as appellant provided neither a transcript nor a written statement of facts, testimony, and other incidents of the case, the record was insufficient to determine fairly and accurately the issues presented. Skeen v. Skeen, No. 0801-00-3, 2001 Va. App. LEXIS 470 (Ct. of Appeals Aug. 7, 2001).

Appeal was dismissed where two developers failed to provide either a transcript from the trial court or a written statement of facts from the trial judge of the court's affirmance of an order from the State Water Control Board denying their application for a permit; although the record on appeal did contain the developers' written petition and brief filed in the trial court, the record in no way reflected what arguments the developers made to the trial court, what evidence was introduced at the hearing, or on what basis the trial court ruled. Ashe v. State Water Control Bd., No. 1268-04-1, 2004 Va. App. LEXIS 624 (Ct. of Appeals Dec. 21, 2004).

Defendant's failure to comply with the provisions of Va. Sup. Ct. R. 5A:8, by failing to file the transcript from his suppression hearing in the trial court within 60 days after entry of the final judgment, was a violation of a non-jurisdictional, though mandatory requirement of the rules governing the processing of appeals and, thus, defendant's motion to dismiss his own appeal was denied. Smith v. Commonwealth, 56 Va. App. 351, 693 S.E.2d 765, 2010 Va. App. LEXIS 242 (2010), aff'd, 281 Va. 464, 706 S.E.2d 889, 2011 Va. LEXIS 59 (2011).

Because the transcript that was provided did not include the hearing during which the issue of whether a witness was "kept away" under subdivision 2 of § 19.2-243, the transcript was insufficient to permit resolution of appellate issues under Va. Sup. Ct. R. 5A:8(b)(4)(ii). Gardner v. Commonwealth, No. 2367-09-1, 2010 Va. App. LEXIS 482 (Ct. of Appeals Dec. 14, 2010).

Requirements for inclusion of written statement of facts in record. — This rule imposes three requirements for a written statement of facts in lieu of a transcript to be included in the record of a case on appeal: (1) It must be filed in the office of the clerk of the trial court within 55 days after entry of judgment; (2) a copy of the statement must be mailed or delivered to opposing counsel along with a notice that the statement will be presented to the trial judge between 15 and 20 days after filing and (3) the trial judge must sign the statement, and the signed statement is to be filed in the office of the clerk. Kyhl v. Kyhl, 32 Va. App. 53, 526 S.E.2d 292 (2000).

Requirements must be strictly adhered to if transcript is indispensable. — If the transcript is indispensable to the determination of the case, then the requirements for making the transcript a part of the record on appeal must be strictly adhered to. Anderson v. Commonwealth, 13 Va. App. 506, 413 S.E.2d 75 (1992).

In a case in which a husband appealed a final divorce decree, asserting that the trial court made six errors, the alleged errors 1, 2, 3, and 6 related to four hearings, however, the record did not contain a timely filed transcript or written statement of facts for those hearing, as required by Va. Sup. Ct. R. 5A:8(a) and (c). A transcript or written statement of facts was indispensable to a determination of the questions presented in alleged errors 1, 2, 3, and 6. Kablach v. Kablach, 2009 Va. App. LEXIS 475 (Oct. 20, 2009).

Failure to comply with procedure for objecting to statement of the facts. — Because defendant failed to utilize the procedure provided by Va. Sup. Ct. R. 5A:8(d) to object to the contents of the statement of facts, he did not preserve his argument regarding the sufficiency of the evidence. Accordingly, Va. Sup. Ct. R. 5A:18 barred the appellate court's consideration of this question on appeal. Delaney v. Commonwealth, 55 Va. App. 64, 683 S.E.2d 834, 2009 Va. App. LEXIS 458 (2009).

The statement of facts did not become a part of the record because the statement was not filed in the office of the clerk within fifty-five days after entry of judgment. Anderson v. Commonwealth, 13 Va. App. 506, 413 S.E.2d 75 (1992).

Purpose of judge's signature on statement of facts. — The requirement that the trial judge sign the statement of facts is designed to ensure an accurate and complete statement of the facts and procedural history of the proceeding in the trial court. This requirement does not provide a means by which the trial judge, through design, inattention or inadvertence, may thwart an appeal by neglecting or refusing to sign the statement of facts. Clary v. Clary, 15 Va. App. 598, 425 S.E.2d 821 (1993).

In a divorce case, the husband failed to comply with Va. Sup. Ct. R. 5A:8(c)(2). His written statement of facts and incidents of trial, included in the appendix he provided on appeal, was not signed by the trial court as required by the Rule. Gopalakrishnan Subramanian v. Ranjeetha Ravichandran, No. 2617-11-4, 2012 Va. App. LEXIS 330 (Oct. 16, 2012).

Court not required to sign statement when record complete. — The trial court is not obligated under this rule to sign a defendant's written statement of facts where the record is complete on its own. Accordingly, there was no abuse of discretion in a trial court's refusal to sign a defendant's written statement of facts in lieu of transcript where the trial court noted that the record was complete and explained on the record what had transpired when the defendant met in the judge's chambers with the Commonwealth attorney and the judge. Harter v. Commonwealth, 31 Va. App. 743, 525 S.E.2d 606 (2000).

Consideration of transcript was not precluded by failure to give written notice to opposing counsel. — Where appellant filed the transcript of proceedings in the trial court in a timely fashion, under Rule 5A:8(a), but did not give written notice of that filing to opposing counsel, with a copy filed in the trial court, this did not preclude the appellate court's consideration of the transcript of proceedings in the trial court, as appellee did not allege that this failure prevented appellee from raising legitimate objections to the contents of the transcript, misled appellee about the contents of the record, or disadvantaged appellee in any other way that would constitute material prejudice under Rule 5A:8(b). M. G. v. Albemarle County Dep't of Soc. Servs., 41 Va. App. 170, 583 S.E.2d 761, 2003 Va. App. LEXIS 406 (2003).

Failure to comply with subdivision (b) of this rule does not invalidate the filing of a transcript which complies with subdivision (a) of this rule. Gollehon v. Gollehon, No. 2178-92-4 (Ct. of Appeals Nov. 23, 1993).

Because defendant juvenile did not provide a transcript or refer to it in the appellate brief, as required by Va. Sup. Ct. R. 5A:8(b) and 5A:20(c), the appellate court was unable to consider whether the proper underlying offense was present to commit defendant to the Department of Juvenile Justice under § 16.1-278.8(A)(14). Williams v. Commonwealth, 2005 Va. App. LEXIS 378 (Oct. 4, 2005).

Court of appeals was unable to review defendant's claim that the trial court violated his right to a trial by jury when it failed to give an instruction for misdemeanor eluding because there was no record of the argument defendant made in chambers requesting the instruction or the trial court's ruling; because there was no transcript in the record including the argument in chambers, the court of appeals could not ascertain the parties' arguments and the basis of the trial court's ruling. Stockman v. Commonwealth, 2008 Va. App. LEXIS 143 (Mar. 25, 2008).

Because appellant failed to file a transcript of a

hearing, the issues presented on appeal by the appellant were waived pursuant to Va. Sup. Ct. R. 5A:8 as that transcript was indispensable to the resolution of the issues. Soliman v. Soliman, No. 0030-10-4, 2010 Va. App. LEXIS 277 (Ct. of Appeals July 20, 2010).

Permitting the adoption of the child by the adoptive parent was appropriate because the putative biological father failed to comply with Va. Sup. Ct. R. 5A:8(b)(4)(ii). Thus, the appellate court did not consider on appeal his argument that the trial court abused its discretion in denying his motion for a continuance. Campos v. Hinsch, 2011 Va. App. LEXIS 313 (Oct. 11, 2011).

Because defendant failed to provide a record that sufficiently established that defendant was convicted of traffic infractions and not crimes, pursuant to Va. Sup. Ct. R. 5A:8(b)(4)(ii), defendant waived the argument on appeal that the trial court erred in imposing a fine under § 19.2-358. Turnbull v. County of Spotsylvania, 2012 Va. App. LEXIS 24 (Jan. 31, 2012).

Failure to submit transcript or statement of facts from the hearing. — In a divorce action, the husband's argument that the trial court erred in denying his motion for accounting in equity and in not considering whether he should have been awarded rental income for the period in which the wife lived in the marital residence during the separation of the parties was improper because there was no transcript or statement of facts from the hearing in which the trial court considered his motion. Harnois v. Riley-Harnois, 2011 Va. App. LEXIS 311 (Oct. 11, 2011).

Husband's argument that the trial court erred in ordering the sale of the marital residence and the disbursement of the proceeds was without merit because he failed to provide a transcript or statement of facts for the hearing at which the trial court appointed the commissioner and ordered the sale of the marital residence. Harnois v. Riley-Harnois, 2011 Va. App. LEXIS 311 (Oct. 11, 2011).

Based on a father's failure to comply with Va. Sup. Ct. R. 5A:8(c), the trial court did not err in refusing to accept the father's written statement of facts; the father did not prove that a copy of the statement was mailed or delivered to opposing counsel along with a notice that the statement would be presented to the trial court between fifteen and twenty days after filing. Lilley v. Wilson, 2012 Va. App. LEXIS 302 (Sept. 25, 2012).

Trial court did not err in failing to impute income to a mother because there was no record of the father's argument to the trial court, and without a transcript or written statement of facts, the court of appeals was unable to determine whether the father's assignment of error was preserved pursuant to Va. Sup. Ct. R. 5A:18; the trial court held that the father's written statement of facts was erroneous and incomplete, argumentative, and did not comply with Va. Sup. Ct. R. 5A:8(c). Lilley v. Wilson, 2012 Va. App. LEXIS 302 (Sept. 25, 2012).

Judge had authority even though not trial judge. — Judge had authority to determine the contents of the statement of facts even though he was not the trial judge; if the trial judge is not available, any judge authorized to act under Rule 5A:9, including a judge having authority to enter orders in the court in which the case was heard, may take appropriate actions as provided by this rule. Dedes v. Dedes, No. 0703-89-2 (Ct. of Appeals Aug. 21, 1990).

Counsel did not establish prima facie compliance. — Counsel did not establish prima facie compliance with the requirements of subdivision (c)(1) where he did not deliver the requisite notice to opposing counsel, and did not present the statement of facts to the trial judge. Clary v. Clary, 15 Va. App. 598, 425 S.E.2d 821 (1993).

B. Timeliness.

Timeliness determined by date order entered. — In determining the date of entry of a final order, a court speaks only through its orders and orders speak as of the day they were entered; the court will presume that the order, as the final pronouncement on the subject, rather than a transcript that may be flawed by omissions, accurately reflects what transpired. Smith v. Commonwealth, 32 Va. App. 766, 531 S.E.2d 11, 2000 Va. App. LEXIS 499 (2000).

Absence or late filing of transcript does nothing to diminish jurisdiction. — If the record on appeal is sufficient in the absence of the transcript to determine the merits of the appellant's allegations, the court is free to proceed to hear the case. Turner v. Commonwealth, 2 Va. App. 96, 341 S.E.2d 400 (1986).

Court could proceed to merits of appeal despite absence of hearing transcript or written statement of facts, where trial judge's order contained sufficient detail concerning evidence produced at hearing. Cummins v. Cummins, No. 2736-98-2 (Ct. of Appeals May 4, 1999).

When a grandmother appealed the denial of her petition for visitation with her granddaughter, her failure to file a transcript of the trial court proceedings or a statement of facts did not require dismissal of the appeal, as a transcript was not indispensable and the trial court's detailed opinion provided sufficient facts. Harris v. Boxler, No. 0604-03-3, 2003 Va. App. LEXIS 461 (Ct. of Appeals Sept. 2, 2003).

Defendant waived defendant's challenge to the trial court's denial of defendant's motion to suppress certain evidence because defendant failed to timely file a transcript necessary to resolve the issue pursuant to Va. Sup. Ct. R. 5A:8. Furthermore, defendant's failure to timely file the transcript did not deprive the intermediate appellate court of its active jurisdiction to proceed to judgment in the appeal and there was no error in the intermediate appellate court entering judgment affirming defendant's convictions, rather than dismissing the appeal for lack of jurisdiction. Smith v. Commonwealth, 281 Va. 464, 706 S.E.2d 889, 2011 Va. LEXIS 59 (2011).

Timely filing of transcript is not mandatory. — Unlike the Supreme Court Rule 5:5(a), Rule 5A:3(a) contains no language which makes the time for filing of the transcript mandatory. Likewise, Rule 5A:7 does not require that the transcript be made a part of the record on appeal. Rule 5A:7 states that the transcript will be included in the record on appeal if it is properly made a part of the record in accordance with the provisions of this rule. There is nothing in the Rules which makes timely filing of the transcript mandatory; rather, the clear objective of these Rules is to ensure that an accurate record, complete to the degree necessary to adjudicate the appeal, is transmitted to the court. Turner v. Commonwealth, 2 Va. App. 96, 341 S.E.2d 400 (1986).

Although wife moved to dismiss the appeal because of the husband's failure to timely file the transcripts of the various ore tenus hearings, and the transcript was indispensable to some of the issues the husband has presented for review, record on appeal provided a sufficient basis upon which the court could fully and adequately consider the jurisdictional questions raised by the husband. Price v. Price, 17 Va. App. 105, 435 S.E.2d 652 (1993).

Transcript from previous hearing was not required for adjudication of issues raised by husband on appeal, where husband conceded there was no transcript, no evidence was taken at hearing, and husband's exceptions were preserved elsewhere. Morris v. Morris, No. 0850-99-2 (Ct. of Appeals Oct. 26, 1999).

Order extending time for filing must be prospective. — The transcript must be timely filed, or leave extending the filing date must be granted, before the deadline occurs, and not after. Orders extending the time for filing must be prospective and not retrospective. Jordan v. Price, 3 Va. App. 672, 353 S.E.2d 168 (1987).

Leave to extend date for filing transcript must be granted before deadline occurs and where the nunc pro tunc order entered by the trial court attempted to accomplish that result, it failed to do so. An order entered nunc pro tunc cannot create a fiction that an act not yet performed has already occurred. Holley v. City of Newport News, 6 Va. App. 567, 370 S.E.2d 320 (1988).

Where trial court entered order purporting to grant extension of filing deadline nunc pro tunc, order had no effect, since nothing in the record indicated that the trial court actually granted the extension. Williams v. Commonwealth, 7 Va. App. 516, 375 S.E.2d 364 (1988).

Order held not to extend filing deadline. — Where trial transcripts were not filed until more than 60 days after entry of judgments, and where although there was no request for extension of time, the record contained an order which stated that the transcript was made a part of the record, this rule did not authorize an open-ended suspension of the deadline or provide that the transcript be deemed part of the record before it was prepared and filed, and thus, the order was not a valid exercise of the trial court's authority under subdivision (a) of this rule to extend the deadline for filing transcripts. Williams v. Commonwealth, 7 Va. App. 516, 375 S.E.2d 364 (1988).

In a case in which defendant appealed his convictions for abduction with intent to defile, rape and use of a firearm in the commission of rape, arguing that the Commonwealth's use of its peremptory strikes to strike three African-American jurors violated the Equal Protection Clause of the Fourteenth Amendment, defendant failed to comply with both Va. Sup. Ct. R. 5A:8 and § 19.2-321.1. Defendant, who had been granted a delayed appeal, was required to file the transcripts by June 24, 2008, which was 60 days after counsel had been appointed, and he did not file the transcript of the voir dire until August 27, 2008, which was 124 days after counsel was appointed. Gilliam v. Commonwealth, 2009 Va. App. LEXIS 450 (Oct. 6, 2009).

Motion to extend the deadline for filing transcripts. — Appellate court erred in requiring defendant to show good cause why her motion to extend the deadline for filing transcript was not filed within 60 days from the entry of final judgment because Va. Sup. Ct. R. 5A:8(a) provided a party 90 days from the entry of final judgment to file a motion to extend the 60-day period to file the transcripts; because the lower court considered and gave significant weight to an irrelevant and improper factor, it abused its discretion. Defendant had shown good cause to extend the period for filing transcripts. LaCava v. Commonwealth, 283 Va. 465, 722 S.E.2d 838, 2012 Va. LEXIS 45 (2012).

When, after defendant appealed defendant's criminal conviction, defendant discovered that the proceedings during one day of defendant's trial had not been transcribed and successfully moved the trial court to correct this error and include the missing transcript in the appellate record, it was error for the appellate court to decline to consider the missing transcript, due to the transcript not having been filed within the 60-day time limit in Va. Sup. Ct. R. 5A:8(a), because (1) a court reporter's failure to transcribe the transcript was an "oversight," under subsection B of § 8.01-428, and (2) the trial court made the missing transcript part of the record before defendant's petition for appeal was filed, while the trial court had jurisdiction, so the trial court's order was authorized under Va. Sup. Ct. R. 5A:9, and Va. Sup. Ct. R. 5A:8(a) did not require defendant to move the appellate court for an extension of time, and the trial court's authority to correct the record superseded Va. Sup. Ct. R. 5A:8(a). Belew v. Commonwealth, 284 Va. 173, 726 S.E.2d 257, 2012 Va. LEXIS 137 (2012).

Requirement of this rule as to filing transcript or written statement is jurisdictional and Rule 5A:3 does not empower the Court of Appeals to extend the time. Barrett v. Barrett, 1 Va. App. 378, 339 S.E.2d 208 (1986).

Untimely transcript was not considered. — Because defendant's filing of the transcript of a pre-trial suppression hearing was untimely, and because no extension of time for filing was granted, defendant's appeal was dismissed for failing to comply with the mandatory provisions of Va. Sup. Ct. R. 5A:8. Fuller v. Commonwealth, 2006 Va. App. LEXIS 222 (May 23, 2006).

Because the transcript was not filed until after its due date, and because the wife failed to request an extension of time for filing prior to that date, the transcript was not timely and could not be considered in the appeal. Roberts v. Roberts, 2006 Va. App. LEXIS 244 (May 30, 2006).

Rule 5A:9. Judge Authorized to Act.

The judge authorized to act in all matters relating to the record on appeal shall be any judge having authority to enter orders in the case or in the court in which the case was heard or, in a case heard by three judges, any one of them.

Cross references. — For applicability of this rule to appeals from the Virginia Workers' Compensation Commission, see Rule 5A:11.

Law Review. — For annual survey of Virginia law article, "Criminal Law and Procedure," see 47 U. Rich. L. Rev. 143 (2012).

CASE NOTES

Judge had authority even though not trial judge. — Judge had authority to determine the contents of the statement of facts even though he was not the trial judge; if the trial judge is not available, any judge authorized to act under this rule, including a judge having authority to enter orders in the court in which the case was heard, may take appropriate actions as provided by Rule 5A:8. Dedes v. Dedes, No. 0703-89-2, (Ct. of Appeals Aug. 21, 1990).

Trial court's authority to correct clerical error. — When, after defendant appealed defendant's criminal conviction, defendant discovered that the proceedings during one day of defendant's trial had not been transcribed and successfully moved the trial court to correct this error and include the missing transcript in the appellate record, it was error for the appellate court to decline to consider the missing transcript, due to the transcript not having been filed within the 60-day time limit in Va. Sup. Ct. R. 5A:8(a), because (1) a court reporter's failure to transcribe the transcript was an "oversight," under Va. Code Ann. § 8.01-428(B), and (2) the trial court made the missing transcript part of the record before defendant's petition for appeal was filed, while the trial court had jurisdiction, so the trial court's order was authorized under Va. Sup. Ct. R. 5A:9, and Va. Sup. Ct. R. 5A:8(a) did not require defendant to move the appellate court for an extension of time, and the trial court's authority to correct the record superseded Va. Sup. Ct. R. 5A:8(a). Belew v. Commonwealth, 284 Va. 173, 726 S.E.2d 257, 2012 Va. LEXIS 137 (2012).

Rule 5A:10. Record on Appeal: Preparation and Transmission.

(a) *Preparation.* — The clerk of the trial court shall prepare the record as soon as possible after notice of appeal is filed. In the event of multiple appeals in the same case, or in cases tried together, only one record need be prepared and transmitted.

(b) *Form of the Record.* — (1) The record shall be compiled in the following order:

(i) a front cover setting forth the name of the court and the short style of the case;

(ii) a table of contents listing each paper included in the record and the page on which it begins;

(iii) each paper constituting a part of the record in chronological order; and

(iv) the certificate of the clerk of the trial court that the foregoing constitutes the true and complete record, except omitted exhibits as hereinafter provided.

(2) Each page of the record shall be numbered at the bottom.

(3) Transcripts, depositions, and reports of commissioners may be included in separate volumes identified by the clerk of the trial court if referred to in the table of contents and at the appropriate place in the record.

(4) Exhibits, other than those filed with pleadings, may be included in a separate volume or envelope certified by the clerk of the trial court, except that any exhibit that cannot be conveniently placed in a volume or envelope shall be identified by a tag. Each such volume or envelope shall include, on its cover or inside, a descriptive list of exhibits contained therein. Reference shall be made to exhibits in the table of contents and at the appropriate place in the record referred to in paragraph (b)(1) of this Rule. The clerk of the trial court shall not transmit the following types of exhibits, unless requested to do so by the clerk of this Court: drugs, guns and other weapons, ammunition, blood vials and other bio-hazard type materials, money, jewelry, articles of clothing, and bulky items such as large graphs and maps. The omission of any such exhibit shall be noted on the descriptive list of exhibits. Upon motion by counsel, this Court may order the trial court to transmit any of these prohibited exhibits.

(5) Any transcript or statement that the clerk of the trial court deems not a part of the record because of untimely filing shall be certified as such and transmitted with the record.

(c) *Abbreviated Record.* — When the assignments of error presented by an appeal can be determined without examination of all the pleadings, facts, testimony, and other incidents of the case, all counsel with the approval of the trial court may prepare for submission an abbreviated record, stating how the assignments of error in the case arose and were decided, and setting forth only so much of the pleadings, facts, testimony, and other incidents of the case as are essential to a determination of the issues on appeal. Such abbreviated record shall be signed by all counsel and the trial judge and filed in the office of the clerk of the trial court. It will be assumed that the abbreviated record contains everything germane to the assignments of error. The Court of Appeals may, however, consider other parts of the record to enable this Court to attain the ends of justice.

(d) *Transmission.* — The clerk of the trial court shall retain the record for 21 days after the notice of appeal has been filed with him pursuant to Rule 5A:6. If the notice of appeal states that a transcript or statement will thereafter be filed, the clerk of the trial court shall retain the record for 21 days after the filing in his office of such transcript or statement or, if objection is made to the transcript or statement pursuant to Rule 5A:8 (d), the clerk of the trial court shall retain the record for five days after the objection is acted upon by the trial judge. The clerk of the trial court shall then forthwith transmit the record to the clerk of this Court; provided, however, that, notwithstanding that the foregoing periods of retention may not have expired, the clerk of the trial court shall transmit the record sooner if requested in writing by counsel for all parties to the appeal and shall, whether or not so requested, transmit the record in time for delivery to the clerk of this Court within three months after entry of the judgment appealed from. The failure of the clerk of the trial court to transmit the record as herein provided shall not be a ground for dismissal of the appeal by this Court.

(e) *Notice of Filing.* — The clerk of this Court shall promptly notify all counsel of the date on which the record is filed in the office of the clerk of the Court of Appeals.

(f) *Disposition of Record.* — When the mandate is issued by this Court, the clerk of this Court shall return the record to the clerk of the trial court. The record shall be returned by that clerk upon the request of the clerk of this Court.

Cross references. — For applicability of this rule to appeals from the Virginia Workers' Compensation Commission, see Rule 5A:11.

The amendment, effective May 2, 2011, adopted March 1, 2011, deleted "or commission in which the proceeding originated" at the end of the first sentence of subdivision (f).

CASE NOTES

Abbreviated record. — Husband's appeal would not be dismissed for his alleged violation of subdivision (c) of this rule, where wife failed to establish that she was prejudiced thereby. Morris v. Morris, No. 0850-99-2 (Ct. of Appeals Oct. 26, 1999).

Applied in Barrett v. Barrett, 1 Va. App. 378, 339 S.E.2d 208 (1986); Watkins v. Fairfax County Dep't of Family Servs., 42 Va. App. 760, 595 S.E.2d 19, 2004 Va. App. LEXIS 164 (2004); Williams Steel Erection Co. v. DOL & Indus., 42 Va. App. 814, 595 S.E.2d 45, 2004 Va. App. LEXIS 166 (2004).

D. PROCEDURE FOR FILING AN APPEAL FROM THE WORKERS' COMPENSATION COMMISSION.

Rule 5A:11. Special Rule Applicable to Appeals From the Virginia Workers' Compensation Commission.

(a) *Non-Application of Other Rules.* — Rules 5A:6 through 5A:10 do not apply to appeals from the Virginia Workers' Compensation Commission except as otherwise specified in this Part Five A.

(b) *Notice of Appeal.* — No appeal from an order of the Commission shall be allowed unless, within 30 days after entry of the order appealed from, or within 30 days after receipt of notice by priority mail with delivery confirmation or equivalent mailing option of the order appealed from, counsel files with the clerk of the Virginia Workers' Compensation Commission a notice of appeal which shall state the names and addresses of all appellants and appellees, the name, Virginia State Bar number, mailing address, telephone number (including any applicable extension), facsimile number (if any), and e-mail address (if any) of counsel for each party, and the mailing address, telephone number, facsimile number (if any), and e-mail address (if any) of any party not represented by counsel, and whether the appellant challenges the sufficiency of the evidence to support the findings of the Commission. A copy of the notice of appeal also shall be filed in the office of the clerk of this Court, and except as otherwise provided by law, must be accompanied by a check or money order in the amount of $50 payable to the "Clerk of the Court of Appeals," for the filing fee required by statute. The fee shall be due at the time the notice of appeal is presented. The clerk of this Court may file any notice of appeal that is not accompanied by such fee if the fee is received by the clerk within ten days of the date the notice of appeal is filed. If the fee is not received within such time, the appeal shall be dismissed.

(c) *Record on Appeal.* — The record on appeal from the Commission shall consist of the originals or copies of the notice of appeal, the employer's first report, medical reports, applications for hearings, the transcript of any hearing, depositions, interrogatories and answer to interrogatories, and opinions of a commissioner or deputy commissioner and opinions of the Commission, together with such other material as may be certified by the clerk of the Commission and shall conform as nearly as practicable to the requirements of Rule 5A:10 (b), provided, that, unless it is stated in the notice of appeal that the appellant challenges the sufficiency of the evidence to support the findings of the Commission, the clerk of the Commission need not prepare or certify the transcript of any hearing.

(d) *Transmission of Record.* — The record shall, as soon as it is certified by the clerk of the Commission, be transmitted by him to the clerk of this Court. It shall be so transmitted within 30 days after filing of the notice of appeal.

(e) *Notice of Filing.* — The clerk of this Court shall promptly notify all counsel of the date on which the record is filed in the office of the clerk of this Court.

(f) *Separate Cases.* — Whenever two or more cases were tried together in the Virginia Workers' Compensation Commission, one notice of appeal and one record may be used to bring all such cases before this Court even though such cases were not consolidated by formal order.

(g) *Record Returned to Commission.* — When the mandate is issued by this Court, the clerk of this Court shall return the record to the clerk of the Commission. The clerk of the Commission shall return the record upon request of the clerk of this Court.

Cross references. — As to appeal bonds, see § 8.01-676.1.

Michie's Jurisprudence. — For related discussion, see 1B M.J. Appeal and Error, §§ 124, 135, 139, 141, 176, 212; 8A M.J. Exceptions, Bill of, § 1; 21 M.J. Workers' Compensation, §§ 78, 80.

CASE NOTES

Purpose. — The purpose of this rule is to facilitate the preparation of the record on appeal. Harrison v. Nabisco Brands, Inc., No. 1149-9-2, (Ct. of Appeals Apr. 27, 1993).

Absence of actual transcript due to malfunction of tape recording equipment or agreed upon account of the evidence foreclosed the Commission's ability to discharge its duty to review the evidence as required by this section, and further prevented the Court of Appeals from examining a complete record for the purpose of appellate review. Burkholder & Kreig, Inc. v. Hughes, No. 0125-84, (Ct. of Appeals Aug. 29, 1985).

Malfunction of tape recorder resulting in incomplete record. — Where the full Commission did not review all the evidence because a nine-minute portion of the proceedings was missing due to a mechanical malfunction of the tape recording equipment, it could not be said as a matter of law that the nine minutes of evidence, which were not presented to the full Commission or to the Court of Appeals, had no effect on the outcome of the case. Flavin v. J.C. Penney Co., 1 Va. App. 1, 332 S.E.2d 805 (1985).

The time requirement for filing is mandatory, and failure of the appellant to file the notice of appeal timely requires dismissal of the appeal. Zion Church Designers & Bldrs. v. McDonald, 18 Va. App. 580, 445 S.E.2d 704 (1994).

Appellant's failure to include the addresses of both parties, the phone number of claimant's attorney, and whether appellant was challenging the sufficiency of the evidence was a mere failure to perform a directory act and was not fatal to its appeal. Teagle & Little, Inc. v. Balchunis, No. 2270-94-1, (Ct. of Appeals July 25, 1995).

Notice of appeal. — Provision of Rule 5A:1(10) that a copy of the notice of appeal be mailed or delivered to opposing counsel does not defeat the filing of notice of appeal with the clerk of the Commission under paragraph (b) of this rule; this provision is directory rather than mandatory, because appellee is put on notice of the appeal when the clerk of court sends notice that the record has been filed and because appellee has no reason to assume that an appeal will not follow a favorable decision by the Commission, since such appeals are a matter of right rather than by petition. Johnson v. City of Clifton Forge, 7 Va. App. 538, 375 S.E.2d 540 (1989).

Applied in Greif Cos./Genesco, Inc. v. Hensley, 22 Va. App. 546, 471 S.E.2d 803 (1996); Watkins v. Fairfax County Dep't of Family Servs., 42 Va. App. 760, 595 S.E.2d 19, 2004 Va. App. LEXIS 164 (2004).

E. PROCEDURE ON PETITION FOR APPEAL IN CRIMINAL CASES AND TRAFFIC INFRACTIONS.

Rule 5A:12. Petition for Appeal.

(a) *When the Petition Must be Filed.* — When an appeal to the Court of Appeals does not lie as a matter of right, a petition for appeal must be filed with the clerk of this Court not more than 40 days after the filing of the record with the Court of Appeals. An extension of 30 days may be granted on motion in the discretion of this Court upon a showing of good cause sufficient to excuse the delay.

(b) *Copy to Opposing Counsel.* — At the time the petition for appeal is filed, a copy of the petition shall be mailed or delivered to the Commonwealth's attorney or the city, county, or town attorney, as the case may be.

(c) *What the Petition Must Contain.* — A petition for appeal must contain the following:

(1) Assignments of Error. The provisions of Rule 5A:18 shall apply to limit those assignments of error which this Court will rule upon on appeal. Under a heading entitled "Assignments of Error," the petition shall list, clearly and concisely and without extraneous argument, the specific errors in the rulings below upon which the party intends to rely. An exact reference to the pages of the transcript, written statement of facts, or record where the alleged error has been preserved in the trial court or other tribunal from which the appeal is taken shall be included with each assignment of error.

(i) Effect of Failure to Assign Error. Only assignments of error assigned in the petition for appeal will be noticed by this Court. If the petition for appeal does not contain assignments of error, it shall be dismissed.

(ii) Insufficient Assignments of Error. An assignment of error which does not address the findings or rulings in the trial court or other tribunal from which an appeal is taken, or which merely states that the judgment or award is contrary to the law and the evidence is not sufficient. If the assignments of error are insufficient or otherwise fail to comply with the requirements of this Rule, the petition for appeal shall be dismissed.

(2) Table of Contents and Table of Authorities. A table of contents and table of authorities with cases alphabetically arranged. Citations of all authorities shall include the year thereof.

(3) Nature of the Case and Material Proceedings Below. A brief statement of the nature of the case and of the material proceedings in the trial court or commission in which the case originated. This statement shall omit references to any paper filed or action taken that does not relate to the assignments of error.

(4) Statement of Facts. A clear and concise statement of the facts that relate to the assignments of error, with references to the pages of the record, transcript, or written statement of facts. Any quotation from the record should be brief. When the facts are in dispute, the petition shall so state. The testimony of individual witnesses should not be summarized seriatim unless the facts are in dispute and such a summary is necessary to support the appellant's version of the facts.

(5) Authorities and Argument. With respect to each assignment of error, the standard of review and the argument — including principles of law and the authorities — shall be stated in one place and not scattered through the petition. At the option of counsel, the argument may be preceded by a short summary.

(6) Conclusion. A short conclusion stating the precise relief sought.

(7) Contact Information. The signature of at least one counsel, counsel's name, Virginia State Bar number, mailing address, telephone number, facsimile number (if any), and email address (if any).

(8) Certificate. A certificate stating the date of mailing or delivery of the petition to opposing counsel and whether or not the appellant desires to state orally the reasons why the petition for appeal should be granted.

(d) *Number of Copies to File.* — Four copies of the petition shall be filed with the clerk of this Court.

(e) *Length.* — Except by leave of a Judge of this Court, a petition shall not exceed 12,300 words. The word limit does not include the cover page, table of contents, table of authorities, and certificate.

(f) *Single Petition in Separate Cases.* — Whenever two or more cases were tried together in the trial court or commission below, one petition for appeal may be used to bring all such cases before the Court of Appeals even though the cases were not consolidated below by formal order.

(g) *Oral Argument.* — When the appeal is not granted by the Judge of this Court to whom the petition for appeal is originally presented, the petitioner shall be entitled to state orally, in person or by conference telephone call, to a panel of this Court the reasons the petition for appeal should be granted. The appellant may waive the right to oral argument on the petition for appeal before a panel by notifying the clerk of this Court and opposing counsel in writing, or by filing a reply brief. Any lawyer not licensed to practice in Virginia who seeks to appear pro hac vice to present oral argument to this Court must comply with the requirements of Rule 1A:4.

(h) *Procedure for an Anders appeal.* — If counsel for appellant finds his client's appeal to be without merit, he must comply with the requirements of *Anders v. California,* 386 U.S. 738 (1967), and *Akbar v. Commonwealth,* 7 Va. App. 611, 376 S.E.2d 545 (1989). In compliance therewith, counsel is required to file (1) a petition for appeal which refers to anything in the record which might arguably support the appeal and which demonstrates to the Court of Appeals counsel's conscientious examination of the merits of the appeal; (2) a motion for leave to withdraw as counsel; and (3) a motion for an extension of time to allow the appellant to file a supplemental petition for appeal. The petition for appeal and the motion for leave to withdraw as counsel should specifically cite to *Anders.* All three pleadings must be served on opposing counsel and upon the client and must contain a certificate providing evidence of such service. The Court of Appeals will rule upon the motion for extension of time upon its receipt, but will not rule on the motion to withdraw as counsel until this Court considers the case in its entirety, including any supplemental petition for appeal that may be filed.

Cross references. — For procedures on appeal, see § 17.1-407. For time for filing notice of appeal and petition, see § 17.1-408. As to appeals by the Commonwealth from certain pretrial rulings, see § 19.2-398 et seq.

The amendment, effective May 2, 2011, adopted March 1, 2011, added subdivision (c)(7) and redesignated former subdivision (c)(7) as (c)(8).

Law Review. — For 1985 survey of Virginia civil procedure and practice, see 19 U. Rich. L. Rev. 679 (1985).

Michie's Jurisprudence. — For related discussion, see 1B M.J. Appeal and Error, § 124.

CASE NOTES

Filing requirement is unambiguous, mandatory, and jurisdictional. — The filing requirement of this rule is unambiguous, mandatory, and jurisdictional. Haywood v. Commonwealth, 15 Va. App. 297, 423 S.E.2d 202 (1992).

Petition filed by first class mail held untimely. — Where petition was due on December 2, 1987, and was received in the clerk's office of the Court of Appeals on December 7, and where the petition was mailed by first class mail, not by registered or certified mail, the petition was not timely filed and would be dismissed, since Rule 5A:3(c) specifically lists appropriate mailing methods that are deemed timely filed without mentioning first class mail as an alternative. Long v. Commonwealth, 7 Va. App. 503, 375 S.E.2d 368 (1988).

Order granting delayed appeal did not affect filing requirement. — Filing requirement for the petition for appeal was not accomplished until petition was physically delivered to the clerk on December 3, a day late. It made no difference that appeal was sought pursuant to an order from the Supreme Court granting a delayed appeal. That order merely authorized the delayed initiation of the appeal. It did not otherwise vary the jurisdictional and procedural time constraints. Haywood v. Commonwealth, 15 Va. App. 297, 423 S.E.2d 202 (1992).

Petition denied where no timely motion for extension filed. — Petition for appeal would be dismissed where although paragraph (a) of this rule vests the court with discretionary authority to grant a 30-day extension of the filing deadline, no timely motion for such action was made, and motions to extend the filing deadline for petitions must be filed and granted before the original deadline has passed. Long v. Commonwealth, 7 Va. App. 503, 375 S.E.2d 368 (1988).

Time requirements for interlocutory appeals by the Commonwealth in criminal cases. — In reading §§ 17.1-408 and 19.2-402 and Va. Sup. Ct. R. 5A:12 together and giving effect to as much of their respective provisions as possible, in any interlocutory appeal by the Commonwealth in a criminal case, a petition for appeal that is compliant with the provisions of Va. Sup. Ct. R. 5A:12(c)(1) must be filed within fourteen days of the receipt by the clerk of the trial court of the transcript or written statement of facts or, if there are objections thereto, within fourteen days after the judge signs the transcript or written statement of facts, and, in such cases, the Virginia Court of

Appeals has no authority to grant an extension of time for any reason, and any grant of such authority to that Court must come from the general assembly. Commonwealth v. Square, No. 2526-11-2, 2012 Va. App. LEXIS 202 (June 12, 2012).

Incorporation of Va. Sup. Ct. R. 5A:12 in § 19.2-402 did not include authority to grant Commonwealth extension of time to file petition for interlocutory appeal. — While § 19.2-402 incorporates by reference the requirements of the Rules of the Supreme Court of Virginia applicable to the Virginia Court of Appeals, the authority to grant an extension of time as found in Va. Sup. Ct. R. 5A:12(a) does not apply to interlocutory appeals by the Commonwealth because the statute's plain language incorporates by reference only the substantive requirements for the petition as found in other subsections of Va. Sup. Ct. R. 5A:12. Commonwealth v. Square, No. 2526-11-2, 2012 Va. App. LEXIS 202 (June 12, 2012).

Only questions presented in petition will be noticed. — Only questions presented in the petition for appeal will be noticed by the Court of Appeals. Lester v. Commonwealth, No. 0538-89-1, (Ct. of Appeals June 12, 1990); Alexander v. Commonwealth, 28 Va. App. 771, 508 S.E.2d 912 (1999).

Unlike Rule 5A:18, this rule contains no "good cause" or "ends of justice" exception. Lane v. Commonwealth, No. 2161-98-2 (Ct. of Appeals Sept. 28, 1999).

Court of Appeals would not consider issues other than one on which appeal was granted. Pollard v. Commonwealth, No. 2638-98-2 (Ct. of Appeals Sept. 21, 1999).

When defendant in a drunk driving case failed to present the issue of his sentence enhancement to the trial court, it was not preserved for appeal, and the trial court would not consider sua sponte the ends-of-justice exception to Va. Sup. Ct. R. 5A:18 when defendant had failed to raise it. Moreover, the issue was defaulted because even if defendant had preserved the issue, he had not presented it in his petition for appeal as required by Va. Sup. Ct. R. 5A:12(c) or briefed it as required by Va. Sup. Ct. R. 5A:20. Luginbyhl v. Commonwealth, 48 Va. App. 58, 628 S.E.2d 74, 2006 Va. App. LEXIS 170 (2006).

Intermediate appellate court improperly relied entirely on defendant's "access to justice" rationale in support of his denial of cross-examination argument, which defendant had not asserted on appeal, because only arguments presented in the petition for appeal and granted were to have been considered on appeal; an issue abandoned at trial may not have been resurrected on appeal, and an appellate court was not allowed to "recast" an argument made below into a different argument upon which to base its decision. Clifford v. Commonwealth, 274 Va. 23, 645 S.E.2d 295, 2007 Va. LEXIS 93 (2007).

Because defendant's "Statement of Questions Presented" did not maintain that the evidence was insufficient for his conviction, but rather maintained that the challenged evidence on which that conviction was based was improperly admitted, given that the appeals court determined that said evidence was properly admitted, it declined to address defendant's sufficiency claim. Guerara-Sandoval v. Commonwealth, 2007 Va. App. LEXIS 296 (Aug. 7, 2007).

In a case in which defendant listed all of his convictions on his notice of appeal, the appellate court would consider only those convictions that related to the question he presented since Va. Sup. Ct. R. 5A:12(c) provided that only questions presented in the petition for appeal would be noticed by the appellate court. Drew v. Commonwealth, 2009 Va. App. LEXIS 415 (Sept. 22, 2009).

Court of appeals could not consider the terms of a plea agreement in defendant's appeal of an order finding that he violated his probation because the terms were not a basis for reversal permitted by the Rules of Court when defendant did not ask the court of appeals to consider whether the trial court's decision was a breach of the terms of the plea agreement he made with the Commonwealth; the plea agreement and defendant's Alford plea questions did not involve the same evidence because the former required attention to the text of the written agreement, and the latter did not, and the questions did not require similar legal analyses. Carroll v. Commonwealth, 54 Va. App. 730, 682 S.E.2d 92, 2009 Va. App. LEXIS 392 (2009), aff'd, 280 Va. 641, 701 S.E.2d 414, 2010 Va. LEXIS 277 (2010).

In a case in which defendant appealed his convictions for breaking and entering, in violation of § 18.2-91, and grand larceny, in violation of § 18.2-95, asserting that the evidence was insufficient to support his convictions, but he arguing in his brief on appeal, and at oral argument, that the trial court erred in admitting the stolen items' serial numbers into evidence, asserting that those numbers were inadmissible hearsay, the admissibility of evidence and the sufficiency of evidence were distinct issues. Va. Sup. Ct. R. 5A:12(c) provided that only questions presented in the petition for appeal will be noticed by the Virginia Court of Appeals. Lunsford v. Commonwealth, 55 Va. App. 59, 683 S.E.2d 831, 2009 Va. App. LEXIS 461 (2009).

Appellate court's judgment reversing defendant's conviction was itself reversed because under Va. Sup. Ct. R. 5A:12 the appellate court could not reverse a circuit court's judgment on a basis not argued on appeal by defendant. Commonwealth v. Brown, 279 Va. 235, 687 S.E.2d 742, 2010 Va. LEXIS 16 (2010).

Where there were two alternative holdings on a motion to set aside a verdict and where defendant failed to challenge the trial court's finding that he was procedurally barred from attacking his convictions and instead challenged only the finding that the evidence was sufficient to support his convictions, defendant waived any claim of error with respect to the motion to set aside the verdict because defendant's failure to address one of the holdings resulted in the waiver of any claim of error with respect to the trial court's decision on that issue. Parrish v. Commonwealth, 2010 Va. App. LEXIS 186 (May 11, 2010).

Appellate court declined to consider defendant's argument that a requirement of sex-offender therapy making defendant admit guilt to the crime of rape was a breach of defendant's Alford plea agreement because defendant's statement of the questions presented did not contain the words "breach" or "plea agreement." Carroll v. Commonwealth, 280 Va. 641, 701 S.E.2d 414, 2010 Va. LEXIS 277 (2010).

Defendant failed to significantly comply with Va. Sup. Ct. R. 5A:12(c) when she phrased her question presented on appeal as whether the trial court erred by not allowing the cross-examination of the Commonwealth's witnesses concerning their bias. Since the question presented did not cover the excluded testimony of defendant and a defense witness on direct examination, defendant waived her contention that testimony as to these two witnesses was improperly excluded. Escalante v. Commonwealth, 2010 Va. App. LEXIS 338 (Aug. 17, 2010).

Failure to address trial court's findings or rulings. — Appellate court lacked active jurisdiction to consider defendant's sole assignment of error because it did not address the findings or rulings in the trial court, and was, therefore, insufficient under Va. Sup. Ct. R. 5A:12(c)(1)(ii). Coleman v. Commonwealth, 60 Va. App. 618, 731 S.E.2d 22, 2012 Va. App. LEXIS 260 (Aug. 14, 2012).

Where the question presented relied on the wrong standard. — Where the question presented on appeal erroneously relied on the wrong standard governing a fourth amendment claim, "probable cause" rather than "reasonable suspicion," but the question was restated by the Commonwealth and agreed to by the parties, as well as being fully briefed, argued and decided on appeal, the court erred by foreclosing the petitioner's right to defend the decision of the panel. Moore v. Commonwealth, 276 Va. 747, 668 S.E.2d 150, 2008 Va. LEXIS 106 (2008).

Issue not considered in absence of allegation of trial court error. — Defendant did not allege a trial court error in either question presented to the appellate court, and thus the substantive issue was not considered. Kilby v. Commonwealth, 2007 Va. App. LEXIS 364 (Ct. of Appeals Oct. 2, 2007).

Because defendant's "questions presented" in her opening brief failed to allege any trial court error, the court of appeals would not consider them on appeal; none of the questions presented invoked assertions of error on the part of the trial court. Newman v. Commonwealth, 2009 Va. App. LEXIS 360 (Aug. 11, 2009).

Enlargement of petition. — Va. Sup. Ct. R. 5A:12 does not prevent the Court of Appeals of Virginia, in its discretion and pursuant to its inherent authority, from considering additional issues not raised in a notice of appeal as long as the court has acquired jurisdiction over the appeal via timely filing of the original petition for appeal. Riner v. Commonwealth, 40 Va. App. 440, 579 S.E.2d 671, 2003 Va. App. LEXIS 287 (2003), aff'd, 268 Va. 296, 601 S.E.2d 555 (2004).

Dismissal not required for Va. Sup. Ct. R. 5A:12(c)(1). — Remedies short of dismissal are available in the event an appellant fails to note where the issue was preserved as required by Va. Sup. Ct. R. 5A:12(c)(1) as counsel may seek, or the appellate court may compel, the filing of an amended brief that complies with Rule 5A:12(c)(1)(ii); although dismissal is not required it nonetheless may constitute an appropriate exercise of discretion in some situations, whether at the petition stage or after an appeal has been granted, where counsel for an appellant, despite multiple opportunities to cure the defect in his petition for appeal, does not do so.. Brooks v. Commonwealth, No. 2708-10-1, 61 Va. App. 576, 739 S.E.2d 224, 2013 Va. App. LEXIS 99 (Mar. 26, 2013).

Dismissal available for Va. Sup. Ct. R. 5A:12(c)(1) violation. — Dismissal of an appeal is available after a petition for appeal is granted as: (1) once the appellate court grants a petition for appeal, Va. Sup. Ct. R. 5A:20 and 5A:26, rather than Va. Sup. Ct. R. 5A:12, govern the opening brief; (2) Rule 5A:20(c) provides that an opening brief must contain a statement of the assignments of error with a clear and exact reference to the pages of the transcript, written statement, record, or appendix where each assignment of error was preserved in the trial court; and (3) Rule 5A:26 provides that the appellate court may dismiss the appeal whenever the appellant fails to file a brief in compliance with the Virginia Supreme Court Rules. Brooks v. Commonwealth, No. 2708-10-1, 61 Va. App. 576, 739 S.E.2d 224, 2013 Va. App. LEXIS 99 (Mar. 26, 2013).

Two distinct requirements in Va. Sup. Ct. R. 5A:12(c)(1). — Appellate court declines to conflate the two distinct requirements of Va. Sup. Ct. R. 5A:12(c)(1) of the assignment of error and the separate but related requirement that an appellant point out where the alleged error was preserved in the trial court as the two separate requirements serve different functions; the purpose of the assignment of error is to alert the appellate court and opposing counsel to the precise error allegedly committed below and to limit review to that issue, and the requirement of providing an exact reference to where the issue was preserved helps the appellate court grant review only for cases where the issue was preserved, or where the ends of justice exception applies. Brooks v. Commonwealth, No. 2708-10-1, 61 Va. App. 576, 739 S.E.2d 224, 2013 Va. App. LEXIS 99 (Mar. 26, 2013).

Assignment of error separate from requirement of citation to where alleged error preserved. — Appellate court refused to conflate the requirements of Va. Sup. Ct. R. 5A:12(c)(1) of an assignment of error and the separate but related requirement that an appellant point out where the alleged error was preserved in the trial court; these two separate requirements serve different roles as the purpose of the assignment of error is to alert the appellate court and opposing counsel to the precise error allegedly committed below and to limit review to that issue, and the requirement of providing an exact reference to where the issue was preserved helps the appellate court to grant review only for cases where the issue was preserved, or where the ends of justice exception applies. Chatman v. Commonwealth, No. 0858-11-2, 61 Va. App. 618, 739 S.E.2d 245, 2013 Va. App. LEXIS 98 (Mar. 26, 2013).

Appeal dismissed for failure to comply with Va. Sup. Ct. R. 5A:12(c)(1). — Defendant's appeal was dismissed as his assignments of error cited the transcript pages containing the entire suppression hearing and nearly the entire trial in violation of Va. Sup. Ct. R. 5A:12(c)(1); dismissal was proper since defendant's counsel, despite multiple opportunities to cure the defect in his petition for appeal, did not do so, or seek leave to file an amended brief to correct the defect. Brooks v. Commonwealth, No. 2708-10-1, 61 Va. App. 576, 739 S.E.2d 224, 2013 Va. App. LEXIS 99 (Mar. 26, 2013).

Defect may be corrected after deadline for filing petition for appeal has passed. — Appellant, who timely files a petition for appeal, can file an amended petition for appeal, even after the deadline for filing the petition for appeal has passed, which corrects a defect under Va. Sup. Ct. R. 5A:12(c)(1); neither § 17.1-408 nor Rule 5A:12(a) specifies that the petition for appeal must be free of all defects in order to be timely filed, and the statute and the rule do not prohibit an appellate court from considering, and where appropriate, granting, a motion to correct a defect with regard to pointing out where in the record the issue raised on appeal was preserved. Chatman v. Commonwealth, No. 0858-11-2, 61 Va. App. 618, 739 S.E.2d 245, 2013 Va. App. LEXIS 98 (Mar. 26, 2013).

Amendment of assignments of error. — Appellate court exercised its discretion to grant defendant's motion to amend the petition for appeal and, in turn, the court addressed the merits of the appeal because (1) defendant's request for the amendment at issue was made after defendant filed a timely notice of appeal and a timely petition for appeal; (2) the requested amendment was consistent with arguments presented at trial and did not constitute a broadening of the scope of the original assignment of error; and (3) the Commonwealth of Virginia did not articulate any prejudice that would follow from such an amendment. Whitt v. Commonwealth, No. 0885-11-3, 61 Va. App. 637, 739 S.E.2d 254, 2013 Va. App. LEXIS 100 (Mar. 26, 2013).

Failure to comply with Va. Sup. Ct. R. 5A:12(c)(1) did not deprive appellate court of active jurisdiction. — Defendant's failure to comply with Va. Sup. Ct. R. 5A:12(c)(1) in a timely petition for appeal could be corrected in an amended petition filed after the deadline for filing a petition for appeal had passed; defendant's initial failure to comply with Rule 5A:12(c)(1) did not deprive the appellate court of active jurisdiction. Chatman v. Commonwealth, No. 0858-11-2, 61 Va. App. 618, 739 S.E.2d 245, 2013 Va. App. LEXIS 98 (Mar. 26, 2013).

Petition not timely filed. — Petition to Court of Appeals was considered a review pursuant to § 18.2-308 D, and thus its filing more than 30 days after the decision was untimely. It was not treated as a "petition for appeal" under this rule whereby the filing would have followed the record within 40 days and been timely. In re Cummins, 19 Va. App. 128, 449 S.E.2d 263 (1994).

When the Commonwealth's petition for an interlocutory appeal appealing an order granting a motion to suppress did not contain assignments of error, the appellate court erroneously granted an extension of time within which to file a proper petition and had no jurisdiction to consider the petition because (1) the requirement of assignments of error was jurisdictional, (2) the legislature intended in §§ 19.2-402 and 17.1-408 to expeditiously dispose of such appeals, (3) § 19.2-402 did not let the appellate court grant an extension in such cases, (4) § 19.2-402, reducing the time to file an interlocutory petition for appeal to fourteen days, governed, as the statute was a more specific and more recent expression of legislative intent, and (5) § 19.2-402's incorporation of Va. Sup. Ct. R. 5A:12 did not include authority to grant extensions of time, so (6) the general assembly did not intend to grant extensions to file a petition for appeal in these cases. Commonwealth v. Square, No. 2526-11-2, 2012 Va. App. LEXIS 202 (June 12, 2012).

Actual ruling required. — Court of Appeals would not consider assertion that trial court erred in ruling, as a matter of law, that statute could not be applied, because trial court made no such ruling. Terrell v. Commonwealth, No. 2476-98-4 (Ct. of Appeals Dec. 28, 1999).

Provisions of what petition "shall contain" were not jurisdictional. — In termination of parental rights case, a cover letter, signed by the mother's guardian ad litem, did, in fact, indicate that the children's guardian ad litem received a copy of the notice of appeal, even though the certificate attached to the notice did not so indicate, and thus, the mother complied with Va. Sup. Ct. R. 5A:6(a); as long as the petition for appeal was timely filed, the provisions of Va. Sup. Ct. R. 5A:12(c), stating what the petition "shall contain" were not jurisdictional and did not prevent appellate courts from exercising jurisdiction over assignments of error added to the petition, with leave of court, at a later date. M. G. v. Albemarle County Dep't of Soc. Servs., 41 Va. App. 170, 583 S.E.2d 761, 2003 Va. App. LEXIS 406 (2003).

Court of Appeals of Virginia erred by dismissing a portion of petitions for appeal filed separately by two defendants, upon their failure to comply with the requirements of Va. Sup. Ct. R. 5A:20(e), as: (1) the rule did not impose jurisdictional requirements; and (2) the Court of Appeals could have explored other options, short of dismissal, and should have considered whether any failure to strictly adhere to the requirements of the rule was insignificant, thus allowing the court to address the merits of a question presented. Jay v. Commonwealth, 275 Va. 510, 659 S.E.2d 311, 2008 Va. LEXIS 53 (2008).

Inadequate statement of authority. — Averment in a petition for appeal in a criminal case that under "well settled law" the evidence was insufficient gave no supporting case citation, in violation of subsection (c) of Rule 5A:12. Jacobs v. Commonwealth, 2002 Va. App. LEXIS 589 (Oct. 8, 2002).

Preservation for review. — Because defendant never argued that defendant's probation should not be revoked or that defendant involuntarily left an alternative sentencing program because of an unforeseen medical condition, defendant failed to preserve the issues for appeal. Hubbard v. Commonwealth, 2005 Va. App. LEXIS 194 (May 17, 2005).

Defendant was precluded from seeking review of the trial court's admission into evidence of recorded 911 calls because the calls were unduly prejudicial as defendant never made that argument in the trial court and, thus, could not seek to overturn defendant's conviction on that ground. Ellis v. Commonwealth, 2008 Va. App. LEXIS 439 (Sept. 30, 2008).

Appellant's attempts at making an as-applied challenge in an appellate brief to the constitutionality of an ordinance, where an as-applied challenge was not alleged in the assignment of error on appeal, were barred under Va. Sup. Ct. R. 5A:12(c)(1)(i). Pearson v. City of Falls Church, 2012 Va. App. LEXIS 12 (Jan. 17, 2012).

Defendant's argument made on appeal was actually raised in his appellate brief; thus, it was properly preserved and was not procedurally barred pursuant to Va. Sup. Ct. R. 5A:12. Simmons

v. Commonwealth, 2012 Va. App. LEXIS 204 (June 19, 2012).

Appellate court declined to consider defendant's appeal pursuant to Va. Sup. Ct. R. 5A:12(c)(1)(ii) because the trial court did not admit a purported certified copy of marriage record into evidence pursuant to subsection B of § 8.01-391, and defendant did not raise an argument regarding subsection A of § 8.01-390 with the trial court. Jernigan v. Commonwealth, No. 2245-11-1, 2012 Va. App. LEXIS 319 (Oct. 9, 2012).

Appeal dismissed for failure to comply with Va. Sup. Ct. R. 5A:12(c)(1). — Defendant's appeal was dismissed for failure to comply with Va. Sup. Ct. R. 5A:12(c)(1) because (1) defendant's assignment of error alleging a general insufficiency of the evidence did not list clearly and concisely the specific errors on which defendant intended to rely, and (2) the failure to comply deprived the appellate court of active jurisdiction to consider the appeal. Chatman v. Commonwealth, 60 Va. App. 622, 731 S.E.2d 24, 2012 Va. App. LEXIS 263 (Aug. 14, 2012).

Dismissal required for failure to comply with Va. Sup. Ct. R. 5A:12(c)(1). — With the amendment of Va. Sup. Ct. R. 5A:12(c) to mandate dismissal of a petition for appeal if the assignments of error fail to comply with the requirements of the Rule, Va. Sup. Ct. R. 5A:12(c)(1)(ii), coupled with the Virginia Supreme Court's recent interpretation and application of such mandatory dismissal language in Va. Sup. Ct. R. 5:17(c)(1)(iii), the Virginia Court of Appeals now must dismiss a petition for appeal containing assignments of error that fail to comply with the requirements of Va. Sup. Ct. R. 5A:12(c)(1). Chatman v. Commonwealth, 60 Va. App. 622, 731 S.E.2d 24, 2012 Va. App. LEXIS 263 (Aug. 14, 2012).

Defendant's appeal was dismissed for failure to comply with Va. Sup. Ct. R. 5A:12(c)(1) because (1) defendant's citations to the entire transcripts of a hearing on defendant's motion to suppress and defendant's trial did not point out specific errors "with reasonable certainty," and (2) the failure to comply deprived the appellate court of active jurisdiction to consider the appeal. Chatman v. Commonwealth, 60 Va. App. 622, 731 S.E.2d 24, 2012 Va. App. LEXIS 263 (Aug. 14, 2012).

Assignments of error. — Defendant's appeal was dismissed for failure to comply with Va. Sup. Ct. R. 5A:12(c)(1) because (1) assignments of error in defendant's only timely petition for appeal did not refer to where defendant preserved alleged errors in the trial court, (2) since this petition was non-compliant, defendant's untimely amended petition could not be considered, and (3) the failure to comply deprived the court of active jurisdiction to consider the appeal. Chatman v. Commonwealth, 60 Va. App. 622, 731 S.E.2d 24, 2012 Va. App. LEXIS 263 (Aug. 14, 2012).

Court of appeals had jurisdiction to consider defendant's claim of trial error because defendant's petition for appeal sufficiently invoked the jurisdiction of the court of appeals to consider the asserted trial court errors; both parties were aware of the asserted trial court errors presented by defendant on appeal and fully briefed those issues for consideration by the court of appeals. Herring v. Commonwealth, No. 1430-12-3, 2013 Va. App. LEXIS 123 (Ct. of Appeals Apr. 16, 2013).

Multiple assignments of error. — When the Virginia Court of Appeals addresses multiple assignments of error in a case on appeal, the Court of Appeals cannot believe that the Virginia Supreme Court intended in the newly revised Va. Sup. Ct. R. 5A:12(c)(1)(ii) for the Court of Appeals to dismiss the entire appeal when only one assignment of error fails to comply with Rule 5A:12(c)(1)(ii), even though all of the other assignments of error in that appeal are properly stated. Sexton v. Commonwealth, No. 0352-12-2, 2013 Va. App. LEXIS 119 (Ct. of Appeals Apr. 16, 2013).

No assignment of error. — Appellate court, under Va. Sup. Ct. R. 5A:12(c)(1)(i) and Va. Sup. Ct. R. 5:20(c), will not consider claims of error for which there is no assignment of error. Zedan v. Westheim, 60 Va. App. 556, 729 S.E.2d 785, 2012 Va. App. LEXIS 257 (2012).

Claim not raised in petition for appeal. — Court declined to rule on defendant's claim that the statute of conviction was unconstitutionally vague because this issue was not included in his pettiion for appeal, as required by Va. Sup. Ct. R. 5A:12(c). Nelson v. Commonwealth, 2010 Va. App. LEXIS 42 (2010), aff'd, 281 Va. 212, 707 S.E.2d 815, 2011 Va. LEXIS 27 (2011).

In a case in which defendant appealed his conviction for violating §§ 18.2-51, 18.2-53.1, and 18.2-286.1, he argued that evidence of other crimes was inadmissible. The appellate court lacked jurisdiction to consider his argument as it was not presented in the assignment of error on his brief, as required by Va. Sup. Ct. R. 5A:12(c)(1), and was not included as part of the assignment of error on which the appeal was granted at the petition stage. Wyche v. Commonwealth, 2012 Va. App. LEXIS 227 (July 10, 2012).

Defendant's petition for appeal, had to be dismissed in accordance with Va. Sup. Ct. R. 5A:12(c)(1)(i) because the assignments of error in defendant's opening brief were not contained in the petition and the single assignment of error noted in the petition was inadequate and did not comply with Rule 5A:12(c)(1)(ii). Mack v. Commonwealth, No. 1584-11-1, 2012 Va. App. LEXIS 354 (Nov. 6, 2012).

Applied in Iglesias v. Commonwealth, 7 Va. App. 93, 372 S.E.2d 170 (1988); Gray v. Commonwealth, 28 Va. App. 227, 503 S.E.2d 252 (1998); Humbert v. Commonwealth, 29 Va. App. 783, 514 S.E.2d 804 (1999); McLean v. Commonwealth, 30 Va. App. 322, 516 S.E.2d 717 (1999); Fogg v. Commonwealth, 31 Va. App. 722, 525 S.E.2d 596 (2000); Megel v. Commonwealth, 37 Va. App. 676, 561 S.E.2d 21, 2002 Va. App. LEXIS 267 (2002); Parker v. Commonwealth, 42 Va. App. 358, 592 S.E.2d 358, 2004 Va. App. LEXIS 54 (2004); Hoyt v. Commonwealth, 44 Va. App. 489, 605 S.E.2d 755, 2004 Va. App. LEXIS 599 (2004); Peake v. Commonwealth, 46 Va. App. 35, 614 S.E.2d 672, 2005 Va. App. LEXIS 238 (2005); Gregory v. Commonwealth, 46 Va. App. 683, 621 S.E.2d 162, 2005 Va. App. LEXIS 442 (2005); Logan v. Commonwealth, 50 Va. App. 518, 651 S.E.2d 403, 2007 Va. App. LEXIS 393 (2007); Henderson v. Commonwealth, 59 Va. App. 641, 722 S.E.2d 275, 2012 Va. App. LEXIS 116 (2012).

Rule 5A:13. Brief in Opposition.

(a) *Filing Time.* — A brief in opposition to granting the appeal may be filed with the clerk of this Court by the appellee within 21 days after the petition for appeal is served on counsel for the appellee. Within the same time he shall mail or deliver a copy to counsel for appellant. Four copies shall be filed. Motions for an extension to this briefing deadline shall be filed no later than 10 days after the expiration of the deadline.

(b) *Form and Content.* — The brief in opposition shall conform in all respects to the requirements of the brief of appellee (Rule 5A:21).

(1) Length. Except by leave of a Judge of this Court, the brief shall not exceed 8,800 words.

(2) Table of Contents and Table of Authorities. If the brief exceeds 3,500 words, it shall contain a table of contents and table of authorities with cases alphabetically arranged.

(3) Criminal or Traffic Cases. In a criminal or traffic case, a brief may be filed by the Commonwealth's attorney, city, county, or town attorney, as the case may be.

(c) *Expedited Review.* — When it clearly appears that an appeal ought to be granted without further delay, an appeal may be granted before the filing of the brief in opposition.

Rule 5A:14. Reply Brief.

When a brief in opposition to the petition for appeal has been filed, the appellant may, within 14 days thereafter, in lieu of oral argument, file with the clerk of this Court a reply brief not to exceed 5,300 words in length. Four copies shall be filed. Motions for an extension to this briefing deadline shall be filed no later than 10 days after the expiration of the deadline.

Rule 5A:15. Denial of Petition for Appeal; Petition for Rehearing.

(a) *Denial by a Single Judge.* — When a petition for appeal is denied by a Judge of this Court pursuant to Code § 17.1-407(C), the clerk of this Court shall send a copy of the order denying the petition to counsel for the appellant and counsel for the appellee. Pro se prisoners and those with leave of this Court to proceed under this Rule may demand consideration of the petition by three-judge panel pursuant to Code § 17.1-407(D). The demand shall be filed in writing. Four copies must be filed with the clerk of this Court within fourteen days after the date of the order by which the petition was denied. The demand, which shall include a statement identifying how the one-judge order is in error, shall not exceed 350 words. Oral argument shall not be permitted on consideration of a petition by a three-judge panel unless oral argument was requested in the petition for appeal pursuant to Rule 5A:12(c). A petitioner who has previously requested oral argument may waive oral argument by so stating in the demand for review. All petitioners other than pro se prisoners and those with leave of this Court to proceed under this Rule must follow the provisions of Rule 5A:15A(a) when filing a demand for three-judge review pursuant to Code § 17.1-407(D).

(b) *Denial by a Three-Judge Panel.* — When a petition for appeal is denied by a three-judge panel, the clerk of this Court shall send a copy of the order or memorandum opinion denying the appeal to counsel for the appellant and counsel for the appellee. Pro se prisoners and those with leave of this Court to proceed under this Rule may, within 14 days after the date of this notice, file a petition for rehearing in writing in the office of the clerk of this Court unless the denial was by a three-Judge panel after its consideration of a petition denied by a Judge of this Court pursuant to Code § 17.1-407. The petition for rehearing shall not exceed 5,300 words in length. The petition shall state that a copy has been mailed or delivered to counsel for the appellee. Four copies shall be filed. Oral argument on the petition for rehearing will not be allowed. The petition for rehearing shall be referred to the panel of this Court that considered the petition for appeal. No responsive brief shall be filed unless requested by this Court. The clerk of this Court shall notify counsel for the appellant and counsel for the appellee of the action taken by this Court on the petition for rehearing. All petitioners other than pro se prisoners and those with leave of this Court to proceed under this Rule must follow the provisions of Rule 5A:15A(b) when filing a petition for a rehearing of an order of a three-judge panel denying a petition for appeal.

Law Review. — For article reviewing recent developments and changes in legislation, case law, and Virginia Supreme Court Rules affecting civil litigation, see "Civil Practice and Procedure," 40 U. Rich. L. Rev. 95 (2005).

Rule 5A:15A. Denial of Petition for Appeal; Petition for Rehearing Filed by Electronic Means.

(a) *Proceedings After Denial of Petition by Single Judge.* — (1) When a petition for appeal is denied by a Judge of this Court pursuant to Code § 17.1-407(C), the clerk of this Court shall send a copy of the order denying the petition to counsel for the appellant and counsel for the appellee. The appellant may demand consideration of the petition by three-judge panel pursuant to Code § 17.1-407(D). Demands for three-judge review filed by pro se prisoners or by those with leave of this Court to proceed under Rule 5A:15(a) shall be filed in accordance with the provisions of Rule 5A:15(a).

(2) Except for demands for three-judge review filed by pro se prisoners or by those with leave of this Court to proceed under Rule 5A:15(a), the demand shall be filed as a single Adobe Acrobat Portable Document Format (PDF) document attached to an e-mail addressed to cavpfr@courts.state.va.us and will be timely filed if received by the clerk's office at or before 11:59 p.m. on the fourteenth day after the date of the order by which the petition was denied.

(3) The demand, which shall include a statement identifying how the one-judge order is in error, must be formatted to print on a page 8 ½ x 11 inches, must be in 12-point font or larger, must be double-spaced, and must not exceed 350 words. The demand must include a certificate of service to opposing counsel and the certificate shall specify the manner of service and the date of service. If opposing counsel has an e-mail address, service on opposing counsel shall be by electronic means and such address shall be included in the certificate of service. The demand must also include a certificate of compliance with the word count limit. The demand will be considered filed on the date and time that it is received by cavpfr@courts.state.va.us. If the demand does not meet the requirements of this rule as to format, the clerk of this Court shall so notify counsel and provide a specific amount of time for a corrected copy of the demand to be filed. A person who files a document electronically shall have the same responsibility as a person filing a document in paper form for ensuring that the document is properly filed, complete, and readable. However, if technical problems at the Court of Appeals result in a failure to timely receive the electronically filed demand for three-judge review, counsel shall provide to the clerk of this Court on the next business day all documentation which exists demonstrating the attempt to file the demand by e-mail, any delivery failure notice received in response to the attempt, and a copy of the demand for three-judge review.

(4) The e-mail message to which the demand is attached shall recite in the subject line the style of the case and the Court of Appeals record number. The body of the e-mail message shall contain a paragraph stating that a demand for three-judge review is being filed, the style of the case, the Court of Appeals record number, the name and Virginia State Bar number of counsel filing the demand, as well as the law firm name, mailing address, telephone number, facsimile number (if any), and e-mail address (if any) of counsel filing the demand. The message shall also state whether a copy of the demand has been served by e-mail or another means on opposing counsel and the date of such service. If the demand has been served on opposing counsel by e-mail, the e-mail address for opposing counsel shall also be included. Upon receipt of the demand for three-judge review in the e-mail box of the clerk's office, an acknowledgment will be forwarded by e-mail to counsel seeking the rehearing.

(5) Oral argument shall not be permitted on consideration of a petition by a three-judge panel unless oral argument was requested in the petition for appeal pursuant to Rule 5A:12(c). An appellant who has previously requested oral argument may waive oral argument by so stating in the demand for review.

(b) *Proceedings After Denial of Petition by Three-Judge Panel.* — (1) When a petition for appeal is denied by a three-judge panel, the clerk of this Court shall send a copy of the order or memorandum opinion denying the appeal to counsel for the appellant and counsel for the appellee. Counsel for the appellant may file a petition for rehearing in the office of the clerk of this Court unless the denial was by a three-judge panel after its consideration of a petition denied by a Judge of this Court pursuant to Code § 17.1-407. Petitions for rehearing filed by pro se prisoners or by those with leave of court to proceed under Rule 5A:15(b) shall be in accordance with the provisions of Rule 5A:15(b).

(2) Except for petitions for rehearing filed by pro se prisoners or by those with leave of this Court to proceed under Rule 5A:15(b), the petition shall be filed as a single PDF document attached to an email addressed to cavpfr@courts.state.va.us and will be timely filed if received by the clerk's office at or before 11:59 p.m. on the fourteenth day after the date of the order by which the petition was denied.

(3) The petition must be formatted to print on a page 8 ½ x 11 inches, must be in 12-point font or larger, must be double-spaced, and must not exceed 5,300 words. The petition must include a certificate of service to opposing counsel and the certificate shall specify the manner of service and the date of service. If opposing counsel has an e-mail address, service on opposing counsel shall be by electronic means and such address shall be included in the certificate of service. The petition must also include a certificate of compliance with the word count limit. Petitions filed by e-mail will be considered filed on the date and time that it is received by cavpfr@courts.state.va.us. If the petition does not meet the requirements of this rule as to format, the clerk of this Court shall so notify counsel and provide a specific amount of time for a corrected copy of the petition to be filed. A person who files a document electronically shall have the same responsibility as a person filing a document in paper form for ensuring that the document is properly filed, complete, and readable. However, if technical problems at the Court of Appeals result in a failure to timely receive the electronically filed petition for rehearing, counsel shall provide to the clerk of this Court on the next business day all documentation which exists demonstrating the attempt to file the petition by e-mail, any delivery failure notice received in response to the attempt, and a copy of the petition for rehearing.

(4) The e-mail message to which the petition is attached shall recite in the subject line the style of the case and the Court of Appeals record number. The body of the e-mail message shall contain a paragraph stating that a petition for rehearing is being filed, the style of the case, the Court of Appeals record number, the name and Virginia State Bar number of counsel filing the petition, as well as the law firm name, mailing address, telephone number, facsimile number (if any), and e-mail address (if any) of counsel filing the petition. The message shall also state whether a copy of the petition has been served by e-mail or another means on opposing counsel and the date of such service. If the petition has been served on opposing counsel by e-mail, the e-mail address for opposing counsel shall also be included. Upon receipt of the petition for rehearing in the e-mail box of the clerk's office, an acknowledgment will be forwarded by e-mail to counsel seeking the rehearing.

(5) Oral argument on the petition for rehearing will not be allowed. The petition for rehearing shall be referred to the panel of this Court that considered the petition for appeal. No responsive brief shall be filed unless requested by this Court. The clerk of this Court shall notify counsel for the appellant and counsel for the appellee of the action taken by the Court of Appeals on the petition for rehearing via e-mail, if e-mail addresses for both counsel have been provided, or via U.S. Mail to any counsel or party who has not provided an e-mail address.

Law Review. — For article reviewing recent developments and changes in legislation, case law, and Virginia Supreme Court Rules affecting civil litigation, see "Civil Practice and Procedure," 40 U. Rich. L. Rev. 95 (2005).

F. PROCEDURE FOLLOWING PERFECTION OF APPEAL.

Rule 5A:16. Perfection of Appeal; Docketing.

(a) *Appeals as a Matter of Right.* — In cases when an appeal lies as a matter of right to the Court of Appeals, such appeal shall be perfected by the timely filing of a notice of appeal pursuant to Rule 5A:6. Such case shall be considered mature for purposes of further proceedings from the date the record is filed in the office of the clerk of the Court of Appeals. A party filing a notice of an appeal of right to the Court of Appeals shall simultaneously file in the trial court an appeal bond in compliance with Code § 8.01-676.1.

(b) *Grant of Petition for Appeal.* — Promptly after a petition for appeal has been granted by the Court of Appeals, the clerk of the Court of Appeals shall certify this action to the trial court and all counsel. Such case shall be considered mature for purposes of further proceedings from the date of such certificate.

(c) *Docketing.* — Cases shall be placed on the docket in the order in which they mature, provided that precedence shall be given to the following cases:

(1) criminal cases;
(2) cases from the Virginia Workers' Compensation Commission;
(3) cases involving termination of parental rights;
(4) cases of original jurisdiction;
(5) cases to be reheard; and
(6) any other cases required by statute to be given precedence.

The Court of Appeals may, however, for good cause shown or for reasons appearing sufficient to the Court, give preference to other cases.

Law Review. — For 1985 survey of Virginia civil procedure and practice, see 19 U. Rich. L. Rev. 679 (1985). For 1995 survey of civil practice and procedure, see 29 U. Rich. L. Rev. 897 (1995).

CASE NOTES

Failure to name indispensable party. — Mother's appeal of the termination of her parental rights was dismissed due to her failure to timely name the children's guardian ad litem, an indispensable party under § 16.1-266, as an appellee in either the notice of appeal or the accompanying certificate of service; the failure to name the guardian ad litem as an appellee meant that the appeal was not perfected under Rule 5A:16, and the appellate court never acquired jurisdiction over the guardian ad litem. Watkins v. Fairfax County Dep't of Family Servs., 42 Va. App. 760, 595 S.E.2d 19, 2004 Va. App. LEXIS 164 (2004).

Petition for rehearing cannot keep appeal alone where bond not filed in time. — Where wife failed to file the required bond within the 30-day appeal period prescribed by § 8.01-676.1 A and this rule, which period expired long before § 8.01-676.1 L ever became effective, therefore, that appeal was dead, and any effort to keep it alive by way of a petition for rehearing, or otherwise, was unavailing. Foster v. Foster, 237 Va. 484, 378 S.E.2d 826 (1989).

Nunc pro tunc order valid. — Case was mature, and therefore "docketed," when the record was filed in the office of the clerk of the appellate court; therefore, the trial court was not required to seek leave of the appellate court to correct an error in the record arising from oversight or from an inadvertent omission. Goodwin v. Flinn, 2012 Va. App. LEXIS 189 (June 5, 2012).

Applied in Barrett v. Barrett, 1 Va. App. 378, 339 S.E.2d 208 (1986).

Rule 5A:17. Security for Appeal.

(a) *Form for Security.* — All security for appeal required under Code § 8.01-676.1 shall substantially conform to the forms set forth in the Appendix to this Part Five A.

(b) *Security for Appeal; Defects.* — Whenever an appellant files an appeal bond or irrevocable letter of credit, he shall contemporaneously give notice in writing of said filing to counsel for appellee. No appeal shall be dismissed because of defect in any bond or irrevocable letter of credit unless an appellee, within 21 days after the giving of such notice, files with the clerk of the Court of Appeals a statement in writing of the defects in the bond or irrevocable letter of credit, and unless the appellant fails to correct such defects, if any, within 21 days after such statement is filed. If the appellant fails to correct such defects within 21 days, an appellee may move that the appeal be dismissed and it shall be dismissed unless the appellant satisfies the Court of Appeals that the bond or irrevocable letter of credit, either as originally given or as amended, has been filed as required by law.

CASE NOTES

Supreme Court requirements are substantially same. — The appeal bond required by statute and the rules applicable to their filing are substantially the same in the Court of Appeals and the Supreme Court. Duckett v. Duckett, 1 Va. App. 279, 337 S.E.2d 759 (1985).

Subdivision (b) applicable only when bond filed. — Subdivision (b) of this rule (which corresponds to Rule 5:24 relating to Supreme Court appeals) clearly only applies "whenever an appellant files an appeal bond." Burns v. C.W. Wright Constr. Co., 1 Va. App. 256, 336 S.E.2d 908 (1985).

State agency not required to file appeal bond. — Pursuant to § 53.1-8, the Virginia Department of Corrections is an administrative subdivision of the Commonwealth of Virginia; therefore, under § 8.01-676.1, it was not required to post an appeal bond in its appeal from the reversal of its termination of a corrections officer. Va. Dep't of Corr. v. Compton, 47 Va. App. 202, 623 S.E.2d 397, 2005 Va. App. LEXIS 517 (2005).

Lack of appeal bond not curable. — The requirement of a timely appeal bond under former Va. Code § 8.01-676 (see now § 8.01-676.1) is jurisdictional, and is not a defect which may be cured pursuant to this rule. Lipscomb v. Rosenthal Chevrolet, No. 0404-85, (Ct. of Appeals Dec. 10, 1985); O'Brien v. O'Brien, No. 0335-85, (Ct. of Appeals Dec. 23, 1985).

Failure to file an appeal bond as required by Va. Code § 8.01-676.1 requires that an appeal be dismissed and neither Rule 5A:3(b) nor subdivision (b) of this rule can be used to extend the time for filing of bonds when none has been given. Burns v. C.W.

Wright Constr. Co., 1 Va. App. 256, 336 S.E.2d 908 (1985).

Failure to post the appeal bond by the last day on which appellant could file his notice of appeal, is a defect, which cannot be cured under this rule. This rule is applicable when there is a defect in the bond that has been filed, not when no bond is posted at all. Adams v. Adams, Nos. 0064-84 and 0347-85, (Ct. of Appeals Feb. 28, 1986).

Applied in Jay v. Commonwealth, 275 Va. 510, 659 S.E.2d 311, 2008 Va. LEXIS 53 (2008).

Rule 5A:18. Preservation of Issues for Appellate Review.

No ruling of the trial court or the Virginia Workers' Compensation Commission will be considered as a basis for reversal unless an objection was stated with reasonable certainty at the time of the ruling, except for good cause shown or to enable the Court of Appeals to attain the ends of justice. A mere statement that the judgment or award is contrary to the law and the evidence is not sufficient to preserve the issue for appellate review.

Law Review. — For 2003/2004 survey of civil practice and procedure, see 39 U. Rich. L. Rev. 87 (2004). For 2003/2004 survey of criminal law and procedure, see 39 U. Rich. L. Rev. 133 (2004).

Michie's Jurisprudence. — For related discussion, see 1B M.J. Appeal and Error, § 103; 7B M.J. Evidence, § 55; 8A M.J. Exceptions, Bill of, § 1.

CASE NOTES

I. General Consideration.
II. Statement of Objections.
  A. In General.
  B. Contemporaneous Objection Rule.
  C. Specificity of Objection.
III. Ends of Justice.
IV. Contrary to the Law and Evidence.
V. Illustrations.

I. GENERAL CONSIDERATION.

Editor's note. — *Campbell v. Commonwealth*, 12 Va. App. 476, 405 S.E.2d 1 (1991), overruled *Williams v. Commonwealth*, 6 Va. App. 412, 368 S.E.2d 293 (1988), to the extent that *Williams* held an appeal of the sufficiency of the evidence was barred by the failure to move to strike the Commonwealth's evidence at the conclusion of the defendant's evidence even if the issue of sufficiency is clearly presented to the trial court by a motion to strike at the conclusion of the Commonwealth's evidence and in a closing argument to the trial court.

Primary purpose of contemporaneous objection rule is to advise the trial judge of the action complained of so that the court can consider the issue intelligently and, if necessary, take corrective action to avoid unnecessary appeals, reversals, and mistrials. Head v. Commonwealth, 3 Va. App. 163, 348 S.E.2d 423 (1986), overruled on other grounds, Cruz v. Commonwealth, 24 Va. App. 454, 482 S.E.2d 880 (1997).

The purpose of this rule is to allow correction of an error if possible during the trial, thereby avoiding the necessity of mistrials and reversals. Gardner v. Commonwealth, 3 Va. App. 418, 350 S.E.2d 229 (1986).

The purpose of this rule is to allow correction of an error if possible during the trial, thereby avoiding the necessity of mistrials and reversals. To avoid this result, the rule places an affirmative duty on the parties to enter timely objections to rulings made during the trial. Wineman v. Agee, No. 0794-89-1 (Ct. of Appeals June 12, 1990).

The purpose of this rule is to allow the trial judge to correct in the trial court any error that is called to his attention. It has been argued that it is unfair to reverse the trial judge for an error which was not called to his attention in the trial court in time for him to take corrective action. A perhaps more compelling reason for the rule is that it is unfair to the opposing party, who may have been able to offer an alternative to the objectionable ruling, but did not do so, believing there was no problem. Lee v. Lee, 394 S.E.2d 490 (1990), aff'd on reh'g en banc, 12 Va. App. 512, 404 S.E.2d 736 (1991); Taylor v. Caccia, No. 1733-02-2, 2003 Va. App. LEXIS 238 (Ct. of Appeals Apr. 22, 2003).

The purpose of the contemporaneous objection rule is to inform the trial judge of the action complained of in order to give the judge the opportunity to consider the issue and to take timely corrective action, if warranted, in order to avoid unnecessary appeals, reversals and mistrials. Robinson v. Commonwealth, 13 Va. App. 574, 413 S.E.2d 885 (1992).

The primary function of this rule is to alert the trial judge to possible error so that the judge may consider the issue intelligently and take any corrective actions necessary to avoid unnecessary appeals, reversals and mistrials. Martin v. Commonwealth, 13 Va. App. 524, 414 S.E.2d 401 (1992).

Rule prevents building error into record and promotes efficiency. — This rule prevents building error into the record, and promotes efficient judicial administration because it results in fewer new trials. Lee v. Lee, 394 S.E.2d 490 (1990), aff'd on reh'g en banc, 12 Va. App. 512, 404 S.E.2d 736 (1991).

Economy requires enforcement of rule. — Economy, both of litigation costs and of judicial time, requires enforcement of this rule in all cases. Lee v. Lee, 394 S.E.2d 490 (1990), aff'd on reh'g en banc, 12 Va. App. 512, 404 S.E.2d 736 (1991).

Requirements applied to all cases. — The requirements of this rule are applied to all cases, law and equity, including divorce. Lee v. Lee, 394 S.E.2d 490 (1990), aff'd on reh'g en banc, 12 Va. App. 512, 404 S.E.2d 736 (1991).

Rule equally applicable to pro se party. — Challenge to a ruling of the trial court was precluded by Va. Sup. Ct. R. 5A:18, even though the mother proceeded pro se, because Rule 5A:18 applied equally to the mother, a pro se litigant in a termination of parental rights action, and the good cause and ends-of-justice exceptions did not apply. Brazell v. Fairfax County Dep't of Family Servs., 2008 Va. App. LEXIS 388 (Aug. 12, 2008).

Pro se status not good cause for failing to object. — Even pro se litigants must comply with the rules of court and the mere fact that a litigant was proceeding pro se is not good cause such as would excuse his failure to make a contemporaneous objection. Penn v. Penn, No. 2403-99-1, 2000 Va. App. LEXIS 275 (Ct. of Appeals Apr. 11, 2000).

On appeal, the court considers only those issues raised before the full commission and properly appealed to it from the decision of the deputy commissioner. Best Masonry, Inc. v. Wilkins, No. 1121-92-4 (Ct. of Appeals Oct. 15, 1992).

In a proceeding before the Virginia Workers' Compensation Commission under the Virginia Birth-Related Neurological Injury Compensation Act, § 38.2-5000 et seq., a health care provider did not properly preserve the issue of whether a recovery could be had both under the Act and in a medical malpractice action when the issue was not raised or addressed at a hearing before the deputy commissioner, and the provider's motion for reconsideration asking the Commission to address the issue did not cure this defect, so an appellate court would not address it on review. Ctr. for Obstetrics & Gynecology, Inc. v. Va. Birth-Related Neurological Injury Comp. Fund, No. 2430-02-1, 2003 Va. App. LEXIS 72 (Ct. of Appeals Feb. 11, 2003)

Defendant cannot invite error. — Defendant's claim of error regarding his sentence lacked merit where he was granted the precise relief requested. Woodson v. Commonwealth, No. 0081-03-1, 2004 Va. App. LEXIS 61 (Ct. of Appeals Feb. 10, 2004).

No ruling of the trial court will be considered as a basis for reversal unless the objection was stated together with the grounds therefor at the time of the ruling, except for good cause shown or to enable the Court of Appeals to attain the ends of justice. Carcamo v. Commonwealth, No. 1554-95-4 (Ct. of Appeals Sept. 17, 1996).

Applicability. — This rule does not require an appellee to raise an issue at trial before it may be considered on appeal where the issue is not offered to support reversal of the trial court ruling. An appellee is subject to the limitations of this rule only where it asserts an error that seeks to reverse a judgment. Jones v. Commonwealth, No. 1419-93-2 (Ct. of Appeals Jan. 24, 1995).

Husband's vague argument in his brief regarding "setting child support" failed to articulate any specific error in the trial court's calculation of retroactive child support, and, thus, the appellate court could not address whether retroactive child support was properly calculated. McClure v. McClure, 2006 Va. App. LEXIS 294 (July 5, 2006).

Because defendant's "Statement of Questions Presented" did not maintain that the evidence was insufficient for his conviction, but rather maintained that the challenged evidence on which that conviction was based was improperly admitted, given that the appeals court determined that said evidence was properly admitted, it declined to address defendant's sufficiency claim. Guerara-Sandoval v. Commonwealth, 2007 Va. App. LEXIS 296 (Aug. 7, 2007).

Because the trial court, in the order on appeal, had already determined the issues raised by father by finding that his appearance and participation in the October 1996 hearing was a general appearance that waived all questions about service of process and notice, and he had abandoned his only remedy of an appeal from said order, his further attempt to litigate those same issues was barred by res judicata. Star v. Commonwealth, 2007 Va. App. LEXIS 417 (Nov. 20, 2007).

Rule not bar to jurisdiction challenge. — The law is well established that this rule may not be invoked to bar consideration of an appeal which attacks the jurisdiction of the circuit court. Jones v. Division of Child Support Enforcement ex rel. Owens, 19 Va. App. 184, 450 S.E.2d 172 (1994).

But lack of "notice" jurisdiction barred. — Argument that a workers' compensation deputy commissioner lacked "notice" jurisdiction, which was not made before the Workers' Compensation Commission, could not be considered on appeal because, even though it addressed jurisdiction, it was an argument in favor of jurisdiction, and was, thus, capable of being waived by not being raised before the Commission; only arguments that a tribunal did not have subject matter jurisdiction could not be waived. Weikle v. Southland Corp., No. 1346-02-3, 2003 Va. App. LEXIS 126 (Ct. of Appeals Mar. 11, 2003).

Issue not preserved or briefed was not considered on appeal. — Where the parties failed to preserve or brief an issue for appellate review, under Rule 5A:18, the appellate court did not consider whether the husband's father's one third undivided interest in the parties' marital residence passed by devise under the father's will or passed in equal shares to the husband and wife as tenants in common, pursuant to § 20-111, by virtue of the joint survivorship under the grantee clause of the deed. Binhammer v. Reilly, No. 1907-01-2, 2003 Va. App. LEXIS 71 (Ct. of Appeals Feb. 11, 2003).

Defendant's failure to raise his public confidence argument at trial regarding the seating of the jurors barred consideration of the same on appeal, pursuant to Va. Sup. Ct. R. 5A:18 and 5:25; moreover, it was fundamentally unfair to overturn the valid decision of a jury for reasons never given to the trial court and which do not go to the merits of the case or the actual bias of a juror. Townsend v. Commonwealth, 270 Va. 325, 619 S.E.2d 71, 2005 Va. LEXIS 81 (2005), cert. denied, 547 U.S. 1008, 126 S. Ct. 1477, 164 L. Ed. 2d 257, 2006 U.S. LEXIS 2118 (2006).

Because the Uninsured Employer's Fund did not object to the Virginia Workers' Compensation Commission's review of the deputy commissioner's sua sponte ruling on a doctor, it did not preserve for appeal the argument that the Commission had no authority to reconsider the deputy's finding regarding the doctor; the issue was before the Commission because the workers' compensation claimant clearly noted that she objected to the deputy's decision to ignore the reports of the doctor, and she presented the argument in her brief to the Commission. Uninsured Employer's Fund v. Wiredu, 2009 Va. App. LEXIS 393 (Sept. 8, 2009).

Court of appeals could not consider the terms of a plea agreement in defendant's appeal of an order finding that he violated his probation because the terms were not a basis for reversal permitted by the Rules of Court when defendant did not ask the court of appeals to consider whether the trial court's decision was a breach of the terms of the plea agreement he made with the Commonwealth; the plea agreement and defendant's Alford plea questions did not involve the same evidence because the former required attention to the text of the written agreement, and the latter did not, and the questions did not require similar legal analyses. Carroll v. Commonwealth, 54 Va. App. 730, 682 S.E.2d 92, 2009 Va. App. LEXIS 392 (2009), aff'd, 280 Va. 641, 701 S.E.2d 414, 2010 Va. LEXIS 277 (2010).

Appellate court summarily rejected the former wife's arguments regarding the trial court's equitable distribution award pursuant to Va. Sup. Ct. R. 5A:27 because Va. Sup. Ct. R. 5A:21(b) required an appellee to provide a clear and exact reference to the pages of the transcript, written statement, record, or appendix where each additional question was preserved in the trial court, and the former wife's brief failed to identify in the record where she preserved the issues she raised on appeal. Although Va. Sup. Ct. R. 5A:21(b) allowed an appellee to raise additional issues on brief, it did not dispense with the requirements of Va. Sup. Ct. R. 5A:18; a litigant seeking to reverse a trial court, therefore, had to either prove where the issue was preserved below or demonstrate an equitable basis for suspending the waiver rule, and having done neither, the former wife could not prevail on appeal. Williams v. Williams, 2009 Va. App. LEXIS 553 (Dec. 15, 2009).

Virginia Sup. Ct. R. 5A:18 barred consideration of defendant's argument on appeal because defendant made no argument in the circuit court that § 19.2-176, although repealed in 2010, still applied to defendant's case. Gill v. Commonwealth, 2012 Va. App. LEXIS 137 (May 1, 2012).

Issue not required to be raised at trial where issue is not offered to support reversal. — This rule does not require an appellee to raise an issue at trial before it may be considered on appeal where the issue is not offered to support reversal of a trial court ruling. Driscoll v. Commonwealth, 14 Va. App. 449, 417 S.E.2d 312 (1992); Harris v. Commonwealth, 39 Va. App. 670, 576 S.E.2d 228, 2003 Va. App. LEXIS 39 (2003).

No bar to appeal of issue where law changed between trial and appeal. — This rule does not bar an appeal of an issue where the law has changed between trial and appeal. Darnell v. Commonwealth, 12 Va. App. 948, 408 S.E.2d 540 (1991).

No bar to review on appeal where the trial court could have corrected the error. — The record established that the trial court had the opportunity to correct its error in regard to the sufficiency of the evidence to prove constructive possession of the cocaine and firearm found inside the residence. Pitchford v. Commonwealth, No. 1582-01-1, 2002 Va. App. LEXIS 565 (Ct. of Appeals Sept. 24, 2002).

Section 8.01-384 and rule not limited to evidentiary rule or other rulings. — Both the Code (§ 8.01-384) and this rule, by their terms, are not limited to evidentiary rule or other rulings relating to incidents of the trial. The Code is applicable to any "rulings or order of the court." This rule includes the phrase that "a mere statement that the judgment or award is contrary to the law and the evidence is not sufficient." Both provisions negated appellant's contention that this rule is applicable only to evidentiary and similar rulings and not legal decisions and findings. The myriad of cases interpreting Rule 5:25, this rule's counterpart for the Supreme Court, also belies that contention. Lee v. Lee, 12 Va. App. 512, 404 S.E.2d 736 (1991).

Failure to object to Virginia Board of Dentistry. — Since a dentist, who had appealed sanctions imposed by the Virginia Board of Dentistry, did not raise several arguments until his appeal to the circuit court, those questions were not preserved for appeal and were thus procedurally defaulted pursuant to Va. Sup. Ct. R. 5A:18. Doe v. Va. Bd. of Dentistry, 50 Va. App. 626, 652 S.E.2d 794, 2007 Va. App. LEXIS 418 (2007).

Trial court must have opportunity to rule on dispute. — This rule places the parties on notice that they must give the trial court the first opportunity to rule on disputed questions. Gardner v. Commonwealth, 3 Va. App. 418, 350 S.E.2d 229 (1986); Wineman v. Agee, No. 0794-89-1 (Ct. of Appeals June 12, 1990).

This rule requires that the trial judge be given the first opportunity to rule on disputed evidentiary and procedural questions. Gilchrist v. Commonwealth, No. 1496-91-1 (Ct. of Appeals Oct. 27, 1992).

Appellate court refused to hear defendant's argument that the trial court erred when it revoked his probation for possessing cocaine and sentenced him to incarceration for one year and six months without giving him credit for time he spent in a detention center's incarceration program because defendant did not make that argument to the trial court. Keeling v. Commonwealth, No. 1876-02-1, 2003 Va. App. LEXIS 626 (Ct. of Appeals Dec. 9, 2003).

Local practice and consent of counsel no grounds to disregard rules. — Where counsel for both parties agreed that it was their local practice not to object with specificity to a trial judge's final decision in divorce matters or to include in the final order any objection to specific parts of the order, and judges in the locale apparently believed that "seen and objected to" preserved all issues for appeal, local practice and consent of counsel provided no grounds to disregard the Rules of the Supreme Court. Lee v. Lee, 394 S.E.2d 490 (1990), aff'd on reh'g en banc, 12 Va. App. 512, 404 S.E.2d 736 (1991).

Supreme Court Rule 5:25 and this rule are equivalent, virtually identical, and both are included as part of the Rules of Virginia Supreme Court; under such circumstances, decisions pertaining to the construction and application of one rule inextricably relate to the other. Johnson v.

Commonwealth, No. 0259-91-1 (Ct. of Appeals Nov. 10, 1992).

Applied in Audobon Tree Serv. v. Childress, 2 Va. App. 35, 341 S.E.2d 211 (1986); Bell v. Commonwealth, 2 Va. App. 48, 341 S.E.2d 654 (1986); Snurkowski v. Commonwealth, 2 Va. App. 532, 348 S.E.2d 1 (1986); Cunningham v. Commonwealth, 2 Va. App. 358, 344 S.E.2d 389 (1986); Johnson v. Commonwealth, 2 Va. App. 447, 345 S.E.2d 303 (1986); Stotler v. Commonwealth, 2 Va. App. 481, 346 S.E.2d 39 (1986); Parham v. Commonwealth, 2 Va. App. 633, 347 S.E.2d 172 (1986); Wright v. Commonwealth, 2 Va. App. 743, 348 S.E.2d 9 (1986); Martin v. School Bd., 3 Va. App. 197, 348 S.E.2d 857 (1986); Chrisman v. Commonwealth, 3 Va. App. 371, 349 S.E.2d 899 (1986); M.E.D. v. J.P.M., 3 Va. App. 391, 350 S.E.2d 215 (1986); Smith v. Commonwealth, 3 Va. App. 650, 353 S.E.2d 159 (1987); Vescuso v. Commonwealth, 4 Va. App. 32, 354 S.E.2d 68 (1987); Yates v. Commonwealth, 4 Va. App. 140, 355 S.E.2d 14 (1987); Arnold v. Commonwealth, 4 Va. App. 275, 356 S.E.2d 847 (1987); McCormick v. City of Va. Beach, 5 Va. App. 369, 363 S.E.2d 124 (1987); Howard v. Commonwealth, 6 Va. App. 132, 367 S.E.2d 527 (1988); Scott v. Commonwealth, 7 Va. App. 252, 372 S.E.2d 771 (1988); Miller v. Commonwealth, 7 Va. App. 367, 373 S.E.2d 721 (1988); Bennett v. Commonwealth, 8 Va. App. 228, 380 S.E.2d 17 (1989); Tomlinson v. Commonwealth, 8 Va. App. 218, 380 S.E.2d 26 (1989); Jewell v. Commonwealth, 8 Va. App. 353, 382 S.E.2d 259 (1989); Zipf v. Zipf, 8 Va. App. 387, 382 S.E.2d 263 (1989); Kelly v. Commonwealth, 8 Va. App. 359, 382 S.E.2d 270 (1989); Kauffman v. Commonwealth, 8 Va. App. 400, 382 S.E.2d 279 (1989); Murphy v. Commonwealth, 9 Va. App. 139, 384 S.E.2d 125 (1989); Hope v. Commonwealth, 8 Va. App. 491, 386 S.E.2d 807 (1989); Gay v. Commonwealth, 10 Va. App. 229, 391 S.E.2d 737 (1990); Johns v. Commonwealth, 10 Va. App. 283, 392 S.E.2d 487 (1990); Moreno v. Commonwealth, 10 Va. App. 408, 392 S.E.2d 836 (1990); Stewart v. Commonwealth, 10 Va. App. 563, 394 S.E.2d 509 (1990); Joyner v. Commonwealth, 10 Va. App. 290, 392 S.E.2d 822 (1990); McIntosh v. Commonwealth, 15 Va. App. 314, 394 S.E.2d 333 (1990); Simms v. Commonwealth, 10 Va. App. 723, 395 S.E.2d 475 (1990); Low v. Commonwealth, 11 Va. App. 48, 396 S.E.2d 383 (1990); Martin v. Commonwealth, 11 Va. App. 397, 399 S.E.2d 623 (1990); Stein v. Commonwealth, 12 Va. App. 65, 402 S.E.2d 238 (1991); Hervey v. Newport News Shipbuilding & Dry Dock Co., 12 Va. App. 88, 402 S.E.2d 688 (1991); Soliman v. Soliman, 12 Va. App. 234, 402 S.E.2d 922 (1991); Alatishe v. Commonwealth, 12 Va. App. 376, 404 S.E.2d 81 (1991); Commonwealth v. Holtz, 12 Va. App. 1151, 408 S.E.2d 561 (1991); Virginia Bd. of Medicine v. Fetta, 12 Va. App. 1173, 408 S.E.2d 573 (1991); Morris v. Commonwealth, 13 Va. App. 77, 408 S.E.2d 588 (1991); Crump v. Commonwealth, 13 Va. App. 286, 411 S.E.2d 238 (1991); Mason v. Commonwealth, 14 Va. App. 609, 419 S.E.2d 856 (1992); Singleton v. Commonwealth, 14 Va. App. 947, 419 S.E.2d 866 (1992); Miller v. Commonwealth, 15 Va. App. 301, 422 S.E.2d 795 (1992); Gaynor v. Hird, 15 Va. App. 379, 424 S.E.2d 240 (1992); Nesbit v. Commonwealth, 15 Va. App. 391, 424 S.E.2d 239 (1992); Schlimme v. Commonwealth, 16 Va. App. 15, 427 S.E.2d 431 (1993); Huger v. Huger, 16 Va. App. 785, 433 S.E.2d 255 (1993); Whitt v. Race Fork Coal Corp., 18 Va. App. 71, 441 S.E.2d 357 (1994); Davis v. Commonwealth, 17 Va. App. 666, 440 S.E.2d 426 (1994); King v. Commonwealth, 18 Va. App. 57, 441 S.E.2d 704 (1994); Knight v. Commonwealth, 18 Va. App. 207, 443 S.E.2d 165 (1994); Rodriguez v. Commonwealth, 18 Va. App. 277, 443 S.E.2d 419 (1994); Pavlicek v. Jerabek, Inc., 21 Va. App. 50, 461 S.E.2d 424 (1995); Briggs v. Commonwealth, 21 Va. App. 338, 464 S.E.2d 512 (1995); Bullis v. Bullis, 21 Va. App. 394, 464 S.E.2d 538 (1995); Jones v. Commonwealth, 21 Va. App. 435, 464 S.E.2d 558 (1995); Garcia v. Commonwealth, 21 Va. App. 445, 464 S.E.2d 563 (1995); Taylor v. Commonwealth, 21 Va. App. 557, 466 S.E.2d 118 (1996); Gilley v. Commonwealth, 21 Va. App. 740, 467 S.E.2d 312 (1996); Bullis v. Bullis, 22 Va. App. 24, 467 S.E.2d 830 (1996); Miller v. Commonwealth, 22 Va. App. 497, 471 S.E.2d 780 (1996); Cudjoe v. Commonwealth, 23 Va. App. 193, 475 S.E.2d 821 (1996); Allard v. Commonwealth, 24 Va. App. 57, 480 S.E.2d 139 (1997); Wilson v. Commonwealth, 25 Va. App. 263, 487 S.E.2d 857 (1997); Moore v. Commonwealth, 25 Va. App. 277, 487 S.E.2d 864 (1997); Canipe v. Commonwealth, 25 Va. App. 629, 491 S.E.2d 747 (1997); Hodges v. Commonwealth, 26 Va. App. 43, 492 S.E.2d 846 (1997); Holden v. Commonwealth, 26 Va. App. 403, 494 S.E.2d 892 (1998); Allen v. Commonwealth, 27 Va. App. 726, 501 S.E.2d 441 (1998); Martin v. Martin, 27 Va. App. 745, 501 S.E.2d 450 (1998); Douglas v. Hammett, 28 Va. App. 517, 507 S.E.2d 98 (1998); Ramadan v. Commonwealth, 28 Va. App. 708, 508 S.E.2d 357 (1998); Hartless v. Commonwealth, 29 Va. App. 172, 510 S.E.2d 738 (1999); Dickerson v. Commonwealth, 29 Va. App. 252, 511 S.E.2d 434 (1999); Woolridge v. Commonwealth, 29 Va. App. 339, 512 S.E.2d 153 (1999); Crawley v. Commonwealth, 29 Va. App. 372, 512 S.E.2d 169 (1999); Newton v. Commonwealth, 29 Va. App. 433, 512 S.E.2d 846; Jones v. Commonwealth, 29 Va. App. 503, 513 S.E.2d 431 (1999); Yiaadey v. Commonwealth, 29 Va. App. 535, 513 S.E.2d 446 (1999); Rogers v. Commonwealth, 29 Va. App. 580, 513 S.E.2d 876 (1999); Humbert v. Commonwealth, 29 Va. App. 783, 514 S.E.2d 804 (1999); Batts v. Commonwealth, 30 Va. App. 1, 515 S.E.2d 307 (1999); Scott v. Rutherfoord, 30 Va. App. 176, 516 S.E.2d 225 (1999); McLean v. Commonwealth, 30 Va. App. 322, 516 S.E.2d 717 (1999); Elkins v. Commonwealth, 30 Va. App. 460, 517 S.E.2d 728 (1999); Lester v. Commonwealth, 30 Va. App. 495, 518 S.E.2d 318 (1999); Mitchell v. Commonwealth, 30 Va. App. 520, 518 S.E.2d 330 (1999); Francis v. Francis, 30 Va. App. 584, 518 S.E.2d 842 (1999); Cottee v. Commonwealth, 31 Va. App. 546, 525 S.E.2d 25 (2000); Fogg v. Commonwealth, 31 Va. App. 722, 525 S.E.2d 596 (2000); Harter v. Commonwealth, 31 Va. App. 743, 525 S.E.2d 606 (2000); McLean v. Commonwealth, 32 Va. App. 200, 527 S.E.2d 443, 2000 Va. App. LEXIS 280 (2000); Dickerson v. Commonwealth, 36 Va. App. 8, 548 S.E.2d 230, 2001 Va. App. LEXIS 398 (2001); Wolfe v. Commonwealth, 37 Va. App. 136, 554 S.E.2d 695, 2001 Va. App. LEXIS 629 (2001); Morrison v. Commonwealth, 37 Va. App. 273, 557 S.E.2d 724, 2002 Va. App. LEXIS 1 (2002); Esser v. Commonwealth, 38 Va. App. 520, 566 S.E.2d 876, 2002 Va. App. LEXIS 438 (2002); M. Morgan Cherry & Assocs. v.

Cherry, 38 Va. App. 693, 568 S.E.2d 391, 2002 Va. App. LEXIS 588 (2002); Raja v. Commonwealth, 40 Va. App. 710, 581 S.E.2d 237, 2003 Va. App. LEXIS 318 (2003); Askew v. Commonwealth, 40 Va. App. 104, 578 S.E.2d 58, 2003 Va. App. LEXIS 135 (2003); Commonwealth v. Hudson, 265 Va. 505, 578 S.E.2d 781, 2003 Va. LEXIS 49 (2003); Roberts v. Roberts, 41 Va. App. 513, 586 S.E.2d 290, 2003 Va. App. LEXIS 486 (2003); Williams v. Gloucester Sheriff's Dep't, 266 Va. 409, 587 S.E.2d 546, 2003 Va. LEXIS 109 (2003); Edwards v. Commonwealth, 41 Va. App. 752, 589 S.E.2d 444, 2003 Va. App. LEXIS 637 (2003); Va. Imps., Ltd. v. Kirin Brewery of Am., LLC, 41 Va. App. 806, 589 S.E.2d 470, 2003 Va. App. LEXIS 650 (2003); Kelly v. Commonwealth, 42 Va. App. 347, 592 S.E.2d 353, 2004 Va. App. LEXIS 47 (2004); Estate of Hackler v. Hackler, 44 Va. App. 51, 602 S.E.2d 426, 2004 Va. App. LEXIS 454 (2004); Cirrito v. Cirrito, 44 Va. App. 287, 605 S.E.2d 268, 2004 Va. App. LEXIS 574 (2004); Hoyt v. Commonwealth, 44 Va. App. 489, 605 S.E.2d 755, 2004 Va. App. LEXIS 599 (2004); McBride v. Commonwealth, 44 Va. App. 526, 605 S.E.2d 773, 2004 Va. App. LEXIS 597 (2004); Wheeler v. Commonwealth, 44 Va. App. 689, 607 S.E.2d 133, 2005 Va. App. LEXIS 8 (2005); Gregory v. Commonwealth, 46 Va. App. 683, 621 S.E.2d 162, 2005 Va. App. LEXIS 442 (2005); Singson v. Commonwealth, 46 Va. App. 724, 621 S.E.2d 682, 2005 Va. App. LEXIS 452 (2005); Corado v. Commonwealth, 47 Va. App. 315, 623 S.E.2d 452, 2005 Va. App. LEXIS 528 (2005); Mason v. Commonwealth, 49 Va. App. 39, 636 S.E.2d 480, 2006 Va. App. LEXIS 505 (2006); Wright v. Commonwealth, 49 Va. App. 58, 636 S.E.2d 489, 2006 Va. App. LEXIS 503 (2006); Alston v. Commonwealth, 49 Va. App. 115, 637 S.E.2d 344, 2006 Va. App. LEXIS 544 (2006); McDuffie v. Commonwealth, 49 Va. App. 170, 638 S.E.2d 139, 2006 Va. App. LEXIS 573 (2006); Logan v. Commonwealth, 50 Va. App. 518, 651 S.E.2d 403, 2007 Va. App. LEXIS 393 (2007); Johnson v. Commonwealth, 50 Va. App. 600, 652 S.E.2d 156, 2007 Va. App. LEXIS 406 (2007); George v. Commonwealth, 51 Va. App. 137, 655 S.E.2d 43, 2008 Va. App. LEXIS 12; Bunch v. Commonwealth, 51 Va. App. 491, 658 S.E.2d 724, 2008 Va. App. LEXIS 169 (2008); Williams v. Commonwealth, 52 Va. App. 194, 662 S.E.2d 627, 2008 Va. App. LEXIS 301 (2008); Cobbins v. Commonwealth, 53 Va. App. 28, 668 S.E.2d 816, 2008 Va. App. LEXIS 523 (2008); Mabe v. Wythe County Dep't of Soc. Servs., 53 Va. App. 325, 671 S.E.2d 425, 2009 Va. App. LEXIS 35 (2009); Garcia v. Commonwealth, 60 Va. App. 262, 726 S.E.2d 359, 2012 Va. App. LEXIS 186 (2012); Fox v. Fox, 61 Va. App. 185, 734 S.E.2d 662, 2012 Va. App. LEXIS 395 (2012); Wright v. Wright, 61 Va. App. 432, 737 S.E.2d 519, 2013 Va. App. LEXIS 53 (Feb. 19, 2013).

II. STATEMENT OF OBJECTIONS.

A. In General.

Purpose. — The purpose behind this rule is to require that objections be promptly brought to the attention of the trial court with sufficient specificity that the alleged error could be dealt with and timely addressed and corrected when necessary; this rule promotes orderly and efficient justice and is to be strictly enforced, the ends of justice exception is narrow and should be used sparingly. Wade v. Commonwealth, No. 1790-00-3, 2002 Va. App. LEXIS 121 (Ct. of Appeals Feb. 26, 2002). See also, Ames v. Commonwealth, No. 1524-02-1, 2003 Va. App. LEXIS 186 (Ct. of Appeals Apr. 1, 2003).

Counsel may meet the mandates of this rule in many ways. — For instance, counsel may make clear the ground for his objection in a motion to strike the evidence or in closing argument. Counsel may also state the grounds therefor during a motion to set aside the verdict or a motion to reconsider. Likewise, counsel may, if he or she has previously failed to do so, include an objection and reasons therefor in the final order or at least tender such an order to the trial judge. Lee v. Lee, 12 Va. App. 512, 404 S.E.2d 736 (1991).

A specific procedure is not mandated. — Neither the Code (§ 8.01-384) nor this rule mandate a specific procedure to preserve for appeal an issue objected to in the trial court. A simple statement that embodies the objection and reason therefor suffices. However, neither the Code nor this rule is complied with merely by objecting generally to an order. Lee v. Lee, 12 Va. App. 512, 404 S.E.2d 736 (1991).

Where defense counsel had repeatedly objected to evidence as being inadmissible hearsay, it was unnecessary in order to preserve the issue for appeal under this rule for counsel again to object after the court gave its last admonition to the jury in response to defense counsel's objection and motion to strike the evidence. Jones v. Commonwealth, 11 Va. App. 75, 396 S.E.2d 844 (1990).

Defendant did not waive claim where he did not insist judge rule on motion taken under advisement. — Having raised the issue on three separate occasions before the court reached its verdict, and having taken no action that might be construed as a waiver, the defendant did all that was required to preserve the issue for appeal and did not waive his claim by not insisting that the trial judge rule on the motion he had taken under advisement. Robinson v. Commonwealth, 13 Va. App. 574, 413 S.E.2d 885 (1992).

Commonwealth's argument at trial preserved for appeal its argument that cocaine was discovered pursuant to an independent source, and that any taint resulting from initial warrantless entry dissipated prior to discovery of cocaine. Commonwealth v. Lane, No. 0318-99-2 (Ct. of Appeals Aug. 3, 1999).

Argument must be preserved in the record. — Where appellate court could not determine from the record whether appellant husband had preserved his argument that he was denied due process when the trial court failed to address the issue of a witness's duty to honor a subpoena duces tecum (the husband had filed only a partial trial transcript), the appellate court declined to address the argument. Motley v. Motley, 2007 Va. App. LEXIS 133 (Apr. 3, 2007), overruled in part on other grounds by Jay v. Commonwealth, 275 Va. 510, 659 S.E.2d 311, 2008 Va. LEXIS 53 (2008).

Failure to present argument. — Since a husband did not include an argument in his questions presented, as required by Va. Sup. Ct. R. 5A:18 and 5A:20, the argument was not addressed on appeal; accordingly, because he failed to pay a lump sum alimony payment, the trial court's contempt finding under subdivision K 2 of § 20-107.3 was summarily affirmed. Stoneman v. Stoneman, 2008 Va. App. LEXIS 458 (Oct. 14, 2008).

In a case in which a mother appealed the trial court's termination of her parental rights to her four children, arguing that the trial court erred because it was the children's father who was convicted of felony child neglect and he was the individual accused of molesting two of her children, pursuant to Va. Sup. Ct. R. 5A:18, the appellate court was barred from hearing that claim since there was no evidence in the statement of facts that the mother presented that argument to the trial court. Strother v. Petersburg Dep't of Soc. Servs., 2009 Va. App. LEXIS 455 (Oct. 13, 2009).

In a case in which defendant argued on appeal that he lacked the mens rea to violate § 18.2-279, he had not presented that argument to the trial court, and he did not argue that the appellate court should invoke the good cause or to meet the ends of justice exceptions, the appellate court would not consider that argument. Berger v. Commonwealth, 2006 Va. App. LEXIS 609 (Nov. 17, 2006).

Mother failed to specify a basis for her challenge to the trial court's decision to terminate her parental rights because the agreed statement of facts the parties submitted pursuant to Va. Sup. Ct. R. 5A:8(c) did not recite the mother's arguments, if any, or any objections she made to the trial court's rulings; the record fell far short of affirmatively demonstrating a miscarriage of justice. Sutton v. Shenandoah Valley Dep't of Soc. Servs., 2012 Va. App. LEXIS 27 (Feb. 7, 2012).

Court of appeals would not address defendant's assertion that the trial court erred in overruling his motion to strike the Commonwealth's evidence because defendant failed to preserve the argument of error for appeal. Johnson v. Commonwealth, 2012 Va. App. LEXIS 239 (July 24, 2012).

The requirement of noting an exception to a final adverse ruling of the trial judge has been eliminated. Martin v. Commonwealth, 13 Va. App. 524, 414 S.E.2d 401 (1992).

Exception need not be noted on face of order. — The court of appeals rejected appellee's contention that appellant did not comply with this rule and their decision in Lee v. Lee, 12 Va. App. 512, 404 S.E.2d 736 (1991), in that she did not note the exception to the court's order on the face of the order; neither Lee nor this rule require such when the record makes clear that the appellant has brought the matter to the attention of the trial judge and the trial judge has ruled thereon. Howard v. Howard, No. 0735-91-4 (Ct. of Appeals Mar. 31, 1992).

Defendant did not waive his right to stand on his original motion to strike because the sole issue, from the outset, was whether defendant was "involved" in the accident. Thus, the trial court throughout the trial was aware of the only issue in the case and the requirements of Va. Sup. Ct. R. 5A:18 were fulfilled and the sufficiency issue was preserved for appeal. Campbell v. Commonwealth, 2008 Va. App. LEXIS 325 (July 15, 2008).

Withdrawal of objections. — Defendant did not preserve his evidentiary objection for appeal where he withdrew his motion to suppress during argument on the motion. Beverly v. Commonwealth, No. 0852-98-2 (Ct. of Appeals June 29, 1999).

No relief sought. — While defendant complained to the trial court of the Commonwealth's refusal to disclose witness' criminal record prior to trial, he sought no consequential relief; thus, the trial court denied no requested relief. Allen v. Commonwealth, No. 1201-98-2, 2002 Va. App. LEXIS 363 (Ct. of Appeals June 25, 2002), cert. denied, 539 U.S. 949, 123 S. Ct. 2624, 156 L. Ed. 2d 640 (2003).

Waiver of issues. — Where husband did not present the grounds of his objection and failed to object to the presentation of wife's affidavit in lieu of direct testimony, husband waived the issues for appeal. Lord v. Lord, No. 0049-02-4, 2002 Va. App. LEXIS 362 (Ct. of Appeals June 25, 2002).

Defense counsel waived an objection to the trial court's response to the jury's request for clarification of the concert of action and principal in the second degree instructions and was barred from raising the issue on appeal under Rule 5A:18. Paxton v. Commonwealth, No. 3063-01-2, 2002 Va. App. LEXIS 785 (Ct. of Appeals Dec. 31, 2002).

Revocation of defendant's sentence was properly based on a nunc pro tunc sentencing order (which was signed at the revocation hearing because the trial court had forgotten to sign it when the defendant's sentence was first pronounced) since the defendant waived and was procedurally barred under Rules 5:25 and 5A:18 from making his argument that the order was invalid, because he had admitted the validity of the original sentence pronouncement. Jefferson v. Commonwealth, 269 Va. 136, 607 S.E.2d 107, 2005 Va. LEXIS 15 (2005).

Defendant's appellate claim that a ballistic test of a gun to show that the gun was not used in the crimes should have been provided to him before trial since a photo of the gun was first admitted, then not admitted, at trial. Defendant's claim was barred by Va. Sup. Ct. R. 5A:18 as he failed to make a clear objection to the trial court and did not move for a mistrial on that basis. Boone v. Commonwealth, 2005 Va. App. LEXIS 455 (Nov. 15, 2005).

Whether trial court erred in admitting a statement made by the victim about where the sexual assault of her occurred could not be considered on appeal, as defense counsel had not objected to the police officer's testimony about the victim's identification of a nearby school as the location of the incident; accordingly, defendant had waived the issue and no exception applied that would allow the appellate court to consider it. Mejia-Martinez v. Commonwealth, 2006 Va. App. LEXIS 80 (Mar. 7, 2006).

Because: (1) a father failed to comply with Va. Sup. Ct. R. 5A:8 and 5A:18 in order to adequately preserve the issues he raised on appeal from an order terminating his residual parental rights to his minor child pursuant to § 16.1-283(C)(1) and (C)(2); and (2) the trial court's ruling was not narrow enough to make obvious the basis of the father's objection, said order was affirmed on appeal. Stewart v. Hopewell Dep't of Soc. Servs., 2007 Va. App. LEXIS 320 (Aug. 28, 2007).

Defendant's claims that the trial court engaged in improper conduct in imposing post release supervision in defendant's voluntary manslaughter case had to be rejected, as defendant did not make timely objections with grounds for the objections, as required by the Virginia Supreme Court rules, and, thus, those claims raised later on were waived. Alston v. Commonwealth, 274 Va. 759, 652 S.E.2d 456, 2007 Va. LEXIS 133 (2007).

Defendant waived the issue in defendant's failure to appear case about whether the Commonwealth showed that defendant's failure to appear was willful. Defendant did not raise that issue in the trial court, and, thus, the issue was waived on appeal. Bowling v. Commonwealth, 51 Va. App. 102, 654 S.E.2d 354, 2007 Va. App. LEXIS 461 (2007).

Defendant's failure to ask the trial court for a cautionary instruction or argue to the court that the failure to give such an instruction would impair defendant's right to a jury free from bias waived the issue for appellate review. Although defendant claimed that handcuffing defendant for security purposes due to a disturbance outside the courtroom during voir dire possibly could have influenced prospective jurors, defendant's failure to object did not give the trial court a chance to resolve any issues arising from the incident. Carter v. Commonwealth, 2008 Va. App. LEXIS 90 (Feb. 19, 2008).

Defendant's argument that the trial court's jury instruction on felony eluding under subsection B of § 46.2-817 was deficient was waived, and the court of appeals refused to consider it on appeal because defendant made no objection to the instruction at any time. Stockman v. Commonwealth, 2008 Va. App. LEXIS 143 (Mar. 25, 2008).

Because the Commonwealth did not articulate an argument that the trial court did not have the authority to impose a juvenile sentence upon defendant, the issue was not preserved for appeal, as required by Va. Sup. Ct. R. 5A:18. Brown v. Commonwealth, 279 Va. 210, 688 S.E.2d 185, 2010 Va. LEXIS 9 (2010).

As a wife failed to present any argument regarding the duration of the spousal support award, and even though the defect was significant, the appellate court did not consider the issue on appeal. Grimes v. Grimes, 2008 Va. App. LEXIS 413 (Sept. 2, 2008).

In an appeal from a decision upholding disciplinary action by an employer, an employee failed to make a timely objection or timely raise any of her contentions in the circuit court, and, thus, her claims could not be considered pursuant to Va. Sup. Ct. R. 5A:18; the judgment was, therefore, summarily affirmed under Va. Sup. Ct. R. 5A:27. Winfield v. Southside Va. Training Ctr., 2008 Va. App. LEXIS 484 (Oct. 28, 2008).

Although defendant claimed that the court of appeals had to review a trial court's evidentiary rulings strictly on the ground that the rulings violated his constitutional rights to confrontation and due process, defendant never contended at trial that the rulings implicated any constitutional rights; therefore, defendant waived consideration of any constitutional error in the appeal. Cable v. Commonwealth, 2009 Va. App. LEXIS 409 (Sept. 15, 2009).

Trial court did not abuse its discretion in excluding the testimony of a father's neighbor regarding a son's relationship with the father and the father's new wife on the ground that the son would have to tell the trial court what he had to say because the father did not object or argue with the reasoning and did not preserve his objection under Va. Sup. Ct. R. 5A:18; even if the neighbor had testified about the son's relationship with the father and the father's neighbors those observations would not have influenced the outcome of the case. Christovich v. Christovich, 2009 Va. App. LEXIS 404 (Sept. 15, 2009).

Court of appeals did not address a father's claim that a trial court abused its discretion by suggesting that opening statements be waived and then limiting opening statements to three minutes because the father did not preserve the argument for appeal pursuant to Va. Sup. Ct. R. 5A:18; the father did not make his objection known to the trial court when it announced the time limit. Christovich v. Christovich, 2009 Va. App. LEXIS 404 (Sept. 15, 2009).

Because defendant failed to object to a physician's testimony during trial, he was procedurally barred by Va. Sup. Ct. R. 5A:18 from raising the issue for the first time on appeal; despite having had the opportunity to do so, defendant did not raise below, and the trial court was not given the opportunity to address, the claim defendant raised on appeal. Gainov v. Commonwealth, 2009 Va. App. LEXIS 387 (Sept. 1, 2009).

As Va. Sup. Ct. R. 5A:18 barred consideration of defendant's claims that the trial court improperly admitted a draft promissory note on appeal and abused its discretion by admitting the copy of the draft promissory note under the best evidence rule, because these claims were raised for the first time on appeal. Cardinal v. Commonwealth, 2009 Va. App. LEXIS 478 (Oct. 27, 2009).

Where defendant asserted in his written motion to dismiss the indictments for lack of speedy trial that his constitutional speedy trial rights had been violated, but he made no argument in support of that assertion in his written motion or at the hearing on that motion, this was insufficient to preserve this issue on appeal under Va. Sup. Ct. R. 5A:18. Hall v. Commonwealth, 2009 Va. App. LEXIS 467 (Oct. 20, 2009).

As a father informed a trial court that he would be willing to transport the parties' child to therapy every other week, he expressly waived his argument on appeal that the trial court erred by ordering him to take the child to therapy during his visitation time with her; accordingly, the claim was not preserved for review pursuant to subsection A of § 8.01-384. Freeman v. Golden, 2011 Va. App. LEXIS 54 (Feb. 15, 2011).

Because defendant neither argued why defendant's motion to withdraw a plea of nolo contendere should be granted, nor proffered the evidence defendant intended to elicit or the argument defendant made on appeal, defendant's argument was waived pursuant to Va. Sup. Ct. R. 5A:18. Stone v. Commonwealth, 2011 Va. App. LEXIS 288 (Sept. 27, 2011).

Former spouse failed to adequately preserve the spouse's assigned errors for review by the appellate court, pursuant to Va. Sup. Ct. R. 5A:18, because the spouse objected to the trial court's order finding the spouse in contempt, for violating the terms of a property settlement agreement, by writing, on the face of the order, "Seen and Objected to. I do not have the funds to pay for the $383,226.70 annuity," and, there was no basis for the court to apply the ends of justice exception to the assignments of error. Accordingly, the spouse's arguments on appeal were waived pursuant to Va. Sup. Ct. R. 5A:18. Nelson v. Nelson, 2012 Va. App. LEXIS 210 (June 26, 2012).

Probation revocation proceeding. — Defendant's argument that his probation revocation was improperly based on conduct previously considered by the trial court and found to be a violation of his probation in contravention of the Double Jeopardy Clause of the Fifth Amendment was not preserved for appeal and consideration of the argument on appeal was barred by Va. Sup. Ct. R. 5A:18 because defendant made this argument for the first time on appeal; Va. Sup. Ct. R. 5A:18 applied to bar even constitutional claims. Miles v. Commonwealth, 2007 Va. App. LEXIS 330 (Sept. 4, 2007).

Rule applied to uphold exclusion of evidence. — Forged time sheets were properly admitted into evidence at trial where there was no timely objection to their admissibility and where the company records keeper testified that they were original records, entered in the regular course of the company's business, and that they were obtained from the place where they were properly kept. Barr v. Commonwealth, No. 1150-01-3, 2002 Va. App. LEXIS 218 (Ct. of Appeals Apr. 9, 2002).

B. Contemporaneous Objection Rule.

Purpose of the contemporaneous objection rule. — This rule serves an important function during the conduct of a trial by placing the parties on notice that they must give the trial court the first opportunity to rule on disputed evidentiary and procedural questions. The purpose of this rule is to allow correction of an error if possible during the trial, thereby avoiding the necessity of mistrials and reversals. To hold otherwise would invite parties to remain silent at trial, possibly resulting in the trial court committing needless error. Taylor v. Commonwealth, No. 1673-89-2 (Ct. of Appeals Sept. 29, 1992).

Among the purposes underlying the contemporaneous objection rule are to enable the trial court to prevent error, to cure alleged error with prompt and decisive instruction, and to prevent compounding any harmful consequences by dwelling on irrelevant matters. Harward v. Commonwealth, 5 Va. App. 468, 364 S.E.2d 511 (1988).

The purpose of this rule is self-evident. Any potential error should be brought to the trial court's attention so that the court may consider the issue and take corrective action to avoid unnecessary appeals, reversals and mistrials. Wolfe v. Commonwealth, 6 Va. App. 640, 371 S.E.2d 314 (1988).

The laudatory purpose behind this rule, and its equivalent Supreme Court Rule 5:25, frequently referred to as the contemporaneous objection rules, is to require that objections be promptly brought to the attention of the trial court with sufficient specificity that the alleged error can be dealt with and timely addressed and corrected when necessary and the rules promote orderly and efficient justice and are to be strictly enforced except where the error has resulted in manifest injustice. Brown v. Commonwealth, 8 Va. App. 126, 380 S.E.2d 8 (1989).

Purpose of this rule is to afford trial court an opportunity to rule intelligently on issues presented, thus avoiding unnecessary appeals and reversals. In addition, a specific, contemporaneous objection gives opposing party opportunity to meet objection at that stage of proceeding. Kost v. Kost, No. 0116-99-1 (Ct. of Appeals Dec. 14, 1999).

This rule places parties on notice that they must give trial court the first opportunity to rule on disputed evidentiary and procedural questions. The purpose of the rule is to allow correction of an error if possible during trial, thereby avoiding necessity of mistrials and reversals. Bottoms v. Bottoms, No. 0589-98-2 (Ct. of Appeals June 29, 1999).

This rule serves to protect the trial court from appeals based on undisclosed grounds, to prevent the setting of traps on appeal, to enable the trial judge to rule intelligently and to avoid unnecessary reversals and mistrials. Gary v. Commonwealth, No. 0720-99-2, 2000 Va. App. LEXIS 311 (Ct. of Appeals May 2, 2000).

Where the trial judge never had an opportunity to intelligently consider arguments, the arguments were procedurally barred on appeal by Rule 5A:18. Byrd v. Commonwealth, No. 2550-02-1, 2003 Va. App. LEXIS 708 (Ct. of Appeals Dec. 30, 2003).

Defendant's contention that the trial court erred in answering a jury's question in the affirmative because the response was contrary to the law and led directly to an inconsistent verdict was not properly preserved for review. Pursuant to Va. Sup. Ct. R. 5A:18, to preserve an issue for appeal, an objection had to be stated together with the grounds at the time of the ruling in order for the trial court to consider it, and defendant did not object to the trial court's response prior to the response being submitted to the jury. Ludwig v. Commonwealth, 52 Va. App. 1, 660 S.E.2d 679, 2008 Va. App. LEXIS 227 (2008).

Timeliness of objection to evidence. — Where the inadmissibility and objectionable nature of the evidence are not immediately obvious to counsel, the objection will be timely if made as soon as the dangerous drift of the examination becomes apparent. Simmons v. Commonwealth, 6 Va. App. 445, 371 S.E.2d 7 (1988), rev'd on other grounds, 238 Va. 200, 380 S.E.2d 656 (1989).

Objection raised at the end of a series of voir dire questions was properly preserved for appeal. Hazel v. Commonwealth, 31 Va. App. 403, 524 S.E.2d 134 (2000).

Where the defense counsel objected to seating the entire jury during voir dire based on improper voir dire questioning, counsel did not need to reassert the objection when the jury was sworn in to preserve the issue for appeal. Hazel v. Commonwealth, 31 Va. App. 403, 524 S.E.2d 134 (2000).

Because Va. Sup. Ct. R. 5A:18 precluded consideration of challenges to admissibility of evidence to which there was no timely objection, the court did not consider defendant's challenge to the evidence. Despite trial court's tentative ruling at a pretrial hearing, defendant both failed to object to the admission of the testimony at the time it was offered and failed to present the arguments to the trial court that he made on appeal. Osman v. Commonwealth, 2010 Va. App. LEXIS 30 (Jan. 26, 2010).

Timeliness of objection to identification evidence. — Objections to identification evidence must be made by motion or objection either before or at the time the identification evidence is unfolded to the jury. Scott v. Commonwealth, No. 1589-00-3, 2001 Va. App. LEXIS 293 (Ct. of Appeals May 29, 2001).

Counsel adequately stated objection to relevance of testimony. — Where the record established that the appellant objected to the testimony in question on the ground of hearsay and requested a bench conference, where the appellant then changed his objection to relevancy, stating "[W]hat relevance is the statement that the man says the family wants the tools and then he has the tools two days later have to do with the killing of William Johnson? I mean we feel its extremely prejudicial," where counsel further added, "[W]e want to note that we strenuously object," and where the trial judge responded "I understand your objection, and you are on the record, and I overrule it," counsel adequately stated his objection to the relevance of the testimony. Witt v. Commonwealth, No. 0938-89-3 (Ct. of Appeals Apr. 2, 1991).

Objection to expert witness testimony. — Mother, pursuant to Va. Sup. Ct. R. 5A:18, waived her right to raise on appeal her contention that the father's expert witness impermissibly commented on the veracity of a witness when he expressed an opinion that the child was not being truthful in her allegations that her father had abused her. The mother failed to raise this issue prior to trial at the time that she raised other objections to the expert's testimony. Jaouni v. Said Samir Ibrahim Salah, 2012 Va. App. LEXIS 15 (Jan. 24, 2012).

Mother, pursuant to Va. Sup. Ct. R. 5A:18, waived her right to raise on appeal her contention that the father's expert witness was never qualified as an expert as the mother never objected on this basis in the trial court. Jaouni v. Said Samir Ibrahim Salah, 2012 Va. App. LEXIS 15 (Jan. 24, 2012).

Former wife's objections to the former husband's expert were not timely in an annulment action, since she waited twenty-one days after the entry of the order to note her objections as to whether the witness was properly offered as an expert and whether he could opine about the ultimate issue in the case. Naseer v. Moghal, 2012 Va. App. LEXIS 259 (Aug. 14, 2012).

In order for objection to be preserved for appeal, it must be timely made and the grounds stated with specificity. To be timely, an objection must be made at the time the occasion arises, i.e., at the time the evidence is offered. Ingram v. Commonwealth, 1 Va. App. 335, 338 S.E.2d 657 (1986).

Pursuant to this rule, the court of appeals may consider only the questions presented in defendant's petition for appeal. Riggs v. Commonwealth, No. 1892-95-2, 1996 Va. App. LEXIS 591 (Ct. of Appeals Sept. 10, 1996).

A trial court must be alerted to the precise issue to which a party objects. Clark v. Commonwealth, No. 2427-97-2 (Ct. of Appeals Aug. 3, 1999).

This rule requires that objections to a trial court's action or ruling be made with specificity in order to preserve an issue for appeal. Wilkerson v. Commonwealth, No. 1287-98-1 (Ct. of Appeals June 8, 1999); Childers v. Childers, No. 2659-98-3 (Ct. of Appeals June 29, 1999).

Issue of whether codefendants' statements were unreliable hearsay was not preserved for appeal because, although defense counsel objected to the statements, he objected on the grounds that the court should not consider the statements of codefendants against each other, not on the grounds of hearsay. Scott v. Commonwealth, 31 Va. App. 461, 524 S.E.2d 162 (2000).

Defendant was limited, on appeal, to the specific objection he raised at trial. Caprio v. Commonwealth, No. 2225-98-1 (Ct. of Appeals Mar. 14, 2000).

Trial court, by ruling electronic incarceration was not an option for legal reasons, implicitly concluded it was not a practical impossibility due to the fact that the appellant resided in another jurisdiction and the absence of an express statement to this effect in the record did not bar appeal. Cuffee-Smith v. Commonwealth, 39 Va. App. 476, 574 S.E.2d 294, 2002 Va. App. LEXIS 771 (2002).

Defendant's argument that the testimony of a rebuttal witness was inadmissible because it did not rebut defendant's testimony was not raised in the trial court, and, thus, defendant was not entitled to raise that argument for the first time on appeal. Tory v. Commonwealth, No. 0756-02-1, 2003 Va. App. LEXIS 124 (Ct. of Appeals Mar. 11, 2003).

Failure to raise issue at trial barred consideration on appeal. — Party was barred from raising issue on appeal since the record failed to show any instance where the party raised the issue at trial and no good cause was shown that in order to attain the ends of justice, court should have considered this issue. Dixon v. Pugh, No. 1647-90-2 (Ct. of Appeals Aug. 13, 1991).

A matter not in dispute before the trial court will not be considered for the first time on appeal. Connelly v. Commonwealth, 14 Va. App. 888, 420 S.E.2d 244 (1992).

The court of appeals will not consider an argument on appeal which was not presented to the trial court. Michaels v. Commonwealth, 32 Va. App. 601, 529 S.E.2d 822, 2000 Va. App. LEXIS 463 (2000).

Where defendant failed, without good cause, to raise before the trial court the due process argument he made on appeal, and was unable to prove that a manifest injustice resulted, consideration of the merits of the argument was barred on appeal. Andrews v. Commonwealth, 37 Va. App. 479, 559 S.E.2d 401, 2002 Va. App. LEXIS 89 (2002).

Defendant, convicted of operating a food manufacturing plant without inspection, in violation of § 3.1-398.1 [see now § 3.2-5130], and offering misbranded food for sale, in violation of § 3.1-388(a) [see now § 3.2-5123], contended that cheeses were merely placed in bags for the purchaser's convenience, and that because the cheeses were sold by the pound, they were not pre-packaged for distribution purposes; however, defendant failed to preserve the argument for appeal, because there was no evidence presented to that effect at trial, and accordingly, the appellate court did not consider such evidence or argument for purposes of appeal, under Rule 5A:18. McClellan v. Commonwealth, 39 Va. App. 759, 576 S.E.2d 785, 2003 Va. App. LEXIS 95 (2003).

An employer's res judicata claim could not be considered because it had not been raised as a bar to the change in condition application pursuant to Va. Sup. Ct. R. 5A:18. Wellmont Lonesome Pine Hosp. v. Cantor, No. 0665-03-3, 2003 Va. App.

LEXIS 435 (Ct. of Appeals Aug. 12, 2003).

Appellate court could not consider defendant's assertion of error on appeal that the trial court erred in limiting the testimony of an acquaintance who was recalled to the witness stand to clarify one central point, as defendant's counsel agreed with the limitation and did not otherwise object; accordingly, defendant did not properly preserve for review any issue regarding the trial court's limitation on that questioning. Lawson v. Commonwealth, No. 1495-03-4, 2004 Va. App. LEXIS 372 (Ct. of Appeals Aug. 3, 2004).

Despite having had the opportunity to do so, a husband did not alert the trial court to his claim that the court erred in failing to account for his personal goodwill in dividing the value of the parties' business, a newspaper; thus, the trial court was not timely advised of the alleged error and had no opportunity to consider, address, or correct it. Pearson v. Pearson, 2006 Va. App. LEXIS 334 (July 25, 2006).

Because the record contained no arguments or objections concerning the trial court proceedings, the record did not show that the father argued to the trial court, as he did on appeal, that the trial court erred by failing to consider father's objections addressing the juvenile and domestic relations district court proceedings, or that the father argued to the trial court that his due process rights were denied when his guardian ad litem failed to appear for the trial court hearing. Accordingly, the arguments were barred by Va. Sup. Ct. R. 5A:18 because they were not raised in the trial court. Harris v. Burd, 2006 Va. App. LEXIS 393 (Aug. 22, 2006).

Mother claimed the trial court erred by terminating her parental rights without a ruling as to whether or not proper procedure was followed, but at trial she never argued that the trial court failed to issue a ruling. Because the requirements of Va. Sup. Ct. R. 5A:18 had not been met, the appeals court would not consider the question on appeal. Cox v. Wise County Dep't of Soc. Servs., 2006 Va. App. LEXIS 429 (Sept. 26, 2006).

In an appeal of a marital property division in a divorce suit, appellant husband failed to make a specific argument to the trial court in order to preserve his appellate contention that the trial court erred in finding that an investment account was marital property; he did not assert his argument regarding the classification of the investment account in his written argument to the trial court, nor did he object to the finding in his written "Objections to Final Decree of Divorce." Patel v. Patel, 2006 Va. App. LEXIS 418 (Sept. 12, 2006).

Appellate consideration of defendant's argument that the testimony of two officers during the penalty phase of his criminal case was improperly admitted was barred because defendant never raised this argument below; defendant objected to the officers' testimony based on relevance and prejudice, but the trial court was not presented with the issue of whether the officers were "victims" under the victim impact statute, § 19.2-299.1, and, thus, defendant's objection lacked the requisite specificity to preserve his appellate argument that the officers' testimony was inadmissible under that statute. Defendant also did not argue in the trial court, as he did on appeal, that the testimony was barred under the bifurcated sentencing statute, § 19.2-295.1, and this argument was also barred on appeal. Macklin v. Commonwealth, 2007 Va. App. LEXIS 269 (June 26, 2007).

Mother's arguments on appeal of an order terminating her parental rights were barred from consideration pursuant to Va. Sup. Ct. R. 5A:18 because the mother failed to present her arguments to the trial court; the mother did not argue that any of the exceptions should have been invoked and the record did not establish a basis for applying any of the exceptions. The termination order was summarily affirmed. Clinton-Williams v. Newport News Dep't of Soc. Servs., 2007 Va. App. LEXIS 361 (Oct. 2, 2007).

Defendant did not raise at trial his appellate argument that the trial judge improperly participated in the prosecution and that the trial judge should have accepted the Commonwealth's attorney's concession that the evidence was insufficient and dismissed the case; thus, consideration of those arguments on appeal was barred. Castilloux v. Commonwealth, 2007 Va. App. LEXIS 358 (Oct. 2, 2007).

Because an employer failed to assert a "termination for cause" objection upon its appeal to the full Workers' Compensation Commission, pursuant to Va. Sup. Ct. R. 5A:18, the objection could not be considered on appeal; therefore, the employer's arguments on appeal were defaulted and the Commission's holding was affirmed. City of Norfolk Sch. Bd. v. Mitchell, 2008 Va. App. LEXIS 334 (July 22, 2008).

Because an employer's claims on appeal were not presented to the Workers' Compensation Commission, Va. Sup. Ct. R. 5A:18 barred consideration of the claims for the first time on appeal; in any event, a review of the record and the commission's opinion showed that the employer's appeal was without merit. Euro Composites Corp. v. William Frederick Lekebusch, 2008 Va. App. LEXIS 423 (Sept. 16, 2008).

In a case in which defendant appealed her conviction for felony child neglect in violation of subsection B of § 18.2-371.1, she argued unsuccessfully that the evidence was insufficient because it failed to show that: (1) she withheld her son's medication; (2) her behavior caused a substantial risk to his life or health; and (3) she knew withholding his medication was likely to cause such a risk. The record on appeal failed to establish the defendant preserved any of her arguments for appeal as required by Va. Sup. Ct. R. 5A:18. Thornton v. Commonwealth, 2009 Va. App. LEXIS 413 (Sept. 15, 2009).

In a conviction of two counts of use of a firearm during the commission of a felony, defendant procedurally defaulted a claim that he did not display a firearm in a threatening manner because he did not raise this claim in the trial court. Startin v. Commonwealth, 54 Va. App. 778, 682 S.E.2d 115, 2009 Va. App. LEXIS 394 (2009).

In a case in which defendant argued that the evidence was insufficient to prove what month the sexual assaults began, he did not raise that issue in the trial court but rather argued the Commonwealth of Virginia failed to prove the number of counts charged in the indictments; thus, his argument regarding a failure to prove the initial time frame as set forth in the indictments was waived.

Moreover, time was not of essence in the sexual assault charges. Laines v. Commonwealth, 2009 Va. App. LEXIS 373 (Aug. 18, 2009).

Because a mother waited until her motion for reconsideration to note her objection to the trial court's consideration of a psychological evaluation report, the mother did not provide the trial court with an opportunity to address the issue until after its decision on the merits. Thus, Va. Sup. Ct. R. 5A:18 barred consideration of the issue on appeal. Mercurio v. Mercurio, 2009 Va. App. LEXIS 492 (Nov. 3, 2009).

Appellate court was unable to review claim of defendant, who was convicted of assault of his domestic partner, that the trial court erroneously disallowed the testimony of a certain witness because defendant did not object that the trial court's ruling violated his constitutional rights, he did not challenge the trial court's implicit ruling that the disputed testimony was hearsay, and he did not provide an offer of proof to preserve the ruling for appellate review. Pitt v. Commonwealth, 2009 Va. App. LEXIS 470 (Oct. 20, 2009).

Defendant failed to satisfy the contemporaneous objection requirement of Va. Sup. Ct. R. 5A:18 because he did not contend in the trial court, as he argued on appeal, that Virginia's statutory scheme, specifically § 19.2-187.1, impermissibly shifted to him the burden of calling the forensic analyst. Miller v. Commonwealth, 2009 Va. App. LEXIS 421 (Sept. 22, 2009).

Defendant's convictions for distributing cocaine were proper, in part because her argument that testimony of her prior criminal behavior was impermissible evidence of her prior bad acts and served no other purpose than to prejudice her in the eyes of the jury was not presented to the trial court; thus, the appellate court refused to consider it on appeal. Defendant had based both of her objections on relevancy grounds and not once did she argue at trial that the evidence that she sought to exclude constituted impermissible other crimes or bad acts evidence. Terry v. Commonwealth, 2010 Va. App. LEXIS 216 (May 25, 2010).

Because a claimant for workers' compensation benefits failed to point a discrepancy out to the Virginia Workers' Compensation Commission, despite two opportunities to do so, the claimant was now barred by Va. Sup. Ct. R. 5A:18 from raising it in the appellate court. Avila-Rivera v. Excel Masonry, Inc., 2011 Va. App. LEXIS 338 (Nov. 8, 2011).

Defendant's drug convictions and conviction for contributing to the delinquency of a minor were proper because, although he argued on brief that the trial court abused its discretion in failing to make an express finding on the record that the probative value of the evidence outweighed any prejudice to the accused, he failed to object to the admissibility of the evidence at trial as being more prejudicial than probative and thus, he waived that specific objection on appeal. Pinnix v. Commonwealth, 2011 Va. App. LEXIS 149 (May 3, 2011).

Since a wife made no timely objection, the court of appeals would not consider her assignment of error that she did not receive a fair and impartial trial. Canedo v. Canedo, No. 0851-12-4, 2013 Va. App. LEXIS 61 (Feb. 26, 2013).

Failure to raise argument before Workers' Compensation Commission. — Court of appeals could not consider on appeal the deputy commissioner's decision to terminate a temporary total disability award because the employee never sought full review by the Virginia Workers' Compensation Commission of that decision; because the full Commission never considered the termination of the temporary total disability award on the merits, the court of appeals had no Commission ruling to review on the issue. Windsor v. Loomis Fargo & Co., 2011 Va. App. LEXIS 407 (Dec. 20, 2011).

Counsel's objection sufficient. — On appeal from his convictions, the record established that defendant's counsel objected on hearsay grounds to the admissibility of defense counsel's testimony as to what a friend of the victim had testified at the preliminary hearing. Thus, the issue was preserved for appellate consideration. Turner v. Commonwealth, 58 Va. App. 567, 712 S.E.2d 28, 2011 Va. App. LEXIS 248 (2011).

On appeal from his convictions, the record established that defendant's counsel objected to the admissibility of testimony on the basis of the duty and obligation that defendant's prior counsel owed him regarding anything that transpired during his representation of defendant. Thus, the objection by defendant's counsel was specific and timely, and the issue is preserved for appellate consideration. Turner v. Commonwealth, 58 Va. App. 567, 712 S.E.2d 28, 2011 Va. App. LEXIS 248 (2011).

Failure to proffer document at trial barred consideration on appeal. — Record failed to show that a wife proffered a copy of an assessment of the value of the parties' marital property or that the commissioner refused a proffer, and, thus, the wife failed preserved this issue below. Roman v. Price, 2008 Va. App. LEXIS 501 (Nov. 12, 2008).

Reargument not required to preserve issue on appeal from remand. — Va. Sup. Ct. R. 5A:18 did not require the mother to repeat arguments to the trial court, during the remand for an explanation of the deviation from the child support guidelines, in order to preserve the issue for appeal. Olson v. Olson, 2009 Va. App. LEXIS 6 (Jan. 13, 2009).

Failure to raise jury selection issue. — Although defendant argued on appeal that he established a prima facie case of both racial and gender discrimination in the Commonwealth's exercise of peremptory strikes to remove two African-American women in his criminal trial, defendant did not raise an issue of gender discrimination in the trial court; therefore, appellate consideration of the gender issue was barred. Lightfoot v. Commonwealth, 50 Va. App. 723, 653 S.E.2d 615, 2007 Va. App. LEXIS 443 (2007).

Requests for admission of videotape during trial and post-trial motion challenging exclusion preserved issue for appellate review. — Challenge to exclusion of evidence was properly preserved for appellate review where defendant asked the trial court to show a videotape twice during trial and then raised the challenge again in a post-trial motion; defendant placed sufficient information before the trial court about the nature of the request when defendant tried to show the videotape to the jury before concluding defendant's case and repeated the request before the jury began deliberating, when the trial court still could have taken action to correct its error. Jones v. Commonwealth, 50 Va. App. 437, 650 S.E.2d 859, 2007 Va. App. LEXIS 356 (2007).

Statement made in mitigation at sentencing insufficient to preserve the issue for appeal. — Issue of whether the legislature intended the concealed weapon offense to be a strict liability offense or whether scienter or mens rea was a necessary element of the offense was not raised during trial and appellate consideration of the issue was barred; defendant's statement made in mitigation at sentencing was insufficient to preserve the issue for appeal. Pruitt v. Commonwealth, 2006 Va. App. LEXIS 597 (May 24, 2006).

Objection to prosecutor's comments must be accompanied by motion for cautionary instruction or mistrial. — It is well-settled that errors assigned because of a prosecutor's alleged improper comments or conduct during argument will not be considered on appeal unless an accused timely moves for a cautionary instruction or for a mistrial. The motions must be made timely if the accused desires to take advantage of his objection on appeal. Moore v. Commonwealth, 14 Va. App. 83, 414 S.E.2d 859 (1992).

Correction of instruction omitting element of crime. — The proper description of the elements of an offense is vital to a defendant, and attaining the "ends of justice" requires correction of an instruction which allows a jury to convict a defendant without proof of an element of a crime. Herbert v. Commonwealth, No. 0888-00-4, 2001 Va. App. LEXIS 184 (Ct. of Appeals Apr. 10, 2001).

Refusal of proffered instructions. — In a first-degree murder prosecution, defendant's proffer of a correct instruction on self-defense was sufficient to preserve for appeal the question of whether the trial court erred in refusing that instruction. It was not necessary for her to expressly articulate each element necessary to her defense, because the trial court heard the evidence and could evaluate its application to the proffered instruction. Commonwealth v. Cary, 271 Va. 87, 623 S.E.2d 906, 2006 Va. LEXIS 22 (2006).

Failure to object to a jury instruction. — Because defendant did not object to a jury instruction, pursuant to Va. Sup. Ct. R. 3A:16 and Va. Sup. Ct. R. 5A:18, any previous objection by defendant was trumped by his acquiescence to jury instruction number 7, which allowed the jury to consider his prior statement. Younger v. Commonwealth, No. 1775-11-2, 2012 Va. App. LEXIS 328 (Oct. 16, 2012).

Objections during opening statement are no substitute for timely objections to evidence subsequently offered at trial. Brandon v. Commonwealth, No. 2434-98-2 (Ct. of Appeals Jan. 11, 2000).

Parties chose not to make a part of the record their closing arguments or any other communication with the court. Therefore, this record failed to establish that the issues appealed by appellant were raised in the trial court by an objection with a statement of the reasons therefor. The court could not assume that appellant's objection and reasons were proffered but not made a part of the record. Rule 5A:8 requires appellant to present a complete transcript for this court to consider his or her issues on appeal. Lee v. Lee, 12 Va. App. 512, 404 S.E.2d 736 (1991).

Objections at the close of all evidence. — At the conclusion of defendant's bench trial for grand larceny, in order to preserve his objections that neither the victim's lack of consent nor defendant's fraudulent intent had been shown, defendant had to make a motion to strike at the close of the evidence, present an appropriate argument in summation, or move to set aside the verdict, and he failed to do so. McCullough v. Commonwealth, No. 1155-02-1, 2003 Va. App. LEXIS 127 (Ct. of Appeals Mar. 11, 2003).

Objection presented via motion to set aside verdict is sufficiently timely to satisfy this rule. Akers v. Commonwealth, 31 Va. App. 521, 525 S.E.2d 13 (2000).

Any objection in the circuit court to the status of the record of an administrative proceeding was not timely and would not be considered on appeal where the objecting party had filed a timely motion for reconsideration with the circuit court but withdrawn it and filed a second motion requiring completion of the record after the time had passed within which the circuit court could entertain such a motion. Smith v. Department of Mines, Minerals & Energy, 28 Va. App. 677, 508 S.E.2d 342 (1998).

Objection to court order not timely. — Former husband could not claim that his First Amendment rights were violated by a court order that the husband not post materials regarding a dissolution case on the Internet as no objection was made until three days after the order was entered; thus, the husband failed to comply with Va. Sup. Ct. R. 5A:18. Jagannathan v. Jagannathan, 2008 Va. App. LEXIS 88 (Feb. 19, 2008).

Objection to court order timely. — Mother preserved for review her claim that the trial court denied her an impartial de novo standard of review on appeal from a juvenile and domestic relations district court order because although the mother did not note her objection within the ten days as requested by the trial court in a pendente lite order, she did note her objections a few weeks after the trial court issued its order and reiterated them, and the trial court was given an opportunity to address the issue if it felt that it needed to. Huston v. Huston, 2010 Va. App. LEXIS 407 (Oct. 19, 2010).

Constitutional question waived because not raised at trial. — The defendant contended that if the revocation of the suspended sentence was based upon any other condition of the plea agreement than his agreement to testify truthfully, revocation was arbitrary, capricious, and constitutionally impermissible. The appellate court properly refused to address the constitutional question because the defendant did not raise it in the trial court. Cottrell v. Commonwealth, 12 Va. App. 570, 405 S.E.2d 438 (1991).

On appeal, the defendant contended that the trial court's refusal to admit tax records of the witness violated her right to confront and cross-examine her accuser in derogation of the Sixth Amendment to the United States Constitution and Article I, § 8 of the Virginia Constitution. Because the defendant did not raise these issues at trial she was barred from asserting them for the first time on appeal. Evans v. Commonwealth, No. 0771-96-4 (Ct. of Appeals Feb. 4, 1997).

Defendant failed to preserve for review defendant's constitutional challenge to the trial court's decision to allow child victims to testify about defendant via two-way closed-circuit television, as defendant did not raise the constitutional claim in the trial court. Civitello v. Commonwealth, No. 1963-01-2, 2003 Va. App. LEXIS 2 (Ct. of Appeals Jan. 7, 2003).

Defendant's convictions for first-degree murder and use of a firearm in the commission of a felony were proper because he failed to state questions that he would have asked and the eyewitness's expected answers to those questions for the record, and because he did not specifically raise an objection to the court's decision based upon the U.S. Const., Amend. VI right to confrontation. Thus, the issue regarding the trial court's refusal to allow re-cross-examination was not properly preserved for appeal. Cortez-Hernandez v. Commonwealth, 58 Va. App. 66, 706 S.E.2d 893, 2011 Va. App. LEXIS 114 (2011).

Failure to preserve issue. — Judgment terminating a mother's parental rights was affirmed because the mother did not preserve her due process issue for appeal as required by Va. Sup. Ct. R. 5A:18; the mother's endorsement of the termination order gave no indication of a due process argument. The mother did not argue to invoke the exceptions for good cause or to meet the ends of justice. Dolak v. Va. Beach Dep't of Human Servs., 2012 Va. App. LEXIS 244 (July 31, 2012).

Husband's assertion that the trial court in the husband's divorce proceeding failed to accommodate him under the Americans With Disabilities Act after his counsel was allowed to withdraw on the first day of trial was untimely and would not be considered on appeal where the husband failed to provide a transcript of the trial and the records that were provided indicated the issue was raised months after the trial concluded. Cahill v. Cahill, No. 0305-12-1, 2012 Va. App. LEXIS 409 (Dec. 18, 2012).

Constitutional question not presented to trial court. — Where the appellant argued that § 19.2-83 proscribed the search of his car, and this issue was not presented to the trial court, the appellant's motion to suppress was based on constitutional grounds and was not considered for the first time on appeal. Jacques v. Commonwealth, 12 Va. App. 591, 405 S.E.2d 630 (1991).

After defendant's motion to suppress was denied, he was not required to except to the trial court's ruling to preserve the issue raised in his suppression motion for appeal. Belmer v. Commonwealth, 36 Va. App. 448, 553 S.E.2d 123, 2001 Va. App. LEXIS 531 (2001).

Appellate court declined to consider defendant's argument that he was entitled to full faith and credit of a West Virginia court's restoration of his civil rights with respect to the use of that state's underlying felony for purposes of defendant's conviction in Virginia, as defendant failed to raise the issue before the trial court, as required by 5A:18. Farnsworth v. Commonwealth, 43 Va. App. 490, 599 S.E.2d 482, 2004 Va. App. LEXIS 358 (2004), aff'd, 270 Va. 1, 613 S.E.2d 459 (2005).

Denial of fair and impartial trial had to be conveyed to trial judge. — At a minimum, at some point during the trial, counsel had to notify the trial judge of the problem or assert in some way his belief that the defendant was being denied a fair and impartial trial. Neal v. Commonwealth, 15 Va. App. 416, 425 S.E.2d 521 (1992).

Failure to object to juror inattention. — Defendant's failure to object or request relief after a juror's alleged inattention was brought to defendant's attention at trial constituted a failure to timely demand a mistrial and a failure to preserve the issue for appellate review. Perry v. Commonwealth, 58 Va. App. 655, 712 S.E.2d 765, 2011 Va. App. LEXIS 262 (2011).

Defendant was procedurally barred by this rule from making a claim based on Miranda rights, where he failed to raise a Miranda based objection anywhere during trial. Bivins v. Commonwealth, No. 1872-89-1 (Ct. of Appeals Oct. 2, 1990).

Defendant's habeas claim that the Commonwealth of Virginia failed to correct false testimony of its witness was barred because this nonjurisdictional issue could have been raised by defendant at trial and on appeal. Bowman v. Johnson, 282 Va. 359, 718 S.E.2d 456, 2011 Va. LEXIS 218 (2011).

No good cause shown for failure to raise objection. — The Court of Appeals will not consider a question raised for the first time on appeal, even a constitutional question. Furthermore, it is not necessary to apply one of the exceptions to this rule in order to correct a miscarriage of justice. Appellant did not demonstrate good cause for having failed to raise his objection at trial. Singleton v. Commonwealth, 19 Va. App. 728, 453 S.E.2d 921 (1995).

This rule barred appellate consideration of husband's challenges to the child support ruling. Moreover, the record did not reflect any reason to invoke the good cause or ends of justice exceptions to this rule. Norman v. Norman, No. 1044-96-1 (Ct. of Appeals Jan. 7, 1997).

Defendant's claim that the evidence was insufficient to establish that he maintained a "custodial or supervisory relationship" with victim on April 18, 1995 was procedurally barred; the court of appeals' review is limited to the record on appeal, and defendant's failure to transcribe his motion to strike and closing argument prevented review in this case. Conner v. Commonwealth, No. 1720-96-2 (Ct. of Appeals Mar. 25, 1997).

Wife's appeal from the trial court's ruling granting the husband spousal support lacked merit; as the wife failed to timely submit any objections, the trial court no longer had jurisdiction over the case, and Rule 5A:18 precluded the appellate court from addressing the wife's issues on appeal. Gantt v. Gantt, No. 1973-02-3, 2003 Va. App. LEXIS 112 (Ct. of Appeals Mar. 4, 2003).

Under Va. Sup. Ct. R. 5A:18, the appellate court would not consider an argument on appeal which was not presented to the trial court as the record did not reflect any reason to invoke the good cause or ends of justice exceptions to Va. Sup. Ct. R. 5A:18. Baxani v. Baxani, No. 2945-02-2, 2003 Va. App. LEXIS 380 (Ct. of Appeals July 1, 2003).

Father's argument that the time limit imposed at the child custody hearing was improper was waived, as the trial court at the beginning of the hearing set forth the total amount of time that would be spent hearing the matter and the amount of time allotted to each side for presenting evidence;

the father's failure to object and state the grounds for that objection at trial waived that issue for review, and exceptions where good cause was shown for not raising the issue or to attain the ends of justice did not apply. Lanzalotti v. Lanzalotti, 41 Va. App. 550, 586 S.E.2d 881, 2003 Va. App. LEXIS 497 (2003).

Defendant's claim that he did not abduct a victim because the detention was incidental to the restraint employed in a rape was not preserved for appeal and did not fall within the "ends of justice" exception of Rule 5A:18; as the victim testified that defendant grabbed her wrists and pulled her to a bedroom, and those actions were not inherent to the commission of rape or forcible sodomy, defendant failed to establish than an element of the offense did not occur. Payne v. Commonwealth, No. 0678-03-1, 2004 Va. App. LEXIS 135 (Ct. of Appeals Mar. 30, 2004).

City of Norfolk Department of Human Services lacked good cause to overcome its failure to raise its appellate issues in the trial court pursuant to Va. Sup. Ct. R. 5A:18; nothing in the record indicated that the Department could not have objected to the trial court's oral ruling after the trial judge orally dismissed the petitions, and nothing in the record showed that the clerk failed to send copies of the decree to the parties, at which time the Department could have objected. City of Norfolk Dep't of Human Servs. v. Harris, 2005 Va. App. LEXIS 301 (Aug. 2, 2005).

Defendant conceded the failure to object to a police detective's hearsay testimony at trial, but contended it would have been futile given the court's earlier ruling regarding the admissibility of the testimony of a police officer. However, the futility of presenting an objection could not alone constitute cause for a failure to object at trial. Henh Chu Ngo v. Commonwealth, 2008 Va. App. LEXIS 285 (June 17, 2008).

Good cause shown. — "Good cause" exception to the procedural bar of Va. Sup. Ct. R. 5A:18 applied after a guardian ad litem sought an aware of fees in a custody case and appeared in another proceeding to orally request an award of her fees, the trial courts remarks from the bench arguably suggested all issues, including the guardian ad litem's fees request would be decided no earlier than 21 days later, and the trial court then entered the guardian ad litem's drafter order 15 days after the hearing, before the wife had a chance to object. Neither the parties nor counsel were aware the order had been entered in the wrong case and the wife filed a timely notice of appeal upon discovering the order. Gudino v. Gudino, 2012 Va. App. LEXIS 195 (June 12, 2012).

C. Specificity of Objection.

Specificity. — Contemporaneous objection requirement of this rule requires that objections be specifically stated so trial courts have opportunity to maturely consider issues and correct problems immediately, rather than encourage unnecessary delays. Bartz v. Commonwealth, No. 1374-98-2 (Ct. of Appeals June 29, 1999).

Where defendant objected at trial to the hearsay nature of the witness's testimony of an intermediary's description of defendant, but defendant argued on appeal that the trial court erred by considering the intermediary's hearsay description of the dealer as substantive evidence, the argument was not preserved for appeal pursuant to Rule 5A:18, as defendant did not specify at trial, or at any time later in the trial, that the trial court was inappropriately considering that evidence to weigh defendant's guilt or innocence, and the record did not reflect any reason to invoke the good cause or ends of justice exceptions to the preservation rule. Martin v. Commonwealth, No. 1484-03-1, 2004 Va. App. LEXIS 122 (Ct. of Appeals Mar. 23, 2004).

When a husband seeking to void a separation agreement's child support provisions argued, on appeal, that the agreement's child support formula was not specific and clear and might change monthly, the argument was not considered because the husband did not raise this argument with specificity before the trial court, as required by Va. Sup. Ct. R. 5A:18, and the record did not reflect any reason to invoke the good cause or ends of justice exceptions to Rule 5A:18. Owata v. Owata, No. 2927-03-1, 2004 Va. App. LEXIS 223 (Ct. of Appeals May 11, 2004).

Where defendant appealed his conviction for stalking, claiming that the evidence was insufficient to support the conviction, the appellate court did not consider the argument on the merits because it was barred by Va. Sup. Ct. R. 5A:18, as the issue was not properly preserved for review; although defendant had made two motions to strike against the Commonwealth's evidence, those motions were not supported with any specificity as to the grounds of the objections and accordingly, the trial court did not have an opportunity to consider the issue of sufficiency of the evidence. Hurley v. Commonwealth, No. 1332-03-3, 2004 Va. App. LEXIS 255 (Ct. of Appeals June 1, 2004).

Making one specific argument on an issue does not preserve a separate legal point on the same issue for review. Young v. Commonwealth, No. 0007-03-3, 2004 Va. App. LEXIS 323 (Ct. of Appeals July 13, 2004).

Specific argument must be made to the trial court at the appropriate time, or the allegations of error will not be considered on appeal; a general argument or an abstract reference to the law is not sufficient to preserve an issue. Young v. Commonwealth, No. 0007-03-3, 2004 Va. App. LEXIS 323 (Ct. of Appeals July 13, 2004).

Mere notation of objection to final order insufficient. — A notation of "Seen and Objected To" by counsel when signing the final order does not preserve an issue for appeal unless the record further reveals that the issue was properly raised for consideration by the trial court. Clark v. Clark, No. 0827-99-2, 2000 Va. App. LEXIS 469 (Ct. of Appeals June 27, 2000).

Father failed to preserve for appellate review his argument that the trial court erred by ruling that the child was not of reasonable and sufficient intelligence to express his personal preference under circumstances in which the father failed to object at the time the court made the ruling; additionally, the father did not raise this argument on the final order, which he endorsed "Seen and objected to," but stated no specific objections. Masters v. Sutton, 2007 Va. App. LEXIS 136 (Apr. 3, 2007).

Wife in a divorce case failed to preserve her appellate argument that the trial court erred in rejecting a commissioner's findings relating to the distribution of property because her endorsement of the final divorce decree as "seen and objected to for reasons previously stated" failed to provide a specific objection regarding the distribution of property. Williams v. Williams, 2007 Va. App. LEXIS 379 (Oct. 9, 2007).

General argument or abstract reference is insufficient to preserve issue. — Because defendant's arguments for severance of the charges under Va. Sup. Ct. R. 3A:6,á3A:10(c) relied entirely upon the assumption that the testimony defendant would have given represented exculpatory evidence on the failure to appear charge, because the arguments were unpreserved under Va. Sup. Ct. R. 5A:18, and because defendant did not preserve a complete and proper record for review, the arguments were procedurally barred. Jackson v. Commonwealth, 2008 Va. App. LEXIS 80 (Feb. 19, 2008).

Objections to sufficiency of evidence. — When considering sufficiency of evidence arguments on appeal, only specific objections advanced at trial will be considered. White v. Commonwealth, No. 1086-98-2 (Ct. of Appeals Dec. 21, 1999).

A challenge to sufficiency of the Commonwealth's evidence is waived if not raised with some specificity in the trial court. Steward v. Commonwealth, No. 2829-98-1 (Ct. of Appeals Dec. 21, 1999).

Father failed to preserve for appeal his argument that the evidence was insufficient to support a trial court's child custody decision because, although he objected generally to the sufficiency of the evidence, he failed to specify his objections; objections were required to be made with specificity in order to preserve an issue for appeal. Naaman v. Larrazabal, 2007 Va. App. LEXIS 189 (May 8, 2007).

In a case in which defendant appealed his convictions for attempted robbery and use or attempted use of a firearm in the commission of a felony, arguing that the evidence was not sufficient to convict him of the two crimes because the victim was not present and because no circumstances independent of the will of defendant interrupted him and his companions, the Commonwealth argued unsuccessfully that much of defendant's argument was not preserved pursuant to Va. Sup. Ct. R. 5A:18. While the words used in defendant's motion to strike before the trial court were somewhat different from the particular language that he used on appeal, the meaning and intention of his argument is clearly the same on appeal as the argument that he made to the trial court; therefore, his argument was preserved under Rule 5A:18. Rogers v. Commonwealth, 55 Va. App. 20, 683 S.E.2d 311, 2009 Va. App. LEXIS 449 (2009).

Although defendant did not state his objection to the sufficiency of the evidence regarding causation with the precision or particularity that was generally desirable, he did state his concern with the minimum amount of specificity necessary to fulfill the requirements of Va. Sup. Ct. R. 5A:18, in that he did reference the issue of causation in his closing argument. Johnson v. Commonwealth, 58 Va. App. 303, 709 S.E.2d 175, 2011 Va. App. LEXIS 185 (2011).

Defendant's suggestion that the testmiony regarding someone in camouflage was something that would have to go to the finder of fact and that there was no direct evidence where someone saw defendant in possession of that particular firearm was sufficient to preserve challenge to the sufficiency of the evidence for appellate review. Henderson v. Commonwealth, 2011 Va. App. LEXIS 301 (Oct. 4, 2011).

Objection preserved where patent. — Where the defendant's counsel made an unambiguous request for an assault instruction based upon the evidence, the objection was patent and the defendant's objection that the jury was not instructed as to an essential element was preserved. Martin v. Commonwealth, 13 Va. App. 524, 414 S.E.2d 401 (1992).

When no objection with specificity is made at trial, on appeal the Court of Appeals may not consider alleged error except to correct an obvious miscarriage of justice. Buchanan v. Commonwealth, No. 0960-88-3 (Ct. of Appeals May 8, 1990).

Where a defendant fails to state the alleged error with specificity to the trial court, he or she will not be heard to complain on appeal. Winter v. Commonwealth, No. 0172-96-1 (Ct. of Appeals Mar. 11, 1997).

Specificity of objections. — Counsel's endorsement of decree as "seen and objected to" gave no indication what husband's specific objections were, and endorsement was therefore insufficient to preserve question raised by husband on appeal. Yates v. Yates, No. 1282-99-3 (Ct. of Appeals Nov. 30, 1999).

Defendant's claim on appeal that his detention in connection with a search warrant was unlawful because it was effected outside the curtilage of defendant's home could not be considered as a basis for reversal of his conviction for possession of cocaine with intent to distribute and possession of a firearm while in possession of cocaine where defendant did not specifically raise the issue at trial, as required by Va. Sup. Ct. R. 5A:18 but merely alleged that his statements to police and the subsequent evidence obtained should be excluded on the grounds that the officer did not have the search warrant at the time that defendant was detained and the warrant incorrectly identified the occupant of the home to be searched. Wilson v. Commonwealth, No. 0003-04-1, 2005 Va. App. LEXIS 12 (Ct. of Appeals Jan. 11, 2005).

Defendant's objection at trial was insufficiently specific to encompass his appellate claim that the judge at sentencing erred by refusing to continue the hearing to permit sentencing by the judge who presided at trial where the extent of defendant's objection was that he was moving for a continuance to a day when the trial judge was present; further, while defendant contended that communications by the bailiff and the clerk with the jury at the sentencing phase at trial were improper, at no point during the proceedings below did defendant raise any of these arguments or contend the sentencing phase of the trial was flawed, and did not satisfy the requirements to preserve these arguments for appeal. Grandison v. Commonwealth, 2005 Va. App. LEXIS 420 (Oct. 25, 2005).

Defendant's objection to the introduction of evidence in the trial of her child endangerment case that defendant told a police officer that she was on her way to collect another child from school was specific and timely as defendant objected to the statement on the basis that the statement was not relevant to her conduct in the parking lot, which was the incident that was at issue in the case. Thus, defendant's claim of error was not waived pursuant to Va. Sup. Ct. R. 5A:18. Wood v. Commonwealth, 57 Va. App. 286, 701 S.E.2d 810, 2010 Va. App. LEXIS 454 (2010).

Defendant's challenge to the admission of the challenged statements under the confrontation clause of the Sixth Amendment was not a basis for reversal, as defendant failed to preserve the issue for review by making a specific, timely objection at trial. Perry v. Commonwealth, 58 Va. App. 655, 712 S.E.2d 765, 2011 Va. App. LEXIS 262 (2011).

Defendant's objection did not specifically present the question of prejudice to the trial judge where the defense counsel objected to a photo of a heart, saying "I don't think it adds anything." Carmouche v. Commonwealth, No. 1757-92-4 (Ct. of Appeals Mar. 15, 1994).

Issue not raised with sufficient specificity. — Where defendant's objection at trial went to qualifications of expert to give opinion, not admissibility of opinion on an ultimate issue of fact, Court of Appeals would not address the latter issue. Neale v. Commonwealth, No. 1822-98-3, 1997 Va. App. LEXIS 619 (Ct. of Appeals Sept. 28, 1999).

Without a complete transcript or written statement of facts from a commissioner's hearing concerning the wife's spousal support, the appellate court had no knowledge of the arguments subsequently made by husband to a trial court. Bryan v. Bryan, No. 1919-02-1, 2002 Va. App. LEXIS 662 (Ct. of Appeals Nov. 5, 2002).

Commonwealth had a limited right to appeal the trial court's granting of defendant's motion to suppress, but the trial court's judgment had to be affirmed, as the Commonwealth's argument that the motion to suppress should not have been denied because the evidence showed that there was probable cause to make an arrest and to search incident to that arrest had to be rejected because that objection to the granting of the motion to suppress had not been raised in the trial court and, therefore, could not be considered for the first time on appeal. Commonwealth v. Flythe, No. 0759-03-1, 2003 Va. App. LEXIS 410 (Ct. of Appeals July 18, 2003).

Appellate court could not review defendant's conviction for using profane/vulgar language over the telephone, as defendant's appeal presented three specific objections why the evidence was insufficient to support his conviction, but defendant never presented those objections to the trial court; rather, defendant merely presented a general insufficiency of the evidence argument at trial and, thus, his specific objections raised for the first time on appeal were procedurally barred. Strong v. Commonwealth, No. 0926-02-2, 2003 Va. App. LEXIS 458 (Ct. of Appeals Sept. 2, 2003).

Sentence imposed by a trial court in revoking defendant's suspended sentence was affirmed on appeal because defense counsel failed to properly object to the sentence imposed by the trial court or to state the grounds for such an objection but merely questioned whether the trial court's failure to credit defendant with time already served was appropriate. Widdifield v. Commonwealth, 43 Va. App. 559, 600 S.E.2d 159, 2004 Va. App. LEXIS 379 (2004).

Appellate court could not address the underlying issues asserted by a husband premised on dismissal order entered by the juvenile and domestic relations court, where the husband failed to preserve for appeal any issue concerning support and visitation through a specific statement of objections; thus, dismissal was summarily affirmed. Hernandez v. Pao, Nos. 1017-04-4, 1018-04-4, 2004 Va. App. LEXIS 475 (Ct. of Appeals Oct. 5, 2004).

Because a mother never made an objection or argument to the trial court on the grounds that the court made its decision on a "compelling reason" standard instead of a "best interests" standard, and there was no appreciable difference between the broad statement, "seen and objected to" and mother's broad endorsement, "objected to for reasons argued at trial and in plaintiff's memorandum of law," particularly since none of the issues raised by the mother in the memorandum or at trial related to her claim on appeal that the court made its decision on a "compelling reason" standard instead of a "best interests" standard, said action was insufficient to preserve the mother's argument for appeal. Newsome v. Neary, 2005 Va. App. LEXIS 328 (Aug. 30, 2005).

Because a husband's opening brief did not direct the appellate court to the place in the record where he stated the reasons for his objection to the trial court's property distribution, in accordance with Va. Sup. Ct. R. 5A:20(c), the husband did not preserve the objections for review under Va. Sup. Ct. R. 5A:18. Huffman v. Huffman, 2005 Va. App. LEXIS 369 (Sept. 27, 2005).

Father did not make a specific, contemporaneous objection to the trial court's failure to make explicit findings regarding a material change in circumstances before the trial court transferred custody of the mother and father's minor child to the mother, and, thus, the father did not properly preserve that issue for appeal. Reid v. Reid, 2006 Va. App. LEXIS 317 (July 18, 2006).

Because a husband's endorsement of an order denying his motion for a reduction in or termination of his spousal support as "seen and objected to" was insufficient to alert the trial court to any of his claimed errors on appeal, and absent any allegation that an exception to Va. Sup. Ct. R. 5A:18 applied, the appeals court refused to assume that the husband's objection and reasons were proffered but not made a part of the record, as required by Va. Sup. Ct. R. 5A:8. As a result, his appeal lacked merit, entitling his ex-wife to her attorney's fees and costs, including any attorney's fees and costs incurred at the remand hearing Williams v. Williams, 2007 Va. App. LEXIS 415 (Nov. 20, 2007).

Defendant's claim that a trial court erred in violating her constitutional right to confront a confidential informant who was not present at trial was procedurally barred because defendant only offered a general hearsay objection at trial and she neither alleged nor sought a ruling as to a Confrontation Clause violation. Corsaro v. Commonwealth, 2007 Va. App. LEXIS 488 (Nov. 6, 2007).

Husband did not argue in the husband's pleadings in a divorce case, as the husband did on appeal, that the trial court erroneously included certain items as part of the wife's living expenses in calculating spousal support nor did the husband assert in the husband's pleadings that the trial court erroneously calculated the parties' gross incomes when determining child support. Since the husband did not raise the required specific and timely objection required by Va. Sup. Ct. R. 5A:18, the appellate court could not consider those issues on appeal. Eisert v. Eisert, 2008 Va. App. LEXIS 134 (Mar. 18, 2008).

Appellate court would not consider an argument on appeal which was not presented to the trial court, and a review of the appendix pages, and the exceptions and objections cited by the appellant, failed to show that the appellant made a specific argument at trial. Duke v. Duke, 2008 Va. App. LEXIS 258 (May 27, 2008).

Grandmother's "seen and objected to" endorsement did not specify her objections to the findings that the mother voluntarily relinquished the child and that the mother was immature and was not sufficient to preserve the grandmother's issues for appeal, pursuant to Va. Sup. Ct. R. 5A:18, of the decision awarding custody of her grandchild to the putative adoptive mother. Jones v. Jones, 2008 Va. App. LEXIS 366 (July 29, 2008).

Even assuming counsel's objection could be construed to question the trial court's earlier ruling on the scope of cross-examination (rather than merely a comment on the weight of the victim's testimony), pursuant to Va. Sup. Ct. R. 5A:18, the stated objection did not raise with specificity a Sixth Amendment Confrontation Clause argument. Golden v. Commonwealth, 2009 Va. App. LEXIS 69 (Feb. 10, 2009).

In a conviction of felony receipt of stolen goods, defendant failed to preserve his claim regarding the sufficiency of the evidence regarding the value of the goods because in his motion to strike the charge, which he summarily renewed after presenting evidence in his case in chief, defendant only challenged whether the evidence showed that he knowingly received stolen property with dishonest intent, but he never questioned the value of the stolen items or sought to discredit the testimony of the Commonwealth's witness on this matter. Palmer v. Commonwealth, 2009 Va. App. LEXIS 533 (Dec. 1, 2009).

Defendant was precluded under Va. Sup. Ct. R. 5A:18 from claiming an error regarding a requested jury instruction because he did not make the same argument for the inclusion of the requested instruction at trial. Patillo v. Commonwealth, 2010 Va. App. LEXIS 14 (Jan. 12, 2010).

Defendant's failure to raise objection's to the denial of a motion to strike the Commonwealth's evidence at trial precluded appellate review; the "ends of justice" exception did not apply. Parker v. Commonwealth, 2010 Va. App. LEXIS 252 (June 22, 2010).

Va. Sup. Ct. R. 5A:18 precluded the court of appeals from considering a father's argument that the trial court erred in allowing a Child Protective Services worker to give her opinion as to why Child Protective Services amended its findings concerning the identity of an abuser and further give her opinion that the father abused his children because although the father objected to the mother's question to the worker about whether she believed that the father was the abuser, the father's objection was that the question was leading; the father did not object to the worker answering the question because it was a conclusion of law, which was what he argued for the first time in his brief. Olson v. Conlon, 2010 Va. App. LEXIS 374 (Sept. 21, 2010).

Issue raised sufficiently for court's consideration. — After the trial court ruled, defense counsel noted an exception to the ruling, but did not object specifically to the standard used by the court in deciding sentence. However, before the trial court ruled, defense counsel had cited cases and argued his position regarding the proper standard to be used to the trial judge. Thus, the issue was adequately raised for the trial court's consideration, and the appellate court was not barred from considering the issue on appeal. Draper v. Commonwealth, No. 1385-93-3 (Ct. of Appeals Dec. 6, 1994).

Appellant preserved for appeal his argument that the victim's pretrial statement was Brady information. Appellant's Brady argument was absent from his written motion for a new trial. However, during oral argument on his motion, appellant's counsel stated that he considered the pretrial statement to be "Brady material." Because the trial court was sufficiently placed on notice of this ground for appellant's motion for a new trial, this rule did not bar the court's consideration of it on appeal. Roark v. Commonwealth, No. 2544-96-2 (Ct. of Appeals Sept. 23, 1997).

The combination of oral argument reduced to transcript and an objection noted by the trial court in the final decree was sufficient to make known husband's objection to the valuation of his business. Street v. Street, No. 1940-95-4 (Ct. of Appeals Jan. 21, 1997).

Exchange, albeit brief, preserved issue for appeal where it was sufficient to inform trial court of defendant's belief that convictions for unlawful wounding and use of a firearm in the commission of a malicious wounding were inconsistent. Akers v. Commonwealth, 31 Va. App. 521, 525 S.E.2d 13 (2000).

Wife properly objected to trial court's order requiring wife to execute a qualified domestic relations order mandating a transfer of funds to the ex-husband and to pay ex-husband's attorney's fees and costs, thus preserving the issue for appeal. McManus v. Neuschulz, No. 0731-02-4, 2002 Va. App. LEXIS 695 (Ct. of Appeals Nov. 19, 2002).

While the defendant did not specifically use the words "public confidence" at trial as a ground for striking a prospective juror for cause, the defendant did ask the trial court to strike the juror for cause based on the juror's relationship with the county sheriff's department and the information the juror received from members of that department. Therefore, the issue of public confidence was not procedurally barred on appeal. Patterson v. Commonwealth, 39 Va. App. 658, 576 S.E.2d 222, 2003 Va. App. LEXIS 38 (2003).

In a criminal prosecution for attempted capital murder for hire and solicitation of capital murder for hire, defendant requested the Commonwealth to elect between the charges and renewed his motion after the jury announced its verdict. Defendant's objections at trial satisfied Va. Sup. Ct. R. 5A:18 and the issue was preserved for review. Ashford v. Commonwealth, 47 Va. App. 676, 626 S.E.2d 464, 2006 Va. App. LEXIS 70 (2006).

Record sufficiently showed that a father specifically voiced his objection to the appropriate court at the appropriate time for purposes of appeal; the father moved the the juvenile and domestic relations district court to reconsider the custody order, and filed a motion to modify the entry date of the custody order in the circuit court, requesting the circuit court to grant leave to appeal and adjust the computation of time of the entry of the order, for appeal purposes only. Eklund v. Eklund, 2011 Va. App. LEXIS 171 (May 17, 2011).

Father preserved his arguments for appeal because he laid out a specific argument in the trial court that he pursued on appeal; the trial court addressed father's arguments in the letter opinion and final order, and the father's appeal was based on the trial court's rulings on his arguments. McPhail v. McPhail, 2012 Va. App. LEXIS 301 (Sept. 25, 2012).

Father properly complied with Va. Sup. Ct. R. 5A:18 and properly preserved his issue for appeal because the father made the trial court aware of his position; the father filed written pleadings setting forth his objections and arguments, and he made clear the grounds for his objections in his closing argument. Moncrief v. Div. of Child Support Enforcement ex rel. Joyner, 60 Va. App. 721, 732 S.E.2d 714, 2012 Va. App. LEXIS 320 (2012).

Issue not supported by law or evidence. — Because a wife's claim that the parties had lived together within the time period allowed by §§ 20-91 and 20-121.02, the claim was unpreserved and barred by Va. Sup. Ct. R. 5A:18; because the wife's case was not supported by law or evidence, the husband was entitled to attorney's fees and costs. Mayo v. Mayo, 2006 Va. App. LEXIS 443 (Oct. 10, 2006).

III. ENDS OF JUSTICE.

Requirements. — Ends of justice exception to rule barring review where no timely objection was made requires that the record must affirmatively show that a miscarriage of justice has occurred, not merely might have occurred; therefore exception does not apply where record fails to show that trial court mistakenly convicted defendant in child sodomy case for animate object penetration rather than inanimate object penetration. Marshall v. Commonwealth, 26 Va. App. 627, 496 S.E.2d 120 (1998).

For the "ends of justice" exception to apply, defendant must prove that a miscarriage of justice has actually occurred. Jonathan v. Commonwealth, No. 1983-98-1 (Ct. of Appeals Nov. 9, 1999); See also. Jennings v. Commonwealth, No. 2848-00-2, 2001 Va. App. LEXIS 664 (Ct. of Appeals Dec. 4, 2001).

Application of the ends of justice exception requires proof of an error that was clear, substantial and material. Akers v. Commonwealth, 31 Va. App. 521, 525 S.E.2d 13 (2000).

The "ends of justice" exception to this rule is narrow and is to be used sparingly. A defendant must affirmatively show that a miscarriage of justice has occurred, not that a miscarriage might have occurred. Kost v. Kost, No. 0116-99-1 (Ct. of Appeals Dec. 14, 1999).

To satisfy the burden of establishing that a miscarriage of justice has occurred in a criminal prosecution, a defendant must show more than that the Commonwealth failed to prove an element of the offense; the defendant must demonstrate that he was convicted for conduct that was not a criminal offense or the record must affirmatively prove that an element of the offense did not occur. Lima v. Commonwealth, No. 1263-99-3, 2000 Va. App. LEXIS 344 (Ct. of Appeals May 9, 2000).

Claim that the imposition of a two-year term of post release supervision under § 19.2-295.2 violated the separation of powers doctrine was barred by Va. Sup Ct. R. 5A:18 where defendant failed to make his argument before the trial court. The ends of justice exception to Rule 5A:18 did not apply where defendant did not show that a miscarriage of justice actually occurred. Fitzpatrick v. Commonwealth, 2008 Va. App. LEXIS 52 (Feb. 5, 2008).

"Ends of justice" exception not applicable. — Ends of justice exception to the requirement that an appellate issue be first raised before the trial court did not apply to a defendant's objection to being bound and gagged before the jury at the penalty phase of his trial, after he had been disruptive. Showalter v. Commonwealth, No. 1718-00-3, 2001 Va. App. LEXIS 642 (Ct. of Appeals Nov. 20, 2001).

Ends of justice exception to the requirement to first raise an appellate issue before the trial court did not apply when the trial court brought a defendant who had requested to proceed pro se before it, without his appointed standby counsel, to advise him against proceeding pro se. Showalter v. Commonwealth, No. 1718-00-3, 2001 Va. App. LEXIS 642 (Ct. of Appeals Nov. 20, 2001).

Father's appeal from a contempt order for the father's failure to provide support, was properly dismissed, as the father failed to raise the issues contained in the opening brief as required by Rule 5A:18, and the record reflected no reason to invoke the good cause or ends of justice exceptions. Switzer v. Smith, No. 0779-02-3, 2002 Va. App. LEXIS 648 (Ct. of Appeals Oct. 29, 2002).

Neither the issue of whether the trial court should have considered the home study reports that had not been admitted into evidence, nor the issue of custody of the daughter born during the parties' separation, would be considered under the "ends of justice" exception, because the home studies did not have an effect on the outcome of the case and the custody determination did not involve a miscarriage of justice. Broccuto v. Broccuto, No. 0661-02-1, 2002 Va. App. LEXIS 651 (Ct. of Appeals Oct. 29, 2002).

Trial court did not err in awarding sole custody of children to the mother and not the father, as the trial court stated that the award was based on the evidence presented and the best interests of the children, and the evidence presented by the mother and the social worker related to the enumerated factors in § 20-124.3 and supported the trial court's sole custody award to the mother; thus, the record did not reflect any reason to invoke the good cause or ends of justice exceptions. Gaione v. Gaione, No. 1315-02-2, 2002 Va. App. LEXIS 692 (Ct. of Appeals Nov. 19, 2002).

"Ends of justice" exception was inapplicable to allow defendant to assert for the first time on appeal a claim that the evidence was insufficient to establish the corpus delicti of rape, as his confession was corroborated by testimony that he had been seen kissing and lying in bed with the 11-year-old victim. Navarrette v. Commonwealth, No. 0403-01-4, 2002 Va. App. LEXIS 590 (Ct. of Appeals Oct. 8, 2002).

Rule 5A:18 precluded the consideration of mother's due process and substantial justice claims arising from the denial of her motion for unsupervised visitation with her son and for court-ordered therapy as her arguments were not presented to the trial court; neither the good cause nor ends of justice exceptions applied. Rutledge v. Rutledge, No. 1961-02-4, 2003 Va. App. LEXIS 78 (Ct. of Appeals Feb. 19, 2003).

Victim's detention was separate and apart from the restraint employed in the taking indecent liberties with a minor and object sexual penetration offenses, and the "ends of justice" exception in Rule 5A:18 did not apply; defendant's sufficiency argument was improper. Dade v. Commonwealth, No. 2042-02-1, 2003 Va. App. LEXIS 368 (Ct. of Appeals June 24, 2003).

When a grandmother argued in her appeal of the denial of her petition for visitation with her granddaughter that the trial court applied the wrong standard, this claim was not considered because it had not been raised before the trial court, and, as the trial court applied the correct standard, there was no reason to invoke the good cause or ends of justice exceptions to Rule 5A:18. Harris v. Boxler, No. 0604-03-3, 2003 Va. App. LEXIS 461 (Ct. of Appeals Sept. 2, 2003).

Where the defendant contended that the police did not have grounds to arrest him under § 19.2-81 and his arrest and detention were unlawful, but failed to properly preserve this issue at trial, this precluded review under Rule 5A:18 and the ends of justice exception did not apply. Benton v. Commonwealth, 40 Va. App. 136, 578 S.E.2d 74, 2003 Va. App. LEXIS 150 (2003).

Where defendant asserted on appeal that the trial court made a finding before all of the evidence was presented and that the trial court abandoned the presumption of innocence when the trial court stopped the Commonwealth's questioning of the investigator, who was giving an expert opinion as to whether defendant was selling the drugs in the bag or whether defendant was personally using them, and asked the relevance of the issue given that the investigator saw defendant selling the drugs out of the bag when this fact had not yet been entered into evidence, defendant's argument was waived pursuant to Rule 5A:18, as defendant did not object on this ground at trial, instead defendant merely pointed out the trial court's error of fact; the good cause and ends of justice exception was inapplicable, because the trial court, which conceded its error, was concerned about the cumulative nature of the evidence, and it did not abandon the presumption of innocence. Martin v. Commonwealth, No. 1484-03-1, 2004 Va. App. LEXIS 122 (Ct. of Appeals Mar. 23, 2004).

Defendant did not preserve claim that double jeopardy barred him from being convicted on both involuntary manslaughter and aggravated involuntary manslaughter, as defendant did not, when objecting to his convictions, inform the trial court that he objected on general constitutional or double jeopardy grounds, and, thus, he did not make a specifically sufficient statement of his objection such that his claim could be reviewed on appeal; too, because the alleged error was not "clear, substantial, and material" and the record did not show that a miscarriage of justice had occurred, the "ends of justice" exception to the waiver rule did not apply. West v. Commonwealth, 43 Va. App. 327, 597 S.E.2d 274, 2004 Va. App. LEXIS 276 (2004).

Ends of justice did not require an appellate court to address the issue of an alleged trial court error on defendant's appeal of his sexual battery conviction where defendant failed to affirmatively show that a miscarriage of justice had occurred; defendant's argument that the trial court erred in preliminarily instructing the jury that it was permitted to accept or disregard all or part of the testimony of the alleged victim was barred on appeal as a result of defendant's failure to make any objection at trial to the rulings of the trial court. Yarborough v. Commonwealth, No. 0352-03-4, 2004 Va. App. LEXIS 186 (Ct. of Appeals Mar. 2, 2004).

To compel a trial judge to give a cautionary instruction in the face of defense counsel's express request that he not do so would compromise the trial court's objectivity and interfere with the prerogative of trial counsel to the detriment of the adversarial system. The ends-of-justice exception, therefore, cannot be invoked under these circumstances. Thomas v. Commonwealth, 44 Va. App. 741, 607 S.E.2d 738, 2005 Va. App. LEXIS 31 (2005).

Defendant's argument that the trial court's perjury warnings given to her alibi witnesses violated her Sixth Amendment right to call witnesses was not preserved for review and did not rise to the level necessary to invoke the ends of justice exception to Va. Sup. Ct. R. 5A:18. Because of the overwhelming evidence against her, defendant did not demonstrate that the error was a "clear, substantial, and material" error which created a grave injustice. Dasey v. Commonwealth, 2005 Va. App. LEXIS 454 (Nov. 15, 2005).

Omission of the intent element from a finding instruction did not require reversal of defendant's conviction for damaging property under § 18.2-137 because defendant did not object to the finding instruction, the verdict form, or the sentencing instruction, and the verdict correctly included the intent element; the ends of justice exception to Va. Sup. Ct. R. 5A:18 did not apply because the evidence was overwhelming that defendant acted intentionally when he threw a brick through a window. Perry v. Commonwealth, 2006 Va. App. LEXIS 270 (June 20, 2006).

Wife's appeal of an order enjoining her from proceeding with her Massachusetts divorce action was summarily affirmed; although Va. Sup. Ct. R. 5A:18 provided for consideration of a ruling that was not objected to at trial to enable the appellate court to attain the ends of justice, no reason was found to invoke the ends of justice exception. Cherin v. Cherin, 2006 Va. App. LEXIS 462 (Oct. 17, 2006).

Because the police found a concealed weapon in defendant's possession that, as a convicted felon, defendant could not lawfully carry in a concealed manner, and because defendant failed to prove that a miscarriage of justice had occurred after failing to preserve a claim, Va. Sup. Ct. R. 5A:18 barred review of the issue. Davis v. Commonwealth, 2006 Va. App. LEXIS 444 (Oct. 10, 2006).

Defendant's contention that the trial court erred in entering the jury room to answer a written question the jury posed about sentencing was waived and would not be considered the "ends-of-justice" exception to the requirement that objections to be reviewed on appeal had to be raised at trial; defendant and defense counsel's silence when the trial court asked whether the response should be phrased in open court with the jury or whether the trial court could step into the jury room and respond meant defendant on appeal was trying to take advantage of an error for which he was responsible since his failure to object at trial and his subsequent objection on appeal was inviting error and then trying to benefit from it, which the appellate court would not allow. Pope v. Commonwealth, 2006 Va. App. LEXIS 500 (Nov. 7, 2006).

Because the court was unable to determine that a miscarriage of justice occurred under the facts and circumstances of the case, the court did not consider the merits of defendant's due process claim under the ends of justice exception to Va. Sup. Ct. R. 5A:18 when defendant had failed to raise the issue of prosecution vindictiveness at trial. Wolford v. Commonwealth, 2006 Va. App. LEXIS 513 (Nov. 14, 2006).

Appellate court declined to grant relief to defendant under the "ends of justice" exception to Va. Sup. Ct. R. 5A:18 where defendant contended on appeal that the trial court erred in imposing two years of prison upon defendant and resuspended three years of defendant's original five-year sentence after defendant violated the terms of that five-year suspended sentence; defendant did not object in the trial court when the trial court entered a sentencing order that failed to grant defendant credit for time defendant spent in a diversion program and defendant did not affirmatively show that a miscarriage of justice occurred, especially since the time defendant would have served, two years in prison and three years resuspended, did not exceed the originally imposed five-year sentence. Goode v. Commonwealth, 2007 Va. App. LEXIS 118 (Mar. 27, 2007).

Because the record contained ample credible evidence to support the trial judge's finding under § 16.1-283 that a father's substance abuse rendered his residence unsafe for his child, the "ends of justice" exception to Va. Sup. Ct. R. 5A:18 did not require consideration of the father's argument on appeal. Ridley v. Chesapeake Dep't of Human Servs., 2007 Va. App. LEXIS 167 (Apr. 24, 2007).

Even assuming that defendant's right against double jeopardy was violated, the "ends of justice exception" did not apply because defendant failed to preserve the issue for appeal under Va. Sup. Ct. R. 5A:18. Tinsley v. Commonwealth, 2007 Va. App. LEXIS 207 (May 15, 2007).

Attorney's joint representation of defendant and her husband in a criminal case did not impose a duty on the trial court to raise a conflict of interest issue sua sponte; the conflict issue was not raised in the trial court, and, because defendant failed to point to any particular manifestation of a specific conflict, the ends of justice exception to Va. Sup. Ct. R. 5A:18 did not apply. Despite defendant's denial, her appeal clearly raised an ineffective assistance of counsel claim, which could not have been considered on direct appeal. Kilby v. Commonwealth, 2007 Va. App. LEXIS 364 (Ct. of Appeals Oct. 2, 2007).

Where defendant failed to object to jury instruction's definition of firearm and the definition that included a BB gun was correct under § 18.2-53.1, the issue was procedurally defaulted on appeal and no miscarriage of justice warranted application of "ends of justice" exception to Va. Sup Ct. R. 5A:18. Wubneh v. Commonwealth, 51 Va. App. 224, 656 S.E.2d 418, 2008 Va. App. LEXIS 56 (2008), overruled in part by Startin v. Commonwealth, 56 Va. App. 26, 690 S.E.2d 310, 2010 Va. App. LEXIS 115 (2010).

Because defendant did not ask the trial court to voir dire the jurors during the trial or allege any specific misconduct by any juror in discussing the case with someone outside of the jury room, those issues were not properly and timely raised; the court of appeals declined to apply the ends of justice exception to Va. Sup. Ct. R. 5A:18 because defendant failed to identify any alleged error to which the "good cause" or "ends of justice" exceptions applied. Nixon v. Commonwealth, 2008 Va. App. LEXIS 148 (Mar. 25, 2008).

Given that the record on appeal adequately demonstrated that the sentencing judge correctly understood his discretion and sentenced defendant within the lawful scope of that discretion, the Court of Appeals of Virginia declined to apply the ends of justice exception to Va. Sup. Ct. R. 5A:18. Scalf v. Commonwealth, 2008 Va. App. LEXIS 230 (May 13, 2008).

Defendant was not entitled to invoke the ends of justice exception to Va. Sup. Ct. R. 5A:18 after failing to object to jurisdiction based on absence of arraignment and entry of pleas, because the trial court's order referring the matter for a presentence report recited that defendant appeared in person and waived arraignment. Dizon v. Commonwealth, 2008 Va. App. LEXIS 507 (Nov. 18, 2008).

Ends of justice exception did not apply to defendant's challenge to the credit card theft conviction, because defendant did not claim that the conduct for which defendant was convicted was not a crime, nor did defendant contend that the record affirmatively proved that defendant lacked the requisite intent. Hollie v. Commonwealth, 2009 Va. App. LEXIS 5 (Jan. 13, 2009).

Defendant's attempt to invoke the ends of justice exception to Va. Sup. Ct. R. 5A:18 failed, because the evidence showed defendant signed a written plea agreement and verbally acknowledged that defendant understood the charges, had spoken with counsel, and had the right to a jury trial. Thus, the record showed that defendant voluntarily, intelligently, and knowingly entered the nolo contendere plea. Vesley v. Commonwealth, 2009 Va. App. LEXIS 49 (Feb. 3, 2009).

Court of appeals declined to apply the ends of justice exception to defendant's claim that the trial court erred by convicting him of seven counts of forgery based upon multiple signatures on two documents in violation of § 18.2-168 because an allegation that defendant's guarantee against double jeopardy could have been violated was not enough to invoke the ends of justice exception to Va. Sup. Ct. R. 5A:18; each of the signatures documented a separate transaction, either the receipt or return of property, and,therefore, had a separate existence with separate consequences. Word v. Commonwealth, No. 2660-07-3, 2009 Va. App. LEXIS 330 (Ct. of Appeals July 21, 2009).

Court of appeals declined to apply the ends of justice exception to defendant's claim that certain documents were not public records within the meaning of § 18.2-168 because jail/annex property issued/returned sheets, police department advice of rights forms, advice of right form, and written statement to the police were all public records; those documents were made in connection with transaction of public business, admitting a prisoner to jail and investigating a crime, and were made by an authorized public officer to serve as evidence of things that were written, said or done, the receipt of defendant's personal property at the jail and the distribution of jail property to defendant in the context of the property records, or legal proof that defendant had been advised of his Miranda rights and had given a statement to the police. Word v. Commonwealth, No. 2660-07-3, 2009 Va. App. LEXIS 330 (Ct. of Appeals July 21, 2009).

In an appeal of a child custody and visitation order in which a father did not comply with Va. Sup. Ct. R. 5A:18 as to three issues and a question that he raised on appeal, he had not preserved them for appeal, and his failure to comply with rule 5A:18 was fatal. There was no miscarriage of justice, and the ends of justice exception did not apply. Libron v. Branch, 2009 Va. App. LEXIS 371 (Aug. 18, 2009).

As defendant did not raise a challenge to the a petit larceny, third offense sentence under §§ 18.2-103 and 18.2-104 below, and because the sentence to to five years of imprisonment with three years' suspended was not excessive on its face, there was no reason to invoke the ends of justice exception under Va. Sup. Ct. R. 5A:18. Brittle v. Commonwealth, 54 Va. App. 505, 680 S.E.2d 335, 2009 Va. App. LEXIS 359 (2009).

Defendant's failure to object to the introduction of the prior convictions and failure to challenge the sufficiency of the evidence precluded appellate review of defendant's third offense petit larceny conviction under §§ 18.2-103 and 18.2-104 as: (1) Va. Sup. Ct. R. 5A:18 did not apply as defendant did not dispute that defendant concealed steaks in a grocery store, or challenge a 2005 order stating that defendant pled guilty to second offense petit larceny; (2) although the two 1997 orders did not prove the convictions, they did not establish the non-existence of the predicate offenses; (3) the pre-sentence report proved that defendant was sentenced in 1993 for petit larceny; and (4) defendant did not show that an element of the offense did not occur or that he was convicted of a non-offense. Brittle v. Commonwealth, 54 Va. App. 505, 680 S.E.2d 335, 2009 Va. App. LEXIS 359 (2009).

Father claimed that the Virginia Department of Social Services (DSS) committed reversible error by not tape recording the interviews with the alleged victim, conceded that the issue was not preserved at trial but asserted there is good cause shown and the ends of justice exception to Va. Sup. Ct. R. 5A:18 applied; however, because the law applicable to the father's claim that the DSS interviews with the minor should have been recorded did not change, the court could not find that the ends of justice or good cause exceptions to Rule 5A:18 allowed the appellate court's consideration of the issue on appeal. Comm'r v. Fulton, 55 Va. App. 69, 683 S.E.2d 837, 2009 Va. App. LEXIS 464 (2009).

Defendant's argument that the evidence was not sufficient to corroborate her confession was not properly before the court of appeals because the issue was not raised in the trial court; although defendant asked the court of appeals to apply the ends of justice exception, the application of the exception was not warranted because the record did not show affirmative evidence of innocence or lack of a criminal offense. Durand v. Commonwealth, 2009 Va. App. LEXIS 419 (Sept. 22, 2009).

In a case in which: (1) at trial, defendant objected to the witness's testimony identifying the victim of the attempted robbery; (2) he specifically stated that his objection did not apply to his conspiracy and use of a firearm during the commission of a felony charges; and (3) on appeal, defendant argued that the appellate court should apply either the ends of justice or the good cause shown exceptions to Va. Sup. Ct. R. 5A:18 so that he was not punished for his counsel's error at trial, he made no argument as to why either exception was applicable. Nothing in the record indicated that defendant was convicted for conduct that was not a criminal offense or the record affirmatively proved that an element of the offense did not occur; similarly, nothing indicated why the good cause shown exception was applicable. Drew v. Commonwealth, 2009 Va. App. LEXIS 415 (Sept. 22, 2009).

Defendant's sentences after he was convicted of leaving the scene of an accident in which a person was killed, driving under the influence of drugs, driving on a suspended license (third or subsequent offense), and possession of more than one-half ounce but not more than five pounds of marijuana with the intent to distribute were appropriate because, by failing to object to either the written victim impact statements or the corresponding testimony at the time they were tendered to the trial court, defendant waived any argument with respect to their admissibility on appeal. Additionally, the "ends of justice" exception was inapplicable because he did not establish that the conduct for which he was convicted was not a criminal offense, nor that the sentence imposed exceeded the statutory limitations. Tillery v. Commonwealth, 2010 Va. App. LEXIS 213 (May 25, 2010).

Defendant was not able to show that the conviction for a lesser-included offense than that charged in the amended indictment prejudiced his defense, and the appellate court declined to invoke the ends of justice exception to Va. Sup. Ct. R. 5A:18 to set aside defendant's conviction due to his asserted constructive amendment of the indictment. Woodruff v. Commonwealth, 2010 Va. App. LEXIS 439 (Nov. 9, 2010).

Court refused to apply the ends of justice exception in Va. Sup. Ct. R. 5A:18 because defendant, who was convicted of misdemeanor child neglect when she was indicted for felony child neglect, failed to establish that she was convicted of conduct that was not a criminal offense, nor did she point to evidence that affirmatively established that an element of the offense did not occur. McKinnon v. Commonwealth, 2011 Va. App. LEXIS 372 (Nov. 29, 2011).

Virginia Sup. Ct. R. 5A:18 ends-of-justice exception was inapplicable because defendant invited the trial court's alleged error in imposing successful completion of a drug treatment court program as a condition of her suspended sentence; at sentencing, defendant asked that she be allowed to participate in the drug treatment court program with jail time over her head, and her request for leniency in sentencing was premised on her request that the trial court allow her to participate in the program. In the memorandum of plea agreement, defendant noted that the Commonwealth would not object to her participation in the program if she were accepted and if the trial court allowed her to do so, and defendant proffered evidence that she had, in fact, been accepted into the program, and that she thought she would be successful in it. Dunn-Brinkley v. Commonwealth, 2012 Va. App. LEXIS 128 (Apr. 24, 2012).

Because the record did not show that a miscarriage of justice occurred, the court would not consider under the "ends of justice" exception to Va. Sup. Ct. R. 5A:18 defendant's assertion that the trial court erred in considering letter reports from his probation officer. If defendant had objected, the trial court could have considered his objection. Vogt v. Commonwealth, 2012 Va. App. LEXIS 170 (May 22, 2012).

As defendant did not move to strike the charge of possession of a concealed weapon by a felon, he failed to preserve his claim that the evidence was insufficient to convict him. And as he claimed the prosecution failed to prove an element of the crime, i.e., that the knives he possessed were not of "like kind" to those enumerated weapons in § 18.2-308, not that there was affirmative evidence that an element of the crime did not occur, he did not show that the ends of justice exception to Va. Sup. Ct. R. 5A:18 should apply to his conviction. Massa v. Commonwealth, 2012 Va. App. LEXIS 300 (Sept. 25, 2012).

Defendant waived his non-jurisdictional challenges to the continuance of the initial hearing that put his hearing outside of the § 16.1-285.2 time constraints and the ruling that was made outside of the time constraints as he did not object at either the initial or the continued hearing; the ends of justice exception to Va. Sup. Ct. R. 5A:18 did not apply as: (1) the order revoking defendant's suspended sentence was voidable, not void as the trial court had jurisdiction; (2) the trial court scheduled and initiated a hearing on May 4, 2011, during which it granted a continuance and scheduled a date for the review hearing; and (3) both of these actions took place 28 days after the April 6, 2011, petition, and were within the § 16.1-285.2 time period for scheduling and holding the initial hearing, and scheduling the continued hearing. Edmonds v. Commonwealth, No. 1577-11-4, 2013 Va. App. LEXIS 71 (Mar. 5, 2013).

Defendant could not rely on a post-sentencing letter he sent to the trial court requesting that the sentences imposed on him for two driving violations be set to run concurrently to invoke the "ends of justice" exception, allowing him to raise a double jeopardy claim for the first time on appeal. The trial court had not considered the letter, so it was not part of the appellate record and could not be considered by the appellate court. Webb v. Commonwealth, No. 0954-12-3, 2013 Va. App. LEXIS 177 (Ct. of Appeals June 11, 2013).

Father's failure to raise any issue in the trial court of the trial court's authority to exercise its jurisdiction precluded the court's review of the issue on appeal. The father did not demonstrate any grave injustice or denial of essential rights that would occur if the court declined to address the issue on appeal. Kolmetz v. Hitchcock, No. 1464-12-2, 2013 Va. App. LEXIS 133 (Ct. of Appeals Apr. 30, 2013).

Motion to strike the evidence without specifically asserting any grounds upon which the alleged evidence was insufficient precluded defendant from raising that issue, with regard to the particular element of intent, for the first time on appeal, and finding no "good cause" supporting defendant's failure to raise the specific issue, nor justification to apply the ends of justice exception in Va. Sup. Ct. R. 5A:18, the trial court's judgment convicting him of assaulting a police officer was affirmed. Bowman v. Commonwealth, No. 2169-02-1, 2003 Va. App. LEXIS 379 (Ct. of Appeals July 1, 2003).

"Ends of justice" provision is a narrow one that allows consideration when the record affirmatively shows that a miscarriage of justice has occurred; it is not sufficient that the record show that a miscarriage of justice might have occurred. Reed v. Commonwealth, 6 Va. App. 65, 366 S.E.2d 274 (1988).

Where the error was not stated with the required specificity, yet the evidence clearly failed to show that the accused was guilty of the crime of which he or she was convicted, the court of appeals will invoke the ends of justice provision of this rule and reverse the conviction. Winter v. Commonwealth, No. 0172-96-1 (Ct. of Appeals Mar. 11, 1997).

Because errors can usually be corrected in the trial court, appellate courts will notice error for which there has been no timely objection only when necessary to satisfy the ends of justice. Redman v. Commonwealth, 25 Va. App. 215, 487 S.E.2d 269 (1997).

The ends of justice exception is narrow and is to be used sparingly when an error at trial is clear, substantial and material. Michaels v. Commonwealth, 32 Va. App. 601, 529 S.E.2d 822, 2000 Va. App. LEXIS 463 (2000). See also Clark v. Clark, No. 0827-99-2, 2000 Va. App. LEXIS 469 (Ct. of Appeals June 27, 2000).

Exception justified only when error clear, substantial, and material. — Although both this rule and Supreme Court Rule 5:25 provide exceptions to accommodate "good cause" and "obtain the ends of justice," this is justified only when the record reflects error which is clear, substantial, and material. Johnson v. Commonwealth, No. 0259-91-1 (Ct. of Appeals Nov. 10, 1992).

In this case, although the Commonwealth may have failed to prove that principal had committed a burglary and destroyed property or that the defendant knew that principal had committed the crimes, the evidence did not affirmatively show that a burglary had not occurred or that the defendant did not know that the principal had committed these acts; the Commonwealth's failure to present sufficient evidence to prove these two elements demonstrates only that a miscarriage of justice may have occurred, not that a miscarriage of justice did occur. Redman v. Commonwealth, 25 Va. App. 215, 487 S.E.2d 269 (1997).

When defendant failed to object on Confrontation Clause grounds to a detective's testimony about the victim's out-of-court identification, his Confrontation Clause argument could not be considered on appeal because it did not meet the "ends of justice" exception to Va. Sup. Ct. R. 5A:18 by establishing an error that was clear, substantial, and material. The Confrontation Clause was satisfied when a hearsay declarant testified at trial and was available for cross-examination; here, the victim testified at trial and was available for cross-examination, although defendant's counsel chose not to question him about his pretrial identification of defendant. King v. Commonwealth, 2006 Va. App. LEXIS 151 (Apr. 25, 2006).

"Ends of justice" exception applicable. — Appellant's obstruction of justice conviction was reversed because, although appellant failed to properly preserve the issue for appellate review, the "ends of justice" exception applied since a miscarriage of justice occurred because appellant could not have been convicted of violating subsection A of § 18.2-460 based solely upon appellant's flight from the scene. Yancey v. Commonwealth, 2008 Va. App. LEXIS 29 (Jan. 15, 2008).

Court of appeals invoked the ends of justice exception to defendant's claim that the trial court erred in convicting him of forging a juvenile and domestic relations district court guilty plea form because a miscarriage of justice took place, and defendant showed affirmative evidence in the record establishing that an element of the offense of forging a public document did not exist and that he did not commit the crime of forging a public record; the juvenile and domestic relations district court guilty plea form was not a public record because it was not prepared in connection with a legitimate legal proceeding, and that form was replaced with a general district court form before final judgment was entered in the general district court. Word v. Commonwealth, No. 2660-07-3, 2009 Va. App. LEXIS 330 (Ct. of Appeals July 21, 2009).

Evidence clearly and affirmatively showed that an element of one of the crimes of which defendant was convicted did not occur. Accordingly, there was error in the judgment appealed from and application of the ends of justice exception was necessary to avoid a grave injustice. Ali v. Commonwealth, 280 Va. 665, 701 S.E.2d 64, 2010 Va. LEXIS 273 (2010).

Judgment was reversed and the case was remanded for a new sentencing hearing on defendant's robbery, conspiracy, and wearing a mask in public convictions as the ends of justice exception in Va. Sup. Ct. R. 5A:18 applied because defendant was sentenced to a maximum total sentence of 33 years' in violation of § 19.2-295, when the jury imposed a maximum total sentence of 15 years of imprisonment. Gibbs v. Commonwealth, No. 1726-11-1, 2012 Va. App. LEXIS 324 (Oct. 16, 2012).

Appellate court considered defendant's challenge to defendant's sentence under the ends of justice exception to Va. Sup. Ct. R. 5A:18, because defendant failed to object to the trial court's sentencing order and the trial court imposed terms of incarceration that were beyond that authorized by law. Gordon v. Commonwealth, No. 0940-12-2, 61 Va. App. 682, 739 S.E.2d 276, 2013 Va. App. LEXIS 102 (Apr. 2, 2013).

"Ends of justice" exception inapplicable. — Since defendant invited any error in jury instructions given by the trial court by agreeing to the jury instructions he challenged on appeal, Va. Sup. Ct. R. 5A:18's ends-of-justice exception was inapplicable. Lucas v. Commonwealth, No. 0805-11-2, 2012 Va. App. LEXIS 411 (Dec. 18, 2012).

Sentence exceeding that set by jury a manifest injustice. — A manifest injustice occurred justifying consideration of the issue on appeal even though not objected to at trial where the trial court sentenced a defendant to a term in excess of that fixed by the jury. Williams v. Commonwealth, No. 1114-00-2, 2001 Va. App. LEXIS 334 (Ct. of Appeals June 12, 2001).

Possibility of miscarriage of justice insufficient. — See Lima v. Commonwealth, No. 1263-99-3, 2000 Va. App. LEXIS 344 (Ct. of Appeals May 9, 2000).

Defendant was not entitled to review of his claims that his Fifth Amendment and Va. Const., Art. I, § 8, rights to remain silent and his privilege against self-incrimination were violated under the ends of justice exception to Rule 5A:18 as the evidence showed only that a miscarriage of justice might have occurred where: (1) defense counsel did not object to the testimony, (2) a deputy sheriff testified that defendant was not questioned and did not make a statement, (3) however, the evidence of defendant's guilt was not limited to his silence as the deputy sheriff also testified that defendant hung his head when the spoon was seized, and (4) this was conduct that the jury could have found sufficient to support a knowing possession. Day v. Commonwealth, No. 0193-03-2, 2004 Va. App. LEXIS 50 (Ct. of Appeals Feb. 3, 2004).

To satisfy this burden, an appellant must show more than that the Commonwealth failed to prove an element of the offense; the appellant must demonstrate that he or she was convicted for conduct that was not a criminal offense, or the record must affirmatively prove that an element of the offense did not occur. Young v. Commonwealth, No. 0007-03-3, 2004 Va. App. LEXIS 323 (Ct. of Appeals July 13, 2004).

Voidable order valid until set aside. — The ends of justice exception to the rule does not negate the principle that a voidable order remains valid until set aside. Green v. Commonwealth, No. 1724-97-3 (Ct. of Appeals Nov. 24, 1998).

Failure to reduce terms to writing or disclose in open court. — "Ends of justice" did not require review of the failure to reduce terms of the plea agreement to writing or disclose it in open court where the defendant's substantial rights were not implicated by the fact that the plea agreement was not in writing or disclosed in open court and the record showed that the terms of the plea agreement were fully presented to the trial court and that the defendant acknowledged that the oral presentation of the plea agreement was consistent with his understanding of the agreement. Hairston v. Commonwealth, 16 Va. App. 941, 434 S.E.2d 350 (1993).

When "the ends of justice" require consideration of issue for first time on appeal. — Under what circumstances "the ends of justice" require the Supreme Court to consider an issue for the first time on appeal depends upon whether a miscarriage of justice has clearly occurred. Mounce v. Commonwealth, 4 Va. App. 433, 357 S.E.2d 742 (1987).

The "ends of justice" provision may be used when the record affirmatively shows that a miscarriage of justice has occurred, not when it merely shows that a miscarriage might have occurred. Obviously, the applicability of this exception cannot be determined on the mere assertion of the general rule, but necessarily requires the review of the record. Johnson v. Commonwealth, 5 Va. App. 529, 365 S.E.2d 237 (1988).

When defendant was convicted of two violations of § 46.2-894, requiring him to stop and render assistance in an accident in which he was involved, because there were two occupants injured in a vehicle he caused to go off the road, this was a miscarriage of justice, because defendant was convicted twice for conduct that was but one criminal offense, so his failure to object did not bar the appellate court, under Va. Sup. Ct. R. 5A:18, from finding that the ends of justice exception to that Rule applied. Tooke v. Commonwealth, 47 Va. App. 759, 627 S.E.2d 533, 2006 Va. App. LEXIS 110 (2006).

Although defendant failed to contemporaneously object to the trial court's imposition of a ten-year incarceration for a use of a firearm conviction, the ends of justice exception applied because the sentence imposed was in excess of that prescribed by law and denying defendant her liberty on the basis of a void sentence would have imposed a grave injustice upon her. Hines v. Commonwealth, 59 Va. App. 567, 721 S.E.2d 792, 2012 Va. App. LEXIS 45 (2012).

Where the defendant was sentenced for a crime other than that for which he was convicted, and the error was clear, material and substantial and the error was so contrary to fundamental notions of justice that to permit it to pass uncorrected would seriously undermine the integrity of the judicial system, and the ends of justice exception permits redress in those limited instances of obvious injustice. Brown v. Commonwealth, 8 Va. App. 126, 380 S.E.2d 8 (1989).

A miscarriage of justice occurred when the trial court sentenced the defendant for a crime other than that for which he had been convicted. While strict enforcement of court rules and procedure is essential to the orderly administration of justice, the error in this case was so manifestly unjust that the court must overlook the failure to make a contemporaneous objection and exercise its authority to consider this issue on appeal in order to attain the ends of justice since the defendant was, in fact, sentenced for a crime other than that for which he was convicted and accordingly, the sentence was vacated. Brown v. Commonwealth, 8 Va. App. 126, 380 S.E.2d 8 (1989).

Commonwealth's attorney's improper statement made ends of justice exception applicable. — The appellant's motion for a mistrial was not timely made as required by this rule; however, the ends of justice exception to this rule was applicable. Where the Commonwealth's attorney's improper statement undermined the integrity of the trial, and its effect on the jury and the resulting prejudice to the appellant appeared plainly from the verdict, the trial court should have declared a mistrial. Morgan v. Commonwealth, No. 0477-91-1 (Ct. of Appeals Mar. 31, 1992).

When a principle of law is vital to a defendant in a criminal case, a trial court has an affirmative duty properly to instruct a jury about the matter. That principle applies even when an objection has not been stated. Johnson v. Commonwealth, 20 Va. App. 547, 458 S.E.2d 599 (1995).

Instruction which allows jury to convict without necessary element. — The "ends of justice" exception to this rule should have been invoked because an erroneous jury instruction could have deprived defendant of a fair trial; instruction eight was so defective that it allowed the jury to convict defendant of forgery even if the jury concluded that defendant lacked an intent to defraud. Intent to defraud, however, is a necessary element of forgery. Campbell v. Commonwealth, 14 Va. App. 988, 421 S.E.2d 652 (1992), aff'd, 246 Va. 174, 431 S.E.2d 648 (1993).

The Virginia Supreme Court and the Court of Appeals have invoked the "ends of justice" exception in cases where elements of the offense have been omitted from jury instructions at trial without objection from counsel. Phoung v. Commonwealth, 15 Va. App. 457, 424 S.E.2d 712 (1992).

When an instruction allows a jury to convict a defendant without proof of an essential and necessary element of the charged offense, the Commonwealth is not entitled to an appellate affirmance based solely on application of this rule. Campbell v. Commonwealth, 14 Va. App. 988, 421 S.E.2d 652 (1992), aff'd, 246 Va. 174, 431 S.E.2d 648 (1993).

"Ends of justice" exception not applicable when requested instruction was not vital to the defense. — Appellate court declined to invoke the "ends of justice" exception where defendant failed to request a jury instruction limiting the jury's consideration of defendant's prior drug use to impeachment because the limiting instruction requested did not related to an element of the crime charged and was not vital to defendant's defense. Pearce v. Commonwealth, 53 Va. App. 113, 669 S.E.2d 384, 2008 Va. App. LEXIS 545 (2008).

Rule controlled where failure to instruct jury was harmless error. — Where the failure to instruct the jury properly was harmless error and did not result in a miscarriage of justice, the contemporaneous objection rule, this rule, controlled. Phoung v. Commonwealth, 15 Va. App. 457, 424 S.E.2d 712 (1992).

Error in jury instruction not material. — Where the error in the jury instruction was that the instruction omitted the requirement of violence or intimidation as an element of the offense charged in the indictment, it essentially permitted a conviction on a finding that defendant broke and entered the dwelling with only the intent to commit larceny rather than robbery, contrary to the statutory law. Because the erroneous instruction related to the elements of the crime charged, the error also was "substantial." However, the error in the jury instruction was not material because it did not affect the outcome of the trial; while error, it was harmless. Phoung v. Commonwealth, 15 Va. App. 457, 424 S.E.2d 712 (1992).

Defendant, who was convicted of possessing with intent to distribute marijuana, did not establish a miscarriage of justice under Va. Sup. Ct. R. 5A:18, permitting consideration of the trial court's error in omitting a jury instruction regarding conspiracy, because there was sufficient evidence supporting the conspiracy and defendant presented his defense to this charge to the jury. Cameron v. Commonwealth, 2009 Va. App. LEXIS 398 (Sept. 8, 2009).

Where court failed to provide written findings. — Where court, while refusing to terminate child support because 18-year-old child was mentally retarded, did reduce the amount of monthly support from $357.50 to $157.50, and where counsel's objection was insufficient to satisfy the requirement of this rule because the entry of a support order without any written findings as to why the guideline amount was unjust or inappropriate and without justifying the deviation would not provide an adequate basis for setting support in the future, the court of appeals reviewed the modification of the child support award under the "ends of justice" exception to this rule. Miller v. Miller, No. 1935-92-1 (Ct. of Appeals Dec. 28, 1993).

Failure to follow child support statute. — Pursuant to § 20-108.1(B), when determining child support, a court has an affirmative duty to calculate expressly the presumptive amount of child support under the guidelines, and if it deviates from that presumptive amount, to explain adequately the basis for such deviation; if the Court fails to expressly calculate the guideline amount or to make the written findings required to justify its deviation from that amount, the ends of justice exception applies and permits a challenge to the award even though not objected to with particularity below. Herring v. Herring, 33 Va. App. 281, 532 S.E.2d 923, 2000 Va. App. LEXIS 610 (2000).

Termination of parental rights. — Because mother's claims of breach of contract and application of the law of the case doctrine related to juvenile and domestic relations court decree and were not raised in de novo hearing in the circuit court, and because trial courts are vested with broad discretion in making decisions regarding a child's best interests, the record reflected no reason to invoke the good cause or ends of justice exceptions on challenge to the circuit court's termination of mother's parental rights. Swearengin v. Department of Social Servs., No. 1798-00-3, 2001 Va. App. LEXIS 377 (Ct. of Appeals June 26, 2001).

IV. CONTRARY TO THE LAW AND EVIDENCE.

The phrase in this rule that "a mere statement that the judgment or award is contrary to the law and the evidence is not sufficient," negates the contention that the rule is only applicable to evidentiary and procedural rulings and not legal decisions and findings. Dowell v. Commonwealth, No. 1567-87-2 (Ct. of Appeals May 21, 1991).

Challenge to sufficiency of Commonwealth's evidence is waived if not raised with some specificity in the trial court. Mounce v. Commonwealth, 4 Va. App. 433, 357 S.E.2d 742 (1987).

Where defendant contended for the first time on appeal that his conviction for shooting at an occupied structure in violation of § 18.2-279 was "contrary to the law and the evidence"; and where the record reflected that at no time in the trial court did he move to strike the Commonwealth's evidence at the close of the Commonwealth's case, or to strike the evidence at the close of his evidence and the Commonwealth's rebuttal, or to set aside the verdict after the jury rendered its verdict, defendant was barred from raising the issue for the first time on appeal. Parnell v. Commonwealth, 15 Va. App. 342, 423 S.E.2d 834 (1992).

If the argument of an accused before the trial court fails to specify in what respects the evidence is insufficient to prove the offense, the issue is not properly preserved for appeal. Olgers v. Commonwealth, No. 0856-99-2, 2000 Va. App. LEXIS 342 (Ct. of Appeals May 9, 2000).

A general objection to the sufficiency of the evidence that does not specify the manner in which the evidence was insufficient to prove the charged offense fails to preserve the issue for appeal. Lima v. Commonwealth, No. 1263-99-3, 2000 Va. App. LEXIS 344 (Ct. of Appeals May 9, 2000).

Renewal of motion to strike prerequisite to challenge of sufficiency of evidence. — A defendant is barred on appeal from challenging the sufficiency of the evidence when he fails to renew his motion to strike the evidence after presenting his case, unless the record demonstrates that good cause exists or that consideration of this issue would enable the Court of Appeals to attain the ends of justice. White v. Commonwealth, 3 Va. App. 231, 348 S.E.2d 866 (1986).

By presenting evidence, a defendant waives his motion to strike the evidence and by failing to present the sufficiency issue to the trial court in the context of all the evidence, he fails to preserve that issue for appeal. McQuinn v. Commonwealth, 20 Va. App. 753, 460 S.E.2d 624 (1995).

Sufficiency of evidence considered on appeal where raised in motion to set aside verdict. — Where the defendant's written motion to set aside the verdict articulated specific objections to the sufficiency of the evidence of possession and manufacturing of controlled substances, the sufficiency of the evidence could be considered on appeal, even though the defendant made no motion to strike the Commonwealth's evidence in the trial court. McGee v. Commonwealth, 4 Va. App. 317, 357 S.E.2d 738 (1987).

Where issue raised in appeal was sufficiency of evidence to support conviction where no motion to strike was made and where after jury returned its verdicts, defendant moved court to set them aside as being contrary to law and evidence, motion to set aside verdict was proper method of testing sufficiency of evidence since defendant's closing argument was viewed as raising question of sufficiency of evidence to sustain convictions. Lewis v. Commonwealth, 7 Va. App. 596, 376 S.E.2d 295, aff'd, 8 Va. App. 574, 383 S.E.2d 736 (1989).

Sufficiency of evidence held not required to be considered for first time on appeal. — Where, in prosecution for the felonious unauthorized use of an automobile in violation of § 18.2-102, the evidence did not clearly show that the automobile in working condition could not have a value of more than $200.00, the ends of justice did not require that the Supreme Court consider the issue of the sufficiency of the evidence to prove that the value of the automobile was over $200.00 for the first time on appeal. Mounce v. Commonwealth, 4 Va. App. 433, 357 S.E.2d 742 (1987).

Counsel's statement held to raise issue of sufficiency of evidence. — Where an issue of sufficiency of evidence is presented to a trial court, sitting without a jury, in a motion to strike at the conclusion of the Commonwealth's evidence, and upon its denial and upon conclusion of the defendant's evidence, the same issue is presented in the defendant's final argument to the court, the defendant has preserved his right to appeal this issue, even though he did not make a motion to strike at the conclusion of his own evidence. Campbell v. Commonwealth, 12 Va. App. 476, 405 S.E.2d 1 (1991).

Insufficient evidence of contempt. — The "ends of justice" exception was applicable where the defendant, a deputy sheriff, had been held in criminal contempt for failing to transport a prisoner, but the underlying order did not expressly impose a duty on the defendant or any other personnel from the sheriff's office to transport the prisoner. Michaels v. Commonwealth, 32 Va. App. 601, 529 S.E.2d 822, 2000 Va. App. LEXIS 463 (2000).

Conviction for conduct that was not a criminal offense. — In order to show that a miscarriage of justice has occurred, thereby invoking the ends of justice exception, the defendant must demonstrate that he was convicted for conduct that was not a criminal offense or the record must affirmatively prove that an element of the offense did not occur. Bennett v. Commonwealth, 35 Va. App. 442, 546 S.E.2d 209, 2001 Va. App. LEXIS 262 (2001).

Evidence insufficient as matter of law. — The "ends of justice" exception was applicable where the evidence was insufficient, as a matter of law, to prove that a defendant assaulted two police officers in the course of a confrontation in which the defendant insisted that the officers leave his house; both officers testified that the defendant was not armed and made no threatening gestures with his hands and, although the defendant stood within inches of the officers, he made no overt act or attempt to physically harm either officer during the time the officers remained in his home after being asked to leave. Bennett v. Commonwealth, 35 Va. App. 442, 546 S.E.2d 209, 2001 Va. App. LEXIS 262 (2001).

Insufficient evidence. — Where the court found that a miscarriage of justice had occurred, the court, in order to attain the ends of justice, did not invoke the procedural bar of this rule because the evidence was insufficient, as a matter of law, to convict the defendant as a principal either in the first or second degree to robbery. Ellis v. Commonwealth, No. 1252-89-2 (Ct. of Appeals Jan. 8, 1991).

V. ILLUSTRATIONS.

Applicability. — Va. Sup. Ct. R. 5A:18 did not prevent consideration of defendant's appeal of a trial court's denial of his motion to withdraw his guilty pleas because defendant made the same argument on appeal that he made to the trial court; the trial court considered defendant's request to withdraw the plea agreement as a motion to withdraw his guilty pleas, and defendant's arguments to the court of appeals were basically the same as the arguments he made during the sentencing hearing. Booker v. Commonwealth, 2008 Va. App. LEXIS 171 (Apr. 8, 2008).

Because § 18.2-91 did not require the use or display of a firearm during a burglary, and because defendant's challenge to the sufficiency of the evidence under § 18.2-53.1 for use of a firearm in the commission of a breaking and entering was waived, the ends of justice exception in Va. Sup. Ct. R. 5A:18 did not apply. Blackwell v. Commonwealth, 2012 Va. App. LEXIS 9 (Jan. 17, 2012).

Requirements of Va. Sup. Ct. R. 5A:18 did not apply to a claimant's notice of appeal from a decision of the Virginia Workers' Compensation Commission. Furthermore, the issue which the claimant raised on appeal was preserved under Rule 5A:18 because the issue was presented and argued to the Full Commission and the Full Commission ruled on the issue. Whitt v. Halliburton Energy Servs., 2012 Va. App. LEXIS 156 (May 15, 2012).

Failure to object at pretrial hearing. — Defendant's claim that the trial court violated his right to counsel when it required him to appear at a pretrial hearing without representation was not properly preserved for appeal because defendant did not object to the procedure at the hearing. Showalter v. Commonwealth, No. 2224-00-3, 2001 Va. App. LEXIS 644 (Ct. of Appeals Nov. 20, 2001).

Pretrial motion made in order to avoid objecting in jury's presence complied with rule. — Where evidence that defendant had threatened to beat his girlfriend was the subject of a motion in limine made prior to the start of trial, on the morning of trial counsel advised the court that he did not wish to object to this issue before the jury and asked that the court note a continuing objection, and the court indicated it would, the trial court thus had an informed opportunity to rule on the issue and the purpose of this rule was satisfied. Chappell v. Commonwealth, No. 0465-85 (Ct. of Appeals Oct. 10, 1986).

Objections to rulings made during the voir dire of prospective jurors must be preserved by a subsequent objection to the seating of the jurors. Spencer v. Commonwealth, 238 Va. 295, 384 S.E.2d 785 (1989), cert. denied, 493 U.S. 1093, 110 S. Ct. 1171, 107 L. Ed. 2d 1073 (1990); Mu'Min v. Commonwealth, 239 Va. 433, 389 S.E.2d 886 (1990), aff'd on other grounds, 500 U.S. 415, 111 S. Ct. 1899, 114 L. Ed. 2d 493 (1991); defendant's contention that *Spencer* and *Mu'Min* were not controlling because these cases applied Supreme Court Rule 5:25, which relates to "proceedings in the Supreme Court of Virginia," rather than this rule of this court, was without merit. Johnson v. Commonwealth, No. 0259-91-1 (Ct. of Appeals Nov. 10, 1992).

Defendant's claim that he was deprived of a fair trial was not procedurally barred by his failure to reassert his objection to seating the jury when the jury was sworn as defendant made a contemporaneous objection and a timely motion for mistrial at the first opportunity after the trial court's allegedly improper question on voir dire; thus, counsel objected to seating the entire jury panel based on allegedly improper comments during voir dire. Nelson v. Commonwealth, No. 3408-02-2, 2004 Va. App. LEXIS 224 (Ct. of Appeals May 18, 2004).

Time impeachment evidence offered. — A defendant was not required, under this rule, to offer impeachment evidence regarding a hearsay declarant at the time the Commonwealth introduced the declarant's statement. Luck v. Commonwealth, 30 Va. App. 36, 515 S.E.2d 325 (1999).

Where procedure set up to allow parties to make objections out of court's presence, rule inapplicable. — Where husband contended that appellant allowed in evidence, without objection, all of the expenditures made by the husband from the date of separation until the date of hearing, and where, when the court entered its order, it stated that the parties could file exceptions up to ten days after the entry of the decree, and appellant then filed an objection to the decree arguing that the court should not have considered the post-divorce expenditures, if the trial court sets up a procedure allowing parties to make objections out of its presence, it is, insofar as the contemporaneous objection rule is concerned, the same as denying a party the right to make objections; thus, this rule was not applicable. McClemons v. McClemons, No. 1290-91-4 (Ct. of Appeals Apr. 14, 1992).

Requests to have court reporter present. — In camera proceedings are proceedings excluding the public. The defendant is entitled to be present and to have a court reporter present except under narrowly defined circumstances. Where defense counsel requested the trial court several times to have a court reporter present, these requests were a sufficient objection to notify the trial court of its content; therefore, this rule was complied with. Brittingham v. Commonwealth, 10 Va. App. 530, 394 S.E.2d 336 (1990).

Where questions asked by trial judge demonstrated that he was aware of the nature of defendant's objection, the objection was sufficient to notify the trial court of its content; therefore, it complied with this rule. Coone v. Commonwealth, No. 1003-85 (Ct. of Appeals Aug. 31, 1987).

Actions of trial judge indicated awareness of defendant's motion. — Although defendant presented evidence, he failed to renew his motion to strike or move to set aside the verdict; nevertheless, the sufficiency issue was preserved for appeal, where the record revealed that after counsel for each side presented closing arguments, the trial court, sitting without a jury, stated that it needed to recess court until a further day to allow it the opportunity to examine the issue of the victim's physical helplessness. Howard v. Commonwealth, 21 Va. App. 473, 465 S.E.2d 142 (1995).

Issue was preserved for appeal where defendant objected to testimony and grounds on which it was offered, and trial court considered and ruled on that specific issue. Broggin v. Commonwealth, No. 0131-98-3 (Ct. of Appeals Oct. 5, 1999).

Actions of trial court satisfied rule. — Notwithstanding the assertion that by failing to state a specific objection to the trial court's ruling striking his testimony, the defendant failed to preserve that issue for appeal, by ruling on its own motion and noting defense counsel's exception without affording counsel the opportunity to specify an objection, the trial court itself satisfied the requirement of the rule and preserved the issue for appeal. Tate, Jr. v. Commonwealth, No. 3017-97-2 (Ct. of Appeals Mar. 30, 1998).

Where appellant failed to specify basis, court considered basis and error preserved. — Although defendant failed to specify a basis for his objection to the "target" testimony, in response to his motion for a new trial, the court stated that it was rejecting the motion because it did not find the testimony to be prejudicial. Because the court considered the basis on which defendant now appealed, defendant's assertion of error was not barred by this rule. Newton v. Commonwealth, No. 1708-96-3, 1997 Va. App. LEXIS 619 (Ct. of Appeals Oct. 7, 1997).

Continuing objection sufficient to preserve issue for review. — Defendant sufficiently preserved a challenge to the legality of a warrantless search for appeal by moving to suppress the heroin the officers found and making a continuing objection to its admission at trial. Byrd v. Commonwealth, 50 Va. App. 542, 651 S.E.2d 414, 2007 Va. App. LEXIS 394 (2007).

Issue heard on appeal absent formal objection where it was discussed at trial. — Where the court and counsel knew that defendant was not present for trial, and although no immediate formal objection was made to proceeding without him, the trial went forward only after much discussion about trying him in his absence, and the trial court could have done nothing to produce him for trial at that time, the Court of Appeals addressed the issue of the trial of defendant in his absence. Head v. Commonwealth, 3 Va. App. 163, 348 S.E.2d 423 (1986), overruled on other grounds, Cruz v. Commonwealth, 24 Va. App. 454, 482 S.E.2d 880 (1997).

Where defendant failed to object to the testimony by the expert that allegedly opined as to the victim's credibility, the issue was not waived under Rule 5A:18 because the trial court had a chance to rule on its merits in defendant's Rule 3A:15 motion to set aside the verdict. Riffle v. Commonwealth, No. 0145-03-1, 2004 Va. App. LEXIS 446 (Ct. of Appeals Sept. 14, 2004).

Failure to preserve a ground for the motion. — Where the trial court denied motion to sever the robbery involving the firearm from the other robbery charges, under Rule 5A:18 the appellate court would only review the ground for this motion which defendant stated at trial, which was that the jury could become confused and believe that a firearm was involved in all the robberies. Valery v. Commonwealth, No. 2381-01-1, 2003 Va. App. LEXIS 133 (Ct. of Appeals Mar. 11, 2003).

In challenging the trial court's granting of defendant's motion to suppress, the Commonwealth was barred from arguing that the game warden affected a custodial arrest because that argument was not presented before the trial court. Commonwealth v. Wilkins, 2008 Va. App. LEXIS 302 (June 24, 2008).

Trial court properly denied defendant's pre-trial motion for the appointment of a special prosecutor, seeking the appointment on the basis that the assigned prosecutor had first-hand knowledge of evidence impeaching an eyewitness and, therefore, was a potential witness himself. The trial court properly denied the motion initially because the testimony of the prosecutor would have been admissible only if the witness denied making the conflicting statement, and at trial, once the witness denied making the statement, defendant did not renew his motion to disqualify and did not request a mistrial; thus, defendant failed to preserve for appeal this aspect of his request for the appointment of a special prosecutor. Campbell v. Commonwealth, No. 0269-12-1, 2012 Va. App. LEXIS 413 (Dec. 18, 2012).

Failure to seek ruling from trial court. — Under Rule 5A:18, a wife failed to preserve for appeal her claim to attorney's fees for a discovery dispute resolved in her favor because simply including a request for fees and costs in a motion, without mentioning that request at the hearing or seeking a ruling thereon from the trial court, was not sufficient to bring it to the trial court's attention and to preserve the matter for appeal. Ash v. Ash, No. 1943-03-2, 2004 Va. App. LEXIS 120 (Ct. of Appeals Mar. 23, 2004).

Va. Sup. Ct. R. 5A:18 barred the court of appeals from considering defendant's contention that the presentence report contained an error relating to a mental health issue because defendant did not present that argument to the trial court. Knight v. Commonwealth, 2006 Va. App. LEXIS 607 (Sept. 15, 2006).

When defense counsel failed to specifically challenge the sufficiency of the evidence proving an element of sexual battery, and had not affirmatively shown that a miscarriage of justice had occurred so that the "ends of justice" exception to Va. Sup. Ct. R. 5A:18 applied, the court would not consider the argument on appeal. Patrick v. Commonwealth, 2006 Va. App. LEXIS 457 (Oct. 17, 2006).

Where defendant conceded at oral argument that her statement to police constituted a full confession to the crime of conspiracy to distribute cocaine, and, consequently, only slight corroborative evidence was necessary to establish veracity of the confession, defendant's failure to assign error to one of the trial court's alternate holdings resulted in a waiver of any claim of error with respect to the decision on that issue. Corsaro v. Commonwealth, 2007 Va. App. LEXIS 488 (Nov. 6, 2007).

Commonwealth's claim that a police officer had a reasonable articulable suspicion that criminal activity was afoot and that defendant was armed and dangerous was barred under Va. Sup. Ct. R. 5A:18 as the Commonwealth's argument was based on the application of a reasonableness standard — a standard the Commonwealth never asked the trial court to apply. Commonwealth v. Blount, 2008 Va. App. LEXIS 3 (Jan. 4, 2008).

Defendant was precluded from arguing for the first time on appeal that the evidence was insufficient to prove that he broke into his former girlfriend's apartment with the intent to commit assault and battery because defendant never requested further review of the issue until filing his appeal; when the trial court found that defendant broke into the dwelling with the intent to commit assault defendant did not object that under the indictment, the trial court had to find that he broke in with the intent to commit an assault and battery, not a simple assault. Thomas v. Commonwealth, 2008 Va. App. LEXIS 161 (Apr. 8, 2008).

In a termination of parental rights action, the mother's argument that the trial court erred by admitting testimony of a doctor because its prejudicial effect outweighed its probative value was not reviewable because the mother failed to raise the issue before the trial court. Douglas v. Alexandria Dep't of Human Servs., 2008 Va. App. LEXIS 407 (Aug. 26, 2008).

Mother's challenge to the sufficiency of the evidence supporting the termination of the mother's parental rights was precluded by Va. Sup. Ct. R. 5A:18, because the mother made no motion to strike, to set aside, or to reconsider based on sufficiency grounds before the trial court. Brazell v. Fairfax County Dep't of Family Servs., 2008 Va. App. LEXIS 388 (Aug. 12, 2008).

Defendant's convictions for second-degree murder and use of a firearm in the commission of murder were proper because, although he contended that the trial court "effectively" denied him the opportunity to make his own proffer of the evidence, he failed to make that argument to the trial court and as such, the argument is barred from appellate consideration. Taylor v. Commonwealth, 2011 Va. App. LEXIS 187 (May 31, 2011).

Father's arguments were not preserved pursuant to Va. Sup. Ct. R. 5A:18 because the trial court waived the father's endorsement to the final order but included his objections to the ruling that the trial court did not have jurisdiction to determine custody and support pursuant to the Uniform Child Custody Jurisdiction and Enforcement Act, and his objection to the denial of his motion for show cause; the father did not file a motion to reconsider. Sowers v. Walker, 2011 Va. App. LEXIS 155 (May 10, 2011).

Defendant failed to preserve an objection to the scope of a search because defendant never asked the trial court for a ruling on defendant's motion once defendant had filed it. Clark v. Commonwealth, 2011 Va. App. LEXIS 219 (July 5, 2011).

Va. Sup. Ct. R. 5A:18 precluded the court of appeals from considering a husband's argument because the husband failed to object to the trial court's ruling regarding reinstatement of the case to the active docket. West v. West, 59 Va. App. 225, 717 S.E.2d 831, 2011 Va. App. LEXIS 390 (2011).

Because an appellant failed to present an argument to the trial court, the appellate court would not consider it for the first time on appeal. Breit v. Mason, 59 Va. App. 322, 718 S.E.2d 482, 2011 Va. App. LEXIS 414 (2011).

Defendant failed to preserve for appeal his claim that his sentencing as a second offender was error because, by failing to provide the trial court with argument, including legal authority, to support his objection, defendant denied the trial court the opportunity to address and correct the alleged error; Va. Sup. Ct. R. 5A:18 required objection in trial court. Defendant did not argue that either the good cause or ends of justice exceptions to Rule 5A:18 should have been invoked, and the appellate court did not consider Rule 5A:18 exceptions sua sponte. Elliott v. Commonwealth, 2012 Va. App. LEXIS 75 (Mar. 20, 2012).

Mother waived her claim of error in the apportionment of guardian ad litem fees in a change in physical custody dispute as although the mother stated her objection in a document of objections to the final order, she did not argue or obtain a ruling from the trial court on the issue; the mother did not argue that the exceptions to Va. Sup. Ct. R. 5A:18 for good cause or to meet the ends of justice applied, and the record did not reflect any reason to invoke the good cause or ends of justice exceptions since guardian ad litem fees could properly be assigned as costs to the parties under §§ 20-79(b), 20-99(5), and 17.1-600. Turpin v. McGowan, 2012 Va. App. LEXIS 125 (Apr. 24, 2012).

Failure to raise argument before Workers' Compensation Commission. — In rejecting an employer's appeal of a Workers' Compensation Commission decision to award a claimant temporary total disability benefits, the court of appeals did not consider the employer's argument that the commission erroneously considered certain documents that were not a part of the record because the employer never raised this argument before the commission; therefore, it failed to provide the commission with the opportunity to correct any perceived error. Thus, the employer failed to preserve for appellate review its assertion that the commission erroneously considered those documents, and the court of appeals refused to address the argument for the first time on appeal. Angler Constr. Co. L.L.C. v. Blankenberg, 2008 Va. App. LEXIS 272 (June 10, 2008).

In a workers' compensation case in which the claimant alleged that reflex sympathetic dystrophy in the claimant's right arm related to a 1994 work injury had spread to her left arm, the statute of limitations that applied was § 65.2-708, which related to a claim based on a change of condition, rather than § 65.2-601, which related to original claims; because the employer did not base its argument on § 65.2-708, any argument regarding the statute of limitations was waived under Va. Sup. Ct. R. 5A:20(e) for failure to discuss the relevant legal principles and under Va. Sup. Ct. R. 5A:18 because no statute of limitations argument was made before the Workers' Compensation Commission. Mount Vernon Hosp. v. Devers, 2008 Va. App. LEXIS 494 (Nov. 4, 2008).

Employee could not raise his argument that an employer did not seek to promptly terminate his benefits because the employee did not raise his timeliness argument before the full Virginia Workers' Compensation Commission. Urias v. Winkler's, Inc., 2011 Va. App. LEXIS 397 (Dec. 13, 2011).

Employee's argument seeking to have the Canons of Judicial Conduct apply to deputy commissioners of the Virginia Workers' Compensation Commission were not timely presented because the employee failed on multiple occasions to ask the Commission to adopt the Canons of Judicial Conduct for deputy commissioners; the Commission's decision to refuse to consider the employee's due process argument that the Canons had to apply to deputy commissioners was proper since the employee could have earlier raised the legal arguments. Urias v. Winkler's, Inc., 2011 Va. App. LEXIS 397 (Dec. 13, 2011).

Because an employee did not appeal a deputy commissioner's decision on an issue to the Virginia Workers' Compensation Commission, Va. Sup. Ct. R. 5A:18 barred consideration of the issue for the first time on appeal. County of Henrico v. Henry, 2012 Va. App. LEXIS 31 (Feb. 7, 2012).

Since workers' compensation claimant never argued before the Virginia Workers' Compensation Commission that the employer was bound by the specific order or progression of the disciplinary sanctions listed in the employer's written policy, the court did not need to address this assertion by the employer. Mouhssine v. Crystal City Laundry, 62 Va. App. 65, 741 S.E.2d 804, 2013 Va. App. LEXIS 153 (2013).

Appellate review of the issue of whether the workers' compensation claim was compensable because the claimant fell on the "concrete" sidewalk, which the employer contended was an extension of the parking lot, and not on the "brick" sidewalk, which led to the building's entrance, was barred by Va. Sup. Ct. R. 5A:18 because the employer did not make this specific argument to the Workers' Compensation Commission, and the Commission did not make a ruling on it. Capital Area Pediatrics, Inc. v. Eken, No. 1557-12-4, 2013 Va. App. LEXIS 141 (Ct. of Appeals May 7, 2013).

Failure to offer evidence. — Since defendant never sought to offer any evidence of the reasons he was terminated from the drug court program, the court could not say that the circuit court erred in refusing evidence when no evidence was offered or refused. As a result, Va. Sup. Ct. R. 5A:18 barred the court's consideration of this argument. Harris v. Commonwealth, 2009 Va. App. LEXIS 218 (May 12, 2009).

Closing argument met requirements of rule. — Where the defense's closing argument emphasized that the jury should not believe witness because he was a robber and a liar, this argument could be viewed as raising the question of the sufficiency of the evidence to sustain the convictions, and the requirements of this rule were met. Lewis v. Commonwealth, 8 Va. App. 574, 383 S.E.2d 736 (1989).

The contemporaneous objection requirement of this rule was satisfied when counsel informed the trial judge in closing argument of the relief that was sought. Harris v. Commonwealth, 13 Va. App. 593, 413 S.E.2d 354 (1992).

Failure to make argument during closing argument. — Denial of the wife's request for equitable distribution of the husband's military retirement was appropriate because her argument that the language of the parties' separation agreement constituted a full and final accounting of all claims, rights, or other interests existent in 1982 was waived because she failed to make that argument in her closing argument. Savedge v. Barbour, 2010 Va. App. LEXIS 259 (June 29, 2010).

Wife's first, second, and third assignments of error were not preserved as she did not file a motion to set aside the verdict or a motion to reconsider, and in her closing argument, she argued for sole legal and physical custody, but did not mention the husband's alleged abusive behavior and alleged drinking issues, which were the subjects of her first three assignments of error. Smith v. Smith, No. 2069-11-2, 2012 Va. App. LEXIS 308 (Oct. 2, 2012).

Where the trial judge has overruled an objection to the Commonwealth attorney's closing argument, defense counsel is not required to request a cautionary instruction or a mistrial in order to preserve the issue for appeal. Martinez v. Commonwealth, 10 Va. App. 664, 395 S.E.2d 467 (1990), aff'd, 241 Va. 557, 403 S.E.2d 358 (1991).

Where evidence was not proffered until after defendant had been convicted, its tender was not timely and its rejection was not preserved for appeal. Hancock v. Commonwealth, No. 0182-99-1 (Ct. of Appeals Jan. 27, 2000).

The words "seen and objected to" over counsel's signature do not alert the trial judge to the nature of the alleged error, much less provide a statement of the grounds therefor. Lee v. Lee, 394 S.E.2d 490 (1990), aff'd on reh'g en banc, 12 Va. App. 512, 404 S.E.2d 736 (1991).

Where only objection to trial court's ruling contained in the record is counsel's endorsement of the final decree under the phrase "Seen and Objected to," such an endorsement, without more, fails to meet the requirements of this rule. Boyd v. Boyd, No. 2010-92-3 (Ct. of Appeals May 25, 1993); Bailey v. Duncan, No. 2573-92-3 (Ct. of Appeals Sept. 14, 1993).

Statement that order "seen and objected to." — Ordinarily, endorsement of an order "Seen and objected to" is not specific enough to meet the requirements of this rule because it does not sufficiently alert the trial court to the claimed error; such an endorsement is sufficient to satisfy the rule only if the ruling made by the trial court was narrow enough to make obvious the basis of the objection. Herring v. Herring, 33 Va. App. 281, 532 S.E.2d 923, 2000 Va. App. LEXIS 610 (2000).

Statement "seen and objected to" is insufficient. — Since this rule provides that "[a] mere statement that the judgment or award is contrary to the law and the evidence is not sufficient," it follows that a statement that an order is "seen and objected to" must also be insufficient. Lee v. Lee, 12 Va. App. 512, 404 S.E.2d 736 (1991).

For other cases holding that simply endorsing order as "seen and objected to" is insufficient to satisfy the requirements of this rule, see Miller v. Miller, No. 1935-92-1 (Ct. of Appeals Dec. 28, 1993); Street v. Street, No. 1940-95-4 (Ct. of Appeals Jan. 21, 1997); Simmons v. Darden, No. 2596-03-1, 2004 Va. App. LEXIS 86 (Ct. of Appeals Feb. 24, 2004); Eubank v. Chesterfield-Colonial Heights Dep't of Soc. Servs., No. 1357-04-2, 2005 Va. App. LEXIS 71 (Ct. of Appeals Feb. 15, 2005).

Although father's counsel endorsed final termination order "Have Seen and Objected to," the written statement filed as the record did not recite the father's arguments or any objections he made to the trial court's ruling terminating his parental rights, and, thus, the reviewing court had to conclude that the father did not properly preserve any specific objection to the trial court's termination of his parental rights. Rivera v. City of Hampton Dep't of Soc. Servs., No. 1857-03-1, 2004 Va. App. LEXIS 221 (Ct. of Appeals May 11, 2004).

Order granting custody of the parties five children to a mother was upheld on appeal, as the father: (1) endorsed the final order "seen and objected to" without stating his reasons for his objections; (2) failed to present a request for further explanation of the trial court's decision; and (3) failed to preserve any claim of error for appellate review with respect to said order; thus, the decision of the trial court was summarily affirmed. Hooper v. Odle, 2005 Va. App. LEXIS 162 (Apr. 26, 2005).

Because a husband's endorsement of an order denying his motion for a reduction in or termination of his spousal support as "seen and objected to" was insufficient to alert the trial court to any of his claimed errors on appeal, and absent any allegation that an exception to Va. Sup. Ct. R. 5A:18 applied, he failed to satisfy the rule. As a result, his appeal lacked merit, entitling his ex-wife to her attorney's fees and costs, including any attorney's fees and costs incurred at the remand hearing Williams v. Williams, 2007 Va. App. LEXIS 415 (Nov. 20, 2007).

In an annulment case in which a pro se wife appealed, contending that the trial court denied her a fair hearing and erroneously entered a final order, which was drafted by the husband's attorney who allegedly inserted her opinion in the order, the wife did not make those objections at the trial court level. Although she signed the order as "Except that defendant intends to appeal the honorable court's decision," a statement of "seen and objected to" was insufficient to preserve an issue for appeal. Odocha v. Sarago, 2009 Va. App. LEXIS 457 (Oct. 13, 2009).

Father did not preserve his claim that he was deprived of his right to due process under the Fifth and Fourteenth Amendments, U.S. Const. amends. V and XIV, and Va. Const. art. I, § 11 when his parental rights were terminated under § 16.1-283, in absentia, as required by Va. Sup. Ct. R. 5A:18 where: (1) the order was signed "seen and objected to" by the father's counsel; (2) no grounds for the objection were given; (3) the father's endorsement of the order terminating his parental rights gave no indication of a due process argument; (4) the father and the mother were given proper notice of the termination proceedings; and (5) counsel for both parties appeared at the hearing. Dolak v. Va. Beach Dep't of Human Servs., 2012 Va. App. LEXIS 245 (July 31, 2012).

As the trial court made numerous rulings, a parent's endorsement of an order as "seen and objected to" was not sufficient on appeal, and would not be considered; the parent did not object to the ruling in closing argument, did not note any objections to the final order, did not file a motion to reconsider, and the page that the parent cited to in an appendix as to where the parent preserved the issue did not include the argument the parent presented in the parent's brief. Wilson v. Britton, 2012 Va. App. LEXIS 291 (Sept. 4, 2012).

Failure to object and endorsement as "seen and agreed" barred review. — See Saunders v. Saunders, No. 0393-03-2, 2003 Va. App. LEXIS 553 (Ct. of Appeals Nov. 4, 2003); Courembis v. Courembis, 43 Va. App. 18, 595 S.E.2d 505, 2004 Va. App. LEXIS 203 (2004).

Rule complied with although order merely endorsed "objected to." — Where employer contended that employee's appeal was barred because the court's order was merely endorsed "objected to" in violation of this rule, since the trial court was aware of employee's objections and could rule on them during trial, employee complied with the requirements of this rule. Helmick v. Martinsville-Henry County Economic Dev. Corp., 14 Va. App. 853, 421 S.E.2d 23 (1992).

Appeal was not barred by this rule where, although the statement of facts submitted in lieu of the transcript contained no mention of any objection to the trial court's ruling, the final order as signed by counsel for appellant, read "Seen and Objected to." Although counsel failed to include any specific grounds for the objection, as is generally required by this rule, the ruling made by the trial court was narrow enough to make obvious the basis of appellant's objection. Mackie v. Hill, 16 Va. App. 229, 429 S.E.2d 37 (1993).

Venue question not stated with sufficient particularity. — When appellant made his motion to set aside the verdict, there was no identified point "to save." The motion to set aside the verdict did not state the venue question with sufficient particularity to submit that issue to the trial court. Day v. Commonwealth, 12 Va. App. 1078, 407 S.E.2d 52 (1991).

Failure to object to certificate of analysis. — Defendant's claim that the trial judge erred in admitting the certificate of analysis into evidence, as an exception to the hearsay rule in the absence of the breathalyzer operator whom the Commonwealth unilaterally excused from appearing at trial was not preserved for appellate review because there was nothing in the record showing that a hearsay objection was made to the admission of said evidence. Gupta v. Commonwealth, 2007 Va. App. LEXIS 264 (July 10, 2007).

Evidence concerning photographic identification correctly admitted where objection lacked required specificity. — Where defendant objected to a mug shot on relevancy grounds the trial court correctly admitted evidence concerning the photographic identification because defendant did not state in the trial court his reason for objection with the specificity required by this rule. Irving v. Commonwealth, 15 Va. App. 178, 422 S.E.2d 471 (1992).

Objection to jury instructions. — Because defense counsel did not object to instruction, given in response to jury's question, until after jury left to deliberate further, counsel's objection came too late and would not be considered on appeal. Djelebova v. Commonwealth, No. 1748-98-2 (Ct. of Appeals Mar. 7, 2000).

Because defendant did not request that the jury be instructed that parole had been abolished, did not object to the trial judge's jury instructions or to the trial judge's reply to the jury's inquiry regarding what percentage of the sentence had to be served, and made no showing that review of the issue was necessary to serve the ends of justice, defendant was procedurally barred pursuant to Rule 5A:18 from arguing on appeal that the trial court erred in failing to instruct the jury that parole had been abolished in Virginia. Warren v. Commonwealth, No. 2831-00-3, 2002 Va. App. LEXIS 200 (Ct. of Appeals Apr. 2, 2002).

In a case in which an Allen charge was given in a criminal trial, and defendant objected to the giving of the instruction, defendant's argument on appeal, objecting to the contents of the instruction, was not properly preserved for review, and its consideration by the appellate court was barred. Roberts v. Commonwealth, No. 2401-01-2, 2003 Va. App. LEXIS 249 (Ct. of Appeals Apr. 29, 2003).

Defendant did not properly preserve the defendant's objection to the denial of the defendant's proffered self-defense jury instructions for appeal by specifying the grounds for the defendant's objections, the defendant merely read the defendant's proffered instructions into the record; consequently, the defendant was procedurally barred from raising the denied jury instruction claim on appeal. Moreover, the record did not reflect any reason to invoke the good cause or ends of justice exceptions to Rule 5A:18. Johnson v. Commonwealth, No. 2517-01-2, 2003 Va. App. LEXIS 240 (Ct. of Appeals Apr. 22, 2003).

When the trial court erroneously instructed the jury that the Commonwealth had to prove defendant willfully or wantonly disregarded an officer's signal, rather than proving defendant willfully and wantonly disregarded the signal, under § 46.2-817, the ends of justice exception to Rule 5A:18 did not allow the appellate court to consider defendant's argument that he was entitled to a reversal of his conviction, despite his failure to object to the instruction, because his case did not represent an "extraordinary" circumstance, as the evidence that he "willfully and wantonly" disregarded an officer's signal, so as to "endanger any person" was overwhelming, he never contested the elements of "willfulness" or "wantonness" at trial, and the erroneous instruction did not allow the jury to convict defendant of otherwise innocent behavior. Bazemore v. Commonwealth, 42 Va. App. 203, 590 S.E.2d 602, 2004 Va. App. LEXIS 19 (2004).

Defendant's argument that the jury should have been instructed as to the consequences of a verdict of not guilty by reason of insanity was preserved for appeal under Va. Sup. Ct. R. 5A:18. The Commonwealth's motion in limine sought to exclude references to the consequences of an insanity finding "in any stage of the trial," including voir dire, and the trial court's ruling clearly encompassed whether defendant could address an insanity disposition in a jury instruction. Holmes v. Commonwealth, 2008 Va. App. LEXIS 515 (Nov. 25, 2008).

Failure to raise constitutional claims related to jury instructions. — Defendant's argument that the giving of one instruction and the refusal of others violated his constitutional rights was procedurally barred because defendant had not raised the constitutional claim at trial. His oblique statement had not sufficiently alerted the trial court to defendant's present constitutional claim. Murray v. Commonwealth, 2006 Va. App. LEXIS 409 (Aug. 29, 2006).

Objection at time of examination of jury instructions timely. — Where the defendant could not have known that the Commonwealth would seek to use previous rape as a predicate for attempted capital murder charge until the proposed jury instructions were examined, and at that time, he promptly objected, this issue was presented timely to the trial court. Curtis v. Commonwealth, 13 Va. App. 622, 414 S.E.2d 421 (1992).

Failure to object to how the polling of the jury was conducted. — Because the defendant failed to object to the individual polling of the jury at the time the poll was taken, thus preventing the trial court from correcting any error or determining if any individual juror opposed the sentencing verdicts, the defendant could not raise the issue of the alleged failure to poll one of the jurors for the first time on appeal. Turner v. Commonwealth, No. 1641-01-3, 2002 Va. App. LEXIS 707 (Ct. of Appeals Nov. 26, 2002).

Objection to expert testimony. — Defendant's motion in limine seeking to exclude expert testimony on the ground that it invaded the province of the jury preserved the question for appellate review. Yeldell v. Commonwealth, 2006 Va. App. LEXIS 359 (Aug. 8, 2006).

Trial court did not abuse its discretion in allowing

an expert to give an opinion regarding the probable distance a shell casing would be ejected by a nine-millimeter auto-loading pistol. Despite having had the opportunity to do so, defendant did not raise below, and the trial court was not given the opportunity to address, the claim defendant raised on appeal, as defendant's counsel stated only "Your honor I'm going to object. I would say that that is speculation as to how or what it would do, eject"; no other grounds for the objection were given. Jones v. Commonwealth, 2007 Va. App. LEXIS 265 (July 17, 2007).

In an annulment case in which a pro se wife appealed, contending that the trial court erred by relying on the husband's expert witness regarding Nigerian marriages and divorces, pursuant to Va. Sup. Ct. R. 5A:18, the appellate court could not consider that argument. The wife did not object to the witness being offered as an expert in the trial court. Odocha v. Sarago, 2009 Va. App. LEXIS 457 (Oct. 13, 2009).

Failure to preserve objections to divorce decree. — This rule barred consideration of issues presented by wife on appeal from divorce decree, where husband's counsel provided wife with copies of depositions and draft final decree more than two months prior to entry of decree, neither wife nor her counsel appeared at hearing on final decree, and wife noted no exceptions to final decree. King v. King, No. 1827-99-2 (Ct. of Appeals Feb. 8, 2000).

Appeal filed by an executrix from the trial court's order sustaining the demurrer of the decedent's first wife was dismissed pursuant to Rule 5A:18 as the executrix failed to present her argument, that the divorce decree regarding the decedent's first marriage was ambiguous, to the trial court. Addenbrook v. Addenbrook, No. 2612-03-1, 2004 Va. App. LEXIS 218 (Ct. of Appeals May 11, 2004).

Because a husband did not note any objection to the trial court's ruling that child support payments would be retroactive, the court of appeals could not consider the claim pursuant to Va. Sup. Ct. R. 5A:18. Brown v. Brown, 2012 Va. App. LEXIS 233 (2012).

Wife did not preserve her claim that her request for equitable distribution of her husband's retirement under § 20-107.3 was improperly denied because she did not note her objection to the final decree or in her motion to reconsider under Va. Sup. Ct. R. 5A:18; it could not be determined whether the wife preserved the issue in her closing argument because there was no transcript or written statement of facts. Wang v. Crumpacker, No. 0263-12-4, 2012 Va. App. LEXIS 401 (Dec. 11, 2012).

Failure to object to child support order. — Husband had not preserved the right to appeal a trial court order increasing husband's child support obligation so that husband's son could attend a private military school as the husband did not object to the order in the trial court but merely signed off on the trial court's order indicating that the order had been seen. Dick v. Dick, No. 0966-01-2, 2001 Va. App. LEXIS 596 (Ct. of Appeals Oct. 30, 2001).

Failure to object to guardian ad litem appointment. — Award of primary physical custody of the children to the father was proper, in part because the mother was not permitted to complain on appeal of error in the circuit court where she herself failed to follow through with her motion to exclude the guardian ad litem and where she failed to properly notify the court of the statutory requirements for the appointment. The issue was waived. Gudino v. Gudino, 2011 Va. App. LEXIS 327 (Nov. 1, 2011).

Failure to object to equitable distribution rulings. — Where the record contained no indication that appellant objected to rulings on equitable distribution or the award of attorney's fees, either at the hearing or by endorsement of the decree itself, and his attempt to raise these issues in a motion to reconsider was not timely filed, his assignments of error were barred. Newsome v. Newsome, 18 Va. App. 22, 441 S.E.2d 346 (1994).

Having failed to timely object to trial court's use of a fifty-percent figure throughout proceedings when division of marital property was made, and to court's award of in-kind marital property, husband waived any objection to court's equitable distribution award. Kost v. Kost, No. 0116-99-1 (Ct. of Appeals Dec. 14, 1999).

Failure to raise argument at suppression hearing. — Where a game warden confiscated jet skis from appellant's property and appellant argued on appeal that the warden did not have probable cause to seize the jet skis because the warden could not observe the hull identification numbers when the warden confiscated them, appellant's motion to suppress was properly denied because appellant was procedurally barred from raising the argument for the first time on appeal since appellant never raised this specific argument at the suppression hearing. Branch v. Commonwealth, 2007 Va. App. LEXIS 484 (Dec. 27, 2007).

Failure to object at trial will bar review on appeal. — Where appellant conceded at oral argument that she failed to object at trial to the valuation date used to value the marital share of husband's pension, the Court of Appeals would not consider the issue on appeal. Gollehon v. Gollehon, No. 2178-92-4 (Ct. of Appeals Nov. 23, 1993).

Contention by appellant, who was convicted of pandering, regarding the erroneous use of the term "sexual acts" instead of "unlawful sexual intercourse" or one of the acts specified in Code § 18.2-361, was barred from appellate review because it was never raised in the trial court. Haitham Shurbaji v. Commonwealth, No. 1822-92-4 (Ct. of Appeals Mar. 29, 1994).

Where, at trial, appellant voiced no objection to a unitary trial, and in fact acquiesced in the court's proposal to hold the two stages of the trial "at the same time," appellant was barred on appeal from challenging the court's failure to hold a bifurcated trial. Coleman v. Commonwealth, No. 1331-94-2 (Ct. of Appeals Aug. 1, 1995).

Because defendant never specifically raised the void-for-vagueness issue at the trial court level, this rule barred her from raising it on appeal. Riggs v. Commonwealth, No. 1892-95-2, 1996 Va. App. LEXIS 591 (Ct. of Appeals Sept. 10, 1996).

Because defendant failed to specifically move to strike the evidence or to set aside the verdict, this rule barred appellate consideration of his insufficient evidence claim. Redman v. Commonwealth, 25 Va. App. 215, 487 S.E.2d 269 (1997).

If there shall appear to be any variance between the allegations therein and the evidence offered in proof thereof, the court may permit amendment of such indictment at any time before the jury returns a verdict or the court finds the accused guilty or not guilty, provided the amendment does not change the nature or character of the offense charged; here, any objection to deficiencies in arraignment on the amended indictment was not presented to the trial court and, therefore, was not before the court of appeals. Barnett v. Commonwealth, No. 2622-95-1 (Ct. of Appeals Sept. 24, 1996).

Where the wife failed to object to the husband's calculation of interest earnings of his separate contributions to a retirement plan at trial, she was procedurally barred from raising this issue on appeal. Mann v. Mann, 22 Va. App. 459, 470 S.E.2d 605 (1996).

Employer in workers' compensation matter failed to file motion to reconsider or set aside full commission's decision, and since employer's arguments were not raised before commission they could not be considered for first time on appeal. Mary Washington Health Ctr. v. Jones, No. 0959-99-2 (Ct. of Appeals Sept. 21, 1999).

Because defendant acquiesced in court's erroneous finding at trial, he was barred from raising that issue on appeal. Fowler v. Commonwealth, No. 2116-99-3 (Ct. of Appeals Sept. 28, 1999).

Defendant waived any argument as to admission of pornographic videotapes, where he offered no objection to their admission or to testimony concerning their discovery and contents. Lee v. Commonwealth, No. 2588-98-2 (Ct. of Appeals Feb. 15, 2000).

Because defendant failed to raise the issues before the trial court of either a lack of probable cause to arrest or whether the evidence was sufficient to convict defendant of obstruction of justice, defendant was barred from raising those issues for the first time on appeal. Fricke v. Commonwealth, No. 0035-01-2, 2001 Va. App. LEXIS 632 (Ct. of Appeals Nov. 13, 2001).

Because the defendant failed to raise the issue that his right to due process was violated when the State added charges prior to his second trial, he was barred from raising that issue on appeal. Andrews v. Commonwealth, 37 Va. App. 479, 559 S.E.2d 401, 2002 Va. App. LEXIS 89 (2002).

While the trial court had a general obligation to instruct the jury on the abolition of parole, where defendant did not request such an instruction or otherwise raise the issue, the jury did not inquire about the possibility of parole, and no evidence or argument place the issue of parole before the jury, Rule 5A:18 precluded the Court of Appeals from considering the issue. Waters v. Commonwealth, 39 Va. App. 72, 569 S.E.2d 763, 2002 Va. App. LEXIS 559 (2002).

Appellate court would not consider defendant's argument that certain hearsay evidence was improperly excluded by the trial court because it was admissible under certain exceptions to the hearsay rule, because those exceptions were first asserted on appeal, rather than before the trial court. Cousins v. Commonwealth, No. 1553-01-2, 2002 Va. App. LEXIS 606 (Ct. of Appeals Oct. 8, 2002).

As defendant did not put the trial court on notice that defendant was challenging the sufficiency of the evidence as to whether defendant was driving recklessly, the trial court could not consider defendant's specific argument or take corrective action; thus, defendant's claim was procedurally defaulted under Rule 5A:18. Frazier v. Commonwealth, No. 1082-01-3, 2002 Va. App. LEXIS 577 (Ct. of Appeals Oct. 1, 2002).

Appellate court declined to consider an injured firefighter's claim that a fire department failed to provide the firefighter with a panel of physicians, because the Virginia Workers' Compensation Commission had not decided this issue and has ruled that a hearing was necessary. Carter v. Arlington County Fire Dep't, No. 1328-02-4, 2002 Va. App. LEXIS 623 (Ct. of Appeals Oct. 15, 2002).

Defendant's contentions that the victim's statements to her cousin as to the identity of the robber were admissible under the dying declaration exception to the hearsay rule and were exculpatory were not considered by the appellate court as defendant failed to raise the issues before the trial court at the time the evidcnce was offered and the trial court made its ruling; defendant failed to properly preserve the issues for purposes of appeal. Gent v. Commonwealth, No. 0429-02-3, 2003 Va. App. LEXIS 66 (Ct. of Appeals Feb. 11, 2003).

Rule 5A:18 precluded the consideration of an argument that was not presented to the trial court; Rule 5A:18 also applied to constitutional claims. Rutledge v. Rutledge, No. 1961-02-4, 2003 Va. App. LEXIS 78 (Ct. of Appeals Feb. 19, 2003).

Rule 5A:18 barred defendant's appeal of a trial court's grant of a continuance during trial under subsection C of § 19.2-183, so that defendant could receive his lab analysis of the drugs at issue 10 days before trial under § 19.2-187; defendant failed to raise his arguments that § 19.2-183(C) related only to preliminary hearings and that the grant of a continuance violated his constitutional right to due process in the trial court, and there was no cause to invoke the ends of justice exception to Rule 5A:18. Chambers v. Commonwealth, No. 1302-02-3, 2003 Va. App. LEXIS 28 (Ct. of Appeals Jan. 28, 2003).

Where the trial court did not rely solely upon a husband's constructive desertion and the husband did not preserve his claims, the trial court did not abuse its discretion in awarding lump sum alimony and attorneys' fees to the wife. Turner v. Turner, No. 2926-02-3, 2003 Va. App. LEXIS 258 (Ct. of Appeals Apr. 29, 2003).

Defendant's failure specifically to object to the standard he believed the trial court erroneously applied to his motion for a change of venue barred him from challenging this ruling on appeal. Riner v. Commonwealth, 40 Va. App. 440, 579 S.E.2d 671, 2003 Va. App. LEXIS 287 (2003), aff'd, 268 Va. 296, 601 S.E.2d 555 (2004).

Where a defendant made no objection when the Commonwealth reminded the trial court at a revocation hearing that a term of defendant's probation was to remain drug and alcohol free, or when the trial court noted that defendant had been under the influence of alcohol contrary to the terms of his probation, and made no argument at the hearing that the trial court's consideration of his consumption of alcohol was a violation of his due process rights or otherwise improper, he was barred under Rule 5A:18 from raising this issue for the first time on appeal. Cappell v. Commonwealth, No. 0807-02-3, 2003 Va. App. LEXIS 313 (Ct. of Appeals May 27, 2003).

Where attorney did not file any objections with the workers' compensation commission to the claimant's request to review the attorney fee award that was rendered in the claimant's workers' compensation case and did not file a motion for reconsideration after the workers' compensation commission reduced the attorney fee award, the attorney could not argue, for the first time on appeal, that reduction of the attorney fee award was improper. Kidd v. Thomas, No. 2675-02-3, 2003 Va. App. LEXIS 177 (Ct. of Appeals Apr. 1, 2003).

As the record failed to show that the husband ever objected to the trial court's decision in the final decree to award the wife a divorce on a fault ground after earlier indicating that the divorce would be based on § 20-91(A)(9), the appellate court was barred from considering those arguments for the first time on appeal, and a transcript of the motions for reconsideration and show cause was not included; thus, the trial court could have reconsidered its earlier finding or corrected a typographical error and, regardless, the evidence supported the finding of cruelty. Brown v. Brown, No. 0580-03-2, 2003 Va. App. LEXIS 528 (Ct. of Appeals Oct. 21, 2003).

When defendant argued on appeal that the trial court failed to advise him that all 12 members of the jury would have to unanimously find him guilty, so he did not knowingly waive his right to a jury trial, this argument could not be considered because it was not raised in the trial court. Steward v. Commonwealth, No. 0052-03-4, 2003 Va. App. LEXIS 694 (Ct. of Appeals Dec. 30, 2003).

Because defendant did not argue to the trial court that the Commonwealth's reason for striking an African-American juror was pretextual, Rule 5A:18 barred the appellate court's review of the argument. Martinez v. Commonwealth, 42 Va. App. 9, 590 S.E.2d 57, 2003 Va. App. LEXIS 678 (2003).

Defendant's argument that the evidence was insufficient to establish that he traveled onto school property with the intent to distribute the cocaine while on the property was procedurally barred because defendant failed to raise it at trial where defendant argued only that no evidence was presented that the parking lot was within 1,000 feet of a school zone; furthermore, the ends of justice exception did not apply. Copeland v. Commonwealth, 42 Va. App. 424, 592 S.E.2d 391, 2004 Va. App. LEXIS 62 (2004).

Defendant's claim that the trial court applied the incorrect evidentiary standard of "preponderance of the evidence" when it concluded that he had violated the terms and conditions of a peace bond was not considered as: (1) defendant failed to present the argument to the trial court and the trial court lacked the opportunity to assess the merits of his objection, (2) the Commonwealth was deprived of the opportunity to address the claimed error in the trial court, and (3) defendant failed in his brief to demonstrate good cause for his failure to raise the issue in the trial court or to request that the appellate court invoke the ends of justice exception to Rule 5A:18. Stallings v. Commonwealth, No. 1692-03-4, 2004 Va. App. LEXIS 343 (Ct. of Appeals July 13, 2004).

Appeals court refused to address defendant's arguments stated on appeal as to the improper admission of certain evidence on hearsay grounds, as he alleged at trial that said evidence was irrelevant; therefore, the court also refused to address that the victim's statements regarding fear of defendant were admissible to rebut claims of self-defense, suicide, or accidental death, as applied to a case in which the defense of manslaughter was raised. Harris v. Commonwealth, No. 2153-03-2, 2005 Va. App. LEXIS 74 (Ct. of Appeals Feb. 22, 2005).

Defendant's failure to raise the issue at trial about whether he was able to financially comply with the terms of his probation meant that he could not assert that issue for the first time on appeal. Myers v. Commonwealth, 2005 Va. App. LEXIS 165 (Apr. 26, 2005).

In a divorce case, when a husband argued at trial that he was entitled to half the equity from the sale of the marital home, but did not argue until appeal that the failure to award him the equity impermissibly modified the final divorce decree, his appeal was procedurally barred under Va. Sup. Ct. R. 5A:18. The "ends of justice" exception did not apply, as there was no indication that the trial court believed it was substantively modifying the terms of the final decree. Staples v. Staples, 2006 Va. App. LEXIS 230 (Apr. 18, 2006).

Defendant's claim that defendant's rights to due process, confrontation of accusers and witnesses, and effective counsel were violated was barred by Va. Sup. Ct. R. 5A:18, because the issue was not raised, directly or indirectly, at trial. Gupta v. Commonwealth, 2007 Va. App. LEXIS 264 (July 10, 2007).

Commonwealth was barred by Va. Sup. Ct. R. 5A:18 from raising its claim that a trial court erred by dismissing an indictment for object sexual penetration for the first time on appeal because: (1) the Commonwealth did not present the specific argument to the trial court; (2) at defendant's hearing on his motion to dismiss, the Commonwealth addressed only an indictment for aggravated sexual battery, the nolle prosse of that indictment, and the effect of the nolle prosse on speedy trial issues; (3) despite having had the opportunity to do so, the Commonwealth did not raise below the claim now argued on appeal, and (4) although Rule 5A:18 allowed exceptions for good cause or to meet the ends of justice, the Commonwealth did not argue that the court should invoke the exceptions. Commonwealth v. Phillip, 2007 Va. App. LEXIS 424 (Nov. 28, 2007).

Where appellant challenged the denial of a motion to suppress evidence, but appellant did not argue that an officer's seizure of "plain view" weapons during a second entry was illegal, the issue was not considered on appeal. Stallings v. Commonwealth, 2007 Va. App. LEXIS 451 (Dec. 18, 2007).

Defendant's failure to object to the deailed contents of a letter the victim wrote to a school counselor waived any challenge to the letter's admission at trial. Furthermore, defendant's failure to specifically object to the admission of the letter on the grounds of prior bad acts precluded appellate review on that ground; at trial, defendant only argued that the letter was unsigned, undated, duplicative, and prejudicial. Williams v. Commonwealth, 2008 Va. App. LEXIS 460 (Oct. 14, 2008).

Effect of failure to raise argument at trial or in a motion to reconsider. — In a spousal support case, where a wife argued on brief that the trial court erred in finding that the wife caused the dissolution of the marriage because Virginia law did not permit a divorce to be entered based upon the gradual breakdown of the marital relationship, this argument was not considered on appeal because the wife did not make this argument at trial or in the motion to reconsider. Morgan v. Watkins, 2007 Va. App. LEXIS 412 (Nov. 13, 2007).

Objection not specific and timely. — Va. Sup. Ct. R. 5A:18 precluded appellate review of the father's motion to appoint a new guardian ad litem, where the father failed to give specific and timely notice to the trial court of the father's objection to the trial court's failure to rule on the father's pretrial motion to disqualify the guardian ad litem. Otey v. Roanoke City Dep't of Soc. Servs., 2006 Va. App. LEXIS 324 (July 18, 2006).

Brief inadequate for appellate review. — In a dissolution of marriage action, where the wife's appellate brief submitted 10 questions referencing objections appended to the final decree, the appellate court was not required to comb through the record of seven days of testimony in order to properly assess the wife's claims on appeal. Catlett v. Catlett, Nos. 3031-03-2, 3057-03-2, 2004 Va. App. LEXIS 401 (Ct. of Appeals Aug. 24, 2004).

In a child custody dispute, a father's argument regarding interference of interstate commerce was not considered on appeal, because the father failed to present this argument to the trial court, develop the argument on brief, or cite any case law in support of the assertion. D'Ambrosio v. Fowler, 2008 Va. App. LEXIS 89 (Feb. 19, 2008).

Appellant did not preserve an issue for appeal because the appellant, at trial, did not make any argument relating to the issue, as the appellant did in the appellant's opening brief on appeal. Moreover, the ends of justice exception did not apply because the appellant did not show that a miscarriage of justice occurred. Lewis v. Bailey, 2011 Va. App. LEXIS 253 (Aug. 2, 2011).

Award of sole legal and physical custody of the parties' child to the mother was appropriate because his arguments regarding his "unique" circumstances were not preserved and the appellate court did not consider any arguments on appeal that were not presented to the trial court. Dajani v. Dajani, 2011 Va. App. LEXIS 383 (Dec. 6, 2011).

Issue of refusal of treatment not reviewable when not raised before Industrial (now Workers' Compensation) Commission. — Where the issue of unjustifiable refusal of medical treatment, for whatever reasons, was not raised before the Industrial (now Workers' Compensation) Commission, and in the absence of a ruling by the Commission on this issue, there was no foundation for appellate review. Catalytic, Inc. v. Mitchell, No. 0421-85 (Ct. of Appeals Dec. 13, 1985).

No previous opportunity to object. — Where the trial court on its own motion instructed the jury to ignore parts of an instruction without previous consultation with counsel, defense counsel did not have an opportunity to object to the trial court's ruling, and was not precluded from raising the issue on appeal. Mason v. Commonwealth, 7 Va. App. 339, 373 S.E.2d 603 (1988).

Objection to lesser included offense. — Where appellant failed to object to the trial court's ruling in convicting him of assault and battery based on an indictment for robbery at any time during the 21-day-period in which the court retained jurisdiction over the case, he was barred from raising the lesser included issue on appeal for the first time. Wetherington v. Commonwealth, No. 1836-92-1 (Ct. of Appeals July 19, 1994).

Failure to provide sufficient record. — Trial court's order pursuant to § 37.1-134.21 requiring a mental patient to undergo medical treatment was affirmed, because the patient failed to provide a sufficient record as required by Rule 5A:18 in order to allow the appellate court to consider the patient's arguments that the evidence was insufficient for the trial court to find that he was incapable of making an informed decision on his own behalf, and that the trial court failed to make certain findings required by § 37.1-134.21(H). Mullins v. Commonwealth, 39 Va. App. 728, 576 S.E.2d 770, 2003 Va. App. LEXIS 94 (2003).

When a defendant alleged, on appeal, that the trial court did not afford him the opportunity to present evidence that he had complied with his plea agreement, contrary to the representations of the state, the question was not preserved for appeal because, when the state advised the trial court, at sentencing, that defendant had not complied with his plea agreement, defendant only objected to the trial court's refusal to allow him to withdraw his guilty plea and did not attempt to present evidence of his compliance or seek a later hearing at which to present such evidence. Wright v. Commonwealth, No. 2214-02-1, 2003 Va. App. LEXIS 685 (Ct. of Appeals Dec. 23, 2003).

Although appellant stated that he would explain that his failure to appear at a contempt hearing was not his fault, neither the trial court's opinion letter nor anything in the record showed that the trial court ruled on whether the failure to appear was excusable neglect; therefore, there was nothing for the appellate court to review on appeal, and appellate consideration was barred. Walker v. Walker, 2007 Va. App. LEXIS 70 (Feb. 27, 2007).

Trial court did not err in failing to impute income to a mother because there was no record of the father's argument to the trial court, and without a transcript or written statement of facts, the court of appeals was unable to determine whether the father's assignment of error was preserved pursuant to Va. Sup. Ct. R. 5A:18; the trial court held that the father's written statement of facts was erroneous and incomplete, argumentative, and did not comply with Va. Sup. Ct. R. 5A:8(c). Lilley v. Wilson, 2012 Va. App. LEXIS 302 (Sept. 25, 2012).

Wife did not file objections or a motion to reconsider the trial court's order refusing to certify the written statement of facts as required by Va. Sup. Ct. R. 5A:18 and her claim of error was not preserved; as she did not provide a transcript of the hearing and the trial court was unable to certify the written statement of facts, her claims that the trial court included irrelevant, self-contradicting and defaming allegations in the final decree, that her evidence of her husband's desertion was improperly excluded, and that his improper testimony was admitted could not be considered since it could not be determined whether the claims were preserved under Va. Sup. Ct. R. 5A:8 and 5A:18. Wang v. Crumpacker, No. 0263-12-4, 2012 Va. App. LEXIS 401 (Dec. 11, 2012).

Defendant's failure to file a trial transcript or statement of facts did not mandate that his appeal be dismissed, since the purposes of this rule had been fulfilled, and the record establishes that the issue defendant raised was properly preserved for appellate review. Wolfe v. Commonwealth, 6 Va. App. 640, 371 S.E.2d 314 (1988).

Inadvertent failure to redact evidence. — Although inadvertent, defendant failed to avail himself of opportunity to redact objectionable portion of transcript before trial, and thus his objection was not timely and trial court did not err by granting a cautionary instruction and refusing to grant a mistrial. Shifflett v. Commonwealth, No. 2600-98-2 (Ct. of Appeals Feb. 29, 2000).

Failure to receive abstract into evidence. — Where defendant never contested the accuracy of the abstract not formally marked and received into evidence by the trial court upon which the show cause order was based, but instead contested the underlying validity of one entry on the abstract, and never objected to the trial court's consideration of the abstract, or the accuracy of its contents, the appellate court would not further consider defendant's claim that the evidence was insufficient because the abstract was not received into evidence. Myers v. Commonwealth, No. 0778-87-4 (Ct. of Appeals Jan. 24, 1989).

Argument on admission of chemical analysis certificate had to appear in transcript. — The transcript of a trial for driving while intoxicated submitted by appellant showed that he objected to the certificate of analysis and that the trial court allowed him to cross-examine the arresting officer before arguing the objection. However, the transcript does not contain any argument on the objection or the trial court's ruling. Thus, this rule bars appellant's regarding the certificate arguments on appeal. Sullivan v. County of Arlington, No. 2004-94-4 (Ct. of Appeals Oct. 17, 1995).

Failure to seek action after objection prevented consideration of error. — Merely stating an objection to "the irregularity of the jury" failed to indicate what action the defendant wanted the trial court to take; thus, defendant's failure to seek a mistrial or other action by the trial court prevented considering the error as a basis for a reversal. Parker v. Commonwealth, 14 Va. App. 592, 421 S.E.2d 450 (1992).

Defendant's acquiescence in the trial judge's statement of the law precludes reversal on the ground that an uncertified transcript could be used for the purpose of refreshing recollection. Jones v. Commonwealth, No. 1071-94-2 (Ct. of Appeals, Aug. 1, 1995).

Criminal procedure. — Because defendant lodged no objection to trial court's deferring adjudication on his guilty plea and placing him on probation, his argument that procedure was erroneous would not be considered for first time on appeal. Harris v. Commonwealth, No. 2986-98-4 (Ct. of Appeals Mar. 7, 2000).

Defendant's contention that the trial court erred in admitting an unauthenticated report could not be considered on appeal pursuant to Va. Sup. Ct. R. 5A:18 because defendant failed to specifically object as to the report's admission in the trial court. Farrar v. Commonwealth, 2006 Va. App. LEXIS 301 (July 5, 2006).

Defendant's plea was valid because the trial court conducted an extensive colloquy with him to ensure his plea of guilty was made knowingly, intelligently, and voluntarily and defendant, at no time, raised any issues regarding the voluntary nature of his plea. During the 15 months following his plea, defendant never challenged the trial court's acceptance of his plea; there was also no merit to his contention that he had little or no opportunity to challenge the voluntary nature of his plea in the trial court. Swilling v. Commonwealth, 2009 Va. App. LEXIS 24 (Jan. 27, 2009).

Motion was sufficient to properly raise issue. — Where Commonwealth contended that the defendant was procedurally barred by this rule from raising the issue on appeal because the motion to set aside the verdict was too vague and general and where the defendant did not move to strike the evidence after the Commonwealth's case or at the conclusion of all the evidence, but did move to set aside the verdict as contrary to the law and evidence since the trial court considered and ruled after a timely motion whether the evidence was sufficient to support the convictions, the motion was sufficient to properly raise the issue. Brown v. Commonwealth, 8 Va. App. 474, 382 S.E.2d 296 (1989).

Where appellant husband made several motions for the trial court to appoint a guardian ad litem, both orally and in written form, and the trial court denied all of husband's motions, because the trial court and the opposing party were given the opportunity to intelligently address, examine, and resolve the issue in the trial court, the appellate court was satisfied that the husband preserved the issue for appeal. Westfall v. Westfall, 2008 Va. App. LEXIS 34 (Jan. 22, 2008).

Appellants' motions to stay execution of sentence and the supporting grounds alleged therein, filed before the trial court entered the final order of contempt, were more effective at alerting the trial court to the appellants' objections than would have been the commonly accepted practice of endorsing the final order seen and objected to for the same reasons. Accordingly, the goals of Va. Sup. Ct. R. 5A:18 were met because the appellants afforded the circuit court an opportunity to rule intelligently on the due process issues that the appellants raised, thereby satisfying the requirements of Rule 5A:18. Scialdone v. Commonwealth, 51 Va. App. 679, 660 S.E.2d 317, 2008 Va. App. LEXIS 202 (2008).

Argument preserved. — Wife's claim that a husband did not preserve his assignments of error because he sent in his objections to the final order more than 21 days after the entry of the order for Va. Sup. Ct. R. 1:1 purposes was rejected as the husband properly preserved his objections under Va. Sup. Ct. R. 5A:18 in his closing argument and motion for rehearing on the sale of his separate property. Parsons v. Parsons, Nos. 2184-12-4, 2352-12-4, 2013 Va. App. LEXIS 169 (Ct. of Appeals June 4, 2013).

Because a motion for rehearing was both filed and ruled upon within the 21-day-period, wife properly preserved assignment of error for appeal. Smith v. Smith, 18 Va. App. 427, 444 S.E.2d 269 (1994).

Objection renewed in motion to reconsider. — Since wife raised issue in her exceptions to the commissioner's report and renewed her objection, although not quite so articulately, in her motion to reconsider, the dictates of this rule were satisfied. Smith v. Smith, 18 Va. App. 427, 444 S.E.2d 269 (1994).

Employer failed to move for reconsideration or to vacate opinion during 30-day period that decision remained within jurisdiction of Workers' Compensation Commission, and therefore issue of commission's compliance with review process would not be considered on appeal. Marley Mouldings, Inc. v. McGhee, No. 2272-99-3 (Ct. of Appeals Feb. 15, 2000).

Issue not preserved for appeal where objection was insufficiently specific. — Because defendant failed to make a contemporaneous objection to the Commonwealth's attorneys' question about nature and details of a prior felony conviction for unauthorized use to show the defendant's propensity to commit the charged offense of unauthorized use of an automobile with sufficient specificity for the trial judge to have intelligently considered and ruled upon the issue, the defendant had not preserved the issue for appeal. Henry v. Commonwealth, No. 1154-92-2 (Ct. of Appeals Nov. 9, 1993).

Where defendant argued that the officer's response misled him by suggesting that the officer was required only to ask, rather than to obtain, permission to search, and defendant failed to articulate this specific argument at the hearing on his motion to suppress, and the trial court had no opportunity to address the issue in the context of defendant's more general complaint, defendant's argument was procedurally barred. Temple v. Commonwealth, No. 2838-95-2 (Ct. of Appeals Mar. 11, 1997).

Defendant's argument concerning right to exercise peremptory challenge was not presented to trial court with specificity required by this rule, and therefore it would not be considered on appeal. Caprio v. Commonwealth, No. 2225-98-1 (Ct. of Appeals Mar. 14, 2000).

Wife in divorce matter failed to preserve any issues for appeal, she did not specify her objections or state her grounds as required. Jackson v. Jackson, No. 0995-01-2, 2001 Va. App. LEXIS 610 (Ct. of Appeals Nov. 6, 2001).

Where appellant husband objected to the trial court's child support award simply on the grounds that it was too high and that he could not afford it, but he mentioned nothing about the deviation being unsupported by "relevant evidence" and did not mention § 20-108.1, because the husband did not raise the "relevant evidence" argument in the trial court, the issue was not preserved for appeal. Westfall v. Westfall, 2008 Va. App. LEXIS 34 (Jan. 22, 2008).

Since defendant's only objection at trial was an objection to an expert's general qualifications as an expert and did not address whether delayed disclosure was a sufficiently proven scientific theory, defendant waived the defendant's objection on that basis under Rule 5A:18. Kilby v. Commonwealth, 52 Va. App. 397, 663 S.E.2d 540, 2008 Va. App. LEXIS 365 (2008).

Since defendant did not raise in his motion to strike or in his closing argument the issue of whether the evidence was sufficient to support the finding that he simultaneously possessed a firearm and cocaine, defendant waived the issue for appeallate review under Va. Sup. Ct. R. 5A:18. Scott v. Commonwealth, 2010 Va. App. LEXIS 458 (Nov. 23, 2010).

Decree lacked specificity necessary to save issue for appeal. — Although a notation on a decree recited that "[t]he defendant, by his attorney, noted an exception to the court's ruling based upon the fact that error was committed in computing the marital assets," this decree lacked the specificity necessary to save an issue for appeal. Appellant's generalized exception did not sufficiently state his objection together with the grounds therefor. Rose v. Rose, No. 0256-92-3 (Ct. of Appeals Sept. 15, 1992).

Query not sufficient to preseve error for review. — Appellate court refused to consider defendant's contention that the trial court erred in not giving her credit for 12 months served in jail where she failed to raise the issue in the trial court; the record showed only that counsel queried whether defendant would receive such credit. Widdifield v. Commonwealth, No. 3100-02-2, 2004 Va. App. LEXIS 63 (Ct. of Appeals Feb. 10, 2004), aff'd, 43 Va. App. 559, 600 S.E.2d 159 (2004).

Issue not preserved or briefed was not considered on appeal. — Because there were no transcript or statement of facts complying with Va. Sup. Ct. R. 5A:8, the record failed to establish that appellant presented the issues he raised on appeal to the trial court, as required by Va. Sup. Ct. R. 5A:18. Bowser v. Guenard, 2009 Va. App. LEXIS 266 (June 16, 2009).

Indigent defendant's claim on petition for appeal that the trial court violated defendant's constitutional and statutory rights by providing only a limited amount of funds to hire an investigator to locate alibi witness was barred by Va. Sup. Ct. R. 5A:18 because defendant failed to raise the constitutional and statutory arguments in the trial court. Dowdy v. Commonwealth, 2008 Va. App. LEXIS 588 (May 30, 2008).

Issue not preserved for appeal because no proffer was made. — Appellant did not preserve a line of questioning for review because the appellant did not specifically proffer what the answer or series of answers to the line of questioning would be, and the appellant's counsel did not represent that the particular line of questioning was relevant to establish an issue. The appellant's counsel also did not contend that the trial court's ruling resulted in a violation of the appellant's due process rights. Mosteller v. Brooks, 2008 Va. App. LEXIS 565 (Dec. 23, 2008).

Court of appeals had no basis for adjudication of defendant's claim that a trial court erred in prohibiting his attempts to impeach a victim and her mother because defendant did not make a proper proffer of the expected responses of the victim and mother to cross-examination questions; in the absence of such a proffer, the court of appeals was unable to determine whether the trial court's decision to exclude that testimony, if erroneous, prejudiced defendant. Cable v. Commonwealth, 2009 Va. App. LEXIS 409 (Sept. 15, 2009).

Failure to raise sentencing issue. — Because defendant did not object to a sentence of 29 years, 11 months with a suspended sentence of 25 years, five months conditioned upon the completion of a transitional program, and because the sentence did not exceed the maximum sentence in § 18.2-248, defendant's challenge to the sentencing order was barred by Va. Sup. Ct. R. 5A:18. Johnson v. Commonwealth, 2007 Va. App. LEXIS 257 (July 3, 2007).

Sentencing issue preserved for review. — Commonwealth had sufficiently preserved for appeal under Va. Sup. Ct. R. 5A:18 its argument that the sentences imposed on defendants were contrary to mandatory minimum sentencing terms. With regard to the first defendant, requiring the Commonwealth to "except" to the court's denial of its request to impose the mandatory minimum sentences would, in effect, re-create the requirement of noting an exception to a final adverse ruling of the trial judge; with regard to the second defendant, the Commonwealth's argument asking the trial court to impose the mandatory minimum sentences, coupled with the identical nature of the wording in the sentencing orders, made it clear that the trial judge understood that the Commonwealth's objection on this ground was continuing. Commonwealth v. Brown, 2008 Va. App. LEXIS 517 (2008), aff'd in part and rev'd in part, 279 Va. 210, 688 S.E.2d 185, 2010 Va. LEXIS 9 (2010).

Failure to raise issue of shifting burden of proof. — The court of appeals treated appellee's motion to dismiss as a motion for summary affirmance pursuant to Rule 5A:27; affirmance, not dismissal, is the proper appellate disposition when faced with a violation under this rule. Rose v. Rose, No. 0256-92-3 (Ct. of Appeals Sept. 15, 1992).

Calculation of pendente lite support. — Husband's argument that his income was overstated was barred on appeal because, even if trial court mistakenly failed to credit husband the claimed amount, he agreed to and signed the order for pendente lite support without objection. Kost v. Kost, No. 0116-99-1 (Ct. of Appeals Dec. 14, 1999).

Sexual penetration. — Appellant in first-degree murder case arising out of death of infant son, although moving to strike, failed to specifically assert that the evidence was insufficient to prove sexual penetration with an inanimate rather than an animate object, as required to preserve the issue for appeal. Marshall v. Commonwealth, 26 Va. App. 627, 496 S.E.2d 120 (1998).

The court of appeals would not address the appellant's argument that the Commonwealth had failed to prove that he had accomplished unlawful sexual penetration by force, threat or intimidation where this issue had not been raised with specificity at trial; the objections that were made related to the Commonwealth's failure to prove the absence of a marital relationship between the appellant and the victim and that the evidence failed to support the wording of the indictment. Clark v. Commonwealth, 30 Va. App. 406, 517 S.E.2d 260 (1999).

Right to speedy trial. — Although counsel and trial judge informally discussed speedy trial requirements, record failed to show that defendant alleged a speedy trial violation or moved to dismiss indictments based on § 19.2-243, and therefore this rule barred consideration of speedy trial issue on appeal. Laidler v. Commonwealth, No. 0161-99-4 (Ct. of Appeals Mar. 28, 2000).

Mother in child custody case was not estopped to show a change of circumstance because father did not raise the argument in the trial court. Parish v. Spaulding, 26 Va. App. 566, 496 S.E.2d 91 (1998), aff'd, 257 Va. 357, 513 S.E.2d 391 (1999).

Sufficiency of evidence to terminate parental rights. — Where mother, who appealed termination of her parental rights, argued issues on appeal, other than the sufficiency of the evidence to prove the necessary elements under § 16.1-283 to terminate her parental rights, the appellate court was barred from consideration of the other issues raised on appeal. Swearengin v. Department of Social Servs., No. 1798-00-3, 2001 Va. App. LEXIS 377 (Ct. of Appeals June 26, 2001).

Because a father failed to challenge the termination of his parental rights under subsection B and subdivision C 2 of § 16.1-283, and because nothing in the record or the written statement of facts filed in lieu of a transcript indicated that the father alleged a violation of his due process rights before the trial court, Va. Sup. Ct. R. 5A:18 barred consideration of his claims on appeal. Carr v. Pulaski County Dep't of Soc. Servs., 2008 Va. App. LEXIS 337 (July 22, 2008).

Exceptions not applicable. — On appeal from the termination of parental rights, the parents due process arguments were not considered by the appellate court because they did not make the arguments to the trial court and the good cause and/or ends of justice exceptions to Va. Sup. Ct. R. 5A:18 were not applicable. The parents did not argue why the exceptions should be applied, which they were required to do. Birchfield v. Scott County Dep't of Soc. Servs., 2011 Va. App. LEXIS 376 (Nov. 29, 2011).

Miscarriage of justice shown. — Defendant made an affirmative showing that a miscarriage of justice had occurred in his case even though he did not raise the specific argument concerning revocation of his suspended sentence and probation for distributing imitation cocaine during his subsequent malicious wounding trial, as no evidence in the record showed that defendant committed any violation that would render his suspended sentence and probation subject to revocation; indeed, the conduct that was the basis for the revocation occurred before the sentence was imposed on defendant for cocaine distribution, not after as was required. Oliver v. Commonwealth, 38 Va. App. 845, 568 S.E.2d 465, 2002 Va. App. LEXIS 522 (2002).

Miscarriage of justice not shown. — In a case in which defendant was alleged to have sexually abused his six-year-old daughter, who was allowed to testify by closed-circuit television, defendant did not object to the child having a coloring book while she testified, and nothing suggested that the coloring book clearly, substantially, and materially contributed to the child's confusing, inexact, and inconsistent testimony, such that the "miscarriage of justice" exception to the requirement that an error be raised in the trial court would apply. Parrish v. Commonwealth, 38 Va. App. 607, 567 S.E.2d 576, 2002 Va. App. LEXIS 487 (2002).

Defendant, who failed to object to certain testimony regarding his alleged sexual abuse of a seven year old girl, failed to preserve the issue under Rule 5A:18, and the court would not consider his objection because he failed to show that a miscarriage of justice, or a clear, substantial, or material error had occurred. Almond v. Commonwealth, No. 3071-01-2, 2002 Va. App. LEXIS 746 (Ct. of Appeals Dec. 17, 2002).

In a termination of parental rights case, the mother whose parental rights were terminated by the trial court could not argue initially on appeal that the department of social services did not make reasonable efforts to reunify her with her children, and, as she showed no good cause for her failure to comply with the reasonable efforts the department did make, there was no reason to invoke the good cause or ends of justice exceptions to Va. Sup. Ct. R. 5A:18's preclusion of the appellate consideration of an argument not first raised before the trial court. Hansberry v. Charlottesville Dep't of Soc. Servs., Nos. 0117-03-2 - 0120-03-2, 2003 Va. App. LEXIS 336 (Ct. of Appeals June 17, 2003).

Because none of defendant's arguments on appeal were raised before the trial court, and because defendant did not argue that the exceptions for good cause or to meet the ends of justice should be invoked, Va. Sup. Ct. R. 5A:18 barred consideration of the issues for the first time on appeal. Lara v. Commonwealth, 2007 Va. App. LEXIS 154 (Apr. 17, 2007).

Court was unconvinced that a miscarriage of justice has occurred, where the circuit court used appellant husband's adultery as grounds for uneven distribution of marital property. Westfall v. Westfall, 2008 Va. App. LEXIS 34 (Jan. 22, 2008).

Rule 5A:19. General Requirements for All Briefs.

(a) *Length.* — Except by permission of a Judge of this Court, neither the opening brief of appellant, nor the brief of appellee, nor a brief amicus curiae shall exceed 12,300 words. No reply brief shall exceed 3,500 words. Word limits under this Rule do not include appendices, or the cover page, table of contents, table of authorities, and certificate. There shall be no exception to these limits except by permission of this Court on motion for extension of the limits.

(b) *Filing Time: Appeal as a Matter of Right.* — In cases when appeal lies as a matter of right to the Court of Appeals, briefs shall be filed as follows:

(1) The appellant shall file the opening brief in the office of the clerk of the Court of Appeals within 40 days after the date of the filing of the record in such office.

(2) The brief of appellee and the brief of the guardian ad litem shall be filed in the office of the clerk of the Court of Appeals within 25 days after filing of the opening brief.

(3) The appellant may file a reply brief in the office of the clerk of the Court of Appeals within 14 days after filing of the brief of appellee or guardian ad litem.

(4) Motions for extensions to these briefing deadlines shall be filed no later than 10 days after the expiration of the deadline.

(c) *Filing Time: Grant of Petition for Appeal.* — In cases when a petition for appeal has been granted by the Court of Appeals, briefs shall be filed as follows:

(1) The appellant shall file the opening brief in the office of the clerk of the Court of Appeals within 40 days after the date of the certificate of appeal issued by the clerk of the Court of Appeals pursuant to Rule 5A:16(b).

(2) The brief of appellee shall be filed in the office of the clerk of the Court of Appeals within 25 days after filing of the opening brief.

(3) The appellant may file a reply brief in the office of the clerk of the Court of Appeals within 14 days after filing of the brief of appellee.

(4) Motions for extensions to these briefing deadlines shall be filed no later than 10 days after the expiration of the deadline.

(d) *Participation by Guardian Ad Litem.* — If a guardian ad litem joins with either appellant or appellee, the guardian ad litem must notify the Clerk's Office, in writing, which side it joins. Thereafter, the guardian ad litem may rely on the brief of that party and is entitled to oral argument under Rule 5A:26.

(e) *Arguments Made by Reference.* — Attempts to incorporate arguments made below by reference to pleadings, motions, memorandum, or other filings are prohibited.

(f) *Copies.* — Seven copies of each brief shall be filed and one copy shall be mailed or delivered to opposing counsel on or before the date of filing.

Cross references. — See Rule 5A:10 regarding filing of the record.

Law Review. — For 2003/2004 survey of family and juvenile law, see 39 U. Rich. L. Rev. 241 (2004).

Michie's Jurisprudence. — For related discussion, see 1B M.J. Appeal and Error, § 233.

CASE NOTES

Compliance. — Appellate court denied the motion to dismiss filed by the parents that claimed the compensation program did not comply with Va. Sup. Ct. R. 5A:19(f); the compensation program mailed a copy of its opening brief to the parents at the time it filed its brief with the appellate court and it was only because of an improper address that the brief was delayed in getting to the parents, but the rule did not require timely receipt of the brief by opposing counsel as a prerequisite for compliance with the rule. Va. Birth-Related Neurological Injury Comp. Program v. McGrady, 2006 Va. App. LEXIS 79 (Mar. 7, 2006).

Rule 5A:20. Requirements for Opening Brief of Appellant.

The opening brief of appellant shall contain:

(a) A table of contents and table of authorities with cases alphabetically arranged. Citations of all authorities shall include the year thereof.

(b) A brief statement of the nature of the case and of the material proceedings in the trial court, which shall omit references to any paper filed or action taken that does not relate to the assignments of error.

(c) A statement of the assignments of error with a clear and exact reference to the page(s) of the transcript, written statement, record, or appendix where each assignment of error was preserved in the trial court.

(d) A clear and concise statement of the facts that relate to the assignments of error, with references to the pages of the transcript, written statement, record, or appendix. Any quotation from the record should be brief. When the facts are in dispute, the brief shall so state. The testimony of individual witnesses should not be summarized seriatim unless the facts are in dispute and such a summary is necessary to support the appellant's version of the facts.

(e) The standard of review and the argument (including principles of law and authorities) relating to each assignment of error. When the assignment of error was not preserved in the trial court, counsel shall state why the good cause and/or ends of justice exceptions to Rule 5A:18 are applicable. With respect to each assignment of error, the standard of review and the argument — including principles of law and the authorities — shall be stated in one place and not scattered through the brief. At the option of counsel, the argument may be preceded by a short summary.

(f) A short conclusion stating the precise relief sought.

(g) The signature (which need not be in handwriting) of at least one counsel and counsel's Virginia State Bar number, address, telephone number, facsimile number (if any), and email address (if any).

(h) A certificate (which need not be signed in handwriting) stating (1) that Rule 5A:19(f) has been complied with, and (2) whether counsel desires to waive oral argument. The certificate must also state the number of words (headings, footnotes, and quotations count towards the word limitation; the cover page, table of contents, table of authorities, and certificate do not count towards the word count). Additionally, any party may waive oral argument without leave of this Court by written notification to the clerk of this Court within 21 days after the date on which the appellee's brief is due to be filed or has been filed.

Comment. — In their briefs and oral argument, counsel should avoid references to parties by such designations as "appellant" and "appellee." Clarity is promoted by the use of the names of the parties, or descriptive terms such as "the employee," "the injured person," "the driver" or "the husband," or the designations used in the lower court or commission.

Law Review. — For annual survey article, "Family Law," see 46 U. Rich. L. Rev. 145 (2011).

CASE NOTES

Failure to include issue in statement of questions presented. — Although issue was briefed by appellants, it would not be reached where it was not included in their statement of questions presented. Toombs v. Smith, No. 0109-99-2 (Ct. of Appeals Nov. 9, 1999).

Where defendant failed to brief the specific issue upon which the appeal was awarded, pursuant to Rule 5A:20(e), the appeal was not addressed. Chubbick v. Commonwealth, No. 2554-02-1, 2003 Va. App. LEXIS 534 (Ct. of Appeals Oct. 28, 2003).

Virginia Uninsured Employer's Fund's issues as

to whether the Virginia Workers' Compensation Commission erred in finding that a workers' compensation claimant was an employee, that the employer was subject to the Virginia Workers' Compensation Act, § 65.2-100 et seq., and that the claimant made a reasonable effort to market the claimant's residual work capacity were not raised in the Fund's first question presented, and were not addressed on appeal pursuant to Va. Sup. Ct. R. 5A:20(c)-(e). Uninsured Employer's Fund v. Chaney, 2007 Va. App. LEXIS 335 (Sept. 11, 2007).

On appeal from a drug-related conviction, defendant's argument regarding chain of custody requirements was not considered as it was not included in the "questions presented" in defendant's opening brief as required by Va. Sup. Ct. R. 5A:20. Smith v. Commonwealth, 2007 Va. App. LEXIS 457 (Dec. 18, 2007).

Arguments attached as appendix are not considered on appeal. — Appellate court would not consider defendant's additional arguments attached to his brief as an appendix in violation of Rule 5A:20(e); it is not the function of the appellate court to comb through the record to ferret-out for itself the validity of the parties' claims. Parks v. Commonwealth, No. 2780-02-1, 2003 Va. App. LEXIS 385 (Ct. of Appeals July 8, 2003).

Failure to provide supporting law, argument or authorities. — Court would not address question supported by neither argument nor precedent. Henderson v. VEC, No. 1056-99-2 (Ct. of Appeals Sept. 14, 1999).

Counsel provided not a single case citation in support of his position. Jacobs v. Commonwealth, 2002 Va. App. LEXIS 589 (Oct. 8, 2002).

Because a wife presented no legal authority on appeal that she was legally obligated to assign rental income to her mother and that a trial court erroneously considered that income in establishing child support, an appellate court declined to consider it on appeal. Holohan v. Holohan, No. 1387-03-4, 2004 Va. App. LEXIS 121 (Ct. of Appeals Mar. 23, 2004).

In a husband's appeal of the award of alimony to his former wife, when he did not cite authority supporting four of the six assignments of error he raised, the appellate court was precluded, under Va. Sup. Ct. R. 5A:20, from considering those assignments. Driskill v. Driskill, No. 2625-03-1, 2004 Va. App. LEXIS 311 (Ct. of Appeals July 6, 2004).

Trial court declined to consider defendant's appeal as she failed to meet the requirements of Rule 5A:20(e) that her opening brief include the principles of law, the argument, and the authorities relating to each question presented. Marsh v. Commonwealth, No. 2865-02-1, 2004 Va. App. LEXIS 68 (Ct. of Appeals Feb. 10, 2004).

Because she presented no citations or authority in her brief in support of her question on appeal, a mother waived her claim of error that the trial court applied improper legal standards and burdens of proof and law. Nelson v. Petersburg Dep't of Soc. Servs., No. 1343-04-2, 2005 Va. App. LEXIS 72 (Ct. of Appeals Feb. 22, 2005).

Because defendant made no argument and did not cite to any authority in support of an assertion that the trial court lacked authority to assess costs for the victim's funeral expenses, defendant violated the provisions of Va. Sup. Ct. R. 5A:20; consequently, the trial court's judgment was affirmed. Bridges v. Commonwealth, 2005 Va. App. LEXIS 498 (Dec. 13, 2005).

Appeals court rejected a husband's six claims of error from a QDRO, awarding a wife the gains earned on the portion of his retirement account distributed to her in the couple's divorce decree, as the husband failed to comply with Va. Sup. Ct. R. 5A:20(c) and (e), and despite his pro se status, he was required to comply with the rules of court. Blythe v. Blythe, 2006 Va. App. LEXIS 392 (Aug. 22, 2006).

Husband waived his claim that the trial court erred by failing to issue a written statement explaining its deviation from the child support guidelines as he failed to cite any authority or argument for the proposition that a trial court was required to issue a written statement in a modification of child support proceeding. Towner v. Towner, 2006 Va. App. LEXIS 430 (Sept. 26, 2006).

An attempt to comply with Va. Sup. Ct. R. 5A:20(e) in a reply brief filed pursuant to Va. Sup. Ct. R. 5A:22 could not excuse a defendant's failure to comply with Va. Sup. Ct. R. 5A:20. Bennett v. Commonwealth, 2007 Va. App. LEXIS 155 (Apr. 17, 2007).

Father's failure to cite authority for the father's argument that the trial court by not specifically including in its final order a provision affirming that the father was entitled to retain a child dependency income tax exemption provided for the father in a property settlement agreement waived the father's argument on appeal, as the father was required to cite authority in support of the father's argument in order to merit appellate consideration. Ericson v. Ericson, 2007 Va. App. LEXIS 258 (July 3, 2007).

Because an employer/carrier's opening brief failed to comply with Va. Sup. Ct. R. 5A:20(e), its claims relating to the Workers' Compensation Commission's findings that an employee proved various periods of disability and that the employee's injuries, disability, and medical treatment were causally related to an injury by accident were dismissed. Inova Fair Oaks Hosp. v. Epps, 2007 Va. App. LEXIS 289 (July 31, 2007).

Defendant waived a challenge to the alleged multifariousness of the charge against defendant by failing to cite to cases, statutes, treatises, or other informative legal sources addressing any aspect of defendant's argument. Morin v. Commonwealth, 2007 Va. App. LEXIS 346 (Sept. 18, 2007).

Appellant wife's argument that a trial court erred by failing to award her attorney's fees in divorce proceedings was not considered on appeal because the wife did not comply wtih Va. Sup. Ct. R. 5A:20(e) as her opening brief did not contain sufficient principles of law, argument, or citation to legal authorities or the record to fully develop her arguments. Ulka Ghulam v. Ghulam Ali Sidiqi, 2007 Va. App. LEXIS 452 (Dec. 18, 2007).

In a child custody dispute, a father's argument regarding interference of interstate commerce was not considered on appeal, because the father failed to present this argument to the trial court, develop the argument on brief, or cite any case law in support of the assertion. D'Ambrosio v. Fowler, 2008 Va. App. LEXIS 89 (Feb. 19, 2008).

Appellate court did not consider defendant's allegation of a Sixth Amendment violation on appeal, pursuant to Va. Sup. Ct. R. 5A:20(c), because, although defendant included a Sixth Amendment violation in his question presented, defendant did not make any argument that defendant's Sixth Amendment right to counsel was violated or cite to any authority to support a Sixth Amendment violation. Jones v. Commonwealth, 2008 Va. App. LEXIS 84 (Feb. 19, 2008).

Defendant waived his argument that the circuit court erred in refusing to allow him to admit evidence of the victim's bad character during the sentencing proceedings because defendant violated Va. Sup. Ct. R. 5A:20(e) by failing to cite any authority in support of that argument in his opening brief. Rambo v. Commonwealth, 51 Va. App. 418, 658 S.E.2d 688, 2008 Va. App. LEXIS 149 (2008).

Because defendant cited no authority for the proposition he put forth in his brief that the police were required to advise him of his Miranda rights specifically pertaining to the victim's murder, after questioning him about a stolen car, the appellate court did not review that argument. Eleazer v. Commonwealth, 2008 Va. App. LEXIS 133 (Mar. 18, 2008).

Court of appeals was procedurally barred from considering a husband's claim that a court's illegible handwritten orders violated due process because the husband's opening brief with respect to that issue did not comply with Va. Sup. Ct. R. 5A:20(e); the husband failed to include any principles of law or authorities related to the question in support of his argument. Smith v. Smith, 2008 Va. App. LEXIS 184 (Apr. 15, 2008).

Defendant's argument that a principal in the second degree had to adopt the criminal intent of an actual, not conditional, threat by the principal in the first degree was procedurally defaulted because defendant did not cite any legal authority for the claim or make a legal argument beyond ambiguous and conclusory statements. McKinney v. Commonwealth, 2008 Va. App. LEXIS 344 (July 8, 2008).

Since a husband did not include an argument in his questions presented, as required by Va. Sup. Ct. R. 5A:18 and 5A:20, the argument was not addressed on appeal; accordingly, because he failed to pay a lump sum alimony payment, the trial court's contempt finding under subdivision K 2 of § 20-107.3 was summarily affirmed. Stoneman v. Stoneman, 2008 Va. App. LEXIS 458 (Oct. 14, 2008).

Because an owner's opening brief contained no argument, principles of law, or authorities related to the owner's questions presented on appeal, the owner's failure to comply with Va. Sup. Ct. R. 5A:20(e) was significant; accordingly, the questions were waived. Meadows v. Smith, 2008 Va. App. LEXIS 419 (Sept. 16, 2008).

Because an employee presented no argument and cited no authorities in support of the employee's question regarding medical causation for the employee's disability, as required by Va. Sup. Ct. R. 5A:20(e), the employee's failure to comply with Rule 5A:20(e) was significant, and the question was waived. Kohut v. Piedmont Reg'l Educ. Program, 2008 Va. App. LEXIS 420 (Sept. 16, 2008).

Former wife did not comply with Va. Sup. Ct. R. 5A:20(e) because her opening brief did not contain any principles of law, argument, or citation to legal authorities or the record to fully develop her arguments; because the wife's failure to comply with Rule 5A:20(e) was significant, the court of appeals would not consider the questions she presented. Deluca v. Katchmeric, 2009 Va. App. LEXIS 267 (June 16, 2009).

Father's appeals of circuit court orders awarding a mother attorney's fees, dismissing rules to show cause, and calculating child support and arrears were procedurally barred because the father failed to comply with Va. Sup. Ct. R. 5A:20(e) when his opening briefs did not contain any principles of law or citation to legal authorities or the record to fully develop his arguments; the husband's failure to comply with Rule 5A:20(e) was significant, and the court of appeals would not consider the issues he raised on appeal. Salah v. Commonwealth ex rel. Jaouni, 2009 Va. App. LEXIS 233 (May 19, 2009).

Defendant's failure to strictly adhere to the requirements of Va. Sup. Ct. R. 5A:20(e) was significant, and defendant's claim was waived as defendant did not testify and never specifically articulated how the evidence supported the proffered self-defense instructions in relation to defendant's hitting a bouncer as: (1) defendant's witness testified that defendant never hit anyone after the bouncers brought defendant outside; and (2) none of the versions indicated that the bouncer was engaged in any behavior that entitled defendant to act in self-defense after the bouncers had deposited defendant on the ground and ended their physical contact with defendant. Bufford v. Commonwealth, 2009 Va. App. LEXIS 335 (July 28, 2009).

In a child custody case in which a pro se father failed to comply with the requirements of Va. Sup. Ct. R. 5A:20(e) as to his claims that the trial court erred in finding that there was a change in circumstances warranting a change in custody and that the change was in the child's best interests, that failure was significant, and the appellate court would not consider those questions. Serdah v. Serdah, 2009 Va. App. LEXIS 410 (Sept. 15, 2009).

Mother did not comply with Va. Sup. Ct. R. 5A:20(e) because her opening brief did not contain any principles of law, or citation to legal authorities or to the record to fully develop her argument that the trial court erred in reviewing a guardian ad litem's addendum. Because the mother's failure to comply with Rule 5A:20(e) was significant, the issue was not considered on appeal. Mercurio v. Mercurio, 2009 Va. App. LEXIS 492 (Nov. 3, 2009).

On appeal from a divorce action, the husband's argument that the trial court used an incorrect date of separation, which affected the division of his military retirement, and that trial court erred in ruling that the wife was not responsible for a portion of the student loan used for the benefit of their child was improper because the husband failed to comply with Va. Sup. Ct. R. 5A:20(e). His opening brief did not contain any principles of law or citation to legal authorities to fully develop his arguments. Holmes v. Holmes, 2010 Va. App. LEXIS 40 (Feb. 2, 2010).

In an appeal from an order finding a husband in contempt of a final divorce decree and ordering the husband to pay the wife an arrearage, three issues were not preserved for appeal because the husband failed to comply with Va. Sup. Ct. R. 5A:20(e) in his opening brief where the husband failed to develop the arguments and the citation to legal authorities did not support the questions presented. Jackson v. Jackson, 2010 Va. App. LEXIS 221 (June 1, 2010).

Husband did not comply with Va. Sup. Ct. R. 5A:20(e) because his opening brief did not contain any principles of law or citation to legal authorities to support his asserted trial court error in the denial of the motions to modify judgment. Cook v. Cross, 2010 Va. App. LEXIS 234 (June 8, 2010).

Appellant did not comply with Va. Sup. Ct. R. 5A:20(e) in that the appellant's opening brief did not contain any principles of law or citation to legal authorities to fully develop the appellant's argument. Because the appellant's failure to comply with Rule 5A:20(e) was significant, the appellate court did not consider the issue which the appellant sought to raise on appeal. Pramagioulis v. Pramagioulis, 2011 Va. App. LEXIS 20 (Jan. 25, 2011).

Since a husband had not provided the court of appeals with any argument or legal support in his brief for why the trial court erred in deferring to a Hungarian court's jurisdiction over the divorce, the court of appeals would not consider that particular issue. Prizzia v. Prizzia, 58 Va. App. 137, 707 S.E.2d 461, 2011 Va. App. LEXIS 124 (2011).

Husband failed to comply with Va. Sup. Ct. R. 5A:20(e) because his opening brief did not contain any principles of law, or citation to legal authorities, to fully develop his arguments for some of the issues he raised on appeal; the husband's failure to comply with Rule 5A:20(e) was significant, so the court of appeals would not consider those issues. Kirkendale v. Kirkendale, 2011 Va. App. LEXIS 109 (Mar. 29, 2011).

Father did not comply with Va. Sup. Ct. R. 5A:20(e) because his opening brief did not contain any principles of law, or citation to legal authorities, or the record to fully develop his arguments for his assignment of error; the father's failure to comply with Rule 5A:20(e) was significant, so the court of appeals would not consider the assignment of error. Sowers v. Walker, 2011 Va. App. LEXIS 155 (May 10, 2011).

Because the record did not contain copies of the protective orders at issue and the trial court's orders from a husband's divorce, because the husband was not a "party defendant" entitled to appointment of a guardian ad litem under § 8.01-9, and because his opening brief did not comply with Va. Sup. Ct. R. 5A:20(e), the appeal lacked merit. Harnois v. Commonwealth, 2011 Va. App. LEXIS 285 (Sept. 27, 2011).

Appellate court found defendant's failure to explain, develop, or support an argument in defendant's brief was significant. Therefore, the court did not address it pursuant to Va. Sup. Ct. R. 5A:20(e). Epps v. Commonwealth, 59 Va. App. 71, 717 S.E.2d 151, 2011 Va. App. LEXIS 351 (2011).

While an employee received notice of the deficiencies in the employee's brief and appendix under Va. Sup. Ct. R. 5A:4, 5A:18, 5A:20, 5A:24, 5A:25, because the employee failed to correct any of the defects, which in totality were significant, and never actually challenged the ruling of the issue on appeal, the employee's appeal lacked merit. Adams v. Va. Empl. Comm'n, 2012 Va. App. LEXIS 67 (Mar. 6, 2012).

Since defendant failed to provide any argument, principles of law, or legal authority in her brief to support her contention that the trial court erred in convicting her of conspiracy to commit abduction and robbery, as required by Va. Sup. Ct. R. 5A:20(e), the trial court refused to address defendant's sufficiency argument as it related to her conviction. Wade v. Commonwealth, 2012 Va. App. LEXIS 161 (May 15, 2012).

Court did not address defendant's contention that the jury was allowed to presume fraud in the absence of evidence demonstrating fraud when it was not provided with a legal definition of the term "fraud" as defendant did not develop the argument, as required by Va. Sup. Ct. R. 5A:20. Wells v. Commonwealth, 60 Va. App. 111, 724 S.E.2d 225, 2012 Va. App. LEXIS 131 (2012).

Trial court did not err in awarding a mother for the attorney's fees she incurred in her challenge to a father's written statement of facts because the mother appeared before the trial court to argue her objections to the written statement of facts, and she presented an affidavit, indicating the amount of attorney's fees she incurred for reviewing and addressing the issues regarding the written statement of facts; the father did not present any legal authority to support his argument that he should have received a copy of the attorney's fees affidavit even though he was late to the hearing. Lilley v. Wilson, 2012 Va. App. LEXIS 302 (Sept. 25, 2012).

Father did not comply with Va. Sup. Ct. R. 5A:20(e) because his opening brief did not contain any principles of law, or citation to legal authorities, or the record to fully develop his arguments regarding alleged fraud; the father's failure to comply with Rule 5A:20(e) was significant, so the court of appeals would will not consider the assignment of error. Quincer v. Dep't of Soc. Servs., Div. of Child Support Enforcement, No. 0693-12-4, 2012 Va. App. LEXIS 339 (Oct. 23, 2012).

Husband's claim that lay opinion testimony on the ultimate issue was improperly admitted was waived under Va. Sup. Ct. R. 5A:20(e) as it was not supported by authority, even though a statute, subsection B of § 8.01-401.3, governed the issue. Harris v. Harris, No. 1957-11-2, 2012 Va. App. LEXIS 361 (Nov. 13, 2012).

Court of appeals would not consider defendant's alleged error because defendant failed to make any argument or to cite any authority in support of his contention as required under Va. Sup. Ct. R. 5A:20(e). Mayo v. Commonwealth, 2013 Va. App. LEXIS 57 (Feb. 19, 2013).

Husband's claims that the trial court erred in not awarding him custody and in decreasing his visitation and that the trial court demonstrated its prejudice against the husband by rendering unfair and unworkable orders were waived as he did not cite relevant legal authority for his claims as required by Va. Sup. Ct. R. 5A:20(e). Kramer v. Kramer, 2013 Va. App. LEXIS 48 (Feb. 12, 2013).

Arguments in a mother's brief regarding her claim of error in the adoption of the father's proposed order did not contain any principles of law or citations to legal authorities as required by Va. Sup. Ct. R. 5A:20(e) and were not considered. Richards v. Richards, No. 1326-12-2, 2013 Va. App. LEXIS 106 (Ct. of Appeals Apr. 2, 2013).

Mother's brief fell short of the threshold showing

of advocacy necessary to warrant serious appellate review because the mother failed to cite any authority or develop the argument related to the assignments of error related to a hearing wherein the mother was found to have violated an order to return the child to the father. Wandell v. Connelly, No. 2225-12-2, 2013 Va. App. LEXIS 178 (Ct. of Appeals June 11, 2013).

Failure to cite cases addressing issues. — Defendant violated the provisions of Va. Sup. Ct. R. 5A:20(e) by failing to cite any cases addressing the substantive issues of his appeal; an appellate court thus declined to address defendant's arguments as to sufficiency of the evidence or as to denial of his motion to suppress. Palmer v. Commonwealth, 2006 Va. App. LEXIS 543 (Dec. 5, 2006).

Appellate court declined to consider the father's contentions in a case involving the mother and father's divorce, and related rulings, that the tribal court in Minnesota that was determined to be a better forum to consider the issues had no jurisdiction over the father, as the father did not present authority to support that position. Swalef v. Anderson, 50 Va. App. 100, 646 S.E.2d 458, 2007 Va. App. LEXIS 245 (2007).

Court of Appeals of Virginia erred by dismissing a portion of petitions for appeal filed separately by two defendants, upon their failure to comply with the requirements of Va. Sup. Ct. R. 5A:20(e), as: (1) the rule did not impose jurisdictional requirements; and (2) the Court of Appeals could have explored other options, short of dismissal, and should have considered whether any failure to strictly adhere to the requirements of the rule was insignificant, thus allowing the court to address the merits of a question presented. Jay v. Commonwealth, 275 Va. 510, 659 S.E.2d 311, 2008 Va. LEXIS 53 (2008).

Appellate court refused to reconsider a husband's argument concerning a $331,294 payment to his ex-wife under Va. Sup. Ct. R. 5A:18 because he should not be penalized for his attorney's error as the ends of justice exception applied to Rule 5A:18 and objections made at trial; it did not apply to Va. Sup. Ct. R. 5A:20(e) and an attorney's failure to cite legal authorities to support an argument. Parsons v. Parsons, Nos. 2184-12-4, 2352-12-4, 2013 Va. App. LEXIS 169 (Ct. of Appeals June 4, 2013).

Failure to provide reference to arguments or objections. — Husband failed to preserve the issues for appeal, where the appendix pages referenced in the husband's brief did not refer to arguments or objections made to the trial court regarding the issues; nor did the record reflect any reason to invoke the good cause or ends of justice exceptions to the Rules. Brown v. Brown, No. 0580-03-2, 2003 Va. App. LEXIS 528 (Ct. of Appeals Oct. 21, 2003).

Husband's argument that he objected to the alteration of any provision of an earlier protective order other than the rescission of the grant of the exclusive use of the former marital residence was not supported by references to the pages of the appendix where such an objection was preserved in the trial court, and, thus, the trial court's action in not modifying a "no contact" provision from a prior protective order when a new protective order was entered was affirmed. Shaffer v. Shaffer, No. 1945-03-2, 2004 Va. App. LEXIS 269 (Ct. of Appeals June 8, 2004).

Husband's brief on appeal failed to include any reference to the trial court's finding that the husband failed to cooperate with his former counsel, which resulted in counsel's withdrawal and a delay in the proceedings; that oversight warranted a reminder to counsel about what to include in an opening brief. True v. True, No. 0141-04-1, 2004 Va. App. LEXIS 350 (Ct. of Appeals July 20, 2004).

Because a husband's opening brief did not direct the appellate court to the place in the record where he stated the reasons for his objection to the trial court's property distribution, in accordance with Va. Sup. Ct. R. 5A:20(c), the husband did not preserve the objections for review under Va. Sup. Ct. R. 5A:18. Huffman v. Huffman, 2005 Va. App. LEXIS 369 (Sept. 27, 2005).

Appellate court denied the motion to dismiss filed by the parents since the compensation program's complied with Va. Sup. Ct. R. 20(c); the plain language of Va. Sup. Ct. R. 20(c) did not require the compensation program to cite to the transcript, appendix, or record within the "Questions Presented" section of the compensation program's opening brief, and, thus, the compensation program could not violate that rule for not having done so. Va. Birth-Related Neurological Injury Comp. Program v. McGrady, 2006 Va. App. LEXIS 79 (Mar. 7, 2006).

Because an employee's brief failed to include sufficient principles of law or any citation to legal authorities in support of the extent and duration of the employee's disability, it did not comply with Va. Sup. Ct. R. 5A:20(e). Washington v. Stanford Enterprises/Upscale Healthcare Servs., 2007 Va. App. LEXIS 160 (Apr. 17, 2007).

Court of appeals refused to address questions a husband presented on appeal because the record did not reflect two of the rulings to which the husband assigned error, and the fact that the husband's opening brief indicated that the issues were preserved at certain transcript pages was hardly the clear and exact reference required by Va. Sup. Ct. R. 5A:20(c). Showalter v. Showalter, 2009 Va. App. LEXIS 78 (Feb. 17, 2009).

Defendant's convictions for statutory burglary, attempted robbery, unlawful wounding, and use of a firearm in the commission of a felony were proper because, although he asserted that the trial court abused its discretion when it failed to grant his motions for mistrial following arguably improper testimony by three other witnesses, defendant failed to make a legal argument in support of those assertions of error as required by Va. Sup. Ct. R. 5A:20(e). Clatterbaugh v. Commonwealth, 2010 Va. App. LEXIS 289 (July 27, 2010).

Because it did not appear that an objection was ever presented to the trial court, Va. Sup. Ct. R. 5A:18 barred consideration on appeal of the mother's argument that the trial court erred in refusing to allow disclosures of sexual abuse as evidence of a child's state of mind; the mother's brief did not direct the court of appeals to the place in the record where she preserved the specific issue for appeal, and there was no evidence in the record indicating that the mother informed the trial court of the error she presented to the court of appeals. Anonymous C v. Anonymous B, No. 2232-09-2, 2011 Va. App. LEXIS 14 (Ct. of Appeals Jan. 11, 2011).

Husband's argument was barred by Va. Sup. Ct.

R. 5A:20(c) because he did not preserve the argument in his breif. West v. West, 59 Va. App. 225, 717 S.E.2d 831, 2011 Va. App. LEXIS 390 (2011).

Father's failure to strictly adhere to the requirements of Va. Sup. Ct. R. 5A:20(c) were insignificant and were not so substantial as to preclude the court of appeals from addressing the merits of the case because the father's references to where he preserved the alleged error for appeal adequately encompass his arguments and objections to the trial court as well as the trial court's ruling. Moncrief v. Div. of Child Support Enforcement ex rel. Joyner, 60 Va. App. 721, 732 S.E.2d 714, 2012 Va. App. LEXIS 320 (2012).

Failure to support argument. — Since a wife failed to cite even a single principle of law or authority to support her argument that the trial court's allegedly erroneous evaluation of the evidence required a reversal of the judgment insofar as it related to the award of spousal support, the wife waived her right to have these assignments of error reviewed by the court. Willson v. Willson, No. 1187-12-2, 2013 Va. App. LEXIS 128 (Ct. of Appeals Apr. 23, 2013).

Failure to comply with certification requirement. — Appellate court denied the motion to dismiss filed by the parents that claimed the compensation program's certificate appended to the compensation program's opening brief was inadequate to comply with the certificate requirement of Va. Sup. Ct. R. 5A:20(h) because the certificate was improperly dated; while the certification did contain a typographical error regarding the date, such an error did not invalidate the certification required by Va. Sup. Ct. R. 5A:20(h) and the compensation program complied with the requirement by the mere fact of certification. Va. Birth-Related Neurological Injury Comp. Program v. McGrady, 2006 Va. App. LEXIS 79 (Mar. 7, 2006).

Failure to comply with rule. — Where a wife's appellate brief did not present principles of law or argue the issue of spousal support with specificity, did not cite to controlling authority, and did not preserve the issue of future spousal support pursuant to Rule 5A:18, and where the trial court complied with subsection F of § 20-107.1 by identifying the factors supporting its property distribution, the wife's appeal and request for attorney's fees did not meet the requirements of Rule 5A:20(e) and were procedurally barred or without merit. Claure v. Murray, No. 2516-02-4, 2003 Va. App. LEXIS 498 (Ct. of Appeals Sept. 30, 2003).

Where father's opening brief on appeal from a trial court's decision modifying child support failed to comply with Va. Sup. Ct. Rule 5A:20, in that it did not contain an exact reference to the page of the record where each question was preserved in the trial court and did not show that he preserved his objections to the trial court's decision, the appellate court refused to consider the father's arguments because, under Va. Sup. Ct. Rule 5A:18, the court will not consider an argument on appeal that was not presented to the trial court, and the ends of justice exception did not apply because the record did not affirmatively show that a miscarriage of justice had occurred. Hylton v. Hylton, 2005 Va. App. LEXIS 146 (Apr. 12, 2005).

Because defendant juvenile did not provide a transcript or refer to it in the appellate brief, as required by Va. Sup. Ct. R. 5A:8(b) and 5A:20(c), the appellate court was unable to consider whether the proper underlying offense was present to commit defendant to the Department of Juvenile Justice under § 16.1-278.8(A)(14). Williams v. Commonwealth, 2005 Va. App. LEXIS 378 (Oct. 4, 2005).

When defendant in a drunk driving case failed to present the issue of his sentence enhancement to the trial court, it was not preserved for appeal, and the trial court would not consider sua sponte the ends-of-justice exception to Va. Sup. Ct. R. 5A:18 when defendant had failed to raise it. Moreover, the issue was defaulted because even if defendant had preserved the issue, he had not presented it in his petition for appeal as required by Va. Sup. Ct. R. 5A:12(c) or briefed it as required by Va. Sup. Ct. R. 5A:20. Luginbyhl v. Commonwealth, 48 Va. App. 58, 628 S.E.2d 74, 2006 Va. App. LEXIS 170 (2006).

Because defendant failed to present his equal protection argument in his writ petition or his brief, the appellate court would not consider it. McDonald v. Commonwealth, 48 Va. App. 325, 630 S.E.2d 754, 2006 Va. App. LEXIS 259 (2006), aff'd, 645 S.E.2d 918, 2007 Va. LEXIS 87 (Va. 2007).

Appellate court could not consider the husband's argument on appeal that the trial court did not consider each of the factors enumerated in § 20-107.1 E in determining whether to modify the wife's spousal support award, as the husband failed to provide the appellate court with a sufficient record, as required by Va. Sup. Ct. R. 5A:20, from which the appellate court could determine whether the wife satisfied her burden of proof that changed circumstances warranted the trial court's modification of spousal support in a decreased amount that was less than the decrease the husband would have preferred. McClure v. McClure, 2006 Va. App. LEXIS 294 (July 5, 2006).

Defendant had not complied with Va. Sup. Ct. R. 5A:20 when he provided no analytical support for his argument that he had rebutted a presumption. Murray v. Commonwealth, 2006 Va. App. LEXIS 409 (Aug. 29, 2006).

Because a wife's brief made no reference to the page(s) of the transcript, record, or appendix where each question was preserved in the trial court, the wife did not comply with Va. Sup. Ct. R. 5A:20(c); because the wife's motion for reconsideration was untimely, Va. Sup. Ct. R. 5A:18 barred consideration of her appeal. Tribble v. Tribble, 2006 Va. App. LEXIS 522 (Nov. 21, 2006).

In a divorce case, the court refused to consider arguments of the husband when the husband had not cited to case law or authority to support them. Brannon v. Brannon, 2007 Va. App. LEXIS 381 (Oct. 9, 2007).

While § 20-155 allowed the parties to a divorce action to enter a valid, written, property settlement agreement, signed by both parties to settle the rights and obligations of either or both of them with regard to temporary support, because the husband failed to introduce the agreement into evidence at trial, the trial court had no way to know its content or provisions, to interpret it, or to enforce its terms. Thus, due to the lack of an adequate record, the husband's claim of error regarding the agreement, which allowed for temporary support, was not reviewed. Robinson v. Robinson, 50 Va. App. 189, 648 S.E.2d 314, 2007 Va. App. LEXIS 291 (2007).

Defendant argued the trial court erred in revoking his suspension because he committed no additional acts of misconduct after the prior hearing and his later release from incarceration, but he failed to cite to any legal authority for this argument; by failing to cite any authority in support of this argument in his opening brief, defendant violated the provisions of Va. Sup. Ct. R. 5A:20(e). Miles v. Commonwealth, 2007 Va. App. LEXIS 330 (Sept. 4, 2007).

Appeal was dismissed under Va. Sup. Ct. R. 5A:20(e) with respect to the Virginia Uninsured Employer's Fund's claim as to its first question presented as the Fund's brief failed to include any argument in its brief related to the specific issue raised by its first question presented. Uninsured Employer's Fund v. Chaney, 2007 Va. App. LEXIS 335 (Sept. 11, 2007).

Court of appeals refused to address a husband's argument that the trial court erred in granting a wife a lump sum award of one-half of the husband's accumulated annual leave because the husband did not provide a legal basis for his claim; the husband's brief failed to comply with Va. Sup. Ct. R. 5A:20(e) because the brief solely relied on unpublished opinions as authority, and the husband failed to present any legal argument predicated on the legal analyses in those opinions and relied on conclusory statements. Buch v. Buch, 2008 Va. App. LEXIS 147 (Mar. 25, 2008).

Argument that a parent made in the parent's brief on appeal from the termination of the parent's parental rights was inadequate for appellate review. While the parent broadly asserted that termination was not in the best interests of the child and that the parent had remedied the situation leading to foster care, the parent pointed to no specific errors of the trial court, advanced no argument in support of the parent's contention, and cited no authorities for this contention. Devin v. Charlottesville Dep't of Soc. Servs., 2008 Va. App. LEXIS 254 (May 27, 2008).

Because a husband's opening brief did not contain sufficient principles of law, argument, or citation to legal authorities or the record to fully develop his argument, the appellate court did not consider the argument as the failure to comply was significant. Greene v. Greene, 2008 Va. App. LEXIS 266 (June 3, 2008).

Appellants' motions to stay execution of sentence and the supporting grounds alleged therein, filed before the trial court entered the final order of contempt, were more effective at alerting the trial court to the appellants' objections than would have been the commonly accepted practice of endorsing the final order seen and objected to for the same reasons. Accordingly, the goals of Va. Sup. Ct. R. 5A:18 were met because the appellants afforded the circuit court an opportunity to rule intelligently on the due process issues that the appellants raised, thereby satisfying the requirements of Rule 5A:18. Scialdone v. Commonwealth, 51 Va. App. 679, 660 S.E.2d 317, 2008 Va. App. LEXIS 202 (2008).

In a workers' compensation case in which the claimant alleged that reflex sympathetic dystrophy in the claimant's right arm related to a 1994 work injury had spread to her left arm, the statute of limitations that applied was § 65.2-708, which related to a claim based on a change of condition, rather than § 65.2-601, which related to original claims; because the employer did not base its argument on § 65.2-708, any argument regarding the statute of limitations was waived under Va. Sup. Ct. R. 5A:20(e) for failure to discuss the relevant legal principles and under Va. Sup. Ct. R. 5A:18 because no statute of limitations argument was made before the Workers' Compensation Commission. Mount Vernon Hosp. v. Devers, 2008 Va. App. LEXIS 494 (Nov. 4, 2008).

In a case in which defendant appealed his convictions for abduction with intent to defile, rape and use of a firearm in the commission of rape, arguing that the Commonwealth's use of its peremptory strikes to strike three African-American jurors violated the Equal Protection Clause of the Fourteenth Amendment, defendant failed to comply with Va. Sup. Ct. R. 5A:20(e). While defendant provided a statement of facts in his opening brief, none of the facts in that section related to the issue presented in his appeal. Gilliam v. Commonwealth, 2009 Va. App. LEXIS 450 (Oct. 6, 2009).

Decree of divorce was summarily upheld because a former wife waived her arguments on appeal by failing to comply with Va. Sup. Ct. R. 5A:20(c) and (e) since she failed to provide the appellate court with a list of issues with a clear reference to pages in the transcript, and she did not cite any legal authority or fully develop the arguments in her brief. Obst v. Obst, 2010 Va. App. LEXIS 95 (Mar. 16, 2010).

In an annulment case in which a pro se wife appealed, contending that the trial court erred in annulling her marriage, she failed to comply with Va. Sup. Ct. R. 5A:20 because her opening brief did not contain any principles of law or citation to legal authorities. Odocha v. Sarago, 2009 Va. App. LEXIS 457 (Oct. 13, 2009).

In a case in which a husband appealed a final divorce decree and he contended that the trial court erred in its equitable distribution and spousal support awards, he did not comply with Va. Sup. Ct. R. 5A:20(e) because his opening brief did not contain any principles of law, or citation to legal authorities, or the record to fully develop his arguments regarding the equitable distribution and spousal support awards. The husband's failure to comply with Rule 5A:20(e) was significant, and the appellate court would not consider those two alleged errors. Kablach v. Kablach, 2009 Va. App. LEXIS 475 (Oct. 20, 2009).

In an appeal from a final divorce decree, the wife waived arguments by failing to comply with Va. Sup. Ct. R. 5A:20 where the wife did not list any questions presented, recited portions of the parties' testimony and then stated the issues with the trial court's ruling in the section requesting relief, and failed to cite to any legal authority or principles of law. Joseph v. George, 2010 Va. App. LEXIS 173 (May 4, 2010).

On appeal from a final decree that awarded the wife spousal support and attorney fees, the husband failed to comply with Va. Sup. Ct. R. 5A:20(e) and his failure to comply was so significant that the appellate court refused to consider the question presented regarding the effective date for the spousal support. Harrison v. Harrison, 2010 Va. App. LEXIS 158 (Apr. 27, 2010).

Because a wife's failure to comply with the mandates of Va. Sup. Ct. R. 5A:20(e) was significant, the wife's claim that the trial court erred in excluding the wife's estimated income taxes based on the wife's request for $7,000 monthly in spousal support was waived; the wife's opening brief contained a single citation to a footnote in a previously decided case in support of a two-page argument that the trial court erred in excluding the estimated income taxes as hearsay. Buniva v. Buniva, 2010 Va. App. LEXIS 222 (June 1, 2010).

Court refused to consider the issue raised by the husband with respect to whether the trial court erred in granting the wife, not the husband, a divorce on the grounds of living separate and apart for more than one year, as the husband's brief did not contain the standard of review or any principles of law or citation to legal authorities to fully develop his argument, as required by Va. Sup. Ct. R. 5A:20(e). Blackwell v. Blackwell, 2010 Va. App. LEXIS 479 (Dec. 14, 2010).

Appellate court declined to consider the sufficiency of the evidence concerning the nurse's lack of care for patient B, because the nurse's brief did not contain any principles of law, citation to legal authorities, or the record to fully develop his arguments. Maristela v. Va. Bd. of Nursing, No. 1203-10-3, 2010 Va. App. LEXIS 457 (Ct. of Appeals Nov. 23, 2010).

Appellate court did not consider issues on appeal because the appellant failed to comply with Va. Sup. Ct. R. 5A:20(e) as the appellant did not address assignments of error in the appellant's brief, or else did not cite any legal authority to support an argument. Lewis v. Bailey, 2011 Va. App. LEXIS 253 (Aug. 2, 2011).

On appeal from the termination of parental rights, the appellate court did not consider the parents' argument that the trial court erred in not finding that the Department of Social Services was required to provide them services up to and until the actual termination hearing or that the trial court erred in not admitting into evidence a home study from Tennessee since they failed to comply with Va. Sup. Ct. R. 5A:20(e). Birchfield v. Scott County Dep't of Soc. Servs., 2011 Va. App. LEXIS 376 (Nov. 29, 2011).

On appeal from his convictions, the appellate court did not consider his argument that the trial court improperly sustained the Commonwealth's objection when counsel attempted to question defendant's son because that evidentiary ruling was not included in the assignments of error, Va. Sup. Ct. R. 5A:20(c). Flowers v. Commonwealth, 2011 Va. App. LEXIS 310 (Oct. 11, 2011).

Court of appeals would not consider an employee's argument that an employer's nurse care manager failed to schedule the employee with all the physicians he needed to see because blaming the nurse case manager for failing to schedule appointments fell outside the employee's assignment of error and was a significant non-compliance. Urias v. Winkler's, Inc., 2011 Va. App. LEXIS 397 (Dec. 13, 2011).

Husband's failure to present authority to support his contention that the trial court erred in failing to reduce the value of a second company partially owned by him by the debt to the husband's brother was significant, and pursuant to Va. Sup. Ct. R. 5A:20(e), appellate consideration of the issue was not merited. Sfreddo v. Sfreddo, 59 Va. App. 471, 720 S.E.2d 145, 2012 Va. App. LEXIS 13 (2012).

On appeal of defendant's conviction for attempted aggravated sexual battery, his appellate brief did not address the assertion that the trial court erred in misstating the rule regarding rehabilitating a witness with prior consistent statements. Because his brief contained no argument relating to the assignment of error as required by Va. Sup. Ct. R. 5A:20(e), the court of appeals did not address the issue. Gallier v. Commonwealth, 2012 Va. App. LEXIS 60 (Mar. 6, 2012).

As a former wife's opening brief did not comply with the requirements in Va. Sup. Ct. R. 5A:20(b)-(e), and as she did not file a replacement brief despite being given the opportunity to do so, the wife's arguments regarding her spousal support award would not be considered on appeal. Swanson v. Taylor, 2012 Va. App. LEXIS 196 (June 12, 2012).

Father's appeal was without merit because he failed to comply with Va. Sup. Ct. R. 5A:20(c)-(e) by including references to pages of the written statement, record, or appendix to support his statement of facts, and the appendix that was filed did not contain a part of the record that was essential to the resolution of the issues on appeal. Bilski v. Bilski, 2012 Va. App. LEXIS 191 (June 12, 2012).

Wife's brief did not comply with Va. Sup. Ct. R. 5A:20 as she raised issues that had not been presented to the trial court, and did not include the standard of review and the argument relating to each assignment of error. Smith v. Smith, No. 2069-11-2, 2012 Va. App. LEXIS 308 (Oct. 2, 2012).

Appellate court summarily affirmed an order under Va. Sup. Ct. R. 5A:27, which awarded the custody of two children to the City of Roanoke Department of Social Services as the children's great-aunt did not include her motion to reconsider in her appendix as required by Va. Sup. Ct. R. 5A:25(c)(6), or include a clear and exact reference to the pages of the transcript, written statement, record, or appendix where each assignment of error was preserved in the trial court as required by Va. Sup. Ct. R. 5A:20(c). Hustead v. City of Roanoke Dep't of Soc. Servs., No. 0331-12-3, 2012 Va. App. LEXIS 403 (Dec. 11, 2012).

Dismissal of an appeal is available after a petition for appeal is granted as: (1) once the appellate court grants a petition for appeal, Va. Sup. Ct. R. 5A:20 and 5A:26, rather than Va. Sup. Ct. R. 5A:12, govern the opening brief; (2) Rule 5A:20(c) provides that an opening brief must contain a statement of the assignments of error with a clear and exact reference to the pages of the transcript, written statement, record, or appendix where each assignment of error was preserved in the trial court; and (3) Rule 5A:26 provides that the appellate court may dismiss the appeal whenever the appellant fails to file a brief in compliance with the Virginia Supreme Court Rules. Brooks v. Commonwealth, No. 2708-10-1, 61 Va. App. 576, 739 S.E.2d 224, 2013 Va. App. LEXIS 99 (Mar. 26, 2013).

Failure to comply. — Denial of workers' compensation benefits was proper because the claimant failed to comply with Va. Sup. Ct. R. 5A:20(e). The opening brief did not contain any principles of law, argument, or citation to legal authorities or the record to develop her arguments. Stone v. Allstate Ins. Co., 2011 Va. App. LEXIS 150 (May 3, 2011).

Defendant's drug convictions and conviction for contributing to the delinquency of a minor were proper because he cited no legal authority on brief for his proposition that the trial court must sua sponte make an express finding as to the probative/prejudicial nature of the evidence. Thus, he waived that specific assertion, Va. Sup. Ct. R. 5A:20(e). Pinnix v. Commonwealth, 2011 Va. App. LEXIS 149 (May 3, 2011).

Award of sole legal and physical custody of the parties' child to the mother was appropriate because the father cited to no legal authority, as mandated by Va. Sup. Ct. R. 5A:20(e), to support his argument that his right to cross-examine witnesses and present evidence were violated. Dajani v. Dajani, 2011 Va. App. LEXIS 383 (Dec. 6, 2011).

City of Norfolk School Board's claim that a permanent impairment rating had to be based on objective findings was not considered as it was not supported by authority; the issue was waived under Va. Sup. Ct. R. 5A:20. City of Norfolk Sch. Bd. v. Vaughan, 2012 Va. App. LEXIS 124 (Apr. 24, 2012).

Workers' compensation claimant waived her claim that an employer was not entitled to a credit for an overpayment under § 65.2-520 where she did not argue the issue with any specificity, relying instead on a few broad, conclusory assertions, and she failed to provide any citation to controlling legal authority that supported her position as required by Va. Sup. Ct. R. 5A:20(e). Waters v. TGI Friday's, 2012 Va. App. LEXIS 129 (Apr. 24, 2012).

Former husband's argument that the trial court erred in awarding the former wife $500 in attorney's fees was not considered by the appellate court because the former husband did not specifically challenge the trial court's award of attorney's fees based on the arguments presented on appeal; further, the former husband failed to cite any legal authorities to support his argument. Dickover v. Seaton, 2012 Va. App. LEXIS 121 (Apr. 17, 2012).

Spouse's argument regarding the divorce court's distribution of retirement assets was not addressed on appeal because it was not included as an assignment of error pursuant to Va. Sup. Ct. R. 5A:20(c) and the spouse did not preserve the argument in the trial court as required by Va. Sup. Ct. R. 5A:18 as it was not one of the spouse's objections to the trial court's final order. Laing v. Laing, 2012 Va. App. LEXIS 165 (May 15, 2012).

Husband waived several of his assignments of error because he did not raise them in the trial court or address them in his brief; opening brief did not contain any principles of law or citation to legal authorities to fully develop some of his arguments; the husband's failure to comply with Rule 5A:20(e) was significant. Brown v. Brown, 2012 Va. App. LEXIS 233 (2012).

Trial court's order was summarily affirmed because the trial court examined all of the factors in subsection E of § 20-107.3, including a husband's contributions, in determining an equitable distribution award, the husband's opening brief did not contain the standard of review, principles of law, or citations to legal authorities or the record required by Va. Sup. Ct. R. 5A:20(e). Taylor v. Taylor, Nos. 0077-12-4, 0084-12-4, 2012 Va. App. LEXIS 362 (Nov. 13, 2012).

Compliance with rule. — Defendant complied with Va. Sup. Ct. R. 5A:20 because in her opening brief, she clearly exceeded the minimum requirements of Rule 5A:20 when the argument section of her brief was replete with citations to and analysis of cases and code sections, and her application of § 19.2-303 was a question of first impression; when a question is of first impression, it is generally sufficient that an appellant's opening brief contain citations to the statute in question, well-reasoned arguments from the plain language of the statute, and any informative or illustrative cases, and Rule 5A:20 does not require appellants to cite cases where no precedent exists or to cite a set number of cases or code sections. Wilson v. Commonwealth, 54 Va. App. 631, 681 S.E.2d 74, 2009 Va. App. LEXIS 363 (2009).

Because defendant's "questions presented" in her opening brief failed to allege any trial court error, the court of appeals would not consider them on appeal; none of the questions presented invoked assertions of error on the part of the trial court. Newman v. Commonwealth, 2009 Va. App. LEXIS 360 (Aug. 11, 2009).

Father complied with Va. Sup. Ct. R. 5A:20(d) becuase on brief, he cited to pages in the record after each paragraph in his statement of facts; thus, the father did not err when he cited to pages of the record rather than to pages in the appendix. Moncrief v. Div. of Child Support Enforcement ex rel. Joyner, 60 Va. App. 721, 732 S.E.2d 714, 2012 Va. App. LEXIS 320 (2012).

Failure to discuss questions. — Because two of a husband's questions were not really even discussed in his amended brief, the questions were not considered on appeal, in accordance with Va. Sup. Ct. R. 5A:20(e). Roberts v. Roberts, 2007 Va. App. LEXIS 477 (Dec. 27, 2007).

Because a county never addressed an assignment of error on brief separate from its first assignment of error, the court of appeals did not address it outside the context of the first assignment of error. County of Henrico v. Henry, 2012 Va. App. LEXIS 31 (Feb. 7, 2012).

Inadequate record on appeal. — Order directing a husband to designate the parties' minor child as beneficiary of his life insurance policy was affirmed because, under subsection D of § 20-108.1, the trial court had the authority to enter the order, and, as the husband provided no indication that the trial court abused its discretion, the order was presumed correct; the burden was upon the husband to provide a record that substantiated his claim of error. Watson v. Watson, 2009 Va. App. LEXIS 323 (July 21, 2009).

Brief's inadequacies did not require dismissal of appeal. — Wife's claim that her husband's appeal should be dismissed for his citation in his brief to facts that were not part of the record, for misconstruing other facts, and for inadequately citing the record in his statement of facts was rejected as although the husband's brief contained a few inadequacies, most were inconsequential, and none related to any matter of substantive importance; further, the wife did not claim that the failures affected her ability to prepare a response, and if she disagreed with the husband's statement of facts, she could include her own under Rule 5A:21(b). Courembis v. Courembis, 43 Va. App. 18, 595 S.E.2d 505, 2004 Va. App. LEXIS 203 (2004).

Husband's questions on appeal were not preserved pursuant to Rule 5A:18 despite the husband's failure to cite to the appropriate pages in the appendix as required by this rule, as they were either not raised at trial, or because the husband failed to make the same argument on appeal that he made at the trial court. Courembis v. Courembis, 43 Va. App. 18, 595 S.E.2d 505, 2004 Va. App. LEXIS 203 (2004).

Although the argument in a mother's brief that a trial court erred in terminating her parental rights when it did not terminate the father's parental rights because the mother and father intended to remain living together as a couple was supported by only a few citations to authority, as the brief was not entirely lacking in such citations, the appellate court declined to consider the issue waived. Campbell County Dep't of Soc. Servs. v. Roberts, 2008 Va. App. LEXIS 225 (May 6, 2008).

Assignments of error not considered on appeal. — In his brief, the father restated his argument and the trial court's rulings, but did not offer any legal authority to support his argument, so the appellate court declined to consider the father's first two assignments of error. Jonathan v. Jonathan, 2011 Va. App. LEXIS 334 (Nov. 8, 2011).

Husband argued that the trial court erred in not dividing transportation, but the husband did not raise transportation in his assignments of error and did not provide any legal authority to support his argument; therefore, pursuant to Va. Sup. Ct. R. 5A:20, the court of appeals would not consider the assignment of error. Brown v. Brown, 2012 Va. App. LEXIS 233 (2012).

Applied in Fitzgerald v. Bass, 4 Va. App. 371, 358 S.E.2d 576 (1987); Littlejohn v. Commonwealth, 24 Va. App. 401, 482 S.E.2d 853 (1997); Megel v. Commonwealth, 37 Va. App. 676, 561 S.E.2d 21, 2002 Va. App. LEXIS 267 (2002); Kane v. Szymczak, 41 Va. App. 365, 585 S.E.2d 349, 2003 Va. App. LEXIS 445 (2003); Roberts v. Roberts, 41 Va. App. 513, 586 S.E.2d 290, 2003 Va. App. LEXIS 486 (2003); Steadman v. Liberty Fabrics, Inc., 41 Va. App. 796, 589 S.E.2d 465, 2003 Va. App. LEXIS 643 (2003); Via v. Commonwealth, 42 Va. App. 164, 590 S.E.2d 583, 2004 Va. App. LEXIS 14 (2004); Cirrito v. Cirrito, 44 Va. App. 287, 605 S.E.2d 268, 2004 Va. App. LEXIS 574 (2004); Jeter v. Commonwealth, 44 Va. App. 733, 607 S.E.2d 734, 2005 Va. App. LEXIS 27 (2005); Barrs v. Barrs, 45 Va. App. 500, 612 S.E.2d 227, 2005 Va. App. LEXIS 174 (2005); Fields v. Dinwiddie County Dep't of Soc. Servs., 46 Va. App. 1, 614 S.E.2d 656, 2005 Va. App. LEXIS 236 (2005); Mason v. Commonwealth, 49 Va. App. 39, 636 S.E.2d 480, 2006 Va. App. LEXIS 505 (2006); Stokes v. Commonwealth, 49 Va. App. 401, 641 S.E.2d 780, 2007 Va. App. LEXIS 89 (2007); Klein v. Klein, 49 Va. App. 478, 642 S.E.2d 313, 2007 Va. App. LEXIS 114 (2007); Hoffman v. Carter, 50 Va. App. 199, 648 S.E.2d 318, 2007 Va. App. LEXIS 298 (2007); Winston v. Commonwealth, 51 Va. App. 74, 654 S.E.2d 340, 2007 Va. App. LEXIS 485 (2007); Fadness v. Fadness, 52 Va. App. 833, 667 S.E.2d 857, 2008 Va. App. LEXIS 496 (2008); Masonite Holdings, Inc. v. Cubbage, 53 Va. App. 13, 668 S.E.2d 809, 2008 Va. App. LEXIS 510 (2008); Doering v. Doering, 54 Va. App. 162, 676 S.E.2d 353, 2009 Va. App. LEXIS 227 (2009); Duncan v. Commonwealth, 55 Va. App. 175, 684 S.E.2d 838, 2009 Va. App. LEXIS 515 (2009); Shiembob v. Shiembob, 55 Va. App. 234, 685 S.E.2d 192, 2009 Va. App. LEXIS 520 (2009); Davis v. Davis, 2010 Va. App. LEXIS 26 (Jan. 26, 2010); Commonwealth v. Brown, 279 Va. 235, 687 S.E.2d 742, 2010 Va. LEXIS 16 (2010); Murillo-Rodriguez v. Commonwealth, 279 Va. 64, 688 S.E.2d 199, 2010 Va. LEXIS 18 (2010); Montalbano v. Richmond Ford, LLC, 57 Va. App. 235, 701 S.E.2d 72, 2010 Va. App. LEXIS 448 (2010); Smith v. Commonwealth, 281 Va. 464, 706 S.E.2d 889, 2011 Va. LEXIS 59 (2011); Ceres Marine Terminals v. Armstrong, 59 Va. App. 694, 722 S.E.2d 301, 2012 Va. App. LEXIS 59 (2012); Henderson v. Commonwealth, 59 Va. App. 641, 722 S.E.2d 275, 2012 Va. App. LEXIS 116 (2012); Griffin v. Griffin, 2012 Va. App. LEXIS 179 (May 29, 2012); Fox v. Fox, 61 Va. App. 185, 734 S.E.2d 662, 2012 Va. App. LEXIS 395 (2012).

Rule 5A:21. Requirements for Brief of Appellee or Guardian Ad Litem.

The brief of appellee or the brief of the guardian ad litem shall contain:

(a) A table of contents and table of authorities with cases alphabetically arranged. Citations of all authorities shall include the year thereof.

(b) A statement of the case if the appellee disagrees with the statement presented by the appellant and a statement of any additional assignments of error the appellee wishes to present with a clear and exact reference to the page(s) of the transcript, written statement, record, or appendix where each additional assignment of error was preserved in the trial court.

(c) A statement of the facts necessary to correct or amplify the statement in the brief of appellant with appropriate references to the pages of the transcript, written statement, record, or appendix. The testimony of individual witnesses should not be summarized seriatim unless the facts are in dispute and such a summary is necessary to support the appellee's version of the facts.

(d) The standard of review and the argument (including principles of law and authorities) relating to each assignment of error. For any additional assignment of error by appellee which was not preserved in the trial court, counsel shall state why the good cause and/or ends of justice exceptions to Rule 5A:18 are applicable. With respect to each assignment of error, the standard of review and the argument — including principles of law and the authorities — shall be stated in one place and not scattered through the brief. At the option of counsel, the argument may be preceded by a short summary.

(e) A statement of the precise relief sought, if any.

(f) The signature (which need not be in handwriting) of at least one counsel and counsel's Virginia State Bar number, address, telephone number, facsimile number (if any), and email address (if any).

(g) A certificate (which need not be signed in handwriting) stating (1) that Rule 5A:19(f) has been complied with, and (2) whether counsel desires to waive oral argument. The certificate must also state the number of words (headings, footnotes, and quotations count towards the word limitation; the cover page, table of contents, table of authorities, and certificate do not count towards the word count). Additionally, any party may waive oral argument without leave of this Court by written notification to the clerk of this Court within 21 days after the date on which the appellee's brief is due to be filed or has been filed.

Comment. — In their briefs and oral argument, counsel should avoid references to parties by such designations as "appellant" and "appellee." Clarity is promoted by the use of the names of the parties, or descriptive terms such as "the employee," "the injured person," "the driver" or "the husband," or the designations used in the lower court or commission.

CASE NOTES

Additional questions raised and relief sought by appellee. — Subdivisions (b) and (e) of this rule considered together clearly provide that additional questions separate from those presented by the appellant, and any additional relief sought separate from that requested by the appellant, may be raised by the appellee in his brief. D'Auria v. D'Auria, 1 Va. App. 455, 340 S.E.2d 164 (1986).

Workers' Compensation Commission did not err in finding that claimant failed in his duty to market his residual work capacity, where he made a limited search for work, failed to register with the Commission, and failed to inquire about light-duty work. Goodyear Tire & Rubber Co. v. McGinnis, No. 3253-01-3, 2002 Va. App. LEXIS 226 (Ct. of Appeals Apr. 9, 2002).

In a cross-appeal from a final divorce decree, the husband waived arguments by failing to comply with Va. Sup. Ct. R. 5A:21 where the husband did not list additional questions presented and did not include any citations to legal authority or principles of law to support the arguments, and where the husband merely responded to the wife's summary of the parties' testimony and then recited the relief that was sought at the end of the brief. Joseph v. George, 2010 Va. App. LEXIS 173 (May 4, 2010).

Deficient brief. — Although appellee prevailed on appeal, as her brief failed to comply with Va. Sup. Ct. R. 5A:21(b), (c), or (d), the quality of her advocacy did not warrant an award of appellate attorneys' fees. Griffin v. Griffin, 2012 Va. App. LEXIS 179 (May 29, 2012).

Issue not raised in prior appeal. — There is no merit to employer's argument that the commission was required to reopen the record and hold an evidentiary hearing prior to issuing an order under the mandate the appellate court's opinion where that issue was not raised by employer in the prior appeal. O'Sullivan Corp. v. Timbrook, 20 Va. App. 113, 455 S.E.2d 720 (1995).

Issue not preserved. — Appellate court summarily rejected the former wife's arguments regarding the trial court's equitable distribution award pursuant to Va. Sup. Ct. R. 5A:27 because Va. Sup. Ct. R. 5A:21(b) required an appellee to provide a clear and exact reference to the pages of the transcript, written statement, record, or appendix where each additional question was preserved in the trial court, and the former wife's brief failed to identify in the record where she preserved the issues she raised on appeal. Although Va. Sup. Ct. R. 5A:21(b) allowed an appellee to raise additional issues on brief, it did not dispense with the requirements of Va. Sup. Ct. R. 5A:18; a litigant seeking to reverse a trial court, therefore, had to either prove where the issue was preserved below or demonstrate an equitable basis for suspending the waiver rule, and having done neither, the former wife could not prevail on appeal. Williams v. Williams, 2009 Va. App. LEXIS 553 (Dec. 15, 2009).

Appellate court considered only assignments of error and, as such, would not consider additional issues listed as questions presented. Furthermore, the court found that an appellee's failure to comply with Va. Sup. Ct. R. 5A:21 was significant and, therefore, would not consider the additional issue the appellee raised. Garner v. Ruckman, 2011 Va. App. LEXIS 369 (Nov. 29, 2011).

Issue properly raised by appellee. — Department, as appellee, was permitted to present as an issue whether the trial court erred in finding that its letter was a case decision. Frederick County Bus. Park, LLC v. Va. Dep't of Envtl. Quality, 52 Va. App. 40, 660 S.E.2d 698, 2008 Va. App. LEXIS 244 (2008), aff'd, 278 Va. 207, 677 S.E.2d 42, 2009 Va. LEXIS 64 (2009).

Where order in primary appeal was not appealable. — As a trial court's order remanding to Virginia Department of Professional and Occupational Regulation, Real Estate Board, for further reconsideration of a sanction it imposed against real estate agents was not a "final decision" under § 17.1-405, the agents' designation of a default judgment ruling as an additional question on appeal under Va. Ct. R. 5A:21(b) was also an interlocutory appeal that the court of appeals lacked jurisdiction to hear. Commonwealth v. Lancaster, 45 Va. App. 723, 613 S.E.2d 828, 2005 Va. App. LEXIS 226 (2005).

Citation to authority for position. — Court could not entertain a former wife's challenge to the former husband's release from jail by the trial court on contempt charges because the wife failed to cite any authority for her position in her brief as required by Va. Sup. Ct. 5A-21(b). Jagannathan v. Jagannathan, 2008 Va. App. LEXIS 88 (Feb. 19, 2008).

Applied in Schwab Constr. v. McCarter, 25 Va. App. 104, 486 S.E.2d 562 (1997); TBC Corp. v. Stephens, 49 Va. App. 650, 644 S.E.2d 84, 2007 Va. App. LEXIS 181 (2007); Mabe v. Wythe County Dep't of Soc. Servs., 53 Va. App. 325, 671 S.E.2d 425, 2009 Va. App. LEXIS 35 (2009); Prizzia v. Prizzia, 58 Va. App. 137, 707 S.E.2d 461, 2011 Va. App. LEXIS 124 (2011).

Rule 5A:22. Requirements for Reply Brief.

The reply brief, if any, shall contain argument in reply to contentions made in the brief of appellee. No reply brief is necessary if the contentions have been adequately answered in the opening brief of appellant. The reply brief shall contain a certificate (which need not be signed in handwriting) that Rule 5A:19(f) has been complied with. The certificate must also state the number of words (headings, footnotes, and quotations count towards the word limitation; the cover page, table of contents, table of authorities, and certificate do not count towards the word count).

Rule 5A:23. Briefs Amicus Curiae.

(a) A brief amicus curiae may be filed at the petition, perfected appeal and rehearing stages of the appellate proceedings:

(1) on behalf of the United States or the Commonwealth of Virginia without the prior consent of this Court or counsel; and

(2) by any other person if it is accompanied by the written consent of all counsel; and

(3) otherwise only on motion (which may be accompanied by the proposed brief) and the consent of this Court.

(b) A brief amicus curiae will be accepted only if filed on or before the date on which the brief of the party supported is required to be filed. A brief amicus curiae may be filed at the time of filing of the reply brief of the appellant only if an opening brief amicus curiae has been filed.

(c) A brief amicus curiae shall comply with the rules applicable to the brief of the party supported.

(d) Notwithstanding the provisions of paragraphs (a) and (b) of this Rule, the Court of Appeals may request that a brief amicus curiae be filed at any time.

CASE NOTES

Motion to file brief amicus curiae was properly denied. — The Court of Appeals denied defendant's motion to file a brief amicus curiae. The brief did not purport to be filed by Transportation Safety Programs Manager of Virginia Department of Motor Vehicles in his individual capacity. Instead, it named the manager as representative of the Transportation Safety Program of Virginia Division of Motor Vehicles. Because the brief did not purport to be filed on behalf of the manager individually, it did not comply with subdivision (c) and Rule 5A:20(g). Duggan v. Commonwealth, No. 1258-91-4 (Ct. of Appeals Feb. 23, 1993).

Rule 5A:24. Covers of Documents.

(a) To facilitate identification, documents shall bear covers colored as follows:

Document	*Color of Cover*
Appendix	Red
Brief of the Appellant	White
Brief of the Appellee	Blue
Brief of Guardian Ad Litem (if separate from appellant and appellee)	Brown
Reply Brief of the Appellant	Green
Brief Amicus Curiae	Gray
Petition for Rehearing	Yellow
Petition for Rehearing En Banc	Yellow

(b) No appeal shall be dismissed for failure to comply with the provisions of this rule; however, the clerk of the Court of Appeals may require that a document be redone in compliance with this Rule.

CASE NOTES

Failure to comply. — While an employee received notice of the deficiencies in the employee's brief and appendix under Va. Sup. Ct. R. 5A:4, 5A:18, 5A:20, 5A:24, 5A:25, because the employee failed to correct any of the defects, which in totality were significant, and never actually challenged the ruling of the issue on appeal, the employee's appeal lacked merit. Adams v. Va. Empl. Comm'n, 2012 Va. App. LEXIS 67 (Mar. 6, 2012).

Rule 5A:25. Appendix.

(a) *When Required.* — An appendix shall be filed by the appellant in all cases no later than the time of filing his opening brief.

(b) *Filing.* — If the combined lengths of the appendix and the opening brief of the appellant do not exceed the limitation prescribed in Rule 5A:19, the appendix may be filed as an addendum to the opening brief and within the same cover. If the combined lengths of the appendix and the opening brief exceed the limitation prescribed in Rule 5A:19, the appellant shall file the appendix as a separate volume. The number of copies filed and mailed to opposing counsel shall conform to Rule 5A:19(f).

(c) *Contents.* — An appendix shall include:

(1) the basic initial pleading (as finally amended);

(2) the judgment appealed from, and any memorandum or opinion relating thereto;

(3) any testimony and other incidents of the case germane to the assignments of error;

(4) the title (but not the caption) of each paper contained in the appendix, and its filing date;

(5) the names of witnesses printed at the beginning of excerpts from their testimony and at the top of each page thereof; and

(6) exhibits necessary for an understanding of the case that can reasonably be reproduced.

(d) *Determination of Contents.* — Within ten days after the filing of the record with the Court of Appeals or, in a case in which a petition for appeal has been granted, within ten days after the date of the certificate of appeal issued by the clerk of the Court of Appeals, counsel for appellant shall file in the office of the clerk of the Court of Appeals a written statement signed by all counsel setting forth an agreed designation of the parts of the record to be included in the appendix. In the absence of such an agreement, counsel for appellant shall file with the clerk of the Court of Appeals a statement of the assignments of error and a designation of the contents to be included in the appendix within fifteen days after the filing of the record or, in a case in which a petition for appeal has been granted, within fifteen days after the date of the certificate of appeal; not more than ten days after this designation is filed, counsel for appellee shall file with the clerk of the Court of Appeals a designation of any additional contents to be included in the appendix. The appellant shall include in the appendix the parts thus designated, together with any additional parts he considers germane.

(e) *Table of Contents; Form of Presentation.* — At the beginning of the appendix there shall be a table of contents, which shall include the name of each witness whose testimony is included in the appendix and the page number of the appendix at which each portion of the testimony of the witness begins. Thereafter, the parts of the record to be reproduced shall be set out in chronological order. When matter contained in the transcript of proceedings is set out in the appendix, the page of the transcript or of the record at which such matter may be found shall be indicated in brackets immediately before the matter which is set out. Omissions in the text of papers or of the transcript must be indicated by asterisks. Immaterial matters (such as captions, subscriptions and acknowledgements) shall be omitted. A question and its answer may be contained in a single paragraph.

(f) *Costs.* — Unless counsel otherwise agree, the cost of producing the appendix shall initially be paid by the appellant, but if the appellant considers that parts of the record designated by the appellee for inclusion are unnecessary for the determination of the issue presented, he may so advise the appellee, and the appellee shall advance the cost of including such parts. The cost of producing the appendix shall be taxed as costs in the case.

(g) *Penalty.* — Nothing shall be included in the appendix that is not germane to an assignment of error. As examples, no pleadings (other than the basic initial pleading as finally amended) shall be included unless an assignment of error is presented relating to it, and then only the portion thereof to which the assignment relates; and testimony relating solely to the amount of damages shall not be included unless error is assigned relating to the amount of damages. If parts of the record are included in the appendix unnecessarily at the direction of a party, this Court may impose the cost of producing such parts on that party.

(h) *Assumptions.* — It will be assumed that the appendix contains everything germane to the assignments of error. The Court of Appeals may, however, consider other parts of the record.

Law Review. — For 2003/2004 survey of civil practice and procedure, see 39 U. Rich. L. Rev. 87 (2004).

CASE NOTES

Untimely designation of appendix's contents not grounds for dismissal. — Failure to timely designate the contents of the appendix under subdivision (d) of this rule is not ground for dismissal if an appellant includes in his appendix everything germane to the disposition of his appeal and the appellee has not been prejudiced by the failure. Gollehon v. Gollehon, No. 2178-92-4, (Ct. of Appeals Nov. 23, 1993).

Failure to designate the contents of the record under subdivision (d) is not ground for dismissal if an appellant includes in his appendix everything germane to the disposition of his appeal and the appellee has not been prejudiced by the failure. Teagle & Little, Inc. v. Balchunis, No. 2270-94-1 (Ct. of Appeals July 25, 1995).

Failure to provide tape or transcript of material used to refresh memory of witness. — Defendant's conviction of first-degree murder was affirmed, because the trial court did not allow the Commonwealth to impeach its own witness, but rather properly allowed the Commonwealth to refresh the memory of the witness after the witness stated that she was unable to recall certain statements she had made to police investigators, and defendant failed to include either the tape played to refresh the witness's memory or the contents of the tape in the record on appeal as required by Va. Sup. Ct. R. 5A:25, so the appellate court had no basis for determining whether the trial court committed error in permitting the tape to be played in the presence of the jury, and therefore the appellate court determined that the evidence was clearly sufficient to sustain the jury's finding of guilt. Brockenbrough v. Commonwealth, No. 3023-01-2, 2003 Va. App. LEXIS 243 (Ct. of Appeals Apr. 22, 2003).

No prejudice where claimant familiar with issue. — Where claimant was familiar with the issue being appealed because there had been only one issue throughout the case, failure by appellant to file a statement of questions presented did not prejudice claimant. Teagle & Little, Inc. v. Balchunis, No. 2270-94-1 (Ct. of Appeals July 25, 1995).

Appendix was deficient. — Two contentions of defendant could not be reviewed, due to deficiencies in the appendix before the appellate court, as the appendix had to include any testimony and other incidents of the case germane to the questions presented under Rule 5A:25(c)(3); the judgment of the lower court was presumed to be correct and the burden was on defendant, as the appellant, to present to the appellate court a sufficient record from which the appellate court could determine whether the lower court had erred in the respect complained of, which defendant failed to do, resulting in the judgment being affirmed. Patterson v. City of Richmond, 39 Va. App. 706, 576 S.E.2d 759, 2003 Va. App. LEXIS 74 (2003).

When a mother appealed a trial court's finding that she had neglected her child, the trial court's ruling was affirmed because the appendix which the mother filed with her appeal contained only the mother's testimony, so the appellate court could not determine why it was alleged that the child was neglected or what evidence was presented to support that allegation, and the mother did not meet her burden of presenting the appellate court with an adequate record. Cooper v. Va. Beach Dep't of Soc. Servs., No. 0645-03-1, 2003 Va. App. LEXIS 491 (Ct. of Appeals Sept. 30, 2003).

Where neither a settlement agreement nor any of the parties' respective requests regarding modification of a protective order were part of the appendix, and it was unclear from the appendix whether any of the parties' modification requests were submitted in writing, the appendix was deficient; however, the appellate court was authorized to look beyond the appendix and into the record although it was not required to do so, and upon doing so, it was entitled to determine that the husband's appeal was procedurally barred because the husband had not first raised his appellate claim that the "no contact" provision from the prior protective order should have been deleted from the new, modified order in the trial court, as he was required to do. Shaffer v. Shaffer, No. 1945-03-2, 2004 Va. App. LEXIS 269 (Ct. of Appeals June 8, 2004).

Appendix of husband's brief did not include portions of the hearing transcript containing the trial court's fact findings and rulings regarding the issue raised on appeal, which warranted a reminder to counsel about what a proper appendix should contain. True v. True, No. 0141-04-1, 2004 Va. App. LEXIS 350 (Ct. of Appeals July 20, 2004).

Record in a child custody case was insufficient to decide certain issues because the father's appendix failed to contain everything germane to them as required by Va. Sup. Ct. R. 5A:25. The father's stated justification that it would be cost-prohibitive to include all the pertinent transcript pages in the appendix did not excuse his failure to do so. Barrett v. Barrett, 2006 Va. App. LEXIS 463 (Oct. 17, 2006).

In a case in which defendant appealed his convictions for abduction with intent to defile, rape and use of a firearm in the commission of rape, arguing that the Commonwealth's use of its peremptory strikes to strike three African-American jurors violated the Equal Protection Clause of the Fourteenth Amendment, defendant did not comply with Va. Sup. Ct. R. 5A:25(c)(3) by failing to include the transcript of the voir dire in the joint appendix. The transcript was clearly germane to the question presented and should have been timely filed and included in the joint appendix. Gilliam v. Commonwealth, 2009 Va. App. LEXIS 450 (Oct. 6, 2009).

Husband failed to provide the court of appeals with the necessary documents in the appendix to consider the issues he raised on appeal because the appendix did not contain the husband's motion for reconsideration, the order denying his motion, and those portions of the transcript necessary for the court of appeals to review the husband's arguments as required by Va. Sup. Ct. R. 5A:25; the husband failed to provide the court of appeals with an adequate appendix to enable it to address his assignments of error. Kirkendale v. Kirkendale, 2011 Va. App. LEXIS 109 (Mar. 29, 2011).

While an employee received notice of the deficiencies in the employee's brief and appendix under Va. Sup. Ct. R. 5A:4, 5A:18, 5A:20, 5A:24, 5A:25, because the employee failed to correct any of the defects, which in totality were significant, and never actually challenged the ruling of the issue on appeal, the employee's appeal lacked merit. Adams v. Va. Empl. Comm'n, 2012 Va. App. LEXIS 67 (Mar. 6, 2012).

Where the record on appeal consisted of thousands of pages of documents, as appellant's failure to file a proper appendix had a substantial impact on the appellate court's ability to rule on the merits of his arguments, he defaulted them. Griffin v. Griffin, 2012 Va. App. LEXIS 179 (May 29, 2012).

Husband failed to provide the court with an adequate record from which it could determine whether the trial court erred in denying his request for a divorce. The appendix did not contain records from the trial court necessary to support his assertions of where he preserved his assignments of error, as required by Va. Sup. Ct. R. 5A:25(c)(3). Gopalakrishnan Subramanian v. Ranjeetha Ravichandran, No. 2617-11-4, 2012 Va. App. LEXIS 330 (Oct. 16, 2012).

Wife violated Va. Sup. Ct. R. 5:25(d) as she failed to include all of the husband's documents in the appendix; she violated Rule 5A:25(c) as the documents in the appendix were not in chronological order. Smith v. Smith, No. 2069-11-2, 2012 Va. App. LEXIS 308 (Oct. 2, 2012).

Appellate court summarily affirmed an order under Va. Sup. Ct. R. 5A:27, which awarded the custody of two children to the City of Roanoke Department of Social Services as the children's great-aunt did not include her motion to reconsider in her appendix as required by Va. Sup. Ct. R. 5A:25(c)(6), or include a clear and exact reference to the pages of the transcript, written statement, record, or appendix where each assignment of error was preserved in the trial court as required by Va. Sup. Ct. R. 5A:20(c). Hustead v. City of Roanoke Dep't of Soc. Servs., No. 0331-12-3, 2012 Va. App. LEXIS 403 (Dec. 11, 2012).

Cost of preparation of appendix. — Denial of the employer's request to assess the cost of preparing the joint appendix against the employee was proper because the extensive medical records designated by the employee were plausibly necessary to defend the employer's claim that the injuries resulted from the employee's pre-existing conditions. Heartland Hospice Manor Care, Inc. v. Patton, 2010 Va. App. LEXIS 162 (Apr. 27, 2010).

Record held sufficient. — Wife's claim that a husband's appeal from a decree of divorce on grounds that he failed to present the court with a complete record was rejected, as the transcript of a hearing presenting argument to the trial court was not required in order to decide the issues on appeal, and she failed to explain what information was presented at that hearing that was germane to the questions presented. Didio v. Didio, 2007 Va. App. LEXIS 453 (Dec. 18, 2007).

Meritless appeal. — Where an untimely appeal was without merit, and thus summarily affirmed, the appeals court denied a motion filed by the Virginia Employment Commission to dismiss on the ground that an employee failed to comply with Rule 5A:25 with respect to the filing of the appendix. Jones v. Va. Empl. Comm'n, No. 0362-04-4, 2004 Va. App. LEXIS 571 (Ct. of Appeals Nov. 23, 2004).

Husband's appeal of a trial court's final decree granting a divorce to his wife was dismissed; the husband failed to provide the appellate court with an adequate appendix to enable it to address the issue raised by the husband. Montakhabi v. Montakhabi, No. 1531-04-4, 2005 Va. App. LEXIS 25 (Ct. of Appeals Jan. 18, 2005).

Applied in Rhodes v. Commonwealth, 41 Va. App. 195, 583 S.E.2d 773, 2003 Va. App. LEXIS 418 (2003); Reid v. Commonwealth, 57 Va. App. 42, 698 S.E.2d 269, 2010 Va. App. LEXIS 349 (2010).

Rule 5A:26. Effect of Noncompliance With Rules Regarding Briefs.

If an appellant fails to file a brief in compliance with these Rules, the Court of Appeals may dismiss the appeal. If an appellee fails to file a brief in compliance with these Rules, the Court of Appeals may disregard any additional assignments of error raised by the appellee. If one party has complied with the Rules governing briefs, but the other has not, the party in default will not be heard orally if the case proceeds to oral argument, except for good cause shown.

Law Review. — For 2003/2004 survey of family and juvenile law, see 39 U. Rich. L. Rev. 241 (2004).

Michie's Jurisprudence. — For related discussion, see 1B M.J. Appeal and Error, § 233.

CASE NOTES

Dismissal available. — Dismissal of an appeal is available after a petition for appeal is granted as: (1) once the appellate court grants a petition for appeal, Va. Sup. Ct. R. 5A:20 and 5A:26, rather than Va. Sup. Ct. R. 5A:12, govern the opening brief; (2) Rule 5A:20(c) provides that an opening brief must contain a statement of the assignments of error with a clear and exact reference to the pages of the transcript, written statement, record, or appendix where each assignment of error was preserved in the trial court; and (3) Rule 5A:26 provides that the appellate court may dismiss the appeal whenever the appellant fails to file a brief in compliance with the Virginia Supreme Court Rules. Brooks v. Commonwealth, No. 2708-10-1, 61 Va. App. 576, 739 S.E.2d 224, 2013 Va. App. LEXIS 99 (Mar. 26, 2013).

Applied in Rusty's Welding Serv., Inc. v. Gibson, 29 Va. App. 119, 510 S.E.2d 255 (1999).

Rule 5A:27. Summary Disposition.

In cases in which appeal lies as a matter of right, if all the Judges of the panel of the Court of Appeals to which a pending appeal has been referred conclude from a review of the record and the briefs of the parties that the appeal is without merit, the panel shall forthwith affirm the judgment of the trial court or commission.

CASE NOTES

Workers' Compensation Commission. — Virginia Workers' Compensation Commission could reasonably infer from the evidence that the claimant's employment-related need to hurry to catch the shoplifters resulted in his knee injury, which constituted injury by accident arising out of his employment, and the appellate court summarily affirmed the commission's decision. Food Lion, Inc. v. Seals, No. 1734-01-1, 2001 Va. App. LEXIS 631 (Ct. of Appeals Nov. 13, 2001).

Pursuant to Rule 5A:27, the Virginia Workers' Compensation Commission properly summarily denied an injured firefighter's claim seeking reimbursement for medical bills, mileage expenses, vehicle repairs, and home air conditioning repairs, because the record supported the Commission's findings that the disputed items had either been paid by a fire department, not proven by the firefighter to be medically reasonable or necessary, and/or were barred by the doctrine of res judicata. Carter v. Arlington County Fire Dep't, No. 1328-02-4, 2002 Va. App. LEXIS 623 (Ct. of Appeals Oct. 15, 2002).

Court of Appeals found that there was no merit to a home improvement company's claim that a worker it hired was an independent contractor, not an employee, and it summarily affirmed a decision by the Virginia Workers' Compensation Commission which granted the worker's claim for workers' compensation benefits, but denied his claim for temporary total disability benefits. North Star Home Improvement, Inc. v. Heddings, No. 2350-03-4, 2004 Va. App. LEXIS 81 (Ct. of Appeals Feb. 17, 2004).

Virginia Workers' Compensation commission awarded a claimant temporary partial disability benefits and found she made a good faith effort to market her residual work capacity; the court summarily affirmed pursuant to § 17.1-403 and Rule 5A:27 because the facts and legal contentions were adequately presented and argument would not have aided the decisional process. Family Care Home Health, Inc. v. Nye, No. 0823-04-3, 2004 Va. App. LEXIS 388 (Ct. of Appeals Aug. 10, 2004).

Spousal support. — Where a trial court considered, inter alia, the parties' earning capacities, obligations, needs, and financial resources in accordance with subsection E of § 20-107.1, there was an evidentiary foundation supporting the award of permanent spousal support to a wife; as a result, the husband's appeal lacked merit and the trial court's decision could be summarily affirmed pursuant to Rule 5A:27. Whitehead v. Whitehead, No. 3219-02-1, 2003 Va. App. LEXIS 139 (Ct. of Appeals Mar. 18, 2003).

Equitable distribution award. — Appellate court summarily rejected the former wife's arguments regarding the trial court's equitable distribution award pursuant to Va. Sup. Ct. R. 5A:27 because Va. Sup. Ct. R. 5A:21(b) required an appellee to provide a clear and exact reference to the pages of the transcript, written statement, record, or appendix where each additional question was preserved in the trial court, and the former wife's brief failed to identify in the record where she preserved the issues she raised on appeal. Although Va. Sup. Ct. R. 5A:21(b) allowed an appellee to raise additional issues on brief, it did not dispense with the requirements of Va. Sup. Ct. R. 5A:18; a litigant seeking to reverse a trial court, therefore, had to either prove where the issue was preserved below or demonstrate an equitable basis for suspending the waiver rule, and having done neither, the former wife could not prevail on appeal. Williams v. Williams, 2009 Va. App. LEXIS 553 (Dec. 15, 2009).

Custody decision. — Appellate court summarily affirmed an order under Va. Sup. Ct. R. 5A:27, which awarded the custody of two children to the City of Roanoke Department of Social Services as the children's great-aunt did not include her motion to reconsider in her appendix as required by Va. Sup. Ct. R. 5A:25(c)(6), or include a clear and exact reference to the pages of the transcript, written statement, record, or appendix where each assignment of error was preserved in the trial court as required by Va. Sup. Ct. R. 5A:20(c). Hustead v. City of Roanoke Dep't of Soc. Servs., No. 0331-12-3, 2012 Va. App. LEXIS 403 (Dec. 11, 2012).

Meritless appeal was subject to summary affirmance. — Res judicata prevented a husband from relitigating issues that were fully adjudicated on prior appeals, so the husband could only challenge circuit court orders finding him in contempt for failure to pay his wife prior attorney fee awards and determining an amount to award the wife in attorney fees that were incurred in the wife's defense of the husband's appeals. However, the husband's failure to provide any argument, legal authority, or citation to the record waived those issues under Va. Sup. Ct. R. 5A:20(e); therefore, the court found the husband's appeal was meritless and it entered a summary affirmance under Va. Sup. Ct. R. 5A:27. Simpson v. Simpson, 2005 Va. App. LEXIS 391 (Oct. 11, 2005).

Because the trial court, in the order on appeal, had already determined the issues raised by father by finding that his appearance and participation in the October 1996 hearing was a general appearance that waived all questions about service of process and notice, and he had abandoned his only remedy of an appeal from said order, his further attempt to litigate those same issues was barred by res judicata. Thus, the appeals court found the father's appeal to be meritless. Star v. Commonwealth, 2007 Va. App. LEXIS 417 (Nov. 20, 2007).

Based on the parties' briefs, the record, and the Workers' Compensation Commission's opinion, the court found that the claimant's appeal was without merit; the court dispensed with oral argument and summarily affirmed pursuant to § 17.1-403 and Va. Sup. Ct. R. 5A:27 because the facts and legal contentions were adequately presented in the materials before the court and argument would not aid the decisional process. Grantham v. B & S Landscaping, Inc., 2008 Va. App. LEXIS 433 (Sept. 23, 2008).

Meritless appeals. — Husband's appeal from the trial court's finding that he was in contempt for not paying a lump sum settlement to his wife, representing pension proceeds, as he was was ordered to do was without merit and could be summarily dismissed. The husband's interpretation of the trial court's order to read that a qualified domestic relations order first had to be in place before he was required to pay was at odds with the plain language of the trial court's order, and merely invited a finding of error in an attempt to take advantage of his deliberate misreading of the order, which was not permitted. Martin v. Goodwin, No. 1886-03-4, 2004 Va. App. LEXIS 34 (Ct. of Appeals Jan. 28, 2004).

Despite a grandson's expressed willingness to resolve a visitation matter with his grandparents amicably, when the grandparents insisted on communicating via counsel and resolving the matter in a contested court proceeding with counsel, resulting in the grandson incurring over $9,000 in attorney's fees, the trial court did not abuse its discretion in ordering the grandparents to contribute towards the cost of said fees; thus, on appeal, the matter was summarily affirmed. Hoppe v. Scholz, No. 0495-04-4, 2004 Va. App. LEXIS 451 (Ct. of Appeals Sept. 21, 2004).

Trial court's decision denying a wife's show cause petition alleging that the husband be ordered to pay her for the room and board she expended on behalf of their daughter while the daughter lived with her and attended college full time, and decision ordering the wife to pay one-half of the daughter's college-related expenses to attend a different school, was summarily affirmed because under the Hawaiian support agreement sought to be enforced: (1) the husband had no duty to help pay for the parties' daughter's living expenses while she attended college, to which the wife conceded; and (2) the daughter's less-than-full-time status in school did not obviate any duty to help pay for related expenses. Wesner v. Wesner, No. 2433-04-1, 2005 Va. App. LEXIS 139 (Ct. of Appeals Apr. 5, 2005).

In a father's custody modification action, the trial court did not err in finding that a mother was entitled to relief and in determining the amount of the sanction imposed against the father, as: (1) the evidence clearly showed that the father's motion for a change in custody was unsupported; (2) after initiating an appeal to the circuit court, the father attempted to non-suit the case days before the scheduled trial; (3) the juvenile court permissibly inferred from the record that the father used his pending appeal as leverage, in offering a settlement to mother; and (4) the financial burden of the instant litigation was far more burdensome on the mother, and the father knew it; hence, as a resut of the aforementioned, the circuit court's affirmance of the juvenile court's findings was summarily affirmed and the wife was awarded her appellate attorney's fees. Ottosen v. Saunders, 2005 Va. App. LEXIS 484 (Dec. 6, 2005).

In light of the fact that appellant had filed six appeals with the court and that those appeals were pending at the time of the hearing, the trial court lacked jurisdiction to revisit its earlier order during the pendency of the other appeals and properly refused to do so. Thus, the appeal was without merit, and the court summarily affirmed the decision of the trial court pursuant to Va. Sup. Ct. R. 5A:27. Russell v. Russell, 2007 Va. App. LEXIS 47 (Feb. 13, 2007).

On appeal from an equitable distribution award, while evidence was introduced that both parties had numerous credit card accounts and they transferred balances from old accounts to new accounts, because the commissioner was unable to determine the source and the nature of the debts and whether they were indeed marital debts, the Appeals Court had no choice but to affirm the findings against the husband and find that his appeal from the order entered against him was meritless. Harrison v. Allegretto, 2007 Va. App. LEXIS 32 (Jan. 30, 2007).

Because neither party requested the trial court to retain jurisdiction over the distribution of their property, the husband failed to timely request an equitable distribution hearing during the 21-day period following entry of the decree during which the trial court retained jurisdiction over the case and, the trial court properly held that it lacked jurisdiction to reopen the divorce proceedings in order to equitably distribute the parties' marital property, the husband appeal from the judgment of the trial court lacked merit. Miller v. Miller, 2007 Va. App. LEXIS 212 (May 22, 2007).

In an appeal and cross-appeal from a final divorce decree, the wife waived her arguments by failing to comply with Va. Sup. Ct. R. 5A:20 in her brief and the husband waived his arguments by failing to comply with Va. Sup. Ct. R. 5A:21 in his brief and, thus, the court entered a summary disposition pursuant to Va. Sup. Ct. R. 5A:27. Joseph v. George, 2010 Va. App. LEXIS 173 (May 4, 2010).

Failure to comply with briefing and appendix requirements. — Applying Va. Sup. Ct. R. 5A:27, an appellate court summarily affirmed a trial court's denial of a husband's motion to correct a retirement distribution because the untimely appendix did not comply with Va. Sup. Ct. R. 5A:25 and the brief did not comply with Va. Sup. Ct. R. 5A:20. Cragg v. Cragg, 2010 Va. App. LEXIS 133 (Apr. 6, 2010).

Termination order subject to summary affirmance. — Mother's arguments on appeal of an order terminating her parental rights were barred from consideration pursuant to Va. Sup. Ct. R. 5A:18 because the mother failed to present her arguments to the trial court; the mother did not argue that any of the exceptions should have been invoked and the record did not establish a basis for applying any of the exceptions. The termination order was summarily affirmed. Clinton-Williams v. Newport News Dep't of Soc. Servs., 2007 Va. App. LEXIS 361 (Oct. 2, 2007).

In light of the conflicting medical opinions presented to the Virginia Workers' Compensation Commission, the Commission, as fact finder, was entitled to conclude that a doctor and a hospital failed to sustain their burden of proof that the decedent infant qualified for inclusion under the Virginia Birth-Related Neurological Injury Compensation Act. Hence, because the Commission's decision hinged on its resolution of the conflicting medical evidence, and there was credible evidence in the record to support it, it was binding and conclusive upon the Court of Appeals of Virginia. Inova Fairfax Hosp. v. Yost, 2007 Va. App. LEXIS 293 (Aug. 7, 2007).

Attorney's fees allowed. — Since a wife's attempts to relitigate issues that properly were raised or could have been raised in a prior appeal of a divorce decree were barred by the doctrine of res judicata, and since she did not preserve her other arguments, the exceptions in Va. Sup. Ct. R. 5A:18 did not apply; therefore, the husband was entitled to attorney's fees under Va. Sup. Ct. R. 5A:27. Sharp v. Sharp, 2010 Va. App. LEXIS 317 (Aug. 10, 2010).

Applied in National Fruit Prod. Co. v. Staton, 28 Va. App. 650, 507 S.E.2d 667 (1998); Gross v. Gross, No. 2214-12-3, 2013 Va. App. LEXIS 180 (Ct. of Appeals June 11, 2013).

Rule 5A:28. Oral Argument.

(a) *Notice.* — Whenever appeal lies as a matter of right or a petition for appeal has been granted, oral argument shall be permitted except in those cases disposed of pursuant to Rule 5A:27. The Clerk of the Court of Appeals, except in extraordinary circumstances, shall give at least 15 days notice to counsel of the date, approximate time, and location for oral argument.

(b) *Length.* — Except as otherwise directed by the Court of Appeals, argument for a party shall not exceed 15 minutes in length. Such time may be apportioned among counsel for the same side at their discretion, except that only one counsel may present the opening argument for the appellant. If a guardian ad litem joins with either appellant or appellee, the guardian ad litem shall share the time for oral argument with the party. If a guardian ad litem requests additional time to argue, the guardian ad litem must state that application in its brief, subject to approval of this Court.

(c) *Appearance Pro Hac Vice.* — Any lawyer not licensed in Virginia who seeks to appear pro hac vice to present oral argument to the Court of Appeals must comply with the requirements of Rule 1A:4.

(d) *Amicus Curiae.* — No oral argument is permitted by amicus curiae except by leave of this Court. Leave may be granted upon the joint written request of amicus curiae and the party whose position amicus curiae supports. The request shall specify the amount of its allotted time the supported party is willing to yield to amicus curiae.

(e) *Waiver.* — During oral argument, it shall not be necessary for any party to expressly reserve any argument made on brief, and the failure to raise any such argument shall not constitute a waiver. Any party may, without waiving the arguments made on brief, waive oral argument. See Rules 5A:20(h) and 5A:21(g).

Law Review. — For 2003/2004 survey of family and juvenile law, see 39 U. Rich. L. Rev. 241 (2004).

G. DECISION, COSTS, AND MANDATE.

Rule 5A:29. Notice of Decision.

Promptly after the Court of Appeals has decided a case, the clerk of the Court of Appeals shall send a copy of the decision to all counsel of record and to the court or commission from which the appeal proceeded.

Cross references. — As to opinions and reporting and printing thereof, see § 17.1-413.

Rule 5A:30. Costs and Notarized Bill of Costs.

(a) *To Whom Allowed.* — Except as otherwise provided by law, if an appeal is dismissed, costs shall be taxed against the appellant unless otherwise agreed by the parties or ordered by the Court of Appeals; if a judgment is affirmed, costs shall be taxed against the appellant unless otherwise ordered; if a judgment is reversed, costs shall be taxed against the appellee unless otherwise ordered; if a judgment is affirmed in part or reversed in part, or is vacated, costs shall be allowed as ordered by the Court of Appeals.

(b) *Taxable Costs.* — Costs, including the filing fee and costs incurred in the printing or producing of necessary copies of briefs, appendices, and petitions for rehearing, shall be taxable in this Court. Costs incurred in the preparation of transcripts may be taxable in this Court. See, Code § 17.1-128.

(c) *Notarized Bill of Costs.* — Counsel for a party who desires costs to be taxed shall itemize them in a notarized bill of costs, which shall be filed with the clerk of this Court within 14 days after the date of the decision in the case. Objections to the bill of costs must be filed with the clerk of this Court within 10 days after the date of filing the bill of costs.

(d) *Award.* — The clerk of this Court shall prepare and certify an itemized statement of costs taxed in this Court for insertion in the mandate, but the issuance of the mandate shall not be delayed for taxation of costs. If the mandate has been issued before final determination of costs, the statement, or any amendment thereof, shall be added to the mandate on request by the clerk of this Court to the clerk of the trial court or the clerk of the Virginia Workers' Compensation Commission.

The amendment effective January 1, 2013, adopted December 14, 2012, added the last two sentences in (b).

CASE NOTES

Construction with other law. — A trial court does not err by failing or refusing to deduct costs awarded on appeal from trial court's monetary equitable distribution award in divorce. Estate of Cummings v. Greenwood, No. 1361-99-3 (Ct. of Appeals Feb. 29, 2000).

Rule 5A:31. Mandate.

(a) *Time.* — When there can be no further proceedings in the Court of Appeals or in the Supreme Court with respect to a decision of the Court of Appeals, the clerk of the Court of Appeals shall forward its mandate promptly to the clerk of the court or commission from which the appeal proceeded.

(b) *Opinions.* — If the judgment or order is supported by an opinion, a certified copy of the opinion shall accompany the mandate.

H. REHEARING.

Rule 5A:32. Scope.

The provisions of Rules 5A:33 through 5A:35 do not apply to the denial of a petition for appeal.

Rule 5A:33. Rehearing — On Motion of a Party After Final Disposition of a Case.

(a) *Requirements for Pro Se Prisoners and By Leave of Court.* — Pro se prisoners and those with leave of Court to proceed under this paragraph of the Rule desiring a rehearing of a decision or order of the Court of Appeals finally disposing of a case shall within 14 days following such decision or order, file seven copies of a petition for rehearing with the clerk of the Court of Appeals. The petition for rehearing shall not exceed 5,300 words in length. All petitioners other than pro se prisoners and those with leave of Court to proceed under this paragraph of the Rule must follow the provisions of paragraph (b) of this Rule when filing a petition for rehearing.

(b) *Requirements for All Others.* — Any party, other than pro se prisoners or those with leave of Court to proceed under paragraph (a) of this Rule, desiring a rehearing of a decision or order of the Court of Appeals finally disposing of a case shall, within 14 days following such decision, file a petition for rehearing with the clerk of the Court of Appeals.

(1) The petition shall be filed as a single Adobe Acrobat Portable Document Format (PDF) document attached to an e-mail addressed to cavpfr@courts.state.va.us and will be timely filed if received by the clerk's office at or before 11:59 p.m. on the fourteenth day after the date of the decision or order sought to be reheard.

(2) The petition must be formatted to print on a page 8 ½ x 11 inches, must be in 12-point font or larger, must be double-spaced, and must not exceed 5,300 words. The petition must include a certificate of service to opposing counsel and the certificate

shall specify the manner of service and the date of service. If opposing counsel has an e-mail address, service on opposing counsel shall be by electronic means and such address shall be included in the certificate of service. The petition must also include a certificate of compliance with the word count limit. The petition will be considered filed on the date and time that it is received by cavpfr@courts.state.va.us. If the petition does not meet the requirements of this rule as to format, the clerk of the Court of Appeals shall so notify counsel and provide a specific amount of time for a corrected copy of the petition to be filed. A person who files a document electronically shall have the same responsibility as a person filing a document in paper form for ensuring that the document is properly filed, complete, and readable. However, if technical problems at the Court of Appeals result in a failure to timely receive the electronically filed petition for rehearing, counsel shall provide to the clerk of this Court on the next business day all documentation which exists demonstrating the attempt to file e-mail the petition by e-mail, any delivery failure notice received in response to the attempt, and a copy of the petition for rehearing.

(3) The e-mail message to which the petition is attached shall recite in the subject line the style of the case and the Court of Appeals record number. The body of the e-mail message shall contain a paragraph stating that a petition for rehearing is being filed, the style of the case, the Court of Appeals record number, the name and Virginia State Bar number of counsel filing the petition, as well as the law firm name, mailing address, telephone number, facsimile number (if any), and e-mail address (if any) of counsel filing the petition. The message shall also state whether a copy of the petition has been served by e-mail or another means on opposing counsel and the date of such service. If the petition has been served on opposing counsel by e-mail, the e-mail address for opposing counsel shall also be included. Upon receipt of the petition for rehearing in the e-mail box of the clerk's office, an acknowledgment will be forwarded by e-mail to counsel filing the petition for rehearing.

(c) *Response.* — No response to a petition for rehearing will be received unless requested by the Court of Appeals.

(d) *No Oral Argument.* — No oral argument on the petition will be permitted.

(e) *Grounds.* — No petition for rehearing will be granted unless one of the Judges who decided the case adversely to the petitioner determines that there is good cause for such rehearing. The clerk of the Court of Appeals shall notify counsel for the appellant and counsel for the appellee of the action taken by the Court of Appeals on the petition for rehearing via e-mail, if e-mail addresses for both counsel have been provided, or via U.S. Mail to any counsel or party who has not provided an e-mail address.

Law Review. — For article reviewing recent developments and changes in legislation, case law, and Virginia Supreme Court Rules affecting civil litigation, see "Civil Practice and Procedure," 40 U. Rich. L. Rev. 95 (2005).

CASE NOTES

Applied in Rusty's Welding Serv., Inc. v. Gibson, 29 Va. App. 119, 510 S.E.2d 255 (1999).

Rule 5A:34. Rehearing En Banc After Final Disposition of a Case.

(a) *Who May File.* — Any party wishing to raise any issue decided by a panel of this Court must file a petition for rehearing en banc pursuant to this Rule.

(b) *Requirements for Pro Se Prisoners and By Leave of Court.* — A pro se prisoner or a party who has leave of Court to proceed under this paragraph of the Rule aggrieved by a decision of a panel of this Court may file a petition for rehearing en banc within 14 days after the date of the order sought to be reheard. Twelve copies of any such petition shall be filed with the clerk of the Court of Appeals. The petition for rehearing en banc shall not exceed 5,300 words in length. All petitioners other than pro se prisoners and those with leave of this Court to proceed under this paragraph of the Rule must follow the provisions of paragraph (c) of this Rule when filing a petition for rehearing en banc.

(c) *Requirements for All Others.* — (1) Except for petitions for rehearing en banc filed by pro se prisoners or by those with leave of Court to proceed under paragraph (b) of this Rule, the petition shall be filed as a single Adobe Acrobat Portable Document Format (PDF) document attached to an e-mail addressed to cavpfr@courts.state.va.us and will be timely filed if received by the clerk's office at or before 11:59 p.m. on the fourteenth day after the date of the decision or order sought to be reheard.

(2) The petition must be formatted to print on a page 8 ½ x 12 inches, must be in 12-point font or larger, must be double-spaced, and must not exceed 5,300 words. The petition must include a certificate of service to opposing counsel and the certificate shall specify the manner of service and the date of service. If opposing counsel has an e-mail address, service on opposing counsel shall be by electronic means and such address shall be included in the certificate of service. The petition must also include a certificate of compliance with the word count limit. The petition will be considered filed on the date and time that it is received by cavpfr@courts.state.va.us. If the petition does not meet the requirements of this rule as to format, the clerk of the Court of Appeals shall so notify counsel and provide a specific amount of time for a corrected copy of the petition to be filed. A person who files a document electronically shall have the same responsibility as a person filing a document in paper form for ensuring that the document is properly filed, complete, and readable. However, if technical problems at the Court of Appeals result in a failure to timely receive the electronically filed petition for rehearing, counsel shall provide to the clerk of this Court on the next business day all documentation which exists demonstrating the attempt to file the petition by e-mail, any delivery failure notice received in response to the attempt, and a copy of the petition for rehearing.

(3) The e-mail message to which the petition is attached shall recite in the subject line the style of the case and the Court of Appeals record number. The body of the e-mail message shall contain a paragraph stating that a petition for rehearing en banc is being filed, the style of the case, the Court of Appeals record number, the name and Virginia State Bar number of counsel filing the petition, as well as the law firm name, mailing address, telephone number, facsimile number (if any), and e-mail address (if any) of counsel filing the petition. The message shall also state whether a copy of the petition has been served by e-mail or another means on opposing counsel and the date of such service. If the petition has been served on opposing counsel by e-mail, the e-mail address for opposing counsel shall also be included. Upon receipt of the petition for rehearing in the e-mail box of the clerk's office, an acknowledgment will be forwarded by e-mail to counsel filing the petition.

(d) *Proceedings After Petition for Rehearing.* — No answer to a petition for a rehearing en banc will be received unless requested by the Court of Appeals. A rehearing en banc on motion of the Court of Appeals shall be ordered no later than 20 days after the date of rendition of the order to be reheard. The clerk of the Court of Appeals shall promptly notify counsel for both parties of the action taken by this Court on the petition for rehearing en banc via e-mail, if e-mail addresses for both counsel have been provided, or via U.S. Mail to any counsel or party who has not provided an e-mail address.

The amendment, effective May 2, 2011, adopted March 1, 2011, added "After Final Disposition of a Case" to the Rule heading.

Law Review. — For article reviewing recent developments and changes in legislation, case law, and Virginia Supreme Court Rules affecting civil litigation, see "Civil Practice and Procedure," 40 U. Rich. L. Rev. 95 (2005).

CASE NOTES

Weight and sufficiency. — Upon rehearing en banc it was determined that where a prior stalking conviction provided only a historical context in which defendant's subsequent conduct was adjudged, neither double jeopardy nor res judicata applied; the evidence abundantly supported the reasonableness of the victim's fear. Burwell v. Commonwealth, No. 1777-99-2, 2001 Va. App. LEXIS 711 (Ct. of Appeals Apr. 17, 2001).

Applied in Rusty's Welding Serv., Inc. v. Gibson, 29 Va. App. 119, 510 S.E.2d 255 (1999).

Rule 5A:35. Procedure for Rehearing.

(a) *Rehearing by a Panel.* — When rehearing by a panel is granted on petition of a party, the clerk of the Court of Appeals shall notify all counsel promptly. No brief in addition to the petition may be filed by petitioner. Respondent may file in the office of the clerk seven copies of an answering brief, which shall not exceed 5,300 words in length, within 21 days following the date of the order of this Court granting a rehearing. Three copies of the respondent's answering brief shall be mailed or delivered to opposing counsel on or before the date the answering brief is filed.

Respondent may be heard orally whether or not an answering brief is filed. The case will be placed on the docket for oral argument. When practicable, such a rehearing will be heard by the same panel that rendered the final decision in the case.

(b) *Rehearing En Banc.* — When all or part of a petition for rehearing en banc is granted, the clerk of this Court shall notify all counsel promptly. The mandate entered is stayed as to all issues decided by the panel pending the decision of the Court en banc. The appeal is reinstated on the docket of the Court for oral argument only as to issues granted. Briefing and oral argument shall proceed in the same order as before the three judge panel. The Court of Appeals may require any party to whom rehearing en banc has been granted to file 20 copies of an appendix, prepared in conformity with the provisions of Rule 5A:25, with the clerk of the Court within such time as the Court of Appeals shall specify.

(1) Issues Considered Upon Rehearing En Banc. Only issues raised in the petition for rehearing en banc and granted for rehearing or included in the grant by the Court on its own motion are available for briefing, argument, and review by the en banc Court. The Court may grant a petition in whole or in part. Any issue decided by a panel of this Court not subject to a petition for rehearing en banc remains undisturbed by an en banc decision.

(2) Appellant's Opening Brief Upon Rehearing En Banc. The party who was the appellant before the panel of this Court shall file in the office of the clerk 20 copies of a brief, which shall not exceed 12,300 words in length. Such brief shall be filed within 21 days following the date of the order of this Court granting rehearing en banc, and shall be accompanied by a certificate that three copies were mailed or delivered to opposing counsel on or before the date of filing. The brief shall bear a white cover.

(3) Appellee's Answering Brief Upon Rehearing En Banc. The party who was the appellee before the panel of this Court may file in the office of the clerk 20 copies of an answering brief not to exceed 12,300 words in length, within 14 days after the opening brief has been filed. Three copies of appellee's answering brief shall be mailed or delivered to opposing counsel on or before the date the answering brief is filed. The brief shall bear a blue cover. Appellee may be heard orally whether or not the answering brief is filed.

(4) Appellant's Reply Brief Upon Rehearing En Banc. The party who was the appellant before the panel may file in the office of the clerk a reply brief, not to exceed 3,500 words, within 14 days after the answering brief has been filed. Twenty copies of the reply brief shall be filed. Three copies of such brief shall be mailed or delivered to opposing counsel on or before the date the answering brief is filed. The brief shall bear a green cover.

The amendment, effective May 2, 2011, adopted March 1, 2011, in subdivision (a), divided the former first sentence into the present first and sixth sentences, and added the second through fifth sentences.

I. SETTLEMENT, WITHDRAWAL, AND MEDIATION.

Rule 5A:36. Settlement or Withdrawal of Pending Appeal.

When a case has been settled or the appeal withdrawn at any time after the notice of appeal has been filed, it shall be the duty of counsel to notify the clerk of the Court of Appeals by filing a written notice that the case has been settled or the appeal withdrawn. If counsel certifies that the terms of the settlement or withdrawal require further proceedings in the trial court, a single Judge of the Court of Appeals may approve entry of an order of remand.

Rule 5A:37. Appellate Settlement Conference in the Court of Appeals.

(a) *Settlement Conference.* — Upon motion or sua sponte, this Court may order counsel, and clients in appropriate cases, to participate in a settlement conference. An informal motion requesting a settlement conference may be filed at any time while the matter is on appeal and should state briefly why a settlement conference would be useful. The motion shall state whether all parties concur. If a party objects, that party shall file within 7 days a short response explaining the grounds for the objection. All motions and responses may be in letter format addressed to the clerk of this Court. If this Court orders a settlement conference, it will ordinarily be held by telephone conference call and, in the discretion of the settlement judge, may be held in person at a convenient location.

(b) *Settlement Judge.* — A senior or retired appellate judge will conduct all settlement conferences at no cost to the litigants.

(c) *Excluded Cases.* — No settlement conference shall be conducted in appeals of criminal judgments or orders terminating parental rights or in any other case arising under this Court's original jurisdiction.

(d) *Conferences.* — Prior to participating in a settlement conference, all counsel shall consult with their respective clients about settlement options and ask for express authority to settle within any parameters acceptable to the client. The settlement judge may conduct more than one conference if, in his discretion, he deems it advisable. During a conference, the settlement judge may consult ex parte with counsel, or with counsel and that counsel's client, but shall not consult ex parte with any represented client without counsel's agreement.

(e) *Conference Orders.* — A settlement conference, if ordered in a case, shall not automatically affect any time deadline otherwise applicable. The settlement judge, however, may direct the clerk of court to enter orders tolling any non-mandatory time deadline before or after the deadline has passed. If any party advises the settlement judge that all or part of an appeal has been settled, the settlement judge shall direct the parties to prepare and sign a settlement agreement setting forth all agreed-upon terms. Upon receiving a copy of the settlement agreement, the settlement judge shall thereafter direct the clerk of court to enter an order dismissing with prejudice all or part of the appeal subject to the agreement.

(f) *Confidentiality.* — The provisions of the settlement agreement shall not be considered confidential except to the extent the agreement specifically requires it. No confidentiality provision, however, shall prejudice any party's ability to seek judicial enforcement of a settlement agreement. In any case in which a settlement conference does not result in a settlement agreement, no statement made during a settlement conference or in motions requesting a settlement conference or responses to such motions shall be disclosed by the settlement judge, the parties, or counsel to any (i) appellate judge who may be called upon to decide the merits of the appeal or any related appeal, or (ii) lower court judge who may be called upon to decide the merits of the case if remanded or the merits of any related case.

(g) *Cross-Appeals and Related Appeals.* — Appeals and cross-appeals will ordinarily be addressed in a single settlement conference. At the discretion of the settlement judge, related appeals may be consolidated for settlement conference purposes.

Effective date. — This rule became effective July 1, 2010, by order adopted April 30, 2010.

APPENDIX OF FORMS.

Form 1. Bond for Costs Alone — Appeal of Right From Circuit Court to Court of Appeals (including further appeal to the Supreme Court).

KNOW ALL MEN BY THESE PRESENTS, That we,

______________________________, principal, and
______________________________, surety, are held
and firmly bound unto ______________________________
appellee(s)
in the sum of ______________________________
to the payment of which we bind ourselves, our heirs, successors, personal representatives and assigns, jointly and severally, firmly by these presents.

The condition of this obligation is such that:

Whereas judgment was rendered by the Circuit Court of ______________
on the __________ day of ______________, ____,
in the case of ______________________________
______________________________;

And whereas it is the intention of ______________________________
__________ to appeal said judgment to the Court of Appeals of Virginia;

Now, therefore, if ______________________________
appellant(s)
shall pay all damages, costs, and fees which may be awarded against (him) (her) (them) (it) in the Court of Appeals and Supreme Court if it takes cognizance of the claim, then this obligation shall be void, otherwise to remain in full force and virtue.

Form 2. Bond for Costs and Suspension — Appeal From Circuit Court to Appellate Court.

KNOW ALL MEN BY THESE PRESENTS, That we,

______________________________, principal, and
______________________________, surety, are held
and firmly bound unto ______________________________
appellee(s)
in the sum of ______________________________
to the payment of which we bind ourselves, our heirs, successors, personal representatives and assigns, jointly and severally, firmly by these presents.

The condition of this obligation is such that:

Whereas judgment was rendered by the Circuit Court of ______________
on the __________ day of ______________, ____,
in the case of ______________________________
______________________________;

And whereas it is the intention of ______________________________
to appeal said judgment to the (Supreme Court) (Court of Appeals) of Virginia, and suspension of execution of the judgment is sought;

Now, therefore, if ______________________________
appellant(s)
shall perform and satisfy and said judgment or the part thereof proceedings on which are stayed, in case such judgment or such part be affirmed in whole or in part, or the appeal be dismissed, refused or not timely prosecuted, and shall pay all damages, costs, and fees which may be awarded against (him) (her) (them) (it) in the (Supreme Court) (Court of Appeals and Supreme Court if it takes cognizance of the claim) and all actual damages incurred in consequence of the suspension, then this obligation shall be void, otherwise to remain in full force and virtue.

Form 3. Bond for Costs Alone Required by Appellate Court on Appeal From Circuit Court.

KNOW ALL MEN BY THESE PRESENTS, That we,

______________________________, principal, and
______________________________, surety, are held

and firmly bound unto ______________________________
appellee(s)
in the sum of ______________________________
to the payment of which we bind ourselves, our heirs, successors, personal representatives and assigns, jointly and severally, firmly by these presents.

The condition of this obligation is such that:

Whereas the (Supreme Court of Virginia) (Court of Appeals of Virginia) on the ____________ day of ________________, ______, awarded an appeal from a judgment rendered against ____________________ by
appellant(s)
the Circuit Court of ________________, on the ____________ day of ________________, ______, upon ____________________ ______________________________, or some one for (him) (her) (them) (it),
appellant(s)
filing an appeal bond with sufficient security in the clerk's office of the Circuit Court of ______________________________, in the penalty of ____________________ within fifteen (15) days of the date of the certificate of appeal, with condition as the law directs;

Now, therefore, if ______________________________
appellant(s)
shall pay all damages, costs, and fees which may be awarded against (him) (her) (them) (it) in the (Supreme Court) (Court of Appeals and Supreme Court if it takes cognizance of the claim), then this obligation shall be void, otherwise to remain in full force and virtue.

Form 4. Bond for Suspension Alone Required by Appellate Court on Appeal From Circuit Court.

KNOW ALL MEN BY THESE PRESENTS, That we,

______________________________, principal, and
______________________________, surety, are held
and firmly bound unto ______________________________
appellee(s)
in the sum of ______________________________
to the payment of which we bind ourselves, our heirs, successors, personal representatives and assigns, jointly and severally, firmly by these presents.

The condition of this obligation is such that:

Whereas the (Supreme Court of Virginia) (Court of Appeals of Virginia) on the ____________ day of ____________, ______, suspended execution of a judgment rendered against ____________________ by the Circuit
appellant(s)
Court of __________, on the ________ day of __________, ______, upon ____________ ______________________________, or some one for
appellant(s)
for (him) (her) (them) (it), filing an appeal bond with sufficient security in the clerk's office of the Circuit Court of ____________, in the penalty of ____________ within fifteen (15) days of the date of the certificate of appeal, with condition as the law directs;

Now, therefore, if ______________________________
appellant(s)
shall perform and satisfy said judgment or the part thereof proceedings on which are stayed, in case such judgment or such part be affirmed in whole or in part, and shall pay all actual damages incurred in consequence of the suspension, then this obligation shall be void, otherwise to remain in full force and virtue.

Form 5. Bond for Costs and Suspension Required by Appellate Court on Appeal From Circuit Court.

KNOW ALL MEN BY THESE PRESENTS, That we,

______________________________, principal, and
______________________________, surety, are held

and firmly bound unto ____
appellee(s)
in the sum of ____
to the payment of which we bind ourselves, our heirs, successors, personal representatives and assigns, jointly and severally, firmly by these presents.

The condition of this obligation is such that:

Whereas the (Supreme Court of Virginia) (Court of Appeals of Virginia) on the ________ day of ________________, ______, awarded an appeal and (suspension of judgment) (supersedeas) from a judgment rendered against ____________________________________ by the Circuit
appellant(s)
Court of __________, on the ________ day of ________, ______, upon ________
____, or some one for
appellant(s)
(him)(her)(them)(it) filing an appeal bond with sufficient security in the clerk's office of the Circuit Court of ______________, in the penalty of __________ within fifteen (15) days of the date of the certificate of appeal, with condition as the law directs;

Now, therefore, if ____
appellant(s)
shall perform and satisfy said judgment or the part thereof proceedings on which are stayed, in case such judgment or such part be affirmed in whole or in part, and shall pay all damages, costs, and fees which may be awarded against (him) (her) (them) (it) in the (Supreme Court) (Court of Appeals and Supreme Court if it takes cognizance of the claim) and all actual damages incurred in consequence of the suspension, then this obligation shall be void, otherwise to remain in full force and virtue.

Form 6. Additional Bond Required by Appellate Court on Appeal From Circuit Court.

KNOW ALL MEN BY THESE PRESENTS, That we,

____, principal, and
____, surety, are held
and firmly bound unto ____
appellee(s)
in the sum of ____
to the payment of which we bind ourselves, our heirs, successors, personal representatives and assigns, jointly and severally, firmly by these presents.

The condition of this obligation is such that:

Whereas the (Supreme Court of Virginia) (Court of Appeals of Virginia) on the ________ day of ________________, ______, required additional bond on this appeal from a judgment rendered against ______________________________ by the
appellant(s)
Circuit Court of ________, on the ________ day of ______________, ______, such additional bond to be filed in the clerk's office of the Circuit Court of ______ in the penalty of ________________, and
with the following additional requirements: ______________________________
____
within fifteen (15) days of the date of the order requiring additional bond, with condition as the law directs;

Now, therefore, if ____
appellant(s)
shall perform and satisfy said judgment or the part thereof proceedings on which are stayed, in case such judgment or such part be affirmed in whole or in part, and shall pay all actual damages incurred in consequence of the suspension, then this obligation shall be void, otherwise to remain in full force and virtue.

Form 7. Bond for Costs Alone — Appeal of Right From Virginia Workers' Compensation Commission to Court of Appeals (including further appeal to the Supreme Court).

KNOW ALL MEN BY THESE PRESENTS, That we,

__________________________________, principal, and __________________________________, surety, are held and firmly bound unto ______________________________
appellee(s)
in the sum of __________________________________
to the payment of which we bind ourselves, our heirs, successors, personal representatives and assigns, jointly and severally, firmly by these presents.

The condition of this obligation is such that:

Whereas an award was entered by the Virginia Workers' Compensation Commission on the ________ day of ________________, ______, in the case of ____;

And whereas it is the intention of ____________________________________ to appeal said award to the Court of Appeals of Virginia;

Now, therefore, if __________________________________
appellant(s)
shall pay all damages, costs, and fees which may be awarded against (him) (her) (them) (it) in the Court of Appeals and Supreme Court if it takes cognizance of the claim, then this obligation shall be void, otherwise to remain in full force and virtue.

Form 8. Bond for Costs Alone — Required by Supreme Court on Appeal of Right From State Corporation Commission.

KNOW ALL MEN BY THESE PRESENTS, That we,

__________________________________, principal, and __________________________________, surety, are held and firmly bound unto ______________________________
appellee(s)
in the sum of __________________________________
to the payment of which we bind ourselves, our heirs, successors, personal representatives and assigns, jointly and severally, firmly by these presents.

The condition of this obligation is such that:

Whereas the Supreme Court of Virginia on the ________________ day of ________________, ______, awarded an appeal from a final order entered in Case No. ________________________ under the style of ____________________ by the State Corporation Commission of Virginia, on the ________________ day of ____________________________, ______, on the condition that __________________________________
appellant(s)
or someone for (him) (her) (them) (it), file an appeal bond with sufficient security in the clerk's office of the State Corporation Commission, in the penalty of ____ within fifteen (15) days of the date of the certificate of appeal, with condition as the law directs;

Now, therefore, if __________________________________
appellant(s)
shall pay all damages, costs, and fees which may be awarded against (him) (her) (them) (it) in the Supreme Court, then this obligation shall be void, otherwise to remain in full force and virtue.

Form 9. Bond for Costs and Suspension — Required by Supreme Court on Appeal of Right From State Corporation Commission.

KNOW ALL MEN BY THESE PRESENTS, That we,

__________________________________, principal, and __________________________________, surety, are held

and firmly bound unto ______________________________
appellee(s)
in the sum of ______________________________
to the payment of which we bind ourselves, our heirs, successors, personal representatives and assigns, jointly and severally, firmly by these presents.

The condition of this obligation is such that:

Whereas the Supreme Court of Virginia on the ______________ day of ______________, ______, awarded an appeal and suspension from a final order entered in Case No. ______________ under the style of ______________ by the State Corporation Commission of Virginia, on the ______________ day of ______________, ______, on the condition that ______________, or some one for (him) (her) (them) (it), file an
appellant(s)
appeal bond with sufficient security in the clerk's office of the State Corporation Commission, in the penalty of ______________ within fifteen (15) days of the date of the certificate of appeal, with condition as the law directs;

Now, therefore, if ______________________________
appellant(s)
shall perform and satisfy said order or the part thereof proceedings on which are stayed, in case such order or such part be affirmed in whole or in part, and shall pay all damages, costs, and fees which may be awarded against (him) (her) (them) (it) in the Supreme Court and all actual damages incurred in consequence of the suspension, then this obligation shall be void, otherwise to remain in full force and virtue.

Form 10. Form for Execution and Acknowledgment of All Bonds.

In witness whereof, the said ______________ ______________, principal, and ______________ ______________, surety, have hereunto set their hands and seals, this ______ day of ______________, ______.

______________________________ (SEAL)
______________________________ (SEAL)

State of Virginia
City/County of ______________

The foregoing instrument was acknowledged before me this ______________ day of ______________, ______, by ______________________________.

____
Notary Public

My commission expires: ______________________________

Form 11. Irrevocable Letters of Credit.

(Name and Address of Bank)

______________, 20____

U.S. $____________

On all communications please refer to (No. of Letter of Credit)

(Name and address of appellee(s))

Dear ______________:

We hereby establish our Irrevocable Letter of Credit No. __________ in your favor, for the account of (name and address of appellant(s)), and hereby undertake to honor your draft at sight on us, not exceeding in the aggregate U.S. $ ___(amount in words)___. A draft drawn under this letter of credit must be marked "Drawn under ___(Name of Bank)___ Letter of Credit No. __________, dated ______________, 20____." Funds under this letter of credit will be available to you in a single drawing by presentation of your sight draft drawn on us, accompanied by:

(For Costs Alone)

1. The original of this letter of credit.
2. Your verified statement that ______________________ (has)(have) failed to
appellant(s)
pay all damages, costs and fees assessed against (him)(her)(them)(it) in the Court of Appeals of Virginia in the case of ______________________.
3. A certified copy of an order or itemized statement of costs from the Court of Appeals assessing such damages, costs and fees against ______________________.
appellant(s)

(For Suspension Alone)

1. The original of this letter of credit.
2. Your verified statement that ______________________ (has)(have) failed to
appellant(s)
perform and satisfy the judgment rendered against (him)(her)(them)(it) on ______________________ by the Circuit Court of ______________________ in the case of ______________________, and (has)(have) failed to pay all actual damages incurred in consequence of the suspension of judgment.
3. A copy of the trial court judgment order, attested by its clerk.
4. A copy of an order of the Court of Appeals of Virginia, attested by its clerk, affirming said judgment or refusing, dismissing or allowing withdrawal of the appeal of said judgment, or certification by the clerk of the Court of Appeals that the appeal of said judgment was not prosecuted timely.
5. A copy of an order, if any, of the Court of Appeals or trial court, attested by the clerk, assessing actual damages in consequence of the suspension of judgment.

(For Costs and Suspension)

1. The original of this letter of credit.
2. Your verified statement that ______________________ (has)(have) failed to
appellant(s)
perform and satisfy the judgment rendered against (him)(her)(them)(it) on ______________________ by the Circuit Court of ______________________ in the case of ______________________, and (has)(have) failed to pay all damages, costs and fees assessed against (him)(her)(them)(it) in the Court of Appeals of Virginia, and all actual damages incurred in consequence of the suspension of judgment.
3. A copy of the trial court judgment order, attested by its clerk.
4. A copy of an order of the Court of Appeals, attested by its clerk, affirming said judgment or refusing, dismissing or allowing withdrawal of the appeal of said judgment, or certification by the clerk of the Court of Appeals that the appeal of said judgment was not prosecuted timely.
5. A copy of an order, if any, of the Court of Appeals, attested by its clerk, assessing damages, costs and fees against ______________________.
appellant(s)
6. A copy of an order, if any, of the Court of Appeals or trial court, attested by the clerk, assessing actual damages in consequence of the suspension of judgment.

This letter of credit is valid until ____ p.m. local time ________, 20____, and a draft drawn hereunder, if accompanied by documents as specified above, will be honored if presented to (Presentation Address of Bank) on or before that date. However, this letter of credit automatically will be renewed for successive one (1) year periods from the initial expiration date or any renewal period expiration date hereunder, unless at least sixty (60) days prior to any such expiration date (Name of Bank) notifies you that it has elected not to renew this letter of credit for such additional one (1) year period. The notice required hereunder will be deemed to have been given when received by you.

In the event that (Name of Bank) elects not to renew this letter of credit as required above, the full amount of this letter of credit shall be payable to the Clerk of the Circuit Court of ______________________ upon presentation of your verified statement that:

1. A final order of the Court of Appeals of Virginia has not been entered in the case of ______________________ (or, where there has been suspension of

judgment, a final order has not been entered by the Court of Appeals or trial court assessing actual damages in consequence of the suspension).

2. Thirty (30) days have elapsed since notice of non-renewal was given and appellant(s) (has)(have) not filed acceptable substitute security.

In the event of non-renewal, within fifteen (15) days after payment to the clerk under the previous paragraph, the appellant(s) or someone for (him)(her)(them)(it) shall file with said clerk an appeal bond in substantial conformance with the appropriate form in the Appendix to Part Five A of the Rules of the Supreme Court of Virginia. The bond shall be in the penalty of the amount paid to said clerk under this letter of credit, and said funds shall be in lieu of surety.

Except as otherwise expressly stated herein, this letter of credit is subject to the Uniform Customs and Practice for Documentary Credits as most recently published by the International Chamber of Commerce.

Very truly yours,

______________________________ Bank

By ______________________________

Authorized Signature

Form 12. Petition for a Writ of Actual Innocence Based on Nonbiological Evidence.

PETITION FOR A WRIT OF ACTUAL INNOCENCE BASED ON NONBIOLOGICAL EVIDENCE

THE COURT OF APPEALS OF VIRGINIA

______________________________ Record No. ____________________

(FULL NAME OF PETITIONER AND PRISONER NO., IF APPLICABLE)

(TO BE SUPPLIED BY THE CLERK OF THE COURT OF APPEALS)

v.

Commonwealth of Virginia

(RESPONDENT)

____

(PETITIONER'S ADDRESS)

____

____

Pursuant to the provisions of Chapter 19.3 of Title 19.2 of the Code of Virginia, I, ____

NAME OF PETITIONER

hereby petition this Court for a WRIT OF ACTUAL INNOCENCE BASED ON NONBIOLOGICAL EVIDENCE. In support of this petition, I state under oath that the following information is true:

1. On ______________________________, I was convicted or

DATE

adjudicated delinquent in the

______________________________ Circuit Court of the following offense(s):

JURISDICTION (CITY/COUNTY)

Description of Felony Offense	Virginia Code	Circuit Court Case No.	Plea
______________	______________	______________	____________
______________	______________	______________	____________
______________	______________	______________	____________
______________	______________	______________	____________
______________	______________	______________	____________

2. I am innocent of the offense(s) that are the subject of this petition.

3. I understand that I can file only one petition for any felony (a) conviction or (b) adjudication of delinquency and I have not previously filed a Petition For A Writ Of Actual Innocence Based On Nonbiological Evidence with regard to the above conviction(s) or adjudication(s) of delinquency in the Court of Appeals of Virginia.

4. My claim of innocence is based upon the following evidence:

____

____

[ ] ATTACHED ADDITIONAL SHEET(S)

5. This evidence was previously unknown or unavailable to either me or my attorney at the time the conviction(s) or adjudication(s) of delinquency became final in the circuit court.

6. This evidence became known or available to me on ______________________.

DATE

7. The circumstances under which the evidence was discovered were

____

____

[ ] ATTACHED ADDITIONAL SHEET(S)

8. This evidence could not have been discovered or obtained by the exercise of diligence before the expiration of 21 days following entry of the final order(s) of conviction or adjudication of delinquency by the court.

9. The evidence upon which I base my claim is material and when considered with all of the other evidence in the record, will prove that no rational trier of fact would have found me to be guilty or delinquent beyond a reasonable doubt of the charge(s) described above because

____

____

[ ] ATTACHED ADDITIONAL SHEET(S)

10. In support of this petition, I have attached the following documents:

____

____

[ ] ATTACHED ADDITIONAL SHEET(S)

11. I understand that this petition must contain all relevant allegations of facts that are known to me at this time.

12. I understand that it must include all previous records, applications, petitions, and appeals and their dispositions related to this/these conviction(s) or adjudication(s) of delinquency, as well as a copy of any documents or evidence in support of the facts that I assert above.

13. I understand that if this petition is not complete, this Court may dismiss the petition or return the petition to me pending the completion of such form.

14. I understand that I am responsible for all statements contained in this petition.

15. I understand that any knowingly or willfully made false statement shall be a ground for prosecution and conviction of perjury as provided for in Virginia Code § 18.2-434.

16. Counsel. Check the appropriate box.

[ ] I am being represented by an attorney on the filing of this petition. My attorney's name and address are

____

____

____

____

[ ] I am not being represented by an attorney on the filing of this petition.

17. Exemption from filing fee. Check box below if claiming in forma pauperis status and seeking to file this petition without payment of fees.

[ ] I claim *in forma pauperis* status and I request that this Court accept this petition without the payment of filing fees. I affirm under oath that I am eligible for *in forma pauperis* status. My assets amount to $________ (which sum includes my institutional inmate account which has a balance of $__________), and my liabilities amount to $__________.

18. Request for counsel. Check box below if claiming eligibility for court-appointed counsel and requesting appointment of counsel.

[ ] I am requesting that the Court appoint counsel to represent me in this action. I affirm under oath that I am unable to pay for an attorney to represent me in this action, as set forth in item No. 17 above.

Based on the above, I petition this Court pursuant to the provisions of Chapter 19.3 of Title 19.2 of the Code of Virginia for a Writ of Actual Innocence Based on Nonbiological Evidence.

______________________________ ______________________________

DATE SIGNATURE OF PETITIONER

Commonwealth/State of ______________________________

[ ] City [ ] County of ______________________

Subscribed and sworn to/affirmed before me on this date by the above-named person.

____

DATE NOTARY PUBLIC

My commission expires: ____________

____

DATE SIGNATURE OF ATTORNEY (IF APPLICABLE)

____

VIRGINIA STATE BAR NUMBER

Pro se (self-represented) petitioners: You are required to send copies of the PETITION FOR A WRIT OF ACTUAL INNOCENCE BASED ON NONBIOLOGICAL EVIDENCE and all attachments to the Commonwealth's Attorney of the jurisdiction where the conviction(s) or adjudication(s) of delinquency occurred and to the Attorney General of Virginia by certified mail. You must complete the form entitled Court of Appeals Form CAV-104, CERTIFICATE OF MAILING — PETITION FOR A WRIT OF ACTUAL INNOCENCE BASED ON NONBIOLOGICAL EVIDENCE.

Petitioners represented by counsel: You are required to serve copies of the PETITION FOR A WRIT OF ACTUAL INNOCENCE BASED ON NONBIOLOGICAL EVIDENCE and all attachments on the Commonwealth's Attorney of the jurisdiction where the conviction(s) or adjudication(s) of delinquency occurred and on the Attorney General of Virginia. You must include the forms entitled Court of Appeals Form CAV-103CA, ACCEPTANCE OF SERVICE OR RETURN OF SERVICE BY THE COMMONWEALTH'S ATTORNEY — PETITION FOR A WRIT OF ACTUAL INNOCENCE BASED ON NONBIOLOGICAL EVIDENCE Court of Appeals Form CAV-103AG, ACCEPTANCE OF SERVICE OR RETURN OF SERVICE BY THE ATTORNEY GENERAL — PETITION FOR A WRIT OF ACTUAL INNOCENCE BASED ON NONBIOLOGICAL EVIDENCE.

Effective date. — This form, adopted July 21, 2005, became effective August 15, 2005; and has been amended by order adopted June 21, 2013, effective July 1, 2013.

PART SIX
INTEGRATION OF THE STATE BAR

Section I. Unauthorized Practice Rules and Considerations.

Introduction.
Practice of Law in the Commonwealth of Virginia.

Rule
1. Practice Before Tribunals.
2. Lay Adjusters.
3. Collection Agencies.
4. Estate Planning and Settlement.
5. Tax Practice.
6. Real Estate Practice.
7. Title Insurance.
8. Trade Associations.
9. Administrative Agency Practice.

Section II. Virginia Rules of Professional Conduct.

Preamble.

CLIENT-LAWYER RELATIONSHIP.

Rule
1.1. Competence.
1.2. Scope of Representation.
1.3. Diligence.
1.4. Communication.
1.5. Fees.
1.6. Confidentiality of Information.
1.7. Conflict of Interest: General Rule.
1.8. Conflict of Interest: Prohibited Transactions.
1.9. Conflict of Interest: Former Client.
1.10. Imputed Disqualification: General Rule.
1.11. Special Conflicts of Interest for Former and Current Government Officers and Employees.
1.12. Former Judge or Arbitrator.
1.13. Organization as Client.
1.14. Client With Impairment.
1.15. Safekeeping Property.
1.16. Declining Or Terminating Representation.
1.17. Sale of Law Practice.
1.18. Duties To Prospective Client.

COUNSELOR AND THIRD-PARTY NEUTRAL.

2.1. Advisor.
2.2. [Deleted.]
2.3. Evaluation For Use By Third Persons.
2.10. Third Party Neutral.
2.11. Mediator.

ADVOCATE.

3.1. Meritorious Claims And Contentions.
3.3. Candor Toward The Tribunal.
3.4. Fairness To Opposing Party And Counsel.
3.5. Impartiality and Decorum of the Tribunal.
3.6. Trial Publicity.
3.7. Lawyer As Witness.
3.8. Additional Responsibilities of a Prosecutor.

TRANSACTIONS WITH PERSONS OTHER THAN CLIENTS.

Rule
4.1. Truthfulness in Statement to Others.
4.2. Communication with Persons Represented by Counsel.
4.3. Dealing with Unrepresented Persons.
4.4. Respect for Rights of Third Persons.

LAW FIRMS AND ASSOCIATIONS.

5.1. Responsibilities of Partners and Supervisory Lawyers.
5.3. Responsibilities Regarding Nonlawyer Assistants.
5.4. Professional Independence Of A Lawyer.
5.5. Unauthorized Practice of Law; Multijurisdictional Practice of Law.
5.6. Restrictions on Right to Practice.

PUBLIC SERVICE.

6.1. Voluntary Pro Bono Publico Service.
6.2. Accepting Appointments.
6.3. Membership in Legal Services Organization.
6.5. Nonprofit and Court-Annexed Limited Legal Services Programs.

INFORMATION ABOUT LEGAL SERVICES.

7.1. Communications Concerning a Lawyer's Services.
7.2. Advertising [DELETED].
7.3. Direct Contact with Potential Clients.
7.4. Communication of Fields of Practice and Certification.
7.5. Lawyer and Firm Names and Letterheads.

MAINTAINING THE INTEGRITY OF THE PROFESSION.

8.1. Bar Admission and Disciplinary Matters.
8.2. Judicial Officials.
8.3. Reporting Misconduct.
8.4. Misconduct.
8.5. Disciplinary Authority; Choice of Law.
Cross Reference Tables.

Section III. Canons of Judicial Conduct for the State of Virginia.

Preamble.

Canon
1. A Judge Shall Uphold the Integrity and Independence of the Judiciary.
2. A Judge Shall Avoid Impropriety and the Appearance of Impropriety in All of the Judge's Activities.
3. A Judge Shall Perform The Duties Of Judicial Office Impartially And Diligently.
4. A Judge May Engage in Extra-Judicial Activities Designed to Improve the Law, the Legal System, and the Administration of Justice, and Shall Conduct Any Such Extra-Judi-

Canon
cial Activities in a Manner That Minimizes the Risk of Conflict With Judicial Obligations.
5. A Judge Shall Refrain From Political Activity Inappropriate to the Judicial Office.
6. Judges Pro Tempore, Retired Judges, Substitute Judges and Persons Selected for Judgeship Are Required to Comply With the Canons.
7. Effective Date.
Establishment of Judicial Ethics Advisory Committee.

Section IV. Organization and Government.

Para.
1. Name.
2. Membership and Registration.
3. Classes of Membership.
4. Officers.
5. The Council.
6. Election to Council.
7. Meetings of the Council.
8. Annual Meeting of the Virginia State Bar.
9. Powers of the Council.
10. Promulgation of Legal Ethics, Unauthorized Practice of Law Opinions, and Rules of Court; Informal Staff Opinions of Ethics Counsel; and Complaints of Unauthorized Practice of Law.
11. Dues.
12. Disbursements.

Para.
13. Procedure for Disciplining, Suspending, and Disbarring Attorneys.
13.1. Suspension for Failure to Complete Professionalism Course.
13.2. Suspension for Failure to Complete Continuing Legal Education Requirement.
13.3. Reserved.
14. Professional Corporations, Professional Limited Liability Companies and Limited Liability Partnerships (Limited Liabilities Entities).
15. Third Year Student Practice Rule.
16. Clients' Protection Fund.
17. Mandatory Continuing Legal Education Rule.
18. Financial Responsibility.
19. Procedure for the Administrative Suspension of a Member.
20. Maintenance of Trust Accounts; Notice of Election Requirements.
21. Computerized Legal Research Services Rule.
A. Appendix A.

Section V. Bylaws of the Council of the Virginia State Bar. [Deleted.]

Section VI. Virginia State Bar Bylaws. [Deleted.]

Section VII. Acts of the General Assembly (The Bar Act of 1938 and Appendix).

Editor's note. — On October 21, 1938, the Virginia Supreme Court first adopted, promulgated and published the Rules for Integration of the State Bar as Part Six of the Rules of the Supreme Court. See 171 Va. xvii (1938). At that time, the divisions of Part Six were designated Rule I through Rule IV. In subsequent publications of Part Six in the Virginia Reports, the Rules were variously referred to as "sections" and "articles." For purposes of uniformity, the divisions within Part Six will be referred to herein as Sections I through VII.

Section I, pertaining to the definition of the practice of law and advisory opinions on the unauthorized practice of law, has been published as follows to provide guidance to the practitioner. Additionally, Section IV, pertaining to the organization and government of the Virginia State Bar, has been published.

Section II of Part Six, the Canons of Professional Ethics, was revised by the order adopted June 1, 1983, and effective Oct. 1, 1983.

Effective January 1, 2000, the Rules of Professional Conduct replaced the Code of Professional Responsiblity in Section II.

Section V of Part Six, the Bylaws of the Council of the Virginia State Bar, and Section VI of Part Six, the Virginia State Bar Bylaws, were deleted effective Dec. 1, 1983, by the order adopted Sept. 9, 1983.

The following table is provided to facilitate reference to Sections II, III, and VII and former Sections V and VI in the Virginia Reports:

CROSS REFERENCE TO PART SIX OF THE RULES OF THE SUPREME COURT

Sections I, II, III, and IV: 171 Va. xvii (1938); 173 Va. xviii (1939); 174 Va. xviii (1940); 198 Va. cxxxiii (1951); 215 Va. 859 (1975); 216 Va. 1061 (1975).

Section II: 171 Va. xvii (1938); 173 Va. xviii (1939); 174 Va. xviii (1939); 211 Va. 295 (1971); 214 Va. 420 (1973); 215 Va. 246 (1974); 218 Va. 192 (1977); 220 Va. 616 (1980); March 30, 1983, orders of the Supreme Court of Virginia.

Section III: 213 Va. 572 (1973).

Section IV: April 26, 1983, orders of the Supreme Court of Virginia.

Section V (deleted effective December 1, 1983).

Section VI (deleted effective December 1, 1983).

Section VII: Chapter 410 of the 1938 Acts of the General Assembly, as amended, was set out in former §§ 54-48 through 54-52.2:1 of the Code of Virginia (see now §§ 54.1-3909 through 54.1-3918).

SECTION I. UNAUTHORIZED PRACTICE RULES AND CONSIDERATIONS.

INTRODUCTION.

The right of individuals to represent themselves is an inalienable right common to all natural persons. But no one has the right to represent another; it is a privilege to be granted and regulated by law for the protection of the public.

The Supreme Court of Virginia has the inherent power to make rules governing the practice of law in the Commonwealth of Virginia. The Court has promulgated the definition of the practice of law. See "PRACTICE OF LAW IN THE COMMONWEALTH OF VIRGINIA," *infra.*

The public is best served in legal matters by lawyers. A client is entitled to be served disinterestedly by a lawyer who is not motivated or influenced by any allegiance other than to the client and our system of justice.

The services of a lawyer are essential and in the public interest whenever the exercise of professional legal judgment is required. The essence of such judgment is the lawyer's educated ability to relate the general body and philosophy of law to a specific legal problem. The public is better served by those who have met rigorous educational requirements, have been certified of honest demeanor and good moral character, and are subject to high ethical standards and strict disciplinary rules in the conduct of their practice.

By statute, any person practicing law without being duly authorized or licensed is guilty of a misdemeanor. The Attorney General of Virginia may leave the prosecution to the local attorney for the Commonwealth, or he may in his discretion institute and conduct such proceedings.

The courts of the Commonwealth have the inherent power, apart from statute, to inquire into the conduct of any person to determine whether he is illegally engaged in the practice of law, and to enjoin such conduct. The State Corporation Commission of Virginia may order the dissolution of any corporation or revoke its certificate of authority to transact business in the Commonwealth upon a finding that any officer, member, agent or employee thereof has been engaged in the unauthorized practice of law.

Any fees charged by a person engaged in the unauthorized practice of law are not collectible in court.

Any lawyer who aids a non-lawyer in the unauthorized practice of law is subject to discipline and disbarment. A lawyer has an affirmative duty to report unprivileged knowledge of such misconduct by another lawyer to the appropriate District Committee, and to discontinue his representation of a client when he discovers that his employment furthers the unauthorized practice of law by the client. Advisory opinions on the unauthorized practice of law, therefore, are as much intended to assist lawyers in fulfilling their ethical responsibilities as to inform and deter those who are engaged, or would engage, in such practice in derogation of the public's interest in a trained and regulated legal profession.

With the increase in the complexity of our society and its laws, the independence and integrity of a strong legal profession, devoted disinterestedly to those requiring legal services, are crucial to a free and democratic society. Allegiance to this principle, rather than the preservation of economic benefits for lawyers, is the basis upon which the Virginia State Bar, as the Administrative agency of the Supreme Court of Virginia, carries forward the responsibility for the discipline of lawyers and the investigation of persons practicing law in the Commonwealth without proper authority.

PRACTICE OF LAW IN THE COMMONWEALTH OF VIRGINIA.

(A) No non-lawyer shall engage in the practice of law in the Commonwealth of Virginia or in any manner hold himself out as authorized or qualified to practice law in the Commonwealth of Virginia except as may be authorized by rule or statute.

(B) *Definition of the Practice of Law.* — The principles underlying a definition of the practice of law have been developed through the years in social needs and have received recognition by the courts. It has been found necessary to protect the relation of attorney and client against abuses. Therefore, it is from the relation of attorney and client that any practice of law must be derived.

The relation of attorney and client is direct and personal, and a person, natural or artificial, who undertakes the duties and responsibilities of an attorney is nonetheless practicing law though such person may employ others to whom may be committed the actual performance of such duties.

The gravity of the consequences to society resulting from abuses of this relation demands that those assuming to advise or to represent others shall be properly trained and educated, and be subject to a peculiar discipline. That fact, and the necessity for protection of society in its affairs and in the ordered proceedings of its tribunals, have developed the principles which serve to define the practice of law.

Generally, the relation of attorney and client exists, and one is deemed to be practicing law whenever he furnishes to another advice or service under circumstances which imply his possession and use of legal knowledge or skill.

Specifically, the relation of attorney and client exists, and one is deemed to be practicing law whenever —

(1) One undertakes for compensation, direct or indirect, to advise another, not his regular employer, in any matter involving the application of legal principles to facts or purposes or desires.

(2) One, other than as a regular employee acting for his employer, undertakes, with or without compensation, to prepare for another legal instruments of any character, other than notices or contracts incident to the regular course of conducting a licensed business.

(3) One undertakes, with or without compensation, to represent the interest of another before any tribunal — judicial, administrative, or executive — otherwise than in the presentation of facts, figures, or factual conclusions, as distinguished from legal conclusions, by an employee regularly and bona fide employed on a salary basis, or by one specially employed as an expert in respect to such facts and figures when such representation by such employee or expert does not involve the examination of witnesses or preparation of pleadings.

(4) One holds himself or herself out to another as qualified or authorized to practice law in the Commonwealth of Virginia.

(C) *Definition of "Non-lawyer."* — the term "non-lawyer" means any person, firm, association or corporation not duly licensed or authorized to practice law in the Commonwealth of Virginia. However, any lawyer not licensed to practice law in Virginia, but licensed in any other state or territory of the United States or the District of Columbia, or a foreign nation, who provides legal advice or services to clients in Virginia, shall not be subject to these Unauthorized Practice rules but shall be subject to the laws, rules and regulations of the jurisdiction(s) in which he/she is licensed to practice, as well as otherwise applicable Virginia Law including the Virginia Rules of Professional Conduct.

(D) The Unauthorized Practice rules which follow represent a nonexclusive list of specific types of practice which would violate these rules.

Cross references. — For authority of Attorney General to institute proceedings, see § 2.2-511. For penalty provisions for the unauthorized practice of law, see § 54.1-3904. For unauthorized practice of law opinions, see the Legal Ethics and Unauthorized Practice Opinions volumes of the Code of Virginia.

Editor's note. — The unauthorized practice considerations and rules which follow are derived from the Virginia Rules of Court, Part Six, § I; 171 Va. xvii (1938); 216 Va. 1062 (1976). Part Six, § IV, Paragraph 10 of the Rules of Court prescribes the procedures governing petitions for and promulgation and publication of advisory unauthorized practice of law opinions by the council of the Virginia State Bar.

Section Ia (now Section I) of Part Six of the Rules was originally published as an Appendix to Paragraph 10 of Section IV. See 221 Va. 381 (1980). The designation for each UPL advisory opinion as "Rule 6.1-1, Rule 6.1-2" etc., has been amended; they are now designated "Unauthorized Practice Rule 1," etc. Unauthorized Practice Rules 8 and 9 were published at 221 Va. 1147 (1981). Unauthorized Practice Rules 6 and 7 were adopted by the Supreme Court on Oct. 16, 1981, effective Jan. 1, 1982, but were not originally published in the Virginia Reports.

The amendment, effective November 22, 1999, added subdivision (B)(4).

The amendment effective January 11, 2010, adopted January 11, 2010, rewrote subdivision (C).

Law Review. — For article, "Virginia: The Unauthorized Practice of Law Experience," see 19 U. Rich. L. Rev. 499 (1985).

Michie's Jurisprudence. — For related discussion, see 2A M.J. Attorney and Client, § 57.

CASE NOTES

Representation of client at bankruptcy proceeding. — Appearance on behalf of a client at a § 341 bankruptcy proceeding constitutes the practice of law in Virginia. Duncan v. Garrett (In re Tanksley), 174 Bankr. 434 (Bankr. W.D. Va. 1994).

Applied in Commonwealth Virginia State Bar v. Jones & Robins, Inc., 186 Va. 30, 41 S.E.2d 720 (1947); NLRB v. Harvey, 349 F.2d 900 (4th Cir. 1965).

Unauthorized Practice Rule 1. Practice Before Tribunals.

Note. — The unauthorized practice considerations and rules stated herein are derived from Va. Rules of Court Part Six, § I; 171 Va. xvii (1938); 216 Va. 1062 (1976), and the principles referred to in the Introduction, supra, and such authorities are hereby incorporated by reference herein.

UPR 1-101. Representation Before Tribunals. — (A) A non-lawyer, with or without compensation, shall not represent the interest of another before a tribunal, otherwise than in the presentation of facts, figures or factual conclusions, as distinguished from legal conclusions, except:

(1) A non-lawyer under the supervision of a lawyer who is a regular employee of a legal aid society approved by the Virginia State Bar in accordance with its rules and regulations adopted under § 54-52.1 of the Code of Virginia may represent an indigent patron of such society before such a tribunal when authorized to do so by the governing body of such society and when such representation is permitted by the rules of practice of such tribunal. The supervising attorney shall assume personal professional responsibility for any work undertaken by the non-lawyer.

(2) A law student may appear and represent others before such a tribunal in accordance with the third-year student practice rule.

(B) A non-lawyer regularly employed on a salary basis by a corporation appearing on behalf of his employer before a tribunal shall not engage in activities involving the examination of witnesses, the preparation and filing of briefs or pleadings or the presenting of legal conclusions.

(C) A non-lawyer regularly employed by a corporation or partnership may appear and file certain pleadings on behalf of his or her employer as authorized by Virginia Code § 16.1-88.03.

Cross references. — See Paragraph 15 of Section IV of this Part Six of the Rules of Court for the Third-Year Student Practice Rule referred to in UPR 1-101(2).

Editor's note. — Section 54-52.1, referred to in this rule, was repealed, effective January 1, 1989. For similar provision, effective January 1, 1989, see § 54.1-3916.

The amendment effective September 29, 1999, adopted September 29, 1999, added subdivision (C).

UNAUTHORIZED PRACTICE CONSIDERATIONS.

UPC 1-1. — The term "tribunal" shall include, in addition to the courts and judicial officers of Virginia or of the United States of America, the State Corporation Commission of Virginia and its various divisions, the Virginia Workers' Compensation Commission, and the Alcoholic Beverage Control Board, or any agency, authority, board, or commission when it determines the rights and obligations of parties to proceedings before it, as opposed to promulgating rules and regulations of general applicability. Such term does not include a tribunal established by virtue of the Constitution or laws of the United States, to the extent that the regulation of practice before such tribunal has been preempted by federal law, nor does it include a tribunal established under the Constitution or laws of Virginia before which the practice or appearance by a non-lawyer on behalf of another is authorized by statute.

Editor's note. — UPC 1-1 and UPC 1-2 have been modified by amendments to Rule 3D:5 adopted by the Supreme Court effective Feb. 15, 1983, and by action of the 1983 Session of the General Assembly in adopting § 55-246.1.

CASE NOTES

Treatment of federal tribunals. — Virginia Unauthorized Practice Consideration 1-1 defines the term "tribunal" to include various state agencies in addition to the state and federal courts. It does not, however, exclude other, non-judicial federal proceedings. Nor does any language in Virginia UPC 9-2 or 9-5 imply that federal administrative proceedings are not to be considered tribunals for purposes of the Virginia definition of the practice of law when the Virginia rules are otherwise applicable. Duncan v. Garrett (In re Tanksley), 174 Bankr. 434 (Bankr. W.D. Va. 1994).

UPC 1-2. — A non-lawyer may represent himself, but not the interest of another, before any tribunal. A non-lawyer regularly employed on a salary basis or one specially retained as an expert (whether as an independent contractor or an employee of another) may present facts, figures, or factual conclusions, as distinguished from legal conclusions, when such presentation does not involve the examination of witnesses or preparation of briefs or pleadings.

UPC 1-3. — A corporation (other than a duly registered law corporation) does not have the same right of appearance before a tribunal as an individual and may not be represented before a tribunal by its officers, employees or agents who are not duly authorized or licensed to practice law in Virginia. A corporation can be represented only by a lawyer before a tribunal, with respect to matters involving legal conclusions, examination of witnesses or preparation of briefs or pleadings.

UPC 1-4. — A lawyer who is duly authorized or licensed to practice law in Virginia and who is also regularly employed on a salary basis by a corporation may represent such corporation before a tribunal as lawyer for the corporation, with the same privileges of a lawyer in private practice (including confidential communications with his employer when he is acting as a lawyer in connection with such communication).

UPC 1-5. — A lawyer who is duly authorized or licensed to practice law in Virginia and who is regularly employed on a salary basis by a corporation may also represent before a tribunal the interest of a subsidiary or affiliated corporation when requested to do so by his employer and when not otherwise in conflict with the Virginia Code of Professional Responsibility. Such lawyer (unless a regular employee of a duly registered law corporation) in the course of his employment may not normally represent before a tribunal customers or patrons of his employer.

Unauthorized Practice Rule 2. Lay Adjusters.

Note. — The unauthorized practice considerations and rules stated herein are derived from Va. Rules of Court Part Six, § I; 171 Va. xvii (1938); 216 Va. 1062 (1976), and the principles referred to in the Introduction, supra; and such authorities are hereby incorporated by reference herein.

UPR 2-101. Definitions. — (A) "Lay adjuster" refers to a non-lawyer retained by a principal as an employee, independent contractor, or employee of an independent contractor, for the purposes of:

(1) investigating facts and circumstances related to a personal injury and/or property claim;

(2) reporting such facts to his principal; or

(3) assisting his principal in the handling, negotiation and settlement of such claim.

(B) "Principal" refers to:

(1) an insurance company as defined in Title 38.2 of the Code of Virginia;

(2) a self-insured; or

(3) any insured individual, business entity or governmental organization asserting a right to payment under an insurance policy or insurance contract issued to such individual, business entity or governmental organization arising out of the occurrence of the contingency or loss covered by such policy or contract.

(C) A business entity shall include but not be limited to a sole proprietorship, firm, partnership, corporation, joint venture, association or unincorporated association engaged in a commercial, charitable or professional activity.

(D) "Self-insured" refers to any person, business entity (as defined hereinabove) or governmental organization which is potentially liable for claims and which does not elect to insure against loss or, to the extent such organization retains by way of a percentage or deductible, a portion of its risk.

UPR 2-102. Investigation. — (A) A non-lawyer shall not for compensation, direct or indirect, advise another as to the law governing the facts as disclosed by his investigation, except:

(1) A lay adjuster may investigate the facts relative to a claim, and make a report thereon and an estimate of its monetary value to his principal.

(2) A lay adjuster may give his opinion to his principal as to liability with respect to a claim investigated by him.

UPR 2-103. Negotiation of a Settlement. — (A) A non-lawyer shall not for compensation, direct or indirect, negotiate or settle a claim on behalf of another party not represented by a lawyer except:

(1) A lay adjuster may secure and convey factual data and information, transmit settlement offers made by either party, determine and express his opinion on the extent of damage or injury and its monetary value, deliver releases or other documents, and assist the lawyer for his principal in the efficient performance of ministerial acts arising out of the settlement negotiations.

(2) A lay adjuster may, in the course of negotiating a settlement for his principal, make statements to the claimant or others as to his principal's liability or as to the law governing the facts to the extent consistent with the principles enunciated in the Rules Governing Unfair Claim Settlement Practices as from time to time promulgated by the State Corporation Commission of Virginia, § 38.2-510 of the Code of Virginia, provided that:

(a) the lay adjuster has informed the claimant or other person that his principal may be adversarial to the claimant or other person;

(b) it is clear that the claimant or other person recognizes the lay adjuster as an adversary; and

(c) it is apparent that the claimant or other person is otherwise competent to manage his own affairs.

(B) A non-lawyer shall not for compensation, direct or indirect, conduct negotiations to settle a claim pending in court except with the approval of the lawyer for his principal.

UPR 2-104. Preparation of Documents. — (A) A non-lawyer shall not, with or without compensation, direct or indirect, prepare or deliver legal instruments of any character except a lay adjuster may prepare a form of release or other document prepared or approved by his principal as to which the lay adjuster may fill in blanks supplying factual data.

UPR 2-105. Third Party Claims. — (A) The activities authorized under UPR 2-102, 2-103 and 2-104 are permitted only on behalf of a principal:

(1) which is making a claim against its own insurance carrier; or

(2) which is subject to a claim which may be paid by the principal or its insurance carrier; or

(3) which is pursuing its subrogation rights.

(B) Except as permitted in (A)(3) above, neither a non-lawyer nor a lay adjuster may engage in any of the activities described in UPR 2-102, 2-103 and 2-104, on behalf of any principal or other party which is making or may make a claim against a third party or against an insurance carrier or other potential guarantor or payor of third party liability to the principal or other party. Claims against an insured's insurance carrier for Uninsured Motorists or Under Insured Motorists coverage shall be deemed to be third party claims.

UNAUTHORIZED PRACTICE CONSIDERATIONS.

UPC 2-1. — For example, the activities of a lay adjuster in claims may consist of acting on behalf of his principal in identifying the facts and parties, securing witness statements, estimating the costs of repair, and compiling other information about the claim. Statements are given by the lay adjuster to his principal from whom he receives instructions as to the disposition of the claim. The lay adjuster then may attempt to settle the claim at the monetary value his principal is willing to pay or accept.

UPC 2-2. — As a part of his factual analysis, a lay adjuster may express his opinion on the extent of damage or injury and the monetary value of any claim investigated by him.

UPC 2-3. — A lay adjuster may, incident to his investigation of the facts, give to his principal his opinion of liability as disclosed by his investigation. Such lay adjuster is authorized to make a settlement on behalf of his principal and, in the course of such negotiations, make statements as to his principal's liability or as to the law governing the facts to the extent consistent with the Rules Governing Unfair Claim Settlement Practices, as applicable. A lay adjuster not now covered by such Rules may make statements as to his principal's legal liability, or as to the law governing the facts to the extent consistent with the principles enunciated in such Rules, and with the requirements of UPR 2-103(A)(2).

Editor's note. — The Rules Governing Unfair Claim Settlement Practices referred to in UPC 2-3 are promulgated by the State Corporation Commission. See also UPR 2-101 through 2-105.

UPC 2-4. — In a claim pending in court, a lay adjuster may properly secure factual data and transmit settlement offers made on behalf of his principal when acting with the consent of the lawyers for both plaintiff and defendant. With such consent, he may also assist in the settlement negotiations with the approval of the lawyer for his principal.

UPC 2-5. — A lawyer who is regularly employed on a salary basis as a lay adjuster is deemed to be acting on behalf of his employer and is subject to the same limitations with respect to representing his employer's customers or patrons as are imposed on his employer hereunder.

UPC 2-6. — If a lay adjuster in any case attempts to draft legally binding settlement papers, he is engaged in the unauthorized practice of law. A lay adjuster may draft a receipt or fill in blanks supplying factual data in a form of release or other document prepared or approved by his principal, but he may not otherwise undertake to draft particular provisions intended to have legally binding effect in a specific case.

Unauthorized Practice Rule 3. Collection Agencies.

Note. — The unauthorized practice considerations and rules stated herein are derived from Va. Rules of Court Part Six, § I; 171 Va. xvii (1938); 216 Va. 1062 (1976), and the principles referred to in the Introduction, supra; and such authorities are hereby incorporated by reference herein.

UPR 3-101. Attorney-Client Relationship. — (A) An agency shall not disrupt the relationship of confidence and trust which must exist between a lawyer and his client.

(B) An agency shall not prevent a lawyer from exercising independent professional judgment on behalf of his client by attempting to fix the lawyer's compensation, or sharing in a percentage of his compensation, or prescribing the terms of his employment, or attempting in any way to control or direct his actions.

(C) An agency shall not place itself between the lawyer and the creditor in an attempt to act as the only conduit of information between the two, since this would prevent the establishment of the fundamental relationship of trust and direct personal responsibility which ought to exist between a lawyer and his client.

UPR 3-102. Referral and Control of Claims. — (A) An agency may refer claims to a lawyer on behalf of the creditor subject to the following:

(1) The creditor shall first have the opportunity to select a lawyer of his own choosing.

(2) If the creditor does not so select a lawyer, the agency shall submit a list of lawyers from which the creditor may make his selection, which list may include the customary fee of each attorney. The creditor may subsequently authorize the agency to refer his account to the lawyer so selected by the creditor.

(3) The lawyer shall be free at all times to communicate directly with the creditor; and, upon receipt of the initial referral, as well as upon receipt of any subsequent referral unacceptable to the lawyer on the basis of the prior fee arrangement, the lawyer shall communicate with the creditor for the purpose of establishing the fee arrangement, in which arrangement the agency shall not participate.

(4) The agency may thereafter, if authorized by the creditor, continue correspondence of a routine nature with the lawyer on behalf of the creditor.

(B) An agency shall not exercise or attempt to exercise any control or imply that it has any right to control the actions of the lawyer in the handling of the creditor's claim. All decisions are to be those of the lawyer acting on behalf of his client, the creditor.

UPR 3-103. Preparation of Documents. — (A) An agency may prepare statements of accounts and affidavits of facts relating to accounts and may file the same with personal representatives and trustees in bankruptcy.

(B) An agency shall not prepare a proof of claim or file such a claim as agent for the creditor with the bankruptcy court except to the extent it is permitted to do so by the Bankruptcy Rules.

(C) An agency shall not prepare for others any document which requires legal training or the application of legal principles to factual situations except as authorized under these Rules.

(D) An agency shall not use any letters or forms which threaten the institution of legal proceedings or simulate judicial process or notice of judicial process.

UNAUTHORIZED PRACTICE CONSIDERATIONS.

UPC 3-1. — A collection agency (herein referred to as "an agency") is a business involved in the collection of past-due accounts for its customer (herein referred to as "the creditor"). The efforts of an agency to collect such a claim through correspondence or personal contacts, or both, are not the unauthorized practice of law. It is, however, improper for an agency to refer an account to a lawyer in a manner which disrupts the fundamental lawyer-client relationship.

UPC 3-2. — It is critical to the lawyer-client relationship that the lawyer remain in a position that will enable him to exercise independent judgment on behalf of his client, the creditor. A lawyer should not accept a claim from an agency under circumstances or pursuant to an arrangement that would render his judgment susceptible to control by the agency.

UPC 3-3. — A referral by an agency which permits the agency to fix the lawyer's compensation, or share in a percentage of his compensation, or prescribe the terms of his employment, or control and direct his actions, is improper. The lawyer, while handling such a claim, would not be governed by his independent judgment of what would best benefit his client, the creditor, but would be influenced, if not controlled, by the provisions of the agreement by which the referral was made. Since an agency itself cannot directly provide the creditor with legal advice, it cannot be permitted to provide such advice indirectly by influencing the actions of the lawyer.

UPC 3-4. — With regard to referrals by an agency to a lawyer, any arrangement or understanding requiring that communications between the lawyer and the creditor be handled only through the agency is improper. Such an arrangement could disrupt the relationship of trust and direct personal responsibility which ought to exist between a lawyer and his client. With direct communications, the lawyer can better perceive and analyze the individual needs of his client, and the creditor's direct contact with his lawyer lessens the possibility of misunderstanding and affords him the opportunity to determine for himself the quality of service that he is receiving. Furthermore, if the agency is the sole conduit of information, the lawyer is unable to preserve the confidences and secrets of his client. There can be no effective representation of a client if the client is reluctant to provide his lawyer with a complete and accurate statement of the facts because of his concern that this information might be divulged to some third party without his permission. It is the responsibility of both the lawyer and the agency to abide by these considerations and to avoid arrangements contrary thereto.

UPC 3-5. — The decision to bring suit on a claim involves the application of legal principles to a factual situation. An agency threatening the institution of legal proceedings is engaged in the unauthorized practice of law, but the mere statement that the claim is being or will be referred to a lawyer, without more, is not deemed to be threatening the institution of legal proceedings as long as the lawyer remains free to exercise his independent professional judgment on behalf of the creditor. Likewise, the use by an agency of letters or forms that simulate or are intended to simulate judicial process or notice of judicial process is improper.

UPC 3-6. — Statements of account and affidavits of facts relating to accounts and other matters are not legal instruments, and the preparation of the same by an agency is not the unauthorized practice of law. Such preparation does not require legal training or the application of legal principles; nor is the mere filing of such accounts or affidavits with personal representatives, trustees in bankruptcy and the like representing the interest of another before a tribunal.

UPC 3-7. — A non-lawyer may properly act as a trustee in bankruptcy but may not prepare pleadings in the bankruptcy court except as authorized by the Bankruptcy Rules.

Unauthorized Practice Rule 4. Estate Planning and Settlement.

Note. — The unauthorized practice considerations and rules stated herein are derived from Va. Rules of Court Part Six, § I; 171 Va. xvii (1938); 216 Va. 1062 (1976), and the principles referred to in the Introduction, supra; and such authorities are hereby incorporated by reference herein.

UPR 4-101. Estate Planning Advice. — (A) A non-lawyer shall not advise another for compensation, direct or indirect, in any matter involving the application of legal principles to particular facts or purposes or desires, except:

(1) A non-lawyer may collect information and analyze the facts and assets of a particular estate in relation to its economic or investment needs.

(2) A non-lawyer may, incident to the sale or transfer of a particular investment asset, give information about the laws affecting the holding or disposition of such asset, such as making projections of possible tax effects arising from a transfer of ownership of a life insurance policy, security or other investment.

(3) A non-lawyer may specifically recommend dispositive provisions for a will or trust.

UPR 4-102. Holding Out With Regard to Estate Planning. — (A) Except to the extent estate planning advice is permitted under UPR 4-101, a non-lawyer shall not hold himself out as authorized to furnish another advice or service under circumstances which imply his possession of legal knowledge or skill in the application of any law, federal, state or local, to a specific set of facts for a particular person.

(B) A non-lawyer shall not be excused from any violation of these Rules by any disclaimer or other statement that his unauthorized advice or conduct should be reviewed by his customer's own lawyer.

UPR 4-103. Preparation of Documents. — (A) A non-lawyer shall not, with or without compensation, prepare or draft, or cause his own lawyer to prepare or draft, for another legal instruments of any character, including the filling out of a form for any will or trust, except:

(1) A non-lawyer may prepare forms of wills or trusts of general application.

(2) A non-lawyer, as an incident to the regular course of conducting his business, may submit to his customer's lawyer specimen language for inclusion in a legal instrument to be prepared by such lawyer, subject to acceptance, modification or rejection by such lawyer.

(3) A non-lawyer, as an incident to the regular course of conducting his business, may furnish his customer with routine forms or contracts of generally accepted application which do not go beyond the legitimate interest of the non-lawyer and do not involve a selection by the customer as between alternative with materially different legal results not generally understood in the community. For example, the offering by a savings institution of a joint account with right of survivorship, a simple revocable trust account or a custodial account under the Virginia Uniform Gifts to Minors Act would normally not constitute the unauthorized practice of law.

UPR 4-104. Settlement of Estates. — (A) A non-lawyer shall not give legal advice with respect to a person's domicile.

(B) A non-lawyer shall not prepare or draft instruments, or give legal advice, with respect to the disclaimer of all or part of a person's interest in property, or a person's right to renounce all or part of any interest due under the will of such person's spouse.

(C) A non-lawyer shall not undertake in the settlement of an estate or trust to represent the interest of another before any tribunal, judicial, administrative or executive, otherwise than in the presentation of facts, figures or factual conclusions, except:

(1) A non-lawyer may offer to the proper clerk of court a will for probate or qualify as a fiduciary in any uncontested proceeding.

(2) A non-lawyer may prepare and file accountings and confer with the Commissioner of Accounts in any uncontested proceeding.

(3) With respect to tax matters, as set forth in Unauthorized Practice Rule 5, *infra.*

UNAUTHORIZED PRACTICE CONSIDERATIONS.

UPC 4-1. — "Estate planning," as that term is generally used and understood today, refers to the orderly arrangement of an individual's assets so as to provide most effectively for his economic needs while living, and for the personal and economic needs of those he may wish to benefit after his death. Estate planning necessarily involves, among other things, a knowledge and application of principles of the law relating to wills and descents and distribution, trusts and future interests, real and personal property, gifts, and taxation. In addition, effective post-mortem estate planning requires an intimate familiarity with probate procedure and practice.

UPC 4-2. — The proper planning of an individual's estate is often aided by the services of non-lawyers skilled in insurance, investments, accounting services, and the like. An analysis of the facts and assets of an estate in relation to its economic or investment needs, and the giving of general information as to the laws affecting the disposition of estates without any specific application thereof to a particular situation, other than mathematical computations to support a hypothetical analysis, is not the unauthorized practice of law.

UPC 4-3. — The holding out to the public, directly or indirectly, overtly or subtly, by any non-lawyer of his willingness to give advice as to the legal consequences of a particular plan which goes beyond matters incident to the sale or transfer of a particular investment asset, such as a life insurance policy or security, in the regular course of the non-lawyer's business, or his willingness to perform legal services in the field of estate planning, is a holding out to engage in the unauthorized practice of law. A non-lawyer cannot solicit such services and then hire a lawyer to perform them. A non-lawyer consultant or adviser cannot offer the legal services of his own lawyer. Such practices are not purged or purified by an acknowledgment that the consultant or adviser is not authorized to give legal advice, or by any disclaimer or suggestion that such advice should be reviewed by the customer's own lawyer.

UPC 4-4. — Activities geared to motivating an individual to give consideration to his estate, and to seek the advice of a lawyer of his own choosing as early as possible, preferably from the outset, with regard to the development of an overall estate plan, are in the public interest. Advice on matters of law with respect to the particular factual situation of the individual concerned, however, is the unauthorized practice of law whenever it goes beyond advice on matters incident to the sale or transfer of a particular investment asset, such as a life insurance policy or security, in the regular course of the non-lawyer's business.

UPC 4-5. — The preparation of legal instruments such as wills, codicils and trusts by a non-lawyer for another, with or without compensation, goes beyond the area of permitted advice incident to the regular course of a non-lawyer's business. There is nothing improper, however, in the submission of suggested forms for various types of wills or trusts to lawyers for present or prospective customers of a non-lawyer. Distributing forms of separate administrative or dispositive provisions setting forth the proper name of a fiduciary, a charity or the like is not improper.

UPC 4-6. — Selecting or filling out a form of will or trust for another is an exercise in legal judgment. As an aid to a customer's lawyer, a non-lawyer may submit to such lawyer, and only to him, specimen language for technical provisions to be included in his client's will, codicil or trust; but such non-lawyer is not entitled to hold himself out as the responsible draftsman of such provisions.

UPC 4-7. — Advice by a non-lawyer as to the use of his "standard form trust," "plain English trust," "mini-trust," or the like constitutes the unauthorized practice of law when the provisions of such instrument go beyond the legitimate interest of the non-lawyer therein, seek to do more than the normal agency or deposit contract, or affect the legal rights of persons not parties to the contract. For example, the furnishing by a non-lawyer to his customer of a power of attorney which extends the authority of the attorney-in-fact to deal on behalf of his principal with all his principal's assets or accounts, whether or not maintained by that particular non-lawyer, goes beyond the area of that non-lawyer's legitimate interest.

UPC 4-8. — The settlement of a decedent's estate invariably poses problems of a legal nature. Such settlement may involve the practice of law in such areas, among others, as the offering of writings for probate, the qualification of fiduciaries, the preparation of accountings, and the determination of legal rights and liabilities with respect to the assets of the estate. In administering and settling the affairs of an estate, a fiduciary is not acting primarily for himself; and the drafting of instruments and appearance at probate hearings by a non-lawyer, as contrasted to the preparation and filing of a list of heirs, inventory or accountings, whether in person or through lawyers who are salaried employees, ordinarily constitutes the unauthorized practice of law.

Unauthorized Practice Rule 5. Tax Practice.

Note. — The unauthorized practice considerations and rules stated herein are derived from Va. Rules of Court Part Six, § I; 171 Va. xvii (1938); 216 Va. 1062 (1976), and the principles referred to in the Introduction, supra; and such authorities are hereby incorporated by reference herein.

UPR 5-101. Holding Out as a Tax Expert. — (A) A non-lawyer shall not hold himself out as authorized to furnish to another advice or service under circumstances which imply his possession of legal knowledge or skill in the application of any law, federal, state or local, dealing with taxes, except:

(1) A non-lawyer may hold himself out as an expert in the preparation of tax returns.

(2) A certified public accountant or a person duly enrolled may hold himself out as authorized to practice before the Internal Revenue Service, as those terms are defined by the then applicable federal regulations and to the extent permitted therein.

(3) A person admitted to practice before the United States Tax Court may hold himself out as such to the extent permitted by the rules of such Court.

(4) As permitted by UPR 5-102.

UPR 5-102. Practicing Law in Tax Matters. — (A) A non-lawyer shall not furnish to another for compensation, direct or indirect, advice or service under circumstances which require his use of legal knowledge or skill in the application of any law, federal, state or local, dealing with taxes, except:

(1) A non-lawyer may prepare tax returns.

(2) A certified public accountant or a person duly enrolled may practice before the Internal Revenue Service, as those terms are defined by the then applicable federal regulations and to the extent permitted therein.

(3) A non-lawyer may render such advice or service in connection with his representation of his employer or others before a tribunal, judicial, administrative, or executive, (i) in the presentation of facts, figures or factual conclusions, (ii) as authorized before the Internal Revenue Service, in (2) above, or (iii) as permitted by the rules of practice of the United States Tax Court.

(4) A non-lawyer may render such advice or service incident to an engagement to provide products or services which he is otherwise authorized to provide, where such advice or service arises out of the providing of such other products or services and was not the principal purpose of the engagement.

(5) A non-lawyer may render such advice or service to his regular employer other than in aid of such employer's unauthorized rendition of legal advice or services to another.

Law Review. — For article discussing representation of taxpayers before an administrative board of tax appeals by persons other than attorneys, see 38 Wash. & Lee L. Rev. 1115 (1981).

UNAUTHORIZED PRACTICE CONSIDERATIONS.

UPC 5-1. — Taxation affects almost every phase of modern life. The giving of tax advice necessarily involves many branches of law and requires a familiarity with many nontax legal principles on which the tax issues depend. In addition, the legal and accounting phases of tax practice are often so interrelated and overlapping that they are difficult to distinguish.

UPC 5-2. — The preparation of a tax return does not necessarily involve the practice of law. It may often be accomplished by one having only incidental legal knowledge.

UPC 5-3. — A non-lawyer otherwise entitled to do so may hold himself out as a tax return preparer or as enrolled to practice before the Internal Revenue Service; but he may not hold himself out as qualified to deal with difficult and involved questions of tax law, wholly apart from any engagement to prepare tax returns or practice before the Internal Revenue Service.

UPC 5-4. — In general, tax planning is not considered to be the unauthorized practice of law. Attempting to resolve uncertainties as to the interpretation or application of tax or general law to a particular transaction, however, involves the practice of law unless it is incidental to a tax return preparer's engagement or the regular course of conducting a licensed business, for example, an investment business, or is limited to an analysis of merely the facts and assets of an estate.

UPC 5-5. — Only a lawyer may prepare legal instruments for others or take the necessary steps to create, amend or dissolve a partnership, corporation or other business entity. Suggesting that any such legal work should be reviewed by the taxpayer's lawyer will not cure any unauthorized practice. In general, a lawyer working for a corporation not engaged in the practice of law as a registered law corporation is not entitled in the course of his employment to provide such services for customers or patrons of his employer.

UPC 5-6. — Non-lawyers authorized by statute or Treasury Department regulations to represent taxpayers may do so in accordance with the existing law, rules and regulations governing such practice.

UPC 5-7. — When a taxpayer is being investigated for a possible criminal violation of the tax laws, he should be promptly advised to seek advice from a lawyer. The lawyer-client privilege is a unique relationship to which the taxpayer is entitled at the earliest stage of the investigation.

UPC 5-8. — Nothing herein is intended to modify or limit the right of a certified public accountant to certify, attest or express an opinion that financial data comply with conditions established by law or contract. Certified public accountants are members of a profession regulated by law who must meet certain minimal education requirements and observe certain rules of professional conduct. As such, certified public accountants engaged in the practice of their profession are entitled to a greater degree of latitude in the resolution of issues involving overlapping legal and accounting principles.

Unauthorized Practice Rule 6. Real Estate Practice.

UPR 6-101. Giving Legal Advice. — (A) A non-lawyer shall not undertake for compensation, direct or indirect, to advise another in any matter involving the application of legal principles to the ownership, use, disposition or encumbrance of real estate, except that, incident to his investigation of factual matters, he may give advice to his regular employer, other than in aid of his employer's unauthorized practice of law, or to a lawyer upon request by the lawyer therefor.

(B) A non-lawyer or lay entity may not employ a lawyer, directly or indirectly, to advise a customer in any matter involving the application of legal principles to the ownership, use, disposition or encumbrance of real estate. A non-lawyer or lay entity may, however, refer its customer to a lawyer for legal services.

(C) If a non-lawyer or lay entity refers its customer to a lawyer for legal services involving the application of legal principles to the ownership, use, disposition or encumbrance of real estate, such a non-lawyer or lay entity shall not exercise or attempt to exercise any control over, or imply that the non-lawyer or lay entity has any right to control, the actions of the lawyer in the handling of the transaction. All decisions are to be those of the lawyer acting on behalf of his client.

The amendment effective June 24, 2002, added subsections (B) and (C).

UPR 6-102. Holding Out With Regard to Real Estate Services. — (A) Except as specifically provided in UPR 6-101(A), a non-lawyer shall not hold himself out as authorized to furnish to another advice or service with respect to real estate transactions under circumstances which imply his possession of legal knowledge or skill in the application of any law, federal, state, or local, to a specific set of facts for a particular person.

(B) Notwithstanding any rule of this Court to the contrary, a settlement agent authorized by law to provide escrow, closing or settlement services for real estate transactions may hold himself out as authorized to provide such services in the purchase or financing of real estate in the Commonwealth of Virginia.

(C) A non-lawyer shall not be excused from any violation of these Rules by any disclaimer, admonition to seek the advice of an attorney, or waiver by the customer.

The amendment effective June 24, 2002, added present subsection (B) and redesignated former subsection (B) as present (C).

UPR 6-103. Preparation of Legal Instruments. — (A) Unless a party to the transaction, a non-lawyer shall not, with or without compensation, prepare for another legal instruments of any character affecting the title to or use of real estate.

(1) A non-lawyer may prepare a deed for any real estate owned by him. A non-lawyer may prepare a deed of trust or deed of trust note for any real estate owned by him or in connection with any transaction to which he is a party involving its purchase, sale, transfer or encumbrance.

(2) A regular employee may prepare legal instruments for use by his employer for which no separate charge shall be made. However, such employee may not assist his employer in the unauthorized practice of law.

(3) A real estate agent, or his regular employee, involved in the negotiation of a transaction and incident to the regular course of conducting his licensed business, may prepare a contract of sale, exchange, option or lease with respect to such transaction, for which no separate charge shall be made.

(4) A lending institution may in the regular course of conducting its business prepare a deed of trust or mortgage on real estate securing the payment of its loan, for which no separate charge shall be made.

(5) A settlement agent authorized to provide escrow, closing or settlement services for real estate transactions under the Consumer Real Estate Settlement Protection Act (CRESPA), Va. Code §§ 6.1-2.19, et seq. or the Real Estate Settlement Agent Registration Act (RESARA), Va. Code §§ 6.1-2.30, et seq. or any other Virginia statute now existing or hereafter enacted may complete form documents and instruments selected by and in accordance with the instructions of the parties to the transaction.

(B) A non-lawyer or lay entity may not employ a lawyer, directly or indirectly, for the purpose of drafting legal instruments affecting the title to or use of real estate for a customer of the non-lawyer or lay entity. A non-lawyer or lay entity may, however, refer its customer to a lawyer for legal services.

The amendment effective June 24, 2002, inserted "[u]nless a party to the transaction" at the beginning of subsection (A); rewrote subdivisions (A)(1) and (2); and added subdivision (A)(5) and subsection (B).

UPR 6-104. Real Estate Closings. — (A) In connection with a real estate closing, a non-lawyer shall not give legal advice to another, or prepare for or advise another in the preparation of legal instruments, for compensation, direct or indirect. A non-lawyer may:

(1) Act as a settlement agent if registered under and in compliance with CRESPA.

(2) Provide such services of a clerical or ministerial nature as may assist the parties in the settlement of a contract, commitment or other agreement with respect to the sale or encumbrance of property including administrative and clerical services as authorized under CRESPA and RESARA.

(3) Act as an agent or broker in connection with issuance of title insurance commitments, binders and policies.

(4) Perform searches of public land and related records, make abstracts of title (i.e., copy salient portions of what the public records show as distinguished from expressing an opinion on the legal consequences of such records), prepare title reports and, to the extent licensed to do so, underwrite for and prepare title insurance commitments or binders and policies.

The amendment effective June 24, 2002, rewrote this rule.

UPR 6-105. Lawyer-Client Relationship. — (A) A real estate agent, closing agent, lender or other party interested in a real estate transaction shall not:

(1) Disrupt the relationship of confidence and trust which must exist between a lawyer and his client.

(2) Prevent a lawyer from exercising independent judgment on behalf of his client by attempting to fix the lawyer's compensation, or sharing in a percentage of his compensation, or prescribing the terms of his employment, or attempting in any way to control or direct his actions.

(3) Place himself between the lawyer and the owner or landlord in an attempt to act as the only conduit of information between the two, since this would prevent the

establishment of the fundamental relationship of trust and direct personal responsibility which ought to exist between a lawyer and his client.

UPR 6-106. Referral of Business. — (A) A real estate agent, closing agent, lender or other party interested in a real estate transaction may refer its customer to a lawyer subject to the following:

(1) The customer shall first have the opportunity to select a lawyer of his own choosing.

(2) If the customer does not so select a lawyer, the agency shall submit a list of lawyers from which the customer may make his selection and subsequently authorize the agent to refer the representation of such customer to the lawyer so selected.

(3) The lawyer shall be free at all times to communicate directly with such customer, now his client; and, upon receipt of the initial referral, as well as upon the receipt of any subsequent business unacceptable to the lawyer on the basis of the prior fee arrangement, the lawyer shall communicate with his client for the purpose of establishing the fee arrangement, in which arrangement the agent shall not participate.

(B) A real estate agent, closing agent, lender or other party interested in a real estate transaction shall not exercise or attempt to exercise any control over or imply that he has any right to control the actions of the lawyer in the handling of the transaction. All decisions are to be those of the lawyer acting on behalf of his client.

UNAUTHORIZED PRACTICE CONSIDERATIONS.

UPC 6-1. — A non-lawyer may not express to any person, an opinion as to the validity or legal status of title to real estate or as to the legal effect of anything found in the chain of title such as, for example, a suit, will, judgment, release deed or extension agreement or as to the effect on title of matters not necessarily appearing of record such as, for example, adverse possession, the statute of limitations, or the disabilities of parties. A lawyer employed by a lay agency to render services for others is restricted to the doing of acts in the course of his employment that a non-lawyer can lawfully do. Nothing herein shall be construed to impair the right to practice of duly licensed house counsel, see Unauthorized Practice Rule 1, Practice Before Tribunals; or to impair rights guaranteed by the Constitution; or to impair the rights of a subscriber under a legal services plan licensed under Chapter 23 of Title 38.2 of the Code of Virginia.

The amendment, effective June 24, 2002, rewrote this rule.

UPC 6-2. — A non-lawyer may not hold out to the public, directly or indirectly, his willingness to give legal advice or perform legal services, nor solicit such services and then hire a lawyer to perform them. Such practices are not validated by an acknowledgment that the non-lawyer is not authorized to give legal advice, or by any disclaimer or suggestion that such advice should be reviewed by the customer's own lawyer. A settlement agent registered under and in compliance with CRESPA or RESARA, may hold himself or herself out as providing escrow, closing or settlement services in the purchase or financing of real estate in the Commonwealth of Virginia.

The amendment effective June 24, 2002, substituted "validated" for "purged or purified" in the second sentence and added the last sentence.

UPC 6-3. — A non-lawyer may compile and report factual information as disclosed by the public records, sometimes referred to as making an abstract of title; but he may not express an opinion or issue a certificate as to the legal consequences of what his investigation of the public records may show. Incident to his investigation of the facts, an abstracter may give to his regular employer or, upon request, to a lawyer his opinion as to the status of legal title as disclosed by his investigation; but neither he nor his employer, unless a lawyer or registered law corporation, may give a certificate of title or opinion to a third party, or otherwise hold themselves out as possessing legal knowledge or skill.

UPC 6-4. — The drawing or preparation of deeds, deeds of trust, mortgages, deeds of release, and other instruments affecting title to real estate requires the possession and use of legal knowledge and skill. Such instruments are extraordinary contracts and muniments of title to real estate. This is nonetheless true where a form of deed or deed of trust prepared by a lawyer may be followed or filled in, and whether the instrument is deemed simple or complex. Legal knowledge and skill are required, in any event, in the selection and completion of the proper form to fit the facts of the particular case. Notwithstanding the foregoing, a settlement agent registered under and in compliance with CRESPA may complete form documents and instruments selected by and in accordance with the instructions of the parties to the transaction. However, a non-lawyer settlement agent may not draft the deed or deed of trust or select the form of the deed or deed of trust to be used for a particular transaction.

The amendment effective June 24, 2002, added the last two sentences.

UPC 6-5. — An individual, if he chooses to do so, may draw or attempt to draw legal instruments for himself or affecting his property. A corporation acting through its employees may do the same with respect to its own property.

UPC 6-6. — A non-lawyer licensed real estate agent may, pursuant to Virginia Code § 54.1-2101.1, prepare for another contracts incident to the regular course of conducting a licensed real estate business. Whether in a particular case the preparation of a contract by a non-lawyer is incident to the regular course of conducting such licensed business must, of necessity, be determined on the facts of that particular case. Preparation, in this context, includes not only the drafting of a form but also the filling in of a previously prepared form. In making such a determination, the following facts, not necessarily listed in the order of their importance, are among those which should be considered:

A. Whether the preparer is a party to the contract;

B. Whether the object to be accomplished by the contract is essential to the regular conduct of the real estate business of the preparer or merely ancillary thereto or an indirect by-product;

C. Whether a separate charge is made for preparation of the contract;

D. Whether the implication of legal knowledge and skill on the part of the drafter is minimal;

E. Whether the reliance on such service as a legal service is minimal;

F. The extent to which the licensed purpose of the business would be frustrated if preparation of the contract were not permitted;

G. The likelihood that legal advice will in fact be given by a non-lawyer, in connection with the execution of the contract by the parties;

H. The extent to which preparation of the contract by a non-lawyer reduces cost, saves time and avoids inconvenience to the parties; and

I. The custom and practice in the industry.

The amendment effective June 24, 2002, rewrote the first sentence of the first paragraph.

UPC 6-7. — In connection with a real estate closing, a non-lawyer settlement agent may not give legal advice to another, or prepare for or advise another in the preparation of legal instruments, for compensation, direct or indirect. A non-lawyer may, however:

A. Order a survey, but not give an opinion as to the adequacy of such survey or with respect to matters reflected therein.

B. Obtain copies of leases, easements, restrictions, building codes, zoning ordinances and the like, but not give an opinion as to the legal effects thereof or any party's legal obligation to comply therewith.

C. Order termite or other inspections, but not give an opinion as to whether the results thereof comply with the terms of the contract.

D. Ascertain the status of utility services and assist in their transfer, but not give advice as to a party's legal obligation with respect thereto.

E. Arrange for the issuance of casualty insurance coverage, as requested by a party in interest.

F. Provide lien payoff figures as asserted by the lienholder, but not give advice as to a party's legal obligation to pay the amount claimed.

G. Make mathematical computations involving the proration of taxes, insurance, rents, interest and the like in accordance with the terms of the contract or local custom.

H. Obtain lien waivers from mechanics or materialmen in form acceptable to the party in interest.

I. Prepare settlement statements and complete form documents and instruments selected by and in accordance with the instructions of the parties to the transaction and prepare settlement statements, such as the HUD-1, and other form documents such as the Owner's/Seller's Affidavit, Notice of Availability (of Owner's Title Insurance), and tax reporting forms including FIRPTA, Form 1099, VA R-5, and VA R-5E.

J. Receive and disburse settlement funds, and serve as escrow agent, to the extent licensed to do so.

K. Prepare receipts and certificates of satisfaction, but not deeds, deeds of trust, deeds of trust notes, or deeds of release.

L. Create or prepare a title abstract or title report, and to the extent licensed to do so, underwrite for and prepare title insurance commitments or binders and policies.

The foregoing list of examples would not be considered to be the unauthorized practice of law; it is intended only to provide guidance and is thus non-exclusive.

The amendment effective June 24, 2002, inserted "settlement agent" following "non-lawyer" in the first paragraph; deleted "but not prepare such waiver or give advice as to the legal sufficiency thereof" in subsection (H); substituted "satisfaction" for "release" in subsection (K); and added subsection (L) and the final paragraph.

UPC 6-8. — While a lay agency may recommend to its customers the employment of a lawyer, the lawyer so employed should in all matters be employed, controlled and paid by his client, the customer. The lay agency may refer its customer to a lawyer and may consult with that lawyer or any other lawyer engaged by its customer. The lawyer, however, owes his undivided loyalty to his client, the customer, and not to the lay agency, and should be especially sensitive in real estate transactions to the ethical constraints governing conflicts of interest. To the extent the lawyer considers the lay agency to be his client and, in the preparation of legal instruments for the lay agency, he knows, or should know, that the lay agency intends to use such legal instruments in the closing of a real estate transaction for another, such lawyer is aiding such lay agency in the unauthorized practice of law. A lawyer may, however, in representing his or her lay agency client, advise the lay agency as to compliance with applicable law including the legal sufficiency and accuracy of legal documents or instruments. A direct and personal lawyer-client relationship must be established and preserved at all times; otherwise, through its own lawyer, such lay agency becomes engaged in the business of providing legal services to others.

The amendment effective June 24, 2002, rewrote this rule.

UPC 6-9. — If legal advice is requested by a party, the non-lawyer settlement agent should take care to refer the party to a lawyer. Defining what is legal advice is difficult; however, a non-lawyer acting as a settlement agent is engaged in the unauthorized practice of law if he or she:

A. Recommends or urges a course of action to a party to the transaction under circumstances which require the exercise of legal judgment;

B. Drafts a legal instrument for a party to the transaction, other than completing form documents selected by and in accordance with the instructions of the parties to the transaction; or selects or assists a party in selecting a form document, if such selection or assistance requires the exercise of legal judgment;

C. Assists a party to the transaction in the completion of a legal document, other than a form document selected by and in accordance with the instruction of the parties, if such assistance requires the exercise of legal judgment;

D. Advises or instructs a party to the transaction of which way to take title to the property or the legal consequences of taking title in a particular manner, except that providing a description of the various tenancies recognized under Virginia law shall be permitted;

E. Attempts to settle or resolve a dispute between the parties to the transaction which requires the exercise of legal judgment to a particular situation;

F. Explains the legal effect of an item reported as an exception in a title commitment except as necessary to underwrite a policy of insurance and except that a licensed title insurer, agency or agent may explain an underwriting decision to an insured or prospective insured including providing the reason for such decision;

G. Provides a legal opinion in response to inquiries regarding rights and obligations under legal documents provided that a layman's description of the purpose or intent of a document shall not constitute a legal opinion.

The foregoing list of examples considered to be the unauthorized practice of law is intended only to provide guidance and is thus non-exclusive.

The amendment effective June 24, 2002, rewrote this rule.

Unauthorized Practice Rule 7. Title Insurance.

Note. — The unauthorized practice considerations and rules stated herein are derived from Va. Rules of Court Part Six, § I; 171 Va. xvii (1938); 216 Va. 1062 (1976), and the principles referred to in the Introduction printed at 28 Va. Bar News No. 2, pp. 39-42 (Aug. 1979); and such authorities are hereby incorporated herein.

UPR 7-101. Title Insurance Practice. — (A) A title insurance company, through its employees, agents or other representatives acting as such, shall not give legal advice or express an opinion to any person other than, upon request, to a lawyer, as to the status or marketability of title to real property in Virginia, or as to the legal effect of documents comprising the chain of title or matters revealed by a title search or examination.

(B) A title insurance commitment, binder or policy, or any of the provisions thereof, shall not be held out, directly or indirectly, by any person as constituting the equivalent of, or as tantamount to, a legal opinion based upon an examination of title.

(C) A title insurance company may in the regular course of conducting its business, issue directly to an insured or prospective insured its title insurance commitments, binders and policies, as otherwise permitted by law.

(D) A title insurance company, its employees, agents and other representatives are subject in all respects to the Rules set forth in Unauthorized Practice Rule 6, Real Estate Practice.

UNAUTHORIZED PRACTICE CONSIDERATIONS.

UPC 7-1. — Title insurance is insurance indemnifying the insured from loss if the status of title on a certain date is other than as stated in the policy, subject to the exclusions and exceptions from coverage set out in the policy.

UPC 7-2. — The abstracting of title to real property located in Virginia by a non-lawyer from public records does not, standing alone, constitute the practice of law; but the interpretation of the meaning of documents comprising and affecting the chain of title, and the concepts attendant thereto, require a knowledge of statutes, general law in the field, and judicial decisions not generally possessed by non-lawyers. It is not improper, however, for an employee of a title insurance company to search the title records and report his findings to his employer, and express his conclusions to his employer or, upon request, to a lawyer as to which liens, encumbrances and the like relate to or affect the status of a particular title.

UPC 7-3. — Although legal knowledge and skill may be utilized in the preparation and issuance of a title insurance policy, this does not make such policy a legal opinion. The policy is one of indemnity against loss issued in the regular course of its business by a title insurance company subject to inspection, supervision and regulation by the State Corporation Commission of Virginia.

UPC 7-4. — If an employee, agent or other representative of a title insurance company attempts to advise another, other than such company or, upon request, a lawyer, on the legal effect of matters affecting the chain of title to real estate located in Virginia and the concepts attendant thereto, he then engages in the unauthorized practice of law since he would be furnishing to another advice or service under circumstances which imply his possession and use of legal knowledge and skill.

Unauthorized Practice Rule 8. Trade Associations.

Note. — The unauthorized practice considerations and rules stated herein are derived from Va. Rules of Court Part Six, § I; 171 Va. xvii (1938); 216 Va. 1062 (1976), and the principles referred to in the Introduction, 29 Va. Bar News No. 2, pp. 10-12 (Aug. 1980); and such authorities are hereby incorporated by reference herein.

UPR 8-101. Giving Legal Advice. — (A) A trade association shall not give legal advice or provide legal services to its members, directly or through its employed or retained lawyer, except that a trade association may:

(1) Distribute to its members any legal opinion rendered to the trade association by its lawyer on a matter which affects or may affect the general membership of the association.

(2) Appear through its lawyer as an intervenor or amicus curiae in any case involving a member, to the extent otherwise permitted by the court.

(3) Refer one or more of its members to its lawyer with respect to any legal matter so long as such lawyer is recognized throughout by all concerned as representing solely the interest of such member or members, free of control by or interference from the trade association.

(4) Solicit the comments of its members on proposed legislation or regulations drafted by its lawyer which affect or may affect the general membership of the association.

(5) Provide legal advice and the services of its lawyer to one or more of its members preliminary to and in connection with any matter that may seek to:

(a) Further the political goals of the association;

(b) Obtain meaningful access to the courts; or

(c) Vindicate civil liberties guaranteed by the Constitutions of Virginia or the United States.

CIRCUIT COURT OPINIONS

Wrongful termination claim. — Narrow exceptions to the at-will employment doctrine did not permit a wrongful termination claim by an attorney against a trade association for the attorney's discharge by the trade association because of the attorney's refusal to engage in conduct prohibited by Va. Sup. Ct. R. pt. 6, § I, R. 8-101 and § 54.1-3904. Rubin v. Am. Soc'y of Travel Agents, Inc., 78 Va. Cir. 1, 2008 Va. Cir. LEXIS 197 (Alexandria 2008).

UPR 8-102. Holding Out With Regard to Legal Services. — (A) Except to the extent legal advice or services are permitted to be provided under UPR 8-101, a trade association shall not hold itself out as authorized to furnish its members legal advice or services.

UPR 8-103. Attorney-Client Relationship. — (A) A trade association shall not:

(1) Disrupt the relationship of confidence and trust which must exist between a lawyer and his client.

(2) Prevent a lawyer from exercising independent judgment on behalf of his client by attempting to fix the lawyer's compensation, or sharing in a percentage of his compensation, or prescribing the terms of his employment, or attempting in any way to control or direct his actions, except that in matters of collective interest a trade association may negotiate on behalf of its members with respect to the legal fees to be charged.

(3) Place itself between the lawyer and the member in an attempt to act as the only conduit of information between the two, since this would prevent the establishment of the fundamental relationship of trust and direct personal responsibility which ought to exist between a lawyer and his client.

UPR 8-104. Referral of Business. — (A) A trade association may refer its member to a lawyer subject to the following:

(1) The member shall first have the opportunity to select a lawyer of his own choosing.

(2) If the member does not so select a lawyer, the trade association shall submit a list of lawyers from which the member may make his selection, which list may include the customary fee of each lawyer on the list.

(3) The lawyer shall be free at all times to communicate directly with such member, now his client; and upon receipt of the initial referral, as well as upon the receipt of any

subsequent business unacceptable to the lawyer on the basis of the prior fee arrangement, the lawyer shall communicate with his client for the purpose of establishing the fee arrangement, in which arrangement the trade association, in pursuit of its associational goals, may participate as a negotiator or contributor, or both.

(B) A trade association shall not exercise or attempt to exercise any control or imply that it has any right to control the action of the lawyer in the handling of the transaction. All decisions are to be those of the lawyer acting on behalf of his client.

UNAUTHORIZED PRACTICE CONSIDERATIONS.

UPC 8-1. — The term "trade association" as used herein means a nonprofit organization formed for the principal purpose of furthering the common business or professional interest of its members. Any organization that qualifies as a business league or chamber of commerce under § 501(c)(6) of the Internal Revenue Code shall be presumed to be a trade association for purposes of this Rule. The conduct of a prepaid legal services plan is not to be considered governed by this Rule.

UPC 8-2. — A trade association may recommend to its members the services of a lawyer. A trade association should not interfere with the personal lawyer-client relationship that should exist between a member and such member's own lawyer.

UPC 8-3. — If a trade association offers to provide or provides its members with the services of a lawyer subject to the trade association's direction and control, it is engaged in the unauthorized practice of law unless such services seek to further the political or ideological goals of their associational activity. For example, a trade association may provide its members with its views, including the legal opinions of its employed or retained lawyer, on legislative, administrative and judicial developments or other matters of general interest to some or all of its members, but may not advise, or hold itself out as permitted to advise, an individual member as to the application of a statute, regulation or decision to such member's particular set of facts, unless such advice is incident to or part of the association's collective activity undertaken to obtain meaningful access to the courts or other fundamental rights within the protection of Article I, § 12 of the Virginia Constitution or the First Amendment to the United States Constitution.

UPC 8-4. — Incident to his normal duties as a lobbyist or otherwise, a non-lawyer representative of a trade association may discuss with a member of the trade association the possible application of a proposed or enacted statute, regulation or decision to a particular set of facts; provided that such discussion does not constitute the giving of legal advice.

Unauthorized Practice Rule 9. Administrative Agency Practice.

Note. — The unauthorized practice considerations and rules stated herein are derived from Va. Rules of Court Part Six, § I; 171 Va. xvii (1938); 216 Va. 1062 (1976), and the principles referred to in the Introduction, 29 Va. Bar News No. 2, pp. 10-12 (Aug. 1980); and such authorities are hereby incorporated by reference herein.

UPR 9-101. Holding Out as an Expert. — (A) A non-lawyer shall not hold himself out as authorized to furnish to another advice or service under circumstances which imply his possession of legal knowledge or skill in the application of any law, federal, state or local, or administrative regulation or ruling applicable thereto, except that a person admitted to practice by an administrative agency may hold himself out as such to the extent permitted by such agency as long as he does not misrepresent the scope of his practice authorized by such agency.

(B) A person duly licensed or authorized to practice law in another state or before any administrative agency shall not use the descriptive term "law office" or its equivalent on any signs or listings in Virginia, unless he is an employee or member of a firm with one or more lawyers duly licensed to practice law in Virginia.

UPR 9-102. Agency Practice. — (A) A non-lawyer shall not furnish to another for compensation, direct or indirect, advice or service under circumstances which require his use of legal knowledge or skill in the application of any law, federal, state or local, or administrative regulation or ruling applicable thereto, except:

(1) As an employee to his regular employer.

(2) As permitted by the rules of such agency and reasonably within the scope of his practice authorized by such agency.

(B) A non-lawyer shall not undertake, with or without compensation, to prepare for another legal instruments of any character incident to his practice before an administrative agency, except:

(1) As an employee for his regular employer.

(2) In the regular course and reasonably within the scope of his practice authorized by such agency.

(C) As to representing the interest of another before an administrative tribunal, see Unauthorized Practice Rule 1, Practice Before Tribunals.

Law Review. — For article discussing representation of taxpayers before an administrative board of tax appeals by persons other than attorneys, see 38 Wash. & Lee L. Rev. 1115 (1981).

UPR 9-103. Immigration Practice. — (A) The preceding provisions of UPR 9 also apply to unauthorized nonlawyers who represent persons, with or without compensation, before federal administrative agencies in connection with petitions or applications for benefits under the Immigration and Nationality Act and other federal immigration and nationality statutes and regulations.

(B) For purposes of UPR 9-103(A):

(1) "Unauthorized" means unable to show specific authorization by the appropriate federal agency to practice before it. With respect to matters before the Immigration and Naturalization Service, this means unable to show recognition as an authorized nonlawyer representative pursuant to 8 CFR Part 292, to wit: providing for representation by law students, law graduates not yet admitted to the bar, "reputable individuals" appearing without direct or indirect remuneration, accredited representatives, accredited officials, and certain attorneys residing outside the United States.

(2) "Represent" means to engage in "practice" or "preparation" as those terms are defined, respectively, in 8 CFR §§ 1.1(i) and (k), to wit: "practice" means the act or acts of any person appearing in any case, either in person or through the preparation or filing of any brief or other document, paper, application, or petition on behalf of another person or client before or with the Service ...; "preparation" means the study of the facts of a case and the applicable laws, coupled with the giving of advice and auxiliary activities, including the incidental preparation of papers, but does not include the lawful functions of a notary public or service consisting solely of assistance in the completion of blank spaces on printed Service forms by one whose remuneration, if any, is nominal and who does not hold himself out as qualified in legal matters or in immigration and naturalization procedure or as 8 CFR Part 292 may be amended from time to time.

(C) The provisions of (A) and (B) above are not intended to prohibit an unauthorized nonlawyer from assisting an individual in the completion of forms which had been personally selected by the individual, to the extent that such assistance involves only the taking and transcription of dictation or the translation of such dictation into English. However, the referenced provisions are intended to prohibit such an unauthorized nonlawyer from selecting specific forms for completion or from advising the individual as to which forms are appropriate for completion and submission to the Service provided such activities require the use of legal knowledge and skill.

UNAUTHORIZED PRACTICE CONSIDERATIONS.

UPC 9-1. — Representing another before an administrative agency normally constitutes the practice of law.

UPC 9-2. — Regulation of the practice of law before federal administrative agencies is the responsibility of Congress. When Congress grants authority to an agency to prescribe regulations governing the recognition and conduct of a person representing the interest of another before such agency, the State is preempted from enforcing its own rules of practice while such person is acting reasonably within the scope of the practice authorized by the agency. As to rules of practice before Virginia administrative agencies, see Unauthorized Practice Rule 1, Practice Before Tribunals.

CASE NOTES

Treatment of federal tribunals. — Virginia Unauthorized Practice Consideration 1-1 defines the term "tribunal" to include various state agencies in addition to the state and federal courts. It does not, however, exclude other, non-judicial federal proceedings. Nor does any language in Virginia UPC 9-2 or 9-5 imply that federal administrative proceedings are not to be considered tribunals for purposes of the Virginia definition of the practice of law when the Virginia rules are otherwise applicable. Duncan v. Garrett (In re Tanksley), 174 Bankr. 434 (Bankr. W.D. Va. 1994).

UPC 9-3. — Normally, a person authorized to practice before an administrative agency may give advice to others informing them of their rights and obligations as to matters pending before, to be presented to or otherwise within the jurisdiction of such agency; prepare applications, exhibits and other documents as required by such agency in the submission of matters to it and in the performance of its regulatory functions; appear before such agency at any hearing, formal or informal, within Virginia and, as otherwise permitted by such agency, represent the interests of others before such agency, including filing motions and briefs, cross-examining witnesses, and making oral arguments as to matters of law; and hold himself out as qualified to perform such services before such agency within the scope of his agency license.

UPC 9-4. — A person authorized to practice before an administrative agency may not prepare for another, not his regular employer, legal instruments not reasonably within the scope of his agency practice. For example, the preparation of a lease or contract to be approved by an administrative agency may facially appear to be incident to the regular course of conducting an approved agency practice; but such a document normally creates substantive rights and obligations for the parties under state law, and to prepare such documents and give advice concerning their significance beyond their compliance with federal law or regulations may constitute the unauthorized practice of law.

UPC 9-5. — The privilege of practicing before most federal administrative agencies is not restricted to lawyers. The federal Administrative Procedure Act grants to an individual who is a member in good standing of the Bar of the highest court of any state an initial right to represent others before any federal agency; but if such person is not duly licensed or authorized to practice law in Virginia or has not obtained the requisite revenue license required by § 58-371 of the Code of Virginia, he is subject to the same rules as a non-lawyer when his activities in Virginia extend beyond the scope of the practice authorized by the federal agency.

Editor's note. — Section 58-371, referred to in UPC 9-5, has been repealed.

CASE NOTES

Treatment of federal tribunals. — Virginia Unauthorized Practice Consideration 1-1 defines the term "tribunal" to include various state agencies in addition to the state and federal courts. It does not, however, exclude other, non-judicial federal proceedings. Nor does any language in Virginia UPC 9-2 or 9-5 imply that federal administrative proceedings are not to be considered tribunals for purposes of the Virginia definition of the practice of law when the Virginia rules are otherwise applicable. Duncan v. Garrett (In re Tanksley), 174 Bankr. 434 (Bankr. W.D. Va. 1994).

UPC 9-6. — A person who is authorized to practice before an administrative agency and who is duly licensed or authorized to practice law in another state presumably has met certain minimal educational requirements and is subject to discipline for violations of a code of professional responsibility similar to that governing the conduct of lawyers licensed to practice in Virginia. As such, a person licensed or authorized to practice law in another state is entitled to a greater degree of latitude in the resolution of issues involving whether his activity is within the scope of the practice authorized by such agency and whether any legal instruments prepared by him are properly incident thereto.

UPC 9-7. — Aliens are especially vulnerable to the unauthorized practice of law. Such unauthorized practice, which may include incompetent or fraudulent legal services, can cause serious economic harm, may result in the separation of families, and may even result in the death of an individual forcibly repatriated to another country if asylum is denied to him in the United States.

The Virginia State Bar recognizes that certain nonlawyers may be authorized to practice before a federal immigration agency. However, nonlawyers who are not so authorized are limited to providing assistance to an alien resident for such limited services as translation of documents, and assistance in the transcription of documents or answers provided by the alien, for a fee commensurate with such limited services. However, the selection of appropriate immigration forms, the assistance to the alien in the information to be provided on such forms, and other related services by an unauthorized nonlawyer may constitute the unauthorized practice of law.

Furthermore, in addition to engaging in the unauthorized practice of law, an individual who holds himself or herself out as qualified to render such legal services and performs such services, may also be subject to criminal prosecution, to civil remedies such as quo warranto actions, and to such discipline and sanctions as may be imposed under federal statutes and regulations.

SECTION II. VIRGINIA RULES OF PROFESSIONAL CONDUCT.

Cross references. — For legal ethics opinions, see the Legal Ethics and Unauthorized Practice Opinions volumes of the Code of Virginia.

Editor's note. — The Virginia Rules of Professional Conduct were adopted January 25, 1999, effective January 1, 2000.

Research References. — Altman and Weil, How to Manage Your Law Office (Matthew Bender).

Burke and Bradbury, Accounting Systems for Law Offices (Matthew Bender).

D. Edward Martin, Attorney's Handbook of Accounting, Auditing, and Financial Reporting (Matthew Bender).

PREAMBLE: A LAWYER'S RESPONSIBILITIES

A lawyer is a representative of clients or a neutral third party, an officer of the legal system and a public citizen having special responsibility for the quality of justice.

A lawyer may perform various functions. As advisor, a lawyer provides a client with an informed understanding of the client's legal rights and obligations and explains their practical implications. As advocate, a lawyer zealously asserts the client's position under the rules of the adversary system. As negotiator, a lawyer seeks a result advantageous to the client but consistent with requirements of honest dealing with others. As intermediary between clients, a lawyer seeks to reconcile their divergent interests as an advisor and, to a limited extent, as a spokesperson for each client. As third party neutral, a lawyer represents neither party, but helps the parties arrive at their own solution. As evaluator, a lawyer examines a client's legal affairs and reports about them to the client or to others.

In all professional functions a lawyer should be competent, prompt and diligent. A lawyer should maintain communication with a client concerning the representation. A lawyer should keep in confidence information relating to representation of a client except so far as disclosure is required or permitted by the Rules of Professional Conduct or other law.

A lawyer's conduct should conform to the requirements of the law, both in professional service to clients and in the lawyer's business and personal affairs. A lawyer should use the law's procedures only for legitimate purposes and not to harass or intimidate others. A lawyer should demonstrate respect for the legal system and for those who serve it, including judges, other lawyers and public officials. While it is a lawyer's duty, when necessary, to challenge the rectitude of official action, it is also a lawyer's duty to uphold legal process.

As a public citizen, a lawyer should seek improvement of the law, the administration of justice and the quality of service rendered by the legal profession. As a member of a learned profession, a lawyer should cultivate knowledge of the law beyond its use for clients, employ that knowledge in reform of the law and work to strengthen legal education. A lawyer should be mindful of deficiencies in the administration of justice and of the fact that the poor, and sometimes persons who are not poor, cannot afford adequate legal assistance, and should therefore devote professional time and civic influence in their behalf. A lawyer should aid the legal profession in pursuing these objectives and should help the bar regulate itself in the public interest.

Many of a lawyer's professional responsibilities are prescribed in the Rules of Professional Conduct, as well as substantive and procedural law. However, a lawyer is also guided by personal conscience and the approbation of professional peers. A lawyer should strive to attain the highest level of skill, to improve the law and the legal profession, and to exemplify the legal profession's ideals of public service.

A lawyer's responsibilities as a representative of clients, an officer of the legal system and a public citizen are usually harmonious. Thus, when an opposing party is well represented, a lawyer can be a zealous advocate on behalf of a client and at the same time assume that justice is being done. So also, a lawyer can be sure that preserving client confidences ordinarily serves the public interest because people are more likely to seek legal advice, and thereby heed their legal obligations, when they know their communications will be private.

In the nature of law practice, however, conflicting responsibilities are encountered. Virtually all difficult ethical problems arise from conflict between a lawyer's responsibilities to clients, to the legal system and to the lawyer's own interest in remaining an upright person while earning a satisfactory living. The Rules of Professional Conduct prescribe terms for resolving such conflicts. Within the framework of these Rules, many difficult issues of professional discretion can arise. Such issues must be resolved through the exercise of sensitive professional and moral judgment guided by the basic principles underlying the Rules.

The legal profession is largely self-governing. Although other professions also have been granted powers of self-government, the legal profession is unique in this respect because of the close relationship between the profession and the processes of government and law enforcement. This connection is manifested in the fact that ultimate authority over the legal profession is vested largely in the courts.

To the extent that lawyers meet the obligations of their professional calling, the occasion for government regulation is obviated. Self-regulation also helps maintain the legal profession's independence from government domination. An independent legal profession is an important force in preserving government under law, for abuse of legal authority is more readily challenged by a profession whose members are not dependent on government for the right to practice.

The legal profession's relative autonomy carries with it special responsibilities of self-government. The profession has a responsibility to assure that its regulations are conceived in the public interest and not in furtherance of parochial or self-interested concerns of the bar. Every lawyer is responsible for observance of the Rules of Professional Conduct. A lawyer should also aid in securing their observance by other lawyers. Neglect of these responsibilities compromises the independence of the profession and the public interest which it serves.

Lawyers play a vital role in the preservation of society. The fulfillment of this role requires an understanding by lawyers of their relationship to our legal system. The Rules of Professional Conduct, when properly applied, serve to define that relationship.

Scope

The Rules of Professional Conduct are rules of reason. They should be interpreted with reference to the purposes of legal representation and of the law itself. Some of the Rules are imperatives, cast in the terms "shall" or "shall not." These define proper conduct for purposes of professional discipline. Others, generally cast in the term "may," are permissive and define areas under the Rules in which the lawyer has professional discretion. No disciplinary action should be taken when the lawyer chooses not to act or acts within the bounds of such discretion. Other Rules define the nature of relationships between the lawyer and others. The Rules are thus partly obligatory and disciplinary and partly constitutive and descriptive in that they define a lawyer's professional role. Many of the Comments use the term "should." Comments do not add obligations to the Rules but provide guidance for practicing in compliance with the Rules.

These Rules follow the same format as the current American Bar Association Model Rules of Professional Conduct ("ABA Model Rules"), rather than the former American Bar Association Model Code of Professional Responsibility ("ABA Model Code"), or the former Virginia Code of Professional Responsibility ("Virginia Code"). Although interpretation of similar language in the ABA Model Rules by other states' courts and bars might be helpful in understanding Virginia's Rules, those foreign interpretations should not be binding in Virginia.

The Rules presuppose a larger legal context shaping the lawyer's role. That context includes court rules and statutes relating to matters of licensure, laws defining specific obligations of lawyers and substantive and procedural law in general. Compliance with the Rules, as with all law in an open society, depends primarily upon understanding and voluntary compliance, secondarily upon reinforcement by peer and public opinion and finally, when necessary, upon enforcement through disciplinary proceedings. The Rules do not, however, exhaust the moral and ethical considerations that should inform a lawyer, for no worthwhile human activity can be completely defined by legal rules. The Rules simply provide a framework for the ethical practice of law.

Furthermore, for purposes of determining the lawyer's authority and responsibility, principles of substantive law external to these Rules determine whether a client-lawyer relationship exists. Most of the duties flowing from the client-lawyer relationship attach only after the client has requested the lawyer to render legal services and the lawyer has agreed to do so. But there are some duties, such as that of confidentiality under Rule 1.6, that may attach when the lawyer agrees to consider whether a client-lawyer relationship shall be established. Whether a client-lawyer relationship exists for any specific purpose can depend on the circumstances and may be a question of fact.

These Rules apply to all lawyers, whether practicing in the private or the public sector. However, under various legal provisions, including constitutional, statutory and common law, the responsibilities of government lawyers may include authority concerning legal matters that ordinarily reposes in the client in private client-lawyer relationships. For example, a lawyer for a government agency may have authority on behalf of the government to decide upon settlement or whether to appeal from an adverse judgment. Such authority in various respects is generally vested in the Attorney General and the commonwealth attorneys in state government, and their federal counterparts, and the same may be true of other government law officers. Also, lawyers under the supervision of these officers may be authorized to represent several government agencies in intragovernmental legal controversies in circumstances where a private lawyer could not represent multiple private clients. They also may have authority to represent the "public interest" in circumstances where a private lawyer would not be authorized to do so. These Rules do not abrogate any such authority.

Failure to comply with an obligation or prohibition imposed by a Rule is a basis for invoking the disciplinary process. The Rules presuppose that disciplinary assessment of a lawyer's conduct will be made on the basis of the facts and circumstances as they existed at the time of the conduct in question and in recognition of the fact that a lawyer often has to act upon uncertain or incomplete evidence of the situation. Moreover, the Rules presuppose that whether or not discipline should be imposed for a violation, and the severity of a sanction, depend on all the circumstances, such as the willfulness and seriousness of the violation, extenuating factors and whether there have been previous violations.

Violation of a Rule should not give rise to a cause of action nor should it create any presumption that a legal duty has been breached. The Rules are designed to provide guidance to lawyers and to provide a structure for regulating conduct through disciplinary agencies. They are not designed to be a basis for civil liability. Furthermore, the purpose of the Rules can be subverted when they are invoked by opposing parties as procedural weapons. The fact that a Rule is a just basis for a lawyer's self-assessment, or for sanctioning a lawyer under the administration of a disciplinary authority, does not imply that an antagonist in a collateral proceeding or transaction has standing to seek enforcement of the Rule. Accordingly, nothing in the Rules should be deemed to augment any substantive legal duty of lawyers or the extra-disciplinary consequences of violating such a duty.

Moreover, these Rules are not intended to govern or affect judicial application of either the attorney-client or work product privilege. Those privileges were developed to promote compliance with law and fairness in litigation. In reliance on the attorney-client privilege, clients are entitled to expect that communications within the scope of the privilege will be protected against compelled disclosure. The attorney-client privilege is that of the client and not of the lawyer. The fact that in exceptional situations the lawyer under the Rules has either a limited discretion or a limited obligation to disclose a client confidence does not vitiate the proposition that, as a general matter, the client has a reasonable expectation that information relating to the client will not be voluntarily disclosed and that disclosure of such information may be judicially compelled only in accordance with recognized exceptions to the attorney-client and work product privileges.

The lawyer's exercise of discretion not to disclose information under Rule 1.6 should not be subject to reexamination. Permitting such reexamination would be incompatible with the general policy of promoting compliance with law through assurances that communications will be protected against disclosure.

The Preamble and this note on Scope provide general orientation. The text of each Rule and the following Terminology section are authoritative and the Comments accompanying each Rule are interpretive.

Terminology

"Belief" or "believes" denotes that the person involved actually supposed the fact in question to be true. A person's belief may be inferred from circumstances.

"Consult" or "consultation" denotes communication of information reasonably sufficient to permit the client to appreciate the significance of the matter in question.

"Firm" or "law firm" denotes a professional entity, public or private, organized to deliver legal services, or a legal department of a corporation or other organization. See Comment, Rule 1.10.

"Fraud" or "fraudulent" denotes conduct having a purpose to deceive and not merely negligent misrepresentation or failure to apprise another of relevant information.

"Knowingly," "known," or "knows" denotes actual knowledge of the fact in question. A person's knowledge may be inferred from circumstances.

"Partner" denotes a member of a partnership or a shareholder or member of a professional entity, public or private, organized to deliver legal services, or a legal department of a corporation or other organization.

"Reasonable" or "reasonably" when used in relation to conduct by a lawyer denotes the conduct of a reasonably prudent and competent lawyer.

"Reasonable belief" or "reasonably believes" when used in reference to a lawyer denotes that the lawyer believes the matter in question and that the circumstances are such that the belief is reasonable.

"Reasonably should know" when used in reference to a lawyer denotes that a lawyer of reasonable prudence and competence would ascertain the matter in question.

"Should" when used in reference to a lawyer's action denotes an aspirational rather than a mandatory standard.

"Substantial" when used in reference to degree or extent denotes a material matter of clear and weighty importance.

CLIENT-LAWYER RELATIONSHIP.

Rule 1.1. Competence.

A lawyer shall provide competent representation to a client. Competent representation requires the legal knowledge, skill, thoroughness and preparation reasonably necessary for the representation.

COMMENT

Legal Knowledge and Skill

[1] In determining whether a lawyer employs the requisite knowledge and skill in a particular matter, relevant factors include the relative complexity and specialized nature of the matter, the lawyer's general experience, the lawyer's training and experience in the field in question, the preparation and study the lawyer is able to give the matter and whether it is feasible to refer the matter to, or associate or consult with, a lawyer of established competence in the field in question. In many instances, the required proficiency is that of a general practitioner. Expertise in a particular field of law may be required in some circumstances.

[2] A lawyer need not necessarily have special training or prior experience to handle legal problems of a type with which the lawyer is unfamiliar. A newly admitted lawyer can be as competent as a practitioner with long experience. Some important legal skills, such as the analysis of precedent, the evaluation of evidence and legal drafting, are required in all legal problems. Perhaps the most fundamental legal skill consists of determining what kind of legal problems a situation may involve, a skill that necessarily transcends any particular specialized knowledge. A lawyer can provide adequate representation in a wholly novel field through necessary study. Competent representation can also be provided through the association of a lawyer of established competence in the field in question.

[2a] Another important skill is negotiating and, in particular, choosing and carrying out the appropriate negotiating strategy. Often it is possible to negotiate a solution which meets some of the needs and interests of all the parties to a transaction or dispute, i.e., a problem-solving strategy.

[3] In an emergency a lawyer may give advice or assistance in a matter in which the lawyer does not have the skill ordinarily required where referral to or consultation or association with another lawyer would be impractical. Even in an emergency, however, assistance should be limited to that reason ably necessary in the circumstances, for ill-considered action under emergency conditions can jeopardize the client's interest.

[4] A lawyer may accept representation where the requisite level of competence can be achieved by reasonable preparation. This applies as well to a lawyer who is appointed as counsel for an unrepresented person. See also Rule 6.2.

Thoroughness and Preparation

[5] Competent handling of a particular matter includes inquiry into and analysis of the factual and legal elements of the problem, and use of methods and procedures meeting the standards of competent practitioners. It also includes adequate preparation. The required attention and preparation are determined in part by what is at stake; major litigation and complex transactions ordinarily require more elaborate treatment than matters of lesser consequence.

Maintaining Competence

[6] To maintain the requisite knowledge and skill,

a lawyer should engage in continuing study and education. The Mandatory Continuing Legal Education requirements of the Rules of the Supreme Court of Virginia set the minimum standard for continuing study and education which a lawyer licensed and practicing in Virginia must satisfy. If a system of peer review has been established, the lawyer should consider making use of it in appropriate circumstances.

Virginia Code Comparison

Rule 1.1 is substantially similar to DR 6-101(A). DR 6-101(A)(1) provided that a lawyer "shall undertake representation only in matters in which . . . [t]he lawyer can act with competence and demonstrate the specific legal knowledge, skill, efficiency, and thoroughness in preparation employed in acceptable practice by lawyers undertaking similar matters." DR 6-101(A)(2) also permitted representation in matters if a lawyer "associated with another lawyer who is competent in those matters."

Committee Commentary

The Committee adopted the ABA Model Rule verbatim, but added the third paragraph of the Comment to make it clear that legal representation, in which a lawyer is expected to be competent, involves not only litigation but also negotiation techniques and strategies.

In addition, the Committee added the second sentence under Maintaining Competence Comment section to note Virginia's Mandatory Continuing Legal Education requirements.

Law Review. — For article, "Professional Responsibility," see 39 U. Rich. L. Rev. 315 (2004). For article, "Professional Responsibility," see 43 U. Rich. L. Rev. 379 (2008).

CASE NOTES

Conduct punishable as contempt of court may also be considered as evidence that an attorney is unfit to practice law. Matthews v. Virginia State Bar ex rel. Third Dist. Comm., 231 Va. 308, 343 S.E.2d 79 (1986) (decided under former DR 6-101).

Neglect of matters entrusted to attorney. — The language of former subdivision (A)(3) of this rule encompasses neglect of legal matters entrusted to a lawyer, whether entrusted by a client or a third party. Pickus v. Virginia State Bar, 232 Va. 5, 348 S.E.2d 202 (1986) (decided under former DR 6-101).

Failure to prepare. — Finding that the attorney violated Va. Sup. Ct. R. pt. 6, § II, R. 1.1 was proper because, during the prosecution of a criminal defendant, the attorney, a prosecutor, failed to provide the thoroughness and preparation reasonably necessary for the representation of his client, the Commonwealth. Even if an attorney has the necessary legal knowledge and skill, thoroughness and preparation required the competent handling of a particular matter, which included inquiry into and analysis of the factual and legal elements of the problem and use of methods and procedures meeting the standards of competent practitioners. Livingston v. Va. State Bar, 286 Va. 1, 744 S.E.2d 220, 2013 Va. LEXIS 75 (2013).

Lending institutions entrusted legal matters to the closing attorney, within the meaning of former subdivision (A)(3) of this rule, when they delivered the loan proceeds to him with directions to satisfy prior liens and to obtain mortgagee title insurance policies insuring that the new loans constituted first liens. Where he not only failed to satisfy the prior liens in all three cases but also failed in one instance to obtain title insurance, he neglected the matters entrusted to him by the lending institutions. Pickus v. Virginia State Bar, 232 Va. 5, 348 S.E.2d 202 (1986) (decided under former DR 6-101).

Filing in wrong court. — Attorney violated Va. Sup. Ct. R. pt. 6, § II, R. 1.1 by filing an appeal on behalf of a client in the wrong court, which was dismissed, and by filing an untimely appeal in a separate case, which was dismissed, and then not informing the client of the dismissals. Additionally, the attorney paid himself from his clients funds before little, if any, work was accomplished on the matters. Green v. Va. State Bar ex rel. Seventh Dist. Comm., 274 Va. 775, 652 S.E.2d 118, 2007 Va. LEXIS 134 (2007).

Inexperience no excuse. — Inexperience was no excuse for plaintiff's counsel's conduct where counsel had been on notice for over 21 days that her clients' lawsuit was frivolous and that she and they faced Rule 11 sanctions if they persisted in suing defendants, but during oral argument of the motion to dismiss, counsel continued to ignore the First Amendment issue and argued law that was irrelevant. Gibson v. City of Alexandria, 855 F. Supp. 133 (E.D. Va. 1994) (decided under former DR 6-101).

Incompetence not shown. — Attorney's failure to read responsive pleadings in a timelier manner and the attorney's delay in withdrawing a special plea, while not the preferred way of practicing law, did not support a finding of incompetent representation. Barrett v. Va. State Bar, 272 Va. 260, 634 S.E.2d 341, 2006 Va. LEXIS 84 (2006).

Applied in Weatherbee v. Va. State Bar ex rel. Fourth Dist., 279 Va. 303, 689 S.E.2d 753, 2010 Va. LEXIS 37 (2010).

Rule 1.2. Scope of Representation.

(a) A lawyer shall abide by a client's decisions concerning the objectives of representation, subject to paragraphs (b), (c), and (d), and shall consult with the client as to the means by which they are to be pursued. A lawyer shall abide by a client's decision, after consultation with the lawyer, whether to accept an offer of settlement of a matter. In a criminal case, the lawyer shall abide by the client's decision, after consultation with the lawyer, as to a plea to be entered, whether to waive jury trial and whether the client will testify.

(b) A lawyer may limit the objectives of the representation if the client consents after consultation.

(c) A lawyer shall not counsel a client to engage, or assist a client, in conduct that the lawyer knows is criminal or fraudulent, but a lawyer may discuss the legal consequences of any proposed course of conduct with a client and may counsel or assist a client to make a good faith effort to determine the validity, scope, meaning, or application of the law.

(d) A lawyer may take such action on behalf of the client as is impliedly authorized to carry out the representation.

(e) When a lawyer knows that a client expects assistance not permitted by the Rules of Professional Conduct or other law, the lawyer shall consult with the client regarding the relevant limitations on the lawyer's conduct.

COMMENT

Scope of Representation

[1] Both lawyer and client have authority and responsibility in the objectives and means of representation. The client has ultimate authority to determine the purposes to be served by legal representation, within the limits imposed by the law and the lawyer's professional obligations. Within those limits, a client also has a right to consult with the lawyer about the means to be used in pursuing those objectives. In that context, a lawyer shall advise the client about the advantages, disadvantages, and availability of dispute resolution processes that might be appropriate in pursuing these objectives. At the same time, a lawyer is not required to pursue objectives or employ means simply because a client may wish that the lawyer do so. A clear distinction between objectives and means sometimes cannot be drawn, and in many cases the client/lawyer relationship partakes of a joint undertaking. In questions of means, the lawyer should assume responsibility for technical and legal tactical issues, but should defer to the client regarding such questions as the expense to be incurred and concern for third persons who might be adversely affected. These Rules do not define the lawyer's scope of authority in litigation.

[2-3] *ABA Model Rule* Comments not adopted.

[4] In a case in which the client appears to be suffering mental disability, the lawyer's duty to abide by the client's decisions is to be guided by reference to Rule 1.14.

Independence from Client's Views or Activities

[5] Legal representation should not be denied to people who are unable to afford legal services, or whose cause is controversial or the subject of popular disapproval. By the same token, a lawyer's representation of a client, including representation by appointment, does not constitute an endorsement of the client's political, economic, social or moral views or activities.

Services Limited in Objectives or Means

[6] The objectives or scope of services provided by a lawyer may be limited by agreement with the client or by the terms under which the lawyer's services are made available to the client. For example, a retainer may be for a specifically defined purpose. Representation provided through a legal aid agency may be subject to limitations on the types of cases the agency handles. When a lawyer has been retained by an insurer to represent an insured, the representation may be limited to matters related to the insurance coverage. The terms upon which representation is undertaken may exclude specific objectives or means. Such limitations may exclude objectives or means that the lawyer regards as repugnant or imprudent.

[7] An agreement concerning the scope of representation must accord with the Rules of Professional Conduct and other law. Thus, the client may not be asked to agree to representation so limited in scope as to violate Rule 1.1, or to surrender the right to terminate the lawyer's services or the right to settle litigation that the lawyer might wish to continue.

[8] *ABA Model Rule* Comment not adopted.

Criminal, Fraudulent and Prohibited Transactions

[9] A lawyer is required to give an honest opinion about the actual consequences that appear likely to result from a client's conduct. The fact that a client uses advice in a course of action that is criminal or fraudulent does not, of itself, make a lawyer a party to the course of action. However, a lawyer may not knowingly assist a client in criminal or fraudulent conduct. There is a critical distinction between presenting an analysis of legal aspects of questionable conduct and recommending the means by which a crime or fraud might be committed with impunity.

[10] When the client's course of action has already begun and is continuing, the lawyer's responsibility is especially delicate. The lawyer is not permitted to reveal the client's wrongdoing, except where permitted or required by Rule 1.6. However, the lawyer is required to avoid furthering the purpose, for example, by suggesting how it might be concealed. A lawyer shall not continue assisting a client in conduct that the lawyer originally supposes is legally proper but then discovers is criminal or fraudulent. See Rule 1.16.

[11] Where the client is a fiduciary, the lawyer may be charged with special obligations in dealings with a beneficiary.

[12] Paragraph (c) applies whether or not the defrauded party is a party to the transaction. Hence, a lawyer should not participate in a sham transaction; for example, a transaction to effectuate criminal or fraudulent escape of tax liability. Paragraph (c) does not preclude undertaking a criminal defense incident to a general retainer for legal services to a lawful enterprise. The last clause of paragraph (c) recognizes that determining the validity or interpretation of a statute or regulation may require a course of action involving disobedi-

ence of the statute or regulation or of the interpretation placed upon it by governmental authorities. See also Rule 3.4(d).

Virginia Code Comparison

Paragraph (a) has no direct counterpart in the Disciplinary Rules of the Virginia Code. EC 7-7 stated: "In certain areas of legal representation not affecting the merits of the cause or substantially prejudicing the rights of a client, a lawyer is entitled to make decisions on his own. But otherwise the authority to make decisions is exclusively that of the client...." EC 7-8 stated that "[I]n the final analysis, however, the ... decision whether to forego legally available objectives or methods because of nonlegal factors is ultimately for the client.... In the event that the client in a nonadjudicatory matter insists upon a course of conduct that is contrary to the judgment and advice of the lawyer but not prohibited by Disciplinary Rules, the lawyer may withdraw from the employment." DR 7-101(A)(1) provided that a lawyer "shall not intentionally ... [f]ail to seek the lawful objectives of his client through reasonably available means permitted by law.... A lawyer does not violate this Disciplinary Rule, however, by ... avoiding offensive tactics...."

With regard to paragraph (b), DR 7-101(B)(1) provided that a lawyer may, "with the express or implied authority of his client, exercise his professional judgment to limit or vary his client's objectives and waive or fail to assert a right or position of his client."

With regard to paragraph (c), DR 7-102(A)(7) provided that a lawyer shall not "counsel or assist his client in conduct that the lawyer knows to be illegal or fraudulent." DR 7-102(A)(6) provided that a lawyer shall not "participate in the creation or preservation of evidence when he knows or it is obvious that the evidence is false." DR 7-105(A) provided that a lawyer shall not "advise his client to disregard a standing rule of a tribunal or a ruling of a tribunal ... but he may take appropriate steps in good faith to test the validity of such rule or ruling." EC 7-5 stated that a lawyer "should never encourage or aid his client to commit criminal acts or counsel his client on how to violate the law and avoid punishment therefor."

Paragraph (d) had no counterpart in the Virginia Code.

With regard to paragraph (e), DR 2-108(A)(1) provided that a lawyer shall withdraw from representation if "continuing the representation will result in a course of conduct by the lawyer that is illegal or inconsistent with the Disciplinary Rules." DR 9-101(C) provided that "[a] lawyer shall not state or imply that he is able to influence improperly ... any tribunal, legislative body or public official."

Committee Commentary

The Committee adopted this Rule as a more succinct and useful statement regarding the scope of the relationship between a lawyer and the client. However, the Committee moved the language of paragraph (b) of the ABA Model Rule to the Comment section styled "Independence from Client's Views or Activities" since it appears more appropriate as a Comment than a Rule. Subsequent paragraphs were redesignated accordingly.

The Committee added the fourth sentence in Comment [1] requiring lawyers to advise clients of dispute resolution processes that might be "appropriate."

In Comment [7], the Committee used the verb "shall" to match the mandatory standard of the Virginia Code and these Rules.

The amendment effective January 1, 2004, adopted September 24, 2003, added present paragraph (d) and redesignated former paragraph (d) as present paragraph (e).

Law Review. — For article, "Professional Responsibility," see 43 U. Rich. L. Rev. 255 (2008). For essay, "A Distinction Without a Difference? An Examination of the Legal and Ethical Difference Between Asset Protection and Fraudulent Transfers Under Virginia Law," see 47 U. Rich. L. Rev. 381 (2012).

CASE NOTES

Debtor-in-possession. — Where debtor-in-possession, authorized to manage its affairs under 11 U.S.C.S. § 1107, sought to employ general counsel, pursuant to 11 U.S.C.S. § 327, the applicant was required to disclose the compensation paid, under 11 U.S.C.S. § 329(a), and show that it waived any conflicting claim as a pre-petition creditor of the debtor. The retainer fee had to comply with Va. Sup. Ct. R. pt. 6, § II, R. 1.15(a)(2), 1.16(d), and the authorization to settle claims could not conflict with Va. Sup. Ct. R. pt. 6, § II, R. 1.2. In re Circle T Pipeline, Inc., 2011 Bankr. LEXIS 2490 (Bankr. W.D. Va. Apr. 27, 2011).

Applied in BP Prods. N. Am., Inc. v. Dagra, 232 F.R.D. 263, 2005 U.S. Dist. LEXIS 27452 (E.D. Va. 2005).

CIRCUIT COURT OPINIONS

Attorney-client privilege. — Doctor's motion to quash a duces tecum a patient served upon the president of the medical practice that employed the doctor was denied to the extent that the attorney-client privilege did not apply because there was no agency relationship between the doctor and the president when the doctor did not possess the power to control the president's actions. Campbell v. Dastoor, 79 Va. Cir. 569, 2009 Va. Cir. LEXIS 141 (Salem Dec. 9, 2009).

Attorney acting without authority. — Accident victim was not bound by the actions of her attorney in settling her claims against certain defendants because there was no evidence that the attorney was acting with actual authority, implied authority, or apparent authority in settling the claims. The victim was unaware of his actions and received none of the funds tendered by defendants. Andrews v. Andrews, 80 Va. Cir. 279, 2010 Va. Cir. LEXIS 55 (Prince William County Apr. 14, 2010).

Rule 1.3. Diligence.

(a) A lawyer shall act with reasonable diligence and promptness in representing a client.

(b) A lawyer shall not intentionally fail to carry out a contract of employment entered into with a client for professional services, but may withdraw as permitted under Rule 1.16.

(c) A lawyer shall not intentionally prejudice or damage a client during the course of the professional relationship, except as required or permitted under Rule 1.6 and Rule 3.3.

COMMENT

[1] A lawyer should pursue a matter on behalf of a client despite opposition, obstruction or personal inconvenience to the lawyer, and may take whatever lawful and ethical measures are required to vindicate a client's cause or endeavor. A lawyer should act with commitment and dedication to the interests of the client and with zeal in advocacy upon the client's behalf. However, a lawyer is not bound to press for every advantage that might be realized for a client. A lawyer has professional discretion in determining the means by which a matter should be pursued. See Rule 1.2. A lawyer's work load should be controlled so that each matter can be handled adequately.

[2] Additionally, lawyers have long recognized that a more collaborative, problem-solving approach is often preferable to an adversarial strategy in pursuing the client's needs and interests. Consequently, diligence includes not only an adversarial strategy but also the vigorous pursuit of the client's interest in reaching a solution that satisfies the interests of all parties. The client can be represented zealously in either setting.

[3] Perhaps no professional shortcoming is more widely resented than procrastination. A client's interests often can be adversely affected by the passage of time or the change of conditions; in extreme instances, as when a lawyer overlooks a statute of limitations, the client's legal position may be destroyed. Even when the client's interests are not affected in substance, however, unreasonable delay can cause a client needless anxiety and undermine confidence in the lawyer's trustworthiness.

[4] Unless the relationship is terminated as provided in Rule 1.16, a lawyer should carry through to conclusion all matters undertaken for a client. If a lawyer's employment is limited to a specific matter, the relationship terminates when the matter has been resolved. If a lawyer has served a client over a substantial period in a variety of matters, the client sometimes may assume that the lawyer will continue to serve on a continuing basis unless the lawyer gives notice of withdrawal. Doubt about whether a client-lawyer relationship still exists should be clarified by the lawyer, preferably in writing, so that the client will not mistakenly suppose the lawyer is looking after the client's affairs when the lawyer has ceased to do so. For example, if a lawyer has handled a judicial or administrative proceeding that produced a result adverse to the client but has not been specifically instructed concerning pursuit of an appeal, the lawyer should advise the client of the possibility of appeal before relinquishing responsibility for the matter.

[5] A lawyer should plan for client protection in the event of the lawyer's death, disability, impairment, or incapacity. The plan should be in writing and should designate a responsible attorney capable of making, and who has agreed to make, arrangements for the protection of client interests in the event of the lawyer's death, impairment, or incapacity.

Virginia Code Comparison

With regard to paragraph (a), DR 6-101(B) required that a lawyer "attend promptly to matters undertaken for a client until completed or until the lawyer has properly and completely withdrawn from representing the client." EC 6-4 stated that a lawyer should "give appropriate attention to his legal work." Canon 7 stated that "a lawyer should represent a client zealously within the bounds of the law."

Paragraphs (b) and (c) adopt the language of DR 7-101(A)(2) and DR 7-101(A)(3) of the Virginia Code.

Committee Commentary

The Committee added DR 7-101(A)(2) and DR 7-101(A)(3) from the Virginia Code as paragraphs (b) and (c) of this Rule in order to make it a more complete statement about fulfilling one's obligations to a client. Additionally, the Committee added the second paragraph to the Comment as a reminder to lawyers that there is often an appropriate collaborative component to zealous advocacy.

The amendment effective January 1, 2004, adopted September 24, 2003, set out the rule with no apparent change to text or commentary.

The amendment, effective February 28, 2006, added [5] to the commentary.

Law Review. — For article, "Professional Responsibility," see 43 U. Rich. L. Rev. 255 (2008).

CASE NOTES

Attorney's obligation continued until permission to withdraw was granted. — Until plaintiff's counsel was granted permission to withdraw, counsel was obliged to zealously represent plaintiff. RZS Holdings AVV v. PDVSA Petroleo S.A., 506 F.3d 350, 2007 U.S. App. LEXIS 25548 (4th Cir. 2007).

Evidence was sufficient to show attorney prejudiced his client's rights. — See El-Amin v. Virginia State Bar ex rel. Third Dist. Committee, 257 Va. 608, 514 S.E.2d 163 (1999) (decided under former DR 7-101).

Lack of reasonable diligence. — Averment in a petition for appeal in a criminal case that under "well settled law" the evidence was insufficient gave no supporting case citation, in violation of Rules 5A:12(c) and 5A:20(e), as well as Va. Sup. Ct. R., pt. 6, § II, Rules 1.3(a) or 3.3(a)(3). Jacobs v. Commonwealth, 2002 Va. App. LEXIS 589 (Oct. 8, 2002).

Although an attorney did not promptly represent a client and violated Sup. Ct. R., pt. 6, § II, Rule 1.3(a), there was no finding that a disciplinary committee was unable to gather information as a result of the attorney's failure to appear at a subsequent disciplinary hearing; therefore, the violation of Sup. Ct. R., pt. 6, § II, Rule 8.1(c) was reversed and remanded for reconsideration of the sanction. Rice v. Va. State Bar, 267 Va. 299, 592 S.E.2d 643, 2004 Va. LEXIS 27 (2004).

Where an attorney failed to pay a filing fee with a debtor's bankruptcy petition, and asserted that the failure was due to inadvertence on the part of a paralegal, the attorney failed to act with the requisite commitment and dedication to the interests of the debtor, and could not be absolved of such responsibilities by claiming to have delegated them to a subordinate. Office of the United States Trustee v. Jones (In re Alvarado), 363 B.R. 484, 2007 Bankr. LEXIS 533 (Bankr. E.D. Va. 2007).

Attorney violated Va. Sup. Ct. R. pt. 6, § II, R. 1.3 because, although he was paid to file a habeas corpus petition on behalf of a client, he did not file the petition, he refused to refund the fee, and he claimed that his associate was actually retained to file the petition. Green v. Va. State Bar ex rel. Seventh Dist. Comm., 274 Va. 775, 652 S.E.2d 118, 2007 Va. LEXIS 134 (2007).

Not acting in a client's best interest. — Where the grandmother and father of an 18-year-old Chapter 13 debtor used the debtor as part of a scheme to hinder, delay, and defraud their own creditors, the attorney for the debtor, who had represented the grandmother and father in prior bankruptcy cases, was a willing and active participant in the scheme, in violation of Fed. R. Bankr. P. 9011 and several rules of the Virginia Rules of Professional Conduct, including Va. Sup. Ct. R. pt. 6, § II, R. 1.3. In re Johnson, 2008 Bankr. LEXIS 164 (Bankr. E.D. Va. Jan. 18, 2008).

Rule 1.4. Communication.

(a) A lawyer shall keep a client reasonably informed about the status of a matter and promptly comply with reasonable requests for information.

(b) A lawyer shall explain a matter to the extent reasonably necessary to permit the client to make informed decisions regarding the representation.

(c) A lawyer shall inform the client of facts pertinent to the matter and of communications from another party that may significantly affect settlement or resolution of the matter.

COMMENT

[1] This continuing duty to keep the client informed includes a duty to advise the client about the availability of dispute resolution processes that might be more appropriate to the client's goals than the initial process chosen. For example, information obtained during a lawyer-to-lawyer negotiation may give rise to consideration of a process, such as mediation, where the parties themselves could be more directly involved in resolving the dispute.

[2-4] *ABA Model Rule* Comments not adopted.

[5] The client should have sufficient information to participate intelligently in decisions concerning the objectives of the representation and the means by which they are to be pursued, to the extent the client is willing and able to do so. For example, a lawyer negotiating on behalf of a client should provide the client with facts relevant to the matter, inform the client of communications from another party and take other reasonable steps that permit the client to make a decision regarding an offer from another party. A lawyer who receives from opposing counsel an offer of settlement in a civil controversy or a proffered plea agreement in a criminal case should promptly inform the client of its substance unless prior discussions with the client have left it clear that the proposal will be unacceptable. See Rule 1.2(a). Even when a client delegates authority to the lawyer, the client should be kept advised of the status of the matter.

[6] Ordinarily, the information to be provided is that appropriate for a client who is a comprehending and responsible adult. However, fully informing the client according to this standard may be impracticable, for example, where the client is a child or suffers from mental disability. See Rule 1.14. When the client is an organization or group, it is often impossible or inappropriate to inform every one of its members about its legal affairs; ordinarily, the lawyer should address communications to the appropriate officials of the organization. See Rule 1.13. Where many routine matters are involved, a system of limited or occasional reporting may be arranged with the client. Practical exigency may also require a lawyer to act for a client without prior consultation.

Withholding Information

[7] In some circumstances, a lawyer may be justified in delaying transmission of information

when the client would be likely to react imprudently to an immediate communication. Thus, a lawyer might withhold a psychiatric diagnosis of a client when the examining psychiatrist indicates that disclosure would harm the client. A lawyer may not withhold information to serve the lawyer's own interest or convenience. Rules or court orders governing litigation may provide that information supplied to a lawyer may not be disclosed to the client. Rule 3.4(d) directs compliance with such rules or orders.

Virginia Code Comparison

Rule 1.4(a) is substantially similar to DR 6-101(C) of the Virginia Code which stated: "A lawyer shall keep a client reasonably informed about matters in which the lawyer's services are being rendered."

Paragraph (b) has no direct counterpart in the Virginia Code. EC 7-8 stated that a lawyer "should exert his best efforts to insure that decisions of his client are made only after the client has been informed of relevant considerations." EC 9-2 stated that "a lawyer should fully and promptly inform his client of material developments in the matters being handled for the client."

Paragraph (c) is identical to DR 6-101(D) of the Virginia Code.

Committee Commentary

The Virginia Code had already substituted the essential notion of paragraph (a) as DR 6-101(C), thus specifically addressing a responsibility omitted from the ABA Model Code. The Committee believed that paragraph (b) specifically addressed a responsibility only implied in the Virginia Code and that adding DR 6-101(D) as paragraph (c) made the Rule a more complete statement regarding a lawyer's obligation to communicate with a client. Additionally, the Committee added a new second paragraph to the Comment to remind lawyers of their continuing duty to help clients choose the most appropriate settlement process.

Law Review. — For article, "Professional Responsibility," see 39 U. Rich. L. Rev. 315 (2004). For article, "Professional Responsibility," see 43 U. Rich. L. Rev. 255 (2008).

CASE NOTES

Duty to convey settlement offers to insured. — During their representation of both insurer and insured, attorneys have the duty to convey settlement offers to the insured that may significantly affect settlement or resolution of the matter. State Farm Mut. Auto. Ins. Co. v. Floyd, 235 Va. 136, 366 S.E.2d 93 (1988) (decided under former DR 6-101).

Failure to communicate effectively. — Attorney failed to communicate effectively with a bankruptcy debtor where the attorney failed to advise the debtor concerning the dismissal of the debtor's bankruptcy petition for the attorney's failure to pay the filing fee, which was prepaid by the debtor, and the attorney then filed a second petition without consulting the debtor or advising the debtor of the adverse consequences of a second petition. Office of the United States Trustee v. Jones (In re Alvarado), 363 B.R. 484, 2007 Bankr. LEXIS 533 (Bankr. E.D. Va. 2007).

Attorney violated Va. Sup. Ct. R., Pt. 6, § II, R. 1.4 because, although he was paid to file a habeas corpus petition on behalf of a client, he did not file the petition, he refused to refund the fee, and he claimed that his associate was actually retained to file the petition. Green v. Va. State Bar ex rel. Seventh Dist. Comm., 274 Va. 775, 652 S.E.2d 118, 2007 Va. LEXIS 134 (2007).

Failure to advise against filing bankruptcy. — Where the grandmother and father of an 18-year-old Chapter 13 debtor used the debtor as part of a scheme to hinder, delay, and defraud their own creditors, the attorney for the debtor, who had represented the grandmother and father in prior bankruptcy cases, was a willing and active participant in the scheme, in violation of Fed. R. Bankr. P. 9011 and several rules of the Virginia Rules of Professional Conduct, including Va. Sup. Ct. R., Pt. 6, § II, R. 1.4(b). In re Johnson, 2008 Bankr. LEXIS 164 (Bankr. E.D. Va. Jan. 18, 2008).

Lack of communication. — Clear and convincing evidence supported the Board's determination that the attorney in one case violated the professional conduct rule about handling client funds, Va. Sup. Ct. R. pt. 6, § II, R. 1.15(a)(2), by putting the client's retainer in a trust account and almost immediately withdrawing those funds when they had not been earned, and in a second case violated rules regarding client communication and termination of representation, Va. Sup. Ct. R. pt. 6, § II, R. 1.4(a), (b), and (c), and Va. Sup. Ct. R. pt. 6, § II, R. 1.16(d), respectively, by not keeping the clients informed about the status of their case and not informing them when the attorney stopped representing them. As a result, an 18-month suspension of the attorney's law license was warranted. Green v. Va. State Bar, 278 Va. 162, 677 S.E.2d 227, 2009 Va. LEXIS 67 (2009).

Applied in BP Prods. N. Am., Inc. v. Dagra, 232 F.R.D. 263, 2005 U.S. Dist. LEXIS 27452 (E.D. Va. 2005).

Rule 1.5. Fees.

(a) A lawyer's fee shall be reasonable. The factors to be considered in determining the reasonableness of a fee include the following:

(1) the time and labor required, the novelty and difficulty of the questions involved, and the skill requisite to perform the legal service properly;

(2) the likelihood, if apparent to the client, that the acceptance of the particular employment will preclude other employment by the lawyer;

(3) the fee customarily charged in the locality for similar legal services;

(4) the amount involved and the results obtained;
(5) the time limitations imposed by the client or by the circumstances;
(6) the nature and length of the professional relationship with the client;
(7) the experience, reputation, and ability of the lawyer or lawyers performing the services; and
(8) whether the fee is fixed or contingent.

(b) The lawyer's fee shall be adequately explained to the client. When the lawyer has not regularly represented the client, the amount, basis or rate of the fee shall be communicated to the client, preferably in writing, before or within a reasonable time after commencing the representation.

(c) A fee may be contingent on the outcome of the matter for which the service is rendered, except in a matter in which a contingent fee is prohibited by paragraph (d) or other law. A contingent fee agreement shall state in writing the method by which the fee is to be determined, including the percentage or percentages that shall accrue to the lawyer in the event of settlement, trial or appeal, litigation and other expenses to be deducted from the recovery, and whether such expenses are to be deducted before or after the contingent fee is calculated. Upon conclusion of a contingent fee matter, the lawyer shall provide the client with a written statement stating the outcome of the matter and, if there is a recovery, showing the remittance to the client and the method of its determination.

(d) A lawyer shall not enter into an arrangement for, charge, or collect a contingent fee:
(1) in a domestic relations matter, except in rare instances; or
(2) for representing a defendant in a criminal case.

(e) A division of a fee between lawyers who are not in the same firm may be made only if:
(1) the client is advised of and consents to the participation of all the lawyers involved;
(2) the terms of the division of the fee are disclosed to the client and the client consents thereto;
(3) the total fee is reasonable; and
(4) the division of fees and the client's consent is obtained in advance of the rendering of legal services, preferably in writing.

(f) Paragraph (e) does not prohibit or regulate the division of fees between attorneys who were previously associated in a law firm or between any successive attorneys in the same matter. In any such instance, the total fee must be reasonable.

COMMENT

Basis or Rate of Fee

[1] *ABA Model Rule* Comment not adopted.

[2] When the lawyer has regularly represented a client, they ordinarily will have evolved an understanding concerning the basis or rate of the fee. In a new client-lawyer relationship, however, an understanding as to the amount, basis, or rate of the fee should be promptly established. It is not necessary to recite all the factors that underlie the basis of the fee, but only those that are directly involved in its computation. It is sufficient, for example, to state that the basic rate is an hourly charge or a fixed amount or an estimated amount, or to identify the factors that may be taken into account in finally fixing the fee. A written statement concerning the fee reduces the possibility of misunderstanding. Furnishing the client with a simple letter, memorandum, receipt or a copy of the lawyer's customary fee schedule may be sufficient if the basis or rate of the fee is set forth.

[3] *ABA Model Rule* Comment not adopted.

Terms of Payment

[4] A lawyer may require advance payment of a fee, but is obliged to return any unearned portion. See Rule 1.16(d). A lawyer may accept property in payment for services, such as an ownership interest in an enterprise, providing this does not involve acquisition of a proprietary interest in the cause of action or subject matter of the litigation contrary to Rule 1.8(j). However, a fee paid in property instead of money may be subject to special scrutiny because it involves questions concerning both the value of the services and the lawyer's special knowledge of the value of the property.

[5] An agreement may not be made whose terms might induce the lawyer improperly to curtail services for the client or perform them in a way contrary to the client's interest. For example, a lawyer should not enter into an agreement whereby services are to be provided only up to a stated amount when it is foreseeable that more extensive services probably will be required, unless the situation is adequately explained to the client. Otherwise, the client might have to bargain for further assistance in the midst of a proceeding or transaction. However, it is proper to define the extent of services in light of the client's ability to pay. A lawyer should not exploit a fee arrangement based primarily on hourly charges by using wasteful procedures. When considering whether a contingent fee is consistent with the client's best interest, the lawyer should offer the client alternative bases

for the fee and explain their implications. Applicable law may impose limitations on contingent fees, such as a ceiling on the percentage. In any event, a fee should not be imposed upon a client, but should be the result of an informed decision concerning reasonable alternatives.

Contingent Fees in Domestic Relations Cases

[6] An arrangement for a contingent fee in a domestic relations matter has been previously considered appropriate only in those rare instances where:

(a) the contingent fee is for the collection of, and is to be paid out of (i) accumulated arrearages in child or spousal support; (ii) an asset not previously viewed or contemplated as a marital asset by the parties or the court; (iii) a monetary award pursuant to equitable distribution or under a property settlement agreement;

(b) the parties are divorced and reconciliation is not a realistic prospect;

(c) the children of the marriage are or will soon achieve the age of maturity and the legal services rendered pursuant to the contingent fee arrangement are not likely to affect their relationship with the non-custodial parent;

(d) the client is indigent or could not otherwise obtain adequate counsel on an hourly fee basis; and

(e) the fee arrangement is fair and reasonable under the circumstances.

Division of Fee

[7] A division of fee refers to a single billing to a client covering the fee of two or more lawyers who are not in the same firm. A division of fee facilitates association of more than one lawyer in a matter in which neither alone could serve the client as well, and most often is used when the fee is contingent and the division is between a referring lawyer and a trial specialist.

[8] *ABA Model Rule* Comment not adopted.

Disputes over Fees

[9] If a procedure has been established for resolution of fee disputes, such as an arbitration or mediation procedure established by the bar, the lawyer should conscientiously consider submitting to it. Law may prescribe a procedure for determining a lawyer's fee, for example, in representation of an executor or administrator, a class or a person entitled to a reasonable fee as part of the measure of damages. The lawyer entitled to such a fee and a lawyer representing another party concerned with the fee should comply with the prescribed procedure.

Virginia Code Comparison

With regard to paragraph (a), DR 2-105(A) required that a "lawyer's fees . . . be reasonable and adequately explained to the client." The factors involved in assessing the reasonableness of a fee listed in Rule 1.5(a) are substantially similar to those listed in EC 2-20.

Paragraph (b) emphasizes the lawyer's duty to adequately explain fees (which appears in DR 2-105(A)) but stresses the lawyer's duty to disclose fee information to the client rather than merely responding to a client's request for information (as in DR 2-105(B)).

Paragraph (c) is substantially the same as DR 2-105(C). EC 2-22 provided that "[c]ontingent fee arrangements in civil cases have long been commonly accepted in the United States," but that "a lawyer generally should decline to accept employment on a contingent fee basis by one who is able to pay a reasonable fixed fee...."

With regard to paragraph (d), DR 2-105(C) prohibited a contingent fee in a criminal case. EC 2-22 provided that "contingent fee arrangements in domestic relation cases are rarely justified."

With regard to paragraph (e), DR 2-105(D) permitted division of fees only if: "(1) The client consents to employment of additional counsel; (2) Both attorneys expressly assume responsibility to the client; and (3) The terms of the division of the fee are disclosed to the client and the client consents thereto."

There was no counterpart to paragraph (f) in the Virginia Code.

Committee Commentary

The Committee believes that DR 2-105 placed greater emphasis than the ABA Model Rule on the Full Disclosure of Fees and Fee Arrangements to Clients and therefore added language from DR 2-105(A) to paragraph (a) and from DR 2-105(D)(3) to paragraph (e). The Comment to paragraph (d)(1) reflects the Committee's conclusion that the public policy concerns which preclude contingent fee arrangements in certain domestic relations cases do not apply when property division, support matters or attorney's fee awards have been previously determined. Paragraph (e) eliminates the requirement in the Virginia Code that each lawyer involved in a fee-splitting arrangement assume full responsibility to the client, regardless of the degree of the lawyer's continuing participation. The requirement in the Virginia Code was deleted to encourage referrals under appropriate circumstances by not requiring the lawyer making the referral to automatically assume ethical responsibility for all of the activities of the other lawyers involved in the arrangement. However, such an arrangement is acceptable only if the client consents after full disclosure, which must include a delineation of each lawyer's responsibilities to the client.

The amendment effective January 1, 2004, adopted September 24, 2003, inserted present paragraph (e)(2) and redesignated former paragraphs (e)(2) and (e)(3) as present (e)(3) and (e)(4); and added paragraph (f).

Law Review. — For article, "Professional Responsibility," see 43 U. Rich. L. Rev. 255 (2008).

CASE NOTES

Fees as percent of pro rata distribution. — Absent a showing of exceptional circumstances, any fee exceeding 10 percent of a pro rata distribution in the instant case is "per se" unreasonable, shocks the conscience of the court, and will be disallowed pursuant to this court's inherent powers to supervise the bar. In re A.H. Robins Co., 182 Bankr. 128 (Bankr. E.D. Va. 1995), aff'd sub nom. Bergstrom v. Dalkon Shield Claimants Trust, 86 F.3d 364 (4th Cir.), cert. denied, 519 U.S. 993, 117 S. Ct. 483, 136 L. Ed. 2d 377 (1996) (decided under former DR 2-105).

Ethical considerations were properly considered where court awarded deceased attorney's estate a $100,000 fee for approximately 52 hours of legal work. Fambrough v. Estate of Nunley (In re Mullins), 190 Bankr. 812 (Bankr. W.D. Va. 1995) (decided under former DR 2-105).

CIRCUIT COURT OPINIONS

Alleged ethical violations not grounds for reducing attorney's fee award. — Where property owners prevailed in a condemnation action, even assuming that a referral fee arrangement involving the owner's attorneys violated Va. Sup. Ct. R. pt. 6, § II, R. 1.5(e), this was not grounds for reducing the fees the attorneys were entitled to under § 25.1-419. Norfolk Redevelopment & Hous. Auth. v. C & C Real Estate, Inc., 72 Va. Cir. 464, 2007 Va. Cir. LEXIS 162 (Norfolk 2007).

Violation of Va. Sup. Ct. R., pt. 6, § II, R. 1.5(c), which required that contingency fee agreements be in writing, was not a bar to recovery of attorney's fees under § 59.1-207.14 of the Motor Vehicle Warranty Enforcement Act as the manufacturer did not have standing in a collateral proceeding to argue reduction of attorney's fees to the vehicle purchasers' counsel on that basis. Dickerson v. Ford Motor Co., 74 Va. Cir. 509, 2008 Va. Cir. LEXIS 4 (Roanoke 2008).

Rule 1.6. Confidentiality of Information.

(a) A lawyer shall not reveal information protected by the attorney-client privilege under applicable law or other information gained in the professional relationship that the client has requested be held inviolate or the disclosure of which would be embarrassing or would be likely to be detrimental to the client unless the client consents after consultation, except for disclosures that are impliedly authorized in order to carry out the representation, and except as stated in paragraphs (b) and (c).

(b) To the extent a lawyer reasonably believes necessary, the lawyer may reveal:

(1) such information to comply with law or a court order;

(2) such information to establish a claim or defense on behalf of the lawyer in a controversy between the lawyer and the client, to establish a defense to a criminal charge or civil claim against the lawyer based upon conduct in which the client was involved, or to respond to allegations in any proceeding concerning the lawyer's representation of the client;

(3) such information which clearly establishes that the client has, in the course of the representation, perpetrated upon a third party a fraud related to the subject matter of the representation;

(4) such information reasonably necessary to protect a client's interests in the event of the representing lawyer's death, disability, incapacity or incompetence;

(5) such information sufficient to participate in a law office management assistance program approved by the Virginia State Bar or other similar private program

(6) information to an outside agency necessary for statistical, bookkeeping, accounting, data processing, printing, or other similar office management purposes, provided the lawyer exercises due care in the selection of the agency, advises the agency that the information must be kept confidential and reasonably believes that the information will be kept confidential.

(c) A lawyer shall promptly reveal:

(1) the intention of a client, as stated by the client, to commit a crime and the information necessary to prevent the crime, but before revealing such information, the attorney shall, where feasible, advise the client of the possible legal consequences of the action, urge the client not to commit the crime, and advise the client that the attorney must reveal the client's criminal intention unless thereupon abandoned, and, if the crime involves perjury by the client, that the attorney shall seek to withdraw as counsel;

(2) information which clearly establishes that the client has, in the course of the representation, perpetrated a fraud related to the subject matter of the representation upon a tribunal. Before revealing such information, however, the lawyer shall request that the client advise the tribunal of the fraud. For the purposes of this paragraph and paragraph (b)(3), information is clearly established when the client acknowledges to the attorney that the client has perpetrated a fraud; or

(3) information concerning the misconduct of another attorney to the appropriate professional authority under Rule 8.3. When the information necessary to report the

misconduct is protected under this Rule, the attorney, after consultation, must obtain client consent. Consultation should include full disclosure of all reasonably foreseeable consequences of both disclosure and non-disclosure to the client.

COMMENT

[1] The lawyer is part of a judicial system charged with upholding the law. One of the lawyer's functions is to advise clients so that they avoid any violation of the law in the proper exercise of their rights.

[2] The common law recognizes that the client's confidences must be protected from disclosure. The observance of the ethical obligation of a lawyer to hold inviolate confidential information of the client not only facilitates the full development of facts essential to proper representation of the client but also encourages people to seek early legal assistance.

[2a] Almost without exception, clients come to lawyers in order to determine what their rights are and what is, in the maze of laws and regulations, deemed to be legal and correct. Based upon experience, lawyers know that clients usually follow the advice given, and the law is upheld.

[2b] A fundamental principle in the client-lawyer relationship is that the lawyer maintain confidentiality of information relating to the representation. The client is thereby encouraged to communicate fully and frankly with the lawyer even as to embarrassing or legally damaging subject matter.

[3] The principle of confidentiality is given effect in two related bodies of law, the attorney-client privilege (which includes the work product doctrine) in the law of evidence and the rule of confidentiality established in professional ethics. The attorney-client privilege applies in judicial and other proceedings in which a lawyer may be called as a witness or otherwise required to produce evidence concerning a client. The rule of client-lawyer confidentiality applies in situations other than those where evidence is sought from the lawyer through compulsion of law. The confidentiality rule applies not merely to matters communicated in confidence by the client but also to all information protected by the attorney-client privilege under applicable law or other information gained in the professional relationship that the client has requested be held inviolate or the disclosure of which would be embarrassing or would be likely to be detrimental to the client, whatever its source. A lawyer may not disclose such information except as authorized or required by the Rules of Professional Conduct or other law.

[3a] The rules governing confidentiality of information apply to a lawyer who represents an organization of which the lawyer is an employee.

[4] The requirement of maintaining confidentiality of information relating to representation applies to government lawyers who may disagree with the policy goals that their representation is designed to advance.

Authorized Disclosure

[5] A lawyer is impliedly authorized to make disclosures about a client when appropriate in carrying out the representation, except to the extent that the client's instructions or special circumstances limit that authority. In litigation, for example, a lawyer may disclose information by admitting a fact that cannot properly be disputed, or in negotiation by making a disclosure that facilitates a satisfactory conclusion.

[5a] Lawyers frequently need to consult with colleagues or other attorneys in order to competently represent their clients' interests. An overly strict reading of the duty to protect client information would render it difficult for lawyers to consult with each other, which is an important means of continuing professional education and development. A lawyer should exercise great care in discussing a client's case with another attorney from whom advice is sought. Among other things, the lawyer should consider whether the communication risks a waiver of the attorney-client privilege or other applicable protections. The lawyer should endeavor when possible to discuss a case in strictly hypothetical or abstract terms. In addition, prior to seeking advice from another attorney, the attorney should take reasonable steps to determine whether the attorney from whom advice is sought has a conflict. The attorney from whom advice is sought must be careful to protect the confidentiality of the information given by the attorney seeking advice and must not use such information for the advantage of the lawyer or a third party.

[5b] Compliance with Rule 1.6(a) might include fulfilling duties under Rule 1.14, regarding a client with an impairment.

[5c] Compliance with Rule 1.6(b)(5) might require a written confidentiality agreement with the outside agency to which the lawyer discloses information.

[6] Lawyers in a firm may, in the course of the firm's practice, disclose to each other information relating to a client of the firm, unless the client has instructed that particular information be confined to specified lawyers.

[6a] Lawyers involved in insurance defense work that includes submission of detailed information regarding the client's case to an auditing firm must be extremely careful to gain consent from the client after full and adequate disclosure. Client consent to provision of information to the insurance carrier does not equate with consent to provide the information to an outside auditor. The lawyer must obtain specific consent to disclose the information to that auditor. Pursuant to the lawyer's duty of loyalty to the client, the lawyer should not recommend that the client provide such consent if the disclosure to the auditor would in some way prejudice the client. Legal Ethics Opinion #1723, approved by the Supreme Court of Virginia, September 29, 1999.

Disclosure Adverse to Client

[6b] The confidentiality rule is subject to limited exceptions. However, to the extent a lawyer is required or permitted to disclose a client's confidences, the client will be inhibited from revealing facts which would enable the lawyer to counsel against a wrongful course of action. The public is

better protected if full and open communication by the client is encouraged than if it is inhibited.

[7] Several situations must be distinguished.

[7a] First, the lawyer may not counsel or assist a client in conduct that is criminal or fraudulent. See Rule 1.2(c). Similarly, a lawyer has a duty under Rule 3.3(a)(4) not to use false evidence. This duty is essentially a special instance of the duty prescribed in Rule 1.2(c) to avoid assisting a client in criminal or fraudulent conduct.

[7b] Second, the lawyer may have been innocently involved in past conduct by the client that was criminal or fraudulent. In such a situation the lawyer has not violated Rule 1.2(c), because to "counsel or assist" criminal or fraudulent conduct requires knowing that the conduct is of that character.

[7c] Third, the lawyer may learn that a client intends prospective criminal conduct. As stated in paragraph (c)(1), the lawyer is obligated to reveal such information. Some discretion is involved as it is very difficult for a lawyer to "know" when proposed criminal conduct will actually be carried out, for the client may have a change of mind.

[8] The lawyer's exercise of discretion requires consideration of such factors as the nature of the lawyer's relationship with the client, the nature of the client's intended conduct, the lawyer's own involvement in the transaction, and factors that may extenuate the conduct in question. Where practical, the lawyer should seek to persuade the client to take appropriate action. In any case, a disclosure adverse to the client's interest should be no greater than the lawyer reasonably believes necessary to the purpose.

Withdrawal

[9] If the lawyer's services will be used by the client in materially furthering a course of criminal or fraudulent conduct, the lawyer must withdraw, as stated in Rule 1.16(a)(1).

[9a] After withdrawal the lawyer is required to refrain from making disclosure of the client's confidences, except as otherwise provided in Rule 1.6. Neither this Rule nor Rule 1.8(b) nor Rule 1.16(d) prevents the lawyer from giving notice of the fact of withdrawal, and the lawyer may also withdraw or disaffirm any opinion, document, affirmation, or the like.

[9b] Where the client is an organization, the lawyer may be in doubt whether contemplated conduct will actually be carried out by the organization. Where necessary to guide conduct in connection with this Rule, the lawyer may make inquiry within the organization as indicated in Rule 1.13(b).

Dispute Concerning a Lawyer's Conduct

[10] Where a legal claim or disciplinary charge alleges complicity of the lawyer in a client's conduct or other misconduct of the lawyer involving representation of the client, the lawyer may respond to the extent the lawyer reasonably believes necessary to establish a defense. The same is true with respect to a claim involving the conduct or representation of a former client. The lawyer's right to respond arises when an assertion of such complicity has been made. Paragraph (b)(2) does not require the lawyer to await the commencement of an action or proceeding that charges such complicity, so that the defense may be established by responding directly to a third party who has made such an assertion. The right to defend, of course, applies where a proceeding has been commenced. Where practicable and not prejudicial to the lawyer's ability to establish the defense, the lawyer should advise the client of the third party's assertion and request that the client respond appropriately. In any event, disclosure should be no greater than the lawyer reasonably believes is necessary to vindicate innocence, the disclosure should be made in a manner which limits access to the information to the tribunal or other persons having a need to know it, and appropriate protective orders or other arrangements should be sought by the lawyer to the fullest extent practicable.

[10a] If the lawyer is charged with wrongdoing in which the client's conduct is implicated, the rule of confidentiality should not prevent the lawyer from defending against the charge. Such a charge can arise in a civil, criminal or professional disciplinary proceeding, and can be based on a wrong allegedly committed by the lawyer against the client, or on a wrong alleged by a third person; for example, a person claiming to have been defrauded by the lawyer and client acting together. A lawyer entitled to a fee is permitted by paragraph (b)(2) to prove the services rendered in an action to collect it. This aspect of the Rule expresses the principle that the beneficiary of a fiduciary relationship may not exploit it to the detriment of the fiduciary. As stated above, the lawyer must make every effort practicable to avoid unnecessary disclosure of information relating to a representation, to limit disclosure to those having the need to know it, and to obtain protective orders or make other arrangements minimizing the risk of disclosure.

Disclosures Otherwise Required or Authorized

[11] If a lawyer is called as a witness to give testimony concerning a client, absent waiver by the client, paragraph (a) requires the lawyer to invoke the attorney-client privilege when it is applicable. Except as permitted by Rule 3.4(d), the lawyer must comply with the final orders of a court or other tribunal of competent jurisdiction requiring the lawyer to give information about the client.

[12] The Rules of Professional Conduct in various circumstances permit or require a lawyer to disclose information relating to the representation. See Rules 2.3, 3.3 and 4.1. In addition to these provisions, a lawyer may be obligated or permitted by other provisions of law to give information about a client. Whether another provision of law supersedes Rule 1.6 is a matter of interpretation beyond the scope of these Rules, but a presumption should exist against such a supersession.

Attorney Misconduct

[13] Self-regulation of the legal profession occasionally places attorneys in awkward positions with respect to their obligations to clients and to the profession. Paragraph (c)(3) requires an attorney who has information indicating that another attorney has violated the Rules of Professional Conduct, learned during the course of representing a client and protected as a confidence or secret under Rule 1.6, to request the permission of the client to disclose the information necessary to report the misconduct to disciplinary authorities. In requesting consent, the attorney must inform the client of all reasonably foreseeable consequences of both

disclosure and non-disclosure.

[14] Although paragraph (c)(3) requires that authorized disclosure be made promptly, a lawyer does not violate this Rule by delaying in reporting attorney misconduct for the minimum period of time necessary to protect a client's interests. For example, a lawyer might choose to postpone reporting attorney misconduct until the end of litigation when reporting during litigation might harm the client's interests.

[15-17] *ABA Model Rule* Comments not adopted.

Former Client

[18] The duty of confidentiality continues after the client-lawyer relationship has terminated.

Virginia Code Comparison

Rule 1.6 retains the two-part definition of information subject to the lawyer's ethical duty of confidentiality. EC 4-4 added that the duty differed from the evidentiary privilege in that it existed "without regard to the nature or source of information or the fact that others share the knowledge." However, the definition of "client information" as set forth in the ABA Model Rules, which includes all information "relating to" the representation, was rejected as too broad.

Paragraph (a) permits a lawyer to disclose information where impliedly authorized to do so in order to carry out the representation. Under DR 4-101(B) and (C), a lawyer was not permitted to reveal "confidences" unless the client first consented after disclosure.

Paragraph (b)(1) is substantially the same as DR 4-101(C)(2).

Paragraph (b)(2) is substantially similar to DR 4-101(C)(4) which authorized disclosure by a lawyer of "[c]onfidences or secrets necessary to establish the reasonableness of his fee or to defend himself or his employees or associates against an accusation of wrongful conduct."

Paragraph (b)(3) is substantially the same as DR 4-101(C)(3).

Paragraph (b)(4) had no counterpart in the Virginia Code.

Paragraphs (c)(1) and (c)(2) are substantially the same as DR 4-101(D).

Paragraph (c)(3) had no counterpart in the Virginia Code.

Committee Commentary

The Committee added language to this Rule from DR 4-101 to make the disclosure provisions more consistent with current Virginia policy. The Committee specifically concluded that the provisions of DR 4-101(D) of the Virginia Code, which required broader disclosure than the ABA Model Rule even permitted, should be added as paragraph (c). Additionally, to promote the integrity of the legal profession, the Committee adopted new language as paragraph (c)(3) setting forth the circumstances under which a lawyer must report the misconduct of another lawyer when such a report may require disclosure of privileged information.

The amendment effective January 1, 2004, adopted September 24, 2003, inserted present paragraph (b)(4) and redesignated former paragraphs (b)(4) and (b)(5) as present (b)(5) and (b)(6); and in paragraph (c)(3), deleted "but only if the client consents after consultation," inserted the present second sentence, and deleted the former last sentence, which read: "Under this paragraph, an attorney is required to request the consent of a client to disclose information necessary to report the misconduct of another attorney."

Law Review. — For article, "Professional Responsibility," see 43 U. Rich. L. Rev. 255 (2008). For article, "Professional Responsibility," see 45 U. Rich. L. Rev. 347 (2010).

CASE NOTES

Disqualification where confidential information exchanged in prior matter. — There is an irrebuttable presumption that confidential information is exchanged as a result of an attorney-client relationship. The existence of an attorney-client relationship and the concomitant presumption of an exchange of confidences is not enough, however, to require disqualification. In addition to the foregoing, there must be a substantial relationship between the matters in that the information must be relevant to the pending litigation. Chantilly Constr. Corp. v. John Driggs Co., 39 Bankr. 466 (Bankr. E.D. Va. 1984) (decided under DR 4-101).

Representation of defendant accused of murder of other client. — An attorney representing a defendant in a criminal case has a duty to consider and pursue all reasonable areas of investigation, but where the attorney representing the defendant in a murder case had represented the victim up until his death, the petitioner challenging his conviction on conflict of interest grounds is still required to establish that his attorney's conflict of interest adversely affected his lawyer's performance, even where the court has failed to inquire into a potential conflict about which it reasonably should have been aware. Mickens v. Taylor, 240 F.3d 348 (4th Cir. 2001), aff'd 535 U.S. 162, 152 L. Ed. 2d 291, 122 S. Ct. 1237 (2002) (decided under former DR 4-101).

Attorney's familiarity with corporation's workings or personality of its representatives is totally insufficient as basis for disqualification, where it cannot reasonably be said that in the course of the former representation the attorney might have acquired information related to the subject of the present litigation. Chantilly Constr. Corp. v. John Driggs Co., 39 Bankr. 466 (Bankr. E.D. Va. 1984) (decided under DR 4-101).

Attorney's testimony permitted. — On appeal from his convictions, the circuit court did not abuse its discretion by permitting the defense counsel at the preliminary hearing to testify regarding information that was not obtained confidentially from defendant. Neither Va. Sup. Ct. R. pt. 6, § II, R. 1.6 nor 1.9 prohibited a lawyer from testifying in court regarding what occurred at a former public court proceeding when such testimony did not involve communications solely between an attorney and his client and the testimony concerned information that had become generally known. Turner v. Commonwealth, 58 Va. App. 567, 712 S.E.2d 28, 2011 Va. App. LEXIS 248 (2011).

Subdivision (C)(3)'s standard and standard of crime-fraud exception to attorney-client privilege. — Subdivision (C)(3)'s [see now subdivisions (c)(1) and (c)(2)] "clearly establishes" standard imposes a heavier burden on the party seeking disclosure than the prima facie standard of the crime-fraud exception to the attorney-client privilege. X Corp. v. Doe, 805 F. Supp. 1298 (E.D. Va. 1992), aff'd sub nom. Under Seal v. Under Seal, 17 F.3d 1435 (4th Cir. 1994). (decided under DR 4-101).

Attorney must show more than mere suspicion of fraud. — When the burden shifts to attorney to show that the material and information he voluntarily disclosed or seeks to disclose clearly establish that during the course of attorney's representation, client perpetrated a fraud related to the subject matter of the representation upon a third party, attorney must demonstrate more than mere suspicion of fraud; he must show that a reasonable attorney in his position would find the communications at issue to be convincing evidence of the perpetration of a fraud on the third party during the course of his representation related to the subject matter of that representation. But the fraud itself need not be conclusively proved. X Corp. v. Doe, 805 F. Supp. 1298 (E.D. Va. 1992), aff'd sub nom. Under Seal v. Under Seal, 17 F.3d 1435 (4th Cir. 1994) (decided under DR 4-101).

Disqualification. — Where an employee shared the employer's confidential information with the employee's attorney while asserting a discrimination claim, the attorney and the firm were disqualified because the attorney viewed at least one privileged document; the attorney could be disqualified for reasons other than a violation of the duty of loyalty to his or her client. Lewis v. Capital One Servs., 2004 U.S. Dist. LEXIS 26978 (E.D. Va. June 10, 2004).

Court granted defendant's motion to disqualify plaintiffs' counsel under Va. Sup. Ct. R. pt. 6, § II, R. 1.9(a) and 1.6 because it previously represented defendant in other matters where, inter alia, the cases were substantially related, the parties were essentially the same, and the allegations were inextricably intertwined. The most important factor in granting defendant's motion was that the present suit sought to prevent what the law firm was hired by defendant to accomplish, to collect money from the debtor's subsidiary and to collect a supplemental assessment from the debtor, by hindering, delaying, or preventing a settlement of the disputes between plaintiff and the debtor that was currently scheduled before the bankruptcy court for approval under Fed. R. Bankr. P. 9019. Sobel v. Sells (In re Gordon Props., LLC), 2013 Bankr. LEXIS 728 (Bankr. E.D. Va. Feb. 25, 2013).

CIRCUIT COURT OPINIONS

Reasonable expectation of confidentiality. — Law firm that represented both defendant's company and plaintiff was disqualified pursuant to Va. Sup. Ct. R. pt. 6, § II, R. 1.6, 1.9, and 1.13. Though there was no express attorney-client relationship between defendant, who was plaintiff's officer, and the firm's attorney, defendant had a reasonable expectation that what he told the attorney about plaintiff's claims against him would remain confidential. Arriba Corp. v. Bostic, 69 Va. Cir. 505, 2002 Va. Cir. LEXIS 464 (Norfolk 2002).

Rule 1.7. Conflict of Interest: General Rule.

(a) Except as provided in paragraph (b), a lawyer shall not represent a client if the representation involves a concurrent conflict of interest. A concurrent conflict of interest exists if:

(1) the representation of one client will be directly adverse to another client; or

(2) there is significant risk that the representation of one or more clients will be materially limited by the lawyer's responsibilities to another client, a former client or a third person or by a personal interest of the lawyer.

(b) Notwithstanding the existence of a concurrent conflict of interest under paragraph (a), a lawyer may represent a client if each affected client consents after consultation, and:

(1) the lawyer reasonably believes that the lawyer will be able to provide competent and diligent representation to each affected client;

(2) the representation is not prohibited by law;

(3) the representation does not involve the assertion of a claim by one client against another client represented by the lawyer in the same litigation or other proceeding before a tribunal; and

(4) the consent from the client is memorialized in writing.

COMMENT

Loyalty to a Client

[1] Loyalty and independent judgment are essential elements in the lawyer's relationship to a client. An impermissible conflict of interest may exist before representation is undertaken, in which event the representation should be declined.

[2] *ABA Model Rule* Comment not adopted.

[3] The lawyer should adopt reasonable proce-

dures, appropriate for the size and type of firm and practice, to determine in both litigation and non-litigation matters the parties and issues involved and to determine whether there are actual or potential conflicts of interest.

[4] If such a conflict arises after representation has been undertaken, the lawyer should withdraw from the representation. See Rule 1.16. Where more than one client is involved and the lawyer withdraws because a conflict arises after representation, whether the lawyer may continue to represent any of the clients is determined by Rule 1.9. As to whether a client-lawyer relationship exists or, having once been established, is continuing, see Comment to Rule 1.3 and Scope.

[5] *ABA Model Rule* Comment not adopted.

[6] As a general proposition, loyalty to a client prohibits undertaking representation directly adverse to that client without that client's consent. Paragraph (a) expresses that general rule. Thus, a lawyer ordinarily may not act as advocate against a person the lawyer represents in some other matter, even if it is wholly unrelated. On the other hand, simultaneous representation in unrelated matters of clients whose interests are only generally adverse, such as competing economic enterprises, does not require consent of the respective clients.

[7] *ABA Model Rule* Comment not adopted.

[8] Loyalty to a client is also impaired when a lawyer cannot consider, recommend or carry out an appropriate course of action for the client because of the lawyer's other responsibilities or interests. The conflict in effect forecloses alternatives that would otherwise be available to the client. A possible conflict does not itself preclude the representation. The critical questions are the likelihood that a conflict will eventuate and, if it does, whether it will materially interfere with the lawyer's independent professional judgment in considering alternatives or foreclose courses of action that reasonably should be pursued on behalf of the client. Nevertheless, a lawyer can never adequately provide joint representation in certain matters relating to divorce, annulment or separation — specifically, child custody, child support, visitation, spousal support and maintenance or division of property.

Conflict Charged by an Opposing Party

[9] Resolving questions of conflict of interest is primarily the responsibility of the lawyer undertaking the representation. In litigation, a court may raise the question when there is reason to infer that the lawyer has neglected the responsibility. In a criminal case, inquiry by the court is generally required when a lawyer represents multiple defendants. Where the conflict is such as clearly to call in question the fair or efficient administration of justice, opposing counsel may properly raise the question. Such an objection should be viewed with caution, however, for it can be misused as a technique of harassment.

Lawyer's Interests

[10] A lawyer may not allow business or personal interests to affect representation of a client. For example, a lawyer's need for income should not lead the lawyer to undertake matters that cannot be handled competently and at a reasonable fee. See Rules 1.1 and 1.5. Similarly, a lawyer may not refer clients to an enterprise in which the lawyer has an undisclosed interest. A lawyer's romantic or other intimate personal relationship can also adversely affect representation of a client.

Interest of Person Paying for a Lawyer's Service

[11-12] *ABA Model Rule* Comments not adopted.

[13] A lawyer may be paid from a source other than the client if the client is informed of that fact and consents and the arrangement does not compromise the lawyer's duty of loyalty to the client. See Rule 1.8(f). For example, when an insurer and its insured have conflicting interests in a matter arising from a liability insurance agreement, and the insurer is required to provide special counsel for the insured, the arrangement should assure the special counsel's professional independence. So also, when a corporation and its directors or employees are involved in a controversy in which they have conflicting interests, the corporation may provide funds for separate legal representation of the directors or employees, if the clients consent after consultation and the arrangement ensures the lawyer's professional independence.

[14-18] *ABA Model Rule* Comments not adopted.

Consultation and Consent

[19] A client may consent to representation notwithstanding a conflict. However, when a disinterested lawyer would conclude that the client should not agree to the representation under the circumstances, the lawyer involved cannot properly ask for such agreement or provide representation on the basis of the client's consent. When more than one client is involved, the question of conflict must be resolved as to each client. Moreover, there may be circumstances where it is impossible to make the disclosure necessary to obtain consent. For example, when the lawyer represents different clients in related matters and one of the clients refuses to consent to the disclosure necessary to permit the other client to make an informed decision, the lawyer cannot properly ask the latter to consent. A lawyer's obligations regarding conflicts of interest are not present solely at the onset of the attorney-client relationship; rather, such obligations are ongoing such that a change in circumstances may require a lawyer to obtain new consent from a client after additional, adequate disclosure regarding that change in circumstances.

[20] Paragraph (b) requires that client consent be memorialized in writing. Preferably, the attorney should present the memorialization to the client for signature or acknowledgement; however, any writing will satisfy this requirement, including, but not limited to, an attorney's notes or memorandum, and such writing need not be signed by, reviewed with, or delivered to the client.

[21-22] *ABA Model Rule* Comments not adopted.

Conflicts in Litigation

[23] Paragraph (a)(1) prohibits representation of opposing parties in litigation. Simultaneous representation of parties whose interests in litigation may conflict, such as co-plaintiffs or co-defendants, is governed by paragraph(a)(2). An impermissible conflict may exist by reason of substantial discrepancy in the parties' testimony, incompatibility in positions in relation to an opposing party or the fact that there are substantially different possibilities of settlement of the claims or liabilities in question. Such conflicts can arise in criminal cases as well as civil. The potential for conflict of interest in repre-

senting multiple defendants in a criminal case is so grave that ordinarily a lawyer should decline to represent more than one co-defendant. On the other hand, common representation of persons having similar interests is proper if the risk of adverse effect is minimal and the requirements of paragraph (b) are met.

[23a] Ordinarily, a lawyer may not act as advocate against a client the lawyer represents in some other matter, even if the other matter is wholly unrelated. However, there are circumstances in which a lawyer may act as advocate against a client. For example, a lawyer representing an enterprise with diverse operations may accept employment as an advocate against the enterprise in an unrelated matter if doing so will not adversely affect the lawyer's relationship with the enterprise or conduct of the suit and if both clients consent upon consultation. By the same token, government lawyers in some circumstances may represent government employees in proceedings in which a government agency is the opposing party. The propriety of concurrent representation can depend on the nature of the litigation. For example, a suit charging fraud entails conflict to a degree not involved in a suit for a declaratory judgment concerning statutory interpretation.

[24] A lawyer may represent parties having antagonistic positions on a legal question that has arisen in different cases, unless representation of either client would be materially limited. Thus, it is ordinarily not improper to assert such positions in cases pending in different trial courts, but it may be improper to do so in cases pending at the same time in an appellate court.

[25] *ABA Model Rule* Comment not adopted.

Other Conflict Situations

[26] Conflicts of interest in contexts other than litigation sometimes may be difficult to assess. Relevant factors in determining whether there is a potential conflict include the duration and intimacy of the lawyer's relationship with the client or clients involved, the functions being performed by the lawyer, the likelihood that actual conflict will arise and the likely prejudice to the client from the conflict if it does arise. The question is often one of proximity and degree.

[27] For example, a lawyer may not represent multiple parties to a negotiation whose interests are fundamentally antagonistic to each other, but common representation is permissible where the clients are generally aligned in interest even though there is some difference of interest among them.

[28] Conflict questions may also arise in estate planning and estate administration. A lawyer may be called upon to prepare wills for several family members, such as husband and wife, and, depending upon the circumstances, a conflict of interest may arise. The lawyer should make clear his relationship to the parties involved.

Special Considerations in Common Representation

[29] In considering whether to represent multiple clients in the same matter, a lawyer should be mindful that if the common representation fails because the potentially adverse interests cannot be reconciled, the result can be additional cost, embarrassment and recrimination. Ordinarily, the lawyer will be forced to withdraw from representing all of the clients if the common representation fails. In some situations, the risk of failure is so great that multiple representation is plainly impossible. For example, a lawyer cannot undertake common representation of clients where contentious litigation or negotiations between them are imminent or contemplated. Moreover, because the lawyer is required to be impartial between commonly represented clients, representation of multiple clients is improper when it is unlikely that impartiality can be maintained. Generally, if the relationship between the parties has already assumed antagonism, the possibility that the client's interests can be adequately served by common representation is not very good. Other relevant factors are whether the lawyer subsequently will represent both parties on a continuing basis and whether the situation involves creating or terminating a relationship between the parties.

[30] A particularly important factor in determining the appropriateness of common representation is the effect on client-lawyer confidentiality and the attorney-client privilege. With regard to the attorney-client privilege, the prevailing rule is that, as between commonly represented clients, the privilege does not attach. Hence, it must be assumed that if litigation eventuates between the clients, the privilege will not protect any such communications, and the clients should be so advised.

[31] As to the duty of confidentiality, continued common representation will almost certainly be inadequate if one client asks the lawyer not to disclose to the other client information relevant to the common representation. This is so because the lawyer has an equal duty of loyalty to each client, and each client has the right to be informed of anything bearing on the representation that might affect the client's interests and the right to expect that the lawyer will use that information to that client's benefit. See Rule 1.4. The lawyer should, at the outset of the common representation and as part of the process of obtaining each client's informed consent, advise each client that information will be shared and that the lawyer will have to withdraw if one client decides that some matter material to the representation should be kept from the other. In limited circumstances, it may be appropriate for the lawyer to proceed with the representation when the clients have agreed, after being properly informed, that the lawyer will keep certain information confidential. For example, the lawyer may reasonably conclude that failure to disclose one client's trade secrets to another client will not adversely affect representation involving a joint venture between the clients and agree to keep that information confidential with the informed consent of both clients.

[32] When seeking to establish or adjust a relationship between clients, the lawyer should make clear that the lawyer's role is not that of partisanship normally expected in other circumstances and, thus, that the clients may be required to assume greater responsibility for decisions than when each client is separately represented. Any limitations on the scope of the representation made necessary as a result of the common representation should be fully explained to the clients at the outset of the representation. See Rule 1.2(b).

[33] Subject to the above limitations, each client in the common representation has the right to loyal and diligent representation and the protection of Rule 1.9 concerning the obligations to a former client. The client also has the right to discharge the lawyer as stated in Rule 1.16.

[34] *ABA Model Rule* Comment not adopted.

[35] A lawyer for a corporation or other organization who is also a member of its board of directors should determine whether the responsibilities of the two roles may conflict. The lawyer may be called on to advise the corporation in matters involving actions of the directors. Consideration should be given to the frequency with which such situations may arise, the potential intensity of the conflict, the effect of the lawyer's resignation from the board and the possibility of the corporation's obtaining legal advice from another lawyer in such situations. If there is material risk that the dual role will compromise the lawyer's independence of professional judgment, the lawyer should not serve as a director.

Virginia Code Comparison

This Rule is similar to DR 5-101(A) and DR 5-105(C). DR 5-101(A) provided that "[a] lawyer shall not accept employment if the exercise of his professional judgment on behalf of his client may be affected by his own financial, business, property, or personal interests, except with the consent of his client after full and adequate disclosure under the circumstances." DR 5-105(C) provided that "a lawyer may represent multiple clients if it is obvious that he can adequately represent the interest of each and if each consents to the representation after full disclosure of the possible effect of such representation on the exercise of his independent professional judgment on behalf of each."

Rule 1.7(b) clarifies DR 5-105(A) by requiring that, when the lawyer's other interests are involved, not only must the client consent after consultation but also that, independent of such consent, the lawyer must believe that he can provide competent and diligent representation, that the representation must be lawful, and the representation must not involve asserting a claim on behalf of one client against another client in the same litigation or other proceeding before a tribunal. This requirement appears to be the intended meaning of the provision in DR 5-105(C) that "it [be] obvious that [the lawyer] can adequately represent" the client, and was implicit in EC 5-2, which stated that a lawyer "should not accept proffered employment if his personal interests or desires may affect adversely the advice to be given or services to be rendered the prospective client."

Committee Commentary

Although there are few substantive differences between this Rule and corresponding provisions in the Virginia Code, the Committee concluded that the ABA Model Rule provides a more succinct statement of a general conflicts rule.

The amendment, effective June 30, 2005, adopted June 30, 2005, rewrote the Rule and the Commentary thereto.

Law Review. — For article, "Professional Responsibility," see 43 U. Rich. L. Rev. 255 (2008).

CASE NOTES

Procedure. — Where a party alerts the trial court to a potential conflict of interest due to an attorney's previous representation of a witness, the proper course of action is for the trial court to investigate, in some fashion, the potential conflict of interest, focusing primarily on whether the attorney received any confidential information from the former client that is beneficial to the current client. If the investigation reveals that the attorney does not possess any such information, there is no significant risk that the attorney's representation of the current client will be materially affected, and therefore, no conflict of interest exists; however, if the investigation reveals that the attorney does possess such information, there is a significant risk that the attorney's representation of the current client will be materially affected, and therefore, a conflict of interest exists. Samuels v. Commonwealth, 2010 Va. App. LEXIS 466 (Nov. 30, 2010).

Burden of moving party. — Disqualification is a serious matter which cannot be based on imagined scenarios of conflict, and the moving party has a high standard of proof to meet in order to prove that counsel should be disqualified; however, in a close case the trial court should not engage in "hair-splitting" niceties but instead resolve all doubts in favor of disqualification. Stokes v. Firestone, 156 Bankr. 181 (Bankr. E.D. Va. 1993) (decided under former DR 5-105).

Joint representation does not impose duty on trial court to raise the issue. — Attorney's joint representation of defendant and her husband in a criminal case did not impose a duty on the trial court to raise a conflict of interest issue sua sponte; the conflict issue was not raised in the trial court, and, because defendant failed to point to any particular manifestation of a specific conflict, the ends of justice exception to Va. Sup. Ct. R. 5A:18 did not apply. Despite defendant's denial, her appeal clearly raised an ineffective assistance of counsel claim, which could not have been considered on direct appeal. Kilby v. Commonwealth, 2007 Va. App. LEXIS 364 (Ct. of Appeals Oct. 2, 2007).

Representation of clients with potential conflicts of interest. — Trial counsel's conduct in representing two or more clients with potential conflicting interests is not necessarily in contravention of the Code of Professional Responsibility. When there is a full disclosure to the parties and counsel can adequately represent all parties, he may do so and not violate the Code of Professional Responsibility. Dowell v. Commonwealth, 3 Va. App. 555, 351 S.E.2d 915 (1987) (decided under former DR 5-105).

Representation of defendant charged with murder of other client. — An attorney representing a defendant in a criminal case has a duty to consider and pursue all reasonable areas of investigation, but where the attorney representing the defendant in a murder case had represented the victim up until his death, the petitioner challenging his conviction on conflict of interest grounds is still required to establish that his attorney's conflict of interest adversely affected his lawyer's performance, even where the court has failed to inquire into a potential conflict about which it reasonably should have been aware. Mickens v. Taylor, 240 F.3d 348 (4th Cir. 2001), aff'd 535 U.S. 162, 152 L. Ed. 2d 291, 122 S. Ct. 1237 (2002) (decided under former DR 5-105).

All clients must waive potential conflicts of interest. — Where one lawyer represents multiple clients with divergent interests, all clients must waive the potential conflict of interest in order for the attorney to proceed. O'Dell v. Commonwealth, 234 Va. 672, 364 S.E.2d 491, cert. denied, 488 U.S. 871, 109 S. Ct. 186, 102 L. Ed. 2d 154, cert. denied, 488 U.S. 977, 109 S. Ct. 521, 102 L. Ed. 2d 554 (1988) (decided under former DR 5-105).

If witness' testimony will incriminate both witness and defendant, the attorney must choose between negotiating concessions in exchange for the witness' testimony or deterring the witness from testifying in order to protect the defendant. Consequently, the effect of such testimony would be to create a conflict of interest. Dowell v. Commonwealth, 3 Va. App. 555, 351 S.E.2d 915 (1987) (decided under former DR 5-105).

If witness' testimony is expected to incriminate witness but exculpate defendant, the attorney must either assert the witness' right to remain free from self-incrimination at the sacrifice of the defendant's best interest or allow the defendant to be exonerated at the risk of the witness incriminating himself. A conflict of interest would exist. Dowell v. Commonwealth, 3 Va. App. 555, 351 S.E.2d 915 (1987) (decided under former DR 5-105).

If witness' testimony is expected to exonerate witness and incriminate defendant, the attorney, if he does not use the witness' fifth amendment right to protect the defendant, will be forced to cross-examine the witness, his own client. If he must cross-examine the witness as an adverse witness, he cannot be expected to zealously attempt to discredit one of his clients to protect another. A conflict of interest would exist. Dowell v. Commonwealth, 3 Va. App. 555, 351 S.E.2d 915 (1987) (decided under former DR 5-105).

Defendant did not have right to force attorney to continue representing clients with conflicting interests. — Where attorney requested to withdraw because of a potential conflict of interest in his representation of defendant and another of his clients, who, according to defendant, had confessed to the same murder, and while defendant was willing to waive the conflict, there was no showing that his attorney was, defendant had no right to force the attorney to continue as counsel under these circumstances. O'Dell v. Commonwealth, 234 Va. 672, 364 S.E.2d 491, cert. denied, 488 U.S. 871, 109 S. Ct. 186, 102 L. Ed. 2d 154, cert. denied, 488 U.S. 977, 109 S. Ct. 521, 102 L. Ed. 2d 554 (1988) (decided under former DR 5-105).

All doubts are to be resolved in favor of disqualification. Rogers v. Pittston Co., 800 F. Supp. 350 (W.D. Va. 1992), aff'd, 996 F.2d 1212 (1993) (decided under former DR 5-105).

Impact of appearance of impropriety on criminal defendant. — A criminal defendant is denied due process only when his former counsel joins a Commonwealth's Attorney office and is not effectively screened from contact with the Commonwealth's attorneys who are handling the defendant's case on a related matter Lux v. Commonwealth, 24 Va. App. 561, 484 S.E.2d 145 (1997) (decided under former DR 5-105).

While an ethical rule that strives to avoid the appearance of impropriety is a worthy standard for professional conduct, a criminal defendant's constitutional right to due process does not entitle him to a prosecution free of such appearances. Lux v. Commonwealth, 24 Va. App. 561, 484 S.E.2d 145 (1997) (decided under former DR 5-105).

Motives of attorney irrelevant. — Although the court had no doubt that present attorney for plaintiff and former attorney for defendant testified truthfully to his lack of knowledge of any confidences, and furthermore, the court was convinced that attorney made every effort to ensure that he was acting in an ethical manner, however, it was not for the court to consider whether the motives of counsel in seeking to appear despite his conflict were pure or corrupt; in either case the disqualification was plain. Rogers v. Pittston Co., 800 F. Supp. 350 (W.D. Va. 1992), aff'd, 996 F.2d 1212 (1993) (decided under former DR 5-105).

In camera submission of documents. — Because moving party is not required to publicly reveal actual confidences, in camera submission of documents is a recognized way of establishing that the two matters are substantially related. Rogers v. Pittston Co., 800 F. Supp. 350 (W.D. Va. 1992), aff'd, 996 F.2d 1212 (1993) (decided under former DR 5-105).

Attorney's familiarity with corporation's workings or personality of its representatives is totally insufficient as a basis for disqualification, where it cannot reasonably be said that in the course of the former representation the attorney might have acquired information related to the subject to the present litigation. Chantilly Constr. Corp. v. John Driggs Co., 39 Bankr. 466 (Bankr. E.D. Va. 1984) (decided under former DR 5-105).

Role as registered agent for other party not grounds for disqualification. — The fact that an attorney acted as registered agent for a party does not support its motion to disqualify him from representing the other party. A registered agent may be any person over 18 who is either an officer or director of the corporation or a member of the Virginia State Bar or an appropriately registered professional corporation. As a practical matter, the single function of a registered agent is to act as the recipient of any process, notice, order or demand required or permitted by law, to be served upon the corporation. Such a function does not constitute the establishment of an attorney-client relationship. Chantilly Constr. Corp. v. John Driggs Co., 39 Bankr. 466 (Bankr. E.D. Va. 1984) (decided under former DR 5-105).

Mere fact that law firm representing trustee in bankruptcy was a judgment lien creditor of defendants in an adversary proceeding did not alone establish a sufficient basis to disqualify them as attorneys for the trustee, where no friendly alliance existed between counsel for the trustee and the defendants in the adversary proceeding. The interests of the trustee to independently select his own counsel and the trustee's interest to hire counsel already familiar with the facts and circumstances of this case overrode any possible taint upon the appointment of that law firm to represent the trustee. In re Stancraft Corp., 39 Bankr. 748 (Bankr. E.D. Va. 1984) (decided under former DR 5-105).

Bankruptcy trustee's counsel disqualified by cause of action against former client for benefit of estate. — Where the law firm representing the trustee in bankruptcy (the plaintiff) also represented the minority shareholders of the defendant corporation in another action and such shareholders have an interest that may be adverse to the interests of the trustee in that the trustee has a cause of action against those minority shareholders to disgorge part of the settlement obtained by the minority shareholders for the benefit of bankrupt's creditors, disqualification is mandated. In re Stancraft Corp., 39 Bankr. 748 (Bankr. E.D. Va. 1984) (decided under former DR 5-105).

Representing debtor in possession in Chapter 11 and creditor asserting claim. — Claim by a law firm, even if true, that its dual representation of a debtor in possession and a creditor in the case did not violate Va. Sup. Ct. R. pt. 6, § II, 1.7(b) (2010) was not a defense and did not forestall a determination that the firm's conduct was improper under 11 U.S.C.S. § 327, which governed such an issue in a bankruptcy case. In re Lewis Road, LLC, 2011 Bankr. LEXIS 4827 (Bankr. E.D. Va. Dec. 9, 2011).

Mere payment of fees to ex-husband's attorney by ex-wife did not establish attorney-client relationship. — There was no attorney-client relationship between ex-wife and attorney for ex-husband based upon the fact that she and her ex-husband personally paid the legal bills of ex-husband's attorney, therefore ex-husband's attorney would not be disqualified from representing the ex-husband in adversary proceeding. Stokes v. Firestone, 156 Bankr. 181 (Bankr. E.D. Va. 1993) (decided under former DR 5-105).

Representing two clients. — Though counsel concurrently represented plaintiff in a separate action and the union in plaintiff's action against the union for eleven weeks, the conflict of interest did not justify disqualification from representation of the union but did justify referral to the Virginia State Bar for Va. Sup. Ct. R. pt. 6, § II, R. 1.7(a)(1) and 1.10(a) violations. Reese v. Va. Int'l Terminals, Inc., 2012 U.S. Dist. LEXIS 109372 (E.D. Va. Aug. 2, 2012).

Representation on unrelated matter. — Attorney for a murder defendant was properly denied his motion to withdraw where he had previously represented one of Commonwealth's witnesses on an unrelated matter. Mackall v. Commonwealth, 236 Va. 240, 372 S.E.2d 759 (1988), cert. denied, 492 U.S. 925, 109 S. Ct. 3261, 106 L. Ed. 2d 607 (1989) (decided under former DR 5-105).

Representing the interests of others. — Where the grandmother and father of an 18-year-old Chapter 13 debtor used the debtor as part of a scheme to hinder, delay, and defraud their own creditors, the attorney for the debtor, who had represented the grandmother and father in prior bankruptcy cases, was a willing and active participant in the scheme, in violation of Fed. R. Bankr. P. 9011 and several rules of the Virginia Rules of Professional Conduct, including Va. Sup. Ct. R. pt. 6, § II, R. 1.7. In re Johnson, 2008 Bankr. LEXIS 164 (Bankr. E.D. Va. Jan. 18, 2008).

Disqualification of entire office unwarranted. — Where two attorneys, who formerly represented and had a connection with defendant, joined U.S. Attorney's Office and had no involvement in investigation since they had recused themselves and had erected a "Chinese wall," there was no basis to disqualify the entire U.S. Attorney's Office. In re Grand Jury, 790 F. Supp. 109 (E.D. Va. 1992) (decided under former DR 5-105).

Use of stipulation of violation in federal criminal case. — State bar investigation led to a stipulation that defendant had mismanaged client trust accounts in violation of Va. Sup. Ct. R. pt. 6, § II, R. 1.7, subsection A of § 55-548.02, and § 55-525.24, as well as an agreement to surrender his law license, an FBI investigation, and criminal charges; in the federal criminal case, the district court thoughtfully balanced the probative value of the stipulation to revocation of defendant's law license against its potential for prejudice, and the appellate court declined to second-guess that balancing. United States v. Titus, 2012 U.S. App. LEXIS 7507 (4th Cir. Apr. 13, 2012).

Representing bankruptcy trustee. — Where the financial and personal interests of the attorney for the bankruptcy trustee can be seen to possibly affect the exercise of his independent professional judgment on behalf of the trustee, the attorney is prohibited from accepting the employment except on consent of the trustee after full and adequate disclosure. In re Porter, 52 Bankr. 692 (Bankr. E.D. Va. 1985) (decided under former DR 5-101).

No conflict of interest. — Trial court did not err in denying defendant's motion for a continuance and his counsel's motion to withdraw when it was discovered that defendant's attorney had previously represented the informant and possibly her estranged husband in other cases as there was no conflict of interest. The record established that the attorney did not recall anything about his previous representation of the informant, and a voir dire of the informant about the attorney's previous representation revealed that the informant had only a five-minute meeting with the attorney and did not reveal anything that she would consider to be a personal confidence to him; thus, there was no risk that the attorney's representation of defendant was materially affected. Samuels v. Commonwealth, 2010 Va. App. LEXIS 466 (Nov. 30, 2010).

Where there was no conflict of interest in representation of three injured parties, who had filed separate suits based on injuries incurred while on an amusement park ride because counsel had obtained a written waiver, in any event, the representation did not violate of Rule 1.7(1) since there was no showing that the clients should not have agreed to the representation since, based on the specific facts of the case, the plaintiffs' interests did not conflict and there was no scenario under which the parties' interest were adverse and it was not likely that there would be a conflict even after a jury verdict. Simms v. Deggeller Attractions, Inc., 2013 U.S. Dist. LEXIS 448 (W.D. Va. Jan. 2, 2013).

Where there was no conflict of interest in representation of three injured parties, who had filed separate suits based on injuries incurred while on an amusement park ride because counsel had obtained a written waiver, in any event, the representation did not violate of Rule 1.7(4), since it did not involve the assertion of a claim by one client against another client represented by the lawyer in the same litigation. Simms v. Deggeller Attractions, Inc., 2013 U.S. Dist. LEXIS 448 (W.D. Va. Jan. 2, 2013).

There was no conflict of interest in representation of three injured parties, who had filed separate suits based on injuries incurred while on an amusement park ride because counsel had obtained a written waiver of any possible conflict from all three plaintiffs, and those waivers adequately and clearly inform the plaintiffs of the potential risks of the concurrent conflict. Simms v. Deggeller Attractions, Inc., 2013 U.S. Dist. LEXIS 448 (W.D. Va. Jan. 2, 2013).

CIRCUIT COURT OPINIONS

Representing two clients. — Motions to disqualify legal counsel, for an alleged conflict of interest in representing two clients under Va. Sup. Ct. R. pt. 6, § . II, 1.7 in separate lawsuits against an attorney, were denied because there was no concurrent conflict of interest and a written waiver signed by the clients cured any conflict. Wright v. Kincheloe, 81 Va. Cir. 277, 2010 Va. Cir. LEXIS 121 (Fairfax Oct. 20, 2010).

Representing class and individuals. — Motions to disqualify home owners' counsel based on a conflict of interest in representing class action and individual plaintiffs seeking a limited fund in violation of Va. Sup. Ct. R. pt. 6, § II, R. 1.7 was denied because there was no inherent conflict between representation of a class and representation of individual claimants as lawyers who represented only entire classes with no responsibility to individual class members would in effect have no clients and no one with whom to consult. Chinese Drywall Cases, 80 Va. Cir. 69, 2010 Va. Cir. LEXIS 14 (Norfolk Jan. 22, 2010).

Rule 1.8. Conflict of Interest: Prohibited Transactions.

(a) A lawyer shall not enter into a business transaction with a client or knowingly acquire an ownership, possessory, security or other pecuniary interest adverse to a client unless:

(1) the transaction and terms on which the lawyer acquires the interest are fair and reasonable to the client and are fully disclosed and transmitted in writing to the client in a manner which can be reasonably understood by the client;

(2) the client is given a reasonable opportunity to seek the advice of independent counsel in the transaction; and

(3) the client consents in writing thereto.

(b) A lawyer shall not use information relating to representation of a client for the advantage of the lawyer or of a third person or to the disadvantage of the client unless the client consents after consultation, except as permitted or required by Rule 1.6 or Rule 3.3.

(c) A lawyer shall not solicit, for himself or a person related to the lawyer, any substantial gift from a client including a testamentary gift. A lawyer shall not accept any such gift if solicited at his request by a third party. A lawyer shall not prepare an instrument giving the lawyer or a person related to the lawyer any substantial gift from a client, including a testamentary gift, unless the lawyer or other recipient of the gift is related to the client. For purposes of this paragraph, a person related to a lawyer includes a spouse, child, grandchild, parent, or other relative or individual with whom the lawyer or the client maintains a close, familial relationship.

(d) Prior to the conclusion of all aspects of a matter giving rise to the representation of a client, a lawyer shall not make or negotiate an agreement giving the lawyer literary or media rights to a portrayal or account based in substantial part on information relating to the representation.

(e) A lawyer shall not provide financial assistance to a client in connection with pending or contemplated litigation, except that:

(1) a lawyer may advance court costs and expenses of litigation, provided the client remains ultimately liable for such costs and expenses; and

(2) a lawyer representing an indigent client may pay court costs and expenses of litigation on behalf of the client.

(f) A lawyer shall not accept compensation for representing a client from one other than the client unless:

(1) the client consents after consultation;

(2) there is no interference with the lawyer's independence of professional judgment or with the client-lawyer relationship; and

(3) information relating to representation of a client is protected as required by Rule 1.6.

(g) A lawyer who represents two or more clients shall not participate in making an aggregate settlement of the claims of or against the clients, or in a criminal case an aggregated agreement as to guilty or nolo contendere pleas, unless each client consents after consultation, including disclosure of the existence and nature of all the claims or pleas involved and of the participation of each person in the settlement.

(h) A lawyer shall not make an agreement prospectively limiting the lawyer's liability to a client for malpractice, except that a lawyer may make such an agreement with a client of which the lawyer is an employee as long as the client is independently represented in making the agreement.

(i) A lawyer related to another lawyer as parent, child, sibling or spouse, or who is intimately involved with another lawyer, shall not represent a client in a representation directly adverse to a person whom the lawyer knows is represented by the other lawyer except upon consent by the client after consultation regarding the relationship.

(j) A lawyer shall not acquire a proprietary interest in the cause of action or subject matter of litigation the lawyer is conducting for a client, except that the lawyer may:

(1) acquire a lien granted by law to secure the lawyer's fee or expenses; and

(2) contract with a client for a reasonable contingent fee in a civil case, unless prohibited by Rule 1.5.

(k) While lawyers are associated in a firm, none of them shall knowingly enter into any transaction or perform any activity when one of them practicing alone would be prohibited from doing so by paragraphs (a), (b), (c), (d), (e), (f), (g), (h), or (j) of this Rule.

COMMENT

Transactions Between Client and Lawyer

[1] As a general principle, all transactions between client and lawyer should be fair and reasonable to the client. In such transactions a review by independent counsel on behalf of the client is often advisable. Furthermore, a lawyer may not exploit information relating to the representation to the client's disadvantage. For example, a lawyer who has learned that the client is investing in specific real estate may not, without the client's consent, seek to acquire nearby property where doing so would adversely affect the client's plan for investment. Paragraph (a) does not, however, apply to standard commercial transactions between the lawyer and the client for products or services that the client generally markets to others, for example, banking or brokerage services, medical services, products manufactured or distributed by the client, and utilities services. In such transactions, the lawyer has no advantage in dealing with the client, and the restrictions in paragraph (a) are unnecessary and impracticable. Similarly, paragraph (b) does not limit an attorney's use of information obtained independently outside the attorney-client relationship.

[2-5] *ABA Model Rule* Comments not adopted.

[6] A lawyer may accept ordinary gifts from a client. For example, an ordinary gift such as a present given at a holiday or as a token of appreciation is permitted. If effectuation of a substantial gift requires preparing a legal instrument such as a will or conveyance, however, the client should have the detached advice that another lawyer can provide. Paragraph (c) recognizes an exception where the client is a relative of the donee or the gift is not substantial.

[7-8] *ABA Model Rule* Comments not adopted.

Literary Rights

[9] An agreement by which a lawyer acquires literary or media rights concerning the conduct of the representation creates a conflict between the interests of the client and the personal interests of the lawyer. Measures suitable in the representation of the client may detract from the publication value of an account of the representation. Paragraph (d) does not prohibit a lawyer representing a client in a transaction concerning literary property from agreeing that the lawyer's fee shall consist of a share in ownership in the property, if the arrangement conforms to Rule 1.5 and paragraph (j).

[10] *ABA Model Rule* Comment not adopted.

Person Paying for a Lawyer's Services

[11] Paragraph (f) requires disclosure of the fact that the lawyer's services are being paid for by a third party. Such an arrangement must also conform to the requirements of Rule 1.6 concerning confidentiality, Rule 1.7 concerning conflict of interest, and Rule 5.4(c) concerning the professional independence of a lawyer. Where the client is a class, consent may be obtained on behalf of the class by court-supervised procedure.

Family Relationships Between Lawyers

[12] Paragraph (i) applies to related lawyers who are in different firms. Related lawyers in the same firm are governed by Rules 1.7, 1.9, and 1.10. The disqualification stated in paragraph (i) is personal and is not imputed to members of firms with whom the lawyers are associated.

[13-15] *ABA Model Rule* Comments not adopted.

Acquisition of Interest in Litigation

[16] Paragraph (j) states the traditional general rule that lawyers are prohibited from acquiring a proprietary interest in litigation. This general rule, which has its basis in common law champerty and maintenance, is subject to specific exceptions developed in decisional law and continued in these Rules, such as the exception for reasonable contingent fees set forth in Rule 1.5 and the exception for certain advances or payment of the costs of litigation set forth in paragraph (e).

Virginia Code Comparison

With regard to paragraph (a), DR 5-104(A) provided that a lawyer "shall not enter into a business transaction with a client if they have differing interests therein and if the client expects the lawyer to exercise his professional judgment therein for the protection of the client, unless the client has consented after full and adequate disclosure . . . ." EC 5-3 stated that a lawyer "should not seek to persuade his client to permit him to invest in an undertaking of his client nor make improper use of his professional relationship to influence his client to invest in an enterprise in which the lawyer is interested."

Paragraph (b) is substantially similar to DR 4-101(B)(3) which provided that a lawyer should not use "a confidence or secret of his client for the advantage of himself, or a third person, unless the client consents after full disclosure."

Paragraph (c) is substantially similar to DR 5-104(B) which stated that a lawyer "shall not prepare an instrument giving the lawyer or a member of the lawyer's family any gift from a client, including a testamentary gift, except where the client is a relative of the donee." EC 5-5 stated that a lawyer "should not suggest to his client that a gift be made to himself or for his benefit. If a lawyer accepts a gift from his client, he is peculiarly susceptible to the charge that he unduly influenced or overreached the client. If a client voluntarily offers to make a gift to his lawyer, the lawyer may accept the gift, but before doing so, he should urge that the client secure disinterested advice from an independent, competent person who is cognizant of all the circumstances. Except in those instances in which the client is related to the donee, a lawyer may not prepare an instrument by which the client gives a gift to the lawyer or to a member of his family."

Paragraph (d) has no direct counterpart in the Virginia Code. EC 5-4 stated that in order to avoid "potentially differing interests" a lawyer should "scrupulously avoid [literary arrangements with a client] prior to the termination of all aspects of the matter giving rise to the employment, even though [the lawyer's] employment has previously ended."

Paragraph (e)(1) incorporates the provisions of DR 5-103(B), including the requirement that the client remain "ultimately liable" for such advanced expenses.

Paragraph (e)(2) has no direct counterpart in the Virginia Code, although DR 5-103(B) allowed a lawyer to advance or guarantee expenses of litigation as long as the client remained ultimately liable.

Paragraph (f) is substantially similar to DR 5-106(A)(1) and DR 5-106(B). DR 5-106(A)(1) stated: "Except with the consent of his client after full and adequate disclosure under the circumstances, a lawyer shall not . . . [a]ccept compensation for his legal services from one other than his client." DR 5-106(B) stated that "[a] lawyer shall not permit a person who recommends, employs, or pays him to render legal services for another to direct or regulate his professional judgment in rendering such legal services."

Paragraph (g) is substantially similar to DR 5-107, but also covers aggregated plea agreements in criminal cases.

The first portion of Paragraph (h) is essentially the same as DR 6-102(A), but the second portion of Paragraph (h) has no counterpart in the Virginia Code. The new provision allows in-house lawyers to arrange for the same indemnity available to other officers and employees, as long as their employers are independently represented in making the arrangement.

Paragraph (i) has no counterpart in the Virginia Code.

Paragraph (j) is substantially the same as DR 5-103(A).

Paragraph (k) had no counterpart in the Virginia Code.

Committee Commentary

The Committee added "for the advantage of himself or a third person" from DR 4-101(B)(3) to paragraph (b) as a further limitation on a lawyer's use of information relating to representation of a client.

The Committee added a further time limitation to paragraph (d)'s restriction. Borrowing language from EC 5-4, the restriction on agreements giving a lawyer literary or media rights extends through the conclusion of "all aspects of a matter giving rise to the representation."

In Rule 1.8(e)(1), the Committee retained the requirement in DR 5-103(B) that a client must "remain ultimately liable for [litigation] expenses." However, the Committee adopted the limited exception for indigent clients that appears in Rule 1.8(e)(2).

After lengthy debate, the Committee adopted 1.8(h), which retains the general prohibition on lawyers prospectively limiting their malpractice liability to clients (which appeared in Virginia Code DR 6-102). However, the Committee added a limited exception that allows in-house lawyers to arrange for the type of indemnity that other officers and employees of entities may obtain. The Committee voted to insist that the client be independently represented in agreeing to any such arrangement.

In 1.8(i), the Committee adopted the ABA Model Rule approach, which permits lawyers who are members of the same nuclear family to represent clients adverse to each other, as long as both clients consent after full disclosure. The Virginia Code was interpreted to create a non-waivable per se conflict of interest in these circumstances. See LEO 190 (April 1, 1985).

The amendment effective January 1, 2004, adopted September 24, 2003, rewrote paragraph (c) and added paragraph (k).

CASE NOTES

This rule is intended and designed to maintain the independent judgment of counsel in the representation of clients. Shea v. Virginia State Bar, 236 Va. 442, 374 S.E.2d 63 (1988) (decided under former DR 5-103).

Independent judgment of counsel. — This rule is intended and designed to maintain the independent judgment of counsel in the representation of clients. Shea v. Virginia State Bar, 236 Va. 442, 374 S.E.2d 63 (1988) (decided under former DR 5-103).

The policy embodied in subdivision (B) of this rule is that a lawyer simply should not face this risk to independent judgment. Shea v. Virginia State Bar, 236 Va. 442, 374 S.E.2d 63 (1988) (decided under former DR 5-103).

Consideration of past record. — In a proceeding for violation of this rule, the State Bar Disciplinary Board could consider attorney's past record of disciplinary violations and decide to suspend him for 90 days. Shea v. Virginia State Bar, 236 Va. 442, 374 S.E.2d 63 (1988) (decided under former DR 5-103).

Conduct fit within policy exclusion. — Asserted damages in an underlying complaint against plaintiff insureds, a law firm and attorneys, resulted from conflicts of interests between the insureds and the underlying plaintiffs, their clients, and fell within the business enterprise exclusion in a policy of insurance. The insureds allegedly obtained complete ownership and control of their clients' assets and exploited those assets for personal benefit, which conduct violated any number of Virginia professional ethics rules. Minn. Lawyers Mut. Ins. Co. v. Antonelli, Terry, Stout & Kraus, LLP, 2012 U.S. App. LEXIS 6504 (4th Cir. Mar. 29, 2012).

Rule 1.9. Conflict of Interest: Former Client.

(a) A lawyer who has formerly represented a client in a matter shall not thereafter represent another person in the same or a substantially related matter in which that person's interests are materially adverse to the interests of the former client unless both the present and former client consent after consultation.

(b) A lawyer shall not knowingly represent a person in the same or a substantially related matter in which a firm with which the lawyer formerly was associated had previously represented a client

(1) whose interests are materially adverse to that person; and

(2) about whom the lawyer had acquired information protected by Rules 1.6 and 1.9(c) that is material to the matter; unless both the present and former client consent after consultation.

(c) A lawyer who has formerly represented a client in a matter or whose present or former firm has formerly represented a client in a matter shall not thereafter:

(1) use information relating to or gained in the course of the representation to the disadvantage of the former client except as Rule 1.6 or Rule 3.3 would permit or require with respect to a client, or when the information has become generally known; or

(2) reveal information relating to the representation except as Rule 1.6 or Rule 3.3 would permit or require with respect to a client.

COMMENT

[1] After termination of a client-lawyer relationship, a lawyer may not represent another client except in conformity with this Rule. The principles in Rule 1.7 determine whether the interests of the present and former client are adverse. Thus, a lawyer could not properly seek to rescind on behalf of a new client a contract drafted on behalf of the former client. So also a lawyer who has prosecuted an accused person could not properly represent the accused in a subsequent civil action against the government concerning the same transaction.

[2] The scope of a "matter" for purposes of this Rule may depend on the facts of a particular situation or transaction. The lawyer's involvement in a matter can also be a question of degree. When a lawyer has been directly involved in a specific transaction, subsequent representation of other clients with materially adverse interests clearly is prohibited. On the other hand, a lawyer who recurrently handled a type of problem for a former client is not precluded from later representing another client in a wholly distinct problem of that type even though the subsequent representation involves a position adverse to the prior client. Similar considerations can apply to the reassignment of military lawyers between defense and prosecution functions within the same military jurisdiction. The underlying question is whether the lawyer was so involved in the matter that the subsequent representation can be justly regarded as a changing of sides in the matter in question.

[3] The second aspect of loyalty to a client is the lawyer's obligation to decline subsequent representations involving positions adverse to a former client arising in substantially related matters. This obligation requires abstention from adverse representation by the individual lawyer involved and other lawyers may be subject to imputed disqualification under Rule 1.10. If a lawyer left one firm for another, the new affiliation would not preclude the firms involved from continuing to represent clients with adverse interests in the same or related matters, so long as the conditions of paragraphs 1.9 (b) and (c) concerning confidentiality have been met.

Lawyers Moving Between Firms

[4] When lawyers have been associated within a firm but then end their association, the question of whether a lawyer should undertake representation is more complicated. There are several competing considerations. First, the client previously represented by the former firm must be reasonably assured that the principle of loyalty to the client is not compromised. Second, the Rule should not be so broadly cast as to preclude other persons from having reasonable choice of legal counsel. Third, the Rule should not unreasonably hamper lawyers from forming new associations and taking on new clients after having left a previous association. In this connection, it should be recognized that today many lawyers practice in firms, that many lawyers to some degree limit their practice to one field or another, and that many move from one association to another several times in their careers. If the concept of imputation were applied with unqualified rigor, the result would be radical curtailment of the opportunity of lawyers to move from one practice setting to another and of the opportunity of clients to change counsel.

[4a] Reconciliation of these competing principles in the past has been attempted under two rubrics. One approach has been to seek per se rules of disqualification. For example, it has been held that a partner in a law firm is conclusively presumed to have access to all confidences concerning all clients of the firm. Under this analysis, if a lawyer has been a partner in one law firm and then becomes a partner in another law firm, there may be a presumption that all confidences known by the partner in the first firm are known to all partners in the second firm. This presumption might properly be applied in some circumstances, especially where the client has been extensively represented, but may be unrealistic where the client was represented only for limited purposes. Furthermore, such a rigid rule exaggerates the difference between a partner and an associate in modern law firms.

[4b] The other rubric formerly used for dealing with disqualification is the appearance of impropriety proscribed in Canon 9 of the Virginia Code. This rubric has a twofold problem. First, the appearance of impropriety can be taken to include any new client-lawyer relationship that might make a former client feel anxious. If that meaning were adopted, disqualification would become little more than a question of subjective judgment by the former client. Second, since "impropriety" is undefined, the term "appearance of impropriety" is question-begging. It therefore has to be recognized that the problem of disqualification cannot be properly resolved either by simple analogy to a lawyer practicing alone or by the very general concept of appearance of impropriety. A rule based on a functional analysis is more appropriate for determining the question of vicarious disqualification. Two functions are involved: preserving confidentiality and avoiding positions adverse to a client.

[5] Paragraph (b) operates to disqualify the lawyer only when the lawyer involved has actual knowledge of information protected by Rules 1.6 and 1.9(b). Thus, if a lawyer while with one firm acquired no knowledge or information relating to a particular client of the firm, and that lawyer later joined another firm, neither the lawyer individually nor the second firm is disqualified from representing another client in the same or a related matter even though the interests of the two clients conflict. *See* Rule 1.10(b) for the restrictions on a firm once a lawyer has terminated association with the firm; and Rule 1.11(d) for restrictions regarding a lawyer moving from private employment to public employment.

Confidentiality

[6] Preserving confidentiality is a question of access to information. Access to information, in turn, is essentially a question of fact in particular circumstances, aided by inferences, deductions or working presumptions that reasonably may be made about the way in which lawyers work together. A lawyer may have general access to files of all clients of a law firm and may regularly participate in discussions of their affairs; it should be inferred that such a lawyer in fact is privy to all information about all the firm's clients. In contrast, another lawyer may have access to the files of only a limited number of clients and participate in discussions of the affairs of no other clients; in the absence of information to the contrary, it should be inferred that such a lawyer in fact is privy to information about the clients actually served but not those of other clients.

[6a] Application of paragraph (b) depends on a situation's particular facts. In such an inquiry, the burden of proof should rest upon the firm whose disqualification is sought.

[7] Independent of the question of disqualification of a firm, a lawyer changing professional association has a continuing duty to preserve confidentiality of information about a client formerly represented. See Rules 1.6 and 1.9.

Adverse Positions

[8] Information acquired by the lawyer in the course of representing a client may not subsequently be used or revealed by the lawyer to the disadvantage of the client. However, the fact that a lawyer has once served a client does not preclude the lawyer from using non-confidential information about that client when later representing another client.

[9] Disqualification from subsequent representation is primarily for the protection of former clients but may also affect current clients. This protection, however, can be waived by both. A waiver is effective only if there is full disclosure of the circumstances, including the lawyer's intended role in behalf of the new client.

[10] With regard to an opposing party's raising a question of conflict of interest, see Comment to Rule 1.7. With regard to disqualification of a firm with which a lawyer is or was formerly associated, see Rule 1.10.

Virginia Code Comparison

Paragraph (a) is substantially the same as DR 5-105(D), although the Rule requires waiver by both a lawyer's current and former client, rather than just the former client.

There was no direct counterpart to paragraph (b) in the Virginia Code. Representation by a lawyer adverse to a client of a law firm with which a lawyer was previously associated was sometimes dealt with under the rubric of Canon 9 of the Virginia Code which provided: "A lawyer should avoid even the appearance of impropriety."

There was no counterpart to paragraph (c) in the Virginia Code. The exception in the last clause of paragraph (c)(1) permits a lawyer to use information relating to a former client that is in the "public domain," a use that also was not prohibited by the Virginia Code which protected only "confidences and secrets." Since the scope of paragraphs (a) and (b) is much broader than "confidences and secrets," it is necessary to define when a lawyer may make use of information about a client after the client-lawyer relationship has terminated.

Committee Commentary

The Committee believed that, in an era when lawyers frequently move between firms, this Rule provided more specific guidance than the implicit provisions of the Disciplinary Rules. However, the Committee added language to paragraph (a) requiring consent of both present and former clients. Additionally, the Committee adopted broader language in paragraph (c) precluding the use of any information "relating to or gained in the course of" the representation of a former client, rather than precluding the use only of information "relating to" the former representation.

The amendment effective January 4, 2010, adopted November 2, 2009, combined the former concluding phrase of subdivision (b) with paragraph (2) thereof; and added "and Rule 1.11(d) for restrictions regarding a lawyer moving from private employment to public employment" at the end of Comment [5].

Law Review. — For article, "Professional Responsibility," see 43 U. Rich. L. Rev. 255 (2008). For annual survey of Virginia law article, "Criminal Law and Procedure," see 47 U. Rich. L. Rev. 143 (2012).

CASE NOTES

Disqualification test. — The correct test for disqualification does not require an actual dispute between the parties; instead, the standard is substantial relatedness. Rogers v. Pittston Co., 800 F. Supp. 350 (W.D. Va. 1992), aff'd, 996 F.2d 1212 (1993) (decided under former DR 5-105).

Under the "substantially related" test, the movant must establish both: (1) that an attorney-client relationship existed between the alleged former client, and (2) that the former representation and the current controversy are substantially related. Tessier v. Plastic Surgery Specialists, Inc., 731 F. Supp. 724 (E.D. Va. 1990) (decided under former DR 5-105).

Substantially related has been interpreted to mean "identical" or essentially the same. Rogers v. Pittston Co., 800 F. Supp. 350 (W.D. Va. 1992), aff'd, 996 F.2d 1212 (1993) (decided under former DR 5-105).

Substantial relationship test is a measure of quantum of evidence. — The substantial relationship test is not a rule of substantive law but a measure of the quantum of evidence required for proof of the existence of the professional obligation. Rogers v. Pittston Co., 800 F. Supp. 350 (W.D. Va. 1992), aff'd, 996 F.2d 1212 (1993) (decided under former DR 5-105).

Substantial relationship found. — In a patent infringement suit, plaintiff's law firm was disqualified under Va. Sup. Ct. Rules, Part 6, § II, R. 1.9 and 1.10 because there was a substantial relationship between prior and successive representation of a particular defendant due to the involvement in patent prosecution work for defendant by an attorney employed in plaintiff's law firm. Sunbeam Prods. v. Hamilton Beach Brands, Inc., 2010 U.S. Dist. LEXIS 74001 (E.D. Va. July 22, 2010).

Where a debtor transferred property to its sole member, also a debtor in bankruptcy, in a transaction that was potentially avoidable, an attorney's representation of both debtors was substantially related, and the attorney could not represent both debtors simultaneously, nor could he represent one debtor after he terminated his representation of the other debtor. In re Dickson Props., LLC, 2012 Bankr. LEXIS 2520 (Bankr. E.D. Va. June 5, 2012).

Exposure to confidences in former case. — In determining whether two cases are "substantially related," the court must decide whether the attorney could reasonably have been exposed to client confidences in the former case. Rogers v. Pittston Co., 800 F. Supp. 350 (W.D. Va. 1992), aff'd, 996 F.2d 1212 (1993) (decided under former DR 5-105).

When irrebuttable presumption arises that confidences were exchanged. — Where the matters are determined to be substantially related, and there was a reasonable chance that the attorney received confidences in the first matter, an irrebuttable presumption arises that confidences were exchanged. Rogers v. Pittston Co., 800 F. Supp. 350 (W.D. Va. 1992), aff'd, 996 F.2d 1212 (1993) (decided under former DR 5-105).

Once it is determined that an attorney-client relationship existed and that the matters are determined to be substantially related, then an irrebuttable presumption arises that relevant confidences were exchanged so that the attorney and attorney's law firm must be disqualified. Stokes v. Firestone, 156 Bankr. 181 (Bankr. E.D. Va. 1993) (decided under former DR 5-105).

No actual receipt of confidences must be shown; such a standard would place an unreasonable burden on the moving party. Rogers v. Pittston Co., 800 F. Supp. 350 (W.D. Va. 1992), aff'd, 996 F.2d 1212 (1993) (decided under former DR 5-105).

Demonstration of actual confidences not required. — Where former attorney of defendant company and present attorney of plaintiff was copied to a document prepared by a legal colleague at defendant company dealing with one of the issues in later case, while attorney testified that he did not recall this document, defendant companies were not required to demonstrate actual confidences. Rogers v. Pittston Co., 800 F. Supp. 350 (W.D. Va. 1992), aff'd, 996 F.2d 1212 (1993) (decided under former DR 5-105).

Continued representation by counsel presented conflicts of interest. — Where government argued that an actual conflict of interest was present because members or employees of private law firm, which represented defendant, would be called to testify at defendant's trial regarding the cash payment of legal fees by a third-party unindicted co-conspirator as possible evidence of the existence of a drug conspiracy, where the government also argued that an actual conflict of interest existed because the private firm represented both defendant and an alleged member of conspiracy in a substantially related matter, and where firm argued that it could continue to represent defendant through his trial if the potential testimony of its members or employees could be stipulated, and if members or employees of the firm were forced to testify at trial, then the firm would disqualify itself at that point, continued representation by current counsel presented actual and potential conflicts of interest and would give the appearance of impropriety. United States v. Scott, 980 F. Supp. 165 (E.D. Va. 1997) (decided under former DR 5-105).

Duty of loyalty. — Where an attorney continued to file pleadings on behalf of Chapter 11 debtor after his employment application was denied and also represented creditors of the debtor in connection with adversary proceedings filed by the Chapter 11 trustee against the creditors, his representation of the creditor violated his continuing duty of loyalty to the bankruptcy estate. In re Dickson Props., LLC, 2012 Bankr. LEXIS 2520 (Bankr. E.D. Va. June 5, 2012).

Representation of defendant accused of murder of other client. — An attorney representing a defendant in a criminal case has a duty to consider and pursue all reasonable areas of investigation, but where the attorney representing the defendant in a murder case had represented the victim up until his death, the petitioner challenging his conviction on conflict of interest grounds is still required to establish that his attorney's conflict of interest adversely affected his lawyer's performance, even where the court has failed to inquire into a potential conflict about which it reasonably should have been aware. Mickens v. Taylor, 240 F.3d 348 (4th Cir. 2001), aff'd 535 U.S. 162, 152 L. Ed. 2d 291, 122 S. Ct. 1237 (2002) (decided under DR 4-101 and DR 5-105).

Attorney's testimony permitted. — On appeal from his convictions, the circuit court did not abuse its discretion by permitting the defense counsel at the preliminary hearing to testify regarding information that was not obtained confidentially from defendant. Neither Va. Sup. Ct. R. pt. 6, § II, R. 1.6 nor 1.9 prohibited a lawyer from testifying in court regarding what occurred at a former public court proceeding when such testimony did not involve communications solely between an attorney and his client and the testimony concerned information that had become generally known. Turner v. Commonwealth, 58 Va. App. 567, 712 S.E.2d 28, 2011 Va. App. LEXIS 248 (2011).

Disqualification required. — Court granted defendant's motion to disqualify plaintiffs' counsel under Va. Sup. Ct. R. pt. 6, § II, R. 1.9(a) and 1.6 because it previously represented defendant in other matters where, inter alia, the cases were substantially related, the parties were essentially the same, and the allegations were inextricably intertwined. The most important factor in granting defendant's motion was that the present suit sought to prevent what the law firm was hired by defendant to accomplish, to collect money from the debtor's subsidiary and to collect a supplemental assessment from the debtor, by hindering, delaying, or preventing a settlement of the disputes between plaintiff and the debtor that was currently scheduled before the bankruptcy court for approval under Fed. R. Bankr. P. 9019. Sobel v. Sells (In re Gordon Props., LLC), 2013 Bankr. LEXIS 728 (Bankr. E.D. Va. Feb. 25, 2013).

CIRCUIT COURT OPINIONS

Disqualification test. — Landowners' current counsel was disqualified, based on counsel's prior representation of the opposing party's subsidiary, in a substantially related matter and an irrefutable presumption that the attorney had confidential information about the opposing party, given that both the subsidiary and its principal had the same interests. United Leasing Corp. v. Lehner, 75 Va. Cir. 18, 2008 Va. Cir. LEXIS 28 (Hanover County 2008).

Lack of substantial relationship between current action and prior representation. — Company's motion to disqualify a doctor's defense counsel on the basis of conflict was denied, because there was no relationship between the present litigation and past services rendered by the defense firm on behalf of the company which would constitute a conflict pursuant to Va. Sup. Ct. R., Pt. 6, § II, Rule 1.9, and there was no imputed conflict of interest pursuant to Va. Sup. Ct. R., Pt. 6, § II, Rule 1.10. Softwise, Inc. v. Goodrich, 62 Va. Cir. 301, 2003 Va. Cir. LEXIS 91 (Roanoke 2003).

No conflict of interest shown. — Former client's motion to disqualify a present client's counsel was denied because the mere fact that the present client's law firm had represented the former client in two totally unrelated matters over five years ago was insufficient for disqualification because no conflict of interest was shown. Jerome v. Farmer, 62 Va. Cir. 294, 2003 Va. Cir. LEXIS 159 (Chesterfield County 2003).

Developer's motion to disqualify opposing counsel's representation of a sanitation authority under Va. Sup. Ct. R. pt. 6, § II, R. 1.9(a) was denied, as insufficient evidence was presented that said counsel's representation of a former client would compromise its representation of the sanitation authority in the instant litigation; moreover, while those interests might have been adverse to those of the sanitation authority, anxiety or subjective judgment of a former client were not the basis for which the court could grant disqualification. Brookside Dev., L.L.C. v. Fauquier Water & Sanitation Auth., 68 Va. Cir. 76, 2005 Va. Cir. LEXIS 199 (Fauquier County 2005).

Commonwealth's motion to disqualify defense counsel under Va. Sup. Ct. R. pt. 6, § II, R. 1.9(c) was denied because although counsel represented a former client, who was involved in the underlying prosecution, such occurred seven years earlier, and counsel represented to the court that the former client's filed contained no impeachable information. Although criminal jury trial was an unpredictable thing and it was certainly possible that some unforeseen conflict could arise, the court did not believe that possibility justified depriving defendant of the assistance of counsel of his choice under the facts presented. Commonwealth v. Dudley, 78 Va. Cir. 242, 2009 Va. Cir. LEXIS 151 (Norfolk Mar. 24, 2009).

Plaintiff's attorney previously represented defendant in an unrelated matter. — Where the wife's attorney previously represented the husband in a personal injury matter, Va. Sup. Ct. R., pt. 6, § II, Rule 1.9(a) did not require the wife's attorney's withdrawal in the wife's action against the husband, as the husband's previous action was unrelated to the instant matter; the wife's attorney, however, had to be mindful of the mandate under Va. Sup. Ct. R., pt. 6, § II, Rule 1.9(c). Parker v. Parker, 61 Va. Cir. 670, 2002 Va. Cir. LEXIS 318 (Roanoke 2002).

Representation by former law firm partner of party opponent in substantially related matter. — Although a member of the wife's attorney's former law firm represented the husband in a substantially related matter, the husband's first divorce, the wife's attorney was not required to withdraw; the wife's attorney did not participate in the case, and the wife, who worked at the law firm, did not have access to the file. Parker v. Parker, 61 Va. Cir. 670, 2002 Va. Cir. LEXIS 318 (Roanoke 2002).

Disqualification required. — Law firm that represented both defendant's company and plaintiff was disqualified pursuant to Va. Sup. Ct. R. pt. 6, § II, R. 1.6, 1.9, and 1.13. Though there was no express attorney-client relationship between defendant, who was plaintiff's officer, and the firm's attorney, defendant had a reasonable expectation that what he told the attorney about plaintiff's claims against him would remain confidential. Arriba Corp. v. Bostic, 69 Va. Cir. 505, 2002 Va. Cir. LEXIS 464 (Norfolk 2002).

Because there was a "relatedness" in the current proceeding involving a business trust suing a corporation and an individual and a proceeding where the counsel for the business trust represented an alleged "dummy company" and there was a common thread of facts and issues that were identical or essentially the same, in addition to the high likelihood that the attorney acquired information about a "dummy company" during his prior representation that would assist him in the course of this litigation because he argued a directly contrary position in the previous case, counsel's representation of the business trust would violate Va. Sup. Ct. R. pt. 6, § II, R. 1.9. Lehner Family Bus. Trust v. United Leasing Corp., 71 Va. Cir. 150, 2006 Va. Cir. LEXIS 227 (Richmond 2006).

In a pending lawsuit between a buyer and a seller, because a law firm failed in its burden of communicating to the buyer that its prior representation had been terminated, and hence, its representation of the seller had commenced, and failed to clarify its relationship to the buyer, the buyer's motion to disqualify the law firm from representing the seller was granted. Comstock Lake Pelham, L.C. v. Clore Family, LLC, 74 Va. Cir. 35, 2007 Va. Cir. LEXIS 46 (Fairfax County 2007).

Rule 1.10. Imputed Disqualification: General Rule.

(a) While lawyers are associated in a firm, none of them shall knowingly represent a client when any one of them practicing alone would be prohibited from doing so by Rules 1.6, 1.7, 1.9, or 2.10(e).

(b) When a lawyer has terminated an association with a firm, the firm is not prohibited from thereafter representing a person with interests materially adverse to those of a client represented by the formerly associated lawyer and not currently represented by the firm, unless:

(1) the matter is the same or substantially related to that in which the formerly associated lawyer represented the client; and

(2) any lawyer remaining in the firm has information protected by Rules 1.6 and 1.9(c) that is material to the matter.

(c) A disqualification prescribed by this Rule may be waived by the affected client under the conditions stated in Rule 1.7.

(d) The imputed prohibition of improper transactions is governed by Rule 1.8(k).

(e) The disqualification of lawyers associated in a firm with former or current government lawyers is governed by Rule 1.11.

COMMENT

Definition of "Firm"

[1] Whether two or more lawyers constitute a firm as defined in the Terminology section can depend on the specific facts. For example, two practitioners who share office space and occasionally consult or assist each other ordinarily would not be regarded as constituting a firm. However, if they present themselves to the public in a way suggesting that they are a firm or conduct themselves as a firm, they should be regarded as a firm for the purposes of the Rules. The terms of any formal agreement between associated lawyers are relevant in determining whether they are a firm, as is the fact that they have mutual access to information concerning the clients they serve. Furthermore, it is relevant in doubtful cases to consider the underlying purpose of the Rule that is involved. A group of lawyers could be regarded as a firm for purposes of the Rule that the same lawyer should not represent opposing parties in litigation, while it

might not be so regarded for purposes of the Rule that information acquired by one lawyer is attributed to the other.

[1a] With respect to the law department of an organization, there is ordinarily no question that the members of the department constitute a firm within the meaning of the Rules of Professional Conduct. However, there can be uncertainty as to the identity of the client. For example, it may not be clear whether the law department of a corporation represents a subsidiary or an affiliated corporation, as well as the corporation by which the members of the department are directly employed. A similar question can arise concerning an unincorporated association and its local affiliates.

[1b] Similar questions can also arise with respect to lawyers in legal aid. Lawyers employed in the same unit of a legal service organization constitute a firm, but not necessarily those employed in separate units. As in the case of independent practitioners, whether the lawyers should be treated as associated with each other can depend on the particular rule that is involved, and on the specific facts of the situation.

[1c] Where a lawyer has joined a private firm after having represented the government, the situation is governed by Rule 1.11(b) and (c); where a lawyer represents the government after having served private clients, the situation is governed by Rule 1.11(d)(1). The individual lawyer involved is bound by the Rules generally, including Rules 1.6, 1.7 and 1.9.

[1d] Different provisions are thus made for movement of a lawyer from one private firm to another and for movement of a lawyer between a private firm and the government. The government is entitled to protection of its client confidences and, therefore, to the protections provided in Rules 1.6, 1.9 and 1.11. However, if the more extensive disqualification in Rule 1.10 were applied to former government lawyers, the potential effect on the government would be unduly burdensome. The government deals with all private citizens and organizations and, thus, has a much wider circle of adverse legal interests than does any private law firm. In these circumstances, the government's recruitment of lawyers would be seriously impaired if Rule 1.10 were applied to the government. On balance, therefore, the government is better served in the long run by the protections stated in Rule 1.11.

Principles of Imputed Disqualification

[2] The rule of imputed disqualification stated in paragraph (a) gives effect to the principle of loyalty to the client as it applies to lawyers who practice in a law firm. Such situations can be considered from the premise that a firm of lawyers is essentially one lawyer for purposes of the rules governing loyalty to the client, or from the premise that each lawyer is vicariously bound by the obligation of loyalty owed by each lawyer with whom the lawyer is associated. Paragraph (a) operates only among the lawyers currently associated in a firm. When a lawyer moves from one firm to another, the situation is governed by Rules 1.9(b) and 1.10(b).

[3 - 4] *ABA Model Rule* Comments not adopted.

[5] Rule 1.10(b) operates to permit a law firm, under certain circumstances, to represent a person with interests directly adverse to those of a client represented by a lawyer who formerly was associated with the firm. The Rule applies regardless of when the formerly associated lawyer represented the client. However, the law firm may not represent a person with interests adverse to those of a present client of the firm, which would violate Rule 1.7. Moreover, the firm may not represent the person where the matter is the same or substantially related to that in which the formerly associated lawyer represented the client and any other lawyer currently in the firm has material information protected by Rules 1.6 and 1.9(c).

Virginia Code Comparison

There was no direct counterpart to this Rule in the Virginia Code. DR 5-105(E) provided that "[i]f a lawyer is required to decline employment or to withdraw from employment under DR 5-105, no partner of his or his firm may accept or continue such employment."

Committee Commentary

The ABA Model Code contained a broadly inclusive imputation rule, prohibiting representation by a partner, associate, or any affiliated lawyer when a lawyer would be required to decline employment under any Disciplinary Rule. See ABA Model Code DR 5-105(D). The Virginia Code limited imputation to disqualification under DR 5-105. See Virginia Code DR 5-105(E). The Committee concluded that the provisions of the ABA Model Rule struck the appropriate balance between the confidentiality needs of clients and the professional needs of lawyers.

The amendment effective January 1, 2004, adopted September 24, 2003, substituted "Rules 1.6, 1.7, 1.9, or 2.10(e)" for "Rules 1.7, 1.8(c), 1.9 or 2.2" at the end of paragraph (a); and added paragraphs (d) and (e).

Law Review. — For article, "Professional Responsibility," see 43 U. Rich. L. Rev. 255 (2008).

CASE NOTES

Substantial relationship found. — In a patent infringement suit, plaintiff's law firm was disqualified under Va. Sup. Ct. Rules, Part 6, § II, R. 1.9 and 1.10 because there was a substantial relationship between prior and successive representation of a particular defendant due to the involvement in patent prosecution work for defendant by an attorney employed in plaintiff's law firm. Sunbeam Prods. v. Hamilton Beach Brands, Inc., 2010 U.S. Dist. LEXIS 74001 (E.D. Va. July 22, 2010).

Disqualification not justified. — Though counsel concurrently represented plaintiff in a separate action and the union in plaintiff's action against the union for eleven weeks, the conflict of interest did not justify disqualification from representation of the union but did justify referral to the Virginia State Bar for Va. Sup. Ct. R. pt. 6, § II, R. 1.7(a)(1) and 1.10(a) violations. Reese v. Va. Int'l Terminals, Inc., 2012 U.S. Dist. LEXIS 109372 (E.D. Va. Aug. 2, 2012).

Construction. — Va. Sup. Ct. R. pt. 6, § II, R. 1.10(a) (Rule 1.10(a)) is not a rule of strict liability. The use of "knowingly" in Rule 1.10(a) is not without purpose, but is a separate and distinct element of the Rule that must be proven before a violation can be imposed. Northam v. Va. State Bar, 285 Va. 429, 737 S.E.2d 905, 2013 Va. LEXIS 36 (Feb. 28, 2013).

CIRCUIT COURT OPINIONS

Lack of substantial relationship between current action and prior representation. — Company's motion to disqualify a doctor's defense counsel on the basis of conflict was denied, because there was no relationship between the present litigation and past services rendered by the defense firm on behalf of the company which would constitute a conflict pursuant to Va. Sup. Ct. R. Pt. 6, § II, R. 1.9, and there was no imputed conflict of interest pursuant to Va. Sup. Ct. R. Pt. 6, § II, R. 1.10. Softwise, Inc. v. Goodrich, 62 Va. Cir. 301, 2003 Va. Cir. LEXIS 91 (Roanoke 2003).

Rule 1.11. Special Conflicts of Interest for Former and Current Government Officers and Employees.

(a) A lawyer who holds public office shall not:

(1) use the public position to obtain, or attempt to obtain, a special advantage in legislative matters for the lawyer or for a client under circumstances where the lawyer knows or it is obvious that such action is not in the public interest;

(2) use the public position to influence, or attempt to influence, a tribunal to act in favor of the lawyer or of a client; or

(3) accept anything of value from any person when the lawyer knows or it is obvious that the offer is for the purpose of influencing the lawyer's action as a public official.

(b) Except as law may otherwise expressly permit, a lawyer shall not represent a private client in connection with a matter in which the lawyer participated personally and substantially as a public officer or employee, unless the private client and the appropriate government agency consent after consultation. No lawyer in a firm with which that lawyer is associated may knowingly undertake or continue representation in such a matter unless:

(1) the disqualified lawyer is screened from any participation in the matter and is apportioned no part of the fee therefrom; and

(2) written notice is promptly given to the appropriate government agency to enable it to ascertain compliance with the provisions of this Rule.

(c) Except as law may otherwise expressly permit, a lawyer having information that the lawyer knows is confidential government information about a person acquired when the lawyer was a public officer or employee, may not represent a private client whose interests are adverse to that person in a matter in which the information could be used to the material disadvantage of that person. A firm with which that lawyer is associated may undertake or continue representation in the matter only if the disqualified lawyer is screened from any participation in the matter and is apportioned no part of the fee therefrom.

(d) Except as law may otherwise expressly permit, a lawyer serving as a public officer or employee shall not:

(1) participate in a matter in which the lawyer participated personally and substantially while in private practice or nongovernmental employment, unless under applicable law no one is, or by lawful delegation may be, authorized to act in the lawyer's stead in the matter; or

(2) negotiate for private employment with any person who is involved as a party or as attorney for a party in a matter in which the lawyer is participating personally and substantially, except that a lawyer serving as a law clerk to a judge, other adjudicative officer, mediator or arbitrator may negotiate for private employment as permitted by Rule 1.12(b) and subject to the conditions stated in Rule 1.12(b).

(e) Paragraph (d) does not disqualify other lawyers in the disqualified lawyer's agency.

(f) As used in this Rule, the term "matter" includes:

(1) any judicial or other proceeding, application, request for a ruling or other determination, contract, claim, controversy, investigation, charge, accusation, arrest or other particular matter involving a specific party or parties; and

(2) any other matter covered by the conflict of interest rules of the appropriate government agency.

(g) As used in this Rule, the term "confidential government information" means information which has been obtained under governmental authority and which, at the time this Rule is applied, the government is prohibited by law from disclosing to the public or has a legal privilege not to disclose, and which is not otherwise available to the public.

COMMENT

[1] This Rule prevents a lawyer from exploiting public office for the advantage of the lawyer or a private client. A lawyer who is a public officer should not engage in activities in which his personal or professional interests are or foreseeably may be in conflict with official duties or obligations to the public.

[2] A lawyer representing a government agency, whether employed or specially retained by the government, is subject to the Rules of Professional Conduct, including the prohibition against representing adverse interests stated in Rule 1.7 and the protections afforded former clients in Rule 1.9. In addition, such a lawyer is subject to Rule 1.11 and to statutes and government regulations regarding conflict of interest. Such statutes and regulations may circumscribe the extent to which the government agency may give consent under this Rule.

[3] *ABA Model Rule* Comment not adopted.

[4] Where the successive clients are a public agency and a private client, the risk exists that power or discretion vested in public authority might be used for the special benefit of a private client. A lawyer should not be in a position where benefit to a private client might affect performance of the lawyer's professional functions on behalf of public authority. Also, unfair advantage could accrue to the private client by reason of access to confidential government information about the client's adversary obtainable only through the lawyer's government service. However, the rules governing lawyers presently or formerly employed by a government agency should not be so restrictive as to inhibit transfer of employment to and from the government. The government has a legitimate need to attract qualified lawyers as well as to maintain high ethical standards. The provisions for screening and waiver are necessary to prevent the disqualification rule from imposing too severe a deterrent against entering public service. The private client should be informed of the lawyer's prior relationship with a public agency at the time of engagement of the lawyer's services.

[5] When the client is an agency of one government, that agency should be treated as a private client for purposes of this Rule if the lawyer thereafter represents an agency of another government, as when a lawyer represents a city and subsequently is employed by a federal agency.

[6] Paragraphs (b)(1) and (c) do not prohibit a lawyer from receiving a salary or partnership share established by prior independent agreement. They prohibit directly relating the attorney's compensation to the fee in the matter in which the lawyer is disqualified.

[7] Paragraph (b)(2) does not require that a lawyer give notice to the government agency at a time when premature disclosure would injure the client; a requirement for premature disclosure might preclude engagement of the lawyer. Such notice is, however, required to be given as soon as practicable in order that the government agency will have a reasonable opportunity to ascertain that the lawyer is complying with Rule 1.11 and to take appropriate action if it believes the lawyer is not complying.

[8] Paragraph (c) operates only when the lawyer in question has knowledge of the information, which means actual knowledge; it does not operate with respect to information that merely could be imputed to the lawyer.

[9] Paragraphs (b) and (d) do not prohibit a lawyer from jointly representing a private party and a government agency when doing so is permitted by Rule 1.7 and is not otherwise prohibited by law.

Virginia Code Comparison

Paragraph (a) is identical to DR 8-101(A).

Paragraph (b) is substantially similar to DR 9-101(B), except that the latter used the terms "in which he had substantial responsibility while he was a public employee." The Rule also requires consent of both a current client and the former agency.

Paragraphs (c), (d), (e) [now (f)] and (f) [now (g)] have no counterparts in the Virginia Code.

Committee Commentary

The Committee believed that the ABA Model Rule provides more complete guidance regarding lawyers' movement between the public and private sectors. However, the Committee added the language of DR 8-101(A) as paragraph (a) in order to make this Rule a more complete statement regarding the particular responsibilities of lawyers who are public officials. Additionally, to make paragraph (b) consistent with similar provisions under Rule 1.9(a) and (b), the Committee modified the paragraph to require consent to representation by both the current client and the lawyer's former government agency.

The amendment effective January 1, 2004, adopted September 24, 2003, rewrote the rule heading.

The amendment effective January 4, 2010, adopted November 2, 2009, added subdivision (e) and redesignated former subdivisions (e) and (f) as (f) and (g); and deleted Paragraph [10] of the Comments.

Law Review. — For article, "Professional Responsibility," see 43 U. Rich. L. Rev. 255 (2008).

CASE NOTES

Attorney for the Commonwealth may not represent crime victim in civil action. — Even in jurisdictions in which the Attorney for the Commonwealth is permitted to engage in the part-time practice of law, he may not undertake the civil representation of a victim, or the family of a victim, of a crime whose perpetrator he must prosecute. Cantrell v. Commonwealth, 229 Va. 387, 329 S.E.2d 22 (1985), cert. denied, 496 U.S. 911, 110 S. Ct. 2600, 110 L. Ed. 2d 280 (1990) (decided under former DR 8-101).

Sufficient evidence of violation. — Where, as part of plea agreement, defendant's father agreed to make charitable contributions totaling $25,000 and where, at the direction of commonwealth's attorney who knew he would face a reelection campaign, defense counsel issued and delivered to commonwealth's attorney checks totaling nearly $25,000 payable to the various charities named by the commonwealth's attorney, and where the commonwealth's attorney never failed to let donee charity know that he had selected that charity as the donee of the gift, the commonwealth's attorney's carefully orchestrated scheme was designed to secure something of value for him—the possibility that members of the donee charities would express their gratitude in the form of political support in the forthcoming election. Accordingly, the evidence clearly supported the trial court's conclusion that the commonwealth's attorney violated subdivision (A)(3) of this rule. Morrissey v. Virginia State Bar, 248 Va. 334, 448 S.E.2d 615 (1994) (decided under former DR 8-101).

Disqualification of entire office unwarranted. — Where two attorneys, who formerly represented and had a connection with defendant, joined U.S. Attorney's Office and had no involvement in investigation since they had recused and had erected a "Chinese wall," there was no basis to disqualify the entire U.S. Attorney's Office. In re Grand Jury, 790 F. Supp. 109 (E.D. Va. 1992) (decided under former DR 9-101).

Continued representation by counsel would give appearance of impropriety. — Where government argued that an actual conflict of interest was present because members or employees of private law firm, which represented defendant, would be called to testify at defendant's trial regarding the cash payment of legal fees by a third-party unindicted co-conspirator as possible evidence of the existence of a drug conspiracy, where the government also argued that an actual conflict of interest existed because the private firm represented both defendant and an alleged member of conspiracy in a substantially related matter, and where firm argued that it could continue to represent defendant through his trial if the potential testimony of its members or employees could be stipulated, and if members or employees of the firm were forced to testify at trial, then the firm would disqualify itself at that point, continued representation by current counsel presented actual and potential conflicts of interest and would give the appearance of impropriety. United States v. Scott, 980 F. Supp. 165 (E.D. Va. 1997) (decided under former DR 9-101).

Rule 1.12. Former Judge or Arbitrator.

(a) Except as stated in paragraph (d), a lawyer shall not represent anyone in connection with a matter in which the lawyer participated personally and substantially as a judge, other adjudicative officer, arbitrator or a law clerk to such a person, unless all parties to the proceeding consent after consultation.

(b) A lawyer shall not negotiate for employment with any person who is involved as a party or as attorney for a party in a matter in which the lawyer is participating personally and substantially as a judge, other adjudicative officer or arbitrator. A lawyer serving as a law clerk to a judge, other adjudicative officer, or arbitrator may negotiate for employment with a party or attorney involved in a matter in which the clerk is participating personally and substantially, but only after the lawyer has notified the judge, other adjudicative officer, or arbitrator.

(c) If a lawyer is disqualified by paragraph (a), no lawyer in a firm with which that lawyer is associated may knowingly undertake or continue representation in the matter unless:

(1) the disqualified lawyer is timely screened from any participation in the matter and is apportioned no part of the fee therefrom; and

(2) written notice is promptly given to the parties and any appropriate tribunal to enable them to ascertain compliance with the provisions of this Rule.

(d) An arbitrator selected as a partisan of a party in a multimember arbitration panel is not prohibited from subsequently representing that party.

COMMENT

[1] This Rule generally parallels Rule 1.11. The term "personally and substantially" signifies that a judge who was a member of a multimember court, and thereafter left judicial office to practice law, is not prohibited from representing a client in a matter pending in the court, but in which the former judge did not participate. So also the fact that a former judge exercised administrative responsibility in a court does not prevent the former judge from acting as a lawyer in a matter where the judge had previously exercised remote or incidental administrative responsibility that did not affect the

merits. Compare the Comment to Rule 1.11. The term "adjudicative officer" includes such officials as judges pro tempore, referees, special masters, hearing officers and other parajudicial officers, and also lawyers who serve as part-time judges. Compliance Canons A (2), B (2) and C of the Virginia Code of Judicial Conduct provide that a part-time judge, judge pro tempore or retired judge recalled to active service, may not "act as a lawyer in any proceeding in which he served as a judge or in any other proceeding related thereto." Although phrased differently from this Rule, those rules correspond in meaning.

[2] Like former judges, lawyers who have served as arbitrators, may be asked to represent a client in a matter in which the lawyer participated personally and substantially. This Rule forbids such representation unless all of the parties to the proceedings give their consent after consultation. Other law or codes of ethics governing these roles may impose more stringent standards of personal or imputed disqualification.

[3] Although lawyers who serve as judges and arbitrators do not have information concerning the parties that is protected under Rule 1.6, they typically owe the parties an obligation of confidentiality under law or codes of ethics governing their roles. Thus, paragraph (c) provides that conflicts of the personally disqualified lawyer will be imputed to other lawyers in a law firm unless the conditions of paragraph (c) are met.

[4] *ABA Model Rule* Comment not adopted.

[5] Notice, including a description of the screened lawyer's representation and of the screening procedures employed, generally should be given as soon as practicable after the need for screening becomes apparent.

Virginia Code Comparison

Paragraph (a) is substantially similar to DR 9-101(A), which provided that a lawyer "shall not accept private employment in a matter upon the merits of which he has acted in a judicial capacity." Paragraph (a) differs, however, in that it is broader in scope and states more specifically the persons to whom it applies. There was no counterpart in the Virginia Code to paragraphs (b), (c) or (d).

With regard to arbitrators and mediators, EC 5-20 stated that "a lawyer [who] has undertaken to act as an impartial arbitrator or mediator ... should not thereafter represent in the dispute any of the parties involved." DR 9-101(A) did not permit a waiver of the disqualification applied to former judges by consent of the parties. However, DR 5-105(C) was similar in effect and could be construed to permit waiver.

Committee Commentary

The Committee adopted the ABA Model Rule essentially verbatim for former judges and arbitrators since it clearly provides more complete guidance to judicial officials than DR 9-101(A). However, the committee chose not to extend these provisions to mediators and other third-party neutrals, as those roles are distinguishable.

The amendment effective January 1, 2004, adopted September 24, 2003, deleted a comma following "other adjudicative officer" near the end of the first sentence of paragraph (b); and in paragraph (c)(2), inserted "parties and any" and substituted "them" for "it."

Rule 1.13. Organization as Client.

(a) A lawyer employed or retained by an organization represents the organization acting through its duly authorized constituents.

(b) If a lawyer for an organization knows that an officer, employee or other person associated with the organization is engaged in action, intends to act or refuses to act in a matter related to the representation that is a violation of a legal obligation to the organization, or a violation of law which reasonably might be imputed to the organization, and is likely to result in substantial injury to the organization, the lawyer shall proceed as is reasonably necessary in the best interest of the organization. In determining how to proceed, the lawyer shall give due consideration to the seriousness of the violation and its consequences, the scope and nature of the lawyer's representation, the responsibility in the organization and the apparent motivation of the person involved, the policies of the organization concerning such matters and any other relevant considerations. Any measures taken shall be designed to minimize disruption of the organization and the risk of revealing information relating to the representation to persons outside the organization. Such measures may include among others:

(1) asking for reconsideration of the matter;

(2) advising that a separate legal opinion on the matter be sought for presentation to appropriate authority in the organization;

(3) referring the matter to higher authority in the organization, including, if warranted by the seriousness of the matter, referral to the highest authority that can act in behalf of the organization as determined by applicable law.

(c) If, despite the lawyer's efforts in accordance with paragraph (b), the highest authority that can act on behalf of the organization insists upon action, or a refusal to act, that is clearly a violation of law and is likely to result in substantial injury to the organization, the lawyer may resign or may decline to represent the client in that matter in accordance with Rule 1.16.

(d) In dealing with an organization's directors, officers, employees, members, shareholders or other constituents, a lawyer shall explain the identity of the client when it is apparent that the organization's interests are adverse to those of the constituents with whom the lawyer is dealing.

(e) A lawyer representing an organization may also represent any of its directors, officers, employees, members, shareholders or other constituents, subject to the provisions of Rule 1.7. If the organization's consent to the dual representation is required by Rule 1.7, the consent shall be given by an appropriate official of the organization other than the individual who is to be represented, or by the shareholders.

COMMENT

The Entity as the Client

[1] An organizational client is a legal entity, but it cannot act except through its officers, directors, employees, shareholders and other constituents. These persons are referred to herein as the constituents of the corporate organizational client. The duties defined in this Comment apply equally to unincorporated associations. "Other constituents" as used in this Comment means the positions equivalent to officers, directors, employees and shareholders held by persons acting for organizational clients that are not corporations.

[2] When one of the constituents of an organizational client communicates with the organization's lawyer in that person's organizational capacity, the communication is protected by Rule 1.6. Thus, by way of example, if an organizational client requests its lawyer to investigate allegations of wrongdoing, interviews made in the course of that investigation between the lawyer and the client's employees or other constituents are covered by Rule 1.6. This does not mean, however, that constituents of an organizational client are the clients of the lawyer. The lawyer may not disclose to such constituents information relating to the representation except for disclosures explicitly or impliedly authorized by the organizational client in order to carry out the representation or as otherwise permitted by Rule 1.6.

[3] The decisions of constituents of the organization ordinarily must be accepted by the lawyer even if their utility or prudence is doubtful. Decisions concerning policy and operations, including ones entailing serious risk, are not as such in the lawyer's province. However, different considerations arise when the lawyer knows that the organization may be substantially injured by action of a constituent that is in violation of law. In such a circumstance, it may be reasonably necessary for the lawyer to ask the constituent to reconsider the matter. If that fails, or if the matter is of sufficient seriousness and importance to the organization, it may be reasonably necessary for the lawyer to take steps to have the matter reviewed by a higher authority in the organization. Substantial justification should exist for seeking review over the head of the constituent normally responsible for it. The stated policy of the organization may define circumstances and prescribe channels for such review, and a lawyer should encourage the formulation of such a policy. Even in the absence of organization policy, however, the lawyer may have an obligation to refer a matter to higher authority, depending on the seriousness of the matter and whether the constituent in question has apparent motives to act at variance with the organization's interest. Review by the chief executive officer or by the board of directors may be required when the matter is of importance commensurate with their authority. At some point it may be useful or essential to obtain an independent legal opinion.

[4] *ABA Model Rule* Comment not adopted.

[5] In an extreme case, it may be reasonably necessary for the lawyer to refer the matter to the organization's highest authority. Ordinarily, that is the board of directors or similar governing body. However, applicable law may prescribe that under certain conditions highest authority reposes elsewhere; for example, in the independent directors of a corporation.

Relation to Other Rules

[6] The authority and responsibility provided in paragraph (b) are concurrent with the authority and responsibility provided in other Rules. In particular, this Rule does not limit or expand the lawyer's responsibility under Rules 1.6, 1.8, 1.16, 3.3 or 4.1. If the lawyer's services are being used by an organization to further a crime or fraud by the organization, Rule 1.2(c) can be applicable.

[7-8] *ABA Model Rule* Comments not adopted.

Government Agency

[9] The duty defined in this Rule applies to government organizations. However, when the client is a governmental organization, a different balance may be appropriate between maintaining confidentiality and assuring that the wrongful official act is prevented or rectified, for public business is involved. In addition, duties of lawyers employed by the government or lawyers in military service may be defined by statutes and regulation. Therefore, defining precisely the identity of the client and prescribing the resulting obligations of such lawyers may be more difficult in the government context. Government lawyers, in many situations, are asked to represent diverse client interests. The government lawyer may be authorized by the organization to represent subordinate, internal clients in the interest of the organization subject to the other Rules relating to conflicts.

Although in some circumstances the client may be a specific agency, it is generally the government as a whole. For example, if the action or failure to act involves the head of a bureau, either the department of which the bureau is a part or the government as a whole may be the client for purpose of this Rule. Moreover, in a matter involving the conduct of government officials, a government lawyer may have authority to question such conduct more extensively than that of a lawyer for a private organization in similar circumstances. This Rule does not limit that authority. See note on Scope.

Clarifying the Lawyer's Role

[10] When the organization's interest may be or become adverse to those of one or more of its constituents, the lawyer should advise any constituent, whose interest the lawyer finds adverse to that of the organization of the conflict or potential conflict of interest, that the lawyer cannot represent such constituent, and that such person may wish to obtain independent representation. Care must be taken to assure that the individual understands that, when there is such adversity of interest, the lawyer for the organization cannot provide legal representation for that constituent individual, and that discussions between the lawyer for the organization and the individual may not be privileged.

[11] Whether such a warning should be given by the lawyer for the organization to any constituent individual may turn on the facts of each case.

Dual Representation

[12] Paragraph (e) recognizes that a lawyer for an organization may also represent individuals within the organization. When an organization's lawyer is assigned or authorized to represent such an individual, the lawyer has an attorney-client relationship with both that individual and the organization. Accordingly, the lawyer's representation of both is controlled by the confidentiality and conflicts provisions of these Rules.

Derivative Actions

[13] Under generally prevailing law, the shareholders or members of a corporation may bring suit to compel the directors to perform their legal obligations in the supervision of the organization. Members of unincorporated associations have essentially the same right. Such an action may be brought nominally by the organization, but usually is, in fact, a legal controversy over management of the organization.

[14] The question can arise whether counsel for the organization may defend such an action. The proposition that the organization is the lawyer's client does not alone resolve the issue. Most derivative actions are a normal incident of an organization's affairs, to be defended by the organization's lawyer like any other suit. However, if the claim involves serious charges of wrongdoing by those in control of the organization, a conflict may arise between the lawyer's duty to the organization and the lawyer's relationship with the board. In those circumstances, Rule 1.7 governs who should represent the directors and the organization.

Virginia Code Comparison

There was no direct counterpart to this Rule in the Disciplinary Rules of the Virginia Code. EC 5-18 stated that a "lawyer employed or retained by a corporation or similar entity owes his allegiance to the entity and not to a stockholder, director, officer, employee, representative, or other person connected with the entity. In advising the entity, a lawyer should keep paramount its interests and the lawyer's professional judgment should not be influenced by the personal desires of any person or organization. Occasionally, a lawyer for an entity is requested by a stockholder, director, officer, employee, representative, or other person connected with the entity to represent the individual in an individual capacity; in such case the lawyer may serve the individual only if the lawyer is convinced that differing interests are not present." EC 5-24 stated that although a lawyer "may be employed by a business corporation with non-lawyers serving as directors or officers, and they necessarily have the right to make decisions of business policy, a lawyer must decline to accept direction of his professional judgment from any layman." DR 5-106(B) provided that a lawyer "shall not permit a person who ... employs ... him to render legal services for another to direct or regulate his professional judgment in rendering such legal services."

Committee Commentary

The Committee adopted this Rule because it directly addresses matters only implicitly addressed in Ethical Considerations of the Virginia Code.

The amendment effective January 1, 2004, adopted September 24, 2003, inserted "for" in paragraph (b)(1).

CIRCUIT COURT OPINIONS

Reasonable expectation of confidentiality. — Law firm that represented both defendant's company and plaintiff was disqualified pursuant to Va. Sup. Ct. R. pt. 6, § II, R. 1.6, 1.9, and 1.13. Though there was no express attorney-client relationship between defendant, who was plaintiff's officer, and the firm's attorney, defendant had a reasonable expectation that what he told the attorney about plaintiff's claims against him would remain confidential. Arriba Corp. v. Bostic, 69 Va. Cir. 505, 2002 Va. Cir. LEXIS 464 (Norfolk 2002).

When an attorney became aware of ill will among plaintiff's principals, it was his duty to tell defendant, plaintiff's officer and director, that he represented plaintiff, not him, and that he should not discuss matters related to plaintiff. His failure to do so, and defendant's reasonable expectation that his communications would be confidential, mandated the disqualification of the attorney's firm. Arriba Corp. v. Bostic, 69 Va. Cir. 505, 2002 Va. Cir. LEXIS 464 (Norfolk 2002).

Rule 1.14. Client With Impairment.

(a) When a client's capacity to make adequately considered decisions in connection with a representation is diminished, whether because of minority, mental impairment or some other reason, the lawyer shall, as far as reasonably possible, maintain a normal client-lawyer relationship with the client.

(b) When the lawyer reasonably believes that the client has diminished capacity, is at risk of substantial physical, financial or other harm unless action is taken and cannot adequately act in the client's own interest, the lawyer may take reasonably necessary protective action, including consulting with individuals or entities that have the ability to take action to protect the client and, in appropriate cases, seeking the appointment of a guardian ad litem, conservator or guardian.

(c) Information relating to the representation of a client with diminished capacity is protected by Rule 1.6. When taking protective action pursuant to paragraph (b), the lawyer is impliedly authorized under Rule 1.6(a) to reveal information about the client, but only to the extent reasonably necessary to protect the client's interests.

COMMENT

[1] The normal client-lawyer relationship is based on the assumption that the client, when properly advised and assisted, is capable of making decisions about important matters. When the client is a minor or suffers from a diminished mental capacity, however, maintaining the ordinary client-lawyer relationship may not be possible in all respects. In particular, an incapacitated person may have no power to make legally binding decisions. Nevertheless, a client with diminshed capacities often has the ability to understand, deliberate upon, and reach conclusions about matters affecting the client's own well-being. For example, children as young as five or six years of age, and certainly those of ten or twelve, are regarded as having opinions that are entitled to weight in legal proceedings concerning their custody. So also, it is recognized that some persons of advanced age can be quite capable of handling routine financial matters while needing special legal protection concerning major transactions.

[2] The fact that a client suffers a disability does not diminish the lawyer's obligation to treat the client with attention and respect. If the person has no guardian or legal representative, the lawyer often must act as de facto guardian. Even if the person does have a legal representative, the lawyer should as far as possible accord the represented person the status of client, particularly in maintaining communication.

[3] *ABA Model Rule* Comment not adopted.

[4] If the client has a legal representative, the lawyer should ordinarily look to the representative for decisions on behalf of the client. If there is no legal representative, the lawyer should seek such an appointment where it would serve the client's best interests. Thus, if a disabled client has substantial property that should be sold for the client's benefit, effective completion of the transaction ordinarily requires appointment of a legal representative. In many circumstances, however, appointment of a legal representative may be expensive or traumatic for the client. Evaluation of these considerations is a matter of professional judgment on the lawyer's part. If the lawyer represents the guardian as distinct from the ward, and is aware that the guardian is acting adversely to the ward's interest, the lawyer may have an obligation to prevent or rectify the guardian's misconduct. See Rule 1.2(d).

Disclosure of the Client's Condition

[5-7] *ABA Model Rule* Comments not adopted.

[8] Court Rules generally provide that minors or persons suffering mental disability shall be represented by a guardian or next friend if they do not have a guardian. However, disclosure of the client's disability can adversely affect the client's interests. For example, raising the question of disability could, in some circumstances, lead to proceedings for involuntary commitment. The lawyer's position in such cases is an unavoidably difficult one. The lawyer may seek guidance from an appropriate diagnostician.

Virginia Code Comparison

There was no direct counterpart to this Rule in the Disciplinary Rules of the Virginia Code. EC 7-11 stated that the "responsibilities of a lawyer may vary according to the intelligence, experience, mental condition or age of a client. . . . Examples include the representation of an illiterate or an incompetent. . . ." EC 7-12 stated that "[a]ny mental or physical condition of a client that renders him incapable of making a considered judgment on his own behalf casts additional responsibilities upon his lawyer. Where an incompetent is acting through a guardian or other legal representative, a lawyer must look to such representative for those decisions which are normally the prerogative of the client to make. If a client under disability has no legal representative, his lawyer may be compelled in court proceedings to make decisions on behalf of the client. If the client is capable of understanding the matter in question or of contributing to the advancement of his interests, regardless of whether he is legally disqualified from performing certain acts, the lawyer should obtain from him all possible aid. If the disability of a client and the lack of a legal representative compel the lawyer to make decisions for his client, the lawyer should consider all circumstances then prevailing and act with care to safeguard and advance the interests of his client. But obviously a lawyer cannot perform any act or make any decision which the law requires his client to perform or make, either acting for himself if competent, or by a duly constituted representative if legally incompetent."

Committee Commentary

The Committee adopted this Rule because it directly addresses matters only implicitly addressed in Ethical Considerations of the Virginia Code.

The amendment effective January 1, 2004, adopted September 24, 2003, rewrote the rule.

Law Review. — For article, "Professional Responsibility," see 39 U. Rich. L. Rev. 315 (2004). For article, "Professional Responsibility," see 43 U. Rich. L. Rev. 255 (2008).

Rule 1.15. Safekeeping Property.

(a) *Depositing Funds.* — (1) All funds received or held by a lawyer or law firm on behalf of a client or a third party, or held by a lawyer as a fiduciary, other than reimbursement of advances for costs and expenses, shall be deposited in one or more identifiable trust accounts or placed in a safe deposit box or other place of safekeeping as soon as practicable.

(2) For lawyers or law firms located in Virginia, a lawyer trust account shall be maintained only at a financial institution approved by the Virginia State Bar, unless otherwise expressly directed in writing by the client for whom the funds are being held.

(3) No funds belonging to the lawyer or law firm shall be deposited or maintained therein except as follows:

(i) funds reasonably sufficient to pay service or other charges or fees imposed by the financial institution or to maintain a required minimum balance to avoid the imposition of service fees, provided the funds deposited are no more than necessary to do so; or

(ii) funds in which two or more persons (one of whom may be the lawyer) claim an interest shall be held in the trust account until the dispute is resolved and there is an accounting and severance of their interests. Any portion finally determined to belong to the lawyer or law firm shall be promptly withdrawn from the trust account.

(b) *Specific Duties.* — A lawyer shall:

(1) promptly notify a client of the receipt of the client's funds, securities, or other properties;

(2) identify and label securities and properties of a client, or those held by a lawyer as a fiduciary, promptly upon receipt;

(3) maintain complete records of all funds, securities, and other properties of a client coming into the possession of the lawyer and render appropriate accountings to the client regarding them;

(4) promptly pay or deliver to the client or another as requested by such person the funds, securities, or other properties in the possession of the lawyer that such person is entitled to receive; and

(5) not disburse funds or use property of a client or of a third party with a valid lien or assignment without their consent or convert funds or property of a client or third party, except as directed by a tribunal.

(c) *Record-Keeping Requirements.* — A lawyer shall, at a minimum, maintain the following books and records demonstrating compliance with this Rule:

(1) Cash receipts and disbursements journals for each trust account, including entries for receipts, disbursements, and transfers, and also including, at a minimum: an identification of the client matter; the date of the transaction; the name of the payor or payee; and the manner in which trust funds were received, disbursed, or transferred from an account.

(2) A subsidiary ledger containing a separate entry for each client, other person, or entity from whom money has been received in trust.

The ledger should clearly identify:

(i) the client or matter, including the date of the transaction and the payor or payee and the means or methods by which trust funds were received, disbursed or transferred; and

(ii) any unexpended balance.

(3) In the case of funds or property held by a lawyer as a fiduciary, the required books and records shall include an annual summary of all receipts and disbursements and changes in assets comparable in detail to an accounting that would be required of a court-supervised fiduciary in the same or similar capacity, including all source documents sufficient to substantiate the annual summary.

(4) All records subject to this Rule shall be preserved for at least five calendar years after termination of the representation or fiduciary responsibility.

(d) *Required Trust Accounting Procedures.* — In addition to the requirements set forth in Rule 1.15 (a) through (c), the following minimum trust accounting procedures are applicable to all trust accounts:

(1) Insufficient Fund Reporting. All accounts are subject to the requirements governing insufficient fund check reporting as set forth in the Virginia State Bar Approved Financial Institution Agreement.

(2) Deposits. All trust funds received shall be deposited intact. Mixed trust and non-trust funds shall be deposited intact into the trust fund and the non-trust portion shall be withdrawn upon the clearing of the mixed fund deposit instrument. All such deposits should include a detailed deposit slip or record that sufficiently identifies each item.

(3) Reconciliations.

(i) At least quarterly, a reconciliation shall be made that reflects the trust account balance for each client, person or other entity.

(ii) A monthly reconciliation shall be made of the cash balance that is derived from the cash receipts journal, cash disbursements journal, the trust account checkbook balance, and the trust account bank statement balance.

(iii) At least quarterly, a reconciliation shall be made that reconciles the cash balance from (d)(3)(ii) above and the subsidiary ledger balance from (d)(3)(i).

(iv) Reconciliations must be approved by a lawyer in the law firm.

(4) The purpose of all receipts and disbursements of trust funds reported in the trust journals and ledgers shall be fully explained and supported by adequate records.

COMMENT

[1] A lawyer should hold property of others with the care required of a professional fiduciary. Securities should be kept in a safe deposit box, except when some other form of safekeeping is warranted by special circumstances. For purposes of this Rule, the term "fiduciary" includes personal representative, trustee, receiver, guardian, committee, custodian, and attorney-in-fact. All property that is the property of clients or third persons should be kept separate from the lawyer's business and personal property and, if monies, in one or more trust accounts. Separate trust accounts may be warranted when administering estate monies or acting in similar fiduciary capacities.

[2] Separation of the funds of a client from those of the lawyer not only serves to protect the client but also avoids even the appearance of impropriety and, therefore, commingling of such funds should be avoided.

[2a] In relation to (b)(5), consent can be inferred from the engagement agreement or any consequential agreement between the lawyer and the client regarding the disbursement of fees, i.e., when earned fees are routinely withdrawn from the lawyer's trust account upon an accounting to the client, when costs and expenses of litigation are routinely withdrawn, or when other fees/costs or expenses are agreed upon in advance.

[3] Lawyers often receive funds from third parties from which the lawyer's fee will be paid. If there is risk that the client may divert the funds without paying the fee, the lawyer is not required to remit the portion from which the fee is to be paid. However, a lawyer may not hold funds to coerce a client into accepting the lawyer's contention. The disputed portion of the funds should be kept in trust and the lawyer should suggest means for prompt resolution of the dispute, such as arbitration or mediation. The undisputed portion of the funds shall be promptly distributed.

[4] Paragraphs (b)(4) and (b)(5) do not impose an obligation upon the lawyer to protect funds on behalf of the client's general creditors who have no valid claim to an interest in the specific funds or property in the lawyer's possession. However, a lawyer may be in possession of property or funds claimed both by the lawyer's client and a third person; for example, a previous lawyer of the client claiming a lien on the client's recovery or a person claiming that the property deposited with the lawyer was taken or withheld unlawfully from that person. Additionally, a lawyer may have a duty under applicable law to protect such third-party claims against wrongful interference by the client, and accordingly may refuse to surrender the property to the client. For example, if a lawyer has actual knowledge of a third party's lawful claim to an interest in the specific funds held on behalf of a client, then by virtue of a statutory lien (e.g., medical, workers' compensation, attorneys' lien, a valid assignment executed by the client, or a lien on the subject property created by a recorded deed of trust) the lawyer has a duty to secure the funds claimed by the third party. Under the above-described circumstances, paragraphs (b)(4) and (b)(5) require the lawyer either to deliver the funds or property to the third party or, if a dispute to the third party's claim exists, to safeguard the contested property or funds until the dispute is resolved. If the client has a non-frivolous dispute with the third party's claim, then the lawyer cannot release those funds without the agreement of all parties involved or a court determination of who is entitled to receive them, such as an interpleader action. A lawyer does not violate paragraphs (b)(4) and (b)(5) if he has acted reasonably and in good faith to determine the validity of a third-party's claim or lien.

[5] The obligations of a lawyer under this Rule are independent of those arising from activity other than rendering legal services. For example, a lawyer who serves as an escrow agent is governed by the applicable law relating to fiduciaries even though the lawyer does not render legal services in the transaction.

[6] Nothing in this Rule is intended to prohibit an attorney from using electronic checking for his trust account so long as all requirements in this Rule are fulfilled. It is the lawyer's responsibility to assure that complete and accurate records of the receipt and disbursement of entrusted property are maintained in accordance with this Rule. Many businesses are now converting paper checks to automated clearinghouse (ACH) debits. Authorized ACH debits that are electronic transfers of funds (in which no checks are involved) are allowed provided

the lawyer maintains a record of the transaction as required by this Rule. The record, whether consisting of the instructions or authorization to debit the account, a record or receipt from the financial institution, or the lawyer's independent record of the transaction, must show the amount, date, recipient of the transfer or disbursement, and the name of the client or other person to whom the funds belong.

Prior Rule Comparison

This rule is substantially the same as the original Rule 1.15 adopted January 1, 2000 except that the language has been substantially simplified for ease of understanding and the portions regarding the Financial Institutions duties redacted as they are appropriately incorporated into the "Trust Account Notification Agreement" signed by all Virginia-approved financial institutions.

Committee Commentary

The Committee chose to modify the rule for ease of understanding and enforcement with no substantive changes to a lawyer's safekeeping property and record-keeping requirements.

The amendment effective January 1, 2004, adopted September 24, 2003, deleted "subsidiary ledger" at the beginning of paragraph (e)(1)(iii); substituted "paragraph" for "subsection" in paragraphs (e)(1)(v) and (e)(2)(iii); deleted "subsection" preceding "(i)" in paragraph (e)(2)(ii); and rewrote the second paragraph of paragraph (f)(1)(ii).

The amendment effective June 21, 2011, adopted June 21, 2011, rewrote the Rule.

Law Review. — For article, "Professional Responsibility," see 45 U. Rich. L. Rev. 347 (2010).

CASE NOTES

This rule was promulgated to protect third parties as well as clients. Pickus v. Virginia State Bar, 232 Va. 5, 348 S.E.2d 202 (1986) (decided under former DR 9-102).

When suspension of license appropriate. — Suspension is generally appropriate when a lawyer knows or should know that he is dealing improperly with client property. Delk v. Virginia State Bar, 233 Va. 187, 355 S.E.2d 558 (1987) (decided under former DR 9-102).

Clear and convincing evidence supported the Board's determination that the attorney in one case violated the professional conduct rule about handling client funds, Va. Sup. Ct. R. pt. 6, § II, R. 1.15(a)(2), by putting the client's retainer in a trust account and almost immediately withdrawing those funds when they had not been earned, and in a second case violated rules regarding client communication and termination of representation, Va. Sup. Ct. R. pt. 6, § II, R. 1.4(a), (b), and (c), and Va. Sup. Ct. R. pt. 6, § II, R. 1.16(d), respectively, by not keeping the clients informed about the status of their case and not informing them when the attorney stopped representing them. As a result, an 18-month suspension of the attorney's law license was warranted. Green v. Va. State Bar, 278 Va. 162, 677 S.E.2d 227, 2009 Va. LEXIS 67 (2009).

Misappropriation of client funds. — Attorney violated Va. Sup. Ct. R. pt. 6, § II, R. 1.15 because, although he was paid to file a habeas corpus petition on behalf of a client, he did not file the petition, he refused to refund the fee, and he claimed that his associate was actually retained to file the petition. Green v. Va. State Bar ex rel. Seventh Dist. Comm., 274 Va. 775, 652 S.E.2d 118, 2007 Va. LEXIS 134 (2007).

Attorney violated Va. Sup. Ct. R. pt. 6, § II, R. 1.15 because he was paid in advance to represent a client in a divorce matter, immediately removed the money from his trust account before little, if any, work was done, worked on the case sporadically, and did not respond to a request for itemization of his work after his services were terminated. Green v. Va. State Bar ex rel. Seventh Dist. Comm., 274 Va. 775, 652 S.E.2d 118, 2007 Va. LEXIS 134 (2007).

"Funds" is not confined to items such as money or cash. El-Amin v. Virginia State Bar ex rel. Third Dist. Committee, 257 Va. 608, 514 S.E.2d 163 (1999) (decided under former DR 9-102).

Where attorney held client's car as a bailee for the purpose of securing the payment of legal fees to be incurred in the future by the client, and attorney converted the car into a credit which he received on the purchase of his new car, the credit represented the retainer fee and it became a "fund " set aside for a specific purpose. Therefore, the attorney had an obligation to deposit the funds. El-Amin v. Virginia State Bar ex rel. Third Dist. Committee, 257 Va. 608, 514 S.E.2d 163 (1999) (decided under former DR 9-102).

Moral turpitude need not be shown for suspension of license. — It is not necessary in a disciplinary proceeding to show that moral turpitude exists before a lawyer's license may be suspended for mishandling client funds. Whether the attorney's failure to pay the association resulted from mere inadvertence, or from intentional wrongdoing, is immaterial. Delk v. Virginia State Bar, 233 Va. 187, 355 S.E.2d 558 (1987) (decided under former DR 9-102).

Loss of money by a client is not a prerequisite to suspension of an attorney's license for mishandling the client's funds. Delk v. Virginia State Bar, 233 Va. 187, 355 S.E.2d 558 (1987) (decided under former DR 9-102).

Closing attorney represents all parties where no other attorney involved. — The lending institutions were more than third parties in their relationship with the closing attorney, where the institutions were not represented by their own attorneys, so he acted alone in closing the loans in question. When a lawyer acts as a closing or settlement attorney and no other lawyer is involved, the closing or settlement attorney represents all the parties and, in this limited sense, all the parties are his clients. In such a situation, the settlement attorney assumes the duties of a fiduciary and must properly handle and dispose of any funds not his own which he may receive in connection with the settlement. Pickus v. Virginia State Bar, 232 Va. 5, 348 S.E.2d 202 (1986) (decided under former DR 9-102).

Making loans from trust account. — An attorney who makes loans from a trust account, obviously treating the money as his own, violates this rule. Cogdill v. First Dist. Comm., 221 Va. 376, 269 S.E.2d 391 (1980) (decided under former DR 9-102).

Retainer fee. — Where debtor-in-possession, authorized to manage its affairs under 11 U.S.C.S. § 1107, sought to employ general counsel, pursuant to 11 U.S.C.S. § 327, the applicant was required to disclose the compensation paid, under 11 U.S.C.S. § 329(a), and show that it waived any conflicting claim as a pre-petition creditor of the debtor. The retainer fee had to comply with Va. Sup. Ct. R. pt. 6, § II, R. 1.15(a)(2), 1.16(d), and the authorization to settle claims could not conflict with Va. Sup. Ct. R. pt. 6, § II, R. 1.2. In re Circle T Pipeline, Inc., 2011 Bankr. LEXIS 2490 (Bankr. W.D. Va. Apr. 27, 2011).

Rule 1.16. Declining Or Terminating Representation.

(a) Except as stated in paragraph (c), a lawyer shall not represent a client or, where representation has commenced, shall withdraw from the representation of a client if:

(1) the representation will result in violation of the Rules of Professional Conduct or other law;

(2) the lawyer's physical or mental condition materially impairs the lawyer's ability to represent the client; or

(3) the lawyer is discharged.

(b) Except as stated in paragraph (c), a lawyer may withdraw from representing a client if withdrawal can be accomplished without material adverse effect on the interests of the client, or if:

(1) the client persists in a course of action involving the lawyer's services that the lawyer reasonably believes is illegal or unjust;

(2) the client has used the lawyer's services to perpetrate a crime or fraud;

(3) a client insists upon pursuing an objective that the lawyer considers repugnant or imprudent;

(4) the client fails substantially to fulfill an obligation to the lawyer regarding the lawyer's services and has been given reasonable warning that the lawyer will withdraw unless the obligation is fulfilled;

(5) the representation will result in an unreasonable financial burden on the lawyer or has been rendered unreasonably difficult by the client; or

(6) other good cause for withdrawal exists.

(c) In any court proceeding, counsel of record shall not withdraw except by leave of court after compliance with notice requirements pursuant to applicable Rules of Court. In any other matter, a lawyer shall continue representation notwithstanding good cause for terminating the representation, when ordered to do so by a tribunal.

(d) Upon termination of representation, a lawyer shall take steps to the extent reasonably practicable to protect a client's interests, such as giving reasonable notice to the client, allowing time for employment of other counsel, refunding any advance payment of fee that has not been earned and handling records as indicated in paragraph (e).

(e) All original, client-furnished documents and any originals of legal instruments or official documents which are in the lawyer's possession (wills, corporate minutes, etc.) are the property of the client and, therefore, upon termination of the representation, those items shall be returned within a reasonable time to the client or the client's new counsel upon request, whether or not the client has paid the fees and costs owed the lawyer. If the lawyer wants to keep a copy of such original documents, the lawyer must incur the cost of duplication. Also upon termination, the client, upon request, must also be provided within a reasonable time copies of the following documents from the lawyer's file, whether or not the client has paid the fees and costs owed the lawyer: lawyer/client and lawyer/third-party communications; the lawyer's copies of client-furnished documents (unless the originals have been returned to the client pursuant to this paragraph); transcripts, pleadings and discovery responses; working and final drafts of legal instruments, official documents, investigative reports, legal memoranda, and other attorney work product documents prepared or collected for the client in the course of the representation; research materials; and bills previously submitted to the client. Although the lawyer may bill and seek to collect from the client the costs associated with making a copy of these materials, the lawyer may not use the client's refusal to pay for such materials as a basis to refuse the client's request. The lawyer, however, is not required under this Rule to provide the client copies of billing records and documents intended only for internal use, such as memoranda prepared by the lawyer discussing conflicts of interest, staffing considerations, or difficulties arising from the lawyer-client relationship. The lawyer has met his or her obligation under this paragraph by furnishing these items one time at client request upon termination; provision of multiple copies is not required. The lawyer has not met his or her obligation under this paragraph by the mere provision of copies of documents on an item-by-item basis during the course of the representation.

COMMENT

[1] A lawyer should not accept or continue representation in a matter unless it can be performed competently, promptly, without improper conflict of interest and to completion.

Mandatory Withdrawal

[2] A lawyer ordinarily must decline or withdraw from representation if the client demands that the lawyer engage in conduct that is illegal or violates the Rules of Professional Conduct or other law. The lawyer is not obliged to decline or withdraw simply because the client suggests such a course of conduct; a client may make such a suggestion in the hope that a lawyer will not be constrained by a professional obligation.

[3] When a lawyer has been appointed to represent a client, withdrawal ordinarily requires approval of the appointing authority. See also Rule 6.2. Difficulty may be encountered if withdrawal is based on the client's demand that the lawyer engage in unprofessional conduct. The court may wish an explanation for the withdrawal, while the lawyer may be bound to keep confidential the facts that would constitute such an explanation. The lawyer's statement that professional considerations require termination of the representation ordinarily should be accepted as sufficient.

Discharge

[4] A client has a right to discharge a lawyer at any time, with or without cause. Where future dispute about the withdrawal may be anticipated, it may be advisable to prepare a written statement reciting the circumstances.

[5] Whether a client can discharge appointed counsel may depend on applicable law. A client seeking to do so should be given a full explanation of the consequences. These consequences may include a decision by the appointing authority that appointment of successor counsel is unjustified, thus requiring the client to proceed pro se.

[6] If the client is mentally incompetent, the client may lack the legal capacity to discharge the lawyer, and in any event the discharge may be seriously adverse to the client's interests. The lawyer should make special effort to help the client consider the consequences and, in an extreme case, may initiate proceedings for a conservatorship or similar protection of the client. See Rule 1.14.

Optional Withdrawal

[7] A lawyer may withdraw from representation in some circumstances. The lawyer has the option to withdraw if it can be accomplished without material adverse effect on the client's interests. Withdrawal is also justified if the client persists in a course of action that the lawyer reasonably believes is illegal or unjust, for a lawyer is not required to be associated with such conduct even if the lawyer does not further it. Withdrawal is also permitted if the lawyer's services were misused in the past even if that would materially prejudice the client. The lawyer also may withdraw where the client insists on a repugnant or imprudent objective.

[8] A lawyer may withdraw if the client refuses to abide by the terms of an agreement relating to the representation, such as an agreement concerning fees or court costs or an agreement limiting the objectives of the representation.

Assisting the Client upon Withdrawal

[9] Even if the lawyer has been unfairly discharged by the client, a lawyer must take all reasonable steps to mitigate the consequences to the client. Whether or not a lawyer for an organization may under certain unusual circumstances have a legal obligation to the organization after withdrawing or being discharged by the organization's highest authority is beyond the scope of these Rules.

Retention of Client Papers or File When Client Fails or Refuses to Pay Fees/Expenses Owed to Lawyer

[10] Paragraph (e) eschews a "prejudice" standard in favor of a more objective and easily-applied rule governing specific kinds of documents in the lawyer's files.

[11] The requirements of paragraph (e) should not be interpreted to require disclosure of materials where the disclosure is prohibited by law.

Virginia Code Comparison

Paragraph (a) is substantially the same as DR 2-108(A).

Paragraph (b) is substantially similar to DR 2-108(B) which provided that a lawyer "may withdraw from representing a client if: (1) Withdrawal can be effected without material prejudice to the client; or (2) The client persists in a course of conduct involving the lawyer's services that the lawyer reasonably believes is illegal or unjust; or (3) The client fails to fulfill an obligation to the lawyer regarding the lawyer's services and such failure continues after reasonable notice to the client; or (4) The representation will result in an unreasonable financial burden on the lawyer or has been rendered unreasonably difficult by the client."

Paragraph (c) is identical to DR 2-108(C).

Paragraph (d) is based on DR 2-108(D), but does not address documents in the lawyer's files (which are handled under paragraph (e).

Paragraph (e) is new.

Committee Commentary

The provisions of DR 2-108 of the Virginia Code derived more from ABA Model Rule 1.16 than from its counterpart in the ABA Model Code, DR 2-110. Accordingly, the Committee generally adopted the ABA Model Rule, but substituted the "illegal or unjust" language from DR 2-108(B)(2) for the "criminal or fraudulent" language of the ABA Model Rule. Additionally, the Committee substituted the language of DR 2-108(C) for that of paragraph (c) of the ABA Model Rule to make it clear that a lawyer, in circumstances involving court proceedings, has an affirmative duty to request leave of court to withdraw. The Committee recommended paragraph (e) instead of a "prejudice" standard as being more easily understood and applied by lawyers.

The amendment effective January 1, 2004, adopted September 24, 2003, in paragraph (e), inserted "therefore, upon termination of the representation, those items," "within a reasonable time" and "or the client's new counsel" in the first sentence; inserted "also upon termination, the client" preceding, and deleted "the client" following, "upon request," inserted "within a reasonable time," inserted "transcripts" and "or collected" in the third sentence; and added the sixth sentence.

Law Review. — For article, "Professional Responsibility," see 39 U. Rich. L. Rev. 315 (2004). For essay, "A Distinction Without a Difference? An Examination of the Legal and Ethical Difference Between Asset Protection and Fraudulent Transfers Under Virginia Law," see 47 U. Rich. L. Rev. 381 (2012).

CASE NOTES

Communicating termination of representation to client. — Clear and convincing evidence supported the Board's determination that the attorney in one case violated the professional conduct rule about handling client funds, Va. Sup. Ct. R. pt. 6, § II, R. 1.15(a)(2), by putting the client's retainer in a trust account and almost immediately withdrawing those funds when they had not been earned, and in a second case violated rules regarding client communication and termination of representation, Va. Sup. Ct. R. pt. 6, § II, R. 1.4(a), (b), and (c), and Va. Sup. Ct. R. pt. 6, § II, R. 1.16(d), respectively, by not keeping the clients informed about the status of their case and not informing them when the attorney stopped representing them. As a result, an 18 month suspension of the attorney's law license was warranted. Green v. Va. State Bar, 278 Va. 162, 677 S.E.2d 227, 2009 Va. LEXIS 67 (2009).

Discharged attorney may recover reasonable value of services. — That the client may at any time, for any reason or without any reason, discharge his attorney, is a firmly-established rule. The attorney may recover the reasonable value of the services which he has rendered, but he cannot recover for damages for the breach of contract. The discharge of the attorney by his client does not constitute a breach of the contract, because it is a term of such contract, implied from the peculiar relationship which the contract calls into existence, that the client may terminate the contract at any time with or without cause. Heinzman v. Fine, Fine, Legum & Fine, 217 Va. 958, 234 S.E.2d 282 (1977), decided under former DR 2-110.

Discharged attorney entitled to quantum meruit recovery and lien for fees. — When an attorney employed under a contingent fee contract is discharged without just cause and the client employs another attorney who effects a recovery, the discharged attorney is entitled to a fee based upon quantum meruit for services rendered prior to discharge and, as security for such fee, to the lien granted by former § 54-70 (see now § 54.1-3932). Heinzman v. Fine, Fine, Legum & Fine, 217 Va. 958, 234 S.E.2d 282 (1977), decided under former DR 2-110.

Refund of fee to a debtor-in-possession. — Where debtor-in-possession, authorized to manage its affairs under 11 U.S.C.S. § 1107, sought to employ general counsel, pursuant to 11 U.S.C.S. § 327, the applicant was required to disclose the compensation paid, under 11 U.S.C.S. § 329(a), and show that it waived any conflicting claim as a pre-petition creditor of the debtor. The retainer fee had to comply with Va. Sup. Ct. R. pt. 6, § II, R. 1.15(a)(2), 1.16(d), and the authorization to settle claims could not conflict with Va. Sup. Ct. R. pt. 6, § II, R. 1.2. In re Circle T Pipeline, Inc., 2011 Bankr. LEXIS 2490 (Bankr. W.D. Va. Apr. 27, 2011).

Withdrawal not allowed. — Counsel was not allowed to withdraw from a Chapter 11 bankruptcy case under Bankr. E.D. Va. R. 2090-1(G) and Va. Sup. Ct. R. pt. 6, § II, R. 1.16. The debtors had to quickly sell their real property or face relief from stay, and it would severely prejudice them and interfere with the administration of justice to release counsel at this stage of the case. In re Schley, 2012 Bankr. LEXIS 2135 (Bankr. E.D. Va. May 9, 2012).

CIRCUIT COURT OPINIONS

Law firm failed in its burden of communicating termination of representation to client. — In a pending lawsuit between a buyer and a seller, because a law firm failed in its burden of communicating to the buyer that its prior representation had been terminated, and hence, its representation of the seller had commenced, and failed to clarify its relationship to the buyer, the buyer's motion to disqualify the law firm from representing the seller was granted. Comstock Lake Pelham, L.C. v. Clore Family, LLC, 74 Va. Cir. 35, 2007 Va. Cir. LEXIS 46 (Fairfax County 2007).

Rule 1.17. Sale of Law Practice.

A lawyer or a law firm may sell or purchase a law practice, partially or in its entirety, including good will, if the following conditions are satisfied:

(a) The seller ceases to engage in the private practice of law, or in the area of practice that has been sold, in the geographic area in which the practice has been conducted, except the lawyer may practice law while on staff of a public agency or legal services entity which provides legal services to the poor, or as in-house counsel to a business.

(b) The entire practice, or the entire area of practice, is sold to one or more lawyers or law firms;

(c) Actual written notice is given by the seller to each of the seller's clients (as defined by the terms of the proposed sale) regarding:

(1) the proposed sale and the identity of the purchaser;

(2) any proposed change in the terms of the future representation including the fee arrangement;

(3) the client's right to consent or to refuse to consent to the transfer of the client's matter, and that said right must be exercised within ninety (90) days of receipt of the notice;

(4) the client's right to retain other counsel and/or take possession of the file; and

(5) the fact that the client's refusal to consent to the transfer of the client's matter will be presumed if the client does not take any action or does not otherwise consent within ninety (90) days of receipt of the notice.

(d) If a client involved in a pending matter cannot be given notice, the representation of that client may be transferred to the purchaser only upon entry of an order so authorizing by a court having jurisdiction. The seller may disclose to the court *in camera* information relating to the representation only to the extent necessary to obtain an order authorizing the transfer of a file.

(e) The fees charged clients shall not be increased by reason of the sale.

COMMENT

[1] The practice of law is a profession, not merely a business. Clients are not commodities that can be purchased and sold at will. Pursuant to this Rule, when a lawyer or an entire firm ceases to practice and another lawyer or firm takes over the representation, the selling lawyer or firm may obtain compensation for the reasonable value of the practice as may withdrawing partners of law firms. *See* Rules 5.4 and 5.6.

Termination of Practice by Seller

[2] The fact that a number of the seller's clients decide not to be represented by the purchaser but take their matters elsewhere does not result in a violation. Neither does the seller's return to private practice after the sale as a result of an unanticipated change in circumstances result in a violation. For example, a lawyer who has sold the practice to accept an appointment to judicial office does not violate the requirement that the sale be attendant to cessation of practice if the lawyer later resumes private practice upon leaving the office.

[3] Comment [3] to *ABA Model Rule* 1.17 substantially appears in paragraph (a) of this Rule.

[4] The Rule permits a sale of an entire practice attendant upon retirement from the private practice of law within the jurisdiction.

[5] This Rule also permits a lawyer or law firm to sell an area of practice. If an area of practice is sold and the lawyer remains in the active practice of law, the lawyer must cease accepting any matters in the area of practice that has been sold, either as counsel or co-counsel or by assuming joint responsibility for a matter in connection with the division of a fee with another lawyer as would otherwise be permitted by Rule 1.5(e). For example, a lawyer with a substantial number of estate planning matters and a substantial number of probate administration cases may sell the estate planning portion of the practice but remain in the practice of law by concentrating on probate administration; however, that practitioner may not thereafter accept any estate planning matters. Although a lawyer who leaves a jurisdiction or geographical area typically would sell the entire practice, this Rule permits the lawyer to limit the sale to one or more areas of the practice, thereby preserving the lawyer's right to continue practice in the areas of the practice that were not sold.

Sale of Entire Practice or Entire Area of Practice

[6] The Rule requires that the seller's entire practice, or an entire area of practice, be sold. The prohibition against sale of less than an entire practice area protects those clients whose matters are less lucrative and who might find it difficult to secure other counsel if a sale could be limited to substantial fee-generating matters. The purchasers are required to undertake all client matters in the practice or practice area, subject to client consent. This requirement is satisfied, however, even if a purchaser is unable to undertake a particular client matter because of a conflict of interest.

Client Confidences, Consent and Notice

[7] Negotiations between seller and prospective purchaser prior to disclosure of information relating to a specific representation of an identifiable client no more violate the confidentiality provisions of Rule 1.6 than do preliminary discussions concerning the possible association of any lawyer or mergers between firms, with respect to which client consent is not required. Providing the purchaser access to client-specific information relating to the representation and to the file, however, requires client consent. The Rule provides that before such information can be disclosed by the seller to the purchaser the client must be given actual written

notice of the contemplated sale, including the identity of the purchaser and any proposed change in the terms of future representation, and must be told that the decision to consent or to make other arrangements must be made within 90 days. If nothing is heard from the client within that time, the client's refusal to consent to the sale is presumed.

[8] A lawyer or law firm ceasing to practice cannot be required to remain in practice because some clients cannot be given actual notice of the proposed purchase. Since these clients cannot themselves consent to the purchase or direct any other disposition of their files, the Rule requires an order from a court having jurisdiction authorizing their transfer or other disposition. The Court can be expected to determine whether reasonable efforts to locate the client have been exhausted, and whether the absent client's legitimate interest will be served by authorizing the transfer of the file so that the purchaser may continue the representation. Preservation of client confidences requires that the petition for a court order be considered *in camera*.

[9] All the elements of client autonomy, including the client's absolute right to discharge a lawyer and transfer the representation to another, survive the sale of the practice.

Fee Arrangements Between Client and Purchaser

[10] The sale may not be financed by increases in fees charged the clients of the practice. Existing agreements between the seller and the client as to fees and the scope of work must be honored by the purchaser, unless the client consents after consultation.

Other Applicable Ethical Standards

[11] Lawyers participating in the sale of a law practice are subject to the ethical standards applicable to involving another lawyer in the representation of a client. These include, for example, the seller's obligation to assure that the purchaser is qualified to assume the practice and the purchaser's obligation to undertake the representation competently (*see* Rule 1.1); the obligation to avoid disqualifying conflicts, and to secure client consent after consultation for those conflicts which can be agreed to (*see* Rule 1.7); and the obligation to protect information relating to the representation (*see* Rules 1.6 and 1.9).

[12] If approval of the substitution of the purchasing attorney for the selling attorney is required by the rules of any tribunal in which a matter is pending, such approval must be obtained before the matter can be concluded in the sale (*see* Rule 1.16).

Applicability of the Rule

[13] This Rule applies to the sale of a law practice by representatives of a deceased, disabled or disappeared lawyer. Thus, the seller may be represented by a nonlawyer representative not subject to these Rules. Since, however, no lawyer may participate in a sale of a law practice which does not conform to the requirements of this Rule, the representatives of the seller as well as the purchasing lawyer shall see to it that they are met.

[14] Admission to or retirement from a law partnership or professional association, retirement plans and similar arrangements, and a sale of tangible assets of a law practice, do not constitute a sale or purchase governed by this Rule.

[15] This Rule does not apply to the transfers of legal representation between lawyers when such transfers are unrelated to the sale of a practice.

Virginia Code Comparison

Ethical Consideration 4-6 states that a lawyer should not attempt to sell a law practice as a going business because, among other things, to do so would involve the disclosure of confidences and secrets.

Committee Commentary

The Committee was persuaded to eliminate the prohibition of the sale of a law practice currently set forth in Ethical Consideration 4-6 by several arguments, the first being that sole practitioners and their clients are often unreasonably discriminated against when the attorney's practice is terminated. When lawyers who are members of firms retire, the transition for the client is usually smooth because another attorney of the firm normally takes over the matter. Such a transition is usually more difficult for the clients of a sole practitioner, who must employ another attorney or firm.

Another persuasive argument is that some attorneys leaving practice, firm members and sole practitioners alike, indirectly "sell" their practices, including its good will, by utilizing various arrangements. For example, firm members sometimes receive payments from their firm pursuant to retirement agreements that have the effect of rewarding the lawyer for the value of his/her practice. Sole practitioners contemplating leaving the practice of law may sell their tangible assets at an inflated price or bring in a partner prior to retirement, then allow the partner to take over the practice pursuant to a compensation agreement. Such arrangements do not always involve significant client participation or consent.

In addition, an attorney's practice has value that is recognized in the law. Under Virginia divorce law, for example, a professional's practice, including its good will, may be subject to equitable distribution. (*Russell v. Russell,* 11 Va. App. 411, 399 S.E.2d 166 (1990)). Therefore, under the *Virginia Code*, an attorney in a divorce proceeding may be required to compensate his/her spouse for the value of the practice, yet be forbidden to sell it.

The Committee recommended, after considering all of these factors, that adopting a carefully crafted rule allowing such sales without resort to these alternate methods would be preferable and would assure maximum protection of clients. This recommended Rule is based on the *ABA Model Rule* 1.17 with several significant changes, the chief ones relating to consent and fees.

The amendment effective January 1, 2004, adopted September 24, 2003, added the exception at the end of paragraph (a).

The amendment effective January 4, 2010, adopted November 2, 2009, inserted "or in the area of practice that has been sold" in subdivision (a); added present subdivision (b), and redesignated the following subdivisions accordingly; and in the Comments, inserted paragraphs [4] through [6].

Rule 1.18. Duties To Prospective Client.

(a) A person who discusses with a lawyer the possibility of forming a client-lawyer relationship with respect to a matter is a prospective client.

(b) Even when no client-lawyer relationship ensues, a lawyer who has had discussions with a prospective client shall not use or reveal information learned in the consultation, except as Rule 1.9 would permit with respect to information of a former client.

(c) A lawyer subject to paragraph (b) shall not represent a client with interests materially adverse to those of a prospective client in the same or a substantially related matter if the lawyer received information from the prospective client that could be significantly harmful to that person in the matter, except as provided in paragraph (d). If a lawyer is disqualified from representation under this paragraph, no lawyer in a firm with which that lawyer is associated may knowingly undertake or continue representation in such a matter, except as provided in paragraph (d).

(d) When the lawyer has received disqualifying information as defined in paragraph (c), representation is permissible if:

(1) both the affected client and the prospective client have given informed consent, confirmed in writing, or

(2) the lawyer who received the information took reasonable measures to avoid exposure to more disqualifying information than was reasonably necessary to determine whether to represent the prospective client; and

(i) the disqualified lawyer is timely screened from any participation in the matter; the disqualified lawyer reasonably believes that the screen would be effective to sufficiently protect information that could be significantly harmful to the prospective client; and

(ii) written notice that includes a general description of the subject matter about which the lawyer was consulted and the screening procedures employed is promptly given to the prospective client.

COMMENT

[1] Prospective clients, like clients, may disclose information to a lawyer, place documents or other property in the lawyer's custody, or rely on the lawyer's advice. A lawyer's discussions with a prospective client usually are limited in time and depth and leave both the prospective client and the lawyer free (and sometimes required) to proceed no further. The principle of loyalty diminishes in importance if the sole reason for an individual lawyer's disqualification is the lawyer's initial consultation with a prospective new client with whom no client-lawyer relationship is formed, either because the lawyer detected a conflict of interest as a result of an initial consultation, or for some other reason (e.g., the prospective client decided not to retain the firm). Hence, prospective clients should receive some but not all of the protection afforded clients.

[2] Not all persons who communicate information to a lawyer are entitled to protection under this Rule. A person who unilaterally communicates information to a lawyer, without any reasonable expectation that the lawyer is willing to discuss the possibility of forming a client-lawyer relationship, is not a "prospective client" within the meaning of paragraph (a).

[3] It is often necessary for a prospective client to reveal information to the lawyer during an initial consultation prior to the decision about formation of a client-lawyer relationship. The client may disclose such information as part of the process of determining whether the client wishes to form a client-lawyer relationship. The lawyer often must learn such information to determine whether there is a conflict of interest with an existing client and whether the matter is one that the lawyer is willing to undertake. Paragraph (b) prohibits the lawyer from using or revealing that information, except as permitted by Rule 1.9, even if the client or lawyer decides not to proceed with the representation. The duty exists regardless of how brief the initial conference may be.

[4] In order to avoid acquiring disqualifying information from a prospective client, a lawyer considering whether or not to undertake a new matter should limit the initial interview to only such information as reasonably appears necessary for that purpose. Where the information indicates that a conflict of interest or other reason for non-representation exists, the lawyer should so inform the prospective client or decline the representation. If the prospective client wishes to retain the lawyer, and if consent is possible under Rule 1.7, then consent from all affected present or former clients must be obtained before accepting the representation.

[5] A lawyer may condition conversations with a prospective client on the person's informed consent that no information disclosed during the consultation will prohibit the lawyer from representing a different client in the matter. If the agreement expressly so provides, the prospective client may also consent to the lawyer's subsequent use of

information received from the prospective client.

[6] Even in the absence of an agreement, under paragraph (c), the lawyer is not prohibited from representing a client with interests adverse to those of the prospective client in the same or a substantially related matter unless the lawyer has received from the prospective client information that could be significantly harmful if used in the matter and the lawyer believes that an effective screen could not be engaged to protect the prospective client.

[7] Under paragraph (c), the prohibition in this Rule is imputed to other lawyers as provided in Rule 1.10, but, under paragraph (d)(1), imputation may be avoided if the lawyer obtains the informed consent, confirmed in writing, of both the prospective and affected clients. In the alternative, imputation may be avoided if the conditions of paragraph (d)(2) are met and all disqualified lawyers are timely screened and written notice is promptly given to the prospective client and the lawyer reasonably believes that an effective screen will protect the confidential information of the prospective client.

[8] Notice, including a general description of the subject matter about which the lawyer was consulted, and of the screening procedures employed, generally should be given as soon as practicable after the need for screening becomes apparent.

[9] For the duty of competence of a lawyer who gives assistance on the merits of a matter to a prospective client, see Rule 1.1. For a lawyer's duties when a prospective client entrusts valuables or papers to the lawyer's care, see Rule 1.15.

Effective date. — This rule, adopted June 21, 2011, became effective June 21, 2011.

COUNSELOR AND THIRD-PARTY NEUTRAL.

Rule 2.1. Advisor.

In representing a client, a lawyer shall exercise independent professional judgment and render candid advice. In rendering advice, a lawyer may refer not only to law but to other considerations such as moral, economic, social and political factors, that may be relevant to the client's situation.

COMMENT

Scope of Advice

[1] A client is entitled to straightforward advice expressing the lawyer's honest assessment. Legal advice often involves unpleasant facts and alternatives that a client may be disinclined to confront. In presenting advice, a lawyer endeavors to sustain the client's morale and may put advice in as acceptable a form as honesty permits. However, a lawyer should not be deterred from giving candid advice by the prospect that the advice will be unpalatable to the client.

[2] Advice couched in narrowly legal terms may be of little value to a client, especially where practical considerations, such as cost or effects on other people, are predominant. Purely technical legal advice, therefore, can sometimes be inadequate. It could also ignore, to the client's disadvantage, the relational or emotional factors driving a dispute. In such a case, advice may include the advantages, disadvantages and availability of other dispute resolution processes that might be appropriate under the circumstances.

[2a] It is proper for a lawyer to refer to relevant moral and ethical considerations in giving advice. Although a lawyer is not a moral advisor as such, moral and ethical considerations impinge upon most legal questions and may decisively influence how the law will be applied.

[3] A client may expressly or impliedly ask the lawyer for purely technical advice. When such a request is made by a client experienced in legal matters, the lawyer may accept it at face value. When such a request is made by a client inexperienced in legal matters, however, the lawyer's responsibility as advisor may include indicating that more may be involved than strictly legal considerations.

[4] Matters that go beyond strictly legal questions may also be in the domain of another profession. Family matters can involve problems within the professional competence of psychiatry, clinical psychology or social work; business matters can involve problems within the competence of the accounting profession or of financial specialists. Where consultation with a professional in another field is itself something a competent lawyer would recommend, the lawyer should make such a recommendation. At the same time, a lawyer's advice at its best often consists of recommending a course of action in the face of conflicting recommendations of experts.

Offering Advice

[5] In general, a lawyer is not expected to give advice until asked by the client. However, when a lawyer knows that a client proposes a course of action that is likely to result in substantial adverse legal, moral or ethical consequences to the client or to others, duty to the client under Rule 1.4 may require that the lawyer act if the client's course of action is related to the representation. A lawyer ordinarily has no duty to initiate investigation of a client's affairs or to give advice that the client has indicated is unwanted, but a lawyer may initiate advice to a client when doing so appears to be in the client's interest.

Virginia Code Comparison

There was no direct counterpart to this Rule in the Disciplinary Rules of the Virginia Code. DR

5-106(B) provided that a lawyer "shall not permit a person who recommends, employs, or pays him to render legal services for another to direct or regulate his professional judgment in rendering such legal services." EC 7-8 stated that "[a]dvice of a lawyer to his client need not be confined to purely legal considerations.... In assisting his client to reach a proper decision, it is often desirable for a lawyer to point out those factors which may lead to a decision that is morally just as well as legally permissible.... In the final analysis, however, ... the decision whether to forego legally available objectives or methods because of nonlegal factors is ultimately for the client...."

Committee Commentary

The Committee adopted the ABA Model Rule verbatim because it sets forth more clearly than the Disciplinary Rules the scope of a lawyer's advisory role.

CASE NOTES

Failure to advise against filing bankruptcy. — Where the grandmother and father of an 18-year-old Chapter 13 debtor used the debtor as part of a scheme to hinder, delay, and defraud their own creditors, the attorney for the debtor, who had represented the grandmother and father in prior bankruptcy cases, was a willing and active participant in the scheme, in violation of Fed. R. Bankr. P. 9011 and several rules of the Virginia Rules of Professional Conduct, including Va. Sup. Ct. R. pt. 6, § II, R. 2.1. In re Johnson, 2008 Bankr. LEXIS 164 (Bankr. E.D. Va. Jan. 18, 2008).

Rule 2.2. Intermediary.

Editor's note. — Deleted by order adopted September 24, 2003, effective January 1, 2004.

Rule 2.3. Evaluation For Use By Third Persons.

(a) A lawyer acts as evaluator by examining a client's legal affairs and reporting about them to the client or to others.

(b) A lawyer may undertake an evaluation of a matter affecting a client for the use of someone other than the client if:

(1) the lawyer reasonably believes that making the evaluation is compatible with other aspects of the lawyer's relationship with the client; and

(2) the client consents after consultation.

(c) Except as disclosure is required in connection with a report of an evaluation information relating to the evaluation is otherwise protected by Rule 1.6.

COMMENT

Definition

[1] An evaluation may be performed at the client's direction but for the primary purpose of establishing information for the benefit of third parties; for example, an opinion concerning the title of property rendered at the behest of a vendor for the information of a prospective purchaser, or at the behest of a borrower for the information of a prospective lender. In some situations, the evaluation may be required by a government agency; for example, an opinion concerning the legality of the securities registered for sale under the securities laws. In other instances, the evaluation may be required by a third person, such as a purchaser of a business.

[1a] Lawyers for the government may be called upon to give a formal opinion on the legality of contemplated government agency action. In making such an evaluation, the government lawyer acts at the behest of the government as the client but for the purpose of establishing the limits of the agency's authorized activity. Such an opinion is to be distinguished from confidential legal advice given agency officials. The critical question is whether the opinion is to be made public.

[2] A legal evaluation should be distinguished from an investigation of a person with whom the lawyer does not have a client-lawyer relationship. For example, a lawyer retained by a purchaser to analyze a vendor's title to property does not have a client-lawyer relationship with the vendor. So also, an investigation into a person's affairs by a government lawyer, or by special counsel employed by the government, is not an evaluation as that term is used in this Rule. The question is whether the lawyer is retained by the person whose affairs are being examined. When the lawyer is retained by that person, the general rules concerning loyalty to client and preservation of confidences apply, which is not the case if the lawyer is retained by someone else. For this reason, it is essential to identify the person by whom the lawyer is retained. This should be made clear not only to the person under examination, but also to others to whom the results are to be made available.

Duty to Third Person

[3] When the evaluation is intended for the information or use of a third person, a legal duty to that person may or may not arise. That legal question is beyond the scope of this Rule. However, since such an evaluation involves a departure from the normal client-lawyer relationship, careful analysis of the situation is required. The lawyer must be satisfied as a matter of professional judgment that making the evaluation is compatible with other functions undertaken in behalf of the client. For

example, if the lawyer is acting as advocate in defending the client against charges of fraud, it would normally be incompatible with that responsibility for the lawyer to perform an evaluation for others concerning the same or a related transaction. Assuming no such impediment is apparent, however, the lawyer should advise the client of the implications of the evaluation, particularly the lawyer's responsibilities to third persons and the duty to disseminate the findings.

Access to and Disclosure of Information

[4] The quality of an evaluation depends on the freedom and extent of the investigation upon which it is based. Ordinarily a lawyer should have whatever latitude of investigation seems necessary as a matter of professional judgment. Under some circumstances, however, the terms of the evaluation may be limited. For example, certain issues or sources may be categorically excluded, or the scope of search may be limited by time constraints or the noncooperation of persons having relevant information. Any such limitations which are material to the evaluation should be described in the report. If after a lawyer has commenced an evaluation, the client refuses to comply with the terms upon which it was understood the evaluation was to have been made, the lawyer's obligations are determined by law, having reference to the terms of the client's agreement and the surrounding circumstances.

[5] *ABA Model Rule* Comment not adopted.

Financial Auditors' Requests for Information

[6] When a question concerning the legal situation of a client arises at the instance of the client's financial auditor and the question is referred to the lawyer, the lawyer's response may be made in accordance with procedures recognized in the legal profession. Such a procedure is set forth in the American Bar Association Statement of Policy Regarding Lawyers' Responses to Auditors' Requests for Information, adopted in 1975.

Virginia Code Comparison

There was no counterpart to this Rule in the Virginia Code.

Committee Commentary

The Committee adopted this Rule because it addressed matters not addressed in the Virginia Code. This Rule generally follows ABA Model Rule 2.3, but the Committee added subparagraph 2.3(c) in recognition of the statutory requirement of confidentiality in the dispute resolution process. See Code of Virginia Section 8.01-576.10.

Rule 2.10. Third Party Neutral.

(a) A third party neutral assists parties in reaching a voluntary settlement of a dispute through a structured process known as a dispute resolution proceeding. The third party neutral does not represent any party.

(b) A lawyer who serves as a third party neutral

(1) shall inform the parties of the difference between the lawyer's role as third party neutral and the lawyer's role as one who represents a client;

(2) shall encourage unrepresented parties to seek legal counsel before an agreement is executed; and

(3) may encourage and assist the parties in reaching a resolution of their dispute; but

(4) may not compel or coerce the parties to make an agreement.

(c) A lawyer may serve as a third party neutral only if the lawyer has not previously represented and is not currently representing one of the parties in connection with the subject matter of the dispute resolution proceeding.

(d) A lawyer may serve as a third party neutral in a dispute resolution proceeding involving a client whom the lawyer has represented or is representing in a matter unrelated to the dispute resolution proceeding, provided:

(1) there is full disclosure of the prior or present representation;

(2) in light of the disclosure, the third party neutral obtains the parties' informed consent;

(3) the third party neutral reasonably believes that a prior or present representation will not compromise or adversely affect the ability to act as a third party neutral; and

(4) there is no unauthorized disclosure of information in violation of Rule 1.6.

(e) A lawyer who serves or has served as a third party neutral may not serve as a lawyer on behalf of any party to the dispute, nor represent one such party against the other in any legal proceeding related to the subject of the dispute resolution proceeding.

(f) A lawyer shall withdraw as third party neutral if any of the requirements stated in this Rule is no longer satisfied or if any of the parties in the dispute resolution proceeding so requests. If the parties are participating pursuant to a court referral, the third party neutral shall report the withdrawal to the authority issuing the referral.

(g) A lawyer who serves as a third party neutral shall not charge a fee contingent on the outcome of the dispute resolution proceeding.

(h) This Rule does not apply to joint representation, which is covered by Rule 1.7.

COMMENT

[1] This Rule sets forth conflicts of interest and other ethical guidelines for a lawyer who serves as a third party neutral. Dispute resolution proceedings that are conducted by a third party neutral include mediation, conciliation, early neutral evaluation, non-binding arbitration and non-judicial settlement conferences.

[2] A lawyer who serves as a third party neutral under this Rule or as a mediator under Rule 2.11 is engaged in the provision of a law-related service that may involve the application of a lawyer's particular legal expertise and skills. The standards set forth in this Rule, however, do not amount to a determination that a lawyer who serves as a third party neutral pursuant to this Rule or as a mediator pursuant to Rule 2.11 is engaged in the practice of law. The determination of whether a particular activity constitutes the practice of law is beyond the scope and purpose of these Rules.

[3] A lawyer serving as third party neutral shall not offer any of the parties legal advice, which is a function of the lawyer who is representing a client (See Preamble: A Lawyer's Responsibilities). A third party neutral may, however, offer neutral evaluations, if requested by the parties. Special provisions under which a lawyer-mediator can offer certain neutral evaluations are contained in Rule 2.11.

[4] Confidentiality of information revealed in the dispute resolution process is governed by Code of Virginia Sections 8.01-576.9 and 8.01-576.10.

[5] A third party neutral as defined in these Rules does not include a lawyer providing binding arbitration services (See Code of Virginia Section 8.01-577 et. seq.).

[6] The imputation of conflicts arising under paragraph (e) is addressed in Rule 1.10.

Virginia Code Comparison

There was no counterpart to this Rule in the Virginia Code.

Committee Commentary

The Committee adopted this Rule, not part of the ABA Model Rules, to provide guidelines for lawyers who serve as neutrals and who do not represent a party to a dispute or transaction. Following adoption of Virginia Rule 2.10, the ABA adopted Model Rule 2.4 governing third-party neutrals. The Virginia and ABA Rules are substantially different.

The amendment effective January 1, 2004, adopted September 24, 2003, substituted "joint representation" for "intermediation" and "Rule 1.7" for "Rule 2.2" in paragraph (h).

Law Review. — For article, "Professional Responsibility," see 43 U. Rich. L. Rev. 255 (2008).

Rule 2.11. Mediator.

(a) A lawyer-mediator is a third party neutral (See Rule 2.10) who facilitates communication between the parties and, without deciding the issues or imposing a solution on the parties, enables them to understand and resolve their dispute.

(b) Prior to agreeing to mediate and throughout the mediation process a lawyer-mediator should reasonably determine that:

(1) mediation is an appropriate process for the parties;

(2) each party is able to participate effectively within the context of the mediation process; and

(3) each party is willing to enter and participate in the process in good faith.

(c) A lawyer-mediator may offer legal information if all parties are present or separately to the parties if they consent. The lawyer-mediator shall inform unrepresented parties or those parties who are not accompanied by legal counsel about the importance of reviewing the lawyer-mediator's legal information with legal counsel.

(d) A lawyer-mediator may offer evaluation of, for example, strengths and weaknesses of positions, assess the value and cost of alternatives to settlement or assess the barriers to settlement (collectively referred to as evaluation) only if such evaluation is incidental to the facilitative role and does not interfere with the lawyer-mediator's impartiality or the self-determination of the parties.

(e) Prior to the mediation session a lawyer-mediator shall:

(1) consult with prospective parties about

(i) the nature of the mediation process;

(ii) the limitations on the use of evaluation, as set forth in subparagraph (d) above;

(iii) the lawyer-mediator's approach, style and subject matter expertise; and

(iv) the parties' expectations regarding the mediation process; and

(2) enter into a written agreement to mediate which references the choice and expectations of the parties, including whether the parties have chosen, permit or expect the use of neutral evaluation or evaluative techniques during the course of the mediation.

(f) A lawyer-mediator shall conduct the mediation in a manner that is consistent with the parties' choice and expectations.

COMMENT

[1] Offering assessments, evaluations, and advice are traditional lawyering functions for the lawyer who represents a client. A lawyer-mediator, who does not represent any of the parties to the mediation, should not assume that these functions are appropriate. Although these functions are not specifically prohibited in the statutory definition of mediation which is set forth as subparagraph (a) of this Rule, an evaluative approach which interferes with the parties' self-determination and the mediator's impartiality would be inconsistent with this definition of mediation.

[2] Defining mediation to exclude an evaluative approach is difficult not only because practice varies widely but because no consensus exists as to what constitutes an evaluation. Also, the effects of an evaluation on the mediation process depend upon the attitude and style of the mediator and the context in which it is offered. Thus, a question by a lawyer-mediator to a party that might be considered by some as "reality testing" and facilitative, might be viewed by others as evaluative. On the other hand, an evaluation by a facilitative mediator could help free the parties from the narrowing effects of the law and help empower them to resolve their dispute.

Informed Consent to Mediator's Approach

[3] The Rule focuses on the informed consent of the prospective mediation clients to the particular approach, style and subject matter expertise of the lawyer-mediator. This begins with consultation about the nature of the mediation process, the limitations on evaluation, the lawyer-mediator's approach, style and subject matter expertise and the parties' expectations regarding the mediation process. If the parties request an evaluative approach, the lawyer-mediator shall explain the risk that evaluation might interfere with mediator impartiality and party self-determination. Following this consultation the lawyer-mediator and the parties shall sign a written agreement to mediate which reflects the choice and expectation of the parties. The lawyer-mediator shall then conduct the mediation in a manner that is consistent with the parties' choice and expectations. This is similar to the lawyer-client consultation about the means to be used in pursuing a client's objectives in Rule 1.2.

Continuing Responsibility to Examine Potential Impact of Evaluation

[4] If the parties choose a lawyer-mediator who is willing and able to offer evaluation during the mediation process and has met the requirements of paragraph (e), a lawyer-mediator has a continuing responsibility under paragraphs (b) and (d) to assess the situation and consult with the parties before offering or responding to a request for an evaluation. Consideration shall be given again to whether mediator impartiality and party self-determination are at risk. Consideration should also be given as to whether an evaluation could detract from the willingness of the parties to work at understanding their own and each other's situation and at considering a broader range of interests, issues and options. Also, with an evaluation the parties may miss out on opportunities to maintain or improve relationships or to create a higher quality and more satisfying result.

[5] On the other hand, the parties may expect the lawyer-mediator to offer an evaluation in helping the parties reach agreement, especially when the most important issues are the strengths or weaknesses of legal positions, or the significance of commercial or financial risks. This is particularly useful after parties have worked at possible solutions and have built up confidence in the mediator's impartiality or where widely divergent party evaluations are major barriers to settlement.

[6] The presence of attorneys for the parties offers additional protection in minimizing the risk of a poor quality evaluation and of too strong an influence on the parties' self-determination. An evaluation, coupled with a reminder to the parties that the evaluation is but one of the factors to be considered as they deliberate on the outcome, may in certain cases be the most appropriate way to assure that the parties are making fully informed decisions.

Legal Advice, Legal Information and Neutral Evaluation

[7] A lawyer-mediator shall not offer any of the parties legal advice which is a function of the lawyer who is representing a client. However, a lawyer-mediator may offer legal information under the conditions outlined in paragraph (c). Offering legal information is an educational function which aids the parties in making informed decisions. Neutral evaluations in the mediation process consist of, for example, opining as to the strengths and weaknesses of positions, assessing the value and costs of alternatives to settlement or assessing the barriers to settlement.

[8] The lawyer-mediator shall not, however, make decisions for any party to the mediation process nor shall the lawyer-mediator use a neutral evaluation to coerce or influence the parties to settle their dispute or to accept a particular solution to their dispute. Paragraphs (d), (e), and (f) restrict the use of evaluative techniques by the lawyer-mediator to situations where the parties have given their informed consent to the use of such techniques and where a neutral evaluation will assist, rather than interfere with the ability of the parties to reach a mutually agreeable solution to their dispute.

Mediation

[9] While a lawyer is cautioned in Rule 1.7 regarding the special considerations in common representation, these should not deter a lawyer-mediator from accepting clients for mediation. In mediation, a lawyer-mediator represents none of the parties and should be trained to deal with strong emotions. In fact, mediation can be especially useful in a case where communication and relational breakdown have made negotiation or litigation of legal issues more difficult.

Confidentiality and Professional Responsibility Standards

[10] Confidentiality of information revealed in the mediation process is governed by Code of Virginia Sections 8.01-576.9 and 8.01-576.10 and Section 8.01-581.22.

Virginia Code Comparison

There was no counterpart to this Rule in the Virginia Code.

Committee Commentary

The Committee adopted this Rule, not part of the ABA Model Rules, to give further guidance to lawyers who serve as mediators. Although Legal Ethics Opinions (e.g., LEO 590 (May 17, 1985)) have approved of lawyers serving as mediators, different approaches to and styles of mediation ranging from pure facilitation to evaluation of positions are being offered. This Rule requires lawyer-mediators to consult with prospective parties about the lawyer-mediators' approach, style and subject matter expertise and to honor the parties' choice and expectations.

ADVOCATE.

Rule 3.1. Meritorious Claims And Contentions.

A lawyer shall not bring or defend a proceeding, or assert or controvert an issue therein, unless there is a basis for doing so that is not frivolous, which includes a good faith argument for an extension, modification or reversal of existing law. A lawyer for the defendant in a criminal proceeding, or the respondent in a proceeding that could result in incarceration, may nevertheless so defend the proceeding as to require that every element of the case be established.

COMMENT

[1] The advocate has a duty to use legal procedure for the fullest benefit of the client's cause, but also a duty not to abuse legal procedure. The law, both procedural and substantive, establishes the limits within which an advocate may proceed. However, the law is not always clear and is never static. Accordingly, in determining the proper scope of advocacy, account must be taken of the law's ambiguities and potential for change.

[2] The filing of an action or defense or similar action taken for a client is not frivolous merely because the facts have not first been fully substantiated or because the lawyer expects to develop vital evidence only by discovery. Such action is not frivolous even though the lawyer believes that the client's position ultimately will not prevail. The action is frivolous, however, if the client desires to have the action taken primarily for the purpose of harassing or maliciously injuring a person, or if the lawyer is unable either to make a good faith argument on the merits of the action taken or to support the action taken by a good faith argument for an extension, modification or reversal of existing law.

Virginia Code Comparison

Rule 3.1 is similar to DR 7-102(A)(1), but with three differences. First, the test of improper conduct is changed from "merely to harass or maliciously injure another" to the requirement that there be a basis for the litigation measure involved that is "not frivolous." This includes the concept stated in DR 7- 102(A)(2) that a lawyer may advance a claim or defense unwarranted by existing law if "it can be supported by good faith argument for an extension, modification, or reversal of existing law." Second, the test in Rule 3.1 is an objective test, whereas DR 7-102(A)(1) applied only if the lawyer "knows or when it is obvious" that the litigation is frivolous. Third, Rule 3.1 has an exception that in a criminal case, or a case in which incarceration of the client may result (for example, certain juvenile proceedings), the lawyer may put the prosecution to its proof even if there is no nonfrivolous basis for defense.

Committee Commentary

Although Rule 3.1 is similar in substance to existing Virginia Code provisions, the Committee concluded that the objective standard of the ABA Model Rule was preferable and more closely paralleled Section 8.01-271.1 of the Code of Virginia, dealing with lawyer sanctions.

Law Review. — For article, "Professional Responsibility," see 43 U. Rich. L. Rev. 255 (2008).

CASE NOTES

Fraudulently signed bankruptcy petition. — Attorney's conduct in electronically filing a bankruptcy petition containing the electronic signatures of the debtor and the attorney, when in fact the attorney did not have the debtor's physical signature on a hard copy of the petition, violated the dictates for electronic filing in Fed. R. Bankr. P. 5005(a)(2), and E.D. Va. Bankr. R. 5005-1, violated the attorney's obligation in Va. Sup. Ct. R., pt. 6, § II, Rules 3.1 and 3.3 to bring only non-frivolous matters before the court, amounted to fraud on the court in violation of Fed. R. Bankr. P. 9011, and was sanctionable under the equitable powers granted to the court under 11 U.S.C.S. § 105. In re Wenk, 296 Bankr. 719, 2002 Bankr. LEXIS 1733 (Bankr. E.D. Va. 2002).

Rule violated. — Attorney violated Va. Sup. Ct. R., Pt. 6, § II, Rule 3.1 when he claimed he was not married to the plaintiff in the divorce action based on alleged error in her name in the pleadings. Barrett v. Va. State Bar, 269 Va. 583, 611 S.E.2d 375, 2005 Va. LEXIS 45 (2005).

Attorney violated Va. Sup. Ct. R. pt. 6, § II, R. 3.1 and 3.4(j) when the attorney attempted to call opposing counsel as a witness in the attorney's divorce case because the attorney allegedly thought the attorney's wife was having a romantic relationship with opposing counsel. Barrett v. Va. State Bar, 272 Va. 260, 634 S.E.2d 341, 2006 Va. LEXIS 84 (2006).

Because a suspended attorney was being treated like other suspended lawyers, and because the Rules of Professional Conduct applied to the attorney, the attorney was properly disbarred for violating Va. Sup. Ct. R., Pt. 6, § II, R. 3.1 by asserting that because the attorney's ex-wife was awarded sole custody of their children, the attorney was no longer required to support the attorney's children. Barrett v. Va. State Bar ex rel. Second Dist. Comm., 277 Va. 412, 675 S.E.2d 827, 2009 Va. LEXIS 56 (2009).

Judgment finding that an attorney violated Va. Sup. Ct. R. pt. 6, § II, R. 3.1 was affirmed because the record demonstrated by clear and convincing evidence that the attorney's medical malpractice action against a doctor was frivolous as the lawsuit had no basis in law or fact since the doctor had no legal duty to the attorney's client. Weatherbee v. Va. State Bar ex rel. Fourth Dist., 279 Va. 303, 689 S.E.2d 753, 2010 Va. LEXIS 37 (2010).

Rule not violated. — Finding that the attorney violated Va. Sup. Ct. R. pt. 6, § II, R. 3.1 was improper because the argument he asserted in response to a criminal defendant's motion to amend the language of the order dismissing the second indictment was not frivolous. The attorney did not oppose the amendment of the order dismissing the second indictment; instead, he stated to the trial court that the Commonwealth did not oppose the motion to modify but opposed the motion to modify as written. Livingston v. Va. State Bar, 286 Va. 1, 744 S.E.2d 220, 2013 Va. LEXIS 75 (2013).

Rule 3.3. Candor Toward The Tribunal.

(a) A lawyer shall not knowingly:

(1) make a false statement of fact or law to a tribunal;

(2) fail to disclose a fact to a tribunal when disclosure is necessary to avoid assisting a criminal or fraudulent act by the client, subject to Rule 1.6;

(3) fail to disclose to the tribunal controlling legal authority in the subject jurisdiction known to the lawyer to be adverse to the position of the client and not disclosed by opposing counsel; or

(4) offer evidence that the lawyer knows to be false. If a lawyer has offered material evidence and comes to know of its falsity, the lawyer shall take reasonable remedial measures.

(b) A lawyer may refuse to offer evidence that the lawyer reasonably believes is false.

(c) In an ex parte proceeding, a lawyer shall inform the tribunal of all material facts known to the lawyer which will enable the tribunal to make an informed decision, whether or not the facts are adverse.

(d) A lawyer who receives information clearly establishing that a person other than a client has perpetrated a fraud upon a tribunal shall promptly reveal the fraud to the tribunal.

COMMENT

[1] The advocate's task is to present the client's case with persuasive force. Performance of that duty while maintaining confidences of the client is qualified by the advocate's duty of candor to the tribunal. However, an advocate does not vouch for the evidence submitted in a cause; the tribunal is responsible for assessing its probative value.

[2] *ABA Model Rule* Comment not adopted.

Representations by a Lawyer

[3] An advocate is responsible for pleadings and other documents prepared for litigation, but is usually not required to have personal knowledge of matters asserted therein, for litigation documents ordinarily present assertions by the client, or by someone on the client's behalf, and not assertions by the lawyer. Compare Rule 3.1. However, Section 8.01-271.1 of the Code of Virginia states that a lawyer's signature on a pleading constitutes a certification that the lawyer believes, after reasonable inquiry, that there is a factual and legal basis for the pleading. Additionally, an assertion purporting to be on the lawyer's own knowledge, as in an affidavit by the lawyer or in a statement in open court, may properly be made only when the lawyer knows the assertion is true or believes it to be true on the basis of a reasonably diligent inquiry. There are circumstances where failure to make a disclosure is the equivalent of an affirmative misrepresentation. The obligation prescribed in Rule 1.2(c) not to counsel a client to commit or assist the client in committing a fraud applies in litigation. Regarding compliance with Rule 1.2(c), see the Comment to that Rule. See also the Comment to Rule 8.4(b).

Misleading Legal Argument

[4] Legal argument based on a knowingly false representation of law constitutes dishonesty toward the tribunal. Furthermore, the complexity of law often makes it difficult for a tribunal to be fully informed unless pertinent law is presented by the lawyers in the cause. A tribunal that is fully informed on the applicable law is better able to make a fair and accurate determination of the matter before it. The underlying concept is that legal argument is a discussion seeking to determine the legal premises properly applicable to the case. A lawyer is not required to make a disinterested exposition of the law, but must recognize the existence of pertinent legal authorities. Furthermore, as stated in paragraph (a)(3), an advocate has a duty to disclose controlling adverse authority in the subject jurisdiction which has not been disclosed by the opposing party.

False Evidence

[5] When evidence that a lawyer knows to be false is provided by a person who is not the client, the lawyer must refuse to offer it regardless of the client's wishes.

[6] When false evidence is offered by the client, however, a conflict may arise between the lawyer's duty to keep the client's revelations confidential and the duty of candor to the court. Upon ascertaining that material evidence is false, the lawyer should seek to persuade the client that the evidence should not be offered or, if it has been offered, that its false character should immediately be disclosed. If the persuasion is ineffective, the lawyer must take reasonable remedial measures.

[7-9] *ABA Model Rule* Comments not adopted.

Remedial Measures

[10] *ABA Model Rule* Comment not adopted.

[11] Except in the defense of a criminal accused, the rule generally recognized is that, if necessary to rectify the situation, an advocate must disclose the existence of the client's deception to the court or to the other party. Such a disclosure can result in grave consequences to the client, including not only a sense of betrayal but also loss of the case and perhaps a prosecution for perjury. But the alternative is that the lawyer cooperate in deceiving the court, thereby subverting the truth-finding process which the adversary system is designed to implement. See Rule 1.2(c). Furthermore, unless it is clearly understood that the lawyer will act upon the duty to disclose the existence of false evidence, the client can simply reject the lawyer's advice to reveal the false evidence and insist that the lawyer keep silent. Thus the client could in effect coerce the lawyer into being a party to fraud on the court.

Perjury by a Criminal Defendant

[12] Whether an advocate for a criminally accused has the same duty of disclosure has been intensely debated. While it is agreed that the lawyer should seek to persuade the client to refrain from perjurious testimony, there has been dispute concerning the lawyer's duty when that persuasion fails. If the confrontation with the client occurs before trial, the lawyer ordinarily can withdraw. Withdrawal before trial may not be possible, however, either because trial is imminent, or because the confrontation with the client does not take place until the trial itself, or because no other counsel is available.

[13] The most difficult situation, therefore, arises in a criminal case where the accused insists on testifying when the lawyer knows that the testimony is perjurious. The lawyer's effort to rectify the situation can increase the likelihood of the client's being convicted as well as opening the possibility of a prosecution for perjury. On the other hand, if the lawyer does not exercise control over the proof, the lawyer participates, although in a merely passive way, in deception of the court.

[13a] Three resolutions of this dilemma have been proposed. One is to permit the accused to testify by a narrative without guidance through the lawyer's questioning. This compromises both contending principles; it exempts the lawyer from the duty to disclose false evidence but subjects the client to an implicit disclosure of information imparted to counsel. Another suggested resolution, of relatively recent origin, is that the advocate be entirely excused from the duty to reveal perjury if the perjury is that of the client. This is a coherent solution but makes the advocate a knowing instrument of perjury.

[13b] The ultimate resolution of the dilemma, however, is that the lawyer must reveal the client's perjury if necessary to rectify the situation. A criminal accused has a right to the assistance of an advocate, a right to testify and a right of confidential communication with counsel. However, an accused should not have a right to assistance of counsel in committing perjury. Furthermore, an advocate has an obligation, not only in professional ethics but under the law as well, to avoid implication in the commission of perjury or other falsification of evidence. See Rule 1.2(c).

Ex Parte Proceedings

[14] Ordinarily, an advocate has the limited responsibility of presenting one side of the matters that a tribunal should consider in reaching a decision; the conflicting position is expected to be presented by the opposing party. However, in an ex parte proceeding, such as an application for a temporary restraining order, there is no balance of presentation by opposing advocates. The object of an ex parte proceeding is nevertheless to yield a substantially just result. The judge has an affirmative responsibility to accord the absent party just consideration. The lawyer for the represented party has the correlative duty to make disclosures of material facts known to the lawyer and that the lawyer reasonably believes are necessary to an informed decision. For purposes of this Rule, ex parte proceedings do not include grand jury proceedings or proceedings which are non-adversarial, including various administrative proceedings in which a party chooses not to appear. However, a particular tribunal (including an administrative tribunal) may have an explicit rule or other controlling precedent which requires disclosure even in a non-adversarial proceeding. If so, the lawyer must comply with a disclosure demand by the tribunal or challenge the action by available legal means. The failure to disclose information as part of a legal challenge to a demand for disclosure will not constitute a violation of this Rule.

Virginia Code Comparison

Paragraph (a)(1) is substantially similar to DR 7-102(A)(5), which provided that "[i]n his representation of a client, a lawyer shall not knowingly make a false statement of law or fact."

With regard to paragraph (a)(2), DR 7-102(A)(3) provided that "[i]n his representation of a client, a lawyer shall not conceal or knowingly fail to disclose that which he is required by law to reveal."

Paragraph (a)(3) has no direct counterpart in the Virginia Code. EC 7-20 stated: "Where a lawyer knows of legal authority in the controlling jurisdiction directly adverse to the position of his client, he should inform the tribunal of its existence unless his adversary has done so; but, having made such disclosure, he may challenge its soundness in whole or in part."

With regard to paragraph (a)(4), the first sentence of this subparagraph is similar to DR 7-102(A)(4), which provided that a lawyer shall not "knowingly use perjured testimony or false evidence." DR 4-101(D)(2), adopted here as Rule 1.6(c)(2), made it clear that the "remedial measures" referred to in the second sentence of paragraph (a)(4) could include disclosure of the fraud to the tribunal.

Paragraph (b) confers discretion on the lawyer to refuse to offer evidence that the lawyer "reasonably believes" is false. This gives the lawyer more latitude than DR 7-102(A)(4), which prohibited the lawyer from offering evidence the lawyer "knows" is false.

There was no counterpart in the Virginia Code to paragraph (c).

Paragraph (d) is identical to DR 7-102(B).

Committee Commentary

The Committee generally adopted the ABA Model Rule, but it deleted the word "material" from paragraph (a)(1) to make it identical to DR 7-102(A)(5) and from paragraph (a)(2) because it appeared to be redundant. Additionally, the word "directly," preceding "adverse" was deleted from paragraph (a)(3).

With respect to paragraph (a)(3), the Committee believed it advisable to adopt a provision requiring the disclosure of controlling adverse legal authority. While there was no corresponding provision within the Disciplinary Rules of the Virginia Code, there is a corresponding provision within the ABA Model Code, DR 7-106(B)(1). However, the Committee deleted the word "directly" from the paragraph in the belief that the limiting effect of that term could seriously dilute the paragraph's meaning.

The Committee determined to retain the obligation to report a non-client's fraud on the tribunal, and therefore repeated the provisions of DR 7-102(B) in paragraph (d).

CASE NOTES

Motion for sentencing departure based on truthful representations did not constitute ethical violation. — Lawyer could have requested a self-defense departure for defendant at sentencing for his violation of 18 U.S.C.S. § 922(g) (possession of a firearm and ammunition by a felon), without compromising his ethical duties under Va. Sup. Ct. R. pt. 6, § II, R. 3.3 and 4.1 because a motion for a self-defense departure would not have required the lawyer to make a false statement of fact or law to the sentencing court, to offer evidence that he knew or reasonably believed to be false, or to otherwise contravene the applicable ethics rules. Rather, the lawyer could have made a self-defense departure motion on the strength of the truthful and undisputed evidence that another client also represented by the lawyer had posed a genuine threat to defendant's life, that defendant had claimed to the authorities that he possessed a firearm at the time of his arrest for protection from the other client, and that the authorities believed him. United States v. Nicholson, 611 F.3d 191, 2010 U.S. App. LEXIS 14185 (4th Cir. July 12, 2010).

Failure to give authority. — Averment in a petition for appeal in a criminal case that under "well settled law" the evidence was insufficient gave no supporting case citation, in violation of Rules 5A:12(c) and 5A:20(e), as well as Va. Sup. Ct. R. pt. 6, § II, Rule 1.3(a) or 3.3(a)(3). Jacobs v. Commonwealth, 2002 Va. App. LEXIS 589 (Oct. 8, 2002).

Fraudulently signed bankruptcy petition. — Attorney's conduct in electronically filing a bankruptcy petition containing the electronic signatures of the debtor and the attorney, when in fact the attorney did not have the debtor's physical signature on a hard copy of the petition, violated the dictates for electronic filing in Fed. R. Bankr. P. 5005(a)(2), and E.D. Va. Bankr. R. 5005-1, violated the attorney's obligation in Va. Sup. Ct. R., pt. 6, § II, Rules 3.1 and 3.3 to bring only non-frivolous matters before the court, amounted to fraud on the court in violation of Fed. R. Bankr. P. 9011, and was sanctionable under the equitable powers granted to the court under 11 U.S.C.S. § 105. In re Wenk, 296 Bankr. 719, 2002 Bankr. LEXIS 1733 (Bankr. E.D. Va. 2002).

CIRCUIT COURT OPINIONS

Unsubstantiated claim. — Counsel violated Va. Sup. Ct. R. pt. 6, § II, R. 3.3(a) and § 8.01-271.1 by maintaining that defense counsel "hacked into" or made unauthorized access to plaintiff's Facebook account during a hearing in open court, based on no inquiry into the relevant facts beyond the bare, unsubstantiated assertions of his client. Lester v. Allied Concrete Co., 80 Va. Cir. 454, 2010 Va. Cir. LEXIS 153 (Charlottesville June 28, 2010).

Sanctions. — Attorney violated § 8.01-271.1, Va. Sup. Ct. R. 4:1(g), and Va. Sup. Ct. R. 4:12 by omitting an e-mail and by his failure to submit the subject e-mail to the court for in camera inspection. The attorney conceded that his behavior also violated Va. Sup. Ct. R. pt. 6, § II, R. 3.3 and 3.4; thus, he was liable for attorney fees. Lester v. Allied Concrete Co., 38 Va. Cir. 308, 2011 Va. Cir. LEXIS 245 (Charlottesville Sept. 6, 2011).

Rule 3.4. Fairness To Opposing Party And Counsel.

A lawyer shall not:

(a) Obstruct another party's access to evidence or alter, destroy or conceal a document or other material having potential evidentiary value for the purpose of obstructing a party's access to evidence. A lawyer shall not counsel or assist another person to do any such act.

(b) Advise or cause a person to secrete himself or herself or to leave the jurisdiction of a tribunal for the purpose of making that person unavailable as a witness therein.

(c) Falsify evidence, counsel or assist a witness to testify falsely, or offer an inducement to a witness that is prohibited by law. But a lawyer may advance, guarantee, or pay:

(1) reasonable expenses incurred by a witness in attending or testifying;

(2) reasonable compensation to a witness for lost earnings as a result of attending or testifying;

(3) a reasonable fee for the professional services of an expert witness.

(d) Knowingly disobey or advise a client to disregard a standing rule or a ruling of a tribunal made in the course of a proceeding, but the lawyer may take steps, in good faith, to test the validity of such rule or ruling.

(e) Make a frivolous discovery request or fail to make reasonably diligent effort to comply with a legally proper discovery request by an opposing party.

(f) In trial, allude to any matter that the lawyer does not reasonably believe is relevant or that will not be supported by admissible evidence, assert personal knowledge of facts in issue except when testifying as a witness, or state a personal opinion as to the justness of a cause, the credibility of a witness, the culpability of a civil litigant or the guilt or innocence of an accused.

(g) Intentionally or habitually violate any established rule of procedure or of evidence, where such conduct is disruptive of the proceedings.

(h) Request a person other than a client to refrain from voluntarily giving relevant information to another party unless:

(1) the information is relevant in a pending civil matter;

(2) the person in a civil matter is a relative or a current or former employee or other agent of a client; and

(3) the lawyer reasonably believes that the person's interests will not be adversely affected by refraining from giving such information.

(i) Present or threaten to present criminal or disciplinary charges solely to obtain an advantage in a civil matter.

(j) File a suit, initiate criminal charges, assert a position, conduct a defense, delay a trial, or take other action on behalf of the client when the lawyer knows or when it is obvious that such action would serve merely to harass or maliciously injure another.

COMMENT

[1] The procedure of the adversary system contemplates that the evidence in a case is to be marshaled competitively by the contending parties. Fair competition in the adversary system is secured by prohibitions against destruction or concealment of evidence, improperly influencing witnesses, obstructive tactics in discovery procedure, and the like.

[2] Documents and other items of evidence are often essential to establish a claim or defense. Subject to evidentiary privileges, the right of an opposing party, including the government, to obtain evidence through discovery or subpoena is an important procedural right. The exercise of that right can be frustrated if relevant material is altered, concealed or destroyed. Applicable law makes it an offense to destroy material for purpose of impairing its availability in a pending proceeding or one whose commencement can be foreseen. Paragraph (a) applies to evidentiary material generally, including computerized information.

[3] With regard to paragraph (c), it is not improper to pay a witness's reasonable expenses or to pay a reasonable fee for the services of an expert witness. The common law rule is that it is improper to pay an occurrence witness any fee for testifying and that it is improper to pay an expert witness a contingent fee.

[3a] The legal system depends upon voluntary compliance with court rules and rulings in order to function effectively. Thus, a lawyer generally is not justified in consciously violating such rules or rulings. However, paragraph (d) allows a lawyer to take measures necessary to test the validity of a rule or ruling, including open disobedience. See also Rule 1.2(c).

[4] Paragraph (g) prohibits lawyers from requesting persons other than clients to refrain from voluntarily giving relevant information. The Rule contains an exception permitting lawyers to advise current or former employees or other agents of a client to refrain from giving information to another party, because such persons may identify their interests with those of the client. The exception is limited to civil matters because of concerns with allegations of obstruction of justice (including perceived intimidation of witnesses) that could be made in a criminal investigation and prosecution. See also Rule 4.2.

[5] Although a lawyer is prohibited by paragraph (h) from presenting or threatening to present criminal or disciplinary charges solely to obtain an advantage in a civil matter, a lawyer may offer advice about the possibility of criminal prosecution and the client's rights and responsibilities in connection with such prosecution.

[6] Paragraph (i) deals with conduct that could harass or maliciously injure another. Dilatory practices bring the administration of justice into dispute. Delay should not be indulged merely for the convenience of the advocates, or solely for the purpose of frustrating an opposing party's attempt to obtain rightful redress or repose. It is not a justification that similar conduct is tolerated by the bench and the bar. The question is whether a competent lawyer acting in good faith would regard the course of action as having some substantial purpose other than delay.

[7] In the exercise of professional judgment on those decisions which are for the lawyer's determination in the handling of a legal matter, a lawyer

should always act in a manner consistent with the best interests of a client. However, when an action in the best interest of a client seems to the lawyer to be unjust, the lawyer may ask the client for permission to forego such action. The duty of lawyer to represent a client with zeal does not militate against his concurrent obligation to treat, with consideration, all persons involved in the legal process and to avoid the infliction of needless harm. Under this Rule, it would be improper to ask any question that the lawyer has no reasonable basis to believe is relevant to the case and that is intended to degrade any witness or other person.

[8] In adversary proceedings, clients are litigants and though ill feeling may exist between the clients, such ill feeling should not influence a lawyer's conduct, attitude or demeanor towards opposing counsel. A lawyer should not make unfair or derogatory personal reference to opposing counsel. Haranguing and offensive tactics by lawyers interfere with the orderly administration of justice and have no proper place in our legal system. A lawyer should be courteous to opposing counsel and should accede to reasonable requests regarding court proceedings, settings, continuances, waiver of procedural formalities, and similar matters which do not prejudice the rights of the client. A lawyer should follow the local customs of courtesy or practice, unless the lawyer gives timely notice to opposing counsel of the intention not to do so. A lawyer should be punctual in fulfilling all professional commitments.

Virginia Code Comparison

With regard to paragraph (a), DR 7-108(A) provided that a lawyer "shall not suppress any evidence that he or his client has a legal obligation to reveal or produce."

Paragraph (b) is identicial to DR 7-108(B).

Paragraph (c) is substantially similar to DR 7-108(C) which provided that a lawyer "shall not pay, offer to pay, or acquiesce in the payment of compensation to a witness contingent upon the content of his testimony or the outcome of the case. But a lawyer may advance, guarantee or acquiesce in the payment of: (1) Expenses reasonably incurred by a witness in attending or testifying; (2) Reasonable compensation to a witness for his loss of time in attending or testifying; (or) (3) A reasonable fee for the professional services of an expert witness. EC 7-25 stated that witnesses "should always testify truthfully and should be free from any financial inducements that might tempt them to do otherwise."

Paragraph (d) is substantially the same as DR 7-105(A).

Paragraph (e) is new.

Paragraph (f) is substantially similar to DR 7-105(C)(1), (2), (3) and (4) which stated:

In appearing in his professional capacity before a tribunal, a lawyer shall not: (1) State or allude to any matter that he has no reasonable basis to believe is relevant to the case or that will not be supported by admissible evidence. (2) Ask any question that he has no reasonable basis to believe is relevant to the case and that is intended to degrade a witness or other person. (3) Assert his personal knowledge of the facts in issue, except when testifying as a witness. (4) Assert his personal opinion as to the justness of a cause, as to the credibility of a witness, as to the culpability of a civil litigant, or as to the guilt or innocence of an accused, but he may argue, on his analysis of the evidence, for any position or conclusion with respect to the matters stated herein.

Paragraph (g) is identical to DR 7-105 (C)(5).

Paragraph (h) is new.

Paragraph (i) is similar to DR 7-104, although a lawyer is no longer prohibited from "participat[ing] in presenting" criminal charges and therefore may freely offer advice to the client about the client's rights under the criminal law.

Paragraph (j) is identical to DR 7-102(A)(1).

Committee Commentary

The Committee attempted to join the best of both the Virginia Code and ABA Model Rule 3.4 in this Rule. For example, paragraph (a) was adopted because it appears to place a broader obligation on lawyers than DR 7-108(A), but DR 7-108(B) was added to the Rule as paragraph (b) because it states explicitly what is only implicit in paragraph (a).

Language from DR 7-108(C) was added to paragraph (c) to make it clear that certain witness compensation is permitted — something not clear from the language of the ABA Model Rule, although it is stated in the ABA Model Rule's Comment.

The language of DR 7-105(A) was adopted as paragraph (d) in lieu of the ABA Model Rule language because it states more clearly what is apparently intended by the Rule. However, the Committee deleted as unnecessary the word "appropriate" preceding "steps."

With respect to paragraph (e), the Committee saw no reason to limit the discovery request provisions to the pretrial period, as is explicitly the case in the ABA Model Rule.

Paragraph (f) parallels similar provisions in DR 7-105(C) and paragraph (h) covers a subject not addressed in the Virginia Code.

Paragraph (i) is similar to DR 7-104, although the Committee voted to delete the reference to "participate in presenting." This deletion allows a lawyer to offer advice to the client about the client's rights under the criminal law without violating this Rule.

The Committee determined that the existing language of DR 7-102(A)(1) should appear as paragraph (j), although the ABA Model Rules do not contain this section.

The amendment effective January 1, 2004, adopted September 24, 2003, added present paragraph (g) and redesignated former paragraphs (g) through (i) as present paragraphs (h) through (j).

Law Review. — For article, "Professional Responsibility," see 43 U. Rich. L. Rev. 255 (2008).

CASE NOTES

Threats against opposing counsel in attempt to force withdrawal. — Attorney violated Va. Sup. Ct. R., Pt. 6, § II, Rule 3.4(i) and (j) when he personally attacked opposing counsel, making threats in an attempt to force opposing counsel to withdraw from representing the attorney's wife in a divorce action. Barrett v. Va. State Bar, 269 Va. 583, 611 S.E.2d 375, 2005 Va. LEXIS 45 (2005).

Agreements to pay witnesses more than statutory fee for expenses not improper. — Agreements to pay witnesses for lost time and expenses incurred, in excess of the statutory fees, are not unusual, extraordinary or improper. Slayton v. Weinberger, 213 Va. 690, 194 S.E.2d 703 (1973) (decided under former EC 7-28).

But are not encouraged nor legally enforceable. — Agreements to pay witnesses for lost time and expenses incurred, in excess of the statutory fees are not to be encouraged and, for that reason, they are not legally enforceable. Slayton v. Weinberger, 213 Va. 690, 194 S.E.2d 703 (1973), (decided under former EC 7-28).

Existence of agreement may be shown to impeach. — While the existence of an agreement to pay witnesses for lost time and expenses incurred, in excess of the statutory fees, may be shown as affecting the weight and credibility of the witness' testimony, the existence of an agreement is not ordinarily sufficient grounds to set aside a verdict and award a new trial. Slayton v. Weinberger, 213 Va. 690, 194 S.E.2d 703 (1973) (decided under former EC 7-28).

Prosecutor may not deny intention to call witness to avoid discovery. — Where the Commonwealth's attorney knows that an informant's appearance as a witness is impending, or intends in all likelihood to call the witness, the prosecutor may not deny his or her intention to call the witness as a pretext to avoid discovery. Courts have the responsibility to monitor the conduct of those attorneys who appear before them and assure adherence to professional standards. Moreno v. Commonwealth, 10 Va. App. 408, 392 S.E.2d 836 (1990) (decided under former DR 7-105).

Reasonable belief that conduct occurred required for impeachment attempt. — One may not attempt to impeach a witness by asking about the witness's alleged misconduct without having a reasonable belief that the allegations of misconduct are true. Therefore, the trial court erred in permitting the prosecutor to ask a defense witness if he had threatened the Commonwealth's witness without determining whether the question was based on a reasonable belief that the witness had made such threats, and allowing this unsubstantiated question was not harmless error. Scott v. Commonwealth, 18 Va. App. 692, 446 S.E.2d 619 (1994) (decided under former DR 7-105).

Rule violated. — Attorney violated Va. Sup. Ct. R. pt. 6, § II, R. 3.1 and 3.4(j) when the attorney attempted to call opposing counsel as a witness in the attorney's divorce case because the attorney allegedly thought the attorney's wife was having a romantic relationship with opposing counsel. Barrett v. Va. State Bar, 272 Va. 260, 634 S.E.2d 341, 2006 Va. LEXIS 84 (2006).

Violation of local federal rule. — An attorney was subject to discipline for holding a press conference concerning the testimony of a prospective witness in a pending federal criminal case and for making statements to a newspaper reporter concerning the alleged lack of merit in the government's case where a local rule of the federal court, of which the attorney was aware, expressly prohibited lawyers from making public statements about the identity, testimony or credibility of prospective witnesses, or from giving any opinion about the merits of a pending case. Morrissey v. Virginia State Bar ex rel. Third Dist. Comm., 260 Va. 472, 538 S.E.2d 677, 2000 Va. LEXIS 148 (2000) (decided under former 7-105(A)).

CIRCUIT COURT OPINIONS

Rule violated. — Attorney violated Va. Code § 8.01-271.1, Va. Sup. Ct. R. 4:1(g), and Va. Sup. Ct. R. 4:12 by omitting an e-mail and by his failure to submit the subject e-mail to the court for in camera inspection. The attorney conceded that his behavior also violated Va. Sup. Ct. R. pt. 6, § II, R. 3.3 and 3.4; thus, he was liable for attorney fees. Lester v. Allied Concrete Co., 38 Va. Cir. 308, 2011 Va. Cir. LEXIS 245 (Charlottesville Sept. 6, 2011).

Rule 3.5. Impartiality and Decorum of the Tribunal.

(a) A lawyer shall not:

(1) before or during the trial of a case, directly or indirectly, communicate with a juror or anyone the lawyer knows to be a member of the venire from which the jury will be selected for the trial of the case, except as permitted by law;

(2) after discharge of the jury from further consideration of a case:

(i) ask questions of or make comments to a member of that jury that are calculated merely to harass or embarrass the juror or to influence the juror's actions in future jury service;

(ii) communicate with a member of that jury if the communication is prohibited by law or court order; or

(iii) communicate with a member of that jury if the juror has made known to the lawyer a desire not to communicate; or

(3) conduct or cause, by financial support or otherwise, another to conduct a vexatious or harassing investigation of either a juror or a member of a venire.

(b) All restrictions imposed by paragraph (a) upon a lawyer also apply to communications with or investigations of members of the immediate family or household of a juror or a member of a venire.

(c) A lawyer shall reveal promptly to the court improper conduct by a member of a venire or a juror, or by another toward a venireman or a juror or a member of the juror's family, of which the lawyer has knowledge.

(d) A lawyer shall not give or lend anything of value to a judge, official, or employee of a tribunal under circumstances which might give the appearance that the gift or loan is made to influence official action.

(e) In an adversary proceeding, a lawyer shall not communicate, or cause another to communicate, as to the merits of the cause with a judge or an official before whom the proceeding is pending, except:

(1) in the course of official proceedings in the cause;

(2) in writing if the lawyer promptly delivers a copy of the writing to opposing counsel or to the adverse party who is not represented by a lawyer;

(3) orally upon adequate notice to opposing counsel or to the adverse party who is not represented by a lawyer; or

(4) as otherwise authorized by law.

(f) A lawyer shall not engage in conduct intended to disrupt a tribunal.

COMMENT

[1] *ABA Model Rule* Comment not adopted.

[2] To safeguard the impartiality that is essential to the judicial process, veniremen and jurors should be protected against extraneous influences. When impartiality is present, public confidence in the judicial system is enhanced. There should be no extra-judicial communication with veniremen prior to trial or with jurors during trial by or on behalf of a lawyer connected with the case. Furthermore, a lawyer who is not connected with the case should not communicate with or cause another to communicate with a venireman or juror about the case. After the trial, communication by a lawyer with jurors is permitted so long as the lawyer refrains from asking questions or making comments that tend to harass or embarrass the juror or to influence actions of the juror in future cases. Were a lawyer to be prohibited from communicating after trial with a juror, the lawyer could not ascertain if the verdict might be subject to legal challenge, in which event the invalidity of a verdict might go undetected. When an extra-judicial communication by a lawyer with a juror is permitted by law, it should be made considerately and with deference to the personal feelings of the juror.

[3] All litigants and lawyers should have access to tribunals on an equal basis. Generally, in adversary proceedings a lawyer should not communicate with a judge relative to a matter pending before, or which is to be brought before, a tribunal over which the judge presides in circumstances which might have the effect or give the appearance of granting undue advantage to one party. For example, a lawyer should not communicate with a tribunal by a writing unless a copy thereof is promptly delivered to opposing counsel or to an adverse party proceeding pro se. Ordinarily an oral communication by a lawyer with a judge or hearing officer should be made only upon adequate notice to opposing counsel, or, if there is none, to the opposing party. A lawyer should not condone or lend himself or herself to private importunities by another with a judge or hearing officer on behalf of the lawyer or the client.

[4] The advocate's function is to present evidence and arguments so that the cause may be decided according to law. Refraining from abusive or obstreperous conduct is a corollary of the advocate's right to speak on behalf of litigants. A lawyer must stand firm against abuse by a judge but should avoid reciprocation; the judge's default is no justification for similar dereliction by an advocate. An advocate can present the cause, protect the record for subsequent review and preserve professional integrity by patient firmness no less effectively than by belligerence or theatrics. Rule 8.3(b) also requires a lawyer to report such conduct by a judge to the appropriate authority and with this duty and recourse there is no reason for a lawyer to reciprocate.

Virginia Code Comparison

Paragraphs (a)-(c) are substantially the same as DR 7-107(A) - 7-107(F). Paragraph (a)(2)(ii) and (iii) are new.

Paragraph (d) is identical to DR 7-109(A).

Paragraph (e) is identical to DR 7-109(B).

Paragraph (f) is new.

Committee Commentary

The Committee believed that the adopted language of DR 7-107 and DR 7-109 provides better guidance to lawyers than that of paragraphs (a) and (b) of the ABA Model Rule. In paragraph (f) of this Rule, the Committee adopted the language of paragraph (c) of the ABA Model Rule, which prohibits "conduct intended to disrupt a tribunal," because the Committee considered the general admonition against "conduct prejudicial to the administration of justice" to be vague.

The amendment effective January 1, 2004, adopted September 24, 2003, in (a)(2), inserted the (i) designator and added subparagraphs (ii) and (iii).

CASE NOTES

Mailing order of confirmation to judge and not mailing copy to counsel. — Bankruptcy trustee's actions in mailing order of confirmation to bankruptcy judge and not mailing copy to opposing counsel were practices that were custom, and were ethical and beyond reproach, and did not violate this rule. In re Endicott, 157 Bankr. 255 (W.D. Va. 1993) (decided under former DR 7-109).

Mailing order of argument to judge and not mailing copy to counsel. — Attorney violated Va. Sup. Ct. R., Pt. 6, § II, Rule 3.5 when he sent a letter to the judge in his divorce action arguing that his wife was unfit to have custody of the children and that he should be awarded custody, and then failed to send a copy to opposing counsel. Barrett v. Va. State Bar, 269 Va. 583, 611 S.E.2d 375, 2005 Va. LEXIS 45 (2005).

Rule 3.6. Trial Publicity.

(a) A lawyer participating in or associated with the investigation or the prosecution or the defense of a criminal matter that may be tried by a jury shall not make or participate in making an extrajudicial statement that a reasonable person would expect to be disseminated by means of public communication that the lawyer knows, or should know, will have a substantial likelihood of interfering with the fairness of the trial by a jury.

(b) A lawyer shall exercise reasonable care to prevent employees and associates from making an extrajudicial statement that the lawyer would be prohibited from making under this Rule.

COMMENT

[1] It is difficult to strike a balance between protecting the right to a fair trial and safeguarding the right of free expression. In a criminal matter which may be tried by a jury, preserving the right to a fair trial necessarily entails some curtailment of the information that may be disseminated about a defendant or witnesses prior to trial. If there were no such limits, the result would be the practical nullification of the protective effect of the rules of forensic decorum and the exclusionary rules of evidence. On the other hand, there are vital social interests served by the free dissemination of information about events having legal consequences and about legal proceedings themselves. In addition to its legitimate interest in the conduct of judicial proceedings, the public has a right to know about threats to its safety and measures aimed at assuring its security.

Virginia Code Comparison

Rule 3.6 is substantially the same as DR 7-106, except that paragraph (a) adopts a "substantial likelihood of material prejudice" standard rather than the "clear and present danger" standard of DR 7-106(A).

Committee Commentary

The Committee believed that one lesson of *Hirschkop v. Snead*, 594 F.2d 356 (4th Cir. 1979) is that a rule, such as the ABA Model Rule, which sets forth a specific list of prohibited statements by lawyers in connection with a trial, is constitutionally suspect. Accordingly, the more succinct language of DR 7-106 was adopted. However, the Committee changed the standard to the arguably broader "substantial likelihood of material prejudice," in accord with the language approved by the Supreme Court of the United States in *Gentile v. State Bar, 501 U.S. 1030 (1991)*.

Rule 3.7. Lawyer As Witness.

(a) A lawyer shall not act as an advocate in an adversarial proceeding in which the lawyer is likely to be a necessary witness except where:

(1) the testimony relates to an uncontested issue;

(2) the testimony relates to the nature and value of legal services rendered in the case; or

(3) disqualification of the lawyer would work substantial hardship on the client.

(b) If, after undertaking employment in contemplated or pending litigation, a lawyer learns or it is obvious that the lawyer may be called as a witness other than on behalf of the client, the lawyer may continue the representation until it is apparent that the testimony is or may be prejudicial to the client.

(c) A lawyer may act as advocate in an adversarial proceeding in which another lawyer in the lawyer's firm is likely to be called as witness unless precluded from doing so by Rule 1.7 or 1.9.

COMMENT

[1] Combining the roles of advocate and witness can prejudice the opposing party and can involve a conflict of interest between the lawyer and client.

[2] The opposing party has proper objection where the combination of roles may prejudice that party's rights in the litigation. A witness is required

to testify on the basis of personal knowledge, while an advocate is expected to explain and comment on evidence given by others. It may not be clear whether a statement by an advocate—witness should be taken as proof or as an analysis of the proof.

[3] Paragraph (a)(1) recognizes that if the testimony will be uncontested, the ambiguities in the dual role are purely theoretical. Paragraph (a)(2) recognizes that where the testimony concerns the extent and value of legal services rendered in the action in which the testimony is offered, permitting the lawyers to testify avoids the need for a second trial with new counsel to resolve that issue. Moreover, in such a situation the judge has firsthand knowledge of the matter in issue; hence, there is less dependence on the adversary process to test the credibility of the testimony.

[4] Apart from these two exceptions, paragraph (a)(3) recognizes that a balancing is required between the interests of the client and those of the opposing party. Whether the opposing party is likely to suffer prejudice depends on the nature of the case, the importance and probable tenor of the lawyer's testimony, and the probability that the lawyer's testimony will conflict with that of other witnesses. Even if there is risk of such prejudice, in determining whether the lawyer should be disqualified, due regard must be given to the effect of disqualification on the lawyer's client. It is relevant that one or both parties could reasonably foresee that the lawyer would probably be a witness. The principle of imputed disqualification stated in Rule 1.10 has no application to this aspect of the problem.

[5] *ABA Model Rule* Comment not adopted.

[6] Whether the combination of roles involves an improper conflict of interest with respect to the client is determined by Rule 1.7 or 1.9. For example, if there is likely to be substantial conflict between the testimony of the client and that of the lawyer or a member of the lawyer's firm, the representation is improper. The problem can arise whether the lawyer is called as a witness on behalf of the client or is called by the opposing party. Where a lawyer may be called as a witness other than on behalf of the client, paragraph (b) allows the lawyer to continue representation until it becomes apparent that the testimony may be prejudicial to the client. Determining whether or not such a conflict exists is primarily the responsibility of the lawyer involved. See Comment to Rule 1.7. If a lawyer who is a member of a firm may not act as both advocate and witness by reason of conflict of interest, Rule 1.10 disqualifies the firm also.

Virginia Code Comparison

With regard to paragraph (a), DR 5-101(B) prohibited a lawyer, or the lawyer's firm, from serving as advocate if the lawyer "knows or it is obvious that he or a lawyer in his firm ought to be called as a witness" unless "(1) . . . the testimony will relate solely to an uncontested matter or to a matter of formality and there is no reason to believe that substantial evidence will be offered in opposition to the testimony; (2) . . . the testimony will relate solely to the nature and value of legal services rendered in the case by the lawyer or his firm to the client; (3) . . . refusal would work a substantial hardship on the client because of the distinctive value of the lawyer or his firm as counsel in the particular case." Similarly, DR 5-102(A) stated: "If, after undertaking employment in contemplated or pending litigation, a lawyer learns or it is obvious that he or a lawyer in his firm ought to be called as a witness on behalf of his client, he shall withdraw from the conduct of the trial and his firm, if any, shall not continue representation in the trial, except that he may continue the representation and he or a lawyer in his firm may testify in the circumstances enumerated in DR 5-101(B)(1) through (3)," quoted above.

Paragraph (b) is substantially the same as DR 5-102(B).

Paragraph (c) had no counterpart in the *Virginia Code*.

Committee Commentary

The Committee concluded that the test in the ABA Model Rule, i.e., whether a lawyer "is likely to be a necessary witness," is more instructive than that in DR 5-101(B), i.e., whether the lawyer "knows or it is obvious that he . . . ought to be called as a witness." The Committee did, however, conclude that the ABA Model Rule should be modified to apply not just to trials but to any "adversarial proceeding." Additionally, the ABA Model Rule applies only to individual lawyers and not, in general, to an entire firm—providing a flexibility which the Committee believed is needed. Additionally, the Committee incorporated the language of DR 5-102(B) as paragraph (b) to give the Rule additional flexibility. With respect to paragraph (b), the Committee deleted the DR 5-102(B)'s reference to "a lawyer in his firm" since that situation is now addressed by paragraph (c) and the conflicts provisions of these Rules.

CASE NOTES

"Witness-advocate" rule. — Together, subdivision (B) and DR 5-102(A) comprise what is commonly referred to as the "witness-advocate" rule under which lawyers are prohibited from serving as an advocate and a witness in the same proceeding, except in the limited circumstances set forth in subdivisions (B)(1)-(3) [see now (a)(1)-(3) of this rule]. Moreover, as these DRs plainly indicate, disqualification of a lawyer is imputed to that lawyer's firm as well. Estate of Andrews v. United States, 804 F. Supp. 820 (E.D. Va. 1992) (decided under former DR 5-101).

Testimony of law partner as to preparation of deeds. — The law partner of defendant's counsel was permitted to testify that he prepared certain deeds and as to their contents and execution, where such testimony involved only formal matters, and substantial evidence disputing the preparation, execution, or contents of the deeds was not offered. Matney v. Cedar Land Farms, Inc., 216 Va. 932, 224 S.E.2d 162 (1976) (decided under former DR 5-101).

Disqualification of counsel with whom party had long-established relationship would be hardship. — Where counsel for a party has approximately 1,000 hours of services performed in its representations, any disqualification on grounds that an attorney affiliated with the firm is to be called as a witness would represent an extreme hardship on that party. In addition to being deprived of counsel with which it has a well-founded relationship, the party would have the very heavy burden of educating replacement counsel on all the activity which has transpired previously. Chantilly Constr. Corp. v. John Driggs Co., 39 Bankr. 466 (Bankr. E.D. Va. 1984) (decided under former DR 5-101).

Firm not disqualified where testimony of attorney would be cumulative and redundant. — A law firm should not be disqualified from representing a party to an action on grounds that the other party plans to call attorneys affiliated with the firm as witnesses, where their testimony would be cumulative and in some instances redundant. Chantilly Constr. Corp. v. John Driggs Co., 39 Bankr. 466 (Bankr. E.D. Va. 1984) (decided under former DR 5-102).

Disqualification under this rule must be accompanied by a showing that the testimony of the lawyer is (1) relevant; (2) necessary; and (3) is or may be prejudicial to the client whose lawyer is to be called as a witness by the adverse party; the moving party bears the substantial burden of demonstrating specifically how and as to what issues in the action the prejudice exists or is likely to occur. Personalized Mass Media Corp. v. Weather Channel, Inc., 899 F. Supp. 239 (E.D. Va. 1995) (decided under former DR 5-102).

Disqualification denied as plaintiff did not prove necessary elements. — Plaintiff failed to prove that the witness-advocate rule applied to her situation; plaintiff's description of the law firm partner's likely knowledge did not represent such testimony as genuinely unique so as to be strictly necessary. In short, plaintiff had to overcome a substantial burden to prove the necessary elements of the witness-advocate rule, and she did not meet this burden. Sutherland v. Jagdmann, 2005 U.S. Dist. LEXIS 25878 (E.D. Va. Oct. 31, 2005).

Motion for appointment of special prosecutor properly denied. — Trial court properly denied defendant's pre-trial motion for the appointment of a special prosecutor, seeking the appointment on the basis that the assigned prosecutor had first-hand knowledge of evidence impeaching an eyewitness and, therefore, was a potential witness himself. The trial court properly denied the motion initially because the testimony of the prosecutor would have been admissible only if the witness denied making the conflicting statement, and at trial, once the witness denied making the statement, defendant did not renew his motion to disqualify and did not request a mistrial; thus, defendant failed to preserve for appeal this aspect of his request for the appointment of a special prosecutor. Campbell v. Commonwealth, No. 0269-12-1, 2012 Va. App. LEXIS 413 (Dec. 18, 2012).

Burden of proof. — Party seeking to invoke the witness-advocate rule for disqualification purposes must prove that the proposed witness-advocate's testimony is strictly necessary, not merely relevant and useful. Sutherland v. Jagdmann, 2005 U.S. Dist. LEXIS 25878 (E.D. Va. Oct. 31, 2005).

Continued representation by counsel presented conflicts of interest. — Where government argued that an actual conflict of interest was present because members or employees of private law firm, which represented defendant, would be called to testify at defendant's trial regarding the cash payment of legal fees by a third-party unindicted co-conspirator as possible evidence of the existence of a drug conspiracy, where the government also argued that an actual conflict of interest existed because the private firm represented both defendant and an alleged member of conspiracy in a substantially related matter, and where firm argued that it could continue to represent defendant through his trial if the potential testimony of its members or employees could be stipulated, and if members or employees of the firm were forced to testify at trial, then the firm would disqualify itself at that point, continued representation by current counsel presented actual and potential conflicts of interest and would give the appearance of impropriety. United States v. Scott, 980 F. Supp. 165 (E.D. Va. 1997) (decided under former DR 5-102).

CIRCUIT COURT OPINIONS

No conflict of interest. — Where a law firm had represented the executor of a trust, the beneficiary's motion to disqualify the law firm on ground that an attorney with firm was a witness, was denied; there was no conflict of interest for which a client could be adversely affected by the law firm's continued representation of the executor. Old Dominion Trust Co. v. Geiger, 56 Va. Cir. 522, 2001 Va. Cir. LEXIS 494 (Norfolk 2001).

Withdrawal unnecessary. — Where the wife's attorney participated in the wife's termination from the law firm, which was allegedly caused by the wife's unstable behavior, the wife's attorney was arguably a potential witness in the wife's action against the husband; the wife's attorney was not required to withdraw pursuant to Va. Sup. Ct. R., pt. 6, § II, Rule 3.7(b), as there was no allegation that the wife's attorney's testimony would be prejudicial to the wife's interests. Parker v. Parker, 61 Va. Cir. 670, 2002 Va. Cir. LEXIS 318 (Roanoke 2002).

Though defendant's counsel stated he would probably have to depose plaintiff's attorney, as the evidence did not establish that the attorney would be a "necessary" witness or that his testimony would be prejudicial to defendant, the attorney's firm was not disqualified under Va. Sup. Ct. R., pt. 6, § II, Rule 3.7. Arriba Corporation v. Bostic, 69 Va. Cir. 505, 2002 Va. Cir. LEXIS 464 (Norfolk 2002).

Rule 3.8. Additional Responsibilities of a Prosecutor.

A lawyer engaged in a prosecutorial function shall:

(a) not file or maintain a charge that the prosecutor knows is not supported by probable cause;

(b) not knowingly take advantage of an unrepresented defendant;

(c) not instruct or encourage a person to withhold information from the defense after a party has been charged with an offense;

(d) make timely disclosure to counsel for the defendant, or to the defendant if he has no counsel, of the existence of evidence which the prosecutor knows tends to negate the guilt of the accused, mitigate the degree of the offense, or reduce the punishment, except when disclosure is precluded or modified by order of a court; and

(e) not direct or encourage investigators, law enforcement personnel, employees or other persons assisting or associated with the prosecutor in a criminal case to make an extrajudicial statement that the prosecutor would be prohibited from making under Rule 3.6.

COMMENT

[1] A prosecutor has the responsibility of a minister of justice and not simply that of an advocate. This responsibility carries with it specific obligations to see that the defendant is accorded procedural justice and that guilt is decided upon the basis of sufficient evidence.

[1a] Paragraph (a) prohibits a prosecutor from initiating or maintaining a charge once he knows that the charge is not supported by even probable cause. The prohibition recognizes that charges are often filed before a criminal investigation is complete.

[1b] Paragraph (b) is intended to protect the unrepresented defendant from the overzealous prosecutor who uses tactics that are intended to coerce or induce the defendant into taking action that is against the defendant's best interests, based on an objective analysis. For example, it would constitute a violation of the provision if a prosecutor, in order to obtain a plea of guilty to a charge or charges, falsely represented to an unrepresented defendant that the court's usual disposition of such charges is less harsh than is actually the case, e.g., that the court usually sentences a first-time offender for the simple possession of marijuana under the deferred prosecution provisions of Code of Virginia Section 18.2-251 when, in fact, the court has a standard policy of not utilizing such an option.

[2] At the same time, the prohibition does not apply to the knowing and voluntary waiver by an accused of constitutional rights such as the right to counsel and silence which are governed by controlling case law. Nor does (b) apply to an accused appearing pro se with the ultimate approval of the tribunal. Where an accused does appear pro se before a tribunal, paragraph (b) does not prohibit discussions between the prosecutor and the defendant regarding the nature of the charges and the prosecutor's intended actions with regard to those charges. It is permissible, therefore, for a prosecutor to state that he intends to reduce a charge in exchange for a guilty plea from a defendant if nothing in the manner of the offer suggests coercion and the tribunal ultimately finds that the defendant's waiver of his right to counsel and his guilty plea are knowingly made and voluntary.

[3] The qualifying language in paragraph (c), i.e., ". . . after a party has been charged with an offense," is intended to exempt the rule from application during the investigative phase (including grand jury) when a witness may be requested to maintain secrecy in order to protect the integrity of the investigation and support concerns for safety. The term "encourage" in paragraph (c) is intended to prevent a prosecutor from doing indirectly what cannot be done directly. The exception in paragraph (d) also recognizes that a prosecutor may seek a protective order from the tribunal if disclosure of information to the defense could result in substantial harm to an individual or to the public interest.

[4] Paragraphs (d) and (e) address knowing violations of the respective provisions so as to allow for better understanding and easier enforcement by excluding situations (paragraph (d)), for example, where the lawyer/prosecutor does not know the theory of the defense so as to be able to assess the exculpatory nature of evidence or situations (paragraph (e)) where the lawyer/prosecutor does not have knowledge or control over the ultra vires actions of law enforcement personnel who may be only minimally involved in a case.

Virginia Code Comparison

With respect to paragraphs (a), DR 8-102(A)(1) provided that a "public prosecutor or other government lawyer shall . . . refrain from prosecuting a charge that [he] . . . knows is not supported by probable cause."

Paragraph (b) is derived from DR 8-102(A)(2) which prohibited prosecutors from inducing an unrepresented defendant to "surrender important procedural rights."

The counterpart to paragraph (c) is DR 8-102(A)(3) which proscribed "discouraging" a person from giving relevant information to the defendants.

Paragraph (d) is similar to DR 8 102(A)(4), but requires actual knowledge on the part of prosecuting lawyers that they are in possession of exculpatory evidence as opposed to simply being in knowing possession of evidence that may be determined to be of such a nature, although acknowledging that such disclosure may be affected by court orders.

Paragraph (e) has no direct counterpart in Virginia Code, but it generally parallels DR 7-106 (B), now Rule 3.6(b), which directed that a lawyer "exercise reasonable care to prevent his employees and associates from making a [prohibited] extrajudicial statement."

Paragraph DR 8-102(A)(5), which prohibited the subpoena of an attorney as a witness in a criminal prosecution regarding a present or past client without prior judicial approval, has been deleted in light of prevailing case law.

Committee Commentary

The Committee retitled this Rule "Additional Responsibilities of a Prosecutor," rather than "Special Responsibilities of a Prosecutor," as in the ABA Model Rule, to make it clear that the Rule's provisions are in addition to the obligations of the attorney acting in a prosecutorial role as set forth in the remaining Rules. The Committee also thought it appropriate to address the proscriptions of the Rule to any "lawyer engaged in a prosecutorial function" as opposed to just a "prosecutor in a criminal case" so as to eliminate any confusion on the part of any lawyer (such as a County Attorney or assistant Attorney General) who may be acting in the role of a prosecutor without being a member of a Commonwealth's Attorney's office.

The Committee believed that paragraph (a) in which actual knowledge is required is more understandable and more susceptible to ready enforcement where any more subjective standard (such as "or it is obvious") is too vague. At the same time, the Committee wanted to strengthen the proscription set forth in the Virginia Code ("shall refrain") so as to make clear that the prosecutor should not even file a charge if it is not supported by "probable cause" and should certainly not pursue a charge to trial, even if initially supported by the minimum standard of "probable cause," if it cannot reasonably expected to survive a motion to strike the evidence or motion for judgment of acquittal. The original ABA Model Rule language only proscribed "prosecuting a charge that... is not supported by probable cause."

The Committee did not include the language of ABA Model Rule 3.8(b) in which the prosecutor is required to "make reasonable efforts to assure that the accused has been advised of the right to, and the procedure for obtaining, counsel and has been given reasonable opportunity to obtain counsel" because the Committee did not believe that such an obligation should formally be placed on the lawyer-prosecutor.

The Committee concluded that the language of proposed paragraph (b) more accurately focuses on the type of prosecutorial conduct that is prohibited, rather than the provision of the existing DR and ABA Model Rule 3.8(c) which address the waiver of important procedural rights which, in fact, can be knowingly waived as the Comment attempts to explain. In addition, the Committee felt that the example of the waiver of such a procedural right as that of a preliminary hearing as set forth in the existing DR and ABA Model Rule is misleading at best, since it is exceedingly rare that a defendant charged with a felony would insist on proceeding pro se and then agree to waive the hearing.

The Committee felt that it was appropriate to strengthen the provisions of DR 8-102(A)(3) to provide that the lawyer acting in a prosecutorial function shall not "instruct or encourage a person to withhold information from the defense" as opposed to the more subjective and less enforceable "shall not discourage". In addition, in recognition of the reality of the investigative stage of a matter in which a witness may be asked to "keep quiet" in order to protect the witness and the integrity of the investigation, the Committee felt it appropriate to restrict application of the prohibition to that point in the process after formal charge when the "person" becomes a "party."

The Committee felt a change from existing DR 8-102(A)(4) concerning the disclosure of exculpatory evidence to the defense was appropriate by clarifying that it would apply only to that evidence which the prosecutor knows is exculpatory as opposed to a more subjective analysis of evidence which may be in the knowing possession of the prosecutor but which he does not have reason to believe would be exculpatory.

The Committee felt that the language of the ABA Model Rule which speaks in terms of "exercising reasonable care" to prevent others involved in a prosecution from making prohibited extrajudicial statements placed an unreasonable affirmative duty on the attorney acting in a prosecutorial role whereby the attorney would be held responsible for attempting to control the conduct of others.

Finally, the Committee decided to recommend deletion of DR 8-102(5) prohibiting the subpoena of an attorney as a witness in a criminal matter involving a present or former client without prior judicial approval because of prevailing case law and judicial fiat (the United States District Court for the Eastern District of Virginia) which does not require same.

CASE NOTES

Failure of Commonwealth to comply with discovery order. — When it is brought to the attention of a court that the Commonwealth has failed to comply with a discovery order, the court may prohibit the Commonwealth from introducing the evidence or enter such other order as it deems just under the circumstances. Certain circumstances may dictate a citation for contempt and/or require referral of the matter to the appropriate ethics committee of the bar. Stotler v. Commonwealth, 2 Va. App. 481, 346 S.E.2d 39 (1986) (decided under former DR 8-102).

Sanctions, etc., for deliberate attempt to introduce inadmissible evidence. — When it appears to a trial court that a party has deliberately attempted to introduce evidence which it knows is improper or inadmissible, either because it was not disclosed during discovery or because it otherwise is inadmissible under rules of evidence, it is the duty and responsibility of the court to deter such inappropriate tactics by taking such action, imposing such sanctions, or granting such relief as it deems appropriate. Stotler v. Commonwealth, 2 Va. App. 481, 346 S.E.2d 39 (1986) (decided under former DR 8-102).

Court order that Commonwealth refrain from interfering with attempts to interview witnesses. — Article I, Section 8 of the Virginia Constitution protects "the right to prepare for trial which, in turn, includes the right to interview material witnesses and to ascertain the truth," and is reinforced by the Virginia Code of Professional Responsibility. "The prosecutor in a criminal case ... shall ... [n]ot discourage a person from giving relevant information to the defendants." DR 8-102 (A)(3) (1987). As qualified by writ of prohibition, the trial judge's order that the Commonwealth refrain from any interference with attempts by defense counsel to interview witnesses is fully consistent with those principles. Epperly v. Booker, 235 Va. 35, 366 S.E.2d 62 (1988) (decided under former DR 8-102).

Rule not violated. — Finding that the attorney violated Va. Sup. Ct. R. pt. 6, § II, R. 3.8(a) was improper because it could not be inferred from the circumstances that the attorney had actual knowledge that the third indictment lacked probable cause to support it. Livingston v. Va. State Bar, 286 Va. 1, 744 S.E.2d 220, 2013 Va. LEXIS 75 (2013).

Prosecutor may not deny intention to call witness to avoid discovery. — Where the Commonwealth's attorney knows that an informant's appearance as a witness is impending, or intends in all likelihood to call the witness, the prosecutor may not deny his or her intention to call the witness as a pretext to avoid discovery. Courts have the responsibility to monitor the conduct of those attorneys who appear before them and assure adherence to professional standards. Moreno v. Commonwealth, 10 Va. App. 408, 392 S.E.2d 836 (1990) (decided under former DR 8-102).

TRANSACTIONS WITH PERSONS OTHER THAN CLIENTS.

Rule 4.1. Truthfulness in Statement to Others.

In the course of repersenting a client a lawyer shall not knowingly:

(a) Make a false statement of fact or law; or

(b) Fail to disclose a fact when disclosure is necessary to avoid assisting a criminal or fraudulent act by a client.

COMMENT

Misrepresentation

[1] A lawyer is required to be truthful when dealing with others on a client's behalf, but generally has no affirmative duty to inform an opposing party of relevant facts. A misrepresentation can occur if the lawyer incorporates or affirms a statement of another person that the lawyer knows is false. Misrepresentations can also occur by failure to act or by knowingly failing to correct false statements made by the lawyer's client or someone acting on behalf of the client.

Statements of Fact

[2] This Rule refers to statements of fact. Whether a particular statement should be regarded as one of fact can depend on the circumstances. Under generally accepted conventions in negotiation, certain types of statements ordinarily are not taken as statements of material fact. Estimates of price or value placed on the subject of a transaction and a party's intentions as to an acceptable settlement of a claim are in this category, and so is the existence of an undisclosed principal except where nondisclosure of the principal would constitute fraud.

Fraud by Client

[3] Paragraph (b) recognizes that substantive law may require a lawyer to disclose certain information to avoid being deemed to have assisted the client's crime or fraud. The requirement of disclosure is governed by Rule 1.6.

Virginia Code Comparison

Paragraph (a) is substantially similar to DR 7-102(A)(5), which stated, "[I]n his representation of a client, a lawyer shall not ... [k]nowingly make a false statement of law or fact."

With regard to paragraph (b), DR 7-102(A)(3) provided, "In his representation of a client, a lawyer shall not. . . [c]onceal or knowingly fail to disclose that which he is required by law to reveal."

Committee Commentary

The Committee deleted the ABA Model Rule's references to a "third person" in the belief that such language merely confused the Rule. Additionally, the Committee deleted the word "material" preceding "fact or law" from paragraph (a) to make it more closely parallel DR 7-102(A)(5). The word "material" was similarly deleted from paragraph (b) as it appears somewhat redundant. Finally, the modified Comment expands the coverage of the Rule to constructive misrepresentation — i.e., the knowing failure of a lawyer to correct a material misrepresentation by the client or by someone on behalf of the client.

CASE NOTES

Motion for sentencing departure based on truthful representations did not constitute ethical violation. — Lawyer could have requested a self-defense departure for defendant at sentencing for his violation of 18 U.S.C.S. § 922(g) (possession of a firearm and ammunition by a felon), without compromising his ethical duties under Va. Sup. Ct. R., Pt. 6, § II, Rules 3.3 and 4.1 because a motion for a self-defense departure would not have required the lawyer to make a false statement of fact or law to the sentencing court, to offer evidence that he knew or reasonably believed to be false, or to otherwise contravene the applicable ethics rules. Rather, the lawyer could have made a self-defense departure motion on the strength of the truthful and undisputed evidence that another client also represented by the lawyer had posed a genuine threat to defendant's life, that defendant had claimed to the authorities that he possessed a firearm at the time of his arrest for protection from the other client, and that the authorities believed him. United States v. Nicholson, 611 F.3d 191, 2010 U.S. App. LEXIS 14185 (4th Cir. July 12, 2010).

CIRCUIT COURT OPINIONS

Certification requirements for discovery. — Though literally "other papers" as used in Va. Sup. Ct. Rule 4.1 falls within the ambit of § 8.01-271.1, certification requirements for discovery papers should be governed by new Rule 4.1(g), the specific provision for pretrial discovery. Lester v. Allied Concrete Co., 80 Va. Cir. 454, 2010 Va. Cir. LEXIS 153 (Charlottesville June 28, 2010).

Rule 4.2. Communication with Persons Represented by Counsel.

In representing a client, a lawyer shall not communicate about the subject of the representation with a person the lawyer knows to be represented by another lawyer in the matter, unless the lawyer has the consent of the other lawyer or is authorized by law to do so.

COMMENT

[1-2] *ABA Model Rule* Comments not adopted.

[3] The Rule applies even though the represented person initiates or consents to the communication. A lawyer must immediately terminate communication with a person if, after commencing communication, the lawyer learns that the person is one with whom communication is not permitted by this Rule. A lawyer is permitted to communicate with a person represented by counsel without obtaining the consent of the lawyer currently representing that person, if that person is seeking a "second opinion" or replacement counsel.

[4] This Rule does not prohibit communication with a represented person, or an employee or agent of a represented person, concerning matters outside the representation. For example, the existence of a controversy between an organization and a private party, or between two organizations, does not prohibit a lawyer for either from communicating with nonlawyer representatives of the other regarding a separate matter. Also, parties to a matter may communicate directly with each other and a lawyer having independent justification or legal authorization for communicating with the other party is permitted to do so.

[5] In circumstances where applicable judicial precedent has approved investigative contacts prior to attachment of the right to counsel, and they are not prohibited by any provision of the United States Constitution or the Virginia Constitution, they should be considered to be authorized by law within the meaning of the Rule. Similarly, communications in civil matters may be considered authorized by law if they have been approved by judicial precedent. This Rule does not prohibit a lawyer from providing advice regarding the legality of an interrogation or the legality of other investigative conduct.

[6] ABA Model Rule Comment not adopted.

[7] In the case of an organization, this Rule prohibits communications by a lawyer for one party concerning the matter in representation with persons in the organization's "control group" as defined in Upjohn v. United States, 449 U.S. 383 (1981) or persons who may be regarded as the "alter ego" of the organization. The "control group" test prohibits ex parte communications with any employee of an organization who, because of their status or position, have the authority to bind the corporation. Such employees may only be contacted with the consent of the organization's counsel, through formal discovery or as authorized by law. An officer or director of an organization is likely a member of that organization's "control group." The prohibition does not apply to former employees or agents of the organization, and an attorney may communicate ex parte with such former employee or agent even if he or she was a member of the organization's "control group." If an agent or employee of the organization is represented in the matter by separate counsel, the consent by that counsel to a communication will be sufficient for purposes of this Rule.

[8] This Rule covers any person, whether or not a party to a formal proceeding, who is represented by counsel concerning the matter in question. Neither the need to protect uncounselled persons against being taken advantage of by opposing counsel nor the importance of preserving the client-attorney relationship is limited to those circumstances where the represented person is a party to an adjudicative or other formal proceeding. The interests sought to be protected by the Rule may equally well be involved when litigation is merely under consideration, even though it has not actually been instituted, and the persons who are potentially parties to the litigation have retained counsel with respect to the matter in dispute.

[9] Concerns regarding the need to protect uncounselled persons against the wiles of opposing counsel and preserving the attorney-client relationship may also be involved where a person is a target of a criminal investigation, knows this, and has retained counsel to receive advice with respect to the investigation. The same concerns may be involved where a "third-party" witness furnishes testimony in an investigation or proceeding, and although not a formal party, has decided to retain counsel to receive advice with respect thereto. Such concerns are equally applicable in a non-adjudicatory context, such as a commercial transaction involving a sale, a lease or some other form of contract.

Virginia Code Comparison

This Rule is substantially the same as DR 7-103(A)(1), except for the change of "party" to "person" to emphasize that the prohibition on certain communications with a represented person applies outside the litigation context.

Committee Commentary

The Committee believed that substituting "person" for "party" more accurately reflected the intent of the Rule, as shown in the last sentence of the Comment, and was preferable to the apparent limitation of DR 7-103(A)(1) which referred to "[c]ommunicat[ion] on the subject of the representation with a party . . . ."

Law Review. — For article, "Professional Responsibility," see 43 U. Rich. L. Rev. 255 (2008).

Michie's Jurisprudence. — For related discussion, see 2A M.J. Attorney and Client, § 33.

CASE NOTES

Interpretation. — The bar must prove three separate facts to establish a violation of the Va. Sup. Ct. R. pt. 6, § II, R. 4.2 of the Virginia Rules of Professional Conduct: (1) that the attorney knew that he or she was communicating with a person represented by another lawyer; (2) that the communication was about the subject of the representation; and (3) that the attorney (a) did not have the consent of the lawyer representing the person and (b) was not otherwise authorized by law to engage in the communication. While the first two facts may occur in any order, both must occur before an attorney violates the rule. Zaug v. Va. State Bar, 285 Va. 457, 737 S.E.2d 914, 2013 Va. LEXIS 35 (Feb. 28, 2013).

"Immediately" does not mean "instantaneously," and Va. Sup. Ct. R. pt. 6, § II, R. 4.2 of the Virginia Rules of Professional Conduct does not obligate an attorney to hang up on a represented person without regard to courtesy. Zaug v. Va. State Bar, 285 Va. 457, 737 S.E.2d 914, 2013 Va. LEXIS 35 (Feb. 28, 2013).

Attorneys must understand that they are ethically prohibited from communicating about the subject of representation with a person represented by another attorney unless they have that attorney's consent or are authorized by law to do so. Va. Sup. Ct. R. pt. 6, § II, R. 4.2 of the Virginia Rules of Professional Conduct categorically and unambiguously forbids an attorney from initiating such communications and requires an attorney to disengage from such communications when they are initiated by others. But the rule does not require attorneys to be discourteous or impolite when they do so. Zaug v. Va. State Bar, 285 Va. 457, 737 S.E.2d 914, 2013 Va. LEXIS 35 (Feb. 28, 2013).

This rule does not prohibit, even after the commencement of an action, a party from interviewing those individuals with whom the lawyer cannot communicate. Tucker v. Norfolk & W. Ry., 849 F. Supp. 1096 (E.D. Va. 1994) (decided under former DR 7-103).

Ex parte communications with defendant's employees are barred by this rule, absent prior consent of defendant's counsel, unless such communications are otherwise authorized by law. Queensberry v. Norfolk & W. Ry., 157 F.R.D. 21 (E.D. Va. 1993) (decided under former DR 7-103).

Corporate party. — When one of the parties is a corporation, this disciplinary rule prohibits ex parte communication with: (1) Persons having managerial responsibility for the corporate party; (2) any other person whose act or omission in connection with that matter may be imputed to the corporate party for purposes of civil or criminal liability or (3) any other person whose statement may constitute an admission on the part of the corporate party. Armsey v. Medshares Mgt. Servs., Inc., 184 F.R.D. 569 (W.D. Va. 1998) (decided under former DR 7-103).

Former employee of corporation. — Former employees may no longer bind their corporate employer by their current statements, acts or admissions. Yet, this does not prevent liability being imposed upon their former employer based on the statements, acts or omissions of these individuals which occurred during the course of their employment. Under these facts, ex parte communications with former employees is not proper. Armsey v. Medshares Mgt. Servs., Inc., 184 F.R.D. 569 (W.D. Va. 1998) (decided under former DR 7-103).

Contact with defendant's employees. — Communications between plaintiff's counsel and defendant's employees which occurred before the filing of the instant action are not prohibited. Tucker v. Norfolk & W. Ry., 849 F. Supp. 1096 (E.D. Va. 1994) (decided under former DR 7-103).

CIRCUIT COURT OPINIONS

Contact with limited partners of opposing party. — Defense counsel were disqualified after conducting ex parte communications with certain limited partners who were alter egos of the opposing party. Counsel violated Va. Sup. Ct. R. pt. 6, § II, R. 4.2, and R. 8.4(c) by concealing their role in the litigation and by communicating with the partners without notifying their counsel; defense counsel's unethical conduct also tainted the underlying trial and violated Va. Sup. Ct. R. pt. 6, § II, R. 4.4. Yukon Pocahontas Coal Co. v. Consolidation Coal Co., 72 Va. Cir. 75, 2006 Va. Cir. LEXIS 195 (Buchanan County 2006).

Rule 4.3. Dealing with Unrepresented Persons.

(a) In dealing on behalf of a client with a person who is not represented by counsel, a lawyer shall not state or imply that the lawyer is disinterested. When the lawyer knows or reasonably should know that the unrepresented person misunderstands the lawyer's role in the matter, the lawyer shall make reasonable efforts to correct the misunderstanding.

(b) A lawyer shall not give advice to a person who is not represented by a lawyer, other than the advice to secure counsel, if the interests of such person are or have a reasonable possibility of being in conflict with the interest of the client.

COMMENT

[1] An unrepresented person, particularly one not experienced in dealing with legal matters, might assume that a lawyer is disinterested in loyalties or is a disinterested authority on the law even when the lawyer represents a client. During the course of a lawyer's representation of a client, the lawyer should not give advice to an unrepresented person other than the advice to obtain counsel.

Virginia Code Comparison

Paragraph (a) is identical to DR 7-103(B) and paragraph (b) is similar to DR 7-103(A)(2).

Committee Commentary

The Virginia Code had deviated from the ABA Model Code by using the language of ABA Model Rule 4.3(a) as DR 7-103(B). This provision continues unchanged in Rule 4.3.

CASE NOTES

Communications did not purport to give legal advice. — Attorney's communications with his wife before she retained counsel during a divorce action did not violate Va. Sup. Ct. R., Pt. 6, § II, Rule 4.3(b) because they merely expressed opinions that he held a superior legal position as to certain issues and did not purport to give legal advice. Barrett v. Va. State Bar, 269 Va. 583, 611 S.E.2d 375, 2005 Va. LEXIS 45 (2005).

Rule 4.4. Respect for Rights of Third Persons.

In representing a client, a lawyer shall not use means that have no purpose other than to embarrass, delay, or burden a third person, or use methods of obtaining evidence that violate the legal rights of such a person.

COMMENT

[1] Responsibility to a client requires a lawyer to subordinate the interests of others to those of the client, but that responsibility does not imply that a lawyer may disregard the rights of third persons. It is impractical to catalogue all such rights, but they include legal restrictions on methods of obtaining evidence from third persons.

Virginia Code Comparison

Rule 4.4 has no direct counterpart in the Virginia Code. DR 7-105(C)(2) provided that a lawyer shall not "[a]sk any question that he has no reasonable basis to believe is relevant to the case and that is intended to degrade a witness or other person." DR 7-102(A)(1) provided that a lawyer shall not "take ... action on behalf of his client when he knows or when it is obvious that such action would serve merely to harass or maliciously injure another." DR 7-107(C) provided that "[a]fter discharge of the jury ... the lawyer shall not ask questions or make comments to a member of that jury that are calculated merely to harass or embarrass the juror...." DR 7-107(D) provided that a lawyer "shall not conduct ... a vexatious or harassing investigation of either a venireman or a juror."

Committee Commentary

The Committee adopted this Rule, for which there was no specific corresponding Disciplinary Rule, as a reminder that there is some limitation placed upon activities for which "zealous representation" might be offered as an excuse. For the same reason, the Committee deleted the word "substantial" from the ABA Model Rules provision.

Law Review. — For article, "Professional Responsibility," see 43 U. Rich. L. Rev. 255 (2008).

CASE NOTES

Attempt to subpoena as way to get lien released. — Attorney violated Va. Sup. Ct. R. pt. 6, § II, R. 4.4 and 8.4(b) when the attorney attempted to subpoena a former employer to testify in the attorney's divorce action for no purpose other than to get the employer to release a lien claim against the attorney. Barrett v. Va. State Bar, 272 Va. 260, 634 S.E.2d 341, 2006 Va. LEXIS 84 (2006).

CIRCUIT COURT OPINIONS

Contact with limited partners of opposing party without notifying their counsel. — Defense counsel were disqualified after conducting ex parte communications with certain limited partners who were alter egos of the opposing party. Counsel violated Va. Sup. Ct. R. pt. 6, § II, R. 4.2, and R. 8.4(c) by concealing their role in the litigation and by communicating with the partners without notifying their counsel; defense counsel's unethical conduct also tainted the underlying trial and violated Va. Sup. Ct. R. pt. 6, § II, R. 4.4. Yukon Pocahontas Coal Co. v. Consolidation Coal Co., 72 Va. Cir. 75, 2006 Va. Cir. LEXIS 195 (Buchanan County 2006).

LAW FIRMS AND ASSOCIATIONS.

Rule 5.1. Responsibilities of Partners and Supervisory Lawyers.

(a) A partner in a law firm, or a lawyer who individually or together with other lawyers possesses managerial authority, shall make reasonable efforts to ensure that the firm has in effect measures giving reasonable assurance that all lawyers in the firm conform to the Rules of Professional Conduct.

(b) A lawyer having direct supervisory authority over another lawyer shall make reasonable efforts to ensure that the other lawyer conforms to the Rules of Professional Conduct.

(c) A lawyer shall be responsible for another lawyer's violation of the Rules of Professional Conduct if:

(1) the lawyer orders or, with knowledge of the specific conduct, ratifies the conduct involved; or

(2) the lawyer is a partner or has managerial authority in the law firm in which the other lawyer practices, or has direct supervisory authority over the other lawyer, and knows of the conduct at a time when its consequences can be avoided or mitigated but fails to take reasonable remedial action.

COMMENT

[1] Paragraph (a) applies to lawyers who have managerial authority over the professional work of a firm. This includes members of a partnership and the shareholders in a law firm organized as a professional corporation; lawyers having managerial authority in the law department of an enterprise or government agency; and lawyers who have intermediate managerial responsibilities in a firm. See the "partner" definition in the Terminology section at the beginning of these Rules. Paragraph (b) applies to lawyers who have supervisory authority over the work of other lawyers.

[2] Paragraph (a) requires lawyers with a managerial authority within a firm to make reasonable efforts to establish internal policies and procedures designed to provide reasonable assurance that all lawyers in the firm will conform to the Rules of Professional Conduct. Such policies and procedures include those designed to detect and resolve conflicts of interest, identify dates by which actions must be taken in pending matters, account for client funds and property and ensure that inexperienced lawyers are properly supervised.

[3] Other measures that may be required to fulfill the responsibility prescribed in paragraph (a) can depend on the firm's structure and the nature of its practice. In a small firm, informal supervision and periodic review ordinarily will suffice. In a large firm, or in practice situations in which difficult ethical problems frequently arise, more elaborate measures may be necessary. Firms, whether large or small, may also rely on continuing legal education in professional ethics. In any event, the ethical atmosphere of a firm can influence the conduct of all its members and the partners or those lawyers with managerial authority may not assume that all lawyers associated with the firm will inevitably conform to the Rules.

[4] Paragraph (c) expresses a general principle of personal responsibility for acts of another. See also Rule 8.4(a).

[5] Paragraph (c)(2) defines the duty of a lawyer having direct supervisory authority over performance of specific legal work by another lawyer. Whether a lawyer has such supervisory authority in particular circumstances is a question of fact. Partners of a private firm have at least indirect responsibility for all work being done by the firm, while a partner in charge of a particular matter ordinarily has responsibility for the work of other firm lawyers engaged in the matter. Appropriate remedial action by a partner would depend on the immediacy of the partner's involvement and the seriousness of the misconduct. The supervisor is required to intervene to prevent avoidable consequences of misconduct if the supervisor knows that the misconduct occurred. Thus, if a supervising lawyer knows that a subordinate misrepresented a matter to an opposing party in negotiation, the supervisor as well as the subordinate has a duty to correct the resulting misapprehension.

[6] Professional misconduct by a lawyer under supervision could reveal a violation of paragraph (b) on the part of the supervisory lawyer even though it does not entail a violation of paragraph (c) because there was no direction, ratification or knowledge of the violation.

[7] Apart from this Rule and Rule 8.4(a), a lawyer does not have disciplinary liability for the conduct of a partner, associate or subordinate. Whether a lawyer may be liable civilly or criminally for another lawyer's conduct is a question of law beyond the scope of these Rules.

Virginia Code Comparison

There was no direct counterpart to this Rule in the Virginia Code. DR 1-103(A) provided that "[a] lawyer having information indicating that another lawyer has committed a violation of the Disciplinary Rules that raises a substantial question as to that lawyer's honesty, trustworthiness, or fitness to practice law in other respects, shall report such information to the appropriate professional authority . . . ."

Committee Commentary

The Committee adopted the language of ABA Model Rule 5.1 because lawyers who practice in firms should have an affirmative obligation to assure adherence to the Rules of Professional Conduct by those with whom they professionally associate.

The amendment effective January 1, 2004, adopted September 24, 2003, substituted "Partners and Supervisory Lawyers" for "Partner or Supervisory Lawyer" in the rule heading; inserted "or a lawyer who individually or together with other lawyers possesses managerial authority" in paragraph (a); and inserted "or has managerial authority" in paragraph (c)(2).

Rule 5.3. Responsibilities Regarding Nonlawyer Assistants.

With respect to a nonlawyer employed or retained by or associated with a lawyer:

(a) a partner or a lawyer who individually or together with other lawyers possesses managerial authority in a law firm shall make reasonable efforts to ensure that the firm has in effect measures giving reasonable assurance that the person's conduct is compatible with the professional obligations of the lawyer;

(b) a lawyer having direct supervisory authority over the nonlawyer shall make reasonable efforts to ensure that the person's conduct is compatible with the professional obligations of the lawyer; and

(c) a lawyer shall be responsible for conduct of such a person that would be a violation of the Rules of Professional Conduct if engaged in by a lawyer if:

(1) the lawyer orders or, with the knowledge of the specific conduct, ratifies the conduct involved; or

(2) the lawyer is a partner or has managerial authority in the law firm in which the person is employed, or has direct supervisory authority over the person, and knows or should have known of the conduct at a time when its consequences can be avoided or mitigated but fails to take reasonable remedial action.

COMMENT

[1] Lawyers generally employ assistants in their practice, including secretaries, investigators, law student interns, and paraprofessionals. Such assistants, whether employees or independent contractors, act for the lawyer in rendition of the lawyer's professional services. A lawyer should give such assistants appropriate instruction and supervision concerning the ethical aspects of their employment, particularly regarding the obligation not to disclose information relating to representation of the client, and should be responsible for their work product. The measures employed in supervising nonlawyers should take account of the fact that they do not have legal training and are not subject to professional discipline. At the same time, however, the Rule is not intended to preclude traditionally permissible activity such as misrepresentation by a nonlawyer of one's role in a law enforcement investigation or a housing discrimination "test".

Virginia Code Comparison

Rule 5.3(a) and (b) are similar to DR 3-104(C). The Virginia Code also addressed a supervising lawyer's responsibilities in DR 4-101(E) and DR 7-106(B). The Virginia Code did not contain any explanation of a lawyer's responsibility for a nonlawyer assistant's wrongdoing, which is addressed in Rule 5.3(c).

Committee Commentary

The Committee adopted this Rule as a parallel companion to Rule 5.1 which applies similar provisions to lawyers with supervisory authority over other lawyers. The Committee inserted the phrase "or should have known" in Rule 5.3(c)(2) to reflect a negligence standard. The Committee also deemed it appropriate to add the language in the last sentence of the Comment to cover such recognized and accepted activities as those described.

The amendment effective January 1, 2004, adopted September 24, 2003, inserted "or a lawyer who individually or together with other lawyers possesses managerial authority" following "partner" in paragraph (a); and in paragraph (c)(2), inserted "or has managerial authority" following "the lawyer is a partner."

CASE NOTES

Delegation. — Where an attorney failed to pay a filing fee with a debtor's bankruptcy petition, and asserted that the failure was due to inadvertence on the part of a paralegal, the attorney failed to act with the requisite commitment and dedication to the interests of the debtor, and could not be absolved of such responsibilities by claiming to have delegated them to a subordinate. Office of the United States Trustee v. Jones (In re Alvarado), 363 B.R. 484, 2007 Bankr. LEXIS 533 (Bankr. E.D. Va. 2007).

Debtor attorney's responsibility for paralegal and title examiner. — Creditor's objection to a debtor's exemption in wages earned by the debtor for personal services performed, with the assistance of a paralegal and title examiner, as the sole attorney for a professional corporation under § 34-29 was overruled because the creditor failed to show that the debtor did no work to earn the difference between the amount the debtor was paid by her client and the amount she paid to her two contractors and because Va. Sup. Ct. R. pt. 6, § II, R. 5.3 required the debtor to be responsible for nonlawyers in her employ. In re Sheeran, 369 B.R. 910, 2007 Bankr. LEXIS 2052 (Bankr. E.D. Va. 2007).

Rule 5.4. Professional Independence Of A Lawyer.

(a) A lawyer or law firm shall not share legal fees with a nonlawyer, except that:

(1) an agreement by a lawyer with the lawyer's firm, partner, or associate may provide for the payment of money, over a reasonable period of time after the lawyer's death, to the lawyer's estate or to one or more specified persons;

(2) a lawyer who undertakes to complete unfinished legal business of a deceased, disabled, or disappeared lawyer may pay to the estate or other representative of that lawyer that portion of the total compensation that fairly represents the services rendered by the deceased, disabled or disappeared lawyer;

(3) a lawyer or law firm may include nonlawyer employees in a compensation or retirement plan, even though the plan is based in whole or in part on a profit-sharing arrangement; and

(4) a lawyer may accept discounted payment of his fee from a credit card company on behalf of a client.

(b) A lawyer shall not form a partnership with a nonlawyer if any of the activities of the partnership consist of the practice of law.

(c) A lawyer shall not permit a person who recommends, employs, or pays the lawyer to render legal services for another to direct or regulate the lawyer's professional judgment in rendering such legal services.

(d) A lawyer shall not practice with or in the form of a professional corporation or association authorized to practice law for a profit, if:

(1) a nonlawyer owns any interest therein, except as provided in (a)(3) above, or except that a fiduciary representative of the estate of a lawyer may hold the stock or interest of the lawyer for a reasonable time during administration;

(2) a nonlawyer is a corporate director or officer thereof; or

(3) a nonlawyer has the right to direct or control the professional judgment of a lawyer.

COMMENT

[1] The provisions of this Rule express traditional limitations on sharing fees. These limitations are to protect the lawyer's professional independence of judgment. Where someone other than the client pays the lawyer's fee or salary or recommends employment of the lawyer, that arrangement does not modify the lawyer's obligation to the client. As stated in paragraph (c), such arrangements should not interfere with the lawyer's professional judgment. See also Rule 1.8(f).

Virginia Code Comparison

Paragraph (a)(1) is identical to DR 3-102(A)(1).

Paragraph (a)(2) is substantially similar to DR 3-102(A)(2) which stated: "A lawyer who undertakes to complete unfinished legal business of a deceased lawyer may pay to the estate of the deceased lawyer that proportion of the total compensation that fairly represents the services rendered by the deceased lawyer."

Paragraph (a)(3) is substantially the same as DR 3-102(A)(3).

Paragraph (a)(4) had no counterpart in the Virginia Code.

Paragraph (b) is identical to DR 3-103(A).

Paragraph (c) is identical to DR 5-106(B).

Paragraph (d) is identical to DR 5-106(C).

Committee Commentary

The ABA Model Rule generally paralleled various Disciplinary Rules.

The amendment effective January 1, 2004, adopted September 24, 2003, added paragraph (a)(4).

Law Review. — For article, "Professional Responsibility," see 43 U. Rich. L. Rev. 255 (2008).

CASE NOTES

Subdivision (b) intended to prevent improper influence by nonlawyer. — Subdivision (b) is intended to prevent a nonlawyer from improperly influencing the professional judgment of a lawyer. It has no application to the relationship between one lawyer and another. Ortiz v. Barrett, 222 Va. 118, 278 S.E.2d 833 (1981) (decided under former DR 5-107).

Agreements among attorneys for same client do not violate subdivision (b). — In any case where two or more attorneys perform legal services for the same client in one case or legal transaction, there may be differences of opinion as to the appropriate actions to be taken. Each lawyer may attempt to persuade the others to his view, but the final decision of lead counsel will not bring those who accede to the decision into violation of subdivision (b) of this rule. Ortiz v. Barrett, 222 Va. 118, 278 S.E.2d 833 (1981) (decided under former DR 5-107).

Rule 5.5. Unauthorized Practice of Law; Multijurisdictional Practice of Law.

(a) A lawyer, law firm or professional corporation shall not employ in any capacity a lawyer whose license has been suspended or revoked for professional misconduct, during such period of suspension or revocation, if the disciplined lawyer was associated with such lawyer, law firm, or professional corporation at any time on or after the date of the acts which resulted in suspension or revocation.

(b) A lawyer, law firm or professional corporation employing a lawyer as a consultant, law clerk, or legal assistant when that lawyer's license is suspended or revoked for professional misconduct shall not represent any client represented by the disciplined lawyer or by any lawyer with whom the disciplined lawyer practiced on or after the date of the acts which resulted in suspension or revocation.

(c) A lawyer shall not practice law in a jurisdiction in violation of the regulation of the legal profession in that jurisdiction, or assist another in doing so.

(d) Foreign Lawyers:

(1) "Foreign Lawyer" is a person authorized to practice law by the duly constituted and authorized governmental body of any State or Territory of the United States or the District of Columbia, or a foreign nation, but is neither licensed by the Supreme Court of Virginia or authorized under its rules to practice law generally in the Commonwealth of Virginia, nor disbarred or suspended from practice in any jurisdiction.

(2) A Foreign Lawyer shall not, except as authorized by these Rules or other law:

(i) establish an office or other systematic and continuous presence in Virginia for the practice of law, which may occur even if the Foreign Lawyer is not physically present in Virginia; or

(ii) hold out to the public or otherwise represent that the Foreign Lawyer is admitted to practice law in Virginia.

(3) A Foreign Lawyer shall inform the client and interested third parties in writing:

(i) that the lawyer is not admitted to practice law in Virginia;

(ii) the jurisdiction(s) in which the lawyer is licensed to practice; and

(iii) the lawyer's office address in the foreign jurisdiction.

(4) A Foreign Lawyer may, after informing the client as required in 3(i)-(iii) above, provide legal services on a temporary and occasional basis in Virginia that:

(i) are undertaken in association with a lawyer who is admitted to practice without limitation in Virginia or admitted under Part I of Rule 1A:5 of this Court and who actively participates in the matter;

(ii) are in or reasonably related to a pending or potential proceeding before a tribunal in Virginia or another jurisdiction, if the Foreign Lawyer, or a person the Foreign Lawyer is assisting, is authorized by law or order to appear in such proceeding or reasonably expects to be so authorized;

(iii) are in or reasonably related to a pending or potential arbitration, mediation, or other alternative dispute resolution proceeding in Virginia or another jurisdiction, if the services arise out of or are reasonably related to the Foreign Lawyer's practice in a jurisdiction in which the Foreign Lawyer is admitted to practice and are not services for which the forum requires pro hac vice admission; or

(iv) are not within paragraphs (4)(ii) or (4)(iii) and arise out of or are reasonably related to the representation of a client by the Foreign Lawyer in a jurisdiction in which the Foreign Lawyer is admitted to practice or, subject to the foregoing limitations, are governed primarily by international law.

(5) A foreign legal consultant practicing under Rule 1A:7 of this Court and a corporate counsel registrant practicing under Part II of Rule 1A:5 of this Court are not authorized to practice under this rule.

COMMENT

[1] A lawyer may practice law only in a jurisdiction in which the lawyer is authorized to practice. A lawyer may be admitted to practice law in a jurisdiction on a regular basis or may be authorized by court rule or order or by law to practice for a limited purpose or on a restricted basis. Paragraph (c) applies to unauthorized practice of law by a lawyer, whether through the lawyer's direct action or by the lawyer assisting another person.

[1a] For purposes of paragraphs (a), (b), and (c) "Lawyer," denotes a person authorized by the Supreme Court of Virginia or its Rules to practice law in the Commonwealth of Virginia including persons admitted to practice in this state pro hac vice.

[2] The definition of the practice of law is established by law and varies from one jurisdiction to another. Whatever the definition, limiting the practice of law to members of the bar protects the public against rendition of legal services by unqualified persons. Paragraph (c) does not prohibit a lawyer

from employing the services of paraprofessionals and delegating functions to them, so long as the lawyer supervises the delegated work and retains responsibility for their work. *See* Rule 5.3.

[3] Likewise, the definition of the practice of law does not prohibit lawyers from providing professional advice and instruction to nonlawyers whose employment requires knowledge of law — for example, claims adjusters, employees of financial or commercial institutions, social workers, accountants, and persons employed in government agencies.

[4] Other than as authorized by law or this Rule, a Foreign Lawyer violates paragraph (d)(2)(i) if the Foreign Lawyer establishes an office or other systematic and continuous presence in Virginia for the practice of law. Presence may be systematic and continuous even if the Foreign Lawyer is not physically present here. Such "non-physical" presence includes, but is not limited to, the regular interaction with residents of Virginia for delivery of legal services in Virginia through exchange of information over the Internet or other means. Such Foreign Lawyer must not hold out to the public or otherwise represent that the Foreign Lawyer is admitted to practice law in Virginia. See also, Rules 7.1(a) and 7.5(b). Despite the foregoing general prohibition, a Foreign Lawyer may establish an office or other systematic and continuous presence in Virginia if the Foreign Lawyer's practice is limited to areas which by state or federal law do not require admission to the Virginia State Bar. Examples of lawyers admitted in another United States jurisdiction include those lawyers whose practices are limited to federal tax practice before the IRS and Tax Court, patent law before the Patent and Trademark Office, or immigration law. A Foreign Lawyer admitted to practice in a jurisdiction outside the United States may be authorized to practice under Rule 1A:7 as a foreign legal consultant and may likewise establish an office or other systematic and continued presence in Virginia.

[5] Paragraphs (d)(4)(i), (ii) and (iii) identify circumstances in which a Foreign Lawyer may provide legal services on a temporary basis in Virginia that do not create an unreasonable risk to the interests of their clients, the public, or the courts. The fact that conduct is not so identified does not imply that the conduct is or is not authorized. Except as authorized by this rule or other law, a Foreign Lawyer may not establish an office or other systematic and continuous presence in Virginia without being admitted to practice generally here.

[6] There is no single test to determine whether a Foreign Lawyer's services are provided on a "temporary basis" in Virginia, and may therefore be permissible under paragraph (d)(4). Services may be "temporary" even though the Foreign Lawyer provides services in Virginia on a recurring basis, or for an extended period of time, as when the Foreign Lawyer is representing a client in a single lengthy negotiation or litigation. "Temporary" refers to the duration of the Foreign lawyer's presence and provision of services, while "occasional" refers to the frequency with which the Foreign lawyer comes into Virginia to provide legal services.

[7] Paragraph (d)(1) requires that the Foreign Lawyer be authorized to practice in the jurisdiction in which the Foreign Lawyer is admitted and excludes a Foreign Lawyer who, while technically admitted, is not authorized to practice because, for example, the Foreign Lawyer is on inactive status.

[8] Paragraph (d)(4)(i) recognizes that the interests of clients and the public are protected if a Foreign Lawyer associates with a lawyer licensed to practice Virginia. For this paragraph to apply, however, the lawyer admitted to practice in Virginia must actively participate in and share responsibility for the representation of the client.

[9] Foreign Lawyers not admitted to practice generally in this jurisdiction may be authorized by law or order of a tribunal or an administrative agency to appear before the tribunal or agency. Under paragraph (d)(4)(ii), a Foreign Lawyer does not violate this Rule when the Foreign Lawyer appears before a tribunal or agency pursuant to such authority. To the extent that a court rule or other law of Virginia requires a Foreign Lawyer to obtain admission pro hac vice before appearing before a tribunal or administrative agency, this Rule requires the Foreign Lawyer to obtain that authority.

[10] Paragraph (d)(4)(ii) also provides that a Foreign Lawyer rendering services in Virginia on a temporary basis does not violate this Rule when the Foreign Lawyer engages in conduct in anticipation of a proceeding or hearing in a jurisdiction in which the Foreign Lawyer is authorized to practice law or in which the Foreign Lawyer reasonably expects to be admitted pro hac vice. Examples of such conduct include meetings with the client, interviews of potential witnesses, and the review of documents. Similarly, a Foreign Lawyer may engage in conduct temporarily in Virginia in connection with pending litigation in another jurisdiction in which the Foreign Lawyer is or reasonably expects to be authorized to appear, including taking depositions in Virginia.

[11] *ABA Model Rule* Comment not adopted.

[12] Paragraph (d)(4)(iii) permits a Foreign Lawyer to perform services on a temporary basis in Virginia if those services are in or reasonably related to a pending or potential arbitration, mediation, or other alternative dispute resolution proceeding in this or another jurisdiction, if the services arise out of or are reasonably related to the Foreign Lawyer's practice in a jurisdiction in which the Foreign Lawyer is admitted to practice. The Foreign Lawyer, however, must obtain admission pro hac vice in the case of a court-annexed arbitration or mediation or otherwise if court rules or law so require.

[13] Paragraph (d)(4)(iv) permits a Foreign Lawyer to provide certain legal services on a temporary basis in Virginia that arise out of or are reasonably related to that lawyer's practice in a jurisdiction in which the Foreign Lawyer is admitted but are not within paragraphs (d)(4)(ii) or (d)(4)(iii). These services include both legal services and services that nonlawyers may perform but that are considered the practice of law when performed by lawyers. Paragraph (d)(4)(iv) applies to a Foreign Lawyer admitted to practice only in a foreign nation.

[14] Paragraphs (d)(4)(ii), (d)(4)(iii), and (d)(4)(iv) require that the services arise out of or be reasonably related to the Foreign Lawyer's practice in a jurisdiction in which the Foreign Lawyer is admitted to practice. A variety of factors evidence such a

relationship. The Foreign Lawyer's client may have been previously represented by the Foreign Lawyer, or may be resident in or have substantial contacts with the jurisdiction in which the Foreign Lawyer is admitted. The matter, although involving other jurisdictions, may have a significant connection with that jurisdiction. In other cases, significant aspects of the Foreign Lawyer's work might be conducted in that jurisdiction or a significant aspect of the matter may involve the law of that jurisdiction. The necessary relationship might arise when the client's activities or the legal issues involve multiple jurisdictions, such as when the officers of a multinational corporation survey potential business sites and seek the services of their Foreign Lawyer in assessing the relative merits of each. In addition, the services may draw on the Foreign Lawyer's recognized expertise developed through the regular practice of law on behalf of clients in matters involving a particular body of federal, nationally-uniform, foreign, or international law.

[14a] Paragraph (d)(4)(iv) recognizes that a Foreign Lawyer may provide legal services when the services provided are governed by international law or the law of a foreign jurisdiction in which the Foreign Lawyer is admitted to practice.

[15-18] it ABA Model Rule Comments not adopted.

[19] A Foreign Lawyer who practices law in Virginia pursuant to this Rule is subject to the disciplinary authority of Virginia. See Rule 8.5(a).

[20] *ABA Model Rule* Comment not adopted.

[21] Paragraph (d)(4) does not authorize communications advertising legal services to prospective clients in Virginia by Foreign Lawyers who are admitted to practice in other jurisdictions. Whether and how Foreign Lawyers may communicate the availability of their services to prospective clients in Virginia is governed by Rules 7.1 to 7.5.

Prior Rule Comparison

Neither former Rule 5.5 nor any other of the Virginia Rules of Professional Conduct provided any criteria for practice in Virginia by a foreign lawyer (non-Virginia or non-U.S.). Such practice was controlled by Part 6, §I (C) of the Rules of the Virginia Supreme Court which defined "on-lawyer' and set out the parameters for temporary practice in Virginia by a "oreign lawyer,' defined only as admitted to practice and in good standing in any state in the U.S. There was no provision for practice by a foreign, non-U.S. lawyer. Enforcement of Part 6, §I (C) fell within the authority of the Virginia State Bar's Standing Committee on the Unauthorized Practice of Law. Rule 5.5 allows for temporary and occasional practice in Virginia by both non-Virginia and non-U.S. lawyers and places enforcement within the Virginia State Bar's disciplinary system.

Committee Commentary

The Committee adopted this Rule in light of the recommendation of the American Bar Association (ABA) that the states adopt more specific rules governing multi-jurisdictional practice. This rule adopts language similar to ABA Model Rule 5.5 allowing for circumstances of temporary and occasional practice by lawyers licensed in other U.S. jurisdictions, but expands such practice to include lawyers licensed in non-U.S. jurisdictions. Paragraphs (a) and (b) are identical to paragraphs (b) and (c) in former Virginia Rule 5.5.

The amendment effective March 1, 2009, adopted December 30, 2008, rewrote the Rule and Commentary thereto.

CASE NOTES

Availability of declaratory determination as to whether practice unauthorized. — The fact that the unauthorized practice of law is a misdemeanor did not preclude declaratory relief to attorneys who sought determination as to whether a title insurance company's activities constituted the unauthorized practice of law, where their goal was not solely to stop the illegal conduct of others, but to insure their own conduct conformed to the law and the tenets of the legal profession. The availability of criminal proceedings under former § 54-44 (see now § 54.1-3904), a writ of quo warranto, under § 8.01-636 and advisory opinions under the Rules of Court, Part Six, § IV, ¶ 10 did not preclude the use of declaratory judgment. Blodinger v. Broker's Title, Inc., 224 Va. 201, 294 S.E.2d 876 (1982) (decided under former DR 3-101).

CIRCUIT COURT OPINIONS

No cause of action for negligent supervision. — See Lockney v. Vroom, 61 Va. Cir. 359, 2003 Va. Cir. LEXIS 263 (Norfolk 2003).

Rule 5.6. Restrictions on Right to Practice.

A lawyer shall not participate in offering or making:

(a) a partnership or employment agreement that restricts the right of a lawyer to practice after termination of the relationship, except an agreement concerning benefits upon retirement; or

(b) an agreement in which a restriction on the lawyer's right to practice is part of the settlement of a controversy, except where such a restriction is approved by a tribunal or a governmental entity.

COMMENT

[1] An agreement restricting the right of lawyers to practice after leaving a firm not only limits their professional autonomy but also limits the freedom of clients to choose a lawyer. Paragraph (a) prohibits such agreements except for restrictions incident to provisions concerning retirement benefits for service with the firm.

[2] Paragraph (b) prohibits lawyers from agreeing to a restriction on their right to practice, unless approved by a tribunal (in such situations as the settlement of mass tort cases) or a governmental entity. However, the lawyer must fully disclose the extent of any restriction to any future client and refer the client to another lawyer if requested to do so.

Virginia Code Comparison

This Rule is similar to DR 2-106, although it specifically permits a restriction if it is approved by a tribunal or a governmental entity.

Committee Commentary

After a lengthy debate about the merits of settlements and the public policy favoring clients' unrestricted choice of legal representation, the Committee decided to generally prohibit provisions in settlement agreements that restricted a lawyer's right to practice, but added an exception if a tribunal or a governmental entity approves the restriction. The Comment emphasizes that lawyers whose right to practice has been restricted by a court-approved settlement should advise all future clients of the restriction and refer them to other counsel, if necessary.

Originally, Rule 5.6(b) prohibited only *broad* restrictions on an attorney's right to practice in settlement agreements. However, in line with the recommendations of the Boyd-Graves Conference Report of August 2004, the prohibition in Rule 5.6(b) is now expanded to reach *all* restrictions on the right to practice in settlement agreements, other than those within the exception afforded for settlement agreements approved by a tribunal or governmental entity. The current more expansive prohibition is in line with both the ABA's Model Rule 5.6 and with provisions in other jurisdictions.

The amendment effective January 1, 2004, substituted "lawyers" for "partners or associates" in the first sentence of the first comment.

The amendment effective September 1, 2006, adopted July 20, 2006, deleted "broad" preceding "restriction" in subdivision (b), in Comment [2], and in the Virginia Code Comparison; and in the Committee Commentary, deleted "broadly" preceding "restricted" in the first sentence of the first paragraph, and added the second paragraph.

Law Review. — For article, "Professional Responsibility," see 43 U. Rich. L. Rev. 255 (2008).

CASE NOTES

Provision in addendum to employment contract did not violate code. — Where provision in an addendum to an employment contract entered into between law firm and employee which stated that upon the voluntary or involuntary termination of his employment with law firm employee would remain liable on a monthly basis for his "proportionate share" of the lease payments, the disputed addendum provision did not violate the Virginia Code of Professional Responsibility. Shuttleworth, Ruloff & Giordano v. Nutter, 254 Va. 494, 493 S.E.2d 364 (1997) (decided under former DR 2-106).

PUBLIC SERVICE.

Rule 6.1. Voluntary Pro Bono Publico Service.

(a) A lawyer should render at least two percent per year of the lawyer's professional time to pro bono publico legal services. Pro bono publico services include poverty law, civil rights law, public interest law, and volunteer activities designed to increase availability of pro bono legal services.

(b) A law firm or other group of lawyers may satisfy their responsibility collectively under this Rule.

(c) Direct financial support of programs that provide direct delivery of legal services to meet the needs described in (a) above is an alternative method for fulfilling a lawyer's responsibility under this Rule.

COMMENT

[1] Every lawyer, regardless of professional prominence or professional work load, has a personal responsibility to provide legal services to those unable to pay, and personal involvement in the problems of the disadvantaged can be one of the most rewarding experiences in the life of a lawyer.

The Council for the Virginia State Bar urges all Virginia lawyers to contribute a minimum of two percent of their professional time annually to pro bono services. Pro bono legal services consist of any professional services for which the lawyer would ordinarily be compensated, including dispute resolution as a mediator or third party neutral.

[2] Pro bono services in poverty law consist of free or nominal fee professional services for people who do not have the financial resources to compensate a lawyer. Private attorneys participating in legal aid referral programs are typical examples of "poverty law." Legal services for persons whose incomes exceed legal aid guidelines, but who nevertheless have insufficient resources to compensate counsel, would also qualify as "poverty law," provided the free or nominal fee nature of any such legal work is established in advance.

[3] Pro bono publico legal services in civil rights law consists of free or nominal fee professional services to assert or protect rights of individuals in which society has an interest. Professional services to assert or protect for victims of discrimination based on race, sex, age or handicap would be typical examples of "civil rights law," provided the free or nominal nature of any such legal work is established in advance.

[4] Free or nominal fee provision of legal services to religious, charitable or civic groups in efforts such as setting up a shelter for the homeless, operating a hotline for battered spouses or providing public service information would be examples of "public interest law."

[5] Training and mentoring lawyers who have volunteered to take legal aid referrals or helping recruit lawyers for pro bono referral programs would be examples of "volunteer activities designed to increase availability of pro bono legal services."

[6] Service in any of the categories described is not pro bono publico if provided on a contingent fee basis. Because service must be provided without fee or expectation of fee, the intent of the lawyer to render free or nominal fee legal services is essential. Accordingly, services for which fees go uncollected would not qualify.

Collective Fulfillment of Pro Bono Publico Service

[7] Although every lawyer has an individual responsibility to provide pro bono publico services, some legal matters require the application of considerably greater effort and resources than a lawyer, acting alone, could reasonably provide on a pro bono basis. In fulfilling their obligation under this Rule, a group of two or more lawyers may pool their resources to ensure that individuals in need of such assistance, who would otherwise be unable to afford to compensate counsel, receive needed legal services. The designation of one or more lawyers to work on pro bono publico matters may be attributed to other lawyers within the firm or group who support the representation.

[8] *ABA Model Rule* Comment not adopted.

Financial Support in Lieu of Direct Pro Bono Publico Services

[9] The provision of free or nominally priced legal services to those unable to pay continues to be the obligation of each lawyer as well as the profession generally, but the efforts of individual lawyers are often not enough to meet the need Not only do these needs far exceed the capacity of the collective bar, the nature of legal practice for many lawyers places constraints on their ability to render pro bono publico legal services. For example, some lawyers (e.g., some government lawyers) are prohibited by the terms of their employment from engaging in any outside practice. Other lawyers lack the experience and access to resources necessary to provide competent legal assistance.

[10] To provide legal services beyond those available through the pro bono efforts of individual lawyers, the legal profession and government have established additional programs to provide such services. Lawyers who are unable to fulfill their pro bono publico obligation through direct, legal representation should support programs that provide legal services for the purposes described in (a) through financial contributions in proportion to their professional income.

Virginia Code Comparison

There was no direct counterpart to this Rule in the Disciplinary Rules of the Virginia Code. EC 2-27 stated that the "basic responsibility for providing legal services for those unable to pay ultimately rests upon the individual lawyer. . . . Every lawyer, regardless of professional prominence or professional work load, should find time to participate in serving the disadvantaged." EC 8-9 stated that "[t]he advancement of our legal system is of vital importance in maintaining the rule of law . . . [and] lawyers should encourage, and should aid in making, needed changes and improvements." EC 8-3 stated that "[t]hose persons unable to pay for legal services should be provided needed services."

Committee Commentary

The subject matter of this Rule was not specifically addressed in the Disciplinary Rules of the Virginia Code. The Committee drafted language different from that of the ABA Model Rule to bring the Rule in line with Ethical Considerations approved by the Supreme Court of Virginia on June 17, 1994 (specifically EC 2-28 and 2-29). The Committee then adopted the new versions of EC 2-27 and EC 2-30, EC 2-31, and EC 2-32 as the Rule's Comment for section (a). Sections (b) and (c) permit greater flexibility in the manner in which lawyers fulfill their pro bono obligations.

Rule 6.2. Accepting Appointments.

A lawyer should not seek to avoid appointment by a tribunal to represent a person except for good cause, such as:

(a) representing the client is likely to result in violation of the Rules of Professional Conduct or other law;

(b) representing the client is likely to result in an unreasonable financial burden on the lawyer; or

(c) the client or the cause is so repugnant to the lawyer as to be likely to impair the client-lawyer relationship or the lawyer's ability to represent the client.

COMMENT

[1] A lawyer ordinarily is not obliged to accept a client whose character or cause the lawyer regards as repugnant. The lawyer's freedom to select clients is, however, qualified. All lawyers have a responsibility to assist in providing pro bono publico service. See Rule 6.1. An individual lawyer fulfills this responsibility by accepting a fair share of unpopular matters or indigent or unpopular clients. A lawyer may also be subject to appointment by a court to serve unpopular clients or persons unable to afford legal services.

Appointed Counsel

[2] For good cause a lawyer may seek to decline an appointment to represent a person who cannot afford to retain counsel or whose cause is unpopular. Good cause exists if the lawyer could not handle the matter competently, see Rule 1.1, or if undertaking the representation would result in an improper conflict of interest, for example, when the client or the cause is so repugnant to the lawyer as to be likely to impair the client-lawyer relationship or the lawyer's ability to represent the client. A lawyer may also seek to decline an appointment if acceptance would be unreasonably burdensome, for example, when it would impose a financial sacrifice so great as to be unjust.

[3] An appointed lawyer has the same obligations to the client as retained counsel, including the obligations of loyalty and confidentiality, and is subject to the same limitations on the client-lawyer relationship, such as the obligation to refrain from assisting the client in violation of the Rules.

Virginia Code Comparison

There was no counterpart to this Rule in the Disciplinary Rules of the Virginia Code. EC 2-38 stated that when a lawyer is "appointed by a court or requested by a bar association to undertake representation of a person unable to obtain counsel, whether for financial or other reasons, he should not seek to be excused from undertaking the representation except for compelling reasons. Compelling reasons do not include such factors as the repugnance of the subject matter of the proceeding, the identity or position of a person involved in the case, the belief of the lawyer that the defendant in a criminal proceeding is guilty, or the belief of the lawyer regarding the merits of the civil case." EC 2-39 stated that "a lawyer should decline employment if the intensity of his personal feelings, as distinguished from a community attitude, may impair his effective representation of a prospective client."

Committee Commentary

The Committee adopted this Rule as an appropriate companion to Rule 6.1 because it emphasizes the responsibility of lawyers to increase the availability of legal services by accepting court appointed clients.

Rule 6.3. Membership in Legal Services Organization.

A lawyer may serve as a director, officer or member of a legal services organization, apart from the law firm in which the lawyer practices, notwithstanding that the organization serves persons having interests adverse to a client of the lawyer. The lawyer shall not knowingly participate in a decision or action of the organization:

(a) if participating in the decision or action would be incompatible with the lawyer's obligations to a client under Rule 1.7; or

(b) where the decision or action could have a material adverse effect on the representation of a client of the organization whose interests are adverse to a client of the lawyer.

COMMENT

[1] Lawyers should be encouraged to support and participate in legal service organizations. A lawyer who is an officer or a member of such an organization does not thereby have a client-lawyer relationship with persons served by the organization. However, there is potential conflict between the interests of such persons and the interests of the lawyer's clients. If the possibility of such conflict disqualified a lawyer from serving on the board of a legal services organization, the profession's involvement in such organizations would be severely curtailed.

[2] It may be necessary in appropriate cases to reassure a client of the organization that the representation will not be affected by conflicting loyalties of a member of the board. Established, written policies in this respect can enhance the credibility of such assurances.

Virginia Code Comparison

There was no counterpart to this Rule in the Virginia Code.

Committee Commentary

The Committee adopted this Rule to recognize and address the potential tension between private clients and participation by their lawyers in legal services organizations — which was not addressed by the Virginia Code.

Rule 6.5. Nonprofit and Court-Annexed Limited Legal Services Programs.

(a) A lawyer who, under the auspices of a program sponsored by a nonprofit organization or court, provides short-term limited legal services to a client without expectation by either the lawyer or the client that the lawyer will provide continuing representation in the matter:

(1) is subject to Rules 1.7 and 1.9(a) only if the lawyer knows that the representation of the client involves a conflict of interest; and

(2) is subject to Rule 1.10 only if the lawyer knows that another lawyer associated with the lawyer in a law firm is disqualified by Rule 1.7 or 1.9(a) with respect to the matter.

(b) Except as provided in paragraph (a)(2), Rule 1.10 is inapplicable to a representation governed by this Rule.

COMMENT

[1] Legal services organizations, courts and various nonprofit organizations have established programs through which lawyers provide short-term limited legal services — such as advice or the completion of legal forms — that will assist persons to address their legal problems without further representation by a lawyer. In these programs, such as legal-advice hotlines, advice-only clinics or pro se counseling programs, a client-lawyer relationship is established, but there is no expectation that the lawyer's representation of the client will continue beyond the limited consultation. Such programs are normally operated under circumstances in which it is not feasible for a lawyer to systematically screen for conflicts of interest as is generally required before undertaking a representation. See, e.g., Rules 1.7, 1.9 and 1.10.

[2] A lawyer who provides short-term limited legal services pursuant to this Rule must secure the client's informed consent to the limited scope of the representation. See Rule 1.2(b). If a short-term limited representation would not be reasonable under the circumstances, the lawyer may offer advice to the client but must also advise the client of the need for further assistance of counsel. Except as provided in this Rule, the Rules of Professional Conduct, including Rules 1.6 and 1.9(c), are applicable to the limited representation.

[3] Because a lawyer who is representing a client in the circumstances addressed by this Rule ordinarily is not able to check systematically for conflicts of interest, paragraph (a) requires compliance with Rules 1.7 or 1.9(a) only if the lawyer knows that the representation presents a conflict of interest for the lawyer, and with Rule 1.10 only if the lawyer knows that another lawyer in the lawyer's firm is disqualified by Rules 1.7 or 1.9(a) in the matter.

[4] Because the limited nature of the services significantly reduces the risk of conflicts of interest with other matters being handled by the lawyer's firm, paragraph (b) provides that Rule 1.10 is inapplicable to a representation governed by this Rule except as provided by paragraph (a)(2). Paragraph (a)(2) requires the participating lawyer to comply with Rule 1.10 when the lawyer knows that the lawyer's firm is disqualified by Rules 1.7 or 1.9(a). By virtue of paragraph (b), however, a lawyer's participation in a short-term limited legal services program will not preclude the lawyer's firm from undertaking or continuing the representation of a client with interests adverse to a client being represented under the program's auspices. Nor will the personal disqualification of a lawyer participating in the program be imputed to other lawyers participating in the program.

[5] If, after commencing a short-term limited representation in accordance with this Rule, a lawyer undertakes to represent the client in the matter on an ongoing basis, Rules 1.7, 1.9(a) and 1.10 become applicable.

Virginia Code Comparison

This Rule had no counterpart in the Virginia Code.

Committee Commentary

The committee adopted this specific conflicts of interest rule in recognition of the distinctive nature of services provided in this context.

Effective date. — This rule and the commentary thereto became effective January 1, 2004, by order adopted September 24, 2003.

INFORMATION ABOUT LEGAL SERVICES.

Rule 7.1. Communications Concerning a Lawyer's Services.

(a) A lawyer shall not make a false or misleading communication about the lawyer or the lawyer's services. A communication is false or misleading if it contains a material misrepresentation of fact or law, or omits a fact when omission of such fact makes the statement materially false or misleading as a whole.

(b) A communication violates this rule if it advertises specific or cumulative case results, without a disclaimer that (i) puts the case results in a context that is not misleading; (ii) states that case results depend upon a variety of factors unique to each case; and (iii) further states that case results do not guarantee or predict a similar result in any future case undertaken by the lawyer. The disclaimer shall precede the communication of the case results. When the communication is in writing, the disclaimer shall be in bold type face and uppercase letters in a font size that is at least as large as the largest text used to advertise the specific or cumulative case results and in the same color and against the same colored background as the text used to advertise the specific or cumulative case results.

(c) Any advertising pursuant to this Rule shall include the name and office address of at least one lawyer responsible for its content; or, in the alternative, a law firm may file with the Virginia State Bar a current written statement identifying the lawyer responsible for the law firm's advertising and its office address. The law firm shall promptly update the written statement if there is any change in status.

(d) A lawyer shall timely respond to and fully cooperate with any requests for information by Ethics Counsel regarding the lawyer's advertising.

COMMENT

[1] This Rule governs all communications about a lawyer's services, including advertising. The purpose of lawyer advertising is to promote or propose the hiring of the lawyer. Communications about a lawyer's services are statements or claims made about the lawyer or lawyer's services that are intended, in whole or in part, to inform others about the availability of the lawyer's services. Communications through public media as well as communications targeted to one or more persons are subject to this Rule. This Rule is not intended to regulate forms of non-commercial speech by lawyers such as political or religious commentary. Whatever means are used to communicate regarding a lawyer's services, statements about them must be truthful and not misleading. A statement or claim is misleading if it is likely to mislead the public or a prospective client. For example, a statement that "you pay nothing unless we win" is false and misleading if the client is held responsible for payment or reimbursement of costs or expenses related to the client's case, as required by Rule 1.8(e). Similarly, a statement or claim that a lawyer handles a particular type of case, i.e., products liability, is false and misleading if the lawyer does not practice in that area of law and the lawyer's only involvement is to intake the client and then refer the client to another lawyer outside the firm.

[2] Advertisements and other communications about a lawyer or a lawyer's services that are not false or misleading will make it apparent that the necessity and advisability of legal action depends on variant factors that must be evaluated individually. Due to fee information that may frequently be incomplete and misleading to a layperson, a lawyer should exercise great care that fee information is complete and accurate. Due to the individuality of each legal problem, statements regarding average, minimum, or estimated fees may be misleading, as will commercial publicity conveying information as to results previously achieved, general or average solutions, or expected outcomes. It would be misleading to advertise a set fee for a specific type of case without adhering to the stated fee in charging clients. Advertisements or other claims that convey an impression that the ingenuity of the lawyer, rather than the justice of the claim is determinative are similarly likely to be misleading. Advertising and other communications stating specific or aggregate case results should disclose the impossibility of assuring any particular result. Not only must a communication be truthful, but its meaning must be capable of being understood by the reasonably prudent layperson.

[3] Truthful statements that are misleading are also prohibited by this Rule. A truthful statement is misleading if it omits a fact necessary to make the lawyer's communication considered as a whole not materially misleading. A truthful statement is also misleading if there is a substantial likelihood that it will lead a reasonable person to formulate a specific conclusion about the lawyer or the lawyer's services for which there is no reasonable factual foundation. A good example of a truthful statement that is misleading by omission of a material fact is the statement "We won a $2 million verdict in this case" when in fact the verdict had been overturned by the court. The omission of that key fact makes the statement itself misleading.

[4] A statement or claim that an outcome was not or will not be related to the facts or merits of the particular matter is false or misleading and, therefore, improper. An advertisement that truthfully reports a lawyer's achievements on behalf of clients or former clients may be misleading if presented so as to lead a reasonable person to form an unjustified expectation that the same results could be obtained for other clients in similar matters without reference to the specific factual and legal circumstances of each client's case. Further, any statement or claim that is likely to create an unjustified expectation about the results the lawyer can achieve is misleading. The inclusion of the disclaimer required by paragraph (b) of this Rule is necessary to avoid creating unjustified expectations or misleading a potential client. The required disclaimer must precede each and every statement of specific or cumulative case results.

[5] Similarly, an unsubstantiated comparison of the lawyer's services or fees with the services or fees of other lawyers may be misleading if presented with such specificity as would lead a reasonable person to conclude that the comparison can be substantiated.

[6] Statements or claims made by others about the lawyer's services are governed by this rule if the lawyer adopts them in his or her communications. See also Rule 8.4(a) regarding violations of the Rules of Professional Conduct through the agency of another.

[7] This Rule permits public dissemination of information concerning, for example, a lawyer's name or firm name, address, and telephone number; the kinds of services the lawyer will undertake; the basis on which the lawyer's fees are determined, including prices for specific services and payment and credit arrangements; a lawyer's foreign language ability; names of references and, with their consent, names of clients regularly represented; and other information that might invite the attention of those seeking legal assistance.

Committee Commentary

The Committee has revised Rules 7.1-7.5 in their entirety. Rule 7.2 has been eliminated and relevant parts of Rule 7.2 regarding lawyer advertising are incorporated within Rule 7.1 as that Rule covers all communications including lawyer advertising; relevant parts of Rule 7.2 regarding solicitation and paying others to recommend a lawyer have been incorporated within Rule 7.3.

Editor's note. — This rule was amended by court order September 18, 2012, to become effective December 1, 2012. The amendments were vacated by court order effective November 29, 2012, and therefore, never took effect.

The amendment effective November 1, 2002, adopted November 1, 2002, rewrote the Rule and commentary thereto.

The amendment effective July 1, 2013, adopted April 15, 2013, rewrote the Rule and commentary thereto.

Law Review. — For article, "Professional Responsibility," see 43 U. Rich. L. Rev. 255 (2008).

CASE NOTES

Comparative claims. — Where a state bar committee issued advisory opinions regarding the possibility that plaintiffs' legal advertisements violated a prohibition on comparative claims, plaintiffs had standing as to their First Amendment claims, the claims were ripe and not moot, and plaintiffs were entitled to a preliminary injunction. Allen v. Williams, 254 F. Supp. 2d 614, 2003 U.S. Dist. LEXIS 5124 (E.D. Va. 2003).

Rule 7.2. Advertising [DELETED].

Editor's note. — This rule was amended by court order September 18, 2012, to become effective December 1, 2012. The amendments were vacated by court order effective November 29, 2012, and therefore, never took effect.

The amendment effective July 1, 2013, adopted April 15, 2013, deleted the Rule and commentary thereto.

Rule 7.3. Direct Contact with Potential Clients.

(a) A lawyer shall not solicit employment from a potential client if:

(1) the potential client has made known to the lawyer a desire not to be solicited by the lawyer; or

(2) the solicitation involves harassment, undue influence, coercion, duress, compulsion, intimidation, threats or unwarranted promises of benefits.

(b) A lawyer shall not give anything of value to a person for recommending the lawyer's services except that a lawyer may:

(1) pay the reasonable costs of advertisements or communications permitted by this Rule and Rule 7.1;

(2) pay the usual charges of a legal service plan or a not-for-profit qualified lawyer referral service;

(3) pay for a law practice in accordance with Rule 1.17; and

(4) give nominal gifts of gratitude that are neither intended nor reasonably expected to be a form of compensation for recommending a lawyer's services.

(c) Every written, recorded or electronic communication from a lawyer soliciting professional employment from a potential client known to be in need of legal services in a particular matter shall conspicuously display the words "ADVERTISING MATERIAL" on the outside envelope, if any, and at the beginning and ending of any recorded or electronic communication, unless the recipient of the communication:

(1) is a lawyer; or

(2) has a familial, personal, or prior professional relationship with the lawyer; or

(3) is one who has had prior contact with the lawyer.

COMMENT

Direct Contact between Lawyers and Laypersons

[1] A solicitation is a targeted communication initiated by the lawyer that is directed to a specific potential client and that offers to provide, or can reasonably be understood as offering to provide, legal services. In contrast, a lawyer's communication typically does not constitute a solicitation if it is directed to the general public, such as through a billboard, an Internet banner advertisement, a website or a television commercial, or if it is in response to a request for information or is automat-

ically generated in response to Internet searches.

[2] There is far less likelihood that a lawyer would engage in abusive practices against an individual who is a former client, or with whom the lawyer has a close personal or family relationship; nor is there a serious potential for abuse when the person contacted is a lawyer or when the person has already initiated contact with the lawyer. Consequently, the requirements of Rule 7.3(c) are not applicable in those situations.

[3] Even permitted forms of solicitation can be abused; thus, any solicitation that contains information that is false or misleading within the meaning of Rule 7.1, which involves coercion, duress or harassment within the meaning of Rule 7.3(a), or which involves contact with a potential client who has made known to the lawyer a desire not to be solicited by the lawyer within the meaning of Rule 7.3(a), is prohibited. Moreover, if after sending a letter or other communication to a potential client the lawyer receives no response, continued repeated efforts to communicate with the potential client may constitute harassment and therefore violate the provisions of Rule 7.3(a). Regardless of the form of the communication, its propriety will be judged by the totality of the circumstances under which it is made, including the potential client's sophistication and physical, emotional, and mental state, the nature and characterization of the legal matter, the parties' previous relationship, the lawyer's conduct, and the words spoken.

Paying Others to Recommend a Lawyer

[4] Lawyers are not permitted to pay others for channeling professional work. However, Paragraph (b)(1) allows a lawyer to pay for advertising and communications permitted by this Rule, including the costs of print directory listings, on-line directory listings, newspaper ads, television and radio airtime, domain-name registrations, sponsorship fees, banner ads, and group advertising. A lawyer may compensate employees, agents, and vendors who are engaged to provide marketing or client-development services, such as publicists, public-relations personnel, business-development staff, and website designers. See Rule 5.3 for the duties of lawyers and law firms with respect to the conduct of nonlawyers who prepare marketing materials for them.

[5] Selection of a lawyer by a layperson should be made on an informed basis. Advice and recommendation of third parties — relatives, friends, acquaintances, business associates, or other lawyers — and publicity and personal communications from lawyers may help to make this possible. A lawyer should not compensate another person for recommending him or her, for influencing a potential client to employ him or her, or to encourage future recommendations.

[6] A lawyer may pay the usual charges of a legal service plan or a not-for-profit lawyer referral service. A legal service plan is a prepaid or group legal service plan or a similar delivery system that assists potential clients to secure legal representation. Not-for-profit lawyer referral services are consumer-oriented organizations that provide unbiased referrals to lawyers with appropriate experience in the subject matter of the representation and afford other client protections, such as complaint procedures or malpractice insurance requirements. Consequently, this Rule permits a lawyer to pay only the usual charges of a not-for-profit lawyer referral service.

[7] A lawyer who accepts assignments or referrals from a legal service plan or referrals from a not-for-profit lawyer referral service must act reasonably to assure that the activities of the plan or service are compatible with the lawyer's professional obligations. See Rule 5.3. Legal service plans and not-for-profit lawyer referral services may communicate with potential clients, but such communication must be in conformity with these Rules. Thus, advertising must not be false or misleading, as would be the case if the communications of a group advertising program or a group legal services plan would mislead potential clients to think that it was a lawyer referral service sponsored by a state agency or bar association. Nor could the lawyer allow in-person, telephonic, or real time contacts that would violate Rule 7.3.

[8] The requirement in Rule 7.3(c) that certain communications be marked "ADVERTISING MATERIAL" does not apply to communications sent in response to requests of potential clients or their spokespersons or sponsors; however, prior contact from the lawyer in the form of advertising material does not circumvent the need to include the words "ADVERTISING MATERIAL" in future contacts. General announcements by lawyers, including changes in personnel or office location, do not constitute communications soliciting professional employment from a potential client known to be in need of legal services within the meaning of this Rule.

Committee Commentary

The Committee changed the rule to refer to the "potential" client as a result of the recent adoption of Rule 1.18 which narrowly defines the "prospective" client.

Editor's note. — This rule was amended by court order September 18, 2012, to become effective December 1, 2012. The amendments were vacated by court order effective November 29, 2012, and therefore, never took effect.

The amendment effective November 1, 2002, adopted November 1, 2002, changed the style of the designations throughout; substituted "over persuasion" for "overpersuasion" in paragraphs a. 2. and c. 2.; and added "and 7.2" following "Rule 7.1" once in subdivision b. and twice in subdivision d.; and changed the designations for the commentary from [1] through [7] to 1. through 7.

The amendment effective July 1, 2013, adopted April 15, 2013, rewrote the Rule and commentary thereto.

Rule 7.4. Communication of Fields of Practice and Certification.

Lawyers may state, announce or hold themselves out as limiting their practice in a particular area or field of law so long as the communication of such limitation of practice is in accordance with the standards of this Rule, Rule 7.1 and Rule 7.3, as appropriate. A lawyer shall not state or imply that the lawyer has been recognized or certified as a specialist in a particular field of law except as follows:

(a) A lawyer admitted to engage in patent practice before the United States Patent and Trademark Office may use the designation "Patent Attorney" or a substantially similar designation;

(b) A lawyer engaged in Admiralty practice may use as a designation "Admiralty," "Proctor in Admiralty" or a substantially similar designation;

(c) A lawyer who has been certified by the Supreme Court of Virginia as a specialist in some capacity may use the designation of being so certified, e.g., "certified mediator" or a substantially similar designation;

(d) A lawyer may communicate the fact that the lawyer has been certified as a specialist in a field of law by a named organization, provided that the communication clearly states that there is no procedure in the Commonwealth of Virginia for approving certifying organizations.

COMMENT

[1] This Rule permits a lawyer to indicate areas of practice in communications about the lawyer's services. If a lawyer practices only in certain fields, or will not accept matters in a specified field or fields, the lawyer is permitted to so indicate. A lawyer is generally permitted to state that the lawyer is a "specialist," practices a "specialty," or "specializes in" particular fields, but such communications are subject to the "false and misleading" standard applied in Rule 7.1 to public communications concerning a lawyer's services.

[2] However, a lawyer may not communicate that the lawyer has been recognized or certified as a specialist in a particular field of law, except as provided by this Rule. Recognition of specialization in patent matters is a matter of long established policy of the Patent and Trademark Office as reflected in paragraph (a). Paragraph (b) recognizes that designation of admiralty practice has a long historical tradition associated with maritime commerce and the federal courts.

[3] Because Virginia has no procedure for approving organizations granting certifications of other specialties, lawyers communicating the fact that they have been certified as specialists in a field of law by a named organization (other than the Supreme Court of Virginia as provided in paragraph (c)) must clearly disclose that there is no procedure in Virginia for approving certifying organizations (paragraph (d)).

Virginia Code Comparison

Rule 7.4(a) and (b) are substantially the same as DR 2-104(A). Paragraph (c) is new, and paragraph (d) follows one of the two options in ABA Model Rule 7.4(c).

Committee Commentary

The Committee maintained the current DR 2-104(A) approach in the first two paragraphs of this Rule.

Because national organizations are increasingly certifying specialists in different areas of the law, the Committee determined to permit Virginia lawyers to describe such certifications. However, Virginia has no procedure for state approval of such certifications. For this reason, the Committee adopted the alternative ABA Model Rule 7.4(c) that requires lawyers communicating certified specializations to make the additional clear disclosure that Virginia has no procedure for approving certifying organizations. This additional disclosure balances Virginia clients' interest in receiving additional information about lawyers and the need to avoid misleading clients by implying some government-approved certification. At the same time, it was deemed that any certification process implemented by the Supreme Court of Virginia (under (d)) would obviously be reliable, so as to eliminate the necessity for any disclaimer.

Editor's note. — This rule was amended by court order September 18, 2012, to become effective December 1, 2012. The amendments were vacated by court order effective November 29, 2012, and therefore, never took effect.

The amendment effective November 1, 2002, adopted November 1, 2002, inserted "Rule 7.2" in the introductory language; and inserted "and 7.2" in 1.

The amendment effective July 1, 2013, adopted April 15, 2013, rewrote the Rule and commentary thereto.

Rule 7.5. Lawyer and Firm Names and Letterheads.

(a) A lawyer shall not use a name, firm name, letterhead, or other professional designation that violates Rule 7.1. A trade name may be used by a lawyer in private practice if it does not imply a connection with a government agency or with a public or charitable legal services organization and is not otherwise in violation of Rule 7.1.

(b) A law firm with offices in more than one jurisdiction may use the same name or other professional designation in each jurisdiction, but identification of the lawyers in an office of the firm shall indicate the jurisdictions in which they are licensed to practice if they are not licensed to practice in the jurisdiction where the office is located.

(c) The name of a lawyer holding a public office shall not be used in the name of a law firm, or in communications on its behalf, during any substantial period in which the lawyer is not actively and regularly practicing with the firm.

(d) Lawyers may state or imply that they practice in a partnership or other organization only when that is the fact.

COMMENT

[1] A firm may be designated by the names of all or some of its members, by the names of deceased members where there has been a continuing succession in the firm's identity or by a trade name such as the "ABC Legal Clinic." A lawyer or law firm may also be designated by a distinctive website address or comparable professional designation. Although the Supreme Court of the United States has held that legislation may prohibit the use of trade names in professional practice, use of such names in law practice is acceptable so long as it is not misleading. If a private firm uses a trade name that includes a geographical name such as "Springfield Legal Clinic," an express disclaimer that it is not a public legal aid agency may be required to avoid a misleading implication. It may be observed that any firm name including the name of a retired or deceased partner is, strictly speaking, a trade name. The use of such names to designate law firms has proven a useful means of identification. However, it is misleading to use the name of a lawyer not associated with the firm or a predecessor of the firm, or the name of a nonlawyer.

[2] With regard to paragraph (d), lawyers sharing office facilities, but who are not in fact partners associated with each other in a law firm, may not denominate themselves as, for example, "Smith and Jones," for that title suggests that they are practicing law together in a firm.

[3] Lawyers should practice using the official name under which they are licensed or seek an appropriate and legal change of name from the Supreme Court of Virginia. The lawyer's use of a name other than the lawyer's name on record with the Virginia State Bar may be a misleading communication about the lawyer's services to the public in violation of Rule 7.1.

Editor's note. — This rule was amended by court order September 18, 2012, to become effective December 1, 2012. The amendments were vacated by court order effective November 29, 2012, and therefore, never took effect.

The amendment effective November 1, 2002, adopted November 1, 2002, in subdivision a., inserted "website" in the first sentence, and added "and 7.2" at the end of the second sentence; inserted the present second sentence in [1]; and substituted "ABA Model Rule" for "Rule" preceding "7.5 more in line with DR 2-102" at the end of the Committee Commentary.

The amendment effective June 30, 2005, adopted June 30, 2005, in paragraph [1] of the commentary, inserted "retired or" preceding "deceased" in the fifth sentence, and substituted the present last two sentences for the former last sentence, which read: "However, it is misleading to use the name of a lawyer not associated with the firm or a predecessor of the firm."

The amendment effective July 1, 2013, adopted April 15, 2013, rewrote the Rule and commentary thereto.

Law Review. — For article, "Professional Responsibility," see 43 U. Rich. L. Rev. 255 (2008).

MAINTAINING THE INTEGRITY OF THE PROFESSION.

Rule 8.1. Bar Admission and Disciplinary Matters.

An applicant for admission to the bar, or a lawyer already admitted to the bar, in connection with a bar admission application, any certification required to be filed as a condition of maintaining or renewing a license to practice law, or in connection with a disciplinary matter, shall not:

(a) knowingly make a false statement of material fact;

(b) fail to disclose a fact necessary to correct a misapprehension known by the person to have arisen in the matter;

(c) fail to respond to a lawful demand for information from an admissions or disciplinary authority, except that this Rule does not require disclosure of information otherwise protected by Rule 1.6; or

(d) obstruct a lawful investigation by an admissions or disciplinary authority.

COMMENT

[1] The duty imposed by this Rule extends to persons seeking admission to the bar as well as to lawyers. Hence, if a person makes a materially false statement in connection with an application for admission or a certification necessary for license renewal, it may be the basis for disciplinary action

once that person has been admitted to the Bar. The duty imposed by this Rule applies to a lawyer's own admission or discipline as well as that of others. Thus, it is a separate professional offense for a lawyer to knowingly make a misrepresentation or omission in connection with a disciplinary investigation of the lawyer's own conduct. This Rule also requires affirmative clarification of any material misstatement, of which the person involved becomes aware, that could lead to a misunderstanding on the part of the admissions or disciplinary authority.

[2] This Rule is subject to the provisions of the Fifth Amendment of the United States Constitution, corresponding provisions of state constitutions, or other lawfully recognized matters of privilege. A person relying on such a provision in response to a question should openly assert the basis for nondisclosure.

[3] A lawyer representing an applicant for admission to the bar, or representing a lawyer who is the subject of a disciplinary inquiry or proceeding, is governed by the rules applicable to the attorney-client relationship.

[4] The Rule also prohibits the obstruction of either an admissions or disciplinary inquiry. "Obstruction" is used in the ordinary sense and includes, among other intentional acts, purposeful delay, attempts to improperly influence others who are requested to provide information, and the falsification or destruction of relevant documentation.

Virginia Code Comparison

Rule 8.1 is broader than DR 1-101 of the Virginia Code. DR 1-101(A) provided that a lawyer is "subject to discipline if he has made a materially false statement in, or if he has deliberately failed to disclose a material fact requested in connection with, his or another's application for admission to the bar." DR 1-101(B) provided that a lawyer is "subject to discipline if he has made a materially false statement in any certification required to be filed as a condition of maintaining or renewing his license to practice law."

Committee Commentary

The Committee preferred the broader coverage of the ABA Model Rule to that of DR 1-101 and made it even broader by adding language to the opening sentence covering required certifications and license renewal. Additionally, the Committee added paragraph (c) to impose an affirmative duty of cooperation with lawful demands for information, and added paragraph (d) to make it a separate violation to obstruct any investigation by a disciplinary or admissions authority.

The amendment effective September 26, 2002, adopted September 26, 2002, inserted a comma following "or a lawyer" near the beginning of the introductory language.

The amendment effective January 1, 2004, adopted September 24, 2003, inserted "already admitted to the bar" and deleted "in connection with" following "admission application" in the introductory paragraph.

Law Review. — For an essay, "Upping the Ante: Curricular and Bar Exam Reform in Professional Responsibility," see 56 Wash. & Lee L. Rev. 1023 (1999). For article, "Professional Responsibility," see 39 U. Rich. L. Rev. 315 (2004). For article, "Professional Responsibility," see 43 U. Rich. L. Rev. 255 (2008).

CASE NOTES

Failure to respond to demand for information. — Although an attorney did not promptly represent a client and violated Sup. Ct. R., pt. 6, § II, Rule 1.3(a), there was no finding that a disciplinary committee was unable to gather information as a result of the attorney's failure to appear at a subsequent disciplinary hearing; therefore, the violation of Sup. Ct. R., pt. 6, § II, Rule 8.1(c) was reversed and remanded for reconsideration of the sanction. Rice v. Va. State Bar, 267 Va. 299, 592 S.E.2d 643, 2004 Va. LEXIS 27 (2004).

Rule 8.2. Judicial Officials.

A lawyer shall not make a statement that the lawyer knows to be false or with reckless disregard as to its truth or falsity concerning the qualifications or integrity of a judge or other judicial officer.

COMMENT

[1] False statements by a lawyer concerning the qualifications or integrity of a judge can unfairly undermine public confidence in the administration of justice. To maintain the fair and independent administration of justice, lawyers are encouraged to continue traditional efforts to defend judges and courts unjustly criticized.

Virginia Code Comparison

There was no direct counterpart to Rule 8.2 in the Virginia Code. EC 8-6 stated: "While a lawyer as a citizen has a right to criticize [judges and other judicial officers], he should be certain of the merit of his complaint, use appropriate language, and avoid petty criticisms, for unrestrained and intemperate statements tend to lessen public confidence in our legal system."

Committee Commentary

The Committee adopted this Rule because it addressed a subject not explicitly addressed by the Virginia Code. However, the Committee deleted ABA Model Rule language which brought candidates for judicial office under the protection of this Rule and which required such candidates to abide by applicable provisions of the Virginia Code —

concluding that such requirements and protections were neither necessary nor advisable for lawyers who are being considered for judicial office. While the dignity of courts and the attendant requirement that judicial officials be treated with respect acts as a restraint on lawyer criticism of those officials, the Committee concluded that to extend this Rule to those being considered for judicial office might have a chilling effect on free discussion of judicial candidates' qualifications.

Law Review. — For article, "Professional Responsibility," see 43 U. Rich. L. Rev. 255 (2008).

CASE NOTES

Accusations. — Because an attorney personally attacked a judge by accusing the judge of lying and other professional misconduct, and the attorney's statements were made with reckless disregard as to their truth or falsity; consequently, the Virginia State Bar Disciplinary Board properly suspended the attorney's license to practice law for 90 days. Pilli v. Va. State Bar, 269 Va. 391, 611 S.E.2d 389, 2005 Va. LEXIS 34, cert. denied, 546 U.S. 977, 126 S. Ct. 555, 163 L. Ed. 2d 461 (2005).

Rule 8.3. Reporting Misconduct.

(a) A lawyer having reliable information that another lawyer has committed a violation of the Rules of Professional Conduct that raises a substantial question as to that lawyer's honesty, trustworthiness or fitness to practice law shall inform the appropriate professional authority.

(b) A lawyer having reliable information that a judge has committed a violation of applicable rules of judicial conduct that raises a substantial question as to the judge's fitness for office shall inform the appropriate authority.

(c) If a lawyer serving as a third party neutral receives reliable information during the dispute resolution process that another lawyer has engaged in misconduct which the lawyer would otherwise be required to report but for its confidential nature, the lawyer shall attempt to obtain the parties' written agreement to waive confidentiality and permit disclosure of such information to the appropriate professional authority.

(d) This Rule does not require disclosure of information otherwise protected by Rule 1.6 or information gained by a lawyer or judge who is a member of an approved lawyer's assistance program, or who is a trained intervenor or volunteer for such a program or committee, or who is otherwise cooperating in a particular assistance effort, when such information is obtained for the purposes of fulfilling the recognized objectives of the program.

(e) A lawyer shall inform the Virginia State Bar if:

(1) the lawyer has been disciplined by a state or federal disciplinary authority, agency or court in any state, U.S. territory, or the District of Columbia, for a violation of rules of professional conduct in that jurisdiction;

(2) the lawyer has been convicted of a felony in a state, U.S. territory, District of Columbia, or federal court;

(3) the lawyer has been convicted of either a crime involving theft, fraud, extortion, bribery or perjury, or an attempt, solicitation or conspiracy to commit any of the foregoing offenses, in a state, U.S. territory, District of Columbia, or federal court.

COMMENT

[1] Self-regulation of the legal profession requires that members of the profession initiate disciplinary investigation when they know of a violation of the Rules of Professional Conduct. Lawyers have a similar obligation with respect to judicial misconduct. An apparently isolated violation may indicate a pattern of misconduct that only a disciplinary investigation can uncover. Reporting a violation is especially important where the victim is unlikely to discover the offense.

[2] A report about misconduct is not required where it would involve violation of Rule 1.6. See Rule 1.6(c)(3).

[3] If a lawyer were obliged to report every violation of the Rules, the failure to report any violation would itself be a professional offense. Such a requirement existed in many jurisdictions but proved to be unenforceable. This Rule limits the reporting obligation to those offenses that a self-regulating profession must vigorously endeavor to prevent. A measure of judgment is, therefore, required in complying with the provisions of this Rule. The term "substantial" refers to the seriousness of the possible offense and not the quantum of evidence of which the lawyer is aware. A report should be made to the bar disciplinary agency unless some other agency, such as a peer review agency, is more appropriate in the circumstances. Similar considerations apply to the reporting of judicial misconduct.

[3a] In court-related dispute resolution proceedings, a third party neutral cannot disclose any information exchanged or observations regarding the conduct and demeanor of the parties and their counsel during the proceeding. Mediation sessions are covered by another statute, which is less restrictive, covering "any communication made in or in connection with the mediation which relates to the controversy being mediated." Thus a lawyer serving as a mediator or third party neutral may not be able to discharge his or her obligation to report the misconduct of another lawyer if the reporting lawyer's information is based on information protected as confidential under the statutes. However, both statutes permit the parties to agree in writing to waive confidentiality.

[3b] The Rule requires a third party neutral lawyer to attempt to obtain the parties' written consent to waive confidentiality as to professional misconduct, so as to permit the lawyer to reveal information regarding another lawyer's misconduct which the lawyer would otherwise be required to report.

[4] The duty to report professional misconduct does not apply to a lawyer retained to represent a lawyer or judge whose professional conduct is in question. Such a situation is governed by the rules applicable to the client-lawyer relationship.

[5] Information about a lawyer's or judge's misconduct or fitness may be received by a lawyer in the course of that lawyer's participation in or cooperation with an approved lawyers or judges assistance program. In that circumstance, providing for the confidentiality of such information encourages lawyers and judges to seek treatment through such program. Conversely, without such confidentiality, lawyers and judges may hesitate to seek assistance from these programs, which may then result in additional harm to their professional careers and additional injury to the welfare of clients and the public. The duty to report, therefore, does not apply to a lawyer who is participating in or cooperating with an approved lawyer assistance program such as the Virginia Bar Association's Committee on Substance Abuse and who learns of the confidences and secrets of another lawyer who is the object of a particular assistance effort when such information is obtained for the purpose of fulfilling the recognized objectives of the program. Such confidences and secrets are to be protected to the same extent as the confidences and secrets of a lawyer's client in order to promote the purposes of the assistance program. On the other hand, a lawyer who receives such information would nevertheless be required to comply with the Rule 8.3 reporting provisions to report misconduct if the impaired lawyer or judge indicates an intent to engage in illegal activity, for example, the conversion of client funds to personal use.

[6] The duty of a lawyer to self-report a criminal conviction or professional discipline under paragraph (e) of this rule is triggered only after the conviction or decision has become final. Whether an offense is a felony shall be governed by the state, U.S. territory, District of Columbia or federal law under which the conviction is obtained. Thus, it is possible that an offense in another jurisdiction may be a misdemeanor crime for which there is no duty to self-report, even though under Virginia law the offense is a felony.

Virginia Code Comparison

Paragraph (a) is substantially similar to DR 1-103(A) when coupled with the reference to Rule 1.6 in paragraph (d). DR 1-103(A) stated: "A lawyer having information indicating that another lawyer has committed a violation of the Disciplinary Rules that raises a substantial question as to that lawyer's honesty, trustworthiness, or fitness to practice law in other respects, shall report such information to the appropriate professional authority, except as provided in DR 4-101."

Paragraph (c) has no counterpart in the Virginia Code.

With respect to paragraph (d), DR 1-103(B) effectively excluded from the disclosure requirements of DR 1-103(A) "any information gained in the performance of . . . duties" by "a lawyer who is a member of The Virginia Bar Association's Committee on Substance Abuse and/or who is a trained intervenor for the Committee."

Committee Commentary

These attorney misconduct reporting requirements do not differ substantially from those of the corresponding Disciplinary Rule, DR 1-103. Although paragraph (b), requiring the reporting of judicial misconduct, and paragraph (c), requiring reporting of lawyer misconduct by a third party neutral, have no counterpart in the Virginia Code, the Committee believed them to be appropriate additions. With respect to both paragraphs (a) and (b) and (c), the Committee believed that the phrase "reliable information" indicated more clearly than the ABA Model Rule's "knowledge" the sort of information which should support a report of attorney misconduct.

The amendment, effective September 26, 2002, adopted September 26, 2002, substituted "to practice law" for "as a lawyer" near the end of subdivision (a), added subdivision (e), and added comment 6.

CASE NOTES

Attorneys have continuing duty to disclose violations. — As officers of the court all attorneys have a continuing obligation to disclose to the court violations of the Rules of Professional Conduct. In re Stancraft Corp., 39 Bankr. 748 (Bankr. E.D. Va. 1984) (decided under former DR 1-103).

Standing to move to disqualify counsel. — Although the court recognized that the defendant's reasons in bringing the motion for disqualification of attorneys for the trustee in bankruptcy may not have been purely for preserving the integrity of the judicial system, it held that the defendants had standing to bring the motion. Moreover, once a violation of the ethical standards of conduct were brought to the attention of the court by any party, it had an independent duty to consider and resolve the matter. In re Stancraft Corp., 39 Bankr. 748 (Bankr. E.D. Va. 1984) (decided under former DR 1-103).

Rule 8.4. Misconduct.

It is professional misconduct for a lawyer to:

(a) violate or attempt to violate the Rules of Professional Conduct, knowingly assist or induce another to do so, or do so through the acts of another;

(b) commit a criminal or deliberately wrongful act that reflects adversely on the lawyer's honesty, trustworthiness or fitness as a lawyer;

(c) engage in conduct involving dishonesty, fraud, deceit or misrepresentation which reflects adversely on the lawyer's fitness to practice law;

(d) state or imply an ability to influence improperly or upon irrelevant grounds any tribunal, legislative body, or public official; or

(e) knowingly assist a judge or judicial officer in conduct that is a violation of applicable rules of judicial conduct or other law.

COMMENT

[1] *ABA Model Rule* Comment not adopted.

[2] Many kinds of illegal conduct reflect adversely on fitness to practice law, such as offenses involving fraud and the offense of willful failure to file an income tax return. However, some kinds of offense carry no such implication. Traditionally, the distinction was drawn in terms of offenses involving "moral turpitude." That concept can be construed to include offenses concerning some matters of personal morality, such as adultery and comparable offenses, that have no specific connection to fitness for the practice of law. Although a lawyer is personally answerable to the entire criminal law, a lawyer should be professionally answerable only for offenses that indicate lack of those characteristics relevant to law practice. Offenses involving violence, dishonesty, breach of trust, or serious interference with the administration of justice are in that category. A pattern of repeated offenses, even ones of minor significance when considered separately, can indicate indifference to legal obligation.

[3] *ABA Model Rule* Comment not adopted.

[4] A lawyer may refuse to comply with an obligation imposed by law upon a good faith belief that no valid obligation exists. The provisions of Rule 1.2(c) concerning a good faith challenge to the validity, scope, meaning or application of the law apply to challenges of legal regulation of the practice of law. *See* also Rule 3.1, Rule 3.4(d).

[5] Lawyers holding public office assume legal responsibilities going beyond those of other citizens. A lawyer's abuse of public office can suggest an inability to fulfill the professional role of attorney. The same is true of abuse of positions of private trust such as trustee, executor, administrator, guardian, agent and officer, director or manager of a corporation or other organization.

Virginia Code Comparison

With regard to paragraphs (a) through (c), DR 1-102(A) provided that a lawyer shall not:

"(1) Violate a Disciplinary Rule or knowingly aid another to do so.

(2) Circumvent a Disciplinary Rule through actions of another.

(3) Commit a crime or other deliberately wrongful act that reflects adversely on the lawyer's fitness to practice law.

(4) Engage in conduct involving dishonesty, fraud, deceit, or misrepresentation which reflects adversely on a lawyer's fitness to practice law."

Paragraph (d) is substantially the same as DR 9-101(C).

There was no direct counterpart to paragraph (e) in the Disciplinary Rules of the Virginia Code. EC 7-31 stated in part that "[a] lawyer ... is never justified in making a gift or a loan to a [judicial officer] under circumstances which might give the appearance that the gift or loan is made to influence official action." EC 9-1 stated that a lawyer "should promote public confidence in our [legal] system and in the legal profession."

Committee Commentary

Much of this Rule parallels provisions of the Disciplinary Rules of the Virginia Code. Paragraph (e), however, sets forth a prohibition not in the Virginia Code, and the Committee believed it is an appropriate addition.

The amendment, effective March 25, 2003, adopted March 25, 2003, deleted "professional" preceding "conduct involving" and added "which reflects adversely on the lawyer's fitness to practice law" in subsection (c).

Michie's Jurisprudence. — For related discussion, see 2A M.J. Attorney and Client, § 26.

CASE NOTES

Construction with federal law. — While an United States District Court utilizes the Code of Professional Responsibility as adopted by the Supreme Court of Virginia, it must nevertheless look to federal law in order to interpret and apply those rules and should not abdicate to the state's view of what constitutes professional conduct even in diversity cases. Armsey v. Medshares Mgt. Servs., Inc., 184 F.R.D. 569 (W.D. Va. 1998) (decided under former DR 1-102).

Attorney's knowing and intentional misrepresentation satisfies scienter requirement. — It is an attorney's knowing and intentional misrepresentation, not a wrongful intent to defraud his client, which satisfies the scienter requirement. Gay v. Virginia State Bar ex rel. Second Dist. Comm., 239 Va. 401, 389 S.E.2d 470 (1990) (decided under former DR 1-102).

Removal of goods from premises of employer. — Removal by an attorney of office equipment from the office of the real estate corporation that employed him as its agent constituted misconduct. Smolka v. Second Dist. Comm., 224 Va. 161, 295 S.E.2d 267 (1982) (decided under former DR 1-102).

Fabrication of charges for legal services in order to avoid repayment to client of client's overpayment constitutes misconduct. Blue v. Seventh Dist. Comm., 220 Va. 1056, 265 S.E.2d 753, stay denied, 448 U.S. 904, 100 S. Ct. 3045, 65 L. Ed. 2d 1134 (1980) (decided under former DR 1-102).

Sending of letter with forged signature. — Where attorney sent an undated letter, purportedly signed by another, requesting cancellation of the insurance, and the attorney required his wife, who was also his secretary, to forge his signature, the evidence was sufficient to support the finding of the disciplinary board that the attorney violated this rule. Gibbs v. Virginia State Bar, 232 Va. 39, 348 S.E.2d 209 (1986) (decided under former DR 1-102).

Recording third-party conversations. — The recordation, by a lawyer by his authorization, of conversation between third persons, to which he is not a party, without the consent or prior knowledge of each party to the conversation, is conduct involving dishonesty, fraud, or deceit under this section. Gunter v. Virginia State Bar, 238 Va. 617, 385 S.E.2d 597 (1989), cert. denied, 500 U.S. 953, 111 S. Ct. 2260, 114 L. Ed. 2d 712 (1991) (decided under former DR 1-102).

Failure to ascertain that liens satisfied before certifying so. — Certification to a title insurance company that the prior liens had been satisfied and released of record was certainly a knowing and intentional act. Necessarily implicit in the attorney's certification was the representation that he, or someone for whom he was responsible, had satisfied the prior liens and ascertained from the land records that those liens had been released. The attorney performed the same sort of knowing and intentional act and made the same type of representation when he showed on a settlement statement that the prior deed of trust had been satisfied. Where neither he nor anyone for whom he was responsible had satisfied any of the prior liens or ascertained whether the liens had been released of record, and he knew that neither he nor anyone for whom he was responsible had performed any of these necessary acts, the board did not err in finding the attorney had violated subdivision (A)(4) of this rule. Pickus v. Virginia State Bar, 232 Va. 5, 348 S.E.2d 202 (1986) (decided under former DR 1-102).

Prosecutor may not deny intention to call witness to avoid discovery. — Where the Commonwealth's attorney knows that an informant's appearance as a witness is impending, or intends in all likelihood to call the witness, the prosecutor may not deny his or her intention to call the witness as a pretext to avoid discovery. Courts have the responsibility to monitor the conduct of those attorneys who appear before them and assure adherence to professional standards. Moreno v. Commonwealth, 10 Va. App. 408, 392 S.E.2d 836 (1990) (decided under former DR 1-102).

Disputing propriety of sentence. — An attorney was subject to discipline where, after the court pronounced his client's sentence, the attorney vociferously expressed his disagreement with the sentence and, after having been held in contempt, took several steps towards the bench while raising his voice and continuing to express his view that the sentence was unjustified and outrageous. Morrissey v. Virginia State Bar ex rel. Third Dist. Comm., 260 Va. 472, 538 S.E.2d 677 (2000) (decided under former DR 1-102(A)(3)).

Virginia State Bar could discipline one who violated former § 51-179. — Because violations of former § 51-179 bore a substantial relationship to an attorney's fitness to practice law, the Virginia State Bar has authority to discipline a violator. Thompson v. Walker, 583 F. Supp. 175 (E.D. Va. 1984), aff'd, 758 F.2d 1004 (4th Cir. 1985) (decided under former DR 1-102).

Duties not limited to dealings with clients. — Where commonwealth's attorney deliberately concealed from complainant in abduction and rape case that defendant was willing to pay up to $50,000 to complainant as part of plea agreement, and where commonwealth's attorney misled complainant into believing that psychiatric evidence about her might be admissible in order to influence her to settle for $25,000, and where commonwealth's attorney contended that neither of these acts violated this rule because he was not complainant's attorney, the court stated that an attorney's duty not to practice deceit or misrepresentation is not confined to dealings with his client; it also extends to others who may be adversely affected by such conduct. Morrissey v. Virginia State Bar, 248 Va. 334, 448 S.E.2d 615 (1994) (decided under former DR 1-102).

Necessity of disclosure of charitable contribution as part of plea agreement. — When commonwealth's attorney, during presentation of plea agreement to judge for his acceptance, deliberately concealed the $25,000 charitable contributions to be made by defendant's father, and also asked defense counsel not to disclose it, the court rejected his contention that a prosecutor is not required to inform the sentencing court of any such condition. Morrissey v. Virginia State Bar, 248 Va. 334, 448 S.E.2d 615 (1994) (decided under former DR 1-102).

Where attorney used client's retainer without earning it, and attempted to deceive an investigator in claiming the retainer had been earned, the attorney's conduct involved dishonesty, fraud, deceit, or misrepresentation which reflected adversely on his fitness to practice law. El-Amin v. Virginia State Bar ex rel. Third Dist. Committee, 257 Va. 608, 514 S.E.2d 163 (1999) (decided under former DR 1-102).

Similarly, where attorney cashed his client's

$4,000 retainer, used the proceeds without earning the fee, and delayed refunding the retainer, his conduct sufficiently supported the finding that he committed a deliberately wrongful act that reflected adversely on his fitness to practice law. El-Amin v. Virginia State Bar ex rel. Third Dist. Committee, 257 Va. 608, 514 S.E.2d 163 (1999) (decided under former DR 1-102).

Where attorney was supposed to hold proceeds of sale of client's Lincoln Continental as a retainer fee pending client's appeal, but instead personally used client's car, and then traded it for a newer one without reflecting the resulting credit on the title to the newer car or in his records, his conduct sufficiently supported the trial court's findings of violations of both subsection (A)(3) and (A)(4) of these rules. El-Amin v. Virginia State Bar ex rel. Third Dist. Committee, 257 Va. 608, 514 S.E.2d 163 (1999) (decided under former DR 1-102).

Attempt to subpoena as way to get lien released. — Attorney violated Va. Sup. Ct. R. pt. 6, § II, R. 4.4 and 8.4(b) when the attorney attempt to subpoena a former employer to testify in the attorney's divorce action for no purpose other than to get the employer to release a lien claim against the attorney. Barrett v. Va. State Bar, 272 Va. 260, 634 S.E.2d 341, 2006 Va. LEXIS 84 (2006).

Dishonesty not shown by clear and convincing proof. — Virginia State Bar Disciplinary Board erred in finding that an attorney violated Va. Sup. Ct. R. pt. 6, § II, R. 4.3(b), 8.4(c) by representing both a driver and a passenger in legal proceedings arising out of an automobile accident; its findings of fact did not prove by clear and convincing evidence that he acted with dishonesty, fraud, deceit, or misrepresentation. Pappas v. Va. State Bar, 271 Va. 580, 628 S.E.2d 534, 2006 Va. LEXIS 51 (2006).

CIRCUIT COURT OPINIONS

Contact with limited partners of opposing party without notifying their counsel. — Defense counsel were disqualified after conducting ex parte communications with certain limited partners who were alter egos of the opposing party. Counsel violated Va. Sup. Ct. R. pt. 6, § II, R. 4.2, and R. 8.4(c) by concealing their role in the litigation and by communicating with the partners without notifying their counsel; defense counsel's unethical conduct also tainted the underlying trial and violated Va. Sup. Ct. R. pt. 6, § II, R. 4.4. Yukon Pocahontas Coal Co. v. Consolidation Coal Co., 72 Va. Cir. 75, 2006 Va. Cir. LEXIS 195 (Buchanan County 2006).

Notarizing documents without being duly authorized notary public. — Attorney was suspended from the practice of law for two years because the Virginia State Bar proved by clear and convincing evidence that the attorney violated Va. Sup. Ct. R. pt. 6, § II, R. 8.4(a), (b), and (c); the attorney admitted in court that he notarized certain documents, that at the time he was not a duly authorized Virginia notary public, and that at no time had he ever applied to become a notary public in the Commonwealth of Virginia, and the attorney further admitted that he was improperly in possession of a notary seal declaring him to be a duly authorized Virginia notary and that he personally used that seal when notarizing the signature of another attorney's client. Va. State Bar ex rel. Fourth District v. Duncan, 2011 Va. Cir. LEXIS 20 (Alexandria Mar. 15, 2011).

Rule 8.5. Disciplinary Authority; Choice of Law.

(a) Disciplinary Authority. A lawyer admitted to practice in this jurisdiction is subject to the disciplinary authority of Virginia, regardless of where the lawyer's conduct occurs. A lawyer not admitted in Virginia is also subject to the disciplinary authority of Virginia if the lawyer provides, holds himself out as providing, or offers to provide legal services in Virginia. By doing so, such lawyer consents to the appointment of the Clerk of the Supreme Court of Virginia as his or her agent for purposes of notices of any disciplinary action by the Virginia State Bar. A lawyer may be subject for the same conduct to the disciplinary authority of Virginia and any other jurisdiction where the lawyer is admitted.

(b) Choice of Law. In any exercise of the disciplinary authority of Virginia, the rules of professional conduct to be applied shall be as follows:

(1) for conduct in connection with a proceeding in a court, agency, or other tribunal before which a lawyer appears, the rules to be applied shall be the rules of the jurisdiction in which the court, agency, or other tribunal sits, unless the rules of the court, agency, or other tribunal provide otherwise;

(2) for any other conduct, the rules of the jurisdiction in which the lawyer's conduct occurred; and

(3) notwithstanding subparagraphs (b)(1) and (b)(2), for conduct in the course of providing, holding out as providing, or offering to provide legal services in Virginia, the Virginia Rules of Professional Conduct shall apply.

COMMENT

Disciplinary Authority

[1] In the past, a jurisdiction's authority to discipline a lawyer has been based upon whether the lawyer is admitted in that jurisdiction. Subparagraph (a) is a significant change in that a lawyer not admitted in Virginia is nonetheless subject to

the disciplinary authority of Virginia for conduct occurring in the course of providing, holding himself out as providing, or offering to provide legal services in Virginia. Subparagraph (a) adopts the scope of jurisdiction recommended by the ABA Model Rules for Lawyer Disciplinary Enforcement, as amended in 1996, by extending Virginia's disciplinary authority to any lawyer who commits misconduct within Virginia.

It is longstanding law that the conduct of a lawyer admitted to practice in this jurisdiction is subject to the disciplinary authority of this jurisdiction. Extension of the disciplinary authority of this jurisdiction to other lawyers who provide or offer to provide legal services in this jurisdiction is for the protection of the citizens of this jurisdiction. Reciprocal enforcement of a jurisdiction's disciplinary findings and sanctions will further advance the purposes of this Rule. A lawyer who is subject to the disciplinary authority of this jurisdiction under Rule 8.5(a) appoints the Clerk of the Supreme Court of Virginia to receive service of process in this jurisdiction.

Choice of Law

[2-7] *ABA Model Rule* Comments not adopted.

[8] Subparagraph (b) seeks to resolve conflicts that may arise when a lawyer is subject to the rules of more than one jurisdiction. The rules of one jurisdiction may prohibit the questioned conduct while the rules of another jurisdiction may permit it. A lawyer admitted in only one jurisdiction may also be subject to the rules of another jurisdiction in which he is not admitted to practice for conduct occurring in the course of providing, holding himself out as providing, or offering to provide legal services in the non-admitting jurisdiction. Also, a lawyer admitted in one jurisdiction may be subject to the rules of another jurisdiction if he appears before a court, agency, or other tribunal in that jurisdiction.

[9] If the lawyer appears before a court, agency, or other tribunal in another jurisdiction, subparagraph (b)(1) applies the law of the jurisdiction in which the court, agency, or other tribunal sits. In some instances, the court, agency, or other tribunal may have its own lawyer conduct rules and disciplinary authority. For example, the United States Patent and Trademark Office ("PTO'), through the Office of Enrollment and Discipline, enforces its own rules of conduct and disciplines practitioners under its own procedures. A lawyer admitted in Virginia who engages in misconduct in connection with practice before the PTO is subject to the PTO rules, and in the event of a conflict between the rules of Virginia and the PTO rules with respect to the questioned conduct, the latter would control.

[10] As to other conduct, if jurisdictions have conflicting rules regarding the questioned conduct, subparagraph (b)(2) resolves the conflict by choosing the rules of the jurisdiction where the conduct occurred. The physical presence of the lawyer is not dispositive in determining where the questioned conduct occurred. Determining where the lawyer's conduct occurred in the context of transactional work may require the appropriate disciplinary tribunal to consider other factors, including the residence and place of business of any client, third person, or public institution such as a court, tribunal, public body, or administrative agency, the interests of which are materially affected by the lawyer's actions.

Prior Rule Comparison

Virginia Rule 8.5 made no provision for disciplinary authority over a lawyer not admitted to practice in Virginia. Rather, a non-lawyer who committed misconduct in Virginia was subject to Virginia's unauthorized practice of law rules and the authority of the Virginia State Bar's Standing Committee on the Unauthorized Practice of Law.

Under former Rule 8.5 (b)(2), if a lawyer was subject to the rules of more than one jurisdiction, the rules of the jurisdiction in which the lawyer principally practiced applied unless the conduct had its predominant effect in another jurisdiction in which the lawyer was admitted to practice. The former rule, however, did not provide clear guidance if the lawyer's conduct occurred in a jurisdiction where the lawyer was not admitted.

Committee Commentary

The Committee adopted this Rule in light of the ABA recommendation that the states adopt more specific rules governing multi-jurisdictional practice. Like ABA Model Rule 8.5 (a), this rule states that for conduct occurring in the course of providing, holding oneself out as providing, or offering to provide legal services in Virginia the Virginia State Bar may exercise disciplinary authority over a lawyer not admitted in Virginia. Consistent with ABA Model Rule 8.5, the Virginia rule adopts choice of law rules for circumstances in which the lawyer is subject to the professional conduct rules of more than one jurisdiction and they conflict. The Virginia rule adopts verbatim ABA Model Rule 8.5 (b)(1), applying the rules of the jurisdiction in which the court, agency, or other tribunal sits. The Committee, however, did not adopt the "predominant effect" test used in ABA Model Rule 8.5 (b)(2), favoring instead the application of the rules of the jurisdiction in which the lawyer's conduct occurred. Virginia Rule 8.5 (b)(3) is new. The Committee did not adopt ABA Model Rule Comments 2-7.

The amendment effective March 1, 2009, adopted December 30, 2008, rewrote the Rule and Commentary thereto.

CROSS REFERENCE TABLE: VIRGINIA RULES OF PROFESSIONAL CONDUCT TO VIRGINIA CODE OF PROFESSIONAL RESPONSIBILITY

NOTE: Please observe the symbol (***) for rules which have no direct counterpart in the Virginia Code of Professional Responsibility. While often the case, a cross-reference to a provision in the Code of Professional Responsibility does not necessarily mean that the cited provision is identical or even substantially similar to a particular rule. A citation may simply mean that a provision in the Code of Professional Responsibility applies to the same issue covered by the rule. In some instances, an area covered by a rule was addressed in an Ethical Consideration (EC), but not a Disciplinary Rule (DR), and, therefore, only the EC is cited.

Virginia Rules of Professional Conduct	Issue or Topic	Virginia Code of Professional Responsibility
1.1	Competence	DR 6-101 (A)(2)
1.2 (a)	Scope of Representation	*** EC 7-7; EC 7-8
1.2 (b)	" " " "	DR 7-101 (B)(1)
1.2 (c)	" " " "	DR 7-102 (A)(7); DR 7-102 (A)(6); DR 7-105 (A); EC 7-5
1.2 (d)	" " " "	***
1.2 (e)	" " " "	DR 2-108 (A)(1)
1.3 (a)	Diligence	DR 6-101 (B)
1.3 (b)	" " " "	DR 7-101 (A)(2)
1.3 (c)	" " " "	DR 7-101 (A)(3)
1.4 (a)	Communication	DR 6-101 (C)
1.4 (b)	" " " "	*** EC 7-8; EC 9-2
1.4 (c)	" " " "	DR 6-101 (D)
1.5 (a)	Fees	DR 2-105 (A); EC 2-20
1.5 (b)	Contingent Fees	DR 2-105 (C); EC 2-22
1.5 (c)	Fee Splitting	DR 2-105 (D)
1.5 (d)	Contingent Fees	DR 2-105 (C)
1.5 (e)	Fee Sharing	DR 2-105 (D)
1.5 (f)	" " " "	***
1.6 (a)	Confidentiality	DR 4-101 (A), (B)
1.6 (b)(1)	Disclosure Required By Law or Court Order	DR 4-101 (C)(2)
1.6 (b)(2)	Disclosure to Protect Lawyer's Legal Rights	DR 4-101 (C)(4)
1.6 (b)(3)	Disclosure of Client Fraud on Third Party	DR 4-101 (C)(3)
1.6 (b)(4)	Disclosure of Client Information for Attorney's Death or Disability	***
1.6 (b)(5)	Disclosure of Client Information for LOMAP	***
1.6 (b)(6)	Disclosure of Client Information to Outside Auditor	*** EC 4-3
1.6 (c)(1)	Disclosure of Client's Intent to Commit Crime	DR 4-101 (D)
1.6 (c)(2)	Disclosure of Client Fraud on Tribunal	DR 4-101 (D)
1.6 (c)(3)	Reporting Misconduct of Another Attorney	***
1.7 (a), (b)	Conflict of Interest	DR 5-105 (A), (C)
1.8 (a)	Business Transaction With Client	DR 5-104 (A)
1.8 (b)	Improper Use of Client Confidences or Secrets	DR 4-101 (B)(3)
1.8 (c)	Client Gifts to Lawyer	DR 5-104 (B)
1.8 (d)	Literary Rights in Subject Matter of Representation	*** EC 5-4
1.8 (e)	Financial Assistance to Client	DR 5-103(B)
1.8 (f)	Nonclient Paying Lawyer's Fee	DR 5-106
1.8 (g)	Aggregate Settlements	DR 5-107
1.8 (h)	Limitation of Malpractice Liability	DR 6-102)A)
1.8 (i)	Interfamily Conflicts	***

Virginia Rules of Professional Conduct	Issue or Topic	Virginia Code of Professional Responsibility
1.8 (j)	Proprietary Interest in Client Matter	***
1.8 (k)	Imputation of Conflicts	***
1.9 (a)	Conflict of Interest: Former Client	DR 5-105 (D)
1.9 (b)	" " " "	***
1.9 (c)	" " " "	***
1.10 (a)	Imputed Disqualification	*** DR 5-105 (E)
1.11 (a)	Public Officials: Conflicts	DR 8-101 (A)
1.11 (b)	" " " "	DR 9-101 (B)
1.11 (c)	" " " "	***
1.11 (d)	" " " "	***
1.11 (e)	" " " "	***
1.11 (f)	" " " "	***
1.12 (a)	Former Judge, Arbitrator or Mediator	DR 9-101 (A); EC 5-20
1.12 (b)	" " " "	***
1.12 (c)	" " " "	***
1.12 (d)	" " " "	***
1.13	Organization as a Client	*** EC 5-18; EC 5-24
1.14	Client With Impairment	*** EC 7-11: EC 7-12
1.15 (a)	Safekeeping Property	DR 9-102 (A)
1.15 (b)	" " " "	***
1.15 (c)	" " " "	DR 9-102 (B)
1.15 (d)	" " " "	***
1.15 (e)(1)	Recordkeeping Requirements for Trust Accounts	DR 9-103
1.15 (e)(2)	Recordkeeping Requirements for Lawyers Serving as Fiduciaries	***
1.15 (f)	Accounting Procedures	DR 9-103 (B)
1.16 (a)	Terminating or Declining Representation	DR 2-108 (A)
1.16 (b)	" " " "	DR 2-108 (B)
1.16 (c)	" " " "	DR 2-108 (C)
1.16 (d)	" " " "	DR 2-108 (D)
1.16 (e)	Delivery of Former Client's File	***
1.17	Sale of a Law Practice	*** EC 4-6
2.1	Lawyer as Advisor	*** EC 7-8
2.3	Lawyer as Evaluator	*** EC 5-20
2.10	Third Party Neutral	***
2.11	Mediator	***
3.1	Meritorious Claims	DR 7-102 (A)(1), (2)
3.3 (a)(1)	Candor Toward Tribunal	DR 7-102 (A)(5)
3.3 (a)(2)	" " " "	DR 7-102 (A)(3)
3.3 (a)(3)	Controlling Legal Authority	*** EC 7-20
3.3 (a)(4)	False Evidence	DR 7-102 (A)(4)
3.3 (b)	" " " "	***
3.3 (c)	Ex Parte Proceedings	***
3.3 (d)	Reporting Third Party Fraud on Tribunal	DR 7-102 (B)
3.4 (a)	Fairness To Opposing Party & Counsel; Obstructing Access to Evidence	DR 7-108 (A)
3.4 (b)	Secreting Witnesses	DR 7-108 (B)
3.4 (c)	Compensating Witnesses	DR 7-108 (C); EC 7-25
3.4 (d)	Disregarding Court Rules or Orders	DR 7-105 (A)
3.4 (e)	Discovery Abuse	***
3.4 (f)	Improper Trial Conduct	DR 7-105 (C)(1)-(4)
3.4 (g)	Disruptive Rule Violations	DR 7-105 (C)(5)
3.4 (h)	Discouraging Witnesses	***
3.4 (i)	Threatening Criminal or Disciplinary Action	DR 7-104
3.4 (j)	Harassing or Injuring Others	DR 7-102 (A)(1)
3.5 (a), (b), (c)	Communications With Jurors	DR 7-107 (A)-(F), ***
3.5 (d)	Influencing Judges	DR 7-109 (A)

Virginia Rules of Professional Conduct	Issue or Topic	Virginia Code of Professional Responsibility
3.5 (e)	Ex Parte Communication With Judge	DR 7-109 (B)
3.5 (f)	Disruptive Conduct Toward Tribunal	***
3.6 (a), (b)	Trial Publicity	DR 7-106
3.7 (a)	Lawyer as Witness	DR 5-101 (B); DR 5-102 (A)
3.7 (b)	" " " "	DR 5-102 (B)
3.7 (c)	" " " "	***
3.8 (a)	Additional Responsibilities of a Prosecutor	DR 8-102 (A)(1)
3.8 (b)	" " " "	DR 8-102 (A)(1)
3.8 (c)	" " " "	DR 8-102 (A)(2)
3.8 (d)	" " " "	DR 8-102 (A)(3)
3.8 (e)	" " " "	DR 7-106 (B)
4.1 (a)	Truthfulness in Statements to Others	DR 7-102 (A)(5)
4.1 (b)	" " " "	*** DR 7-102 (A)(3); DR 7-102 (A)(7)
4.2	Ex Parte Communication With Represented Person	DR 7-103 (A)(1)
4.3 (a)	Dealing With Unrepresented Persons	DR 7-103 (B)
4.3 (b)	" " " "	DR 7-103 (A)(2)
4.4	Respect for Rights of Third Persons	*** DR 7-102 (A)(1); DR 7-105 (C)(2); DR 7-107 (C); DR 7-107 (D)
5.1	Responsibilities of a Supervising Lawyer	*** DR 1-103 (A); DR 4-101 (E); DR 7-106 (B)
5.3 (a), (b)	Nonlawyer Assistants	DR 3-104 (C); DR 4-101 (E)
5.3 (c)	" " " "	***
5.4 (a)	Sharing Fees With Nonlawyer	*** DR 3-102 (A)
5.4 (b)	Partnership with Nonlawyer	DR 3-103 (A)
5.4 (c)	Avoiding Influence By Non-clients	DR 5-106(B)
5.4 (d)	Professional Corporations Owned by Nonlawyers	DR 5-106 (C)
5.5 (a)(1)	Unauthorized Practice of Law	*** EC 3-9
5.5 (a)(2)	" " " "	DR 3-101 (A)
5.5 (b)	Employment of Suspended or Disbarred Lawyers	DR 3-101 (B)
5.5 (c)	" " " "	DR 3-101 (C)
5.6 (a), (b)	Agreements Restricting Practice of Law	DR 2-106
6.1	Voluntary Pro Bono Publico Service	*** ECs 2-26, 2-27, 2-28, 2-29, 2-30, 2-31, 2-32, 2-33, 2-34
6.2	Accepting Appointments	*** EC 2-38; EC 2-39
6.3	Membership in Legal Services Organization	***
6.5	Nonprofit Limited Legal Services	***
7.1	Communications Concerning A Lawyer's Services	DR 2-101
7.2	Advertising	DR 2-101, ***
7.3	Recommendation or Solicitation of Professional Employment	DR 2-103
7.4 (a), (b)	Communication of Fields of Practice & Certification	DR 2-104 (A), (B)
7.4 (c)	" " " "	***
7.4 (d)	" " " "	***
7.5	Firm Names & Letterheads	DR 2-102
8.1	Bar Admission & Disciplinary Matters	DR 1-101
8.2	Judicial Officials	*** EC 8-6
8.3 (a)	Reporting Professional Misconduct	DR 1-103 (A)
8.3 (b)	" " " "	***
8.3 (c)	" " " "	***
8.3 (d)	" " " "	***

Virginia Rules of Professional Conduct	Issue or Topic	Virginia Code of Professional Responsibility
8.3 (e)	Reporting Lawyer's Own Professional Misconduct	***
8.4 (a)	Misconduct	DR 1-102 (A)(1)
8.4 (b)	" " " "	DR 1-102 (A)(3)
8.4 (c)	" " " "	DR 1-102 (A)(4)
8.4 (d)	Misconduct	DR 9-101 (C)
8.4 (e)	" " " "	EC 7-31, EC 9-1
8.5 (a)	Disciplinary Authority; Choice of Law	DR 1-102 (B)
8.5 (b)	" " " "	***

CROSS REFERENCE TABLE: VIRGINIA CODE OF PROFESSIONAL RESPONSIBILITY TO VIRGINIA RULES OF PROFESSIONAL CONDUCT

Virginia Code of Professional Responsibility (DR)	Issue or Topic	Virginia Rule of Professional Conduct
DR 1-101	Bar Admissions or Renewal	Rule 8.1
DR 1-102	Misconduct	Rule 8.4
DR 1-103	Reporting Professional Misconduct	Rule 8.3
DR 2-101	Publicity and Advertising	Rule 7.1, 7.2
DR 2-102	Professional Letterheads, Offices, Notices	Rule 7.5
DR 2-103	Recommendation or Solicitation of Employment	Rule 7.3
DR 2-104	Specialists; Limitation of Practice	Rule 7.4
DR 2-105	Fees	Rule 1.5
DR 2-106	Agreements Restricting Practice of Law	Rule 5.6
DR 2-107	Acceptance of Employment	***
DR 2-108	Terminating Representation	Rule 1.16
DR 3-101	Aiding Unauthorized Practice of Law	Rule 5.5 (a)(2)
DR 3-102	Dividing Fees With a Nonlawyer	Rule 5.4 (a)
DR 3-103	Forming Partnership With a Nonlawyer	Rule 5.4 (b), (d)
DR 3-104	Supervising Nonlawyer Personnel	Rule 5.3
DR 4-101	Preservation of Confidences & Secrets of a Client	Rule 1.6
DR 5-101 (A)	Personal Interests Affecting Professional Judgment	Rule 1.7 (b)
DR 5-101 (B)	Lawyer as Witness	Rule 3.7
DR 5-102 (A), (B)	" " " "	" " " "
DR 5-103 (A)	Acquiring Proprietary Interest in Subject Matter of Litigation	Rule 1.8 (d), Rule 1.8 (j)
DR 5-103 (B)	Financial Assistance to Client	Rule 1.8 (e)
DR 5-104 (A)	Business Transactions with Client	Rule 1.8 (a)
DR 5-104 (B)	Preparing Instrument in Which Lawyer Receives Gift	Rule 1.8 (c)
DR 5-105	Representing Multiple Clients Whose Interests Conflict	Rule 1.7
DR 5-106	Avoiding Influence by Persons Other Than Client	Rule 1.8 (f), Rule 5.4 (c)
DR 5-107	Settling Similar Claims of Clients	Rule 1.8 (g)
DR 6-101 (A)	Competence	Rule 1.1
DR 6-101 (B)	Promptness	Rule 1.3 (a)
DR 6-101 (C)	Communication	Rule 1.4 (a), (b)
DR 6-101 (D)	" " " "	Rule 1.4 (c)
DR 6-102	Limiting Liability to Client	Rule 1.8 (h)
DR 7-101 (A)	Representing Client Zealously	Rule 1.3 (b), (c)
DR 7-101 (B)	Limitations on Zealous Representation	Rule 1.2 (b), (c)

Virginia Code of Professional Responsibility (DR)	Issue or Topic	Virginia Rule of Professional Conduct
DR 7-102 (A)	Representing Client Within Bounds of Law	Rule 3.1, Rule 3.3, Rule 3.4 (j), Rule 4.4
DR 7-102 (B)	Reporting Third Party Fraud on Tribunal	Rule 3.3 (d)
DR 7-103 (A)(1)	Communication with Persons Represented by Counsel	Rule 4.2
DR 7-103 (A)(2)	Advising Unrepresented Persons	Rule 4.3
DR 7-103 (B)	Dealing with Unrepresented Persons	Rule 4.3
DR 7-104	Threatening Criminal or Disciplinary Charges	Rule 3.4 (h)
DR 7-105 (A)	Trial Conduct: Disregarding Court Rule or Order	Rule 3.4 (d)
DR 7-105 (B)	Disclosing Representation to Court	***
DR 7-105 (C)	Trial Conduct	Rule 3.4
DR 7-106	Trial Publicity	Rule 3.6
DR 7-107	Communication With or Investigation of Jurors	Rule 3.5 (a)-(c)
DR 7-108	Contact With Witnesses	Rule 3.4
DR 7-109	Contact With Officials	Rule 3.5 (d), (e)
DR 8-101	Action as Public Official	Rule 1.11 (a)
DR 8-102	Special Responsibilities of a Prosecutor	Rule 3.8
DR 9-101	Avoiding Even the Appearance of Impropriety	Rule 1.11
DR 9-102	Preserving Identity of Funds and Property of Client	Rule 1.15
DR 9-103	Record Keeping Requirements	Rule 1.15

SECTION III. CANONS OF JUDICIAL CONDUCT FOR THE STATE OF VIRGINIA.

PREAMBLE

Our legal system is based on the principle that an independent, fair and competent judiciary will interpret and apply the laws that govern us. The role of the judiciary is central to American concepts of justice and the rule of law. Intrinsic to all sections of these Canons are the precepts that judges, individually and collectively, must respect and honor the judicial office as a public trust and strive to enhance and maintain confidence in our legal system. The judge is an arbiter of facts and law for the resolution of disputes and a highly visible symbol of government under the rule of law.

The Canons of Judicial Conduct are intended to establish standards for ethical conduct of judges. They consist of broad statements called Canons, specific rules set forth in Sections under each Canon and Commentary. The text of the Canons and the Sections is authoritative. Each Commentary, by explanation and example, is advisory and provides guidance with respect to the purpose and meaning of the Canons and Sections. The Commentary is not intended as a statement of additional rules. When the text uses "shall" or "shall not" or "must" or "must not" it is intended to impose binding obligations the violation of which can result in disciplinary action. When "should" or "should not" is used, the text is intended as a statement of what is or is not appropriate conduct but not as a binding rule under which a judge may be disciplined. When "may" is used, it denotes permissible discretion or, depending on the context, it refers to action that is not covered by specific proscriptions.

The Canons and Sections are rules of reason. They should be applied consistent with constitutional requirements, statutes, other court rules and decisional law and in the context of all relevant circumstances. The Canons are to be construed so as not to impinge on the essential independence of judges in making judicial decisions.

The Canons are designed to provide guidance to judges and candidates for judicial office and to provide a structure for regulating conduct through the Judicial Inquiry and Review Commission. They are not designed or intended as a basis for civil liability or criminal prosecution. Furthermore, the purpose of the Canons would be subverted if the Canons were invoked by lawyers for mere tactical advantage in a proceeding.

The text of the Canons and Sections is intended to govern conduct of judges and to be binding upon them. It is not intended, however, that every transgression will result in disciplinary action. Whether disciplinary action is appropriate, and the degree of discipline to be imposed, should be determined through a reasonable and reasoned application of the text and should depend on such factors as the seriousness of the transgression, whether there is a pattern of improper activity and the effect of the improper activity on others or on the judicial system.

These Canons apply to (1) all active Justices of the Supreme Court of Virginia, and Judges of the Court of Appeals of Virginia, Circuit Courts, General District Courts, Juvenile and Domestic Relations District Courts, Members of the State Corporation Commission and the Virginia Workers' Compensation Commission; (2) retired Judges and Members eligible for recall to judicial service; (3) substitute Judges and Special Justices; (4) persons selected for a full-time judgeship either by election by both houses of the General Assembly or appointment by the appropriate authority who are not already justices, judges or retired judges, but who have not taken the oath of office as a justice or judge; and (5) Judges pro tempore while acting as a Judge pro tempore. Magistrates are not bound by these Canons. However, Canons of Conduct for Virginia Magistrates were adopted by the Committee on District Courts effective January 1, 1980.

Effect of amendments. — The order adopted April 12, 2001, effective July 1, 2001, in the second paragraph, substituted "are intended to establish" for "is intended to establish" in the first sentence and substituted "They consist of broad" for "It consists of broad" in the second sentence; substituted "They are not designed" for "It is not designed" in the second sentence in the fourth paragraph; and inserted (5) in the last paragraph.

Law Review. — For an article, "Racial Diversity on the Bench: Beyond Role Models and Public Confidence," see 57 Wash. & Lee L. Rev. 405 (2000).

Canon 1. A Judge Shall Uphold the Integrity and Independence of the Judiciary.

A. An independent and honorable judiciary is indispensable to justice in our society. A judge should participate in establishing, maintaining and enforcing high standards of conduct, and shall personally observe those standards so that the integrity and independence of the judiciary will be preserved. The provisions of these Canons are to be construed and applied to further that objective.

Comment. — Deference to the judgments and rulings of courts depends upon public confidence in the integrity and independence of judges. The integrity and independence of judges depends in turn upon their acting without fear or favor. Although judges should be independent, they must comply with the law, including the provisions of these Canons. Public confidence in the impartiality of the judiciary is maintained by the adherence of each judge to this responsibility. Conversely, violation of this Canon diminishes public confidence in the judiciary and thereby does injury to the system of government under law.

CASE NOTES

Not unconstitutionally vague as applied. — In a case brought pursuant to Va. Const., Art. VI, § 10 and § 17.1-902 in which the Judicial Inquiry and Review Commission proved by clear and convincing evidence that a judge violated Canons of Judicial Conduct 1, 2A, and 3B(2) when she ruled that her order denying a juvenile's written motion for bond and release pending the sentencing hearing was interlocutory and nonappealable, the judge unsuccessfully argued that the Canons were unconstitutionally vague and without appropriately definite standards as applied to the facts in the complaint against her, and that vague and indefinite laws and regulations offended due process rights. Judicial Inquiry & Review Comm'n of Va. v. Taylor, 278 Va. 699, 685 S.E.2d 51, 2009 Va. LEXIS 114 (2009), cert. denied, 177 L. Ed. 2d 304, 130 S.Ct. 3396, 2010 U.S. LEXIS 4645 (2010).

Judicial integrity. — Trial judge's conduct in a custody hearing in which the trial court decided a custody issue through the flip of a coin failed to uphold the integrity of the judiciary because it suggested that serious legal issues were to be decided in a whimsical manner, the trial judge's conduct in a separate custody hearing of having the wife lower her pants in the courtroom twice so that the trial judge could examine a wound was demeaning to the wife, and the trial judge's conduct in the same custody hearing of placing an ex parte telephone call to the hospital to resolve a factual matter failed to promote impartiality in the decision making process, all of which constituted violations of the Canons of Judicial Conduct. Judicial Inquiry & Review Comm'n v. Shull, 274 Va. 657, 651 S.E.2d 648, 2007 Va. LEXIS 123 (2007).

Making an order denying bond and release interlocutory and nonappealable was improper. — In a case brought pursuant to Va. Const., Art. VI, § 10 and § 17.1-902, the Judicial Inquiry and Review Commission proved by clear and convincing evidence that a judge violated Canons of Judicial Conduct 1, 2A, and 3B(2) when she ruled that her order denying a juvenile's written motion for bond and release pending the sentencing hearing was interlocutory and nonappealable. The judge could not prevent the appeal of her decision by ruling that the order was interlocutory and nonappealable; the judge's violations of Canons 1, 2A, and 3B(2) constituted conduct prejudicial to the administration of justice. Judicial Inquiry & Review Comm'n of Va. v. Taylor, 278 Va. 699, 685 S.E.2d 51, 2009 Va. LEXIS 114 (2009), cert. denied, 177 L. Ed. 2d 304, 130 S.Ct. 3396, 2010 U.S. LEXIS 4645 (2010).

Trial judge's discretion to determine bias or prejudice. — It is within the trial judge's discretion to determine whether he harbors bias or prejudice which will impair his ability to give the defendant a fair trial. Terrell v. Commonwealth, 12 Va. App. 285, 403 S.E.2d 387 (1991).

Violation not found. — When a judge, whose nephew sought his party's nomination to run for office, sent a court employee a text message asking if the judge's mother could contact the employee's mother, who, the judge thought, would be attending a political convention the next day, clear and convincing evidence did not show a violation of Va. Sup. Ct. R. pt. 6, § III, Canons 1, 2, or 5 because (1) there was nothing in the language of the messages that was overtly political, and (2) nothing showed the employee understood the messages as being political in nature, so the judge did not use the "prestige of judicial office." Judicial Inquiry & Review Comm'n v. Waymack, 284 Va. 527, 745 S.E.2d 410, 2012 Va. LEXIS 199 (2012).

When a judge attended a close personal friend's hearing, clear and convincing evidence did not show a violation of Va. Sup. Ct. R. pt. 6, § III, Canons 1, 2, or 5 because (1) the judge attended the hearing as a member of the public, and (2) the judge left the hearing as soon as requested by the presiding judge. Judicial Inquiry & Review Comm'n v. Waymack, 284 Va. 527, 745 S.E.2d 410, 2012 Va. LEXIS 199 (2012).

Canon 2. A Judge Shall Avoid Impropriety and the Appearance of Impropriety in All of the Judge's Activities.

A. A judge shall respect and comply with the law and shall act at all times in a manner that promotes public confidence in the integrity and impartiality of the judiciary.

B. A judge shall not allow family, social, political or other relationships to influence the judge's judicial conduct or judgment. A judge shall not lend the prestige of judicial office to advance the private interests of the judge or others; nor shall a judge convey or permit others to convey the impression that they are in a special position to influence the judge. A judge shall not testify as a character witness.

C. A judge shall not hold membership in any organization that practices invidious discrimination on the basis of race, sex, religion or national origin.

Comment on subdivision A. — Public confidence in the judiciary is eroded by irresponsible or improper conduct by judges. A judge must avoid all impropriety and appearance of impropriety. A judge must expect to be the subject of constant public scrutiny. A judge must therefore accept restrictions on the judge's conduct that might be viewed as burdensome by the ordinary citizen and should do so freely and willingly.

The prohibition against behaving with impropriety or the appearance of impropriety applies to both the professional and personal conduct of a judge. Because it is not practicable to list all prohibited acts, the proscription is necessarily cast in general terms that extend to conduct by judges that is harmful although not specifically mentioned in the Canons. Actual improprieties under this standard include violations of law, court rules or other specific provisions of these Canons. The test for appearance of impropriety is whether the conduct would create in reasonable minds a perception that the judge's ability to carry out judicial responsibilities with integrity and impartiality is impaired.

See also Commentary under Section 2C.

A judge may vote in a primary election conducted by the State Board of Elections that is open to all registered voters qualified to vote pursuant to Code § 24.2-530. Voting in such a primary election does not constitute an act of partiality by a judge as prohibited by subdivision A. The act of a judge voting in a primary election is the discharge of an honorable civic duty, an obligation of responsible citizenship, and does not give the "appearance of impropriety."

The statutory requirements for voting in a primary election reflect voting in a primary election by a judge as an act of "impartiality" as used in subdivision A(1)(c) because there is no registration by political affiliation, no loyalty or political party oath required to vote, and no pledge of support for any person or political group. It is the impartial nature of such a primary election that enables judges to avoid an "appearance of impropriety."

See also Commentary under Canon 5A.

Comment on subdivision B. — Maintaining the prestige of judicial office is essential to a system of government in which the judiciary functions independently of the executive and legislative branches. Respect for the judicial office facilitates the orderly conduct of legitimate judicial functions. Judges should distinguish between proper and improper use of the prestige of office in all of their activities. For example, it would be improper for a judge to allude to his or her judgeship to gain a personal advantage such as deferential treatment when stopped by a police officer for a traffic offense. Similarly, judicial letterhead must not be used for conducting a judge's personal business.

A judge must avoid lending the prestige of judicial office for the advancement of the private interests of others. For example, a judge must not use the judge's judicial position to gain advantage in a civil suit involving a member of the judge's family. As to the acceptance of awards, see Section 4D(5)(a) and Commentary.

In a criminal case, a judge may not approve a plea agreement or disposition that requires or permits the defendant to make a charitable contribution or donation, or any other monetary payment other than a statutorily authorized fine or restitution or payment in satisfaction of an injury pursuant to Code § 19.2-151, as a condition of a suspended sentence or the reduction or dismissal of charges.

Although a judge should be sensitive to possible abuse of the prestige of office, a judge may, based on the judge's personal knowledge, serve as a reference or provide a letter of recommendation. When using court stationery for letters of reference an indication should be made that the opinion expressed is personal and not an opinion of the court. However, a judge must not initiate the communication of information to a sentencing judge or a probation or corrections officer but may provide to such person information for the record in response to a formal request.

Judges may participate in the process of judicial selection by cooperating with appointing authorities and screening committees seeking names for consideration, and by responding to official inquiries concerning a person being considered for a judgeship.

Comment on subdivision C. — Membership of a judge in an organization that practices invidious discrimination gives rise to perceptions that the judge's impartiality is impaired. Section 2C refers to the current practices of the organization. Whether an organization practices invidious discrimination is often a complex question to which judges should be sensitive. The answer cannot be determined from a mere examination of an organization's current membership rolls but rather depends on how the organization selects members and other relevant factors, such as that the organization is dedicated to the preservation of religious, ethnic or cultural values of legitimate common interest to its members, or that it is in fact and effect an intimate, purely private organization whose membership limitations could not be constitutionally prohibited. Absent such factors, an organization is generally said to discriminate invidiously if it arbitrarily excludes from membership on the basis of race, religion, sex or national origin persons who would otherwise be admitted to membership.

Although Section 2C relates only to membership in organizations that invidiously discriminate on the basis of race, sex, religion or national origin, a judge's membership in an organization that engages in any discriminatory membership practices prohibited by the law of the jurisdiction also violates Canon 2 and Section 2A and gives the appearance of impropriety. In addition, it would be a violation of Canon 2 and Section 2A for a judge to arrange a meeting at a club that the judge knows practices invidious discrimination on the basis of race, sex, religion or national origin in its membership or other policies, or for the judge to regularly use such a club. Moreover, public manifestation by a judge of the judge's knowing approval of invidious discrimination on any basis gives the appearance of impropriety under Canon 2 and diminishes public confidence in the integrity and impartiality of the judiciary, in violation of Section 2A.

The amendment, effective February 6, 2004, adopted February 6, 2004, added the third paragraph of the Comment on subdivision B.

The amendment, effective November 2, 2004, added the fourth through sixth paragraphs to the Comment on subdivision A.

CASE NOTES

Not unconstitutionally vague as applied. — In a case brought pursuant to Va. Const., Art. VI, § 10 and § 17.1-902 in which the Judicial Inquiry and Review Commission proved by clear and convincing evidence that a judge violated Subsection A of Canon 2 of the Canons of Judicial Conduct when she ruled that her order denying a juvenile's written motion for bond and release pending the sentencing hearing was interlocutory and nonappealable, the judge unsuccessfully argued that the Canons were unconstitutionally vague and without appropriately definite standards as applied to the facts in the complaint against her, and that vague and indefinite laws and regulations offended due process rights. Judicial Inquiry & Review Comm'n of Va. v. Taylor, 278 Va. 699, 685 S.E.2d 51, 2009 Va. LEXIS 114 (2009), cert. denied, 177 L. Ed. 2d 304, 130 S.Ct. 3396, 2010 U.S. LEXIS 4645 (2010).

Making an order denying bond and release interlocutory and nonappealable was improper. — In a case brought pursuant to Va. Const., Art. VI, § 10 and § 17.1-902, the Judicial Inquiry and Review Commission proved by clear and convincing evidence that a judge violated subsection A of Canon 2 of the Canons of Judicial Conduct when she ruled that her order denying a juvenile's written motion for bond and release pending the sentencing hearing was interlocutory and nonappealable. The judge could not prevent the appeal of her decision by ruling that the order was interlocutory and nonappealable; the judge's violations of Canons 1, 2A, and 3B(2) constituted conduct prejudicial to the administration of justice. Judicial Inquiry & Review Comm'n of Va. v. Taylor, 278 Va. 699, 685 S.E.2d 51, 2009 Va. LEXIS 114 (2009), cert. denied, 177 L. Ed. 2d 304, 130 S.Ct. 3396, 2010 U.S. LEXIS 4645 (2010).

Impropriety. — Trial judge's conduct in a custody hearing in which the trial court decided a custody issue through the flip of a coin failed to uphold the integrity of the judiciary because it suggested that serious legal issues were to be decided in a whimsical manner, the trial judge's conduct in a separate custody hearing of having the wife lower her pants in the courtroom twice so that the trial judge could examine a wound was demeaning to the wife, and the trial judge's conduct in the same custody hearing of placing an ex parte telephone call to the hospital to resolve a factual matter failed to promote impartiality in the decision making process, all of which constituted violations of the Canons of Judicial Conduct. Judicial Inquiry & Review Comm'n v. Shull, 274 Va. 657, 651 S.E.2d 648, 2007 Va. LEXIS 123 (2007).

Trial judge's discretion to determine bias or prejudice. — It is within the trial judge's discretion to determine whether he harbors bias or prejudice which will impair his ability to give the defendant a fair trial. Terrell v. Commonwealth, 12 Va. App. 285, 403 S.E.2d 387 (1991).

Violation not found. — When a judge, whose nephew sought his party's nomination to run for office, sent a court employee a text message asking if the judge's mother could contact the employee's mother, who, the judge thought, would be attending a political convention the next day, clear and convincing evidence did not show a violation of Va. Sup. Ct. R. pt. 6, § III, Canons 1, 2, or 5 because (1) there was nothing in the language of the messages that was overtly political, and (2) nothing showed the employee understood the messages as being political in nature, so the judge did not use the "prestige of judicial office." Judicial Inquiry & Review Comm'n v. Waymack, 284 Va. 527, 745 S.E.2d 410, 2012 Va. LEXIS 199 (2012).

When a judge attended a close personal friend's hearing, clear and convincing evidence did not show a violation of Va. Sup. Ct. R. pt. 6, § III, Canons 1, 2, or 5 because (1) the judge attended the hearing as a member of the public, and (2) the judge left the hearing as soon as requested by the presiding judge. Judicial Inquiry & Review Comm'n v. Waymack, 284 Va. 527, 745 S.E.2d 410, 2012 Va. LEXIS 199 (2012).

CIRCUIT COURT OPINIONS

No bias shown. — Fact that counsel for a creditor was a member of the Virginia Legislature did not mean that there was even an appearance of impropriety; therefore, a motion seeking recusal of a judge in a debtor/creditor case was denied. Belfort Furniture, Inc. v. Stewart, 64 Va. Cir. 461, 2004 Va. Cir. LEXIS 154 (Loudoun County 2004).

Canon 3. A Judge Shall Perform The Duties Of Judicial Office Impartially And Diligently.

A. *Judicial Duties in General.* — The judicial duties of a judge take precedence over all the judge's other activities. The judge's judicial duties include all the duties of the judge's office prescribed by law. In the performance of these duties, the following standards apply.

B. *Adjudicative Responsibilities.* — (1) A judge shall hear and decide promptly matters assigned to the judge except those in which disqualification is required.

(2) A judge shall be faithful to the law and maintain professional competence in it. A judge shall not be swayed by partisan interests, public clamor or fear of criticism.

(3) A judge shall require order, decorum, and civility in proceedings before the judge.

(4) A judge shall be patient, dignified and courteous to litigants, jurors, witnesses, lawyers and others with whom the judge deals in an official capacity, and shall require similar conduct of lawyers, and of staff, court officials and others subject to the judge's direction and control.

(5) A judge shall perform judicial duties without bias or prejudice. A judge shall not, in the performance of judicial duties, by words or conduct manifest bias or prejudice, including but not limited to bias or prejudice based upon race, sex, religion, national origin, disability, age, sexual orientation or socioeconomic status, and shall not permit staff, court officials and others subject to the judge's direction and control to do so. This Section 3B(5) does not preclude proper judicial consideration when race, sex, religion, national origin, disability, age, sexual orientation or socioeconomic status, or similar factors, are issues in the proceeding.

(6) A judge shall require all persons appearing in proceedings before the judge to refrain from manifesting, by words or conduct, bias or prejudice based upon race, sex, religion, national origin, disability, age, sexual orientation or socioeconomic status, against parties, witnesses, counsel or others. This Section 3B(6) does not preclude legitimate advocacy when race, sex, religion, national origin, disability, age, sexual orientation or socioeconomic status, or other similar factors, are issues in the proceeding.

(7) A judge shall accord to every person who has a legal interest in a proceeding, or that person's lawyer, the right to be heard according to law. A judge shall not initiate, permit, or consider ex parte communications, or consider other communications made to the judge outside the presence of the parties concerning a pending or impending proceeding except that:

(a) Where circumstances require, ex parte communications for scheduling, administrative purposes or emergencies that do not deal with substantive matters or issues on the merits are authorized; provided:

(i) The judge reasonably believes that no party will gain a procedural or tactical advantage as a result of the ex parte communication, and

(ii) The judge makes provision promptly to notify all other parties of the substance of the ex parte communication and allows an opportunity to respond.

(b) A judge may obtain the advice of a disinterested expert on the law applicable to a proceeding before the judge if the judge gives notice to the parties of the person consulted and the substance of the advice, and affords the parties reasonable opportunity to respond.

(c) A judge may consult with law clerks whose function is to aid the judge in carrying out the judge's adjudicative responsibilities or with other judges.

(d) A judge may, with the consent of the parties, confer separately with the parties and their lawyers in an effort to settle matters pending before the judge.

(e) A judge may initiate or consider any ex parte communications when expressly authorized by law to do so.

(8) A judge shall dispose promptly of the business of the court.

(9) A judge shall abstain from public comment about a pending or impending proceeding in any court, and should direct similar abstention on the part of court personnel subject to his direction and control. This subsection does not prohibit judges or court personnel from speaking on the legal system or the administration of justice or from explaining for public information the procedures of the court. This Section does not apply to proceedings in which the judge is a litigant in a personal capacity.

(10) A judge shall not commend or criticize jurors for their verdict other than in a court order or opinion in a proceeding, but may express appreciation to jurors for their service to the judicial system and the community.

(11) A judge shall not disclose or use, for any purpose unrelated to judicial duties, nonpublic information acquired in a judicial capacity.

C. *Administrative Responsibilities.* — (1) A judge shall diligently discharge the judge's administrative responsibilities without bias or prejudice and maintain professional competence in judicial administration, and shall cooperate with other judges and court officials in the administration of court business.

(2) A judge shall require staff, court officials and others subject to the judge's direction and control to observe the standards of fidelity and diligence that apply to the judge and to refrain from manifesting bias or prejudice in the performance of their official duties.

(3) The chief judge shall take reasonable measures to assure the prompt disposition of matters before the court.

(4) A judge shall not make unnecessary appointments. A judge shall exercise the power of appointment impartially and on the basis of merit. A judge shall avoid nepotism and favoritism. A judge shall not approve compensation of appointees beyond the fair value of services rendered.

D. *Disciplinary Responsibilities.* — (1) A judge who receives reliable information indicating a substantial likelihood that another judge has committed a violation of these Canons should take appropriate action. A judge having knowledge that another judge has committed a violation of these Canons that raises a substantial question as to the other judge's fitness for office should inform the Judicial Inquiry and Review Commission.

(2) A judge who receives reliable information indicating a substantial likelihood that a lawyer has committed a violation of the Code of Professional Responsibility should take appropriate action. A judge having knowledge that a lawyer has committed a violation of the Code of Professional Responsibility that raises a substantial question as to the lawyer's honesty, trustworthiness or fitness as a lawyer in other respects should inform the Virginia State Bar.

(3) A judge shall have absolute immunity from civil action with respect to the discharge of disciplinary responsibilities required or permitted by Sections 3D(1) and 3D(2).

E. *Disqualification.* — (1) A judge shall disqualify himself or herself in a proceeding in which the judge's impartiality might reasonably be questioned, including but not limited to instances where:

(a) The judge has a personal bias or prejudice concerning a party or a party's lawyer, or personal knowledge of disputed evidentiary facts concerning the proceeding;

(b) The judge served as a lawyer in the matter in controversy, or a lawyer with whom the judge previously practiced law served during such association as a lawyer concerning the matter, or the judge has been a material witness concerning it;

(c) The judge knows that he or she, individually or as a fiduciary, or the judge's spouse, parent, or child wherever residing, or any other member of the judge's family residing in the judge's household, has an economic interest in the subject matter in controversy or in a party to the proceeding or has more than a de minimis interest that could be substantially affected by the proceeding;

(d) The judge or the judge's spouse, or a person within the third degree of relationship to either of them, or the spouse of such a person:

(i) is a party to the proceeding, or an officer, director or trustee of a party;

(ii) is acting as a lawyer in the proceeding;

(iii) is known by the judge to have a more than de minimis interest that could be substantially affected by the proceeding;

(iv) is to the judge's knowledge likely to be a material witness in the proceeding.

(2) A judge shall keep informed about the judge's personal and fiduciary economic interests, and make a reasonable effort to keep informed about the personal economic interests of the judge's spouse and minor children residing in the judge's household.

F. *Remittal of Disqualification.* — A judge who may be disqualified by the terms of Section 3E may ask, or have the clerk of court ask, the parties and their lawyers to consider, out of the presence of the judge, whether to waive disqualification. If following disclosure of any basis for disqualification other than personal bias or prejudice concerning a party, the parties and lawyers, without participation by the judge, all agree that the judge should not be disqualified, and the judge is then willing to participate, the judge may participate in the proceeding. Written evidence of the agreement shall be incorporated in the record of the proceeding.

Comment on subdivision B(3). — "Require." The rules prescribing that a judge "require" certain conduct of others are, like all of the rules in these Canons, rules of reason. The use of the term "require" in that context means a judge is to exercise reasonable direction and control over the conduct of those persons subject to the judge's direction and control.

Comment on subdivision B(4). — The duty to hear all proceedings fairly and with patience is not inconsistent with the duty to dispose promptly of the business of the court. Judges can be efficient and businesslike while being patient and deliberate.

Comment on subdivision B(5). — A judge must refrain from speech, gestures or other conduct that could reasonably be perceived as sexual harassment and must require the same standard of conduct of others subject to the judge's direction and control.

A judge must perform judicial duties impartially and fairly. A judge who manifests bias on any basis in a proceeding impairs the fairness of the proceeding and brings the judiciary into disrepute. Facial expression and body language, in addition to oral communication, can give to parties or lawyers in the proceeding, jurors, the media and others an appearance of judicial bias. A judge must be alert to avoid behavior that may be perceived as prejudicial.

Comment on subdivision B(7). — The proscription against communications concerning a proceeding includes communications from lawyers, law teachers, and other persons who are not participants in the proceeding, except to the limited extent permitted.

To the extent reasonably possible, all parties or their lawyers shall be included in communications with a judge. A judge should always be cautious with regard to the possibility of prejudice or the appearance of such when communicating with a probation officer or a similarly situated person without the involvement of all parties.

Whenever presence of a party or notice to a party is required by Section 3B(7), it is the party's lawyer or if the party is unrepresented, the party who is to be present or to whom notice is to be given.

An appropriate and often desirable procedure for a court to obtain the advice of a disinterested expert on legal issues is to invite the expert to file a brief amicus curiae.

Certain ex parte communication is approved by Section 3B(7) to facilitate scheduling and other administrative purposes and to accommodate emergencies. In general, however, a judge must discourage ex parte communication and allow it only if all the criteria stated in Section 3B(7) are clearly met. A judge must disclose to all parties all ex parte communications described in Sections 3B(7)(a) and 3B(7)(b) regarding a proceeding pending or impending before the judge.

A judge must not independently investigate facts in a case and must consider only the evidence presented.

A judge may request a party to submit proposed findings of fact and conclusions of law, so long as the other parties are apprised of the request and are given an opportunity to respond to the proposed findings and conclusions.

A judge must make reasonable efforts, including the provision of appropriate supervision, to ensure that Section 3B(7) is not violated through law clerks or other personnel on the judge's staff.

A judge may consult with the Legal Research Assistance Project of the Supreme Court of Virginia for aid in carrying out the judge's adjudicative responsibilities.

If communication between the trial judge and the appellate court with respect to a proceeding is permitted, a copy of any written communication or the substance of any oral communication should be provided to all parties.

Judges have historically played an important role in providing instruction, advice and mentoring to lawyers as they begin and continue to develop their practice skills. Judges should insure that the instruction and advice they provide will not result in unfair advantage to the recipient or prejudice to other parties in a pending proceeding.

Comment on subdivision B(8). — In disposing of matters promptly, a judge must demonstrate due regard for the rights of the parties to be heard and to have issues resolved without unnecessary cost or delay.

Containing costs while preserving fundamental rights of parties also protects the interests of witnesses and the general public.

Prompt disposition of the court's business requires a judge to devote adequate time to judicial duties, to be punctual in attending court and expeditious in determining matters under submission, and to insist that court officials, litigants and their lawyers cooperate with the judge to that end.

Comment on subdivision B(9). — The requirement that judges abstain from public comment regarding a pending or impending proceeding continues during any appellate process and until final disposition. This Section does not prohibit a judge from commenting on proceedings in which the judge is a litigant in a personal capacity, but in cases such as a writ of mandamus where the judge is a litigant in an official capacity, the judge must not comment publicly.

See also Commentary under Canon 6C.

Comment on subdivision B(10). — Commending or criticizing jurors for their verdict may imply a judicial expectation in future cases and may impair a juror's ability to be fair and impartial in a subsequent case.

Comment on subdivision C(4). — Appointees of a judge include assigned counsel, officials such as commissioners, receivers and guardians and personnel such as clerks, and secretaries. Consent by the parties to an appointment or an award of compensation does not relieve the judge of the obligation prescribed by Section 3C(4).

Comment on subdivision D. — Appropriate action may include direct communication with the judge or lawyer who has committed the violation, other direct action if available, and reporting the violation to the appropriate authority or other agency or body.

Comment on subdivision E(1). — Under this rule, a judge is disqualified whenever the judge's impartiality might reasonably be questioned, regardless whether any of the specific rules in Section 3E(l) apply.

A judge should disclose information that the

judge believes the parties or their lawyers might consider relevant to the question of disqualification, even if the judge believes there is no real basis for disqualification.

By decisional law, the rule of necessity may override the rule of disqualification. For example, a judge might be required to participate in judicial review of a judicial salary statute, or might be the only judge available in a matter requiring immediate judicial action, such as a hearing on probable cause or a temporary restraining order. In the latter case, the judge must disclose the basis for possible disqualification and use reasonable efforts to transfer the matter to another judge as soon as practicable.

Comment on subdivision E(1)(b). — A lawyer in a government agency does not ordinarily have an association with other lawyers employed by that agency within the meaning of Section 3E(l)(b); a judge formerly employed by a government agency, however, should disqualify himself or herself in a proceeding if the judge's impartiality might reasonably be questioned because of such association.

Comment on subdivision E(1)(d). — "Third degree of relationship." The following persons are relatives within the third degree of relationship: great-grandparent, grandparent, parent, uncle, aunt, brother, sister, child, grandchild, great-grandchild, nephew or niece.

Comment on subdivision E(1)(d)(iv). — The fact that a lawyer in a proceeding is affiliated with a law firm or governmental agency with which a relative of the judge is affiliated does not of itself disqualify the judge. Under appropriate circumstances, the fact that "the judge's impartiality might reasonably be questioned" under Section 3E(1), or that the relative is known by the judge to have an interest in the law firm or governmental agency that could be "substantially affected by the outcome of the proceeding" under Section 3E(1)(d)(iii) may require the judge's disqualification.

Comment on subdivision E(2). — "Economic interest" denotes ownership of a more than de minimis legal or equitable interest, or a relationship as officer, director, advisor or other active participant in the affairs of a party, except that:

(i) ownership of an interest in a mutual or common investment fund that holds securities is not an economic interest in such securities unless the judge participates in the management of the fund or a proceeding pending or impending before the judge could substantially affect the value of the interest;

(ii) service by a judge as an officer, director, advisor or other active participant in an educational, religious, charitable, fraternal or civic organization, or service by a judge's spouse, parent or child as an officer, director, advisor or other active participant in any organization does not create an economic interest in securities held by that organization.

(iii) a deposit in a financial institution, the proprietary interest of a policy holder in a mutual insurance company, of a depositor in a mutual savings association or of a member in a credit union, or a similar proprietary interest, is not an economic interest in the organization unless a proceeding pending or impending before the judge could substantially affect the value of the interest;

(iv) ownership of government securities is not an economic interest in the issuer unless a proceeding pending or impending before the judge could substantially affect the value of the securities.

"Member of the judge's family residing in the judge's household" denotes any relative of a judge by blood or marriage, or a person treated by a judge as a member of the judge's family, who resides in the judge's household.

Comment on subdivision F. — A remittal procedure provides the parties an opportunity to proceed without delay if they wish to waive the contemplated disqualification. To assure that consideration of the question of remittal is made independently of the judge, a judge may ask, or have the clerk of court ask, the parties and their lawyers to consider, out of the presence of the judge, whether to waive disqualification.

Editor's note. — The Rule is set out above to correct the text of subdivision B (6). In the first sentence, "all persons appearing" was substituted for "all person's appearing."

The amendment, effective March 9, 2000, rewrote subdivision B(9) of this Rule.

Michie's Jurisprudence. — For related discussion, see 11A M.J. Judges, § 14.

CASE NOTES

Not unconstitutionally vague as applied. — In a case brought pursuant to Va. Const., Art. VI, § 10 and § 17.1-902 in which the Judicial Inquiry and Review Commission proved by clear and convincing evidence that a judge violated subdivision B(2) of Canon 3 of the Canons of Judicial Conduct when she ruled that her order denying a juvenile's written motion for bond and release pending the sentencing hearing was interlocutory and nonappealable, the judge unsuccessfully argued that the Canons were unconstitutionally vague and without appropriately definite standards as applied to the facts in the complaint against her, and that vague and indefinite laws and regulations offended due process rights. Judicial Inquiry & Review Comm'n of Va. v. Taylor, 278 Va. 699, 685 S.E.2d 51, 2009 Va. LEXIS 114 (2009), cert. denied, 177 L. Ed. 2d 304, 130 S.Ct. 3396, 2010 U.S. LEXIS 4645 (2010).

Courts have responsibility to monitor conduct of Commonwealth's attorney. — Where the Commonwealth's attorney knows that an informant's appearance as a witness is impending, or intends in all likelihood to call the witness, the prosecutor may not deny his or her intention to call the witness as a pretext to avoid discovery. Courts have the responsibility to monitor the conduct of those attorneys who appear before them and assure adherence to professional standards. Moreno v. Commonwealth, 10 Va. App. 408, 392 S.E.2d 836 (1990).

Making an order denying bond and release interlocutory and nonappealable was improper. — In a case brought pursuant to Va. Const. art. VI, § 10 and § 17.1-902, the Judicial Inquiry and Review Commission proved by clear and convincing evidence that a judge violated subdivision B(2) of Canon 3 of the Canons of Judicial Conduct when she ruled that her order denying a juvenile's written motion for bond and release pending the sentencing hearing was interlocutory and nonappealable. The judge could not prevent the appeal of her decision by ruling that the order was interlocutory and nonappealable; the judge's violations of Canons 1, 2A, and 3B(2) constituted conduct prejudicial to the administration of justice. Judicial Inquiry & Review Comm'n of Va. v. Taylor, 278 Va. 699, 685 S.E.2d 51, 2009 Va. LEXIS 114 (2009), cert. denied, 177 L. Ed. 2d 304, 130 S.Ct. 3396, 2010 U.S. LEXIS 4645 (2010).

Question of impartiality lies within sound discretion of judge. — The requirement of this canon is clear; a judge must diligently avoid not only impropriety but a reasonable appearance of impropriety as well. Exactly when a judge's impartiality might reasonably be called into question is a determination to be made by that judge in the exercise of his or her sound discretion. Davis v. Commonwealth, 21 Va. App. 587, 466 S.E.2d 741 (1996).

Failing to promote impartiality. — Trial judge's conduct in a custody hearing in which the trial court decided a custody issue through the flip of a coin failed to uphold the integrity of the judiciary because it suggested that serious legal issues were to be decided in a whimsical manner, the trial judge's conduct in a separate custody hearing of having the wife lower her pants in the courtroom twice so that the trial judge could examine a wound was demeaning to the wife, and the trial judge's conduct in the same custody hearing of placing an ex parte telephone call to the hospital to resolve a factual matter failed to promote impartiality in the decision making process, all of which constituted violations of the Canons of Judicial Conduct. Judicial Inquiry & Review Comm'n v. Shull, 274 Va. 657, 651 S.E.2d 648, 2007 Va. LEXIS 123 (2007).

Judges are presumed to be aware of the provisions of this canon, and their decisions will not be disturbed absent an abuse of that discretion. Davis v. Commonwealth, 21 Va. App. 587, 466 S.E.2d 741 (1996).

Prejudicial conduct. — Judge's inclusion of a purge clause in his contempt order could only be construed as directly contrary to, and in disregard of, a circuit court's stay order, and as a violation of Va. Sup. Ct. R., Pt. 6, § III, Canons 1, 2, 2A, and 3B(2). Judicial Inquiry & Review Comm'n v. Lewis, 264 Va. 401, 568 S.E.2d 687, 2002 Va. LEXIS 95 (2002).

Judge must avoid appearance of impropriety. — The requirement of subdivision E of this canon is clear; a judge must diligently avoid not only impropriety but a reasonable appearance of impropriety as well. Kreiger v. Commonwealth, No. 2317-99-2, 2000 Va. App. LEXIS 374 (Ct. of Appeals May 16, 2000).

Recusal within trial court's discretion. — Whether a trial judge should recuse himself is measured by whether he harbors such bias or prejudice as would deny the defendant a fair trial, and is a matter left to the reasonable discretion of the trial court. Kreiger v. Commonwealth, No. 2317-99-2, 2000 Va. App. LEXIS 374 (Ct. of Appeals May 16, 2000).

Absent any showing of actual bias or prejudice by a trial judge, it was not an abuse of discretion to fail to recuse himself from presiding over a jury trial, which resulted in defendant's convictions. Morris v. Commonwealth, No. 3071-02-2, 2004 Va. App. LEXIS 185 (Ct. of Appeals Mar. 2, 2004).

In a mother's termination of parental rights action, the trial judge did not abuse his discretion when he did not recuse himself pursuant to Va. Sup. Ct. R. pt. 6, § III, Canon 3(E)(1) because the mother failed to show actual prejudice or bias that resulted from the judge's presiding over a prior appeal and the evidence in question was presented at two separate hearings involving different statutes and different burdens of proof. Green v. City of Hampton Dep't of Soc. Servs., 2006 Va. App. LEXIS 510 (Nov. 7, 2006).

With regard to defendant's convictions on two capital murder counts and the imposition of two death sentences against him, the trial court judge did not abuse his discretion by refusing to recuse himself from the case because the record did not support defendant's allegation that the judge entirely discounted his mitigating evidence, he offered no evidence or even allegation of extrajudicial influence that would suggest bias, and in the course of his judicial duty to evaluate the jury's death sentences, the judge was required by the laws of the Commonwealth of Virginia to consider the vileness of the crime and, given the task set before him, it was neither surprising nor inappropriate that the record contained emotional language. Prieto v. Commonwealth, 283 Va. 149, 721 S.E.2d 484, 2012 Va. LEXIS 20 (2012).

Subdivisions C(1) and C(2) [now subdivisions E(1) and E(2)] specify particular situations when a judge's impartiality might reasonably be called into question. While these subdivisions do not provide an exhaustive list, they certainly provide insight into the type of situations which give rise to a reasonable appearance of impropriety. What is certain is that subdivision C does not require a judge to recuse himself or herself and disrupt the orderly flow of the docket at the whim or unsupported suggestion of a party. Davis v. Commonwealth, 21 Va. App. 587, 466 S.E.2d 741 (1996).

Where appearance of bias, court's determination not reversed unless conduct affected outcome. — Subdivision C [now subdivision E] requires that a judge must diligently avoid not only impropriety but a reasonable appearance of impropriety as well. Nevertheless, even when circumstances create an appearance of bias, unless the conduct of the judge is shown to have affected the outcome of the case, the court's determination will not be reversed. Harley v. Commonwealth, No. 2734-96-2 (Ct. of Appeals Nov. 4, 1997).

Recusal required. — Trial judge's failure to recuse himself was an abuse of discretion because the record showed that the judge's actions in ordering defendant's attorney removed from the list of court-appointed attorneys on the ground that the attorney counseled defendant to ask for a jury trial specifically because the case was transferred from one judge to the second judge reflected a personal bias and prejudice against defense counsel and raised concerns about the judge's impartiality in the case and about the public's perception of his fairness in the case. Wilson v. Commonwealth, 272 Va. 19, 630 S.E.2d 326, 2006 Va. LEXIS 60 (2006).

Recusal issue waived. — In a case brought by the Judicial Inquiry and Review Commission pursuant to Va. Const., Art. VI, § 10 and § 17.1-902, the judge unsuccessfully argued that subsection E of Canon of Judicial Conduct 3 required the recusal of the Commission's chairman due to his status as complainant in a prior contact with the Commission. Since she had not presented that argument at the Commission hearing, she had waived it. Judicial Inquiry & Review Comm'n of Va. v. Taylor, 278 Va. 699, 685 S.E.2d 51, 2009 Va. LEXIS 114 (2009), cert. denied, 177 L. Ed. 2d 304, 130 S.Ct. 3396, 2010 U.S. LEXIS 4645 (2010).

Review of presentence report of co-defendant from related case. — Defendant was not entitled to have defendant's sentence set aside because the trial court's sua sponte review of the presentence report of the defendant in a related case was not improper pursuant to Va. Sup. Ct. R. pt. 6, § III, Canon 3(B)(7), which forbid judges from engaging in certain ex parte communications, in that the report, which was included in the records of the court, did not represent an ex parte communication under Va. Sup. Ct. R. pt. 6, § III, Canon 3(B)(7). Moreover, Va. Sup. Ct. R. pt. 6, § III, Canon 3(B)(7)(3) allowed the court to consider ex parte communications if they were expressly authorized by law and § 19.2-299 expressly provided that presentence reports were available to courts. Stewart v. Commonwealth, No. 2453-11-4, 2012 Va. App. LEXIS 327 (Oct. 16, 2012).

CIRCUIT COURT OPINIONS

Recusal denied. — Because a court's receipt of financial support from governmental entities did not create doubt as to the court's impartiality, the board of zoning appeals' motion for recusal under Va. Sup. Ct. R. pt. 6, § III, Canon 3(3)(1) was denied. Bd. of Zoning Appeals v. Bd. of Supervisors, 72 Va. Cir. 362, 2006 Va. Cir. LEXIS 282 (Fairfax County 2006).

Record of the proceedings demonstrated that throughout the court's service as presiding judge of the matter, the court sought to be fair and impartial to all sides; in particular, the sentencing statements made by the court were made in the performance of the court's official duties, involved matters that lay at the core of the court's sentencing responsibilities, and were based solely and exclusively on evidence and other material properly before the court. Commonwealth v. Prieto, 84 Va. Cir. 567, 2010 Va. Cir. LEXIS 33 (Fairfax County Mar. 8, 2010).

Defendant asserted that the words the court used during sentencing were evidence of bias and prejudice, but this argument was without merit; there was no doubt the court used strong and descriptive language but the law was clear that this was not a basis for recusal. Moreover, it was not at all unusual for courts to characterize crimes of such as those at issue — capital murder and rape — in explicit terms Commonwealth v. Prieto, 84 Va. Cir. 567, 2010 Va. Cir. LEXIS 33 (Fairfax County Mar. 8, 2010).

Recusal decision must be based on the entire record. — Recusal decision must be based on the entire record, and not just isolated excerpts from it; thus, in determining the public perception of the court's fairness, a party cannot simply pick and choose a particular event in a trial but, rather, must examine the whole record. It is for that reason that many cases have stated that a judge should recuse himself or herself whenever a reasonable person, with knowledge of all the facts of the case, would question the judge's impartiality. Commonwealth v. Prieto, 84 Va. Cir. 567, 2010 Va. Cir. LEXIS 33 (Fairfax County Mar. 8, 2010).

Judge may speak with emotion without providing any basis for recusal. — Judge may speak with emotion without providing any basis for recusal; judges are not required to shed their humanity when they don their robes. What a judge may not do is to be swayed or driven by emotion in his decisions. Commonwealth v. Prieto, 84 Va. Cir. 567, 2010 Va. Cir. LEXIS 33 (Fairfax County Mar. 8, 2010).

Public's perception of bias. — It is the public's perception of bias, not a litigant's personal perception, that a judge must consider when determining whether recusal is necessary to preserve the integrity of the judicial system. Commonwealth v. Prieto, 84 Va. Cir. 567, 2010 Va. Cir. LEXIS 33 (Fairfax County Mar. 8, 2010).

Trial judge asked to recuse himself must exercise reasonable discretion to determine whether he possesses such bias or prejudice as would deny the defendant a fair trial; in exercising his or her discretion in this regard, the judge must be guided not only by the true state of his or her impartiality, but also by the public perception of his or her fairness, in order that public confidence in the integrity of the judiciary may be maintained. Commonwealth v. Prieto, 84 Va. Cir. 567, 2010 Va. Cir. LEXIS 33 (Fairfax County Mar. 8, 2010).

Canon 4. A Judge May Engage in Extra-Judicial Activities Designed to Improve the Law, the Legal System, and the Administration of Justice, and Shall Conduct Any Such Extra-Judicial Activities in a Manner That Minimizes the Risk of Conflict With Judicial Obligations.

A. *Extra Judicial Activities in General.* — A judge shall conduct all of the judge's extra judicial activities so that they do not:

(1) cast reasonable doubt on the judge's capacity to act impartially as a judge;

(2) demean the judicial office; or

(3) interfere with the proper performance of judicial duties.

B. *Avocational Activities.* — A judge may speak, write, lecture, teach and participate in other extra judicial activities concerning the law, the legal system, the administration of justice and non-legal subjects, subject to the requirements of these Canons.

C. *Governmental, Civic or Charitable Activities.* — (1) A judge shall not appear at a public hearing before, or otherwise consult with, an executive or legislative body or official except on matters concerning the law, the legal system or the administration of justice or except when acting pro se in a matter involving the judge or the judge's interests.

(2) A judge shall not accept appointment to a governmental committee or commission or other governmental position that is concerned with issues of fact or policy on matters other than the improvement of the law, the legal system or the administration of justice. A judge may, however, represent a country, state or locality on ceremonial occasions or in connection with historical, educational or cultural activities.

(3) A judge may serve as an officer, director, trustee or non legal advisor of an organization or governmental agency devoted to the improvement of the law, the legal system or the administration of justice or of an educational, religious, charitable, fraternal or civic organization not conducted for profit, subject to the following limitations and the other requirements of this Code.

(a) A judge shall not serve as an officer, director, trustee or non legal advisor of a governmental, civic, or charitable organization if it is likely that the organization:

(i) will be engaged in proceedings that would ordinarily come before the judge, or

(ii) will be engaged frequently in adversary proceedings in the court of which the judge is a member or in any court subject to the appellate jurisdiction of the court of which the judge is a member.

(b) A judge as an officer, director, trustee or non legal advisor, or as a member or otherwise:

(i) may assist such an organization in planning fund raising and may participate in the management and investment of the organization's funds, but shall not personally participate in the solicitation of funds, except that a judge may solicit funds from other judges over whom the judge does not exercise supervisory or appellate authority;

(ii) may make recommendations to public and private fund granting organizations on projects and programs concerning the law, the legal system or the administration of justice so long as one organization is not favored over another;

(iii) shall not personally participate in membership solicitation if the solicitation might reasonably be perceived as coercive or, except as permitted in Section 4C(3)(b)(i), if the membership solicitation is essentially a fund raising mechanism;

(iv) shall not use or permit the use of the prestige of judicial office for fund raising or membership solicitation; and

(v) shall not be a speaker or guest of honor at an organization's fund raising events, but may attend such events.

D. *Financial Activities.* — (1) A judge shall not engage in financial and business dealings that:

(a) may reasonably be perceived to exploit the judge's judicial position, or

(b) involve the judge in frequent transactions or continuing business relationships with those lawyers or other persons likely to come before the court on which the judge serves.

(2) A judge may, subject to the requirements of this Canon, hold and manage investments of the judge and members of the judge's family, including real estate.

(3) A judge shall not serve as an officer, director, manager, general partner, advisor or employee of any business entity except that a judge may, subject to the requirements of this Canon, manage and participate in:

(a) a business closely held by the judge or members of the judge's family, or

(b) a business entity primarily engaged in investment of the financial resources of the judge or members of the judge's family.

(4) A judge shall manage the judge's investments and other financial interests to minimize the number of cases in which the judge is disqualified. As soon as the judge can do so without serious financial detriment, the judge shall divest himself or herself of investments and other financial interests that might require frequent disqualification.

(5) A judge shall not accept, and shall urge members of the judge's family residing in the judge's household not to accept, a gift, favor or loan from anyone except for:

(a) a gift incident to a public testimonial, books, tapes and other resource materials supplied by publishers on a complimentary basis for official use, or an invitation to the judge and the judge's spouse or guest to attend a bar related function or an activity devoted to the improvement of the law, the legal system or the administration of justice;

(b) a gift, award or benefit incident to the business, profession or other separate activity of a spouse or other family member of a judge residing in the judge's household, including gifts, awards and benefits for the use of both the spouse or other family member and the judge (as spouse or family member), provided the gift, award or benefit could not reasonably be perceived as intended to influence the judge in the performance of judicial duties;

(c) ordinary social hospitality;

(d) a gift from a relative or friend, for a special occasion, such as a wedding, anniversary or birthday, if the gift is fairly commensurate with the occasion and the relationship;

(e) a gift, favor or loan from a relative or close personal friend whose appearance or interest in a case would in any event require disqualification under Section 3E;

(f) a loan from a lending institution in its regular course of business on the same terms generally available to persons who are not judges;

(g) a scholarship or fellowship awarded on the same terms and based on the same criteria applied to other applicants.

E. *Fiduciary Activities.* — (1) A judge shall not serve as executor, administrator or other personal representative, trustee, guardian, attorney in fact or other fiduciary, except for the estate, trust or person of a member of the judge's family, and then only if such service will not interfere with the proper performance of judicial duties.

(2) A judge shall not serve as a fiduciary if it is likely that the judge as a fiduciary will be engaged in proceedings that would ordinarily come before the judge, or if the estate, trust or ward becomes involved in adversary proceedings in the court on which the judge serves or one under its appellate jurisdiction.

(3) The same restrictions on financial activities that apply to a judge personally also apply to the judge while acting in a fiduciary capacity.

F. *Service as Arbitrator or Mediator.* — A judge shall not act as an arbitrator or mediator or otherwise perform judicial functions in a private capacity.

G. *Practice of Law.* — A judge shall not practice law. Notwithstanding this prohibition, a judge may act pro se and may, without compensation, give legal advice to and draft or review documents for a member of the judge's family.

H. *Compensation, Reimbursement and Reporting.* — (1) Compensation and Reimbursement. A judge may receive compensation and reimbursement of expenses for the extra judicial activities permitted by these Canons, if the source of such payments does not give the appearance of influencing the judge's performance of judicial duties or otherwise give the appearance of impropriety.

(a) Compensation shall not exceed a reasonable amount nor shall it exceed what a person who is not a judge would receive for the same activity.

(b) Expense reimbursement shall be limited to the actual cost of travel, food and lodging reasonably incurred by the judge and, where appropriate to the occasion, by the judge's spouse or guest. Any payment in excess of such an amount is compensation.

(2) Public Reports. A Judge shall report compensation as required by § 2.2-3114 of the Code of Virginia.

Comment on subdivision A. — Complete separation of a judge from extra judicial activities is neither possible nor wise; a judge should not become isolated from the community in which the judge lives.

Expressions of bias or prejudice by a judge, even outside the judge's judicial activities, may cast reasonable doubt on the judge's capacity to act impartially as a judge. Expressions which may do so include jokes or other remarks demeaning individuals on the basis of their race, sex, religion, national origin, disability, age, sexual orientation or socioeconomic status.

See Section 2C and accompanying Commentary.

Comment on subdivision B. — As a judicial officer and person specially learned in the law, a judge is in a unique position to contribute to the improvement of the law, the legal system, and the administration of justice. To the extent that time permits, a judge is encouraged to do so, either independently or through a bar association, judicial conference or other organization dedicated to the improvement of the law. Judges may participate in efforts to promote the fair administration of justice, the independence of the judiciary and the integrity of the legal profession.

Comment on subdivision C(1). — See Section 2B regarding the obligation to avoid improper influence.

Comment on subdivision C(3)(a). — Nothing

contained in these Canons shall be deemed to prohibit a judge from serving in a nonvoting capacity on the Board of Directors of Lawyers Helping Lawyers, or any committees of Lawyers Helping Lawyers.

Comment on subdivision C(3)(b). — A judge may solicit membership or endorse or encourage membership efforts for an organization devoted to the improvement of the law, the legal system or the administration of justice or a nonprofit educational, religious, charitable, fraternal or civic organization as long as the solicitation cannot reasonably be perceived as coercive and is not essentially a fund raising mechanism. Solicitation of funds for an organization and solicitation of memberships similarly involve the danger that the person solicited will feel obligated to respond favorably to the solicitor if the solicitor is in a position of influence or control. A judge must not engage in direct, individual solicitation of funds or memberships in person, in writing or by telephone except in the following cases: 1) a judge may solicit funds or memberships from other judges over whom the judge does not exercise supervisory or appellate authority, 2) a judge may solicit other persons for membership in the organizations described above if neither those persons nor persons with whom they are affiliated are likely ever to appear before the court on which the judge serves and 3) a judge who is an officer of such an organization may send a general membership solicitation mailing over the judge's signature.

This Canon is not intended to prohibit judges from participating in all charitable events. Judges are encouraged to be involved in community activities so long as the judge does not participate in the solicitation of funds and the prestige of the office is not used for fund raising.

Use of an organization letterhead for fund raising or membership solicitation does not violate Section 4C(3)(b) provided the letterhead lists only the judge's name and office or other position in the organization, and, if comparable designations are listed for other persons, the judge's judicial designation. In addition, a judge must also make reasonable efforts to ensure that the judge's staff, court officials and others subject to the judge's direction and control do not solicit funds on the judge's behalf for any purpose, charitable or otherwise.

Comment on subdivision D(1). — A judge must avoid financial and business dealings that involve the judge in frequent transactions or continuing business relationships with persons likely to come either before the judge personally or before other judges on the judge's court. In addition, a judge should discourage members of the judge's family from engaging in dealings that would reasonably appear to exploit the judge's judicial position. This rule is necessary to avoid creating an appearance of exploitation of office or favoritism and to minimize the potential for disqualification.

Comment on subdivision D(2). — This Section provides that, subject to the requirements of this Canon, a judge may hold and manage investments owned solely by the judge, investments owned solely by a member or members of the judge's family, and investments owned jointly by the judge and members of the judge's family. A judge may own real estate or other property with others, who are not family members, so long as the judge complies with Section 4D(1) and (2).

Comment on subdivision D(3). — Subject to the requirements of this Canon, a judge may participate in a business in which at least fifty percent is held either by the judge alone, by members of the judge's family, or by the judge and members of the judge's family.

Although participation by a judge in a closely held family business might otherwise be permitted by Section 4D(3), a judge may be prohibited from participation by other provisions of these Canons when, for example, the business entity frequently appears before the judge's court or the participation requires significant time away from judicial duties. Similarly, a judge must avoid participating in a closely held family business if the judge's participation would involve misuse of the prestige of judicial office, subject the judge to public criticism or give the appearance of impropriety.

"Member of the judge's family" denotes a spouse, child, grandchild, parent, grandparent, or other relative or person with whom the judge maintains a close familial relationship.

Comment on subdivision D(5). — Because a gift, favor or loan to a member of the judge's family residing in the judge's household might be viewed as intended to influence the judge, a judge must inform those family members of the relevant ethical constraints upon the judge in this regard and discourage those family members from violating them. A judge cannot, however, reasonably be expected to know or control all of the financial or business activities of all family members residing in the judge's household.

Comment on subdivision D(5)(a). — Acceptance of an invitation to a law related function is governed by Section 4D(5)(a).

Comment on subdivision D(5)(d). — A gift to a judge, or to a member of the judge's family living in the judge's household, that is excessive in value raises questions about the judge's impartiality and the integrity of the judicial office and might require disqualification of the judge where disqualification would not otherwise be required. See, however, Section 4D(5)(e).

Comment on subdivision E. — The restrictions imposed by this Canon may conflict with the judge's obligation as a fiduciary. For example, a judge should resign as trustee if detriment to the trust would result from divestiture of holdings the retention of which would place the judge in violation of Section 4D(4).

Comment on subdivision F. — Section 4F does not prohibit a judge from participating in settlement conferences performed as part of judicial duties.

Comment on subdivision G. — This prohibition refers to the practice of law in a representative capacity and not in a pro se capacity. A judge may act for himself or herself in all legal matters, including matters involving litigation and matters involving appearances before or other dealings with legislative and other governmental bodies. However, in so doing, a judge must not abuse the prestige of office to advance the interests of the judge or the judge's family. See Section 2(B).

These Canons allow a judge to give legal advice to and draft legal documents for members of the judge's family, so long as the judge receives no compensation. A judge must not, however, act as an advocate or negotiator for a member of the judge's family in a legal matter.

Section 51.1-309 of the Virginia Code prohibits a retired judge who is receiving benefits under the Judicial Retirement System from appearing as counsel in any case in any court in the Commonwealth.

Comment on subdivision H. — The Canons do not prohibit a judge from accepting honoraria or speaking fees provided that the compensation is reasonable and commensurate with the task performed. A judge should ensure, however, that no conflicts are created by the arrangement. A judge must not appear to trade on the judicial position for personal advantage. Nor should a judge spend significant time away from court duties to meet speaking or writing commitments for compensation. In addition, the source of the payment must not raise any question of undue influence or the judge's ability or willingness to be impartial.

The amendment, effective April 13, 2004, adopted April 13, 2004, added the Comment on subdivision C(3)(a).

The amendment effective November 2, 2009, adopted November 2, 2009, substituted "§ 2.2-3114" for "2.1-639.13" in subdivision H(2).

Canon 5. A Judge Shall Refrain From Political Activity Inappropriate to the Judicial Office.

A. *Political Conduct in General.* — (1) A judge shall not:

(a) act as a leader or hold any office in a political organization;

(b) make speeches for a political organization or candidate or publicly endorse or oppose a candidate for public office; or

(c) solicit funds for or pay an assessment or make a contribution to a political organization or candidate, attend political gatherings, or purchase tickets for political party dinners, or other political functions.

(2) A judge shall resign his office when he becomes a candidate either in a party primary or in a general election for a public office, except that he may continue to hold his judicial office while being a candidate for election to or serving as a delegate in a state constitutional convention, if he is otherwise permitted by law to do so.

(3) A judge shall not engage in any other political activity except in behalf of measures to improve the law, the legal system, or the administration of justice.

Comment on subdivision A. — A judge may vote in a primary election conducted by the State Board of Elections that is open to all registered voters qualified to vote pursuant to Code § 24.2-530. Voting in such a primary election does not constitute attending a "political gathering" as prohibited by subdivision A(1)(c) or constitute engaging "in any other political activity" as prohibited by subdivision A(3). The act of a judge voting in a primary election is the discharge of an honorable civic duty and an obligation of responsible citizenship.

The statutory requirements for voting in a primary election distinguish voting in a primary election by a judge from a "political gathering" as used in subdivision A(1)(c) because there is no registration by political affiliation, no loyalty or political party oath required to vote, and no pledge of support for any person or political group. For the same reasons, voting in a primary election by a judge is not engaging "in any other political activity" as used in subdivision A(3).

See also Commentary under Canon 2A.

The 2004 amendment, effective November 2, 2004, added the comment on subdivision A.

CASE NOTES

Violation not found. — When a judge, whose nephew sought his party's nomination to run for office, sent a court employee a text message asking if the judge's mother could contact the employee's mother, who, the judge thought, would be attending a political convention the next day, clear and convincing evidence did not show a violation of Va. Sup. Ct. R. pt. 6, § III, Canons 1, 2, or 5 because (1) there was nothing in the language of the messages that was overtly political, and (2) nothing showed the employee understood the messages as being political in nature, so the judge did not use the "prestige of judicial office." Judicial Inquiry & Review Comm'n v. Waymack, 284 Va. 527, 745 S.E.2d 410, 2012 Va. LEXIS 199 (2012).

When a judge attended a close personal friend's hearing, clear and convincing evidence did not show a violation of Va. Sup. Ct. R. pt. 6, § III, Canons 1, 2, 2(B), or 5(A)(3) because (1) the judge attended the hearing as a member of the public, and (2) the judge left the hearing as soon as requested by the presiding judge. Judicial Inquiry & Review Comm'n v. Waymack, 284 Va. 527, 745 S.E.2d 410, 2012 Va. LEXIS 199 (2012).

Canon 6. Judges Pro Tempore, Retired Judges, Substitute Judges and Persons Selected for Judgeship Are Required to Comply With the Canons.

A. *Judge Pro Tempore.* — A judge pro tempore is a person who is appointed pursuant to §§ 17.1-109, 17.1-110, and 17.1-111 of the Code of Virginia to act temporarily as a judge.

(1) While acting as such, a judge pro tempore is required to comply with the Canons as they apply to the case before him.

(2) A person who has been a judge pro tempore shall not act as a lawyer in a proceeding in which he has served as a judge or in any proceeding related thereto.

B. *Retired Judge, Senior Judge Or Justice.* — The provisions of § 51.1-309 of the Code of Virginia and of these Canons shall apply to all retired judges. Such judges, however, are not required to comply with Canon 4C(2), D(3), E, F, G, and H(2).

C. *Substitute Judge Or Special Justice.* — A substitute judge or special justice shall not act as a lawyer in a proceeding in which he has served as a judge or in any other proceeding related thereto but otherwise may practice law in the court on which he serves. A substitute judge or special justice is not required to comply with 4C(l)(2) and (3) except that he shall not use or permit the use of the prestige of judicial office for fund raising or membership solicitation. A substitute judge or special justice is not required to comply with 4D(3), E, F, and G.

D. *Person Selected for Judgeship.* — A person selected for a full-time position subject to the provisions of these Canons who is not already a justice or judge, from either election by both houses of the General Assembly or appointment by the appropriate authority until taking the oath of office as a justice or judge, is required to comply with Canons 1, 2, 2A, 2B, 4A, 4B, 4C(2), 4C(3)(b)(i, iii, and iv), 4D(1)(a), 4D(5), 4H(1), and 5. Such person shall arrange his or her affairs to be in compliance with the other appropriate parts of the Canons of Judicial Conduct at the time that he or she takes the oath of office.

Comment on subdivision A. — A judge pro tempore appointed under the provisions of Section 16.1-69.9:2 or 17-120 [17.1-509] of the Code shall be bound by the same Canons as a full time judge.

Comment on subdivision B. — A retired judge who both receives retirement benefits and appears in Virginia courts violates Va. Code § 51.1-309 and subdivision B of this Canon.

Retired judges may be listed as such or be referred to as "Honorable" in materials distributed by alternative dispute resolution groups and they may list their judicial service on resumes distributed by such organizations. When the term "Honorable" is used, however, the materials shall make clear that the judge is a retired judge.

Comment on subdivision C. — When sitting as a substitute judge or special justice, the substitute judge or special justice shall be bound by the Canons in the same manner as a full time judge. When a substitute judge is acting as a practicing attorney, he or she will not be precluded from those activities otherwise authorized as a practicing attorney.

Comment on subdivision D. — A person who has been selected as a judge but who has not yet taken the oath of office is perceived by the public as a person who should adhere to the high standards of conduct applicable to a judge. However, such a person needs time to arrange his or her affairs to be in compliance with these Canons at the time of taking the oath of office, and to wind down his or her practice prior to taking the oath of office. This provision applies the rule of reason to this transition process. During this period, such person should act in a manner appropriate to, and should not take advantage of, his or her status of impending judicial position.

The 2001 amendment, effective July 1, 2001, adopted April 12, 2001, in C., inserted "or special justice" in four places; and added D.

CASE NOTES

Virginia acted reasonably in setting up its recall system, whether it be obligatory or merely discretionary, for retired judges under 70 years of age. Thompson v. Walker, 758 F.2d 1004 (4th Cir. 1985).

Retired judge who both receives retirement benefits and appears in Virginia courts violates former Va. Code § 51-179 (now § 51.1-309) and subdivision C (now subdivision B) of this canon, which incorporates and interprets former Va. Code § 51-178. Thompson v. Walker, 583 F. Supp. 175 (E.D. Va. 1984), aff'd, 758 F.2d 1004 (4th Cir. 1985).

Canon 7. Effective Date.

These Canons shall become effective July 1, 1999.

ESTABLISHMENT OF JUDICIAL ETHICS ADVISORY COMMITTEE

A Judicial Ethics Advisory Committee is hereby established to render advisory opinions concerning the compliance of proposed future conduct with the Canons of Judicial Conduct. The committee shall have nine members. Five members shall be active or retired judges; two members shall be attorneys; and two members shall be lay persons. All members shall be appointed by the Chief Justice of the Virginia Supreme Court. Committee members shall serve for three-year terms from the date of appointment.

A request for an advisory opinion may be made by any judge or any person whose conduct is subject to the Canons of Judicial Conduct. The committee may not issue an opinion in response to a request where the facts are known to be the subject of a past or pending litigation or disciplinary proceeding or investigation. The committee may also issue opinions at its own initiative on matters of interest to the judiciary.

All opinions shall be advisory only, and no opinion shall be binding on the Judicial Inquiry and Review Commission or the Supreme Court in the exercise of its judicial discipline responsibilities. However, the Judicial Inquiry and Review Commission and the Supreme Court may in their discretion consider compliance with an advisory opinion by the requesting individual to be evidence of a good faith effort to comply with the Canons of Judicial Conduct provided that compliance with an opinion issued to one judge shall not be considered evidence of good faith of another judge unless the underlying facts are substantially the same.

Membership

1. The committee shall have nine members appointed by the Chief Justice of the Supreme Court. Members of the Judicial Inquiry and Review Commission may not serve simultaneously on the Judicial Ethics Advisory Committee.

2. Five members shall be either active or retired judges. One judge member shall be appointed from the Circuit, General District and Juvenile and Domestic Relations Courts and from the Court of Appeals. No member of the Supreme Court may be appointed to the Judicial Ethics Advisory Committee.

3. Two members shall be attorneys admitted to the practice of law in Virginia for at least ten years, who shall not be judges nor ever have been judges. The attorney members shall not be employees or officers within any branch of government except that they may be employees of educational institutions.

4. Two members shall be citizens who are not admitted to practice law in any state and who are not employees or officers within any branch of government except that they may be employees of educational institutions.

5. Committee members shall serve for three-year terms from the date of appointment, except that, to achieve staggered terms, three of the members first appointed shall be appointed for one year, three shall be appointed for two years, and three shall be appointed for three years. Committee members may be reappointed, but no member shall serve for more than two full consecutive terms.

6. A vacancy shall occur when a committee member resigns, ceases to be a member of the category from which the member was appointed, or becomes unable to serve for any reason. Vacancies shall be filled in the same manner as the original appointment, and appointments to fill a vacancy shall be for the balance of the term vacated. A member whose term expires shall continue to serve until a successor is appointed.

General Provisions

7. Members should be reimbursed for expenses actually and necessarily incurred in the performance of their duties for the committee.

8. To encourage judges to seek advice from the committee, the judge members of the committee, when acting in their advisory capacity, shall be exempt from the provisions regarding disciplinary responsibilities in the Canons of Judicial Conduct. The attorney members of the committee, when acting in their advisory capacity, shall be exempt from the provisions regarding reporting misconduct in the Code of Professional Responsibility.

9. By the concurrence of a majority of its members and subject to approval by the Supreme Court, the committee may promulgate additional rules of procedure not inconsistent with these rules.

10. The chair of the committee shall be elected by the members of the committee. The chair shall serve for a term of one year and shall not serve more than two

successive terms. The chair is authorized to call meetings as needed, to preside over those meetings, and to coordinate the work of the committee. A vice chair shall be elected in the same manner.

11. No member of the committee shall participate in any request for advice in which he or she has a direct or indirect interest, including his or her personal inquiry.

12. The committee may submit to the Supreme Court recommendations for amendments to the Canons of Judicial Conduct.

13. Each year, the committee shall submit to the Supreme Court a report of its activities.

14. Counsel to the Judicial Inquiry and Review Commission shall provide administrative and research support sufficient to carry out the committee's functions.

Jurisdiction

15. Any judge or any person whose conduct is subject to the Canons of Judicial Conduct may request an advisory opinion about the propriety of his or her own conduct. The committee may decline to respond to an inquiry from someone who is not a member of the judiciary.

16. The committee shall not render opinions regarding the proposed conduct of someone other than the inquirer, except the committee may respond to requests from a judge about a person subject to the judge's direction and control, from a judge about the judge's relatives, or from a judge with supervisory responsibilities.

17. The committee shall only issue opinions that address contemplated or proposed future conduct and shall not issue opinions addressing past or current conduct unless the past or current conduct relates to future conduct or is continuing. The committee may not issue an opinion in response to a request when the facts are known to be the subject of a past or pending litigation or disciplinary investigation or proceeding.

18. The committee may in its discretion decline to respond to any inquiry where the committee determines that a response would be inappropriate or that an opinion will not aid the judge, benefit the judiciary as a whole, or serve the public interest.

19. The committee may not issue an advisory opinion that interprets any constitutional provision, statute, rule, or regulation that does not relate to judicial ethics.

20. Notwithstanding any other provision of these rules, the committee may also issue opinions at its own initiative on matters of interest to the judiciary.

Procedures

21. A request for an advisory opinion must be in writing, signed by the person requesting the opinion, and sent to Counsel for the Judicial Inquiry and Review Commission.

22. A request shall contain a statement describing in detail all relevant facts and circumstances pertaining to the conduct for which an opinion is being sought. The request shall also include a clear, concise statement of the question of judicial ethics for which an opinion is sought and include references to the relevant section(s) of the Canons of Judicial Conduct, advisory opinions, case law, and other authority that the inquirer has already consulted.

23. Counsel shall review the request for an advisory opinion and notify the inquirer if it does not comply with these rules.

24. If an existing opinion answers the question presented in a request, Counsel may send a copy of the opinion to the inquirer, and the committee need not issue a new advisory opinion.

25. If an existing opinion does not answer the question presented in a request, Counsel shall send the request and any accompanying documents to all members of the committee.

26. If the facts or circumstances provided by the requesting individual are unclear, vague, or insufficient in detail, the chair or any member of the committee shall request supplemental information. If the supplemental information provided is still insufficient or is not provided within a reasonable time, the chair shall inform the inquirer, and the committee shall not render an advisory opinion.

27. After discussion and consideration of the request, the chair shall assign the responsibility for drafting an opinion to members of the committee. The assigned member will have 30 days to prepare a proposed opinion and circulate it to the other members.

28. Committee members will have 15 days to indicate their approval or disapproval of a proposed opinion and to make comments. The failure to respond within 15 days

shall be deemed an assent to the proposed opinion. Each committee member will send his or her response to all other committee members, including the chair, and to staff. Members will have an additional 15 days to respond to the comments of other members.

29. A telephone conference call may be arranged to discuss the proposed opinion and any comments.

30. A majority of the members shall be required to concur in any advisory opinion issued by the committee.

31. Any member of the committee may submit a minority opinion to be circulated for comment.

Formal Opinions

32. Formal opinions shall set forth the facts upon which the opinion is based and provide advice only with regard to those facts. Formal opinions shall cite the rules, cases, and other authorities that bear upon the advice rendered and shall quote the applicable provisions of the Canons of Judicial Conduct.

33. Formal opinions shall contain a discussion section that analyzes the issues and provides the rationale for the advice given by the committee. If the opinion responds to more than one issue, each issue shall be answered separately.

34. If the request raises issues under constitutional provisions, statutes, rules, or regulations other than the Canons of Judicial Conduct, the formal opinion may note the issues but shall indicate that the committee is not authorized to interpret a judge's obligations under any law other than the Canons of Judicial Conduct.

35. Formal opinions shall state the authority of the committee and explain the effect of compliance with the opinion in disciplinary proceedings.

Informal Opinions

36. Counsel for the Judicial Inquiry and Review Commission may issue informal opinions. An informal advisory opinion may be issued if the opinion is not inconsistent with prior formal opinions and Counsel finds that the subject is not of general substantial interest and continuing concern to the judiciary or the public.

37. If a request is made that requires only an informal opinion, Counsel may render an informal opinion at once or solicit the advice of the chair and other members before rendering an informal opinion.

38. Informal opinions may be oral. A written record shall be maintained by Counsel and a copy of the memorandum shall be promptly forwarded to the chair.

39. Counsel shall report in writing at the next meeting of the committee, on all informal opinions. If one-third of the members of the committee disagree with an informal opinion, that opinion shall be resubmitted for further study and issuance of a formal opinion.

40. Compliance with an informal opinion shall have the same effect as compliance with a formal opinion in judicial discipline proceedings.

41. Informal opinions will not be distributed or published in the same manner as formal opinions.

Distribution and Publication

42. The original formal opinion shall be mailed to the person requesting the opinion, and copies shall be mailed to all committee members.

43. The committee shall cause to be prepared an edited version of a formal opinion that omits the names of persons, courts, places, and any other information that might tend to identify either the person making the request or any other person. The edited opinion shall use neutral gender references. The chair shall review the edited opinion and add a heading.

44. Copies of edited opinions as they are prepared shall be sent to the Supreme Court, the Judicial Inquiry and Review Commission, the Executive Secretary of the Supreme Court, the Supreme Court Law Library, all law school libraries in Virginia, and the American Judicature Society.

45. Copies of edited opinions shall be published in a publication generally available to judges.

46. Copies of all edited opinions shall be sent by the Executive Secretary of the Supreme Court to all judges at least once a year. An index shall be distributed to all judges annually. A complete set of the committee's edited opinions shall be provided to each new judge.

47. A minority opinion shall be distributed and published in the same manner as the majority opinion of the committee.

48. The committee will release a copy of any edited opinion upon request.

Reconsideration and Modification

49. Any determination of the propriety of particular conduct by the Judicial Inquiry and Review Commission or the Supreme Court shall supersede any conflicting opinion of the committee. The committee shall examine and reconsider any of its opinions upon the request of the Judicial Inquiry and Review Commission or the Supreme Court.

50. At any time, a majority of the committee may modify or reverse any advisory opinion. The committee shall periodically review all of its opinions to determine if any are obsolete.

51. Within thirty days after the distribution of an edited opinion to all judges, any person, court, or agency authorized to request an opinion may petition the committee to reconsider the opinion by letter or memorandum explaining the basis for the request. The committee shall respond to the request by either reaffirming or revising the opinion. Revised opinions shall be distributed and published in the same manner as the original opinion.

SECTION IV. ORGANIZATION AND GOVERNMENT.

Research References. — Altman and Weil, How to Manage Your Law Office (Matthew Bender).

Burke and Bradbury, Accounting Systems for Law Offices (Matthew Bender).

D. Edward Martin, Attorney's Handbook of Accounting, Auditing, and Financial Reporting (Matthew Bender).

1. Name.

The name of the Association shall be the Virginia State Bar.

2. Membership and Registration.

(a) Every person licensed by the Virginia Board of Bar Examiners or admitted by the Supreme Court of Virginia is a member of the Virginia State Bar. Such persons shall register with the Virginia State Bar within one year after licensure or admission. Attorneys who are seeking active membership in the Virginia State Bar under Virginia Supreme Court Rule 1A:5, Part I (Virginia Corporate Counsel) must complete their registration requirements with the Virginia State Bar and their admission before the Supreme Court of Virginia within six months; otherwise such attorneys will be required to initiate a new application process.

(b) Every lawyer making application to the Virginia State Bar as a Corporate Counsel Registrant under Virginia Supreme Court Rule 1A:5 Part II, and every lawyer issued a certificate by the Virginia Board of Bar Examiners under Virginia Supreme Court Rules 1A:6 or 1A:7 must complete their registration requirements with the Virginia State Bar within six months; otherwise such attorneys will be required to initiate a new application process.

The amendment effective January 4, 2010, adopted November 2, 2009, rewrote the Rule.

3. Classes of Membership.

Members of the Virginia State Bar shall be divided into five classes, namely: (a) Active Members, (b) Associate Members, (c) Judicial Members, and (d) Disabled and Retired Members; and (e) Emeritus Members. Each member shall submit in writing to the membership department of the Virginia State Bar an address of record which will be used for all membership and regulatory purposes, including official mailings and notices of disciplinary proceedings. If a member's address of record is not a physical address where process can be served, the member must submit in writing to the membership department an alternate address where process can be served. The alternate address is personal information and shall not be disclosed pursuant to Section 2.2-3704, *Code of Virginia*. Members have a duty promptly to notify the membership department in writing of any changes in either the address of record or any alternate address. Members, by request, may have their names and addresses removed from the Virginia State Bar's membership list when it is distributed for other than official purposes.

(a) *Active Members.* — Those attorneys who are admitted to practice law in this state and who are engaged in the practice of law, either full-time or part-time, salaried or non-salaried, shall be active members of the Virginia State Bar. Those attorneys who are admitted to practice law in this state, but who are not presently so engaged, may acquire active status by paying the dues prescribed for active members and satisfying any other required membership obligations. Each active member's address of record will establish the judicial circuit in which the member is entitled to vote and hold office in the Virginia State Bar.

(b) *Associate Members.* — Those attorneys who have heretofore or may hereafter be admitted to practice law in the courts of this state but who are not presently so engaged and all persons on the law faculties of any law schools of this state that have been approved by the American Bar Association may become associate members of the Virginia State Bar upon application to the secretary and payment of the required dues. Associate members shall be entitled to all the privileges of active members except that they may not practice law, vote or hold office (other than as members of committees) in the Virginia State Bar.

(c) *Judicial Members.* — All full-time judges of the State (including federal judges), other officers qualified but forbidden by statute to practice law, and all retired judges who are receiving retirement benefits and are prohibited from appearing as counsel in any case in any court of the Commonwealth under section 51.1-309 of the *Code of Virginia*shall constitute the Judicial Membership of the Virginia State Bar. They shall pay no dues but shall be entitled to all of the privileges of active members except that they may not vote or hold office in the Virginia State Bar, and shall comply with any statutory limitations regulating their practice of the law.

(d) *Disabled and Retired Members.* — Any member of the Virginia State Bar, upon attaining the age of 70 or on the basis of a permanent disability, may submit to the executive director of the Virginia State Bar a written request to be transferred to the disabled and retired class of membership. Members who are electing this status based on a permanent disability must submit adequate medical and/or psychological documentation with the request. Members qualifying for transfer to the disabled and retired class shall not be entitled to practice law. Further, such members shall not be eligible to vote or hold office in the Virginia State Bar. Disabled and retired members may submit a petition to the executive director in writing for reinstatement to active or associate membership and state in the petition each circumstance that has changed since the member elected disabled or retired status. Adequate medical and/or psychological documentation must be submitted with the petition showing that the member is fit and capable of practicing law. If there are any misconduct complaints or proceedings pending when the executive director receives a petition for reinstatement, or if the member appears to suffer from a disability, the executive director shall defer consideration of the petition until the misconduct or disability issues are resolved. The Executive Committee of the Virginia State Bar shall consider and act on any such petition, taking into account the recommendation of the executive director. The Executive Director may deny a petition for reinstatement if the member is publicly disciplined or is determined to have a disability raising a serious question as to the member's fitness or capacity to practice law. If the Executive Committee approves the petition, the member shall be returned to active or associate status upon payment of the appropriate dues, satisfaction of any other required membership obligations, and payment of any outstanding financial obligations to the bar. Medical and/or psychological information provided pursuant to this subparagraph (d) is confidential and shall not be disclosed by the bar.

(e) *Emeritus Members.* — Those attorneys who are admitted to practice law in the Commonwealth of Virginia may, upon request to the Virginia State Bar with the supporting materials specified in this subparagraph, become emeritus members and provide *pro bono* legal services to the poor and working poor as emeritus members subject to the terms and conditions stated in this subparagraph. They shall pay no dues, may not practice law except in the limited manner specified in this subparagraph, and may not vote or hold office in the Virginia State Bar.

(1) Definitions.

(A) Active practice of law, for the purposes of this subparagraph, means that an attorney has been engaged in the practice of law, which includes private practice, house counsel, public employment as a lawyer, or full-time teaching at an American Bar Association approved law school.

(B) Emeritus member is any person who is admitted to practice law in the Commonwealth of Virginia, who is retiring or has retired from the active practice of law, and who intends to provide pro bono services under this subparagraph; and

(i) Has been engaged in the active practice of law for a minimum of ten out of the fifteen years immediately preceding the application to become an emeritus member; and

(ii) Is, at the time of requesting emeritus member status, an active member in good standing of the Virginia State Bar and has not been disciplined for professional misconduct by the bar or courts of any jurisdiction within the past fifteen years; and

(iii) Signs a statement that he or she has read and will comply with the Virginia Rules of Professional Conduct and as an emeritus member submits to the continuing jurisdiction of the Virginia Supreme Court and the Virginia State Bar for disciplinary purposes; and

(iv) Agrees to neither ask for nor receive any compensation of any kind, except for out-of-pocket expenses, for the legal service to be rendered under this subparagraph.

(C) Approved legal assistance organization, for the purposes of this subparagraph, is a Virginia licensed legal aid society or other not for profit entity organized in whole or in part, to provide legal services to the poor and/or working poor in Virginia and receiving funds for that purpose from an agency or entity of the federal government or the Commonwealth of Virginia, or from the Virginia Law Foundation.

(D) Supervising attorney, for purposes of this subparagraph, is an attorney who directs and supervises an emeritus member engaged in activities permitted by this subparagraph. The supervising attorney must:

(i) Be an active member of the Virginia State Bar in good standing employed by or participating as a volunteer for an approved legal assistance organization; and

(ii) Assume personal professional responsibility for supervising the conduct of the litigation, administrative proceeding, or other legal service in which the emeritus member engages; and

(iii) Direct and assist the emeritus member in his or her preparation to the extent the supervising attorney considers it necessary.

(2) Activities.

(A) An emeritus member, in association with an approved legal assistance organization and only under the supervision of a supervising attorney, may perform only the following activities:

(i) The emeritus member may appear in any court or before an administrative tribunal or arbitrator in the Commonwealth of Virginia on behalf of a client of an approved legal assistance organization if the person on whose behalf the emeritus member is appearing has consented in writing to that appearance and a supervising attorney has given written approval for that appearance. The written consent and approval shall be filed in the record of each case and shall be brought to the attention of the presiding judge or presiding officer in any administrative or arbitration proceeding.

(ii) The emeritus member may prepare and sign pleadings and other documents to be filed in any court or with any administrative tribunal or arbitrator in this state in any matter in which the emeritus member is involved.

(iii) The emeritus attorney may render legal advice and perform other appropriate legal services, but only with the express approval of the supervising attorney.

(iv) The emeritus attorney may engage in such other preparatory activities as are necessary for any matter in which he or she is properly involved.

(B) The presiding judge, hearing officer, or arbitrator may, in his or her discretion, determine the extent of the emeritus member's participation in any proceeding.

(3) Supervision and Limitations

(A) An emeritus member must perform all activities authorized by this subparagraph under the direct supervision of a supervising attorney.

(B) Emeritus members permitted to perform services under this subparagraph are not, and shall not represent themselves to be, active members of the Virginia State Bar licensed to practice law generally in the Commonwealth of Virginia.

(C) The prohibition against compensation for the emeritus member contained in Section (1)(B)(iv) of this subparagraph shall not prevent the approved legal assistance organization from reimbursing the emeritus member for actual expenses incurred while rendering service under this subparagraph, nor shall it prevent the approved legal assistance organization from charging for its services as it may otherwise properly charge. The approved legal assistance organization shall be entitled to receive all court awarded attorney's fees for any representation rendered by an emeritus member.

(4) Certification. Permission for an emeritus member to perform services under this subparagraph shall become effective upon filing with and approval by the Virginia State Bar of:

(A) A determination by the Virginia State Bar that the emeritus member has fulfilled the requirements of such membership and has a clear disciplinary record as required by Section (1)(B) of this subparagraph; and

(B) A certification by an approved legal assistance organization stating that the emeritus member is currently associated with that approved legal assistance organization and that an attorney employed by or participating as a volunteer with that organization will assume the duties of the supervising attorney required under this subparagraph.

(5) Withdrawal of Certification.

(A) Permission to perform services under this subparagraph shall cease immediately upon the filing with the Virginia State Bar of a notice either:

(i) By the approved legal assistance organization stating that:

(a) The emeritus member has ceased to be associated with the organization, which notice must be filed within five days after such association has ceased, or

(b) That the certification of such attorney is withdrawn. An approved legal assistance organization may withdraw certification at any time and it is not necessary that the notice state the cause for such withdrawal. A copy of the notice filed with the Virginia State Bar shall be mailed by the organization to the emeritus member concerned.

(ii) By the Virginia State Bar, or the Virginia Supreme Court, at any time, stating that permission to perform service under this subparagraph is revoked. A copy of such notice shall be mailed to the emeritus member involved and to the approved legal assistance organization by which he or she has been certified. The emeritus member may apply to the Virginia State Bar or the Virginia Supreme Court for review of such revocation.

(B) If an emeritus member's certification is withdrawn, for any reason, the supervising attorney shall promptly file a notice of such action in the official file of each matter pending before any court or tribunal in which the emeritus member was involved.

(6) Discipline. In addition to any appropriate investigation or proceeding instituted, or any discipline that may be imposed by the Virginia Supreme Court or the Virginia State Bar, the emeritus member shall be subject to the following disciplinary measures:

(A) The presiding judge or hearing officer for any matter in which the emeritus member has participated may hold the emeritus member in civil contempt for any failure to abide by such tribunal's orders; and

(B) The Virginia Supreme Court, the Virginia State Bar, or the approved legal assistance organization may, at any time, with or without cause, withdraw certification under this subparagraph.

(7) Mandatory Continuing Legal Education. Emeritus members must satisfy the Mandatory Continuing Legal Education (MCLE) obligations required of active members under Part 6, § IV, Paragraph 17 of the Rules of the Supreme Court of Virginia. Failure to satisfy the MCLE requirements shall subject the emeritus members to the fees and sanctions specified in Part 6, Section IV, Paragraph 19 of the Rules the Virginia Supreme Court.

(8) Change of Membership Status. An emeritus member may petition for reinstatement to active membership under the procedure prescribed in subparagraph (d) of this rule for disabled and retired members.

Editor's note. — Paragraph 3(b) of § IV was amended in 1939 (see 172 Va. xvi). Paragraph 3(d) was added in 1941 (see 177 Va. vii), readopted in 1950 (see 191 Va. lxxiii) and amended in 1973 (see 214 Va. 420).

The amendment effective September 29, 1999, adopted September 29, 1999, substituted "51.1-309" for "51-179" in the first sentence of subdivision (c).

The amendment effective September 26, 2002, adopted September 26, 2002, added the second through fifth sentences to the introductory paragraph; in subdivision (a), substituted "in this state" for "in the courts of this State" and "nonsalaried" for "nonsalaried" in the first sentence, and substituted "in this state for "in the courts of this State" in the second sentence, and substituted the present third sentence for the former third through sixth sentences; and rewrote subdivision (d).

The amendment effective September 1, 2004, adopted August 2, 2004, added subdivision (e). who retires from the practice of law may, either at age 70 or over,

The amendment effective January 4, 2010, adopted November 2, 2009, in the introductory paragraph, substituted "five" for "four" and added "and (e) Emeritus Members" in the first sentence, and added the last sentence thereof; in subdivision (a), substitued "dues" for "fee" and inserted "and satisfying any other required membership obligations" in the second sentence; in subdivision (b) substituted "have been" for "have heretofore or may hereafter be" near the beginning of the first sentence; in subdivision (d), substituted "Any member of the Virginia State Bar, upon attaining the age of 70" for "Any active member of the bar who retires from the practice of law may, either at age 70 or over" and inserted "may" in the first sentence, substituted "Disabled and retired members may" for "Those retired members who, after removal from active membership on account of age or disability, desire to return to the practice of law must" at the beginning of the fifth sentence, and inserted "or associate" therein, and in the tenth sentence, inserted "or associate," substituted "the appropriate" for "active member" and deleted "tender of sufficient MCLE credits to satisfy the requirements for one bar year"; and substituted "attorneys" for "persons" and made stylistic changes throughout the Rule.

4. Officers.

The officers of the Virginia State Bar shall be a President, a President-elect, an Immediate Past President and a Secretary-Treasurer. The President-elect shall be elected annually for a term to commence immediately upon the adjournment of the Annual Meeting of the Virginia State Bar and to continue until adjournment of the next Annual Meeting of the Virginia State Bar, at which time he or she shall take office as President. The President shall continue in office until adjournment of the next Annual Meeting, at which time he or she shall become the Immediate Past-President until adjournment of the following Annual Meeting.

To be eligible for nomination as President-elect, the candidate must, at the time of nomination, have been an active member of the Virginia State Bar for a period of seven years and must have served on the Council for a minimum of two years within the five-year period next preceding his or her election.

The method of election of the President-elect shall be in the manner prescribed by the Bylaws of the Council.

Vacancies in the office of President or President-elect shall be filled by the Council.

The President, the President-elect and the Immediate Past President shall be ex officio members of the Council; the President shall preside over the Council. In the absence of the President, the President-elect shall preside.

The Secretary-Treasurer shall also bear the title of Executive Director and Chief Operating Officer. The Council shall recommend its nominee as Secretary-Treasurer to the Supreme Court of Virginia which shall approve or reject the Council's recommendation. If the Supreme Court rejects Council's recommendation, Council shall submit another recommendation to the Court for its consideration. The Secretary-Treasurer shall keep all records of the Council and the Virginia State Bar. Accounts of the Secretary-Treasurer shall be audited annually.

The Secretary-Treasurer may be removed from office by the Council with the approval of the Supreme Court or by the Supreme Court, acting *sua sponte*.

Editor's note. — Amendments to paragraph 4 of § IV are published at 180 Va. lxvii (1942); 1981 Va. lxxxi (1942); 201 Va. lxxxiii (1960); 208 Va. 350 (1967); 214 Va. 420 (1974); 215 Va. 589 (1975). Paragraph 4 was also amended by reference in amendments to paragraph 8 of § IV. See, 190 Va. cxxxvii (1949).

The amendment, effective February 6, 2004, adopted February 6, 2004, in the sixth paragraph, deleted "and shall be elected annually by the Council" at the end of the first sentence, substituted the present second sentence for the former second and third sentences, substituted "The Secretary-Treasurer" for "He or she" at the beginning of the present fourth sentence, deleted the former fourth sentence, and substituted "Accounts of the Secretary-Treasurer" for "His or her accounts" at the beginning of the last sentence; and deleted the former seventh paragraph; and added the seventh paragraph.

The amendment, effective January 1, 2006, adopted December 21, 2005, in the first paragraph, inserted "an Immediate Past President" in the first sentence and "adjournment of" in the second and third sentences, and added "at which time he or she shall become the Immediate Past-President until adjournment of the following Annual Meeting" at the end of the third sentence.

5. The Council.

The powers of the Virginia State Bar shall be exercised by a Council composed of at least thirty-seven members in addition to the President, President-elect and Immediate Past President, as ex officio members, elected and appointed as follows:

At least one active member from each of the thirty-one judicial circuits, elected for a term of three years by the members of the Bar of each circuit, and nine members appointed by the Supreme Court of Virginia from the active members of the bar of the state at large. The Court shall appoint the at-large members to serve for a term of three years and, further, shall appoint in such a manner as to ensure that three members are appointed annually. A person who has served two successive full three-year terms as an elected or appointed member of Council shall not be eligible for election or appointment to a third successive term.

For each additional judicial circuit, whenever created, there shall be a member of the Council, who shall be an active member of the bar of that circuit. An election shall be held in such circuit within sixty (60) days after the creation of such circuit or as soon thereafter as may be feasible in the manner provided at Paragraph 6. The Council at its meeting next thereafter shall determine the length of the term of the first member from that circuit so that, as nearly as possible, the terms of one-third of the members of the Council expire each year.

Any circuit having as of the 1st day of February in any year more than 500 active members in good standing who are domiciled or principally practice their profession in such circuit shall be entitled to one additional member of the Council for each additional 500 members or major fraction thereof. In the event that the membership in a circuit as of February 1 is such that it is no longer entitled to one or more additional members, the term of such additional member[s] of the Council shall end at the expiration of the term for which the member[s] was elected. Provided, however, that the number of Council members from each circuit as of July 1, 2008, shall not be reduced unless the active membership in the circuit first increases to the number which will sustain its allocation of Council members as of July 1, 2008, under the above formula, and subsequently falls below that number.

Whenever a judicial circuit shall be abolished, the term of any member of the Council from that circuit shall end forthwith.

The President of the Young Lawyers Conference shall serve as an ex officio member of the Council.

The Chair of the Conference of Local Bar Associations shall serve as an ex officio member of the Council.

The Chair of the Senior Lawyers Conference shall serve as an ex officio member of the Council.

The Chair of the Diversity Conference shall serve as an ex officio member of the Council.

Editor's note. — Amendments to paragraph 5 of § IV are published at 180 Va. lxvii (1942); 181 Va. lxxxi (1942); 183 Va. vii (1944); 201 Va. lxxxiii (1959); 213 Va. 334, 718 (1973); and 218 Va. 452 (1977). Paragraph 5 was also amended by reference in amendments to paragraph 8 of § IV. See, 190 Va. cxxxvii (1949).

The amendment effective July 1, 1999, adopted April 23, 1999, in the first paragraph, substituted "nine members" for "six members" in the first sentence and substituted "three members" for "two members" in the second sentence.

The amendment effective July 1, 2000, deleted "if not already regular members" following "as ex officio members" in the first sentence of the first paragraph.

The amendment effective October 1, 2001, adopted October 1, 2001, added the present next-to-last paragraph.

The amendment effective October 31, 2008, adopted October 31, 2008, in the fourth paragraph, substituted "1st day of February" for "fifteenth day of March," "500" for "400" twice, "February 1" for "March 1," "July 1, 2008" for "July 1, 1992" twice, and "allocation of Council members" for "allocation of Council member"; and made stylistic changes thoughout the Rule.

The amendment effective January 22, 2010, adopted January 22, 2010, added the last paragraph.

6. Election to Council.

Prior to the expiration of a term of a Council member from a circuit, or when it appears that such a position has otherwise become vacant, or the circuit becomes entitled to an additional Council member under other provisions of this section, the Executive Director shall initiate the election process for the election of a Council member in the manner prescribed by the Bylaws of the Council.

Editor's note. — Amendments to paragraph 6 of § IV are published at 194 Va. clxx (1952) and 213 Va. 334, 718 (1973). Paragraph 6 was also amended by reference in amendments to paragraph 8 of § VI. See, 190 Va. cxxxvii (1949).

7. Meetings of the Council.

The Council shall hold meetings at such regular times and upon such call as it may specify. A quorum at any meeting shall consist of not less than twenty members. Between meetings of the Council its duties and functions may be performed by such Executive Committee of members or officers as the Council may designate.

Editor's note. — Paragraph 7 was amended by reference in amendments to paragraph 8 of § IV. See 190 Va. cxxxvii (1949).

8. Annual Meeting of the Virginia State Bar.

Annually, on or before July 1st, there shall be held a meeting of the members of the Virginia State Bar at a time and place designated by the Council or Executive

Committee and presided over by the President. All officers elected at the annual meeting or by the Council shall take office immediately upon adjournment of the annual meeting except in cases where vacancies are filled for an unexpired term. At such meeting there shall be a report from the officers and from the Council, and there shall be elected the President and President-Elect for the ensuing year.

A quorum at such meeting shall be those members of the Virginia State Bar present and voting.

There may be transacted also such other business as may come before the meeting.

A special meeting of the Virginia State Bar may be called by the Council.

Editor's note. — Amendments to paragraph 8 are published at 190 Va. cxxxvii (1949) and 201 Va. lxxxiii (1959). The purpose of the 1949 amendment, which amended paragraphs 4, 5, 6 and 7 by reference, was to change the date for commencement of the administrative year for the Bar from Sept. 1 to July 1.

9. Powers of the Council.

The Council shall have general charge of the administration of the affairs of the Virginia State Bar, and shall have the power:

(a) To adopt Bylaws for the Council and the Virginia State Bar not in conflict with these rules.

(b) To elect the officers provided for by these rules.

(c) To fill vacancies in the Council for unexpired terms if there should be a failure for sixty days to elect as provided in Paragraph 6 and to fill vacancies in any office for unexpired terms.

(d) To appoint Committees and prescribe their duties.

(e) To employ such assistants as it deems necessary and to fix their duties and compensation and the compensation of the Secretary-Treasurer.

(f) To make allocations of funds within the amounts available.

(g) To conduct such investigations and make such reports as may be directed by the Supreme Court or by the Bar.

(h) To render advisory opinions as provided in Paragraph 10.

(i) To establish an Administration and Finance Fund from which expenses related to meetings of the Council, meetings of the Executive Committee, the Annual and Midyear Meetings, and other official functions of the Virginia State Bar may be paid. The Fund shall be composed of funds appropriated to it by Council, or otherwise received. Such funds may be held, managed and invested as authorized or directed by Council. Disbursements from the fund shall be made as authorized by Council to pay the necessary expenses related to official functions of the Virginia State Bar as authorized by these Rules including, but not limited to, those expenses resulting from the exercise of the Council's powers under these Rules.

(j) The Council may, at its discretion or upon a written request of the majority of the members of the Virginia State Bar or pursuant to a resolution duly adopted at a regular or called meeting, exercise the necessary powers:

To promote reforms in judicial procedure and the judicial system that are intended to improve the quality and fairness of the system;

To recommend to the Supreme Court procedures for the disciplining, suspending and disbarring of attorneys;

To recommend to the Supreme Court the adoption of, modifications to, amendments to or the repeal of any rule of the Rules of the Supreme Court of Virginia;

To regulate the legal profession;

To improve the quality of the legal services made available to the people of Virginia;

To investigate, evaluate or endorse judicial candidates on a nonpartisan, merit basis;

To uphold and elevate the standards of honor, of integrity and of courtesy in the legal profession;

To encourage higher and better education for membership in the profession;

To encourage and promote diversity in the profession and the judiciary; and

To perform all duties imposed by law.

The amendment effective January 22, 2010, adopted January 22, 2010, added the next-to-last paragraph and made a related change.

CASE NOTES

Supreme Court had power to adopt subparagraph 9(j). — The Supreme Court possessed the inherent power to include in its rules for the integration of the Bar the provisions of subparagraph 9(j). Button v. Day, 204 Va. 547, 132 S.E.2d 292 (1963).

Continuing legal education programs within scope of subparagraph 9(j). — The Virginia continuing legal education program tends to advance the science of jurisprudence and facilitate the administration of justice. It is clearly within the scope and purpose of subparagraph 9(j). Button v. Day, 204 Va. 547, 132 S.E.2d 292 (1963).

10. Promulgation of Legal Ethics, Unauthorized Practice of Law Opinions, and Rules of Court; Informal Staff Opinions of Ethics Counsel; and Complaints of Unauthorized Practice of Law.

10-1. DEFINITIONS

As used in this Paragraph, the following terms shall have the meaning herein stated unless the context clearly requires otherwise:

"Advisory Opinion" means a written statement of the subject involved, the question presented, the Rule of Court or other precedents relied upon, the opinion reached, and the reasons therefore.

"Bar" means the Virginia State Bar.

"Committee" means the Standing Committee on Legal Ethics or the Standing Committee on Unauthorized Practice of Law.

"Council" means the Council of the Virginia State Bar.

"Court" means the Supreme Court of Virginia.

"Ethics Counsel" means the Ethics Counsel or an assistant ethics counsel of the Virginia State Bar.

"Member" means any active member of the Virginia State Bar or a Foreign Lawyer as defined under Rule 5.5(d)(1) of the *Rules of Professional Conduct*.

"Notice" means publishing in the *Virginia Lawyer Register* and at a minimum posting on the Virginia State Bar's website for at least 30 calendar days.

"Rule" means any proposed new Rule of Court or any modification, amendment, or proposed repeal of any existing Rule of Court promulgated by either the Standing Committee on Legal Ethics or the Standing Committee on Unauthorized Practice of Law.

10-2. ADVISORY OPINIONS OR RULES.

A. Request for Advisory Opinion. Any Member may request a legal ethics opinion or unauthorized practice of law opinion. The request shall be submitted as a hypothetical on a form approved by the Committee. A request for an Advisory Opinion will be reviewed by Ethics Counsel and forwarded to the appropriate Committee for consideration. In its discretion, the Committee may decline to render an Advisory Opinion regarding a previously resolved issue, or any matter that is currently the subject of any disciplinary proceeding or litigation.

B. Rules. The Committee may propose a new Rule or propose amendments, modifications, or repeal of existing Rules at its discretion. For rule changes that declare conduct as the unauthorized practice of law, the Bar shall seek comment from the Attorney General's office analyzing any restraint on competition that might result from the adoption of the proposed change.

C. Notice and Comments. The Committee shall provide Notice and opportunity for public comment on proposed Advisory Opinions or proposed Rules. Public comments shall be directed to the Executive Director of the Virginia State Bar. For proposed Advisory Opinions, the Committee will consider any comments received and either publish the opinion as an Advisory Opinion or ask for Council review in accordance with section 10-3. Advisory Opinions express the judgment of the Committee and are not binding on any judicial or administrative tribunal. In the case of a Rule, the Committee will consider any comments received and then submit the Rule to Council for consideration in accordance with section 10-3.

D. Appeal. After the comment period, any party requesting an Advisory Opinion who disagrees with the result may appeal the opinion to Council for approval, modification, or disapproval.

E. Unauthorized Practice of Law Advisory Opinions. An unauthorized practice of law Advisory Opinion in which the Committee concludes that the conduct in question constitutes or would constitute the unauthorized practice of law shall be sent to

Council in accordance with section 10-3. For these Advisory Opinions, the Bar shall seek comment from the Attorney General's office analyzing any restraint on competition that might result from the promulgation and implementation of the opinion.

F. Confidentiality. All Committee deliberations, memoranda, correspondence, and work product shall be confidential and privileged from discovery or subpoena and will not be provided to anyone absent a court order.

10-3. ADVISORY OPINION OR RULE CONSIDERATION BY COUNCIL.

A. Review. After considering all materials and written comments, Council may approve, modify, or disapprove any Advisory Opinion or Rule by a majority vote of those present and voting. If Council approves or modifies an Advisory Opinion it may be published as an Advisory Opinion of the Bar and have the same legal effect as a Committee-issued opinion. Council may determine to submit the Advisory Opinion or Rule to the Court for review along with copies of all public comments.

B. Unauthorized Practice of Law Advisory Opinions. If Council concurs by a majority vote of those present and voting that the proposed conduct in any unauthorized practice of law Advisory Opinion constitutes the unauthorized practice of law, the Advisory Opinion shall be sent to the Court for review along with copies of all public comments.

10-4. ADVISORY OPINION OR RULE REVIEW BY THE SUPREME COURT OF VIRGINIA.

A. Review. After considering all materials submitted to it, the Court shall approve, modify, or disapprove any Advisory Opinion or Rule.

10-5. INFORMAL STAFF OPINIONS OF ETHICS COUNSEL.

A. Informal Advice. At the request of a Member, Ethics Counsel shall provide informal advice or opinion based on the facts provided.

B. Protection. Ethics Counsel shall not be compelled to testify, via subpoena or otherwise, in any judicial or adjudicative proceeding, except on behalf of a respondent in disciplinary proceedings of the Virginia State Bar, regarding any advice or opinion provided to that attorney. Except as stated herein, Ethics Counsel shall not be subject to subpoena or otherwise compelled to testify or to produce any documents in any judicial or adjudicative proceeding or to testify as an expert witness regarding legal ethics or the practice of law. In a disciplinary proceeding, testimony of Ethics Counsel shall be limited to the substance of any communications by and between Ethics and the Member, where such communications are an issue in the proceeding.

C. Confidentiality. All communications between Ethics Counsel and any Member requesting advice or opinion shall be confidential. Ethics Counsel shall not disclose the content of any such discussion without the express written consent of the Member to whom Ethics Counsel provided such advice or opinion. No Member shall withhold consent if the Member is claiming, in the course of a disciplinary investigation or hearing, that the Member relied on the advice of Ethics Counsel.

D. Use of Informal Advice in Collateral Litigation. Informal advice of Ethics Counsel is advisory only and expresses the judgment of the Ethics Counsel and is not binding on the Court, Council, Committee or any judicial or administrative tribunal. Except as provided herein in connection with attorney disciplinary proceedings, informal advice of Ethics Counsel shall not be used, admitted, introduced, argued or cited in any litigation or before any judicial or administrative tribunal for the purpose of seeking disqualification of a lawyer or law firm.

10-6. COMPLAINTS OF UNAUTHORIZED PRACTICE OF LAW.

A. Review of Complaints. Any written complaint alleging the unauthorized practice of law shall be reviewed by Ethics Counsel and either dismissed or referred for investigation with full report to the Committee. After reviewing a report of investigation, the Committee may conduct a hearing to take testimony from witnesses and review evidence. By majority vote the Committee may dismiss the complaint due to insufficient evidence or other good cause, dismiss the complaint with cautionary language, or enter a finding of probable cause to believe there is unauthorized practice of law.

B. Referral. If a majority of the Committee finds probable cause to believe there is unauthorized practice of law, the Committee may dismiss the complaint by letter agreement in which the party against whom the complaint is pending agrees to cease the activity; or refer the complaint to the Attorney General, a Commonwealth's Attorney, or other appropriate agency for action.

C. Summons or Subpoena. If a summons or subpoena is necessary for investigation of a matter outlined in section 10-6.A., Ethics Counsel may issue such a summons or subpoena in the name of the Commonwealth. The Committee or a Virginia State Bar investigator may use a summons to examine a witness or to obtain statements from persons having knowledge about the subject of the complaint.

D. Enforcement of Summons or Subpoena. Every Circuit Court shall have power to enforce a summons or subpoena issued by the Ethics Counsel and to adjudge disobedience thereof as contempt.

The amendment, effective January 27, 1998, adopted January 27, 1998, rewrote subdivisions (e) and (g).

The amendment effective September 29, 1999, adopted September 29, 1999, added subdivision (a)(viii); substituted "appropriate Committee" for "Executive Director" in subdivision (b)(ii); in subdivision (c)(i), in the first sentence, substitued "Ethics Counsel shall review" for "Executive Director shall transmit" and inserted "to determine whether the request should be referred," and substituted "Ethics Counsel or Committee" for "Chairman" in the second sentence; added "or which presents an issue beyond its purview" at the end of subdivision (c)(ii); substituted "*Virginia Lawyer Register*" for "Virginia Bar News" in subdivision (d)(ii); substituted "Ethics Counsel" for "Executive Director" in subdivision (h)(i); rewrote subdivision (h)(ii), which formerly read "Within sixty days from the receipt of any complaint the Executive Director shall present a report to the Committee detailing his findings and the results of his investigation"; added subdivisions (h)(iii) and (h)(iv); in subdivision (i)(i), in the first sentence, substituted "complaint" for "written application from a Virginia State Bar investigator or counsel or from the Chair of the Committee," inserted "provided," inserted "summons or" in three places, and substituted "Ethics Counsel may" for "Executive Director shall," and added the second sentence; in subdivision (i)(ii), deleted "Enforcement:" at the beginning and substituted "Ethics Counsel" for "Executive Director"; in subdivision (j)(i), substituted "Ethics Counsel's" for "Executive Director's" and substituted "may" for "shall"; and substituted "may direct the Ethics Counsel" for "shall direct the Executive Director" in subdivision (j)(ii).

The amendment, effective January 1, 2005, adopted October 1, 2004, rewrote the Rule.

The amendment effective January 22, 2010, adopted January 22, 2010, deleted "Lawyer Advertising, Solicitation" in the Rule heading; in (a)(ii), deleted "the Committee on Lawyer Advertising and Solicitation, or all of them," and made a related change; and in (a)(ix), deleted "the Standing Committee on Lawyer Advertising and Solicitation" and the punctuation surrounding.

The amendment, effective March 19, 2010, adopted March 19, 2010, rewrote the Rule.

Law Review. — For article, "Virginia: The Unauthorized Practice of Law Experience," see 19 U. Rich. L. Rev. 499 (1985).

CASE NOTES

Availability of declaratory determination as to whether practice unauthorized. — The fact that the unauthorized practice of law is a misdemeanor did not preclude declaratory relief to attorneys who sought determination as to whether a title insurance company's activities constituted the unauthorized practice of law, where their goal was not solely to stop the illegal conduct of others, but to insure their own conduct conformed to the law and the tenets of the legal profession. The availability of criminal proceedings under former § 54-44 (see now § 54.1-3904), a writ of quo warranto, under § 8.01-636 and advisory opinions under this paragraph did not preclude the use of declaratory judgment. Blodinger v. Broker's Title, Inc., 224 Va. 201, 294 S.E.2d 876 (1982).

11. Dues.

Each active member shall pay to the Treasurer of the Virginia State Bar, annual dues not to exceed $250, and each associate member shall pay to the Treasurer of the Virginia State Bar annual dues not to exceed $125, on or before the 31st day of July of each fiscal year, provided that persons admitted to practice by examination or under Rule 1A:1 of the Supreme Court of Virginia shall not be liable for dues in the year of admission if admitted during the last three months of any fiscal year. Persons admitted to practice under Rule 1A:1 at any other point during any fiscal year shall pay the full amount of dues as specified above at the time they register with the Virginia State Bar. Persons admitted to practice by examination at any other point during any fiscal year shall pay one-half the amount of dues as specified above at the time they register with the Virginia State Bar. On or before April 1st, the Bar shall report to the Court the annual dues amount proposed for the next fiscal year.

No increase in the annual dues above $250 for active members or $125 for associate members will be authorized by the Court whenever the total combined cash balances of the State Bar Fund and the Virginia State Bar's Administration and Finance

Account shall exceed fifteen (15) percent of the total annual operating expenditures of the Virginia State Bar for the year preceding the year in which the dues increase is sought.

All monies collected hereunder shall be accounted for and paid into the State Treasury of Virginia.

Failure to comply with this Rule shall subject the member to penalties set forth in Paragraph 19 herein.

Editor's note. — Amendments to paragraph 11 of § IV are published at 186 VA. xcv (1947); 201 Va. lxxxiii (1959); 205 Va. 1011 (1965); 211 Va. 116 (1970); 213 Va. 334 (1973); 216 Va. 305 (1975); and 220 Va. 469 (1979).

The amendment, effective July 1, 2000, adopted February 4, 2000, in the first paragraph, substituted "$250" for "$169," and substituted "$125" for "$84.50."

The amendment, effective April 12, 2001, rewrote the first paragraph.

The amendment, effective March 9, 2011, aopted March 9, 2011, substituted "Each active member shall pay to the Treasurer of the Virginia State Bar, annual dues not to exceed $250, and each associate member shall pay to the Treasurer of the Virginia State Bar annual dues not to exceed $125," for "Effective July 1, 2000, each active member shall pay to the Treasurer of the Virginia State Bar, annual dues of $250, and associate members shall pay annual dues of $125," at the beginning of the first sentence, and added the last sentence, of the first paragraph, and inserted "above $250 for active members or $125 for associate members" near the beginning of the second paragraph.

Law Review. — For survey on professional responsibility in Virginia for 1989, see 23 U. Rich. L. Rev. 751 (1989).

12. Disbursements.

Disbursements shall be paid out of the state treasury in accordance with allocations of the Council and on requisitions signed by the President, President-Elect, or Secretary-Treasurer, and upon the warrant of the State Comptroller. No member of the Council, and no member or officer of the Virginia State Bar except the Secretary-Treasurer, shall receive compensation for his or her services as such, nor shall any member of the Council or of the Virginia State Bar receive compensation for service on any Committee, but such Council member or Committeeman shall be reimbursed for his or her necessary and actual traveling and subsistence expenses incurred in the performance of his or her duties. The Council shall cause proper books of account to be kept, and have them audited annually. At each annual meeting of the Virginia State Bar, the Council shall cause to be presented a financial statement of the receipts and expenditures of the Virginia State Bar, which shall be published in the next volume of reports.

Editor's note. — Amendments to paragraph 12 of § IV are published at 201 Va. lxxxiii (1959) and 205 Va. 1011 (1964).

13. Procedure for Disciplining, Suspending, and Disbarring Attorneys.

13-1. DEFINITIONS

As used in this Paragraph, the following terms shall have the meaning herein stated unless the context clearly requires otherwise:

"Adjudication of a Crime Proceeding" means the proceeding which follows the summary Suspension of an Attorney after receipt by the Clerk of the Disciplinary System of initial notification from any court of competent jurisdiction stating that an Attorney has been found guilty of a Crime, irrespective of whether sentencing has occurred.

"Admonition" means a private sanction imposed by a Subcommittee *sua sponte,* a private or public sanction based upon an Agreed Disposition approved by a Subcommittee, or a public sanction imposed by a District Committee or the Board upon a finding that Misconduct has been established, but that no substantial harm to the Complainant or the public has occurred, and that no further disciplinary action is necessary.

"Agreed Disposition" means the disposition of a Disciplinary Proceeding agreed to by Respondent and Bar Counsel and approved by a Subcommittee, District Committee, the Board or a Circuit Court.

"Attorney" means a member of the Bar, a Corporate Counsel Registrant, Foreign Lawyer, Foreign Legal Consultant, and any member of the bar of any other jurisdiction while engaged, *pro hac vice* or otherwise, in the practice of law in Virginia.

"Bar" means the Virginia State Bar.

"Bar Counsel" means the Attorney who is appointed as such by Council and who is approved by the Attorney General pursuant to Va. Code § 2.1-122(c) and such deputies, assistants, and Investigators as may be necessary to carry out the duties of the office, except where the duties must specifically be performed by the individual appointed pursuant to Va. Code § 2.1-122(c).

"Bar Official" means any Bar officer or any member, employee, or counsel of Council, the Board, a District Committee, or COLD.

"Board" means the Bar Disciplinary Board.

"Certification" means the document issued by a Subcommittee or a District Committee when it has elected to certify allegations of Misconduct to the Board for its consideration, which document shall include sufficient facts to reasonably notify Bar Counsel and Respondent of the basis for such Certification and the Disciplinary Rules alleged to have been violated.

"Certification for Sanction Determination" means the document issued by a District Committee to certify to the Board that a sanction within the power of the Board is in order where the District Committee has found that Respondent failed to fulfill the terms of a Public Reprimand with Terms issued either by a Subcommittee on the basis of an Agreed Disposition or by a District Committee.

"Chair," unless otherwise specified, means the Chair, Vice Chair, or Acting Chair of a District Committee, or a Section, Panel, or Subcommittee of a District Committee, or of the Board or any Panel of the Board.

"Charge of Misconduct" means the notice given by the Bar to a Respondent, setting forth generally the Misconduct alleged to have been committed by the Respondent, and identifying the specific Disciplinary Rule(s) alleged to have been violated by the Respondent. The Charge of Misconduct shall also include the date, time, and place of the hearing.

"Circuit Court" means a court designated as such by Va. Code § 17.1-500.

"Clerk of the Disciplinary System" means the employee of the Bar who, together with such assistants as may be required, provides administrative support to the disciplinary system and serves as official custodian of the Disciplinary Records.

"COLD" means the Standing Committee on Lawyer Discipline.

"Complainant" means the initiator of a Complaint.

"Complaint" means any written communication to the Bar alleging Misconduct or from which allegations of Misconduct reasonably may be inferred.

"Committee Counsel" means an Attorney District Committee member assigned to prosecute a Complaint.

"Corporate Counsel Registrant" means a person who has been recorded by the Virginia State Bar as a Corporate Counsel Registrant pursuant to Rule 1A:5.

"Costs" means reasonable costs paid by the Bar to outside experts or consultants; reasonable travel and out-of-pocket expenses for witnesses; Court Reporter and transcript fees; electronic and telephone conferencing and recording costs, if such procedures are requested by Respondent; copying, mailing, and required publication costs, translator fees and an administrative charge determined by Council.

"Council" means the Council of the Bar.

"Court Reporter" means a person who is qualified to transcribe proceedings in a Circuit Court.

"CRESPA" means the Virginia Consumer Real Estate Settlement Protection Act, Va. Code, Title 6.1, Chapter 1.3, and any regulations promulgated thereunder.

"Crime" means:

1. Any offense declared to be a felony by federal or state law;
2. Any other offense involving theft, fraud, forgery, extortion, bribery, or perjury;
3. An attempt, solicitation or conspiracy to commit any of the foregoing; or
4. Any of the foregoing found by a foreign jurisdiction.

"Disbarment" has the same meaning as Revocation.

"Disciplinary Proceeding" means any proceeding governed by this Paragraph.

"Disciplinary Record" means any tangible or electronic record of:

1. Any proceeding in which the Respondent has been found guilty of Misconduct, including those proceedings in which (a) the Board's or Court's finding of Misconduct has been appealed to this Court; (b) the Respondent's License has been revoked upon consent to revocation or Respondent has been found guilty of a Crime; or (c) the Respondent has received a sanction pursuant to this Paragraph; and

2. Any proceeding which has been resolved by (a) a *De Minimis* Dismissal; (b) a Dismissal for Exceptional Circumstances; or (c) an Admonition; and

3. Any proceeding in which the Respondent has been found guilty of a violation of CRESPA; and

4. Any proceeding which resulted in a sanction which created a disciplinary record at the time it was imposed.

"Disciplinary Rules" means:

1. the Virginia Rules of Professional Conduct and Virginia Code of Professional Responsibility, as applicable; and

2. the disciplinary rules of any other jurisdiction applicable under Rule 8.5 of the Virginia Rules of Professional Conduct.

"Dismissal" means the dismissal of a Complaint or Disciplinary Proceeding by Bar Counsel, a Subcommittee, a District Committee, the Board or a Circuit Court.

"Dismissal *De Minimis*" means a finding that the Respondent has engaged in Misconduct that is clearly not of sufficient magnitude to warrant disciplinary action, and Respondent has taken reasonable precautions against a recurrence of same.

"Dismissal for Exceptional Circumstances" means a finding that the Respondent has engaged in Misconduct but there exist exceptional circumstances mitigating against further proceedings, which circumstances shall be set forth in writing.

"District Committee" means one of the District Committees appointed as hereinafter provided or, where the context requires, a Panel, a Section, or a Subcommittee thereof.

"District Committee Determination" means the written decision of a District Committee or a Subcommittee of a District Committee, relating to a Complaint or Charge of Misconduct.

"Executive Committee" means the Executive Committee of the Bar.

"Executive Director" means the Executive Director of the Bar and any deputy or assistant designated by Council to act as Executive Director.

"Files" means those files maintained by the Clerk of the Disciplinary System, and office of Bar Counsel with respect to each Complaint.

"Foreign Lawyer" means a person authorized to practice law by the duly constituted and authorized governmental body of any State or Territory of the United States or the District of Columbia, or a foreign nation, but is neither licensed by the Court or authorized under its rules to practice law generally in the Commonwealth of Virginia, nor disbarred or suspended from practice in any jurisdiction.

"Foreign Legal Consultant" means a person who has been issued a foreign legal consultant certificate by the Virginia Board of Bar Examiners pursuant to Rule 1A:7.

"Impairment" means any physical or mental condition that materially impairs the fitness of an Attorney to practice law.

"Impairment Proceeding" means the proceeding:

1. Initiated by Bar Counsel to petition the Board to order the Respondent to undergo examination(s) and provide releases for records;

2. Initiated by Bar Counsel to determine whether an Attorney has an Impairment;

3. That follows the summary Suspension of an Attorney who may have an Impairment; or

4. That follows a request by Respondent to terminate an Impairment Suspension.

"Investigation" means any inquiry by Bar Counsel, Committee Counsel, or the Bar's designee concerning any alleged Misconduct or Crime committed by an Attorney or any Impairment of an Attorney.

"Investigative Report" means the report prepared as a result of an Investigation.

"Investigator" means a person designated by the Bar to conduct an Investigation.

"Judge" means a judge within the meaning of Va. Code § 2.1-37.1, and any judge appointed or elected under the laws of any other jurisdiction.

"License" means the license or authority to practice law granted by this Court.

"Memorandum Order" means the opinion and order of the Board entered following a Disciplinary Proceeding that shall contain a brief statement of the findings of fact; the nature of the Misconduct shown by such finding of facts; the Disciplinary Rules found to have been violated by clear and convincing evidence; the sanction imposed; the notice requirements, if any, imposed upon Respondent; the time in which Terms are required to be satisfied by Respondent, if Terms are imposed; the alternative sanction, if Respondent fails to comply with any Terms that are imposed; the name and address of the Court Reporter who served at the hearing; the names of the members of the Board that constituted the Panel; and that Costs shall be reimbursed by Respondent.

"Misconduct" means any:

1. Unlawful conduct described in Va. Code § 54.1-3935;
2. Violation of the Disciplinary Rules;
3. Conviction of a Crime;
4. Conviction of any other criminal offense or commission of a deliberately wrongful act that reflects adversely on the Attorney's honesty, trustworthiness, or fitness as an Attorney; or
5. Violation of CRESPA or any regulations adopted pursuant thereto.

"Panel" means a group of members of a Section, District Committee, or the Board hearing a disciplinary matter that constitutes the quorum required by this Paragraph.

"Paragraph" means Paragraph 13 of the Rules of this Court, Part Six, Section IV.

"Petitioner" means:

1. An Attorney seeking Reinstatement after a Revocation; or
2. An Attorney seeking termination of an Impairment Suspension; or
3. A Bar Counsel or District Committee Chair seeking an expedited hearing before the Board and alleging that an Attorney is engaging in Misconduct likely to result in injury to or loss of property of a client or other entity, or alleging an Attorney poses imminent danger to the public.

"Private Discipline" means an Admonition without Terms issued by a Subcommittee *sua sponte,* a Private Reprimand or any form of discipline which is not public.

"Private Reprimand" means a form of non-public discipline that declares privately the conduct of the Respondent improper but does not limit the Respondent's right to practice law.

"Proceeding" means the same as Disciplinary Proceeding.

"Public Reprimand" means a form of public discipline that declares publicly the conduct of the Respondent improper, but does not limit the Respondent's right to practice law.

"Receivership" means a receivership created pursuant to Va. Code § 54.1-3900.01or § 54.1-3936.

"Reinstatement" means the restoration by this Court of an Attorney's License in the manner provided in this Paragraph.

"Reinstatement Proceeding" means the proceeding which takes place upon referral from this Court of a Petition for Reinstatement by an Attorney whose License was previously revoked.

"Respondent" means any Attorney:

1. Who is the subject of a Complaint;
2. Who is the subject of any proceeding under this Paragraph, Va. Code §§ 54.1-3900.01, 54.1-3935, 54.1-3936, or CRESPA; or
3. Who is the subject of an Adjudication of a Crime Proceeding, Proceedings upon Disbarment, Revocation or Suspension in another jurisdiction, Impairment Proceeding, or Reinstatement Proceeding.

"Revocation" means any revocation of an Attorney's License and, when applied to a lawyer not admitted or authorized to practice law in Virginia, means the exclusion from the admission to, or the exercise of any privilege to, practice law in Virginia.

"Section" means a subgroup of a District Committee that has the same powers, authority, and duties as the District Committee.

"Subcommittee" means a subgroup of a District Committee or any Section thereof, convened for the purpose of performing the functions of a Subcommittee as described in this Paragraph.

"Summary Order" means a bench order entered by the Chair following a Disciplinary Proceeding that outlines in summary form the findings as to the allegations of Misconduct, the sanctions to be imposed, the effective date of any sanctions imposed, and any notice requirements.

"Suspension" means the temporary suspension of an Attorney's License for either a fixed or indefinite period of time and, when applied to a lawyer not admitted or authorized to practice law in Virginia, means the temporary or indefinite exclusion from the admission to, or the exercise of any privilege to, practice law in Virginia.

"Terms" shall mean those conditions imposed on the Respondent by a Subcommittee, District Committee, Board, or Circuit Court, that require the Respondent to perform certain remedial actions as a necessary condition for the imposition of an Admonition, a Private or Public Reprimand, or a Suspension pursuant to this Paragraph.

"Va. Code" means the 1950 Code of Virginia, as amended.

13-2. AUTHORITY OF THE COURTS

Nothing in this Paragraph shall be interpreted so as to eliminate, restrict or impair the jurisdiction of the courts of this Commonwealth to deal with the disciplining of Attorneys as provided by law. Every Judge shall have authority to take such action as may be necessary or appropriate to protect the interests of clients of any Attorney whose License is subject to a Suspension or Revocation. Every Circuit Court shall have power to enforce any order, summons or subpoena issued by the Board, a District Committee or Bar Counsel and to adjudge disobedience thereof as contempt.

13-3. GENERAL ADMINISTRATIVE AUTHORITY OF COUNCIL

Council shall have general administrative authority over and responsibility for the disciplinary system created pursuant to this Paragraph.

13-4. ESTABLISHMENT OF DISTRICT COMMITTEES

A. Creation of District Committees. Council shall appoint a sufficient number of District Committees to carry out the purposes of this Paragraph. District Committees shall be established in geographical areas consisting of one or more judicial circuits. In creating the District Committee areas, Council shall give due consideration to Attorney population and the community of interest among different judicial circuits within a District Committee area. Each District Committee shall consist of ten, or in the discretion of Council, 20, 30 or 40 members. Three members of a ten-member District Committee, six members of a 20-member District Committee, nine members of a 30-member District Committee, and 12 members of a 40-member District Committee shall be nonlawyers. All other members shall be active members of the Bar. Former members of a District Committee may serve on a District Committee Subcommittee or participate in a District Committee hearing whenever the District Committee Chair determines that such service is necessary for the orderly administration of the District Committee's work.

B. Panel Quorum. A Panel quorum shall consist of five or more persons. One person assigned to a District Committee Panel shall be a present or former nonlawyer member of a District Committee. If the scheduled nonlawyer is unable to attend, and if an alternate nonlawyer is not reasonably available, participation by a nonlawyer member shall not be required in a proceeding if a quorum is otherwise present. The action of a majority of a quorum shall be the action of the District Committee Panel.

C. Geographic Criteria. Each member of a District Committee shall be a resident of or have his or her office in the District Committee area for which such member is appointed. Members shall, to the extent practicable, be appointed from different geographical sections of their districts.

D. Term of Office. Council shall appoint members of each District Committee for such terms of service as will allow for the retirement from the District Committee, or completion of the existing terms, of one-third of the District Committee membership at the end of each fiscal year. A District Committee member's term shall be for three years, and, upon completion of such term, such member is eligible for appointment to a second successive three-year term. A member who has served two full successive terms of three years each on a District Committee shall not be eligible to serve again until one year after the expiration of the second term.

E. Qualification of Members. Before nominating any individual for membership on a District Committee, the Council members making such recommendation shall first determine that the nominee is willing to serve on the District Committee and will conscientiously discharge the responsibility as a member of the District Committee. Council members making the nominations shall also obtain a statement from the nominees, in writing, that the nominees are willing to serve on the District Committee, if elected. In order to be considered as a potential appointee to a District Committee, each potential appointee shall execute the following: (1) a waiver of confidentiality with respect to his or her Disciplinary Record and any pending Complaints and a release allowing production of his or her Disciplinary Record and any pending Complaints from any jurisdiction for purposes of the appointment process; and (2) an authorization for the Bar to conduct a criminal records check of all jurisdictions for any conviction of a Crime and provide the results to the members of Council and the staff of the Bar for purposes of the appointment process. No member of Council shall be a member of a District Committee.

F. Persons Ineligible for Appointment. Any potential appointee shall be ineligible for appointment to a District Committee if such potential appointee has: (1) ever been convicted in any jurisdiction of a Crime; (2) ever committed any criminal act that reflects adversely on the potential appointee's honesty, trustworthiness or fitness as a member of a District Committee; (3) a Disciplinary Record in any jurisdiction consisting of a Disbarment, Revocation, Suspension imposed at any time or Public Reprimand imposed within the ten years immediately preceding the proposed appointment date; or (4) a Disciplinary Record in any jurisdiction consisting of Private Discipline, except for a *de minimis* dismissal or a dismissal for exceptional circumstances, or an Admonition imposed within the five years immediately preceding the proposed appointment date. The Standing Committee on Lawyer Discipline shall have the sole discretion to determine whether a *de minimis* dismissal or a dismissal for exceptional circumstances shall disqualify a potential appointee.

G. Interim Vacancies. Whenever a vacancy occurs on a District Committee, the Executive Committee may fill the vacancy. Bar Counsel or a majority of the members of a District Committee may request the Executive Committee to declare that a District Committee position held by any particular District Committee member has become vacant when, in the judgment of Bar Counsel or the Committee majority, such member has become, or has been for any reason, unavailable for or delinquent in the conduct of the District Committee's business. Similarly, upon request of Bar Counsel, the Executive Committee shall have the power to declare such vacancy. Before such vacancy is declared, the particular District Committee member shall be afforded notice and a reasonable opportunity to be heard.

13-5. AUTHORITY AND DUTIES OF COLD

All powers and duties of Council, with respect to the Disciplinary System, except the power to appoint District Committee members, may be exercised by COLD, subject to the direction and control of Council. Notwithstanding any rule to the contrary, any member of COLD may attend proceedings of the Subcommittees, District Committees or the Board. Service by an Attorney on COLD shall be deemed to be a professional relationship within the meaning of Disciplinary Rules 1.6, 1.7, 1.9, 1.10 and 3.7. Such service shall be deemed the holding of public office within the meaning of Disciplinary Rules 1.11 and 1.12. Consent under Disciplinary Rules 1.6, 1.7 and 1.9 shall be deemed to include Bar Counsel's consent on behalf of the Bar. The membership of COLD shall consist of twelve persons, ten of whom shall be active members of the Bar and two shall be nonlawyers. In addition, a vice chair of the Board shall be an ex-officio, nonvoting member.

13-6. DISCIPLINARY BOARD

A. Appointment of Members. This Court shall appoint, upon recommendation of Council, 20 members of the Board, 16 of whom shall be active members of the Bar and four of whom shall be nonlawyers. One Attorney member shall be designated by the Court as Chair and two Attorney members as Vice Chairs, upon recommendations of Council. Before nominating any individual for membership on the Board, the Bar's nominating committee shall first determine that the nominee is willing to serve on the Board and will conscientiously discharge the responsibilities as a member of the Board. All nominees shall have previously served on a district committee. The Bar nominating committee shall also obtain a statement from the nominees, in writing, that the nominees are willing to serve on the Board, if elected and appointed. In order to be considered as a potential appointee to the Board, each potential appointee shall execute the following: (1) a waiver of confidentiality with respect to his or her Disciplinary Record and any pending Complaints and a release allowing production of his or her Disciplinary Record and pending Complaints from any jurisdiction for purposes of the appointment process; and (2) an authorization for the Bar to conduct a criminal records check of all jurisdictions for any conviction of a Crime and provide the results to the members of Council and the staff of the Bar for purposes of the appointment process.

B. Persons Ineligible for Appointment. Any potential appointee shall be ineligible for appointment to the Board if such potential appointee has (1) ever been convicted in any jurisdiction of a Crime; (2) ever committed any criminal act that reflects adversely on the potential appointee's honesty, trustworthiness, or fitness as a Board member; (3) a Disciplinary Record in any jurisdiction of a Disbarment, Revocation, Suspension or Public Reprimand imposed within the ten years immediately preceding the proposed appointment date; (4) a Disciplinary Record in any jurisdiction consisting of Private Discipline, except for a *de minimis* dismissal or a dismissal for exceptional circumstances, or an Admonition within the five years immediately preceding the proposed appointment date. The Standing Committee on Lawyer Discipline shall have the sole discretion to determine whether a *de minimis* dismissal or a dismissal for exceptional circumstances shall disqualify a potential appointee.

C. Term of Office. Members shall serve staggered terms of three years each. No member shall serve more than two consecutive three-year terms but shall be eligible for reappointment after the lapse of one or more years following expiration of the previous three-year term. At the expiration of the initial term of any member so appointed for less than a three-year term, such member shall be eligible for immediate reappointment to the Board for two additional consecutive three-year terms.

D. Meetings and Quorum. The Board shall meet on reasonable notice by the Chair or a Vice Chair. A Panel of five members shall constitute a quorum, and the action of a majority of a Panel shall constitute action of the Board. One of the five persons assigned to any Panel shall be a present or former nonlawyer member. If the scheduled nonlawyer is unable to attend and an alternate nonlawyer member or former member is not reasonably available, participation by a nonlawyer shall not be required in any Proceeding if a quorum is otherwise present.

E. Roster. The Clerk of the Disciplinary System shall establish a roster of Board members sufficient to constitute a quorum for action on the matter to which they are being assigned. Former members of the Board may serve on a Panel of the Board or participate in Board matters whenever the Chair, Vice Chair or Clerk of the Disciplinary System determines that such service is necessary for the orderly administration of the Board's work.

F. Jurisdiction. The Board shall have jurisdiction to consider: (1) Appeals from Public or Private Reprimands, with or without Terms, or Admonitions, with or without Terms, imposed by District Committees or Dismissals that otherwise create a Disciplinary Record; (2) Complaints and Certifications submitted to it by a Subcommittee or a District Committee; (3) Misconduct by reason of conviction of a Crime; (4) Impairment Proceedings; (5) Revocation or Suspension in another jurisdiction; (6) Petitions from Bar Counsel or the Chair of a District Committee seeking summary Suspension upon a belief that an Attorney is engaging in Misconduct likely to result in injury to or loss of property of a client or other entity or alleging an Attorney poses imminent danger to the public; (7) Petitions for Reinstatement referred to the Board for its recommendation to this Court; (8) Violations of CRESPA or any regulations adopted pursuant thereto; (9) Failure of Respondent to make a complete transcript part of the Record, as provided in this Paragraph; (10) Failure of an Attorney to comply with an order, summons or subpoena issued in connection with a Disciplinary Proceeding; and (11) Failure of Respondent to fulfill the terms of a Public Reprimand with Terms certified to it by a District Committee for sanction determination.

G. Additional Board Powers. The Board shall have the following powers in addition to all other powers granted to the Board:

1. To sanction a Respondent for failing to comply with an order issued by the Board. This sanction can include an interim Suspension. Before imposing an interim Suspension, the Board shall issue a notice to the Respondent advising the Respondent that he or she may petition the Board within ten days after service of the notice to withhold entry of an interim Suspension order and to hold an evidentiary hearing. If ten days after service of the notice the Respondent has not petitioned the Board to withhold entry of an interim Suspension order, the Board shall enter an Order suspending the Attorney's License until such time as the Attorney remedies the failure to comply or a determination is made as to whether the Attorney has violated any Disciplinary Rules. An Attorney suspended pursuant to this subparagraph G.1. is subject to the provisions of subparagraph 13-29;

2. On its own motion or upon request by Bar Counsel or the Respondent, to summon and examine witnesses under oath or affirmation administered by any member of the Board and to compel the attendance of witnesses and the production of documents necessary or material to any proceeding. Any summons or subpoena may be issued by any Board member or the Clerk of the Disciplinary System and shall have the force of and may be enforced as a summons or subpoena issued by a Circuit Court. A subpoena duces tecum which compels the Respondent to produce documents may be served upon the Respondent by certified mail at the Respondent's last address of record for membership purposes with the Bar or, if service cannot be effected at the Respondent's last address on record, and if the Respondent is a Foreign Lawyer, a lawyer engaged

pro hac vice in the practice of law in Virginia, or a lawyer not admitted in Virginia, when mailed by first class mail to the Clerk of the Supreme Court of Virginia.

3. To impose an interim Suspension if an Attorney fails to comply with a summons or subpoena issued by any member of the Board, the Clerk of the Disciplinary System, Bar Counsel or any lawyer member of a District Committee for trust account, estate account, fiduciary account, operating account or other records maintained by the Attorney or the Attorney's law firm. In the event of alleged noncompliance, Bar Counsel may file with the Board and serve on the Attorney a notice of noncompliance requesting the Board to suspend the Attorney's License. The noncompliance notice must advise the Attorney that he or she may petition the Board within 10 days of service of the notice to withhold entry of a Suspension order and to hold a hearing, at which time the Attorney shall have the burden of proving good cause for the alleged noncompliance. If 10 days after service of the notice of noncompliance the Attorney has not petitioned the Board to withhold entry of an interim Suspension order, the Board shall enter an Order suspending the Attorney's License until such time as the Attorney fully complies with the summons or subpoena or a determination is made as to whether the Attorney's noncompliance violated the Disciplinary Rules. An Attorney suspended pursuant to this subparagraph G.3. is subject to the provisions of subparagraph 13-29;

4. To rule on the admissibility of evidence, through a panel Chair, which rulings may be overruled by a majority of the Panel; and

5. To act through its Chair or one of the Vice Chairs (an officer) on any non-dispositive pre-hearing matters and on any dispositive matters where all parties are in agreement, subject to the following qualification and exception: (1) any pre-hearing ruling on a non-dispositive matter made by an officer of the Board shall be subject to being overruled by a majority vote of the Panel which actually hears the matter; and (2) Agreed Dispositions must be approved by a Panel.

H. Agreed Disposition. Whenever Bar Counsel and Respondent are in agreement as to the disposition of a Disciplinary Proceeding, the parties may submit a proposed Agreed Disposition to five members of the Board selected by the Chair. The five members so selected will constitute a Panel. If the proposed Agreed Disposition is accepted by a majority of the Panel so selected, the Agreed Disposition will be adopted by order of the Board. If the Agreed Disposition is not accepted by the Panel, the Disciplinary Proceeding will then be set for hearing before another Panel of the Board at the earliest possible date. No member of the Panel which considered the proposed Agreed Disposition shall be assigned to the Panel which hears the Disciplinary Proceeding.

13-7. DISTRICT COMMITTEES

A. Powers. Each District Committee and Section thereof shall have the power to:

1. Elect a Chair, Vice Chair and Secretary, and such other officers as it considers appropriate;

2. Conduct hearings and adjudicate Charges of Misconduct as provided in this Paragraph;

3. Summon and examine witnesses under oath to be administered by any member of the District Committee;

4. Issue, through any of its Attorney members or through Bar Counsel, any summons or subpoena necessary to compel the attendance of witnesses and the production of documents or evidence necessary or material to any Investigation or Disciplinary Proceeding. Any such summons or subpoena issued to a non-Attorney shall have the force of and be enforced as a summons or subpoena issued by a Circuit Court. A subpoena duces tecum which compels the Respondent to produce documents may be served upon the Respondent by certified mail at the Respondent's last address of record for membership purposes with the Bar or, if service cannot be effected at the Respondent's last address on record, and if the Respondent is a Foreign Lawyer, a lawyer engaged *pro hac vice* in the practice of law in Virginia, or a lawyer not admitted in Virginia, when mailed by first class mail to the Clerk of the Supreme Court of Virginia.

5. Direct Bar Counsel to file a notice of noncompliance requesting the Board to suspend an Attorney's License until such time as the Attorney fully complies with a subpoena requiring production of trust account, estate account, fiduciary account, operating account or other records maintained by the Attorney or the Attorney's law firm;

6. Rule on the admissibility of evidence and other matters relating to the conduct of a Disciplinary Proceeding;

7. Rule on motions to limit or quash any summons or subpoena;

8. Maintain order in all its proceedings through its Chair; and

9. Approve, through a Subcommittee acting by a unanimous vote, an Agreed Disposition of a Complaint or Charge of Misconduct submitted by Bar Counsel and the Respondent.

B. Creation of Subcommittees. The Chair shall appoint one or more Subcommittees of each District Committee. Where a District Committee is divided into two or more Sections, there shall be one or more Subcommittees of each Section, as determined by the respective District Committee Section Chair. Each Subcommittee shall consist of three members of that District Committee or that Section of the District Committee. Two members of a Subcommittee shall be members of the Bar, one of whom shall be appointed by the District Committee or Section Chair to act as Chair of that Subcommittee, and one member of the Subcommittee shall be a non-lawyer member.

C. Subcommittee Quorums. A quorum of a Subcommittee shall consist of three members, who may act in a meeting in person or through any means of communication by which all three members participating may simultaneously hear each other during the meeting.

D. District Committee Jurisdiction. A District Committee shall have jurisdiction over all Complaints referred to it.

E. Limitation on Private Discipline. Private Discipline shall be imposed only in cases of minor Misconduct, when there is little or no injury to any of the following: a client, the public, the legal system or the profession, and when there is little likelihood of repetition by the Respondent. When any Respondent has received two determinations of Private Discipline, excepting only *de minimis* Dismissals, during any ten-year period, it shall be presumed that further Private Discipline is not an appropriate disposition. Any Respondent who has received two determinations of Private Discipline within the ten-year period immediately preceding the Bar's receipt of the oldest Complaint that the Subcommittee is considering, shall receive public discipline for any violation of the Disciplinary Rules, unless there are sufficient facts and circumstances to rebut such presumption.

F. Venue. Venue shall not be jurisdictional, but venue shall lie with the District Committee, in the following order of preference, where:

1. Any portion of the alleged Misconduct occurred;
2. The Respondent resides;
3. The Respondent maintains an office;
4. The Respondent has an address on record with the Bar as the Respondent's address for membership purposes; or
5. The Complainant resides.

G. Preferred Venue. If preferred venue does not lie with any District Committee able to adjudicate the Complaint against a Respondent, such Complaint may be filed with and adjudicated by a District Committee designated by the Clerk of the Disciplinary System. In determining to which District Committee a Complaint should be referred, the Clerk of the Disciplinary System shall consider the volume of Complaints pending before the District Committee and the inconvenience imposed upon the Respondent and the witnesses by the location of the District Committee.

H. Objections to Venue. Either the Respondent or Bar Counsel may object to venue by filing a notice of objection with the Clerk of the Disciplinary System within ten days of notification of the referral of the Complaint to a District Committee. Objections to venue shall be deemed waived unless made within this ten-day time period. Upon receipt of a timely filed notice of objection, the Clerk of the Disciplinary System shall forward the notice of objection to the Chair of the Board for decision.

I. Complaints Referred to District Committee or Subcommittee. A District Committee or Subcommittee shall consider, adjudicate and dispose of Complaints referred to the District Committee pursuant to this Paragraph. Where appropriate, the District Committee or Subcommittee shall also counsel Respondents concerning their conduct. In addition, members of a District Committee, other than nonlawyer members, may participate in the Investigation of Complaints, provided that a member participating in such Investigation shall not participate in a District Committee's consideration, adjudication and disposition of such Complaint or Charge of Misconduct.

J. Service by a Member of the Bar and Professional Relationship. Service by a member of the Bar on a District Committee shall be deemed to be a professional relationship within the meaning of Disciplinary Rules 1.6, 1.7, 1.9, 1.10 and 3.7. Such service shall be deemed the holding of public office within the meaning of Disciplinary Rules 1.11 and 1.12.

K. Consent by Bar Counsel. Consent under Disciplinary Rules 1.6, 1.7 and 1.9 shall be deemed to include Bar Counsel's consent on behalf of the Bar.

L. Recusal or Disqualification of District Committee Members. In the event of recusal or disqualification of so many District Committee members that the District Committee is unable to discharge its responsibilities under this Rule, the District Committee may supplement its membership with members from other District Committees to achieve a quorum. If every member of a District Committee is recused or is disqualified from considering Charges of Misconduct, the Clerk of the Disciplinary System shall assign the Charges of Misconduct to another District Committee.

13-8. BAR COUNSEL

A. Authority. Bar Counsel shall have the authority, to the extent provided in this Paragraph and subject to the general supervision of COLD, to:

1. Initiate, investigate, present or prosecute Complaints or other Proceedings before Subcommittees, District Committees, the Board and Circuit Courts. Bar Counsel may represent the Bar in matters pending in this Court. In the course of performing such functions, Bar Counsel shall act independently and exercise prosecutorial autonomy and discretion;

2. Examine criminal history record information relating to any Attorney or former Attorney from any state or federal law enforcement agency;

3. Examine financial books and records, once a Complaint has been filed, including, without limitation, any and all escrow accounts, trust accounts, estate accounts, fiduciary accounts and operating or other accounts, maintained by the Attorney, the Attorney's law firm or any other third party organization by whom the Attorney is employed or with whom the Attorney is associated;

4. Examine the accounts described in the preceding subparagraph A.3. at any time when Bar Counsel reasonably believes that such accounts may not be in compliance with the Disciplinary Rules. In every instance in which Bar Counsel initiates examination of accounts or issues any summons or subpoena in the conduct of an examination or an Investigation concerning accounts, other than on the basis of a Complaint against the Attorney, Bar Counsel shall file a written statement as part of the record setting forth the reasons supporting the belief that the accounts may not comply with the Disciplinary Rules. A copy of this written statement shall be served upon the Attorney who is the subject of the Investigation when an examination has begun or any summons or subpoena has been issued;

5. Issue such summons for the attendance of witnesses and subpoenae for the production of documents necessary or material to any Investigation, District Committee or Board proceeding; and

6. File a notice of noncompliance requesting the Board to suspend the Attorney's License until such time as the Attorney fully complies with a subpoena issued by the Bar Counsel, a District Committee or the Board, for the production of trust account, estate account, fiduciary account, operating account or other records maintained by the Attorney or the Attorney's law firm.

B. Acting Bar Counsel. In the event of disqualification or recusal of Bar Counsel in any Proceeding, the allegation of Misconduct shall be prosecuted by a District Committee member designated by the District Committee Chair if the Proceeding is before a District Committee, or by the Attorney General or his designee if the Proceeding is before the Board or a three-judge Circuit Court.

13-9. CLERK OF THE DISCIPLINARY SYSTEM

A. Current Dockets. The Clerk of the Disciplinary System shall maintain a docket of current Attorney discipline and CRESPA matters pending before the District Committees, the Board or courts of this Commonwealth.

B. Records Retention. The Clerk of the Disciplinary System shall retain all Files with respect to any Disciplinary Record for a period of at least five years from the date of the final Order in the Disciplinary Proceeding that created that Disciplinary Record. The Clerk may destroy all other Files upon the expiration of one year after the Dismissal.

C. File Destruction. Whenever a File is destroyed, the following information shall be preserved:

1. The name and Bar identification number of Respondent;
2. The name and last known address of the Complainant;
3. The date the matter was initially received by the Bar;
4. A summary of the Complaint or allegation of Misconduct;
5. The date of the Dismissal or any sanction(s) imposed; and
6. The disposition of the matter, including the basis for Dismissal or the sanction(s) imposed.

Such summary information shall be retained for at least five years whenever the Complaint or allegation of Misconduct is dismissed with no Disciplinary Record having been created, and for at least ten years whenever a Disciplinary Record has been created, an Impairment determined, a Reinstatement Proceeding held, or a finding of Misconduct involving a CRESPA violation made.

D. Preservation of Determinations and Orders. The Clerk of the Disciplinary System shall preserve a copy of all District Committee Determinations and Board or court orders in which an Attorney has been found to have engaged in Misconduct, to be impaired, to have committed a violation of CRESPA or requested Reinstatement.

E. Costs. The Clerk of the Disciplinary System shall assess Costs against the Respondent in the following cases:

1. All cases in which a final determination of Misconduct is made by a Subcommittee, District Committee, three-judge Circuit Court, the Board or this Court;
2. All cases against a Respondent who consents to revocation;
3. All proceedings under this Paragraph in which there is a finding that a Respondent has been found guilty of a Crime;
4. All reciprocal cases under this Paragraph in which a final determination imposing discipline is made;
5. All Reinstatement cases under this Paragraph; and
6. All cases before the Board in which sanctions were imposed for violations of CRESPA and/or the Bar's CRESPA regulations.

F. Review of Costs Assessment. If the Respondent disagrees with the amount of Costs as calculated by the Clerk, or if the Respondent asserts that the immediate payment thereof would constitute a hardship, the Respondent may petition the Board for review within ten days of the notice assessing Costs. The Chair, upon written request of Respondent, included with his petition, may grant Respondent a hearing on the Costs issue. The decision of the Chair shall be final and non-appealable. Interest at the judgment rate shall commence on the Costs assessed 30 days after the issuance of the notice of assessment, unless otherwise prescribed by the Board. If the Respondent fails to pay the Costs and interest so assessed within 30 days of the notice of assessment or within such other time as the Board may order, then the Costs assessed and interest shall be a debt subject to collection by the Bar, and the Board shall issue an order of Suspension against the Respondent until such time as Respondent shall pay all of the Costs and accrued interest.

G. Public Notification of Sanctions. The Clerk shall issue a statement to the communications media summarizing each public Admonition, Public Reprimand, Suspension or Revocation. The Clerk shall notify the following individuals and entities of each public Admonition, Public Reprimand, Suspension or Revocation:

1. The Clerk of the Supreme Court;
2. Clerks of the Circuit and District Courts in each judicial circuit in the Commonwealth where the Attorney resides or maintains an office; and
3. Disciplinary authorities for jurisdictions, federal or state, wherein it is reasonable to expect that the Attorney may be licensed.

13-10. PROCESSING OF COMPLAINTS BY BAR COUNSEL.

A. Review. Bar Counsel shall review all Complaints. If, following review of a Complaint, Bar Counsel determines that the conduct questioned or alleged does not present an issue under the Disciplinary Rules, Bar Counsel shall not open an Investigation, and the Complaint shall be dismissed.

B. No Dismissal by Complainant. No Complaint or allegation of Misconduct shall be dismissed at any stage of the process solely upon a request by a Complainant to withdraw his or her Complaint.

C. Summary Resolution. Bar Counsel shall decide whether a Complaint is appropriate for an informal or abbreviated Investigation. When a Complaint involves minor allegations of Misconduct susceptible to early resolution, Bar Counsel may assign the Complaint to a staff member, a District Committee member, or use any other means practicable to speedily investigate and resolve the allegations of Misconduct. If the Complaint is resolved through this process, Bar Counsel shall then dismiss the Complaint. Such dismissal shall not become a part of the Respondent's Disciplinary Record. If Bar Counsel chooses not to proceed under this subsection, or, having elected to proceed under this subsection, the Complaint is not resolved within 90 days from the date of filing, Bar Counsel shall proceed pursuant to the following subsections.

D. Preliminary Investigation. A preliminary Investigation may consist of obtaining a response, in writing, from the Respondent to the Complaint and sharing the response, if any, with the Complainant, so the Complainant may have an opportunity to provide additional information.

E. Disposition by Bar Counsel after Preliminary Investigation. Bar Counsel may conduct a preliminary Investigation of any Complaint to determine whether it should be referred to the District Committee. Bar Counsel shall not file a Complaint with a District Committee following a preliminary Investigation when, in Bar Counsel's judgment:

1. As a matter of law, the conduct questioned or alleged does not constitute Misconduct;

2. The evidence available shows that the Respondent did not engage in the Misconduct questioned or alleged;

3. There is no credible evidence to support any allegation of Misconduct by the Respondent; or

4. The evidence available could not reasonably be expected to support any allegation of Misconduct under a clear and convincing evidentiary standard.

F. Referral to District Committee. Bar Counsel shall notify the District Committee Chair that a Complaint has been referred to a District Committee for investigation. Thereafter, the Complaint shall be investigated and a report thereof made to a Subcommittee.

G. Report to Subcommittee. When submitting an Investigative Report to the Subcommittee, Bar Counsel or Committee Counsel may also send a recommendation as to the appropriate disposition of the Complaint.

13-11. LIMITED RIGHT TO DISCOVERY.

There shall be no right to discovery in connection with disciplinary matters, including matters before three-judge Circuit Courts, except:

A. Issuance of such summonses and subpoenae as are authorized; and

B. Bar Counsel shall furnish to Respondent a copy of the Investigative Report considered by the Subcommittee when the Subcommittee set the Complaint for hearing before the District Committee or certified the Complaint to the Board, with the following limitations:

1. Bar Counsel shall not be required to produce any information or document obtained in confidence from any law enforcement or disciplinary agency, or any documents that are protected by the attorney-client privilege or work product doctrine, unless attached to or referenced in the Investigative Report;

2. Bar Counsel shall not be required to reveal other communications between the Investigator and Bar Counsel, or between Bar Counsel and the Subcommittee; and

3. Bar Counsel shall make a timely disclosure to the Respondent of all known evidence that tends to negate the Misconduct of the Respondent or mitigate its severity or which, upon a finding of Misconduct, would tend to support imposition of a lesser sanction than might be otherwise imposed.

13-12. SUBSTANTIAL COMPLIANCE, NOTICE AND EVIDENTIARY RULINGS, AND ADDRESS NOTIFICATION.

A. Substantial Compliance. Except where this Paragraph provides specific time deadlines, substantial compliance with the provisions hereof shall be sufficient, and no allegation of Misconduct shall be dismissed on the sole ground that any such provision has not been strictly complied with.

B. Time Deadlines. Where specific time deadlines are provided, such deadlines shall be jurisdictional, except when the Clerk of the Disciplinary System, Bar Counsel, a District Committee or the Board is granted specific authority herein to extend or otherwise modify any such deadline.

C. Service. Whenever any notice or other writing directed to the Respondent is required or permitted under this Rule, such notice or other writing shall be deemed effective and served when mailed by certified mail to the Respondent at the Respondent's last address on record for membership purposes with the Bar or, if service cannot be effected at the Respondent's last address on record, and if the Respondent is a Foreign Lawyer, a lawyer engaged *pro hac vice* in the practice of law in Virginia, or a lawyer not admitted in Virginia, when mailed by first class mail to the Clerk of the Supreme Court of Virginia.

D. Evidentiary Rulings. In any Disciplinary Proceeding, evidentiary rulings shall be made favoring receipt into evidence of all reasonably probative evidence to satisfy the ends of justice. The weight given such evidence received shall be commensurate with its evidentiary foundation and likely reliability.

E. Rights of Counsel for Complainant or Witness. Neither counsel for the Complainant, if there is one, nor counsel for any witnesses, may examine or cross-examine any witness, introduce any evidence or present any argument.

F. Notice of Impairment Evidence. A Respondent who intends to rely upon evidence of an Impairment in mitigation of Misconduct shall, absent good cause excusing his or her failure to do so, provide notice not less than 14 days prior to the hearing to Bar Counsel and the District Committee or Board of his or her intention to do so.

G. English Required. All communication with the Bar, whether written or oral, shall be in English.

13-13. PARTICIPATION AND DISQUALIFICATION OF COUNSEL.

A. Attorney for Respondent. A Respondent may be represented by a member of the Bar, or any member of the bar of any other jurisdiction while engaged *pro hac vice* in the practice of law in Virginia, at any time with respect to a Complaint.

B. Signature Required by Respondent. A Respondent must sign his or her written response to any Complaint, allegation of Misconduct or Certification.

C. Disqualification. An Attorney shall not represent a Respondent at any time with respect to a Complaint or allegation of Misconduct:

1. While such Attorney is a current employee or current officer of the Bar or is a member of Council, COLD, the Board, or a District Committee;

2. For 90 days after such Attorney ceases to be an employee or officer of the Bar or a member of Council, COLD, the Board, or a District Committee;

3. At any time, after such Attorney ceases to be an employee or officer of the Bar or a member of Council, COLD, the Board or a District Committee, if such Attorney was personally involved in the subject matter of the Complaint, allegation of Misconduct or any related matter while acting as such employee, officer or member;

4. At any time after such Attorney ceased to be a liaison from COLD to a District Committee before which the Disciplinary Proceeding involving such Complaint or Charge of Misconduct was pending during the time such Attorney was such liaison; or

5. If such Attorney is a partner or an associate of, or is a member, shareholder or has a similar relation with any Attorney described in the preceding subparagraphs C.1. through C.4.

13-14. DISQUALIFICATION OF DISTRICT COMMITTEE MEMBER OR BOARD MEMBER

A. Personal or Financial Interest. A member or former member of a District Committee or the Board shall be disqualified from adjudicating any matter with respect to which the member has any personal or financial interest that might affect or reasonably be perceived to affect the member's ability to be impartial. The Chair shall rule on the issue of disqualification, subject to being overruled by a majority of the Panel or Subcommittee.

B. Complaint Against a Member. Upon the referral of any Complaint against a member or former member of a District Committee or the Board to a District Committee for Investigation, the member shall be recused from any service on the District Committee or the Board until the Dismissal of the Complaint without the imposition of any form of discipline.

C. Imposition of Discipline. Upon the final imposition of a Private Reprimand, a Public Reprimand, an Admonition, a Suspension or a Revocation against a member or former member of a District Committee or the Board, the member shall automatically be terminated from membership or further service on the District Committee or Board. Upon the final imposition of any other form of Attorney discipline, COLD shall have sole discretion to determine whether the member shall be terminated from membership or further service on the District Committee or the Board.

D. Interpretation. Unless otherwise stated, all questions of interpretation under this subparagraph 13-14 shall be decided by the tribunal before which the proceeding is pending, except that COLD shall determine discretionary termination of membership or further service.

E. Ineligibility. Any member or former member of a District Committee or the Board shall be ineligible to serve in a Disciplinary Proceeding in which:

1. The District Committee or Board member or any member of his or her firm is involved in any significant way with the matter on which the District Committee or Board would act;

2. The Board member or any member of the Board member's firm was serving on the District Committee that certified the matter to the Board or has otherwise acted on the matter;

3. A Judge would be required to withdraw from consideration of, or presiding over, the matter under the Canons of Judicial Conduct adopted by this Court;

4. The District Committee or Board member previously represented the Respondent; or

5. The District Committee or Board member, upon reasonable notice to the Clerk of the Disciplinary System or to the Chair, presiding over a matter, disqualifies himself or herself from participation in the matter, because such member believes that he or she is unable to participate objectively in consideration of the matter or for any other reason.

13-15. SUBCOMMITTEE ACTION

A. Referral. Following receipt of the report of Investigation and Bar Counsel's recommendation, the Subcommittee may refer the matter to Bar Counsel for further Investigation.

B. Other Actions. Once the Investigation is complete to the Subcommittee's satisfaction, it will take one of the following actions.

1. Dismiss. It shall dismiss the Complaint when:

a. As a matter of law the conduct questioned or alleged does not constitute Misconduct; or

b. The evidence available shows that the Respondent did not engage in the Misconduct questioned or alleged, or there is no credible evidence to support any allegation of Misconduct by Respondent, or the evidence available could not reasonably be expected to support any allegation of Misconduct under a clear and convincing evidentiary standard; or

c. The Subcommittee concludes that a Dismissal *De Minimis* should be imposed; or

d. The Subcommittee concludes that a Dismissal for Exceptional Circumstances should be imposed; or

e. The action alleged to be Misconduct is protected by superseding law.

In making the determination in the preceding subparagraphs B.1.c. and B.1.d., the Subcommittee shall have access to Respondent's prior Disciplinary Record. Respondent, within ten days after the issuance of a dismissal which creates a Disciplinary Record, may request a hearing before the District Committee.

2. Impose an Admonition without Terms. In making this determination, the Subcommittee shall have access to Respondent's prior Disciplinary Record. Respondent, within ten days after the issuance of an Admonition without Terms, may request a hearing before the District Committee.

3. Certify to the Board. Certify the Complaint to the Board pursuant to this Paragraph or file a complaint in a Circuit Court, pursuant to Va. Code § 54.1-3935. Certification shall be based on a reasonable belief that the Respondent has engaged or is engaging in Misconduct that, if proved, would justify a Suspension or Revocation. In making this determination, the Subcommittee shall have access to Respondent's prior Disciplinary Record.

4. Approve an Agreed Disposition. Approve an Agreed Disposition imposing one of the following conditions or sanctions:

a. Admonition, with or without Terms; or

b. Private Reprimand, with or without Terms; or

c. Public Reprimand, with or without Terms.

5. Set the Complaint for Hearing before the District Committee. In making this determination, the Subcommittee shall have access to Respondent's prior Disciplinary Record.

C. Vote Required for Action. All actions taken by Subcommittees, except for approval of Agreed Dispositions, shall be by majority vote.

D. Report of the Subcommittee. All decisions of the Subcommittee shall be reported to the District Committee in a timely fashion.

E. Notice of Action of the Subcommittee. If a Subcommittee has dismissed the Complaint, the Chair shall promptly provide written notice to the Complainant, the Respondent and Bar Counsel of such Dismissal and the factual and legal basis therefor. If a Subcommittee determines to issue an Admonition with or without Terms, or a Private or Public Reprimand with or without Terms, the Chair shall promptly send the Complainant, the Respondent and Bar Counsel a copy of the Subcommittee's determination. If a Subcommittee elects to certify a Complaint to the Board, the Subcommittee Chair shall promptly mail a copy of the Certification to the Clerk of the Disciplinary System, Bar Counsel, the Respondent and the Complainant.

F. Procedure in All Terms Cases. If a Subcommittee imposes Terms, the Subcommittee shall specify the time period within which compliance with the Terms shall be completed. If Terms have been imposed against a Respondent, that Respondent shall deliver a certification of compliance with such Terms to Bar Counsel within the time period specified by the Subcommittee. If a Subcommittee issues an Admonition with Terms, a Private Reprimand with Terms, or a Public Reprimand with Terms based on an Agreed Disposition, the Agreed Disposition shall specify the alternative disposition to be imposed if the Terms are not complied with or if the Respondent does not certify compliance with Terms to Bar Counsel. If the Respondent does not comply with the Terms imposed or does not certify compliance with Terms to Bar Counsel within the time period specified, Bar Counsel shall serve notice requiring the Respondent to show cause why the alternative disposition should not be imposed. Such show cause proceeding shall be set for hearing before the District Committee at its next available hearing date as determined in the discretion of the District Committee Chair. The burden of proof shall be on the Respondent to show timely compliance and timely certification by clear and convincing evidence. If the District Committee determines that the Respondent failed to comply with the Terms or failed to certify compliance within the stated time period, the alternative disposition shall be imposed. Bar Counsel shall be responsible for monitoring compliance with Terms and reporting any noncompliance to the District Committee.

G. Alternative Disposition for Public Reprimand with Terms. The alternative disposition for a Public Reprimand with Terms shall be a Certification For Sanction Determination unless the Respondent has entered into an Agreed Disposition for the imposition of an alternative disposition of a specific period of Suspension of License.

13-16. DISTRICT COMMITTEE PROCEEDINGS.

A. Charge of Misconduct. If the Subcommittee determines that a hearing should be held before a District Committee, Bar Counsel shall, at least 42 days prior to the date fixed for the hearing, serve upon the Respondent by certified mail the Charge of Misconduct, a copy of the Investigative Report considered by the Subcommittee and any exculpatory materials in the possession of Bar Counsel.

B. Response by Respondent Required. After the Respondent has been served with the Charge of Misconduct, the Respondent shall, within 21 days after service of the Charge of Misconduct:

1. File an answer to the Charge of Misconduct, which answer shall be deemed consent to the jurisdiction of the District Committee; or

2. File an answer to the Charge of Misconduct and a demand with the Clerk of the Disciplinary System that the proceedings before the District Committee be terminated and that further proceedings be conducted pursuant to Va. Code § 54.1-3935; and simultaneously provide available dates for a hearing not less than 30 nor more than 120 days from the date of the demand. Upon such demand and provision of available dates as specified above, further proceedings before the District Committee shall terminate, and Bar Counsel shall file the complaint required by Va. Code § 54.1-3935. The hearing shall be scheduled as soon as practicable. However, the 30 to 120 day time frame shall not constitute a deadline for the hearing to be held.

C. Failure of Respondent to Respond. If the Respondent fails to file an answer, or an answer and a demand, and provide available dates, as specified above, the Respondent shall be deemed to have consented to the jurisdiction of the District Committee.

D. Pre-Hearing Orders. The Chair may, *sua sponte* or upon motion of the Respondent or Bar Counsel, enter such pre-hearing order as is necessary for the orderly conduct of the hearing before the District Committee. Such order may establish time limits and:

1. Direct Bar Counsel and Respondent to provide to each other, with a copy to the Chair, a list of and copies of all exhibits proposed to be introduced at the Misconduct stage of the hearing;

2. Encourage Bar Counsel and Respondent to confer and discuss stipulations; and

3. Direct Bar Counsel and Respondent to serve on each other, with a copy to the Chair, lists setting forth the name of each witness the party intends to call.

E. Subpoenae, Summonses and Counsel. The Respondent may be represented by counsel. The Respondent may request Bar Counsel or the Chair of the District Committee to issue summonses or subpoenae for witnesses and documents. Requests for summonses and subpoenae shall be granted, unless, in the judgment of the Chair of the District Committee, such request is unreasonable. Either Bar Counsel or Respondent may move the District Committee to quash such summonses or subpoenae.

F. Continuances. Once a District Committee has scheduled a hearing, no continuance shall be granted unless in the judgment of the Chair the continuance is necessary to prevent injustice.

G. Public Hearings. District Committee hearings, except deliberations, shall be open to the public.

H. Public Docket. The Clerk's Office shall maintain a public docket of all matters set for hearing before a District Committee or certified to the Board. For every matter before a District Committee for which a Charge of Misconduct has been mailed by the Office of the Bar Counsel, the Clerk shall place it on the docket 21 days after the date of the Charge of Misconduct. For every Complaint certified to the Board by a Subcommittee, the Clerk shall place it on the docket on receipt of the statement of the certified charges from the Subcommittee.

I. Oral Testimony and Exhibits. Oral testimony shall be taken and preserved by a Court Reporter. All exhibits or copies thereof received in evidence or marked refused by the District Committee shall be preserved in the District Committee file on the matter.

J. Opening Remarks by the Chair. After swearing the Court Reporter, who thereafter shall administer oaths or affirmations to witnesses, the Chair shall make opening remarks in the presence of the Respondent and the Complainant, if present. The Chair shall also inquire of the members present whether any member has any personal or financial interest that may affect, or be reasonably perceived to affect, his or her ability to be impartial. Any member answering in the affirmative shall be excused from participation in the matter.

K. Motion to Exclude Witnesses. Witnesses other than the Complainant and the Respondent shall be excluded until excused from a public hearing on motion of Bar Counsel, the Respondent or the District Committee.

L. Presentation of the Bar's Evidence. Bar Counsel or Committee Counsel shall present witnesses and other evidence supporting the Charge of Misconduct. Respondent shall be afforded the opportunity to cross-examine the Bar's witnesses and to challenge any evidence introduced on behalf of the Bar. District Committee members may also examine witnesses offered by Bar Counsel or Committee Counsel.

M. Presentation of the Respondent's Evidence. Respondent shall be afforded the opportunity to present witnesses and other evidence on behalf of Respondent. Bar Counsel or Committee's Counsel shall be afforded the opportunity to cross-examine Respondent's witnesses and to challenge any evidence introduced on behalf of Respondent. District Committee members may also examine witnesses offered on behalf of Respondent.

N. No Participation by Other Counsel. Neither counsel for the Complainant, if there be one, nor counsel for any witness, may examine or cross-examine any witness, introduce any other evidence, or present any argument.

O. Depositions. Depositions may be taken only when witnesses are unavailable, in accordance with Rule 4:7(a)(4) of the Rules of this Court.

P. Testimony by Videoconferencing and Telephone. Testimony by videoconferencing and/or telephonic means may be utilized, if in compliance with the Rules of this Court.

Q. Admissibility of Evidence. The Chair shall rule on the admissibility of evidence, which rulings may be overruled by a majority of the remaining District Committee members participating in the hearing.

R. Motion to Strike. At the conclusion of the Bar's evidence or at the conclusion of all of the evidence, the District Committee on its own motion, or the Respondent or the Respondent's counsel may move to strike the Bar's evidence as to one or more allegations of Misconduct contained in the Charge of Misconduct. A motion to strike an allegation of Misconduct shall be sustained if the Bar has failed to introduce sufficient evidence that would under any set of circumstances support the conclusion that the Respondent engaged in the alleged Misconduct that is the subject of the motion to strike. If the Chair sustains the motion to strike an allegation of Misconduct, subject to being overruled by a majority of the remaining members of the Committee, that allegation of Misconduct shall be dismissed.

S. Argument. The District Committee shall afford a reasonable opportunity for argument on behalf of the Respondent and Bar Counsel on the allegations of Misconduct.

T. Deliberations. The District Committee members shall deliberate in private on the allegations of Misconduct. After due deliberation and consideration, the District Committee shall vote on the allegations of Misconduct.

U. Change in District Committee Composition. When a hearing has been adjourned for any reason and any of the members initially constituting the quorum for the hearing cannot be present, the hearing of the matter may be completed by furnishing a transcript of the subsequent proceedings conducted in one or more member's absence to any such absent member or members; or substituting another District Committee member for any absent member or members and furnishing a transcript of the prior proceedings in the matter to such substituted member or members.

V. Show Cause for Compliance with Terms. Any show cause proceeding involving the question of compliance with Terms shall be deemed a new hearing and not a continuation of the hearing that resulted in the imposition of Terms.

W. Dismissal. After due deliberation and consideration, the District Committee may dismiss the Charge of Misconduct, or any allegation thereof, as not warranting further action when in the judgment of the District Committee:

1. As a matter of law the conduct questioned or alleged does not constitute Misconduct;

2. The evidence presented shows that the Respondent did not engage in the Misconduct alleged, or there is no credible evidence to support any allegation of Misconduct by Respondent, or the evidence does not reasonably support any allegation of Misconduct under a clear and convincing evidentiary standard;

3. The action alleged to be Misconduct is protected by superseding law; or

4. The District Committee is unable to reach a decision by a majority vote of those constituting the hearing panel, the Charge of Misconduct, or any allegation thereof, shall be dismissed on the basis that the evidence does not reasonably support the Charge of Misconduct, or one or more allegations thereof, under a clear and convincing evidentiary standard.

X. Sanctions. If the District Committee finds that Misconduct has been shown by clear and convincing evidence, then the District Committee shall, prior to determining the appropriate sanction to be imposed, inquire whether the Respondent has been the subject of any Disciplinary Proceedings in this or any other jurisdiction and shall give Bar Counsel and the Respondent an opportunity to present material evidence in aggravation or mitigation, as well as argument. In determining what disposition of the Charge of Misconduct is warranted, the District Committee shall consider the Respondent's Disciplinary Record. A District Committee may:

1. Conclude that a Dismissal *De Minimis* should be imposed;

2. Conclude that a Dismissal for Exceptional Circumstances should be imposed;

3. Conclude that an Admonition, with or without Terms, should be imposed;

4. Issue a Public Reprimand, with or without Terms; or

5. Certify the Charge of Misconduct to the Board or file a complaint in a Circuit Court, pursuant to Va. Code § 54.1-3935.

Y. District Committee Determinations. If the District Committee finds that the evidence shows the Respondent engaged in Misconduct by clear and convincing evidence, then the Chair shall issue the District Committee's Determination, in writing, setting forth the following:

1. Brief findings of the facts established by the evidence;

2. The nature of the Misconduct shown by the facts so established, including the Disciplinary Rules violated by the Respondent; and

3. The sanctions imposed, if any, by the District Committee.

Z. Notices.

If the District Committee:

1. Issues a Dismissal, the Chair shall promptly provide written notice to the Complainant, the Respondent and Bar Counsel of such Dismissal and the factual and legal basis therefor.

2. Issues a Public Reprimand, with or without Terms; an Admonition, with or without Terms; a Dismissal *De Minimis*; or a Dismissal for Exceptional Circumstances, the Chair shall promptly send the Complainant, the Respondent and Bar Counsel a copy of the District Committee's Determination.

3. Finds that the Respondent failed to comply with the Terms imposed by the District Committee, the Chair shall notify the Complainant, the Respondent and Bar Counsel of the imposition of the alternative disposition.

4. Has elected to certify the Complaint, the Chair of the District Committee shall promptly mail to the Clerk of the Disciplinary System a copy of the Certification. A copy of the Certification shall be sent to Bar Counsel, Respondent and the Complainant.

AA. District Committee Determination Finality and Public Statement. Upon the expiration of the ten-day period after service on the Respondent of a District Committee Determination, if either a notice of appeal or a notice of appeal and a written demand that further Proceedings be conducted before a three-judge Circuit Court pursuant to Va. Code § 54.1-3935 has not been filed by the Respondent, the District Committee Determination shall become final, and the Clerk of the Disciplinary System shall issue a public statement as provided for in this Paragraph for the dissemination of public disciplinary information.

BB. Enforcement of Terms. In all cases where Terms are included in the disposition, the District Committee shall specify the time period within which compliance shall be completed and, if required, the time period within which the Respondent shall deliver a written certification of compliance to Bar Counsel. The District Committee shall specify the alternative disposition if the Terms are not complied with or, if required, compliance is not certified to Bar Counsel. Bar Counsel shall be responsible for monitoring compliance and reporting any noncompliance to the District Committee. Whenever it appears that the Respondent has not complied with the Terms imposed, including written certification of compliance if required, Bar Counsel shall serve notice requiring the Respondent to show cause why the alternative disposition should not be imposed. Such show cause proceeding shall be set for hearing before the District Committee at its next available hearing date as determined in the discretion of the District Committee Chair. The burden of proof shall be on the Respondent to show compliance by clear and convincing evidence. If the Respondent has failed to comply with the Terms, including written certification of compliance if required, within the stated time period as determined by the District Committee, the alternative disposition shall be imposed. Any show cause proceeding involving the question of compliance shall be deemed a new matter and not a continuation of the matter that resulted in the imposition of Terms.

CC. Alternative Disposition and Procedure for Public Reprimand with Terms. The alternative disposition for a Public Reprimand with Terms shall be a Certification for Sanction Determination. Upon a decision to issue a Certification for Sanction Determination, Bar Counsel shall order the transcript of the show cause hearing and file it and a true copy of the Public Reprimand with Terms determination with the Clerk of the Disciplinary System.

DD. Reconsideration of Action by the District Committee.

1. A Charge of Misconduct dismissed by a District Committee may be reconsidered only upon:

(a) A finding by a majority vote of the Panel that heard the matter originally that material evidence not known or available when the matter was originally presented has been discovered; or

(b) A unanimous vote of the Panel that heard the matter originally.

2. No action by a District Committee imposing a sanction or certifying a matter to the Board shall be reconsidered unless a majority of the Panel that heard the matter votes to reconsider the sanction.

3. No member shall vote to reconsider a District Committee action unless it appears to such member that reconsideration is necessary to prevent an injustice or warranted by specific exceptional circumstances militating against adherence to the initial action of the District Committee.

4. District Committee members may be polled on the issue of whether to reconsider an earlier District Committee action.

5. Any reconsideration of an earlier District Committee action must occur at a District Committee meeting, whether in person or by any means of communication which allows all members participating to simultaneously hear each other.

13-17. PERFECTING AN APPEAL OF A DISTRICT COMMITTEE DETERMINATION BY THE RESPONDENT

A. Notice of Appeal; Demand. Within ten days after service on the Respondent of the District Committee Determination, the Respondent may file with the Clerk of the Disciplinary System either a notice of appeal to the Board or a notice of appeal and a written demand that further Proceedings be conducted pursuant to Va. Code § 54.1-3935. In either case, the Respondent shall send copies to the District Committee Chair and to Bar Counsel. Upon such demand, further proceedings before the Board shall terminate, and Bar Counsel shall file the complaint required by Va. Code § 54.1-3935. The hearing shall be scheduled as soon as practicable. If the Respondent fails to file a demand, as specified above, the Respondent shall be deemed to have consented to the jurisdiction of the Board.

B. Staying of Discipline. If the Clerk of the Disciplinary System receives a timely notice of appeal from a Public Reprimand, with or without Terms, or an Admonition, with or without Terms, the sanction shall be stayed during the pendency of the appeal.

C. Filing the Transcript and Record on Appeal. The Respondent shall certify in the notice of appeal or written demand that he or she has ordered from the Court Reporter a complete transcript of the proceedings before the District Committee, at the Respondent's cost. Upon receipt of the notice of appeal or written demand, Bar Counsel shall forward those portions of the record in his or her possession to the Clerk of the Disciplinary System. The transcript is a part of the record when it is received in the office of the Clerk of the Disciplinary System within 40 days after filing of the notice of appeal or written demand. The Clerk of the Disciplinary System shall retain the records until the transcript has been received or for 40 days after the notice of appeal or written demand has been received, whichever occurs first, and shall then dispose of the record as prescribed in the records retention policy set forth in this Paragraph. Failure of the Respondent to make the complete transcript a part of the Record as specified herein shall result in Dismissal of the appeal by the Board, whether initiated by notice of appeal or written demand, and affirmance of the sanction imposed by the District Committee. Bar Counsel shall initiate the three-judge Circuit Court process for the appeal only after receipt of the transcript by the Clerk of the Disciplinary System.

D. Appeal to a Circuit Court. An appeal to a Circuit Court pursuant to Va. Code § 54.1-3935 shall be conducted before a duly convened three-judge Circuit Court as an appeal on the record using the same procedure prescribed for an appeal of a District Committee Determination before the Board under this Paragraph. The Clerk of the Disciplinary System shall forward the record to the clerk of the designated Circuit Court only upon receipt of the transcript as provided in the preceding subparagraph C.

E. Appeal from Agreed Sanction Prohibited. No appeal shall lie from any sanction to which the Respondent has agreed.

13-18. BOARD PROCEEDINGS UPON CERTIFICATION.

A. Filing by Respondent. After a Subcommittee or District Committee certifies a matter to the Board, and the Respondent has been served with the Certification, the Respondent shall, within 21 days after service of the Certification:

1. File an answer to the Certification with the Clerk of the Disciplinary System, which answer shall be deemed consent to the jurisdiction of the Board; or file an answer to the Certification and a demand with the Clerk of the Disciplinary System that the proceedings before the Board be terminated and that further proceedings be conducted pursuant to Va. Code § 54.1-3935; and simultaneously provide available dates for a hearing not less than 30 nor more than 120 days from the date of the demand.

2. Upon such demand and provision of available dates as specified above, further proceedings before the Board shall terminate, and Bar Counsel shall file the complaint required by Va. Code § 54.1-3935. The hearing shall be scheduled as soon as practicable. However, the 30 to 120 day time frame shall not constitute a deadline for the hearing to be held.

B. No Filing by Respondent. If the Respondent fails to file an answer, or an answer and a demand, and provide available dates, as specified above, the Respondent shall be deemed to have consented to the jurisdiction of the Board.

C. Notice of Hearing. The Board shall set a date, time, and place for the hearing, and shall serve notice of such hearing upon the Respondent at least 21 days prior to the date fixed for the hearing.

D. Expedited Hearings.

1. If Bar Counsel or a District Committee Chair has reasonable cause to believe that an Attorney is engaging in Misconduct which is likely to result in injury to, or loss of property of, one or more of the Attorney's clients or any other person, and that the continued practice of law by the Attorney poses an imminent danger to the public, Bar Counsel or the District Committee Chair may petition the Board to issue an order requiring the Attorney to appear before the Board for a hearing in accordance with the procedures set forth below.

2. The petition shall be under oath and shall set forth the nature of the alleged Misconduct, the factual basis for the belief that immediate action by the Board is reasonable and necessary and any other facts which may be relevant to the Board's consideration of the matter, including any prior Disciplinary Record of the Attorney.

3. Upon receipt of the petition, the Chair or Vice-Chair of the Board shall issue an order requiring the Respondent to appear before the Board not less than 14 nor more than 30 days from the date of the order for a hearing to determine whether the Misconduct has occurred and the imposition of sanctions is appropriate. The Board's order shall be served on the Respondent no fewer than ten days prior to the date set for hearing.

4. If the Respondent, at the time the petition is received by the Board, is the subject of an order then in effect by a Circuit Court pursuant to Va. Code § 54.1-3936 appointing a receiver for his accounts, the Board shall issue a further order summarily suspending the License of the Respondent until the Board enters its order following the expedited hearing.

5. At least five days prior to the date set for hearing, the Respondent shall either file an answer to the petition with the Clerk of the Disciplinary System, which answer shall be conclusively deemed consent to the jurisdiction of the Board; or file an answer and a demand with the Clerk of the Disciplinary System that proceedings before the Board be terminated and that further proceedings be conducted pursuant to Va. Code § 54.1-3935; and simultaneously provide available dates for a hearing not less than 30 days nor more than 120 days from the date of the Board order. Upon such demand and provision of available dates as specified above, further proceedings before the Board shall be terminated and Bar Counsel shall file the complaint required by Va. Code § 54.1-3935. The hearing shall be scheduled as soon as practicable. However, the 30 to 120 day time frame shall not constitute a deadline for the hearing to be held. If any order of summary Suspension has been entered, such Suspension shall remain in effect until the court designated under Va. Code § 54.1-3935 enters a final order disposing of the issue before it. If the Respondent fails to file an answer, or an answer and a demand, and provide available dates, as specified above, the Respondent shall be deemed to have consented to the jurisdiction of the Board.

E. Pre-Hearing Orders. The Chair may, *sua sponte* or upon motion of the Respondent or Bar Counsel, enter such pre-hearing order as is necessary for the orderly conduct of the hearing before the Board in Misconduct cases. Such order may establish time limits and:

1. Direct Bar Counsel and the Respondent to provide to each other, with a copy to the Clerk of the Disciplinary System, a list of and copies of all exhibits proposed to be introduced at the Misconduct stage of the hearing;

2. Encourage Bar Counsel and the Respondent to confer and discuss stipulations; and

3. Direct Bar Counsel and the Respondent to provide to each other, with a copy to the Clerk of the Disciplinary System, lists setting forth the name of each witness the party intends to call.

F. Continuance of a Hearing. Absent exceptional circumstances, once the Board has scheduled a hearing, no continuance shall be granted unless, in the judgment of the Chair, the continuance is necessary to prevent injustice. No continuance will be granted because of a conflict with the schedule of the Respondent or the Respondent's counsel unless such continuance is requested in writing by the Respondent or the Respondent's counsel within 14 days after mailing of a notice of hearing. Any request for a continuance shall be filed with the Clerk of the Disciplinary System.

G. Preliminary Explanation. The Chair shall state in the presence of the Respondent and the Complainant, if present, a summary of the alleged Misconduct, the nature and purpose of the hearing, the procedures to be followed during the hearing, and the dispositions available to the Board following the hearing. The Chair shall also inquire of the members present whether any member has any personal or financial interest that may affect, or be reasonably perceived to affect, his or her ability to be impartial. Any member answering in the affirmative shall be excused from participation in the matter.

H. Attendance at Hearing. Witnesses other than the Complainant and the Respondent shall be excluded until excused from a public hearing on motion of Bar Counsel, the Respondent or the Board.

I. Order of Hearing.

1. Brief opening statements by Bar Counsel and by the Respondent or the Respondent's counsel shall be permitted but are not required.

2. Bar Counsel shall present witnesses and other evidence supporting the Certification. The Respondent shall be afforded the opportunity to cross-examine the Bar's witnesses and to challenge any evidence introduced on behalf of the Bar. Board members may also examine witnesses offered by Bar Counsel.

3. Respondent shall be afforded the opportunity to present witnesses and other evidence. Bar Counsel shall be afforded the opportunity to cross-examine Respondent's witnesses and to challenge any evidence introduced on behalf of Respondent. Board members may also examine witnesses offered on behalf of a Respondent.

4. Bar Counsel may rebut the Respondent's evidence.

5. Bar Counsel may make the initial closing argument.

6. The Respondent or the Respondent's counsel may then make a closing argument.

7. Bar Counsel may then make a rebuttal closing argument.

J. Motion to Strike. At the conclusion of the Bar's evidence or at the conclusion of all the evidence, the Board on its own Motion, or the Respondent or the Respondent's counsel, may move to strike the Bar's evidence as to one or more allegations of Misconduct contained in the Certification. A motion to strike an allegation of Misconduct shall be sustained if the Bar has failed to introduce sufficient evidence that would under any set of circumstances support the conclusion that the Respondent engaged in the alleged Misconduct that is the subject of the motion to strike. If the Chair sustains the motion to strike an allegation of Misconduct, subject to being overruled by a majority of the remaining members of the Board, that allegation of Misconduct shall be dismissed from the Certification.

K. Deliberations. As soon as practicable after the conclusion of the evidence and arguments as to the issue of Misconduct, the Board shall deliberate in private. If the Board finds by clear and convincing evidence that the Respondent has engaged in Misconduct, the Board shall, prior to determining the appropriate sanction to be imposed, inquire whether the Respondent has been the subject of any Disciplinary Proceeding in this or any other jurisdiction and shall give Bar Counsel and the Respondent an opportunity to present material evidence and arguments in aggravation or mitigation. The Board shall deliberate in private on the issue of sanctions. The Board may address any legal questions to the Office of the Attorney General.

L. Dismissal for Failure of the Evidence. If the Board concludes that the evidence fails to show under a clear and convincing evidentiary standard that the Respondent engaged in the Misconduct, the Board shall dismiss any allegation of Misconduct not so proven.

M. Disposition Upon a Finding of Misconduct. If the Board concludes that there has been presented clear and convincing evidence that the Respondent has engaged in Misconduct, after considering evidence and arguments in aggravation and mitigation, the Board shall impose one of the following sanctions and state the effective date of the sanction imposed:

1. Admonition, with or without Terms;

2. Public Reprimand, with or without Terms;

3. Suspension of the License of the Respondent for a stated period not exceeding five years; provided, however, if the Suspension is for more than one year, the Respondent must apply for Reinstatement as provided in this Paragraph; or

4. Revocation of the Respondent's License.

N. Dismissal for Failure to Reach a Majority Decision. If the Board is unable to reach a decision by a majority vote of those constituting the hearing panel, the Certification, or any allegation thereof, shall be dismissed on the basis that the evidence does not reasonably support the Certification, or one or more allegations thereof, under a clear and convincing evidentiary standard.

O. Enforcement of Terms. In all cases where Terms are included in the disposition, the Board shall specify the time period within which compliance shall be completed and, if required, the time period within which the Respondent shall deliver a written certification of compliance to Bar Counsel. The Board shall specify the alternative disposition if the Terms are not complied with or, if required, compliance is not certified to Bar Counsel. Bar Counsel shall be responsible for monitoring compliance and reporting any noncompliance to the Board. Whenever it appears that the Respondent has not complied with the Terms imposed, including written certification of compliance if required, Bar Counsel shall serve notice requiring the Respondent to show cause why the alternative disposition should not be imposed. Such show cause proceeding shall be set for hearing before the Board at its next available hearing date. The burden of proof shall be on the Respondent to show compliance by clear and convincing evidence. If the Respondent has failed to comply with the Terms, including written certification of compliance if required, within the stated time period, as determined by the Board, the alternative disposition shall be imposed. Any show cause proceeding involving the question of compliance shall be deemed a new matter and not a continuation of the matter that resulted in the imposition of Terms.

P. Orders, Findings, and Opinions. Upon disposition of a matter, the Board shall issue the Summary Order. Thereafter, the Board shall issue the Memorandum Order. A Board member shall prepare the Summary Order and Memorandum Order for the signature of the Chair or the Chair's designee. Dissenting opinions may be filed.

Q. Change in Composition of Board Hearing Panel. Whenever a hearing has been adjourned for any reason and one or more of the members initially constituting the quorum for the hearing are unable to be present, the hearing of the matter may be completed by furnishing a transcript of the subsequent proceedings conducted in one or more member's absence to such absent member, or substituting another Board member for any absent member and furnishing a transcript of the prior proceedings in the matter to such substituted member(s).

R. Reconsideration of Board Action. No motion for reconsideration or modification of the Board's decision shall be considered unless it is filed with the Clerk of the Disciplinary System within 10 days after the hearing before the Board. The moving party shall file an original and six copies of both the motion and all supporting exhibits with the Clerk of the Disciplinary System. Such motion shall be granted only to prevent manifest injustice upon the ground of:

1. Illness, injury or accident which prevented the Respondent or a witness from attending the hearing and which could not have been made known to the Board within a reasonable time prior to the hearing; or

2. Evidence which was not known to the Respondent at the time of the hearing and could not have been discovered prior to, or produced at, the hearing in the exercise of due diligence and would have clearly produced a different result if the evidence had been introduced at the hearing.

3. If such a motion is timely filed, the Clerk of the Disciplinary System shall promptly forward copies to each member of the hearing panel. The panel may deny the motion without response from Bar Counsel. No relief shall be granted without allowing Bar Counsel an opportunity to oppose the motion in writing. If no relief is granted, the Board shall enter its order disposing of the case.

13-19. BOARD PROCEEDINGS UPON APPEAL.

A. Docketing An Appeal. Upon receipt of notice from the Clerk of the Disciplinary System that a Respondent has filed an appeal from a District Committee Determination the Board shall place such matter on its docket for review.

B. Notice to the Appellant. The Clerk of the Disciplinary System shall notify the appellant when the entire record of the Proceeding before the District Committee has been received or when the time for appeal has expired.

C. Record on Appeal. The record shall consist of the Charge of Misconduct, the complete transcript of the Proceeding, any exhibits received or refused by the District Committee, the District Committee Determination, and all briefs, memoranda or other papers filed with the District Committee by the Respondent or the Bar. Upon petition of the Respondent, for good cause shown, the Board may permit the record to be supplemented to prevent injustice, such supplement to be in such form as the Board may deem appropriate.

D. Briefing. Thereafter, briefs shall be filed in the office of the Clerk of the Disciplinary System, as follows:

1. The appellant shall file an opening brief within 40 days after the mailing of the notice to the appellant regarding the record by the Clerk of the Disciplinary System. Failure of the appellant to file an opening brief within the time specified herein shall result in the Dismissal of the appeal and affirmance of the decision by the District Committee.

2. The appellee shall file its brief within 25 days after filing of the opening brief.

3. The appellant may file a reply brief within 14 days after filing of the appellee's brief.

E. Standard of Review. In reviewing a District Committee Determination, the Board shall ascertain whether there is substantial evidence in the record upon which the District Committee could reasonably have found as it did.

F. Oral Argument. Oral argument shall be granted, unless waived by the appellant.

G. Imposition of Sanctions. Upon review of the record in its entirety, the Board may:

1. Dismiss the Charge of Misconduct upon a finding that the District Committee Determination is contrary to the law or is not supported by substantial evidence;

2. Affirm the District Committee Determination, in which instance the Board may impose the same or any lesser sanction as that imposed by the District Committee. In no case shall it increase the severity of the sanction imposed by the District Committee; or

3. Reverse the decision of the District Committee and remand the Charge of Misconduct to the District Committee for further proceedings.

13-20. BOARD PROCEEDINGS UPON CERTIFICATION FOR SANCTION DETERMINATION

A. Initiation of Proceeding. Upon receipt of the Certification for Sanction Determination from a District Committee, the Clerk of the Disciplinary System shall issue a notice of hearing on the Certification for Sanction Determination giving Respondent the date, time and place of the Proceeding and a copy of the Certification for Sanction Determination.

B. Proceedings Upon the Record. The proceeding shall be conducted upon the record which shall consist of the Public Reprimand with Terms determination issued by either a Subcommittee or a District Committee, the transcript of the District Committee show cause hearing, and the Certification for Sanction Determination.

C. Evidence. Evidence only of mitigation and aggravation with respect to compliance or certification shall be permitted in the proceeding.

D. Argument. Argument shall be conducted as in the sanction phase of a Misconduct case.

E. Sanctions. The Board may impose a sanction of Suspension or Revocation of License.

13-21. BOARD PROCEEDINGS UPON A FIRST OFFENDER PLEA

A. Action Upon Receipt of Notification. Whenever the Clerk of the Disciplinary System receives written notification from any court of competent jurisdiction stating that an Attorney has entered a plea to a Crime under a first offender statute, and that the court has found facts that would justify a finding of guilt and ordered that the Attorney be put on probation, the Board shall forthwith enter an order requiring the Attorney to appear at a specified time and place for a hearing before the Board to determine whether the Attorney's License should be revoked or suspended or, if not, whether the Attorney should be required to give notice, by certified mail, of the plea and probation ordered by the court, including the terms and duration of the probation, to all clients for whom the Attorney is currently handling matters, and to all opposing attorneys and the presiding judges in pending litigation. A copy of the written notification from the court shall be served with the order fixing the time and place of the hearing. The hearing shall be set not less than 14 or more than 30 days after the date of the Board's order.

B. Burden of Proof. At the hearing, the Attorney shall have the burden of proving why his or her License should not be suspended or revoked and why he or she should not be required to give notice of the plea and probation ordered by the court.

C. Demand for Three Judge Court. If the Attorney elects to have further proceedings conducted pursuant to Va. Code § 54.1-3935, the Attorney shall file a demand with the Clerk of the Disciplinary System not later than ten days prior to the date set for the Board hearing, and simultaneously provide available dates for a hearing not less than 30 nor more than 120 days from the date of the demand. Upon such demand and provision of available dates as specified above, further proceedings before the Board shall be terminated and Bar Counsel shall file the complaint required by Va. Code § 54.1-3935. The hearing shall be scheduled as soon as practicable. However, the 30 to 120 day time frame shall not constitute a deadline for the hearing to be held. If the Respondent fails to file a demand, and provide available dates, as specified above, the Respondent shall be deemed to have consented to the jurisdiction of the Board.

D. Attorney Compliance with Notice Requirements. If the Board or court suspends or revokes the Attorney's License, the Attorney must comply with the notice requirements set out in subparagraph 13-29. If the Board or court orders the Attorney to give notice of the plea and court ordered probation, the Attorney shall give such notice within 14 days after the effective date of the Board's order and furnish proof to the Bar within 60 days of the effective date of the order that such notices have been timely given. Issues concerning the adequacy of the notice shall be determined by the Board, which may suspend or revoke the Attorney's License for failure to comply with the above notice requirements.

13-22. BOARD PROCEEDINGS UPON A GUILTY PLEA OR AN ADJUDICATION OF A CRIME.

A. Action Upon Receipt of Notification. Whenever the Clerk of the Disciplinary System receives written notification from any court of competent jurisdiction stating that an Attorney (the "Respondent") has been found guilty or convicted of a Crime by a Judge or jury, pled guilty to a Crime or entered a plea wherein the facts found by a court would justify a finding of guilt, irrespective of whether sentencing has occurred, a member of the Board shall forthwith and summarily enter an order of Suspension requiring the Respondent to appear at a specified time and place for a hearing before the Board to show cause why the Respondent's License to practice law should not be further suspended or revoked. A copy of the written notification from the court shall be served upon the Respondent with the Board's order of Suspension.

B. Time of Hearing, Continuance and Interim Hearing. The hearing shall be set not less than 14 or more than 30 days after the date of the Board's order. Upon written request of the Respondent, the hearing may be continued until any probation ordered by a court has ended or after sentencing has occurred. Upon receipt by the Board of a certified copy of a notice of appeal from the conviction, proceedings before the Board shall, upon request of the Respondent, be continued pending disposition of such appeal. The Board shall, upon request of the Respondent, hold an interim hearing and shall terminate such Suspension while the probation, sentencing, or appeal is pending, if the Board finds that such Suspension, if not terminated, would be likely to exceed the discipline imposed by the Board upon a hearing on the merits of the case.

C. Reversal of Conviction. Upon presentation to the Board of a certified copy of an order setting aside the verdict or reversing the conviction on appeal, any Suspension shall be automatically terminated and any Revocation shall be vacated, and the License shall be deemed automatically reinstated. Discharge or Dismissal of a guilty plea or termination of probation shall not result in the automatic termination of the Suspension or vacation of the Revocation. Nothing herein shall preclude further proceedings against the Respondent upon allegations of Misconduct arising from the facts leading to such conviction.

D. Burden of Proof. At the hearing, the Respondent shall have the burden of proving why his or her License should not be further suspended or revoked.

E. Action by the Board and Notice to Respondent. If the Board finds at the hearing that the Respondent has been found guilty or convicted of a Crime by a Judge or jury, pled guilty to a Crime or entered a plea wherein the facts found by a court would justify a finding of guilt, an order shall be issued, and a copy thereof served upon the Respondent in which the Board shall continue the Suspension or issue an order of Suspension against the Respondent for a stated period not in excess of five years; or issue an order of Revocation against the Respondent.

F. Procedure. The procedure applicable to Proceedings related to Misconduct shall apply to Proceedings relating to guilty pleas or Adjudication of a Crime. If the Respondent elects to have further Proceedings conducted pursuant to Va. Code § 54.1-3935, the Respondent shall file a demand with the Clerk of the Disciplinary System not later than ten days prior to the date set for the hearing before the Board, and simultaneously provide available dates for a hearing not less than 30 nor more than 120 days from the date of the demand. Upon such demand and provision of available dates as specified above, further proceedings before the Board shall be terminated and Bar Counsel shall file the complaint required by Va. Code § 54.1-3935. The hearing shall be scheduled as soon as practicable. However, the 30 to 120 day time frame shall not constitute a deadline for the hearing to be held. The order of Suspension issued by the Board shall remain in effect until the court designated under Va. Code § 54.1-3935 enters a final order disposing of the issue before it. If the Respondent fails to file a demand, and provide available dates, as specified above, the Respondent shall be deemed to have consented to the jurisdiction of the Board.

13-23. BOARD PROCEEDINGS UPON IMPAIRMENT.

A. Suspension for Impairment. The Board shall have the power to issue an order of Suspension to a Respondent who has an Impairment. The term of such Suspension shall be indefinite and, except as provided below, shall be terminated only upon determination by the Board that Respondent no longer has the Impairment. A Respondent who intends to rely upon evidence of an Impairment in mitigation of Misconduct shall, absent good cause excusing his or her failure to do so, provide notice not less than 14 days prior to the hearing to Bar Counsel and the District Committee or Board of his or her intention to do so. A finding of Impairment may be utilized by Bar Counsel to dismiss any pending Complaints or allegations of Misconduct on the basis of the existence of exceptional circumstances militating against further proceedings, which circumstances of Impairment shall be set forth in the Dismissal.

B. Burden of Proof. Whenever the existence of an Impairment is alleged in a Proceeding under this Rule or in mitigation of allegations of Misconduct, the burden of proving such an Impairment shall rest with the party asserting its existence. The issue of the existence of an Attorney's Impairment may be raised by any person at any time, and if a District Committee or the Board, during the course of a hearing on allegations of Misconduct against a Respondent, believes that the Respondent may then have an Impairment, the District Committee or the Board may postpone the hearing and initiate an Impairment Proceeding under this Rule. In Proceedings to terminate a Suspension for Impairment, the burden of proving the termination of an Impairment shall be on the Respondent.

C. Investigation. Upon receipt of notice or evidence that an Attorney has or may have an Impairment, Bar Counsel shall cause an Investigation to be made to determine whether there is reason to believe that the Respondent has the Impairment. As a part of the Investigation of whether an Impairment exists, and for good cause shown in the interest of public protection Bar Counsel may petition the Board to order the Respondent:

1. To undergo a psychiatric, physical or other medical examination by qualified physicians or other health care provider selected by the Board; and

2. To provide appropriate releases to health care providers authorizing the release of Respondent's psychiatric, physical or other medical records to Bar Counsel and the Board for purposes of the Investigation and any subsequent Impairment proceedings.

Upon notice to the Respondent, the Board shall hold a hearing to determine whether any such examination or release is appropriate.

D. Summary Suspension. Upon receipt of a notice from the Clerk of the Disciplinary System with supporting documentary evidence that an Attorney has been adjudicated by a court of competent jurisdiction to have an Impairment, or that an Attorney has been involuntarily admitted to a hospital (as defined in Va. Code § 37.1-1) for treatment of any addiction, inebriety, insanity or mental illness, any member of the Board shall summarily issue on behalf of the Board an order of Suspension against the Respondent and cause the order to be served on such Respondent.

E. Action by Board after a Hearing.

1. If Bar Counsel determines that there is reason to believe that an Attorney has an Impairment, Bar Counsel shall file a petition with the Board, and the Board shall promptly hold a hearing to determine whether such Impairment exists. A copy of the petition shall be served on the Respondent. If the Board determines that an Impairment exists, it shall enter an order of Suspension.

2. The Board shall hold a hearing upon petition of a Respondent who is subject to a Suspension for Impairment that alleges that the Impairment no longer exists. Evidence that the Respondent is no longer hospitalized shall not be conclusive to the Board's determination of the Respondent's ability to resume the practice of law.

F. Procedure. Such hearing shall be conducted substantially in accordance with the procedures established in proceedings related to Misconduct, except that the public and witnesses, other than the Complainant and the Respondent, shall be excluded throughout an Impairment Proceeding when not testifying.

G. Guardian *Ad Litem*. The notice of any hearing to determine whether the Respondent has an Impairment shall order Respondent to advise the Board whether Respondent has retained counsel for the hearing. Unless counsel for such Respondent enters an appearance with the Board within ten days of the date of the notice, the Board shall appoint a guardian *ad litem* to represent such Respondent at the hearing.

H. Examination. Following a psychiatric, physical or other medical examination, written reports of the results of such examination, along with written reports from other qualified physicians or other health care providers who have examined Respondent, may be considered as evidence by the Board. Such reports shall be filed with the Clerk of the Disciplinary System.

I. Termination of Suspension. In cases where a Suspension is based upon an adjudication of an Impairment by a court, upon receipt of documentary evidence of adjudication by a court of competent jurisdiction that the Respondent's Impairment has terminated, the Board shall promptly enter an order terminating such Suspension.

J. Enforcement. The Board shall have the power to sanction an Attorney for failure to comply with its orders and subpoenae issued in connection with an Impairment Proceeding. The sanction can include a summary Suspension in a case where it is determined that the public and/or the clients of the Attorney are in jeopardy; such action can be *sua sponte* or on motion by Bar Counsel, with appropriate notice to the Attorney and the Attorney's counsel or guardian *ad litem*.

13-24. BOARD PROCEEDINGS UPON DISBARMENT, REVOCATION OR SUSPENSION IN ANOTHER JURISDICTION.

A. Initiation of Proceedings. Upon receipt of a notice from the Clerk of the Disciplinary System that another jurisdiction has suspended or revoked the License of the Respondent and that such action has become final (the "Suspension or Revocation Notice"), any Board member shall enter on behalf of the Board an order of Suspension against such Respondent to show cause why the same discipline imposed in the other jurisdiction should not be imposed by the Board. The Board shall serve upon such Respondent by certified mail: a copy of the Suspension or Revocation Notice; a copy of the Board's order; and a notice fixing the date, time and place of the hearing before the Board to determine what action should be taken in response to the Suspension or Revocation Notice and stating that the purpose of the hearing is to provide Respondent an opportunity to show cause why the same discipline that was imposed in the other jurisdiction should not be imposed by the Board.

B. Opportunity for Response. Within 14 days of the date of mailing of the Board order, via certified mail, return receipt requested, to the last address of record of the Respondent with the Bar, Respondent shall file with the Clerk of the Disciplinary System an original and six copies of any written response and any communications or other materials, which shall be confined to allegations that:

1. The record of the proceeding in the other jurisdiction would clearly show that such proceeding was so lacking in notice or opportunity to be heard as to constitute a denial of due process;

2. The imposition by the Board of the same discipline upon the same proof would result in a grave injustice; or

3. The same conduct would not be grounds for disciplinary action or for the same discipline in Virginia.

C. Scheduling and Continuance of Hearing. Unless continued by the Board for good cause, the hearing shall be set not less than 21 nor more than 30 days after the date of the Board's order of Suspension.

D. Provision of Copies. The Clerk of the Disciplinary System shall furnish to the Board members designated for the hearing and make available to Respondent copies of the Suspension or Revocation Notice, the Board's order of Suspension against the Respondent, the notice of hearing, any notice of continuance of the hearing, and any response or materials filed by Respondent.

E. Hearing Procedures. Insofar as applicable, the procedures for Proceedings on allegations of Misconduct shall govern Proceedings under this subparagraph 13-24.

F. Burden of Proof. The Respondent shall have the burden of proof, by a clear and convincing evidentiary standard, and the burden of producing the Record upon which the Respondent relies to support the Respondent's contentions, and shall be limited at the hearing to proof of the specific contentions raised in any written response. Except to the extent the allegations of the written response are established, the findings in the other jurisdiction shall be conclusive of all matters for purposes of the Proceeding before the Board.

G. Action by the Board. If Respondent has not filed a timely written response, or does not appear at the hearing or if the Board, after a hearing, determines that the Respondent has failed to establish the contentions of the written response by clear and convincing evidence, the Board shall impose the same discipline as was imposed in the other jurisdiction. If the Board determines that the Respondent has established such contentions by clear and convincing evidence, the Board may dismiss the proceeding or impose a lesser discipline than was imposed in the other jurisdiction. A copy of any order imposing discipline shall be served upon the Respondent via certified mail, return receipt requested. Any such order shall be final and binding, subject only to appeal as provided in this Paragraph.

13-25. BOARD PROCEEDINGS FOR REINSTATEMENT

A. Waiver of Confidentiality. The filing by a former Attorney of a petition for Reinstatement shall constitute a waiver of all confidentiality relating to the petition, and to the Complaint or Complaints that resulted in, or were pending at, the time the former Attorney resigned or his or her License was revoked.

B. Readmission After Resignation. If after resigning from the Bar, a former Attorney wishes to resume practicing law in the Commonwealth of Virginia, the former Attorney must apply to the Board of Bar Examiners, satisfy the character and fitness requirements and pass the Bar examination. Before being readmitted to the Bar, the former Attorney must also satisfy any membership obligations that were delinquent when the former Attorney resigned.

C. Petition for Reinstatement After Revocation. After a Revocation, a Petitioner may petition this Court for Reinstatement, setting forth in that petition the reasons why his or her License should be reinstated. The following requirements shall apply: the petition shall be filed under oath or affirmation with penalty of perjury; no petition may be filed sooner than five years from the effective date of the Revocation; and the Petitioner must certify in the petition that he or she has met the requirements of the following subparagraph D. This Court may deny the petition or refer it to the Board for recommendation, together with the record before the clerk of this Court. The Board may recommend approval or disapproval of the petition. Final action on the petition shall be taken by this Court.

D. Evidence Required for Reinstatement After Revocation. After a Revocation, Petitioner's License shall not be reinstated unless the Petitioner proves by clear and convincing evidence that Petitioner:

1. Within five years prior to filing the petition has attended 60 hours of continuing legal education, of which at least ten hours shall be in the area of legal ethics or professionalism;

2. Has taken the Multistate Professional Responsibility Examination and received a scaled score of 85 or higher;

3. Has reimbursed the Bar's Clients' Protection Fund for any sums of money it may have paid as a result of Petitioner's Misconduct;

4. Has paid the Bar all Costs that have been previously assessed against Petitioner, together with any interest due thereon at the judgment rate;

5. Has reimbursed the Bar for any sums of money it may have paid as a result of a receivership involving Petitioner's law practice; and

6. Is a person of honest demeanor and good moral character and possesses the requisite fitness to practice law.

E. Bond Required for Reinstatement After Revocation. The Petitioner shall post with his or her petition for Reinstatement a $5,000 cash bond for payment of Costs resulting from the Reinstatement Proceedings.

F. Determination of Costs for Reinstatement After Revocation. At the conclusion of the Reinstatement Proceeding, the Board or the Clerk of the Disciplinary System shall determine the Costs associated with such proceeding and submit that determination to the clerk of this Court as part of the Board's findings of fact.

G. Additional Requirements After Approval of Petition. Upon approval of a petition by this Court, the Petitioner shall meet the following requirements prior to and as a condition of his or her Reinstatement:

1. Pay to the Bar any Costs assessed in connection with the Reinstatement Proceeding;

2. Take and pass the written portion of the Virginia State Bar examination;

3. If required by the Board, obtain and maintain a professional liability insurance policy issued by a company authorized to write such insurance in Virginia at the cost of the Petitioner in an amount and for such term as set by the Board; and

4. If required by the Board, obtain and maintain a blanket fidelity bond or dishonesty insurance policy issued by a company authorized to write such bonds or insurance in Virginia at the Petitioner's cost in an amount and for such term as set by the Board.

H. Reinstatement After Disciplinary Suspension for More than One Year. After a Suspension for more than one year, the License of the Attorney subject to the Suspension shall not be reinstated unless the Attorney demonstrates to the Board that he or she has:

1. Attended 12 hours of continuing legal education, of which at least two hours shall be in the area of legal ethics or professionalism, for every year or fraction thereof of the Suspension;

2. Taken the Multistate Professional Responsibility Examination since imposition of discipline and received a scaled score of 85 or higher;

3. Reimbursed the Bar's Clients' Protection Fund for any sums of money it may have paid as a result of the Attorney's Misconduct;

4. Paid to the Bar all Costs that have been assessed against him or her, together with any interest due thereon at the judgment rate at the time the Costs are paid; and

5. Reimbursed the Bar for any sums of money it may have paid as a result of a receivership involving Petitioner's law practice.

I. Investigation of Impairment in Reinstatement Matters. Upon receipt of notice or evidence that an individual seeking Reinstatement has or may have an Impairment, Bar Counsel shall cause an Investigation to be made to determine whether there is reason to believe that the Impairment exists. As part of the Investigation of whether an Impairment exists, and for good cause shown in the interest of public protection, Bar Counsel may petition the Board to order the individual:

1. To undergo at his or her expense a psychiatric, physical or other medical examination by a qualified physician or other health care provider selected by the Board; and

2. To provide appropriate releases to health care providers authorizing the release of his or her psychiatric, physical or other medical records to Bar Counsel and the Board for purposes of the Investigation and any subsequent Reinstatement Proceedings.

The Board shall hold a hearing to determine whether such examination(s) and releases(s) are appropriate, upon notice to the individual petitioning for Reinstatement.

J. Reinstatement Hearings. The Clerk of the Disciplinary System shall advise the Petitioner in writing upon receipt of a petition for Reinstatement from the clerk of this Court and arrange a hearing date with the Petitioner and Bar Counsel.

1. Quorum. A quorum shall be five members of the Board.

2. Powers of the Board in Reinstatement Cases. The Board is empowered to hold a hearing and make its recommendation to this Court either to approve or disapprove the petition.

3. Hearing Date. The date of the hearing shall be determined by the Chair. Upon the scheduling of a hearing date, the Clerk of the Disciplinary System shall file six copies of the available transcript, exhibits, pleadings, and orders from the original Disciplinary Proceeding.

4. Investigation. Bar Counsel shall conduct such Investigation and make such inquiry as it deems appropriate. On request of Bar Counsel, the Petitioner shall promptly sign such forms and give such permission as are necessary to permit inquiry of the Petitioner's background through the Internal Revenue Service, the National Criminal Information Center, the National Criminal Information Network and any other similar information network or system.

5. Notice. Reasonable notice of filing of the petition and the date of the hearing shall be mailed by the Clerk of the Disciplinary System to all members of the Bar of the circuit in the jurisdictions in which the Petitioner resided, and of the circuit in which the Petitioner maintained a principal office, at the time of the Revocation or Suspension. The Clerk of the Disciplinary System shall also mail the notice to the members of the District Committee who heard the original Complaint, to members of

the Board who heard the original Complaint, to the members of the District Committee for the judicial circuit in which the Petitioner currently resides, to the complaining witness or witnesses on all Complaints pending against the Petitioner before the Board, a District Committee or a court at the date of the Revocation or Suspension and to such other individuals as the Clerk of the Disciplinary System deems appropriate. The Clerk of the Disciplinary System shall publish a synopsis of the petition in the Virginia Lawyer Register and in a newspaper of general circulation in the judicial circuit where the Petitioner currently resides and where the Petitioner maintained a principal office at the time of the Revocation or Suspension. The entire petition and exhibits together with the documents referred to in subparagraph 13-25.D. above, shall be available for inspection and copying by interested persons at the office of the Bar on reasonable notice and on payment of costs incurred to make the copies.

6. Bill of Particulars. On written request by Bar Counsel, served by certified mail, return receipt requested, a Petitioner seeking Reinstatement shall file with the Clerk of the Disciplinary System within 21 days after receipt of the request, an original and six copies of a bill of particulars setting forth the grounds for Reinstatement.

7. Hearing. On the date set for the hearing, the Petitioner shall have the right to representation by counsel, to examine and cross-examine witnesses and to present evidence. The testimony and other incidents of the hearing shall be transcribed and preserved, together with all exhibits (or copies thereof) received into evidence or refused. Bar Counsel shall appear and represent the Commonwealth and its citizens. Bar Counsel shall have the right to cross-examine, call witnesses and present evidence in opposition to the petition. Board members may examine witnesses called by either party. Legal advice to the Board, if required, shall be rendered by the Office of the Attorney General.

8. Factors to be Considered. In considering the matter prior to making a recommendation to this Court the Board may consider, but is not bound by, the factors spelled out *In the Matter of Alfred Lee Hiss,* VSB Docket No. 83-26 (Va. Sup. Ct. July 2, 1984).

9. Character Witnesses. Up to five character witnesses supporting and up to five character witnesses opposing the petition shall be heard. In addition, the Board may consider any letters submitted regarding the Petitioner's character and fitness.

10. Determination by the Board. The Board shall, within 60 days after the receipt of the transcript, forward the record and its recommendations to this Court with a copy to the Petitioner and Bar Counsel. A recommendation of approval may be conditioned upon Petitioner obtaining malpractice insurance coverage and/or a blanket fidelity bond or dishonesty insurance coverage in amount(s) set by the Board from an approved professional insurance carrier for a definite term or on an ongoing basis.

13-26. APPEAL FROM BOARD DETERMINATIONS

A. Right of Appeal. As a matter of right any Respondent may appeal to this Court from an order of Admonition, Public Reprimand, Suspension, or Disbarment imposed by the Board. An appeal shall lie once the Memorandum Order described in this Paragraph has been served on the Respondent. No appeal shall lie from a Summary Order.

B. Notice of Appeal. The Respondent shall file with the Clerk of the Disciplinary System a notice of appeal and assignments of error within 30 days after the Memorandum Order of the Board is served on the Respondent. This action within the time prescribed is jurisdictional.

C. Further Proceedings. Further proceedings shall be as provided in this Court's procedure for filing an appeal from a trial court and procedure following perfection of appeal. For the purposes of determining dates of filing, the date of filing the record with the clerk of this Court shall be deemed to be the date of the issuance of the certificate of the clerk of this Court under Rule 5:23. The Clerk of the Disciplinary System shall immediately notify the Respondent and his counsel, if any, by certified mail, of the date on which the record is filed.

D. Determination. This Court shall hear the case and make such determination in connection therewith as it shall deem right and proper.

E. Office of the Attorney General. In all appeals to this Court, the Office of the Attorney General, or the Bar Counsel, if so requested by the Attorney General, shall represent the interests of the Commonwealth and its citizens as appellees.

F. Stay Pending Appeal. Upon the entry by the Board of either a Summary or Memorandum Order of Suspension, this Court may, upon petition of the Respondent, stay the effect of such an order of Suspension prior to or during the pendency of the appeal. Any order of Admonition or Public Reprimand shall be automatically stayed prior to or during the pendency of an appeal therefrom. No stay shall be granted in cases where the Respondent's License has been revoked by either the Summary or Memorandum Order of the Board.

13-27. RESIGNATION

A. Application. A sworn and notarized application to resign from the practice of law shall be submitted to the Clerk of the Disciplinary System. The application shall state that the resignation is not being offered to avoid disciplinary action and that the Attorney has no knowledge of any complaint, investigation, action, or proceeding in any jurisdiction involving allegations of Misconduct by the Attorney. An application to resign will not prevent or preclude any disciplinary proceeding or action against an Attorney.

B. Procedure. The Clerk of the Disciplinary System shall submit applications for resignation to Bar Counsel, who shall investigate each application and determine whether, based upon the information available, the statements in the sworn application appear to be true and complete. If Bar Counsel files a written objection to the application with the Clerk of the Disciplinary System, the Board shall hold a hearing on whether the application should be accepted. If Bar Counsel does not file an objection, the Board may enter an order accepting the Attorney's resignation without a hearing. A resignation shall be effective only upon entry of an order accepting it. Upon entry of an order accepting an Attorney's resignation, the former Attorney shall immediately cease the practice of law and make appropriate arrangements for the disposition of matters in the Attorney's care in conformity with the wishes of the Attorney's clients.

C. When Not Permitted. An Attorney may not resign while the Attorney is the subject of a disciplinary complaint, investigation, action, or proceeding involving allegations of Misconduct.

13-28. CONSENT TO REVOCATION.

A. When Permitted. An Attorney who is the subject of a disciplinary complaint, investigation or Proceeding involving allegations of Misconduct may consent to Revocation, but only by delivering to the Clerk of the Disciplinary System an affidavit declaring the Attorney's consent to Revocation and stating that:

1. The consent is freely and voluntarily rendered, that the Attorney is not being subjected to coercion or duress, and that the Attorney is fully aware of the implications of consenting to Revocation;

2. The Attorney is aware that there is currently pending a complaint, an investigation into, or a Proceeding involving, allegations of Misconduct, the nature of which shall be specifically set forth in the affidavit;

3. The Attorney acknowledges that the material facts upon which the allegations of Misconduct are predicated are true; and

4. The Attorney submits the consent to Revocation because the Attorney knows that if disciplinary Proceedings based on the alleged Misconduct were brought or prosecuted to a conclusion, the Attorney could not successfully defend them.

B. Admissions. The admissions offered in the affidavit consenting to Revocation shall not be deemed an admission in any proceeding except one relating to the status of the Attorney as a member of the Bar.

C. Procedure. The Clerk of the Disciplinary System shall submit the affidavit to Bar Counsel, who shall investigate the affidavit and determine whether, based upon the information available, the statements in the sworn application appear to be true and complete. If Bar Counsel files a written objection to the affidavit with the Clerk of the Disciplinary System, the Board shall hold a hearing on whether the affidavit and consent to Revocation should be accepted. If Bar Counsel does not file an objection, the Board shall enter an order revoking the Attorney's License by consent without a hearing.

D. Attorney Action Required upon Revocation. Upon entry of such an order of Revocation by consent, the revoked Attorney shall immediately cease the practice of law and shall comply with the notice requirements set forth in subparagraph 13-29.

E. Dismissal of Complaints or Allegations of Misconduct. When an Attorney's License is revoked by consent, Bar Counsel, in his or her discretion, may dismiss without prejudice any and all Complaints or allegations of Misconduct then pending by notifying the Clerk of the Disciplinary System and the District Committee, Board or court wherein the matter or matters lie.

13-29. DUTIES OF DISBARRED OR SUSPENDED RESPONDENT.

After a Suspension against a Respondent is imposed by either a Summary or Memorandum Order and no stay of the Suspension has been granted by this Court, or after a Revocation against a Respondent is imposed by either a Summary Order or Memorandum Order, that Respondent shall forthwith give notice, by certified mail, of his or her Revocation or Suspension to all clients for whom he or she is currently handling matters and to all opposing Attorneys and the presiding Judges in pending litigation. The Respondent shall also make appropriate arrangements for the disposition of matters then in his or her care in conformity with the wishes of his or her clients. The Respondent shall give such notice within 14 days of the effective date of the Revocation or Suspension, and make such arrangements as are required herein within 45 days of the effective date of the Revocation or Suspension. The Respondent shall also furnish proof to the Bar within 60 days of the effective date of the Revocation or Suspension that such notices have been timely given and such arrangements made for the disposition of matters. The Board shall decide all issues concerning the adequacy of the notice and arrangements required herein, and the Board may impose a sanction of Revocation or additional Suspension for failure to comply with the requirements of this subparagraph 13-29.

13-30. CONFIDENTIALITY OF DISCIPLINARY RECORDS AND PROCEEDINGS.

A. Confidential Matters. Except as otherwise provided in this subparagraph 13-30, the following Disciplinary Proceedings, records, and information are confidential and shall not be disclosed:

1. Complaints, unless introduced at a public hearing or incorporated in a pending Charge of Misconduct, when the matter is placed on the public District Committee hearing docket, or a Certification;

2. Investigations, except that Investigative Reports admitted as exhibits at a public hearing are public;

3. Impairment proceedings, except that final orders are public;

4. Notes, memoranda, research, and all other work product of Bar Counsel;

5. Records, communications, and information protected by Disciplinary Rule 1.6;

6. Subcommittee records and proceedings, except determinations imposing public discipline; and

7. Deliberations and working papers of District Committees, the Board or a three-judge Circuit Court.

B. Timing of Disclosure of Disciplinary Record in Sanctions Proceedings. If an Attorney has a Disciplinary Record and is subsequently found by a Subcommittee, a District Committee, the Board or a three-judge Circuit Court empaneled under Va. Code § 54.1-3935 to have engaged in Misconduct, the facts and circumstances giving rise to such Disciplinary Record may be disclosed (i) to the Subcommittee, District Committee, Board or three-judge Circuit Court prior to the imposition of any sanction and (ii) by the Subcommittee, District Committee, Board or three-judge Circuit Court in its findings of fact set forth in its order. The facts and circumstances giving rise to such Disciplinary Record may also be disclosed to the Board during a hearing concerning whether an affidavit and consent to Revocation should be accepted.

C. Timing of Public Access to Disciplinary Information. All records of a matter set for public hearing remain confidential until the matter is dismissed or a public sanction is imposed except:

1. A Charge of Misconduct is public when the matter is placed on the public District Committee hearing docket; and

2. A Certification is public when filed with the Clerk of the Disciplinary System.

D. Public Statements Concerning Disciplinary Information. To the extent necessary to exercise their official duties, Bar Officials have access to all confidential information; however, except for Bar Counsel, no Bar Official shall communicate with a member of the media or the public concerning a matter that is confidential under this Paragraph. If an inquiry is made about a matter that, although confidential under this Paragraph, has become a matter of public record or has become known to the public, Bar Counsel may confirm whether the Bar is conducting an Investigation or if an Investigation resulted in a determination that further proceedings were not warranted.

E. Protection of the Public. Bar Counsel may transmit confidential information to persons or agencies outside of the disciplinary system if such disclosure is necessary to protect the public or the administration of justice.

F. Disclosure to Other Jurisdictions. Bar Counsel may share information regarding an Investigation with his or her counterparts in other jurisdictions provided that such jurisdiction agrees to maintain the confidentiality of the information as provided in this Paragraph.

G. Disclosure of Criminal Activity. If Bar Counsel or a Chair of the Board or a Chair of a District Committee discovers evidence of criminal activity by an Attorney, Bar Counsel, the Chair of the Board or a Chair of a District Committee shall forward such evidence to the appropriate Commonwealth's Attorney, United States Attorney or other law enforcement agency. The Attorney concerned shall be notified whenever this information is transmitted pursuant to this subparagraph 13-30 unless Bar Counsel decides that giving such notice will prejudice a disciplinary investigation.

H. Disclosure of Information to Government Entities. By order of this Court, confidential information may be disclosed to the Joint Legislative Audit and Review Commission or other governmental entities incident to their discharge of official duties, provided the entity is required or agrees to maintain the confidentiality of the information provided.

I. Waiver of Confidentiality. Confidential information, excluding notes, memoranda, research, and all other work product of Bar Counsel, may upon written request be disclosed when and to the extent confidentiality is waived by the Respondent, by the Complainant, and, if protected by Disciplinary Rule 1.6, by Respondent's client.

J. Testimony about Disciplinary Proceedings.

1. In no case shall Bar Counsel, a member of COLD, a member of a District Committee, a member of the Board, or a Committee Counsel be subject to a subpoena or otherwise compelled to testify in any proceeding regarding any matter investigated or considered in such person's official capacity, except that an Investigator may be compelled to testify in a Disciplinary Proceeding, subject to rulings of the court or Chair.

2. In no case shall the Clerk of the Disciplinary System be subject to a subpoena or otherwise compelled to testify regarding any matter investigated or considered in the disciplinary system, or the records of any such matter, dealt with by the Clerk of the Disciplinary System in his or her official capacity, except that the Clerk of the Disciplinary System may be compelled to testify in a Disciplinary Proceeding in order to authenticate records of the Clerk of the Disciplinary System.

K. Records of the Disciplinary System. In no case shall confidential records of the attorney disciplinary system be subject to subpoena.

L. Virginia Lawyer Referral Service. Bar Counsel shall notify the Virginia Lawyer Referral Service when a Complaint involving any Attorney member of the service is referred to a District Committee for Investigation or when any Attorney member of the service is disciplined. Bar Counsel shall also notify the Virginia Lawyer Referral Service when any Complaint involving an Attorney member of the service is dismissed following Investigation or when any Attorney member of the service complies with Terms imposed.

13-31. DISMISSAL OF COMPLAINTS AND ALLEGATIONS OF MISCONDUCT UPON REVOCATION WITHOUT CONSENT, OR UPON DEATH.

When an Attorney's License is revoked without consent, or upon the death of an Attorney, Bar Counsel, in his or her discretion, may dismiss without prejudice any and all Complaints or allegations of Misconduct then pending against said Attorney by notifying the Clerk of the Disciplinary System, the Complainant(s) and the District Committee, Board or court wherein the matter(s) lies.

Cross references. — As to transmittal to House and Senate Committees for Courts of Justice of evidence in the possession of the Virginia State Bar relating to pending disciplinary proceedings involving a licensed attorney being considered for election as a judge, see § 54.1-3911. As to proceedings pending disciplinary action, see § 54.1-3936.

Editor's note. — Amendments to former paragraphs 13(c) and 13(d) of Section IV are published at 202 Va. lxi (1961). Amendments to paragraphs 13G(6) and 13J(5) are published at 221 Va. 381 (1980). Paragraph 13B(1)(d) was amended in 1981 (see 221 Va. 1147). Paragraphs 13A(9), 13D(1), 13D(2) and 13D(3) were amended effective July 1, 1983. Additional amendments to paragraph 13 are published at 210 Va. 411 (1970); 211 Va. cxxxiii (1971); and 217 Va. 173 (1976).

In subdivision 13-1, the reference to § 2.1-122(c) in the definition of "Bar Counsel" should refer to

§ 2.2-510, and the reference to § 2.1-37.1 in the definition of "Judge" should refer to § 17.1-900.

The amendment effective January 27, 1998, adopted January 27, 1998, rewrote the paragraph defining "Disciplinary Record" in subdivision A and rewrote subdivisions K (1) and K (4).

The amendment effective September 23, 1998, adopted September 23, 1998, in subdivision C (5), in the first sentence, substituted "Procedure on Certification to the Board" for "Procedure on Charges of Misconduct"; and in subdivision C (5) (a), rewrote the introductory paragraph which formerly read: "Upon certification by a Subcommittee of a Complaint or a District Committee of a Charge of Misconduct, Bar Counsel shall cause to be served on the Respondent a statement of the certified charges. The Respondent may, within twenty-one days after such service," and deleted the first sentence in the concluding paragraph which formerly read: "After the answer has been filed, or the time has expired for either filing an answer or demanding that the proceeding be terminated, the Board shall set a time and place for hearing and shall, at least twenty-one days prior to the date fixed for the hearing, serve notice thereof upon the Respondent."

The amendment effective July 1, 1999, adopted April 23, 1999, in B (2) d, substituted "ten, or in the discretion of Council, twenty, thirty or forty members" for "nine, or in the discretion of Council, eighteen, twenty-seven or thirty-six members" in the first sentence, substituted "Three members of a ten-member District Committee, six members of a twenty-member District Committee, nine members of a thirty member District Committee, and twelve members of a forty-member" for "Two members of a nine-member District Committee and four members of an eighteen-member District Committee and six members of a twenty-seven member District Committee and eight members of a thirty-six member" in the second sentence and substituted "twenty members or more, ten members" for "eighteen members or more, nine" in the third sentence; redesignated the last three sentences in subdivision B (10) (a) as the first three sentences in subdivision B (10) (b) and in subdivision B (10) (b), inserted "or written demand" following "notice of appeal" in the first, second, fourth, fifth and sixth sentences, added "When proceeding by notice of appeal or a written demand that further proceedings be conducted pursuant to Article 6 of Chapter 39 of Title 54.1 of the Code of Virginia" in the first sentence, inserted "by the Clerk of the Disciplinary System, the imposition of any" in the second sentence, inserted "of" following "after filing" in the fifth sentence, substituted "subparagraph (c) below in the case of an appeal to a three-judge court" for "statute in case of an appeal to the Court" in the sixth sentence, in the seventh sentence, deleted "Except as provided in Paragraph 13.D.(1)" preceding "failure of the Respondent" and inserted "by the Disciplinary Board, whether initiated by notice of appeal or written demand" and added the last sentence; inserted subdivision B (10) (c); inserted subdivision C (3) (i); in subdivision K (10), in the first sentence, inserted "The Clerk of the Disciplinary system shall assess costs against the Respondent in the following cases," inserted the subdivision (a) designator, substituted "All" for "In a" and deleted "the Clerk of the Disciplinary System shall assess costs against the Respondent-attorney," in the second sentence, deleted "The Clerk shall also assess costs in those cases in which the Respondent-attorney," inserted the subdivision (b) designator and inserted "All cases against a Respondent who," inserted subdivisions (c) and (d), inserted the subdivision (e) designator, inserted the first sentence in subdivision (e), and in the former third sentence, inserted "reasonable costs paid by the Bar to outside experts or consultants" and substituted "and transcript fees, copying, mailing and required publication costs" for "fees, copy costs."

The amendment effective September 29, 1999, adopted September 29, 1999, substituted "with his petition for reinstatement a bond of $3,500 for payment of costs" for "a bond of $1,000 for payment of costs with his petition for reinstatement" in the first sentence of the third paragraph of subdivision K (10) (e).

The amendment effective February 4, 2000, substituted "Rules of Professional Conduct" for "Code of Professional Responsibility" throughout subdivisions A through 5 B of this rule; in the second sentence in subdivision K (b), inserted "Attorney's disciplinary record or any disciplinary," inserted "for bar admission or enforcement purposes," and deleted "but" preceding "only if" in the present third sentence of subdivision K (b), substituted "District Committee Chair discovers" for "District Committee discovers" and substituted "Chair" for "Chairman"; rewrote subdivision K (5) (d); in subdivision K (5) (e), deleted "three-judge Circuit Court" following "District Committee" and deleted "shall be public, and" preceding "shall be certified to the Clerk"; and in subdivision K (5) (f), inserted "and its dispositive orders" preceding "except Disability proceedings" and deleted "and appeals of private reprimands or Terms" thereafter.

The amendment effective March 29, 2000, inserted "or the Code of Professional Responsibility" following "Rules of Professional Conduct" in this rule.

The amendment effective July 1, 2000, inserted the paragraph defining "Revocation" in subdivision A; in subdivision B(5)(c)(ii), substituted "i." for "(i)" and "ii." for "(ii)" in (d), and in (e), deleted the language following "before the District Committee," and in the third paragraph of (e), inserted "(ii)" preceding "(d)"; in subdivision H(2), substituted "thirty" for "twenty-one"; and in subdivision J, in the first paragraph, inserted "(1) Reinstatement After Revocation," and inserted the present second and fifth sentences, inserted the present second, fourth and fifth paragraphs, and added subdivisions (2) and (3).

The amendment effective December 18, 2000, in subdivision B(3), inserted the present second sentence; in the present third sentence, inserted "but is not limited to" and "examine criminal history record information relating to any Respondent from any state or federal law enforcement agency, and to"; in the present fourth sentence, deleted "the Rules of Professional Conduct or" preceding "the Code of Professional Responsibility"; and in the present sixth sentence, substituted "summonses or subpoenas" for "summons or subpoena" and deleted "the Rules of Professional Conduct or" preceding "the Code of Professional Responsibility."

The amendment effective January 1, 2001, adopted October 23, 2000, in subdivision I, in the first sentence, inserted "notarized" preceding "resignation" and substituted "Board, or a District Committee, or a Court, shall" for "Board, District Committee, or a Court shall"; and substituted "Paragraph K(1)" for "paragraph K.(1)" near the end of the fifth sentence.

The amendment effective April 12, 2001, adopted April 12, 2001, added present subdivision 13B(2)(a) and redesignated former subdivsions 13B(2)(a) through (2)(d) as present subdivisions (2)(b) through (2)(e); added present subdivision C(1) and redesignated former subdivisions C(1) through C(6) as present subdivisions C(2) through C(7); and rewrote K(9)(b) and K(9)(e).

The amendment effective June 5, 2001, adopted June 5, 2001, added the second sentence of subdivision 13K(5)(c).

The amendment effective October 1, 2001, adopted October 1, 2001, in subdivision F, redesignated former subdivision (1) as present subdivision (2) and former (2) as present (1); in present subdivision (1), substituted "(7)(c)(i)" for "(6)(a)" in the second sentence, inserted "a" and "a District Committee or" in the second sentence, and added the third sentence; in present subdivision (2), deleted "for the suspension of the license fo an Attorney" following "this Rule" in the first sentence, inserted "a" preceding "Disability" twice and substituted "proceeding" for "proceedings" in the second sentence, and inserted "a" preceding "Disability" twice in the third sentence; rewrote former subdivision (3) and created present subdivisions (4) and (5); redesignated former subdivisions (4) and (5) as present subdivision (6) and (7); in present subdivision (6)(a), substituted "Counsel, a District Committee or the Disciplinary Board" for "Counsel or a District Committee"' in present subdivision (6)(b), inserted "a" preceding "Disability" in the first sentence, deleted "as provided in (3)(a) above" following "hospitalized" and "to the Board's determination" following "conclusive" in the second sentence; rewrote present subdivision (7); redesignated former subparagraph (6) as present (7)(c) and rewrote it.

The amendment effective November 2, 2001, adopted November 2, 2001, in subdivision C(3), substituted "Chair" for "Chairman" and "Vice-Chair" for "Vice-Chairman" in the first sentence, and inserted the present third sentence.

The amendment effective January 1, 2002, adopted October 1, 2001, amended subdivisions B and K(5)(f) as follows:

Subdivision B(4)(b)(iv) — in the concluding paragraph, substituted "Chair of the Board" for "Chairmain of the Board."

Subdivision B(4)(c)(i) — substituted "chair, vice-chair" for "chairman, vice-chairman."

Subdivision B(4)(c)(iii) — deleted "and to compel the attendance of witnesses and the production of documents necessary or material to any inquiry" and "and."

Subdivision B(4)(c)(iv) — inserted.

Subdivision B(4)(c)(v) — redesignated from former B(4)(c)(iv).

Subdivision B(4)(c)(vi) — inserted.

Subdivision B(5)(a) — deleted "Virginia" preceding "Code of Professional Responsibility" in the heading.

Subdivision B(5)(c)(i) — substituted "Investigation, Filing" for "Investigation and Filing" in the heading; and in the concluding paragraph, substituted "chair" for "Chairman" three times.

Subdivision B(5)(c)(ii)(e) — deleted the former first paragraph following and inserted the present second paragraph.

Subdivision B(6)(a) — substituted "Counsel shall, at least forty-two days prior" for "Counsel shall at least twenty-one days prior."

Subdivision B(6)(b) — inserted the present first sentence, in the present third sentence, substituted "exhibits" for "witnesses"; and inserted the concluding paragraph.

Subdivision B(6)(c) — substituted "chair" for "Chairman" in the second paragraph.

Subdivision B(7) — deleted former sub-subparagraph (b), redesignated sub-paragraphs (c) and (d) as (b) and (c), and in (c), substituted "Section" for "§."

Subdivisions B(8) and B(9)(a) — substituted "chair" for "Chairman."

Subdivision B(9)(b) — deleted "If the Subcommittee or District Committee determines to issue a private or public reprimand, with or without Terms, or a dismissal upon Terms, then" at the beginning and substituted "chair" for "Chairman" twice.

Subdivision B(9)(c) — redesignated former second sentence of (b) as (c), and substituted "chair" for "Chairman" twice.

Subdivision B(10)(a) — deleted "private or" preceding "public reprimand" in the first sentence and substituted "chair" for "Chairman" in the second sentence.

Subdivision B(10)(b) — inserted "the" preceding "notice of appeal" in the fourth sentence and deleted "a" preceding "part of" in the fifth sentence.

Subdivision B(10)(c) — deleted "except that all such proceedings shall be public" at the end of the first sentence and substituted "reference" for "references" at the beginning of the third sentence.

Subdivision B(11) — inserted "public" preceding "reprimand" and deleted "if the reprimand is a public reprimand" preceding "Bar Counsel."

Subdivision K(5)(f) — Rewrote.

The amendment effective September 18, 2002, adopted September 18, 2002, completely rewrote the Rule; in subdivision (A), substituted "Paragraph" for "Rule" in the introductory language; amended, or rewrote, the paragraphs defining "Admonition," "Attorney," "Bar Counsel," "Board," "Charge of Misconduct," "Clerk of the Disciplinary System," "Complaint," "Committee Counsel," "Crime," "Disability," "Disciplinary Record," "District Committee," "Executive Director," "Judge," "Misconduct," "Public Reprimand," "Respondent," "Revocation," "Standing Committee," "Subcommittee," and "Terms"; added the paragraphs defining, "Adjudication of a Crime Proceeding," "Agreed Disposition," "Bar Official," "Certification," "Chair," "COLD," "Costs," "Court Reporter," "CRESPA," "De minimis Dismissal," "Disability Proceeding," "Disability Rules," "Dismissal," "Dismissal for Exceptional Circumstances," "Dismissal With Terms," "District Committee Determination," "Executive Director," "Files," "Investigation," "Investigative Report," "Investigator," "License," "Memorandum Order," "Panel," "Paragraph," "Petitioner," "Private Discipline," "Private Reprimand,"

"Proceeding," "Receivership," "Reinstatement," "Reinstatement Proceeding," "Section," "Summary Order," "Suspension," and "Va. Code"; and rewrote the remainder of the Rule, by substituting present subdivisions B through N for former subdivisions B through K.

The amendment effective January 1, 2004, adopted November 6, 2003, by three orders of the Virginia Supreme Court, rewrote the Rule.

The amendment effective April 15, 2004, adopted February 6, 2004, in subdivision M, substituted "Suspension against a Respondent is imposed by either a Summary or Memorandum Order and no stay of the Suspension has been granted by this Court, or after a Revocation against a Respondent is imposed by either a Summary Order or Memorandum Order, that" for "Suspension or Revocation against a Respondent becomes final and nonappealable, that" at the beginning of the first sentence, and in the last sentence, substituted "Unless the matter is being considered by a three-judge panel, a sanction" for "The Board shall decide all issues concerning the adequacy of the notice and arrangements required herein, and the Board may impose a sanction" and "Suspension may be imposed for the failure" for "Suspension for failure."

The amendment effective November 1, 2004, adopted October 8, 2004, in subdivision A, inserted the paragraphs defining "Impairment" and "Impairment Proceeding"; made stylistic changes throughout the Rule in order to substitute "Impairment" for "Disability"; rewrote subdivision C.6.; added subdivision E.5.; rewrote subdivision H.1.a.(2)(b), H.2.p.(1), and I.1.a.(1)(b); added subdivision I.2.g., redesignated former subdivisions I.2.g. and I.2.h. as present subdivisions I.2.h. and I.2.I., and added subdivision I.2.j.; and substituted "provide notice not less than 14 days prior" for "provide reasonable notice prior" in subdivision I.6.a.

The amendment effective January 1, 2005, adopted September 30, 2004, in subdivision G, deleted former subdivision G.1.a.(4), redesignated former subdivisions G.1.a.(5) and G.1.a.(6) as present subdivisions G.1.a.(4) and G.1.a.(5), inserted present G.1.b., redesignated former subdivisions G.1.b. through G.1.d. as present subdivisions G.1.c. through G.1.e.; and in subdivision H, rewrote subdivision H.3.a.

The amendment effective January 1, 2005, adopted December 22, 2004, in subdivision H, substituted "to the Charge of Misconduct, which answer shall be deemed" for "that shall be conclusively deemed to be" in subdivision H.1.a.(2)(a), inserted "an answer to the Charge of Misconduct and" near the beginning of subdivision H.1.a.(2)(b), and substituted "answer, or an answer and a demand" for "answer or demand" in subdivision H.1.a.(3); and in subdivision I, substituted "to the Certification, which answer shall be deeme" for "that shall be conclusively deemed to be a" in subdivisions I.1.a.(1)(a) and inserted "an answer to the Certification and" near the beginning of subdivision I.1.a.(1)(b) and substituted "answer, or an answer and a demand'" for "answer or demand" in subdivision I.1.a.(2); and substituted "this Paragraph" for "paragraph 13.M. of these Rules" at the end of subdivision I.7.f.

The amendment effective July 1, 2005, adopted April 26, 2005, added the last two sentences of subdivision H.2.d.; inserted "Admonition," in the first sentence of subdivision J.1.; inserted "Admonition or" in the second sentence of subdivision J.6.; and added the last sentence of subdivision N.2.

The amendment effective September 1, 2005, adopted August 26, 2005, inserted "has reimbursed the Bar for any sums of money it may have paid as a result of a receivership involving Petitioner's law practice" near the end of the first sentence of subdivision I.8.b.; and added "and has reimbursed the Bar for any sums of money it may have paid as a result of a receivership involving Petitioner's law practice" at the end of subdivision I.8.c.

The amendment effective January 1, 2006, adopted December 21, 2005, in subdivision F.1., added the a. designator and subdivision F.1.b.

The amendment effective January 1, 2007, adopted October 31, 2006, in subdivision B.6., deleted former subdivision B.6.h., and redesignated former subdivision B.6.i. as present subdivision B.6.h., deleted "or panel" throughout and deleted the last sentence thereof; and in subdivision F.3., added the last sentence of subdivision F.3.a., added "Unless otherwise stated" at the beginning of subdivision F.3.d., and rewrote subdivision F.3.e.

The amendment effective March 1, 2007, adopted March 1, 2007, in subdivision H.2.b., deleted "for which a Notice of Hearing" preceding, and inserted "for which a Charge of Misconduct," following "before a District Committee" near the middle, and substituted "Charge of Misconduct" for "Notice" at the end, of the first sentence; in subdivision I.3.a., substituted "Upon" for "on" in the 3. heading, and in a., substituted "Charge of Misconduct" for "notice of hearing" in the third sentence, and deleted a comma preceding "as follows" at the end of the fifth sentence; in subdivision I.4.a., inserted a comma following "District Committee" and "the" preceding "Certification for Sanction Determination"; and in subdivision N.3.a., substituted "Charge of Misconduct" for "Notice of Hearing."

The amendment effective February 29, 2008, adopted February 29, 2008, in subdivision A, in the paragraph defining "Certification," substituted "allegations" for "the charges of."

The first amendment effective May 1, 2008, adopted February 29, 2008, in subdivision H.1.a.(2), substituted "hearing not less than 30 nor more than 120 days from the date of the demand" for "hearing to be scheduled not less than 30 nore more than 120 days form the damand" in (a), and added the present second sentence of (b); rewrote subdivision H.4.a.(1); in subdivision H.4.a.(4), inserted "of a District Committee Determination"; added the last sentence of subdivision I.1.a.; rewrote subdivisions I.1.b.(5) and I.5.a.(3); inserted the subdivision I.5.b.(1) designation and added subdivision I.5.b.(2)

The second amendment effective May 1, 2008, adopted February 29, 2008, in subdivision H.2.n., added "of District Committee Decision" to the catchline, in the second paragraph, inserted "a Dismissal *De Minimus*; or a Dismissal for Exceptional Circumstances" and made related changes; rewrote subdivision H.2.o.; purported to amend subdivision H.4.a.(1), but effect was given to the other amendment adopted February 29, 2008, and effective May 1, 2008; and in subdivision H.4.a.(4), inserted "of a District Committee Determination" near the end of the first sentence.

The amendment effective March 1, 2009, adopted December 30, 2008, rewrote subdivision I. 2. f. (2) (c).

The amendment effective May 1, 2009, adopted February 27, 2009, rewrote the Rule, by adding the division headings — 13-1 through 13-31 — and changing the style and format of the text.

The amendment effective August 1, 2009, adopted May 29, 2009, in 13-1, in the definition of "Costs," inserted "electronic and telephonic conferencing and recording costs, if such procedures are requested by Respondent," and in the paragraph defining "Terms," deleted "the Dismissal of a Complaint or Charge of Misconduct, or" following "condition for the" and "or" following "Admonition," and added "or a Suspension pursuant to this Paragraph"; and in subsection E of 13-25, substituted "$5,000" for "$3,500."

The first amendment effective March 19, 2010, adopted March 19, 2010, in 13-10, deleted "to the satisfaction of the Complainant, the Respondent and the Bar" following "through this process" in the third sentence of C, and in 13-22, rewrote A, added D, and redesignated former D and E as E and F.

The second amendment effective March 19, 2010, adopted March 19, 2010, in 13-1, substituted "Disciplinary Proceeding" for "Complaint or Charge of Misconduct" and "Committee, the Board or a Circuit Court" for "Committee, or the Board" in the paragraph defining "Agreed Disposition," substituted "which" for "in which a Complaint or Charge of Misconduct" in paragraph 2. of the definition of "Disciplinary Record," rewrote the definition of "Dismissal," and in the definition of "Summary Order," deleted "Board" preceding "Chair" and "Board's" preceding "findings" and substituted "allegations" for "Charge"; in 13-6, substituted "Certifications submitted" for "Charges of Misconduct certified" in clause (1) of F, and in H, substituted "the disposition of a Disciplinary Proceeding" for "a Charge of Misconduct or a Certification for Sanction Determination and desire to enter into an Agreed Disposition of the Charge of Misconduct or Certification for Sanction Determination" in the first sentence, and "Disciplinary Proceeding" for "Charge of Misconduct or Certification for Sanction Determination" in the fourth and fifth sentences; in 13-8, substituted "allegation of Misconduct" for "charge of Misconduct" in B; in 13-9, substituted "allegation of Misconduct" for "charge of Misconduct" in 4. and the concluding paragraph, and inserted a comma following "Proceeding held" in the concluding paragraph; in 13-10, substituted "allegation of Misconduct" for "Charge of Misconduct" in B; in 13-12, substituted "allegation of Misconduct" for "Charge of Misconduct" in A; in 13-13, substituted "allegation of Misconduct" for "Charge of Misconduct" in the introductory paragraph and 3.; in 13-16 X 5., substituted "Charge" for "Charges"; in 13-18, substituted "Certification" for "Charge of Misconduct" at the end of the first sentence of I 2, inserted a comma following "Respondent's counsel" and substituted "Certification for "Charge of Misconduct" in the first sentence of J, substituted "Certification for "Charge of Misconduct" at the end of the third sentence of J; substituted "allegation of Misconduct" for "Charge of Misconduct" in L, and substituted "Certification" for "Charge of Misconduct" twice in N; in 13-19, substituted "Charge of Misconduct" for "Charges of Misconduct" in G 1 and G 3; in 13-22, substituted "allegations of Misconduct" for "Charges of Misconduct" in C; in 13-23, deleted a comma following "indefinite" in the second sentence and substituted "allegations of Misconduct" for "Charges of Misconduct" in the fourth sentence of A, and substituted "allegations of Misconduct" for "Charges of Misconduct" twice in B; in 13-24, substituted "allegations of Misconduct" for "Charges of Misconduct" in E; in 13-28, substituted substituted "allegations of Misconduct" for "Charges of Misconduct" twice in E; in 13-30, inserted ", when the matter is placed on the public District Committee hearing docket,"; in 13-31, substituted "allegations of Misconduct" for "Charges of Misconduct" twice.

The amendment effective February 17, 2011, adopted February 17, 2011, in 13-1, inserted ", a Corporate Counsel Registrant, Foreign Lawyer, Foreign Legal Consultant," in the paragraph defining "Attorney," added the paragraph defining "Corporate Counsel Registrant," substituted "costs, translator fees and" for "costs; and" near the end of the paragraph defining "Costs," deleted ", whether federal or state," in paragraph 2., added paragraph 4., and made related changes in the definition of "Crime," substituted "License has been revoked upon consent to revocation or Respondent" for "License to practice law has been surrendered with charges pending or Respondent" in paragraph 1. of the definition of "Disciplinary Record," rewrote the definition of "Disciplinary Rules," added the paragraphs defining "Foreign Lawyer" and "Foreign Legal Consultant," inserted "or authority" in the definition of "License," deleted "to practice law" in the definition of "Reinstatement," rewrote the definition of "Revocation" and "Suspension"; in 13-4, inserted the present sixth sentence of A, and in E, substituted "Qualification" for "Qualifications" in the heading, and added the last sentence; added the last two sentences of 13-5; in 13-6, inserted "active" near the middle of the first sentence of A, and rewrote the third sentence of paragraph 2. of G; in 13-7, rewrote the third sentence of paragraph 4. of A, substituted "members of the Bar" for "Attorneys" and "non-lawyer" for "non-attorney" in the last sentence of B, and in J, substitued "a member of the Bar" for "an Attorney" in the heading and in the first sentence; in 13-8, substituted "served upon" for "delivered to" in the last sentence of paragraph 4. of A; in 13-9, rewrote paragraph 2. of E; in 13-12, rewrote C and added G; in 13-13, rewrote A; in 13-21, deleted "to practice law" following "Attorney's License" in the first sentence of A and D, and in D, substituted "Attorney's License" for "Attorney" near the end of the last sentence; in 13-25, inserted a comma following "pending at" and made a stylistic change in A, and deleted "to practice law in Virginia" following "her License" in the first sentence of C, deleted "to practice law" following "License" in the introductory paragraph of D, substituted "the Internal Revenue Service, the National Criminal Information Center, the National Criminal Information Network" for "IRS, NCIC, NCIN" near the end of paragraph 4. of J, and inserted "served by certified mail, return receipt requested," in paragraph 6. of J; in 13-26, made a stylsitic change in the first sentence, and deleted "to practice law" following "License" near the end of the second sentence of F; and in 13-28, deleted "to practice law" following "Licence" near the end of C.

The amendment effective April 13, 2012, adopted April 13, 2012, in 13-6, inserted the present fourth sentence of A.

The amendment effective December 14, 2012, adopted December 14, 2012, in 13-16, amended DD, by relocating the 1. designator to precede "A Charge of Misconduct," and adding the (a) and (b) designators.

Law Review. — For article, "Professional Responsibility," see 39 U. Rich. L. Rev. 315 (2004). For article, "Professional Responsibility," see 43 U. Rich. L. Rev. 255 (2008).

Michie's Jurisprudence. — For related discussion, see 2A M.J. Attorney and Client, §§ 56 — 58.

CASE NOTES

Editor's note. — Many of the cases below were decided under prior law.

Purpose of preliminary investigation. — A duly constituted committee of the Virginia State Bar is authorized in any case of alleged unprofessional conduct by an attorney, to "make such preliminary investigation as may be appropriate." Through the medium of such investigation a number of frivolous and groundless complaints preferred against attorneys are dismissed. The attorney involved is thereby spared the embarrassment and the unwarranted publicity that attends the filing of a formal complaint and a hearing. Seventh Dist. Comm. v. Gunter, 212 Va. 278, 183 S.E.2d 713 (1971).

"Certification." — The Virginia State Bar Disciplinary Board improperly allowed the amendment of a statement in a certification against an attorney after he had admitted the statement's correctness; the amended charge was tantamount to a new charge without notice, review by the district committee, or opportunity to be heard, and the attorney was denied the procedural protections of Va. Sup. Ct. R., pt. 6, § IV, R. 13. Pappas v. Va. State Bar, 271 Va. 580, 628 S.E.2d 534, 2006 Va. LEXIS 51 (2006).

Although the actual mailing of a subcommittee's certification determination may have been done by Bar Counsel instead of a subcommittee chair, it was of no legal significance and represented substantial compliance with Va. Sup. Ct. R. pt. 6, § IV, R. 13(E). Green v. Va. State Bar ex rel. Seventh Dist. Comm., 274 Va. 775, 652 S.E.2d 118, 2007 Va. LEXIS 134 (2007).

Notice of certification was prompt under Va. Sup. Ct. R. pt. 6, § IV, R. 13(G)(4) because an attorney showed no prejudice caused to him by virtue of the inaccuracies in the Virginia Bar's pleadings or the two-week period that elapsed between the subcommittee action and the mailing. Green v. Va. State Bar ex rel. Seventh Dist. Comm., 274 Va. 775, 652 S.E.2d 118, 2007 Va. LEXIS 134 (2007).

Although the Bar did not mail to the attorney the certification of charges of misconduct for more than a year after its subcommittee certified the charges despite a "prompt mailing provision" at Va. Sup. Ct. R. pt. 6, § IV, R. 13-15(E), the attorney was still not entitled to relief in the Bar's disciplinary proceedings against the attorney. Pursuant to Va. Sup. Ct. R. pt. 6, § IV, R. 13-12(A) and (B), only substantial compliance with the rule regarding certification of charges was required and the attorney was not entitled to relief because the attorney could not show how the delay in mailing the certification prejudiced the attorney. Green v. Va. State Bar, 278 Va. 162, 677 S.E.2d 227, 2009 Va. LEXIS 67 (2009).

Disciplinary proceedings may be conducted administratively or before three judge court. — Read together, § 54.1-3935 and paragraph 13 vest Bar Counsel and a district committee with the option of conducting disciplinary proceedings either administratively or before a three-judge court; there is no due process defect in such an option. Gunter v. Virginia State Bar ex rel. Seventh Dist. Comm., 241 Va. 186, 399 S.E.2d 820, cert. denied, 500 U.S. 953, 111 S. Ct. 2260, 114 L. Ed. 2d 712 (1991).

Request for three judge court. — Attorney's remanded appeal to a Disciplinary Board for reconsideration did not trigger any new right for him to then request a three-judge court under § 54.1-3915 and Va. Sup. Ct. R. pt. 6, § IV, R. 13(I)(1)(a)(1)(a). Green v. Va. State Bar ex rel. Seventh Dist. Comm., 274 Va. 775, 652 S.E.2d 118, 2007 Va. LEXIS 134 (2007).

District committee may instigate a disciplinary proceeding on its own. Delk v. Virginia State Bar, 233 Va. 187, 355 S.E.2d 558 (1987).

No attorney has right to insist proceedings be confined to administrative forum. — Although an attorney, like a district committee, is given a right to remove disciplinary proceedings from the administrative forum to a circuit court, no attorney has a right to insist that the proceedings be confined to the administrative forum. Gunter v. Virginia State Bar ex rel. Seventh Dist. Comm., 241 Va. 186, 399 S.E.2d 820, cert. denied, 500 U.S. 953, 111 S. Ct. 2260, 114 L. Ed. 2d 712 (1991).

Acquittal in a criminal proceeding presents no bar to a disciplinary proceeding arising out of substantially the same facts. The rationale which underlies this distinction is that the purpose of the disciplinary proceeding is not to punish, but to protect the public from unfit members of the bar. Smolka v. Second Dist. Comm., 224 Va. 161, 295 S.E.2d 267 (1982).

A circuit court's conclusion that an attorney's offense in removing office equipment from another's business and placing it in his own law office did not rise above trespass in no way precluded the State Bar Disciplinary Board from independently examining the matter and reaching a determination of misconduct. Smolka v. Second Dist. Comm., 224 Va. 161, 295 S.E.2d 267 (1982).

Disciplinary proceedings are judicial in nature for purposes of applying *Rooker-Feldman* doctrine.— In finding that it lacked subject matter jurisdiction under the *Rooker-Feldman* doctrine, the court found that the disbarment proceedings of the Virginia State Bar and its committees, as well as the right of appeal before the Virginia Supreme Court, were judicial in nature and that granting relief on an attorney's challenges to his disbarment proceeding and the disciplinary and Supreme Court's findings would have rendered ineffectual the state decisions. Motley v. Va. State Bar, 403 F. Supp. 2d 468, 2005 U.S. Dist. LEXIS 29605 (E.D. Va. 2005).

Jurisdictional requirements involve venue, not subject-matter jurisdiction. — A provision may use the word "jurisdiction" in the sense that the court has territorial jurisdiction over the subject matter, meaning that the court is the proper venue. Smolka v. Second Dist. Comm., 224 Va. 161, 295 S.E.2d 267 (1982).

The use of "jurisdiction" in subparagraph B(4) establishes the territorial jurisdiction, or venue, of the district committee. The provision in no way limits the Board's authority to determine cases of attorney misconduct. Smolka v. Second Dist. Comm., 224 Va. 161, 295 S.E.2d 267 (1982).

Under paragraph 13, it is the duty of a district committee to investigate charges of misconduct against an attorney when the misconduct occurs in that district or the attorney resides in or maintains an office in the district. However, this paragraph establishes venue rather than subject-matter jurisdiction. Stith v. Virginia State Bar, 233 Va. 222, 355 S.E.2d 310 (1987).

Failure to timely object to venue in disciplinary action. — Ordinarily, venue is waived if the defendant does not make a timely objection. This concept is implicit in subparagraph C(5). Smolka v. Second Dist. Comm., 224 Va. 161, 295 S.E.2d 267 (1982).

Under former subparagraph C(5), when an attorney files his answer to a charge of misconduct, he waives his privilege to assert lack of venue. If he waits until after the adverse decision of the Virginia State Bar Disciplinary Board to state his objection to venue, his objection is untimely. Smolka v. Second Dist. Comm., 224 Va. 161, 295 S.E.2d 267 (1982).

Venue is waived if timely objection is not made. Stith v. Virginia State Bar, 233 Va. 222, 355 S.E.2d 310 (1987).

Where attorney's first objection to venue of record was his motion to dismiss filed with the disciplinary board, this objection came too late in the disciplinary proceedings to afford him relief, and the disciplinary board properly overruled this motion. Stith v. Virginia State Bar, 233 Va. 222, 355 S.E.2d 310 (1987).

Where attorney appeared before the district committee on the first complaint and did not raise objection to the venue, this was equivalent to an express waiver. Where he did not appear on the second complaint and did no more than communicate by telephone with a member of the committee, his failure to object either in person or in writing again waived any objection to venue. Stith v. Virginia State Bar, 233 Va. 222, 355 S.E.2d 310 (1987).

The attorney's failure to make a timely demand for a three-judge court constituted a conclusive waiver of the right to subsequently file such demand. Wright v. Virginia State Bar, 233 Va. 491, 357 S.E.2d 518, cert. denied, 484 U.S. 930, 108 S. Ct. 300, 98 L. Ed. 2d 259 (1987).

Provision of former Va. Sup. Ct. R. pt. 6, § IV, R. 13(C)(6) (now Va. Sup. Ct. R. pt. 6, § IV, R. 13(I)(1)(a)(1)(a)) does not conflict with the mandate of § 54.1-3915 that an attorney who demands to be tried for disciplinary charges before a court of competent jurisdiction is to be tried before no other forum; nothing in § 54.1-3915 suggests that the right to be tried by a three-judge court cannot be waived, and an attorney who fails to file a timely demand for a trial before a three-judge court effectively waives the right to demand such a forum for the charges against the attorney. Fails v. Va. State Bar, 265 Va. 3, 574 S.E.2d 530, 2003 Va. LEXIS 11 (2003).

Procedure for disciplining, suspending, and disbarring attorneys. — When an attorney timely demanded his alleged violations be tried before a three-judge court, the Virginia State Bar Disciplinary Board's authority terminated and it had no authority to enter its order suspending the attorney's license. Cilman v. Va. State Bar, 266 Va. 66, 580 S.E.2d 830, 2003 Va. LEXIS 63 (2003).

Because the Virginia State Bar submitted itself to the jurisdiction of a three-judge panel when it stipulated that an attorney's former Va. Sup. Ct. R. pt. 6, § IV, para. 13(I)(1)(a)(1)(b) demand was timely, the Virginia State Bar Disciplinary Board lacked jurisdiction to suspend the attorney's license to practice law for a period of one year. Brown v. Va. State Bar, 270 Va. 409, 621 S.E.2d 106, 2005 Va. LEXIS 94 (2005).

Procedure. — Attorney was not entitled to relief from the Board's determinations, and resulting suspension of the attorney's law license, in disciplinary proceedings the Bar brought against the attorney for violation of professional conduct rules, as the attorney could not show a procedural irregularity pursuant to Va. Sup. Ct. R. pt. 6, § IV, R. 13-18 that merited relief. Although the Board substituted some members at a second hearing on the attorney's disciplinary matter, it could do so because it provided new members with a transcript of the earlier hearing and a complete record, and the chairman's designate could enter the suspension order against the attorney because the attorney waived any allegation of impropriety by not timely objecting. Green v. Va. State Bar, 278 Va. 162, 677 S.E.2d 227, 2009 Va. LEXIS 67 (2009).

Timeliness of hearing. — Time provision of Va. Sup. Ct. R. pt. 6, § IV, R. 13(I)(1)(b) operated as a scheduling mechanism rather than a jurisdictional bar such as a statute of limitations or statute of repose. Thus, the failure to schedule a hearing within the 30 to 120 day window of the rule did not divest a three judge panel of jurisdiction to consider a disciplinary matter. Green v. Va. State Bar ex rel. Seventh Dist. Comm., 274 Va. 775, 652 S.E.2d 118, 2007 Va. LEXIS 134 (2007).

Petition merely repeating untimely venue objection was properly denied. — Where attorney filed with the Disciplinary Board a petition for review of its decision and remand of the case to the Fourth District Committee for a hearing de novo on the ground that the Fifth District Committee lacked jurisdiction to investigate the complaints against him, and his petition merely repeated his untimely objection to venue, the Disciplinary Board did not err in denying it. Stith v. Virginia State Bar, 233 Va. 222, 355 S.E.2d 310 (1987).

Attorney's untimely demand for trial before a three-judge court did not deprive board of jurisdiction. — Contrary to an attorney's argument, the attorney's demand to have the charges of misconduct in the attorney's case tried before a three-judge court did not deprive the Virginia State Bar Disciplinary Board of subject matter jurisdiction to determine the charges, as the limitation in former Va. Sup. Ct. R. pt. 6, § IV, R. 13(C)(6) (now Va. Sup. Ct. R. pt. 6, § IV, R. 13(I)(1)(a)(1)(a)) was a limit only on territorial jurisdiction or venue, and not on subject matter jurisdiction, and the attorney's failure to file a timely demand for a trial before a three-judge court acted as a waiver of that right. Fails v. Va. State Bar, 265 Va. 3, 574 S.E.2d 530, 2003 Va. LEXIS 11 (2003).

Committee for district to which attorney improperly removes goods has jurisdiction. — Where attorney takes office equipment from one district and uses it in his law office in another district, the committee for the latter district has jurisdiction to investigate this misconduct. Larceny is a continuing offense and use of the equipment by the attorney in his law office constituted misconduct in the district in which it was located. Smolka v. Second Dist. Comm., 224 Va. 161, 295 S.E.2d 267 (1982).

Use of bar funds to pay counsel in suits to enjoin unauthorized practice of law. — Payment from bar funds of reasonable counsel fees for the prosecution of suits on behalf of the Virginia State Bar to enjoin the unauthorized practice of law is within the authority of the Bar Rules and the Bar Act; but such payments shall be limited to attorneys specially employed for that purpose and only in cases in which special counsel is requested by the Attorney General. Button v. Day, 204 Va. 547, 132 S.E.2d 292 (1963).

Attorney's failure to handle a legal matter in a timely fashion and failure to keep his client reasonably informed as to the status of the matter was misconduct in violation of subsection (C) of DR 6-101, and the State Bar Disciplinary Board did not abuse its discretion in ordering disbarment. Tucker v. Virginia State Bar, 233 Va. 526, 357 S.E.2d 525 (1987).

Sanctions for misconduct. — Upon finding misconduct proved, the State Bar Disciplinary Board may (a) deliver a private reprimand; (b) deliver a public reprimand; (c) suspend the attorney's license for a stated period up to five years; or (d) revoke the attorney's license. Tucker v. Virginia State Bar, 233 Va. 526, 357 S.E.2d 525 (1987).

Disciplinary Board did not abuse its discretion under Va. Sup. Ct. R. pt. 6, § IV, R. 13(I)(2)(f)(2) in imposing a sanction of 45 days or in its setting of that sanction to commence on the date immediately following a separate six-month suspension of the attorney on other unrelated charges. Green v. Va. State Bar ex rel. Seventh Dist. Comm., 274 Va. 775, 652 S.E.2d 118, 2007 Va. LEXIS 134 (2007).

Refusal to admit mitigation evidence error. — Disciplinary board's refusal to admit evidence he proffered regarding bar's press release regarding his professional discipline and devastating impact it had on his law practice and family was error pursuant to Va. Sup. Ct. R. pt. 6, § IV, R. 13(I)(2)(f)(2). Evidence was relevant as to whether disciplinary board should lessen severity of sanction. Green v. Va. State Bar, 272 Va. 612, 636 S.E.2d 412, 2006 Va. LEXIS 97 (2006).

Mitigation evidence properly considered. — Attorney was provided a full and fair opportunity to present evidence in mitigation, and a Disciplinary Board heard and considered the aggravating and mitigating factors, including the attorney's argument of a de facto suspension because of the improper dissemination of information about the attorney under Va. Sup. Ct. R. pt. 6, § IV, R. 13(N)(4), before announcing its decision. Green v. Va. State Bar ex rel. Seventh Dist. Comm., 274 Va. 775, 652 S.E.2d 118, 2007 Va. LEXIS 134 (2007).

Foreign adjudication on merits held conclusive. — This rule does not permit the respondent attorney to relitigate any issues of fact which were expressly or implicitly decided in the foreign jurisdiction. The board, therefore, correctly held that the foreign adjudication on the merits was conclusive. Cummings v. Virginia State Bar, 233 Va. 363, 355 S.E.2d 588 (1987).

Appellate review of Disciplinary Board findings and conclusions. — On review the Supreme Court will make an independent examination of the whole record, giving the factual findings of the Disciplinary Board substantial weight and viewing them as prima facie correct. While not given the weight of a jury verdict, those conclusions will be sustained unless it appears they are not justified by a reasonable view of the evidence or are contrary to law. Blue v. Seventh Dist. Comm., 220 Va. 1056, 265 S.E.2d 753, stay denied, 448 U.S. 904, 100 S. Ct. 3045, 65 L. Ed. 2d 1134 (1980).

The penalty imposed by the State Bar Disciplinary Board in a disciplinary proceeding will be viewed on appeal as prima facie correct and will not be disturbed unless, upon the Supreme Court's independent examination of the whole record, it appears unjustified by a reasonable view of the evidence or is contrary to law. Tucker v. Virginia State Bar, 233 Va. 526, 357 S.E.2d 525 (1987).

A sanction imposed by the Disciplinary Board will be viewed on appeal as prima facie correct and will not be disturbed unless, upon independent examination of the whole record, it appears unjustified by a reasonable view of the evidence or is contrary to law. Shea v. Virginia State Bar, 236 Va. 442, 374 S.E.2d 63 (1988).

Applied in Tucker v. Seventh Dist. Comm., 202 Va. 840, 120 S.E.2d 366 (1961); Maddy v. First Dist. Comm., 205 Va. 652, 139 S.E.2d 56 (1964); Blum v. Tenth Dist. Comm., 210 Va. 5, 168 S.E.2d 121 (1969); Greene v. Virginia State Bar Ass'n, 411 F. Supp. 512 (E.D. Va. 1976).

13.1. Suspension for Failure to Complete Professionalism Course.

Each person admitted to the Virginia State Bar on or after July 1, 1988, as an active member shall complete the course of study prescribed by the Executive Committee of the Virginia State Bar and approved by the Supreme Court of Virginia on the Rules of Professional Conduct and the lawyer's broader professional obligations, and any active member who fails to complete the course shall be suspended unless a waiver is obtained for good cause shown. Such course of study shall be funded by attendance fees paid by those attending the course.

Any active member licensed after June 30, 1988, and any other member who changes his or her membership to active status shall complete the required course within twelve months of becoming an active member. Failure to comply with this Rule shall subject the active member to the penalties set forth in Paragraph 19 herein.

"Good cause shown" as used herein shall include illness, hospitalization or such other cause as may be determined by the Executive Committee, whose determination shall be final. Any determination by the Executive Committee may be reviewed by the Supreme Court on request of the member seeking a waiver.

The amendment, effective February 4, 2000, substituted "Rules of Professional Conduct" for "Code of Professional Responsibility" in the first sentence of the first paragraph.

Michie's Jurisprudence. — For related discussion, see 2A M.J. Attorney and Client, § 56.

13.2. Suspension for Failure to Complete Continuing Legal Education Requirement.

Each active member of the Virginia State Bar shall complete the Continuing Legal Education requirement prescribed by Paragraph 17 of these Rules, and any active member who fails to complete the requirement shall be suspended unless a waiver is obtained for good cause shown. Any active member licensed on or after July 1, 1986, shall thereafter annually file prior to, but no later than, December 15, certifications that he or she has completed the mandatory continuing legal education programs required by Paragraph 17, or obtain a waiver for good cause shown; provided, however, the next certification deadline following July 31, 2001, shall be December 15, 2002. Failure to comply with this Rule shall subject the active member to the penalties set forth in Paragraph 19 herein.

"Good cause shown" as used herein shall include illness, hospitalization, or such other cause as may be determined by the Continuing Legal Education Board whose determination shall be final. Any determination by the Continuing Legal Education Board may be reviewed by the Supreme Court upon request of the member seeking a waiver.

The amendment, effective October 1, 2001, adopted October 1, 2001, in the second sentence of the first paragraph, substituted "December 15" for "July 31" and added the proviso at the end thereof.

Michie's Jurisprudence. — For related discussion, see 2A M.J. Attorney and Client, § 56.

13.3. Reserved.

Editor's note. — This paragraph, which was adopted by order of April 25, 1989, effective July 1, 1989, was deleted by order of September 21, 1989, effective January 1, 1990.

14. Professional Corporations, Professional Limited Liability Companies and Limited Liability Partnerships (Limited Liabilities Entities).

The rules and regulations in the following provisions of this Paragraph 14 shall constitute a Code of Ethics governing the professional conduct of the practice of law through professional law corporations, professional limited liability companies and registered limited liability partnerships in Virginia.

(a) *Scope.* — All applications, reports and other documents required to be filed with the Virginia State Bar by this Paragraph 14 shall be signed and verified by an officer, director, partner, or manager of the applicant who is a duly licensed, active member of the Virginia State Bar or who is otherwise legally authorized to practice law in Virginia and filed at the office of the Virginia State Bar.

(b) *Certificate of Registration.* — An applicant for registration as a limited liability entity shall file with the Virginia State Bar an application for a Certificate of Registration, on a form furnished by the Virginia State Bar, and pay a fee of $100. The term "limited liability entity," as used in this Paragraph 14 shall include a professional law corporation, professional limited liability company, and a registered limited liability partnership.

(i) The Executive Director of the Virginia State Bar, or a person or persons designated by him, shall review such application for registration and, within 15 days after receipt of such application, approve the application and issue a Certificate of Registration provided the application conforms to the requirements of law and this Paragraph 14. If the application fails to include the information required in subparagraphs (c)(i) through (c)(v) of this Paragraph 14, the Executive Director shall refuse to approve the application and notify the applicant of the reasons therefore. A request by the Executive Director for further information to comply with the requirement of said subparagraph (c) of this Paragraph 14, or a request that the application be amended, may be deemed by the applicant to be a refusal to approve the application for purposes of initiating review under subparagraph (b)(iii) of this Paragraph 14.

(ii) The effective date of the Certificate of Registration shall be the date on which the applicant has filed with the Virginia State Bar all material required for approval of the application; provided, however, that (1) a later effective date may be granted if requested by the applicant prior to the issuance of the Certificate of Registration, or (2) in the discretion of the Executive Director an earlier effective date may be granted if good cause appears therefore.

(iii) An applicant may request a review of a refusal to approve its application within sixty days after the date of the notice of such refusal. Such request shall be heard by the Executive Committee of the Virginia State Bar. Upon completion of review, which may include examination of all information submitted by the applicant and a hearing, the Committee shall either (1) approve the application and order the issuance of a Certificate of Registration, or (2) request further information required by subparagraph (c) of this Paragraph 14 or amendments not theretofore supplied by the applicant, or (3) refuse to approve the application in any case where the applicant fails or refuses to supply the required information or has made a material misrepresentation of fact. The Committee shall report in writing its findings of fact and the reasons for its order, whether approving or refusing to approve the application. Notice of the order and a copy of the report shall be mailed to the applicant.

(iv) Insofar as applicable, the rules of procedure of the Virginia State Bar shall apply to the procedure in (b)(iii) above. An aggrieved applicant may proceed in a court of competent jurisdiction by motion for declaratory judgment for review of matters relating to its application.

(c) *Application for Certificates.* — A Certificate of Registration as a limited liability entity shall be issued if the application shows:

(i) The applicant is organized and qualified under the provisions of Chapter 7 (Section 13.1-542 et seq.) of Title 13.1 of the Code of Virginia (the Virginia Professional Corporations Act), organized and qualified under the provisions of Chapter 13 (Section 13.1-1100 et seq.) of Title 13.1 of the Code of Virginia (the Virginia Professional Limited Liability Company Act), organized and qualified under the provisions of Article 9.1 (Section 50-73.132 et seq.) of Chapter 2.2 of Title 50 (the Virginia Registered Limited Liability Partnership Act), or organized and qualified under the laws of a jurisdiction other than the Commonwealth of Virginia to perform a professional service of the type defined in Section 13.1-543(A) of the Code of Virginia.

(ii) All of the applicant's shareholders, directors, officers, partners, members or managers and their names and addresses are set forth in full in the application.

(iii) Each member, manager, partner, employee or agent of the applicant who will practice law in Virginia, the names and addresses of whom are set forth in full in the application, whether or not a director, officer, shareholder, partner, member or manager of the applicant, is an active member of the Virginia State Bar or otherwise legally authorized to practice law in Virginia. Nothing in this Paragraph 14(c)(iii) shall be deemed to prohibit a non-licensed individual from serving as secretary, treasurer, office manager or business manager of any limited liability entity, provided, however, that such individual shall not be held out to be qualified or otherwise authorized to practice law or give advice on a legal or related matter to the clients of the entity. Any employee or agent of the applicant who is duly licensed to practice law in Virginia and who is not held out to the public to be so authorized shall be deemed for the purposes of these Rules to be a non-licensed individual.

(iv) A trade name may be used by a limited liability entity if it does not imply a connection with a government agency or with a public or charitable organization and is not otherwise in violation of Virginia Rules of Professional Condut 7.1(a). The name of a lawyer holding a public office shall not be used in the name of the entity, or in communications on its behalf, during any substantial period in which the lawyer is not actively and regularly practicing with the entity.

(v) The applicant has advised or intends to advise the clients of any predecessor organization, and the clients of any shareholder, director, officer, member, partner, manager, employee or agent of the applicant who will practice law, of the transfer of such organization's or lawyer's practice to a limited liability entity.

(d) *Ownership.* — An interest in or shares of a professional law corporation or professional limited liability company may be owned only in accordance with the provisions of Chapter 7 or Chapter 13 of Title 13.1. Ownership of shares of a professional law corporation or professional limited liability company for the purpose of construing this subparagraph (d) shall mean both legal and beneficial ownership. All the trustees of any voting trust which may be entered into by any shareholder shall be duly licensed or otherwise legally authorized to practice law in Virginia, and no proxy to vote any of such shares shall be valid unless granted to and voted by an individual or individuals duly licensed or otherwise legally authorized to practice law in Virginia.

(e) *Control Over and Rendition of Legal Services; Letterhead.* — No person not a member of the Virginia State Bar and duly licensed to practice law in Virginia shall have the right to direct or control the professional judgment of any employee of a limited liability entity or the conduct of employees of the entity with respect to the practice of law in Virginia. Any limited liability entity practicing law in a foreign jurisdiction and which enumerates its employees on its letterhead and in other permissible listings shall do so in a manner which will make clear the jurisdictional limitations on those employees and agents of the entity not licensed to practice in all listed jurisdictions.

(f) *Correspondence, Pleadings and Documents.* — Correspondence, pleadings and other documents, the execution of which constitutes the practice of law in Virginia, shall be executed on behalf of a limited liability entity by an employee who is an active member of the Virginia State Bar and duly licensed to practice law in Virginia. Corporate documents, the execution of which does not constitute the practice of law, may be executed on behalf of a limited liability entity by any authorized employee, whether or not licensed to practice law.

(g) *Division of Fees.* — It shall be lawful, ethical and proper for a lawyer employed by a limited liability entity, as part of the terms of his employment, to agree to turn over to the entity by which he is employed all fees, compensation or reimbursement which he may be entitled to receive for his professional services, regardless of where such professional services are rendered. No limited liability entity with a Certificate of Registration in effect shall be deemed a lay agency, nor shall any employee of such entity be deemed to be practicing law through an intermediary during any period for which such entity maintains a Certificate of Registration in effect.

(h) *Professional Responsibility.* — Nothing in this Paragraph 14 shall be deemed to diminish or change the obligation of any lawyer employed by a limited liability entity to conduct the practice of law in accordance with any specific standards promulgated by the Supreme Court of Virginia. Any lawyer who by act or omission causes the entity by which he is employed to act or fail to act in a manner which violates any applicable standard of professional conduct, including any of the provisions of this Paragraph 14, shall be personally responsible for such act or omission and subject to discipline therefore.

(i) *Attorney-Client Privilege.* — Nothing in this Paragraph 14 shall be deemed to modify, abrogate or reduce the attorney-client privilege or any comparable privilege or relationship, whether derived by statute or from common law.

(j) *Discipline.* — A Certificate of Registration shall continue in effect until it is suspended or revoked as provided herein. Such certificate may be suspended or revoked if a limited liability entity fails at any time to comply fully with the provisions of this Paragraph 14, the Rules of Professional Conduct, the Code of Professional Responsibility, the applicable Virginia Professional Corporation Act, the Virginia Professional Limited Liability Company Act, or the Virginia Registered Limited Liability Partnership Act, after notice and an opportunity to be heard as provided in 14(j)(ii) below; provided that, if the violation be such as can be corrected upon notice to the entity of its violation, or if the violation be that of one or several persons only, suspension or revocation of the certificate need not be invoked if the interest of justice and the protection of the public can be fairly served by appropriate disciplinary proceedings against the individual(s) involved.

(i) Upon receipt of a resolution of the board of directors or the written statement of the manager(s) or partner(s) of a limited liability entity requesting the cancellation of the Certificate of Registration of that entity, such certificate shall be cancelled by the Executive Director of the Virginia State Bar, or by a person or persons designated by him. The cancellation of a Certificate of Registration at the request of a limited liability entity shall be effective as of the date such request is received at the office of the Virginia State Bar, except that a later effective date shall be granted upon request of the entity or, in the discretion of the Executive Director of the Virginia State Bar, an earlier effective date may be granted if good cause appears therefor.

(ii) Where a limited liability entity has violated or is about to violate any pertinent statute, rule or any provision of this Paragraph 14, the Executive Director of the Virginia State Bar, or a person or persons designated by him, may issue a notice directing Bar Counsel to investigate the alleged violation. Bar Counsel may issue such summons and subpoenas, and/or compel the production of such documents as he/she may reasonably deem necessary or material for the effective conduct of an investigation. Every Circuit Court shall have power to enforce any summons or subpoena issued by Bar Counsel and to adjudge disobedience thereof as contempt.

If the report of Bar Counsel concludes either that the allegation is without merit or that specific corrective action has been or will be taken, the Executive Director shall dismiss the matter forthwith. If Bar Counsel concludes that the allegation has merit warranting court action, Bar Counsel shall file with the Circuit Court having jurisdiction in the premises a verified complaint. The court shall issue a rule against the limited liability entity concerned and conduct further proceedings in the matter in accordance with Section 54.1-3937 of the Code of Virginia, as amended, which is incorporated herein by reference. In addition to or in lieu of a Circuit Court complaint against the entity, Bar Counsel may refer the matter to the appropriate District Committee pursuant to Part 6, Section IV, Para. 13, B.(5)(a) et seq. of these Rules. After the court has held its hearing pursuant to its rule, it shall enter an order reprimanding the entity or revoking or suspending its Certificate of Registration if it finds that the circumstances of the violation warrant such action; otherwise the court shall dismiss the matter.

(k) *Certificate Renewal.* — On the date two years after the effective date of its initial Certificate of Registration and biennially thereafter, each limited liability entity shall pay a fee of $50 whereupon its Certificate of Registration shall be automatically renewed.

(*l*) *Annual Report; Corporate or Partnership Changes.* — Each limited liability entity shall file with the Virginia State Bar a copy of any document or report required to be filed with the State Corporation Commission. In addition, each such entity shall file a special report on a form provided by the Virginia State Bar within thirty days after any change in its shareholders, directors, officers, members, managers, partners, employees or agents duly licensed to practice law. Each such change in personnel of a limited liability entity shall be brought to the attention of each of its clients, so that such client may know by whom he is represented or may be represented and with whom his confidences may be shared, in the same manner as is customary with partnerships.

(m) *Effective Dates.* — This Paragraph 14 shall become effective on [to be effective after the proposed statutory change goes into effect] and shall apply in like manner to professional corporations theretofore or thereafter organized under the provisions of Chapter 7 (Section 13.1-542 et seq.) of Title 13.1 of the Code of Virginia to practice law, and to professional limited liability companies theretofore or thereafter organized under the provisions of Chapter 13 (Section 13.1-1100 et seq.) of Title 13.1 of the Code of Virginia to practice law, and to registered limited liability partnerships theretofore or thereafter organized under the provisions of Article 9.1 (§ 50-73.132 et seq.) of Chapter 2.2 of Title 50 of the Code of Virginia to practice law, except where inconsistent with the provisions of such laws.

The amendment, effective February 4, 2000, substituted "Rules of Professional Conduct" for "Code of Professional Responsibility" in the second sentence of subsection (j).

The amendment, effective March 29, 2000, substituted "the Code of Professional Responsibility" for "or" preceding "the applicable Virginia Professional Corporation Act" in the second sentence of subsection (j).

The amendment, effective January 1, 2005, adopted December 22, 2004, rewrote subdivision (l).

The amendment effective July 1, 2006, adopted June 2, 2006, substituted "Section" preceding "§" throughout the Rule; rewrote subdivision (a);

substituted "therefore" for "therefor" at the end of subdivisions (b)(iii) and (h); in subdivision (c)(i) and near the end of subdivision (m), substituted "Article 9 (Section 50-73.132 et seq.) of Chapter 2.2 of Title 50" for "Article (§ 50- et seq.) of Chapter of Title 50"; in the first sentence of subdivision (c)(iii), inserted "member, manager, partner," substituted "is an active member" for "is a member" and "Bar of otherwise legally authorized to practice" for "Bar and duly licensed to practice"; in subdivision (c)(iii), substituted "Virginia Rules of Professional Conduct 7.1(a)" for "DR 2-101(A)" at the end of the first sentence; in subdivision (c)(iv), substituted "such organization's or lawyer's practice" for "such"; in subdivision (d), inserted "or otherwise legally authorized" twice; rewrote subdivision (l); and in subdivision (m), substituted "[to be effective after the proposed statutory change goes into effect]" for "July 1, 1995."

15. Third Year Student Practice Rule.

(a) *Activities.* — (i) An eligible law student may, in the presence of a supervising lawyer, appear in any court or before any administrative tribunal in this Commonwealth in any civil, criminal or administrative matter on behalf of any person if the person on whose behalf he is appearing has indicated in writing his consent to that appearance. The eligible law student must obtain written approval from the court or administrative tribunal prior to any appearance before the court or administrative tribunal.

(ii) An eligible law student may also, in the presence of a supervising lawyer, appear in any criminal matter on behalf of the Commonwealth with the written approval of the prosecuting attorney or his authorized representative, provided the student obtains the written authorization from the court or administrative tribunal prescribed in paragraph (a)(i) of this Rule.

(iii) The written consent and approval of the person or entity on whose behalf the student appears shall be filed in the record of the case and shall be brought to the attention of the judge of the court or the presiding officer of the administrative tribunal.

(b) *Requirements and Limitations.* — In order to qualify pursuant to this Rule, the law student must:

(i)a. Be duly enrolled and in good standing in a law school that is approved by the American Bar Association, but if such school is located in another state that permits law student practice, only if such other state permits a student of a law school in this State to engage in such practice; or

b. Be duly enrolled in a program of study in the office of an attorney as authorized in subdivision 2. of § 54.1-3926, Code of Virginia, and in accordance with the Rules of the Virginia Board of Bar Examiners.

(ii)a. Have completed satisfactorily legal studies amounting to at least four semesters, or the equivalent if the school is on a basis other than a semester basis; or

b. Be certified by the Virginia Board of Bar Examiners as being in the final year of a program of study in the office of an attorney as authorized in subdivision 2. of § 54.1-3926, Code of Virginia, and in accordance with the Rules of the Virginia Board of Bar Examiners.

(iii) Be certified by the dean of his law school, or by the attorney under whom he is studying in the case of a law reader, as being of good character and competent ability, and as having completed satisfactorily a course or program of study in each of the following: criminal law, professional ethics, evidence and procedure.

(iv) Be introduced to the court or agency in which he is appearing by an attorney admitted to practice in that court or agency.

(v) Neither ask for nor receive any compensation or remuneration of any kind for his services from the person on whose behalf he renders services but this shall not prevent a lawyer or law firm, legal aid bureau, public defender agency, or the Commonwealth from paying compensation to the eligible law student, nor shall it prevent charges by a lawyer or law firm for such services as may otherwise be proper.

(c) *Certification.* — The certification of a student by the Virginia Board of Bar Examiners, the law school dean, or the attorney under whom the student is studying in compliance with Paragraph 15(b)(ii) and (iii) above:

(i) Shall be filed with the Executive Director of the Virginia State Bar and, unless it is sooner withdrawn, shall remain in effect until the expiration of eighteen months after it is filed, or until the announcement of the results of the first examination given by the Virginia Board of Bar Examiners following the student's graduation or completion of the program of study, whichever date is earlier. Thereafter, the certification shall lapse and be of no further force or effect.

(ii) May be withdrawn by the Board, dean or attorney under whom the student is studying at any time by mailing a notice to that effect to the Executive Director of the Virginia State Bar. It is not necessary that the notice state the cause for withdrawal.

(d) *Supervision.* — The supervising attorney under whose supervision an eligible law student performs any of the activities permitted by this Rule (Paragraph) 15 shall:

(i) Be an active member of the Virginia State Bar who practices before, and whose service as a supervising lawyer for this program is approved by, each court or administrative body in which the eligible law student engages in limited practice.

(ii) Assume personal professional responsibility for the student's guidance in any work undertaken and for supervising the quality of the student's work.

(iii) Assist the student in his preparation to the extent the supervising lawyer considers it necessary.

(iv) The approval of the court designated in (a)(i) or (d)(i) above may be withdrawn at any time without stating the cause for withdrawal.

(e) *Miscellaneous.* — Nothing contained in this Rule (Paragraph) shall affect the right of any person who is not admitted to practice law to do anything that he might lawfully do before the adoption of this Rule (Paragraph).

Editor's note. — Paragraph 15 was added to § IV in 1975 (see 216 Va. 158).

The amendment effective July 1, 1999, adopted April 23, 1999, added the last sentence in subdivision (a)(i), added "provided the student obtains the written authorization from the court or administrative tribunal prescribed in paragraph (a)(i) of this Rule" at the end of subdivision (a)(ii), substituted "The written consent and approval of the person or entity on whose behalf the student appears" for "In each case the written consent and approval referred to above" in subdivision (a)(iii), in the first sentence of subdivision (c)(i), inserted "be" following "examination" and inserted "date," and inserted "(a)(i) or" in subdivision (d)(iv).

The amendment, effective October 1, 2001, adopted October 1, 2001, in subdivision (c)(i), deleted "be" following "examination" in the first sentence, rewrote the second sentence, and deleted the former third sentence.

The amendment, effective October 26, 2007, adopted October 26, 2007, inserted "prior to" preceding "any appearance" in the last sentence of subdivision (a)(i).

Law Review. — For article on third-year practice rules in Virginia, see 11 U. Rich. L. Rev. 69 (1976). For article, "A Model Rule for Student Practice in the United States Courts," see 37 Wash. & Lee L. Rev. 1101 (1980).

16. Clients' Protection Fund.

The Council may establish a Clients' Protection Fund for the purposes of reimbursing all or part of losses sustained by a client or other person or entity to whom a fiduciary duty is owed as a result of dishonest conduct of a member of the Virginia State Bar. The Board shall be appointed by Council, and shall receive, hold, manage, invest and distribute funds appropriated to it by Council or otherwise received, in accordance with procedures established by Council.

Effective July 1, 2007, each active member of the Virginia State Bar shall be assessed a required fee of $25 for the Clients' Protection Fund on the bar's annual dues statement. The fee shall be in addition to each member's annual dues as prescribed in Part 6, Section IV, Paragraph 11 of these rules, and it shall be paid on or before the 31st day of July each fiscal year.

All monies collected under this Paragraph 16 shall be accounted for and paid into the State Treasury of Virginia and transferred by the bar from the Treasury to the Clients' Protection Fund. The bar shall report annually on or about January 15 to the Supreme Court of Virginia on the financial condition of the Clients' Protection Fund, and the assessment will be reduced or discontinued whenever directed by the Court.

Failure to comply with the requirements of this Paragraph 16 shall subject the active member to penalties set forth in Part 6, Section IV, Paragraph 19 of these rules.

The amendment, effective July 1, 2007, adopted April 1, 2007, substituted "Clients' Protection Fund" for "Clients' Security Fund" in the catchline and in the first paragraph; substituted "lossess" for "injury," inserted "or other person or entity to whom a fiduciary duty is owed" and deleted "improper or" preceding "dishonest conduct" in the first sentence of the first paragraph; and added the second, third, and fourth paragraphs.

17. Mandatory Continuing Legal Education Rule.

The Virginia Supreme Court hereby establishes a Mandatory Continuing Legal Education Program in the Commonwealth of Virginia.

A. *Purpose.* — Continuing professional education of lawyers serves to improve the administration of justice and benefit the public interest. Regular participation in Continuing Legal Education programs will enhance the professional skills of practicing lawyers, afford them periodic opportunities for professional self-evaluation and improve the quality of legal services rendered to the public. All active members of the Virginia State Bar shall participate in an additional amount of further legal study throughout the period of their active practice of law, and failure to do so shall result in their suspension from membership in the Virginia State Bar.

B. *Continuing Legal Education Board.* — A Continuing Legal Education Board shall be established for the purpose of administering the program.

(1) Appointment: The Chief Justice of the Supreme Court shall appoint, after consultation with the Council, the members of the board who shall be members of the bar and twelve in number. One member shall be designated by the Chief Justice as Chairman and another as Vice-chairman. Members shall serve terms of three years each, except that, initially, four members shall be appointed for terms of one year, four for terms of two years, and four for terms of three years. No member shall serve more than two consecutive terms but shall be eligible for reappointment after the lapse of one or more years following expiration of the previous term. The Executive Director of the Virginia State Bar shall be an ex-officio member of the board.

(2) Notice of Meetings/Quorum: The board shall meet on reasonable notice by the Chairman, Vice-chair or the Executive Director. Five members shall constitute a quorum and the action of a majority of a quorum shall constitute action of the board; however, new regulations or amendments shall be approved by a majority of the full membership of the board.

(3) Powers: The board shall have those general administrative and supervisory powers necessary to effectuate the purposes of this Rule, including the power to adopt, following the advice and comment of Council, reasonable and necessary regulations consistent with this Rule. The effective date of any regulations or amendments to the regulations adopted by the board shall be as prescribed by the board, but in no event earlier than one hundred twenty (120) days following such adoption. The Council may reject any regulations or amendments to the regulations adopted by the board on or after July 1, 2010, by a 2/3 vote of those members of Council present and voting. Council's rejection of any regulations or amendments to the regulations shall have the effect of suspending the regulation or amendment until the Supreme Court has reviewed and approved, rejected, or modified the proposed regulation or amendment. The Virginia State Bar shall have the responsibility for funding the board and for enforcing Mandatory Continuing Legal Education requirements.

The board shall specifically have the following powers and duties:

(a) To approve, on an individual basis, CLE programs and sponsors and publish a list of those approved. The publication shall include the number of credits earned for completion of a particular program;

(b) To establish procedures for the approval of Continuing Legal Education courses, whether those courses are offered within the Commonwealth or elsewhere. These procedures should include the method by which CLE sponsors could make application to the board for approval, and if necessary, make amendments to their application;

(c) To authorize sponsors of Continuing Legal Education programs to advertise that participation in their program fulfills the CLE requirements of this Rule;

(d) To formulate and distribute to all members of the Virginia State Bar appropriate information regarding the requirements of this Rule, including the distribution of a certification form to be filed annually by each active member.

C. *Continuing Legal Education Requirements.* — (1) All active members of the Virginia State Bar shall annually complete and certify attendance at a minimum of twelve (12) credit hours of approved Continuing Legal Education courses of which at least two (2) hours shall be in the area of legal ethics or professionalism, except those lawyers expressly exempted from the requirement by this Rule or by decision of the Continuing Legal Education Board; provided, however, that for the period July 1, 2001 through October 31, 2002, active members shall complete and certify attendance at a minimum of fifteen (15) credit hours of approved Continuing Legal Education courses of which at least two (2) hours shall be in the area of legal ethics or professionalism, except those lawyers expressly exempted from the requirement by this rule or by decision of the Continuing Legal Education Board. Each active member shall complete the required Continuing Legal Education courses each year during the period

November 1 through October 31 of the following year; provided, however, the next completion period following June 30, 2001, shall be July 1, 2001 through October 31, 2002.

(2) In order to provide flexibility in fulfilling the annual requirement, a one-year carryover of credit hours is permitted, so that accrued credit hours in excess of one year's requirement may be carried forward from one year to meet the requirement for the next year. A member may carry forward a maximum of twelve (12) credit hours, two (2) of which, if earned in legal ethics or professionalism, may be counted toward the two (2) hours required in legal ethics or professionalism.

(3) Each active member of the Virginia State Bar shall be responsible for ascertaining whether or not a particular course satisfies the requirements of this Rule. Each member should exercise discretion in choosing those approved programs which are most likely to enhance professional skills and improve delivery of legal services.

D. *Certificate of Attendance.* — (1) Each active member of the Virginia State Bar shall certify prior to December 15 each year that such lawyer attended approved Mandatory Continuing Legal Education programs for the minimum number of hours required during the previous calendar year ending October 31; provided, however, the next certification deadline following July 31, 2001, shall be December 15, 2002. The failure to certify shall cause suspension of such lawyer's license to practice law. An untruthful certification shall subject the lawyer to appropriate disciplinary action.

E. *Exemptions.* — Each active member of the Virginia State Bar shall comply with this Rule except as follows:

(1) A newly admitted member shall be exempted from filing a certification for the completion period in which he or she is first admitted.

(2) A member who has obtained a waiver for good cause shown, as may be determined by the board, shall be exempted from filing a certification for the completion period for which the waiver is granted.

F. *Activation or Reactivation.* — A member of any category who wishes to become an active member of the Virginia State Bar shall furnish to the Secretary an affidavit stating that he or she has completed twelve (12) hours of Continuing Legal Education, including two (2) hours in legal ethics or professionalism within the previous twelve months. Thereafter, that member shall have the same completion period and certification deadline as other active members.

G. *Credits.* — (1) Credit will be given only for Continuing Legal Education courses or activities approved by the board.

(2) Hours in excess of the minimum requirements defined in this Rule may not be carried forward for credit beyond the one year provided for in the Rule.

(3) Credit will not be given for Continuing Legal Education hours accumulated prior to admission to the Virginia State Bar.

(4) Credit shall be given to active members of the Virginia State Bar who prepare course materials and who personally participate as instructors. The credit, as determined by the Board, will reflect the time reasonably required for preparation of materials, as well as the actual time spent instructing.

H. *Standards.* — The board shall evaluate, and where appropriate, approve, those programs which serve to satisfy the requirements of this Rule. In evaluating the specific programs, the board shall consider the following factors:

(1) Whether the course tends to increase the participant's professional competence as a lawyer.

(2) The number of hours of actual presentation, lecture, or participation, so that the appropriate number of credit hours can be identified and published.

(3) The usage of written educational materials which reflect a thorough preparation by the provider of the course, and which assist course participants in improving their legal competence.

(4) To qualify for mandatory continuing legal education credit, a course is not required to have a component on legal ethics or professionalism, although such components are encouraged. When topics on legal ethics or professionalism are offered, either as an entire course or component thereof, they must be clearly identified as such.

The amendment, effective February 4, 2000, in subdivision C(1), inserted "and certify attendance at" near the beginning of the first sentence and added the second sentence; in subdivision C(2), substituted "one year's requirement" for "one-year's requirement" near the middle of the first sentence, deleted the former second sentence, which read: "However, from the 1990-91 reporting period, an active member may carry forward a maximum of 10 credit hours toward the 1991-92 requirement, none of which may be counted toward the two (2) hours required in legal ethics or professionalism," and deleted "Thereafter," from the beginning of the present second sentence; and in subdivision D(1), in the first sentence, inserted "each year" and "required" and substitued "year ended June 30" for "reporting period."

The amendment, effective December 18, 2000, in subdivision E, substituted "newly admitted" for "newly-admitted" in paragraph (1) and deleted former paragraph (3).

The amendment, effective October 1, 2001, adopted October 1, 2001, in subdivision C, added the proviso at the end of the first sentence, and in the second sentence, substituted "November 1" for "July 1" and "October 31" for "June 30" and added the proviso at the end thereof; in subdivision D, in the first sentence, substituted "December 15" for "July 31" and "calendar year ending October 31" for "year ended June 30" and added the proviso at the end thereof; in subdivisions E(1) and E(2), substituted "completion period" for "reporting period"; and in subdivision F, substituted "completion period" for "reporting period" and inserted "and certification deadline" in the second sentence.

The amendment, effective January 7, 2011, adopted January 7, 2011, in subdivision B, in subsubdivision (2), substituted "Vice-chair" for "Vice-chairman" in the first sentence and added "however, new regulations or amendments shall be approved by a majority of the full membership of the board" at the end of the second sentence, and in subdivision (3), added "following the advice and comment of Council" in first sentence, and added the present second through fourth sentences.

18. Financial Responsibility.

In order to make available to the public information about the financial responsibility of each active member of the Virginia State Bar for professional liability claims, each such member shall, upon admission to the Bar, and with each application for renewal thereof, submit the certification required herein or obtain a waiver for good cause shown. The active member shall certify to the Bar on or before July 31 of each year: a) whether or not such member is currently covered by professional liability insurance, other than an extended reporting endorsement; b) whether or not such member is engaged in the private practice of law involving representation of clients drawn from the public, and, if so, whether the member intends to maintain professional liability insurance coverage during the period of time the member remains engaged in the private practice of law; and c) the date, amount, and court where rendered, of any unsatisfied final judgment(s) against such member, or any firm or professional corporation in which he or she has practiced, for acts, errors, or omissions (including, but not limited to, acts of dishonesty, fraud, or intentional wrongdoing) arising out of the performance of legal services by such member.

The foregoing shall be certified by each active member of the Virginia State Bar in such form as may be prescribed by the Virginia State Bar and shall be made available to the public by such means as may be designated by the Virginia State Bar.

Each active member who certifies to the Bar that such member is covered by professional liability insurance shall notify the Bar in writing within thirty (30) days if the insurance policy providing coverage lapses, is no longer in effect or terminates for any reason, unless the policy is replaced with another policy and no lapse in coverage occurs.

Failure to comply with this Rule shall subject the active member to the penalties set forth in Paragraph 19 herein. An untruthful certification or unjustified failure to notify the Bar of a lapse or termination of coverage shall subject the member to appropriate disciplinary action.

"Good cause shown" as used herein shall include illness, absence from the Commonwealth of Virginia, or such cause as may be determined by the Executive Committee of the Virginia State Bar whose determination shall be final. Any determination by the Executive Committee may be reviewed by the Supreme Court upon request of the member seeking a waiver.

The amendment, effective July 1, 2005, adopted April 26, 2005, inserted "and, if so, whether the member intends to maintain professional liability insurance coverage during the period of time the member remains engaged in the private practice of law" in clause b) of the first paragraph; added the present third paragraph; and inserted "or unjustified failure to notify the Bar of a lapse or termination of coverage" in the present fourth paragraph.

19. Procedure for the Administrative Suspension of a Member.

Whenever it appears that a member of the Virginia State Bar has failed to comply with any of the Rules of Court relating to such person's membership in the bar, the Secretary-Treasurer shall mail a notice to the member advising of the member's noncompliance and demanding (1) compliance within sixty (60) days of the date of such notice and (2) payment of a delinquency fee of $50, for each Rule violated, provided, however, that the delinquency fee for an attorney who does not comply with the timely completion requirements of Paragraphs 13.2 and 17(C) of these rules shall be $100, and the delinquency fee for an attorney who does not comply with the certification requirements of Paragraphs 13.2 and 17(D) of these rules shall be $100, and shall increase by $100 on February 1 for noncompliance with the certification requirements. The notice shall be mailed to the member at his last address on file at the Virginia State Bar.

In the event the member fails to comply with the directive of the Secretary-Treasurer within the time allowed, the Secretary-Treasurer will then mail a notice to the member by certified mail to advise (1) that the attorney's membership in the bar has been suspended and (2) that the attorney may no longer practice law in the Commonwealth of Virginia or in any way hold himself or herself out as a member of the Virginia State Bar. Thereafter the attorney's membership in the Virginia State Bar may be reinstated only upon showing to the Secretary-Treasurer (1) that the attorney has complied with all the Court's rules relating to his or her membership in the bar and (2) upon payment of a reinstatement fee of $150 for each Rule violated, provided, however, that the reinstatement fee for an attorney who was suspended for noncompliance with Paragraphs 13.2 and 17 of these rules shall be $250, and shall increase by $50 for each subsequent such suspension, not to exceed a maximum of $500.

Whenever the Secretary-Treasurer notifies a member that his or her membership in the bar has been administratively suspended, the Secretary-Treasurer shall also (1) advise the Chief Judges of the circuit and district in which the attorney has his or her office, as well as the clerks of those courts and the Clerk of the Supreme Court of Virginia, of such suspension and (2) publish notice of the suspension in the next issue of the *Virginia Lawyer Register*.

An administrative suspension shall not relieve the delinquent member of his or her annual responsibility to attend continuing legal education programs or to pay his or her dues to the Virginia State Bar.

The amendment effective February 4, 2000, in the first paragraph, substituted "the timely completion requirements of Paragraphs 13.2 and 17 C. of these rules shall be $50, and the delinquency fee for an attorney who does not comply with the certification requirements of Paragraphs 13.2 and 17 D. of these rules" for "the requirements of Section 13.2 herein"; and, in the second paragraph, in the second sentence, substituted "noncompliance with Paragraphs 13.2 and 17 of these rules shall be $250, and shall increase by $50 for each subsequent such suspension, not to exceed a maximum of $500" for "noncompliance with section 13.2 herein shall be $250."

The amendment effective July 1, 2007, adopted April 13, 2007, increased the fee amounts, and made stylistic changes in the first paragraph; in the second paragraph, inserted "or herself" in clause (2) of the first sentence and in clause (1) of the second sentence, substituted "$150" for "$75" in clause (2) of the second sentence, and made minor stylistic changes; and inserted "or her" twice in the third and fourth paragraphs.

The amendment effective August 1, 2009, adopted May 29, 2009, in the first paragraph, inserted "and shall increase by $100 on February 1 for noncompliance with the certification requirements" at the end of the first sentence, and deleted "by certified mail" following "shall be mailed" in the second sentence; and in the third paragraph, inserted "of Virginia" in clause (1).

20. Maintenance of Trust Accounts; Notice of Election Requirements.

Every trust account maintained by an active member of the VSB under Rules of Professional Conduct 1.15 shall also be maintained at a "financial institution approved by the Virginia State Bar" and maintained in accordance with this paragraph and Rule 1.15. A "financial institution approved by the Virginia State Bar" includes regulated state or federal chartered banks, savings institutions, and credit unions that are properly licensed and authorized to do business, have federal insurance on deposits, and have entered into and agreed to abide by a Virginia State Bar Approved Financial Institution Agreement. (See Appendix A which the Virginia State Bar reserves the right to amend or modify upon notice to all approved financial institutions.) The Virginia State Bar shall maintain and publish from time to time a list of approved financial institutions.

(A) *Interest-bearing Trust Accounts.* — A lawyer may maintain funds of clients in one or more interest-bearing accounts in one or more financial institutions, whenever the lawyer has established and follows record-keeping, accounting, clerical, and administrative procedures to compute and credit or pay periodically, but at least quarterly, pro rata to each client the interest on such client's funds less fees, costs, or expenses charged by the lawyer for the record-keeping, accounting, clerical, and administrative procedures associated with computing and crediting or paying such amounts.

(B) *IOLTA Accounts.* — A lawyer may deposit funds of a client in an identifiable interest-bearing trust (IOLTA) account for which the lawyer has not established procedures to compute and credit or pay pro rata net earnings to such client whenever:

(1) At the time of such deposit the lawyer reasonably expects that the fees, costs, or expenses which the lawyer would be entitled to charge under Paragraph 20(A) would equal or exceed the pro rata interest on such client's funds (the determination of whether the funds of a client or third person can earn income in excess of fees, costs or expenses the lawyer would be entitled to charge under paragraph 20(A) shall rest in the sound judgment of the lawyer or law firm, and no lawyer shall be charged with an ethical impropriety or breach of professional conduct based on the good faith exercise of such judgment); and

(2) The financial institution has agreed to:

(a) Periodically, but at least quarterly, remit to the Legal Services Corporation of Virginia (LSCV) interest or dividends on the average monthly balance of each such account or as otherwise computed in accordance with such bank's standard accounting practice, provided that such rate of interest shall not be less than the rate paid by such bank to regular, non-attorney depositors;

(b) Transmit with each remittance to LSCV a statement identifying the name of the lawyer or law firm from whose account the remittance is sent, the rate of interest applied, the period for which the remittance is made, the total amount of interest earned, the service charges or other fees assessed against the account, if any, and the net amount of interest remitted;

(c) Transmit to the depositing lawyer or law firm at the same time a report showing the amount paid to LSCV from such interest-bearing account, the rate of interest applied, the fees assessed, if any, and the average account balance for the period for which the report is made;

(d) Charge no fees against an IOLTA trust account that are greater than the fees charged to non-attorney depositors, except that an IOLTA remittance fee may be charged to defray the depository institution's administrative costs attributable to calculating and remitting the interest to LSCV; other allowable fees are per check charges, per deposit charges, a fee in lieu of a minimum balance and sweep fees. Allowable, reasonable fees may be deducted from interest or dividends earned on an IOLTA account, provided that such charges or fees shall be calculated in accordance with the Financial Institutions' standard practice for non-IOLTA customers. Fees or charges in excess of the interest or dividends earned on the IOLTA account, for any month or quarter, shall not be taken from the interest or dividends of any other IOLTA account. Fees for wire transfers, insufficient funds, bad checks, stop payment, account reconciliation, negative collected balances, and check printing are not considered customary account maintenance charges and are not deductible from the interest or dividends earned on the IOLTA account. All other fees including those non-customary fees just listed are the responsibility of the lawyer or law firm, who in turn may absorb these specific costs or pass along those fees to the client(s) being served by the transaction in accordance with attorney/client agreements. Financial Institutions may elect to waive any or all fees on IOLTA accounts in recognition of their charitable nature;

(e) Collect no fees from the principal deposited in the IOLTA trust account;

(f) Pay all or part of the funds deposited in such interest-bearing trust account upon demand or order. An IOLTA account may be an interest-bearing check account, a money market account with or tied to check-writing, a sweep account which is a government money market fund or daily overnight financial institution repurchase agreement invested solely in or fully collateralized by United States government securities, or an open-end money market fund solely invested in or fully collateralized by the United States government securities; and

(g) Agree and abide by all provisions in the Virginia State Bar Approved Financial Institution Agreement.

(3) Interest accruing on such accounts and paid by the financial institution to LSCV shall be used for funding 1) civil legal services to the poor in Virginia, 2) LSCV's administrative expenses, and 3) the creation and augmentation of a reserve fund for the same purposes.

(C) *Non-interest-bearing Trust Accounts.* — A lawyer may deposit funds of a client in an identifiable non-interest-bearing trust account for which the account accrues no interest or dividends so long as the attorney or law firm receives no consideration or benefit from the Financial Institution for opening a non-interest bearing trust account or for converting from an IOLTA account to a non-interest bearing trust account. A lawyer who elects not to participate in the maintenance of an interest-bearing trust account as described in Paragraph 20(B) must submit such an election in accordance with the procedures set forth in Paragraph 20(F) of this rule.

(D) *Reporting to Client.* — A lawyer who elects to deposit funds of a client in an account pursuant to Paragraph 20(B) or (C) shall not be required to seek permission from such client in making the election. As to funds deposited in accordance with Paragraph 20(B), a lawyer shall not be required to compute or report to such client any payment to LSCV of interest or dividends by the banking institution on funds in any such account wherein the client's funds have been deposited by the lawyer.

(E) *Law Firm Trust Accounts.* — A law firm of which any participating lawyer is a member may maintain the account(s) on behalf of any or all lawyers in the firm.

(F) *Opt-Out of IOLTA Account.* — A lawyer who elects to open an IOLTA account shall obtain a "Request to Establish IOLTA Account" form from LSCV. A lawyer who elects not to maintain an IOLTA account shall make such election on a "Request to Opt-Out" form provided by LSCV.

The amendment, effective February 4, 2000, substituted "Rules of Professional Conduct 1.15" for "DR 9-102 and DR 9-103" in the introductory paragraph.

The amendment effective June 21, 2011, adopted June 21, 2011, rewrote the Rule.

CASE NOTES

Only the Virginia State Bar has the ability to pursue violations of paragraph 20. In re Palumbo Family Ltd. Partnership, 182 Bankr. 447 (Bankr. E.D. Va. 1995).

21. Computerized Legal Research Services Rule.

The Supreme Court of Virginia hereby authorizes and directs the Virginia State Bar to contract to provide online computerized legal research services to its members.

A. *Purpose* — It is the policy and objective of the Commonwealth of Virginia to improve the quality and reduce the costs of legal services available to the citizens of Virginia. It is also the policy of this Commonwealth to enhance the availability of legal services to poor litigants and indigent criminal defendants. The provision of online computerized legal research tools to all Virginia lawyers will further these policies by increasing and improving the available knowledge and information base for attorneys, enhancing the quality of legal research and advice, making legal research more efficient for many attorneys, reducing the costs of legal services to the poor, and providing additional resources to lawyers who are appointed by courts to represent indigent criminal defendants. The provision of online computerized legal research services to all lawyers in Virginia will reduce the time spent and costs incurred in performing legal research, which will decrease the costs of legal services to consumers in Virginia and thereby increase access to attorneys. In addition, the provision of online computerized legal research will enable more lawyers to provide pro bono services since this research tool will lower their costs and reduce the amount of research time required.

B. *Procedure* — For these reasons, the Virginia State Bar, through its governing body, is authorized to contract to provide online computerized legal research services to its members. In connection therewith, the Virginia State Bar is authorized and directed to solicit proposals from providers of online computerized legal research services, enter into contracts for those services, and expend funds for the purchase of online computerized legal research services for its members. The Virginia State Bar shall supervise and periodically review the provision of online computerized legal research services to its members to ensure the continued quality of those services and that the policies and objectives of the Commonwealth are being met. The Virginia State Bar also shall submit to the Supreme Court of Virginia an annual report that describes and analyzes the status of the Bar's contracts for online computerized legal research services, the online computerized legal research services that are being provided, and the utilization of those services.

Effective date. — This rule, adopted June 13, 2005, became effective July 13, 2005.

A.

APPENDIX A

Virginia State Bar Approved Financial Institution Agreement

This Virginia State Bar Financial Institution Agreement ("Agreement") is made this ________ day of ________________, by and between the Virginia State Bar and 10, ("Financial Institution").

WITNESS:

The undersigned, an officer of the Financial Institution executing this Agreement, being duly authorized to bind said institution by this Agreement, hereby applies to be approved as a depository to receive escrow, trust, or client funds, as defined in Part 6, § IV, Para. 20, of the Rules of the Supreme Court of Virginia, or any successor provision(s), from attorneys for deposit in what are hereinafter referred to as "Trust Accounts." The Financial Institution agrees to comply with the following requirements, or any successor provisions:

1. **Notification to Attorneys or Law Firm.** To promptly notify the attorney or law firm of an overdraft in any Trust Account or the dishonor for insufficient funds of any instrument drawn on any Trust Account held by it.
2. **Notification to Bar Counsel.** To report the overdraft or dishonor to Bar Counsel of the Virginia State Bar, as set forth in Paragraph 5 of this Agreement.
3. **Audit of Trust Account.** To provide reasonable access to the Virginia State Bar of all records of the Trust Account if an audit of such account is ordered pursuant to court order, or upon receipt of a subpoena therefor. The financial institution may charge for the reasonable costs of producing these records.
4. **Interest Calculation.** The financial institution shall not engage in the practice of "negative netting" as to IOLTA trust accounts.
5. **Form of Report.** That all such reports shall be substantially in the following format:

   In either case of a dishonored instrument or an instrument presented against insufficient funds in a Trust Account, but honored by the financial institution, the report shall be identical to the notice customarily forwarded to the depositor and shall include the name and address of the depositor notified, including the name of the lawyer responsible for the account, as well as a copy of the dishonored instrument, if such copy is normally provided to the depositor. In addition, the report shall identify the financial institution reporting the overdraft, the account number, the date of the overdraft, the name of the person making the report, their address and telephone number and date. The report shall be made simultaneously with and within the time provided by law for notice of dishonor to the depositor or, in the case of instruments that are honored by the financial institution, within five (5) banking days after the date of presentation for payment against insufficient funds.
6. **Consent of Attorneys or Law Firms.** The Financial Institution may require, as a condition to opening an attorney Trust Account, the written consent of the attorney or law firm opening such account to the notification to Bar Counsel of the Virginia State Bar as set forth in Paragraph 2 of this Agreement.
7. **Change of Name or Corporate Form.** If a Financial Institution changes its name, merges or otherwise affiliates with, or is acquired by another entity, the successor Financial Institution shall promptly notify Bar Counsel of the change and whether the successor institution wishes to serve as a financial institution approved by the Virginia State Bar for attorney Trust Accounts and enter into an Agreement.
8. **Termination of Agreement.** This Agreement may terminate upon thirty (30) days notice from the Financial Institution in writing to Bar Counsel that the institution intends to terminate the Agreement on a stated date and that copies of the termination notice have been mailed to all attorneys and law firms that maintain Trust Accounts with the Financial Institution or any branch thereof. Notice to the Bar Counsel shall be sent by certified mail to the Virginia State

Bar, Attention: Bar Counsel, 707 E. Main Street, Suite 1500, Richmond, Virginia 23219-2800. This agreement may also be canceled without prior notice by Bar Counsel of the Virginia State Bar if the financial institution fails to abide by the terms of the agreement.

9. **Binding Effect.** This Agreement shall be binding upon the Financial Institution and any branch thereof receiving Trust Accounts.

10. **Definitions.** For purposes of this agreement the following definitions will apply:
   a. "Notice of Dishonor" refers to the notice which, pursuant to Uniform Commercial Code Section 3-508(2), must be given by a drawee bank before its midnight deadline.
   b. "Insufficient funds" refers to a state of affairs in which there is an insufficient collected balance in an account as reflected in the financial institution's accounting records, so that an otherwise properly payable item presented for payment cannot be paid without creating an overdraft in the account.
   c. "Dishonored" shall refer to instruments that have been dishonored because of insufficient funds as defined above.
   d. "Negative Netting" refers to the practice of a financial institution collecting some part or all of the fees assessed during a stated period of time against any IOLTA account that has failed to generate enough interest to pay assessed fees from the positive interest generated by other IOLTA accounts and deducting those fees from the total interest remitted to the Legal Services Corporation of Virginia for that time period.

IN WITNESS WHEREOF, the Financial Institution has executed this Agreement on the date and year written above.

ATTEST:

____
Name of Financial Institution

____
Address of Financial Institution

____
By ____________________________
Officer's Name
(Please print)

____
Officer's Signature

____
Corporate Office Held

Effective date. — This Appendix A, adopted June 21, 2011, became effective June 21, 2011.

SECTION V. BYLAWS OF THE COUNCIL OF THE VIRGINIA STATE BAR.

The order effective Dec. 1, 1983, adopted Sept. 9, 1983, deleted Section V.

SECTION VI. VIRGINIA STATE BAR BYLAWS.

The order effective Dec. 1, 1983, adopted Sept. 9, 1983, deleted Section VI.

SECTION VII. ACTS OF THE GENERAL ASSEMBLY (THE BAR ACT OF 1938 AND APPENDIX).

Editor's note. — This section is not set out. For the text of this section, refer to the sources listed in the Editor's note at the beginning of Part Six.

PART SEVEN A
GENERAL DISTRICT COURTS — IN GENERAL

Rule
7A:1. Scope.
7A:2. Computation of Time.
7A:3. Counsel.
7A:4. Reporters and Transcripts of Proceedings in Court.
7A:5. Discretion of Court.
7A:6. Preservation of the Record.
7A:7. Filing Format and Procedure.
7A:8. General Provisions as to Pleadings.
7A:9. Amendments.
7A:10. Copies of Pleadings and Requests for Subpoenas Duces Tecum to be Furnished.

Rule
7A:11. Endorsements.
7A:12. Requests for Subpoenas for Witnesses and Records.
7A:13. What Constitutes Noting an Appeal.
7A:14. Continuances.
7A:15. General Information Relating to Each Court.
7A:16. Isolation Proceedings under Article 3.01 of Title 32.1 of the Code of Virginia; Communicable Diseases of Public Health Significance.

Editor's note. — The order effective July 1, 1989, adopted Nov. 21, 1988, adopted new Part Seven A.

Rule 7A:1. Scope.

Part Seven-A of the Rules shall apply to all proceedings in the General District Courts.

Cross references. — See also § 8.01-3.
Source. — Former Rule 3D:1.

Michie's Jurisprudence. — For related discussion, see 4A M.J. Continuances, § 3.

Rule 7A:2. Computation of Time.

Whenever a party is required or permitted under these Rules to do an act within a prescribed time after receipt or delivery of a paper and the paper is sent by mail, three days shall be added to the prescribed period.

Cross references. — See also Rule 1:7 and Rule 3A:20.

Rule 7A:3. Counsel.

When used in these Rules, the word "counsel" or "attorney" includes a partnership, a professional corporation or an association of members of the Virginia State Bar practicing under a firm name.

"Counsel of record" in any case includes an attorney who has signed a pleading in the case or who has notified the clerk or judge that the attorney appears in the case and shall also include a party who appears in court pro se. Except as provided in § 16.1-69.32:1, counsel of record shall not withdraw from a case except by leave of court with such notice as the court may require to the client of the time and place of a motion for leave to withdraw.

Cross references. — See also Rule 1:5, § 8.01-314 and § 16.1-69.32:1.
Source. — This is present [former] Rule 3D:2, moved to Section [7]A so that it will be applicable to civil, criminal and traffic cases.

Rule 7A:4. Reporters and Transcripts of Proceedings in Court.

Reporters, when present, shall be first duly sworn to take down and transcribe the proceedings faithfully and accurately to the best of their ability and shall be subject to the control and discipline of the judge.

When a reporter is present and takes down any proceeding in a court, any person interested shall be entitled to obtain a transcript of the proceedings or any part thereof upon terms and conditions to be fixed in each case by the judge.

The proceedings may be taken down by means of any recording device approved by the judge.

Cross references. — See also Rule 1:3 and § 16.1-69.35:2.

Rule 7A:5. Discretion of Court.

All steps and procedures in the clerk's office touching the filing of pleadings and the maturing of suits or actions may be reviewed and corrected by the court.

The time allowed for filing pleadings may be extended by the court in its discretion and such extension may be granted although the time fixed already has expired.

Cross references. — See also Rule 1:9 and § 8.01-428 B.

Rule 7A:6. Preservation of the Record.

A court may authorize the use of electronic or photographic means for the preservation of the record or parts thereof.

Cross references. — See also Rules 1:14 and 8:12, § 16.1-69.35:2, Canons of Judicial Conduct Canon 3 B (7) and § 19.2-266.

Rule 7A:7. Filing Format and Procedure.

(a) Except as provided in subdivision (c) of this Rule and in Rule 1:17 pertaining to Electronically Filed Cases,

(1) All pleadings, motions, briefs and all other documents filed in any clerk's office in any proceeding pursuant to the Rules or statutes shall be 8-1/2 by 11 inches in size. All typed material shall be double spaced except for quotations.

(2) Subdivision (a)(1) of this Rule shall not apply to tables, charts, plats, photographs, and other material that cannot be reasonably reproduced on paper of that size.

(b) No paper shall be refused for failure to comply with the provisions of this Rule, but the clerk or judge may require that the paper be redone in compliance with this Rule and substituted for the paper initially filed. Counsel shall certify that the substituted paper is identical in content to the paper initially filed.

(c) *Electronic Filing.* — In any general district court which has established an electronic filing system pursuant to Rule 1:17:

(1) Any proceeding may be designated as an Electronically Filed Case upon consent of all parties in the case.

(2) Except where service and/or filing of an original paper document is expressly required by these rules, all pleadings, motions, notices and other instruments in an Electronically Filed Case shall be formatted, served and filed as specified in the requirements and procedures of Rule 1:17; provided, however, that when any document listed below is filed in the case, the filing party shall notify the clerk of court that the original document must be retained.

(i) Any pleading or affidavit required by statute or rule to be sworn, verified or certified as provided in Rule 1:17(e)(5).

(ii) Any contract or deed.

(iii) Any prenuptial agreement or written settlement agreement, including any property settlement agreement.

(iv) Any check or other negotiable instrument.

(v) Any handwritten statement, waiver, or consent by a defendant or witness in a criminal proceeding.

(vi) Any form signed by a defendant in a criminal proceeding, including any typed statements or a guilty plea form.

(vii) Any document that cannot be converted into an electronic document in such a way as to produce a clear and readable image.

Cross references. — See also Rule 1:16.

The amendment, effective May 2, 2011, adopted March 1, 2011, rewrote the Rule heading, added the introductory paragraph of subdivision (a), redesignated former subdivisions (a) and (b) as paragraphs (1) and (2) of subdivision (a), added "Subdivision (a)(1) of" at the beginning of subdivision (a)(2), redesignated former subdivision (c) as (b), and added subdivision (c).

Rule 7A:8. General Provisions as to Pleadings.

(a) Counsel of Record tendering a pleading gives assurances that it is filed in good faith and not for delay.

(b) A pleading that is sworn to is an affidavit for all purposes for which an affidavit is required or permitted.

(c) Counsel of Record who files a pleading shall sign it and state counsel's address and phone number.

(d) The mention in a pleading of an accompanying exhibit shall, of itself and without more, make such exhibit a part of the pleading.

Cross references. — See also Rule 1:4 and § 8.01-271.1.

Rule 7A:9. Amendments.

No amendment shall be made to any pleading after it is filed with the clerk, except by leave of court. Leave to amend shall be liberally granted in furtherance of the ends of justice.

In granting leave to amend, the court may make such provision for notice thereof and opportunity to make response as the court may deem reasonable and proper.

Cross references. — See also Rule 1:8.

Rule 7A:10. Copies of Pleadings and Requests for Subpoenas Duces Tecum to be Furnished.

All pleadings not otherwise required to be served and requests for subpoenas duces tecum shall be served on each counsel of record by delivering, dispatching by commercial delivery service, transmitting by facsimile or mailing a copy to each on or before the day of filing.

At the foot of such pleadings and requests shall be appended either acceptance of service or a certificate of counsel that copies were served as this rule requires, showing the date of delivery, dispatching, transmitting or mailing.

Cross references. — See also Rule 1:12, Rule 3A:21(a), § 16.1-89 and § 16.1-131.

The amendment, effective February 1, 1999, adopted November 23, 1998, inserted "dispatching by commercial delivery service, transmitting by facsimile" in the first paragraph and inserted "dispatching, transmitting" in the second paragraph.

Rule 7A:11. Endorsements.

Drafts of orders shall be endorsed by counsel of record, or reasonable notice of the time and place of presenting such drafts together with copies thereof shall be served by delivering, dispatching by commercial delivery service, transmitting by facsimile or mailing to all counsel of record who have not endorsed them. Compliance with this rule and with Rule 7A:10 may be modified or dispensed with by the court in its discretion. In an Electronically Filed Case, endorsement and specification of any objections to the draft order shall be accomplished as provided in Rule 1:17.

Cross references. — See also Rule 1:13.

The amendment, effective February 1, 1999, adopted November 23, 1998, inserted "dispatching by commercial delivery service, transmitting by facsimile" in the first sentence.

The amendment, effective May 2, 2011, adopted March 1, 2011, added the last sentence.

Rule 7A:12. Requests for Subpoenas for Witnesses and Records.

(a) *Subpoenas for Witnesses:*

(1) Requests for subpoenas for witnesses should be filed at least ten days prior to trial.

(2) Requests for subpoenas for witnesses not timely filed should not be honored except when authorized by the court for good cause.

(b) *Subpoenas Duces Tecum:*

(1) Requests for subpoenas duces tecum should be filed at least 15 days prior to trial.

(2) Requests for subpoenas duces tecum not timely filed should not be honored except when authorized by a judge for good cause.

(c) *Meaning of Filed:*

The term filed as used in this Rule means received in the appropriate clerk's office or by an appropriate magistrate.

(d) *Exception:* — This Rule does not apply to subpoenas for witnesses and subpoenas duces tecum issued by attorneys in civil cases as authorized by Virginia Code §§ 8.01-407 and 16.1-89.

Cross references. — See also Rule 3A:12(a), Rule 4:9(c), § 8.01-407, § 8.01-506.1, § 16.1-69.25, § 16.1-89 and § 16.1-131.

The amendment effective July 1, 2000, adopted June 16, 2000, added subdivision (d).

Rule 7A:13. What Constitutes Noting an Appeal.

All appeals shall be noted in writing. An appeal is noted only upon timely receipt in the clerk's office of the writing. An appeal may be noted by a party or by the attorney for such party. In addition, in civil cases, an appeal may be noted by a party's regular and bona fide employee or by a person entitled to ask for judgment under any statute.

Cross references. — See also Rule 3A:19(b), § 8.01-129, § 16.1-106, § 16.1-107, § 16.1-132 and § 16.1-135.

Comment. — Forms are available in the clerk's office for noting an appeal: DC-370, Notice of Appeal (Criminal) and DC-475, Civil Appeal Notice.

Rule 7A:14. Continuances.

(a) *Continuances Granted for Good Cause.* — Continuances should not be granted except by, and at the discretion of, a judge for good cause shown, or unless otherwise provided by law. The judge may, by order, delegate to the clerk the power to grant continuances consented to by all parties under such circumstances as are set forth in the order. Such an order of delegation should be reasonably disseminated and posted so as to inform the bar and the general public.

(b) *All Parties Agree to Continuance.* — If all parties to a proceeding agree to seek a continuance, the request may be made orally by one party as long as that party certifies to the judge that all other parties know of the request and concur. Such a request should be made as far in advance of the scheduled hearing or trial as is practicable. If granted, the moving party shall be responsible for assuring that notice of the continuance is given to all subpoenaed witnesses and that they are provided with the new court date. This obligation may be met by (i) an agreement between the parties that each side will notify its own witnesses; or (ii) any other arrangement that is reasonably calculated to get prompt notice to all witnesses.

(c) *All Parties Do Not Agree to Continuance.* — If a request for continuance is not agreed to by all parties, such request should be made to the court prior to the time originally scheduled for the hearing or trial. If the court determines that a hearing on the request should be conducted prior to the time originally scheduled for the trial, all parties shall be given notice of such hearing by the requesting party.

(d) *Continuances Requested At the Time of Hearing.* — Where a request for a continuance has not been made prior to the hearing or trial and other parties or witnesses are present and prepared for trial, a continuance should be granted only upon a showing that to proceed with the trial would not be in the best interest of justice.

(e) *Parties.* — For purposes of this Rule, the term "parties" shall mean all plaintiffs, defendants and third party defendants in a civil case and the prosecution and the defendant in a criminal or traffic infraction case.

Source. — Former Rule 3D:7.

Michie's Jurisprudence. — For related discussion, see 4A M.J. Continuances, §§ 4, 24 — 27, 49.

CASE NOTES

Continuance properly denied. — Because there was no foreseeable date at which a codefendant's case would be final and the codefendant's Fifth Amendment right extinguished, the trial court did not abuse its discretion in refusing to grant defendant's motion for a continuance. Jackson v. Commonwealth, 2005 Va. App. LEXIS 197 (May 17, 2005).

Implied waiver of speedy trial provisions. — Because defense counsel was not prepared for trial due to defendant's change of mind concerning a plea, defendant's actions and representations were an implicit request for a continuance that effectively waived the statutory speedy trial provisions in § 19.2-243. Richardson v. Commonwealth, 2007 Va. App. LEXIS 170 (Apr. 24, 2007).

Rule 7A:15. General Information Relating to Each Court.

The chief judges of the general district courts shall, on or before December 31 of each year, furnish the Executive Secretary of the Supreme Court current general information relating to the management of the courts within each district. This information shall be assembled and published electronically by the Executive Secretary.

Cross references. — See also Rule 1:15.

Editor's note. — The appendix of current general information relating to the management of the courts, referred to in this rule, is on file with the clerks of the circuit and district courts throughout the State. The appendix lists the judges, clerks, addresses, telephone numbers, office hours, terms and other information for all of the circuit and district courts in the State.

The amendment effective July 1, 2009, adopted June 12, 2009, deleted "on forms provided by him" following "Supreme Court" in the first sentence and substituted "electronically by the Executive Secretary" for "on or before July 1 of each year" in the last sentence.

Rule 7A:16. Isolation Proceedings under Article 3.01 of Title 32.1 of the Code of Virginia; Communicable Diseases of Public Health Significance.

A. Upon any petition by the State Health Commissioner, or that official's designee, for an order that a person or persons appear before the court to determine whether isolation is necessary to protect the public health from the risk of infection with a communicable disease of public health significance, the provisions of §§ 32.1-48.03, 32.1-48.04, and related sections of Article 3.01 of Title 32.1 of the Code of Virginia shall be followed.

B. The court shall hold hearings under this rule in a manner to protect the health and safety of individuals subject to any such order or quarantine or isolation, court personnel, counsel, witnesses, and the general public. To this end, the court may take measures including, but not limited to, ordering the hearing to be held by telephone or video conference or ordering those present to take appropriate precautions, including wearing personal protective equipment.

Effective date. — This rule, adopted February 28, 2006, became effective May 1, 2006.

PART SEVEN B
GENERAL DISTRICT COURTS — CIVIL

Rule
7B:1. Scope.
7B:2. Specific Rule for Pleadings in General District Courts.
7B:3. General Provisions as to Pleadings.
7B:4. Trial of Action.
7B:5. Production of Written Agreement.
7B:6. Verification.
7B:7. Appearance by Plaintiff.
7B:8. Failure of Plaintiff to Appear.
7B:9. Failure of Defendant to Appear.
7B:10. Third-Party Practice and Consolidation of Actions.
7B:11. Motions to Transfer.

Editor's note. — The order effective July 1, 1989, adopted Nov. 21, 1988, adopted new Part Seven B.

Rule 7B:1. Scope.

These Rules apply to all civil cases in the General District Courts.

Cross references. — See also § 8.01-3.

Source. — Former Rule 3D:1.

Rule 7B:2. Specific Rule for Pleadings in General District Courts.

The judge of any General District Court may require the plaintiff to file and serve a written bill of particulars and the defendant to file and serve a written grounds of defense within the periods of time specified in the order so requiring; the failure of either party to comply may be grounds for awarding summary judgment in favor of the adverse party. Upon trial, the judge may exclude evidence as to matters not described in any such pleading.

Cross references. — See also § 16.1-69.25:1.

Source. — Former Rule 3D:4.

CASE NOTES

Eviction proceeding. — In an eviction proceeding, as a discretionary matter, a general district court in Virginia could provide the tenant discovery by ordering a bill of particulars, and issue subpoenas duces tecum, and had the power to issue a final order that would satisfy the requirements for a written decision. Kennedy v. Block, 784 F.2d 1220 (4th Cir. 1986), decided under repealed Rule 3D:4.

Rule 7B:3. General Provisions as to Pleadings.

(a) A party asserting either a claim, counterclaim, cross-claim or a defense may plead alternative facts and theories of recovery against alternative parties, provided that such claims, defenses, or demands for relief so joined arise out of the same transaction or occurrence. Subject to the jurisdictional limits of the General District Court, a party may also state separate related claims or defenses regardless of consistency and whether based on legal or equitable grounds.

(b) The warrant, summons or complaint or an attachment thereto shall contain a statement, approved by the Committee on District Courts, explaining how any party may object to venue.

(c) The warrant, summons or complaint, or an attachment thereto shall contain a statement, approved by the Committee on District Courts, explaining that if the case is contested, how a trial date will be set.

(d) All civil warrants and complaints shall contain on their face language in substantially the following form: "The defendant is not required to appear pursuant to this document, but if the defendant does not appear, judgment may be granted in favor of the plaintiff."

Cross references. — See also Rule 1:4, § 8.01-271 et seq., § 8.01-281, § 16.1-88.01 and § 16.1-88.02.

Source. — Former Rules 3D:3(b) and 3D:6.

The amendment, effective February 28, 2006, adopted February 28, 2006, substituted "complaint" for "motion for judgment" in subdivisions (b) and (c) and "complaints" for "motions for judgment" in subdivision (d).

The amendment effective July 1, 2008, adopted April 9, 2008, substituted "any party" for "a defendant" near the end of subdivision (b).

Rule 7B:4. Trial of Action.

(a) *Method of bringing action.* — A civil action in a general district court may be brought by warrant, summons or complaint directed to the sheriff or to any other person authorized to serve process, requiring such individual to summon the person against whom the claim is asserted to appear before the court on a certain day to answer the complaint of the plaintiff set out in the warrant, summons or complaint.

(b) *When action heard.* — If all parties appear and are ready for trial on the return date of the warrant, summons or complaint, the court may proceed with the trial of the case.

Cross references. — See also §§ 16.1-79 through 16.1-83, § 16.1-86 and § 16.1-93.

Source. — Former Rule 3D:3.

The amendment, effective February 28, 2006, adopted February 28, 2006, substituted "complaint" for "motion for judgment" twice in subdivision (a) and once in subdivision (b).

Rule 7B:5. Production of Written Agreement.

When a suit is brought on a written contract, note or other instrument, the original document shall be tendered to the court for entry of judgment thereon unless the production of the original is excused by the court for good cause or by statute.

Cross references. — See also § 8.01-32 and § 16.1-94.

Source. — Former Rule 3D:8.

Rule 7B:6. Verification.

If a statute requires a pleading to be sworn to, and it is not, or requires a pleading to be accompanied by an affidavit, and it is not, but contains all the allegations required, objection on either ground must be made within seven days after the pleading is filed by a motion to strike; otherwise the objection is waived. At any time before the court passes on the motion or within such time thereafter as the court may prescribe, the pleading may be sworn to or the affidavit filed. In an Electronically Filed Case, verification shall be subject to the provisions of Rule 1:17.

Cross references. — See also Rule 1:10, § 8.01-279, § 8.3A-308, § 16.1-88 and § 16.1-88.2.

The amendment, effective May 2, 2011, adopted March 1, 2011, added the last sentence.

Rule 7B:7. Appearance by Plaintiff.

Except as may be permitted by statute, no judgment for plaintiff shall be granted in any case except on request made in person in court by the plaintiff, plaintiff's attorney, or plaintiff's regular and bona fide employee.

Cross references. — See also § 55-246.1.
Source. — Former Rule 3D:5.

Rule 7B:8. Failure of Plaintiff to Appear.

(a) If neither the plaintiff nor the defendant appears, the Court shall dismiss the action without prejudice to the right of the plaintiff to refile.

(b) If the defendant, but not the plaintiff, appears on the return date and the case is not before the Court for trial, the Court shall dismiss the action without prejudice to the right of the plaintiff to refile.

(c) If the defendant, but not the plaintiff, appears on the trial date and:

(1) The defendant admits owing all or some portion of the claim, the Court shall dismiss the action without prejudice to the right of the plaintiff to refile; but if

(2) The defendant denies under oath owing anything to the plaintiff, the Court shall enter judgment for the defendant with prejudice to the right of the plaintiff to refile.

Cross references. — See also § 16.1-97.1, granting the Court the authority to grant a rehearing.

The amendment, effective March 1, 1998, adopted December 9, 1997, rewrote subdivision (b) and added subdivision (c).

Rule 7B:9. Failure of Defendant to Appear.

Except as may be provided by statute, a defendant who fails to appear in person or by counsel is in default and;

(a) Waives all objections to the admissibility of evidence; and

(b) Is not entitled to notice of any further proceeding in the case, except that when service is by posting pursuant to § 8.01-296(2)(b), the ten day notice required by that section shall be complied with; and

(c) On request made in person in court by the plaintiff, plaintiff's attorney, plaintiff's regular and bona fide employee, or any other person authorized by law, judgment shall be entered for the amount appearing to the judge to be due. If the relief demanded is unliquidated damages, the court shall hear evidence and fix the amount thereof.

Cross references. — See also § 16.1-97.1, granting the Court authority to grant a rehearing.

See Title II of the Servicemembers Civil Relief Act, 50 U.S.C. Appx. § 520 et seq. (as affecting the validity of default judgments entered against defendants in military service). Also see, Va. Code § 8.01 15.2.

See Section 200 of the Soldiers' and Sailors' Civil Relief Act of 1940, 50 U.S.C.App., § 520 (as affecting the validity of default judgments entered against defendants in military service).

Source. — Former Rule 3D:6.

Rule 7B:10. Third-Party Practice and Consolidation of Actions.

(a) *When Defendant May Bring in Third Party:* Whenever a party is served with a warrant, summons, complaint, counterclaim or cross-claim, such party may within 10 days after service or up to the trial date, whichever is sooner, file a third-party civil warrant or complaint on a person not a party to the action who is or may be liable to the party for all or part of the claim being asserted against such party. After such time period, such third-party claim may be asserted only with leave of court.

Any party may move to strike the third-party warrant or complaint, or move for its severance for a separate trial. A third-party defendant may proceed under this rule against any person not a party to the action who is or may be liable to him for all or part of the claim made in the action against the third-party defendant.

(b) *Consolidation of Actions:* The Court may, in its discretion, consolidate for trial separate suits which could be treated as counterclaims, cross-claims, and third-party claims. The judge may enter such orders as may be appropriate to effect a prompt and fair disposition of such cases.

The amendment, effective February 28, 2006, adopted February 28, 2006, in subdivision (a), substituted "complaint" for "motion for judgment" twice in the first paragraph and once in the first sentence of the second paragraph.

Rule 7B:11. Motions to Transfer.

(a) When a written motion to transfer objecting to venue is filed by any party, the party objecting shall mail a copy of such motion to all counsel of record. Failure to comply with this requirement shall not be a ground for denying the motion, but the court may grant a deferral of any hearing on the motion to transfer if it finds that the interest of justice would be served by such deferral.

(b) If any party who has filed a motion to transfer objecting to venue is not present when the court rules on such motion:

(1) If the motion is granted, the Clerk shall transmit the files in accordance with such order and shall send a copy of the letter of transmittal or order of transfer to all parties along with information as to any costs awarded under § 8.01-266; or

(2) If the motion is denied, the court shall set a date for the trial of the case and the Clerk shall notify the absent objecting party by first class mail of such date and of any costs awarded any other party under § 8.01-266.

Cross references. — See also § 8.01-257 et seq. and § 16.1-76.

The amendment, effective January 1, 2002, adopted October 1, 2001, in subdivision (b)(1), substituted "the Clerk shall transmit" for "the court shall direct the Clerk to transmit" and "order and shall send" for "order after the appeal period has run and to send."

The amendment, effective July 1, 2008, adopted April 9, 2008, substituted "by any party, the party objecting shall" for "by a defendant, the defendant shall" in subdivision (a); and in subdivision (b), substituted "any party" for "a defendant" near the beginning of the introductory language, and in (2), substituted "absent objecting party" for "defendant" and "any other party" for "the plaintiff."

The amendment, effective May 2, 2011, adopted March 1, 2011, substituted "transmit the files" for "transmit the papers" in subdivision (b)(1).

PART SEVEN C
GENERAL DISTRICT COURTS — CRIMINAL AND TRAFFIC

Rule
7C:1. Scope.
7C:2. Venue.
7C:3. The Complaint, Warrant, Summons and Capias.
7C:4. Trial Together of More Than One Accused or More Than One Offense and Joint Preliminary Hearings.
7C:5. Discovery.
7C:6. Pleas.
7C:7. Service and Filing.

Editor's note. — The order effective July 1, 1989, adopted Nov. 21, 1988, adopted new Part Seven C.

Rule 7C:1. Scope.

These rules shall apply to all criminal and traffic cases [infractions and others] in the General District Courts.

Cross references. — See also Rule 3A:1 and § 8.01-3.

Rule 7C:2. Venue.

Questions of venue must be raised before a finding of guilty or venue shall be deemed waived.

Cross references. — See also § 19.2-244 et seq.

Rule 7C:3. The Complaint, Warrant, Summons and Capias.

(a) The complaint shall consist of sworn statements of a person or persons of facts relating to the commission of an alleged offense. The statements shall be made upon oath before a judicial officer empowered to issue arrest warrants. The judicial officer may require the sworn statements to be reduced to writing if the complainant is a law-enforcement officer, but shall require the sworn statements to be reduced to writing if the complainant is not a law-enforcement officer.

(b) More than one warrant, summons or capias may issue on the same complaint. A warrant may be issued by a judicial officer if the accused fails to appear in response to a summons.

(c) A separate warrant, summons or capias shall be issued for each charge.

(d) A summons, whether issued by a judicial officer or a law-enforcement officer, shall command the accused to appear at a stated time and place before a court of appropriate jurisdiction. It shall (i) state the name of the accused or, if this name is unknown, set forth a description by which he can be identified with reasonable certainty, (ii) describe the offense charged and state whether the offense is a violation of state, county, city or town law, and (iii) be signed by the magistrate or the law-enforcement officer, as the case may be.

(e) If the warrant has been issued but the officer does not have the warrant in his possession at the time of the arrest, he shall (i) inform the accused of the offense charged and that a warrant has been issued, and (ii) deliver a copy of the warrant to the accused as soon thereafter as practicable.

Cross references. — See also Rule 3A:3, Rule 3A:4 and § 16.1-129.2.

The amendment effective March 1, 2012, adopted December 22, 2011, added "if the complainant is a law-enforcement officer, but shall require the sworn statements to be reduced to writing if the complainant is not a law-enforcement officer" at the end of subdivision (a).

Rule 7C:4. Trial Together of More Than One Accused or More Than One Offense and Joint Preliminary Hearings.

(a) *More Than One Accused — Joinder of Defendants.* — On motion of the Commonwealth, for good cause shown, the court, in its discretion, may order persons charged with participation in related acts or occurrences or in a series of acts or occurrences constituting an offense or offenses to be tried jointly unless such joint trial would constitute prejudice to a defendant.

(b) *More Than One Accused — Severance of Defendants.* — If the court finds that a joint trial would constitute prejudice to a defendant, the court shall order severance as to that defendant or provide such other relief as justice requires.

(c) *An Accused Charged With More Than One Offense.* — The Court may direct that an accused be tried at one time for all offenses then pending against him, if justice does not require separate trials and (a) the offenses are based on the same act or transaction, or on two or more acts or transactions that are connected or constitute parts of a common scheme or plan, or (b) the accused and the Commonwealth's Attorney consent thereto.

(d) *Joint Preliminary Hearing.* — Upon motion of the Commonwealth's Attorney, preliminary hearings for persons alleged to have participated in contemporaneous and related acts or occurrences or in a series of such acts or occurrences constituting an offense or offenses may be heard jointly, if jurisdiction over each person and offense lies in the same court, unless the court finds that such joint preliminary hearing would constitute prejudice to a defendant.

Cross references. — See also Rule 3A:6(c) and Rule 3A:10.

Rule 7C:5. Discovery.

(a) *Application of Rule.* — This Rule applies only to the prosecution for a misdemeanor which may be punished by confinement in jail and to a preliminary hearing for a felony.

(b) *Definitions.* — For purposes of discovery under this Rule 1) the prosecuting attorney is the attorney for the Commonwealth or the city attorney, county attorney, or town attorney, who is responsible for prosecuting the case; 2) if no prosecuting attorney prosecutes the case, the representative of the Commonwealth shall be the law enforcement officer, or, if none, such person who appears on behalf of the Commonwealth, county, city or town in the case.

(c) *Discovery by the Accused.* — Upon motion of an accused, the court shall order the prosecuting attorney or representative of the Commonwealth to permit the accused to hear, inspect and copy or photograph the following information or material when the existence of such is known or becomes known to the prosecuting attorney or representative of the Commonwealth and such material or information is to be offered in evidence against the accused in a General District Court:

(1) any relevant written or recorded statements or confessions made by the accused, or copies thereof and the substance of any oral statements and confessions made by the accused to any law enforcement officer; and

(2) any criminal record of the accused.

(d) *Time of Motion.* — A motion by the accused under this Rule shall be made in writing and filed with the Court and a copy thereof mailed, faxed, or otherwise delivered to the prosecuting attorney and, if applicable, to the representative of the Commonwealth at least 10 days before the day fixed for trial or preliminary hearing. The motion shall include the specific information or material sought under this Rule.

(e) *Time, Place and Manner of Discovery and Inspection.* — An order granting relief under this Rule shall specify the time, place and manner of making the discovery and inspection permitted and may prescribe such terms and conditions as are just.

(f) *Failure to Comply.* — If at any time during the course of the proceedings, it is brought to the attention of the court that the prosecuting attorney or representative of the Commonwealth has failed to comply with this Rule or with an order issued pursuant to this Rule, the court shall order the prosecuting attorney or representative of the Commonwealth to permit the discovery or inspection of the material not previously disclosed, and may grant such continuance to the accused as it deems appropriate.

Cross references. — See also Rule 3A:11, § 16.1-69.25:1 and § 16.1-131.

The amendment, effective July 1, 2000, adopted February 4, 2000, rewrote subsection (b); in subsection (c), inserted "or representative of the Commonwealth" twice in the introductory paragraph, and substituted "confessions" for "confession" near the end of subdivision (1); in subsection (d), inserted "and a copy thereof mailed, faxed, or otherwise delivered to the prosecuting attorney and, if applicable, to the representative of the Commonwealth" near the middle of the first sentence; and in subsection (f), inserted "or representative of the Commonwealth" twice.

Law Review. — For 2003/2004 survey of criminal law and procedure, see 39 U. Rich. L. Rev. 133 (2004).

Michie's Jurisprudence. — For related discussion, see 4A M.J. Continuances, § 47.

Rule 7C:6. Pleas.

(a) A court shall not accept a plea of guilty or nolo contendere to any misdemeanor charge punishable by confinement in jail without first determining that the plea is made voluntarily with an understanding of the nature of the charge and the consequences of the plea. Before accepting a plea to such a charge, the court shall inform the accused that such a plea constitutes a waiver of the right to confront one's accusers and the right against compulsory self-incrimination.

(b) A corporation, acting by counsel or through an agent, may enter the same pleas as an individual.

Cross references. — See also Rule 3A:8.

The amendment, effective June 1, 2005, adopted March 1, 2005, adds subdivision (a) and the subdivision (b) designator.

Rule 7C:7. Service and Filing.

(a) *Copies of Written Motions to be Furnished.* — All written motions and notices not required to be served otherwise shall be served on each counsel of record by delivering, dispatching by commercial delivery service, transmitting by facsimile, or mailing, a copy to him on or before the day of filing.

Service pursuant to this Rule shall be effective upon such delivery, dispatch, transmission or mailing, except that papers served by facsimile transmission completed after 5:00 p.m. shall be deemed served on the next day that is not a Saturday, Sunday, or legal holiday.

At the foot of such pleadings and requests shall be appended either acceptance of service or a certificate of counsel that copies were served as this Rule requires, showing the date of delivery and method of service, dispatching, transmitting, or mailing.

(b) *Filing.* — Pleadings, motions, notices, and other materials required to be served shall be filed with the clerk. In an Electronically Filed Case, the provisions of Rule 1:17 shall be applicable.

Effective date. — This rule, adopted April 9, 2008, became effective July 1, 2008.

The amendment, effective May 2, 2011, adopted March 1, 2011, deleted "of Papers" at the end of the Rule heading; substituted "Pleadings, motions, notices, and other materials" for "Papers" at the beginning, and added the second sentence, of subdivision (b).

PART EIGHT
JUVENILE AND DOMESTIC RELATIONS DISTRICT COURTS

Rule
8:1. Scope.
8:2. Definitions.
8:3. Contents of Petitions in Certain Proceedings.
8:4. Service of Process — Motion to Reduce Support Arrearages to Judgment.
8:5. Court-Ordered Reports.
8:6. The Roles of Counsel and of Guardians Ad Litem When Representing Children.
8:7. Format for Filing.
8:8. Pleadings and Filing.
8:9. Discretion of Court.
8:10. Motions to Transfer Venue.
8:11. Reporters and Transcripts of Proceedings in Court.

Rule
8:12. Preservation of the Record.
8:13. Requests for Subpoenas for Witnesses and Records.
8:14. Continuances.
8:15. Discovery.
8:16. Arraignment in Juvenile Delinquency Cases.
8:17. Notification and Waiver of Trial Rights of Parties.
8:18. Pleas.
8:19. Endorsements of Orders.
8:20. Appeals.
8:21. [Deleted.]
8:22. Judicial Consent.

Editor's note. — Comments in Part 8 as provided by the Advisory Committee on Rules of Court, were substantially revised in July 2010.

Effective date. — This part was adopted January 22, 1992, and became effective July 1, 1992.

Rule 8:1. Scope.

Part Eight of the Rules shall apply to all proceedings in the Juvenile and Domestic Relations District Courts.

Law Review. — For article, "Legal Issues Involving Children," see 26 U. Rich. L. Rev. 797 (1992).

Rule 8:2. Definitions.

(a) *Statutory Definitions.* — The definitions stated in § 16.1-228 are applicable to this Part.

(b) *Additional Definitions.* — The following words and phrases used in this Part are defined as follows:

(1) "Counsel" or "attorney" includes a partnership, a professional corporation or an association of members of the Virginia State Bar practicing under a firm name or governmental agency name.

(2) "Counsel of Record" in any pending case includes an attorney who has signed a pleading in the case or who has notified the clerk or judge that the attorney appears in the case and shall also include a guardian ad litem and a party who appears in court pro se. Except as provided by statute, counsel of record shall not withdraw from a case except by leave of court with such notice as the court may require to the client of the time and place of a motion for leave to withdraw.

CASE NOTES

Derogatory statement concerning judge. — Derogatory statement concerning the qualifications or integrity of a judge, made by a lawyer with knowing falsity or with reckless disregard of its truth or falsity, created a substantial likelihood of material prejudice to the administration of justice, and was not, therefore, constitutionally protected speech. Anthony v. Va. State Bar, 270 Va. 601, 621 S.E.2d 121, 2005 Va. LEXIS 103 (2005), cert. denied, 547 U.S. 1193, 126 S. Ct. 2871, 165 L. Ed. 2d 897 (2006).

Signature. — Holding that a wife did not sign a notice of appeal and that it was not signed on her behalf as required by Va. Sup. Ct. R. 8:8(a) and 8:2(b)(2) was a finding of fact supported by the evidence as: (1) a husband testified that the wife's name as printed on the notice of appeal did not appear to be her signature; and (2) the printed name on the notice of appeal was unmistakably different from the cursive imprint of her name on a notice of change of address. Piatt v. Colvin, 2007 Va. App. LEXIS 470 (Dec. 27, 2007).

OPINIONS OF THE ATTORNEY GENERAL

Access to court files of cases must be given to self-represented individuals by juvenile and domestic relations district courts. However, juvenile courts are not required to provide such self-represented litigants with notice regarding their rights of access. See opinion of Attorney General to The Honorable Onzlee Ware, Member, House of Delegates, 06-107 (2/20/07).

Rule 8:3. Contents of Petitions in Certain Proceedings.

(a) *Proceedings for the Ordering of Services.* — (1) Motion or Petition. When a party to a matter pending before the court, or a petition filed for the purpose, proposes that the court enter an order pursuant to § 16.1-278, directing that a governmental officer, employee, agency, or institution render information, assistance, services or cooperation, the petition or motion shall contain:

a) The information, assistance, services, or cooperation sought;

b) The state or federal law or regulation or city, county, or town ordinance that provides for the rendering of such information, assistance, services, or cooperation sought; and

c) The officer, employee, agency, or institution to whom the order should be directed.

(2) Notice. The motion or petition prescribed in paragraph (a)(1) of this Rule shall be served on the governmental officer, employee, agency, or institution in question pursuant to § 16.1-264.

(3) Hearing. The governmental officer, employee, agency, or institution against whom an order is sought shall be entitled to a hearing on the issues raised by the petition or motion. The hearing may be held at such time as the court deems appropriate.

(b) *Proceedings for Judicial Consent to Emergency Surgical or Medical Treatment for a Juvenile.* — When a petition is filed for the purpose of seeking judicial consent for emergency surgical or medical treatment of a juvenile, the petition shall contain:

(1) The juvenile's name, date of birth, residence, and a statement as to whether or not the juvenile has ever been married;

(2) The names and residence of the juvenile's parents, guardian or legal custodian;

(3) The name and residence of the nearest known relative if no parent or guardian can be found;

(4) The name and address of the physician petitioning the court for authorization of surgical or medical treatment for the juvenile;

(5) The name and address of the hospital or medical facility petitioning for authorization of surgical or medical treatment for the juvenile;

(6) A statement of the diagnosis of the juvenile's physical condition, and the recommended medical, surgical, and nursing care; and

(7) A statement of the willingness of the physician and the hospital or medical facility to provide the necessary medical, surgical, and nursing care if judicial consent is given as requested.

(c) *Proceedings for Support.* — Except for temporary child support orders issued pursuant to Va. Code § 16.1-279.1, when a petition is filed seeking a court order for support of a spouse or child, the petition shall contain:

(1) The name and residential address of the person seeking support;

(2) The name and residential address of the person from whom support is sought;

(3) The name, date of birth, and residential address of the person or persons for whom support is sought and the relationship of that person or those persons to the respondent;

(4) A statement whether the Division of Child Support Enforcement is involved in the case;

(5) If child support is at issue, a statement whether or not the petitioner and respondent are presently or have ever been married to each other and, if not, whether paternity has ever been adjudicated;

(6) If child support is at issue, a statement whether the child's custody has been adjudicated;

(7) If known, the name, date of birth, and social security number of each parent or spouse and, if different and if known, the name, date of birth, and social security

number of the person responsible for support and, unless otherwise ordered, the residential and, if different, mailing address, residential and employer telephone number, driver's license number, and the name and address of the employer of each such parent or responsible person;

(8) As an attachment, a copy of the most recent court order, if any, concerning support of the person for whom support is sought in this petition; and

(9) A statement whether either or both parents hold a license, certificate, registration, or other authorization to engage in a profession, trade, business, occupation or recreational activity issued by the Commonwealth and, if so, the type of authorization held.

In the case of a petition for support, if a protective order has been issued or if a party asserts that the party is at risk of physical or emotional harm from the other party, information other than the name of the party at risk shall not be required on the petition; however, the information shall be provided to the court and shall not be disclosed except by order of the court.

Comment. — For subdivision (a) Proceedings for the Ordering of Services, see § 16.1-278. For subdivision (b) Proceedings for Judicial Consent to Emergency Surgery or Medical Treatment for a Juvenile, see § 16.1-241(D), and Rule 8:22 for time requirement. For subdivision (c) Proceedings for Support, see § 20-60.3 and § 20-107.1 for the statutory requirements for the content of support orders.

The amendment effective March 1, 1998, adopted December 9, 1997, in subdivision (c)(7), substituted "residential and, if different, mailing address, residential and employer telephone number, driver's license number, and the name and address of the employer" for "current address and place of employment"; and added the concluding paragraph.

The amendment effective September 30, 2004, adopted September 30, 2004, added "Except for temporary child support orders issued pursuant to Va. Code § 16.1-279.1," at the beginnning of the introductory paragraph of subsection (c).

The amendment effective July 1, 2009, adopted June 1, 2009, substituted "business, occupation or recreational activity" for "business or occupation" in subdivision (c)(9).

Rule 8:4. Service of Process — Motion to Reduce Support Arrearages to Judgment.

Any motion to enter judgment for support arrearages pursuant to § 16.1-278.18 shall be served upon the respondent in accordance with the provisions of §§ 8.01-296, 8.01-327, 8.01-329, or by (1) certified mail, return receipt requested, and (2) first class mail. Upon sufficient showing that a diligent effort was made to ascertain the location of a party, that party may be served with any required notice by delivery of the written notice to that party's residential or business address as filed with the court pursuant to Code § 20-60.3 or the Department of Social Services, or if changed, as shown in the records of the Department of Social Services.

The amendment, effective March 1, 1998, adopted December 9, 1997, added the last sentence.

Rule 8:5. Court-Ordered Reports.

Copies of all studies and reports pursuant to §§ 16.1-269.2, 16.1-273, 16.1-274, 16.1-275 and 63.2-1524, when received by the court shall be furnished by the court to counsel of record, and upon request shall be mailed to such counsel. Counsel of record shall return such reports to the clerk upon the conclusion of the hearing and shall not make copies of such report or amended report or any portion of either.

Comment. — The statutes cited in the rule refer to reports for transfer hearings; social history reports; custody, visitation, or support reports; and reports of physical and mental evaluations. Reports generated pursuant to subsection A of § 16.1-237, § 16.1- 273, or § 9.1-153, or an evaluation pursuant to § 16.1-278.5 shall be returned to the clerk upon the conclusion of the hearing and counsel of record shall not make copies of any such report or amended report or any portion of either. The chief judge of each juvenile and domestic relations district court may provide for an alternative means of copying and distributing reports or amended reports filed pursuant to § 9.1- 153. See Virginia Code § 16.1-274.

For the right to and limitations on access to juvenile records generally, including the authority of the judge to regulate the photocopying of juvenile records, see Virginia Code § 16.1-305.

For a definition of "counsel of record," see Rule 8:2(b)(2), which incorporates both pro se parties and guardians ad litem into the term.

The amendment, effective May 2, 2011, adopted March 1, 2011, substituted "63.2-1524" for "63.1-248.14."

Rule 8:6. The Roles of Counsel and of Guardians Ad Litem When Representing Children.

The role of counsel for a child is the representation of the child's legitimate interests. When appointed for a child, the guardian ad litem shall vigorously represent the child, fully protecting the child's interest and welfare. The guardian ad litem shall advise the court of the wishes of the child in any case where the wishes of the child conflict with the opinion of the guardian ad litem as to what is in the child's interest and welfare.

Comment. — See also Virginia Code § 16.1-266 regarding appointment of a guardian ad litem or counsel for a child. The Judicial Council of Virginia has adopted STANDARDS TO GOVERN THE PERFORMANCE OF GUARDIANS AD LITEM FOR CHILDREN, which may be found on the Internet at http://www.courts.state.va.us/court-admin/aoc/cip/programs/gal/chil dren/gal]-performance]standards]children.pdf. The Virginia Indigent Defense Commission has established STANDARDS OF PRACTICE FOR INDIGENT DEFENSE COUNSEL, which include standards for counsel appointed to represent juveniles in either delinquency proceedings or proceedings to determine whether a juvenile is in need of services or supervision. The STANDARDS OF PRACTICE FOR INDIGENT DEFENSE COUNSEL may be found on the Internet at http://www.indigent-defense.virginia.gov/PDF%20documents/Standards%20 of%20Practice.pdf.

Law Review. — For annual survey article on legal issues involving children, see 38 U. Rich. L. Rev. 161 (2003).

CASE NOTES

Guardian ad litem's recommendation due to be considered. — The recommendation of the guardian ad litem in instant child custody case, while not binding or controlling, should not be disregarded. The duty of a guardian ad litem in a child custody dispute is to see that the interest of the child is represented and protected. This child had no other independent participant in the proceeding, aside from the trial court, to protect his interests. Thus, this diligent guardian ad litem's recommendation that custody be awarded to the grandmother was entitled to be considered by the court in reaching a decision on the issue. Bottoms v. Bottoms, 249 Va. 413, 457 S.E.2d 102 (1995).

Guardian ad litem fees. — Record supported the trial court's findings that the services of a guardian ad litem were required in the contentious custody dispute, and that mother was in contempt for failing to pay one-half the fees as ordered; the trial court did not violate the Thirteenth Amendment, as to involuntary servitude, in finding the mother in contempt. Walker-Duncan v. Duncan, No. 1752-03-1, 2004 Va. App. LEXIS 26 (Ct. of Appeals Jan. 20, 2004).

Rule 8:7. Format for Filing.

(a) Except as provided in Rule 8:8(f) and Rule 1:17 pertaining to Electronically Filed Cases,

(1) All pleadings, motions, briefs and all other documents filed in any clerk's office in any proceeding pursuant to the Rules or statutes shall be 8-1/2 by 11 inches in size. All typed material shall be double spaced except for quotations.

(2) Subdivision (a)(1) of this Rule shall not apply to tables, charts, plats, photographs, and other material that cannot be reasonably reproduced on paper of that size.

(b) No paper shall be refused for failure to comply with the provisions of this Rule, but the clerk or judge may require that the paper be redone in compliance with this Rule and substituted for the paper initially filed. Counsel shall certify that the substituted paper is identical in content to the paper initially filed.

Comment. — See also Rules 1:16 and 7A:7.

The amendment, effective May 2, 2011, adopted March 1, 2011, substituted "Format for Filing" for "Size of Paper" in the Rule heading, redesignated former subdivisions (a) and (b) as paragraphs (1) and (2) of subdivision (a), added the introductory paragraph of subdivision (a), added

"Subdivision (a)(1) of" at the beginning of subdivision (a)(2), and redesignated former subdivision (c) as (b).

Rule 8:8. Pleadings and Filing.

(a) *General.* — Counsel of record tendering a pleading gives assurances that it is filed in good faith and not for delay, and counsel of record who files a pleading shall sign it and state counsel's address and telephone number. A pleading that is sworn to is an affidavit for all purposes for which an affidavit is required or permitted. The mention in a pleading of an accompanying exhibit shall, of itself and without more, make such an exhibit a part of the pleading.

(b) *Denial, Admission, Objection.* — A party respondent need not file a pleading or may file a pleading denying or admitting all or any facts alleged in the petition, motion, or summons, or the respondent may file a motion raising objections. Any allegation not admitted is deemed denied. If a respondent fails to file a pleading, the failure will be taken as a denial of the allegations in the petition, motion, or summons.

(c) *Amendment of Written Pleading.* — Except as hereinafter provided, or as provided pursuant to §§ 16.1-129.2, 16.1-93 and 16.1-259, no amendment shall be made to any pleading after it is filed with the clerk, except by leave of court. Leave to amend a pleading shall be liberally granted in furtherance of the ends of justice. In granting leave to amend, the court may make such provision for notice thereof and opportunity to make response as the court may deem reasonable and proper.

In delinquency, child in need of services, child in need of supervision, and status offense proceedings, the court may permit amendment of the written pleading at any time before adjudication, provided that the amendment does not change the nature or character of the matter alleged. If the amendment is made after the respondent pleads or is made after any evidence is heard, the amended pleading shall be read to him and he shall be allowed to change his plea. If the court finds that the amendment operates as a surprise to the respondent, it shall upon request grant a continuance for a reasonable time.

(d) *Bill of Particulars.* — The court may direct the filing of a bill of particulars at any time before trial.

(e) *Copies of Pleadings to be Furnished.* — Except as provided in subdivision (f) of this Rule, all pleadings not otherwise required to be served shall be served on each counsel of record by delivering, dispatching by commercial delivery service, transmitting by facsimile or mailing a copy to each on or before the day of filing. At the foot of such pleadings shall be appended either acceptances of service or a certificate that copies were served as this Rule requires, showing the date of delivery, dispatching, transmitting or mailing.

(f) *Electronic Filing.* — In any juvenile and domestic relations district court which has established an electronic filing system pursuant to Rule 1:17:

(1) Any proceeding may be designated as an Electronically Filed Case upon consent of all parties in the case.

(2) Except where service and/or filing of an original paper document is expressly required by these rules, all pleadings, motions, notices and other instruments in an Electronically Filed Case shall be formatted, served and filed as specified in the requirements and procedures of Rule 1:17; provided, however, that when any document listed below is filed in the case, the filing party shall notify the clerk of court that the original document must be retained.

(i) Any pleading or affidavit required by statute or rule to be sworn, verified or certified as provided in Rule 1:17(e)(5).

(ii) Any contract or deed.

(iii) Any prenuptial agreement or written settlement agreement, including any property settlement agreement.

(iv) Any check or other negotiable instrument.

(v) Any handwritten statement, waiver, or consent by a defendant or witness in a criminal proceeding.

(vi) Any form signed by a defendant in a criminal proceeding, including any typed statements or a guilty plea form.

(vii) Any document that cannot be converted into an electronic document in such a way as to produce a clear and readable image.

Comment. — Paragraph (b) provides that any allegation of a pleading which is not admitted is deemed denied. This is the converse of the rule applied in other courts (see Rule 1:4(e)).

Paragraph (d) is adapted from § 16.1-69.25:1.

The amendment, effective February 1, 1999, adopted November 23, 1998, in subdivision (e), inserted "dispatching by commercial delivery service, transmitting by facsimile" in the first sentence and inserted "dispatching, transmitting" in the second sentence.

The amendment, effective May 2, 2011, adopted March 1, 2011, added "and Filing" at the end of the Rule heading; added "Except as provided in subdivision (f) of this Rule" at the beginning of subdivision (e); and added subdivision (f).

CASE NOTES

Signature. — Holding that a wife did not sign a notice of appeal and that it was not signed on her behalf as required by Va. Sup. Ct. R. 8:8(a) and 8:2(b)(2) was a finding of fact supported by the evidence as: (1) a husband testified that the wife's name as printed on the notice of appeal did not appear to be her signature; and (2) the printed name on the notice of appeal was unmistakably different from the cursive imprint of her name on a notice of change of address. Piatt v. Colvin, 2007 Va. App. LEXIS 470 (Dec. 27, 2007).

Rule 8:9. Discretion of Court.

All steps and procedures in the clerk's office touching the filing of pleadings and the maturing of suits or actions may be reviewed and corrected by the court.

The time allowed for filing pleadings may be extended by the court in its discretion, and such extension may be granted although the time fixed already has expired.

Rule 8:10. Motions to Transfer Venue.

A motion to transfer venue shall be made in writing or in court with the parties present. When a written motion is filed, it shall be set for hearing, and the motion and notice of hearing shall be served on all other parties or on counsel of record, if any.

Comment. — This Rule applies to both pending and inactive cases.

Rule 8:11. Reporters and Transcripts of Proceedings in Court.

Any party shall have the right to have a court reporter present to take down or record the proceedings. In all proceedings not open to the public it shall be within the sound discretion of the judge as to whether a court reporter may take down or record the proceedings on behalf of a person not a party. In all other proceedings, any person not a party may bring a court reporter to take down the proceedings. Court reporters, when present, shall be first duly sworn to take down and transcribe the proceedings faithfully and accurately to the best of their ability and shall be subject to the control and discipline of the judge.

In proceedings open to the public, when a court reporter is present and takes down or records the proceeding, any interested person shall be entitled to obtain a transcript, unless the court records remain confidential pursuant to § 16.1-305. In proceedings not open to the public, when a court reporter is present and takes down or records the proceeding, a party shall be entitled to obtain a transcript without prior court order, but the court may limit the circulation of the transcript by a party. In such proceedings not open to the public, other than (i) proceedings closed for good cause pursuant to subsection C of § 16.1-302 and which result in an adjudication of delinquency of a juvenile, who was fourteen years or older at the time of the offense, on the basis of an act which would be a felony if committed by an adult or (ii) proceedings resulting in a subsequent adjudication of delinquency as described in subsection B1 of § 16.1-305, all other interested persons shall only be entitled to a transcript by order of court which shall state for whom such transcript shall be prepared and what restrictions, if any, are imposed on the use and distribution of the transcript, its contents or any part. In delinquency proceedings which are closed for good cause pursuant to subsection C of § 16.1-302 and which result in an adjudication of delinquency of a juvenile, who was fourteen years or older at the time of the offense, on the basis of an act which would be a felony if committed by an adult, when a court reporter is present and takes down or records the proceeding, any interested person shall be entitled to a transcript, except for those transcripts or portions of transcripts which the judge has ordered shall remain confidential pursuant to subsection B1 of § 16.1-305. In proceedings resulting in an adjudication of delinquency which is subsequent to a prior adjudication of delinquency of a juvenile who was fourteen years or older at the time of the prior offense and whose prior adjudication was on the basis of an act which would be a felony if committed by an adult, when a court reporter is present and takes down or records the proceeding, any interested person shall be entitled to obtain a transcript, except for those transcripts or portions of transcripts which the judge has ordered shall remain confidential pursuant to subsection B1 of § 16.1-305.

The proceedings may be taken down by means of any recording device approved by the court.

Rule 8:12. Preservation of the Record.

A court may authorize the use of electronic or photographic means for the preservation of the record or parts thereof.

Comment. — See also Rule 7A:6.

Rule 8:13. Requests for Subpoenas for Witnesses and Records.

(a) *Subpoenas for Witnesses.* — (1) Requests for subpoenas for witnesses should be filed at least ten days prior to hearing.

(2) Requests for subpoenas for witnesses not timely filed should not be honored except when authorized by the court for good cause.

(b) *Subpoenas Duces Tecum.* — (1) Requests for subpoenas duces tecum should be filed at least 15 days prior to hearing.

(2) Requests for subpoenas duces tecum not timely filed should not be honored except when authorized by a judge for good cause.

(c) *Meaning of Filed.* — The term "filed" as used in this Rule means received in the appropriate clerk's office or by an appropriate magistrate.

(d) *Copies of Requests for Subpoenas Duces Tecum.* — All requests for subpoenas duces tecum shall be served on each counsel of record by delivering, dispatching by commercial delivery service, transmitting by facsimile or mailing a copy to each on or before the day of filing. At the foot of such requests shall be appended either acceptance of service or a certificate that copies were served as this Rule requires, showing the date of delivery, dispatching, transmitting or mailing.

(e) *Exception.* — This Rule does not apply to subpoenas for witnesses and subpoenas duces tecum issued by attorneys in civil cases as authorized by Virginia Code §§ 8.01-407 and 16.1-265.

The amendment, effective February 1, 1999, adopted November 23, 1998, in subdivision (d), inserted "dispatching by commercial delivery service, transmitting by facsimile" in the first sentence and inserted "dispatching, transmitting" in the second sentence.

The amendment effective July 1, 2000, adopted June 16, 2000, added subdivision (e).

Rule 8:14. Continuances.

(a) *Continuance Granted for Good Cause.* — Continuances should not be granted except by, and at the discretion of, a judge for good cause shown, or unless otherwise provided by law. The judge may, by order, delegate to the clerk the power to grant continuances consented to by all parties under such circumstances as are set forth in the order. Such an order of delegation should be reasonably disseminated and posted so as to inform the bar and the general public.

(b) *All Parties Agree to Continuance.* — If all parties to a proceeding agree to seek a continuance, the request may be made orally by one party as long as that party certifies to the judge that all other parties know of the request and concur. Such a request should be made as far in advance of the scheduled hearing or trial as is practicable. If granted, the moving party shall be responsible for assuring that notice of the continuance is given to all subpoenaed witnesses and that they are provided with the new court date. This obligation may be met by (i) an agreement between the parties that each side will notify its own witnesses; or (ii) any other arrangement that is reasonably calculated to get prompt notice to all witnesses.

(c) *All Parties Do Not Agree to Continuance.* — If a request for continuance is not agreed to by all parties to a proceeding, such request should be made to the court prior to the time originally scheduled for the hearing or trial. If the court determines that a hearing on the request should be conducted prior to the time originally scheduled for the trial, all parties shall be given notice of such hearing by the requesting party.

(d) *Continuances Requested at the Time of Hearing.* — Where a request for a continuance has not been made prior to the hearing or trial and other parties or witnesses are present and prepared for trial, a continuance should be granted only upon a showing that to proceed with the trial would not be in the best interest of justice.

(e) *Parties.* — For purposes of this Rule, the term "parties" shall mean all plaintiffs, petitioners, the prosecution, defendants, respondents and any person who is the subject of the proceeding.

Michie's Jurisprudence. — For related discussion, see 4A M.J. Continuances, §§ 4, 24, 25, 27, 49.

Rule 8:15. Discovery.

(a) *Adult Criminal Case.* — In any cases involving adults charged with crime, the provisions of Rule 7C:5 shall govern discovery.

(b) *Juvenile Delinquency Cases.* — In juvenile delinquency cases, when the juvenile is charged with an act that would be a felony if committed by an adult, or in a transfer hearing or a preliminary hearing to certify charges pursuant to § 16.1-269.1, the court shall, upon motion timely made by the juvenile or the Commonwealth's Attorney, and for good cause, enter such orders in aid of discovery and inspection of evidence as provided under Rule 3A:11.

In juvenile delinquency cases when the juvenile is charged with an act that would be a misdemeanor if committed by an adult, the court shall, upon motion timely made and for good cause, enter such orders for discovery as provided under Rule 7C:5.

(c) *Other Cases.* — In all other proceedings, the court may, upon motion timely made and for good cause, enter such orders in aid of discovery and inspection of evidence as permitted under Part Four of the Rules, except that no depositions may be taken.

(d) In proceedings concerning civil support, the judge may require parties to file a statement of gross income together with documentation in support of the statement.

Rule 8:16. Arraignment in Juvenile Delinquency Cases.

Arraignment in a delinquency proceeding shall consist of reading to the juvenile the charge on which the juvenile will be tried and calling on the juvenile to plead thereto, and it shall be conducted in court. Arraignment may be waived by the juvenile in court, or by counsel.

Rule 8:17. Notification and Waiver of Trial Rights of Parties.

Upon a juvenile's first appearance in court in a delinquency case, the juvenile shall be advised by the judge of the following trial rights: the right to counsel, to a public hearing, to the privilege against self-incrimination, to confront and cross-examine witnesses, to present evidence, and the right to appeal a final decision of the court. In determining whether a waiver of the right to counsel, of the right to a public hearing, and of the privilege against self-incrimination, is knowingly, voluntarily, and intelligently made, the court must find after a thorough inquiry that the juvenile is capable of making an intelligent and understanding decision in light of the child's age, mental condition, education, and experience, considering the nature and complexity of the case. Such waiver of trial rights shall be made orally in open court, and the waiver of the right to counsel shall also be reduced to writing, signed by the juvenile and filed with the court records of the case.

Rule 8:18. Pleas.

(a) *Permissible Pleas by Child.* — A child may admit the allegations of the petition or summons by pleading guilty, or the child may plead not guilty, nolo contendere, or enter no plea. If the child enters no plea, the court will proceed as if a denial were entered to the allegations of the petition or summons.

(b) *Determining Voluntariness, Understanding, and Intelligence of a Plea of Guilty by a Juvenile.* — The court shall not accept a plea of guilty or nolo contendere to a charge of delinquency by a child without first determining that the plea is made voluntarily with an understanding of the nature of the allegations in the petition or summons and the consequences of the plea, including that such a plea constitutes a waiver of the right to confront one's accusers and the right against compulsory self-incrimination.

(c) *Determining Voluntariness, Understanding, and Intelligence of a Plea of Guilty by an Adult.* — In any case involving an adult charged with a crime, the court shall not accept a plea of guilty or nolo contendere to a misdemeanor charge except in compliance with Rule 7C:6.

The amendment, adopted March 1, 2005, effective June 1, 2005, added "including that such a plea constitutes a waiver of the right to confront one's accusers and the right against compulsory self-incrimination" at the end of subdivision (b), and added subdivision (c).

Rule 8:19. Endorsements of Orders.

Drafts of orders prepared by counsel of record shall be endorsed by all counsel of record, or reasonable notice of the time and place of presenting such drafts together with copies thereof shall be served by delivering, dispatching by commercial delivery service, transmitting by facsimile or mailing to all counsel of record who have not endorsed them. Compliance with this Rule may be modified or dispensed with by the court in its discretion. In an Electronically Filed Case, endorsement and specification of any objections to the draft order shall be accomplished as provided in Rule 1:17.

The amendment, effective February 1, 1999, adopted November 23, 1998, inserted "dispatching by commercial delivery service, transmitting by facsimile" in the first sentence.

The amendment, effective May 2, 2011, adopted March 1, 2011, added the last sentence.

Rule 8:20. Appeals.

All appeals shall be noted in writing. An appeal is noted only upon timely receipt in the clerk's office of the writing. An appeal may be noted by a party or by the attorney for such party.

CASE NOTES

Jurisdiction absent where improper party filed appeal. — Nothing in this rule permits the notice of appeal to be filed by a person who is a regular and bona fide employee of the party. Therefore, because the notice of appeal was not filed by the Division of Child Support Enforcement's attorney, the requirement of this rule was not followed in filing the notice of appeal and, the circuit court never acquired jurisdiction over the appeal of the child support matter, from the juvenile court. Jones v. Division of Child Support Enforcement ex rel. Owens, 19 Va. App. 184, 450 S.E.2d 172 (1994).

Final order requirement. — Circuit court did not err in dismissing a mother's appeals of a juvenile and domestic relations (JDR) district court's adjudicatory orders that her children were abused and neglected because the JDR court's dispositional orders, the final orders, were not entered until July 16, 2010, but the mother never appealed those orders, and the filing of the dispositional order appeal forms on June 1, 2010, was premature since there were no final orders from which the mother could appeal at that time; pursuant to subsection A of § 16.1-296, only final orders of the JDR court could be appealed to the circuit court, and adjudicatory orders entered by a JDR district court in child abuse and neglect cases are not final orders for purposes of appeal because they are not entered pursuant to § 16.1-278.2 as required by the General Assembly. Chavis v. Hopewell Dep't of Soc. Servs., 2011 Va. App. LEXIS 118 (Apr. 5, 2011).

Jurisdiction proper. — Trial court had jurisdiction to hear an appeal of the juvenile and domestic relations district court's ruling on the biological mother's petition to modify custody and visitation; the biological mother filed a proper civil appeal notice in the case, was not required to serve the husband with it in order for the trial court to have jurisdiction over the appeal, and, in any event, the husband did not contend that he never received notice that the biological mother filed an appeal. Albert v. Ramirez, 45 Va. App. 799, 613 S.E.2d 865, 2005 Va. App. LEXIS 225 (2005).

Rule 8:21. Violations of Court Orders.

[Deleted.]

The amendment, effective May 2, 2011, adopted March 1, 2011, deleted this Rule.

Rule 8:22. Judicial Consent.

In any instance where the court is called upon in an emergency situation to give judicial consent as provided for by statute, the request and court consent may be oral, but a written request shall be filed in the clerk's office within five days of such consent, and the consent of the court shall also be reduced to a written order as soon as reasonably possible.

Comment. — See also Virginia Code § 16.1-241 (D) and Rule 8:3 (b).

Index to Rules of Supreme Court of Virginia

A

ACTIONS.
Attorneys' fees.
Claims for attorneys' fees, VA SCt Rule 3:25.
Scheduling civil cases for trial, VA SCt Rule 1:20.

ACTUAL INNOCENCE.
Petition for writ of actual innocence, VA SCt Rule 5:7B, VA SCt Rule Pt 5A Appx Form 12, VA SCt Rule Pt 5 Appx Form 12.

ADMINISTRATIVE PROCESS ACT.
See APPEALS.

ADMISSIONS IN EVIDENCE.
Best evidence rule exceptions.
Testimony or written admission of a party, VA SCt Rule 2:1007.
Hearsay exceptions.
Admission by party-opponent, VA SCt Rule 2:803.
Part of record, VA SCt Rule 4:11.
Request for admission, VA SCt Rule 4:11.
Service of request for admission, VA SCt Rule 4:11.

ADVERTISING.
Attorneys at law.
Rules of professional conduct.
Communications and advertising concerning lawyers services, VA SCt Rule Pt 6 §II Rule 7.1.

AFFIDAVITS.
Verification, VA SCt Rule 1:10.
Electronic filing and service, VA SCt Rule 1:17.

AMBULANCE CHASING.
Professional responsibility, VA SCt Rule Pt 6 §II Rule 7.3.

AMENDMENTS.
Pleadings, VA SCt Rule 1:8.

AMICUS CURIAE BRIEFS.
Supreme court, VA SCt Rule 5:30.
Oral argument, VA SCt Rule 5:33.

ANSWERS.
Civil actions, VA SCt Rule 3:8.
Interrogatories to parties, VA SCt Rule 4:8(d).

APPEALS.
Administrative process act.
Application of rules, VA SCt Rule 2A:1.
Authorization, VA SCt Rule 2A:1.
Definitions, VA SCt Rule 2A:1.
Further proceedings, VA SCt Rule 2A:5.
Notice of appeal, VA SCt Rule 2A:2.
Petition for appeal, VA SCt Rule 2A:4.
Record on appeal, VA SCt Rule 2A:3.
Small business challenges, VA SCt Rule 2A:6.
Amicus curiae briefs, VA SCt Rule 5:30.
Oral argument by amicus curiae, VA SCt Rule 5:33.

APPEALS —Cont'd
Assignments of error.
Death sentence imposed, VA SCt Rule 5:22.
Petition for appeal, VA SCt Rule 5:17.
Attorney discipline.
Board proceedings, VA SCt Rule Pt 6 §IV Pars 13-19, 13-26.
District committees.
Appeals from determinations, VA SCt Rule Pt 6 §IV Par 13-17.
State bar disciplinary actions, VA SCt Rule 5:21.
Attorneys' fees.
Circuit courts.
Recovery of appellate attorney's fees, VA SCt Rule 1:1A.
Briefs.
See BRIEFS AND OTHER PAPERS.
Circuit courts.
Attorneys' fees.
Recovery of appellate attorney's fees, VA SCt Rule 1:1A.
Costs, VA SCt Rule 5:35.
Court of appeals, appeals from.
Notice of appeal.
Certification, VA SCt Rule 5:14.
Record on appeal.
Certification for review, VA SCt Rule 5:15.
Disposition, VA SCt Rule 5:16.
Court of appeals generally.
See COURT OF APPEALS.
Criminal procedure, VA SCt Rule 3A:19.
Death imposed.
Special rules, VA SCt Rule 5:22.
Definitions.
Supreme court rules, VA SCt Rule 5:1.
Denial of appeal.
Court of appeals, VA SCt Rule 5A:15.
Supreme court rules, VA SCt Rule 5:20.
Format of petition for rehearing, VA SCt Rules 5:20, 5:20A.
Depositions.
Pending appeal, VA SCt Rule 4:2.
District courts.
Noting an appeal.
What constitutes noting an appeal, VA SCt Rule 7A:13.
Filing date.
Death sentence imposed, VA SCt Rule 5:22.
Health.
Public health threats, order of quarantine or isolation, VA SCt Rule 3:24.
Appeal of circuit court order, VA SCt Rule 5:41.
Inmates.
Petition for appeal to supreme court.
Considered without oral argument, not represented by counsel, VA SCt Rule 5:17.
Timely filing of paper, VA SCt Rule 5A:3.
Jurisdiction.
Supreme court.
Original jurisdiction, VA SCt Rule 5:7.
Juvenile and domestic relations district courts.
Briefs, VA SCt Rule 8:7.

APPEALS —Cont'd
Juvenile and domestic relations district courts —Cont'd
Writing requirement, VA SCt Rule 8:20.
Multi-party cases, appeal from partial final judgment, VA SCt Rule 5:8A.
Non-compliance with rules, sanctions, VA SCt Rule 5:1A.
Notice of appeal.
See NOTICE OF APPEAL.
Oral argument, VA SCt Rule 5:33.
Perfecting the appeal.
See PERFECTING THE APPEAL.
Petition for appeal, VA SCt Rule 5:17.
Petition for rehearing.
Denial of appeal by court of appeals, VA SCt Rule 5A:15.
Format, VA SCt Rules 5:20, 5:20A.
Public health threats.
Order of quarantine or isolation, VA SCt Rule 3:24.
Appeal of circuit court order, VA SCt Rule 5:41.
Quarantine.
Public health threats, order of quarantine or isolation, VA SCt Rule 3:24.
Appeal of circuit court order, VA SCt Rule 5:41.
Questions presented.
Petition for appeal, VA SCt Rule 5:17.
Record on appeal.
Court of appeals, appeals from.
Certification for review, VA SCt Rule 5:15.
Disposition, VA SCt Rule 5:16.
Trial court, appeals from.
Contents, VA SCt Rule 5:10.
Disagreement on contents, VA SCt Rule 5:10.
Judge authorized to act, VA SCt Rule 5:12.
Preparation and transmission, VA SCt Rule 5:13.
Transcript or written statement, VA SCt Rule 5:11.
Record relevant for review.
Death sentence imposed, VA SCt Rule 5:22.
Rehearing.
Petition, denial of appeal by court of appeals, VA SCt Rule 5A:15.
Format, VA SCt Rules 5:20, 5:20A.
Security for appeal, VA SCt Rule 5:24.
Serving counsel for appellee.
Petition for appeal, VA SCt Rule 5:17.
Settlement of pending appeals, VA SCt Rule 5:38.
State bar disciplinary actions, VA SCt Rule 5:21.
State corporation commission.
Special rules applicable to appeals from the state corporation commission, VA SCt Rule 5:21.
Supreme court.
Multi-party cases, appeal from partial final judgment, VA SCt Rule 5:8A.
Non-compliance with rules, sanctions, VA SCt Rule 5:1A.
United States supreme court.
Certification of questions of law.
Briefs, VA SCt Rule 5:40.
Time.
Assignments of error.
Filing in cases when death sentence imposed, VA SCt Rule 5:22.

APPEALS —Cont'd
Time —Cont'd
Filing petition for appeal, VA SCt Rule 5:17.
Petition for rehearing, filing.
Denial of appeal by court of appeals, VA SCt Rule 5A:15.
Record relevant for review.
Filing in cases when death sentence imposed, VA SCt Rule 5:22.
Trial court, appeals from.
Applicability of rules, VA SCt Rule 5:8.
Attorneys' fees.
Recovery of appellate attorney's fees, VA SCt Rule 1:1A.
Judge authorized to act, VA SCt Rule 5:12.
Multi-party cases, appeal from partial final judgment, VA SCt Rule 5:8A.
Notice of appeal, VA SCt Rule 5:9.
Record on appeal.
Contents, VA SCt Rule 5:10.
Disagreement on contents, VA SCt Rule 5:10.
Judge authorized to act, VA SCt Rule 5:12.
Preparation and transmission, VA SCt Rule 5:13.
Transcript or written statement, VA SCt Rule 5:11.
United States supreme court.
Certification of questions of law.
Briefs, VA SCt Rule 5:40.
Procedure upon appeal or petition to, VA SCt Rule 5:39.
Workers' compensation commission.
Provisions for appeals from commission, VA SCt Rule 5A:11.

APPEARANCES.
District courts.
Civil procedure.
Defendant's appearance.
Failure of defendant to appear, VA SCt Rule 7B:9.
Plaintiff's appearance, VA SCt Rule 7B:7.
Failure of plaintiff to appear, VA SCt Rule 7B:8.

APPLICABILITY OF RULES, VA SCt Rule 5:1.

ARBITRATION.
Attorneys at law.
Rules of professional conduct.
Former arbitrator, VA SCt Rule Pt 6 §II Rule 1.12.
Third party neutral service, VA SCt Rule Pt 6 §II Rule 2.10.

ARRAIGNMENT.
Juvenile and domestic relations district courts.
Juvenile delinquency cases, VA SCt Rule 8:16.
Pleas, VA SCt Rule 8:18.
Trial rights of parties.
Notification and waiver, VA SCt Rule 8:17.

ASSIGNMENTS OF ERROR.
Death sentence imposed, VA SCt Rule 5:22.
Petition for appeal, VA SCt Rule 5:17.

ASSOCIATIONS.
Deposition of organization, VA SCt Rule 4:5(b).

ATTORNEY-CLIENT PRIVILEGE.
Evidence, VA SCt Rule 2:502.

ATTORNEY-CLIENT PRIVILEGE —Cont'd
Prospective clients.
Duties to, VA SCt Rule Pt 6 §II Rule 1.18.
Trust accounts, VA SCt Rule Pt 6 §II Rule 1.15.

ATTORNEY DISCIPLINE.
Admonition.
Appeals from board proceedings, VA SCt Rule Pt 6 §IV Par 13-26.
Appeals.
Board proceedings, VA SCt Rule Pt 6 §IV Pars 13-19, 13-26.
Disciplinary board or circuit court determination, VA SCt Rule 5:21.
District committees.
Appeals from determinations, VA SCt Rule Pt 6 §IV Par 13-17.
State bar disciplinary actions, VA SCt Rule 5:21.
Attorney for respondent.
Participation and disqualification of counsel, VA SCt Rule Pt 6 §IV Par 13-13.
Attorneys at law.
District committees proceedings, VA SCt Rule Pt 6 §IV Par 13-16.
Audio-visual depositions.
District committees proceedings, VA SCt Rule Pt 6 §IV Par 13-16.
Bar counsel.
Complaints, processing, VA SCt Rule Pt 6 §IV Par 13-10.
Defined, VA SCt Rule Pt 6 §IV Par 13-1.
District committees, VA SCt Rule Pt 6 §IV Par 13-7.
Limited right to discovery, VA SCt Rule Pt 6 §IV Par 13-11.
Powers and duties, VA SCt Rule Pt 6 §IV Par 13-8.
Bill of particulars.
Reinstatement, VA SCt Rule Pt 6 §IV Par 13-25.
Board.
Another jurisdiction, board proceedings upon disbarment, revocation or suspension in, VA SCt Rule Pt 6 §IV Par 13-24.
Crimes.
Proceedings upon guilty plea or adjudication of a crime, VA SCt Rule Pt 6 §IV Par 13-22.
Disqualification of members, VA SCt Rule Pt 6 §IV Par 13-14.
First offender pleas.
Proceedings upon, VA SCt Rule Pt 6 §IV Par 13-21.
Guilty plea.
Proceedings upon, VA SCt Rule Pt 6 §IV Par 13-22.
Impairment.
Proceedings upon, VA SCt Rule Pt 6 §IV Par 13-23.
Members, terms, meetings and quorum, VA SCt Rule Pt 6 §IV Par 13-6.
Proceedings upon certification, VA SCt Rule Pt 6 §IV Par 13-18.
Appeals, VA SCt Rule Pt 6 §IV Par 13-19.
Reinstatement procedures, VA SCt Rule Pt 6 §IV Par 13-25.
Sanctions.
Proceedings upon certification for sanction determinations, VA SCt Rule Pt 6 §IV Par 13-20.

ATTORNEY DISCIPLINE —Cont'd
Burden of proof.
Board proceedings upon guilty plea or adjudication of a crime, VA SCt Rule Pt 6 §IV Par 13-22.
Clerk of the disciplinary system, VA SCt Rule Pt 6 §IV Par 13-9.
COLD.
Defined, VA SCt Rule Pt 6 §IV Par 13-1.
Disqualification of members, VA SCt Rule Pt 6 §IV Par 13-14.
Powers and duties, VA SCt Rule Pt 6 §IV Par 13-5.
Complaints.
Bar counsel, processing, VA SCt Rule Pt 6 §IV Par 13-10.
Dismissal of complaints, VA SCt Rule Pt 6 §IV Par 13-31.
Confidentiality of information.
Disciplinary records and proceedings, VA SCt Rule Pt 6 §IV Par 13-30.
Consent to revocation, VA SCt Rule Pt 6 §IV Par 13-28.
Council.
Defined, VA SCt Rule Pt 6 §IV Par 13-1.
General administrative authority, VA SCt Rule Pt 6 §IV Par 13-3.
Court authority.
Effect of rules, VA SCt Rule Pt 6 §IV Par 13-2.
Crimes.
Board proceedings upon guilty plea or adjudication of a crime, VA SCt Rule Pt 6 §IV Par 13-22.
Death of respondent.
Dismissal of complaints, VA SCt Rule Pt 6 §IV Par 13-31.
Definitions, VA SCt Rule Pt 6 §IV Par 13-1.
Disbarment.
Another jurisdiction, board proceedings upon, VA SCt Rule Pt 6 §IV Par 13-24.
Appeals from board proceedings, VA SCt Rule Pt 6 §IV Par 13-26.
Duties of disbarred or suspended respondents, VA SCt Rule Pt 6 §IV Par 13-29.
Disciplinary board.
Members, terms, meetings and quorum, VA SCt Rule Pt 6 §IV Par 13-6.
Discovery.
District committees proceedings, VA SCt Rule Pt 6 §IV Par 13-16.
Limited right to discovery, VA SCt Rule Pt 6 §IV Par 13-11.
Dismissal of complaints, VA SCt Rule Pt 6 §IV Par 13-31.
Dismissal of proceedings.
Board proceedings upon certification, VA SCt Rule Pt 6 §IV Par 13-18.
District committees.
Appeals from determinations, VA SCt Rule Pt 6 §IV Par 13-17.
Bar counsel, VA SCt Rule Pt 6 §IV Par 13-7.
Complaints, processing by bar counsel.
Referral to district committee, VA SCt Rule Pt 6 §IV Par 13-10.
Disqualification of members, VA SCt Rule Pt 6 §IV Par 13-14.
Established, VA SCt Rule Pt 6 §IV Par 13-4.
Panel quorum, VA SCt Rule Pt 6 §IV Par 13-4.
Powers, VA SCt Rule Pt 6 §IV Par 13-7.

ATTORNEY DISCIPLINE —Cont'd
District committees —Cont'd
Private discipline, limitation, VA SCt Rule Pt 6 §IV Par 13-7.
Proceedings before, VA SCt Rule Pt 6 §IV Par 13-16.
Subcommittees, VA SCt Rule Pt 6 §IV Par 13-7.
Actions by, VA SCt Rule Pt 6 §IV Par 13-15.
Enforcement of terms.
Board proceedings upon certification, VA SCt Rule Pt 6 §IV Par 13-18.
District committees proceedings, VA SCt Rule Pt 6 §IV Par 13-16.
Evidentiary rulings, VA SCt Rule Pt 6 §IV Par 13-12.
District committees proceedings, VA SCt Rule Pt 6 §IV Par 13-16.
Notice of impairment evidence, VA SCt Rule Pt 6 §IV Par 13-12.
Reinstatement, VA SCt Rule Pt 6 §IV Par 13-25.
First offender pleas.
Board proceedings upon, VA SCt Rule Pt 6 §IV Par 13-21.
Guardian ad litem.
Impairment, VA SCt Rule Pt 6 §IV Par 13-23.
Guilty pleas.
Board proceedings upon, VA SCt Rule Pt 6 §IV Par 13-22.
Hearings.
Board proceedings upon certification, VA SCt Rule Pt 6 §IV Par 13-18.
Criminal adjudication or guilty plea, VA SCt Rule Pt 6 §IV Par 13-22.
Disbarment, revocation or suspension in another jurisdiction, VA SCt Rule Pt 6 §IV Par 13-24.
Reinstatement, VA SCt Rule Pt 6 §IV Par 13-25.
Impairment.
Board proceedings upon, VA SCt Rule Pt 6 §IV Par 13-23.
Reinstatement, VA SCt Rule Pt 6 §IV Par 13-25.
Investigations.
Impairment, VA SCt Rule Pt 6 §IV Par 13-23.
Preliminary investigations.
Complaints, processing by bar counsel, VA SCt Rule Pt 6 §IV Par 13-10.
Reinstatement, VA SCt Rule Pt 6 §IV Par 13-25.
Jurisdiction of courts.
Effect of rules, VA SCt Rule Pt 6 §IV Par 13-2.
Notice, VA SCt Rule Pt 6 §IV Par 13-12.
Appeal of board determination, VA SCt Rule Pt 6 §IV Par 13-19.
Appeals from board proceedings, VA SCt Rule Pt 6 §IV Par 13-26.
Criminal adjudication or guilty plea, VA SCt Rule Pt 6 §IV Par 13-22.
District committees proceedings, VA SCt Rule Pt 6 §IV Par 13-16.
Notice of impairment evidence, VA SCt Rule Pt 6 §IV Par 13-12.
Reinstatement, VA SCt Rule Pt 6 §IV Par 13-25.
Subcommittee actions, VA SCt Rule Pt 6 §IV Par 13-15.
Oral argument.
District committees proceedings, VA SCt Rule Pt 6 §IV Par 13-16.
Pre-hearing orders.
Board proceedings upon certification, VA SCt Rule Pt 6 §IV Par 13-18.

ATTORNEY DISCIPLINE —Cont'd
Private discipline.
District committees, limitation, VA SCt Rule Pt 6 §IV Par 13-7.
Public reprimand with terms.
Appeals from board proceedings, VA SCt Rule Pt 6 §IV Par 13-26.
District committees proceedings.
Alternative disposition and procedure, VA SCt Rule Pt 6 §IV Par 13-16.
Records.
Clerk of the disciplinary system, VA SCt Rule Pt 6 §IV Par 13-9.
Confidentiality, VA SCt Rule Pt 6 §IV Par 13-30.
Reinstatement.
Board procedures, VA SCt Rule Pt 6 §IV Par 13-25.
Resignation, VA SCt Rule Pt 6 §IV Par 13-27.
Reinstatement after resignation, VA SCt Rule Pt 6 §IV Par 13-25.
Revocation.
Another jurisdiction, board proceedings upon, VA SCt Rule Pt 6 §IV Par 13-24.
Consent to revocation, VA SCt Rule Pt 6 §IV Par 13-28.
Dismissal of complaints, VA SCt Rule Pt 6 §IV Par 13-31.
Reinstatement, VA SCt Rule Pt 6 §IV Par 13-25.
Sanctions.
Appeal of board determination, VA SCt Rule Pt 6 §IV Par 13-19.
Board proceedings upon certification for sanction determinations, VA SCt Rule Pt 6 §IV Par 13-20.
District committees proceedings, VA SCt Rule Pt 6 §IV Par 13-16.
Service of notice, process and other papers, VA SCt Rule Pt 6 §IV Par 13-12.
Show cause orders.
District committees proceedings, VA SCt Rule Pt 6 §IV Par 13-16.
Stays pending appeals.
Appeals from board proceedings, VA SCt Rule Pt 6 §IV Par 13-26.
Subcommittees, VA SCt Rule Pt 6 §IV Par 13-7.
Actions by, VA SCt Rule Pt 6 §IV Par 13-15.
Subpoenas.
District committees proceedings, VA SCt Rule Pt 6 §IV Par 13-16.
Limited right to discovery, VA SCt Rule Pt 6 §IV Par 13-11.
Substantial compliance.
Effect, VA SCt Rule Pt 6 §IV Par 13-12.
Summary resolution.
Complaints, processing by bar counsel, VA SCt Rule Pt 6 §IV Par 13-10.
Summary suspensions.
Impairment, VA SCt Rule Pt 6 §IV Par 13-23.
Summons.
District committees proceedings, VA SCt Rule Pt 6 §IV Par 13-16.
Limited right to discovery, VA SCt Rule Pt 6 §IV Par 13-11.
Suspension.
Another jurisdiction, board proceedings upon, VA SCt Rule Pt 6 §IV Par 13-24.
Appeals from board proceedings, VA SCt Rule Pt 6 §IV Par 13-26.

ATTORNEY DISCIPLINE —Cont'd
Suspension —Cont'd
Duties of disbarred or suspended respondents, VA SCt Rule Pt 6 §IV Par 13-29.
Impairment, VA SCt Rule Pt 6 §IV Par 13-23.
Reinstatement, VA SCt Rule Pt 6 §IV Par 13-25.
Terms.
Board proceedings upon certification.
Enforcement of terms, VA SCt Rule Pt 6 §IV Par 13-18.
District committees proceedings.
Enforcement of terms, VA SCt Rule Pt 6 §IV Par 13-16.
Time deadlines, VA SCt Rule Pt 6 §IV Par 13-12.
Witnesses.
District committees proceedings, VA SCt Rule Pt 6 §IV Par 13-16.
Reinstatement.
Character witnesses, VA SCt Rule Pt 6 §IV Par 13-25.

ATTORNEY ISSUED SUBPOENA DUCES TECUM, VA SCt Rule 4:9.

ATTORNEYS AT LAW.
Active members of state bar, VA SCt Rule Pt 6 §IV Par 3.
Actual innocence.
Petition for writ of actual innocence.
Duties of attorney, VA SCt Rule 5:7B.
Address of record.
Each member to submit, VA SCt Rule Pt 6 §IV Par 3.
Admiralty practice.
Rules of professional conduct.
Use of designation, VA SCt Rule Pt 6 §II Rule 7.4.
Admission to bar, VA SCt Rule Pt 6 §II Rule 8.1.
Admission to practice in state without examination, VA SCt Rule 1A:1.
Filing fee.
Admission to practice in state without examination, VA SCt Rule 1A:1.
Revocation of certificates issued, VA SCt Rule 1A:3.
Revocation of certificates to practice in state without examination, VA SCt Rule 1A:3.
Advertising, VA SCt Rule Pt 6 §II Rule 7.1.
Advisory role, VA SCt Rule Pt 6 §II Rule 2.1.
Ambulance chasing, VA SCt Rule Pt 6 §II Rule 7.3.
Appointments to representation.
Accepting, VA SCt Rule Pt 6 §II Rule 6.2.
Actual innocence.
Petition for writ of actual innocence, VA SCt Rule 5:7B.
Associate members of state bar, VA SCt Rule Pt 6 §IV Par 3.
Attorney discipline.
Attorney for respondent.
Participation and disqualification of counsel, VA SCt Rule Pt 6 §IV Par 13-13.
District committees proceedings, VA SCt Rule Pt 6 §IV Par 13-16.
Generally, VA SCt Rule Pt 6 §IV Par 13.
See ATTORNEY DISCIPLINE.
Bar counsel.
Disciplining, suspending and disbarring attorneys, VA SCt Rule Pt 6 §IV Par 13.
Bar disciplinary board.
Disciplining, suspending and disbarring attorneys, VA SCt Rule Pt 6 §IV Par 13.

ATTORNEYS AT LAW —Cont'd
Business cards, VA SCt Rule Pt 6 §II Rule 7.5.
Candor towards tribunal, VA SCt Rule Pt 6 §II Rule 3.3.
Cards.
Professional or business cards, VA SCt Rule Pt 6 §II Rule 7.5.
Change of address or other contact information, VA SCt Rules 5:1, 5A:1.
Classes of membership of state bar, VA SCt Rule Pt 6 §IV Par 3.
Clerk of the disciplinary system.
Disciplining, suspending and disbarring attorneys, VA SCt Rule Pt 6 §IV Par 13.
Client-attorney relationship.
Communication with client, VA SCt Rule Pt 6 §II Rule 1.4.
Competent representation of client, VA SCt Rule Pt 6 §II Rule 1.1.
Conflicts of interest, VA SCt Rule Pt 6 §II Rule 1.7.
Former clients, VA SCt Rule Pt 6 §II Rule 1.9.
Government and private employment in succession, VA SCt Rule Pt 6 §II Rule 1.11.
Imputed disqualification, VA SCt Rule Pt 6 §II Rule 1.10.
Judge or arbitrator service as conflict, VA SCt Rule Pt 6 §II Rule 1.12.
Transactions prohibited, VA SCt Rule Pt 6 §II Rule 1.8.
Declining representation, VA SCt Rule Pt 6 §II Rule 1.16.
Diligent representation, VA SCt Rule Pt 6 §II Rule 1.3.
Disability, client under, VA SCt Rule Pt 6 §II Rule 1.14.
Escrow accounts, VA SCt Rule Pt 6 §II Rule 1.15.
Fees, VA SCt Rule Pt 6 §II Rule 1.5.
Privileged information.
Confidentiality, VA SCt Rule Pt 6 §II Rule 1.6.
Safekeeping property, VA SCt Rule Pt 6 §II Rule 1.15.
Sale of practice, VA SCt Rule Pt 6 §II Rule 1.17.
Scope of representation, VA SCt Rule Pt 6 §II Rule 1.2.
Withdrawal from representation, VA SCt Rule Pt 6 §II Rule 1.16.
Clients' protection fund.
Establishment, VA SCt Rule Pt 6 §IV Par 16.
Client's security fund.
Administrative agency practice.
Immigration law, VA SCt Rule Pt 6 §I UPR 9-103.
Trust accounting procedures.
Maintenance of trust account, VA SCt Rule Pt 6 §IV Par 20.
Reporting requirements, VA SCt Rule Pt 6 §IV Par 20.

COLD.
Standing committee on lawyer discipline.
Disciplining, suspending and disbarring attorneys, VA SCt Rule Pt 6 §IV Par 13.
Commonwealth's attorneys.
Professional responsibility, VA SCt Rule Pt 6 §II Rule 3.8.
Communication with client, VA SCt Rule Pt 6 §II Rule 1.4.

ATTORNEYS AT LAW —Cont'd
Communication with non-client.
Persons represented by counsel.
Presence of other counsel, VA SCt Rule Pt 6 §II Rule 4.2.
Third persons' rights to be respected, VA SCt Rule Pt 6 §II Rule 4.4.
Truthfulness in statements to others, VA SCt Rule Pt 6 §II Rule 4.1.
Unrepresented person, VA SCt Rule Pt 6 §II Rule 4.3.
Competent representation of client, VA SCt Rule Pt 6 §II Rule 1.1.
Computerized legal research.
Virginia state bar ordered to contract to provide, VA SCt Rule Pt 6 §IV Par 21.
Confidentiality of information.
Rules of professional conduct, VA SCt Rule Pt 6 §II Rule 1.6.
Evaluation for use by third persons, VA SCt Rule Pt 6 §II Rule 2.3.
Former client, VA SCt Rule Pt 6 §II Rule 1.9.
Government information.
Successive government and private employment, VA SCt Rule Pt 6 §II Rule 1.11.
Prospective clients, VA SCt Rule Pt 6 §II Rule 1.18.
Third party neutral, VA SCt Rule Pt 6 §II Rule 2.10.
Conflicts of interest.
Organization as client, VA SCt Rule Pt 6 §II Rule 1.13.
Rules of professional conduct.
Former client, VA SCt Rule Pt 6 §II Rule 1.9.
Generally, VA SCt Rule Pt 6 §II Rule 1.7.
Imputed disqualification, VA SCt Rule Pt 6 §II Rule 1.10.
Lawyer as witness, VA SCt Rule Pt 6 §II Rule 3.7.
Prohibited transactions, VA SCt Rule Pt 6 §II Rule 1.8.
Prospective clients, VA SCt Rule Pt 6 §II Rule 1.18.
Consultants.
Foreign legal consultants, registration, VA SCt Rule 1A:7.
Contingent fees.
Rules of professional conduct, VA SCt Rule Pt 6 §II Rule 1.5.
Continuing legal education.
Mandatory continuing legal education rule, VA SCt Rule Pt 6 §IV Par 17.
Suspension for failure to complete, VA SCt Rule Pt 6 §IV Par 13.2.
Requirements. See within this heading, "Education."
Corporations.
Corporate counsel, VA SCt Rule 1A:5.
Corporate counsel registrants, VA SCt Rule 1A:5.
Counsel of record.
Withdrawing from case, VA SCt Rule 1:5.
Crimes.
Honesty or fitness of attorney questionable as result, VA SCt Rule Pt 6 §II Rule 8.4.
Criminal procedure.
Subpoena directed to member of bar.
Proceedings for approval, VA SCt Rule 3A:12.

ATTORNEYS AT LAW —Cont'd
Criminal procedure —Cont'd
Subpoena duces tecum.
Compelling production of testimony concerning present or former client of member of bar.
Proceedings for approval, VA SCt Rule 3A:12.
Declining representation, VA SCt Rule Pt 6 §II Rule 1.16.
Diligent representation, VA SCt Rule Pt 6 §II Rule 1.3.
Disabled and retired members of state bar, VA SCt Rule Pt 6 §IV Par 3.
Disciplinary rules.
Procedure for disciplining, suspending and disbarring attorneys, VA SCt Rule Pt 6 §IV Par 13.
Rules of professional conduct.
Lawyers subject to disciplinary authority, VA SCt Rule Pt 6 §II Rule 8.5.
Discipline, VA SCt Rule Pt 6 §II Rule 8.1.
Attorney for respondent.
Participation and disqualification of counsel, VA SCt Rule Pt 6 §IV Par 13-13.
Authority for discipline, VA SCt Rule Pt 6 §II Rule 8.5.
Choice of law, VA SCt Rule Pt 6 §II Rule 8.5.
Generally, VA SCt Rule Pt 6 §IV Par 13.
See ATTORNEY DISCIPLINE.
Reporting professional misconduct, VA SCt Rule Pt 6 §II Rule 8.3.
District committees.
Disciplining, suspending and disbarring attorneys, VA SCt Rule Pt 6 §IV Par 13.
District courts.
Construction of term, VA SCt Rule 7A:3.
Counsel of record.
Construction of term, VA SCt Rule 7A:3.
Education.
Continuing education requirements.
Certificate of attendance, VA SCt Rule Pt 6 §IV Par 17.
Continuing legal education board, VA SCt Rule Pt 6 §IV Par 17.
Credits, VA SCt Rule Pt 6 §IV Par 17.
Exemptions, VA SCt Rule Pt 6 §IV Par 17.
Purpose, VA SCt Rule Pt 6 §IV Par 17.
Reactivation from inactive status, VA SCt Rule Pt 6 §IV Par 17.
Standards, VA SCt Rule Pt 6 §IV Par 17.
Statement of requirements, VA SCt Rule Pt 6 §IV Par 17.
Suspension for failure to complete continuing legal education requirements, VA SCt Rule Pt 6 §IV Par 13.2.
Legal ethics.
Suspension for failure to complete legal ethics course, VA SCt Rule Pt 6 §IV Par 13.1.
Emeritus members of state bar, VA SCt Rule Pt 6 §IV Par 3.
Evaluation role of attorney, VA SCt Rule Pt 6 §II Rule 2.3.
Fairness to opposition, VA SCt Rule Pt 6 §II Rule 3.4.
Fees.
Foreign attorney admitted to practice without examination, VA SCt Rule 1A:1.
Patent and trademark attorneys, VA SCt Rule 1A:2.

ATTORNEYS AT LAW —Cont'd
Fees —Cont'd
Rules of professional conduct, VA SCt Rule Pt 6 §II Rule 1.5.
Firm name.
Rules of professional conduct.
Use of firm names and letterheads, VA SCt Rule Pt 6 §II Rule 7.5.
Signatures, VA SCt Rule 1:5.
Electronic filing and service, VA SCt Rule 1:17.
Foreign attorneys, VA SCt Rules 1A:1 to 1A:7.
Comity.
When allowed by comity to participate in trial of case, VA SCt Rule 1A:4.
Corporate counsel.
Registration, VA SCt Rule 1A:5.
Foreign legal consultants, registration, VA SCt Rule 1A:7.
Patent and trademark attorneys.
Limitations on practice, VA SCt Rule 1A:2.
Pleading.
Comity.
Pleading or notice to be signed by member of Virginia bar or party, VA SCt Rule 1A:4.
Registered military legal assistance attorneys, VA SCt Rule 1A:6.
Service not required on, VA SCt Rule 1:5.
Service on associate counsel equivalent to service on nonresident attorney, VA SCt Rule 1A:4.
Signatures.
Pleading or notice.
Signing by member of state bar, VA SCt Rule 1A.4.
Trial.
Comity.
When allowed by comity to participate in trial of case, VA SCt Rule 1A:4.
Former clients.
Conflicts of interest, VA SCt Rule Pt 6 §II Rule 1.9.
Frivolous pleadings.
Rules of professional conduct.
Requirements as to meritorious claims and contentions, VA SCt Rule Pt 6 §II Rule 3.1.
Honesty of attorney.
Crimes or acts calling into question, VA SCt Rule Pt 6 §II Rule 8.4.
Impairment proceedings.
Disciplining, suspending and disbarring attorneys, VA SCt Rule Pt 6 §IV Par 13.
IOLTA accounts generally, VA SCt Rule Pt 6 §IV Par 20.
Judgments and decrees.
Drafts of orders and decrees.
Endorsed by counsel of record, VA SCt Rule 1:13.
Electronic filing and service, VA SCt Rule 1:17.
Notice of presentation or entry, VA SCt Rule 1:13.
Judicial members of state bar, VA SCt Rule Pt 6 §IV Par 3.

ATTORNEYS AT LAW —Cont'd
Jury.
Rules of professional conduct.
Communications with jurors.
Restrictions relating to impartiality and decorum of the tribunal, VA SCt Rule Pt 6 §II Rule 3.5.
Juvenile and domestic relations district courts.
"Counsel" defined, VA SCt Rule 8:2.
"Counsel of record" defined, VA SCt Rule 8:2.
Endorsements of orders, VA SCt Rule 8:19.
Juvenile delinquency cases.
Waiver of arraignment, VA SCt Rule 8:16.
Noting of appeal, VA SCt Rule 8:20.
Roles of counsel when representing children, VA SCt Rule 8:6.
Law firms and associations.
Rules of professional conduct.
Firm names and letterheads, VA SCt Rule Pt 6 §II Rule 7.5.
Multijurisdictional practice of law, VA SCt Rule Pt 6 §II Rule 5.5.
Noncompete clauses, employment contracts or settlement agreements, VA SCt Rule Pt 6 §II Rule 5.6.
Nonlawyer assistants.
Responsibilities regarding, VA SCt Rule Pt 6 §II Rule 5.3.
Partner.
Responsibilities, VA SCt Rule Pt 6 §II Rule 5.1.
Professional independence of lawyer, VA SCt Rule Pt 6 §II Rule 5.4.
Restrictions on right to practice, VA SCt Rule Pt 6 §II Rule 5.6.
Supervisory lawyer.
Responsibilities, VA SCt Rule Pt 6 §II Rule 5.1.
Unauthorized practice of law, VA SCt Rule Pt 6 §II Rule 5.5.
Voluntary pro bono publico service, VA SCt Rule Pt 6 §II Rule 6.1.
Legal consultants.
Foreign legal consultants, registration, VA SCt Rule 1A:7.
Legal ethics.
Suspension for failure to complete legal ethics course, VA SCt Rule Pt 6 §IV Par 13.1.
Legal services organizations.
Membership, VA SCt Rule Pt 6 §II Rule 6.3.
Legal services programs, VA SCt Rule Pt 6 §II Rule 6.5.
Letterheads, VA SCt Rule Pt 6 §II Rule 7.5.
Local rules of court.
Duty of attorney as to, VA SCt Rule 1:15.
Mediation.
Rules of professional conduct.
Acting as mediator, VA SCt Rule Pt 6 §II Rule 2.11.
Military attorneys.
Registered military legal assistance attorneys, VA SCt Rule 1A:6.
Multijurisdictional practice of law.
Rules of professional conduct, VA SCt Rule Pt 6 §II Rule 5.5.

ATTORNEYS AT LAW —Cont'd
Non-compliance with rules, sanctions, VA SCt Rule 5:1A.
Online legal research.
Virginia state bar ordered to contract to provide, VA SCt Rule Pt 6 §IV Par 21.
Out-of-state attorneys.
Pro hac vice, VA SCt Rule 1A:4.
Application to appear pro hac vice before a Virginia tribunal, VA SCt Rule Pt 1A Appx Form 1.
Patent and trademark attorneys.
Limitations on practice, VA SCt Rule 1A:2.
Patent attorneys.
Rules of professional conduct.
Use of designation, VA SCt Rule Pt 6 §II Rule 7.4.
Pleading.
Foreign attorneys.
Comity.
Pleading or notice to be signed by member of Virginia bar or party, VA SCt Rule 1A:4.
Office address and telephone number of counsel submitting pleading.
Pleadings to contain, VA SCt Rule 1:4(l).
Service on counsel of record after initial process, VA SCt Rule 1:12.
Signature and address required, VA SCt Rule 1:4(c).
Pro bono public service, VA SCt Rule Pt 6 §II Rule 6.1.
Professional cards, VA SCt Rule Pt 6 §II Rule 7.5.
Professional misconduct.
Elements, VA SCt Rule Pt 6 §II Rule 8.4.
Prosecuting attorneys.
Professional responsibility, VA SCt Rule Pt 6 §II Rule 3.8.
Prosecutors.
Rules of professional conduct.
Additional responsibilities of prosecutor, VA SCt Rule Pt 6 §II Rule 3.8.
Prospective clients.
Duties to, VA SCt Rule Pt 6 §II Rule 1.18.
Public office.
Rules of professional conduct.
Successive government and private employment, VA SCt Rule Pt 6 §II Rule 1.11.
Records.
Rules of professional conduct.
Safekeeping property, VA SCt Rule Pt 6 §II Rule 1.15.
Reinstatement after revocation, VA SCt Rule Pt 6 §IV Par 13.
Reports.
Rules of professional conduct.
Professional misconduct, VA SCt Rule Pt 6 §II Rule 8.3.
Safekeeping property, VA SCt Rule Pt 6 §II Rule 1.15.
Resignation, VA SCt Rule Pt 6 §IV Par 13.
Rules of professional conduct.
Admiralty practice.
Use of designation, VA SCt Rule Pt 6 §II Rule 7.4.
Advertising.
Communications and advertising concerning lawyer's services, VA SCt Rule Pt 6 §II Rule 7.1.

ATTORNEYS AT LAW —Cont'd
Rules of professional conduct —Cont'd
Advisor.
Duties as, VA SCt Rule Pt 6 §II Rule 2.1.
Ambulance chasing.
Direct contact with prospective clients, VA SCt Rule Pt 6 §II Rule 7.3.
Appointment by tribunal to represent person.
Accepting appointment, VA SCt Rule Pt 6 §II Rule 6.2.
Arbitrators.
Former judge or arbitrator, VA SCt Rule Pt 6 §II Rule 1.12.
Bar admissions.
Prohibited acts by applicants, VA SCt Rule Pt 6 §II Rule 8.1.
Business transactions.
Conflicts of interest.
Prohibited transactions, VA SCt Rule Pt 6 §II Rule 1.8.
Candor toward the tribunal, VA SCt Rule Pt 6 §II Rule 3.3.
Choice of law.
Disciplinary authority, VA SCt Rule Pt 6 §II Rule 8.5.
Client papers and files, return upon termination of representation, VA SCt Rule Pt 6 §II Rule 1.16.
Communication of fields of practice and certification, VA SCt Rule Pt 6 §II Rule 7.4.
Communications and advertising concerning lawyers services, VA SCt Rule Pt 6 §II Rule 7.1.
Communication with client, VA SCt Rule Pt 6 §II Rule 1.4.
Communication with jurors.
Restrictions relating to impartiality and decorum of the tribunal, VA SCt Rule Pt 6 §II Rule 3.5.
Communication with persons represented by counsel, VA SCt Rule Pt 6 §II Rule 4.2.
Competent representation of client, VA SCt Rule Pt 6 §II Rule 1.1.
Confidentiality of information, VA SCt Rule Pt 6 §II Rule 1.6.
Evaluation for use by third persons, VA SCt Rule Pt 6 §II Rule 2.3.
Former client, VA SCt Rule Pt 6 §II Rule 1.9.
Government information.
Successive government and private employment, VA SCt Rule Pt 6 §II Rule 1.11.
Prospective clients, VA SCt Rule Pt 6 §II Rule 1.18.
Third party neutral, VA SCt Rule Pt 6 §II Rule 2.10.
Conflicts of interest.
Former client, VA SCt Rule Pt 6 §II Rule 1.9.
Generally, VA SCt Rule Pt 6 §II Rule 1.7.
Imputed disqualification, VA SCt Rule Pt 6 §II Rule 1.10.
Lawyer as witness, VA SCt Rule Pt 6 §II Rule 3.7.
Prohibited transactions, VA SCt Rule Pt 6 §II Rule 1.8.
Prospective clients, VA SCt Rule Pt 6 §II Rule 1.18.
Contingent fees, VA SCt Rule Pt 6 §II Rule 1.5.

ATTORNEYS AT LAW —Cont'd
Rules of professional conduct —Cont'd
Court-annexed limited legal services programs, VA SCt Rule Pt 6 §II Rule 6.5.
Declining representation, VA SCt Rule Pt 6 §II Rule 1.16.
Decorum of the tribunal.
Requirements as to, VA SCt Rule Pt 6 §II Rule 3.5.
Diligence in representing client, VA SCt Rule Pt 6 §II Rule 1.3.
Direct contact with prospective clients, VA SCt Rule Pt 6 §II Rule 7.3.
Disability of client, VA SCt Rule Pt 6 §II Rule 1.14.
Discharge by client.
Termination of representation generally, VA SCt Rule Pt 6 §II Rule 1.16.
Disciplinary authority.
Lawyers subject to, VA SCt Rule Pt 6 §II Rule 8.5.
Disciplinary matters.
Prohibited acts in connection with, VA SCt Rule Pt 6 §II Rule 8.1.
Disqualification.
Former judge or arbitrator, VA SCt Rule Pt 6 §II Rule 1.12.
Imputed disqualification, VA SCt Rule Pt 6 §II Rule 1.10.
Domestic relations cases.
Contingent fees in, VA SCt Rule Pt 6 §II Rule 1.5.
Evaluations for use by third persons, VA SCt Rule Pt 6 §II Rule 2.3.
Evidence.
False evidence.
Requirements as to candor toward the tribunal, VA SCt Rule Pt 6 §II Rule 3.3.
Ex parte proceedings.
Candor toward the tribunal, VA SCt Rule Pt 6 §II Rule 3.3.
Fairness to opposing party and counsel, VA SCt Rule Pt 6 §II Rule 3.4.
False evidence.
Requirements as to candor toward the tribunal, VA SCt Rule Pt 6 §II Rule 3.3.
Requirements as to fairness to opposing party and counsel, VA SCt Rule Pt 6 §II Rule 3.4.
Fees, VA SCt Rule Pt 6 §II Rule 1.5.
Firm name.
Use of firm names and letterheads, VA SCt Rule Pt 6 §II Rule 7.5.
Former clients.
Conflicts of interest, VA SCt Rule Pt 6 §II Rule 1.9.
Fraud upon the tribunal.
Requirements as to candor toward the tribunal, VA SCt Rule Pt 6 §II Rule 3.3.
Impartiality of the tribunal.
Requirements as to, VA SCt Rule Pt 6 §II Rule 3.5.
Imputed disqualification, VA SCt Rule Pt 6 §II Rule 1.10.
Independent professional judgment of lawyer.
Advisor to client, VA SCt Rule Pt 6 §II Rule 2.1.
Judges.
Former judge or arbitrator, VA SCt Rule Pt 6 §II Rule 1.12.

ATTORNEYS AT LAW —Cont'd
Rules of professional conduct —Cont'd
Judicial officials.
False statements concerning qualifications or integrity of, VA SCt Rule Pt 6 §II Rule 8.2.
Jury.
Communications with jurors.
Restrictions related to impartiality and decorum of the tribunal, VA SCt Rule Pt 6 §II Rule 3.5.
Law firms and associations.
Firm names and letterheads, VA SCt Rule Pt 6 §II Rule 7.5.
Multijurisdictional practice of law, VA SCt Rule Pt 6 §II Rule 5.5.
Noncompete clauses, employment contracts or settlement agreements, VA SCt Rule Pt 6 §II Rule 5.6.
Non lawyer assistants.
Responsibilities regarding, VA SCt Rule Pt 6 §II Rule 5.3.
Partner.
Responsibilities, VA SCt Rule Pt 6 §II Rule 5.1.
Professional independence of lawyer, VA SCt Rule Pt 6 §II Rule 5.4.
Restrictions on right to practice, VA SCt Rule Pt 6 §II Rule 5.6.
Supervisory lawyer.
Responsibilities, VA SCt Rule Pt 6 §II Rule 5.1.
Unauthorized practice of law, VA SCt Rule Pt 6 §II Rule 5.5.
Voluntary pro bono publico service, VA SCt Rule Pt 6 §II Rule 6.1.
Legal services organizations.
Membership in, VA SCt Rule Pt 6 §II Rule 6.3.
Letterheads.
Firm names and letterheads, VA SCt Rule Pt 6 §II Rule 7.5.
Limited legal services programs, VA SCt Rule Pt 6 §II Rule 6.5.
Mediator.
Acting as, VA SCt Rule Pt 6 §II Rule 2.11.
Meritorious claims and contentions, VA SCt Rule Pt 6 §II Rule 3.1.
Misconduct of another attorney.
Revealing of information concerning, VA SCt Rule Pt 6 §II Rule 1.6.
Multijurisdictional practice of law, VA SCt Rule Pt 6 §II Rule 5.5.
Nonprofit limited legal services programs, VA SCt Rule Pt 6 §II Rule 6.5.
Notice of sale of law practice, VA SCt Rule Pt 6 §II Rule 1.17.
Notice of termination of representation, VA SCt Rule Pt 6 §II Rule 1.16.
Opposing party and counsel.
Fairness to, VA SCt Rule Pt 6 §II Rule 3.4.
Patent attorneys.
Use of designation, VA SCt Rule Pt 6 §II Rule 7.4.
Pro bono publico service, VA SCt Rule Pt 6 §II Rule 6.1.
Professional independence of lawyer.
Law firms and associations, VA SCt Rule Pt 6 §II Rule 5.4.

ATTORNEYS AT LAW —Cont'd
Rules of professional conduct —Cont'd
Professional misconduct.
Reporting, VA SCt Rule Pt 6 §II Rule 8.3.
What constitutes, VA SCt Rule Pt 6 §II Rule 8.4.
Property of client.
Safekeeping property, VA SCt Rule Pt 6 §II Rule 1.15.
Prosecutors.
Additional responsibilities of prosecutor, VA SCt Rule Pt 6 §II Rule 3.8.
Prospective clients.
Duties to, VA SCt Rule Pt 6 §II Rule 1.18.
Publicity.
Trial publicity, VA SCt Rule Pt 6 §II Rule 3.6.
Public office.
Successive government and private employment, VA SCt Rule Pt 6 §II Rule 1.11.
Recommendation of professional employment, VA SCt Rule Pt 6 §II Rule 7.3.
Records.
Safekeeping property, VA SCt Rule Pt 6 §II Rule 1.15.
Reports.
Professional misconduct, VA SCt Rule Pt 6 §II Rule 8.3.
Safekeeping property, VA SCt Rule Pt 6 §II Rule 1.15.
Representation of client.
Advisor, VA SCt Rule Pt 6 §II Rule 2.1.
Appointment by tribunal to represent person.
Accepting appointment, VA SCt Rule Pt 6 §II Rule 6.2.
Communication with client, VA SCt Rule Pt 6 §II Rule 1.4.
Competence, VA SCt Rule Pt 6 §II Rule 1.1.
Conflicts of interest, VA SCt Rule Pt 6 §II Rule 1.7 to VA SCt Rule Pt 6 §II Rule 1.10.
Lawyer as witness, VA SCt Rule Pt 6 §II Rule 3.7.
Declining representation, VA SCt Rule Pt 6 §II Rule 1.16.
Diligence, VA SCt Rule Pt 6 §II Rule 1.3.
Discharge by client.
Termination of representation generally, VA SCt Rule Pt 6 §II Rule 1.16.
Organization as client, VA SCt Rule Pt 6 §II Rule 1.13.
Safekeeping property, VA SCt Rule Pt 6 §II Rule 1.15.
Scope of representation, VA SCt Rule Pt 6 §II Rule 1.2.
Terminating representation, VA SCt Rule Pt 6 §II Rule 1.16.
Truthfulness in statements to others, VA SCt Rule Pt 6 §II Rule 4.1.
Withdrawal from representation, VA SCt Rule Pt 6 §II Rule 1.16.
Return of client papers and files upon termination of representation, VA SCt Rule Pt 6 §II Rule 1.16.
Sale of law practice, VA SCt Rule Pt 6 §II Rule 1.17.
Specialization.
Communication of fields of practice and certification, VA SCt Rule Pt 6 §II Rule 7.4.

ATTORNEYS AT LAW —Cont'd
Rules of professional conduct —Cont'd
Successive government and private employment, VA SCt Rule Pt 6 §II Rule 1.11.
Terminating representation, VA SCt Rule Pt 6 §II Rule 1.16.
Third party neutral.
Acting as, VA SCt Rule Pt 6 §II Rule 2.10.
Mediator, VA SCt Rule Pt 6 §II Rule 2.11.
Third persons.
Communication with persons represented by counsel, VA SCt Rule Pt 6 §II Rule 4.2.
Evaluation for use by, VA SCt Rule Pt 6 §II Rule 2.3.
Respect for rights of, VA SCt Rule Pt 6 §II Rule 4.4.
Truthfulness in statements to persons other than client, VA SCt Rule Pt 6 §II Rule 4.1.
Unrepresented persons.
Dealing with, VA SCt Rule Pt 6 §II Rule 4.3.
Trial publicity, VA SCt Rule Pt 6 §II Rule 3.6.
Trust accounts.
Maintenance generally, VA SCt Rule Pt 6 §IV Par 20.
Safekeeping property, VA SCt Rule Pt 6 §II Rule 1.15.
Unauthorized practice of law.
Law firms and associations, VA SCt Rule Pt 6 §II Rule 5.5.
Unrepresented persons.
Dealings with, VA SCt Rule Pt 6 §II Rule 4.3.
Prosecutors.
Duty not to knowingly take advantage of unrepresented defendant, VA SCt Rule Pt 6 §II Rule 3.8.
Voluntary pro bono publico service, VA SCt Rule Pt 6 §II Rule 6.1.
Withdrawal from representation of client, VA SCt Rule Pt 6 §II Rule 1.16.
Witnesses.
Lawyer as witness, VA SCt Rule Pt 6 §II Rule 3.7.
Sale of practice, VA SCt Rule Pt 6 §II Rule 1.17.
Scope of representation, VA SCt Rule Pt 6 §II Rule 1.2.
Service of process.
Foreign attorneys, VA SCt Rules 1:5, 1A:4.
On firm, VA SCt Rule 1:5.
Signatures.
Firm name, VA SCt Rule 1:5.
Electronic filing and service, VA SCt Rule 1:17.
Soliciting employment.
Direct contact to recommend professional employment, VA SCt Rule Pt 6 §II Rule 7.3.
Specialization.
Rules of professional conduct.
Communication of fields of practice and certification, VA SCt Rule Pt 6 §II Rule 7.4.
Standing committee on lawyer discipline (COLD).
Disciplining, suspending and disbarring attorneys, VA SCt Rule Pt 6 §IV Par 13.
State bar association rules, VA SCt Rule Pt 6 §IV.
See STATE BAR.
Subpoena duces tecum.
Issuance by attorney, VA SCt Rule 4:9.

ATTORNEYS AT LAW —Cont'd
Supreme court rules non-compliance, sanctions, VA SCt Rule 5:1A.
Suspension.
Administrative suspension.
Procedure, VA SCt Rule Pt 6 §IV Par 19.
Trial publicity.
Rules of professional conduct, VA SCt Rule Pt 6 §II Rule 3.6.
Trust accounts.
IOLTA accounts generally, VA SCt Rule Pt 6 §IV Par 20.
Maintenance of trust accounts generally, VA SCt Rule Pt 6 §IV Par 20.
Rules of professional conduct.
Safekeeping property, VA SCt Rule Pt 6 §II Rule 1.15.
Virginia State Bar approved financial institution agreement, VA SCt Rule Pt 6 §IV Appx A.
Trustworthiness of attorney.
Crimes or acts calling into question, VA SCt Rule Pt 6 §II Rule 8.4.
Truthfulness in statements to others, VA SCt Rule Pt 6 §II Rule 4.1.
Unauthorized practice of law.
Administrative agency practice, VA SCt Rule Pt 6 §I UPR 9.
Holding out as an expert, VA SCt Rule Pt 6 §I UPR 9.
Immigration law, VA SCt Rule Pt 6 §I UPR 9-103.
Collection agencies, VA SCt Rule Pt 6 §I UPR 3.
Attorney-client relationship, VA SCt Rule Pt 6 §I UPR 3.
Preparation of documents, VA SCt Rule Pt 6 §I UPR 3.
Referral and control claims, VA SCt Rule Pt 6 §I UPR 3.
Estate planning and settlement, VA SCt Rule Pt 6 §I UPR 4.
Holding out with regard to estate planning, VA SCt Rule Pt 6 §I UPR 4.
Preparation of documents, VA SCt Rule Pt 6 §I UPR 4.
Immigration practice, VA SCt Rule Pt 6 §I UPC 9-7.
Lay adjusters, VA SCt Rule Pt 6 §I UPR 2.
Definition, VA SCt Rule Pt 6 §I UPR 2.
Investigation, VA SCt Rule Pt 6 §I UPR 2.
Negotiation of settlement, VA SCt Rule Pt 6 §I UPR 2.
Preparation of documents, VA SCt Rule Pt 6 §I UPR 2.
Third-party claims, VA SCt Rule Pt 6 §I UPR 2.
Opinions.
Promulgation of unauthorized practice of law opinions, VA SCt Rule Pt 6 §IV Par 10.
Real estate practice, VA SCt Rule Pt 6 §I UPR 6.
Giving legal advice, VA SCt Rule Pt 6 §I UPR 6.
Holding out with regard to real estate services, VA SCt Rule Pt 6 §I UPR 6.
Lawyer-client relationship, VA SCt Rule Pt 6 §I UPR 6.
Preparation of legal instruments, VA SCt Rule Pt 6 §I UPR 6.
Referral of business, VA SCt Rule Pt 6 §I UPR 6.

ATTORNEYS AT LAW —Cont'd
Unauthorized practice of law —Cont'd
Rules of professional conduct.
Law firms and associations, VA SCt Rule Pt 6 §II Rule 5.5.
Tax practice, VA SCt Rule Pt 6 §I UPR 5.
Holding out as a tax expert, VA SCt Rule Pt 6 §I UPR 5.
Title insurance, VA SCt Rule Pt 6 §I UPR 7.
Trade associations, VA SCt Rule Pt 6 §I UPR 8.
Attorney-client relationship, VA SCt Rule Pt 6 §I UPR 8.
Giving legal advice, VA SCt Rule Pt 6 §I UPR 8.
Holding out with regard to legal services, VA SCt Rule Pt 6 §I UPR 8.
Referral of business, VA SCt Rule Pt 6 §I UPR 8.
Tribunals.
Representation before tribunals, VA SCt Rule Pt 6 §I UPR 1.
Virginia state bar.
Foreign attorneys.
When allowed by comity to participate in trial of case, VA SCt Rule 1A:4.
State bar association rules, VA SCt Rule Pt 6 §IV.
See STATE BAR.
Withdrawal from representation, VA SCt Rule Pt 6 §II Rule 1.16.
Witnesses.
Procuring unavailability, VA SCt Rule Pt 6 §II Rule 3.4.

ATTORNEYS' FEES.
Circuit courts.
Recovery of appellate attorney's fees, VA SCt Rule 1:1A.
Civil procedure.
Recovery of appellate attorney's fees, VA SCt Rule 1:1A.
Claims for attorneys' fees.
Demand, waiver, procedure, VA SCt Rule 3:25.
Foreign attorneys admitted to practice without examination.
Filing fee, VA SCt Rule 1A:1.
Professional responsibility, VA SCt Rule Pt 6 §II Rule 1.5.

AUDIO-VISUAL DEPOSITIONS, VA SCt Rule 4:7A.
Attorney discipline.
District committees proceedings, VA SCt Rule Pt 6 §IV Par 13-16.

AUTHENTICATION OF EVIDENCE.
Required, VA SCt Rule 2:901.
Self-authentication, VA SCt Rule 2:902.
Subscribing witness testimony not necessary, VA SCt Rule 2:903.

B

BAIL AND RECOGNIZANCE.
Defined, VA SCt Rule 3A:2.

BALLISTIC TESTS.
Discovery, VA SCt Rule 3A:11.

BENCH TRIAL.
Scheduling civil cases for trial, VA SCt Rule 1:20.

BENCH TRIAL —Cont'd
Witnesses.
Exclusion of witnesses in criminal trials, VA SCt Rule 2:615.

BEST EVIDENCE RULE, VA SCt Rules 2:1001 to 2:1006.
Definitions, VA SCt Rule 2:1001.
Original required, VA SCt Rule 2:1002.
Civil cases, general district court, VA SCt Rule 7B:5.

BEST EVIDENCE RULE EXCEPTIONS, VA SCt Rules 2:1003 to 2:1006.
Admissions.
Testimony or written admission of a party, VA SCt Rule 2:1007.
Checks.
Substitute checks, VA SCt Rule 2:1003.
Collateral matters, VA SCt Rule 2:1004.
Copies, admissibility, VA SCt Rule 2:1005.
Destroyed originals, VA SCt Rule 2:1004.
Issues of law or fact, VA SCt Rule 2:1008.
Judges.
Issues of law or fact, VA SCt Rule 2:1008.
Jury.
Issues of law or fact, VA SCt Rule 2:1008.
Lost originals, VA SCt Rule 2:1004.
Original in possession of opponent, VA SCt Rule 2:1004.
Original unobtainable, VA SCt Rule 2:1004.
Summaries, VA SCt Rule 2:1006.
Testimony of a party, VA SCt Rule 2:1007.
Voluminous writings.
Summaries, VA SCt Rule 2:1006.

BIAS.
Witnesses, VA SCt Rule 2:610.

BIFURCATED PROCEEDINGS.
Criminal jury trials of non-capital felonies, VA SCt Rule 3A:17.1.

BILL OF PARTICULARS.
Attorney discipline.
Reinstatement, VA SCt Rule Pt 6 §IV Par 13-25.
Circuit courts.
Civil actions, VA SCt Rule 3:7.

BIOLOGICAL EVIDENCE.
Actual innocence.
Petition for writ of actual innocence, VA SCt Rule 5:7B, VA SCt Rule Pt 5A Appx Form 12, VA SCt Rule Pt 5 Appx Form 12.

BLOOD TESTS.
Discovery, VA SCt Rule 3A:11.

BONDS, SURETY.
Appeal bond.
Security for appeal, VA SCt Rule 5:24.
Forms.
See FORMS.

BOUNDARIES.
Hearsay exceptions, reputation concerning boundaries, VA SCt Rule 2:803.

BRIEFS AND OTHER PAPERS, VA SCt Rule 5:26.
Amicus curiae briefs, VA SCt Rule 5:30.
Oral argument, VA SCt Rule 5:33.
Appellee's brief, VA SCt Rule 5:28.
Court of appeals.
Brief of appellee or guardian ad litem, VA SCt Rule 5A:21.

BRIEFS AND OTHER PAPERS —Cont'd
Court of appeals —Cont'd
Rehearing.
See COURT OF APPEALS.
Cross-error.
Reply briefs, VA SCt Rule 5:19.
District courts.
Filing format and procedures, VA SCt Rule 7A:7.
Forms, VA SCt Rule 5:6.
Motions, filing and serving, VA SCt Rule 4:15.
Oral argument, VA SCt Rule 5:33.
Reply brief, VA SCt Rules 5:19, 5:29.
United States supreme court.
Certification of questions of law, VA SCt Rule 5:40.

BURDEN OF PROOF.
Attorney discipline.
Board proceedings upon guilty plea or adjudication of a crime, VA SCt Rule Pt 6 §IV Par 13-22.

BUSINESS CARDS.
Attorneys at law, VA SCt Rule Pt 6 §II Rule 7.5.

BUSINESS RECORDS.
Hearsay exceptions, VA SCt Rule 2:803.

C

CANONS OF JUDICIAL CONDUCT.
See JUDGES.

CAPIAS.
Circuit courts, VA SCt Rule 3A:1.
District courts.
Criminal procedure, VA SCt Rule 7C:3.
Form, VA SCt Rule Pt 3A Appx Form 5.
Juvenile and domestic relations district courts, VA SCt Rule 3A:7.

CAPTIONS.
Civil procedure, VA SCt Rule 3:2.

CERTIFICATION OF QUESTIONS OF LAW, VA SCt Rule 5:40.

CHECKS.
Best evidence rule exceptions.
Substitute checks, VA SCt Rule 2:1003.

CHILD ABUSE AND NEGLECT.
Marriage and family therapist-client privilege, VA SCt Rule 2:506.
Psychologist-client privilege, VA SCt Rule 2:506.
Social worker-client privilege, VA SCt Rule 2:506.

CHILD SUPPORT.
Juvenile and domestic relations district courts.
Motion to reduce support arrearages to judgment.
Service of process, VA SCt Rule 8:4.
Petition for support.
Contents, VA SCt Rule 8:3.

CHOICE OF LAW.
Attorneys at law.
Rules of professional conduct.
Disciplinary authority, VA SCt Rule Pt 6 §II Rule 8.5.

CHURCHES.
Cleric-penitent privilege, VA SCt Rule 2:503.

CIRCUIT COURTS.
Civil actions.
Scheduling cases for trial, VA SCt Rule 1:20.
Discovery.
Electronically stored information, VA SCt Rule 4:1.
Production by a person not party, VA SCt Rule 4:9A.
Production of, VA SCt Rule 4:9.
Production of documents and things.
Production by a person not party, VA SCt Rule 4:9A.
Trial preparation materials, claims of privilege or protection, VA SCt Rule 4:1.
Dockets.
Scheduling civil cases for trial, VA SCt Rule 1:20.
Production of documents and things.
Production by a person not party, VA SCt Rule 4:9A.

CIVIL PROCEDURE, VA SCt Rules 3:1 to 3:25.
Ad damnum clause required, VA SCt Rule 3:2.
Answers, VA SCt Rule 3:8.
Applicability of rules, VA SCt Rule 3:1.
Bill of particulars, VA SCt Rule 3:7.
Captions, VA SCt Rule 3:2.
Commencement, VA SCt Rule 3:2.
Commissioners in chancery.
Proceedings before, VA SCt Rule 3:23.
Complaints.
Ad damnum clause required, VA SCt Rule 3:2.
Contributory negligence, VA SCt Rule 3:18.
Copies of complaint, VA SCt Rule 3:4.
Counterclaims, VA SCt Rule 3:9.
Cross-claims, VA SCt Rule 3:10.
Default judgments, VA SCt Rule 3:19.
Demurrers, VA SCt Rule 3:8.
District courts.
Appearances.
Defendant's appearance.
Failure of defendant to appear, VA SCt Rule 7B:9.
Plaintiff's appearance, VA SCt Rule 7B:7.
Failure of plaintiff to appear, VA SCt Rule 7B:8.
Consolidation of actions, VA SCt Rule 7B:10.
Pleadings.
Allowable pleadings, VA SCt Rule 7B:3.
Contents of pleadings, VA SCt Rule 7B:3.
Requirements that judge may impose, VA SCt Rule 7B:2.
Verification, VA SCt Rule 7B:6.
Scope of rules, VA SCt Rule 7B:1.
Third-party practice, VA SCt Rule 7B:10.
Trial of action, VA SCt Rule 7B:4.
Venue.
Motions to transfer, VA SCt Rule 7B:11.
Verification, VA SCt Rule 7B:6.
Written agreements.
Production of written agreement, VA SCt Rule 7B:5.
Electronic filing and service, VA SCt Rule 3:3(b).
Exhibits, copies, VA SCt Rule 3:4(b).
Exhibits.
Copies, VA SCt Rule 3:4

CIVIL PROCEDURE —Cont'd
Failure to timely respond.
Default judgments, VA SCt Rule 3:19.
Filing of pleadings, VA SCt Rule 3:3.
Interpleader, statutory, VA SCt Rule 3:15.
Intervention, VA SCt Rule 3:14.
Joinder of parties, VA SCt Rule 3:12.
Jury trial.
Right to trial by jury, VA SCt Rule 3:21.
Trial by jury or by court, VA SCt Rule 3:22.
Matters not covered by rules.
Continuance of established practices and procedures, VA SCt Rule 3:1.
Motions.
Responsive pleadings, VA SCt Rule 3:8.
Negligence, allegations, VA SCt Rule 3:18.
New parties, VA SCt Rule 3:16.
Petitions.
Ad damnum clause required, VA SCt Rule 3:2.
Commencement of actions, VA SCt Rule 3:2.
Form and content, VA SCt Rule 3:2.
Pleadings.
Ad damnum clause required, VA SCt Rule 3:2.
Commencement of proceedings, VA SCt Rule 3:2.
District courts.
Allowable pleadings, VA SCt Rule 7B:3.
Contents of pleadings, VA SCt Rule 7B:3.
Requirements that judge may impose, VA SCt Rule 7B:2.
Verification, VA SCt Rule 7B:6.
General provisions, VA SCt Rule 3:18.
Proof of service, VA SCt Rule 3:6.
Reply, VA SCt Rule 3:11.
Responsive pleadings, VA SCt Rule 3:8.
Return of writs, VA SCt Rule 3:3.
Scope of rules, VA SCt Rule 3:1.
Service of process.
Proof of service, VA SCt Rule 3:6.
Summons, VA SCt Rule 3:5.
Statute of limitations.
Pleading, VA SCt Rule 3:18.
Substitution of parties, VA SCt Rule 3:17.
Summary judgment, VA SCt Rule 3:20.
Summons.
Form, VA SCt Rule 3:5.
Third party claims, VA SCt Rule 3:13.
District courts, VA SCt Rule 7B:10.

CLERGY-PENITENT PRIVILEGE, VA SCt Rule 2:503.

CLERKS OF COURT.
Competency to testify.
Criminal or civil proceedings, VA SCt Rule 2:605.
Discretion of court, VA SCt Rule 1:9.
Local rules of court.
Procedure for clerk, VA SCt Rule 1:15.

CLIENTS' PROTECTION FUND.
Attorneys at law.
Establishment, VA SCt Rule Pt 6 §IV Par 16.
Generally, VA SCt Rule Pt 6 §IV Par 16.

CLINICAL PSYCHOLOGISTS.
Physician-patient privilege, VA SCt Rule 2:505.

CODE OF PROFESSIONAL RESPONSIBILITY.
See ATTORNEYS AT LAW.

COMMENCEMENT OF CIVIL ACTIONS, VA SCt Rule 3:2.

COMMISSIONERS IN CHANCERY.
Proceedings before, VA SCt Rule 3:23.

COMMONWEALTH'S ATTORNEYS.
Professional responsibility, VA SCt Rule Pt 6 §II Rule 3.8.

COMMUNICABLE DISEASES.
Public health threats, order of quarantine or isolation.
Appeal of circuit court order, VA SCt Rule 5:41.
Circuit court proceedings, VA SCt Rule 3:24.
Isolation proceedings, VA SCt Rule 7A:16.

COMPETENCY OF WITNESSES.
Certain judicial officials in criminal cases, VA SCt Rule 2:605.
Clerks of court, VA SCt Rule 2:605.
General rule, VA SCt Rule 2:601.
Judges, VA SCt Rule 2:605.
Magistrates.
Criminal or civil proceedings, VA SCt Rule 2:605.

COMPLAINTS.
Civil procedure.
Captions, VA SCt Rule 3:2.
Commencement of actions, VA SCt Rule 3:2.
Copies of complaint, VA SCt Rule 3:4.
Filing of pleadings, VA SCt Rule 3:3.
Form and content, VA SCt Rule 3:2.

COMPROMISE.
Evidence.
Relevancy, VA SCt Rule 2:408.
Supreme court.
Settlement of pending appeal, VA SCt Rule 5:38.

CONFIDENTIAL INFORMATION.
Attorney-client information, VA SCt Rule 1:6, VA SCt Rule Pt 6 §II.
Attorney discipline.
Disciplinary records and proceedings, VA SCt Rule Pt 6 §IV Par 13-30.
Attorneys.
Rules of professional conduct.
Prospective clients, VA SCt Rule Pt 6 §II Rule 1.18.
Criminal procedure.
Confidentiality of juror personal information, VA SCt Rule 3A:14.1.
Research, development or commercial information.
Discovery, protection from disclosure, VA SCt Rule 4:1.

CONFLICTS OF INTEREST.
Attorneys at law.
Client-attorney relationship.
Former clients, VA SCt Rule Pt 6 §II Rule 1.9.
General rule, VA SCt Rule Pt 6 §II Rule 1.7.
Government and private employment in succession, VA SCt Rule Pt 6 §II Rule 1.11.
Imputed disqualification, VA SCt Rule Pt 6 §II Rule 1.10.
Judge or arbitrator service as conflict, VA SCt Rule Pt 6 §II Rule 1.12.
Prospective clients, VA SCt Rule Pt 6 §II Rule 1.18.
Transactions prohibited, VA SCt Rule Pt 6 §II Rule 1.8.

CONFLICTS OF INTEREST —Cont'd
Attorneys at law —Cont'd
Witness, lawyer as, VA SCt Rule Pt 6 §II Rule 3.7.

CONFUSION.
Evidence.
Exclusion of relevant evidence, VA SCt Rule 2:403.

CONSENT.
Attorney discipline.
Consent to revocation, VA SCt Rule Pt 6 §IV Par 13-28.
Trial without jury, VA SCt Rule 3A:13.

CONSOLIDATION OF ACTIONS.
District courts, VA SCt Rule 7B:10.
Criminal procedure.
Trial together of more than one offense, VA SCt Rule 7C:4.

CONSULTANTS.
Attorneys.
Foreign legal consultants, registration, VA SCt Rule 1A:7.

CONTEMPT.
Criminal procedure.
Failure to obey subpoena, VA SCt Rule 3A:12.

CONTINUANCES.
District courts.
Agreement among all parties to continuance, VA SCt Rule 7A:14.
Good cause, VA SCt Rule 7A:14.
Parties not in agreement, VA SCt Rule 7A:14.
Requests at time of hearing, VA SCt Rule 7A:14.
Juvenile and domestic relations district courts.
Criteria for granting, VA SCt Rule 8:14.
Good cause as grounds for granting, VA SCt Rule 8:14.

CONTINUING LEGAL EDUCATION REQUIREMENTS.
Certificate of attendance, VA SCt Rule Pt 6 §IV Par 17.
Continuing legal education board, VA SCt Rule Pt 6 §IV Par 17.
Credits, VA SCt Rule Pt 6 §IV Par 17.
Exemptions, VA SCt Rule Pt 6 §IV Par 17.
Purpose, VA SCt Rule Pt 6 §IV Par 17.
Reactivation from inactive status, VA SCt Rule Pt 6 §IV Par 17.
Standards, VA SCt Rule Pt 6 §IV Par 17.
Statement of requirements, VA SCt Rule Pt 6 §IV Par 17.
Suspension for failure to complete, VA SCt Rule Pt 6 §IV Par 13.2.

CONTRACTS.
District courts.
Production of written agreement, VA SCt Rule 7B:5.

CONTRIBUTORY NEGLIGENCE, VA SCt Rule 3:18.

CONVENING OF COURT.
When in banc, VA SCt Rule 5:3.
When in division, VA SCt Rule 5:3.

CONVICTED FELONS.
Witnesses.
Impeachment of witnesses, conviction of crime, VA SCt Rule 2:609.

CONVICTIONS.
Impeachment of witnesses.
Conviction of crime, VA SCt Rule 2:609.
Witnesses.
Impeachment of witnesses, conviction of crime, VA SCt Rule 2:609.

COPIES OF COMPLAINT.
Civil procedure, VA SCt Rule 3:4.

COPY OF SUBPOENAED DOCUMENTS.
Subpoenaing party to supply copies, upon request, to court and other parties, VA SCt Rule 4:9.

CORPORATIONS.
Attorneys at law.
Client-attorney relationship.
Organization as client, VA SCt Rule Pt 6 §II Rule 1.13.
Corporate counsel, VA SCt Rule 1A:5.
Corporate counsel registrants, VA SCt Rule 1A:5.
Deposition of organization, VA SCt Rule 4:5(b).

COSTS.
Court of appeals, VA SCt Rule 5A:30.
Supreme court, VA SCt Rule 5:35.
United States supreme court.
Certification of questions of law, VA SCt Rule 5:40.

COUNSEL.
See ATTORNEYS AT LAW.

COUNTERCLAIMS.
Civil actions, VA SCt Rule 3:9.

COURT OF APPEALS.
Amicus curiae.
Oral argument, VA SCt Rule 5A:28.
Appendix.
Assumption, VA SCt Rule 5A:25.
Contents, VA SCt Rule 5A:25.
Costs, VA SCt Rule 5A:25.
Covers, VA SCt Rule 5A:24.
Determination of contents, VA SCt Rule 5A:25.
Filing, VA SCt Rule 5A:25.
Penalty, VA SCt Rule 5A:25.
Table of contents, VA SCt Rule 5A:25.
When required, VA SCt Rule 5A:25.
Briefs.
Amicus curiae, VA SCt Rule 5A:23.
Appellee's brief, VA SCt Rule 5A:21.
Brief in opposition, VA SCt Rule 5A:13.
Copies, VA SCt Rule 5A:19.
Covers, VA SCt Rule 5A:24.
Extension of time for filing, VA SCt Rule 5A:19.
Filing time, VA SCt Rule 5A:19.
Appeal as matter of right, VA SCt Rule 5A:19.
Extension, VA SCt Rule 5A:19.
Grant of petition for appeal, VA SCt Rule 5A:19.
Form of briefs, VA SCt Rule 5A:4.
Guardian ad litem's brief, VA SCt Rule 5A:21.
Length, VA SCt Rule 5A:19.
Noncompliance with rules, VA SCt Rule 5A:26.
Opening brief of appellant, VA SCt Rule 5A:20.
Rehearing, VA SCt Rule 5A:35.
Reply briefs, VA SCt Rules 5A:14, 5A:22.
Contemporaneous objection rule.
Preservation of issues for appeal, VA SCt Rule 5A:18.

COURT OF APPEALS —Cont'd
Costs.
Award of costs, VA SCt Rule 5A:30.
Taxable costs, VA SCt Rule 5A:30.
To whom allowed, VA SCt Rule 5A:30.
Covers of documents, VA SCt Rule 5A:24.
Criminal cases and traffic infractions.
Denial of appeal, VA SCt Rule 5A:15A.
Petition for appeal, VA SCt Rule 5A:12.
Anders appeal, VA SCt Rule 5A:12.
Content, VA SCt Rule 5A:12.
Copy to opposing counsel, VA SCt Rule 5A:12.
Electronic filing, VA SCt Rule 5A:15A.
Form, VA SCt Rule 5A:12.
Format, VA SCt Rule 5A:15.
Oral argument, VA SCt Rule 5A:12.
Single petition in separate cases, VA SCt Rule 5A:12.
When required, VA SCt Rule 5A:12.
Petition for rehearing, VA SCt Rule 5A:15A.
Decision.
Citing unpublished dispositions, VA SCt Rule 5A:1.
Notice of decision, VA SCt Rule 5A:29.
Definitions, VA SCt Rule 5A:1.
Denial of appeal, VA SCt Rule 5A:15.
Documents.
Cover, VA SCt Rule 5A:24.
Errors.
Preservation of issues for appeal, VA SCt Rule 5A:18.
Forms.
Additional bond required by appellate court on appeal from circuit court, VA SCt Rule Pt 5A Appx Form 6.
Bond for costs alone, VA SCt Rule Pt 5A Appx Form 1.
Appellate court on appeal from circuit court, VA SCt Rule Pt 5A Appx Form 3.
Industrial commission on appeal of right to court of appeals, VA SCt Rule Pt 5A Appx Form 7.
Supreme court on appeal of right from state corporation commission, VA SCt Rule Pt 5A Appx Form 8.
Bond for costs and suspension, VA SCt Rule Pt 5A Appx Form 2.
Appellate court on appeal from circuit court, VA SCt Rule Pt 5A Appx Form 5.
Supreme court on appeal of right from state corporation commission, VA SCt Rule Pt 5A Appx Form 9.
Bond for suspension alone required by appellate court on appeal from circuit court, VA SCt Rule Pt 5A Appx Form 4.
Execution and acknowledgment of bonds, VA SCt Rule Pt 5A Appx Form 10.
Irrevocable letters of credit, VA SCt Rule Pt 5A Appx Form 11.
Guardian ad litem, brief by.
Contents, VA SCt Rule 5A:21.
Judges.
Authority to act, VA SCt Rule 5A:9.
Mandate, VA SCt Rule 5A:31.
Motions, VA SCt Rule 5A:2.
Notice of appeal, VA SCt Rule 5A:6.
Notice of decision, VA SCt Rule 5A:29.
Opinions.
Copy of opinion to accompany mandate, VA SCt Rule 5A:31.

COURT OF APPEALS —Cont'd
Oral argument, VA SCt Rule 5A:28.
Petition for rehearing, VA SCt Rule 5A:33(d).
Orders, VA SCt Rule 5A:2.
Original jurisdiction, VA SCt Rule 5A:5.
Proceedings pursuant to.
Applicable rules, VA SCt Rule 5A:5.
Perfection of appeal.
Appeal as matter of right, VA SCt Rule 5A:16.
Docketing, VA SCt Rule 5A:16.
Grant of petition, VA SCt Rule 5A:16.
Petition for rehearing, VA SCt Rule 5A:15.
Covers, VA SCt Rule 5A:24.
Format, VA SCt Rule 5A:33(a).
Grounds, VA SCt Rule 5A:33(e).
Oral argument, VA SCt Rule 5A:33(d).
Time for filing, VA SCt Rule 5A:33(b).
Procedure for filing an appeal from the court of appeals.
Notice of appeal.
Certification, VA SCt Rule 5:14.
Record on appeal.
Certification for review, VA SCt Rule 5:15.
Disposition, VA SCt Rule 5:16.
Record on appeal.
Contents, VA SCt Rule 5A:7.
Disagreement with contents, VA SCt Rule 5A:7.
Preparation, VA SCt Rule 5A:10.
Transcript or written statement, VA SCt Rule 5A:8.
Transmission, VA SCt Rule 5A:10.
Rehearing, VA SCt Rules 5A:32 to 5A:35.
Answering brief, VA SCt Rule 5A:35.
En banc, VA SCt Rule 5A:34.
Petition, VA SCt Rule 5A:34.
Procedure, VA SCt Rule 5A:35(b).
Grounds, VA SCt Rule 5A:33(e).
On motion of party, VA SCt Rule 5A:33.
Oral argument.
Petition for rehearing, VA SCt Rule 5A:33(d).
Panel, VA SCt Rule 5A:35(a).
Petition for rehearing, VA SCt Rule 5A:15.
En banc, VA SCt Rule 5A:34.
Format, VA SCt Rule 5A:33(a).
Grounds, VA SCt Rule 5A:33(e).
Oral argument, VA SCt Rule 5A:33(d).
Time for filing, VA SCt Rule 5A:33(b).
Procedure, VA SCt Rule 5A:35.
Reply brief, VA SCt Rule 5A:35.
Response to petition, VA SCt Rule 5A:33(c).
Scope of rules, VA SCt Rule 5A:32.
Rehearings, VA SCt Rules 5A:32 to 5A:35.
Petition for rehearing.
Criminal cases and traffic infractions, VA SCt Rules 5A:15, 5A:15A.
En banc, VA SCt Rules 5A:34, 5A:35.
Extension of time, VA SCt Rule 5A:3.
On motion of party, VA SCt Rule 5A:33.
Procedure, VA SCt Rule 5A:35.
Scope of rules, VA SCt Rule 5A:32.
Responsive pleading.
Proceedings pursuant to court's original jurisdiction, VA SCt Rule 5A:5.
Scope of rules, VA SCt Rule 5A:1.
Security for appeal, VA SCt Rule 5A:17.
Service of papers, VA SCt Rule 5A:1.
Settlement.
Conference, VA SCt Rule 5A:37.
Pending appeal, VA SCt Rule 5A:36.

COURT OF APPEALS —Cont'd
Summary disposition, VA SCt Rule 5A:27.
Time.
Extension of time, VA SCt Rule 5A:3.
Mandate, VA SCt Rule 5A:31.
Unpublished dispositions, citing, VA SCt Rule 5A:1.
Waiver.
Oral argument, VA SCt Rule 5A:28.
Workers' compensation commission.
Procedure for filing appeal, VA SCt Rule 5A:11.

COURT ROOM.
Preservation of records by electronic or photographic means, VA SCt Rule 1:14.
District courts, VA SCt Rule 7A:6.
Juvenile and domestic relations district courts, VA SCt Rule 8:12.

CRIMES.
Attorneys at law.
Honesty or fitness of attorney questionable as result, VA SCt Rule Pt 6 §II Rule 8.4.

CRIME VICTIM AND WITNESS ASSISTANCE.
Exclusion from criminal trials, VA SCt Rule 2:615.

CRIMINAL PROCEDURE.
Accused.
Discovery, VA SCt Rule 3A:11.
More than one accused.
Trial together, VA SCt Rule 3A:10.
More than one offense.
Trial together, VA SCt Rule 3A:10.
Acquittal.
Judgment of acquittal, VA SCt Rule 3A:15.
Appeals.
Circuit court.
Conviction in, VA SCt Rule 3A:19.
Juvenile and domestic relations district courts.
Procedure, VA SCt Rule 3A:19.
Attorney discipline.
Board proceedings upon guilty plea or adjudication of a crime, VA SCt Rule Pt 6 §IV Par 13-22.
Attorneys at law.
Subpoena directed to member of bar.
Proceedings for approval, VA SCt Rule 3A:12.
Subpoena duces tecum.
Compelling production of testimony concerning present or former client of member of bar.
Proceedings for approval, VA SCt Rule 3A:12.
Autopsy examinations.
Discovery, VA SCt Rule 3A:11.
Bail and recognizance.
Defined, VA SCt Rule 3A:2.
Ballistic tests, VA SCt Rule 3A:11.
Bifurcated jury trials of non-capital felonies, VA SCt Rule 3A:17.1.
Blood analyses.
Discovery, VA SCt Rule 3A:11.
Breath analyses.
Discovery, VA SCt Rule 3A:11.
Capias.
Execution, VA SCt Rule 3A:7.
Form, VA SCt Rule 3A:7.
Sample form, VA SCt Rule Pt 3A Appx Form 5.

CRIMINAL PROCEDURE —Cont'd
Capias —Cont'd
Return, VA SCt Rule 3A:7.
Upon indictment or information, VA SCt Rule 3A:7.
Circuit courts.
Scope, VA SCt Rule 3A:1.
Clerk.
Defined, VA SCt Rule 3A:2.
Commonwealth.
Discovery, VA SCt Rule 3A:11.
Commonwealth's attorney.
Defined, VA SCt Rule 3A:2.
Competency of witnesses.
Certain judicial officials, VA SCt Rule 2:605.
Complaint.
Contents, VA SCt Rule 3A:3.
District court, VA SCt Rule 7C:3.
Form, VA SCt Rule Pt 3A Appx Form 1.
Confidentiality of information.
Jury, confidentiality of juror personal information, VA SCt Rule 3A:14.1.
Contempt.
Failure to obey subpoena, VA SCt Rule 3A:12.
Continuance.
Defined, VA SCt Rule 3A:2.
Death penalty, VA SCt Rule 3A:18.
Appeals in cases death sentence imposed.
Special rules, VA SCt Rule 5:22.
Definitions, VA SCt Rule 3A:2.
Discovery.
Application of rule, VA SCt Rule 3A:11.
By the accused, VA SCt Rule 3A:11.
By the Commonwealth, VA SCt Rule 3A:11.
Continuing duty to disclose, VA SCt Rule 3A:11.
District court procedure, VA SCt Rule 7C:5.
Failure to comply, VA SCt Rule 3A:11.
Manner, VA SCt Rule 3A:11.
Motion.
Time, VA SCt Rule 3A:11.
Place, VA SCt Rule 3A:11.
Protective order, VA SCt Rule 3A:11.
Time.
General provisions, VA SCt Rule 3A:11.
Time of motion, VA SCt Rule 3A:11.
District courts, VA SCt Rules 7C:1 to 7C:7.
Applicability of rules, VA SCt Rule 7C:1.
Capias, VA SCt Rule 7C:3.
Complaints, VA SCt Rule 7C:3.
Discovery, VA SCt Rule 7C:5.
Pleas, VA SCt Rule 7C:6.
Summons, VA SCt Rule 7C:3.
Trial.
Multiple defendants or multiple offenses, VA SCt Rule 7C:4.
Venue, VA SCt Rule 7C:2.
Warrants, VA SCt Rule 7C:3.
Electronic filing and service, VA SCt Rule 3A:23.
Evidence.
Incompetency of certain judicial officials to testify, VA SCt Rule 2:605.
Motion to strike.
General provisions, VA SCt Rule 3A:15.
Granting.
Summary judgment or partial summary judgment entered in conformity with ruling on motion to strike, VA SCt Rule 1:11.

CRIMINAL PROCEDURE —Cont'd
Evidence —Cont'd
Motion to strike —Cont'd
Procedure, VA SCt Rule 1:11.
Prior inconsistent statements reduced to writing, VA SCt Rule 2:613.
Exclusion of witnesses, VA SCt Rule 2:615.
Filing of papers.
Electronic filing and service, VA SCt Rule 3A:23.
General district courts.
Service and filing, VA SCt Rule 7C:7.
General provisions, VA SCt Rule 3A:21.
Fingerprints.
Discovery, VA SCt Rule 3A:11.
Forms.
Accused who has pleaded guilty.
Suggested questions, VA SCt Rule Pt 3A Appx Form 6.
Accused who has pleaded not guilty.
Suggested questions, VA SCt Rule Pt 3A Appx Form 7.
Arrest warrant.
Statement of witness, VA SCt Rule Pt 3A Appx Form 2.
Capias, VA SCt Rule Pt 3A Appx Form 5.
Criminal complaint, VA SCt Rule Pt 3A Appx Form 1.
Illustrative nature of forms, VA SCt Rule 3A:22.
Indictment, VA SCt Rule Pt 3A Appx Form 4.
Sentencing orders, VA SCt Rule Pt 3A Appx Form 10.
Subpoena, VA SCt Rule Pt 3A Appx Form 8.
Subpoena duces tecum, VA SCt Rule Pt 3A Appx Form 9.
Suggested questions by court to accused pleading guilty.
Misdemeanor proceedings, VA SCt Rule Pt 3A Appx Form 11.
Summons, VA SCt Rule Pt 3A Appx Form 3.
Warrants.
Arrest warrant.
Statement of witness, VA SCt Rule Pt 3A Appx Form 2.
General district courts.
Service and filing, VA SCt Rule 7C:7.
Grand jury.
Dismissal.
Motion to dismiss, VA SCt Rule 3A:5.
Secrecy of proceeding, VA SCt Rule 3A:5.
Who may be present, VA SCt Rule 3A:5.
Indictment.
Capias, VA SCt Rule 3A:7.
Form, VA SCt Rule Pt 3A Appx Form 5.
Contents, VA SCt Rule 3A:6.
Defined, VA SCt Rule 3A:2.
Form, VA SCt Rule 3A:6.
Sample form, VA SCt Rule Pt 3A Appx Form 4.
Joinder of offenses, VA SCt Rule 3A:6.
Summons. See within this heading, "Summons."
Information.
Capias, VA SCt Rule 3A:7.
Form, VA SCt Rule Pt 3A Appx Form 5.
Contents, VA SCt Rule 3A:6.
Form, VA SCt Rule 3A:6.
Joinder of offenses, VA SCt Rule 3A:6.
Summons. See within this heading, "Summons."
Inspection.
Application of rule, VA SCt Rule 3A:11.

CRIMINAL PROCEDURE —Cont'd
Inspection —Cont'd
Continuing duty to inspect, VA SCt Rule 3A:11.
Failure to comply, VA SCt Rule 3A:11.
Motion.
Written motion, VA SCt Rule 3A:11.
Protective order, VA SCt Rule 3A:11.
Time, place and manner of inspection, VA SCt Rule 3A:11.
Judgments and decrees.
Finality of judgments, orders and decrees, VA SCt Rule 1:1.
Jury.
Challenges.
For cause, VA SCt Rule 3A:14.
Confidentiality of juror personal information, VA SCt Rule 3A:14.1.
Examination.
Trial jurors, VA SCt Rule 3A:14.
Grand jury.
Dismissal.
Motion to dismiss, VA SCt Rule 3A:5.
Secrecy of proceeding, VA SCt Rule 3A:5.
Who may be present, VA SCt Rule 3A:5.
Instructions.
Bifurcated jury trials of non-capital felonies, VA SCt Rule 3A:17.1.
Giving instructions, VA SCt Rule 3A:16.
Objections, VA SCt Rule 3A:16.
Proposed instructions, VA SCt Rule 3A:16.
Verdicts.
Alternate forms of verdicts, VA SCt Rule 3A:16.
Separate verdicts, VA SCt Rule 3A:16.
Right to jury, VA SCt Rule 3A:13.
Trial by jury, VA SCt Rule 3A:13.
Waiver of jury.
In circuit court, VA SCt Rule 3A:13.
Juvenile and domestic relations district courts.
Appeals.
Procedure, VA SCt Rule 3A:19.
Arraignment.
Juvenile delinquency cases, VA SCt Rule 8:16.
Trial rights of parties.
Notification and waiver, VA SCt Rule 8:17.
Discovery.
Adult criminal cases, VA SCt Rule 8:15.
Juvenile delinquency cases, VA SCt Rule 8:15.
Exception, VA SCt Rule 3A:1.
Juvenile delinquency cases.
Arraignment, VA SCt Rule 8:16.
Pleas, VA SCt Rule 8:18.
Trial rights of parties.
Notification and waiver, VA SCt Rule 8:17.
Pleas.
Juvenile delinquency cases, VA SCt Rule 8:18.
Scope of provisions, VA SCt Rule 3A:1.
Magistrates.
Complaint.
Requirements, VA SCt Rule 3A:3.
Defined, VA SCt Rule 3A:2.
Scope, VA SCt Rule 3A:1.
Motions.
Copies of written motions to be furnished, VA SCt Rule 3A:21.
Evidence.
Motion to strike evidence.
Effect of sustaining motion, VA SCt Rule 1:11.

CRIMINAL PROCEDURE —Cont'd
Motions —Cont'd
Evidence —Cont'd
Motion to strike evidence —Cont'd
Summary judgment or partial summary judgment entered in conformity with ruling on motion to strike, VA SCt Rule 1:11.
Motions before trial.
Defenses.
Motion raising, VA SCt Rule 3A:9.
Effect of determination, VA SCt Rule 3A:9.
Form of motion, VA SCt Rule 3A:9.
General provisions, VA SCt Rule 3A:9.
Hearing on motion, VA SCt Rule 3A:9.
Objections.
Defenses.
Time of making, VA SCt Rule 3A:9.
Time.
Filing notice or making motion, VA SCt Rule 3A:9.
Waiver.
Relief from waiver, VA SCt Rule 3A:9.
New trial.
General provisions, VA SCt Rule 3A:15.
Nolo contendere.
General district court, VA SCt Rule 7C:6.
Trial without jury, VA SCt Rule 3A:13.
Pleading.
Bifurcated jury trials of non-capital felonies, VA SCt Rule 3A:17.1.
District court pleas, VA SCt Rule 7C:6.
Entering of pleas.
Before trial, VA SCt Rule 3A:9.
General district court, VA SCt Rule 7C:6.
Guilty.
Determining voluntary pleas of guilty, VA SCt Rule 3A:8.
Trial without jury, VA SCt Rule 3A:13.
Nolo contendere.
Determining voluntariness, VA SCt Rule 3A:8.
Plea agreement procedure, VA SCt Rule 3A:8.
Suggested question by court to accused pleading.
Misdemeanor proceedings, VA SCt Rule Pt 3A Appx Form 11.
Voluntary pleas of guilty or nolo contendere.
Determining voluntariness, VA SCt Rule 3A:8.
General district court, VA SCt Rule 7C:6.
Postconviction proceedings.
Filings by inmates confined to institutions.
Timely filing, what constitutes, VA SCt Rule 3A:25.
Purpose and interpretation, VA SCt Rule 3A:2.
Scientific tests.
Discovery, VA SCt Rule 3A:11.
Scope, VA SCt Rule 3A:1.
Sentencing orders, VA SCt Rule Pt 3A Appx Form 10.
Service of process.
Electronic filing and service, VA SCt Rule 3A:23.
General district courts.
Service and filing, VA SCt Rule 7C:7.
Subpoena, VA SCt Rule 3A:12.
Written motions, VA SCt Rule 3A:21.
Subpoena.
Attendance of witnesses, VA SCt Rule 3A:12.
Attorneys at law, VA SCt Rule 3A:12.
Attorneys at law.
Subpoena directed to member of bar.
Proceedings for approval, VA SCt Rule 3A:12.

CRIMINAL PROCEDURE —Cont'd
Subpoena —Cont'd
Contempt, VA SCt Rule 3A:12.
Documentary evidence.
Production, VA SCt Rule 3A:12.
Form, VA SCt Rule Pt 3A Appx Form 8.
Objects.
Production, VA SCt Rule 3A:12.
Return, VA SCt Rule 3A:12.
Service, VA SCt Rule 3A:12.
Subpoena duces tecum.
Attorneys at law.
Compelling production or testimony concerning present or former client of member of bar.
Proceedings for approval, VA SCt Rule 3A:12.
Copying documents, VA SCt Rule 3A:12.
Form, VA SCt Rule Pt 3A Appx Form 9.
Production of documentary evidence and objects, VA SCt Rule 3A:12.
Attorneys at law, VA SCt Rule 3A:12.
Summons.
District court, VA SCt Rule 7C:3.
Execution, VA SCt Rule 3A:7.
By whom, VA SCt Rule 3A:4.
Manner, VA SCt Rule 3A:4.
Form, VA SCt Rule Pt 3A Appx Form 3.
Return, VA SCt Rules 3A:4, 3A:7.
Upon indictment or information, VA SCt Rule 3A:7.
Time.
Extension, VA SCt Rule 3A:20.
Unaffected by expiration of term of court, VA SCt Rule 3A:20.
Trial.
Bifurcated jury trials of non-capital felonies, VA SCt Rule 3A:17.1.
By court.
Duty of court in nonjury trial, VA SCt Rule 3A:13.
Nolo contendere.
Trial without jury, VA SCt Rule 3A:13.
Plea of guilty.
Trial without jury, VA SCt Rule 3A:13.
District court.
Multiple offenses or multiple defendants, VA SCt Rule 7C:4.
Urine analyses.
Discovery, VA SCt Rule 3A:11.
Venue.
District court, VA SCt Rule 7C:2.
Questions to be raised before verdict of finding of guilt, VA SCt Rule 3A:2.1.
When questions raised, VA SCt Rule 3A:2.1.
Verdicts.
Accused.
Several accused, VA SCt Rule 3A:17.
Conviction of lesser offenses, VA SCt Rule 3A:17.
Instructions.
Alternate forms of verdicts, VA SCt Rule 3A:16.
Separate verdicts, VA SCt Rule 3A:16.
Motion to set aside verdict, VA SCt Rule 3A:15.
Poll of jury, VA SCt Rule 3A:17.
Return, VA SCt Rule 3A:17.
Warrant.
District court, VA SCt Rule 7C:3.

CRIMINAL PROCEDURE —Cont'd
Warrant —Cont'd
Execution.
By whom, VA SCt Rule 3A:4.
Manner, VA SCt Rule 3A:4.
Form, VA SCt Rule 3A:4.
Arrest warrant forms, VA SCt Rule Pt 3A Appx Form 2.
Issuance.
General provisions, VA SCt Rule 3A:4.
Return, VA SCt Rule 3A:4.
Witnesses.
Judicial officers, competency to testify, VA SCt Rule 2:605.
Prior inconsistent statements reduced to writing, VA SCt Rule 2:613.
Subpoena, VA SCt Rule 3A:12.

CROSS-CLAIMS.
Civil actions, VA SCt Rule 3:10.

D

DEAD MAN ACT.
Hearsay exceptions.
Statement by person incapable of testifying, VA SCt Rule 2:804.

DEAF OR HEARING IMPAIRED.
Interpreters.
Privilege, evidence, VA SCt Rule 2:507.

DEATH.
Attorney discipline.
Death of respondent.
Dismissal of complaints, VA SCt Rule Pt 6 §IV Par 13-31.
Hearsay exceptions.
Statement under belief of impending death, VA SCt Rule 2:804.
Witness.
Use of deposition, VA SCt Rule 4:7.

DEATH PENALTY, VA SCt Rule 3A:18.
Actual innocence.
Petition for writ of actual innocence, VA SCt Rule 5:7B, VA SCt Rule Pt 5A Appx Form 12, VA SCt Rule Pt 5 Appx Form 12.
Appeals in cases death sentence imposed.
Special rules, VA SCt Rule 5:22.
Habeas corpus, VA SCt Rule 5:7A.
Petition for habeas corpus, VA SCt Rule 5:7A.

DECISIONS.
Notice of decision and order, VA SCt Rule 5:34.

DEFAULT JUDGMENTS.
Civil actions, VA SCt Rule 3:19.
District courts.
Failure of defendant to appear, VA SCt Rule 7B:9.

DEFINITIONS, VA SCt Rule 5:1.
Appeals, VA SCt Rule 2A:1.
Supreme court rules, VA SCt Rule 5:1.
Attorney discipline, VA SCt Rule Pt 6 §IV Par 13-1.
Counsel, VA SCt Rule 5:1.
Criminal procedure, VA SCt Rule 3A:2.
Confidentiality of juror personal information.
Personal information defined, VA SCt Rule 3A:14.1.

DEFINITIONS —Cont'd
Electronic filing and service, VA SCt Rule 1:17(b).
Juvenile and domestic relations district courts, VA SCt Rule 8:2.
Continuances.
Meaning of "parties,"VA SCt Rule 8:14.
Request for subpoenas.
Meaning of "file,"VA SCt Rule 8:13.

DEMURRERS.
Civil actions, VA SCt Rule 3:8.

DEPOSITIONS AND INTERROGATORIES.
Audio-visual depositions, VA SCt Rule 4:7A.
Criminal discovery.
See CRIMINAL PROCEDURE.
Disposition of discovery material, VA SCt Rule 4:14.
Paper.
Size of paper, VA SCt Rule 1:16.
Pretrial procedure.
Depositions for discovery and use as evidence.
See PRETRIAL PROCEDURES.
Teleconferencing used to take depositions, VA SCt Rules 4:5(b), 4:7A.
Authorized use, VA SCt Rule 4:7A(a).
Editing, VA SCt Rule 4:7A(c).
Filing, VA SCt Rule 4:7A(g).
Procedure, VA SCt Rule 4:7A(b).
Recording and transcription, VA SCt Rule 4:7A(d).
Submission to witness, changes and signing, VA SCt Rule 4:7A(f).
Use, VA SCt Rule 4:7A(e).
Uniform interstate depositions and discovery act.
Electronically stored information.
Production of, subject to act, VA SCt Rule 4:9.
Taking of depositions, subject to act, VA SCt Rule 4:5.
Video conferencing used to take depositions, VA SCt Rules 4:5(b), 4:7A.
Authorized use, VA SCt Rule 4:7A(a).
Editing, VA SCt Rule 4:7A(c).
Filing, VA SCt Rule 4:7A(g).
Procedure, VA SCt Rule 4:7A(b).
Recording and transcription, VA SCt Rule 4:7A(d).
Submission to witness, changes and signing, VA SCt Rule 4:7A(f).
Use, VA SCt Rule 4:7A(e).

DILATORY PLEADINGS, VA SCt Rule 1:4.
District courts.
Counsel of record assuring that pleading not filed for delay, VA SCt Rule 7A:8.

DISBARRING ATTORNEYS, VA SCt Rule Pt 6 §IV Par 13.

DISCOVERY.
Attorney disciplinary proceedings, VA SCt Rule Pt 6 §IV Par 13.
Attorney discipline.
District committees proceedings, VA SCt Rule Pt 6 §IV Par 13-16.
Limited right to discovery, VA SCt Rule Pt 6 §IV Par 13-11.
Criminal procedure.
See CRIMINAL PROCEDURE.

DISCOVERY —Cont'd
Disposition of discovery material, VA SCt Rule 4:14.
District courts.
Criminal procedure, VA SCt Rule 7C:5.
Electronically stored information, VA SCt Rule 4:1.
Production by a person not party, VA SCt Rule 4:9A.
Production of, VA SCt Rule 4:9.
Juvenile and domestic relations district courts.
Adult criminal cases, VA SCt Rule 8:15.
Juvenile delinquency cases, VA SCt Rule 8:15.
Other cases, VA SCt Rule 8:15.
Pretrial procedures.
See PRETRIAL PROCEDURES.
Trial preparation materials, claims of privilege or protection, VA SCt Rule 4:1.
Uniform interstate depositions and discovery act.
Electronically stored information.
Production of, subject to act, VA SCt Rule 4:9.
Work-product doctrine, VA SCt Rule 4:1.

DISCRETION OF COURT.
Circuit courts, VA SCt Rule 1:9.

DISCRIMINATION.
Witnesses.
Bias or prejudice, VA SCt Rule 2:610.

DISMISSAL, DISCONTINUANCE AND NONSUIT.
Appearance by plaintiff.
Failure to appear, VA SCt Rule 7B:8.

DISPOSITION OF CASES.
Default judgments, VA SCt Rule 3:19.

DISTRICT COURTS.
Appeals.
Noting an appeal.
What constitutes noting an appeal, VA SCt Rule 7A:13.
Appearances.
Civil procedure.
Defendant's appearance.
Failure of defendant to appear, VA SCt Rule 7B:9.
Plaintiff's appearance, VA SCt Rule 7B:7.
Failure of plaintiff to appear, VA SCt Rule 7B:8.
Applicability of provisions, VA SCt Rule 7A:1.
Attorneys at law.
Construction of term, VA SCt Rule 7A:3.
Counsel of record.
Construction of term, VA SCt Rule 7A:3.
Briefs.
Filing format and procedures, VA SCt Rule 7A:7.
Capias.
Criminal procedure, VA SCt Rule 7C:3.
Civil procedure.
Appearances.
Defendant's appearance.
Failure of defendant to appear, VA SCt Rule 7B:9.
Plaintiff's appearance, VA SCt Rule 7B:7.
Failure of plaintiff to appear, VA SCt Rule 7B:8.
Consolidation of actions, VA SCt Rule 7B:10.

DISTRICT COURTS —Cont'd
Civil procedure —Cont'd
Pleadings.
Allowable pleadings, VA SCt Rule 7B:3.
Contents of pleadings, VA SCt Rule 7B:3.
Requirements that judge may impose, VA SCt Rule 7B:2.
Verification, VA SCt Rule 7B:6.
Scope of rules, VA SCt Rule 7B:1.
Third-party practice, VA SCt Rule 7B:10.
Trial of action, VA SCt Rule 7B:4.
Venue.
Motions to transfer, VA SCt Rule 7B:11.
Verification, VA SCt Rule 7B:6.
Written agreements.
Production of written agreement, VA SCt Rule 7B:5.
Complaints.
Criminal procedure, VA SCt Rule 7C:3.
Consolidation of actions, VA SCt Rule 7B:10.
Criminal procedure.
Trial together of more than one offense, VA SCt Rule 7C:4.
Continuances.
Agreement among all parties to continuance, VA SCt Rule 7A:14.
Good cause, VA SCt Rule 7A:14.
Parties not in agreement, VA SCt Rule 7A:14.
Requests at time of hearing, VA SCt Rule 7A:14.
Contracts.
Production of written agreement, VA SCt Rule 7B:5.
Counsel.
Construction of term, VA SCt Rule 7A:3.
Counsel of record.
Construction of term, VA SCt Rule 7A:3.
Criminal procedure, VA SCt Rules 7C:1 to 7C:7.
Applicability of rules, VA SCt Rule 7C:1.
Capias, VA SCt Rule 7C:3.
Complaints, VA SCt Rule 7C:3.
Discovery, VA SCt Rule 7C:5.
Guilty plea.
Voluntariness of plea, determination, VA SCt Rule 7C:6.
Nolo contendere plea
Voluntariness of plea, determination, VA SCt Rule 7C:6.
Pleas, VA SCt Rule 7C:6.
Suggested question by court to accused pleading guilty or nolo contendere.
Misdemeanor proceedings, VA SCt Rule Pt 3A Appx Form 11.
Summons, VA SCt Rule 7C:3.
Trial.
Multiple defendants or multiple offenses, VA SCt Rule 7C:4.
Venue, VA SCt Rule 7C:2.
Warrants, VA SCt Rule 7C:3.
Default judgments.
Failure of defendant to appear, VA SCt Rule 7B:9.
Dilatory pleadings.
Counsel of record assuring that pleading not filed for delay, VA SCt Rule 7A:8.
Discovery.
Criminal procedure, VA SCt Rule 7C:5.
Discretion of court, VA SCt Rule 7A:5.
Electronic filing and service, VA SCt Rule 7A:7.

DISTRICT COURTS —Cont'd
Filing format and procedures, VA SCt Rule 7A:7.
Frivolous pleadings.
Counsel of record assuring that pleading not filed for delay, VA SCt Rule 7A:8.
Good faith.
Counsel of record assuring that pleading filed in good faith, VA SCt Rule 7A:8.
Joinder of actions, VA SCt Rule 7B:10.
Joinder of additional parties.
Criminal procedure.
Trial together of more than one accused, VA SCt Rule 7C:4.
Juvenile and domestic relations district courts.
See JUVENILE AND DOMESTIC RELATIONS DISTRICT COURTS.
Local rules.
General information relating to each court to be furnished to executive secretary of supreme court, VA SCt Rule 7A:15.
Motions.
Civil procedure.
Transfer.
Motions to transfer, VA SCt Rule 7B:11.
Filing format and procedures, VA SCt Rule 7A:7.
Orders of court.
Endorsements.
Counsel of record to endorse, VA SCt Rule 7A:11.
Transcripts of proceedings, VA SCt Rule 7A:4.
Photography.
Preservation of records.
Use of photographic means, VA SCt Rule 7A:6.
Pleadings.
Amendments, VA SCt Rule 7A:9.
Civil procedure.
Authorized pleadings, VA SCt Rule 7B:3.
Contents of pleadings, VA SCt Rule 7B:3.
Requirements that judge may impose, VA SCt Rule 7B:2.
Verification, VA SCt Rule 7B:6.
Copies, VA SCt Rule 7A:10.
Criminal pleas in district courts, VA SCt Rule 7C:6.
Dilatory pleadings.
Counsel of record.
Tendering pleading gives assurance that delay not intended, VA SCt Rule 7A:8.
Discretion of court as to pleadings, VA SCt Rule 7A:5.
Effect of sworn pleading, VA SCt Rule 7A:8.
Exhibits.
Incorporation as part of pleading, VA SCt Rule 7A:8.
Filing format and procedures, VA SCt Rule 7A:7.
Good faith.
Assured by counsel of record, VA SCt Rule 7A:8.
Signature, VA SCt Rule 7A:8.
Pleas.
Criminal procedure, VA SCt Rule 7C:6.
Records.
Preservation of records.
Use of electronic or photographic means, VA SCt Rule 7A:6.
Scope of provisions, VA SCt Rule 7A:1.
Size of paper, VA SCt Rule 7A:7.

DISTRICT COURTS —Cont'd
Subpoenas.
Witnesses.
Requests for subpoenas, VA SCt Rule 7A:12.
Subpoenas duces tecum.
Request for subpoenas duces tecum, VA SCt Rule 7A:12.
Copies to be furnished, VA SCt Rule 7A:10.
Summons.
Criminal procedure, VA SCt Rule 7C:3.
Third-party practice, VA SCt Rule 7B:10.
Time.
Computation of time, VA SCt Rule 7A:2.
Traffic infractions.
Applicability of rules, VA SCt Rule 7C:1.
Complaint, warrant, summons and capias, VA SCt Rule 7C:3.
Venue, VA SCt Rule 7C:2.
Trial.
Consolidation of actions, VA SCt Rule 7B:10.
Criminal procedure.
Multiple defendants or multiple offenses, VA SCt Rule 7C:4.
Method of bringing action, VA SCt Rule 7B:4.
Preservation of records by electronic or photographic means, VA SCt Rule 7A:6.
When action heard, VA SCt Rule 7B:4.
Venue.
Civil procedure.
Motion to transfer, VA SCt Rule 7B:11.
Criminal procedure, VA SCt Rule 7C:2.
Verification.
Civil procedure, VA SCt Rule 7B:6.
Warrant.
Criminal procedure, VA SCt Rule 7C:3.
Witnesses.
Subpoenas.
Requests for subpoenas, VA SCt Rule 7A:12.

DNA.
Actual innocence.
Petition for writ of actual innocence, VA SCt Rule 5:7B, VA SCt Rule Pt 5A Appx Form 12, VA SCt Rule Pt 5 Appx Form 12.

DOCKET.
Appeals.
See APPEALS.

DOCKET CALL.
Setting civil cases for trial, VA SCt Rule 1:20.

DOCKETS.
Circuit courts.
Scheduling civil cases for trial, VA SCt Rule 1:20.

DOMESTIC RELATIONS DISTRICT COURTS.
See JUVENILE AND DOMESTIC RELATIONS DISTRICT COURTS.

E

EDUCATION.
Attorneys at law.
Continuing education requirements.
Certificate of attendance, VA SCt Rule Pt 6 §IV Par 17.
Continuing legal education board, VA SCt Rule Pt 6 §IV Par 17.
Credits, VA SCt Rule Pt 6 §IV Par 17.

EDUCATION —Cont'd
Attorneys at law —Cont'd
Continuing education requirements —Cont'd
Exemptions, VA SCt Rule Pt 6 §IV Par 17.
Purpose, VA SCt Rule Pt 6 §IV Par 17.
Reactivation from inactive status, VA SCt Rule Pt 6 §IV Par 17.
Standards, VA SCt Rule Pt 6 §IV Par 17.
Statement of requirements, VA SCt Rule Pt 6 §IV Par 17.
Suspension for failure to complete continuing legal education requirements, VA SCt Rule Pt 6 §IV Par 13.2.
Legal ethics.
Suspension for failure to complete legal ethics course, VA SCt Rule Pt 6 §IV Par 13.1.
Legal education.
Continuing legal education.
Legal ethics.
Suspension for failure to complete legal ethics course, VA SCt Rule Pt 6 §IV Par 13.2.
Mandatory continuing legal education rule, VA SCt Rule Pt 6 §IV Par 17.
Suspension for failure to complete continuing legal education requirement, VA SCt Rule Pt 6 §IV Par 13.2.

ELECTRONIC COMMUNICATIONS.
Discovery.
Electronically stored information, VA SCt Rule 4:1.
Production by a person not party, VA SCt Rule 4:9A.
Production of, VA SCt Rule 4:9.
District courts.
Electronic filing and service, VA SCt Rule 7A:7.
Electronic filing and service, VA SCt Rule 1:17.
Applicability of and compliance with other rules, VA SCt Rule 1:17(e).
Civil procedure, VA SCt Rule 3:3(b).
Exhibits, copies, VA SCt Rule 3:4(b).
Computation of time after service by electronic mail, VA SCt Rule 1:7.
Court of appeals.
Criminal cases and traffic infractions, petition for rehearing, VA SCt Rule 5A:15A.
Criminal procedure, VA SCt Rule 3A:23.
Definitions, VA SCt Rule 1:17(b).
District courts, VA SCt Rule 7A:7.
Juvenile and domestic relations district courts, VA SCt Rules 8:7, 8:8.
Practice and procedure, VA SCt Rule 1:17(d).
Scope of electronic filing rules, VA SCt Rule 1:17(a).
Service of pleadings not otherwise required to be served, VA SCt Rule 1:12.
System operational standards, VA SCt Rule 1:17(c).
Electronic means to preserve record, VA SCt Rule 1:14.
General district courts, VA SCt Rule 7A:6.
Juvenile and domestic relations district court, VA SCt Rule 8:12.
Record on appeal.
Administrative process act.
Electronic or digital records, VA SCt Rule 2A:3(d).
Subpoena duces tecum.
Criminal cases, VA SCt Rule 3A:12.

E-MAIL.
Electronic filing and service, VA SCt Rule 1:17.

EMOTIONAL CONDITION.
Evidence.
Hearsay exceptions.
Then existing mental, emotional, or physical condition, VA SCt Rule 2:803.

ENDORSEMENT OR RECOMMENDATION OF LAWYER SERVICES.
Compensation for recommendations, VA SCt Rule Pt 6 §II Rule 7.3.

EQUITABLE ACTIONS.
Applicability of rules, VA SCt Rule 3:1.
Circuit courts.
Civil actions, VA SCt Rules 3:1 to 3:25.
Defensive pleading, VA SCt Rule 1:4.
Equitable defenses.
Applicable, VA SCt Rule 1:4(g).
Requirements as to legal defenses.
Applicable, VA SCt Rule 1:4(g).
Judgments and decrees.
Draft endorsed by counsel on notice given of presentation, VA SCt Rule 1:13.
Electronic filing and service, VA SCt Rule 1:17.

EVIDENCE, VA SCt Rules 2:101 to 2:1101.
Abuse, certain criminal trials, VA SCt Rule 2:409.
Accused, testimony by.
Preliminary determinations, limitations, VA SCt Rule 2:104.
Admissibility for limited purposes, VA SCt Rule 2:105.
Applicability of rules, VA SCt Rule 2:1101.
Attorney-client privilege, VA SCt Rule 2:502.
Attorney discipline.
District committees proceedings, VA SCt Rule Pt 6 §IV Par 13-16.
Evidentiary rulings, VA SCt Rule Pt 6 §IV Par 13-12.
Notice of impairment evidence, VA SCt Rule Pt 6 §IV Par 13-12.
Reinstatement, VA SCt Rule Pt 6 §IV Par 13-25.
Authentication.
Required, VA SCt Rule 2:901.
Self-authentication, VA SCt Rule 2:902.
Subscribing witness testimony not necessary, VA SCt Rule 2:903.
Best evidence rule, VA SCt Rules 2:1001 to 2:1006, 7B:5.
Definitions, VA SCt Rule 2:1001.
Exceptions.
See BEST EVIDENCE RULE EXCEPTIONS.
Original required, VA SCt Rule 2:1002.
Bifurcated jury trials of non-capital felonies, VA SCt Rule 3A:17.1.
Biological evidence.
Actual innocence.
Petition for writ of actual innocence, VA SCt Rule 5:7B, VA SCt Rule Pt 5A Appx Form 12, VA SCt Rule Pt 5 Appx Form 12.
Burden of proof.
Presumptions, VA SCt Rule 2:301.
Character evidence.
Generally inadmissible, VA SCt Rule 2:404.
Hearsay exceptions.
Reputation as to character trait, VA SCt Rule 2:803.

EVIDENCE —Cont'd
Character evidence —Cont'd
Impeachment of witnesses.
Cross-examination of character witnesses, VA SCt Rule 2:608.
Methods of proving character traits, VA SCt Rule 2:405.
Other crimes, wrongs or acts.
Character evidence, admissibility, VA SCt Rule 2:404.
Citation of rules, VA SCt Rule 2:101.
Cleric-penitent privilege, VA SCt Rule 2:503.
Complex documents.
Use of portions of documents in evidence, VA SCt Rule 2:106.
Compromise.
Relevancy, VA SCt Rule 2:408.
Conduct, specific instances.
Methods of proving character traits, VA SCt Rule 2:405.
Confusion.
Exclusion of relevant evidence, VA SCt Rule 2:403.
Construction and interpretation of rules, VA SCt Rule 2:102.
Credibility.
Preliminary determinations, VA SCt Rule 2:104.
Criminal procedure.
Abuse, certain criminal trials, VA SCt Rule 2:409.
Incompetency of certain judicial officials to testify, VA SCt Rule 2:605.
Prior inconsistent statements reduced to writing, VA SCt Rule 2:613.
Cumulative evidence, needless presentation, VA SCt Rule 2:403.
Depositions for discovery and use as evidence.
See PRETRIAL PROCEDURES.
False evidence.
Rules of professional conduct.
Lawyer not to offer evidence known to be false, VA SCt Rule Pt 6 §II Rule 3.3.
Requirements as to fairness to opposing party and counsel by lawyer, VA SCt Rule Pt 6 §II Rule 3.4.
Federal law.
Presumptions, VA SCt Rule 2:302.
Habit, VA SCt Rule 2:406.
Hearsay exceptions, VA SCt Rules 2:801 to 2:806.
Admission by party-opponent, VA SCt Rule 2:803.
Ancient document, VA SCt Rule 2:803.
Baptismal certificates, VA SCt Rule 2:803.
Boundaries, reputation concerning, VA SCt Rule 2:803.
Business records, VA SCt Rule 2:803.
Credibility.
Attacking and supporting credibility of hearsay declarant, VA SCt Rule 2:806.
Dead man rule.
Statement by person incapable of testifying, VA SCt Rule 2:804.
Death, statement under belief of impending.
Declarant unavailable, VA SCt Rule 2:804.
Declarant availability irrelevant, VA SCt Rule 2:803.
Declarant unavailable, VA SCt Rule 2:804.

EVIDENCE —Cont'd
Hearsay exceptions —Cont'd
Definitions, VA SCt Rule 2:801.
Excited utterance, VA SCt Rule 2:803.
Family records, VA SCt Rule 2:803.
Personal or family history, statement regarding, VA SCt Rule 2:804.
Former testimony.
Declarant unavailable, VA SCt Rule 2:804.
Hearsay rule, generally, VA SCt Rule 2:802.
Hearsay within hearsay, VA SCt Rule 2:805.
Identification, statement by witness, VA SCt Rule 2:803.
Interest in property, records or documents affecting, VA SCt Rule 2:803.
Judgments, VA SCt Rule 2:803.
Learned treatises, VA SCt Rule 2:803.
Market quotations, VA SCt Rule 2:803.
Marriage licenses and certificates, VA SCt Rule 2:803.
Medical treatment, statement for purposes of, VA SCt Rule 2:803.
Personal or family history, statement regarding, VA SCt Rule 2:804.
Present sense impression, VA SCt Rule 2:803.
Price of goods, VA SCt Rule 2:803.
Public records or reports, VA SCt Rule 2:803.
Absence of entries where expected, VA SCt Rule 2:803.
Recorded recollection, VA SCt Rule 2:803.
Religious organizations, records, VA SCt Rule 2:803.
Reputation as to character trait, VA SCt Rule 2:803.
Sexual assault.
Recent complaints, VA SCt Rule 2:803.
Statement against interest, VA SCt Rule 2:804.
Then existing mental, emotional, or physical condition, VA SCt Rule 2:803.
Unavailable witness.
Statement by person incapable of testifying, VA SCt Rule 2:804.
Vital records, VA SCt Rule 2:803.
Hearsay rule, generally, VA SCt Rule 2:802.
Insurance.
Existence of, admissibility, VA SCt Rule 2:411.
Interpreters for deaf or non-English speaking persons.
Privilege, VA SCt Rule 2:507.
Irrelevant evidence inadmissible, VA SCt Rule 2:402.
Judicial notice, VA SCt Rules 2:201 to 2:203.
Law, VA SCt Rule 2:202.
Official publications, VA SCt Rule 2:203.
Opportunity to be heard, VA SCt Rule 2:201.
Subjects, VA SCt Rule 2:201.
Time for taking, VA SCt Rule 2:201.
Jury trials.
Confessions, admissibility, out of the hearing of the jury, VA SCt Rule 2:104.
Inadmissible hearing, prevent jury from hearing, VA SCt Rule 2:103.
Preliminary matters.
Out of the hearing of the jury, VA SCt Rule 2:104.
Law.
Judicial notice, VA SCt Rule 2:202.
Presumptions.
Federal law, applicability, VA SCt Rule 2:302.

EVIDENCE —Cont'd
Lengthy documents.
Use of portions of documents in evidence, VA SCt Rule 2:106.
Limiting instructions, VA SCt Rule 2:105.
Marriage and family therapist-client privilege, VA SCt Rule 2:506.
Misleading.
Exclusion of relevant evidence, VA SCt Rule 2:403.
Motion to strike.
Criminal procedure.
General provisions, VA SCt Rule 3A:15.
Granting motion.
Summary judgment entered in conformity with granting of motion to strike, VA SCt Rule 1:11.
Procedure, VA SCt Rule 1:11.
Depositions as basis for motion, VA SCt Rule 4:7.
Overruling motion.
Renewal after discharge of hung jury, VA SCt Rule 1:11.
Objections.
Required, VA SCt Rule 2:103.
Offers to compromise.
Relevancy, VA SCt Rule 2:408.
Official publications.
Judicial notice, VA SCt Rule 2:203.
Other crimes, wrongs or acts.
Character evidence, admissibility, VA SCt Rule 2:404.
Physician-patient privilege, VA SCt Rule 2:505.
Pleas.
Withdrawn pleas and offers to plead, VA SCt Rule 2:410.
Polygraph examinations.
Admissibility, VA SCt Rule 2:402.
Prejudice.
Exclusion of relevant evidence, VA SCt Rule 2:403.
Preliminary determinations, VA SCt Rule 2:104.
Presumptions.
Burden of proof, VA SCt Rule 2:301.
Federal law, applicability, VA SCt Rule 2:302.
Privilege, VA SCt Rules 2:501 to 2:507.
Attorney-client privilege, VA SCt Rule 2:502.
Cleric-penitent privilege, VA SCt Rule 2:503.
Common law interpretation, VA SCt Rule 2:501.
General rule, VA SCt Rule 2:501.
Interpreters for deaf or non-English speaking persons, VA SCt Rule 2:507.
Marriage and family therapist-client privilege, VA SCt Rule 2:506.
Physician-patient privilege, VA SCt Rule 2:505.
Preliminary determinations, VA SCt Rule 2:104.
Professional counselor-client privilege, VA SCt Rule 2:506.
Psychologist-client privilege, VA SCt Rule 2:506.
Social worker-client privilege, VA SCt Rule 2:506.
Spousal privilege, VA SCt Rule 2:504.
Professional counselor-client privilege, VA SCt Rule 2:506.
Proffers, VA SCt Rule 2:103.
Psychologist-client privilege, VA SCt Rule 2:506.

EVIDENCE —Cont'd
Publications.
Official publications.
Judicial notice, VA SCt Rule 2:203.
Recorded statements.
Portions of recording, admissibility of remainder, VA SCt Rule 2:106.
Records.
Hearsay exceptions, VA SCt Rule 2:803.
Self-authentication, VA SCt Rule 2:902.
Relevancy, VA SCt Rules 2:401 to 2:412.
Abuse, certain criminal trials, VA SCt Rule 2:409.
Admissibility, general rule, VA SCt Rule 2:402.
Character evidence.
Generally inadmissible, VA SCt Rule 2:404.
Methods of proving character traits, VA SCt Rule 2:405.
Compromise, VA SCt Rule 2:408.
Conditioned on proof of connecting facts, VA SCt Rule 2:104.
Conduct, specific instances.
Methods of proving character traits, VA SCt Rule 2:405.
Confusion.
Exclusion of relevant evidence, VA SCt Rule 2:403.
Cumulative evidence, needless presentation, VA SCt Rule 2:403.
Defined, VA SCt Rule 2:401.
Habit, VA SCt Rule 2:406.
Insurance, existence of, VA SCt Rule 2:411.
Irrelevant evidence inadmissible, VA SCt Rule 2:402.
Misleading.
Exclusion of relevant evidence, VA SCt Rule 2:403.
Offers to compromise, VA SCt Rule 2:408.
Other crimes, wrongs or acts.
Character evidence, admissibility, VA SCt Rule 2:404.
Past behavior, VA SCt Rule 2:412.
Polygraph examinations, admissibility, VA SCt Rule 2:402.
Prejudice.
Exclusion of relevant evidence, VA SCt Rule 2:403.
Prior sexual conduct, VA SCt Rule 2:412.
Reputation.
Methods of proving character traits, VA SCt Rule 2:405.
Routine practice, VA SCt Rule 2:406.
Subsequent remedial measures, VA SCt Rule 2:407.
Withdrawn pleas and offers to plead, VA SCt Rule 2:410.
Reputation.
Hearsay exceptions.
Reputation as to character trait, VA SCt Rule 2:803.
Impeachment of witnesses, reputation for truthtelling, VA SCt Rule 2:608.
Methods of proving character traits, VA SCt Rule 2:405.
Routine practice, VA SCt Rule 2:406.
Scope of rules, VA SCt Rule 2:102.
Applicability of rules, VA SCt Rule 2:1101.
Self-authentication, VA SCt Rule 2:902.

EVIDENCE —Cont'd
Sexual assault.
Hearsay exceptions.
Recent complaints, VA SCt Rule 2:803.
Social worker-client privilege, VA SCt Rule 2:506.
Subsequent remedial measures.
Relevancy, VA SCt Rule 2:407.
Sustaining motion.
Summary judgment or partial summary judgment entered in conformity with ruling on motion, VA SCt Rule 1:11.
Use of portions of documents in evidence, VA SCt Rule 2:106.
Virginia rules of evidence, citation, VA SCt Rule 2:101.
Voluminous documents.
Use of portion of documents in evidence, VA SCt Rule 2:106.
Weight of evidence.
Preliminary determinations, VA SCt Rule 2:104.
Witnesses.
Expert witnesses, VA SCt Rules 2:701 to 2:706.
Generally, VA SCt Rules 2:601 to 2:615.
Written statements.
Portions of writing, admissibility of remainder, VA SCt Rule 2:106.

EXAMINATIONS.
Physical and mental examination of persons, VA SCt Rule 4:10.

EXCITED UTTERANCE.
Hearsay exceptions, VA SCt Rule 2:803.

EXCLUSION OF WITNESSES.
Civil trials, VA SCt Rule 2:615.
Criminal trials, VA SCt Rule 2:615.

EXHIBITS.
Copies, VA SCt Rule 3:4.
District courts.
Incorporation as part of pleading, VA SCt Rule 7A:8.
Pleading, VA SCt Rule 1:4(i).
Pretrial procedures.
Depositions for discovery and use as evidence, VA SCt Rule 4:5(f).

EXPERT WITNESSES, VA SCt Rules 2:701 to 2:706.
Basis of expert testimony, VA SCt Rule 2:703.
Exclusion from civil trials, VA SCt Rule 2:615.
Facts or data used in testimony, VA SCt Rule 2:705.
Learned treatises, VA SCt Rule 2:706.
Hearsay exceptions, VA SCt Rule 2:803.
Opinion testimony, VA SCt Rule 2:702.
Lay witnesses, VA SCt Rule 2:701.
Ultimate issue, VA SCt Rule 2:704.
Ultimate fact in issue rule, VA SCt Rule 2:704.
Use of experts generally, VA SCt Rule 2:702.

F

FAILURE TO TIMELY RESPOND.
Default judgments, VA SCt Rule 3:19.

FEES.
Attorneys at law.
Foreign attorney admitted to practice without examination, VA SCt Rule 1A:1.
Filing fee, VA SCt Rule 1A:1.

FEES —Cont'd
Attorneys at law —Cont'd
Foreign attorney admitted to practice without examination —Cont'd
Patent and trademark attorneys, VA SCt Rule 1A:2.
Rules of professional conduct, VA SCt Rule Pt 6 §II Rule 1.5.
See ATTORNEYS AT LAW.
Court of appeals.
Filing notice of appeal, VA SCt Rule 5A:6.
Foreign attorney admitted to practice without examination, VA SCt Rule 1A:1.
Patent and trademark attorneys, VA SCt Rule 1A:2.
Supreme court.
Petition for appeal, VA SCt Rule 5:17.
Grant or refusal of injunction, VA SCt Rule 5:17A.

FILING DATE.
Death sentence imposed.
Review of conviction and sentence, VA SCt Rule 5:22.

FILING OF PLEADINGS.
Appeals.
United States supreme court.
Deferred mandate by Virginia supreme court, VA SCt Rule 5:39.
Civil procedure, VA SCt Rule 3:3.
Bill of particulars, VA SCt Rule 3:7.
Copies of complaint, VA SCt Rule 3:4.
Criminal procedure.
General district courts, VA SCt Rule 7C:7.

FINES.
Uniform fine schedule.
Non-traffic prepayable offenses, VA SCt Rule 3C:2.
Traffic infractions, VA SCt Rule 3B:2.

FINGERPRINTS.
Discovery, VA SCt Rule 3A:11.

FIREWOOD.
Importing into state park.
Uniform fine schedule, VA SCt Rule 3C:2.

FOREIGN ATTORNEYS, VA SCt Rules 1A:1 to 1A:7.
Admission to practice in state without examination, VA SCt Rules 1A:1 to 1A:7.
Revocation of certificates issued, VA SCt Rule 1A:3.
Allowed by comity to participate in trial, VA SCt Rule 1A:4.
Corporate counsel.
Registration, VA SCt Rule 1A:5.
Foreign legal consultants, registration, VA SCt Rule 1A:7.
Patent and trademark attorneys.
Limitations on practice, VA SCt Rule 1A:2.
Registered military legal assistance attorneys, VA SCt Rule 1A:6.

FORMS.
Actual innocence, petition for writ of based on biological evidence, VA SCt Rule Pt 5A Appx Form 12, VA SCt Rule Pt 5 Appx Form 12.
Additional bond required by appellate court on appeal from circuit court, VA SCt Rule Pt 5 Appx Form 6.

FORMS —Cont'd
Bond for costs alone, VA SCt Rule Pt 5 Appx Form 1.
Appellate court on appeal from circuit court, VA SCt Rule Pt 5 Appx Form 3.
Industrial commission on appeal of right to court of appeals, VA SCt Rule Pt 5 Appx Form 7.
Supreme court on appeal for right from state corporation commission, VA SCt Rule Pt 5 Appx Form 8.
Bond for costs and suspension, VA SCt Rule Pt 5 Appx Form 2.
Appellate court on appeal from circuit court, VA SCt Rule Pt 5 Appx Form 5.
Supreme court on appeal of right from state corporation commission, VA SCt Rule Pt 5 Appx Form 9.
Bond for suspension alone required by appellate court on appeal from circuit court, VA SCt Rule Pt 5 Appx Form 4.
Briefs and other papers, VA SCt Rule 5:6.
Court of appeals, VA SCt Rule Pt 5A Appx.
See COURT OF APPEALS.
Criminal procedure.
See CRIMINAL PROCEDURE.
Execution and acknowledgment of bonds, VA SCt Rule Pt 5 Appx Form 10.
Innocence.
Actual innocence, petition for writ of based on biological evidence, VA SCt Rule Pt 5A Appx Form 12, VA SCt Rule Pt 5 Appx Form 12.
Instructions, VA SCt Rule Pt 1 Appx Form 2.
Interrogatories to parties, VA SCt Rule 4:8(b).
Irrevocable letters of credit, VA SCt Rule Pt 5 Appx Form 11.
Jury instructions, VA SCt Rule Pt 1 Appx Form 2.
Praecipe, VA SCt Rule Pt 1 Appx Form 1.
Supreme court, VA SCt Rule Pt 5A Appx.

FRIVOLOUS PLEADINGS, VA SCt Rule 1:4.
Attorneys at law.
Rules of professional conduct.
Requirements as to meritorious claims and contentions, VA SCt Rule Pt 6 §II Rule 3.1.
District courts.
Counsel of record assuring that pleading not filed for delay, VA SCt Rule 7A:8.

G

GENERAL PROVISIONS, VA SCt Rule 5:1.

GENETIC TESTING.
Actual innocence.
Petition for writ of actual innocence, VA SCt Rule 5:7B, VA SCt Rule Pt 5A Appx Form 12, VA SCt Rule Pt 5 Appx Form 12.

GOOD FAITH, VA SCt Rule 1:4.
District courts.
Counsel of record assuring that pleading filed in good faith, VA SCt Rule 7A:8.

GOVERNMENTAL AGENCIES.
Attorneys at law.
Conflicts of interest.
Successive government and private employment, VA SCt Rule Pt 6 §II Rule 1.11.

GOVERNMENTAL AGENCIES —Cont'd
Deposition of organizations, VA SCt Rule 4:5(b).

GRAND JURY.
Criminal procedure.
See CRIMINAL PROCEDURE.

GUARDIANS AD LITEM.
Attorney discipline.
Impairment, VA SCt Rule Pt 6 §IV Par 13-23.
Attorneys.
Diminished capacity client.
Appointment of guardian ad litem, VA SCt Rule Pt 6 §II Rule 1.14.
Briefs.
Court of appeals practice and procedure, VA SCt Rule 5A:21.
Juvenile and domestic relations district courts.
Roles of guardians when representing children, VA SCt Rule 8:6.

GUILTY PLEA.
Attorney discipline.
Board proceedings upon, VA SCt Rule Pt 6 §IV Par 13-22.
Entry by accused at anytime prior to return of verdict, VA SCt Rule 3A:17.1.
Evidence of guilty plea later withdrawn or offer to plead guilty, VA SCt Rule 3A:8.
Juvenile and domestic relations district court, VA SCt Rule 8:18.
Non-traffic offenses.
Written appearance, waiver of hearing, plea of guilty, payment of fine, VA SCt Rule 3C:2.
Plea agreement procedure, VA SCt Rule 3A:8.
Traffic offenses.
Entry of written appearance, waiver of hearing, plea of guilty, payment of fine and costs, VA SCt Rule 3B:2.
Voluntariness determination before accepting, VA SCt Rule 3A:8.
General district court, VA SCt Rule 7C:6.
Withdrawal.
Rejection of plea agreement by court, VA SCt Rule 3A:8.

H

HABEAS CORPUS.
Exclusion of witnesses, VA SCt Rule 2:615.
Inmate filing papers.
Timely filing, VA SCt Rule 3A:25.
Petitions.
Denial of petition for habeas corpus.
Contents of orders denying, VA SCt Rule 3A:24.
Jurisdiction of court, VA SCt Rules 5:7, 5:7A.
Rule on witnesses, VA SCt Rule 2:615.
Supreme court.
Jurisdiction.
Death sentence cases, VA SCt Rule 5:7A.
Generally, VA SCt Rule 5:7.
Original jurisdiction, VA SCt Rule 5:7A.

HEALTH THREATS.
Public health threats, order of quarantine or isolation.
Appeal of circuit court order, VA SCt Rule 5:41.
Circuit court proceedings, VA SCt Rule 3:24.

HEALTH THREATS —Cont'd
Public health threats, order of quarantine or isolation —Cont'd
Isolation proceedings, VA SCt Rule 7A:16.

HEARINGS.
Attorney discipline.
Board proceedings upon certification, VA SCt Rule Pt 6 §IV Par 13-18.
Criminal adjudication or guilty plea, VA SCt Rule Pt 6 §IV Par 13-22.
Disbarment, revocation or suspension in another jurisdiction, VA SCt Rule Pt 6 §IV Par 13-24.
Reinstatement, VA SCt Rule Pt 6 §IV Par 13-25.
Motions, VA SCt Rule 4:15.

HEARSAY EXCEPTIONS, VA SCt Rules 2:801 to 2:806.
Admission by party-opponent, VA SCt Rule 2:803.
Ancient document, VA SCt Rule 2:803.
Baptismal certificates, VA SCt Rule 2:803.
Boundaries, reputation concerning, VA SCt Rule 2:803.
Business records, VA SCt Rule 2:803.
Credibility.
Attacking and supporting credibility of hearsay declarant, VA SCt Rule 2:806.
Dead man rule.
Statement by person incapable of testifying, VA SCt Rule 2:804.
Death, statement under belief of impending.
Declarant unavailable, VA SCt Rule 2:804.
Definitions, VA SCt Rule 2:801.
Excited utterance, VA SCt Rule 2:803.
Family records, VA SCt Rule 2:803.
Personal or family history, statement regarding, VA SCt Rule 2:804.
Former testimony.
Declarant unavailable, VA SCt Rule 2:804.
Hearsay rule, generally, VA SCt Rule 2:802.
Hearsay within hearsay, VA SCt Rule 2:805.
Identification, statement by witness, VA SCt Rule 2:803.
Interest in property, records or documents affecting, VA SCt Rule 2:803.
Judgments, VA SCt Rule 2:803.
Learned treatises, VA SCt Rule 2:803.
Market quotations, VA SCt Rule 2:803.
Marriage licenses and certificates, VA SCt Rule 2:803.
Medical treatment, statement for purposes of, VA SCt Rule 2:803.
Party as witness.
Admission by party-opponent, VA SCt Rule 2:803.
Personal or family history, statement regarding, VA SCt Rule 2:804.
Present sense impression, VA SCt Rule 2:803.
Price of goods, VA SCt Rule 2:803.
Prior inconsistent statements.
Criminal cases, VA SCt Rule 2:613.
Public records, VA SCt Rule 2:803.
Absence of entries where expected, VA SCt Rule 2:803.
Recorded recollection, VA SCt Rule 2:803.
Religious organizations, records, VA SCt Rule 2:803.
Reputation as to character trait, VA SCt Rule 2:803.

HEARSAY EXCEPTIONS —Cont'd
Sexual assault.
Recent complaint exception, VA SCt Rule 2:803.
Statement against interest, VA SCt Rule 2:804.
Then existing mental, emotional, or physical condition, VA SCt Rule 2:803.
Unavailable witness.
Statement by person incapable of testifying, VA SCt Rule 2:804.
Vital records, VA SCt Rule 2:803.

HUSBAND AND WIFE.
Privileged communications.
Evidence, VA SCt Rule 2:504.

I

IDENTIFICATION.
Hearsay exceptions.
Statements by witnesses, VA SCt Rule 2:803.

IMMIGRATION PRACTICE.
Attorneys at law.
Unauthorized practice of law, VA SCt Rule Pt 6 §I UPC 9-7, VA SCt Rule Pt 6 §I UPR 9-103.

IMPAIRMENT PROCEEDINGS.
State bar procedure, VA SCt Rule Pt 6 §IV Par 13.

IMPEACHMENT OF WITNESSES, VA SCt Rule 2:607.
Adverse interests, VA SCt Rule 2:607.
Character witness, cross-examination, VA SCt Rule 2:608.
Conviction of crime, VA SCt Rule 2:609.
Grounds, VA SCt Rule 2:607.
Perjury, unadjudicated, VA SCt Rule 2:608.
Prior false accusations, sexual assault cases, VA SCt Rule 2:608.
Prior inconsistent statements, VA SCt Rule 2:613.
Criminal cases, VA SCt Rule 2:613.
Reputation for truthtelling, VA SCt Rule 2:608.
Specific instances of conduct, VA SCt Rule 2:608.

INDICTMENT.
Criminal procedure.
See CRIMINAL PROCEDURE.

INFORMATION.
Criminal procedure.
See CRIMINAL PROCEDURE.

IN-HOUSE COUNSEL.
Corporate counsel, VA SCt Rule 1A:5.
Corporate counsel registrants, VA SCt Rule 1A:5.

INMATES.
Notice of appeal to supreme court.
Timely filing, VA SCt Rule 5:5.
Petition for appeal to supreme court.
Considered without oral argument, not represented by counsel, VA SCt Rule 5:17.
Timely filing of paper by inmate, VA SCt Rule 5A:3.
Postconviction proceedings, VA SCt Rule 3A:25.

INNOCENCE, ACTUAL.
Actual innocence.
Petition for writ of actual innocence, VA SCt Rule 5:7B, VA SCt Rule Pt 5A Appx Form 12, VA SCt Rule Pt 5 Appx Form 12.

INSTRUCTIONS.
Criminal procedure, VA SCt Rule 3A:16.
Bifurcated jury trials of non-capital felonies, VA SCt Rule 3A:17.1.
Forms, VA SCt Rule Pt 1 Appx Form 2.

INSURANCE.
Evidence.
Existence of, admissibility, VA SCt Rule 2:411.

INTERPLEADER.
Statutory interpleader.
Civil actions, VA SCt Rule 3:15.

INTERPRETERS.
Oath or affirmation, VA SCt Rule 2:604.
Privilege, evidence, VA SCt Rule 2:507.
Witnesses, VA SCt Rule 2:604.

INTERVENTION.
Civil actions, VA SCt Rule 3:14.

IOLTA, VA SCt Rule Pt 6 §IV Par 20.

J

JOINDER OF ACTIONS.
District courts, VA SCt Rule 7B:10.
Criminal procedure.
Trial together of more than one action, VA SCt Rule 7C:4.

JOINDER OF PARTIES.
Circuit courts.
Civil actions, VA SCt Rule 3:12.
Third party claims, VA SCt Rule 3:13.
Civil actions, VA SCt Rule 3:12.
District courts.
Criminal procedure.
Trial together of more than one accused, VA SCt Rule 7C:4.

JUDGES.
Attorneys at law.
Rules of professional conduct.
Former judge or arbitrator, VA SCt Rule Pt 6 §II Rule 1.12.
Best evidence rule exceptions.
Issues of law or fact, VA SCt Rule 2:1008.
Canons of judicial conduct.
Adjudicative responsibilities, VA SCt Rule Pt 6 §III Canon 3.
Administrative responsibilities, VA SCt Rule Pt 6 §III Canon 3.
Appearance of impropriety.
Avoidance, VA SCt Rule Pt 6 §III Canon 2.
Arbitration.
Judges not to act as arbitrators or mediators, VA SCt Rule Pt 6 §III Canon 4.
Avocational activities, VA SCt Rule Pt 6 §III Canon 4.
Campaign conduct, VA SCt Rule Pt 6 §III Canon 5.
Civic and charitable activities, VA SCt Rule Pt 6 §III Canon 4.
Disciplinary responsibilities, VA SCt Rule Pt 6 §III Canon 3.
Disqualification, VA SCt Rule Pt 6 §III Canon 3.
Remittal of disqualification, VA SCt Rule Pt 6 §III Canon 3.
Effective date of canons, VA SCt Rule Pt 6 §III Canon 7.

JUDGES —Cont'd
Canons of judicial conduct —Cont'd
Extra-judicial activities, VA SCt Rule Pt 6 §III Canon 4.
Compensation for, VA SCt Rule Pt 6 §III Canon 4.
Fiduciary activities, VA SCt Rule Pt 6 §III Canon 4.
Financial activities, VA SCt Rule Pt 6 §III Canon 4.
Impropriety.
Avoidance in all activities, VA SCt Rule Pt 6 §III Canon 2.
Integrity and independence of judiciary.
Duty to uphold, VA SCt Rule Pt 6 §III Canon 1.
Judges pro tempore.
Compliance with canons, VA SCt Rule Pt 6 §III Canon 6.
Political activity, VA SCt Rule Pt 6 §III Canon 5.
Reports.
Compensation received for extra-judicial activities, VA SCt Rule Pt 6 §III Canon 4.
Retired judges.
Compliance with canons, VA SCt Rule Pt 6 §III Canon 6.
Senior judge or justice.
Compliance with canons, VA SCt Rule Pt 6 §III Canon 6.
Substitute judges.
Compliance with canons, VA SCt Rule Pt 6 §III Canon 6.
Civil or criminal proceedings.
Competency to testify, VA SCt Rule 2:605.
Competency to testify.
Civil or criminal proceedings, VA SCt Rule 2:605.
Evidence.
Best evidence rule exceptions.
Issues of law or fact, VA SCt Rule 2:1008.
Rules of professional conduct.
False statement by lawyer concerning qualifications or integrity of judicial official, VA SCt Rule Pt 6 §II Rule 8.2.

JUDGMENTS AND DECREES.
Civil procedure.
Default judgments, VA SCt Rule 3:19.
Summary judgment, VA SCt Rule 3:20.
Criminal cases.
Finality of judgments, VA SCt Rule 1:1.
Drafts of orders and decrees.
Endorsement by counsel of record, VA SCt Rule 1:13.
Electronic filing and service, VA SCt Rule 1:17.
Modified or dispensed with by court in its discretion, VA SCt Rule 1:13.
Endorsement.
Drafts by counsel of record.
Electronic filing and service, VA SCt Rule 1:17.
Modified or dispensed with by court in its discretion, VA SCt Rule 1:13.
Evidence.
Hearsay exceptions, VA SCt Rule 2:803.
Finality of judgment and decree.
Civil cases.
Time to remain under control of court, VA SCt Rule 1:1.

JUDGMENTS AND DECREES —Cont'd
Finality of judgment and decree —Cont'd
Criminal cases.
Time to remain under control of trial court, VA SCt Rule 1:1.
Hearsay exceptions, VA SCt Rule 2:803.
Juvenile and domestic relations district courts.
Motion to reduce support arrearages to judgment.
Service of process, VA SCt Rule 8:4.
Summary judgment.
Depositions.
Limitation on use, VA SCt Rule 4:7.

JURISDICTION.
Appeals.
Supreme court.
Original jurisdiction, VA SCt Rule 5:7.
Attorney discipline.
Effect of rules, VA SCt Rule Pt 6 §IV Par 13-2.
Supreme court, VA SCt Rule 5:7.

JURY TRIAL.
Attorneys at law.
Rules of professional conduct.
Communications with jurors.
Restrictions relating to impartiality and decorum of the tribunal, VA SCt Rule Pt 6 §II Rule 3.5.
Best evidence rule exceptions.
Issues of law or fact, VA SCt Rule 2:1008.
Challenge for cause, VA SCt Rule 1:22.
Circuit courts.
Right to trial by jury, VA SCt Rule 3:21.
Trial by jury or by court, VA SCt Rule 3:22.
Civil procedure.
Right to trial by jury, VA SCt Rule 3:21.
Trial by jury or by court, VA SCt Rule 3:22.
Competency of jurors as witnesses, VA SCt Rule 2:606.
Criminal procedure.
See CRIMINAL PROCEDURE.
Evidence.
Best evidence rule exceptions.
Issues of law or fact, VA SCt Rule 2:1008.
Exclusion of witnesses, VA SCt Rule 2:615.
Expert witnesses.
Exclusion of witnesses in civil cases, VA SCt Rule 2:615.
Jurors as witnesses.
Competency, VA SCt Rule 2:606.
Note-taking by jurors, VA SCt Rule 1:23.
Rule on witnesses, VA SCt Rule 2:615.
Scheduling civil cases for trial, VA SCt Rule 1:20.
Voir dire examination.
Preliminary instructions, VA SCt Rule 1:21.
Witnesses.
Exclusion of witnesses, VA SCt Rule 2:615.
Jurors as witnesses.
Competency, VA SCt Rule 2:606.

JUVENILE AND DOMESTIC RELATIONS DISTRICT COURTS, VA SCt Rule 1:15.
Adult criminal cases.
Discovery, VA SCt Rule 8:15.
Appeals.
Briefs, VA SCt Rule 8:7.
Writing requirement, VA SCt Rule 8:20.

JUVENILE AND DOMESTIC RELATIONS DISTRICT COURTS —Cont'd
Applicability of rules, VA SCt Rule 8:1.
Definitions, VA SCt Rule 8:2.
Arraignment.
Juvenile delinquency cases, VA SCt Rule 8:16.
Pleas, VA SCt Rule 8:18.
Trial rights of parties.
Notification and waiver, VA SCt Rule 8:17.
Attorneys at law.
"Counsel" defined, VA SCt Rule 8:2.
"Counsel of record" defined, VA SCt Rule 8:2.
Endorsements of orders, VA SCt Rule 8:19.
Juvenile delinquency cases.
Waiver of arraignment, VA SCt Rule 8:16.
Noting of appeal, VA SCt Rule 8:20.
Roles of counsel when representing children, VA SCt Rule 8:6.
Bill of particulars, VA SCt Rule 8:8.
Briefs.
Format, VA SCt Rule 8:7.
Child support.
Motion to reduce support arrearages to judgment.
Service of process, VA SCt Rule 8:4.
Petition for support.
Contents, VA SCt Rule 8:3.
Consent.
Emergency medical or surgical treatment for a juvenile.
Judicial consent, VA SCt Rule 8:3.
Emergency situations.
Judicial consent, VA SCt Rule 8:22.
Construction of rules, VA SCt Rule 8:1.
Definitions, VA SCt Rule 8:2.
Continuances.
Criteria for granting, VA SCt Rule 8:14.
Good cause as grounds for granting, VA SCt Rule 8:14.
Court discretion, VA SCt Rule 8:9.
Juvenile delinquency cases.
Waiver of arraignment, VA SCt Rule 8:16.
Preservation of records by photographic means, VA SCt Rule 8:12.
Court-ordered reports, VA SCt Rule 8:5.
Criminal procedure.
Appeals.
Procedure, VA SCt Rule 3A:19.
Arraignment.
Juvenile delinquency cases, VA SCt Rule 8:16.
Trial rights of parties.
Notification and waiver, VA SCt Rule 8:17.
Discovery.
Adult criminal cases, VA SCt Rule 8:15.
Juvenile delinquency cases, VA SCt Rule 8:15.
Exception, VA SCt Rule 3A:1.
Juvenile delinquency cases.
Arraignment, VA SCt Rule 8:16.
Pleas, VA SCt Rule 8:18.
Trial rights of parties.
Notification and waiver, VA SCt Rule 8:17.
Pleas.
Juvenile delinquency cases, VA SCt Rule 8:18.
Scope of provisions, VA SCt Rule 3A:1.
Definitions, VA SCt Rule 8:2.
Continuances.
Meaning of "parties,"VA SCt Rule 8:14.
Request for subpoenas.
Meaning of "file,"VA SCt Rule 8:13.

JUVENILE AND DOMESTIC RELATIONS DISTRICT COURTS —Cont'd
Discovery.
Adult criminal cases, VA SCt Rule 8:15.
Juvenile delinquency cases, VA SCt Rule 8:15.
Other cases, VA SCt Rule 8:15.
Discretion of court, VA SCt Rule 8:9.
Juvenile delinquency cases.
Waiver of arraignment, VA SCt Rule 8:16.
Preservation of records by electronic or photographic means, VA SCt Rule 8:12.
Electronic filing and service, VA SCt Rules 8:7, 8:8.
Electronic preservation of records, VA SCt Rule 8:12.
Guardians ad litem.
Roles of guardians when representing children, VA SCt Rule 8:6.
Judgments and decrees.
Motion to reduce support arrearages to judgment.
Service of process, VA SCt Rule 8:4.
Judicial consent.
Emergency situations, VA SCt Rule 8:22.
Medical or surgical treatment for a juvenile.
Petition, VA SCt Rule 8:3.
Judicial discretion, VA SCt Rule 8:9.
Juvenile delinquency cases.
Waiver of arraignment, VA SCt Rule 8:16.
Preservation of records by electronic or photographic means, VA SCt Rule 8:12.
Juvenile delinquency cases.
Arraignment, VA SCt Rule 8:16.
Discovery, VA SCt Rule 8:15.
Guilty pleas, VA SCt Rule 8:18.
Trial rights of parties.
Notification and waiver, VA SCt Rule 8:17.
Local rules of court, VA SCt Rule 1:15.
Medical or surgical treatment.
Judicial consent to emergency medical or surgical treatment for juvenile.
Petition.
Contents, VA SCt Rule 8:3.
Motions.
Court-ordered services.
Proceedings, VA SCt Rule 8:3.
Format, VA SCt Rule 8:7.
Support and maintenance.
Motion to reduce support arrearages to judgment.
Service of process, VA SCt Rule 8:4.
Venue.
Motions to transfer venue, VA SCt Rule 8:10.
Orders.
Endorsements of orders, VA SCt Rule 8:19.
Parties.
Juvenile delinquency cases.
Trial rights of parties.
Notification and waiver, VA SCt Rule 8:17.
Noting of appeal, VA SCt Rule 8:20.
Petitions.
Contents of petitions, VA SCt Rule 8:3.
Photography.
Preservation of records by, VA SCt Rule 8:12.
Pleadings.
Admission, denial or objection, VA SCt Rule 8:8.
Amendment of written pleading, VA SCt Rule 8:8.
Bill of particulars, VA SCt Rule 8:8.

JUVENILE AND DOMESTIC RELATIONS DISTRICT COURTS —Cont'd
Pleadings —Cont'd
Electronic filing and service, VA SCt Rule 8:8.
Format, VA SCt Rule 8:7.
Furnishing copies of pleadings, VA SCt Rule 8:8.
Plea of guilty by juvenile, VA SCt Rule 8:18.
Determining voluntariness, understanding and intelligence of plea, VA SCt Rule 8:18.
Pleas.
Juvenile delinquency cases.
Permissible pleas by child, VA SCt Rule 8:18.
Voluntariness, understanding and intelligence of plea of guilty.
Determining by a juvenile, VA SCt Rule 8:18.
Production of documents.
Subpoenas duces tecum, VA SCt Rule 8:13.
Records.
Request for production.
Subpoenas duces tecum, VA SCt Rule 8:13.
Reporters.
Transcripts of proceedings, VA SCt Rule 8:11.
Reports.
Court-ordered reports, VA SCt Rule 8:5.
Scope of rules, VA SCt Rule 8:1.
Service of process.
Child support.
Motion to reduce support arrearages to judgment, VA SCt Rule 8:4.
Services.
Ordering of services.
Motion or petition, VA SCt Rule 8:3.
Size of paper, VA SCt Rule 8:7.
Pleadings, motions, etc., VA SCt Rule 8:7.
Subpoenas.
Production of documents, VA SCt Rule 8:13.
Witnesses, VA SCt Rule 8:13.
Subpoenas duces tecum.
Production of documents, VA SCt Rule 8:13.
Support and maintenance.
Motion to reduce support arrearages to judgment.
Service of process, VA SCt Rule 8:4.
Petition for support of spouse or child.
Contents, VA SCt Rule 8:3.
Spousal support.
Motion to reduce support arrearages to judgment.
Service of process, VA SCt Rule 8:4.
Technology in courts.
Preservation of records by electronic or photographic means, VA SCt Rule 8:12.
Transcripts.
Court proceedings, VA SCt Rule 8:11.
Venue.
Motions to transfer venue, VA SCt Rule 8:10.
Witnesses.
Subpoenas for witnesses, VA SCt Rule 8:13.

L

LAW FIRMS AND ASSOCIATIONS.
See ATTORNEYS AT LAW.

LESSER INCLUDED OFFENSE.
Bifurcated jury trial on finding of guilt for non-capital felony.
Instructions at punishment phase, VA SCt Rule 3A:17.1.

LESSER INCLUDED OFFENSE —Cont'd
Bifurcated jury trial on finding of guilt for non-capital felony —Cont'd
Mistrial, non-unanimous verdict, retrial on offense, VA SCt Rule 3A:17.1.

LIMITED LIABILITY ENTITIES, VA SCt Rule Pt 6 §IV Par 14.

LOCAL RULES OF COURT.
District courts.
General information relating to each court to be furnished to executive secretary of supreme court, VA SCt Rule 7A:15.
General provisions, VA SCt Rule 1:15.
Instructions, VA SCt Rule 1:15.
Praecipe.
Form, VA SCt Rule 1:15.

M

MAGISTRATES.
Competency to testify.
Criminal or civil proceedings, VA SCt Rule 2:605.

MAIL FILING AND SERVICE.
Prisoners.
Timely filing of paper by inmate.
Postconviction proceedings, VA SCt Rule 3A:25.

MANDAMUS.
Supreme court.
Jurisdiction, VA SCt Rule 5:7.

MANDATES, VA SCt Rule 5:36.

MARKET ANALYSES.
Hearsay exceptions.
Market quotations, VA SCt Rule 2:803.

MARRIAGE AND FAMILY THERAPISTS.
Privileged communications, VA SCt Rule 2:506.

MARRIAGE LICENSES AND CERTIFICATES.
Hearsay exceptions, VA SCt Rule 2:803.

MEDIATION.
Attorneys at law.
Rules of professional conduct.
Acting as mediator, VA SCt Rule Pt 6 §II Rule 2.11.
Third party neutral service, VA SCt Rule Pt 6 §II Rule 2.10.

MEDICAL EXAMINATIONS.
Physical and mental examination of persons, VA SCt Rule 4:10.

MEDICAL TREATMENT.
Hearsay exceptions.
Medical treatment, statement for purposes of, VA SCt Rule 2:803.

MENTAL DISABILITY.
Attorneys at law.
Rules of professional conduct.
Client under a disability, VA SCt Rule Pt 6 §II Rule 1.14.

MENTAL EXAMINATIONS.
Physical and mental examination of persons, VA SCt Rule 4:10.

MENTAL HEALTH.
Hearsay exceptions.
Then existing mental, emotional, or physical condition, VA SCt Rule 2:803.
Physician-patient privilege.
Clinical psychologists as healing art practitioners, VA SCt Rule 2:505.

MILITARY ATTORNEYS.
Registered military legal assistance attorneys, VA SCt Rule 1A:6.

MINISTERS.
Cleric-penitent privilege, VA SCt Rule 2:503.

MINORS.
Attorneys at law.
Rules of professional conduct.
Client under a disability, VA SCt Rule Pt 6 §II Rule 1.14.

MISLEADING EVIDENCE.
Exclusion of relevant evidence, VA SCt Rule 2:403.

MISTRIALS.
Bifurcated jury trials of non-capital felonies, VA SCt Rule 3A:17.1.

MOTION FOR JUDGMENT.
Endorsement of drafts of orders and decrees, VA SCt Rule 1:13.
Electronic filing and service, VA SCt Rule 1:17.
Evidence.
Striking the evidence, VA SCt Rule 1:11.
Summary judgment or partial summary judgment entered in conformity with ruling on motion to strike, VA SCt Rule 1:11.

MOTIONS.
Circuit courts.
Civil actions.
Responsive pleadings, VA SCt Rule 3:8.
Civil actions.
Responsive pleadings, VA SCt Rule 3:8.
Criminal procedure.
Jury.
Confidentiality of juror personal information, VA SCt Rule 3A:14.1.
District courts.
Civil procedure.
Transfer.
Motions to transfer, VA SCt Rule 7B:11.
Filing format and procedures, VA SCt Rule 7A:7.
Juvenile and domestic relations district courts.
Court-ordered services.
Proceedings, VA SCt Rule 8:3.
Format, VA SCt Rule 8:7.
Support and maintenance.
Motion to reduce support arrearages to judgment.
Service of process, VA SCt Rule 8:4.
Venue.
Motions to transfer venue, VA SCt Rule 8:10.
Paper.
Size of paper, VA SCt Rule 1:16.
Scheduling and hearing, procedure, VA SCt Rule 4:15.
Service of process.
Service of papers after initial process, VA SCt Rule 1:12.

MOTIONS —Cont'd
Supreme court, VA SCt Rule 5:4.

MOVE OVER LAW.
Failure to yield right of way.
Fine schedule, VA SCt Rule 3B:2.

MULTI-PARTY CASES.
Appeal from partial final judgment, VA SCt Rule 5:8A.

N

NEGLIGENCE.
Civil procedure.
Allegations of negligence, VA SCt Rule 3:18.

NEW TRIAL.
Mistrial upon non-unanimous verdict at penalty phase, VA SCt Rule 3A:17.1.

NON-COMPLIANCE WITH RULES, SANCTIONS, VA SCt Rule 5:1A.

NON-ENGLISH SPEAKING PERSONS.
Interpreter privilege, VA SCt Rule 2:507.

NON-TRAFFIC PREPAYABLE OFFENSES AND UNIFORM FINE SCHEDULE, VA SCt Rules 3C:1, 3C:2.

NOTICE OF APPEAL.
Extension of time for filing, VA SCt Rule 5:5.
Filing by mail, VA SCt Rule 5:5.
Inmate filing, timely filing, VA SCt Rule 5:5.
Procedure for filing an appeal from a trial court, VA SCt Rule 5:9.
Procedure for filing an appeal from the court of appeals, VA SCt Rule 5:14.

NOTICE OF DECISION AND ORDER, VA SCt Rule 5:34.

O

OATHS AND AFFIRMATIONS.
Interpreters, VA SCt Rule 2:604.
Witnesses, VA SCt Rule 2:603.

OFFERS TO COMPROMISE.
Evidence, relevancy, VA SCt Rule 2:408.

OPINIONS OF COURT, VA SCt Rule 5:36.
Citing unpublished judicial dispositions, VA SCt Rule 5:1.
United States supreme court.
Certification of questions of law, VA SCt Rule 5:40.

ORAL ARGUMENT, VA SCt Rule 5:33.
Attorney discipline.
District committees proceedings, VA SCt Rule Pt 6 §IV Par 13-16.
Supreme court.
Length, VA SCt Rule 5:33.
Notice, VA SCt Rule 5:33.
Waiver, VA SCt Rule 5:33.

ORDERS OF COURT, VA SCt Rule 5:4.
District courts.
Endorsements.
Counsel of record to endorse, VA SCt Rule 7A:11.
Transcripts of proceedings, VA SCt Rule 7A:4.

ORDERS OF COURT —Cont'd
Drafts of orders.
Endorsed by counsel of record, VA SCt Rule 1:13.
District courts, VA SCt Rule 7A:11.
Electronic filing and service, VA SCt Rule 1:17.
Endorsement.
Drafts endorsed by counsel, VA SCt Rule 1:13.
District courts, VA SCt Rule 7A:11.
Electronic filing and service, VA SCt Rule 1:17.
Juvenile and domestic relations district courts.
Endorsements of orders, VA SCt Rule 8:19.
Pretrial procedure.
Order arising from pretrial conference, VA SCt Rule 4:13.
Sentencing orders, VA SCt Rule Pt 3A Appx Form 10.

ORIGINAL JURISDICTION, VA SCt Rules 5:7, 5:7A.

P

PAPER.
Size of paper, VA SCt Rule 1:16(a).
District court papers, VA SCt Rule 7A:7.
Electronic filing and service.
Applicability of provisions, VA SCt Rule 1:17.
Nonconforming paper may be required to be redone to comply, VA SCt Rule 1:16(b).

PARTIES.
Circuit courts.
Intervention, VA SCt Rule 3:14.
Joinder of parties, VA SCt Rule 3:12.
New parties, VA SCt Rule 3:16.
Statutory interpleader, VA SCt Rule 3:15.
Substitution of parties, VA SCt Rule 3:17.
Third party claims, VA SCt Rule 3:13.
Civil procedure.
Intervention, VA SCt Rule 3:14.
Joinder of parties, VA SCt Rule 3:12.
New parties, VA SCt Rule 3:16.
Statutory interpleader, VA SCt Rule 3:15
Substitution of parties, VA SCt Rule 3:17.
Third party claims, VA SCt Rule 3:13.
Juvenile and domestic relations district courts.
Juvenile delinquency cases.
Trial rights of parties.
Notification and waiver, VA SCt Rule 8:17.
Noting of appeal, VA SCt Rule 8:20.

PARTNERSHIPS.
Depositions of organizations, VA SCt Rule 4:5(b).

PERFECTING THE APPEAL.
Brief in opposition, VA SCt Rule 5:18.
Denial of appeal, VA SCt Rule 5:20.
Petition for rehearing, VA SCt Rule 5:20.
Petition for appeal, VA SCt Rule 5:17.
Grant or refusal of injunction, VA SCt Rule 5:17A.
Procedure following.
Appendices.
When required, VA SCt Rule 5:32.
Brief of appellee, VA SCt Rule 5:28.
Briefs, VA SCt Rule 5:26.

PERFECTING THE APPEAL —Cont'd
Procedure following —Cont'd
Briefs amicus curiae, VA SCt Rule 5:30.
Contemporaneous objection rule, VA SCt Rule 5:25.
Covers of documents, VA SCt Rule 5:31.
Docketing, VA SCt Rule 5:23.
Grant of petition for appeal, VA SCt Rule 5:23.
Opening brief of appellant, VA SCt Rule 5:27.
Oral argument, VA SCt Rule 5:33.
Reply brief, VA SCt Rule 5:29.
Security for appeal, VA SCt Rule 5:24.
Reply brief, VA SCt Rule 5:19.

PERJURY.
Impeachment of witnesses.
Unadjudicated perjury, VA SCt Rule 2:608.

PETITIONS.
Actual innocence.
Petition for writ of actual innocence, VA SCt Rule 5:7B, VA SCt Rule Pt 5A Appx Form 12, VA SCt Rule Pt 5 Appx Form 12.
Administrative process act.
Petition for appeal, VA SCt Rule 2A:4.
Contents, VA SCt Rule 2A:4(b).
Time for filing, VA SCt Rule 2A:4(a).
Appeal, VA SCt Rule 5:17.
Rehearing, VA SCt Rule 5:37.
Court of appeals.
Petition for rehearing, VA SCt Rules 5A:32 to 5A:35.
Death row prisoners.
Habeas corpus writs.
Petition for writ in cases where death sentence imposed, VA SCt Rule 5:7A.
Habeas corpus.
Denial of petition for habeas corpus.
Contents of orders denying, VA SCt Rule 3A:24.
Juvenile and domestic relations district courts.
Contents of petitions, VA SCt Rule 8:3.
Rehearing, VA SCt Rule 5:37.
Denial of appeal by court of appeals, VA SCt Rule 5A:15.
Format, VA SCt Rules 5:20, 5:20A.

PHOTOGRAPHY.
District courts.
Preservation of records by photographic means, VA SCt Rule 7A:6.
Juvenile and domestic relations district courts.
Preservation of records by photographic means, VA SCt Rule 8:12.
Preservation of records.
Use of photographic means, VA SCt Rule 1:14.
District courts, VA SCt Rule 7A:6.

PHYSICAL CONDITION.
Hearsay exceptions.
Then existing mental, emotional, or physical condition, VA SCt Rule 2:803.

PHYSICAL EXAMINATIONS.
Physical and mental examination of persons, VA SCt Rule 4:10.

PHYSICIAN-PATIENT PRIVILEGE, VA SCt Rule 2:505.

PHYSICIANS.
Hearsay exceptions.
Medical treatment, statement for purposes of, VA SCt Rule 2:803.

PLEA AGREEMENTS.
Evidence.
Withdrawn pleas and offers to plead, VA SCt Rule 2:410.

PLEADINGS.
Abatement.
Filing pleas in abatement, VA SCt Rule 1:9.
Admission of fact, VA SCt Rule 1:4(e).
Affidavit.
Verification, VA SCt Rule 1:10.
Electronic filing and service, VA SCt Rule 1:17.
Amendments, VA SCt Rule 1:8.
District court, VA SCt Rule 7A:9.
Attorneys at law.
Foreign attorneys.
Comity.
Pleading or notice to be signed by member of Virginia bar or party, VA SCt Rule 1A:4.
Office address and telephone number of counsel submitting pleading.
Pleadings to contain, VA SCt Rule 1:4(l).
Service on counsel of record after initial process, VA SCt Rule 1:12.
Signature and address required, VA SCt Rule 1:4(c).
Brevity required, VA SCt Rule 1:4(j).
Circuit courts.
Answers, VA SCt Rule 3:8.
Bill of particulars, VA SCt Rule 3:7.
Captions, VA SCt Rule 3:2.
Counterclaims, VA SCt Rule 3:9.
Cross-claims, VA SCt Rule 3:10.
Demurrers, VA SCt Rule 3:8.
Filing of pleadings, VA SCt Rule 3:3.
General provisions, VA SCt Rule 3:18.
Negligence, allegations, VA SCt Rule 3:18.
Reply.
Civil actions, VA SCt Rule 3:11.
Responsive pleadings, VA SCt Rule 3:8.
Civil procedure.
Ad damnum clause required, VA SCt Rule 3:2.
Answers, VA SCt Rule 3:8.
Bill of particulars, VA SCt Rule 3:7.
Captions, VA SCt Rule 3:2.
Commencement of proceedings, VA SCt Rule 3:2.
Counterclaims, VA SCt Rule 3:9.
Cross-claims, VA SCt Rule 3:10.
Demurrers, VA SCt Rule 3:8.
Filing of pleadings, VA SCt Rule 3:3.
General provisions, VA SCt Rule 3:18.
Negligence, allegations, VA SCt Rule 3:18.
Reply.
Civil actions, VA SCt Rule 3:11.
Responsive pleadings, VA SCt Rule 3:8.
Clerk of court.
Note and attest filing date, VA SCt Rule 1:4(h).
Copies.
District court, VA SCt Rule 7A:10.
Criminal procedure.
See CRIMINAL PROCEDURE.
Denial of fact, VA SCt Rule 1:4(e).
Dilatory pleadings, VA SCt Rule 1:4(a).
District courts, VA SCt Rule 7A:8.

PLEADINGS —Cont'd
Discretion of court, VA SCt Rule 1:9.
District court, VA SCt Rule 7A:5.
District courts, VA SCt Rule 7C:6.
Amendments, VA SCt Rule 7A:9.
Civil procedure.
Authorized pleadings, VA SCt Rule 7B:3.
Contents of pleadings, VA SCt Rule 7B:3.
Requirements that judge may impose, VA SCt Rule 7B:2.
Verification, VA SCt Rule 7B:6.
Copies, VA SCt Rule 7A:10.
Criminal pleas in district court, VA SCt Rule 7C:6.
Dilatory pleadings.
Counsel of record.
Tendering pleading gives assurance that delay not intended, VA SCt Rule 7A:8.
Discretion of court as to pleadings, VA SCt Rule 7A:5.
Effect of sworn pleading, VA SCt Rule 7A:8.
Exhibits.
Incorporation as part of pleading, VA SCt Rule 7A:8.
Filing format and procedures, VA SCt Rule 7A:7.
Good faith.
Assured by counsel of record, VA SCt Rule 7A:8.
Signature, VA SCt Rule 7A:8.
Electronic filing and service, VA SCt Rule 1:17.
Applicability of and compliance with other rules, VA SCt Rule 1:17(e).
Definitions, VA SCt Rule 1:17(b).
Practice and procedure, VA SCt Rule 1:17(d).
Scope of electronic filing rules, VA SCt Rule 1:17(a).
System operational standards, VA SCt Rule 1:17(c).
Exhibits, VA SCt Rule 1:4(i).
District court, VA SCt Rule 7A:8.
Filing.
Discretion of court, VA SCt Rule 1:9.
Frivolous pleadings, VA SCt Rule 1:4(a).
District courts, VA SCt Rule 7A:8.
General provisions, VA SCt Rule 1:4.
Good faith of counsel, VA SCt Rule 1:4(a).
District courts, VA SCt Rule 7A:8.
Juvenile and domestic relations district courts.
Admission, denial or objection, VA SCt Rule 8:8.
Amendment of written pleading, VA SCt Rule 8:8.
Bill of particulars, VA SCt Rule 8:8.
Furnishing copies of pleadings, VA SCt Rule 8:8.
Size of paper, VA SCt Rule 8:8.
Motion for judgment.
See MOTION FOR JUDGMENT.
Paper.
Size of paper, VA SCt Rule 1:16.
Electronic filing and service.
Applicability of provisions, VA SCt Rule 1:17.
Sealed instruments.
Requirements, VA SCt Rule 1:4(f).
Service of process.
Service of papers after initial process, VA SCt Rule 1:12.
Signature, VA SCt Rule 1:4.
District court, VA SCt Rule 7A:8.

PLEADINGS —Cont'd
State true nature of claim or defense, VA SCt Rule 1:4(d).
Verification.
Affidavit, VA SCt Rule 1:4(b).
District court, VA SCt Rule 7B:6.

PLEAS.
Bifurcated jury trials of non-capital felonies, VA SCt Rule 3A:17.1.
District courts, VA SCt Rule 7C:6.
Evidence.
Withdrawn pleas and offers to plead, VA SCt Rule 2:410.
Juvenile and domestic relations district courts.
Juvenile delinquency cases.
Permissible pleas by child, VA SCt Rule 8:18.
Voluntariness, understanding and intelligence of plea of guilty.
Determining by a juvenile, VA SCt Rule 8:18.

POLYGRAPH TESTS.
Evidence.
Admissibility, VA SCt Rule 2:402.

POSTMORTEM EXAMINATIONS.
Discovery, VA SCt Rule 3A:11.

PRAECIPE.
Local rules of court.
Form, VA SCt Rule Pt 1 Appx Form 1.

PREJUDICE.
Evidence.
Exclusion of relevant evidence, VA SCt Rule 2:403.
Witnesses, VA SCt Rule 2:610.

PRESENT SENSE IMPRESSION.
Hearsay exceptions, VA SCt Rule 2:803.

PRETRIAL CONFERENCES, VA SCt Rule 1:19.

PRETRIAL PROCEDURES.
Admissibility.
Documents.
Admission of facts and genuineness of documents, VA SCt Rule 4:11.
Application of part four, VA SCt Rule 4:0.
Attorneys at law.
Conference.
Formulating issues, VA SCt Rule 4:13.
Conference.
Order arising from pretrial conference, VA SCt Rule 4:13.
Pretrial conference, VA SCt Rule 4:13.
When held, VA SCt Rule 4:13.
Copying.
Discovery and production of documents and things for copying, VA SCt Rule 4:9.
Depositions for discovery and use as evidence.
Action.
Before action, VA SCt Rule 4:2(a).
Notice and service, VA SCt Rule 4:2(a).
Admissibility.
Objections, VA SCt Rule 4:7(b).
Answers to interrogatories.
Failure of party to serve, VA SCt Rule 4:12(d).
Appeal.
Pending appeal, VA SCt Rule 4:2(b).

PRETRIAL PROCEDURES —Cont'd
Depositions for discovery and use as evidence —Cont'd
Associations.
Deposition of organization, VA SCt Rule 4:5(b).
Audio-visual depositions, VA SCt Rule 4:7A.
Certification by officer, VA SCt Rule 4:5(f).
Changes.
General provisions, VA SCt Rule 4:5(e).
Completion of deposition.
General provisions, VA SCt Rule 4:7(d).
Convicts.
Taken by leave of court, VA SCt Rule 4:5(a).
Copies, VA SCt Rule 4:5(f).
Discovery and production of documents and things for copying, VA SCt Rule 4:9.
Corporations.
Deposition of organization, VA SCt Rule 4:5(b).
Disposition of discovery material, VA SCt Rule 4:14.
Errors.
Effect of errors, VA SCt Rule 4:7(d).
Examination.
Before action.
Notice and service, VA SCt Rule 4:2(a).
Order and examination, VA SCt Rule 4:2(a).
Cross-examination, VA SCt Rule 4:5(c).
General provisions, VA SCt Rule 4:5(c).
Limitation.
Motion to limit, VA SCt Rule 4:5(d).
Notice, VA SCt Rule 4:5(b).
Objections, VA SCt Rule 4:5(c).
Records, VA SCt Rule 4:5(c).
Termination.
Motion to terminate, VA SCt Rule 4:5(d).
Exhibits.
General provisions, VA SCt Rule 4:5(f).
Expenses.
Upon failure to attend or serve subpoena, VA SCt Rule 4:5(g).
Filing.
By officer, VA SCt Rule 4:5(f).
Notice, VA SCt Rule 4:5(f).
Written questions, VA SCt Rule 4:6.
Foreign countries, VA SCt Rule 4:3(d).
Form of presentation, VA SCt Rule 4:7(b).
Governmental agencies.
Deposition of organization, VA SCt Rule 4:5(b).
Inspection.
Discovery and production of documents and things for inspection, VA SCt Rule 4:9.
Failure to respond to request for inspection, VA SCt Rule 4:12(d).
Interrogatories to parties.
Answers, VA SCt Rule 4:8(d).
Availability, VA SCt Rule 4:8(a).
Business records.
Option to produce, VA SCt Rule 4:8(f).
Filing, VA SCt Rule 4:8(c).
Form, VA SCt Rule 4:8(b).
Procedures for use, VA SCt Rule 4:8(a).
Scope, VA SCt Rule 4:8(e).
Use, VA SCt Rule 4:8(e).
Irregularities.
Effect, VA SCt Rule 4:7(d).
Leave of court.
Required when, VA SCt Rule 4:5(a).
Limitation on depositions, VA SCt Rule 4:6A.
Limitation on use of depositions, VA SCt Rule 4:7(e).

PRETRIAL PROCEDURES —Cont'd
Depositions for discovery and use as evidence —Cont'd
Limitation on interrogatories.
Interrogatories to parties, VA SCt Rule 4:8(g).
Notice.
Effect of errors and irregularities, VA SCt Rule 4:7(d).
Examination, VA SCt Rule 4:5(b).
Filing, VA SCt Rule 4:5(f).
Service, VA SCt Rule 4:1(f).
Special notice, VA SCt Rule 4:5(b).
Written questions, VA SCt Rule 4:6.
Oath.
General provisions, VA SCt Rule 4:5(c).
Officer taking.
Effect of errors and irregularities as to disqualification, VA SCt Rule 4:7(d).
Organization.
Deposition of organization, VA SCt Rule 4:5(b).
Outside state.
Certificate, VA SCt Rule 4:3(e).
Parties.
Failure of party to attend at own deposition, VA SCt Rule 4:12(d).
Interrogatories to parties, VA SCt Rule 4:8.
Partnerships.
Deposition of organization, VA SCt Rule 4:5(b).
Perpetuation by action, VA SCt Rule 4:2(c).
Person before whom taken, VA SCt Rule 4:3.
Petition.
Before action, VA SCt Rule 4:2(a).
Production of documents and tangible things.
Request, VA SCt Rule 4:5(b).
Questions to parties, VA SCt Rule 4:6.
Record.
Part of record only to extent that offered in evidence, VA SCt Rule 4:7(f).
Requirements.
General requirements, VA SCt Rule 4:5(b).
Return of depositions, VA SCt Rule 4:7(d).
Serving questions, VA SCt Rule 4:6.
Signing, VA SCt Rule 4:5(e).
Stipulations, VA SCt Rule 4:4.
Subpoena.
Failure to serve subpoena, VA SCt Rule 4:5(g).
Taking.
Effect of errors and irregularities, VA SCt Rule 4:7(d).
Effect of taking, VA SCt Rule 4:7(c).
Persons before whom depositions may be taken, VA SCt Rule 4:3.
Stipulations, VA SCt Rule 4:4.
Where taken, VA SCt Rule 4:5(a1).
Teleconferencing used to take depositions, VA SCt Rules 4:5(b), 4:7A.
Authorized use, VA SCt Rule 4:7A(a).
Editing, VA SCt Rule 4:7A(c).
Filing, VA SCt Rule 4:7A(g).
Procedure, VA SCt Rule 4:7A(b).
Recording and transcription, VA SCt Rule 4:7A(d).
Submission to witness, changes and signing, VA SCt Rule 4:7A(f).
Use, VA SCt Rule 4:7A(e).
Telephones used to take depositions, VA SCt Rule 4:5(b).
Time.
When depositions may be taken, VA SCt Rule 4:5(a).

PRETRIAL PROCEDURES —Cont'd
Depositions for discovery and use as evidence —Cont'd
United States.
Within the United States, VA SCt Rule 4:3(b).
Use of depositions.
As basis for motion for summary judgment, VA SCt Rule 4:7.
Effect of using, VA SCt Rule 4:7(c).
Video conferencing used to take depositions, VA SCt Rules 4:5(b), 4:7A.
Authorized use, VA SCt Rule 4:7A(a).
Editing, VA SCt Rule 4:7A(c).
Filing, VA SCt Rule 4:7A(g).
Procedure, VA SCt Rule 4:7A(b).
Recording and transcription, VA SCt Rule 4:7A(d).
Submission to witness, changes and signing, VA SCt Rule 4:7A(f).
Use, VA SCt Rule 4:7A(e).
Where depositions taken, VA SCt Rule 4:5(a1).
Within this state, VA SCt Rule 4:3(a).
Witnesses.
Failure to attend, VA SCt Rule 4:5(g).
Submission to witness, VA SCt Rule 4:5(e).
Upon written questions, VA SCt Rule 4:6.
Discovery.
Compelling discovery.
Appropriate court, VA SCt Rule 4:12(a).
Failure to admit.
Expenses, VA SCt Rule 4:12(c).
Failure to comply with order, VA SCt Rule 4:12(b).
Inspection.
Failure of party to respond to request for inspection, VA SCt Rule 4:12(d).
Interrogatories.
Failure of party to serve answer to interrogatories, VA SCt Rule 4:12(d).
Motion for order, VA SCt Rule 4:12(a).
Party.
Failure of party to attend at own deposition, VA SCt Rule 4:12(d).
Sanctions by court in which action is pending, VA SCt Rule 4:12(b).
Disclosures.
Supplementation, VA SCt Rule 4:1(e).
Disposition of discovery material, VA SCt Rule 4:14.
Experts, VA SCt Rule 4:1(b).
Insurance agreements, VA SCt Rule 4:1(b).
Materials, VA SCt Rule 4:1(b).
Methods, VA SCt Rule 4:1(a).
Production of documents and things for inspection, copying or photographing, VA SCt Rule 4:9.
Protective orders, VA SCt Rule 4:1(c).
Responses.
Signing, VA SCt Rule 4:1(g).
Supplementation, VA SCt Rule 4:1(e).
Scope of discovery, VA SCt Rule 4:1(b).
Sequence, VA SCt Rule 4:1(d).
Signing of request, responses and objections, VA SCt Rule 4:1(g).
Time, VA SCt Rule 4:1(d).
Trial preparation, VA SCt Rule 4:1(b).
Disposition of discovery material, VA SCt Rule 4:14.

PRETRIAL PROCEDURES —Cont'd
Documents.
Admission of facts and genuineness of documents, VA SCt Rule 4:11.
Production for inspection, copying or photographing, VA SCt Rule 4:9.
Examination.
Depositions for discovery and use as evidence. See within this heading, "Depositions for discovery and use as evidence."
Physical and mental examination, VA SCt Rule 4:10.
Inspection.
Discovery and production of documents for inspection, VA SCt Rule 4:9.
Failure to respond to request for inspection, VA SCt Rule 4:12(d).
Interrogatories to parties.
Answers, VA SCt Rule 4:8(d).
Availability, VA SCt Rule 4:8(a).
Business records.
Option to produce, VA SCt Rule 4:8(f).
Filing, VA SCt Rule 4:8(c).
Forms, VA SCt Rule 4:8(b).
Limitation on interrogatories, VA SCt Rule 4:8(g).
Options to produce business records, VA SCt Rule 4:8(f).
Procedures for use, VA SCt Rule 4:8(a).
Scope, VA SCt Rule 4:8(e).
Use, VA SCt Rule 4:8(e).
Issues.
Formulating issues, VA SCt Rule 4:13.
Limitation on depositions, VA SCt Rule 4:6A.
Limitation on interrogatories.
Interrogatories to parties, VA SCt Rule 4:8(g).
Limitations for discovery and use as evidence.
Interrogatories to parties.
Limitation on interrogatories, VA SCt Rule 4:8(g).
Maps.
Discovery and production for inspection, copying or photographing, VA SCt Rule 4:9.
Motions.
Production of documents and things by party, VA SCt Rule 4:9(a).
Motions practice, VA SCt Rule 4:15.
Notices.
Depositions for discovery and use as evidence. See within this heading, "Depositions for discovery and use as evidence."
Orders of court.
Order arising from pretrial conference, VA SCt Rule 4:13.
Production of documents and things by persons not a party, VA SCt Rule 4:9(b).
Parties.
Discovery and production of documents and things for inspection, VA SCt Rule 4:9(a).
Interrogatories to parties. See within this heading, "Interrogatories to parties."
Photographing.
Discovery and production of documents and things for photographing, VA SCt Rule 4:9.
Physical examination.
Order for examination, VA SCt Rule 4:10.
Production of documents, VA SCt Rule 4:9.
By a party, VA SCt Rule 4:9(a).
Procedure, VA SCt Rule 4:9(b).

PRETRIAL PROCEDURES —Cont'd
Production of documents —Cont'd
By person not a party, VA SCt Rule 4:9.
Failure or refusal to comply.
Proceedings, VA SCt Rule 4:9(c).
Scope, VA SCt Rule 4:9(a).
Reports.
Physical and mental examination of persons.
Report of findings, VA SCt Rule 4:10.
Service of process.
Generally, VA SCt Rule 4:1(f).
Subpoenas.
Production of documents and things for inspection, copying or photographing.
By person not a party, VA SCt Rule 4:9(b).

PRETRIAL SCHEDULING ORDER, VA SCt Rule 1:18.
Uniform pretrial scheduling order, VA SCt Rule Pt 1 Appx Form 3.

PRICE OF GOODS.
Hearsay exceptions, VA SCt Rule 2:803.

PRIEST-PENITENT PRIVILEGE, VA SCt Rule 2:503.

PRIOR INCONSISTENT STATEMENTS.
Criminal cases, VA SCt Rule 2:613.
Impeachment of witness, VA SCt Rule 2:613.

PRISONERS.
Actual innocence.
Petition for writ of actual innocence, VA SCt Rule 5:7B, VA SCt Rule Pt 5A Appx Form 12, VA SCt Rule Pt 5 Appx Form 12.
Notice of appeal to supreme court.
Timely filing, VA SCt Rule 5:5.
Petition for appeal to supreme court.
Considered without oral argument.
Inmate not represented by counsel, VA SCt Rule 5:17.
Timely filing of paper by inmate, VA SCt Rule 5A:3.
Postconviction proceedings, VA SCt Rule 3A:25.

PRIVILEGE.
Attorney-client privilege.
Duty to protect information, VA SCt Rule 1:6, VA SCt Rule Pt 6 §II.
Evidence, VA SCt Rule 2:502.
Professional corporations and limited liability entities, VA SCt Rule Pt 6 §IV Par 14.
Attorney-work product privilege, VA SCt Rule 4:1.
Cleric-penitent privilege, VA SCt Rule 2:503.
Evidence, VA SCt Rules 2:501 to 2:507.
Attorney-client privilege, VA SCt Rule 2:502.
Cleric-penitent privilege, VA SCt Rule 2:503.
Common law interpretation, VA SCt Rule 2:501.
General rule, VA SCt Rule 2:501.
Interpreters for deaf or non-English speaking persons, VA SCt Rule 2:507.
Marriage and family therapist-client privilege, VA SCt Rule 2:506.
Physician-patient privilege, VA SCt Rule 2:505.
Preliminary determinations, VA SCt Rule 2:104.
Professional counselor-client privilege, VA SCt Rule 2:506.
Psychologist-client privilege, VA SCt Rule 2:506.
Social worker-client privilege, VA SCt Rule 2:506.
Spousal privilege, VA SCt Rule 2:504.

PRIVILEGE —Cont'd
Healing arts privilege.
Communications between physicians and patients, VA SCt Rule 2:505.
Husband and wife, VA SCt Rule 2:504.
Evidence, VA SCt Rule 2:504.
Interpreters for deaf or non-English speaking persons, VA SCt Rule 2:507.
Marriage and family therapist-client privilege, VA SCt Rule 2:506.
Physician-patient privilege, VA SCt Rule 2:505.
Priest-penitent privilege, VA SCt Rule 2:503.
Professional counselor-client privilege, VA SCt Rule 2:506.
Psychologist-client privilege, VA SCt Rule 2:506.
Clinical psychologists, VA SCt Rule 2:505.
Rabbi-penitent privilege, VA SCt Rule 2:503.
Social worker-client privilege, VA SCt Rule 2:506.
Spousal privilege, VA SCt Rule 2:504.

PRIVITY.
Res judicata, preclusion of claims, effect, VA SCt Rule 1:6.

PRO BONO PUBLIC SERVICE, VA SCt Rule Pt 6 §II Rule 6.1.

PRODUCTION OF DOCUMENTS AND THINGS.
Criminal cases, VA SCt Rule 3A:12.
Juvenile and domestic relations district courts.
Subpoenas duces tecum, VA SCt Rule 8:13.
Non-parties.
Production by a person not party, VA SCt Rule 4:9A.
Pretrial procedures.
Generally, VA SCt Rule 4:9.
Uniform interstate depositions and discovery act.
Electronically stored information.
Production of, subject to act, VA SCt Rule 4:9.

PROFESSIONAL COUNSELOR-CLIENT PRIVILEGE, VA SCt Rule 2:506.

PRO HAC VICE.
Out-of-state attorneys, VA SCt Rule 1A:4.
Application to appear pro hac vice before a Virginia tribunal, VA SCt Rule Pt 1A Appx Form 1.

PROHIBITION.
Supreme court.
Jurisdiction, VA SCt Rule 5:7.

PROOF OF SERVICE.
Civil actions, VA SCt Rule 3:6.

PROSECUTING ATTORNEYS.
Professional responsibility, VA SCt Rule Pt 6 §II Rule 3.8.

PSYCHOLOGIST-CLIENT PRIVILEGE, VA SCt Rule 2:506.
Clinical psychologist, VA SCt Rule 2:505.

PUBLIC HEALTH THREATS.
Order of quarantine or isolation.
Appeal of circuit court order, VA SCt Rule 5:41.
Circuit court proceedings, VA SCt Rule 3:24.
Isolation proceedings, VA SCt Rule 7A:16.

PUNISHMENT PHASE OF TRIAL.
Bifurcated proceeding upon jury finding of guilt, VA SCt Rule 3A:17.1.

Q

QUARANTINE.
Public health threats, order of quarantine or isolation.
Appeal of circuit court order, VA SCt Rule 5:41.
Circuit court proceedings, VA SCt Rule 3:24.
Isolation proceedings, VA SCt Rule 7A:16.

QUESTIONS OF LAW.
Certification, VA SCt Rule 5:40.

QUESTIONS PRESENTED.
Petition for appeal, VA SCt Rule 5:17.

R

RABBI-PENITENT PRIVILEGE, VA SCt Rule 2:503.

RAILROAD CARS.
Boarding or riding without paying fare.
Uniform fine schedule, VA SCt Rule 3C:2.

REAL PROPERTY.
Hearsay exceptions.
Interest in property, records or documents affecting, VA SCt Rule 2:803.

RECORD ON APPEAL.
Administrative process act, VA SCt Rule 2A:3.
Contents, VA SCt Rule 2A:3(c).
Electronic or digital records, VA SCt Rule 2A:3(d).
Large or burdensome records, leave to file index of record, VA SCt Rule 2A:3(e).
Preparation and certification of record, VA SCt Rule 2A:3(b).
Transcript of formal hearing, VA SCt Rule 2A:3(a).

RECORD RELEVANT FOR REVIEW.
Death sentence imposed, VA SCt Rule 5:22.

RECORDS.
Attorney discipline.
Clerk of the disciplinary system, VA SCt Rule Pt 6 §IV Par 13-9.
Confidentiality, VA SCt Rule Pt 6 §IV Par 13-30.
Attorneys at law.
Rules of professional conduct.
Safekeeping property, VA SCt Rule Pt 6 §II Rule 1.15.
Evidence.
Hearsay exceptions.
Business records, VA SCt Rule 2:803.
Family records, VA SCt Rule 2:803.
Public records or reports, VA SCt Rule 2:803.
Recorded recollection, VA SCt Rule 2:803.
Self-authentication, VA SCt Rule 2:902.
Hearsay exceptions.
Business records, VA SCt Rule 2:803.
Family records, VA SCt Rule 2:803.
Public records or reports, VA SCt Rule 2:803.
Recorded recollection, VA SCt Rule 2:803.
Juvenile and domestic relations district courts.
Request for production.
Subpoenas duces tecum, VA SCt Rule 8:13.

RECORDS —Cont'd
Preservation of records.
Photographic or electronic means, VA SCt Rule 1:14.
District courts, VA SCt Rule 7A:6.
Juvenile and domestic relations district courts, VA SCt Rule 8:12.

REHEARINGS, VA SCt Rule 5:37.
Court of appeals.
Petition for rehearing.
Criminal cases and traffic infractions, VA SCt Rule 5A:15A.
Scope of rules, VA SCt Rule 5A:32.
Petition for appeal, VA SCt Rule 5:37.
Petition for rehearing.
Court of appeals.
En banc, VA SCt Rule 5A:34.
Format, VA SCt Rule 5A:33(a).
Denial of appeal by court of appeals, VA SCt Rule 5A:15.
Format of petition, VA SCt Rules 5:20, 5:20A.
Supreme court, VA SCt Rule 5:37.
Petition on denial of appeal.
Format, VA SCt Rules 5:20, 5:20A.
Supreme court.
Petition for rehearing, VA SCt Rule 5:37.

RELIGION.
Hearsay exceptions.
Baptismal certificates, VA SCt Rule 2:803.
Religious organizations, records, VA SCt Rule 2:803.
Privileged communications.
Penitent privilege, VA SCt Rule 2:503.

REMEDIAL MEASURES.
Evidence.
Subsequent remedial measures, relevancy, VA SCt Rule 2:407.

REMOVAL OF CAUSES.
Civil procedure.
Application of rules in cases removed to circuit courts, VA SCt Rule 3:1.

REPLIES.
Civil actions, VA SCt Rule 3:11.

REPORTERS.
Circuit courts.
Transcripts of proceedings.
Oath, VA SCt Rule 1:3.
Oath of reporter, VA SCt Rule 1:3.
Persons entitled to transcript, VA SCt Rule 1:3.
Procedure, VA SCt Rule 1:3.
Recording device, VA SCt Rule 1:3.
Juvenile and domestic relations district courts.
Transcripts of proceedings, VA SCt Rule 8:11.

REPORTS.
Attorneys at law.
Rules of professional conduct.
Professional misconduct, VA SCt Rule Pt 6 §II Rule 8.3.
Safekeeping property, VA SCt Rule Pt 6 §II Rule 1.15.
Hearsay exceptions.
Public records or reports, VA SCt Rule 2:803.
Juvenile and domestic relations district courts.
Court-ordered reports, VA SCt Rule 8:5.

REPUTATION EVIDENCE.
Hearsay exceptions.
Reputation as to character trait, VA SCt Rule 2:803.
Impeachment of witnesses.
Reputation for truthtelling, VA SCt Rule 2:608.

RES JUDICATA.
Preclusion of claims, VA SCt Rule 1:6.

RETRIAL.
Mistrial upon non-unanimous verdict at penalty phase, VA SCt Rule 3A:17.1.

RETURN OF WRITS.
Civil procedure, VA SCt Rule 3:3.

RULE ON WITNESSES, VA SCt Rule 2:615.

RULES OF PRACTICE AND PROCEDURE.
Non-compliance, sanctions, VA SCt Rule 5:1A.

S

SANCTIONS.
Discovery, VA SCt Rule 4:12.

SCHEDULING CIVIL CASES FOR TRIAL, VA SCt Rule 1:20.

SCHEDULING HEARINGS ON WRITTEN MOTIONS, VA SCt Rule 4:15.

SCOPE OF RULES, VA SCt Rule 5:1.

SENTENCE.
Bifurcated jury trial on finding of guilt for non-capital felony, VA SCt Rule 3A:17.1.
Sentencing orders, VA SCt Rule Pt 3A Appx Form 10.

SEPARATE TRIALS.
Civil procedure.
Cross-claims, VA SCt Rule 3:10.

SEQUESTRATION OF WITNESSES, VA SCt Rule 2:615.

SERVICE OF PROCESS.
Actual innocence.
Petition for writ of actual innocence, VA SCt Rule 5:7B.
Admissions in evidence.
Service of request for admission, VA SCt Rule 4:11.
Attorney discipline, VA SCt Rule Pt 6 §IV Par 13-12.
Attorneys at law.
Firm.
Service on one member or associate, VA SCt Rule 1:5.
Foreign attorneys, VA SCt Rule 1A:4.
Not required to be served, VA SCt Rule 1:5.
Briefs.
Motions practice, filing and serving, VA SCt Rule 4:15.
Circuit courts.
Civil actions.
Proof of service, VA SCt Rule 3:6.
Summons, VA SCt Rule 3:5.
Civil actions.
Proof of service, VA SCt Rule 3:6.
Summons, VA SCt Rule 3:5.
Computation of time, VA SCt Rule 1:7.
Electronic filing and service, VA SCt Rule 1:17.

SERVICE OF PROCESS —Cont'd
Court of appeals, VA SCt Rule 5A:1.
Criminal procedure.
See CRIMINAL PROCEDURE.
Electronic filing and service, VA SCt Rule 1:17.
Practice and procedure, VA SCt Rule 1:17(d).
Juvenile and domestic relations district courts.
Child support.
Motion to reduce support arrearages to judgment, VA SCt Rule 8:4.
Motions.
Definition of served for purposes of motions practice, VA SCt Rule 4:15.
Service of papers after initial process, VA SCt Rule 1:12.
Pleading.
Service of papers after initial process, VA SCt Rule 1:12.
Pretrial procedures, VA SCt Rule 4:1(f).
Proof of service.
Circuit courts.
Civil actions, VA SCt Rule 3:6.
Subpoena.
Criminal procedure, VA SCt Rule 3A:12.
Summons.
Civil actions.
Circuit courts, VA SCt Rule 3:5.
Supreme court.
Generally, VA SCt Rule 5:1.

SESSIONS, VA SCt Rule 5:2.

SETTLEMENTS.
Court of appeals.
Pending appeal, VA SCt Rule 5A:36.
Settlement conference, VA SCt Rule 5A:37.
Supreme court.
Settlement of pending appeal, VA SCt Rule 5:38.

SEVERANCE.
Severance of trials, VA SCt Rule 3A:10.

SEXUAL ASSAULT.
Evidence.
Hearsay exceptions.
Recent complaints, VA SCt Rule 2:803.
Prior sexual conduct, VA SCt Rule 2:412.
False accusations.
Impeachment of witnesses, prior false accusations in sexual assault cases, VA SCt Rule 2:608.
Prior sexual conduct.
Evidence, VA SCt Rule 2:412.
Witnesses.
Impeachment, prior false accusations in sexual assault cases, VA SCt Rule 2:608.

SIZE OF PAPER, VA SCt Rule 1:16(a).
District court papers, VA SCt Rule 7A:7.
Electronic filing and service.
Applicability of provisions, VA SCt Rule 1:17.
Juvenile and domestic relations district courts, VA SCt Rule 8:7.
Nonconforming paper may be required to be redone to comply, VA SCt Rule 1:16(b).

SMALL BUSINESSES.
Administrative process act.
Small business challenges, VA SCt Rule 2A:6.

SOCIAL WORKER-CLIENT PRIVILEGE, VA SCt Rule 2:506.

SPECIAL RULES.
Appeals from the state corporation commission, VA SCt Rule 5:21.
Cases in which sentence of death has been imposed, VA SCt Rule 5:22.

SPEECH-IMPAIRED PERSONS.
Interpreters.
Privilege, evidence, VA SCt Rule 2:507.

SPOUSAL PRIVILEGE, VA SCt Rule 2:504.

STATE BAR.
Active members, VA SCt Rule Pt 6 §IV Par 3.
Address of record.
Each member to submit, VA SCt Rule Pt 6 §IV Par 3.
Annual meeting of the Virginia state bar, VA SCt Rule Pt 6 §IV Par 8.
Appeals from disciplinary board or circuit court determination, VA SCt Rule 5:21.
Associate members, VA SCt Rule Pt 6 §IV Par 3.
Bar counsel.
Disciplining, suspending and disbarring attorneys, VA SCt Rule Pt 6 §IV Par 13.
Bar disciplinary board.
Appeals from, VA SCt Rule 5:21.
Disciplining, suspending and disbarring attorneys, VA SCt Rule Pt 6 §IV Par 13.
Classes of membership, VA SCt Rule Pt 6 §IV Par 3.
Clerk of the disciplinary system.
Disciplining, suspending and disbarring attorneys, VA SCt Rule Pt 6 §IV Par 13.
Clients' protection fund.
Council may establish, VA SCt Rule Pt 6 §IV Par 16.
COLD.
Standing committee on lawyer discipline.
Disciplining, suspending and disbarring attorneys, VA SCt Rule Pt 6 §IV Par 13.
Continuing legal education rule, VA SCt Rule Pt 6 §IV Par 17.
Suspension for failure to complete requirement, VA SCt Rule Pt 6 §IV Par 13.2.
Council, VA SCt Rule Pt 6 §IV Par 5.
Election of council, VA SCt Rule Pt 6 §IV Par 6.
Meetings of the council, VA SCt Rule Pt 6 §IV Par 7.
Powers of the council, VA SCt Rule Pt 6 §IV Par 9.
Disabled and retired members, VA SCt Rule Pt 6 §IV Par 3.
Disbarring attorneys.
Procedure for disbarring, VA SCt Rule Pt 6 §IV Par 13.
Disbursements, VA SCt Rule Pt 6 §IV Par 12.
Disciplinary rules of the code of professional responsibility.
See ATTORNEYS AT LAW.
Disciplining attorneys.
Appeals from disciplinary board or circuit court determination, VA SCt Rule 5:21.
Procedure for disciplining, VA SCt Rule Pt 6 §IV Par 13.
District committees.
Disciplining, suspending and disbarring attorneys, VA SCt Rule Pt 6 §IV Par 13.
Dues, VA SCt Rule Pt 6 §IV Par 11.

STATE BAR —Cont'd
Education.
Continuing legal education requirements, VA SCt Rule Pt 6 §IV Par 17.
Suspension for failure to complete, VA SCt Rule Pt 6 §IV Par 13.2.
Election of council, VA SCt Rule Pt 6 §IV Par 6.
Emeritus members, VA SCt Rule Pt 6 §IV Par 3.
Financial responsibility.
Required of members, VA SCt Rule Pt 6 §IV Par 18.
Impairment proceedings.
Disciplining, suspending and disbarring attorneys, VA SCt Rule Pt 6 §IV Par 13.
Interest on lawyers' trust accounts, VA SCt Rule Pt 6 §IV Par 20.
Judicial members, VA SCt Rule Pt 6 §IV Par 3.
Law corporations, VA SCt Rule Pt 6 §IV Par 14.
Legal ethics.
Promulgation of legal ethics opinions, VA SCt Rule Pt 6 §IV Par 10.
Suspension for failure to complete legal ethics course, VA SCt Rule Pt 6 §IV Par 13.1.
Meetings of the council, VA SCt Rule Pt 6 §IV Par 7.
Membership, VA SCt Rule Pt 6 §IV Par 2.
Classes of membership, VA SCt Rule Pt 6 §IV Par 3.
Name, VA SCt Rule Pt 6 §IV Par 1.
Officers, VA SCt Rule Pt 6 §IV Par 4.
Powers of the council, VA SCt Rule Pt 6 §IV Par 9.
Resignation of attorney.
Procedure, VA SCt Rule Pt 6 §IV Par 13.
Rules of court.
Promulgation of rules of court, VA SCt Rule Pt 6 §IV Par 10.
Standing committee on lawyer discipline (COLD).
Disciplining, suspending and disbarring attorneys, VA SCt Rule Pt 6 §IV Par 13.
Suspending attorneys.
Administrative suspension.
Procedure, VA SCt Rule Pt 6 §IV Par 19.
Procedure for suspending, VA SCt Rule Pt 6 §IV Par 13.
Third year student practice rule, VA SCt Rule Pt 6 §IV Par 15.
Trust accounts, VA SCt Rule Pt 6 §IV Par 20.
Unauthorized practice of law.
Attorneys at law.
See ATTORNEYS AT LAW.
Promulgation of unauthorized practice of law opinions, VA SCt Rule Pt 6 §IV Par 10.

STATE CORPORATION COMMISSION.
Appeals.
Special rules applicable to appeals from the state corporation commission, VA SCt Rule 5:21.
Notice of decision and order, VA SCt Rule 5:34.

STATE HEALTH COMMISSIONER.
Public health threats, order of quarantine or isolation.
Appeal of circuit court order, VA SCt Rule 5:41.
Circuit court proceedings, VA SCt Rule 3:24.
Isolation proceedings, VA SCt Rule 7A:16.

STATE PARKS.
Uniform fine schedule, VA SCt Rule 3C:2.

STATUTE OF LIMITATIONS.
Circuit courts.
Pleading, VA SCt Rule 3:18.
Civil procedure.
Pleading, VA SCt Rule 3:18.

STRIKING EVIDENCE.
Motion to strike.
See EVIDENCE.

SUBPOENAS.
Attorney discipline.
District committees proceedings, VA SCt Rule Pt 6 §IV Par 13-16.
Limited right to discovery, VA SCt Rule Pt 6 §IV Par 13-11.
Attorney issued subpoena duces tecum, VA SCt Rule 4:9.
Criminal procedure, VA SCt Rule 3A:12.
Forms, VA SCt Rule Pt 3A Appx Form 8.
District courts.
Witnesses.
Requests for subpoenas, VA SCt Rule 7A:12.
Form, VA SCt Rule Pt 3A Appx Form 8.
Juvenile and domestic relations district courts.
Production of documents, VA SCt Rule 8:13.
Witnesses, VA SCt Rule 8:13.

SUBPOENAS DUCES TECUM.
Attorney issued, VA SCt Rule 4:9.
Clerks of court, subpoenas issued by.
Production by a person not party, VA SCt Rule 4:9A.
Copies.
Subpoenaing party to supply copies, upon request, to court and other parties, VA SCt Rule 4:9.
Criminal procedure, VA SCt Rule 3A:12.
Copying documents, VA SCt Rule 3A:12.
Forms, VA SCt Rule Pt 3A Appx Form 9.
District courts.
Request for subpoenas duces tecum, VA SCt Rule 7A:10.
Copies to be furnished, VA SCt Rule 7A:10.
Form, VA SCt Rule Pt 3A Appx Form 9.
Juvenile and domestic relations district courts.
Production of documents, VA SCt Rule 8:13.
Production by a person not party.
Subpoenas issued by clerk of court, VA SCt Rule 4:9A.

SUBSEQUENT REMEDIAL MEASURES.
Evidence, relevancy, VA SCt Rule 2:407.

SUBSTITUTION OF PARTIES.
Circuit courts, VA SCt Rule 3:17.
Civil procedure, VA SCt Rule 3:17.

SUMMARY JUDGMENT.
Circuit courts, VA SCt Rule 3:20.
Civil procedure, VA SCt Rule 3:20.
Depositions.
Limitation on use, VA SCt Rule 4:7.

SUMMONS.
Attorney discipline.
District committees proceedings, VA SCt Rule Pt 6 §IV Par 13-16.
Limited right to discovery, VA SCt Rule Pt 6 §IV Par 13-11.

SUMMONS —Cont'd
Civil procedure.
Form, VA SCt Rule 3:5.
Criminal procedure.
See CRIMINAL PROCEDURE.
District courts.
Criminal procedure, VA SCt Rule 7C:3.
Form, VA SCt Rule Pt 3A Appx Form 3.

SUPPORT AND MAINTENANCE.
Juvenile and domestic relations district courts.
Motion to reduce support arrearages to judgment.
Service of process, VA SCt Rule 8:4.
Petition for support of spouse or child.
Contents, VA SCt Rule 8:3.
Spousal support.
Motion to reduce support arrearages to judgment.
Service of process, VA SCt Rule 8:4.

SUPREME COURT OF UNITED STATES.
Certification of questions of law.
Certification procedures, VA SCt Rule 5:40.
Virginia supreme court.
Procedure upon appeal or petition to United States supreme court, VA SCt Rule 5:39.

SYNAGOGUES.
Rabbi-penitent privilege, VA SCt Rule 2:503.

T

TELECONFERENCING.
Depositions, VA SCt Rules 4:5(b), 4:7A.
Authorized use, VA SCt Rule 4:7A(a).
Editing, VA SCt Rule 4:7A(c).
Filing, VA SCt Rule 4:7A(g).
Procedure, VA SCt Rule 4:7A(b).
Recording and transcription, VA SCt Rule 4:7A(d).
Submission to witness, changes and signing, VA SCt Rule 4:7A(f).
Use, VA SCt Rule 4:7A(e).

TELEPHONES.
Depositions taken by telephone, VA SCt Rule 4:5(b).

TERMS OF COURT.
Circuit courts.
Times for commencing regular terms, VA SCt Rule 1:15 Sched.

THIRD-PARTY CLAIMS.
Circuit courts, VA SCt Rule 3:13.
Civil procedure, VA SCt Rule 3:13.
District courts, VA SCt Rule 7B:10.

TIME.
Actual innocence.
Petition for writ of actual innocence, VA SCt Rule 5:7B.
Assignments or error.
Filing in cases when death sentence imposed, VA SCt Rule 5:22.
Computation of time, VA SCt Rule 1:7.
District courts, VA SCt Rule 7A:2.
Electronic filing and service, VA SCt Rule 1:17.
Criminal procedure.
Extension, VA SCt Rule 3A:20.

TIME —Cont'd
Criminal procedure —Cont'd
Unaffected by expiration of term of court, VA SCt Rule 3A:20.
Death sentence imposed.
Filing assignments of error and record relevant for review, VA SCt Rule 5:22.
District courts.
Computation of time, VA SCt Rule 7A:2.
Inmate filing paper.
Timely filing, VA SCt Rule 5A:3.
Postconviction proceedings, VA SCt Rule 3A:25.
Petition for appeal, filing, VA SCt Rule 5:17.
Petition for rehearing, filing.
Denial of appeal by court of appeals, VA SCt Rule 5A:15.
Record relevant for review.
Filing in cases when death sentence imposed, VA SCt Rule 5:22.
Supreme court of United States.
Appeals to.
Deferred mandate by Virginia supreme court, VA SCt Rule 5:39.

TRAFFIC INFRACTIONS.
District courts.
Applicability of rules, VA SCt Rule 7C:1.
Complaint, warrant, summons and capias, VA SCt Rule 7C:3.
Venue, VA SCt Rule 7C:2.
Purpose, VA SCt Rule 3B:1.
Uniform fine schedule, VA SCt Rule 3B:2.

TRANSCRIPTS.
Administrative process act.
Transcript of formal hearing, VA SCt Rule 2A:3(a).
Circuit courts, VA SCt Rule 1:3.
District courts, VA SCt Rule 7A:4.
Juvenile and domestic relations district courts.
Court proceedings, VA SCt Rule 8:11.

TRIAL.
Criminal cases, VA SCt Rule 3A:13.
Bifurcated jury trials of non-capital felonies, VA SCt Rule 3A:17.1.
District courts, VA SCt Rule 7C:4.
Joinder of defendants, VA SCt Rules 3A:10, 7C:4.
Severance of defendants, VA SCt Rules 3A:10, 7C:4.
District courts.
Consolidation of actions, VA SCt Rule 7B:10.
Criminal procedure.
Multiple defendants or multiple offenses, VA SCt Rule 7C:4.
Method of bringing action, VA SCt Rule 7B:4.
Preservation of records by photographic or electronic means, VA SCt Rule 7A:6.
When action heard, VA SCt Rule 7B:4.
Publicity.
Attorneys at law.
Professional responsibility, VA SCt Rule Pt 6 §II Rule 3.5.
Scheduling civil cases for trial, VA SCt Rule 1:20.

TRIAL DATE.
Pretrial scheduling conference, VA SCt Rule 1:18.
Uniform pretrial scheduling order, VA SCt Rule Pt 1 Appx Form 3.
Scheduling civil cases for trial, VA SCt Rule 1:20.

TRUST ACCOUNTS.
Attorneys at law.
IOLTA accounts generally, VA SCt Rule Pt 6 §IV Par 20.
Maintenance of trust accounts generally, VA SCt Rule Pt 6 §IV Par 20.
Virginia State Bar approved financial institution agreement, VA SCt Rule Pt 6 §IV Appx A.

TRUTHFULNESS.
Impeachment of witnesses.
Reputation for truthtelling, VA SCt Rule 2:608.

U

UNAUTHORIZED PRACTICE OF LAW.
See ATTORNEYS AT LAW.

UNIFORM FINE SCHEDULE.
Non-traffic prepayable offenses and uniform fine schedule, VA SCt Rule 3C:2.
Traffic infractions, VA SCt Rule 3B:2.

UNIFORM PRETRIAL SCHEDULING ORDER, VA SCt Rule 1:18.
Uniform pretrial scheduling order, VA SCt Rule Pt 1 Appx Form 3.

UNITED STATES SUPREME COURT.
Certification of questions of law, VA SCt Rule 5:40.
Procedure upon appeal or petition to supreme court of the United States, VA SCt Rule 5:39.

UNPUBLISHED DISPOSITIONS, CITING, VA SCt Rule 5:1.
Court of appeals, VA SCt Rule 5A:1.

URINE TESTS.
Discovery, VA SCt Rule 3A:11.

V

VENUE.
Criminal procedure.
District courts, VA SCt Rule 7C:2.
When questions raised, VA SCt Rule 3A:2.1.
District courts.
Civil procedure.
Motion to transfer, VA SCt Rule 7B:11.
Criminal procedure, VA SCt Rule 7C:2.
Juvenile and domestic relations district courts.
Motions to transfer venue, VA SCt Rule 8:10.

VERDICT.
Criminal procedure.
See CRIMINAL PROCEDURE.

VERIFICATION.
District courts.
Civil procedure, VA SCt Rule 7B:6.
Pleading.
Electronic filing and service, VA SCt Rule 1:17.

VERIFICATION —Cont'd
Pleading —Cont'd
General provisions, VA SCt Rule 1:10.

VICTIMS OF CRIME.
Exclusion from criminal trials, VA SCt Rule 2:615.

VIDEO CONFERENCING.
Depositions, VA SCt Rules 4:5(b), 4:7A.
Authorized use, VA SCt Rule 4:7A(a).
Editing, VA SCt Rule 4:7A(c).
Filing, VA SCt Rule 4:7A(g).
Procedure, VA SCt Rule 4:7A(b).
Recording and transcription, VA SCt Rule 4:7A(d).
Submission to witness, changes and signing, VA SCt Rule 4:7A(f).
Use, VA SCt Rule 4:7A(c).

VIRGINIA STATE BAR.
Computerized legal research.
Virginia state bar ordered to contract to provide, VA SCt Rule Pt 6 §IV Par 21.
Online legal research.
Virginia state bar ordered to contract to provide, VA SCt Rule Pt 6 §IV Par 21.

VITAL RECORDS.
Hearsay exceptions, VA SCt Rule 2:803.

VOLUNTARY PRO BONO PUBLIC SERVICE, VA SCt Rule Pt 6 §II Rule 6.1.

W

WARRANT.
Arrest warrant, VA SCt Rule 3A:4.
Forms, VA SCt Rule Pt 3A Appx Form 2.
District courts.
Criminal procedure, VA SCt Rule 7C:3.

WITNESSES, VA SCt Rules 2:601 to 2:615.
Adverse interests.
Impeachment, VA SCt Rule 2:607.
Affirmation, VA SCt Rule 2:603.
Attorney discipline.
District committees proceedings, VA SCt Rule Pt 6 §IV Par 13-16.
Reinstatement.
Character witnesses, VA SCt Rule Pt 6 §IV Par 13-25.
Attorneys at law.
Rules of professional conduct.
Lawyer as witness, VA SCt Rule Pt 6 §II Rule 3.7.
Bias, VA SCt Rule 2:610.
Calling by court, VA SCt Rule 2:614.
Cleric-penitent privilege, VA SCt Rule 2:503.
Competency.
Certain judicial officers in criminal cases, VA SCt Rule 2:605.
Clerks of court, VA SCt Rule 2:605.
Court personnel, VA SCt Rule 2:605.
General rule, VA SCt Rule 2:601.
Judges, VA SCt Rule 2:605.
Jurors, VA SCt Rule 2:606.
Rulings, incompetency, VA SCt Rule 2:601.
Contradiction.
Prior inconsistent statements, VA SCt Rule 2:613.

WITNESSES —Cont'd
Court personnel.
Competency, VA SCt Rule 2:605.
Credibility.
Hearsay exceptions.
Attacking and supporting credibility of hearsay declarant, VA SCt Rule 2:806.
Preliminary determinations, VA SCt Rule 2:104.
Criminal cases.
Judicial officers.
Competency to testify, VA SCt Rule 2:605.
Prior inconsistent statements reduced to writing, VA SCt Rule 2:613.
Subpoena, VA SCt Rule 3A:12.
Cross-examination.
Scope, VA SCt Rule 2:611.
District courts.
Subpoenas.
Requests for subpoenas, VA SCt Rule 7A:12.
Evidence rules, VA SCt Rules 2:601 to 2:615.
Exclusion of witnesses, VA SCt Rule 2:615.
Expert witnesses, VA SCt Rules 2:701 to 2:706.
Basis of expert testimony, VA SCt Rule 2:703.
Exclusion, VA SCt Rule 2:615.
Facts or data used in testimony, VA SCt Rule 2:705.
Learned treatises, VA SCt Rule 2:706.
Hearsay exceptions, VA SCt Rule 2:803.
Opinion testimony, VA SCt Rule 2:702.
Lay witnesses, VA SCt Rule 2:701.
Ultimate issue, VA SCt Rule 2:704.
Use of experts generally, VA SCt Rule 2:702.
Hearsay exceptions.
Credibility.
Attacking and supporting credibility of hearsay declarant, VA SCt Rule 2:806.
Dead man rule, VA SCt Rule 2:805.
Identification, statement by witness, VA SCt Rule 2:803.
Identification, statement by witness.
Hearsay exceptions, VA SCt Rule 2:803.
Impeachment, VA SCt Rule 2:607.
Adverse interests, VA SCt Rule 2:607.
Character witness, cross-examination, VA SCt Rule 2:608.
Conviction of crime, VA SCt Rule 2:609.
Grounds, VA SCt Rule 2:607.
Perjury, unadjudicated, VA SCt Rule 2:608.
Prior false accusations, sexual assault cases, VA SCt Rule 2:608.
Prior inconsistent statement, VA SCt Rule 2:613.
Reputation for truthtelling, VA SCt Rule 2:608.
Specific instances of conduct, VA SCt Rule 2:608.
Interpreters, VA SCt Rule 2:604.
Interrogation.
By court, VA SCt Rule 2:614.
Mode and order of interrogation and presentation, VA SCt Rule 2:611.
Jurors as witnesses.
Competency, VA SCt Rule 2:606.
Juvenile and domestic relations district courts.
Subpoenas for witnesses, VA SCt Rule 8:13.
Lack of personal knowledge, VA SCt Rule 2:602.

WITNESSES —Cont'd
Leading questions, VA SCt Rule 2:611.
Learned treatises.
Expert witnesses, VA SCt Rule 2:706.
Mode and order of interrogation and presentation, VA SCt Rule 2:611.
Oaths, VA SCt Rule 2:603.
Opinion testimony.
Expert witnesses, VA SCt Rule 2:702.
Ultimate issue, VA SCt Rule 2:704.
Lay witnesses, VA SCt Rule 2:701.
Ultimate fact in issue, VA SCt Rule 2:704.
Order of interrogation and presentation, VA SCt Rule 2:611.
Personal knowledge or experience.
Lack of, VA SCt Rule 2:602.
Opinion testimony by lay witnesses, VA SCt Rule 2:701.
Physician-patient privilege, VA SCt Rule 2:505.
Prejudice, VA SCt Rule 2:610.
Presentation of evidence.
Mode and order of interrogation and presentation, VA SCt Rule 2:611.
Priest-penitent privilege, VA SCt Rule 2:503.
Prior inconsistent statements.
Impeaching witness proving adverse, VA SCt Rule 2:613.
Prior sexual conduct.
Evidence, VA SCt Rule 2:412.
Professional counselor-client privilege, VA SCt Rule 2:506.
Psychologist-client privilege, VA SCt Rule 2:506.
Clinical psychologist, VA SCt Rule 2:505.
Qualifications.
Preliminary determinations, VA SCt Rule 2:104.
Rabbi-penitent privilege, VA SCt Rule 2:503.
Refreshing memory, use of writings, VA SCt Rule 2:612.
Rule on witnesses, VA SCt Rule 2:615.
Sequestration, VA SCt Rule 2:615.
Social worker-client privilege, VA SCt Rule 2:506.
Writing used to refresh memory, VA SCt Rule 2:612.

WORKERS' COMPENSATION COMMISSION.
Appeals.
Provisions for appeals from commission, VA SCt Rule 5A:11.

WORK-PRODUCT.
Discovery of trial preparation materials, VA SCt Rule 4:1.

WRITINGS USED TO REFRESH MEMORY.
Witnesses, VA SCt Rule 2:612.

WRITS.
Actual innocence.
Petition for writ of actual innocence, VA SCt Rule 5:7B, VA SCt Rule Pt 5A Appx Form 12, VA SCt Rule Pt 5 Appx Form 12.
Civil procedure.
Return of writs, VA SCt Rule 3:3.
Mandamus and prohibition.
Jurisdiction of court, VA SCt Rule 5:7.

MEDICAL MALPRACTICE RULES OF PRACTICE

Rule
1. Applicability; Definitions.
2. Request for Medical Malpractice Review Panel.
3. Designation of Panel; Certificate of Parties.
4. Convening of Panel.
5. Request for Ore Tenus Hearing.
6. Conduct of an Ore Tenus Hearing.

Rule
7. Expenses and Costs.

Appendix of Forms.

Subpoena.
Subpoena Duces Tecum.
Index.

Note. — These are the rules promulgated by the Chief Justice of the Supreme Court of Virginia pursuant to § 8.01-581.11 of the Code of Virginia to carry out the provisions of Chapter 21.1 of Title 8.01 of the Virginia Code as added by Chapter 611 of the Acts of Assembly of 1976. They were promulgated by the Chief Justice on June 20, 1977, and became effective on July 1, 1977, and were revised effective July 1, 1978, and effective Aug. 15, 1979. They were amended February 28, 2006.

Rule 1. Applicability; Definitions.

(a) These Rules are promulgated in accordance with Section 8.01-581.11 of the Code of Virginia and shall govern all formal proceedings instituted pursuant to the provisions of Chapter 21.1 of Title 8.01 with respect to the activities of a duly constituted Medical Malpractice Review Panel. The Rules shall not apply to any cause of action which arose prior to July 1, 1976, the effective date of Chapter 21.1 of Title 8.01 unless the claimant has filed* notice under § 8.01-581.2 and such filing occurred prior to the expiration of any applicable statute of limitation.

(b) References herein to "it" and "its" shall apply equally to "him," "his," or "her." The singular shall include the plural. Terms used in this part that are defined in Chapter 21.1 of Title 8.01 are used with the definitions therein contained.

Law Review. — For an article, "The Quiet Demise of Deference to Custom: Malpractice Law at the Millenium," see 57 Wash. & Lee L. Rev. 163 (2000). For annual survey article discussing the state of health care law in Virginia, see 38 U. Rich. L. Rev. 137 (2003).

Research References. — Roscoe N. Gray, Attorneys' Textbook of Medicine (Matthew Bender).

Rule 2. Request for Medical Malpractice Review Panel.

(a) *Request for Panel.* — The plaintiff or any defendant health care provider may, within thirty days from the filing of the responsive pleading in any action brought for malpractice against a health care provider, file a written request for a review by a panel with the clerk of the Supreme Court of Virginia. The request for review of such claim by a panel shall be deemed to be filed when delivered or mailed by registered or certified mail to the clerk of the Supreme Court of Virginia. The request shall include a copy of the complaint and a copy of all responsive pleadings. A copy of the request shall be filed with the clerk of the circuit court wherein the malpractice action has been filed, and a copy of such request shall be mailed to the opposing party and its counsel, if known. The request shall include the name of the judge to whom the case is assigned. Upon receipt of the request the circuit court clerk shall immediately advise the judge to whom the case has been assigned.

(b) *Contents of Request.* — The request for the appointment of a medical review panel shall contain the following (to the extent known):

(1) The name, address and telephone number of the plaintiff.

(2) The name, address and telephone number of the attorney of record for the plaintiff.

---

* Chapter 262 of the Acts of Assembly of 1978 provides that the term "has filed" is deemed to include the filing of notice under § 8.01-581.2 where such filing occurred prior to the expiration of any applicable statute of limitation when the causes of action arose prior to July 1, 1976.

(3) The name, address and telephone number of the defendant health care provider(s).

(4) The name, address and telephone number of the attorney of record for the health care provider.

(5) A statement specifying the classification of the health care provider in accordance with Section 8.01-581.1 of the Code and, in the case of a physician, his specialty or subspecialty.

(6) A certification that a copy of the request for a review panel has been mailed to all other parties and their counsel, if known.

(7) The name of the judge to whom the case is assigned.

(c) *Multiple Parties.* — Any health care provider named as a defendant shall have the right to request a panel and, in that event, shall mail copies of its request to the other health care providers named in the complaint as well as to the plaintiff and his counsel of record. When a request for a panel is made by any party, a single panel shall be designated and all health care providers against whom a claim is asserted shall be subject to the jurisdiction of such panel.

The amendment effective July 1, 2000, adopted June 16, 2000, in subdivision (a), substituted "Supreme Court of Virginia" for "circuit court wherein the malpractice action has been filed" at the end of the first sentence, substituted "clerk of the Supreme Court of Virginia" for "circuit court clerk of such court" at the end of the second sentence, added the present third sentence, in the present fourth sentence, substituted "the request" for "such request" and inserted "filed with the clerk of the circuit court wherein the malpractice action has been filed, and a copy of such request shall be," and added the present fifth sentence; and added subdivision (b)(7).

The amendment, effective February 28, 2006, adopted February 28, 2006, substituted "complaint" for "motion for judgment" in the third sentence of subdivision (a) and in the first sentence of subdivision (c).

Law Review. — For article, "Medical Malpractice Review Panels in Operation in Virginia," see 19 U. Rich. L. Rev. 273 (1985).

CASE NOTES

Subdivision (c) does not conflict with Medical Malpractice Act. — The provisions of subdivision (c) of this rule do not conflict with the provisions of the Medical Malpractice Act (Va. Code § 8.01-581.1 et seq.), in violation of Va. Const., Art. VII, § 5. The authors of the act expressly empowered the Chief Justice to promulgate rules necessary to carry out its provisions. Subdivision (c) of this rule merely particularizes the mechanics of the filing requirements of Va. Code §§ 8.01-581.2 and 8.01-581.9. Horn v. Abernathy, 231 Va. 228, 343 S.E.2d 318 (1986).

Rule 3. Designation of Panel; Certificate of Parties.

(a) *Designation of Panel.* — Upon receipt of a request for the appointment of a medical review panel, the Supreme Court of Virginia shall designate the panel within sixty days after receipt of the request.

(b) *Composition.* — The panel so designated shall consist of two impartial attorneys and two impartial health care providers, licensed and actively practicing their professions and a circuit court judge of the court in which the action was filed who shall preside over the panel but need not attend or participate in the deliberations of the panel.

(c) *Attorney Members.* — The Supreme Court of Virginia shall select the attorney members of each panel from a list provided by the Virginia State Bar. The Virginia State Bar shall provide to the Executive Secretary of the Supreme Court of Virginia a list of two hundred forty actively practicing attorneys. Such list shall include the office address and telephone number of each attorney. One third of such list shall be replaced each year but members may be reappointed to the list without limit in time.

(d) *Health Care Provider Members.* — The Supreme Court of Virginia shall select the health care provider members of the panel from a list provided by the State Board of Medicine. The State Board of Medicine shall provide to the Executive Secretary of the Supreme Court of Virginia a list of nine hundred fifteen health care providers. Such a list shall include the office address and telephone number of each health care provider. The list furnished by the State Board of Medicine shall be by classification, as stated in Section 8.01-581.1 of the Code, and, where practical, by specialty as follows:

(1) Physicians (605). Seventy-five in General Practice; sixty in Surgery; fifty in Internal Medicine; thirty in Orthopedic Surgery; sixty in Obstetrics and Gynecology; thirty in Anesthesiology; forty in Emergency Medicine; and twenty in each of the

following: Dermatology, Neurology, Neurosurgery, Ophthalmology, Otorhinolaryngology, Pediatrics, Pathology, Physical Medicine, Plastic Surgery, Radiology, Urology, Psychiatry and Osteopathy.

(2) Hospitals (40). Forty hospital administrators.

(3) Dentists (60). Twenty in General Practice. Ten in each of the following specialties: Oral Surgery, Endodontics, Orthodontics and Periodontics.

(4) Pharmacists (40). Twenty each in community pharmacy and hospital pharmacy.

(5) Registered or Licensed Practical Nurses or Nurse Practitioners (40).

(6) Optometrists (20).

(7) Podiatrists (20).

(8) Chiropractors (10).

(9) Physical Therapists (10).

(10) Physical Therapy Assistants (10).

(11) Clinical Psychologists (10).

(12) Nursing homes (20). Twenty nursing home administrators.

(13) Clinical Social Workers (10).

(14) Professional Counselors (10).

(15) Dental Hygientists (10).

It shall be the responsibility of the State Board of Medicine to coordinate with the State Board of Health, State Board of Dentistry, State Board of Pharmacy, State Board of Nursing, State Board of Optometry, and such other regulatory boards as may be necessary to compile this list. A new list shall be provided every three years but members may be reappointed to the list without limit in time.

(e) *Withdrawal from List.* — (1) An individual whose name is included on any list may have his or her name withdrawn from the list by notifying the Virginia State Bar or the State Board of Medicine. Upon receipt of such notification, the Virginia State Bar or the State Board of Medicine shall advise the Executive Secretary of the Supreme Court of Virginia of this change and submit a replacement.

(2) Any person subject to disciplinary action by his or her profession shall be automatically removed from the list by the appropriate regulatory body and a replacement submitted to the Executive Secretary of the Supreme Court.

(3) Any person who is unable through sickness, disability, or for any other reason to serve regularly on a panel shall be removed from the list and a replacement submitted to the Executive Secretary of the Supreme Court.

(4) The Executive Secretary of the Supreme Court may request that a name be removed from the list because of constant refusal to serve.

(f) *Manner of Selection.* — (1) Selection from the lists by the Supreme Court of Virginia will be rotated based on availability with due regard to the nature of the claim.

(2) Unless it shall prove impracticable, one health care provider on the panel shall represent the medical specialty involved in the claim.

(3) Any member of the panel may disqualify himself if he believes that his presence constitutes a conflict of interest or gives the appearance of impropriety. A party may move for such disqualification for cause within ten days after receiving notice of designation of the panel. The motion shall be in writing addressed to the judge presiding over the panel and served by mail on the opposing party or its counsel. The judge shall act on the motion unless the panel member in question disqualifies himself. In the event of such disqualification, the Supreme Court of Virginia shall designate a new panel member.

(g) *Rescission.* — A party may rescind a request for review by a panel at any time prior to the selection of the panel, in which event, if no other party had also requested the panel, the presiding judge shall dismiss the panel. After the selection of the members of the review panel, the requesting party may rescind a request for review by the panel only with the consent of all parties or with leave of the judge presiding over the panel. The Executive Secretary of the Supreme Court of Virginia shall be notified of any dismissal.

The amendment, effective July 1, 2000, adopted June 16, 2000, substituted "shall designate the panel within sixty days after receipt of the request" for "shall forthwith designate the panel" at the end of subdivision (a).

The amendment, effective January 1, 2002, adopted October 1, 2001, in subdivision (g), substituted "selection of the panel" for "panel decision" in the first sentence, redesignated the former second sentence as the present third sentence, inserted the present second sentence and substituted "any" for "this" in the present third sentence.

Law Review. — For article, "Medical Malpractice Review Panels in Operation in Virginia," see 19 U. Rich. L. Rev. 273 (1985).

Rule 4. Convening of Panel.

(a) *Notice of Appointment.* — Upon selection of the panel members by the Supreme Court, the Executive Secretary shall mail a letter to the panel members advising them of their selection to the panel and of the names and addresses of the parties and attorneys involved in this proceeding. A brief description of the claim shall be included in this letter. The panelists, within ten days thereafter, shall advise the Executive Secretary if they will be unable to serve. Upon expiration of the ten days, the Supreme Court will issue an official designation specifying the style of the proceeding and each panel member. A copy of this designation shall be mailed together with the names, addresses and professional practice of each panel member to the plaintiff and the health care provider and their counsel. This designation shall recite that the date, time, and place for the convening of the panel shall be fixed by the judge presiding over the panel in consultation with the members of the panel.

(b) *Additional Parties.* — Upon request, the judge of the circuit court hearing the case may grant leave to amend the request for a review panel to add additional parties or causes of action in furtherance of the ends of justice except where (i) the request for leave to amend is made less than ten days before the date set for the review panel to convene or (ii) the judge finds that the request for leave to amend is without merit. If leave to amend is granted, the judge may, upon motion of either party, stay the review panel proceedings, extend the time for completion of discovery, filing of submissions and other procedural limitation periods, or enter such orders as are appropriate to avoid prejudice to the parties and to avoid unnecessary delay and duplication in the proceedings. Leave to add additional parties shall not be granted if the judge finds that the applicable statute of limitations has expired with respect to the new or additional parties or causes of action.

(c) *Notification.* — At the time the panel is designated the Supreme Court shall advise the clerk of the circuit court in which the matter is filed of the names of the panel members. The Supreme Court shall also notify the parties of the name, address and professional practice of each panel member and shall also notify the panel members, in writing, of their appointment.

(d) *Completion of Discovery.* — Within ten days of receipt of the request for the panel the judge shall advise the parties of the date set for the completion of discovery. Except for good cause shown, the date for completion of discovery shall not be set beyond one hundred twenty days from the date on which the panel was requested. Procedures for the taking of depositions shall be governed by Part Four of the Rules of the Supreme Court and the provisions of Section 8.01-581.4 of the Code of Virginia, 1950, as amended.

(e) *Submission by Plaintiff.* — The plaintiff within ten days after the date set for completion of discovery, shall submit to each member of the panel, including the judge, a statement of facts together with all documentary evidence he or she desires to introduce. The plaintiff shall submit to the panel members only those portions of deposition transcripts, medical records, treatises and other documents which are relevant to the claim. However, upon request of the judge, the plaintiff shall produce all or part of any such document submitted. These materials shall be accompanied by a certificate stating that a copy of all such materials has been mailed to the health care provider and its counsel. All costs attendant to the submission of these materials shall be borne by the plaintiff. If the plaintiff fails to comply with this subsection, the judge shall prescribe a time within which the health care provider may submit evidence and shall order that the matter be considered solely upon the evidence. If the health care provider fails to comply with such order, the judge shall order the panel discharged.

(f) *Submission by Health Care Provider.* — Within ten days after receipt of the materials filed by the plaintiff, the health care provider shall submit to each panel member, including the judge, a counter statement of facts and all materials that it desires to introduce. The health care provider shall submit to the panel members only those portions of deposition transcripts, medical records, treatises and other documents which are relevant to the claim. However, upon request of the judge, the health care provider shall produce all or part of any such document submitted. These materials shall be accompanied by a certificate stating that a copy of all such materials has been mailed to the plaintiff and his counsel. All costs attendant to the submission of these materials shall be borne by the health care provider.

(g) *Extension of Time.* — The time periods stated in Rules Four (e) and Four (f) above may be extended by the judge for good cause shown.

(h) *Convening of Panel.* — The circuit judge presiding over the panel, within the period set for the taking of discovery and upon consultation with the panel members, shall notify all parties of the date, time and place for a hearing by the review panel, if any, or the date on which the panel will convene, having given due regard to the location of the other panel members and the parties involved and the time periods granted the parties to file their submissions. Such date shall not be set sooner than ten days after the date set for filing of the submission by the health care provider.

(i) *Oath.* — Upon convening of the panel, the judge shall swear in each panel member as follows:

> I do solemnly swear (or affirm) that I have no past or present relationship with the parties nor am I aware of anything that would prevent me from being impartial in my deliberations. I further swear (or affirm) that I will render an opinion faithfully and fairly on the basis of the evidence presented, applying any professional expertise I may have, giving due regard to the nature of the claim and the nature of the practice of the health care provider.

Law Review. — For article, "Medical Malpractice Review Panels in Operation in Virginia," see 19 U. Rich. L. Rev. 273 (1985).

Rule 5. Request for Ore Tenus Hearing.

Either party may request the panel to conduct an ore tenus hearing and, when such a hearing is requested, it shall be held. Such a request shall be made in writing to the judge within ten days after the receipt of the designation of a panel. A copy of the request for an ore tenus hearing shall be sent to each panel member, the opposing party and its counsel. The panel may, in the absence of a request from either party, determine that an ore tenus hearing shall be held. If an ore tenus hearing is held, the judge shall notify all parties and panel members of the date, time and place for such a hearing. If no ore tenus hearing is held, the judge may, on the request of any party, extend the time for the submission of evidence in order to permit the parties to take and file depositions, and, in any such case, the panel shall convene at the direction of the judge in executive session for the purpose of conducting its review of the written evidence; provided, however, that when the panel chooses to act only in executive session, counsel for all parties shall be notified of the date, time and place of that session.

Rule 6. Conduct of an Ore Tenus Hearing.

(a) *Subpoenas.* — The judge upon the oral or written request of any party, without notice, or upon motion of the panel, may issue subpoenas for the attendance of witnesses and for the production of books, records, documents, and other evidence. When so issued, such subpoenas and subpoenas duces tecum shall be in the form prescribed in the Appendix of Forms attached hereto and shall be returnable to the office of the Clerk of the Circuit Court where the action was filed. Any expense incurred in the service of such subpoenas shall be borne by the requesting party except in the case of subpoenas requested by the panel in which case the expense will be distributed as costs.

(b) Reserved.

(c) *Copies.* — Any party may obtain from the clerk of the court to which subpoenas are returnable copies of any books, records or documents and other tangible evidence, upon paying to the clerk the reasonable cost of the copy.

(d) *Assembly of Record.* — The judge shall see to the transportation to the panel's meeting place of such books, records and documents as have been lodged in such clerk's office. The judge, upon request of any party, shall, for the purpose of depositions, permit such books, records and documents to be transported by counsel for such party to the place for the taking of depositions after such counsel has given an appropriate receipt to the clerk, and such counsel shall be responsible for the return of such materials to the clerk's office. Upon conclusion of deliberations and rendering of an opinion by the panel, all documentary evidence submitted to the panel, a transcript of the ore tenus hearing, if any, and a copy of the written opinion of the panel shall be filed in the office of the clerk in which the action was filed. The clerk shall mail a copy of the written opinion to the plaintiff and the defendant within five days of the date of rendering. A copy of such opinion shall also be mailed to the Executive Secretary of the Supreme Court of Virginia together with the apportionment of the costs as may be determined by the judge.

(e) *Quorum.* — All members of the panel must be present at a hearing unless waived by both parties.

(f) *Decision.* — A majority vote of the panel members may decide any question and determine the ultimate opinion. The judge shall have no vote.

(g) *Evidence.* — The judge shall rule upon the admissibility of all evidence, but strict rules of evidence need not be observed. Caution should be taken to insure that an opinion is not based entirely on hearsay evidence. Evidence should be material, but should be excluded only when it does not contribute to the development of a fair record.

(h) *Exclusion of Witnesses.* — Witnesses other than the parties or one representative of each may be excluded at the discretion of the judge.

(i) *Reporter.* — Upon application of either party, a court reporter may be present to prepare a transcript of the proceeding. The cost of such reporter shall be borne by the party or parties using the services of the court reporter.

(j) *Procedure at Hearing.* — The following general procedure shall be followed at an ore tenus hearing:

(1) The judge shall convene the hearing, state the style of the case, and state any general rules adopted by the panel.

(2) The judge shall swear in all panel members as provided in Rule Four (i).

(3) Preliminary motions may be made except that no demurrers, motions to dismiss or motions to strike will be permitted.

(4) All testimony shall be taken under oath.

(5) The counsel for the plaintiff may make an opening statement giving a chronological account of events, stating the acts or omissions that he believes constitute the professional negligence and specifying the evidence that he expects to produce.

(6) The counsel for the health care provider may make an opening statement setting forth his statement of facts and the evidence that he expects to produce.

(7) The counsel for the plaintiff shall then produce his evidence. All witnesses are subject to cross-examination and may be questioned by the panel.

(8) The counsel for the health care provider shall then produce his evidence. All witnesses are subject to cross-examination and may be questioned by the panel.

(9) The panel may call any witnesses that it desires to hear including expert witnesses. Any expense incurred by the panel in the calling of expert witnesses shall be apportioned as costs.

(10) Counsel for the plaintiff may present oral argument.

(11) Counsel for the health care provider may present oral argument.

(12) If oral argument is presented by the health care provider, counsel for the plaintiff shall be allowed rebuttal.

(13) At the conclusion of the hearing, the panel will deliberate in executive session and render its decision pursuant to Section 8.01-581.7 of the Code. The judge presiding over the panel need not attend or participate in the deliberations.

CASE NOTES

Discovery of panel deliberations. — The requirement of this rule that the panel deliberate in "executive session" does not support limiting discovery of those deliberations. That contention, if valid, would bring this rule into conflict with the foregoing statutes. On the contrary, the rule is consistent with the statutory scheme. It merely provides for the procedure to be followed at the conclusion of a hearing and for consideration of the merits of the claim to be in private. The rule does not attempt to control the procedure to be followed during the subsequent legal action, which is governed by applicable statutes and rules of practice and procedure. Klarfeld v. Salsbury, 233 Va. 277, 355 S.E.2d 319 (1987).

Rule 7. Expenses and Costs.

(a) *Expenses.* — Each member of the panel including the judge shall be reimbursed for his actual and necessary expenses.

(b) *Compensation.* — Each member of the panel except the judge shall be paid at a rate of fifty dollars per day for service as a member of the panel.

(c) *Claims.* — The Executive Secretary of the Supreme Court of Virginia shall provide a form of voucher to each member of the panel for reimbursement and compensation. All vouchers shall be submitted by panel members to the Executive Secretary not later than thirty days after the rendering of the decision by the panel.

(d) *Costs.* — The judge shall apportion to the parties the expenses of conducting the panel in such proportions as may be determined by the judge in his discretion. When apportioning the costs, the judge shall add to the per diem and other expenses of the panel a fee of twenty-five dollars to cover administrative costs incurred by the Commonwealth with respect to proceedings under Chapter 21.1 of Title 8.01 of the Code of Virginia.

(e) *Expert Witness.* — The charges of any expert witness called by any party shall be paid by such party.

(f) *Payment.* — The Executive Secretary shall invoice the costs as apportioned by the judge. Within thirty days after the date of the invoice, each party shall send to the Executive Secretary of the Supreme Court of Virginia a check or money order payable to the Treasurer of Virginia in payment of all sums due and owing as that party's respective share of the costs. It shall be the duty of the counsel of record to insure that such payments are forwarded to the Executive Secretary.

APPENDIX OF FORMS.

Subpoena.
COMMONWEALTH OF VIRGINIA
COUNTY OF (OR CITY OF) ...., to-wit:

To the Sheriff of said City/County Greeting:

We command you in the name of the Commonwealth of Virginia at the instance of a Medical Malpractice Review Panel duly constituted in accordance with §§ 8.01-581.2 and 8.01-581.3 of the Virginia Code to summon ....
....
to appear before the Medical Malpractice Review Panel, at ....
.........., Virginia, at .... a.m./p.m. on ...., 20..., to give evidence in connection with a claim pending before the Medical Malpractice Review Panel brought by ......
....
against ....
and make return how you have executed this subpoena.

Given under my hand this .... day of ...., 20 .....

Medical Malpractice Review Panel
By ....
Judge or Clerk

Subpoena Duces Tecum.
COMMONWEALTH OF VIRGINIA
COUNTY OF (OR CITY OF) ...., to-wit:

To the Sheriff of said City/County Greeting:

We command you in the name of the Commonwealth of Virginia at the instance of a Medical Malpractice Review Panel duly constituted in accordance with §§ 8.01-581.2 and 8.01-581.3 of the Virginia Code to summon ....
....
....
to produce on or before ...., 20 ...., at the office of the Clerk of the Circuit Court of ....
the following written material, to-wit:
....
....
....
such material to remain in such office until further ordered and to be available for review and copy, and make return how you have executed this subpoena.

Medical Malpractice Review Panel
By ....
Judge or Clerk

Index to Medical Malpractice Rules of Practice

A

APPLICABILITY OF RULES, MedMal Rule 1.

C

COSTS.
Review panel.
Costs of conducting panel, MedMal Rule 7.
Witnesses.
Expert witnesses.
Charges to be paid by party, MedMal Rule 7.

D

DEFINITIONS, MedMal Rule 1.
DEPOSITIONS, MedMal Rule 6.
Witnesses.
Charges to be paid by party, MedMal Rule 7.

E

EVIDENCE.
Ore tenus hearings, MedMal Rule 6.

H

HEARINGS.
Conduct of ore tenus hearing, MedMal Rule 6.
Request for ore tenus hearing, MedMal Rule 5.

N

NOTICE.
Request for review by medical malpractice review panel, MedMal Rule 2.
Review panel.
Appointment, MedMal Rule 4.
Claims.
Amendment of notice of claim, MedMal Rule 4.
Notice of claim included with notice of appointment, MedMal Rule 4.

O

OATHS.
Review panel.
Members' oaths, MedMal Rule 4.

R

REQUEST FOR REVIEW BY MEDICAL MALPRACTICE REVIEW PANEL, MedMal Rule 2.

REVIEW PANEL.
Appointment, MedMal Rule 3.
Attorney members, MedMal Rule 3.
Compensation, MedMal Rule 7.
Composition, MedMal Rule 3.
Convening panel, MedMal Rule 4.
Costs, MedMal Rule 7.
Designation of panel, MedMal Rule 3.
Discovery.
Completion of discovery.
When required, MedMal Rule 4.
Expenses, MedMal Rule 7.
Health care provider members, MedMal Rule 3.
Hearings.
Ore tenus hearing.
Conduct, MedMal Rule 6.
Procedure, MedMal Rule 6.
Request, MedMal Rule 5.
Request for hearing.
Ore tenus hearing, MedMal Rule 5.
Members, MedMal Rule 3.
Notice.
Appointment, MedMal Rule 4.
Claims.
Amendment of notice of claim, MedMal Rule 4.
Notice of claim included with notice of appointment, MedMal Rule 4.
Oaths.
Members' oaths, MedMal Rule 4.
Ore tenus hearing.
Conduct of hearing, MedMal Rule 6.
Request for hearing, MedMal Rule 5.
Quorum, MedMal Rule 6.
Record.
Assembly of record, MedMal Rule 6.
Removal of record for inspection and copying, MedMal Rule 6.
Request for review by panel, MedMal Rule 2.
Rescission of request, MedMal Rule 3.
Selection of members.
Manner of selection, MedMal Rule 3.
Submission by claimant, MedMal Rule 4.
Submission by health care provider, MedMal Rule 4.
Time.
Extension of time, MedMal Rule 4.

S

SUBPOENAS, MedMal Rule 6.

T

TIME.
Review panel.
Extension of time, MedMal Rule 4.

W

WITNESSES.
Depositions.
Charges to be paid by party, MedMal Rule 7.

WITNESSES —Cont'd
Expert testimony.
Charges to be paid by party, MedMal Rule 7.

RULES OF THE JUDICIAL INQUIRY AND REVIEW COMMISSION

Adopted and effective November 10, 1998; amended effective February 14, 2006.

Pursuant to Section 17.1-902, Code of Virginia (1950), as amended, the following rules shall apply to govern investigations and hearings conducted by the Commission.

Rule
1. General.
2. Definitions.
3. Procedures for Handling Complaints/Inquiries.
4. Informal Conferences.
5. Formal Specification of Pleadings.
6. General Requirements as to Pleadings.
7. Filing of Documents.
8. Service.
9. Time for Filing Documents.

Rule
10. Computation of Time.
11. Preliminary Matters.
12. Subpoenas.
13. Hearings.
14. Waiver of Procedural Rules.
15. Disposition of Charges.
16. Preservation of Files.
17. Effective Date.
Index.

Rule 1. General.

A. *Applicability.* — These rules shall govern proceedings before the Judicial Inquiry and Review Commission.

B. *Gender.* — The words "he", "him", "his", or similar words as used in these Rules are intended to include both the feminine and the masculine.

C. *Exceptions.* — When the interests of justice require and for good cause shown, the Commission may waive the requirements of any rule.

Law Review. — For comment, "Guarding the Guardians: Judge's Rights and Virginia's Judicial Inquiry and Review Commission," see 43 U. Rich. L. Rev. 473 (2008).

Rule 2. Definitions.

A. "Commission" shall mean the Judicial Inquiry and Review Commission.

B. "Member or Members" shall mean members of the Judicial Inquiry and Review Commission and substitute members appointed pursuant to Va. Code § 17.1-901.

C. "Judge" shall mean the person who is under investigation by the Commission.

D. "Formal hearing" shall mean an investigative hearing to determine whether a judge has violated the Canons of Judicial Conduct and, if so, what sanctions should be imposed. A formal proceeding is initiated by a Notice of Hearing. Formal hearings may be conducted at such times and places in the Commonwealth as the Commission shall determine.

E. "Informal Conference" is a meeting between the judge and the Commission or one or more of its members to discuss alleged improper conduct by the judge.

F. "Document" shall mean any writing, including but not limited to a pleading, exhibit, chart, table or photograph.

G. "Presiding member" shall mean the Chairman or the commission member who presides at a prehearing conference or at any meeting, conference or formal hearing conducted by the Commission.

H. "Investigation" shall mean the process by which the Commission investigates charges coming before it pursuant to Va. Code § 17.1-902. An investigation may or may not include a formal hearing or informal conference. The Commission or the chairman may order an investigation to be made in such manner as is deemed appropriate. The judge may or may not be notified of the investigation.

I. "Complaint" shall mean information alleging any misconduct by a judge whether or not the alleged misconduct violates the Canons of Judicial Conduct.

J. "Inquiry" shall mean any complaint alleging misconduct which is in violation of the Canons of Judicial Conduct or which would be the basis for retirement, censure, or removal of a judge.

K. "Evidence" shall mean the findings of fact contained in the Commission's order that support the determination that the judge has violated the Canons of Judicial Conduct or that the judge's conduct would be the basis for retirement, censure, or removal.

L. "Charge" shall mean an Inquiry that the Commission determines, after a preliminary investigation by counsel and upon the recommendation of counsel, could be a violation of the Canons of Judicial Conduct or the basis for retirement, censure, or removal of a judge.

M. "Well Founded" shall mean that the Commission has found based upon clear and convincing evidence and supported by facts and sound judgment that the misconduct has occurred.

Rule 3. Procedures for Handling Complaints/Inquiries.

A. Receipt of Complaints:

(1) The Commission requests that all Complaints be submitted in writing to the Commission Office by mail at Post Office Box 367, Richmond, Virginia 23218-0367. Verbal complaints may be considered.

(2) Counsel for the Commission shall promptly acknowledge receipt of initial letters of Complaint.

(3) Any Complaint not stating a violation of the Canons of Judicial Conduct or which would not be the basis for retirement, censure, or removal of a judge need not be presented to the Commission and the sender will be notified by Commission Counsel.

(4) Any Complaint, which Commission Counsel believes to allege a violation of the Canons of Judicial Conduct, or which would be the basis for retirement, censure or removal of a judge, shall be presented to the Commission as an Inquiry.

(5) Each Inquiry presented to the Commission shall be numbered and considered by the Commission, along with Commission Counsel's findings and recommendation after a preliminary investigation.

(6) If the Commission determines that the Inquiry has no merit, the Inquiry shall be dismissed and Commission Counsel will notify the sender.

B. Establishment of Charges:

(1) If the Commission determines that the Inquiry may have merit, it shall establish the Inquiry as a charge and the Commission may direct further investigation or propose an informal conference with the judge.

(2) Upon determination that the charge, if well founded, would be the basis for retirement, censure, or removal of a judge, the Commission may proceed with a formal hearing.

(3) Disposition of charges shall be as provided in Rule 15 of the Rules of the Commission, or as may be provided by statute.

C. Temporary Suspension/Mental and Physical Examination:

(1) In any pending investigation or formal hearing, the Commission may suspend a judge with pay pursuant to Va. Code § 17.1-911.

(2) Whenever the Commission has probable cause to believe that a judge is unable to perform his duties because of excessive use of alcohol or drugs or physical or mental illness, the Commission may direct a physical or mental examination pursuant to Va. Code § 17.1-912.

D. Termination of Charges:

(1) The Commission may terminate the charge or charges at any time when it determines that the investigation is complete and the charge or charges are without merit or not sufficient to constitute the basis of retirement, censure or removal.

(2) The charge or charges against a judge shall be terminated with a finding and an order, signed by the Commission Chairperson and Commission Counsel, and a copy of the finding and order shall be forwarded to the judge if the judge has been made aware of the charge.

(3) The finding shall state whether the charge was well-founded and whether of sufficient gravity to constitute the basis for retirement, censure or removal, or whether the charge was well-founded and, with the consent of the judge, an agreement for supervision was reached under terms and conditions approved by the Commission.

(4) The order shall state the action taken by the Commission, including the status of the charge on the Commission's docket.

(5) Commission Counsel shall notify the complainant when the charge is terminated.

Rule 4. Informal Conferences.

In the discretion of the Commission, a judge who is alleged to have violated the Canons of Judicial Conduct may be invited to meet with the Commission or a member or members to discuss informally the allegations and possible solutions. Counsel may represent the judge but no witnesses will be permitted to testify. If the judge and the Commission do not resolve the matter at such an informal conference, the Commission may remove the matter from the Commission's docket or give the judge notice of a formal proceeding. The Commission may proceed directly to a formal proceeding without first holding an informal conference. Informal conferences shall not be governed by these rules.

Rule 5. Formal Specification of Pleadings.

A. *Number of Copies.* — Unless otherwise specified, an executed original and eight (8) true copies of each document required or permitted to be filed under these rules shall be filed with the Commission. The copies need not be signed but the name of the person signing the document, as distinguished from the firm he represents, shall also be typed or printed on all copies below the space provided for signature.

B. *Facsimile Transmission.* — Pleadings may not be filed by facsimile transmission.

Rule 6. General Requirements as to Pleadings.

A. *Contents.* — All pleadings shall contain a proper identification of the case and a concise but complete statement of the facts relied upon and the relief sought.

B. *Subscription.* — Every pleading submitted to the Commission shall be signed by the judge filing same and his attorney. The signature of an attorney or party constitutes a certificate by him that (i) he has read the pleading, motion, or other paper, (ii) to the best of his knowledge, information and belief, formed after reasonable inquiry, it is well grounded in fact and is warranted by existing law or a good faith argument for the extension, modification, or reversal of existing law, and (iii) it is not interposed for any improper purpose, such as to harass or to cause unnecessary delay or needless increase in the cost of litigation. If a pleading, written motion, or other paper is not signed, it shall be stricken unless it is signed promptly after the omission is called to the attention of the pleader or movant.

An oral motion made by an attorney or party before the Commission constitutes a representation by him that (i) to the best of his knowledge, information and belief formed after reasonable inquiry it is well grounded in fact and is warranted by existing law or a good faith argument for the extension, modification or reversal of existing law, and (ii) it is not interposed for any improper purpose, such as to harass or to cause unnecessary delay or needless increase in the cost of litigation.

C. *Answers.* — A judge who receives a Notice of Hearing shall file his answer within 21 days of service. For good cause the Commission or the Presiding Member may shorten or extend the time in which the Answer must be filed. The Answer shall fully and completely state the nature of the defense and shall admit or deny specifically and in detail each allegation of the Notice of Hearing unless the judge is without knowledge, in which case, his Answer shall so state and the statement shall operate as a denial. Matters alleged as affirmative defenses shall be separately stated and numbered.

Rule 7. Filing of Documents.

A. *Where Filed.* — All documents shall be filed with the Commission either by personal delivery at 100 North Ninth Street, Suite 661, Richmond, Virginia 23219 or by mail at Post Office Box 367, Richmond, Virginia 23218-0367. Documents shall be deemed filed on the date of actual receipt by the Commission.

B. *Name of Person Filing.* — Every document shall include the name, address, telephone number and signature of the person filing same.

Rule 8. Service.

A. *Persons To Be Served.* — The Commission shall serve its Notice by personal delivery upon the judge. Thereafter documents will be served upon the judge unless he is represented by an attorney in which case succeeding documents shall be served upon his attorney. Documents shall be served upon the Commission by delivering such documents to the Commission's Counsel.

B. *Where Served.* — The Notice shall be served upon the judge at his home, if possible, in order to protect the confidentiality of the proceeding. If the judge cannot be served at his home, he may be served at any place where he may be found.

C. *Proof of Service.* — Proof of service shall accompany all documents when they are filed and shall consist of a certificate of mailing executed by the person mailing the document, an acknowledgement of service, or a certificate of service.

Rule 9. Time for Filing Documents.

A. *Amendments.* — An amendment to any pleading may be made prior to the filing of answers thereto, or if no answer be filed, prior to its hearing date. The Commission may permit amendments to the pleadings prior to the close of the hearing for the sole purpose of insuring that the pleadings conform to the evidence.

B. *Other Documents.* — All other documents shall be filed within the period established by the Commission or its Presiding Member.

Rule 10. Computation of Time.

A. *Effect of Holidays.* — When any period of time fixed by these rules shall expire on a Saturday, Sunday or legal holiday, it shall be extended to the next day not a Saturday, Sunday or legal holiday.

B. *Extensions of time.* — Upon good cause shown the Commission or its Presiding Member may grant extensions of time. Motions to continue hearings are regarded with disfavor and will be granted only for extraordinary reasons.

Rule 11. Preliminary Matters.

A. *Motions.* — At least fourteen (14) days before the hearing, preliminary motions must be filed. If a prehearing conference is held, such motions must be filed at least fourteen (14) days before the prehearing conference.

B. *Prehearing Conference.* — The Commission or the Presiding Member may on its own motion, the motion of the Commission's Counsel, or the judge's motion, hold prehearing conferences to consider:

(1) The simplification of the issues.
(2) The necessity or desirability of amendments to the pleadings.
(3) The possibility of obtaining admissions of fact and of documents which will avoid unnecessary proof.
(4) The limitation of the number of witnesses.
(5) Lists of witnesses.
(6) Stipulations of evidence.
(7) Admissibility of evidence.
(8) Any preliminary motion filed.
(9) Any other procedural matters, which will expedite the hearing, process.

The prehearing conference will be held at a specified place and date before the Presiding Member after notice or at the beginning of the hearing, as the Presiding Member shall determine. An official reporter may record prehearing conferences.

C. *Prehearing Conference Order.* — The Presiding Member shall prepare a written order which recited the action taken at the prehearing conference, the amendments allowed to the pleadings, and the agreements made by counsel as to any of the matters considered, and any ruling made by the Presiding Member. Such order when entered controls the subsequent course of the action unless modified by the Commission to prevent manifest injustice. The official transcript, if any, of the prehearing conference may serve as the order to the extent that it includes rulings and agreements on material questions raised at the prehearing conference.

D. *Discovery.* — When a judge is formally charged with a violation of the Canons, once the judge obtains the services of an attorney, Commission Counsel promptly will contact the judge's attorney and offer to meet in order to discuss the case. Upon request by the judge's attorney, Commission Counsel will meet with the judge's attorney, outline the Commission's case, summarize what each of the Commission's witnesses is expected to say, and provide copies of all documents that the Commission intends to present at the hearing. It is the intent of the Commission that the judge and the judge's attorney have a clear understanding of the Commission's case in advance of the hearing and that they not be surprised by any of the Commission's evidence presented at the hearing. Any testimony or documents to be presented that come to the attention of Commission Counsel after the initial meeting with the judge's attorney will be disclosed promptly to the judge's attorney.

Rule 12. Subpoenas.

A. *Application for Subpoenas.* — An application for a subpoena shall be made at least fourteen (14) days before the hearing.

B. *Issuance of Subpoenas.* — The Commission's Counsel shall issue the subpoenas requested if the application complies with these rules.

C. *Service of Subpoenas; Motions to Quash.* — Subpoenas issued under this section shall be served upon the person to whom directed. Within seven (7) days after service of a subpoena, a motion to quash or modify the subpoena may be filed with the Commission.

Rule 13. Hearings.

A. *Order of Presentation.* — The Commission's Counsel shall present the case in chief against the judge, which shall be followed by the case on behalf of the judge. The judge shall be required to attend unless the Commission excuses his appearance.

B. *Evidence.* — Evidence must be material and relevant to the issues. Hearsay evidence is admissible so long as it is material, relevant, and probative. Irrelevant, immaterial, insubstantial, and repetitive evidence shall not be permitted.

C. *Objections.* — Objections to the admission or exclusion of evidence shall be in short form, stating the grounds relied upon. Objections may be stated in writing before the hearing commences. When the hearing is convened, all objections may be orally stated.

D. *Exhibits.* — When written exhibits are offered in evidence, the original and eight (8) copies shall be presented. If the Commission or Presiding Member has not fixed a time for the exchange of exhibits, each party shall exchange copies of exhibits not later than fourteen (14) days before the hearing convenes.

E. *Substitution of Copies for Originals.* — In its discretion, the Commission may permit the withdrawal of original documents offered in evidence and the substitution of true copies.

F. *Records in Other Proceedings.* — If any portion of the record in any other proceeding is offered in evidence, a true copy of the same shall become an exhibit.

G. *Transcript.* — An official reporter shall record hearings.

Rule 14. Waiver of Procedural Rules.

Waivers of any procedural rules shall be in writing and signed by the judge and his attorney and by the Commission's Counsel. If the hearing has been convened, such waivers may be stated on the record rather than in writing.

Rule 15. Disposition of Charges.

A. After an investigation has been concluded, the Commission may take any of the following actions:

(1) Remove the charges from Commission's the docket.

(2) If the Commission finds the charges against the judge to be well founded and of sufficient gravity to constitute the basis for retirement, censure or removal, it shall file a complaint against the judge in the Supreme Court of Virginia.

(3) If the Commission finds the charges against the judge to be well founded but not of sufficient gravity to constitute the basis for retirement, censure or removal, it may summon the judge before the Commission or designated Commission members, and advise the judge of its findings. The charges shall then be removed from the Commission's docket but may, nevertheless, be considered with any other future charges against the judge.

(4) If the Commission finds the charges against the judge to be well founded, the Commission may, with the consent of the judge, place the judge on a period of supervision under such terms and conditions as the Commission shall determine.

Violation of such terms and conditions shall be grounds for a new charge of failure to cooperate with the Commission.

(5) If the Commission finds the charges against the judge to be well founded under 15.A. (2), (3), or (4), the Commission shall transmit its findings and final order to the legislature in accordance with Va. Code § 17.1-918 and such information shall be sent to the judge.

B. The Commission may take any of the actions listed in the foregoing sections of this Rule after an informal conference with the judge, provided that the judge consents to such actions.

CASE NOTES

Commission not required to file complaint. — While the Judicial Inquiry and Review Commission, believed that it had grounds to file a complaint in the Supreme Court of Virginia, pursuant to Va. Const., Art. VI, § 10, and § 17.1-902, against a district judge who was found to have violated the Canons of Judicial Conduct, the Commission was not required to do so. Under Va. Const., Art. VI, § 10, and § 17.1-902, the provisions of Va. Jud. Inq. and Rev. R. 15(A)(2), which allowed a complaint to be filed, were necessarily permissive rather than mandatory. Judicial Inquiry & Review Comm'n of Va. v. Elliott, 272 Va. 97, 630 S.E.2d 485, 2006 Va. LEXIS 58 (2006).

Supervision agreement. — Despite the claims of the Judicial Inquiry and Review Commission that the terms discussed in a judge's disciplinary hearings had not yet been approved and were never reduced to a formal supervision agreement, the Commission had no right to file a complaint against the judge in the Supreme Court of Virginia pursuant to Va. Const., Art. VI, § 10, and § 17.1-902. A statement was made that the terms would be reduced to writing, but the Chairman also indicated that the judge could inform others that he would return to the bench; thus, no gag order was imposed, the judge's statements to others that "everything would be OK" did not constitute a breach of the agreement, and he made no representation that the Commission had exonerated him or vindicated him. Judicial Inquiry & Review Comm'n of Va. v. Elliott, 272 Va. 97, 630 S.E.2d 485, 2006 Va. LEXIS 58 (2006).

Despite the claims of the Judicial Inquiry and Review Commission that it had a right when it did to file a complaint in the Supreme Court of Virginia against a district judge, seeking his censure or removal because of his judicial conduct, that Court determined that under Va. Const., Art. VI, § 10, and § 17.1-902, the complaint should not have been filed. The judge and the Commission had reached a valid supervision agreement under Va. Jud. Inq. and Rev. R. 15(A)(4), in which the judge's return to the bench was conditioned, in part, on certain terms, but the Commission indicated that immediately after the hearing, he could tell people that he was returning to the bench; the judge thus did not violate the terms, and the Commission, in the absence of a breach by the judge, was bound by the agreement and foreclosed from revoking it and filing a complaint in the supreme court pursuant to Va. Jud. Inq. and Rev. R. 15(A)(2). Judicial Inquiry & Review Comm'n of Va. v. Elliott, 272 Va. 97, 630 S.E.2d 485, 2006 Va. LEXIS 58 (2006).

Rule 16. Preservation of Files.

A. It shall be the responsibility of Counsel to maintain the records of the Commission in the following manner:

B. Proceedings that are disposed of by Counsel or the Commission without an adverse finding by the Commission against a judge.

C. All records related to such proceedings shall be maintained in the Commission's confidential files. Counsel shall destroy such records upon the judge's death, resignation, or retirement not subject to recall.

D. Proceedings that are disposed of by the Commission after an adverse finding by the Commission against a judge.

E. All records related to such proceedings shall be maintained in the Commission's confidential files. Any adverse finding by the Commission against a judge shall be reported by Counsel to the General Assembly pursuant to Rule 15A(5), but shall not be re-reported upon any subsequent election or re-election of the judge. Counsel shall destroy all records relating to an adverse finding by the Commission against a judge upon the judge's death, resignation, or retirement not subject to recall.

F. Proceedings that are disposed of by filing a formal complaint in the Supreme Court of Virginia.

G. All records related to such proceedings shall be maintained in the Commission's confidential files. Counsel shall destroy such records upon the judge's death, resignation, or retirement not subject to recall. A copy of the record and briefs filed in the Supreme Court of Virginia, however, and any order issued by that Court in such proceedings, shall be retained permanently in the Commission's files.

H. All agendas and annotated agendas of the Commission's meetings shall be retained in the Commission's confidential files.

I. Counsel shall report to the Commission on an annual basis as to any records destroyed pursuant to this Rule.

CASE NOTES

Waiver of challenge to admission of evidence. — In a case brought by the Judicial Inquiry and Review Commission pursuant to Va. Const., Art. VI, § 10 and § 17.1-902, citing to § 17.1-913, the judge unsuccessfully argued that it was improper for the Commission to admit and consider evidence of her prior contacts with the Commission; she contended that neither § 17.1-913 nor VA. Jud. Inq. and Rev. R. 16 allowed for the removal of the confidentiality of records of complaints that were not deemed well founded and that her two prior contacts were not determined to be well founded. At the outset of the Commission hearing, counsel for the Commission stated that the exhibits were all in the red binder there on the witness desk and that both the sides were in agreement that there was no objection to the admission of any of the exhibits; pursuant to Va. Sup. Ct. R. 5:25, the judge's agreement to the Commission's admission of the exhibits was fatal to her argument that the Commission erred in admitting those same exhibits. Judicial Inquiry & Review Comm'n of Va. v. Taylor, 278 Va. 699, 685 S.E.2d 51, 2009 Va. LEXIS 114 (2009), cert. denied, 177 L. Ed. 2d 304, 130 S.Ct. 3396, 2010 U.S. LEXIS 4645 (2010).

Rule 17. Effective Date.

These rules shall be effective February 14, 2006.

Index to Rules of Judicial Inquiry and Review Commission

A

ANSWERS, JIRC Rule 6.

APPLICABILITY OF RULES, JIRC Rule 1.

C

CHARGES.
Defined, JIRC Rule 2.
Disposition of charges, JIRC Rule 15.
Establishment of charges, JIRC Rule 3.
Termination of charges, JIRC Rule 3.

COMPLAINTS.
Defined, JIRC Rule 2.
Receipt of complaints, JIRC Rule 3.

COMPUTATION OF TIME.
Extensions of time, JIRC Rule 10.
Holidays, JIRC Rule 10.

D

DEFINITIONS, JIRC Rule 2.

DISCOVERY, JIRC Rule 11.

DISPOSITION OF CHARGES, JIRC Rule 15.

E

EFFECTIVE DATE OF RULES, JIRC Rule 17.

EVIDENCE.
Defined, JIRC Rule 2.
Hearings, JIRC Rule 13.

F

FILES.
Preservation, JIRC Rule 16.

FILING OF DOCUMENTS.
Name of person filing, JIRC Rule 7.
Time for filing, JIRC Rule 9.
Where filed, JIRC Rule 7.

G

GENDER, JIRC Rule 1.

H

HEARINGS.
Evidence, JIRC Rule 13.

HEARINGS —Cont'd
Exhibits, JIRC Rule 13.
Formal hearing, defined, JIRC Rule 2.
Objections, JIRC Rule 13.
Order of presentation, JIRC Rule 13.
Transcripts, JIRC Rule 13.

I

INFORMAL CONFERENCES, JIRC Rule 4.
Defined, JIRC Rule 2.

M

MOTIONS, JIRC Rule 11.

P

PLEADINGS.
Amendments.
Time for filing, JIRC Rule 8.
Answers, JIRC Rule 6.
Contents, JIRC Rule 6.
Facsimile transmission, JIRC Rule 5.
Number of copies, JIRC Rule 5.
Subscription, JIRC Rule 6.

PREHEARING CONFERENCE, JIRC Rule 11.

PRELIMINARY MATTERS, JIRC Rule 11.

PRESERVATION OF FILES, JIRC Rule 16.

S

SERVICE OF PROCESS.
Persons to be served, JIRC Rule 8.
Proof of service, JIRC Rule 8.
Subpoenas, JIRC Rule 12.
Where served, JIRC Rule 8.

SUBPOENAS.
Application for subpoena, JIRC Rule 12.
Issuance, JIRC Rule 12.
Service of subpoenas, JIRC Rule 12.

T

TRANSCRIPTS.
Hearings, JIRC Rule 13.

W

WAIVER OF RULES, JIRC Rules 1, 14.

BYLAWS OF THE VIRGINIA STATE BAR AND COUNCIL

As revised October 19, 2012.

Part I — Bylaws of the Virginia State Bar.

Article
I. Members.
II. Officers.
III. Election of President-Elect.
IV. Meetings.
V. Committees.

Part II — Bylaws of the Council.

I. Members.
II. Election of Council.
Article
III. Secretary-Treasurer [Executive Director].
IV. Notices of Meetings.
V. Meetings.
VI. Executive Committee.
VII. District Committees and the Disciplinary Board.
VIII. Standing Committees.
IX. Votes by Mail or Telephone.
X. Vacancies in Committees.
XI. Sections.
Index.

PART I — BYLAWS OF THE VIRGINIA STATE BAR.

Article I. Members.

The Virginia State Bar is comprised of all attorneys licensed to practice law in Virginia.

Article II. Officers.

The officers of the Virginia State Bar shall be a President, a President-Elect, an immediate Past President and a Secretary-Treasurer.

Article III. Election of President-Elect.

Section 1. Nominations. — In order to qualify for election to the office of president-elect for the ensuing bar year, a candidate must be duly qualified as set forth in Paragraph 4 of the Rules of Court, Part Six, Section IV and must file a nominating petition with the executive director.

Section 2. Petition. — The nominating petition shall be signed by at least 50 members of the Virginia State Bar and shall be signed by the candidate, who shall certify that he or she is qualified to run for the office. The nominating petition must be received by the executive director on or before October 1 of each year.

Section 3. Method of Election. — In the event only one nominating petition is received by the executive director on or before October 1 of any year, the election for the office of president-elect shall be held at the next annual meeting in accordance with the provisions of Article IV, below.

In the event two or more nominating petitions are received by the executive director on or before October 1 of any year, the election of the president-elect will be in accordance with the provisions of Sections 4 and 5, below.

Section 4. Ballots. — In the event nominating petitions for two or more candidates are received by the executive director, then:

(a) The executive director shall prepare a ballot which shall list in alphabetical order the names of those persons nominated to the office of president-elect.

(b) The ballot shall be distributed by mail or made available by electronic means to all members on or before November 5. The form of the ballot and the procedure for distribution, collection and tabulation of ballots shall be determined by the executive director.

(c) If any member fails to receive a ballot within ten (10) days of distribution, or by November 15, whichever is later, the intended recipient shall be given a replacement ballot upon executing an affidavit, in a form to be prescribed by the Executive Committee, averring (i) that no ballot has been received and (ii) that in the event the original ballot is subsequently received, it will promptly be returned unmarked to the executive director. The affidavit and request for a replacement ballot must be received by the executive director not later than November 22, and the replacement ballot must be returned to the executive director by December 1.

(d) If any member receives more than one ballot, he or she shall return the excess ballot or ballots, unmarked, to the executive director in the same envelope provided for return of his or her marked ballot.

Section 5. Ballot Elections. — The ballots shall be collected and counted in a manner which assures the confidentiality of the members' votes. A plurality of the votes cast by all members shall elect. No ballot received by the executive director after December 1 shall be counted. Write-in votes shall be permitted, but the executive director may exclude illegible write-in votes and shall exclude write-in votes for any candidate ineligible to serve pursuant to these bylaws, if elected.

Section 6. General Provisions. — The following provisions shall be applicable to any election of the president-elect under this Article III.

(a) For purposes of these provisions, a "member" is an active member in good standing of the Virginia State Bar. Only such person may nominate, be nominated, vote or be elected in any election for the office of president-elect.

(b) Records maintained by the executive director as to membership and good-standing status shall be controlling.

(c) The failure to comply with the dates designated for the occurrence or completion of certain acts shall not invalidate any election, unless substantial prejudice can be shown to have resulted therefrom.

(d) For purposes of determining voter and candidate eligibility, the membership list maintained by the executive director as of October 1 shall be controlling. Except to correct clerical errors in records maintained as of that date, no revisions or additions to the membership list for purposes of the election shall be made after October 1.

(e) The executive director shall announce to the bar the results of the election for the office of president-elect.

(f) Any responsibility assigned herein to be discharged by the executive director may be assumed and discharged by the Executive Committee, at its discretion.

(g) Any challenge to an election shall be resolved by a committee which shall be chaired by the president and shall include the president-elect, the immediate past president and two members of Council appointed by the president who shall not be current members of the Executive Committee.

Article IV. Meetings.

Section 1. — The Secretary shall give thirty days' notice by mail of annual meetings of the bar, and such written notice of special meetings of the bar as the Executive Committee shall prescribe in its call. Meetings of the organization shall be held at such times and places and after such notices as may be prescribed by the appropriate provisions of Section IV, Rules of the Supreme Court for the Integration of the Virginia State Bar and Council Bylaws.

Section 2. — A quorum at any such meeting shall be as set forth in the Court Rules.

Section 3. — The program and order of business at any meeting of the Virginia State Bar, unless otherwise ordered by the Council, shall be determined by the president in consultation with the president-elect and the executive director.

Section 4. — Proceedings at any such meeting shall be governed by Roberts Rules of Order, except that no member shall without unanimous consent speak more than twice on any one subject nor more than five minutes at any one time.

Section 5. — Voting at any such meeting shall be *viva voce* with each active member present entitled to vote, unless at least ten active members shall either before or immediately after such vote demand a vote by judicial circuits on a roll called in numerical order. In the latter event, each circuit shall be entitled to one vote for each twenty-five active members or fraction of twenty-five registered in that circuit. When a vote by circuits is ordered, the active members present from each circuit shall cast the entire vote to which such circuit is entitled. If there be a division among the active members present from any circuit as to how the vote of such circuit shall be cast, the vote of such circuit shall be divided and cast in proportion to the vote on such division, unless such circuit at a meeting of its members shall have adopted and caused to be certified to the Secretary a resolution providing that the entire vote of such circuit shall be cast as a majority of the active members from that circuit present and voting shall determine.

Provided, however, that in any election for the office of president-elect, voting shall be viva voce unless more than one candidate shall be duly nominated, in which event voting shall be by written ballot by judicial circuits as provided in Article III above.

Section 6. — An active member shall be deemed to be registered in the circuit where he or she is entitled to vote for a member of Council provided that for the purpose of this section, no member may change his or her registration within five days preceding a meeting of the organization. At the opening of the meeting the Secretary shall post in a conspicuous place a list showing the number of votes to which each circuit is entitled and shall, upon the request of a member of any circuit, also post a list of the active members officially registered in that circuit. The lists so posted shall be conclusive as to the number of votes to which each circuit is entitled and as to the active members registered in each circuit, provided that any interested active member challenging the correctness of any such list, either as to the number of votes to which a circuit is entitled or as to the circuit in which an active member is registered, may appeal to the floor; but the circuits or members affected shall not vote on such appeal.

Article V. Committees.

Section 1. — Unless otherwise provided in the Supreme Court Rules, by action of Council, or elsewhere in these by-laws or the by-laws of Council, all committees shall be appointed by the president, who shall have power to determine the size and composition of the committee and to designate the chair thereof and to fill any vacancy therein.

Section 2. — A majority of any committee shall constitute a quorum.

Section 3. — In addition to the Executive Committee, district committees, and standing committees specified in the by-laws of Council, there shall be special committees to carry out the other ongoing work of the bar, and study committees, where appropriate in the judgment of the president, to examine and make recommendations on specific proposals or programs within a reasonably brief and discrete period of time.

Section 4. — Members of special committees shall be appointed to three-year terms, with the exception of the Special Committee on Lawyer Malpractice Insurance whose members shall be appointed to five-year terms. No member shall serve more than two consecutive terms on such a committee. A member appointed to fill an unexpired term shall be eligible to serve two additional full terms. An eligible member wishing to be reappointed to a special committee shall be required to reapply in writing prior to the end of his or her current term under procedures established by Council and administered by the executive director. If any member of a committee fails to attend either three meetings during any bar year or two successive meetings of the committee without providing an explanation satisfactory to the committee chair, or in the case of a lawyer member, is declared not in good standing with the Virginia State Bar, such person's position shall automatically be considered vacated and filled as in the case of other vacancies.

Section 5. — In making initial appointments to new special committees, the president shall appoint members to one, two and three-year terms so as to allow for the retirement or re-appointment of one-third of the membership of each special committee at the end of each bar year.

Section 6. — Effective July 1, 1996, the size of special committees shall be as specified by Council. A list of the committees and their respective sizes shall be maintained by the executive director. Changes in the size of special committees may be approved by the Executive Committee.

PART II — BYLAWS OF THE COUNCIL.

Article I. Members.

The Council is comprised of attorneys elected or appointed in accordance with applicable provisions of Section IV, Rules of the Supreme Court for the Organization and Government of the Virginia State Bar.

Article II. Election of Council.

The election of members of Council for each circuit shall be by one of the two following methods.

Section 1. Circuit Bar Meeting. — Prior to March 1 of any year in which a Council member from the circuit is to be elected, the executive director shall notify the Chief Judge of the circuit of the need for a meeting of the bar of the circuit and the number of vacancies to be filled. The executive director shall obtain from the Chief Judge the date and location for a meeting of the members of the circuit which shall be held prior to May 1. The executive director shall give at least fourteen days notice to the members of the meeting.

All members whose Virginia State Bar membership mailing addresses are maintained in the circuit may attend and vote at the meeting. A quorum shall consist of those members who vote at the meeting. No member shall vote by proxy. Prior to the meeting, the executive director shall transmit to the Chief Judge or the designated presiding officer a list of the members whose names appear on the membership roster for such circuit. The Chief Judge shall either preside at the meeting, designate another active or retired judge of the circuit to preside, or designate an attorney to preside who is neither a candidate for election to Council nor associated in the practice of law with a candidate nominated for election.

At the circuit meeting, any member eligible to vote in the circuit who is not then serving a second successive full term on Council shall be eligible for election. Nominations may be made at the circuit meeting or by any member eligible to vote in the circuit. No supporting petition or second for such nomination will be required. After the nominations are closed, an election by written ballot shall be conducted. In the event of a tie vote, the winner shall be chosen by lot drawn by the presiding judge or his designee.

Within ten days after the meeting, the presiding officer or the Chief Judge shall communicate the names of the person or persons elected to the executive director.

Section 2. Ballot. — On or about March 1, the executive director shall cause to be distributed by mail or electronic means to every member eligible to vote in the circuit a notice of any vacancy or vacancies on Council, and a brief description of the method of nomination and voting. All members whose Virginia State Bar membership mailing addresses are maintained in the circuit are eligible to vote.

Nominations for election to Council shall be by petition filed by the candidate with the executive director. Such petition shall be signed by not fewer than ten other members eligible to vote in the circuit, and shall be accompanied by a statement of qualifications not exceeding one hundred and fifty words. Nominations must be filed in the office of the executive director on or before April 1. Any petition failing to comply with these requirements shall be rejected.

On or before April 15, the executive director shall distribute by mail or electronic means to all eligible members of the circuit a ballot containing the names of all persons nominated, along with each nominee's statement of qualifications.

The form of the ballot and the procedure for distribution, collection and tabulation of ballots shall be determined by the executive director. In the event of a tie vote, the executive director shall pick the winner by lot. No ballot received by the executive director after May 1 shall be counted.

Write-in votes shall be permitted, but the executive director may exclude illegible write-in votes and shall exclude write-in votes for any candidate ineligible to serve pursuant to these bylaws, if elected. In those instances where there are more candidates for Council positions than there are positions to be filled from the circuit, the ballot will contain instructions to vote only for the same number of persons as there are positions to be filled; ballots which do not conform to this requirement will not be counted.

Section 3. General Provisions. — The following provisions shall be applicable to both methods of election:

(a) The timeline for special elections to fill vacancies on Council shall be determined by the executive director.

(b) For purposes of these provisions, a "member" is an active member in good standing of the Virginia State Bar. Only such person may nominate, be nominated, vote or be elected in any Council election.

(c) Records maintained by the executive director as to membership, good-standing status and assignment of a member to a particular circuit shall be controlling.

(d) The failure to comply with the dates designated for the occurrence or completion of certain acts shall not invalidate any election unless substantial prejudice can be shown to have resulted therefrom.

(e)(1) In all elections the candidate receiving the highest number of votes shall be elected.

(2) In the event that more than one full term is to be filled by a circuit at any single election, the candidates receiving the highest number of votes shall be elected.

(3) In the event that a regular election and special election to fill an unexpired term are held simultaneously in the same circuit, they shall be conducted as a single election and the successful candidate receiving the highest number of votes shall be entitled to choose either a regular term or the unexpired term, with the choice passing down in order until the unexpired term is selected. The successful candidate(s) receiving the lower number of votes shall be elected to fill the term(s) not chosen. In the event two or more unexpired terms are to be filled in the same election, the longer unexpired term(s) shall go to the successful candidate(s) receiving the highest number of votes who choose(s) to fill an unexpired term.

(4) As a part of the election process in each circuit under these bylaws, the voting members of the circuit shall prescribe the method for that circuit's next election and, in the event of a meeting, shall determine the length of time during which ballots may be cast in the next election, not to exceed one business day. A vote to change the method of election shall be by majority of votes cast. The ballot in each circuit's election shall provide a space for the voting member to indicate a preference for one of the two election methods described by these bylaws. For the meeting method, the ballot shall also provide a space to indicate whether voting shall be allowed all day, half day or only during the meeting. No quorum call shall be required for any meeting.

(5) For purposes of determining voter and candidate eligibility, the membership list maintained by the executive director as of March 15 shall be controlling. Except to correct clerical errors in records maintained as of that date, no changes in circuit membership, revisions or additions to the membership list for purposes of the election shall be made after March 15.

(6) The executive director shall announce to the bar the results of the election for the office of Council.

(7) Any challenge to an election shall be resolved by a committee which shall be chaired by the president and shall include the president-elect, the immediate past president, and two members of Council appointed by the president who shall not be current members of the Executive Committee.

(8) Should a member of Council change his or her address of record from the circuit he or she represents, his or her seat shall be declared vacant. A vacancy among the elected members of Council shall be cause for a special election to occur for the unexpired term of the vacant seat.

Article III. Secretary-Treasurer [Executive Director].

Section 1. — The Secretary-Treasurer [Executive Director] shall perform all duties prescribed by the Rules and these by-laws, and in addition such other duties as may be delegated to him from time to time by the Council or Executive Committee. He or she shall act as Secretary of the Bar, of the Council and of the Executive Committee.

Section 2. — The Secretary-Treasurer [Executive Director] shall give bond of $250,000 with corporate surety conditioned for the faithful performance of his or her duties, the premium of which shall be paid by the bar.

Article IV. Notices of Meetings.

The Secretary shall give twenty days' notice by mail of all meetings of the Council, and five days' notice by mail of all meetings of the Executive Committee. Notice of mailing shall commence on the date of mailing.

Article V. Meetings.

Section 1. — In the absence of specific action by the Council, the Executive Committee shall fix the time and place of the annual meeting of the bar, and may call any special meetings of the bar at such time and place as it shall designate.

Section 2. — In the absence of specific action by the Council, the Executive Committee shall fix the time and place of all meetings of the Council. There shall be at least two meetings annually. Special meetings of the Council may be called at any time by the Executive Committee. The Executive Committee shall call a special meeting at the written request of twelve members of the Council.

Section 3. — The Executive Committee shall meet on the call of the president or of the president-elect and a meeting shall be called at the written request of three members of the committee.

Section 4. — Proceedings at all meetings shall be governed by Roberts Rules of Order, except that no member shall without unanimous consent speak more than twice on any one subject or more than five minutes at any one time.

Article VI. Executive Committee.

Section 1. — There shall be an Executive Committee consisting of twelve members, six of whom shall be elected annually by and from the Council, with the president, president-elect, immediate past president, President of the Young Lawyers Conference, Chair of the Senior Lawyers Conference and Chair of the Conference of Local Bar Associations serving as ex officio members.

Section 2. — A quorum of the Executive Committee shall consist of six members thereof.

Section 3. — The Executive Committee shall have authority to:

(a) Allocate funds as required for authorized bar purposes and functions within amounts available to the bar;

(b) Employ such staff as it deems necessary and fix the duties and compensation of such staff;

(c) Cause proper books and records of account to be kept and audited annually, and cause proper financial statements of receipts and expenditures to be prepared and regularly presented to Council;

(d) Review annually the performance of the Executive Director, Deputy Executive Director and Bar Counsel and set the compensation of each;

(f) Review matters which are placed on the agenda for Council meetings and make recommendations to Council when appropriate; and

(e) Between meetings of Council, perform any other duties and powers prescribed for Council under any of the rules of the Supreme Court of Virginia, except such duties and powers as Council may reserve to itself or delegate to other committees.

Editor's note. — Paragraphs (f) and (e) are set out in the order in which they appear in the original.

Article VII. District Committees and the Disciplinary Board.

Sec. 1. District Committees — The several district committees provided for by Part 6, Section IV, Paragraph 13 of the Rules of Court and elected by the Council shall be known as District Committees under numerical designation of the respective districts, for example, First District Committee, etc. A district committee shall consist of ten or, in the discretion of Council, twenty, thirty or forty members. Three members of a ten-member district committee, six members of a twenty-member district committee, nine members of a thirty member district committee, and twelve members of a forty member district committee shall be non-lawyers. All other district committee members shall be active members of the bar. No member of the Council shall be a member of a district committee. All potential district committee appointees shall fulfill the qualification requirements provided for in Paragraph 13 before appointment.

Effective July 1, 1992, the District Committees shall be comprised of the following judicial circuits:

First District Committee: Circuits 1, 3, 5, 7 and 8
Second District Committee: Circuits 2 and 4 (2 sections)
Third District Committee: Circuits 6, 11, 12, 13 and 14 (3 sections)
Fourth District Committee: Circuits 17 and 18 (2 sections)
Fifth District Committee: Circuits 19 and 31 (3 sections)
Sixth District Committee: Circuits 9 and 15
Seventh District Committee: Circuits 16, 20 and 26
Eighth District Committee: Circuits 23 and 25
Ninth District Committee: Circuits 10, 21, 22 and 24
Tenth District Committee: Circuits 27, 28, 29 and 30 (2 sections)

The Secretary shall notify the members of each district committee of their appointments and each district committee shall meet within forty (40) days thereafter and shall elect from their attorney members a Chair, Vice-Chair, and Secretary and such other officers as they deem necessary.

Sec. 2. Disciplinary Board — The Council shall recommend persons to the Court for appointment as members of the Disciplinary Board. The Disciplinary Board shall consist of twenty members, four of whom shall be non-lawyers and sixteen of whom shall be active members of the bar. The Council shall also recommend attorney members of the Disciplinary Board to the Court to serve as Chair and two Vice Chairs. All potential Disciplinary Board appointees shall fulfill the qualification requirements provided for in Paragraph 13 before appointment.

Article VIII. Standing Committees.

Section 1. Committee on Legal Ethics. — There shall be a standing committee to be appointed by the president and to be known as the Committee on Legal Ethics. The committee shall consist of nine active members of the bar, at least two of whom shall be members of the Council. All powers and duties of the Council with respect to legal ethics, not otherwise delegated or reserved, shall be exercised and discharged by the committee.

Members shall be appointed to three-year terms. No member shall serve more than two consecutive three-year terms. A member appointed to fill an unexpired term shall be eligible to serve two additional full three-year terms. An eligible member wishing to be reappointed shall be required to reapply in writing prior to the end of his or her current term under procedures established by Council and administered by the executive director.

Section 2. Committee on Unauthorized Practice of Law. — There shall be a standing committee to be appointed by the president and to be known as the Committee on the Unauthorized Practice of Law. The committee shall consist of nine members. Seven of the members shall be active members of the bar, at least two of whom shall be members of the Council. Two of the members shall be non-lawyers. All powers and duties of the Council with respect to the unauthorized practice of the law, not otherwise delegated or reserved, shall be exercised and discharged by the committee.

Members shall be appointed to three-year terms. No member shall serve more than two consecutive three-year terms. A member appointed to fill an unexpired term shall be eligible to serve two additional full three-year terms. An eligible member wishing to be reappointed shall be required to reapply in writing prior to the end of his or her current term under procedures established by Council and administered by the executive director.

Section 3. Committee on Lawyer Discipline. — There shall be a standing committee to be appointed by the president and to be known as the Committee on Lawyer Discipline. The committee shall consist of twelve persons, ten of whom shall be active members of the bar and two shall be non-lawyers. In addition, the vice-chairman of the Virginia State Bar Disciplinary Board shall be an ex-officio, non voting member of the committee. At least two of the lawyers who are members shall be members of the Council. All members shall serve a three-year term and the president shall appoint members to the committee so as to allow for the retirement from the committee of one third of its membership at the end of each fiscal year. No member shall serve more than two consecutive three-year terms. A member appointed to fill an unexpired term shall be eligible to serve two additional full three-year terms. An eligible member wishing to be reappointed shall be required to reapply in writing under procedures established by Council and administered by the executive director. All powers and duties of the Council with respect to operation of the bar's disciplinary system, not otherwise delegated or reserved, shall be exercised and discharged by the committee.

Section 4. Committee on Professionalism. — There shall be a standing committee to be appointed by the president and to be known as the Committee on Professionalism. The committee shall consist of fifteen members, each of whom shall be an active or judicial member of the bar. At least two of the committee members shall be members of the Council, at least three shall be current or former members of the faculty of the mandatory course on professionalism, and at least one shall, when initially appointed, be an officer or member of the board of governors of the Young Lawyers Conference. In addition, the Virginia State Bar Counsel shall be an ex officio member of the committee. All members shall serve for a three-year term. No member may serve more than two consecutive three-year terms. A member appointed to fill an unexpired term shall be eligible to serve two additional full three-year terms. An eligible member wishing to be reappointed shall be required to reapply in writing under procedures established by Council and administered by the executive director. All powers and duties of Council with respect to the implementation of Paragraph 13.1 of Part Six, Section IV of the Rules of the Supreme Court of Virginia, and with respect to professionalism in the practice of law in Virginia, not otherwise delegated or reserved, shall be exercised and discharged by the Committee.

Section 5. Budget and Finance Committee. — There shall be a standing committee to be appointed by the president and to be known as the Budget and Finance Committee. The committee shall consist of nine active members of the bar, three of whom shall be elected members of the Executive Committee and three of whom shall be other members of Council. In addition, the president-elect shall serve as an ex officio member.

All members, other than the president-elect, shall serve three-year terms. No member shall serve more than two consecutive three-year terms. A member appointed to fill an unexpired term shall be eligible to serve two additional full three-year terms. An eligible member wishing to be reappointed shall be required to re-apply in writing under procedures established by Council and administered by the Executive Director.

The committee shall perform such tasks as are delegated or assigned by the Executive Committee and/or the Bar Council. The committee shall work with appropriate members of the bar staff to develop the bar's annual budget and present the budget to the Executive Committee and Council for approval. The committee shall also be responsible for reviewing and making recommendations with respect to the bar's appropriation requests prior to their submission to the Commonwealth of Virginia, Department of Planning and Budget. The committee shall also be responsible for assessing and making recommendations to the Executive Committee and Council regarding other budget matters, including personnel issues which are budget-related or budget-driven.

Article IX. Votes by Mail or Telephone.

By unanimous consent of the members of any committee, all questions before such committee may be settled by mail ballot or telephone call.

Article X. Vacancies in Committees.

All vacancies in committees appointed by the president shall be filled by him. Vacancies in other committees shall be temporarily filled by the president, his or her appointees to act until the next meeting of the Council.

Article XI. Sections.

The Council may create and abolish sections as it may consider necessary or desirable to accomplish the purposes and serve the interests of the Virginia State Bar and of the sections and shall prescribe the powers and duties of the sections. The bylaws of any section shall be subject to approval of Council.

Index to Bylaws of the Virginia State Bar

B

BAR COMMITTEES, VSB Bylaw Pt I Art V.
Committee on resolutions, VSB Bylaw Pt I Art VI.

BAR COMPOSITION, VSB Bylaw Pt I Art I.

BAR MEETINGS, VSB Bylaw Pt I Art IV.

BAR OFFICERS, VSB Bylaw Pt I Art II.

BONDS, SURETY.
Secretary-treasurer, VSB Bylaw Pt II Art III.

C

COMMITTEES.
Budget and finance committee, VSB Bylaw Pt II Art VIII.
Committee on lawyer advertising and solicitation, VSB Bylaw Pt II Art VIII.
Committee on lawyer discipline, VSB Bylaw Pt II Art VIII.
Committee on legal ethics, VSB Bylaw Pt II Art VIII.
Committee on professionalism, VSB Bylaw Pt II Art VIII.
Committee on unauthorized practice of law, VSB Bylaw Pt II Art VIII.
District committees, VSB Bylaw Pt II Art VII.
Executive committee, VSB Bylaw Pt II Art VI.
Mail votes, VSB Bylaw Pt II Art IX.
Standing committees, VSB Bylaw Pt II Art VIII.
Telephone votes, VSB Bylaw Pt II Art IX.
Vacancies, VSB Bylaw Pt II Art X.

COMMITTEES OF BAR, VSB Bylaw Pt I Art V.
Committee on resolutions, VSB Bylaw Pt I Art VI.

COUNCIL ELECTION, VSB Bylaw Pt II Art II.

COUNCIL MEETINGS, VSB Bylaw Pt II Art V.
Notice, VSB Bylaw Pt II Art IV.

COUNCIL MEMBERS, VSB Bylaw Pt II Art I.

COUNCIL SECTIONS, VSB Bylaw Pt II Art XI.

D

DISCIPLINARY BOARD.
District committees, VSB Bylaw Pt II Art VII.

DISTRICT COMMITTEES, VSB Bylaw Pt II Art VII.

E

ELECTION OF COUNCIL, VSB Bylaw Pt II Art II.

EXECUTIVE COMMITTEE, VSB Bylaw Pt II Art VI.

EXECUTIVE DIRECTOR, VSB Bylaw Pt II Art III.

M

MEETINGS OF BAR, VSB Bylaw Pt I Art IV.

MEETINGS OF COUNCIL, VSB Bylaw Pt II Art V.
Notice, VSB Bylaw Pt II Art IV.

MEMBERS OF BAR, VSB Bylaw Pt I Art I.

MEMBERS OF COUNCIL, VSB Bylaw Pt II Art I.

N

NOTICE.
Council meetings, VSB Bylaw Pt II Art IV.

O

OFFICERS OF BAR, VSB Bylaw Pt I Art II.

P

PRESIDENT.
Election, VSB Bylaw Pt I Art III.

S

SECRETARY-TREASURER, VSB Bylaw Pt II Art III.

SECTIONS WITHIN COUNCIL, VSB Bylaw Pt II Art XI.

STANDING COMMITTEES, VSB Bylaw Pt II Art VIII.

MANDATORY CONTINUING LEGAL EDUCATION REGULATIONS

Purpose

The Virginia Supreme Court has established, by Rule of Court, a mandatory continuing legal education program in the Commonwealth of Virginia, which requires each active member of the Virginia State Bar annually to complete a minimum of twelve (12) hours of approved continuing legal education courses, of which at least two (2) hours shall be in the area of legal ethics or professionalism, unless expressly exempted from such requirement.

The Virginia Supreme Court has established a Continuing Legal Education Board to administer the program and has given to it those general administrative and supervisory powers necessary to effectuate the purposes of the Rule, including the power to adopt reasonable and necessary regulations consistent with the Rule.

Pursuant to this authority, these regulations have been adopted by the Continuing Legal Education Board.

Effective July 1, 2001; amended effective November 1, 2011.

Regulation
101. Definitions.
102. Requirements and Computations.
103. Standards for Approval of Programs.
104. Procedure for Approval of Programs.
105. Procedure for Accreditation of Sponsors.
106. Delegation.
107. Board's Determination and Review.
108. Reporting of Certification Procedures.
109. Noncompliance, Restoration and Reinstatement.
110. Exemptions.
111. Waivers, Extensions and Extensions.
112. Representations by Members.

Appendix of Forms.

Regulation 101. Definitions.

As used in these regulations, the following definitions shall apply:

(a) The "Rule" shall mean the provisions of the Mandatory Continuing Legal Education (also referred to as "MCLE") Rule established by Paragraph 17 of Section IV, Part Six, Rules of Virginia Supreme Court.

(b) The "Board" shall mean the Virginia State Bar Mandatory Continuing Legal Education Board established by Paragraph B of the Rule.

(c) A "Member" as defined by Paragraph 2 of Section IV, Part Six, Rules of Virginia Supreme Court, shall comprise all attorneys-at-law in this Commonwealth.

(d) An "Active Member," shall mean an Active or Emeritus Member as defined by Paragraph 3 of Section IV, Part Six, Rules of Virginia Supreme Court.

(e) A "newly-admitted member" shall mean a person first admitted to practice during the current completion period.

(f) A "program sponsor" or "sponsor" is any person or entity presenting or offering to present one or more continuing legal education programs.

(g) The terms "course" and "program" mean a discrete continuing legal education (also referred to as "CLE") offering, regardless of length or daily schedule, provided that the course or program is a minimum of 30 minutes in length.

(h) An "accredited sponsor" shall mean an organization which, based on a history of providing approved courses and pursuant to Regulation 105, has been granted approval for its programs. The programs must meet the approval standards of Regulation 103 and are not subject to the individual course application procedures of Regulation 104(a).

(i) An "approved course" means a course expressly approved by the Board for the relevant completion period or a course offered by an accredited sponsor during the completion period for which the sponsor is accredited and meets the approval standards of Regulation 103.

(j) A "pre-recorded course" means a program where a live presentation has been recorded and presented via any electronic media (e.g. videotaped, DVD or CD-ROM presentations, audiotaped or CD presentations, pre-recorded telephone seminars or webcasts, on-demand online courses, etc.) that does not include simultaneous, live interaction with the presenter.

(k) A "specially approved course or program" means a course which does not meet the standards of regulation 103(b) and (c) but which, because of its significant value to the practice of a member who has sought approval, has been approved by the Board for such member. As to such member, the term "approved course" includes a specially approved course or program.

(*l*) The term "panel(s)" shall mean a committee or committees organized by the Board for the purpose of expeditiously considering and deciding matters arising under the Rule and these regulations.

(m) The term "Director of MCLE" or "MCLE Director" shall mean the head of the Mandatory Continuing Legal Education Department of the Virginia State Bar who acts as the liaison and administrative staff for the Board.

(n) A course or program offered "in-house" means one sponsored by a single private law firm, a single corporate law department or a single federal, state or local governmental agency or military branch for lawyers who are members or employees of the firm, department, agency or branch.

(o) The term "completion period" shall mean a period of one year beginning on November 1, of one year and ending on October 31 of the next year; provided, however, that the next completion period following June 30, 2001, shall be July 1, 2001, to October 31, 2002.

(p) The term "faculty member" shall mean a person qualified by practical or academic experiences to teach the subject he or she covers.

(q) "Credit hours" (also referred to in context as "hours," "credits," and "hours credit") are the 60-minute units used for measuring completion of Mandatory Continuing Legal Education as required by the Rule.

(r) "Ethics credits" are credit hours which apply toward Mandatory Continuing Legal Education in the area of legal ethics or professionalism as required by the Rule.

(s) A "qualified ethics course or component" is a clearly identified segment of a course or program which meets the requirements of Regulation 103(d) and is devoted to one or more topics embraced in recognized formulations of rules of professional conduct or codes of professional responsibility applicable to attorneys and/or to the systems and procedures which have been established for enforcement and interpretation of those rules or codes. An ethics component in a course or program involving a substantive area of law may constitute a "clearly identified segment" if the integration of the substantive material is necessary to understand the ethical topic, and if the ethical topic is the primary focus of the segment. Such a segment must be appropriately described or entitled in the course materials and must have a defined duration in the course or program schedule.

(t) A "qualified professionalism course or component" is a clearly identified segment of a course or program which meets the requirements of Regulation 103(d) and is devoted to one or more topics designed to educate and encourage attorneys to aspire to and achieve higher and more noble standards of professional conduct than the minimum standards set forth in recognized formulations of rules of professional conduct or codes of professional responsibility. All or part of a malpractice program may qualify as a professionalism course or component if it is devoted to one or more topics designed to educate and encourage attorneys to take measures in the conduct of the practice of law to serve the interests of the client, consistent with the attorney's fiduciary duty to the client, and to endeavor to maintain an appropriate standard of care in the practice of the profession. Such a course or component will not be approved if the primary focus is malpractice litigation tactics or strategy. A professionalism component in a course or program involving a substantive area of law may constitute a "clearly identified segment" if the integration of the substantive material is necessary to understand the professionalism topic, and if the professionalism topic is the primary focus of the segment. Such a segment must be appropriately described or entitled in the course materials and must have a defined duration in the course or program schedule.

(u) A "course presented by distance learning methods" includes any course in which the participant seeking credit received the instruction at a location different from the location from which the instruction was presented or at a time different from the time when the instruction was presented. Thus, all courses presented to participants from pre-recorded media (e.g. videotape, DVD or CD-ROM presentations, audiotape or CD presentations, pre-recorded telephone seminars or webcasts, on-demand online courses, etc.) are "courses presented by distance learning methods." Similarly, any course taken by a participant at a location separate from the instructor (e.g. live telephone seminars, live webcasts, live videoconferences, etc.) are "courses presented by distance learning methods." (Comment: See MCLE Board Opinion 16.)

(v) The term "online MCLE record" shall mean the electronic access to the individual attorney's MCLE record maintained by the MCLE Department of the Virginia State Bar.

Regulation 102. Requirements and Computations.

(a) Each active member, other than a newly-admitted member as defined in Regulation 101, shall complete, during each completion period in which he or she is an active member for any part thereof, a minimum of twelve (12) credit hours of approved continuing legal education (also referred to as CLE) courses, of which at least two (2) hours shall be in the area of legal ethics or professionalism. Of the twelve credit hours required, no more than eight (8) may be earned from pre-recorded courses. Credit must be obtained in the manner hereinafter provided, unless expressly exempted therefrom pursuant to the provisions of Regulation 110 or waived pursuant to Regulation 111.

(b) Credit will be given to a member who personally attends an approved course and to a member who prepares written materials for an approved course and to a member who personally participates as an instructor for such course. Credit in the area of legal ethics or professionalism will be given a member who attends a course approved for credit in such area and to a member who personally prepares materials for a qualified ethics or professionalism component of such course and to a member who personally participates as an instructor for such a component.

(c) Credits for attendance will be awarded on the basis of time spent in personal attendance at an approved course which meets the standards of these regulations. Credits for teaching will be awarded on the basis of time spent in personal participation as an instructor at an approved course. However, no credit will be awarded for teaching and preparation of a "specially approved course or program." Credit hours will be computed by calculating the total instructional minutes attended or taught for the course, rounded to the nearest half hour. Credit will not be given for time spent in meal or coffee breaks. Credit will not be given for keynote speeches or introductory remarks or time spent on any subject matter which is not directly related to instruction pertinent to that course.

EXAMPLES:

(1) A member attends a one-day course or seminar with seven (7) segments, each lasting 50 minutes. Two of the segments are in the area of legal ethics or professionalism under the standards set forth in Regulation 103. Credit hours will be computed by calculating the total instructional minutes rounded to the nearest half hour. Since there are 350 total instructional minutes (5 hours, 50 minutes) the Board will round this time to the nearest half hour and the member will receive six (6) hours credit, not seven (7). Of such six (6) hours credit, one and one-half (1 ½) hours (100 minutes rounded to the nearest half hour) will be in the area of legal ethics or professionalism.

(2) A member attends a course or program which is presented all day Friday and on Saturday morning. The member attends a 3 hour, 15 minute Friday morning session; a 2 hour, 15 minute Friday afternoon session; and a 3 hour, 10 minute Saturday morning session. Since the total instruction time is eight (8) hours and 40 minutes for the two-day program, the Board will round this time to the nearest half hour and the member will receive 8 ½ hours of credit.

(3) A member attends a course or program which is advertised as having been "approved by the Virginia Mandatory Continuing Legal Education Board" for six (6) credit hours, of which one and one-half (1 ½) apply in the area of legal ethics or professionalism. No further computation need be made by the member if he attends the entire course or program.

(4) A member personally teaches any of the courses in the previous examples. The teaching member will receive credit hours for teaching time computed in the same fashion as the credit hours are computed for the attending member.

(5) A member is a teacher at a one-day course or program with seven (7) segments, each lasting 50 minutes. Application forms are filed certifying that the member taught one segment and also attended one segment. The member did not attend or teach the other five segments. Since the member attended or taught 100 total instructional minutes for the course, the Board will round this time to the nearest half hour and the member will receive 1 ½ hours of credit. The member does not receive one credit hour for 50 minutes teaching plus one credit hour for the other 50 minutes attending.

(d) Credits for preparation will be awarded on the basis of time spent by a member (i) in preparing written materials which meet the standards of these regulations for use in the presentation of an approved course; and (ii) in preparing a personal presentation as an instructor for an approved course. The number of preparation minutes eligible for credit shall not exceed four times the number of instructional minutes in the presentation which is being prepared. Credit hours will be computed by calculating the total minutes spent in preparation for the course, rounded to the nearest half hour. In no event shall more than eight (8) hours of credit be awarded for preparing a single course or program.

EXAMPLES:

(1) A member prepares thorough, high-quality instructional written materials which appropriately cover the subject matter for an approved program which lasts 120 minutes. The member certifies that eight (8) hours or more was spent preparing the written materials. The Board will award eight (8) credit hours for preparation time. This does not exceed the maximum limit of four times the presentation time of the program and is consistent with the maximum limit of eight (8) hours of credit for preparing a single course or program.

(2) Same as example 1 above except the member also taught the entire program and certifies that an additional eight (8) hours or more was spent preparing for the presentation as an instructor. This is a total preparation time of sixteen (16) hours. The Board will still award eight (8) credit hours for preparation time because this is the maximum limit of four times the presentation time and also because this is the maximum limit of credit for preparing a single course or program. However, the member will be awarded two (2) credit hours for teaching time and will therefore receive a total of ten (10) credit hours for the activities in preparing and teaching the program.

(3) A member teaches at a course approved for five (5) credits including one (1) ethics credit. The member certifies that he taught the morning ethics segment of twenty (20) minutes. The member further certifies that one hour and twenty minutes was spent preparing for the presentation. Since the member taught twenty (20) minutes eighty (80) minutes (four (4) times the presentation time) of the member's preparation time is eligible for credit. The Board will total the minutes and round this time to the nearest half hour and the member will therefore receive a total of one and one half (1.5) hours CLE credit including one and one half (1.5) hours ethics credit for teaching and preparing the ethics segment.

(e) A one-year carryover of credit hours will be permitted, so that accrued credit hours in excess of one year's requirement may be carried forward to meet the requirement of the following year. A member may carry forward a maximum of twelve (12) credit hours, not more than two (2) of which, if earned in the area of legal ethics or professionalism, may be counted toward credit hours required in such area. No more than eight (8) credit hours, of which not more than two (2) ethics or professionalism credit hours, may be carried forward from pre-recorded programs.

(f) A member shall not receive credit for any course attended in preparation for admission to practice law in any state. A member shall not receive credit for teaching that is directed primarily to persons preparing for admission to practice law. Regular full time, part-time and adjunct academic faculty shall not receive credit for teaching any law school courses (undergraduate or graduate) or bar review courses. A member attending law classes, for a purpose other than preparing for admission to practice law, may receive credit in accordance with the manner described in Regulation 102(c). A member may not receive credit for any course which is not materially different in substance from a course for which the same member received credit during the same completion period or the completion period immediately prior to the one for which credit is sought.

(g) A member may receive credit for attending a course delivered by distance learning methods which otherwise satisfies the requirements of these Regulations. No more than eight (8) credit hours may be earned in any twelve hour period attending pre-recorded courses. (Comment: See MCLE Board Opinion 16.)

Regulation 103. Standards for Approval of Programs.

(a) Subject to the provisions of Regulation 105(d), a course is approved for credit if it has been specifically approved by the Board or is presented by an accredited sponsor previously designated by the Board under the provisions of Regulation 105. A course is approved for credit in the area of legal ethics or professionalism if and to the extent specifically approved by the Board. Subject to the provisions of Regulation 105(d), a course presented by an accredited sponsor is also approved for credit in the area of legal ethics or professionalism if and to the extent so represented by such sponsor.

(b) The course must have significant intellectual or practical content. Its primary objective must be to increase the attendee's professional competence and skills as an attorney, and to improve the quality of legal services rendered to the public.

(c) The course must pertain to a recognized legal subject or other subject matter which integrally relates to the practice of law, or to the professional responsibility or ethical obligations of the participants.

(d) A course may be approved for credit in the area of legal ethics or professionalism only to the extent that the course constitutes or contains one or more qualified ethics or professionalism components as defined in Regulation 101. Topics which will not generally be approved for ethics credit include ethics standards of conduct applicable to other professions such as government employees, government contractors, accountants and businesses including corporate compliance. Also, rules of procedure, rules of evidence and litigation tactics will not generally be approved for ethics credit. (Comment: See MCLE Board Opinion 13.) A minimum scheduling of thirty (30) minutes in the aggregate of one or more qualified ethics or professionalism components is required before an approved course can be approved for credit in the area of legal ethics or professionalism.

EXAMPLES:

(1) A sponsor's application for approval of a one-day program comprising seven 50 minute segments states in relevant part "each speaker will devote ten minutes of allotted time to ethical considerations." The program does not contain a qualified ethics component and is not eligible for approval for credit in the area of legal ethics. The requirement that a qualified component be a "clearly defined segment" is not met. Such segment must be capable of identification on the schedule and have a defined beginning and end.

(2) A sponsor's application for approval of a one-day program reveals in relevant part that the opening 30 minute morning segment is clearly identified as devoted to ethical considerations and that the concluding 20 minutes of the afternoon session is also clearly identified as devoted to ethical considerations. Assuming that other requirements for course approval are met, the Board will approve the program for one (1) hour credit in the area of legal ethics or professionalism. (See Regulation 102.)

(e) Courses must be conducted in a setting physically suitable to the educational course or program, free from distractions and conducive to learning.

(f) No credit will be allowed (or "be granted") for any course or part thereof taken simultaneously with any other course or part thereof.

(g) Thorough, high quality instructional written materials which appropriately cover the subject matter must be distributed to all attendees at or before the time the course is presented. A mere agenda or topical outline will not be sufficient. (Comment: See MCLE Board Opinion 14.)

(h) Each course shall be presented by a faculty member or members qualified by academic or practical experience to teach the subjects covered. Consistent with Virginia State Bar policy, course sponsors should exercise care to ensure that faculty members, where possible, reflect the racial and gender diversity of the State Bar as a whole.

(i) A course presented by distance learning methods which otherwise satisfies the requirements of these Regulations may be approved provided the speakers and attendees are participating simultaneously. Pre-recorded courses in any electronic form which otherwise satisfy the requirements of these regulations may be approved however no other form of self-study will be approved. (Comment: See MCLE Board Opinion 16.)

(j) A program offered "in-house" may be approved by the Board provided the subject matter of the program does not primarily focus on internal policies, practices and procedures. An in-house program will be approved if it otherwise meets the standards of these regulations and if the approval procedures prescribed by these regulations are followed. (Comment: See MCLE Board Opinion 17.)

(k) Participation in deliberative groups concerned with political activism, law reform, judicial administration, or regulation of the profession generally will not be approved for credit. Activities associated with membership or attendance at committee meetings, business meetings or work sessions will generally not be approved for credit.

(*l*) To be accredited, a course must have no attendance restrictions based on race, color, national origin, religion, creed, gender, age, disability, sexual orientation or marital status.

(m) No credit will be given for any course primarily focused on marketing a particular product or service. (Comment: See MCLE Board Opinion 15.)

(n) A course that does not meet the requirements of subsections (b) and (c) of this Regulation may, on application of a member, be approved as a "specially approved course or program" for the applicant where the Board is satisfied that the course has significant value to the applicant's practice. Thus, for example, in appropriate cases courses on engineering, accounting or medical topics may be approved for a particular member.

Regulation 104. Procedure for Approval of Programs.

(a) A member or course sponsor desiring approval of a course or program shall submit to the Board all information called for by the "Application for Approval of a Continuing Legal Education Course." The content of this application has been promulgated by the Board and may be changed from time to time. A member seeking approval of a course as a "specially approved course or program" should include on the Application for Approval of a Continuing Legal Education Course, or as an attachment thereto, a statement of why the course has significant value to the member's practice. The Board shall then determine whether or not the course or program satisfies the requirements of Regulation 103. If the course or program is approved, the Board also shall determine the number of credit hours to be awarded. The Board shall notify the requesting member or sponsor of its decision within 90 days after receipt of the completed application. The Board shall maintain and make available a list of all approved courses and programs for each completion period. An approved course or program is accredited only for the completion period for which it is approved. A "specially approved course or program" is accredited only for the member for whom approved.

(b) The sponsor of an approved course or program should include in its brochures or course descriptions the information contained in the following illustrative statement: "This course or program has been approved by the Virginia Mandatory Continuing Legal Education Board for ________ hours of credit, of which ________ hours will also apply in the area of legal ethics or professionalism." An announcement is permissible only after the course or program has been specifically approved pursuant to an application submitted directly by the sponsor.

(c) The sponsor of an approvable course or program that has not yet been approved after application should announce: "Application for approval for this course or program is pending with the Virginia Mandatory Continuing Legal Education Board."

(d) At each presentation of an approved course or program or one for which approval is pending, the sponsor shall make available copies of the Board's Certification of Attendance for completion by the attendees and the Board's Certification of Teaching for completion by the instructors, copies of which will be provided by the Board with the course approval notification. The content of these certifications has been promulgated by the Board and may change from time to time. Where some portion of the program has not been approved for CLE or ethics credit, the sponsor shall provide that information to the attendees with the certification of attendance.

(e) In the instance of a course or program presented while an application for approval is pending, it will be the responsibility of the sponsor to provide the attendees with the Board's Certification of Attendance or Teaching as required in Regulation 104(d) immediately upon receipt of the approval notification. If such course or program is not approved, the sponsor shall immediately notify the attendees that credit for the course has been denied. Under certain circumstances a member may seek approval for a specially approved course or program as defined in Regulation 101(k) in the manner specified in Regulation 104(f).

(f) Any member seeking credit for attendance at a course or program shall submit to the Board immediately following such attendance all information called for on the Application for Approval of a Continuing Legal Education Course. The Board will then determine whether the program qualifies under these Regulations and, if so, how many credit hours are approved. The Board will promptly notify the applicant of its decision. Applications received more than 90 days following the date of the program shall be subject to a late application fee.

(g) Any sponsor seeking approval after presenting a course or program, shall submit to the Board within 30 days after the date of the program all information called for on the Application for Approval of a Continuing Legal Education Course. The Board will then determine whether the program qualifies under these Regulations and, if so, how many credit hours are approved. The Board will promptly notify the applicant of its decision.

(h) Failure to comply with the sponsor requirements of Regulation 104 or Regulation 105 may result in fines; revocation of course approval; denial of future course credit; suspension or revocation of accreditation; or any other sanction deemed fit by and in the discretion of the Board.

Regulation 105. Procedure for Accreditation of Sponsors.

(a) Any sponsor may apply for approval of individual courses by complying with the criteria of Regulation 103 and the procedures of Regulation 104.

(b) If the Board determines that a sponsor regularly provides a significant volume of continuing legal education courses, that these courses uniformly meet the approval criteria of Regulation 103, and that the sponsor will maintain and submit the records directed by these Regulations, the Board may designate such a course provider as an "accredited sponsor" under the Rule. Such designation shall be effective for a period of no more than two years unless renewed.

(c) A sponsor applying for status as an accredited sponsor shall submit to the Board all information called for on the Application for Status as Accredited Sponsor of Continuing Legal Education.

(d) An accredited sponsor shall be subject to and governed by the applicable provisions of the Rule and these regulations, including the quality standards of Regulation 103 and the record-keeping and reporting requirements of this Regulation 105. The Board may at any time review an accredited sponsor program and reserves the right to deny CLE or ethics credit when the standards for approval are not met. Accordingly, for example, an accredited sponsor may represent in its descriptive literature that a course or program generates credits in the area of legal ethics or professionalism only to the extent the course contains one or more qualified ethics components as provided in Regulation 103.

(e) The approval procedure of Regulation 104 does not apply to accredited sponsors. An accredited sponsor shall provide the Board at least thirty days in advance of a program with a descriptive course agenda or brochure which includes the name, date, location and credit hours requested for a particular course pursuant to the approval standards of Regulation 103, including, where appropriate, credit hours requested in the area of legal ethics or professionalism and a description of the content of the ethics session(s). The Board may request additional information regarding a course or program. The Board will provide the sponsor with copies of the Board's Certification of Attendance and Certification of Teaching for each course or program and the sponsor shall make available, collect and transmit such forms in accordance with the requirements of Regulation 104(d).

(f) The Board may at any time reevaluate and revoke the status of an accredited sponsor. If the Board finds there is a basis for revocation of the accreditation granted to an accredited sponsor, the Board shall send notice by certified mail to that sponsor of the revocation within thirty (30) days of the Board's decision.

(g) Law firms, professional corporations, and corporate law departments are not eligible to become accredited sponsors.

Regulation 106. Delegation.

(a) The Board may organize itself into panels to facilitate course approval, sponsor accreditation, interpretation of these regulations and to consider and decide matters arising under the Rule and under these regulations.

(b) To facilitate the orderly and prompt administration of the Rule and these regulations, and to expedite the processes of course approval the Board may, under its supervision and direction, delegate to the Director of MCLE (hereafter referred to as the MCLE Director) general authority to act on behalf of the Board to review applications and approve or deny programs for credit pursuant to the approval standards of Regulation 103.

Regulation 107. Board's Determination and Review.

(a) Pursuant to directions established by the Board, a panel or the MCLE Director on behalf of the Board shall, in response to written requests for approval of courses or programs or for awarding of credit for the attendance at or teaching in approved courses, waivers, extensions of time deadlines and interpretations of these regulations, make a written response describing the action taken. A Panel or the MCLE Director may seek a determination of the Board before taking action. Upon request of the Board, the panel or MCLE Director shall report on all determinations made since the last meeting of the Board.

(b) An aggrieved party may file with the Board a written appeal of an adverse decision by a panel or the MCLE Director within thirty (30) days after notice of the adverse decision has been mailed to him or her. No form of appeal is required but the affected person or program sponsor shall state in narrative form the action complained of and all of the reasons he or she believes the decision is erroneous.

(c) The Board shall review any adverse determination of a panel or the MCLE Director which has been appealed to it pursuant to Regulation 107(b). The aggrieved party may present information to the Board in writing or in person, and at such time and place as the Board may direct. If the Board finds that a panel or the MCLE Director has incorrectly interpreted the facts, the provisions of the Rule or the provisions of these regulations, it may take such action as may be appropriate. The Board shall advise the affected party or program sponsor of its findings and any action taken.

(d) Pursuant to Paragraph 17 of Section IV, Part Six, Rules of the Virginia Supreme Court, the Virginia State Bar may from time to time establish fees for processing applications, approving courses and accrediting sponsors; the remittance of any of these may be required before action is taken by the Board.

(e) All decisions of the Board under this Regulation 107 and any other of these regulations shall be final and binding on all persons affected thereby and no appeal or other relief therefrom shall lie, except as specifically provided in Regulation 109.

Regulation 108. Reporting of Certification Procedures.

(a) Where a sponsor makes copies of the Certification of Attendance and the Certification of Teaching available at a course or program, each active member who wishes credit may certify attendance electronically as instructed on the MCLE attendance reporting site of the Virginia State Bar's internet website.

(b) Where a member attends a course or program, and for any reason the member is unable to certify his or her attendance or teaching credit electronically, the member who wishes the Board to record credit may obtain a copy of the Certification of Attendance or Certification of Teaching from the sponsor, complete it and forward it to the Board.

(c) On or before October 31 of each year each active member shall certify attendance online or submit the Certification of Attendance or Certification of Teaching for the minimum educational requirement.

(d) The MCLE Board shall provide ongoing access to each individual attorney's MCLE record for the current compliance year on the Virginia State Bar's internet website. The record shall include carryover hours from the previous reporting period, identifying course information including the number of hours reported for each course and the total hours of CLE, including the totals for those CLE hours designated as ethics or professionalism and those hours for pre-recorded courses which are limited to eight (8) hours per reporting period. Attorneys shall periodically review this online MCLE record to ensure accuracy and timely compliance.

(e) Following the end of each completion period, the Board shall advise each active member of his or her status respecting completion of the annual educational requirements. This notice shall be entitled the "MCLE END OF YEAR REPORT" and shall include the information reflected on the individual attorney's MCLE record as of October 31 and instructions for completion and timely compliance.

(f) If the active member accepts the MCLE END OF YEAR REPORT as accurately reflecting his or her credit hours for the period, including any carryover hours from the previous reporting period, and the form lists 12.0 or more CLE credits of which 2.0 or more are ethics or professionalism credits, the member does not need to file his form with the MCLE Board. If a member believes that the information reflected on the Board's records is erroneous or incomplete, then additions and corrections to the MCLE END OF YEAR REPORT must be filed as instructed and received by the MCLE office no later than close of business on December 15 of the year in which the credit is sought.

(g) To the extent not completed online, the MCLE End of Year Report must accompany any request for credit or corrections submitted after October 31.

(h) Delinquency fees for failure to timely complete the MCLE requirements are set forth in Paragraph 19 of Section IV, Part Six, Rules of Virginia Supreme Court. Members who have attended an insufficient number of required credits by the October 31 deadline shall remit a delinquency fee hereto referred to as a "noncompliance fee." Members who certify attendance after the December 15 certification deadline shall remit the appropriate delinquency fee hereto referred to as a "late filing fee." The late filing fee amount shall be doubled for members who fail to comply with the certification requirements by February 1 following the completion period.

(i) After December 15, a member who wishes to receive credit for credit hours earned during the previous completion period whether for compliance or additional carryover credit may forward to the Board a certification on the appropriate forms together with remittance of the late filing fee. Any credits approved shall be recorded for the previous completion period and shall be eligible for the one year carryover into the current completion period in the same fashion as other credits. A member may not apply for credits earned earlier than the next preceding completion period.

Regulation 109. Noncompliance, Restoration and Reinstatement.

(a) *Noncompliance.* — (1) An active member who fails to comply with the educational and certification requirements of the Rule and these regulations, including payment of any required fees, and has not obtained a waiver or extension for good cause shown by December 15 of each year, shall be subject to suspension of such active member's license to practice law as is provided by Paragraph 13.2 of Section IV, Part Six, Rules of Virginia Supreme Court.

(2) Pursuant to Paragraph 13.2 of Section IV, Part Six, Rules of Virginia Supreme Court, whenever the Board determines that an active member has failed to (i) complete the mandatory continuing legal education requirements as required by Regulation 102 and/or (ii) failed to certify attendance and pay any required fees as required by Regulation 108 without first obtaining a waiver or extension in accordance with Regulation 111, the member shall be deemed to be delinquent.

(b) *Restoration and Reinstatement.* — (1) A delinquent member may be restored to good standing only following (i) his or her certifying to the Secretary-Treasurer of the Virginia State Bar of compliance with the requirements of the Rule in the manner provided by Regulation 108 and as instructed in the notice of impending suspension provided pursuant to Paragraph 19 of Section IV, Part Six, Rules of Virginia Supreme Court, and a determination by the Board that he or she has completed the mandatory continuing legal education requirements of the Rule and paying any required fees, or (ii) the obtaining of a waiver or extension in accordance with Regulation 111.

(2) A delinquent member who is suspended pursuant to Paragraph 13.2 shall not further engage in the active practice of law until he or she has been reinstated. A suspended member may be reinstated only after paying any required fees and certifying compliance with the Rule as provided in Paragraph 13.2 and these regulations.

(3) Where a default in compliance is cured by earning credit hours in a subsequent completion period, credit hours applied to correct the default shall not be applied to satisfy the requirements of any other period.

(4) A member suspended for an entire completion period must show attendance at 12.0 CLE credit hours including 2.0 ethics credits earned within the previous 12 months. This member cannot rely on credits earned through carryover in the previous

completion period or credits used to satisfy the requirement of any previous compliance year.

Regulation 110. Exemptions.

The Rule exempts from the certification requirement a newly admitted member for the completion period in which he or she is first admitted to practice in Virginia. A newly admitted member will not receive credit under these regulations for attending or teaching any course prior to his or her admission to the Virginia State Bar.

EXAMPLE:

Attorney A is first licensed to practice law in October 2009. Attorney A is not required to comply with the minimum continuing legal education requirement of the Rule and these regulations by taking or teaching approved courses until on and after November 1, 2009. Attorney A also shall not be required to file the certification required by Regulation 108 until December 15, 2010. If Attorney A attends or teaches approved courses between October 2009 and November 1, 2009, he may "carry over" to the next completion period credits in accordance with Regulation 102. Attorney A, beginning on November 1, 2009, will be subject to said requirement as long as he or she is an active member of the Virginia State Bar.

Regulation 111. Waivers, Extensions and Extensions.

(a) *Waivers.* — (1) A waiver of the MCLE requirement or of any fees associated with MCLE noncompliance may be sought by filing a request with the Board, together with any appropriate or required supporting material or documentation (e.g. doctors' letters, medical records). The filing of any waiver request does not toll the running of any time limit set forth in these regulations or the Rule regarding suspension.

(2) A waiver shall be valid for a single completion period, unless renewed or extended by the Board. A waiver will be granted only for good cause.

(3) If the waiver is based on medical reason, condition, illness or hospitalization, then the application for waiver shall be a completed form entitled "Request for Waiver Based on Hospitalization, Illness or Medical Reason." It must be completed and signed by the admitting, family or attending health care provider and it must set forth the medical condition, hospitalization or illness which prevents the member from completing the required MCLE courses for the period for which the Waiver is being requested and have attached to it any appropriate supporting material or documentation.

(4) If the waiver is based on non-medical reasons, then the grounds shall be stated in a letter to the Board and any appropriate supporting material or documentation shall be attached.

(5) A member who is unable to satisfy the MCLE requirement due to extraordinary or extenuating circumstances beyond the control of the member may apply as prescribed in Regulation 111(a)(1) to have all or part of the eight-hour limitation on pre-recorded courses waived.

(6) All waiver requests should be promptly submitted when the grounds for the waiver request become known to the applicant or applicant's representative. Failure to file a waiver request in a timely manner may be considered by the Board in determining whether to grant a waiver. A prudent lawyer will use the carryover of credits provision of the Rule to avoid most non-medical based waiver requests.

(b) *Extensions.* — (1) An extension may be sought by filing with the Board a request, together with any appropriate or required supporting material or documentation (e.g. physicians' letters, medical records, military deployment orders). The filing of an extension request does not toll the running of any time limit set forth in these regulations or the Rule regarding suspension.

(2) An extension shall be valid for the specific time period granted by the Board unless renewed or extended. An extension will be granted only for good cause.

(3) If the extension is based on medical reason, condition, illness or hospitalization, then the application for extension shall be a completed form entitled "Request for an Extension Based on Hospitalization, Illness or Medical Reason." It must be completed and signed by the admitting, family or attending health care provider and it must set forth the medical condition, hospitalization or illness which prevents the member from completing the required MCLE courses for the period for which an extension is being requested and have attached to it any appropriate supporting material or documentation.

(4) If the extension is based on non-medical reasons, then the grounds should be stated in a letter to the Board and any appropriate supporting material or documentation should be attached.

(5) All extension requests should be promptly submitted when the grounds for the extension request become known to the applicant or the applicant's representative. Failure to file an extension request in a timely manner may be considered by the Board in determining whether to grant an extension. A prudent lawyer will use the carryover of credits provision of the Rule to avoid most non-medical based extension requests.

(c) *Deferrals.* — (1) Members who change their class of membership from Active or Emeritus Member to any other class of membership, as defined in Paragraph 3 of Section IV, Part Six, Rules of Virginia Supreme Court, during the course of the compliance year may defer the completion of any remaining MCLE requirements (including payment of any outstanding MCLE delinquency fee obligations) for that compliance year including any MCLE deficiencies for any previous year(s). Prior to reactivation of their membership status, members shall satisfy all deferred MCLE requirements in addition to the requirement for the current compliance year. Credit hours reported for compliance with the current year's requirement must have been completed within the previous twelve months prior to reactivation.

Regulation 112. Representations by Members.

A member who makes a materially false statement in any document filed with the Board shall be subject to appropriate disciplinary action.

APPENDIX OF FORMS.

Form 2.

Virginia MCLE Board
Virginia State Bar
707 East Main Street, 15th Floor
Richmond, VA 23219-2800
(804) 775-0577 · (804) 775-0544 · Web site: www.vsb.org

CERTIFICATION OF ATTENDANCE (FORM 2)

Pursuant to Paragraph 17B, C and D of Section IV, Part Six, Rules of the Supreme Court of Virginia. The information provided will be available for inspection by the public under the Freedom of Information Act. Complete all requested information and sign certification.

Contact the Sponsor First for Virginia Approval Information and Form.
When provided, also attach any sponsor generated attendance form. The Virginia certification of attendance and/or Virginia course approval ID# has been provided to the sponsor for all Virginia approved programs.

Member Name: ______________________ VSB Member Number: ______________

Official Address of Record: ______________________

______________________ Daytime Phone (   ) ______________

______________________ E-Mail Address: ______________
City State Zip

Course ID Number:

Sponsor:

Course/Program Title:

CLE (Ethics) Credits: (   ) Ethics

CERTIFICATION

Date(s) Attended: ______________________ Location(s): ______________________

Delivery method: _____Live or Group Video _____*Live Telephone or live Webcast _____ *Videoconference or Satellite
_____* Internet on-demand _____*CD-rom _____♦ Video/DVD _____♦Audio/CD _____Other______________
Setting: _____Group (with other attendees) _____* Individual attendance at my location

****Distance Learning Programs Require Attendance Form Verified and Provided by the Course Sponsor when done in an Individual Setting.***
♦Video and Audio programs require at least 2 attorneys in attendance

By my signature below I certify

___ I attended a total of ____________ (hrs/mins) of **approved CLE**, of which (_______) (hrs/mins) were in **approved Ethics**.
___ The sessions I am claiming had written instructional materials to cover the subject.
___ I participated in this program in a setting physically suitable to the course and a suitable writing surface was available.
___ I was given the opportunity to participate in discussions with other attendees and/or the presenter.
___ I understand I may not receive credit for any course/segment which is not materially different in substance than a course/segment for which credit has been previously given during the same completion period or the completion period immediately prior.
___ I understand that a materially false statement shall be subject to appropriate disciplinary action.

NOTE: Credit is awarded for actual time in attendance rounded to the nearest half hour.

______________________ ______________________
Date Signature

You may certify your MCLE attendance online at www.vsb.org

MCLE Completion Deadline - October 31
Deadline to Certify MCLE Approved Hours - December 15
A $100 fee will be charged for failure to comply with either deadline

Fax transmissions are subject to receipt by the MCLE office of complete and legible forms.

Form 3.

Virginia MCLE Board

CERTIFICATION OF TEACHING (FORM 3)

MCLE requirement pursuant to Paragraph 17, of Section IV, Part Six, Rules of the Supreme Court of Virginia and the MCLE Board Regulations.

INSTRUCTIONS

E-mail this form to mymcle@vsb.org

Complete this Certification to Include Both Teaching and Attendance hours. Retain copy for two years.
MCLE Compliance Deadline - October 31. MCLE Reporting Deadline - December 15.
A $100 fee will be assessed for failure to comply with either deadline.

Member Name: ____________________ **VSB Member Number:** ____________

Address: ____________________ **Daytime Phone:** ____________

____________________ **E-mail Address:** ____________

____
City **State** **Zip**

Course ID Number:

Sponsor:

Course/Program Title:

CLE (Ethics) Credits: ______ (______) Ethics

Date(s) of Teaching: ____________________ Location(s): ____________________

ONLY SESSIONS WITH WRITTEN INSTRUCTIONAL MATERIALS ARE APPROVABLE FOR CREDIT

- My teaching segment was ______ (hrs/mins) of CLE, of which (______) (hrs/mins) were in Ethics.
- In addition, I attended *other* segments totaling ______ (hrs/mins) of CLE, of which (______) (hrs/mins) were in Ethics.
- I spent ______ hours preparing for teaching my segment of the course.
- No more than four (4) hours of preparation credit may be claimed per one hour of instructional time in your presentation, and no more than eight (8) hours total for any one course. Total credit is awarded for actual time spent teaching, attendance and preparation rounded to the nearest half hour. (Example: 1hr 15min = 1.5hr)
- A materially false statement shall be subject to appropriate disciplinary action.

____________________ ____________________
Date **Signature**

Questions? Contact the MCLE Department at (804) 775-0577 or E-mail questions to mcle@vsb.org

If not e-mailed, this form may be mailed or faxed (fax disabled Nov 2-Dec 31)
Virginia MCLE Board
Virginia State Bar
707 East Main Street, 15th Floor
Richmond, VA 23219-2800
Web site: www.vsb.org Fax: (804) 775-0544

Form 4.

Virginia MCLE Board
Virginia State Bar
707 East Main Street, Suite 1500
Richmond, VA 23219-2800
(804) 775-0577
Website: http://www.vsb.org

BOARD USE ONLY	
Course ID# ________	**Letter#** ________
CLE hours ________	**Decision** ________
Ethics hours ________	**Decision** ________

APPLICATION FOR CLE COURSE APPROVAL (FORM 4)
MCLE Deadline October 31

1. Applicant: VSB member # ____________ Course Sponsor: ____________
   Name: ____________ Sponsor Representative: ____________
   Address: ____________ Address: ____________
   ____________ ____________
   Daytime phone: (____) ____________ Phone: (____) ____________
   FAX #: (____) ____________ FAX #: ____________
   E-mail Address: ____________ E-mail Address: ____________
2. Title of Program: ____________
3. Total CLE hours: ______ including (____) Ethics hours (Only sessions with written materials are approvable)
   To qualify for credit <u>Ethics components must be clearly identified on the course schedule</u> and total a minimum of 30 minutes. A SAMPLE OF THE ETHICS MATERIAL DISTRIBUTED MUST BE ATTACHED.
4. CIRCLE all that apply to this presentation:
   TYPE: LIVE *ON-DEMAND
   SETTING: Group Setting *Delivered to Individuals In-house **ATTENDANCE:** OPEN CLOSED
   DELIVERY METHOD: Speaker in Room *Internet *Telephone/Webcast *CD-Rom Video Audio
   Satellite/Videoconference Other: ____________ ***See Opinion 16***
5. Date(s): ____________
   Location(City & Venue): ____________
6. Course Registration Fee: $ ______ **TARGET AUDIENCE:** CLIENTS ______ ATTORNEYS ______ OTHER ______
7. **REQUIRED ATTACHMENTS: MCLE Board will only consider applications with required attachments.**
   a. Program Time Schedule or Agenda (times are required to compute approvable credit hours)
   b. Table of Contents AND a sample of materials from each session (2-3 pgs each)
8. Description of materials: **Total pages** ______ Printed ______ Other ______
   Materials are distributed: Before program ______ At program ______ Other ______
   I am only requesting credit for sessions which had substantive written materials YES____ Unknown____
9. Physical Facilities: Conference room ______ Classroom ______ Theater style ______ Writing surface ______
10. Number of attorneys present or anticipated: ______ (Clients: ______) Number of non-attorneys: ______
11. If the program does not cover a recognized legal topic, attach a statement of how this course relates to your practice.
12. **ATTENDANCE CERTIFICATION:**
    I certify that I attended ______ CLE hours, including (______) Ethics hours, of the above-named course.
13. **Attorneys MUST FILE A $50 FEE ONLY WITH IN-HOUSE AUDIO/VIDEO or CD-ROM APPLICATION.**

Signature ____________
(VSB Member Applicant)

FAX & E-MAIL TRANSMISSIONS NOT ACCEPTED
Please allow 4 to 6 weeks for board decision on all applications

A materially false statement shall be subject to appropriate disciplinary action.

DEFINITION OF COURSE TYPES AND EXPLANATION OF VIRGINIA CRITERIA FOR APPROVAL

OPEN—Course advertised and open to all attorneys

CLOSED—Course open only to law firm, in-house law department, government agency, or members of a professional organization.

LIVE—Instructor and attendees participate simultaneously

IN-HOUSE—Program offered to attorneys within a firm, corporation or government agency.

GROUP SETTING—Program offered in group of 2 or more attorneys. (Where individual attendees are conferenced into a program you must meet Opinion 16 standards)

TELECONFERENCE, SATELLITE, VIDEOCONFERENCE, OR LIVE WEBCAST—To meet Virginia regulations the course must
(1) have a means to connect audience with faculty and/or other attendees to allow for live interaction and discussion.
(2) written materials must be available to participants prior to the broadcast.
(3) have attendance tracking - See OPINION 16

VIDEO, AUDIO, CD-ROM—To meet Virginia regulations the course must
(1) have at least 2 attorney participants (not restricted to only VA attorneys)
(2) be conducted in an educational setting (conference room)
(3) have written materials provided to each participant prior to the presentation.

INTERNET, CD-ROM ON-DEMAND programming—(SELF-STUDY NOT APPROVABLE.)
To meet Virginia regulations the course must
(1) be in audio or audio/video format. Text based courses are not approvable
(2) allow the participant to interact with the presenter and/or other attendees
(3) have written materials available to participants for reference during and subsequent to program
(4) have attendance tracking—See OPINION 16

INSTRUCTIONS FOR COMPLETING ATTORNEY APPLICATION FOR CLE APPROVAL (FORM 4)
MCLE DEADLINE—October 31

1. Complete attorney information on left hand side. Complete identifying sponsor information on right hand side of application.
2. Give Title of Program
3. **Total CLE hours** are the number of 60 minute hours of course presentation excluding introductory remarks, breaks, meals, closing remarks. **ONLY SESSIONS WITH WRITTEN INSTRUCTIONAL MATERIALS ARE APPROVABLE.** Keynote, mealtime speakers, judicial presentations or roundtable discussions are considered for CLE credit only when written handout materials are provided to appropriately cover the topic.

   Total Ethics hours are the number of 60 minute hours devoted to Ethics as it applies to Attorneys. Ethics relating to other professions, government employees, business professionals or general ethics are not approvable for Ethics credit. The Ethics time segment must be clearly defined on the course schedule and be accompanied by specific ethics materials. A sample of the ethics material must be included with this application. (See Opinion #13 for approvable ethics topics)
4. Indicate type of course, setting and delivery method specific to your application. Presentations resulting from the rental or purchase of video or audio programs require 2 or more attorneys in attendance and accompanied by appropriate written instructional materials. **Please contact the MCLE office for special instructions and forms.**
5. Give all dates and locations. The MCLE completion period is November 1–October 31. Courses are approved for the compliance period they are presented and **must be reported during that period.**
6. Enter the price you paid for course attendance. Target audience: Courses must be directed primarily to attorneys and address a legal topic to be approved. Special approval is given for non-legal courses if pertinent to the attorney's practice. (See #11 below)
7. **Warning!** Application must include the following:
   a. Program time schedule or agenda (TIMES ARE NEEDED TO COMPUTE APPROVABLE CREDIT HOURS)
   b. Table of contents, if available **AND** a sample of the written material for each session (2–3 pages) distributed to the attendees at the program. Ethics materials must be submitted to receive ethics credit. (See Opinion #14 on Written Materials) The MCLE Board reserves the right to request a complete set of materials.
   d. Applicable fees for in-house audio/video or CD-Rom program.
8. **Description of materials**—Give approximate total pages and check type of materials and when distributed. **ONLY SESSIONS WITH WRITTEN INSTRUCTIONAL MATERIALS ARE APPROVABLE**
9. Physical Facilities—select applicable type. A writing surface must be provided.
10. Enter approximate number of attorneys and non-attorneys present or anticipated.
11. Attach a statement of how a non-legal course relates to your practice if applicable.
12. Complete certification of attendance. For teaching credit please use the Form #3 Certification of Teaching.
13. In-house Video, Audio or CD-Rom programs require a $50 Application fee. Make payable to Treasurer of Virginia.

Index to Mandatory Regulations of Continuing Legal Education

A

ACCREDITATION OF SPONSORS.
Accredited sponsor defined, MCLE Reg 101.
Procedure, MCLE Reg 105.

ACCREDITED SPONSOR.
Procedure for accreditation, MCLE Reg 105.

ACCRUED CREDIT HOURS.
Carryover, MCLE Reg 102.

ACTIVE MEMBERS.
Defined, MCLE Reg 101.

ADVERSE DETERMINATION.
Appeal of panel decisions to board, MCLE Reg 107.

APPEALS TO BOARD.
Panel decisions, MCLE Reg 107.

APPLICATION FOR APPROVAL OF COURSE, MCLE Form 4, MCLE Reg 104.
Pending application.
Announcement by sponsor, MCLE Reg 104.
Notice to attendees as to approval, MCLE Reg 104.

APPLICATION FOR STATUS AS ACCREDITED SPONSOR, MCLE Reg 105.

APPROVAL OF PROGRAMS.
Application for approval, MCLE Form 4.
Approved course defined, MCLE Reg 101.
Procedure, MCLE Reg 104.
Standards, MCLE Reg 103.

APPROVAL PENDING.
Announcement by sponsor, MCLE Reg 104.
Notification to attendees as to approval, MCLE Reg 104.

AUDIO PROGRAMS.
Standards for approval, MCLE Reg 103.

AWARDING CREDITS, MCLE Reg 102.

B

BOARD.
Defined, MCLE Reg 101.

BROCHURES.
Information included by sponsor of program, MCLE Reg 104.

C

CALCULATING CREDITS, MCLE Reg 102.

CARRYOVER OF CREDIT HOURS, MCLE Reg 102.

CERTIFICATION OF ATTENDANCE AT APPROVED COURSE OR PROGRAM, MCLE Form 2, MCLE Reg 108.
Attendees to fill out, sponsor to collect and submit to board, MCLE Reg 104.
End of year report, MCLE Form 1, MCLE Reg 108.

CERTIFICATION OF TEACHING AT APPROVED COURSE OR PROGRAM.
Attendees to fill out, sponsor to collect and submit to board, MCLE Form 3, MCLE Reg 104.
Reporting procedures, MCLE Reg 108.

COFFEE BREAKS.
Credits not given for time spent, MCLE Reg 102.

COMPLETION PERIOD.
Defined, MCLE Reg 101.

COMPUTING CREDITS, MCLE Reg 102.

CORPORATE LAW DEPARTMENTS.
Ineligibility to become accredited sponsors, MCLE Reg 105.

CORRECTED MCLE END OF YEAR REPORT.
Member's information in error.
Filing by member, time, MCLE Reg 108.

COURSE DESCRIPTIONS.
Information included by sponsor of program, MCLE Reg 104.

COURSE PRESENTED BY DISTANCE LEARNING METHODS.
Defined, MCLE Reg 101.

COURSES.
Defined, MCLE Reg 101.

CREDIT HOURS.
Defined, MCLE Reg 101.

D

DECISION ON APPROVAL OF PROGRAM.
Time board to notify of decision, MCLE Reg 104.

DEFERRALS, MCLE Reg 111.

DEFINITIONS, MCLE Reg 101.

DELEGATION TO BOARD PANELS, MCLE Reg 106.

DELINQUENT.
Active member deemed, MCLE Reg 109.

DESCRIPTION OF COURSE.
Information included by sponsor of program, MCLE Reg 104.

DETERMINATIONS BY PANELS, MCLE Reg 107.

DIRECTOR OF MCLE.
Defined, MCLE Reg 101.

DISTANCE LEARNING.
Course presented by distance learning methods, defined, MCLE Reg 101.

E

ETHICS CREDITS.
Defined, MCLE Reg 101.
Minimum number, MCLE Reg 102.
Qualified ethics course or component, defined, MCLE Reg 101.

EXEMPTION OF NEWLY ADMITTED MEMBERS, MCLE Reg 110.

EXTENSIONS, MCLE Reg 111.

F

FACULTY.
Faculty member defined, MCLE Reg 101.
No credits for teaching law school course or bar review, MCLE Reg 102.

FALSE STATEMENTS BY MEMBERS, MCLE Reg 112.

H

HOSPITALIZATION, ILLNESS OR MEDICAL REASON.
Extension based on, MCLE Reg 111.
Waiver based on, MCLE Reg 111.

I

INELIGIBILITY TO BECOME ACCREDITED SPONSORS, MCLE Reg 105.

IN-HOUSE PROGRAMS.
In-house defined, MCLE Reg 101.
Standards for approval, MCLE Reg 103.

INSTRUCTOR OF APPROVED COURSE.
Credits given, MCLE Reg 102.

INTRODUCTORY REMARKS.
Credit not given for, MCLE Reg 102.

K

KEYNOTE SPEECHES.
Credit not given for, MCLE Reg 102.

L

LAW FIRMS.
Ineligibility to become accredited sponsors, MCLE Reg 105.

LAW SCHOOL FACULTY.
No credits for teaching law school course or bar review, MCLE Reg 102.

LEGAL ETHICS.
Minimum credit hours, MCLE Reg 102.

LEGAL ETHICS —Cont'd
Standards for approval of programs, MCLE Reg 103.
When credits given, MCLE Reg 102.

LIST OF APPROVED COURSES AND PROGRAMS.
Board to maintain, MCLE Reg 104.

M

MCLE DIRECTOR.
Defined, MCLE Reg 101.

MCLE END OF YEAR REPORT, MCLE Form 1.
Status respecting completion of CLE requirement, MCLE Reg 108.

MEALS.
Credits not given for time spent, MCLE Reg 102.

MEMBERS.
Defined, MCLE Reg 101.

MINIMUM CREDIT HOURS, MCLE Reg 102.

MISREPRESENTATIONS, MCLE Reg 112.

N

NAME, DATE, LOCATION AND CREDIT HOURS OF PROGRAM.
Notice by accredited sponsor, MCLE Reg 105.

NEWLY-ADMITTED MEMBERS.
Defined, MCLE Reg 101.
Exemption, MCLE Reg 110.

NONCOMPLIANCE, MCLE Reg 109.

O

ONE-YEAR CARRYOVER OF CREDIT HOURS, MCLE Reg 102.

ONLINE MCLE RECORD.
Defined, MCLE Reg 101.

P

PANELS.
Board may organize into, MCLE Reg 106.
Defined, MCLE Reg 101.

PENDING APPROVAL.
Announcement by sponsor, MCLE Reg 104.
Notice to attendees as to approval, MCLE Reg 104.

PERSONAL ATTENDANCE AT APPROVED COURSE.
Credits given, MCLE Reg 102.

PREPARING WRITTEN MATERIALS FOR APPROVED COURSE.
Credits given, MCLE Reg 102.

PRE-RECORDED COURSES.
Defined, MCLE Reg 101.
Limitation on number of hours by, MCLE Reg 102.

PROCEDURE FOR ACCREDITATION OF SPONSORS, MCLE Reg 105.

PROCEDURE FOR APPROVAL OF PROGRAMS.
Application for approval, MCLE Form 4.
Procedure, MCLE Reg 104.

PROFESSIONAL CORPORATIONS.
Ineligibility to become accredited sponsors, MCLE Reg 105.

PROFESSIONALISM.
Minimum credit hours, MCLE Reg 102.
Qualified professionalism course or component, defined, MCLE Reg 101.
Standards for approval of programs, MCLE Reg 103.
When credits given, MCLE Reg 102.

PROGRAMS.
Defined, MCLE Reg 101.

PROGRAM SPONSOR.
Defined, MCLE Reg 101.

Q

QUALIFIED ETHICS COURSE OR COMPONENT.
Defined, MCLE Reg 101.

QUALIFIED PROFESSIONALISM COURSE OR COMPONENT.
Defined, MCLE Reg 101.

R

REINSTATEMENT OF SUSPENDED MEMBER, MCLE Reg 109.

REPORT ON STATUS OF CLE REQUIREMENT.
MCLE end of year report, MCLE Form 1, MCLE Reg 108.

REQUEST FOR EXTENSION BASED ON HOSPITALIZATION, ILLNESS OR MEDICAL REASON, MCLE Reg 111.

REQUEST FOR WAIVER BASED ON HOSPITALIZATION, ILLNESS OR MEDICAL REASON, MCLE Reg 111.

REQUIREMENTS, MCLE Reg 102.

RESTORATION TO GOOD STANDING.
Delinquent members, MCLE Reg 109.

REVIEW BY BOARD.
Panel decisions, MCLE Reg 107.

REVOCATION OF ACCREDITATION, MCLE Reg 105.

RULE.
Defined, MCLE Reg 101.

S

SPECIALLY APPROVED COURSE OR PROGRAM, MCLE Reg 103.
Application for approval, MCLE Form 4, MCLE Reg 104.
Calculation of credit hours, MCLE Reg 102.
Defined, MCLE Reg 101.

SPEECHES.
Credit not given for, MCLE Reg 102.

SPONSORS.
Defined, MCLE Reg 101.

STANDARDS FOR APPROVAL OF PROGRAMS, MCLE Reg 103.

SUSPENSION OF LICENSE TO PRACTICE LAW.
Noncompliance, MCLE Reg 109.

T

TEACHING APPROVED COURSE.
Credits given, MCLE Reg 102.

TIME.
Appeal to board of panel decision, MCLE Reg 107.
Application for approval pending during presentation.
Notice to attendees as to approval, MCLE Reg 104.
Certification of attendance or teaching at approved course or program.
Submission by active members, MCLE Reg 108.
Submission by sponsor to board, MCLE Reg 104.
Corrected MCLE end of year report.
Member's information in error.
Filing by member, MCLE Reg 108.
Decision on approval of program.
Time board to notify of decision, MCLE Reg 104.
Extension, MCLE Reg 111.
Name, date location and credit hours of program.
Notice by accredited sponsor, MCLE Reg 105.

V

VIDEO PROGRAMS.
Standards for approval, MCLE Reg 103.

W

WAIVERS, MCLE Reg 111.

WHEN CREDITS GIVEN, MCLE Reg 102.

CLIENTS' PROTECTION FUND RULES

(As revised effective February 23, 2013)

RESOLUTION OF THE COUNCIL OF THE VIRGINIA STATE BAR

Establishing a Clients' Protection Fund

WHEREAS, it is the desire of the lawyers of Virginia acting through the State Bar to preserve and protect the honor and integrity of the profession, and;

WHEREAS, it is recognized that despite the high standards of ethical conduct required of and generally maintained by the Virginia State Bar, a member of the Virginia State Bar may engage in dishonest conduct and that such conduct may result in losses to clients, and;

WHEREAS, it is the desire of the Virginia State Bar to alleviate the injury to persons so sustaining loss or damage in certain cases.

NOW, THEREFORE, BE IT RESOLVED BY THE VIRGINIA STATE BAR:

1. That there is hereby established a special Board of the Virginia State Bar to be known as the Clients' Protection Fund Board (hereinafter called the "Board") whose function it shall be to receive, hold, manage and distribute, pursuant to the terms herein contained, such funds as may from time to time be appropriated to it by the Council of the Virginia State Bar or through voluntary contribution or otherwise for the purpose of maintaining the integrity and protecting the good name of the legal profession by reimbursing to the extent deemed proper and feasible by the Board losses caused by the dishonest conduct of members of the Virginia State Bar.
2. The Board shall consist of fourteen members, one of whom shall be a nonlawyer, appointed by the Council. One member shall be from each of the ten (10) Disciplinary Districts in Virginia, and four (4) shall be appointed from the State at large. All appointments shall be for a term of three years. No appointees shall serve more than two consecutive full terms until after the expiration of at least one year. Vacancies shall be filled by appointment by the President of the Virginia State Bar for the unexpired term.
3. The Board shall be authorized to consider petitions for reimbursement of losses arising after January 1, 1976 and caused by the dishonest conduct of a member of the Virginia State Bar, acting either as a lawyer or as a fiduciary in the matter in which the loss arose except to the extent to which they are bonded or to the extent such losses are otherwise covered, provided such member has been disbarred or suspended from the practice of law pursuant to any provision of Paragraph 13 of Part 6, Section IV of the Rules of the Supreme Court of Virginia, has voluntarily resigned from the practice of law in Virginia, has died, has been adjudicated incompetent, has been the subject of a bankruptcy case that would stay, reduce or discharge the claims of the lawyer's past or present clients, or whose whereabouts is unknown to the Virginia State Bar. The Board shall be authorized and empowered to admit or reject such petitions in whole or in part, and the Board shall have complete discretion in determining the order, extent, and manner of payment. On establishing the Clients' Protection Fund, the Virginia State Bar does not create or acknowledge any legal responsibility for the acts of individual lawyers in the practice of law. All reimbursements of losses from the Clients' Protection Fund shall be in the sole discretion of the Board and not as a matter of right. No client or member of the public shall have any right in the Clients' Protection Fund as a third party beneficiary or otherwise. No attorney shall be compensated for presenting a petition except as authorized by the Board.
4. The Board shall operate pursuant to rules of procedure approved by the Council of the Virginia State Bar for the management of the Board's funds and affairs, for the presentation of petitions, and the processing and payment thereof.

5. All sums appropriated by the Council of the Virginia State Bar for the use of the Board shall be held and invested as a separate account known as Clients' Protection Fund, subject to the written direction of the Board under written Board rules approved by the Council of the Virginia State Bar; the interest or other income thereby received to be added to and automatically become a part of the Fund.
6. The Board may use or employ the Clients' Protection Fund for any of the following purposes within the scope of the Board's objectives, as heretofore outlined:
   (a) To make payments or reimbursements on approved petitions as herein provided to clients and members of the public;
   (b) To purchase insurance to cover such losses in whole or in part, provided that such insurance is obtainable at reasonable costs and is deemed appropriate and provided that the purchase of such insurance is approved by the Council of the Virginia State Bar;
   (c) To reimburse to the Virginia State Bar those costs of receiverships initiated by the Virginia State Bar occasioned by the need for the receiver to administer, pursue or defend assets, the recovery or preservation of which would inure to the benefit of one or more clients or other members of the public who have suffered losses as a result of the dishonest conduct of the Virginia State Bar member who is the subject of the receivership, acting as either a lawyer or as a fiduciary in the matter or matters in which the loss or losses occurred.
7. The administrative expenses of the Board shall be paid out of the general fund of the Virginia State Bar in accordance with policies established by the Council. However, the board annually at its discretion may contribute to the cost of administration by designating a sum to be paid out of the Clients' Protection Fund to the Virginia State Bar.
8. The Board shall provide a full report of its activities at least yearly to the Council of the Virginia State Bar, and it shall make such other report of its activities and give only such publicity to same as the Council may deem advisable.
9. The Council at any time may abolish the Board and the Fund. In the event of such abolition, all assets of the Fund shall be and remain the property of the Virginia State Bar to be used for its general purposes, as determined by the Council.
10. The financial condition of the Clients' Protection Fund shall be reviewed annually in conjunction with the State Bar's annual budgeting process. The Council of the Virginia State Bar shall make appropriations adequate to maintain the funding of the Clients' Protection Fund at a reasonable level, provided, however, that no appropriation may be made which will increase the assets of the fund to an amount in excess of $5,000,000.00.
11. Payment shall be made from the Fund only upon condition that the Virginia State Bar receive a pro tanto assignment from the payee of the payee's assignable rights against the lawyer or others involved, their personal representatives, heirs, devisees and assigns, and upon condition that the Fund shall be entitled to reimbursement on such terms as the Board may deem proper under the circumstances, including reimbursement of costs incurred in prosecuting a claim against said lawyer, his personal representatives, etc. The net proceeds collected by reason of such assignment shall be for the sole benefit of the Fund and applied thereto, and enforcement of this right shall be within the sole discretion of the Board.
12. The Board may give such publicity to awards made or to the work, procedures, and existence of the Clients' Protection Fund as it shall deem proper, except that in no case shall the name of the payee be stated in any release to the media. Copies of all releases shall be sent to the Executive Director of the Virginia State Bar to ensure conformity with this rule. No publicity shall be given to pending claims without the express approval of the Council of the Virginia State Bar.

RULES OF PROCEDURE OF THE CLIENTS' PROTECTION FUND OF THE VIRGINIA STATE BAR

I. Definitions

For the purpose of these Rules of Procedure, the following definitions shall apply:

1. The "Board" shall mean the Clients' Protection Fund Board.

2. The "Fund" shall mean the Clients' Protection Fund of the Virginia State Bar.

3. A "Lawyer," "Attorney" or "Respondent" shall mean one who, at the time of the act complained of, was a member of the Virginia State Bar, was domiciled in Virginia, and was actually engaged in the practice of law in Virginia. The fact that the act complained of took place outside of the Commonwealth of Virginia does not necessarily mean that the Lawyer was not engaged in the practice of law in Virginia.

4. A "Petitioner" or "Claimant" shall mean a person or entity that applies to the Clients' Protection Fund Board for payment pursuant to the rules applicable to the Fund.

5. "Reimbursable Losses" are limited to actual, out-of-pocket or quantifiable losses, supported by documentation, of money or other property that meet the following tests:

(a) The conduct which occasioned the loss occurred on or after January 1, 1976.

(b) The loss must be caused by the dishonest conduct of the Lawyer and shall have arisen out of and by reason of a lawyer-client relationship or a fiduciary relationship between the Lawyer and the Claimant.

(c) The Lawyer has been disbarred or suspended from the practice of law pursuant to any provision of Paragraph 13 of Part 6, Section IV of the Rules of the Supreme Court of Virginia, has voluntarily resigned from the practice of law in Virginia, has died, has been adjudicated incompetent, has been the subject of a bankruptcy case that would stay, reduce or discharge the claims of the lawyer's past or present clients, or whose whereabouts is unknown to the Virginia State Bar.

5.1. The following shall be excluded from "Reimbursable Losses":

(a) Losses of spouses, other close relatives, partners, associates and employees of Lawyers causing the losses;

(b) Losses covered by any bond, surety agreement, or insurance contract to the extent covered thereby, including any loss to which any bonding agent, surety or insurer is subrogated;

(c) Losses of any financial institution which are recoverable under a "banker's blanket bond" or similar commonly available insurance or surety contract;

(d) Losses by any business entity controlled by the Lawyer;

(e) Losses incurred by any governmental entity or agency;

(f) Losses occasioned by a loan or an investment transaction with a Lawyer, unless it arose out of and in the course of the attorney-client relationship and but for the fact that the dishonest attorney enjoyed an attorney-client relationship with the Claimant such loss could not have occurred. In considering whether that standard has been met, the following factors will be considered:

1. The disparity in bargaining power between the attorney and the client and their respective educational backgrounds and business sophistication.
2. The extent to which the attorney-client relationship overcame the normal prudence of the applicant.
3. The extent to which the attorney, by virtue of the attorney-client relationship with the applicant, became privy to information as to the applicant's financial affairs.
4. Whether a principal part of the service arose out of a relationship requiring a license to practice law.

(g) Claims by a Petitioner for damages for a cause of action in which a Lawyer represented a Petitioner and that never resulted in a settlement or judgment;

(h) Claims for interest, late fees, penalties, surcharges or other consequential damages, even if such damages arise out of Reimbursable Losses.

6. "Dishonest Conduct" may include, but is not necessarily limited to:

(a) Any act committed by a Lawyer in the nature of theft, conversion, embezzlement or withholding of money or property from its rightful owner, recipient or person entitled to receive such money or property;

(b) Any act committed by a Lawyer in the nature of failure, refusal or inability to refund unearned fees received in advance where the Lawyer performed no legal services or such an insignificant service that the failure, refusal or inability to refund the unearned fees constitutes a wrongful taking or conversion. Where the Board finds that the legal services performed by the Lawyer are more than insignificant, but the Lawyer has not fully earned the entire fee, the failure, refusal or inability to refund the unearned fees may still constitute a wrongful taking or conversion, and the Board may reimburse fifty percent of the total fees paid by the Petitioner.

6.1. The Board shall exercise its discretion in deciding whether a Lawyer committed Dishonest Conduct. In making its determination, the Board may consider as compelling evidence of such Dishonest Conduct, in addition to other factors:

(a) an order from any court or disciplinary tribunal disciplining a Lawyer for the same act or conduct alleged in a Petition or otherwise finding that a Lawyer committed Dishonest Conduct; or

(b) a final judgment imposing civil or criminal liability upon a Lawyer for such conduct.

II. Application for Reimbursement

1. The Board shall prepare a form of Petition for reimbursement; in its discretion the Board may waive a requirement that a Petition be filed on such form.

2. At a minimum, the form shall require the Petitioner to state:

(a) The name, address and telephone number of the Petitioner.

(b) The name and last known address of the Lawyer allegedly responsible for the claimed loss.

(c) The amount of the loss claimed.

(d) Documentation supporting the loss, including proof of payment for monies the Petitioner or anyone on his behalf paid directly to the Lawyer.

(e) The date or period of time the alleged loss occurred.

(f) A description of the efforts by the Petitioner to recover the alleged loss from the Lawyer or from other sources of payment besides the Virginia State Bar.

(g) The notarized signature of the Petitioner.

3. The Petition shall contain the following statement in bold type:

"IN ESTABLISHING THE CLIENTS' PROTECTION FUND, THE VIRGINIA STATE BAR DID NOT CREATE OR ACKNOWLEDGE ANY LEGAL RESPONSIBILITY FOR THE ACTS OF INDIVIDUAL LAWYERS IN THE PRACTICE OF LAW. ALL REIMBURSEMENTS OF LOSSES FROM THE CLIENTS' PROTECTION FUND SHALL BE IN THE SOLE DISCRETION OF THE BOARD ADMINISTERING THE FUND AND NOT AS A MATTER OF RIGHT. NO CLIENT OR MEMBER OF THE PUBLIC SHALL HAVE ANY RIGHT IN THE CLIENTS' PROTECTION FUND AS A THIRD PARTY BENEFICIARY OR OTHERWISE."

4. Petitions shall be submitted to the central office of the Virginia State Bar in Richmond, Virginia. If the staff of the Virginia State Bar determines that the Petition complies with the minimum requirements of these Rules, the Petition shall be investigated and approved or denied by the Board.

III. Processing Petitions

1. The Chair of the Board or such bar staff as the Chair designates shall cause each Petition to be sent to a member of the Board or other member of the Virginia State Bar for investigation and report. A copy shall be sent to the Lawyer at his address of record maintained by the membership department of the bar. The Lawyer or his representative may respond to the Petition within thirty (30) days of the date of the letter or letters transmitting the Petition to him.

Petitions shall be assigned considering the workload of each Board member, and, when possible, by giving preference for assignment to a Board member who works or lives in the jurisdiction in which the Lawyer maintained his office, place of employment, or address of record with the Virginia State Bar.

2. A member to whom a Petition is referred for investigation shall conduct such investigation as to him seems necessary and desirable in order to determine whether the same is for a Reimbursable Loss and in order to guide the Board in determining the extent, if any, to which the loss should be reimbursed from the Fund.

3. When, in the opinion of the member to whom the Petition has been referred, the Petition is clearly not for a reimbursable loss, no further investigation need be conducted, but a report with respect to such Petition shall be made by the member to whom the Petitioner was referred, as hereinafter specified.

4. The Board member who investigates a Petition shall prepare a written report and recommendation as to whether the Petition should be paid or denied. Such report shall be available for inspection by the Board members attending the meeting at which the Petition is reviewed.

5. No Petition with respect to which an inadequate opportunity for investigation has been afforded need be considered by the Board for reimbursement in the year in which such claim is presented.

6. In those instances where the reporting member in his report suggests or any other member of the Board, after studying the reports of Petitions to be processed, requests that the Board hear evidence, the Board shall hear the Petitioner, the Lawyer and such other evidence as may be presented. Absent such recommendation or request, Petitions may be processed on the basis of information contained therein and in the report of the member who investigated each Petition. The Lawyer or his personal representative, or the Petitioner or his personal representative, may request to address the Board at a meeting at which the Board is considering the claim. Any such request must be made to the Chair or his designee, and the Chair may place restrictions and/or limitations on the length or subject matter of any statements allowed.

7. The Board shall, in its sole discretion and by a majority vote, determine the amount of loss, if any, for which any Petitioner shall be reimbursed from the Fund. Although only a majority vote is required to approve or deny a Petition, the Board should aspire to come to a consensus on every Petition. In making such determination, the Board shall consider *inter alia*, the following:

(a) Any conduct of the Petitioner which contributed to the loss.

(b) The loss to be paid to any one Petitioner shall not exceed $50,000 for losses incurred on or after July 1, 2000, or $25,000 for losses incurred prior to July 1, 2000. For purposes of this provision, the Board may regard two or more persons, firms or entities as one Petitioner with respect to a Lawyer's Dishonest Conduct in handling a given matter where the facts and entities are found to justify such a conclusion.

(c) The total amount of losses reimbursable hereunder on account of the misconduct of any one lawyer or association of lawyers (including, without limitation, a law firm, professional corporation, or an office-sharing arrangement among lawyers) shall be limited to ten percent (10%) of the net worth of the Clients' Protection Fund at the time the first claim is made. In the event of multiple claims on account of the misconduct of any one lawyer or association of lawyers, claims may be considered in any order or grouping which the Board, in its discretion, finds appropriate, taking into account the equities and timeliness of each claim, and no further payment shall be made in respect to misconduct of any one lawyer or association of lawyers once the ten percent limit has been reached.

(d) The total amount of Reimbursable Losses in previous years for which payment has not been made and the total assets of the Fund.

(e) The Board may, in its sole discretion, allow further payment in any year on account of a reimbursable loss allowed by it in prior years which has not been fully paid; provided such further payment would not be inconsistent or in conflict with any previous determination with respect to such loss.

(f) No payment shall be made upon any Petition, a summary of which has not been submitted to the members in accordance with these Rules of Procedure. No payment shall be made to any Petitioner unless said payment is duly approved by the Board.

(g) No claim shall be considered by the Board unless the same shall have been filed within seven years from the time the Claimant knew or should have known of the Lawyer's Dishonest Conduct, or within one year after the first occurrence of one of the following events, whichever date is later:

i. the Lawyer has been disbarred or suspended from the practice of law pursuant to any provision of Part 6, Section IV, Paragraph 13 of the Rules of the Supreme Court of Virginia;

ii. the Lawyer has voluntarily resigned from the practice of law in Virginia;
iii. the Lawyer has died;
iv. the Lawyer has been adjudicated incompetent;
v. the Lawyer has been the subject of a bankruptcy that would stay, reduce or discharge the claims of the Lawyer's past or present clients; or
vi. the whereabouts of the Lawyer is unknown to the Virginia State Bar.

(h) The Board may make a finding of Dishonest Conduct for purposes of adjudicating a claim. Such a determination is not a finding of Dishonest Conduct for purposes of professional discipline.

8. A member who has or has had a lawyer-client relationship or financial relationship with a Claimant or Lawyer who is the subject of a claim shall not participate in the investigation or adjudication of a claim involving that Claimant or Lawyer. A member with any other past or present relationship with a Claimant or the Lawyer whose alleged conduct is the subject of the claim, shall disclose such relationship to the Board and, if the Board deems appropriate, that member shall not participate in any proceeding relating to such claim.

9. The Claimant or Respondent may request reconsideration in writing within 30 days of the denial or determination of the amount of a claim. If the Claimant or Respondent fails to make a request or the request is denied, the decision of the Board is final. There shall be no appeal from a decision of the Board.

10. A Lawyer whose Dishonest Conduct has resulted in reimbursement to a Claimant shall make restitution to the Fund including interest and the expense incurred by the Fund in processing the claim.

IV. Assignment When Payment Made

In the event payment is made from the Fund to a Petitioner, the Fund shall require an assignment from the Petitioner of such claim as he may have against the Lawyer complained of and may bring such action thereon in the name of the Petitioner as is deemed advisable against the Lawyer, his assets or his estate. The Petitioner shall be required to execute such an assignment. Prior to the commencement of an action by the Board, it shall advise the Petitioner thereof at his last known address. The Petitioner may then join in such action to press a claim for his loss in excess of the amount of the payment made by the Fund or for any other claims. The Board may impose such other conditions and requirements as it may deem appropriate in connection with payment to any Petitioner.

V. Payment of Receivership Costs

Costs of any Virginia State Bar receivership occasioned by the need for the receiver to administer, pursue or defend assets, the recovery or preservation of which would inure to the benefit of one or more clients or other members of the public who have suffered losses as a result of the dishonest conduct of the Virginia State Bar member who is the subject of the receivership, acting as either a lawyer or as a fiduciary in the matter or matters in which the loss or losses occurred, shall be documented and certified to the Board by the Virginia State Bar staff for consideration of payment from the Fund by the Board as an agenda item at a meeting of the Board.

VI. Meeting of the Board

1. The Board shall meet at least one time during each fiscal year. The first meeting of any fiscal year shall be designated the "Annual Meeting." The Annual Meeting shall take place after the beginning of the fiscal year, but not later than September 30. In addition, the Board shall meet from time to time upon call of the Chair or any two members of the Board.

2. The members shall be given not less than 15 days' written notice of the time and place of the annual meeting and not less than 5 days' written notice of each special meeting. Notice of any meeting may be waived by a member either before or after the meeting.

3. A quorum at any meeting of the Board shall be six (6) members. No action shall be taken by the Board in the absence of a quorum; except that any action which might be taken at a meeting may be taken without a meeting if a consent in writing, setting forth the action so to be taken, shall be signed before such action by all the members of the Board.

4. Written minutes of each meeting shall be prepared and permanently maintained.

5. The Chair and Vice Chair of the Board shall be elected by a majority of the Board at the last meeting of the fiscal year. Their terms shall extend until the last meeting of the next fiscal year and until their successors are elected and qualified. Should a vacancy occur in the office of Chair or Vice Chair, such vacancy shall be filled by majority vote of the members of the Board at the meeting next following the occurrence of the vacancy.

VII. General Purposes

These Rules of Procedure shall be liberally interpreted and, in any given case, the Board may waive technical adherence to these Rules of Procedure in order to achieve the objectives of the Fund, as contained in the enabling Resolution establishing the Fund.

VIII. Authorized Investments

Investment of monies of the Clients' Protection Fund shall be restricted to the following:

(a) Interest-bearing deposits (including as well certificates of deposit) in federally insured banks and savings institutions located in the state of Virginia.

(b) Direct obligations of the Commonwealth of Virginia and the United States Government, and securities of entities created by Congress and authorized to issue such securities; provided that no such deposit, certificate or obligation shall have a maturity beyond ten years from the date of the investment; and provided further that the interest, discount or other gain or income realized from any such investment, net of any bank or brokerage charges incurred in connection therewith, shall automatically become a part of the Fund.

IX. Amendments

These Rules may be changed at any time by a majority vote of the Board at a duly held meeting at which a quorum is present, and subject to the approval of the Council of the Virginia State Bar.

Index to Clients' Protection Fund Rules

A

AMENDMENTS TO RULES, VSB CPF Rule IX.

AMOUNT OF LOSS.
Determination, VSB CPF Rule III.

APPLICATION FOR REIMBURSEMENT, VSB CPF Rule II.

B

BOARD.
Amendments to rules, VSB CPF Rule IX.
Construction and interpretation of rules, VSB CPF Rule VII.
Defined, VSB CPF Rule I.
Meetings, VSB CPF Rule VI.

C

CLAIMANT.
Defined, VSB CPF Rule I.

CONSTRUCTION AND INTERPRETATION OF RULES, VSB CPF Rule VII.

D

DEFINITIONS, VSB CPF Rule I.

DISHONEST CONDUCT.
Defined, VSB CPF Rule I.

F

FUND.
Authorized investments, VSB CPF Rule VIII.
Defined, VSB CPF Rule I.
Payments from fund.
Assignment of claim, VSB CPF Rule IV.
Receivership costs, VSB CPF Rule V.

I

INVESTIGATIONS.
Processing petitions, VSB CPF Rule III.

L

LAWYER.
Defined, VSB CPF Rule I.

M

MEETINGS OF BOARD, VSB CPF Rule VI.

P

PAYMENTS FROM FUND.
Assignment of claim, VSB CPF Rule IV.

PETITIONER.
Defined, VSB CPF Rule I.

PETITIONS.
Application for reimbursement, VSB CPF Rule II.
Processing petitions, VSB CPF Rule III.

R

RECEIVERSHIP.
Payment of costs, VSB CPF Rule V.

REIMBURSABLE LOSSES.
Defined, VSB CPF Rule I.
Right to reimbursement, VSB CPF Rule III

REIMBURSEMENT.
Application for reimbursement, VSB CPF Rule II.
Reimbursable losses.
Defined, VSB CPF Rule I.
Right to reimbursement, VSB CPF Rule III.

REPORTS.
Processing petitions, VSB CPF Rule III.

RULES OF THE VIRGINIA WORKERS' COMPENSATION COMMISSION

Revised effective January 1, 1994; amended effective July 13, 2010.

Rule
1. Prehearing Procedures.
2. Hearing Procedures.
3. Posthearing Procedures.
4. Filing Documents.
5. Cost of Medical Services.
6. Award of Attorney's Fees Under § 65.2-714 of the Code of Virginia.
7. Employer Responsibilities.
8. Self-Insurance.

Rule
9. Payment of Compensation.
10. X-ray Evidence for Coal Workers' Pneumoconiosis Claims.
11. Pneumoconiosis Table.
12. Hearing Loss Table.
13. Table of Percentage of Loss of Visual Acuity.
14. Definition of Community.
Index.

These rules are issued to provide procedures to identify and resolve disputed issues promptly through informal dispute resolution or hearing.

The following words and terms, when used in these rules, shall have the following meaning, unless the context clearly indicates otherwise:

"Act" means the Virginia Workers' Compensation Act.

"Commission" means the Virginia Workers' Compensation Commission.

"Employer" includes the employer's insurance carrier unless the context otherwise requires.

Editor's note. — For website of the Virginia Workers' Compensation Commission, see http://www.vwc.state.va.us

Rule 1. Prehearing Procedures.

1.1 Employee's Original Claim for Benefits. — An employee's original claim for benefits shall be filed within the applicable statutes of limitation.

An original claim for benefits shall be in writing, signed and should set forth:

1. Employee's name and address;
2. Employer's name and address;
3. Date of accident or date of communication of occupational disease;
4. Nature of injury or occupational disease;
5. Benefits sought: temporary total, temporary partial, permanent total, permanent partial or medical benefits;
6. Periods of disability, if appropriate.

Research References. — Daniel J. Stone, Occupational Injuries and Illnesses (Matthew Bender).

CASE NOTES

Facsimile transmission did not constitute a notice for a claim of benefits. — Facsimile inquiry an employee sent to the Chief Deputy Commissioner failed to meet the criteria for a claim for benefits. While it contained the name and address of the employer, it did not specify it was the employer at the time the injury was sustained nor did it request any benefits; it merely contained questions concerning the time frame for filing a claim for benefits that the Chief Deputy Commissioner answered clearly and unambiguously. Thus, credible evidence supported the Virginia Workers' Compensation Commission's finding that the facsimile was not a claim for benefits. Remington v. Global One Communs., LLC, No. 2099-02-4, 2003 Va. App. LEXIS 116 (Ct. of Appeals Mar. 4, 2003).

Filing of memorandum of agreement satisfied claim filing requirements. — Memorandum of Agreement, which was mailed by an employer to the Workers' Compensation Commission, constituted a notice of claim pursuant to the requirements of § 65.2-701, where an award that had been entered thereon was vacated, but the actual memorandum was not withdrawn or dismissed; the court noted that the memorandum contained the essential filing requirements of claims, pursuant to Va. Workers' Comp. Comm'n R. 1.1(A). Fairfax County Sch. Bd. v. Humphrey, 41 Va. App. 147, 583 S.E.2d 65, 2003 Va. App. LEXIS 396 (2003).

NOTES FROM THE WORKERS' COMPENSATION COMMISSION

An executed Agreement to Pay Benefits form that was filed with the Commission within two years of the accident constituted a timely claim for benefits because it contained all the information typically expected of a claim even though an Award could not be entered because of the need to clarify the seven-day waiting period. Belmonte-Arwood v. Net2000 Group, Inc., VWC File No. 206-54-65 (July 26, 2005).

Where award was entered without the filing of an original claim for benefits, claimant's next correspondence with the Commission, entitled "application for hearing" served as both the claim for medical benefits and the request for a hearing. Therefore, the deputy commissioner properly dismissed the claim when the claimant withdrew his application for hearing. Hartley v. G & T Conveyor Co., VWC File No. 210-60-29 (March 4, 2005).

A claimant may amend her claim at the hearing to include a claim for lifetime medical benefits. Such a claim is implicit in an initial claim that alleges disability from work. Woodson v. County of Nelson School Bd., VWC File No. 216-72-04 (Oct. 26, 2004).

A certified letter must be posted at the United States Post Office in order to be considered "filed". The marking of a letter as "certified mail" and placing it in a mail box is considered filed only when received by the Commission. Smallwood v. Overbrook Landscaping, Inc., 70 O.I.C. 56 (1991).

Dismissal of a claim, with a condition that a new claim will be accepted only if outstanding discovery interrogatories are answered, is an appropriate sanction where there is chronic failure to file discovery responses. After a claim is dismissed without prejudice, it is treated as if no claim had been filed. Bryant v. Fieldcrest Cannon, Inc., 75 O.W.C. 184 (1996).

No statutory provision sets forth a specific statute of limitations for responding to a letter decision from a Claims Examiner. Rule 1.6 provides that a request for review of a decision accepting or rejecting a change in condition claim or application must be filed within twenty days from the date of the decision, but that Rule specifically does not refer to initial claims for benefits. The Commission's Rule 1.1 states that an employee's original claim for benefits shall be filed within the applicable statutes of limitations; however, this Rule does not establish a specific time in which the employee must respond if the Claims Examination Department questions whether his claim has been filed within the statute of limitation period. The Commission found that the employee's response to the Claims Examiner thirty-three days after the claim was rejected was timely filed. Tang v. Progressive Engineering Co., 77 O.W.C. 276 (1998).

Timely submission to the Commission of a letter, advising that the *pro se* claimant's condition is still being treated, and that further surgical correction was anticipated, satisfied the requirements of Commission Rule 1.1. The Rule mandates that the employee's original claim for benefits be in writing, but only suggests such additional information that "should" be included. It is clear from the wording of the rule that the Commission did not intend for a claim to fail merely because one or more of the listed items was inadvertently left off a claim. The key determination to be made is whether the claimant fairly apprised the Commission that a claim was being made. Colgan v. Massey Builders Supply Corp., VWC File No. 188-97-98 (January 4, 2001) *aff'd sub nom.* Massey Bldrs. Supply Corp. v. Colgan, 30 Va. App. 496, 553 S.E.2d 146 (2001).

1.2 Employee's Claim on the Ground of Change in Condition or Other Relief. — A. A change in condition claim must be in writing and state the change in condition relied upon. A copy of the claim should be sent to the employer.

B. Additional compensation may not be awarded more than 90 days before the filing of the claim with the Commission. Requests for cost of living supplements are not subject to this limitation.

Comment. — Most of the cases cited herein were decided under former Rule 13.

CASE NOTES

Generally. — See Bristol Door & Lumber Co. v. Hinkle, 157 Va. 474, 161 S.E. 902 (1932); Wise Coal & Coke Co. v. Roberts, 157 Va. 782, 161 S.E. 911 (1932); Gray v. Underwood Bros., 164 Va. 344, 180 S.E. 317 (1935); Parker v. Manchester Bd. & Paper Co., 201 Va. 328, 111 S.E.2d 453 (1959).

Writing requirement not complied with. — Where an employer defended a worker's claim for increased temporary partial disability benefits on the grounds of the worker's physical ability to work and the causation of his alleged ongoing disability, the argument did not comply with the writing requirement of Va. Workers' Comp. Comm'n R. 1.2(A); as a result, the worker had no notice of the argued issues, the issues were not before the workers' compensation commission, and, pursuant to Va.

Sup. Ct. R. 5A:27, the employer's appeal thereof lacked merit. UPS of Am. v. Bradshaw, No. 1643-03-2, 2003 Va. App. LEXIS 532 (Ct. of Appeals Oct. 28, 2003).

Former subdivision B of Rule 13 promotes the purpose of the Workers' Compensation Act and does not conflict with it. Whitten v. Mead Paperboard Prods., 4 Va. App. 182, 355 S.E.2d 349 (1987).

Former Rule 13 applied equally to both employers and employees. — It furthered the purpose of the Workers' Compensation Act with respect to both employers and employees without taking away substantive rights. Whitten v. Mead Paperboard Prods., 4 Va. App. 182, 355 S.E.2d 349 (1987).

Former subdivision B of Rule 13 merely limits retrospective period of recovery. — Former subdivision B of Rule 13 does not reduce the number of weeks of disability from 500 weeks. It also does not reduce the 24-month period allowed to file for a change in condition under § 65.1-99 (now § 65.2-708). Former subdivision B of the rule merely required that a claimant timely exercise his right to compensation by limiting the retrospective period of recovery to not more than 90 days prior to the filing of the application. Whitten v. Mead Paperboard Prods., 4 Va. App. 182, 355 S.E.2d 349 (1987).

Former subdivision B of Rule 13 allows employer to provide light work or rehabilitation. — Former subdivision B of Rule 13 facilitated the purpose of the Workers' Compensation Act, encouraging a claimant to obtain compensation as it becomes due. It afforded the opportunity for the employer to provide light work or rehabilitation in order to reduce liability, as the employer had the right to do under § 65.1-88 (now § 65.2-603). If the employee could wait the full 24-month period without notifying the employer of the claimed change in condition, the employer's rights under § 65.1-88 (now § 65.2-603) would be lost. Whitten v. Mead Paperboard Prods., 4 Va. App. 182, 355 S.E.2d 349 (1987).

Former subdivision B of Rule 13 was not intended as statute of limitation to prevent valid claims. — Former subdivision B was not intended as a statute of limitation to prevent the assertion of valid claims. It was designed to encourage early filing to further the purpose of the Workers' Compensation Act: to get compensation and treatment to injured persons. Crystal Oil Co. v. Dotson, 12 Va. App. 1014, 408 S.E.2d 252 (1991).

Cost-of-living supplements were not compensation within meaning of former subdivision B of Rule 13. Commonwealth Dep't of Hwys. & Transp. v. Williams, 1 Va. App. 349, 338 S.E.2d 660 (1986).

Former subdivision B of Rule 13 did not apply to cost-of-living supplements, because of the distinctions which existed between such payments and the compensation paid for actual disability. Commonwealth Dep't of Hwys. & Transp. v. Williams, 1 Va. App. 349, 338 S.E.2d 660 (1986).

Limitation precluding award of benefits for more than 90 days prior to filing of a claim was not applicable to cost-of-living supplements. ARA Health Servs. v. Flax, No. 1660-99-1 (Ct. of Appeals Mar. 28, 2000).

The purposes of former subdivision B of Rule 13 were not violated by allowing an amendment to relate back to the time of filing, where on the date of filing, the employer had all of the information it needed to protect its interest. Crystal Oil Co. v. Dotson, 12 Va. App. 1014, 408 S.E.2d 252 (1991).

Claim was time barred. — Where an employee argued that a claim for total disability benefits was erroneously characterized as one for additional compensation, implicating the 90-day deadline of subsection B of Rule 1.2, rather than an enforcement action of an earlier award, the appellate court could not consider the employee's claim, as the employee did not make the argument to the Virginia Workers' Compensation Commission. Morissette v. Custom Tel. Serv., No. 1820-02-2, 2003 Va. App. LEXIS 82 (Ct. of Appeals Feb. 19, 2003).

NOTES FROM THE WORKERS' COMPENSATION COMMISSION

General:

Employee not prevented from filing "protective" claim for benefits, although she was under an open award of benefits at the time of the filing, when employer had filed application to terminate benefits. Simons v. Tartan Textile Serv., Inc., VWC File No. 201-42-52 (July 7, 2003).

The Commission vacated an Agreed Statement of Fact upon finding that it was invalid because the employer was aware the claimant was represented by counsel but did not submit the agreement to him; the claimant was not receiving wages equal to his pre-injury wage; and the nature of the document was misrepresented to the injured worker. The Commission held that the 90 day provision of Rule 1.2 was inapplicable. Eudailey v. Fairfield Williamsburg Property, 73 O.W.C. 57 (1994).

The Deputy Commissioner may consider medical evidence obtained by either party after the filing of an application but prior to the time of the hearing. Lay v. Baldindos Lock & Key Service, Inc., 71 O.W.C. 110 (1992).

Rule 1.2 (A):

Rule 1.2(A) of the Rules of the Virginia Workers' Compensation Commission provides that a change in condition claim must be in writing and state the change in condition relied upon. Gatling v. Siemen's Corporation, 77 O.W.C. 95 (1998).

A "generic" change in condition claim for "all benefits to which an employee is or may be entitled pursuant to the Virginia Workmens [sic] Compensation Act" is not sufficient to enable the employer to determine the nature of the change in condition for which benefits are sought. It provides no information to which the employer might respond with its defenses, if medical benefits have already been awarded. Gatling v. Siemen's Corporation, 77 O.W.C. 95 (1998).

Rule 1.2 (B):

Employee's change-in-condition claim filed in right-knee injury case did not satisfy Rule 1.2(B) as to separate left-knee injury case, although employer the same for both injuries; December 2002 claim in left-knee injury case could not be seen as providing notice to employer of claim for additional wage loss associated with right-knee injury case.

Barker v. Virginia Elec. & Power Co., VWC File No. 173-08-48 (Dec. 17, 2003).

Rule 1.2(B) did not apply to employee's claim for initial period of disability benefits following accident, when parties agreed that accident was compensable and that a de facto award for a later period was appropriate; Rule 1.2(B) does not apply to an initial period of claimed benefits. Young v. Young's Welding, Inc., VWC File No. 204-86-50 (Aug. 4, 2003).

It is proper to apply Rule 13 (now Rule 1.2B) even though the employer did not raise the issue at the hearing. Chowdhury v. Hyatt Regency Crystal City, 67 O.I.C. 192 (1988).

"We uphold the Industrial Commission's decision that its Rule 13(B) (now Rule 1.2B) prohibits an award of compensation to [claimant] upon his application alleging a change of condition. In so doing we reaffirm our holding in *Whitten v. Mead Paperboard Products* that Rule 13(B) (now Rule 1.2B) is a valid rule." Graham v. Peoples Life Ins. Co., 7 Va. App. 61, 372 S.E.2d 161 (1988).

Rule 13(B) (now Rule 1.2B) which limits the award of benefits to ninety days prior to the date of the change in condition application, does not apply to claims for permanent partial loss of use of a member. The date for commencement of compensation benefits under § 65.1-56 (now § 65.2-503) is the date on which medical maximum improvement was reached. Wolf v. Baskin & Robbins, Inc., 70 O.I.C. 227 (1991).

Where an employee files a change in condition application for temporary partial benefits and amends it at the time of the hearing to allege temporary total incapacity, Rule 13(B) (now Rule 1.2B) was not violated by allowing the amendment to relate to the earlier filing because on that date the employer possessed all the information required to protect its interest since the period of recovery for which benefits was sought by the amendment fell within the ninety day period. Crystal Oil Co. v. Dotson, 12 Va. App. 1014, 407 S.E.2d 919 (1991).

Where an employee was advised that the employer would forward lost time slips to the carrier and compensation would be paid as in the past, the employer is estopped from asserting the limitation period of § 65.1-99 (now § 65.2-708) and Rule 13(B) (now Rule 1.2B). The claimant timely submitted time slips and is not precluded by Rule 13(B) (now Rule 1.2B) (from receiving benefits more than ninety days prior to the filing of her applications. Nabisco Brands, Inc. v. Jones, 12 Va. App. 1028, 407 S.E.2d 919 (1991), 69 O.I.C. 37 (1990).

Where an employee has failed to notify the employer of a change in earnings, a request for credit is not limited to ninety days before the filing of the application but extends for the whole period of overpayment. Ruffin v. Casey Chevrolet, 70 O.I.C. 247 (1991).

Where the employee alleges entitlement to more than one period of compensation benefits in his claim for benefits, but proceeds at an evidentiary hearing only as to the latter period, a subsequent claim for the earlier period is precluded by the doctrine of *res judicata,* not merely limited by the 90-day rule of Commission Rule 1.2(B). In such a case, it was reasonable for the employer and the Deputy Commissioner to conclude that the employee was no longer claiming benefits for the earlier periods omitted. Since the claim was fully litigated, and the omitted periods of disability could have been litigated at the hearing, the subsequent claim for such periods is barred by the doctrine of *res judicata.* If this were not the case, disputes over accrued compensation benefits would be litigated in a piece-meal fashion. Basham v. Lillian Vernon Corp., VWC File No. 193-57-46 (January 8, 2001).

The limitation against awarding "additional compensation" for any period more than ninety days before the date the claim was filed, does not apply in cases where a medical-only award is outstanding. The express language of the rule refers to claims for "additional compensation." Because an award of medical benefits is not an award of "compensation," the ninety-day provision of Rule 1.2(B) does not limit the claim for compensation to periods within ninety days of the filing. Kim v. Fairfax (County of) School Bd., VWC File No. 193-03-06 (April 17, 2001).

Where the employee is under an open award of compensation benefits, he has no legal obligation to file an application for hearing to enforce that award. Therefore, the ninety-day limitation of Rule 1.2(B) is inapplicable. In this case, the employee was under an open award when the employer unilaterally ceased paying benefits. Six months later, the employee submitted a claim to the Commission, seeking reinstatement of the discontinued benefits. The Commission declined to apply the ninety-day limitation of Rule 1.2(B), noting that to do so would penalize the employee for the employer's unilateral suspension of benefits and failure to file an application for hearing. It is the employer's duty, not the employee's, to submit a timely application for suspension of an outstanding award. Luong v. Wash. Metro Area Transit Auth., VWC File No. 195-73-54 (April 5, 2001).

Rule 1.2 (C):

Senior Claims Examiner's decision to refer employee's change-in-condition Claim to hearing docket upheld; in previous proceeding, employee's marketing efforts, based on restrictions in February 2003 medical report, found to be insufficient; in present proceeding, employee sought benefits based on marketing efforts, and included February 2003 report; employer's objection to further consideration of February 2003 rejected because present Claim based on continuing restrictions and marketing efforts, and medical report relevant to such inquiry. Beard v. Rogar Int'l Corp., VWC File No. 213-76-96 (Apr. 30, 2004).

1.3 Dismissal Upon Failure to File Supporting Evidence. — If supporting evidence is not filed within 90 days after an employee's claim is filed, it may be dismissed upon motion of the employer after notice by the Commission to the parties.

CASE NOTES

Applicability. — This rule provides that an employee's claim "may be dismissed upon motion of the employer after notice by the Commission to the parties" if the employee does not file supporting evidence within ninety days after the claim is filed. Eastman Kodak Co. v. Stremovihtg, No. 1406-95-2 (Ct. of Appeals Mar. 26, 1996).

NOTES FROM THE WORKERS' COMPENSATION COMMISSION

If supporting evidence is not filed within 90 days after an employee's claim is filed, the claim may be dismissed after notice is given by the Commission to the parties. Corley v. Lafferty, 75 O.W.C. 30 (1996).

1.4 Employer's Application for Hearing. — A. An employer's application for hearing shall be in writing and shall state the grounds and the relief sought. At the time the application is filed with the Commission, a copy of the application and supporting documentation shall be sent to the employee and a copy to the employee's attorney, if represented.

B. Each change in condition application filed by an employer under § 65.2-708 of the Code of Virginia shall:

1. Be in writing;
2. Be under oath;
3. State the grounds for relief; and
4. State the date for which compensation was last paid.

C. Compensation shall be paid through the date the application was filed, unless:

1. The application alleges the employee returned to work, in which case payment shall be made to the date of the return.

2. The application alleges a refusal of selective employment or medical attention or examination, in which case payment shall be made to the date of the refusal or 14 days before filing, whichever is later.

3. The application alleges a failure to cooperate with vocational rehabilitation, in which case payment must be made through the date the application is filed.

4. An employer files successive applications, in which case compensation shall be paid through the date required by the first application. If the first application is rejected, payment shall be made through the date required by the second application.

5. The same application asserts multiple allegations, in which case payment is determined by the allegation that allows the earliest termination date.

D. An employer may file a change in condition application while an award is suspended.

E. No change in condition application under § 65.2-708 of the Code of Virginia shall be accepted unless filed within two years from the date compensation was last paid pursuant to an award.

F. A change in condition application may be accepted and docketed when payment of compensation continues.

Comment. — Most of the cases cited herein were decided under former Rule 13.

CASE NOTES

Generally. — See Bristol Door & Lumber Co. v. Hinkle, 157 Va. 474, 161 S.E. 902 (1932); Wise Coal & Coke Co. v. Roberts, 157 Va. 782, 161 S.E. 911 (1932); Gray v. Underwood Bros., 164 Va. 344, 180 S.E. 317 (1935); Parker v. Manchester Bd. & Paper Co., 201 Va. 328, 111 S.E.2d 453 (1959).

Employer seeking a hearing on whether a workers' compensation claimant had been medically released to return to work showed probable cause allowing the matter to be scheduled for a hearing when it submitted a physician's report stating that the claimant could return to her former employment, even though the job description the physician reviewed in making this determination was not attached to the physician's report, as the accuracy of the job description reviewed by the physician was a matter for the hearing. Gallahan v. Free Lance Star Publ'g Co., 41 Va. App. 694, 589 S.E.2d 12, 2003 Va. App. LEXIS 607 (2003).

Purpose of rule. — Former Rule 13 was designed to protect employees, not to deprive them of rights existing under the Workmen's (now Workers') Compensation Act. It established barriers that an employer or insurer had to surmount before it could obtain the hearing under § 65.1-99 (now § 65.2-708), that was a prerequisite to extinguishing a claimant's right to enforce an award or agreement in the state court. This former rule was designed to serve as a screening device for eliminating obviously unmeritorious applications for hearings filed by insurers and employers. It was not an authorization for an employer or insurer to suspend payments with assurance that a claimant could not have them reinstated under former § 65.1-100. Dillard v. Industrial Comm'n, 416 U.S. 783, 94 S. Ct. 2028, 40 L. Ed. 2d 540 (1974), vacating and remanding 347 F. Supp. 71 (E.D. Va. 1972).

Effect of failure to file application. — The plain language of subdivision (C)(1) allows an employer to cease payment of compensation on the date an employee returns to work only when the employer files an application alleging the employee returned to work. Here, employer never filed an application alleging that claimant returned to work. Rather, it did nothing. Odin, Inc. v. Price, 23 Va. App. 66, 474 S.E.2d 162 (1996).

When a workers' compensation claimant notified the Workers' Compensation Commission that his employer's carrier was not paying workers' compensation benefits he had been awarded, and sought additional compensation due to a change in condition, to which the employer responded that the claimant had returned to work and any change in his condition was unrelated to his compensable injury, the issue of causation of the change in condition was improperly considered by the Commission because the claimant did not concede it was properly before the Commission, it was not mentioned in the hearing notice, nor did the Commission say it was considering terminating the claimant's award based on his change in condition application, under § 65.2-708(A), and the carrier did not seek permission to terminate the claimant's benefits, so the only issue properly before the Commission was whether the carrier should be assessed a penalty under § 65.2-524 for not paying benefits, and, as the claimant's award was valid and not paid, the Commission erred in not awarding this penalty. Washington v. UPS of Am., 267 Va. 539, 593 S.E.2d 229, 2004 Va. LEXIS 31 (2004).

Time limitations. — Employer's application to terminate temporary partial disability compensation was timely filed as the employer made a lump sum payment on the day that it filed the application, bringing its compensation payments current to two years prior to the date of filing its application to terminate, as required by § 65.2-708 and Va. Workers' Comp. Comm'n R. 1.4(E). Davis v. City of Lynchburg Waste Mgmt. & Liberty Mut. Ins. Co., 57 Va. App. 278, 701 S.E.2d 93, 2010 Va. App. LEXIS 445 (2010).

Employer's continuing liability. — Because an employer had a continuing liability to pay wage benefits under an open award in favor of an injured employee, and it failed to timely file a changed-circumstance application, despite the fact that the employee failed to file for termination of said benefits, the Virginia Workers' Compensation Commission properly assessed a 20 percent nonpayment penalty against it for its failure to pay the injured employee unpaid wage benefits. Wal-Mart Assocs. v. Cannon, 2007 Va. App. LEXIS 387 (Oct. 23, 2007).

To raise the issue of causation, the employer must do more. — This rule mandates that an application for a change of condition shall state the grounds for relief. One purpose of this portion of the rule is to provide due process notice to the claimant so that he or she can prepare to be heard on the issues raised in the application. To raise the issue of causation, an employer must do more than allege that the claimant is able to return to work, or by application state that the claimant is able to return to work and include a standard physician's form from the attending physician which states that the employee can return to work. Keen Drilling Co. v. Smith, No. 1225-94-3, (Ct. of Appeals June 20, 1995).

Probable cause for employer requested hearing. — Workers' Compensation Commission erred in refusing to hear an employer's allegation that a claimant receiving temporary partial disability unjustifiably refused selective employment under § 65.2-510 on the ground there was insufficient probable cause for a hearing under Va. Workers' Comp. Comm'n R. 1.4 and 1.5 because the employer did not submit medical evidence. Because the only allegation was a change in the conditions under which compensation was awarded, not a change in the claimant's physical condition or work capacity, the employer was not required to submit medical evidence; the open award for itself provided the requisite probable cause. Food Lion, LLC v. Dalton, 50 Va. App. 713, 653 S.E.2d 611, 2007 Va. App. LEXIS 441 (2007).

Employer was entitled to a hearing, pursuant to Va. Workers' Comp. Comm'n R. 1.4 and § 65.2-708, based on the medical evidence, which consisted of reports written by doctors who had examined the employee, that was submitted with the employer's application to suspend the disability benefits awarded to an employee based upon a change in the employee's condition. Advanced Finishing Sys. v. Brown-Snyder, 2008 Va. App. LEXIS 76 (Feb. 12, 2008).

Reasonable notice. — An employer must allege that the effects of the injury have fully dissipated and the disability is the result of another cause. While such allegations do not have to appear on the face of the application, the employer must at least reference the documents from which the employee could gain notice of the issue and attach the documents to the application. Referencing and attaching the documents must be done in such a way as to provide reasonable notice to the employee that the issue of causation will be raised. Keen Drilling Co. v. Smith, No. 1225-94-3, (Ct. of Appeals June 20, 1995).

Although the workers' compensation commission did not err in deciding that the claimant's benefits should be terminated because she voluntarily quit her employment without justification, it should have decided that the termination was effective on the date the employer filed its third application for termination, rather than the date her treating physician released her to return to work, as doing so prevented the workers' compensation commission from issuing a ruling having a retroactive effect on benefits paid prior to the filing of the application to terminate. Mileos v. Venus Pizza, No. 3132-02-4, 2003 Va. App. LEXIS 416 (Ct. of Appeals July 29, 2003).

Simultaneous payment and notification. — Check postmarked the day after an employer and insurer notified an employee of termination of her benefits and application for a rehearing on a changed condition did not violate the rule that payment and notification must be simultaneous. Boyd v. People, Inc., 43 Va. App. 82, 596 S.E.2d 100, 2004 Va. App. LEXIS 233 (2004).

No change in condition application under § 65.2-708 shall be accepted unless filed within two years from the date compensation was last paid pursuant to an award. — An employer was clearly in violation of that rule where it admitted it stopped paying its employee on July 30, 2000, but did not file its application to terminate payments until August, 2002, despite two letters from the Virginia Worker's Compensation Commission to the employer's insurer notifying it of its obligation to apply for a hearing to terminate benefits; the commission properly rejected the employer's application. Genesis Health Ventures, Inc. v. Pugh, 42 Va. App. 297, 591 S.E.2d 706, 2004 Va. App. LEXIS 21 (2004).

Insurer did not act under color of state law by suspending award pursuant to Workers' Compensation Commission Rules 1.4 and 1.5. Fleming v. Workers' Comp. Comm'n, 878 F. Supp. 852 (E.D. Va. 1995), aff'd, 78 F.3d 578 (4th Cir. 1996).

Failure to pay open benefits award when employee returned to work. — Employer was required to pay compensation pursuant to an award of the Virginia Workers' Compensation Commission, and assessed a 20 percent penalty on unpaid compensation pursuant to § 65.2-524 because the employer unilaterally ceased paying an employee benefits due and owed under an open award. The employer stopped paying the employee compensation benefits when he returned to full-duty work, and did not file appropriate paperwork or an application to terminate the award until well outside the two-year period provided for doing so under § 65.2-708, and in violation of Va. Workers' Comp. Comm'n R. 1.4. Washington Post v. Fox, 49 Va. App. 692, 644 S.E.2d 105, 2007 Va. App. LEXIS 185 (2007).

Retroactive modification of award not authorized. — When an employer sought the retroactive modification of a claimant's award of temporary total disability benefits, based on the claimant's return to light-duty work, § did not authorize such a modification because there was no evidence the claimant had misrepresented or failed to report her earnings, and no language in § 65.2-712, § 65.2-708, or Va. Workers' Comp. Comm'n R. 1.4(C)(1) allowed a retroactive modification, under these facts. Newport News Shipbuilding & Dry Dock Co. v. Bailey, No. 1782-03-1, 2003 Va. App. LEXIS 681 (Ct. of Appeals Dec. 23, 2003).

Calculation based on when employee returned to work. — Employer was erroneously required to pay the employee two years additional temporary total disability benefits after the Workers' Compensation Commission mistakenly concluded that the employer failed to show that the employee returned to work when he accepted the employer's offer to work in the mailroom. Newport News Shipbuilding & Dry Dock Co. v. Richardson, No. 1756-02-1, 2004 Va. App. LEXIS 32 (Ct. of Appeals Jan. 28, 2004).

Suspension of benefits. — Without seeking an order from the Virginia Workers' Compensation Commission, the fund ceased paying the claimant his benefits because the fund was informed that the claimant was incarcerated. Upon entry of the temporary partial disability award, the claimant became vested with the right to receive compensation benefits because the award remained outstanding and he violated no duty imposed by the Commission's rules and the Act; thus, the Commission improperly invoked the doctrine of imposition to uphold the fund's unilateral suspension of benefits in violation of Va. Workers' Comp. Comm'n R. 1.4(C). Uninsured Employer's Fund v. Peters, 43 Va. App. 731, 601 S.E.2d 687, 2004 Va. App. LEXIS 417 (2004).

Employer's burden where injury not subject of enforceable award. — As the parties' agreement to pay benefits did not mention the employee's hand injury, which prevented his cooperation with vocational rehabilitation, it was not the subject of an enforceable award. Therefore, the employer, which applied for a hearing to terminate benefits under subsection B of § 65.2-603, did not have the burden to show that the hand injury was not work-related. UPS v. Ilg, 54 Va. App. 366, 679 S.E.2d 545, 2009 Va. App. LEXIS 329 (2009).

NOTES FROM THE WORKERS' COMPENSATION COMMISSION

General:

A Deputy Commissioner does not have jurisdiction or authority to overrule a decision of the Senior Claims Examiner which accepts or rejects an Employer's Application. Estate of Giers v. Francis N. Sanders Nursing Home, Inc., VWC File No. 200-72-25 (Jan. 30, 2008), aff'd, No. 0332-0801 (Ct. of Appeals, June 3, 2008, unpublished).

Employer's application based on claimant's alleged refusal to cooperate with vocational rehabilitation properly dismissed where the rehabilitation services were not provided by a certified rehabilitation provider. It is not sufficient that the provider's supervisor was a certified rehabilitation consultant. Copeland v. Stone Container Corp., VWC File No. 206-01-65 (July 19, 2004).

Deputy Commissioner properly modified award of temporary total benefits to provide temporary partial benefits, although employer's Application sought termination of award; employee defended Application and requested entry of partial award; Commission found that employer had burden to prove change in condition and extent of change, and only proved that employee's total wage loss did not continue and that partial wage loss did continue; thus, entry of partial award appropriate, based on uncontradicted evidence of partial wage loss. Perrin v. Tri Cities Beverage Corp., VWC File No. 210-59-81 (Apr. 29, 2004).

Senior Claims Examiner's rejection of employer's application to terminate benefits for employee's refusal to attend an employer's medical examination overturned; although employer failed to provide documentary evidence showing that employee received notice of the scheduled examination, employer filed evidence from a physician stating that employee did not attend an examination, and employee did not object to the application on the basis that he did not receive notice of the examination. Cutlip v. Precision Fabricators, Inc., VWC File No. 203-34-60 (Aug. 19, 2003).

When claimant failed to notify the Commission of

a change of address, benefits were appropriately suspended as of date that Commission became aware of faulty address, and not date that employer knew of faulty address; employer may not unilaterally suspend benefits without filing application with the Commission. Hakimi v. K-Mart Corp., VWC File No. 189-35-70 (June 5, 2003).

The Deputy Commissioner may consider medical evidence obtained by either party after the filing of an application but prior to the time of the hearing. Lay v. Baldindos Lock & Key Service, Inc., 71 O.W.C. 110 (1992).

Where an employer files an application alleging an employee has returned to work and seeks a credit but does not request that an outstanding award be vacated, a finding that the employee briefly returned to light work at reduced wages does not require that the award be suspended until the claimant files a change in condition application. While a credit may be allowed for the period in which the claimant worked, compensation is reinstated thereafter on the basis that there is no further grounds for suspension under Rule 13 (now Rule 1.4 & 1.5) or § 65.1-100.3 (now § 65.2- 712). Telesystems, Inc. v. Hill, 12 Va. App. 466, 404 S.E.2d 523 (1991), 69 O.I.C. 46 (1990).

Rule 1.4(B) only requires that an application for hearing be under oath. There is no requirement that supporting documentation that alleges a refusal of vocational rehabilitation must be filed under oath. Blackwell v. SSI Services, Inc., VWC File No. 214-10-71 (Feb. 23, 2005).

Where the issue alleged in the Employee's Application For Hearing was that the claimant had returned to light duty work at earnings less than his pre-injury average weekly wage, the Deputy Commissioner property terminated the outstanding Award and entered an Award for temporary partial disability. McRea v. Int'l Sewer Service, Inc., 75 O.W.C. 71 (1996).

In rejecting an employer's application for failing to pay compensation pursuant to Rule 1.4, the Commission held that a facsimile transmission is not "filed" until actually received by the Commission. Sistare v. W. Logan Rowse, 73 O.W.C. 54 (1994).

The employer's cover letter indicated its application was sent by certified mail, but a postal receipt subsequently filed did not include that portion with the date, nor was any receipt filed that showed it was delivered to the Commission. The Commission held that the cover letter and the partial receipt was insufficient evidence to establish that the application was in fact filed. Hamilton v. Ramada Inn, 76 O.W.C. 74 (1997).

An employer, who filed a second application for hearing after requesting review of the Claims Division's rejection of its first application, must comply with Rule 13 (Rule 1.4) when the first rejection is affirmed on Review. Rachel v. Clintwood Garment Company, Inc., 69 O.I.C. 43 (1990).

It would be error for a Deputy Commissioner to dismiss an Application for Hearing on the ground that it was not supported by sufficient documentation. In such a situation, the Deputy Commissioner must hold a Hearing on the merits. However, the Deputy Commissioner has jurisdiction to determine as a preliminary matter that an issue is properly before him and whether an application is defective as not in conformity with Commission Rules. Silvious v. General Excavation, Inc., 77 O.W.C. 42 (1998).

When the employer alleges a change in condition, the Commission is charged with the responsibility of determining whether probable cause exists to suspend benefits pending a hearing on the issue raised in the application. Arzola v. Cherner Lincoln Mercury, Inc., 77 O.W.C. 12 (1998).

Where the work allegedly refused by a claimant exceeds permanent restrictions imposed by the treating physician, a release to such work that is approved by the employer's medical examiner does not establish sufficient probable cause to suspend compensation benefits pending a hearing. Arzola v. Cherner Lincoln Mercury, Inc., 77 O.W.C. 12 (1998).

With an Application for Hearing pursuant to Commission Rule 1.4, the employer must submit information sufficient to allow the Commission to assess whether probable cause exists to refer the application to the docket. Submission of a list of names, numbers and dates, purporting to be a work "ineligibility" list, without more, is insufficient to establish probable cause that the employee unjustifiably refused appropriate selective employment. On Review of the claims examiner's rejection of the application, the employer tried to explain the information submitted in support of its application and proffered the evidence it intended to introduce at the hearing. Commission Rule 1.6 (D) precludes consideration of anything beyond the information in the file at the time the probable cause determination was made, along with the Review request and response of the opposing party. The Commission affirmed the rejection, finding that there was neither documentary evidence available to the claims examiner nor sufficient evidence on Review upon which to find that the claimant was offered selective employment or that he refused it. Ward v. Ceres Marine Terminal, VWC File No. 166-37-83 (January 5, 2001).

Whether a *de facto* award has already been recognized by the Commission, or it simply appears from the record that one would be so recognized, an employer is required to file an application for hearing to be heard on the question of whether ongoing payment of benefits should be terminated or suspended. The Senior Claims Technician rejected the employer's application in this case because there was no open award, and the Commission reversed this decision. Although a *de facto* award had not yet been recognized, both parties acknowledged that compensation benefits had been paid over a long period of time. Where the facts suggest the reasonable possibility that a Deputy Commissioner might find that a *de facto* award exists, the employer should be allowed to file an application to her heard on the issue of suspension or termination of the ongoing payment of benefits. Tate v. United Parcel Service of America, VWC File No. 198-42-59 (August 17, 2001).

Rule 1.4 A & B:

Senior Claims Examiner correctly referred employer's application to hearing docket; employer filed application with Commission on January 31st, and certified on application that it also delivered application to counsel for claimant; evidence showed, however, application mailed to counsel on February 3rd; Commission determined employer attempted to deliver application as certified, and no evidence of willful intention to delay delivery. Madison v. Sam's Club, VWC File No. 193-21-10 (Apr. 29, 2003).

Rule 1.4(A) states that, at the time an employer's application is filed with the Commission, a copy of the application and supporting documentation shall be sent to the claimant and to the claimant's attorney, if represented. Rule 1.4(B) requires that the employer's application be under oath and state the date through which compensation was last paid. Rule 1.4(C) requires that compensation be paid through the date the application was filed, except for specific exceptions. Davis v. E. T. Bricklaying, Inc., 76 O.W.C. 303 (1997).

Rule 1.4(A) requires that a copy of the defendants' application and supporting documentation must be sent to the employee, and a copy to the employee's attorney if the employee is represented. Logically, since the defendants do not know the employee's address, they cannot possibly provide him with a copy of the application. However, because the employee was represented by an attorney at the time of the last hearing on this matter, and the defendants were certainly aware of that representation, the Commission held that the due process rights of the claimant had been violated, and the Commission rejected the Employer's Application on that ground. Jones v. Goodwill Industries, 79 O.W.C. 1 (2000).

An employer's application for hearing is defective and properly rejected by the Commission if it is not certified or submitted under oath, or where there is no evidence on the face of the document that compensation was paid pursuant to Rule 1.4(C). Davis v. E. T. Bricklaying, Inc., 76 O.W.C. 303 (1997).

When an employer files an application seeking to suspend compensation benefits on the basis that the claimant has refused vocational rehabilitation or medical treatment, the application must specify the dates and the nature of such refusal. Phelps v. J.B. Eurell Company, 67 O.I.C. 28 (1988).

Rule of the Commission 1.4(B) provides that each change in condition application filed by the employer under § 65.2-708 must be in writing and under oath. Rule 1.4(B) also states that the defendants shall state the grounds for relief as well as the date for which compensation was last paid. However, Rule 1.4(B) applies only to employer's applications filed under § 65.2-708, not to those filed under § 65.2-711 for failure to report a change in address. Jones v. Goodwill Industries, 79 O.W.C. 1 (2000).

The Employer's Application For Hearing form does not on its face specifically require an applicant's signature, because the form leaves a blank in which the applicant is supposed to insert the "Applicant's name and title." By way of contrast, we note that the Commission's form for a memorandum of agreement specifically calls for the signatures of the employer, the employee, and the insurer or authorized representative. Griffin v. Allied Auto Parts, Inc., 76 O.W.C. 511 (1997).

By creating an Employer's Application For Hearing form which does not on its face require a signature but only a name and title, while at the same time using the words "subscribed and sworn before me," the Commission has created a complex document, partially in the form of an acknowledgement and partially in the form of a jurat. There is a difference between acknowledging a signature and signing a document under oath. An acknowledgment verifies that the person named executed the document in question. By swearing to a document, the person vouches that the contents are true. A signature is not absolutely required by the form, so long as the applicant acknowledges in the presence of a notary that he executed the form. Griffin v. Allied Auto Parts, Inc., 76 O.W.C. 511 (1997).

The requirement that an Employer's Application For Hearing must be under oath is in Rule 1.4(B)(2). By the terms of that Rule, it only applies to a change in condition application filed by an employer under Code § 65.2-708. Nuttall v. Autozone, 79 O.W.C. 195 (2000).

Where an Employer's Application For Hearing is filed pursuant to Code § 65.2-712, the requirements of Rule 1.4(A) apply. However, the application need not be submitted under oath, as is required by Rule 1.4(B) for applications submitted under Code § 65.2-708. Nuttall v. Autozone, 79 O.W.C. 195 (2000).

The Employer's Application For Hearing showed that the notary filled in the date September 30, 1997, whereas the date typed after the name of the applicant is October 1, 1997, so that the date of the notary's action actually predated the acknowledgement. While this discrepancy might be only a scrivener's error, it is a critical element of the acknowledgment. Griffin v. Allied Auto Parts, Inc., 76 O.W.C. 511 (1997).

A report of a private investigator submitted in support of a hearing application must be signed, notarized and indicate direct knowledge of the allegations for which it is submitted. Dorey v. Anderson & Cramer, Inc., 70 O.I.C. 75 (1991).

An employer seeking to suspend payments under an outstanding award pursuant to Rule 13(a) (now Rule 1.4), must file medical evidence along with the application. Hartman v. Avtex Fibers, Inc., 67 O.I.C. 30 (1988).

Where an employer fails to furnish medical reports upon the filing of its application as required by Rule 13 (now Rule 1.4) and Rule 17 (now Rule 4.2), the application is void *ab initio*. It is also appropriate to assess a penalty under § 65.1-75.1 (now § 65.2-524) and a fine under § 65.1-124 (now § 65.2-900) and § 65.1-127 (now § 65.2-902). Marrow v. Addington Beaman Lumber Company, Inc., 69 O.I.C. 195 (1990).

In order to determine whether probable cause exists to suspend benefits and refer the matter to the docket for a hearing on the merits, the Commission's claims examiner must make a determination of whether there is a reasonable probability that the employer will succeed on the merits of its claim. The Commission held that a claims examiner could properly find probable cause that the claimant refused selective employment from (1) a medical report releasing the claimant to return to work; (2) a job description approved by the physician; and (3) the employer's statement under oath in the application that offered employment was refused. Berry v. Aramark Corporation, 78 O.W.C. 22 (1999).

A treating physician's release to "return to work" without listing any restrictions to be observed at work is sufficient documentation to refer the case to the docket and to suspend compensation payments pending a hearing. Jenkins v. Loudoun Hospital Center, 75 O.W.C. 140 (1996).

Deference is given to the opinions of a treating physician, especially in situations where the treating physician has been responsible for the claimant's care for several years and when the opposing opinion is asserted by an employer's medical examiner who had little contact with the employee. Silvious v. General Excavation, Inc., 77 O.W.C. 42 (1998).

The employer, as the proponent of an application that the claimant has been released to regular work, must prove by a preponderance of the evidence that the claimant is capable of performing all the duties of his pre-injury work. Meekins v. Heritage Golf Club, 77 O.W.C. 81 (1998).

Prospective releases to return to work are looked upon with disfavor by the Commission. Leech v. G. M. Clements Co., Inc., 77 O.W.C. 10 (1998).

Where the employee was still symptomatic and under lifting restrictions when last examined by the treating physician, his release to regular work ten days later was prospective and did not satisfy the employer's burden to prove the employee could return to work as of that date. Leech v. G. M. Clements Co., Inc., 77 O.W.C. 10 (1998).

The medical evidence showed that the claimant was able to perform light-duty work, and the issue was whether the light-duty restriction would allow the claimant to perform all the duties of his pre-injury work. Evidence of the claimant's pre-injury work duties necessary to resolve this issue was absent from the record. Since the employer, as the proponent of the change in condition application, had the burden to supply evidence to prove its claim by a preponderance of the evidence, and since evidence of the claimant's pre-injury work was not presented, the Commission held that the employer failed to prove the claimant could return to his pre-injury work. Meekins v. Heritage Golf Club, 77 O.W.C. 81 (1998).

Where the employer alleges in its Application that the claimant can return to her pre-injury work, but does not allege that any residual disability is unrelated to the work accident, the issue of causation is not before the Commission, only the narrow issue of whether the claimant is able to return to her pre-injury work. Martinez v. Embassy Suites, 76 O.W.C. 126 (1997).

Rule 1.4 C:

Employer filed an application alleging that the claimant had returned to pre-injury work. Two months later the employer sought to amend the application by asserting that the claimant had been released to return to pre-injury work. A Deputy Commissioner dismissed the employer's application, finding that it was defective on its face, because when the application was amended from "returned" to work to "released" to return to work, the employer was required to pay the claimant through the date the amended application was filed, and failed to do so. The Full Commission affirmed, ruling that the employer abandoned the allegation in the initial application when it sought to amend it to "released" to return to work. Hayes v. Action Home Construction, Inc., VWC File No. 222-72-36 (Sept. 17, 2010).

An employer is not required to seek a credit for payments made through an employer funded disability plan at the hearing. The employer may make such a request post hearing. The request is not barred if the lower opinion fails to address the issue. A request for a credit for payments made under a disability plan pursuant to § 65.2-520 is not a change in condition and is not governed by Rule 1.4. Pieters v. Wegman's Food Markets, Inc., #4007, VWC File No. 227-86-93 (Oct. 4, 2007).

Where the carrier issued the check the day after filing the Application for Hearing, the requirement of Rule 1.4 C that "payment must be through the date the application was filed" has not been met and the application is void. Johnston v. Giant Food, Inc., VWC File No. 213-96-83 (May 1, 2007).

When payment was processed on the Friday that an Employer's Application for Hearing was filed, but the check was not mailed to the claimant until Monday, it was appropriate to reject the Application because compensation was not paid to the date of filing. Cromer v. Unifirst Corp., VWC File Nos. 218-55-41 & 219-71-37 (July 31, 2006).

Where employee's check was mailed the day after the employer's application was filed, compensation was considered paid as required by Rule 1.4(C), and application to terminate benefits may go forward. O'Quinn v. J&J Contractors, Inc., VWC File No. 212-87-93 (March 25, 2005).

Rule 1.4(C) does not apply to Code § 65.2-712 violations. An application that only alleges a § 65.2-712 violation is not subject to the technical requirements of Rule 1.4(B) or payment requirements of Rule 1.4(C). Whitehead v. Lamberts Point Docks, Inc., VWC File Nos. 186-79-31, 204-38-00 (Feb. 18, 2005).

Denial of employer's Application to terminate benefits, based on refusal of medical treatment, affirmed; Application filed November 2003 and was supported by alleged refusal in April and August 2002 and March 2003; evidence showed compliance with treating physician's treatment as of November 2003, and thus, at time employer's Application was filed, there was no evidence of refusal. Gray v. Wal Mart Associates, Inc., VWC File No. 208-04-10 (Apr. 9, 2004).

Employer who proved that employee's compensation should be terminated because he was able to return to pre-injury work, based on a May 10, 2002, examination by the employee's treating physician, not entitled to credit for benefits paid to employee between May 10, 2002, and May 29, 2002, the date the employer filed an application to terminate benefits; benefits were owed under the open award until the date the application was properly filed, not the date of the release to pre-injury work. Gillis v. Enterprise Rent A Car Co., VWC File No. 205-20-70 (Aug. 26, 2003).

Senior Claims Examiner's rejection of employer's April 18, 2003, Application to terminate benefits based on December 3, 2002, release to return to work upheld, when Application certified that employer paid benefits only through December 5, 2002; although employer argued that employee refused to execute agreement forms, there was no evidence that employee actually had returned to work while still on an open award and had refused to execute appropriate agreement forms. Atkinson v. Penske Logistics, Inc., VWC File No. 201-39-53 (July 15, 2003).

Employer's application to terminate benefits, alleging full-duty release, complied with Rule 1.4(C) although payment not mailed to claimant until day after application filed; employer filed application and paid compensation to claimant through July 18, 2002; check issued on July 18, 2002, but not mailed until July 19, 2002; Commission found that application not defective. Boyd v. People, Inc., VWC File No. 206-40-00 (June 24, 2003), aff'd, 43 Va. App. 82, 596 S.E.2d 100 (2004).

Employer that unsuccessfully litigated application alleging release to return to pre-injury work precluded from later litigating return to light-duty work on same date, followed by alleged unjustified refusal shortly thereafter; employer knew of facts surrounding later application at time of prior application. Barton v. McDonald's, VWC File No. 196-30-27 (May 27, 2003).

Rule 1.4(C) requires that compensation shall be paid through the date the application was filed, unless, *inter alia*, the application alleges a refusal of selective employment or medical attention or examination, in which case payment shall be made to the date of the refusal or 14 days before filing, whichever is later. Campbell v. Perdue Foods, Inc., 76 O.W.C. 157 (1997).

The Commission has held that an employer's application alleging the claimant's failure to report a change of address under Code § 65.2-711 may be made without payment of benefits to the date of application as required by Rule 1.4(C), since the essence of the defendants' application is to complain that they are unable to locate the claimant in order to pay benefits. Jones v. Goodwill Industries, 79 O.W.C. 1 (2000).

Since an alleged change in condition would be made effective by an order or award as of the date compensation pursuant to an award was last paid and suspended pursuant to Rule 1.4(C), the medical evidence must show that the claimant was able to return to his pre-injury work at a time proximate to the date that the employer filed its application for hearing. Meekins v. Heritage Golf Club, 77 O.W.C. 81 (1998).

While an allegation of refusal of employment, medical attention or examination requires that compensation be paid through the date of the refusal or fourteen days prior to the filing, whichever is later, an assertion of failure to cooperate with vocational rehabilitation efforts requires payment to be made to the date on which the application is received in the Commissioner's offices or posted by certified mail. Hadjuducsek v. Ames Department Stores, Inc., 71 O.W.C. 256 (1992).

Where the employer alleges that the employee was released to return to light duty and that he is incarcerated, compensation must be paid through the date the Employer's Application For Hearing is filed, or it will be rejected. Campbell v. Perdue Foods, Inc., 76 O.W.C. 157 (1997).

Code § 65.2-510.1 sets forth the provisions for the suspension of benefits when a claimant is imprisoned and is medically released to perform selective employment, upon filing of a proper application to the Commission. A proper application under Code Ann. § 65.2-708 requires compliance with Rule 1.4(C). Campbell v. Perdue Foods, Inc., 76 O.W.C. 157 (1997).

Compensation paid "to" the date the claimant returns to or refuses work requires payment through the day before the alleged refusal or return. Payment for the date of alleged refusal or return to work is not required, since that would require payment for a day on which the claimant worked or refused to work. Rule v. Southside Regional Medical Center, 74 O.W.C. 40 (1995).

An application is void *ab initio* where an employer fails to pay compensation through the date of filing as required by Rule 13 (now Rule 1.4). In addition to upholding the validity of Rule 13 (now Rule 1.4), the Court found that the employee was not required to alert the employer to the defect in the application prior to the hearing. Specialty Auto Body v. Cook, 14 Va. App. 327, 416 S.E.2d 233 (1992).

Compensation must be paid pursuant to Rule 1.4 (C) either before or with the filing of an Employer's Application For Hearing. Compensation mailed to the claimant three days after the application was filed and eight days after the date through which payment was required does not comply with Rule 1.4 (C). Rule v. Southside Regional Medical Center, 74 O.W.C. 40 (1995).

Where the employer three days after filing to encompass the period up to the date of filing, the Commission in rejecting the application held that Rule 1.4(C) requires that compensation must be paid to the employee at the time of filing. Mullins v. T & J Trucking, 73 O.W.C. 56 (1994).

Where the employer voluntarily pays compensation for eight months without submitting a Supplemental Memorandum of Agreement, the Commission found a *de facto* award. Testimony challenging causation was not be allowed. To terminate benefits the employer must comply with § 65.2-708 and Rule 1.4(C). Anderson v. City of Roanoke Fire Department, 73 O.W.C. 34 (1994).

Where an employer was entitled to suspend payments pursuant to Rule 13 (now Rule 1.4 C) at an earlier date but paid through the date of filing, there is no provision for a credit for compensation paid during the period in which it was not required. Williams v. Richfood, Inc., 71 O.W.C. 286 (1992).

An employer is obligated to pay compensation pursuant to an open Award until its application is filed, and it cannot suspend payments under the outstanding award without a penalty. Thus, continuing payments that satisfied its obligation to pay the Award were not "overpayments" for which it could claim reimbursement. Pavlicek v. Jerabek, Inc., 76 O.W.C. 17 (1997).

Where a deputy commissioner in earlier proceedings awarded the employer a credit for all overpayments of benefits it had paid to the claimant, because of a miscalculation of average weekly wage, which opinion was not appealed, the employer was entitled to a credit against its future obligations through the date on which it filed its change in condition application. Phares v. Big Meadows Lodge, 76 O.W.C. 154 (1997).

An employer who files a subsequent application while benefits are suspended pending adjudication of a previous application is not required to pay compensation to the date of the second application unless the first application is dismissed. Day v. Shenandoah Fiberglass Products Co., Inc., 70 O.I.C. 73 (1991).

The employer properly filed an Application for

Hearing on February 12, 1997, seeking suspension of benefits due to the claimant's refusal of medical care. It subsequently wrote seeking to amend the application by adding two issues. The hearing Deputy Commissioner chose not to hear the new allegations, but indicated that it would be referred to the hearing docket. The senior claims examiner construed the amendment as a new claim and held it to the technical requirements of Commission Rule 1.4. The Commission held that the line between an amendment and a new claim is not always clear, but given that the Deputy Commissioner announced at the hearing that she would send the request to the hearing docket, together with the fact that the amendment was filed with the Commission more than three months before the hearing, it was error to reject the application because it technically did not comply with Rule 1.4. Colindres v. Jay Swigart Construction, 76 O.W.C. 503 (1997).

An employer, who filed a second application for hearing after requesting review of the Claims Division's rejection of its first application, must comply with Rule 13 (now Rule 1.4) when the first rejection is affirmed on Review. Rachel v. Clintwood Garment Company, Inc., 69 O.I.C. 43 (1990).

Until the issue of a change in treating physicians has been determined in an opinion no longer subject to review or appeal, the claimant is not required to select from a panel of physicians. Until there has been a final decision on the issue of a change in physicians, an employer may not demand that a claimant select from a panel and terminate benefits for a failure to do so. Such a rule would require the claimant to disrupt her medical treatment for a period when she may ultimately be able to return to her treating physician. Cubbage v. Wrangler, 78 O.W.C. 166 (1999).

Virginia Code § 65.2-711 states that failure to disclose a change of address without reasonable justification may result in suspension of compensation payments until the employee complies with this duty. Anderson v. Shenandoah's Pride Dairy, 76 O.W.C. 255 (1997).

An appropriate response to a party's failure to respond to discovery is a motion for sanctions under Rule 1.8(K). The filing of a motion for sanctions does not entitle an employer to suspend benefits pending a ruling on the motion, and an employer's motion for sanctions would also be considered defective if the claimant is not provided a copy as required by Rule 1.8(K). Davis v. E. T. Bricklaying, Inc., 76 O.W.C. 303 (1997).

Interest due and payable on an award is not "compensation" for purposes of Commission Rule 1.4(C). The employee urged the Commission to reject the employer's application for hearing, arguing that the employer failed to pay all "compensation" owed through the date the application was filed. The employee noted that interest had accrued on the benefits previously awarded before the employer's present application was filed. The employee alleged that the employer's application was defective because this interest amount was not paid. The Commission disagreed, finding that interest is not "compensation" because it is not wage reimbursement paid because of the employee's incapacity. The employer's application conformed to Rule 1.4(C). Kelley v. Midway Trucking, Inc., VWC File No. 197-69-19 (April 23, 2001).

Rule 1.4 E:

Despite several letters from the Commission advising employer that it assumed claimant was continuing to receive benefits under an open award, employer failed to file an application to terminate benefits until several years after claimant returned to work for employer. However, since the parties agreed to address issues in addition to the penalty issue at the hearing, these issues constituted an employer's application for benefits, and under Rule 1.4(E) the employer is required to pay compensation within two years from the date of the hearing, and a 20% penalty applies to all past due compensation. Johnson v. Federal Express Corp., VWC File No. 200-18-74 (Dec. 13, 2004).

Claims technician improperly rejected employer's application as not complying with Rule 1.4(E); although employee under outstanding award, and employer stopped payments under award in 2001, and did not file application until 2003, employer submitted evidence that employee returned to work in 2001 and also had been incarcerated since then, but was unable to be located; Commission found that employer unduly prejudiced by Commission's refusal to hear application because employer cannot determine exact whereabouts of employee. Cowan v. Glass Protection Services, Inc., VWC File No. 205-48-82 (Feb. 23, 2004).

While an employer who files a change of condition application under § 65.2-708 must pay compensation within two years prior to the date of the filing, an allegation of failure to provide a current address pursuant to § 65.2-711 allows for the suspension of benefits until an address is provided and proper notice of adjudication of the claim on the merits can be given. Ross v. Pony Express, 71 O.W.C. 99 (1992).

An employer who unilaterally suspends compensation benefits when a claimant returns to work without submitting the appropriate signed agreement forms to the Commission must comply with Virginia Code Ann. § 65.2-708 by paying compensation benefits to within two years from the date which compensation was last paid in order to have a change of condition application placed on the hearing docket. Umphlett v. Tidewater Container Corp., 76 O.W.C. 371 (1997).

An employer who unilaterally suspends compensation benefits when an employee returns to work without submitting the appropriate signed agreement forms to the Commission must comply with § 65.1-99 (now § 65.2-708) by paying compensation benefits to within two years from the date which compensation was last paid to have a change of condition application placed on the hearing docket. The employer is also estopped from asserting Rule 13(B) (now Rule 1.2 B) because the employee, who remained under an outstanding award, had no basis for filing an application for additional benefits until the employer filed an application to terminate the outstanding award. Middleton v. Howat Concrete, 69 O.W.C. 40 (1990).

On June 9, 1977, the employer filed an Application For Hearing alleging that the claimant had returned to his pre-injury work on April 1, 1991. The employer averred that it had paid compensation through April 15, 1991. The Commission held that the employer must pay compensation to within two years of the date of the application to have the matter referred to the docket. Umphlett v. Tidewater Container Corp., 76 O.W.C. 371 (1997).

See Notes to § 65.2-708 for additional cases on change in condition.

Rule 1.4(F):

A change in condition application may be accepted and docketed without a finding of probable cause when the payment of compensation continues. Hux v. Ball Corporation, 77 O.W.C. 226 (1998).

Where the employer's application was not based upon a change in condition, but merely sought to modify the average weekly wage and did not seek to suspend compensation payments pending a hearing, the acceptance or rejection of the application would not be based upon the usual probable cause standard. Hux v. Ball Corporation, 77 O.W.C. 226 (1998).

See Notes to § 65.2-708 for additional cases on change in condition.

1.5 Acceptance or Rejection of Claim or Application. — A. After receipt the Commission shall review the claim or application for compliance with the Workers' Compensation Act and Rules of the Commission.

B. The Commission may order the employer to advise whether the employee's claim is accepted or to provide reasons for denial.

1. Response to the order shall be considered a required report pursuant to § 65.2-902 of the Code of Virginia.

2. The employer's response to this order shall not be considered part of the hearing record.

C. If the employer's application is technically acceptable, the opposing party shall be permitted up to 15 days from the date the application was filed to present evidence in opposition to the application.

1. Pending acceptance or rejection of the application, the employer may suspend or modify compensation payments as of the date for which compensation was last paid.

2. If rejected, the Commission shall advise the employer of the reason for rejection and compensation shall be reinstated immediately.

3. If accepted, the application shall be referred:

a. For dispute resolution,

b. For decision on the record, or

c. For an evidentiary hearing.

CASE NOTES

Insurer did not act under color of state law by suspending award pursuant to Workers' Compensation Commission Rules 1.4 and 1.5. Fleming v. Workers' Comp. Comm'n, 878 F. Supp. 852 (E.D. Va. 1995), aff'd, 78 F.3d 578 (4th Cir. 1996).

Probable cause for employer requested hearing. — Workers' Compensation Commission erred in refusing to hear an employer's allegation that a claimant receiving temporary partial disability unjustifiably refused selective employment under § 65.2-510 on the ground there was insufficient probable cause for a hearing under Va. Workers' Comp. Comm'n R. 1.4 and 1.5 because the employer did not submit medical evidence. Because the only allegation was a change in the conditions under which compensation was awarded, not a change in the claimant's physical condition or work capacity, the employer was not required to submit medical evidence; the open award for itself provided the requisite probable cause. Food Lion, LLC v. Dalton, 50 Va. App. 713, 653 S.E.2d 611, 2007 Va. App. LEXIS 441 (2007).

Applied in Gallahan v. Free Lance Star Publ'g Co., 41 Va. App. 694, 589 S.E.2d 12, 2003 Va. App. LEXIS 607 (2003).

NOTES FROM THE WORKERS' COMPENSATION COMMISSION

An employer is not estopped from asserting a statute of limitations defense because of its responses to the Commission's "20-day Orders." Such responses are intended to promote identification and resolution of workers' compensation disputes and are not binding at hearing under Rule 1.5(B)(2). Moore v. Ross Store, Inc., VWC File No. 205-86-06 (Sept. 30, 2004).

Senior Claims Examiner's decision that there was no probable cause to refer to docket employer's Application to terminate benefits, alleging an unreported return to work by the employee, affirmed; Application based on investigator's report providing hearsay information from homeowner who purportedly hired employee, but homeowner's statement not included; Application did not include direct information of return to work that was sufficient to support probable cause finding. Ralda v. Wheat's Lawn & Custom Landscape, VWC File No. 215-55-91 (Apr. 2, 2004).

Senior Claims Examiner's rejection of employer's application upheld; only evidence showing release to pre-injury work was one-time employer's medical examination, whereas employee submitted substantial medical documentation, including treating physician's opinion, showing continued incapacity; Examiner allowed to weigh evidence in determining probable cause. Shelton v. Froehling & Robertson, Inc., VWC File No. 211-48-67 (Dec. 31, 2003).

Senior Claims Examiner's rejection of employer's

application to terminate benefits because of a release to return to regular work upheld; evidence supporting application consisted of opinion of employer's medical examiner; employee objected to application and supplied evidence from long-time treating physician showing that employee was restricted to light-duty and restrictions were supported by medical evidence. Reed v. Shoppers Food Warehouse, VWC File No. 199-64-13 (Sept. 8, 2003).

Senior Claims Examiner correctly referred employer's application to hearing docket; employer filed application with Commission on January 31st, and certified on application that it also delivered application to counsel for claimant; evidence showed, however, application mailed to counsel on February 3rd; Commission determined employer attempted to deliver application as certified, and no evidence of willful intention to delay delivery. Madison v. Sam's Club, VWC File No. 193-21-10 (Apr. 29, 2003).

Rule 1.5 of the Rules of the Commission states that after the Commission receives a claim or application, it shall review the document for compliance with the Workers' compensation Act and the Rules of the Commission, including whether the application raises sufficient probable cause to justify suspending payment of compensation pending a hearing. Chase v. Beverly Manor of Portsmouth, 76 O.W.C. 257 (1997).

When the employer alleges a change in condition, the Commission is charged with the responsibility of determining whether probable cause exists to suspend benefits pending a hearing on the issue raised in the application. Arzola v. Cherner Lincoln Mercury, Inc., 77 O.W.C. 12 (1998).

Where the employer al released to her pre-injury employment, but medical records show the claimant could not perform all the tasks of her pre-injury work that were identified in the job description filed by the claimant in response to the employer's application, the employer has presented insufficient evidence to establish probable cause to suspend the award and refer the matter to the evidentiary hearing docket. Chase v. Beverly Manor of Portsmouth, 76 O.W.C. 257 (1997).

1.6 Review of Decision Accepting or Rejecting Claim or Application. — A. A request for review of a decision accepting or rejecting a change in condition claim or application shall be filed within thirty (30) days from date of the decision. No oral argument is permitted.

B. The letter requesting a review should specify each determination of fact and law to which exception is taken. A copy of the request shall be sent to the opposing party.

C. The opposing party shall have 10 days from the date the review request is filed to provide a written response to the Commission.

D. Only information contained in the file at the time of the original decision along with the review request and any response from the opposing party will be considered. Additional evidence will not be accepted.

E. If rejection of a claim or application is affirmed on review, the penalty and interest provisions of §§ 65.2-524 and 65.2-707 of the Code of Virginia shall apply from the date the application was initially rejected.

CASE NOTES

Generally. — See, Thomas v. Nordstrom Pentagon City/Nordstrom, Inc., 22 Va. App. 626, 472 S.E.2d 288 (1996).

NOTES FROM THE WORKERS' COMPENSATION COMMISSION

No statutory provision sets forth a specific statute of limitations for responding to a letter decision from a Claims Examiner. Rule 1.6 provides that a request for review of a decision accepting or rejecting a change in condition claim or application must be filed within twenty days from the date of the decision, but that Rule specifically does not refer to initial claims for benefits. The Commission's Rule 1.1 states that an employee's original claim for benefits shall be filed within the applicable statutes of limitations; however, this Rule does not establish a specific time in which the employee must respond if the Claims Examination Department questions whether his claim has been filed within the statute of limitation period. The Commission found that the employee's response to the Claims Examiner thirty-three days after the claim was rejected was timely filed. Tang v. Progressive Engineering Co., 77 O.W.C. 256 (1998).

A decision by the Claims Department to place an application on hold until supporting documentation is received is not a judicial action and, therefore, Commission Rule 2, and its requirement that a party file a request for Review within twenty days from the date of the decision does not apply. Kibler v. Alger Brothers Construction Co., 73 O.W.C. 157 (1994).

Although Rule 13(C) (now Rule 1.6) does not specifically refer to the right of Review before the Full Commission of a Claims Division's decision not to place a case on the docket, this procedure is allowed recognizing that the claimant's benefits are suspended pending the hearing but also noting that if the employer prevails there is no means of recovering payments made during the review process. Stiltner v. Doris Coal Company, 68 O.I.C. 41 (1989).

The procedure regarding the review of a decision to accept or reject a claim or application does not provide for a written statement to be filed. The letter requesting a review should specify each determination of fact and law to which exception is taken. Rule 1.6 (D) provides that "[o]nly information contained in the file at the time of the original decision, along with the review request and any response from the opposing party, will be considered. Additional evidence will not be accepted." Campbell v. Perdue Foods, Inc., 76 O.W.C. 157 (1997).

Where an employer requests a Review of the Claims Division's rejection of an application, the outstanding award remains in effect pending the Review decision. If the employer does not prevail at Review, a penalty may be assessed on all compensation more than two weeks in arrears commencing on the day the application was rejected. Wadley v. Camelot Hall Nursing Home, 69 O.I.C. 191 (1990).

An employer, who filed a second application for hearing after requesting review of the Claims Division's rejection of its first application, must comply with Rule 13 (now Rule 1.4) when the first rejection is affirmed on Review. Rachel v. Clintwood Garment Company, Inc., 69 O.I.C. 43 (1990).

With an Application for Hearing pursuant to Commission Rule 1.4, the employer must submit information sufficient to allow the Commission to assess whether probable cause exists to refer the application to the docket. Submission of a list of names, numbers and dates, purporting to be a work "ineligibility" list, without more, is insufficient to establish probable cause that the employee unjustifiably refused appropriate selective employment. On Review of the claims examiner's rejection of the application, the employer tried to explain the information submitted in support of its application and proffered the evidence it intended to introduce at the hearing. Commission Rule 1.6 (D) precludes consideration of anything beyond the information in the file at the time the probable cause determination was made, along with the Review request and response of the opposing party. The Commission affirmed the rejection, finding that there was neither documentary evidence available to the claims examiner nor sufficient evidence on Review upon which to find that the claimant was offered selective employment or that he refused it. Ward v. Ceres Marine Terminal, VWC File No. 166-37-83 (January 5, 2001).

1.7 Compromise Settlement; Lump Sum Payment. — A. A proposed compromise settlement shall be submitted to the Commission in the form of a petition setting forth:

1. The matters in controversy;
2. The proposed terms of settlement;
3. The total of medical and indemnity payments made to date of submission and the date through which all medical expenses will be paid;
4. The proposed method of payment;
5. Such other facts as will enable the Commission to determine if approval serves the best interests of the claimant or the dependents.

B. The petition shall be signed by the claimant and, if represented, an attorney and by the other parties or their attorneys. An endorsing attorney must be licensed to practice in Virginia.

C. The petition shall be accompanied by:

1. A medical report stating the claimant's current condition and whether the injuries have stabilized;
2. An informational letter from the claimant or counsel stating whether the claimant is competent to manage the proceeds of the settlement and describing the plan for managing the proceeds;
3. A notarized affidavit attesting the claimant's understanding of and voluntary compliance with the terms of the settlement; and
4. A fee statement endorsed by the claimant and the claimant's attorney.

D. If the proposed settlement contemplates payment in a lump sum, the petition shall set forth in detail the facts relied upon to show that the best interests of the employee or the dependents will be served thereby.

If the proposed settlement contemplates an annuity, the petition shall state that the company issuing the annuity is authorized by the State Corporation Commission to transact the business of insurance in the Commonwealth and that, in case of default, the employer or carrier shall remain responsible for payment.

E. The parties shall submit an original proposed order, properly endorsed.

F. Payment shall be due within 10 days after entry of the order approving the compromise.

NOTES FROM THE WORKERS' COMPENSATION COMMISSION

The parties reached an agreement in mediation to settle the case. This agreement was not approved as it did not comply with the rules of the Commission. The plaintiff appealed, arguing that Rule 1.9 required the Commission to enforce the agreement reached at the mediation. The Full Commission held that Rule 1.7 and Section 65.2-701 require that certain documentation is required before the Commission will enforce agreements reached in mediation. Brown v. Pepsi Bottling Group, Inc., VWC File No. 209-73-44 (June 4, 2010).

Where payment is required pursuant to an Award

or Order that would be subject to the Review period set forth in § 65.2-705 of the Act, including an Order for a compromise settlement, payment is due within 14 days of the expiration of the Review period. The period begins to run from the date that counsel for the defendants receives the settlement Order not the date the carrier receives the Order. Swartz v. Home Depot, VWC File No. 200-65-49 (July 7, 2006).

A compromise settlement may be approved when the Commission is clearly of the opinion that the best interests of the employee will be served thereby. Herring v. Shotgun Express, Inc., 76 O.W.C. 135 (1997).

Commission may extend medical treatment under settlement agreement due to employer/carrier's delay in authorizing the treatment. Fraysier v. Clinch River Health Services, Inc., VWC File No. 193-86-15 (May 28, 2004).

Code § 65.2-701 requires that all compromise settlements between the parties shall be filed with the Commission for approval, and such agreement may be approved only when the Commission is clearly of the opinion that the best interests of the employee will be served thereby. If the agreement is not approved, it shall be void. Vercoe v. Air Wisconsin, 76 O.W.C. 288 (1997).

Before approving a settlement proposal, the Commission must determine that the compromise is in the best interest of the claimant. Isner v. Griffith Commercial Interiors, 76 O.W.C. 249 (1997).

The particular facts and circumstances of each case determine whether a compromise settlement proposal is in the best interests of the employee. The Commission will not approve a compromise settlement that it finds is not in the claimant's best interests. Jocham v. Retired Persons Services, Inc., 76 O.W.C. 433 (1997).

Code § 65.2-701 is clear in its purpose and mandatory in its language. Vercoe v. Air Wisconsin, 76 O.W.C. 288 (1997).

The Deputy Commissioner did not err in failing to address whether the parties had reached a binding compromise of the claim, because there can be no "binding" settlement of a claim until it is approved by the Commission. Stone v. Fairfax County Bd. of Sup'rs, 76 O.W.C. 109 (1997).

Whenever either party withdraws its agreement to a compromise settlement and so advises the Commission before the entry of the settlement order, the Commission will not enter the order. If the order has been entered prior to the receipt of the party's withdrawal of agreement, the party may petition for review of the order in a timely manner without the necessity of establishing fraud, mutual mistake, or imposition. Damewood v. Lanford Brothers Co., Inc., 77 O.W.C. 101 (1998).

The claimant and the carrier negotiated a compromise settlement of the claim, and it was submitted to the Commission. The carrier was thereafter advised that the claimant had since died from causes unrelated to his work injuries, and it withdrew its agreement to the settlement. The Commission held that the carrier's request was timely and declined to enter the compromise settlement order. Damewood v. Lanford Brothers Co., Inc., 77 O.W.C. 101 (1998).

In order for a lump sum settlement to be approved, the Commission must be furnished sufficient information to determine if it is in the best interest of the employee. The information must include evidence that the employee's injuries are stabilized, permanency exists, evidence of the employee's capabilities to handle the funds, and a detailed plan of how the proceeds will be used or invested. Warrick v. Goodyear Tire & Rubber Company, 69 O.I.C. 131 (1990); Herring v. Shotgun Express, Inc., 76 O.W.C. 135 (1997).

In the absence of requested medical reports, the Commission cannot find a compromise settlement to be in the best interest of the claimant. Lewis v. K-Mart Corporation, 73 O.W.C. 227 (1994); Herring v. Shotgun Express, Inc., 76 O.W.C. 135 (1997).

Where documents filed with the Commission failed to show that the claimant had fully recovered and had been released to his pre-injury work, but suggest that he continues under a doctor's care, and no provision is made to pay for the claimant's health care providers, the Commission could not find that approval would be in the claimant's best interests. Herring v. Shotgun Express, Inc., 76 O.W.C. 135 (1997).

Where surgery is delayed while the carrier obtains other opinions to determine whether it is reasonable and necessary treatment of the work injury, the agreed period during which medical care is to be provided by the employer pursuant to a compromise settlement may be extended to the extent of such delay. Fox v. W. G. Enterprises, 75 O.W.C. 243 (1996).

The Commission requires that the parties identify the specific claims which are being compromised. A general release of all claims, without specific reference to a date of injury or a specific claim, cannot operate in the best interest of the claimant. Isner v. Griffith Commercial Interiors, 76 O.W.C. 249 (1997).

The Commission recommends language that limits a release to injuries or disabilities sustained by the employee in the course of employment before the date of settlement. Jocham v. Retired Persons Services, Inc., 76 O.W.C. 433 (1997).

General blanket releases for past accidental injuries or diseases will not be approved unless the Commission is convinced that the circumstances indicate that the parties have thoughtfully contemplated both the reason for the release and the consideration given for it. Jocham v. Retired Persons Services, Inc., 76 O.W.C. 433 (1997).

Where the compromise settlement incorporates a "blanket release" from liability for all claims, including future claims, it may not be sufficient that both parties, even though represented by counsel, bargained for and carefully considered the proposed settlement. Jocham v. Retired Persons Services, Inc., 76 O.W.C. 433 (1997).

The Commission applies a high standard of scrutiny to all settlement proposals that contain "blanket release" language, and it believes that the best interests of the claimant are served when the parties identify the specific date or time period when accidents to be released are alleged to have occurred. Jocham v. Retired Persons Services, Inc., 76 O.W.C. 433 (1997).

The claimant filed a claim for benefits in Virginia, and was awarded compensation and medical benefits. He subsequently filed a claim for Illinois workers' compensation, which was settled for a lump sum in an agreement that provided "the settlement of this matter will close all matters in all jurisdictions and specifically Illinois and Virginia." Neither party filed the settlement proposal with the Virginia Commission. The Virginia Workers' Compensation Commission held that the claimant's rights under the Virginia Act were not extinguished and that the Award in this case remained outstanding. Vercoe v. Air Wisconsin, 76 O.W.C. 288 (1997).

An employee's claim for permanent total disability benefits held not barred by an Order of the Commission approving a compromise settlement of his permanent partial disability claim, even though the Order provided that the employer would also pay up to 500 weeks of temporary total disability. The settlement agreement did not indicate that the employee intended a final settlement of his claim, to the exclusion of a claim for permanent total disability, but only for his permanent partial disability claim. Holt v. Wood Brokers Co., 76 O.W.C. 13 (1997).

Rule 1.7, effective January 1, 1994, provides that payments must be made within 10 days after entry of an order approving a compromise settlement. However, that Rule was superseded by the amendment to Code § 65.2-524, effective July 1, 1994, providing that payments shall not be subject to a penalty until two weeks after the period within which a party may request review of such order. Hunt v. Southern Industrial At Union Camp, 76 O.W.C. 215 (1997).

The Commission approved a compromise settlement to be paid within a reasonable time after the order entered on June 25, 1996. The 20 days allowed for an appeal of that order expired on July 15, 1996, and the employer had an additional two weeks to make payment, to July 30, 1996, even if the order was not appealed. Hunt v. Southern Industrial At Union Camp, 76 O.W.C. 215 (1997).

The Commission approved a compromise settlement on June 25, 1996. The employer mailed payment to the claimant's attorney on July 22, 1996. Counsel, in turn, mailed the check to the claimant on July 29, 1996, and claimant received it on July 31, 1996 or August 1, 1996. The Commission held that payment was made on July 29, 1996 when counsel placed the check for the claimant in the regular mail. Because payment was therefore made before July 30, 1996, the last date it was due, no penalty could be assessed against the employer. Hunt v. Southern Industrial At Union Camp, 76 O.W.C. 215 (1997).

1.8 Discovery. — A. Scope and Method. — The scope of discovery shall extend only to matters which are relevant to issues pending before the Commission and which are not privileged. It is not ground for objection that the information sought will be inadmissible at the trial if the information sought appears reasonably calculated to lead to the discovery of admissible evidence. Discovery may be obtained by oral or written deposition, interrogatories to parties, production of documents or things, requests for admission, inspection of premises or other means of inquiry approved by the Commission.

B. Limiting Discovery. — The Commission may limit the frequency or extent of discovery if it is unreasonably cumulative, duplicative, expensive or if the request was not timely made. The Commission will consider the nature and importance of the contested issues, limitations on the parties' resources and whether the information may be obtained more conveniently and economically from another source.

C. Stipulation to Discovery. — Except as specifically provided by these rules, the parties may by written stipulation agree to other methods of discovery or provide that depositions may be taken before any person, at any time or place, upon any notice and in any manner and when so taken may be used like other depositions.

D. Supplementation of Responses. — A party who has responded to a request for discovery with a response that was complete when made is under no duty to supplement a response to include information thereafter acquired unless such information materially affects a prior response.

E. Protective Order. — Upon good cause shown, the Commission may enter an order limiting discovery to protect a party, a witness, or other person from embarrassment, oppression, or undue burden or expense.

F. Subpoenas. — A party requesting a subpoena for witness or subpoena duces tecum shall prepare the subpoena and submit it to the Commission for insertion of return date and Clerk certification; a check or money order for service fee, payable to the appropriate sheriff's office, shall accompany the request. The Commission shall forward the subpoena and service fee to the designated sheriff's office, unless requested to do otherwise.

Subpoenaed records may be made returnable to the requesting party or, at the direction of the Commission, to the Clerk of the Commission or to a regional office. If subpoenaed records contain medical reports they must be filed with the Commission pursuant to Rule 4.2.

Requests for subpoenas may be filed with the Commission at Richmond or in the regional office assigned to hear the case.

1. Subpoenas for Witnesses. — Requests should be filed at least 10 days prior to hearing.

2. Subpoenas Duces Tecum. — Requests should be filed at least 15 days before hearing and the subpoena shall describe with particularity the materiality of the documents or articles to be produced.

All requests for subpoenas duces tecum shall be served on each counsel of record, or the unrepresented party, by delivering or mailing a copy to each on or before the day of filing. Each request shall have appended either acceptance of service or a certificate that copies were served in accordance with the law, showing the date of delivery or mailing.

G. Depositions. — After a claim or application has been filed, any party may take the testimony of any person, including a party, by deposition upon oral examination or upon written questions.

The attendance of witnesses may be compelled by subpoena. The deposition of a party or physician may be taken without permission of the Commission. Leave of the Commission shall be obtained to take the deposition of any other persons. Depositions shall be taken in accordance with the requirements and limitations of the Rules of the Supreme Court of Virginia governing actions at law unless the parties stipulate to discovery as set forth in Rule 1.8(C), supra.

For good cause shown the deposition of an attending panel physician may be ordered to be taken at the expense of the employer if the physician has not prepared and completed an Attending Physician's Report (Form 6) or has not otherwise prepared written reports which are sufficient to answer questions concerning injury, diagnosis, causation, disability and other matters not stipulated and deemed by the Commission to be material to a claim or to a defense. The expenses of such depositions are subject to the approval of the Commission.

Depositions shall be filed with the Commission and be made a part of the record.

H. Interrogatories to Parties. — After a claim or application has been filed, interrogatories limited to contested issues may be served by one party on another party, more than 21 days before hearing without prior Commission approval.

Answers under oath to each interrogatory are to be filed within 21 days after service. Objections must be included with answers. If there is objection to an interrogatory and the party serving the interrogatory moves the Commission for relief, the hearing officer shall enter an order resolving the issue, after giving the parties an opportunity to state their positions in writing.

No party shall serve upon any other party, at one time or cumulatively, more than 15 interrogatories, including all parts and subparts, without leave of the Commission for good cause shown. Leave shall be timely requested in writing. Relevant interrogatories should be served promptly upon commencement of a contested claim.

It is not necessary to file interrogatories or answers with the Commission unless they are the subject of a motion.

I. Request for Admission. — After a claim or application has been filed, a party may serve upon any other party a written request for the admission of the truth of any material matter.

Each request must be numbered and set forth separately. Copies of documents shall be served with the request unless they have been furnished or made available for inspection and copying.

An admission under this rule may be used only for providing evidence in the proceeding for which the request was made and shall not have force or effect with respect to any other claim or proceeding. An admission or denial must be offered in evidence to be made part of the record. A party is required to respond within 30 days or be subject to compliance under Rule 1.8(K) or sanctions under Rule 1.12.

J. Production of Wage Information. — If the average weekly wage is contested, the employer shall timely file a wage chart showing all wages earned by an employee in its employment for the term of employment, not to exceed one year before the date of injury.

If an employee has earned wages in more than one employment, the employee shall have responsibility for filing information concerning wages earned in an employment other than the one in which claim for injury is made.

K. Failure to Make Discovery; To Produce Documentary Evidence; To Comply With Request for Admission. — A party, upon reasonable notice to other parties and all persons affected thereby, may request an order compelling discovery as follows:

A timely request in writing in the form of a motion to compel discovery may be made to the Commission or to such regional office of the Commission where an application is assigned to be heard.

Failure of a deponent to appear or to testify; failure of a party on whom interrogatories have been served to answer; failure of a party or other person to respond to a subpoena for production of documents or other materials; or failure to respond to a request for admission shall be the basis for an order addressing a request to compel compliance or for sanctions, or both.

L. Disposition of Discovery Material. — Any discovery material not admitted in evidence and filed in the Commission may be destroyed by the Clerk of the Commission after one year from entry of a final decision of the Commission or appellate court.

CASE NOTES

Discovery of basis for claim of employee status. — Pursuant to this rule, an employer or insurer is free to propound interrogatories to a claimant seeking the basis for his claim that he is a covered employee under § 65.2-101, but in the absence of such an interrogatory, the employee is not required to elect the subsection or subsections under which he claims coverage. Thacker v. TNT Insulations Co., No. 3111-99-4, 2000 Va. App. LEXIS 507 (Ct. of Appeals July 11, 2000).

Failure to make discovery. — Commission did not err in dismissing claimant's pending claims without prejudice, due to his failure to attend deposition as ordered by commission. Craft v. Commercial Courier Express, No. 1517-99-2 (Ct. of Appeals Dec. 7, 1999).

Failure to respond to discovery request. — Virginia Workers' Compensation Commission did not abuse its discretion in dismissing a workers' compensation claimant's third claim without prejudice under Va. Workers' Comp. Comm'n R. 1.12 where: (1) the claimant was well aware of the Commission's rules as he had filed multiple motions and discovery requests, (2) the Commission had granted the claimant's motion for a continuance for a reasonable time, since the claimant was incarcerated, (3) pursuant to Va. Workers' Comp. Comm'n R. 1.8(K), the deputy commissioner had ordered the claimant to respond to the employer's request for admissions within seven days, and (4) the claimant failed to respond to the request for admissions or to offer an alternative method of presenting his case. Taylor v. MJRW, Inc., No. 2923-03-1, 2004 Va. App. LEXIS 192 (Ct. of Appeals Apr. 27, 2004).

Social security records. — No authority permitted the Workers' Compensation Commission to order an employee to sign a release authorizing employer to get the employee's records from the Social Security Administration, and the Commission exceeded its authority ordering the signing of the release. Arvizu v. Gold, 38 Va. App. 641, 567 S.E.2d 592, 2002 Va. App. LEXIS 491 (2002).

Filing of wage chart. — Requirement that employer timely file a wage chart showing all wages earned by an employee in its employment for the term of employment not to exceed one year before the date of the injury did not equate to entering a document into evidence by which the claimant would demonstrate what his average weekly wage was, and, thus, the workers' compensation commission erred in allowing the claimant to belatedly submit average weekly wage information when he was granted the opportunity to timely submit that information and did not do so. Gwaltney of Portsmouth v. Scales, 2005 Va. App. LEXIS 474 (Nov. 22, 2005).

NOTES FROM THE WORKERS' COMPENSATION COMMISSION

General:

A claimant's on-going award of medical benefits constitutes a sufficient issue or proceeding to allow the defendants to propound discovery concerning medical treatment. Greenwood v. B W I Distribution, VWC File No. 194-35-98 (May 13, 2005).

Where the claimant is on an outstanding award there is a proceeding under the title such as to allow for discovery, and the Commission has the authority to require the production of documents and other things. Habina v. Jasper Construction, VWC File No. 173-22-55 (Aug. 26, 2005).

The 21 day time frame contained in Rule 1.8 for providing answers to interrogatories also applies to request for production of documents. After a party has been provided the initial 21 days, it is within the discretion of the deputy commissioner to determine the time frame for responses to an Order to Compel. Habina v. Jasper Construction, VWC File No. 173-22-55 (Aug. 26, 2005).

Employer allowed to conduct discovery despite employee's request that claim be considered "inactive" while third-party lawsuit pursued; evidence showed that third-party lawsuit ripe for settlement and employer requested discovery to assist in decision on approval thereof. Viar v. Raytheon Constructors, Inc., VWC File No. 189-75-51 (Apr. 4, 2003).

Code § 65.2-703 asserts, *inter alia,* that all interrogatories, depositions, or any other discovery shall conform to rules governing discovery promulgated by the Commission, and that such rules shall conform as nearly as practicable to the Rules of the Virginia Supreme Court regarding discovery. The Commission has interpreted this Section to allow reasonable discretion to most efficiently administer the Act and to do justice for all parties, as may be suggested by the facts of a particular case. Magana v. Sosa, 79 O.W.C. 136 (2000).

Where the determination of a discovery issue may have great impact on an employee's claim, interlocutory review may be appropriate. Handlovitch v. Chesapeake General Hosp., 75 O.W.C. 293 (1996).

An employee should not be compelled to seek out and obtain a document pursuant to a motion for production filed by an adverse party, absent evidence that the document to be produced is otherwise unavailable to the requesting party. Zeballos v. Mendez, 75 O.W.C. 229 (1996).

The Commission may compel the employee to answer discovery requests regarding Social Security Administration information, and/or provide a release for such information. The Act gives the Commission the discretion to order the employee to obtain and present Social Security information when it is relevant to a claim for workers' compensation benefits. The employee's legal work status was clearly at issue in the case. Therefore, the Commission found that it was appropriate for the hearing officer to order the employee to obtain information regarding his work status in the United States from the Social Security Administration. Arvizu v. Archie D. Gold, VWC File No. 202-92-84 (August 29, 2001).

The employer must produce in discovery any surveillance videotape or film upon which it intends to rely at the hearing of the matter. However, the employer need not produce such evidence to the employee until after it has an opportunity to take the employee's deposition. Noting that the purpose of Commission hearings is to adduce the truth, the Commission held that allowing the employer to depose the employee before production of surveillance materials encourages truthfulness by the parties at the hearing. Hairston v. Sentara Hampton General Hospital, VWC File No. 203-57-10 (August 6, 2001).

An employee's ongoing award of medical benefits constitutes a sufficient "issue" or "proceeding" before the Commission to allow discovery requests under Rule 1.8(A). The employer sought leave to issue a subpoena to a third party entity, on whose premises the accident occurred, seeking information regarding the accident and a possible claim against the third-party. The employee was under a medical award, but no other matter was pending before the Commission, and the third party argued that the subpoena exceeded the scope of discovery under Commission rules. The Commission disagreed, finding that the claim remained before it on the open medical award, noting the impact that the discovery could have on the award and subrogation rights under Code §§ 65.2-309 and 65.2-310. Johnson v. Laurel Trucking, Inc., VWC File No. 200-18-25 (August 29, 2001). See also Fields v. Labor Ready, Inc., VWC File No. 203-70-99 (November 16, 2001) (applying the same rule to demand for answers to interrogatories).

Rule 1.8(D):

Deputy Commissioner properly refused to allow employer to call witness not identified in discovery; employer's discovery response was that it had not decided whom to call as witness; Commission agreed with Deputy Commissioner's finding that this response was not complete when made and thus employer required to supplement response. Crowe v. Lowe's of South Boston Va., VWC File No. 208-09-67 (Oct. 16, 2003).

Rule 1.8(E):

Statements taken by employer's counsel of three witnesses are privileged work product, unless the employee can show substantial need for the information requested and that he is unable to obtain the substantial equivalent of the information. Baugh v. Rust Industrial Cleaning Service, 75 O.W.C. 307 (1996).

A third party claim accident report is discoverable, inasmuch as it directly relates to the workers' compensation claim and could reasonably lead to other discoverable information. Zeballos v. Mendez, 75 O.W.C. 229 (1996).

Rule 1.8 (F):

Electronic Communications Privacy Act (18 U.S.C. section 2702) protects information on the Facebook website, and the Commission lacks authority to compel Facebook to provide such information in response to a *subpoena duces tecum.* Hensley v. Colgan Air, Inc., VWC File No. 232-16-19 (Apr. 9, 2010).

Where the subpoena is limited to encompass only records relevant to the proceeding before the Commission, the agency has the authority to require Child Support Enforcement to comply with the subpoena duces tecum, and produce the requested wage and child support payment information. Dignazio, Jr., v. Continental Commercial Corporation/Hillsborough Vineyards, VWC File No. 222-30-88 (Nov. 1, 2005).

Deputy Commissioner properly denied DMV's motion to quash subpoena for medical information concerning employee's application for disabled parking permit; medical information in question found to be material and relevant and neither employee nor physician supplying information had expectation of privacy; protective order issued to allow Deputy Commissioner to examine records in camera before ruling on admissibility. Seeman v. Belfort Furniture, Inc., VWC File No. 213-79-35 (Nov. 18, 2003).

The Commission is vested with the authority of courts and judges to enforce the production of records. Since the Commission can enforce the production of records, the Commission may also determine what records are to be produced. Morgan v. Eastern State Hospital, 78 O.W.C. 192 (1999).

Commission Rule 4.2 provides that a medical care provider attending an injured employee shall furnish a copy of required reports to the employer or employee. The physician-patient privilege as to all physicians is waived in all proceedings under the Act. Hassell v. Arlington County Human Services, 79 O.W.C. 141 (2000).

The Commission has authority to exclude medical evidence. However, the employer has the right to see all the medical records, because this information is, or might lead to, admissible evidence. In this case, the Commission found that the Deputy Commissioner erred by allowing the claimant's treating physician to submit redacted and summarized records relevant to the claimant's post traumatic stress disorder claim, and that the employer was entitled to review all of the physician's records for his treatment of the claimant, unredacted and unsummarized. Hassell v. Arlington County Human Services, 79 O.W.C. 141 (2000).

The parties have a right to receive and review all medical documents which are or may be related to the claimant's condition. The claimant calls his medical condition into question by filing a claim for medical benefits, and the defendants have a right to subpoena documents which may be relevant in the defense of the claim, even though the claim had been accepted as compensable, and even though there is no pending claim for additional benefits. Smith v. Mullins Coal Company, Inc. of Va., 78 O.W.C. 202 (1999).

Even if a claim is found to be compensable, the

employer is not responsible for the cost of a physician's treatment if the physician declines to produce the records of treatment. Hassell v. Arlington County Human Services, 79 O.W.C. 141 (2000).

Counsel in workers' compensation cases under § 65.2-402 (involving the presumption as to death or disability from respiratory disease, hypertension, or heart disease in regard to certain workers) are entitled to discover underlying facts and assumptions upon which an expert opinion is based in such cases, but the physician-patient confidentiality must also be protected. The Commission held that an expert witness identified in the case was required to produce, pursuant to a subpoena duces tecum, all opinion reports issued in cases before the Virginia Workers' Compensation Commission during the period from January 1, 1998 to the present, with the claimants' names redacted, in which the report was requested by a claimant or an employer and in which the expert witness was not the treating physician. Brandon v. City of Richmond Fire Department, 78 O.W.C. 216 (1999).

Where the employee alleges a disease [Hepatitis] contracted incidental to an accidental event and linked to the medical condition of a patient hospitalized with the employer, employee's counsel is entitled to access to the patient's medical records by *in camera* review. The limited physician-patient privilege of § 8.01-399], is not applicable to cases where the physical or mental condition of the patient is at issue. It is inapplicable where "a court, in the exercise of sound discretion, deems disclosure necessary to the proper administration of justice." This exception extends to the Commission, which is vested with the authority of courts and judges to enforce the production of records. Handlovitch v. Chesapeake General Hosp., 75 O.W.C. 293 (1996).

The claimant alleged that certain patient records of the employer were necessary to establish the hazards to which she was exposed in the employment, because they would establish that the patient was prescribed medicine for aggressive tendencies. The Commission held that it was not vital that the specific records be produced, because evidence was already available that patients were prescribed medication and the Commission acknowledged that patients were hospitalized at the hospital for certain identifiable diagnoses, and that this case did not override the need to preserve the confidentiality of the medical records of the patient, who was not a party to the case. Morgan v. Eastern State Hospital, 78 O.W.C. 192 (1999).

The rule in civil cases and the standard of practice adopted by the Commission is that counsel cannot rely upon a witness subpoena of opposing counsel, whether the subpoena was issued by opposing counsel or by the Commission itself. The defendants asked the Commission to issue a witness subpoena, compelling the attendance of one of its employees at a hearing. The witness did not appear at the hearing, and claimant's counsel sought to keep the record open so that additional evidence from the witness could be introduced. The employer objected and the Deputy Commissioner denied the request. The Commission affirmed, noting that claimant's counsel did not identify the witness in response to interrogatories, and did not separately subpoena her attendance at the hearing. Bledsoe v. Wise (County of) Sheriff's Office, VWC File No. 204-29-06 (March 13, 2002).

Rule 1.8 (G):

The deputy commissioner did not err in failing to admit claimant's discovery deposition where employer objected, and claimant testified extensively at the hearing regarding the events surrounding his injury. Thaxton v. United Parcel Service, Inc., VWC File No. 218-71-85 (Feb. 1, 2005).

Employer not required to transcribe deposition taken at employer's request absent showing of good cause; until deposition is transcribed there is no requirement to file deposition with Commission; contrary holding in Pretlow v. Peninsula Regional Jail , VWC File No. 203-16-24 (2/19/02) overruled. Browne v. Aureus Group, VWC File No. 201-28-86 (Mar. 10, 2003).

An employee is not required to attend a discovery or de bene esse deposition of an expert witness called by the employer. Foster v. Hooker Furniture Corp., 75 O.W.C. 355 (1996).

Although statements obtained by an employer from witnesses are deemed work product, the employer may not withhold the documents under privilege and then use them at trial. Baugh v. Rust Industrial Cleaning Service, 75 O.W.C. 309 (1996).

Witness statements obtained without leave of the Commission under Rule 1.8(G) may be used for rebuttal purposes only, after the statement is made available to the employee. Baugh v. Rust Industrial Cleaning Service, 75 O.W.C. 307 (1996).

A doctor's deposition is similar to a medical report, and the party taking the deposition is required to file it with the Commission. Because the defendants took the doctor's deposition, and a transcript is necessary to have the deposition made a part of the Commission's record, the defendants are financially responsible for ordering a transcript and filing it with the Commission. Pretlow v. Virginia Peninsula Regional Jail Authority, VWC File No. 203-16-24 (February 19, 2002).

Rule 1.8 (H):

The scope of discovery in a Commission proceeding is determined not only by Commission Rule 1.8 but also by Supreme Court Rule 4:1(b)(1), which in part provides that, "[p]arties may obtain discovery regarding any matter, not privileged, which is relevant to the subject matter involved in the pending action, whether it relates to the claim or defense of the party seeking discovery or to the claim or defense of any other party." Craft v. Commercial Courier Express, Inc., 78 O.W.C. 270 (1999).

The employer disclosed in its discovery responses to the claimant the results of tests taken after the work accident that showed recent use of marijuana and alcohol by the employee. However, the employer did not disclose that the laboratory that had performed the tests was a certified laboratory, pursuant to Code § 65.2-306(B). The Commission agreed with the Deputy Commissioner that, because the cover letter from the laboratory for the tests had not been disclosed to the claimant in discovery as a potential hearing exhibit, the employer could not offer the letter at the hearing to establish proof of such certification. The Commission also agreed that the Deputy Commissioner properly excluded testimony from the employer's clinic manager that the laboratory was a certified laboratory, and that the Deputy properly refused to take judicial notice of the certification, because the documentation had not been provided in discovery. Foster v. Smithfield Packing Co., Inc., 79 O.W.C. 184 (2000).

So long as a claimant remains under an open award, the employer has the right to discover medical evidence relevant to the claimant's physical and medical condition. Discovery is permissible while a claimant is under an open award even in the absence of a pending application for hearing. Craft v. Commercial Courier Express, Inc., 78 O.W.C. 270 (1999).

Claimant's ongoing award for medical benefits constitutes an "issue" or "proceeding" pending before the Commission as those terms are used in Commission Rule 1.8 and in Virginia Code § 65.2-703. Also, Virginia Code § 65.2-711 requires a claimant under an open award to inform the employer of his current residential address unless there is reasonable justification for refusing to do so. A residential address is not equivalent to a post office box address. Craft v. Commercial Courier Express, Inc., 78 O.W.C. 270 (1999).

The Commission denied the claimant's demand that the employer identify, in response to interrogatories, the names of each person who spoke with the claimant's treating physician in the employer's behalf, and the substance of each such meeting or conversation. The employer carried its burden to prove that the substance of what was discussed with the physician, memorialized in the defendants' notes but not in the physician's treatment records, was information prepared in anticipation of litigation and protected by the work product doctrine. The Commission observed that the claimant failed to take advantage of standard discovery devices that would have revealed the same information. Accordingly, the claimant failed to prove a substantial need for the information recorded by the defendants' representatives. Rose v. Interim Healthcare, VWC File No. 207-16-00 (March 22, 2002).

Rule 1.8 (I):

Regarding discovery admissions, the Commission has held that Rule 1.8(I) requires responses within 30 days, or the party failing to answer is subject to compliance under Rule 1.8(K) or sanctions under Rule 1.12. Rule 1.8(K) allows a party to request an Order compelling the discovery, and Rule 1.12 sets out sanctions for failure to comply with Orders or Rules of the Commission, including fines, attorney's fees, rejection of pleadings, exclusion of evidence, or dismissal of a claim or application. Magana v. Sosa, 79 O.W.C. 136 (2000).

While the Commission encourages stipulations to narrow disputed issues and avoid unnecessarily litigious hearings, an employee is not obligated to admit facts not within his personal knowledge. Foster v. Hooker Furniture Corp., 75 O.W.C. 355 (1996).

In the present case, where the claimant was unrepresented, the Commission held that the sanctions would appear unduly harsh if the claim was dismissed, or if the request for admissions were deemed admitted without the claimant having at least the benefit of an explanation of her requirement to respond to discovery. Instead, the Commission admonished the claimant to respond or to object to the request for admissions, lest the Commission at some later date deem her failure to respond as admissions to the requested information, or to order that her claim be dismissed. Magana v. Sosa, 79 O.W.C. 136 (2000).

There is no provision in Commission Rules 1.8(I), 1.8(K) and 1.12 that would specifically allow the Commission to deem requests for admissions "admitted" when the party to whom they were directed fails to respond to them in a timely manner. The Commission observed that Rule 4:11 of the Rules of the Supreme Court is much broader than the Commission rules, and Rule 4:11 is self-executing. Determining all disputed facts in favor of the moving party, merely because of the passage of time, is a harsh result not contemplated by the drafters of the Commission rules. The Deputy Commissioner has the discretion to impose an appropriate sanction for failure to respond to discovery, and the Commission agreed that striking the claimant's defenses to the employer's application was an appropriate sanction. Hunt v. R M Thorton, Inc., VWC File No. 201-73-17 (July 30, 2002).

Rule 1.8 (K):

Where employer showed blatant disregard for Commission's discovery orders, deputy commissioner properly struck defense to the compensability of the accident and prohibited testimony of witnesses on this issue. Branham v. Runk & Pratt of Forest, VWC File No. 213-15-02 (Sept. 1, 2004).

Deputy Commissioner properly excluded video surveillance evidence because evidence was in existence prior to employer's responses to discovery seeking such evidence and employer did not produce evidence, as requested; employer's assertion that employee would not be prejudiced by late admission of evidence not relevant to question of whether employer failed to comply with pre-hearing discovery. Davis v. Lasco Bathware, VWC File No. 211-12-03 (Nov. 24, 2003).

Deputy Commissioner properly refused to allow employer to call witness not identified in discovery; employer's discovery response was that it had not decided whom to call as witness; Commission agreed with Deputy Commissioner's finding that this response was not complete when made and thus employer required to supplement response. Crowe v. Lowe's of South Boston Va., VWC File No. 208-09-67 (Oct. 16, 2003).

An employee cannot ignore or neglect proper discovery requests, but must answer them substantively within the time period allowed by discovery rules, or within that period challenge requests she considers objectionable. Where a party disregards discovery orders of the Commission with impunity, dismissal of the claim is an appropriate sanction for such conduct. Zeballos v. Mendez, 75 O.W.C. 229 (1996).

A party seeking to enforce discovery must file a timely motion to compel discovery in the office where the case is assigned to be heard. Wright v. CBI Na-Con, Inc., 77 O.W.C. 31 (1998).

Where the claim was filed January 15, 1997, but interrogatories were not propounded by the employer until April 21, 1997, and the Motion to Compel was not filed until May 20, 1997, the Deputy Commissioner did not abuse his discretion in finding that the filing of the motion just ten days before the hearing left him insufficient time to issue an order compelling the claimant to respond and for counsel to receive the answers, and the Deputy Commissioner did not abuse his discretion in refusing the employer's request for a continuance. Wright v. CBI Na-Con, Inc., 77 O.W.C. 31 (1998).

While the Act does not contain specific authority to impose sanctions as provided in Virginia Supreme Court Rule 4:12, Va. Ann. Code § 65.2-202 does grant the Commission the same authority to enforce its orders as is vested in the circuit courts of Virginia. This Section has been interpreted to include the sanctions set out in Rule 4:12. The Commission's authority to impose sanctions for failure to discover are stated in Rule 1.12 of the Rules of the Commission. Foster v. Hooker Furniture Corp., 75 O.W.C. 355 (1996).

Dismissal of a claim is the most severe sanction that the Commission may impose for a claimant's failure to cooperate with discovery. Both Rule 1.12 and the general principles of due process require that the Commission give notice of its intent to impose this sanction and provide an opportunity for each party to be heard on this issue. May v. Mount Vernon Hospital, 77 O.W.C. 228 (1998).

Dismissal of a claim, with a condition that a new claim will be accepted only if outstanding discovery interrogatories are answered, is an appropriate sanction where there is chronic failure to file discovery responses. Bryant v. Fieldcrest Cannon, Inc., 75 O.W.C. 184 (1996).

Dismissal of a claim is not an appropriate sanction for dilatory conduct during discovery that obstructs the efficient administration of the claim, where the claimant has finally complied. A more appropriate sanction for repeated dilatory conduct that obstructs the administration of the proceedings may be found in the Commission's power to punish for contempt, which may be enforced at an interlocutory show cause hearing and may be more easily tailored to the degree of offense. Foster v. Hooker Furniture Corp., 75 O.W.C. 355 (1996).

An appropriate sanction for repeated dilatory conduct that obstructs the administration of a claim proceeding is found in the Commission's power to punish for contempt, which may be enforced at an interlocutory show cause hearing and may be more easily tailored to the degree of offense. Dismissal of the claim may produce a result which is too harsh in light of the circumstances. May v. Mount Vernon Hospital, 77 O.W.C. 228 (1998).

There is no provision in Commission Rules 1.8(I), 1.8(K) and 1.12 that would specifically allow the Commission to deem requests for admissions "admitted" when the party to whom they were directed fails to respond to them in a timely manner. The Commission observed that Rule 4:11 of the Rules of the Supreme Court is much broader than the Commission rules, and Rule 4:11 is self-executing. Determining all disputed facts in favor of the moving party, merely because of the passage of time, is a harsh result not contemplated by the drafters of the Commission rules. The Deputy Commissioner has the discretion to impose an appropriate sanction for failure to respond to discovery, and the Commission agreed that striking the claimant's defenses to the employer's application was an appropriate sanction. Hunt v. R M Thorton, Inc., VWC File No. 201-73-17 (July 30, 2002).

1.9 Informal Dispute Resolution. — At the request of either party, or at the Commission's direction, contested claims and applications for hearing will be evaluated and may be referred for informal dispute resolution. When it appears that a claim may be resolved by informal dispute resolution, the Commission will refer the case to a Commission representative who may schedule the parties for personal appearance or telephone conference. The Commission will attempt to identify disputed issues and to bring about resolution through agreement. Parties need not be represented by counsel. If agreement is reached it shall be reduced to writing and shall be binding.

Examples of limited issues often subject to prompt resolution are:

A. Average weekly wage;
B. Closed periods of disability;
C. Change in treating physician;
D. Contested medical issues including bills;
E. Permanent disability ratings;
F. Return to work;
G. Failure to report incarceration, change in address or return to work;
H. Attorney fee disputes.

If there is no agreement between the parties and there is no material fact in dispute, issues may be referred for decision on the record. If it is determined that material issues of fact are in dispute or that oral testimony will be required, the case will be referred to the docket for evidentiary hearing.

NOTES FROM THE WORKERS' COMPENSATION COMMISSION

The parties reached an agreement in mediation to settle the case. This agreement was not approved as it did not comply with the rules of the Commission. The plaintiff appealed, arguing that Rule 1.9 required the Commission to enforce the agreement reached at the mediation. The Full Commission held that Rule 1.7 and Section 65.2-701 require that certain documentation is required before the Commission will enforce agreements reached in mediation. Brown v. Pepsi Bottling Group, Inc., VWC File No. 209-73-44 (June 4, 2010).

For Appellate cases upholding the Commission's on the record procedure see Williams v. Virginia Electric and Power Company, 18 Va. App. 569, 445 S.E.2d 693 (1994); Duncan v. ABF Freight System, Unpublished Opinion, Record No. 1320-94-3 (1995).

Certain issues, such as those involving medical questions, can be fully and fairly determined from documentary evidence and do not require an evidentiary hearing. Contested matters that involve the credibility of a witness or party are not appropriate for on the record determinations. Where inconsistent medical opinions are based on different assessments of the employee's subjective statements, the employee's credibility is in issue and an on the record determination is inappropriate. Stanley v. Westmoreland Coal Co., 75 O.W.C. 91 (1996).

Proceedings before the Commission constitute practice before a tribunal, so only attorneys licensed to practice law in Virginia may represent another person before the Commission. A nonlawyer may request a hearing or submit a petition for review for another person, and the provisions of Rule 1.9 of the Rules of the Commission allows nonlawyers to submit arguments for a party in Informal Dispute Resolution proceedings. Pannell v. Gerdy Construction Co., Inc., 75 O.W.C. 219 (1996).

A nonlawyer employee/agent of a corporate party may request a hearing or review, and offer written argument in a matter before the Commission's Informal Dispute Resolution Department, pursuant to Rule 1.9 of the Rules of the Commission. However, nonlawyers may not represent a party in *ore tenus* proceedings before the Commission, or file written argument or other pleadings in a case referred for review. Washington v. City of Richmond Fire Dept., 75 O.W.C. 347 (1996).

1.10 Willful Misconduct. — If the employer intends to rely upon a defense under § 65.2-306 of the Act, it shall give to the employee and file with the Commission no less than 15 days prior to the hearing, a notice of its intent to make such defense together with a statement of the particular act relied upon as showing willful misconduct.

CASE NOTES

Giving notice and burden of proving case. — Former Rule 4 and § 65.1-38 (now § 65.2-306) merely required the giving of notice if the employer intended to interpose an affirmative defense to bar an otherwise meritorious claim. Neither provision relieved the claimant of the burden of proving his case. Anderson v. East Coast Fish & Scallop Co., 10 Va. App. 215, 391 S.E.2d 347 (1990).

Failure to give notice. — Virginia Workers' Compensation Commission's sua sponte exercise of its authority to correct any error or decision on review deemed necessary for a just determination of the issues was not an abuse of discretion under the facts because under Va. Workers' Comp. Comm'n R. 2.2 and 3.1, a workers' compensation benefits claimant's failure to object to an employer's testimony did not prevent the Virginia Workers' Compensation Commission from applying Va. Workers' Comp. Comm'n R. 1.10 notice provisions. Jenkins v. Webb, 52 Va. App. 206, 662 S.E.2d 633, 2008 Va. App. LEXIS 300 (2008).

Virginia Workers' Compensation Commission properly awarded a workers' compensation claimant benefits because an employer offered no excuse or explanation for its failure to comply with the notice requirements of Va. Workers' Comp. Comm'n R. 1.10; the employer never asserted a self-inflicted injury defense under § 65.2-306, and the failure to give proper notice deprived the claimant of the opportunity to subpoena witnesses and gather evidence in response to the defense. Jenkins v. Webb, 52 Va. App. 206, 662 S.E.2d 633, 2008 Va. App. LEXIS 300 (2008).

Hockey player. — Where the workers' compensation claimant, a professional hockey player, was injured in a fight that the claimant was ordered by the claimant's coach to instigate, the employer, in a workers' compensation case, did not show that the claimant's injury was the result of willful misconduct under § 65.2-306, as the employer failed to rebut the evidence that the claimant was engaged in an activity required by the claimant's employment; furthermore, the employer failed to rely on the willful misconduct defense in accordance with Va. Workers' Comp. Comm'n R. 1.10. Norfolk Admirals v. Jones, 2005 Va. App. LEXIS 443 (Nov. 1, 2005).

NOTES FROM THE WORKERS' COMPENSATION COMMISSION

Compensation benefits will be denied where there is a willful failure to perform a duty required by statute only if the violation was the proximate cause of the injury. Carter v. American Cleaning Services, 67 O.I.C. 209 (1988).

An employee was precluded from receiving compensation benefits because of willful misconduct in wearing sunglasses rather than protective eye wear as required by the employer's safety rule. Watford v. Colonial Williamsburg Foundation, 13 Va. App. 501, 413 S.E.2d 69 (1992).

Where a claimant who was repeatedly admonished by the employer not to do heavy lifting continues to perform this duty and was not disciplined, willful misconduct has not been established. Pellerin v. Hematology & Oncology Associates, Ltd., 67 O.I.C. 212 (1988).

While the claimant may have selected an inappropriate method to perform his work by standing on a small stool to cut electrical wires with a knife, this was not a bar to compensation benefits. Tickle v. Douglas Shelor t/a Ledo Painting & Repairs, 67 O.I.C. 216 (1988).

An employee will be estopped from asserting Rule 4 (now Rule 1.10) when his testimony at the hearing indicated a willful violation of a safety rule but prior to the hearing he denied a material fact that was critical to a safety violation defense. A party will not be denied the benefit of a statutory right by enforcement of an administrative rule when the rule could not have reasonably been pursued due to a false statement by the opposing party. Wyle v. Professional Services Industries, 12 Va. App. 684, 406 S.E.2d 410 (1991), 69 O.I.C. 77 (1990) (case was remanded on other grounds).

Code § 65.1-38 (now § 54.2-306) and Rule 4 (now

Rule 1.10) merely require that an employer give notice if he intends to interpose an affirmative defense to bar an otherwise meritorious claim. It does not relieve an employee from the burden of proving his case. Therefore, the Commission acted properly in denying benefits on the basis that the employee's gunshot wound was self-inflicted despite the employer's failure to allege willful misconduct. Anderson v. East Coast Fish & Scallop, 10 Va. App. 215, 391 S.E.2d 347 (1991).

The Commission has interpreted Code § 65.2-306 and Commission Rule 1.10 as requiring that the employer provide a specific written statement of its intent to rely upon one of the defenses set out in Code § 65.2-306, detailing the particular act(s) upon which it bases its defense. Rule 1.10 is not satisfied by mere discovery responses, and proof of "actual notice" of the defense is insufficient for compliance with the rule. Rule 1.10 requires that "a notice" of the defense be timely provided to the claimant, and that a copy of the notice be "filed" with the Commission. Failure to comply with the rule may result in rejection of the defense, as was the case here. Campbell v. Lowes of Short Pump Virginia, VWC File No. 201-91-57 (August 10, 2001) *aff'd sub nom.* Lowes of Short Pump Virginia, 38 Va. App. 55, 561 S.E.2d 757 (2002).

See Notes to § 65.2-306 for additional cases on misconduct.

1.11 Prehearing Statement. — The Commission may require a prehearing statement by the parties as to the particulars of a claim and the grounds of defense.

1.12 Enforcement of the Act and Rules of the Commission; Sanctions. — In addition to the statutory authority of the Commission to levy fines, to assess attorney fees and punish contempt, the Commission may enforce its rules and the provisions of the Workers' Compensation Act upon motion of a party, or upon its own motion, after giving a party or other interested person the opportunity to be heard, by imposition of the following sanctions:

A. Rejection of a pleading including, but not limited to, all or part of a claim and grounds of defense;

B. Exclusion of evidence from the record;

C. Dismissal of a claim or application.

CASE NOTES

Dismissal of claim. — Commission did not err in dismissing employee's claim for benefits without prejudice, as a sanction for employee's failure to submit to telephonic deposition. Wingate v. Assett Protection Team, Inc., No. 2569-98-4 (Ct. of Appeals Oct. 5, 1999).

Virginia Workers' Compensation Commission did not abuse its discretion in dismissing a workers' compensation claimant's third claim without prejudice under Va. Workers' Comp. Comm'n R. 1.12 where: (1) the claimant was well aware of the Commission's rules as he had filed multiple motions and discovery requests, (2) the Commission had granted the claimant's motion for a continuance for a reasonable time, since the claimant was incarcerated, (3) pursuant to Va. Workers' Comp. Comm'n R. 1.8(K), the deputy commissioner had ordered the claimant to respond to the employer's request for admissions within seven days, and (4) the claimant failed to respond to the request for admissions or to offer an alternative method of presenting his case. Taylor v. MJRW, Inc., No. 2923-03-1, 2004 Va. App. LEXIS 192 (Ct. of Appeals Apr. 27, 2004).

Va. Workers' Comp. Comm'n R. 1.12 expressly permitted the Virginia Workers' Compensation Commission to act sua sponte to dismiss a claim, with or without prejudice; the commission's sua sponte dismissal of a claim without prejudice was not an abuse of discretion where the claimant worker and his counsel had missed a scheduled hearing. Jenkins v. Webb, 47 Va. App. 404, 624 S.E.2d 115, 2006 Va. App. LEXIS 8 (2006).

Punishment for contempt. — When a judicial body punishes for contempt, it is obliged to use the least possible power adequate to the end proposed. Thus, when a contemnor is subjected to Draconian punitive measures, such as the outright dismissal of a case with prejudice or the striking of evidence central to a claim or defense, the record must support the assertion that no lesser sanction could have adequately compelled compliance and preserved the dignity of the tribunal. Mason v. Danis Enters. Corp., No. 2370-93-4, (Ct. of Appeals April 11, 1995).

Where fault could be charged to claimant other than on account of his selection of counsel, and in light of the deputy commissioner's letter directing that counsel was "alone" responsible for rescheduling the deposition, the commission had within its power less extreme sanctions, which it should have imposed upon counsel as the responsible party, before imposing the most severe sanction of striking the medical records. Mason v. Danis Enters. Corp., No. 2370-93-4, (Ct. of Appeals April 11, 1995).

NOTES FROM THE WORKERS' COMPENSATION COMMISSION

Deputy commissioner's dismissal without prejudice vacated where dismissal would effectively preclude pursuit of the case because the statute of limitations would bar re-filing the claim and claimant's conduct did not show deliberate disregard for the Commission's authority. Thomas v. Newport

News (City of) School Bd., VWC File No. 213-03-31 (Dec. 13, 2004).

Dismissal with prejudice affirmed due to claimant's pattern of non-cooperation with discovery, failure to comply with Commission's discovery rules and orders, and failure to appear at hearing. Harris v. Williamsburg Honda Dodge, VWC File No. 206-30-08 (Sept. 8, 2004).

When an order of the Commission is ignored, the contempt is against the Commission and not against the claimant or any other party to the underlying claim. There is no provision allowing any party to the underlying claim to use the Commission's enforcement powers to obtain attorney fees or costs. Harrington v. Food Lion DC2, VWC File No. 196-40-35 (Aug. 10, 2004).

While the Act does not contain specific authority to impose sanctions as provided in Virginia Supreme Court Rule 4:12, Va. Ann. Code § 65.2-202 does grant the Commission the same authority to enforce its orders as is vested in the circuit courts of Virginia. This Section has been interpreted to include the sanctions set out in Rule 4:12. The Commission's authority to impose sanctions for failure to discover are stated in Rule 1.12 of the Rules of the Commission. Foster v. Hooker Furniture Corp., 75 O.W.C. 355 (1996).

An employee cannot ignore or neglect proper discovery requests, but must answer them substantively within the time period allowed by discovery rules, or within that period challenge requests she considers objectionable. Where a party disregards discovery orders of the Commission with impunity, dismissal of the claim is an appropriate sanction for such conduct. Zeballos v. Mendez, 75 O.W.C. 229 (1996).

A claimant who fails to cooperate with discovery as defined by Rule 1.8(K) of the Rules of the Commission becomes subject to the sanctions of Rule 1.12. May v. Mount Vernon Hospital, 77 O.W.C. 228 (1998).

In addition to its statutory authority to levy fines, to assess attorney fees, and to punish contempt, the Commission may enforce its rules and the provisions of the Workers' Compensation Act upon motion of a party, or upon its own motion, after giving a party or other interested person the opportunity to be heard, by rejection of a pleading, including a claim or a defense; exclusion of evidence; or dismissal of a claim or application. May v. Mount Vernon Hospital, 77 O.W.C. 228 (1998).

The imposition of sanctions under Rule 1.12 must comport with the concept of "minimal due process," which requires that the Commission afford to all parties notice and an opportunity to be heard on the issues it decides. May v. Mount Vernon Hospital, 77 O.W.C. 228 (1998).

Dismissal of a claim is the most severe sanction that the Commission may impose for a claimant's failure to cooperate with discovery. Both Rule 1.12 and the general principles of due process require that the Commission give notice of its intent to impose this sanction and provide an opportunity for each party to be heard on this issue. May v. Mount Vernon Hospital, 77 O.W.C. 228 (1998).

Dismissal of a claim, with a condition that a new claim will be accepted only if outstanding discovery interrogatories are answered, is an appropriate sanction where there is chronic failure to file discovery responses. Bryant v. Fieldcrest Cannon, Inc., 75 O.W.C. 184 (1996).

Dismissal of a claim is not an appropriate sanction for dilatory conduct during discovery that obstructs the efficient administration of the claim, where the claimant has finally complied. A more appropriate sanction for repeated dilatory conduct that obstructs the administration of the proceedings may be found in the Commission's power to punish for contempt, which may be enforced at an interlocutory show cause hearing and may be more easily tailored to the degree of offense. Foster v. Hooker Furniture Corp., 75 O.W.C. 355 (1996).

An appropriate sanction for repeated dilatory conduct that obstructs the administration of a claim proceeding is found in the Commission's power to punish for contempt, which may be enforced at an interlocutory show cause hearing and may be more easily tailored to the degree of offense. Dismissal of the claim may produce a result which is too harsh in light of the circumstances. May v. Mount Vernon Hospital, 77 O.W.C. 228 (1998).

After a claim is dismissed without prejudice, it is treated as if no claim had been filed. Bryant v. Fieldcrest Cannon, Inc., 75 O.W.C. 184 (1996).

There is no provision in Commission Rules 1.8(I), 1.8(K) and 1.12 that would specifically allow the Commission to deem requests for admissions "admitted" when the party to whom they were directed fails to respond to them in a timely manner. The Commission observed that Rule 4:11 of the Rules of the Supreme Court is much broader than the Commission rules, and Rule 4:11 is self-executing. Determining all disputed facts in favor of the moving party, merely because of the passage of time, is a harsh result not contemplated by the drafters of the Commission rules. The Deputy Commissioner has the discretion to impose an appropriate sanction for failure to respond to discovery, and the Commission agreed that striking the claimant's defenses to the employer's application was an appropriate sanction. Hunt v. R M Thorton, Inc., VWC File No. 201-73-17 (July 30, 2002).

Rule 2. Hearing Procedures.

At the request of either party, or at the Commission's direction, contested issues not resolved informally through prehearing procedures will be referred for decision on the record or evidentiary hearing.

2.1 Decision on the Record. — When it appears that there is no material fact in dispute as to any contested issue, determination will proceed on the record. After each party has been given the opportunity to file a written statement of the evidence supporting a claim or defense, the Commission shall enter a decision on the record.

A. Written Statements. — When the Commission determines that decision on the record is appropriate, the parties shall be given 20 days to submit written statements and evidence. Ten additional days shall be given to respond. For good cause shown additional time may be allowed. Copies of all written statements and evidence shall be furnished to the Commission and all parties.

B. Review. — Request for review of decision on the record shall proceed under § 65.2-705 of the Code of Virginia and Rule 3.

2.2 Evidentiary Hearing. — An evidentiary hearing by the Commission shall be conducted as a judicial proceeding. All witnesses shall testify under oath and a record of the proceeding shall be made. Except for rules which the Commission promulgates, it is not bound by statutory or common law rules of pleading or evidence nor by technical rules of practice.

The Commission will take evidence at hearing and make inquiry into the questions at issue to determine the substantial rights of the parties, and to this end hearsay evidence may be received. The party having the burden of proof shall have the right to open and close. Each party shall be allowed 20 minutes in which to present evidence unless prior arrangement is made through the Commission to extend hearing time.

A. Continuances. — The parties should be prepared to present evidence at the time and place scheduled for hearing. A motion to continue will be granted only when it appears that material or irreparable harm may result if not granted.

B. Evidence.

1. Stipulations to agreed facts shall be included in the record. Each exhibit offered shall be marked and identified, and the record shall show whether it was admitted in evidence.

2. Reports and records of physicians and reports of medical care directed by physicians may be admitted in evidence as testimony by physicians or medical care providers. Upon timely motion, any party shall have the right to cross-examine the source of a medical document offered for admission in evidence.

3. The parties shall specifically designate, by author, deponent and date, medical reports, records or depositions to be received in evidence. Those portions of a deposition to be included in the record must be specifically identified by page and line.

4. Medical reports, records or deposition portions designated by the parties or included by the Commission will be admitted into evidence.

CASE NOTES

Dismissal was proper where claimant missed hearing. — Virginia Workers' Comp. Comm'n R. 1.12 expressly permitted the Virginia Workers' Compensation Commission to act sua sponte to dismiss a claim, with or without prejudice; the commission's sua sponte dismissal of a claim without prejudice was not an abuse of discretion where the claimant worker and his counsel had missed a scheduled hearing. Jenkins v. Webb, 47 Va. App. 404, 624 S.E.2d 115, 2006 Va. App. LEXIS 8 (2006).

Consideration of hearsay evidence. — Virginia Workers' Compensation Commission committed no error in assessing a doctor's testimony because the Commission was able to consider hearsay evidence, including medical reports of a hearsay nature. Stokes v. Monogram Snacks Martinsville, LLC, 2012 Va. App. LEXIS 90 (Mar. 27, 2012).

Waiver of objection to evidence. — When a nurse's memorandum was designated as a medical record, a worker waived any objection he might have had to the Workers' Compensation Commission's consideration of it when on review before the full Commission, he did not challenge a deputy commissioner's designation of the documents submitted under Rule 2.2 as part of the evidence of record. Sherwin Williams Co. v. England, 2006 Va. App. LEXIS 157 (Apr. 25, 2006).

Failure to object. — Virginia Workers' Compensation Commission's sua sponte exercise of its authority to correct any error or decision on review deemed necessary for a just determination of the issues was not an abuse of discretion under the facts because under Va. Workers' Comp. Comm'n R. 2.2 and 3.1, a workers' compensation benefits claimant's failure to object to an employer's testimony did not prevent the Virginia Workers' Compensation Commission from applying Va. Workers' Comp. Comm'n R. 1.10. Jenkins v. Webb, 52 Va. App. 206, 662 S.E.2d 633, 2008 Va. App. LEXIS 300 (2008).

Employee log of job leads properly admitted. — Although admission of an employee's log of job leads was not barred by the best evidence rule, its admission was appropriate because the Virginia Workers' Compensation Commission was not bound by the rules of evidence or the technical rules of practice. Kmart Mgmt. Corporation/Sears Holdings Mgmt. Corp. v. Zelones, 2010 Va. App. LEXIS 119 (Mar. 30, 2010).

NOTES FROM THE WORKERS' COMPENSATION COMMISSION

The Deputy Commissioner did not abuse her discretion in denying the defendants' continuance request where the hearing notices had been mailed; the insurer was advised to retain counsel; after the letter of representation from defense counsel there was no inquiry of the hearing date or request for a copy of the file; and the claimant's counsel copied defense counsel on need for a translator, which referenced the date and time of hearing. Nogales-Sanchex v. Forever 21, Inc., VWC File No. 235-99-03 (Aug. 18, 2008).

It is within the discretionary power of the deputy commissioner to grant or deny motions to continue a case to allow for mediation. Surrett v. Paramont Coal Co., VWC File No. 211-17-53 (May 9, 2007).

2.3 Expedited Hearing. — An employee may request an expedited hearing before the Commission when the employer has submitted an Application for Hearing pursuant to Rule 1.4 and probable cause has been found to suspend benefits pending a hearing on the matter. An employee may also seek expedited determination of any disputed claim arising after the initial compensability of the accident has been determined by the Commission.

A. Written Request. — An employee seeking an expedited hearing must file a written request with the Clerk's office, and a copy of the request shall be sent to the employer. The request must include, by way of description, attachment or enclosure, evidence sufficient to find that, without an expedited proceeding to determine the merits of the dispute, the employee will be caused to suffer severe economic hardship. What constitutes severe economic hardship will be determined by the Commission on a case-by-case basis. A copy of the employee's accepted request will be sent to the employer's counsel of record, the designated third-party administrator and the carrier, along with a Notice of Request For Expedited Hearing.

B. Loss of Income. — When the employee alleges that he/she is not receiving compensation benefits, and is unemployed, unable to work, or only partially employed because of an injury compensable under the Act, the employee must establish that failure to grant an expedited hearing will result in severe, immediate economic hardship. In this regard, the Commission will consider, but is not limited in considering the following evidence:

1. Whether, and to what extent, the employee is presently employed, and what other sources of income are available to support the employee;
2. Whether the employee has dependents for whom the employee's wages, salary and/or other income were the sole or primary source of financial support;
3. Whether the employee has received notices of imminent or threatened foreclosure or eviction actions, or the employee is in a state of homelessness;
4. Whether the employee has received notices of imminent repossession of personal vehicles necessary for employment or medical treatment visits;
5. Whether the employee's financial difficulties were caused by the termination of workers' compensation benefits by prior adjudication, caused by other circumstances, or both; and
6. Any other evidence demonstrating that the employee's immediate ability to provide food, clothing and shelter will be threatened by failure to grant an expedited hearing.

C. Medical Expenses. — When the employee seeks an expedited hearing, asserting that authorization of, or payment for recommended medical treatment has been denied by the employer or insurer, the employee must establish that failure to grant an expedited hearing will result in severe economic hardship. In this regard, the Commission will consider, but is not limited in considering the following evidence:

1. The general nature of the employee's injuries;
2. Whether, if authorization is being sought for recommended treatment not already obtained, the employee's physician has stated that the procedure must be performed on an emergent basis, and failure to do so will threaten the employee's life or result in immediate and severe deterioration of the employee's physical or mental condition;
3. Whether, if payment or reimbursement for medical expenses already incurred is being sought, reasonable and necessary ongoing medical treatment will be withheld for failure to pay for prior medical treatment, and that the withholding of such treatment will threaten the employee's life or result in immediate and severe deterioration of the employee's physical or mental condition;
4. The cost of the medical treatment in dispute, and the employee's ability to pay for it; and
5. Any other evidence demonstrating that failure to grant an expedited hearing on this issue will result in severe economic hardship.

D. Employer Response. — Upon issuance of the Commission's Notice of Request for Expedited Hearing, the employer shall have fourteen (14) days to investigate the basis for the employee's expedited hearing request. Prior to, or at the expiration of the fourteenth day, the employer shall file with the Commission, by hand-delivery, electronic filing or certified mail, a written statement indicating whether the employer will or will not agree to the employee's request for expedited hearing. If the employer will not agree to proceed on an expedited basis, it must state, with specificity, the basis for its inability to proceed pursuant to an expedited hearing schedule. Filing shall be effective upon receipt by the Commission or its agent, or by placing the statement in certified mail.

E. Informal Conference — Once the Commission has received the employer's response statement, or fourteen (14) days pass without a filed response from the employer, the Commission shall schedule, as expeditiously as possible, an informal conference with the parties, whether in person, by teleconference or by other electronic transmission. With regard to expedited claims for payment of medical expenses pursuant to Rule 2.2 (D), no informal conference will be scheduled until the employee submits medical evidence to the employer and the Commission supporting both the underlying claim and the necessity of expedited proceedings. During the informal conference, the Commission will discuss issues relevant to the grant or denial of an expedited hearing including, but not limited to, discovery between the parties, the timing and scheduling of depositions and the parties' ability to secure other relevant evidence in an expedited manner. The Commission will discuss the issues raised by the claim, and try to limit the scope of any matter ultimately referred to the expedited hearing docket by facilitating agreements between the parties. The Commission will confer with the parties about scheduling a hearing date at the informal conference, or by teleconference after the informal conference.

F. Grant or Denial of Expedited Hearing. — During the informal conference, or within seven (7) days of its completion, the Commission will determine whether the claim underlying the request for expedited hearing is appropriate for the expedited hearing docket. If the request for an expedited hearing is granted, the Commission will advise the parties of this decision during the informal conference, or in writing within seven (7) days, by priority mail. If the Commission determines that the matter is not appropriate for the expedited docket, the parties will be advised of the Commission's determination, and the matter will be referred for regular processing.

G. Scheduling and Continuances. — The matter will be set for a hearing no less than ten (10) days, and no more than twenty-eight (28) days after the expedited hearing was granted. Ordinarily, once the matter is set down for an expedited hearing, neither party will be granted a continuance. A continuance will be granted only for good cause shown, involving exceptional circumstances beyond the control of the party, or the party's attorney. Any claim pending on the expedited docket that is continued or non-suited at the request of the employee will be removed from the expedited docket, and shall not be reinstated for expedited proceedings.

H. Closing the Record. — The record shall close at the end of the expedited hearing unless, for good cause shown, one or both parties are unable to present necessary medical or factual evidence.

I. Decision. — The Deputy Commissioner hearing the case will issue an opinion within fourteen (14) days after the record closes in an expedited hearing proceeding.

J. Expedited Review. — Either party may seek an expedited Review of the decision to grant or deny an expedited hearing. Parties seeking expedited Review must file a written request within seven (7) days of the date of the decision to grant or deny an expedited hearing. The written request must include a statement explaining the grounds for review, and must enclose all information the party believes is necessary for consideration of the request. A copy of the Request for Expedited Review shall be furnished to the opposing party. The Commission shall provide Notice of the request for expedited review within three (3) days of its receipt. The opposing party shall have seven (7) days from the date of the Commission's Notice to file a written statement addressing the merits of the review request, and enclosing all information it believes is necessary for consideration on review. The Commission shall review the decision to grant or deny an expedited hearing, and will issue a decision by Order within seven (7) days.

K. Review After Expedited Hearing. — Review of a Deputy Commissioner's decision following an expedited hearing shall proceed according to the provisions of Rule 3.1 and § 65.2-705 of the Code of Virginia.

Comment. — Some of the cases cited herein were decided under former Rule 1.

CASE NOTES

Rules of pleading, evidence, and practice not rigid or technical. — While some degree of formality or the use of standardized uniform procedures and forms may be more conducive to an orderly and expeditious process, rigid or technical rules of pleading, evidence, or practice in the conduct of hearings shall not apply so long as the procedures adopted protect the substantial rights of the parties. Sergio's Pizza v. Soncini, 1 Va. App. 370, 339 S.E.2d 204 (1986).

As a general matter, while procedures before the Industrial (now Workers' Compensation) Commission must ensure that the parties are accorded due process of law, the Commission is afforded considerable latitude in adapting the conduct of hearings to the circumstances of the case. Kum Ja Kim v. Sportswear, 10 Va. App. 460, 393 S.E.2d 418 (1990).

In light of the rules according the commission wide discretion in determining the evidence it will receive and consider, the commission did not abuse its discretion in allowing the documents, some of which were employer's own records, into evidence. Department of Health/Commonwealth v. Keene, No. 1732-96-1 (Ct. of Appeals Jan. 7, 1997).

Request for proffer of evidence not an abuse of discretion. — Given the difficulties encountered in the conduct of workers' compensation hearing where the witnesses all spoke little or no English, the deputy commissioner did not abuse his discretion by requesting a proffer of the evidence concerning decedent's parents' circumstances, subject to cross-examination. Kum Ja Kim v. Sportswear, 10 Va. App. 460, 393 S.E.2d 418 (1990).

Hearsay evidence permitted without corroboration. — Section 8.01-397 does not apply to hearings before the Commission, and this rule, enacted pursuant to § 65.1-18 (now § 65.2-201), correctly permits the use of hearsay evidence without corroboration. Franklin Mtg. Corp. v. Walker, 5 Va. App. 95, 360 S.E.2d 861 (1987), aff'd, 6 Va. App. 108, 367 S.E.2d 191 (1988).

Commission's broad statement that it could not rely on history taken from a claimant to determine how an accident occurred was contrary to the common law principles enunciated in appellate court decisions but more importantly, was contrary to Workers' Compensation Rule 2.2 which gives the Commission the discretion to give probative weight to hearsay statements in arriving at its finding of facts. Pence Nissan Oldsmobile v. Oliver, 20 Va. App. 314, 456 S.E.2d 541 (1995).

Consolidation of matters for hearing. — It is a matter within the Commission's discretion and compatible with a longstanding approved worker's compensation practice that all possible relevant aspects of a matter be considered and determined in one hearing proceeding. Sergio's Pizza v. Soncini, 1 Va. App. 370, 339 S.E.2d 204 (1986).

Decision to award benefits on record did not violate due process. — The commission's decision to award benefits to claimant "on the record" was not a violation of appellant's due process rights. Pursuant to the commission's rules, appellant had opportunities to attempt to introduce evidence regarding claimant's scar prior to the full commission's award. The record established that appellant failed to act on these opportunities. City of Roanoke v. Guilliams, No. 1218-97-3 (Ct. of Appeals Dec. 23, 1997).

Witnesses. — Commission did not err in allowing claimant to testify, notwithstanding fact he did not identify himself as a witness in his answers to interrogatories. Norton's Marina v. Gill, No. 0579-99-2 (Ct. of Appeals July 20, 1999).

Based on this rule and lack of any evidence of prejudice to employer, commission did not err in refusing to permit employer to call claimant's wife as a witness to testify regarding a calendar she kept of days claimant worked. Norton's Marina v. Gill, No. 0579-99-2 (Ct. of Appeals July 20, 1999).

Workers' compensation commission applied the "not reasonably available" standard in determining that the deputy commissioner had not abused his discretion by taking witness testimony when the record had been left open for medical evidence; the commission had authority to decide how its hearings shall be conducted. Estate of Kiser v. Pulaski Furniture Co., 41 Va. App. 293, 584 S.E.2d 464, 2003 Va. App. LEXIS 423 (2003).

NOTES FROM THE WORKERS' COMPENSATION COMMISSION

General:

Proceedings before the Commission constitute practice before a tribunal, so only attorneys licensed to practice law in Virginia may represent another person before the Commission. A nonlawyer may request a hearing or submit a petition for review for another person, and the provisions of Rule 1.9 of the Rules of the Commission allows nonlawyers to submit arguments for a party in Informal Dispute Resolution proceedings. Pannell v. Gerdy Construction Co., Inc., 75 O.W.C. 219 (1996).

Representation of parties before the Virginia Workers' Compensation Commission constitutes the practice of law. A proper person may appear *pro se*, but a corporate party may appear only through an attorney licensed to practice law in Virginia. A nonlawyer employee/agent of a corporate party may request a hearing or review, and offer written argument in a matter before the Commission. However, nonlawyers may not represent a party in *ore tenus* proceedings before the Commission, or file written argument or other pleadings in a case referred for review. Washington v. City of Richmond Fire Dept., 75 O.W.C. 347 (1996).

A nonlawyer representative of the carrier may request review of a Commission decision, but arguing the case *ore tenus* or by brief constitutes the practice of law and will be heard only from licensed attorneys. Smith v. Orange Livestock Market, Inc., 75 O.W.C. 129 (1996).

Illinois counsel advised that he would not associate Virginia counsel regarding this claim, and he refused to allow defense counsel to contact the claimant. The Commission held that the claimant was therefore deemed to be proceeding *pro se* in Virginia, and the employer was therefore granted permission to contact the claimant directly, until he retained Virginia counsel. Vercoe v. Air Wisconsin, 76 O.W.C. 288 (1997).

Rule 2.1:

Dismissal with prejudice affirmed due to claimant's pattern of non-cooperation with discovery, failure to comply with Commission's discovery rules and orders, and failure to appear at hearing. Harris v. Williamsburg Honda Dodge, VWC File No. 206-30-08 (Sept. 8, 2004).

Commission did not violate employer's due process rights by failing to send hearing notice to its third party administrator where the Commission notified both employer and insurer of scheduled hearing. Hayes v. Cadmus Specialty Publication, VWC File No. 215-94-05 (June 29, 2004).

Certain issues, such as those involving medical questions, can be fully and fairly determined from documentary evidence and do not require an evidentiary hearing. Contested matters that involve the credibility of a witness or party are not appropriate for on the record determinations. Where inconsistent medical opinions are based on different assessments of the employee's subjective statements, the employee's credibility is in issue and an on the record determination is inappropriate. Stanley v. Westmoreland Coal Co., 75 O.W.C. 91 (1996).

Non-designated medical reports and records are automatically a part of the hearing record. Lowery v. Globe Iron Const. Co., Inc., 76 O.W.C. 221 (1997).

Rule 2.2:

Because a list of job contacts and the claimant's deposition are not medical records, they are not part of the record unless they were moved into evidence. Even in on-the-record hearings the entirety of the file does not become part of the record. Owens v. Miners and Merchants Bank and Trust, VWC File No. 219-47-41 (Jan. 10, 2006).

Whether asthma may be caused by dust and mites and is therefore an ordinary disease of life is not a fact commonly known from human experience, and the Commission may not take judicial notice of such "fact." Ruiz v. Abbotts Upholstery, 75 O.W.C. 213 (1996).

A claimant is not limited by statements in her Claim For Benefits form that allege only a cumulative trauma injury, and she may present evidence at an evidentiary hearing of a specific injury by accident. Isbell v. Bank of America Mortgage Co., 76 O.W.C. 103 (1997).

A party's evidence can rise no higher than his own testimony. Calloway v. Dept. of Corrections, 77 O.W.C. 35 (1998).

A damaging statement in one part of testimony must be considered in view of a later explanation in another part of the testimony. Kimberly I. Bell v. Sara Lee Knit Products, 74 O.W.C. 67 (1995).

The Commission is not bound by statutory or common law rules of pleading or evidence, nor by technical rules of practice. Statements on a Claim For Benefits form may be used to impeach or corroborate testimony, but the Commission's jurisdiction is determined by the entire record. Isbell v. Bank of America Mortgage Co., 76 O.W.C. 103 (1997).

The claimant died from unrelated causes prior to the evidentiary hearing. The employer argued that it would be severely prejudiced if the claim was allowed, because it could not cross-examine the claimant. The Commission disagreed that the contested issues could not be decided without the claimant's testimony, since the Act's liberal hearsay rule would allow the evidence to be presented through the testimony of other witnesses and other evidence in the record. The Commission acknowledged that the absence of a significant witness would affect the quality of the evidence in the record, but that such an obstacle was not so critical as to render the proceedings fundamentally unfair. Echols v. Rite Aid Corporation, 78 O.W.C. 16 (1999).

Although the Commission is not bound by statutory rules of evidence, it is guided by them. Thus, Rule 2.2 allows the Commission to accept hearsay evidence, but hearing officers may exclude such evidence not considered reasonably reliable. Wright v. Harrison's Supermarket, 75 O.W.C. 195 (1996).

Declarations not offered for truth of the matters asserted, but offered solely to show that it was uttered, without regard to the truth or falsity of its content, are not excluded as hearsay. Butcher v. Abex Friction Products, 77 O.W.C. 279 (1998).

A party that alleges material evidentiary fraud in the case presented to the Commission must raise the issue at the evidentiary hearing or within the time allowed for review or appeal. Pollard v. First General Services, 77 O.W.C. 259 (1998).

The admission of hearsay in the form of company records was within the sound discretion of the Deputy Commissioner. Edmond v. Delta Air Lines, Inc., 68 O.I.C. 224 (1989).

Hearsay evidence was properly expunged from the police reports admitted in evidence. Burch-Rishel v. Canterbury Square Apartments, 69 O.I.C. 102 (1990).

Code § 8.01-398, which provides that a spouse shall not testify without the consent of the other "as to any communication privately made by one to the other while married," even if and after the marriage relation ceases, must be observed in cases before the Workers' Compensation Commission. The spousal privilege to exclude private communications applies to words and acts intended to be concealed, even if witnessed by a third party. Wright v. Harrison's Supermarket, 75 O.W.C. 195 (1996).

There is no provision in the Rules of the Commission regarding a nonsuit. The Commission has followed § 8.01-380 and allowed a party to nonsuit a claim at any time prior to its being submitted for decision. While Code § 8.01-380 states that only one nonsuit may be taken against a party to the proceedings, it also provides that the court may allow additional nonsuits. However, a party may not obtain two nonsuits as a matter of right, and nonsuits are not condoned on the day before hearing. The standard for review as to nonsuits is whether the Deputy Commissioner abused her discretion by granting it. Where the record fails to state the reason the nonsuit was requested or the rationale for granting it, the Commission cannot state that discretion was abused. Norman v. Reynolds Metal Co., 75 O.W.C. 353 (1996).

Va. Code Ann. § 8.01-380(B) provides that a

claimant may have one voluntary non-suit as a matter of right. When the claimant petitions for relief to withdraw his claim a second time, it is left to the discretion of the hearing officer to determine whether the dismissal will be with prejudice or without prejudice. Zirkle v. Rocco Farms, 78 O.W.C. 36 (1999).

The Commission has historically conformed to the Civil Nonsuit Section, Virginia Code § 8.01-308, and allowed a nonsuit any time before the hearing record was closed and the claim submitted to the Deputy Commissioner for a decision. A nonsuit is not allowed after a decision has been rendered. Worrell v. Samax Eggleston, et al., 75 O.W.C. 158 (1996).

The claimant sought to withdraw his request for nonsuit 22 hours after it was communicated to the Deputy Commissioner, when he realized that the effect of such nonsuit would be to extinguish his claim. This harsh result is inconsistent with the beneficent purposes of the Act. The purpose of the Workers' compensation Act is to protect the employee and avoid harsh results inconsistent with such purposes, and the Deputy Commissioner erred in denying the motion to vacate. Leeson v. Washington County School Board, 76 O.W.C. 193 (1997).

Rule 1 (now Rule 2) of the Commission releases it from complying with the statutory or common law rules of pleading or technical rules of practice. Therefore, it is not appropriate for the Commission to grant a motion to strike/summary judgment until after the entire record has been reviewed. Francisco v. O'Sullivan Industries Virginia, Inc., 70 O.I.C. 132 (1991).

The Deputy Commissioner retains jurisdiction over Orders and Awards for twenty days from issuance, during which time he may vacate, amend, or reconsider his decision. Leeson v. Washington County School Board, 76 O.W.C. 193 (1997).

Rule 2.2 (A):

Counsel for employee and employee's own representations that neither received notice of hearing accepted; dismissal for failure to appear at hearing vacated and new hearing ordered. Lewis v. D.A. Foster Co., VWC File No. 191-21-58 (Dec. 30, 2003).

It is within the discretionary power of the Deputy Commissioner to grant or deny motions to continue a case. Leeson v. Washington County School Board, 76 O.W.C. 193 (1997).

Deputy Commissioners are given considerable discretion to grant or deny a continuance. Rule 2.2(A) advises that the parties should be prepared to present evidence at the time and place scheduled for hearing. The employer's application suspended benefits based on an allegation of fraud in the procurement of the award. After many months, the issue was finally heard. The employer's witnesses were absent, and employer's counsel sought a continuance. The Deputy Commissioner denied the continuance request, noting that the employer would have to re-file and bring compensation benefits current. He weighed the prejudice to the employee due to a further delay in compensation, against the prejudice to the employer, determining that granting a continuance would be more prejudicial to the employee. On Review, the Commission agreed. Todd v. Mobil Oil Corp., VWC File No. 198-47-54 (September 25, 2001).

Rule 2.2 (B) (2):

Medical depositions are in the nature of medical reports since they represent a physician's verbal testimony as recorded and transcribed, as opposed to dictated or written testimony as contained in medical reports. Lowery v. Globe Iron Const. Co., Inc., 76 O.W.C. 221 (1997).

Under common law rules of evidence, medical histories are admissible substantively as party admissions. McMurphy Coal Co. v. Miller, 20 Va. App. 57, 455 S.E.2d 265 (1995).

Under Rule 2.2 the Commission has the discretion to give probatice weight to hearsay statments in arrriving at its findings of fact. Therefore, it may rely on medical histories to determine how an accident occurred under common law principles. Pence Nissan Oldsmobile v. Oliver, 20 Va. App. 314, 456 S.E.2d 541 (1995).

A party has the right to have the entire deposition testimony of a doctor received into the evidentiary record, notwithstanding the requirement in Rule 2.2 (B)(3) that the transcript must be specifically identified by page and line. Lowery v. Globe Iron Const. Co., Inc., 76 O.W.C. 221 (1997).

The report of a clinical psychologist may be admitted as evidence under Rule 1 (now Rule 2). Landy v. Eastern State Hospital, 68 O.I.C. 212 (1989).

The notes, reports and opinions of a licensed clinical psychologist who does not have a Ph.D. are not, by themselves, competent evidence under the Act. Medical reports and opinions rendered by physicians and clinical psychologists holding a Ph.D. degree are accepted into evidence as exceptions to the hearsay rule. The opinions of licensed clinical psychologists without a Ph.D. may become competent evidence only to the extent that such opinions have been expressly ratified, and incorporated in the medical reports of licensed physicians as their own opinions. Price v. Sodexho Marriott Services, Inc., VWC File No. 197-76-40 (May 14, 2002).

Mental health records are not admissible without testimony of the counselor unless the care has been rendered by or at the direction of a practitioner of the healing arts licensed under § 54.1-2929, Code of Virginia. Potter v. Island Creek Coal Company, 69 O.I.C. 67 (1990).

A doctor's office note stating that the claimant failed to attend a medical appointment was admissible as a record of the physician's care of the patient. Griffith v. Commonwealth Steel Erectors, Inc., 68 O.I.C. 218 (1989).

Rule 2.2 (B) (3):

Employer not required to transcribe deposition taken at employer's request absent showing of good cause; until deposition is transcribed there is no requirement to file deposition with Commission; contrary holding in Pretlow v. Peninsula Regional Jail , VWC File No. 203-16-24 (2/19/02) overruled. Browne v. Aureus Group, VWC File No. 201-28-86 (Mar. 10, 2003).

A request to depose a physician first made at or close in time to the evidentiary hearing is untimely where there was ample time after the physician's report was issued and before the hearing to cross examine the physician by deposition. Clay v. Ogden Allied Building Services, 75 O.W.C. 83 (1996).

Rule 2.2 (B) (4):

The Deputy Commissioner may consider medical

evidence obtained by either party after the filing of an application but prior to the time of the hearing. Lay v. Baldindos Lock & Key Service, Inc., 71 O.W.C. 110 (1992).

See Notes to § 65.2-704 for additional cases on procedure.

Rule 3. Posthearing Procedures.

3.1 Request for Review. — A request for review of a decision, order or award of the Commission shall be filed by a party in writing with the Clerk of the Commission within thirty (30) days of the date of such decision, order or award.

A request for review should assign as error specific findings of fact and conclusions of law. Failure of a party to assign any specific error in its request for review may be deemed by the Commission to be a waiver of the party's right to consideration of that error. The Commission may, however, on its own motion, address any error and correct any decision on review if such action is considered to be necessary for just determination of the issues.

A copy of the request for review shall be furnished to the opposing party. Upon request to the Clerk, a party may obtain a copy of the hearing transcript subject to an appropriate charge.

Comment. — Some of the cases cited herein were decided under former Rule 2(A).

CASE NOTES

Commission must adhere to its own rules. — See Pittston Co. v. Fulks, 201 Va. 128, 109 S.E.2d 387 (1959).

Commission's authority to correct an error on review. — Virginia Workers' Compensation Commission's sua sponte exercise of its authority to correct any error or decision on review deemed necessary for a just determination of the issues was not an abuse of discretion under the facts because under Va. Workers' Comp. Comm'n R. 2.2 and 3.1, a workers' compensation benefits claimant's failure to object to an employer's testimony did not prevent the Virginia Workers' Compensation Commission from applying Va. Workers' Comp. Comm'n R. 1.10. Jenkins v. Webb, 52 Va. App. 206, 662 S.E.2d 633, 2008 Va. App. LEXIS 300 (2008).

Failure to seek full review by commission. — Court of appeals could not consider on appeal the deputy commissioner's decision to terminate a temporary total disability award because the employee never sought full review by the Virginia Workers' Compensation Commission of that decision; because the full commission never considered the termination of the temporary total disability award on the merits, the court of appeals had no commission ruling to review on the issue. Windsor v. Loomis Fargo & Co., 2011 Va. App. LEXIS 407 (Dec. 20, 2011).

Requirement that parties specify each determination of fact or law. — Subdivision A of former Rule 2 did not create an absolute requirement that parties specify each determination of fact or law to which exception is taken. However, the rule had to be applied equally to all parties irrespective of whether they be claimant or employer/insurer. Seneca Falls Greenhouse & Nursery v. Layton, 9 Va. App. 482, 389 S.E.2d 184 (1990).

Party need not specify every issue. — Former Rule 2(A) did not require that a party specify every contested issue in the application for review or that a prevailing party take exception to an adverse finding of fact or conclusion of law; consequently, the failure of a party to specify certain issues did not deprive the commission of jurisdiction to consider issues that are necessary to a resolution of the claim. Greif Cos. v. Sipe, 16 Va. App. 709, 434 S.E.2d 314 (1993).

Interpretation of word "should" in subdivision A of former Rule 2. — Former Rule 2(A) stated that a request for review "should" specify each issue of law or fact. "The word 'should' ... denotes duty or obligation, [but] implies no more than expediency." "It is not mandatory, but directory only." Thus, the requirement that the request for review specify all issues to which exception was taken was not jurisdictional in nature, mandating that the commission disregard other errors that could be made by the deputy commissioner. Greif Cos. v. Sipe, 16 Va. App. 709, 434 S.E.2d 314 (1993).

Sanctions for failure to follow subdivision A of former Rule 2. — If the Commission imposed sanctions for the failure to follow the specific provisions of subdivision A of former Rule 2 dealing with specification of the exceptions, the sanctions could not be applied arbitrarily to parties based upon their position in the case or whether they were represented by counsel. Seneca Falls Greenhouse & Nursery v. Layton, 9 Va. App. 482, 389 S.E.2d 184 (1990).

Necessity of a written statement. — Once a request for review has been filed, Rule 3.2, in conjunction with this rule, permits the Workers' Compensation Commission to address and correct, sua sponte, any errors of the Deputy Commissioner, whether or not written statements are submitted. Russell Stover Candies v. Alexander, 30 Va. App. 812, 520 S.E.2d 404 (1999).

When an issue is not raised at the review stage, pursuant to subdivision A of former Rule 2, that issue cannot be raised or heard by the Full Commission or by the court of appeals. Delta Airlines v. Smith, No. 0890-89-4, (Ct. of Appeals May 8, 1990).

Because employer did not request full commission review of deputy's decision failing to award it credit for certain payments to claimant, deputy's denial of relief to employer for such payments was not before full commission on review. The court could therefore not subsequently entertain error in attendant decision of commission for a failure to address that issue. Newport News Shipbuilding & Dry Dock v. Lawrence, No. 0086-99-1 (Ct. of Appeals Aug. 3, 1999).

Award cannot be broken into separate parts. — A single award may not be segmented into component parts, some of which are final dispositions and others of which are not; an appeal of a deputy commissioner's award empowers the Industrial Commission to reexamine all of the deputy commissioner's conclusions. Greif Cos. v. Sipe, 16 Va. App. 709, 434 S.E.2d 314 (1993) (decided under former Rule 2(A)).

Granting of request to reconsider vacated original opinion. — Deputy commissioner's letter to counsel, granting request to reconsider earlier opinion, acted to vacate his original opinion, and thus deputy had jurisdiction to issue later opinion despite passage of more than 20 days since original opinion. Basic Constr. Co. v. Hamilton, No. 2844-98-1 (Ct. of Appeals Aug. 17, 1999).

Timeliness of request for review. — A request for review of a decision or award of the Commission must be filed in writing by a party within twenty days of the date of such decision or award. Workers' Compensation Commission erred in holding that the actual notice provision of § 65.2-705 applied only to awards that were entered following an evidentiary hearing and did not apply to awards entered upon agreement; therefore, the Commission erred in holding that a worker's request to review an award was untimely under Va. Sup. Ct. R. 3.1 because it was not filed within 20 days of the date of the award rather than within 20 days of when the worker received notice of the award. Since the worker's request for review of the award was filed within 20 days of the date he received notice from the Commission of the award being entered, the worker's request was timely under Va. Sup. Ct. R. 3.1. Ashby v. Ramar Coal Co., 47 Va. App. 8, 622 S.E.2d 230, 2005 Va. App. LEXIS 472 (2005).

Applied in Peacock v. Browning Ferris, Inc., 38 Va. App. 241, 563 S.E.2d 368, 2002 Va. App. LEXIS 294 (2002).

NOTES FROM THE WORKERS' COMPENSATION COMMISSION

The filing of an interlocutory request for Review does not automatically stay the underlying evidentiary, on the-the-record or show cause proceeding. Proceedings in those cases may go forward absent a preliminary Order or substantive Opinion from the Commission specifically imposing a stay. It remains within the Deputy Commissioner's discretion to determine whether to continue a scheduled proceeding pending a decision from the Commission on the interlocutory matter. Boylan v. Cunningham Tires, VWC File No. 223-87-08 (September 8, 2010).

The 20-day Review period began to run with the delivery of the Opinion to the attorney's post office box rather than the date the mail is actually received. It is irrelevant that the attorney's office was closed on the Saturday that the Opinion was delivered and that it was not retrieved until the following Tuesday. Prunty v. Goodyear Tire & Rubber Co., VWC File No. 212-77-70 (June 6, 2005).

The Commission has no jurisdiction to vacate an award based on agreement where the carrier alleged unilateral mistake of claims representative who thought he was agreeing to a medical only award, and the Request for Review of the award was untimely. Hamilton v. Quebecor World, Inc., VWC File No. 218-22-73 (Oct. 22, 2004).

The confirmation of delivery to the claimant's address of record is all that is required for an Opinion to be considered "received" by a party and begin the twenty-day period for a review request. The fact that the claimant was traveling and did not actually receive the Opinion does not negate that the review request was untimely. Lee v. County of Fairfax School Bd., VWC File No. 581-804 (May 10, 2005).

The Commission has no jurisdiction over issues on appeal to the Virginia Supreme Court, but it retains jurisdiction over issues not on appeal. The jurisdiction of a court initially considering a matter is limited to the issues framed in the pleadings, and the same is true for the jurisdiction of the Supreme Court on appeal. Dancy v. Georgia Pacific Corporation, 76 O.W.C. 446 (1997).

In general, a right of review lies only to a final decision or award "that is, a decision of the [Workers' Compensation Commission] granting or denying, or changing or refusing to change some benefit payable or allowable under the Workers' Compensation Act and leaving nothing to be done except to superintend ministerially the execution of the award." Morgan v. Eastern State Hospital, 78 O.W.C. 192 (1999).

A review of right exists only to a final decision or award of the Commission regarding a benefit allowable under the Act, and the Commission usually declines interlocutory reviews on evidentiary or procedural matters except for good cause. Dancy v. Georgia Pacific Corporation, 76 O.W.C. 446 (1997).

The Commission has the discretionary authority to allow interlocutory review of evidentiary or procedural matters. However, requests for such interlocutory reviews are usually denied, except for good cause. Morgan v. Eastern State Hospital, 78 O.W.C. 192 (1999).

The "decision or award" from which a right of review lies is to a *final* decision or award granting or denying, or changing or refusing to change, some benefit payable or allowable under the Workers' Compensation Act and leaving nothing to be done except to superintend ministerially the execution of the award. A decision to refer the case to the review docket is not a final decision as contemplated § 65.2-705, but it is merely a procedural and interlocutory order not addressing the merits of a claim, and a petition on review to vacate such decision is not untimely. Saunders v. Management Consulting, Inc., 75 O.W.C. 22 (1996).

In general, a right of review lies only to a final decision or award that grants, denies, or changes a benefit payable under the Workers' Compensation Act and leaves nothing to be done except to superintend ministerially the execution of the award.

However, the Commission has the discretionary authority to allow interlocutory review of evidentiary or procedural matters. Where the determination of a discovery issue may have great impact on an employee's claim, interlocutory review may be appropriate. Handlovitch v. Chesapeake General Hosp., 75 O.W.C. 293 (1996).

The claimant appealed a discovery order issued by the deputy commissioner for information deemed to be relevant and material. The claimant made no showing that the ruling of the deputy commissioner was clearly wrong or that it would result in substantial prejudice, and the Commission declined to consider the issue on review, but deferred to the deputy commissioner, who had jurisdiction. Dancy v. Georgia Pacific Corporation, 76 O.W.C. 446 (1997).

An appeal places the entire award before the Commission, and it may on review address any error and correct any decision if necessary for a just determination of the issues. Perrigan v. Clinchfield Coal Co., 75 O.W.C. 324 (1996).

A Motion For Reconsideration does not substitute for a request for a review. Ferguson v. Olsten Kimberly Quality Care, 76 O.W.C. 52 (1997).

The Commission permits parties to file requests for reconsideration. However, requests for reconsideration are different from requests for review. A request for reconsideration does not toll the statute for filing a review request. Hamilton v. Basic Construction Company, 77 O.W.C. 245 (1998).

An application for review must be made within twenty days after receipt of notice of an award. The twenty-day period established by Code § 65.2-705 and Rule 3.1 is jurisdictional, and the Commission has no jurisdiction to review a case if the request for review is not filed within that time period, except to correct for fraud or mistake. Markham v. City of Norfolk Fire & Paramedical, 78 O.W.C. 189 (1999).

Res judicata is not applicable where fraud or misrepresentation is alleged. Even where an award has become final, the Commission has the authority to reconsider such awards that are entered through fraud, mistake or imposition. The Commission has the implied power to entertain and hear an application, seasonably presented, to vacate and set aside an award procured through fraud or mistake. Quezada v. P M M C Associates, Inc., 79 O.W.C. 46 (2000).

Where the employer establishes by clear and convincing evidence that the claimant was not legally eligible to work in the United States at the time of her hire and accident, that the claimant intentionally and fraudulently misrepresented her employment status to the employer, and that the employer reasonably and justifiably relied upon those representations to its detriment when it hired her and later agreed to the entry of an award of compensation benefits, the claimant's fraud and misrepresentation resulted in an imposition on the Commission, and the Commission lacked subject matter jurisdiction to enter the award of compensation benefits. Quezada v. P M M C Associates, Inc., 79 O.W.C. 46 (2000).

An application for review is deemed "filed" on the date it is hand delivered to the Commission's office in Richmond, or any regional office maintained by the Commission; or the date on which it is posted through the United States Postal Service by certified or registered mail. Filing by first-class mail, telegraph, electronic mail, or facsimile transmission shall be deemed completed only when the application actually reaches a Commission office. Markham v. City of Norfolk Fire & Paramedical, 78 O.W.C. 189 (1999).

Where the claimant intentionally and fraudulently misrepresented her employment status to the employer, that employer was under no obligation to make further independent inquiry as to the claimant's legal status, as it had no reason to question the representations and documents produced by the claimant. If an employer were to make such an investigation without reasonable justification, it might well face a legitimate claim of discrimination. In this case, the Commission found that the employer acted seasonably in filing its application upon learning that the claimant had misrepresented her legal work status. Quezada v. P M M C Associates, Inc., 79 O.W.C. 46 (2000).

The employer mailed its original request for review in a timely manner. However, by electing to send the notice by first-class mail, the employer risked the possibility, however remote, that it would not be actually delivered to the Commission within the twenty-day period necessary to perfect the review request. Because no notice or request for review was received by a Commission office within the period required by law, the Commission held that it had no jurisdiction to hear the employer's petition subsequently, but untimely, filed. Markham v. City of Norfolk Fire & Paramedical, 78 O.W.C. 189 (1999).

An application to vacate is not, strictly speaking, an application for a review. A request that a deputy reconsider to vacate an order does not preserve the claimant's rights to challenge the deputy's decision on review if the deputy denies or does not consider the motion within the twenty-day period before the order becomes final. Therefore, unless counsel files a motion for reconsideration or a motion to vacate in the alternative with a petition for review, the Commission's jurisdiction to act upon its order expires with the passing of the twenty-day period. Asanakis v. Ice Follies & Holiday On Ice, Inc., 76 O.W.C. 278 (1997).

A Deputy Commissioner maintains control and retains jurisdiction over a claim only for twenty days after issuing an Opinion. However, where the deputy commissioner vacates his original opinion, he has jurisdiction to issue a subsequent opinion, even a year later. Hamilton v. Basic Construction Company, 77 O.W.C. 245 (1998).

Where the Deputy Commissioner writes that he grants the request for reconsideration and will issue a new opinion on the merits, the effect of such language is to vacate his original decision and to preserve his jurisdiction to issue another opinion. Hamilton v. Basic Construction Company, 77 O.W.C. 245 (1998).

Where either party withdraws its approval of a Memorandum of Agreement after the award has been entered, a request for review must be made within twenty days, and the award may then be Vacated by the Commission without the necessity of establishing fraud, mistake, or imposition. Cornish v. Anheuser Busch Co., Inc., 76 O.W.C. 47 (1997).

Whenever either party withdraws its agreement to a compromise settlement and so advises the

Commission before the entry of the settlement order, the Commission will not enter the order. If the order has been entered prior to the receipt of the party's withdrawal of agreement, the party may petition for review of the order in a timely manner without the necessity of establishing fraud, mutual mistake, or imposition. Damewood v. Lanford Brothers Co., Inc., 77 O.W.C. 101 (1998).

The claimant and the carrier negotiated a compromise settlement of the claim, and it was submitted to the Commission. The carrier was thereafter advised that the claimant had since died from causes unrelated to his work injuries, and it withdrew its agreement to the settlement. The Commission held that the carrier's request was timely and declined to enter the compromise settlement order. Damewood v. Lanford Brothers Co., Inc., 77 O.W.C. 101 (1998).

A decision by the Claims Department to place an application on hold until supporting documentation is received is not a judicial action and, therefore, Commission Rule 3, and its requirement that a party file a request for Review within twenty days from the date of the decision does not apply. Kibler v. Alger Brothers Construction Co., 73 O.W.C. 157 (1994).

A request for review of a decision or award of the Commission must be filed in writing by a party within twenty days of the date of such decision or award. A request filed by the claimant's father was not a valid request for review by a party. The Commission noted that the father was not a member of the claimant's household or even living in the State. Barrett v. University of Virginia, 74 O.W.C. 49 (1995).

The twenty day period to file a review request is not tolled where the employer does not receive a copy of the deputy commissioner's opinion. Hyman v. U. S. Air, Inc., 74 O.W.C. 153 (1995).

The Commission has the discretion to hear a petition for Review without a specification of each determination of fact or law and to determine all issues involved in the case. The provision in Rule 2A (now Rule 3.1) that a request for Review should specify each determination of fact or law to which exception is taken is not mandatory, but directory only. Brushy Ridge Coal Co. v. Blevins, 6 Va. App. 73, 367 S.E.2d 204 (1988).

While Rule 2(A) (now Rule 3.1) which requires the specification of issues in a Review request is not mandatory, it must be equally applied to both employees and employer/insurers. Seneca Falls Greenhouse & Nursery v. Layton, 9 Va. App. 482, 389 S.E.2d 184 (1990).

The requirement that a party requesting a Review specify each determination of law or fact is not jurisdictional and does not mandate that the Commission disregard other areas that may be apparent in the record. Thornton v. Virginia Concrete Co., Inc., 67 O.I.C. 240 (1988).

The purpose of Rule 3.1 is to apprise opposing parties and the Commission of alleged errors to be considered. Where a case involves no factual disputes and the only issue is the applicability of the time limitation in Code § 65.2-708, the issue under consideration is obvious to all. The Commission held that the employer's request for review adequately apprised all parties of the error assigned, that no party was prejudiced by any lack of specificity, and that the request for review filed on behalf of the employer/insurer was adequate. Attia v. W9Y Construction Co., Inc., 76 O.W.C. 332 (1997).

Where there has been an evidentiary hearing, a transcript of that hearing is necessary for Commission and appellate review of the Opinion of the hearing officer. Unless the parties can stipulate to factual evidence presented at the hearing, loss of the record requires remand for a new hearing. Saunders v. Management Consulting, Inc., 75 O.W.C. 22 (1996).

The Commission has the discretion to undertake interlocutory review of a discovery decision when failure to do so might result in substantial prejudice. The Deputy Commissioner ruled that the claimant did not have to attend an independent medical evaluation (IME) scheduled by the defendants shortly before the evidentiary hearing. The Commission reversed the Deputy Commissioner, finding that the IME had the potential of being outcome-determinative in the case. The Commission held that good cause and the potential for substantial prejudice exists when resolution of an interlocutory issue could provide the Commission with outcome-determinative testimony. Lavender v. City of Richmond Police Dep't, VWC File No. 201-96-35 (January 25, 2001).

The parties and their counsel are responsible for reviewing the applicable statute or rule governing requests for review, and the period within which one must be filed. A party or attorney who relies upon informal information regarding filing deadlines, given to him over the telephone by someone in the Clerk's office, does so at their peril. The Commission dismissed the Petitioner's request for review, finding that it was filed untimely. Even though counsel was apparently misinformed about the filing deadline, the Commission found the law is clear that relying on inaccurate information does not toll a review statute. In Re: Camay Alcira, VWC File No. B-00-10 (March 13, 2002).

Where the claimant fails to identify in her request for review, specific findings of fact or conclusions of law she believes to be erroneous, and thereafter fails to submit a written statement supporting the request for review, the Commission may conclude that she waived her right to review. Stanley v. Heritage Hall/Genesis Health Ventures, Inc., VWC File No. 200-15-83 (April 5, 2002).

3.2 Written Statements. — The Commission will advise the parties of the schedule for filing brief written statements supporting their respective positions. The statements shall address all errors assigned, with particular reference to those portions of the record which support a party's position. No schedules for written statements shall be issued in connection with interlocutory appeals, appeals of award orders issued pursuant to agreements or appeals of decisions accepting or rejecting a change in condition claim or application. However, where a decision accepting or rejecting a change in condition claim or application has been appealed, the non-appealing party shall have ten days from the date the Request for Review was filed to provide a written response.

CASE NOTES

Necessity of a written instrument. — Once a request for review has been filed, Virginia Workers' Compensation Commission Rule 3.2, in conjunction with Rule 3.1, permits the Workers' Compensation Commission to address and correct, sua sponte, any errors of the Deputy Commissioner, whether or not written statements are submitted. Russell Stover Candies v. Alexander, 30 Va. App. 812, 520 S.E.2d 404 (1999).

Failure to file. — Claimant's failure to file written statement did not require that his appeal be dismissed, since his request for review provided sufficient detail to determine issues on review and there was no resulting prejudice to employer. B & R Contractors v. Wethington, No. 0087-99-1 (Ct. of Appeals June 15, 1999).

An issue may be deemed waived or abandoned where a party assigns error to an issue in its request for review, but then does not argue that issue in its written statement. Graham v. Consolidated Stores Corp., No. 1464-98-3 (Ct. of Appeals Dec. 8, 1998).

NOTES FROM THE WORKERS' COMPENSATION COMMISSION

An employer who failed to appeal a hearing opinion but raised issues in a reply brief to claimant's appeal was not entitled to have the issue heard. In the absence of a timely appeal, the Commission is not required to review each ruling made by the Deputy Commissioner that is unrelated to the issues on appeal. It is each party's responsibility to make a timely request for review of any contested issue. Classic Floors, Inc. v. Guy, 9 Va. App. 90, 383 S.E.2d 761 (1989).

A nonlawyer representative of the carrier may request review of a Commission decision, but arguing the case *ore tenus* or by brief constitutes the practice of law and will be heard only from licensed attorneys. Smith v. Orange Livestock Market, Inc., 75 O.W.C. 129 (1996).

A nonlawyer employee/agent of a corporate party may request a hearing or review, and offer written argument in the matter before the Commission's Informal Dispute Resolution department, pursuant to Rule 1.9 of the Rules of the Commission. However, nonlawyers may not represent a party in *ore tenus* proceedings before the Commission, or file written argument or other pleadings in a case referred for review. Washington v. City of Richmond Fire Dept., 75 O.W.C. 347 (1996).

Written statements on review must be filed by an attorney licensed to practice law in Virginia, unless the person filing the statement is a *pro se* litigant. McRea v. Int'l Sewer Service, Inc., 75 O.W.C. 71 (1996).

The procedure regarding the review of a decision to accept or reject a claim or application does not provide for a written statement to be filed. The letter requesting a review should specify each determination of fact and law to which exception is taken. Rule 1.6 (D) provides that "[o]nly information contained in the file at the time of the original decision, along with the review request and any response from the opposing party, will be considered. Additional evidence will not be accepted." Campbell v. Perdue Foods, Inc., 76 O.W.C. 157 (1997).

Where the employer does not argue an issue in its written statement on review, the Commission may deem it waived or abandoned. Leon v. Lewis-Gale Clinic, 76 O.W.C. 350 (1997).

3.3 Additional Testimony. — No new evidence may be introduced by a party at the time of review except upon agreement of the parties. A petition to reopen or receive after-discovered evidence may be considered only upon request for review.

A petition to reopen the record for additional evidence will be favorably acted upon by the full Commission only when it appears to the Commission that such course is absolutely necessary and advisable and also when the party requesting the same is able to conform to the rules prevailing in the courts of this State for the introduction of after-discovered evidence.

Comment. — Some of the cases cited herein were decided under former Rule 2.

CASE NOTES

Purpose. — Former Rule 2 served important goals. It assured an opposing party the opportunity to rebut additional testimony introduced after the hearing of a case. It also supported finality in the decision making process. Charcoal Hearth Restaurant v. Kandetzki, 1 Va. App. 327, 338 S.E.2d 352 (1986).

Reopening case on grounds of newly-discovered evidence. — In order to entitle a litigant to reopen a case on the ground of newly-discovered evidence, the evidence must be discovered after the trial and be such as could not have been discovered before, by the exercise of reasonable diligence; must be material and not merely cumulative; and such, if true, as ought at another hearing produce a different result on the merits. Chenault v. Blue Roofing,

Inc., No. 0405-85, (Ct. of Appeals Feb. 12, 1986).

As appellants' case was still pending decision by the deputy commissioner when he decided to reconvene the evidentiary hearing to take the witness's testimony, and therefore was not under "review," as contemplated in Va. Workers' Comp. Comm'n R. 3.3 and *Williams v. People's Life Ins. Co.*, 19 Va. App. 530, 452 S.E.2d 881 (1995), the after-discovered evidence rule did not apply. Estate of Kiser v. Pulaski Furniture Co., 41 Va. App. 293, 584 S.E.2d 464, 2003 Va. App. LEXIS 423 (2003).

Workers' compensation commission erred in allowing the claimant to introduce evidence as to his average weekly wage after the original hearing on his case had ended and after the extended time for presenting evidence had passed, as the workers' compensation commission was not permitted to accept evidence after those two periods had passed; while a claimant could file a motion to re-open the record, the claimant filed no such motion and the motion would not likely have been granted because the average weekly wage evidence did not qualify as evidence that could not have been obtained prior to the hearing through the exercise of reasonable diligence. Gwaltney of Portsmouth v. Scales, 2005 Va. App. LEXIS 474 (Nov. 22, 2005).

No error occurred when the state workers' compensation commission denied the employer's motion to reconsider and/or vacate the workers' compensation commission's decision, on the ground of mootness, that affirmed the deputy commissioner's findings that the employer was responsible for a pain clinic evaluation for the claimant; at the time that the issue was heard on the merits, there was an actual controversy between the parties and the employer's attempt after the hearing on the merits to submit medical records to establish mootness had to fail because the records were not "after-discovered evidence" that reasonably could not have been obtained prior to the relevant hearing. Wal-Mart Assocs., Inc. v. Jones, 2007 Va. App. LEXIS 49 (Feb. 13, 2007).

Doctor's report not after-discovered evidence where he was not unavailable. — A doctor's report could not be termed after-discovered evidence under former Rule 2, where there was no evidence that the doctor was unavailable to the claimant prior to the hearing. Flavin v. J.C. Penney Co., 1 Va. App. 1, 332 S.E.2d 805 (1985).

Where no evidence showed that claimant was precluded from obtaining doctor's opinion or that doctor was unavailable before December 13, 1999 hearing, and November 1, 1999 recorded statement was given by claimant before the hearing, and he offered no explanation as to why he could not have offered the statement into evidence at the hearing, doctor's opinion was not after-discovered evidence. Taylor v. Pocahontas Correctional Unit/Commonwealth, No. 1216-00-2, 2000 Va. App. LEXIS 650 (Ct. of Appeals Sept. 12, 2000).

Hospital discharge summary held not after-discovered evidence. — See Lewis v. Lynchburg Foundry Co., 204 Va. 303, 130 S.E.2d 429 (1963).

Co-worker's notes not after discovered evidence. — Co-worker's notes were not after-discovered evidence and the Virginia Workers' Compensation Commission did not err by refusing to consider the notes when it considered an employee's request that it review its decision denying compensation. Blankenship v. CSI/Archstone Communities Trust, No. 0249-02-3, 2002 Va. App. LEXIS 368 (Ct. of Appeals July 2, 2002).

Letters from two doctors regarding appropriateness of medical treatment by doctor under whose care claimant placed herself after becoming dissatisfied with the treating physician's treatment were not admissible, although the letters involved were authored after the hearing before the deputy commissioner, where consideration of the letters would not have produced a different result even if allowed into evidence, since, in essence, both letters confirmed that treatment by the doctor chosen by the claimant was proper, but the issue before the Commission was not whether his treatment was proper, but whether the claimant was justified in refusing to continue treatment with the treating physician. The Commission found no such justification. Horne v. Northern Va. Training Ctr., No. 0351-85, (Ct. of Appeals Feb. 7, 1986).

Refusal to grant claimant's motion to reopen case not error. — It was not error for the Commission to refuse to grant claimant's motion to reopen the case to receive additional evidence, where no specific documents had been produced which could be considered as after-discovered evidence under the provisions of Subdivision C. Edelblute v. Edelblute's Serv. Ctr., No. 1752-89-1, (Ct. of Appeals June 26, 1990).

NOTES FROM THE WORKERS' COMPENSATION COMMISSION

Employer's request to admit evidence after the hearing regarding a credit for short-term disability payments made during the period of disability is not subject to the rule governing after-discovered evidence. An employer may seek credit for benefits paid at the hearing or by post-hearing application. Juhl v. Monumental Life, Inc., VWC File No. 217-76-00 (Feb. 1, 2005).

Since case was still pending a decision by the deputy commissioner when he issued his decision to reconvene the hearing, the case was not "under review" as contemplated by Rule 3.3, and deputy commissioner retained discretion to hear and review additional evidence. Collick v. Batey Enterprises II, Inc., VWC File No. 216-57-38 (Oct. 22, 2004).

Deputy commissioner's opinion vacated and remanded for consideration of evidence that claimant and his wife pled guilty to certain federal criminal charges where credibility was central issue in case. Martin v. Groome Transp., Inc., VWC File No. 209-63-38 (Oct. 15, 2004).

The party requesting admission of additional testimony or evidence must be able to conform to the rules prevailing in the courts of Virginia for the introduction of after-discovered evidence. Miller v. Dixon Lumber Company, 67 O.I.C. 71 (1988).

Failure to obtain known and available medical records prior to a hearing does not constitute due diligence such as to require the reopening of a claim for submission of after-discovered evidence. An employee's mistaken belief that all medical records were submitted to the Commission is not a basis to reopen a claim to receive additional evidence. Mize

v. Rocky Mount Ready Mix, Inc., 11 Va. App. 601, 401 S.E.2d 200 (1991).

Where a second medical opinion is approved for the employer by the Commission, but the results of the completed examination are not thereafter filed with the Commission by the employer, such evidence is significant to the deliberations of the Commission and the Award entered without it may be vacated upon Motion by the claimant on the grounds of imposition. Cornish v. Anheuser Busch Co., Inc., 76 O.W.C. 47 (1997).

Where evidence of additional medical treatment resulting in diagnosis or other findings that would be material to determining the nature of the employee's condition, incapacity or origin of any disability is obtained after the hearing before the Deputy Commissioner but pending the Review hearing, the Commission is required to reopen the hearing to consider such evidence because a finding adverse to the claimant's change in condition application would be *res judicata* with the employee forever barred from proving that the specific disability was a result of a compensable accidental injury. Mize v. Rocky Mount Ready Mix, Inc., 11 Va. App. 601, 401 S.E.2d 200 (1991).

A request to introduce after-discovered evidence was denied on the basis that the medical reports were available at the time of the hearing and would not produce a different result. Ellis v. City of Norfolk, 68 O.I.C. 47 (1989).

Counsel's request to present additional evidence rebutting the veracity of witnesses at hearing was denied on the basis that it did not meet the requirement for after-discovered evidence. Sams v. The Goodyear Tire & Rubber Company, 73 O.W.C. 124 (1994).

Evidence that could have been obtained prior to the hearing with the exercise of due diligence is not a proper basis for reopening the hearing record. Ruiz v. Abbotts Upholstery, 75 O.W.C. 213 (1996).

Where the employer failed to sufficiently explain why a medical report could not have been obtained before the hearing by the exercise of due diligence, the Commission declined to receive the report as after-discovered evidence. Custer v. Wampler Longacre Turkey, Inc., 76 O.W.C. 176 (1997).

The requirements to be met before after-discovered evidence may be accepted are that (1) the evidence was obtained after the hearing; (2) such evidence could not have been obtained prior to the hearing through the exercise of reasonable diligence; (3) the evidence is not merely cumulative, corroborative, or collateral; and (4) the evidence is material and should produce an opposite result before the Commission. The fact that the employer would submit the claimant's current medical records to earlier treating physicians for review and evaluation should not have been unanticipated. The claimant was entitled to cross-examine the opinions, but she was not entitled to seek out and develop additional evidence to bolster her own case to rebut those opinions. Pollard v. First General Services, 77 O.W.C. 259 (1998).

A party that alleges material evidentiary fraud in the case presented to the Commission must raise the issue at the evidentiary hearing or within the time allowed for review or appeal. Pollard v. First General Services, 77 O.W.C. 259 (1998).

3.4 Oral Argument. — A party may request oral argument at the time of application for review. Otherwise, the review shall proceed on the record.

If oral argument is requested and the Commission considers it necessary or of probable benefit to the parties or to the Commission in adjudicating the issues, the parties will be scheduled to present oral argument.

Any party may request the Commission to schedule argument by telephone conference by giving notice to the Clerk of the Commission and to opposing counsel at least five days before the scheduled date for argument.

Each side will be limited to no more than 15 minutes for presentation of oral argument.

If oral argument is requested and the requesting party fails to appear in person or by scheduled telephone conference, the Commission may impose sanctions in the absence of good cause shown.

CASE NOTES

The Commission is not required to allow oral argument, but may do so when it is determined to be necessary and helpful. Barnes v. Wise Fashions, 16 Va. App. 108, 428 S.E.2d 301 (1993).

NOTES FROM THE WORKERS' COMPENSATION COMMISSION

Unless oral argument is deemed necessary by the Full Commission, an employer's appeal of the Claims Division's refusal to place a case on the docket will be determined on the record and without oral argument. Sexton v. South Mountain Coal Company, Inc., 69 O.I.C. 53 (1990).

Oral argument will be allowed on Review only if requested by a party and the Commission deems it to be helpful in determining the issues to be reviewed. Williams v. Virginia Electric & Power Company, 18 Va. App. 569, 445 S.E.2d 693 (1994); 71 O.W.C. 101 (1992).

Rule 4. Filing Documents.

4.1 Agreements. — All agreements as to payment of compensation shall be reduced to writing by the employer and promptly filed with the Commission. If the claim is denied the employer shall notify the employee and the Commission promptly in writing.

Cross references. — As to filing of settlement agreements and filing of memorandum of agreement between employer and employee, see § 65.2-701.

CASE NOTES

Failure to promptly file memorandum of agreements is violative of the statute and frustrates a primary purpose behind the Workers' Compensation Act — to expedite the entry of awards in cases where the parties agree as to the compensability of the employee's injury. National Linen Serv. v. McGuinn, 5 Va. App. 265, 362 S.E.2d 187 (1987) (decided under former Rule 15).

4.2 Medical Reports. — Each party shall promptly provide the other parties with copies of any medical records they receive as they receive them. Unless otherwise directed by the Commission or these Rules, the parties shall not file medical records with the Commission until a hearing request is filed. The requesting party shall promptly file medical records supporting the request, if applicable. After a hearing request has been filed, the parties shall file with the Commission only medical records that are related to the hearing request. These records shall be filed upon receipt by the party filing them, and are required reports subject to the provisions of 65.2-902. A party is not required to file copies of medical records that another party has already filed.

A medical care provider attending an injured employee shall, upon request from an employer or an employee, furnish a copy of required reports, at no cost except for a nominal copying charge.

A medical care provider is entitled to a reasonable fee for preparation of a narrative report written in response to a request from a party if the report requires significant professional research or preparation.

CASE NOTES

Notice sufficient. — Finding that the employee was entitled to ongoing workers' compensation benefits was appropriate because evidence of prejudice from the settlement as to injuries other than the compensable brain injury did not justify termination of the award for that injury. The evidence, viewed in the light most favorable to claimant, established that claimant suffered no exacerbation of his compensable 2004 brain injury in the 2006 auto accident and continued to be temporarily and totally disabled as a result of the 2004 brain injury after the 2006 auto accident. United Airlines, Inc. v. Hayes, 58 Va. App. 220, 708 S.E.2d 418, 2011 Va. App. LEXIS 163 (2011).

NOTES FROM THE WORKERS' COMPENSATION COMMISSION

Employer not required to pay for narrative report accompanying physician's permanent impairment rating, but also not allowed to obtain report through subpoena without payment. Kingery v. Bandy & Son, Inc., VWC File No. 209-43-42 (Mar. 1, 2004).

Employer not required to transcribe deposition taken at employer's request absent showing of good cause; until deposition is transcribed there is no requirement to file deposition with Commission; contrary holding in Pretlow v. Peninsula Regional Jail, VWC File No. 203-16-24 (2/19/02) overruled. Browne v. Aureus Group, VWC File No. 201-28-86 (Mar. 10, 2003).

Commission Rule 4.2 provides that a medical care provider attending an injured employee shall furnish a copy of required reports to the employer or employee. The physician-patient privilege as to all physicians is waived in all proceedings under the Act. Hassell v. Arlington County Human Services, 79 O.W.C. 141 (2000).

The parties have a right to receive and review all medical documents which are or may be related to the claimant's condition. The claimant calls his medical condition into question by filing a claim for medical benefits, and the defendants have a right to subpoena documents which may be relevant in the defense of the claim, even though the claim had been accepted as compensable, and even though there is no pending claim for additional benefits. Smith v. Mullins Coal Company, Inc. of Va., 78 O.W.C. 202 (1999).

Rule 4.2 of the Rules of the Virginia Workers' Compensation Commission requires that legible copies of all medical reports shall be filed immediately with the Commission. All medical reports relevant to a claim are required reports. Eames v. Williamsburg Soap & Candle Co., 76 O.W.C. 7 (1997).

Medical reports must be filed under Rule 17 and are not a work product. Hughes v. Goodyear Tire & Rubber Co., 60 O.I.C. 219 (1981).

Non-designated medical reports and records are automatically a part of the hearing record. Lowery v. Globe Iron Const. Co., Inc., 76 O.W.C. 221 (1997).

Medical depositions are in the nature of medical

reports since they represent a physician's verbal testimony as recorded and transcribed, as opposed to dictated or written testimony as contained in medical reports. Lowery v. Globe Iron Const. Co., Inc., 76 O.W.C. 221 (1997).

A party has the right to have the entire deposition testimony of a doctor received into the evidentiary record, notwithstanding the requirement in Rule 2.2 (B)(3) that the transcript must be specifically identified by page and line. Lowery v. Globe Iron Const. Co., Inc., 76 O.W.C. 221 (1997).

A doctor's deposition is similar to a medical report, and the party taking the deposition is required to file it with the Commission. Because the defendants took the doctor's deposition, and a transcript is necessary to have the deposition made a part of the Commission's record, the defendants are financially responsible for ordering a transcript and filing it with the Commission. Pretlow v. Virginia Peninsula Regional Jail Authority, VWC File No. 203-16-24 (February 19, 2002).

Where an employer fails to furnish medical reports upon the filing of its application as required by Rule 13 (now Rule 1.4) and Rule 17 (now Rule 4.2), the application is void *ab initio*. It is also appropriate to assess a penalty under § 65.1-75.1 (now § 65.2-524) and a fine under § 65.1-124 (now § 65.2-900) and 65.1-127 (now § 65.2-902). Marrow v. Addington Beaman Lumber Company, Inc., 69 O.I.C. 195 (1990).

The Commission may assess fines under § 65.1-127 (now § 65.2-902), for failure to file medical reports as required by Rule 17 (now Rule 4.2). A fine will not be assessed when the medical report in question has no specific bearing on the issues or outcome of the case. Whitehair v. American Industrial Contracting, 67 O.I.C. 181 (1988).

There is no requirement that the Commission fine an employee for failure to file a medical report. Since Rule 17 (now Rule 4.2) treats all parties in the same class equally, it does not violate the Equal Protection Clause of the Constitution. Whitehair v. American Industrial Contracting, 67 O.I.C. 181 (1988).

The Commission denied a physician's demand for fees related to medical "case management." The physician demanded a fee for telephone communications he had with defense counsel and the insurer's representatives. In denying the claim, the Commission noted that approved physicians are entitled to reasonable reimbursement for services that provide the claimant with necessary care. An approved physician may be entitled to a reasonable fee for the preparation of any special reports required by the parties, and the costs associated with the time the physician may have to spend offering testimony, whether at a hearing or by deposition. However, the physician may not necessarily be reimbursed for all the time spent related to the employee's treatment. By statute, certain types of reports must be provided by the physician, the preparation of which constitutes medical "case management." The costs associated with preparing these reports are subsumed within the totality of the fee paid to the physician and the medical care he is expected to provide. Fox v. Waffle House, VWC File No. 194-57-70 (April 30, 2001).

The Commission ordered a change in the approved treating physician due to the physician's consistent failure to cooperate with the insurer's reasonable efforts to collect information regarding the claimant's medical status. While Code § 65.2-603 grants the approved treating physician the exclusive right to manage the injured worker's medical treatment, the Act provides a concomitant obligation on the part of the physician reasonably to cooperate with the insurer's requests for information regarding the claimant's condition and ongoing treatment. Code § 65.2-604 and Commission Rule 4.2 require that physicians attending injured workers provide medical reports upon request. In this case, the treating physician's consistent refusal to cooperate prejudiced the insurer's ability to evaluate the employee's ongoing condition and treatment, thereby justifying his removal. Newton v. Hunt Country Nursing Service, VWC File No. 196-43-73 (June 12, 2002).

Rule 5. Cost of Medical Services.

A claimant under an award shall not be liable for the cost of medical services payable under the Act.

CASE NOTES

Applied in Herbert Clements & Sons, Inc. v. Harris, 52 Va. App. 447, 663 S.E.2d 564, 2008 Va. App. LEXIS 362 (2008).

Rule 6. Award of Attorney's Fees Under § 65.2-714 of the Code of Virginia.

6.1 Agreement Between Parties as to a Fee. — An attorney's fee shall be awarded from sums recovered for the benefit of a third-party insurance carrier or a health care provider pursuant to § 65.2-714 of the Code of Virginia, if agreement is reached and an order, endorsed by counsel and the carrier or provider, identifying the amount of medical charges recovered and the agreed fee, is submitted to the Commission.

6.2 Parties Fail to Agree on a Fee. — A. An Attorney's fee shall be awarded from sums recovered for the benefit of a third-party insurance carrier or a health care provider pursuant to § 65.2-714 of the Code of Virginia, if the parties cannot agree, upon filing of a statement including the name and address of each carrier or provider from whom the fee is requested, the amount of the medical charge recovered for each carrier or provider and the amount of the fee requested, and certification that:

1. The claim was contested or that the defense was abandoned;

2. Prior to the filing of a request with the Commission the attorney and carrier or provider made a reasonable good faith effort to resolve the matter;

3. The insurance carrier or health care provider was given reasonable notice that a motion for an award of such fee would be made;

4. A copy of the motion has been sent to each carrier and health care provider identified.

B. If the request is referred to the evidentiary hearing docket, counsel must provide notice of the hearing to each carrier or provider. The notice must state the amount of the medical charge recovered for the carrier or provider, the amount of the attorney's fee requested and the time and place of the hearing.

NOTES FROM THE WORKERS' COMPENSATION COMMISSION

An attorney's fee against the health care providers may not be assessed if there is no hearing on the issue of compensability and no abandonment of any defense prior to a hearing. Thornton v. Virginia Concrete Company, Inc., 67 O.I.C. 240 (1988).

An attorney's request for fees under § 65.2-714(B) was denied because the case was not "contested." While there may have been a delay in investigating and providing a Memorandum of Agreement, the case was never denied and any subsequent disagreement involving reasonableness of health care charges did not affect the employee. Gamble v. PA Coal Company, Inc., 71 O.W.C. 299 (1992).

Section 65.1-102 (now § 65.2-714) and Rule 18 (now Rule 6) are constitutional exercises of State Governmental authority and do not deprive any party of a property right without due process of law. Sines v. Better Homes Realty, Inc., 66 O.I.C. 158 (1987). (Aff'd by Ct. of App. Unpublished Memorandum Opinion March 14, 1989).

An award of attorney's fees under § 65.2-714 (B) may result from a separate procedure or from the initial hearing to determine compensability of the case. Gamble v. PA Coal Company, Inc., 71 O.W.C. 299 (1992). See also *Blackburn v. Adrian Clevinger*, VWC # 143-34-32 decided June 12, 1992.

An attorney who seeks a fee for services from a health care provider must within a reasonable time, either before or after a final award or order providing for medical benefits is entered, give notice to the health care provider that an award for fees for legal services will be sought. The notice must state the time and place of the hearing on the motion before the Commission, the amount of payment or reimbursement upon which the fee is based, the manner of service and refer to the Commission's case (or Award/Order if already entered) upon which the motion is based. Sines v. Better Homes Realty, Inc., 66 O.I.C. 162 (1987).

Section 65.2-714 (B) requires payment by the health care provider of its pro rata share of an award of attorney's fees only after the provider has received reimbursement from the employer or its insurer. Danville Radiologists, Inc. Raymond Perkins, 22 Va. App. 454, 470 S.E.2d 602 (1996).

Counsel for the employee is entitled to an award of attorney's fees from the hospital even though Blue Cross/Blue Shield would have paid the bill if compensability were denied. Shelton v. PA Coal Company,, 71 O.W.C. 296 (1992).

An insurance company merely acting as a servicing agency with no funds of its own at risk is not a "third party insurance carrier" contemplated by the Act and is not liable for payment of an attorney's fee. Eveland v. Commonwealth of Virginia/Department of Transportation, 74 O.W.C. 189 (1995).

Rule 7. Employer Responsibilities.

7.1 Proof of Insurance Coverage. — Every employer subject to the Act shall file with the Commission proof of compliance with the insurance provisions (§§ 65.2-800 and 65.2-801) of the Act. A notice from the insurer (Form No. 45F) certifying this fact will be received as acceptable proof.

CASE NOTES

Applied in Hampton Inn & Selective Ins. Co. of Am. v. King, 58 Va. App. 286, 708 S.E.2d 450, 2011 Va. App. LEXIS 176 (2011).

7.2 Posting Notices. — Every employer subject to the Act shall post and keep posted, conspicuously, in the plant, shop or place of business at a location frequented by employees, notice of compliance with the provisions of the Act. Such notice shall follow substantially the form prescribed by the Commission. The Commission will supply employers with printed notices upon request. Failure by an employer to give such notice to an employee may constitute waiver of the notice defense pursuant to § 65.2-600 of the Code of Virginia.

CASE NOTES

Commission has discretion to find employer has waived "notice defense." — Under this rule, the commission has discretion to find that an employer has waived its "notice defense" under Section 65.2-600 as a sanction for failing to "post and keep posted, conspicuously, in the ... place of business at a location frequented by employees, notice of compliance with the provisions of the Act." Family Health Care Assocs. v. Perkins, Nos. 1238-97-3, 1290-97-3 (Ct. of Appeals Dec. 23, 1997).

NOTES FROM THE WORKERS' COMPENSATION COMMISSION

Every employer is responsible for posting notice of coverage and reporting requirements, pursuant to Rule 7.2 of the Rules of the Virginia Workers' Compensation Commission. Perkins v. Family Health Care Assoc., 76 O.W.C. 84 (1997).

The failure of an employer to post notices may constitute a waiver of the notice defense. Perkins v. Family Health Care Assoc., 76 O.W.C. 84 (1997).

Rule 8. Self-Insurance.

8.1 The Commonwealth of Virginia, Its Municipalities and Political Subdivisions. — Permission for self-insurance will be granted by the Commission to the Commonwealth and its political subdivisions and to Virginia municipalities upon application for certification, without submission of proof of financial ability and without deposit of bond or other security. However, the premium tax provided for in § 65.2-1006 of the Act shall be paid.

8.2 Confidentiality of Self-Insurer Information. — No record of any information concerning the solvency and financial ability of any employer acquired by a Commissioner or his agent by virtue of his powers under the Act shall be subject to inspection; nor shall any information in any way acquired for such purposes by virtue of such powers be divulged by a Commissioner or his agent, unless by order of the court, so long as said employer shall continue solvent and the compensation legally due from him, in accordance with provisions of the Act, shall continue to be paid.

Rule 9. Payment of Compensation.

9.1 Waiting Period. — If the employee is not paid wages for the entire day on which the injury occurred, the seven-day waiting period prescribed by the Act shall include the day of injury regardless of the hour of the injury.

All days or parts of days when the injured employee is unable to earn a full day's wages, or is not paid a full day's wages, due to injury, shall be counted in computing the waiting period even though the days may not be consecutive.

9.2 Direct Payment. — All compensation due an injured employee or compensation awarded on account of death under the Act must be paid directly to the beneficiary in accordance with the award. This ruling applies whether or not the employee is represented.

Compensation awarded shall be paid promptly and in strict accordance with the award issued by the Commission. When an award provides for an attorney fee, the employer shall pay the fee directly to the attorney unless there is alternative provision in the award.

CASE NOTES

Under § 65.1-75.1 (now § 65.2-524) a benefit is "paid" when payment is mailed directly to claimant, at his current residential address, within two weeks after it becomes due. Audobon Tree Serv. v. Childress, 2 Va. App. 35, 341 S.E.2d 211 (1986) (decided under former Rule 12).

NOTES FROM THE WORKERS' COMPENSATION COMMISSION

Rule 9.2 requires that all compensation due must be paid or mailed directly to the claimant, but neither the Code nor the Commission Rules make any distinction as to who makes the payment. Hunt v. Southern Industrial At Union Camp, 76 O.W.C. 215 (1997).

The Commission approved a compromise settlement on June 25, 1996. The employer mailed payment to the claimant's attorney on July 22, 1996. Counsel, in turn, mailed the check to the claimant on July 29, 1996, and claimant received it on July 31, 1996 or August 1, 1996. The Commission held that payment was made on July 29, 1996 when counsel placed the check for the claimant in the regular mail. Because payment was therefore made before July 30, 1996, the last date it was due, no penalty could be assessed against the employer. Hunt v. Southern Industrial At Union Camp, 76 O.W.C. 215 (1997).

Rule 10. X-ray Evidence for Coal Workers' Pneumoconiosis Claims.

10.1 Limitation on X-ray Submissions. — In any claim for first, second, or third stage pneumoconiosis under § 65.2-504 of the Code of Virginia, the employer and the employee each shall be limited to submission of not more than three medical interpretations (readings) of x-ray evidence without regard to the number of x-rays. For good cause shown, additional interpretations may be received as evidence if deemed necessary by the Commission.

10.2 Reading by Pulmonary Committee. — Any party to a contested claim, or the parties upon agreement, may submit the x-ray evidence to the Commission for interpretation by the Pulmonary Committee. If a party agrees to accept the x-ray reading of the Pulmonary Committee as the binding classification, the costs of evaluation shall be borne by the Commission.

10.3 Appointment of Pulmonary Committee. — The Commission shall appoint a Pulmonary Committee to be composed of at least three qualified physicians certified as B readers under standards promulgated by the International Labour Organization (ILO).

NOTES FROM THE WORKERS' COMPENSATION COMMISSION

Stipulations are binding on a party. Parties who enter into stipulations may not set aside those stipulations except in very limited circumstances. Where a claimant, by counsel, agrees to accept the reading of the Pulmonary Committee as the binding classification regarding his claim for coal workers pneumoconiosis, he is thereafter bound by the findings of the Committee. Short v. Island Creek Coal Company, 78 O.W.C. 137 (1999).

Rule 11. Pneumoconiosis Table.

A table for conversion of medically-classified categories of pneumoconiosis (under ILO standards) into stages of pneumoconiosis shall be promulgated by the Commission and information from the table shall be the basis for determining the amount of compensation due, if any, under § 65.2-504 of the Code of Virginia for coal workers' pneumoconiosis and under § 65.2-503 of the Code of Virginia for other pneumoconioses.

TABLE

Medical interpretations of radiographic evidence, for the purpose of conversion to stages under this table, shall be based upon the ILO 1980 International Classification of Radiographs of the Pneumoconioses.

First Stage :	Category	1 and 2	p,s
	"	1	q,t
Second Stage :	Category	3	p,s
	"	2 and 3	q,t
	"	1, 2 and 3	r,u
Third Stage :	Category	A, B and C	

NOTES FROM THE WORKERS' COMPENSATION COMMISSION

Although employee did not show a level of coal-workers' pneumoconiosis that would support an award of benefits under Code § 65.2-504, the evidence showed the existence of pneumoconiosis, and therefore the employee was awarded medical benefits for this condition. Wheeler v. Paramount Coal Corp., VWC File No. 209-75-07 (July 7, 2003).

A mere diagnosis and communication is not sufficient to prove an occupational disease. A preponderance of the evidence must establish the disease to be at a compensable level, *i.e.*, Category I. Wood v. Todd Marine Enterprises, 74 O.W.C. 137 (1995).

The mere fact that pneumoconiosis does not rise to the level of a ratable permanent loss under Code § 65.2-503(B)(17) does not automatically preclude entry of an award for medical benefits only. The Commission noted that the Court of Appeals earlier ordered entry of an award for medical benefits in a nearly identical case involving "asbestosis." See *Jones v. E.I. DuPont De Nemours*, 24 Va. App. 36, 480 S.E.2d 129 (1997). Observing that "asbestosis" is but one of several occupationally-induced forms of pneumoconioses, the Commission refused to recognize a distinction between the different forms the disease may take. While not entitled to permanency, the claimant established the presence of compensable pneumoconiosis and was entitled to entry of an award of medical benefits. Reed v. Clinchfield Coal Company, VWC File No. 205-30-74 (June 6, 2002).

Pneumoconiosis diseases as defined in Code § 65.2-503 specifically include silicosis and asbestosis. White v. C. J. Coakley Co., Inc., 77 O.W.C. 209 (1998).

Rule 12. Hearing Loss Table.

A table for determining compensable percentage of hearing loss shall be promulgated by the Commission.

All determinations are to be made (i) without the use of a hearing aid; and (ii) with a pure-tone audiometer by air conduction alone.

Hearing loss in decibels is to be recorded at 500, 1,000, 2,000 and 3,000 cycles per second. The audiometer must be calibrated to the ANSI 1969 standard.

The average decibel loss is to be translated into percentage of compensable hearing loss of each ear according to the following table:

Average Decibel Loss	Percent of Compensable Hearing Loss	Average Decibel Loss	Percent of Compensable Hearing Loss
27	.8	60	55
28	2.2	61	56.7
29	3.6	62	58.3
30	5	63	60
31	6.7	64	61.7
32	8.3	65	63.3
33	10	66	65
34	11.7	67	66.7
35	13.3	68	68.3
36	15	69	70
37	16.7	70	71.7
38	18.3	71	73.3
39	20	72	75
40	21.7	73	76.4
41	23.3	74	77.8
42	25	75	79.2
43	26.7	76	80.6
44	28.3	77	82
45	30	78	83.4
46	31.7	79	84.8
47	33.3	80	86.2
48	35	81	87.6
49	36.7	82	89
50	38.3	83	90.4
51	40	84	91.8
52	41.7	85	93.2
53	43.3	86	94.6
54	45	87	96
55	46.7	88	97.4
56	48.3	89	98.8
57	50	90 and over	100
58	51.7		
59	53.3		

No allowance for presbycusis is to be made

NOTES FROM THE WORKERS' COMPENSATION COMMISSION

The claimant, who had pre-existing hearing loss, suffered a compensable injury by accident when gunfire resulted in hearing loss. In determining claimant's hearing loss from the accident the normal or non-material 26 decibel is subtracted from the pre-existing hearing loss. This number is then subtracted from the post-accident hearing loss. The resulting decibel loss is then compared to the chart in Rule 12 to determine the percent of hearing loss related to the compensable work accident. Macudzinski v. Omniplex World Service, Inc., VWC File No. 218-73-91 (Feb. 21, 2007).

The Virginia Court of Appeals on September 3, 1996 held that a hearing loss caused by prolonged exposure to noise at work is a noncompensable gradually incurred injury. Although the General Assembly changed the law so that hearing loss caused by cumulative trauma may be compensable as of July 1, 1997, that law was not made retroactive. Jost v. Pohanka Acura, 76 O.W.C. 106 (1997).

Rule 13. Table of Percentage of Loss of Visual Acuity.

SNELLEN'S CHART

Snellen's Chart Readings	Percentage of Loss of Visual Acuity
20/20	0
20/25	5
20/30	10
20/40	20
20/50	25
20/60	33½
20/70	40
20/80	50
20/90	62½
20/100	75
20/110	80
20/120	85
20/130	87
20/140	89
20/150	91
20/160	93
20/170	95
20/180	97
20/190	99
20/200	100

Any other deviation from normal vision caused by the injury shall be considered.

CASE NOTES

Basis of change must be stated. — Under this rule, the application must state the "change in the condition relied upon." Danville Sch. Bd. v. Chilton, No. 2168-95-2 (Ct. of Appeals Mar. 26, 1996).

By subtracting worker's pre-existing vision acuity reading (20/80) from his post-injury vision acuity reading (20/300), the employer was given the benefit of the provision of § 65.2-505 and worker was given the benefit of the deviation from normal vision as required by this rule. Accordingly, under a proper application of this rule and § 65.2-505, worker's loss of visual acuity resulting from the injury far exceeded the minimum threshold for industrial blindness and entitled him to one hundred percent permanent partial disability. Sinclair v. Shelter Constr. Corp., 23 Va. App. 154, 474 S.E.2d 856 (1996).

Rule 14. Definition of Community.

For purposes of Code of Virginia Section 65.2-605, the word "community" shall mean one or more planning districts as set forth below:

Community	Planning District(s)
1	Districts 1 & 2
2	District 3
3	District 4
4	District 5
5	District 11 & 13
6	District 12
7	District 6
8	District 7
9	District 16

10	District 9 & 10
11	District 8
12	District 17 & 18
13	District 22 & 23
14	District 14 & 15
15	District 19

Whenever an employee receives treatment outside of the Commonwealth, the Commission will determine the appropriate community in the state or territory where the treatment is rendered upon application of either the employee, employer (or its representative), or medical provider.

When the commission deems appropriate, it may consider additional data to determine the prevailing community rate. (Effective July 1, 1996.)

NOTES FROM THE WORKERS' COMPENSATION COMMISSION

The Tennessee fee schedule applies only to individuals seeking benefits under the Tennessee Workers' Compensation Act, not those who seek benefits under the Virginia Act, even where the medical services are rendered in Tennessee; the prevailing community rate standard applies to such services of the Virginia Act. Mullins, Highlands Neurosurgery, P.C. v. Kyn Coal Corporation, VWC File No. 236-10-44 (Sept. 2, 2009).

Where a carrier pays a medical bill and it is later found that the payment exceeded the prevailing community rate, pursuant to Rule 14, the carrier is entitled to repayment or a credit for the overpayment. Bush v. Sure Kick Battery Co., VWC File No. 156-69-22 (March 5, 2008).

The employer was not responsible for the full payment of the bill because the pharmacy charges exceeded the prevailing community rate and it included charges for ancillary services that are not included under the Act, such as advocacy services in achieving reimbursement and the shifting of risk of non-payment away from the patient. Riggleman, Jr. v. Donald L. Riggleman, VWC File No. 138-66-10 (Aug. 30, 2005).

Medical bills received by a claimant are prima facie evidence that they are both reasonable and necessary. An employer or carrier alleging excessive medical charges must prove that such costs exceed the prevailing rate of the community for the same services. A mere statement by a carrier that their administrator recommended a different community rate payment does not satisfy the insurer's burden to show that the charges in question are higher than the prevailing community rate. Moorefield v. Cooperative Supply Inc., 79 O.W.C. 29 (2000).

An employer alleging excessive doctors' fees must prove that such costs exceed the prevailing rate of the community for the same or comparable services. Korsh v. Builders Hardware & Architectural Prods., Inc., 76 O.W.C. 76 (1997).

The employer has the burden of showing that the physician's charges did not fall within the prevailing community rate as set forth in § 65.2-605, and that the carrier's reimbursement did meet that standard. The employer retains this burden whether the claim is brought by the employer or the medical care provider. Korsh v. Builders Hardware & Architectural Prods., Inc., 76 O.W.C. 76 (1997).

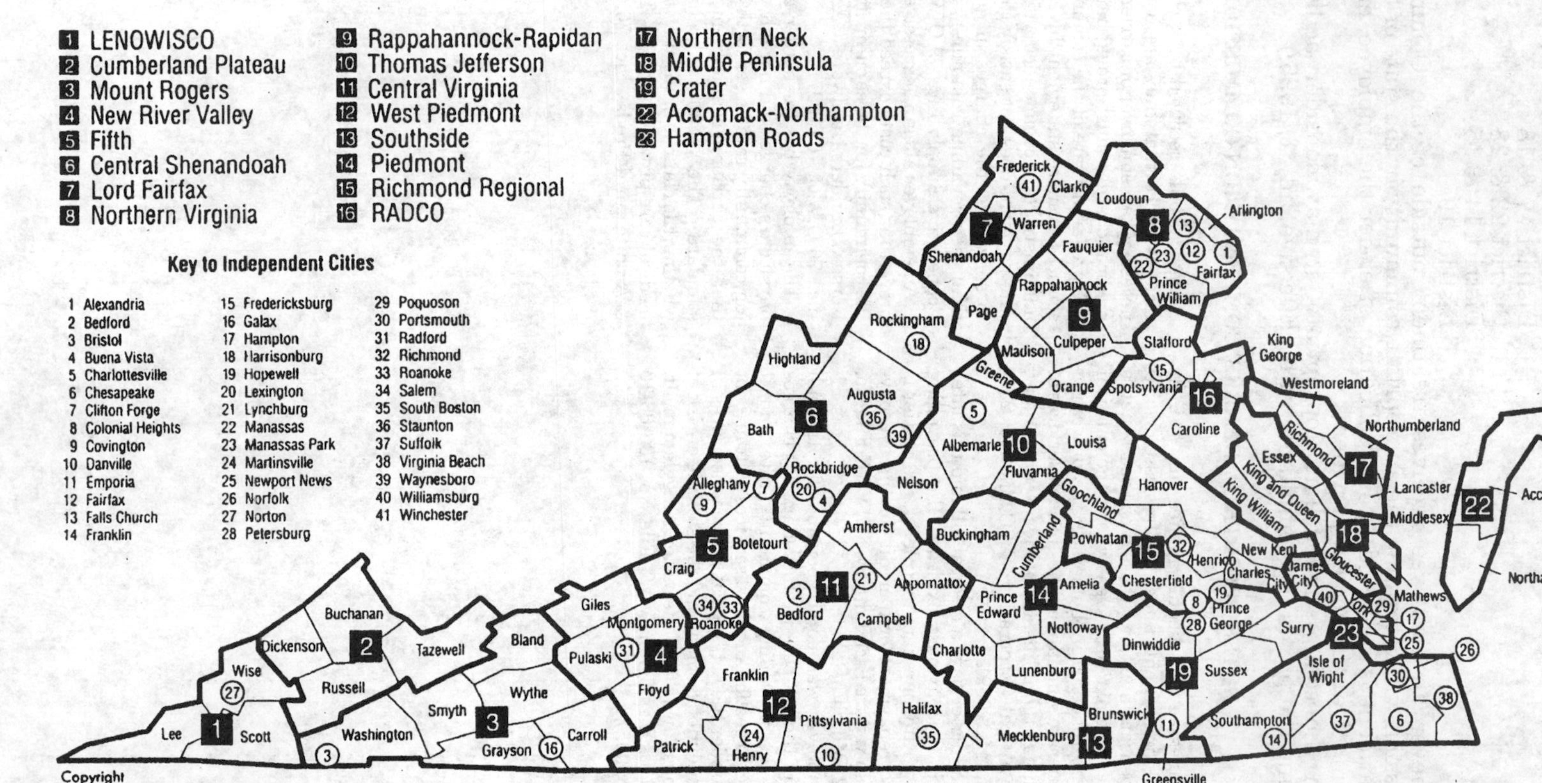
Virginia Planning District Commissions (PDCs)
1 LENOWISCO
2 Cumberland Plateau
3 Mount Rogers
4 New River Valley
5 Fifth
6 Central Shenandoah
7 Lord Fairfax
8 Northern Virginia
9 Rappahannock-Rapidan
10 Thomas Jefferson
11 Central Virginia
12 West Piedmont
13 Southside
14 Piedmont
15 Richmond Regional
16 RADCO
17 Northern Neck
18 Middle Peninsula
19 Crater
22 Accomack-Northampton
23 Hampton Roads
Key to Independent Cities
1 Alexandria
2 Bedford
3 Bristol
4 Buena Vista
5 Charlottesville
6 Chesapeake
7 Clifton Forge
8 Colonial Heights
9 Covington
10 Danville
11 Emporia
12 Fairfax
13 Falls Church
14 Franklin
15 Fredericksburg
16 Galax
17 Hampton
18 Harrisonburg
19 Hopewell
20 Lexington
21 Lynchburg
22 Manassas
23 Manassas Park
24 Martinsville
25 Newport News
26 Norfolk
27 Norton
28 Petersburg
29 Poquoson
30 Portsmouth
31 Radford
32 Richmond
33 Roanoke
34 Salem
35 South Boston
36 Staunton
37 Suffolk
38 Virginia Beach
39 Waynesboro
40 Williamsburg
41 Winchester
Copyright
1992 Virginia Employment Commission

Index to Virginia Workers' Compensation Commission Rules

C

COMPENSATION.
Direct payment, VWCC Rule 9.2.
Waiting period, VWCC Rule 9.1.

COSTS.
Medical service costs, VWCC Rule 5.

E

EMPLOYERS.
Employer responsibilities.
Insurance coverage proof, VWCC Rule 7.1.
Posting notices, VWCC Rule 7.2.

F

FILING OF MEDICAL REPORTS, VWCC Rules 4.1, 4.2.

H

HEARING LOSS TABLE, VWCC Rule 12.

HEARINGS.
Hearing procedures.
Decision on the record, VWCC Rule 2.1.
Evidentiary hearings, VWCC Rule 2.2.
Expedited hearing, VWCC Rule 2.3.
Review of decisions, VWCC Rule 2.1.
Posthearing procedures.
Additional testimony, VWCC Rule 3.3.
Oral argument, VWCC Rule 3.4.
Request for review, VWCC Rule 3.1.
Written statements, VWCC Rule 3.2.
Prehearing procedures, VWCC Rules 1.1 to 1.12.
Acceptance or rejection of claims, VWCC Rule 1.5.
Change of condition claims, VWCC Rule 1.2.
Compromise and settlement, VWCC Rule 1.7.
Discovery generally, VWCC Rule 1.8.
Dismissal for failure to file supporting evidence, VWCC Rule 1.3.
Employer's application for hearing, VWCC Rule 1.4.

HEARINGS —Cont'd
Prehearing procedures —Cont'd
Enforcement of rules, VWCC Rule 1.12.
Informal dispute resolution, VWCC Rule 1.9.
Lump sum payments, VWCC Rule 1.7.
Original claim for benefits, VWCC Rule 1.1.
Prehearing statement, VWCC Rule 1.11.
Review of decisions, VWCC Rule 1.6.
Willful misconduct, VWCC Rule 1.10.

I

INSURANCE.
Employers.
Proof of insurance coverage, VWCC Rule 7.1.
Self-insurance, VWCC Rules 8.1, 8.2.

M

MEDICAL REPORTS.
Filing required, VWCC Rules 4.1, 4.2.

N

NOTICE.
Employer posting of notices, VWCC Rule 7.2.

P

PNEUMOCONIOSIS CLAIMS.
Coal workers.
X-ray evidence, VWCC Rules 10.1 to 10.3.

PNEUMOCONIOSIS TABLE, VWCC Rule 11.

S

SELF-INSURANCE, VWCC Rules 8.1, 8.2.

V

VISUAL ACUITY.
Percentage of loss table, VWCC Rule 13.

RULES OF PRACTICE AND PROCEDURE OF THE STATE CORPORATION COMMISSION

Part I. General Provisions.

Rule
5 VAC 5-20-10. Applicability.
5 VAC 5-20-20. Good faith pleading and practice.
5 VAC 5-20-30. Counsel.
5 VAC 5-20-40. Photographs and broadcasting of proceedings.
5 VAC 5-20-50. Consultation by parties with Commissioners and Hearing Examiners.
5 VAC 5-20-60. Commission staff.
5 VAC 5-20-70. Informal complaints.

Part II. Commencement of Formal Proceedings.

5 VAC 5-20-80. Regulatory Proceedings.
5 VAC 5-20-90. Adjudicatory proceedings.
5 VAC 5-20-100. Other proceedings.

Part III. Procedures in Formal Proceedings.

5 VAC 5-20-110. Motions.
5 VAC 5-20 120. Procedure Before Hearing Examiners.
5 VAC 5-20-130. Amendment of pleadings.

Rule
5 VAC 5-20-140. Filing and service.
5 VAC 5-20-150. Copies and format.
5 VAC 5-20-160. Memorandum of completeness.
5 VAC 5-20-170. Confidential information.
5 VAC 5-20-180. Official transcript of hearing.
5 VAC 5-20-190. Rules of evidence.
5 VAC 5-20-200. Briefs.
5 VAC 5-20-210. Oral argument.
5 VAC 5-20-220. Petition for rehearing or reconsideration.
5 VAC 5-20-230. Extension of time.

Part IV. Discovery and Hearing Preparation Procedures.

5 VAC 5-20-240. Prepared testimony and exhibits.
5 VAC 5-20-250. Process, witnesses, and production of documents and things.
5 VAC 5-20-260. Interrogatories or requests for production of documents and things.
5 VAC 5-20-270. Hearing preparation.
5 VAC 5-20-280. Discovery applicable only to 5 VAC 5 20-90 proceedings.
Index.

Editor's note. — The following rules of the State Corporation Commission are effective for cases established on and after March 11, 2009.

For constitutional and statutory provisions relating to the promulgation of rules by the State Corporation Commission, see art. IX, § 3, Va. Const., and § 12.1-25.

For website of the State Corporation Commission, see http://www.state.va.us/scc.

PART I. GENERAL PROVISIONS.

5 VAC 5-20-10. Applicability.

The State Corporation Commission Rules of Practice and Procedure are promulgated pursuant to the authority of § 12.1-25 of the Code of Virginia and are applicable to the regulatory and adjudicatory proceedings of the State Corporation Commission except where superseded by more specific rules for particular types of cases or proceedings. When necessary to serve the ends of justice in a particular case, the commission may grant, upon motion or its own initiative, a waiver or modification of any of the provisions of these rules, except 5 VAC 5-20-220, under terms and conditions and to the extent it deems appropriate. These rules do not apply to the internal administration or organization of the commission in matters such as the procurement of goods and services, personnel actions, and similar issues, nor to matters that are being handled administratively by a division or bureau of the commission.

Law Review. — For article, "Legislative and Executive Veto of Rules of Administrative Agencies: Models and Alternatives," see 24 Wm. & Mary L. Rev. 79 (1982).

5 VAC 5-20-20. Good faith pleading and practice.

Every pleading, written motion, or other document presented for filing by a party represented by an attorney shall be signed by at least one attorney of record in the attorney's individual name, and the attorney's mailing address and telephone number, and where available, telefax number and email address, shall be stated. An individual not represented by an attorney shall sign the individual's pleading, motion, or other document, and shall state the individual's mailing address and telephone number. A partnership not represented by an attorney shall have a partner sign the partnership's pleading, motion, or other document, and shall state the partnership's mailing address and telephone number. A nonlawyer may only represent the interests of another before the commission in the presentation of facts, figures, or factual conclusions, as distinguished from legal arguments or conclusions. In the case of an individual or entity not represented by counsel, each signature shall be that of the individual or a qualified officer or agent of the entity. Documents signed pursuant to this rule need not be under oath unless so required by statute.

The commission allows electronic filing. Before filing electronically, the filer shall complete an electronic document filing authorization form, establish a filer authentication password with the Clerk of the State Corporation Commission and otherwise comply with the electronic filing procedures adopted by the commission. Upon establishment of a filer authentication password, a filer may make electronic filings in any case. All documents submitted electronically must be capable of being printed as paper documents without loss of content or appearance.

The signature of an attorney or party constitutes a certification that (i) the attorney or party has read the pleading, motion, or other document; (ii) to the best of the attorney's or party's knowledge, information, and belief formed after reasonable inquiry, the pleading, motion or other document is well grounded in fact and is warranted by existing law or a good faith argument for the extension, modification, or reversal of existing law; and (iii) the pleading, motion or other document is not interposed for any improper purpose, such as to harass or to cause unnecessary delay or needless increase in the cost of litigation. A pleading, written motion, or other document will not be accepted for filing by the Clerk of the Commission if it is not signed.

An oral motion made by an attorney or party in a commission proceeding constitutes a representation that the motion (i) is well grounded in fact and is warranted by existing law or a good faith argument for the extension, modification, or reversal of existing law; and (ii) is not interposed for any improper purpose, such as to harass or to cause unnecessary delay or needless increase in the cost of litigation.

5 VAC 5-20-30. Counsel.

Except as otherwise provided in 5 VAC 5-20-20, no person other than a properly licensed attorney at law shall file pleadings or papers or appear at a hearing to represent the interests of another person or entity before the commission. An attorney admitted to practice in another jurisdiction, but not licensed in Virginia, may be permitted to appear in a particular proceeding pending before the commission in association with a member of the Virginia State Bar. The Virginia State Bar member will be counsel of record for every purpose related to the conduct and disposition of the proceeding.

In all appropriate proceedings before the Commission, the Division of Consumer Counsel, Office of the Attorney General, may appear and represent and be heard on behalf of consumers' interests, and investigate matters relating to such appearance, and otherwise may participate to the extent reasonably necessary to discharge its statutory duties.

5 VAC 5-20-40. Photographs and broadcasting of proceedings.

Electronic media and still photography coverage of commission hearings will be allowed at the discretion of the commission.

5 VAC 5-20-50. Consultation by parties with Commissioners and Hearing Examiners.

No commissioner or hearing examiner shall consult with any party or any person acting on behalf of any party with respect to a pending formal proceeding without giving adequate notice and opportunity for all parties to participate.

5 VAC 5-20-60. Commission staff.

The commissioners and hearing examiners shall be free at all times to confer with any member of the commission staff. However, no facts nor legal arguments likely to influence a pending formal proceeding and not of record in that proceeding shall be furnished ex parte to any commissioner or hearing examiner by any member of the commission staff.

5 VAC 5-20-70. Informal complaints.

All correspondence and informal complaints shall be referred to the appropriate division or bureau of the commission. The head of the division or bureau receiving this correspondence or complaint shall attempt to resolve the matter presented. Matters not resolved to the satisfaction of all participating parties by the informal process may be reviewed by the full commission upon the proper filing of a formal proceeding in accordance with the rules by any party to the informal process.

PART II. COMMENCEMENT OF FORMAL PROCEEDINGS.

5 VAC 5-20-80. Regulatory Proceedings.

A. *Application.* — Except where otherwise provided by statute, rule or commission order, a person or entity seeking to engage in an industry or business subject to the commission's regulatory authority, or to make changes in any previously authorized service, rate, facility, or other aspect of such industry or business that, by statute or rule, must be approved by the Commission, shall file an application requesting authority to do so. The application shall contain: (i) a specific statement of the action sought; (ii) a statement of the facts that the applicant is prepared to prove that would warrant the action sought; (iii) a statement of the legal basis for such action; and (iv) any other information required by law or regulation. Any person or entity filing an application shall be a party to that proceeding.

B. *Participation as a respondent.* — A notice of participation as a respondent is the proper initial response to an application. A notice of participation shall be filed within the time prescribed by the commission and shall contain: (i) a precise statement of the interest of the respondent; (ii) a statement of the specific action sought to the extent then known; and (iii) the factual and legal basis for the action. Any person or entity filing a notice of participation as a respondent shall be a party to that proceeding.

C. *Public witnesses.* — Any person or entity not participating in a matter pursuant to 5 VAC 5-20-80 A or 5 VAC 5-20-80 B may make known their position in any regulatory proceeding by filing written comments in advance of the hearing if provided for by commission order or by attending the hearing, noting an appearance in the manner prescribed by the commission, and giving oral testimony. Public witnesses may not otherwise participate in the proceeding, be included in the service list, or be considered a party to the proceeding.

D. *Commission staff.* — The commission staff may appear and participate in any proceeding in order to see that pertinent issues on behalf of the general public interest are clearly presented to the commission. The staff may, inter alia, conduct investigations and discovery, evaluate the issues raised, testify and offer exhibits, file briefs and make argument, and be subject to cross-examination when testifying. Neither the commission staff collectively nor any individual member of the commission staff shall be considered a party to the case for any purpose by virtue of participation in a proceeding.

5 VAC 5-20-90. Adjudicatory proceedings.

A. *Initiation of proceedings.* — Investigative, disciplinary, penal, and other adjudicatory proceedings may be initiated by motion of the commission staff or upon the commission's own motion. Further proceedings shall be controlled by the issuance of a rule to show cause, which shall give notice to the defendant, state the allegations against the defendant, provide for a response from the defendant and, where appropriate, set the matter for hearing. A rule to show cause shall be served in the manner provided by § 12.1-19.1 or § 12.1-29 of the Code of Virginia. The commission staff shall prove the case by clear and convincing evidence.

B. *Answer.* — An answer or other responsive pleading shall be filed within 21 days of service of the rule to show cause, unless the commission shall order otherwise. The answer shall state, in narrative form, each defendant's responses to the allegations in the rule to show cause and any affirmative defenses asserted by the defendant. Failure to file a timely answer or other responsive pleading may result in the entry of judgment by default against the party failing to respond.

5 VAC 5-20-100. Other proceedings.

A. *Promulgation of general orders, rules, or regulations.* — Before promulgating a general order, rule, or regulation, the commission shall, by order upon an application or upon its own motion, require reasonable notice of the contents of the proposed general order, rule, or regulation, including publication in the Virginia Register of Regulations, and afford interested persons an opportunity to comment, present evidence, and be heard. A copy of each general order, rule, and regulation adopted in final form by the commission shall be filed with the Registrar of Regulations for publication in the Virginia Register of Regulations.

B. *Petitions in other matters.* — Persons having a cause before the commission, whether by statute, rule, regulation, or otherwise, against a defendant, including the commission, a commission bureau, or a commission division, shall proceed by filing a written petition containing: (i) the identity of the parties; (ii) a statement of the action sought and the legal basis for the commission's jurisdiction to take the action sought; (iii) a statement of the facts, proof of which would warrant the action sought; (iv) a statement of the legal basis for the action; and (v) a certificate showing service upon the defendant.

Within 21 days of service of a petition under this rule, the defendant shall file an answer or other responsive pleading containing, in narrative form, (i) a response to each allegation of the petition and (ii) a statement of each affirmative defense asserted by the defendant. Failure to file a timely answer may result in entry of judgment by default against the defendant failing to respond. Upon order of the commission, the commission staff may participate in any proceeding under this rule in which it is not a defendant to the same extent as permitted by 5 VAC 5-20-80 D.

C. *Declaratory judgments.* — Persons having no other adequate remedy may petition the commission for a declaratory judgment. The petition shall meet the requirements of 5 VAC 5-20-100 B and, in addition, contain a statement of the basis for concluding that an actual controversy exists. In the proceeding, the commission shall by order provide for the necessary notice, responsive pleadings, and participation by interested parties and the commission staff.

PART III. PROCEDURES IN FORMAL PROCEEDINGS.

5 VAC 5-20-110. Motions.

Motions may be filed for the same purposes recognized by the courts of record in the Commonwealth. Unless otherwise ordered by the commission, any response to a motion must be filed within 14 days of the filing of the motion, and any reply by the moving party must be filed within ten days of the filing of the response.

5 VAC 5-20-120. Procedure Before Hearing Examiners.

A. *Assignment.* — The commission may, by order, assign a matter pending before it to a hearing examiner. Unless otherwise ordered, the hearing examiner shall conduct all further proceedings in the matter on behalf of the commission in accordance with these rules. In the discharge of his duties, the hearing examiner shall exercise all the adjudicatory powers possessed by the commission including, inter alia, the power to administer oaths; require the attendance of witnesses and parties; require the production of documents; schedule and conduct pre-hearing conferences; admit or exclude evidence; grant or deny continuances; and rule on motions, matters of law, and procedural questions. The hearing examiner shall, upon conclusion of all assigned duties, issue a written final report and recommendation to the commission at the conclusion of the proceedings.

B. *Objections and certification of issues.* — An objection to a ruling by the hearing examiner during a hearing shall be stated with the reasons therefore at the time of the ruling. Any objection to a hearing examiner's ruling may be argued to the commission as part of a response to the hearing examiner's report. A ruling by the hearing examiner that denies further participation by a party in interest or the commission staff in a proceeding that has not been concluded may be immediately appealed to the commission by filing a written motion with the commission for review. Upon the motion of any party or the staff, or upon the hearing examiner's own initiative, the hearing examiner may certify any other material issue to the commission for its consideration and resolution. Pending resolution by the commission of a ruling appealed or certified, the hearing examiner shall retain procedural control of the proceeding.

C. *Responses to hearing examiner reports.* — Unless otherwise ordered by the hearing examiner, responses supporting or objecting to the hearing examiner's final report must be filed within 21 days of the issuance of the report. A reply to a response to the hearing examiner's report may only be filed with leave of the commission. The commission may accept, modify, or reject the hearing examiner's recommendations in any manner consistent with law and the evidence, notwithstanding an absence of objections to the hearing examiner's report.

5 VAC 5-20-130. Amendment of pleadings.

No amendment shall be made to any pleading after it is filed except by leave of the commission, which leave shall be liberally granted in the furtherance of justice. The commission shall make such provision for notice and for opportunity to respond to the amended pleadings as it may deem necessary and proper.

5 VAC 5-20-140. Filing and service.

A pleading or other document shall be considered filed with the commission upon receipt of the original and required copies by the Clerk of the Commission no later than the time established for the closing of business of the clerk's office on the day the item is due. The original and copies shall be stamped by the Clerk to show the time and date of receipt.

Electronic filings may be submitted at any time and will be deemed filed on the date and at the time the electronic document is received by the commission's database; provided, that if a document is received when the clerk's office is not open for public business, the document shall be deemed filed on the next regular business day. A filer will receive an electronic notification identifying the date and time the document was received by the commission's database. An electronic document may be rejected if it is not submitted in compliance with these rules.

When a filing would otherwise be due on a day when the clerk's office is not open for public business during all or part of a business day, the filing will be timely if made on the next regular business day that the office is open to the public. Except as otherwise ordered by the commission, when a period of 15 days or fewer is permitted to make a filing or take other action pursuant to commission rule or order, intervening weekends or holidays shall not be counted in determining the due date.

Service of a pleading, brief, or other document filed with the commission required to be served on the parties to a proceeding or upon the commission staff, shall be effected by delivery of a true copy to the party or staff, or by deposit of a true copy into the United States mail or overnight express mail delivery service properly addressed and postage prepaid, or via hand-delivery, on or before the date of filing. Service on a party may be made by service on the party's counsel. Alternatively, electronic service shall be permitted on parties or staff in cases where all parties and staff have agreed to such service, or where the commission has provided for such service by order. At the foot of a formal pleading, brief, or other document required to be served, the party making service shall append a certificate of counsel of record that copies were mailed or delivered as required. Notices, findings of fact, opinions, decisions, orders, or other documents to be served by the commission may be served by United States mail. However, all writs, processes, and orders of the commission, when acting in conformity with § 12.1-27 of the Code of Virginia, shall be attested by the Clerk of the Commission and served in compliance with § 12.1-19.1 or 12.1-29 of the Code of Virginia.

5 VAC 5-20-150. Copies and format.

Applications, petitions, motions, responsive pleadings, briefs, and other documents filed by parties must be filed in an original and 15 copies unless otherwise directed by the commission. Except as otherwise stated in these rules, submissions filed electronically are exempt from the copy requirement. One copy of each responsive pleading or brief must be served on each party and the commission staff counsel assigned to the matter, or, if no counsel has been assigned, on the general counsel.

Each document must be filed on standard size white opaque paper, 8-1/2 by 11 inches in dimension, must be capable of being reproduced in copies of archival quality, and only one side of the paper may be used. Submissions filed electronically shall be made in portable document format (PDF).

Each document shall be bound or attached on the left side and contain adequate margins. Each page following the first page shall be numbered. If necessary, a document may be filed in consecutively numbered volumes, each of which may not exceed three inches in thickness. Submissions filed electronically may not exceed 100 pages of printed text of 8-1/2 by 11 inches.

Each document containing more than one exhibit should have dividers separating each exhibit and should contain an index. Exhibits such as maps, plats, and photographs not easily reduced to standard size may be filed in a different size, as necessary. Submissions filed electronically that otherwise would incorporate large exhibits impractical for conversion to electronic format shall be identified in the filing and include a statement that the exhibit was filed in hardcopy and is available for viewing at the commission or that a copy may be obtained from the filing party. Such exhibit shall be filed in an original and 15 copies.

All filed documents shall be fully collated and assembled into complete and proper sets ready for distribution and use, without the need for further assembly, sorting, or rearrangement.

The Clerk of the Commission may reject the filing of any document not conforming to the requirements of this rule.

5 VAC 5-20-160. Memorandum of completeness.

With respect to the filing of a rate application or an application seeking actions that by statute or rule must be completed within a certain number of days, a memorandum shall be filed by an appropriate member of the commission staff within ten days of the filing of the application stating whether all necessary requirements imposed by statute or rule for filing the application have been met and all required information has been filed. If the requirements have not been met, the memorandum shall state with specificity the remaining items to be filed. The Clerk of the Commission immediately shall serve a copy of the memorandum on the filing party. The first day of the period within which action on the application must be concluded shall be set forth in the memorandum and shall be the initial date of filing of applications that are found to be complete upon filing. Applications found to require supplementation shall be complete upon the date of filing of the last item identified in the Staff memorandum. Applications shall be deemed complete upon filing if the memorandum of completeness is not timely filed.

5 VAC 5-20-170. Confidential information.

A person who proposes in good faith in a formal proceeding that information to be filed with or delivered to the commission be withheld from public disclosure on the ground that it contains trade secrets, privileged, or confidential commercial or financial information shall file this information under seal with the Clerk of the Commission, or otherwise deliver the information under seal to the commission staff, or both, as may be required. Items filed or delivered under seal shall be securely sealed in an opaque container that is clearly labeled "UNDER SEAL," and, if filed, shall meet the other requirements for filing contained in these rules. An original and 15 copies of all such information shall be filed with the clerk. One additional copy of all such information shall also be delivered under seal to the commission staff counsel assigned to the matter, or, where no counsel has been assigned, to the general counsel who, until ordered otherwise by the commission, shall disclose the information only to the members of the commission staff directly assigned to the matter as necessary in the discharge of their duties. Staff counsel and all members of the commission staff, until otherwise ordered by the commission, shall maintain the information in strict confidence and shall not disclose its contents to members of the public, or to other staff members not assigned to the matter. The commission staff or any party may object to the proposed withholding of the information.

When an application (including supporting documents and prefiled testimony) contains information that the applicant claims to be confidential, the filing shall be made under seal and accompanied by a motion for protective order or other confidential treatment. The provision to a party of information claimed to be trade secrets, privileged, or confidential commercial or financial information shall be governed by a protective order or other individual arrangements for confidential treatment.

On every document filed or delivered under seal, the producing party shall mark each individual page of the document that contains confidential information, and on each such page shall clearly indicate the specific information requested to be treated as confidential by use of highlighting, underscoring, bracketing or other appropriate marking. All remaining materials on each page of the document shall be treated as nonconfidential and available for public use and review. If an entire document is confidential, or if all information provided in electronic format under Part IV (5 VAC 5-20-240 et seq.) of these rules is confidential, a marking prominently displayed on the first page of such document or at the beginning of any information provided in electronic format, indicating that the entire document is confidential shall suffice.

Upon challenge, the information shall be treated as confidential pursuant to these rules only where the party requesting confidential treatment can demonstrate to the satisfaction of the commission that the risk of harm of publicly disclosing the information outweighs the presumption in favor of public disclosure. If the commission determines that the information should be withheld from public disclosure, it may nevertheless require the information to be disclosed to parties to a proceeding under appropriate protective order.

Whenever a document is filed with the clerk under seal, an original and one copy of an expurgated or redacted version of the document deemed by the filing party or determined by the commission to be confidential shall be filed with the clerk for use and review by the public. A document containing confidential information shall not be submitted electronically. An expurgated or redacted version of the document may be filed electronically. Documents containing confidential information must be filed in hardcopy and in accordance with all requirements of these rules. Upon a determination by the commission or a hearing examiner that all or portions of any materials filed under seal are not entitled to confidential treatment, the filing party shall file one original and one copy of the expurgated or redacted version of the document reflecting the ruling.

When the information at issue is not required to be filed or made a part of the record, a party who wishes to withhold confidential information from filing or production may move the commission for a protective order without filing the materials. In considering such a motion, the commission may require production of the confidential materials for inspection in camera, if necessary.

A party may request additional protection for extraordinarily sensitive information by motion filed pursuant to 5 VAC 5-20-110, and filing the information with the Clerk of the Commission under seal and delivering a copy of the information to commission staff counsel under seal as directed above. Whenever such treatment has been requested under Part IV of these rules, the commission may make such orders as necessary to permit parties to challenge the requested additional protection.

The commission, hearing examiners, any party and the commission staff may make use of confidential material in orders, filing pleadings, testimony, or other documents, as directed by order of the commission. When a party or commission staff uses confidential material in a filed pleading, testimony, or other document, the party or commission staff must file both confidential and nonconfidential versions of the pleading, testimony, or other document. Confidential versions of filed pleadings, testimony, or other documents shall clearly indicate the confidential material contained within by highlighting, underscoring, bracketing or other appropriate marking. When filing confidential pleadings, testimony, or other documents, parties must submit the confidential version to the Clerk of the Commission securely sealed in an opaque container that is clearly labeled "UNDER SEAL." Nonconfidential versions of filed pleadings, testimony, or other documents shall expurgate, redact, or otherwise omit all references to confidential material.

The commission may issue such order as it deems necessary to prevent the use of confidentiality claims for the purpose of delay or obstruction of the proceeding.

A person who proposes in good faith that information to be delivered to the commission staff outside of a formal proceeding be withheld from public disclosure on the ground that it contains trade secrets, privileged, or confidential commercial or financial information may deliver the information under seal to the commission staff, subject to the same protections afforded confidential information in formal proceedings.

5 VAC 5-20-180. Official transcript of hearing.

The official transcript of a hearing before the commission or a hearing examiner shall be that prepared by the court reporters retained by the commission and certified by the court reporter as a true and correct transcript of the proceeding. Transcripts of proceedings shall not be prepared except in cases assigned to a hearing examiner, when directed by the commission, or when requested by a party desiring to purchase a copy. Parties desiring to purchase copies of the transcript shall make arrangement for purchase with the court reporter. When a transcript is prepared, a copy thereof shall be made available for public inspection in the clerk's office. If the transcript includes confidential information, an expurgated or redacted version of the transcript shall be made available for public inspection in the clerk's office. Only the parties who have executed an agreement to adhere to a protective order or other arrangement for access to confidential treatment in such proceeding and the commission staff shall be entitled to access to an unexpurgated or unredacted version of the transcript. By agreement of the parties, or as the commission may by order provide, corrections may be made to the transcript.

5 VAC 5-20-190. Rules of evidence.

In proceedings under 5 VAC 5-20-90, and all other proceedings in which the commission shall be called upon to decide or render judgment only in its capacity as a court of record, the common law and statutory rules of evidence shall be as observed and administered by the courts of record of the Commonwealth. In other proceedings, evidentiary rules shall not be unreasonably used to prevent the receipt of evidence having substantial probative effect.

5 VAC 5-20-200. Briefs.

Written briefs may be authorized at the discretion of the commission, except in proceedings under 5 VAC 5-20-100 A, where briefs may be filed by right. The time for filing briefs and reply briefs, if authorized, shall be set at the time they are authorized. The commission may limit the length of a brief. The commission may by order provide for the electronic filing or service of briefs.

5 VAC 5-20-210. Oral argument.

The commission may authorize oral argument, limited as the commission may direct, on any pertinent matter at any time during the course of the proceeding.

5 VAC 5-20-220. Petition for rehearing or reconsideration.

Final judgments, orders, and decrees of the commission, except judgments prescribed by § 12.1-36 of the Code of Virginia, and except as provided in §§ 13.1-614 and 13.1-813 of the Code of Virginia, shall remain under the control of the commission and subject to modification or vacation for 21 days after the date of entry. Except for good cause shown, a petition for rehearing or reconsideration must be filed not later than 20 days after the date of entry of the judgment, order, or decree. The filing of a petition will not suspend the execution of the judgment, order, or decree, nor extend the time for taking an appeal, unless the commission, within the 21 day period following entry of the final judgment, order or decree, shall provide for a suspension in an order or decree granting the petition. A petition for rehearing or reconsideration must be served on all parties and delivered to commission staff counsel on or before the day on which it is filed. The commission will not entertain responses to, or requests for oral argument on, a petition. An order granting a rehearing or reconsideration will be served on all parties and commission staff counsel by the Clerk of the Commission.

5 VAC 5-20-230. Extension of time.

The commission may, at its discretion, grant a continuance, postponement, or extension of time for the filing of a document or the taking of an action required or permitted by these rules, except for petitions for rehearing or reconsideration filed pursuant to 5 VAC 5-20-220. Except for good cause shown, motions for extensions shall be made in writing, served on all parties and commission staff counsel, and filed with the commission at least three days prior to the date the action sought to be extended is due.

PART IV. DISCOVERY AND HEARING PREPARATION PROCEDURES.

5 VAC 5-20-240. Prepared testimony and exhibits.

Following the filing of an application dependent upon complicated or technical proof, the commission may direct the applicant to prepare and file the testimony and exhibits by which the applicant expects to establish its case. In all proceedings in which an applicant is required to file testimony, respondents shall be permitted and may be directed by the commission or hearing examiner to file, on or before a date certain, testimony and exhibits by which they expect to establish their case. Any respondent that chooses not to file testimony and exhibits by that date may not thereafter present testimony or exhibits except by leave of the commission, but may otherwise fully participate in the proceeding and engage in cross-examination of the testimony and exhibits of commission staff and other parties. The commission staff also shall file testimony and exhibits when directed to do so by the commission. Failure to comply with the directions of the commission, without good cause shown, may result in rejection of the testimony and exhibits by the commission. With leave of the commission and unless a timely objection is made, the commission staff or a party may correct or supplement any prepared testimony and exhibits before or during the hearing. In all proceedings, all evidence must be verified by the witness before introduction into the record, and the admissibility of the evidence shall be subject to the same standards as if the testimony were offered orally at hearing, unless, with the consent of the commission, the staff and all parties stipulate the introduction of testimony without need for verification. An original and 15 copies of prepared testimony and exhibits shall be filed unless otherwise specified in the commission's scheduling order and public notice, or unless the testimony and exhibits are filed electronically and otherwise comply with these rules. Documents of unusual bulk or weight and physical exhibits other than documents need not be filed in advance, but shall be described and made available for pretrial examination.

5 VAC 5-20-250. Process, witnesses, and production of documents and things.

A. *Subpoenas.* — Commission staff and any party to a proceeding shall be entitled to process, to convene parties, to compel the attendance of witnesses, and to compel the production of books, papers, documents, or things provided in this rule.

B. *Commission issuance and enforcement of other regulatory agency subpoenas.* — Upon motion by commission staff counsel, the commission may issue and enforce subpoenas at the request of a regulatory agency of another jurisdiction if the activity for which the information is sought by the other agency, if occurring in the Commonwealth, would be a violation of the laws of the Commonwealth that are administered by the commission.

A motion requesting the issuance of a commission subpoena shall include:

1. A copy of the original subpoena issued by the regulatory agency to the named defendant;

2. An affidavit of the requesting agency administrator stating the basis for the issuance of the subpoena under that state's laws; and

3. A memorandum from the commission's corresponding division director providing the basis for the issuance of the commission subpoena.

C. *Document subpoenas.* — In a pending proceeding, at the request of commission staff or any party, the Clerk of the Commission shall issue a subpoena. When a matter is under investigation by commission staff, before a formal proceeding has been established, whenever it appears to the commission by affidavit filed with the Clerk of the Commission by the commission staff or an individual, that a book, writing, document, or thing sufficiently described in the affidavit, is in the possession, or under the control, of an identified person and is material and proper to be produced, the commission may order the Clerk of the Commission to issue a subpoena and to have the subpoena duly served, together with an attested copy of the commission's order compelling production at a reasonable place and time as described in the commission's order.

D. *Witnesse subpoenas.* — In a pending proceeding, at the request of commission staff or any party, the Clerk of the Commission shall issue a subpoena.

5 VAC 5-20-260. Interrogatories or requests for production of documents and things.

The commission staff and any party in a formal proceeding before the commission, other than a proceeding under 5 VAC 5-20-100 A, may serve written interrogatories or requests for production of documents upon a party, to be answered by the party served, or if the party served is an entity, by an officer or agent of the entity, who shall furnish to the staff or requesting party information as is known. Interrogatories or requests for production of documents, including workpapers pursuant to 5 VAC 5-20-270, that cannot be timely answered before the scheduled hearing date may be served only with leave of the commission for good cause shown and upon such conditions as the commission may prescribe. Such otherwise untimely interrogatories or requests for production of documents, including workpapers pursuant to 5 VAC 5-20-270, may not be served until such leave is granted. Interrogatories or requests for production of documents may be served upon a member of the commission staff, or an expert or consultant filing testimony on behalf of the commission staff, in a proceeding under 5 VAC 5-20-80 to discover: (i) factual information that supports the workpapers submitted by the staff pursuant to 5 VAC 5-20-270, including electronic spreadsheets that include underlying formulas and assumptions; (ii) any other documents relied upon as a basis for recommendations or assertions in prefiled testimony, staff reports or exhibits filed by staff, or by an expert or consultant filing testimony on behalf of the staff; or (iii) the identity of other formal proceedings in which an expert or consultant filing testimony on behalf of the staff testified regarding the same or a substantially similar subject matter. The disclosure of communications within the commission shall not be required and, except for good cause shown, no interrogatories or requests for production of documents may be served upon a member of the commission staff, or an expert or consultant filing testimony on behalf of the staff, prior to the filing of staff's testimony. All interrogatories and requests for production of documents shall be filed with the Clerk of the Commission. Responses to interrogatories and requests for production of documents shall not be filed with the Clerk of the Commission.

The response to each interrogatory or document request shall identify by name the person making the response. Any objection to an interrogatory or document request shall identify the interrogatory or document request to which the objection is raised, and shall state with specificity the basis and supporting legal theory for the objection. Objections shall be served with the list of responses or in such manner as the commission may designate by order. Responses and objections to interrogatories or requests for production of documents shall be served within 10 days of receipt, unless otherwise ordered by the commission. Upon motion promptly made and accompanied by a copy of the interrogatory or document request and the response or objection that is subject to the motion, the commission will rule upon the validity of the objection; the objection otherwise will be considered sustained.

Interrogatories or requests for production of documents may relate to any matter not privileged, which is relevant to the subject matter involved, including the existence, description, nature, custody, condition, and location of any books, documents, or other tangible things, and the identity and location of persons having knowledge of evidentiary value. It is not grounds for objection that the information sought will be inadmissible at the hearing if the information appears reasonably calculated to lead to the discovery of admissible evidence.

Where the response to an interrogatory or document request may only be derived or ascertained from the business records of the party questioned, from an examination, audit, or inspection of business records, or from a compilation, abstract, or summary of business records, and the burden of deriving or ascertaining the response is substantially the same for one entity as for the other, a response is sufficient if it: (i) identifies by name and location all records from which the response may be derived or ascertained; and (ii) tenders to the inquiring party reasonable opportunity to examine, audit, or inspect the records subject to objection as to their proprietary or confidential nature. The inquiring party bears the expense of making copies, compilations, abstracts, or summaries.

5 VAC 5-20-270. Hearing preparation.

In a formal proceeding, a party or the commission staff may serve on a party a request to examine the workpapers supporting the testimony or exhibits of a witness whose prepared testimony has been filed in accordance with 5 VAC 5-20-240. The movant may request abstracts or summaries of the workpapers, and may request copies of the workpapers upon payment of the reasonable cost of duplication or reproduction. Copies requested by the commission staff shall be furnished without payment of copying costs. In actions pursuant to 5 VAC 5-20-80 A, the commission staff shall, upon the filing of its testimony, exhibits, or report, provide (in either paper or electronic format) a copy of any workpapers that support the recommendations made in its testimony or report to any party upon request and may additionally file a copy of such workpapers with the Clerk of the Commission. The Clerk of the Commission shall make any filed workpapers available for public inspection and copying during regular business hours.

5 VAC 5-20-280. Discovery applicable only to 5 VAC 5-20-90 proceedings.

This rule applies only to a proceeding in which a defendant is subject to a monetary penalty or injunction, or revocation, cancellation, or curtailment of a license, certificate of authority, registration, or similar authority previously issued by the commission to the defendant.

1. *Discovery of material in possession of the Commission staff.* Upon written motion of the defendant, the commission shall permit the defendant to inspect and, at the defendant's expense, copy or photograph (exclusive of investigative notes): (i) any relevant written or recorded statements, the existence of which is known, after reasonable inquiry, by the commission staff counsel assigned to the matter to be within the custody, possession, or control of commission staff, made by (a) the defendant, or representatives or agents of the defendant if the defendant is other than an individual, or (b) any witness whom the commission staff intends, or does not intend, to call to testify at the hearing, to a commission staff member or law enforcement officer; (ii) designated books, tangible objects, papers, documents, or copies or portions thereof, that are within the custody, possession, or control of commission staff and that commission staff intends to introduce into evidence at the hearing or that the commission staff obtained for the purpose of the instant proceeding; and (iii) the list of the witnesses that commission staff intends to call to testify at the hearing. Upon good cause shown to protect the identity of persons not named as a defendant, the commission or hearing examiner may direct the commission staff to withhold disclosure of material requested under this rule. The term "statement" as used in relation to any witness (other than a defendant) described in clause (i) of this subdivision includes a written statement made by said witness and signed or otherwise adopted or approved by him, and verbatim transcriptions or recordings of a witness' statement that are made contemporaneously with the statement by the witness.

A motion by the defendant or staff under this rule shall be filed and served at least 30 days before the hearing date. The motion shall include all relief sought. A subsequent motion may be made only upon a showing of cause as to why the motion would be in the interest of justice. An order or ruling granting relief under this rule shall specify the time, place, and manner of making discovery and inspection permitted, and may prescribe such terms and conditions as the commission may determine.

Upon written motion of the commission staff, staff may also obtain the list of witnesses that the defendant intends to call to testify at the hearing, and inspect, copy, and photograph, at commission staff's expense, the evidence that the defendant intends to introduce into evidence at the hearing.

The commission staff and the defendant shall be required to produce the information described above as directed by the commission or hearing examiner, but not later than 10 days prior to the scheduled hearing; and the admission of any additional evidence not provided in accordance herewith shall not be denied solely on the basis that it was not produced timely, provided the additional evidence was produced to commission staff or the defendant as soon as practicable prior to the hearing, or prior to the introduction of such evidence at the hearing. The requirement to produce the information described in this section shall be in addition to any requirement by commission staff or the defendant to timely respond to an interrogatory or document request made pursuant to 5 VAC 5-20-260.

Nothing in this rule shall require the disclosure of any information, the disclosure of which is prohibited by statute or other legal privilege. The disclosure of the results of a commission staff investigation or work product of commission staff counsel shall not be required.

2. *Depositions.* After commencement of a proceeding to which this rules applies, the commission staff or a party may take the testimony of (i) a party, or (ii) a person not a party for good cause shown to the commission or hearing examiner, other than a member of the commission staff, by deposition on oral examination or by written questions. Depositions may be used for any purpose for which they may be used in the courts of record of the Commonwealth. Except where the commission or hearing examiner finds that an emergency exists, no deposition may be taken later than 10 days in advance of the formal hearing. The attendance of witnesses at depositions may be compelled by subpoena. Examination and cross-examination of the witness shall be as at hearing. Depositions may be taken in the City of Richmond or in the town, city, or county in which the deposed person resides, is employed, or does business. The parties and the commission staff, by agreement, may designate another place for the taking of the deposition. Reasonable notice of the intent to take a deposition must be given in writing to the commission staff counsel and to each party to the action, stating the time and place where the deposition is to be taken. A deposition may be taken before any person (the "officer") authorized to administer oaths by the laws of the jurisdiction in which the deposition is to be taken. The officer shall certify his or her authorization in writing, administer the oath to the deponent, record or cause to be recorded the testimony given, and note any objections raised. In lieu of participating in the oral examination, a party or the commission staff may deliver sealed written questions to the officer, who shall propound the questions to the witness. The officer may terminate the deposition if convinced that the examination is being conducted in bad faith or in an unreasonable manner. Costs of the deposition shall be borne by the party noticing the deposition, unless otherwise ordered by the commission.

3. *Requests for admissions.* The commission staff or a party to the proceeding may serve upon a party written requests for admission. Each matter on which an admission is requested shall be stated separately. A matter shall be deemed admitted unless within 21 days of the service of the request, or some other period the commission may designate, the party to whom the request is directed serves upon the requesting party a written answer addressing or objecting to the request. The response shall set forth in specific terms a denial of the matter set forth or an explanation as to the reasons the responding party cannot truthfully admit or deny the matter set forth. Requests for admission shall be filed with the Clerk of the Commission and simultaneously served on commission staff counsel and on all parties to the proceeding.

Index to Rules of State Corporation Commission

A

ADMISSIBILITY OF EVIDENCE.
Exhibits and testimony, 5 VAC 5-20-240.

ADMISSIONS.
Discovery in adjudicatory proceedings, 5 VAC 5-20-280.

AFFIDAVITS.
Subpoenas, 5 VAC 5-20-250.

AGENTS.
Interrogatories, answer, 5 VAC 5-20-260.
Pleadings.
Signatures required, 5 VAC 5-20-20.
Requests for production of documents, answer, 5 VAC 5-20-260.

ANSWER TO REQUESTS FOR ADMISSIONS, 5 VAC 5-20-280.

ANSWER TO RULE TO SHOW CAUSE, 5 VAC 5-20-90.

APPLICABILITY OF RULES, 5 VAC 5-20-10.

APPLICATIONS, 5 VAC 5-20-80.
Copies and format, 5 VAC 5-20-150.
Exhibits and testimony, 5 VAC 5-20-240.
Memorandum of completeness, 5 VAC 5-20-160.
Rate applications, 5 VAC 5-20-160.

ATTORNEYS AT LAW.
Authorized to appear, 5 VAC 5-20-30.
Commission counsel.
Subpoenas, 5 VAC 5-20-250.
Consumer counsel, 5 VAC 5-20-30.
Pleadings.
Signatures required, 5 VAC 5-20-20.

B

BRIEFS.
Copies and format, 5 VAC 5-20-150.
Written briefs, 5 VAC 5-20-200.

BROADCASTING OF PROCEEDINGS, 5 VAC 5-20-40.

BURDEN OF PROOF.
Adjudicatory proceedings, 5 VAC 5-20-90.

BUSINESS RECORDS, 5 VAC 5-20-260.

C

CALENDARS.
Extension of time, 5 VAC 5-20-230.
Holidays and weekends.
Filing of pleadings, 5 VAC 5-20-140.

COMMISSION STAFF.
Commission and hearing examiners may confer with, 5 VAC 5-20-50.
Discovery in adjudicatory proceedings, 5 VAC 5-20-280.

COMMISSION STAFF —Cont'd
Exhibits and testimony, 5 VAC 5-20-240.
Ex parte proceedings, 5 VAC 5-20-40, 5 VAC 5-20-60.
Memorandum of completeness, 5 VAC 5-20-160.
Participation in proceedings, 5 VAC 5-20-80, 5 VAC 5-20-100.
Subpoenas, 5 VAC 5-20-250.
Work papers, 5 VAC 5-20-260.
Requests to examine work papers, 5 VAC 5-20-270.

CONFIDENTIAL INFORMATION, 5 VAC 5-20-170.

CONSULTANTS.
Interrogatories or requests for production of documents, service upon, 5 VAC 5-20-260.
Subpoena of witnesses.
Discovery in adjudicatory proceedings, 5 VAC 5-20-280.

CONTINUANCES, 5 VAC 5-20-230.

D

DECLARATORY JUDGMENTS, 5 VAC 5-20-100.

DEFAULT JUDGMENTS.
Failure to answer petitions, 5 VAC 5-20-100.
Failure to answer rule to show cause, 5 VAC 5-20-90.

DEFENSES.
Petitions, 5 VAC 5-20-100.
Rule to show cause, 5 VAC 5-20-90.

DEPOSITIONS.
Discovery in adjudicatory proceedings, 5 VAC 5-20-280.

DISCOVERY.
Adjudicatory proceedings, 5 VAC 5-20-280.

E

ELECTRONIC MEDIA, 5 VAC 5-20-40.

ELECTRONIC PLEADINGS, 5 VAC 5-20-20.
Briefs, 5 VAC 5-20-200.
Confidential information.
Expurgated or redacted versions, 5 VAC 5-20-170.
Copies and format, 5 VAC 5-20-150.
Filing and service, 5 VAC 5-20-140.

EXHIBITS, 5 VAC 5-20-240.
Copies and format, 5 VAC 5-20-150.

EXPERTS.
Interrogatories or requests for production of documents, service upon, 5 VAC 5-20-260.
Subpoena of witnesses.
Discovery in adjudicatory proceedings, 5 VAC 5-20-280.

EXTENSION OF TIME, 5 VAC 5-20-230.

F

FACSIMILE PLEADINGS, 5 VAC 5-20-140.

H

HEARING EXAMINERS.
Proceedings before hearing examiners, 5 VAC 5-20-120.
Transcripts, 5 VAC 5-20-180.

I

INFORMAL COMPLAINTS, 5 VAC 5-20-70.

INTERROGATORIES, 5 VAC 5-20-260.

M

MEMORANDUM OF COMPLETENESS, 5 VAC 5-20-160.

MOTIONS.
Adjudicatory proceedings, initiation of, 5 VAC 5-20-90.
Discovery in adjudicatory proceedings.
Material in possession of commission staff, 5 VAC 5-20-280.
Extension of time, 5 VAC 5-20-230.
Generally, 5 VAC 5-20-110.
Interrogatories, objection to, 5 VAC 5-20-260.
Oral motions, 5 VAC 5-20-20.
Request for production of documents, objection to, 5 VAC 5-20-260.
Subpoenas for other regulatory agencies, 5 VAC 5-20-250.

N

NOTICE AND PUBLICATION.
Promulgation of general orders, rules or regulations, 5 VAC 5-20-100.

NOTICE OF PARTICIPATION AS A RESPONDENT.
Regulatory proceedings, 5 VAC 5-20-80.

O

OATHS.
Depositions.
Discovery in adjudicatory proceedings, 5 VAC 5-20-280.

ORAL ARGUMENT, 5 VAC 5-20-210.
Petitions for rehearing or reconsideration, 5 VAC 5-20-220.

P

PARTNERSHIPS.
Pleadings.
Signatures required, 5 VAC 5-20-20.

PETITIONS.
Copies and format, 5 VAC 5-20-150.

PETITIONS —Cont'd
Non-adjudicatory proceedings, 5 VAC 5-20-100.
Rehearing or reconsideration, 5 VAC 5-20-220.
Extension of time, 5 VAC 5-20-230.

PHOTOGRAPHS, 5 VAC 5-20-40.

PLEADINGS.
Amendments, 5 VAC 5-20-130.
Copies and format, 5 VAC 5-20-150.
Electronic pleadings, 5 VAC 5-20-20, 5 VAC 5-20-140.
Exhibits and testimony, 5 VAC 5-20-240.
Extension of time, 5 VAC 5-20-230.
Filing, 5 VAC 5-20-140.
Good faith, 5 VAC 5-20-20.
Signatures required, 5 VAC 5-20-20.

PROCEEDINGS.
Adjudicatory proceedings, 5 VAC 5-20-90.
Applications.
Exhibits and testimony, 5 VAC 5-20-240.
Filing of applications, 5 VAC 5-20-80, 5 VAC 5-20-150.
Memorandum of completeness, 5 VAC 5-20-160.
Briefs, 5 VAC 5-20-150, 5 VAC 5-20-200.
Confidential information, 5 VAC 5-20-170.
Discovery in adjudicatory proceedings, 5 VAC 5-20-280.
Evidence rules, 5 VAC 5-20-190.
Exhibits and testimony, 5 VAC 5-20-240.
Extension of time, 5 VAC 5-20-230.
Hearing examiners, 5 VAC 5-20-120.
Interrogatories, 5 VAC 5-20-260.
Motions generally, 5 VAC 5-20-110.
Objections to rulings by hearing examiners, 5 VAC 5-20-120.
Oral argument, 5 VAC 5-20-210.
Petitions for rehearing or reconsideration, 5 VAC 5-20-220.
Petitions in non-adjudicatory proceedings, 5 VAC 5-20-100.
Pleadings.
Amendment of pleadings, 5 VAC 5-20-130.
Exhibits and testimony, 5 VAC 5-20-240.
Extension of time, 5 VAC 5-20-230.
Filing of pleadings, 5 VAC 5-20-140, 5 VAC 5-20-150.
Signatures required, 5 VAC 5-20-20.
Promulgation of general orders, rules or regulations, 5 VAC 5-20-100.
Regulatory proceedings, 5 VAC 5-20-80.
Requests for production of documents, 5 VAC 5-20-260.
Requests to examine work papers, 5 VAC 5-20-270.
Rule to show cause, 5 VAC 5-20-90.
Subpoenas, 5 VAC 5-20-250.
Witnesses, 5 VAC 5-20-280.
Transcripts, 5 VAC 5-20-180.

PRODUCTION OF DOCUMENTS, 5 VAC 5-20-260.
Subpoenas, 5 VAC 5-20-250.

PROMULGATION OF GENERAL ORDERS, RULES OR REGULATIONS, 5 VAC 5-20-100.

PRO SE REPRESENTATION.
Hearings, 5 VAC 5-20-30.
Pleadings.
Signatures required, 5 VAC 5-20-20.

PROTECTIVE ORDERS.
Confidential information, 5 VAC 5-20-170.

PUBLIC WITNESSES, 5 VAC 5-20-80.

R

REPORTS.
Response to hearing examiners' reports, 5 VAC 5-20-120.

RULES OF EVIDENCE, 5 VAC 5-20-190.

RULE TO SHOW CAUSE.
Initiation of proceedings, 5 VAC 5-20-90.

S

SELF REPRESENTATION.
Hearings, 5 VAC 5-20-30.
Pleadings.
Signatures required, 5 VAC 5-20-20.

SERVICE OF PROCESS.
Electronic service, 5 VAC 5-20-140.
Petitions, 5 VAC 5-20-100.
Pleadings, 5 VAC 5-20-140.

SIGNATURES.
Pleadings, 5 VAC 5-20-20.

SUBPOENAS.
Generally, 5 VAC 5-20-250.

SUBPOENAS —Cont'd
Other regulatory agency subpoenas, 5 VAC 5-20-250.
Witnesses, 5 VAC 5-20-280.

T

TRANSCRIPTS, 5 VAC 5-20-180.

V

VENUE.
Depositions.
Discovery in adjudicatory proceedings, 5 VAC 5-20-280.

W

WAIVER OR MODIFICATION OF RULES, 5 VAC 5-20-10.

WITNESSES.
Public witnesses, 5 VAC 5-20-80.
Requests to examine work papers supporting witnesses' testimony, 5 VAC 5-20-270.
Subpoena of witnesses, 5 VAC 5-20-250.
Discovery in adjudicatory proceedings, 5 VAC 5-20-280.

FEDERAL RULES OF CIVIL PROCEDURE

The following rules were adopted by order of the Supreme Court on December 20, 1937, and became effective on September 16, 1938. They have been amended since their adoption.

Title I. Scope of Rules — Form of Action.

Rule
1. Scope and Purpose.
2. One Form of Action.

Title II. Commencing an Action; Service of Process, Pleadings, Motions, and Orders

3. Commencing an Action.
4. Summons.
4.1. Serving Other Process.
5. Serving and Filing Pleadings and Other Papers.
5.1. Constitutional Challenge to a Statute — Notice, Certification, and Intervention.
5.2. Privacy Protection For Filings Made with the Court.
6. Computing and Extending Time; Time for Motion Papers.

Title III. Pleadings and Motions.

7. Pleadings Allowed; Form of Motions and Other Papers.
7.1. Disclosure Statement.
8. General Rules of Pleading.
9. Pleading Special Matters.
10. Form of Pleadings.
11. Signing Pleadings, Motions, and Other Papers; Representations to the Court; Sanctions.
12. Defenses and Objections: When and How Presented; Motion for Judgment on the Pleadings; Consolidating Motions; Waiving Defenses; Pretrial Hearing.
13. Counterclaim and Crossclaim.
14. Third-Party Practice.
15. Amended and Supplemental Pleadings.
16. Pretrial Conferences; Scheduling; Management.

Title IV. Parties.

17. Plaintiff and Defendant; Capacity; Public Officers.
18. Joinder of Claims.
19. Required Joinder of Parties.
20. Permissive Joinder of Parties.
21. Misjoinder and Nonjoinder of Parties.
22. Interpleader.
23. Class Actions.
23.1. Derivative Actions.
23.2. Actions Relating to Unincorporated Associations.
24. Intervention.
25. Substitution of Parties.

Title V. Disclosures and Discovery.

26. Duty to Disclose; General Provisions Governing Discovery.

Rule
27. Depositions to Perpetuate Testimony.
28. Persons Before Whom Depositions May Be Taken.
29. Stipulations About Discovery Procedure.
30. Depositions by Oral Examination.
31. Depositions by Written Questions.
32. Using Depositions in Court Proceedings.
33. Interrogatories to Parties.
34. Producing Documents, Electronically Stored Information, and Tangible Things, or Entering onto Land, for Inspection and Other Purposes.
35. Physical and Mental Examinations.
36. Requests for Admission.
37. Failure to Make Disclosures or to Cooperate in Discovery; Sanctions.

Title VI. Trials.

38. Right to a Jury Trial; Demand.
39. Trial by Jury or by the Court.
40. Scheduling Cases for Trial.
41. Dismissal of Actions.
42. Consolidation; Separate Trials.
43. Taking Testimony.
44. Proving an Official Record.
44.1. Determining Foreign Law.
45. Subpoena.
46. Objecting to a Ruling or Order.
47. Selecting Jurors.
48. Number of Jurors; Verdict; Polling.
49. Special Verdict; General Verdict and Questions.
50. Judgment as a Matter of Law in a Jury Trial; Related Motion for a New Trial; Conditional Ruling.
51. Instructions to the Jury; Objections; Preserving a Claim of Error.
52. Findings and Conclusions by the Court; Judgment on Partial Findings.
53. Masters.

Title VII. Judgment.

54. Judgments; Costs.
55. Default; Default Judgment.
56. Summary Judgment.
57. Declaratory Judgment.
58. Entering Judgment.
59. New Trial; Altering or Amending a Judgment.
60. Relief from a Judgment or Order.
61. Harmless Error.
62. Stay of Proceedings to Enforce a Judgment.
62.1. Indicative Ruling on a Motion for Relief That is Barred by a Pending Appeal.
63. Judge's Inability to Proceed.

Title VIII. Provisional and Final Remedies.

Rule
64. Seizing a Person or Property.
65. Injunctions and Restraining Orders.
65.1. Proceedings Against a Surety.
66. Receivers.
67. Deposit into Court.
68. Offer of Judgment.
69. Execution.
70. Enforcing a Judgment for a Specific Act.
71. Enforcing Relief For or Against a Nonparty.

Title IX. Special Proceedings.

71.1. Condemning Real or Personal Property.
72. Magistrate Judges: Pretrial Order.
73. Magistrate Judges: Trial by Consent; Appeal.
74. — 76. (Abrogated.)

Title X. District Courts and Clerks: Conducting Business; Issuing Orders.

77. Conducting Business; Clerk's Authority; Notice of an Order or Judgment.
78. Hearing Motions; Submission on Briefs.
79. Records Kept by the Clerk.
80. Stenographic Transcript as Evidence.

Title XI. General Provisions.

81. Applicability of the Rules in General; Removed Actions.
82. Jurisdiction and Venue Unaffected.
83. Rules by District Courts; Judge's Directives.
84. Forms.
85. Title.
86. Effective Dates.

Forms.

Form
1. Caption.
2. Date, Signature, Address, E-mail Address, and Telephone Number.
3. Summons.
4. Summons on a Third-Party Complaint.
5. Notice of a Lawsuit and Request to Waive Service of a Summons.
6. Waiver of the Serivce of Summons.
7. Statement of Jurisdiction.
8. Statement of Reasons for Omitting a Party.
9. Statement Noting a Party's Death.
10. Complaint to Recover a Sum Certain.
11. Complaint for Negligence.
12. Complaint for Negligence When the Plaintiff Does Not Know Who Is Responsible.
13. Complaint for Negligence Under the Federal Employers' Liability Act.
14. Complaint for Damages Under the Merchant Marine Act.
15. Complaint for the Conversion of Property.
16. Third-Party Complaint.
17. Complaint for Specific Performance of a Contract to Convey Land.
18. Complaint for Patent Infringement.
19. Complaint for Copyright Infringement and Unfair Competition.
20. Complaint for interpleader and Declaratory Relief.
21. Complaint on a Claim for a Debt and to Set Aside a Fradulent Conveyance Under Rule 18(b).
30. Answer Presenting Defenses Under Rule 12(b).
31. Answer to a Complaint for Money Had and Received with a Counterclaim for Interpleader.
40. Motion to Dismiss Under Rules 12(b) for Lack of Jurisdiction, Improper Venue, Insufficient Service of Process, or Failure to State a Claim.
41. Motion to Bring in a Third-Party Defendant.
42. Motion to Intervene as a Defendant Under Rule 24.
50. Request to Produce Documents and Tangible Things, or to Enter onto Land Under Rule 34.
51. Request for Admissions Under Rule 36.
52. Report of the Parties' Planning Meeting.
60. Notice of Condemnation.
61. Complaint for Condemnation.
70. Judgment on a Jury Verdict.
71. Judgment by the Court without a Jury.
80. Notice of a Magistrate Judge's Availability.
81. Consent to an Assignment to a Magistrate Judge.
82. Order of Assignment to a Magistrate Judge.

Supplemental Rules for Admiralty or Maritime Claims and Asset Forfeiture Actions.

A. Scope of Rules.
B. In Personam Actions: Attachment and Garnishment.
C. In Rem Actions: Special Provisions.
D. Possessory, Petitory and Partition Actions.
E. Actions in Rem and Quasi in Rem: General Provisions.
F. Limitation of Liability.
G. Forfeiture Actions In Rem.
Index.

Cross references. — See **www.uscourts.gov/rules**.

TITLE I. SCOPE OF RULES — FORM OF ACTION.

Rule 1. Scope and Purpose.

These rules govern the procedure in all civil actions and proceedings in the United States district courts, except as stated in Rule 81. They should be construed and administered to secure the just, speedy, and inexpensive determination of every action and proceeding. (Amended by order adopted December 29, 1948, effective October 20, 1949, by order adopted February 28, 1966, effective July 1, 1966, by order adopted April 22, 1993, effective December 1, 1993, and by order adopted April 30, 2007, effective December 1, 2007.)

Comment. — The language of Rule 1 has been amended as part of the general restyling of the Civil Rules to make them more easily understood and to make style and terminology consistent throughout the rules. These changes are intended to be stylistic only.

The merger of law, equity, and admiralty practice is complete. There is no need to carry forward the phrases that initially accomplished the merger.

The former reference to "suits of a civil nature" is changed to the more modern "actions and proceedings." This change does not affect such questions as whether the Civil Rules apply to summary proceedings created by statute. See *SEC v. McCarthy,* 322 F.3d 650 (9th Cir. 2003); see also *New Hampshire Fire Ins. Co. v. Scanlon,* 362 U.S. 404 (1960).

Law Review. — For article, "Amending the Federal Rules of Civil Procedure," see 4 Wash. & Lee L. Rev. 1 (1946). For a survey of Civil Procedure in the 4th Cir., see 39 Wash. & Lee L. Rev. 479 (1982). For article discussing the idea that the Federal Rules of Civil Procedure are trans-substantive, see "The Transformation of Trans-Substantivity," 49 Wash. & Lee. L. Rev. 1501 (1992).

CASE NOTES

Rules govern questions of procedure. — Ordinarily, questions of procedure in the federal courts are governed by the federal rules and by federal decisions interpreting and supplementing them, and questions of substantive law by the rules prevailing in the courts of the several states. Lachman v. Pennsylvania Greyhound Lines, 160 F.2d 496 (4th Cir. 1947).

Rule recognizes distinction in nature of suits. — This rule, while providing for uniformity of procedure in all civil suits, recognizes the distinction in the nature of such suits. Carter Coal Co. v. Litz, 54 F. Supp. 115 (W.D. Va. 1943), aff'd, 140 F.2d 934 (4th Cir. 1944).

Rules are followed in bankruptcy proceedings. — The Federal Rules of Civil Procedure are to be followed in bankruptcy proceedings in accordance with General Order No. 37, so long as they are not inconsistent with the Bankruptcy Act. In re W. Auto Assoc. Store, 295 F. Supp. 566 (W.D. Va. 1968).

Burden of proving rule to be substantive in nature. — A strong presumption exists that the Supreme Court, in prescribing the federal rules, acted within the scope of its power. Anyone contending that a rule having been prescribed by the Supreme Court as a rule of procedure is substantive in nature, and a constitutional attack amounts to such a contention, carries a heavy burden. Helms v. Richmond-Petersburg Tpk. Auth., 52 F.R.D. 530 (E.D. Va. 1971).

Rules of civil procedure applicable in proceeding to recover personal property where no criminal proceeding pending. In re J.W. Schonfeld, Ltd., 460 F. Supp. 332 (E.D. Va. 1978).

Applied in United States v. Schlitz, 9 F.R.D. 259 (E.D. Va. 1949); American Gen. v. Equitable Gen., 87 F.R.D. 736 (E.D. Va. 1980); Jop v. City of Hampton, 163 F.R.D. 486 (E.D. Va. 1995); Plett v. United States, 185 F.3d 216 (4th Cir. 1999).

Rule 2. One Form of Action.

There is one form of action — the civil action. (Amended by order adopted April 30, 2007, effective December 1, 2007.)

Comment. — The language of Rule 2 has been amended as part of the general restyling of the Civil Rules to make them more easily understood and to make style and terminology consistent throughout the rules. These changes are intended to be stylistic only.

CASE NOTES

Under the rules there is only one action — a civil action — in which all claims may be joined and all remedies are available. Sperry Rand Corp. v. A-T-O, Inc., 447 F.2d 1387 (4th Cir. 1971), vacating in part Sperry Rand Corp. v. Electronic Concepts, Inc., 325 F. Supp. 1209 (E.D. Va. 1970), cert. denied, 405 U.S. 1017, 92 S. Ct. 1292, 31 L. Ed. 2d 479, 409 U.S. 892, 93 S. Ct. 117, 34 L. Ed. 2d 150 (1972).

Principles of equity have not been discarded. — The Federal Rules of Civil Procedure have abolished the procedural distinctions between law and equity by providing for one form of action in all civil cases, and have largely discarded the terms "at law" or "in equity" as legal nomenclature. But they have not abolished or discarded the principles of equity, nor their application in appropriate cases. Carter Coal Co. v. Litz, 54 F. Supp. 115 (W.D. Va. 1943), aff'd, 140 F.2d 934 (4th Cir. 1944).

TITLE II. COMMENCING AN ACTION; SERVICE OF PROCESS, PLEADINGS, MOTIONS, AND ORDERS.

Rule 3. Commencing an Action.

A civil action is commenced by filing a complaint with the court. (Amended by order adopted April 30, 2007, effective December 1, 2007.)

Comment. — The caption of Rule 3 has been amended as part of the general restyling of the Civil Rules to make them more easily understood and to make style and terminology consistent throughout the rules. These changes are intended to be stylistic only.

CASE NOTES

Delivering complaint to officer of court is sufficient. — It is sufficient that the complaint is delivered to an officer of the court who is authorized to receive it. Greeson v. Sherman, 265 F. Supp. 340 (W.D. Va. 1967).

Hence, delivery to deputy clerk at home at night is proper. — There was no impropriety in plaintiff's method of filing his complaint, where his counsel delivered the complaint at night to the home of the deputy clerk, who marked it "filed" and accepted the filing fee by check. Greeson v. Sherman, 265 F. Supp. 340 (W.D. Va. 1967).

Delivery to prison authorities. — The complaint was "filed" within the meaning of this rule and Federal Rules of Civil Procedure 5(e) when the prisoner delivered the complaint to prison authorities for mailing to the clerk of the district court. Lewis v. Richmond City Police Dep't, 947 F.2d 733 (4th Cir. 1991).

For statute of limitation purposes, complaint may be considered "filed" as of the date of its receipt, even if it is not docketed, and summons will not issue until the appropriate fee is paid. Wells v. Apfel, 103 F. Supp. 2d 893 (W.D. Va. 2000).

Filing in forma pauperis. — A complaint was considered filed the date it was received by the clerk's office, even though the filing fee was not included and plaintiff's in forma pauperis application was denied. Wells v. Apfel, 103 F. Supp. 2d 893 (W.D. Va. 2000).

Applied in Austin v. Reynolds Metals Co., 327 F. Supp. 1145 (E.D. Va. 1970); Leathers v. Serrell, 376 F. Supp. 983 (W.D. Va. 1974); Greene v. Brown, 451 F. Supp. 1266 (E.D. Va. 1978); Keith v. Heckler, 603 F. Supp. 150 (E.D. Va. 1985); Unsecured Creditors Comm. v. Marepcon Fin. Corp., 907 F.2d 1430 (4th Cir. 1990).

Rule 4. Summons.

(a) *Contents, Amendments.* — (1) Contents. A summons must:

(A) name the court and the parties;

(B) be directed to the defendant;

(C) state the name and address of the plaintiff's attorney or — if unrepresented — of the plaintiff;

(D state the time within which the defendant must appear and defend;

(E) notify the defendant that a failure to appear and defend will result in a default judgment against the defendant for the relief demanded in the complaint;

(F) be signed by the clerk; and

(G) bear the court's seal.

(2) Amendments. The court may permit a summons to be amended.

(b) *Issuance.* — On or after filing the complaint, the plaintiff may present a summons to the clerk for signature and seal. If the summons is properly completed, the clerk must sign, seal, and issue it to the plaintiff for service on the defendant. A summons — or a copy of a summons that is addressed to multiple defendants — must be issued for each defendant to be served.

(c) *Service.* — (1) In General. A summons must be served with a copy of the complaint. The plaintiff is responsible for having the summons and complaint served within the time allowed by Rule 4(m) and must furnish the necessary copies to the person who makes service.

(2) By Whom. Any person who is at least 18 years old and not a party may serve a summons and complaint.

(3) By a Marshal or Someone Specially Appointed. At the plaintiff's request, the court may order that service be made by a United States marshal or deputy marshal or by a person specially appointed by the court. The court must so order if the plaintiff is authorized to proceed in forma pauperis under 28 U.S.C. § 1915 or as a seaman under 28 U.S.C. § 1916.

(d) *Waiving Service.* — (1) Requesting a Waiver. An individual, corporation, or association that is subject to service under Rule 4(e), (f), or (h) has a duty to avoid unnecessary expenses of serving the summons. The plaintiff may notify such a defendant that an action has been commenced and request that the defendant waive service of a summons. The notice and request must:

(A) be in writing and be addressed:

(i) to the individual defendant; or

(ii) for a defendant subject to service under Rule 4(h), to an officer, a managing or general agent, or any other agent authorized by appointment or by law to receive service of process;

(B) name the court where the complaint was filed;

(C) be accompanied by a copy of the complaint, 2 copies of a waiver form, and a prepaid means for returning the form;

(D) inform the defendant, using text prescribed in Form 5, of the consequences of waiving and not waiving service;

(E) state the date when the request is sent;

(F) give the defendant a reasonable time of at least 30 days after the request was sent — or at least 60 days if sent to the defendant outside any judicial district of the United States — to return the waiver; and

(G) be sent by first-class mail or other reliable means.

(2) Failure to Waive. If a defendant located within the United States fails, without good cause, to sign and return a waiver requested by a plaintiff located within the United States, the court must impose on the defendant:

(A) the expenses later incurred in making service; and

(B) the reasonable expenses, including attorney's fees, of any motion required to collect those service expenses.

(3) Time to Answer After a Waiver. A defendant who, before being served with process, timely returns a waiver need not serve an answer to the complaint until 60 days after the request was sent — or until 90 days after it was sent to the defendant outside any judicial district of the United States.

(4) Results of Filing a Waiver. When the plaintiff files a waiver, proof of service is not required and these rules apply as if a summons and complaint had been served at the time of filing the waiver.

(5) Jurisdiction and Venue Not Waived. Waiving service of a summons does not waive any objection to personal jurisdiction or to venue.

(e) *Serving an Individual Within a Judicial District of the United States.* — Unless federal law provides otherwise, an individual — other than a minor, an incompetent person, or a person whose waiver has been filed — may be served in a judicial district of the United States by:

(1) following state law for serving a summons in an action brought in courts of general jurisdiction in the state where the district court is located or where service is made; or

(2) doing any of the following:

(A) delivering a copy of the summons and of the complaint to the individual personally;

(B) leaving a copy of each at the individual's dwelling or usual place of abode with someone of suitable age and discretion who resides there; or

(C) delivering a copy of each to an agent authorized by appointment or by law to receive service of process.

(f) *Serving an Individual in a Foreign Country.* — Unless federal law provides otherwise, an individual — other than a minor, an incompetent person, or a person whose waiver has been filed — may be served at a place not within any judicial district of the United States:

(1) by any internationally agreed means of service that is reasonably calculated to give notice, such as those authorized by the Hague Convention on the Service Abroad of Judicial and Extrajudicial Documents;

(2) if there is no internationally agreed means, or if an international agreement allows but does not specify other means, by a method that is reasonably calculated to give notice:

(A) as prescribed by the foreign country's law for service in that country in an action in its courts of general jurisdiction;

(B) as the foreign authority directs in response to a letter rogatory or letter of request; or

(C) unless prohibited by the foreign country's law, by:

(i) delivering a copy of the summons and of the complaint to the individual personally; or

(ii) using any form of mail that the clerk addresses and sends to the individual and that requires a signed receipt; or

(3) by other means not prohibited by international agreement, as the court orders.

(g) *Serving a Minor or an Incompetent Person.* — A minor or an incompetent person in a judicial district of the United States must be served by following state law for serving a summons or like process on such a defendant in an action brought in the courts of general jurisdiction of the state where service is made. A minor or an incompetent person who is not within any judicial district of the United States must be served in the manner prescribed by Rule 4(f)(2)(A), (f)(2)(B), or (f)(3).

(h) *Serving a Corporation, Partnership, or Association.* — Unless federal law provides otherwise or the defendant's waiver has been filed, a domestic or foreign corporation, or a partnership or other unincorporated association that is subject to suit under a common name, must be served:

(1) in a judicial district of the United States:

(A) in the manner prescribed by Rule 4(e)(1) for serving an individual; or

(B) by delivering a copy of the summons and of the complaint to an officer, a managing or general agent, or any other agent authorized by appointment or by law to receive service of process and — if the agent is one authorized by statute and the statute so requires — by also mailing a copy of each to the defendant; or

(2) at a place not within any judicial district of the United States, in any manner prescribed by Rule 4(f) for serving an individual, except personal delivery under (f)(2)(C)(i).

(i) *Serving the United States and Its Agencies, Corporations, Officers, or Employees.* — (1) United States. To serve the United States, a party must:

(A)(i) deliver a copy of the summons and of the complaint to the United States attorney for the district where the action is brought — or to an assistant United States attorney or clerical employee whom the United States attorney designates in a writing filed with the court clerk — or

(ii) send a copy of each by registered or certified mail to the civil-process clerk at the United States attorney's office;

(B) send a copy of each by registered or certified mail to the Attorney General of the United States at Washington, D.C.; and

(C) if the action challenges an order of a nonparty agency or officer of the United States, send a copy of each by registered or certified mail to the agency or officer.

(2) Agency; Corporation; Officer or Employee Sued in an Official Capacity. To serve a United States agency or corporation, or a United States officer or employee sued only in an official capacity, a party must serve the United States and also send a copy of the summons and of the complaint by registered or certified mail to the agency, corporation, officer, or employee.

(3) Officer or Employee Sued Individually. To serve a United States officer or employee sued in an individual capacity for an act or omission occurring in connection with duties performed on the United States' behalf (whether or not the officer or employee is also sued in an official capacity), a party must serve the United States and also serve the officer or employee under Rule 4(e), (f), or (g).

(4) Extending Time. The court must allow a party a reasonable time to cure its failure to:

(A) serve a person required to be served under Rule 4(i)(2), if the party has served either the United States attorney or the Attorney General of the United States; or

(B) serve the United States under Rule 4(i)(3), if the party has served the United States officer or employee.

(j) *Serving a Foreign, State, or Local Government.* — (1) Foreign State. A foreign state or its political subdivision, agency, or instrumentality must be served in accordance with 28 U.S.C. § 1608.

(2) State or Local Government. A state, a municipal corporation, or any other state-created governmental organization that is subject to suit must be served by:

(A) delivering a copy of the summons and of the complaint to its chief executive officer; or

(B) serving a copy of each in the manner prescribed by that state's law for serving a summons or like process on such a defendant.

(k) *Territorial Limits of Effective Service.* — (1) In General. Serving a summons or filing a waiver of service establishes personal jurisdiction over a defendant:

(A) who is subject to the jurisdiction of a court of general jurisdiction in the state where the district court is located;

(B) who is a party joined under Rule 14 or 19 and is served within a judicial district of the United States and not more than 100 miles from where the summons was issued; or

(C) when authorized by a federal statute.

(2) Federal Claim Outside State-Court Jurisdiction. For a claim that arises under federal law, serving a summons or filing a waiver of service establishes personal jurisdiction over a defendant if:

(A) the defendant is not subject to jurisdiction in any state's courts of general jurisdiction; and

(B) exercising jurisdiction is consistent with the United States Constitution and laws.

(*l*) *Proving Service.* — (1) Affidavit Required. Unless service is waived, proof of service must be made to the court. Except for service by a United States marshal or deputy marshal, proof must be by the server's affidavit.

(2) Service Outside the United States. Service not within any judicial district of the United States must be proved as follows:

(A) if made under Rule 4(f)(1), as provided in the applicable treaty or convention; or

(B) if made under Rule 4(f)(2) or (f)(3), by a receipt signed by the addressee, or by other evidence satisfying the court that the summons and complaint were delivered to the addressee.

(3) Validity of Service; Amending Proof. Failure to prove service does not affect the validity of service. The court may permit proof of service to be amended.

(m) *Time Limit for Service.* — If a defendant is not served within 120 days after the complaint is filed, the court — on motion or on its own after notice to the plaintiff — must dismiss the action without prejudice against that defendant or order that service be made within a specified time. But if the plaintiff shows good cause for the failure, the court must extend the time for service for an appropriate period. This subdivision (m) does not apply to service in a foreign country under Rule 4(f) or 4(j)(1).

(n) *Asserting Jurisdiction over Property or Assets.* — (1) Federal Law. The court may assert jurisdiction over property if authorized by a federal statute. Notice to claimants of the property must be given as provided in the statute or by serving a summons under this rule.

(2) State Law. On a showing that personal jurisdiction over a defendant cannot be obtained in the district where the action is brought by reasonable efforts to serve a summons under this rule, the court may assert jurisdiction over the defendant's assets found in the district. Jurisdiction is acquired by seizing the assets under the circumstances and in the manner provided by state law in that district. (Amended by order adopted January 21, 1963, effective July 1, 1963, by order adopted February 28, 1966, effective July 1, 1966, by order adopted April 29, 1980, effective August 1, 1980, by P.L. 97-462, approved January 12, 1983, effective February 28, 1983, by order adopted March 2, 1987, effective August 1, 1987, by order adopted April 22, 1993, effective December 1, 1993, by order adopted April 17, 2000, effective December 1, 2000, and by order adopted April 30, 2007, effective December 1, 2007.)

Comment. — The language of Rule 4 has been amended as part of the general restyling of the Civil Rules to make them more easily understood and to make style and terminology consistent throughout the rules. These changes are intended to be stylistic only.

Rule 4(d)(1)(C) corrects an inadvertent error in former Rule 4(d)(2)(G). The defendant needs two copies of the waiver form, not an extra copy of the notice and request.

Rule 4(g) changes "infant" to "minor." "Infant" in the present rule means "minor." Modern word usage suggests that "minor" will better maintain the intended meaning. The same change from "infant" to "minor" is made throughout the rules. In addition, subdivision (f)(3) is added to the description of methods of service that the court may order; the addition ensures the evident intent that the court not order service by means prohibited by international agreement.

Rule 4(i)(4) corrects a misleading reference to "the plaintiff" in former Rule 4(i)(3). A party other than a plaintiff may need a reasonable time to effect service. Rule 4(i)(4) properly covers any party.

Former Rule 4(j)(2) refers to service upon an "other governmental organization subject to suit." This is changed to "any other state-created governmental organization that is subject to suit." The change entrenches the meaning indicated by the caption ("Serving a Foreign, State, or Local Government"), and the invocation of state law. It excludes any risk that this rule might be read to govern service on a federal agency, or other entities not created by state law.

Law Review. — For article, "Service of Process: Rethinking the Theory and Procedure of Serving Process under Federal Rule 4(c)," see 73 Va. L. Rev 1183 (1987). For article, "Federalism, Forum Shopping, and the Foreign Injury Paradox," see 51 Wm. and Mary L. Rev. 87 (2009).

CASE NOTES

Effect of the 1979 amendments to subdivision (a) of this rule is that a motion to extend the time must be filed no later than 30 days after the expiration of the original appeal period in order for a court of appeals to have jurisdiction over the appeal. A bare notice of appeal should not be construed as a motion for extension of time, where no request for additional time is manifest. Shah v. Hutto, 722 F.2d 1167 (4th Cir. 1983), cert. denied, 466 U.S. 975, 104 S. Ct. 2354, 80 L. Ed. 2d 827 (1984).

Effect of 1993 amendment. — Under subdivision (m), plaintiff must show good cause for his failure to effect service within 120 day period to defeat defendant's motion to dismiss. The 1993 amendment to subdivision (m) has not changed this concept. Sullivan v. Hall, 222 Bankr. 275 (Bankr. E.D. Va. 1998).

Actual notice of action. — While the Federal Rules of Civil Procedure are to be followed and not ignored, actual notice of an action will cause the rules governing service of process to be "liberally interpreted," meaning that every "technical violation of the rule or failure of strict compliance may not invalidate the service of process." Selman v. American Sports Underwriters, Inc., 697 F. Supp. 225 (W.D. Va. 1988).

Actual notice does not cure defects in service. Notice of an adversary proceeding received by means other than those authorized by statute or rule cannot serve to bring defendant within the Court's jurisdiction. Sullivan v. Hall, 222 Bankr. 275 (Bankr. E.D. Va. 1998).

Service must be in manner prescribed by applicable state laws. — Defendants who are not residents of, or found within, the state in which the district court is held must be served with process in the manner prescribed by the applicable laws of the state in which the district court is held. Barry v. Whalen, 796 F. Supp. 885 (E.D. Va. 1992).

Failure to diligently serve results in dismissal with prejudice. — Pursuant to this rule, a summons and complaint in an adversary proceeding are to be served on the defendant and counsel within 120 days or such further time period as ordered by the court for cause; if a plaintiff is not diligent and fails to serve the complaint, the case shall be dismissed without prejudice unless plaintiff demonstrates good cause not to dismiss the action; once plaintiff fails to establish good cause, dismissal is mandatory, and plaintiff must refile the action before the court can consider plaintiff's claim; then upon refiling, plaintiff is subject to all time defenses even if the effect of dismissal "is to bar plaintiff's claim," as in this case. Mrochek v. Oprean, 189 Bankr. 616 (Bankr. E.D. Va. 1995).

Even though considering complaint "filed" as of date of receipt could pose problems with securing service in a timely fashion under subsection (m) of this rule, an action may still be subject to dismissal if the plaintiff delayed payment of the filing fee and did not serve the defendant with the complaint within the 120-period required by subsection (m). Wells v. Apfel, 103 F. Supp. 2d 893 (W.D. Va. 2000).

Service may be in manner authorized by state statute. — A party not an inhabitant or not found within the state in which the district court is held may be served with a summons in federal court in the manner prescribed by a statute of the state in which the court is sitting. Olin Mathieson Chem. Corp. v. Molins Orgs., Ltd., 261 F. Supp. 436 (E.D. Va. 1966).

Such as "long-arm" statute. — Under new subdivision (e), entitled "Service upon Party Not Inhabitant of or Found Within State," there is no question but that a federal court can use the new Virginia "long-arm" statute, § 8.01-328.1, to extend its jurisdiction over nonresident defendants. Jackson v. National Linen Serv. Corp., 248 F. Supp. 962 (W.D. Va. 1965); Etzler v. Dille & McGuire Mfg. Co., 249 F. Supp. 1 (W.D. Va. 1965).

Where service is effectuated under a state long-arm statute, the permissible reach of process rendering jurisdiction over the person is to be determined by the applicable standard as proclaimed by that state. Alabama Great S.R.R. v. Allied Chem. Co., 312 F. Supp. 3 (E.D. Va. 1970), rev'd on other grounds, 467 F.2d 679 (4th Cir. 1972).

Where plaintiff seaman attempted service of process upon the foreign owner of a vessel under the Virginia long-arm statute, subdivision (e) required the federal court to look to the state law to determine if service was valid. Elefteriou v. Tanker Archontissa, 443 F.2d 185 (4th Cir. 1971).

An individual may be served in a federal suit by utilizing the state long arm statutes, so long as the individual has certain "minimum contacts" with the forum state. Awalt v. Whalen, 809 F. Supp. 414 (E.D. Va. 1992).

Although case involves federal question. — Service of process in accordance with the state statute is available although the case concerns a federal question, such as a patent infringement action. Olin Mathieson Chem. Corp. v. Molins Orgs., Ltd., 261 F. Supp. 436 (E.D. Va. 1966).

Federal rule as to service of process inapplicable to suit in state court. — Nothing in the United States Code, or more particularly in the Federal Tort Claims Act, required plaintiff to comply with the Federal Rules of Civil Procedure regarding service of process in filing his suit in state court. Therefore, it cannot successfully be argued that the 30-day period for removal of actions did not begin to run because plaintiff did not comply with this rule in serving process upon the defendant. Williams v. Farmers Home Admin., 623 F. Supp. 1175 (E.D. Va. 1985).

Validity of actual service of complaint pursuant to this rule may be determined by reference to state law. Allied Towing Corp. v. Great E. Petro. Corp., 642 F. Supp. 1339 (E.D. Va. 1986).

Validity of service on nonresident defendant controlled by law of forum state. — Absent a federal statute expressly authorizing nationwide service of process, the validity of service on a nonresident defendant is controlled by the law of the forum state. Allied Towing Corp. v. Great E. Petro. Corp., 642 F. Supp. 1339 (E.D. Va. 1986).

Generally, the application of long-arm statutes involves two steps. — It is necessary to determine first whether the statute permits service of process on the nonresident defendant, and second, whether service under the statute violates the due process clause of the federal constitution. Haynes v. James H. Carr, Inc., 427 F.2d 700 (4th Cir. 1970), aff'g, 307 F. Supp. 1228 (E.D. Va. 1969), cert. denied, 400 U.S. 942, 91 S. Ct. 238, 27 L. Ed. 2d 245 (1970).

Unless expressly provided, service can only be made within state where court sits. — The provisions of subdivision (f) require that, unless otherwise provided by a federal statute or other federal rule of procedure, process can be served only within the territorial limits of the state in which the district court is held. This rule is merely an enunciation of the principle that it is a basic tenet of justice and due process that the power of a court to render a judgment in personam is limited and dependent on the presence of the defendant within the territorial jurisdiction of the court. V & V Mining Supply, Inc. v. Matway, 295 F. Supp. 643 (W.D. Va. 1969).

Unless it be waived, jurisdiction in personam requires valid service of process within the territorial limits of Virginia. While § 8.01-301, provides for service on a foreign corporation, and former § 13.1-111 (see now § 13.1-766) provides how such process may be served, it is required both by Virginia and federal law that the corporation be doing business or transacting affairs in Virginia under the facts of this case to constitute valid service. Goldrick v. D.M. Picton Co., 56 F.R.D. 639 (E.D. Va. 1971).

Service on successors or representatives of deceased party. — The nonparties for whom Rule 25(a)(1) and subdivision (d)(1) of this rule mandate personal service are evidently the "successors or representatives of the deceased party." This conclusion follows both from the language of Rule 25(a)(1), which refers to no other nonparties, and from the rule's underlying policies. Rule 25(a)(1) directs that both parties and appropriate nonparties be served with the suggestion of death to commence the 90-day substitution period, for the rule seeks "to assure the parties to the action and other concerned persons of notice of the death so that they may take appropriate action to make substitution for the deceased party." Fariss v. Lynchburg Foundry, 769 F.2d 958 (4th Cir. 1985).

Subdivision (e) permits service on person not within state pursuant to state statute. — Subdivision (e) allows process to be served on a person not found within the state in which the district court is held if such service is made under the circumstances and in the manner prescribed by an applicable statute of such state. V & V Mining Supply, Inc. v. Matway, 295 F. Supp. 643 (W.D. Va. 1969).

But if service cannot be made within state or pursuant to state "long-arm" statute, jurisdiction is lacking. — Where it is obvious that the defendant was not personally present in the State of Virginia to accept service of process pursuant to subdivision (f), nor has the defendant transacted business in the State of Virginia such as would make him amenable to service under § 8.01-329, the proceeding should be dismissed for lack of jurisdiction. V & V Mining Supply, Inc. v. Matway, 295 F. Supp. 643 (W.D. Va. 1969).

Under subdivisions (e) and (f) of this rule, a Michigan corporation that was directed by a bankruptcy referee in the eastern district of Virginia to turn over monies allegedly owed a bankrupt estate, was amenable to process outside Virginia only if a federal or Virginia statute so provided, and then only if there were minimal contacts. Collins v. Carmen Cosmetics, Inc., 465 F.2d 693 (4th Cir. 1972).

Service of process outside the Commonwealth does not provide the court with jurisdiction over defendants where they have no contacts with the Commonwealth. Awalt v. Whalen, 809 F. Supp. 414 (E.D. Va. 1992).

Subsection (j) does not apply to service properly effected pursuant to subsection (i). Selman v. American Sports Underwriters, Inc., 697 F. Supp. 225 (W.D. Va. 1988).

Service in class action against unions and members. — In a suit against an unincorporated brotherhood of railroad employees the inquiry was not whether the service was sufficient in a suit against the brotherhood as an entity under its common name (where the provision of subdivision (d)(3) would be applicable), but whether the joinder and service upon members of the brotherhood was sufficient to bring them as a class before the court in a class suit under Rule 23(a). Two subordinate lodges within the court's jurisdiction were joined, one was unquestionably served, and service was made upon the local chairman of the other. The member who was served was not only chairman of a subordinate lodge but was also representative of the brotherhood, as bargaining agent, in enforcing the rights of employees under their trade agreement with the railway company. This service, as a matter of fact, did bring the brotherhood in, fighting. It cannot be contended with any show of reason that the chairman and the subordinate lodge, who were admittedly served, were not fairly representative of the membership of the brotherhood, or that service upon them would not give adequate notice to the class sued to come in and defend; and this is the criterion as to the sufficiency of joinder and service in a class suit. Tunstall v. Brotherhood of Locomotive Firemen & Enginemen, 148 F.2d 403 (4th Cir. 1945).

Service on federal agency. — Where the federal housing administration is doing business within a district and has present an agent in charge of its affairs, there is no reason why service of process cannot be made upon it and upon the United States, whose representative it is, in accordance with the provisions of subdivision (d)(4) and (5). Seven Oaks, Inc. v. Federal Hous. Admin., 171 F.2d 947 (4th Cir. 1948).

In a suit against the federal housing administration, the agency is duly served with process by service upon the state director and upon the United States attorney and the Attorney General of the United States. Seven Oaks, Inc. v. Federal Hous. Admin., 171 F.2d 947 (4th Cir. 1948).

Method of service not explicitly authorized under local law invalid. — The Hague Convention is appropriately and sensibly read as allowing only those methods of service explicitly sanctioned by the contracting state, and since service of a summons upon a Quebec resident via hand delivery by a private process server is not explicitly authorized, such service is insufficient for a federal district court to obtain personal jurisdiction over the person so served. ePlus Tech., Inc. v. Aboud, 155 F. Supp. 2d 692, 2001 U.S. Dist. LEXIS 11799 (E.D. Va. 2001).

Good cause. — Courts have consistently held inadvertence of counsel does not constitute good cause. Sullivan v. Hall, 222 Bankr. 275 (Bankr. E.D. Va. 1998).

Agents who may be served for associations or corporations. — An association or corporation certainly ought not be heard to say that agents through which it transacts the very business for which it is organized and through which it collects funds in a given territory are not agents of such character that process may be served upon them. Tunstall v. Brotherhood of Locomotive Firemen & Enginemen, 148 F.2d 403 (4th Cir. 1945).

Service on parent or subsidiary corporations. — The doing of business of a subsidiary corporation in a state does not, without more confer jurisdiction over the nonresident parent corporation. Nor does service of process on the parent company permit the court to exercise personal jurisdiction over a wholly owned subsidiary, if they are two separate distinct entities and so operate. Goldrick v. D.M. Picton Co., 56 F.R.D. 639 (E.D. Va. 1971).

Attorney General was not empowered to accept service for unnamed state officials. — Where plaintiff's complaint referred to unnamed officials of the Commonwealth of Virginia, and where plaintiff had apparently attempted to complete service by serving the Attorney General of Virginia, this official was not empowered to accept service of process on behalf of other officials of the Commonwealth, and accordingly, plaintiff failed to adequately provide for service of process on unnamed officials. Jeffress v. Titius, 756 F. Supp. 255 (W.D. Va. 1990), aff'd, 925 F.2d 1456 (4th Cir. 1991).

Patent infringement. — Personal service may be effected under the Virginia long-arm statute in a case involving allegations of patent infringement, since a patent infringement is a tort. Marston v. Gant, 351 F. Supp. 1122 (E.D. Va. 1972).

Amendment cannot be permitted to prejudice substantial rights of parties. — Under subdivision (h) of this rule, the court cannot permit an amendment when it would materially prejudice the substantial rights of the defendant. Phillip v. Sam Finley, Inc., 270 F. Supp. 292 (W.D. Va. 1967).

Plaintiffs could seek leave of court to amend their complaint to add a new party where motion to amend was filed at a very early stage in the litigation and would not prejudice the newly joined defendant, who was notified of this action within the period for service of a summons and complaint. United States ex rel. Tucker v. Thomas Howell Kiewit (USA) Inc., 149 F.R.D. 125 (E.D. Va. 1993).

"Single act" within state is sufficient for application of rule in conjunction with state long-arm statute. — See Darden v. Heck's, Inc., 459 F. Supp. 727 (W.D. Va. 1978).

Defective summons held harmless error. — Although a summons was defective because its caption indicated the parties only by the reference "see complaint," such error was harmless, where a copy of the complaint, with the names of all parties, was attached to the summons, and defendant was not prejudiced by the defect. Newman v. Prior, 518 F.2d 97 (4th Cir. 1975), overruled on other grounds, Newcome v. Esrey, 862 F.2d 1099 (4th Cir. 1988).

Harmless error in form of summons. — Although a summons was defective because its caption indicated the parties only by the reference "see complaint" such error was harmless, where a copy of the complaint, with the names of all parties was attached to the summons, and the defendant, contrary to the preliminary pretrial order, neither moved to dismiss for defective process nor sought to have the summons amended. Although the summons did not literally comply with subdivision (b) of this rule, the defendant has and therefore was not prejudiced by the defect. Newman v. Prior, 518 F.2d 97 (4th Cir. 1975), overruled on other grounds, Newcome v. Esrey, 862 F.2d 1099 (4th Cir. 1988).

Third-party defendant served without destroying diversity jurisdiction. — Where the plaintiff in his action refused to join a party who was jointly and severally liable with the defendant because such joinder would have destroyed the diversity jurisdiction of the federal district court, if the defendant felt apprehensive that it could have been held liable as principle for the acts of the party not joined, the defendant was free to bring that party into the action as a third-party defendant and have him served with process under subdivision (f) of this rule. Such action would have protected the defendant without depriving the court of the subject matter jurisdiction over the diversity action. Willis v. Semmes, Bowen & Semmes, 441 F. Supp. 1235 (E.D. Va. 1977).

Mere return receipt will not satisfy acknowledgement requirement. — A plaintiff may certainly use registered or certified mail to effect service under subsection (c)(2)(C)(ii); however, a mere return receipt for the registered mail will not satisfy the "acknowledgement" requirement of the rule. Selman v. American Sports Underwriters, Inc., 697 F. Supp. 225 (W.D. Va. 1988).

Service not prescribed by foreign law is not prohibited by that law. — A mode of service of process that is not prescribed by foreign law is not "prohibited" by that law within the meaning of subdivision (f)(2)(C). Dee-K Enters. Inc. v. Heveafil SDN. BHD., 174 F.R.D. 376 (E.D. Va. 1997).

Invalid form of service is not necessarily prohibited form of service. — An ineffective or invalid form of service is not necessarily a prohibited form of service, i.e., a form of service that violates a foreign country's law. Dee-K Enters. Inc. v. Heveafil SDN. BHD., 174 F.R.D. 376 (E.D. Va. 1997).

Applied in Devier v. George Cole Motor Co., 27 F. Supp. 978 (W.D. Va. 1939); Trueblood v. Grayson Shops of Tenn., Inc., 32 F.R.D. 190 (E.D. Va. 1963); Snow v. Clark, 263 F. Supp. 66 (W.D. Va. 1967); Atkins v. Schmutz Mfg. Co., 268 F. Supp. 406 (W.D. Va. 1967); Willis v. Weinberger, 385 F. Supp. 1092 (E.D. Va. 1974); Davis H. Elliot Co. v. Caribbean Utils. Co., 64 F.R.D. 594 (W.D. Va. 1974); Causey v. Pan Am. World Airways, Inc., 66 F.R.D. 392 (E.D.

Va. 1975); American Gen. v. Equitable Gen., 87 F.R.D. 736 (E.D. Va. 1980); United Coal Co. v. Land Use Corp., 575 F. Supp. 1148 (W.D. Va. 1983); Crosson v. Conlee, 745 F.2d 896 (4th Cir. 1984); National Trust for Historic Preservation v. 1750 K Inv. Partnership, 100 F.R.D. 483 (E.D. Va. 1984); Philipp Bros. v. M/V Ocea, 144 F.R.D. 312 (E.D. Va. 1992); Board of Trustees v. McD Metals, Inc., 964 F. Supp. 1040 (E.D. Va. 1997); Johnson v. United Steel Workers, 172 F.R.D. 185 (W.D. Va. 1997); In re Motorsports Merchandise Antitrust Litig., 186 F.R.D. 344 (W.D. Va. 1999); American Chiropractic Ass'n v. Trigon Healthcare, Inc., 151 F. Supp. 2d 723, 2001 U.S. Dist. LEXIS 10348 (W.D. Va. 2001).

Rule 4.1. Serving Other Process.

(a) *In General.* — Process — other than a summons under Rule 4 or a subpoena under Rule 45 — must be served by a United States marshal or deputy marshal or by a person specially appointed for that purpose. It may be served anywhere within the territorial limits of the state where the district court is located and, if authorized by a federal statute, beyond those limits. Proof of service must be made under Rule 4(l).

(b) *Enforcing Orders: Committing for Civil Contempt.* — An order committing a person for civil contempt of a decree or injunction issued to enforce federal law may be served and enforced in any district. Any other order in a civil-contempt proceeding may be served only in the state where the issuing court is located or elsewhere in the United States within 100 miles from where the order was issued. (Added by order adopted April 22, 1993, effective December 1, 1993; amended by order adopted April 30, 2007, effective December 1, 2007.)

Comment. — The language of Rule 4.1 has been amended as part of the general restyling of the Civil Rules to make them more easily understood and to make style and terminology consistent throughout the rules. These changes are intended to be stylistic only.

Rule 5. Serving and Filing Pleadings and Other Papers.

(a) *Service: When Required.* — (1) In General. Unless these rules provide otherwise, each of the following papers must be served on every party:

(A) an order stating that service is required;

(B) a pleading filed after the original complaint, unless the court orders otherwise under Rule 5(c) because there are numerous defendants;

(C) a discovery paper required to be served on a party, unless the court orders otherwise;

(D) a written motion, except one that may be heard ex parte; and

(E) a written notice, appearance, demand, or offer of judgment, or any similar paper.

(2) If a Party Fails to Appear. No service is required on a party who is in default for failing to appear. But a pleading that asserts a new claim for relief against such a party must be served on that party under Rule 4.

(3) Seizing Property. If an action is begun by seizing property and no person is or need be named as a defendant, any service required before the filing of an appearance, answer, or claim must be made on the person who had custody or possession of the property when it was seized.

(b) *Service: How Made.* — (1) Serving an Attorney. If a party is represented by an attorney, service under this rule must be made on the attorney unless the court orders service on the party.

(2) Service in General. A paper is served under this rule by:

(A) handing it to the person;

(B) leaving it:

(i) at the person's office with a clerk or other person in charge or, if no one is in charge, in a conspicuous place in the office; or

(ii) if the person has no office or the office is closed, at the person's dwelling or usual place of abode with someone of suitable age and discretion who resides there;

(C) mailing it to the person's last known address — in which event service is complete upon mailing;

(D) leaving it with the court clerk if the person has no known address;

(E) sending it by electronic means if the person consented in writing — in which event service is complete upon transmission, but is not effective if the serving party learns that it did not reach the person to be served; or

(F) delivering it by any other means that the person consented to in writing — in which event service is complete when the person making service delivers it to the agency designated to make delivery.

(3) Using Court Facilities. If a local rule so authorizes, a party may use the court's transmission facilities to make service under Rule 5(b)(2)(E).

(c) *Serving Numerous Defendants.* — (1) In General. If an action involves an unusually large number of defendants, the court may, on motion or on its own, order that:

(A) defendants' pleadings and replies to them need not be served on other defendants;

(B) any crossclaim, counterclaim, avoidance, or affirmative defense in those pleadings and replies to them will be treated as denied or avoided by all other parties; and

(C) filing any such pleading and serving it on the plaintiff constitutes notice of the pleading to all parties.

(2) Notifying Parties. A copy of every such order must be served on the parties as the court directs.

(d) *Filing.* — (1) Required Filings; Certificate of Service. Any paper after the complaint that is required to be served — together with a certificate of service — must be filed within a reasonable time after service. But disclosures under Rule 26(a)(1) or (2) and the following discovery requests and responses must not be filed until they are used in the proceeding or the court orders filing: depositions, interrogatories, requests for documents or tangible things or to permit entry onto land, and requests for admission.

(2) How Filing Is Made — In General. A paper is filed by delivering it:

(A) to the clerk; or

(B) to a judge who agrees to accept it for filing, and who must then note the filing date on the paper and promptly send it to the clerk.

(3) Electronic Filing, Signing, or Verification. A court may, by local rule, allow papers to be filed, signed, or verified by electronic means that are consistent with any technical standards established by the Judicial Conference of the United States. A local rule may require electronic filing only if reasonable exceptions are allowed. A paper filed electronically in compliance with a local rule is a written paper for purposes of these rules.

(4) Acceptance by the Clerk. The clerk must not refuse to file a paper solely because it is not in the form prescribed by these rules or by a local rule or practice. (Amended by order adopted January 21, 1963, effective July 1, 1963, by order adopted March 30, 1970, effective July 1, 1970, by order adopted April 29, 1980, effective August 1, 1980, by order adopted March 2, 1987, effective August 1, 1987, by order adopted April 30, 1991, effective December 1, 1991, by order adopted April 22, 1993, effective December 1, 1993, by order adopted April 23, 1996, effective December 1, 1996, by order adopted April 17, 2000, effective December 1, 2000, by order adopted April 23, 2001, effective December 1, 2001, by order adopted April 12, 2006, effective December 1, 2006, and by order adopted April 30, 2007, effective December 1, 2007.)

Comment. — The language of Rule 5 has been amended as part of the general restyling of the Civil Rules to make them more easily understood and to make style and terminology consistent throughout the rules. These changes are intended to be stylistic only.

Rule 5(a)(1)(E) omits the former reference to a designation of record on appeal. Appellate Rule 10 is a self-contained provision for the record on appeal, and provides for service.

Former Rule 5(b)(2)(D) literally provided that a local rule may authorize use of the court's transmission facilities to make service by non-electronic means agreed to by the parties. That was not intended. Rule 5(b)(3) restores the intended meaning—court transmission facilities can be used only for service by electronic means.

Rule 5(d)(2)(B) provides that "a" judge may accept a paper for filing, replacing the reference in former Rule 5(e) to "the" judge. Some courts do not assign a designated judge to each case, and it may be important to have another judge accept a paper for filing even when a case is on the individual docket of a particular judge. The ministerial acts of accepting the paper, noting the time, and transmitting the paper to the court clerk do not interfere with the assigned judge's authority over the action.

CASE NOTES

Delivering complaint to court officer is sufficient. — It is sufficient that the complaint is delivered to an officer of the court who is authorized to receive it. Greeson v. Sherman, 265 F. Supp. 340 (W.D. Va. 1967).

Hence, delivery to deputy clerk at home at night is proper. — There was no impropriety in plaintiff's method of filing his complaint, where his counsel delivered the complaint at night to the home of the deputy clerk, who marked it "filed" and accepted the filing fee by check. Greeson v. Sherman, 265 F. Supp. 340 (W.D. Va. 1967).

Delivery to prison authorities. — The complaint was "filed" within the meaning of Federal Rules of Civil Procedure 3 and subdivision (e) of this rule when the prisoner delivered the complaint to prison authorities for mailing to the clerk of the district court. Lewis v. Richmond City Police Dep't, 947 F.2d 733 (4th Cir. 1991).

For statute of limitation purposes, complaint may be considered "filed" as of the date of its receipt, even if it is not docketed, and summons will not issue until the appropriate fee is paid. Wells v. Apfel, 103 F. Supp. 2d 893 (W.D. Va. 2000).

Filing in forma pauperis. — A complaint was considered filed the date it was received by the clerk's office, even though the filing fee was not included and plaintiff's in forma pauperis application was denied. Wells v. Apfel, 103 F. Supp. 2d 893 (W.D. Va. 2000).

Motion held timely filed. — See Fleming v. Citizens for Albemarle, Inc., 577 F.2d 236 (4th Cir. 1978), cert. denied, 439 U.S. 1071, 99 S. Ct. 842, 59 L. Ed. 2d 37 (1979).

Filing by facsimile transmission. — Implicit within subdivision (e) is the concept that, absent a local rule authorizing filing by facsimile, such filings are null. In re Fisherman's Wharf Fillet, Inc., 83 F. Supp. 2d 651 (E.D. Va. 1999).

Applied in United States v. O'Day, 667 F.2d 430 (4th Cir. 1981); Keith v. Heckler, 603 F. Supp. 150 (E.D. Va. 1985).

Rule 5.1. Constitutional Challenge to a Statute — Notice, Certification, and Intervention.

(a) *Notice by a Party.* — A party that files a pleading, written motion, or other paper drawing into question the constitutionality of a federal or state statute must promptly:

(1) file a notice of constitutional question stating the question and identifying the paper that raises it, if:

(A) a federal statute is questioned and the parties do not include the United States, one of its agencies, or one of its officers or employees in an official capacity; or

(B) a state statute is questioned and the parties do not include the state, one of its agencies, or one of its officers or employees in an official capacity; and

(2) serve the notice and paper on the Attorney General of the United States if a federal statute is questioned — or on the state attorney general if a state statute is questioned — either by certified or registered mail or by sending it to an electronic address designated by the attorney general for this purpose.

(b) *Certification by the Court.* — The court must, under 28 U.S.C. § 2403, certify to the appropriate attorney general that a statute has been questioned.

(c) *Intervention; Final Decision on the Merits.* — Unless the court sets a later time, the attorney general may intervene within 60 days after the notice is filed or after the court certifies the challenge, whichever is earlier. Before the time to intervene expires, the court may reject the constitutional challenge, but may not enter a final judgment holding the statute unconstitutional.

(d) *No Forfeiture.* — A party's failure to file and serve the notice, or the court's failure to certify, does not forfeit a constitutional claim or defense that is otherwise timely asserted. (Added by order adopted April 12, 2006, effective December 1, 2006; amended by order adopted April 30, 2007, effective December 1, 2007.)

Comment. — The language of Rule 5.1 has been amended as part of the general restyling of the Civil Rules to make them more easily understood and to make style and terminology consistent throughout the rules. These changes are intended to be stylistic only.

Rule 5.2. Privacy Protection For Filings Made with the Court.

(a) *Redacted Filings.* — Unless the court orders otherwise, in an electronic or paper filing with the court that contains an individual's social-security number, taxpayer-identification number, or birth date, the name of an individual known to be a minor, or a financial-account number, a party or nonparty making the filing may include only:

(1) the last four digits of the social-security number and taxpayer-identification number;

(2) the year of the individual's birth;

(3) the minor's initials; and

(4) the last four digits of the financial-account number.

(b) *Exemptions from the Redaction Requirement.* — The redaction requirement does not apply to the following:

(1) a financial-account number that identifies the property allegedly subject to forfeiture in a forfeiture proceeding;

(2) the record of an administrative or agency proceeding;

(3) the official record of a state-court proceeding;

(4) the record of a court or tribunal, if that record was not subject to the redaction requirement when originally filed;

(5) a filing covered by Rule 5.2(c) or (d); and

(6) a pro se filing in an action brought under 28 U.S.C. §§ 2241, 2254, or 2255.

(c) *Limitations on Remote Access to Electronic files; Social-Security Appeals and Immigration Cases.* — Unless the court orders otherwise, in an action for benefits under the Social Security Act, and in an action or proceeding relating to an order of removal, to relief from removal, or to immigration benefits or detention, access to an electronic file is authorized as follows:

(1) the parties and their attorneys may have remote electronic access to any part of the case file, including the administrative record;

(2) any other person may have electronic access to the full record at the courthouse, but may have remote electronic access only to:

(A) the docket maintained by the court; and

(B) an opinion, order, judgment, or other disposition of the court, but not any other part of the case file or the administrative record.

(d) *Filings Made Under Seal.* — The court may order that a filing be made under seal without redaction. The court may later unseal the filing or order the person who made the filing to file a redacted version for the public record.

(e) *Protective Orders.* — For good cause, the court may by order in a case:

(1) require redaction of additional information; or

(2) limit or prohibit a nonparty's remote electronic access to a document filed with the court.

(f) *Option for Additional Unredacted Filing Under Seal.* — A person making a redacted filing may also file an unredacted copy under seal. The court must retain the unredacted copy as part of the record.

(g) *Option for Filing a Reference List.* — A filing that contains redacted information may be filed together with a reference list that identifies each item of redacted information and specifies an appropriate identifier that uniquely corresponds to each item listed. The list must be filed under seal and may be amended as of right. Any reference in the case to a listed identifier will be construed to refer to the corresponding item of information.

(h) *Waiver of Protection of Identifiers.* — A person waives the protection of Rule 5.2(a) as to the person's own information by filing it without redaction and not under seal. (Added by order adopted April 30, 2007, effective December 1, 2007.)

Comment. — The rule is adopted in compliance with section 205(c)(3) of the E-Government Act of 2002, Public Law 107-347. Section 205(c)(3) requires the Supreme Court to prescribe rules "to protect privacy and security concerns relating to electronic filing of documents and the public availability . . . of documents filed electronically." The rule goes further than the E-Government Act in regulating paper filings even when they are not converted to electronic form. But the number of filings that remain in paper form is certain to diminish over time. Most districts scan paper filings into the electronic case file, where they become available to the public in the same way as documents initially filed in electronic form. It is electronic availability, not the form of the initial filing, that raises the privacy and security concerns addressed in the E-Government Act.

The rule is derived from and implements the policy adopted by the Judicial Conference in September 2001 to address the privacy concerns resulting from public access to electronic case files. *See* http://www.privacy.uscourts.gov/Policy.htm. The Judicial Conference policy is that documents in case files generally should be made available electronically to the same extent they are available at the courthouse, provided that certain "personal data identifiers" are not included in the public file.

While providing for the public filing of some information, such as the last four digits of an account number, the rule does not intend to establish a presumption that this information never could or should be protected. For example, it may well be necessary in individual cases to prevent remote access by nonparties to any part of an account number or social security number. It may also be necessary to protect information not covered by the redaction requirement — such as driver's license numbers and alien registration numbers — in a particular case. In such cases, protection may be sought under subdivision (d) or (e). Moreover, the Rule does not affect the protection available under other rules, such as Civil Rules 16 and 26(c), or under other sources of protective authority.

Parties must remember that any personal information not otherwise protected by sealing or redaction will be made available over the internet. Counsel should notify clients of this fact so that an informed decision may be made on what information is to be included in a document filed with the court.

The clerk is not required to review documents filed with the court for compliance with this rule. The responsibility to redact filings rests with counsel and the party or nonparty making the filing.

Subdivision (c) provides for limited public access in Social Security cases and immigration cases. Those actions are entitled to special treatment due to the prevalence of sensitive information and the volume of filings. Remote electronic access by nonparties is limited to the docket and the written dispositions of the court unless the court orders otherwise. The rule contemplates, however, that nonparties can obtain full access to the case file at the courthouse, including access through the court's public computer terminal.

Subdivision (d) reflects the interplay between redaction and filing under seal. It does not limit or expand the judicially developed rules that govern sealing. But it does reflect the possibility that redaction may provide an alternative to sealing.

Subdivision (e) provides that the court can by order in a particular case for good cause require more extensive redaction than otherwise required by the Rule. Nothing in this subdivision is intended to affect the limitations on sealing that are otherwise applicable to the court.

Subdivision (f) allows a person who makes a redacted filing to file an unredacted document under seal. This provision is derived from section 205(c)(3)(iv) of the E-Government Act.

Subdivision (g) allows the option to file a register of redacted information. This provision is derived from section 205(c)(3)(v) of the E-Government Act, as amended in 2004. In accordance with the E-Government Act, subdivision (g) refers to "redacted" information. The term "redacted" is intended to govern a filing that is prepared with abbreviated identifiers in the first instance, as well as a filing in which a personal identifier is edited after its preparation.

Subdivision (h) allows a person to waive the protections of the rule as to that person's own personal information by filing it unsealed and in unredacted form. One may wish to waive the protection if it is determined that the costs of redaction outweigh the benefits to privacy. If a person files an unredacted identifier by mistake, that person may seek relief from the court.

Trial exhibits are subject to the redaction requirements of Rule 5.2 to the extent they are filed with the court. Trial exhibits that are not initially filed with the court must be redacted in accordance with the rule if and when they are filed as part of an appeal or for other reasons.

Rule 6. Computing and Extending Time; Time for Motion Papers.

(a) *Computing Time.* — The following rules apply in computing any time period specified in these rules, in any local rule or court order, or in any statute that does not specify a method of computing time.

(1) Period Stated in Days or a Longer Unit. When the period is stated in days or a longer unit of time:

(A) exclude the day of the event that triggers the period;

(B) count every day, including intermediate Saturdays, Sundays, and legal holidays; and

(C) include the last day of the period, but if the last day is a Saturday, Sunday, or legal holiday, the period continues to run until the end of the next day that is not a Saturday, Sunday, or legal holiday.

(2) Period Stated in Hours. When the period is stated in hours:

(A) begin counting immediately on the occurrence of the event that triggers the period;

(B) count every hour, including hours during intermediate Saturdays, Sundays, and legal holidays; and

(C) if the period would end on a Saturday, Sunday, or legal holiday, the period continues to run until the same time on the next day that is not a Saturday, Sunday, or legal holiday.

(3) Inaccessibility of the Clerk's Office. Unless the court orders otherwise, if the clerk's office is inaccessible:

(A) on the last day for filing under Rule 6(a)(1), then the time for filing is extended to the first accessible day that is not a Saturday, Sunday, or legal holiday; or

(B) during the last hour for filing under Rule 6(a)(2), then the time for filing is extended to the same time on the first accessible day that is not a Saturday, Sunday, or legal holiday.

(4) "Last Day" Defined. Unless a different time is set by a statute, local rule, or court order, the last day ends:

(A) for electronic filing, at midnight in the court's time zone; and

(B) for filing by other means, when the clerk's office is scheduled to close.

(5) "Next Day" Defined. The "next day" is determined by continuing to count forward when the period is measured after an event and backward when measured before an event.

(6) "Legal Holiday" Defined. "Legal holiday" means:

(A) the day set aside by statute for observing New Year's Day, Martin Luther King Jr.'s Birthday, Washington's Birthday, Memorial Day, Independence Day, Labor Day, Columbus Day, Veterans' Day, Thanksgiving Day, or Christmas Day;

(B) any day declared a holiday by the President or Congress; and

(C) for periods that are measured after an event, any other day declared a holiday by the state where the district court is located.

(b) *Extending Time.* — (1) In General. When an act may or must be done within a specified time, the court may, for good cause, extend the time:

(A) with or without motion or notice if the court acts, or if a request is made, before the original time or its extension expires; or

(B) on motion made after the time has expired if the party failed to act because of excusable neglect.

(2) Exceptions. A court must not extend the time to act under Rules 50(b) and (d), 52(b), 59(b), (d), and (e), and 60(b).

(c) *Motions, Notices of Hearing, and Affidavits.* — (1) In General. A written motion and notice of the hearing must be served at least 14 days before the time specified for the hearing, with the following exceptions:

(A) when the motion may be heard ex parte;

(B) when these rules set a different time; or

(C) when a court order — which a party may, for good cause, apply for ex parte — sets a different time.

(2) Supporting Affidavit. Any affidavit supporting a motion must be served with the motion. Except as Rule 59(c) provides otherwise, any opposing affidavit must be served at least 7 days before the hearing, unless the court permits service at another time.

(d) *Additional Time After Certain Kinds of Service.* — When a party may or must act within a specified time after service and service is made under Rule 5(b)(2)(C), (D), (E), or (F), 3 days are added after the period would otherwise expire under Rule 6(a). (Amended by order adopted December 27, 1946, effective March 19, 1948, by order adopted January 21, 1963, effective July 1, 1963, by order adopted February 28, 1966, effective July 1, 1966, by order adopted December 4, 1967, effective July 1, 1968, by order adopted March 1, 1971, effective July 1, 1971, by order adopted April 28, 1983, effective August 1, 1983, by order adopted April 29, 1985, effective August 1, 1985, by order adopted March 2, 1987, effective August 1, 1987, by order adopted April 26, 1999, effective December 1, 1999, by order adopted April 23, 2001, effective December 1, 2001; by order April 25, 2005, effective December 1, 2005; by order adopted April 30, 2007, effective December 1, 2007; and by order adopted March 26, 2009, effective December 1, 2009.)

Comment. — The language of Rule 6 has been amended as part of the general restyling of the Civil Rules to make them more easily understood and to make style and terminology consistent throughout the rules. These changes are intended to be stylistic only.

CASE NOTES

Monthly or yearly periods run from numerical date to numerical date. Poston v. Ford, 34 Bankr. 93 (Bankr. W.D. Va. 1983), aff'd, 53 Bankr. 444 (Bankr. W.D. Va. 1984), 773 F.2d 52 (4th Cir. 1985).

Time of date immaterial. — In computing yearly periods, the time of day at which any event occurred is immaterial. Poston v. Ford, 34 Bankr. 93 (Bankr. W.D. Va. 1983), aff'd, 53 Bankr. 444 (Bankr. W.D. Va. 1984), 773 F.2d 52 (4th Cir. 1985).

Regardless of nature of time limit terminating on Sunday, performance on Monday is timely. — The federal courts of appeals have consistently held conduct timely if performed on the subsequent Monday when the applicable time limit terminated on Sunday, regardless of the nature of the time limit. Wirtz v. Peninsula Shipbuilders Ass'n, 382 F.2d 237 (4th Cir. 1967).

Presumption of receipt after three days. — This rule provides the presumption that if the date of receipt is unknown or in dispute, courts will presume receipt three days after mailing; however, such a presumption is not automatic, but rather is only applicable if the parties dispute the date of receipt. Williams v. Enterprise Leasing Co., 911 F. Supp. 988 (E.D. Va. 1995).

Subdivision (a) applies to time allowed by any statute. — Subdivision (a) provides that where the last day for performance of an act falls on a Sunday or a legal holiday, performance on the next day which is not a Sunday or legal holiday is timely. That rule provides the method for computation of time prescribed or allowed not only by the rules or by order of court but by "any applicable statute." Wirtz v. Peninsula Shipbuilders Ass'n, 382 F.2d 237 (4th Cir. 1967).

And has been applied to statutes of limitation. — It has been suggested that subdivision (a) of this rule is a rule of procedure relating to acts done or proceedings had after the commencement of action and to any statutes expressly applicable to such proceedings and that it is not intended to modify and change existing statutes of limitation. But this holding has been questioned by the Fourth Circuit Court of Appeals and rejected by it, at least where the time limitation on commencing an action has been enacted long after the enactment of the rule. Wirtz v. Peninsula Shipbuilders Ass'n, 382 F.2d 237 (4th Cir. 1967).

This rule is applicable to pleadings and statutes of limitations. In computing time, the first day should be excluded and the last day included. Paynter v. C & O Ry., 60 F.R.D. 153 (W.D. Va. 1973).

For statute of limitation purposes, a complaint may be considered "filed" as of the date of its receipt, even if it is not docketed, and summons will not issue until the appropriate fee is paid. Wells v. Apfel, 103 F. Supp. 2d 893 (W.D. Va. 2000).

Such as time limit under Labor-Management Reporting and Disclosure Act. — Computation of the 60-day time limit for bringing action under § 402(b) of the Labor-Management Reporting and Disclosure Act, 29 U.S.C. § 482(b) (1964), in the manner prescribed by subdivision (a) of this rule where the last day of the period falls on Sunday is both consistent with the express language and purpose of the rule and in accord with the policy underlying the act — the vindication of union members' rights. Wirtz v. Peninsula Shipbuilders Ass'n, 382 F.2d 237 (4th Cir. 1967).

And statute of limitations under Federal Employees Liability Act. — See Paynter v. C & O Ry., 60 F.R.D. 153 (W.D. Va. 1973).

And one-year provision for commencing action under Truth-in-Lending Act. — Regardless of whether the one-year provision for commencing an action under the federal Truth-in-Lending Act is viewed as a condition of liability or a period of limitation, the method for computing the passage of one year should be that prescribed by the Federal Rules of Civil Procedure wherein in computing the one-year period the day of the transaction is excluded and the last day of the period is included. McMillon v. Budget Plan, 510 F. Supp. 17 (E.D. Va. 1980).

Rule applied to state statute of limitations applicable to § 1983 actions. — See Bulls v. Holmes, 403 F. Supp. 475 (E.D. Va. 1975).

This rule applies to admiralty proceedings. Muse v. Freeman, 197 F. Supp. 67 (E.D. Va. 1961).

A district court has discretion to consider a late affidavit if it chooses to do so; however, these exceptions should generally be used only if cause or excusable neglect has been shown by the party failing to comply with the time provisions. Orsi v. Kirkwood, 999 F.2d 86 (4th Cir. 1993).

"Excusable neglect." — Excuse that defendant was seeking legal assistance before filing his petition did not constitute "excusable neglect" under subsection (b)(2) of this rule. Bilodeau v. Angelone, 39 F. Supp. 2d 652 (E.D. Va. 1999).

Substitution proper although not timely where no prejudice suffered. — Where party had not originally opposed the motion for an enlargement of time and had suffered no prejudice from a failure to timely substitute parties but had continued representing its interests through court appearances and responses to pleadings and motions, the district court correctly ruled that the substitution was proper. Capital Investors Co. v. Executors of Estate of Morrison, 800 F.2d 424 (4th Cir. 1986).

Determining when transfer of realty occurred for purposes of bankruptcy proceedings. — Subdivision (a) of this rule is used in a bankruptcy proceeding in computing the one-year time period within which a transfer of real property occurred. The transfer is the act from which the "designated period of time begins to run." Determining the period within which the transfer occurred requires a counting from the act forward to the date of the bankruptcy petition commencing a case. Poston v. Ford, 34 Bankr. 93 (Bankr. W.D. Va. 1983), aff'd, 53 Bankr. 444 (Bankr. W.D. Va. 1984), 773 F.2d 52 (4th Cir. 1985).

Motion to modify taxation of costs held untimely. — The plaintiff's motion to modify taxation of costs, filed more than six months after the judgment was entered and after the sworn statement of costs was filed, and 45 days after the costs were taxed by the clerk, was not timely. No application to extend the time for filing having been submitted, and no motion for relief from judgment having been filed, the plaintiff's motion was denied. Person v. Omni Int'l Hotel-Norfolk, 106 F.R.D. 7 (E.D. Va. 1984).

Answer allowed to be filed four days late. — See Redmond v. O'Sullivan Rubber Co., 10 F.R.D. 519 (W.D. Va. 1943).

Filing in forma pauperis. — A complaint was considered filed the date it was received by the clerk's office, even though the filing fee was not included, and plaintiff's in forma pauperis application was denied. Wells v. Apfel, 103 F. Supp. 2d 893 (W.D. Va. 2000).

Applied in Dabney v. Cunningham, 317 F. Supp. 57 (E.D. Va. 1970); Raether v. Phillips, 401 F. Supp. 1393 (W.D. Va. 1975); Marshall v. Ampthill Rayon Workers, Inc., 454 F. Supp. 84 (E.D. Va. 1978); United States v. O'Day, 667 F.2d 430 (4th Cir. 1981); United States ex rel. Magna Masonry, Inc. v. R.T. Woodfield, Inc., 709 F.2d 249 (4th Cir. 1983); Vecco Constr. Indus., Inc. v. Century Constr. Co., 33 Bankr. 757 (Bankr. E.D. Va. 1983); Miners & Merchants Bank & Trust Co. v. Mullins, 55 Bankr. 618 (Bankr. W.D. Va. 1985); Bryant v. Smith, 165 Bankr. 176 (W.D. Va. 1994).

TITLE III. PLEADINGS AND MOTIONS.

Rule 7. Pleadings Allowed; Form of Motions and Other Papers.

(a) *Pleadings.* — Only these pleadings are allowed:

(1) a complaint;

(2) an answer to a complaint;

(3) an answer to a counterclaim designated as a counterclaim;

(4) an answer to a crossclaim;

(5) a third-party complaint;

(6) an answer to a third-party complaint; and

(7) if the court orders one, a reply to an answer.

(b) *Motions and Other Papers.* — (1) In General. A request for a court order must be made by motion. The motion must:

(A) be in writing unless made during a hearing or trial;

(B) state with particularity the grounds for seeking the order; and

(C) state the relief sought.

(2) Form. The rules governing captions and other matters of form in pleadings apply to motions and other papers. (Amended by order adopted December 27, 1946, effective March 19, 1948, by order adopted January 21, 1963, effective July 1, 1963, by order adopted April 28, 1983, effective August 1, 1983; and by order adopted April 30, 2007, effective December 1, 2007.)

Comment. — The language of Rule 7 has been amended as part of the general restyling of the Civil Rules to make them more easily understood and to make style and terminology consistent throughout the rules. These changes are intended to be stylistic only.

Former Rule 7(a) stated that "there shall be * * * an answer to a cross-claim, if the answer contains a cross-claim * * *." Former Rule 12(a)(2) provided more generally that "[a] party served with a pleading stating a cross-claim against that party shall serve an answer thereto * * *." New Rule 7(a) corrects this inconsistency by providing for an answer to a crossclaim.

For the first time, Rule 7(a)(7) expressly authorizes the court to order a reply to a counterclaim answer. A reply may be as useful in this setting as a reply to an answer, a third-party answer, or a crossclaim answer.

Former Rule 7(b)(1) stated that the writing requirement is fulfilled if the motion is stated in a written notice of hearing. This statement was deleted as redundant because a single written document can satisfy the writing requirements both for a motion and for a Rule 6(c)(1) notice.

The cross-reference to Rule 11 in former Rule 7(b)(3) is deleted as redundant. Rule 11 applies by its own terms. The force and application of Rule 11 are not diminished by the deletion.

Former Rule 7(c) is deleted because it has done its work. If a motion or pleading is described as a demurrer, plea, or exception for insufficiency, the court will treat the paper as if properly captioned.

CASE NOTES

Notice of motion has replaced rule to show cause. — Since the effective date of the new rules of civil procedure, rules to show cause have not been properly a part of civil practice. Subdivision (b) provides that all applications to the court for orders shall be by motion. The rules and forms then clearly indicate that motions are brought before the court by means of "notice of motion" which serves the purpose of a rule to show cause, and obviates the necessity for obtaining such a rule. Walling v. Moore Milling Co., 62 F. Supp. 378 (W.D. Va. 1945).

And is standard procedure for hearing on preliminary injunction. — Subdivision (b) of this rule and Rule 65 are perfectly clear, and set out the standard procedure for bringing on for hearing a motion for a preliminary injunction. A plaintiff, who desires a preliminary injunction, need only give his notice of such motion, as provided in the rules. Walling v. Moore Milling Co., 62 F. Supp. 378 (W.D. Va. 1945).

Under Rule 38(b), a demand for jury trial must be in writing and served "not later than 10 days after the service of the last pleading directed to" the "issue triable of right by a jury." Plaintiffs attempted to escape their dilemma of having failed to follow the rule by claiming that their filing, on or about March 8, 1979, of a response to defendant's answer and grounds of defense amounted to the last pleading for Rule 38(b) purposes. However, the "response" was clearly a superfluous document, not provided for in these rules, and consequently did not qualify as a pleading under subdivision (a). The possibility of an escape under a provision in Rule 81(c), which applies to removed actions, and governs the situation where "state law applicable in the court from which the case is removed does not require the parties to make express demands in order to claim trial by jury" was foreclosed, since the rules applicable in the circuit court of the City of Virginia Beach, did require an express jury trial demand, prior to trial. Malbon v. Pennsylvania Millers Mut. Ins. Co., 636 F.2d 936 (4th Cir. 1980).

Applied in Davenport v. Deseret Pharmaceutical Co., 321 F. Supp. 659 (E.D. Va. 1971); Grayson-Carroll-Wythe Mut. Ins. Co. v. Allstate Ins. Co., 582 F. Supp. 560 (W.D. Va. 1984); International Longshoremen's Ass'n v. Virginia Int'l Terms., Inc., 904 F. Supp. 500 (E.D. Va. 1995).

Rule 7.1. Disclosure Statement.

(a) *Who Must File; Contents.* — A nongovernmental corporate party must file 2 copies of a disclosure statement that:

(1) identifies any parent corporation and any publicly held corporation owning 10% or more of its stock; or

(2) states that there is no such corporation.

(b) *Time to File; Supplemental Filing.* — A party must:

(1) file the disclosure statement with its first appearance, pleading, petition, motion, response, or other request addressed to the court; and

(2) promptly file a supplemental statement if any required information changes. (Amended by order adopted April 29, 2002, effective December 1, 2002, and by order adopted April 30, 2007, effective December 1, 2007.)

Comment. — The language of Rule 7.1 has been amended as part of the general restyling of the Civil Rules to make them more easily understood and to make style and terminology consistent throughout

the rules. These changes are intended to be stylistic only.

Rule 8. General Rules of Pleading.

(a) *Claim for Relief.* — A pleading that states a claim for relief must contain:

(1) a short and plain statement of the grounds for the court's jurisdiction, unless the court already has jurisdiction and the claim needs no new jurisdictional support;

(2) a short and plain statement of the claim showing that the pleader is entitled to relief; and

(3) a demand for the relief sought, which may include relief in the alternative or different types of relief.

(b) *Defenses; Admissions and Denials.* — (1) In General. In responding to a pleading, a party must:

(A) state in short and plain terms its defenses to each claim asserted against it; and

(B) admit or deny the allegations asserted against it by an opposing party.

(2) Denials — Responding to the Substance. A denial must fairly respond to the substance of the allegation.

(3) General and Specific Denials. A party that intends in good faith to deny all the allegations of a pleading — including the jurisdictional grounds — may do so by a general denial. A party that does not intend to deny all the allegations must either specifically deny designated allegations or generally deny all except those specifically admitted.

(4) Denying Part of an Allegation. A party that intends in good faith to deny only part of an allegation must admit the part that is true and deny the rest.

(5) Lacking Knowledge or Information. A party that lacks knowledge or information sufficient to form a belief about the truth of an allegation must so state, and the statement has the effect of a denial.

(6) Effect of Failing to Deny. An allegation — other than one relating to the amount of damages — is admitted if a responsive pleading is required and the allegation is not denied. If a responsive pleading is not required, an allegation is considered denied or avoided.

(c) *Affirmative Defenses.* — (1) In General. In responding to a pleading, a party must affirmatively state any avoidance or affirmative defense, including:

- accord and satisfaction;
- arbitration and award;
- assumption of risk;
- contributory negligence;
- duress;
- estoppel;
- failure of consideration;
- fraud;
- illegality;
- injury by fellow servant;
- laches;
- license;
- payment;
- release;
- res judicata;
- statute of frauds;
- statute of limitations; and
- waiver.

(2) Mistaken Designation. If a party mistakenly designates a defense as a counterclaim, or a counterclaim as a defense, the court must, if justice requires, treat the pleading as though it were correctly designated, and may impose terms for doing so.

(d) *Pleading to Be Concise and Direct; Alternative Statements; Inconsistency.* — (1) In General. Each allegation must be simple, concise, and direct. No technical form is required.

(2) Alternative Statements of a Claim or Defense. A party may set out 2 or more statements of a claim or defense alternatively or hypothetically, either in a single count or defense or in separate ones. If a party makes alternative statements, the pleading is sufficient if any one of them is sufficient.

(3) Inconsistent Claims or Defenses. A party may state as many separate claims or defenses as it has, regardless of consistency.

(e) *Construing Pleadings.* — Pleadings must be construed so as to do justice. (Amended by order adopted February 28, 1966, effective July 1, 1966, by order adopted March 2, 1987, effective August 1, 1987, by order adopted April 30, 2007, effective December 1, 2007, and by order adopted April 28, 2010, effective December 1, 2010.)

Comment. — The language of Rule 8 has been amended as part of the general restyling of the Civil Rules to make them more easily understood and to make style and terminology consistent throughout the rules. These changes are intended to be stylistic only.

The former Rule 8(b) and 8(e) cross-references to Rule 11 are deleted as redundant. Rule 11 applies by its own terms. The force and application of Rule 11 are not diminished by the deletion.

Former Rule 8(b) required a pleader denying part of an averment to "specify so much of it as is true and material and * * * deny only the remainder." "[A]nd material" is deleted to avoid the implication that it is proper to deny something that the pleader believes to be true but not material.

Deletion of former Rule 8(e)(2)'s "whether based on legal, equitable, or maritime grounds" reflects the parallel deletions in Rule 1 and elsewhere. Merger is now successfully accomplished.

Law Review. — For note, "The Specificity of Pleading in Modern Civil Practice: Addressing Common Misconceptions," see 25 U. Rich. L. Rev. 135 (1991).

CASE NOTES

Claim may be stated in general terms. — The antitrust claims in plaintiff's complaint needed to give defendant sufficient notice that it was complaining of territorial restrictions, tying arrangements, and an alleged antitrust conspiracy. Plaintiff was not required to set out all the facts upon which it based its claims. All it needed to do was provide defendant with a "short and plain statement of the claims," under subdivision (a)(2) of this rule. If defendant wished to probe more deeply the basis of plaintiff's claims, it could have availed itself of the liberal discovery procedures provided by the federal rules. Material Handling Indus., Inc. v. Eaton Corp., 391 F. Supp. 977 (E.D. Va. 1975).

This rule's liberal pleading standards requires that the complaint need only state sufficient facts to enable the defendant to draft a responsive pleading. Jetform Corp. v. Unisys Corp., 11 F. Supp. 2d 788 (E.D. Va. 1998).

Detailed facts underlying claims not required. — A section 1983 plaintiff seeking to impose municipal liability must satisfy only the usual requirements of notice to provide nothing more than a short and plain statement of the claim that will give the defendant fair notice of what the plaintiff's claim is and the grounds upon which it rests and there is no requirement that he detail the facts underlying his claims, or that he plead the multiple incidents of constitutional violations that may be necessary at later stages to establish the existence of an official policy or custom and causation. Jordan v. Jackson, 15 F.3d 333 (4th Cir. 1994).

Subdivision (a), which requires a statement of jurisdiction, contemplates reference to a federal statute, since the federal constitution does not confer jurisdiction on district courts. Atkins v. School Bd., 379 F. Supp. 1060 (W.D. Va. 1974), aff'd, 511 F.2d 1398 (4th Cir. 1975).

Grounds for jurisdiction must be stated. — The complaint must state on its face the grounds for jurisdiction, regardless of whether the case is one of diversity or "federal question" jurisdiction. Bowman v. White, 388 F.2d 756 (4th Cir.), cert. denied, 393 U.S. 891, 89 S. Ct. 214, 21 L. Ed. 2d 172 (1968).

The complaint must state on its face the grounds for jurisdiction. Haynes v. James H. Carr, Inc., 307 F. Supp. 1228 (E.D. Va. 1969), aff'd, 427 F.2d 700 (4th Cir.), cert. denied, 400 U.S. 942, 91 S. Ct. 238, 27 L. Ed. 2d 245 (1970).

Plaintiffs must affirmatively plead the jurisdiction of the federal court. Dracos v. Hellenic Lines, 762 F.2d 348 (4th Cir.), cert. denied, 474 U.S. 945, 106 S. Ct. 311, 88 L. Ed. 2d 288 (1985) (on petition for rehearing en banc).

Subdivision (a) allows inconsistent alternative claims. — Subdivision (a) allows alternative claims by the use of distinct and alternative counts, n'importe their inconsistency. Biggs v. Norfolk Dredging Co., 360 F.2d 360 (4th Cir. 1966), rev'g 237 F. Supp. 590 (E.D. Va. 1965) and Clowers v. Tidewater-Raymond-Kiewit, 237 F. Supp. 1015 (E.D. Va. 1965).

Election of remedies. — This rule does not require an election of remedies. Ambrose Branch Coal Co. v. Tankersley, 106 Bankr. 462 (Bankr. W.D. Va. 1989).

Construction of complaint of pro se litigant. — A court has a duty to assist a pro se litigant who may not understand concepts of legal responsibility. A pro se litigant may not understand that under this rule he may set forth two or more statements of a claim alternately or hypothetically, and may also state as many separate claims as he has regardless of consistency. Therefore, a court will construe a plaintiff's complaint to have included a statement of his claim based on a theory of negligence where this seems more appropriate than the intentional tort theory on which the plaintiff based his claim. Frazier v. Collins, 538 F. Supp. 603 (E.D. Va. 1982).

Defense within statutory exceptions to incontestability of registered trademarks is affirmative. — When the commissioner of patents accepts a manufacturer's affidavits with respect to trademark registrations that makes the registrations incontestable under 15 U.S.C. §§ 1065, 1115(b) (1964), and the burden of establishing a defense which falls within one of the exceptions mentioned in the federal statute, 15 U.S.C. § 1115(b) (1964), is upon the one disputing the registrant's right to the marks. The defense must be pleaded affirmatively. Philip Morris, Inc. v. Imperial Tobacco Co., 251 F. Supp. 362 (E.D. Va. 1965), aff'd, 401 F.2d 179 (4th Cir. 1968), cert. denied, 393 U.S. 1094, 89 S. Ct. 875, 21 L. Ed. 2d 784 (1969).

Laches is an affirmative defense under subdivision (c). Giddens v. Isbrandtsen Co., 355 F.2d 125 (4th Cir. 1966); White v. Johns-Manville Corp., 662 F.2d 234 (4th Cir. 1981), cert. denied, 454 U.S. 1163, 102 S. Ct. 1037, 71 L. Ed. 2d 319 (1982), 474 U.S. 970, 106 S. Ct. 351, 88 L. Ed. 2d 319 (1985).

But laches properly relevant only where claims characterized as equitable. — Laches is one of the affirmative defenses generally allowable under subsection (c), although it is properly relevant only where the claims presented may be characterized as equitable, rather than legal. White v. Daniel, 909 F.2d 99 (4th Cir. 1990), cert. denied, 501 U.S. 1260, 111 S. Ct. 2916, 115 L. Ed. 2d 1079 (1991).

Laches imposes on the defendant the ultimate burden of proving (1) lack of diligence by the party against whom the defense is asserted, and (2) prejudice to the party asserting the defense. White v. Daniel, 909 F.2d 99 (4th Cir. 1990), cert. denied, 501 U.S. 1260, 111 S. Ct. 2916, 115 L. Ed. 2d 1079 (1991).

And defendant has burden of proving delay, plus prejudice. — The pattern to be followed for decision upon a plea of laches is this: The defendant has the burden of ultimately proving inexcusable or inadequately excused delay, plus prejudice, inasmuch as laches is an affirmative defense. Giddens v. Isbrandtsen Co., 355 F.2d 125 (4th Cir. 1966).

A complaint is not an anagrammatic exercise in which the pleader must find just exactly the prescribed combination of words and phrases. However, the Federal Rules of Civil Procedure do require, "'a short and plain statement of the claim' that will give the defendant fair notice of what the plaintiff's claim is and the grounds upon which it rests." Miller v. Holiday Inns, Inc., 436 F. Supp. 460 (E.D. Va. 1977).

For purposes of motion to dismiss, material allegations of complaint taken as admitted and the complaint is to be liberally construed in favor of plaintiff. MacKethan v. Peat, Marwick, Mitchell & Co., 439 F. Supp. 1090 (E.D. Va. 1977).

Use of Fifth Amendment to avoid subdivision (d). — When properly invoked, the Fifth Amendment privilege against self-incrimination, which applies to civil proceedings as well as criminal, can avoid the operation of subdivision (d). The privilege applies not only at trial but also at the pleading stage. However, the mere blanket refusal to answer questions does not suffice to raise constitutional questions. Nor does a proper invocation of the privilege mean that a defendant is excused from the requirement to file a responsive pleading; he is obliged to answer those allegations that he can and to make a specific claim of the privilege as to the rest. North River Ins. Co. v. Stefanou, 831 F.2d 484 (4th Cir. 1987), cert. denied, 486 U.S. 1007, 108 S. Ct. 1733, 100 L. Ed. 2d 196 (1988).

Failure to plead defense in original action. — See United States v. Snepp, 595 F.2d 926 (4th Cir. 1979), rev'd on other grounds, 444 U.S. 507, 100 S. Ct. 763, 62 L. Ed. 2d 704 (1980).

Rule 9(b) must be read in conjunction with the notice pleading requirement. — See Picture Lake Campground, Inc. v. Holiday Inns, Inc., 497 F. Supp. 858 (E.D. Va. 1980).

Although the court recognizes that Rule 9(b) must be read in conjunction with this rule, which contains the "notice" pleading provisions of the federal rules, a court need not accept inferences drawn by plaintiffs if such inferences are unsupported by the facts set out in the complaint. Weill v. Dominion Resources, Inc., 875 F. Supp. 331 (E.D. Va. 1994).

When a party challenges the sufficiency of a complaint under Rule 9(b) it is the duty of the court to balance the pleading requirement of notice pleading under Rule 8 against the requirement of particularity under Rule 9(b). Picture Lake Campground, Inc. v. Holiday Inns, Inc., 497 F. Supp. 858 (E.D. Va. 1980).

The requirements of Rule 9(b) must be read in conjunction with this rule which establishes the general rules of pleading. Subsections (a) and (e) of this rule require a short and plain statement of the claim and that each averment be simple, concise, and direct. When the sufficiency of a complaint under Rule 9(b) is challenged, it is the duty of the court to balance the requirements of each of the rules. Sweeney Co. v. Engineers-Constructors, Inc., 109 F.R.D. 358 (E.D. Va. 1986).

Complaint filed by foreign attorney did not warrant dismissal. — Complaint filed by an attorney who was not admitted to practice before district court should not be dismissed for he subsequently associated himself with local counsel and was admitted pro hac vice. Wolford v. Budd Co., 149 F.R.D. 127 (W.D. Va. 1993).

Greater degree of specificity required in claim asserting copyright violation. — An exception to this general rule that plaintiff generally only needs to set forth a short and plain statement of the alleged wrong which apprises the defendant of the charge and enables him to prepare a responsive pleading has been recognized when the claimant is asserting a copyright violation; in such cases, courts have required a greater degree of specificity but requiring the claimant to state: (1) which specific original works are the subject of the claim; (2) that plaintiff owns the copyrights in issue; (3) that the works in issue have been registered; and (4) by what acts and during what time frame defendants have infringed the copyright. Paragon Servs., Inc. v. Hicks, 843 F. Supp. 1077 (E.D. Va. 1994).

Applied in Dairyland Ins. Co. v. Hughes, 317 F. Supp. 928 (W.D. Va. 1970); Austin v. Reynolds Metals Co., 327 F. Supp. 1145 (E.D. Va. 1970); Davenport v. Deseret Pharmaceutical Co., 321 F. Supp. 659 (E.D. Va. 1971); Richmond Educ. Ass'n v. Crockford, 55 F.R.D. 362 (E.D. Va. 1972); EEOC v. GE Co., 370 F. Supp. 1258 (W.D. Va. 1973); Greene v. Virginia State Bar Ass'n, 411 F. Supp. 512 (E.D. Va. 1976); Grayson-Carroll-Wythe Mut. Ins. Co. v. Allstate Ins. Co., 582 F. Supp. 560 (W.D. Va. 1984); Northwestern Bank v. First Va. Bank, 585 F. Supp. 425 (W.D. Va. 1984); Harrison v. KVAT Food Mgt., Inc., 766 F.2d 155 (4th Cir. 1985); Music City Music v. Alfa Foods, Ltd., 616 F. Supp. 1001 (E.D. Va. 1985); In re Dodd, 46 Bankr. 335 (Bankr. E.D. Va. 1985); Simmons v. Frank, 731 F. Supp. 1289 (E.D. Va. 1989); Williams-El v. Dunning, 816 F. Supp. 418 (E.D. Va. 1993); Blizzard v. Dalton, 876 F. Supp. 95 (E.D. Va. 1995); Keegan v. Dalton, 899 F. Supp.

1503 (E.D. Va. 1995); Childress v. City of Richmond, 907 F. Supp. 934 (E.D. Va. 1995); Brzonkala v. Virginia Polytechnic & State Univ., 935 F. Supp. 779 (W.D. Va. 1996); Affordable Efficiencies, Inc. v. Bane, 228 Bankr. 835 (Bankr. W.D. Va. 1998); Paul v. Gomez, 190 F.R.D. 402 (W.D. Va. 2000).

Rule 9. Pleading Special Matters.

(a) *Capacity or Authority to Sue; Legal Existence.* — (1) In General. Except when required to show that the court has jurisdiction, a pleading need not allege:

(A) a party's capacity to sue or be sued;

(B) a party's authority to sue or be sued in a representative capacity; or

(C) the legal existence of an organized association of persons that is made a party.

(2) Raising Those Issues. To raise any of those issues, a party must do so by a specific denial, which must state any supporting facts that are peculiarly within the party's knowledge.

(b) *Fraud or Mistake; Conditions of Mind.* — In alleging fraud or mistake, a party must state with particularity the circumstances constituting fraud or mistake. Malice, intent, knowledge, and other conditions of a person's mind may be alleged generally.

(c) *Conditions Precedent.* — In pleading conditions precedent, it suffices to allege generally that all conditions precedent have occurred or been performed. But when denying that a condition precedent has occurred or been performed, a party must do so with particularity.

(d) *Official Document or Act.* — In pleading an official document or official act, it suffices to allege that the document was legally issued or the act legally done.

(e) *Judgment.* — In pleading a judgment or decision of a domestic or foreign court, a judicial or quasi-judicial tribunal, or a board or officer, it suffices to plead the judgment or decision without showing jurisdiction to render it.

(f) *Time and Place.* — An allegation of time or place is material when testing the sufficiency of a pleading.

(g) *Special Damages.* — If an item of special damage is claimed, it must be specifically stated.

(h) *Admiralty or Maritime Claim.* — (1) How Designated. If a claim for relief is within the admiralty or maritime jurisdiction and also within the court's subject-matter jurisdiction on some other ground, the pleading may designate the claim as an admiralty or maritime claim for purposes of Rules 14(c), 38(e), and 82 and the Supplemental Rules for Admiralty or Maritime Claims and Asset Forfeiture Actions. A claim cognizable only in the admiralty or maritime jurisdiction is an admiralty or maritime claim for those purposes, whether or not so designated.

(2) Designation for Appeal. A case that includes an admiralty or maritime claim within this subdivision (h) is an admiralty case within 28 U.S.C. § 1292(a)(3). (Added by order adopted February 28, 1966, effective July 1, 1966, amended by order adopted December 4, 1967, effective July 1, 1968, by order adopted March 30, 1970, effective July 1, 1970, by order adopted March 2, 1987, effective August 1, 1987, by order adopted April 11, 1997, effective December 1, 1997, by order adopted April 12, 2006, effective December 1, 2006, and by order adopted April 30, 2007, effective December 1, 2007.)

Comment. — The language of Rule 9 has been amended as part of the general restyling of the Civil Rules to make them more easily understood and to make style and terminology consistent throughout the rules. These changes are intended to be stylistic only.

Law Review. — For a note, "The Definition and Pleading of Special Damage Under the Federal Rules of Civil Procedure," see 55 Va. L. Rev. 542 (1969).

CASE NOTES

Purpose of requirements as to averment of fraud. — Subdivision (b) of this rule provides that in averments of fraud, "the circumstances constituting fraud or mistake shall be stated with particularity." The purposes advanced by this requirement are to insure that allegations are specified enough to inform defendant and enable him to prepare an effective response and defense, to eliminate complaints filed in order to find unknown wrongs through discovery, and to protect defendants from unfounded charges that involve moral turpitude. Sweeney Co. v. Engineers-Constructors, Inc., 109 F.R.D. 358 (E.D. Va. 1986).

The particularity requirement is (1) to provide defendants with fair notice of plaintiff's claim; (2) to protect defendants from harm to their reputation or good will; and (3) to reduce the number of nuisance or "strike" suits. Weill v. Dominion Resources, Inc., 875 F. Supp. 331 (E.D. Va. 1994).

Specificity required in alleging fraud. — This rule requires that the complaint set forth the facts constituting the alleged fraud in sufficient detail to inform the defendant fairly of the charges made against him. If, therefore, under the circumstances of the case, it appears that the defendant does in fact have notice of the matters of which the plaintiff complains, the complaint may be deemed sufficient. Jensen Elecs., Inc. v. American Computer & Telecommunications Corp., 26 Bankr. 512 (Bankr. E.D. Va. 1983).

Under subdivision (b) and Virginia law, a fraud complaint must allege with particularity a false representation by defendant of a material fact with the intent to mislead, and the plaintiff reasonably relied on the representation to her detriment. Kline v. Nationsbank, 886 F. Supp. 1285 (E.D. Va. 1995).

To survive a motion of this rule, plaintiffs who were purchasers of corporation's common stock must point in complaint to some reason that the difference between the rosy projections made by the corporation and later results was attributable to fraud. Borow v. nVIEW Corp., 829 F. Supp. 828 (E.D. Va. 1993), aff'd, 27 F.3d 562 (4th Cir. 1994).

Alleging that defendant did not take the proper action concerning her trust property, after discovering its existence, and caused her damages does not meet the requirement of alleging with specificity how she reasonably relied on a particular, intentionally false statement to her detriment. Kline v. Nationsbank, 886 F. Supp. 1285 (E.D. Va. 1995).

Where complainant went to the government and said, "I think there's something fishy going on in connection with Government Contract A and Contractor B," this was not enough to file a fraud complaint, and thus was not enough to earn qui tam relator status. United States ex rel. Detrick v. Daniel F. Young, Inc., 909 F. Supp. 1010 (E.D. Va. 1995).

Under subdivision (b) and Virginia law, a fraud complaint must allege with particularity a false representation by defendant of a material fact with the intent to mislead, and the plaintiff reasonably relied on the representation to her detriment. Kline v. Nationsbank, 886 F. Supp. 1285 (E.D. Va. 1995).

Where plaintiff's amended complaint provided defendant with sufficient information to determine who made the alleged misrepresentations, plaintiff satisfied the requirements of the rule. Tidewater Beverage Servs., Inc. v. Coca Cola Co., 907 F. Supp. 943 (E.D. Va. 1995).

Mere allegations of fraud by hindsight will not withstand a motion of this rule. Borow v. nVIEW Corp., 829 F. Supp. 828 (E.D. Va. 1993), aff'd, 27 F.3d 562 (4th Cir. 1994).

Subdivision (b) carves an exception out of the general rule of notice pleading embraced by the Federal Rules of Civil Procedure. Steyhr Daimler Puch of Am. Corp. v. Pappas, 35 Bankr. 1001 (E.D. Va. 1983).

Although the court recognizes that subsection (b) must be read in conjunction with Rule 8, which contains the "notice" pleading provisions of the federal rules, a court need not accept inferences drawn by plaintiffs if such inferences are unsupported by the facts set out in the complaint. Weill v. Dominion Resources, Inc., 875 F. Supp. 331 (E.D. Va. 1994).

Subdivision (b) directs that federal courts are not to countenance "fishing expeditions" on bare allegations of fraud. Ginsberg v. Pomponio, 95 F.R.D. 156 (E.D. Va. 1982).

Fraudulent misrepresentation. — The purposes of this rule are accomplished when a plaintiff alleges the time, place, and content of the false misrepresentation, the fact misrepresented and what was gained or given up as a consequence of the fraud. Sweeney Co. v. Engineers-Constructors, Inc., 109 F.R.D. 358 (E.D. Va. 1986).

Failure to plead and insufficient evidence of fraud. — See United States v. Snepp, 595 F.2d 926 (4th Cir. 1979), rev'd on other grounds, 444 U.S. 507, 100 S. Ct. 763, 62 L. Ed. 2d 704 (1980).

Subdivision (b) must be read in conjunction with the notice pleading requirement. — See Picture Lake Campground, Inc. v. Holiday Inns, Inc., 497 F. Supp. 858 (E.D. Va. 1980).

When a party challenges the sufficiency of a complaint under subdivision (b) it is the duty of the court to balance the pleading requirement of notice pleading under Rule 8 against the requirement of particularity under subdivision (b). Picture Lake Campground, Inc. v. Holiday Inns, Inc., 497 F. Supp. 858 (E.D. Va. 1980).

The focal point of a subdivision (b) inquiry should be whether, given the nature and facts of the case and circumstances of the parties, the pleading in question is sufficiently particular to satisfy the purposes of subdivision (b). Picture Lake Campground, Inc. v. Holiday Inns, Inc., 497 F. Supp. 858 (E.D. Va. 1980).

The requirements of subdivision (b) of this rule must be read in conjunction with Rule 8 which establishes the general rules of pleading. Subdivisions (a) and (e) of Rule 8 require a short and plain statement of the claim and that each averment be simple, concise, and direct. When the sufficiency of a complaint under subdivision (b) of this rule is challenged, it is the duty of the court to balance the requirements of each of the rules. Sweeney Co. v. Engineers-Constructors, Inc., 109 F.R.D. 358 (E.D. Va. 1986).

Securities fraud action. — In securities fraud action, in order to attack projections or beliefs about company's future, plaintiff must plead facts that tend to show that, at the time they were made, the statements either weren't genuinely believed or that there were no reasonable grounds for the belief, or that the proponent knew facts that seriously undermined the grounds for the belief to satisfy "particularity" requirement of subdivision (b). Borow v. nView Corp., 829 F. Supp. 828 (E.D. Va. 1993), aff'd, 27 F.3d 562 (4th Cir. 1994).

To satisfy "the circumstances constituting fraud" element of subsection (b) in a federal securities case, a plaintiff must plead who, what, when, where and how. Weill v. Dominion Resources, Inc., 875 F. Supp. 331 (E.D. Va. 1994).

Complaint failed to state circumstances constituting fraud with requisite particularity. — Where plaintiff claimed that prospective employer had a duty to inform him that employment offer could be revoked at will and thus employer breached that duty by willfully suppressing this fact, leading plaintiff to rely upon misrepresentation, such claim was insufficient because it failed to allege a false representation by the employer; he neither alleged nor presented any evidence to support an inference that employer intended to mislead him, and thus complaint failed to state the circumstances constituting the fraud with the requisite particularity. Sneed v. American Bank Stationary Co., 764 F. Supp. 65 (W.D. Va. 1991).

Shareholders failed to provide separate facts in support of fraud claims. — Where shareholders claimed that banking corporation maintained grossly inadequate loan loss reserves, understated nonperforming loans, and overconcentrated the loan portfolio in the real estate sector, that the corporation's credit review and authorization standards and policies were not functioning properly, and that their lending practices and controls had become unmanageable, and where to support these claims, shareholders merely quoted corporation's representations concerning banking corporation's financial status from Jan., 1989 to July, 1990, and then stated that the inverse was true, shareholders failed to provide any separate facts in support of their claims of fraud. Dubowski v. Dominion Bankshares Corp., 763 F. Supp. 169 (W.D. Va. 1991).

No right to jury trial if claim identified as admiralty or maritime. — The merger of civil and admiralty procedure in 1966 does not affect the right to jury trial. If the only basis for jurisdiction is that the case is an admiralty case, there is no right to a jury. If jurisdiction can alternatively be based on a federal question, or on diversity and the necessary jurisdictional amount, either party may demand a jury trial unless plaintiff has chosen to identify the claim as an admiralty or maritime claim, as permitted by subdivision (h) of this rule. If he exercises that option, Rule 38(e) provides that there is no right to trial by jury. Sanderlin v. Old Dominion Stevedoring Corp., 281 F. Supp. 1015 (E.D. Va. 1968).

Subdivision (h) effectively precludes trial by jury for cases in which the court has jurisdiction through admiralty or some other means and the plaintiff identifies the claim as one brought in admiralty, and those in which the court's exclusive jurisdiction is in admiralty. Gaines v. Ampro Fisheries, Inc., 836 F. Supp. 347 (E.D. Va. 1993).

Applied in Gulf-Caribbean Nav. Co. v. Sea Bird Nav., Inc., 340 F. Supp. 1156 (E.D. Va. 1971); J.M. Huber & Co. v. M/V Plym, 468 F.2d 166 (4th Cir. 1972); M.W. Zack Metal Co. v. International Nav. Corp., 510 F.2d 451 (4th Cir. 1975); Pierside Term. Operators, Inc. v. M/V Floridian, 423 F. Supp. 962 (E.D. Va. 1976); Scheel v. Conboy, 551 F.2d 41 (4th Cir. 1977); W.F. Magann Corp. v. The Tug Delilah, 434 F. Supp. 517 (E.D. Va. 1977); Moore v. Northern Homes of Pa., Inc., 80 F.R.D. 278 (W.D. Va. 1978); Atkinson Indus., Inc. v. Yacht My Jan, 651 F.2d 936 (4th Cir. 1981); Coley v. Dragon Ltd., 138 F.R.D. 460 (E.D. Va. 1990); Lewis v. United States, 812 F. Supp. 620 (E.D. Va. 1993); Settle v. S.W. Rodgers Co., 998 F. Supp. 657 (E.D. Va. 1998); Vanguard Military Equip. Corp. v. David B. Finestone Co., 6 F. Supp. 2d 488 (E.D. Va. 1997); R.M.S. Titanic, Inc. v. Haver, 171 F.3d 943 (4th. Cir. 1999); King v. Donnkenny, Inc., 84 F. Supp. 2d 736 (W.D. Va. 2000); Stone Castle Fin., Inc. v. Friedman, Billings, Ramsey & Co., 191 F. Supp. 2d 652, 2002 U.S. Dist. LEXIS 3764 (E.D. Va. 2002).

Rule 10. Form of Pleadings.

(a) *Caption; Names of Parties.* — Every pleading must have a caption with the court's name, a title, a file number, and a Rule 7(a) designation. The title of the complaint must name all the parties; the title of other pleadings, after naming the first party on each side, may refer generally to other parties.

(b) *Paragraphs; Separate Statements.* — A party must state its claims or defenses in numbered paragraphs, each limited as far as practicable to a single set of circumstances. A later pleading may refer by number to a paragraph in an earlier pleading. If doing so would promote clarity, each claim founded on a separate transaction or occurrence — and each defense other than a denial — must be stated in a separate count or defense.

(c) *Adoption by Reference; Exhibits.* — A statement in a pleading may be adopted by reference elsewhere in the same pleading or in any other pleading or motion. A copy of a written instrument that is an exhibit to a pleading is a part of the pleading for all purposes. (Amended by order adopted April 30, 2007, effective December 1, 2007.)

Comment. — The language of Rule 10 has been amended as part of the general restyling of the Civil Rules to make them more easily understood and to make style and terminology consistent throughout the rules. These changes are intended to be stylistic only.

CASE NOTES

Resolution of conflicting evidence. — Where there is conflict between any exhibit attached pursuant to subdivision (c) of this rule and bare allegations of the complaint, the exhibit prevails. Davis v. Cole, 999 F. Supp. 809 (E.D. Va. 1998).

Noncompliance as grounds for sustaining motion to dismiss. — There is some authority in support of the view that failure to comply with this rule, which is addressed to matters of form, will sustain a motion to dismiss. Doe v. Boyle, 60 F.R.D. 507 (E.D. Va. 1973), aff'd, 494 F.2d 1279 (4th Cir. 1974).

Rule 11. Signing Pleadings, Motions, and Other Papers; Representations to the Court; Sanctions.

(a) *Signature.* — Every pleading, written motion, and other paper must be signed by at least one attorney of record in the attorney's name — or by a party personally if the party is unrepresented. The paper must state the signer's address, e-mail address, and telephone number. Unless a rule or statute specifically states otherwise, a pleading need not be verified or accompanied by an affidavit. The court must strike an unsigned paper unless the omission is promptly corrected after being called to the attorney's or party's attention.

(b) *Representations to the Court.* — By presenting to the court a pleading, written motion, or other paper — whether by signing, filing, submitting, or later advocating it — an attorney or unrepresented party certifies that to the best of the person's knowledge, information, and belief, formed after an inquiry reasonable under the circumstances:

(1) it is not being presented for any improper purpose, such as to harass, cause unnecessary delay, or needlessly increase the cost of litigation;

(2) the claims, defenses, and other legal contentions are warranted by existing law or by a nonfrivolous argument for extending, modifying, or reversing existing law or for establishing new law;

(3) the factual contentions have evidentiary support or, if specifically so identified, will likely have evidentiary support after a reasonable opportunity for further investigation or discovery; and

(4) the denials of factual contentions are warranted on the evidence or, if specifically so identified, are reasonably based on belief or a lack of information.

(c) *Sanctions.* — (1) In General. If, after notice and a reasonable opportunity to respond, the court determines that Rule 11(b) has been violated, the court may impose an appropriate sanction on any attorney, law firm, or party that violated the rule or is responsible for the violation. Absent exceptional circumstances, a law firm must be held jointly responsible for a violation committed by its partner, associate, or employee.

(2) Motion for Sanctions. A motion for sanctions must be made separately from any other motion and must describe the specific conduct that allegedly violates Rule 11(b). The motion must be served under Rule 5, but it must not be filed or be presented to the court if the challenged paper, claim, defense, contention, or denial is withdrawn or appropriately corrected within 21 days after service or within another time the court sets. If warranted, the court may award to the prevailing party the reasonable expenses, including attorney's fees, incurred for the motion.

(3) On the Court's Initiative. On its own, the court may order an attorney, law firm, or party to show cause why conduct specifically described in the order has not violated Rule 11(b).

(4) Nature of a Sanction. A sanction imposed under this rule must be limited to what suffices to deter repetition of the conduct or comparable conduct by others similarly situated. The sanction may include nonmonetary directives; an order to pay a penalty into court; or, if imposed on motion and warranted for effective deterrence, an order directing payment to the movant of part or all of the reasonable attorney's fees and other expenses directly resulting from the violation.

(5) Limitations on Monetary Sanctions. The court must not impose a monetary sanction:

(A) against a represented party for violating Rule 11(b)(2); or

(B) on its own, unless it issued the show-cause order under Rule 11(c)(3) before voluntary dismissal or settlement of the claims made by or against the party that is, or whose attorneys are, to be sanctioned.

(6) Requirements for an Order. An order imposing a sanction must describe the sanctioned conduct and explain the basis for the sanction.

(d) *Inapplicability to Discovery.* — This rule does not apply to disclosures and discovery requests, responses, objections, and motions under Rules 26 through 37.

(Amended by order adopted April 28, 1983, effective August 1, 1983, by order adopted March 2, 1987, effective August 1, 1987, by order adopted April 22, 1993, effective December 1, 1993, and by order adopted April 30, 2007, effective December 1, 2007.)

Comment. — The language of Rule 11 has been amended as part of the general restyling of the Civil Rules to make them more easily understood and to make style and terminology consistent throughout the rules. These changes are intended to be stylistic only.

Law Review. — For note, "The Specificity of Pleading in Modern Civil Practice: Addressing Common Misconceptions," see 25 U. Rich. L. Rev. 135 (1991). For note, "Application of Rule 11 in the Fourth Circuit," see 48 Wash. & Lee L. Rev. 621 (1991).

CASE NOTES

I. In General.
II. Representations to Court.
III. Sanctions.

I. IN GENERAL.

Purpose of rule. — This rule and related local rules are promulgated for the purpose of regulating attorneys and not for the purpose of penalizing innocent litigants. Wolford v. Budd Co., 149 F.R.D. 127 (W.D. Va. 1993).

This rule does not authorize one party to make representations or file pleadings on behalf of another. Creekmore v. Food Lion, Inc., 797 F. Supp. 505 (E.D. Va. 1992).

"Snapshot view" does not obviate need to reevaluate case. — The "snapshot" view, i.e., the signer's conduct is to be judged as of the time the pleading or other paper is signed, does not obviate the need to reevaluate one's case. Many papers are signed and filed during the course of the proceedings, and counsel must ensure that each paper filed has merit in order to avoid sanctions. A paper signed and filed in opposition to a motion for summary judgment when development of the facts has made it clear that summary judgment must be granted, for example, will violate this rule. Brubaker v. City of Richmond, 943 F.2d 1363 (4th Cir. 1991).

Effect of attorney's signature. — Implicit in a lawyer's signature on a pleading is the representation that, after appropriate investigation and inquiry, he reasonably believes that a proper legal claim or defense is stated. Chu v. Griffith, 771 F.2d 79 (4th Cir. 1985).

Attorneys who put their names to pleadings must be cognizant of the fact, too, that they are vouching for the paper's good faith. In re Shiu Hung Leung, 8 Bankr. 242 (Bankr. E.D. Va. 1981).

A lack of formal "verification" should not be allowed to defeat a prisoner's constitutional claims in his habeas corpus petition. Morris v. United States, 399 F. Supp. 720 (E.D. Va. 1975).

Habeas corpus petition signed by agent for prisoner. — Where the petitioner in his federal habeas corpus complaint alleges that federal prison authorities restricted his ability to communicate by mail or verbally with the codefendant, who was assisting the petitioner in drafting his petition and was clearly operating with the consent of and in the best interests of the petitioner, and expediency may have required that the codefendant and not the petitioner sign and mail the complaint, the petitioner need not demonstrate a physical or mental handicap to justify an agent's signature. Morris v. United States, 399 F. Supp. 720 (E.D. Va. 1975).

Rule applies to every paper signed during course of proceedings. — This rule as amended applies to every paper signed during the course of the proceedings and not only to the pleadings; while the drafters of the rule could easily have further extended its application by referring to the entire conduct of the proceedings, they failed to do so and instead chose to expand only the categories of papers to which the rule applies. Brubaker v. City of Richmond, 943 F.2d 1363 (4th Cir. 1991).

Sanctioning conduct which does not involve signing of papers. — This rule does not purport to be a means for district courts to sanction conduct in the course of a lawsuit, such as failure to comply with court orders, that does not involve the signing of pleadings, motions, or other papers. Simpson v. Welch, 900 F.2d 33 (4th Cir. 1990); Sowards v. Switch Energy Co., 744 F. Supp. 1399 (W.D. Va. 1990).

Applied in Misegades, Douglas & Levy v. Sonnenberg, 76 F.R.D. 384 (E.D. Va. 1976); Brown v. Cameron-Brown Co., 652 F.2d 375 (4th Cir. 1981); Reasor v. City of Norfolk, 606 F. Supp. 788 (E.D. Va. 1984); Cohen v. VEPCO, 617 F. Supp. 619 (E.D. Va. 1985); Hoover Universal, Inc. v. Brockway Imco, Inc., 809 F.2d 1039 (4th Cir. 1987); LaVay Corp. v. Dominion Fed. Sav. & Loan Ass'n, 830 F.2d 522 (4th Cir. 1987); United States v. Hirschfeld, 911 F. Supp. 200 (E.D. Va. 1995); In re Atlas Mach. & Iron Works, Inc., 190 Bankr. 796 (Bankr. E.D. Va. 1995); Laremont-Lopez v. Southeastern Tidewater Opportunity Project, 968 F. Supp. 1075 (E.D. Va. 1997); Bright v. Norshipco, 187 F.R.D. 536 (E.D. Va. 1998); Stewart v. Angelone, 186 F.R.D. 342 (E.D. Va. 1999).

II. REPRESENTATIONS TO COURT.

Duty to conduct prefiling examination of facts and law. — From both the plain language of the rule itself and the notes of the Advisory Committee, it is clear that the rule imposes upon an attorney a duty to conduct a prefiling examination of both the facts and the law before instituting legal process. Cabell v. Petty, 810 F.2d 463 (4th Cir. 1987).

The proper inquiry in ruling on this rule motion is whether a reasonable attorney in like circumstances would believe his actions to be factually and legally justified. Artco Corp. v. Lynnhaven Dry Storage Marina, Inc., 898 F.2d 953 (4th Cir. 1990).

To be reasonable, the prefiling factual investigation must uncover some information to support the allegations in the complaint; a complaint containing allegations unsupported by any information obtained prior to filing violates the required prefiling factual investigation; that is, where there is no factual basis for a plaintiff's allegations, the complaint violates this Rule's factual inquiry requirement. Brubaker v. City of Richmond, 943 F.2d 1363 (4th Cir. 1991).

The prefiling investigation must uncover some basis in law to support the claims in the complaint; a prefiling investigation of the law will not pass muster under this rule where the complaint has absolutely no chance of success under the existing precedent. Brubaker v. City of Richmond, 943 F.2d 1363 (4th Cir. 1991).

Attorney must conduct objectively reasonable investigation. — Under this rule, attorneys are required to investigate the factual and legal basis for the claim before filing a lawsuit. The 1972 amendments underscored this duty by eliminating the subjective "good faith" harbor and requiring an attorney to conduct an objectively reasonable investigation. Cleveland Demolition Co. v. Azcon Scrap Corp., 827 F.2d 984 (4th Cir. 1987); Sowards v. Switch Energy Co., 744 F. Supp. 1399 (W.D. Va. 1990).

Basic requirement of this rule is that an unrepresented party or a represented party's attorney conduct a prefiling investigation of law and fact which is objectively reasonable under the circumstances. Harmon v. O'Keefe, 149 F.R.D. 114 (E.D. Va. 1993).

Attorney's actions examined under standard of objective reasonableness. — If an attorney's conduct appears to fall within the scope of this rule, the court must first examine the actions at issue according to a standard of objective reasonableness. At this stage, the inquiry focuses only on whether a reasonable attorney in like circumstances could believe his actions to be factually and legally justified. Cabell v. Petty, 810 F.2d 463 (4th Cir. 1987); Sowards v. Switch Energy, Co. 744 F. Supp. 1399, (W.D. Va. 1990).

This rule provides for sanctions by the court if the court determines that the rule has been violated "after notice and a reasonable opportunity to respond;" an inquiry into a party's conduct under this rule is guided by an objective standard of reasonableness under the circumstances rather than an assessment of the party's subjective intent. Davis v. Hudgins, 896 F. Supp. 561 (E.D. Va. 1995), aff'd, 87 F.3d 1308 (4th Cir. 1996).

The reasonableness of the inquiry depends, to a large extent, on the circumstances that existed at the time the attorney filed the pleading. Sowards v. Switch Energy Co., 744 F. Supp. 1399 (W.D. Va. 1990).

If standard of objective reasonableness is unsatisfied, sanctions are mandatory. Cabell v. Petty, 810 F.2d 463 (4th Cir. 1987); Artco Corp. v. Lynnhaven Dry Storage Marina, Inc., 898 F.2d 953 (4th Cir. 1990).

Court refused to find that plaintiffs had continuing obligation to reevaluate merits of case. — Had the court of appeals found that plaintiffs had a continuing obligation to reevaluate the merits of their case and to dismiss the case once it lacked merit, the court would have concluded — contrary to Simpson v. Welch, 900 F.2d 33 (4th Cir. 1990) — that Rule 11 could be the basis for sanctions for failure to file certain papers. The court of appeals could not overrule a prior panel of the Fourth Circuit. Brubaker v. City of Richmond, 943 F.2d 1363 (4th Cir. 1991).

Motion violated rule where moving party planned to withdraw it if defendant opposed it. — Where the plaintiff's attorney did not act in bad faith in filing the pleading, because there was a legal basis for the claims he asserted, but the evidence before the district court established that plaintiff and his attorney decided in advance that if defendant indicated any opposition to their motion, they would withdraw it, the district court did not abuse its discretion in finding that the motion for leave to amend was filed for an improper purpose in violation of this rule. Defendant went to considerable expense in opposing the motion after it was filed, a burden that it need not have undertaken. If it were the plan of plaintiff and his attorney to withdraw the motion immediately upon discovering that there would be opposition to it, defendant's attorneys could have been informally contacted in order to ascertain whether they would object. Cohen v. VEPCO, 788 F.2d 247 (4th Cir. 1986).

Plaintiff's argument utilizing "stream of commerce" theory of personal jurisdiction was not so lacking in legal foundation as to warrant the imposition of sanctions under this rule. Sowards v. Switch Energy Co., 744 F. Supp. 1399 (W.D. Va. 1990).

Sanctions not avoided merely because defense is affirmative one. — A plaintiff cannot avoid sanctions merely because a defense to the claim is an affirmative one; this rule does not concern itself with the failure to assert an available defense; the rule does not permit a plaintiff to avoid sanctions merely because the opposing party or the judge might not immediately recognize that the assertion is groundless; where an attorney knows that a claim is time-barred and has no intention of seeking reversal of existing precedent, he makes a claim groundless in law and is subject to sanctions under this rule. Brubaker v. City of Richmond, 943 F.2d 1363 (4th Cir. 1991).

This rule does not require that a judge or jury agree with a plaintiff's allegation; for this rule's purposes, the allegation merely must be supported by some evidence. Brubaker v. City of Richmond, 943 F.2d 1363 (4th Cir. 1991).

Whether plaintiffs' complaint makes only a conclusory allegation of municipal custom or policy is irrelevant to an inquiry under this rule; the factual support for the allegation is relevant, however, because the concept of a municipal policy or custom is a legal one, and the court must assess the factual support in light of the legal standards. Brubaker v. City of Richmond, 943 F.2d 1363 (4th Cir. 1991).

Case remanded where circumstances and record do not reflect reasons. — In cases where the circumstances and the record do not clearly reflect the reasons for the district court's disposition of a motion under this rule, the case will be remanded with instruction that the district court make findings of fact concerning the frivolousness of the nonmovant's action. Miltier v. Beorn, 896 F.2d 848 (4th Cir. 1990).

Absence of deliberate "harassment." — Although the absence of deliberate "harassment" may be a consideration in choosing an appropriate sanction, it is not a factor in determining a violation. This rule does not prohibit merely intentional misconduct. Inexperience, incompetence, willfulness or deliberate choice may all contribute to a violation. Cabell v. Petty, 810 F.2d 463 (4th Cir. 1987).

Duty of disclosure in defective product case. — The cause of the product's deterioration stands on a different footing; it is not so much an objectively observable fact as it is a matter of expert opinion. Thus, a defendant may decline to admit the defectiveness of a product, even though some objective facts may suggest otherwise, provided there are reasonable grounds for the denial. Board of Dirs. v. Anden Group, 136 F.R.D. 100 (E.D. Va. 1991).

No abuse of discretion to find plaintiffs had no factual support when they filed memorandum opposing summary judgment. — It was not an abuse of discretion for the district court to find that when plaintiffs filed their memorandum opposing summary judgment, they had no factual support for their allegation that defendant was involved in the decision making process they claimed deprived them of their constitutional rights; the district court properly could hold plaintiffs and their attorney responsible for defendant's reasonable expenses incurred because of the filing of this memorandum in opposition to summary judgment. Brubaker v. City of Richmond, 943 F.2d 1363 (4th Cir. 1991).

District court erred in sanctioning plaintiffs. — Where district judge awarded sanctions to city since plaintiffs should have known that the city was incapable of forming the criminal intent necessary for liability under the Virginia Conspiracy Act, where the Virginia Conspiracy Act itself does not clearly state whether cities can be subjected to liability, where the Virginia Supreme Court has not been confronted directly with whether a city is a person within the meaning of the Virginia Conspiracy Act, and where a recent pronouncement of the Supreme Court in a Virginia Conspiracy Act case seemed to have left open the possibility that a city could be sued under that act, the district court abused its discretion in sanctioning plaintiffs since the court of appeals was unable to say that plaintiffs had "absolutely no chance of success" in bringing a Virginia Conspiracy Act claim against the city. Brubaker v. City of Richmond, 943 F.2d 1363 (4th Cir. 1991).

Where district court awarded sanctions to city on the ground that plaintiffs had no evidence to support their allegations that the city was involved in a scheme to prevent them from obtaining MBE certification or securing investment business, when plaintiffs filed their complaint, the Virginia Supreme Court had not rejected the concept of vicarious liability in the Virginia Conspiracy Act context and, in fact, seemed to leave open at least the possibility of this theory; because plaintiffs had a sufficient factual basis for implicating the city in the scheme, the district court abused its discretion in awarding sanctions to the city on the Virginia Conspiracy Act count. Brubaker v. City of Richmond, 943 F.2d 1363 (4th Cir. 1991).

Where district court awarded sanctions to city on Racketeer Influenced and Corrupt Organizations Act (RICO) count on the basis that plaintiffs should have known that the city could not form the criminal intent necessary under RICO, the district court should not have based sanctions on the city's incapacity to form criminal intent because the Fourth Circuit case law in this area was nonexistent and there was not enough other authority to conclude that it was objectively unreasonable to believe that the city could form criminal intent. Brubaker v. City of Richmond, 943 F.2d 1363 (4th Cir. 1991).

III. SANCTIONS.

Rule provides that court "shall" impose sanctions. — If an attorney signs a complaint without undertaking the necessary investigation, this rule provides that the district court "shall" impose sanctions. Cleveland Demolition Co. v. Azcon Scrap Corp., 827 F.2d 984 (4th Cir. 1987).

Sanctions proper where factual inquiry minimal and legal research cursory. — To fulfill his duty, an attorney must investigate the facts, examine the law, and then decide whether the complaint is justified. Plaintiff failed to discharge this duty, where it conducted only a minimal factual inquiry and a cursory legal investigation, and the district court properly imposed sanctions. Cleveland Demolition Co. v. Azcon Scrap Corp., 827 F.2d 984 (4th Cir. 1987).

Sanction cannot bankrupt party. — Court must avoid imposing a monetary award for purposes of imposing a sanction so great that it will bankrupt the offending party. Harmon v. O'Keefe, 149 F.R.D. 114 (E.D. Va. 1993).

Discretion of court as to sanctions. — It is always within the trial court's discretion to sanction attorneys for actions which lack a reasonable foundation in fact or in law. Van Arsdale v. Clemo, 825 F.2d 794 (4th Cir. 1987).

While some sanction is required when an infraction occurs, the determination of what is "appropriate" is still a matter left to the sound discretion of the district court. Cabell v. Petty, 810 F.2d 463 (4th Cir. 1987).

Decision to impose sanctions will be reversed only for abuse of discretion. Cleveland Demolition Co. v. Azcon Scrap Corp., 827 F.2d 984 (4th Cir. 1987).

A district court's ultimate decision to impose sanctions under this rule, and the quality and amount of the sanctions imposed, is reviewed under an abuse of discretion standard. Miltier v. Downes, 935 F.2d 660 (4th Cir. 1991).

Severity of sanction. — In choosing a sanction the basic principle is that the least severe sanction adequate to serve the purpose should be imposed. Cabell v. Petty, 810 F.2d 463 (4th Cir. 1987).

In choosing a sanction, the guiding principle is that the least severe sanction adequate to serve the purposes of this rule should be imposed. Miltier v. Downes, 935 F.2d 660 (4th Cir. 1991).

Sanctions in cases removed to federal court. — In removed cases sanctions may only be imposed under this rule, for actions or proceedings had after removal to federal court and may not be imposed for the filing of such action in the state court or for any proceedings or actions of the parties in that court. Meadow Ltd. Partnership v. Meadow Farm Partnership, 816 F.2d 970 (4th Cir. 1987).

A district judge cannot grant sanctions for the mere filing of a nonmeritorious case in a state court simply because that case was later removed to the federal court, nor can he grant sanctions for any action of the appellee in the state court. But if after removal of the case, the appellee continues to prosecute its claim and forces the appellant to take appropriate steps to defend the action in the federal court, whether this later action of the appellee in the federal court after removal warrants sanctions is a matter to be resolved by the district judge. Meadow Ltd. Partnership v. Meadow Farm Partnership, 816 F.2d 970 (4th Cir. 1987).

Monetary sanction imposed without consideration of ability to pay is abuse of discre-

tion. — Although the burden is on the sanctioned parties to offer evidence of their financial status, a monetary sanction imposed without any consideration of ability to pay is an abuse of discretion. Brubaker v. City of Richmond, 943 F.2d 1363 (4th Cir. 1991).

Court should give those sanctioned opportunity to submit affidavits on financial status. — If the court on remand is contemplating a large monetary sanction, the court should give those to be sanctioned the opportunity to submit affidavits on their financial status, or to submit such other evidence as the court in its discretion deems appropriate; the evidence offered should enable the district court to determine what amount of sanction would be so great as to restrict unfairly plaintiffs' access to the courts, to cause plaintiffs or attorney great financial distress, or to curtail attorney's ability to practice law. Brubaker v. City of Richmond, 943 F.2d 1363 (4th Cir. 1991).

Courts may require counsel to pay attorneys' fees under the inherent equitable powers possessed by a court. — In order for attorneys' fees to be assessed against counsel, however, a court must find that counsel acted in bad faith either in filing or in pursuing the claim. Tanner's Transf. & Storage of Va., Inc. v. Florance, 39 Bankr. 835 (Bankr. E.D. Va. 1984).

Court need not do more than state whether fee is reasonable. — This rule permits the district court to award a reasonable attorney's fee, and the court need not do more in its order than state whether the fee is reasonable; such a statement indicates that the court has undertaken an analysis of the reasonableness of the fee. Brubaker v. City of Richmond, 943 F.2d 1363 (4th Cir. 1991).

In determining the amount of sanctions, a district court should expressly consider the four factors adopted by this circuit in In re Kuntsler, 914 F.2d 505 (4th Cir. 1990), cert. denied, 499 U.S. 969, 111 S. Ct. 1607, 113 L. Ed. 2d 669 (1991): (1) The reasonableness of the opposing party's attorney's fees; (2) the minimum to deter; (3) the ability to pay; and (4) factors related to the severity of the Rule 11 violation. Brubaker v. City of Richmond, 943 F.2d 1363 (4th Cir. 1991).

In determining the amount of sanctions, the district court on remand should consider factors related to the severity of the violation under this rule, such as the offending party's history, experience, and ability, the severity of the violation, the degree to which malice or bad faith contributed to the violation, the risk of chilling the type of litigation involved and other factors as deemed appropriate. Brubaker v. City of Richmond, 943 F.2d 1363 (4th Cir. 1991).

Attorneys' fees and costs reasonably incurred to defend a claim filed in bad faith are recoverable. — Of course, attorneys' fees and costs generated by steps taken only to protract the litigation would not be incurred reasonably and, therefore, would not be recoverable. Tanner's Transf. & Storage of Va., Inc. v. Florance, 39 Bankr. 835 (Bankr. E.D. Va. 1984).

Sanctions not imposed. — Where each side had caused the other to incur approximately the same expense, the court considered it appropriate to let the matter rest where it was as to the offending pleadings and no sanctions were awarded under this rule. St. Jarre v. Heidelberger Druckmaschinen, 816 F. Supp. 424 (E.D. Va. 1993).

Fees usually assessed against both party and counsel. — Usually, an assessment of attorneys' fees is made jointly and severally against a party and his counsel, both of whom have acted in bad faith. Such an assessment is the result of the general understanding that a party is bound by the actions of his attorney. Tanner's Transf. & Storage of Va., Inc. v. Florance, 39 Bankr. 835 (Bankr. E.D. Va. 1984).

Error in award from date prior to when court denied motion to dismiss charge. — Where August 7 was the first day that one defendant's attorneys billed defendant for reviewing plaintiffs' memorandum in opposition to that defendant's Motion to Dismiss, the district court erred in awarding attorneys' fees from August 7, because on August 24, the district court denied defendant's motion to dismiss the § 1983 count, finding that the § 1983 charge against defendant was at that time supported by sufficient allegations. Brubaker v. City of Richmond, 943 F.2d 1363 (4th Cir. 1991).

Where a filing concerning an opposing party's motion for sanctions does not itself violate this rule, it is an abuse of discretion for a district court to award expenses incurred in connection with the sanctions motion. Brubaker v. City of Richmond, 943 F.2d 1363 (4th Cir. 1991).

Sanction imposed in amount of $500.00 was appropriate. — Sanction of plaintiff who failed to establish a legitimate discriminatory claim in the amount of $500.00 paid in monthly installments of $20.00 per month was appropriate in light of fact plaintiff, a pro se plaintiff, committed violation under this rule without malice or bad faith and plaintiff anticipated having no household income in the foreseeable future except food stamps and his wife's wages of approximately $200.00 biweekly. Harmon v. O'Keefe, 149 F.R.D. 114 (E.D. Va. 1993).

Rule 12. Defenses and Objections: When and How Presented; Motion for Judgment on the Pleadings; Consolidating Motions; Waiving Defenses; Pretrial Hearing.

(a) *Time to Serve a Responsive Pleading.* — (1) In General. Unless another time is specified by this rule or a federal statute, the time for serving a responsive pleading is as follows:

(A) A defendant must serve an answer:

(i) within 21 days after being served with the summons and complaint; or

(ii) if it has timely waived service under Rule 4(d), within 60 days after the request for a waiver was sent, or within 90 days after it was sent to the defendant outside any judicial district of the United States.

(B) A party must serve an answer to a counterclaim or crossclaim within 21 days after being served with the pleading that states the counterclaim or crossclaim.

(C) A party must serve a reply to an answer within 21 days after being served with an order to reply, unless the order specifies a different time.

(2) United States and Its Agencies, Officers, or Employees Sued in an Official Capacity. The United States, a United States agency, or a United States officer or employee sued only in an official capacity must serve an answer to a complaint, counterclaim, or crossclaim within 60 days after service on the United States attorney.

(3) United States Officers or Employees Sued in an Individual Capacity. A United States officer or employee sued in an individual capacity for an act or omission occurring in connection with duties performed on the United States' behalf must serve an answer to a complaint, counterclaim, or crossclaim within 60 days after service on the officer or employee or service on the United States attorney, whichever is later.

(4) Effect of a Motion. Unless the court sets a different time, serving a motion under this rule alters these periods as follows:

(A) if the court denies the motion or postpones its disposition until trial, the responsive pleading must be served within 14 days after notice of the court's action; or

(B) if the court grants a motion for a more definite statement, the responsive pleading must be served within 14 days after the more definite statement is served.

(b) *How to Present Defenses.* — Every defense to a claim for relief in any pleading must be asserted in the responsive pleading if one is required. But a party may assert the following defenses by motion:

(1) lack of subject-matter jurisdiction;

(2) lack of personal jurisdiction;

(3) improper venue;

(4) insufficient process;

(5) insufficient service of process;

(6) failure to state a claim upon which relief can be granted; and

(7) failure to join a party under Rule 19.

A motion asserting any of these defenses must be made before pleading if a responsive pleading is allowed. If a pleading sets out a claim for relief that does not require a responsive pleading, an opposing party may assert at trial any defense to that claim. No defense or objection is waived by joining it with one or more other defenses or objections in a responsive pleading or in a motion.

(c) *Motion for Judgment on the Pleadings.* — After the pleadings are closed — but early enough not to delay trial — a party may move for judgment on the pleadings.

(d) *Result of Presenting Matters Outside the Pleadings.* — If, on a motion under Rule 12(b)(6) or 12(c), matters outside the pleadings are presented to and not excluded by the court, the motion must be treated as one for summary judgment under Rule 56. All parties must be given a reasonable opportunity to present all the material that is pertinent to the motion.

(e) *Motion for a More Definite Statement.* — A party may move for a more definite statement of a pleading to which a responsive pleading is allowed but which is so vague or ambiguous that the party cannot reasonably prepare a response. The motion must be made before filing a responsive pleading and must point out the defects complained of and the details desired. If the court orders a more definite statement and the order is not obeyed within 14 days after notice of the order or within the time the court sets, the court may strike the pleading or issue any other appropriate order.

(f) *Motion to Strike.* — The court may strike from a pleading an insufficient defense or any redundant, immaterial, impertinent, or scandalous matter. The court may act:

(1) on its own; or

(2) on motion made by a party either before responding to the pleading or, if a response is not allowed, within 21 days after being served with the pleading.

(g) *Joining Motions.* — (1) Right to Join. A motion under this rule may be joined with any other motion allowed by this rule.

(2) Limitation on Further Motions. Except as provided in Rule 12(h)(2) or (3), a party that makes a motion under this rule must not make another motion under this rule raising a defense or objection that was available to the party but omitted from its earlier motion.

(h) *Waiving and Preserving Certain Defenses.* — (1) When Some Are Waived. A party waives any defense listed in Rule 12(b)(2)-(5) by:

(A) omitting it from a motion in the circumstances described in Rule 12(g)(2); or

(B) failing to either:

(i) make it by motion under this rule; or

(ii) include it in a responsive pleading or in an amendment allowed by Rule 15(a)(1) as a matter of course.

(2) When to Raise Others. Failure to state a claim upon which relief can be granted, to join a person required by Rule 19(b), or to state a legal defense to a claim may be raised:

(A) in any pleading allowed or ordered under Rule 7(a);

(B) by a motion under Rule 12(c); or

(C) at trial.

(3) Lack of Subject-Matter Jurisdiction. If the court determines at any time that it lacks subject-matter jurisdiction, the court must dismiss the action.

(i) *Hearing Before Trial.* — If a party so moves, any defense listed in Rule 12(b)(1)-(7) — whether made in a pleading or by motion — and a motion under Rule 12(c) must be heard and decided before trial unless the court orders a deferral until trial. (Amended by order adopted December 27, 1946, effective March 19, 1948, by order adopted January 21, 1963, effective July 1, 1963, by order adopted February 28, 1966, effective July 1, 1966, by order adopted March 2, 1987, effective August 1, 1987, by order adopted April 22, 1993, effective December 1, 1993, by order adopted April 17, 2000, effective December 1, 2000, by order adopted April 30, 2007, effective December 1, 2007, and by order adopted March 26, 2009, effective December 1, 2009.)

Comment. — The language of Rule 12 has been amended as part of the general restyling of the Civil Rules to make them more easily understood and to make style and terminology consistent throughout the rules. These changes are intended to be stylistic only.

Former Rule 12(a)(4) referred to an order that postpones disposition of a motion "until the trial on the merits." Rule 12(a)(4) now refers to postponing disposition "until trial." The new expression avoids the ambiguity that inheres in "trial on the merits," which may become confusing when there is a separate trial of a single issue or another event different from a single all-encompassing trial.

CASE NOTES

I. In General.
II. Jurisdictional Issues.
III. Rule 12(b)(6) Motion.
A. In General.
B. When Treated as Motion for Summary Judgment.

I. IN GENERAL.

Sources of power to dismiss complaint. — A district court has the power to dismiss a complaint, sua sponte, either by noting the inadequacy of the complaint and then dismissing it for failure to state a claim under this rule, by way of the court's "inherent power" to take such action under the proper circumstances, or by way of 28 U.S.C. § 1915(d), through a finding that the complaint, filed in forma pauperis pursuant to 28 U.S.C. 1915(a), is frivolous on its face. Johnson v. Baskerville, 568 F. Supp. 853 (E.D. Va. 1983).

Time for service of answer by United States may be limited by other provisions. — It is true that subdivision (a) of this rule allows the United States 60 days after service to answer a complaint. But such a general provision must be inapplicable in an action required by law to be wholly determined within 20 days after it is commenced. Clarke v. United States, 553 F. Supp. 382 (E.D. Va. 1983), aff'd, 587 F. Supp. 674 (E.D. Va. 1984).

Answer allowed to be filed four days late. — See Redmond v. O'Sullivan Rubber Co., 10 F.R.D. 519 (W.D. Va. 1943).

Pro se complaint to be read liberally. — A complaint will not be dismissed for failure to state a cause of action where it is likely that facts may be adduced to support the claim of threatening a prison inmate for pursuing judicial relief where the inmate was threatened, transferred to a road gang with an armed guard and the penal officer making the threat was subsequently dismissed. Hudspeth v. Figgins, 584 F.2d 1345 (4th Cir. 1978), cert. denied, 441 U.S. 913, 99 S. Ct. 2013, 60 L. Ed. 2d 386 (1979).

A pro se complaint raising civil rights issues is particularly entitled to liberal construction. Islam v. Jackson, 782 F. Supp. 1111 (E.D. Va. 1992); Terry v. Bobb, 827 F. Supp. 366 (E.D. Va. 1993).

Allegations by a pro se plaintiff, however inartfully pleaded, are sufficient to call for an opportunity to offer supporting evidence, unless it is beyond a doubt that plaintiff could prove no set of facts that would entitle him to relief. Torcasio v. Murray, 862 F. Supp. 1482 (E.D. Va. 1994), aff'd in part, rev'd in part, 57 F.3d 1340 (4th Cir. 1995), cert. denied, 516 U.S. 1071, 116 S. Ct. 772, 133 L. Ed. 2d 724 (1996).

Motion to dismiss complaint denied with leave to renew. — Plaintiffs were entitled to be heard on the paramount question raised by the amended supplemental complaint as to whether or not the defendants, individually or in concert with each other, were deliberately circumventing or attempting to circumvent or frustrate the order of the district court. Therefore, the motions to dismiss were denied, without prejudice to the rights of the defendants or any of them to renew their motions upon the conclusion of the hearing if they are then so advised. Allen v. County Sch. Bd., 28 F.R.D. 367 (E.D. Va. 1961).

Burden of proving proper venue. — When a defendant moves to dismiss under subdivision (b)(3), plaintiff bears the burden of establishing that venue is proper. Wood v. Barnette, Inc., 648 F. Supp. 936 (E.D. Va. 1986).

Failure to renew motion to dismiss for improper venue, after initial motion to dismiss was denied without prejudice because motion did not comply with local rule 11(F), resulted in waiver regarding venue. Alderman v. Chrysler Corp., 480 F. Supp. 600 (E.D. Va. 1979).

Whether car was operated by agent so as to permit substituted service on nonresident held issue best disposed of at trial. — See Powell v. Knight, 74 F. Supp. 191 (E.D. Va. 1947).

Motion for more definite statement is expeditious. — To send the parties as well as the court into a pretrial conference on the subject, to make necessary an exchange of interrogatories and answers, or to force resort to discovery depositions, just to ascertain the bases of the complaint, is hardly expedition within the intent of the rules. Surely less involved is an immediate and direct motion by the defendant for the particulars he needs. McComb v. Hardy, 8 F.R.D. 28 (E.D. Va. 1948).

But such motion does not lie to procure evidence. McComb v. Hardy, 8 F.R.D. 28 (E.D. Va. 1948).

Jurisdictional amount may be raised by motion. — The jurisdictional amount may be properly challenged by a motion to dismiss under subdivision (b). Payton v. Freeze, 49 F.R.D. 11 (E.D. Va. 1969).

As may statute of limitations. — The defense of the statute of limitations, where the limitation appears on the face of the complaint, is properly raised by a motion to dismiss — but not by a "plea." Davenport v. Deseret Pharmaceutical Co., 321 F. Supp. 659 (E.D. Va. 1971).

Plaintiff has burden to prove jurisdictional facts placed in issue. — Although a plaintiff cannot normally be put to his proof on a motion to dismiss, if jurisdictional facts are placed in issue, it is up to plaintiff to prove their existence. Willis v. Semmes, Bowen & Semmes, 441 F. Supp. 1235 (E.D. Va. 1977).

Where personal jurisdiction is challenged pursuant to this rule, the parties asserting personal jurisdiction have the burden of proving the facts necessary to the assertion of such jurisdiction by a preponderance of the evidence. Abel v. Montgomery Ward Co., 798 F. Supp. 322 (E.D. Va. 1992).

Allegations were sufficient to provide the defendants notice of the nature of the claim against them and the grounds on which it rested, and it did not appear beyond a doubt that there was no set of facts which the plaintiffs could prove in support of claim which would entitle them to relief. Jordan v. Jackson, 15 F.3d 333 (4th Cir. 1994).

Allegations must be taken as true on motion to dismiss. — The facts set forth in the complaint must be assumed to be true in passing on a motion to dismiss for failure to state a claim. Johnson v. Mueller, 415 F.2d 354 (4th Cir. 1969); Lucas v. Kale, 364 F. Supp. 1345 (W.D. Va. 1973).

For purposes of a motion to dismiss, the material allegations of the complaint must be taken as admitted and the complaint is to be liberally construed in favor of the plaintiff. MacKethan v. Peat, Marwick, Mitchell & Co., 439 F. Supp. 1090 (E.D. Va. 1977).

The allegations of the complaint and the exhibits, for the purposes of a motion to dismiss under subdivision (b), must be taken as true. Deward & Rich, Inc. v. Bristol Sav. & Loan Corp., 29 F. Supp. 777 (W.D. Va. 1939).

Court must accept as true all material allegations of complaint. — See Puerto Rico ex rel. Quiros v. Alfred L. Snapp & Sons, 632 F.2d 365 (4th Cir. 1980), cert. granted, 454 U.S. 1079, 102 S. Ct. 631, 70 L. Ed. 2d 612 (1981), aff'd, 458 U.S. 592, 102 S. Ct. 3260, 73 L. Ed. 2d 995 (1982).

Court may consider matters of public record, orders, items appearing in the record of the case, and exhibits attached to the complaint, when ruling on a motion to dismiss for failure to state a claim upon which relief can be granted under subdivision (b)(6). Moore v. Flagstar Bank, 6 F. Supp. 2d 496 (E.D. Va. 1997).

No presumptive truthfulness attaches to the plaintiff's allegations and the existence of disputed material facts will not preclude the trial court from evaluating for itself the merits of jurisdictional claims. Materson v. Stokes, 166 F.R.D. 368 (E.D. Va. 1996).

Allegation not sufficient. — A mere allegation that defendants violated the antitrust laws as to a particular plaintiff and commodity is insufficient to survive a Rule 12(b)(6) motion. Estate Constr. Co. v. Miller & Smith Holding Co., 14 F.3d 213 (4th Cir. 1994).

Restriction on use of motion for more definite statement. — The motion for a more definite statement is restricted to pleadings so vague or ambiguous that the opposing party could not frame an appropriate response. EEOC v. GE Co., 370 F. Supp. 1258 (W.D. Va. 1973).

When the complaint conforms to Rule 8(a) and it is neither so vague nor so ambiguous that the defendant cannot reasonably be required to answer, the district court should deny a motion for a more definite statement and require the defendant to bring the case to issue by filing a response within the time provided by the rules. Hodgson v. Virginia Baptist Hosp., 482 F.2d 821 (4th Cir. 1973).

Motion to strike is not a favored motion because it is a drastic remedy, and courts will deny a motion to strike a defense that fairly presents a question of law or fact that a court ought to consider. In re J.W. Schonfeld, Ltd., 460 F. Supp. 332 (E.D. Va. 1978).

Impertinent or immaterial. — A matter is "impertinent" or "immaterial" under subdivision (f) if it is not relevant to the issues involved in the action. Paul v. Gomez, 190 F.R.D. 402 (W.D. Va. 2000).

Complaint held sufficient to require defendant to respond. — See Hodgson v. Virginia Baptist Hosp., 482 F.2d 821 (4th Cir. 1973).

Purpose of subdivision (f) is not to test legal sufficiency of affirmative defense. — Where, before filing their motion for summary judgment, plaintiffs filed, and defendants responded to, a motion to strike the defendants' affirmative defenses pursuant to subdivision (f) of this rule, but plaintiffs did not bring this motion on for hearing or request a decision on it, and it appears that they intended to accomplish the same thing by a motion for summary judgment, the plaintiffs in effect were attempting to create a plaintiff's version of subdivision (b)(6) to test the legal sufficiency of the defendants' assertions, which is not the intended purpose of subdivision (f). Watkins v. Cantrell, 568 F. Supp. 1225 (E.D. Va. 1983), aff'd, 736 F.2d 933 (4th Cir. 1984).

Purpose of subdivision (g) is to prevent unnecessary delay at pleading stage. Jetform Corp. v. Unisys Corp., 11 F. Supp. 2d 788 (E.D. Va. 1998).

District court had no jurisdiction regarding handling of appeal by Supreme Court of Virginia. — The United States District Court had no jurisdiction to determine whether the Supreme Court of Virginia erred in its handling of an appeal from the Circuit Court of Gloucester County. It therefore dismissed the action pursuant to subdivision (h)(3) of this rule. Snow v. Nevada Dep't of Prisons, 582 F. Supp. 53 (E.D. Va. 1984).

When Rule 83 cannot be basis for dismissal. — Where dismissal for want of a meritorious claim is provided for by rules other than Rule 83 and dismissal under Rule 83 for lack of a meritorious claim would be inconsistent with those other provisions, specifically Rule 12(b) and Rule 56, Rule 83 could not be the basis for a dismissal of a cause of action deemed not meritorious. Brown v. Cameron-Brown Co., 652 F.2d 375 (4th Cir. 1981).

Dismissal held improper. — In a case where the plaintiffs sought an injunction against annexation proceedings on the basis of infringement of voting rights, the Fourth Circuit Court of Appeals held that the injunction was properly denied below but that the district court should retain jurisdiction until proposals designed to prevent potentially unconstitutional effects on voting were put into effect. Citizens Comm. to Oppose Annexation v. City of Lynchburg, 528 F.2d 816 (4th Cir.), modifying 400 F. Supp. 68 (W.D. Va. 1975).

The district court improperly dismissed plaintiffs' claim for the loss of use and enjoyment of their real property resulting from the exposure to vapors under the federal preemption doctrine, since "wafting vapors" were not an insufficient impact as a matter of law. Cavallo v. Star Enter., 100 F.3d 1150 (4th Cir. 1996), cert. denied, 522 U.S. 1044, 118 S. Ct. 684, 139 L. Ed. 2d 631 (1998).

Courts will not reconsider a motion to dismiss where such "Request for Reconsideration of a Motion" has no statutory authority and such motion merely cites authority and factual matter which was available to the litigant and easily could have been included in the original brief. Shepherd v. Health Drinks of Am., Inc., 69 F.R.D. 607 (E.D. Va. 1976).

Suit against Equal Employment Opportunity Commission for release of information as stated cause of action. — See Associated Dry Goods Corp. v. EEOC, 419 F. Supp. 814 (E.D. Va. 1976).

Applied in Railway Labor Executives' Ass'n v. Wheeling & L.E. Ry., 741 F. Supp. 595 (E.D. Va. 1990); Flinders v. Datasec Corp., 742 F. Supp. 929 (E.D. Va. 1990); First Am. Nat'l Bank v. Straight Creek Processing Co., 756 F. Supp. 945 (E.D. Va. 1991); Hammar v. Cost Control Mktg. & Sales Mgt. of Va., Inc., 757 F. Supp. 698 (W.D. Va. 1990); Lester Mobile Home Sales, Inc. v. Woods, 130 Bankr. 204 (W.D. Va. 1990); Rountree v. Fairfax County Sch. Bd., 933 F.2d 219 (4th Cir. 1991); Kiernan v. Agency Rent A Car, Inc., 940 F.2d 917 (4th Cir. 1991); Dubowski v. Dominion Bankshares Corp., 763 F. Supp. 169 (W.D. Va. 1991); Jones v. United States, 763 F. Supp. 852 (W.D. Va. 1991); Newton v. State Farm Fire & Cas. Co., 138 F.R.D. 76 (E.D. Va. 1991); Stevens v. Jackson, 800 F. Supp. 344 (W.D. Va. 1992); Lewis v. United States, 802 F. Supp. 1419 (E.D. Va. 1992); Eckstein v. Cullen, 803 F. Supp. 1107 (E.D. Va. 1992); Portsmouth Redevelopment & Hous. Auth. v. BMI Apts. Assocs., 827 F. Supp. 354 (E.D. Va. 1993); United States ex rel. Owens v. Olympic Marine Servs., 827 F. Supp. 1232 (E.D. Va. 1993); Simmons v. Baker, 842 F. Supp. 883 (E.D. Va. 1994); Kramer v. United States, 843 F. Supp. 1066 (E.D. Va. 1994); Adams v. Star Enters., 851 F. Supp. 770 (E.D. Va. 1994); Weill v. Dominion Resources, Inc., 875 F. Supp. 331 (E.D. Va. 1994); Smith v. Richels, 163 Bankr. 760 (Bankr. E.D. Va. 1994); John S. Clark Co. v. Faggert & Frieden, 65 F.3d 26 (4th Cir. 1995); Pittston Coal Co. v. Babbitt, 66 F.3d 714 (4th Cir. 1995); Mayo v. Kiwest Corp., 898 F. Supp. 335 (E.D. Va. 1995); Mitchell v. RJK of Gloucester, Inc., 899 F. Supp. 246 (E.D. Va. 1995); George v. Angelone, 901 F. Supp. 1070 (E.D. Va. 1995); International Longshoremen's Ass'n v. Virginia Int'l Terms., Inc., 904 F. Supp. 500 (E.D. Va. 1995); Cate v. Transcontinental Gas Pipe Line Corp., 904 F. Supp. 526 (W.D. Va. 1995); Childress v. City of Richmond, 907 F. Supp. 934 (E.D. Va. 1995); Tidewater Beverage Servs., Inc. v. Coca Cola Co., 907 F. Supp. 943 (E.D. Va. 1995); Williams v. Enterprise Leasing Co., 911 F. Supp. 988 (E.D. Va. 1995); Moeller v. D'Arrigo, 163 F.R.D. 489 (E.D. Va. 1995); Cochran v. Morris, 73 F.3d 1310 (4th Cir. 1996); Robb v. United States, 80 F.3d 884 (4th Cir. 1996); International Longshoremen's Ass'n v. Virginia Int'l Terms., Inc., 914 F. Supp. 1335 (E.D. Va. 1996); Rutherford v. City of Newport News, 919 F. Supp. 885 (E.D. Va. 1996); Porter v. United States, 919 F. Supp. 927 (E.D. Va. 1996); Reynolds & Reynolds Co. v. Hardee, 932 F. Supp. 149 (E.D. Va. 1996); Estate of Morgan v. Mayor of Hampton, 936 F. Supp. 343 (E.D. Va. 1996); Wichlacz v. United States Dep't of Interior, 938 F. Supp. 325 (E.D. Va. 1996); Brown v. Angelone, 938 F. Supp. 340 (W.D. Va. 1996); Michael v. Sentara Health Sys., 939 F. Supp. 1220 (E.D. Va. 1996); Starr v. United States, 940 F. Supp. 916 (E.D. Va. 1996); Garrett v. Angelone, 940 F. Supp. 933 (W.D. Va. 1996); Hinch v. Duncan, 941 F. Supp. 62 (W.D. Va. 1996); White v. CMA Constr. Co., 947 F. Supp. 231 (E.D. Va. 1996); Comet Enters. Ltd. v. Air-A-Plane Corp., 128 F.3d 855 (4th Cir. 1997); Taylor v. Virginia, DOT, 170 F.R.D. 10 (E.D. Va. 1996); Lugo v. Immigration & Naturalization Serv., 950 F. Supp. 743 (E.D. Va. 1997); Royal Meadows Stables, Inc. v. Colonial Farm Credit, 207 Bankr. 1003 (E.D. Va. 1997); Board of Trustees v. McD Metals, Inc., 964 F. Supp. 1040 (E.D. Va. 1997); Sculthorpe v. Virginia Retirement Sys., 952 F. Supp. 307 (E.D. Va. 1997); GTE S. Inc. v. Morrison, 957 F. Supp. 800 (E.D. Va. 1997); African Dev. Co. v. Keene Eng'g, 963 F. Supp. 522 (E.D. Va. 1997); Sellers v. School Bd., 141 F.3d 524 (4th Cir. 1998); Settle v. S.W. Rodgers Co., 998 F. Supp. 657 (E.D. Va. 1998); Davis v. Cole, 999 F.

Supp. 809 (E.D. Va. 1998); Chisholm v. UHP Projects, Inc., 1 F. Supp. 2d 581 (E.D. Va. 1998); Litman v. George Mason Univ., 5 F. Supp. 2d 366 (E.D. Va. 1998); Vanguard Military Equip. Corp. v. David B. Finestone Co., 6 F. Supp. 2d 488 (E.D. Va. 1997); Sullivan v. Hall, 222 Bankr. 275 (Bankr. E.D. Va. 1998); Affordable Efficiencies, Inc. v. Bane, 228 Bankr. 835 (Bankr. W.D. Va. 1998); Evans v. B.F. Perkins Co., a Div. of Standex Intern Corp., 166 F.3d 642 (4th. Cir. 1999); Manning ex rel. Manning v. Fairfax School, 176 F.3d 235 (4th Cir. 1999); Sumner v. Tucker, 9 F. Supp. 2d 641 (E.D. Va. 1998); Frontline Test Equip., Inc. v. Greenleaf Software, Inc., 10 F. Supp. 2d 583 (W.D. Va. 1998); Barron v. Runyon, 11 F. Supp. 2d 676 (E.D. Va. 1998); Fanney v. Trigon Ins. Co., 11 F. Supp. 2d 829 (E.D. Va. 1998); Norfolk & W. Ry. v. Brotherhood of R.R. Signalmen, 11 F. Supp. 2d 833 (W.D. Va. 1998); Patient v. Corbin, 37 F. Supp. 2d 433 (E.D. Va. 1998); Russo v. United States, 37 F. Supp. 2d 450 (E.D. Va. 1999); Lincoln Nat'l Life Ins. Co. v. Johnson, 38 F. Supp. 2d 440 (E.D. Va. 1999); Chaudhry v. Mobil Oil Corp., 186 F.3d 502 (4th Cir. 1999); Lovern v. Edwards, 190 F.3d 648 (4th Cir. 1999); King v. Donnkenny, Inc., 84 F. Supp. 2d 736 (W.D. Va. 2000); United States v. Elliot, 83 F. Supp. 2d 637 (E.D. Va. 1999); Women in Military Serv. for Am. Mem. Found. v. Hartford Fire Ins. Co., 215 F.3d 1324, 2000 U.S. App. LEXIS 12223 (4th Cir. 2000); Puryear v. County of Roanoke, 214 F.3d 514, 2000 U.S. App. LEXIS 13677 (4th Cir. 2000); American Chiropractic Ass'n v. Trigon Healthcare, Inc., 151 F. Supp. 2d 723, 2001 U.S. Dist. LEXIS 10348 (W.D. Va. 2001); Hager v. First Va. Banks, Inc., 2002 U.S. Dist. LEXIS 412 (W.D. Va. 2002).

II. JURISDICTIONAL ISSUES.

Manner of presenting motion to dismiss for lack of subject matter jurisdiction. — There are two critically different ways in which to present a motion to dismiss for lack of subject matter jurisdiction. First, it may be contended that a complaint simply fails to allege facts upon which subject matter jurisdiction can be based. In that event, all the facts alleged in the complaint are assumed to be true and the plaintiff, in effect, is afforded the same procedural protection as he would receive under a Rule 12(b)(6) consideration. Second, it may be contended that the jurisdictional allegations of the complaint were not true. A trial court may then go beyond the allegations of the complaint and in an evidentiary hearing determine if there are facts to support the jurisdictional allegations. Adams v. Bain, 697 F.2d 1213 (4th Cir. 1982).

A motion to dismiss for lack of subject matter jurisdiction may attack the complaint on its face or the truth of the underlying jurisdictional allegations contained in the complaint; the nonmovant has the burden to allege and prove such jurisdiction. Marks v. United States Social Sec. Admin., 906 F. Supp. 1017 (E.D. Va. 1995), aff'd in part and vacated in part, 92 F.3d 1180 (4th Cir. 1996).

A plaintiff carries the burden of proving that federal subject matter jurisdiction is proper; as the party asserting jurisdiction, he continues to shoulder this burden where defendant objects to a federal district court's assertion of jurisdiction. Materson v. Stokes, 166 F.R.D. 368 (E.D. Va. 1996).

Noncompliance with notice requirement of statute raised by motion. — Compliance with the notice requirement of the Age Discrimination in Employment Act is a condition precedent to acquiring federal-question jurisdiction under the Age Discrimination in Employment Act, and where the complaint on its face shows that such was not complied with, a motion to dismiss is proper. Raynor v. Great Atl. & Pac. Tea Co., 400 F. Supp. 357 (E.D. Va. 1975).

Disposition of motion based on jurisdictional amount. — Where defendant challenged the jurisdictional amount required for federal jurisdiction, and plaintiff had proposed to file an affidavit to support his claim, but no such affidavit had been filed, the district court allowed a brief time for filing the affidavit before dismissing, and reserved the right to apply sanctions if the recovery on trial proved less than the jurisdictional amount where on the facts the claimed recovery seemed doubtful. Dykstra v. Rich Neck Corp., 68 F.R.D. 572 (E.D. Va. 1975).

Guarding ship in port sufficient maritime activity. — Plaintiff's guarding of public vessel during its repairs in port was conduct sufficiently connected to traditional maritime activity to confer jurisdiction on the federal courts. White v. United States, 53 F.3d 43 (4th Cir. 1995).

Court may look beyond allegations where subject matter jurisdiction challenged. — In this case, the motion under this rule challenges the actual existence of the district court's subject matter jurisdiction. In such a situation the court may look beyond the jurisdictional allegations of the complaint and view whatever evidence has been submitted on the issue to determine whether in fact subject matter jurisdiction exists. Virginia v. United States, 926 F. Supp. 537 (E.D. Va. 1995).

Where subject matter jurisdiction is challenged, factual allegations assumed true. — Where a motion under this rule constitutes a facial attack upon the complaint's allegations of subject matter jurisdiction, the district court must assume that all factual allegations in the complaint are true. Virginia v. United States, 926 F. Supp. 537 (E.D. Va. 1995).

Motions under subsection (b)(1) do not go to the merits of the claim, but address only jurisdictional issues. Shoemaker v. Metro Info. Servs., 910 F. Supp. 259 (E.D. Va. 1996).

Invocation of "lessened burden standard" in Rule 12(b)(2) challenge. — While the burden of demonstrating that in personam jurisdiction exists rests ultimately on the plaintiff, that burden is lessened considerably when a court declines to hold an evidentiary hearing on the matter, instead relying on the parties' pleadings, affidavits, and other relevant legal documents. Under this "lessened burden standard," the plaintiff need only make a prima facie case for jurisdiction to forestall his complaint's demise. Dismissal is appropriate only when, construing all relevant allegations in the light most favorable to the plaintiff, assuming credibility, and drawing the most favorable inferences for the existence of jurisdiction, the court finds the plaintiff's stated case deficient. Klockner-Pentaplast of Am., Inc. v. Roth Display Corp., 860 F. Supp. 1119 (W.D. Va. 1994).

There is an important difference between subdivisions (b)(1) and (b)(6). — On a motion to dismiss pursuant to subdivision (b)(1), unlike subdivision (b)(6), courts may consider evidence outside of the complaint to resolve factual disputes concerning jurisdiction without converting the motion into one for summary judgment. Carter v. Arlington Pub. Sch. Sys., 82 F. Supp. 2d 561 (E.D. Va. 2000).

Facts considered in ruling on Rule 12(b)(1) motion. — Unlike the procedure in a Rule 12(b)(6) motion where there is a presumption reserving the truth finding role to the ultimate factfinder, the court in a Rule 12(b)(1) hearing weighs the evidence to determine its jurisdiction. This does not usually present a serious problem except in those cases where the jurisdictional facts are intertwined with the facts central to the merits of the dispute. In such cases the entire factual dispute is appropriately resolved only by a proceeding on the merits. Adams v. Bain, 697 F.2d 1213 (4th Cir. 1982).

Dismissal under subdivision (b)(1) has two consequences: one, the court may consider the evidence beyond the scope of the pleadings to resolve factual disputes concerning jurisdiction; and two, dismissal for jurisdictional defects has no res judicata effect. Williams v. United States, 50 F.3d 299 (4th Cir. 1995).

The differing procedural standards of dismissal under Rule 12(b)(1) and summary judgment under Rule 56(c) are more than academic. Williams v. United States, 50 F.3d 299 (4th Cir. 1995).

Burden of proving subject matter jurisdiction on a motion to dismiss is on the plaintiff, the party asserting jurisdiction. A trial court may consider evidence by affidavit, depositions or live testimony without converting the proceeding to one for summary judgment. Adams v. Bain, 697 F.2d 1213 (4th Cir. 1982).

On a motion to dismiss under this rule, the plaintiff bears the burden to establish subject matter jurisdiction; when the issue turns on a factual dispute, the court may weigh conflicting evidence and resolve the dispute. Vick v. Foote, Inc., 898 F. Supp. 330 (E.D. Va. 1995), aff'd, 82 F.3d 411 (4th Cir. 1996), cert. denied, 519 U.S. 935, 117 S. Ct. 311, 136 L. Ed. 2d 228 (1996).

Issue of jurisdiction raised in petition for rehearing. Cook v. Arentzen, 582 F.2d 870 (4th Cir. 1978).

Declaratory Judgment Act not a grant of jurisdiction to federal court but merely makes available additional remedy where jurisdiction already exists. El-Amin v. Wilkinson, 454 F. Supp. 804 (E.D. Va. 1978).

Immunity from civil suit for damages for acts done in official capacity. — See Burke v. Miller, 580 F.2d 108 (4th Cir. 1978), cert. denied, 440 U.S. 930, 99 S. Ct. 1268, 59 L. Ed. 2d 487 (1979).

Waiver of sovereign immunity. — Absent a waiver of sovereign immunity, jurisdiction is defective, and an action against the United States is barred. Bay Sav. Bank v. IRS, 837 F. Supp. 150 (E.D. Va. 1993).

III. RULE 12(B)(6) MOTION.

A. In General.

Duty of the court. — In reviewing a Rule 12(b)(6) motion to dismiss, the court must accept all allegations of the complaint as true, construe it in a light most favorable to the plaintiff, and determine whether, under any reasonable reading of the complaint, the plaintiff might be entitled to relief. Broad St. Assocs. v. United Cos. Life Ins. Co., 163 Bankr. 68 (Bankr. E.D. Va. 1993).

This holding properly balances the plaintiffs' right to notice of those matters which may be addressed by the court, and the defendants' right to test swiftly the legal soundness of the charges made against them. Gasner v. County of Dinwiddie, 162 F.R.D. 280 (E.D. Va. 1995), aff'd, 103 F.3d 351 (4th Cir. 1996).

A court cannot consider matters outside the pleadings when determining a motion pursuant to subsection (b)(6) which goes to the merits of the claim. Shoemaker v. Metro Info. Servs., 910 F. Supp. 259 (E.D. Va. 1996).

Jurisdictional challenge compared with Rule 12(b)(6) motion. — A Rule 12(b)(6) motion to dismiss for failure to state a claim does not permit the court to look outside the complaint, and is thus distinguishable from a challenge to the court's subject matter jurisdiction, which allows the court to "look beyond the jurisdictional allegations of the complaint and view whatever evidence has been submitted on the issue to determine whether in fact subject matter jurisdiction exists." Gasner v. County of Dinwiddie, 162 F.R.D. 280 (E.D. Va. 1995), aff'd, 103 F.3d 351 (4th Cir. 1996).

Generally, motion to dismiss under Rule 12(b)(6) must be assessed in light of Rule 8's liberal pleading standards. Therefore, the complaint need only state sufficient facts to enable the defendant to draft a responsive pleading. Jetform Corp. v. Unisys Corp., 11 F. Supp. 2d 788 (E.D. Va 1998).

A Rule 12(b)(6) motion cannot be raised for first time after trial, and Rule 60(b) may not serve as a surrogate to a tardy Rule 12(b)(6) motion. Eberhardt v. Integrated Design & Constr., Inc., 167 F.3d 861 (4th. Cir. 1999).

Raising affirmative defenses. — A motion under subdivision (b)(6) of this rule is intended to test the legal adequacy of the complaint, and not to address the merits of any affirmative defenses; in the limited circumstances where the allegations of the complaint give rise to an affirmative defense, the defense may be raised but only if it clearly appears on the face of the complaint. Richmond, F. & P.R.R. v. Forst, 4 F.3d 244 (4th Cir. 1993).

A defendant admits facts alleged in a complaint when he files a motion to dismiss a complaint for failure to state a claim upon which relief can be granted, and a court should not dismiss a complaint unless it is certain that the plaintiff can produce no set of facts which would entitle him to relief. Herman Cantor Corp. v. Central Fid. Bank, 15 Bankr. 747 (Bankr. E.D. Va. 1981).

Standard of review. — In ruling on a motion to dismiss for failure to state a claim upon which relief can be granted, the complaint is construed in the light most favorable to the plaintiffs and their allegations are taken as true. Higgins v. Medical College, 849 F. Supp. 1113 (E.D. Va. 1994).

Complaint viewed in light most favorable to plaintiff. — For purposes of granting a motion to dismiss, the complaint is construed in the light most favorable to plaintiff and its allegations are taken as true. However, more detail often is required than the bold statement by plaintiff that he has a valid claim of some type against defendant. Davis v. City of Portsmouth, 579 F. Supp. 1205 (E.D. Va. 1983), aff'd, 742 F.2d 1448 (4th Cir. 1984).

In ruling on a motion to dismiss, the court must ascertain whether the factual allegations in the complaint, taken as true and viewed in the light most favorable to the plaintiff, constitute a short and plain statement of the claim showing that the pleader is entitled to relief. Oxford House, Inc. v. City of Va. Beach, 825 F. Supp. 1251 (E.D. Va. 1993).

The complaint should not be dismissed unless it appears beyond doubt that the plaintiffs can prove no set of facts in support of their claim which would entitle them to relief. Higgins v. Medical College, 849 F. Supp. 1113 (E.D. Va. 1994).

The function of a motion to dismiss is to test "the sufficiency of a complaint; importantly, it does not resolve contests surrounding the facts, the merits of a claim, or the applicability of defenses." Thus, the standard approach to a motion to dismiss requires the court to presume that all factual allegations in a plaintiff's complaint are true, to make all reasonable inferences in favor of the nonmoving party, and not to dismiss any count unless it appears beyond a doubt that recovery would be impossible under any set of facts which could be proven. Gasner v. County of Dinwiddie, 162 F.R.D. 280 (E.D. Va. 1995), aff'd, 103 F.3d 351 (4th Cir. 1996).

A motion to dismiss for failure to state a claim for relief should not be granted unless it appears to a certainty that the plaintiff would be entitled to no relief under any state of facts which could be proved in support of his claim. Samuel v. Rose's Stores, Inc., 907 F. Supp. 159 (E.D. Va. 1995).

A complaint should survive a motion to dismiss if it sets out facts sufficient for the court to infer that all of the required elements of the cause of action are present. Oram v. Dalton, 927 F. Supp 180 (E.D. Va. 1996).

A court should not dismiss a complaint even if it appears on the face of the pleadings that the chance of recovery is very remote. Higgins v. Medical College, 849 F. Supp. 1113 (E.D. Va. 1994).

Dismissal of complaint. — Complaint should not be dismissed unless it appears beyond doubt that the plaintiffs can prove no set of facts in support of their claim which would entitle them to relief. B.M.H. ex rel. C.B. v. School Bd., 833 F. Supp. 560 (E.D. Va. 1993).

A motion to dismiss should be denied unless it appears beyond doubt that the plaintiff can prove no set of facts in support of his claim which would entitle him to relief. Oram v. Dalton, 927 F. Supp 180 (E.D. Va. 1996).

A motion to dismiss for failure to state a claim for relief should not be granted unless it appears to a certainty that the plaintiff would be entitled to no relief under any state of facts which could be proved in support of his claim. Lewin v. Medical College, 931 F. Supp. 443 (E.D. Va. 1996).

A court should not dismiss a complaint even if it appears on the face of the pleadings that the chance of recovery is very remote. B.M.H. ex rel. C.B. v. School Bd., 833 F. Supp. 560 (E.D. Va. 1993); Mazur v. Woodson, 932 F. Supp. 144 (E.D. Va. 1996).

Dismissal involving "complex litigation." — Contention that dismissal should be granted sparingly in "complex antitrust litigation" was without merit where case did not entail "complex antitrust litigation," but instead at issue was a single real estate foreclosure. Estate Constr. Co. v. Miller & Smith Holding Co., 14 F.3d 213 (4th Cir. 1994).

When dismissal for failure to state claim granted. — A motion to dismiss for failure to state a claim for relief should not be granted unless it appears to a certainty that the plaintiff would be entitled to no relief under any state of facts which could be proved in support of his claim. Johnson v. Mueller, 415 F.2d 354 (4th Cir. 1969); Taliaferro v. State Council of Higher Educ., 372 F. Supp. 1378 (E.D. Va. 1974); Adams v. Bain, 697 F.2d 1213 (4th Cir. 1982).

A motion to dismiss will not be granted unless it appears to a certainty that the plaintiff would be entitled to no relief under any state of facts which could be proved in support of his claim. Wolford v. Budd Co., 149 F.R.D. 127 (W.D. Va. 1993).

A complaint should not be dismissed for failure to state a claim for relief unless it appears beyond doubt that the plaintiff can prove no set of facts in support of his claim which would entitle him to relief. Austin v. Reynolds Metals Co., 327 F. Supp. 1145 (E.D. Va. 1970); Doby v. Safeway Stores, Inc., 523 F. Supp. 1162 (E.D. Va. 1981).

To warrant dismissal of the complaint for failure to state a claim it would have to appear from the papers addressed to the court that a cause of action does not exist and that the plaintiff, if given every chance to sharpen his allegations, could not cure the defects. Austin v. Reynolds Metals Co., 327 F. Supp. 1145 (E.D. Va. 1970).

A motion to dismiss for failure to state a claim should not be granted unless it appears that plaintiffs are entitled to no relief under any state of facts which could be proven in support of their claim. Grossberg v. Deusebio, 380 F. Supp. 285 (E.D. Va. 1974).

A complaint, no matter how unartfully pleaded, must survive a motion to dismiss under subdivision (b)(6) of this rule for failure to state a claim unless it appears beyond doubt that the plaintiff can prove no set of facts in support of his claim which would entitle him to relief. Islam v. Jackson, 782 F. Supp. 1111 (E.D. Va. 1992).

Unless it appears beyond a reasonable doubt that the plaintiff can prove no set of facts in support of his claim which would entitle him to relief, a court should not dismiss a complaint for failure to state a claim. Moore v. Flagstar Bank, 6 F. Supp. 2d 496 (E.D. Va. 1997).

Complaint should not be dismissed merely because the court doubts that plaintiff will ultimately prevail; so long as a plaintiff colorably states facts which, if proven, would entitle him to relief, the motion to dismiss should not be granted. Adams v. Bain, 697 F.2d 1213 (4th Cir. 1982).

In deciding a motion to dismiss for failure to state a claim upon which relief can be granted, pursuant to this rule, a court must accept the facts pleaded by the plaintiff as true; the court should not dismiss the claim unless it appears to a certainty that the plaintiff can prove no facts in support of his claims which would entitle him to relief. Davis v. Hudgins,

896 F. Supp. 561 (E.D. Va. 1995), aff'd, 87 F.3d 1308 (4th Cir. 1996).

Motion to dismiss for failure to state a claim was particularly inappropriate in a case where resolution involves a delicate factual balance and the court's initial ruling was deliberately tentative. Grossberg v. Deusebio, 380 F. Supp. 285 (E.D. Va. 1974).

Where defendants' motion to dismiss for failure to state a claim on which relief could be granted, if granted, would transpose what was explicitly a preliminary hearing into a final adjudication on the merits, this would cut against the spirit of Rule 65(a) (2), which contemplates that such an intention be made known to plaintiffs while they still may present further evidence. Grossberg v. Deusebio, 380 F. Supp. 285 (E.D. Va. 1974).

A complaint should not be dismissed for failure to state a claim unless it appears beyond doubt that the plaintiff can prove no set of facts in support of his claim which would entitle him to relief. Marshall v. Spangler, 397 F. Supp. 200 (W.D. Va. 1975).

Where plaintiff's complaint contains no facts at all, rather, it is a bare recital of the statutory language that does nothing more than list various bars to discharge contained in section 727 of the United States Bankruptcy Code, it lacks a foundation of operative facts which give rise to the plaintiff's claim, and the pleading must fail under subdivision (b)(6) of this rule. Mason v. Allen, 150 Bankr. 21 (Bankr. E.D. Va. 1993).

Lack of overall reasonableness constitutes grounds for dismissal. — Even if the court finds that there is a basis for personal jurisdiction under the minimum contacts theory or the stream of commerce theory, the lack of overall reasonableness in the assertion of personal jurisdiction constitutes an independent ground for dismissal under this rule. Abel v. Montgomery Ward Co., 798 F. Supp. 322 (E.D. Va. 1992).

Dismissal under Rule 12(b)(6) is with prejudice unless otherwise specified. — A district court's dismissal under Rule 12(b)(6) is with prejudice unless it specifically orders dismissal without prejudice. That determination is within the district court's discretion. Carter v. Norfolk Community Hosp. Ass'n, 761 F.2d 970 (4th Cir. 1985).

Remand for determination whether to dismiss with or without prejudice. — Where circuit court affirmed on Rule 12(b)(6) grounds which were not the basis for dismissal by the district court, the court would remand for the district court's decision whether to dismiss with or without prejudice. Carter v. Norfolk Community Hosp. Ass'n, 761 F.2d 970 (4th Cir. 1985).

Complaint looked to for undisputed facts. — Under Rule 12(b)(6), Fed. R. Civ. P. the complaint, as supplemented, may be looked to for the undisputed facts. Continental Properties, Inc. v. Ullman Co., 436 F. Supp. 538 (E.D. Va. 1977).

Generalized allegations containing no factual support and no specific incidents cannot give rise to a claim upon which relief may be granted. Feazell v. Augusta County Jail, 401 F. Supp. 405 (W.D. Va. 1975).

To state a claim under the First Amendment, plaintiff must first identify some speech or expressive conduct that implicates the First Amendment, and second, demonstrate that this speech merits constitutional protection. Roper v. County of Chesterfield, 807 F. Supp. 1221 (E.D. Va. 1992).

Applicability of Rule 12(b)(6) motion in bankruptcy. — A motion to dismiss a proceeding for failure to state a claim for which relief may be granted under subdivision (b)(6) of this rule is made applicable to adversary proceedings in bankruptcy by Rule 7012(b) of the Rules of Bankruptcy Procedure. Janssen v. Washington Hosp. Ctr., 42 Bankr. 294 (Bankr. E.D. Va. 1984).

Court properly granted sheriff's motion to dismiss for failure to state a claim in a civil rights action against sheriff for supervisory liability for actions of a deputy where the alleged facts, even liberally construed, made no allegation of deliberate indifference to or tacit authorization of, pervasive misconduct on behalf of sheriff's deputies; at most the complaint alleged an isolated incident of possible misconduct by one of sheriff's deputies. McNeal v. Harper, 816 F. Supp. 421 (E.D. Va. 1993).

Debtor's motion for a lien avoidance, although not joined with a motion for a declaratory judgment that the lien had been avoided, stated a claim upon which relief could be granted. Webb v. Robert A. Boroughs, Ltd., 49 Bankr. 646 (Bankr. E.D. Va. 1984).

Failure to satisfy element did not automatically defeat discrimination claim. — Where defendants contended that plaintiff had not alleged sufficient facts to establish racially motivated termination and failure to rehire under Title VII and 42 U.S.C. Section 1981, although it was true that the elements missing in complaint were generally required to state a prima facie case of discriminatory discharge or failure to rehire, these elements were not always essential. But failure to satisfy one element of an organizational framework does not automatically defeat a discrimination claim, particularly at the Rule 12(b)(6) stage. Thus, plaintiff had alleged sufficient facts in her complaint to state claims for discriminatory termination at least. Carter v. Rental Uniform Serv. of Culpeper, Inc., 977 F. Supp. 753 (W.D. Va. 1997).

Third party beneficial claim. — Until plaintiffs' complaint is formally amended to reflect the third party beneficiary claim, the third party, who only made an allegation in a brief opposing a motion to dismiss, has not stated a claim for which relief can be granted. Picture Lake Campground, Inc. v. Holiday Inns, Inc., 497 F. Supp. 858 (E.D. Va. 1980).

Claim based on maggot contaminated food dismissed for failure to state a claim. — Inmate's cruel and unusual punishment claim, based on service of maggot contaminated food and unsanitary conditions, was dismissed for failure to state a claim where the complaint failed to allege adequately that defendants acted with the state of mind necessary to establish a claim under the Eighth Amendment. Islam v. Jackson, 782 F. Supp. 1111 (E.D. Va. 1992).

Rule held not automatically applicable to action involving governmental secrets for proof of both plaintiff's case and certain defenses. — See Farnsworth Cannon, Inc. v. Grimes, 635 F.2d 268 (4th Cir. 1980).

B. When Treated as Motion for Summary Judgment.

Motion for summary judgment compared with Rule 12(b)(6) motion. — Unlike a Rule 12(b)(6) motion, which limits the court's inquiry to the adequacy of the content of the complaint, a motion for summary judgment involves a determination from the pleadings, depositions, answers to interrogatories, and affidavits whether there is a genuine issue of fact. Morgan v. American Family Life Assurance Co., 559 F. Supp. 477 (W.D. Va. 1983).

Although judgment is made as a matter of law, the standard for entry of summary judgment is slightly different than that for granting a motion to dismiss under subdivision (b)(6). Summary judgment is entered when a plaintiff fails to make a showing sufficient to establish the existence of an element essential to that party's case, and on which that party will bear the burden of proof at trial. Moore v. Flagstar Bank, 6 F. Supp. 2d 496 (E.D. Va. 1997).

Motion to dismiss treated as motion for summary judgment. — See Bowring v. Chairman, Va. Parole Bd., 436 F. Supp. 339 (W.D. Va. 1977), aff'd, 573 F.2d 1304 (4th Cir. 1978).

The motion to dismiss for failure to state a claim for which relief can be granted may be treated as a motion for summary judgment when matters outside the pleadings are considered by the court. Kipps v. Ewell, 538 F.2d 564 (4th Cir. 1976), aff'g 391 F. Supp. 1285 (W.D. Va. 1975).

Where the parties have submitted materials in addition to their pleadings, the court will treat defendants' preliminary motion to dismiss and/or for summary judgment as one for summary judgment. Eldridge v. Bouchard, 620 F. Supp. 678 (W.D. Va. 1985).

The rules require that if the court does consider "matters outside the complaint" it must convert the motion into a motion for summary judgment, affording the parties a "reasonable opportunity to present all material made pertinent to such a motion." Gasner v. County of Dinwiddie, 162 F.R.D. 280 (E.D. Va. 1995), aff'd, 103 F.3d 351 (4th Cir. 1996).

Motions to dismiss and for summary judgment are not considered responsive pleadings for purposes of Rule 15(a). Williams v. Wilkerson, 90 F.R.D. 168 (E.D. Va. 1981).

Defendant's motion to dismiss will not be treated as motion for summary judgment. — Motion to dismiss may not be considered as a motion for summary judgment where not only was issue not ripe for disposition, not having had oral argument presented, but defendants had not set forth such facts as would be admissible in evidence. Wolford v. Budd Co., 149 F.R.D. 127 (W.D. Va. 1993).

When a party is aware that material outside the pleadings is before the court, the party is on notice that a Rule 12(b)(6) motion may be treated as a motion for summary judgment. Gay v. Wall, 761 F.2d 175 (4th Cir. 1985).

Notification of conversion and opportunity for discovery. — Notification that a Rule 12(b)(6) motion may be converted is only one of the requirements of this rule; once notified, a party must be afforded a reasonable opportunity for discovery before a Rule 12(b)(6) motion may be converted and summary judgment granted. Gay v. Wall, 761 F.2d 175 (4th Cir. 1985).

The term "reasonable opportunity" in Rule 12(b)(6) requires that all parties be given some indication by the court that it is treating the 12(b)(6) motion as a motion for summary judgment, with the consequent right in the opposing party to file counter affidavits or pursue reasonable discovery. Gay v. Wall, 761 F.2d 175 (4th Cir. 1985).

Where plaintiff was not afforded an opportunity for reasonable discovery, the district court's treatment of defendants' motion to dismiss as a motion for summary judgment was an abuse of discretion. Gay v. Wall, 761 F.2d 175 (4th Cir. 1985).

Motions for summary judgment treated as motions requesting judgment on pleadings. — Although both parties termed their respective motions as ones for summary judgment, since neither party had offered matters outside the pleadings and the parties stipulated to the relevant facts, the court treated the parties' motions as requesting judgment on the pleadings under subsection (c). Old Bridge Estates Community Ass'n v. Lozada, 214 Bankr. 558 (Bankr. E.D. Va. 1997), aff'd, 176 F.3d 475 (4th Cir. 1999).

Judgment on pleadings under subsection (c) should be granted if the defendant is entitled to judgment as a matter of law. In re Bryant, 235 Bankr. 581 (W.D. Va. 1998).

Amended complaint went beyond bare conclusory allegations. — See Beasley v. Motor Freight Express, Inc., 401 F. Supp. 662 (E.D. Va. 1975).

Motion to dismiss held in abeyance so plaintiff could tender amended complaint. — See Miller v. Holiday Inns, Inc., 436 F. Supp. 460 (E.D. Va. 1977).

When a plaintiff fails to introduce a pertinent document as part of his complaint, the defendant may attach the document to a motion to dismiss the complaint and the court may consider the same without converting the motion to one for summary judgment. This ruling encompasses not only documents quoted, relied upon, or incorporated by reference in the complaint, but also official public records pertinent to the plaintiffs' claims. Gasner v. County of Dinwiddie, 162 F.R.D. 280 (E.D. Va. 1995), aff'd, 103 F.3d 351 (4th Cir. 1996).

Motion for dismissal treated as one for summary judgment where matters outside pleadings attached. — See Wooldridge v. Virginia, 453 F. Supp. 1333 (E.D. Va. 1978).

Requiring limited expansion of complaint is matter generally left to district court's discretion. — See Hodgson v. Virginia Baptist Hosp., 482 F.2d 821 (4th Cir. 1973).

CIRCUIT COURT OPINIONS

Motion to dismiss was granted with leave to replead. — Motion to dismiss was granted because the corporation could not maintain the breach of contract action as it was not a party to the contract.

The language of the contract supported the architect's testimony that he thought that he was in contract with the owner as an individual and not a corporation. Berglund Chevrolet v. Thor, Inc., 63 Va. Cir. 334, 2003 Va. Cir. LEXIS 251 (Roanoke 2003).

Rule 13. Counterclaim and Crossclaim.

(a) *Compulsory Counterclaim.* — (1) In General. A pleading must state as a counterclaim any claim that — at the time of its service — the pleader has against an opposing party if the claim:

(A) arises out of the transaction or occurrence that is the subject matter of the opposing party's claim; and

(B) does not require adding another party over whom the court cannot acquire jurisdiction.

(2) Exceptions. The pleader need not state the claim if:

(A) when the action was commenced, the claim was the subject of another pending action; or

(B) the opposing party sued on its claim by attachment or other process that did not establish personal jurisdiction over the pleader on that claim, and the pleader does not assert any counterclaim under this rule.

(b) *Permissive Counterclaim.* — A pleading may state as a counterclaim against an opposing party any claim that is not compulsory.

(c) *Relief Sought in a Counterclaim.* — A counterclaim need not diminish or defeat the recovery sought by the opposing party. It may request relief that exceeds in amount or differs in kind from the relief sought by the opposing party.

(d) *Counterclaim Against the United States.* — These rules do not expand the right to assert a counterclaim — or to claim a credit — against the United States or a United States officer or agency.

(e) *Counterclaim Maturing or Acquired After Pleading.* — The court may permit a party to file a supplemental pleading asserting a counterclaim that matured or was acquired by the party after serving an earlier pleading.

(f) [Abrogated.]

(g) *Crossclaim Against a Coparty.* — A pleading may state as a crossclaim any claim by one party against a coparty if the claim arises out of the transaction or occurrence that is the subject matter of the original action or of a counterclaim, or if the claim relates to any property that is the subject matter of the original action. The crossclaim may include a claim that the coparty is or may be liable to the crossclaimant for all or part of a claim asserted in the action against the crossclaimant.

(h) *Joining Additional Parties.* — Rules 19 and 20 govern the addition of a person as a party to a counterclaim or crossclaim.

(i) *Separate Trials; Separate Judgments.* — If the court orders separate trials under Rule 42(b), it may enter judgment on a counterclaim or crossclaim under Rule 54(b) when it has jurisdiction to do so, even if the opposing party's claims have been dismissed or otherwise resolved. (Amended by order adopted December 27, 1946, effective March 19, 1948, by order adopted January 21, 1963, effective July 1, 1963, by order adopted February 28, 1966, effective July 1, 1966, by order adopted March 2, 1987, effective August 1, 1987, by order adopted April 30, 2007, effective December 1, 2007, and by order adopted March 26, 2009, effective December 1, 2009.)

Comment. — The language of Rule 13 has been amended as part of the general restyling of the Civil Rules to make them more easily understood and to make style and terminology consistent throughout the rules. These changes are intended to be stylistic only.

The meaning of former Rule 13(b) is better expressed by deleting "not arising out of the transaction or occurrence that is the subject matter of the opposing party's claim." Both as a matter of intended meaning and current practice, a party may state as a permissive counterclaim a claim that does grow out of the same transaction or occurrence as an opposing party's claim even though one of the exceptions in Rule 13(a) means the claim is not a compulsory counterclaim.

CASE NOTES

Failure to assert compulsory counterclaim precludes assertion in later action. — Although this rule does not explicitly so state, the effect of a defendant's failure to assert a counterclaim made compulsory by subdivision (a) is to preclude its assertion in a later action against the former plaintiff. Mesker Bros. Iron Co. v. Donata Corp., 401 F.2d 275 (4th Cir. 1968).

The failure to file a compulsory counterclaim as required by subdivision (a) constitutes a waiver, and the party is precluded by res judicata from ever suing upon it again. There is some ground for argument supporting relief for failure to file a compulsory counterclaim, but not as applied to the facts of a case where the matter was fully tried and final judgment entered. Kennedy v. Jones, 44 F.R.D. 52 (E.D. Va. 1968).

Where the plaintiff had failed to file a compulsory counterclaim under subdivision (a) in a prior action arising out of a motor vehicle accident tried in the same federal district court between the same parties, which was tried to a jury with a resulting verdict in favor of the now plaintiff and his employer, defendants in the first action, the defense of the prior action being conducted by the attorneys for the employer's liability insurance carrier, it was held that the now plaintiff's failure to file his counterclaim for personal injuries precluded the present action. Kennedy v. Jones, 44 F.R.D. 52 (E.D. Va. 1968).

A litigant who fails to file a compulsory counterclaim as required by this rule is thereafter barred from asserting that claim. Balbir Brar Assocs. v. Consolidated Trading and Servs. Corp., 252 Va. 341, 477 S.E.2d 743 (1996).

Subdivision (a) does not come into play when a defendant files only a motion to dismiss, instead of a pleading. Mellon Bank v. Ternisky, 999 F.2d 791 (4th Cir. 1993).

Party treated as brought in under third-party practice to preserve diversity jurisdiction. — Where an impleader under Rule 19 or an order under subdivision (h) of this rule would have destroyed the jurisdiction of the court because the impleaded party and the plaintiff were both residents of Virginia, the court treated the procedure as an ancillary proceeding under subdivision (a) of Rule 14, not requiring diversity of citizenship. Lumbermens Mut. Cas. Co. v. Harleysville Mut. Cas. Co., 367 F.2d 250 (4th Cir. 1966).

Counterclaim treated as affirmative defense by way of recoupment. — Where the facts supporting the government's counterclaim for salvage undeniably arose out of the same cause of action which gave rise to a shipowner's suit for damages resulting from the alleged negligent conduct of rescue operations, the counterclaim was treated as an affirmative defense by way of recoupment, even though, as an affirmative cause of action, the counterclaim was barred by limitations. Basic Boats, Inc. ex rel. Lumbermens Mut. Cas. Co. v. United States, 311 F. Supp. 596 (E.D. Va. 1970).

The burden is upon the defendant to demonstrate a cause of action upon which a pending counterclaim may be maintained. Defendant's failure to do so would result in the dismissal of the counterclaim. Gilbert v. GE Co., 59 F.R.D. 273 (E.D. Va. 1973).

Effect of compulsory counterclaim on state court jurisdiction. — The necessity of pleading a cause of action as a compulsory counterclaim in a federal action does not deprive the state court of jurisdiction of a claim created by state law. The counterclaim cannot alter the basis of the cause of action; it has its genesis in state law and therefore is inadequate to confer federal removal jurisdiction. APCO v. Region Properties, Inc., 364 F. Supp. 1273 (W.D. Va. 1973).

Where federal antitrust litigation has been followed by state court litigation involving the transaction which formed the basis of the antitrust action, and additionally the plaintiff in the state court suit has counterclaimed in the federal action, the courts have consistently refused to enjoin the state court proceeding. APCO v. Region Properties, Inc., 364 F. Supp. 1273 (W.D. Va. 1973).

The filing of a compulsory counterclaim does not waive defects in personal jurisdiction and venue, as would the filing of a permissive counterclaim. Medicenters of Am., Inc. v. T & V Realty & Equip. Corp., 371 F. Supp. 1180 (E.D. Va. 1974).

Counterclaim rules held inapplicable. — When trustee commences an adversary proceeding based on an action belonging to the trustee in the trustee's own capacity, such as an avoidance action, if defendant has a claim against the debtor, the compulsory counterclaim rules are inapplicable. In re Williams Contract Furn., Inc., 148 Bankr. 799 (Bankr. E.D. Va. 1992).

Counterclaim held compulsory. — See Stone v. Stone, 330 F. Supp. 1026 (W.D. Va. 1971), rev'd in part, 460 F.2d 64 (4th Cir.), cert. denied, 409 U.S. 1000, 93 S. Ct. 315, 34 L. Ed. 2d 261 (1972).

Although these rules favor the determination of all pending issues between parties at one time, and subdivision (a) of this rule makes the assertion of certain counterclaims compulsory, yet these rules do not seem to in anywise alter the situation regarding counterclaims against the United States. United States v. Heard, 32 F. Supp. 39 (W.D. Va. 1940).

Holding claim compulsory did not chill prosecution of § 1983 actions. — Plaintiff's argument, that holding counterclaim to be compulsory would impermissibly chill prosecution of actions under 42 U.S.C. § 1983, failed because subdivision (a) is neutral in its terms and does not suggest that characterization of counterclaims should be made to depend upon type of cause of action alleged in complaint and because substantial evidence test employed to find counterclaim compulsory was, inclusive in its application. Painter v. Harvey, 863 F.2d 329 (4th Cir. 1988).

Rights of jointly liable insurers may be determined before payment. — Notwithstanding the substantive rule of law requiring payment by a surety before the right to subrogation arises, subdivision (g) of this rule and Rule 14(a) allow a constitutional order determining the rights of jointly liable insurers to be entered before payment. Lumbermen's Mut. Ins. Co. v. Massachusetts Bonding & Ins. Co., 310 F.2d 627 (4th Cir. 1962).

Cross-claim not dismissed with original claim if it has independent jurisdictional basis. — Generally, dismissal of the original claim out of which the cross-claim arises does not result in dismissal of the cross-claim if it stands on independent jurisdictional grounds. National Trust for Historic Preservation v. 1750 K Inv. Partnership, 100 F.R.D. 483 (E.D. Va. 1984), aff'd sub nom. Fisher v. Beauchamp, 755 F.2d 927 (4th Cir.), aff'd, 755 F.2d 929 (4th Cir. 1985).

Dismissal of the original claim does not automatically result in the dismissal of the cross-claim where there is independent jurisdiction established for the cross-claim. National Trust for Historic Preservation v. 1750 K Inv. Partnership, 100 F.R.D. 483 (E.D. Va. 1984), aff'd sub nom. Fisher v.

Beauchamp, 755 F.2d 927 (4th Cir.), aff'd, 755 F.2d 929 (4th Cir. 1985).

Cross-claim involving question of ownership of vessel. — Where the resolution of the question of the ownership of a vessel would necessarily turn on the contract of sale, and the issue was one in which the general maritime law was not controlling, a court of admiralty would not normally have jurisdiction over such a claim; but since it was only brought as a cross-claim, subdivision (g) of this rule applied. Puamier v. Barge BT 1793, 395 F. Supp. 1019 (E.D. Va. 1974).

Independent basis of federal jurisdiction not required for compulsory counterclaim. — Compulsory counterclaims are ancillary to the claim asserted in the complaint and no independent basis of federal jurisdiction is required. Wigglesworth v. Teamsters Local 592, 68 F.R.D. 609 (E.D. Va. 1975).

Or where counterclaim qualifies as valid set-off. — If a defendant's counterclaims qualify as a valid set-off, then they constitute an exception to the permissive counterclaim jurisdictional requirement, and no independent jurisdictional basis is necessary. In order for a counterclaim to qualify as a valid set-off, the claim must be liquidated or capable of liquidation and grow out of a contract or judgment. Wigglesworth v. Teamsters Local 592, 68 F.R.D. 609 (E.D. Va. 1975).

Permissive counterclaims without independent jurisdictional support may be dismissed. — Where the plaintiff's complaint qualified for federal jurisdiction, but the defendant's counterclaims were permissive, were between nondiverse parties, and were grounded solely in state law, they were without independent jurisdictional support, and were therefore dismissed. Wigglesworth v. Teamsters Local 592, 68 F.R.D. 609 (E.D. Va. 1975).

Permissive counterclaims must have an independent jurisdictional base in order to be considered by a federal district court. If there is no independent jurisdictional base to hear defendant's counterclaim, a federal court must decline to consider it. Campbell v. General Fin. Corp., 523 F. Supp. 989 (W.D. Va. 1981).

Exercise of pendent jurisdiction is discretionary. — The judicial power to hear and decide counterclaims exists in pendent jurisdiction; however, the jurisdictional doctrine is discretionary in nature with respect to permissive counterclaims. Wigglesworth v. Teamsters Local 592, 68 F.R.D. 609 (E.D. Va. 1975).

The test of compulsoriness requires that there be not so much an absolute identity of factual backgrounds for the two claims, but only a logical relationship between them. Wigglesworth v. Teamsters Local 592, 68 F.R.D. 609 (E.D. Va. 1975).

Four inquiries to determine if counterclaim is compulsory: (1) Are issues of fact and law raised in claim and counterclaim largely same? (2) Would res judicata bar subsequent suit on party's counterclaim, absent compulsory counterclaim rule? (3) Will substantially same evidence support or refute claim as well as counterclaim? and (4) Is there any logical relationship between claim and counterclaim?; a court need not answer all these questions in affirmative for counterclaim to be compulsory. Painter v. Harvey, 863 F.2d 329 (4th Cir. 1988).

When determining whether a claim must be asserted as a compulsory counterclaim, the focus is on the original court's construction of its compulsory counterclaim rule. Balbir Brar Assocs. v. Consolidated Trading and Servs. Corp., 252 Va. 341, 477 S.E.2d 743 (1996).

A defendant's counterclaim is permissive where it does not arise out of the transaction or occurrence that is the subject matter of plaintiff's claim. Campbell v. General Fin. Corp., 523 F. Supp. 989 (W.D. Va. 1981).

"Transaction" is a word of flexible meaning. It may comprehend a series of many occurrences, depending not so much upon the immediateness of their connection as upon their logical relationship. Wigglesworth v. Teamsters Local 592, 68 F.R.D. 609 (E.D. Va. 1975).

Cross claim in admiralty. — Where the resolution of the question of the ownership of a vessel necessarily turned on a contract of sale and the issue was one in which the general maritime law was not controlling, a court of admiralty would not normally have jurisdiction over such a claim, but where it was only brought as a cross claim subsection (g) of this rule applies. Puamier v. Barge BT 1793, 395 F. Supp. 1019 (E.D. Va. 1974).

Counterclaim held compulsory despite assertion events relevant only by affirmative defense. — Plaintiff's assertion that counterclaim was permissive because events in question became relevant to libel counterclaim only when plaintiff responded to that counterclaim with affirmative defense of truth failed; plaintiff could not have withheld affirmative defense without repudiating version of events as set forth in her original complaint, and since counterclaim itself was not subject to the federal face of the complaint rule, status of counterclaim could not be made to depend on fact that issue was joined over events in question only by way of affirmative defense. Painter v. Harvey, 863 F.2d 329 (4th Cir. 1988).

Counterclaim held permissive. — Where the counterclaim was an action for libel and slander in response to a complaint alleging violation of a union member's rights under the Labor-Management Reporting Disclosure Act, there was no connection between the events giving rise to the counterclaims asserted by defendants and the transaction or occurrence upon which plaintiff's claim was based, and therefore the counterclaims were permissive. Wigglesworth v. Teamsters Local 592, 68 F.R.D. 609 (E.D. Va. 1975).

Fact counterclaim based on state law not relevant in relationship to federal claim. — Where plaintiff's claim involved federal law and defendant's counterclaim involved state libel law, fact that counterclaim was one of state law said nothing about its logical relationship to federal claim or to evidentiary overlap between them, and where plaintiff asserted claim based on federal law, counterclaim based on state law was adjudicated as matter of ancillary jurisdiction since counterclaim arose from same transaction. Painter v. Harvey, 863 F.2d 329 (4th Cir. 1988).

Counterclaims against United States. — The United States by commencing a suit to quiet title does not consent to be sued on a counterclaim based upon a cause of action for which it has not otherwise given its consent to be sued. The Federal Rule of Civil Procedure governing compulsory counterclaims does not expand this court's jurisdiction. United States v. Drinkwater, 434 F. Supp. 457 (E.D. Va. 1977).

Filing of cross-claims by third-party defendants. — Subdivision (a) of Rule 14 does not specifically permit or prohibit the filing of cross-claims by a third-party defendant against co-defendants of the third-party plaintiffs. An examination of the history of Rule 14(a) does not indicate a clear intention to prohibit such cross-claims. Barring some prejudice to the movants, the court is thus not specifically prohibited by rule from permitting the filing of third-party defendant's cross-claims against the movants. American Gen. v. Equitable Gen., 87 F.R.D. 736 (E.D. Va. 1980).

Motion to dismiss on ground of statute of limitations where counterclaim does not set forth any dates from which it could be concluded that the claim is time-barred would be denied with direction to amend counterclaim to set forth dates. Haynes v. Anderson & Strudwick, Inc., 508 F. Supp. 1303 (E.D. Va. 1981).

Res judicata test not controlling to distinguish counterclaim. — Where plaintiff sued defendant on 42 U.S.C. § 1983 claim, plaintiff's argument that defendant's counterclaim, based on state libel law was permissive because withheld counterclaim would face no res judicata bar in subsequent state proceeding failed; res judicata test was not controlling because limitation of test would make subdivision (a) superfluous, and because res judicata test, to distinguish between permissive and compulsory counterclaims was difficult to use. Painter v. Harvey, 863 F.2d 329 (4th Cir. 1988).

Burden of multiple trials. — Where defendant counterclaimed with state libel law action to plaintiff's 42 U.S.C. § 1983 claim and where plaintiff wanted state claim pursued independent of federal action, plaintiff's argument, that adverse verdict on her § 1983 claim would collaterally estop her on issue of liability in libel in state court and would restrict any future state trial to the matter of damages, failed since to require defendant to pursue state libel claim independently of action, in which only determination to have been made would have centered on damages, was to ignore value of having same factfinder resolve all issues with eye for consistency and appreciation for total context of case. Painter v. Harvey, 863 F.2d 329 (4th Cir. 1988).

Notice requirement applicable. — Apartment partnership's argument that its claim was exempt from the notice requirement because it was presented as a compulsory claim under this rule was erroneous because the notice requirement was jurisdictional and its application was not a mere formality. Portsmouth Redevelopment & Hous. Auth. v. BMI Apts. Assocs., 847 F. Supp. 380 (E.D. Va. 1994).

Applied in Bates v. Devers, 214 Va. 667, 202 S.E.2d 917 (1974); Wittersheim v. General Transp. Servs., Inc., 378 F. Supp. 762 (E.D. Va. 1974); EEOC v. Allied Chem. Corp., 69 F.R.D. 62 (E.D. Va. 1975); Cosgrove v. First & Merchants Nat'l Bank, 68 F.R.D. 555 (E.D. Va. 1975); Berger v. City of N. Miami, 820 F. Supp. 989 (E.D. Va. 1993); Laughlin v. Edwards Bus. Machs., Inc., 155 F.R.D. 543 (W.D. Va. 1994); Pneumo Abex Corp. v. Bessemer & L.E.R.R., 936 F. Supp. 1274 (E.D. Va. 1996).

Rule 14. Third-Party Practice.

(a) *When a Defending Party May Bring in a Third-Party.* — (1) Timing of the Summons and Complaint. A defending party may, as third-party plaintiff, serve a summons and complaint on a nonparty who is or may be liable to it for all or part of the claim against it. But the third-party plaintiff must, by motion, obtain the court's leave if it files the third-party complaint more than 14 days after serving its original answer.

(2) Third-Party Defendant's Claims and Defenses. The person served with the summons and third-party complaint — the "third-party defendant":

(A) must assert any defense against the third-party plaintiff's claim under Rule 12;

(B) must assert any counterclaim against the third-party plaintiff under Rule 13(a), and may assert any counterclaim against the third-party plaintiff under Rule 13(b) or any crossclaim against another third-party defendant under Rule 13(g);

(C) may assert against the plaintiff any defense that the third-party plaintiff has to the plaintiff's claim; and

(D) may also assert against the plaintiff any claim arising out of the transaction or occurrence that is the subject matter of the plaintiff's claim against the third-party plaintiff.

(3) Plaintiff's Claims Against a Third-Party Defendant. The plaintiff may assert against the third-party defendant any claim arising out of the transaction or occurrence that is the subject matter of the plaintiff's claim against the third-party plaintiff. The third-party defendant must then assert any defense under Rule 12 and any counterclaim under Rule 13(a), and may assert any counterclaim under Rule 13(b) or any crossclaim under Rule 13(g).

(4) Motion to Strike, Sever, or Try Separately. Any party may move to strike the third-party claim, to sever it, or to try it separately.

(5) Third-Party Defendant's Claim Against a Nonparty. A third-party defendant may proceed under this rule against a nonparty who is or may be liable to the third-party defendant for all or part of any claim against it.

(6) Third-Party Complaint In Rem. If it is within the admiralty or maritime jurisdiction, a third-party complaint may be in rem. In that event, a reference in this

rule to the "summons" includes the warrant of arrest, and a reference to the defendant or third-party plaintiff includes, when appropriate, a person who asserts a right under Supplemental Rule C(6)(a)(i) in the property arrested.

(b) *When a Plaintiff May Bring in a Third-Party.* — When a claim is asserted against a plaintiff, the plaintiff may bring in a third-party if this rule would allow a defendant to do so.

(c) *Admiralty or Maritime Claim.* — (1) Scope of Impleader. If a plaintiff asserts an admiralty or maritime claim under Rule 9(h), the defendant or a person who asserts a right under Supplemental Rule C(6)(a)(i) may, as a third-party plaintiff, bring in a third-party defendant who may be wholly or partly liable — either to the plaintiff or to the third-party plaintiff — for remedy over, contribution, or otherwise on account of the same transaction, occurrence, or series of transactions or occurrences.

(2) Defending Against a Demand for Judgment for the Plaintiff. The third-party plaintiff may demand judgment in the plaintiff's favor against the third-party defendant. In that event, the third-party defendant must defend under Rule12 against the plaintiff's claim as well as the third-party plaintiff's claim; and the action proceeds as if the plaintiff had sued both the third-party defendant and the third-party plaintiff. (Amended by order adopted December 27, 1946, effective March 19, 1948, by order adopted January 21, 1963, effective July 1, 1963, by order adopted February 28, 1966, effective July 1, 1966, and by order adopted March 2, 1987, effective August 1, 1987, by order adopted April 17, 2000, effective December 1, 2000, by order adopted April 12, 2006, effective December 1, 2006, by order adopted April 30, 2007, effective December 1, 2007, and by order adopted March 26, 2009, effective December 1, 2009.)

Comment. — The language of Rule 14 has been amended as part of the general restyling of the Civil Rules to make them more easily understood and to make style and terminology consistent throughout the rules. These changes are intended to be stylistic only.

Former Rule 14 twice refers to counterclaims under Rule 13. In each case, the operation of Rule 13(a) depends on the state of the action at the time the pleading is filed. If plaintiff and third-party defendant have become opposing parties because one has made a claim for relief against the other, Rule 13(a) requires assertion of any counterclaim that grows out of the transaction or occurrence that is the subject matter of that claim. Rules 14(a)(2)(B) and (a)(3) reflect the distinction between compulsory and permissive counterclaims.

Law Review. — For note, "Rule 14 Claims and Ancillary Jurisdiction," see 57 Va. L. Rev. 265 (1971). For comment, "Extension of Ancillary Jurisdiction to Plaintiff's Claims Against Nondiverse Third-Party Defendants," see 30 Wash. & Lee L. Rev. 295 (1973). For note on third-party removal of an entire case: who can remove, who cannot, see 41 Wash. & Lee L. Rev. 1533 (1984). For article on Finley v. United States and ancillary jurisdiction, see 76 Va. L. Rev. 539 (1990).

CASE NOTES

This rule should be liberally construed. Weaver v. Marcus, 165 F.2d 862, 175 A.L.R. 1305 (4th Cir. 1948), rev'g 73 F. Supp. 736 (W.D. Va. 1947).

The purpose of third-party procedure is to prevent circuity of action by drawing into one proceeding all parties who may become ultimately liable, so that they may therein assert and have a determination of their various claims inter sese. This is intended to save the time and cost of duplicating evidence and to obtain consistent results from identical or similar evidence, as well as to avoid the serious handicap of a time lag between a judgment against the original defendant and a judgment in his favor against the third-party defendant. American Export Lines v. Revel, 262 F.2d 122 (4th Cir. 1958), aff'd, 266 F.2d 82 (4th Cir. 1959).

This rule does not provide a basis for subject matter jurisdiction. Lewis v. United States, 816 F. Supp. 1097 (E.D. Va. 1993).

This rule does not create any new substantive rights. Jennings v. Franz Torwegge Mach. Works, 347 F. Supp. 1288 (W.D. Va. 1972).

Impleader merely accelerates determination of liability and does not have the effect of enlarging any substantive rights. Rambone v. Critzer, 548 F. Supp. 660 (W.D. Va. 1982).

Time period for service of third-party complaint. — Although subdivision (c) of this rule is silent on the period within which a third-party complaint may be served without notice or motion, the timing appears to be governed by subdivision (a) of this rule. Lewis v. United States, 816 F. Supp. 1097 (E.D. Va. 1993).

Rule does not establish right to reimbursement, indemnity or contribution. — This rule does not establish a right of reimbursement, indemnity or contribution. American Tobacco Co. v. Transport Corp., 277 F. Supp. 457 (E.D. Va. 1967).

Court to assess jurisdiction by considering voluntary and involuntary claims. — Where a defendant impleads a third-party and tenders it to the plaintiff on the theory that the third-party is wholly liable to the plaintiff, and thereby seeks to have the action proceed as if the plaintiff had commenced it against the third-party defendant as well as the third-party plaintiff, it seems logical and consistent with the basic prnciples of federal jurisdiction generally applicable to third-party practice that the court should assess subject matter jurisdiction by considering all of the plaintiff's claims, both voluntary and involuntary. Lewis v. United States, 816 F. Supp. 1097 (E.D. Va. 1993).

The rule does not compel defendant to bring third parties into the litigation; rather, it simply permits the addition of anyone who meets the standard set forth in the rule. In many instances, tactical considerations will lead a party to pursue an independent action against a possible third-party defendant rather than resorting to impleader. Valley Landscape Co. v. Rolland, 218 Va. 257, 237 S.E.2d 120 (1977).

A possibility of indemnification is the only basis upon which a third party may be impleaded under this rule. Kenrose Mfg. Co. v. Fred Whitaker Co., 512 F.2d 890 (4th Cir. 1972), aff'g 53 F.R.D. 491 (W.D. Va. 1971).

State law, not rule, governs reimbursement, indemnity or contribution. — This rule does not establish a right of reimbursement, indemnity or contribution. The court looks to the state law in such a situation. Uptagrafft v. United States, 315 F.2d 200 (4th Cir.), cert. denied, 375 U.S. 818, 84 S. Ct. 54, 11 L. Ed. 2d 52 (1963).

Although federal law provides the procedures to be used in an impleader action, it is necessary to look to state law, in a diversity case, for the requisite right of indemnification. Kenrose Mfg. Co. v. Fred Whitaker Co., 512 F.2d 890 (4th Cir. 1972), aff'g 53 F.R.D. 491 (W.D. Va. 1971).

Claim based upon theory of contract indemnification. — Where an action had been brought against a federal reserve bank for the wrongful death of plaintiff's decedent in an elevator accident at the bank, the bank was not precluded from maintaining its third-party claim against the decedent's employer upon the theory of contract indemnification, notwithstanding the employer's contention that the claim was barred by the provisions of the Virginia workmen's compensation act. Bell v. Federal Reserve Bank, 57 F.R.D. 632 (E.D. Va. 1972), distinguishing Brooks v. Brown, 307 F. Supp. 907 (E.D. Va. 1969).

Independent basis of jurisdiction is necessary to support a plaintiff's action against a third-party defendant and is a prerequisite to the maintenance of such a claim. Kenrose Mfg. Co. v. Fred Whitaker Co., 512 F.2d 890 (4th Cir. 1972), aff'g 53 F.R.D. 491 (W.D. Va. 1971).

No independent grounds of jurisdiction are needed to entertain an ancillary third-party claim. Hobbs v. Buckeye Union Cas. Co., 212 F. Supp. 349 (W.D. Va. 1962).

Only person secondarily liable to defendant may be joined. — The right to bring in a third party exists only when the third party "is or may be liable to him [the defendant] for all or part of plaintiff's claim against him." It is not enough that the third-party defendant may be liable to the plaintiff. Uptagrafft v. United States, 315 F.2d 200 (4th Cir.), cert. denied, 375 U.S. 818, 84 S. Ct. 54, 11 L. Ed. 2d 52 (1963).

A third-party claim may be asserted under the rule only when the third party's liability is in some way dependent on the outcome of the main claim or when the third party is secondarily liable to defendant. The secondary or derivative liability notion is central and it is irrelevant whether the basis of the third-party claim is indemnity, subrogation, contribution, express or implied warranty, or some other theory. But impleader is proper only when a right to relief exists under the applicable substantive law. Valley Landscape Co. v. Rolland, 218 Va. 257, 237 S.E.2d 120 (1977).

A defendant cannot compel the plaintiff, who has sued him, to sue also a third party whom he does not wish to sue, by tendering in a third-party complaint the third party as an additional defendant directly liable to the plaintiff. Herman Cantor Corp. v. Central Fid. Bank, 17 Bankr. 612 (Bankr. E.D. Va. 1982).

Defendant may implead a third party of the same citizenship as plaintiff where there is diversity between plaintiff and defendant. In such case, it may be said that ancillary jurisdiction confers power upon the court over the third-party action. Kenrose Mfg. Co. v. Fred Whitaker Co., 512 F.2d 890 (4th Cir. 1972), aff'g 53 F.R.D. 491 (W.D. Va. 1971).

Though the plaintiff and the third party defendant are citizens of Virginia, impleading him as a third party defendant under this rule did not require diversity of citizenship. Semler v. Psychiatric Inst., 538 F.2d 121 (4th Cir.), cert. denied, 429 U.S. 827, 97 S. Ct. 83, 50 L. Ed. 2d 90 (1976).

Where the plaintiff in his action refused to join a party who was jointly and severally liable with the defendant because such joinder would have destroyed the diversity jurisdiction of the federal district court, if the defendant felt apprehensive that it could have been held liable as principle for the acts of the party not joined, the defendant was free to bring that party into the action as a third party defendant and have him served with process under Rule 4 (f), Fed. R. Civ. P. Such action would have protected the defendant without depriving the court of the subject matter jurisdiction over the diversity action. Willis v. Semmes, Bowen & Semmes, 441 F. Supp. 1235 (E.D. Va. 1977).

Although this Rule permits a defendant to implead a third-party of the same citizenship as the plaintiff, the plaintiff cannot assert a claim directly against the third-party defendant unless complete diversity pursuant to 28 U.S.C. § 1332 is maintained or an independent form of jurisdiction is available. Coley v. Dragon Ltd., 138 F.R.D. 460 (E.D. Va. 1990).

Party treated as brought in under third-party practice to preserve diversity jurisdiction. — Where an impleader under Rule 19 or an order under subdivision (h) of Rule 13 would have destroyed the jurisdiction of the court because the impleaded party and the plaintiff were both residents of Virginia, the court treated the procedure as an ancillary proceeding under subdivision (a) of this rule, not requiring diversity of citizenship. Lumbermens Mut. Cas. Co. v. Harleysville Mut. Cas. Co., 367 F.2d 250 (4th Cir. 1966).

Claim by plaintiff against guarantors of loan held different from guarantors' claim for improperly closing debtor's business. — Where the question is whether a third-party complaint against a bank and a warehouse company to the effect that they improperly closed down the business of the debtor is the same claim as the claim of the plaintiff, the United States, against the defendants, who were guarantors for the payment of the balance due on a loan to the business, the answer is obvious. Such claim as the defendants may have against the warehouse and the bank is obviously an entirely different claim from the claim of the United States against the defendants. The claim of the United States is upon the note given it by the defendant guarantors, while the defendants' claim against the bank and warehouse is for alleged tortious action on their part. Plainly the third-party complaint does not seek recovery against the bank and warehouse for any part of the claim of the United States against the defendants but is upon an entirely independent claim. United States v. Mullins, 228 F. Supp. 748 (W.D. Va. 1964).

Rights of jointly liable insurers may be determined before payment. — Notwithstanding the substantive rule of law requiring payment by a surety before the right to subrogation arises, subdivision (a) of this rule and Rule 13(g) allow a constitutional order determining the rights of jointly liable insurers to be entered before payment. Lumbermen's Mut. Ins. Co. v. Massachusetts Bonding & Ins. Co., 310 F.2d 627 (4th Cir. 1962).

Vacating order impleading third party when no federal question or diversity of citizenship exists between third-party plaintiff and defendant. — See United States v. Houff, 202 F. Supp. 471 (W.D. Va.), aff'd, 312 F.2d 6 (4th Cir. 1962).

The burden is upon the defendant to demonstrate a cause of action upon which proposed third-party claims may be maintained. Defendant's failure to do so would result in the denial of his motion for leave to file a third-party complaint. Gilbert v. GE Co., 59 F.R.D. 273 (E.D. Va. 1973).

Rule 41, governing the voluntary dismissal of actions, applies in terms to third-party claims also. Kenrose Mfg. Kenrose Mfg. Co. v. Fred Whitaker Co., 512 F.2d 890 (4th Cir. 1972), aff'g 53 F.R.D. 491 (W.D. Va. 1971).

Consolidation used to achieve same result as third party practice. — Consolidation under Rule 42(a), Fed. R. Civ. P. may be used to achieve the same result as could be reached by means of third-party practice under Rule 14(a), Fed.R.Civ.P. A/S J. A/S J. Ludwig Mowinckles Rederi v. Tidewater Constr. Corp., 559 F.2d 928 (4th Cir. 1977).

Filing of cross-claims. — Subdivision (a) does not specifically permit or prohibit the filing of cross-claims by a third-party defendant against co-defendants of the third-party plaintiffs. An examination of the history of subdivision (a) does not indicate a clear intention to prohibit such cross-claims. Barring some prejudice to the movants, the court is thus not specifically prohibited by rule from permitting the filing of third-party defendant's cross-claims against the movants. American Gen. v. Equitable Gen., 87 F.R.D. 736 (E.D. Va. 1980).

The significance of the election to proceed in admiralty or as an ordinary civil action relates to distinctive procedural requirements and remedies available in admiralty claims and the fact that there is no right to trial by jury of an admiralty claim. Coley v. Dragon Ltd., 138 F.R.D. 460 (E.D. Va. 1990).

Applied in Kenrose Mfg. Co. v. Fred Whitaker Co., 53 F.R.D. 491 (W.D. Va. 1971); Eden Corp. v. Utica Mut. Ins. Co., 350 F. Supp. 637 (W.D. Va. 1972); Garrison v. Newell, 55 F.R.D. 550 (W.D. Va. 1972); Gilbert v. GE Co., 59 F.R.D. 267 (E.D. Va. 1973); Wittersheim v. General Transp. Servs., Inc., 378 F. Supp. 762 (E.D. Va. 1974).

Rule 15. Amended and Supplemental Pleadings.

(a) *Amendments Before Trial.* — (1) Amending as a Matter of Course. A party may amend its pleading once as a matter of course within:

(A) 21 days after serving it, or

(B) if the pleading is one to which a responsive pleading is required, 21 days after service of a responsive pleading or 21 days after service of a motion under Rule 12(b), (e), or (f), whichever is earlier.

(2) Other Amendments. In all other cases, a party may amend its pleading only with the opposing party's written consent or the court's leave. The court should freely give leave when justice so requires.

(3) Time to Respond. Unless the court orders otherwise, any required response to an amended pleading must be made within the time remaining to respond to the original pleading or within 14 days after service of the amended pleading, whichever is later.

(b) *Amendments During and After Trial.* — (1) Based on an Objection at Trial. If, at trial, a party objects that evidence is not within the issues raised in the pleadings, the court may permit the pleadings to be amended. The court should freely permit an amendment when doing so will aid in presenting the merits and the objecting party fails to satisfy the court that the evidence would prejudice that party's action or defense on the merits. The court may grant a continuance to enable the objecting party to meet the evidence.

(2) For Issues Tried by Consent. When an issue not raised by the pleadings is tried by the parties' express or implied consent, it must be treated in all respects as if raised in the pleadings. A party may move — at any time, even after judgment — to amend the pleadings to conform them to the evidence and to raise an unpleaded issue. But failure to amend does not affect the result of the trial of that issue.

(c) *Relation Back of Amendments.* — (1) When an Amendment Relates Back. An amendment to a pleading relates back to the date of the original pleading when:

(A) the law that provides the applicable statute of limitations allows relation back;

(B) the amendment asserts a claim or defense that arose out of the conduct, transaction, or occurrence set out — or attempted to be set out — in the original pleading; or

(C) the amendment changes the party or the naming of the party against whom a claim is asserted, if Rule 15(c)(1)(B) is satisfied and if, within the period provided by Rule 4(m) for serving the summons and complaint, the party to be brought in by amendment:

(i) received such notice of the action that it will not be prejudiced in defending on the merits; and

(ii) knew or should have known that the action would have been brought against it, but for a mistake concerning the proper party's identity.

(2) Notice to the United States. When the United States or a United States officer or agency is added as a defendant by amendment, the notice requirements of Rule 15(c)(1)(C)(i) and (ii) are satisfied if, during the stated period, process was delivered or mailed to the United States attorney or the United States attorney's designee, to the Attorney General of the United States, or to the officer or agency.

(d) *Supplemental Pleadings.* — On motion and reasonable notice, the court may, on just terms, permit a party to serve a supplemental pleading setting out any transaction, occurrence, or event that happened after the date of the pleading to be supplemented. The court may permit supplementation even though the original pleading is defective in stating a claim or defense. The court may order that the opposing party plead to the supplemental pleading within a specified time. (Amended by order adopted January 21, 1963, effective July 1, 1963, by order adopted February 28, 1966, effective July 1, 1966, by order adopted March 2, 1987, effective August 1, 1987, by order adopted April 30, 1991, effective December 1, 1991, by order adopted April 22, 1993, effective December 1, 1993, by order adopted April 30, 2007, effective December 1, 2007, and by order adopted March 26, 2009, effective December 1, 2009.)

Comment. — The language of Rule 15 has been amended as part of the general restyling of the Civil Rules to make them more easily understood and to make style and terminology consistent throughout the rules. These changes are intended to be stylistic only.

Former Rule 15(c)(3)(A) called for notice of the "institution" of the action. Rule 15(c)(1)(C)(i) omits the reference to "institution" as potentially confusing. What counts is that the party to be brought in have notice of the existence of the action, whether or not the notice includes details as to its "institution."

Law Review. — For comment on standing to amend in light of Summit Office Park v. United States Steel Corp., 639 F.2d 1278 (5th Cir. 1981), see 69 Va. L. Rev. 205 (1983).

CASE NOTES

I. In General.
II. Amendments as a Matter of Course.
III. Amendments to Conform to Evidence.
IV. Relation Back of Amendments.

I. IN GENERAL.

This rule provides liberal practice in allowance of amendments to formal pleadings. Coral v. Gonse, 330 F.2d 997 (4th Cir. 1964).

In federal practice leave to amend is to be granted with liberality. Austin v. Reynolds Metals Co., 327 F. Supp. 1145 (E.D. Va. 1970).

Leave to amend is granted liberally, and to justify a denial of such leave, it must appear to the Court that the amendment is futile, offered in bad faith, prejudicial or otherwise contrary to the interests of justice. Roper v. County of Chesterfield, 807 F. Supp. 1221 (E.D. Va. 1992).

Subsection (a) of this rule emcompasses a preference for liberal leave to amend even when the movant must seek leave to do so. Stewart v. Angelone, 186 F.R.D. 342 (E.D. Va. 1999).

Burden under this rule rests primarily on plaintiff to amend complaint, not upon defendant to anticipate a new claim. Davis v. Virginia Commonwealth Univ., 180 F.3d 626 (4th Cir. 1999).

Discretion of court. — Within the guidelines provided by the language of the rule and its interpretation by the court, the grant or denial of leave to amend is within the discretion of the trial court. First Va. Bank v. McClellan, 60 Bankr. 719 (Bankr. E.D. Va. 1986).

This rule permits a party to amend a pleading by leave of the court; such leave "shall be freely given when justice so requires," and the decision to grant leave to amend is within the discretion of the trial court. Hart v. Riverside Hosp., 899 F. Supp. 264 (E.D. Va. 1995).

A court's discretion to deny leave to amend is constrained by the dictate of this rule that "leave shall be freely given when justice so requires;" a court may not "use its discretion either arbitrarily, or in a way that undermines the basic policy of the rule." Keegan v. Dalton, 899 F. Supp. 1503 (E.D. Va. 1995).

The disposition of a motion to amend is within the sound discretion of the district court, and the appellate court reviews for abuse of that discretion. Davis v. Virginia Commonwealth Univ., 180 F.3d 626 (4th Cir. 1999).

Bankruptcy court's determination as to whether to grant leave to amend a proof of claim is a matter wholly within its discretion. Jackson v. IRS, 220 Bankr. 273 (Bankr. W.D. Va. 1998).

This rule allows the district court to exercise its discretion in granting or denying leave to amend pleading as justice requires. Manuel v. United States, 846 F. Supp. 478 (E.D. Va. 1994), aff'd, 50 F.3d 1253 (4th Cir. 1995).

Courts should generally grant leave to amend unless an amendment would cause undue prejudice or undue delay to the nonmoving party, or unless the motion was filed in bad faith or with an improper motive. Stewart v. Angelone, 186 F.R.D. 342 (E.D. Va. 1999).

It must also appear that successive amendments are futile, offered in bad faith, prejudicial, or otherwise contrary to interests of justice to justify denials of leave to amend. Ward Elecs. Serv., Inc. v. First Commercial Bank, 819 F.2d 496 (4th Cir. 1987), aff'd in part and rev'd in part, 856 F.2d 188 (4th Cir. 1988).

Subsequent events may be covered by supplemental amendments and necessary parties added. — Subdivision (d) of this rule plainly permits supplemental amendments to cover events happening after suit, and it follows, of course, that persons participating in these new events may be added if necessary. Such amendments are well within the basic aim of the rules to make pleadings a means to achieve an orderly and fair administration of justice. Griffin v. County Sch. Bd., 377 U.S. 218, 84 S. Ct. 1226, 12 L. Ed. 2d 256 (1964), rev'g Griffin v. Board of Supvrs., 322 F.2d 332 (4th Cir. 1963).

Applied in Dairyland Ins. Co. v. Hughes, 317 F. Supp. 928 (W.D. Va. 1970); Scruggs v. C & O Ry., 320 F. Supp. 1248 (W.D. Va. 1970); Eden Corp. v. Utica Mut. Ins. Co., 350 F. Supp. 637 (W.D. Va. 1972); Joseph v. House, 353 F. Supp. 367 (E.D. Va. 1973); Leathers v. Serrell, 376 F. Supp. 983 (W.D. Va. 1974); Kirtley v. Armentrout, 405 F. Supp. 575 (W.D. Va. 1975); Pizzuto v. Hall's Motor Transit Co., 409 F. Supp. 427 (E.D. Va. 1976); In re Steuart Transp. Co., 435 F. Supp. 798 (E.D. Va. 1977); Davidson v. Cook, 567 F. Supp. 225 (E.D. Va. 1983); Davis v. City of Portsmouth, 579 F. Supp. 1205 (E.D. Va. 1983); American Honda Fin. Corp. v. Tester, 56 Bankr. 208 (W.D. Va. 1985); Sweeney Co. v. Engineers-Constructors, Inc., 109 F.R.D. 358 (E.D. Va. 1986); Selman v. American Sports Underwriters, Inc., 697 F. Supp. 225 (W.D. Va. 1988); Minnick v. United States, 767 F. Supp. 115 (E.D. Va. 1990); Natural Resources Defense Council, Inc. v. United States EPA, 770 F. Supp. 1093 (E.D. Va. 1991); St. Jarre v. Heidelberger Druckmaschinen, 816 F. Supp. 424 (E.D. Va. 1993); Feikema v. Texaco, Inc., 16 F.3d 1408 (4th Cir. 1994); Weill v. Dominion Resources, Inc., 875 F. Supp. 331 (E.D. Va. 1994); Jacobi v. Blocker, 153 F.R.D. 84 (E.D. Va. 1994); NAACP Labor Comm. v. Laborers' Int'l Union, 902 F. Supp. 688 (W.D. Va. 1995); Gambelli v. United States, 904 F. Supp. 494 (E.D. Va. 1995); Young v. James, 168 F.R.D. 24 (E.D. Va. 1996); Phillips v. United Fixtures Co., 168 F.R.D. 183 (W.D. Va. 1996); Morrel v. Nationwide Mut. Fire Ins. Co., 188 F.3d 218 (4th Cir. 1999); Blagman v. White, 112 F. Supp. 2d 534, 2000 U.S. Dist. LEXIS 13799 (E.D. Va. 2000).

II. AMENDMENTS AS A MATTER OF COURSE.

One amendment is permitted of course before a responsive pleading is filed. Coral v. Gonse, 330 F.2d 997 (4th Cir. 1964); Wallace v. Chrysler Credit Corp., 743 F. Supp. 1228 (W.D. Va. 1990).

And defective jurisdictional averments are correctible to conform to proof. — Defective jurisdictional averments are readily correctible in the light of proof even after the proofs are in. Coral v. Gonse, 330 F.2d 997 (4th Cir. 1964).

But court has discretion to disallow plaintiff's attempt to show citizenship other than originally alleged. — In a diversity action, for the purpose of founding the jurisdiction of the court, the plaintiff had solemnly and formally asserted that he was not only a resident of Virginia but a citizen of Virginia. Such averment is in the nature of a judicial admission, for it was a formal declaration of fact peculiarly within his own knowledge. He might have been unaware of some legal principle affecting an ultimate determination of his citizenship, or of his legal residency, but he could not have been unaware of the underlying facts. Under these circumstances, after having been confronted with almost conclusive proof that the defendant was a resident of the same state of which he claimed to be a resident, he ought not lightly to be allowed to reverse his field and take an inconsistent position. Considering the nature of the averment, its probable truth even in the light of the present claim, the fact that this averment was not at issue, and the fact that there was no suggestion of mistake until after the defendant's status as a resident of Virginia was established and the motion to dismiss was about to be granted, it was well within the district court's discretion to refuse to hear the plaintiff's proffered testimony and to dismiss the action for want of diversity of citizenship. Coral v. Gonse, 330 F.2d 997 (4th Cir. 1964).

Term "responsive pleading" is defined by reference to Rule 7(a), which distinguishes between pleadings and motions, and provides an exclusive list of what is a pleading: a complaint, an answer, a reply to a counterclaim, an answer to a cross-claim, a third party complaint, and an answer. Vanguard Military Equip. Corp. v. David B. Finestone Co., 6 F. Supp. 2d 488 (E.D. Va. 1997).

Just because answer does not respond to all allegations in the complaint does not make it any more or less a "pleading" for 15(a) and Rule 7(a) purposes. Vanguard Military Equip. Corp. v. David B. Finestone Co., 6 F. Supp. 2d 488 (E.D. Va. 1997).

Motions to dismiss and for summary judgment are not considered responsive pleadings for purposes of this rule. Williams v. Wilkerson, 90 F.R.D. 168 (E.D. Va. 1981); United States ex rel. Tucker v. Thomas Howell Kiewit (USA) Inc., 149 F.R.D. 125 (E.D. Va. 1993).

Motions to dismiss are not considered responsive pleadings for the purposes of this rule. Wallace v. Chrysler Credit Corp., 743 F. Supp. 1228 (W.D. Va. 1990).

Where defendants did not file an answer to plaintiff's original complaint, but rather filed motions to dismiss, such pre-answer Rule 12(b) motions not being responsive pleadings, plaintiff was not required to obtain leave of court before filing his amended complaint. Sohns v. Dahl, 392 F. Supp. 1208 (W.D. Va. 1975).

Defendant's motions were not responsive pleadings. — Defendant's motion to quash service of process and motion to dismiss did not constitute responsive pleadings, thus plaintiff could "amend his pleading once as a matter of course." United States ex rel. Tucker v. Thomas Howell Kiewit (USA) Inc., 149 F.R.D. 125 (E.D. Va. 1993).

Plaintiff entitled to amend complaint. — Although defendant had moved to dismiss complaint, he had not answered it, and accordingly, plaintiff was entitled to amend the complaint to replead claim. Battle v. Whitehurst, 831 F. Supp. 522 (E.D. Va. 1993), aff'd, 36 F.3d 1091 (4th Cir. 1994).

III. AMENDMENTS TO CONFORM TO EVIDENCE.

Once the complaint has been dismissed (or disposed of on summary judgment) whether to grant leave to amend is in the discretion of the trial court. Wallace v. Chrysler Credit Corp., 743 F. Supp. 1228 (W.D. Va. 1990).

A motion to amend a complaint is not held to the summary judgment standard defendant implicitly invoked by arguing the sufficiency of the evidence, but rather only to that of a motion to dismiss under Federal Rules of Civil Procedure, Rule 12(b)(6). Unless a proposed amendment may clearly be seen to be futile because of substantive or procedural considerations, conjecture about the merits of the litigation should not enter into the decision whether to allow amendment. Burns v. AAF-McQuay, Inc., 980 F. Supp. 175 (W.D. Va. 1997), aff'd, 166 F.3d 292 (4th Cir. 1999).

An informa pauperis litigant is entitled to the opportunity under this rule to amend his complaint before dismissal. Church v. Attorney Gen., 125 F.3d 210 (4th Cir. 1997).

Subdivision (b) of this rule is in effect a "deeming" rule which permits pleadings to be amended after the fact. Frazier v. Collins, 538 F. Supp. 603 (E.D. Va. 1982).

It should be liberally interpreted. — Subdivision (b) of this rule is intended to promote the objective of deciding cases on their merits, and a court should interpret the rule liberally and permit an amendment whenever doing so will effectuate the underlying purpose of the rule. Burke & Herbert Bank & Trust Co. v. Crockett, 11 Bankr. 822 (Bankr. E.D. Va. 1981).

Subdivision (b) authorizes determination of issue made by evidence. — Subdivision (b) authorizes and permits the court's determination of an issue as to a defendant's primary negligence, not definitely made by the pleadings nor included in the pretrial order, but clearly presented by the evidence, provided that such determination has not prejudiced the defendant in his defense upon the merits. Carroll v. Harrison, 49 F. Supp. 283 (W.D. Va.), aff'd, 139 F.2d 427 (4th Cir. 1943).

Under subdivision (b) of this rule, a liberal provision is made for amendments to conform the pleadings to the evidence, and a court may consider issues so raised even though no formal application is made to amend. The fact that this involves a change in the legal theory of the action is immaterial so long as the opposing party has not been prejudiced in presenting his case. EEOC v. GE Co., 532 F.2d 359 (4th Cir. 1976).

The court will not imply consent to try a claim merely because evidence relevant to a properly pleaded issue incidentally tends to establish an unpleaded claim. McClam v. City of Norfolk Police Dep't, 877 F. Supp. 277 (E.D. Va. 1995).

Formal amendment is needed only when evidence is objected to at trial as not within the scope of the pleadings. EEOC v. GE Co., 532 F.2d 359 (4th Cir. 1976).

Copy of proposed amended pleading should be submitted. — When a plaintiff seeks leave to amend his complaint or any other pleading, a copy of the proposed amended pleading, and not simply the proposed amendment, must be attached to the motion; otherwise, the motion will be denied, without prejudice. Williams v. Wilkerson, 90 F.R.D. 168 (E.D. Va. 1981).

Virginia Supreme Court Rule 3:16(d) (see now Rule 3:18) does not supersede this rule. — The trial court's decision to permit a party to amend its complaint at trial to incorporate the defense theory of contributory negligence was a proper exercise of its discretion under subdivision (b) of this rule. Virginia Supreme Court Rule 3:16(d) does not create substantive law which supersedes the liberal amendment provisions of subdivision (b) of this rule. For the purpose of determining whether the Federal Rules of Civil Procedure apply, the Virginia rules are clearly procedural. A constitutionally valid federal rule must be given effect in district court, even if it would supply a different result than would state law. Seidman v. Fishburne-Hudgins Educ. Found., Inc., 724 F.2d 413 (4th Cir. 1984).

Consent to try claim not implied merely because evidence tends to prove it. — A court will not imply consent to try a claim merely because evidence relevant to a properly pleaded issue incidentally tends to establish an unpleaded claim. Quillen v. International Playtex, Inc., 789 F.2d 1041 (4th Cir. 1986).

Changing plaintiff's theory of case. — The fact that an amendment changes the plaintiff's theory of the case will not suffice as a reason for denial absent a showing of prejudice, bad faith, futility, or dilatoriness associated with the motion. Ward Elecs. Serv., Inc. v. First Commercial Bank, 819 F.2d 496 (4th Cir. 1987), aff'd in part and rev'd in part, 856 F.2d 188 (4th Cir. 1988).

Change in theory of recovery and one prior amendment of the complaint, early in the pretrial process, were not sufficient to justify denial of leave to amend. Ward Elecs. Serv., Inc. v. First Commercial Bank, 819 F.2d 496 (4th Cir. 1987), aff'd in part and rev'd in part, 856 F.2d 188 (4th Cir. 1988).

Court in exercise of discretion may permit amendment defeating jurisdiction. — See Pierside Term. Operators, Inc. v. M/V Floridian, 423 F. Supp. 962 (E.D. Va. 1976).

Amendment not changing cause of action. — An original complaint under the Federal Employers' Liability Act for an employee's death alleged a failure to provide a proper lookout for deceased, to give him proper warning of the approach of the train, to keep the head car properly lighted, and to warn the deceased of an unprecedented and unexpected change in the manner of shifting cars. The amended complaint charged the failure to have the locomotive properly lighted as required by the Boiler Inspection Act. Both of them related to the same general conduct, transaction and occurrence which involved the death of the deceased. There was therefore no departure. The cause of action now, as it was in the beginning, is the same — it is a suit to recover damages for the alleged wrongful death of the deceased. The amendment was thus not barred by the limitation statute provided in the Federal Employers' Liability Act. Tiller v. Atlantic Coast Line R.R., 323 U.S. 574, 65 S. Ct. 421, 89 L. Ed. 465 (1945), rev'g 142 F.2d 718 (4th Cir. 1944).

Plaintiff not entitled to amend complaint. — The court was unpersuaded by plaintiff's argument that pendent Virginia law claims for intentional infliction of emotional distress and negligent infliction of emotional distress could not have been pled at the time of the original complaint. Plaintiff's claimed emotional distress damages, while not recoverable "under" the Age Discrimination in Employment Act, 29 U.S.C. Section 626, potentially were recoverable in 1994 "under" pendent state law infliction of emotional distress causes of action. Therefore, plaintiff's motion for leave to amend was denied. Burns v. AAF-McQuay, Inc., 980 F. Supp. 175 (W.D. Va. 1997), aff'd, 166 F.3d 292 (4th Cir. 1999).

Where plaintiff wanted leave to amend her complaint to plead the Sixth Circuit novel holding in *Crawford v. Medina General Hospital*, 96 F.3d 830 (6th Cir. 1996) that Title VII's hostile work environment doctrine applies to an Age Discrimination in Employment Act (ADEA) cause of action, because Fourth Circuit law does not recognize the applicability of Title VII's hostile work environment doctrine in age discrimination actions under the ADEA, the court denied plaintiff leave to amend her complaint. Burns v. AAF-McQuay, Inc., 980 F. Supp. 175 (W.D. Va. 1997), aff'd, 166 F.3d 292 (4th Cir. 1999).

Refusal to permit filing of amended and supplemental complaint held abuse of discretion. — Where the sole objective of the plaintiffs, in both their original complaint and a tendered amendment and supplement thereto, was to recover from their insurer the excess of their judgments over and above the limits of their judgment debtor's policy, and the one real issue for trial would be the negligence and bad faith of the insurer in failing to settle claims, it was held an abuse of discretion to refuse to permit plaintiffs, who originally sued as third-party beneficiaries of the insurance contract and as judgment creditors of the insured, to file the proposed amended and supplemental complaint, by which they sought to recover as assignees of the insured's cause of action against the insurer for failure to settle. Rowe v. United States Fid. & Guar. Co., 421 F.2d 937 (4th Cir. 1970).

Plaintiff's attempt to amend held not abuse of court's processes. — Plaintiff's conduct in attempting further amendment was not an abuse of the court's processes calling for the visitation of sanctions upon the plaintiff who was, himself, an attorney, where plaintiff contended that the evidence before the court would support an alternative theory of recovery based upon the common law and irrespective of the statutes upon which he had theretofore relied as the basis of his claim for damages and civil penalty, and that, in asking leave to amend, after hearing, he was attempting to proceed according to subdivision (b) to amend the pleadings to conform to the evidence. Williams v. Lewis, 342 F.2d 727 (4th Cir.), cert. denied, 382 U.S. 814, 86 S. Ct. 30, 15 L. Ed. 2d 61, reh'g denied, 382 U.S. 933, 86 S. Ct. 306, 15 L. Ed. 2d 345 (1965).

Bankruptcy court did not abuse its discretion in allowing a creditor to submit, at the close of trial, an amended complaint asserting bailment as a theory of recovery in a secured creditor's action to establish that it had a perfected lien on some of debtor's equipment. Ingersoll-Rand Fin. Corp. v. Nunley, 11 Bankr. 528 (Bankr. W.D. Va. 1981).

Leave to amend after hearing held properly denied. — See Williams v. Lewis, 342 F.2d 727 (4th Cir.), cert. denied, 382 U.S. 814, 86 S. Ct. 30, 15 L. Ed. 2d 61, reh'g denied, 382 U.S. 933, 86 S. Ct. 306, 15 L. Ed. 2d 345 (1965).

Amendment to answer in Age Discrimination in Employment Act properly allowed to assert defense omitted in answer. — See Smallwood v. United Air Lines, 661 F.2d 303 (4th Cir. 1981), cert. denied, 456 U.S. 1007, 102 S. Ct. 2299, 73 L. Ed. 2d 1302 (1982), 469 U.S. 832, 105 S. Ct. 120, 83 L. Ed. 2d 62 (1984).

Motion to amend denied pending compliance with local rules. — Where after plaintiff's original motion was denied, plaintiff submitted a copy of the proposed amended complaint, but did not renew his motion for leave to amend, nor did he file a supporting brief in accordance with local Rule 11(A) and (F), under such circumstances, the motion would be denied pending plaintiff's compliance with the local rules. Williams v. Wilkerson, 90 F.R.D. 168 (E.D. Va. 1981).

IV. RELATION BACK OF AMENDMENTS.

Three elements must be met before subdivision (c) relation back will be allowed, even when the result could be extinguishment of the claim: (1) Same transaction or occurrence; (2) the new party had notice of the action prior to the expiration of the statute of limitations; and (3) he knew or should have known that but for a mistake in identity the action would have been brought against him. Weisgal v. Smith, 774 F.2d 1277 (4th Cir. 1985).

Relation back of amendment which merely expands or amplifies cause of action. — Where an amendment merely expands or amplifies the cause of action already asserted, it relates back to the commencement of the action and is not affected by the intervening lapse of time. Paynter v. C & O Ry., 60 F.R.D. 153 (W.D. Va. 1973).

Amendment of a complaint enjoining violation of the Fair Labor Standards Act to restrain defendant from withholding wages due to present and former employees was permitted even though at the time the amendment was filed the statute of limitations could bar collection of most of the money sought to be obtained in back wages, and the amendment related back to the date of the original pleadings. Wirtz v. Atkins, 247 F. Supp. 503 (E.D. Va. 1965).

Where defendant, through first amended complaint, was on notice with regard to disability discrimination claim, and second amended complaint merely added additionally obtained facts, the district court erred when it held that the 90-day statute of limitations jurisdictionally barred consideration of the second amended complaint. Davis v. Virginia Commonwealth Univ., 180 F.3d 626 (4th Cir. 1999).

Amendment does not relate back where based on different theories or facts. — Plaintiff's amended complaint could not relate back, where his original and amended complaints were based on entirely different theories, facts and occurrences. Painter v. Mohawk Rubber Co., 636 F. Supp. 453 (W.D. Va. 1986).

Relation back doctrine applied on case-by-case basis. — Courts have generally examined the facts of each case to ascertain whether application of the relation back doctrine would be inconsistent with the notice safeguards of clauses (1) and (2) of subdivision (c). Bruce v. Smith, 581 F. Supp. 902 (W.D. Va. 1984).

"Action" as used in subdivision (c) pertains to the actual filing of the lawsuit, not the incident giving rise to that suit. Bruce v. Smith, 581 F. Supp. 902 (W.D. Va. 1984).

"Period provided by law for commencing the action" as used in subdivision (c) obviously refers to the applicable statute of limitations period. Bruce v. Smith, 581 F. Supp. 902 (W.D. Va. 1984).

Informal notice to new party of commencement of action is sufficient. Bruce v. Smith, 581 F. Supp. 902 (W.D. Va. 1984).

Rule does not include reasonable allowance for service beyond limitations period. — The language of the rule requires, in plain and clear terms, that the notice be given "within the limitations period." It includes no reasonable allowance for service beyond that "limitations period." To include "time for service" as an addition to the six-months' limit in the rule in a Federal Tort Claims Act action would demand a rewriting of the rule. Weisgal v. Smith, 774 F.2d 1277 (4th Cir. 1985).

Subdivision (c)(2) does not require notice. — The plain language of subdivision (c)(2) contains no notice requirement. Authority once to the contrary has been recognized as having been overruled. Carter v. Rental Uniform Serv. of Culpeper, Inc., 977 F. Supp. 753 (W.D. Va. 1997).

No relation back where plaintiff sued wrong party. — Absent a mistake by plaintiff as to identification of proper defendants, the addition of a new defendant did not relate back to the filing of the initial complaint as there was no mistake as to the identity of the new party; the plaintiff did not misname the defendants in the original complaint but, rather, he sued the wrong parties. Fitzpatrick v. Marion Corr. Treatment Ctr., — F. Supp. 2d —, 2001 U.S. Dist. LEXIS 19882 (W.D. Va. 2001).

Absent a mistake by plaintiff as to identification of proper defendants, it is irrelevant whether the new party had constructive notice that the suit would have been brought against him. Bruce v. Smith, 581 F. Supp. 902 (W.D. Va. 1984).

Identity of interest between old and new plaintiffs is an appropriate guide in measuring possible prejudices to these newly named parties. This concept, a judicial gloss on clause (1) of subdivision (c), provides that when the original and added parties are so closely related in business or other activities that it is fair to presume that the added parties learned of the institution of the suit shortly after it was commenced. Bruce v. Smith, 581 F. Supp. 902 (W.D. Va. 1984).

Naming unknown, fictitious, or "John Doe" defendants in a complaint does not toll the statute of limitations until such time as the names of these parties can be secured. Instead, it amounts to a change of parties under subdivision (c) and the newly named defendant sought to be substituted for the previously unknown defendant becomes a new party. Bruce v. Smith, 581 F. Supp. 902 (W.D. Va. 1984).

Amendment held to relate back despite misnomer in complaint. — The plaintiff's amendments charging the defendant with defectively manufacturing the glass related back to the date of the original complaint and were not barred by the statute of limitations, where despite the misnomer in the complaint, the defendant received notice of the products liability claim when it was served with the plaintiff's initial timely, and otherwise correct, complaint. Kast v. PPG Indus., Inc., 664 F. Supp. 237 (W.D. Va. 1987).

Amendments held to relate back although some original claims lacked jurisdiction. — Where defendants objected that plaintiff's 42 U.S.C. Section 1981 claims could not relate back to the Title VII claims because some of the latter claims were jurisdictionally barred, the district court stopped short of "bootstrapping" from Title VII claims which lacked jurisdiction altogether to save an otherwise time-barred Section 1981 claim. Here, the court had jurisdiction over several of plaintiff's Title VII counts; they were squarely before this tribunal. That plaintiff's Section 1981 claims should relate back to them was proper under subsection (c). Carter v. Rental Uniform Serv. of Culpeper, Inc., 977 F. Supp. 753 (W.D. Va. 1997).

Standard for determining whether Section 1981 claim relates back to Title VII complaint. — Where defendants argued that plaintiff's 42 U.S.C. Section 1981 claims did not relate back because they constituted new legal theories not alleged in plaintiff's original complaint, under subsection (c) this was not the standard for determining whether a claim should relate back. Provided that the requisite "factual nexus" between the amendment and the original complaint is present, a Section 1981 claim relates back by subsection (c) to an original Title VII complaint for limitations purposes. Carter v. Rental Uniform Serv. of Culpeper, Inc., 977 F. Supp. 753 (W.D. Va. 1997).

Inexcusable neglect as possible prejudice to defense on merits. — As to possible prejudice to defendants maintaining a defense on the merits, plaintiff's own inexcusable neglect is a proper consideration. Bruce v. Smith, 581 F. Supp. 902 (W.D. Va. 1984).

Where plaintiff's original pleading was drawn without the assistance of counsel and, like the great majority of pro se complaints, it did not track with technical precision the pleading requirements for antitrust causes of action, but did give defendant adequate notice that the plaintiff wished to litigate the validity of certain territorial restrictions and tying arrangements contained in its franchise agreement with the defendant, because the territorial restriction and tying arrangement causes of action were in substance the same causes of action as were set forth in the original complaint, plaintiff was entitled to have the filing date relate back to the date of filing the original complaint under subdivision (c) of this rule. Material Handling Indus., Inc. v. Eaton Corp., 391 F. Supp. 977 (E.D. Va. 1975).

Amended complaint cannot relate back to claim filed with administrative agency. — An amended complaint filed in a federal district court cannot relate back to a charge filed with an administrative agency regardless of whether the facts alleged therein support the additional causes in the amended complaint. Beasley v. Motor Freight Express, Inc., 401 F. Supp. 662 (E.D. Va. 1975).

Relation back provision not applied. — Where even when the original complaint was given the benefit of liberal construction, the court could nowhere find in it a hint that plaintiff was complaining, or even attempting to complain, of an antitrust conspiracy involving defendant, plaintiff could not have the benefit of subdivision (c)'s relation back provision because relation back would prejudice defendant by depriving it of the protection of the statute of limitations with respect to the conspiracy count. Material Handling Indus., Inc. v. Eaton Corp., 391 F. Supp. 977 (E.D. Va. 1975).

Leave to include party where class not designated. — Where an unnamed plaintiff did not join as a named plaintiff on the assumption that her interests would be protected as a member of the class, but no class was designated in the action, and it was not clear at the time that it would be proper or appropriate to designate a class, leave was granted plaintiffs to file an amended complaint or through otherwise appropriate pleading to bring the individual in as an additional party plaintiff. Howard v. Aluminum Workers Int'l Union, 418 F. Supp. 1058 (E.D. Va. 1976), aff'd, 589 F.2d 771 (4th Cir. 1978).

Amendment adding defense of statute of frauds allowed. — The addition of the statutes of frauds question did not prejudice plaintiff where it did not arise from additional evidence to which plaintiff had lodged objection and it was not outside his knowledge of the true facts. Pierside Term. Operators, Inc. v. M/V Floridian, 423 F. Supp. 962 (E.D. Va. 1976).

Rule 16. Pretrial Conferences; Scheduling; Management.

(a) *Purposes of a Pretrial Conference.* — In any action, the court may order the attorneys and any unrepresented parties to appear for one or more pretrial conferences for such purposes as:

(1) expediting disposition of the action;

(2) establishing early and continuing control so that the case will not be protracted because of lack of management;

(3) discouraging wasteful pretrial activities;

(4) improving the quality of the trial through more thorough preparation; and

(5) facilitating settlement.

(b) *Scheduling.* — (1) Scheduling Order. Except in categories of actions exempted by local rule, the district judge — or a magistrate judge when authorized by local rule — must issue a scheduling order:

(A) after receiving the parties' report under Rule 26(f); or

(B) after consulting with the parties' attorneys and any unrepresented parties at a scheduling conference or by telephone, mail, or other means.

(2) Time to Issue. The judge must issue the scheduling order as soon as practicable, but in any event within the earlier of 120 days after any defendant has been served with the complaint or 90 days after any defendant has appeared.

(3) Contents of the Order. (A) Required Contents. The scheduling order must limit the time to join other parties, amend the pleadings, complete discovery, and file motions.

(B) Permitted Contents. The scheduling order may:

(i) modify the timing of disclosures under Rules 26(a) and 26(e)(1);

(ii) modify the extent of discovery;

(iii) provide for disclosure or discovery of electronically stored information;

(iv) include any agreements the parties reach for asserting claims of privilege or of protection as trial-preparation material after information is produced;

(v) set dates for pretrial conferences and for trial; and

(vi) include other appropriate matters.

(4) Modifying a Schedule. A schedule may be modified only for good cause and with the judge's consent.

(c) *Attendance and Matters for Consideration at a Pretrial Conference.* — (1) Attendance. A represented party must authorize at least one of its attorneys to make stipulations and admissions about all matters that can reasonably be anticipated for discussion at a pretrial conference. If appropriate, the court may require that a party or its representative be present or reasonably available by other means to consider possible settlement.

(2) Matters for Consideration. At any pretrial conference, the court may consider and take appropriate action on the following matters:

(A) formulating and simplifying the issues, and eliminating frivolous claims or defenses;

(B) amending the pleadings if necessary or desirable;

(C) obtaining admissions and stipulations about facts and documents to avoid unnecessary proof, and ruling in advance on the admissibility of evidence;

(D) avoiding unnecessary proof and cumulative evidence, and limiting the use of testimony under Federal Rule of Evidence 702;

(E) determining the appropriateness and timing of summary adjudication under Rule 56;

(F) controlling and scheduling discovery, including orders affecting disclosures and discovery under Rule 26 and Rules 29 through 37;

(G) identifying witnesses and documents, scheduling the filing and exchange of any pretrial briefs, and setting dates for further conferences and for trial;

(H) referring matters to a magistrate judge or a master;

(I) settling the case and using special procedures to assist in resolving the dispute when authorized by statute or local rule;

(J) determining the form and content of the pretrial order;

(K) disposing of pending motions;

(L) adopting special procedures for managing potentially difficult or protracted actions that may involve complex issues, multiple parties, difficult legal questions, or unusual proof problems;

(M) ordering a separate trial under Rule 42(b) of a claim, counterclaim, crossclaim, third-party claim, or particular issue;

(N) ordering the presentation of evidence early in the trial on a manageable issue that might, on the evidence, be the basis for a judgment as a matter of law under Rule 50(a) or a judgment on partial findings under Rule 52(c);

(O) establishing a reasonable limit on the time allowed to present evidence; and

(P) facilitating in other ways the just, speedy, and inexpensive disposition of the action.

(d) *Pretrial Orders.* — After any conference under this rule, the court should issue an order reciting the action taken. This order controls the course of the action unless the court modifies it.

(e) *Final Pretrial Conference and Orders.* — The court may hold a final pretrial conference to formulate a trial plan, including a plan to facilitate the admission of evidence. The conference must be held as close to the start of trial as is reasonable, and must be attended by at least one attorney who will conduct the trial for each party and by any unrepresented party. The court may modify the order issued after a final pretrial conference only to prevent manifest injustice.

(f) *Sanctions.* — (1) In General. On motion or on its own, the court may issue any just orders, including those authorized by Rule 37(b)(2)(A)(ii)-(vii), if a party or its attorney:

(A) fails to appear at a scheduling or other pretrial conference;

(B) is substantially unprepared to participate — or does not participate in good faith — in the conference; or

(C) fails to obey a scheduling or other pretrial order.

(2) Imposing Fees and Costs. Instead of or in addition to any other sanction, the court must order the party, its attorney, or both to pay the reasonable expenses — including attorney's fees — incurred because of any noncompliance with this rule, unless the noncompliance was substantially justified or other circumstances make an award of expenses unjust. (Amended by order adopted April 28, 1983, effective August 1, 1983, by order adopted March 2, 1987, effective August 1, 1987, by order adopted April 22, 1993, effective December 1, 1993, by order adopted April 12, 2006, effective December 1, 2006, and by order adopted April 30, 2007, effective December 1, 2007.)

Comment. — The language of Rule 16 has been amended as part of the general restyling of the Civil Rules to make them more easily understood and to make style and terminology consistent throughout the rules. These changes are intended to be stylistic only.

Law Review. — For note, "Pretrial Conference: A Critical Examination of Local Rules Adopted by Federal District Courts," see 64 Va. L. Rev. 467 (1978). For note on judicial authority in the settlement of federal civil cases, see 42 Wash. & Lee L. Rev. 171 (1985).

CASE NOTES

Trial court's authority to permit dismissal of party derives from Rules 15 and 21 F.R.Civ.P., not Rule 19. Caperton v. Beatrice Pocahontas Coal Co., 585 F.2d 683 (4th Cir. 1978).

Applied in Williams v. Howard Johnson's, Inc., 323 F.2d 102 (4th Cir. 1963); Pierside Term. Operators, Inc. v. M/V Floridian, 423 F. Supp. 962 (E.D. Va. 1976); Jesselson v. Outlet Assocs., 784 F. Supp. 1223 (E.D. Va. 1991).

TITLE IV. PARTIES.

Rule 17. Plaintiff and Defendant; Capacity; Public Officers.

(a) *Real Party in Interest.* — (1) Designation in General. An action must be prosecuted in the name of the real party in interest. The following may sue in their own names without joining the person for whose benefit the action is brought:

(A) an executor;

(B) an administrator;

(C) a guardian;

(D) a bailee;

(E) a trustee of an express trust;

(F) a party with whom or in whose name a contract has been made for another's benefit; and

(G) a party authorized by statute.

(2) Action in the Name of the United States for Another's Use or Benefit. When a federal statute so provides, an action for another's use or benefit must be brought in the name of the United States.

(3) Joinder of the Real Party in Interest. The court may not dismiss an action for failure to prosecute in the name of the real party in interest until, after an objection, a reasonable time has been allowed for the real party in interest to ratify, join, or be substituted into the action. After ratification, joinder, or substitution, the action proceeds as if it had been originally commenced by the real party in interest.

(b) *Capacity to Sue or Be Sued.* — Capacity to sue or be sued is determined as follows:

(1) for an individual who is not acting in a representative capacity, by the law of the individual's domicile;

(2) for a corporation, by the law under which it was organized; and

(3) for all other parties, by the law of the state where the court is located, except that:

(A) a partnership or other unincorporated association with no such capacity under that state's law may sue or be sued in its common name to enforce a substantive right existing under the United States Constitution or laws; and

(B) 28 U.S.C. §§ 754 and 959(a) govern the capacity of a receiver appointed by a United States court to sue or be sued in a United States court.

(c) *Minor or Incompetent Person.* — (1) With a Representative. The following representatives may sue or defend on behalf of a minor or an incompetent person:

(A) a general guardian;

(B) a committee;

(C) a conservator; or

(D) a like fiduciary.

(2) Without a Representative. A minor or an incompetent person who does not have a duly appointed representative may sue by a next friend or by a guardian ad litem. The court must appoint a guardian ad litem — or issue another appropriate order — to protect a minor or incompetent person who is unrepresented in an action.

(d) *Public Officer's Title and Name.* — A public officer who sues or is sued in an official capacity may be designated by official title rather than by name, but the court may order that the officer's name be added. (Amended by order adopted December 27, 1946, effective March 19, 1948, by order adopted December 29, 1948, effective October 20, 1949, by order adopted February 28, 1966, effective July 1, 1966, by order adopted March 2, 1987, effective August 1, 1987, by order adopted April 25, 1988, effective August 1, 1988, by P.L. 100-690, § 7049, effective November 18, 1988, and by order adopted April 30, 2007, effective December 1, 2007.)

Comment. — The language of Rule 17 has been amended as part of the general restyling of the Civil Rules to make them more easily understood and to make style and terminology consistent throughout the rules. These changes are intended to be stylistic only.

Rule 17(d) incorporates the provisions of former Rule 25(d)(2), which fit better with Rule 17.

Law Review. — For note on joinder of partially subrogated insurers, see 40 Wash. & Lee L. Rev. 756 (1983).

CASE NOTES

Subdivision (a) merely defines real parties in interest. — Subdivision (a) of this rule is properly interpreted only as defining — either directly or by incorporation of state law — those persons who, as real parties in interest, have substantive rights of action, and not as enabling those parties then to avoid joinder of other parties in interest. Travelers Ins. Co. v. Riggs, 671 F.2d 810 (4th Cir. 1982).

The meaning and object of the "real party in interest" principle is that the action must be brought by a person who possesses the right to enforce the claim and who has a significant interest in the litigation. It also enables a defendant to present defenses he has against the real party in interest, to protect the defendant against a subsequent action by the party actually entitled to relief, and to ensure that the judgment will have proper res judicata effect. VEPCO v. Westinghouse Elec. Corp., 485 F.2d 78 (4th Cir. 1973), cert. denied, 415 U.S. 935, 94 S. Ct. 1450, 39 L. Ed. 2d 493 (1974).

The question of the authority of a personal representative must be raised, if at all, in the initial answer. Scruggs v. C & O Ry., 320 F. Supp. 1248 (W.D. Va. 1970).

Non-lawyer parent suing as next friend represented by counsel. — This rule concerns the capacity to sue and be sued. Subdivision (c) of that rule says that an infant can sue through a next friend. This means that the next friend is trusted to make decisions for the minor child—whether to sue, when to sue, when and on what terms to settle, and the like. But this rule does not address the question whether a non-lawyer parent, when suing as next friend of the child, must be represented by legal counsel. Brown v. Ortho Diagnostic Sys., 868 F. Supp. 168 (E.D. Va. 1994).

Where there is partial subrogation, there are two real parties in interest. Either party may bring suit — the insurer-subrogee to the extent it has reimbursed the subrogor, or the subrogor for either the entire loss or only its unreimbursed loss. VEPCO v. Westinghouse Elec. Corp., 485 F.2d 78 (4th Cir. 1973), cert. denied, 415 U.S. 935, 94 S. Ct. 1450, 39 L. Ed. 2d 493 (1974).

A partial subrogee is a real party in interest within the meaning of subdivision (a) of this rule. Ingram v. Link Belt Power Shovel Co., 94 F.R.D. 196 (W.D. Va. 1982).

But not an indispensable party. — Partial subrogees are not indispensable parties within the meaning of Rule 19(b). Accordingly, federal courts will deny a defendant's motion to join a partial subrogee when to do so would destroy diversity jurisdiction. Ingram v. Link Belt Power Shovel Co., 94 F.R.D. 196 (W.D. Va. 1982).

Employer and workmen's compensation insurance carrier as real parties in interest. — In an action by an employee to recover for personal injury, where the injured employee has received workmen's compensation benefits, the employer and, in turn, his workmen's compensation insurance carrier should be considered the real parties in interest under this rule, since under Va. Code, §§ 65.1-41 and 65.1-112 they are subrogated to the rights of the injured employee and are thus entitled to seek recovery of the amount of the benefits from a third party tortfeasor. Ingram v. Link Belt Power Shovel Co., 94 F.R.D. 196 (W.D. Va. 1982).

Question of capacity to sue raises issue of jurisdiction over person. — See Goranson v. Capital Airlines, 221 F. Supp. 820 (E.D. Va. 1963), cert. denied, 382 U.S. 984, 86 S. Ct. 560, 15 L. Ed. 2d 473 (1966).

Jurisdictional questions can be raised at any time. — See Goranson v. Capital Airlines, 221 F. Supp. 820 (E.D. Va. 1963), cert. denied, 382 U.S. 984, 86 S. Ct. 560, 15 L. Ed. 2d 473 (1966).

Although jurisdiction over person may be waived. — See Goranson v. Capital Airlines, 221 F. Supp. 820 (E.D. Va. 1963), cert. denied, 382 U.S. 984, 86 S. Ct. 560, 15 L. Ed. 2d 473 (1966).

Capacity of state prisoner to sue for deprivation of civil right. — Insofar as there is any conflict between the federal Civil Rights Act, which affords the right to sue to any citizen of the United States who has been deprived of any right, privilege or immunity, and subdivision (b) of this rule, which provides that the capacity of an individual to sue or be sued shall be determined by the law of his domicile, the Fourth Circuit Court of Appeals has held that, in the case of a Virginia prisoner's suit for deprivation of civil rights, the act should prevail over the policy expressed in the rule, particularly when applied in the light of the rationale of Virginia statutes restricting the right of prisoners to sue or be sued except by their committee. Almond v. Kent, 459 F.2d 200 (4th Cir. 1972), rev'g 321 F. Supp. 1225 (W.D. Va. 1970), commented on in 30 Wash. & Lee L. Rev. 329 (1973).

Capacity of a governmental unit to be sued in federal court is to be determined by reference to state law. Hearn v. Hudson, 549 F. Supp. 949 (W.D. Va. 1982).

City's Department of Economic Development held not a proper defendant. — Under subdivision (a) of this rule the capacity to be sued, where the party is not an individual or a corporation, must be determined by the law of the state. A municipal corporation has the authority under state law to establish a Department of Economic Development and determine its powers and duties. Therefore, where the city code does not bestow the capacity to be sued upon the Department of Economic Development, that body is not a proper defendant. Davis v. City of Portsmouth, 579 F. Supp. 1205 (E.D. Va. 1983), aff'd, 742 F.2d 1448 (4th Cir. 1984).

Action under Tort Claims Act must be brought by insured for insurer and himself. — In an action against the United States under the Federal Tort Claims Act the insured and insurer can be compelled to join, and the action brought in the name of the insured for the use of himself and of his insurer. If such procedure is deemed advisable, then the plaintiff may amend by adding the insured or insurer, as the case may be, as a party plaintiff, to meet the requirements of subdivision (a). Insurance Co. of N. Am. v. United States, 76 F. Supp. 951 (E.D. Va. 1948).

Rule gives voluntary unincorporated association right to sue in common name. — This rule provided in voluntary unincorporated association, composed of Negro teachers and principals in the public colored schools of Norfolk, the right to sue in its common name for the purpose of enforcing substantive rights under the Constitution of the United States. Alston v. School Bd., 112 F.2d 992, 130 A.L.R. 1506 (4th Cir.), cert. denied, 311 U.S. 693, 61 S. Ct. 75, 85 L. Ed. 448 (1940).

But it is permissive. — The language of subdivision (b) relating to suits against partnerships and unincorporated associations is permissive. So also is the language of Rule 23(a). Together they provide alternative methods of bringing unincorporated associations into court. Tunstall v. Brotherhood of Locomotive Firemen & Enginemen, 148 F.2d 403 (4th Cir. 1945).

And intended to add to facilities for suing associations. — The manifest purpose of the provision of subdivision (b) relating to suits against partnerships and unincorporated associations is to add to, not to detract from, the existing facilities for obtaining jurisdiction over them. Tunstall v. Brotherhood of Locomotive Firemen & Enginemen, 148 F.2d 403 (4th Cir. 1945).

So that class suits against associations are still proper. — There is nothing in subdivision (b) which limits the right to bring a class suit under Rule 23(a) in proper cases. Subdivision (b) relates to capacity to sue or be sued; and it provides that, where a partnership or unincorporated association has no such capacity by the law of the state where the court is held, it may nevertheless sue or be sued in its common name for the purpose of enforcing for or against it a substantive right existing under the Constitution or laws of the United States. There is nothing in this that limits the right to bring the unincorporated association into court by means of a class suit in accordance with the prior practice. Tunstall v. Brotherhood of Locomotive Firemen & Enginemen, 148 F.2d 403 (4th Cir. 1945).

Standing of unincorporated association to maintain civil rights action. — Subdivision (b) of this rule directs that the capacity of an unincorporated association to sue or be sued shall be determined by the law of the state in which the federal district court sits. Section 8.01-15, Code of Virginia (1950) specifically confers upon an unincorporated association the capacity to sue or be sued. But the fact that the association has capacity to sue does not necessarily imply that it also has standing to maintain a particular action. Therefore, where there is no allegation that the association itself suffered either an injury in fact or a deprivation of any constitutionally protected right, the association does not have the proper standing to maintain a civil rights suit on its own behalf. Richmond Black Police Officers Ass'n v. City of Richmond, 386 F. Supp. 151 (E.D. Va. 1974).

Standard for production of information in grand jury proceedings. — In order to require production of information prior to trial, a party must make a reasonably specific request for information that would be both relevant and admissible at trial, but this standard does not apply in the context of grand jury proceedings. United States v. R. Enters., Inc., 498 U.S. 292, 111 S. Ct. 722, 112 L. Ed. 2d 795 (1991).

Grand jury subpoenas. — A grand jury subpoena issued through normal channels is presumed to be reasonable, and the burden of showing unreasonableness must be on the recipient who seeks to avoid compliance. United States v. R. Enters., Inc., 498 U.S. 292, 111 S. Ct. 722, 112 L. Ed. 2d 795 (1991).

Where a subpoena is challenged on relevancy grounds, the motion to quash must be denied unless the district court determines that there is no reasonable possibility that the category of materials the government seeks will produce information relevant to the general subject of the grand jury's investigation. United States v. R. Enters., Inc., 498 U.S. 292, 111 S. Ct. 722, 112 L. Ed. 2d 795 (1991).

Father, an unlicensed layman, attempt to act as daughter's lawyer was not a violation of this rule or Rule 41. And dismissal of her claim on this ground is certainly unwarranted. Rather, all that is required is for the court to appoint counsel for her. Brown v. Ortho Diagnostic Sys., 868 F. Supp. 168 (E.D. Va. 1994).

Applied in Railway Employees' Dep't of Am. Fed'n of Labor v. Virginian Ry., 39 F. Supp. 354 (E.D. Va. 1941); Davi v. Laird, 318 F. Supp. 478 (W.D. Va. 1970); Laws v. Spain, 51 F.R.D. 307 (E.D. Va. 1970); Willis v. Semmes, Bowen & Semmes, 441 F. Supp. 1235 (E.D. Va. 1977); Hereth v. Jones, 544 F. Supp. 111 (E.D. Va. 1982); National Union Fire Ins. Co. v. Hutcherson, 50 Bankr. 845 (Bankr. E.D. Va. 1985); McCoy v. Chesapeake Correctional Ctr., 788 F. Supp. 890 (E.D. Va. 1992); Kollsman, Div. of Sequa Corp. v. Cubic Corp., 800 F. Supp. 1381 (E.D. Va. 1992); Fair Oaks Dodge v. Skinner, 175 Bankr.

613 (Bankr. E.D. Va. 1994); NAACP Labor Comm. v. Laborers' Int'l Union, 902 F. Supp. 688 (W.D. Va. 1995).

Rule 18. Joinder of Claims.

(a) *In General.* — A party asserting a claim, counterclaim, crossclaim, or third-party claim may join, as independent or alternative claims, as many claims as it has against an opposing party.

(b) *Joinder of Contingent Claims.* — A party may join two claims even though one of them is contingent on the disposition of the other; but the court may grant relief only in accordance with the parties' relative substantive rights. In particular, a plaintiff may state a claim for money and a claim to set aside a conveyance that is fraudulent as to that plaintiff, without first obtaining a judgment for the money. (Amended by order adopted February 28, 1966, effective July 1, 1966, by order adopted March 2, 1987, effective August 1, 1987, and by order adopted April 30, 2007, effective December 1, 2007.)

Comment. — The language of Rule 18 has been amended as part of the general restyling of the Civil Rules to make them more easily understood and to make style and terminology consistent throughout the rules. These changes are intended to be stylistic only.

Modification of the obscure former reference to a claim "heretofore cognizable only after another claim has been prosecuted to a conclusion" avoids any uncertainty whether Rule 18(b)'s meaning is fixed by retrospective inquiry from some particular date.

CASE NOTES

Permitting the joinder of claims does not mean that the requisite amount in controversy is present. Stone v. Stone, 405 F.2d 94 (4th Cir. 1968), cert. denied, 409 U.S. 1000, 93 S. Ct. 315, 34 L. Ed. 2d 261 (1972).

But plaintiff may aggregate claims to satisfy monetary requirement. — It is settled law that a plaintiff may aggregate his claims against an opposing party and thereby satisfy the monetary requirement for federal jurisdiction. Stone v. Stone, 405 F.2d 94 (4th Cir. 1968), cert. denied, 409 U.S. 1000, 93 S. Ct. 315, 34 L. Ed. 2d 261 (1972).

Applied in Mason v. Richmond Motor Co., 625 F. Supp. 883 (E.D. Va. 1986).

Rule 19. Required Joinder of Parties.

(a) *Persons Required to Be Joined if Feasible.* — (1) Required Party. A person who is subject to service of process and whose joinder will not deprive the court of subject-matter jurisdiction must be joined as a party if:

(A) in that person's absence, the court cannot accord complete relief among existing parties; or

(B) that person claims an interest relating to the subject of the action and is so situated that disposing of the action in the person's absence may:

(i) as a practical matter impair or impede the person's ability to protect the interest; or

(ii) leave an existing party subject to a substantial risk of incurring double, multiple, or otherwise inconsistent obligations because of the interest.

(2) Joinder by Court Order. If a person has not been joined as required, the court must order that the person be made a party. A person who refuses to join as a plaintiff may be made either a defendant or, in a proper case, an involuntary plaintiff.

(3) Venue. If a joined party objects to venue and the joinder would make venue improper, the court must dismiss that party.

(b) *When Joinder Is Not Feasible.* — If a person who is required to be joined if feasible cannot be joined, the court must determine whether, in equity and good conscience, the action should proceed among the existing parties or should be dismissed. The factors for the court to consider include:

(1) the extent to which a judgment rendered in the person's absence might prejudice that person or the existing parties;

(2) the extent to which any prejudice could be lessened or avoided by:

(A) protective provisions in the judgment;

(B) shaping the relief; or

(C) other measures;

(3) whether a judgment rendered in the person's absence would be adequate; and

(4) whether the plaintiff would have an adequate remedy if the action were dismissed for nonjoinder.

(c) *Pleading the Reasons for Nonjoinder.* — When asserting a claim for relief, a party must state:

(1) the name, if known, of any person who is required to be joined if feasible but is not joined; and

(2) the reasons for not joining that person.

(d) *Exception for Class Actions.* — This rule is subject to Rule 23. (Amended by order adopted February 28, 1966, effective July 1, 1966, by order adopted March 2, 1987, effective August 1, 1987, and by order adopted April 30, 2007, effective December 1, 2007.)

Comment. — The language of Rule 19 has been amended as part of the general restyling of the Civil Rules to make them more easily understood and to make style and terminology consistent throughout the rules. These changes are intended to be stylistic only.

Former Rule 19(b) described the conclusion that an action should be dismissed for inability to join a Rule 19(a) party by carrying forward traditional terminology: "the absent person being thus regarded as indispensable." "Indispensable" was used only to express a conclusion reached by applying the tests of Rule 19(b). It has been discarded as redundant.

Law Review. — For note on joinder of partially subrogated insurers, see 40 Wash. & Lee L. Rev. 756 (1983).

CASE NOTES

The term "necessary parties" means "desirable parties" as distinguished from indispensable parties on the one hand and from proper parties on the other hand. While it is not essential that necessary parties be before the court, it is often desirable to bring them in to dispose effectively of the claims of all parties and interests in one proceeding. The rule leaves no discretion on the matter, but requires the joinder of necessary parties where jurisdiction of them can be obtained and where their joinder will not defeat federal jurisdiction of the case. Bradley v. School Bd., 51 F.R.D. 139 (E.D. Va. 1970).

When action will affect interests of party not before court ultimate question is this: Were the case to proceed, could a decree be crafted in a way that protects the interests of the missing party and that still provides adequate relief to a successful litigant? Teamsters Local Union No. 171 v. Keal Driveaway Co., 173 F.3d 915 (4th Cir. 1999).

"Complete relief" in subdivision (a)(1) of this rule refers to relief as between the persons already parties, not as between a party and the absent person whose joinder is sought. United States v. County of Arlington, 669 F.2d 925 (4th Cir.), appeal dismissed and cert. denied, 459 U.S. 801, 103 S. Ct. 23, 74 L. Ed. 2d 39 (1982).

Questions of compulsory joinder are to be resolved flexibly and with an eye to practical considerations. Fout v. Allegheny Regional Hosp., 111 F.R.D. 467 (W.D. Va. 1986).

Rule contains an initial two-step inquiry. — Initially, the court must determine whether the absent person's joinder is feasible under subdivision (a). If joinder is feasible, a determination of indispensability under subdivision (b) is not required. United Va. Bank v. Cleveland, 53 Bankr. 814 (Bankr. E.D. Va. 1985).

This rule creates a two-step inquiry: first, whether a party is necessary to a proceeding because of its relationship to the matter under consideration; and second, if a necessary party is unavailable, whether the proceeding can continue in that party's absence. Teamsters Local Union No. 171 v. Keal Driveaway Co., 173 F.3d 915 (4th Cir. 1999).

Four factors specifically listed in subdivision (b) are not an exhaustive list of considerations for trial courts. Fout v. Allegheny Regional Hosp., 111 F.R.D. 467 (W.D. Va. 1986).

Feasibility of joining party. — Under this rule, the first inquiry is whether the party is one who should be joined if feasible under subdivision (a). The inquiry is a practical one which demands flexibility. Under the present rule, pragmatic concerns, especially the effect on the parties and on the litigation, control a court's decision on joinder. In the final analysis, joinder is addressed to the sound discretion of the court. Steyhr Daimler Puch of Am. Corp. v. Pappas, 35 Bankr. 1001 (E.D. Va. 1983).

Dismissal of case is drastic remedy which should be employed only sparingly. Teamsters Local Union No. 171 v. Keal Driveaway Co., 173 F.3d 915 (4th Cir. 1999).

When absent parties should be joined. — Absent parties should be joined if it is probable that the relief sought cannot be achieved, or can be achieved only partially or conditionally, without them. Judicial discretion would likewise require that they be joined if it is possible that a decree against current defendants could unduly prejudice them, as it well might if the burden and expense of affording the relief sought should, in law, be shared with others. Bradley v. School Bd., 51 F.R.D. 139 (E.D. Va. 1970).

Under subdivision (a) of this rule, joinder of an absent party is appropriate in either of two instances: (1) When nonjoinder would prevent the court from providing complete relief among those who are parties to the action; or (2) when the absent party claims an interest relating to the subject of the action and is so situated that the disposition of the action in the party's absence may impede or impair that party's ability to protect that interest. If either of the two tests under subdivision (a) of this rule is met, the absent party shall be joined. CSX Transp., Inc. v. Forst, 777 F. Supp. 435 (E.D. Va. 1991).

The absence of a party from an action can result in dismissal of that action, however, only if such party is not subject to service of process, or if the party's joinder would destroy the court's jurisdiction. CSX Transp., Inc. v. Forst, 777 F. Supp. 435 (E.D. Va. 1991).

When person's joinder is feasible, that person is a necessary party rather than an indispensable party. United Va. Bank v. Cleveland, 53 Bankr. 814 (Bankr. E.D. Va. 1985).

Person is indispensable only when his joinder is not feasible under subdivision (a), and in his absence, dismissal of the case is preferable to adjudication. United Va. Bank v. Cleveland, 53 Bankr. 814 (Bankr. E.D. Va. 1985).

Joinder not required when absent person's interests protected. — Subdivision (a)(2)(i) means that joinder is not required when the absent person's interests are fully protected by an existing party. United Va. Bank v. Cleveland, 53 Bankr. 814 (Bankr. E.D. Va. 1985).

Rule not authorizing automatic dismissal of nonessential party. — See Caperton v. Beatrice Pocahontas Coal Co., 585 F.2d 683 (4th Cir. 1978).

Where plaintiffs are given opportunity but refuse to join necessary parties, court's duty to join is moot. — See Thaxton v. Vaughan, 321 F.2d 474 (4th Cir. 1963).

City or council held necessary parties defendant to suit to desegregate city armory. — See Thaxton v. Vaughan, 321 F.2d 474 (4th Cir. 1963).

Since decree against mayor of Virginia city manager system city would be ineffective. — See Thaxton v. Vaughan, 321 F.2d 474 (4th Cir. 1963).

If complete diversity is lacking after joinder of an indispensable party pursuant to this rule, a federal court no longer would have authority to entertain the suit on that basis. The problem is not avoided by simply naming the party as a party defendant, because the court has a duty to look beyond the pleadings and align the joined party according to his real interest. Steyhr Daimler Puch of Am. Corp. v. Pappas, 35 Bankr. 1001 (E.D. Va. 1983).

Because of the divestment of a court's subject matter jurisdiction caused by the existence of an indispensable but nondiverse party, the result under subdivision (b) of this rule would be dismissal of the action or, alternatively, remand to the state court. Coley v. Dragon Ltd., 138 F.R.D. 460 (E.D. Va. 1990).

Party treated as brought in under third-party practice to preserve diversity jurisdiction. — Where an impleader under this rule or an order under subdivision (h) of Rule 13 would have destroyed the jurisdiction of the court because the impleaded party and the plaintiff were both residents of Virginia, the court treated the procedure as an ancillary proceeding under subdivision (a) of Rule 14, not requiring diversity of citizenship. Lumbermens Mut. Cas. Co. v. Harleysville Mut. Cas. Co., 367 F.2d 250 (4th Cir. 1966).

In a personal injury action, joinder of resident co-guardian was not required, where his absence would not prevent the court from granting complete relief among the parties before the court, his absence would not subject any of the parties to a substantial risk of multiple or inconsistent obligations, and his absence would not impair his ability to protect his interest in the suit. While as guardian, he plainly had an interest in the suit, his interest was exactly the same as the interest of his co-guardian. His interest in the suit would be represented by the co-guardian. Fout v. Allegheny Regional Hosp., 111 F.R.D. 467 (W.D. Va. 1986).

Partner is necessary but not indispensable party in action for tort of partnership employee. — See Weaver v. Marcus, 165 F.2d 862, 175 A.L.R. 1305 (4th Cir. 1948), rev'g 73 F. Supp. 736 (W.D. Va. 1947).

And may be omitted or dropped as party. — See Weaver v. Marcus, 165 F.2d 862, 175 A.L.R. 1305 (4th Cir. 1948), rev'g 73 F. Supp. 736 (W.D. Va. 1947).

Nonparty unions not joined in suit for employment discrimination. — Where the interests of nonparty unions sought to be joined were represented by plaintiff union in its action brought against an employer for sex discrimination, and by virtue of the class definition, inconsistent obligations could not arise as a result of the litigation, the court was satisfied that the nonparty unions were not indispensable, and while joinder would be permissible, the court, in the exercise of its discretion, chose not to compel the addition of further parties in what had been ponderous litigation. Gilbert v. GE Co., 59 F.R.D. 273 (E.D. Va. 1973).

Corporation must be party where relief would alter articles of incorporation. — Corporation must be a party to a case where the relief sought would alter the articles of incorporation and direct the duties of the directors. Bates v. Cekada, 130 F.R.D. 52 (E.D. Va. 1990).

Accounting sought of bequest distributed to corporation. — If an accounting is sought of a bequest that was distributed to corporation, then corporation should be made a party; corporation's absence from this litigation would impair its ability to protect its interest with regard to the accounting that the plaintiffs seek. Bates v. Cekada, 130 F.R.D. 52 (E.D. Va. 1990).

Application of rule to situations involving single fund or res. — Cases dealing with subdivision (a)(2) of this rule have addressed themselves particularly to situations where a single fund or res is the subject of contention in the suit and an absent party may have a legal right to all or part of that fund. Under these cases, the interest of the absent party is independent of the interest of parties already in the suit. VEPCO v. Bunker Ramo Corp., 61 F.R.D. 366 (E.D. Va. 1973).

Insured party not indispensable where insurance company is present in action concerning a release procured by insurance company as agent for insured. Hill v. Liberty Mut. Ins. Co., 453 F. Supp. 1342 (E.D. Va. 1978).

Partial subrogees are not indispensable parties within the meaning of subdivision (b) of this rule. Accordingly, federal courts will deny a defendant's motion to join a partial subrogee when to do so would destroy diversity jurisdiction. Ingram v. Link Belt Power Shovel Co., 94 F.R.D. 196 (W.D. Va. 1982).

Joinder of partial subrogee. — See VEPCO v. Westinghouse Elec. Corp., 485 F.2d 78 (4th Cir. 1973), cert. denied, 415 U.S. 935, 94 S. Ct. 1450, 39 L. Ed. 2d 493 (1974).

A debtor having no interest in the real property involved in a foreclosure sale is not a necessary party to an action to enforce a mechanic's lien. Nelson White Constr. Mgt. Corp. v. McConaghy, 15 Bankr. 480 (Bankr. E.D. Va. 1981).

The test for determining indispensability under Rule 19 has been summarized as: (1) Can relief be afforded to the plaintiff without the presence of the other party? (2) Can the case be decided on its merits without prejudicing rights of the other party? Willis v. Semmes, Bowen & Semmes, 441 F. Supp. 1235 (E.D. Va. 1977).

Joint tortfeasors are not necessary but merely permissive parties under this rule. — Their joinder or dismissal, therefore, is a matter for the court's discretion. Jensen Elecs., Inc. v. American Computer & Telecommunications Corp., 26 Bankr. 512 (Bankr. E.D. Va. 1983).

Joint tortfeasors and contractual coobligors not indispensable parties. — Although a strict categorical approach to the question of what constitutes a "necessary" or "indispensable" party under Rule 19, Fed. R. Civ. P. was disapproved by the Supreme Court, it is evident that the traditional rule that joint tort-feasors and contractual coobligors are not indispensable parties is largely the result of just such a pragmatic approach. Such a classification is justified in that such persons are nearly always jointly and severally liable, thereby eliminating prejudice through nonjoinder both to parties to the action and unjoined participants in the alleged wrongdoing. Willis v. Semmes, Bowen & Semmes, 441 F. Supp. 1235 (E.D. Va. 1977).

Local attorney held not indispensable party. — Rule 7 (D) U.S. Distr. Ct. (E.D. Va.), requiring foreign attorneys to be associated with local counsel in order to appear and conduct cases in the Eastern District of Virginia, did not make the local counsel, who might have been a joint obligor or joint tortfeasor with the foreign attorney, an indispensable party to the plaintiff's action against the foreign attorney for breach of contract and malpractice. The purpose of this rule is to give the court effective control of court business by assuring that attorneys involved in litigation will be available and subject to the court's authority. Such a rule cannot make an otherwise dispensable party indispensable. Willis v. Semmes, Bowen & Semmes, 441 F. Supp. 1235 (E.D. Va. 1977).

Foreign nation held not necessary party. — Where the United States did not institute the action simply to assert the claims of the German Democratic Republic that it could not accept a tax judgment obtained by a county because the GDR was immune from the jurisdiction of United States courts and the suit was impermissible according to the principles of international law but, rather, the complaint disclosed that the United States sued to vindicate its own policy and authority, complete resolution of the dispute between the United States and the county did not require the joinder of the GDR, the GDR was not a necessary party to the action, and the district court did not commit error by proceeding without requiring its joinder. United States v. County of Arlington, 669 F.2d 925 (4th Cir.), appeal dismissed and cert. denied, 459 U.S. 801, 103 S. Ct. 23, 74 L. Ed. 2d 39 (1982).

In suit brought by unsuccessful offeror, successful offeror was not indispensable party. — Where a suit was brought by unsuccessful offeror to challenge award of contract and where the government contended that successful offeror had to be joined as an indispensable party to proceeding, while successful offeror may have well qualified under subdivision (a)(2) as a party that should have been joined, successful offeror could not be subjected to court's process. The court after weighing the factors contained in subdivision (b) concluded that successful offeror was not an indispensable party to this proceeding. Howard Cooper Corp. v. United States, 763 F. Supp. 829 (E.D. Va. 1991).

Child not necessary party in action between parents. — A child was not a necessary party in a suit under the Hague Convention on the Civil Aspects of International Child Abduction and the International Child Abduction Remedies Act to secure the return of the child to Colombia, as any relief would be directly solely to the parties, and not the child. Hazbun Escaf v. Rodriquez, 191 F. Supp. 2d 685, 2002 U.S. Dist. LEXIS 4855 (E.D. Va. 2002).

Realignment of parties. — Where no parties' rights would be adversely affected by a realignment, the interests of the party seeking realignment as expressed in the pleading coincide with those of the plaintiff, and the party is equally amenable to claims by the defendant against the party no matter whether it be plaintiff or defendant, there simply is no good reason to refuse the request of the party. EEOC v. Allied Chem. Corp., 69 F.R.D. 62 (E.D. Va. 1975).

Labor organization held indispensable party to defend victory in underlying arbitration. — See Teamsters Local Union No. 171 v. Keal Driveaway Co., 173 F.3d 915 (4th Cir. 1999).

Applied in Rakes v. Coleman, 318 F. Supp. 181 (E.D. Va. 1970); Sun Yeong Lee v. Thompson, 50 F.R.D. 138 (E.D. Va. 1970); Mills v. Roanoke Indus. Loan & Thrift, 70 F.R.D. 448 (W.D. Va. 1975); Fletcher v. Washington & Lee Univ., 706 F.2d 475 (4th Cir. 1983); Forest Hills Early Learning Ctr., Inc. v. Lukhard, 728 F.2d 230 (4th Cir. 1984); Croatan Books, Inc. v. Baliles, 583 F. Supp. 857 (E.D. Va. 1984); Yale II Mining Assocs. v. Gilliam, 586 F. Supp. 893 (W.D. Va. 1984); City of Va. Beach v. Roanoke River Basin Ass'n, 776 F.2d 484 (4th Cir. 1985); United States ex rel. Pittman Mechanical Contractors v. Irvine & Assocs., 645 F. Supp. 845 (E.D. Va. 1986); Selman v. American Sports Underwriters, Inc., 697 F. Supp. 225 (W.D. Va. 1988); Glamorgan Coal Corp. v. Bowen, 742 F. Supp. 308 (W.D. Va. 1990); Middleton & Dugger Plumbing & Heating v. Richardson Bldrs., Inc., 123 Bankr. 736 (Bankr. W.D. Va. 1990); Pasquotank Action Council, Inc. v. City of Va. Beach, 909 F. Supp. 376 (E.D. Va. 1995).

Rule 20. Permissive Joinder of Parties.

(a) *Persons Who May Join or Be Joined.* — (1) Plaintiffs. Persons may join in one action as plaintiffs if:

(A) they assert any right to relief jointly, severally, or in the alternative with respect to or arising out of the same transaction, occurrence, or series of transactions or occurrences; and

(B) any question of law or fact common to all plaintiffs will arise in the action.

(2) Defendants. Persons — as well as a vessel, cargo, or other property subject to admiralty process in rem — may be joined in one action as defendants if:

(A) any right to relief is asserted against them jointly, severally, or in the alternative with respect to or arising out of the same transaction, occurrence, or series of transactions or occurrences; and

(B) any question of law or fact common to all defendants will arise in the action.

(3) Extent of Relief. Neither a plaintiff nor a defendant need be interested in obtaining or defending against all the relief demanded. The court may grant judgment to one or more plaintiffs according to their rights, and against one or more defendants according to their liabilities.

(b) *Protective Measures.* — The court may issue orders — including an order for separate trials — to protect a party against embarrassment, delay, expense, or other prejudice that arises from including a person against whom the party asserts no claim and who asserts no claim against the party. (Amended by order adopted February 28, 1966, effective July 1, 1966, by order adopted March 2, 1987, effective August 1, 1987, and by order adopted April 30, 2007, effective December 1, 2007.)

Comment. — The language of Rule 20 has been amended as part of the general restyling of the Civil Rules to make them more easily understood and to make style and terminology consistent throughout the rules. These changes are intended to be stylistic only.

CASE NOTES

Joinder hereunder is governed by concepts of "same transaction" and "common question." — Under this rule, not only must the plaintiff demonstrate a right to relief against any additional defendants he wishes to join, but the liability of the additional defendants must in addition arise out of the same transaction, occurrence, or series of transactions or occurrences and involve a question of law or fact common to all defendants. Wilkinson v. Hamel, 381 F. Supp. 766 (W.D. Va. 1974).

Joinder held improper. — Joinder of additional parties on the basis of incidents arising almost four years subsequent to those incidents complained of in the original complaint and having no effect on the cause of action previously asserted is improper. Wilkinson v. Hamel, 381 F. Supp. 766 (W.D. Va. 1974).

Joinder held proper. — In plaintiff's claim against the Army, the EEOC could properly have been joined as a defendant under subdivision (a) of this rule, since the plaintiff's requested relief from the EEOC arose from the same occurrence as the case against the Army, and the nature of the EEOC order was unclear and an explanation of its contested actions was helpful to just adjudication. In addition, common questions of law and fact were involved. Nealon v. Stone, 958 F.2d 584 (4th Cir. 1992).

Severance granted. — The administrator of the Lynchburg general hospital, and the hospital authority of the city of Lynchburg were originally made parties to a suit brought by the plaintiffs, as a class action, against them and various officials of the city of Lynchburg, Virginia, in what was termed by plaintiffs' counsel as an "omnibus" suit — designed to end racial segregation in the city in all of its phases. Since the court was unable to perceive how the actions alleged with respect to these two defendants could have arisen "out of the same transaction, occurrence, or series of transactions or occurrences" as those involving the other defendants, it concluded that the "omnibus" had become overcrowded and granted a motion for severance made by counsel for these defendants. Wood v. Hogan, 215 F. Supp. 53 (W.D. Va. 1963).

Applied in Stone v. Stone, 405 F.2d 94 (4th Cir. 1968); Scott v. Aetna Life & Cas. Co., 48 F.R.D. 446 (W.D. Va. 1969); Causey v. Pan Am. World Airways, Inc., 66 F.R.D. 392 (E.D. Va. 1975); Jenkins v. Rumsfeld, 412 F. Supp. 1177 (E.D. Va. 1976); Glover v. Johns-Manville Corp., 662 F.2d 225 (4th Cir. 1981).

Rule 21. Misjoinder and Nonjoinder of Parties.

Misjoinder of parties is not a ground for dismissing an action. On motion or on its own, the court may at any time, on just terms, add or drop a party. The court may also sever any claim against a party. (Amended by order adopted April 30, 2007, effective December 1, 2007.)

Comment. — The language of Rule 21 has been amended as part of the general restyling of the Civil Rules to make them more easily understood and to make style and terminology consistent throughout

the rules. These changes are intended to be stylistic only.

CASE NOTES

Rule does not give relief to plaintiff suing wrong party. — This rule was not adopted to give relief to a plaintiff who sues the wrong party, but to a plaintiff who sues too many parties, or not enough parties. United States v. Swink, 41 F. Supp. 98 (E.D. Va. 1941).

Dropping parties is discretionary with court, not plaintiff. — The fact that this rule provides that parties may be dropped "by order of the court" implies that the matter is one in which the court has the right to exercise some discretion and that it does not follow as a matter of right that a party can be dropped at the mere desire of the plaintiff. Weaver v. Marcus, 165 F.2d 862, 175 A.L.R. 1305 (4th Cir. 1948), rev'g 73 F. Supp. 736 (W.D. Va. 1947).

Court may join party on its own motion. — This rule allows the court to order a party joined to the proceeding on its own motion to serve the purpose of judicial economy and to afford complete relief to the parties. Herman Cantor Corp. v. Central Fid. Bank, 17 Bankr. 612 (Bankr. E.D. Va. 1982).

Discretion of court on motion to add parties. — The court in its determination of a motion to add parties plaintiff pursuant to this rule is duty bound to exercise its sound discretion; however, while the court is required to exercise its judicial discretion, it is not inclined to be influenced by the efforts of plaintiffs to override its jurisdictional and venue determinations by a technical use of pleadings and motion practice. Gilbert v. GE Co., 347 F. Supp. 1058 (E.D. Va. 1972).

Trial court's authority to permit dismissal of party derives from Rules 15 and 21, F. R. Civ. P., not Rule 19. Caperton v. Beatrice Pocahontas Coal Co., 585 F.2d 683 (4th Cir. 1978).

Where plaintiffs are given opportunity but refuse to join necessary parties, court's duty to join is moot. — See Thaxton v. Vaughan, 321 F.2d 474 (4th Cir. 1963).

Partner is necessary but not indispensable party in action for tort of partnership employee. — See Weaver v. Marcus, 165 F.2d 862, 175 A.L.R. 1305 (4th Cir. 1948), rev'g 73 F. Supp. 736 (W.D. Va. 1947).

And may be omitted or dropped as party. — See Weaver v. Marcus, 165 F.2d 862, 175 A.L.R. 1305 (4th Cir. 1948), rev'g 73 F. Supp. 736 (W.D. Va. 1947).

Motion to dismiss complaint on ground all but one plaintiff had no interest in subject matter treated as motion to drop parties. — See Railway Employees' Dep't of Am. Fed'n of Labor v. Virginian Ry., 39 F. Supp. 354 (E.D. Va. 1941).

Plaintiffs may seek leave of court to amend their complaint to add a new party where motion to amend was filed at a very early stage in the litigation and would not prejudice the newly joined defendant, who was notified of this action within the period for service of a summons and complaint. United States ex rel. Tucker v. Thomas Howell Kiewit (USA) Inc., 149 F.R.D. 125 (E.D. Va. 1993).

Adding insurer or insured as plaintiff in action under Tort Claims Act. — In an action against the United States under the Federal Tort Claims Act the insured and insurer can be compelled to join, and the action brought in the name of the insured for the use of himself and of his insurer. If such procedure is deemed advisable, then the plaintiff may amend by adding the insured or insurer, as the case may be, as a party plaintiff, to meet the requirements of Rule 17(a). Insurance Co. of N. Am. v. United States, 76 F. Supp. 951 (E.D. Va. 1948).

Applied in Rakes v. Coleman, 318 F. Supp. 181 (E.D. Va. 1970); Joseph v. House, 353 F. Supp. 367 (E.D. Va. 1973); Willis v. Semmes, Bowen & Semmes, 441 F. Supp. 1235 (E.D. Va. 1977); Harris v. Young, 718 F.2d 620 (4th Cir. 1983).

Rule 22. Interpleader.

(a) *Grounds.* — (1) By a Plaintiff. Persons with claims that may expose a plaintiff to double or multiple liability may be joined as defendants and required to interplead. Joinder for interpleader is proper even though:

(A) the claims of the several claimants, or the titles on which their claims depend, lack a common origin or are adverse and independent rather than identical; or

(B) the plaintiff denies liability in whole or in part to any or all of the claimants.

(2) By a Defendant. A defendant exposed to similar liability may seek interpleader through a crossclaim or counterclaim.

(b) *Relation to Other Rules and Statutes.* — This rule supplements — and does not limit — the joinder of parties allowed by Rule 20. The remedy this rule provides is in addition to — and does not supersede or limit — the remedy provided by 28 U.S.C. §§ 1335, 1397, and 2361. An action under those statutes must be conducted under these rules. (Amended by order adopted December 29, 1948, effective October 20, 1949, by order adopted March 2, 1987, effective August 1, 1987, and by order adopted April 30, 2007, effective December 1, 2007.)

Comment. — The language of Rule 22 has been amended as part of the general restyling of the Civil Rules to make them more easily understood and to make style and terminology consistent throughout the rules. These changes are intended to be stylistic only.

CASE NOTES

Interpleader and action in nature of interpleader are available remedies. — The remedy of interpleader, including the action in the nature of interpleader, has long been available in equity and is available in the United States district courts, as expressly recognized by the rules of court. MFA Mut. Ins. Co. v. Lusby, 295 F. Supp. 660 (W.D. Va. 1969).

Multiplicity of suits is justification for either remedy. — With few exceptions the rule is now accepted that exposure to unnecessary vexation by a multiplicity of suits is a sufficient ground for maintaining either strict interpleader or an action in the nature of interpleader. Multiplicity of suits has been accepted as complete justification in this rule, which provides that "persons having claims against the plaintiff may be joined as defendants and required to interplead when their claims are such that the plaintiff is or may be exposed to double or multiple liability . . . ." MFA Mut. Ins. Co. v. Lusby, 295 F. Supp. 660 (W.D. Va. 1969).

Action in nature of interpleader does not preclude adverse claim by plaintiff. — An action in the nature of interpleader does not preclude a plaintiff from asserting an adverse claim to the money or property in dispute. A plaintiff is allowed by both 28 U.S.C. § 1335 (1964) and this rule to bring an action in the nature of interpleader while averring that he is not liable to any or all of the claimants. MFA Mut. Ins. Co. v. Lusby, 295 F. Supp. 660 (W.D. Va. 1969).

Applied in United States Fid. & Guar. Co. v. Rowe, 249 F. Supp. 993 (E.D. Va. 1966); Pine Bldrs., Inc. v. United States, 413 F. Supp. 77 (E.D. Va. 1976); Weeks v. Angelone, 4 F. Supp. 2d 497 (E.D. Va. 1998); Lincoln Nat'l Life Ins. Co. v. Johnson, 38 F. Supp. 2d 440 (E.D. Va. 1999).

Rule 23. Class Actions.

(a) *Prerequisites.* — One or more members of a class may sue or be sued as representative parties on behalf of all members only if:

(1) the class is so numerous that joinder of all members is impracticable;

(2) there are questions of law or fact common to the class;

(3) the claims or defenses of the representative parties are typical of the claims or defenses of the class; and

(4) the representative parties will fairly and adequately protect the interests of the class.

(b) *Types of Class Actions.* — A class action may be maintained if Rule 23(a) is satisfied and if:

(1) prosecuting separate actions by or against individual class members would create a risk of:

(A) inconsistent or varying adjudications with respect to individual class members that would establish incompatible standards of conduct for the party opposing the class; or

(B) adjudications with respect to individual class members that, as a practical matter, would be dispositive of the interests of the other members not parties to the individual adjudications or would substantially impair or impede their ability to protect their interests;

(2) the party opposing the class has acted or refused to act on grounds that apply generally to the class, so that final injunctive relief or corresponding declaratory relief is appropriate respecting the class as a whole; or

(3) the court finds that the questions of law or fact common to class members predominate over any questions affecting only individual members, and that a class action is superior to other available methods for fairly and efficiently adjudicating the controversy. The matters pertinent to these findings include:

(A) the class members' interests in individually controlling the prosecution or defense of separate actions;

(B) the extent and nature of any litigation concerning the controversy already begun by or against class members;

(C) the desirability or undesirability of concentrating the litigation of the claims in the particular forum; and

(D) the likely difficulties in managing a class action.

(c) *Certification Order; Notice to Class Members; Judgment; Issues Classes; Subclasses.* — (1) Certification Order.

(A) *Time to Issue.* At an early practicable time after a person sues or is sued as a class representative, the court must determine by order whether to certify the action as a class action.

(B) *Defining the Class; Appointing Class Counsel.* An order that certifies a class action must define the class and the class claims, issues, or defenses, and must appoint class counsel under Rule 23(g).

(C) *Altering or Amending the Order.* An order that grants or denies class certification may be altered or amended before final judgment.

(2) Notice.

(A) *For (b)(1) or (b)(2) Classes.* For any class certified under Rule 23(b)(1) or (b)(2), the court may direct appropriate notice to the class.

(B) *For (b)(3) Classes.* For any class certified under Rule 23(b)(3), the court must direct to class members the best notice that is practicable under the circumstances, including individual notice to all members who can be identified through reasonable effort. The notice must clearly and concisely state in plain, easily understood language:

(i) the nature of the action;

(ii) the definition of the class certified;

(iii) the class claims, issues, or defenses;

(iv) that a class member may enter an appearance through an attorney if the member so desires;

(v) that the court will exclude from the class any member who requests exclusion;

(vi) the time and manner for requesting exclusion; and

(vii) the binding effect of a class judgment on members under Rule 23(c)(3).

(3) Judgment. Whether or not favorable to the class, the judgment in a class action must:

(A) for any class certified under Rule 23(b)(1) or (b)(2), include and describe those whom the court finds to be class members; and

(B) for any class certified under Rule 23(b)(3), include and specify or describe those to whom the Rule 23(c)(2) notice was directed, who have not requested exclusion, and whom the court finds to be class members.

(4) Particular Issues. When appropriate, an action may be brought or maintained as a class action with respect to particular issues.

(5) Subclasses. When appropriate, a class may be divided into subclasses that are each treated as a class under this rule.

(d) *Conducting the Action.* — (1) In General. In conducting an action under this rule, the court may issue orders that:

(A) determine the course of proceedings or prescribe measures to prevent undue repetition or complication in presenting evidence or argument;

(B) require — to protect class members and fairly conduct the action — giving appropriate notice to some or all class members of:

(i) any step in the action;

(ii) the proposed extent of the judgment; or

(iii) the members' opportunity to signify whether they consider the representation fair and adequate, to intervene and present claims or defenses, or to otherwise come into the action;

(C) impose conditions on the representative parties or on intervenors;

(D) require that the pleadings be amended to eliminate allegations about representation of absent persons and that the action proceed accordingly; or

(E) deal with similar procedural matters.

(2) Combining and Amending Orders. An order under Rule 23(d)(1) may be altered or amended from time to time and may be combined with an order under Rule 16.

(e) *Settlement, Voluntary Dismissal, or Compromise.* — The claims, issues, or defenses of a certified class may be settled, voluntarily dismissed, or compromised only with the court's approval. The following procedures apply to a proposed settlement, voluntary dismissal, or compromise:

(1) The court must direct notice in a reasonable manner to all class members who would be bound by the proposal.

(2) If the proposal would bind class members, the court may approve it only after a hearing and on finding that it is fair, reasonable, and adequate.

(3) The parties seeking approval must file a statement identifying any agreement made in connection with the proposal.

(4) If the class action was previously certified under Rule 23(b)(3), the court may refuse to approve a settlement unless it affords a new opportunity to request exclusion to individual class members who had an earlier opportunity to request exclusion but did not do so.

(5) Any class member may object to the proposal if it requires court approval under this subdivision (e); the objection may be withdrawn only with the court's approval.

(f) *Appeals.* — A court of appeals may permit an appeal from an order granting or denying class-action certification under this rule if a petition for permission to appeal is filed with the circuit clerk within 14 days after the order is entered. An appeal does not stay proceedings in the district court unless the district judge or the court of appeals so orders.

(g) *Class Counsel.* — (1) Appointing Class Counsel. Unless a statute provides otherwise, a court that certifies a class must appoint class counsel. In appointing class counsel, the court:

(A) must consider:

(i) the work counsel has done in identifying or investigating potential claims in the action;

(ii) counsel's experience in handling class actions, other complex litigation, and the types of claims asserted in the action;

(iii) counsel's knowledge of the applicable law; and

(iv) the resources that counsel will commit to representing the class;

(B) may consider any other matter pertinent to counsel's ability to fairly and adequately represent the interests of the class;

(C) may order potential class counsel to provide information on any subject pertinent to the appointment and to propose terms for attorney's fees and nontaxable costs;

(D) may include in the appointing order provisions about the award of attorney's fees or nontaxable costs under Rule 23(h); and

(E) may make further orders in connection with the appointment.

(2) Standard for Appointing Class Counsel. When one applicant seeks appointment as class counsel, the court may appoint that applicant only if the applicant is adequate under Rule 23(g)(1) and (4). If more than one adequate applicant seeks appointment, the court must appoint the applicant best able to represent the interests of the class.

(3) Interim Counsel. The court may designate interim counsel to act on behalf of a putative class before determining whether to certify the action as a class action.

(4) Duty of Class Counsel. Class counsel must fairly and adequately represent the interests of the class.

(h) *Attorney's Fees and Nontaxable Costs.* — In a certified class action, the court may award reasonable attorney's fees and nontaxable costs that are authorized by law or by the parties' agreement. The following procedures apply:

(1) A claim for an award must be made by motion under Rule 54(d)(2), subject to the provisions of this subdivision (h), at a time the court sets. Notice of the motion must be served on all parties and, for motions by class counsel, directed to class members in a reasonable manner.

(2) A class member, or a party from whom payment is sought, may object to the motion.

(3) The court may hold a hearing and must find the facts and state its legal conclusions under Rule 52(a).

(4) The court may refer issues related to the amount of the award to a special master or a magistrate judge, as provided in Rule 54(d)(2)(D). (Amended by order adopted February 28, 1966, effective July 1, 1966, by order adopted March 2, 1987, effective August 1, 1987, by order adopted April 24, 1998, effective December 1, 1998, by order adopted March 27, 2003, effective December 1, 2003, by order adopted April 30, 2007, effective December 1, 2007, and by order adopted March 26, 2009, effective December 1, 2009.)

Comment. — The language of Rule 23 has been amended as part of the general restyling of the Civil Rules to make them more easily understood and to make style and terminology consistent throughout the rules. These changes are intended to be stylistic only.

Amended Rule 23(d)(2) carries forward the provisions of former Rule 23(d) that recognize two separate propositions. First, a Rule 23(d) order may be combined with a pretrial order under Rule 16. Second, the standard for amending the Rule 23(d) order continues to be the more open-ended standard for amending Rule 23(d) orders, not the more exacting standard for amending Rule 16 orders.

As part of the general restyling, intensifiers that provide emphasis but add no meaning are consistently deleted. Amended Rule 23(f) omits as redundant the explicit reference to court of appeals discretion in deciding whether to permit an interlocutory appeal. The omission does not in any way limit the unfettered discretion established by the original rule.

Law Review. — For note, "Proposed Rule 23: Class Actions Reclassified," see 51 Va. L. Rev. 629 (1965). For note, "Dismissal of Class Actions: The Small Claim Plaintiff and the Doctrine of Finality

Under 28 U.S.C. § 1291," see 29 Wash. & Lee L. Rev. 465 (1972). For comment, "Rule 23 Class Action Enforcement of the Clean Air Act of 1970," see 7 U. Rich. L. Rev. 549 (1973). For comment, "The Class Action and Title VII," see 10 U. Rich. L. Rev. 325 (1976). For article, "Processing the Explosion in Title VII Class Action Suits: Achieving Increased Compliance with Federal Rule of Civil Procedure 23(a)," see 19 Wm. & Mary L. Rev. 469 (1978). For comment, "Can Defendants Use Mootness Doctrine to Buy Off Class Actions?," see 36 Wash. & Lee L. Rev. 167 (1979). For review of civil procedure in the fourth circuit, see 36 Wash. & Lee L. Rev. 421 (1979). For comment, "*Deposit Guar. Nat'l Bank v. Roper* and *United States Parole Comm'n v. Geraghty:* Solution for or Confusion of Class Action Mootness?," see 38 Wash. & Lee L. Rev. 275 (1981). For note on defendant communications with absent class members in Rule 23(b)(3) class action litigation, see 42 Wash. & Lee L. Rev. 145 (1985). As to dealing with mass torts in bankruptcy, see 13 G.M.U. L. Rev. 381 (1990); For note, "Merit-Based Class Action Certification: Old Wine in a New Bottle," see 78 Va. L. Rev. 1001 (1992). As to the role of class counsel in allocating settlement proceeds, see 84 Va. L. Rev. 1465 (1998). For a note, "Who Can Tell the Futures? Protecting Settlement Class Action Members Without Notice," see 85 Va. L. Rev. 531 (1999). For an article, "As Mandatory Binding Arbitration Meets the Class Action, Will the Class Action Survive?," see 42 Wm. & Mary L. Rev. 1 (2000). For article, "Class Certification, the Merits, and Expert Evidence," see 11 G.M.U. L. Rev. 1 (2002). For note, "A Litigation Association Model to Aggregate Mass Tort Claims for Adjudication," see 91 Va. L. Rev. 1463 (2005). For article, "The Challenge to the Individual Causation Requirement in Mass Products Torts," see 62 Wash. & Lee L. Rev. 873 (2005). For article, "Universes Colliding: The Constitutional Implications of Arbitral Class Actions," see 47 Wm. & Mary L. Rev. 1711 (2005).

CASE NOTES

I. General Consideration.
II. Subdivision (a) Prerequisites.
  A. Numerosity.
  B. Commonality.
  C. Typicality.
  D. Fair Protection of Class Interests.
III. Subdivision (b) Analyses.
IV. Subdivision (c).
  A. Certification, Amendments.
  B. Notice, Opting Out.
  C. Judgment.
  D. Issues and Sub-Classes.
V. Orders; Dismissal or Compromise.
VI. Particular Actions.

I. GENERAL CONSIDERATION.

Purpose of rule. — It is well established that this rule was intended to open up the federal courts to the plaintiffs with small but valid claims. Cosgrove v. First & Merchants Nat'l Bank, 68 F.R.D. 555 (E.D. Va. 1975).

Rule interpreted liberally to allow class actions in civil rights cases. — Because civil rights suits, by their nature, are generally not as unmanageable as other types of class actions, this rule has been interpreted liberally to allow a class action in such cases. Moss v. Lane Co., 50 F.R.D. 122 (W.D. Va. 1970), rev'd on other grounds, 471 F.2d 853 (4th Cir. 1973).

This rule simply codified in rule form the existing practices in the federal courts in class action suits and in the giving of notice to members of the class in such actions. Baker v. Michie Co., 93 F.R.D. 494 (W.D. Va. 1982).

Alternatives to the class action device include: the test case, joinder, intervention, consolidation and individual actions. Brown v. Cameron-Brown Co., 92 F.R.D. 32 (E.D. Va.), rev'd and remanded on other grounds, 652 F.2d 375 (4th Cir. 1981).

Commonwealth did not need to identify each consumer harmed. — In consumer fraud case, the Commonwealth did not need to identify each consumer harmed, but could proceed on behalf of the class of purchasers who allegedly suffered damage. The Commonwealth is a unique plaintiff with law-enforcement interests such that it need not comply with the requirements for class actions under this rule. In re Fravel, 143 Bankr. 1001 (Bankr. E.D. Va. 1992).

Class must be determined before ruling on the merits. — See United States v. School Bd., 418 F. Supp. 639 (E.D. Va. 1976).

Discretion of court. — Whether a suit may be maintained as a class action is to some extent within the court's discretion. Frankel v. Wyllie & Thornhill, Inc., 55 F.R.D. 330 (W.D. Va. 1972); Richmond v. Railey's Appliance Ctr., Inc., 59 F.R.D. 641 (E.D. Va. 1973).

Whether the burden of satisfying the requirements for certification of a class action has been met is left to the trial court's discretion and will be reversed only for abuse. Brown v. Cameron-Brown Co., 92 F.R.D. 32 (E.D. Va.), rev'd and remanded on other grounds, 652 F.2d 375 (4th Cir. 1981).

A federal district court has broad discretion in determining whether a particular action complies with the requisites of subdivision (a). This determination is usually predicated on more information than the complaint itself affords. Davis v. City of Portsmouth, 579 F. Supp. 1205 (E.D. Va. 1983), aff'd, 742 F.2d 1448 (4th Cir. 1984).

Trial court's decision on whether class is proper is generally final. — Generally, unless abuse is shown, the trial court's decision as to whether a proper class action has been brought is final. Cypress v. Newport News Gen. & Nonsectarian Hosp. Ass'n, 375 F.2d 648 (4th Cir. 1967), rev'g 251 F. Supp. 667 (E.D. Va. 1966).

In determining whether to certify a class, the court may look beyond the pleadings, may permit discovery relating to issues involved in maintainability, and may schedule a preliminary evidentiary hearing to assist in determining "whether the moving party is asserting a claim which, assuming its merit, will satisfy the requirements of this rule." The court is proscribed, however, from conducting any preliminary inquiry into the merits of the suit. Brown v. Cameron-Brown Co., 92 F.R.D. 32 (E.D. Va.), rev'd and remanded on other grounds, 652 F.2d 375 (4th Cir. 1981).

And may require supplements to pleadings. — While the court may not put the plaintiff to preliminary proof of his claims in determining whether to certify a class action, it may require such supplements to the pleadings to allow an informed judgment on each of this rule's requirements. Brown v. Cameron-Brown Co., 92 F.R.D. 32 (E.D. Va.), rev'd and remanded on other grounds, 652 F.2d 375 (4th Cir. 1981).

But must take substantive allegations as true. — The court, in its determination of whether to certify the class, is bound to take the substantive allegations of the complaint as true. Brown v. Cameron-Brown Co., 92 F.R.D. 32 (E.D. Va.), rev'd and remanded on other grounds, 652 F.2d 375 (4th Cir. 1981).

Though plaintiff may be unable to prove allegations at trial. — That plaintiff may be unable to prove his allegations at trial is not a proper basis for the denial of class certification. Brown v. Cameron-Brown Co., 92 F.R.D. 32 (E.D. Va.), rev'd and remanded on other grounds, 652 F.2d 375 (4th Cir. 1981).

Burden is upon plaintiffs to provide the court sufficient information to determine whether class certification is appropriate. Davis v. City of Portsmouth, 579 F. Supp. 1205 (E.D. Va. 1983), aff'd, 742 F.2d 1448 (4th Cir. 1984).

The proponent of class certification has the burden of establishing the right to such certification under this rule. Butt v. Allegheny Pepsi-Cola Bottling Co., 116 F.R.D. 486 (E.D. Va. 1987).

Doubts should be resolved in favor of class certification. — Where doubts exist as to the advisability of proceeding with a class action, they should be resolved in favor of class certification. Brown v. Cameron-Brown Co., 92 F.R.D. 32 (E.D. Va.), rev'd and remanded on other grounds, 652 F.2d 375 (4th Cir. 1981).

Application of rule depends on circumstances. — Application of this rule is to be considered in light of the particular circumstances of the case. Cypress v. Newport News Gen. & Nonsectarian Hosp. Ass'n, 375 F.2d 648 (4th Cir. 1967), rev'g 251 F. Supp. 667 (E.D. Va. 1966).

This rule is inapplicable to suits filed under the federal Age Discrimination Employment Act because the procedures of § 16(b) of the Fair Labor Standards Act are made applicable to age discrimination suits and direct that the Age Discrimination Employment Act be enforced "in accordance with" the Fair Labor Standards Act. While the Fair Labor Standards Act authorizes "class actions" use of this rule is inappropriate because of the Fair Labor Standards Act requirement of notice to the secretary of labor and its requirement that a consent be filed by each "similarly situated" party. Moreover, "class action" under the Fair Labor Standards Act is statutory and independent of class actions under this rule. Cooke v. Reynolds Metals Co., 65 F.R.D. 539 (E.D. Va. 1975).

To maintain a class action under this rule, one must satisfy all four of the provisions of section (a) and one of the subdivisions of section (b). Lukenas v. Bryce's Mt. Resort, Inc., 538 F.2d 594 (4th Cir. 1976), aff'g 66 F.R.D. 69 (W.D. Va. 1975).

Where the beneficiary population is easily delineated and ascertained, creation of the class is not a complicated matter, and the court will not make it so. McGlothlin v. Connors, 142 F.R.D. 626 (W.D. Va. 1992).

Where judgment would be broad enough to protect potential class members, certification would be refused. — See Ruhe v. Block, 507 F. Supp. 1290 (E.D. Va. 1981).

Estoppel. — Where the class certification issues were virtually the same as those previously before the Ninth Circuit, that is, whether a nationwide punitive damages class met the prerequisites of subdivision (a) of this rule and the requirements of subdivision (b)(1)(B), the fact that the defendant raised the same issues in a set of lawsuits that different plaintiffs had brought elsewhere did not, in and of itself, change the nature of the issues involved for collateral estoppel purposes. Indeed, to have held that it did would have been to impose a mutuality requirement for collateral estoppel. In re Dalkon Shield Punitive Damages Litig., 613 F. Supp. 1112 (E.D. Va. 1985).

Remand for class certification held not to apply to plaintiffs in original action. — Where the district court considered the evidence applicable to plaintiffs as if the action had been tried as a class action and nevertheless found for the defendants, its judgment in this respect was simply affirmed and it was held that should there be any revival of the class action following remand, the plaintiffs could not participate. They have had their day in court. Goodman v. Schlesinger, 584 F.2d 1325 (4th Cir. 1978).

Applied in Mardel Sec., Inc. v. Alexandria Gazette Corp., 320 F.2d 890 (4th Cir. 1963); Rakes v. Coleman, 318 F. Supp. 181 (E.D. Va. 1970); Woolfolk v. Brown, 325 F. Supp. 1162 (E.D. Va. 1971); Jervey v. Martin, 336 F. Supp. 1350 (W.D. Va. 1972); Lawson v. Brown, 349 F. Supp. 203 (W.D. Va. 1972); Joseph v. House, 353 F. Supp. 367 (E.D. Va. 1973); Anderson v. Denny, 365 F. Supp. 1254 (W.D. Va. 1973); Black Bros. Combined of City of Richmond, Inc. v. City of Richmond, 386 F. Supp. 147 (E.D. Va. 1974); Ransom v. Ballou, 399 F. Supp. 191 (W.D. Va. 1975); Franklin v. Shields, 399 F. Supp. 309 (W.D. Va. 1975); Dyson v. Lavery, 417 F. Supp. 103 (E.D. Va. 1976); Woodard v. Virginia Bd. of Bar Exmrs., 420 F. Supp. 211 (E.D. Va. 1976); Jarrell v. Eastern Air Lines, 430 F. Supp. 884 (E.D. Va. 1977); Maclennan v. American Airlines, 440 F. Supp. 466 (E.D. Va. 1977); Lewis v. Tobacco Workers' Int'l Union, 577 F.2d 1135 (4th Cir. 1978); Lee v. City of Richmond, 456 F. Supp. 756 (E.D. Va. 1978); Burwell v. Eastern Air Lines, 458 F. Supp. 474 (E.D.

Va. 1978); White v. City of Suffolk, 460 F. Supp. 516 (E.D. Va. 1978); Harris v. Ballone, 681 F.2d 225 (4th Cir. 1982); Randall v. Lukhard, 536 F. Supp. 723 (W.D. Va. 1982); West v. Costen, 558 F. Supp. 564 (W.D. Va. 1983); Hill v. Hutto, 559 F. Supp. 390 (E.D. Va. 1983); Adams v. Heckler, 566 F. Supp. 1047 (W.D. Va. 1983); Watkins v. Cantrell, 568 F. Supp. 1225 (E.D. Va. 1983); Reed v. Lukhard, 591 F. Supp. 1247 (W.D. Va. 1984); Forest Hills Early Learning Ctr., Inc. v. Lukhard, 789 F.2d 295 (4th Cir. 1986); Forest Hills Early Learning Ctr., Inc. v. Lukhard, 661 F. Supp. 300 (E.D. Va. 1987); Malone v. Microdyne Corp., 148 F.R.D. 153 (E.D. Va. 1993); Simmons v. Poe, 47 F.3d 1370 (4th Cir. 1995); Switzenbaum v. Orbital Sciences Corp., 187 F.R.D. 246 (E.D. Va. 1999).

II. SUBDIVISION (A) PREREQUISITES.

A. Numerosity.

No specified number is needed for class action. — No specified number is needed to maintain a class action under this rule. Cypress v. Newport News Gen. & Nonsectarian Hosp. Ass'n, 375 F.2d 648 (4th Cir. 1967), rev'g 251 F. Supp. 667 (E.D. Va. 1966).

But class must be so numerous that joinder of all members is impracticable. — Where the class is 25 or more, joinder is usually presumed impracticable. Talbott v. GC Servs., Ltd. Partnership, 191 F.R.D. 99 (W.D. Va. 2000).

See Scott v. Aetna Life & Cas. Co., 48 F.R.D. 446 (W.D. Va. 1969); Briggs v. Brown & Williamson Tobacco Corp., 414 F. Supp. 371 (E.D. Va. 1976); Beck v. Mather, 417 F. Supp. 648 (W.D. Va. 1976).

Knowledge of precise size of class not necessary. — It is not necessary that plaintiffs know precisely the size of the class, rather it is necessary only to show that the class is so large as to make joinder impracticable. McGlothlin v. Connors, 142 F.R.D. 626 (W.D. Va. 1992).

The court may certify a class based on a common sense estimation of the class size if the precise number of class members is unknown. Talbott v. GC Servs., Ltd. Partnership, 191 F.R.D. 99 (W.D. Va. 2000).

Joinder of all members of class with similar claims not impracticable. — In the absence of a showing of the number of persons who may have been subjected to the treatment that the party attempting to represent the class complained of, the court cannot conclude that joinder of all members of a class with similar claims is impracticable. Greene v. Brown, 451 F. Supp. 1266 (E.D. Va. 1978).

Requirement of impracticality held satisfied. — Where plaintiffs assert the class to number at least several thousand and the defendants refer to a potential class of 200,000, the requirement that the class be so numerous that joinder of all members would be impracticable has been satisfied. Brown v. Cameron-Brown Co., 92 F.R.D. 32 (E.D. Va.), rev'd and remanded on other grounds, 652 F.2d 375 (4th Cir. 1981).

Three individuals insufficient number for class action. — See Chappelle v. E.I. DuPont de Nemours & Co., 422 F. Supp. 17 (E.D. Va. 1976).

Joinder impracticable where 120,000 members. — There is no question that 120,000 members constitutes a sufficiently large class to make joinder impracticable. McGlothlin v. Connors, 142 F.R.D. 626 (W.D. Va. 1992).

Racial discrimination suit failing to meet requirement of numerosity. — Where all 67 black employees, including the eight identified, lived in the same general area, class certification was properly denied. Kelley v. Norfolk & W. Ry., 584 F.2d 34 (4th Cir. 1978).

With respect to the requirement of numerosity, 88 black police officers, each alleging common questions of law of fact, were too numerous to make practicable their joinder as plaintiffs in a single proceeding, accordingly, the numerosity requirement of subdivision (a)(1) was satisfied. Richmond Black Police Officers Ass'n v. City of Richmond, 386 F. Supp. 151 (E.D. Va. 1974), rev'd on other grounds, 614 F.2d 940 (4th Cir. 1980).

Mayor may not be treated as representative of city council. — It is not a proper case for treating the mayor of a city as representative of a class including the other council members, where there is no showing, as required by the rule, that the parties necessary to be joined as defendants are so numerous as to make joinder impracticable. Where there are seven councilmen, clearly their number is not sufficient to make joinder of all impracticable. Thaxton v. Vaughan, 321 F.2d 474 (4th Cir. 1963).

B. Commonality.

Liberal construction. — The requirement that questions of law or fact must be common to the class is to be liberally construed. McGlothlin v. Connors, 142 F.R.D. 626 (W.D. Va. 1992).

This rule does not require a complete coincidence of legal claims. It requires only that there be some questions of law and fact in common. Crockett v. Virginia Folding Box Co., 61 F.R.D. 312 (E.D. Va. 1974).

When the plaintiff directed his attack at discriminatory policies of defendant's manifested and various actions, and as one who has allegedly been aggrieved by some of those actions, he has demonstrated a sufficient nexus to enable him to represent others who have suffered from different actions motivated by the same policies. Briggs v. Brown & Williamson Tobacco Corp., 414 F. Supp. 371 (E.D. Va. 1976).

There are diverse issues of fact in all class actions. The individual members of a class will invariably reach an adversary posture with the defendant in different ways. But the rule does not require that the factual background of the named plaintiff's case be identical with that of other members of the class, but that the disputed issue occupy essentially the same degree of centrality to the named plaintiffs' claim as to that of other members of their purported class. Cottrell v. VEPCO, 62 F.R.D. 516 (E.D. Va. 1974).

The claims of individual class members do not have to match precisely. Talbott v. GC Servs., Ltd. Partnership, 191 F.R.D. 99 (W.D. Va. 2000).

But there must be a shared question of law or fact. — The commonality requirement of subdivision (a) (2) requires that a question of law or fact be presented which is shared in the grievances of the prospective class as defined. Taliaferro v. State Council of Higher Educ., 372 F. Supp. 1378 (E.D. Va. 1974).

Disparate facts which merely set the stage for alleged common deprivations of rights have not been allowed to defeat the requirement that there must be issues of fact or law common to all class members if litigation is to be given class treatment. Cottrell v. VEPCO, 62 F.R.D. 516 (E.D. Va. 1974).

Some factual variance is permitted. — Commonality does not require that all questions of law or fact be common to every member of the class; some factual variance is permitted. McGlothlin v. Connors, 142 F.R.D. 626 (W.D. Va. 1992).

The fact that questions peculiar to each individual member of the class may remain after the common questions have been resolved does not, by itself, mandate a refusal to grant class certification. Cosgrove v. First & Merchants Nat'l Bank, 68 F.R.D. 555 (E.D. Va. 1975).

A conspiracy allegation as to violation of the antitrust laws involves common questions as to the class of plaintiffs and plaintiffs' proof in this action will generally be the same as to all defendants. Brown v. Cameron-Brown Co., 92 F.R.D. 32 (E.D. Va.), rev'd and remanded on other grounds, 652 F.2d 375 (4th Cir. 1981).

Where a plaintiff alleges a nationwide conspiracy to restrain trade, and he does not have actual dealings with the entire class of defendants, he can still be an adequate class representative where all injuries of the class are the result of a conspiracy or concerted schemes between the defendants at whose hands the class suffered injury. Brown v. Cameron-Brown Co., 92 F.R.D. 32 (E.D. Va.), rev'd and remanded on other grounds, 652 F.2d 375 (4th Cir. 1981).

Antitrust plaintiffs are found to have satisfied the requirement of paragraph (a) that a question be common to members of the class in their complaint since allegation of conspiracy or monopolization will generally be treated as a central or single overriding issue or common nucleus of operative fact sufficient to establish a common question. Brown v. Cameron-Brown Co., 92 F.R.D. 32 (E.D. Va.), rev'd and remanded on other grounds, 652 F.2d 375 (4th Cir. 1981).

A number of courts have found that allegations concerning the existence, scope, and efficacy of an alleged antitrust conspiracy present questions adequately common to class members to satisfy the requirement that there be a question of either law or fact common to the members of the class. Butt v. Allegheny Pepsi-Cola Bottling Co., 116 F.R.D. 486 (E.D. Va. 1987).

Allegation regarding commonality does not attack sufficiency of complaint. — An allegation that an action does not comply with the prerequisites of this rule, because the claims raised are not common to a class, does not attack the sufficiency of the complaint, but rather goes to the court's determination as to whether a class action should be declared. Prior to at least preliminary discovery, such an allegation is premature. Burwell v. Eastern Air Lines, 394 F. Supp. 1361 (E.D. Va. 1975), aff'd in part, rev'd in part, 633 F.2d 361 (4th Cir. 1980).

Standardized collection letter. — Mailing standardized collection letter satisfies commonality and has been the basis for certification. Talbott v. GC Servs., Ltd. Partnership, 191 F.R.D. 99 (W.D. Va. 2000).

An allegation that an action does not comply with the prerequisites of this rule, because the claims raised are not common to a class, does not attack the sufficiency of the complaint, but rather goes to the court's determination as to whether a class action should be declared. Prior to at least preliminary discovery, such an allegation is premature. Burwell v. Eastern Air Lines, 394 F. Supp. 1361 (E.D. Va. 1975), aff'd in part, rev'd in part, 633 F.2d 361 (4th Cir. 1980).

C. Typicality.

"Typicalness" under the rule is not a subjective test, authorizing a judge to dismiss a class action based on a substantial legal claim where he thinks some members of the class may prefer to leave the violation of their rights unremedied. Cottrell v. VEPCO, 62 F.R.D. 516 (E.D. Va. 1974).

Typicality refers to the nature of the claims of the class representative and not necessarily to the specific facts from which the case arose. Brown v. Cameron-Brown Co., 92 F.R.D. 32 (E.D. Va.), rev'd and remanded on other grounds, 652 F.2d 375 (4th Cir. 1981).

Premise of typicality requirement is simply stated: as goes the claim of the named plaintiff, so go the claims of the class. Talbott v. GC Servs., Ltd. Partnership, 191 F.R.D. 99 (W.D. Va. 2000).

And requires alignment of class representative's interests with interests of class. — In considering whether the typicality requirement has been met, the emphasis of the court's examination is on a square alignment with the class representative's interests with the interests of the class. Brown v. Cameron-Brown Co., 92 F.R.D. 32 (E.D. Va.), rev'd and remanded on other grounds, 652 F.2d 375 (4th Cir. 1981).

The typicality requirement necessitates that the class representative's interest ought to be squarely aligned in interest with the represented group. McGlothlin v. Connors, 142 F.R.D. 626 (W.D. Va. 1992).

Typicality requires that the claim arise from the same event or course of conduct which gives rise to the claims of other class members and is based on the same legal theory. McGlothlin v. Connors, 142 F.R.D. 626 (W.D. Va. 1992).

Class members must occupy same degree of centrality to claims. — The typicality requirement demands that the named plaintiffs be proper members of the class with the disputed issue occupying essentially the same degree of centrality to their claim as to that of other members of their purported class. Taliaferro v. State Council of Higher Educ., 372 F. Supp. 1378 (E.D. Va. 1974).

Typicality may be found notwithstanding factual differences. — Where the class representatives' claims are such that they will have to prove the same elements as the remainder of the class, then typicality should be found notwithstanding factual differences between various members of the class. Brown v. Cameron-Brown Co., 92 F.R.D. 32 (E.D. Va.), rev'd and remanded on other grounds, 652 F.2d 375 (4th Cir. 1981).

Courts acknowledge that some factual variations between the class members is not fatal to a finding that the predominant legal claims are similar. McGlothlin v. Connors, 142 F.R.D. 626 (W.D. Va. 1992).

Typicality does not require that the claims be identical. Talbott v. GC Servs., Ltd. Partnership, 191 F.R.D. 99 (W.D. Va. 2000).

Typicality is satisfied when the claim arises from the same event or practice or course of conduct; and similarity of legal theory may control even in the face of differences of fact. Talbott v. GC Servs., Ltd. Partnership, 191 F.R.D. 99 (W.D. Va. 2000).

Typicality requirement can be met in an antitrust case even though there are many products sold at varied prices and conditions, essentially because all class members will seek to prove the same elements: that there was a conspiracy to fix prices in violation of the antitrust laws, that the prices were fixed pursuant thereto, and that the plaintiffs purchased products at prices which, as a result of the conspiracy, were higher than they would have been in a free market. Butt v. Allegheny Pepsi-Cola Bottling Co., 116 F.R.D. 486 (E.D. Va. 1987).

And proofs necessary to establish injury are essentially the same. — As a practical matter, where plaintiffs have been affected by a concerted practice effecting a common course of antitrust conduct, the proofs necessary to establish the fact of injury or impact will be essentially the same for each member of the class notwithstanding the rule that such an issue is individual to each plaintiff. Brown v. Cameron-Brown Co., 92 F.R.D. 32 (E.D. Va.), rev'd and remanded on other grounds, 652 F.2d 375 (4th Cir. 1981).

Legal claims arose from same conduct and were typical. — Although the variety of health care services provided, the degree of injury claimed, or the amount of damages suffered may have varied among plaintiffs, the court found that the named plaintiffs' legal claims arose from the same conduct and were typical of the entire class. McGlothlin v. Connors, 142 F.R.D. 626 (W.D. Va. 1992).

D. Fair Protection of Class Interests.

Two interests in litigation recognized. — A plaintiff seeking class certification may assert an interest either in his individual substantive claim or in shifting the costs of litigation to the remainder of the class. Toms v. Allied Bond & Collection Agency, Inc., 179 F.3d 103 (4th Cir. 1999).

Adequacy of representation should be scrutinized. — The adequacy of representation should be scrutinized with particular care where suit is brought against a purported class of defendants, the obvious reason being that they cannot be protected adequately if the interest of the defendants, or the members of the class, are in conflict. Marston v. L.E. Gant, Ltd., 56 F.R.D. 60 (E.D. Va. 1972).

The adequacy of legal counsel focuses on whether counsel is competent, dedicated, qualified, and experienced enough to conduct the litigation and whether there is an assurance of vigorous prosecution. The burden is on defendants to establish inadequate representation. McGlothlin v. Connors, 142 F.R.D. 626 (W.D. Va. 1992).

Absence of conflict between representative and other class members. — Subdivision (a)(4) requires that the class representative fairly and adequately protect the interests of the class. In evaluating this requirement, courts generally look for an absence of potential conflict between the representative and other class members, and assurances of a vigorous prosecution by competent attorneys. Butt v. Allegheny Pepsi-Cola Bottling Co., 116 F.R.D. 486 (E.D. Va. 1987).

The vigorous prosecution test of subdivision (a)(4) is generally satisfied upon the court's determination that the plaintiff's attorney is professionally competent to conduct the particular litigation. Brown v. Cameron-Brown Co., 92 F.R.D. 32 (E.D. Va.), rev'd and remanded on other grounds, 652 F.2d 375 (4th Cir. 1981).

To meet the two requirements of subdivision (a)(4) of absence of potential conflicts between the representatives and other members of the class and assurances that the case will be prosecuted vigorously, plaintiff must satisfy a two-pronged test: (1) Plaintiff's attorney must be professionally competent to conduct the particular litigation, and (2) the interests of the representative must neither be in conflict with nor antagonistic to those of the class as a whole. Brown v. Cameron-Brown Co., 92 F.R.D. 32 (E.D. Va.), rev'd and remanded on other grounds, 652 F.2d 375 (4th Cir. 1981).

The requirement of adequate representation comprises only two elements: (a) that the interests of the representative party must coincide with those of the class; and (b) that the representative party and his attorney can be expected to prosecute the action vigorously. Cottrell v. VEPCO, 62 F.R.D. 516 (E.D. Va. 1974).

Adequacy of representation is a factual issue in which the court conducts two separate inquiries: The adequacy of the class representative and the adequacy of legal counsel. McGlothlin v. Connors, 142 F.R.D. 626 (W.D. Va. 1992).

Plaintiff must be able to maintain action in his own right. — One cannot redress grievances through membership in a class where he or she would be unable to maintain the action in his or her own right. Burwell v. Eastern Airlines, 68 F.R.D. 495 (E.D. Va. 1975).

To sue on behalf of a class plaintiff must be a member of the class which he purports to represent, he must suffer the same injury as the other members of the class, and he must be able fairly and adequately to represent them. Richmond Black Police Officers Ass'n v. City of Richmond, 386 F. Supp. 151 (E.D. Va. 1974).

Though some cases have been interpreted as indicating that the nexus required to exist between a named plaintiff and a class may be as broad as that they are all of the same sex or race, this expansive interpretation has been substantially restricted in later cases. A class representative must be part of the class and "possess the same interest and suffer the same injury" as the class members. Steur v. ITT Continental Baking Co., 80 F.R.D. 624 (E.D. Va. 1977).

A class representative must be part of the class and "possess the same interest and suffer the same injury" as class members. Wilson v. Allied Chem. Corp., 456 F. Supp. 249 (E.D. Va. 1978).

It is incumbent upon the court to determine that the named plaintiffs are members of the class they seek to represent. A class representative must be part of the class and "possess the same interest and suffer the same injury" as the class members. Belcher v. Bassett Furn. Indus., Inc., 588 F.2d 904 (4th Cir. 1978).

To support a class action which puts in issue a

particular claim, there must be a representative party who has been personally aggrieved. Wilson v. Allied Chem. Corp., 456 F. Supp. 249 (E.D. Va. 1978).

The court must make an initial determination that the representatives in a class action are members of the proposed class. McGlothlin v. Connors, 142 F.R.D. 626 (W.D. Va. 1992).

Plaintiff can bargain away his interest in litigation by negotiating a settlement agreement with the defendant. Toms v. Allied Bond & Collection Agency, Inc., 179 F.3d 103 (4th Cir. 1999).

Plaintiff released his interests in the litigation when he entered into a settlement agreement with defendant that was detailed and specific, and plaintiff expressly relinquished any and all claims of any kind or nature whatsoever that he may have had individually, as well as any and all monetary claims including any claims for attorney's fees, costs, or compensation as class representative, that he may have as a member/representative of the putative class. Toms v. Allied Bond & Collection Agency, Inc., 179 F.3d 103 (4th Cir. 1999).

Considerations of court. — On the issue of adequate class representation, the court may consider the extent to which other class members support the representative parties, and whether a potential conflict exists between the named plaintiffs and the proposed class. McGlothlin v. Connors, 142 F.R.D. 626 (W.D. Va. 1992).

This rule does not require that all members of the class be identically situated. Paxman v. Wilkerson, 390 F. Supp. 442 (E.D. Va. 1975), aff'd in part and rev'd in part, 612 F.2d 848 (4th Cir. 1980).

It has never been the rule that all issues must be identical for all members of the class. So long as it is possible to say that the economy of time, effort and expense, as well as the desirability of uniformity are greater than the burden of determining individual issues, the court will allow a class action as the superior method. The prospect of remaining issues to be resolved by separate trials or other appropriate procedures, after common issues have been adjudicated, provides no particular deterrent in the mind of the court. Mills v. Roanoke Indus. Loan & Thrift, 70 F.R.D. 448 (W.D. Va. 1975).

Nor does the rule require that all persons in the class desire to take advantage of the rights the plaintiffs may have. The fact that some members of the class are personally satisfied with the action complained of is irrelevant, and the injunctive or declaratory relief referred to in the rule does not require the court to look into the particular circumstances of each member of the class. Paxman v. Wilkerson, 390 F. Supp. 442 (E.D. Va. 1975), aff'd in part and rev'd in part, 612 F.2d 848 (4th Cir. 1980).

Plaintiffs' misunderstanding of nature of suit. — Where defendants cited the deposition testimony of and which indicated that plaintiffs did not understand that they were supposedly seeking to represent a class of plaintiffs rather than just themselves, and that they thought the actions concerned price discrimination against small retailers, plaintiffs' misunderstanding concerning the nature of their suit was not fatal; defendants conceded the ability of plaintiffs' counsel to litigate a class action; therefore, plaintiffs were adequate representatives of the class. Meredith v. Mid-Atlantic Coca Cola Bottling Co., 129 F.R.D. 130 (E.D. Va. 1989).

But plaintiff having minimal knowledge and interest may nevertheless represent class. — Even where plaintiffs evidence only a minimal knowledge and interest in the suit, they may be found capable of adequately representing the class. Brown v. Cameron-Brown Co., 92 F.R.D. 32 (E.D. Va.), rev'd and remanded on other grounds, 652 F.2d 375 (4th Cir. 1981).

Named plaintiffs must be able, at a minimum, to make important nondelegable decisions about the course of litigation; also if the named plaintiffs are evasive, untruthful, or lacking credibility, this weighs heavily against them as adequate class representatives. Smyth v. Carter, 168 F.R.D. 28 (W.D. Va. 1996).

Differing degrees of liability of defendants would not preclude class action. — The fact that defendants, in a suit involving securities law violations in connection with the sale of bonds, might have had differing degrees of liability did not preclude maintenance of the suit as a class action, where there were common questions of law and fact, and those questions predominated over any individual issues. Frankel v. Wyllie & Thornhill, Inc., 55 F.R.D. 330 (W.D. Va. 1972).

Class certification of pro se plaintiff is inappropriate. — Unless a party can fairly and adequately protect the interest of the class, he may not represent it and the court generally considers the competence of a layman representing himself to be clearly too limited to allow him to risk the rights of others. Thus, class certification of pro se plaintiffs would be inappropriate, in that the rights of parties included in the class may be jeopardized by unqualified representation. Davis v. City of Portsmouth, 579 F. Supp. 1205 (E.D. Va. 1983), aff'd, 742 F.2d 1448 (4th Cir. 1984).

Complaint alleging discrimination against black policemen. — Plaintiffs qualified under subdivision (a)(3) and (4), as proper representative parties of the class of people comprising present black employees of the Richmond bureau of police in that these plaintiffs are black police officers and as such they necessarily suffer the same harm as other black police officers if there is merit to the plaintiffs' allegations that the black policemen have been injured by the discriminatory practices of the police bureau. Richmond Black Police Officers Ass'n v. City of Richmond, 386 F. Supp. 151 (E.D. Va. 1974), rev'd on other grounds, 614 F.2d 940 (4th Cir. 1980).

Complaint alleging that black policemen presently employed had been injured on account of habitual discriminatory hiring and promotion practices on the part of the Richmond bureau of police satisfied the commonality requisite of subdivision (a)(2) of the rule. Richmond Black Police Officers Ass'n v. City of Richmond, 386 F. Supp. 151 (E.D. Va. 1974), rev'd on other grounds, 614 F.2d 940 (4th Cir. 1980).

Where proposed class consists of all persons who have applied for Medicaid under Supplemental Security Income-related eligibility since February, 1984 or who will apply and who have not or will not be provided an independent determination of disability and the class includes persons who have been found to be disabled by SSI as well as those who have been found not disabled, a second determination of disability could cause some members of the class to lose their Medicaid eligibility. For this reason the plaintiff cannot be said to fairly and adequately protect the interest of the class in seeking independent determinations of disability for the class and motions for leave to amend the pleadings and for certification of the class should be denied. Lester v. Lukhard, 622 F. Supp. 316 (W.D. Va. 1985).

III. SUBDIVISION (B) ANALYSES.

Mass accident litigation is not generally appropriate for class action treatment pursuant to either subdivision (b)(1) or subdivision (b)(2) of this rule. Causey v. Pan Am. World Airways, Inc., 66 F.R.D. 392 (E.D. Va. 1975).

When both subdivisions (b)(2) and (b)(3) apply, court should proceed under subdivision (b)(2). — Although a class action met the requirements of subdivision 23(b)(3) because questions of law or fact were common to the entire class, the class was more appropriately certified under subdivision 23(b)(2). When both provisions apply, the court should proceed under subdivision 23(b)(2) so that all the class members will be bound. McGlothlin v. Connors, 142 F.R.D. 626 (W.D. Va. 1992).

There are two basic factors that must be present under subdivision 23(b)(2): (1) The opposing party's conduct must be "generally applicable" to the class and (2) final injunctive or corresponding declaratory relief must be requested for the class. McGlothlin v. Connors, 142 F.R.D. 626 (W.D. Va. 1992).

"Generally applicable." — In order for the opposing party's conduct to be "generally applicable" to the class, it is not necessary that the party act directly against each member of the class. McGlothlin v. Connors, 142 F.R.D. 626 (W.D. Va. 1992).

Subdivision (b)(2) applicable where relief sought against single defendant. — Subdivision (b)(2) is applicable to situations in which a class of plaintiffs seeks injunctive relief against a single defendant, the party opposing the class. To proceed under subdivision (b)(2) against a class of defendants would constitute the plaintiffs as the party opposing the class. Paxman v. Campbell, 612 F.2d 848 (4th Cir. 1980), cert. denied, 449 U.S. 1129, 101 S. Ct. 951, 67 L. Ed. 2d 117 (1981).

Certification appropriate only where relief exclusively or predominantly injunctive or declaratory. — Certification under subdivision (b)(2) is appropriate only when the relief sought is exclusively or predominantly injunctive or declaratory. McGlothlin v. Connors, 142 F.R.D. 626 (W.D. Va. 1992).

Subdivision (b)(2) does not extend to cases in which the appropriate final relief relates exclusively or predominantly to money damages. Causey v. Pan Am. World Airways, Inc., 66 F.R.D. 392 (E.D. Va. 1975).

Subdivision (b)(2) of this rule was never intended to cover cases where the primary claim is for damages, but is only applicable where the relief sought is exclusively or predominantly injunctive or declaratory. Lukenas v. Bryce's Mt. Resort, Inc., 538 F.2d 594 (4th Cir. 1976), aff'g 66 F.R.D. 69 (W.D. Va. 1975).

Where the plaintiffs spoke of their action as one for rescission, but they actually sought rescission simply as a predicate for a monetary judgment, such an action is not suitable for treatment as a class action. Lukenas v. Bryce's Mt. Resort, Inc., 538 F.2d 594 (4th Cir. 1976), aff'g 66 F.R.D. 69 (W.D. Va. 1975).

Duty of court to consider standards set forth in subdivision (b)(3). — Where the prerequisites set forth in subdivision (a)(1) through (4) have been met, the court must also consider the applicability of the specific standards, and the matters pertinent thereto, set forth in subdivision (b)(3). Causey v. Pan Am. World Airways, Inc., 66 F.R.D. 392 (E.D. Va. 1975).

The court must find that "a class action is superior to other available methods for the fair and efficient adjudication of the controversy." Subdivision (b)(3) of this rule suggests "pertinent" considerations in making this determination. These include the nature of litigation already commenced by members of the class, the desirability of concentrating the litigation of the class claims in a particular forum, and the difficulties in the management of the class. Beard v. King Appliance Co., 61 F.R.D. 434 (E.D. Va. 1973).

Subdivision (b)(3) contemplates a dual test: First, questions of law or fact common to the members of the class must predominate over questions affecting individual members; and, second, the court must be satisfied that a class action is superior to other available methods for the fair and efficient adjudication of the controversy. Brown v. Cameron-Brown Co., 92 F.R.D. 32 (E.D. Va.), rev'd and remanded on other grounds, 652 F.2d 375 (4th Cir. 1981).

Class action must be superior to other available methods. — In order to allow maintenance of a class action, the court must find that the questions of law or fact common to the members of the class predominate over any questions affecting only individual members, and that the action, that is the class action, is superior to other available methods for the fair and efficient adjudication of the controversy. Marston v. L.E. Gant, Ltd., 56 F.R.D. 60 (E.D. Va. 1972).

The superiority issue in this rule involves considerations distinct from those of the predominance issue and involves a determination of whether the class action device is superior to other methods available to the court for a fair and efficient adjudication of the controversy. Brown v. Cameron-Brown Co., 92 F.R.D. 32 (E.D. Va.), rev'd and remanded on other grounds, 652 F.2d 375 (4th Cir. 1981).

A class action is the superior method for adjudicating a controversy where the recovery of many individual class members would be relatively small and therefore as a practical matter the prospect of individual suits is not realistic. Mills v. Roanoke Indus. Loan & Thrift, 70 F.R.D. 448 (W.D. Va. 1975).

Plaintiffs' burden under subdivision (b)(3) is to assure the court that use of the class action device will achieve the economies of time, effort and expense contemplated by the rule, without sacrificing procedural fairness or bringing about other undesirable results. Brown v. Cameron-Brown Co., 92 F.R.D. 32 (E.D. Va.), rev'd and remanded on other grounds, 652 F.2d 375 (4th Cir. 1981).

When subdivision (b)(3) satisfied. — Generally, where a court finds liability to be a question common to the class it holds subdivision (b)(3) satisfied. Brown v. Cameron-Brown Co., 92 F.R.D. 32 (E.D. Va.), rev'd and remanded on other grounds, 652 F.2d 375 (4th Cir. 1981).

Common questions need only predominate. — To establish their right to class certification, plaintiffs need not prove that the common questions are dispositive of the entire litigation as it pertains to each individual. Rather, subdivision (b)(3) requires only a demonstration by plaintiffs of the predominance of common questions. Brown v. Cameron-Brown Co., 92 F.R.D. 32 (E.D. Va.), rev'd and remanded on other grounds, 652 F.2d 375 (4th Cir. 1981).

But requirement of common question is less stringent than requirement of predominance. — The second prerequisite of subdivision (a), that there be either a question of law or fact common to members of the class, is less stringent than the predominance requirement of subdivision (b)(3). Brown v. Cameron-Brown Co., 92 F.R.D. 32 (E.D. Va.), rev'd and remanded on other grounds, 652 F.2d 375 (4th Cir. 1981).

Where common questions do not predominate class action is inappropriate. — In a court's analysis of the predominance test of subdivision (b)(3), a valid concern is whether the class action will splinter into individual trials suggesting that common questions do not predominate over individual questions and that a class action would be inappropriate. Brown v. Cameron-Brown Co., 92 F.R.D. 32 (E.D. Va.), rev'd and remanded on other grounds, 652 F.2d 375 (4th Cir. 1981).

Possibility of subsequently arising inconsistencies does not defeat action at certification stage. — Where all of the plaintiffs appear to be similarly situated at the class certification stage, such inconsistencies as might arise subsequently through the factual developments with respect to possible differences between actions of particular defendants toward individual members of the plaintiff class might suggest the necessity for the creation of subclasses, a factor to be addressed under 23(b). Brown v. Cameron-Brown Co., 92 F.R.D. 32 (E.D. Va.), rev'd and remanded on other grounds, 652 F.2d 375 (4th Cir. 1981).

Questions individual to class members as to liability and damages which may subsequently preclude the use of the class action device do not defeat the applicability of this rule at the certification stage of litigation. Brown v. Cameron-Brown Co., 92 F.R.D. 32 (E.D. Va.), rev'd and remanded on other grounds, 652 F.2d 375 (4th Cir. 1981).

The declaratory judgment should be the equivalent of an injunction. McGlothlin v. Connors, 142 F.R.D. 626 (W.D. Va. 1992).

Requirement that each swindled investor trace funds into bankrupt estate. — In a class action where each investor who was swindled must trace his or her individual funds into the estate, any potential adversarial stance of the investors does not exceed that which would exist in any class action of this nature, and therefore does not destroy the class action. Furthermore, the necessity of the tracing requirement is yet another question of law common to members of the class, further buttressing the case for class certification. Brown v. Goldstein (In re Johnson), 80 Bankr. 791 (Bankr. E.D. Va. 1987), aff'd, 960 F.2d 396 (4th Cir. 1992).

Effect of individualized claims for damages. — In cases where the fact of injury and damage breaks down in what may be characterized as virtually a mechanical task, capable of mathematical or formula calculation, the existence of individualized claims for damages seems to offer no barrier to class certification on grounds of manageability. On the other hand, where the issue of damages and impact does not lend itself to such a mechanical calculation, but requires separate minitrials of an overwhelming large number of individual claims, the staggering problems of logistics thus created make the damage aspect of the case predominate, and render the class unmanageable as a class action. Brown v. Cameron-Brown Co., 92 F.R.D. 32 (E.D. Va.), rev'd and remanded on other grounds, 652 F.2d 375 (4th Cir. 1981).

Individual damage questions will not be held to predominate to the preclusion of a class action where liability has been found to be common to the class, where the issues of liability and individual damages can be treated separately, or where damages are susceptible to mathematical or formula calculation. Brown v. Cameron-Brown Co., 92 F.R.D. 32 (E.D. Va.), rev'd and remanded on other grounds, 652 F.2d 375 (4th Cir. 1981).

Even though criminal trial had been conducted concerning conspiracy to fix prices, defendants had not conceded the existence of the conspiracy, the effect of the conspiracy had to be determined, and the appropriate method to compute damages constituted a class-wide measure of damages to be established at trial; therefore, the common questions of the existence, scope and effect of the conspiracy predominated over individual claims and satisfied the common question requirement of this rule. Meredith v. Mid-Atlantic Coca Cola Bottling Co., 129 F.R.D. 130 (E.D. Va. 1989).

Conflicting interests held to keep all testator's children from falling in same class. — The potentially conflicting interests which the plaintiffs have with the other two children of testator, over the issue of the part played by them in the bank's disbursement of the funds of the residuary estate, prevent the testator's children from falling in the same class. Hyde v. First & Merchants Nat'l Bank, 41 F.R.D. 527 (W.D. Va. 1967).

IV. SUBDIVISION (C).

A. Certification, Amendments.

The party moving for certification of a suit as a class action is charged with the burden of satisfying the "prerequisites" to a class action of subdivision (a) of this rule and the "predominance" and "superiority" criteria of subdivision (b). Brown v. Cameron-Brown Co., 92 F.R.D. 32 (E.D. Va.), rev'd and remanded on other grounds, 652 F.2d 375 (4th Cir. 1981).

When court may consider certification. — Once the court determines that a class exists and the class representatives are properly members of the class, the court may then consider certification of the class action. McGlothlin v. Connors, 142 F.R.D. 626 (W.D. Va. 1992).

Certification left to sound discretion of trial court. — Certification of a class is left to the sound discretion of the trial court and will be reversed only upon a showing of abuse of discretion. McGlothlin v. Connors, 142 F.R.D. 626 (W.D. Va. 1992).

Ruling as to class action may be conditional. — Any ruling as to a class action may be conditional and may be altered or amended before a decision on the merits. Marston v. L.E. Gant, Ltd., 56 F.R.D. 60 (E.D. Va. 1972).

Attack upon merits of claims not proper response to motion for class action certification. — See Wilson v. Allied Chem. Corp., 456 F. Supp. 249 (E.D. Va. 1978).

The certification stage is an inappropriate time to make any determination as to plaintiffs' standing to represent the putative class. Brown v. Cameron-Brown Co., 92 F.R.D. 32 (E.D. Va.), rev'd and remanded on other grounds, 652 F.2d 375 (4th Cir. 1981).

Decision whether plaintiffs should represent class made on full record. — Once a class is certified the claims of the class need not stand or fall with the claims of the individual representative parties. But where the class has not been certified "the decision whether the named plaintiffs should represent a class is appropriately made on the full record." In making its decision on the question of whether the requirements of this rule are met, the court must not close its eyes to the facts that have been established at the time the decision is reached. Greene v. Brown, 451 F. Supp. 1266 (E.D. Va. 1978).

Who may represent class based on facts at time of certification. — A court may not conduct a preliminary inquiry into the merits of a suit in order to determine whether it may be maintained as a class action. However, the determination of who may represent a class shall be based on facts shown at the time the certification is made. Greene v. Brown, 451 F. Supp. 1266 (E.D. Va. 1978).

Certification not necessary prior to issuing preliminary injunction. — Class certification is not necessary prior to issuing a preliminary injunction. McGlothlin v. Connors, 142 F.R.D. 626 (W.D. Va. 1992).

District court prematurely denied class certification. — See Goodman v. Schlesinger, 584 F.2d 1325 (4th Cir. 1978).

Leave to include party where class not designated. — Where an unnamed plaintiff did not join as a named plaintiff on the assumption that her interests would be protected as a member of the class, but no class was designated in the action and it was not clear at the time that it would be proper or appropriate to designate a class, accordingly, leave was granted plaintiffs to file an amended complaint or, through otherwise appropriate pleading, to bring the individual in as an additional party plaintiff. Howard v. Aluminum Workers Int'l Union, 418 F. Supp. 1058 (E.D. Va. 1976), aff'd, 589 F.2d 771 (4th Cir. 1978).

Enlargement of class inappropriate at late date in proceedings. Burwell v. Eastern Air Lines, 458 F. Supp. 474 (E.D. Va. 1978), aff'd in part, rev'd in part, 633 F.2d 361 (4th Cir. 1980).

Parties satisfactorily repudiated withdrawal from class. — Where the parties revoked their previously executed "Request for Exclusion from Class" form before the deadline set by the court for withdrawal from the class and because that revocation unequivocally expressed their desire to be class members once again, the parties had, as a matter of law, satisfactorily repudiated their withdrawal from class membership and were regarded as members of the plaintiffs' class for the purposes of the litigation. Bailey v. Cost Control Mktg. & Sales Mgt. of Va., Inc., 132 F.R.D. 435 (W.D. Va. 1990).

Class action not rendered moot by dismissal of individual claim. — If the plaintiff were a member of the class at the commencement of the action and his competency as a representative of the class then determined or assumed, the subsequent dismissal or mootness of his individual claim, particularly in a discrimination case, will not operate as a dismissal or render moot the action of the class, or destroy the plaintiff's right to litigate the issues on behalf of the class. Moss v. Lane Co., 471 F.2d 853 (4th Cir. 1973). See Hazelgrove v. Ford Motor Co., 428 F. Supp. 1096 (E.D. Va. 1977).

B. Notice, Opting Out.

Notice required as matter of due process. — There is a growing body of authority holding that notice, as a matter of due process, is required in all representative actions if the resulting judgment is to be binding on absent class members. Despite the fact that this rule only specifically requires notice in subdivision (b)(3) class actions, cases have held that due process requires notice in actions brought under subdivisions (b)(1) and (b)(2) also. Richmond Black Police Officers Ass'n v. City of Richmond, 386 F. Supp. 151 (E.D. Va. 1974).

The opt-out provisions of subdivision (c)(2) may not be used to achieve compliance with the prerequisites of subdivision (a). Lukenas v. Bryce's Mt. Resort, Inc., 66 F.R.D. 69 (W.D. Va. 1975), aff'd, 538 F.2d 594 (4th Cir. 1976).

Contents of notice. — Where individual recoveries in an action might be small or eliminated by the administrative costs of the suit, the notice sent to all class members who are identifiable should contain information on the approximation of projected recovery, taking into account prospective attorney fees and other administrative costs. Cosgrove v. First & Merchants Nat'l Bank, 68 F.R.D. 555 (E.D. Va. 1975).

Names and addresses of attorneys who are presently representing class representatives should be included in the notice in order to allow class members to decide whether to retain their own attorney at their own expense or rely on counsel of record. Burwell v. Eastern Airlines, 68 F.R.D. 495 (E.D. Va. 1975).

Circulation of notice to potential class members. — A federal court should not permit the circulation of a court-approved notice to all potential class members informing them of their right to "opt in" to the action under the Fair Labor Standards Act. Baker v. Michie Co., 93 F.R.D. 494 (W.D. Va. 1982).

Aggrieved persons may signify their exclusion from class. — Aggrieved persons who fear that their interests will not be adequately protected by the representative plaintiffs may signify their exclusion from the class. Frankel v. Wyllie & Thornhill, Inc., 55 F.R.D. 330 (W.D. Va. 1972).

Issue of applicability of judgment to member of class regardless of notification of suit not decided where case reversed on other grounds. Lewis v. Tobacco Workers' Int'l Union, 577 F.2d 1135 (4th Cir. 1978), cert. denied, 439 U.S. 1089, 99 S. Ct. 871, 59 L. Ed. 2d 56 (1979).

C. Judgment.

Record and judgment failing to identify members of class. — Where, in a class action, the record did not clearly identify the members of the class, because although plaintiffs' counsel has informally advised the district court that the required notice had been given, the court's files contained neither a copy of the notice nor a certificate that it was sent, and the judgment did not "specify or describe those to whom the notice . . . was directed, and who have not requested exclusion, and whom the court finds to be members of the class," as required by subdivision (c)(3) of this rule, such omission having resulted from the oversight of counsel but being capable of remedy without difficulty, the judgment was affirmed, but the case was remanded to the district court so that the omissions in the record could be corrected and the judgment amended. Newman v. Prior, 518 F.2d 97 (4th Cir. 1975), overruled on other grounds, Newcome v. Esrey, 862 F.2d 1099 (4th Cir. 1988).

Remand for correction of omissions. — Where the record did not clearly identify the members of the class and the judgment did not "specify or describe those to whom the notice . . . was directed, and who have not requested exclusion, and whom the court finds to be members of the class," as required by subdivision (c)(3) of this rule, such omissions having resulted from the oversight of counsel and having been remediable without difficulty, the judgment was affirmed and the case was remanded to the district court so that the omissions in the record could be corrected and the judgment amended. Newman v. Prior, 518 F.2d 97 (4th Cir. 1975), overruled on other grounds, Newcome v. Esrey, 862 F.2d 1099 (4th Cir. 1988).

Defining the class. — Where the issues to be litigated by flight attendants will differ in complexity and detail from those of ground employees, and the interests of the two groups potentially conflict, and a prior suit has been instituted by several ground employees, the scope of the class in the instant suit is best limited to flight attendants. Burwell v. Eastern Airlines, 68 F.R.D. 495 (E.D. Va. 1975).

D. Issues and Sub-Classes.

Treatment of potential rivalry among class members. — Any potential rivalry among class members after the issue of liability is decided can be adequately treated since subdivision (c)(4) of this rule gives the court the power to divide the class into appropriate subclasses or to require the members to bring individual suits for damages. Frankel v. Wyllie & Thornhill, Inc., 55 F.R.D. 330 (W.D. Va. 1972).

Severance of one or more issues may prove advantageous. — If the court determines that individual issues predominate as to the class as a whole, the court should consider whether the severance of one or more issues would prove advantageous. Brown v. Cameron-Brown Co., 92 F.R.D. 32 (E.D. Va.), rev'd and remanded on other grounds, 652 F.2d 375 (4th Cir. 1981).

Or court may consider creation of subclasses. — If the court determines that individual issues predominate as to the class as a whole, the court should consider whether the creation of subclasses would present common questions as to various subclasses. Brown v. Cameron-Brown Co., 92 F.R.D. 32 (E.D. Va.), rev'd and remanded on other grounds, 652 F.2d 375 (4th Cir. 1981).

Consumer protection laws. — Class actions may be particularly useful devices to enforce consumer protection laws. A conditional certification prior to a decision on the merits is appropriate. Talbott v. GC Servs., Ltd. Partnership, 191 F.R.D. 99 (W.D. Va. 2000).

Fraud case may be unsuited as class action. —Although having some common core, a fraud case may be unsuited for treatment as a class action if there was material variation in the representations made or in the kinds of degrees of reliance by the persons to whom they were addressed. Lukenas v. Bryce's Mt. Resort, Inc., 538 F.2d 594 (4th Cir. 1976), aff'g 66 F.R.D. 69 (W.D. Va. 1975).

"Domino theory" of fraudulent misrepresentation allowing purchasers of securities to be represented as class. — The "domino theory" of fraudulent misrepre- sentation has been evolved, allowing purchasers of securities over an extended time period, during which several communications concerning the corporation's financial status may have been issued, to be represented in one class action. According to this formulation, the group of defrauded purchasers may constitute a class if the several misrepresentations were similar or interdependent in content, or if they were all issued as part of an integrated course of manipulative conduct by defendant. Having found that the class members' claims are grounded in one set of defendant's actions, courts view individual variations as unimportant; indeed, defendant's liability may depend predominantly on an elaboration of the background and history of the overall "common scheme." Mills v. Roanoke Indus. Loan & Thrift, 70 F.R.D. 448 (W.D. Va. 1975).

V. ORDERS; DISMISSAL OR COMPROMISE.

Dismissal not justified by differences as to computation of damages. — Differences in parties' claims bearing only upon the ultimate computation of damages do not justify dismissal of the suit as a class action. Frankel v. Wyllie & Thornhill, Inc., 55 F.R.D. 330 (W.D. Va. 1972).

Adjudication on merits not subject to subdivision (e) notice requirements. — An order which is not a voluntary dismissal or compromise but instead represents an adjudication on the merits is not subject to subdivision (e)'s notice requirements. Riddick ex rel. Riddick v. School Bd., 784 F.2d 521 (4th Cir.), cert. denied, 479 U.S. 938, 107 S. Ct. 420, 93 L. Ed. 2d 370 (1986).

Dismissal of action that has become moot as to named plaintiff. — Unless a case has been certified by the trial court as a class action prior to the time that the case has been mooted with respect to the named plaintiff, then dismissal is required by the "case or controversy" provisions of the United States Constitution. McCleary v. Realty Indus., Inc., 405 F. Supp. 128 (E.D. Va. 1975).

In a purported class action, the controversy is between only the named parties until such time as the trial court certifies the action as a class action. And if a resolution of the controversy between the named parties is reached prior to the time class action status is determined, the action must be dismissed. McCleary v. Realty Indus., Inc., 405 F. Supp. 128 (E.D. Va. 1975).

When claim becomes moot. — Where the plaintiff brought a purported class action alleging a denial of procedural due process to herself and persons in her class, her claim became moot when the defendants voluntarily consented to procedures which were in accord with the due process requirements prayed for in her complaint, even though there was in existence a class of persons suffering the deprivation, since that class of persons was not deprived of judicial remedies from mootness due to any inexorable change in their status. Banks v. Multi-Family Mgt., Inc., 406 F. Supp. 876 (E.D. Va. 1975), aff'd, 554 F.2d 127 (4th Cir. 1977).

Effect of settlement offer. — Where the settlement offer of the defendant, if accepted by the court, would vindicate not only the rights of the named plaintiff, but also those of all members of the purported class, the settlement offer would effectively eliminate any further controversy between the defendant and the members of the purported class represented by the named plaintiff. Thus, entry of the settlement offer would render the issues between the parties moot. The same facts which would support a finding of mootness as to plaintiff's claims would also render plaintiff a nonrepresentative party in a class action. Once the representative plaintiff has obtained the relief sought, his interests no longer coincide with those of the members of the class. Additionally, any expectation that such plaintiff would vigorously prosecute the action would be greatly diminished, since his personal stake in the litigation is ended. McCleary v. Realty Indus., Inc., 405 F. Supp. 128 (E.D. Va. 1975).

Review of adequacy of settlement. — If a class action settlement is found to meet fairness criteria, the court must then review the adequacy of the settlement, including: 1. the relative strength of the plaintiffs' case on the merits; 2. the existence of any difficulties of proof or strong defenses the plaintiffs are likely to encounter if the case goes to trial; 3. the anticipated duration and expense of additional litigation; 4. the solvency of the defendants and the likelihood of recovery on a litigated judgment; and 5. the degree of opposition to the settlement. Strang v. JHM Mtg. Sec. Ltd. Partnership, 890 F. Supp. 499 (E.D. Va. 1995).

To determine the fairness of a class action settlement agreement, the court must consider: 1. the posture of the case at the time of settlement; 2. the extent of discovery that had been conducted; 3. the circumstances surrounding the negotiations; and 4. the experience of counsel in the area of securities class action litigation. Strang v. JHM Mtg. Sec. Ltd. Partnership, 890 F. Supp. 499 (E.D. Va. 1995).

Class action consent decree not immune from scrutiny. — Consent decrees, although looked upon favorably by the courts, are not immune from scrutiny in terms of propriety and legality. This principle is especially true in class actions where the effect of the relief usually has widespread and considerable impact both within and outside the class. For good reason the rule requires that "a class action shall not be dismissed or compromised without the approval of the court." Carson v. American Brands, Inc., 446 F. Supp. 780 (E.D. Va. 1977), appeal dismissed, 606 F.2d 420 (4th Cir. 1979), rev'd on other grounds, 450 U.S. 79, 101 S. Ct. 993, 67 L. Ed. 2d 59 (1981).

Consent decree in class action barred later suit by individual. — A consent decree in a class action, alleging that a governmental agency was engaging in various discriminatory disciplinary and promotion practices, was properly entered by a court of competent jurisdiction. The class consisted of ". . . all present and future black police officers . . ." employed by that agency. A later civil rights action by one of these officers, a member of the class, was barred by the principles of res judicata, since the prior decree had specifically resolved his individual claims of discrimination. Ivy v. Dole, 610 F. Supp. 165 (E.D. Va. 1985), aff'd, 811 F.2d 1505 (4th Cir. 1987).

VI. PARTICULAR ACTIONS.

All tenants at a low income housing project who were paying, or would have been subjected to pay under an approved rent increase schedule, in excess of 30% of their adjusted gross income for rent, due to increased utilities costs and local property taxes constituted an appropriate class under Rule 23, Federal Rules of Civil Procedure. Gibson v. Harris, 438 F. Supp. 487 (E.D. Va. 1977).

Resort development property purchasers seeking rescission of contracts. — Where by plaintiffs' own estimation only approximately 190 of the 610 purchasers of property in a resort development would desire to remain within the class represented by plaintiffs and rescind their purchase contracts, the interests of this minority of purchasers in the suit were clearly antagonistic to that of those purchasers who had a continuing interest in the financial viability of the defendant. Denial of class certification under this rule in this case was supported by those cases in which courts have refused to allow a terminated franchisee to represent a class including current franchisees because of the continuing interest of the current franchisee in the economic viability of the defendant franchisor. There is a serious lack of a common interest in the outcome of the suit. Lukenas v. Bryce's Mt. Resort, Inc., 66 F.R.D. 69 (W.D. Va. 1975), aff'd, 538 F.2d 594 (4th Cir. 1976).

Where, from the record before the court, it was clear that there would be numerous individual differences among members of the class which would affect the right to rescission the plaintiffs were seeking to establish, these individual differences among the members of the proposed class and the nature of the legal issue sought to be established, caused subdivision (b)(3) and hence the attendant notice provision of subdivision (c)(2) not to be applicable to the suit. Lukenas v. Bryce's Mt. Resort, Inc., 66 F.R.D. 69 (W.D. Va. 1975), aff'd, 538 F.2d 594 (4th Cir. 1976).

Chairman and subordinate lodge held representative of brotherhood. — In a suit against an unincorporated brotherhood of railroad employees, the inquiry was not whether the service was sufficient in a suit against the brotherhood as an entity under its common name (where the provision of Rule 4(d) (3) would be applicable), but whether the joinder and service upon members of the brotherhood were sufficient to bring them as a class before the court in a class suit under subdivision (a) of this rule. Two subordinate lodges within the court's jurisdiction were joined, one was unquestionably served, and service was made upon the local chairman of the other. The member who was served was not only chairman of a subordinate lodge but was also representative of the brotherhood, as bargaining agent, in enforcing the rights of employees under their trade agreement with the railway company. This service, as a matter of fact, did bring the brotherhood in, fighting. It cannot be contended with any show of reason that the chairman and the subordinate lodge, who were admittedly served, were not fairly representative of the membership of the brotherhood, or that service upon them would not give adequate notice to the class sued to come in and defend; and this is the criterion as to the sufficiency of joinder and service in a class suit. Tunstall v. Brotherhood of Locomotive Firemen & Enginemen, 148 F.2d 403 (4th Cir. 1945).

Action by homosexuals attacking constitutionality of sodomy statute. — The plaintiffs' class action, attacking the constitutionality of the Virginia statute making sodomy a crime, on behalf of themselves as well as of all other homosexuals similarly situated, against all local officers, in addition to the commonwealth's attorney for the City of Richmond, did not fit within the compass of this rule, because actions by or against individual members of the alleged classes would not create a risk of inconsistent or varying adjudications with respect to individual members, since the commonwealth's attorney, as a defendant, would be bound at future local trials by an adjudication upon the validity of the statute. Doe v. Commonwealth's Att'y, 403 F. Supp. 1199 (E.D. Va. 1975), aff'd, 425 U.S. 901, 96 S. Ct. 1489, 47 L. Ed. 2d 751, reh'g denied, 425 U.S. 985, 96 S. Ct. 2192, 48 L. Ed. 2d 810 (1976).

Action by women employees to establish right to compensation for childbirth disabilities. — A class action by certain women employees against their employer to secure affirmative injunctive relief under the equal employment opportunity provisions of the Civil Rights Act of 1964, to establish that childbirth disabilities of women employees were compensable under the employer's employee disability plan which was applicable generally throughout all the employer's plants, fell within the mold of subdivision (b)(2) of this rule. Gilbert v. GE Co., 519 F.2d 661 (4th Cir. 1975), rev'd on other grounds, 429 U.S. 125, 97 S. Ct. 401, 50 L. Ed. 2d 343 (1976).

Environmental suit against dam project held not proper for class action. — Suit seeking injunctive and declaratory relief on environmental grounds against federal dam project was not a proper one for a class action for two reasons: First, the members of the class could not reasonably be determined, and second, there was no reasonable method of giving such people proper notice. Cape Henry Bird Club v. Laird, 359 F. Supp. 404 (W.D. Va.), aff'd, 484 F.2d 453 (4th Cir. 1973).

Federal prisoners attacking conditions in city jail. — Federal prisoners who brought an action attacking various conditions in a city jail where they had been confined did not present a case for class certification, where the prisoners were acting pro se and had been transferred to facilities other than the city jail. Fore v. Godwin, 407 F. Supp. 1145 (E.D. Va. 1976).

Action to prevent incarceration of chronic alcoholics. — The allegations of the complaint and the affidavits that the plaintiff and those he represents shared the following claims: They are chronic alcoholics, they are being and will be incarcerated pursuant to a state law, they are denied the defense of alcoholism, and they are not being afforded rehabilitative treatment, were sufficient to establish standing to maintain class action. Rakes v. Coleman, 359 F. Supp. 370 (E.D. Va. 1973).

Action to compel payment of welfare benefits in accordance with federal standards. — Plaintiffs' motion for leave to proceed as a class action in an action seeking to compel state officials to pay welfare benefits in accordance with federal standards was granted where the members of the class were all 16 and 17-year-old children not regularly attending school and the supporting parents of these children to whom relief had been denied. Frye v. Lukehard, 361 F. Supp. 60 (W.D. Va.), modified, 364 F. Supp. 1379 (W.D. Va. 1973).

All black physicians and their patients held members of class interested in suit on discriminatory hospital practices. — Where a class action was brought by a black physician seeking an injunction against the racially discriminatory policies and practices of a publicly supported hospital, there followed the ineluctable conclusion that all black physicians practicing medicine in the area, and not only two individuals who already had applied for and been denied hospital staff privileges, should be considered members of the interested class. Moreover, it was held that the joining of physicians and patients in such action did not constitute misjoinder of distinct classes, where it was shown that the patients, who desired admission to what was agreed to be the best hospital in the area, were forced to elect either to forego treatment at that hospital or relinquish their personal physicians, since patients could be admitted to the hospital only on referral by members of its staff. Cypress v. Newport News Gen. & Nonsectarian Hosp. Ass'n, 375 F.2d 648 (4th Cir. 1967), rev'g 251 F. Supp. 667 (E.D. Va. 1966).

Class action on behalf of residential customers of electric utility. — A substantive claim that an electric utility's service termination practices resulted in termination of electrical service without adequate notice and a prior evidentiary hearing, thereby denying procedural due process required by the Fourteenth Amendment, was properly maintainable as a class action on behalf of the utility's residential customers. Cottrell v. VEPCO, 62 F.R.D. 516 (E.D. Va. 1974).

Suit by orphans under Ku Klux Klan Act. — A group of orphans possesses no other trait — economic, ethnic, geographic, racial, religious, or sexual. Their commonality of interest to bring a suit under the Ku Klux Klan Act is the only characteristic binding them as a class for the purpose of a class action: their action may suffice for the definition of "class" under this rule, but it is illogical and unreasonable to designate animus against the group as class-based. Dotson v. Mountain Mission Sch., Inc., 590 F. Supp. 583 (W.D. Va. 1984), aff'd, 789 F.2d 915 (4th Cir.), cert. denied, 479 U.S. 886, 107 S. Ct. 279, 93 L. Ed. 2d 255 (1986).

Private antitrust actions are accorded no presumption on the issue of predominance of common questions over individual questions in class actions. Brown v. Cameron-Brown Co., 92 F.R.D. 32 (E.D. Va.), rev'd and remanded on other grounds, 652 F.2d 375 (4th Cir. 1981).

A plaintiff in a private antitrust action must prove three elements to succeed: (1) violation of the antitrust laws; (2) direct injury to the plaintiff from each violation; and (3) damages sustained by the plaintiff. Moreover, in the fourth circuit, courts construe the gravamen of such an action to be the injury to the plaintiff as an individual, rather than issues relating to an overall conspiracy. Brown v. Cameron-Brown Co., 92 F.R.D. 32 (E.D. Va.), rev'd and remanded on other grounds, 652 F.2d 375 (4th Cir. 1981).

Since plaintiffs who were operators of small food markets and the members of the proposed classes were all allegedly harmed by the same conduct of defendants, i.e., by the illegal conspiracy to fix prices, the variance between the size of the class members' operations and the prices they paid, therefore, did not serve as a bar to class certification. Meredith v. Mid-Atlantic Coca Cola Bottling Co., 129 F.R.D. 130 (E.D. Va. 1989).

Suit by college teachers alleging sex discrimination by several schools held not class action. — See Taliaferro v. State Council of Higher Educ., 372 F. Supp. 1378 (E.D. Va. 1974).

Action brought by college students claiming right to vote held not class action. — See Manard v. Miller, 53 F.R.D. 610 (E.D. Va. 1971), aff'd, 405 U.S. 982, 92 S. Ct. 1253, 31 L. Ed. 2d 449 (1972).

Suit alleging unlawful deprivation of custody of children. — See McGhee v. Moyer, 60 F.R.D. 578 (W.D. Va. 1973).

Action brought by pregnant female employees against employer. — See Gilbert v. GE Co., 59 F.R.D. 267 (E.D. Va. 1973).

Usury. — The personal nature of a usury claim does not act to prohibit the aggregation of those claims in a class action suit. Cosgrove v. First & Merchants Nat'l Bank, 68 F.R.D. 555 (E.D. Va. 1975).

In a class action alleging violations of the usury statutes relating to management of Bank Americard accounts, the potential assertion of counterclaims against a few delinquent account holders should not be allowed to defeat an otherwise valid class action on behalf of numerous other class members. Cosgrove v. First & Merchants Nat'l Bank, 68 F.R.D. 555 (E.D. Va. 1975).

Litigation on behalf of a national class over a nationally employed policy affecting all class members in a similar fashion is well suited to class action adjudication. Burwell v. Eastern Airlines, 68 F.R.D. 495 (E.D. Va. 1975).

Magistrates who had power to issue warrants. — Motion for certification of a defendant class of all Virginia magistrates who currently had, or in the future would have, the power to issue search warrants was denied because the incidents of which plaintiff complained were based on unique responses to a specific crime and to the facts known about the circumstances of that crime, therefore, no class existed to represent. Simmons v. Baker, 842 F. Supp. 883 (E.D. Va. 1994), aff'd in part and rev'd in part sub nom., Simmons v. Poe, 47 F.3d 1370 (4th Cir. 1995).

Rule 23.1. Derivative Actions.

(a) *Prerequisites.* — This rule applies when one or more shareholders or members of a corporation or an unincorporated association bring a derivative action to enforce a right that the corporation or association may properly assert but has failed to enforce. The derivative action may not be maintained if it appears that the plaintiff does not fairly and adequately represent the interests of shareholders or members who are similarly situated in enforcing the right of the corporation or association.

(b) *Pleading Requirements.* — The complaint must be verified and must:

(1) allege that the plaintiff was a shareholder or member at the time of the transaction complained of, or that the plaintiff's share or membership later devolved on it by operation of law;

(2) allege that the action is not a collusive one to confer jurisdiction that the court would otherwise lack; and

(3) state with particularity:

(A) any effort by the plaintiff to obtain the desired action from the directors or comparable authority and, if necessary, from the shareholders or members; and

(B) the reasons for not obtaining the action or not making the effort.

(c) *Settlement, Dismissal, and Compromise.* — A derivative action may be settled, voluntarily dismissed, or compromised only with the court's approval. Notice of a proposed settlement, voluntary dismissal, or compromise must be given to shareholders or members in the manner that the court orders. (Added by order adopted February 28, 1966, effective July 1, 1966, amended by order adopted March 2, 1987, effective August 1, 1987, and by order adopted April 30, 2007, effective December 1, 2007.)

Comment. — The language of Rule 23.1 has been amended as part of the general restyling of the Civil Rules to make them more easily understood and to make style and terminology consistent throughout the rules. These changes are intended to be stylistic only.

Law Review. — For article, "Annual Survey of Antitrust Developments — Class Actions, Mergers and Market Definition: A New Trend Toward Neutrality," see 32 Wash. & Lee L. Rev. 299 (1975). For article, "Corporate Governance in the Courtroom: An Empirical Analysis," see 51 Wm. and Mary L. Rev. 1749 (2010).

CASE NOTES

Demand requirements of federal and Virginia law do not differ. — For all practical purposes, there is no difference between the demand requirements of federal and Virginia law. Smith v. Gordon, 668 F. Supp. 520 (E.D. Va. 1987).

A preliminary demand by a shareholder on directors is procedural. Meltzer v. Atlantic Research Corp., 330 F.2d 946 (4th Cir.), cert. denied, 379 U.S. 841, 85 S. Ct. 80, 13 L. Ed. 2d 47 (1964).

And, as such, is governed by federal law. Meltzer v. Atlantic Research Corp., 330 F.2d 946 (4th Cir.), cert. denied, 379 U.S. 841, 85 S. Ct. 80, 13 L. Ed. 2d 47 (1964).

Requirement that stockholders first address their grievance to corporate authority serves numerous practical purposes, such as forcing shareholders to exhaust their intercorporate remedies; permitting the corporation to pursue alternative remedies; permitting the termination of meritless actions designed to vex or harass the corporation; permitting the corporation, with superior knowledge and financial resources, to assume control of the suit; and avoiding unnecessary judicial involvement in the internal affairs of the organization. Reilly Mtg. Group, Inc. v. Mount Vernon Sav. & Loan Ass'n, 568 F. Supp. 1067 (E.D. Va. 1983).

Stockholder must show why directors incapable of performing duty. — Under the demand requirement, which assumes that directors and not stockholders ordinarily conduct the affairs of the company, the stockholder seeking to conduct litigation on the corporation's behalf without first affording the directors the opportunity to occupy their normal status must show that his case is exceptional. His initial burden is to demonstrate why the directors are incapable of doing their duty. Determination of whether plaintiff has carried its burden is within the sound discretion of the trial court. Clark Enters., Inc. v. Holywell Corp., 559 F. Supp. 1307 (E.D. Va. 1983).

Purpose of requiring allegations of efforts made to obtain action from directors. — This rule requires that the complaint in any shareholder's derivative action allege with particularity the efforts made to obtain the action the plaintiffs desire from the directors or comparable authority and the reasons for the failure. Such specificity is necessary to insure that the decision to sue for harm to the corporation initially belongs to the management of a corporation, and not to the shareholders. Womble v. Dixon, 585 F. Supp. 728 (E.D. Va. 1983), modified, 752 F.2d 80 (4th Cir. 1984).

"Hard-boiled" rule as to when demand is excused is also the majority rule, though it is applied with varying degrees of vigor in the different circuits. The rule holds that absent specific allegations of self-dealing or bias on the part of a majority of the board, mere director approval and acquiescence in the alleged misdeeds are insufficient to render demand futile. Reilly Mtg. Group, Inc. v. Mount Vernon Sav. & Loan Ass'n, 568 F. Supp. 1067 (E.D. Va. 1983).

Discretion of court as to determining when demand requirement met. — The question of when demand is required is particularly hard to answer. Because of the difficulty of such analyses, the decision as to whether a plaintiff's allegations of futility are sufficient to excuse demand depends on the particular facts of each case and lies within the discretion of the district court. Reilly Mtg. Group, Inc. v. Mount Vernon Sav. & Loan Ass'n, 568 F. Supp. 1067 (E.D. Va. 1983).

The question whether a plaintiff has shown that the demand requirement is excused is committed to the sound discretion of the trial court. Smith v. Gordon, 668 F. Supp. 520 (E.D. Va. 1987).

Demand requirement applies in diversity actions. — The demand requirement applies to stockholder's derivative actions brought in federal courts where jurisdiction is based on diversity of citizenship. Reilly Mtg. Group, Inc. v. Mount Vernon Sav. & Loan Ass'n, 568 F. Supp. 1067 (E.D. Va. 1983).

Willful or negligent breach of fiduciary duties usually excuses demand. — Demand is almost always excused in derivative suits alleging that the directors have engaged in willful or negligent breach of their fiduciary duties. Clark Enters., Inc. v. Holywell Corp., 559 F. Supp. 1307 (E.D. Va. 1983).

Demand is excused where board of directors is subject to control of alleged wrongdoers. Clark Enters., Inc. v. Holywell Corp., 559 F. Supp. 1307 (E.D. Va. 1983).

Significance of previous actual demand in determining if demand required. — In determining the preliminary issue whether demand is required it is irrelevant that there may have been an actual demand at some point prior to the filing of the complaint. The analysis whether demand is excused involves solely an examination of the complaint. Clark Enters., Inc. v. Holywell Corp., 559 F. Supp. 1307 (E.D. Va. 1983).

The presence of the actual demand in a case is not absolutely insignificant; to a certain extent, it aids the court in reaching its determination that requiring this plaintiff to complete this rule's demand requirements would be an exercise in futility. The actual demand made prior to the filing of the complaint allows the court to see what would happen next if demand were required. Clark Enters., Inc. v. Holywell Corp., 559 F. Supp. 1307 (E.D. Va. 1983).

Demand requirement held excused. — Where the allegations contained in plaintiff's complaint portray the controlling director as having engaged in a pattern of wrongdoing, including allegations that defendant caused the corporation to make improper loans or advances, interest-free and without security, for his personal investments, which investments belonged to the corporation; that he caused the corporation to fix for himself improper and excessive compensation; and that he usurped corporate opportunities, and improperly treated corporate assets as his own and where, in addition, defendant has historically proven obstructive to plaintiff's efforts to inspect the corporation's books and records, forcing plaintiff to resort to judicial compulsion to enforce plaintiff's right to examine the books, the facts alleged are sufficient to excuse demand. Clark Enters., Inc. v. Holywell Corp., 559 F. Supp. 1307 (E.D. Va. 1983).

Allegations held sufficient to excuse plaintiff's failure to make demand. — See Meltzer v. Atlantic Research Corp., 330 F.2d 946 (4th Cir.), cert. denied, 379 U.S. 841, 85 S. Ct. 80, 13 L. Ed. 2d 47 (1964).

Rule 23.2. Actions Relating to Unincorporated Associations.

This rule applies to an action brought by or against the members of an unincorporated association as a class by naming certain members as representative parties. The action may be maintained only if it appears that those parties will fairly and adequately protect the interests of the association and its members. In conducting the action, the court may issue any appropriate orders corresponding with those in Rule 23(d), and the procedure for settlement, voluntary dismissal, or compromise must correspond with the procedure in Rule 23(e). (Added by order adopted February 28, 1966, effective July 1, 1966; amended by order adopted April 30, 2007, effective December 1, 2007.)

Comment. — The language of Rule 23.2 has been amended as part of the general restyling of the Civil Rules to make them more easily understood and to make style and terminology consistent throughout the rules. These changes are intended to be stylistic only.

CASE NOTES

Purpose. — The purpose of this rule is a procedural device that provides a supplementary method for unincorporated associations to litigate in a federal court. Patrician Towers Owners, Inc. v. Fairchild, 513 F.2d 216 (4th Cir. 1975).

Right to sue under this rule has similarity to class derivative suit. — The right of the representative plaintiffs to sue for the benefit of the unincorporated association under this rule has considerable similarity to a class derivative suit. A derivative action would ordinarily not be maintainable if the real party's interest, the corporate principal, for instance, had brought suit in its own name. Why should there be a different rule where, under largely similar circumstances, a class action under this rule is pressed on behalf of an unincorporated association if the very entity the class representative is seeking to represent (i.e. the unincorporated association) is itself a party, asserting in good faith the very same claim that the class representative is asserting? Patrician Towers Owners, Inc. v. Fairchild, 513 F.2d 216 (4th Cir. 1975).

Class representation is denied if the association is legally empowered to sue on its own behalf. Patrician Towers Owners, Inc. v. Fairchild, 513 F.2d 216 (4th Cir. 1975).

Although an action by or against representatives of the membership of an unincorporated association has often been viewed as a class action, the real or main purpose of this characterization has been to give "entity treatment" to the association, when, for formal reasons, it could not sue or be sued as a jural person under Rule 17(b), which restricts the capacity of unincorporated associations, when suing or being sued, to the capacity given them by the law of the state where the district court is held. Patrician Towers Owners, Inc. v. Fairchild, 513 F.2d 216 (4th Cir. 1975).

When the law of the state in a particular case does not provide an unincorporated association with capacity as a jural person to sue or to be sued, then and only then does the mechanism of this rule come into operation and is available as a way of overcoming this lack of capacity by suing the individual representative of the unincorporated association. Patrician Towers Owners, Inc. v. Fairchild, 513 F.2d 216 (4th Cir. 1975).

Rule 24. Intervention.

(a) *Intervention of Right.* — On timely motion, the court must permit anyone to intervene who:

(1) is given an unconditional right to intervene by a federal statute; or

(2) claims an interest relating to the property or transaction that is the subject of the action, and is so situated that disposing of the action may as a practical matter impair or impede the movant's ability to protect its interest, unless existing parties adequately represent that interest.

(b) *Permissive Intervention.* — (1) In General. On timely motion, the court may permit anyone to intervene who:

(A) is given a conditional right to intervene by a federal statute; or

(B) has a claim or defense that shares with the main action a common question of law or fact.

(2) By a Government Officer or Agency. On timely motion, the court may permit a federal or state governmental officer or agency to intervene if a party's claim or defense is based on:

(A) a statute or executive order administered by the officer or agency; or

(B) any regulation, order, requirement, or agreement issued or made under the statute or executive order.

(3) Delay or Prejudice. In exercising its discretion, the court must consider whether the intervention will unduly delay or prejudice the adjudication of the original parties' rights.

(c) *Notice and Pleading Required.* — A motion to intervene must be served on the parties as provided in Rule 5. The motion must state the grounds for intervention and be accompanied by a pleading that sets out the claim or defense for which intervention is sought. (Amended by order adopted December 27, 1946, effective March 19, 1948, by order adopted December 29, 1948, effective October 20, 1949, by order adopted January 21, 1963, effective July 1, 1963, by order adopted February 28, 1966, effective July 1, 1966, by order adopted March 2, 1987, effective August 1, 1987, by order adopted April 30, 1991, effective December 1, 1991, by order adopted April 12, 2006, effective December 1, 2006, and by order adopted April 30, 2007, effective December 1, 2007.)

Comment. — The language of Rule 24 has been amended as part of the general restyling of the Civil Rules to make them more easily understood and to make style and terminology consistent throughout the rules. These changes are intended to be stylistic only.

The former rule stated that the same procedure is followed when a United States statute gives a right to intervene. This statement is deleted because it added nothing.

CASE NOTES

Only legal interest entitles person to intervention of right. — The only interest which will entitle a person to the right of intervention in a case is a legal interest as distinguished from interests of a general and indefinite character which do not give rise to definite legal rights. Jewell Ridge Coal Corp. v. Local No. 6167 UMW, 3 F.R.D. 251 (W.D. Va. 1943); Allen v. County Sch. Bd., 28 F.R.D. 358 (E.D. Va. 1961).

Even intervention of right may properly be made conditional by the exigencies of the particular case. Newport News Shipbuilding & Drydock Co. v. Peninsula Shipbuilders' Ass'n, 646 F.2d 117 (4th Cir. 1981).

This rule need not be strictly applied where, as in this case, there were non-prejudicial technical defects in the motion to intervene. Marshall v. Meadows, 921 F. Supp. 1490 (E.D. Va. 1996), aff'd, 105 F.3d 904 (4th Cir. 1997).

In order to be allowed to intervene as of right the intervenor must show first, an interest sufficient to merit intervention; second, that without intervention, its interest may be impaired; and third, that the present litigants do not adequately represent its interest. All three tests must be met if the intervenor is to prevail. Virginia v. Westinghouse Elec. Corp., 542 F.2d 214 (4th Cir. 1976).

To intervene as a matter of right under subdivision (a)(2) of this rule, the moving party must show that (1) it has an interest in the subject matter of the action, (2) disposition of the action may practically impair or impede the movant's ability to protect that interest, and (3) that interest is not adequately represented by the existing parties. Newport News Shipbuilding & Drydock Co. v. Peninsula Shipbuilders' Ass'n, 646 F.2d 117 (4th Cir. 1981).

The impairment prong of subdivision (a)(2) is met when the disposition of the case would, as a practical matter, impair an intervention applicant's ability to protect his interest in the subject matter of the litigation. NISH v. Cohen, 191 F.R.D. 94 (E.D. Va. 2000).

And government cannot intervene on ground of violation of court orders until violation found. — The United States has no right to intervene as a party plaintiff in a federal school desegregation case on the ground of violation or circumvention of federal court orders until the district court has first determined that its orders are in fact being violated or circumvented. Allen v. County Sch. Bd., 28 F.R.D. 358 (E.D. Va. 1961).

Permissive intervention may be denied where adjudication of the rights of original parties might be delayed or prejudiced. Jewell Ridge Coal Corp. v. Local No. 6167 UMW, 3 F.R.D. 251 (W.D. Va. 1943).

As the district court was of the opinion that the granting of intervention would unduly delay and prejudice the adjudication of the rights of the original parties, the motion of the United States to intervene as a party plaintiff and to add as parties defendant the Prince Edward School Foundation, the Commonwealth of Virginia, and comptroller of Virginia was denied. Allen v. County Sch. Bd., 28 F.R.D. 358 (E.D. Va. 1961).

Intervention after final judgment proper where party's interest not represented at first hearing. — See Fleming v. Citizens for Albemarle,

Inc., 577 F.2d 236 (4th Cir. 1978), cert. denied, 439 U.S. 1071, 99 S. Ct. 842, 59 L. Ed. 2d 37 (1979).

To the extent any more stringent standard for intervention following judgment than that applied before judgment is warranted, it must be based upon heightened prejudice to the parties and more substantial interference with the orderly process of the court in that context, and if neither of these results would occur, the mere fact that judgment already has been entered should not by itself require an application for intervention to be denied. Hill v. Western Elec. Co., 672 F.2d 381 (4th Cir.), cert. denied, 459 U.S. 981, 103 S. Ct. 318, 74 L. Ed. 2d 294 (1982).

Claim must be direct and not remote. — To be protectable, the putative intervenor's claim must bear a close relationship to the dispute between the existing litigants and therefore must be direct, rather than remote or contingent. Dairy Maid Dairy, Inc. v. United States, 147 F.R.D. 109 (E.D. Va. 1993).

Timeliness of motion to intervene in class action. — In a class action, the critical issue with respect to timeliness of motion for intervention is whether the proposed intervenor moved to intervene as soon as it became clear that the interests of the unnamed class members would no longer be protected by the named class representatives. Hill v. Western Elec. Co., 672 F.2d 381 (4th Cir.), cert. denied, 459 U.S. 981, 103 S. Ct. 318, 74 L. Ed. 2d 294 (1982).

Bifurcation of Title VII class action proceedings for hearings on liability and damages is now commonplace, and there is all the more justification for such a procedure when separable claims, subject if necessary to structuring by sub-classes, are involved. Hill v. Western Elec. Co., 672 F.2d 381 (4th Cir.), cert. denied, 459 U.S. 981, 103 S. Ct. 318, 74 L. Ed. 2d 294 (1982).

Intervention in subpoena enforcement action is permissive only, not mandatory, and determination of whether a party should be allowed to intervene requires a court to balance the opposing equities. Court can also consider such factors as whether material is privileged and the interest of the agency requesting the material. In re Oral Testimony of Witness, 1 F. Supp. 2d 587 (E.D. Va. 1998).

Intervention in condemnation proceeding. — See United States v. 1,830.62 Acres of Land, 51 F. Supp. 158 (W.D. Va. 1943) (decided prior to the adoption of Rule 71A).

The test on review of a motion to intervene is whether the district judge abused his discretion in denying the motion for intervention. Virginia v. Westinghouse Elec. Corp., 542 F.2d 214 (4th Cir. 1976).

A district court is entitled to the full range of reasonable discretion in determining whether the requirements for intervention are met. NISH v. Cohen, 191 F.R.D. 94 (E.D. Va. 2000).

Presumption that intervenor's interest adequately represented. — When the party seeking intervention has the same ultimate objective as a party to the suit, a presumption arises that its interests are adequately represented, against which the petitioner must demonstrate adversity of interest, collusion or nonfeasance. Virginia v. Westinghouse Elec. Corp., 542 F.2d 214 (4th Cir. 1976).

A presumption of adequacy arises when the applicant and an existing party have the same interest or ultimate objectives in the litigation. NISH v. Cohen, 191 F.R.D. 94 (E.D. Va. 2000).

Local environmental organizations were not allowed to intervene in a county's action to overturn an Environmental Protection Agency's (EPA) veto of an Army Corps of Engineer's decision to permit the creation of a creek reservoir where the EPA had continually asserted the organizations' position and there was no adversity of interest, collusion, or nonfeasance on the part of the EPA. James City County v. United States EPA, 131 F.R.D. 472 (E.D. Va. 1990).

Citizens advocacy organizations and government entities representing interests of blind business vendors were allowed to intervene as a matter of right in action challenging federal statute designed to ensure that the number of vending facilities operated by licensed blind individuals on federal and other property was maximized. NISH v. Cohen, 191 F.R.D. 94 (E.D. Va. 2000).

Where a party wishes to withdraw his motion to intervene while retaining the ability to file a separate action and toll the statute of limitations, the desired result may be achieved by the court granting the motion and then severing the complaint from the action intervened in. Braxton v. Virginia Folding Box Co., 72 F.R.D. 124 (E.D. Va. 1976).

Motion to intervene was regarded as commencement of action. — Employees' filing of a motion to intervene accompanied by proper pleadings in an employment discrimination suit against their employer was regarded as the commencement of an action for purposes of determining whether their separate action was barred by the running of the statute of limitations. An analogy is drawn between the motion to intervene and a separate timely filed action. Where an action is voluntarily dismissed without prejudice, the parties are left as if the action had never been brought. Consequently, the statute of limitations is not tolled by filing an action that is subsequently voluntarily dismissed. An analogy drawn between the motion to intervene and a separate action would compel the conclusion that the voluntary withdrawal of the motion to intervene likewise does not toll the running of the limitation period. Braxton v. Virginia Folding Box Co., 72 F.R.D. 124 (E.D. Va. 1976).

Intervention by trustee. — Trustee, who came into the suit only at the urging of the court and after his ability to maintain a separate and independent action has expired, could not have it both ways. If claim was distinct and independent such that it was not subject to the defenses asserted against the debtors, the trustee could not use the mechanism of intervention to overcome his failure to comply with the contractual limitation period. United States Fid. & Guar. Co. v. Houska, 184 Bankr. 494 (E.D. Va. 1995), modified, American Bankers Ins. Co. v. Maness, 101 F.3d 358 (4th Cir. 1996).

Intervention held demandable of right. — See Fleming v. Citizens for Albemarle, Inc., 577

F.2d 236 (4th Cir. 1978), cert. denied, 439 U.S. 1071, 99 S. Ct. 842, 59 L. Ed. 2d 37 (1979).

An intervenor is held to take the case as he finds it. Newport News Shipbuilding & Drydock Co. v. Peninsula Shipbuilders' Ass'n, 646 F.2d 117 (4th Cir. 1981).

Surety on bond had "interest" in compromise agreement between bankruptcy trustee and creditor. — See Merritt Com. Savs. & Loan, Inc. v. Guinee, 766 F.2d 850 (4th Cir. 1985).

Contest of agreement settling complaint as to dischargeability in bankruptcy. — Holder of a deed of trust on the debtor's property clearly had the right to intervene and contest an agreement settling a complaint to determine dischargeability of a debt in bankruptcy. United Va. Bank v. Cleveland, 53 Bankr. 814 (Bankr. E.D. Va. 1985).

Discovery. — Once intervention was allowed the court could not effectively deny all discovery. Columbus-America Discovery Group v. Atlantic Mut. Ins. Co., 974 F.2d 450 (4th Cir. 1992), cert. denied, 507 U.S. 1000, 113 S. Ct. 1625, 123 L. Ed. 2d 183 (1993).

Applied in Forest Hills Early Learning Ctr., Inc. v. Lukhard, 728 F.2d 230 (4th Cir. 1984); Lewis v. United States, 812 F. Supp. 629 (E.D. Va. 1993).

CIRCUIT COURT OPINIONS

Petition to intervene denied. — Contractor's petition to intervene in an LLC's action against joint tenants to enforce a mechanic's lien was denied because pursuant to 11 U.S.C.S. § 362, a bankruptcy stay extinguished the contractor's lien as to the entire ownership until the bankruptcy stay was lifted, and the filing of the lien memorandum did not sever the joint tenancy; although the second joint tenant did not file for bankruptcy, he remained an integral part of the lien, as a joint tenant and co-signer, and because the bankruptcy filing did not sever the joint tenancy, a judgment against the second joint tenant during the period of the bankruptcy stay would have amounted to a judgment against the first joint tenant. Heritage Contr., L.L.C. v. Vasquez, 81 Va. Cir. 161, 2010 Va. Cir. LEXIS 116 (Fairfax Sept. 7, 2010).

Rule 25. Substitution of Parties.

(a) *Death.* — (1) Substitution if the Claim Is Not Extinguished. If a party dies and the claim is not extinguished, the court may order substitution of the proper party. A motion for substitution may be made by any party or by the decedent's successor or representative. If the motion is not made within 90 days after service of a statement noting the death, the action by or against the decedent must be dismissed.

(2) Continuation Among the Remaining Parties. After a party's death, if the right sought to be enforced survives only to or against the remaining parties, the action does not abate, but proceeds in favor of or against the remaining parties. The death should be noted on the record.

(3) Service. A motion to substitute, together with a notice of hearing, must be served on the parties as provided in Rule 5 and on nonparties as provided in Rule 4. A statement noting death must be served in the same manner. Service may be made in any judicial district.

(b) *Incompetency.* — If a party becomes incompetent, the court may, on motion, permit the action to be continued by or against the party's representative. The motion must be served as provided in Rule 25(a)(3).

(c) *Transfer of Interest.* — If an interest is transferred, the action may be continued by or against the original party unless the court, on motion, orders the transferee to be substituted in the action or joined with the original party. The motion must be served as provided in Rule 25(a)(3).

(d) *Public Officers; Death or Separation from Office.* — An action does not abate when a public officer who is a party in an official capacity dies, resigns, or otherwise ceases to hold office while the action is pending. The officer's successor is automatically substituted as a party. Later proceedings should be in the substituted party's name, but any misnomer not affecting the parties' substantial rights must be disregarded. The court may order substitution at any time, but the absence of such an order does not affect the substitution. (Amended by order adopted December 29, 1948, effective October 20, 1949, by order adopted April 17, 1961, effective July 19, 1961, by order adopted January 21, 1963, effective July 1, 1963, by order adopted March 2, 1987, effective August 1, 1987, and by order adopted April 30, 2007, effective December 1, 2007.)

Comment. — The language of Rule 25 has been amended as part of the general restyling of the Civil Rules to make them more easily understood and to make style and terminology consistent throughout the rules. These changes are intended to be stylistic only.

Former Rule 25(d)(2) is transferred to become Rule 17(d) because it deals with designation of a public officer, not substitution.

CASE NOTES

"Successors or representatives of the deceased party" contemplated by this rule are those empowered to assert any legal claims of the decedent not extinguished by death, or to defend the estate against others' claims. Personal service of the suggestion of death alerts the nonparty to the consequences of death for a pending suit, signaling the need for action to preserve the claim if so desired. Fariss v. Lynchburg Foundry, 769 F.2d 958 (4th Cir. 1985).

Nonparties for whom subdivision (a)(1) of this rule and Rule 4(d)(1) mandate personal service are evidently the "successors or representatives of the deceased party." This conclusion follows both from the language of subdivision (a)(1) of this rule, which refers to no other nonparties, and from the rule's underlying policies. Subdivision (a)(1) directs that both parties and appropriate nonparties be served with the suggestion of death to commence the 90-day substitution period, for the rule seeks "to assure the parties to the action and other concerned persons of notice of the death so that they may take appropriate action to make substitution for the deceased party." Fariss v. Lynchburg Foundry, 769 F.2d 958 (4th Cir. 1985).

Notice to nonparty representative of deceased. — Absent personal service, there is no reason to presume that the successor or representative, who must decide whether to pursue the claim, is aware of the substitution requirement. The administratrix may well be represented by different counsel. Either a motion to substitute, or the suggestion of death should have been served on the nonparty representative of the deceased, not merely on the deceased's attorney, to satisfy subdivision (a)(1). Fariss v. Lynchburg Foundry, 769 F.2d 958 (4th Cir. 1985).

Service on decedent's attorney alone is inadequate, since the attorney's agency to act ceases with the death of his client, and he has no power to continue or terminate an action on his own initiative. Because the attorney is neither a party, nor a legal successor or representative of the estate, he has no authority to move for substitution under subdivision (a)(1), as the courts have repeatedly recognized. Fariss v. Lynchburg Foundry, 769 F.2d 958 (4th Cir. 1985).

Service on decedent's counsel alone was inadequate to commence running of the 90-day substitution period allowed by subdivision (a)(1). Where a personal representative has been appointed following the death of a party, the suggestion of death must be personally served on that representative. Fariss v. Lynchburg Foundry, 769 F.2d 958 (4th Cir. 1985).

Substitution proper although not timely where no prejudice suffered. — Where party had not originally opposed the motion for an enlargement of time and had suffered no prejudice from a failure to timely substitute parties but had continued representing its interests through court appearances and responses to pleadings and motions, the district court correctly ruled that the substitution was proper. Capital Investors Co. v. Executors of Estate of Morrison, 800 F.2d 424 (4th Cir. 1986).

Applied in United States v. Swink, 41 F. Supp. 98 (E.D. Va. 1941); Seven Oaks, Inc. v. Federal Hous. Admin., 171 F.2d 947 (4th Cir. 1948); Dyson v. Lavery, 417 F. Supp. 103 (E.D. Va. 1976); United States v. Gregory, 582 F. Supp. 1319 (W.D. Va. 1984); City of Va. Beach v. Roanoke River Basin Ass'n, 776 F.2d 484 (4th Cir. 1985); CMF Va. Land v. Brinson, 806 F. Supp. 90 (E.D. Va. 1992); Wills v. Heritage Bank, 226 Bankr. 369 (Bankr. E.D. Va. 1998).

TITLE V. DISCLOSURES AND DISCOVERY.

Rule 26. Duty to Disclose; General Provisions Governing Discovery.

(a) *Required Disclosures.* (1) Initial Disclosure. (A) In General. Except as exempted by Rule 26(a)(1)(B) or as otherwise stipulated or ordered by the court, a party must, without awaiting a discovery request, provide to the other parties:

(i) the name and, if known, the address and telephone number of each individual likely to have discoverable information — along with the subjects of that information — that the disclosing party may use to support its claims or defenses, unless the use would be solely for impeachment;

(ii) a copy — or a description by category and location — of all documents, electronically stored information, and tangible things that the disclosing party has in its possession, custody, or control and may use to support its claims or defenses, unless the use would be solely for impeachment;

(iii) a computation of each category of damages claimed by the disclosing party — who must also make available for inspection and copying as under Rule 34 the documents or other evidentiary material, unless privileged or protected from disclosure, on which each computation is based, including materials bearing on the nature and extent of injuries suffered; and

(iv) for inspection and copying as under Rule 34, any insurance agreement under which an insurance business may be liable to satisfy all or part of a possible judgment in the action or to indemnify or reimburse for payments made to satisfy the judgment.

(B) Proceedings Exempt from Initial Disclosure. The following proceedings are exempt from initial disclosure:

(i) an action for review on an administrative record;

(ii) a forfeiture action in rem arising from a federal statute;

(iii) a petition for habeas corpus or any other proceeding to challenge a criminal conviction or sentence;

(iv) an action brought without an attorney by a person in the custody of the United States, a state, or a state subdivision;

(v) an action to enforce or quash an administrative summons or subpoena;

(vi) an action by the United States to recover benefit payments;

(vii) an action by the United States to collect on a student loan guaranteed by the United States;

(viii) a proceeding ancillary to a proceeding in another court; and

(ix) an action to enforce an arbitration award.

(C) Time for Initial Disclosures — In General. A party must make the initial disclosures at or within 14 days after the parties' Rule 26(f) conference unless a different time is set by stipulation or court order, or unless a party objects during the conference that initial disclosures are not appropriate in this action and states the objection in the proposed discovery plan. In ruling on the objection, the court must determine what disclosures, if any, are to be made and must set the time for disclosure.

(D) Time for Initial Disclosures — For Parties Served or Joined Later. A party that is first served or otherwise joined after the Rule 26(f) conference must make the initial disclosures within 30 days after being served or joined, unless a different time is set by stipulation or court order.

(E) Basis for Initial Disclosure; Unacceptable Excuses. A party must make its initial disclosures based on the information then reasonably available to it. A party is not excused from making its disclosures because it has not fully investigated the case or because it challenges the sufficiency of another party's disclosures or because another party has not made its disclosures.

(2) Disclosure of Expert Testimony. (A) In General. In addition to the disclosures required by Rule 26(a)(1), a party must disclose to the other parties the identity of any witness it may use at trial to present evidence under Federal Rule of Evidence 702, 703, or 705.

(B) Witnesses Who Must Provide a Written Report. Unless otherwise stipulated or ordered by the court, this disclosure must be accompanied by a written report — prepared and signed by the witness — if the witness is one retained or specially employed to provide expert testimony in the case or one whose duties as the party's employee regularly involve giving expert testimony. The report must contain:

(i) a complete statement of all opinions the witness will express and the basis and reasons for them;

(ii) the facts or data considered by the witness in forming them;

(iii) any exhibits that will be used to summarize or support them;

(iv) the witness's qualifications, including a list of all publications authored in the previous 10 years;

(v) a list of all other cases in which, during the previous 4 years, the witness testified as an expert at trial or by deposition; and

(vi) a statement of the compensation to be paid for the study and testimony in the case.

(C) Witnesses Who Do Not Provide a Written Report. Unless otherwise stipulated or ordered by the court, if the witness is not required to provide a written report, this disclosure must state:

(i) the subject matter on which the witness is expected to present evidence under Federal Rule of Evidence 702, 703, or 705; and

(ii) a summary of the facts and opinions to which the witness is expected to testify.

(D) Time to Disclose Expert Testimony. A party must make these disclosures at the times and in the sequence that the court orders. Absent a stipulation or a court order, the disclosures must be made:

(i) at least 90 days before the date set for trial or for the case to be ready for trial; or

(ii) if the evidence is intended solely to contradict or rebut evidence on the same subject matter identified by another party under Rule 26(a)(2)(B) or (C), within 30 days after the other party's disclosure.

(E) Supplementing the Disclosure. The parties must supplement these disclosures when required under Rule 26(e).

(3) Pretrial Disclosures. (A) In General. In addition to the disclosures required by Rule 26(a)(1) and (2), a party must provide to the other parties and promptly file the

following information about the evidence that it may present at trial other than solely for impeachment:

(i) the name and, if not previously provided, the address and telephone number of each witness — separately identifying those the party expects to present and those it may call if the need arises;

(ii) the designation of those witnesses whose testimony the party expects to present by deposition and, if not taken stenographically, a transcript of the pertinent parts of the deposition; and

(iii) an identification of each document or other exhibit, including summaries of other evidence — separately identifying those items the party expects to offer and those it may offer if the need arises.

(B) Time for Pretrial Disclosures; Objections. Unless the court orders otherwise, these disclosures must be made at least 30 days before trial. Within 14 days after they are made, unless the court sets a different time, a party may serve and promptly file a list of the following objections: any objections to the use under Rule 32(a) of a deposition designated by another party under Rule 26(a)(3)(A)(ii); and any objection, together with the grounds for it, that may be made to the admissibility of materials identified under Rule 26(a)(3)(A)(iii). An objection not so made — except for one under Federal Rule of Evidence 402 or 403 — is waived unless excused by the court for good cause.

(4) Form of Disclosures. Unless the court orders otherwise, all disclosures under Rule 26(a) must be in writing, signed, and served.

(b) *Discovery Scope and Limits.* — (1) Scope in General. Unless otherwise limited by court order, the scope of discovery is as follows: Parties may obtain discovery regarding any nonprivileged matter that is relevant to any party's claim or defense — including the existence, description, nature, custody, condition, and location of any documents or other tangible things and the identity and location of persons who know of any discoverable matter. For good cause, the court may order discovery of any matter relevant to the subject matter involved in the action. Relevant information need not be admissible at the trial if the discovery appears reasonably calculated to lead to the discovery of admissible evidence. All discovery is subject to the limitations imposed by Rule 26(b)(2)(C).

(2) Limitations on Frequency and Extent. (A) When Permitted. By order, the court may alter the limits in these rules on the number of depositions and interrogatories or on the length of depositions under Rule 30. By order or local rule, the court may also limit the number of requests under Rule 36.

(B) Specific Limitations on Electronically Stored Information. A party need not provide discovery of electronically stored information from sources that the party identifies as not reasonably accessible because of undue burden or cost. On motion to compel discovery or for a protective order, the party from whom discovery is sought must show that the information is not reasonably accessible because of undue burden or cost. If that showing is made, the court may nonetheless order discovery from such sources if the requesting party shows good cause, considering the limitations of Rule 26(b)(2)(C). The court may specify conditions for the discovery.

(C) When Required. On motion or on its own, the court must limit the frequency or extent of discovery otherwise allowed by these rules or by local rule if it determines that:

(i) the discovery sought is unreasonably cumulative or duplicative, or can be obtained from some other source that is more convenient, less burdensome, or less expensive;

(ii) the party seeking discovery has had ample opportunity to obtain the information by discovery in the action; or

(iii) the burden or expense of the proposed discovery outweighs its likely benefit, considering the needs of the case, the amount in controversy, the parties' resources, the importance of the issues at stake in the action, and the importance of the discovery in resolving the issues.

(3) Trial Preparations: Materials. (A) Documents and Tangible Things. Ordinarily, a party may not discover documents and tangible things that are prepared in anticipation of litigation or for trial by or for another party or its representative (including the other party's attorney, consultant, surety, indemnitor, insurer, or agent). But, subject to Rule 26(b)(4), those materials may be discovered if:

(i) they are otherwise discoverable under Rule 26(b)(1); and

(ii) the party shows that it has substantial need for the materials to prepare its case and cannot, without undue hardship, obtain their substantial equivalent by other means.

(B) Protection Against Disclosure. If the court orders discovery of those materials, it must protect against disclosure of the mental impressions, conclusions, opinions, or legal theories of a party's attorney or other representative concerning the litigation.

(C) Previous Statement. Any party or other person may, on request and without the required showing, obtain the person's own previous statement about the action or its subject matter. If the request is refused, the person may move for a court order, and Rule 37(a)(5) applies to the award of expenses. A previous statement is either:

(i) a written statement that the person has signed or otherwise adopted or approved; or

(ii) a contemporaneous stenographic, mechanical, electrical, or other recording — or a transcription of it — that recites substantially verbatim the person's oral statement.

(4) Trial Preparation: Experts. (A) Deposition of an Expert Who May Testify. A party may depose any person who has been identified as an expert whose opinions may be presented at trial. If Rule 26(a)(2)(B) requires a report from the expert, the deposition may be conducted only after the report is provided.

(B) Trial-Preparation Protection for Draft Reports or Disclosures. Rules 26(b)(3)(A) and (B) protect drafts of any report or disclosure required under Rule 26(a)(2), regardless of the form in which the draft is recorded.

(C) Trial-Preparation Protection for Communications Between a Party's Attorney and Expert Witnesses. Rules 26(b)(3)(A) and (B) protect communications between the party's attorney and any witness required to provide a report under Rule 26(a)(2)(B), regardless of the form of the communications, except to the extent that the communications:

(i) relate to compensation for the expert's study or testimony;

(ii) identify facts or data that the party's attorney provided and that the expert considered in forming the opinions to be expressed; or

(iii) identify assumptions that the party's attorney provided and that the expert relied on in forming the opinions to be expressed.

(D) Expert Employed Only for Trial Preparation. Ordinarily, a party may not, by interrogatories or deposition, discover facts known or opinions held by an expert who has been retained or specially employed by another party in anticipation of litigation or to prepare for trial and who is not expected to be called as a witness at trial. But a party may do so only:

(i) as provided in Rule 35(b); or

(ii) on showing exceptional circumstances under which it is impracticable for the party to obtain facts or opinions on the same subject by other means.

(E) Payment. Unless manifest injustice would result, the court must require that the party seeking discovery:

(i) pay the expert a reasonable fee for time spent in responding to discovery under Rule 26(b)(4)(A) or (D); and

(ii) for discovery under (D), also pay the other party a fair portion of the fees and expenses it reasonably incurred in obtaining the expert's facts and opinions.

(5) Claiming Privilege or Protecting Trial-Preparation Materials. (A) Information Withheld. When a party withholds information otherwise discoverable by claiming that the information is privileged or subject to protection as trial-preparation material, the party must:

(i) expressly make the claim; and

(ii) describe the nature of the documents, communications, or tangible things not produced or disclosed — and do so in a manner that, without revealing information itself privileged or protected, will enable other parties to assess the claim.

(B) Information Produced. If information produced in discovery is subject to a claim of privilege or of protection as trial preparation material, the party making the claim may notify any party that received the information of the claim and the basis for it. After being notified, a party must promptly return, sequester, or destroy the specified information and any copies it has; must not use or disclose the information until the claim is resolved; must take reasonable steps to retrieve the information if the party disclosed it before being notified; and may promptly present the information to the court under seal for a determination of the claim. The producing party must preserve the information until the claim is resolved.

(c) *Protective Orders.* — (1) In General. A party or any person from whom discovery is sought may move for a protective order in the court where the action is pending — or as an alternative on matters relating to a deposition, in the court for the district where the deposition will be taken. The motion must include a certification that the movant has in good faith conferred or attempted to confer with other affected parties in an effort to resolve the dispute without court action. The court may, for good cause, issue an order to protect a party or person from annoyance, embarrassment, oppression, or undue burden or expense, including one or more of the following:

(A) forbidding the disclosure or discovery;

(B) specifying terms, including time and place, for the disclosure or discovery;

(C) prescribing a discovery method other than the one selected by the party seeking discovery;

(D) forbidding inquiry into certain matters, or limiting the scope of disclosure or discovery to certain matters;

(E) designating the persons who may be present while the discovery is conducted;

(F) requiring that a deposition be sealed and opened only on court order;

(G) requiring that a trade secret or other confidential research, development, or commercial information not be revealed or be revealed only in a specified way; and

(H) requiring that the parties simultaneously file specified documents or information in sealed envelopes, to be opened as the court directs.

(2) Ordering Discovery. If a motion for a protective order is wholly or partly denied, the court may, on just terms, order that any party or person provide or permit discovery.

(3) Awarding Expenses. Rule 37(a)(5) applies to the award of expenses.

(d) *Timing and Sequence of Discovery.* — (1) Timing. A party may not seek discovery from any source before the parties have conferred as required by Rule 26(f), except in a proceeding exempted from initial disclosure under Rule 26(a)(1)(B), or when authorized by these rules, by stipulation, or by court order.

(2) Sequence. Unless, on motion, the court orders otherwise for the parties' and witnesses' convenience and in the interests of justice:

(A) methods of discovery may be used in any sequence; and

(B) discovery by one party does not require any other party to delay its discovery.

(e) *Supplementing Disclosures and Responses.* — (1) In General. A party who has made a disclosure under Rule 26(a) — or who has responded to an interrogatory, request for production, or request for admission — must supplement or correct its disclosure or response:

(A) in a timely manner if the party learns that in some material respect the disclosure or response is incomplete or incorrect, and if the additional or corrective information has not otherwise been made known to the other parties during the discovery process or in writing; or

(B) as ordered by the court.

(2) Expert Witness. For an expert whose report must be disclosed under Rule 26(a)(2)(B), the party's duty to supplement extends both to information included in the report and to information given during the expert's deposition. Any additions or changes to this information must be disclosed by the time the party's pretrial disclosures under Rule 26(a)(3) are due.

(f) *Conference of the Parties; Planning for Discovery.* — (1) Conference Timing. Except in a proceeding exempted from initial disclosure under Rule 26(a)(1)(B) or when the court orders otherwise, the parties must confer as soon as practicable — and in any event at least 21 days before a scheduling conference is to be held or a scheduling order is due under Rule 16(b).

(2) Conference Content; Parties' Responsibilities. In conferring, the parties must consider the nature and basis of their claims and defenses and the possibilities for promptly settling or resolving the case; make or arrange for the disclosures required by Rule 26(a)(1); discuss any issues about preserving discoverable information; and develop a proposed discovery plan. The attorneys of record and all unrepresented parties that have appeared in the case are jointly responsible for arranging the conference, for attempting in good faith to agree on the proposed discovery plan, and for submitting to the court within 14 days after the conference a written report outlining the plan. The court may order the parties or attorneys to attend the conference in person.

(3) Discovery Plan. A discovery plan must state the parties' views and proposals on:

(A) what changes should be made in the timing, form, or requirement for disclosures under Rule 26(a), including a statement of when initial disclosures were made or will be made;

(B) the subjects on which discovery may be needed, when discovery should be completed, and whether discovery should be conducted in phases or be limited to or focused on particular issues;

(C) any issues about disclosure or discovery of electronically stored information, including the form or forms in which it should be produced;

(D) any issues about claims of privilege or of protection as trial-preparation materials, including — if the parties agree on a procedure to assert these claims after production — whether to ask the court to include their agreement in an order;

(E) what changes should be made in the limitations on discovery imposed under these rules or by local rule, and what other limitations should be imposed; and

(F) any other orders that the court should issue under Rule 26(c) or under Rule 16(b) and (c).

(4) Expedited Schedule. If necessary to comply with its expedited schedule for Rule 16(b) conferences, a court may by local rule:

(A) require the parties' conference to occur less than 21 days before the scheduling conference is held or a scheduling order is due under Rule 16(b); and

(B) require the written report outlining the discovery plan to be filed less than 14 days after the parties' conference, or excuse the parties from submitting a written report and permit them to report orally on their discovery plan at the Rule 16(b) conference.

(g) *Signing Disclosures and Discovery Requests, Responses, and Objections.* — (1) Signature Required; Effect of Signature. Every disclosure under Rule 26(a)(1) or (a)(3) and every discovery request, response, or objection must be signed by at least one attorney of record in the attorney's own name — or by the party personally, if unrepresented — and must state the signer's address, e-mail address, and telephone number. By signing, an attorney or party certifies that to the best of the person's knowledge, information, and belief formed after a reasonable inquiry:

(A) with respect to a disclosure, it is complete and correct as of the time it is made; and

(B) with respect to a discovery request, response, or objection, it is:

(i) consistent with these rules and warranted by existing law or by a nonfrivolous argument for extending, modifying, or reversing existing law, or for establishing new law;

(ii) not interposed for any improper purpose, such as to harass, cause unnecessary delay, or needlessly increase the cost of litigation; and

(iii) neither unreasonable nor unduly burdensome or expensive, considering the needs of the case, prior discovery in the case, the amount in controversy, and the importance of the issues at stake in the action.

(2) Failure to Sign. Other parties have no duty to act on an unsigned disclosure, request, response, or objection until it is signed, and the court must strike it unless a signature is promptly supplied after the omission is called to the attorney's or party's attention.

(3) Sanction for Improper Certification. If a certification violates this rule without substantial justification, the court, on motion or on its own, must impose an appropriate sanction on the signer, the party on whose behalf the signer was acting, or both. The sanction may include an order to pay the reasonable expenses, including attorney's fees, caused by the violation. (Amended by order adopted December 27, 1946, effective March 19, 1948, by order adopted January 21, 1963, effective July 1, 1963, by order adopted February 28, 1966, effective July 1, 1966, by order adopted March 30, 1970, effective July 1, 1970, by order adopted April 29, 1980, effective August 1, 1980, by order adopted April 28, 1983, effective August 1, 1983, by order adopted March 2, 1987, effective August 1, 1987, by order adopted April 22, 1993, effective December 1, 1993, by order adopted April 17, 2000, effective December 1, 2000, by order adopted April 12, 2006, effective December 1, 2006, by order adopted April 30, 2007, effective December 1, 2007, and by order adopted April 28, 2010, effective December 1, 2010.)

Comment. — The language of Rule 26 has been amended as part of the general restyling of the Civil Rules to make them more easily understood and to make style and terminology consistent throughout

the rules. These changes are intended to be stylistic only.

Former Rule 26(a)(5) served as an index of the discovery methods provided by later rules. It was deleted as redundant. Deletion does not affect the right to pursue discovery in addition to disclosure.

Former Rule 26(b)(1) began with a general statement of the scope of discovery that appeared to function as a preface to each of the five numbered paragraphs that followed. This preface has been shifted to the text of paragraph (1) because it does not accurately reflect the limits embodied in paragraphs (2), (3), or (4), and because paragraph (5) does not address the scope of discovery.

The reference to discovery of "books" in former Rule 26(b)(1) was deleted to achieve consistent expression throughout the discovery rules. Books remain a proper subject of discovery.

Amended Rule 26(b)(3) states that a party may obtain a copy of the party's own previous statement "on request." Former Rule 26(b)(3) expressly made the request procedure available to a nonparty witness, but did not describe the procedure to be used by a party. This apparent gap is closed by adopting the request procedure, which ensures that a party need not invoke Rule 34 to obtain a copy of the party's own statement.

Rule 26(e) stated the duty to supplement or correct a disclosure or discovery response "to include information thereafter acquired." This apparent limit is not reflected in practice; parties recognize the duty to supplement or correct by providing information that was not originally provided although it was available at the time of the initial disclosure or response. These words are deleted to reflect the actual meaning of the present rule.

Former Rule 26(e) used different phrases to describe the time to supplement or correct a disclosure or discovery response. Disclosures were to be supplemented "at appropriate intervals." A prior discovery response must be "seasonably * * * amend[ed]." The fine distinction between these phrases has not been observed in practice. Amended Rule 26(e)(1)(A) uses the same phrase for disclosures and discovery responses. The party must supplement or correct "in a timely manner."

Former Rule 26(g)(1) did not call for striking an unsigned disclosure. The omission was an obvious drafting oversight. Amended Rule 26(g)(2) includes disclosures in the list of matters that the court must strike unless a signature is provided "promptly * * * after being called to the attorney's or party's attention."

Former Rule 26(b)(2)(A) referred to a "good faith" argument to extend existing law. Amended Rule 26(b)(1)(B)(i) changes this reference to a "nonfrivolous" argument to achieve consistency with Rule 11(b)(2).

Law Review. — For article, "Should Virginia Adopt the Federal Rules of Discovery," see 2 U. Rich. L. Notes 187 (1966). For article, "Oral Depositions: The Low Income Litigant and the Federal Rules," see 54 Va. L. Rev. 391 (1968). For comment, "Discovery of Expert Information under the Federal Rules," see 10 U. Rich. L. Rev. 706 (1976). For article, "Electronically Stored Evidence: Answers to Some Recurring Questions Concerning Pretrial Discovery and Trial Usage," see 41 Wash. & Lee L. Rev. 1335 (1984). For note, "The Attorney-Client Privilege," see 19 U. Rich. L. Rev. 559 (1985). For note, "Transnational Discovery: The Balancing Act of American Trial Courts and the New Approach to the Hague Convention," see 42 Wash. & Lee L. Rev. 1285 (1985). For article, "Rethinking Work Product," see 77 Va. L. Rev. 1515 (1991). For essay "Protective Orders in Products Liability Litigation: Striking the Proper Balance," see 48 Wash. & Lee L. Rev. 1503 (1991). For article, "Suggestions for Cir cuit Court Review of Local Procedures," see 52 Wash. & Lee L. Rev. 359 (1995). For a note, "Allocating Discovery Costs in the Computer Age: Deciding Who Should Bear the Costs of Discovery of Electronically Stored Data," see 57 Wash. & Lee L. Rev. 257 (2000). For note, "The Dubious Origins and Dangers of Clawback and Quick-Peek Agreements: An Argument Against Their Codification in the Federal Rules of Civil Procedure," see 47 Wm. & Mary L. Rev. 663 (2005).

CASE NOTES

I. In General.
II. Limitations on Discovery.
A. In General.
B. Trial Preparation.

I. IN GENERAL.

The discovery rules are required to be broadly construed. VEPCO v. Sun Shipbuilding & Dry Dock Co., 68 F.R.D. 397 (E.D. Va. 1975).

The federal rules contemplate the broadest discovery possible in the search for truth. Kline v. Martin, 345 F. Supp. 31 (E.D. Va. 1972).

One method of discovery cannot be arbitrarily demanded over another. — Although the federal rules do not prescribe an order of preference for discovery techniques, one method cannot arbitrarily be demanded over another simply because it is less burdensome to the moving party. Belcher v. Bassett Furn. Indus., Inc., 588 F.2d 904 (4th Cir. 1978).

The disclosure of insurance policies is not a significant invasion of privacy. Helms v. Richmond-Petersburg Tpk. Auth., 52 F.R.D. 530 (E.D. Va. 1971).

Deposition of party admissible as substantive evidence whether party testifies or not. — See Community Counselling Serv., Inc. v. Reilly, 317 F.2d 239 (4th Cir. 1963).

And the deposition of an officer or agent of a corporate party may be used for any purpose. Williams v. Howard Johnson's, Inc., 323 F.2d 102

(4th Cir. 1963), vacating and remanding 210 F. Supp. 295 (E.D. Va. 1962).

But plaintiff's deposition is not part of record if conditions for admission not met. — The deposition of the plaintiff cannot be regarded as part of the record where it is not admissible under this rule because the conditions of subdivision (d)(3) are not met. Williams v. Howard Johnson's, Inc., 323 F.2d 102 (4th Cir. 1963), vacating and remanding 210 F. Supp. 295 (E.D. Va. 1962).

Subdivision (c) of this rule gives the court much leeway in effecting a protective order. Metal Foil Prods. Mfg. Co. v. Reynolds Metals Co., 55 F.R.D. 491 (E.D. Va. 1970).

Under this rule the court has the power as well as the duty to fashion protective orders that enable the movant to secure the needed information at a minimum of public exposure to the subject of the subpoena, and to condition the discovery on reasonable payment for the services rendered. Gilbert v. Allied Chem. Corp., 411 F. Supp. 505 (E.D. Va. 1976).

In determining whether protective order allowing retained counsel access to confidential business data should nevertheless prohibit a competitor's in-house counsel from reviewing the same data, a court should consider: (1) The nature of the litigation and whether that litigation presents difficult or complex issues or claims; (2) whether alternative discovery measures would assist the in-house attorney seeking access to the confidential information in the development of the litigation and (3) whether the in-house attorney is involved in the employer-litigant's "competitive decisionmaking." Volvo Penta of the Ams., Inc. v. Brunswick Corp., 187 F.R.D. 240 (E.D. Va. 1999).

"Competitive decisionmaking" refers to the in-house counsel's role, if any, in making company decisions that affect contracts, marketing, employment, pricing, product design, or any or all of the client's decisions made in light of similar or corresponding information about a competitor. Volvo Penta of the Ams., Inc. v. Brunswick Corp., 187 F.R.D. 240 (E.D. Va. 1999).

Rule 34 contemplates extrajudicial discovery, but provides for determination of the issue when confronted with objections. The court may compel discovery under Rule 37(a) and provide protective provision under subdivision (c) of this rule. Belcher v. Bassett Furn. Indus., Inc., 588 F.2d 904 (4th Cir. 1978).

Pro se litigants are entitled to the use of discovery procedures in civil rights cases on the same terms as litigants represented by counsel. Castle v. Jallah, 142 F.R.D. 618 (E.D. Va. 1992).

Discovery not thwarted by possibility that marketing information might fall into hands of competitors. — Defendant corporation's argument that the divulging of internal marketing information might fall into the hands of substantial competitors, while stating an understandable position, could not be maintained in such a way as to thwart the purpose of the rules of discovery. Metal Foil Prods. Mfg. Co. v. Reynolds Metals Co., 55 F.R.D. 491 (E.D. Va. 1970).

Director conflict claim necessitates no knowledge of substance of advice given. — Irrespective of who carries the initial burden of proof and when during the course of litigation it might shift, the bottom line is that none of the elements of a director conflict claim or defense involves the need for knowing the substance of advice given the director before or during a transaction. WLR Foods, Inc. v. Tyson Foods, Inc., 155 F.R.D. 142 (W.D. Va. 1994), aff'd, 65 F.3d 1172 (4th Cir. 1995), cert. denied, 516 U.S. 1117, 116 S. Ct. 921, 133 L. Ed. 2d 850 (1996).

Section 13.1-690 is process-oriented in that it permits inquiry into the process by which the decision was made rather than the substance of the information processed by the director in making the business decision. WLR Foods, Inc. v. Tyson Foods, Inc., 155 F.R.D. 142 (W.D. Va. 1994), aff'd, 65 F.3d 1172 (4th Cir. 1995), cert. denied, 516 U.S. 1117, 116 S. Ct. 921, 133 L. Ed. 2d 850 (1996).

"Good faith" under § 13.1-690 presents the question of whether a process was engaged that would produce a defensible business decision. The procedural soundness of a business decision may be assessed by examining the qualifications of the persons with whom the director consulted, the general topics, not the substance, of the information sought or imparted and, even whether the advice was followed. WLR Foods, Inc. v. Tyson Foods, Inc., 155 F.R.D. 142 (W.D. Va. 1994), aff'd, 65 F.3d 1172 (4th Cir. 1995), cert. denied, 516 U.S. 1117, 116 S. Ct. 921, 133 L. Ed. 2d 850 (1996).

Limitation on right of access to evidence of experts. — While FRCP, Rule 45 no longer requires the issuance of deposition subpoenas as a basis for subpeona duces tecum, subdivision (b)(4) remains a limitation on the right of access by an opposing party to the evidence of experts who have been retained to testify in the case. Therefore, discovery of the facts and opinions of such experts cannot be obtained solely under Rule 45 where, a bare subpoena duces tecum has been issued for the experts' files. Marsh v. Jackson, 141 F.R.D. 431 (W.D. Va. 1992).

Necessity of expert written report. — If a treating physician forms an opinion of causation of an injury to a patient and the prognosis of the patient's condition during the treatment then such opinion may be expressed by the treating physician without the necessity of a report under subdivision (a)(2)(B). Defendants may still discover those opinions through interrogatories, requests for production of documents, and depositions of the treating physicians. Litman v. George Mason Univ., 5 F. Supp. 2d 366 (E.D. Va. 1998), aff'd, 186 F.3d 544 (4th Cir. 1999).

However, if a physician, even though he may be a treating physician, is specially retained or employed to render a medical opinion based on factors that were not learned in the course of the treatment of the patient, then such a doctor would be required to present an expert written report. Litman v. George Mason Univ., 5 F. Supp. 2d 366 (E.D. Va. 1998), aff'd, 186 F.3d 544 (4th Cir. 1999).

Controlling effect of this rule and FRCP, Rule 30. — None of the methods of discovery allowed under subdivision (b)(4) and FRCP, Rule 30 permit the use of bare FRCP, Rule 45 subpoenas duces tecum. Instead, they operate as a control on the potential runaway use of the subpoena duces tecum to compel the production of the evidence of experts retained by a party to testify at trial. They protect the interests of the expert and the party retaining him in the work that he has produced, while also providing access to the opposing party, though such access might not be as inexpensive as the opponent might desire. Marsh v. Jackson, 141 F.R.D. 431 (W.D. Va. 1992).

In order to be an expert one must be in a position to testify as an expert and not as a partisan. VEPCO v. Sun Shipbuilding & Dry Dock Co., 68 F.R.D. 397 (E.D. Va. 1975).

Expert witness testimony allowed. — District court did not err in its allowance of testimony of expert witness, although identity of the expert witness was not disclosed to other side until the day before trial, for the district court had required the expert witness to be available to other side for an interview prior to his testimony. Nehi Bottling Co. v. All-American Bottling Corp., 8 F.3d 157 (4th Cir. 1993).

For purposes of discovery, the "in house expert" is to be treated as an ordinary witness. — This view does not in any way prohibit any expert, in house or out, from giving an opinion in testimony at trial. It merely opens up that opinion, based on facts gained in the course of his employment, to discovery. VEPCO v. Sun Shipbuilding & Dry Dock Co., 68 F.R.D. 397 (E.D. Va. 1975).

Duty of disclosure in defective product case. — The cause of the product's deterioration stands on a different footing; it is not so much an objectively observable fact as it is a matter of expert opinion. Thus, a defendant may decline to admit the defectiveness of a product, even though some objective facts may suggest otherwise, provided there are reasonable grounds for the denial. Board of Dirs. v. Anden Group, 136 F.R.D. 100 (E.D. Va. 1991).

Common interest rule. — See Front Royal Ins. Co. v. Gold Players, Inc., 187 F.R.D. 252 (W.D. Va. 1999).

Punitive damages. — Where plaintiff sought punitive damages, information concerning defendant's gross sales of merchandise was both relevant to the subject matter of plaintiff's punitive damages claim and reasonable. Vanguard Military Equip. Corp. v. David B. Finestone Co., 6 F. Supp. 2d 488 (E.D. Va. 1997).

Arbitration. — A party confronted with a claim of arbitrability may pursue an order insulating it from discovery that could not be had if the underlying claim is properly the subject of arbitration. Absent a protective order, however, the party seeking arbitration does not lose its contractual right by prudently pursuing discovery in the face of a court-ordered deadline. Maxum Founds., Inc. v. Salus Corp., 779 F.2d 974 (4th Cir. 1985).

Applied in Byers Theater, Inc. v. Murphy, 1 F.R.D. 286 (W.D. Va. 1940); Ivory v. Nichols, 34 F.R.D. 128 (E.D. Va. 1963); Haney v. Woodward & Lothrop, Inc., 330 F.2d 940 (4th Cir. 1964); Adams v. Dan River Mills, Inc., 54 F.R.D. 220 (W.D. Va. 1972); Crockett v. Virginia Folding Box Co., 61 F.R.D. 312 (E.D. Va. 1974); Miners & Merchants Bank & Trust Co. v. Mullins, 55 Bankr. 618 (Bankr. W.D. Va. 1985); Furmanite Am., Inc. v. Durango Assocs., 662 F. Supp. 348 (E.D. Va. 1986); Darnell v. McMurray, 141 F.R.D. 433 (W.D. Va. 1992); Nellis v. Air Line Pilots Ass'n, 144 F.R.D. 68 (E.D. Va. 1992); Hall v. Sykes, 164 F.R.D. 46 (E.D. Va. 1995); Collins v. Mullins, 170 F.R.D. 132 (W.D. Va. 1996); Chaudhry v. Mobil Oil Corp., 186 F.3d 502 (4th Cir. 1999).

II. LIMITATIONS ON DISCOVERY.

A. In General.

Subdivision (b)(2) of this rule is not unconstitutional. Helms v. Richmond-Petersburg Tpk. Auth., 52 F.R.D. 530 (E.D. Va. 1971).

Scope of privilege as to income tax returns. — A "qualified" privilege disfavors the disclosure of income tax returns as a matter of general federal policy. This qualified privilege may be overcome, however, in "appropriate circumstances." In order to compel the disclosure of tax returns, the court must be shown that the information sought from the returns bears some relevance to the subject matter of the litigation; and that the information sought from the returns is not readily obtainable from other sources. Eastern Auto Distribs., Inc. v. Peugeot Motors of Am., Inc., 96 F.R.D. 147 (E.D. Va. 1982).

Rationale for adopting discovery limitations. — See Lykins v. Attorney Gen. of United States, 86 F.R.D. 318 (E.D. Va. 1980).

Good cause requirement upheld. — See Lykins v. Attorney Gen. of United States, 86 F.R.D. 318 (E.D. Va. 1980).

Where institutional security outweighed need for confidential Departmental Operating Procedures. — Where institutional security far outweighed any need plaintiff may have had for the prison's confidential Departmental Operating Procedures, the court denied plaintiff's motion to compel production. Castle v. Jallah, 142 F.R.D. 618 (E.D. Va. 1992).

The burden is on the person objecting to discovery to show that discovery should not be allowed. Castle v. Jallah, 142 F.R.D. 618 (E.D. Va. 1992).

The party opposing discovery bears the burden of showing that information or materials withheld from discovery are protected by an asserted privilege or the work-product doctrine. Front Royal Ins. Co. v. Gold Players, Inc., 187 F.R.D. 252 (W.D. Va. 1999).

Privilege against self-incrimination may be asserted and preserved in the course of discovery proceedings, but in specifics sufficient to provide the court with a record upon which to decide whether the privilege has been properly asserted as to each question. North River Ins. Co. v. Stefanou, 831 F.2d 484 (4th Cir. 1987), cert. denied, 486 U.S. 1007, 108 S. Ct. 1733, 100 L. Ed. 2d 196 (1988).

The "control group" test, with respect to whether an employee of a corporation is a "client" for purposes of the lawyer-client privilege when dealing with communications from such employee to the lawyer for the corporation, requires that the communicant be in a position to control or take a substantial part in a decision about any action to be taken upon the advice of the lawyer, or that the communicant be a member of a group having such authority. VEPCO v. Sun Shipbuilding & Dry Dock Co., 68 F.R.D. 397 (E.D. Va. 1975).

Insufficient basis for invocation of attorney-client privilege. — Claim of attorney-client privilege predicated principally, if not exclusively, on the fact that lawyers were involved in the communication is not a sufficient basis to support application of the privilege. Portsmouth Redevelopment & Hous. Auth. v. BMI Apts. Assocs., 155 F.R.D. 136 (E.D. Va. 1994).

Executive privilege. — The purpose of the common-law executive privilege is to protect the governmental decision-making process. This policy consideration determines the scope of the privilege: Application of the official privilege is founded on the belief that there are certain governmental processes related to legal and policy decisions which cannot be carried out effectively if they must be carried out under the public eye. Government officials would hesitate to offer their candid and conscientious opinions to superiors or coworkers if they knew that their opinions of the moment might be made a matter of public record at some future date. Thus, executive privilege shields from disclosure intra-governmental documents reflecting advisory opinions, recommendations and deliberations comprising part of a process by which governmental decisions and policies are formulated. Greene v. Thalhimer's Dep't Store, 93 F.R.D. 657 (E.D. Va. 1982).

There are two important limitations on the executive privilege doctrine. First, the privilege does not protect communications or reports made after completion of the deliberative process. Discovery of such material does not jeopardize the decision-making function. Second, the privilege does not prohibit disclosure of factual materials. An agency must produce "compiled factual material or purely factual material contained in deliberative memoranda and severable from its context." Greene v. Thalhimer's Dep't Store, 93 F.R.D. 657 (E.D. Va. 1982).

"Substantial need" requirement applies to subdivision (b)(4). — Subdivision (b)(4) of the rule is not explicit in setting forth the requirement that a "substantial need" be shown. However, it is clear that it was drafted as a further limitation on materials and information otherwise discoverable under subdivision (b)(3) of the rule. Subdivision (b)(3) specifically provides for a demonstration of "substantial need." That requirement would therefore apply to subdivision (b)(4) by reference and implication. Crockett v. Virginia Folding Box Co., 61 F.R.D. 312 (E.D. Va. 1974).

A master-servant relationship between a party and his expert was not contemplated within the ambit of subdivision (b)(4). VEPCO v. Sun Shipbuilding & Dry Dock Co., 68 F.R.D. 397 (E.D. Va. 1975).

Members of a board of parole should be subjected to depositions under only exceptional circumstances. — United States Bd. United States Bd. of Parole v. Merhige, 487 F.2d 25 (4th Cir. 1973), cert. denied, 417 U.S. 918, 94 S. Ct. 2625, 41 L. Ed. 2d 224 (1974).

Documents derived from regular employees of a corporate defendant were not entitled to a qualified immunity from discovery simply because the employees were experts and the documents contained their expert opinions, findings and factual analyses. VEPCO v. Sun Shipbuilding & Dry Dock Co., 68 F.R.D. 397 (E.D. Va. 1975).

Reports prepared by a person who is an expert in a trade or science, but who is neither retained nor specially employed but merely is, has been and will be an employee of the litigant without regard to the pendency of the claim, are fully discoverable on a motion to produce. VEPCO v. Sun Shipbuilding & Dry Dock Co., 68 F.R.D. 397 (E.D. Va. 1975).

Though one be an expert, if his contact with the case is not in his capacity as an impartial observer, but is instead as one going about his duties as a loyal employee, then he should be treated as an ordinary witness. VEPCO v. Sun Shipbuilding & Dry Dock Co., 68 F.R.D. 397 (E.D. Va. 1975).

B. Trial Preparation.

The provisions of subdivision (b)(3) are straightforward and easily understood. VEPCO v. Sun Shipbuilding & Dry Dock Co., 68 F.R.D. 397 (E.D. Va. 1975).

The 1970 amendment to this rule extinguished any confusion about whose work product was preserved; a representative of the party, "including his attorney, consultant, surety, indemnitor, insurer, or agent," may file a document that is covered under the work product theory. State Farm Fire & Cas. Co. v. Perrigan, 102 F.R.D. 235 (W.D. Va. 1984).

The work-product doctrine operates in narrow confines: the anticipation of future litigation must have been the primary motivation which led to the creation of the documents in order to qualify for the privilege. Front Royal Ins. Co. v. Gold Players, Inc., 187 F.R.D. 252 (W.D. Va. 1999).

Burden of showing preparation of documents under subdivision (b)(3) circumstances. — The party opposing discovery has the burden of showing, as to each document, that it was prepared under subdivision (b)(3) circumstances. If there be such a showing to the satisfaction of the court, the burden shifts to the party seeking discovery to show, as to each document, the "substantial need" and "undue hardship." VEPCO v. Sun Shipbuilding & Dry Dock Co., 68 F.R.D. 397 (E.D. Va. 1975).

Once the court determines that the documents are within the scope of discovery, the second step is deciding whether they were compiled in anticipation of trial. After the party shows that the documents were put together in preparation of litigation, the burden shifts to the party seeking discovery to show the substantial need and undue hardship. State Farm Fire & Cas. Co. v. Perrigan, 102 F.R.D. 235 (W.D. Va. 1984).

If anyone prepares documents for a party in anticipation of litigation or for trial, documents so prepared are not discoverable except upon a showing of "substantial need" and "undue hardship." VEPCO v. Sun Shipbuilding & Dry Dock Co., 68 F.R.D. 397 (E.D. Va. 1975).

Where the information here is work product but not absolutely immune, plaintiff is entitled to discover it only upon a showing of "substantial need." Duck v. Warren, 160 F.R.D. 80 (E.D. Va. 1995).

Documents generated in anticipation of litigation not work product. — The withheld documents, although generated in anticipation of possible litigation, are not protected by the work product doctrine as company was a nonparty. Johnson v. Standex Int'l Corp., 153 F.R.D. 80 (E.D. Va. 1994).

Document is not created in anticipation of litigation unless the probability of litigating the claim is substantial and imminent or litigation is fairly foreseeable when it is created. Front Royal Ins. Co. v. Gold Players, Inc., 187 F.R.D. 252 (W.D. Va. 1999).

The protection accorded by subdivision (b)(3) of this rule applies only to documents prepared by a party or a party's representative. Rickman v. Deere & Co., 154 F.R.D. 137 (E.D. Va. 1993), aff'd, 36 F.3d 1093 (4th Cir. 1994).

Documents representing witnesses' impressions are not attorney's work product. — Statements and documents which represent the impressions and observations of the witnesses and not those of the attorney or his investigators are not part of the attorney's work product. VEPCO v. Sun Shipbuilding & Dry Dock Co., 68 F.R.D. 397 (E.D. Va. 1975).

In analyzing whether or not information is immune from discovery under the work product doctrine the first question is whether the documents were prepared "in anticipation of litigation." Next it must be decided if the documents are "mental impressions, conclusions, opinions, or legal theories of an attorney or other representative of a party concerning the litigation," and therefore absolutely immune. Duck v. Warren, 160 F.R.D. 80 (E.D. Va. 1995).

Nor are statements filed by employees in regular course of business. — Where the statements made or the reports filed are such as would be made by employees in the usual and regular course of normal business procedure, the corporation being on notice that an accident claim is likely, even though the statement or other document was obtained at the direction of a lawyer, such statement or document is not a part of the lawyer's work product. VEPCO v. Sun Shipbuilding & Dry Dock Co., 68 F.R.D. 397 (E.D. Va. 1975).

Documents which were created in the ordinary course of business under the contractual obligations between insurer and reinsurer were not protected from production by the work-product doctrine. Front Royal Ins. Co. v. Gold Players, Inc., 187 F.R.D. 252 (W.D. Va. 1999).

Work product immunity not available for plaintiff's workers' compensation carrier. — Reports prepared by farm bureau in preparation for its own potential subrogation litigation did not fall within the literal terms of this rule providing for work product immunity; farm bureau was not a party, nor, as the workers' compensation carrier of plaintiff's employer, was it the representative or insurer of plaintiff any more than an insurance carrier of a person sued for negligence would be a representative or insurer of the injured party. Rickman v. Deere & Co., 154 F.R.D. 137 (E.D. Va. 1993), aff'd, 36 F.3d 1093 (4th Cir. 1994).

The work product of the lawyer must be presently a part of his work files to qualify for the protection of the rule. VEPCO v. Sun Shipbuilding & Dry Dock Co., 68 F.R.D. 397 (E.D. Va. 1975).

Blanket assertion that the possibility of litigation was "obvious" was legally insufficient to secure work product protection. Portsmouth Redevelopment & Hous. Auth. v. BMI Apts. Assocs., 155 F.R.D. 136 (E.D. Va. 1994).

In order to secure protection under the work-product doctrine, the document must be prepared because of the prospect of litigation when the preparer faces an actual claim or a potential claim following an actual event or series of events that reasonably could result in litigation. Portsmouth Redevelopment & Hous. Auth. v. BMI Apts. Assocs., 155 F.R.D. 136 (E.D. Va. 1994).

Counsel's statements concerning claim's likely success, even when transcribed by the client, are prime examples of the types of materials entitled to near absolute protection under subdivision (b)(3). Bush Dev. Corp. v. Harbour Place Assocs., 632 F. Supp. 1359 (E.D. Va. 1986).

Annotations on draft complaint reflecting counsel's opinion as to the success of the suit are protectable. Bush Dev. Corp. v. Harbour Place Assocs., 632 F. Supp. 1359 (E.D. Va. 1986).

Insurance investigator's report was discoverable where it was relevant to discover evidence leading to the cause of the fire and the motive, it was prepared during the ordinary course of investigating a fire, at the time of the investigation, the insurer was in the process of adjusting the claim, and the insurer had not decided whether to pay the loss let alone whether to bring an action arising from a payment under the policy. Thus, the probability of litigating the claim was not substantial or imminent at the time of the investigation. The opinions of the investigator likewise were discoverable since the report was prepared during the ordinary course of the insurance company's business and not in anticipation of trial. State Farm Fire & Cas. Co. v. Perrigan, 102 F.R.D. 235 (W.D. Va. 1984).

At some point an insurance company shifts its activity from the ordinary course of business to anticipation of litigation, and no hard and fast rule governs when this change occurs. This distinction lies at the pivotal point where the probability of litigating the claim is substantial and imminent or where litigation was fairly foreseeable at the time the memorandum was prepared. Thus, the decision whether the insurance company's investigatory reports are discoverable depends upon the facts of each case. State Farm Fire & Cas. Co. v. Perrigan, 102 F.R.D. 235 (W.D. Va. 1984).

Discovery of reports containing mental impressions and opinions of investigating agents and employees is conditional upon a strong showing of need and hardship if they were prepared in anticipation of trial. Thus, an insurance company's work product may be discoverable. State Farm Fire & Cas. Co. v. Perrigan, 102 F.R.D. 235 (W.D. Va. 1984).

Rule 27. Depositions to Perpetuate Testimony.

(a) *Before an Action Is Filed.* — (1) Petition. A person who wants to perpetuate testimony about any matter cognizable in a United States court may file a verified petition in the district court for the district where any expected adverse party resides. The petition must ask for an order authorizing the petitioner to depose the named persons in order to perpetuate their testimony. The petition must be titled in the petitioner's name and must show:

(A) that the petitioner expects to be a party to an action cognizable in a United States court but cannot presently bring it or cause it to be brought;

(B) the subject matter of the expected action and the petitioner's interest;

(C) the facts that the petitioner wants to establish by the proposed testimony and the reasons to perpetuate it;

(D) the names or a description of the persons whom the petitioner expects to be adverse parties and their addresses, so far as known; and

(E) the name, address, and expected substance of the testimony of each deponent.

(2) Notice and Service. At least 21 days before the hearing date, the petitioner must serve each expected adverse party with a copy of the petition and a notice stating the time and place of the hearing. The notice may be served either inside or outside the district or state in the manner provided in Rule 4. If that service cannot be made with reasonable diligence on an expected adverse party, the court may order service by publication or otherwise. The court must appoint an attorney to represent persons not served in the manner provided in Rule 4 and to cross-examine the deponent if an unserved person is not otherwise represented. If any expected adverse party is a minor or is incompetent, Rule 17(c) applies.

(3) Order and Examination. If satisfied that perpetuating the testimony may prevent a failure or delay of justice, the court must issue an order that designates or describes the persons whose depositions may be taken, specifies the subject matter of the examinations, and states whether the depositions will be taken orally or by written interrogatories. The depositions may then be taken under these rules, and the court may issue orders like those authorized by Rules 34 and 35. A reference in these rules to the court where an action is pending means, for purposes of this rule, the court where the petition for the deposition was filed.

(4) Using the Deposition. A deposition to perpetuate testimony may be used under Rule 32(a) in any later-filed district-court action involving the same subject matter if the deposition either was taken under these rules or, although not so taken, would be admissible in evidence in the courts of the state where it was taken.

(b) *Pending Appeal.* — (1) In General. The court where a judgment has been rendered may, if an appeal has been taken or may still be taken, permit a party to depose witnesses to perpetuate their testimony for use in the event of further proceedings in that court.

(2) Motion. The party who wants to perpetuate testimony may move for leave to take the depositions, on the same notice and service as if the action were pending in the district court. The motion must show:

(A) the name, address, and expected substance of the testimony of each deponent; and

(B) the reasons for perpetuating the testimony.

(3) Court Order. If the court finds that perpetuating the testimony may prevent a failure or delay of justice, the court may permit the depositions to be taken and may issue orders like those authorized by Rules 34 and 35. The depositions may be taken and used as any other deposition taken in a pending district-court action.

(c) *Perpetuation by an Action.* — This rule does not limit a court's power to entertain an action to perpetuate testimony. (Amended by order adopted December 27, 1946, effective March 19, 1948, by order adopted December 29, 1948, effective October 20, 1949, by order adopted March 1, 1971, effective July 1, 1971, by order adopted March 2, 1987, effective August 1, 1987, by order April 25, 2005, effective December 1, 2005, by order adopted April 30, 2007, effective December 1, 2007, and by order adopted March 26, 2009, effective December 1, 2009.)

Comment. — The language of Rule 27 has been amended as part of the general restyling of the Civil Rules to make them more easily understood and to make style and terminology consistent throughout the rules. These changes are intended to be stylistic only.

Rule 28. Persons Before Whom Depositions May Be Taken.

(a) *Within the United States.* — (1) In General. Within the United States or a territory or insular possession subject to United States jurisdiction, a deposition must be taken before:

(A) an officer authorized to administer oaths either by federal law or by the law in the place of examination; or

(B) a person appointed by the court where the action is pending to administer oaths and take testimony.

(2) Definition of "Officer." The term "officer" in Rules 30, 31, and 32 includes a person appointed by the court under this rule or designated by the parties under Rule 29(a).

(b) *In a Foreign Country.* — (1) In General. A deposition may be taken in a foreign country:

(A) under an applicable treaty or convention;

(B) under a letter of request, whether or not captioned a "letter rogatory";

(C) on notice, before a person authorized to administer oaths either by federal law or by the law in the place of examination; or

(D) before a person commissioned by the court to administer any necessary oath and take testimony.

(2) Issuing a Letter of Request or a Commission. A letter of request, a commission, or both may be issued:

(A) on appropriate terms after an application and notice of it; and

(B) without a showing that taking the deposition in another manner is impracticable or inconvenient.

(3) Form of a Request, Notice, or Commission. When a letter of request or any other device is used according to a treaty or convention, it must be captioned in the form prescribed by that treaty or convention. A letter of request may be addressed "To the Appropriate Authority in [name of country]." A deposition notice or a commission must designate by name or descriptive title the person before whom the deposition is to be taken.

(4) Letter of Request — Admitting Evidence. Evidence obtained in response to a letter of request need not be excluded merely because it is not a verbatim transcript, because the testimony was not taken under oath, or because of any similar departure from the requirements for depositions taken within the United States.

(c) *Disqualification.* — A deposition must not be taken before a person who is any party's relative, employee, or attorney; who is related to or employed by any party's attorney; or who is financially interested in the action. (Amended by order adopted December 27, 1946, effective March 19, 1948, by order adopted January 21, 1963, effective July 1, 1963, by order adopted April 29, 1980, effective August 1, 1980, by order adopted March 2, 1987, effective August 1, 1987, by order adopted April 22, 1993, effective December 1, 1993, and by order adopted April 30, 2007, effective December 1, 2007.)

Comment. — The language of Rule 28 has been amended as part of the general restyling of the Civil Rules to make them more easily understood and to make style and terminology consistent throughout the rules. These changes are intended to be stylistic only.

CASE NOTES

Depositions in foreign countries. — Subdivision (b) of this rule allows depositions in a foreign country on notice before a person authorized to administer oaths at the place of examination, either under a local law or American law, before a person commissioned by the court, or pursuant to a letter rogatory. These methods are sanctioned by the signatories to the Hague Evidence Convention. The letter rogatory technique allows use of the foreign court's compulsory powers for unwilling witnesses. Hodson v. A.H. Robins Co., 528 F. Supp. 809 (E.D. Va. 1981), aff'd, 715 F.2d 142 (4th Cir. 1983).

Rule 29. Stipulations About Discovery Procedure.

Unless the court orders otherwise, the parties may stipulate that:

(a) a deposition may be taken before any person, at any time or place, on any notice, and in the manner specified — in which event it may be used in the same way as any other deposition; and

(b) other procedures governing or limiting discovery be modified — but a stipulation extending the time for any form of discovery must have court approval if it would interfere with the time set for completing discovery, for hearing a motion, or for trial. (Amended by order adopted March 30, 1970, effective July 1, 1970, by order adopted April 22, 1993, effective December 1, 1993, and by order adopted April 30, 2007, effective December 1, 2007.)

Comment. — The language of Rule 29 has been amended as part of the general restyling of the Civil Rules to make them more easily understood and to make style and terminology consistent throughout the rules. These changes are intended to be stylistic only.

CASE NOTES

This rule provides for the taking of deposition evidence abroad in a manner stipulated in writing by the parties. Hodson v. A.H. Robins Co., 528 F. Supp. 809 (E.D. Va. 1981), aff'd, 715 F.2d 142 (4th Cir. 1983).

Applied in Bobrosky v. Vickers, 170 F.R.D. 411 (W.D. Va. 1997).

Rule 30. Depositions by Oral Examination.

(a) *When a Deposition May Be Taken.* — (1) Without Leave. A party may, by oral questions, depose any person, including a party, without leave of court except as provided in Rule 30(a)(2). The deponent's attendance may be compelled by subpoena under Rule 45.

(2) With Leave. A party must obtain leave of court, and the court must grant leave to the extent consistent with Rule 26(b)(2):

(A) if the parties have not stipulated to the deposition and:

(i) the deposition would result in more than 10 depositions being taken under this rule or Rule 31 by the plaintiffs, or by the defendants, or by the third-party defendants;

(ii) the deponent has already been deposed in the case; or

(iii) the party seeks to take the deposition before the time specified in Rule 26(d), unless the party certifies in the notice, with supporting facts, that the deponent is expected to leave the United States and be unavailable for examination in this country after that time; or

(B) if the deponent is confined in prison.

(b) *Notice of the Deposition; Other Formal Requirements.* — (1) Notice in General. A party who wants to depose a person by oral questions must give reasonable written notice to every other party. The notice must state the time and place of the deposition and, if known, the deponent's name and address. If the name is unknown, the notice must provide a general description sufficient to identify the person or the particular class or group to which the person belongs.

(2) Producing Documents. If a subpoena duces tecum is to be served on the deponent, the materials designated for production, as set out in the subpoena, must be listed in the notice or in an attachment. The notice to a party deponent may be accompanied by a request under Rule 34 to produce documents and tangible things at the deposition.

(3) Method of Recording. (A) Method Stated in the Notice. The party who notices the deposition must state in the notice the method for recording the testimony. Unless the court orders otherwise, testimony may be recorded by audio, audiovisual, or stenographic means. The noticing party bears the recording costs. Any party may arrange to transcribe a deposition.

(B) Additional Method. With prior notice to the deponent and other parties, any party may designate another method for recording the testimony in addition to that specified in the original notice. That party bears the expense of the additional record or transcript unless the court orders otherwise.

(4) By Remote Means. The parties may stipulate — or the court may on motion order — that a deposition be taken by telephone or other remote means. For the purpose of this rule and Rules 28(a), 37(a)(2), and 37(b)(1), the deposition takes place where the deponent answers the questions.

(5) Officer's Duties. (A) Before the Deposition. Unless the parties stipulate otherwise, a deposition must be conducted before an officer appointed or designated under Rule 28. The officer must begin the deposition with an on-the-record statement that includes:

(i) the officer's name and business address;

(ii) the date, time, and place of the deposition;

(iii) the deponent's name;

(iv) the officer's administration of the oath or affirmation to the deponent; and

(v) the identity of all persons present.

(B) Conducting the Deposition; Avoiding Distortion. If the deposition is recorded nonstenographically, the officer must repeat the items in Rule 30(b)(5)(A)(i)-(iii) at the beginning of each unit of the recording medium. The deponent's and attorneys' appearance or demeanor must not be distorted through recording techniques.

(C) After the Deposition. At the end of a deposition, the officer must state on the record that the deposition is complete and must set out any stipulations made by the attorneys about custody of the transcript or recording and of the exhibits, or about any other pertinent matters.

(6) Notice or Subpoena Directed to an Organization. In its notice or subpoena, a party may name as the deponent a public or private corporation, a partnership, an association, a governmental agency, or other entity and must describe with reasonable particularity the matters for examination. The named organization must then designate one or more officers, directors, or managing agents, or designate other persons who consent to testify on its behalf; and it may set out the matters on which each person designated will testify. A subpoena must advise a nonparty organization of its duty to make this designation. The persons designated must testify about information known or reasonably available to the organization. This paragraph (6) does not preclude a deposition by any other procedure allowed by these rules.

(c) *Examination and Cross-Examination; Record of the Examination; Objections; Written Questions.* — (1) Examination and Cross-Examination. The examination and cross-examination of a deponent proceed as they would at trial under the Federal Rules of Evidence, except Rules 103 and 615. After putting the deponent under oath or affirmation, the officer must record the testimony by the method designated under Rule 30(b)(3)(A). The testimony must be recorded by the officer personally or by a person acting in the presence and under the direction of the officer.

(2) Objections. An objection at the time of the examination — whether to evidence, to a party's conduct, to the officer's qualifications, to the manner of taking the deposition, or to any other aspect of the deposition — must be noted on the record, but the examination still proceeds; the testimony is taken subject to any objection. An objection must be stated concisely in a nonargumentative and nonsuggestive manner. A person may instruct a deponent not to answer only when necessary to preserve a privilege, to enforce a limitation ordered by the court, or to present a motion under Rule 30(d)(3).

(3) Participating Through Written Questions. Instead of participating in the oral examination, a party may serve written questions in a sealed envelope on the party noticing the deposition, who must deliver them to the officer. The officer must ask the deponent those questions and record the answers verbatim.

(d) *Duration; Sanction; Motion to Terminate or Limit.* — (1) Duration. Unless otherwise stipulated or ordered by the court, a deposition is limited to 1 day of 7 hours. The court must allow additional time consistent with Rule 26(b)(2) if needed to fairly examine the deponent or if the deponent, another person, or any other circumstance impedes or delays the examination.

(2) Sanction. The court may impose an appropriate sanction — including the reasonable expenses and attorney's fees incurred by any party — on a person who impedes, delays, or frustrates the fair examination of the deponent.

(3) Motion to Terminate or Limit. (A) Grounds. At any time during a deposition, the deponent or a party may move to terminate or limit it on the ground that it is being conducted in bad faith or in a manner that unreasonably annoys, embarrasses, or oppresses the deponent or party. The motion may be filed in the court where the action is pending or the deposition is being taken. If the objecting deponent or party so demands, the deposition must be suspended for the time necessary to obtain an order.

(B) Order. The court may order that the deposition be terminated or may limit its scope and manner as provided in Rule 26(c). If terminated, the deposition may be resumed only by order of the court where the action is pending.

(C) Award of Expenses. Rule 37(a)(5) applies to the award of expenses.

(e) *Review by the Witness; Changes.* — (1) Review; Statement of Changes. On request by the deponent or a party before the deposition is completed, the deponent must be allowed 30 days after being notified by the officer that the transcript or recording is available in which:

(A) to review the transcript or recording; and

(B) if there are changes in form or substance, to sign a statement listing the changes and the reasons for making them.

(2) Changes Indicated in the Officer's Certificate. The officer must note in the certificate prescribed by Rule 30(f)(1) whether a review was requested and, if so, must attach any changes the deponent makes during the 30-day period.

(f) *Certification and Delivery; Exhibits; Copies of the Transcript or Recording; Filing.* — (1) Certification and Delivery. The officer must certify in writing that the witness was duly sworn and that the deposition accurately records the witness's testimony. The certificate must accompany the record of the deposition. Unless the court orders otherwise, the officer must seal the deposition in an envelope or package bearing the title of the action and marked "Deposition of [witness's name]" and must promptly send it to the attorney who arranged for the transcript or recording. The attorney must store it under conditions that will protect it against loss, destruction, tampering, or deterioration.

(2) Documents and Tangible Things. (A) Originals and Copies. Documents and tangible things produced for inspection during a deposition must, on a party's request, be marked for identification and attached to the deposition. Any party may inspect and copy them. But if the person who produced them wants to keep the originals, the person may:

(i) offer copies to be marked, attached to the deposition, and then used as originals — after giving all parties a fair opportunity to verify the copies by comparing them with the originals; or

(ii) give all parties a fair opportunity to inspect and copy the originals after they are marked — in which event the originals may be used as if attached to the deposition.

(B) Order Regarding the Originals. Any party may move for an order that the originals be attached to the deposition pending final disposition of the case.

(3) Copies of the Transcript or Recording. Unless otherwise stipulated or ordered by the court, the officer must retain the stenographic notes of a deposition taken stenographically or a copy of the recording of a deposition taken by another method. When paid reasonable charges, the officer must furnish a copy of the transcript or recording to any party or the deponent.

(4) Notice of Filing. A party who files the deposition must promptly notify all other parties of the filing.

(g) *Failure to Attend a Deposition or Serve a Subpoena; Expenses.* — A party who, expecting a deposition to be taken, attends in person or by an attorney may recover reasonable expenses for attending, including attorney's fees, if the noticing party failed to:

(1) attend and proceed with the deposition; or

(2) serve a subpoena on a nonparty deponent, who consequently did not attend.' the court may order the party giving the notice to pay to such other party the reasonable expenses incurred by that party and that party's attorney in attending, including reasonable attorney's fees. (Amended by order adopted January 21, 1963, effective July 1, 1963, by order adopted March 30, 1970, effective July 1, 1970, by order adopted March 1, 1971, effective July 1, 1971, by order adopted November 20, 1972, effective July 1, 1975, by order adopted April 29, 1980, effective August 1, 1980, by order adopted March 2, 1987, effective August 1, 1987, by order adopted April 22, 1993, effective December 1, 1993, by order adopted April 17, 2000, effective December 1, 2000, and by order adopted April 30, 2007, effective December 1, 2007.)

Comment. — The language of Rule 30 has been amended as part of the general restyling of the Civil Rules to make them more easily understood and to make style and terminology consistent throughout the rules. These changes are intended to be stylistic only.

CASE NOTES

Controlling effect of this rule and FRCP, Rule 26. — None of the methods of discovery allowed under Rule 26(b)(4) and this rule permit the use of bare FRCP, Rule 45 subpeonas duces tecum. Instead, they operate as a control on the potential runaway use of the subpeona duces tecum to compel the production of the evidence of experts retained by a party to testify at trial. They protect the interests of the expert and the party retaining him in the work that he has produced, while also providing access to the opposing party, though such access might not be as inexpensive as the opponent might desire. Marsh v. Jackson, 141 F.R.D. 431 (W.D. Va. 1992).

Discovery of party and of nonparty distinguished. — Discovery of a nonparty is a wholly different matter from discovery of a party to an action. Parties to litigation open themselves to the broad discovery practices encompassed in subdivision (b)(5) of this rule and Rule 34. The production of documents or other materials prior to trial by a nonparty, on the other hand, can be compelled only by a subpoena duces tecum issued pursuant to Fed. R. Civ. P. 45(d)(1). Jones v. Continental Cas. Co., 512 F. Supp. 1205 (E.D. Va. 1981).

Allowances not made for attendance at depositions in area or if associate counsel available. — It is fundamental that allowances for attendance at depositions should not be made where the deposition is scheduled to be taken within the general area of the forum, or where the parties have previously retained associate counsel readily available in distant places. Attorneys must anticipate reasonable expenses to be borne by the parties (and by the attorneys). Nagle v. United States Lines Co., 242 F. Supp. 800 (E.D. Va. 1965).

And ordinarily both attorney's fees and travel expenses will not be allowed. — The district court for the eastern district of Virginia does not permit, under ordinary circumstances, the allowance of both attorney's fees and expenses of travel. The expense of litigation should be minimized wherever possible. Frequently it is less expensive to associate counsel for the purpose of attending a deposition. On the other hand, it may be more economical to make an allowance of travel expense. Even in matters where the attendance of trial counsel is deemed to be absolutely necessary, it is generally sufficient to make an allowance of travel expense and reasonable subsistence without an attorney's fee. Nagle v. United States Lines Co., 242 F. Supp. 800 (E.D. Va. 1965).

A signature is required by the deponent only if requested and if changes are made before the 30 day limitation expires. Parker v. Grant, 237 Bankr. 97 (Bankr. E.D. Va. 1999).

Effect of failure to sign. — A failure to read, review and sign within the 30 day limitation constraint constitutes only a waiver of deponent's right to correct mistakes in his deposition testimony and does not affect the original deposition's admissibility. Parker v. Grant, 237 Bankr. 97 (Bankr. E.D. Va. 1999).

Waiver of right to modify transcript. — In a situation where a deponent is requested to read and review his deposition and deponent makes no changes to the deposition transcript, that deponent has effectively waived any right he had to modify his transcript. Parker v. Grant, 237 Bankr. 97 (Bankr. E.D. Va. 1999).

Applied in Ivory v. Nichols, 34 F.R.D. 128 (E.D. Va. 1963); Haney v. Woodward & Lothrop, Inc., 330 F.2d 940 (4th Cir. 1964); McLean v. Prudential S.S. Co., 36 F.R.D. 421 (E.D. Va. 1965).

Rule 31. Depositions by Written Questions.

(a) *When a Deposition May Be Taken.* — (1) Without Leave. A party may, by written questions, depose any person, including a party, without leave of court except as provided in Rule 31(a)(2). The deponent's attendance may be compelled by subpoena under Rule 45.

(2) With Leave. A party must obtain leave of court, and the court must grant leave to the extent consistent with Rule 26(b)(2):

(A) if the parties have not stipulated to the deposition and:

(i) the deposition would result in more than 10 depositions being taken under this rule or Rule 30 by the plaintiffs, or by the defendants, or by the third-party defendants;

(ii) the deponent has already been deposed in the case; or

(iii) the party seeks to take a deposition before the time specified in Rule 26(d); or

(B) if the deponent is confined in prison.

(3) Service; Required Notice. A party who wants to depose a person by written questions must serve them on every other party, with a notice stating, if known, the deponent's name and address. If the name is unknown, the notice must provide a general description sufficient to identify the person or the particular class or group to which the person belongs. The notice must also state the name or descriptive title and the address of the officer before whom the deposition will be taken.

(4) Questions Directed to an Organization. A public or private corporation, a partnership, an association, or a governmental agency may be deposed by written questions in accordance with Rule 30(b)(6).

(5) Questions from Other Parties. Any questions to the deponent from other parties must be served on all parties as follows: cross-questions, within 14 days after being served with the notice and direct questions; redirect questions, within 7 days after being served with cross-questions; and recross-questions, within 7 days after being served with redirect questions. The court may, for good cause, extend or shorten these times.

(b) *Delivery to the Officer; Officer's Duties.* — The party who noticed the deposition must deliver to the officer a copy of all the questions served and of the notice. The officer must promptly proceed in the manner provided in Rule 30(c), (e), and (f) to:

(1) take the deponent's testimony in response to the questions;

(2) prepare and certify the deposition; and

(3) send it to the party, attaching a copy of the questions and of the notice.

(c) *Notice of Completion or Filing.* — (1) Completion. The party who noticed the deposition must notify all other parties when it is completed.

(2) Filing. A party who files the deposition must promptly notify all other parties of the filing. (Amended by order adopted March 30, 1970, effective July 1, 1970, by order adopted March 2, 1987, effective August 1, 1987, by order adopted April 22, 1993, effective December 1, 1993, and by order adopted April 30, 2007, effective December 1, 2007.)

Comment. — The language of Rule 31 has been amended as part of the general restyling of the Civil Rules to make them more easily understood and to make style and terminology consistent throughout the rules. These changes are intended to be stylistic only.

CASE NOTES

Applied in Ivory v. Nichols, 34 F.R.D. 128 (E.D. Va. 1963).

Rule 32. Using Depositions in Court Proceedings.

(a) *Using Depositions.* — (1) In General. At a hearing or trial, all or part of a deposition may be used against a party on these conditions:

(A) the party was present or represented at the taking of the deposition or had reasonable notice of it;

(B) it is used to the extent it would be admissible under the Federal Rules of Evidence if the deponent were present and testifying; and

(C) the use is allowed by Rule 32(a)(2) through (8).

(2) Impeachment and Other Uses. Any party may use a deposition to contradict or impeach the testimony given by the deponent as a witness, or for any other purpose allowed by the Federal Rules of Evidence.

(3) Deposition of Party, Agent, or Designee. An adverse party may use for any purpose the deposition of a party or anyone who, when deposed, was the party's officer, director, managing agent, or designee under Rule 30(b)(6) or 31(a)(4).

(4) Unavailable Witness. A party may use for any purpose the deposition of a witness, whether or not a party, if the court finds:

(A) that the witness is dead;

(B) that the witness is more than 100 miles from the place of hearing or trial or is outside the United States, unless it appears that the witness's absence was procured by the party offering the deposition;

(C) that the witness cannot attend or testify because of age, illness, infirmity, or imprisonment;

(D) that the party offering the deposition could not procure the witness's attendance by subpoena; or

(E) on motion and notice, that exceptional circumstances make it desirable — in the interest of justice and with due regard to the importance of live testimony in open court — to permit the deposition to be used.

(5) Limitations on Use. (A) Deposition Taken on Short Notice. A deposition must not be used against a party who, having received less than 14 days' notice of the deposition, promptly moved for a protective order under Rule 26(c)(1)(B) requesting that it not be taken or be taken at a different time or place — and this motion was still pending when the deposition was taken.

(B) Unavailable Deponent; Party Could Not Obtain an Attorney. A deposition taken without leave of court under the unavailability provision of Rule 30(a)(2)(A)(iii) must not be used against a party who shows that, when served with the notice, it could not, despite diligent efforts, obtain an attorney to represent it at the deposition.

(6) Using Part of a Deposition. If a party offers in evidence only part of a deposition, an adverse party may require the offeror to introduce other parts that in fairness should be considered with the part introduced, and any party may itself introduce any other parts.

(7) Substituting a Party. Substituting a party under Rule 25 does not affect the right to use a deposition previously taken.

(8) Deposition Taken in an Earlier Action. A deposition lawfully taken and, if required, filed in any federal- or state-court action may be used in a later action involving the same subject matter between the same parties, or their representatives or successors in interest, to the same extent as if taken in the later action. A deposition previously taken may also be used as allowed by the Federal Rules of Evidence.

(b) *Objections to Admissibility.* — Subject to Rules 28(b) and 32(d)(3), an objection may be made at a hearing or trial to the admission of any deposition testimony that would be inadmissible if the witness were present and testifying.

(c) *Form of Presentation.* — Unless the court orders otherwise, a party must provide a transcript of any deposition testimony the party offers, but may provide the court with the testimony in nontranscript form as well. On any party's request, deposition testimony offered in a jury trial for any purpose other than impeachment must be presented in nontranscript form, if available, unless the court for good cause orders otherwise.

(d) *Waiver of Objections.* — (1) To the Notice. An objection to an error or irregularity in a deposition notice is waived unless promptly served in writing on the party giving the notice.

(2) To the Officer's Qualification. An objection based on disqualification of the officer before whom a deposition is to be taken is waived if not made:

(A) before the deposition begins; or

(B) promptly after the basis for disqualification becomes known or, with reasonable diligence, could have been known.

(3) To the Taking of the Deposition. (A) Objection to Competence, Relevance, or Materiality. An objection to a deponent's competence — or to the competence, relevance, or materiality of testimony — is not waived by a failure to make the objection before or during the deposition, unless the ground for it might have been corrected at that time.

(B) Objection to an Error or Irregularity. An objection to an error or irregularity at an oral examination is waived if:

(i) it relates to the manner of taking the deposition, the form of a question or answer, the oath or affirmation, a party's conduct, or other matters that might have been corrected at that time; and

(ii) it is not timely made during the deposition.

(C) Objection to a Written Question. An objection to the form of a written question under Rule 31 is waived if not served in writing on the party submitting the question within the time for serving responsive questions or, if the question is a recross-question, within 7 days after being served with it.

(4) To Completing and Returning the Deposition. An objection to how the officer transcribed the testimony — or prepared, signed, certified, sealed, endorsed, sent, or otherwise dealt with the deposition — is waived unless a motion to suppress is made promptly after the error or irregularity becomes known or, with reasonable diligence, could have been known. (Amended by order adopted March 30, 1970, effective July 1, 1970, by order adopted November 20, 1972, effective July 1, 1975, by order adopted April 29, 1980, effective August 1, 1980, by order adopted March 2, 1987, effective August 1, 1987, by order adopted April 22, 1993, effective December 1, 1993, by order adopted April 30, 2007, effective December 1, 2007, and by order adopted March 26, 2009, effective December 1, 2009.)

Comment. — The language of Rule 32 has been amended as part of the general restyling of the Civil Rules to make them more easily understood and to make style and terminology consistent throughout the rules. These changes are intended to be stylistic only.

Former Rule 32(a) applied "[a]t the trial or upon the hearing of a motion or an interlocutory proceeding." The amended rule describes the same events as "a hearing or trial."

The final paragraph of former Rule 32(a) allowed use in a later action of a deposition "lawfully taken and duly filed in the former action." Because of the 2000 amendment of Rule 5(d), many depositions are not filed. Amended Rule 32(a)(8) reflects this change by excluding use of an unfiled deposition only if filing was required in the former action.

CASE NOTES

A party may introduce, as a part of his substantive proof, the deposition of his adversary, and it is quite immaterial that the adversary is available to testify at the trial or has testified there. Lassiter v. United States Lines, 370 F. Supp. 427 (E.D. Va. 1973), aff'd, 490 F.2d 1407 (4th Cir. 1974).

This rule impliedly prohibits the use of a deposition against any party who was not present or represented at the taking of such deposition or who had no reasonable notice thereof. The rule is based on an elementary principle of justice towards the party against whom the deposition is offered. Hewitt v. Hutter, 432 F. Supp. 795 (W.D. Va. 1977), aff'd, 568 F.2d 773 (4th Cir.), 574 F.2d 182 (4th Cir. 1978).

The refusal of the trial court to permit the introduction into evidence of entire depositions did not prejudice the plaintiff, as he was free to explain on recall his prior statements in the deposition and was also free to recall a witness for the same purpose. Padgett v. GMC, 544 F.2d 704 (4th Cir. 1976).

Exceptional circumstances existed. — Subdivision (a)(3)(E) provides for the admission of depositions in exceptional circumstances in the interest of justice. Such exceptional circumstances were present where the absence of the witnesses was a completely unexpected turn of events. There was a report that they were ill. Moreover, the interests of justice were clearly served. All parties had been represented by counsel during the taking of their depositions so that each party had had a full opportunity for cross-examination. Huff v. Marine Tank Testing Corp., 631 F.2d 1140 (4th Cir. 1980).

Defendant waives right against self-incrimination by pleading guilty. — By pleading guilty, a defendant waives his Fifth Amendment right against self-incrimination as to matters germane to the offense for which he has pled guilty and is to be sentenced. Edmundson v. Commonwealth, 13 Va. App. 476, 412 S.E.2d 727 (1992).

Defendant, by pleading guilty, incriminated himself and, by so doing, waived his right against compulsory self-incrimination in regard to matters germane to that offense. Edmundson v. Commonwealth, 13 Va. App. 476, 412 S.E.2d 727 (1992).

The waiver of the right against compulsory self-incrimination is not unlimited; it does not allow the law enforcement authorities to inquire about unrelated matters which have no bearing upon the disposition of the case before the trial court. Edmundson v. Commonwealth, 13 Va. App. 476, 412 S.E.2d 727 (1992).

Inquiry held within scope of waiver of right against self-incrimination. — Where the trial court was considering a presentence report in order to determine an appropriate sentence and disposition, and the defendant had given conflicting reports about the extent of his drug use or habit, the inquiry into the conflicting reports was relevant to the case for which he had pled guilty and within the scope of the waiver of his right against compulsory self-incrimination. Edmundson v. Commonwealth, 13 Va. App. 476, 412 S.E.2d 727 (1992).

Applied in United States v. Barrow, 540 F.2d 204 (4th Cir. 1976); United States v. Lambey, 974 F.2d 1389 (4th Cir. 1992); Bobrosky v. Vickers, 170 F.R.D. 411 (W.D. Va. 1997).

Rule 33. Interrogatories to Parties.

(a) *In General.* — (1) Number. Unless otherwise stipulated or ordered by the court, a party may serve on any other party no more than 25 written interrogatories, including all discrete subparts. Leave to serve additional interrogatories may be granted to the extent consistent with Rule 26(b)(2).

(2) Scope. An interrogatory may relate to any matter that may be inquired into under Rule 26(b). An interrogatory is not objectionable merely because it asks for an opinion or contention that relates to fact or the application of law to fact, but the court may order that the interrogatory need not be answered until designated discovery is complete, or until a pretrial conference or some other time.

(b) *Answers and Objections.* — (1) Responding Party. The interrogatories must be answered:

(A) by the party to whom they are directed; or

(B) if that party is a public or private corporation, a partnership, an association, or a governmental agency, by any officer or agent, who must furnish the information available to the party.

(2) Time to Respond. The responding party must serve its answers and any objections within 30 days after being served with the interrogatories. A shorter or longer time may be stipulated to under Rule 29 or be ordered by the court.

(3) Answering Each Interrogatory. Each interrogatory must, to the extent it is not objected to, be answered separately and fully in writing under oath.

(4) Objections. The grounds for objecting to an interrogatory must be stated with specificity. Any ground not stated in a timely objection is waived unless the court, for good cause, excuses the failure.

(5) Signature. The person who makes the answers must sign them, and the attorney who objects must sign any objections.

(c) *Use.* — An answer to an interrogatory may be used to the extent allowed by the Federal Rules of Evidence.

(d) *Option to Produce Business Records.* — If the answer to an interrogatory may be determined by examining, auditing, compiling, abstracting, or summarizing a party's business records (including electronically stored information), and if the burden of deriving or ascertaining the answer will be substantially the same for either party, the responding party may answer by:

(1) specifying the records that must be reviewed, in sufficient detail to enable the interrogating party to locate and identify them as readily as the responding party could; and

(2) giving the interrogating party a reasonable opportunity to examine and audit the records and to make copies, compilations, abstracts, or summaries. (Amended by order adopted December 27, 1946, effective March 19, 1948, by order adopted March 30, 1970, effective July 1, 1970, by order adopted April 29, 1980, effective August 1, 1980, by order adopted April 22, 1993, effective December 1, 1993, by order adopted April 12, 2006, effective December 1, 2006, and by order adopted April 30, 2007, effective December 1, 2007.)

Comment. — The language of Rule 33 has been amended as part of the general restyling of the Civil Rules to make them more easily understood and to make style and terminology consistent throughout the rules. These changes are intended to be stylistic only.

The final sentence of former Rule 33(a) was a redundant cross-reference to the discovery moratorium provisions of Rule 26(d). Rule 26(d) is now familiar, obviating any need to carry forward the redundant cross-reference.

Former Rule 33(b)(5) was a redundant reminder of Rule 37(a) procedure that is omitted as no longer useful.

Former Rule 33(c) stated that an interrogatory "is not necessarily objectionable merely because an answer * * * involves an opinion or contention * * *." "[I]s not necessarily" seemed to imply that the interrogatory might be objectionable merely for this reason. This implication has been ignored in practice. Opinion and contention interrogatories are used routinely. Amended Rule 33(a)(2) embodies the current meaning of Rule 33 by omitting "necessarily."

Law Review. — For article, "Electronically Stored Evidence: Answers to Some Recurring Questions Concerning Pretrial Discovery and Trial Usage," see 41 Wash. & Lee L. Rev. 1335 (1984).

CASE NOTES

Rule is to be given wide scope. — The distinguished draftsmen who drew this rule, and the courts which have construed it, meant to give it wide scope and eliminate technicalities which would unnecessarily limit its application. Byers Theaters, Inc. v. Murphy, 1 F.R.D. 286 (W.D. Va. 1940).

Names and addresses of agents of corporations may be obtained. — Interrogatories may call for the names and addresses of designated agents of defendant corporations who have, or might have, knowledge of the transactions involved. Byers Theaters, Inc. v. Murphy, 1 F.R.D. 286 (W.D. Va. 1940).

It need not be determined that answer will be admissible in evidence. — In order that an interrogatory be proper, it is not necessary that it be previously determined that the answer thereto will be admissible in evidence. Byers Theaters, Inc. v. Murphy, 1 F.R.D. 286 (W.D. Va. 1940).

Rule authorizes answers by attorney for party. — Rule 33, Fed.R.Civ.P. expressly provides that interrogatories directed to a corporate party may be answered "by any officer or agent, who shall furnish such information as is available to the party." This language has been uniformly construed to authorize "answers by an attorney" for the party. The mere fact that corporate defendants' attorney signed and swore to the interrogatories was accordingly no justification for the trial court's findings, which reflected unfairly on the attorney and his trustworthiness. Wilson v. Volkswagen of Am., Inc., 561 F.2d 494 (4th Cir. 1977), cert. denied, 434 U.S. 1020, 98 S. Ct. 744, 54 L. Ed. 2d 768 (1978).

"Availability" and "control" words of art used to express same thought. — Rule 33, Fed.R.Civ.P. prescribes that, in answering interrogatories, the party "shall furnish such information as is available to the party." Rule 34, Fed.R.Civ.P., which deals with the production of documents, directs that, by way of response to a notice thereunder, the producing party shall produce such documents as are in his "possession, custody, or control." The two Rules are equally inclusive in their scope. "Availability" and "control" are both words of art and are used to express the same thought. There is no basis whatsoever for a trial court to charge a witness at a contempt hearing for failure to make discovery with deception simply because he has used the word "available," a "term of art," which both in common and in legal terms means the same as "control." Wilson v. Volkswagen of Am., Inc., 561 F.2d 494 (4th Cir. 1977), cert. denied, 434 U.S. 1020, 98 S. Ct. 744, 54 L. Ed. 2d 768 (1978).

The meaning of "interest of justice" is largely a matter of discretion for the trial court depending on the circumstances of the case. United States v. Morris, 781 F. Supp. 428 (E.D. Va. 1991).

A general objection that interrogatories constitute a "fishing expedition" is of no avail. Byers Theaters, Inc. v. Murphy, 1 F.R.D. 286 (W.D. Va. 1940).

Interrogatories cannot be used to ask questions to which the answers are well-known by the questioning party. Moss v. Lane Co., 50 F.R.D. 122 (W.D. Va. 1970), rev'd on other grounds, 471 F.2d 853 (4th Cir. 1973).

One party should not be allowed to require another to make investigation, research or compilation of data or statistics for him which he might equally as well make for himself, and it would seem to contravene the provisions of the Fifth Amendment, prior to an adjudication of liability, to require a party to incur expense greater than that ordinarily incident to the prosecution or defense of a suit. Byers Theaters, Inc. v. Murphy, 1 F.R.D. 286 (W.D. Va. 1940).

Number of interrogatories should be few. — The number of interrogatories should be relatively few and related to the important facts of the case rather than very numerous and concerned with relatively minor evidentiary details; and, where a more comprehensive examination of the adverse party is desired, it should be ordinarily done by taking his deposition. Byers Theaters, Inc. v. Murphy, 1 F.R.D. 286 (W.D. Va. 1940).

Communications with counsel and agents should not be pried into. — It does not seem fair or proper to allow one party to pry into and discover the results of conferences and communications between counsel for and agents of a party, or parties similarly situated, after the institution of suit and in preparation for trial. Byers Theaters, Inc. v. Murphy, 1 F.R.D. 286 (W.D. Va. 1940).

Applied in Williams v. Howard Johnson's Inc., 323 F.2d 102 (4th Cir. 1963); Zurenda v. Holloman, 616 F. Supp. 212 (E.D. Va. 1985).

Rule 34. Producing Documents, Electronically Stored Information, and Tangible Things, or Entering onto Land, for Inspection and Other Purposes.

(a) *In General.* — A party may serve on any other party a request within the scope of Rule 26(b):

(1) to produce and permit the requesting party or its representative to inspect, copy, test, or sample the following items in the responding party's possession, custody, or control:

(A) any designated documents or electronically stored information — including writings, drawings, graphs, charts, photographs, sound recordings, images, and other data or data compilations — stored in any medium from which information can be obtained either directly or, if necessary, after translation by the responding party into a reasonably usable form; or

(B) any designated tangible things; or

(2) to permit entry onto designated land or other property possessed or controlled by the responding party, so that the requesting party may inspect, measure, survey, photograph, test, or sample the property or any designated object or operation on it.

(b) *Procedure.* — (1) Contents of the Request. The request:

(A) must describe with reasonable particularity each item or category of items to be inspected;

(B) must specify a reasonable time, place, and manner for the inspection and for performing the related acts; and

(C) may specify the form or forms in which electronically stored information is to be produced.

(2) Responses and Objections. (A) Time to Respond. The party to whom the request is directed must respond in writing within 30 days after being served. A shorter or longer time may be stipulated to under Rule 29 or be ordered by the court.

(B) Responding to Each Item. For each item or category, the response must either state that inspection and related activities will be permitted as requested or state an objection to the request, including the reasons.

(C) Objections. An objection to part of a request must specify the part and permit inspection of the rest.

(D) Responding to a Request for Production of Electronically Stored Information. The response may state an objection to a requested form for producing electronically stored information. If the responding party objects to a requested form — or if no form was specified in the request — the party must state the form or forms it intends to use.

(E) Producing the Documents or Electronically Stored Information. Unless otherwise stipulated or ordered by the court, these procedures apply to producing documents or electronically stored information:

(i) A party must produce documents as they are kept in the usual course of business or must organize and label them to correspond to the categories in the request;

(ii) If a request does not specify a form for producing electronically stored information, a party must produce it in a form or forms in which it is ordinarily maintained or in a reasonably usable form or forms; and

(iii) A party need not produce the same electronically stored information in more than one form.

(c) *Nonparties.* — As provided in Rule 45, a nonparty may be compelled to produce documents and tangible things or to permit an inspection. (Amended by order adopted December 27, 1946, effective March 19, 1948, by order adopted March 30, 1970, effective July 1, 1970, by order adopted April 29, 1980, effective August 1, 1980, by order adopted March 2, 1987, effective August 1, 1987, by order adopted April 30, 1991, effective December 1, 1991, by order adopted April 22, 1993, effective December 1, 1993, by order adopted April 12, 2006, effective December 1, 2006, and by order adopted April 30, 2007, effective December 1, 2007.)

Comment. — The language of Rule 34 has been amended as part of the general restyling of the Civil Rules to make them more easily understood and to make style and terminology consistent throughout the rules. These changes are intended to be stylistic only.

The final sentence in the first paragraph of former Rule 34(b) was a redundant cross-reference to the discovery moratorium provisions of Rule 26(d). Rule 26(d) is now familiar, obviating any need to carry forward the redundant cross-reference.

The redundant reminder of Rule 37(a) procedure in the second paragraph of former Rule 34(b) is omitted as no longer useful.

Law Review. — For article, "Electronically Stored Evidence: Answers to Some Recurring Questions Concerning Pretrial Discovery and Trial Usage," see 41 Wash. & Lee L. Rev. 1335 (1984). For a note, "Allocating Discovery Costs in the Computer Age: Deciding Who Should Bear the Costs of Discovery of Electronically Stored Data," see 57 Wash. & Lee L. Rev. 257 (2000).

CASE NOTES

Inspection and production orders have long been considered constitutional. — See Belcher v. Bassett Furn. Indus., Inc., 588 F.2d 904 (4th Cir. 1978).

Granting or denying motion within court's discretion. — Granting or denying a request under this rule is a matter within the trial court's discretion, and it will be reversed only if the action taken was improvident and affected substantial rights. Belcher v. Bassett Furn. Indus., Inc., 588 F.2d 904 (4th Cir. 1978).

Rule governed by standards of Rule 26. — This rule, concerning the production of documents and tangible things as well as inspection of premises, is governed by the standards of Rule 26(b). There is not, however, a clear indication of which standard defined by Rule 26(b) is to control the proposed inspections. The conflicts in the courts which led to the 1970 amendments centered almost entirely around the production of documents. Consequently, the realignment of this rule and Rule 26, along with the advisory committee's notes, largely concerned documents. Since entry upon a party's premises may entail greater burdens and risks than mere production of documents, a greater inquiry into the necessity for inspection would seem warranted. Rule 26(c) expressly provides that "for good cause shown," the court may "protect a party or person from annoyance, embarrassment, oppression, or undue burden or expense" by either denying inspection or by appropriate restrictions on the inspection. Under this subdivision, the degree to which a proposed inspection will aid in the search for truth must be balanced against the burdens and dangers created by the inspection. Belcher v. Bassett Furn. Indus., Inc., 588 F.2d 904 (4th Cir. 1978).

Scope of discovery under FRCP, Rule 45 coextensive with motion under this rule. — The scope of discovery from a nonparty by means of a subpoena duces tecum under FRCP, Rule 45 is coextensive with that of a motion for production from a party under this rule. Castle v. Jallah, 142 F.R.D. 618 (E.D. Va. 1992).

Discovery of nonparty and of party distinguished. — Discovery of a nonparty is a wholly different matter from discovery of a party to an action. Parties to litigation open themselves to the broad discovery practices encompassed in Fed. R. Civ. P. 30 (b)(5) and this rule. The production of documents or other materials prior to trial by a nonparty, on the other hand, can be compelled only by a subpoena duces tecum issued pursuant to Fed. R. Civ. P. 45(d)(1). Jones v. Continental Cas. Co., 512 F. Supp. 1205 (E.D. Va. 1981).

In the recent more liberalized trend of granting inspection orders, the courts have uniformly scrutinized the problems to insure that the anticipated benefits are real and necessary, and that the burdens will not be intolerable. Belcher v. Bassett Furn. Indus., Inc., 588 F.2d 904 (4th Cir. 1978).

Precision and care are necessary in formulating inspection orders under this rule. Belcher v. Bassett Furn. Indus., Inc., 588 F.2d 904 (4th Cir. 1978).

Some need must be shown. — Neither this rule nor Rule 26, the general discovery rule, permits blanket discovery upon bare skeletal request when confronted with an objection. Some degree of need must be shown. In most cases, this need is demonstrated by simply showing the relevancy of the desired discovery to the cause of action. This, indeed, is the general policy as stated in Rule 26(b)(1). But when the desired discovery concerns materials prepared in anticipation of trial, the moving party must show that he has substantial need of the materials, and that "he is unable without undue hardship to obtain the substantial equivalent of the materials by other means." Belcher v. Bassett Furn. Indus., Inc., 588 F.2d 904 (4th Cir. 1978).

Traditional concepts of good cause important. — Prior to 1970, a showing of "good cause" was a requirement for all discovery under this rule. The advisory committee found that in actual practice, good cause was required only in trial preparation materials cases while mere relevancy was sufficient for production of other documents. The committee accordingly wrote the varying standards into Rule 26 and dropped the good cause requirement from this rule. In so doing, however, it gave no indication as to what standard would govern the second part of this rule, i.e., inspection of a party's premises. Some recent commentators have suggested that upon contest of this rule motion, traditional concepts of "good cause" once again become important. Belcher v. Bassett Furn. Indus., Inc., 588 F.2d 904 (4th Cir. 1978).

Depositions do much to identify the items of discovery and to establish the rights of the parties under this rule. Belcher v. Bassett Furn. Indus., Inc., 588 F.2d 904 (4th Cir. 1978).

Rules should be available to the plaintiff and to an insurer filing pleadings in its own name under the Virginia Uninsured Motorists Law. Ivory v. Nichols, 34 F.R.D. 128 (E.D. Va. 1963).

Computerized payroll file alleged to constitute trade secret. — In an action involving alleged racially discriminatory employment practices by defendant, plaintiffs' request for defendant's current computerized master payroll file and computer printouts for W-2 forms of defendant's employees was not denied on the ground that it constituted a privileged trade secret, although the court expressed its willingness to entertain a motion to put the documents under a protective order. Adams v. Dan River Mills, Inc., 54 F.R.D. 220 (W.D. Va. 1972).

Production of contracts between defendants prior to date of alleged monopoly ordered. — See Byers Theaters, Inc. v. Murphy, 1 F.R.D. 286 (W.D. Va. 1940).

And prices shown by contracts held not trade secrets or confidential. — See Byers Theaters, Inc. v. Murphy, 1 F.R.D. 286 (W.D. Va. 1940).

"Availability" and "control" words of art used to express same thought. — Rule 33, Fed.R.Civ.P. prescribes that, in answering interrogatories, the party "shall furnish such information as is available to the party." Rule 34, Fed.R.Civ.P., which deals with the production of documents, directs that, by way of response to a notice thereunder, the producing party shall produce such documents as are in his "possession, custody, or control." The two Rules are equally inclusive in their scope. "Availability" and "control" are both words of art and are used to express the same thought. There is no basis whatsoever for a trial court to charge a witness at a contempt hearing for failure to make discovery with deception simply because he has used the word "available," a "term of art," which both in common and in legal terms means the same as "control." Wilson v. Volkswagen of Am., Inc., 561 F.2d 494 (4th Cir. 1977), cert. denied, 434 U.S. 1020, 98 S. Ct. 744, 54 L. Ed. 2d 768 (1978).

Applied in Haney v. Woodward & Lothrop, Inc., 330 F.2d 940 (4th Cir. 1964); In re Trinidad Corp., 238 F. Supp. 928 (E.D. Va. 1965); McLean v. Prudential S.S. Co., 36 F.R.D. 421 (E.D. Va. 1965); VEPCO v. Sun Shipbuilding & Dry Dock Co., 68 F.R.D. 397 (E.D. Va. 1975); Lee X v. Casey, 771 F. Supp. 725 (E.D. Va. 1991).

Rule 35. Physical and Mental Examinations.

(a) *Order for an Examination.* — (1) In General. The court where the action is pending may order a party whose mental or physical condition — including blood group — is in controversy to submit to a physical or mental examination by a suitably licensed or certified examiner. The court has the same authority to order a party to produce for examination a person who is in its custody or under its legal control.

(2) Motion and Notice; Contents of the Order. The order:

(A) may be made only on motion for good cause and on notice to all parties and the person to be examined; and

(B) must specify the time, place, manner, conditions, and scope of the examination, as well as the person or persons who will perform it.

(b) *Examiner's Report.* — (1) Request by the Party or Person Examined. The party who moved for the examination must, on request, deliver to the requester a copy of the examiner's report, together with like reports of all earlier examinations of the same condition.The request may be made by the party against whom the examination order was issued or by the person examined.

(2) Contents. The examiner's report must be in writing and must set out in detail the examiner's findings, including diagnoses, conclusions, and the results of any tests.

(3) Request by the Moving Party. After delivering the reports, the party who moved for the examination may request — and is entitled to receive — from the party against whom the examination order was issued like reports of all earlier or later examinations of the same condition. But those reports need not be delivered by the party with custody or control of the person examined if the party shows that it could not obtain them.

(4) Waiver of Privilege. By requesting and obtaining the examiner's report, or by deposing the examiner, the party examined waives any privilege it may have — in that action or any other action involving the same controversy — concerning testimony about all examinations of the same condition.

(5) Failure to Deliver a Report. The court on motion may order — on just terms — that a party deliver the report of an examination. If the report is not provided, the court may exclude the examiner's testimony at trial.

(6) Scope. This subdivision (b) applies also to an examination made by the parties' agreement, unless the agreement states otherwise. This subdivision does not preclude obtaining an examiner's report or deposing an examiner under other rules. (Amended by order adopted March 30, 1970, effective July 1, 1970, by order adopted March 2, 1987, effective August 1, 1987, by P.L. 100-690, § 7047, effective November 18, 1988, by order adopted April 30, 1991, effective December 1, 1991, and by order adopted April 30, 2007, effective December 1, 2007.)

Comment. — The language of Rule 35 has been amended as part of the general restyling of the Civil Rules to make them more easily understood and to make style and terminology consistent throughout the rules. These changes are intended to be stylistic only.

Law Review. — For article, "Compulsory Medical Examinations Under the Federal Rules," see 41 Va. L. Rev. 1059 (1955).

CASE NOTES

Rule should be available to the plaintiff and to an insurer filing pleadings in its own name under the Virginia Uninsured Motorists Law. — See Ivory v. Nichols, 34 F.R.D. 128 (E.D. Va. 1963).

The requirement of "good cause" is not to be treated lightly. — See In re Trinidad Corp., 238 F. Supp. 928 (E.D. Va. 1965).

No right to choose physician. — A defendant does not have an absolute right to choose the doctor who will perform an examination conducted pursuant to this rule; however, absent a "valid objection" to the physician defendant chooses, the defendant's choice is to be respected. Powell v. United States, 149 F.R.D. 122 (E.D. Va. 1993).

Rule restricts independent examinations where prior reports obtained by discovery. — This rule apparently was designed to restrict independent examinations ordered by the court after the party seeking the examination has resorted to the discovery of reports and has successfully obtained same. In re Trinidad Corp., 238 F. Supp. 928 (E.D. Va. 1965).

Independent report is necessary only if specialized field involved or prior report vague. — Only if the report of a claimant's physician indicates the need for an expression of opinion in a specialized field of medical expertise, or there is vagueness or uncertainty in the physician's findings, can a United States district court generally conclude that an independent examination is necessary, or possibly when claimant's physician is not thoroughly qualified in such specialized field. In re Trinidad Corp., 238 F. Supp. 928 (E.D. Va. 1965).

Reports of prior examinations will not be revealed until report under this rule delivered. — The United States district court for the eastern district of Virginia construes the words, "After such request and delivery the party causing the examination to be made shall be entitled upon request to receive from the party examined a like report of any examination, previously or thereafter made, of the same mental or physical condition," to mean that, if an independent examination is ordered by the court, the reports of prior examinations shall not be revealed in advance of the independent examination but shall be produced after the report of the independent examination has been requested and delivered to the party examined or his attorney. In re Trinidad Corp., 238 F. Supp. 928 (E.D. Va. 1965).

Applied in Bowles v. Commercial Cas. Ins. Co., 107 F.2d 169 (4th Cir. 1939).

Rule 36. Requests for Admission.

(a) *Scope and Procedure.* — (1) Scope. A party may serve on any other party a written request to admit, for purposes of the pending action only, the truth of any matters within the scope of Rule 26(b)(1) relating to:

(A) facts, the application of law to fact, or opinions about either; and

(B) the genuineness of any described documents.

(2) Form; Copy of a Document. Each matter must be separately stated. A request to admit the genuineness of a document must be accompanied by a copy of the document unless it is, or has been, otherwise furnished or made available for inspection and copying.

(3) Time to Respond; Effect of Not Responding. A matter is admitted unless, within 30 days after being served, the party to whom the request is directed serves on the requesting party a written answer or objection addressed to the matter and signed by the party or its attorney. A shorter or longer time for responding may be stipulated to under Rule 29 or be ordered by the court.

(4) Answer. If a matter is not admitted, the answer must specifically deny it or state in detail why the answering party cannot truthfully admit or deny it. A denial must fairly respond to the substance of the matter; and when good faith requires that a party qualify an answer or deny only a part of a matter, the answer must specify the part admitted and qualify or deny the rest. The answering party may assert lack of knowledge or information as a reason for failing to admit or deny only if the party states that it has made reasonable inquiry and that the information it knows or can readily obtain is insufficient to enable it to admit or deny.

(5) Objections. The grounds for objecting to a request must be stated. A party must not object solely on the ground that the request presents a genuine issue for trial.

(6) Motion Regarding the Sufficiency of an Answer or Objection. The requesting party may move to determine the sufficiency of an answer or objection. Unless the court finds an objection justified, it must order that an answer be served. On finding that an answer does not comply with this rule, the court may order either that the matter is admitted or that an amended answer be served. The court may defer its final decision until a pretrial conference or a specified time before trial. Rule 37(a)(5) applies to an award of expenses.

(b) *Effect of an Admission; Withdrawing or Amending It.* — A matter admitted under this rule is conclusively established unless the court, on motion, permits the admission to be withdrawn or amended. Subject to Rule 16(e), the court may permit withdrawal or amendment if it would promote the presentation of the merits of the action and if the court is not persuaded that it would prejudice the requesting party in maintaining or defending the action on the merits. An admission under this rule is not an admission for any other purpose and cannot be used against the party in any other proceeding. (Amended by order adopted December 27, 1946, effective March 19, 1948, by order adopted March 30, 1970, effective July 1, 1970, by order adopted March 2, 1987, effective August 1, 1987, by order adopted April 22, 1993, effective December 1, 1993, and by order adopted April 30, 2007, effective December 1, 2007.)

Comment. — The language of Rule 36 has been amended as part of the general restyling of the Civil Rules to make them more easily understood and to make style and terminology consistent throughout the rules. These changes are intended to be stylistic only.

The final sentence of the first paragraph of former Rule 36(a) was a redundant cross-reference to the discovery moratorium provisions of Rule 26(d). Rule 26(d) is now familiar, obviating any need to carry forward the redundant cross-reference. The redundant reminder of Rule 37(c) in the second paragraph was likewise omitted.

CASE NOTES

Rules should be available to the plaintiff and to an insurer filing pleadings in its own name under the Virginia Uninsured Motorists Law. Ivory v. Nichols, 34 F.R.D. 128 (E.D. Va. 1963).

An insurer filing pleadings in its own name under the Virginia Uninsured Motorists Law is an "adverse party." Ivory v. Nichols, 34 F.R.D. 128 (E.D. Va. 1963).

And it will be compelled to answer interrogatories. Ivory v. Nichols, 34 F.R.D. 128 (E.D. Va. 1963).

Facts not denied in manner set out are deemed admitted. — This rule provides that all facts not denied in the manner set out therein are admitted. Durham v. Southern Ry., 256 F. Supp. 879 (W.D. Va. 1966).

Failure to respond where request not mature for response. — Where the requests for admissions are not mature for response, failure to respond cannot be taken as an admission. Johnston Mem. Hosp. v. Hess, 21 Bankr. 465 (Bankr. W.D. Va. 1982), rev'd on other grounds, 44 Bankr. 598 (Bankr. W.D. Va. 1984).

One day delay not an abuse of discretion. — Because the late response was so minimal in time—one day—and work on the date for responding was slowed by the snow storm, the district court did not abuse its discretion in refusing to consider the requests for admission as admitted. Nguyen v. CNA Corp., 44 F.3d 234 (4th Cir. 1995).

Pretrial admission may be withdrawn, amended or challenged. — A party making a pretrial admission may nonetheless amend or withdraw that admission, or challenge the admissibility of that admission into evidence at trial. Johnston Mem. Hosp. v. Hess, 21 Bankr. 465 (Bankr. W.D. Va. 1982), rev'd on other grounds, 44 Bankr. 598 (Bankr. W.D. Va. 1984).

There is no absolute right to withdraw admissions. In re Fisherman's Wharf Fillet, Inc., 83 F. Supp. 2d 651 (E.D. Va. 1999).

The legal principle that guides courts to withdraw deemed admissions when confronted with contrary factual information is at the discretion of the court. In re Fisherman's Wharf Fillet, Inc., 83 F. Supp. 2d 651 (E.D. Va. 1999).

Admissions treated as sworn testimony. — Under this rule, admissions in answer to a request from the other party stand in the same relation to the case as sworn testimony. Williams v. Howard Johnson's Inc., 323 F.2d 102 (4th Cir. 1963), vacating and remanding 210 F. Supp. 295 (E.D. Va. 1962).

Applied in Stephens v. Cox, 315 F. Supp. 821 (W.D. Va. 1970); Eastern Indem. Co. v. J.D. Conti Elec. Co., 573 F. Supp. 1036 (E.D. Va. 1983); Harrison Higgins, Inc. v. AT & T Communications, Inc., 697 F. Supp. 220 (E.D. Va. 1988); White v. United States, 6 F. Supp. 2d 553 (W.D. Va. 1998).

Rule 37. Failure to Make Disclosures or to Cooperate in Discovery; Sanctions.

(a) *Motion for an Order Compelling Disclosure or Discovery.* — (1) In General. On notice to other parties and all affected persons, a party may move for an order compelling disclosure or discovery. The motion must include a certification that the movant has in good faith conferred or attempted to confer with the person or party failing to make disclosure or discovery in an effort to obtain it without court action.

(2) Appropriate Court. A motion for an order to a party must be made in the court where the action is pending. A motion for an order to a nonparty must be made in the court where the discovery is or will be taken.

(3) Specific Motions. (A) To Compel Disclosure. If a party fails to make a disclosure required by Rule 26(a), any other party may move to compel disclosure and for appropriate sanctions.

(B) To Compel a Discovery Response. A party seeking discovery may move for an order compelling an answer, designation, production, or inspection. This motion may be made if:

(i) a deponent fails to answer a question asked under Rule 30 or 31;

(ii) a corporation or other entity fails to make a designation under Rule 30(b)(6) or 31(a)(4);

(iii) a party fails to answer an interrogatory submitted under Rule 33; or

(iv) a party fails to respond that inspection will be permitted — or fails to permit inspection — as requested under Rule 34.

(C) Related to a Deposition. When taking an oral deposition, the party asking a question may complete or adjourn the examination before moving for an order.

(4) Evasive or Incomplete Disclosure, Answer, or Response. For purposes of this subdivision (a), an evasive or incomplete disclosure, answer, or response must be treated as a failure to disclose, answer, or respond.

(5) Payment of Expenses; Protective Orders. (A) If the Motion Is Granted (or Disclosure or Discovery Is Provided After Filing). If the motion is granted — or if the disclosure or requested discovery is provided after the motion was filed — the court must, after giving an opportunity to be heard, require the party or deponent whose conduct necessitated the motion, the party or attorney advising that conduct, or both to pay the movant's reasonable expenses incurred in making the motion, including attorney's fees. But the court must not order this payment if:

(i) the movant filed the motion before attempting in good faith to obtain the disclosure or discovery without court action;

(ii) the opposing party's nondisclosure, response, or objection was substantially justified; or

(iii) other circumstances make an award of expenses unjust.

(B) If the Motion Is Denied. If the motion is denied, the court may issue any protective order authorized under Rule 26(c) and must, after giving an opportunity to be heard, require the movant, the attorney filing the motion, or both to pay the party or deponent who opposed the motion its reasonable expenses incurred in opposing the motion, including attorney's fees. But the court must not order this payment if the motion was substantially justified or other circumstances make an award of expenses unjust.

(C) If the Motion Is Granted in Part and Denied in Part. If the motion is granted in part and denied in part, the court may issue any protective order authorized under Rule 26(c) and may, after giving an opportunity to be heard, apportion the reasonable expenses for the motion.

(b) *Failure to Comply with a Court Order.* — (1) Sanctions Sought in the District Where the Deposition Is Taken. If the court where the discovery is taken orders a deponent to be sworn or to answer a question and the deponent fails to obey, the failure may be treated as contempt of court. If a deposition-related motion is transferred to the court where the action is pending, and that court orders a deponent to be sworn or to answer a question and the deponent fails to obey, the failure may be treated as contempt of either the court where the discovery is taken or the court where the action is pending.

(2) Sanctions Sought in the District Where the Action Is Pending. (A) For Not Obeying a Discovery Order. If a party or a party's officer, director, or managing agent — or a witness designated under Rule 30(b)(6) or 31(a)(4) — fails to obey an order to provide or permit discovery, including an order under Rule 26(f), 35, or 37(a), the court where the action is pending may issue further just orders. They may include the following:

(i) directing that the matters embraced in the order or other designated facts be taken as established for purposes of the action, as the prevailing party claims;

(ii) prohibiting the disobedient party from supporting or opposing designated claims or defenses, or from introducing designated matters in evidence;

(iii) striking pleadings in whole or in part;

(iv) staying further proceedings until the order is obeyed;

(v) dismissing the action or proceeding in whole or in part;

(vi) rendering a default judgment against the disobedient party; or

(vii) treating as contempt of court the failure to obey any order except an order to submit to a physical or mental examination.

(B) For Not Producing a Person for Examination. If a party fails to comply with an order under Rule 35(a) requiring it to produce another person for examination, the court may issue any of the orders listed in Rule 37(b)(2)(A)(i)-(vi), unless the disobedient party shows that it cannot produce the other person.

(C) Payment of Expenses. Instead of or in addition to the orders above, the court must order the disobedient party, the attorney advising that party, or both to pay the reasonable expenses, including attorney's fees, caused by the failure, unless the failure was substantially justified or other circumstances make an award of expenses unjust.

(c) *Failure to Disclose, to Supplement an Earlier Response, or to Admit.* — (1) Failure to Disclose or Supplement. If a party fails to provide information or identify a witness as required by Rule 26(a) or (e), the party is not allowed to use that information or witness to supply evidence on a motion, at a hearing, or at a trial, unless the failure was substantially justified or is harmless. In addition to or instead of this sanction, the court, on motion and after giving an opportunity to be heard:

(A) may order payment of the reasonable expenses, including attorney's fees, caused by the failure;

(B) may inform the jury of the party's failure; and

(C) may impose other appropriate sanctions, including any of the orders listed in Rule 37(b)(2)(A)(i)-(vi).

(2) Failure to Admit. If a party fails to admit what is requested under Rule 36 and if the requesting party later proves a document to be genuine or the matter true, the requesting party may move that the party who failed to admit pay the reasonable expenses, including attorney's fees, incurred in making that proof. The court must so order unless:

(A) the request was held objectionable under Rule 36(a);

(B) the admission sought was of no substantial importance;

(C) the party failing to admit had a reasonable ground to believe that it might prevail on the matter; or

(D) there was other good reason for the failure to admit.

(d) *Party's Failure to Attend Its Own Deposition, Serve Answers to Interrogatories, or Respond to a Request for Inspection.* — (1) In General.

(A) Motion; Grounds for Sanctions. The court where the action is pending may, on motion, order sanctions if:

(i) a party or a party's officer, director, or managing agent — or a person designated under Rule 30(b)(6) or 31(a)(4) — fails, after being served with proper notice, to appear for that person's deposition; or

(ii) a party, after being properly served with interrogatories under Rule 33 or a request for inspection under Rule 34, fails to serve its answers, objections, or written response.

(B) Certification. A motion for sanctions for failing to answer or respond must include a certification that the movant has in good faith conferred or attempted to confer with the party failing to act in an effort to obtain the answer or response without court action.

(2) Unacceptable Excuse for Failing to Act. A failure described in Rule 37(d)(1)(A) is not excused on the ground that the discovery sought was objectionable, unless the party failing to act has a pending motion for a protective order under Rule 26(c).

(3) Types of Sanctions. Sanctions may include any of the orders listed in Rule 37(b)(2)(A)(i)-(vi). Instead of or in addition to these sanctions, the court must require the party failing to act, the attorney advising that party, or both to pay the reasonable expenses, including attorney's fees, caused by the failure, unless the failure was substantially justified or other circumstances make an award of expenses unjust.

(e) *Failure to Provide Electronically Stored Information.* — Absent exceptional circumstances, a court may not impose sanctions under these rules on a party for failing to provide electronically stored information lost as a result of the routine, good-faith operation of an electronic information system.

(f) *Failure to Participate in Framing a Discovery Plan.* — If a party or its attorney fails to participate in good faith in developing and submitting a proposed discovery plan as required by Rule 26(f), the court may, after giving an opportunity to be heard, require that party or attorney to pay to any other party the reasonable expenses, including attorney's fees, caused by the failure. (Amended by order adopted December 29, 1948, effective October 20, 1949, by order adopted March 30, 1970, effective July 1, 1970, by order adopted April 29, 1980, effective August 1, 1980, by order adopted October 21, 1980, effective October 1, 1981, by order adopted March 2, 1987, effective August 1, 1987, by order adopted April 22, 1993, effective December 1, 1993, by order adopted April 17, 2000, effective December 1, 2000, by order adopted April 12, 2006, effective December 1, 2006, by order adopted April 30, 2007, effective December 1, 2007, and by order adopted April 16, 2013, effective December 1, 2013.)

Comment. — The language of Rule 37 has been amended as part of the general restyling of the Civil Rules to make them more easily understood and to make style and terminology consistent throughout the rules. These changes are intended to be stylistic only.

Commitee Note — Subdivision (f). Subdivision (f) is new. It focuses on a distinctive feature of computer operations, the routine alteration and deletion of information that attends ordinary use. Many steps essential to computer operation may alter or destroy information, for reasons that have nothing to do with how that information might relate to litigation. As a result, the ordinary operation of computer systems creates a risk that a party may lose potentially discoverable information without culpable conduct on its part. Under Rule 37(f), absent exceptional circumstances, sanctions cannot be imposed for loss of electronically stored information resulting from the routine, good-faith operation of an electronic information system.

Law Review. — For comment, "Spoliation: Civil Liability for Destruction of Evidence," see 20 U. Rich. L. Rev. 191 (1985). For note, "Transnational Discovery: The Balancing Act of American Trial Courts and the New Approach to the Hague Convention," see 42 Wash. & Lee L. Rev. 1285 (1985).

CASE NOTES

Purpose. — This rule aims at imposing costs on counsel and parties who frustrate the discovery process and occupy the court's time with needless disputes. In re Fisherman's Wharf Fillet, Inc., 83 F. Supp. 2d 651 (E.D. Va. 1999).

Refusal of access to papers is not excused if they might have served in cross-examination. — If the plaintiff was wrongfully refused access to papers or the right to have the court examine them, the defendants cannot exonerate themselves on the ground that the papers were no longer useful anyway, where the documents might have served well in cross-examination. Haney v. Woodward & Lothrop, Inc., 330 F.2d 940 (4th Cir. 1964).

Ex parte subpoenas seeking records from correctional facilities and governmental agencies would be granted. United States v. Beckford, 964 F. Supp. 1010 (E.D. Va. 1997).

Costs and attorney's fees may be recovered for refusal to answer. — A party may apply to the court for an order requiring the other party to answer questions propounded. In the event he obtains such an order and the court requires the other party to answer those questions which had not been answered, the rule provides that the court shall require the refusing party to pay the reasonable costs incurred in obtaining the order requiring the answers, together with reasonable attorney's fees incurred in that connection. Gibbs v. Blackwelder, 346 F.2d 943 (4th Cir. 1965).

But only if order requiring answer has been obtained. — Where the defendants neither sought nor obtained an order requiring the plaintiffs to answer the questions they refused to answer upon the advice of their attorney, they have incurred no costs and have paid no attorney's fees for which they may be reimbursed under the provisions of this rule. And an order which required the plaintiffs' attorney to pay to the defendants $250, plus the cost of transcribing certain depositions, was inappropriate. Gibbs v. Blackwelder, 346 F.2d 943 (4th Cir. 1965).

Absent showing of deliberate concealment, court reluctant to impose sanctions. White v. City of Suffolk, 460 F. Supp. 516 (E.D. Va. 1978).

New trial ordered and defendant required to pay plaintiff's costs and expenses for failure of insurer to produce reports of investigation. — See Haney v. Woodward & Lothrop, Inc., 330 F.2d 940 (4th Cir. 1964).

Sanction must be no more severe than to prevent prejudice. — Even in those cases where it may be found that failure to produce results in the discovering party's case being jeopardized or prejudiced, it is the normal rule that the proper sanction must be no more severe than is necessary to prevent prejudice to the movant. Wilson v. Volkswagen of Am., Inc., 561 F.2d 494 (4th Cir. 1977), cert. denied, 434 U.S. 1020, 98 S. Ct. 744, 54 L. Ed. 2d 768 (1978).

Range of discretion to impose default judgment sanction narrow. — The power to impose sanctions under the rule for failure, after court order in discovery proceedings, to produce documents, is discretionary with the trial court. It is not, however, a discretion without bounds or limits but one to be exercised discreetly and never when it has been established that failure to comply has been due to inability, and not to willfulness, bad faith, or any fault of the noncomplying party. Particularly is the court to act cautiously when the sanction imposed is that of default judgment, which is the most severe in the spectrum of sanctions provided by statute or rule. In that situation the trial court's range of discretion is more narrow than when the court is imposing other less severe sanctions. Wilson v. Volkswagen of Am., Inc., 561 F.2d 494 (4th Cir. 1977), cert. denied, 434 U.S. 1020, 98 S. Ct. 744, 54 L. Ed. 2d 768 (1978).

The reason for a narrower range of discretion is that the sanction of a default judgment, though a rational method of enforcement of the discovery rules, in an appropriate case, represents in effect an infringement upon a party's right to trial by jury under the seventh amendment and runs counter to sound public policy of deciding cases on their merits, and against depriving a party of his fair day in court. Wilson v. Volkswagen of Am., Inc., 561 F.2d 494 (4th Cir. 1977), cert. denied, 434 U.S. 1020, 98 S. Ct. 744, 54 L. Ed. 2d 768 (1978).

While imposition of sanctions under this rule lies within the discretion of the trial court, it is not a discretion without bounds or limits. Hatton v. Spencer, 204 Bankr. 477 (E.D. Va. 1997).

Granting default judgment confined to "flagrant case." — Because of the importance of the constitutional and policy considerations, the exercise of the power should be confined to the "flagrant case" in which it is demonstrated that the failure to produce materially affects the substantial rights of the adverse party and is prejudicial to the presentation of his case. This is so because a default judgment should normally not be imposed so as to foreclose the merits of controversies as punishment for general misbehavior save in that rare case where the conduct represents such flagrant bad faith and callous disregard of the party's obligation under the Rules as to warrant the sanction not simply for the purpose of preventing prejudice to the discovering party but as a necessary deterrent to others. Wilson v. Volkswagen of Am., Inc., 561 F.2d 494 (4th Cir. 1977), cert. denied, 434 U.S. 1020, 98 S. Ct. 744, 54 L. Ed. 2d 768 (1978).

In determining whether to impose the sanction of default judgment the needs of the discovery party must be evaluated as well as the nature of the noncompliance and the trial court must consider how the absence of such evidence not produced would impair the other party's ability to establish their case and whether the noncomplying party's conduct in not producing documents would deprive the other party of a fair trial. Wilson v. Volkswagen of Am., Inc., 561 F.2d 494 (4th Cir. 1977), cert. denied, 434 U.S. 1020, 98 S. Ct. 744, 54 L. Ed. 2d 768 (1978).

Review of trial court's judgment granting sanctions. — Recognizing that the power to grant sanctions under Rule 37(b), Fed.R.Civ.P. is discretionary with the trial court, it follows that the exercise of such power will only be disturbed on appeal for abuse of discretion. This does not mean, though, that an appellate court should automatically affirm such exercise of discretion. On the contrary, it is obligated to consider the full record as well as the reasons assigned by the trial court for its judgment, and to reverse the judgment below, if after such review, the appellate court has a definite and firm conviction that the court below committed a clear error of judgment in the conclusion it reached upon a weighing of the relevant factors. Wilson v. Volkswagen of Am., Inc., 561 F.2d 494 (4th Cir. 1977), cert. denied, 434 U.S. 1020, 98 S. Ct. 744, 54 L. Ed. 2d 768 (1978).

While the discretionary range is "more narrow" when default judgment is entered, a court has a greater degree or range of discretion to impose less onerous sanctions. Hatton v. Spencer, 204 Bankr. 477 (E.D. Va. 1997).

The determination of whether a trial court has abused its discretion is rather case-specific. Hatton v. Spencer, 204 Bankr. 477 (E.D. Va. 1997).

Trial court must clearly state reasons when granting default judgment. — Since every exercise of judicial discretion "must find its basis in good reason," the trial court, when granting a default judgment sanction, should clearly state its reasons so that meaningful review may be had on appeal. Wilson v. Volkswagen of Am., Inc., 561 F.2d 494 (4th Cir. 1977), cert. denied, 434 U.S. 1020, 98 S. Ct. 744, 54 L. Ed. 2d 768 (1978).

Duty of disclosure in defective product case. — The cause of the product's deterioration stands on a different footing; it is not so much an objectively observable fact as it is a matter of expert opinion. Thus, a defendant may decline to admit the defectiveness of a product, even though some objective facts may suggest otherwise, provided there are reasonable grounds for the denial. Board of Dirs. v. Anden Group, 136 F.R.D. 100 (E.D. Va. 1991).

Applied in Lekkas v. Liberian M/V Caledonia, 443 F.2d 10 (4th Cir. 1971); Adams v. Dan River Mills, Inc., 54 F.R.D. 220 (W.D. Va. 1972); Teates v. Kuranda, 122 Bankr. 264 (Bankr. E.D. Va. 1990); Brown v. Black, 260 Va. 305, 534 S.E.2d 727, 2000 Va. LEXIS 117 (2000).

TITLE VI. TRIALS.

Rule 38. Right to a Jury Trial; Demand.

(a) *Right Preserved.* — The right of trial by jury as declared by the Seventh Amendment to the Constitution — or as provided by a federal statute — is preserved to the parties inviolate.

(b) *Demand.* — On any issue triable of right by a jury, a party may demand a jury trial by:

(1) serving the other parties with a written demand — which may be included in a pleading — no later than 14 days after the last pleading directed to the issue is served; and

(2) filing the demand in accordance with Rule 5(d).

(c) *Specifying Issues.* — In its demand, a party may specify the issues that it wishes to have tried by a jury; otherwise, it is considered to have demanded a jury trial on all the issues so triable. If the party has demanded a jury trial on only some issues, any other party may — within 14 days after being served with the demand or within a shorter time ordered by the court — serve a demand for a jury trial on any other or all factual issues triable by jury.

(d) *Waiver; Withdrawal.* — A party waives a jury trial unless its demand is properly served and filed. A proper demand may be withdrawn only if the parties consent.

(e) *Admiralty and Maritime Claims.* — These rules do not create a right to a jury trial on issues in a claim that is an admiralty or maritime claim under Rule 9(h). (Added by order adopted February 28, 1966, effective July 1, 1966, amended by order adopted March 2, 1987, effective August 1, 1987, by order adopted April 1, 1993, effective December 1, 1993, by order adopted April 22, 1993, effective December 1, 1993, by order adopted April 30, 2007, effective December 1, 2007, and by order adopted March 26, 2009, effective December 1, 2009.)

Comment. — The language of Rule 38 has been amended as part of the general restyling of the Civil Rules to make them more easily understood and to make style and terminology consistent throughout the rules. These changes are intended to be stylistic only.

Law Review. — For an article, "The Transformation of the American Civil Trial: The Silent Judge," see 42 Wm. & Mary L. Rev. 195 (2000).

CASE NOTES

No right to jury trial where claim is identified as admiralty or maritime. — The merger of civil and admiralty procedure in 1966 does not affect the right to jury trial. If the only basis for jurisdiction is that the case is an admiralty case, there is no right to a jury. If jurisdiction can alternatively be based on a federal question, or on diversity and the necessary jurisdictional amount, either party may demand a jury trial unless plaintiff has chosen to identify the claim as an admiralty or maritime claim, as permitted by Rule 9(h). If he exercises that option, subdivision (e) of this rule provides that there is no right to trial by jury. Sanderlin v. Old Dominion Stevedoring Corp., 281 F. Supp. 1015 (E.D. Va. 1968).

The significance of the election to proceed in admiralty or as an ordinary civil action relates to distinctive procedural requirements and remedies available in admiralty claims and the fact that there is no right to trial by jury of an admiralty claim. Coley v. Dragon Ltd., 138 F.R.D. 460 (E.D. Va. 1990).

Rule requires written demand served in time. — This rule is explicit in its requirement that demand for trial by jury be in writing and served upon the other party "not later than ten days after the service of the last pleading directed to such issue." Brunwasser v. Suave, 400 F.2d 600 (4th Cir. 1968), cert. denied, 393 U.S. 1083, 89 S. Ct. 868, 21 L. Ed. 2d 777 (1969).

Although the rules preserve the right of trial by jury, a timely demand for a jury trial must be filed. Krodel v. Houghtaling, 468 F.2d 887 (4th Cir. 1972), cert. denied, 414 U.S. 829, 94 S. Ct. 57, 38 L. Ed. 2d 64 (1973).

When request for jury is timely made. — The general rule is that a jury request is timely if made within ten days of the last defendant's answer. However, when a plaintiff adds defendants to a case through an amended complaint, this general precept is superseded by the rule that an amendment to a complaint will revive the plaintiff's right to request a jury trial only when the amendment introduces new issues into the case. Jones v. Boyd, 161 F.R.D. 48 (E.D. Va. 1995).

Changing issues revives right to demand jury trial. — Changing the issues of the complaint determines whether a plaintiff's right to demand a jury trial is revived, not changing the defendants. Gamboa v. Medical College of Hampton Rds., 160 F.R.D. 540 (E.D. Va. 1995).

An amendment which merely adds defendants or changes defendants does not introduce new issues to a case, and therefore does not revive a plaintiff's opportunity to request a jury trial. Jones v. Boyd, 161 F.R.D. 48 (E.D. Va. 1995).

Simply providing names for two previously unidentified defendants did not revive plaintiff's right to request a trial by jury. Jones v. Boyd, 161 F.R.D. 48 (E.D. Va. 1995).

If a party does not make a demand for a jury trial as the rule requires, that constitutes a waiver by that party of a jury trial. Law v. Law, 922 F. Supp. 1106 (E.D. Va. 1996).

Alternative basis for holding that jury demand is proper is plaintiff's introduction of a new issue into litigation. Arguably, the raising of a new issue revives previous jury demand made in an earlier amended complaint. Vanguard Military Equip. Corp. v. David B. Finestone Co., 6 F. Supp. 2d 488 (E.D. Va. 1997).

Copy of answer mailed to one of plaintiff's two attorneys triggered 10-day time limit. — Copy of defendant's answer, which was mailed to, and received by, one of plaintiff's two attorneys of record, was properly delivered for purposes of triggering the 10-day time limit provided in this rule, even though plaintiff claimed the other attorney who did nt receive a copy was his "lead" counsel. Frederick v. Koziol, 130 F.R.D. 620 (E.D. Va. 1990).

Unsigned and undated pleadings. — Pleading sent to an attorney by mail demanding a jury trial was sufficient to trigger the running of the period for filing such a demand, even though the copies were unsigned and undated. Frederick v. Koziol, 130 F.R.D. 620 (E.D. Va. 1990).

It would be a strained construction of subdivision (b) to hold that of necessity no trial may be had within 10 days of the service of the last pleading absent an express waiver of trial by jury. Bills v. Hodges, 628 F.2d 844 (4th Cir. 1980).

Plaintiffs attempted to escape their dilemma of having failed to follow the rule by claiming that their filing, on or about March 8, 1979, of a response to defendant's answer and grounds of defense amounted to the last pleading for subdivision (b) purposes. However, the "response" was clearly a superfluous document, not provided for in the rules, and, consequently, did not qualify as a pleading under Rule 7(a). Malbon v. Pennsylvania Millers Mut. Ins. Co., 636 F.2d 936 (4th Cir. 1980).

But written response to motion is not required and is not "pleading." — The Federal Rules of Civil Procedure do not require that there be a written "pleading" in response to a motion for jury trial. Indeed, where such a document is filed, it is not regarded as a "pleading." Brunwasser v. Suave, 400 F.2d 600 (4th Cir. 1968), cert. denied, 393 U.S. 1083, 89 S. Ct. 868, 21 L. Ed. 2d 777 (1969).

Waiver held sufficient. — When the district court advised the attorneys of the early trial date and was not advised by them in return of any request for a jury, that is sufficient waiver. Bills v. Hodges, 628 F.2d 844 (4th Cir. 1980).

Applied in Lumbermens Mut. Cas. Co. v. Harleysville Mut. Cas. Co., 367 F.2d 250 (4th Cir. 1966); Cook v. Cox, 357 F. Supp. 120 (E.D. Va. 1973); Malbon v. Pennsylvania Millers Mut. Ins. Co., 636 F.2d 936 (4th Cir. 1980); Lewis v. United States, 812 F. Supp. 620 (E.D. Va. 1993); Hall v. Andrews, 189 Bankr. 380 (Bankr. E.D. Va. 1995).

Rule 39. Trial by Jury or by the Court.

(a) *When a Demand Is Made.* — When a jury trial has been demanded under Rule 38, the action must be designated on the docket as a jury action. The trial on all issues so demanded must be by jury unless:

(1) the parties or their attorneys file a stipulation to a nonjury trial or so stipulate on the record; or

(2) the court, on motion or on its own, finds that on some or all of those issues there is no federal right to a jury trial.

(b) *When No Demand Is Made.* — Issues on which a jury trial is not properly demanded are to be tried by the court. But the court may, on motion, order a jury trial on any issue for which a jury might have been demanded.

(c) *Advisory Jury; Jury Trial by Consent.* — In an action not triable of right by a jury, the court, on motion or on its own:

(1) may try any issue with an advisory jury; or

(2) may, with the parties' consent, try any issue by a jury whose verdict has the same effect as if a jury trial had been a matter of right, unless the action is against the United States and a federal statute provides for a nonjury trial. (Amended by order adopted April 30, 2007, effective December 1, 2007.)

Comment. — The language of Rule 39 has been amended as part of the general restyling of the Civil Rules to make them more easily understood and to make style and terminology consistent throughout the rules. These changes are intended to be stylistic only.

CASE NOTES

Utilization of advisory jury does not relieve court of its responsibility to make findings. — Subdivision (c) of this rule specifically authorizes a court in its discretion to employ such procedure in any case "not triable of right by a jury," and the court's exercise of such discretion in these circumstances is not reviewable. The findings of such a jury are, of course, merely advisory; the court must make its own findings, and review on appeal is of the findings of the court as if there had been no verdict from an advisory jury. Cox v. Babcock & Wilcox Co., 471 F.2d 13 (4th Cir. 1972).

Use of advisory jury in Age Discrimination in Employment Act action proper. — The Age Discrimination in Employment Act's provision for legal relief renders actions under the act suits "at common law" under the Seventh Amendment. Thus a plaintiff having a claim for lost wages under the act has a right to a jury trial. Since jury trials have been held appropriate under the act, a federal district court's use of an advisory jury was also proper. Coates v. NCR Co., 433 F. Supp. 655 (W.D. Va. 1977).

Factors considered by courts in decisions as to jury trial. — The factors which courts have weighed when deciding whether to grant a jury trial under subdivision (b) include (1) whether the issues are more appropriate for determination by a jury or a judge (i.e., factual versus legal, legal versus equitable, simple versus complex); (2) any prejudice that granting a jury trial would cause the opposing party; (3) the timing of the motion (early or late in the proceedings) and (4) any effect a jury trial would have on the court's docket and the orderly administration of justice. Malbon v. Pennsylvania Millers Mut. Ins. Co., 636 F.2d 936 (4th Cir. 1980).

The fourth circuit has indicated that district courts should grant untimely jury requests only when the plaintiff demonstrates exceptional circumstances for his delay. Moreover, a district court in the circuit has held that, unless a plaintiff can show some cause beyond mere inadvertence for an untimely jury request, the court should deny such a request. Jones v. Boyd, 161 F.R.D. 48 (E.D. Va. 1995).

Discretion of trial court. — The decision to grant a jury trial pursuant to subdivision (b) is committed to the discretion of the trial court. Malbon v. Pennsylvania Millers Mut. Ins. Co., 636 F.2d 936 (4th Cir. 1980).

Nothing in subdivision (b) suggests that the court is required to commit its exercise of the discretionary power to writing. Malbon v. Pennsylvania Millers Mut. Ins. Co., 636 F.2d 936 (4th Cir. 1980).

Considering plaintiff's failure to request relief under subdivision (b) of this rule for more than four months after removal and more than five weeks after the court first raised the issue, and taking into account the lack of any justification for either failure, the court did not exercise its discretion to grant the untimely jury demand. Vannoy v. Cooper, 872 F. Supp. 1485 (E.D. Va. 1995).

Motions under this rule should be denied, absent some justification beyond inadvertence or "change of mind;" thus to allow parties to change their minds after affirmatively representing to the court a request for a nonjury trial would render a docket unmanageable. Gelardi v. Transamerica Occidental Life Ins. Co., 163 F.R.D. 495 (E.D. Va. 1995).

Suit brought under Veterans Reemployment Rights Act was equitable in nature and should have been tried to the court, and the use of a jury in such case was neither harmless error, nor did it constitute the use of an advisory jury pursuant to subdivision (c) of this rule. Troy v. City of Hampton, 756 F.2d 1000 (4th Cir.), cert. denied, 474 U.S. 864, 106 S. Ct. 182, 88 L. Ed. 2d 151 (1985).

Pro se requests must be timely. — Although courts must liberally construe the pleadings of pro se litigants, a pro se plaintiff must request a jury trial in the same timely manner as other litigants. Jones v. Boyd, 161 F.R.D. 48 (E.D. Va. 1995).

Applied in Lumbermens Mut. Cas. Co. v. Harleysville Mut. Cas. Co., 367 F.2d 250 (4th Cir. 1966); Wright v. Pilot Life Ins. Co., 379 F.2d 409 (4th Cir. 1967); Moss v. Lane Co., 471 F.2d 853 (4th Cir. 1973); Coleman v. Kroger Co., 399 F. Supp. 724 (W.D. Va. 1975); Ramey v. Harber, 431 F. Supp. 657 (W.D. Va. 1977); Law v. Law, 160 F.R.D. 78 (E.D. Va. 1995).

Rule 40. Scheduling Cases for Trial.

Each court must provide by rule for scheduling trials. The court must give priority to actions entitled to priority by a federal statute. (Amended by order adopted April 30, 2007, effective December 1, 2007.)

Comment. — The language of Rule 40 has been amended as part of the general restyling of the Civil Rules to make them more easily understood and to make style and terminology consistent throughout the rules. These changes are intended to be stylistic only.

Rule 41. Dismissal of Actions.

(a) *Voluntary Dismissal.* — (1) By the Plaintiff. (A) Without a Court Order. Subject to Rules 23(e), 23.1(c), 23.2, and 66 and any applicable federal statute, the plaintiff may dismiss an action without a court order by filing:

(i) a notice of dismissal before the opposing party serves either an answer or a motion for summary judgment; or

(ii) a stipulation of dismissal signed by all parties who have appeared.

(B) Effect. Unless the notice or stipulation states otherwise, the dismissal is without prejudice. But if the plaintiff previously dismissed any federal- or state-court action based on or including the same claim, a notice of dismissal operates as an adjudication on the merits.

(2) By Court Order; Effect. Except as provided in Rule 41(a)(1), an action may be dismissed at the plaintiff's request only by court order, on terms that the court considers proper. If a defendant has pleaded a counterclaim before being served with the plaintiff's motion to dismiss, the action may be dismissed over the defendant's objection only if the counterclaim can remain pending for independent adjudication. Unless the order states otherwise, a dismissal under this paragraph (2) is without prejudice.

(b) *Involuntary Dismissal; Effect.* — If the plaintiff fails to prosecute or to comply with these rules or a court order, a defendant may move to dismiss the action or any claim against it. Unless the dismissal order states otherwise, a dismissal under this subdivision (b) and any dismissal not under this rule — except one for lack of jurisdiction, improper venue, or failure to join a party under Rule 19 — operates as an adjudication on the merits.

(c) *Dismissing a Counterclaim, Crossclaim, or Third-Party Claim.* — This rule applies to a dismissal of any counterclaim, crossclaim, or third-party claim. A claimant's voluntary dismissal under Rule 41(a)(1)(A)(i) must be made:

(1) before a responsive pleading is served; or

(2) if there is no responsive pleading, before evidence is introduced at a hearing or trial.

(d) *Costs of a Previously Dismissed Action.* — If a plaintiff who previously dismissed an action in any court files an action based on or including the same claim against the same defendant, the court:

(1) may order the plaintiff to pay all or part of the costs of that previous action; and

(2) may stay the proceedings until the plaintiff has complied. (Amended by order adopted December 27, 1946, effective March 19, 1948, by order adopted January 21, 1963, effective July 1, 1963, by order adopted February 28, 1966, effective July 1, 1966, by order adopted December 4, 1967, effective July 1, 1968, by order adopted March 2, 1987, effective August 1, 1987, by order adopted April 30, 1991, effective December 1, 1991, and by order adopted April 30, 2007, amended, effective December 1, 2007.)

Comment. — The language of Rule 41 has been amended as part of the general restyling of the Civil Rules to make them more easily understood and to make style and terminology consistent throughout the rules. These changes are intended to be stylistic only.

When Rule 23 was amended in 1966, Rules 23.1 and 23.2 were separated from Rule 23. Rule 41(a)(1) was not then amended to reflect the Rule 23 changes. In 1968 Rule 41(a)(1) was amended to correct the cross-reference to what had become Rule 23(e), but Rules 23.1 and 23.2 were inadvertently overlooked. Rules 23.1 and 23.2 are now added to the list of exceptions in Rule 41(a)(1)(A). This change does not affect established meaning. Rule 23.2 explicitly incorporates Rule 23(e), and thus was already absorbed directly into the exceptions in Rule 41(a)(1). Rule 23.1 requires court approval of a compromise or dismissal in language parallel to Rule 23(e) and thus supersedes the apparent right to dismiss by notice of dismissal.

Law Review. — For essay, "Deforming the Federal Rules: An Essay on What's Wrong with the Recent Erie Decisions," see 92 Va. L. Rev. 707 (2006). For article, "Corporate Governance in the Courtroom: An Empirical Analysis," see 51 Wm. and Mary L. Rev. 1749 (2010).

CASE NOTES

Types of pleadings that cut off plaintiff's right to voluntary dismissal. — Although subdivision (a) of this rule sets forth a brightline rule as to what cuts off a plaintiff's right to a voluntary dismissal without prejudice, courts have recognized that certain other pleadings may also bar this right; included in this category are pleadings which effectively join issue on the controversy or bring the court into consideration of the merits of the controversy. Marex Titanic, Inc. v. Wrecked & Abandoned Vessel, 805 F. Supp. 375 (E.D. Va. 1992), rev'd, 2 F.3d 544 (4th Cir. 1993).

The court may dismiss for want of prosecution on its own motion. Reizakis v. Loy, 490 F.2d 1132 (4th Cir. 1974).

Courts possess inherent authority to dismiss cases with prejudice sua sponte. — Federal courts possess the inherent authority to dismiss cases with prejudice sua sponte. Zaczek v. Fauquier County, 764 F. Supp. 1071 (E.D. Va. 1991), aff'd, 16 F.3d 414 (4th Cir. 1993).

Removed action can only be dismissed on terms imposed in order of court. — A dismissal on a motion filed by the plaintiff for permission to dismiss a removed action without prejudice can be had only "upon order of the court and upon such terms and conditions as the court deems proper." Lawson v. Moore, 29 F. Supp. 175 (W.D. Va. 1939).

And court should weigh equities in deciding motion. — On a motion by plaintiff for permission to dismiss without prejudice under subdivision (a)(2), the court should weigh the equities and should make that decision which to the court seems fairest under all the circumstances. Lawson v. Moore, 29 F. Supp. 175 (W.D. Va. 1939).

This rule cannot be automatically or mechanically applied. Reizakis v. Loy, 490 F.2d 1132 (4th Cir. 1974).

Dismissal as sanction for party or attorney who fails to obey court order. — A variety of sanctions, including dismissal, may be imposed upon a party or an attorney who fails or refuses to obey a court order. Zaczek v. Fauquier County, 764 F. Supp. 1071 (E.D. Va. 1991), aff'd, 16 F.3d 414 (4th Cir. 1993).

Dismissal must be exercised with restraint and caution. — Dismissal is a severe sanction which must be exercised with restraint, caution and discretion. Zaczek v. Fauquier County, 764 F. Supp. 1071 (E.D. Va. 1991), aff'd, 16 F.3d 414 (4th Cir. 1993).

Sanction of dismissal only appropriate in most egregious cases. — The sanction of dismissal, when used to punish attorney misbehavior, is only appropriate in the most egregious cases. Doyle v. Murray, 938 F.2d 33 (4th Cir. 1991).

Sanctions to be fixed in proportion to severity of conduct. — In order to ensure that sanctions be fixed in proportion to the severity of a party's or lawyer's misconduct, a court must balance: (1) the degree of personal responsibility of the plaintiff, (2) the amount of prejudice caused the defendant, (3) the existence of a "drawn out history of deliberately proceeding in a dilatory fashion," and (4) the existence of sanctions less drastic than dismissal. Doyle v. Murray, 938 F.2d 33 (4th Cir. 1991).

Public policy must be weighed. — When deciding whether to dismiss for want of prosecution, the sound public policy of deciding cases on their merits must be weighed against the power to prevent delays. Reizakis v. Loy, 490 F.2d 1132 (4th Cir. 1974).

Lack of prejudice to defendant must be considered. — Generally, lack of prejudice to the defendant, though not a bar to dismissal for want of prosecution, is a factor that must be considered in determining whether the trial court exercised sound discretion. Reizakis v. Loy, 490 F.2d 1132 (4th Cir. 1974).

Factors court must examine before sanctioning pro se plaintiff by dismissing complaint. — Before a federal court may invoke its inherent authority to sanction a pro se plaintiff by dismissing a complaint with prejudice sua sponte, the court must examine four factors: (1) the bad faith or deliberate misconduct of the plaintiff; (2) the notice which the plaintiff received concerning the consequences of his continued misconduct; (3) the amount of prejudice caused by the plaintiff; and (4) the existence of an effective sanction which is less drastic. Zaczek v. Fauquier County, 764 F. Supp. 1071 (E.D. Va. 1991), aff'd, 16 F.3d 414 (4th Cir. 1993).

Where a party is not responsible for the fault of his attorney, dismissal for want of prosecution may be invoked only in extreme circumstances. Reizakis v. Loy, 490 F.2d 1132 (4th Cir. 1974).

Dismissal without prejudice of removed action allowed without condition that future litigation be in federal court. — See Lawson v. Moore, 29 F. Supp. 175 (W.D. Va. 1939).

A court will usually permit voluntary dismissal at plaintiff's request, so long as it would not inflict undue hardship upon the defendant. Taylor v. Virginia, DOT, 170 F.R.D. 10 (E.D. Va. 1996).

This rule, governing the voluntary dismissal of actions, applies in terms to third-party claims also. — See Kenrose Mfg. Co. v. Fred Whitaker Co., 512 F.2d 890 (4th Cir. 1972), aff'g 53 F.R.D. 491 (W.D. Va. 1971).

Under this rule, prior to the service of an answer to a third-party complaint, the third-party plaintiff would have been entitled as of right to a voluntary dismissal of his third-party complaint against third-party defendant. Where he did not make its request for dismissal until after third-party defendant had answered, it was for the district court to decide whether dismissal of the third-party action would prejudice any party. If no prejudice appeared, dismissal was in order. Kenrose Mfg. Co. v. Fred Whitaker Co., 512 F.2d 890 (4th Cir. 1972), aff'g 53 F.R.D. 491 (W.D. Va. 1971).

Dismissal of third-party action held not dismissal on merits. — Where a defendant had filed a third-party action alleging a claim by way of contractual indemnity, which third-party action was dismissed in the final judgment of the district court dismissing the original action, but the court of appeals, on appeal by the plaintiff alone, vacated the judgment appealed from and remanded the case for a new trial in which the plaintiff was found entitled to judgment, the district court held that subdivisions (b) and (c) of this rule did not require it, under the circumstances of the case, to construe the order dismissing the third-party action as an adjudication upon the merits, and further held that the third-party defendants were still parties to the action and had to meet the issues raised in the third-party complaint. Stancil v. United States, 200 F. Supp. 36 (E.D. Va. 1961).

When parties moving for voluntary dismissal entitled to attorneys' fees. — Where prevailing parties in a class action which challenged sheriff's department blanket strip search policy, moved for voluntary dismissal under subdivision (a)(1) of this rule, contending that the object of their suit had been achieved, they were properly entitled to an award of attorneys' fees. DeMier v. Gondles, 676 F.2d 92 (4th Cir. 1982).

Requiring compliance with tolling provisions of § 8.01-229(E) is consistent with federal law, and the mere placing of a time constraint on the filing of a § 1983 action is not a consideration sufficient to find an inconsistency. Scoggins v. Douglas, 760 F.2d 535 (4th Cir. 1985).

Virginia state courts required to give effect to Rule 41 dismissals. — The Virginia Code quite clearly requires the state courts to give effect to Rule 41 dismissals as nonsuits, for § 8.01-229(E)(3) provides in terms that it ". . . shall apply irrespective of whether the action is originally filed in a federal or a state court and recommenced in any other court." Scoggins v. Douglas, 760 F.2d 535 (4th Cir. 1985).

Nonsuit under § 8.01-380 compared. — The difference in a Rule 41 dismissal and a Virginia nonsuit under § 8.01-380 goes more to matters of form than substance. While the Virginia statute does not require the consent of the defendant and can be taken at later stages in the proceeding, both the federal rule and the Virginia statute have as their purpose the voluntary dismissal of an action by a plaintiff without prejudice at some stage of a proceeding. Scoggins v. Douglas, 760 F.2d 535 (4th Cir. 1985).

Dismissal under subdivision (a)(1) equated to dismissal under § 8.01-229(E)(3). — The district court was correct when it equated dismissal pursuant to subdivision (a)(1) of this rule to a dismissal under subsection (E)(3) of § 8.01-229 rather than to a dismissal under subsection (E)(1) of § 8.01-229. Scoggins v. Douglas, 760 F.2d 535 (4th Cir. 1985).

Refiling of dismissed § 1983 action held barred by Virginia statute of limitations. — Cause of action under 42 U.S.C. § 1983, which accrued on Dec. 17, 1980, was barred by Virginia's two-year statute of limitations for personal injury actions, where the action was voluntarily dismissed by the plaintiff without prejudice on January 26, 1982, pursuant to subdivision (a)(1) of this rule, and was not refiled until December 27, 1982. Scoggins v. Douglas, 760 F.2d 535 (4th Cir. 1985).

Motion for attorney's fees under Equal Access to Justice Act. — Where a plaintiff requests and is granted a voluntary dismissal pursuant to subdivision (a)(2), and such dismissal is not appealed by the United States, a plaintiff has 90 days from the voluntary dismissal date to file a motion for attorney's fees under the Equal Access to Justice Act, 28 U.S.C. § 2412. Poff v. Gorsuch, 636 F. Supp. 710 (W.D. Va. 1986).

Dismissal under subdivision (b) is matter for court's discretion. — Whether to dismiss a case under subdivision (b) is a matter for the court's discretion. In exercising its discretion, the court balances the sound public policy of deciding cases on their merits against considerations of sound judicial administration. Claitt v. Newcomb, 138 F.R.D. 72 (E.D. Va. 1990).

In determining whether subdivision (b) dismissal is an appropriate sanction, a district court in this circuit must consider—(1) the degree of personal responsibility of the plaintiff, (2) the amount of prejudice caused the defendant, (3) the existence of a "drawn out history of deliberately proceeding in a dilatory fashion," and (4) the existence of sanctions less drastic than dismissal. Claitt v. Newcomb, 138 F.R.D. 72 (E.D. Va. 1990).

Subdivision (b) was not intended to include a dismissal on limitations grounds as an unqualified decision upon the merits. Burgess v. Cohen, 593 F. Supp. 1122 (E.D. Va. 1984).

A dismissal on statute of limitations grounds under § 8.01-243 is not within the intendment of subdivision (b) of this rule and, therefore, is not an adjudication on the merits. The only issue on the merits which would be res judicata in a subsequent action in any court is that the action is time-barred in any action that would necessarily apply § 8.01-243. In all other respects the merits of the claim are unaffected. Burgess v. Cohen, 593 F. Supp. 1122 (E.D. Va. 1984).

Case subject to involuntary dismissal despite presentation of prima facie case. — Subdivision (b) requires the judge, as the trier of fact, to weigh and consider all of the evidence, and he may sustain a motion thereunder even though the plaintiff may have presented a prima facie case. Holmes v. Bevilacqua, 794 F.2d 142 (4th Cir. 1986).

This rule governs withdrawal of a proof of claim. Credit Alliance Corp. v. Penn Hook Coal Co., 68 Bankr. 804 (Bankr. W.D. Va.), modified, 77 Bankr. 57 (Bankr. W.D. Va. 1987), aff'd, 851 F.2d 119 (4th Cir. 1988).

In an unlawful discharge action, denial of defendant's motion for dismissal did not establish the plaintiff's prima facie case as a matter of law, and the burden of proof did not automatically shift to the defendant to prove that it would have fired the plaintiff even absent its discriminatory conduct. EEOC v. Electrolux Corp., 611 F. Supp. 926 (E.D. Va. 1985).

Father, an unlicensed layman, attempt to act as daughter's lawyer was not a violation of Rule 17 or this rule. And dismissal of her claim on this ground is certainly unwarranted. Rather, all that is required is for the court to appoint counsel for her. Brown v. Ortho Diagnostic Sys., 868 F. Supp. 168 (E.D. Va. 1994).

Applied in United States ex rel. Hudson v. Peerless Ins. Co., 374 F.2d 942 (4th Cir. 1967); Katopodis v. Liberian S/T Olympic Sun, 282 F. Supp. 369 (E.D. Va. 1968); Kenrose Mfg. Co. v. Fred Whitaker Co., 53 F.R.D. 491 (W.D. Va. 1971); Krodel v. Houghtaling, 468 F.2d 887 (4th Cir. 1972); Welch v. Evans, 402 F. Supp. 468 (E.D. Va. 1975); Inmates v. Owens, 561 F.2d 560 (4th Cir. 1977); Malbon v. Pennsylvania Millers Mut. Ins. Co., 636 F.2d 936 (4th Cir. 1980); Schnurman v. United States, 490 F. Supp. 429 (E.D. Va. 1980); Lee v. Patel, 564 F. Supp. 755 (E.D. Va. 1983); Croatan Books, Inc. v. Baliles, 583 F. Supp. 857 (E.D. Va. 1984); Holmes v. Bevilacqua, 774 F.2d 636 (4th Cir. 1985); Tingley v. Henson Aviation, Inc., 789 F.2d 275 (4th Cir. 1986); Lucas v. Dole, 835 F.2d 532 (4th Cir. 1987); Simpson v. Welch, 900 F.2d 33 (4th Cir. 1990); James v. Powell, 765 F. Supp. 314 (E.D. Va. 1991); Sumner v. Tucker, 9 F. Supp. 2d 641 (E.D. Va. 1998); United States ex rel. Summit v. Michael Baker Corp., 40 F. Supp. 2d 772 (E.D. Va. 1999); United States v. Dickerson, 166 F.3d 667, 1999 U.S. App. LEXIS 1741 (4th. Cir. 1999); RMD Concessions, L.L.C. v. Westfield Corp., 194 F.R.D. 241, 2000 U.S. Dist. LEXIS 6865 (E.D. Va. 2000).

Rule 42. Consolidation; Separate Trials.

(a) *Consolidation.* — If actions before the court involve a common question of law or fact, the court may:

(1) join for hearing or trial any or all matters at issue in the actions;

(2) consolidate the actions; or

(3) issue any other orders to avoid unnecessary cost or delay.

(b) *Separate Trials.* — For convenience, to avoid prejudice, or to expedite and economize, the court may order a separate trial of one or more separate issues, claims, crossclaims, counterclaims, or third-party claims. When ordering a separate trial, the court must preserve any federal right to a jury trial. (Amended by order adopted February 28, 1966, effective July 1, 1966, and by order adopted April 30, 2007, effective December 1, 2007.)

Comment. — The language of Rule 42 has been amended as part of the general restyling of the Civil Rules to make them more easily understood and to make style and terminology consistent throughout the rules. These changes are intended to be stylistic only.

CASE NOTES

Court must have jurisdiction over actions to be consolidated. — A federal district court has no authority to consolidate an action over which it has jurisdiction with one over which it does not. APCO v. Region Propertics, Inc., 364 F. Supp. 1273 (W.D. Va. 1973); Womble v. Dixon, 585 F. Supp. 728 (E.D. Va. 1983), modified, 752 F.2d 80 (4th Cir. 1984).

Where the court believed removal of an action on certain promissory notes was improper, such action was not "pending before the court," and the court had no authority to consolidate it with pending federal antitrust actions. APCO v. Region Properties, Inc., 364 F. Supp. 1273 (W.D. Va. 1973).

Granting separate trial is discretionary. — The granting of defendant's motion for separate trial on the issue of the validity of a release in an action arising out of injuries sustained by the plaintiff when struck by the defendant's truck was a matter within the sound discretion of the trial judge. Such action did not constitute an abuse of discretion, nor was the plaintiff prejudiced thereby. Bedser v. Horton Motor Lines, 122 F.2d 406 (4th Cir. 1941).

Under this rule whether to grant a severance is a question within the discretion of the trial court. Durham v. Southern Ry., 254 F. Supp. 813 (W.D. Va. 1966).

Where a party wishes to withdraw his motion to intervene while retaining the ability to file a separate action and toll the statute of limitations, the desired result may be achieved by the court granting the motion and then severing the complaint from the action intervened in. Braxton v. Virginia Folding Box Co., 72 F.R.D. 124 (E.D. Va. 1976).

Consolidation may be used to achieve same result as reached by third-party practice. — See A/S J. A/S J. Ludwig Mowinckles Rederi v. Tidewater Constr. Corp., 559 F.2d 928 (4th Cir. 1977).

Standard of review applicable to consolidated actions. — Judicial economy generally favors consolidation, but the court must conduct a careful inquiry in this regard that balances the prejudice and confusion that consolidation might entail against the waste of resources, the burden on the parties and the risk of inconsistent judgments that separate proceedings could engender. Switzenbaum v. Orbital Sciences Corp., 187 F.R.D. 246 (E.D. Va. 1999).

Consolidation of actions arising from train-truck collision under FELA and state wrongful death statute. — See Durham v. Southern Ry., 254 F. Supp. 813 (W.D. Va. 1966).

Consolidation of state and federal actions under swine flu act and federal tort claims act. — See Low v. United States, 463 F. Supp. 948 (E.D. Va. 1978).

Applied in United States Fid. & Guar. Co. v. Rowe, 249 F. Supp. 993 (E.D. Va. 1966); Wooten v. Skibs A/S Samuel Bakke, 431 F.2d 821 (4th Cir. 1969); Bertels v. Sullivan, 312 F. Supp. 63 (E.D. Va. 1970); Calhoun v. United States, 370 F. Supp. 434 (W.D. Va. 1973); Williams v. Norfolk & W. Ry., 530 F.2d 539 (4th Cir. 1975); Dominion Parking Corp. v. B & O R.R., 450 F. Supp. 441 (E.D. Va. 1978); American Gen. v. Equitable Gen., 87 F.R.D. 736 (E.D. Va. 1980); Morgan v. American Family Life Assurance Co., 559 F. Supp. 477 (W.D. Va. 1983); R.M.S. Titanic, Inc. v. Haver, 171 F.3d 943 (4th. Cir. 1999); In re Orbital Sciences Corp. Sec. Litig., 188 F.R.D. 237 (E.D. Va. 1999).

Rule 43. Taking Testimony.

(a) *In Open Court.* — At trial, the witnesses' testimony must be taken in open court unless a federal statute, the Federal Rules of Evidence, these rules, or other rules adopted by the Supreme Court provide otherwise. For good cause in compelling circumstances and with appropriate safeguards, the court may permit testimony in open court by contemporaneous transmission from a different location.

(b) *Affirmation Instead of an Oath.* — When these rules require an oath, a solemn affirmation suffices.

(c) *Evidence on a Motion.* — When a motion relies on facts outside the record, the court may hear the matter on affidavits or may hear it wholly or partly on oral testimony or on depositions.

(d) *Interpreter.* — The court may appoint an interpreter of its choosing; fix reasonable compensation to be paid from funds provided by law or by one or more parties; and tax the compensation as costs. (Amended by order adopted February 28, 1966, effective July 1, 1966, by order adopted November 20, 1972 and December 18, 1972, effective July 1, 1975, by order adopted March 2, 1987, effective August 1, 1987, by order adopted April 23, 1996, effective December 1, 1996, and by order adopted April 30, 2007, effective December 1, 2007.)

Comment. — The language of Rule 43 has been amended as part of the general restyling of the Civil Rules to make them more easily understood and to make style and terminology consistent throughout the rules. These changes are intended to be stylistic only.

Law Review. — For article, "Uniform Evidence Rules in the Federal Courts," see 49 Va. L. Rev. 692 (1963).

CASE NOTES

Since defendant's absence did not change the length of time he could be sentenced, this rule was procedural and sentencing him in absentia did not violate the ex post facto clause. United States v. DePrima, 165 F.R.D. 61 (E.D. Va. 1996).

Applied in Hazelgrove v. Ford Motor Co., 428 F. Supp. 1096 (E.D. Va. 1977).

Rule 44. Proving an Official Record.

(a) *Means of Proving.* — (1) Domestic Record. Each of the following evidences an official record — or an entry in it — that is otherwise admissible and is kept within the United States, any state, district, or commonwealth, or any territory subject to the administrative or judicial jurisdiction of the United States:

(A) an official publication of the record; or

(B) a copy attested by the officer with legal custody of the record — or by the officer's deputy — and accompanied by a certificate that the officer has custody. The certificate must be made under seal:

(i) by a judge of a court of record in the district or political subdivision where the record is kept; or

(ii) by any public officer with a seal of office and with official duties in the district or political subdivision where the record is kept.

(2) Foreign Record. (A) In General. Each of the following evidences a foreign official record — or an entry in it — that is otherwise admissible:

(i) an official publication of the record; or

(ii) the record — or a copy — that is attested by an authorized person and is accompanied either by a final certification of genuineness or by a certification under a treaty or convention to which the United States and the country where the record is located are parties.

(B) Final Certification of Genuineness. A final certification must certify the genuineness of the signature and official position of the attester or of any foreign official whose certificate of genuineness relates to the attestation or is in a chain of certificates of genuineness relating to the attestation. A final certification may be made by a secretary of a United States embassy or legation; by a consul general, vice consul, or consular agent of the United States; or by a diplomatic or consular official of the foreign country assigned or accredited to the United States.

(C) Other Means of Proof. If all parties have had a reasonable opportunity to investigate a foreign record's authenticity and accuracy, the court may, for good cause, either:

(i) admit an attested copy without final certification; or

(ii) permit the record to be evidenced by an attested summary with or without a final certification.

(b) *Lack of a Record.* — A written statement that a diligent search of designated records revealed no record or entry of a specified tenor is admissible as evidence that the records contain no such record or entry. For domestic records, the statement must be authenticated under Rule 44(a)(1). For foreign records, the statement must comply with Rule 44(a)(2)(C)(ii).

(c) *Other Proof.* — A party may prove an official record — or an entry or lack of an entry in it — by any other method authorized by law. (Amended by order adopted February 28, 1966, effective July 1, 1966, by order adopted March 2, 1987, effective August 1, 1987, by order adopted April 30, 1991, effective December 1, 1991, and by order adopted April 30, 2007, effective December 1, 2007.)

Comment. — The language of Rule 44 has been amended as part of the general restyling of the Civil Rules to make them more easily understood and to make style and terminology consistent throughout the rules. These changes are intended to be stylistic only.

CASE NOTES

Applied in United States v. Gilliam, 975 F.2d 1050 (4th Cir. 1992).

Rule 44.1. Determining Foreign Law.

A party who intends to raise an issue about a foreign country's law must give notice by a pleading or other writing. In determining foreign law, the court may consider any relevant material or source, including testimony, whether or not submitted by a party or admissible under the Federal Rules of Evidence. The court's determination must be treated as a ruling on a question of law. (Added by order adopted February 28, 1966, effective July 1, 1966, amended by order adopted November 20, 1972, effective July 1, 1975, by order adopted March 2, 1987, effective August 1, 1987, and by order adopted April 30, 2007, effective December 1, 2007.)

Comment. — The language of Rule 44.1 has been amended as part of the general restyling of the Civil Rules to make them more easily understood and to make style and terminology consistent throughout the rules. These changes are intended to be stylistic only.

CASE NOTES

The purpose of the notice requirement in this rule is simply to avoid surprise. Hodson v. A.H. Robins Co., 528 F. Supp. 809 (E.D. Va. 1981), aff'd, 715 F.2d 142 (4th Cir. 1983).

Plaintiff not required to allege identity and substance of law. — The notice requirement under this rule falls considerably short of a requirement that, in order to survive a Rule 12(b)(6) motion, a plaintiff must allege the identity and substance of the applicable law. Hodson v. A.H.

Robins Co., 528 F. Supp. 809 (E.D. Va. 1981), aff'd, 715 F.2d 142 (4th Cir. 1983).

Time for giving notice. — Where the applicability of foreign law is not obvious at the outset and is a matter of some contention among the parties, the "reasonable written notice," if required at all under this rule, may come at any time sufficient to give the court and the defendants adequate notice of the need to research the foreign rules. Hodson v. A.H. Robins Co., 528 F. Supp. 809 (E.D. Va. 1981), aff'd, 715 F.2d 142 (4th Cir. 1983).

Rule 45. Subpoena.

(a) *In General.* — (1) Form and Contents.

(A) Requirements — In General. Every subpoena must:

(i) state the court from which it issued;

(ii) state the title of the action and its civil-action number;

(iii) command each person to whom it is directed to do the following at a specified time and place: attend and testify; produce designated documents, electronically stored information, or tangible things in that person's possession, custody, or control; or permit the inspection of premises; and

(iv) set out the text of Rule 45(d) and (e).

(B) Command to Attend a Deposition — Notice of the Recording Method. A subpoena commanding attendance at a deposition must state the method for recording the testimony.

(C) Combining or Separating a Command to Produce or to Permit Inspection; Specifying the Form for Electronically Stored Information. A command to produce documents, electronically stored information, or tangible things or to permit the inspection of premises may be included in a subpoena commanding attendance at a deposition, hearing, or trial, or may be set out in a separate subpoena. A subpoena may specify the form or forms in which electronically stored information is to be produced.

(D) Command to Produce; Included Obligations. A command in a subpoena to produce documents, electronically stored information, or tangible things requires the responding person to permit inspection, copying, testing, or sampling of the materials.

(2) Issuing Court. A subpoena must issue from the court where the action is pending.

(3) Issued by Whom. The clerk must issue a subpoena, signed but otherwise in blank, to a party who requests it. That party must complete it before service. An attorney also may issue and sign a subpoena if the attorney is authorized to practice in the issuing court.

(4) Notice to Other Parties Before Service. If the subpoena commands the production of documents, electronically stored information, or tangible things or the inspection of premises before trial, then before it is served on the person to whom it is directed, a notice and a copy of the subpoena must be served on each party.

(b) *Service.* — (1) By Whom and How; Tendering Fees. Any person who is at least 18 years old and not a party may serve a subpoena. Serving a subpoena requires delivering a copy to the named person and, if the subpoena requires that person's attendance, tendering the fees for 1 day's attendance and the mileage allowed by law. Fees and mileage need not be tendered when the subpoena issues on behalf of the United States or any of its officers or agencies.

(2) Service in the United States. A subpoena may be served at any place within the United States.

(3) Service in a Foreign Country. 28 U.S.C. § 1783 governs issuing and serving a subpoena directed to a United States national or resident who is in a foreign country.

(4) Proof of Service. Proving service, when necessary, requires filing with the issuing court a statement showing the date and manner of service and the names of the persons served. The statement must be certified by the server.

(c) *Place of Compliance.* — (1) For a Trial, Hearing, or Deposition. A subpoena may command a person to attend a trial hearing, or deposition only as follows:

(A) within 100 miles of where the person resides, is employed, or regularly transacts business in person; or

(B) within the state where the person resides, is employed, or regularly transacts business in person, if the person

(i) is a party or a party's officer; or

(i) is commanded to attend a trial and would not incur substantial expense.

(2) For Other Discovery. A subpoena may command:

(A) production of documents, electronically stored information, or tangible things at a place within 100 miles of where the person resides, is employed, or regularly transacts business in person; and

(B) inspection of premises at the premises to be inspected.

(d) *Protecting a Person Subject to a Subpoena; Enforcement.* — (1) Avoiding Undue Burden or Expense; Sanctions. A party or attorney responsible for issuing and serving a subpoena must take reasonable steps to avoid imposing undue burden or expense on a person subject to the subpoena. The court for the district where compliance is required must enforce this duty and impose an appropriate sanction — which may include lost earnings and reasonable attorney's fees — on a party or attorney who fails to comply.

(2) Command to Produce Materials or Permit Inspection. (A) Appearance Not Required. A person commanded to produce documents, electronically stored information, or tangible things, or to permit the inspection of premises, need not appear in person at the place of production or inspection unless also commanded to appear for a deposition, hearing, or trial.

(B) Objections. A person commanded to produce documents or tangible things or to permit inspection may serve on the party or attorney designated in the subpoena a written objection to inspecting, copying, testing or sampling any or all of the materials or to inspecting the premises — or to producing electronically stored information in the form or forms requested. The objection must be served before the earlier of the time specified for compliance or 14 days after the subpoena is served. If an objection is made, the following rules apply:

(i) At any time, on notice to the commanded person, the serving party may move the court for the district where compliance is required for an order compelling production or inspection.

(ii) These acts may be required only as directed in the order, and the order must protect a person who is neither a party nor a party's officer from significant expense resulting from compliance.

(3) Quashing or Modifying a Subpoena. (A) When Required. On timely motion, the court for the district where compliance is required must quash or modify a subpoena that:

(i) fails to allow a reasonable time to comply;

(ii) requires a person to comply beyond the geographical limits specified in Rule 45 (c);

(iii) requires disclosure of privileged or other protected matter, if no exception or waiver applies; or

(iv) subjects a person to undue burden.

(B) When Permitted. To protect a person subject to or affected by a subpoena, the court for the district where compliance is required may, on motion, quash or modify the subpoena if it requires:

(i) disclosing a trade secret or other confidential research, development, or commercial information; or

(ii) disclosing an unretained expert's opinion or information that does not describe specific occurrences in dispute and results from the expert's study that was not requested by a party.

(C) Specifying Conditions as an Alternative. In the circumstances described in Rule 45(d)(3)(B), the court may, instead of quashing or modifying a subpoena, order appearance or production under specified conditions if the serving party:

(i) shows a substantial need for the testimony or material that cannot be otherwise met without undue hardship; and

(ii) ensures that the subpoenaed person will be reasonably compensated.

(e) *Duties in Responding to a Subpoena.* — (1) Producing Documents or Electronically Stored Information. These procedures apply to producing documents or electronically stored information:

(A) Documents. A person responding to a subpoena to produce documents must produce them as they are kept in the ordinary course of business or must organize and label them to correspond to the categories in the demand.

(B) Form for Producing Electronically Stored Information Not Specified. If a subpoena does not specify a form for producing electronically stored information, the person responding must produce it in a form or forms in which it is ordinarily maintained or in a reasonably usable form or forms.

(C) Electronically Stored Information Produced in Only One Form. The person responding need not produce the same electronically stored information in more than one form.

(D) Inaccessible Electronically Stored Information. The person responding need not provide discovery of electronically stored information from sources that the person identifies as not reasonably accessible because of undue burden or cost. On motion to compel discovery or for a protective order, the person responding must show that the information is not reasonably accessible because of undue burden or cost. If that showing is made, the court may nonetheless order discovery from such sources if the requesting party shows good cause, considering the limitations of Rule 26(b)(2)(C). The court may specify conditions for the discovery.

(2) Claiming Privilege or Protection. (A) Information Withheld. A person withholding subpoenaed information under a claim that it is privileged or subject to protection as trial-preparation material must:

(i) expressly make the claim; and

(ii) describe the nature of the withheld documents, communications, or tangible things in a manner that, without revealing information itself privileged or protected, will enable the parties to assess the claim.

(B) Information Produced. If information produced in response to a subpoena is subject to a claim of privilege or of protection as trial-preparation material, the person making the claim may notify any party that received the information of the claim and the basis for it. After being notified, a party must promptly return, sequester, or destroy the specified information and any copies it has; must not use or disclose the information until the claim is resolved; must take reasonable steps to retrieve the information if the party disclosed it before being notified; and may promptly present the information under seal to the court for the district where compliance is required for a determination of the claim. The person who produced the information must preserve the information until the claim is resolved.

(f) *Transferring a Subpoena-Related Motion.* — When the court where compliance is required did not issue the subpoena, it may transfer a motion under this rule to the issuing court if the person subject to the subpoena consents or if the court finds exceptional circumstances. Then, if the attorney for the person subject to a subpoena is authorized to practice in the court where the motion is made, the attorney may file papers and appear on the motion as an officer of the issuing court. To enforce its order, the issuing court may transfer the order to the court where the motion was made.

(g) *Contempt.* — The court for the district where compliance is required — and also, after a motion is transferred, the issuing court — may hold in contempt a person who, having been served, fails without adequate excuse to obey the subpoena or an order related to it. (Amended by order adopted December 27, 1946, effective March 19, 1948, by order adopted December 29, 1948, effective October 20, 1949, by order adopted March 30, 1970, effective July 1, 1970, by order adopted April 29, 1980, effective August 1, 1980, by order adopted April 29, 1985, effective August 1, 1985, by order adopted March 2, 1987, effective August 1, 1987, by order adopted April 30, 1991, effective December 1, 1991; by order adopted April 25, 2005, effective December 1, 2005, by order adopted April 12, 2006, effective December 1, 2006, by order adopted April 30, 2007, effective December 1, 2007, and by order adopted April 16, 2013, effective December 1, 2013.)

Comment. — The language of Rule 45 has been amended as part of the general restyling of the Civil Rules to make them more easily understood and to make style and terminology consistent throughout the rules. These changes are intended to be stylistic only.

The reference to discovery of "books" in former Rule 45(a)(1)(C) was deleted to achieve consistent expression throughout the discovery rules. Books remain a proper subject of discovery.

Former Rule 45(b)(1) required "prior notice" to each party of any commanded production of documents and things or inspection of premises. Courts have agreed that notice must be given "prior" to the return date, and have tended to converge on an interpretation that requires notice to the parties before the subpoena is served on the person commanded to produce or permit inspection. That interpretation is adopted in amended Rule 45(b)(1) to give clear notice of general present practice.

The language of former Rule 45(d)(2) addressing the manner of asserting privilege is replaced by adopting the wording of Rule 26(b)(5). The same meaning is better expressed in the same words.

CASE NOTES

Only court, not parties, can dispense with command of subpoena. Parties are not at liberty to dispense with the command of a subpoena. Strictly, this power rests with the court only. In practice the courts generally adopt the wishes of counsel, but the stipulations should be formal to avoid a misunderstanding. Haney v. Woodward & Lothrop, Inc., 330 F.2d 940 (4th Cir. 1964).

FRCP Rule 26 limitation still effective. — While this rule no longer requires the issuance of deposition subpeonas as a basis for subpeona duces tecum, FRCP Rule 26(b)(4) remains a limitation on the right of access by an opposing party to the evidence of experts who have been retained to testify in the case. Therefore, discovery of the facts and opinions of such experts cannot be obtained solely under this rule where, a bare subpeona duces tecum has been issued for the experts' files. Marsh v. Jackson, 141 F.R.D. 431 (W.D. Va. 1992).

Controlling effect of FRCP Rules 26 and 30. — None of the methods of discovery allowed under FRCP Rules 26(b)(4) and 30 permit the use of bare FRCP Rule 45 subpoenas duces tecum. Instead, they operate as a control on the potential runaway use of the subpoena duces tecum to compel the production of the evidence of experts retained by a party to testify at trial. They protect the interests of the expert and the party retaining him in the work that he has produced, while also providing access to the opposing party, though such access might not be as inexpensive as the opponent might desire. Marsh v. Jackson, 141 F.R.D. 431 (W.D. Va. 1992).

Scope of discovery under this rule coextensive with motion under FRCP Rule 34. — The scope of discovery from a nonparty by means of a subpoena duces tecum under this rule is coextensive with that of a motion for production from a party under FRCP Rule 34. Castle v. Jallah, 142 F.R.D. 618 (E.D. Va. 1992).

Discovery of nonparty and of party distinguished. — Discovery of a nonparty is a wholly different matter from discovery of a party to an action. Parties to litigation open themselves to the broad discovery practices encompassed in Fed. R. Civ. P. 30 (b)(5) and 34. The production of documents or other materials prior to trial by a nonparty, on the other hand, can be compelled only by a subpoena duces tecum issued pursuant to subdivision 45(d)(1) of this rule. Jones v. Continental Cas. Co., 512 F. Supp. 1205 (E.D. Va. 1981).

Subdivision (b) aids in actual trial. — The intent and purpose of subdivision (b) was to aid in the actual trial, i.e., in the giving of depositions or the taking of testimony so far as a civil case is concerned. McLean v. Prudential S.S. Co., 36 F.R.D. 421 (E.D. Va. 1965).

And subpoena for discovery in absence of taking deposition is unauthorized. — There is no authority for the service of a subpoena duces tecum on a person not a party for purposes of discovery, in the absence of the taking of a deposition, and therefore, such a subpoena duces tecum is irregular and must be quashed. McLean v. Prudential S.S. Co., 36 F.R.D. 421 (E.D. Va. 1965).

This rule may not be invoked to obtain documentary evidence from nonparties prior to trial if the party invoking the rule has no intention of taking the deposition of the person to whom the subpoena is directed. Jones v. Continental Cas. Co., 512 F. Supp. 1205 (E.D. Va. 1981).

And will be quashed if deposition is not taken. — Where party in a civil action served a subpoena duces tecum on a person not a party, it would be quashed where the deposition of that person was not taken, as the subpoena was being used as an improper shortcut in the judicial process. Jones v. Continental Cas. Co., 512 F. Supp. 1205 (E.D. Va. 1981).

Ordinarily, failure to make timely objection to subpoena duces tecum pursuant to this rule will waive any objection. In unusual circumstances and for good cause, however, the failure to act timely will not bar consideration of objections. Such unusual circumstances and good cause may be shown by a subpoena that is overbroad on its face, a subpoena that would impose significant expense to a nonparty action in good faith, or contact between counsel for the subpoenaed party and the subpoenaing party prior to the challenge to the subpoena. In re Motorsports Merchandise Antitrust Litig., 186 F.R.D. 344 (W.D. Va. 1999).

Cashed checks for one day's witness fees and mileage are taxable costs although witnesses notified not to appear. — Where, prior to the admission of liability by defendant, counsel for plaintiff had caused certain subpoenas to be issued for witnesses deemed necessary to prove liability and subsequently counsel for plaintiff wrote letters to the liability witnesses notifying them that they need not appear on the trial date, and also advising in part: "Unless you have already cashed the check that you received for the witness fee, then this check should be returned to minimize the expenses under the rules of court," as to the witnesses who may have returned checks, it is clear that this is not a taxable item of costs, but as to the witnesses who did not return the checks, the witness fees and mileage are taxable. Plaintiff's counsel does not have the duty to make an additional request for the return of the fee and mileage. Subdivision (c) requires the prepayment of one day's attendance fee and mileage as a condition to the service of a subpoena. There is no statute or rule imposing upon the party or his counsel the duty on recoupment. While it is true that the particular witness receiving said check was not legally entitled to use same unless the witness was required to appear at trial, the most that defendant may require is an assignment of plaintiff's claim against the witness. Oakley v. Norfolk & W. Ry., 42 F.R.D. 653 (E.D. Va. 1967).

Applied in Servo Corp. of Am. v. GE Co., 393 F.2d 551 (4th Cir. 1968); Gilbert v. Allied Chem. Corp., 411 F. Supp. 505 (E.D. Va. 1976); Schultz v. Wills, 126 Bankr. 489 (Bankr. E.D. Va. 1991).

Rule 46. Objecting to a Ruling or Order.

A formal exception to a ruling or order is unnecessary. When the ruling or order is requested or made, a party need only state the action that it wants the court to take or objects to, along with the grounds for the request or objection. Failing to object does not prejudice a party who had no opportunity to do so when the ruling or order was made. (Amended by order adopted March 2, 1987, effective August 1, 1987, and by order adopted April 30, 2007, effective December 1, 2007.)

Comment. — The language of Rule 46 has been amended as part of the general restyling of the Civil Rules to make them more easily understood and to make style and terminology consistent throughout the rules. These changes are intended to be stylistic only.

CASE NOTES

Rule 51 must be read in conjunction with Rule 46; where the district court was fully aware of the plaintiff's position, and the district court had obviously considered and rejected that position, strict enforcement of Rule 51 would exalt form over substance. City of Richmond v. Madison Mgt. Group, Inc., 918 F.2d 438 (4th Cir. 1990).

Rule 47. Selecting Jurors.

(a) *Examining Jurors.* — The court may permit the parties or their attorneys to examine prospective jurors or may itself do so. If the court examines the jurors, it must permit the parties or their attorneys to make any further inquiry it considers proper, or must itself ask any of their additional questions it considers proper.

(b) *Peremptory Challenges.* — The court must allow the number of peremptory challenges provided by 28 U.S.C. § 1870.

(c) *Excusing a Juror.* — During trial or deliberation, the court may excuse a juror for good cause. (Amended by order adopted February 28, 1966, effective July 1, 1966, by order adopted April 30, 1991, effective December 1, 1991, and by order adopted April 30, 2007, effective December 1, 2007.)

Comment. — The language of Rule 47 has been amended as part of the general restyling of the Civil Rules to make them more easily understood and to make style and terminology consistent throughout the rules. These changes are intended to be stylistic only.

Rule 48. Number of Jurors; Verdict; Polling.

(a) *Number of Jurors.* — A jury must begin with at least 6 and no more than 12 members, and each juror must participate in the verdict unless excused under Rule 47(c).

(b) *Verdict.* — Unless the parties stipulate otherwise, the verdict must be unanimous and must be returned by a jury of at least 6 members.

(c) *Polling.* — After a verdict is returned but before the jury is discharged, the court must on a party's request, or may on its own, poll the jurors individually. If the poll reveals a lack of unanimity or lack of assent by the number of jurors that the parties stipulated to, the court may direct the jury to deliberate further or may order a new trial. (Amended by order adopted April 30, 1991, effective December 1, 1991, by order adopted April 30, 2007, effective December 1, 2007, and by order adopted March 26, 2009, effective December 1, 2009.)

Comment. — The language of Rule 48 has been amended as part of the general restyling of the Civil Rules to make them more easily understood and to make style and terminology consistent throughout the rules. These changes are intended to be stylistic only.

Rule 49. Special Verdict; General Verdict and Questions.

(a) *Special Verdict.* — (1) In General. The court may require a jury to return only a special verdict in the form of a special written finding on each issue of fact. The court may do so by:

(A) submitting written questions susceptible of a categorical or other brief answer;

(B) submitting written forms of the special findings that might properly be made under the pleadings and evidence; or

(C) using any other method that the court considers appropriate.

(2) Instructions. The court must give the instructions and explanations necessary to enable the jury to make its findings on each submitted issue.

(3) Issues Not Submitted. A party waives the right to a jury trial on any issue of fact raised by the pleadings or evidence but not submitted to the jury unless, before the jury retires, the party demands its submission to the jury. If the party does not demand submission, the court may make a finding on the issue. If the court makes no finding, it is considered to have made a finding consistent with its judgment on the special verdict.

(b) *General Verdict with Answers to Written Questions.* — (1) In General. The court may submit to the jury forms for a general verdict, together with written questions on one or more issues of fact that the jury must decide. The court must give the instructions and explanations necessary to enable the jury to render a general verdict and answer the questions in writing, and must direct the jury to do both.

(2) Verdict and Answers Consistent. When the general verdict and the answers are consistent, the court must approve, for entry under Rule 58, an appropriate judgment on the verdict and answers.

(3) Answers Inconsistent with the Verdict. When the answers are consistent with each other but one or more is inconsistent with the general verdict, the court may:

(A) approve, for entry under Rule 58, an appropriate judgment according to the answers, notwithstanding the general verdict;

(B) direct the jury to further consider its answers and verdict; or

(C) order a new trial.

(4) Answers Inconsistent with Each Other and the Verdict. When the answers are inconsistent with each other and one or more is also inconsistent with the general verdict, judgment must not be entered; instead, the court must direct the jury to further consider its answers and verdict, or must order a new trial. (Amended by order adopted January 21, 1963, effective July 1, 1963, by order adopted March 2, 1987, effective August 1, 1987, and by order adopted April 30, 2007, effective December 1, 2007.)

Comment. — The language of Rule 49 has been amended as part of the general restyling of the Civil Rules to make them more easily understood and to make style and terminology consistent throughout the rules. These changes are intended to be stylistic only.

CASE NOTES

The furnishing of proper forms of verdict is the duty of the court. Scott v. Isbrandtsen Co., 327 F.2d 113 (4th Cir. 1964).

A trial court has discretion in the use of special verdicts. Scott v. Isbrandtsen Co., 327 F.2d 113 (4th Cir. 1964).

The submission of requests or special issues to the jury rests in the sound discretion of the trial judge. Scarborough v. Atlantic Coast Line R.R., 190 F.2d 935 (4th Cir. 1951).

This rule gives district courts broad discretion in determining the form of verdict, and while whether the district judge has uncontrolled discretion in this regard has not been decided, there apparently has never been a reversal for abuse of discretion in determining the form of verdict. Great Coastal Express, Inc. v. International Bhd. of Teamsters, 511 F.2d 839 (4th Cir. 1975), cert. denied, 425 U.S. 975, 96 S. Ct. 2176, 48 L. Ed. 2d 799 (1976).

Which extends to the form of interrogatories. Scott v. Isbrandtsen Co., 327 F.2d 113 (4th Cir. 1964).

But all material factual issues should be covered by the questions submitted. Scott v. Isbrandtsen Co., 327 F.2d 113 (4th Cir. 1964); Logan v. A/S Havtor, 328 F.2d 84 (4th Cir. 1964).

Jury trial is waived automatically on issue not submitted by court. — Subdivision (a) of this rule works an automatic waiver of jury trial on any issue raised, but not submitted by the court. Scott v. Isbrandtsen Co., 327 F.2d 113 (4th Cir. 1964).

Interrogatory held vague and uncertain and not to present case fairly. — See Scott v. Isbrandtsen Co., 327 F.2d 113 (4th Cir. 1964); Logan v. A/S Havtor, 328 F.2d 84 (4th Cir. 1964).

Questions or special issues submitted to the jury should be simple and clear, with a single issue in each question. Scarborough v. Atlantic Coast Line R.R., 190 F.2d 935 (4th Cir. 1951).

Proper instructions as to legal standards must be given if interrogatory presents mixed question of fact and law. — See Scott v. Isbrandtsen Co., 327 F.2d 113 (4th Cir. 1964).

Sufficiency of objections to court's charge and action on requests to charge. — See Scott v. Isbrandtsen Co., 327 F.2d 113 (4th Cir. 1964).

A federal district court, sitting as chancellor, finds all the facts found by the jury on special verdict as well as all facts reasonably inferable therefrom. As to factual issues not submitted to the jury and factual issues not proper to be submitted to the jury, being exclusively relevant to equitable relief, the court will make its own findings of fact. Davis v. Ampthill Rayon Workers, Inc., 446 F. Supp. 681 (E.D. Va. 1978), aff'd, 594 F.2d 856 (4th Cir. 1979).

Submission of omitted issue. — A vague reference to the plaintiff's jury verdict forms was sufficient to constitute a demand for submission of an omitted issue "before the jury retires" as required by Rule 49(a), Fed.R.Civ.P. Davis v. Ampthill Rayon Workers, Inc., 446 F. Supp. 681 (E.D. Va. 1978), aff'd, 594 F.2d 856 (4th Cir. 1979).

Applied in Wooten v. Skibs A/S Samuel Bakke, 431 F.2d 821 (4th Cir. 1969).

Rule 50. Judgment as a Matter of Law in a Jury Trial; Related Motion for a New Trial; Conditional Ruling.

(a) *Judgment as a Matter of Law.* — (1) In General. If a party has been fully heard on an issue during a jury trial and the court finds that a reasonable jury would not have a legally sufficient evidentiary basis to find for the party on that issue, the court may:

(A) resolve the issue against the party; and

(B) grant a motion for judgment as a matter of law against the party on a claim or defense that, under the controlling law, can be maintained or defeated only with a favorable finding on that issue.

(2) Motion. A motion for judgment as a matter of law may be made at any time before the case is submitted to the jury. The motion must specify the judgment sought and the law and facts that entitle the movant to the judgment.

(b) *Renewing the Motion After Trial; Alternative Motion for a New Trial.* — If the court does not grant a motion for judgment as a matter of law made under Rule 50(a), the court is considered to have submitted the action to the jury subject to the court's later deciding the legal questions raised by the motion. No later than 28 days after the entry of judgment — or if the motion addresses a jury issue not decided by a verdict, no later than 28 days after the jury was discharged — the movant may file a renewed motion for judgment as a matter of law and may include an alternative or joint request for a new trial under Rule 59. In ruling on the renewed motion, the court may:

(1) allow judgment on the verdict, if the jury returned a verdict;

(2) order a new trial; or

(3) direct the entry of judgment as a matter of law.

(c) *Granting the Renewed Motion; Conditional Ruling on a Motion for a New Trial.* — (1) In General. If the court grants a renewed motion for judgment as a matter of law, it must also conditionally rule on any motion for a new trial by determining whether a new trial should be granted if the judgment is later vacated or reversed. The court must state the grounds for conditionally granting or denying the motion for a new trial.

(2) Effect of a Conditional Ruling. Conditionally granting the motion for a new trial does not affect the judgment's finality; if the judgment is reversed, the new trial must proceed unless the appellate court orders otherwise. If the motion for a new trial is conditionally denied, the appellee may assert error in that denial; if the judgment is reversed, the case must proceed as the appellate court orders.

(d) *Time for a Losing Party's New-Trial Motion.* — Any motion for a new trial under Rule 59 by a party against whom judgment as a matter of law is rendered must be filed no later than 28 days after the entry of the judgment.

(e) *Denying the Motion for Judgment as a Matter of Law; Reversal on Appeal.* — If the court denies the motion for judgment as a matter of law, the prevailing party may, as appellee, assert grounds entitling it to a new trial should the appellate court conclude that the trial court erred in denying the motion. If the appellate court reverses the judgment, it may order a new trial, direct the trial court to determine whether a new trial should be granted, or direct the entry of judgment. (Amended by order adopted January 21, 1963, effective July 1, 1963, by order adopted March 2, 1987, effective August 1, 1987, by order adopted April 30, 1991, effective December 1, 1991, by order adopted April 22, 1993, effective December 1, 1993, by order adopted April 27, 1995, effective December 1, 1995, by order adopted April 12, 2006, effective December 1, 2006, by order adopted April 30, 2007, effective December 1, 2007, and by order adopted March 26, 2009, effective December 1, 2009.)

Comment. — The language of Rule 50 has been amended as part of the general restyling of the Civil Rules to make them more easily understood and to make style and terminology consistent throughout the rules. These changes are intended to be stylistic only.

Former Rule 50(b) stated that the court reserves ruling on a motion for judgment as a matter of law made at the close of all the evidence "[i]f, for any reason, the court does not grant" the motion. The words "for any reason" reflected the proposition that the reservation is automatic and inescapable. The ruling is reserved even if the court explicitly denies the motion. The same result follows under the amended rule. If the motion is not granted, the ruling is reserved.

Amended Rule 50(e) identifies the appellate court's authority to direct the entry of judgment. This authority was not described in former Rule 50(d), but was recognized in *Weisgram v. Marley Co.,* 528 U.S. 440 (2000), and in *Neely v. Martin K. Eby Construction Company,* 386 U.S. 317 (1967). When Rule 50(d) was drafted in 1963, the Committee Note stated that "[s]ubdivision (d) does not attempt a regulation of all aspects of the procedure where the motion for judgment n.o.v. and any accompanying motion for a new trial are denied * * *." Express recognition of the authority to direct entry of judgment does not otherwise supersede this caution.

CASE NOTES

Where very little of the evidence was disputed a Rule 50 motion was the appropriate means of resolving the issues in the case. Godfrey v. Boddie-Noell Enters., Inc., 843 F. Supp. 114 (E.D. Va. 1994), aff'd, 46 F.3d 1124 (4th Cir. 1995).

This rule authorizes judgment n.o.v. — The authority to order judgment notwithstanding the verdict in federal courts is provided in this rule. Nuckoles v. F.W. Woolworth Co., 372 F.2d 286 (4th Cir. 1967), rev'g 248 F. Supp. 164 (W.D. Va. 1966).

Motion for judgment n.o.v. in effect renews motion for directed verdict. — A motion for judgment notwithstanding the verdict is, in effect, the same as renewing an earlier motion for a directed verdict. Shelton v. Jones, 272 F. Supp. 139 (W.D. Va. 1967).

Duty of court; test to be applied. — Where a verdict is contrary to the law or the evidence, or without evidence to support it, it is the duty of the court to set the verdict aside. Any other rule would make the verdict final and not subject to question or review. The test to be applied is that when the evidence is such that without weighing the credibility of the witnesses there can be but one reasonable conclusion as to the verdict, a court should set the verdict aside. Jacobs v. College of William & Mary, 517 F. Supp. 791 (E.D. Va. 1980), aff'd, 661 F.2d 922 (4th Cir.), cert. denied, 454 U.S. 1033, 102 S. Ct. 572, 70 L. Ed. 2d 477 (1981).

Judge to direct verdict if only one reasonable conclusion as to verdict. — Subdivision (a) requires the trial judge to direct a verdict if, under controlling law, there can be only one reasonable conclusion as to the verdict. Hicks v. Phipps, 765 F. Supp. 1541 (W.D. Va. 1990).

A district court may grant judgment n.o.v. if there is no legally sufficient evidentiary basis for a reasonable jury to find for the non-moving party. Cline v. Wal-Mart Stores, Inc., 144 F.3d 294 (4th Cir. 1998).

The standard for granting summary judgment is akin to that of granting a directed verdict. — The standard for granting judgment mirrors the standard for a directed verdict under Rule 50(a). Hicks v. Phipps, 765 F. Supp. 1541 (W.D. Va. 1990).

Standard for directing verdict and for entering judgment notwithstanding verdict equivalent. — See Crown Cent. Petro. Corp. v. Brice, 427 F. Supp. 638 (E.D. Va. 1977).

The standard on a judgment as a matter of law is similar to the standard on a summary judgment motion where the court must determine whether the evidence presents a sufficient disagreement to require submission to a jury or whether is so one-sided that one party must prevail as a matter of law. Bentley v. Legent Corp., 849 F. Supp. 429 (E.D. Va. 1994), aff'd sub nom. Herman v. Legent Corp., 50 F.3d 6 (4th Cir. 1995).

Evidence must be viewed in light most favorable to party not moving for directed verdict. — When one party moves for a directed verdict the evidence must be viewed in the light most favorable to the opposite party and courts will take fact questions from the jury only where the necessity for such action is clear and imperative. Southern Fruit Distribs., Inc. v. Fulmer, 107 F.2d 456 (4th Cir. 1939).

On a motion for directed verdict the evidence must be taken in the light most favorable to the party against whom the directed verdict is asked and all conflicts must be resolved in his favor. Aetna Cas. & Sur. Co. v. Yeatts, 122 F.2d 350 (4th Cir. 1941).

In considering a motion for a directed verdict the evidence must be considered in its aspect most favorable to the party against whom the motion is made, with every fair and reasonable inference which the evidence justifies. Mandro v. Vibbert, 170 F.2d 540 (4th Cir. 1948); Smitty Baker Coal Co. v. UMW, 457 F. Supp. 1123 (W.D. Va. 1978), aff'd, 620 F.2d 416 (4th Cir. 1980).

Where the defendants moved for judgment notwithstanding the verdict or, in the alternative, for a new trial, the evidence must be viewed in the light most favorable to the plaintiffs. Azalea Drive-In Theatre, Inc. v. Sargoy, 394 F. Supp. 568 (E.D. Va. 1975), rev'd on other grounds, 540 F.2d 713 (4th Cir. 1976).

All evidentiary conflicts are to be resolved in favor of the successful parties, and they are to be given the benefit of all reasonable inferences. Crown Cent. Petro. Corp. v. Brice, 427 F. Supp. 638 (E.D. Va. 1977).

Where appellant's appeal is from a judgment n.o.v. and directed verdicts, circuit courts of appeals must view the evidence in the light most favorable to him and give him the benefit of all inferences which the evidence fairly supports. Ryan v. Edwards, 592 F.2d 756 (4th Cir. 1979).

A jury verdict is to be viewed in the light most favorable to the party in whose favor it is found, and such party is entitled to the benefit of all inferences which the evidence fairly supports, even though contrary inferences might be drawn. Jacobs v. College of William & Mary, 517 F. Supp. 791 (E.D. Va. 1980), aff'd, 661 F.2d 922 (4th Cir.) cert. denied, 454 U.S. 1033, 102 S. Ct. 572, 70 L. Ed. 2d 477 (1981).

Issues of fact should be left to the determination of the jury, whose duty it is to determine the credibility of the witnesses, and the court should not attempt to substitute its judgment for that of the jury in disputed cases. But, a jury must not be left to speculation or conjecture, or render a verdict based on sympathy. Jacobs v. College of William & Mary, 517 F. Supp. 791 (E.D. Va. 1980), aff'd, 661 F.2d 922 (4th Cir.) cert. denied, 454 U.S. 1033, 102 S. Ct. 572, 70 L. Ed. 2d 477 (1981).

Criteria for judgment n.o.v. and new trial distinguished. — Although some cases have confused the criteria for judgment n.o.v. with those for a new trial the distinction is clear. Where there is substantial evidence in support of plaintiff's case, the judge may not direct a verdict against him, even though he may not believe his evidence or may think that the weight of the evidence is on the other side. He may, however, set aside a verdict supported by substantial evidence where in his opinion it is contrary to the clear weight of the evidence, or is based on evidence which is false; for, even though the evidence be sufficient to preclude the direction of a verdict, it is still his duty to exercise his power over the proceeding before him to prevent a miscarriage of justice. Wyatt v. Interstate & Ocean Transp. Co., 454 F. Supp. 429 (E.D. Va. 1978), rev'd on other grounds, 623 F.2d 888 (1980).

Court may not adopt different standard of proof than that imposed on jury. — See Smitty Baker Coal Co. v. UMW, 457 F. Supp. 1123 (W.D. Va. 1978), aff'd, 620 F.2d 416 (4th Cir. 1980).

Court may not substitute judgment as to proper resolution of facts. — See Smitty Baker Coal Co. v. UMW, 457 F. Supp. 1123 (W.D. Va. 1978), aff'd, 620 F.2d 416 (4th Cir. 1980).

Court may not reweigh evidence or pass on credibility of witnesses. — See Smitty Baker Coal Co. v. UMW, 457 F. Supp. 1123 (W.D. Va. 1978), aff'd, 620 F.2d 416 (4th Cir. 1980).

Initial motion for judgment must be made before verdict. — Defendant's motion for judgment as a matter of law on the ground of legal impossibility was denied because it was not made before the jury's verdict and because the court found no applicable exception to waiver. Ramar Coal Co. v. International Union, UMW, 814 F. Supp. 502 (W.D. Va. 1993).

Judgment n.o.v. entered for insufficiency of evidence only if motion for directed verdict was made. — A judgment non obstante verdicto can be entered on the ground of the insufficiency of the evidence only where a motion for directed verdict has been duly made. Aetna Cas. & Sur. Co. v. Yeatts, 122 F.2d 350 (4th Cir. 1941).

When judgment n.o.v. granted. — Judgment n.o.v. should not be granted unless the evidence is so clear that reasonable men could reach no other conclusion than the one suggested. Azalea Drive-In Theatre, Inc. v. Sargoy, 394 F. Supp. 568 (E.D. Va. 1975), rev'd on other grounds, 540 F.2d 713 (4th Cir. 1976).

Evidence should be so clear that reasonable men could reach no other conclusion. — Judgment n.o.v. should not be granted unless the evidence is so clear that reasonable men could reach no other conclusion than the one suggested. Azalea Drive-In Theatre, Inc. v. Sargoy, 394 F. Supp. 568 (E.D. Va. 1975), rev'd on other grounds, 540 F.2d 713 (4th Cir. 1976).

Sufficiency of evidence to take claim to jury held matter of federal law. — See Nuckoles v. F.W. Woolworth Co., 372 F.2d 286 (4th Cir. 1967), rev'g 248 F. Supp. 164 (W.D. Va. 1966).

Judgment n.o.v. and conditional grant of new trial. — When a court grants judgment notwithstanding the verdict and conditionally grants a motion for a new trial, the finality of the judgment is not affected, and an appellate court can review the conditional grant of a new trial and in an appropriate case reverse the conditional grant of the new trial and direct that judgment be entered on the verdict. United States v. Steed, 674 F.2d 284 (4th Cir.), cert. denied, 459 U.S. 829, 103 S. Ct. 67, 74 L. Ed. 2d 68 (1982).

The fact that the court may resolve the facts in favor of defendants does not mean that there is no evidence to support the verdict of the jury. Azalea Drive-In Theatre, Inc. v. Sargoy, 394 F. Supp. 568 (E.D. Va. 1975), rev'd on other grounds, 540 F.2d 713 (4th Cir. 1976).

Standard of review on appeal. — On appeal, a denial of judgment n.o.v. will be affirmed if, giving the non-movant the benefit of every legitimate inference in his favor, there was evidence upon which a jury could reasonably return a verdict for him. Cline v. Wal-Mart Stores, Inc., 144 F.3d 294 (4th Cir. 1998).

In making a determination whether to affirm a denial of judgment n.o.v. the appellate court is not permitted to retry factual finding or credibility determinations reached by the jury. Rather, it is to assume that testimony in favor of the non-moving party is credible, unless totally incredible on its face and ignore the substantive weight of any evidence supporting the moving party. Cline v. Wal-Mart Stores, Inc., 144 F.3d 294 (4th Cir. 1998).

Sufficiency of evidence not reviewable on appeal unless appropriately challenged at trial. — Where the sufficiency of the evidence has not been challenged by a motion for a directed verdict or by some other appropriate way during trial, a court of appeals has no power to review its sufficiency on appeal. Aetna Cas. & Sur. Co. v. Yeatts, 122 F.2d 350 (4th Cir. 1941).

Appellate court was substantially foreclosed from reviewing the sufficiency of the evidence because plaintiff never moved the district court for judgment as a matter of law pursuant to this rule. Such an absolute failure precludes all but the most deferential appellate review of the evidence. Bristol Steel & Iron Works, Inc. v. Bethlehem Steel Corp., 41 F.3d 182 (4th Cir. 1994).

In reviewing the evidence through the medium of a motion for a new trial after failure to move for judgment as a matter of law, the appellate court does not review "sufficiency" in its technical sense. What is at issue is whether there was an absolute absence of evidence to support the jury's verdict. Bristol Steel & Iron Works, Inc. v. Bethlehem Steel Corp., 41 F.3d 182 (4th Cir. 1994).

Motion for directed verdict necessary to test sufficiency of evidence. — This rule does not do away with but emphasizes the necessity of a motion for a directed verdict to raise the legal question whether the evidence is sufficient. Aetna Cas. & Sur. Co. v. Yeatts, 122 F.2d 350 (4th Cir. 1941).

And motion granted when evidence and inferences therefrom would not support finding. — A motion for a directed verdict should be granted whenever the testimony and all the inferences which the jury could justifiably draw therefrom would be insufficient to support a finding. Southern Fruit Distribs., Inc. v. Fulmer, 107 F.2d 456 (4th Cir. 1939).

Or is overwhelmingly against party not moving. — A verdict can be directed only where there is no substantial evidence to support recovery by the party against whom it is directed or where the evidence is all against him or so overwhelmingly so as to leave no room to doubt what the fact is. Aetna Cas. & Sur. Co. v. Yeatts, 122 F.2d 350 (4th Cir. 1941).

But may not be granted if any substantial evidence supports his case. — Where there is substantial evidence in support of plaintiff's case, the judge may not direct a verdict against him, even though he may not believe his evidence or may think that the weight of the evidence is on the other side; for, under the constitutional guaranty of trial by jury, it is for the jury to weigh the evidence and pass upon its credibility. He may, however, set aside a verdict supported by substantial evidence where in his opinion it is contrary to the clear weight of the evidence, or is based upon evidence which is false; for, even though the evidence be sufficient to preclude the direction of a verdict, it is still his duty to exercise his power over the proceedings before him to prevent a miscarriage of justice. Aetna Cas. & Sur. Co. v. Yeatts, 122 F.2d 350 (4th Cir. 1941).

Test on directing verdict. — The test on directing a verdict is not whether there is any evidence, but whether there are no controverted issues of fact upon which reasonable men could differ. Pogue v. Retail Credit Co., 453 F.2d 336 (4th Cir. 1972), cert. denied, 409 U.S. 1109, 93 S. Ct. 910, 34 L. Ed. 2d 689, reh'g denied, 410 U.S. 960, 93 S. Ct. 1417, 35 L. Ed. 2d 695 (1973).

Court must consider alternative motion for new trial even where judgment n.o.v. granted in action. — See Wyatt v. Interstate & Ocean Transp. Co., 454 F. Supp. 429 (E.D. Va. 1978), rev'd on other grounds, 623 F.2d 888 (4th Cir. 1980).

Grant of new trial where jury verdict excessive. — See Wyatt v. Interstate & Ocean Transp. Co., 454 F. Supp. 429 (E.D. Va. 1978), rev'd on other grounds, 623 F.2d 888 (4th Cir. 1980).

Failure to present sufficient evidence for jury question resulting in judgment n.o.v. — See Wyatt v. Interstate & Ocean Transp. Co., 454 F. Supp. 429 (E.D. Va. 1978), rev'd on other grounds, 623 F.2d 888 (4th Cir. 1980).

Judgment n.o.v. granted only under most unusual circumstances. — The court may not reweigh evidence, pass on credibility of witnesses, nor is it free to substitute its judgment as to the proper resolution of facts, but is limited to a determination as to whether there was but one conclusion as to the verdict that reasonable men could have reached. Smitty Baker Coal Co. v. UMW, 457 F. Supp. 1123 (W.D. Va. 1978), aff'd, 620 F.2d 416 (4th Cir. 1980).

Standard of review. — The court of appeals reviews the grant of a Rule 50(a) motion de novo. Malone v. Microdyne Corp., 26 F.3d 471 (4th Cir. 1994).

Plain error. — Even in the wake of a complete failure to move for judgment as a matter of law, if plain error would result, appellate review is permissible. Singer v. Dungan, 45 F.3d 823 (4th Cir. 1995).

Applied in Eastern Livestock Co-op. Mktg. Ass'n v. Dickenson, 107 F.2d 116 (4th Cir. 1939); Southern Ry. v. Bell, 114 F.2d 341 (4th Cir. 1940); Callander v. Hunter Motor Lines, 327 F.2d 754 (4th Cir. 1964); Marston v. E.I. du Pont de Nemours & Co., 448 F. Supp. 172 (W.D. Va. 1978); Robinson v. Goff, 517 F. Supp. 350 (W.D. Va. 1981); Herold v. Hajoca Corp., 864 F.2d 317 (4th Cir. 1988); United States v. Tobias, 899 F.2d 1375 (4th Cir. 1990); Persinger v. Norfolk & W. Ry., 920 F.2d 1185 (4th Cir. 1990); Flickinger v. School Bd., 799 F. Supp. 586 (E.D. Va. 1992); Nelson v. Watergate at Landmark, 898 F. Supp. 346 (E.D. Va. 1995); Redman v. Sentry Group, Inc., 907 F. Supp. 180 (W.D. Va. 1995); Towler v. Sayles, 76 F.3d 579 (4th Cir. 1996); Konkel v. Bob Evans Farms, Inc., 165 F.3d 275 (4th Cir.); Eberhardt v. Integrated Design & Constr., Inc., 167 F.3d 861 (4th. Cir. 1999); SunTiger, Inc. v. Scientific Research Funding Group, 9 F. Supp. 2d 601 (E.D. Va. 1998); Odetics, Inc. v. Storage Technology Corp., 14 F. Supp. 2d 807 (E.D. Va. 1998); Daniel v. Jones, 39 F. Supp. 2d 635 (E.D. Va. 1999); Baynard v. Lawson, 112 F. Supp. 2d 524, 2000 U.S. Dist. LEXIS 13798 (E.D. Va. 2000); E.I. du Pont de Nemours & Co. v. Kolon Indus., 2011 U.S. Dist. LEXIS 113702 (E.D. Va. Oct. 3, 2011).

Rule 51. Instructions to the Jury; Objections; Preserving a Claim of Error.

(a) *Requests.* — (1) Before or at the Close of the Evidence. At the close of the evidence or at any earlier reasonable time that the court orders, a party may file and furnish to every other party written requests for the jury instructions it wants the court to give.

(2) After the Close of the Evidence. After the close of the evidence, a party may:

(A) file requests for instructions on issues that could not reasonably have been anticipated by an earlier time that the court set for requests; and

(B) with the court's permission, file untimely requests for instructions on any issue.

(b) *Instructions.* — The court:

(1) must inform the parties of its proposed instructions and proposed action on the requests before instructing the jury and before final jury arguments;

(2) must give the parties an opportunity to object on the record and out of the jury's hearing before the instructions and arguments are delivered; and

(3) may instruct the jury at any time before the jury is discharged.

(c) *Objections.* — (1) How to Make. A party who objects to an instruction or the failure to give an instruction must do so on the record, stating distinctly the matter objected to and the grounds for the objection.

(2) When to Make. An objection is timely if:

(A) a party objects at the opportunity provided under Rule 51(b)(2); or

(B) a party was not informed of an instruction or action on a request before that opportunity to object, and the party objects promptly after learning that the instruction or request will be, or has been, given or refused.

(d) *Assigning Error; Plain Error.* — (1) Assigning Error. A party may assign as error:

(A) an error in an instruction actually given, if that party properly objected; or

(B) a failure to give an instruction, if that party properly requested it and — unless the court rejected the request in a definitive ruling on the record — also properly objected.

(2) Plain Error. A court may consider a plain error in the instructions that has not been preserved as required by Rule 51(d)(1) if the error affects substantial rights. (Amended by order adopted March 2, 1987, effective August 1, 1987, by order adopted March 27, 2003, effective December 1, 2003, and by order adopted April 30, 2007, effective December 1, 2007.)

Comment. — The language of Rule 51 has been amended as part of the general restyling of the Civil Rules to make them more easily understood and to make style and terminology consistent throughout the rules. These changes are intended to be stylistic only.

Law Review. — For an article, "The Transformation of the American Civil Trial: The Silent Judge," see 42 Wm. & Mary L. Rev. 195 (2000).

CASE NOTES

Purpose of rule. — The looseness with which some courts, properly, have interpreted this rule remains faithful to the rule's purpose of ensuring that the parties have given the trial judge a chance to resolve disputed issues relating to jury instructions; the requirement for technical compliance with the rule is waived only when the appellate court is sure that the trial court was adequately informed as to a litigant's contentions. City of Richmond v. Madison Mgt. Group, Inc., 918 F.2d 438 (4th Cir. 1990).

Although courts should relax this rule where to do so will not contravene the rule's purpose, they should not do so where a party has merely conclusorily asserted that further objection would have been futile. City of Richmond v. Madison Mgt. Group, Inc., 918 F.2d 438 (4th Cir. 1990).

Rule 51 must be read in conjunction with Rule 46; where the district court was fully aware of the plaintiff's position, and the district court had obviously considered and rejected that position, strict enforcement of this rule would exalt form over substance. City of Richmond v. Madison Mgt. Group, Inc., 918 F.2d 438 (4th Cir. 1990).

This rule constitutes a particular expression of the adversarial theory of justice in which litigants (or, more precisely, their counsel) are to play a central role in generating correct resolutions of disputes. The burden on counsel takes on a special importance where the case is very complex; for as a case's complexity increases, so does the probability that a district court may, in the pressures of trial, overlook something. Congress' decision as expressed in this rule is to impose that burden where litigant is represented by very able, and numerous, counsel. City of Richmond v. Madison Mgt. Group, Inc., 918 F.2d 438 (4th Cir. 1990).

Application of rule to instructions respecting special verdicts under Rule 49. — See Scott v. Isbrandtsen Co., 327 F.2d 113 (4th Cir. 1964).

No duty to charge jury on law not proffered by instructions. — There is no mandatory duty placed upon a trial court by this rule to charge the jury in a civil action upon a point of law not proffered by instructions, unless the failure to so instruct makes the charge so deficient as to constitute plain error. Cicinato v. McPheeters, 542 F.2d 634 (4th Cir. 1976).

Failure to object waived right to complain that action improperly submitted. — Where at trial the plaintiffs made no contention at any point that the law of New Jersey was determinative of the rights of the parties and the plaintiffs agreed in advance to the charge as given by the trial court, and, after the charge had been given, they entered no exceptions thereto, the failure of the plaintiffs to object at any time during trial or to except to the charge waived any right on their part to complain that the action was improperly submitted as one controlled by Virginia law. Bilancia v. GMC, 538 F.2d 621 (4th Cir. 1976).

Applied in Pogue v. Retail Credit Co., 453 F.2d 336 (4th Cir. 1972); Evans v. Wright, 505 F.2d 287 (4th Cir. 1974); Perpetual Real Estate Servs., Inc. v. Michaelson Properties, Inc., 775 F. Supp. 893 (E.D. Va. 1991).

Rule 52. Findings and Conclusions by the Court; Judgment on Partial Findings.

(a) *Findings and Conclusions.* — (1) In General. In an action tried on the facts without a jury or with an advisory jury, the court must find the facts specially and state its conclusions of law separately. The findings and conclusions may be stated on the record after the close of the evidence or may appear in an opinion or a memorandum of decision filed by the court. Judgment must be entered under Rule 58.

(2) For an Interlocutory Injunction. In granting or refusing an interlocutory injunction, the court must similarly state the findings and conclusions that support its action.

(3) For a Motion. The court is not required to state findings or conclusions when ruling on a motion under Rule 12 or 56 or, unless these rules provide otherwise, on any other motion.

(4) Effect of a Master's Findings. A master's findings, to the extent adopted by the court, must be considered the court's findings.

(5) Questioning the Evidentiary Support. A party may later question the sufficiency of the evidence supporting the findings, whether or not the party requested findings, objected to them, moved to amend them, or moved for partial findings.

(6) Setting Aside the Findings. Findings of fact, whether based on oral or other evidence, must not be set aside unless clearly erroneous, and the reviewing court must give due regard to the trial court's opportunity to judge the witnesses' credibility.

(b) *Amended or Additional Findings.* — On a party's motion filed no later than 28 days after the entry of judgment, the court may amend its findings — or make additional findings — and may amend the judgment accordingly. The motion may accompany a motion for a new trial under Rule 59.

(c) *Judgment on Partial Findings.* — If a party has been fully heard on an issue during a nonjury trial and the court finds against the party on that issue, the court may enter judgment against the party on a claim or defense that, under the controlling law, can be maintained or defeated only with a favorable finding on that issue. The court may, however, decline to render any judgment until the close of the evidence. A judgment on partial findings must be supported by findings of fact and conclusions of law as required by Rule 52(a). (Amended by order adopted December 27, 1946, effective March 19, 1948, by order adopted January 21, 1963, effective July 1, 1963, by order adopted April 28, 1983, effective August 1, 1983, by order adopted April 29, 1985, effective August 1, 1985, by order adopted April 30, 1991, effective December 1, 1991, by order adopted April 22, 1993, effective December 1, 1993, by order adopted April 27, 1995, effective December 1, 1995, by order adopted April 30, 2007, effective December 1, 2007, and by order adopted March 26, 2009, effective December 1, 2009.)

Comment. — The language of Rule 52 has been amended as part of the general restyling of the Civil Rules to make them more easily understood and to make style and terminology consistent throughout the rules. These changes are intended to be stylistic only.

Former Rule 52(a) said that findings are unnecessary on decisions of motions "except as provided in subdivision (c) of this rule." Amended Rule 52(a)(3) says that findings are unnecessary "unless these rules provide otherwise." This change reflects provisions in other rules that require Rule 52 findings on deciding motions. Rules 23(e), 23(h), and 54(d)(2)(C) are examples.

Amended Rule 52(a)(5) includes provisions that appeared in former Rule 52(a) and 52(b). Rule 52(a) provided that requests for findings are not necessary for purposes of review. It applied both in an action tried on the facts without a jury and also in granting or refusing an interlocutory injunction. Rule 52(b), applicable to findings "made in actions tried without a jury," provided that the sufficiency of the evidence might be "later questioned whether or not in the district court the party raising the question objected to the findings, moved to amend them, or moved for partial findings." Former Rule 52(b) did not explicitly apply to decisions granting or refusing an interlocutory injunction. Amended Rule 52(a)(5) makes explicit the application of this part of former Rule 52(b) to interlocutory injunction decisions.

Former Rule 52(c) provided for judgment on partial findings, and referred to it as "judgment as a matter of law." Amended Rule 52(c) refers only to "judgment," to avoid any confusion with a Rule 50 judgment as a matter of law in a jury case. The standards that govern judgment as a matter of law in a jury case have no bearing on a decision under Rule 52(c).

Law Review. — For note, "Rule 52(a): Appellate Review of Findings of Fact Based on Documentary or Undisputed Evidence," see 49 Va. L. Rev. 506 (1963).

CASE NOTES

Conciseness is to be striven for, and prolixity avoided, in findings; they must be stated "in such detail and exactness" on all material issues that the reviewing court may understand clearly the factual basis for the trial court's findings and conclusions. Patrician Towers Owners, Inc. v. Fairchild, 513 F.2d 216 (4th Cir. 1975).

When the trial court provides only conclusory findings, illuminated by no subsidiary findings or reasoning on all the relevant facts there is not that "detail and exactness" on the material issues of fact necessary for an understanding by an appellate court of the factual basis for the trial court's findings and conclusions, and for a rational determination of whether the findings of the trial court are clearly erroneous. It was to assure that "detail and exactness" in the trial court's findings as a predicate for intelligent appellate review that this rule was adopted. The failure of the district court to comply with the basic requirement of the rule for detailed findings of fact compels the circuit court of appeals to remand the cause for detailed findings of fact and conclusions of law by the trial court. EEOC v. United Va. Bank/Seaboard Nat'l, 555 F.2d 403 (4th Cir. 1977).

Where at the conclusion of the hearing, the district court orally stated its findings of fact and conclusions of law from the bench, with the written order thereafter entered merely making reference to the "reasons stated from the bench," the district court's oral opinion and subsequent order did not comply with the provisions of the Federal Rules of Civil Procedure relating to findings of fact and conclusions of law in the granting of preliminary injunction. United States v. Virginia, 569 F.2d 1300 (4th Cir. 1978).

Court has power to alter conclusions of law. — While this rule does not expressly refer to reconsideration of legal conclusions, it is clear that the court has the power to alter conclusions of law as well as findings of facts even when doing so results in the reversal of its initial judgment. Central Fid. Bank v. Cooper, 116 Bankr. 469 (Bankr. E.D. Va. 1990).

Requirement of separate findings and conclusions applies to permanent as well as temporary injunctions. — On its face, subdivision (a) would appear to apply only to interlocutory injunctions. However, it has been held that the language of the rule, "[i]n all actions tried upon the facts without a jury ...," encompasses suits in which permanent injunctions are issued. Alberti v. Cruise, 383 F.2d 268 (4th Cir. 1967).

Trial court must do more than announce statements of ultimate fact. — To satisfy the demands of subdivision (a), a trial court must do more than announce statements of ultimate fact. The court must support its rulings by spelling out the subordinate facts on which it relies. Unless the trial court fully complies with subdivision (a), appellate review becomes an exercise in conjecture. United States ex rel. Belcon, Inc. v. Sherman Constr. Co., 800 F.2d 1321 (4th Cir. 1986).

General verdict may prejudice appellate review in close cases. — In close cases, the losing parties' right to appellate review can be prejudiced where there is a general jury verdict and the appellant was entitled to the benefit of the separate findings and conclusions provided by this rule. Troy v. City of Hampton, 756 F.2d 1000 (4th Cir.), cert. denied, 474 U.S. 864, 106 S. Ct. 182, 88 L. Ed. 2d 151 (1985).

Case remanded for detailed and intelligible findings in light of principles set out by court of appeals. — See Servo Corp. of Am. v. GE Co., 393 F.2d 551 (4th Cir. 1968).

Findings on jurisdiction and standing should precede decision on merits. — In resolving material issues of jurisdiction and standing made by the pleadings, the district court is obligated under subdivision (a) of this rule to set forth in a nonjury case its decision in the form of detailed findings of fact and conclusions of law. In the normal course of the proceedings, such findings and conclusions should precede any decision on the substantive merits of the case. Patrician Towers Owners, Inc. v. Fairchild, 513 F.2d 216 (4th Cir. 1975).

Rule not satisfied by single conclusory sentence dismissing motion for new trial. — Subdivision (a) of this rule demands that the district court set forth its factual and legal basis for its final conclusion on standing in such detail that the appellate court may understand the basis for the district court's conclusion. A single conclusory sentence in the order dismissing defendant's motion for a new trial will manifestly not satisfy the mandates of the rule. It provides the court with mere conjectures as to the reasoning, both factually and legally, used by the district court in reaching its conclusion. Patrician Towers Owners, Inc. v. Fairchild, 513 F.2d 216 (4th Cir. 1975).

Findings held sufficient to support judgment. — Although a district judge trying a medical malpractice case erred in failing to clearly state his own conclusions with respect to negligence and proximate cause, even so, his findings of fact were sufficient to support the judgment. And the judgment itself may be treated as a conclusion that there was actionable negligence. Clark v. United States, 402 F.2d 950 (4th Cir. 1968).

Findings and conclusions are not required on motion for judgment on pleadings. — The court is not required by this rule to find the facts and state its conclusions of law where an action is disposed of on a motion for judgment on the pleadings. Harvey v. Early, 66 F. Supp. 761 (W.D. Va. 1946), aff'd, 160 F.2d 836 (4th Cir. 1947).

Nor on motion for summary judgment. — Where the case is to be disposed of upon motions for summary judgment under Rule 56, the court is not required by this rule to find the facts and state separately its conclusions of law thereon. Jordan v. Shelby Mut. Plate Glass & Cas. Co., 51 F. Supp. 240 (W.D. Va. 1943), aff'd, 142 F.2d 52 (4th Cir. 1944).

On a motion for summary judgment, where there is no genuine issue as to any material fact and the defendant is entitled to a judgment as a matter of law, under such circumstances, the court is not required under this rule to make findings. Huffman v. Norfolk & W. Ry., 71 F. Supp. 564 (W.D. Va. 1947).

Where judgment is entered for the defendant upon its motion for summary judgment the court is not required to file findings of fact and conclusions of law under this rule. Jarrett v. Norfolk Redevelopment & Hous. Auth., 74 F. Supp. 585 (E.D. Va. 1947), aff'd, 169 F.2d 409 (4th Cir.), cert. denied, 335 U.S. 886, 69 S. Ct. 238, 93 L. Ed. 425 (1948).

Findings on summary judgment. — On summary judgment, findings of the trial court serve as a determination that a particular fact is not genuinely in dispute. Although such findings are not required on a summary judgment ruling, they are extremely helpful to a reviewing court. The court of appeals does not accord such findings the full measure of deference due after trial. To do so would intrude on the sphere reserved for the ultimate trier of fact. Recent cases of the Supreme Court have made increasingly clear, however, the affirmative obligation of the trial judge to prevent "factually unsupported claims and defenses" from proceeding to trial. Trial court findings are consistent with the role for summary judgment elaborated by the Supreme Court. At a minimum, findings of fact upon summary judgment afford the court of appeals both a surer basis for appellate review and an indication of the care with which the summary judgment record was handled by the district court. Felty v. Graves-Humphreys Co., 818 F.2d 1126 (4th Cir. 1987).

Failure to delineate scope of contract duties. — In an action by a subcontractor against a general contractor for wrongful termination of contract, the district court failed to delineate the scope of the subcontractor's duties under the contract; therefore, the Court of Appeals could not review the propriety of the judgment against the general contractor. Sweeney Co. v. Engineers-Constructors, Inc., 823 F.2d 805 (4th Cir. 1987), aff'd, 869 F.2d 594 (4th Cir. 1989).

A finding not clearly erroneous cannot be set aside on appeal. Carter Coal Co. v. Litz, 140 F.2d 934 (4th Cir. 1944), aff'g 54 F. Supp. 115 (W.D. Va. 1943); Fairfax Hosp. Ass'n v. Mathews, 459 F. Supp. 429 (E.D. Va. 1977), aff'd, 585 F.2d 602 (4th Cir. 1978); Constantino v. American S/T Achilles, 580 F.2d 121 (4th Cir. 1978); Goodman v. Schlesinger, 584 F.2d 1325 (4th Cir. 1978).

The court of appeals is bound by the findings of the district court, in the absence of a showing that such findings are clearly erroneous. D.H. Pritchard v. Nelson, 147 F.2d 939 (4th Cir. 1945).

Where in an action upon a foreign default judgment the return of service in the other state recited that defendant was there personally and appropriately served, but the defendant testified that he was never served and, in truth, was not in that state at the time of the service as returned, which claim the district judge found adequately corroborated by supplementing proof, as his finding was certainly not clearly erroneous, his judgment was affirmed, and the default judgment rendered in the action following such service was not entitled to full faith and credit. Freehill v. Benn, 348 F.2d 911 (4th Cir. 1965).

Under this rule the court of appeals may not set aside findings of fact of the trial court unless they are clearly erroneous, and due regard must be given for the trial court's opportunity to assess the credibility of witnesses. It is not the function of the appellate court to decide factual issues *de novo*; the function of the appellate court is not to determine whether it would have made the findings the trial court made, but whether on the entire evidence it is left with the definite and firm conviction that a mistake has been committed. United States v. Warwick Mobile Home Estates, Inc., 537 F.2d 1148 (4th Cir. 1976).

The findings of fact by the trial judge are entitled to great weight and are not to be disturbed unless they are clearly erroneous. Due regard must be given to opportunity of the trial court to judge credibility. Friend v. Leidinger, 588 F.2d 61 (4th Cir. 1978), aff'g 446 F. Supp. 361 (E.D. Va. 1977).

A federal district court, sitting as chancellor, finds all the facts found by the jury on special verdict as well as all facts reasonably inferable therefrom. As to factual issues not submitted to the jury and factual issues not proper to be submitted to the jury, being exclusively relevant to equitable relief, the court will make its own findings of fact. Davis v. Ampthill Rayon Workers, Inc., 446 F. Supp. 681 (E.D. Va. 1978), aff'd, 594 F.2d 856 (4th Cir. 1979).

No greater scope of review exercised in admiralty cases. — In reviewing a judgment of a trial court, sitting without a jury in admiralty, the court of appeals may not set aside the judgment below unless it is clearly erroneous. No greater scope of review is exercised by the appellate tribunals in admiralty cases than the exercise under Rule 52(a) of the Federal Rules of Civil Procedure. A finding is clearly erroneous when although there is evidence to support it, the reviewing court on the entire evidence is left with a definite and firm conviction that a mistake has been committed. Norfolk Shipbuilding & Drydock Corp. v. The M/Y La Belle Simone, 537 F.2d 1201 (4th Cir. 1976).

Arguments of parties on appeal cannot substitute for findings by trial court. — See EEOC v. United Va. Bank/Seaboard Nat'l, 555 F.2d 403 (4th Cir. 1977).

Particularly after lengthy trial. — The provisions of this rule have special application where the trial has been exceedingly lengthy, many witnesses have been heard orally, and the subject matter concerns a prominent geographical feature of the local district. United States v. Appalachian Elec. Power Co., 107 F.2d 769 (4th Cir. 1939), aff'g 23 F. Supp. 83 (W.D. Va. 1938), rev'd on other grounds, 311 U.S. 377, 61 S. Ct. 291, 85 L. Ed. 243 (1940), reh'g denied, 312 U.S. 712, 61 S. Ct. 548, 85 L. Ed. 1143 (1941).

This rule was applied by courts of equity. — The provisions of this rule, that the findings of fact of the trial judge are to be accepted on appeal unless clearly wrong, are but the formulation of a rule long recognized and applied by courts of equity. United States v. Appalachian Elec. Power Co., 107 F.2d 769 (4th Cir. 1939), aff'g 23 F. Supp. 83 (W.D. Va. 1938), rev'd on other grounds, 311 U.S. 377, 61 S. Ct. 291, 85 L. Ed. 243 (1940), reh'g denied, 312 U.S. 712, 61 S. Ct. 548, 85 L. Ed. 1143 (1941).

And applies to master's findings of fact adopted by court. — Neither the federal district court nor the federal court of appeals is bound by the Virginia law with respect to the weight to be given to the findings of fact by a master. The district court is controlled by the provisions of Rule 53(e)(2), which provides that court shall accept the master's findings of fact unless clearly erroneous. The court of appeals is bound by the provisions of subdivision (a) of this rule, wherein it is provided that in all actions tried upon the facts without a jury, the court shall not set aside the findings of the district court unless clearly erroneous and that the findings of a master, to the extent that the court adopts them, shall be considered to be the findings of the court below. London v. Troitino Bros., 301 F.2d 116 (4th Cir. 1962).

"Clearly erroneous" rule applies although evidence was by deposition. — Subdivision (a) of this rule provides that in a nonjury case, "[f]indings of fact shall not be set aside unless clearly erroneous, and due regard shall be given to the opportunity of the trial court to judge of the credibility of the witnesses." Where much of the testimony is by deposition, the appellate court is as able to judge of credibility as the trial court; nevertheless, the findings still must be tested by the "clearly erroneous" rule. Prendis v. Central Gulf S.S. Co., 330 F.2d 893 (4th Cir. 1963), aff'g 201 F. Supp. 595 (E.D. Va. 1962).

And applies to finding of fact by district court in habeas corpus proceeding. — See Root v. Cunningham, 344 F.2d 1 (4th Cir.), cert. denied, 382 U.S. 866, 86 S. Ct. 135, 15 L. Ed. 2d 104 (1965), But see, United States v. Rhodes, 32 F.3d 867 (4th Cir. 1994), cert. denied, 513 U.S. 1164, 115 S. Ct. 1130, 130 L. Ed. 2d 1092 (1995); Williams v. Peyton, 404 F.2d 528 (4th Cir. 1968).

And is same as rule applied in admiralty. — The scope of review in admiralty appeals has been the same clearly erroneous rule of subdivision (a) of this rule which applies in the ordinary nonjury civil case. Prendis v. Central Gulf S.S. Co., 330 F.2d 893 (4th Cir. 1963), aff'g 201 F. Supp. 595 (E.D. Va. 1962).

A district court's findings regarding unseaworthiness and negligence are generally treated as findings of fact reviewable under the "clearly erroneous" standard. Famous Knitwear Corp. v. Drug Fair, Inc., 493 F.2d 251 (4th Cir. 1974).

Finding of agreement between parties as to extension of time for cleaning of grain storage tanks made after full presentation of facts held not clearly erroneous. Constantino v. American S/T Achilles, 580 F.2d 121 (4th Cir. 1978).

It applies where evidence is conflicting. — Subdivision (a) of this rule comes into play primarily where the trial judge as fact finder has had to reconcile conflicting testimony. Where the veracity of witnesses is in issue, the decision is for the judge who has had the opportunity to see and evaluate the witnesses' demeanor, and the trial court's findings of fact on conflicting evidence will not be disturbed by the appellate court unless clearly erroneous. Hicks v. United States, 368 F.2d 626 (4th Cir. 1966).

But findings cannot be accepted where court of appeals is convinced mistake was made. — Where the court of appeals is convinced that a mistake has been made, it cannot accept the trial court's findings of fact. Tenney v. A.B. & W. Transit Co., 364 F.2d 493 (4th Cir. 1966).

And "clearly erroneous" rule is not violated in not following conclusions of law based on documentary evidence. — Where, in a patent infringement suit, the court of appeals finds a patent invalid, contrary to the holding of the district court, as the criteria governing patentability are standards of law, and since the decision of the district court was largely based on documentary evidence, in not following the conclusions of the trial court the court of appeals does not offend the "clearly erroneous" precept of subdivision (a). Tidewater Patent Dev. Co. v. Kitchen, 371 F.2d 1004 (4th Cir.), cert. denied, 389 U.S. 821, 88 S. Ct. 46, 19 L. Ed. 2d 74 (1967).

When finding "clearly erroneous." — A finding is "clearly erroneous" when although there is evidence to support it, the reviewing court on the entire evidence is left with the definite and firm conviction that a mistake has been committed. Hubbard v. United States, 434 F.2d 62 (4th Cir. 1970), cert. denied, 401 U.S. 1010, 91 S. Ct. 1255, 28 L. Ed. 2d 546 (1971); Famous Knitwear Corp. v. Drug Fair, Inc., 493 F.2d 251 (4th Cir. 1974); Lewis v. Tobacco Workers' Int'l Union, 577 F.2d 1135 (4th Cir. 1978), cert. denied, 439 U.S. 1089, 99 S. Ct. 871, 59 L. Ed. 2d 56 (1979); Ente Nazionale Per L'Energia Electtrica v. Baliwag Nav., Inc., 774 F.2d 648 (4th Cir. 1985).

The appellate court reviews a district court's findings regarding whether a guard has acted with deliberate indifference under a clearly erroneous standard. Brice v. Virginia Beach Correctional Ctr., 58 F.3d 101 (4th Cir. 1995).

Evidence viewed in light favorable to appellee. — In determining whether the district court's findings are clearly erroneous, the court of appeals must construe the evidence in the light most favorable to the appellee. Ente Nazionale Per L'Energia Electtrica v. Baliwag Nav., Inc., 774 F.2d 648 (4th Cir. 1985).

Findings negating applicability of Jones Act not clearly erroneous. — Where only significant American contact was place of contract. Fitzgerald v. Liberian S/T Chryssi P. Goulandris, 582 F.2d 312 (4th Cir. 1978).

Definite and firm conviction that mistake has been committed is test for overturning district court's findings of fact. Goodman v. Schlesinger, 584 F.2d 1325 (4th Cir. 1978).

Where facts are uncontested, "clearly erroneous" rule is inapplicable. — The determination of negligence involves not only the formulation of the legal standard, but more particularly its application to the evidentiary facts as established, and where these are uncontested, there is no basis for applying the "clearly erroneous" rule. Hicks v. United States, 368 F.2d 626 (4th Cir. 1966).

And conclusions on undisputed facts are not entitled to weight of basic findings. — Where the trial court's conclusions are based on undisputed facts, they are not entitled to the finality customarily accorded basic factual findings under this rule. Hicks v. United States, 368 F.2d 626 (4th Cir. 1966).

Where dealing with the testimony of expert witnesses who are not in controversy as to the basic facts, the opportunity of the trial court to observe the witnesses is of limited significance and the trial court's conclusions are not entitled to the finality customarily accorded basic factual findings under this rule. Hicks v. United States, 368 F.2d 626 (4th Cir. 1966).

The appellate court reviews a district court's findings regarding whether a guard has acted with deliberate indifference under a clearly erroneous standard. Brice v. Virginia Beach Correctional Ctr., 58 F.3d 101 (4th Cir. 1995).

Findings regarding agency relationship are reviewed under "clearly erroneous" standard. — The creation, duration, and scope of an agency relationship and the question of the reasonableness of a third party's reliance on a principal's manifestations of the apparent authority of his agent are essentially questions of fact, and are to be reviewed under the "clearly erroneous" standard unless the judge's findings are made in disregard of the applicable principles of law or through gross over-emphasis on one relevant principle to the exclusion of others. Famous Knitwear Corp. v. Drug Fair, Inc., 493 F.2d 251 (4th Cir. 1974).

Reviewing court has limited role. — The role of the Court of Appeals in reviewing factual findings of the district court is quite limited under subdivision (a) of this rule. If the district court's account of the evidence is plausible in light of the record viewed in its entirety, then the court cannot reverse it. Likewise the court can find no clear error if there are two permissible views of the evidence, and the district court as factfinder chooses one over the other. Davis v. Food Lion, 792 F.2d 1274 (4th Cir. 1986).

Findings of fact on conflicting evidence only reversible for plain error. — The trial court's resolutions of questions of fact on conflicting evidence are entitled to great weight and will not be reversed except for plain error. Glasscock v. United States, 323 F.2d 589 (4th Cir. 1963), aff'g 207 F. Supp. 318 (E.D. Va. 1962).

Absent extraordinary circumstances, the circuit court will not disturb a factfinder's credibility determinations. Columbus-America Discovery Group v. Atlantic Mut. Ins. Co., 56 F.3d 556 (4th Cir. 1995), cert. denied, 516 U.S. 938, 116 S. Ct. 352, 133 L. Ed. 2d 248 (1995).

And must be accepted on appeal if supported by substantial evidence. — Although the majority of the court of appeals might be inclined to draw a contrary inference, where it cannot say that the inferences drawn by the district court with respect to the plaintiff's negligence were not supported by substantial evidence and, therefore, clearly permissible, it is required to accept the finding that the plaintiff was guilty of negligence which was the proximate cause of his injury. Glasscock v. United States, 323 F.2d 589 (4th Cir. 1963), aff'g 207 F. Supp. 318 (E.D. Va. 1962).

Findings not reversible merely because reviewing court would have reached different conclusion. — Under the clearly erroneous standard, a reviewing court may not reverse the findings of the trial court simply because it would have decided the case differently. If the district court's account of the evidence is plausible in light of the record viewed in its entirety, the court of appeals may not reverse it even though convinced that had it been sitting as the trier of fact, it would have weighed the evidence differently. Where there are two permissible views of the evidence, the factfinder's choice between them cannot be clearly erroneous. This rule applies even when the district court's findings rest upon physical or documentary evidence. Riddick ex rel. Riddick v. School Bd., 784 F.2d 521 (4th Cir.), cert. denied, 479 U.S. 938, 107 S. Ct. 420, 93 L. Ed. 2d 370 (1986).

Absent extraordinary circumstances, the circuit court will not disturb a factfinder's credibility determinations. Columbus-America Discovery Group v. Atlantic Mut. Ins. Co., 56 F.3d 556 (4th Cir. 1995), cert. denied, 516 U.S. 938, 116 S. Ct. 352, 133 L. Ed. 2d 248 (1995).

Factual findings by a district court in school desegregation cases, especially where the presiding judicial officer has lived with the case for many years, are entitled to great deference on review. Riddick ex rel. Riddick v. School Bd., 784 F.2d 521 (4th Cir.), cert. denied, 479 U.S. 938, 107 S. Ct. 420, 93 L. Ed. 2d 370 (1986).

Findings of fact of a district court sitting without a jury in an admiralty case are reviewed under the "clearly erroneous" standard of subdivision (a). Ente Nazionale Per L'Energia Electtrica v. Baliwag Nav., Inc., 774 F.2d 648 (4th Cir. 1985).

Questions of negligence in admiralty are treated as factual issues and are thus subject to the clearly erroneous standard. Thus, the court of appeals is compelled to review the district court's findings of fact, including its finding as to causation, under the clearly erroneous standard of subdivision (a). Ente Nazionale Per L'Energia Electtrica v. Baliwag Nav., Inc., 774 F.2d 648 (4th Cir. 1985).

District court correctly denied Rule 52(b) motion. — Where in its Rule 52(b) motion, creditor presented its "new value" defense after the trial on the issue of avoidance had been concluded, district court correctly denied the motion, observing that creditor had neither pleaded the "new value" defense nor offered evidence to support it was correct. Counts v. Wang Labs., Inc., 932 F.2d 338 (4th Cir. 1991).

Applied in Kaufman v. United States, 40 F. Supp. 505 (E.D. Va. 1941); Carroll v. Harrison, 49 F. Supp. 283 (W.D. Va. 1943); Hodges v. Johnson, 52 F. Supp. 488 (W.D. Va. 1943); Trueheart v. Eichelberger, 148 F.2d 634 (4th Cir. 1944); Brooks v. United States, 56 F. Supp. 743 (E.D. Va. 1944); Eichelberger v. Mutual Life Ins. Co., 59 F. Supp. 852 (E.D. Va. 1944); Walling v. Moore Milling Co., 62 F. Supp. 378 (W.D. Va. 1945); Walling v. Clinchfield Coal Corp., 64 F. Supp. 347 (W.D. Va. 1946); Walling v. Hamner, 64 F. Supp. 690 (W.D. Va. 1946); United States v. Collins, 78 F. Supp. 259 (E.D. Va. 1948); United States Pipe & Foundry Co. v. Woodward Iron Co., 327 F.2d 242 (4th Cir. 1964); Smith v. Fihelly, 338 F.2d 964 (4th Cir. 1964); Bullard Co. v. GE Co., 348 F.2d 985 (4th Cir. 1965); Philip Morris, Inc. v. Imperial Tobacco Co., 251 F. Supp. 362 (E.D. Va. 1965); Banko v. Continental Motors Corp., 373 F.2d 314 (4th Cir. 1966); NLRB v. Harvey, 250 F. Supp. 639 (W.D. Va. 1966); Allen v. Maryland Cas. Co., 259 F. Supp. 505 (W.D. Va. 1966); Travelers Indem. Co. v. Michigan Mut. Liab. Co., 259 F. Supp. 606 (W.D. Va. 1966); Arrow Wrecking Co. v. Semonian, 375 F.2d 67 (4th Cir. 1967); Mahaffy & Harder Eng'r Co. v. Standard Packaging Corp., 389 F.2d 525 (4th Cir. 1968); Vessella v. United States, 405 F.2d 599 (4th Cir. 1969); Barnes v. Vadico Terms., Inc., 408 F.2d 31 (4th Cir. 1969); Potash Import & Chem. Co. v. M/S Klaus Oldendorff, 422 F.2d 818 (4th Cir. 1969); Whitlock v. United States, 304 F. Supp. 1020 (E.D. Va. 1969); Varga v. United States, 314 F. Supp. 671 (E.D. Va. 1969); Elkins v. United States, 429 F.2d 297 (4th Cir. 1970); Swedish Am. Line v. Evans Prods. Co., 431 F.2d 869 (4th Cir. 1970); Nationwide Mut. Ins. Co. v. Stephens, 313 F. Supp. 890 (W.D. Va. 1970); Stone v. Stone, 330 F. Supp. 1026 (W.D. Va. 1971); Nationwide Mut. Ins. Co. v. United States Fid. & Guar. Co., 450 F.2d 1116 (4th Cir. 1971); Mason v. Brown, 362 F. Supp. 518 (E.D. Va. 1973); American Sec. & Trust Co. v. Fletcher, 490 F.2d 481 (4th Cir. 1974); Alston Studios, Inc. v. Lloyd V. Gress & Assocs., 492 F.2d 279 (4th Cir. 1974); Valley Lumber Corp. v. Geisler, 518 F.2d 1174 (4th Cir. 1975); Johnson v. United States, 528 F.2d 489 (4th Cir. 1975); Smith v. Smith, 391 F. Supp. 443 (W.D. Va. 1975); Phillips v. Puryear, 403 F. Supp. 80 (W.D. Va. 1975); Bituminous Coal Operators' Ass'n v. Hathaway, 406 F. Supp. 371 (W.D. Va. 1975); Semler v. Psychiatric Inst., 538 F.2d 121 (4th Cir. 1976); Cohen v. Boxberger, 544 F.2d 701 (4th Cir. 1976); Bluefield Armature Co. v. R.G. Pope

Constr. Co., 548 F.2d 484 (4th Cir. 1976); Scheel v. Conboy, 551 F.2d 41 (4th Cir. 1977); Grevas v. M/V Olympic Pegasus, 557 F.2d 65 (4th Cir. 1977); Securities & Exch. Comm'n v. American Realty Trust, 429 F. Supp. 1148 (E.D. Va. 1977); Hewitt v. Hutter, 432 F. Supp. 795 (W.D. Va. 1977); Coates v. NCR Co., 433 F. Supp. 655 (W.D. Va. 1977); Hillman v. Elliott, 436 F. Supp. 812 (W.D. Va. 1977); Newell v. Davis, 437 F. Supp. 1059 (E.D. Va. 1976); Johnson v. Hampton, 452 F. Supp. 1 (E.D. Va. 1977); Hewitt v. Hutter, 574 F.2d 182 (4th Cir. 1978); Lewis v. Tobacco Workers' Int'l Union, 577 F.2d 1135 (4th Cir. 1978); Fitzgerald v. Liberian S/T Chryssi P. Goulandris, 582 F.2d 312 (4th Cir. 1978); Virginia Chapter v. Kreps, 444 F. Supp. 1167 (W.D. Va. 1978); Malbon v. Pennsylvania Millers Mut. Ins. Co., 636 F.2d 936 (4th Cir. 1980); National Acceptance Co. of Am. v. Virginia Capital Bank, 498 F. Supp. 1078 (E.D. Va. 1980); Page v. Bolger, 645 F.2d 227 (4th Cir. 1981); EEOC v. American Nat'l Bank, 652 F.2d 1176 (4th Cir. 1981); Smallwood v. United Air Lines, 661 F.2d 303 (4th Cir. 1981); O'Neill Bondholders Comm. v. W.B. Johnson Properties, Inc. (In re O'Neill Enters., Inc.), 11 Bankr. 711 (W.D. Va. 1981); Marcon, Ltd. v. Helena Rubenstein, Inc., 694 F.2d 953 (4th Cir. 1982); Neathery v. M/V Overseas Marilyn, 700 F.2d 140 (4th Cir. 1983); Davidson v. Cook, 567 F. Supp. 225 (E.D. Va. 1983); Vecco Constr. Indus., Inc. v. Century Constr. Co., 33 Bankr. 757 (Bankr. E.D. Va. 1983); Collins v. City of Norfolk, 605 F. Supp. 377 (E.D. Va. 1984); Gazette, Inc. v. Harris, 229 Va. 1, 325 S.E.2d 713 (1985); Corrigan v. United States, 609 F. Supp. 720 (E.D. Va. 1985); Dettmer v. Landon, 617 F. Supp. 592 (E.D. Va. 1985); American Booksellers Ass'n v. Strobel, 617 F. Supp. 699 (E.D. Va. 1985); Monroe v. Burlington Indus., Inc., 784 F.2d 568 (4th Cir. 1986); Tingley v. Henson Aviation, Inc., 789 F.2d 275 (4th Cir. 1986); Holmes v. Bevilacqua, 794 F.2d 142 (4th Cir. 1986); Hellenic Lines v. Prudential Lines, 813 F.2d 634 (4th Cir. 1987); Collins v. City of Norfolk, 816 F.2d 932 (4th Cir 1987); Foremost Guar. Corp. v. Meritor Sav. Bank, 910 F.2d 118 (4th Cir. 1990); Guaranty Sav. & Loan Ass'n v. Ultimate Sav. Bank, 737 F. Supp. 366 (W.D. Va. 1990); Howard Cooper Corp. v. United States, 763 F. Supp. 829 (E.D. Va. 1991); AIG Europe, S.A. v. M/V MSC Lauren, 940 F. Supp. 925 (E.D. Va. 1996); Semiconductor Energy Lab. Co. v. Samsung Elecs. Co., 4 F. Supp. 2d 477 (E.D. Va. 1998).

Rule 53. Masters.

(a) *Appointment.* — (1) Scope. Unless a statute provides otherwise, a court may appoint a master only to:

(A) perform duties consented to by the parties;

(B) hold trial proceedings and make or recommend findings of fact on issues to be decided without a jury if appointment is warranted by:

(i) some exceptional condition; or

(ii) the need to perform an accounting or resolve a difficult computation of damages; or

(C) address pretrial and posttrial matters that cannot be effectively and timely addressed by an available district judge or magistrate judge of the district.

(2) Disqualification. A master must not have a relationship to the parties, attorneys, action, or court that would require disqualification of a judge under 28 U.S.C. § 455, unless the parties, with the court's approval, consent to the appointment after the master discloses any potential grounds for disqualification.

(3) Possible Expense or Delay. In appointing a master, the court must consider the fairness of imposing the likely expenses on the parties and must protect against unreasonable expense or delay.

(b) *Order Appointing a Master.* — (1) Notice. Before appointing a master, the court must give the parties notice and an opportunity to be heard. Any party may suggest candidates for appointment.

(2) Contents. The appointing order must direct the master to proceed with all reasonable diligence and must state:

(A) the master's duties, including any investigation or enforcement duties, and any limits on the master's authority under Rule 53(c);

(B) the circumstances, if any, in which the master may communicate ex parte with the court or a party;

(C) the nature of the materials to be preserved and filed as the record of the master's activities;

(D) the time limits, method of filing the record, other procedures, and standards for reviewing the master's orders, findings, and recommendations; and

(E) the basis, terms, and procedure for fixing the master's compensation under Rule 53(g).

(3) Issuing. The court may issue the order only after:

(A) the master files an affidavit disclosing whether there is any ground for disqualification under 28 U.S.C. § 455; and

(B) if a ground is disclosed, the parties, with the court's approval, waive the disqualification.

(4) Amending. The order may be amended at any time after notice to the parties and an opportunity to be heard.

(c) *Master's Authority.* — (1) In General. Unless the appointing order directs otherwise, a master may:

(A) regulate all proceedings;

(B) take all appropriate measures to perform the assigned duties fairly and efficiently; and

(C) if conducting an evidentiary hearing, exercise the appointing court's power to compel, take, and record evidence.

(2) Sanctions. The master may by order impose on a party any noncontempt sanction provided by Rule 37 or 45, and may recommend a contempt sanction against a party and sanctions against a nonparty.

(d) *Master's Orders.* — A master who issues an order must file it and promptly serve a copy on each party. The clerk must enter the order on the docket.

(e) *Master's Reports.* — A master must report to the court as required by the appointing order. The master must file the report and promptly serve a copy on each party, unless the court orders otherwise.

(f) *Action on the Master's Order, Report, or Recommendations.* — (1) Opportunity for a Hearing; Action in General. In acting on a master's order, report, or recommendations, the court must give the parties notice and an opportunity to be heard; may receive evidence; and may adopt or affirm, modify, wholly or partly reject or reverse, or resubmit to the master with instructions.

(2) Time to Object or Move to Adopt or Modify. A party may file objections to — or a motion to adopt or modify — the master's order, report, or recommendations no later than 21 days after a copy is served, unless the court sets a different time.

(3) Reviewing Factual Findings. The court must decide de novo all objections to findings of fact made or recommended by a master, unless the parties, with the court's approval, stipulate that:

(A) the findings will be reviewed for clear error; or

(B) the findings of a master appointed under Rule 53(a)(1)(A) or (C) will be final.

(4) Reviewing Legal Conclusions. The court must decide de novo all objections to conclusions of law made or recommended by a master.

(5) Reviewing Procedural Matters. Unless the appointing order establishes a different standard of review, the court may set aside a master's ruling on a procedural matter only for an abuse of discretion.

(g) *Compensation.* — (1) Fixing Compensation. Before or after judgment, the court must fix the master's compensation on the basis and terms stated in the appointing order, but the court may set a new basis and terms after giving notice and an opportunity to be heard.

(2) Payment. The compensation must be paid either:

(A) by a party or parties; or

(B) from a fund or subject matter of the action within the court's control.

(3) Allocating Payment. The court must allocate payment among the parties after considering the nature and amount of the controversy, the parties' means, and the extent to which any party is more responsible than other parties for the reference to a master. An interim allocation may be amended to reflect a decision on the merits.

(h) *Appointing a Magistrate Judge.* — A magistrate judge is subject to this rule only when the order referring a matter to the magistrate judge states that the reference is made under this rule. (Amended by order adopted February 28, 1966, effective July 1, 1966, by order adopted April 28, 1983, effective August 1, 1983, by order adopted March 2, 1987, effective August 1, 1987, by order adopted April 30, 1991, effective December 1, 1991, by order adopted April 22, 1993, effective December 1, 1993, by order adopted March 27, 2003, effective December 1, 2003, by order adopted April 30, 2007, effective December 1, 2007, and by order adopted March 26, 2009, effective December 1, 2009.)

Comment. — The language of Rule 53 has been amended as part of the general restyling of the Civil Rules to make them more easily understood and to make style and terminology consistent throughout the rules. These changes are intended to be stylistic only.

CASE NOTES

Proceeding before master should be kept separate and distinct. — Paragraph (2) of subdivision (e) contemplates a separate and distinct proceeding before the master. If it is a genuine reference, it should be strictly followed; otherwise the trial stages before and subsequent to the report become blurred. Of course, the district court has the right on an intricate subject of suit to engage an advisor to attend the trial and assist the court in its comprehension of the case. But when there is a merging of master and advisor the result may have a hybrid status. Bullard Co. v. GE Co., 348 F.2d 985 (4th Cir. 1965), aff'g 234 F. Supp. 995 (W.D. Va. 1964).

Master need not be lawyer where he has demonstrated knowledge of subject matter. — Under subdivision (a) of this rule, there is no requirement that the master appointed by the court must be a lawyer, and in an action involving the validity of a tobacco association's allotment of marketing time, the court properly appointed as a master a person who had demonstrated his marked knowledge of tobacco marketing. Danville Tobacco Ass'n v. Bryant-Buckner Assocs., 333 F.2d 202 (4th Cir. 1964), cert. denied, 387 U.S. 907, 87 S. Ct. 1688, 18 L. Ed. 2d 624 (1967).

Court may modify master's findings. — In accordance with this rule, the master's findings should be accepted as correct unless clearly erroneous; but the court has the power to modify them when deemed equitable to do so. Guaranty Trust Co. v. Seaboard Air Line Ry., 53 F. Supp. 672 (E.D. Va. 1943), aff'd, 145 F.2d 40 (4th Cir. 1944).

Court may reject master's findings in part. — See Bullard Co. v. GE Co., 234 F. Supp. 995 (W.D. Va. 1964), aff'd, 348 F.2d 985 (4th Cir. 1965).

Weight given master's findings. — The court of appeals must give great deference to the judgment of the master in cases which turn in large part upon the credibility of witnesses and on involved questions of accountancy. London v. Troitino Bros., 301 F.2d 116 (4th Cir. 1962).

Neither the federal district court nor the court of appeals is bound by the Virginia law with respect to the weight to be given to the findings of fact by a master. The district court is controlled by the provisions of subdivision (e)(2) of this rule, which provides that court shall accept the master's findings of fact unless clearly erroneous. The court of appeals is bound by Rule 52(a), wherein it is provided that in all actions tried upon the facts without a jury, the court shall not set aside the findings of the district court unless clearly erroneous and that the findings of a master, to the extent that the court adopts them, shall be considered to be the findings of the court below. London v. Troitino Bros., 301 F.2d 116 (4th Cir. 1962).

Paragraph (2) of subdivision (e) expressly provides that in an action tried without a jury the court shall accept findings of fact of a master unless clearly erroneous. Especially imperative is the rule when, in a railroad reorganization case, the master has lived with the case for four years, has patiently studied the complex questions involved and has listened with painstaking care in extended hearings to the arguments and proposals of all the parties who desired to be heard. Badenhausen v. Guaranty Trust Co., 145 F.2d 40 (4th Cir. 1944), aff'g 53 F. Supp. 672 (E.D. Va. 1943), cert. denied, 323 U.S. 797, 65 S. Ct. 440, 89 L. Ed. 636 (1945).

A district court is controlled by the provisions of subdivision (e)(2) of this rule, which provides that the court shall accept the master's findings of fact unless clearly erroneous. Servo Corp. of Am. v. GE Co., 220 F. Supp. 473 (W.D. Va. 1963), rev'd on other grounds, 337 F.2d 716 (4th Cir. 1964), reh'g denied, 342 F.2d 993 (4th Cir. 1965).

In nonjury actions the court shall accept the master's findings of fact unless clearly erroneous. Consolidated Masonry & Fireproofing, Inc. v. Wagman Constr. Corp., 273 F. Supp. 693 (E.D. Va. 1966), aff'd, 383 F.2d 249 (4th Cir. 1967).

Great deference must be accorded the findings of a master where they turn in large measure on the credibility of witnesses who have presented long, involved, and often conflicting testimony. His conclusions of fact must therefore be accepted unless they are clearly erroneous. Swacker v. Southern Ry., 240 F. Supp. 51 (W.D. Va. 1965), aff'd, 360 F.2d 420 (4th Cir.), cert. denied, 385 U.S. 837, 87 S. Ct. 83, 17 L. Ed. 2d 70 (1966); United States Pipe & Foundry Co. v. Woodward Iron Co., 246 F. Supp. 424 (W.D. Va. 1965) (patent infringement case).

Rule 71A(h) incorporates subdivision (e) of this rule, pursuant to which the district court may modify the report on the basis of the record made before the commissioners. United States v. 3.0 Acres of Land, 378 F. Supp. 30 (W.D. Va. 1974).

Weight given commission's findings in eminent domain proceedings. — In eminent domain proceedings in the federal courts, by virtue of Rule 71A and this rule, the commission's findings of fact are clothed in the armor of the "clearly erroneous" rule. Especially is this so where the commission's findings were reviewed and adopted by the district judge, and they will not be disturbed unless a very plain mistake has been made. United States v. Certain Parcels of Land, 384 F.2d 677 (4th Cir. 1967).

Applied in United States v. Moore, 361 F.2d 494 (4th Cir. 1966); United States v. 180.37 Acres of Land, 254 F. Supp. 678 (W.D. Va. 1966); United States v. 615.10 Acres of Land, 327 F. Supp. 691 (W.D. Va. 1971); Western Elec. Co. v. Stewart-Warner Corp., 631 F.2d 333 (4th Cir. 1980); United States v. 452.876 Acres of Land, more or Less, 667 F.2d 442 (4th Cir. 1981); Creasy v. Coleman Furn. Corp., 763 F.2d 656 (4th Cir. 1985).

TITLE VII. JUDGMENT.

Rule 54. Judgments; Costs.

(a) *Definition; Form.* — "Judgment" as used in these rules includes a decree and any order from which an appeal lies. A judgment should not include recitals of pleadings, a master's report, or a record of prior proceedings.

(b) *Judgment on Multiple Claims or Involving Multiple Parties.* — When an action presents more than one claim for relief — whether as a claim, counterclaim, crossclaim, or third-party claim — or when multiple parties are involved, the court may direct entry of a final judgment as to one or more, but fewer than all, claims or parties only if the court expressly determines that there is no just reason for delay.

Otherwise, any order or other decision, however designated, that adjudicates fewer than all the claims or the rights and liabilities of fewer than all the parties does not end the action as to any of the claims or parties and may be revised at any time before the entry of a judgment adjudicating all the claims and all the parties' rights and liabilities.

(c) *Demand for Judgment; Relief to Be Granted.* — A default judgment must not differ in kind from, or exceed in amount, what is demanded in the pleadings. Every other final judgment should grant the relief to which each party is entitled, even if the party has not demanded that relief in its pleadings.

(d) *Costs; Attorney's Fees.* — (1) Costs Other Than Attorney's Fees. Unless a federal statute, these rules, or a court order provides otherwise, costs — other than attorney's fees — should be allowed to the prevailing party. But costs against the United States, its officers, and its agencies may be imposed only to the extent allowed by law. The clerk may tax costs on 14 days' notice. On motion served within the next 7 days, the court may review the clerk's action.

(2) Attorney's Fees. (A) Claim to Be by Motion. A claim for attorney's fees and related nontaxable expenses must be made by motion unless the substantive law requires those fees to be proved at trial as an element of damages.

(B) Timing and Contents of the Motion. Unless a statute or a court order provides otherwise, the motion must:

(i) be filed no later than 14 days after the entry of judgment;

(ii) specify the judgment and the statute, rule, or other grounds entitling the movant to the award;

(iii) state the amount sought or provide a fair estimate of it; and

(iv) disclose, if the court so orders, the terms of any agreement about fees for the services for which the claim is made.

(C) Proceedings. Subject to Rule 23(h), the court must, on a party's request, give an opportunity for adversary submissions on the motion in accordance with Rule 43(c) or 78. The court may decide issues of liability for fees before receiving submissions on the value of services. The court must find the facts and state its conclusions of law as provided in Rule 52(a).

(D) Special Procedures by Local Rule; Reference to a Master or a Magistrate Judge. By local rule, the court may establish special procedures to resolve fee-related issues without extensive evidentiary hearings. Also, the court may refer issues concerning the value of services to a special master under Rule 53 without regard to the limitations of Rule 53(a)(1), and may refer a motion for attorney's fees to a magistrate judge under Rule 72(b) as if it were a dispositive pretrial matter.

(E) Exceptions. Subparagraphs (A)-(D) do not apply to claims for fees and expenses as sanctions for violating these rules or as sanctions under 28 U.S.C. § 1927. (Amended by order adopted December 27, 1946, effective March 19, 1948, by order adopted April 17, 1961, effective July 19, 1961, by order adopted March 2, 1987, effective August 1, 1987, by order adopted April 22, 1993, effective December 1, 1993, by order adopted April 29, 2002, effective December 1, 2002, by order adopted March 27, 2003, effective December 1, 2003, by order adopted April 30, 2007, effective December 1, 2007, and by order adopted March 26, 2009, effective December 1, 2009.)

Comment. — The language of Rule 54 has been amended as part of the general restyling of the Civil Rules to make them more easily understood and to make style and terminology consistent throughout the rules. These changes are intended to be stylistic only.

The words "or class member" have been removed from Rule 54(d)(2)(C) because Rule 23(h)(2) now addresses objections by class members to attorney-fee motions. Rule 54(d)(2)(C) is amended to recognize that Rule 23(h) now controls those aspects of attorney-fee motions in class actions to which it is addressed.

Law Review. — For note, "Federal Rule 54(b): The Multiple Claims Requirement," see 43 Va. L. Rev. 229 (1957). For a note, "Pleading to Stay in State Court: Forum Control, Federal Removal Jurisdiction, and the Amount in Controversy Requirement," see 56 Wash. & Lee L. Rev. 651 (1999).

CASE NOTES

Judgment finally disposing of one cause of action is appealable. — Under this rule, a judgment finally disposing of one cause of action is appealable although other causes of action are not disposed of. Bowles v. Commercial Cas. Ins. Co., 107 F.2d 169 (4th Cir. 1939).

Final judgment determination with appellate courts. — Federal appellate courts are "duty bound" to consider, sua sponte, whether a district court order is a final judgment within the meaning of this rule. Straessle v. Air Line Pilot's Ass'n, Int'l, 253 Va. 349, 485 S.E.2d 387 (1997).

Motion for additional judgment under subdivision (b) disallowed so as not to cut off right of appeal. — See Pierce Oil Corp. v. United States, 9 F.R.D. 619 (E.D. Va. 1949).

Appeal from judgment upon multiple claims or involving multiple parties. — Absent certification by the trial court, as provided by paragraph (b), regarding an order entered by the court, that there is no reason for delay and an express direction by the court for entry of judgment, the court of appeals does not have jurisdiction to hear an appeal. Robinson v. Parke-Davis & Co., 685 F.2d 912 (4th Cir. 1982).

Judgment on fewer than all claims or parties not appealable without express determination and direction for entry. — Where the district court had signed certain default judgments from which an appeal was attempted, but there was no indication in the record that there was ever issued an express direction to the clerk for the entry of such judgments, nor was there any determination that there was no just reason for delay of such entry, it was held that the judgments were not "final decisions" but were instead subject to revision by the terms of subdivision (b), and that, consequently, the court of appeals lacked jurisdiction to consider the judgments on the merits. United States ex rel. Hudson v. Peerless Ins. Co., 374 F.2d 942 (4th Cir. 1967).

Appellant's appeal of the district court ruling denying relief relative to appellant's due process claim was dismissed where the district court, which deferred ruling on appellant's other claims, did not however, make the certification authorized by subdivision (b) of this rule that the ruling on the due process issue was final and appealable. Such a certificate is a jurisdictional prerequisite for an appeal of less than all of the claims in an action. Smith v. Fairfax County Sch. Bd., 497 F.2d 899 (4th Cir. 1974).

Procedure is applicable to joint and joint and/or several liability. — The procedure established for multiple defendants by subdivision (b) is strikingly similar and applicable not only to situations of joint liability but to those where the liability is joint and/or several. United States ex rel. Hudson v. Peerless Ins. Co., 374 F.2d 942 (4th Cir. 1967).

It fixes commencement of running of time for appeal. — The role of the district court in making the certification required by subdivision (b) has been described by the Supreme Court as that of "dispatcher." The district court is permitted to determine under subdivision (b) the appropriate time when each "final decision" upon "one or more but less than all" of the claims in a multiple claims action is ready for appeal. A party adversely affected by a final decision thus knows that his time for appeal will not run against him until this certification has been made. United States ex rel. Hudson v. Peerless Ins. Co., 374 F.2d 942 (4th Cir. 1967), citing Sears, Roebuck & Co. v. Mackey, 351 U.S. 427, 76 S. Ct. 895, 100 L. Ed. 2d 1297 (1956).

And running of time for moving for new trial. — Rule 60(b) requires a motion for new trial on ground of newly discovered evidence to be made within one year. Hence, where the prior judgment of the district court adverse to the applicant was certified as a final judgment under subdivision (b) of this rule and he accepted the certification by himself appealing from it, but it was affirmed, his motion for a new trial, filed more than 15 months after the district court's prior judgment was entered, was filed more than 15 months after final judgment, and it was barred. Capital Investors Co. v. Devers, 387 F.2d 591 (4th Cir. 1967).

Effect of local rule. — Where a local rule mandates that all motions, except those specifically excluded by the rule, shall be accompanied by a written brief setting forth a concise statement of the facts and supporting reasons, along with a citation of the authorities upon which the movant relies, unless a motion is so briefed, it is equivalent under the local rule to not being filed at all. Therefore, failure of the court to adjudicate such a motion does not, in such a case, preclude termination of the action under subdivision (b) of this rule. El-Amin v. Williams, 92 F.R.D. 454 (E.D. Va. 1981).

A party in whose favor judgment is rendered is the prevailing party, regardless of whether he sustains his entire claim or only a part thereof. Sperry Rand Corp. v. A-T-O, Inc., 58 F.R.D. 132 (E.D. Va. 1973), overruled on other grounds, Jop v. City of Hampton, 163 F.R.D. 486 (E.D. Va. 1995), overruled in part on other grounds, Cofield v. Crumpler, 179 F.R.D. 510 (E.D. Va. 1998).

While the trial court exercises considerable discretion in the taxing of costs under Rule 54(d), no reason was given for the district court's departure from the normal practice and therefore the order was vacated on appeal. Constantino v. American S/T Achilles, 580 F.2d 121 (4th Cir. 1978).

Obtaining a trial transcript was necessary to counsel's effective handling of the case in filing post-trial motions, and thus allowable as costs. O'Bryhim v. Reliance Std. Life Ins. Co., 997 F. Supp. 728 (E.D. Va. 1998), aff'd, 188 F.3d 502 (4th Cir. 1999).

Depositions. — A district court should award costs when a deposition is used at trial or the taking of a deposition is reasonably necessary at the time of its taking. O'Bryhim v. Reliance Std. Life Ins. Co., 997 F. Supp. 728 (E.D. Va. 1998), aff'd, 188 F.3d 502 (4th Cir. 1999).

Computer legal research. — The majority of federal courts subscribe to the view that costs of computer legal research are properly reflected as part of the law firm's overhead and, as such, are a factor to be included in the setting of attorneys fees as opposed to ordinary costs. O'Bryhim v. Reliance Std. Life Ins. Co., 997 F. Supp. 728 (E.D. Va. 1998), aff'd, 188 F.3d 502 (4th Cir. 1999).

Costs for processing electronic data. — Former employer had not met its burden of showing that its costs for processing electronic data were allowed by 28 U.S.C.S. § 1920 because, regardless of whether scanning documents should have been viewed as copying materials, the category of taxable costs under § 1920(4) did not include the employer's techniques of processing records, extracting data, and converting files, which served to create searchable documents, rather than merely reproduce paper documents in electronic form. Fells v. Va. DOT, 605 F. Supp. 2d 740, 2009 U.S. Dist. LEXIS 30888 (E.D. Va. 2009).

Postage and long-distance telephone calls are incidental expenses of litigation and therefore not allowable as costs under subdivision (d) or 28 U.S.C. § 1920. O'Bryhim v. Reliance Std. Life Ins. Co., 997 F. Supp. 728 (E.D. Va. 1998), aff'd, 188 F.3d 502 (4th Cir. 1999).

Transportation and parking charges are not recompensable costs under subdivision (d) or 28 U.S.C. § 1920. O'Bryhim v. Reliance Std. Life Ins. Co., 997 F. Supp. 728 (E.D. Va. 1998), aff'd, 188 F.3d 502 (4th Cir. 1999).

Motion to modify taxation of costs held untimely filed. — The plaintiff's motion to modify taxation of costs, filed more than six months after the judgment was entered and after the sworn statement of costs was filed, and 45 days after the costs were taxed by the clerk, was not timely. No application to extend the time for filing having been submitted, and no motion for relief from judgment having been filed, the plaintiff's motion was denied. Person v. Omni Int'l Hotel-Norfolk, 106 F.R.D. 7 (E.D. Va. 1984).

Any final judgment in party's favor may grant any relief to which they are entitled, even if they failed to demand such relief in their pleadings. White v. City of Suffolk, 460 F. Supp. 516 (E.D. Va. 1978).

Final judgment not found. — In was clear that the federal district court order which dismissed plaintiff's claim was not a final judgment, since that order did not contain an express determination that there was no just reason for delay, nor a an express direction for the entry of judgment. Straessle v. Air Line Pilot's Ass'n, Int'l, 253 Va. 349, 485 S.E.2d 387 (1997).

An ad damnum serves no practical purpose in contested case under federal procedure, since the court must award the full relief to which the plaintiff is entitled, regardless of the state of the pleadings. Paul v. Gomez, 190 F.R.D. 402 (W.D. Va. 2000).

Applied in United States ex rel. Mustin v. Al-Con Dev. Corp., 271 F.2d 901 (4th Cir. 1959); Freehill v. Benn, 348 F.2d 911 (4th Cir. 1965); Thornton v. Victory Carriers, Inc., 242 F. Supp. 96 (E.D. Va. 1965); Sperry Rand Corp. v. A-T-O, Inc., 447 F.2d 1387 (4th Cir. 1971); Newport News Fire Fighters Ass'n Local 794 v. City of Newport News, 339 F. Supp. 13 (E.D. Va. 1972); Caperton v. Beatrice Pocahontas Coal Co., 585 F.2d 683 (4th Cir. 1978); Patterson v. American Tobacco Co., 634 F.2d 744 (4th Cir. 1980); Principe v. McDonald's Corp., 95 F.R.D. 34 (E.D. Va. 1982); Coldwell Banker Residential Real Estate v. O'Brien & Assocs., 762 F. Supp. 131 (E.D. Va. 1991); Jop v. City of Hampton, 163 F.R.D. 486 (E.D. Va. 1995).

Rule 55. Default; Default Judgment.

(a) *Entering a Default.* — When a party against whom a judgment for affirmative relief is sought has failed to plead or otherwise defend, and that failure is shown by affidavit or otherwise, the clerk must enter the party's default.

(b) *Entering a Default Judgment.* — (1) By the Clerk. If the plaintiff's claim is for a sum certain or a sum that can be made certain by computation, the clerk — on the plaintiff's request, with an affidavit showing the amount due — must enter judgment for that amount and costs against a defendant who has been defaulted for not appearing and who is neither a minor nor an incompetent person.

(2) By the Court. In all other cases, the party must apply to the court for a default judgment. A default judgment may be entered against a minor or incompetent person only if represented by a general guardian, conservator, or other like fiduciary who has appeared. If the party against whom a default judgment is sought has appeared personally or by a representative, that party or its representative must be served with written notice of the application at least 7 days before the hearing. The court may conduct hearings or make referrals — preserving any federal statutory right to a jury trial — when, to enter or effectuate judgment, it needs to:

(A) conduct an accounting;
(B) determine the amount of damages;
(C) establish the truth of any allegation by evidence; or
(D) investigate any other matter.

(c) *Setting Aside a Default or a Default Judgment.* — The court may set aside an entry of default for good cause, and it may set aside a default judgment under Rule 60(b).

(d) *Judgment Against the United States.* — A default judgment may be entered against the United States, its officers, or its agencies only if the claimant establishes a claim or right to relief by evidence that satisfies the court. (Amended by order adopted March 2, 1987, effective August 1, 1987, by order adopted April 30, 2007, effective December 1, 2007, and by order adopted March 26, 2009, effective December 1, 2009.)

Comment. — The language of Rule 55 has been amended as part of the general restyling of the Civil Rules to make them more easily understood and to make style and terminology consistent throughout the rules. These changes are intended to be stylistic only.

Former Rule 55(a) directed the clerk to enter a default when a party failed to plead or otherwise defend "as provided by these rules." The implication from the reference to defending "as provided by these rules" seemed to be that the clerk should enter a default even if a party did something showing an intent to defend, but that act was not specifically described by the rules. Courts in fact have rejected that implication. Acts that show an intent to defend have frequently prevented a default even though not connected to any particular rule. "[A]s provided by these rules" is deleted to reflect Rule 55(a)'s actual meaning.

Amended Rule 55 omits former Rule 55(d), which included two provisions. The first recognized that Rule 55 applies to described claimants. The list was incomplete and unnecessary. Rule 55(a) applies Rule 55 to any party against whom a judgment for affirmative relief is requested. The second provision was a redundant reminder that Rule 54(c) limits the relief available by default judgment.

CASE NOTES

This rule is similar in effect to Rule 3:17, Sup. Ct. (Va.) (see now Rule 3:19). Chappell v. Smith, 208 Va. 272, 156 S.E.2d 572 (1967).

Where defendant has failed to plead or otherwise defend the action, a default judgment is appropriate and shall be entered. Music City Music v. Alfa Foods, Ltd., 616 F. Supp. 1001 (E.D. Va. 1985).

Defendant in default is in court on hearing limited to damages. — In interpreting this rule, it has been said that a defendant though in default is in court on a hearing limited to the question of the amount of damages, to the same extent that he is in court in a trial on the merits. Chappell v. Smith, 208 Va. 272, 156 S.E.2d 572 (1967).

Where amount of damages alleged is not for a sum certain, the court pursuant to subdivision (b)(2) will determine damages. Music City Music v. Alfa Foods, Ltd., 616 F. Supp. 1001 (E.D. Va. 1985).

Entry of default judgment is discretionary. — Authority to set aside a default judgment is grounded in Federal Rules of Civil Procedure 60(b), where relief may be granted for, among other reasons "mistake, inadvertence, surprise, or excusable neglect." A mere entry of default may be set aside for good cause shown under subdivision (c) of this rule. Under either rule the authority is to be exercised in the sound discretion of the trial court, although the justification for vacating an entry of default is somewhat less stringent than what is required by Federal Rules of Civil Procedure 60(b). Trueblood v. Grayson Shops of Tenn., Inc., 32 F.R.D. 190 (E.D. Va. 1963).

Subdivision (c) of this rule allows an entry of default to be set aside "for good cause shown." The decision whether or not to do so rests in the sound discretion of the court. Since the entry of a default, as opposed to an actual default judgment, is both interlocutory and technical in nature, a court should ordinarily set one aside unless the movant fails to present a reasonable excuse for his neglect or fails to show he has a meritorious defense to the merits of the action. Moran v. Mitchell, 354 F. Supp. 86 (E.D. Va. 1973).

Default judgment should be denied where failure to answer was due to counsel's inadvertence and no prejudice resulted. — See Henry v. Metropolitan Life Ins. Co., 3 F.R.D. 142 (W.D. Va. 1942).

Court's action will not be lightly disturbed. — The disposition of motions made under subdivision (c) of this rule and Rule 60(b) is a matter which lies largely within the discretion of the trial judge, and his action is not likely to be disturbed by an appellate court. Consolidated Masonry & Fireproofing, Inc. v. Wagman Constr. Corp., 383 F.2d 249 (4th Cir. 1967), aff'g 273 F. Supp. 693 (E.D. Va. 1966).

Denying motion is not abuse of discretion unless finding of no good cause is clearly wrong. — There is no abuse of discretion in denying a motion under subdivision (c) of this rule and Rule 60(b) unless it clearly appears that the district court was clearly wrong in finding that good cause had not been shown for setting aside the default. Consolidated Masonry & Fireproofing, Inc. v. Wagman Constr. Corp., 383 F.2d 249 (4th Cir. 1967), aff'g 273 F. Supp. 693 (E.D. Va. 1966).

Court may require disclosure of facts supporting allegation of meritorious defense. While some cases lend support to the proposition that a defendant seeking to set aside a default judgment is required to do no more than merely allege that it has a meritorious defense, where the lower court, in its inquiry into the merits of the case, sought to have the defendant state underlying facts to support its claim of a meritorious defense, the appellate court held that it was not persuaded that a bare allegation of a meritorious defense precludes the court, in its discretion, from requiring disclosure of facts to support such a conclusory assertion. Thus, the lower court did not abuse its discretion, under the circumstances, in denying the motion where the defendant did no more than state that plaintiff breached the contract, a mere conclusion which fell far short of providing the court with a satisfactory explanation of the merits of the defense. Consolidated Masonry & Fireproofing, Inc. v. Wagman Constr. Corp., 383 F.2d 249 (4th Cir. 1967), aff'g 273 F. Supp. 693 (E.D. Va. 1966).

The setting of terms and conditions upon granting of Rule 55c relief is recognized. Wilcox v. Triple D Corp., 78 F.R.D. 5 (E.D. Va. 1978).

Applied in Resorts Int'l Hotel, Inc. v. Agresta, 569 F. Supp. 24 (E.D. Va. 1983); Philipp Bros. v. M/V Ocea, 144 F.R.D. 312 (E.D. Va. 1992); Ontra, Inc. v. Wolfe, 192 Bankr. 679 (W.D. Va. 1996).

Rule 56. Summary Judgment.

(a) *Motion for Summary Judgment or Partial Summary Judgment.* — A party may move for summary judgment, identifying each claim or defense — or the part of each claim or defense — on which summary judgment is sought. The court shall grant summary judgment if the movant shows that there is no genuine dispute as to any material fact and the movant is entitled to judgment as a matter of law. The court should state on the record the reasons for granting or denying the motion.

(b) *Time to File a Motion.* — Unless a different time is set by local rule or the court orders otherwise, a party may file a motion for summary judgment at any time until 30 days after the close of all discovery.

(c) *Procedures.* — (1) Supporting Factual Positions. A party asserting that a fact cannot be or is genuinely disputed must support the assertion by:

(A) citing to particular parts of materials in the record, including depositions, documents, electronically stored information, affidavits or declarations, stipulations (including those made for purposes of the motion only), admissions, interrogatory answers, or other materials; or

(B) showing that the materials cited do not establish the absence or presence of a genuine dispute, or that an adverse party cannot produce admissible evidence to support the fact.

(2) Objection That a Fact Is Not Supported by Admissible Evidence. A party may object that the material cited to support or dispute a fact cannot be presented in a form that would be admissible in evidence.

(3) Materials Not Cited. The court need consider only the cited materials, but it may consider other materials in the record.

(4) Affidavits or Declarations. An affidavit or declaration used to support or oppose a motion must be made on personal knowledge, set out facts that would be admissible in evidence, and show that the affiant or declarant is competent to testify on the matters stated.

(d) *When Facts Are Unavailable to the Nonmovant.* — If a nonmovant shows by affidavit or declaration that, for specified reasons, it cannot present facts essential to justify its opposition, the court may:

(1) defer considering the motion or deny it;

(2) allow time to obtain affidavits or declarations or to take discovery; or

(3) issue any other appropriate order.

(e) *Failing to Properly Support or Address a Fact.* — If a party fails to properly support an assertion of fact or fails to properly address another party's assertion of fact as required by Rule 56(c), the court may:

(1) give an opportunity to properly support or address the fact;

(2) consider the fact undisputed for purposes of the motion;

(3) grant summary judgment if the motion and supporting materials — including the facts considered undisputed — show that the movant is entitled to it; or

(4) issue any other appropriate order.

(f) *Judgment Independent of the Motion.* — After giving notice and a reasonable time to respond, the court may:

(1) grant summary judgment for a nonmovant;

(2) grant the motion on grounds not raised by a party; or

(3) consider summary judgment on its own after identifying for the parties material facts that may not be genuinely in dispute.

(g) *Failing to Grant All the Requested Relief.* — If the court does not grant all the relief requested by the motion, it may enter an order stating any material fact — including an item of damages or other relief — that is not genuinely in dispute and treating the fact as established in the case.

(h) *Affidavit or Declaration Submitted in Bad Faith.* — If satisfied that an affidavit or declaration under this rule is submitted in bad faith or solely for delay, the court — after notice and a reasonable time to respond — may order the submitting party to pay the other party the reasonable expenses, including attorney's fees, it incurred as a result. An offending party or attorney may also be held in contempt or subjected to other appropriate sanctions. (Amended by order adopted December 27, 1946, effective March 19, 1948, by order adopted January 21, 1963, effective July 1, 1963, by order adopted March 2, 1987, effective August 1, 1987, by order adopted April 30, 2007, effective December 1, 2007, by order adopted March 26, 2009, effective December 1, 2009, and by order adopted April 28, 2010, effective December 1, 2010.)

Comment. — The language of Rule 56 has been amended as part of the general restyling of the Civil Rules to make them more easily understood and to make style and terminology consistent throughout the rules. These changes are intended to be stylistic only.

Former Rule 56(a) and (b) referred to summary-judgment motions on or against a claim, counterclaim, or crossclaim, or to obtain a declaratory judgment. The list was incomplete. Rule 56 applies to third-party claimants, intervenors, claimants in interpleader, and others. Amended Rule 56(a) and (b) carry forward the present meaning by referring to a party claiming relief and a party against whom relief is sought.

Former Rule 56(c), (d), and (e) stated circumstances in which summary judgment "shall be rendered," the court "shall if practicable" ascertain facts existing without substantial controversy, and "if appropriate, shall" enter summary judgment. In each place "shall" is changed to "should." It is established that although there is no discretion to enter summary judgment when there is a genuine issue as to any material fact, there is discretion to deny summary judgment when it appears that there is no genuine issue as to any material fact. *Kennedy v. Silas Mason Co.,* 334 U.S. 249, 256-257 (1948). Many lower court decisions are gathered in 10A Wright, Miller & Kane, Federal Practice & Procedure: Civil 3d, § 2728. "Should" in amended Rule 56(c) recognizes that courts will seldom exercise the discretion to deny summary judgment when there is no genuine issue as to any material fact. Similarly sparing exercise of this discretion is appropriate under Rule 56(e)(2). Rule 56(d)(1), on the other hand, reflects the more open-ended discretion to decide whether it is practicable to determine what material facts are not genuinely at issue.

Former Rule 56(d) used a variety of different phrases to express the Rule 56(c) standard for summary judgment—that there is no genuine issue as to any material fact. Amended Rule 56(d) adopts terms directly parallel to Rule 56(c).

CASE NOTES

I. General Consideration.
- A. In General.
- B. Purpose of Summary Judgment.

II. Propriety of Summary Judgment.
- A. In General.
- B. Particular Types of Actions.

III. Burden of Proof.
- A. In General.
- B. Burden of Moving Party.
- C. Burden of Nonmoving Party.

IV. Evidence Considered.
- A. In General.
- B. Affidavits.
- C. Other Evidence.

V. Construction of Evidence.

VI. Function of Trial Court.

VII. Appellate Review.

VIII. Pleading and Practice.

I. GENERAL CONSIDERATION.

A. In General.

The principles governing summary judgment procedures should be applied in a common sense manner to the realities of the litigation at hand. Slusher v. Hercules, Inc., 532 F. Supp. 753 (W.D. Va. 1982).

Test is whether there is no genuine issue as to material fact. — On a motion for summary judgment the test to be applied is whether the pleadings, depositions and admissions on file, together with the affidavits, show that, except as to the amount of damages, there is no genuine issue as to any material fact and that the moving party is entitled to a judgment as a matter of law. Tunstall v. Brotherhood of Locomotive Firemen & Enginemen, 69 F. Supp. 826 (E.D. Va. 1946), aff'd, 163 F.2d 289 (4th Cir. 1947).

This rule permits a party to pierce the allegations of fact in the pleadings and to obtain relief by summary judgment where facts set forth in detail in affidavits, depositions, answers to interrogatories, and admissions on file show that there are no genuine issues of material fact to be tried. Cales v. C & O Ry., 46 F.R.D. 36 (W.D. Va. 1969).

The question presented on a motion for a summary judgment is whether there is a genuine issue as to any material fact in the case. Sherman v. City of Richmond, 543 F. Supp. 447 (E.D. Va. 1982); Via v. City of Richmond, 543 F. Supp. 382 (E.D. Va. 1982).

While it is axiomatic that Rule 56 must be used carefully so as not improperly to foreclose trial on genuinely disputed, material facts, the mere existence of some disputed facts does not require that a case go to trial. The disputed facts must be material to an issue necessary for the proper resolution of the case, and the quality and quantity of the evidence offered to create a question of fact must be adequate to support a jury verdict. Thompson Everett, Inc. v. National Cable Adv., 57 F.3d 1317 (4th Cir. 1995).

An adverse party may not rest on its pleadings when faced with a motion for summary judgment; instead, the opposing party must go beyond its pleadings to demonstrate that a triable issue of fact exists. Dixon v. State Farm Fire & Cas. Ins. Co., 926 F. Supp. 548 (E.D. Va. 1996).

The mere existence of some alleged factual dispute between the parties will not defeat an otherwise properly supported motion for summary judgment; the requirement is that there be no genuine issue of material fact. Garrett v. Gilmore, 926 F. Supp. 554 (W.D. Va.), aff'd, 103 F.3d 117 (4th Cir. 1996).

Under this rule, summary judgment should be granted only if "there is no genuine issue as to any material fact and the ... moving party is entitled to judgment as a matter of law;" for the evidence to present a "genuine" issue of material fact, it must be "such that a reasonable jury could return a verdict for the nonmoving party." Todd Marine Enters., Inc. v. Carter Mach. Co., 898 F. Supp. 341 (E.D. Va. 1995).

To sustain a motion for summary judgment, the court must find that no genuine issue of material fact exists and that the movant is entitled to judgment as a matter of law; the party seeking summary judgment is initially responsible for identifying the absence of a genuine issue of material fact; when this burden is met, the nonmoving party must show, through affidavits or other proof, that a genuine issue of material fact does exist. Adams v. Drew, 906 F. Supp. 1050 (E.D. Va. 1995).

Summary judgment is appropriate where there is no genuine issue as to any material fact and the moving party is entitled to judgment as a matter of law; where the record taken as a whole could not lead a rational trier of fact to find for the nonmoving party, there is no genuine issue for trial and summary judgment is appropriate; in considering a motion for summary judgment, "the court is required to view the facts and draw reasonable inferences in a light most favorable to the nonmoving party; the plaintiff is entitled to have the credibility of all his evidence presumed." Roto-Die Co. v. Lesser, 899 F. Supp. 1515 (W.D. Va. 1995).

A motion for summary judgment shall be granted when there is no genuine dispute as to any material fact, and the moving party is entitled to judgment as a matter of law. CaterCorp, Inc. v. Henicheck, 186 Bankr. 211 (Bankr. E.D. Va. 1995).

When a motion for summary judgment is made and supported with affidavits, "an adverse party may not rest upon the mere allegations or denials of the adverse party's pleading, but the adverse party's response, by affidavits or as otherwise provided in this rule, must set forth specific facts showing that there is a genuine issue for trial." Todd Marine Enters., Inc. v. Carter Mach. Co., 898 F. Supp. 341 (E.D. Va. 1995).

Summary judgment is appropriate when the party seeking judgment has shown that there is no dispute as to any material fact. Long v. First Union Corp., 894 F. Supp. 933 (E.D. Va. 1995), aff'd, 86 F.3d 1151 (4th Cir. 1996).

Once the party moving for summary judgment has demonstrated the absence of a genuine issue of material fact, the non-moving party must come forward with concrete evidence in the form of "specific facts showing that there is a genuine issue for trial." Long v. First Union Corp., 894 F. Supp. 933 (E.D. Va. 1995), aff'd, 86 F.3d 1151 (4th Cir. 1996).

Where a motion for summary judgment is made and properly supported by affidavits, depositions, or answers to interrogatories, the non-moving party may not rest on the mere allegations or denials of the pleadings. Instead the non-moving party must respond by affidavits or otherwise and present specific facts showing there is a genuine issue of disputed fact for trial. Garrett v. Gilmore, 926 F. Supp. 554 (W.D. Va.), aff'd, 103 F.3d 117 (4th Cir. 1996).

Only after the movant's burden is met, and a properly supported motion is before the court, must the party opposing the motion "set forth specific facts showing that there is a genuine issue for trial." Keegan v. Dalton, 899 F. Supp. 1503 (E.D. Va. 1995).

The moving party bears the burden of establishing the absence of any material facts. Once the movant has met this burden, the party opposing the motion must demonstrate that there are genuine disputes of material facts. Mere conclusory statements or conjecture will not suffice. Rather, the party opposing evidence to refute the motion for summary judgment. If the non-moving party fails to meet the burden, summary judgment should be granted. CaterCorp, Inc. v. Henicheck, 186 Bankr. 211 (Bankr. E.D. Va. 1995).

Rule 12(b)(6) motion compared. — Unlike a Rule 12(b)(6) motion, which limits the court's inquiry to the adequacy of the content of the complaint, a motion for summary judgment involves a determination from the pleadings, depositions, answers to interrogatories, and affidavits whether there is a genuine issue of fact. Morgan v. American Family Life Assurance Co., 559 F. Supp. 477 (W.D. Va. 1983).

When Rule 12(b)(6) motion treated as motion for summary judgment. — See Woodard v. Virginia Bd. of Bar Exmrs., 420 F. Supp. 211 (E.D. Va. 1976), aff'd, 598 F.2d 1345 (4th Cir. 1979).

While summary judgment typically is improper when a contract's language is ambiguous, it is appropriate where the evidence indicates that the moving party is entitled to judgment as a matter of law. Bailey v. Blue Cross & Blue Shield, 67 F.3d 53 (4th Cir. 1995), cert. denied, 516 U.S. 1159, 116 S. Ct. 1043, 134 L. Ed. 2d 190 (1996).

Where a defendant's motion for summary judgment attacks, not the sufficency of the plaintiff's evidence but the sufficency of the complaint, the applicable standard is the same as for a motion to dismiss under Rule 12. King v. Speaks, 193 Bankr. 436 (Bankr. E.D. Va. 1995).

When motion to dismiss treated as motion for summary judgment. — Where the parties have submitted materials in addition to their pleadings, the court will treat defendant's preliminary motion to dismiss and/or for summary judgment as one for summary judgment. Eldridge v. Bouchard, 620 F. Supp. 678 (W.D. Va. 1985).

Where the parties have referred to matters outside the pleadings in connection with the motions to dismiss, including declarations and transcripts of deposition testimony, the motions will be treated as ones for summary judgment under this rule. King v. Dalton, 895 F. Supp. 831 (E.D. Va. 1995).

Separate findings and conclusions of law thereon not required. — Where the case is to be disposed of upon motions for summary judgment under this rule, the court is not required by Rule 52 to find the facts and state separately its conclusions of law thereon. Jordan v. Shelby Mut. Plate Glass &

Cas. Co., 51 F. Supp. 240 (W.D. Va. 1943), aff'd, 142 F.2d 52 (4th Cir. 1944). See note to Rule 52.

The standard for granting summary judgment is akin to that of granting a directed verdict: There is no issue for trial unless there is sufficient evidence favoring the nonmoving party for a jury to return a verdict for that party. If the evidence is merely colorable or is not significantly probative, summary judgment may be granted. The judge must ask himself whether a fair-minded jury could return a verdict for plaintiff on the evidence presented. Hicks v. Phipps, 765 F. Supp. 1541 (W.D. Va. 1990); Petra Int'l Banking Corp. v. First Am. Bank, 758 F. Supp. 1120 (E.D. Va. 1991), aff'd sub nom. Petra Int'l Banking Corp. v. Dameron Int'l, Inc., 953 F.2d 1383 (4th Cir. 1992).

1963 amendment of subdivision (c) codified preexisting law. — A 1963 amendment of subdivision (c) of this rule added "answers to interrogatories," but this amendment appears merely to have codified preexisting practice and case law. Williams v. Howard Johnson's, Inc., 323 F.2d 102 (4th Cir. 1963), vacating and remanding 210 F. Supp. 295 (E.D. Va. 1962).

Subdivision (e) was not intended to modify the burden of the moving party under subdivision (c) to show initially the absence of a genuine issue concerning any material fact. Wood v. Kling, 98 F.R.D. 319 (E.D. Va. 1983).

Applied in Pachaly v. City of Lynchburg, 897 F.2d 723 (4th Cir. 1990); Jenkins v. Weatherholtz, 909 F.2d 105 (4th Cir. 1990); Oksanen v. Page Mem. Hosp., 912 F.2d 73 (4th Cir. 1990); Island Creek Coal Co. v. Local 2232, UMW, 732 F. Supp. 666 (W.D. Va. 1990); Chas. H. Tompkins Co. v. Lumbermens Mut. Cas. Co., 732 F. Supp. 1368 (E.D. Va. 1990); Media Gen. Cable of Fairfax, Inc. v. Sequoyah Condominium Council of Co-Owners, 737 F. Supp. 903 (E.D. Va. 1990); Grochowski v. Virginia, 741 F. Supp. 1230 (W.D. Va. 1990); Tyler v. Putman, 110 Bankr. 783 (Bankr. E.D. Va. 1990); R.I.S.E., Inc. v. Kay, 768 F. Supp. 1141 (E.D. Va. 1991); Lee X v. Casey, 771 F. Supp. 725 (E.D. Va. 1991); Flagship Group, Ltd. v. Peninsula Cruise, Inc., 771 F. Supp. 756 (E.D. Va. 1991); Butler v. Navistar Int'l Transp. Corp., 809 F. Supp. 1202 (W.D. Va. 1991); Rountree v. Fairfax County Sch. Bd., 933 F.2d 219 (4th Cir. 1992); Norfolk & W. Ry. v. Accident & Cas. Ins. Co., 796 F. Supp. 925 (W.D. Va. 1992); Norfolk & W. Ry. v. Accident & Cas. Ins. Co., 796 F. Supp. 929 (W.D. Va. 1992); Miller v. United States, 803 F. Supp. 1120 (E.D. Va. 1992); Sentinel Assocs. v. American Mfrs. Mut. Ins. Co., 804 F. Supp. 815 (E.D. Va. 1992); United States v. Ledwith, 805 F. Supp. 371 (E.D. Va. 1992); Verosol B.V. v. Hunter Douglas, Inc., 806 F. Supp. 582 (E.D. Va. 1992); F.P. Corp. v. Golden W. Foods, Inc., 807 F. Supp. 1228 (W.D. Va. 1992); Wellmore Coal Corp. v. Patrick Petro. Corp., 808 F. Supp. 529 (W.D. Va. 1992); Taylor v. Atlas Safety Equip. Co., 808 F. Supp. 1246 (E.D. Va. 1992); Berg v. Commander, Fifth Coast Guard Dist., 810 F. Supp. 703 (E.D. Va. 1992); Ewell v. Murray, 813 F. Supp. 1180 (W.D. Va. 1993); Buko v. American Medical Lab., Inc., 830 F. Supp. 899 (E.D. Va. 1993); Harmer v. VEPCO, 831 F. Supp. 1300 (E.D. Va. 1993); Paterno Imports, Ltd. v. McBee, 159 Bankr. 461 (Bankr. E.D. Va. 1993); Advanced Computer Servs. of Mich., Inc. v. MAI Sys. Corp., 845 F. Supp. 356 (E.D. Va. 1994); In re E. Shore Diving & Marine Servs., Inc., 845 F. Supp. 371 (E.D. Va. 1994); Dillon v. Murray, 853 F. Supp. 199 (W.D. Va. 1994); Austin v. Clark Equip. Co., 48 F.3d 833 (4th Cir. 1995); Multi-Channel TV Cable Co. v. Charlottesville Quality Cable Corp., 65 F.3d 1113 (4th Cir. 1995); Russell v. Microdyne Corp., 65 F.3d 1229 (4th Cir. 1995); Shore v. A.W. Hargrove Ins. Agency, Inc., 873 F. Supp. 992 (E.D. Va. 1995); Dennis v. Aetna Life Ins. & Annuity Co., 873 F. Supp. 1000 (E.D. Va. 1995); Sandhu v. Virginia, Dep't of Conservation & Recreation, 874 F. Supp. 122 (E.D. Va. 1995); Williams v. Air Wisconsin, Inc., 874 F. Supp. 710 (E.D. Va. 1995); Doyle v. Sentry Ins., 877 F. Supp. 1002 (E.D. Va. 1995); Mears v. GMC, 896 F. Supp. 548 (E.D. Va. 1995); Keegan v. Dalton, 899 F. Supp. 1503 (E.D. Va. 1995); Scruggs v. Keen, 900 F. Supp. 821 (W.D. Va. 1995); Burns v. D. Oltmann Maritime PTE Ltd., 901 F. Supp. 203 (E.D. Va. 1995); NAACP Labor Comm. v. Laborers' Int'l Union, 902 F. Supp. 688 (W.D. Va. 1995); International Longshoremen's Ass'n v. Virginia Int'l Terms., Inc., 904 F. Supp. 500 (E.D. Va. 1995); Ramey v. Kingsport Publishing Corp., 905 F. Supp. 355 (W.D. Va. 1995); National Ass'n of Home Bldrs. of United States v. Chesterfield County, 907 F. Supp. 166 (E.D. Va. 1995); Stephens v. Kay Mgt. Co., 907 F. Supp. 169 (E.D. Va. 1995); Cary v. Carmichael, 908 F. Supp. 1334 (E.D. Va. 1995); Religious Technology Ctr. v. Lerma, 908 F. Supp. 1362 (E.D. Va. 1995); Selbe v. United States, 912 F. Supp. 202 (W.D. Va. 1995); Jop v. City of Hampton, 163 F.R.D. 486 (E.D. Va. 1995); Shoemaker v. Metro Info. Servs., 910 F. Supp. 259 (E.D. Va. 1996); Hussain v. Kaiser Found. Health Plan, 914 F. Supp. 1331 (E.D. Va. 1996); David v. Mosley, 915 F. Supp. 776 (E.D. Va. 1996); EEOC v. Kinney Shoe Corp., 917 F. Supp. 419 (W.D. Va. 1996); Rutherford v. City of Newport News, 919 F. Supp. 885 (E.D. Va. 1996); Pneumo Abex Corp. v. Bessemer & L.E.R.R., 921 F. Supp. 336 (E.D. Va. 1996); Hott v. VDO Yazaki Corp., 922 F. Supp. 1114 (W.D. Va. 1996); Reynolds & Reynolds Co. v. Hardee, 932 F. Supp. 149 (E.D. Va. 1996); Virginia Transformer Corp. v. P.D. George Co., 932 F. Supp. 156 (W.D. Va. 1996); Ludwick v. Premier Bank N., Inc., 935 F. Supp. 801 (W.D. Va. 1996); Burke v. Virginia, 938 F. Supp. 320 (E.D. Va. 1996); Wichlacz v. United States Dep't of Interior, 938 F. Supp. 325 (E.D. Va. 1996); International Longshoremen's Ass'n v. Virginia Int'l Terms., 938 F. Supp. 335 (E.D. Va. 1996); Blankenship v. Warren County Sheriff's Dep't, 939 F. Supp. 451 (W.D. Va. 1996); Haines v. Southern Retailers, Inc., 939 F. Supp. 441 (E.D. Va. 1996); Michael v. Sentara Health Sys., 939 F. Supp. 1220 (E.D. Va. 1996); Williams v. Charlottesville Sch. Bd., 940 F. Supp. 143 (W.D. Va. 1996); Garrett v. Angelone, 940 F. Supp. 933 (W.D. Va. 1996); Hinch v. Duncan, 941 F. Supp. 62 (W.D. Va. 1996); National Enters., Inc. v. Moore, 948 F. Supp. 567 (E.D. Va. 1996); Blue v. Jabe, 996 F. Supp. 499 (E.D. Va. 1996); Mathis v. Perry, 996 F. Supp. 503 (E.D. Va. 1997); Wilson v. Wright, 998 F. Supp. 650 (E.D. Va. 1998); Morgan v. Credit Adjustment Bd., Inc., 999 F. Supp. 803 (E.D. Va. 1998); Blankenship v. Buchanan Gen. Hosp., 999 F. Supp. 832 (W.D. Va. 1998); Anderson v. IRS, 228 Bankr. 844 (Bankr. W.D. Va. 1998); Brooks v. Metrica, Inc., 1 F. Supp. 2d 559 (E.D. Va. 1998); Barnett v. Technology Int'l, Inc., 1 F. Supp. 2d 572 (E.D. Va. 1998); Ross v. Keelings, 2 F. Supp. 2d 810

(E.D. Va. 1998); Semiconductor Energy Lab. Co. v. Samsung Elecs. Co., 4 F. Supp. 2d 473 (E.D. Va. 1998); Litman v. George Mason Univ., 5 F. Supp. 2d 366 (E.D. Va. 1998); Childress v. Clement, 5 F. Supp. 2d 384 (E.D. Va. 1998); Moore v. Flagstar Bank, 6 F. Supp. 2d 496 (E.D. Va. 1997); GTE S. Inc. v. Morrison, 6 F. Supp. 2d 517 (E.D. Va. 1998); Hitachi Credit Am. Corp. v. Signet Bank, 166 F.3d 614 (4th. Cir. 1999); Kendall v. City of Chesapeake, 174 F.3d 437 (4th Cir. 1999); Benshoff v. City of Va. Beach, 9 F. Supp. 2d 610 (E.D. Va. 1998); United States v. Smith, 10 F. Supp. 2d 578 (E.D. Va. 1998); Barron v. Runyon, 11 F. Supp. 2d 676 (E.D. Va. 1998); Norfolk & W. Ry. v. Brotherhood of R.R. Signalmen, 11 F. Supp. 2d 833 (W.D. Va. 1998); Turner v. Jack Rabbit, Inc., 12 F. Supp. 2d 529 (E.D. Va. 1998); Harris Corp. v. Atmel Corp., 14 F. Supp. 2d 821 (E.D. Va. 1998); Dawson v. Leewood Nursing Home, Inc., 14 F. Supp. 2d 828 (E.D. Va. 1998); Parents, Alumni, & Friends of Taylor Sch. v. City of Norfolk, 37 F. Supp. 2d 435 (E.D. Va. 1999); Burket v. Angelone, 37 F. Supp. 2d 457 (E.D. Va. 1999); Wolford v. Angelone, 38 F. Supp. 2d 452 (W.D. Va. 1999); Crews v. Shalala, 40 F. Supp. 2d 350 (E.D. Va. 1999); Scheduled Airlines Traffic Offices v. Objective: Inc., 180 F.3d 583 (4th Cir. 1999); Plett v. United States, 185 F.3d 216 (4th Cir. 1999); Mayer v. United States (In re Reasonover), 236 Bankr. 219 (Bankr. E.D. Va. 1999); Matson v. Grease Monkey Int'l, Inc. (In re Bev of Va., Inc.), 237 Bankr. 311 (Bankr. E.D. Va. 1998); Mom's, Inc. v. Weber, 82 F. Supp. 2d 493 (E.D. Va. 2000); Goddard v. Protective Life Corp., 82 F. Supp. 2d 545 (E.D. Va. 2000); In re Fisherman's Wharf Fillet, Inc., 83 F. Supp. 2d 651 (E.D. Va. 1999); Virginia Soc'y for Human Life v. Federal Elect., 83 F. Supp. 2d 668 (E.D. Va. 2000); Franklin v. First Union Corp., 84 F. Supp. 2d 720 (E.D. Va. 2000); McIntyre-Handy v. West Telemarketing Corp., 97 F. Supp. 2d 718, 2000 U.S. Dist. LEXIS 7152 (E.D. Va. 2000); Balthis v. AIG Life Ins. Co., 102 F. Supp. 2d 668 (W.D. Va. 2000); Blagman v. White, 112 F. Supp. 2d 534, 2000 U.S. Dist. LEXIS 13799 (E.D. Va. 2000); Wadkins v. Arnold, 214 F.3d 535, 2000 U.S. App. LEXIS 12102 (4th Cir. 2000); A.T. Massey Coal Co. v. Massanari, 153 F. Supp. 2d 813, 2001 U.S. Dist. LEXIS 10280 (E.D. Va. 2001); Piedmont Envtl. Council v. United States DOT, 159 F. Supp. 2d 260, 2001 U.S. Dist LEXIS 12623 (W.D. Va. 2001).

B. Purpose of Summary Judgment.

Purpose of summary judgment procedure. — Summary judgment is to avoid a useless trial. It is a device to make possible the prompt disposition of controversies on their merits without a trial, if in essence there is no real dispute as to the salient facts. Johnson v. McKee Baking Co., 398 F. Supp. 201 (W.D. Va. 1975), aff'd, 532 F.2d 750 (4th Cir. 1976).

The summary judgment procedure contained in this rule is a tool for ascertaining the facts before the curtain goes up on the trial, because it enables the court to determine whether there should be a trial at all. Johnson v. McKee Baking Co., 398 F. Supp. 201 (W.D. Va. 1975), aff'd, 532 F.2d 750 (4th Cir. 1976).

The purpose of a summary judgment motion is to pierce the allegations of the pleadings, to show that there is no genuine issue of material fact, and that the movant is entitled to judgment as a matter of law. Matney v. First Protection Life Ins. Co., 73 F.R.D. 696 (W.D. Va. 1977).

Summary judgment should not be regarded as a disfavored procedural shortcut but rather as an integral part of the federal rules as a whole which are designed to secure the just, speedy, and inexpensive determination of every action. Crenshaw Assocs. v. Martin, 138 Bankr. 508 (Bankr. E.D. Va. 1992).

II. PROPRIETY OF SUMMARY JUDGMENT.

A. In General.

Several factors must be weighed by the court before deciding upon a motion for summary judgment. The court should consider: The need for cross-examination by the opposing party in relation to evidentiary materials, the general desirability of demeanor testimony, the factor of access to proof by the opposing party and the desirability that the case receive the full exploration of a trial. Other factors to be considered are the complexity of the case and the opposing party's reliance on circumstantial evidence. Such considerations are well within the court's discretion as to whether the granting of summary judgment is judicially proper. Clinch Valley Bank & Trust Co. v. Shortt, 16 Bankr. 813 (Bankr. W.D. Va. 1982); Richardson v. Combs, 40 Bankr. 148 (Bankr. W.D. Va. 1984), aff'd, 838 F.2d 112 (4th Cir. 1988).

When summary judgment should be granted. — The rule in this circuit is that summary judgment should be granted only where it is perfectly clear that no issue of fact is involved and inquiry into the facts is not desirable to clarify the application of the law. And this is true even where there is no dispute as to the evidentiary facts in the case but only as to the conclusions to be drawn therefrom. West v. Costen, 558 F. Supp. 564 (W.D. Va. 1983); Pennsylvania Life Ins. Co. v. Bumbrey, 665 F. Supp. 1190 (E.D. Va. 1987).

A motion for summary judgment may only be granted if the pleadings, depositions, answers to interrogatories and admissions on file, together with the affidavits, if any, show that there is no genuine issue as to any material fact. Powers v. Sims & Levin Realtors, 396 F. Supp. 12 (E.D. Va. 1975), rev'd on other grounds, 542 F.2d 1216 (4th Cir. 1976).

Summary judgment is appropriate if the nonmoving party fails to make a showing sufficient to establish the elements necessary to his or her case. Overstreet v. Kentucky Cent. Life Ins. Co., 950 F.2d 931 (4th Cir. 1991).

Summary judgment should be entered, after adequate time for discovery and upon motion, against a party who fails to demonstrate that evidence exists which would be sufficient to establish an element of that party's case on which that party will bear the burden of proof at trial. RGI, Inc. v. Unified Indus., Inc., 963 F.2d 658 (4th Cir. 1991).

Summary judgment is not to be granted lightly and is not a substitute for the trial of disputed issues of fact. Rather, the use of summary judgment is limited to an exceptional situation where there is no genuine issue as to any material fact and the moving party is entitled to a judgment as a matter of law. Clinch Valley Bank & Trust Co. v. Shortt, 16

Bankr. 813 (Bankr. W.D. Va. 1982); Richardson v. Combs, 40 Bankr. 148 (Bankr. W.D. Va. 1984), aff'd, 838 F.2d 112 (4th Cir. 1988).

Summary judgment on an issue is appropriate when there is no genuine issue of material fact between the parties, and it appears from the pleadings and any supporting affidavits that the moving party is entitled to judgment as a matter of law. Minnick v. United States, 767 F. Supp. 115 (E.D. Va. 1990).

Where plaintiffs did not explain why necessary investigations by their experts could not have been completed many months earlier so that appropriate affidavits of their experts could have been submitted before the hearing, summary judgment against them was appropriate. Gasner v. Board of Supvrs., 103 F.3d 351 (4th Cir. 1996).

Mere existence of some alleged factual dispute between the parties will not defeat an otherwise properly supported motion for summary judgment; the requirement is that there be no genuine issue of material fact. State Farm Mut. Auto. Ins. Co. v. Bright, 850 F. Supp. 493 (W.D. Va. 1994).

While it is axiomatic that Rule 56 must be used carefully so as not improperly to foreclose trial on genuinely disputed, material facts, the mere existence of some disputed facts does not require that a case go to trial. The disputed facts must be material to an issue necessary for the proper resolution of the case, and the quality and quantity of the evidence offered to create a question of fact must be adequate to support a jury verdict. Thompson Everett, Inc. v. National Cable Adv., 57 F.3d 1317 (4th Cir. 1995).

"Material," "genuine," construed. — A fact is material when proof of its existence or nonexistence would affect the outcome of the case, and an issue is genuine if a reasonable jury might return a verdict in favor of the nonmoving party on the basis of such issue. Northwestern Mut. Life Ins. Co. v. Atlantic Research Corp., 847 F. Supp. 389 (E.D. Va. 1994).

The court may grant summary judgment under this rule if, viewing the facts in the light most favorable to the nonmoving party, the record contains no genuine issue of material fact and "the moving party is entitled to judgment as a matter of law." Unlimited Screw Prods., Inc. v. Malm, 781 F. Supp. 1121 (E.D. Va. 1991).

Under this rule, as adopted by Rule 756, Rules of Bankruptcy Procedure, summary judgment properly may be entered only when there is no genuine issue as to any material fact and the movant is entitled to judgment as a matter of law. Docter, Docter & Salus v. United States (In re Abingdon Realty Corp.), 21 Bankr. 290 (Bankr. E.D. Va. 1982).

Disposition by summary judgment is appropriate when the evidence, taken as a whole and viewed in the light most favorable to the party opposing the motion, could not lead a rational trier of fact to find for the nonmoving party. Northwestern Mut. Life Ins. Co. v. Atlantic Research Corp., 847 F. Supp. 389 (E.D. Va. 1994).

Summary judgment is appropriate for "any part" of a claim that presents no triable issues. "Any part" means any portion of the liability or the damages aspects of a claim. Northwestern Mut. Life Ins. Co. v. Atlantic Research Corp., 847 F. Supp. 389 (E.D. Va. 1994).

Summary judgment may be appropriate despite claims of willful or malicious conduct if the depositions and other material in the record do not give substance to the allegations. Johnson v. McKee Baking Co., 398 F. Supp. 201 (W.D. Va. 1975), aff'd, 532 F.2d 750 (4th Cir. 1976).

Prima facie case does not preclude summary judgment. — At a bare minimum, plaintiffs must make out a prima facie case. But even establishment of a prima facie case does not mean the case must be submitted to the jury or that summary judgment is improper. McDaniel v. Mead Corp., 622 F. Supp. 351 (W.D. Va. 1985), aff'd, 818 F.2d 861 (W.D. Va. 1987).

Summary judgment is not appropriate if the evidence is such that a reasonable jury could return a verdict for the nonmoving party, nor is it appropriate even where there is no dispute as to the evidentiary facts but only as to the conclusions to be drawn therefrom. Overstreet v. Kentucky Cent. Life Ins. Co., 950 F.2d 931 (4th Cir. 1991).

Issue of fact precludes summary judgment. — Summary judgment is inappropriate if there is any genuine factual issue or if there is any dispute over the reasonable inferences drawn from the undisputed facts in the record. Cooper v. Ingersoll Rand Co., 628 F. Supp. 1488 (W.D. Va. 1986).

There must be no controversy as to inferences to be drawn from facts. — Summary judgment under this rule should be granted only where it is perfectly clear that no issue of fact is involved and inquiry into the facts is not desirable to clarify the application of the law. This is true even where there is no dispute as to the evidentiary facts but only as to the conclusions or inferences to be drawn therefrom. Not merely must the historic facts be free of controversy but also there must be no controversy as to the inferences to be drawn from them. It is often the case that although the basic facts are not in dispute, the parties nevertheless disagree as to the inferences which may properly be drawn. Under such circumstances, the case is not one to be decided on a motion for summary judgment. Clinch Valley Bank & Trust Co. v. Shortt, 16 Bankr. 813 (Bankr. W.D. Va. 1982).

Even when the evidentiary facts are undisputed, summary judgment should not be granted if conflicting inferences may be drawn from those facts. T.I. Swartz Clothiers, Inc. v. Union Trust Co., 15 Bankr. 590 (Bankr. E.D. Va. 1981).

Summary judgment should be granted if there is no genuine issue as to any material fact. Swacker v. Interstate R.R., 32 F.R.D. 234 (W.D. Va. 1962) (denying motion because of factual issues); American Fid. & Cas. Co. v. London & Edinburgh Ins. Co., 354 F.2d 214 (4th Cir. 1965).

A fact is material if proof of its existence or nonexistence would affect the outcome of the case. Pruitt v. Wilder, 840 F. Supp. 414 (E.D. Va. 1994).

But only where inquiry is not desirable to clarify application of law. — Summary judgment should be granted only where it is perfectly clear that no issue of fact is involved and inquiry into the facts is not desirable to clarify the application of the law. And this is true even where there is no dispute as to the evidentiary facts in the case but only as to the conclusions to be drawn therefrom. Cales v. C & O Ry., 46 F.R.D. 36 (W.D. Va. 1969).

And not where record does not supply basis for assumed facts. — Where the pleadings and the record did not contain the documents which might possibly supply a basis for the assumption that the facts were uncontroverted, and no testimony was taken, and where there was no agreement between the parties upon the facts so assumed, the case was remanded for a full inquiry, since summary judgment was inappropriate under the circumstances. United States v. Mullins, 344 F.2d 128 (4th Cir. 1965), vacating and remanding 234 F. Supp. 819 (W.D. Va. 1964).

Or where judge believes he will have to direct verdict on issues raised. — Even in cases where the judge is of opinion that he will have to direct a verdict for one party or the other on the issues that have been raised, he should ordinarily hear the evidence and direct the verdict rather than attempt to try the case in advance on a motion for summary judgment, which was never intended to enable parties to evade jury trials or have the judge weigh evidence in advance of its being presented. Cales v. C & O Ry., 46 F.R.D. 36 (W.D. Va. 1969).

Or where credibility is crucial. — Where the credibility of depositions is, or may be crucial, summary judgment becomes improper and a trial indispensable. Cales v. C & O Ry., 46 F.R.D. 36 (W.D. Va. 1969).

The summary judgment practice does not become disfavored simply because a case is complex. Thompson Everett, Inc. v. National Cable Adv., 57 F.3d 1317 (4th Cir. 1995).

B. Particular Types of Actions.

Constitutional rights not violated as a matter of law. — Summary judgment was granted where it was held as a matter of law that the parties had no expectations of continued employment as deputies sufficient to confer property interest of constitutional dimension. Hopkins v. Dolinger, 453 F. Supp. 59 (W.D. Va. 1978).

Age discrimination cases. — Summary judgment is not inappropriate in age discrimination cases merely because they involve issues of intent and motive. McDaniel v. Mead Corp., 622 F. Supp. 351 (W.D. Va. 1985), aff'd, 818 F.2d 861 (W.D. Va. 1987).

Employment discrimination cases. — Courts must take special care in considering summary judgment in cases involving questions of motive, such as in an employment discrimination case. However, the fact that motive is often the critical issue in employment discrimination cases does not mean that summary judgment is never an appropriate vehicle for resolution. Where a plaintiff fails to set forth either a prima facie case of discrimination or a genuine factual dispute over the employer's legitimate non-discriminatory explanation, a defendant may prevail on summary judgment. Tyndall v. Dynaric, Inc., 997 F. Supp. 721 (E.D. Va. 1998).

Questions of motive in employment discrimination cases. — Courts must take special care in considering summary judgment in cases involving questions of motive, such as in an employment discrimination case. Chappell v. School Bd., 12 F. Supp. 2d 509 (E.D. Va. 1998).

Fact that motive is often critical issue in employment discriminationcases does not mean that summary judgment is never an appropriate vehicle for resolution. Where a plaintiff fails to set forth either a prima facie case of discrimination or a genuine factual dispute over the employer's legitimate non-discriminatory explanation, a defendant may prevail on summary judgment. Chappell v. School Bd., 12 F. Supp. 2d 509 (E.D. Va. 1998).

Whether employees were told they would not have to work overtime was a material issue of fact in dispute and could not be decided on summary judgment. Belton v. Sigmon, 101 F. Supp. 2d 435 (W.D. Va. 1998).

Motion denied where defense of sovereign immunity found inapplicable. — See Hauth v. Southeastern Tidewater Opportunity Project, Inc., 420 F. Supp. 171 (E.D. Va. 1976).

Proper forum for injured employee is appropriate question for summary judgment. — Whether the state industrial commission or a common-law court is the appropriate forum for the adjudication of rights of an injured claimant is a question peculiarly appropriate for summary judgment. Walker v. United States Gypsum Co., 270 F.2d 857 (4th Cir. 1959), cert. denied, 363 U.S. 805, 80 S. Ct. 1240, 4 L. Ed. 2d 1148 (1960).

Determination of whether employee was supervisor held mixed question of law and fact. — See York County Fire Fighters Ass'n, Local 2498 v. County of York, 589 F.2d 775 (4th Cir. 1978).

In action for wrongful dismissal, genuine issue held to exist as to matters of defense. — See Cales v. C & O Ry., 46 F.R.D. 36 (W.D. Va. 1969) (existence of probable cause for arrest of plaintiff and his discharge from employment for intoxication).

Recital of any fact in a deed conveying interest in real property prima facie evidence of that fact. — In an action to determine the amount of supplementary security income checks where the recipient transferred his title in fee of his homestead to his sons and lived there rent free, testimony of the recipient and his sons as to his intent to retain a life estate was insufficient to overcome the evidence of the deed, and summary judgment was properly entered. Boone v. Califano, 459 F. Supp. 636 (E.D. Va. 1978).

No issue as to material fact in action for damages to property where nuclear power plant, the actual property, was not damaged or diminished in value because of defective supports which were replaced. Stone & Webster Eng'g Corp. v. American Motorist Ins. Co., 458 F. Supp. 792 (E.D. Va. 1978), aff'd, 628 F.2d 1351 (4th Cir. 1980).

Presumption of death. — Where essential element of the plaintiff's case was a showing that the plaintiff's husband, who had been missing for 10 years and was presumed dead under § 64.1-105, died as the result of an accident and not from natural causes, summary judgment was appropriate where there was no circumstantial evidence showing that the deceased died of unexplained, external means. Houchens v. American Home Assurance Co., 927 F.2d 163 (4th Cir. 1991).

Mere allegations of conspiracy, backed up by no factual showing of participation in a conspiracy, are sufficient to support such an action against a motion for summary judgment based on affidavits establishing the absence of any participation. Buschi v. Kirven, 775 F.2d 1240 (4th Cir. 1985).

Defendant may be equitably estopped from pleading statute of limitations. — Assuming that on the summary judgment record the undisputed evidence reveals no conduct amounting to fraud, this does not entitle defendant to judgment as a matter of law, since under Virginia law, one may be estopped to plead the bar of a statute of limitations by conduct short of fraud, under the general doctrine of equitable estoppel. Under that doctrine, estoppel occurs where the aggrieved party reasonably relied on the words and conduct of the person to be estopped in allowing the limitations period to expire. Barry v. Donnelly, 781 F.2d 1040 (4th Cir. 1986).

Summary judgment where state of mind is at issue. — Courts should be particularly circumspect when considering summary judgment in a case where state of mind is at issue, but this rule permits summary judgment in any case, depending on the circumstances. Where there is no probative evidence of material facts creating a genuine issue, summary judgment is proper no matter what the issue. Therefore, even though state of mind is at issue, a summary judgment may be proper. Via v. City of Richmond, 543 F. Supp. 382 (E.D. Va. 1982).

Where states of mind are decisive as elements of a claim or defense, summary judgment ordinarily will not lie. Overstreet v. Kentucky Cent. Life Ins. Co., 950 F.2d 931 (4th Cir. 1991).

Summary judgment is seldom appropriate in cases in which particular states of mind are decisive elements of a claim. Unlimited Screw Prods., Inc. v. Malm, 781 F. Supp. 1121 (E.D. Va. 1991).

Even if a policy be adopted of not granting summary judgment when state of mind is at issue, that policy must be weighed against the policy of protecting public officials from the harassment of frivolous lawsuits. In such a case, a court may properly weigh counter-affidavits and grant summary judgment. Via v. City of Richmond, 543 F. Supp. 382 (E.D. Va. 1982).

Factual question as to parties' intent. — Where a bank applied portions of a secured loan to cover debtor's existing overdraft and claimed that the transfer was a contemporaneous exchange for new value in order to defeat the trustee's preference avoiding power, the bankruptcy court concluded that the issue required the further exploration that trial would provide, since the question involved was a factual one as to parties' intent. T.I. Swartz Clothiers, Inc. v. Union Trust Co., 15 Bankr. 590 (Bankr. E.D. Va. 1981).

Federal courts hesitate to grant summary judgment where motivation is an essential element of the alleged offense. Scallet v. Rosenblum, 911 F. Supp. 999 (W.D. Va. 1996), aff'd, 106 F.3d 391 (4th Cir.), cert. denied, 521 U.S. 1105, 117 S. Ct. 2482, 138 L. Ed. 2d 990 (1997).

Summary judgment granted against debtor who claimed purchaser should have known debtor's psychological problems. — To allow the maker of an instrument to automatically defeat a holder's summary judgment motion by the presentation of evidence of nothing more than the holder's possible knowledge of the maker's or drawer's drinking, psychological, or marital problems, would not only be contrary to the law but would subject innumerable transactions to a level of scrutiny that would have a chilling effect on the transferability of commercial paper, contrary to the general intent of the drafters of Article 3 of the UCC; thus, summary judgment was granted against debtor who claimed purchaser of instrument should have known of debtor's alleged alcohol and psychological problems. Schultz v. Wills, 126 Bankr. 489 (Bankr. E.D. Va. 1991).

Where evidence produced by defendants indicated no contract terms were negotiated and no meeting of the minds ever took place, mere arguments of plaintiff's counsel and pleadings were insufficient evidence to withstand the defendants' motion for summary judgment. Otto Wolff Handelsgesellschaft v. Sheridan Transp. Co., 800 F. Supp. 1359 (E.D. Va. 1992).

Actions pertaining to letters of credit are particularly well suited to determination by motion for summary judgment because they normally present solely legal issues relating to an exchange of documents. Petra Int'l Banking Corp. v. First Am. Bank, 758 F. Supp. 1120 (E.D. Va. 1991), aff'd sub nom. Petra Int'l Banking Corp. v. Dameron Int'l, Inc., 953 F.2d 1383 (4th Cir. 1992).

Bankruptcy court may look behind judgment. — The court has an obligation to search the entire record of the matter before it determines whether to grant summary judgment. When the issue to be determined is the dischargeability of a judgment debt, the bankruptcy court also may look behind the judgment and examine the circumstances that gave rise to the debt. Southern Fed. Sav. & Loan Ass'n v. Fellows, 22 Bankr. 40 (Bankr. E.D. Va. 1982).

Determination of whether reliance was justified. — In a case relating to violations of § 10(b) of the Securities Exchange Act of 1934, determination of whether reliance was justified was a question of law appropriate for resolution by summary judgment. Myers v. Finkle, 758 F. Supp. 1102 (E.D. Va. 1990).

Antitrust cases. — Summary judgment is an important tool for dealing with antitrust cases; in fact, the very nature of antitrust litigation encourages summary disposition of such cases when permissible. Thompson Everett, Inc. v. National Cable Adv., 850 F. Supp. 470 (E.D. Va. 1994), aff'd, 57 F.3d 1317 (4th Cir. 1995).

A party opposing summary judgment in the antitrust context must do more than simply show that there is some metaphysical doubt as to the material facts; the nonmoving party must come forward with specific facts showing that there is a genuine issue for trial. Thompson Everett, Inc. v. National Cable Adv., 850 F. Supp. 470 (E.D. Va. 1994), aff'd, 57 F.3d 1317 (4th Cir. 1995).

In an antitrust case with much complicated and detailed evidence, once the moving party has met its burden, the nonmoving party must do more than simply show that there is some metaphysical doubt as to the material facts, but must come forward with sufficient evidence favoring the nonmoving party for a jury to return a verdict for that party. If the evidence is merely colorable, or is not significantly probative, summary judgment may be granted. Advanced Health-Care Servs., Inc. v. Giles Mem. Hosp., 846 F. Supp. 488 (W.D. Va. 1994).

While Rule 56 is to be applied to antitrust cases no differently from how it is applied to other cases, that is not to say that the summary judgment device is not an appropriate and useful tool for resolving antitrust cases. On the contrary, because of the unusual entanglement of legal and factual issues frequently presented in antitrust cases, the task of sorting them out may be particularly well-suited for Rule 56 utilization. Thompson Everett, Inc. v. National Cable Adv., 57 F.3d 1317 (4th Cir. 1995).

On summary judgment motions in antitrust cases, when there is evidence of conduct that is consistent with both legitimate competition and an illegal conspiracy, courts may not infer that an illegal conspiracy has occurred without other evidence. Thompson Everett, Inc. v. National Cable Adv., 57 F.3d 1317 (4th Cir. 1995).

Summary procedures should be used sparingly in complex antitrust litigation where motive and intent play leading roles, the proof is largely in the hands of the alleged conspirators, and hostile witnesses thicken the plot. Norfolk Monument Co. v. Woodlawn Mem. Gardens, Inc., 394 U.S. 700, 89 S. Ct. 1391, 22 L. Ed. 2d 658 (1969).

The Supreme Court has cautioned that summary procedures should be used sparingly in complex antitrust litigation where motive and intent play leading roles. However, this rule is not to be read out of antitrust cases. Machovec v. Council for Nat'l Register of Health Serv. Providers in Psychology, Inc., 616 F. Supp. 258 (E.D. Va. 1985).

And are usually not appropriate in actions based on negligence. — Where the plaintiff has alleged negligence under the Federal Employers' Liability Act, it is sufficient to say that an action based on negligence is usually not an appropriate action for summary judgment. Cales v. C & O Ry., 46 F.R.D. 36 (W.D. Va. 1969).

But summary judgment is not precluded in every negligence case. Hutchens v. Janssen, 41 F.R.D. 287 (W.D. Va. 1966).

Summary judgment on a contractual claim is appropriate only where there is no ambiguity in the contract or plan, and the question of whether a contract is ambiguous is one of law, which is reviewed de novo. Denzler v. Questech, Inc., 80 F.3d 97 (4th Cir. 1996).

Libel action. — In order to defeat a motion for summary judgment, a public figure libel plaintiff must present evidence to raise a jury question over whether a defendant published a false and defamatory statement with actual malice. Church of Scientology Int'l v. Daniels, 992 F.2d 1329 (4th Cir.), cert. denied, 510 U.S. 869, 1145 S. Ct. 195, 126 L. Ed. 2d 153 (1993).

Moving party in railroad merger conflict held not entitled to judgment as matter of law. — See Swacker v. Interstate R.R., 32 F.R.D. 234 (W.D. Va. 1962).

Special agent who attested to his personal knowledge of the procedures used in handling Freedom of Information Act (FOIA) request and his familiarity with the documents in question demonstrated ample personal knowledge to render him competent to testify regarding the interference posed by disclosure for purposes of subdivision (e) of this rule. Spannaus v. United States Dep't of Justice, 813 F.2d 1285 (4th Cir. 1987).

Rule held not automatically applicable to action involving governmental secrets for proof of both plaintiff's case and certain defenses. — See Farnsworth Cannon, Inc. v. Grimes, 635 F.2d 268 (4th Cir. 1980).

Statements by I.R.S. agents held not to contain conclusions not based on personal knowledge. — In a Freedom of Information Act case, in which taxpayers and their accountant sought access to notes of an interview with I.R.S. agents, the statement provided by agents in support of the government's motion for summary judgment did not contain conclusions not based on the personal knowledge of the maker, since one agent must have known of the types of questions asked, the nature of the answers given, and the manner in which agents were required to record their conversations with appellants, and the other agent's personal knowledge was readily demonstrated by his position as head of the I.R.S.'s Criminal Investigation Division in Richmond and by his statement that he was familiar with the requests for information filed. Willard v. IRS, 776 F.2d 100 (4th Cir. 1985).

Government officials performing discretionary functions are entitled to summary judgment on qualified immunity in civil suits against them if, taking the facts in the light most favorable to the plaintiff, their conduct did not violate clearly established constitutional rights of which a reasonable person would have known. Kane v. Hargis, 987 F.2d 1005 (4th Cir. 1993).

III. BURDEN OF PROOF.

A. In General.

When moving party is entitled to judgment as matter of law. — On a motion for summary judgment, the moving party is entitled to judgment as a matter of law where the nonmoving party has failed to make a sufficient showing of an essential element of his case on which he has the burden of proof. Hicks v. Phipps, 765 F. Supp. 1541 (W.D. Va. 1990).

When opposing party has burden of coming forward with specific controverting facts. — Where on the basis of the materials presented by his affidavits, the moving party, if at trial, would be entitled to a directed verdict unless contradicted, it rests upon the opposing party at least to specify some evidence to show that such contradiction is possible. The burden of coming forward with specific controverting facts shifts to the opponent. It is his duty to expose the existence of a genuine issue which will prevent the trial from being a useless formality. Smith-Johnson Motor Corp. v. Hoffman Motors Corp., 411 F. Supp. 670 (E.D. Va. 1975).

The party bearing the burden of proof on an issue at trial also is required to produce some quantum of evidence at the summary judgment stage. Where that party is the nonmovant, evidence sufficient to support a finding must be adduced to avoid entry of summary judgment. Thompson v. Kings Entertainment Co., 674 F. Supp. 1194 (E.D. Va. 1987).

On motion for summary judgment, the question to be resolved by the court is whether any triable issues of fact exist. Should such factual issues exist, it is not the duty of the court to resolve them at that stage of the proceedings. However, when a motion for summary judgment is made and supported with exhibits and affidavits, the adverse party may not rest upon the mere allegations or denials of his pleading, but his response, by affidavits or otherwise, must set forth specific facts showing that there is a genuine issue for trial. Mickles v. Lynchburg Training Sch. & Hosp., 422 F. Supp. 672 (W.D. Va. 1976).

A "genuine" issue within the scope of subdivision (c) of this rule has been variously described as a "triable," "substantial" or "real" issue of fact. A "genuine" issue is one which can be supported by substantial evidence. Clinch Valley Bank & Trust Co. v. Shortt, 16 Bankr. 813 (Bankr. W.D. Va. 1982); Richardson v. Combs, 40 Bankr. 148 (Bankr. W.D. Va. 1984), aff'd, 838 F.2d 112 (4th Cir. 1988).

An issue is a genuine one if a reasonable jury might return a verdict in favor of the nonmoving party on the basis of such issue. Pruitt v. Wilder, 840 F. Supp. 414 (E.D. Va. 1994).

Affidavits may be used to show no issue of fact. — Summary judgment procedure does not contemplate a trial by affidavits. Nevertheless, this rule authorizes the use of affidavits by both the moving and the opposing party for the purpose of establishing that there is or is not a triable issue of fact. Sage v. Celebrezze, 246 F. Supp. 285 (W.D. Va. 1965).

B. Burden of Moving Party.

Burden on party seeking summary judgment. — It is incumbent on a party seeking summary judgment to show that there is no genuine issue as to any material fact and that the party is entitled to a judgment as a matter of law. United States v. Ball, 326 F.2d 898 (4th Cir. 1964), rev'g 207 F. Supp. 835 (W.D. Va. 1962); Turner v. United States, 553 F. Supp. 347 (W.D. Va. 1982); Walker v. Winchester Mem. Hosp., 585 F. Supp. 1328 (W.D. Va. 1984); McDaniel v. Mead Corp., 622 F. Supp. 351 (W.D. Va. 1985), aff'd, 818 F.2d 861 (W.D. Va. 1987).

Party seeking summary judgment has the initial burden of informing the court of the basis for the motion and of establishing, based on relevant portions of the pleadings, depositions, answers to interrogatories, and admissions on file, together with affidavits, if any, that there is no genuine issue of material fact and that the moving party is entitled to judgment as a matter of law. Clay v. LaPorta, 815 F. Supp. 911 (E.D. Va. 1993), aff'd sub nom. Clay v. Yates, 36 F.3d 1091 (4th Cir. 1994).

In a motion for summary judgment, the initial burden of showing the absence of a genuine issue of material fact rests on the moving party. However, once a motion is made and supported, the nonmoving party must produce evidence showing a genuine issue for trial. RGI, Inc. v. Unified Indus., Inc., 963 F.2d 658 (4th Cir. 1991).

The moving party on a summary judgment motion bears the burden of demonstrating that there is no genuine dispute as to the material facts underlying a claim. The movant has a heavy burden given that the court is directed to read the evidence offered in a light most favorable to the opposing party. Frazier v. Colonial Williamsburg Found., 574 F. Supp. 318 (E.D. Va. 1983).

The burden is on the party moving for summary judgment to produce evidence which negates the opposing party's claim. Richardson v. Combs, 40 Bankr. 148 (Bankr. W.D. Va. 1984), aff'd, 838 F.2d 112 (4th Cir. 1988).

The burden of showing both the absence of a genuine issue of fact and that judgment is warranted as a matter of law is upon the moving party. Cooper v. Ingersoll Rand Co., 628 F. Supp. 1488 (W.D. Va. 1986).

The burden of proving subject matter jurisdiction on a motion to dismiss is on the plaintiff, the party asserting jurisdiction. Oram v. Dalton, 927 F. Supp 180 (E.D. Va. 1996).

Summary judgment places an affirmative burden on the plaintiff to produce concrete evidence on which a trier of fact may reach a reasonable decision; therefore, plaintiff's mere mentioning of prior incidents, without any additional evidence concerning the circumstances, was insufficient to withstand defendant's motion. Cobb v. Rector of UVA, 84 F. Supp. 2d 740 (W.D. Va. 2000).

A party moving for summary judgment is entitled to the sought relief as a matter of law where the party opposing the motion has failed to make sufficient showing of an essential element of his case on which he has the burden of proof. Continental Cas. Co. v. Town of Blacksburg, 846 F. Supp. 483 (W.D. Va. 1993).

Movants did not show that there was no genuine issue of material fact. — See Bartholomew v. Virginia Chiropractors Ass'n, 451 F. Supp. 624 (W.D. Va. 1978), rev'd on other grounds, 612 F.2d 813 (4th Cir. 1979), cert. denied, 446 U.S. 938, 100 S. Ct. 2158, 64 L. Ed. 2d 791 (1980).

Summary judgment movant need not negate his opponent's case; he need only disclose the absence of evidence to support that case. Otto Wolff Handelsgesellschaft v. Sheridan Transp. Co., 800 F. Supp. 1359 (E.D. Va. 1992).

C. Burden of Nonmoving Party.

The burden on the nonmoving party is not a heavy one. He need only demonstrate the existence of specific facts, as opposed to general allegations, that present to the court a genuine issue of material fact. T.I. Swartz Clothiers, Inc. v. Union Trust Co., 15 Bankr. 590 (Bankr. E.D. Va. 1981); Clinch Valley Bank & Trust Co. v. Shortt, 16 Bankr. 813 (Bankr. W.D. Va. 1982); Southern Fed. Sav. & Loan Ass'n v. Fellows, 22 Bankr. 40 (Bankr. E.D. Va. 1982); Richardson v. Combs, 40 Bankr. 148 (Bankr. W.D. Va. 1984), aff'd, 838 F.2d 112 (4th Cir. 1988).

Non-moving party must timely respond. — The non-moving party on a motion for summary judgment may not sit idly by as the deadline to respond approaches; instead, the non-moving party must timely respond to the motion once the moving party has satisfied its initial burden. Nguyen v. CNA Corp., 44 F.3d 234 (4th Cir. 1995).

Issue of material fact on an essential element must be introduced. — To avoid summary judgment, the nonmoving party must introduce evidence to create an issue of material fact on an element essential to the party's case, and on which that party will bear the burden of proof at trial. Olivo v. Mapp. 838 F. Supp. 259, (E.D. Va. 1993).

Party opposing summary judgment must come forward with evidence to show that a genuine issue of material fact exists. Sprague & Henwood v. Johnson, 606 F. Supp. 1564 (W.D. Va. 1985).

The non-moving party must go beyond the pleadings and, by citing its own affidavits or by citing depositions, answers to interrogatories, and admissions on file, designate specific facts showing that there is a genuine issue for trial. Amato v. City of Richmond, 875 F. Supp. 1124 (E.D. Va. 1994), aff'd, 78 F.3d 578 (4th Cir.), cert. denied, 519 U.S. 862, 117 S. Ct. 167, 136 L. Ed. 2d 109 (1996).

Party opposing a properly supported motion for summary judgment may not rest upon mere allegations in his pleading but must set forth specific facts that show there is a genuine issue for trial. Continental Cas. Co. v. Town of Blacksburg, 846 F. Supp. 483 (W.D. Va. 1993).

Nonmoving party must do more than simply show some metaphysical doubt as to material facts. — In summary judgment motion, nonmoving party must do more than simply show that there is some metaphysical doubt as to the material facts; that party must demonstrate that there is a genuine issue for trial. Clay v. LaPorta, 815 F. Supp. 911 (E.D. Va. 1993), aff'd sub nom. Clay v. Yates, 36 F.3d 1091 (4th Cir. 1994).

Issue of fact cannot be created by mere speculation. — The nonmoving party cannot create a genuine issue of material fact through mere speculation or the building of one inference upon another. Beale v. Hardy, 769 F.2d 213 (4th Cir. 1985); Collins v. Allied-Signal, Inc., 128 F.R.D. 643 (E.D. Va.), aff'd, 889 F.2d 1084 (4th Cir. 1989).

Mere assertion that genuine issue exists is insufficient. — The burden on the party opposing the motion to show the existence of a factual dispute is not fulfilled merely by asserting that a genuine issue exists for trial. Cooper v. Ingersoll Rand Co., 628 F. Supp. 1488 (W.D. Va. 1986).

Mere general allegations will not prevent the award of summary judgment. Johnson v. McKee Baking Co., 398 F. Supp. 201 (W.D. Va. 1975), aff'd, 532 F.2d 750 (4th Cir. 1976).

Mere existence of some alleged factual dispute between the parties will not defeat an otherwise properly supported motion for summary judgment; the requirement is that there be no genuine issue of material fact. Lewis v. First Nat'l Bank, 645 F. Supp. 1499 (W.D. Va. 1986), aff'd, 818 F.2d 861 (W.D. Va. 1987); Aliff v. Travelers Ins. Co., 734 F. Supp. 232 (W.D. Va. 1990).

Purpose of subdivision (e). — The portion of subdivision (e) which provides that a party may not rest upon the mere allegations or denials of his pleading was added for the express purpose of overruling the doctrine that well-pleaded claims and defenses were invulnerable to attack by a motion for summary judgment. Johnson v. McKee Baking Co., 398 F. Supp. 201 (W.D. Va. 1975), aff'd, 532 F.2d 750 (4th Cir. 1976).

Subdivision (e) makes it clear that a party cannot rest on the allegations in his complaint in opposition to a properly supported summary judgment motion made against him. Smith-Johnson Motor Corp. v. Hoffman Motors Corp., 411 F. Supp. 670 (E.D. Va. 1975).

In order to resist a motion for summary judgment, plaintiffs cannot rest on the allegations in their complaint, but must counter the evidence produced by the defendants. McDaniel v. Mead Corp., 622 F. Supp. 351 (W.D. Va. 1985), aff'd, 818 F.2d 861 (W.D. Va. 1987).

When a motion for summary judgment is made and supported as provided in this rule, an adverse party may not rest upon the mere allegations or denials of his pleading, but his response, by affidavits or as otherwise provided in this rule, must set forth specific facts showing that there is a genuine issue for trial. If he does not so respond, summary judgment, if appropriate, shall be entered against him. White v. Boyle, 538 F.2d 1077 (4th Cir. 1976), aff'g 390 F. Supp. 514 (W.D. Va. 1975); Matney v. First Protection Life Ins. Co., 73 F.R.D. 696 (W.D. Va. 1977).

The nonmoving party cannot rest on the bald assertions of her pleadings, but must point to specific facts establishing her essential elements. Subdivision (e) therefore requires the nonmoving party to go beyond the pleadings and by her own affidavits, or by the depositions, answers to interrogatories, and admissions on file, designate specific facts showing that there is a genuine issue for trial. Pennsylvania Life Ins. Co. v. Bumbrey, 665 F. Supp. 1190 (E.D. Va. 1987).

Response stating that defendant's facts would be refuted at trial insufficient. — In response to the Rule 56 motion, plaintiff asserted that the facts shown by defendants in support of their summary judgment motion would be refuted at trial. Such a response is insufficient under subdivision (e). Lykins v. Attorney Gen. of United States, 86 F.R.D. 318 (E.D. Va. 1980).

Nonmoving party must introduce evidence beyond mere pleadings. — To avoid entry of summary judgment, the nonmoving party must introduce evidence beyond the mere pleadings to create an issue of material fact on an element essential to that party's case, and on which that party will bear the burden of proof at trial. Unlimited Screw Prods., Inc. v. Malm, 781 F. Supp. 1121 (E.D. Va. 1991); Mayfield v. City of Va. Beach, 780 F. Supp. 1082 (E.D. Va. 1992).

Opportunity to discover. — The requirement that the non-moving party respond specifically to a summary judgment motion is qualified by subdivision (f)'s requirement that summary judgment be refused where the nonmoving party has not had the opportunity to discover information that is essential to his opposition. Nguyen v. CNA Corp., 44 F.3d 234 (4th Cir. 1995).

A party may not simply assert in its brief that discovery was necessary and thereby overturn summary judgment when it failed to comply with the requirement of subdivision (f) to set out reasons for the need for discovery in an affidavit. Nguyen v. CNA Corp., 44 F.3d 234 (4th Cir. 1995).

Petitioner failed to satisfy burden to file responsive material after defendant's summary judgment motion where he relied only on the allegations in his complaint, affidavit, and grievance form that his hand was, on occasions, still swollen and painful and the bare allegation, for which there is likewise no record support, that he suffered psychological harm as a consequence of the incident. Norman v. Taylor, 25 F.3d 1259 (4th Cir. 1994), cert. denied, 513 U.S. 1114, 115 S. Ct. 909, 130 L. Ed. 2d 791 (1995).

Genuine issue of material fact held to exist. — See White v. City of Suffolk, 460 F. Supp. 516 (E.D. Va. 1978).

Genuine issue as to material fact precluding summary judgment. — See Bartholomew v. Virginia Chiropractors Ass'n, 451 F. Supp. 624 (W.D. Va. 1978), rev'd on other grounds, 612 F.2d 812 (4th

Cir. 1979), cert. denied, 446 U.S. 938, 100 S. Ct. 2158, 64 L. Ed. 2d 791 (1980); White v. City of Suffolk, 460 F. Supp. 516 (E.D. Va. 1978).

Genuine issue held to exist as to matter of defense. — See Cales v. C & O Ry., 46 F.R.D. 36 (W.D. Va. 1969).

And as to damages. — Plaintiff's motion for summary judgment cannot be granted because a material fact, the question of the damages he has sustained, is put in issue by the defendant's motion papers. We do not read the defendant's reference to a settlement proposal (defendant's memorandum filed August 14, 1969, at 4, note 3) to constitute an admission of liability. Other language in the same document put the amount of damages directly in issue. The extent of plaintiff's damage will have to be decided on evidence presented at trial. Marsh v. United States, 48 F.R.D. 315 (W.D. Va. 1969).

No genuine issue as to any material fact. — See Jarrett v. Norfolk Redevelopment & Hous. Auth., 74 F. Supp. 585 (E.D. Va. 1947), aff'd, 169 F.2d 409 (4th Cir.), cert. denied, 335 U.S. 886, 69 S. Ct. 238, 93 L. Ed. 425 (1948).

IV. EVIDENCE CONSIDERED.

A. In General.

In ruling on a motion for summary judgment, the court should consider, in addition to the pleadings, all papers of record such as affidavits, answers to interrogatories, admissions and stipulations, documentary and other evidentiary materials, and facts subject to judicial notice, as well as any materials prepared in support of the motion. Evans v. Sturgill, 430 F. Supp. 1209 (W.D. Va. 1977).

A motion for summary judgment may only be granted if the pleadings, depositions, answers to interrogatories and admissions on file, together with the affidavits, if any, show that there is no genuine issue as to any material fact. Powers v. Sims & Levin Realtors, 396 F. Supp. 12 (E.D. Va. 1975), rev'd on other grounds, 542 F.2d 1216 (4th Cir. 1976).

A verified complaint based on personal knowledge serves as the equivalent of an opposing affidavit for the purposes of summary judgment. Boyce v. Fleet Fin., Inc., 802 F. Supp. 1404 (E.D. Va. 1992).

Summary judgment is appropriate if the evidence is merely colorable or is not significantly probative. Amato v. City of Richmond, 875 F. Supp. 1124 (E.D. Va. 1994), aff'd, 78 F.3d 578 (4th Cir.), cert. denied, 519 U.S. 862, 117 S. Ct. 167, 136 L. Ed. 2d 109 (1996).

Where plaintiff's evidence was too insubstantial and speculative to generate an issue of material fact and he presented no evidence that defendant's knew of his political affiliation, defendants were entitled to summary judgment on the First Amendment claim. Pignato v. Virginia Dep't of Envtl. Quality, 948 F. Supp. 532 (E.D. Va 1996).

The court has an obligation to search the entire record, including pleadings, depositions, affidavits, answers to interrogatories and admissions before determining whether to grant summary judgment. Docter, Docter & Salus v. United States (In re Abingdon Realty Corp.), 21 Bankr. 290 (Bankr. E.D. Va. 1982); Richardson v. Combs, 40 Bankr. 148 (Bankr. W.D. Va. 1984), aff'd, 838 F.2d 112 (4th Cir. 1988).

Where a review of opposing documents revealed that the plaintiff supplied factual information as to its business dealings, whereas defendant submitted affidavits based merely on information and belief, there was no issue as to the facts declared by plaintiff, and a motion for summary judgment could be granted. United States ex rel. Acme Limestone Co. v. United States Fid. & Guar. Co., 69 F.R.D. 306 (W.D. Va. 1975).

Court may look to any evidential source to determine if there is issue of fact. — Generally, on a motion for summary judgment, the court is not authorized to try issues of fact, but it does have the power to penetrate allegations of facts in the pleadings and look to any evidential source to determine whether there is an issue of fact to be tried. Cales v. C & O Ry., 46 F.R.D. 36 (W.D. Va. 1969).

Inadmissible evidence. — Inadmissible evidence fails to establish a genuine issue of material fact. West Va. ex rel. West Virginia ex rel. McGraw v. Meadow Gold Dairies, Inc., 875 F. Supp. 340 (W.D. Va. 1994).

For evidence to be properly considered in a summary judgment motion, it must be admissible at trial. Supermarket of Marlinton, Inc. v. Meadow Gold Dairies, Inc., 874 F. Supp. 721 (W.D. Va. 1994), rev'd, 71 F.3d 119 (4th Cir. 1995).

Documents filed are to be used to determine the existence of fact issues, not to decide facts. — See Stanback v. Parke, Davis & Co., 502 F. Supp. 767 (W.D. Va. 1980), aff'd, 657 F.2d 642 (4th Cir. 1981).

Unsworn, unauthenticated documents cannot be considered on a motion for summary judgment; to be admissible at the summary judgment stage, documents must be authenticated by and attached to an affidavit that meets the requirements of subdivision (e) of this rule. Orsi v. Kirkwood, 999 F.2d 86 (4th Cir. 1993).

Where a document has not been authenticated, its contents are unverified hearsay; therefore the document cannot constitute admissible evidence, and it cannot assist the plaintiff in avoiding summary judgment. Jones v. Navix Line, Ltd., 944 F. Supp. 468 (E.D. Va. 1996).

Although the defense of good faith and probable cause in a civil rights action is an affirmative defense which may be properly raised before a jury, summary judgment may be rendered if pleadings and affidavits show that there is no genuine issue as to any material fact and the moving party is entitled to a judgment as a matter of law. Kipps v. Ewell, 538 F.2d 564 (4th Cir. 1976), aff'g 391 F. Supp. 1285 (W.D. Va. 1975).

This rule applies when the magistrate conducts a hearing on a motion for summary judgment. Thus, a party may not "hold back" in the proceeding before the magistrate, hoping to submit additional affidavits or exhibits to the district judge in objection to the magistrate's determination. Callas v. Trane CAC, Inc., 776 F. Supp. 1117 (W.D. Va. 1990).

Unsupported argument of counsel in pleadings cannot preclude the entry of summary judgment because they fail to meet the evidentiary standard necessary to create a genuine issue of material fact. Parkerson v. Federal Home Life Ins. Co., 797 F. Supp. 1308 (E.D. Va. 1992).

Evidentiary ruling under FRCP 72. — Magistrate judge's ruling on defendants' motion in limine could not be analogized to a motion for summary judgment where the subject of the motion in limine was the admissibility of evidence. A motion for summary judgment requires that the court determine that there is no genuine issue as to any material fact and that the moving party is entitled to a judgment as a matter of law. In reaching the evidentiary issue, the magistrate did not make these determinations at the hearing on the motion in limine. Jesselson v. Outlet Assocs., 784 F. Supp. 1223 (E.D. Va. 1991).

Even where the evidence "had a vague aura of a politically motivated patronage firing," such allegations are not sufficient to carry the day if there is no evidence that the defendants knew of the plaintiff's political affiliation. Pignato v. Virginia Dep't of Envtl. Quality, 948 F. Supp. 532 (E.D. Va 1996).

Where the plaintiff's complaint alleged that parole board failed to furnish him with a statement of reasons for parole denials, but the defendant's parole board filed with the court copies of the four letters sent to plaintiff denying him parole, and the copies and the chairman of the parole board's affidavit were unchallenged by plaintiff as such they could have been relied upon in the defendant's motion for summary judgment. Bowring v. Chairman, Va. Parole Bd., 436 F. Supp. 339 (W.D. Va. 1977), aff'd, 573 F.2d 1304 (4th Cir. 1978).

B. Affidavits.

Affidavits may be used to show no issue of fact. — Summary judgment procedure does not contemplate a trial by affidavits. Nevertheless, this rule authorizes the use of affidavits by both the moving and the opposing party for the purpose of establishing that there is or is not a triable issue of fact. Sage v. Celebrezze, 246 F. Supp. 285 (W.D. Va. 1965).

But are useless where there can be no such issue. — See Sage v. Celebrezze, 246 F. Supp. 285 (W.D. Va. 1965).

As in review of administrative order. — See Sage v. Celebrezze, 246 F. Supp. 285 (W.D. Va. 1965).

Under this rule, statements in affidavits as to opinion or belief are of no effect. Saunders v. Sumner, 366 F. Supp. 217 (W.D. Va. 1973).

Response must set forth specific facts. — This rule provides that the judgment sought shall be rendered forthwith if the pleadings and affidavits show there is no genuine issue. The rule provides that the affidavits shall be made on personal knowledge, shall set forth facts which would be admissible in evidence, and shall show affirmatively affiant is competent to testify as to the matters stated therein, and that when a motion is supported as provided in the rule, the adverse party "may not rest upon the mere allegations or denials of his pleading," but his response, by affidavit, or as otherwise provided in the rule, must set forth specific facts. Raynor v. Burroughs Corp., 294 F. Supp. 238 (E.D. Va. 1968).

Failure of opposing party to file counter-affidavits may be waiver. — Failure of a litigant opposing summary judgment to file counter-affidavits may be treated as a conscious waiver. Failure of such litigant, who was an attorney, to conduct any discovery or submit any opposing affidavits in either of his cases, given the time available and the continuances granted, could only be viewed as a waiver of such rights. Morrissey v. William Morrow & Co., 739 F.2d 962 (4th Cir. 1984), cert. denied, 469 U.S. 1216, 105 S. Ct. 1194, 84 L. Ed. 2d 340 (1985).

A verified complaint based on personal knowledge serves as the equivalent of an opposing affidavit for the purposes of summary judgment. Jackson Hewitt, Inc. v. Greene, 865 F. Supp. 1199 (E.D. Va. 1994).

General allegations of opposing affidavit are insufficient. — Subdivision (e), as amended in 1963, deprives a party opposing a motion for summary judgment of the right to stand upon the general allegations of an opposing affidavit. Boddie v. Weakley, 356 F.2d 242 (4th Cir. 1966).

Summary judgment is not inappropriate in age and gender discrimination cases merely because they involve issues of intent and motive. In order to resist a motion for summary judgment, the plaintiff cannot rest on the allegations in his complaint, but must counter the evidence produced by the defendants. Edwards v. Norfolk S. Corp., 872 F. Supp. 277 (W.D. Va.), aff'd, 42 F.3d 1385 (4th Cir. 1994).

Request for discovery need not be a sworn affidavit. — The request for discovery under subdivision (f) of this rule need not be in the form of a sworn affidavit as long as the court is made aware, by outstanding discovery request or other filings with the court, of the need for more discovery. Shortt v. Richlands Mall Assocs., 781 F. Supp. 454 (W.D. Va. 1991).

The onerous and expensive burden of conducting discovery abroad does not relieve a party of the requirement to submit affidavits setting forth specific facts to show that there is a genuine issue for trial. Pelphrey v. United States, 674 F.2d 243 (4th Cir. 1982).

C. Other Evidence.

Motion based solely on pleadings is not functionally different from motion for judgment thereon. — If the motion for summary judgment is based solely on the pleadings, as it may be, then there is no functional difference between that motion and a motion for judgment on the pleadings. Marsh v. United States, 48 F.R.D. 315 (W.D. Va. 1969).

Summary judgment may be awarded on pleadings alone. — Although neither party has submitted affidavits of the type contemplated by this rule, it is proper for a motion for summary judgment to be decided on the basis of the pleadings alone. Marsh v. United States, 48 F.R.D. 315 (W.D. Va. 1969).

Unless allegations show factual dispute. — Allegations in opposing pleadings which show that a factual dispute exists will prevent the award of summary judgment so long as neither side supports its position with affidavits. Marsh v. United States, 48 F.R.D. 315 (W.D. Va. 1969).

Certified court records may be considered. — An objection to the introduction or consideration of certified state court records on the ground that this rule limits the supporting material to affidavits and that court records are not affidavits and not such matter as is contemplated by the rule, is not well taken. Farm Bureau Mut. Ins. Co. v. Hammer, 83 F. Supp. 383 (W.D. Va.), rev'd on other grounds, 177 F.2d 793 (4th Cir. 1949), cert. denied, 339 U.S. 914, 70 S. Ct. 575, 94 L. Ed. 1339 (1950).

Court has discretion to receive supplemental material under subdivision (e). — Subdivision (e) allows the trial court in its discretion to receive supplemental material in support of or in opposition to a motion for summary judgment before ruling on the motion; the underlying purpose of the rule is to assist the court in its deliberation on the summary judgment motion. That purpose would be undercut if the rule were construed to require the court to accept further affidavits after it had already ruled on the motion for summary judgment. RGI, Inc. v. Unified Indus., Inc., 963 F.2d 658 (4th Cir. 1991).

Court has discretion in accepting new evidence under Rule 59. — Under Rule 59 the district court, in its discretion, can accept new evidence if it determines that the moving party's failure to provide the new evidence along with its summary judgment motion was justified. RGI, Inc. v. Unified Indus., Inc., 963 F.2d 658 (4th Cir. 1991).

V. CONSTRUCTION OF EVIDENCE.

Evidence viewed in light most favorable to party opposing motion. — Before summary judgment is granted, the moving party must show that there is no genuine issue as to any material fact, and all pleadings and supporting papers must be viewed in the light most favorable to the party opposing the motion. Greear v. Loving, 538 F.2d 578 (4th Cir. 1976) vacating and remanding 391 F. Supp. 1269 (W.D. Va. 1975); Palmer v. Norfolk & W. Ry., 646 F. Supp. 610 (W.D. Va. 1985).

In passing on a motion for summary judgment, the court must view the facts in the light most favorable to the resisting party and give to that party the benefit of reasonable inferences to be drawn from the underlying facts. Any doubts by the court concerning the existence of a disputed material fact must be resolved against the movant. Southern Fed. Sav. & Loan Ass'n v. Fellows, 22 Bankr. 40 (Bankr. E.D. Va. 1982).

In considering a motion for summary judgment, the court should draw all inferences from the underlying facts in a light most favorable to the nonmoving party. CaterCorp, Inc. v. Henicheck, 186 Bankr. 211 (Bankr. E.D. Va. 1995).

Facts asserted by opposing party taken as true. — Those facts asserted by the party opposing the motion which are supported by affidavits or other evidentiary material must be regarded as true. Richardson v. Combs, 40 Bankr. 148 (Bankr. W.D. Va. 1984), aff'd, 838 F.2d 112 (4th Cir. 1988).

In determining whether a showing of a genuine issue of material fact has been made, the nonmoving party is entitled to have the credibility of his evidence as forecast assumed, his version of all that is in dispute accepted, all internal conflicts in it resolved favorably to him, the most favorable of possible alternative inferences from it drawn in his behalf; and finally, to be given the benefit of all favorable legal theories invoked by the evidence so considered. Pennsylvania Life Ins. Co. v. Bumbrey, 665 F. Supp. 1190 (E.D. Va. 1987).

The inferences to be drawn from the facts contained in the record must be viewed in a light more favorable to the party opposing the motion. Cooper v. Ingersoll Rand Co., 628 F. Supp. 1488 (W.D. Va. 1986).

The court, in passing upon a motion for summary judgment, must view the facts in the light most favorable to the party opposing the motion and give to that party the benefit of reasonable inferences to be drawn from underlying facts. Richardson v. Combs, 40 Bankr. 148 (Bankr. W.D. Va. 1984), aff'd, 838 F.2d 112 (4th Cir. 1988).

The court must draw inferences most favorable to the party opposing the motion when deciding whether a showing of absence of a genuine issue of fact and that judgment is warranted as a matter of law has been made from the documentary materials before it. Furthermore, the opposing party is entitled to be given the benefit of all favorable legal theories invoked by the evidenced so considered. West v. Costen, 558 F. Supp. 564 (W.D. Va. 1983); McDaniel v. Mead Corp., 622 F. Supp. 351 (W.D. Va. 1985), aff'd, 818 F.2d 861 (W.D. Va. 1987).

But inferences must be based on facts. — Although a party opposing a motion for summary judgment is entitled to all favorable inferences to be drawn from the evidence, such inferences must be based on facts; mere hopes or suspicions are not enough. Via v. City of Richmond, 543 F. Supp. 382 (E.D. Va. 1982).

Doubts resolved against movant. — Doubts by the court concerning the existence of a disputed material fact or inference must be resolved against the movant. Richardson v. Combs, 40 Bankr. 148 (Bankr. W.D. Va. 1984), aff'd, 838 F.2d 112 (4th Cir. 1988).

The moving party has the burden of demonstrating that there is no genuine issue of fact, and any doubt as to a dispute over material facts should be resolved against him. Davis v. City of Portsmouth, 579 F. Supp. 1205 (E.D. Va. 1983), aff'd, 742 F.2d 1448 (4th Cir. 1984).

Issue not required to be resolved conclusively in favor of party asserting it. — The issue of material fact required by subdivision (c) of this rule to be present to entitle a party to proceed to trial is not required to be resolved conclusively in favor of the party asserting its existence; rather, all that is required is that sufficient evidence supporting the claimed factual dispute be shown to require a jury, or judge to resolve the parties' differing versions of the truth at trial. Clinch Valley Bank & Trust Co. v. Shortt, 16 Bankr. 813 (Bankr. W.D. Va. 1982).

Evidence in antitrust cases. — On summary judgment motions in antitrust cases, when there is evidence of conduct that is consistent with both legitimate competition and an illegal conspiracy, courts may not infer that an illegal conspiracy has occurred without other evidence. Thompson Everett, Inc. v. National Cable Adv., 57 F.3d 1317 (4th Cir. 1995).

Case did not present "sham" issue of fact. — In a case where question was whether employee's primary duties were administrative, where employee's statements concerning leadership and substantial business development responsibilities came from applications employee prepared for the purpose of gaining admittance to business school, and where at deposition, employee affirmed the accuracy of the statements made in these applications, but stated that the applications focused on a small percentage of her duties while the bulk of her duties were mundane and menial, it is true that a party cannot oppose summary judgment by submitting an affidavit or other declaration which is in conflict with that party's other record testimony, thereby creating a "sham" issue of fact. But this case did not present a "sham" issue of fact. Instead, employee stood by all of her characterizations of duties she performed for employer, contending that the relative significance of these different duties necessarily involved the resolution of certain facts. Yuen v. United States Asia Com. Dev. Corp., 974 F. Supp. 515 (E.D. Va. 1997).

VI. FUNCTION OF TRIAL COURT.

Motion should be carefully scrutinized. — A motion for summary judgment should be scrutinized carefully in order that no litigant may be deprived of the opportunity to present proof in a proper case. Tunstall v. Brotherhood of Locomotive Firemen & Enginemen, 69 F. Supp. 826 (E.D. Va. 1946), aff'd, 163 F.2d 289 (4th Cir. 1947).

On a motion for summary judgment, the function of the federal district court is to determine if there is an issue of fact to be tried and all doubts as to the existence of a genuine issue of material fact will be resolved against the party moving for summary judgment. Thus, the burden of demonstrating that no genuine issue of material fact exists is on the party moving for summary judgment. Saunders v. Sumner, 366 F. Supp. 217 (W.D. Va. 1973).

It is clear that the burden is on the party moving for summary judgment to produce evidence which negatives the opposing party's claim. The court, in passing upon a motion for summary judgment, must view the facts in the light most favorable to the party opposing the motion and give to that party the benefit of reasonable inferences to be drawn from underlying facts. Doubts by the court concerning the existence of a disputed material fact or inference must be resolved against the movant. Clinch Valley Bank & Trust Co. v. Shortt, 16 Bankr. 813 (Bankr. W.D. Va. 1982).

And is not to be lightly granted. — Although this rule provides for summary judgment in appropriate cases, it is not to be lightly granted. However, summary judgment properly may be entered when there is no genuine issue as to any material fact and the movants are entitled to judgment as a matter of law. Southern Fed. Sav. & Loan Ass'n v. Fellows, 22 Bankr. 40 (Bankr. E.D. Va. 1982).

Standard of proof. — The inquiry involved in a ruling on a motion for summay judgment necessarily implicates the substantive evidentiary standard of proof that would apply at the trial on the merits. Petra Int'l Banking Corp. v. First Am. Bank, 758 F. Supp. 1120 (E.D. Va. 1991), aff'd sub nom. Petra Int'l Banking Corp. v. Dameron Int'l, Inc., 953 F.2d 1383 (4th Cir. 1992).

Court must establish which facts are "material." — In determining whether to grant summary judgment, a court must first establish those facts in the case which are "material." Material facts are defined as those facts which, by their nature, tend to prove or disprove elements of a disputed claim for relief. After this preliminary statement, the court must then go beyond and behind the pleadings to find whether issues as to those facts, if any, are genuine. Clinch Valley Bank & Trust Co. v. Shortt, 16 Bankr. 813 (Bankr. W.D. Va. 1982); Richardson v. Combs, 40 Bankr. 148 (Bankr. W.D. Va. 1984), aff'd, 838 F.2d 112 (4th Cir. 1988).

Genuineness and materiality of issues. — The court "must perform a dual inquiry into the genuineness and materiality of any purported factual issues." Drewitt v. Pratt, 999 F.2d 774 (4th Cir. 1993).

Showing of moving party's strong position is not enough. — It is not necessary that the plaintiff come forward with evidence in the form of affidavits or depositions to withstand a motion for summary judgment unless the moving party or parties have shown by their motion and the support thereof that the plaintiff's case is a sham. It is not enough that the record may reveal a strong position on the part of the moving party. The court's task is not to determine a factual issue as presented in the documents before the court, but to determine whether a factual issue exists. The court's task does not include the weighing of evidence. Cales v. C & O Ry., 46 F.R.D. 36 (W.D. Va. 1969).

The district court's function is not to weigh the evidence and determine the truth of the matter but to determine whether there is a genuine issue for trial. Unlimited Screw Prods., Inc. v. Malm, 781 F. Supp. 1121 (E.D. Va. 1991).

VII. APPELLATE REVIEW.

In reviewing a district court's grant of summary judgment, court of appeals applies the same standard as the district court used below. United States v. Ringley, 985 F.2d 185 (4th Cir. 1993).

Appeal. — Where the plaintiff's complaint is dismissed upon the defendant's motion for summary judgment, all issues of fact appearing from the record are, for the purpose of his appeal, resolved in favor of the plaintiff. W.N. Clark Co. v. Miller Mfg. Co., 224 F.2d 660 (4th Cir. 1955).

The circuit court will not review, under any standard, the pretrial denial of a motion for summary judgment after a full trial and final judgment on the merits. Chesapeake Paper Prods. Co. v. Stone & Webster Eng'g Corp., 51 F.3d 1229 (4th Cir. 1995).

Findings on summary judgment. — On summary judgment, findings of the trial court serve as a determination that a particular fact is not genuinely in dispute. Although such findings are not required on a summary judgment ruling, they are extremely helpful to a reviewing court. The court of appeals does not accord such findings the full measure of deference due after trial. To do so would intrude on the sphere reserved for the ultimate trier of fact. Recent cases of the Supreme Court have made increasingly clear, however, the affirmative obligation of the trial judge to prevent "factually unsupported claims and defenses" from proceeding to trial. Trial court findings are consistent with the role for summary judgment elaborated by the Supreme Court. At a minimum, findings of fact upon summary judgment afford the court of appeals both a surer basis for appellate review and an indication of the care with which the summary judgment record was handled by the district court. Felty v. Graves-Humphreys Co., 818 F.2d 1126 (4th Cir. 1987).

Record must establish affirmatively that adverse party cannot prevail. — The Fourth Circuit has explicitly indicated that, unless the entire record shows a right to judgment with such clarity as to leave no room for controversy and establishes affirmatively that the adverse party cannot prevail under any circumstances, summary judgment should not be granted. Clinch Valley Bank & Trust Co. v. Shortt, 16 Bankr. 813 (Bankr. W.D. Va. 1982).

Review of denial of motion. — In reviewing the district court's denial of a motion for summary judgment, the court of appeals must apply the same standards that guided the district court in making its original decisions on that motion. Consequently, it must assess the evidence in the documentary materials before the district court in the light most favorable to the party opposing the motion in order to determine whether the moving party has carried its burden to establish that there is no genuine issue as to any material fact and that the moving party is entitled to judgment as a matter of law. Gill v. Rollins Protective Servs. Co., 773 F.2d 592 (4th Cir. 1985), modified, 788 F.2d 1042 (4th Cir. 1986).

Court of appeals need not consider defenses not passed upon. — Where, in granting defendant's motion for summary judgment, the district court found it unnecessary to pass upon two defenses, there was no occasion for the court of appeals to consider them on affirming the judgment. Booth v. State Farm Mut. Auto. Ins. Co., 138 F.2d 844 (4th Cir.), cert. denied, 321 U.S. 783, 64 S. Ct. 637, 88 L. Ed. 1075 (1943).

Grant of summary judgment on pleadings held error. — Where a liberal construction of plaintiff's pro se complaint required that the judge view all of the allegations not as isolated incidents, but rather as a unit, the grant of summary judgment on the pleadings was error because there clearly was a substantial issue of material fact raised by the pro se complaint. Russell v. Oliver, 552 F.2d 115 (4th Cir. 1977), aff'g in part, vacating in part, 392 F. Supp. 470 (W.D. Va. 1975).

VIII. PLEADING AND PRACTICE.

Procedural requirements must be satisfied before motion granted. — If a Rule 56 motion is to be granted at or before trial, its procedural requirements must be satisfied. These are that the party against whom summary judgment is sought should have ten days' notice before a hearing on the motion and that he should have the right to file affidavits prior to the date of hearing to demonstrate that there is a genuine issue as to any material fact. These procedural protections were denied where the district court did not require the defendant to have ten days' notice of the motion; the motion was received, considered and granted on a single day; the district court did not afford the defendant the opportunity to show that there was a genuine issue as to any material fact; the district court refused to permit the defendant's counsel to cross-examine the witness on whose testimony the plaintiff heavily relied, and it declined to permit the defendant's counsel to adduce his other proofs. Utility Control Corp. v. Prince William Constr. Co., 558 F.2d 716 (4th Cir. 1977).

Procedural standard of dismissal. — The differing procedural standards of dismissal under Rule 12(b)(1) and summary judgment under Rule 56(c) are more than academic. Williams v. United States, 50 F.3d 299 (4th Cir. 1995).

Rule does not provide limited time to party opposing motion. It requires at least 10 days' notice by the movant, but states: "The adverse party prior to the day of hearing may serve opposing affidavits." Morrissey v. William Morrow & Co., 739 F.2d 962 (4th Cir. 1984), cert. denied, 469 U.S. 1216, 105 S. Ct. 1194, 84 L. Ed. 2d 340 (1985).

Notice to pro se litigant of right to file affidavits and responsive material. — Once evidence has been submitted by the movant in a motion for summary judgment, it is the responsibility of the opposing party to introduce its own evidentiary material to the contrary. Plaintiffs proceeding pro se, however, are entitled to have notice of their right to file affidavits and responsive material to prevent summary judgment against them. Davis v. City of Portsmouth, 579 F. Supp. 1205 (E.D. Va. 1983), aff'd, 742 F.2d 1448 (4th Cir. 1984).

Motion not considered a responsive pleading. — For purposes of Rule 15(a), motions to dismiss and for summary judgment are not considered responsive pleadings. Williams v. Wilkerson, 90 F.R.D. 168 (E.D. Va. 1981).

The district court analyzes motions for partial summary judgment by the same standards that govern motions for full summary judgment. Boyd v. Cinmar of Gloucester, Inc., 919 F. Supp. 208 (E.D. Va. 1996).

Effect of inconsistent local rule. — Where dismissal for want of a meritorious claim is provided for by rules other than Rule 83 and that dismissal under Rule 83 for lack of a meritorious claim would be inconsistent with those other provisions, specifically, Rule 12(b) and this rule, Rule 83 could not be the basis for a dismissal of a cause of action deemed not meritorious. Brown v. Cameron-Brown Co., 652 F.2d 375 (4th Cir. 1981).

Motion continued under advisement to afford plaintiffs opportunity to conduct discovery. — Where a union defendant in an employment discrimination case contended that it was not amenable to suit in that it had been completely dissolved, and plaintiffs, in response, contended that they had not had an opportunity to verify the union's allegations, the union's summary judgment motion was continued under advisement until plaintiffs had a reasonable opportunity to conduct discovery with reference to this issue. Burwell v. Eastern Air Lines, 394 F. Supp. 1361 (E.D. Va. 1975), aff'd in part, rev'd in part, 633 F.2d 361 (4th Cir. 1980).

Pleadings without factual dispute treated as cross-motions for summary judgment. — See Seaboard Coast Line R.R. v. United States, 422 F. Supp. 177 (E.D. Va. 1976).

Motions for summary judgment treated as motions requesting judgment on pleadings. — Although both parties termed their respective motions as ones for summary judgment, since neither party had offered matters outside the pleadings and the parties stipulated to the relevant facts, the court treated the parties' motions as requesting judgment on the pleadings under Federal Rules of Civil Procedure, Rule 12 (c). Old Bridge Estates

Community Ass'n v. Lozada, 214 Bankr. 558 (Bankr. E.D. Va. 1997), aff'd, 176 F.3d 475 (4th Cir. 1999).

Rule 57. Declaratory Judgment.

These rules govern the procedure for obtaining a declaratory judgment under 28 U.S.C. § 2201. Rules 38 and 39 govern a demand for a jury trial. The existence of another adequate remedy does not preclude a declaratory judgment that is otherwise appropriate. The court may order a speedy hearing of a declaratory-judgment action. (Amended by order adopted December 29, 1948, effective October 20, 1949, and by order adopted April 30, 2007, effective December 1, 2007.)

Comment. — The language of Rule 57 has been amended as part of the general restyling of the Civil Rules to make them more easily understood and to make style and terminology consistent throughout the rules. These changes are intended to be stylistic only.

CASE NOTES

Granting declaratory relief is a matter resting in the sound discretion of the court. Piedmont Fire Ins. Piedmont Fire Ins. Co. v. Aaron, 138 F.2d 732 (4th Cir.), cert. denied, 321 U.S. 789, 64 S. Ct. 789, 88 L. Ed. 1079 (1943).

And dismissal is proper where a declaratory judgment will serve no useful purpose. Piedmont Fire Ins. Piedmont Fire Ins. Co. v. Aaron, 138 F.2d 732 (4th Cir.), cert. denied, 321 U.S. 789, 64 S. Ct. 789, 88 L. Ed. 1079 (1943).

To obtain declaratory relief, plaintiff would have had to file a separate complaint, and pursue the matter as he would any other cause of action. Plaintiff could not evade this requirement merely by couching his request in the form of a "motion." Assuming a party could seek declaratory relief in the manner attempted by the plaintiff, plaintiff could not obtain the relief he sought. The questions for which he sought declaratory judgment merely constituted preliminary issues before the court. Their resolution would fall well short of terminating the controversy between the parties. Pully v. IRS, 939 F. Supp. 429 (E.D. Va. 1996).

Insurer's liability on binder held question for jury. — The question as to whether an insurance company was liable on a binder was one for trial by jury whether arising in an action on the binder or in a suit for declaratory judgment. Piedmont Fire Ins. Co. v. Aaron, 138 F.2d 732 (4th Cir.), cert. denied, 321 U.S. 789, 64 S. Ct. 789, 88 L. Ed. 1079 (1943).

Pending action does not necessarily preclude declaratory judgment. — The pendency of another proceeding in which relief can be granted does not necessarily preclude the maintenance of a suit for declaratory judgment. Piedmont Fire Ins. Co. v. Aaron, 138 F.2d 732 (4th Cir.), cert. denied, 321 U.S. 789, 64 S. Ct. 789, 88 L. Ed. 1079 (1943).

Applied in United States v. City of Roanoke, 258 F. Supp. 415 (W.D. Va. 1966); Franklin v. Shields, 399 F. Supp. 309 (W.D. Va. 1975); Taliaferro v. Willett, 411 F. Supp. 595 (E.D. Va. 1976).

Rule 58. Entering Judgment.

(a) *Separate Document.* — Every judgment and amended judgment must be set out in a separate document, but a separate document is not required for an order disposing of a motion:

(1) for judgment under Rule 50(b);

(2) to amend or make additional findings under Rule 52(b);

(3) for attorney's fees under Rule 54;

(4) for a new trial, or to alter or amend the judgment, under Rule 59; or

(5) for relief under Rule 60.

(b) *Entering Judgment.* — (1) Without the Court's Direction. Subject to Rule 54(b) and unless the court orders otherwise, the clerk must, without awaiting the court's direction, promptly prepare, sign, and enter the judgment when:

(A) the jury returns a general verdict;

(B) the court awards only costs or a sum certain; or

(C) the court denies all relief.

(2) Court's Approval Required. Subject to Rule 54(b), the court must promptly approve the form of the judgment, which the clerk must promptly enter, when:

(A) the jury returns a special verdict or a general verdict with answers to written questions; or

(B) the court grants other relief not described in this subdivision (b).

(c) *Time of Entry.* — For purposes of these rules, judgment is entered at the following times:

(1) if a separate document is not required, when the judgment is entered in the civil docket under Rule 79(a); or

(2) if a separate document is required, when the judgment is entered in the civil docket under Rule 79(a) and the earlier of these events occurs:

(A) it is set out in a separate document; or

(B) 150 days have run from the entry in the civil docket.

(d) *Request for Entry.* — A party may request that judgment be set out in a separate document as required by Rule 58(a).

(e) *Cost or Fee Awards.* — Ordinarily, the entry of judgment may not be delayed, nor the time for appeal extended, in order to tax costs or award fees. But if a timely motion for attorney's fees is made under Rule 54(d)(2), the court may act before a notice of appeal has been filed and become effective to order that the motion have the same effect under Federal Rule of Appellate Procedure 4(a)(4) as a timely motion under Rule 59. (Amended by order adopted December 27, 1946, effective March 19, 1948, by order adopted January 21, 1963, effective July 1, 1963, by order adopted April 22, 1993, effective December 1, 1993, by order adopted April 29, 2002, effective December 1, 2002, and by order adopted April 30, 2007, effective December 1, 2007.)

Comment. — The language of Rule 58 has been amended as part of the general restyling of the Civil Rules to make them more easily understood and to make style and terminology consistent throughout the rules. These changes are intended to be stylistic only.

CASE NOTES

Purpose of rule is the protection of an appellant from dismissal of his appeal for untimeliness; when the application of the rule does not serve this purpose, it is unnecessary to abort an appeal because of noncompliance with the rule. Hummer v. Dalton, 657 F.2d 621 (4th Cir. 1981).

The purpose of this rule is to clarify when the time for taking an appeal begins to run, since the parties have only 30 days from the entry of judgment in which to file a notice of appeal with the district court. Hughes v. Halifax County Sch. Bd., 823 F.2d 832 (4th Cir. 1987), cert. denied, 488 U.S. 1042, 109 S. Ct. 867, 102 L. Ed. 2d 991 (1989).

Entry of judgment for purposes of notice of appeal. — A notice of appeal must be filed within 30 days of entry of judgment. Entry of judgment consists of two steps: Creation of a document setting out the judgment and a notation of the document on the docket sheet. The 30-day period does not begin to run until after the document is entered on the docket sheet. Wilson v. Murray, 806 F.2d 1232 (4th Cir. 1986), cert. denied, 484 U.S. 870, 108 S. Ct. 197, 98 L. Ed. 2d 149 (1987).

The better procedure is to set forth the decision in a separate document called a judgment. Hummer v. Dalton, 657 F.2d 621 (4th Cir. 1981).

"Judgment" includes any order, such as one dismissing a case for lack of jurisdiction, from which an appeal lies. Caperton v. Beatrice Pocahontas Coal Co., 585 F.2d 683 (4th Cir. 1978).

Primary purpose for defining "entry" is to eliminate uncertainties as to when the time for taking an appeal begins to run. Caperton v. Beatrice Pocahontas Coal Co., 585 F.2d 683 (4th Cir. 1978).

Purpose of requirement that every judgment be set forth on separate document. — The requirement of this rule that every judgment be set forth on a separate document was designed to alleviate the problems that arise when a district court opinion includes seemingly dispositive language, which may or may not constitute an entry of judgment that triggers the 30-day period for filing an appeal. Hughes v. Halifax County Sch. Bd., 823 F.2d 832 (4th Cir. 1987), cert. denied, 488 U.S. 1042, 109 S. Ct. 867, 102 L. Ed. 2d 991 (1989).

In applying requirement of this rule that every judgment be set forth on a separate document to a given situation, the form and content of the document at issue are determinative. Hughes v. Halifax County Sch. Bd., 823 F.2d 832 (4th Cir. 1987), cert. denied, 488 U.S. 1042, 109 S. Ct. 867, 102 L. Ed. 2d 991 (1989).

Brevity is important factor in applying rule that every judgment be set forth on a separate document: an order unaccompanied by a long explanation is likely to be considered a "judgment." Hughes v. Halifax County Sch. Bd., 823 F.2d 832 (4th Cir. 1987), cert. denied, 488 U.S. 1042, 109 S. Ct. 867, 102 L. Ed. 2d 991 (1989).

Document which attempts to combine court's reasoning and its final disposition is not likely to be considered a "separate document" under this rule. Hughes v. Halifax County Sch. Bd., 823 F.2d 832 (4th Cir. 1987), cert. denied, 488 U.S. 1042, 109 S. Ct. 867, 102 L. Ed. 2d 991 (1989).

Order did not comply with separate document requirement of this rule, where it recited the actions factual and procedural background and reasoning for its disposition, and it could be interpreted as an opinion. Hughes v. Halifax County Sch. Bd., 823 F.2d 832 (4th Cir. 1987), cert. denied, 488 U.S. 1042, 109 S. Ct. 867, 102 L. Ed. 2d 991 (1989).

Separate document requirement held not waived. — The separate document requirement was not waived, where the plaintiff filed a motion for entry of judgment, clearly indicating that he did not view the district court's order as its final judgment. Hughes v. Halifax County Sch. Bd., 823 F.2d 832 (4th Cir. 1987), cert. denied, 488 U.S. 1042, 109 S. Ct. 867, 102 L. Ed. 2d 991 (1989).

Absence of separate document not precluding review of merits where parties treat order as validly entered. Caperton v. Beatrice Pocahontas Coal Co., 585 F.2d 683 (4th Cir. 1978).

Delay in seeking entry of judgment held not prejudicial. — The fact that plaintiffs did not seek the entry of a final judgment immediately upon defendant's failure to perform her obligation under a settlement agreement was not a ground for holding the judgment invalid, where defendant failed to make any showing of prejudice growing out of the delay. Hannon v. Hannon, 426 F.2d 771 (4th Cir. 1970).

Unsigned transcription of oral opinion constitutes deviation from rule. — Where no separate document, except for the unsigned transcription of the court's oral opinion, sets forth the judgment, there is a deviation from this rule. But where both parties treat the order as validly entered, the merits of the appeal may be considered. W.G. Cosby Transf. & Storage Corp. v. Froehlke, 480 F.2d 498 (4th Cir. 1973).

Procedure on motion for summary judgment. — A better procedure for handling motions for summary judgment by pro se defendants would involve, first, the issuance of a notice to the plaintiff that he could file counter-affidavits within fifteen (15) days from the date of the notice and warning him that a failure so to do may result in summary judgment, and if no counter-affidavits are filed within the required time by the plaintiff, or if he files counter-affidavits, the district court should under this procedure review the showing made by the defendants in support of the motion and any counter-affidavits filed by the plaintiff and determine from such showings whether there are any genuine issues of fact and decide the proceeding on the record, giving the parties specific notice of the time when either, if dissatisfied, may appeal. Hummer v. Dalton, 657 F.2d 621 (4th Cir. 1981).

Where the decisions of the district court were plainly intended to be "final decisions in the case," were duly recorded on the "clerk's docket," and were understood and accepted by the plaintiff as final for purposes of appeal, and the plaintiff filed a timely appeal, the reason for application of this rule is not present. Hummer v. Dalton, 657 F.2d 621 (4th Cir. 1981).

Where the plaintiff, without seeking to reply to the affidavit filed by defendants within the time allowed by the federal district court, proceeded to appeal, such action on his part constituted a waiver of any right to reply. Hummer v. Dalton, 657 F.2d 621 (4th Cir. 1981).

The federal district judge did not lose authority to direct a verdict after he had orally declared a mistrial. Even though the judge had verbally indicated that he was declaring a mistrial, he retained the power to reconsider his own actions. Marin v. Myers, 665 F.2d 57 (4th Cir. 1981), cert. denied, 456 U.S. 906, 102 S. Ct. 1752, 72 L. Ed. 2d 163 (1982).

Applied in Person v. Omni Int'l Hotel-Norfolk, 106 F.R.D. 7 (E.D. Va. 1984); United States v. Pregent, 190 F.3d 279 (4th Cir. 1999).

Rule 59. New Trial; Altering or Amending a Judgment.

(a) *In General.* — (1) Grounds for New Trial. The court may, on motion, grant a new trial on all or some of the issues — and to any party — as follows:

(A) after a jury trial, for any reason for which a new trial has heretofore been granted in an action at law in federal court; or

(B) after a nonjury trial, for any reason for which a rehearing has heretofore been granted in a suit in equity in federal court.

(2) Further Action After a Nonjury Trial. After a nonjury trial, the court may, on motion for a new trial, open the judgment if one has been entered, take additional testimony, amend findings of fact and conclusions of law or make new ones, and direct the entry of a new judgment.

(b) *Time to File a Motion for a New Trial.* — A motion for a new trial must be filed no later than 28 days after the entry of judgment.

(c) *Time to Serve Affidavits.* — When a motion for a new trial is based on affidavits, they must be filed with the motion. The opposing party has 14 days after being served to file opposing affidavits. The court may permit reply affidavits.

(d) *New Trial on the Court's Initiative or for Reasons Not in the Motion.* — No later than 28 days after the entry of judgment, the court, on its own, may order a new trial for any reason that would justify granting one on a party's motion. After giving the parties notice and an opportunity to be heard, the court may grant a timely motion for a new trial for a reason not stated in the motion. In either event, the court must specify the reasons in its order.

(e) *Motion to Alter or Amend a Judgment.* — A motion to alter or amend a judgment must be filed no later than 28 days after the entry of the judgment. (Amended by order adopted December 27, 1946, effective March 19, 1948, by order adopted February 28, 1966, effective July 1, 1966, by order adopted April 27, 1995, effective December 1, 1995, by order adopted April 30, 2007, effective December 1, 2007, and by order adopted March 26, 2009, effective December 1, 2009.)

Comment. — The language of Rule 59 has been amended as part of the general restyling of the Civil Rules to make them more easily understood and to make style and terminology consistent throughout the rules. These changes are intended to be stylistic only.

Law Review. — For essay, "Deforming the Federal Rules: An Essay on What's Wrong with the Recent Erie Decisions," see 92 Va. L. Rev. 707 (2006).

CASE NOTES

This rule, not state practice, governs granting new trials. — In action in a federal court a motion to set aside the verdict and grant a new trial was a matter of federal procedure, governed by this rule and not subject in any way to the rules of state practice. Aetna Cas. & Sur. Co. v. Yeatts, 122 F.2d 350 (4th Cir. 1941).

Motions for a new trial must comport with proper standards and meet the requirements of the rules. Robinson v. Beneficial Fin. Co., 21 Bankr. 454 (Bankr. W.D. Va. 1982).

A motion for amendment of judgment pursuant to subdivision (e), must show one of three grounds: (1) to accommodate an intervening change in controlling law; (2) to account for new evidence not available at trial; or (3) to correct a clear error of law or prevent manifest injustice. Lux v. Spotswood Constr. Loans, 176 Bankr. 416 (E.D. Va. 1993), aff'd, 43 F.3d 1467 (4th Cir. 1994).

State law standard applicable in motions alleging excessive damages. — Because the doctrine of Erie R.R. Co. v. Tompkins, 304 U.S. 64, 82 L. Ed. 1188, 58 S. Ct. 817 (1938), precludes a recovery in federal court significantly larger than the recovery that would have been tolerated in state court, a district court sitting in diversity must apply state law standards when it considers a motion for a new trial based upon the alleged excessiveness of the jury's compensatory damage award under subdivision (a) of this rule. Konkel v. Bob Evans Farms, Inc., 165 F.3d 275 (4th Cir.), cert. denied, 528 U.S. 877, 120 S. Ct. 184, 145 L. Ed. 2d 155 (1999).

The magistrate judge in diversity case was required to apply Pennsylvania law, not federal law, in determining whether the jury's $ 1,000,000 compensatory damage award in favor of plaintiff was excessive. Because the magistrate judge applied the wrong standard in testing the jury's compensatory damage award for excessiveness, a remand was required unless the court concluded that the magistrate judge would have reached the same result applying Pennsylvania law as he did applying federal law. Konkel v. Bob Evans Farms, Inc., 165 F.3d 275 (4th Cir.), cert. denied, 528 U.S. 877, 120 S. Ct. 184, 145 L. Ed. 2d 155 (1999).

Motion for new trial requires court to consider weight of evidence. — A motion under this rule is unlike a motion for judgment notwithstanding the verdict, which requires the court to view the evidence in the light most favorable to the nonmoving party and that all conflicts be resolved in that party's favor, because the motion for a new trial requires the court to consider the weight of the evidence. Lee v. Adrales, 778 F. Supp. 904 (W.D. Va. 1991).

Unlike a motion for judgment n.o.v., on review of a motion for new trial, the court is permitted to weigh the evidence and consider the credibility of witnesses. Cline v. Wal-Mart Stores, Inc., 144 F.3d 294 (4th Cir. 1998).

However, courts are not free to set aside jury verdict merely because jury could have drawn different conclusion. Nevertheless, in setting aside the verdict as contrary to the clear weight of the evidence, courts are not free to reweigh the evidence and set aside the jury verdict merely because the jury could have redrawn different inferences or conclusions or because judges feel that other results are more reasonable. Lee v. Adrales, 778 F. Supp. 904 (W.D. Va. 1991).

New trial may be granted although verdict is supported by substantial evidence. — A verdict may be set aside and new trial granted, when the verdict is contrary to the clear weight of the evidence, or whenever in the exercise of a sound discretion the trial judge thinks this action necessary to prevent a miscarriage of justice. Aetna Cas. & Sur. Co. v. Yeatts, 122 F.2d 350 (4th Cir. 1941).

It is the duty of the judge to set aside the verdict and grant a new trial, if he is of opinion that the verdict is against the clear weight of the evidence, or is based upon evidence which is false, or will result in a miscarriage of justice, even though there may be substantial evidence which would prevent the direction of a verdict. The exercise of this power is not in derogation of the right of trial by jury but is one of the historic safeguards of that right. Aetna Cas. & Sur. Co. v. Yeatts, 122 F.2d 350 (4th Cir. 1941).

In ruling upon a motion for a new trial, a trial judge has a duty to set aside a verdict and grant a new trial even though it is supported by substantial evidence, if he is of the opinion that the verdict is against the clear weight of the evidence or is based upon evidence which is false or will result in a miscarriage of justice. This standard is very different from the standard employed in granting a motion for judgment notwithstanding the verdict. Gill v. Rollins Protective Servs. Co., 773 F.2d 592 (4th Cir. 1985), modified, 788 F.2d 1042 (4th Cir. 1986).

Where there is substantial evidence in support of plaintiff's case, the judge may not direct a verdict against him, even though he may not believe his evidence or may think that the weight of the evidence is on the other side; for, under the constitutional guaranty of trial by jury, it is for the jury to weigh the evidence and pass upon its credibility. He may, however, set aside a verdict supported by substantial evidence where in his opinion it is contrary to the clear weight of the evidence, or is based upon evidence which is false; for, even though the evidence be sufficient to preclude the direction of a verdict, it is still his duty to exercise his power over the proceedings before him to prevent a miscarriage of justice. Aetna Cas. & Sur. Co. v. Yeatts, 122 F.2d 350 (4th Cir. 1941).

On a motion for a new trial on the merits under this rule, a trial court may weigh the evidence and consider the credibility of the witnesses. Indeed, a trial judge has a duty to set aside a verdict and grant a new trial even though it is supported by substantial evidence, if he is of the opinion that the verdict is against the clear weight of the evidence, or is based upon evidence which is false or will result in a miscarriage of justice. It is not necessary, however, to consider whether under the "new trial" standards the jury verdict should have been set aside as contrary to the clear weight of the evidence. For instance, the court's action granting a new trial was correct because the jury was improperly instructed on the question of liability and reached their decision under an incomplete theory of law. Wyatt v. Interstate & Ocean Transp. Co., 623 F.2d 888 (4th Cir. 1980).

A new trial will be granted if (1) The verdict is against the clear weight of the evidence, or (2) is based upon evidence which is false, (3) or will result in a miscarriage of justice, even though there may be substantial evidence which would prevent the direction of a verdict. Cline v. Wal-Mart Stores, Inc., 144 F.3d 294 (4th Cir. 1998).

The power to set aside verdicts and grant new trials ought to be exercised unflinchingly. — Aetna Cas. & Sur. Aetna Cas. & Sur. Co. v. Yeatts, 122 F.2d 350 (4th Cir. 1941).

While according due respect to the findings of the jury, a federal trial judge should not hesitate to set aside their verdict and grant a new trial in any case where the ends of justice so require. Aetna Cas. & Sur. Co. v. Yeatts, 122 F.2d 350 (4th Cir. 1941).

Substantial evidence to support jury's verdict precluding judgment n.o.v. or new trial. Solvex Corp. v. Freeman, 459 F. Supp. 440 (W.D. Va. 1977).

Unnamed motion. — Where a party submits a motion, such as defendant's to modify review system in order to permit him to maintain two pending cases at one time, which was unnamed and did not refer to a specific Federal Rule of Civil Procedure, the courts have considered that motion either a Rule 59(e) motion to alter or amend a judgment, or a Rule 60(b) motion for relief from a judgment. In this case the question of which rule applied was quickly resolved, for defendant failed to file the motion within 10 days of entry of judgment, and therefore Rule 59(e) was inapplicable. In re Burnley, 988 F.2d 1 (4th Cir. 1992).

Discretion of court to grant or deny new trial. — The granting or refusing of a new trial is a matter resting in the sound discretion of the trial judge, and his action thereon is not reviewable upon appeal, save in the most exceptional circumstances. Aetna Cas. & Sur. Co. v. Yeatts, 122 F.2d 350 (4th Cir. 1941).

The rule that the United States Supreme Court will not review the action of a federal trial court in granting or denying a motion for a new trial for error of fact has been settled by a long and unbroken line of decisions; and has been frequently applied where the ground of the motion was that the damages awarded by the jury were excessive or were inadequate. The rule precludes likewise a review of such action by a court of appeals. Aetna Cas. & Sur. Co. v. Yeatts, 122 F.2d 350 (4th Cir. 1941).

The decision whether to grant or deny a new trial is a discretionary matter with the trial court. Krodel v. Houghtaling, 468 F.2d 887 (4th Cir. 1972), cert. denied, 414 U.S. 829, 94 S. Ct. 57, 38 L. Ed. 2d 64 (1973).

The grant or denial of a motion for new trial is entrusted to the sound discretion of the district court and will be reversed on appeal only upon a showing of abuse of discretion. Cline v. Wal-Mart Stores, Inc., 144 F.3d 294 (4th Cir. 1998).

Court has discretion in accepting new evidence. — Under this rule the district court, in its discretion, can accept new evidence if it determines that the moving party's failure to provide it along with the summary judgment motions is justified. RGI, Inc. v. Unified Indus., Inc., 963 F.2d 658 (4th Cir. 1991).

Motion for new trial on ground of newly discovered evidence. — To be entitled to a new trial upon the ground of newly discovered evidence, the applicant must show that the evidence upon which he relies was in fact newly discovered or unknown to him until after the trial. Robinson v. Beneficial Fin. Co., 21 Bankr. 454 (Bankr. W.D. Va. 1982).

The standards for granting a new trial in the federal courts are clear and exacting. Where a party seeks a new trial on the basis of newly discovered evidence, he must show not only that the evidence is in fact newly discovered, but also that it is not cumulative or merely impeaching, and that its presentation at trial would probably have changed the result. He must also show that he was diligent in the investigation and presentation of his case. Garrick v. Kelly, 649 F. Supp. 607 (E.D. Va. 1986), aff'd, 842 F.2d 1290 (4th Cir. 1990).

Newly-discovered evidence must pertain to facts existing at time of trial. — Motion by defendant in medical malpractice action either to grant a new trial or to open the record to admit new evidence which motion was prompted by the death of the infant plaintiff some six weeks after the trial, on grounds that had she died before trial, the parents could not have recovered certain elements of damages, including her future medical costs, was denied. Under Rules 59 and 60(b)(2), newly discovered evidence must pertain to facts which existed at the time of trial. Were the rule otherwise, litigation would never end. Moreover, § 8.01-21 specifically provides for the entry of judgment when a party dies after the verdict. Boyd v. Bulala, 672 F. Supp. 915 (W.D. Va. 1987).

The standard for granting a new trial is lower than that for judgment as a matter of law. Freeman v. Case Corp., 924 F. Supp. 1456 (W.D. Va. 1996), rev'd on other grounds, 118 F.3d 1011 (4th Cir. 1997), cert. denied, 522 U.S. 1069, 118 S. Ct. 739, 139 L. Ed. 2d 676 (1998).

Notice of appeal period computed from entry of order granting or denying Rule 59(e) relief. — Rule 4(a), Fed. R. App. P. provides that "the notice of appeal . . . shall be filed . . . within 30 days of the date of the entry of the judgment or order appealed from." Where a timely post-judgment motion under subdivision (e) of this rule has been filed, the 30-day period is to be computed "from the entry" of the order granting or denying Rule 59(e), Fed. R. Civ. P. relief. Even the question of whether the Rule 59(e), Fed. R. Civ. P. motion is timely (and therefore capable of tolling the appeal period) depends upon when "entry" of the judgment occurred. Subdivision (a) of this rule provides that such a motion is timely only if served "not later than 10 days after entry of the judgment." Caperton v. Beatrice Pocahontas Coal Co., 585 F.2d 683 (4th Cir. 1978), aff'g 420 F. Supp. 445 (W.D. Va. 1979).

Notice of appeal exceeded maximum allowable extension. — Rule 4(a), Fed. R. App. P. requires that the notice of appeal in a civil case be filed within 30 days of the entry of the judgment from which the appeal is taken. However, where entry of judgment is followed within 10 days by service of a motion under subdivision (e) of this rule to alter or amend the judgment, the 30-day period in which to file an appeal from the judgment begins to run on the date when an order disposing of the motion is entered. Upon a showing of "excusable neglect," the trial court may grant a party additional time to appeal, not to exceed 30 days measured from the date on which the filing period would otherwise have ended. Where September 29 was the date on which the dismissals were entered, a Rule 59(e) motion would have to have been served on October 12 (allowing for a weekend and a holiday) rather than October 13 in order to be timely under subdivision (e) of this rule and to toll the running of the filing period. Since it was not, the plaintiffs had only until October 29 (the 30th day following September 29) to perfect appeals from the dismissals, and the notices filed three months later during a court-granted extension of time were ineffective because the extension exceeded the maximum allowance extension under Rule 4(a), Fed. R. App. P. Caperton v. Beatrice Pocahontas Coal Co., 585 F.2d 683 (4th Cir. 1978), aff'g 420 F. Supp. 445 (W.D. Va. 1977).

A notice of appeal filed prior to the disposition of a Rule 59(e) motion is void and has no effect. Zaczek v. Fauquier County, 764 F. Supp. 1071 (E.D. Va. 1991), aff'd, 16 F.3d 414 (4th Cir. 1993).

New trial limited to one issue. — Where the issues are separable and error is found in the trial of only one, a new trial may be had as to that issue alone where no injustice will result therefrom. Mason v. Mathiasen Tanker Indus., Inc., 298 F.2d 28 (4th Cir.), cert. denied, 371 U.S. 828, 83 S. Ct. 23, 9 L. Ed. 2d 66 (1962).

If an error at the trial requires a new trial on one issue, but this issue is separate from the other issue in the case and the error did not affect the determination of the other issues, the scope of the new trial may be limited to the single issue. Great Coastal Express, Inc. v. International Bhd. of Teamsters, 511 F.2d 839 (4th Cir. 1975), cert. denied, 425 U.S. 975, 96 S. Ct. 2176, 48 L. Ed. 2d 799 (1976) (limiting new trial to issue of damages only).

Move to vacate temporary restraining order qualifies as motion "to alter or amend judgment." — The plaintiff's contention that the notice of appeal, filed February 14, 1975, was filed more than thirty days after entry of the temporary restraining order (TRO) on December 31, 1974 overlooked the fact that defendants moved to vacate the TRO on January 6, 1975, which qualifies as a motion "to alter or amend judgment" within the meaning of Rule 59, Federal Rules of Civil Procedure. By the terms of Rule 4(a), Federal Rules of Appellate Procedure, the "full time for appeal (thirty days) . . . commences to run and is to be computed from the entry of (the) . . . (order) granting or denying a motion under Rule 59 to alter or amend the judgment . . .." January 20, 1975 was thus the date that the appeal period of thirty days began to run, and February 14, 1975 was within the period. Virginia v. Tenneco, Inc., 538 F.2d 1026 (4th Cir. 1976).

Bankruptcy court has discretion to consider motion to alter or amend even though motion raises issues that were argued or could have been argued originally. Citizens Fed. Bank v. Cardigan Mtg. Corp., 122 Bankr. 255 (Bankr. E.D. Va. 1990).

Subdivision (e) not vehicle for obtaining post-judgment reargument. — See Durkin v. Taylor, 444 F. Supp. 879 (E.D. Va. 1977).

Subdivision (e) does not serve the office of providing a disappointed suitor with a post-judgment opportunity to argue that which could have been argued pre-judgment. Johnson v. City of Richmond, 102 F.R.D. 623 (E.D. Va. 1984).

Challenge to summary judgment order. — A timely Rule 59(e) motion is the proper vehicle by which to challenge an order of summary judgment. Thomas v. United States Parole Comm'n, 672 F. Supp. 256 (E.D. Va. 1987).

Pursuant to this section, a damages verdict must be set aside if (1) The verdict is against the clear weight of the evidence, or (2) is based upon evidence which is false, or (3) will result in a miscarriage of justice. Cline v. Wal-Mart Stores, Inc., 144 F.3d 294 (4th Cir. 1998).

Remittitur, which is used in connection with subdivision (a), is a process, dating back to 1822, by which the trial court orders a new trial unless the plaintiff accepts a reduction in an excessive jury award. If a reviewing court concludes that a verdict is excessive, it is the court's duty to require a remittitur or order a new trial, and the failure to do so constitutes an abuse of discretion. Cline v. Wal-Mart Stores, Inc., 144 F.3d 294 (4th Cir. 1998).

Exemplary or punitive damages. — The general rule is that there is no fixed standard for the measurement of exemplary or punitive damages, and the amount of the award is largely within the discretion of the jury. And unless the amount found is so great or small as to evince passion, prejudice, corruption or some mistaken view of law, the jury's verdict should not be set aside. Garrick v. Kelly, 649 F. Supp. 607 (E.D. Va. 1986), aff'd, 842 F.2d 1290 (4th Cir. 1990).

Excessive award of damages. — Where a motion is made for a new trial based on an excessive award of damages, the benefit of every doubt must be given to the judgment of the trial judge, while recognizing that there must be an upper limit to allowable damages. The question of whether that limit has been surpassed is not a question of fact with respect to which reasonable men may differ, but a question of law. Cline v. Wal-Mart Stores, Inc., 144 F.3d 294 (4th Cir. 1998).

A review of whether to grant a motion for a new trial based on excessive punitive damages award, best utilizes the third prong of the Rule 59 standard — whether the jury's award will result in a miscarriage of justice. Cline v. Wal-Mart Stores, Inc., 144 F.3d 294 (4th Cir. 1998).

Judgment in contract action not amended to allow for interest. — See UOP, Inc. v. Infilco Degremont, Inc., 448 F. Supp. 145 (E.D. Va. 1978).

Motion to amend judgment to provide for attorneys' fees. — The ten-day limitation of subdivision (e) of this rule applies to attorneys' fees requests when those requests are based on the bad faith doctrine. El-Amin v. Williams, 92 F.R.D. 454 (E.D. Va. 1981).

Since a judgment granting defendant's motion for

dismissal was a final judgment even though it did not address a "boiler plate" request for attorney's fees made with the motion, a subsequent request for attorney's fees was a motion to alter or amend the judgment. El-Amin v. Williams, 92 F.R.D. 454 (E.D. Va. 1981).

Considerations of new trial on intervention of parties prevented trial judge from protecting their interest in original hearing. Fleming v. Citizens for Albemarle, Inc., 577 F.2d 236 (4th Cir. 1978), cert. denied, 439 U.S. 1071, 99 S. Ct. 842, 59 L. Ed. 2d 37 (1979).

Where timely post-judgment motion under Rule 59, F.R.Civ.P., has been entered, the thirty-day period for application of Rule 4, F.R.App.P., begins to run from the entry of the order granting or denying Rule 59 relief, and such relief depends, in turn, on the entry of original judgment. Caperton v. Beatrice Pocahontas Coal Co., 585 F.2d 683 (4th Cir. 1978).

Three grounds for a retrial may generally exist: Manifest error of law or fact, and newly discovered evidence. In re Kelly, 8 Bankr. 634 (Bankr. E.D. Va. 1981).

Use of wrong standard on motion for new trial is reversible error. — Although the grant or denial of a motion for a new trial may be reversed only upon a showing of abuse of discretion, the application of the wrong standard in considering a motion for a new trial is plainly just such an abuse of discretion. Gill v. Rollins Protective Servs. Co., 773 F.2d 592 (4th Cir. 1985), modified, 788 F.2d 1042 (4th Cir. 1986).

To apply JNOV standard to review of evidence on motion for new trial is reversible error. Gill v. Rollins Protective Servs. Co., 773 F.2d 592 (4th Cir. 1985), modified, 788 F.2d 1042 (4th Cir. 1986).

Appellate review. — In reviewing the evidence through the medium of a motion for a new trial after failure to move for judgment as a matter of law, the appellate court does not review "sufficiency" in its technical sense. What is at issue is whether there was an absolute absence of evidence to support the jury's verdict. Bristol Steel & Iron Works, Inc. v. Bethlehem Steel Corp., 41 F.3d 182 (4th Cir. 1994).

Applied in Great Coastal Express, Inc. v. International Bhd. of Teamsters, 350 F. Supp. 1377 (E.D. Va. 1972); Mays v. Harris, 369 F. Supp. 1348 (W.D. Va. 1973); Smith v. United States, 375 F. Supp. 1244 (E.D. Va. 1974); American Family Life Assurance Co. v. Planned Mktg. Assocs., 389 F. Supp. 1141 (E.D. Va. 1974); Mullins v. Seals, 416 F. Supp. 1098 (W.D. Va. 1976); Wilson v. Volkswagen of Am., Inc., 561 F.2d 494 (4th Cir. 1977); Fleming v. Citizens for Albemarle, Inc., 577 F.2d 236 (4th Cir. 1978); Zaczek v. Hutto, 448 F. Supp. 155 (W.D. Va. 1978); In re Dodd, 46 Bankr. 335 (Bankr. E.D. Va. 1985); Herold v. Hajoca Corp., 864 F.2d 317 (4th Cir. 1988); Natural Resources Defense Council v. United States EPA, 806 F. Supp. 1263 (E.D. Va. 1992); Allred v. Maersk Line, 826 F. Supp. 965 (E.D. Va. 1993); Boykin v. Bergesen D.Y. A/S, 842 F. Supp. 874 (E.D. Va. 1994); United States v. Dickerson, 166 F.3d 667, 1999 U.S. App. LEXIS 1741 (4th. Cir. 1999); Eberhardt v. Integrated Design & Constr., Inc., 167 F.3d 861 (4th. Cir. 1999); SunTiger, Inc. v. Scientific Research Funding Group, 9 F. Supp. 2d 601 (E.D. Va. 1998); Daniel v. Jones, 39 F. Supp. 2d 635 (E.D. Va. 1999); In re U.S. Lan Sys. Corp., 235 Bankr. 847 (Bankr. E.D. Va. 1998).

Rule 60. Relief from a Judgment or Order.

(a) *Corrections Based on Clerical Mistakes; Oversights and Omissions.* — The court may correct a clerical mistake or a mistake arising from oversight or omission whenever one is found in a judgment, order, or other part of the record. The court may do so on motion or on its own, with or without notice. But after an appeal has been docketed in the appellate court and while it is pending, such a mistake may be corrected only with the appellate court's leave.

(b) *Grounds for Relief from a Final Judgment, Order, or Proceeding.* — On motion and just terms, the court may relieve a party or its legal representative from a final judgment, order, or proceeding for the following reasons:

(1) mistake, inadvertence, surprise, or excusable neglect;

(2) newly discovered evidence that, with reasonable diligence, could not have been discovered in time to move for a new trial under Rule 59(b);

(3) fraud (whether previously called intrinsic or extrinsic), misrepresentation, or misconduct by an opposing party;

(4) the judgment is void;

(5) the judgment has been satisfied, released, or discharged; it is based on an earlier judgment that has been reversed or vacated; or applying it prospectively is no longer equitable; or

(6) any other reason that justifies relief.

(c) *Timing and Effect of the Motion.* — (1) Timing. A motion under Rule 60(b) must be made within a reasonable time — and for reasons (1), (2), and (3) no more than a year after the entry of the judgment or order or the date of the proceeding.

(2) Effect on Finality. The motion does not affect the judgment's finality or suspend its operation.

(d) *Other Powers to Grant Relief.* — This rule does not limit a court's power to:

(1) entertain an independent action to relieve a party from a judgment, order, or proceeding;

(2) grant relief under 28 U.S.C. § 1655 to a defendant who was not personally notified of the action; or

(3) set aside a judgment for fraud on the court.

(e) *Bills and Writs Abolished.* — The following are abolished: bills of review, bills in the nature of bills of review, and writs of coram nobis, coram vobis, and audita querela. (Amended by order adopted December 27, 1946, effective March 19, 1948, by order adopted December 29, 1948, effective October 20, 1949, and by order adopted March 2, 1987, effective August 1, 1987, and by order adopted April 30, 2007, effective December 1, 2007.)

Comment. — The language of Rule 60 has been amended as part of the general restyling of the Civil Rules to make them more easily understood and to make style and terminology consistent throughout the rules. These changes are intended to be stylistic only.

The final sentence of former Rule 60(b) said that the procedure for obtaining any relief from a judgment was by motion as prescribed in the Civil Rules or by an independent action. That provision is deleted as unnecessary. Relief continues to be available only as provided in the Civil Rules or by independent action.

Law Review. — For note on remedies for fraud on the court, see 40 Wash. & Lee L. Rev. 554 (1983).

CASE NOTES

I. General Consideration.
II. Clerical Mistakes.
III. Other Mistakes, etc.
  A. In General.
  B. Mistake, Inadvertence, Surprise, and Excusable Neglect.
  C. Newly Discovered Evidence.
  D. Fraud, Misrepresentation, and Other Misconduct.
  E. Other Reasons Justifying Relief.
IV. Appellate Review.
V. Pleading and Practice.

I. GENERAL CONSIDERATION.

The court must balance the competing policies favoring the finality of judgments and justice being done in view of all the facts, to determine, within its discretion, whether relief is appropriate in each case. Square Constr. Co. v. Washington Metro. Area Transit Auth., 657 F.2d 68 (4th Cir. 1981).

Motion is addressed to the sound discretion of the district court and will not be disturbed on appeal save for a showing of abuse. Square Constr. Co. v. Washington Metro. Area Transit Auth., 657 F.2d 68 (4th Cir. 1981); Transportation, Inc. v. Mayflower Servs., Inc., 769 F.2d 952 (4th Cir. 1985); Jones v. City of Richmond, 106 F.R.D. 485 (E.D. Va. 1985).

Scope of rule includes providing relief from final judgment. — It is within the scope of this rule to provide relief from any final judgment, including a previously denied petition for habeas corpus. Jones v. Murray, 802 F. Supp. 1412 (E.D. Va. 1992), aff'd, 976 F.2d 169 (4th Cir. 1992).

Rule supplies no grant of jurisdictional authority. — It merely permits a district court to try the original cause of action when the district court concludes that the ends of justice warrant reinstating the original claim. Fairfax Countywide Citizen's Ass'n, 571 F.2d 1299 (4th Cir.), cert. denied, 439 U.S. 1047, 99 S. Ct. 722, 58 L. Ed. 2d 706 (1978).

Policy of deterring misconduct outweighs considerations of finality. — The policy of deterring misconduct which threatens the fairness and integrity of the fact-finding process must outweigh considerations of finality. Square Constr. Co. v. Washington Metro. Area Transit Auth., 657 F.2d 68 (4th Cir. 1981).

Need to expedite cases cannot thwart objectives of justice. — The need to expedite cases to fully utilize the court's time to reduce overcrowded calendars and to establish finality of judgments should never be used to thwart the objectives of the blind goddess of justice itself. Square Constr. Co. v. Washington Metro. Area Transit Auth., 657 F.2d 68 (4th Cir. 1981).

The court had the authority to raise this matter either sua sponte under this rule or under its inherent power to modify and interpret its original order. R.M.S. Titanic, Inc. v. Wrecked & Abandoned Vessel, 920 F. Supp. 96 (E.D. Va. 1996).

Subdivision (b) of this rule may not serve as surrogate to a tardy Rule 12(b)(6) motion. Eberhardt v. Integrated Design & Constr., Inc., 167 F.3d 861 (4th. Cir. 1999).

Consent order. — A consent order is enforceable as a judicial decree and is therefore subject to subdivision (b) like other judgments and decrees. Roadtechs, Inc. v. MJ Hwy. Technology, Ltd., 83 F. Supp. 2d 677 (E.D. Va. 2000).

Independent action. — Subsection (b) of this rule permits a district court to entertain an independent action to relieve a party from a judgment or suspend its operation. Morrel v. Nationwide Mut.

Fire Ins. Co., 188 F.3d 218 (4th Cir. 1999).

Unlike a motion for relief under subsection (b) of this rule, an "independent action" may be brought by one who was not a party to the original action. Morrel v. Nationwide Mut. Fire Ins. Co., 188 F.3d 218 (4th Cir. 1999).

A federal court can entertain an independent action to enjoin or otherwise grant relief from a judgment rendered not only by it, but also by another federal court. Morrel v. Nationwide Mut. Fire Ins. Co., 188 F.3d 218 (4th Cir. 1999).

Rules may not be used to attack adjudication of bankruptcy. — To allow the use of the Federal Rules of Civil Procedure to allow a creditor to attack an adjudication of bankruptcy under § 18(b) of the Bankruptcy Act, 11 U.S.C. § 41(b) (1964), would be contrary to the intent of Congress in amending that section. In re W. Auto Assoc. Store, 295 F. Supp. 566 (W.D. Va. 1968).

Applied in Scott v. Young, 307 F. Supp. 1005 (E.D. Va. 1969); John W. Johnson, Inc. v. J.A. Jones Constr. Co., 369 F. Supp. 484 (E.D. Va. 1973); American Family Life Assurance Co. v. Planned Mktg. Assoc., 389 F. Supp. 1141 (E.D. Va. 1974); Blackwelder v. Millman, 522 F.2d 766 (4th Cir. 1975); Vander Zee v. Karabatsos, 683 F.2d 832 (4th Cir. 1982); Banks v. Multi-Family Mgt., Inc., 554 F.2d 127 (4th Cir. 1977); Wilson v. Volkswagen of Am., Inc., 561 F.2d 494 (4th Cir. 1977); Caperton v. Beatrice Pocahontas Coal Co., 585 F.2d 683 (4th Cir. 1978); Fowler v. Virginia, 445 F. Supp. 334 (E.D. Va. 1978); Patterson v. American Tobacco Co., 634 F.2d 744 (4th Cir. 1980); Bartl v. Garfinkel (In re Claxton), 30 Bankr. 199 (Bankr. E.D. Va. 1983); Vecco Constr. Indus., Inc. v. Century Constr. Co., 33 Bankr. 757 (Bankr. E.D. Va. 1983); Beneficial Fin. Co. v. Lazrovitch, 47 Bankr. 358 (E.D. Va. 1983); Burgess v. Cohen, 593 F. Supp. 1122 (E.D. Va. 1984); Bartholomew v. Clawson, 594 F. Supp. 1121 (E.D. Va. 1984); A & E Supply Co. v. Nationwide Mut. Fire Ins. Co., 612 F. Supp. 760 (W.D. Va. 1985); United States v. Breit, 754 F.2d 526 (4th Cir. 1985); Alexandria Hosp. v. Bowen, 631 F. Supp. 1237 (W.D. Va. 1986); Boyd v. Bulala, 647 F. Supp. 781 (W.D. Va. 1986); McLawhorn v. John W. Daniel & Co., 924 F.2d 535 (4th Cir. 1991); Creekmore v. Food Lion, Inc., 797 F. Supp. 505 (E.D. Va. 1992); Hutter Assocs. v. Women, Inc., 138 Bankr. 512 (W.D. Va. 1992); Ketaner v. Traditional Indus., Inc., 154 Bankr. 467 (E.D. Va. 1993); Schultz v. Butcher, 24 F.3d 626 (4th Cir. 1994); Moeller v. D'Arrigo, 163 F.R.D. 489 (E.D. Va. 1995); Ontra, Inc. v. Wolfe, 192 Bankr. 679 (W.D. Va. 1996); Taylor v. Virginia, DOT, 170 F.R.D. 10 (E.D. Va. 1996); Marks v. United States Social Sec. Admin., 963 F. Supp. 517 (E.D. Va. 1997); In re Heckert, 226 Bankr. 558 (S.D.W. Va. 1998); United States v. Holland, 214 F.3d 523, 2000 U.S. App. LEXIS 13976 (4th Cir. 2000); Washington-Dulles Transp., Ltd. v. Metropolitan Wash. Airports Auth., 263 F.3d 371, 2001 U.S. App. LEXIS 19298 (4th Cir. 2001).

II. CLERICAL MISTAKES.

Correction of record omissions regarding identification of class members. — Where the record did not clearly identify the members of the class and the judgment did not "specify or describe those to whom the notice . . . was directed, and who have not requested exclusion, and whom the court finds to be members of the class," as required by Rule 23(c)(3), such omissions having resulted from the oversight of counsel and having been remediable without difficulty, the judgment was affirmed and the case was remanded to the district court so that the omissions in the record could be corrected and the judgment amended. Newman v. Prior, 518 F.2d 97 (4th Cir. 1975), overruled on other grounds, Newcome v. Esrey, 862 F.2d 1099 (4th Cir. 1988).

III. OTHER MISTAKES, ETC.

A. In General.

Plaintiff's burden. — To succeed with a subsection (b) motion, plaintiff must as a preliminary matter show that the he has a meritorious defense to the order complained of and that setting aside the order would not unfairly prejudice the opposing parties. Lux v. Spotswood Constr. Loans, 176 Bankr. 416 (E.D. Va. 1993), aff'd, 43 F.3d 1467 (4th Cir. 1994).

If plaintiff moves under subdivision (b)(6), then he must show extraordinary circumstances. Lux v. Spotswood Constr. Loans, 176 Bankr. 416 (E.D. Va. 1993), aff'd, 43 F.3d 1467 (4th Cir. 1994).

Extraordinary circumstances must be shown. — A motion under subdivision (b)(6) of this rule will be granted only in extraordinary circumstances or under circumstances imposing extreme or undue hardship. Holland v. Virginia Lee Co., 188 F.R.D. 241 (W.D. Va. 1999).

Subdivision (b) preserves the court's power to entertain an independent action to set aside the judgment. The independent action rests upon the court's equitable jurisdiction, and has long been an accepted part of federal jurisprudence. Great Coastal Express, Inc. v. International Bhd. of Teamsters, 86 F.R.D. 131 (E.D. Va. 1980), aff'd, 675 F.2d 1349 (4th Cir. 1982), cert. denied, 459 U.S. 1128, 103 S. Ct. 764, 74 L. Ed. 2d 978 (1983).

Fed. R. Civ. P. 60(b) "does not limit the power of a court to entertain an independent action to relieve a party from a judgment ...." A motion may properly be treated as the commencement of such an independent action. Great Coastal Express, Inc. v. International Bhd. of Teamsters, 86 F.R.D. 131 (E.D. Va. 1980), aff'd, 675 F.2d 1349 (4th Cir. 1982), cert. denied, 459 U.S. 1128, 103 S. Ct. 764, 74 L. Ed. 2d 978 (1983).

Subdivision (b) of this rule should be liberally construed and applied to prevent a manifest miscarriage of justice. Stancil v. United States, 200 F. Supp. 36 (E.D. Va. 1961).

Where plaintiff is proceeding pro se, the court must be mindful that it must construe his submissions liberally. Bright v. Norshipco, 187 F.R.D. 536 (E.D. Va. 1998), aff'd, 178 F.3d 1282 (4th Cir. 1999).

Before granting relief, court should consider risk of injustice. — Before granting relief under subsection (b)(6) of this rule, the court should consider the risk of injustice to the parties in the particular case, the risk that the denial of relief will produce injustice in other cases, and the risk of undermining the public's confidence in the judicial process. Bright v. Norshipco, 187 F.R.D. 536 (E.D. Va. 1998), aff'd, 178 F.3d 1282 (4th Cir. 1999).

Motion not authorized when it is request for court to change its mind. — A Rule 60(b) motion is not authorized when it is nothing more than a request for the district court to change its mind. Lee X v. Casey, 771 F. Supp. 725 (E.D. Va. 1991).

Where plaintiff in essence wanted the court to reconsider its previous decision, his request was an inappropriate basis for relief under subsection (b) of this rule. Bright v. Norshipco, 187 F.R.D. 536 (E.D. Va. 1998), aff'd, 178 F.3d 1282 (4th Cir. 1999).

Burden on movant under subdivision (b). — To bring himself within subdivision (b), the movant must make a showing of timeliness, a meritorious defense, a lack of unfair prejudice to the opposing party, and exceptional circumstances. Once the movant has made such a showing, he must proceed to satisfy one or more of the rule's six grounds for relief from judgment. Jones v. City of Richmond, 106 F.R.D. 485 (E.D. Va. 1985).

When making a motion under subsection (b) of this rule, the party moving for relief must clearly establish the grounds therefor to the satisfaction of the district court, and such grounds must be clearly substantiated by adequate proof. In re Burnley, 988 F.2d 1 (4th Cir. 1992).

No abuse of discretion in denying defendant's motion. — Where nowhere in defendant's motion does he set forth any grounds for granting the motion to modify review system in order to permit him to maintain two pending cases at one time, district court did not abuse its discretion in denying the defendant's motion. In re Burnley, 988 F.2d 1 (4th Cir. 1992).

Default judgments are not favored. — Default judgments are not favored in law; courts exist to do justice and are reluctant to enforce an unjust judgment. Trueblood v. Grayson Shops of Tenn., Inc., 32 F.R.D. 190 (E.D. Va. 1963).

Setting aside default is discretionary. — Authority to set aside a default judgment is grounded in subdivision (b) of this rule, where relief may be granted for, among other reasons, "mistake, inadvertence, surprise, or excusable neglect." A mere entry of default may be set aside for good cause shown under Federal Rules of Civil Procedure 55(c). Under either rule the authority is to be exercised in the sound discretion of the trial court although the justification for vacating an entry of default is somewhat less stringent than what is required by subdivision (b) of this rule. Trueblood v. Grayson Shops of Tenn., Inc., 32 F.R.D. 190 (E.D. Va. 1963).

Default judgment vacated on terms subject to defendant's showing existence of meritorious defense. — See Trueblood v. Grayson Shops of Tenn., Inc., 32 F.R.D. 190 (E.D. Va. 1963).

Movant must demonstrate the existence of a meritorious claim or defense. Square Constr. Co. v. Washington Metro. Area Transit Auth., 657 F.2d 68 (4th Cir. 1981).

In order to qualify under the law as meritorious, a movant must demonstrate that granting relief in its case will not have been a futile gesture. Essentially, the law requires a proffer of evidence which would permit a finding for the moving party or which would establish a valid counterclaim. Holland v. Virginia Lee Co., 188 F.R.D. 241 (W.D. Va. 1999).

Both mistake or inadvertence, etc. and meritorious defense must be shown. — Not only must there exist a good reason to set aside the default on the ground of "mistake, inadvertence, surprise, or excusable neglect," but the moving party must show that he has a meritorious defense to the action. The bare wording of subdivision (b) does not require the showing of the existence of a meritorious defense, but this is judicially established and apparently is left within the sound discretion of the trial court. Trueblood v. Grayson Shops of Tenn., Inc., 32 F.R.D. 190 (E.D. Va. 1963).

Court may require disclosure of facts supporting allegation of meritorious defense. — While some cases lend support to the proposition that a defendant seeking to set aside a default judgment is required to do no more than merely allege that it has a meritorious defense, where the lower court, in its inquiry into the merits of the case, sought to have the defendant state underlying facts to support its claim of a meritorious defense, the appellate court held that it was not persuaded that a bare allegation of a meritorious defense precludes the court, in its discretion, from requiring disclosure of facts to support such a conclusory assertion. Thus, the lower court did not abuse its discretion, under the circumstances, in denying the motion where the defendant did no more than state that plaintiff breached the contract, a mere conclusion which fell far short of providing the court with a satisfactory explanation of the merits of the defense. Consolidated Masonry & Fireproofing, Inc. v. Wagman Constr. Corp., 383 F.2d 249 (4th Cir. 1967), aff'g 273 F. Supp. 693 (E.D. Va. 1966).

Exemplary or punitive damages. — The general rule is that there is no fixed standard for the measurement of exemplary or punitive damages, and the amount of the award is largely within the discretion of the jury. Unless the amount found is so great or small as to evince passion, prejudice, corruption or some mistaken view of law, the jury's verdict should not be set aside. Garrick v. Kelly, 649 F. Supp. 607 (E.D. Va. 1986), aff'd, 842 F.2d 1290 (4th Cir. 1988).

Rule may be applied to final order in bankruptcy proceedings. — Control of a bankruptcy court over its orders is generally upheld without reference to subdivision (b) of this rule. However, when a final order is involved, subdivision (b) has been held applicable. In such case, there must be some justification for the party's oversight, inadvertence, or neglect. Also the circumstances surrounding the party's inaction must be considered. In re Perry, 336 F. Supp. 828 (W.D. Va. 1971).

But bankruptcy hearing should not be reopened without compelling reason. — The parties to a bankruptcy proceeding have no absolute right to have hearings reopened, and, in order to promote the prompt and effective settlement of the debtor's estate, a bankruptcy judge should not reopen a hearing without a compelling reason. National Agents Serv. Co. v. Duiser, 12 Bankr. 538 (Bankr. W.D. Va. 1981).

Bankruptcy order of sale may be corrected to state sale was free of liens. — Subdivision (b) furnishes abundant authority to correct the omission in an order of a referee in bankruptcy authorizing acceptance of a private offer for a bankrupt's assets which failed to expressly state the sale was free and clear of all liens as the trustee and purchaser intended. It follows, therefore, that the general rule of law applicable to an order of sale making no mention of liens which, under normal circumstances, would constitute a sale subject to existing liens, is inapplicable. In re Clark, 257 F. Supp. 761 (E.D. Va. 1966).

B. Mistake, Inadvertence, Surprise, and Excusable Neglect.

Court making determination as to whether neglect was "excusable" is to consider the following factors: (1) The danger of prejudice to the other party; (2) the length of the delay and its potential impact on judicial proceedings; (3) the reason for the delay, including whether it was within the reasonable control of the movant; and (4) whether the movant acted in good faith. Copperfield v. Dalkon Shield Claimants Trust (In re A. H. Robins Co.), 221 Bankr. 166 (Bankr. E.D. Va.), aff'd, 166 F.3d 1208 (4th Cir. 1998).

District court should find "excusable neglect" only in extraordinary cases where an injustice would otherwise result. Copperfield v. Dalkon Shield Claimants Trust (In re A. H. Robins Co.), 221 Bankr. 166 (Bankr. E.D. Va.), aff'd, 166 F.3d 1208 (4th Cir. 1998).

Person seeking relief under subdivision (b)(1) bears burden of showing that her neglect was "excusable." That determination is at bottom an equitable one, taking account of all relevant circumstances surrounding the party's omission. Copperfield v. Dalkon Shield Claimants Trust (In re A. H. Robins Co.), 221 Bankr. 166 (Bankr. E.D. Va.), aff'd, 166 F.3d 1208 (4th Cir. 1998).

"Mistake," etc., not capable of precise definition. — There is no uniform interpretation of what constitutes "mistake, inadvertence, surprise, or excusable neglect." Perhaps the terms are not capable of more precise definition. Trueblood v. Grayson Shops of Tenn., Inc., 32 F.R.D. 190 (E.D. Va. 1963).

Failure to answer held result of excusable neglect. — See Trueblood v. Grayson Shops of Tenn., Inc., 32 F.R.D. 190 (E.D. Va. 1963).

Mere assertion that deadline was somehow unfair or "illegal" without any factual support hardly qualifies as "excusable neglect." Copperfield v. Dalkon Shield Claimants Trust (In re A. H. Robins Co.), 221 Bankr. 166 (Bankr. E.D. Va.), aff'd, 166 F.3d 1208 (4th Cir. 1998).

Allegations that claimant was unaware of deadline leading to disallowance of her claim or for some other reason was unable to comply with the deadline constitute a request for relief from disallowance under subdivision (b)(1). Copperfield v. Dalkon Shield Claimants Trust (In re A. H. Robins Co.), 221 Bankr. 166 (Bankr. E.D. Va.), aff'd, 166 F.3d 1208 (4th Cir. 1998).

Party's failure to meet deadline because of inattention, inadvertence, or negligence is "neglect." This holding applies to rules in which the term "excusable neglect" appears, including subdivision (b)(1) of this Rule. Copperfield v. Dalkon Shield Claimants Trust (In re A. H. Robins Co.), 221 Bankr. 166 (Bankr. E.D. Va.), aff'd, 166 F.3d 1208 (4th Cir. 1998).

C. Newly Discovered Evidence.

Burden upon party alleging newly discovered evidence. — To support a motion for rehearing in a bankruptcy proceeding based upon newly discovered evidence, the burden is upon the moving party and such party must show that the evidence was not known and could not have been discovered by due diligence at time of trial and the moving party must also show that the new evidence is material to the issue tried and that it is likely to produce a different result than that originally reached at trial. National Agents Serv. Co. v. Duiser, 12 Bankr. 538 (Bankr. W.D. Va. 1981).

To sustain a Rule 60(b)(2) motion, the court must find that the new evidence actually existed at the time of the trial; that the appellant could not have discovered the evidence earlier by due diligence; that the appellant was diligent; and that consideration of the evidence would be likely to change the result. Fuentes v. Stackhouse, 182 Bankr. 438 (E.D. Va. 1995).

Newly-discovered evidence must pertain to facts existing as time of trial. — Motion by defendant in medical malpractice action either to grant a new trial or to open the record to admit new evidence, which motion was prompted by the death of the infant plaintiff some six weeks after the trial, on grounds that had she died before trial, the parents could not have recovered certain elements of damages, including her future medical costs, was denied. Under Rules 59 and 60(b)(2), newly discovered evidence must pertain to facts which existed at the time of trial. Were the rule otherwise, litigation would never end. Moreover, § 8.01-21 specifically provides for the entry of judgment when a party dies after the verdict. Boyd v. Bulala, 672 F. Supp. 915 (W.D. Va. 1987).

Petitioner's claim was functional equivalent of a "successive petition." — Where substance of petitioner's claim — the constitutionality of Virginia's capital sentencing scheme — had been litigated, evaluated, and affirmed in several different forums, the claim raised no new or colorable issues; as such, it was the functional equivalent of a "successive petition" for habeas corpus within the meaning of Rule 9(b) of the Rules governing 2254 Cases. Jones v. Murray, 802 F. Supp. 1412 (E.D. Va. 1992), aff'd, 976 F.2d 169 (4th Cir. 1992).

D. Fraud, Misrepresentation, and Other Misconduct.

Fraud embraced by subdivision (b)(3) may not be considered proper basis for relief under subdivision (b)(6). Great Coastal Express, Inc. v. International Bhd. of Teamsters, 86 F.R.D. 131 (E.D. Va. 1980), cert. denied, 459 U.S. 1128, 103 S. Ct. 764, 74 L. Ed. 2d 978 (1983).

Power of court to grant relief when court subjected to fraud. — Subdivision (b) recognizes the court's inherent power to grant relief from judgment when the court has been subjected to a fraud. Fraud upon a court is a matter which is so grave that the rules permit relief to be afforded without regard to any time limitation. In fact, a successful movant may be relieved from a judgment procured through fraud upon the court even though the movant has been guilty of laches. Great Coastal Express, Inc. v. International Bhd. of Teamsters, 86 F.R.D. 131 (E.D. Va. 1980), cert. denied, 459 U.S. 1128, 103 S. Ct. 764, 74 L. Ed. 2d 978 (1983).

Fraud must be upon the court. — To succeed with claim of fraud under subsection (b)(6) of this rule, movant must demonstrate that the activity was "fraud upon the court." Bright v. Norshipco, 187

F.R.D. 536 (E.D. Va. 1998), aff'd, 178 F.3d 1282 (4th Cir. 1999).

"Fraud upon the court" defined. — "Fraud upon the court" should embrace only that species of fraud which interferes with the court's discharge of its judicial functions. The most blatant examples of such fraud are bribery or corruption of the court, its officers or the jury. A persuasive definition of "fraud upon the court" emphasizes that the term should embrace only that species of fraud which does or attempts to, defile the court itself, or is a fraud perpetrated by officers of the court so that the judicial machinery cannot perform in the usual manner its impartial task of adjudging cases that are presented for adjudication. Fraud inter partes, without more, should not be a fraud upon the court, but redress should be left to a motion under subdivision 60(b)(3), or to the independent action. Great Coastal Express, Inc. v. International Bhd. of Teamsters, 86 F.R.D. 131 (E.D. Va. 1980), cert. denied, 459 U.S. 1128, 103 S. Ct. 764, 74 L. Ed. 2d 978 (1983).

"Fraud upon the court" is the most egregious species of fraud. Examples of fraud upon the court include the bribing of the judge or a juror or the assertion of improper influence over the court. Bright v. Norshipco, 187 F.R.D. 536 (E.D. Va. 1998), aff'd, 178 F.3d 1282 (4th Cir. 1999).

The concept of "fraud on the court" in the context of subdivision (b) should be construed very narrowly, because it could easily overwhelm the specific provision of subdivision (b)(3) and its time limitation and thereby subvert the balance of equities contained in this rule. Great Coastal Express, Inc. v. International Bhd. of Teamsters, 675 F.2d 1349 (4th Cir. 1982), cert. denied, 459 U.S. 1128, 103 S. Ct. 764, 74 L. Ed. 2d 978 (1983).

Allegation of fraud should be raised in district court. — The proper court in which to raise the allegation that a judgment was obtained by fraud, misrepresentation or other misconduct normally is the district court. It is obvious that a motion under subdivision (b)(1) or (3) or an independent action in equity should be filed in the district court. Furthermore, the proper forum in which to assert that a party has perpetrated a "fraud on the court" is the court which allegedly was a victim of that fraud. Weisman v. Charles E. Smith Mgt., Inc., 829 F.2d 511 (4th Cir. 1987).

The district court is the proper forum to determine in the first instance whether there is sufficient basis to overturn the judgments on the grounds of fraud, misrepresentation, or other misconduct. That court is in the best position to decide whether any fraud was perpetrated upon it or other untoward action occurred, and is the proper forum for the adjudication of claims of plaintiff/appellant which fall under subdivisions (b)(1) and (b)(3). Weisman v. Charles E. Smith Mgt., Inc., 829 F.2d 511 (4th Cir. 1987).

Procedures to overturn judgment obtained by fraud. — Often a party does not seek to overturn a judgment on grounds that it was obtained by fraud, misrepresentation, or other misconduct until sometime after that judgment has been affirmed on appeal or the time for appeal has elapsed, for the simple reason that the basis for such an allegation often is not known until after the judgment has become final. Under such circumstances the party seeking to overturn a federal civil judgment normally can proceed in three ways. That party can file a motion under subdivision (b)(3) for relief on the ground of fraud, misrepresentation or other misconduct. The aggrieved party also can seek to set aside the judgment on the narrower theory that it was obtained by "fraud on the court." Finally, the party that wishes to challenge the judgment can pursue an independent action in equity. Weisman v. Charles E. Smith Mgt., Inc., 829 F.2d 511 (4th Cir. 1987).

Under the intrinsic/extrinsic fraud doctrine, fraud must be "extrinsic" to justify relief, that is, fraud that actually prevented an issue from being joined or a party from making a valid claim or defense; and notwithstanding the considerable criticism leveled against the intrinsic/extrinsic distinction, it is clear that perjury and false testimony are not grounds for relief in an independent action in the fourth circuit. Great Coastal Express, Inc. v. International Bhd. of Teamsters, 675 F.2d 1349 (4th Cir. 1982), cert. denied, 459 U.S. 764, 103 S. Ct. 764, 74 L. Ed. 2d 978 (1983).

Perjured testimony and false evidence obviously interfere with the court's role in discovering the truth. Great Coastal Express, Inc. v. International Bhd. of Teamsters, 86 F.R.D. 131 (E.D. Va. 1980), cert. denied, 459 U.S. 1128, 103 S. Ct. 764, 74 L. Ed. 2d 978 (1983).

But are not grounds for relief. — Perjury or fabricated evidence are not grounds for relief as "fraud on the court." Great Coastal Express, Inc. v. International Bhd. of Teamsters, 675 F.2d 1349 (4th Cir. 1982), cert. denied, 459 U.S. 764, 103 S. Ct. 764, 74 L. Ed. 2d 978 (1983).

Perjury is not a fraud on the court under this rule. Ginsberg v. Pomponio, 95 F.R.D. 156 (E.D. Va. 1982).

Generally, false testimony is not considered fraud upon the court, unless the movant can demonstrate that the witness willfully and purposefully provided false testimony. Bright v. Norshipco, 187 F.R.D. 536 (E.D. Va. 1998), aff'd, 178 F.3d 1282 (4th Cir. 1999).

However, involvement of an attorney, as an officer of the court, in a scheme to suborn perjury would certainly be considered fraud on the court. Great Coastal Express, Inc. v. International Bhd. of Teamsters, 675 F.2d 1349 (4th Cir. 1982), cert. denied, 459 U.S. 764, 103 S. Ct. 764, 74 L. Ed. 2d 978 (1983).

Conspiracy to present perjured testimony. — A verdict may be set aside for fraud on the court if an attorney and a witness have conspired to present perjured testimony. Cleveland Demolition Co. v. Azcon Scrap Corp., 827 F.2d 984 (4th Cir. 1987).

Verdict will be vacated only in the most egregious cases in which the integrity of the court and its ability to function impartially is directly impinged. Although perjury by a witness will not suffice, the involvement of an attorney, as an officer of the court, in a scheme to suborn perjury should certainly be considered fraud on the court. Cleveland Demolition Co. v. Azcon Scrap Corp., 827 F.2d 984 (4th Cir. 1987).

Jury experiments. — Experiments performed by juries, which have the effect of putting them in possession of evidence not offered at trial, constitute jury misconduct requiring a new trial, unless no prejudice results. However, jury experiments that are merely more critical examinations of exhibits than the examinations made during the trial are not objectionable. Konkel v. Bob Evans Farms, Inc., 165 F.3d 275 (4th Cir.), cert. denied, 528 U.S. 877, 120 S. Ct. 184, 145 L. Ed. 2d 155 (1999).

Evidentiary conflicts must be resolved during the initial trial. — If a routine evidentiary dispute, which occurs in virtually all trials, could justify an action for fraud on the court, then any losing party could bring an independent action to set aside the verdict, forcing extended proceedings in almost every case. Because this rule imposes no time limit on these independent actions, they could be brought at any time. Cleveland Demolition Co. v. Azcon Scrap Corp., 827 F.2d 984 (4th Cir. 1987).

Material withheld need not be sufficient to alter district court's judgment. — Setting aside a judgment does not require that the material withheld be sufficient to alter the district court's judgment, and this is especially true when the district court is not the initial fact finder. Square Constr. Co. v. Washington Metro. Area Transit Auth., 657 F.2d 68 (4th Cir. 1981).

Burden on party alleging misconduct. — A party seeking relief under subdivision (b)(3) of the rule must also prove the misconduct complained of by clear and convincing evidence and demonstrate that such misconduct prevented him from fully and fairly presenting his claim or defense. Square Constr. Co. v. Washington Metro. Area Transit Auth., 657 F.2d 68 (4th Cir. 1981).

To prevail on claim of fraud under subsection (b)(6) of this rule, plaintiff must present clear and convincing evidence that misconduct occurred and that the misconduct rose to the level of a fraud upon the court. Bright v. Norshipco, 187 F.R.D. 536 (E.D. Va. 1998), aff'd, 178 F.3d 1282 (4th Cir. 1999).

Facts showing misconduct preventing party from fully and fairly presenting defense. — Where a construction contractor's contract with a transit authority was terminated and the authority claimed reprocurement costs from the construction contractor, the contractor's assertion, that the method of reprocurement was not designed to minimize reprocurement costs, raised a meritorious defense; furthermore, the contractor met its burden of showing the fact of misconduct on the part of an adverse party in the form of the authority's failure to produce the reprocurement estimate pursuant to a proper request, thus this misconduct prevented the contractor from fully and fairly presenting its defense to the assessment of reprocurement costs. Square Constr. Co. v. Washington Metro. Area Transit Auth., 657 F.2d 68 (4th Cir. 1981).

E. Other Reasons Justifying Relief.

Subdivision (b)(6) construed by court. — Subdivision (b)(6) authorizes a court to relieve a party from the operation of a final judgment "for any other reason justifying relief." This provision follows the enumeration of five specific grounds for relief and thus may be properly viewed as a residuary clause intended to encompass contingencies which could not have been foreseen by the rule's drafters. Great Coastal Express, Inc. v. International Bhd. of Teamsters, 86 F.R.D. 131 (E.D. Va. 1980), cert. denied, 459 U.S. 1128, 103 S. Ct. 764, 74 L. Ed. 2d 978 (1983).

It is apparent that the phrase "any other reason" of subdivision (b)(6) is to be accorded its usual meaning; especially in light of the fact that it follows the enumeration of five specific grounds for relief. Great Coastal Express, Inc. v. International Bhd. of Teamsters, 86 F.R.D. 131 (E.D. Va. 1980), cert. denied, 459 U.S. 1128, 103 S. Ct. 764, 74 L. Ed. 2d 978 (1983).

Subdivision (b)(6), on its face, necessitates a ground for relief distinct from those provided in the preceding five subparagraphs. Great Coastal Express, Inc. v. International Bhd. of Teamsters, 86 F.R.D. 131 (E.D. Va. 1980), cert. denied, 459 U.S. 1128, 103 S. Ct. 764, 74 L. Ed. 2d 978 (1983).

Were the court to afford subdivision (b)(6) relief in a situation encompassed by subdivision (b)(3), the one-year limitation of the latter provision would become meaningless. The court cannot adopt an interpretation which is in obvious conflict with the rule's framework. Great Coastal Express, Inc. v. International Bhd. of Teamsters, 86 F.R.D. 131 (E.D. Va. 1980), cert. denied, 459 U.S. 1128, 103 S. Ct. 764, 74 L. Ed. 2d 978 (1983).

Subsection (b)(6) of this rule has been described as the "catch-all" clause, because it provides the court with a grand reservoir of equitable power to do justice in a particular case and vests power in courts adequate to enable them to vacate judgments whenever such action is appropriate to accomplish justice where relief might not be available under any other clause in subsection (b) of this rule. Holland v. Virginia Lee Co., 188 F.R.D. 241 (W.D. Va. 1999).

Public interest sufficient to require relief. — See Marshall v. Ampthill Rayon Workers, Inc., 454 F. Supp. 84 (E.D. Va. 1978).

Intervening and supervening edicts of Supreme Court may justify relief. — Intervening and supervening edicts of the United States Supreme Court qualify under subdivision (b) of this rule as a "reason justifying relief from the operation of the judgment," where they make a substantial change in the law and end further viability of the earlier decision. Griffin v. State Bd. of Educ., 296 F. Supp. 1178 (E.D. Va. 1969).

Neither ignorance nor carelessness of an attorney presents a cognizable ground for relief under subdivision (b) of this rule. Wood v. Kling, 98 F.R.D. 319 (E.D. Va. 1983).

Argument of creditor of bankrupt company, that it was entitled to relief from the judgment because of its counsel's wilful neglect in failing to raise the "new value" defense at trial and it should be relieved of judgment, was properly denied because while attorney malfeasance which actively misleads a client or is comparably culpable might successfully ground a Rule 60(b) motion, a lawyer's ignorance or carelessness does not present cognizable grounds for relief under subdivision (b). Counts v. Wang Labs., Inc., 932 F.2d 338 (4th Cir. 1991).

Change in law. — A supervening change in decisional law on its own is insufficient to afford relief under subsection (b)(6) of this rule. However, where several factors are present in addition to a change in law, the circumstances might be sufficiently extraordinary to warrant relief under subsection (b)(6). Holland v. Virginia Lee Co., 188

F.R.D. 241 (W.D. Va. 1999).

Where a change in law affects a consent decree or permanent injunction, a court may find extraordinary circumstances present. Holland v. Virginia Lee Co., 188 F.R.D. 241 (W.D. Va. 1999).

Where a movant's sole claim is for monies paid based on a change in decisional law, the courts are hard pressed to find extraordinary circumstances or undue hardship under subsection (b)(6) of this rule. Holland v. Virginia Lee Co., 188 F.R.D. 241 (W.D. Va. 1999).

"Good cause" for remand under Social Security Act. — Although in an action under the Social Security Act attacking the denial of disability benefits the proffer of new evidence might not, in and of itself, have been sufficient grounds to vacate a court judgment pursuant to subdivision (b) of this rule, the same was not required to establish "good cause" for a remand under the act. Rather, it was sufficient that no party would be prejudiced by the acceptance of additional evidence and the evidence offered bears directly and substantially on the matter in dispute. Bishop v. Weinberger, 380 F. Supp. 293 (E.D. Va. 1974). See 42 U.S.C. § 405(g).

Settlement agreement is not an extraordinary circumstance that justifies relief under subsection (b)(6) of this rule. Holland v. Virginia Lee Co., 188 F.R.D. 241 (W.D. Va. 1999).

Action available where breach of settlement agreement claimed. — Where federal jurisdiction to sue for a breach of a settlement agreement does not otherwise exist, a plaintiff who claims a breach of his settlement agreement has available two courses of action. First, he may take his contract claim to state court where he may seek enforcement of the settlement agreement. Because enforceability is likely to turn on questions of state law, the state court is an appropriate forum for resolving this dispute. Alternatively, the injured plaintiff may file a Rule 60(b)(6) motion in federal court, requesting that the prior dismissal order be vacated and the case restored to the court's trial docket. This restores the litigants to the status quo ante and allows the plaintiff to prove his case and obtain his relief on the merits of the underlying claim. Fairfax Countywide Citizens Ass'n v. County of Fairfax, 571 F.2d 1299 (4th Cir.), cert. denied, 439 U.S. 1047, 99 S. Ct. 722, 58 L. Ed. 2d 706 (1978).

Upon repudiation of a settlement agreement which had terminated litigation pending before it, a district court has the authority under Rule 60(b)(6) to vacate its prior dismissal order and restore the case to its docket; however, once the proceedings are reopened, the district court is not necessarily empowered to enforce the settlement agreement against the breaching party. The district court is not so empowered unless the agreement had been approved and incorporated into an order of the court, or, at the time the court is requested to enforce the agreement, there exists some independent ground upon which to base federal jurisdiction. Fairfax Countywide Citizens Ass'n v. County of Fairfax, 571 F.2d 1299 (4th Cir.), cert. denied, 439 U.S. 1047, 99 S. Ct. 722, 58 L. Ed. 2d 706 (1978).

Order of confirmation to be vacated. — Counsel's failure to notice creditor's bankruptcy counsel when combined with the unexplained failure of the bank's responsible employees to receive any indication of the impending confirmation of the amended chapter 11 plan clearly present circumstances warranting the vacation of the order of confirmation pursuant to the general provision of subdivision (b)(6). In re Birdneck Apt. Assocs., 152 Bankr. 65 (Bankr. E.D. Va. 1993).

Premature death of infant in medical malpractice action did not justify relief under subdivision (b)(6). Because the weight accorded to the finality of a judgment necessarily increases as time passes, the test, as advanced by the defendant, would allow relief when the plaintiff dies prematurely, but would deny relief when the plaintiff lives longer than expected. Thus, while the balancing test is neutral on its face, in operation it is strongly biased toward defendants and against plaintiffs. Boyd v. Bulala, 672 F. Supp. 915 (W.D. Va. 1987).

Motion for relief denied. — Where, in electing to arbitrate her claim, claimant and her respective counsel signed an arbitration agreement in which she agreed to abide by the Arbitration Rules, and where the Arbitration Rules attached to and incorporated into the signed agreement provided for a single method of seeking relief from an arbitration decision – filing a Motion To Vacate with the court, because claimant knowingly and voluntarily agreed to follow the Arbitration Rules, the district court would not add another avenue of relief that was not contractually agreed upon at the time of the election, and accordingly, the court found that claimant was not entitled to relief under subdivision (b)(6). MacLeod v. Dalkon Shield Claimants Trust (In re A.H. Robins Co.), 213 Bankr. 468 (E.D. Va. 1997).

The court did not abuse its discretion in denying a motion by a physician for relief from judgment in favor of a medical malpractice claimant in light of the claimant's death. Boyd v. Bulala, 905 F.2d 764 (4th Cir. 1990).

Unnamed motion. — Where a party submits a motion such as defendant's to modify review system in order to permit him to maintain two pending cases at one time, which was unnamed and did not refer to a specific Federal Rule of Civil Procedure, the courts have considered that motion either a Rule 59(e) motion to alter or amend a judgment, or a Rule 60(b) motion for relief from a judgment. In this case the question of which rule applied was quickly resolved because the defendant failed to file the motion within 10 days of entry of judgment, and therefore Rule 59(e) was inapplicable. In re Burnley, 988 F.2d 1 (4th Cir. 1992).

Failure to give notice of hearing on amended bankruptcy plan requires vacation of order. — Debtor's admitted failure to give notice to creditor's bankruptcy counsel of the filing of an amended plan and hearing on confirmation requires the court to vacate the confirmation order. In re Birdneck Apt. Assocs., 152 Bankr. 65 (Bankr. E.D. Va. 1993).

IV. APPELLATE REVIEW.

Denying motion is not abuse of discretion unless finding of no good cause is clearly wrong. — There is no abuse of discretion in denying a motion under Rule 55(c) or subdivision (b) of this rule unless it appears that the district court was clearly wrong in finding that good cause had not been shown for setting aside the default. Consolidated Masonry & Fireproofing, Inc. v. Wagman

Constr. Corp., 383 F.2d 249 (4th Cir. 1967), aff'g 273 F. Supp. 693 (E.D. Va. 1966).

And court's action will not be lightly disturbed. — The disposition of motions made under Rule 55(c) and subdivision (b) of this rule is a matter which lies largely within the discretion of the trial judge, and his action is not lightly to be disturbed by an appellate court. Consolidated Masonry & Fireproofing, Inc. v. Wagman Constr. Corp., 383 F.2d 249 (4th Cir. 1967), aff'g 273 F. Supp. 693 (E.D. Va. 1966).

Court of appeals may not review merits of underlying order. — In ruling on an appeal from a denial of a motion pursuant to subsection (b) of this rule, court of appeals may not review the merits of the underlying order; it may only review the denial of the motion with respect to the grounds set forth in subsection (b) of this rule. In re Burnley, 988 F.2d 1 (4th Cir. 1992).

Exhaustion of state remedies. — Where habeas petitioner requested that the Virginia Supreme Court and the federal district court concurrently examine the effect of four recent U.S. Supreme Court cases as they apply to the Virginia death penalty statute, the doctrine of exhaustion required that the federal district court not consider the issue raised in the Rule 60(b) motion until the petitioner had exhausted all available state remedies. Jones v. Murray, 802 F. Supp. 1412 (E.D. Va. 1992), aff'd, 976 F.2d 169 (4th Cir. 1992).

V. PLEADING AND PRACTICE.

A Rule 60(b)(3) motion must be made "not more than one year after the judgment." — See Great Coastal Express, Inc. v. International Bhd. of Teamsters, 86 F.R.D. 131 (E.D. Va. 1980), aff'd, 675 F.2d 1349 (4th Cir. 1982), cert. denied, 459 U.S. 1128, 103 S. Ct. 764, 74 L. Ed. 2d 978 (1983).

A motion under subdivision (b)(6) need only be made within a reasonable time. Great Coastal Express, Inc. v. International Bhd. of Teamsters, 86 F.R.D. 131 (E.D. Va. 1980), cert. denied, 459 U.S. 1128, 103 S. Ct. 764, 74 L. Ed. 2d 978 (1983).

Reasonableness under subsection (b) is essentially judged by looking to delay from the time the party is deemed to have notice of the ground for its motion. Holland v. Virginia Lee Co., 188 F.R.D. 241 (W.D. Va. 1999).

In measuring delay, there is no set time period distinguishing timely from untimely motions outside of the absolute, one-year time frame for motions under subdivisions (b)(1) to (b)(3) of this rule. Holland v. Virginia Lee Co., 188 F.R.D. 241 (W.D. Va. 1999).

And reasonableness depends on facts. — What constitutes a reasonable time will generally depend on the facts of each case. A major consideration in measuring whether a motion was timely filed may well be whether the non-movant was prejudiced by the delay and whether the movant had a good reason for failing to take action sooner. Holland v. Virginia Lee Co., 188 F.R.D. 241 (W.D. Va. 1999).

Plaintiffs held to have proceeded "within a reasonable time." — See Pierce Oil Corp. v. United States, 9 F.R.D. 619 (E.D. Va. 1949).

Plaintiff held to have not proceeded "within a reasonable time." — See Bright v. Norshipco, 187 F.R.D. 536 (E.D. Va. 1998), aff'd, 178 F.3d 1282 (4th Cir. 1999).

Motion allowed to be filed one day late due to public interest. — See Marshall v. Ampthill Rayon Workers, Inc., 454 F. Supp. 84 (E.D. Va. 1978).

Motion to modify taxation of costs held untimely filed. — The plaintiff's motion to modify taxation of costs, filed more than six months after the judgment was entered and after the sworn statement of costs was filed, and 45 days after the costs were taxed by the clerk, was not timely. No application to extend the time for filing having been submitted, and no motion for relief from judgment having been filed, the plaintiff's motion was denied. Person v. Omni Int'l Hotel-Norfolk, 106 F.R.D. 7 (E.D. Va. 1984).

One-year limitation held applicable. — Where a defendant had filed a third-party action which was dismissed by final order of the district court when the original action was dismissed, but on appeal by the plaintiff (the defendant not noting an appeal of the dismissal of the third-party action), the court of appeals vacated the judgment appealed from and remanded the case for a new trial, the district court held that the interpretation of this rule should not be expanded to the point of permitting an appeal from the order dismissing the third-party action by the filing of a motion under subdivision (b) nearly 32 months after the dismissal. Subdivision (b)(1) providing for relief from final judgments entered by "mistake, inadvertence, surprise, or excusable neglect" requires the filing of an appropriate motion within one year, and it is clear that this was the remedy available to the defendant. If the errors of all attorneys are placed under subdivision (b)(5), there would be no need for subdivision (b)(1). Stancil v. United States, 200 F. Supp. 36 (E.D. Va. 1961).

Subdivision (b) requires a motion for new trial on ground of newly discovered evidence to be made within one year. Hence, where the prior judgment of the district court adverse to the applicant was certified as a final judgment under Rule 54(b) and he accepted the certification by himself appealing from it, but it was affirmed, his motion for a new trial, filed more than 15 months after the district court's prior judgment was entered, was filed more than 15 months after final judgment, and it was barred. Capital Investors Co. v. Devers, 387 F.2d 591 (4th Cir. 1967).

One-year limitation held inapplicable. — See Pierce Oil Corp. v. United States, 9 F.R.D. 619 (E.D. Va. 1949).

Standing in admiralty action. — A salvor brought this action under this rule to rescind the court's order naming a competing salvor as the salvor in possession. The salvor who brought this action was not a party to the original action, but had standing because actions in rem apply to admiralty proceedings. R.M.S. Titanic, Inc. v. Wrecked & Abandoned Vessel, 920 F. Supp. 96 (E.D. Va. 1996).

Case remanded to correct omissions in record and amend judgment. — Where, in a class action, the record did not clearly identify the members of the class, because although plaintiffs' counsel had informally advised the district court that the required notice had been given, the court's files contained neither a copy of the notice nor a certificate that it was sent, and the judgment did not "specify or describe those to whom the notice was directed, and who have not requested exclusion, and whom the court finds to be members of the class," as required by Rule 23(c)(3), such omission having resulted from the oversight of counsel but being capable of remedy without difficulty, the judgment was affirmed, but the case was remanded to the district court so that the omissions in the record could be corrected and the judgment amended. Newman v. Prior, 518 F.2d 97 (4th Cir. 1975), overruled on other grounds, Newcome v. Esrey, 862 F.2d 1099 (4th Cir. 1988).

Rule 61. Harmless Error.

Unless justice requires otherwise, no error in admitting or excluding evidence — or any other error by the court or a party — is ground for granting a new trial, for setting aside a verdict, or for vacating, modifying, or otherwise disturbing a judgment or order. At every stage of the proceeding, the court must disregard all errors and defects that do not affect any party's substantial rights. (Amended by order adopted April 30, 2007, effective December 1, 2007.)

Comment. — The language of Rule 61 has been amended as part of the general restyling of the Civil Rules to make them more easily understood and to make style and terminology consistent throughout the rules. These changes are intended to be stylistic only.

CASE NOTES

No right to perfect trial. — Although a person is entitled to a fair trial, he is not entitled to a perfect one. He does not have a right to a new trial merely because harmless error may have been committed. Mills v. Mealey, 274 F. Supp. 4 (W.D. Va. 1967).

Defective summons. — Although a summons was defective because its caption indicated the parties only by the reference "see complaint," such error was harmless, where a copy of the complaint, with the names of all parties, was attached to the summons, and defendant was not prejudiced by the defect. Newman v. Prior, 518 F.2d 97 (4th Cir. 1975), overruled on other grounds, Newcome v. Esrey, 862 F.2d 1099 (4th Cir. 1988).

Misnomer or misapplication of proper procedure. — The court will not reverse a district court's decision based on its misnomer or misapplication of the proper procedure where the error does not affect the substantial rights of the parties. Distaff, Inc. v. Springfield Contracting Corp., 984 F.2d 108 (4th Cir. 1993).

Error in denying jury trial held harmless in age discrimination action. — District court's error in denying worker a jury trial in his claims pursuant to Age Discrimination in Employment Act was harmless where no reasonable jury could have found that he demonstrated by a preponderance of the evidence that his age was a determining factor in his termination because he offered no evidence that his termination was motivated by his age. Sailor v. Hubbell, Inc., 4 F.3d 323 (4th Cir. 1993).

Admission of testimony held not prejudicial in view of instructions to disregard it. — See United States v. Parcel of Land, 54 F. Supp. 901 (E.D. Va. 1944).

Applied in Utica Mut. Ins. Co. v. Rollason, 246 F.2d 105 (4th Cir. 1957); Blum v. Cottrell, 276 F.2d 689 (4th Cir. 1960); Krizak v. W.C. Brooks & Sons, 320 F.2d 37 (4th Cir. 1963); Langley v. Turner's Express, Inc., 375 F.2d 296 (4th Cir. 1967); Rodgers v. Norfolk Sch. Bd., 755 F.2d 59 (4th Cir. 1985).

Rule 62. Stay of Proceedings to Enforce a Judgment.

(a) *Automatic Stay; Exceptions for Injunctions, Receiverships, and Patent Accountings.* — Except as stated in this rule, no execution may issue on a judgment, nor may proceedings be taken to enforce it, until 14 days have passed after its entry. But unless the court orders otherwise, the following are not stayed after being entered, even if an appeal is taken:

(1) an interlocutory or final judgment in an action for an injunction or a receivership; or

(2) a judgment or order that directs an accounting in an action for patent infringement.

(b) *Stay Pending the Disposition of a Motion.* — On appropriate terms for the opposing party's security, the court may stay the execution of a judgment — or any proceedings to enforce it — pending disposition of any of the following motions:

(1) under Rule 50, for judgment as a matter of law;

(2) under Rule 52(b), to amend the findings or for additional findings;

(3) under Rule 59, for a new trial or to alter or amend a judgment; or

(4) under Rule 60, for relief from a judgment or order.

(c) *Injunction Pending an Appeal.* — While an appeal is pending from an interlocutory order or final judgment that grants, dissolves, or denies an injunction, the court may suspend, modify, restore, or grant an injunction on terms for bond or other terms that secure the opposing party's rights. If the judgment appealed from is rendered by a statutory three-judge district court, the order must be made either:

(1) by that court sitting in open session; or

(2) by the assent of all its judges, as evidenced by their signatures.

(d) *Stay with Bond on Appeal.* — If an appeal is taken, the appellant may obtain a stay by supersedeas bond, except in an action described in Rule 62(a)(1) or (2). The bond may be given upon or after filing the notice of appeal or after obtaining the order allowing the appeal. The stay takes effect when the court approves the bond.

(e) *Stay Without Bond on an Appeal by the United States, Its Officers, or Its Agencies.* — The court must not require a bond, obligation, or other security from the appellant when granting a stay on an appeal by the United States, its officers, or its agencies or on an appeal directed by a department of the federal government.

(f) *Stay in Favor of a Judgment Debtor Under State Law.* — If a judgment is a lien on the judgment debtor's property under the law of the state where the court is located, the judgment debtor is entitled to the same stay of execution the state court would give.

(g) *Appellate Court's Power Not Limited.* — This rule does not limit the power of the appellate court or one of its judges or justices:

(1) to stay proceedings — or suspend, modify, restore, or grant an injunction — while an appeal is pending; or

(2) to issue an order to preserve the status quo or the effectiveness of the judgment to be entered.

(h) *Stay with Multiple Claims or Parties.* — A court may stay the enforcement of a final judgment entered under Rule 54(b) until it enters a later judgment or judgments, and may prescribe terms necessary to secure the benefit of the stayed judgment for the party in whose favor it was entered. (Amended by order adopted December 27, 1946, effective March 19, 1948, by order adopted December 29, 1948, effective October 20, 1949, by order adopted April 17, 1961, effective July 19, 1961, by order adopted March 2, 1987, effective August 1, 1987, by order adopted April 30, 2007, effective December 1, 2007, and by order adopted March 26, 2009, effective December 1, 2009.)

Comment. — The language of Rule 62 has been amended as part of the general restyling of the Civil Rules to make them more easily understood and to make style and terminology consistent throughout the rules. These changes are intended to be stylistic only.

The final sentence of former Rule 62(a) referred to Rule 62(c). It is deleted as unnecessary. Rule 62(c) governs of its own force.

CASE NOTES

This rule is made applicable through Bankruptcy Rule of Procedure 7062. — Subdivision (c) of this rule states, in pertinent part, that the court in its discretion may suspend, modify, restore or grant an injunction during the pendency of the appeal upon such terms as to bond or otherwise as it considers proper for the security of the rights of the adverse party. Brookfield Centre Ltd. Partnership v. CFS Mgt. Co., 133 Bankr. 74 (Bankr. E.D. Va. 1991).

The factors to be considered in granting an injunction pending appeal are like those required for a preliminary injunction. The first step is to balance the likelihood of irreparable harm to the plaintiff against the likelihood of irreparable harm to the defendant. If the court determines that the "decided imbalance of hardship" lies with the plaintiff, then the plaintiff need only show he has raised a grave or serious question of law and the court need not address the likelihood of success on appeal. Where a plaintiff fails to demonstrate a decided imbalance of irreparable harm in its favor, the importance of the probability of succeeding on appeal increases as the probability of irreparable harm decreases. Brookfield Centre Ltd. Partnership v. CFS Mgt. Co., 133 Bankr. 74 (Bankr. E.D. Va. 1991).

Supersedeas bond required to stay money judgment. — Under subdivision (d) of this rule and [former] Rule 73(d) bond securing payment of a money judgment must be given, if supersedeas or stay pending appeal is desired. Fidelity & Deposit Co. v. Davis, 127 F.2d 780 (4th Cir. 1942).

Intervention on appeal from denial of injunction denied where case was reversed and intervenors directed to file motions in district court. — See Blakeney v. Fairfax County Sch. Bd., 334 F.2d 239 (4th Cir.), vacating 226 F. Supp. 713 (E.D. Va. 1964).

Where there is an appeal from a federal district court's order granting an injunction, the court loses jurisdiction to amend or vacate its order after the notice of appeal has been filed. The power given the district court by subdivision (c) of this rule only applies to allow for the security of the rights of the adverse party. Lewis v. Tobacco Workers' Int'l Union, 577 F.2d 1135 (4th Cir. 1978), cert. denied, 439 U.S. 1089, 99 S. Ct. 871, 59 L. Ed. 2d 56 (1979).

District court loses jurisdiction to amend or vacate order after notice of appeal has been

filed. — See Lewis v. Tobacco Workers' Int'l Union, 577 F.2d 1135 (4th Cir. 1978), cert. denied, 439 U.S. 1089, 99 S. Ct. 871, 59 L. Ed. 2d (1979).

District court may stay bankruptcy court order pending appeal. — The Rules of Bankruptcy and subdivision (d) of this rule permit a district court to stay enforcement of a bankruptcy court order pending appeal. Under the rules, the district court may condition the granting of the stay upon the filing of a supersedeas bond. In that event, the filing of the petition for review does not effect a stay unless the bond is filed. Alexandria Nat'l Bank v. National Homeowners Sales Serv. Corp., 554 F.2d 636 (4th Cir. 1977).

When an injunction is sought there is no absolute right to a stay pending appeal. Reynolds Metals Co. v. Secretary of Labor, 453 F. Supp. 4 (W.D. Va. 1977).

Applied in Sterling v. Blackwelder, 405 F.2d 884 (4th Cir. 1969); Davis v. Lukhard, 106 F.R.D. 317 (E.D. Va. 1984); United States v. Fourteen Various Firearms, 897 F. Supp. 271 (E.D. Va. 1995); Odetics, Inc. v. Storage Technology Corp., 14 F. Supp. 2d 785 (E.D. Va. 1998).

Rule 62.1. Indicative Ruling on a Motion for Relief That is Barred by a Pending Appeal.

(a) *Relief Pending Appeal.* — If a timely motion is made for relief that the court lacks authority to grant because of an appeal that has been docketed and is pending, the court may:

(1) defer considering the motion;

(2) deny the motion; or

(3) state either that it would grant the motion if the court of appeals remands for that purpose or that the motion raises a substantial issue.

(b) *Notice to the Court of Appeals.* — The movant must promptly notify the circuit clerk under Federal Rule of Appellate Procedure 12.1 if the district court states that it would grant the motion or that the motion raises a substantial issue.

(c) *Remand.* — The district court may decide the motion if the court of appeals remands for that purpose. (Adopted by order March 26, 2009, effective December 1, 2009.)

Rule 63. Judge's Inability to Proceed.

If a judge conducting a hearing or trial is unable to proceed, any other judge may proceed upon certifying familiarity with the record and determining that the case may be completed without prejudice to the parties. In a hearing or a nonjury trial, the successor judge must, at a party's request, recall any witness whose testimony is material and disputed and who is available to testify again without undue burden. The successor judge may also recall any other witness. (Amended by order adopted March 2, 1987, effective August 1, 1987, by order adopted April 30, 1991, effective December 1, 1991, and by order adopted April 30, 2007, effective December 1, 2007.)

Comment. — The language of Rule 63 has been amended as part of the general restyling of the Civil Rules to make them more easily understood and to make style and terminology consistent throughout the rules. These changes are intended to be stylistic only.

Law Review. — For note on death of judge during course of trial, see 40 Wash. & Lee L. Rev. 568 (1983).

TITLE VIII. PROVISIONAL AND FINAL REMEDIES.

Rule 64. Seizing a Person or Property.

(a) *Remedies Under State Law — In General.* — At the commencement of and throughout an action, every remedy is available that, under the law of the state where the court is located, provides for seizing a person or property to secure satisfaction of the potential judgment. But a federal statute governs to the extent it applies.

(b) *Specific Kinds of Remedies.* — The remedies available under this rule include the following — however designated and regardless of whether state procedure requires an independent action:

- arrest;
- attachment;
- garnishment;
- replevin;
- sequestration; and

• other corresponding or equivalent remedies. (Amended by order adopted April 30, 2007, effective December 1, 2007.)

Comment. — The language of Rule 64 has been amended as part of the general restyling of the Civil Rules to make them more easily understood and to make style and terminology consistent throughout the rules. These changes are intended to be stylistic only.

Former Rule 64 stated that the Civil Rules govern an action in which any remedy available under Rule 64(a) is used. The Rules were said to govern from the time the action is commenced if filed in federal court, and from the time of removal if removed from state court. These provisions are deleted as redundant. Rule 1 establishes that the Civil Rules apply to all actions in a district court, and Rule 81(c)(1) adds reassurance that the Civil Rules apply to a removed action "after it is removed."

CASE NOTES

Applied in Sherwood Trucking, Inc. v. Carolina Cas. Ins. Co., 552 F.2d 568 (4th Cir. 1977).

Rule 65. Injunctions and Restraining Orders.

(a) *Preliminary Injunction.* — (1) Notice. The court may issue a preliminary injunction only on notice to the adverse party.

(2) Consolidating the Hearing with the Trial on the Merits. Before or after beginning the hearing on a motion for a preliminary injunction, the court may advance the trial on the merits and consolidate it with the hearing. Even when consolidation is not ordered, evidence that is received on the motion and that would be admissible at trial becomes part of the trial record and need not be repeated at trial. But the court must preserve any party's right to a jury trial.

(b) *Temporary Restraining Order.* — (1) Issuing Without Notice. The court may issue a temporary restraining order without written or oral notice to the adverse party or its attorney only if:

(A) specific facts in an affidavit or a verified complaint clearly show that immediate and irreparable injury, loss, or damage will result to the movant before the adverse party can be heard in opposition; and

(B) the movant's attorney certifies in writing any efforts made to give notice and the reasons why it should not be required.

(2) Contents; Expiration. Every temporary restraining order issued without notice must state the date and hour it was issued; describe the injury and state why it is irreparable; state why the order was issued without notice; and be promptly filed in the clerk's office and entered in the record. The order expires at the time after entry — not to exceed 14 days — that the court sets, unless before that time the court, for good cause, extends it for a like period or the adverse party consents to a longer extension. The reasons for an extension must be entered in the record.

(3) Expediting the Preliminary-Injunction Hearing. If the order is issued without notice, the motion for a preliminary injunction must be set for hearing at the earliest possible time, taking precedence over all other matters except hearings on older matters of the same character. At the hearing, the party who obtained the order must proceed with the motion; if the party does not, the court must dissolve the order.

(4) Motion to Dissolve. On 2 days' notice to the party who obtained the order without notice — or on shorter notice set by the court — the adverse party may appear and move to dissolve or modify the order. The court must then hear and decide the motion as promptly as justice requires.

(c) *Security.* — The court may issue a preliminary injunction or a temporary restraining order only if the movant gives security in an amount that the court considers proper to pay the costs and damages sustained by any party found to have been wrongfully enjoined or restrained. The United States, its officers, and its agencies are not required to give security.

(d) *Contents and Scope of Every Injunction and Restraining Order.* — (1) Contents. Every order granting an injunction and every restraining order must:

(A) state the reasons why it issued;

(B) state its terms specifically; and

(C) describe in reasonable detail — and not by referring to the complaint or other document — the act or acts restrained or required.

(2) Persons Bound. The order binds only the following who receive actual notice of it by personal service or otherwise:

(A) the parties;

(B) the parties' officers, agents, servants, employees, and attorneys; and

(C) other persons who are in active concert or participation with anyone described in Rule 65(d)(2)(A) or (B).

(e) *Other Laws Not Modified.* — These rules do not modify the following:

(1) any federal statute relating to temporary restraining orders or preliminary injunctions in actions affecting employer and employee;

(2) 28 U.S.C. § 2361, which relates to preliminary injunctions in actions of interpleader or in the nature of interpleader; or

(3) 28 U.S.C. § 2284, which relates to actions that must be heard and decided by a three-judge district court.

(f) *Copyright Impoundment.* — This rule applies to copyright-impoundment proceedings. (Amended by order adopted December 27, 1946, effective March 19, 1948, by order adopted December 29, 1948, effective October 20, 1949, by order adopted February 28, 1966, effective July 1, 1966, by order adopted March 2, 1987, effective August 1, 1987, by order adopted April 23, 2001, effective December 1, 2001, by order adopted April 30, 2007, effective December 1, 2007, and by order adopted March 26, 2009, effective December 1, 2009.)

Comment. — The language of Rule 65 has been amended as part of the general restyling of the Civil Rules to make them more easily understood and to make style and terminology consistent throughout the rules. These changes are intended to be stylistic only.

The final sentence of former Rule 65(c) referred to Rule 65.1. It is deleted as unnecessary. Rule 65.1 governs of its own force.

Rule 65(d)(2) clarifies two ambiguities in former Rule 65(d). The former rule was adapted from former 28 U.S.C. § 363, but omitted a comma that made clear the common doctrine that a party must have actual notice of an injunction in order to be bound by it. Amended Rule 65(d) restores the meaning of the earlier statute, and also makes clear the proposition that an injunction can be enforced against a person who acts in concert with a party's officer, agent, servant, employee, or attorney.

CASE NOTES

Rule to show cause abolished. — Since the effective date of the Federal Rules of Civil Procedure, rules to show cause have not been properly a part of civil practice. Rule 7(b) provides that all applications to the court for orders shall be by motion. The rules and forms then clearly indicate that motions are brought before the court by means of "notice of motion" which serves the purpose of a rule to show cause, and obviates the necessity for obtaining such a rule. Walling v. Moore Milling Co., 62 F. Supp. 378 (W.D. Va. 1945).

And only notice of motion required for hearing on preliminary injunction. — Rule 7(b) and this rule are perfectly clear, and set out the standard procedure for bringing on for hearing a motion for a preliminary injunction. A plaintiff, who desires a preliminary injunction, need only give his notice of such motion, as provided in the rules. Walling v. Moore Milling Co., 62 F. Supp. 378 (W.D. Va. 1945).

Basis of injunctive relief in federal courts has always been irreparable harm and inadequacy of legal remedies. — If the plaintiff shows these two elements, the court may grant injunctive relief. Cooper v. Tazewell Square Apts., Ltd., 577 F. Supp. 1483 (W.D. Va. 1984).

Irreparable injury must be shown for temporary restraining order unless granted before notice. — This rule contemplates ex parte applications for temporary restraining orders, but they may be granted only when it appears that the applicant will suffer irreparable injury unless the restraining order is granted before notice to the adverse party and an adversary hearing. Baines v. City of Danville, 337 F.2d 579 (4th Cir. 1964), aff'd on reh'g, 357 F.2d 756 (4th Cir. 1966).

If such order is granted, prompt notice must be given adversary. — See Baines v. City of Danville, 337 F.2d 579 (4th Cir. 1964), aff'd on reh'g, 357 F.2d 756 (4th Cir. 1966).

But if order refused there is no basis for further proceeding without service of process. — If the court refuses a temporary restraining order, no process of any kind having issued, nothing remains before the court unless and until process is served. After service of process, the applicant may apply for a temporary injunction, but, if there has been no service, there is no foundation for further proceedings against unserved parties. Baines v. City of Danville, 337 F.2d 579 (4th Cir. 1964), aff'd on reh'g, 357 F.2d 756 (4th Cir. 1966).

Test for injunctive relief. — The court must decide (1) whether the plaintiff has succeeded on the merits; (2) if so, whether there is an adequate remedy at law; (3) whether the balance of hardship favors the plaintiff; (4) what injunctive relief is appropriate. Cooper v. Tazewell Square Apts., Ltd., 577 F. Supp. 1483 (W.D. Va. 1984).

Need not be shown where injunctive relief authorized by statute. — Where a statute authorizes injunctive relief for its enforcement, plaintiffs need not plead and prove irreparable injury. Environmental Defense Fund, Inc. v. Lamphier, 714 F.2d 331 (4th Cir. 1983).

The standard for determining whether preliminary injunctive relief should issue is the balance-of-hardship test. This test involves the "flexible interplay" of these factors: (1) The likelihood of irreparable harm to the plaintiffs without an injunction; (2) likelihood of harm to the defendant with an injunction; (3) plaintiffs' likelihood of success on the merits; (4) the public interest. Hanky v. City of Richmond, 532 F. Supp. 1298 (E.D. Va. 1982).

The first step of the court's analysis requires a balancing of the likelihood of irreparable harm to the plaintiffs without an injunction against the likelihood of harm to the defendant with an injunction. If a decided imbalance of hardship should appear in plaintiffs' favor, it is enough that grave or serious questions are presented, and plaintiffs do not have to show a likelihood of success on the merits. These are the two most important factors, and the need for plaintiffs to show likelihood of success on the merits increases as the probability of irreparable injury to plaintiffs without an injunction decreases. Also, if the plaintiffs have a strong probability of success on the merits, even a "possible" irreparable injury will suffice to warrant injunctive relief. Hanky v. City of Richmond, 532 F. Supp. 1298 (E.D. Va. 1982).

The issuance of preliminary injunctions in this circuit is governed by a "balance of hardship" test. Bush Dev. Corp. v. Harbour Place Assocs., 632 F. Supp. 1359 (E.D. Va. 1986).

Balance of harms favoring plaintiff. — Defendant insurer cannot seriously argue against finding that the balance of harms analysis strongly favors the plaintiff breast cancer patient: insurer may lose some money; the plaintiff may lose her life. Wilson v. Office of Civilian Health & Medical Program of Uniformed Servs., 866 F. Supp. 903 (E.D. Va. 1994), aff'd, 65 F.3d 361 (4th Cir. 1995).

Balancing not required where activity may endanger public health. — The law of injunctions differs with respect to governmental plaintiffs (or private attorneys general) as opposed to private individuals. Where the plaintiff is a sovereign and where the activity may endanger the public health, injunctive relief is proper, without resort to balancing. Environmental Defense Fund, Inc. v. Lamphier, 714 F.2d 331 (4th Cir. 1983).

Emphasis is on public interest rather than irreparable injury in such cases. — In cases of public health legislation, the emphasis shifts from irreparable injury to concern for the general public interest. The United States is not bound to conform with the requirements of private litigation when it seeks the aid of the courts to give effect to the policy of Congress as manifested in a statute. An injunction is an appropriate means for the enforcement of an act of Congress when it is in the public interest. This rationale applies equally to state enforcement of federal and state health laws. Environmental Defense Fund, Inc. v. Lamphier, 714 F.2d 331 (4th Cir. 1983).

Examination of quantum and quality of likely harm required. — Determination of whether plaintiff faces irreparable harm without an injunction requires examination of the quantum and quality of their likely harm relative to the detriment to the defendant should an injunction issue. Hanky v. City of Richmond, 532 F. Supp. 1298 (E.D. Va. 1982).

Irreparability of harm includes impossibility of ascertaining with any accuracy the extent of the loss. Hanky v. City of Richmond, 532 F. Supp. 1298 (E.D. Va. 1982).

"Concert or participation" sufficient to be bound by order. — Action as an alter ego or in collusion, is required to find "concert or participation" under subdivision (d) of this rule. Thaxton v. Vaughan, 321 F.2d 474 (4th Cir. 1963).

Members of city council held not persons acting in "concert" with mayor. — See Thaxton v. Vaughan, 321 F.2d 474 (4th Cir. 1963).

Purpose of subdivision (d) of this rule is to protect a party subject to an injunction so that he may know precisely what he must refrain from doing in order to comply with the injunction. First Ass'y of God v. City of Alexandria, 739 F.2d 942 (4th Cir.), cert. denied, 469 U.S. 1019, 105 S. Ct. 434, 83 L. Ed. 2d 360 (1984).

Injunction must set forth reasons, be specific, and describe acts enjoined. — Subdivision (d) of this rule clearly requires that every restraining order and order granting an injunction shall (1) set forth the reasons for its issuance, (2) be specific in its terms, and (3) describe in reasonable detail and not by reference to the complaint or other document the act or acts sought to be restrained. These terms are mandatory and must be observed in every instance. Alberti v. Cruise, 383 F.2d 268 (4th Cir. 1967).

Statement that irreparable injury will result is insufficient without findings of fact. — It has been held that a statement by the court that plaintiff would suffer irreparable injury was specific enough to satisfy subdivision (d) when that statement was read along with detailed findings of fact made by the court, but that holding is inapplicable where there were no specific findings of fact as required and no statement of conclusions of law to support the issuance of the injunction. Alberti v. Cruise, 383 F.2d 268 (4th Cir. 1967).

Motion to dismiss not granted where preliminary hearing would be transposed into final adjudication on merits. — Where defendants' motion to dismiss for failure to state a claim on which relief could be granted, if granted, would transpose what was explicitly a preliminary hearing into a final adjudication on the merits, this would cut against the spirit of subdivision (a)(2) of this rule, which contemplates that such an intention be made known to plaintiffs while they still may present further evidence. Grossberg v. Deusebio, 380 F. Supp. 285 (E.D. Va. 1974).

Consideration of public interest. — Although a consideration of the public interest is important in every case requesting a preliminary injunction, it is often most crucial in a suit to halt enforcement of a statute. Virginia Chapter v. Kreps, 444 F. Supp. 1167 (W.D. Va. 1978).

Balance-of-hardship test showed plaintiffs had not suffered irreparable injury. — See Virginia Chapter v. Kreps, 444 F. Supp. 1167 (W.D. Va. 1978).

Court did not comply with rule relating to findings of fact and conclusions of law in granting preliminary injunctions. — See United States v. Virginia, 569 F.2d 1300 (4th Cir. 1978).

Individual defendant properly dismissed where covered by rule. — Where the plaintiff was afforded ample protection from any possible misconduct on the part of a dismissed individual defendant who was an officer of the corporation subject to an injunction, there was no need for reinstating the individual defendant to the action even if the relevant portion of the settlement could be disregarded. Major v. Orthopedic Equip. Co., 496 F. Supp. 604 (E.D. Va. 1980).

Application of preliminary injunction to multiple owners. — Where respondant managed all four multi-dwelling units affected by the preliminary injunction and the contract in question applied to all four multi-dwelling units, all four multi-dwelling unit owners and respondant acted in active concert in arranging the contract in question, thus, the preliminary injunction properly applied to all four multi-dwelling units and their owners. Multi-Channel TV Cable Co. v. Charlottesville Quality Cable Operating Co., 22 F.3d 546 (4th Cir. 1994).

Action for unlawful detainer held not adequate remedy. — Where federal housing laws and regulations established a reviewing process outside the courts and the tenant did not receive a hearing meeting the standards of that process, an unlawful detainer action was not an adequate remedy at law to protect the statutory and regulatory procedures afforded the tenant. Cooper v. Tazewell Square Apts., Ltd., 577 F. Supp. 1483 (W.D. Va. 1984).

Power of bankruptcy court to enjoin collection of penalty by Internal Revenue Service. — A bankruptcy court had the power, regardless of the Anti-Injunction Act, to enjoin the Internal Revenue Service from collecting a penalty assessed against a debtor, because the court had to be able to protect the debtor's opportunity to rehabilitate itself. J.K. Printing Servs., Inc. v. United States, Dep't of Treas., 49 Bankr. 798 (Bankr. W.D. Va. 1985).

Bond amount within court discretion. — While the decision whether to require a bond is strictly circumscribed by subdivision (c) of this rule, the computation of the bond amount is soundly within the court's discretion. Wilson v. Office of Civilian Health & Medical Program of Uniformed Servs., 866 F. Supp. 903 (E.D. Va. 1994), aff'd, 65 F.3d 361 (4th Cir. 1995).

Bond of zero dollars permitted. — Where it was apparent that to require a bond would not only defeat the plaintiff's otherwise meritorious claim and it may also cost the plaintiff her life, plaintiff was required to post a bond of zero dollars. Wilson v. Office of Civilian Health & Medical Program of Uniformed Servs., 866 F. Supp. 903 (E.D. Va. 1994), aff'd, 65 F.3d 361 (4th Cir. 1995).

Applied in Paxman v. Wilkerson, 390 F. Supp. 442 (E.D. Va. 1975); SEC v. American Realty Trust, 429 F. Supp. 1148 (E.D. Va. 1977); Mitchell v. Block, 551 F. Supp. 1011 (W.D. Va. 1982); Fuller v. Hurley, 559 F. Supp. 313 (W.D. Va. 1983); Davis v. Lukhard, 106 F.R.D. 317 (E.D. Va. 1984); Levy v. Runnells, 815 F.2d 969 (4th Cir. 1987); Grundy Nat'l Bank v. Looney, 823 F.2d 788 (4th Cir. 1987); Howard Cooper Corp. v. United States, 763 F. Supp. 829 (E.D. Va. 1991); International Lotto Fund v. Virginia State Lottery Dep't, 800 F. Supp. 337 (E.D. Va. 1992); City Auto, Inc. v. Exxon Co., U.S.A., 806 F. Supp. 567 (E.D. Va. 1992); Lawler v. Schumacher Filters Am., Inc., 832 F. Supp. 1044 (E.D. Va. 1993); Krichbaum v. Kelley, 844 F. Supp. 1107 (W.D. Va. 1994); United States Dep't of HUD v. Cost Control Mktg. & Sales Mgt. of Va., Inc., 64 F.3d 920 (4th Cir. 1995); R.M.S. Titanic, Inc. v. Haver, 171 F.3d 943 (4th. Cir. 1999); R.M.S. Titanic, Inc. v. Wrecked & Abandoned Vessel, 9 F. Supp. 2d 624 (E.D. Va. 1998); CPC Int'l, Inc. v. Skippy, Inc., 214 F.3d 456, 2000 U.S. App. LEXIS 12104 (4th Cir. 2000).

Rule 65.1. Proceedings Against a Surety.

Whenever these rules (including the Supplemental Rules for Admiralty or Maritime Claims and Asset Forfeiture Actions) require or allow a party to give security, and security is given through a bond or other undertaking with one or more sureties, each surety submits to the court's jurisdiction and irrevocably appoints the court clerk as its agent for receiving service of any papers that affect its liability on the bond or undertaking. The surety's liability may be enforced on motion without an independent action. The motion and any notice that the court orders may be served on the court clerk, who must promptly mail a copy of each to every surety whose address is known. (Added by order adopted February 28, 1966, effective July 1, 1966, amended by order adopted March 2, 1987, effective August 1, 1987, by order adopted April 12, 2006, effective December 1, 2006, and by order adopted April 30, 2007, effective December 1, 2007.)

Comment. — The language of Rule 65.1 has been amended as part of the general restyling of the Civil Rules to make them more easily understood and to make style and terminology consistent throughout the rules. These changes are intended to be stylistic only.

Rule 66. Receivers.

These rules govern an action in which the appointment of a receiver is sought or a receiver sues or is sued. But the practice in administering an estate by a receiver or a similar court-appointed officer must accord with the historical practice in federal courts or with a local rule. An action in which a receiver has been appointed may be dismissed only by court order. (Amended by order adopted December 27, 1946, effective March 19, 1948, and by order adopted December 29, 1948, effective October 20, 1949, and by order adopted April 30, 2007, effective December 1, 2007.)

Comment. — The language of Rule 66 has been amended as part of the general restyling of the Civil Rules to make them more easily understood and to make style and terminology consistent throughout the rules. These changes are intended to be stylistic only.

Rule 67. Deposit into Court.

(a) *Depositing Property.* — If any part of the relief sought is a money judgment or the disposition of a sum of money or some other deliverable thing, a party — on notice to every other party and by leave of court — may deposit with the court all or part of the money or thing, whether or not that party claims any of it. The depositing party must deliver to the clerk a copy of the order permitting deposit.

(b) *Investing and Withdrawing Funds.* — Money paid into court under this rule must be deposited and withdrawn in accordance with 28 U.S.C. §§ 2041 and 2042 and any like statute. The money must be deposited in an interest-bearing account or invested in a court-approved, interest-bearing instrument. (Amended by order adopted December 29, 1948, effective October 20, 1949, by order adopted April 28, 1983, effective August 1, 1983, and by order adopted April 30, 2007, effective December 1, 2007.)

Comment. — The language of Rule 67 has been amended as part of the general restyling of the Civil Rules to make them more easily understood and to make style and terminology consistent throughout the rules. These changes are intended to be stylistic only.

Rule 68. Offer of Judgment.

(a) *Making an Offer; Judgment on an Accepted Offer.* — At least 14 days before the date set for trial, a party defending against a claim may serve on an opposing party an offer to allow judgment on specified terms, with the costs then accrued. If, within 14 days after being served, the opposing party serves written notice accepting the offer, either party may then file the offer and notice of acceptance, plus proof of service. The clerk must then enter judgment.

(b) *Unaccepted Offer.* — An unaccepted offer is considered withdrawn, but it does not preclude a later offer. Evidence of an unaccepted offer is not admissible except in a proceeding to determine costs.

(c) *Offer After Liability Is Determined.* — When one party's liability to another has been determined but the extent of liability remains to be determined by further proceedings, the party held liable may make an offer of judgment. It must be served within a reasonable time — but at least 14 days — before the date set for a hearing to determine the extent of liability.

(d) *Paying Costs After an Unaccepted Offer.* — If the judgment that the offeree finally obtains is not more favorable than the unaccepted offer, the offeree must pay the costs incurred after the offer was made. (Amended by order adopted December 27, 1946, effective March 19, 1948, by order adopted February 28, 1966, effective July 1, 1966, by order adopted March 2, 1987, effective August 1, 1987, by order adopted April 30, 2007, effective December 1, 2007, and by order adopted March 26, 2009, effective December 1, 2009.)

Comment. — The language of Rule 68 has been amended as part of the general restyling of the Civil Rules to make them more easily understood and to make style and terminology consistent throughout the rules. These changes are intended to be stylistic only.

CASE NOTES

Difference between normal settlement offer and Rule 68 offer of judgment. — A normal final settlement offer, then, is like an ordinary contract offer in that it leaves the offeree two options: accept it on its terms, or reject it and run the risk of receiving a lesser judgment at trial; an offer of judgment under this rule, on the other hand, presents a more draconian choice to the plaintiff: accept it on its terms, or go to trial and run the risk of obtaining a less favorable judgment and paying the defending party's post-offer costs. Said v. Virginia Commonwealth University/Medical College, 130 F.R.D. 60 (E.D. Va. 1990).

Offeree entitled to construe offer's terms strictly. — The offeree under this rule is entitled to construe the offer's terms strictly, and courts should be reluctant to allow the offeror's extrinsic evidence to affect that construction. Said v. Virginia Commonwealth University/Medical College, 130 F.R.D. 60 (E.D. Va. 1990).

When an offer of judgment uses terms of art, a claimant must be allowed to make his acceptance decision based on the interpretation those terms are commonly given. Said v. Virginia Commonwealth University/Medical College, 130 F.R.D. 60 (E.D. Va. 1990).

How court determines whether attorney's fees included in costs. — When an offeree accepts an offer under this rule stating that judgment shall be entered in a certain amount with costs accrued, the court will not look to the history of negotiations between the parties to divine their intent as to whether attorney's fees are included within that offer; rather, the court will look to the substantive law of the plaintiff's claim to determine what constitutes the pre-offer "costs" he is entitled to. Said v. Virginia Commonwealth University/Medical College, 130 F.R.D. 60 (E.D. Va. 1990).

Costs include attorney's fees in civil rights case. — Where a civil rights plaintiff accepts an offer of judgment under this rule that does not specify whether attorney's fees are included in the offered amount, he shall be entitled to recover his costs, including attorney's fees; this recovery is limited, though, to the costs that had accrued up to the time that offer was made. Said v. Virginia Commonwealth University/Medical College, 130 F.R.D. 60 (E.D. Va. 1990).

Applied in Carr v. Super 8 Motel Developers, Inc., 964 F. Supp. 1046 (E.D. Va. 1997).

Rule 69. Execution.

(a) *In General.* — (1) Money Judgment; Applicable Procedure. A money judgment is enforced by a writ of execution, unless the court directs otherwise. The procedure on execution — and in proceedings supplementary to and in aid of judgment or execution — must accord with the procedure of the state where the court is located, but a federal statute governs to the extent it applies.

(2) Obtaining Discovery. In aid of the judgment or execution, the judgment creditor or a successor in interest whose interest appears of record may obtain discovery from any person — including the judgment debtor — as provided in these rules or by the procedure of the state where the court is located.

(b) *Against Certain Public Officers.* — When a judgment has been entered against a revenue officer in the circumstances stated in 28 U.S.C. § 2006, or against an officer of Congress in the circumstances stated in 2 U.S.C. § 118, the judgment must be satisfied as those statutes provide. (Amended by order adopted December 29, 1948, effective October 20, 1949, by order adopted March 30, 1970, effective July 1, 1970, by order adopted March 2, 1987, effective August 1, 1987, and by order adopted April 30, 2007, effective December 1, 2007.)

Comment. — The language of Rule 69 has been amended as part of the general restyling of the Civil Rules to make them more easily understood and to make style and terminology consistent throughout the rules. These changes are intended to be stylistic only.

Amended Rule 69(b) incorporates directly the provisions of 2 U.S.C. § 118 and 28 U.S.C. § 2006, deleting the incomplete statement in former Rule 69(b) of the circumstances in which execution does not issue against an officer.

CASE NOTES

Use of charging order. — Plaintiff did not cause a writ of execution to issue. Instead, it merely sought the entry of a charging order armed only with what may be best described as a "naked" final judgment. Therefore, until a charging order entered, the judgment debtor virtually was free, as against the instant plaintiff, to encumber intangible property, including her interests to discretionary distributions of a limited partnership. A charging order, without more, does not take priority over a security interest perfected after judgment but before the entry date of the charging order. First Union Nat'l Bank v. Craun, 853 F. Supp. 209 (W.D. Va. 1994).

Applied in Slaughter v. Winston, 347 F. Supp. 1221 (E.D. Va. 1972).

Rule 70. Enforcing a Judgment for a Specific Act.

(a) *Party's Failure to Act; Ordering Another to Act.* — If a judgment requires a party to convey land, to deliver a deed or other document, or to perform any other specific act and the party fails to comply within the time specified, the court may order the act to be done — at the disobedient party's expense — by another person appointed by the court. When done, the act has the same effect as if done by the party.

(b) *Vesting Title.* — If the real or personal property is within the district, the court — instead of ordering a conveyance — may enter a judgment divesting any party's title and vesting it in others. That judgment has the effect of a legally executed conveyance.

(c) *Obtaining a Writ of Attachment or Sequestration.* — On application by a party entitled to performance of an act, the clerk must issue a writ of attachment or sequestration against the disobedient party's property to compel obedience.

(d) *Obtaining a Writ of Execution or Assistance.* — On application by a party who obtains a judgment or order for possession, the clerk must issue a writ of execution or assistance.

(e) *Holding in Contempt.* — The court may also hold the disobedient party in contempt. (Amended by order adopted April 30, 2007, effective December 1, 2007.)

Comment. — The language of Rule 70 has been amended as part of the general restyling of the Civil Rules to make them more easily understood and to make style and terminology consistent throughout the rules. These changes are intended to be stylistic only.

Rule 71. Enforcing Relief For or Against a Nonparty.

When an order grants relief for a nonparty or may be enforced against a nonparty, the procedure for enforcing the order is the same as for a party. (Amended by order adopted March 2, 1987, effective August 1, 1987, and by order adopted April 30, 2007, effective December 1, 2007.)

Comment. — The language of Rule 71 has been amended as part of the general restyling of the Civil Rules to make them more easily understood and to make style and terminology consistent throughout the rules. These changes are intended to be stylistic only.

TITLE IX. SPECIAL PROCEEDINGS.

Rule 71.1. Condemning Real or Personal Property.

(a) *Applicability of Other Rules.* — These rules govern proceedings to condemn real and personal property by eminent domain, except as this rule provides otherwise.

(b) *Joinder of Properties.* — The plaintiff may join separate pieces of property in a single action, no matter whether they are owned by the same persons or sought for the same use.

(c) *Complaint.* — (1) Caption. The complaint must contain a caption as provided in Rule 10(a). The plaintiff must, however, name as defendants both the property — designated generally by kind, quantity, and location — and at least one owner of some part of or interest in the property.

(2) Contents. The complaint must contain a short and plain statement of the following:

(A) the authority for the taking;
(B) the uses for which the property is to be taken;
(C) a description sufficient to identify the property;
(D) the interests to be acquired; and
(E) for each piece of property, a designation of each defendant who has been joined as an owner or owner of an interest in it.

(3) Parties. When the action commences, the plaintiff need join as defendants only those persons who have or claim an interest in the property and whose names are then known. But before any hearing on compensation, the plaintiff must add as defendants all those persons who have or claim an interest and whose names have become known or can be found by a reasonably diligent search of the records, considering both the property's character and value and the interests to be acquired. All others may be made defendants under the designation "Unknown Owners."

(4) Procedure. Notice must be served on all defendants as provided in Rule 71.1(d), whether they were named as defendants when the action commenced or were added later. A defendant may answer as provided in Rule 71.1(e). The court, meanwhile, may order any distribution of a deposit that the facts warrant.

(5) Filing; Additional Copies. In addition to filing the complaint, the plaintiff must give the clerk at least one copy for the defendants' use and additional copies at the request of the clerk or a defendant.

(d) *Process.* — (1) Delivering Notice to the Clerk. On filing a complaint, the plaintiff must promptly deliver to the clerk joint or several notices directed to the named defendants. When adding defendants, the plaintiff must deliver to the clerk additional notices directed to the new defendants.

(2) Contents of the Notice. (A) Main Contents. Each notice must name the court, the title of the action, and the defendant to whom it is directed. It must describe the property sufficiently to identify it, but need not describe any property other than that to be taken from the named defendant. The notice must also state:

(i) that the action is to condemn property;
(ii) the interest to be taken;
(iii) the authority for the taking;

(iv) the uses for which the property is to be taken;

(v) that the defendant may serve an answer on the plaintiff's attorney within 21 days after being served with the notice;

(vi) that the failure to so serve an answer constitutes consent to the taking and to the court's authority to proceed with the action and fix the compensation; and

(vii) that a defendant who does not serve an answer may file a notice of appearance.

(B) Conclusion. The notice must conclude with the name, telephone number, and e-mail address of the plaintiff's attorney and an address within the district in which the action is brought where the attorney may be served.

(3) Serving the Notice. (A) Personal Service. When a defendant whose address is known resides within the United States or a territory subject to the administrative or judicial jurisdiction of the United States, personal service of the notice (without a copy of the complaint) must be made in accordance with Rule 4.

(B) Service by Publication.

(i) A defendant may be served by publication only when the plaintiff's attorney files a certificate stating that the attorney believes the defendant cannot be personally served, because after diligent inquiry within the state where the complaint is filed, the defendant's place of residence is still unknown or, if known, that it is beyond the territorial limits of personal service. Service is then made by publishing the notice — once a week for at least three successive weeks — in a newspaper published in the county where the property is located or, if there is no such newspaper, in a newspaper with general circulation where the property is located. Before the last publication, a copy of the notice must also be mailed to every defendant who cannot be personally served but whose place of residence is then known. Unknown owners may be served by publication in the same manner by a notice addressed to "Unknown Owners."

(ii) Service by publication is complete on the date of the last publication. The plaintiff's attorney must prove publication and mailing by a certificate, attach a printed copy of the published notice, and mark on the copy the newspaper's name and the dates of publication.

(4) Effect of Delivery and Service. Delivering the notice to the clerk and serving it have the same effect as serving a summons under Rule 4.

(5) Proof of Service; Amending the Proof or Notice. Rule 4(l) governs proof of service. The court may permit the proof or the notice to be amended.

(e) *Appearance or Answer.* — (1) Notice of Appearance. A defendant that has no objection or defense to the taking of its property may serve a notice of appearance designating the property in which it claims an interest. The defendant must then be given notice of all later proceedings affecting the defendant.

(2) Answer. A defendant that has an objection or defense to the taking must serve an answer within 21 days after being served with the notice. The answer must:

(A) identify the property in which the defendant claims an interest;

(B) state the nature and extent of the interest; and

(C) state all the defendant's objections and defenses to the taking.

(3) Waiver of Other Objections and Defenses; Evidence on Compensation. A defendant waives all objections and defenses not stated in its answer. No other pleading or motion asserting an additional objection or defense is allowed. But at the trial on compensation, a defendant — whether or not it has previously appeared or answered — may present evidence on the amount of compensation to be paid and may share in the award.

(f) *Amending Pleadings.* — Without leave of court, the plaintiff may — as often as it wants — amend the complaint at any time before the trial on compensation. But no amendment may be made if it would result in a dismissal inconsistent with Rule 71.1(i)(1) or (2). The plaintiff need not serve a copy of an amendment, but must serve notice of the filing, as provided in Rule 5(b), on every affected party who has appeared and, as provided in Rule 71.1(d), on every affected party who has not appeared. In addition, the plaintiff must give the clerk at least one copy of each amendment for the defendants' use, and additional copies at the request of the clerk or a defendant. A defendant may appear or answer in the time and manner and with the same effect as provided in Rule 71.1(e).

(g) *Substituting Parties.* — If a defendant dies, becomes incompetent, or transfers an interest after being joined, the court may, on motion and notice of hearing, order that the proper party be substituted. Service of the motion and notice on a nonparty must be made as provided in Rule 71.1(d)(3).

(h) *Trial of the Issues.* — (1) Issues Other Than Compensation; Compensation. In an action involving eminent domain under federal law, the court tries all issues, including compensation, except when compensation must be determined:

(A) by any tribunal specially constituted by a federal statute to determine compensation; or

(B) if there is no such tribunal, by a jury when a party demands one within the time to answer or within any additional time the court sets, unless the court appoints a commission.

(2) Appointing a Commission; Commission's Powers and Report. (A) Reasons for Appointing. If a party has demanded a jury, the court may instead appoint a three-person commission to determine compensation because of the character, location, or quantity of the property to be condemned or for other just reasons.

(B) Alternate Commissioners. The court may appoint up to two additional persons to serve as alternate commissioners to hear the case and replace commissioners who, before a decision is filed, the court finds unable or disqualified to perform their duties. Once the commission renders its final decision, the court must discharge any alternate who has not replaced a commissioner.

(C) Examining the Prospective Commissioners. Before making its appointments, the court must advise the parties of the identity and qualifications of each prospective commissioner and alternate, and may permit the parties to examine them. The parties may not suggest appointees, but for good cause may object to a prospective commissioner or alternate.

(D) Commission's Powers and Report. A commission has the powers of a master under Rule 53(c). Its action and report are determined by a majority. Rule 53(d), (e), and (f) apply to its action and report.

(i) *Dismissal of the Action or a Defendant.* — (1) Dismissing the Action. (A) By the Plaintiff. If no compensation hearing on a piece of property has begun, and if the plaintiff has not acquired title or a lesser interest or taken possession, the plaintiff may, without a court order, dismiss the action as to that property by filing a notice of dismissal briefly describing the property.

(B) By Stipulation. Before a judgment is entered vesting the plaintiff with title or a lesser interest in or possession of property, the plaintiff and affected defendants may, without a court order, dismiss the action in whole or in part by filing a stipulation of dismissal. And if the parties so stipulate, the court may vacate a judgment already entered.

(C) By Court Order. At any time before compensation has been determined and paid, the court may, after a motion and hearing, dismiss the action as to a piece of property. But if the plaintiff has already taken title, a lesser interest, or possession as to any part of it, the court must award compensation for the title, lesser interest, or possession taken.

(2) Dismissing a Defendant. The court may at any time dismiss a defendant who was unnecessarily or improperly joined.

(3) Effect. A dismissal is without prejudice unless otherwise stated in the notice, stipulation, or court order.

(j) *Deposit and Its Distribution.* — (1) Deposit. The plaintiff must deposit with the court any money required by law as a condition to the exercise of eminent domain and may make a deposit when allowed by statute.

(2) Distribution; Adjusting Distribution. After a deposit, the court and attorneys must expedite the proceedings so as to distribute the deposit and to determine and pay compensation. If the compensation finally awarded to a defendant exceeds the amount distributed to that defendant, the court must enter judgment against the plaintiff for the deficiency. If the compensation awarded to a defendant is less than the amount distributed to that defendant, the court must enter judgment against that defendant for the overpayment.

(k) *Condemnation Under a State's Power of Eminent Domain.* — This rule governs an action involving eminent domain under state law. But if state law provides for trying an issue by jury — or for trying the issue of compensation by jury or commission or both — that law governs.

(*l*) *Costs.* — Costs are not subject to Rule 54(d). (Added by order adopted April 30, 1951, effective August 1, 1951, amended by order adopted January 21, 1963, effective July 1, 1963, by order adopted April 29, 1985, effective August 1, 1985, by order adopted March 2, 1987, effective August 1, 1987, by order adopted April 25, 1988, effective August 1, 1988, by P.L. 100-690, effective November 18, 1988, by order adopted April 1, 1993, effective December 1, 1993, by order adopted April 22, 1993, effective December 1, 1993, by order adopted March 27, 2003, effective December 1, 2003, by order adopted April 30, 2007, effective December 1, 2007, and by order adopted March 26, 2009, effective December 1, 2009.)

Comment. — The language of Rule 71A has been amended as part of the general restyling of the Civil Rules to make them more easily understood and to make style and terminology consistent throughout the rules. These changes are intended to be stylistic only.

Former Rule 71A has been redesignated as Rule 71.1 to conform to the designations used for all other rules added within the original numbering system.

Law Review. — For article, "New Federal Procedure in Condemnation Actions," see 39 Va. L. Re. 1071 (1953).

CASE NOTES

Subdivision (h) of this rule incorporates Rule 53(e), pursuant to which the district court may modify the report on the basis of the record made before the commissioners. United States v. 3.0 Acres of Land, 378 F. Supp. 30 (W.D. Va. 1974).

Judge should subject commission to close supervision. — Under federal practice when a federal district judge uses a commission, he must subject it to close supervision to prevent its becoming a free-wheeling body, taking the law from itself. United States v. 452.876 Acres of Land, more or Less, 667 F.2d 442 (4th Cir. 1981).

The court should carefully instruct the commissioners on the law and the type of report to be filed. United States v. 3.0 Acres of Land, 378 F. Supp. 30 (W.D. Va. 1974).

And litigants have a responsibility to assist the process by specifying their objections to instructions, by offering alternate ones, and by making their timely objections to the report in specific, rather than in generalized form, as required by equity practice. United States v. 3.0 Acres of Land, 378 F. Supp. 30 (W.D. Va. 1974).

What commissioners' report should reveal. — While commissioners, not being trained in the law, need not make detailed findings such as judges who do try a case without a jury, still they can and should be instructed to reveal the reasoning they use in deciding on a particular award, what standard they try to follow, which line of testimony they adopt, and what measure of severance damages they use. United States v. 452.876 Acres of Land, more or Less, 667 F.2d 442 (4th Cir. 1981).

Case remanded for more complete report. — Where the report filed by the commission set forth that the property right taken was a perpetual easement of air rights, the value of the property before the taking, the value of the land after taking the fair market value of the property right and the highest and best use of the property, the unelucidated figure that falls within the highest appraisal advanced by the landowner and the lowest advanced by the government is nothing more than an unexplained result; the mere falling between those extreme limits does nothing to make understandable the process by which the commission arrived at its determinations of values. Therefore, the case would be remanded for a more complete report. United States v. 452.876 Acres of Land, more or Less, 667 F.2d 442 (4th Cir. 1981).

Names and opinions of expert witnesses are not subject to disclosure by discovery. — The federal rule of decision with regard to expert witnesses in eminent domain proceedings is that the names and opinions of such experts are not subject to disclosure by way of discovery. Hornback v. State Hwy. Comm'r, 205 Va. 50, 135 S.E.2d 136 (1964).

The commission's findings must be accepted unless clearly erroneous. United States v. 180.37 Acres of Land, 254 F. Supp. 209 (W.D. Va. 1966); United States v. 180.37 Acres of Land, 254 F. Supp. 678 (W.D. Va. 1966); United States v. Atomic Fuel Coal Co., 383 F.2d 1 (4th Cir. 1967).

A court will be better able to achieve its goal of affording equal justice to all the parties involved if it is able to rely on the judgment of experts in a given field. It is for this reason that the drafters of the federal rules have specified that the opinions and conclusions of the commissioners, arrived at after a thorough consideration of all the facts and evidence introduced, are not to be disturbed unless "clearly erroneous." United States v. 180.37 Acres of Land, 254 F. Supp. 678 (W.D. Va. 1966).

In eminent domain proceedings in the federal courts, by virtue of this rule and Rule 53, the commission's findings of fact are clothed in the armor of the "clearly erroneous" rule. Especially is this so where the commission's findings were reviewed and adopted by the district judge, and they will not be disturbed unless a very plain mistake has been made. United States v. Certain Parcels of Land, 384 F.2d 677 (4th Cir. 1967).

Intervention in condemnation proceeding. — See United States v. 1,830.62 Acres of Land, 51 F. Supp. 158 (W.D. Va. 1943) (decided prior to the adoption of this rule); United States v. 9.85 Acres of Land, 183 F. Supp. 402 (E.D. Va. 1959), aff'd sub nom. Tidewater Dev. & Sales Corp. v. United States, 279 F.2d 890 (4th Cir. 1960).

Refusing motion for mistrial for juror's misconduct is discretionary. — See United States v. Prettyman, 142 F.2d 891 (4th Cir. 1944) (decided prior to adoption of this rule).

And litigants have a responsibility to assist the process by specifying their objections to instructions, by offering alternate ones, and by making their timely objections to the report in specific, rather than in generalized form, as required by equity practice. United States v. 3.0 Acres of Land, 378 F. Supp. 30 (W.D. Va. 1974).

Condemnation proceedings governed by federal law. — The contention of the landowners that, as a matter of absolute right, they were entitled to a trial before a commission in accordance with the laws of Virginia was rejected where the Washington Metr. Area Transportation Compact governed and provides for federal law to govern condemnation proceedings, and Federal Rules of Civil Procedure, Rule 71A provides for the trial to the issue of compensation. Washington Metro. Area Transit Auth. v. Two Parcels of Land, 569 F.2d 816 (4th Cir. 1978).

Applied in United States v. Whitehurst, 337 F.2d 765 (4th Cir. 1964); United States v. Moore, 361 F.2d 494 (4th Cir. 1966); United States v. 23.94 Acres of Land, 325 F. Supp. 330 (W.D. Va. 1970); United States v. 615.10 Acres of Land, 327 F. Supp. 691 (W.D. Va. 1971); United States v. Banisadr Bldg. Joint Venture, 65 F.3d 374 (4th Cir. 1995).

Rule 72. Magistrate Judges: Pretrial Order.

(a) *Nondispositive Matters.* — When a pretrial matter not dispositive of a party's claim or defense is referred to a magistrate judge to hear and decide, the magistrate judge must promptly conduct the required proceedings and, when appropriate, issue a written order stating the decision. A party may serve and file objections to the order within 14 days after being served with a copy. A party may not assign as error a defect in the order not timely objected to. The district judge in the case must consider timely objections and modify or set aside any part of the order that is clearly erroneous or is contrary to law.

(b) *Dispositive Motions and Prisoner Petitions.* — (1) Findings and Recommendations. A magistrate judge must promptly conduct the required proceedings when assigned, without the parties' consent, to hear a pretrial matter dispositive of a claim or defense or a prisoner petition challenging the conditions of confinement. A record must be made of all evidentiary proceedings and may, at the magistrate judge's discretion, be made of any other proceedings. The magistrate judge must enter a recommended disposition, including, if appropriate, proposed findings of fact. The clerk must promptly mail a copy to each party.

(2) Objections. Within 14 days after being served with a copy of the recommended disposition, a party may serve and file specific written objections to the proposed findings and recommendations. A party may respond to another party's objections within 14 days after being served with a copy. Unless the district judge orders otherwise, the objecting party must promptly arrange for transcribing the record, or whatever portions of it the parties agree to or the magistrate judge considers sufficient.

(3) Resolving Objections. The district judge must determine de novo any part of the magistrate judge's disposition that has been properly objected to. The district judge may accept, reject, or modify the recommended disposition; receive further evidence; or return the matter to the magistrate judge with instructions. (Added by order adopted April 28, 1983, effective August 1, 1983, amended by order adopted April 30, 1991, effective December 1, 1991, by order adopted April 22, 1993, effective December 1, 1993, by order adopted April 30, 2007, effective December 1, 2007, and by order adopted March 26, 2009, effective December 1, 2009.)

Comment. — The language of Rule 72 has been amended as part of the general restyling of the Civil Rules to make them more easily understood and to make style and terminology consistent throughout the rules. These changes are intended to be stylistic only.

Editor's note. — As to procedure in appeals to United States courts of appeals generally, see Federal Rules of Appellate Procedure, *infra,* and the rules of the Court of Appeals for the Fourth Circuit, *infra.*

CASE NOTES

Evidentiary ruling. — Magistrate judge's ruling on defendants' motion in limine cannot be analogized to a motion for summary judgment where the subject of the motion in limine was the admissibility of evidence. A motion for summary judgment requires that the court determine that there is no genuine issue as to any material fact and that the moving party is entitled to a judgment as a matter of law. In reaching the evidentiary issue, the magistrate did not make these determinations at the hearing on the motion in limine. Jesselson v. Outlet Assocs., 784 F. Supp. 1223 (E.D. Va. 1991).

Review of a magistrate's ruling before the district court does not permit consideration of issues not raised before the magistrate. The purpose of the rules is to allow magistrates to assume some of the burden imposed on the district courts and to relieve courts of unnecessary work. Allowing plaintiffs to present their case to the magistrate, and then, because they were unsuccessful, present new issues and arguments to the district court would frustrate this purpose. Jesselson v. Outlet Assocs., 784 F. Supp. 1223 (E.D. Va. 1991).

Ruling nondispositive. — Where magistrate did not reach the merits of plaintiffs' case, but merely made evidentiary rulings without regard to the effect of the rulings on the outcome of the litigation, dispositive classification under subsection (b) could not be applied. Jesselson v. Outlet Assocs., 784 F. Supp. 1223 (E.D. Va. 1991).

Applied in Young v. James, 168 F.R.D. 24 (E.D. Va. 1996); Kidwell v. Sheetz, Inc., 996 F. Supp. 552 (W.D. Va. 1998); In re Oral Testimony of Witness, 1 F. Supp. 2d 587 (E.D. Va. 1998); Weeks v. Angelone, 4 F. Supp. 2d 497 (E.D. Va. 1998); Yeatts v. Angelone, 166 F.3d 255 (4th Cir. 1999); Bilodeau v. Angelone, 39 F. Supp. 2d 652 (E.D. Va. 1999); Kyser v. Apfel, 81 F. Supp. 2d 645 (W.D. Va. 2000).

Rule 73. Magistrate Judges: Trial by Consent; Appeal.

(a) *Trial by Consent.* — When authorized under 28 U.S.C. § 636(c), a magistrate judge may, if all parties consent, conduct a civil action or proceeding, including a jury or nonjury trial. A record must be made in accordance with 28 U.S.C. § 636(c)(5).

(b) *Consent Procedure.* — (1) In General. When a magistrate judge has been designated to conduct civil actions or proceedings, the clerk must give the parties written notice of their opportunity to consent under 28 U.S.C. § 636(c). To signify their consent, the parties must jointly or separately file a statement consenting to the referral. A district judge or magistrate judge may be informed of a party's response to the clerk's notice only if all parties have consented to the referral.

(2) Reminding the Parties About Consenting. A district judge, magistrate judge, or other court official may remind the parties of the magistrate judge's availability, but must also advise them that they are free to withhold consent without adverse substantive consequences.

(3) Vacating a Referral. On its own for good cause — or when a party shows extraordinary circumstances — the district judge may vacate a referral to a magistrate judge under this rule.

(c) *Appealing a Judgment.* — In accordance with 28 U.S.C. § 636(c)(3), an appeal from a judgment entered at a magistrate judge's direction may be taken to the court of appeals as would any other appeal from a district-court judgment. (Added by order adopted April 28, 1983, effective August 1, 1983, amended by order adopted March 2, 1987, effective August 1, 1987, by order adopted April 22, 1993, effective December 1, 1993, by order adopted April 11, 1997, effective December 1, 1997, and by order adopted April 30, 2007, effective December 1, 2007.)

Comment. — The language of Rule 73 has been amended as part of the general restyling of the Civil Rules to make them more easily understood and to make style and terminology consistent throughout the rules. These changes are intended to be stylistic only.

Rule 74. Method of Appeal from Magistrate Judge to District Judge Under Title 28, U.S.C. § 636(c)(4) and Rule 73(d). [Abrogated].

Rule 75. Proceedings on Appeal from Magistrate Judge to District Judge Under Rule 73(d). [Abrogated].

Rule 76. Judgment of the District Judge on the Appeal Under Rule 73(d) and Costs. [Abrogated].

TITLE X. DISTRICT COURTS AND CLERKS: CONDUCTING BUSINESS; ISSUING ORDERS.

Rule 77. Conducting Business; Clerk's Authority; Notice of an Order or Judgment.

(a) *When Court Is Open.* — Every district court is considered always open for filing any paper, issuing and returning process, making a motion, or entering an order.

(b) *Place for Trial and Other Proceedings.* — Every trial on the merits must be conducted in open court and, so far as convenient, in a regular courtroom. Any other act or proceeding may be done or conducted by a judge in chambers, without the attendance of the clerk or other court official, and anywhere inside or outside the district. But no hearing — other than one ex parte — may be conducted outside the district unless all the affected parties consent.

(c) *Clerk's Office Hours; Clerk's Orders.* — (1) Hours. The clerk's office — with a clerk or deputy on duty — must be open during business hours every day except Saturdays, Sundays, and legal holidays. But a court may, by local rule or order, require that the office be open for specified hours on Saturday or a particular legal holiday other than one listed in Rule 6(a)(4)(A).

(2) Orders. Subject to the court's power to suspend, alter, or rescind the clerk's action for good cause, the clerk may:

(A) issue process;

(B) enter a default;

(C) enter a default judgment under Rule 55(b)(1); and

(D) act on any other matter that does not require the court's action.

(d) *Serving Notice of an Order or Judgment.* — (1) Service. Immediately after entering an order or judgment, the clerk must serve notice of the entry, as provided in Rule 5(b), on each party who is not in default for failing to appear. The clerk must record the service on the docket. A party also may serve notice of the entry as provided in Rule 5(b).

(2) Time to Appeal Not Affected by Lack of Notice. Lack of notice of the entry does not affect the time for appeal or relieve — or authorize the court to relieve — a party for failing to appeal within the time allowed, except as allowed by Federal Rule of Appellate Procedure (4)(a). (Amended by order adopted December 27, 1946, effective March 19, 1948, by order adopted January 21, 1963, effective July 1, 1963, by order adopted December 4, 1967, effective July 1, 1968, by order adopted March 1, 1971, effective July 1, 1971, by order adopted March 2, 1987, effective August 1, 1987, by order adopted April 30, 1991, effective December 1, 1991, by order adopted April 23, 2001, effective December 1, 2001, and by order adopted April 30, 2007, effective December 1, 2007.)

Comment. — The language of Rule 77 has been amended as part of the general restyling of the Civil Rules to make them more easily understood and to make style and terminology consistent throughout the rules. These changes are intended to be stylistic only.

CASE NOTES

Time for filing. — While the court is deemed "always open" to accept filings under subdivision (a), filing is only complete upon receipt by a judicial official. In re Fisherman's Wharf Fillet, Inc., 83 F. Supp. 2d 651 (E.D. Va. 1999).

Applied in Muse v. Freeman, 197 F. Supp. 67 (E.D. Va. 1961).

Rule 78. Hearing Motions; Submission on Briefs.

(a) *Providing a Regular Schedule for Oral Hearings.* — A court may establish regular times and places for oral hearings on motions.

(b) *Providing for Submission on Briefs.* — By rule or order, the court may provide for submitting and determining motions on briefs, without oral hearings. (Amended by order adopted March 2, 1987, effective August 1, 1987, and by order adopted April 30, 2007, effective December 1, 2007.)

Comment. — The language of Rule 78 has been amended as part of the general restyling of the Civil Rules to make them more easily understood and to make style and terminology consistent throughout the rules. These changes are intended to be stylistic only.

Rule 79. Records Kept by the Clerk.

(a) *Civil Docket.* — (1) In General. The clerk must keep a record known as the "civil docket" in the form and manner prescribed by the Director of the Administrative Office of the United States Courts with the approval of the Judicial Conference of the United States. The clerk must enter each civil action in the docket. Actions must be assigned consecutive file numbers, which must be noted in the docket where the first entry of the action is made.

(2) Items to be Entered. The following items must be marked with the file number and entered chronologically in the docket:

(A) papers filed with the clerk;

(B) process issued, and proofs of service or other returns showing execution; and

(C) appearances, orders, verdicts, and judgments.

(3) Contents of Entries; Jury Trial Demanded. Each entry must briefly show the nature of the paper filed or writ issued, the substance of each proof of service or other return, and the substance and date of entry of each order and judgment. When a jury trial has been properly demanded or ordered, the clerk must enter the word "jury" in the docket.

(b) *Civil Judgments and Orders.* — The clerk must keep a copy of every final judgment and appealable order; of every order affecting title to or a lien on real or personal property; and of any other order that the court directs to be kept. The clerk must keep these in the form and manner prescribed by the Director of the Administrative Office of the United States Courts with the approval of the Judicial Conference of the United States.

(c) *Indexes; Calendars.* — Under the court's direction, the clerk must:

(1) keep indexes of the docket and of the judgments and orders described in Rule 79(b); and

(2) prepare calendars of all actions ready for trial, distinguishing jury trials from nonjury trials.

(d) *Other Records.* — The clerk must keep any other records required by the Director of the Administrative Office of the United States Courts with the approval of the Judicial Conference of the United States. (Amended by order adopted December 27, 1946, effective March 19, 1948, by order adopted December 29, 1948, effective October 20, 1949, by order adopted January 21, 1963, effective July 1, 1963, and by order adopted April 30, 2007, effective December 1, 2007.)

Comment. — The language of Rule 79 has been amended as part of the general restyling of the Civil Rules to make them more easily understood and to make style and terminology consistent throughout the rules. These changes are intended to be stylistic only.

CASE NOTES

"Entry" has a well defined meaning under the rules; it occurs only when the essentials of a judgment or order are set forth in a written document separate from the court's opinion or memorandum and when the substance of this separate document is reflected in an appropriate notation on the docket sheet assigned to the action in the district court. This dual requirement is established by Rule 58, Fed. R. Civ. P. which states that "every judgment shall be set forth on a separate document" and that "a judgment is effective" only when so set forth and when entered as provided in subdivision (a) of this rule. Rule 4(a), Fed. R. App. P. which is derived without change in substance from a former civil rule, incorporates both of these standards. Caperton v. Beatrice Pocahontas Coal Co., 585 F.2d 683 (4th Cir. 1978), aff'g 420 F. Supp. 445 (W.D. Va. 1977).

A notice of appeal must be filed within 30 days of entry of judgment. Entry of judgment consists of two steps: Creation of a document setting out the judgment and a notation of the document on the docket sheet. The 30-day period does not begin to run until after the document is entered on the docket sheet. Wilson v. Murray, 806 F.2d 1232 (4th Cir. 1986), cert. denied, 484 U.S. 870, 108 S. Ct. 197, 98 L. Ed. 2d 149 (1987).

Applied in Gavin v. Department of USAF, No. 00-1144, 2000 U.S. App. LEXIS 12126 (4th Cir. June 2, 2000); Byland v. Cumbia, No. 00-6116, 2000 U.S. App. LEXIS 12257 (4th Cir. June 5, 2000); Gordon v. Angelone, No. 00-6190, 2000 U.S. App. LEXIS 12261 (4th Cir. June 5, 2000); Smith v. Angelone, No. 00-6286, 2000 U.S. App. LEXIS 12311 (4th Cir. June 6, 2000); Smith v. Caldera, No. 00-1160, 2000 U.S. App. LEXIS 14367 (4th Cir. June 21, 2000); Ward v. Virginia, No. 00-6243, 2000 U.S. App. LEXIS 14443 (4th Cir. June 22, 2000); Stephenson v. Angelone, No. 00-6432, 2000 U.S. App. LEXIS 14536 (4th Cir. June 23, 2000); United States v. Singleton, No. 00-6436, 2000 U.S. App. LEXIS 14537 (4th Cir. June 23, 2000); Jones v. Angelone, No. 00-6499, 2000 U.S. App. LEXIS 14540 (4th Cir. June 23, 2000); James v. Braxton, No. 00-6348, 2000 U.S. App. LEXIS 22946 (4th Cir. Sept. 11, 2000); Headley v. Braxton, No. 00-6371, 2000 U.S. App. LEXIS 23338 (4th Cir. Sept. 15, 2000).

Rule 80. Stenographic Transcript as Evidence.

If stenographically reported testimony at a hearing or trial is admissible in evidence at a later trial, the testimony may be proved by a transcript certified by the person who reported it. (Amended by order adopted December 27, 1946, effective March 19, 1948, and by order adopted April 30, 2007, effective December 1, 2007.)

Comment. — The language of Rule 80 has been amended as part of the general restyling of the Civil Rules to make them more easily understood and to make style and terminology consistent throughout the rules. These changes are intended to be stylistic only.

TITLE XI. GENERAL PROVISIONS.

Rule 81. Applicability of the Rules in General; Removed Actions.

(a) *Applicability to Particular Proceedings.* — (1) Prize Proceedings. These rules do not apply to prize proceedings in admiralty governed by 10 U.S.C. §§ 7651-7681.

(2) Bankruptcy. These rules apply to bankruptcy proceedings to the extent provided by the Federal Rules of Bankruptcy Procedure.

(3) Citizenship. These rules apply to proceedings for admission to citizenship to the extent that the practice in those proceedings is not specified in federal statutes and has previously conformed to the practice in civil actions. The provisions of 8 U.S.C. § 1451 for service by publication and for answer apply in proceedings to cancel citizenship certificates.

(4) Special Writs. These rules apply to proceedings for habeas corpus and for quo warranto to the extent that the practice in those proceedings:

(A) is not specified in a federal statute, the Rules Governing Section 2254 Cases, or the Rules Governing Section 2255 Cases; and

(B) has previously conformed to the practice in civil actions.

(5) Proceedings Involving a Subpoena. These rules apply to proceedings to compel testimony or the production of documents through a subpoena issued by a United States officer or agency under a federal statute, except as otherwise provided by statute, by local rule, or by court order in the proceedings.

(6) Other Proceedings. These rules, to the extent applicable, govern proceedings under the following laws, except as these laws provide other procedures:

(A) 7 U.S.C. §§ 292, 499g(c), for reviewing an order of the Secretary of Agriculture;

(B) 9 U.S.C., relating to arbitration;

(C) 15 U.S.C. § 522, for reviewing an order of the Secretary of the Interior;

(D) 15 U.S.C. § 715d(c), for reviewing an order denying a certificate of clearance;

(E) 29 U.S.C. §§ 159, 160, for enforcing an order of the National Labor Relations Board;

(F) 33 U.S.C. §§ 918, 921, for enforcing or reviewing a compensation order under the Longshore and Harbor Workers' Compensation Act; and

(G) 45 U.S.C. § 159, for reviewing an arbitration award in a railway-labor dispute.

(b) *Scire Facias and Mandamus.* — The writs of scire facias and mandamus are abolished. Relief previously available through them may be obtained by appropriate action or motion under these rules.

(c) *Removed Actions.* — (1) Applicability. These rules apply to a civil action after it is removed from a state court.

(2) Further Pleading. After removal, repleading is unnecessary unless the court orders it. A defendant who did not answer before removal must answer or present other defenses or objections under these rules within the longest of these periods:

(A) 21 days after receiving — through service or otherwise — a copy of the initial pleading stating the claim for relief;

(B) 21 days after being served with the summons for an initial pleading on file at the time of service; or

(C) 7 days after the notice of removal is filed.

(3) Demand for a Jury Trial. (A) As Affected by State Law. A party who, before removal, expressly demanded a jury trial in accordance with state law need not renew the demand after removal. If the state law did not require an express demand for a jury trial, a party need not make one after removal unless the court orders the parties to do so within a specified time. The court must so order at a party's request and may so order on its own. A party who fails to make a demand when so ordered waives a jury trial.

(B) Under Rule 38. If all necessary pleadings have been served at the time of removal, a party entitled to a jury trial under Rule 38 must be given one if the party serves a demand within 14 days after:

(i) it files a notice of removal; or

(ii) it is served with a notice of removal filed by another party.

(d) *Law Applicable.* — (1) "State Law" Defined. When these rules refer to state law, the term "law" includes the state's statutes and the state's judicial decisions.

(2) "State" Defined. The term "state" includes, where appropriate, the District of Columbia and any United States commonwealth or territory.

(3) "Federal Statute" Defined in the District of Columbia. In the United States District Court for the District of Columbia, the term "federal statute" includes any Act of Congress that applies locally to the District. (Amended by order adopted December 28, 1939, effective April 3, 1941, by order adopted December 27, 1946, effective March 19, 1948, by order adopted December 29, 1948, effective October 20, 1949, by order adopted April 30, 1951, effective August 1, 1951, by order adopted January 21, 1963, effective July 1, 1963, by order adopted February 28, 1966, effective July 1, 1966, by order adopted December 4, 1967, effective July 1, 1968, by order adopted March 1, 1971, effective July 1, 1971, by order adopted March 2, 1987, effective August 1, 1987, by order adopted April 23, 2001, effective December 1, 2001, by order adopted April 29, 2002, effective December 1, 2002, by order adopted April 30, 2007, effective December 1, 2007, and by order adopted March 26, 2009, effective December 1, 2009.)

Comment. — The language of Rule 81 has been amended as part of the general restyling of the Civil Rules to make them more easily understood and to make style and terminology consistent throughout the rules. These changes are intended to be stylistic only.

Rule 81(c) has been revised to reflect the amendment of 28 U.S.C. § 1446(a) that changed the procedure for removal from a petition for removal to a notice of removal.

Former Rule 81(e), drafted before the decision in *Eric R.R. v. Tompkins,* 304 U.S. 64 (1938), defined state law to include "the statutes of that state and the state judicial decisions construing them." The Erie decision reinterpreted the Rules of Decision Act, now 28 U.S.C. § 1652, recognizing that the "laws" of the states include the common law established by judicial decisions. Long-established practice reflects this understanding, looking to state common law as well as statutes and court rules when a Civil Rule directs use of state law. Amended Rule 81(d)(1) adheres to this practice, including all state judicial decisions, not only those that construe state statutes.

Former Rule 81(f) is deleted. The office of district director of internal revenue was abolished by restructuring under the Internal Revenue Service Restructuring and Reform Act of 1998, Pub.L. 105-206, July 22, 1998, 26 U.S.C. § 1 Note. (Amended by order adopted December 28, 1939, effective April 3, 1941, by order adopted December 27, 1946, effective March 19, 1948, by order adopted December 29, 1948, effective October 20, 1949, by order adopted April 30, 1951, effective August 1, 1951, by order adopted January 21, 1963, effective July 1, 1963, by order adopted February 28, 1966, effective July 1, 1966, by order adopted December 4, 1967, effective July 1, 1968, by order adopted March 1, 1971, effective July 1, 1971, by order adopted March 2, 1987, effective August 1, 1987, by order adopted April 23, 2001, effective December 1, 2001, by order adopted April 29, 2002, effective December 1, 2002; amended, effective December 1, 2007.)

The language of Rule 81 has been amended as part of the general restyling of the Civil Rules to make them more easily understood and to make style and terminology consistent throughout the rules. These changes are intended to be stylistic only.

Rule 81(c) has been revised to reflect the amendment of 28 U.S.C. § 1446(a) that changed the procedure for removal from a petition for removal to a notice of removal.

Former Rule 81(e), drafted before the decision in *Erie R.R. v. Tompkins,* 304 U.S. 64 (1938), defined state law to include "the statutes of that state and the state judicial decisions construing them." The Erie decision reinterpreted the Rules of Decision Act, now 28 U.S.C. § 1652, recognizing that the "laws" of the states include the common law established by judicial decisions. Long-established practice reflects this understanding, looking to state common law as well as statutes and court rules when a Civil Rule directs use of state law. Amended Rule 81(d)(1) adheres to this practice, including all state judicial decisions, not only those that construe state statutes.

Former Rule 81(f) is deleted. The office of district director of internal revenue was abolished by restructuring under the Internal Revenue Service Restructuring and Reform Act of 1998, Pub.L. 105-206, July 22, 1998, 26 U.S.C. § 1 Note.

CASE NOTES

Relief in nature of mandamus confined to ancillary proceedings. — The writ of mandamus in civil actions in federal district courts has been abolished by subdivision (b), and relief in the nature of mandamus is confined to those situations where it is a necessary aid to a court's jurisdiction, as when it is done as an ancillary proceeding in aid of jurisdiction acquired on other grounds. A federal court has no general jurisdiction to issue writs of mandamus where that is the only relief sought. Shelton v. Randolph, 373 F. Supp. 448 (W.D. Va. 1974).

The possibility of an escape under a provision in subdivision (c) was foreclosed, since the rules applicable in the circuit court of the City of Virginia Beach did require an express jury trial demand prior to trial. Malbon v. Pennsylvania Millers Mut. Ins. Co., 636 F.2d 936 (4th Cir. 1980).

Response to defendant's answer and grounds of defense not last pleading. — Under Rule 38(b), a demand for jury trial must be in writing and served "not later than 10 days after the service of the last pleading directed to" the "issue triable of right by a jury." Plaintiffs attempted to escape their dilemma of having failed to follow the rule by claiming that their filing, on or about March 8, 1979, of a response to defendant's answer and grounds of defense amounted to the last pleading for Rule 38(b) purposes. However, the "response" was clearly a superfluous document, not provided for in these rules, and consequently did not qualify as a pleading under Rule 7(a). Malbon v. Pennsylvania Millers Mut. Ins. Co., 636 F.2d 936 (4th Cir. 1980).

Untimely jury demand. — Considering plaintiff's failure to request relief under Rule 39(b) for more than four months after removal and more than five weeks after the court first raised the issue, and taking into account the lack of any justification for either failure, the court did not exercise its discretion to grant the untimely jury demand. Vannoy v. Cooper, 872 F. Supp. 1485 (E.D. Va. 1995).

Applied in Wright v. Pilot Life Ins. Co., 379 F.2d 409 (4th Cir. 1967); Gelardi v. Transamerica Occidental Life Ins. Co., 163 F.R.D. 495 (E.D. Va. 1995).

Rule 82. Jurisdiction and Venue Unaffected.

These rules do not extend or limit the jurisdiction of the district courts or the venue of actions in those courts. An admiralty or maritime claim under Rule 9(h) is not a civil action for purposes of 28 U.S.C. §§ 1391-1392. (Amended by order adopted December 29, 1948, effective October 20, 1949, by order adopted February 28, 1966, effective July 1, 1966, by order adopted April 23, 2001, effective December 1, 2001, and by order adopted April 30, 2007, effective December 1, 2007.)

Comment. — The language of Rule 82 has been amended as part of the general restyling of the Civil Rules to make them more easily understood and to make style and terminology consistent throughout the rules. These changes are intended to be stylistic only.

CASE NOTES

Rules only prescribe how jurisdiction is to be exercised. — The Federal Rules of Civil Procedure prescribe the methods by which the jurisdiction of the federal courts is to be exercised, but do not enlarge the jurisdiction. Fett Roofing & Sheet Metal Co. v. Seaboard Sur. Co., 294 F. Supp. 112 (E.D. Va. 1968).

For purposes of federal diversity jurisdiction, the citizenship of a limited partnership is determined by considering the citizenship of all of its partners, both general and limited. New York State Teachers Retirement Sys. v. Kalkus, 764 F.2d 1015 (4th Cir. 1985).

Claim under Tucker Act exceeding jurisdiction of district court. — See Cook v. Arentzen, 582 F.2d 870 (4th Cir. 1978).

Applied in Weaver v. Marcus, 165 F.2d 862, 175 A.L.R. 1305 (4th Cir. 1948); Kenrose Mfg. Co. v. Fred Whitaker Co., 512 F.2d 890 (4th Cir. 1972); Cook v. Arentzen, 582 F.2d 870 (4th Cir. 1978); Hereth v. Jones, 544 F. Supp. 111 (E.D. Va. 1982).

Rule 83. Rules by District Courts; Judge's Directives.

(a) *Local Rules.* — (1) In General. After giving public notice and an opportunity for comment, a district court, acting by a majority of its district judges, may adopt and amend rules governing its practice. A local rule must be consistent with — but not duplicate — federal statutes and rules adopted under 28 U.S.C. §§ 2072 and 2075, and must conform to any uniform numbering system prescribed by the Judicial Conference of the United States. A local rule takes effect on the date specified by the district court and remains in effect unless amended by the court or abrogated by the judicial council of the circuit. Copies of rules and amendments must, on their adoption, be furnished to the judicial council and the Administrative Office of the United States Courts and be made available to the public.

(2) Requirement of Form. A local rule imposing a requirement of form must not be enforced in a way that causes a party to lose any right because of a nonwillful failure to comply.

(b) *Procedure When There Is No Controlling Law.* — A judge may regulate practice in any manner consistent with federal law, rules adopted under 28 U.S.C. §§ 2072 and 2075, and the district's local rules. No sanction or other disadvantage may be imposed for noncompliance with any requirement not in federal law, federal rules, or the local rules unless the alleged violator has been furnished in the particular case with actual notice of the requirement. (Amended by order adopted April 29, 1985, effective August 1, 1985, by order adopted April 27, 1995, effective December 1, 1995, and by order adopted April 30, 2007, effective December 1, 2007.)

Comment. — The language of Rule 83 has been amended as part of the general restyling of the Civil Rules to make them more easily understood and to make style and terminology consistent throughout the rules. These changes are intended to be stylistic only.

Law Review. — For note on judicial authority in the settlement of federal civil cases, see 42 Wash. & Lee L. Rev. 171 (1985). For article, "Suggestions for Circuit Court Review of Local Procedures," see 52 Wash. & Lee L. Rev. 359 (1995).

CASE NOTES

Local rule inconsistent with Rules 12(b) and 56. — Where dismissal for want of a meritorious claim is provided for by rules other than Rule 83 and that dismissal under Rule 83 for lack of a meritorious claim would be inconsistent with those other provisions, specifically Rule 12(b) and Rule 56, Rule 83 could not be the basis for a dismissal of a cause of action deemed not meritorious. Brown v. Cameron-Brown Co., 652 F.2d 375 (4th Cir. 1981).

Rule 84. Forms.

The forms in the Appendix suffice under these rules and illustrate the simplicity and brevity that these rules contemplate. (Amended by order adopted December 27, 1946, effective March 19, 1948, and by order adopted April 30, 2007, effective December 1, 2007.)

Comment. — The language of Rule 84 has been amended as part of the general restyling of the Civil Rules to make them more easily understood and to make style and terminology consistent throughout the rules. These changes are intended to be stylistic only.

Rule 85. Title.

These rules may be cited as the Federal Rules of Civil Procedure. (Amended by order adopted April 30, 2007, effective December 1, 2007.)

Comment. — The language of Rule 85 has been amended as part of the general restyling of the Civil Rules to make them more easily understood and to make style and terminology consistent throughout the rules. These changes are intended to be stylistic only.

Rule 86. Effective Dates.

(a) *In General.* — These rules and any amendments take effect at the time specified by the Supreme Court, subject to 28 U.S.C. § 2074. They govern:

(1) proceedings in an action commenced after their effective date; and

(2) proceedings after that date in an action then pending unless:

(A) the Supreme Court specifies otherwise; or

(B) the court determines that applying them in a particular action would be infeasible or work an injustice.

(b) *December 1, 2007 Amendments.* — If any provision in Rules 1-5.1, 6-73, or 77-86 conflicts with another law, priority in time for the purpose of 28 U.S.C. § 2072(b) is not affected by the amendments taking effect on December 1, 2007. (Added by order adopted December 27, 1946, effective March 19, 1948, amended by order adopted December 29, 1948, effective October 20, 1949, by order adopted April 17, 1961, effective July 19, 1961, by order adopted January 21, 1963 and March 18, 1963, effective July 1, 1963, and by order adopted April 30, 2007, effective December 1, 2007.)

Comment. — The language of Rule 86 has been amended as part of the general restyling of the Civil Rules to make them more easily understood and to make style and terminology consistent throughout the rules. These changes are intended to be stylistic only.

The subdivisions that provided an incomplete list of the effective dates of the original Civil Rules and amendments made up to 1963 are deleted as no longer useful.

Rule 86(b) is added to clarify the relationship of amendments taking effect on December 1, 2007, to other laws for the purpose of applying the "supersession" clause in 28 U.S.C. § 2072(b). Section 2072(b) provides that a law in conflict with an Enabling Act Rule "shall be of no further force or effect after such rule[] ha[s] taken effect." The amendments that take effect on December 1, 2007, result from the general restyling of the Civil Rules and from a small number of technical revisions adopted on a parallel track. None of these amendments is intended to affect resolution of any conflict that might arise between a rule and another law. Rule 86(b) makes this intent explicit. Any conflict that arises should be resolved by looking to the date the specific conflicting rule provision first became effective.

APPENDIX OF FORMS.

Form 1.

Form 1. Caption. ***(Use on every summons, complaint, answer, motion, or other document.)***

United States District Court
for the
__________District of __________

A B, Plaintiff	)	
	)	
v.	)	
	)	**Civil Action No. _____**
C D, Defendant	)	
	)	
v.	)	
	)	
E F, Third-Party Defendant	)	
(Use if needed.)	)	

(Name of Document)

Form 2.

Form 2. Date, Signature, Address, E-mail Address, and Telephone Number.
(Use at the conclusion of pleadings and other papers that require a signature.)

Date ________

____
(Signature of the attorney or unrepresented party)

____
(Printed name)

____
(Address)

____
(E-mail address)

____
(Telephone number)

Form 3.

Form 3. Summons.

(Caption – See Form 1.)

To *name the defendant*:

A lawsuit has been filed against you.

Within 20 days after service of this summons on you (not counting the day you received it), you must serve on the plaintiff an answer to the attached complaint or a motion under Rule 12 of the Federal Rules of Civil Procedure. The answer or motion must be served on the plaintiff's attorney,__________, whose address is ___________. If you fail to do so, judgment by default will be entered against you for the relief demanded in the complaint. You also must file your answer or motion with the court.

Date _______

____

Clerk of Court

(Court Seal)

(Use 60 days if the defendant is the United States or a United States agency, or is an officer or employee of the United States allowed 60 days by Rule 12(a)(3).)

Form 4.

Form 4. Summons on a Third-Party Complaint.

(Caption – See Form 1.)

To *name the third-party defendant:*

A lawsuit has been filed against defendant _______, who as third-party plaintiff is making this claim against you to pay part or all of what [he] may owe to the plaintiff _______.

Within 20 days after service of this summons on you (not counting the day you received it), you must serve on the plaintiff and on the defendant an answer to the attached third-party complaint or a motion under Rule 12 of the Federal Rules of Civil Procedure. The answer or motion must be served on the defendant's attorney, ____________, whose address is, ____________, and also on the plaintiff's attorney, ______, whose address is, ________________. If you fail to do so, judgment by default will be entered against you for the relief demanded in the third-party complaint. You also must file the answer or motion with the court and serve it on any other parties.

A copy of the plaintiff's complaint is also attached. You may – but are not required to – respond to it.

Date _______

____
Clerk of Court

(Court Seal)

Form 5.

Form 5. Notice of a Lawsuit and Request to Waive Service of a Summons.

(Caption – See Form 1.)

To *(name the defendant – or if the defendant is a corporation, partnership, or association name an officer or agent authorized to receive service):*

Why are you getting this?

A lawsuit has been filed against you, or the entity you represent, in this court under the number shown above. A copy of the complaint is attached.

This is not a summons, or an official notice from the court. It is a request that, to avoid expenses, you waive formal service of a summons by signing and returning the enclosed waiver. To avoid these expenses, you must return the signed waiver within *(give at least 30 days or at least 60 days if the defendant is outside any judicial district of the United States)* from the date shown below, which is the date this notice was sent. Two copies of the waiver form are enclosed, along with a stamped, self-addressed envelope or other prepaid means for returning one copy. You may keep the other copy.

What happens next?

If you return the signed waiver, I will file it with the court. The action will then proceed as if you had been served on the date the waiver is filed, but no summons will be served on you and you will have 60 days from the date this notice is sent (see the date below) to answer the complaint (or 90 days if this notice is sent to you outside any judicial district of the United States).

If you do not return the signed waiver within the time indicated, I will arrange to have the summons and complaint served on you. And I will ask the court to require you, or the entity you represent, to pay the expenses of making service.

Please read the enclosed statement about the duty to avoid unnecessary expenses.

I certify that this request is being sent to you on the date below.

(Date and sign – See Form 2.)

Form 6.

Form 6. Waiver of the Service of Summons.

(Caption – See Form 1.)

To *name the plaintiff's attorney or the unrepresented plaintiff*:

I have received your request to waive service of a summons in this action along with a copy of the complaint, two copies of this waiver form, and a prepaid means of returning one signed copy of the form to you.

I, or the entity I represent, agree to save the expense of serving a summons and complaint in this case.

I understand that I, or the entity I represent, will keep all defenses or objections to the lawsuit, the court's jurisdiction, and the venue of the action, but that I waive any objections to the absence of a summons or of service.

I also understand that I, or the entity I represent, must file and serve an answer or a motion under Rule 12 within 60 days from ______, the date when this request was sent (or 90 days if it was sent outside the United States). If I fail to do so, a default judgment will be entered against me or the entity I represent.

(Date and sign – See Form 2.)

(Attach the following to Form 6.)

Duty to Avoid Unnecessary Expenses of Serving a Summons

Rule 4 of the Federal Rules of Civil Procedure requires certain defendants to cooperate in saving unnecessary expenses of serving a summons and complaint. A defendant who is located in the United States and who fails to return a signed waiver of service requested by a plaintiff located in the United States will be required to pay the expenses of service, unless the defendant shows good cause for the failure.

"Good cause" does *not* include a belief that the lawsuit is groundless, or that it has been brought in an improper venue, or that the court has no jurisdiction over this matter or over the defendant or the defendant's property.

If the waiver is signed and returned, you can still make these and all other defenses and objections, but you cannot object to the absence of a summons or of service.

If you waive service, then you must, within the time specified on the waiver form, serve an answer or a motion under Rule 12 on the plaintiff and file a copy with the court. By signing and returning the waiver form, you are allowed more time to respond than if a summons had been served.

Form 7.

Form 7. Statement of Jurisdiction.

a. *(For diversity-of-citizenship jurisdiction.)* The plaintiff is [a citizen of *Michigan*] [a corporation incorporated under the laws of *Michigan* with its principal place of business in *Michigan*]. The defendant is [a citizen of *New York*] [a corporation incorporated under the laws of *New York* with its principal place of business in *New York*]. The amount in controversy, without interest and costs, exceeds the sum or value specified by 28 U.S.C. § 1332.

b. *(For federal-question jurisdiction.)* This action arises under [the United States Constitution, *specify the article or amendment and the section*] [a United States treaty *specify*] [a federal statute, ___U.S.C. § ___].

c. *(For a claim in the admiralty or maritime jurisdiction.)* This is a case of admiralty or maritime jurisdiction. *(To invoke admiralty status under Rule 9(h) use the following:* This is an admiralty or maritime claim within the meaning of Rule 9(h).)

Form 8.

Form 8. Statement of Reasons for Omitting a Party.
(If a person who ought to be made a party under Rule 19(a) is not named, include this statement in accordance with Rule 19(c).)

This complaint does not join as a party *name* who [is not subject to this court's personal jurisdiction] [cannot be made a party without depriving this court of subject-matter jurisdiction] because *state the reason*.

Form 9.

Form 9. Statement Noting a Party's Death.

(Caption – See Form 1.)

In accordance with Rule 25(a) *name the person*, who is [a party to this action] [a representative of or successor to the deceased party] notes the death during the pendency of this action of *name*, [*describe as party* in this action].

(Date and sign – See Form 2.)

Form 10.

Form 10. Complaint to Recover a Sum Certain.

(Caption – See Form 1.)

1. (Statement of Jurisdiction – See Form 7.)

(Use one or more of the following as appropriate and include a demand for judgment.)

(a) On a Promissory Note

2. On _date_, the defendant executed and delivered a note promising to pay the plaintiff on _date_ the sum of $ ______ with interest at the rate of __ percent. A copy of the note [is attached as Exhibit A] [is summarized as follows: ___________.]

3. The defendant has not paid the amount owed.

(b) On an Account

2. The defendant owes the plaintiff $______ according to the account set out in Exhibit A.

(c) For Goods Sold and Delivered

2. The defendant owes the plaintiff $ _____ for goods sold and delivered by the plaintiff to the defendant from _date_ to _date_.

(d) For Money Lent

2. The defendant owes the plaintiff $ ______ for money lent by the plaintiff to the defendant on _date_.

(e) For Money Paid by Mistake

2. The defendant owes the plaintiff $ _____ for money paid by mistake to the defendant on _date_ under these circumstances: _describe with particularity in accordance with Rule 9(b)._

(f) For Money Had and Received

2. The defendant owes the plaintiff $ ______ for money that was received from _name_ on _date_ to be paid by the defendant to the plaintiff.

Demand for Judgment

Therefore, the plaintiff demands judgment against the defendant for $ _______, plus interest and costs.

(Date and sign – See Form 2.)

Form 11.

Form 11. Complaint for Negligence.

(Caption – See Form 1.)

1. (Statement of Jurisdiction – See Form 7.)

2. On _*date*_, at _*place*_, the defendant negligently drove a motor vehicle against the plaintiff.

3. As a result, the plaintiff was physically injured, lost wages or income, suffered physical and mental pain, and incurred medical expenses of $________.

Therefore, the plaintiff demands judgment against the defendant for $________, plus costs.

(Date and sign – See Form 2).

Form 12.

Form 12. Complaint for Negligence When the Plaintiff Does Not Know Who Is Responsible.

(Caption – See Form 1.)

1. **(Statement of Jurisdiction – See Form 7.)**

2. **On _date_, at _place_, defendant _name_ or defendant _name_ or both of them willfully or recklessly or negligently drove, or caused to be driven, a motor vehicle against the plaintiff.**

3. **As a result, the plaintiff was physically injured, lost wages or income, suffered mental and physical pain, and incurred medical expenses of $ _______.**

Therefore, the plaintiff demands judgment against one or both defendants for $ ____________, plus costs.

(Date and sign – See Form 2.)

Form 13.

Form 13. Complaint for Negligence Under the Federal Employers' Liability Act.

(Caption – See Form 1.)

1. **(Statement of Jurisdiction – See Form 7.)**

2. **At the times below, the defendant owned and operated in interstate commerce a railroad line that passed through a tunnel located at ________.**

3. **On _*date*_, the plaintiff was working to repair and enlarge the tunnel to make it convenient and safe for use in interstate commerce.**

4. **During this work, the defendant, as the employer, negligently put the plaintiff to work in a section of the tunnel that the defendant had left unprotected and unsupported.**

5. **The defendant's negligence caused the plaintiff to be injured by a rock that fell from an unsupported portion of the tunnel.**

6. **As a result, the plaintiff was physically injured, lost wages or income, suffered mental and physical pain, and incurred medical expenses of $ __________.**

Therefore, the plaintiff demands judgment against the defendant for $ ________, and costs.

(Date and sign – See Form 2.)

Form 14.

Form 14. Complaint for Damages Under the Merchant Marine Act.

(Caption – See Form 1.)

1. (Statement of Jurisdiction – See Form 7.)

2. At the times below, the defendant owned and operated the vessel _*name*_ and used it to transport cargo for hire by water in interstate and foreign commerce.

3. On _*date*_, at _*place*_, the defendant hired the plaintiff under seamen's articles of customary form for a voyage from __________ to __________ and return at a wage of $ _____ a month and found, which is equal to a shore worker's wage of $ _____ a month.

4. On _*date*_, the vessel was at sea on the return voyage. *(Describe the weather and the condition of the vessel.)*

5. *(Describe as in Form 11 the defendant's negligent conduct.)*

6. As a result of the defendant's negligent conduct and the unseaworthiness of the vessel, the plaintiff was physically injured, has been incapable of any gainful activity, suffered mental and physical pain, and has incurred medical expenses of $ _____.

Therefore, the plaintiff demands judgment against the defendant for $ _____, plus costs.

(Date and sign — See Form 2.)

Form 15.

Form 15. Complaint for the Conversion of Property.

(Caption — See Form 1.)

1. (Statement of Jurisdiction — See Form 7.)

2. On *date*, at *place*, the defendant converted to the defendant's own use property owned by the plaintiff. The property converted consists of *describe*.

3. The property is worth $________.

Therefore, the plaintiff demands judgment against the defendant for $______, plus costs.

(Date and sign – See Form 2.)

Form 16.

Form 16. Third-Party Complaint.

(Caption – See Form 1.)

1. Plaintiff *name* has filed against defendant *name* a complaint, a copy of which is attached.

2. *(State grounds entitling defendant's name to recover from third-party defendant's name for (all or an identified share) of any judgment for plaintiff's name against defendant's name.)*

Therefore, the defendant demands judgment against *third-party defendant's name* for *all or an identified share* of sums that may be adjudged against the defendant in the plaintiff's favor.

(Date and sign – See Form 2.)

Form 17.

Form 17. Complaint for Specific Performance of a Contract to Convey Land.

(Caption – See Form 1.)

1. **(Statement of Jurisdiction – See Form 7.)**

2. **On *date*, the parties agreed to the contract [attached as Exhibit A][summarize the contract].**

3. **As agreed, the plaintiff tendered the purchase price and requested a conveyance of the land, but the defendant refused to accept the money or make a conveyance.**

4. **The plaintiff now offers to pay the purchase price.**

Therefore, the plaintiff demands that:

(a) **the defendant be required to specifically perform the agreement and pay damages of $ _______, plus interest and costs, or**

(b) **if specific performance is not ordered, the defendant be required to pay damages of $ _______, plus interest and costs.**

(Date and sign – See Form 2.)

Form 18.

Form 18. Complaint for Patent Infringement.

(Caption – See Form 1.)

1. **(Statement of Jurisdiction — See Form 7.)**

2. **On *date*, United States Letters Patent No. _______ were issued to the plaintiff for an invention in an *electric motor*. The plaintiff owned the patent throughout the period of the defendant's infringing acts and still owns the patent.**

3. **The defendant has infringed and is still infringing the Letters Patent by making, selling, and using *electric motors* that embody the patented invention, and the defendant will continue to do so unless enjoined by this court.**

4. **The plaintiff has complied with the statutory requirement of placing a notice of the Letters Patent on all *electric motors* it manufactures and sells and has given the defendant written notice of the infringement.**

Therefore, the plaintiff demands:

(a) a preliminary and final injunction against the continuing infringement;

(b) an accounting for damages; and

(c) interest and costs.

(Date and sign – See Form 2.)

Form 19.

Form 19. Complaint for Copyright Infringement and Unfair Competition.

(Caption – See Form 1.)

1. (Statement of Jurisdiction – See Form 7.)

2. Before *date*, the plaintiff, a United States citizen, wrote a book entitled__________.

3. The book is an original work that may be copyrighted under United States law. A copy of the book is attached as Exhibit A.

4. Between *date* and *date*, the plaintiff applied to the copyright office and received a certificate of registration dated ______ and identified as *date, class, number*.

5. Since *date*, the plaintiff has either published or licensed for publication all copies of the book in compliance with the copyright laws and has remained the sole owner of the copyright.

6. After the copyright was issued, the defendant infringed the copyright by publishing and selling a book entitled __________, which was copied largely from the plaintiff's book. A copy of the defendant's book is attached as Exhibit B.

7. The plaintiff has notified the defendant in writing of the infringement.

8. The defendant continues to infringe the copyright by continuing to publish and sell the infringing book in violation of the copyright, and further has engaged in unfair trade practices and unfair competition in connection with its publication and sale of the infringing book, thus causing irreparable damage.

Therefore, the plaintiff demands that:

(a) until this case is decided the defendant and the defendant's agents be enjoined from disposing of any copies of the defendant's book by sale or otherwise;

(b) the defendant account for and pay as damages to the plaintiff all profits and advantages gained from unfair trade practices and unfair competition in selling the defendant's book, and all profits and advantages gained from infringing the plaintiff's copyright (but no less than the statutory minimum);

(c) the defendant deliver for impoundment all copies of the book in the defendant's possession or control and deliver for destruction all infringing copies and all plates, molds, and other materials for making infringing copies;

(d) the defendant pay the plaintiff interest, costs, and reasonable attorney's fees; and

(e) the plaintiff be awarded any other just relief.

(Date and sign – See Form 2.)

Form 20.

Form 20. Complaint for Interpleader and Declaratory Relief.

(Caption – See Form 1.)

1. (Statement of Jurisdiction – See Form 7.)

2. On *date*, the plaintiff issued a life insurance policy on the life of *name* with *name* as the named beneficiary.

3. As a condition for keeping the policy in force, the policy required payment of a premium during the first year and then annually.

4. The premium due on *date* was never paid, and the policy lapsed after that date.

5. On *date*, after the policy had lapsed, both the insured and the named beneficiary died in an automobile collision.

6. Defendant *name* claims to be the beneficiary in place of *name* and has filed a claim to be paid the policy's full amount.

7. The other two defendants are representatives of the deceased persons' estates. Each defendant has filed a claim on behalf of each estate to receive payment of the policy's full amount.

8. If the policy was in force at the time of death, the plaintiff is in doubt about who should be paid.

Therefore, the plaintiff demands that:

(a) each defendant be restrained from commencing any action against the plaintiff on the policy;

(b) a judgment be entered that no defendant is entitled to the proceeds of the policy or any part of it, but if the court determines that the policy was in effect at the time of the insured's death, that the defendants be required to interplead and settle among themselves their rights to the proceeds, and that the plaintiff be discharged from all liability except to the defendant determined to be entitled to the proceeds; and

(c) the plaintiff recover its costs.

(Date and sign – See Form 2.)

Form 21.

Form 21. Complaint on a Claim for a Debt and to Set Aside a Fraudulent Conveyance Under Rule 18(b).

(Caption – See Form 1.)

1. (Statement of Jurisdiction — See Form 7.)

2. On _date_, defendant _name_ signed a note promising to pay to the plaintiff on _date_ the sum of $ _________ with interest at the rate of ___ percent. [The pleader may, but need not, attach a copy or plead the note verbatim.]

3. Defendant _name_ owes the plaintiff the amount of the note and interest.

4. On _date_, defendant _name_ conveyed all defendant's real and personal property _if less than all, describe it fully_ to defendant _name_ for the purpose of defrauding the plaintiff and hindering or delaying the collection of the debt.

Therefore, the plaintiff demands that:

(a) judgment for $ ______, plus costs, be entered against defendant(s) _name(s)_; and

(b) the conveyance to defendant _name_ be declared void and any judgment granted be made a lien on the property.

(Date and sign – See Form 2.)

Form 30.

Form 30. Answer Presenting Defenses Under Rule 12(b).

(Caption – See Form 1.)

Responding to Allegations in the Complaint

1. Defendant admits the allegations in paragraphs ______.

2. Defendant lacks knowledge or information sufficient to form a belief about the truth of the allegations in paragraphs ________.

3. Defendant admits *identify part of the allegation* in paragraph _______ and denies or lacks knowledge or information sufficient to form a belief about the truth of the rest of the paragraph.

Failure to State a Claim

4. The complaint fails to state a claim upon which relief can be granted.

Failure to Join a Required Party

5. If there is a debt, it is owed jointly by the defendant and *name* who is a citizen of ________. This person can be made a party without depriving this court of jurisdiction over the existing parties.

Affirmative Defense – Statute of Limitations

6. The plaintiff's claim is barred by the statute of limitations because it arose more than _____ years before this action was commenced.

Counterclaim

7. (*Set forth any counterclaim in the same way a claim is pleaded in a complaint. Include a further statement of jurisdiction if needed.*)

Crossclaim

8. (*Set forth a crossclaim against a coparty in the same way a claim is pleaded in a complaint. Include a further statement of jurisdiction if needed.*)

(Date and sign — See Form 2.)

Form 31.

Form 31. Answer to a Complaint for Money Had and Received with a Counterclaim for Interpleader.

(Caption – See Form 1.)

Response to the Allegations in the Complaint
(See Form 30.)

Counterclaim for Interpleader

1. The defendant received from _name_ a deposit of $ _______.
2. The plaintiff demands payment of the deposit because of a purported assignment from _name_, who has notified the defendant that the assignment is not valid and who continues to hold the defendant responsible for the deposit.

Therefore, the defendant demands that:

(a) _name_ be made a party to this action;

(b) the plaintiff and _name_ be required to interplead their respective claims;

(c) the court decide whether the plaintiff or _name_ or either of them is entitled to the deposit and discharge the defendant of any liability except to the person entitled to the deposit; and

(d) the defendant recover costs and attorney's fees.

(Date and sign – See Form 2.)

Form 40.

Form 40. Motion to Dismiss Under Rule 12(b) for Lack of Jurisdiction, Improper Venue, Insufficient Service of Process, or Failure to State a Claim.

(Caption – See Form 1.)

The defendant moves to dismiss the action because:

1. the amount in controversy is less than the sum or value specified by 28 U.S.C. § 1332;

2. the defendant is not subject to the personal jurisdiction of this court;

3. venue is improper (this defendant does not reside in this district and no part of the events or omissions giving rise to the claim occurred in the district);

4. the defendant has not been properly served, as shown by the attached affidavits of ____________; or

5. the complaint fails to state a claim upon which relief can be granted.

(Date and sign – See Form 2.)

Form 41.

Form 41. Motion to Bring in a Third-Party Defendant.

(Caption – See Form 1.)

The defendant, as third-party plaintiff, moves for leave to serve on *name* a summons and third-party complaint, copies of which are attached.

(Date and sign – See Form 2.)

Form 42.

Form 42. Motion to Intervene as a Defendant Under Rule 24.

(Caption – See Form 1.)

1. ___*name*___ moves for leave to intervene as a defendant in this action and to file the attached answer.

(*State grounds under Rule 24(a) or (b).*)

2. The plaintiff alleges patent infringement. We manufacture and sell to the defendant the articles involved, and we have a defense to the plaintiff's claim.

3. Our defense presents questions of law and fact that are common to this action.

(Date and sign – See Form 2.)

[An Intervener's Answer must be attached. See Form 30.]

Form 50.

Form 50. Request to Produce Documents and Tangible Things, or to Enter onto Land Under Rule 34.

(Caption – See Form 1.)

The plaintiff _name_ requests that the defendant _name_ respond within ____ days to the following requests:

1. To produce and permit the plaintiff to inspect and copy and to test or sample the following documents, including electronically stored information:

(Describe each document and the electronically stored information, either individually or by category.)

(State the time, place, and manner of the inspection and any related acts.)

2. To produce and permit the plaintiff to inspect and copy — and to test or sample — the following tangible things:

(Describe each thing, either individually or by category.)

(State the time, place, and manner of the inspection and any related acts.)

3. To permit the plaintiff to enter onto the following land to inspect, photograph, test, or sample the property or an object or operation on the property.

(Describe the property and each object or operation.)

(State the time and manner of the inspection and any related acts.)

(Date and sign – See Form 2.)

Form 51.

Form 51. Request for Admissions Under Rule 36.

(Caption — See Form 1.)

The plaintiff _name_ asks the defendant _name_ to respond within 30 days to these requests by admitting, for purposes of this action only and subject to objections to admissibility at trial:

1. The genuineness of the following documents, copies of which [are attached] [are or have been furnished or made available for inspection and copying].

(*List each document.*)

2. The truth of each of the following statements:

(*List each statement.*)

(Date and sign – See Form 2.)

Form 52.

Form 52. Report of the Parties' Planning Meeting.

(Caption — See Form 1.)

1. The following persons participated in a Rule 26(f) conference on ___*date*___ by ___*state the method of conferring*___ :

2. Initial Disclosures. The parties [have completed] [will complete by ___*date*___] the initial disclosures required by Rule 26(a)(1).

3. Discovery Plan. The parties propose this discovery plan:

   (*Use separate paragraphs or subparagraphs if the parties disagree.*)

   (a) Discovery will be needed on these subjects: (*describe*)
   (b) Disclosure or discovery of electronically stored information should be handled as follows: (*briefly describe the parties' proposals, including the form or forms for production.*)
   (c) The parties have agreed to an order regarding claims of privilege or of protection as trial-preparation material asserted after production, as follows: (*briefly describe the provisions of the proposed order.*)
   (d) (Dates for commencing and completing discovery, including discovery to be commenced or completed before other discovery.)
   (e) (Maximum number of interrogatories by each party to another party, along with dates the answers are due.)
   (f) (Maximum number of requests for admission, along with the dates responses are due.)
   (g) (Maximum number of depositions for each party.)
   (h) (Limits on the length of depositions, in hours.)
   (i) (Dates for exchanging reports of expert witnesses.)
   (j) (Dates for supplementations under Rule 26(e).)

4. Other Items:

   (a) (A date if the parties ask to meet with the court before a scheduling order.)
   (b) (Requested dates for pretrial conferences.)
   (c) (Final dates for the plaintiff to amend pleadings or to join parties.)
   (d) (Final dates for the defendant to amend pleadings or to join parties.)
   (e) (Final dates to file dispositive motions.)
   (f) (State the prospects for settlement.)
   (g) (Identify any alternative dispute resolution procedure that may enhance settlement prospects.)
   (h) (Final dates for submitting Rule 26(a)(3) witness lists, designations of witnesses whose testimony will be presented by deposition, and exhibit lists.)
   (i) (Final dates to file objection under Rule 26(a)(3).)
   (j) (Suggested trial date and estimate of trial length.)
   (k) (Other matters.)

(Date and sign — see Form 2.)

Form 60.

Form 60. Notice of Condemnation.

(Caption – See Form 1.)

To *name the defendant*.

1. A complaint in condemnation has been filed in the United States District Court for the ______ District of ________, to take property to use for *purpose*. The interest to be taken is *describe*. The court is located in the United States courthouse at this address: ____________.

2. The property to be taken is described below. You have or claim an interest in it.

   (*Describe the property.*)

3. The authority for taking this property is *cite*.

4. If you want to object or present any defense to the taking you must serve an answer on the plaintiff's attorney within 21 days [after being served with this notice][from *(insert the date of the last publication of notice)*]. Send your answer to this address: ___________.

5. Your answer must identify the property in which you claim an interest, state the nature and extent of that interest, and state all your objections and defenses to the taking. Objections and defenses not presented are waived.

6. If you fail to answer you consent to the taking and the court will enter a judgment that takes your described property interest.

7. Instead of answering, you may serve on the plaintiff's attorney a notice of appearance that designates the property in which you claim an interest. After you do that, you will receive a notice of any proceedings that affect you. Whether or not you have previously appeared or answered, you may present evidence at a trial to determine compensation for the property and share in the overall award.

(Date and sign – See Form 2.)

Form 61.

Form 61. Complaint for Condemnation.

(Caption – See Form 1; name as defendants the property and at least one owner.)

1. (Statement of Jurisdiction – See Form 7.)

2. This is an action to take property under the power of eminent domain and to determine just compensation to be paid to the owners and parties in interest.

3. The authority for the taking is _______.

4. The property is to be used for _________________.

5. The property to be taken is (*describe in enough detail for identification — or attach the description and state "is described in Exhibit A, attached."*)

6. The interest to be acquired is _________.

7. The persons known to the plaintiff to have or claim an interest in the property are: ____________________________. (*For each person include the interest claimed.*)

8. There may be other persons who have or claim an interest in the property and whose names could not be found after a reasonably diligent search. They are made parties under the designation "Unknown Owners."

Therefore, the plaintiff demands judgment:

(a) condemning the property;

(b) determining and awarding just compensation; and

(c) granting any other lawful and proper relief.

(Date and sign – See Form 2.)

Form 70.

Form 70. Judgment on a Jury Verdict.

(Caption – See Form 1.)

This action was tried by a jury with Judge ________ presiding, and the jury has rendered a verdict.

It is ordered that:

[the plaintiff *name* recover from the defendant *name* the amount of $______ with interest at the rate of __%, along with costs.]

[the plaintiff recover nothing, the action be dismissed on the merits, and the defendant *name* recover costs from the plaintiff *name*.]

Date ________

____
Clerk of Court

Form 71.

Form 71. Judgment by the Court without a Jury.

(Caption – See Form 1.)

This action was tried by Judge _____ without a jury and the following decision was reached:

It is ordered that [the plaintiff _name_ recover from the defendant _name_ the amount of $_______, with prejudgment interest at the rate of ___%, postjudgment interest at the rate of ___%, along with costs.] [the plaintiff recover nothing, the action be dismissed on the merits, and the defendant _name_ recover costs from the plaintiff _name_.]

Date_______

____
Clerk of Court

Form 80.

Form 80. Notice of a Magistrate Judge's Availability.

1. **A magistrate judge is available under title 28 U.S.C. § 636(c) to conduct the proceedings in this case, including a jury or nonjury trial and the entry of final judgment. But a magistrate judge can be assigned only if all parties voluntarily consent.**

2. **You may withhold your consent without adverse substantive consequences. The identity of any party consenting or withholding consent will not be disclosed to the judge to whom the case is assigned or to any magistrate judge.**

3. **If a magistrate judge does hear your case, you may appeal directly to a United States court of appeals as you would if a district judge heard it.**

A form called *Consent to an Assignment to a United States Magistrate Judge* is available from the court clerk's office.

Form 81.

Form 81. Consent to an Assignment to a Magistrate Judge.

(Caption – See Form 1.)

I voluntarily consent to have a United States magistrate judge conduct all further proceedings in this case, including a trial, and order the entry of final judgment. (Return this form to the court clerk — not to a judge or magistrate judge.)

Date__________

____
Signature of the Party

Form 82.

Form 82. Order of Assignment to a Magistrate Judge.

(Caption – See Form 1.)

With the parties' consent it is ordered that this case be assigned to United States Magistrate Judge _________ of this district to conduct all proceedings and enter final judgment in accordance with 28 U.S.C. § 636(c).

Date __________

____
United States District Judge

SUPPLEMENTAL RULES FOR ADMIRALTY OR MARITIME CLAIMS AND ASSET FORFEITURE ACTIONS.

The following supplemental rules were adopted by an order of the Supreme Court effective July 1, 1966, which order also rescinded the former Rules of Practice in Admiralty and Maritime Cases, and have since been further amended.

Rule A. Scope of Rules.

(1) These Supplemental Rules apply to:

(A) the procedure in admiralty and maritime claims within the meaning of Rule 9(h) with respect to the following remedies:

(i) maritime attachment and garnishment,

(ii) actions in rem,

(iii) possessory, petitory, and partition actions, and,

(iv) actions for exoneration from or limitation of liability;

(B) forfeiture actions in rem arising from a federal statute; and

(C) the procedure in statutory condemnation proceedings analogous to maritime actions in rem, whether within the admiralty and maritime jurisdiction or not. Except as otherwise provided, references in these Supplemental Rules to actions in rem include such analogous statutory condemnation proceedings.

(2) The Federal Rules of Civil Procedure also apply to the foregoing proceedings except to the extent that they are inconsistent with these Supplemental Rules. (Added by order adopted February 28, 1966, effective July 1, 1966; amended by order adopted April 12, 2006, effective December 1, 2006.)

Rule B. In Personam Actions: Attachment and Garnishment.

(1) *When Available; Complaint, Affidavit, Judicial Authorization, and Process.* — In an in personam action:

(a) If a defendant is not found within the district when a verified complaint praying for attachment and the affidavit required by Rule B(1)(b) are filed, a verified complaint may contain a prayer for process to attach the defendant's tangible or intangible personal property — up to the amount sued for — in the hands of garnishees named in the process.

(b) The plaintiff or the plaintiff's attorney must sign and file with the complaint an affidavit stating that, to the affiant's knowledge, or on information and belief, the defendant cannot be found within the district. The court must review the complaint and affidavit and, if the conditions of this Rule B appear to exist, enter an order so stating and authorizing process of attachment and garnishment. The clerk may issue supplemental process enforcing the court's order upon application without further court order.

(c) If the plaintiff or the plaintiff's attorney certifies that exigent circumstances make court review impracticable, the clerk must issue the summons and process of attachment and garnishment. The plaintiff has the burden in any post-attachment hearing under Rule E(4)(f) to show that exigent circumstances existed.

(d)(i) If the property is a vessel or tangible property on board a vessel, the summons, process, and any supplemental process must be delivered to the marshal for service.

(ii) If the property is other tangible or intangible property, the summons, process, and any supplemental process must be delivered to a person or organization authorized to serve it, who may be (A) a marshal; (B) someone under contract with the United States; (C) someone specially appointed by the court for that purpose; or, (D) in an action brought by the United States, any officer or employee of the United States.

(e) The plaintiff may invoke state-law remedies under Rule 64 for seizure of person or property for the purpose of securing satisfaction of the judgment.

(2) *Notice to Defendant.* — No default judgment may be entered except upon proof — which may be by affidavit — that:

(a) the complaint, summons, and process of attachment or garnishment have been served on the defendant in a manner authorized by Rule 4;

(b) the plaintiff or the garnishee has mailed to the defendant the complaint, summons, and process of attachment or garnishment, using any form of mail requiring a return receipt; or

(c) the plaintiff or the garnishee has tried diligently to give notice of the action to the defendant but could not do so.

(3) *Answer.* — (a) By Garnishee. — The garnishee shall serve an answer, together with answers to any interrogatories served with the complaint, within 21 days after service of process upon the garnishee. Interrogatories to the garnishee may be served with the complaint without leave of court. If the garnishee refuses or neglects to answer on oath as to the debts, credits, or effects of the defendant in the garnishee's hands, or any interrogatories concerning such debts, credits, and effects that may be propounded by the plaintiff, the court may award compulsory process against the garnishee. If the garnishee admits any debts, credits, or effects, they shall be held in the garnishee's hands or paid into the registry of the court, and shall be held in either case subject to the further order of the court.

(b) By Defendant. — The defendant shall serve an answer within 30 days after process has been executed, whether by attachment of property or service on the garnishee. (Added by order adopted February 28, 1966, effective July 1, 1966, amended by order adopted April 29, 1985, effective August 1, 1985, by order adopted March 2, 1987, effective August 1, 1987, amended by order April 17, 2000, effective December 1, 2000, order April 25, 2005, effective December 1, 2005, and by order adopted March 26, 2009, effective December 1, 2009.)

Rule C. In Rem Actions: Special Provisions.

(1) *When Available.* — An action in rem may be brought:

(a) To enforce any maritime lien;

(b) Whenever a statute of the United States provides for a maritime action in rem or a proceeding analogous thereto.

Except as otherwise provided by law a party who may proceed in rem may also, or in the alternative, proceed in personam against any person who may be liable.

Statutory provisions exempting vessels or other property owned or possessed by or operated by or for the United States from arrest or seizure are not affected by this rule. When a statute so provides, an action against the United States or an instrumentality thereof may proceed on in rem principles.

(2) *Complaint.* — In an action in rem the complaint must:

(a) be verified;

(b) describe with reasonable particularity the property that is the subject of the action; and

(c) state that the property is within the district or will be within the district while the action is pending.

(3) *Judicial Authorization and Process.* — (a) Arrest Warrant.

(i) The court must review the complaint and any supporting papers. If the conditions for an in rem action appear to exist, the court must issue an order directing the clerk to issue a warrant for the arrest of the vessel or other property that is the subject of the action.

(ii) If the plaintiff or the plaintiff's attorney certifies that exigent circumstances make court review impracticable, the clerk must promptly issue a summons and a warrant for the arrest of the vessel or other property that is the subject of the action. The plaintiff has the burden in any post-arrest hearing under Rule E(4)(f) to show that exigent circumstances existed.

(b) Service. (i) If the property that is the subject of the action is a vessel or tangible property on board a vessel, the warrant and any supplemental process must be delivered to the marshal for service.

(ii) If the property that is the subject of the action is other property, tangible or intangible, the warrant and any supplemental process must be delivered to a person or organization authorized to enforce it, who may be: (A) a marshal; (B) someone under contract with the United States; (C) someone specially appointed by the court for that purpose; or, (D) in an action brought by the United States, any officer or employee of the United States.

(c) Deposit in Court. If the property that is the subject of the action consists in whole or in part of freight, the proceeds of property sold, or other intangible property, the clerk must issue — in addition to the warrant — a summons directing any person controlling the property to show cause why it should not be deposited in court to abide the judgment.

(d) Supplemental Process. The clerk may upon application issue supplemental process to enforce the court's order without further court order.

(4) *Notice.* — No notice other than execution of process is required when the property that is the subject of the action has been released under Rule E(5). If the property is not released within 14 days after execution, the plaintiff must promptly — or within the time that the court allows — give public notice of the action and arrest in a newspaper designated by court order and having general circulation in the district, but publication may be terminated if the property is released before publication is completed. The notice must specify the time under Rule C(6) to file a statement of interest in or right against the seized property and to answer. This rule does not affect the notice requirements in an action to foreclose a preferred ship mortgage under 46 U.S.C. §§ 31301 et seq., as amended.

(5) *Ancillary Process.* — In any action in rem in which process has been served as provided by this rule, if any part of the property that is the subject of the action has not been brought within the control of the court because it has been removed or sold, or because it is intangible property in the hands of a person who has not been served with process, the court may, on motion, order any person having possession or control of such property or its proceeds to show cause why it should not be delivered into the custody of the marshal or other person or organization having a warrant for the arrest of the property, or paid into court to abide the judgment; and, after hearing, the court may enter such judgment as law and justice may require.

(6) *Responsive Pleading; Interrogatories.* — (a) Statement of Interest; Answer. In an action in rem:

(i) a person who asserts a right of possession or any ownership interest in the property that is the subject of the action must file a verified statement of right or interest:

(A) within 14 days after the execution of process, or

(B) within the time that the court allows;

(ii) the statement of right or interest must describe the interest in the property that supports the person's demand for its restitution or right to defend the action;

(iii) an agent, bailee, or attorney must state the authority to file a statement of right or interest on behalf of another; and

(iv) a person who asserts a right of possession or any ownership interest must serve an answer within 21 days after filing the statement of interest or right.

(b) Interrogatories. Interrogatories may be served with the complaint in an in rem action without leave of court. Answers to the interrogatories must be served with the answer to the complaint. (Added by order adopted February 28, 1966, effective July 1, 1966, amended by order adopted April 29, 1985, effective August 1, 1985, by order adopted March 2, 1987, effective August 1, 1987, by order adopted April 30, 1991, effective December 1, 1991, by order adopted April 17, 2000, effective December 1, 2000, by order adopted April 29, 2002, effective December 1, 2002, by order adopted April 25, 2005, effective December 1, 2005, by order adopted April 12, 2006, effective December 1, 2006, by order adopted April 23, 2008, effective December 1, 2008, and by order adopted March 26, 2009, effective December 1, 2009.)

CASE NOTES

Suit may be filed and process held in abeyance if absent vessel to return shortly. — If the vessel is absent from the United States, a plaintiff may file suit nonetheless and request the court to hold service of process in abeyance until the vessel returns. However, this request can be granted only if it is clear that the vessel will be within the court's jurisdiction "shortly." Norfolk Shipbuilding & Drydock Corp. v. USNS Truckee, 629 F. Supp. 779 (E.D. Va. 1985).

Vessel must be served before dispositive order issued. — Filing alone will commence the suit and toll the statute of limitations, but the vessel must be served before the court can issue a dispositive order. Norfolk Shipbuilding & Drydock Corp. v. USNS Truckee, 629 F. Supp. 779 (E.D. Va. 1985).

Applied in R.M.S. Titanic, Inc. v. Wrecked & Abandoned Vessel, 9 F. Supp. 2d 624 (E.D. Va. 1998).

Rule D. Possessory, Petitory and Partition Actions.

In all actions for possession, partition, and to try title mantainable according to the course of the admiralty practice with respect to a vessel, in all actions so maintainable with respect to the possession of cargo or other maritime property, and in all actions by one or more part owners against the others to obtain security for the return of the vessel from any voyage undertaken without their consent, or by one or more part owners against the others to obtain possession of the vessel for any voyage on giving security for its safe return, the process shall be by a warrant of arrest of the vessel, cargo, or other property, and by notice in the manner provided by Rule B(2) to the adverse party or parties. (Added by order adopted February 28, 1966, effective July 1, 1966.)

Rule E. Actions in Rem and Quasi in Rem: General Provisions.

(1) *Applicability.* — Except as otherwise provided, this rule applies to actions in personam with process of maritime attachment and garnishment, actions in rem, and petitory, possessory, and partition actions, supplementing Rules B, C, and D.

(2) *Complaint; Security.* — (a) Complaint. — In actions to which this rule is applicable the complaint shall state the circumstances from which the claim arises with such particularity that the defendant or claimant will be able, without moving for a more definite statement, to commence an investigation of the facts and to frame a responsive pleading.

(b) Security for Costs. — Subject to the provisions of Rule 54(d) and of relevant statutes, the court may, on the filing of the complaint or on the appearance of any defendant, claimant, or any other party, or at any later time, require the plaintiff, defendant, claimant, or other party to give security, or additional security, in such sum as the court shall direct to pay all costs and expenses that shall be awarded against the party by any interlocutory order or by the final judgment, or on appeal by any appellate court.

(3) *Process.* — (a) In admiralty and maritime proceedings process in rem or of maritime attachment and garnishment may be served only within the district.

(b) Issuance and Delivery. Issuance and delivery of process in rem, or of maritime attachment and garnishment, shall be held in abeyance if the plaintiff so requests.

(4) *Execution of Process; Marshal's Return; Custody of Property; Procedures for Release.* — (a) In General. — Upon issuance and delivery of the process, or, in the case of summons with process of attachment and garnishment, when it appears that the defendant cannot be found within the district, the marshal or other person or organization having a warrant shall forthwith execute the process in accordance with this subdivision (4), making due and prompt return.

(b) Tangible Property. — If tangible property is to be attached or arrested, the marshal or other person or organization having the warrant shall take it into the marshal's possession for safe custody. If the character or situation of the property is such that the taking of actual possession is impracticable, the marshal or other person executing the process shall affix a copy thereof to the property in a conspicuous place and leave a copy of the complaint and process with the person having possession or the person's agent. In furtherance of the marshal's custody of any vessel the marshal is authorized to make a written request to the collector of customs not to grant clearance to such vessel until notified by the marshal or a deputy marshal or by the clerk that the vessel has been released in accordance with these rules.

(c) Intangible Property. — If intangible property is to be attached or arrested the marshal or other person or organization having the warrant shall execute the process by leaving with the garnishee or other obligor a copy of the complaint and process requiring the garnishee or other obligor to answer as provided in Rules B(3)(a) and C(6); or the marshal may accept for payment into the registry of the court the amount owed to the extent of the amount claimed by the plaintiff with interest and costs, in which event the garnishee or other obligor shall not be required to answer unless alias process shall be served.

(d) Directions with Respect to Property in Custody. — The marshal or other person or organization having the warrant may at any time apply to the court for directions with respect to property that has been attached or arrested, and shall give notice of such application to any or all of the parties as the court may direct.

(e) Expenses of Seizing and Keeping Property; Deposit. — These rules do not alter the provisions of 28 U.S.C. § 1921, as amended, relative to the expenses of seizing and keeping property attached or arrested and to the requirement of deposits to cover such expenses.

(f) Procedure for Release From Arrest or Attachment. — Whenever property is arrested or attached, any person claiming an interest in it shall be entitled to a prompt hearing at which the plaintiff shall be required to show why the arrest or attachment should not be vacated or other relief granted consistent with these rules. This subdivision shall have no application to suits for seamen's wages when process is issued upon a certification of sufficient cause filed pursuant to Title 46, U.S.C. §§ 603 and 604[1] or to actions by the United States for forfeitures for violation of any statute of the United States.

(5) *Release of Property.* — (a) Special Bond. — Whenever process of maritime attachment and garnishment or process in rem is issued the execution of such process shall be stayed, or the property released, on the giving of security, to be approved by the court or clerk, or by stipulation of the parties, conditioned to answer the judgment of the court or of any appellate court. The parties may stipulate the amount and nature of such security. In the event of the inability or refusal of the parties so to stipulate the court shall fix the principal sum of the bond or stipulation at an amount sufficient to cover the amount of the plaintiff's claim fairly stated with accrued interest and costs; but the principal sum shall in no event exceed (i) twice the amount of the plaintiff's claim or (ii) the value of the property on due appraisement, whichever is smaller. The bond or stipulation shall be conditioned for the payment of the principal sum and interest thereon at 6 per cent per annum.

(b) General Bond. — The owner of any vessel may file a general bond or stipulation, with sufficient surety, to be approved by the court, conditioned to answer the judgment of such court in all or any actions that may be brought thereafter in such court in which the vessel is attached or arrested. Thereupon the execution of all such process against such vessel shall be stayed so long as the amount secured by such bond or stipulation is at least double the aggregate amount claimed by plaintiffs in all actions begun and pending in which such vessel has been attached or arrested. Judgments and remedies may be had on such bond or stipulation as if a special bond or stipulation had been filed in each of such actions. The district court may make necessary orders to carry this rule into effect, particularly as to the giving of proper notice of any action against or attachment of a vessel for which a general bond has been filed. Such bond or stipulation shall be indorsed by the clerk with a minute of the actions wherein process is so stayed. Further security may be required by the court at any time.

If a special bond or stipulation is given in a particular case, the liability on the general bond or stipulation shall cease as to that case.

(c) Release by Consent or Stipulation; Order of Court or Clerk; Costs. — Any vessel, cargo, or other property in the custody of the marshal or other person or organization having the warrant may be released forthwith upon the marshal's acceptance and approval of a stipulation, bond, or other security, signed by the party on whose behalf the property is detained or the party's attorney and expressly authorizing such release, if all costs and charges of the court and its officers shall have first been paid. Otherwise no property in the custody of the marshal, other person or organization having the warrant, or other officer of the court shall be released without an order of the court; but such order may be entered as of course by the clerk, upon the giving of approved security as provided by law and these rules, or upon the dismissal or discontinuance of the action; but the marshal or other person or organization having the warrant shall not deliver any property so released until the costs and charges of the officers of the court shall first have been paid.

(d) Possessory, Petitory, and Partition Actions. — The foregoing provisions of this subdivision (5) do not apply to petitory, possessory, and partition actions. In such cases the property arrested shall be released only by order of the court, on such terms and conditions and on the giving of such security as the court may require.

(6) *Reduction or Impairment of Security.* — Whenever security is taken the court may, on motion and hearing, for good cause shown, reduce the amount of security given; and if the surety shall be or become insufficient, new or additional sureties may be required on motion and hearing.

(7) *Security on Counterclaim.* — (a) When a person who has given security for damages in the original action asserts a counterclaim that arises from the transaction or occurrence that is the subject of the original action, a plaintiff for whose benefit the security has been given must give security for damages demanded in the counterclaim unless the court, for cause shown, directs otherwise. Proceedings on the original claim must be stayed until this security is given, unless the court directs otherwise.

(b) The plaintiff is required to give security under Rule E(7)(a) when the United States or its corporate instrumentality counterclaims and would have been required to give security to respond in damages if a private party but is relieved by law from giving security.

(8) *Restricted Appearance.* — An appearance to defend against an admiralty and maritime claim with respect to which there has issued process in rem, or process of attachment and garnishment, may be expressly restricted to the defense of such claim, and in that event is not an appearance for the purposes of any other claim with respect to which such process is not available or has not been served.

(9) *Disposition of Property; Sales.* — (a) Interlocutory Sales; Delivery. (i) On application of a party, the marshal, or other person having custody of the property, the court may order all or part of the property sold — with the sales proceeds, or as much of them as will satisfy the judgment, paid into court to await further orders of the court — if:

(A) the attached or arrested property is perishable, or liable to deterioration, decay, or injury by being detained in custody pending the action;

(B) the expense of keeping the property is excessive or disproportionate; or

[1] Repealed by Pub. L. 98-89, § 4(b), Aug. 26, 1983, 97 Stat. 600, section 1 of which enacted Title 46, Shipping.

(C) there is an unreasonable delay in securing release of the property.

(ii) In the circumstances described in Rule E(9)(a)(i), the court, on motion by a defendant or a person filing a statement of interest or right under Rule C(6), may order that the property, rather than being sold, be delivered to the movant upon giving security under these rules.

(b) Sales; Proceeds. — All sales of property shall be made by the marshal or a deputy marshal, or by other person or organization having the warrant, or by any other person assigned by the court where the marshal or other person or organization having the warrant is a party in interest; and the proceeds of sale shall be forthwith paid into the registry of the court to be disposed of according to law.

(10) *Preservation of Property.* — When the owner or another person remains in possession of property attached or arrested under the provisions of Rule E(4)(b) that permit execution of process without taking actual possession, the court, on a party's motion or on its own, may enter any order necessary to preserve the property and to prevent its removal. (Added by order adopted February 28, 1966, effective July 1, 1966, amended by order adopted April 29, 1985, effective August 1, 1985, by order adopted March 2, 1987, effective August 1, 1987, by order adopted April 30, 1991, effective December 1, 1991, by order adopted April 17, 2000, effective December 1, 2000, and by order adopted April 12, 2006, effective December 1, 2006.)

CASE NOTES

Suit may be filed and process held in abeyance if absent vessel to return shortly. — If the vessel is absent from the United States, a plaintiff may file suit nonetheless and request the court to hold service of process in abeyance until the vessel returns. However, this request can be granted only if it is clear that the vessel will be within the court's jurisdiction "shortly." Norfolk Shipbuilding & Drydock Corp. v. USNS Truckee, 629 F. Supp. 779 (E.D. Va. 1985).

Vessel must be served before dispositive order issued. — Filing alone will commence the suit and toll the statute of limitations, but the vessel must be served before the court can issue a dispositive order. Norfolk Shipbuilding & Drydock Corp. v. USNS Truckee, 629 F. Supp. 779 (E.D. Va. 1985).

Applied in R.M.S. Titanic, Inc. v. Haver, 171 F.3d 943 (4th. Cir. 1999).

Rule F. Limitation of Liability.

(1) *Time for Filing Complaint; Security.* — Not later than six months after receipt of a claim in writing, any vessel owner may file a complaint in the appropriate district court, as provided in subdivision (9) of this rule, for limitation of liability pursuant to statute. The owner (a) shall deposit with the court, for the benefit of claimants, a sum equal to the amount or value of the owner's interest in the vessel and pending freight, or approved security therefor, and in addition such sums, or approved security therefor, as the court may from time to time fix as necessary to carry out the provisions of the statutes as amended; or (b) at the owner's option shall transfer to a trustee to be appointed by the court, for the benefit of claimants, the owner's interest in the vessel and pending freight, together with such sums, or approved security therefor, as the court may from time to time fix as necessary to carry out the provisions of the statutes as amended. The plaintiff shall also give security for costs and, if the plaintiff elects to give security, for interest at the rate of 6 percent per annum from the date of the security.

(2) *Complaint.* — The complaint shall set forth the facts on the basis of which the right to limit liability is asserted and all facts necessary to enable the court to determine the amount to which the owner's liability shall be limited. The complaint may demand exoneration from as well as limitation of liability. It shall state the voyage if any, on which the demands sought to be limited arose, with the date and place of its termination; the amount of all demands including all unsatisfied liens or claims of lien, in contract or in tort or otherwise, arising on that voyage, so far as known to the plaintiff, and what actions and proceedings, if any, are pending thereon; whether the vessel was damaged, lost, or abandoned, and, if so, when and where; the value of the vessel at the close of the voyage or, in case of wreck, the value of her wreckage, strippings, or proceeds, if any, and where and in whose possession they are; and the amount of any pending freight recovered or recoverable. If the plaintiff elects to transfer the plaintiff's interest in the vessel to a trustee, the complaint must further show any prior paramount liens thereon, and what voyages or trips, if any, she has made since the voyage or trip on which the claims sought to be limited arose, and any existing liens arising upon any such subsequent voyage or trip, with the amounts and causes thereof, and the names and addresses of the lienors, so far as known; and whether the vessel sustained any injury upon or by reason of such subsequent voyage or trip.

(3) *Claims Against Owner; Injunction.* — Upon compliance by the owner with the requirements of subdivision (1) of this rule all claims and proceedings against the

owner or the owner's property with respect to the matter in question shall cease. On application of the plaintiff the court shall enjoin the further prosecution of any action or proceeding against the plaintiff or the plaintiff's property with respect to any claim subject to limitation in the action.

(4) *Notice to Claimants.* — Upon the owner's compliance with subdivision (1) of this rule the court shall issue a notice to all persons asserting claims with respect to which the complaint seeks limitation, admonishing them to file their respective claims with the clerk of the court and to serve on the attorneys for the plaintiff a copy thereof on or before a date to be named in the notice. The date so fixed shall not be less than 30 days after issuance of the notice. For cause shown, the court may enlarge the time within which claims may be filed. The notice shall be published in such newspaper or newspapers as the court may direct once a week for four successive weeks prior to the date fixed for the filing of claims. The plaintiff not later than the day of second publication shall also mail a copy of the notice to every person known to have made any claim against the vessel or the plaintiff arising out of the voyage or trip on which the claims sought to be limited arose. In cases involving death a copy of such notice shall be mailed to the decedent at the decedent's last known address, and also to any person who shall be known to have made any claim on account of such death.

(5) *Claims and Answer.* — Claims shall be filed and served on or before the date specified in the notice provided for in subdivision (4) of this rule. Each claim shall specify the facts upon which the claimant relies in support of the claim, the items thereof, and the dates on which the same accrued. If a claimant desires to contest either the right to exoneration from or the right to limitation of liability the claimant shall file and serve an answer to the complaint unless the claim has included an answer.

(6) *Information to Be Given Claimants.* — Within 30 days after the date specified in the notice for filing claims, or within such time as the court thereafter may allow, the plaintiff shall mail to the attorney for each claimant (or if the claimant has no attorney to the claimant) a list setting forth (a) the name of each claimant, (b) the name and address of the claimant's attorney (if the claimant is known to have one), (c) the nature of the claim, i.e., whether property loss, property damage, death, personal injury etc., and (d) the amount thereof.

(7) *Insufficiency of Fund or Security.* — Any claimant may by motion demand that the funds deposited in court or the security given by the plaintiff be increased on the ground that they are less than the value of the plaintiff's interest in the vessel and pending freight. Thereupon the court shall cause due appraisement to be made of the value of the plaintiff's interest in the vessel and pending freight; and if the court finds that the deposit or security is either insufficient or excessive it shall order its increase or reduction. In like manner any claimant may demand that the deposit or security be increased on the ground that it is insufficient to carry out the provisions of the statutes relating to claims in respect of loss of life or bodily injury; and, after notice and hearing, the court may similarly order that the deposit or security be increased or reduced.

(8) *Objections to Claims: Distribution of Fund.* — Any interested party may question or controvert any claim without filing an objection thereto. Upon determination of liability the fund deposited or secured, or the proceeds of the vessel and pending freight, shall be divided pro rata, subject to all relevant provisions of law, among the several claimants in proportion to the amounts of their respective claims, duly proved, saving, however, to all parties any priority to which they may be legally entitled.

(9) *Venue; Transfer.* — The complaint shall be filed in any district in which the vessel has been attached or arrested to answer for any claim with respect to which the plaintiff seeks to limit liability; or, if the vessel has not been attached or arrested, then in any district in which the owner has been sued with respect to any such claim. When the vessel has not been attached or arrested to answer the matters aforesaid, and suit has not been commenced against the owner, the proceedings may be had in the district in which the vessel may be, but if the vessel is not within any district and no suit has been commenced in any district, then the complaint may be filed in any district. For the convenience of parties and witnesses, in the interest of justice, the court may transfer the action to any district; if venue is wrongly laid the court shall dismiss or, if it be in the interest of justice, transfer the action to any district in which it could have been brought. If the vessel shall have been sold, the proceeds shall represent the vessel for the purposes of these rules. (Added by order adopted February 28, 1966, effective July 1, 1966, amended by order adopted March 2, 1987, effective August 1, 1987.)

CASE NOTES

Applied in In re McAllister Towing of Va., Inc., 999 F. Supp. 797 (E.D. Va. 1998).

Rule G. Forfeiture Actions In Rem.

(1) *Scope.* — This rule governs a forfeiture action in rem arising from a federal statute. To the extent that this rule does not address an issue, Supplemental Rules C and E and the Federal Rules of Civil Procedure also apply.

(2) *Complaint.* — The complaint must:

(a) be verified;

(b) state the grounds for subject-matter jurisdiction, in rem jurisdiction over the defendant property, and venue;

(c) describe the property with reasonable particularity;

(d) if the property is tangible, state its location when any seizure occurred and — if different — its location when the action is filed;

(e) identify the statute under which the forfeiture action is brought; and

(f) state sufficiently detailed facts to support a reasonable belief that the government will be able to meet its burden of proof at trial.

(3) *Judicial Authorization and Process.* — (a) Real Property. If the defendant is real property, the government must proceed under 18 U.S.C. § 985.

(b) Other Property; Arrest Warrant. If the defendant is not real property:

(i) the clerk must issue a warrant to arrest the property if it is in the government's possession, custody, or control;

(ii) the court — on finding probable cause — must issue a warrant to arrest the property if it is not in the government's possession, custody, or control and is not subject to a judicial restraining order; and

(iii) a warrant is not necessary if the property is subject to a judicial restraining order.

(c) Execution of Process. (i) The warrant and any supplemental process must be delivered to a person or organization authorized to execute it, who may be: (A) a marshal or any other United States officer or employee; (B) someone under contract with the United States; or (C) someone specially appointed by the court for that purpose.

(ii) The authorized person or organization must execute the warrant and any supplemental process on property in the United States as soon as practicable unless:

(A) the property is in the government's possession, custody, or control; or

(B) the court orders a different time when the complaint is under seal, the action is stayed before the warrant and supplemental process are executed, or the court finds other good cause.

(iii) The warrant and any supplemental process may be executed within the district or, when authorized by statute, outside the district.

(iv) If executing a warrant on property outside the United States is required, the warrant may be transmitted to an appropriate authority for serving process where the property is located.

(4) *Notice.* — (a) Notice by Publication. (i) When Publication Is Required. A judgment of forfeiture may be entered only if the government has published notice of the action within a reasonable time after filing the complaint or at a time the court orders. But notice need not be published if:

(A) the defendant property is worth less than $1,000 and direct notice is sent under Rule G(4)(b) to every person the government can reasonably identify as a potential claimant; or

(B) the court finds that the cost of publication exceeds the property's value and that other means of notice would satisfy due process.

(ii) Content of the Notice. Unless the court orders otherwise, the notice must:

(A) describe the property with reasonable particularity;

(B) state the times under Rule G(5) to file a claim and to answer; and

(C) name the government attorney to be served with the claim and answer.

(iii) Frequency of Publication. Published notice must appear:

(A) once a week for three consecutive weeks; or

(B) only once if, before the action was filed, notice of nonjudicial forfeiture of the same property was published on an official internet government forfeiture site for at least 30 consecutive days, or in a newspaper of general circulation for three consecutive weeks in a district where publication is authorized under Rule G(4)(a)(iv).

(iv) Means of Publication. The government should select from the following options a means of publication reasonably calculated to notify potential claimants of the action:

(A) if the property is in the United States, publication in a newspaper generally circulated in the district where the action is filed, where the property was seized, or where property that was not seized is located;

(B) if the property is outside the United States, publication in a newspaper generally circulated in a district where the action is filed, in a newspaper generally circulated in the country where the property is located, or in legal notices published and generally circulated in the country where the property is located; or

(C) instead of (A) or (B), posting a notice on an official internet government forfeiture site for at least 30 consecutive days.

(b) Notice to Known Potential Claimants. (i) Direct Notice Required. The government must send notice of the action and a copy of the complaint to any person who reasonably appears to be a potential claimant on the facts known to the government before the end of the time for filing a claim under Rule G(5)(a)(ii)(B).

(ii) Content of the Notice. The notice must state:

(A) the date when the notice is sent;

(B) a deadline for filing a claim, at least 35 days after the notice is sent;

(C) that an answer or a motion under Rule 12 must be filed no later than 21 days after filing the claim; and

(D) the name of the government attorney to be served with the claim and answer.

(iii) Sending Notice.

(A) The notice must be sent by means reasonably calculated to reach the potential claimant.

(B) Notice may be sent to the potential claimant or to the attorney representing the potential claimant with respect to the seizure of the property or in a related investigation, administrative forfeiture proceeding, or criminal case.

(C) Notice sent to a potential claimant who is incarcerated must be sent to the place of incarceration.

(D) Notice to a person arrested in connection with an offense giving rise to the forfeiture who is not incarcerated when notice is sent may be sent to the address that person last gave to the agency that arrested or released the person.

(E) Notice to a person from whom the property was seized who is not incarcerated when notice is sent may be sent to the last address that person gave to the agency that seized the property.

(iv) When Notice Is Sent. Notice by the following means is sent on the date when it is placed in the mail, delivered to a commercial carrier, or sent by electronic mail.

(v) Actual Notice. A potential claimant who had actual notice of a forfeiture action may not oppose or seek relief from forfeiture because of the government's failure to send the required notice.

(5) *Responsive Pleadings.* — (a) Filing a Claim. (i) A person who asserts an interest in the defendant property may contest the forfeiture by filing a claim in the court where the action is pending. The claim must:

(A) identify the specific property claimed;

(B) identify the claimant and state the claimant's interest in the property;

(C) be signed by the claimant under penalty of perjury; and

(D) be served on the government attorney designated under Rule G(4)(a)(ii)(C) or (b)(ii)(D).

(ii) Unless the court for good cause sets a different time, the claim must be filed;

(A) by the time stated in a direct notice sent under Rule G(4)(b);

(B) if notice was published but direct notice was not sent to the claimant or the claimant's attorney, no later than 30 days after final publication of newspaper notice or legal notice under Rule G(4)(a) or no later than 60 days after the first day of publication on an official internet government forfeiture site; or

(C) if notice was not published and direct notice was not sent to the claimant or the claimant's attorney;

(1) if the property was in the government's possession, custody, or control when the complaint was filed, no later than 60 days after the filing, not counting any time when the complaint was under seal or when the action was stayed before execution of a warrant issued under Rule G(3)(b); or

(2) if the property was not in the government's possession, custody, or control when the complaint was filed, no later than 60 days after the government complied with 18 U.S.C. § 985(c) as to real property, or 60 days after process was executed on the property under Rule G(3).

(iii) A claim filed by a person asserting an interest as a bailee must identify the bailor, and if filed on the bailor's behalf must state the authority to do so.

(b) Answer. A claimant must serve and file an answer to the complaint or a motion under Rule 12 within 21 days after filing the claim. A claimant waives an objection to in rem jurisdiction or to venue if the objection is not made by motion or stated in the answer.

(6) *Special Interrogatories.* — (a) Time and Scope. The government may serve special interrogatories limited to the claimant's identity and relationship to the defendant property without the court's leave at any time after the claim is filed and before discovery is closed. But if the claimant serves a motion to dismiss the action, the government must serve the interrogatories within 21 days after the motion is served.

(b) Answers or Objections. Answers or objections to these interrogatories must be served within 21 days after the interrogatories are served.

(c) Government's Response Deferred. The government need not respond to a claimant's motion to dismiss the action under Rule G(8)(b) until 21 days after the claimant has answered these interrogatories.

(7) *Preserving, Preventing Criminal Use, and Disposing of Property; Sales.* — (a) Preserving and Preventing Criminal Use of Property. When the government does not have actual possession of the defendant property the court, on motion or on its own, may enter any order necessary to preserve the property, to prevent its removal or encumbrance, or to prevent its use in a criminal offense.

(b) Interlocutory Sale or Delivery. (i) Order to Sell. On motion by a party or a person having custody of the property, the court may order all or part of the property sold if:

(A) the property is perishable or at risk of deterioration, decay, or injury by being detained in custody pending the action;

(B) the expense of keeping the property is excessive or is disproportionate to its fair market value;

(C) the property is subject to a mortgage or to taxes on which the owner is in default; or

(D) the court finds other good cause.

(ii) Who Makes the Sale. A sale must be made by a United States agency that has authority to sell the property, by the agency's contractor, or by any person the court designates.

(iii) Sale Procedures. The sale is governed by 28 U.S.C. §§ 2001, 2002, and 2004, unless all parties, with the court's approval, agree to the sale, aspects of the sale, or different procedures.

(iv) Sale Proceeds. Sale proceeds are a substitute res subject to forfeiture in place of the property that was sold. The proceeds must be held in an interest-bearing account maintained by the United States pending the conclusion of the forfeiture action.

(v) Delivery on a Claimant's Motion. The court may order that the property be delivered to the claimant pending the conclusion of the action if the claimant shows circumstances that would permit sale under Rule G(7)(b)(i) and gives security under these rules.

(c) Disposing of Forfeited Property. Upon entry of a forfeiture judgment, the property or proceeds from selling the property must be disposed of as provided by law.

(8) *Motions.* — (a) Motion To Suppress Use of the Property as Evidence. If the defendant property was seized, a party with standing to contest the lawfulness of the seizure may move to suppress use of the property as evidence. Suppression does not affect forfeiture of the property based on independently derived evidence.

(b) Motion To Dismiss the Action. (i) A claimant who establishes standing to contest forfeiture may move to dismiss the action under Rule 12(b).

(ii) In an action governed by 18 U.S.C. § 983(a)(3)(D) the complaint may not be dismissed on the ground that the government did not have adequate evidence at the time the complaint was filed to establish the forfeitability of the property. The sufficiency of the complaint is governed by Rule G(2).

(c) Motion To Strike a Claim or Answer. (i) At any time before trial, the government may move to strike a claim or answer:

(A) for failing to comply with Rule G(5) or (6), or

(B) because the claimant lacks standing.

(ii) The motion:

(A) must be decided before any motion by the claimant to dismiss the action; and

(B) may be presented as a motion for judgment on the pleadings or as a motion to determine after a hearing or by summary judgment whether the claimant can carry the burden of establishing standing by a preponderance of the evidence.

(d) Petition To Release Property. (i) If a United States agency or an agency's contractor holds property for judicial or nonjudicial forfeiture under a statute governed by 18 U.S.C. § 983(f), a person who has filed a claim to the property may petition for its release under § 983(f).

(ii) If a petition for release is filed before a judicial forfeiture action is filed against the property, the petition may be filed either in the district where the property was seized or in the district where a warrant to seize the property issued. If a judicial forfeiture action against the property is later filed in another district — or if the government shows that the action will be filed in another district — the petition may be transferred to that district under 28 U.S.C. § 1404.

(e) Excessive Fines. A claimant may seek to mitigate a forfeiture under the Excessive Fines Clause of the Eighth Amendment by motion for summary judgment or by motion made after entry of a forfeiture judgment if:

(i) the claimant has pleaded the defense under Rule 8; and

(ii) the parties have had the opportunity to conduct civil discovery on the defense.

(9) *Trial.* — Trial is to the court unless any party demands trial by jury under Rule 38. (Added by order adopted April 12, 2006, effective December 1, 2006, and by order adopted March 26, 2009, effective December 1, 2009.)

Index to Federal Rules of Civil Procedure

A

ADDRESS.
Date, signature, address, email address and telephone number, FRCP Form 2.

ADMIRALTY OR MARITIME AND ASSET FORFEITURE CLAIMS.
Attachment and garnishment, FRCP Admir Rule B.
Forfeiture actions in rem, FRCP Admir Rule G.
In personam actions.
Attachment and garnishment, FRCP Admir Rule B.
In rem actions.
Forfeiture actions in rem, FRCP Admir Rule G.
General provisions, FRCP Admir Rule E.
Special provisions, FRCP Admir Rule C.
Jury trial, right to, FRCP 38(e).
Liability.
Limitation of liability, FRCP Admir Rule F.
Pleading special matters, FRCP 9(h).
Possessory, petitory and partition actions, FRCP Admir Rule D.
Prize proceedings in admiralty.
Applicability of rules, FRCP 81.
Quasi in rem actions.
General provisions, FRCP Admir Rule E.
Scope of rules, FRCP Admir Rule A.
Third-party practice, FRCP 14(c).

ADMISSIONS.
Failure to admit, FRCP 37(c).
Requests for, FRCP 36, FRCP Form 51.
Amendments, FRCP 36(b).
Answer, FRCP 36(a).
Effect of admission, FRCP 36(b).
Failure to admit, FRCP 37(c).
Objections, FRCP 36(a).
Procedure, FRCP 36(a).
Scope of request, FRCP 36(a).
Sufficiency of answer, motions regarding, FRCP 36(a).
Withdrawing, FRCP 36(b).

ADOPTION BY REFERENCE.
Pleadings, FRCP 10(c).

AFFIDAVITS.
Evidence on a motion, FRCP 43(c).
New trial.
Time to serve, FRCP 59(c).
Summary judgment, FRCP 56(c).
Bad faith, submitted in, FRCP 56(h).
Facts unavailable to nonmovant, FRCP 56(d).
Time for service, FRCP 6(c).

AFFIRMATION INSTEAD OF OATH.
Taking testimony, FRCP 43(b).

AFFIRMATIVE DEFENSES.
Pleading, FRCP 8(c).

ALLEGATION OF TIME OR PLACE.
Pleading special matters, FRCP 9(f).

ALTERNATIVE ALLEGATIONS, CLAIM OR DEFENSE, FRCP 8(d).

AMENDMENTS.
Admissions, requests for, FRCP 36(b).
Clerical mistakes, corrections.
Relief from judgment, FRCP 60(a).
Condemnation of property.
Amendment of pleadings, FRCP 71.1(f).
Depositions.
Officer to note in certificate, FRCP 30(e).
Discovery.
Failure to disclose or amend an earlier response, FRCP 37(c).
Judgment, FRCP 59.
Motion to alter or amend judgment, FRCP 59(e).
Pleadings generally, FRCP 15.
Subpoenas, FRCP 45(d).
Summons, FRCP 4(a).
Trials, findings by court.
Amended or additional findings, FRCP 52(b).

ANSWERS.
Admissions, requests for, FRCP 36(a).
Complaint for money had and received with a counterclaim for interpleader, FRCP Form 31.
Condemnation of property, FRCP 71.1(e).
Interrogatories, FRCP 33(b).
Pleadings allowed, FRCP 7(a).
Presenting defense under FRCP 12(b), FRCP Form 30.

APPEALS.
Judgment as a matter of law.
Reversal on appeal, FRCP 50(e).
Magistrate judges, FRCP 73(c).
Relief barred by pending appeal.
Motion for relief, indicative ruling on, FRCP 62.1.
Stays.
Appellate court's powers not limited, FRCP 62(g).
Bond on appeal, FRCP 62(d).
United States, its officers or agencies, FRCP 62(e).
Injunctions pending an appeal, FRCP 62(c).

APPEARANCE.
Condemnation of property, FRCP 71.1(e).

APPLICABILITY OF RULES, FRCP 81.

ARREST.
Remedies available, FRCP 64(b).

ASSET FORFEITURE CLAIMS.
See ADMIRALTY OR MARITIME AND ASSET FORFEITURE CLAIMS.

ASSOCIATIONS AND CLUBS.
Parties.
Actions relating to unincorporated associations, FRCP 23.2.
Service of process and papers.
Summons, FRCP 4(h).

ATTACHMENT.
Enforcing judgment for a specific act.
Writ of attachment or sequestration, obtaining, FRCP 70(c).
Remedies available, FRCP 64(b).

ATTORNEYS AT LAW.
Class actions or proceedings.
Attorneys' fees and nontaxable costs, FRCP 23(h).
Class counsel, FRCP 23(g).
Fees.
Judgment, FRCP 54(d).
Entry of judgment, FRCP 58(e).

AUDITA QUERELA.
Writs abolished, FRCP 60(e).

B

BANKRUPTCY.
Applicability of rules, FRCP 81(a).

BILLS OF REVIEW.
Writs abolished, FRCP 60(e).

BONDS, SURETY.
Injunctions.
Security, FRCP 65(c).
Proceedings against surety, FRCP 65.1.

BRIEFS.
District courts.
Motions, submission and determining without oral hearing, FRCP 78(b).

BUSINESS RECORDS.
Interrogatories.
Option to produce, FRCP 33(d).

C

CAPACITY TO SUE.
Parties, determination of capacity, FRCP 17(b).
Pleading special matters, FRCP 9(a).

CAPTIONS, FRCP Form 1.
Condemnation of property.
Complaints, FRCP 71.1(c).

CHILDREN AND MINORS.
Parties, FRCP 17(c).
Service of process and papers.
Summons, FRCP 4(g).

CITATION OF RULES, FRCP 85.

CITIZENSHIP.
Applicability of rules, FRCP 81(a).

CLASS ACTIONS.
Appeals, FRCP 23(f).
Attorneys at law.
Attorneys' fees and nontaxable costs, FRCP 23(h).
Class counsel, FRCP 23(g).
Certification order, FRCP 23(c).
Class counsel, FRCP 23(g).
Compromise, FRCP 23(e).
Conduct of class actions, FRCP 23(d).
Dismissal.
Voluntary dismissal, FRCP 23(e).

CLASS ACTIONS —Cont'd
Joinder of parties.
Exception, FRCP 19(d).
Judgment, FRCP 23(c).
Notice to class members, FRCP 23(c).
Particular issues, FRCP 23(c).
Prerequisites, FRCP 23(a).
Settlement, FRCP 23(e).
Subclasses, FRCP 23(c).
Types of class actions, FRCP 23(b).
Voluntary dismissal, FRCP 23(e).

CLERICAL MISTAKES, CORRECTION OF.
Relief from judgment, FRCP 60(a).

CLERKS OF COURTS.
Office hours, FRCP 77(c).
Orders, FRCP 77(c).

COMMENCEMENT OF ACTION, FRCP 3.

COMMISSION, APPOINTMENT BY COURT.
Condemnation of property, FRCP 71.1(h).

COMPLAINTS.
Commencement of action, FRCP 3.
Condemnation of property, FRCP 71.1(c), FRCP Form 61.
Merchant marine act, damages under, FRCP Form 14.
Negligence, FRCP Form 11.
Federal employer's liability act, FRCP Form 13.
Plaintiff does not know who is responsible, FRCP Form 12.
Pleadings allowed, FRCP 7(a).
Recovery of a sum certain, FRCP Form 10.
Specific performance of a contract to convey land, FRCP Form 17.
Third-party complaint, FRCP Forms 4, 16.

COMPROMISE.
Class actions, FRCP 23(e).
Derivative actions, FRCP 23.1(c).
Offers of judgment, FRCP 68.

CONCISENESS, PLEADING, FRCP 8(d).

CONDEMNATION OF PROPERTY, FRCP 71.1.
Amendment of pleadings, FRCP 71.1(f).
Answers, FRCP 71.1(e).
Appearance, FRCP 71.1(e).
Applicability of other rules, FRCP 71.1(a).
Commission, appointing, FRCP 71.1(h).
Complaint, FRCP 71.1(c), FRCP Form 61.
Costs, FRCP 71.1(l).
Deposits into court.
Deposit and distribution, FRCP 71.1(j).
Dismissal, FRCP 71.1(i).
Joinder of properties, FRCP 71.1(b).
Notice, FRCP Form 60.
Appearance, FRCP 71.1(e).
Parties.
Complaints, FRCP 71.1(c).
Substitution of parties, FRCP 71.1(g).
Service of process and papers, FRCP 71.1(d).
State's power of eminent domain, FRCP 71.1(k).
Trial of the issues, FRCP 71.1(h).

CONDITIONS PRECEDENT.
Pleading special matters, FRCP 9(c).

CONFLICT OF LAWS.
Applicability of rules, FRCP 81(d).
Foreign law, determining, FRCP 44.1.

CONSENT.
Magistrate judges.
Consent to an assignment to a magistrate judge, FRCP Form 81.
Trial by consent, FRCP 73(a).

CONSOLIDATION OF TRIALS, FRCP 42(a).

CONSTITUTIONAL CHALLENGES.
Notice of filings.
Constitutional challenge to statute, FRCP 5.1.

CONSTRUCTION AND INTERPRETATION OF RULES, FRCP 1.

CONSTRUCTION OF PLEADINGS, FRCP 8(e).

CONTEMPT.
Enforcing judgment for a specific act.
Holding disobedient party in contempt, FRCP 70(e).
Service of process and papers.
Civil contempt, enforcement, FRCP 4.1.
Subpoenas.
Enforcement of subpoenas, FRCP 45(g).

CONVERSION OF PROPERTY.
Complaint for the conversion of property, FRCP Form 15.

COPYRIGHT AND LITERARY PROPERTY.
Complaint for copyright infringement and unfair competition, FRCP Form 19.
Impoundment.
Generally, FRCP 65(f).

CORAM NOBIS.
Writs abolished, FRCP 60(e).

CORAM VOBIS.
Writs abolished, FRCP 60(e).

CORPORATIONS.
Disclosure statements, FRCP 7.1.
Service of notice or process.
Summons, FRCP 4(h).

COSTS.
Condemnation of property, FRCP 71.1(l).
Discovery.
Motion for order compelling disclosure, FRCP 37(a).
Dismissal, FRCP 41(d).
Judgment, FRCP 54(d).
Entry of judgment, FRCP 58(e).
Unaccepted offers of judgment.
Payment of costs, FRCP 68(d).

COUNTERCLAIMS, FRCP 13.
Complaint for money had and received with a counterclaim for interpleader, FRCP Form 31.
Compulsory counterclaims, FRCP 13(a).
Dismissal, FRCP 41(c).
Joining additional parties, FRCP 13(h).
Maturing or acquired after pleading, FRCP 13(e).
Permissive counterclaims, FRCP 13(b).
Pleadings allowed, FRCP 7(a).
Relief sought, differing in amount or kind, FRCP 13(c).
Separate trials or separate judgments, FRCP 13(i).
United States, counterclaim against, FRCP 13(d).

CROSSCLAIMS, FRCP 13.
Coparties, crossclaim against, FRCP 13(g).
Dismissal, FRCP 41(c).
Joining additional parties, FRCP 13(h).
Pleadings allowed, FRCP 7(a).
Separate trials or separate judgments, FRCP 13(i).

CROSS-EXAMINATION.
Depositions, FRCP 30(c).

D

DAMAGES.
Merchant marine act, complaint for damages, FRCP Form 14.
Special damages.
Pleading special matters, FRCP 9(g).

DATE.
Date, signature, address, email address and telephone number, FRCP Form 2.

DEATH.
Statement noting a party's death, FRCP Form 9.
Substitution of parties, FRCP 25(a).
Public officers, death or separation from office, FRCP 25(d).

DECLARATORY JUDGMENT, FRCP 57.

DEFAULT JUDGMENT, FRCP 55.
Entering default, FRCP 55(a).
Entering default judgment, FRCP 55(b).
Setting aside, FRCP 55(c).
United States, judgment against, FRCP 55(d).

DEFENSES, FRCP 12.
Affirmative defenses, FRCP 8(c).
Failure to state a claim upon which relief can be granted.
Assertion of defenses by motion, FRCP 12(b).
Summary judgment, treated as, FRCP 12(d).
Insufficient process.
Assertion of defenses by motion, FRCP 12(b).
Joinder of parties, failure to join.
Assertion of defenses by motion, FRCP 12(b).
Judgment on the pleadings, FRCP 12(c).
Summary judgment, treated as, FRCP 12(d).
Jurisdiction.
Lack of personal jurisdiction.
Assertion of defenses by motion, FRCP 12(b).
Lack of subject matter jurisdiction.
Assertion of defenses by motion, FRCP 12(b).
Motions.
Assertion of defenses by motion, FRCP 12(b).
Judgment on the pleadings, FRCP 12(c).
Summary judgment, treated as, FRCP 12(d).
Pleadings, FRCP 8(b).
Preserving certain defenses, FRCP 12(h).
Pre-trial hearings, FRCP 12(i).
Service of process, insufficient.
Assertion of defenses by motion, FRCP 12(b).
Subject matter jurisdiction, lack of.
Assertion of defenses by motion, FRCP 12(b).
Time to serve a responsive pleading, FRCP 12(a).
Venue, improper.
Assertion of defenses by motion, FRCP 12(b).
Waiving certain defenses, FRCP 12(h).

DEPOSITIONS, FRCP 27.
Actions to perpetuate testimony, FRCP 27(c).
Amendments.
Officer to note in certificate, FRCP 30(e).
Before action, FRCP 27(a).
Certification, FRCP 30(f).
Court proceedings, use in, FRCP 32.
Form of presentation, FRCP 32(c).
Impeachment, FRCP 32(a).
Objections to admissibility, FRCP 32(b).
Waiver of objections, FRCP 32(d).
Unavailable witness, FRCP 32(a).
When used, FRCP 32(a).
Cross-examination of deponent, FRCP 30(c).
Duration, FRCP 30(d).
Failure to attend, FRCP 30(g), 37(d).
Impeachment.
Court proceedings, use in, FRCP 32(a).
Motions.
Terminate or limit examination, FRCP 30(d).
Notice, FRCP 30(b).
Objections, FRCP 30(c).
Court proceedings, use in, FRCP 32(b).
Oral examination, FRCP 30.
Cross-examination, FRCP 30(c).
Notice, FRCP 30(b).
Production of documents and things, FRCP 30(b).
When taken, FRCP 30(a).
Pending appeal, FRCP 27(b).
Production of documents, FRCP 30(b).
Record of the examination, FRCP 30(c).
Certification and delivery, FRCP 30(f).
Review of record by witness, FRCP 30(e).
Sanctions.
Impeding, delaying or frustrating the fair examination of deponent, FRCP 30(d).
Subpoenas.
Failure to serve, FRCP 30(g).
Taking depositions, authority, FRCP 28.
Disqualification, FRCP 28(c).
Foreign countries, FRCP 28(b).
Within United States, FRCP 28(a).
Transcripts, FRCP 30(c).
Certification and delivery, FRCP 30(f).
Court proceedings, use in.
Form of presentation, FRCP 32(c).
Written questions, FRCP 30(c), 31.
Delivery to officer, FRCP 31(b).
Notice, FRCP 31(a).
Filing, FRCP 31(c).
Organizations, questions directed to, FRCP 31(a).
Service, FRCP 31(a).
When taken, FRCP 31(a).

DEPOSITS INTO COURT, FRCP 67.
Condemnation of property.
Deposit and distribution, FRCP 71.1(j).
Investing and withdrawing funds, FRCP 67(b).
Property, FRCP 67(a).

DERIVATIVE ACTIONS.
Dismissal, FRCP 23.1(c).
Parties, FRCP 23.1.
Pleading requirements, FRCP 23.1(b).
Prerequisites, FRCP 23.1(a).
Settlement, dismissal and compromise, FRCP 23.1(c).

DISCHARGE OF JUDGMENT.
Relief from judgment, grounds, FRCP 60(b).

DISCLOSURE STATEMENTS, FRCP 7.1.
Time for filing, FRCP 7.1(b).
Whom must file, FRCP 7.1(a).

DISCOVERY, FRCP 26 to 37.
Admissions, requests for, FRCP 36.
Failure to admit, FRCP 37(c).
Amendments.
Failure to disclose or amend an earlier response, FRCP 37(c).
Conference of parties, FRCP 26(f).
Court order, failure to comply, FRCP 37(b).
Depositions, FRCP 27.
Court proceedings, use in, FRCP 32.
Failure to attend, FRCP 37(d).
Oral examination, FRCP 30.
Taking depositions, authority, FRCP 28.
Written questions, FRCP 31.
Duty to disclose, FRCP 26.
Earlier response, failure to disclose or amend, FRCP 37(c).
Electronically stored information, failure to provide, FRCP 37(e).
Entering onto land, FRCP 34.
Evasive answers, FRCP 37(a).
Execution of judgments.
Obtaining discovery, FRCP 69(a).
Expenses, payment of.
Motion for order compelling disclosure, FRCP 37(a).
Expert witnesses, FRCP 26(b).
Required disclosures, FRCP 26(a).
Supplementing disclosures and responses, FRCP 26(e).
Failure to make disclosures or cooperate in discovery, FRCP 37.
Incomplete disclosures, FRCP 37(a).
Initial disclosures, FRCP 26(a).
Inspections.
Failure to respond to request for inspection, FRCP 37(d).
Interrogatories, FRCP 33.
Failure to serve answers, FRCP 37(d).
Limits, FRCP 26(b).
Motion for order compelling disclosure.
Failure to make disclosures or cooperate in discovery, FRCP 37(a).
Orders.
Failure to comply with a court order, FRCP 37(b).
Physical and mental examinations, FRCP 35.
Plan for discovery.
Conference of parties, FRCP 26(f).
Failure to participate in framing plan, FRCP 37(f).
Report of the parties' planning meeting, FRCP Form 52.
Pretrial disclosures, FRCP 26(a).
Privileged communications.
Claiming privilege or protecting trial preparation materials, FRCP 26(b).
Production of documents and things, FRCP 34.
Depositions, FRCP 30(b).
Protective orders.
Effect, FRCP 26(c).
Motion for order compelling disclosure, FRCP 37(a).
Report of the parties' planning meeting, FRCP Form 52.

DISCOVERY —Cont'd
Requests for admissions, FRCP 36.
Required disclosures, FRCP 26(a).
Sanctions for failure to comply generally, FRCP 37.
Scope of discovery, FRCP 26(b).
Sequence, FRCP 26(d).
Signatures.
Representations, inapplicability, FRCP 11(d).
Required, effect, FRCP 26(g).
Stipulations, FRCP 29.
Supplementing disclosures and responses, FRCP 26(e).
Timing, FRCP 26(d).

DISMISSAL, FRCP 41.
Class actions.
Voluntary dismissal, FRCP 23(e).
Condemnation of property, FRCP 71.1(i).
Costs, FRCP 41(d).
Counterclaims, FRCP 41(c).
Crossclaims, FRCP 41(c).
Derivative actions, FRCP 23.1(c).
Involuntary dismissal, FRCP 41(b).
Motion to dismiss under FRCP 12(b) for lack of jurisdiction, improper venue, insufficient service of process, or failure to state a claim, FRCP Form 40.
Third party claims, FRCP 41(c).
Voluntary dismissal, FRCP 41(a).

DISTRICT COURTS, FRCP 77 to 80.
Calendars.
Records kept by clerk, FRCP 79(c).
Civil docket.
Records kept by clerk, FRCP 79(a).
Civil judgments and orders.
Records kept by clerk, FRCP 79(b).
Clerk's office hours, FRCP 77(c).
Clerk's orders, FRCP 77(c).
Conducting business, FRCP 77.
Hours when court open, FRCP 77(a).
Indexes.
Records kept by clerk, FRCP 79(c).
Judgment.
Civil judgments and orders.
Records kept by clerk, FRCP 79(b).
Local rules, FRCP 83(a).
Motions, FRCP 78.
Briefs, submission and determining without oral hearing, FRCP 78(b).
Regular schedule for oral hearings, FRCP 78(a).
Open court, required, FRCP 77(b).
Orders.
Civil judgments and orders.
Records kept by clerk, FRCP 79(b).
Place for trial, FRCP 77(b).
Procedure when there is no controlling law, FRCP 83(b).
Records kept by clerk, FRCP 79.
Rules by district courts, FRCP 83.
Serving notice of an order or judgment, FRCP 77(d).
Transcripts as evidence, FRCP 80.

DISTRICT OF COLUMBIA.
Applicability of rules, FRCP 81(d).

E

EFFECTIVE DATES, FRCP 86.

ELECTRONICALLY STORED INFORMATOIN.
Discovery sanctions for failure to provide, FRCP 37(e).
Privacy protection for filings with court, FRCP 5.2.

EMAIL.
Date, signature, address, email address and telephone number, FRCP Form 2.

EMINENT DOMAIN.
Condemnation of property generally.
See CONDEMNATION OF PROPERTY.

ENTRY UPON LAND FOR INSPECTION AND OTHER PURPOSES, FRCP 34.
Request to produce documents and tangible things, or to enter onto land, FRCP Form 50.

EQUITY.
Relief from judgment, grounds, FRCP 60(b).

ERROR.
Judgment.
Harmless error, FRCP 61.
Jury instructions.
Assigning error, FRCP 51(d).
Plain error, FRCP 51(d).

EVIDENCE.
Discovery generally.
See DISCOVERY.
District courts.
Transcripts as evidence, FRCP 80.
Newly discovered evidence.
Relief from judgment, grounds, FRCP 60(b).

EXCUSABLE NEGLECT.
Relief from judgment, grounds, FRCP 60(b).

EXECUTION OF JUDGMENTS, FRCP 69.
Discovery, obtaining, FRCP 69(a).
Enforcing judgment for a specific act.
Writ of execution or assistance, obtaining, FRCP 70(d).
Money judgments, FRCP 69(a).
Public officers and employees.
Execution against certain public officers, FRCP 69(b).

EXISTENCE.
Legal existence.
Pleading special matters, FRCP 9(a).

EXPERT WITNESSES.
Discovery, FRCP 26(b).
Required disclosures, FRCP 26(a).
Supplementing disclosures and responses, FRCP 26(e).

F

FAILURE TO MAKE DISCLOSURES OR COOPERATE IN DISCOVERY, FRCP 37.

FAILURE TO STATE A CLAIM UPON WHICH RELIEF CAN BE GRANTED.
Assertion of defenses by motion, FRCP 12(b).
Motion to dismiss under FRCP 12(b) for lack of jurisdiction, improper venue, insufficient service of process, or failure to state a claim, FRCP Form 40.
Summary judgment, treated as, FRCP 12(d).

FEDERAL EMPLOYERS' LIABILITY ACT.
Complaint for negligence under federal employer's liability act, FRCP Form 13.

FILING.
Complaints.
Commencement of action, FRCP 3.
Condemnation of property.
Complaints, FRCP 71.1(c).
Privacy protection for filings with court, FRCP 5.2.
Service of process and papers.
Pleadings and other papers, FRCP 5(d).

FOREIGN COUNTRY.
Depositions, authority to take, FRCP 28(b).
Foreign law, determining, FRCP 44.1.
Service of process and papers.
Foreign governments, summons, FRCP 4(j).
Individuals in foreign countries, summons, FRCP 4(f).

FORFEITURES.
Asset forfeiture claims.
See ADMIRALTY OR MARITIME AND ASSET FORFEIRTURE CLAIMS.

FORM OF ACTION, FRCP 2.

FORMS.
Adoption, FRCP 84.
Answers.
Complaint for money had and received with a counterclaim for interpleader, FRCP Form 31.
Presenting defense under FRCP 12(b), FRCP Form 30.
Caption, FRCP Form 1.
Claim for a debt and to set aside a fraudulent conveyance under FRCP 18(b).
Complaint, FRCP Form 21.
Condemnation.
Complaint, FRCP Form 61.
Consent to an assignment to a magistrate judge, FRCP Form 81.
Conversion of property.
Complaint, FRCP Form 15.
Copyright infringement and unfair competition.
Complaint, FRCP Form 19.
Date, signature, address, email address and telephone number, FRCP Form 2.
Death of party, statement noting, FRCP Form 9.
Dismissal motion under FRCP 12(b) for lack of jurisdiction, improper venue, insufficient service of process, or failure to state a claim, FRCP Form 40.
Interpleader and declaratory relief, FRCP Form 20.
Complaint for money had and received with a counterclaim for interpleader, FRCP Form 31.
Intervention as a defendant under Rule 24, motion, FRCP Form 42.
Judgment by the court without a jury, FRCP Form 71.
Judgment on a jury verdict, FRCP Form 70.
Jurisdiction statement, FRCP Form 7.
Merchant marine act, damages under.
Complaint, FRCP Form 14.

FORMS —Cont'd
Negligence complaint, FRCP Form 11.
Federal employer's liability act, FRCP Form 13.
Plaintiff does not know who is responsible, FRCP Form 12.
Notice.
Condemnation, FRCP Form 60.
Magistrate judge's availability, FRCP Form 80.
Notice of lawsuit and request to waive service of summons, FRCP Form 5.
Omission of party, statement of reasons, FRCP Form 8.
Order of assignment to a magistrate judge, FRCP Form 82.
Patent infringement.
Complaint, FRCP Form 18.
Recover a sum certain.
Complaint, FRCP Form 10.
Report of the parties' planning meeting, FRCP Form 52.
Request for admissions, FRCP Form 51.
Request to produce documents and tangible things, or to enter onto land, FRCP Form 50.
Service of summons, waiver, FRCP Form 6.
Specific performance of a contract to convey land.
Complaint, FRCP Form 17.
Summons, FRCP Form 3.
Third-party complaint, FRCP Form 4.
Third-party complaint, FRCP Form 16.
Summons, FRCP Form 4.
Third-party defendant, motion to bring in, FRCP Form 41.

FRAUD.
Pleading special matters, FRCP 9(b).
Relief from judgment, grounds, FRCP 60(b).

FRAUDULENT CONVEYANCES.
Complaint on a claim for a debt and to set aside a fraudulent conveyance under FRCP 18(b), FRCP Form 21.

G

GARNISHMENT.
Remedies available, FRCP 64(b).

H

HABEAS CORPUS.
Applicability of rules, FRCP 81(a).

HARMLESS ERROR.
Judgment, FRCP 61.

I

IMPEACHMENT.
Depositions.
Court proceedings, use in, FRCP 32(a).

IMPLEADER.
Third party practice generally, FRCP 14.

INADVERTENCE.
Relief from judgment, grounds, FRCP 60(b).

INCOMPETENT PERSONS, PARTIES, FRCP 17(c).
Substitution of parties, party becoming incompetent, FRCP 25(b).

INCONSISTENT PLEADINGS, FRCP 8(d).

INJUNCTIONS, FRCP 65.
Contents, FRCP 65(d).
Copyright impoundment, FRCP 65(f).
Other laws not affected, FRCP 65(e).
Preliminary injunctions, FRCP 65(a).
Scope, FRCP 65(d).
Security, FRCP 65(c).
Stays.
Exception, FRCP 62(a).
Injunctions pending an appeal, FRCP 62(c).
Temporary restraining orders, FRCP 65(b).
Trials.
Interlocutory injunctions.
Findings and conclusions by court, FRCP 52(a).

INSPECTIONS.
Failure to respond to request for inspection, FRCP 37(d).
Subpoenas.
Command to permit, FRCP 45(d).

INSTRUCTIONS TO JURY, FRCP 51.
Assigning error, FRCP 51(d).
Generally, FRCP 51(b).
Objections, FRCP 51(c).
Plain error, FRCP 51(d).
Requests, FRCP 51(a).

INSUFFICIENT PROCESS.
Assertion of defenses by motion, FRCP 12(b).

INTENT.
Pleading special matters, FRCP 9(b).

INTENTIONAL, WILLFUL, OR WANTON ACTS.
Pleading special matters, FRCP 9(b).

INTERLOCUTORY ORDERS.
Stays, exception, FRCP 62(a).

INTERPLEADER, FRCP 22.
Complaint for interpleader and declaratory relief, FRCP Form 20.
Complaint for money had and received with a counterclaim for interpleader, FRCP Form 31.
Grounds, FRCP 22(a).
Relation to other rules and statutes, FRCP 22(b).

INTERPRETERS.
Taking testimony, FRCP 43(d).

INTERROGATORIES, FRCP 33.
Answers, FRCP 33(b).
Business records, option to produce, FRCP 33(d).
Failure to serve answers, FRCP 37(d).
Number, FRCP 33(a).
Objections, FRCP 33(b).
Scope, FRCP 33(a).
Use, FRCP 33(c).

INTERVENTION, FRCP 24.
Intervention of right, FRCP 24(a).
Motion to intervene as a defendant under Rule 24, FRCP Form 42.

INTERVENTION —Cont'd
Permissive intervention, FRCP 24(b).
Procedure, FRCP 24(c).

J

JOINDER OF CLAIMS, FRCP 18.
Contingent claims, FRCP 18(b).
Right to joinder, FRCP 18(a).

JOINDER OF PARTIES.
Class actions.
Exception, FRCP 19(d).
Counterclaims or crossclaims.
Joinder of additional parties, FRCP 13(h).
Failure to join.
Assertion of defenses by motion, FRCP 12(b).
Joinder not feasible, FRCP 19(b).
Misjoinder, FRCP 21.
Nonjoinder, FRCP 21.
Pleading reasons for, FRCP 19(c).
Permissive joinder, FRCP 20.
Persons required to be joined if feasible, FRCP 19(a).
Persons who may join or be joined, FRCP 20(a).
Protective measures, permissive joinder, FRCP 20(b).

JOINDER OF PROPERTIES.
Condemnation of property, FRCP 71.1(b).

JOINT OR SEPARATE ACTION OR TRIAL.
Counterclaims or crossclaims, FRCP 13(i).

JUDGES.
Successor judges.
Judge unable to proceed, FRCP 63.

JUDGMENT, FRCP 54 to 63.
Amendment of judgment, FRCP 59.
Attorneys' fees, FRCP 54(d).
Costs, FRCP 54(d).
Court without a jury, judgment by, FRCP Form 71.
Declaratory judgment, FRCP 57.
Default judgment, FRCP 55.
Entering default, FRCP 55(a).
Entering default judgment, FRCP 55(b).
Setting aside, FRCP 55(c).
United States, judgment against, FRCP 55(d).
Defined, FRCP 54(a).
Demand for judgment, FRCP 54(c).
Discharge.
Relief from judgment, grounds, FRCP 60(b).
District courts.
Civil judgments and orders.
Records kept by clerk, FRCP 79(b).
Serving notice of an order or judgment, FRCP 77(d).
Enforcing judgment for a specific act, FRCP 70.
Contempt, holding party in, FRCP 70(e).
Failure to act, FRCP 70(a).
Vesting title, FRCP 70(b).
Writ of attachment or sequestration, obtaining, FRCP 70(c).
Writ of execution or assistance, obtaining, FRCP 70(d).
Entry of judgment, FRCP 58.
Cost or fee awards, FRCP 58(e).

JUDGMENT —Cont'd
Entry of judgment —Cont'd
Court's approval required, FRCP 58(b).
Request for entry, FRCP 58(d).
Separate document, FRCP 58(a).
Time of entry, FRCP 58(c).
Without court's direction, FRCP 58(b).
Error.
Harmless error, FRCP 61.
Execution of judgments, FRCP 69.
Failure to act, FRCP 70(a).
Generally, FRCP 54.
Harmless error, FRCP 61.
Judge's inability to proceed, FRCP 63.
Jury verdict, FRCP Form 70.
Motions.
Alter or amend judgment, FRCP 59(e).
Multiple claims or parties, FRCP 54(b).
New trial, FRCP 59.
Nonparties.
Enforcing judgment against a nonparty, FRCP 71.
Offer of judgment, FRCP 68.
Partial findings, judgment on, FRCP 52(c).
Pleading special matters, FRCP 9(e).
Release.
Relief from judgment, grounds, FRCP 60(b).
Relief from judgment, FRCP 60.
Clerical mistakes, corrections, FRCP 60(a).
Grounds, FRCP 60(b).
Motion, timing and effect, FRCP 60(c).
Powers to grant relief, generally, FRCP 60(d).
Writs abolished, FRCP 60(e).
Reversal of earlier judgment.
Relief from judgment, grounds, FRCP 60(b).
Satisfaction.
Relief from judgment, grounds, FRCP 60(b).
Stay of proceedings to enforce, FRCP 62.
Summary judgment, FRCP 56.
Affidavits, FRCP 56(c).
Bad faith, submitted in, FRCP 56(h).
Facts unavailable to nonmovant, FRCP 56(d).
Factual positions, supporting assertions, FRCP 56(c).
Failure to grant all requested relief, FRCP 56(g).
Failure to properly support or address a fact, FRCP 56(e).
Judgment independent of motion, FRCP 56(f).
Motion for, FRCP 56(a).
Objections, FRCP 56(c).
Procedure, FRCP 56(c).
Time to file, FRCP 56(b).
Vacation of earlier judgment.
Relief from judgment, grounds, FRCP 60(b).
Vesting title, FRCP 70(b).
Void judgment.
Relief from judgment, grounds, FRCP 60(b).

JUDGMENT AS A MATTER OF LAW, FRCP 50.
Denial of motion, FRCP 50(e).
Motion before case submitted to jury, FRCP 50(a).
Motion for a new trial, alternative motion, FRCP 50(b).
Conditional ruling, FRCP 50(c).
Time for filing, FRCP 50(d).
Renewing motion after trial, FRCP 50(b).
Granting renewed motion, FRCP 50(c).

JUDGMENT AS A MATTER OF LAW —Cont'd
Reversal on appeal, FRCP 50(e).

JURISDICTION.
Motion to dismiss under FRCP 12(b) for lack of jurisdiction, improper venue, insufficient service of process, or failure to state a claim, FRCP Form 40.
Not affected, FRCP 82.
Personal jurisdiction, lack of.
Assertion of defenses by motion, FRCP 12(b).
Statement of jurisdiction, FRCP Form 7.
Subject matter jurisdiction, lack of.
Assertion of defenses by motion, FRCP 12(b).
Summons.
Asserting jurisdiction over property or assets, FRCP 4(n).

JURY TRIAL.
Admiralty and maritime claims, FRCP 38(e).
Advisory jury, FRCP 39(c).
Answers inconsistent with verdict, FRCP 49(b).
Consent, jury trial by, FRCP 39(c).
Demand, FRCP 38(b).
No demand made, FRCP 39(b).
Removed actions, FRCP 81(c).
When made, FRCP 39(a).
Examining jurors, FRCP 47(a).
Excusing a juror, FRCP 47(c).
General verdict, FRCP 49(b).
Instructions to jury, FRCP 51.
Assigning error, FRCP 51(d).
Generally, FRCP 51(b).
Objections, FRCP 51(c).
Plain error, FRCP 51(d).
Requests, FRCP 51(a).
Judgment as a matter of law, FRCP 50.
Denial of motion, FRCP 50(e).
Motion before case submitted to jury, FRCP 50(a).
Motion for a new trial, alternative motion, FRCP 50(b).
Conditional ruling, FRCP 50(c).
Time for filing, FRCP 50(d).
Renewing motion after trial, FRCP 50(b).
Granting renewed motion, FRCP 50(c).
Reversal on appeal, FRCP 50(e).
Judgment on a jury verdict, FRCP Form 70.
Number of jurors, FRCP 48.
Peremptory challenges, FRCP 47(b).
Preservation of right, FRCP 38(a).
Removed actions, FRCP 81(c).
Right to trial by jury, FRCP 38.
Selecting jurors, FRCP 47.
Special verdicts, FRCP 49(a).
Specifying issues to be tried by jury, FRCP 38(c).
Verdicts, FRCP 49.
Requirement for unanimous verdict, FRCP 48.
Waiver, FRCP 38(d).
Issues not submitted, FRCP 49(a).
Withdrawal of demand, FRCP 38(d).
Written questions, answers, FRCP 49(b).

K

KNOWLEDGE.
Pleading special matters, FRCP 9(b).

L

LACK OF JURISDICTION.
Assertion of defenses by motion, FRCP 12(b).

LEGAL EXISTENCE.
Pleading special matters, FRCP 9(a).

M

MAGISTRATE JUDGES, FRCP 72.
Appeals, FRCP 73(c).
Appointment as masters, FRCP 53(h).
Consent.
Assignment to a magistrate judge, FRCP Form 81.
Consent procedures, FRCP 73(b).
Trial by consent, FRCP 73(a).
Dispositive motions, FRCP 72(b).
Nondispositive matters, FRCP 72(a).
Notice of a magistrate judge's availability, FRCP Form 80.
Objections, FRCP 72(b).
Order of assignment to a magistrate judge, FRCP Form 82.
Prisoner petitions, FRCP 72(b).
Trial by consent, FRCP 73(a).
Consent procedures, FRCP 73(b).

MALICE.
Pleading special matters, FRCP 9(b).

MANDAMUS, ABOLITION OF WRIT, FRCP 81(b).

MASTERS, FRCP 53.
Action on master's order, report or recommendations, FRCP 53(f).
Appointment, FRCP 53(a).
Magistrate judge, FRCP 53(h).
Order appointing master, FRCP 53(b).
Authority, FRCP 53(c).
Compensation, FRCP 53(g).
Disqualification, FRCP 53(a).
Findings, FRCP 52(a).
Order appointing master, FRCP 53(b).
Orders of masters, FRCP 53(d).
Action on master's order, report or recommendations, FRCP 53(f).
Reports, FRCP 53(e).
Action on master's order, report or recommendations, FRCP 53(f).
Sanctions, FRCP 53(c).
Scope of duties, FRCP 53(a).

MERCHANT MARINE.
Complaint for damages under the merchant marine act, FRCP Form 14.

MISTAKES.
Pleading special matters, FRCP 9(b).
Relief from judgment.
Clerical mistakes, FRCP 60(a).
Grounds, FRCP 60(b).

MOTIONS.
Admissions, requests for.
Sufficiency of answer, motions regarding, FRCP 36(a).
Affidavits.
Evidence on a motion, FRCP 43(c).

MOTIONS —Cont'd
Appeals.
Relief barred by pending appeal.
Motion for relief, indicative ruling on, FRCP 62.1.
Defenses, assertion by motion, FRCP 12(b).
Depositions.
Terminate or limit examination, FRCP 30(d).
Discovery, motion for order to compel.
Failure to make disclosures or cooperate in discovery, FRCP 37(a).
District courts, FRCP 78.
Briefs, submission and determining without oral hearing, FRCP 78(b).
Regular schedule for oral hearings, FRCP 78(a).
Form of motions, FRCP 7(b).
Joining motions, FRCP 12(g).
Judgment.
Alter or amend judgment, FRCP 59(e).
Relief from judgment.
Timing and effect of motion, FRCP 60(c).
Summary judgment, motion for, FRCP 56(a).
Judgment as a matter of law.
Denial of motion, FRCP 50(e).
Motion before case submitted to jury, FRCP 50(a).
Motion for a new trial, alternative motion, FRCP 50(b).
Conditional ruling, FRCP 50(c).
Time for filing, FRCP 50(d).
Renewing motion after trial, FRCP 50(b).
Granting renewed motion, FRCP 50(c).
Reversal on appeal, FRCP 50(e).
Judgment on the pleadings.
Motion for judgment on the pleadings, FRCP 12(c).
More definite statement, FRCP 12(e).
New trial.
Judgment as a matter of law.
Motion for a new trial, alternative motion, FRCP 50(b).
Time for filing, FRCP 50(d).
Time to file, FRCP 59(b).
Physical and mental examinations.
Order for examination, FRCP 35(a).
Pleadings.
Failure to state a claim or motion for judgment on the pleadings treated as, FRCP 12(d).
Motion for judgment on the pleadings, FRCP 12(c).
Signatures, FRCP 11.
Stay pending disposition of motion, FRCP 62(b).
Striking pleadings.
Motion to strike, FRCP 12(f).
Summary judgment, motion for, FRCP 56(a).
Third-party defendant, motion to bring in, FRCP Form 41.
Time, service, FRCP 6(c).
Trials.
Findings and conclusions by court, FRCP 52(a).

MULTIPLE CLAIMS OR PARTIES.
Joinder of parties generally.
See JOINDER OF PARTIES
Judgment, FRCP 54(b).
Stays, FRCP 62(h).

N

NAMES.
Pleadings, names of parties, FRCP 10(a).

NEGLIGENCE.
Complaint for negligence, FRCP Form 11.
Federal employer's liability act, FRCP Form 13.
Plaintiff does not know who is responsible, FRCP Form 12.
Excusable neglect.
Relief from judgment, grounds, FRCP 60(b).

NEWLY DISCOVERED EVIDENCE.
Relief from judgment, grounds, FRCP 60(b).

NEW TRIAL, FRCP 59.
Affidavits.
Time to serve, FRCP 59(c).
Court's initiative, FRCP 59(d).
Further action after nonjury trial, FRCP 59(a).
Grounds, FRCP 59(a).
Motions.
Alter or amend judgment, FRCP 59(e).
Judgment as a matter of law.
Alternative motion, FRCP 50(b).
Conditional ruling, FRCP 50(c).
Time for filing, FRCP 50(d).
Time to file, FRCP 59(b).

NONPARTIES.
Enforcing judgment against a nonparty, FRCP 71.
Production of documents or things, FRCP 34(c).

NOTICE.
Condemnation of property, FRCP Form 60.
Appearance, FRCP 71.1(e).
Service of process and papers, FRCP 71.1(d).
Constitutional challenge to statute, FRCP 5.1.
Depositions.
Oral examination, FRCP 30(b).
Written questions, FRCP 31(a).
Filing, FRCP 31(c).
District courts.
Serving notice of an order or judgment, FRCP 77(d).
Intervention.
Procedure, FRCP 24(c).
Magistrate judges.
Notice of a magistrate judge's availability, FRCP Form 80.
Masters.
Order appointing master, FRCP 53(b).
Notice of lawsuit and request to waive service of summons, FRCP Form 5.
Physical and mental examinations.
Order for examination, FRCP 35(a).
Time, service, FRCP 6(c).

O

OBJECTIONS, FRCP 12.
Admissions, requests for, FRCP 36(a).
Depositions, FRCP 30(c).
Court proceedings, use in, FRCP 32(b).
Waiver of objections, FRCP 32(d).
Interrogatories, FRCP 33(b).
Judgment on the pleadings, FRCP 12(c).

OBJECTIONS —Cont'd
Jury trial.
Instructions to jury, FRCP 51(c).
Magistrate judges.
Dispositive matters and prisoner petitions, FRCP 72(b).
More definite statement, motion, FRCP 12(e).
Motion to strike, FRCP 12(f).
Pre-trial hearings, FRCP 12(i).
Production of documents or things, FRCP 34(b).
Rulings or orders, FRCP 46.
Summary judgment.
Failure to state a claim or motion for judgment on the pleadings treated as, FRCP 12(d).
Time to serve a responsive pleading, FRCP 12(a).

OFFERS OF JUDGMENT, FRCP 68.
After liability determined, FRCP 68(c).
Judgment on accepted offer, FRCP 68(a).
Making an offer, FRCP 68(a).
Unaccepted offers, FRCP 68(b).
Payment of costs, FRCP 68(d).

OFFICIAL DOCUMENTS OR ACTS.
Pleading special matters, FRCP 9(d).

OFFICIAL RECORD, PROVING, FRCP 44.
Domestic records, FRCP 44(a).
Foreign records, FRCP 44(a).
Lack of record, effect, FRCP 44(b).
Other methods of proving, FRCP 44(c).

ONE FORM OF ACTION, FRCP 2.

ORDERS.
Discovery.
Failure to comply with a court order, FRCP 37(b).
District courts.
Civil judgments and orders.
Records kept by clerk, FRCP 79(b).
Clerk's orders, FRCP 77(c).
Serving notice of an order or judgment, FRCP 77(d).
Magistrate judges.
Order of assignment to a magistrate judge, FRCP Form 82.
Masters, FRCP 53(d).
Action on master's order, report or recommendations, FRCP 53(f).
Appointment of master, FRCP 53(b).
Pretrial conferences, FRCP 16(d).
Final pretrial conference and orders, FRCP 16(e).

P

PARTIAL FINDINGS.
Judgment on partial findings, FRCP 52(c).

PARTIES, FRCP 17 to 25.
Associations.
Actions relating to unincorporated associations, FRCP 23.2.
Capacity to sue or be sued, determination, FRCP 17(b).
Class actions, FRCP 23.
Joinder of parties, exception, FRCP 19(d).
Condemnation of property.
Complaints, FRCP 71.1(c).

PARTIES —Cont'd
Condemnation of property —Cont'd
Substitution of parties, FRCP 71.1(g).
Death.
Statement noting a party's death, FRCP Form 9.
Substitution of parties, FRCP 25(a).
Public officers, death or separation from office, FRCP 25(d).
Defendant, FRCP 17.
Derivative actions, FRCP 23.1.
Incompetent persons, FRCP 17(c).
Substitution of parties, party becoming incompetent, FRCP 25(b).
Interpleader, FRCP 22.
Grounds, FRCP 22(a).
Relation to other rules and statutes, FRCP 22(b).
Intervention, FRCP 24.
Joinder of claims, FRCP 18.
Joinder of parties.
Joinder not feasible, FRCP 19(b).
Misjoinder, FRCP 21.
Nonjoinder, FRCP 21.
Pleading reasons for, FRCP 19(c).
Permissive joinder, FRCP 20.
Persons required to be joined if feasible, FRCP 19(a).
Persons who may join or be joined, FRCP 20(a).
Protective measures, permissive joinder, FRCP 20(b).
Required joinder, FRCP 19.
Minors, FRCP 17(c).
Multiple claims or parties.
Judgment, FRCP 54(b).
Plaintiff, FRCP 17.
Public officers and employees.
Substitution of parties, death or separation from office, FRCP 25(d).
Title and name, FRCP 17(d).
Real party in interest, FRCP 17(a).
Statement of reasons for omitting party, FRCP Form 8.
Substitution, FRCP 25.
Condemnation of property, FRCP 71.1(g).
Transfer of interest.
Substitution of parties, FRCP 25(c).

PARTNERSHIPS.
Service of process and papers.
Summons, FRCP 4(h).

PATENT INFRINGEMENT.
Complaint for patent infringement, FRCP Form 18.
Stays, exceptions, FRCP 62(a).

PHYSICAL AND MENTAL EXAMINATIONS, FRCP 35.
Examiner's report, FRCP 35(b).
Order for examination, FRCP 35(a).

PLACE, ALLEGING.
Pleading special matters, FRCP 9(f).

PLEADINGS, FRCP 7.
Adoption by reference.
Form of pleadings, FRCP 10(c).
Affirmative defenses, FRCP 8(c).
Alternative statements, FRCP 8(d).
Amended pleadings, FRCP 15.
Amendments before trial, FRCP 15(a).
Amendments during and after trial, FRCP 15(b).

PLEADINGS —Cont'd
Amended pleadings —Cont'd
Relation back of amendments, FRCP 15(c).
Answers.
Admissions, requests for, FRCP 36(a).
Complaint for money had and received with a counterclaim for interpleader, FRCP Form 31.
Condemnation of property, FRCP 71.1(e).
Interrogatories, FRCP 33(b).
Pleadings allowed, FRCP 7(a).
Presenting defense under FRCP 12(b), FRCP Form 30.
Attachments.
Form of pleadings, FRCP 10(c).
Caption.
Form of pleadings, FRCP 10(a).
Claim for relief, FRCP 8(a).
Complaints.
Commencement of action, FRCP 3.
Condemnation of property, FRCP 71.1(c), FRCP Form 61.
Merchant marine act, damages under, FRCP Form 14.
Negligence, FRCP Form 11.
Federal employer's liability act, FRCP Form 13.
Plaintiff does not know who is responsible, FRCP Form 12.
Pleadings allowed, FRCP 7(a).
Recover a sum certain, FRCP Form 10.
Specific performance of a contract to convey land, FRCP Form 17.
Third-party complaint, FRCP Forms 4, 16.
Concise and direct, FRCP 8(d).
Construction of pleadings, FRCP 8(e).
Defenses, FRCP 8(b), 12.
Affirmative defenses, FRCP 8(c).
Denials, FRCP 8(b).
Derivative actions, FRCP 23.1(b).
Disclosure statements, FRCP 7.1.
Form of pleadings, FRCP 10.
General rules of pleading, FRCP 8.
Inconsistent claims or defenses, FRCP 8(d).
Joinder of parties.
Nonjoinder, pleading reasons for, FRCP 19(c).
Motion for judgment on the pleadings, FRCP 12(c).
Name of parties.
Form of pleadings, FRCP 10(a).
Separate statements.
Form of pleadings, FRCP 10(b).
Service of process and papers, FRCP 5.
Signatures, FRCP 11.
Special matters, FRCP 9.
Supplemental pleadings, FRCP 15(d).

PRELIMINARY INJUNCTIONS, FRCP 65(a).

PRETRIAL AMENDMENT OF PLEADINGS, FRCP 15(a).

PRETRIAL CONFERENCES, FRCP 16.
Attendance, FRCP 16(c).
Discovery conference, FRCP 26(f).
Final pretrial conference and orders, FRCP 16(e).
Matters for consideration, FRCP 16(c).
Orders, FRCP 16(d).
Final pretrial conference and orders, FRCP 16(e).

PRETRIAL CONFERENCES —Cont'd
Purposes, FRCP 16(a).
Sanctions, FRCP 16(f).
Scheduling order, FRCP 16(b).

PRETRIAL HEARINGS ON DEFENSES AND OBJECTIONS, FRCP 12(i).

PRIVACY PROTECTION FOR FILINGS WITH COURT, FRCP 5.2.

PRIVILEGED COMMUNICATIONS.
Discovery.
Claiming privilege or protecting trial preparation materials, FRCP 26(b).
Physical and mental examinations.
Examiner's report, waiver of privilege, FRCP 35(b).
Privacy protection for filings with court, FRCP 5.2.
Subpoenas.
Claiming privilege, duties in responding, FRCP 45(e).

PRIZE PROCEEDINGS IN ADMIRALTY.
Applicability of rules, FRCP 81.

PRODUCTION OF DOCUMENTS AND THINGS, FRCP 34.
Depositions, FRCP 30(b).
Nonparties, FRCP 34(c).
Objections, FRCP 34(b).
Requests, FRCP 34(b).
Produce documents and tangible things, or to enter onto land, FRCP Form 50.
Service of request, FRCP 34(a).
Subpoenas.
Duties in responding, FRCP 45(e).

PROTECTIVE ORDERS.
Discovery.
Effect, FRCP 26(c).
Motion for order compelling disclosure, FRCP 37(a).

PUBLIC OFFICERS AND EMPLOYEES.
Execution of judgments.
Execution against certain public officers, FRCP 69(b).
Official documents or acts.
Pleading special matters, FRCP 9(d).
Parties.
Substitution of parties, death or separation from office, FRCP 25(d).
Title and name, FRCP 17(d).

PURPOSE OF RULES, FRCP 1.

Q

QUO WARRANTO.
Applicability of rules, FRCP 81(a).

R

REAL PROPERTY.
Complaint for specific performance of a contract to convey land, FRCP Form 17.

RECEIVERSHIPS.
Receivers generally, FRCP 66.
Stays, exceptions, FRCP 62(a).

RECORDS.
District courts.
Records kept by clerk, FRCP 79.
Official record, proving, FRCP 44.
Domestic records, FRCP 44(a).
Foreign records, FRCP 44(a).
Lack of record, effect, FRCP 44(b).
Other methods of proving, FRCP 44(c).

RELEASE.
Relief from judgment, grounds, FRCP 60(b).

RELIEF FROM JUDGMENT, FRCP 60.

REMEDIES.
Provisional and final remedies, FRCP 64 to 71.

REMOVED ACTIONS.
Applicability of rules, FRCP 81(c).

REPLEVIN.
Remedies available, FRCP 64(b).

REPORTS.
Masters, FRCP 53(e).
Action on master's order, report or recommendations, FRCP 53(f).
Physical and mental examinations.
Examiner's report, FRCP 35(b).

REQUESTS FOR ADMISSIONS, FRCP 36.

REVERSAL OF JUDGMENT.
Relief from judgment, grounds, FRCP 60(b).

S

SANCTIONS.
Discovery, FRCP 37.
Masters, authority, FRCP 53(c).

SATISFACTION OF JUDGMENT.
Relief from judgment, grounds, FRCP 60(b).

SCIRE FACIAS.
Abolition of writ, FRCP 81(b).

SCOPE OF RULES, FRCP 1.

SEIZURE, FRCP 64.
Specific remedies, FRCP 64(b).
State law remedies, availability, FRCP 64(a).

SEPARATE JUDGMENTS.
Counterclaims or crossclaims, FRCP 13(i).

SEPARATE TRIALS, FRCP 42(b).
Counterclaims or crossclaims, FRCP 13(i).

SEQUESTRATION.
Enforcing judgment for a specific act.
Writ of attachment or sequestration, obtaining, FRCP 70(c).
Remedies available, FRCP 64(b).

SERVICE OF PROCESS AND PAPERS.
Civil contempt, enforcement, FRCP 4.1.
Condemnation of property, FRCP 71.1(d).
Depositions.
Written questions, FRCP 31(a).
District courts.
Serving notice of an order or judgment, FRCP 77(d).
Filing, FRCP 5(d).
How made, FRCP 5(b).
Insufficient service of process.
Assertion of defenses by motion, FRCP 12(b).

SERVICE OF PROCESS AND PAPERS —Cont'd
Methods of service.
Summons, FRCP 4(e).
Motion to dismiss under FRCP 12(b) for lack of jurisdiction, improper venue, insufficient service of process, or failure to state a claim, FRCP Form 40.
New trial.
Time to serve affidavits, FRCP 59(c).
Numerous defendants, FRCP 5(c).
Pleadings and other papers, FRCP 5.
Process other than summons, FRCP 4.1.
Production of documents or things.
Service of request, FRCP 34(a).
Responsive pleading, time to serve, FRCP 12(a).
Subpoenas, FRCP 45(b).
Summons, FRCP 4(c).
Corporations, partnerships or associations, FRCP 4(h).
Foreign countries, serving foreign governments, FRCP 4(j).
Foreign countries, serving individuals in, FRCP 4(f).
Incompetent persons, FRCP 4(g).
Methods of service, FRCP 4(e).
Minors, FRCP 4(g).
Proof of service, FRCP 4(l).
Territorial limits of effective service, FRCP 4(k).
Time limit for service, FRCP 4(m).
United States and its agencies, corporations, officers or employees, FRCP 4(i).
Waiver of service, FRCP 4(d), FRCP Form 6.
Time.
Computation and extension, FRCP 6.
Waiver of service.
Summons, FRCP 4(d), FRCP Form 6.
When required, FRCP 5(a).

SETTLEMENT.
Class actions, FRCP 23(e).
Derivative actions, FRCP 23.1(c).
Offers of judgment, FRCP 68.

SIGNATURES, FRCP 11.
Date, signature, address, email address and telephone number, FRCP Form 2.
Discovery.
Inapplicability, FRCP 11(d).
Required, effect, FRCP 26(g).
Representation to court, FRCP 11(b).
Required, FRCP 11(a).
Sanctions, FRCP 11(c).

SPECIAL PROCEEDINGS, FRCP 71.1 to 73.

SPECIAL WRITS.
Applicability of rules, FRCP 81(a).

SPECIFIC PERFORMANCE.
Complaint for specific performance of a contract to convey land, FRCP Form 17.

STATE LAW.
Applicability of rules, FRCP 81(d).

STAYS, FRCP 62.
Appellate court's powers not limited, FRCP 62(g).
Automatic stay, FRCP 62(a).
Bond on appeal, FRCP 62(d).
United States, its officers or agencies, FRCP 62(e).

STAYS —Cont'd
Injunctions, exception, FRCP 62(a).
Injunctions pending an appeal, FRCP 62(c).
Interlocutory orders.
Exceptions, FRCP 62(a).
Judgment debtors under state law.
Stay in favor of, FRCP 62(f).
Motions.
Stay pending disposition of motion, FRCP 62(b).
Multiple claims or parties, FRCP 62(h).
Patent infringement.
Exceptions, FRCP 62(a).
Receiverships.
Exceptions, FRCP 62(a).

STIPULATIONS, FRCP 29.

STRIKING PLEADINGS.
Motion to strike, FRCP 12(f).

SUBPOENAS, FRCP 45.
Applicability of rules, FRCP 81(a).
Attendance.
Place of compliance, FRCP 45(c).
Contempt.
Enforcement of subpoenas, FRCP 45(g).
Depositions.
Failure to serve, FRCP 30(g).
Form and contents, FRCP 45(a).
Inspections.
Command to permit, FRCP 45(d).
Issuance, FRCP 45(a).
Modifying, FRCP 45(d).
Motions.
Transfer of subpoena-related motion, FRCP 45(f).
Persons subject to subpoenas, protection, FRCP 45(d).
Place of compliance, FRCP 45(c).
Privileged communications.
Claiming privilege, duties in responding, FRCP 45(e).
Production of documents and things.
Duties in responding, FRCP 45(e).
Protecting person subject to subpoena, FRCP 45(d).
Quashing, FRCP 45(d).
Response, duties in responding, FRCP 45(e).
Service, FRCP 45(b).
Transfer of subpoena-related motion, FRCP 45(f).
Undue burden or expense.
Protecting person subject to subpoena, FRCP 45(d).

SUFFICIENCY OF EVIDENCE.
Trials, findings and conclusions by court, FRCP 52(a).

SUMMARY JUDGMENT, FRCP 56.
Affidavits, FRCP 56(c).
Bad faith, submitted in, FRCP 56(h).
Facts unavailable to nonmovant, FRCP 56(d).
Facts unavailable to nonmovant, FRCP 56(d).
Factual positions, supporting assertions, FRCP 56(c).
Failure to grant all requested relief, FRCP 56(g).
Failure to properly support or address a fact, FRCP 56(e).
Failure to state a claim or motion for judgment on the pleadings treated as, FRCP 12(d).

SUMMARY JUDGMENT —Cont'd
Judgment independent of motion, FRCP 56(f).
Motion for, FRCP 56(a).
Objections, FRCP 56(c).
Procedure, FRCP 56(c).
Time to file, FRCP 56(b).

SUMMONS, FRCP 4, FRCP Form 3.
Amendments, FRCP 4(a).
Contents, FRCP 4(a).
Issuance, FRCP 4(b).
Jurisdiction over property or assets, asserting, FRCP 4(n).
Service of process and papers, FRCP 4(c).
Corporations, partnerships or associations, FRCP 4(h).
Foreign countries, serving foreign governments, FRCP 4(j).
Foreign countries, serving individuals in, FRCP 4(f).
Incompetent persons, FRCP 4(g).
Methods of service, FRCP 4(e).
Minors, FRCP 4(g).
Proof of service, FRCP 4(l).
Territorial limits of effective service, FRCP 4(k).
Time limit for service, FRCP 4(m).
United States and its agencies, corporations, officers or employees, FRCP 4(i).
Waiver of service, FRCP 4(d), FRCP Form 6.
Third-party complaint, FRCP Form 4.

SUPPLEMENTAL PLEADINGS, FRCP 15(d).

SURPRISE.
Relief from judgment, grounds, FRCP 60(b).

T

TELEPHONE NUMBER.
Date, signature, address, email address and telephone number, FRCP Form 2.

TEMPORARY RESTRAINING ORDERS, FRCP 65(b).

THIRD-PARTY PRACTICE, FRCP 14.
Admiralty or maritime claims, FRCP 14(c).
Complaint.
Third-party complaint, FRCP Forms 4, 16.
Defendant bringing in third party, FRCP 14(a).
Dismissal of third-party claims, FRCP 41(c).
Motion to bring in a third-party defendant, FRCP Form 41.
Plaintiff bringing in third party, FRCP 14(b).
Pleadings allowed, FRCP 7(a).
Summons.
Third-party complaint, FRCP Form 4.

TIME, FRCP 6.
Additional time, certain kinds of service, FRCP 6(d).
Affidavits, FRCP 6(c).
Allegation of time or place.
Pleading special matters, FRCP 9(f).
Computation, FRCP 6(a).
Disclosure statements, filing, FRCP 7.1(b).
Discovery, FRCP 26(d).
Extension, FRCP 6(b).
Motions, FRCP 6(c).
New trial.
Motions, time to file, FRCP 59(c).

TIME —Cont'd
New trial —Cont'd
Time to serve affidavits, FRCP 59(c).
Notices of hearings, FRCP 6(c).
Responsive pleading, time to serve, FRCP 12(a).
Service of process and papers.
Summons, FRCP 4(m).
Summons.
Service of process and papers, FRCP 4(m).

TITLE, FRCP 85.

TRANSCRIPTS.
Depositions, FRCP 30(c).
Court proceedings, use in.
Form of presentation, FRCP 32(c).
District courts.
Transcripts as evidence, FRCP 80.

TRANSFER OF INTEREST.
Substitution of parties, FRCP 25(c).

TRIALS, FRCP 38 to 53.
Advisory jury, FRCP 39(c).
Conclusions of court, FRCP 52.
Condemnation of property.
Trial of the issues, FRCP 71.1(h).
Consolidation, FRCP 42(a).
Demand.
No demand made, FRCP 39(b).
Right to trial by jury, FRCP 38(b).
When made, FRCP 39(a).
Dismissal, FRCP 41.
Costs, FRCP 41(d).
Counterclaims, crossclaims or third-party claims, FRCP 41(c).
Involuntary dismissal, FRCP 41(b).
Voluntary dismissal, FRCP 41(a).
Findings by court, FRCP 52.
Amended or additional findings, FRCP 52(b).
Judgment on partial findings, FRCP 52(c).
Setting aside, FRCP 52(a).
Foreign law, determining, FRCP 44.1.
Interlocutory injunctions.
Findings and conclusions by court, FRCP 52(a).
Involuntary dismissal, FRCP 41(b).
Jury trial.
Advisory jury, FRCP 39(c).
Answers inconsistent with verdict, FRCP 49(b).
Consent, jury trial by, FRCP 39(c).
Demand, when made, FRCP 39(a).
Examining jurors, FRCP 47(a).
Excusing a juror, FRCP 47(c).
General verdict, FRCP 49(b).
Instructions to jury, FRCP 51.
Judgment as a matter of law, FRCP 50.
No demand made, FRCP 39(b).
Number of jurors, FRCP 48.
Peremptory challenges, FRCP 47(b).
Right to trial by jury, FRCP 38.
Selecting jurors, FRCP 47.
Special verdicts, FRCP 49(a).
Verdicts, FRCP 49.
Waiver.
Issues not submitted, FRCP 49(a).
Written questions, answers, FRCP 49(b).
Magistrate judges.
Trial by consent, FRCP 73(a).
Consent procedures, FRCP 73(b).
Masters, FRCP 53.
Findings by master, FRCP 52(a).

TRIALS —Cont'd
Motions.
Findings and conclusions by court, FRCP 52(a).
Objections.
Rulings or orders, FRCP 46.
Official record, proving, FRCP 44.
Partial findings.
Judgment on partial findings, FRCP 52(c).
Priority.
Scheduling cases for trial, FRCP 40.
Right to trial by jury, FRCP 38.
Admiralty and maritime claims, FRCP 38(e).
Demand, FRCP 38(b).
Preservation of right, FRCP 38(a).
Specifying issues to be tried by jury, FRCP 38(c).
Waiver, FRCP 38(d).
Withdrawal of demand, FRCP 38(d).
Scheduling cases for trial, FRCP 40.
Separate trials, FRCP 42(b).
Setting aside the findings.
Findings and conclusions by court, FRCP 52(a).
Subpoenas, FRCP 45.
Sufficiency of evidence.
Findings and conclusions by court, FRCP 52(a).
Taking testimony, FRCP 43.
Affidavits.
Evidence on a motion, FRCP 43(c).
Affirmation instead of oath, FRCP 43(b).
In open court, FRCP 43(a).
Interpreters, FRCP 43(d).
Verdicts, FRCP 49.
Requirement for unanimous verdict, FRCP 48.
Voluntary dismissal, FRCP 41(a).

U

UNAVAILABLE WITNESS.
Depositions.
Court proceedings, use in, FRCP 32(a).

UNITED STATES.
Default judgment.
Judgment against United States, FRCP 55(d).
Service of process and papers.
Summons, FRCP 4(i).

V

VENUE.
Improper venue.
Assertion of defenses by motion, FRCP 12(b).
Motion to dismiss, FRCP Form 40.
Not affected, FRCP 82.

VOID JUDGMENT.
Relief from judgment, grounds, FRCP 60(b).

W

WRIT OF AUDITA QUERELA.
Writs abolished, FRCP 60(e).

WRIT OF CORAM NOBIS.
Writs abolished, FRCP 60(e).

WRIT OF CORAM VOBIS.
Writs abolished, FRCP 60(e).

WRITTEN QUESTIONS.
Depositions, FRCP 30(c).

RULES OF CRIMINAL PROCEDURE FOR UNITED STATES DISTRICT COURTS

The following rules were adopted by orders of the Supreme Court on December 26, 1944, and February 8, 1946, and became effective on March 21, 1946. They have been amended since their adoption.

I. Applicability of Rules.

Rule
1. Scope; Definitions.
2. Interpretation.

II. Preliminary Proceedings.

3. The Complaint.
4. Arrest Warrant or Summons on a Complaint.
4.1. Complaint, Warrant, or Summons by Telephone or Other Reliable Electronic Means.
5. Initial Appearance.
5.1. Preliminary Hearing.

III. The Grand Jury, the Indictment, and the Information

6. The Grand Jury.
7. The Indictment and the Information.
8. Joinder of Offenses or Defendants.
9. Arrest Warrant or Summons on an Indictment or Information.

IV. Arraignment and Preparation for Trial.

10. Arraignment.
11. Pleas.
12. Pleadings and Pretrial Motions.
12.1. Notice of an Alibi Defense.
12.2. Notice of an Insanity Defense; Mental Examination.
12.3. Notice of a Public-Authority Defense.
12.4. Disclosure Statement.
13. Joint Trial of Separate Cases.
14. Relief from Prejudicial Joinder.
15. Depositions.
16. Discovery and Inspection.
17. Subpoena.
17.1. Pretrial Conference.

V. Venue.

18. Place of Prosecution and Trial.
19. [Reserved.]
20. Transfer for Plea and Sentence.
21. Transfer for Trial.
22. [Transferred.]

VI. Trial.

23. Jury or Nonjury Trial.
24. Trial Jurors.
25. Judge's Disability.
26. Taking Testimony.
26.1. Foreign Law Determination.
26.2. Producting a Witness's Statement.

Rule
26.3. Mistrial.
27. Proving an Official Record.
28. Interpreters.
29. Motion for a Judgment of Acquittal.
29.1. Closing Argument.
30. Jury Instructions.
31. Jury Verdict.

VII. Post-Conviction Procedures.

32. Sentencing and Judgment.
32.1. Revoking or Modifying Probation or Supervised Release.
32.2. Criminal Forfeiture.
33. New Trial.
34. Arresting Judgment.
35. Correcting or Reducing a Sentence.
36. Clerical Error.
37. (See Editor's note) Indicative Ruling on a Motion for Relief That Is Barred by a Pending Appeal.
38. Staying a Sentence or a Disability.
39. [Reserved.]

VIII. Supplementary and Special Proceedings.

40. Arrest for Failing to Appear in Another District or for Violating Conditions of Release Set in Another District.
41. Search and Seizure.
42. Criminal Contempt.

IX. General Provisions.

43. Defendant's Presence.
44. Right to and Appointment of Counsel.
45. Computing and Extending Time.
46. Release from Custody; Supervising Detention.
47. Motions and Supporting Affidavits.
48. Dismissal.
49. Service and Filing Papers.
49.1. Privacy Protection for Filings Made with the Court.
50. Prompt Disposition.
51. Preserving Claimed Error.
52. Harmless and Plain Error.
53. Courtroom Photographing and Broadcasting Prohibited.
54. [Transferred.]
55. Records.
56. When Court Is Open.
57. District Court Rules.
58. Petty Offenses and Other Misdemeanors.
59. Matters Before a Magistrate Judge.
60. Victim's Rights.

Rule
61. Title.

Rule
Index.

Cross references. — See **www.uscourts.gov/rules.**

I. APPLICABILITY OF RULES.

Rule 1. Scope; Definitions.

(a) *Scope.* — (1) In General. — These rules govern the procedure in all criminal proceedings in the United States district courts, the United States courts of appeals, and the Supreme Court of the United States.

(2) State or Local Judicial Officer. — When a rule so states, it applies to a proceeding before a state or local judicial officer.

(3) Territorial Courts. — These rules also govern the procedure in all criminal proceedings in the following courts:

(A) the district court of Guam;

(B) the district court for the Northern Mariana Islands, except as otherwise provided by law; and

(C) the district court of the Virgin Islands, except that the prosecution of offenses in that court must be by indictment or information as otherwise provided by law.

(4) Removed Proceedings. — Although these rules govern all proceedings after removal from a state court, state law governs a dismissal by the prosecution.

(5) Excluded Proceedings. — Proceedings not governed by these rules include:

(A) the extradition and rendition of a fugitive;

(B) a civil property forfeiture for violating a federal statute;

(C) the collection of a fine or penalty;

(D) a proceeding under a statute governing juvenile delinquency to the extent the procedure is inconsistent with the statute, unless Rule 20(d) provides otherwise;

(E) a dispute between seamen under 22 U.S.C. §§ 256-258; and

(F) a proceeding against a witness in a foreign country under 28 U.S.C. § 1784.

(b) *Definitions.* — The following definitions apply to these rules:

(1) *"Attorney for the government"* means:

(A) the Attorney General or an authorized assistant;

(B) a United States attorney or an authorized assistant;

(C) when applicable to cases arising under Guam law, the Guam Attorney General or other person whom Guam law authorizes to act in the matter; and

(D) any other attorney authorized by law to conduct proceedings under these rules as a prosecutor.

(2) *"Court"* means a federal judge performing functions authorized by law.

(3) *"Federal judge"* means:

(A) a justice or judge of the United States as these terms are defined in 28 U.S.C. § 451;

(B) a magistrate judge; and

(C) a judge confirmed by the United States Senate and empowered by statute in any commonwealth, territory, or possession to perform a function to which a particular rule relates.

(4) *"Judge"* means a federal judge or a state or local judicial officer.

(5) *"Magistrate judge"* means a United States magistrate judge as defined in 28 U.S.C. §§ 631-639.

(6) *"Oath"* includes an affirmation.

(7) *"Organization"* is defined in 18 U.S.C. § 18.

(8) *"Petty offense"* is defined in 18 U.S.C. § 19.

(9) *"State"* includes the District of Columbia, and any commonwealth, territory, or possession of the United States.

(10) *"State or local judicial officer"* means:

(A) a state or local officer authorized to act under 18 U.S.C. § 3041; and

(B) a judicial officer empowered by statute in the District of Columbia or in any commonwealth, territory, or possession to perform a function to which a particular rule relates.

(11) "Telephone" means any technology for transmitting live electronic voice communication.

(12) "Victim" means a "crime victim" as defined in 18 U.S.C. § 3771(e).

(c) *Authority of a Justice or Judge of the United States.* — When these rules authorize a magistrate judge to act, any other federal judge may also act. (Amended by order adopted April 24, 1972, effective October 1, 1972, by order adopted April 28, 1982, effective August 1, 1982, by order adopted April 22, 1993, effective December 1, 1993, by order adopted April 29, 2002, effective December 1, 2002, by order adopted April 23, 2008, effective December 1, 2008, and by order adopted April 26, 2011, effective December 1, 2011.)

Law Review. — For article, "What Next in Federal Criminal Rules?" see 21 Wash. & Lee L. Rev. 1 (1964). For comment, "The Criminal Justice Act of 1964: A Critique," see 7 Wm. & Mary L. Rev. 331 (1966).

CASE NOTES

Rules have force of law. — The Federal Rules of Criminal Procedure were formulated after prolonged, careful and scholarly research and were adopted and promulgated by the Supreme Court of the United States. These rules have the force and effect of law and are binding on district judges conducting criminal trials in the United States courts. United States v. Virginia Erection Corp., 335 F.2d 868 (4th Cir. 1964).

Not applicable to military arrest. — Rule 5 has no application to the arrest of a military person for a violation of military law or regulation. Boeckenhaupt v. United States, 392 F.2d 24 (4th Cir.), cert. denied, 393 U.S. 896, 89 S. Ct. 162, 21 L. Ed. 2d 177 (1968).

Rules should be construed to secure simplicity in procedure. — The rules are not, and were not intended to be, a rigid code to have an inflexible meaning irrespective of the circumstances. They shall be construed to secure simplicity in procedure, fairness in administration and the elimination of unjustifiable expense and delay. Webster v. United States, 330 F. Supp. 1080 (E.D. Va. 1971).

Defendant charged with "petty offense" may elect trial pursuant to rules. — A defendant charged with a crime denominated a "petty offense" is entitled, at his election, to a trial conducted in the district court according to the Federal Rules of Criminal Procedure. United States v. Schembari, 484 F.2d 931 (4th Cir. 1973).

Rule 2. Interpretation.

These rules are to be interpreted to provide for the just determination of every criminal proceeding, to secure simplicity in procedure and fairness in administration, and to eliminate unjustifiable expense and delay. (Amended by order adopted April 29, 2002, effective December 1, 2002.)

II. PRELIMINARY PROCEEDINGS.

Rule 3. The Complaint.

The complaint is a written statement of the essential facts constituting the offense charged. Except as provided in Rule 4.1, it must be made under oath before a magistrate judge or, if none is reasonably available, before a state or local judicial officer. (Amended by order adopted April 24, 1972, effective October 1, 1972, by order adopted April 22, 1993, effective December 1, 1993, by order adopted April 29, 2002, effective December 1, 2002, and by order adopted April 26, 2011, effective December 1, 2011.)

Rule 4. Arrest Warrant or Summons on a Complaint.

(a) *Issuance.* — If the complaint or one or more affidavits filed with the complaint establish probable cause to believe that an offense has been committed and that the defendant committed it, the judge must issue an arrest warrant to an officer authorized to execute it. At the request of an attorney for the government, the judge must issue a summons, instead of a warrant, to a person authorized to serve it. A judge may issue more than one warrant or summons on the same complaint. If a defendant fails to appear in response to a summons, a judge may, and upon request of an attorney for the government must, issue a warrant.

(b) *Form.* — (1) Warrant. — A warrant must:

(A) contain the defendant's name or, if it is unknown, a name or description by which the defendant can be identified with reasonable certainty;

(B) describe the offense charged in the complaint;

(C) command that the defendant be arrested and brought without unnecessary delay before a magistrate judge or, if none is reasonably available, before a state or local judicial officer; and

(D) be signed by a judge.

(2) Summons. — A summons must be in the same form as a warrant except that it must require the defendant to appear before a magistrate judge at a stated time and place.

(c) *Execution or Service, and Return.* — (1) By Whom. — Only a marshal or other authorized officer may execute a warrant. Any person authorized to serve a summons in a federal civil action may serve a summons.

(2) Location. — A warrant may be executed, or a summons served, within the jurisdiction of the United States or anywhere else a federal statute authorizes an arrest.

(3) Manner. — (A) A warrant is executed by arresting the defendant. Upon arrest, an officer possessing the original or a duplicate original warrant must show it to the defendant. If the officer does not possess the warrant, the officer must inform the defendant of the warrant's existence and of the offense charged and, at the defendant's request, must show the original or a duplicate original warrant to the defendant as soon as possible.

(B) A summons is served on an individual defendant:

(i) by delivering a copy to the defendant personally; or

(ii) by leaving a copy at the defendant's residence or usual place of abode with a person of suitable age and discretion residing at that location and by mailing a copy to the defendant's last known address.

(C) A summons is served on an organization by delivering a copy to an officer, to a managing or general agent, or to another agent appointed or legally authorized to receive service of process. A copy must also be mailed to the organization's last known address within the district or to its principal place of business elsewhere in the United States.

(4) Return. — (A) After executing a warrant, the officer must return it to the judge before whom the defendant is brought in accordance with Rule 5. The officer may do so by reliable electronic means. At the request of an attorney for the government, an unexecuted warrant must be brought back to and canceled by a magistrate judge or, if none is reasonably available, by a state or local judicial officer.

(B) The person to whom a summons was delivered for service must return it on or before the return day.

(C) At the request of an attorney for the government, a judge may deliver an unexecuted warrant, an unserved summons, or a copy of the warrant or summons to the marshal or other authorized person for execution or service.

(d) *Warrant by Telephone or Other Reliable Electronic Means.* — In accordance with Rule 4.1, a magistrate judge may issue a warrant or summons based on information communicated by telephone or other reliable electronic means. (Amended by order adopted February 28, 1966, effective July 1, 1966, by order adopted April 24, 1972, effective October 1, 1972, by order adopted April 22, 1974, effective December 1, 1975, by order adopted July 31, 1975, effective December 1, 1975, by order adopted March 9, 1987, effective August 1, 1987, by order adopted April 22, 1993, effective December 1, 1993, by order adopted April 29, 2002, effective December 1, 2002, and by order adopted April 26, 2011, effective December 1, 2011.)

Rule 4.1. Complaint, Warrant, or Summons by Telephone or Other Reliable Electronic Means.

(a) *In General.* — A magistrate judge may consider information communicated by telephone or other reliable electronic means when reviewing a complaint or deciding whether to issue a warrant or summons.

(b) *Procedures.* — If a magistrate judge decides to proceed under this rule, the following procedures apply:

(1) Taking Testimony Under Oath. The judge must place under oath — and may examine — the applicant and any person on whose testimony the application is based.

(2) Creating a Record of the Testimony and Exhibits.

(A) Testimony Limited to Attestation. If the applicant does no more than attest to the contents of a written affidavit submitted by reliable electronic means, the judge must acknowledge the attestation in writing on the affidavit.

(B) Additional Testimony or Exhibits. If the judge considers additional testimony or exhibits, the judge must:

(i) have the testimony recorded verbatim by an electronic recording device, by a court reporter, or in writing;

(ii) have any recording or reporter's notes transcribed, have the transcription certified as accurate, and file it;

(iii) sign any other written record, certify its accuracy, and file it; and

(iv) make sure that the exhibits are filed.

(3) Preparing a Proposed Duplicate Original of a Complaint, Warrant, or Summons. The applicant must prepare a proposed duplicate original of a complaint, warrant, or summons, and must read or otherwise transmit its contents verbatim to the judge.

(4) Preparing an Original Complaint, Warrant, or Summons. If the applicant reads the contents of the proposed duplicate original, the judge must enter those contents into an original complaint, warrant, or summons. If the applicant transmits the contents by reliable electronic means, the transmission received by the judge may serve as the original.

(5) Modification. The judge may modify the complaint, warrant, or summons. The judge must then:

(A) transmit the modified version to the applicant by reliable electronic means; or

(B) file the modified original and direct the applicant to modify the proposed duplicate original accordingly.

(6) Issuance. To issue the warrant or summons, the judge must:

(A) sign the original documents;

(B) enter the date and time of issuance on the warrant or summons; and

(C) transmit the warrant or summons by reliable electronic means to the applicant or direct the applicant to sign the judge's name and enter the date and time on the duplicate original.

(c) *Suppression Limited.* — Absent a finding of bad faith, evidence obtained from a warrant issued under this rule is not subject to suppression on the ground that issuing the warrant in this manner was unreasonable under the circumstances. (Added by order adopted April 26, 2011, effective December 1, 2011.)

Rule 5. Initial Appearance.

(a) *In General.* — (1) Appearance Upon an Arrest.

(A) A person making an arrest within the United States must take the defendant without unnecessary delay before a magistrate judge, or before a state or local judicial officer as Rule 5(c) provides, unless a statute provides otherwise.

(B) A person making an arrest outside the United States must take the defendant without unnecessary delay before a magistrate judge, unless a statute provides otherwise.

(2) Exceptions.

(A) An officer making an arrest under a warrant issued upon a complaint charging solely a violation of 18 U.S.C. § 1073 need not comply with this rule if:

(i) the person arrested is transferred without unnecessary delay to the custody of appropriate state or local authorities in the district of arrest; and

(ii) an attorney for the government moves promptly, in the district where the warrant was issued, to dismiss the complaint.

(B) If a defendant is arrested for violating probation or supervised release, Rule 32.1 applies.

(C) If a defendant is arrested for failing to appear in another district, Rule 40 applies.

(3) Appearance Upon a Summons. — When a defendant appears in response to a summons under Rule 4, a magistrate judge must proceed under Rule 5(d) or (e), as applicable.

(b) *Arrest Without a Warrant.* — If a defendant is arrested without a warrant, a complaint meeting Rule 4(a)'s requirement of probable cause must be promptly filed in the district where the offense was allegedly committed.

(c) *Place of Initial Appearance; Transfer to Another District.* — (1) Arrest in the District Where the Offense Was Allegedly Committed. — If the defendant is arrested in the district where the offense was allegedly committed:

(A) the initial appearance must be in that district; and

(B) if a magistrate judge is not reasonably available, the initial appearance may be before a state or local judicial officer.

(2) Arrest in a District Other Than Where the Offense Was Allegedly Committed. — If the defendant was arrested in a district other than where the offense was allegedly committed, the initial appearance must be:

(A) in the district of arrest; or

(B) in an adjacent district if:

(i) the appearance can occur more promptly there; or

(ii) the offense was allegedly committed there and the ini-tial appearance will occur on the day of arrest.

(3) Procedures in a District Other Than Where the Offense Was Allegedly Committed. — If the initial appearance occurs in a district other than where the offense was allegedly committed, the following procedures apply:

(A) the magistrate judge must inform the defendant about the provisions of Rule 20;

(B) if the defendant was arrested without a warrant, the district court where the offense was allegedly committed must first issue a warrant before the magistrate judge transfers the defendant to that district;

(C) the magistrate judge must conduct a preliminary hearing if required by Rule 5.1;

(D) the magistrate judge must transfer the defendant to the district where the offense was allegedly committed if:

(i) the government produces the warrant, a certified copy of the warrant, or a reliable electronic form of either; and

(ii) the judge finds that the defendant is the same person named in the indictment, information, or warrant; and

(E) when a defendant is transferred and discharged, the clerk must promptly transmit the papers and any bail to the clerk in the district where the offense was allegedly committed.

(4) **(See Editor's note)** Procedure for Persons Extradited to the United States. — If the defendant is surrendered to the United States in accordance with a request for the defendant's extradition, the initial appearance must be in the district (or one of the districts) where the offense is charged.

(d) *Procedure in a Felony Case.* — (1) Advice. — If the defendant is charged with a felony, the judge must inform the defendant of the following:

(A) the complaint against the defendant, and any affidavit filed with it;

(B) the defendant's right to retain counsel or to request that counsel be appointed if the defendant cannot obtain counsel;

(C) the circumstances, if any, under which the defendant may secure pretrial release;

(D) any right to a preliminary hearing; and

(E) the defendant's right not to make a statement, and that any statement made may be used against the defendant.

(2) Consulting with Counsel. — The judge must allow the defendant reasonable opportunity to consult with counsel.

(3) Detention or Release. — The judge must detain or release the defendant as provided by statute or these rules.

(4) Plea. — A defendant may be asked to plead only under Rule 10.

(e) *Procedure in a Misdemeanor Case.* — If the defendant is charged with a misdemeanor only, the judge must inform the defendant in accordance with Rule 58(b)(2).

(f) *Video Teleconferencing.* — Video teleconferencing may be used to conduct an appearance under this rule if the defendant consents. (Amended by order adopted February 28, 1966, effective July 1, 1966, by order adopted April 24, 1972, effective October 1, 1972, by order adopted April 28, 1982, effective August 1, 1982, by P.L. 98-473, Title II, § 209(a), approved October 12, 1984, by order adopted March 9, 1987, effective August 1, 1987, by order adopted May 1, 1990, effective December 1, 1990, by order adopted April 22, 1993, effective December 1, 1993, by order adopted April 27, 1995, effective December 1, 1995, by order adopted April 29, 2002, effective December 1, 2002, by order adopted April 12, 2006, effective December 1, 2006, and by order adopted April 24, 2012, effective December 1, 2012.)

Editor's note. — The Chief Justice signed the letters and orders on April 23, 2012, and the amendments were transmitted to Congress on April 24, 2012. The amendments will take effect on December 1, 2012, unless Congress takes action to reject, modify, or defer them.

CASE NOTES

Rule has no application to military arrest. — This rule has no application to the arrest of a military person for a violation of military law or regulation. Boeckenhaupt v. United States, 392 F.2d 24 (4th Cir.), cert. denied, 393 U.S. 896, 89 S. Ct. 162, 21 L. Ed. 2d 177 (1968).

Military arrest held not subterfuge to evade rule. — A defendant contended that the Air Force and the FBI schemed together in an unlawful working arrangement whereby the Air Force would accomplish his military arrest for the purpose of enabling the FBI to evade this rule of court and the rule excluding admissions made and evidence secured by a consent search while the defendant was detained without being taken before a committing magistrate without unnecessary delay. The argument was that the military charge was trumped up to facilitate the obtaining of admissions and consent to search, but it was held that the argument was factually deficient and that the intent to prosecute on the military charge was both genuine and justifiable. The arrest for violation of the military code was not a subterfuge to permit in-custody interrogation but represented a genuine purpose at the time to prosecute in the military courts. This was not a case of detention being used as the vehicle of investigation, but was, instead, a case of detention having been postponed, as long as national security would permit, for noncustodial investigation. Boeckenhaupt v. United States, 392 F.2d 24 (4th Cir.), cert. denied, 393 U.S. 896, 89 S. Ct. 162, 21 L. Ed. 2d 177 (1968).

Subdivision (a) held inapplicable to FBI questioning during course of reasonable investigation. — Subdivision (a) of this rule is not applicable in a case where FBI questioning of the accused occurred during a period of reasonable investigation to determine whether federal charges should be brought. United States v. McDaniel, 441 F.2d 1160 (4th Cir. 1971).

Second preliminary hearing before reindictment held unnecessary. — A preliminary hearing, although it may serve as a vehicle or pretrial discovery for an accused, has as its principal purpose a determination of whether probable cause exists to bind an accused for action by a grand jury. Thus, where probable cause had been found in an initial hearing before a magistrate, the return of an indictment by a second grand jury (after a previous indictment had been dismissed) was a finding that probable cause existed and obviated the need for another preliminary hearing. United States v. Chase, 372 F.2d 453 (4th Cir. 1967).

Unnecessary delay in arraignment not shown. — See United States v. Swartz, 357 F.2d 322 (4th Cir. 1966); United States v. Ardner, 364 F.2d 719 (4th Cir.), cert. denied, 385 U.S. 884, 87 S. Ct. 177, 17 L. Ed. 2d 112 (1966).

Failure to advise defendant of right to counsel. — See Reed v. United States, 291 F.2d 856 (4th Cir. 1961).

Applied in Fisher v. Washington Metro. Area Transit Auth., 690 F.2d 1133 (4th Cir. 1982).

Rule 5.1. Preliminary Hearing.

(a) *In General.* — If a defendant is charged with an offense other than a petty offense, a magistrate judge must conduct a preliminary hearing unless:

(1) the defendant waives the hearing;

(2) the defendant is indicted;

(3) the government files an information under Rule 7(b) charging the defendant with a felony;

(4) the government files an information charging the defendant with a misdemeanor; or

(5) the defendant is charged with a misdemeanor and consents to trial before a magistrate judge.

(b) *Selecting a District.* — A defendant arrested in a district other than where the offense was allegedly committed may elect to have the preliminary hearing conducted in the district where the prosecution is pending.

(c) *Scheduling.* — The magistrate judge must hold the preliminary hearing within a reasonable time, but no later than 14 days after the initial appearance if the defendant is in custody and no later than 21 days if not in custody.

(d) *Extending the Time.* — With the defendant's consent and upon a showing of good cause — taking into account the public interest in the prompt disposition of criminal cases — a magistrate judge may extend the time limits in Rule 5.1(c) one or more times. If the defendant does not consent, the magistrate judge may extend the time limits only on a showing that extraordinary circumstances exist and justice requires the delay.

(e) *Hearing and Finding.* — At the preliminary hearing, the defendant may cross-examine adverse witnesses and may introduce evidence but may not object to evidence on the ground that it was unlawfully acquired. If the magistrate judge finds probable cause to believe an offense has been committed and the defendant committed it, the magistrate judge must promptly require the defendant to appear for further proceedings.

(f) *Discharging the Defendant.* — If the magistrate judge finds no probable cause to believe an offense has been committed or the defendant committed it, the magistrate judge must dismiss the complaint and discharge the defendant. A discharge does not preclude the government from later prosecuting the defendant for the same offense.

(g) *Recording the Proceedings.* — The preliminary hearing must be recorded by a court reporter or by a suitable recording device. A recording of the proceeding may be made available to any party upon request. A copy of the recording and a transcript may be provided to any party upon request and upon any payment required by applicable Judicial Conference regulations.

(h) *Producing a Statement.* — (1) In General. — Rule 26.2(a)-(d) and (f) applies at any hearing under this rule, unless the magistrate judge for good cause rules otherwise in a particular case.

(2) Sanctions for Not Producing a Statement. — If a party disobeys a Rule 26.2 order to deliver a statement to the moving party, the magistrate judge must not consider the testimony of a witness whose statement is withheld. (Added by order adopted April 24, 1972, effective October 1, 1972, amended by order adopted March 9, 1987, effective August 1, 1987, by order adopted April 22, 1993, effective December 1, 1993, by order adopted April 24, 1998, effective December 1, 1998, by order adopted April 29, 2002, effective December 1, 2002, and by order adopted March 26, 2009, effective December 1, 2009.)

Law Review. — For an article, "Wake Up and Smell the Contraband: Why Courts That do Not Find Probable Cause Based On Odor Are Wrong," see 42 Wm. & Mary L. Rev. 289 (2000).

III. THE GRAND JURY, THE INDICTMENT, AND THE INFORMATION.

Rule 6. The Grand Jury.

(a) *Summoning a Grand Jury.* — (1) In General. — When the public interest so requires, the court must order that one or more grand juries be summoned. A grand jury must have 16 to 23 members, and the court must order that enough legally qualified persons be summoned to meet this requirement.

(2) Alternate Jurors. — When a grand jury is selected, the court may also select alternate jurors. Alternate jurors must have the same qualifications and be selected in the same manner as any other juror. Alternate jurors replace jurors in the same sequence in which the alternates were selected. An alternate juror who replaces a juror is subject to the same challenges, takes the same oath, and has the same authority as the other jurors.

(b) *Objection to the Grand Jury or to a Grand Juror.* — (1) Challenges. — Either the government or a defendant may challenge the grand jury on the ground that it was not lawfully drawn, summoned, or selected, and may challenge an individual juror on the ground that the juror is not legally qualified.

(2) Motion to Dismiss an Indictment. — A party may move to dismiss the indictment based on an objection to the grand jury or on an individual juror's lack of legal qualification, unless the court has previously ruled on the same objection under Rule 6(b)(1). The motion to dismiss is governed by 28 U.S.C. § 1867(e). The court must not dismiss the indictment on the ground that a grand juror was not legally qualified if the record shows that at least 12 qualified jurors concurred in the indictment.

(c) *Foreperson and Deputy Foreperson.* — The court will appoint one juror as the foreperson and another as the deputy foreperson. In the foreperson's absence, the deputy foreperson will act as the foreperson. The foreperson may administer oaths and affirmations and will sign all indictments. The foreperson — or another juror designated by the foreperson — will record the number of jurors concurring in every indictment and will file the record with the clerk, but the record may not be made public unless the court so orders.

(d) *Who May Be Present.* — (1) While the Grand Jury Is in Session. — The following persons may be present while the grand jury is in session: attorneys for the government, the witness being questioned, interpreters when needed, and a court reporter or an operator of a recording device.

(2) During Deliberations and Voting. — No person other than the jurors, and any interpreter needed to assist a hearing-impaired or speech-impaired juror, may be present while the grand jury is deliberating or voting.

(e) *Recording and Disclosing the Proceedings.* — (1) Recording the Proceedings. — Except while the grand jury is deliberating or voting, all proceedings must be recorded by a court reporter or by a suitable recording device. But the validity of a prosecution is not affected by the unintentional failure to make a recording. Unless the court orders otherwise, an attorney for the government will retain control of the recording, the reporter's notes, and any transcript prepared from those notes.

(2) Secrecy. — (A) No obligation of secrecy may be imposed on any person except in accordance with Rule 6(e)(2)(B).

(B) Unless these rules provide otherwise, the following persons must not disclose a matter occurring before the grand jury:

(i) a grand juror;

(ii) an interpreter;

(iii) a court reporter;

(iv) an operator of a recording device;

(v) a person who transcribes recorded testimony;

(vi) an attorney for the government; or

(vii) a person to whom disclosure is made under Rule 6(e)(3)(A)(ii) or (iii).

(3) Exceptions. — (A) Disclosure of a grand-jury matter — other than the grand jury's deliberations or any grand juror's vote — may be made to:

(i) an attorney for the government for use in performing that attorney's duty;

(ii) any government personnel — including those of a state, state subdivision, Indian tribe, or foreign government — that an attorney for the government considers necessary to assist in performing that attorney's duty to enforce federal criminal law; or

(iii) a person authorized by 18 U.S.C. § 3322.

(B) A person to whom information is disclosed under Rule 6(e)(3)(A)(ii) may use that information only to assist an attorney for the government in performing that attorney's duty to enforce federal criminal law. An attorney for the government must promptly provide the court that impaneled the grand jury with the names of all persons to whom a disclosure has been made, and must certify that the attorney has advised those persons of their obligation of secrecy under this rule.

(C) An attorney for the government may disclose any grand-jury matter to another federal grand jury.

(D) An attorney for the government may disclose any grand-jury matter involving foreign intelligence, counterintelligence (as defined in 50 U.S.C. § 401a), or foreign intelligence information (as defined in Rule 6(e)(3)(D)(iii)) to any federal law enforcement, intelligence, protective, immigration, national defense, or national security official to assist the official receiving the information in the performance of that official's duties. An attorney for the government may also disclose any grand jury matter involving, within the United States or elsewhere, a threat of attack or other grave hostile acts of a foreign power or its agent, a threat of domestic or international sabotage or terrorism, or clandestine intelligence gathering activities by an intelligence service or network of a foreign power or by its agent, to any appropriate federal, state, state subdivision, Indian tribal, or foreign government official, for the purpose of preventing or responding to such threat or activities.

(i) Any official who receives information under Rule 6(e)(3)(D) may use the information only as necessary in the conduct of that person's official duties subject to any limitations on the unauthorized disclosure of such information. Any state, state subdivision, Indian tribal, or foreign government official who receives information under Rule 6(e)(3)(D) may use the information only in a manner consistent with any guidelines issued by the Attorney General and the Director of National Intelligence.

(ii) Within a reasonable time after disclosure is made under Rule 6(e)(3)(D), an attorney for the government must file, under seal, a notice with the court in the district where the grand jury convened stating that such information was disclosed and the departments, agencies, or entities to which the disclosure was made.

(iii) As used in Rule 6(e)(3)(D), the term "foreign intelligence information" means:

(a) information, whether or not it concerns a United States person, that relates to the ability of the United States to protect against —

- actual or potential attack or other grave hostile acts of a foreign power or its agent;
- sabotage or international terrorism by a foreign power or its agent; or
- clandestine intelligence activities by an intelligence service or network of a foreign power or by its agent; or

(b) information, whether or not it concerns a United States person, with respect to a foreign power or foreign territory that relates to —

- the national defense or the security of the United States; or
- the conduct of the foreign affairs of the United States.

(E) The court may authorize disclosure — at a time, in a manner, and subject to any other conditions that it directs — of a grand-jury matter:

(i) preliminarily to or in connection with a judicial proceeding;

(ii) at the request of a defendant who shows that a ground may exist to dismiss the indictment because of a matter that occurred before the grand jury;

(iii) at the request of the government, when sought by a foreign court or prosecutor for use in an official criminal investigation;

(iv) at the request of the government if it shows that the matter may disclose a violation of State, Indian tribal, or foreign criminal law, as long as the disclosure is to an appropriate state, state-subdivision, Indian tribal, or foreign government official for the purpose of enforcing that law; or

(v) at the request of the government if it shows that the matter may disclose a violation of military criminal law under the Uniform Code of Military Justice, as long as the disclosure is to an appropriate military official for the purpose of enforcing that law.

(F) A petition to disclose a grand-jury matter under Rule 6(e)(3)(E)(i) must be filed in the district where the grand jury convened. Unless the hearing is ex parte — as it may be when the government is the petitioner — the petitioner must serve the petition on, and the court must afford a reasonable opportunity to appear and be heard to:

(i) an attorney for the government;

(ii) the parties to the judicial proceeding; and

(iii) any other person whom the court may designate.

(G) If the petition to disclose arises out of a judicial proceeding in another district, the petitioned court must transfer the petition to the other court unless the petitioned court can reasonably determine whether disclosure is proper. If the petitioned court decides to transfer, it must send to the transferee court the material sought to be disclosed, if feasible, and a written evaluation of the need for continued grand-jury secrecy. The transferee court must afford those persons identified in Rule 6(e)(3)(F) a reasonable opportunity to appear and be heard.

(4) Sealed Indictment. — The magistrate judge to whom an indictment is returned may direct that the indictment be kept secret until the defendant is in custody or has been released pending trial. The clerk must then seal the indictment, and no person may disclose the indictment's existence except as necessary to issue or execute a warrant or summons.

(5) Closed Hearing. — Subject to any right to an open hearing in a contempt proceeding, the court must close any hearing to the extent necessary to prevent disclosure of a matter occurring before a grand jury.

(6) Sealed Records. — Records, orders, and subpoenas relating to grand-jury proceedings must be kept under seal to the extent and as long as necessary to prevent the unauthorized disclosure of a matter occurring before a grand jury.

(7) Contempt. — A knowing violation of Rule 6, or of any guidelines jointly issued by the Attorney General and the Director of National Intelligence under Rule 6, may be punished as a contempt of court.

(f) *Indictment and Return.* — A grand jury may indict only if at least 12 jurors concur. The grand jury — or its foreperson or deputy foreperson — must return the indictment to a magistrate judge in open court. To avoid unnecessary cost or delay, the magistrate judge may take the return by video teleconference from the court where the grand jury sits. If a complaint or information is pending against the defendant and 12 jurors do not concur in the indictment, the foreperson must promptly and in writing report the lack of concurrence to the magistrate judge.

(g) *Discharging the Grand Jury.* — A grand jury must serve until the court discharges it, but it may serve more than 18 months only if the court, having determined that an extension is in the public interest, extends the grand jury's service. An extension may be granted for no more than 6 months, except as otherwise provided by statute.

(h) *Excusing a Juror.* — At any time, for good cause, the court may excuse a juror either temporarily or permanently, and if permanently, the court may impanel an alternate juror in place of the excused juror.

(i) *"Indian Tribe" Defined.* — "Indian tribe" means an Indian tribe recognized by the Secretary of the Interior on a list published in the Federal Register under 25 U.S.C. § 479a-1. (Amended by order adopted February 28, 1966, effective July 1, 1966, by order adopted April 24, 1972, effective October 1, 1972, by order adopted April 26, 1976 and July 8, 1976, effective August 1, 1976, by order adopted July 30, 1977, effective October 1, 1977, by order adopted April 30, 1979, effective August 1, 1979, by order adopted April 28, 1983, effective August 1, 1983, by order adopted October 12, 1984, effective November 1, 1987, by order adopted April 29, 1985, effective August 1, 1985, by order adopted March 9, 1987, effective August 1, 1987, by P.L. 98-473, Title II, § 215(f), effective November 1, 1987, by order adopted April 22, 1993, effective December 1, 1993, by order adopted April 26, 1999, effective December 1, 1999, by order adopted April 29, 2002, effective December 1, 2002, amended effective Nov. 25, 2002, amended effective December 17, 2004, by order adopted April 12, 2006, effective December 1, 2006, and by order adopted April 26, 2011, effective December 1, 2011.)

Editor's note. — Section 895 of Act Nov. 25, 2002, P. L. 107-296, the Homeland Security Act of 2002, amended this section by adding subdivision (e)(3)(D) and redesignating former subdivisions (e)(3)(D) through (e)(3)(F) as subdivisions (e)(3)(F) through (e)(3)(G).

Law Review. — For note, "Disclosure of Grand Jury Materials to Foreign Authorities Under Federal Rule of Criminal Procedure 6(e)," see 70 Va. L. Rev. 1623 (1984). For article, "Legal Ethics in the Bid Rigging Cases," see 19 U. Rich. L. Rev. 513 (1985).

CASE NOTES

Objection to grand juror must be raised before trial. — In the federal courts an objection to a member of the grand jury, such as that the foreman is the brother of the man whose store was robbed, may be raised only by motion before trial. Rambo v. Peyton, 380 F.2d 363 (4th Cir. 1967).

Veil of secrecy not lifted by rule. — While Rule 6 of the Federal Rules of Criminal Procedure imposes no condition of secrecy on the witness, it is plain that the rule does not lift the general veil of secrecy which covers grand jury proceedings. Bast v. United States, 542 F.2d 893 (4th Cir. 1976).

Purpose of subdivision (e) is to protect the secrecy of grand jury proceedings. It was not intended to cloak individuals under investigation in a protective mantle of concealment. United States v. (Under Seal), 783 F.2d 450 (4th Cir. 1986), cert. denied, 481 U.S. 1032, 107 S. Ct. 1964, 95 L. Ed. 2d 535 (1987).

Showing required for disclosure. — A party seeking disclosure of grand jury materials under subdivision (e) must show that the material they seek is needed to avoid a possible injustice in another judicial proceeding, that the need for disclosure is greater than the need for continued secrecy, and that their request is structured to cover only materials so needed. Conclusory allegations that the public interest will be promoted do not establish that a possible injustice in another judicial proceeding will result unless the subpoenaed documents are disclosed. In re Grand Jury Disclosure, 550 F. Supp. 1171 (E.D. Va. 1982). But see United States v. Reiners, 934 F. Supp. 721 (E.D. Va. 1996).

One's right to disclosure may not rest simply on the weakness of the public interest considerations in favor of secrecy; there must be a showing of some real need on the part of the moving party. And this need, in the case of an application by the government, must be more than a legal conclusion that the Civil Division of the Justice Department was entitled to disclosure on the Division's simple statement "that it has a legitimate interest in the disclosure" and has a "need" for disclosure. In re Grand Jury Proceedings, 800 F.2d 1293 (4th Cir. 1986).

Parties seeking grand jury transcripts under subdivision (e) must show that the material they seek is needed to avoid a possible injustice in another judicial proceeding, that the need for disclosure is greater than the need for continued secrecy, and that their request is structured to cover only material so needed. In re Grand Jury Proceedings, 800 F.2d 1293 (4th Cir. 1986).

The party seeking disclosure must make a strong showing of particularized need for grand jury material before any disclosure will be permitted. That is, the party must prove that without access to the grand jury materials, a defense would be greatly prejudiced or an injustice would be done. Sun Dun Inc. v. United States, 766 F. Supp. 463 (E.D. Va. 1991).

When a party seeks disclosure of immunized testimony, even when the grand jury's investigation has terminated, the party still must make a compelling showing of particularized need before disclosure will be permitted. Sun Dun Inc. v. United States, 766 F. Supp. 463 (E.D. Va. 1991).

Balance of interests in disclosure and secrecy. — The trial court, in determining whether to release grand jury transcripts and materials under subdivision (e) is to balance the petitioner's need for release against the traditional public interest reasons for grand jury secrecy and only in those cases where the need for disclosure outweighs the public interest in secrecy will the requirement of "particularized need" for release be found to exist. In re Grand Jury Proceedings, 800 F.2d 1293 (4th Cir. 1986).

Discovery as prerequisite to disclosure. — Disclosure should not readily be ordered under subdivision (e)(3)(C)(i) if no showing has been made that the usual channels of discovery have proved fruitless or have even been diligently pursued. In re Grand Jury Disclosure, 550 F. Supp. 1171 (E.D. Va. 1982). But see United States v. Reiners, 934 F. Supp. 721 (E.D. Va. 1996).

Effect of disclosure on future grand juries considered. — The trial court, in considering the motion to disclose, should consider as an additional public interest concern, the possible effect upon the functioning of future grand juries by encouraging persons to testify fully and freely before future grand juries. In re Grand Jury Proceedings, 800 F.2d 1293 (4th Cir. 1986).

Strength or weakness of need for secrecy will naturally determine how strong or minimal must be the justification for disclosure made by the party seeking disclosure under the balancing test. If the reasons for secrecy, measured by an assessment of the relevant factors, are weakened or become minimal, the justification for disclosure will be diminished. Such strength or weakness may be resolved by a consideration of a number of factors of varying weight. In re Grand Jury Proceedings, 800 F.2d 1293 (4th Cir. 1986).

Allegation that grand jury materials are rationally related to civil matters within duty of attorney for the government is insufficient standing alone, to support a finding of "particularized need." There must be some additional showing that the disclosure of the "rationally related" grand jury materials would serve the interests of fairness and justice. In re Grand Jury Proceedings, 800 F.2d 1293 (4th Cir. 1986).

"Particularized need" strong in case of prior unlimited disclosure to one party. — The "particularized need" for disclosure becomes "strong" both for purposes of trial preparation and for trial itself, when there has been prior unlimited release to one party in the litigation of the grand jury transcript and materials. In that case, disclosure is in order not merely to assure the accuracy of the testimony but also "to equalize the access to relevant facts which each side possesses" and to eliminate the obvious unfair advantage, arising from affording only one side "exclusive access to a storehouse of relevant fact." In re Grand Jury Proceedings, 800 F.2d 1293 (4th Cir. 1986).

Subdivision (e) is applicable to subpoenaed documents. — Documents subpoenaed by the grand jury are squarely within the cloak of grand jury secrecy and are protected from disclosure, except as provided by subdivision (e). In re Grand Jury Disclosure, 550 F. Supp. 1171 (E.D. Va. 1982). But see United States v. Reiners, 934 F. Supp. 721 (E.D. Va. 1996).

State grand jury investigation is "preliminarily to or in connection with a judicial proceeding" so as to satisfy subdivision (e)(3)(C)(i). In re Grand Jury Disclosure, 550 F. Supp. 1171 (E.D. Va. 1982). But see United States v. Reiners, 934 F. Supp. 721 (E.D. Va. 1996).

Showing required of state agency. — A state agency does not enjoy a reduced standard in showing need under the exception provided in subdivision (e)(3)(C)(i). Rather, the state too must show particularized need and compelling necessity. In re Grand Jury Disclosure, 550 F. Supp. 1171 (E.D. Va. 1982). But see United States v. Reiners, 934 F. Supp. 721 (E.D. Va. 1996).

Possible discrepancies in testimony before two grand juries insufficient reason for inspecting minutes. — The mere possibility that a witness's testimony before two grand juries differed, or the mere possibility that his testimony before a grand jury differed from his testimony at trial, would be insufficient reason to pierce the veil of secrecy which protects the proceedings of such a body. Thus, where the defendant's announced purpose in seeking inspection of the minutes of two grand juries was to discover discrepancies in the testimony of witnesses who appeared before both, he has failed to show a particular need for examination of the minutes, and the district judge does not abuse his discretion under this rule in denying inspection of the grand jury minutes of the grand juries. United States v. Chase, 372 F.2d 453 (4th Cir.), cert. denied, 387 U.S. 913, 87 S. Ct. 1701, 18 L. Ed. 2d 635 (1967).

Where production of grand jury minutes is deemed appropriate, the mechanics of the process calls for defense counsel to determine what is useful. The trial judge functions only in a supervisory capacity. For example, he is to cause the elimination of extraneous matters and to rule upon applications by the government for protective orders in unusual situations. Of course, the search is only to ascertain whether the witness's earlier testimony is inconsistent with the witness's trial affirmations. The truth of the witness's previous evidence is not at stake; any variance is usable only to shake the later testimony. United States v. McGowan, 423 F.2d 413 (4th Cir. 1970).

Supreme Court decisions as to disclosure for use in civil cases held not retroactive. — United States v. Sells Eng'g Co., 463 U.S. 418, 103 S. Ct. 3133, 77 L. Ed. 2d 743 (1983), and United States v. Baggot, 463 U.S. 476, 103 S. Ct. 3164, 77 L. Ed. 2d 785 (1983), which limited the disclosure of grand jury material for use in civil litigation, including civil tax audits, do not apply retroactively so as to prohibit the use of grand jury material which was fully disclosed pursuant to a valid order under subdivision (e) before those cases were decided. United States v. (Under Seal), 783 F.2d 450 (4th Cir. 1986), cert. denied, 481 U.S. 1032, 107 S. Ct. 1964, 95 L. Ed. 2d 535 (1987).

Instructing witnesses as to disclosure of proceedings. — The government attorneys may tell witnesses that, although they have a right to discuss their testimony with third parties, they may also refuse to do so. In addition, the government may indicate to witnesses that it would prefer that they not discuss their testimony with third parties (apart from their own attorneys), although they may do so if they choose. Such a course of action would not violate the proscription in subdivision (e) of this rule against imposing an obligation of secrecy on witnesses; it would merely convey the government's desires. In re Grand Jury Proceedings, 558 F. Supp. 532 (W.D. Va. 1983).

Disclosure pursuant to Antitrust Procedures and Penalties Act. — To the extent an affirmative showing of a particularized need is necessary to require disclosure of grand jury materials, the mandate of Congress, as set out in the Antitrust Procedures and Penalties Act, 15 U.S.C. § 16, is sufficient to meet this need. To claim otherwise would be to allow the parties, if they so desired, to circumvent with impunity the dictates of the act by hiding documents within the penumbra of the grand jury investigation. Accordingly, though the act does not authorize plundering of grand jury records, in a proper case, a determinative document would not necessarily be protected from disclosure because it was obtained during grand jury proceedings. United States v. Central Contracting Co., 537 F. Supp. 571 (E.D. Va. 1982).

Case remanded to permit defense counsel opportunity to inspect minutes of grand jury. — See United States v. McGowan, 423 F.2d 413 (4th Cir. 1970); United States v. Corsi, 425 F.2d 1176 (4th Cir. 1970).

Grant of immunity. — Proceedings on an application before the court under the federal statute for a grant of immunity to a witness before a grand jury should be secret and not open to the public. In re Antitrust Grand Jury Investigation, 508 F. Supp. 397 (E.D. Va. 1980), rev'd on other grounds, 714 F.2d 347 (4th Cir. 1983).

Entry of unauthorized persons held not grounds for dismissal of indictment. — Where each entry of unauthorized persons into the grand jury room brought the proceedings to an abrupt halt, and no testimony was taken in the presence of the unauthorized persons, there was no demonstrable prejudice or substantial threat thereof so that dismissal of the indictment was plainly inappropriate. United States v. Computer Sciences Corp., 689 F.2d 1181 (4th Cir. 1982), cert. denied, 459 U.S. 1105, 103 S. Ct. 729, 74 L. Ed. 2d 953 (1983), overruled on other grounds, Busby v. Crown Supply, Inc., 896 F.2d 833 (4th Cir. 1990).

Applied in United States v. Litton Sys., 573 F.2d 195 (4th Cir. 1978); United States v. Computer Sciences Corp., 689 F.2d 1181 (4th Cir. 1982).

Rule 7. The Indictment and the Information.

(a) *When Used.* — (1) Felony. — An offense (other than criminal contempt) must be prosecuted by an indictment if it is punishable:

(A) by death; or

(B) by imprisonment for more than one year.

(2) Misdemeanor. — An offense punishable by imprisonment for one year or less may be prosecuted in accordance with Rule 58(b)(1).

(b) *Waiving Indictment.* — An offense punishable by imprisonment for more than one year may be prosecuted by information if the defendant — in open court and after being advised of the nature of the charge and of the defendant's rights — waives prosecution by indictment.

(c) *Nature and Contents.* — (1) In General. — The indictment or information must be a plain, concise, and definite written statement of the essential facts constituting the offense charged and must be signed by an attorney for the government. It need not contain a formal introduction or conclusion. A count may incorporate by reference an allegation made in another count. A count may allege that the means by which the defendant committed the offense are unknown or that the defendant committed it by one or more specified means. For each count, the indictment or information must give the official or customary citation of the statute, rule, regulation, or other provision of law that the defendant is alleged to have violated. For purposes of an indictment referred to in section 3282 of title 18, United States Code, for which the identity of the defendant is unknown, it shall be sufficient for the indictment to describe the defendant as an individual whose name is unknown, but who has a particular DNA profile, as that term is defined in section 3282.

(2) Citation Error. — Unless the defendant was misled and thereby prejudiced, neither an error in a citation nor a citation's omission is a ground to dismiss the indictment or information or to reverse a conviction.

(d) *Surplusage.* — Upon the defendant's motion, the court may strike surplusage from the indictment or information.

(e) *Amending an Information.* — Unless an additional or different offense is charged or a substantial right of the defendant is prejudiced, the court may permit an information to be amended at any time before the verdict or finding.

(f) *Bill of Particulars.* — The court may direct the government to file a bill of particulars. The defendant may move for a bill of particulars before or within 14 days after arraignment or at a later time if the court permits. The government may amend a bill of particulars subject to such conditions as justice requires. (Amended by order adopted February 28, 1966, effective July 1, 1966, by order adopted April 24, 1972, effective October 1, 1972, by order adopted April 30, 1979, effective August 1, 1979, by order adopted March 9, 1987, effective August 1, 1987, by order adopted April 17, 2000, effective December 1, 2000, by order adopted April 29, 2002, effective December 1, 2002, amended effective Apr. 30, 2003, and by order adopted March 26, 2009, effective December 1, 2009.)

Editor's note. — Act April 30, 2003, P.L. 108-21, Title VI, § 610(b), 117 Stat. 692, amended subdivision (c)(1) by adding the last sentence.

CASE NOTES

An indictment under subdivision (c) of this rule is sufficient if it: 1) states the essential elements of the offense charged and is sufficiently detailed to apprise a defendant of the charge against him so that he can prepare a defense, and 2) states enough facts and information to allow the indictment to be used as proof to bar subsequent prosecutions of defendant on the same facts. United States v. Brown, 784 F. Supp. 322 (E.D. Va. 1992).

Application and standard of proof. — Subdivision (c)(2) of this rule and Rule 31(e) of the Federal Rules of Criminal Procedure indicate that criminal procedures apply to forfeiture and proof beyond a reasonable doubt is a fundamental element of criminal trials. United States v. Real Property Located at 1808 Diamond Springs Rd., 816 F. Supp. 1077 (E.D. Va. 1993).

Defendant held not misled by incorrect citations of statutes. — Subdivision (c) of this rule, which requires the citation of the appropriate statute the defendant is charged by the indictment to have violated, provides that error in the citation shall not be ground for dismissal of the indictment or reversal of a conviction if the error did not mislead the defendant to his prejudice. In the present case, the defendant was correctly informed of the nature of the charge by the allegations of the second count of the indictment and there was no showing that the defendant or his counsel was in any way misled, much less prejudiced, by the careless miscitations at the end of the second count of the indictment. United States v. Brown, 284 F.2d 89 (4th Cir. 1960); Davis v. United States, 279 F.2d 576 (4th Cir. 1960); Sonnier v. United States, 314 F.2d 69 (4th Cir. 1963).

The purpose of a bill of particulars is to enable a defendant to obtain sufficient information on the nature of the charge against him so that he may prepare for trial, minimize the danger of surprise at trial, and enable him to plead his acquittal or conviction in bar of another prosecution for the same offense. United States v. Schembari, 484 F.2d 931 (4th Cir. 1973).

Bill of particulars may function to apprise defendant of charges against him. — The indictment's function of apprising a defendant of the charge against him so that he may prepare a defense may often be satisfied through a bill of particulars or discovery. United States v. Brown, 784 F. Supp. 322 (E.D. Va. 1992).

Rule drafted to discourage multiplicity. — See United States v. Allied Chem. Corp., 420 F. Supp. 122 (E.D. Va. 1976).

Defendant informed of charges though subsection of statute incorrectly cited in indictment. — See United States v. Stinson, 594 F.2d 982 (4th Cir. 1979).

Indictment held not multiplicitous. — An indictment under the Refuse Act which listed as individual counts the act of discharge of chemicals into navigable waters for each day the act was performed rather than as one act of discharge was held not multiplicitous on its face, and absent a showing that the acts were uninterrupted, the charges would stand as 456 counts. United States v. Allied Chem. Corp., 420 F. Supp. 122 (E.D. Va. 1976).

"Surplusage" defined. — "Surplusage" is any fact or circumstance set forth in the indictment which is not a necessary ingredient of the offense. United States v. Manginen, 565 F. Supp. 1024 (E.D. Va. 1983), aff'd, 788 F.2d 1561 (4th Cir. 1986).

That which is unintelligible is properly regarded as surplusage. United States v. Manginen, 565 F. Supp. 1024 (E.D. Va. 1983), aff'd, 788 F.2d 1561 (4th Cir. 1986).

Defendant has no unconditional right to a bill of particulars. — Instead, the granting or denial of a bill is within the court's discretion. United States v. Bales, 813 F.2d 1289 (4th Cir. 1987).

Denial of bill of particulars held not abuse. — When each count of an indictment contains the official citation of the statute under which the defendant is charged and the evidence constitutes precise proof of the charges in the indictment, denial of a motion for a bill of particulars is not an abuse of discretion. United States v. Bales, 813 F.2d 1289 (4th Cir. 1987).

Applied in Hall v. United States, 410 F.2d 653 (4th Cir. 1969).

Rule 8. Joinder of Offenses or Defendants.

(a) *Joinder of Offenses.* — The indictment or information may charge a defendant in separate counts with 2 or more offenses if the offenses charged — whether felonies or misdemeanors or both — are of the same or similar character, or are based on the same act or transaction, or are connected with or constitute parts of a common scheme or plan.

(b) *Joinder of Defendants.* — The indictment or information may charge 2 or more defendants if they are alleged to have participated in the same act or transaction, or in the same series of acts or transactions, constituting an offense or offenses. The defendants may be charged in one or more counts together or separately. All defendants need not be charged in each count. (Amended by order adopted April 29, 2002, effective December 1, 2002.)

Law Review. — For an article "For the Criminal Practitioner: A review of all 1995 criminal cases decided by the Fourth Circuit," see 53 Wash. & Lee L. Rev. 465 (1996).

CASE NOTES

Subdivision (a) is restatement of existing and familiar law. — See Rakes v. United States, 169 F.2d 739 (4th Cir.), cert. denied, 335 U.S. 826, 69 S. Ct. 51, 93 L. Ed. 380 (1948).

And subdivision (b) states law applicable before its adoption. — See Rakes v. United States, 169 F.2d 739 (4th Cir.), cert. denied, 335 U.S. 826, 69 S. Ct. 51, 93 L. Ed. 380 (1948).

It increases speed and efficiency of justice. — The procedure under subdivision (b) not only increases the speed and efficiency of the administration of justice but also serves to give the jury a complete overall view of the whole scheme and helps them to see how each piece fits into the pattern. Rakes v. United States, 169 F.2d 739 (4th Cir.), cert. denied, 335 U.S. 826, 69 S. Ct. 51, 93 L. Ed. 380 (1948).

Joinder deemed proper. — Although his codefendants appear to have been more deeply involved in the crime, the evidence against the defendant was sufficient to establish his guilt on all three of the counts pertaining to him. The record does not indicate that he was convicted simply by innuendo because his associates were plainly guilty. Accordingly, he was not entitled to a severance. United States v. Hargrove, 647 F.2d 411 (4th Cir. 1981).

Where the defendant was charged with conspiracy and two substantive counts that were also alleged as overt acts of the conspiracy, joinder was proper. United States v. Hargrove, 647 F.2d 411 (4th Cir. 1981).

District court did not commit error in denying the motion to sever two tax charges from trial of 14 drug-related counts; the tax counts charged defendant with wilfully signing income tax returns for the calendar years 1987 and 1988, knowing that the returns omitted the reporting of income which he had received from drug transactions; even if the motion for a severance had been granted, evidence about the drug transactions would have been admissible in the tax case to prove income and show its probable source. United States v. Clark, 928 F.2d 639 (4th Cir. 1991).

Severance is not matter of right as to alleged participants in offense. — Severance is not a matter of right where two defendants are alleged to have participated in the same act or transaction or in the same series of acts or transactions constituting an offense or offenses. United States v. Godel, 361 F.2d 21 (4th Cir.), cert. denied, 385 U.S. 838, 87 S. Ct. 87, 17 L. Ed. 2d 72 (1966).

Severance cures error, if any, in joinder of defendants. — Where defendant claims error in the joinder with him of others as aiders and abettors, the severance, by virtue of which he stood trial with his wife as his only co-defendant, is a sufficient answer to his claim of prejudice in this respect. Rakes v. United States, 169 F.2d 739 (4th Cir.), cert. denied, 335 U.S. 826, 69 S. Ct. 51, 93 L. Ed. 380 (1948).

The mere showing of prejudice is not enough to require severance of a defendant's trial; rather, tailoring of relief, if any, for any potential prejudice resulting from a joint trial is left to the district court's sound discretion. United States v. Hayden, 85 F.3d 153 (4th Cir. 1996).

Offenses came within recognized boundaries of permissive joinder. — Where in a multi-count indictment, the defendant was charged with perjury, unlawfully possessing a stolen United States treasury check, and uttering the same treasury check with intent to defraud the United States, that the three counts came within the recognized boundaries of permissive joinder in the first instance, as defined by Rule 8(a), Fed. R. Crim. P., was manifest, since the transaction out of which Counts II and III arose was the abstraction from the mails by defendant of a treasury check mistakenly sent to her address, her forgery of the endorsement upon the check, and her cashing of it, and the perjury count arose out of the same transaction when questioned under oath at her preliminary hearing on the possession and uttering charges. United States v. Jamar, 561 F.2d 1103 (4th Cir. 1977).

Since the original joinder was proper under subdivision (b), the circuit court of appeals would uphold the denial of the motion to sever since there is no showing that the trial judge abused his discretion. United States v. Mumford, 630 F.2d 1023 (4th Cir. 1980), cert. denied, 450 U.S. 1041, 101 S. Ct. 1759, 68 L. Ed. 2d 238 (1981).

Limiting instruction not necessary. — In a case where three of the narcotics and firearms offenses were all being committed at the same instant—defendant would leave city with guns and come back with drugs—the case was so obviously one for joinder under subsection (a) of this rule a limiting instruction was not necessary absent request or patent prejudice, neither of which was present in the instant case. United States v. Rhodes, 32 F.3d 867 (4th Cir. 1994), cert. denied, 513 U.S. 1164, 115 S. Ct. 1130, 130 L. Ed. 2d 1092 (1995).

Applied in United States v. Larouche, 896 F.2d 815 (4th Cir. 1990); United States v. Gunn, 968 F. Supp. 1089 (E.D. Va. 1997).

Rule 9. Arrest Warrant or Summons on an Indictment or Information.

(a) *Issuance.* — The court must issue a warrant — or at the government's request, a summons — for each defendant named in an indictment or named in an information if one or more affidavits accompanying the information establish probable cause to believe that an offense has been committed and that the defendant committed it. The court may issue more than one warrant or summons for the same defendant. If a defendant fails to appear in response to a summons, the court may, and upon request of an attorney for the government must, issue a warrant. The court must issue the arrest warrant to an officer authorized to execute it or the summons to a person authorized to serve it.

(b) *Form.* — (1) Warrant. — The warrant must conform to Rule 4(b)(1) except that it must be signed by the clerk and must describe the offense charged in the indictment or information.

(2) Summons. — The summons must be in the same form as a warrant except that it must require the defendant to appear before the court at a stated time and place.

(c) *Execution or Service; Return; Initial Appearance.* — (1) Execution or Service. — (A) The warrant must be executed or the summons served as provided in Rule 4(c)(1), (2), and (3).

(B) The officer executing the warrant must proceed in accor-dance with Rule 5(a)(1).

(2) Return. — A warrant or summons must be returned in accordance with Rule 4(c)(4).

(3) Initial Appearance. — When an arrested or summoned defendant first appears before the court, the judge must proceed under Rule 5.

(d) *Warrant by Telephone or Other Means.* — In accordance with Rule 4.1, a magistrate judge may issue an arrest warrant or summons based on information communicated by telephone or other reliable electronic means. (Amended by order adopted April 24, 1972, effective October 1, 1972, by order adopted April 22, 1974, effective December 1, 1975, by order adopted July 31, 1975, by order adopted December 12, 1975, by order adopted April 30, 1979, effective August 1, 1979, by order adopted April 28, 1982, effective August 1, 1982, order adopted April 22, 1993, effective December 1, 1993, by order adopted April 29, 2002, effective December 1, 2002, and by order adopted April 26, 2011, effective December 1, 2011.)

IV. ARRAIGNMENT AND PREPARATION FOR TRIAL.

Rule 10. Arraignment.

(a) *In General.* — An arraignment must be conducted in open court and must consist of:

(1) ensuring that the defendant has a copy of the indictment or information;

(2) reading the indictment or information to the defendant or stating to the defendant the substance of the charge; and then

(3) asking the defendant to plead to the indictment or information.

(b) *Waiving Appearance.* — A defendant need not be present for the arraignment if:

(1) the defendant has been charged by indictment or misdemeanor information;

(2) the defendant, in a written waiver signed by both the defendant and defense counsel, has waived appearance and has affirmed that the defendant received a copy of the indictment or information and that the plea is not guilty; and

(3) the court accepts the waiver.

(c) *Video Teleconferencing.* — Video teleconferencing may be used to arraign a defendant if the defendant consents. (Amended by order adopted March 9, 1987, effective August 1, 1987, and by order adopted April 29, 2002, effective December 1, 2002.)

Law Review. — For article, "Reconceptualizing Competence: An Appeal," see 66 Wash. & Lee L. Rev. 259 (2009).

CASE NOTES

Failure to furnish indictment does not render conviction subject to collateral attack if charges were fully explained. — Where the charges were explained to the defendant in detail before he was called upon to plead thereto and he fully understood the charges against him at the time he entered his pleas, the failure to furnish him with copies of the indictments did not render the judgments subject to collateral attack. Rakes v. United States, 231 F. Supp. 812 (W.D. Va. 1964), aff'd, 352 F.2d 518 (4th Cir. 1965).

Applied in Wilson v. United States, 215 F. Supp. 661 (W.D. Va. 1963).

Rule 11. Pleas.

(a) *Entering a Plea.* — (1) In General. — A defendant may plead not guilty, guilty, or (with the court's consent) nolo contendere.

(2) Conditional Plea. — With the consent of the court and the government, a defendant may enter a conditional plea of guilty or nolo contendere, reserving in

writing the right to have an appellate court review an adverse determination of a specified pretrial motion. A defendant who prevails on appeal may then withdraw the plea.

(3) Nolo Contendere Plea. — Before accepting a plea of nolo contendere, the court must consider the parties' views and the public interest in the effective administration of justice.

(4) Failure to Enter a Plea. — If a defendant refuses to enter a plea or if a defendant organization fails to appear, the court must enter a plea of not guilty.

(b) *Considering and Accepting a Guilty or Nolo Contendere Plea.* — (1) Advising and Questioning the Defendant. — Before the court accepts a plea of guilty or nolo contendere, the defendant may be placed under oath, and the court must address the defendant personally in open court. During this address, the court must inform the defendant of, and determine that the defendant understands, the following:

(A) the government's right, in a prosecution for perjury or false statement, to use against the defendant any statement that the defendant gives under oath;

(B) the right to plead not guilty, or having already so pleaded, to persist in that plea;

(C) the right to a jury trial;

(D) the right to be represented by counsel — and if necessary have the court appoint counsel — at trial and at every other stage of the proceeding;

(E) the right at trial to confront and cross-examine adverse witnesses, to be protected from compelled self-incrimination, to testify and present evidence, and to compel the attendance of witnesses;

(F) the defendant's waiver of these trial rights if the court accepts a plea of guilty or nolo contendere;

(G) the nature of each charge to which the defendant is pleading;

(H) any maximum possible penalty, including imprisonment, fine, and term of supervised release;

(I) any mandatory minimum penalty;

(J) any applicable forfeiture;

(K) the court's authority to order restitution;

(L) the court's obligation to impose a special assessment;

(M) in determining a sentence, the court's obligation to calculate the applicable sentencing-guideline range and to consider that range, possible departures under the Sentencing Guidelines, and other sentencing factors under 18 U.S.C. § 3553(a);

(N) the terms of any plea-agreement provision waiving the right to appeal or to collaterally attack the sentence; and

(O) that, if convicted, a defendant who is not a United States citizen may be removed from the United States, denied citizenship, and denied admission to the United States in the future.

(2) Ensuring That a Plea Is Voluntary. — Before accepting a plea of guilty or nolo contendere, the court must address the defendant personally in open court and determine that the plea is voluntary and did not result from force, threats, or promises (other than promises in a plea agreement).

(3) Determining the Factual Basis for a Plea. — Before entering judgment on a guilty plea, the court must determine that there is a factual basis for the plea.

(c) *Plea Agreement Procedure.* — (1) In General. — An attorney for the government and the defendant's attorney, or the defendant when proceeding pro se, may discuss and reach a plea agreement. The court must not participate in these discussions. If the defendant pleads guilty or nolo contendere to either a charged offense or a lesser or related offense, the plea agreement may specify that an attorney for the government will:

(A) not bring, or will move to dismiss, other charges;

(B) recommend, or agree not to oppose the defendant's request, that a particular sentence or sentencing range is appropriate or that a particular provision of the Sentencing Guidelines, or policy statement, or sentencing factor does or does not apply (such a recommendation or request does not bind the court); or

(C) agree that a specific sentence or sentencing range is the appropriate disposition of the case, or that a particular provision of the Sentencing Guidelines, or policy statement, or sentencing factor does or does not apply (such a recommendation or request binds the court once the court accepts the plea agreement).

(2) Disclosing a Plea Agreement. — The parties must disclose the plea agreement in open court when the plea is offered, unless the court for good cause allows the parties to disclose the plea agreement in camera.

(3) Judicial Consideration of a Plea Agreement. — (A) To the extent the plea agreement is of the type specified in Rule 11(c)(1)(A) or (C), the court may accept the agreement, reject it, or defer a decision until the court has reviewed the presentence report.

(B) To the extent the plea agreement is of the type specified in Rule 11(c)(1)(B), the court must advise the defendant that the defendant has no right to withdraw the plea if the court does not follow the recommendation or request.

(4) Accepting a Plea Agreement. — If the court accepts the plea agreement, it must inform the defendant that to the extent the plea agreement is of the type specified in Rule 11(c)(1)(A) or (C), the agreed disposition will be included in the judgment.

(5) Rejecting a Plea Agreement. — If the court rejects a plea agreement containing provisions of the type specified in Rule 11(c)(1)(A) or (C), the court must do the following on the record and in open court (or, for good cause, in camera):

(A) inform the parties that the court rejects the plea agreement;

(B) advise the defendant personally that the court is not required to follow the plea agreement and give the defendant an opportunity to withdraw the plea; and

(C) advise the defendant personally that if the plea is not withdrawn, the court may dispose of the case less favorably toward the defendant than the plea agreement contemplated.

(d) *Withdrawing a Guilty or Nolo Contendere Plea.* — A defendant may withdraw a plea of guilty or nolo contendere:

(1) before the court accepts the plea, for any reason or no reason; or

(2) after the court accepts the plea, but before it imposes sentence if:

(A) the court rejects a plea agreement under Rule 11(c)(5); or

(B) the defendant can show a fair and just reason for requesting the withdrawal.

(e) *Finality of a Guilty or Nolo Contendere Plea.* — After the court imposes sentence, the defendant may not withdraw a plea of guilty or nolo contendere, and the plea may be set aside only on direct appeal or collateral attack.

(f) *Admissibility or Inadmissibility of a Plea, Plea Discussions, and Related Statements.* — The admissibility or inadmissibility of a plea, a plea discussion, and any related statement is governed by Federal Rule of Evidence 410.

(g) *Recording the Proceedings.* — The proceedings during which the defendant enters a plea must be recorded by a court reporter or by a suitable recording device. If there is a guilty plea or a nolo contendere plea, the record must include the inquiries and advice to the defendant required under Rule 11(b) and (c).

(h) *Harmless Error.* — A variance from the requirements of this rule is harmless error if it does not affect substantial rights. (Amended by order adopted February 28, 1966, effective July 1, 1966, by order adopted April 22, 1974, effective December 1, 1975, by order adopted July 31, 1975, effective August 1, 1975 and December 1, 1975, by order adopted April 30, 1979, effective August 1, 1979 and December 1, 1980, by order adopted April 28, 1982, effective August 1, 1982, by order adopted April 28, 1983, effective August 1, 1983, by order adopted April 29, 1985, effective August 1, 1985, by order adopted March 9, 1987, effective August 1, 1987, by P.L.100-690, § 7076, effective November 18, 1988, by order adopted April 25, 1989, effective December 1, 1989, by order adopted April 26, 1999, effective December 1, 1999, by order adopted April 29, 2002, effective December 1, 2002, by order adopted April 30, 2007, effective December 1, 2007, and by order adopted April 16, 2013, effective December 1, 2013.)

Law Review. — For note on judicial authority in the settlement of federal civil cases, see 42 Wash. & Lee L. Rev. 171 (1985). For article, "Reconceptualizing Competence: An Appeal," see 66 Wash. & Lee L. Rev. 259 (2009).

CASE NOTES

Purpose of this rule requirement is to assure that the accused be not misled as to the nature of the offense with which he stands charged. There is no simple or mechanical rule as to how the court is to determine defendant's understanding of the charge. United States v. Reckmeyer, 786 F.2d 1216 (4th Cir.), cert. denied, 479 U.S. 850, 107 S. Ct. 177, 93 L. Ed. 2d 113 (1986), but see, Libretti v. United States, 516 U.S. 29, 116 S. Ct. 356, 133 L. Ed. 2d 271 (1995).

Purpose of the rule is not to lay a procedural trap for the government and allow a defendant to change his mind after the hearing under this rule and challenge a plea on a technicality. United States v. Reckmeyer, 786 F.2d 1216 (4th Cir.), cert. denied, 479 U.S. 850, 107 S. Ct. 177, 93

L. Ed. 2d 113 (1986), but see, Libretti v. United States, 516 U.S. 29, 116 S. Ct. 356, 133 L. Ed. 2d 271 (1995).

This rule 11 has no application to probation revocation proceedings. United States v. Stehl, 665 F.2d 58 (4th Cir. 1981).

An appropriately conducted Rule 11 proceeding raises a strong presumption that the plea is final and binding. United States v. Puckett, 61 F.3d 1092 (4th Cir. 1995).

Manner of ensuring that defendant is properly informed is committed to the good judgment of the district court, to its calculation of the relative difficulty of comprehension of the charges and of the defendant's sophistication and intelligence. United States v. Reckmeyer, 786 F.2d 1216 (4th Cir.), cert. denied, 479 U.S. 850, 107 S. Ct. 177, 93 L. Ed. 2d 113 (1986), but see, Libretti v. United States, 516 U.S. 29, 116 S. Ct. 356, 133 L. Ed. 2d 271 (1995).

Defendant must be informed of nature of charges, mandatory minimum penalty and maximum possible penalty. — Prior to accepting a guilty plea, a trial court, through colloquy with the defendant, must inform the defendant of, and determine that he understands, the nature of the charges to which the plea is offered, any mandatory minimum penalty, the maximum possible penalty and various rights. United States v. DeFusco, 949 F.2d 114 (4th Cir. 1991), cert. denied, 503 U.S. 997, 112 S. Ct. 1703, 118 L. Ed. 2d 412 (1992).

Subsection (c)(1) of this rule requires that the court inform the defendant of any mandatory minimum penalty provided by law for the charged offense. United States v. DeFusco, 949 F.2d 114 (4th Cir. 1991), cert. denied, 503 U.S. 997, 112 S. Ct. 1703, 118 L. Ed. 2d 412 (1992).

A Rule 11 violation can not be considered harmless if the defendant had no knowledge of the mandatory minimum at the time of the plea. United States v. Goins, 51 F.3d 400 (4th Cir. 1995).

Where there was no evidence in the record that defendant was aware that he was subjecting him self to a mandatory five-year sentence by pleading guilty, the trial court's failure to inform the defendant during the Rule 11 hearing that a guilty plea would result in a mandatory minimum sentence of five years constituted reversible error. United States v. Goins, 51 F.3d 400 (4th Cir. 1995).

No requirement that defendant be informed of sentencing range under guidelines. — Subsection (c)(1) of this rule imposes no requirement that the court determine, and inform, the defendant of the applicable sentencing range under the guidelines before accepting a guilty plea. Under the guidelines, the maximum sentence will never exceed the maximum provided by statute, nor will the defendant be given less than a statutorily provided minimum. So long as the defendant has this information at the time the guilty plea is offered, the dictates of this rule have been met. United States v. DeFusco, 949 F.2d 114 (4th Cir. 1991), cert. denied, 503 U.S. 997, 112 S. Ct. 1703, 118 L. Ed. 2d 412 (1992).

Rule ensures admissions are sufficient to constitute crime. — The rule ensures that the court make clear exactly what a defendant admits to, and whether those admissions are factually sufficient to constitute the alleged crime. United States v. DeFusco, 949 F.2d 114 (4th Cir. 1991), cert. denied, 503 U.S. 997, 112 S. Ct. 1703, 118 L. Ed. 2d 412 (1992).

In reviewing the adequacy of compliance with this rule, the Court of Appeals should accord deference to the trial court's decision as to how best to conduct the mandated colloquy with the defendant. United States v. DeFusco, 949 F.2d 114 (4th Cir. 1991), cert. denied, 503 U.S. 997, 112 S. Ct. 1703, 118 L. Ed. 2d 412 (1992).

A plea of nolo contendere is an admission of guilt which can subject the defendant to the same punishment that he would have received on a plea of guilty. United States v. Dorman, 496 F.2d 438 (4th Cir.), cert. denied, 419 U.S. 945, 95 S. Ct. 214, 42 L. Ed. 2d 168 (1974).

A plea of nolo contendere is not admissible against the defendant in a subsequent civil action, unlike a plea of guilty. United States v. Dorman, 496 F.2d 438 (4th Cir.), cert. denied, 419 U.S. 945, 95 S. Ct. 214, 42 L. Ed. 2d 168 (1974).

A defendant does not have an absolute right to plead nolo contendere simply because he wishes to contest his civil liability. This rule, which provides that the plea can be entered only with the consent of the district court, has been construed to vest the trial judge with broad discretion. United States v. Dorman, 496 F.2d 438 (4th Cir.), cert. denied, 419 U.S. 945, 95 S. Ct. 214, 42 L. Ed. 2d 168 (1974).

A defendant waives his nonjurisdictional claim to plead nolo contendere by his subsequent plea of guilty. United States v. Dorman, 496 F.2d 438 (4th Cir.), cert. denied, 419 U.S. 945, 95 S. Ct. 214, 42 L. Ed. 2d 168 (1974).

Where the judge explained to defendant that he usually did not consent to pleas of nolo contendere except in income tax evasion cases, the reason for the exception, he added, was to enable a defendant to admit his guilt without being estopped to challenge an overstatement of the amount of the tax in the indictment when the government subsequently undertakes collection, and there was no likelihood that the indictments for interstate transportation of forged checks inflated the sums payable ascribed to the forged checks, the district judge's ruling was not arbitrary or capricious. United States v. Dorman, 496 F.2d 438 (4th Cir.), cert. denied, 419 U.S. 945, 95 S. Ct. 214, 42 L. Ed. 2d 168 (1974).

Court has option of whether it will accept plea agreement. — Rule 11(e), Fed. R. Crim. P. spells out the guidelines to be observed by the court and counsel in plea agreement procedures, but the Rule leaves to the court the option of whether it will accept or reject the plea agreement. United States v. Jackson, 563 F.2d 1145 (4th Cir. 1977).

And may decline to countenance any plea bargaining whatsoever. — While the Rule is silent with respect to the authority of the court to decline to countenance any plea bargaining whatsoever, such a prerogative was recognized by the Congress in its consideration of the Federal Rules of Criminal Procedure Act of 1975. United States v. Jackson, 563 F.2d 1145 (4th Cir. 1977).

And refusal will not vitiate knowing and voluntary guilty plea. — Each individual judge is free to decide whether, and to what degree, he will entertain plea bargains, and his refusal to consider any plea bargaining whatsoever will not vitiate a guilty plea which has otherwise been knowingly and voluntarily entered. United States v. Jackson, 563 F.2d 1145 (4th Cir. 1977).

A fair and just reason for withdrawing a guilty plea is one that essentially challenges the fairness of the Rule 11 proceeding. United States v. Puckett, 61 F.3d 1092 (4th Cir. 1995).

Coerced pleas. — If the district court determined that improper persuasion had been used by the prosecutor to compel the plea, the district court could not accept it, or if the issue was raised later, collateral relief under 28 U.S.C. § 2255 would be available. United States v. (Under Seal), 714 F.2d 347 (4th Cir. 1983), appeal dismissed and cert. denied, 464 U.S. 979, 104 S. Ct. 418, 78 L. Ed. 2d 354 (1983), 464 U.S. 978, 104 S. Ct. 1019, 78 L. Ed. 2d 354 (1984).

If the resulting plea is truly coerced, it cannot properly be accepted under subdivision (d) of this rule. Indeed, at the proceeding under this rule, it would be incumbent upon the district court to ascertain the nature of the plea discussions held between the defendant, his counsel and the United States Attorney. United States v. (Under Seal), 714 F.2d 347 (4th Cir. 1983), appeal dismissed and cert. denied, 464 U.S. 979, 104 S. Ct. 418, 78 L. Ed. 2d 354 (1983), 464 U.S. 978, 104 S. Ct. 1019, 78 L. Ed. 2d 354 (1984).

Comparable presumption to presumption of regularity of jury waivers exists in area of guilty pleas. — Both the general rule of presumed regularity of the advance jury waiver and its special application to circumstances personal to the bench trial judge are amply supported in related constitutional doctrine and by reason of practical necessity. So far as the general presumption is concerned, a comparable presumption, though not typically so described, exists in the closely related area of guilty pleas and their subsequent withdrawals. There, after a guilty plea has been entered in accordance with this rule, it may only be withdrawn in the discretion of the district court, and after the imposition of sentence, "only to correct manifest injustice." To employ a similar presumption in respect of jury waivers, where the defendant's interests surely cannot be thought to be more significant, seems clearly justified. Wyatt v. United States, 591 F.2d 260 (4th Cir. 1979).

Unconditional plea waiving right to appeal. — Defendant unsuccessfully sought to exercise a statutory right to appeal his sentence, despite express language in his unconditional plea that waived that very right. United States v. Wiggins, 905 F.2d 51 (4th Cir. 1990).

Immunity under 18 U.S.C. § 6002. — Whatever may be the extent of 18 U.S.C. § 6002 immunity, its scope, when conferred in a plea agreement, must be circumscribed by the words of the plea agreement itself. If the agreement were ambiguous, then the invocation of § 6002 might be useful in determining the scope of the defendant's immunity. United States v. Crisp, 817 F.2d 256 (4th Cir.), cert. denied, 484 U.S. 856, 108 S. Ct. 164, 98 L. Ed. 2d 118 (1987).

The right of direct appeal after judgment on a plea is very limited. — For example, direct review of an adverse ruling on a pre-trial motion is available only if the defendant expressly preserves that right by entering a conditional guilty plea. United States v. Wiggins, 905 F.2d 51 (4th Cir. 1990).

Applied in Reed v. United States, 291 F.2d 856 (4th Cir. 1961); Fee v. United States, 207 F. Supp. 674 (W.D. Va. 1962); Pilkington v. United States, 315 F.2d 204 (4th Cir. 1963); United States v. Roland, 318 F.2d 406 (4th Cir. 1963); Wilson v. United States, 215 F. Supp. 661 (W.D. Va. 1963); Rakes v. United States, 231 F. Supp. 812 (W.D. Va. 1964); Yates v. United States, 245 F. Supp. 147 (E.D. Va. 1965); United States v. Kincaid, 362 F.2d 939 (4th Cir. 1966); United States v. Williams, 407 F.2d 940 (4th Cir. 1969); United States v. Black, 415 F.2d 230 (4th Cir. 1969); Raines v. United States, 423 F.2d 526 (4th Cir. 1970); St. Clair v. Cox, 312 F. Supp. 168 (W.D. Va. 1970); Paige v. United States, 443 F.2d 781 (4th Cir. 1971); United States v. Ready, 460 F.2d 1238 (4th Cir. 1972); Bozeman v. United States, 354 F. Supp. 1262 (E.D. Va. 1973); United States v. Dorman, 496 F.2d 438 (4th Cir. 1974); United States v. Strauss, 563 F.2d 127 (4th Cir. 1977); United States v. Harvey, 791 F.2d 294 (4th Cir. 1986); United States v. Lambey, 949 F.2d 133 (4th Cir. 1991); Nesbitt v. United States, 773 F. Supp. 795 (E.D. Va. 1991); United States v. McDonald, No. 99-4897, 2000 U.S. App. LEXIS 14128 (4th Cir. June 16, 2000); United States v. Ragland, No. 00-4077, 2000 U.S. App. LEXIS 23336 (4th Cir. Sept. 15, 2000).

Rule 12. Pleadings and Pretrial Motions.

(a) *Pleadings.* — The pleadings in a criminal proceeding are the indictment, the information, and the pleas of not guilty, guilty, and nolo contendere.

(b) *Pretrial Motions.* — (1) In General. — Rule 47 applies to a pretrial motion.

(2) Motions That May Be Made Before Trial. — A party may raise by pretrial motion any defense, objection, or request that the court can determine without a trial of the general issue.

(3) Motions That Must Be Made Before Trial. — The following must be raised before trial:

(A) a motion alleging a defect in instituting the prosecution;

(B) a motion alleging a defect in the indictment or information — but at any time while the case is pending, the court may hear a claim that the indictment or information fails to invoke the court's jurisdiction or to state an offense;

(C) a motion to suppress evidence;

(D) a Rule 14 motion to sever charges or defendants; and

(E) a Rule 16 motion for discovery.

(4) Notice of the Government's Intent to Use Evidence. — (A) At the Government's Discretion. — At the arraignment or as soon afterward as practicable, the government may notify the defendant of its intent to use specified evidence at trial in order to afford the defendant an opportunity to object before trial under Rule 12(b)(3)(C).

(B) At the Defendant's Request. — At the arraignment or as soon afterward as practicable, the defendant may, in order to have an opportunity to move to suppress evidence under Rule 12(b)(3)(C), request notice of the government's intent to use (in its evidence-in-chief at trial) any evidence that the defendant may be entitled to discover under Rule 16.

(c) *Motion Deadline.* — The court may, at the arraignment or as soon afterward as practicable, set a deadline for the parties to make pretrial motions and may also schedule a motion hearing.

(d) *Ruling on a Motion.* — The court must decide every pretrial motion before trial unless it finds good cause to defer a ruling. The court must not defer ruling on a pretrial motion if the deferral will adversely affect a party's right to appeal. When factual issues are involved in deciding a motion, the court must state its essential findings on the record.

(e) *Waiver of a Defense, Objection, or Request.* — A party waives any Rule 12(b)(3) defense, objection, or request not raised by the deadline the court sets under Rule 12(c) or by any extension the court provides. For good cause, the court may grant relief from the waiver.

(f) *Recording the Proceedings.* — All proceedings at a motion hearing, including any findings of fact and conclusions of law made orally by the court, must be recorded by a court reporter or a suitable recording device.

(g) *Defendant's Continued Custody or Release Status.* — If the court grants a motion to dismiss based on a defect in instituting the prosecution, in the indictment, or in the information, it may order the defendant to be released or detained under 18 U.S.C. § 3142 for a specified time until a new indictment or information is filed. This rule does not affect any federal statutory period of limitations.

(h) *Producing Statements at a Suppression Hearing.* — Rule 26.2 applies at a suppression hearing under Rule 12(b)(3)(C). At a suppression hearing, a law enforcement officer is considered a government witness. (Amended by order adopted April 22, 1974, effective December 1, 1975, by order adopted July 31, 1975, effective December 1, 1975, by order adopted April 28, 1983, effective August 1, 1983, by order adopted March 9, 1987, effective August 1, 1987, by order adopted April 22, 1993, effective December 1, 1993, and by order adopted April 29, 2002, effective December 1, 2002.)

Law Review. — For an article "For the Criminal Practitioner: A review of all 1995 criminal cases decided by the Fourth Circuit," see 53 Wash. & Lee L. Rev. 465 (1996).

CASE NOTES

Motions to dismiss for improper venue or to sever a count for trial elsewhere. — A motion to dismiss for improper venue must be made pretrial or within any time set by the court for pretrial motions. The same is true of motions to sever a count for trial elsewhere. United States v. Billups, 522 F. Supp. 935 (E.D. Va. 1981), aff'd, 692 F.2d 320 (4th Cir. 1982).

Waiver of right to object to venue. — Defendant, by waiting to object for the first time to venue in a district until just before the jury was impanelled, waived his right to object to venue by failure to comply with the requirement of the Federal Rules of Criminal Procedure that such objection be timely. United States v. Billups, 522 F. Supp. 935 (E.D. Va. 1981), aff'd, 692 F.2d 320 (4th Cir. 1982).

Waiver rule to be applied with rigor. — Like all waiver rules, this one may sometimes operate to a defendant's significant disadvantage—even provable prejudice—but there are significant reasons for applying the rule with rigor. It imposes a fair and minimal burden on defendants to timely inform their counsel of obviously critical inculpatory evidence in police hands and of the circumstances of its acquisition. By this means, difficult suppression issues may be resolved before trial on fair notice to both parties. It would not do to allow the salutary purposes of the waiver rule, which is critical to pre-trial resolution of those issues, to be subverted by a defendant's simply withholding that information until trial. United States v. Ricco, 52 F.3d 58 (4th Cir. 1995), cert. denied, 516 U.S. 898, 116 S. Ct. 254, 133 L. Ed. 2d 179 (1995).

Scope of waiver provisions of subdivision (b) (2). — The waiver provisions of subdivision (b) (2) are operative only with respect to claims of defects in the institution of criminal proceedings. If its time limits are followed, inquiry into an alleged defect may be concluded and, if necessary, cured before the court, the witnesses and the parties have gone to the burden and expense of a trial. If defendants were allowed to flout its time limitations, on the other hand, there would be little incentive to comply with its terms when a successful attack might simply result in a new indictment prior to trial. United States v. Guyette, 382 F. Supp. 1266 (E.D. Va. 1974).

The defenses of lack of jurisdiction and failure of the information to charge an offense "shall be noticed by the court at any time during the pendency of the proceeding"; those defenses are not waived, and may be validly raised for the first time upon appeal. United States v. Guyette, 382 F. Supp. 1266 (E.D. Va. 1974).

To be entitled to relief from the waiver provision the applicant must show not only that there was good cause for his failure timely to assert the claim, but also that he suffered actual prejudice from the alleged improper jury composition. United States v. Williams, 544 F.2d 1215 (4th Cir. 1976).

Decision to grant or deny relief from waiver provision matter left to discretion of judge. — See United States v. Williams, 544 F.2d 1215 (4th Cir. 1976).

Failure to raise double jeopardy claim. — While it is true that the initial burden of raising and pleading a double jeopardy claim lies with the defendant, failure to do so before trial does not result in an automatic forfeiture of the double jeopardy defense. United States v. Jarvis, 7 F.3d 404 (4th Cir. 1993), cert. denied, 510 U.S. 1169, 114 S. Ct. 1200, 127 L. Ed. 2d 549 (1994).

Defenses must be raised before district court. — Such defenses and objections as former jeopardy, former acquittal, former conviction, the statute of limitations, and immunity must be raised some time in the proceeding before the district court on pain of forfeiture. United States v. Jarvis, 7 F.3d 404 (4th Cir. 1993), cert. denied, 510 U.S. 1169, 114 S. Ct. 1200, 127 L. Ed. 2d 549 (1994).

Failure to raise a contemporaneous objection of immunity before a trial does not constitute a forfeiture of the objection because the defendant is not forced by Rule 12(b) to assert the objection before the proceedings against him commence. However, failure to raise the immunity defense at some point during the proceedings before the district court would result in a forfeiture of the objection. United States v. Jarvis, 7 F.3d 404 (4th Cir. 1993), cert. denied, 510 U.S. 1169, 114 S. Ct. 1200, 127 L. Ed. 2d 549 (1994).

Denial of suppression motion abuse of discretion. — Where defendant moved for a suppression hearing 11 days before trial, and where counsel's tardiness was due not to negligence, oversight, or laziness but rather to the fact that the government did not turn over the grand jury transcript, which contained the basis of the informant's knowledge, until one day before the filing, denial of defendant's motion to suppress filed out of time constituted a clear abuse of discretion. United States v. Chavez, 902 F.2d 259 (4th Cir. 1990).

Motion to dismiss for defect in indictment. — In order to prevail on a motion to dismiss subdivision (b) of this rule, the defendants must show a defect in the indictment. United States v. Computer Sciences Corp., 511 F. Supp. 1125 (E.D. Va. 1981), rev'd on other grounds, 689 F.2d 1181 (4th Cir. 1982), cert. denied, 459 U.S. 1105, 103 S. Ct. 729, 74 L. Ed. 2d 953 (1983), overruled on other grounds, Busby v. Crown Supply, Inc., 896 F.2d 833 (4th Cir. 1990).

An indictment that involves essential elements of facts and law which have been tried and decided in an earlier case should be dismissed. United States v. Computer Sciences Corp., 511 F. Supp. 1125 (E.D. Va. 1981), rev'd on other grounds, 689 F.2d 1181 (4th Cir. 1982), cert. denied, 459 U.S. 1105, 103 S. Ct. 729, 74 L. Ed. 2d 953 (1983), overruled on other grounds, Busby v. Crown Supply, Inc., 896 F.2d 833 (4th Cir. 1990).

On a motion to dismiss an indictment, based on a collateral estoppel argument, it is the burden of the moving party to demonstrate that the issue which they urge is foreclosed logically constituted the basis of the earlier jury verdict. United States v. Computer Sciences Corp., 511 F. Supp. 1125 (E.D. Va. 1981), rev'd on other grounds, 689 F.2d 1181 (4th Cir. 1982), cert. denied, 459 U.S. 1105, 103 S. Ct. 729, 74 L. Ed. 2d 953 (1983), overruled on other grounds, Busby v. Crown Supply, Inc., 896 F.2d 833 (4th Cir. 1990).

Notice not required to challenge radar. — Notice pursuant to this rule is not required from a defendant who wishes to challenge the accuracy of radar equipment in a speeding violation case. United States v. Wornom, 754 F. Supp. 517 (W.D. Va. 1991).

The complexity of the other evidence in the case should not have affected defense counsel's ability to challenge the voluntariness of statements by his clients. — See United States v. Badwan, 624 F.2d 1228 (4th Cir. 1980), cert. denied, 449 U.S. 1124, 101 S. Ct. 941, 67 L. Ed. 2d 110 (1981).

Applied in United States v. Semel, 347 F.2d 228 (4th Cir. 1965); United States v. Paolicelli, 505 F.2d 971 (4th Cir. 1974); United States v. Guyette, 382 F. Supp. 1266 (E.D. Va. 1974); United States v. Alexander, 789 F.2d 1046 (4th Cir. 1986); United States v. Jones, 916 F. Supp. 558 (E.D. Va. 1996).

Rule 12.1. Notice of an Alibi Defense.

(a) *Government's Request for Notice and Defendant's Response.* — (1) Government's Request. — An attorney for the government may request in writing that the defendant notify an attorney for the government of any intended alibi defense. The request must state the time, date, and place of the alleged offense.

(2) Defendant's Response. — Within 14 days after the request, or at some other time the court sets, the defendant must serve written notice on an attorney for the government of any intended alibi defense. The defendant's notice must state:

(A) each specific place where the defendant claims to have been at the time of the alleged offense; and

(B) the name, address, and telephone number of each alibi witness on whom the defendant intends to rely.

(b) *Disclosing Government Witnesses.* — (1) Disclosure. — (A) In General. If the defendant serves a Rule 12.1(a)(2) notice, an attorney for the government must disclose in writing to the defendant or the defendant's attorney:

(i) the name of each witness — and the address and telephone number of each witness other than a victim — that the government intends to rely on to establish that the defendant was present at the scene of the alleged offense; and

(ii) each government rebuttal witness to the defendant's alibi defense.

(B) Victim's Address and Telephone Number. If the government intends to rely on a victim's testimony to establish that the defendant was present at the scene of the alleged offense and the defendant establishes a need for the victim's address and telephone number, the court may:

(i) order the government to provide the information in writing to the defendant or the defendant's attorney; or

(ii) fashion a reasonable procedure that allows preparation of the defense and also protects the victim's interests.

(2) Time to Disclose. — Unless the court directs otherwise, an attorney for the government must give its Rule 12.1(b)(1) disclosure within 14 days after the defendant serves notice of an intended alibi defense under Rule 12.1(a)(2), but no later than 14 days before trial.

(c) *Continuing Duty to Disclose.* — (1) In General. Both an attorney for the government and the defendant must promptly disclose in writing to the other party the name of each additional witness — and the address and telephone number of each additional witness other than a victim — if:

(A) the disclosing party learns of the witness before or during trial; and

(B) the witness should have been disclosed under Rule 12.1(a) or (b) if the disclosing party had known of the witness earlier.

(2) Address and Telephone Number of an Additional Victim Witness. The address and telephone number of an additional victim witness must not be disclosed except as provided in Rule 12.1(b)(1)(B).

(d) *Exceptions.* — For good cause, the court may grant an exception to any requirement of Rule 12.1(a)-(c).

(e) *Failure to Comply.* — If a party fails to comply with this rule, the court may exclude the testimony of any undisclosed witness regarding the defendant's alibi. This rule does not limit the defendant's right to testify.

(f) *Inadmissibility of Withdrawn Intention.* — Evidence of an intention to rely on an alibi defense, later withdrawn, or of a statement made in connection with that intention, is not, in any civil or criminal proceeding, admissible against the person who gave notice of the intention. (Added by order adopted April 22, 1974, effective December 1, 1975, amended by order adopted July 31, 1975, effective December 1, 1975, by order adopted April 29, 1985, effective August 1, 1985, by order adopted March 9, 1987, effective August 1, 1987, by order adopted April 29, 2002, effective December 1, 2002, by order adopted April 23, 2008, effective December 1, 2008, and by order adopted March 26, 2009, effective December 1, 2009.)

CASE NOTES

Defendant need not have given notice that he would not take the stand, as he must of his intention to assert an alibi. United States v. Grooms, 2 F.3d 85 (4th Cir. 1993), cert. denied, 511 U.S. 1035, 114 S. Ct. 1550, 128 L. Ed. 2d 199 (1994).

Rule 12.2. Notice of an Insanity Defense; Mental Examination.

(a) *Notice of an Insanity Defense.* — A defendant who intends to assert a defense of insanity at the time of the alleged offense must so notify an attorney for the government in writing within the time provided for filing a pretrial motion, or at any later time the court sets, and file a copy of the notice with the clerk. A defendant who fails to do so cannot rely on an insanity defense. The court may, for good cause, allow the defendant to file the notice late, grant additional trial-preparation time, or make other appropriate orders.

(b) *Notice of Expert Evidence of a Mental Condition.* — If a defendant intends to introduce expert evidence relating to a mental disease or defect or any other mental condition of the defendant bearing on either (1) the issue of guilt or (2) the issue of punishment in a capital case, the defendant must — within the time provided for filing a pretrial motion or at any later time the court sets — notify an attorney for the government in writing of this intention and file a copy of the notice with the clerk. The court may, for good cause, allow the defendant to file the notice late, grant the parties additional trial-preparation time, or make other appropriate orders.

(c) *Mental Examination.* — (1) Authority to Order an Examination; Procedures.

(A) The court may order the defendant to submit to a competency examination under 18 U.S.C. § 4241.

(B) If the defendant provides notice under Rule 12.2(a), the court must, upon the government's motion, order the defendant to be examined under 18 U.S.C. § 4242. If the defendant provides notice under Rule 12.2(b) the court may, upon the government's motion, order the defendant to be examined under procedures ordered by the court.

(2) Disclosing Results and Reports of Capital Sentencing Examination. — The results and reports of any examination conducted solely under Rule 12.2 (c)(1) after notice under Rule 12.2(b)(2) must be sealed and must not be disclosed to any attorney for the government or the defendant unless the defendant is found guilty of one or more capital crimes and the defendant confirms an intent to offer during sentencing proceedings expert evidence on mental condition.

(3) Disclosing Results and Reports of the Defendant's Expert Examination. — After disclosure under Rule 12.2(c)(2) of the results and reports of the government's examination, the defendant must disclose to the government the results and reports of any examination on mental condition conducted by the defendant's expert about which the defendant intends to introduce expert evidence.

(4) Inadmissibility of a Defendant's Statements. — No statement made by a defendant in the course of any examination conducted under this rule (whether conducted with or without the defendant's consent), no testimony by the expert based on the statement, and no other fruits of the statement may be admitted into evidence against the defendant in any criminal proceeding except on an issue regarding mental condition on which the defendant:

(A) has introduced evidence of incompetency or evidence requiring notice under Rule 12.2(a) or (b)(1), or

(B) has introduced expert evidence in a capital sentencing proceeding requiring notice under Rule 12.2(b)(2).

(d) *Failure to Comply.* — (1) Failure to Give Notice or to Submit to Examination. The court may exclude any expert evidence from the defendant on the issue of the defendant's mental disease, mental defect, or any other mental condition bearing on the defendant's guilt or the issue of punishment in a capital case if the defendant fails to:

(A) give notice under Rule 12.2(b); or

(B) submit to an examination when ordered under Rule 12.2(c).

(2) Failure to Disclose. The court may exclude any expert evidence for which the defendant has failed to comply with the disclosure requirement of Rule 12.2(c)(3).

(e) *Inadmissibility of Withdrawn Intention.* — Evidence of an intention as to which notice was given under Rule 12.2(a) or (b), later withdrawn, is not, in any civil or criminal proceeding, admissible against the person who gave notice of the intention. (Added by order adopted April 22, 1974, effective December 1, 1975, amended by order adopted July 31, 1975, effective December 1, 1975, by order adopted April 28, 1983, effective August 1, 1983, by P.L. 98-473, Title II, § 404(a), approved October 12, 1984, by P.L. 98-596, § 11(a)(1), 11(a)(1), effective October 12, 1984, by P.L. 99-646, § 24, by order adopted April 29, 1985, effective August 1, 1985, by order effective November 10, 1986, by order adopted March 9, 1987, effective August 1, 1987, by order adopted April 29, 2002, effective December 1, 2002, and by order adopted April 25, 2005, effective December 1, 2005.)

Editor's note. — Public Law 98-473, Title II, § 404(b) and (d) amended this rule, effective October 12, 1984, but those amendments were repealed by P.L. 98-596, § 11(b), effective October 12, 1984.

Public Law 98-473, Title II, § 404(c), and P.L. 98-596, § 11(a)(1), both amended subdivision (c), effective October 12, 1984. The two amendments substituted identical language, but only the amendment by P.L. 98-596 has been implemented, since the amendment by P.L. 98-473 purported to delete language that was not in subdivision (c).

CASE NOTES

Defense of "stupidity" was "other condition" for purposes of subdivision (b) of this rule. United States v. Edwards, 90 F.R.D. 391 (E.D. Va. 1981).

Where defendant lacked sufficient intellectual capacity to understand the intricacies of federal income tax reporting requirements to enable him to knowingly and wilfully attempt to evade and defeat the payment of the lawful tax, such condition qualified under this rule. United States v. Edwards, 90 F.R.D. 391 (E.D. Va. 1981).

Sufficiency of notice under subdivision (b). — A motion to suppress statements made in an investigation does not constitute sufficient notice under subdivision (b) of this rule of a defense of mental deficiency. The rule contemplates express, forthright notice to the government of an intention to present expert testimony relating to a mental state or condition. United States v. Edwards, 90 F.R.D. 391 (E.D. Va. 1981).

Effect of failure to give notice under subdivision (b). — Subdivision (b) of this rule does not specify a remedy for its violation. It is within the discretion of the trial judge whether to exclude evidence covered by the rule that is introduced without the required notice. United States v. Edwards, 90 F.R.D. 391 (E.D. Va. 1981).

It is not an abuse of discretion for a trial judge to exclude expert testimony under subdivision (d) of this rule for lack of notice of a defense of mental disease, etc., to opposing counsel, even where a continuance is a viable alternative. United States v. Edwards, 90 F.R.D. 391 (E.D. Va. 1981).

Rule 12.3. Notice of a Public-Authority Defense.

(a) *Notice of the Defense and Disclosure of Witnesses.* — (1) Notice in General. — If a defendant intends to assert a defense of actual or believed exercise of public authority on behalf of a law enforcement agency or federal intelligence agency at the time of the alleged offense, the defendant must so notify an attorney for the government in writing and must file a copy of the notice with the clerk within the time provided for filing a pretrial motion, or at any later time the court sets. The notice filed with the clerk must be under seal if the notice identifies a federal intelligence agency as the source of public authority.

(2) Contents of Notice. — The notice must contain the following information:

(A) the law enforcement agency or federal intelligence agency involved;

(B) the agency member on whose behalf the defendant claims to have acted; and

(C) the time during which the defendant claims to have acted with public authority.

(3) Response to the Notice. — An attorney for the government must serve a written response on the defendant or the defendant's attorney within 14 days after receiving the defendant's notice, but no later than 21 days before trial. The response must admit or deny that the defendant exercised the public authority identified in the defendant's notice.

(4) Disclosing Witnesses. — (A) Government's Request. — An attorney for the government may request in writing that the defendant disclose the name, address, and telephone number of each witness the defendant intends to rely on to establish a public-authority defense. An attorney for the government may serve the request when the government serves its response to the defendant's notice under Rule 12.3(a)(3), or later, but must serve the request no later than 21 days before trial.

(B) Defendant's Response. — Within 14 days after receiving the government's request, the defendant must serve on an attorney for the government a written statement of the name, address, and telephone number of each witness.

(C) Government's Reply. — Within 14 days after receiving the defendant's statement, an attorney for the government must serve on the defendant or the defendant's attorney a written statement of the name of each witness — and the address and telephone number of each witness other than a victim — that the government intends to rely on to oppose the defendant's public-authority defense.

(D) Victim's Address and Telephone Number. — If the government intends to rely on a victim's testimony to oppose the defendant's publicauthority defense and the defendant establishes a need for the victim's address and telephone number, the court may:

(i) order the government to provide the information in writing to the defendant or the defendant's attorney; or

(ii) fashion a reasonable procedure that allows for preparing the defense and also protects the victim's interests.

(5) Additional Time. — The court may, for good cause, allow a party additional time to comply with this rule.

(b) *Continuing Duty to Disclose.* — (1) In General. Both an attorney for the government and the defendant must promptly disclose in writing to the other party the name of any additional witness — and the address, and telephone number of any additional witness other than a victim — if:

(A) the disclosing party learns of the witness before or during trial; and

(B) the witness should have been disclosed under Rule 12.3(a)(4) if the disclosing party had known of the witness earlier.

(2) Address and Telephone Number of an Additional Victim-Witness. The address and telephone number of an additional victimwitness must not be disclosed except as provided in Rule 12.3(a)(4)(D).

(c) *Failure to Comply.* — If a party fails to comply with this rule, the court may exclude the testimony of any undisclosed witness regarding the public-authority defense. This rule does not limit the defendant's right to testify.

(d) *Protective Procedures Unaffected.* — This rule does not limit the court's authority to issue appropriate protective orders or to order that any filings be under seal.

(e) *Inadmissibility of Withdrawn Intention.* — Evidence of an intention as to which notice was given under Rule 12.3(a), later withdrawn, is not, in any civil or criminal proceeding, admissible against the person who gave notice of the intention. (Adopted in P.L.100-690, signed by president on November 18, 1988, amended by order adopted April 29, 2002, effective December 1, 2002,by order adopted March 26, 2009, effective December 1, 2009, and by order adopted April 28, 2010, effective December 1, 2010.)

Rule 12.4. Disclosure Statement.

(a) *Who Must File.* — (1) Nongovernmental Corporate Party. — Any nongovernmental corporate party to a proceeding in a district court must file a statement that identifies any parent corporation and any publicly held corporation that owns 10% or more of its stock or states that there is no such corporation.

(2) Organizational Victim. — If an organization is a victim of the alleged criminal activity, the government must file a statement identifying the victim. If the organizational victim is a corporation, the statement must also disclose the information required by Rule 12.4(a)(1) to the extent it can be obtained through due diligence.

(b) *Time for Filing; Supplemental Filing.* — A party must:

(1) file the Rule 12.4(a) statement upon the defendant's initial appearance; and

(2) promptly file a supplemental statement upon any change in the information that the statement requires. (Added by order adopted April 29, 2002, effective December 1, 2002.)

Rule 13. Joint Trial of Separate Cases.

The court may order that separate cases be tried together as though brought in a single indictment or information if all offenses and all defendants could have been joined in a single indictment or information. (Amended by order adopted April 29, 2002, effective December 1, 2002.)

Rule 14. Relief from Prejudicial Joinder.

(a) *Relief.* — If the joinder of offenses or defendants in an indictment, an information, or a consolidation for trial appears to prejudice a defendant or the government, the court may order separate trials of counts, sever the defendants' trials, or provide any other relief that justice requires.

(b) *Defendant's Statements.* — Before ruling on a defendant's motion to sever, the court may order an attorney for the government to deliver to the court for in camera inspection any defendant's statement that the government intends to use as evidence. (Amended by order adopted February 28, 1966, effective July 1, 1966, and by order adopted April 29, 2002, effective December 1, 2002.)

CASE NOTES

Severance cures error, if any, in joinder of defendants. — Where defendant claims error in the joinder with him of others as aiders and abettors, the severance, by virtue of which he stood trial with his wife as his only co-defendant, is a sufficient answer to his claim of prejudice in this respect. Rakes v. United States, 169 F.2d 739 (4th Cir.), cert. denied, 335 U.S. 826, 69 S. Ct. 51, 93 L. Ed. 380 (1948).

Severance is within the discretion of the court. — Whether to grant a severance under Rule 14 of the Federal Rules of Criminal Procedure is a matter within the discretion of the district court, and the denial of such a motion will be overturned only in the case of a clear abuse of discretion. United States v. Cofield, 11 F.3d 413 (4th Cir. 1993), cert. denied, 510 U.S. 1140, 114 S. Ct. 1125, 127 L. Ed. 2d 433 (1994).

Decision to sever reviewed under "abuse of discretion" standard. — A trial court's decision not to sever is reviewed under the "abuse of discretion" standard. United States v. Larouche, 896 F.2d 815 (4th Cir.), cert. denied, 496 U.S. 927, 110 S. Ct. 2621, 110 L. Ed. 2d 642 (1990).

Discretion in denying severance held not abused. — See United States v. Fersner, 416 F.2d 403 (4th Cir. 1969), cert. denied, 397 U.S. 954, 90 S. Ct. 982, 25 L. Ed. 2d 137 (1970).

Prejudice from denial of severance not shown. — Where, on appeal, a defendant complains about the court's denial of a severance and the admission of testimony implicating a co-defendant, but the co-defendant did not confess, and he testified and was available for cross-examination by the defendant's counsel, the defendant has failed to demonstrate that he was prejudiced by the joinder. United States v. Fersner, 416 F.2d 403 (4th Cir. 1969), cert. denied, 397 U.S. 954, 90 S. Ct. 982, 25 L. Ed. 2d 137 (1970).

Where the trial court carefully labeled the evidence as being admissible only against the codefendants of the defendant and repeatedly admonished the jury to disregard the evidence as implicating him in any way, not only was the evidence confined solely to implicating the codefendants, but clearly its use in the joint trial did not raise even that degree of prejudice required to sever the defendant's trial under this rule. United States v. Peterson, 524 F.2d 167 (4th Cir. 1975), cert. denied, 423 U.S. 1088, 96 S. Ct. 881, 47 L. Ed. 2d 99, 424 U.S. 925, 96 S. Ct. 1136, 47 L. Ed. 2d 334 (1976).

Severance of counts from indictment. — Where defendant was charged in a six-count indictment, count one charged him with solicitation to commit murder, count two charged him with solicitation to commit abduction, count three charged wire fraud, count five sought a forfeiture of currency derived from that alleged fraud, count four charged him with structuring certain financial transactions for the purpose of evading the reporting requirements, and count six sought forfeiture of the proceeds of that alleged structuring, and to prove fraud claim, the government must establish that items submitted on property loss report were either nonexistent or that their value was overstated, and that evidence will have little in common with the evidence proving that the defendant solicited someone to commit abduction and murder, therefore, much of the evidence relating to counts three through six would be substantially prejudicial to the defendant and of little probative value as to the two solicitation counts, thus, counts three through six will be severed from the indictment. United States v. Stone, 826 F. Supp. 173 (W.D. Va. 1993).

Compelling reasons may relieve joinder. — Absent compelling reasons, persons indicted together should be tried together. United States v. Cofield, 11 F.3d 413 (4th Cir. 1993), cert. denied, 510 U.S. 1140, 114 S. Ct. 1125, 127 L. Ed. 2d 433 (1994).

In seeking a reversal of the trial court's denial of the defendant's motion to sever offenses in the indictment under Rule 14, Fed. R. Crim. P., the defendant must overcome the burden imposed by a stringent standard of review. In ruling on a motion for severance, the trial court is vested with discretion; it must carefully weigh the possible prejudice to the accused against the often equally compelling interests of the judicial process, which include the avoidance of needlessly duplicative trials involving substantially similar proof. The exercise of this discretion will be overturned only for clear abuse affecting substantial rights of the accused. United States v. Jamar, 561 F.2d 1103 (4th Cir. 1977).

Applied in United States v. Clark, 928 F.2d 639 (4th Cir. 1991); United States v. Gunn, 968 F. Supp. 1089 (E.D. Va. 1997).

Rule 15. Depositions.

(a) *When Taken.* — (1) In General. — A party may move that a prospective witness be deposed in order to preserve testimony for trial. The court may grant the motion because of exceptional circumstances and in the interest of justice. If the court orders the deposition to be taken, it may also require the deponent to produce at the deposition any designated material that is not privileged, including any book, paper, document, record, recording, or data.

(2) Detained Material Witness. — A witness who is detained under 18 U.S.C. § 3144 may request to be deposed by filing a written motion and giving notice to the parties. The court may then order that the deposition be taken and may discharge the witness after the witness has signed under oath the deposition transcript.

(b) *Notice.* — (1) In General. — A party seeking to take a deposition must give every other party reasonable written notice of the deposition's date and location. The notice must state the name and address of each deponent. If requested by a party receiving the notice, the court may, for good cause, change the deposition's date or location.

(2) To the Custodial Officer. — A party seeking to take the deposition must also notify the officer who has custody of the defendant of the scheduled date and location.

(c) **(See Editor's note)** *Defendant's Presence.* — (1) Defendant in Custody. — Except as authorized by Rule 15(c)(3), the officer who has custody of the defendant must produce the defendant at the deposition and keep the defendant in the witness's presence during the examination, unless the defendant:

(A) waives in writing the right to be present; or

(B) persists in disruptive conduct justifying exclusion after being warned by the court that disruptive conduct will result in the defendant's exclusion.

(2) Defendant Not in Custody. — Except as authorized by Rule 15(c)(3), a defendant who is not in custody has the right upon request to be present at the deposition, subject to any conditions imposed by the court. If the government tenders the defendant's expenses as provided in Rule 15(d) but the defendant still fails to appear, the defendant — absent good cause — waives both the right to appear and any objection to the taking and use of the deposition based on that right.

(3) Taking Depositions Outside the United States Without the Defendant's Presence. — The deposition of a witness who is outside the United States may be taken without the defendant's presence if the court makes casespecific findings of all the following:

(A) the witness's testimony could provide substantial proof of a material fact in a felony prosecution;

(B) there is a substantial likelihood that the witness's attendance at trial cannot be obtained;

(C) the witness's presence for a deposition in the United States cannot be obtained;

(D) the defendant cannot be present because:

(i) the country where the witness is located will not permit the defendant to attend the deposition;

(ii) for an in-custody defendant, secure transportation and continuing custody cannot be assured at the witness's location; or

(iii) for an out-of-custody defendant, no reasonable conditions will assure an appearance at the deposition or at trial or sentencing; and

(E) the defendant can meaningfully participate in the deposition through reasonable means.

(d) *Expenses.* — If the deposition was requested by the government, the court may — or if the defendant is unable to bear the deposition expenses, the court must — order the government to pay:

(1) any reasonable travel and subsistence expenses of the defendant and the defendant's attorney to attend the deposition; and

(2) the costs of the deposition transcript.

(e) *Manner of Taking.* — Unless these rules or a court order provides otherwise, a deposition must be taken and filed in the same manner as a deposition in a civil action, except that:

(1) A defendant may not be deposed without that defendant's con-sent.

(2) The scope and manner of the deposition examination and cross-examination must be the same as would be allowed during trial.

(3) The government must provide to the defendant or the defendant's attorney, for use at the deposition, any statement of the deponent in the government's possession to which the defendant would be entitled at trial.

(f) **(See Editor's note)** *Admissibility and Use as Evidence.* — An order authorizing a deposition to be taken under this rule does not determine its admissibility. A party may use all or part of a deposition as provided by the Federal Rules of Evidence.

(g) *Objections.* — A party objecting to deposition testimony or evidence must state the grounds for the objection during the deposition.

(h) *Depositions by Agreement Permitted.* — The parties may by agreement take and use a deposition with the court's consent. (Amended by order adopted April 22, 1974, effective December 1, 1975, by order adopted July 31, 1975, effective December 1, 1975, by P.L. 98-473, Title II, § 209(b), approved October 12, 1984, by order adopted March 9, 1987, effective August 1, 1987, by order adopted April 29, 2002, effective December 1, 2002, and by order adopted April 24, 2012, effective December 1, 2012.)

Editor's note. — The Chief Justice signed the letters and orders on April 23, 2012, and the amendments were transmitted to Congress on April 24, 2012. The amendments will take effect on December 1, 2012, unless Congress takes action to reject, modify, or defer them.

Rule 16. Discovery and Inspection.

(a) *Government's Disclosure.* — (1) Information Subject to Disclosure. — (A) Defendant's Oral Statement. — Upon a defendant's request, the government must disclose to the defendant the substance of any relevant oral statement made by the defendant, before or after arrest, in response to interrogation by a person the defendant knew was a government agent if the government intends to use the statement at trial.

(B) Defendant's Written or Recorded Statement. — Upon a defendant's request, the government must disclose to the defendant, and make available for inspection, copying, or photographing, all of the following:

(i) any relevant written or recorded statement by the defendant if:

• the statement is within the government's possession, custody, or control; and

• the attorney for the government knows — or through due diligence could know — that the statement exists;

(ii) the portion of any written record containing the substance of any relevant oral statement made before or after arrest if the defendant made the statement in response to interrogation by a person the defendant knew was a government agent; and

(iii) the defendant's recorded testimony before a grand jury relating to the charged offense.

(C) Organizational Defendant. — Upon a defendant's request, if the defendant is an organization, the government must disclose to the defendant any statement described in Rule 16(a)(1)(A) and (B) if the government contends that the person making the statement:

(i) was legally able to bind the defendant regarding the subject of the statement because of that person's position as the defendant's director, officer, employee, or agent; or

(ii) was personally involved in the alleged conduct constituting the offense and was legally able to bind the defendant regarding that conduct because of that person's position as the defendant's director, officer, employee, or agent.

(D) Defendant's Prior Record. — Upon a defendant's request, the government must furnish the defendant with a copy of the defendant's prior criminal record that is within the government's possession, custody, or control if the attorney for the government knows — or through due diligence could know — that the record exists.

(E) Documents and Objects. — Upon a defendant's request, the government must permit the defendant to inspect and to copy or photograph books, papers, documents, data, photographs, tangible objects, buildings or places, or copies or portions of any of these items, if the item is within the government's possession, custody, or control and:

(i) the item is material to preparing the defense;

(ii) the government intends to use the item in its case-in-chief at trial; or

(iii) the item was obtained from or belongs to the defendant.

(F) Reports of Examinations and Tests. — Upon a defendant's request, the government must permit a defendant to inspect and to copy or photograph the results or reports of any physical or mental examination and of any scientific test or experiment if:

(i) the item is within the government's possession, custody, or control;

(ii) the attorney for the government knows — or through due diligence could know — that the item exists; and

(iii) the item is material to preparing the defense or the government intends to use the item in its case-in-chief at trial.

(G) Expert Witnesses. — At the defendant's request, the government must give to the defendant a written summary of any testimony that the government intends to use under Rules 702, 703, or 705 of the Federal Rules of Evidence during its case-in-chief at trial. If the government requests discovery under subdivision (b)(1)(C)(ii) and the defendant complies, the government must, at the defendant's request, give to the defendant a written summary of testimony that the government intends to use under Rules 702, 703, or 705 of the Federal Rules of Evidence as evidence at trial on the issue of the defendant's mental condition. The summary provided under this subparagraph must describe the witness's opinions, the bases and reasons for those opinions, and the witness's qualifications.

(2) Information Not Subject to Disclosure. — Except as permitted by Rule 16(a)(1)(A)-(D), (F), and (G), this rule does not authorize the discovery or inspection of reports, memoranda, or other internal government documents made by an attorney for the government or other government agent in connection with investigating or prosecuting the case. Nor does this rule authorize the discovery or inspection of statements made by prospective government witnesses except as provided in 18 U.S.C. § 3500.

(3) Grand Jury Transcripts. — This rule does not apply to the discovery or inspection of a grand jury's recorded proceedings, except as provided in Rules 6, 12(h), 16(a)(1), and 26.2.

(b) *Defendant's Disclosure.* — (1) Information Subject to Disclosure. — (A) Documents and Objects. — If a defendant requests disclosure under Rule 16(a)(1)(E) and the government complies, then the defendant must permit the government, upon request, to inspect and to copy or photograph books, papers, documents, data, photographs, tangible objects, buildings or places, or copies or portions of any of these items if:

(i) the item is within the defendant's possession, custody, or control; and

(ii) the defendant intends to use the item in the defendant's case-in-chief at trial.

(B) Reports of Examinations and Tests. — If a defendant requests disclosure under Rule 16(a)(1)(F) and the government complies, the defendant must permit the government, upon request, to inspect and to copy or photograph the results or reports of any physical or mental examination and of any scientific test or experiment if:

(i) the item is within the defendant's possession, custody, or control; and

(ii) the defendant intends to use the item in the defendant's case-in-chief at trial, or intends to call the witness who prepared the report and the report relates to the witness's testimony.

(C) Expert Witnesses. — The defendant must, at the government's request, give to the government a written summary of any testimony that the defendant intends to use under Rules 702, 703, or 705 of the Federal Rules of Evidence as evidence at trial, if —

(i) the defendant requests disclosure under subdivision (a)(1))G) and the government complies; or

(ii) the defendant has given notice under Rule 12.2(b) of an intent to present expert testimony on the defendant's mental condition.

This summary must describe the witness's opinions, the bases and reasons for those opinions, and the witness's qualifications.

(2) Information Not Subject to Disclosure. — Except for scientific or medical reports, Rule 16(b)(1) does not authorize discovery or inspection of:

(A) reports, memoranda, or other documents made by the defendant, or the defendant's attorney or agent, during the case's investigation or defense; or

(B) a statement made to the defendant, or the defendant's attorney or agent, by:

(i) the defendant;

(ii) a government or defense witness; or

(iii) a prospective government or defense witness.

(c) *Continuing Duty to Disclose.* — A party who discovers additional evidence or material before or during trial must promptly disclose its existence to the other party or the court if:

(1) the evidence or material is subject to discovery or inspection under this rule; and

(2) the other party previously requested, or the court ordered, its production.

(d) *Regulating Discovery.* — (1) Protective and Modifying Orders. — At any time the court may, for good cause, deny, restrict, or defer discovery or inspection, or grant other appropriate relief. The court may permit a party to show good cause by a written statement that the court will inspect ex parte. If relief is granted, the court must preserve the entire text of the party's statement under seal.

(2) Failure to Comply. — If a party fails to comply with this rule, the court may:

(A) order that party to permit the discovery or inspection; specify its time, place, and manner; and prescribe other just terms and conditions;

(B) grant a continuance;

(C) prohibit that party from introducing the undisclosed evidence; or

(D) enter any other order that is just under the circumstances. (Amended by order adopted February 28, 1966, effective July 1, 1966, by order adopted April 22, 1974, effective December 1, 1975, by order adopted July 31, 1975, effective December 1, 1975, by order adopted December 12, 1975, by order adopted April 28, 1983, effective August 1, 1983, by order adopted March 9, 1987, effective August 1, 1987, by order adopted April 30, 1991, effective December 1, 1991, by order adopted April 22, 1993, effective December 1, 1993, by order adopted April 29, 1994, effective December 1, 1994, by order adopted April 11, 1997, effective December 1, 1997, by order adopted April 29, 2002, effective December 1, 2002, by order adopted November 2, 2002, effective December 1, 2002, and by order adopted April 16, 2013, effective December 1, 2013.)

CASE NOTES

Jencks Act request inappropriate in pretrial motion for discovery. — Although the defendant's counsel made a broad pretrial discovery motion arguably encompassing Jencks Act material, a Jencks Act request is wholly inappropriate in a pretrial motion for discovery, and the defense counsel, in order to invoke the benefits of the act (18 U.S.C. § 3500), is obligated at the very least to alert the trial judge during the course of the trial to his request by demanding the production and inspection of the material when its existence becomes known and not simply by means of some multipronged pretrial motion. United States v. Peterson, 524 F.2d 167 (4th Cir. 1975), cert. denied, 423 U.S. 1088, 96 S. Ct. 881, 47 L. Ed. 2d 99, 424 U.S. 925, 96 S. Ct. 1136, 47 L. Ed. 2d 334 (1976).

Where an agent intended to incorporate the substance of a memorandum into a written report of the investigation which had not been compiled at the time of the defendant's bank robbery trial and the report, apparently prepared after an interview with a prosecution witness, contained the agent's version of the interview, this memorandum, if producible at all, is to be governed by the provisions of the Jencks Act (18 U.S.C. § 3500), and not by a discovery motion made pursuant to this rule. However, nothing in the act compels the production of FBI memoranda prepared by an agent as a result of and after the interview of a witness. United States v. Peterson, 524 F.2d 167 (4th Cir. 1975), cert. denied, 423 U.S. 1088, 96 S. Ct. 881, 47 L. Ed. 2d 99, 424 U.S. 925, 96 S. Ct. 1136, 47 L. Ed. 2d 334 (1976).

Failure to specifically request production. — Defendant's Rule 16 claim that the government should have produced the computer printouts and programs used to complete "peer-group" analyses prepared and presented at trial by Medicaid and Blue Cross investigators was waived by his failure to specifically request production of the computer materials before trial. United States v. Alexander, 789 F.2d 1046 (4th Cir. 1986).

Failure to provide grand jury witness' testimony did not deny due process. — The government's failure to provide the defendant with the transcript of a potential government witness' grand jury testimony and government interview notes was not a denial of due process. The defendant's request for exculpatory evidence set forth a 15-page, single-spaced pleading entitled, "General Motion for Discovery and Inspection under Rule 16 and Motion for Exculpatory Evidence and Memorandum in Support Thereof," and not mentioning the witness by name, was not specific enough to put the government on notice of exactly what the defense desired. United States v. Breit, 767 F.2d 1084 (4th Cir. 1985).

For oral statement to be within purview of subdivision (a)(1)(A), it must be made in response to interrogation. United States v. Cooper, 800 F.2d 412 (4th Cir. 1986).

Denial of discovery motion was not abuse of discretion. — In prosecution for conversion and unauthorized conveyance of governmental information and mail fraud, where government adequately provided the material required by this rule and where items court did not require to be furnished were immaterial to the issues in the case and not subject to discovery under this rule, court's denial of discovery motion was not abuse of discretion. United States v. Fowler, 932 F.2d 306 (4th Cir. 1991).

Applied in United States v. Jordan, 466 F.2d 99 (4th Cir. 1972); United States v. Schembari, 484 F.2d 931 (4th Cir. 1973); Bast v. United States, 542 F.2d 893 (4th Cir. 1976).

Rule 17. Subpoena.

(a) *Content.* — A subpoena must state the court's name and the title of the proceeding, include the seal of the court, and command the witness to attend and testify at the time and place the subpoena specifies. The clerk must issue a blank subpoena — signed and sealed — to the party requesting it, and that party must fill in the blanks before the subpoena is served.

(b) *Defendant Unable to Pay.* — Upon a defendant's ex parte application, the court must order that a subpoena be issued for a named witness if the defendant shows an inability to pay the witness's fees and the necessity of the witness's presence for an adequate defense. If the court orders a subpoena to be issued, the process costs and witness fees will be paid in the same manner as those paid for witnesses the government subpoenas.

(c) *Producing Documents and Objects.* — (1) In General. — A subpoena may order the witness to produce any books, papers, documents, data, or other objects the subpoena designates. The court may direct the witness to produce the designated items in court before trial or before they are to be offered in evidence. When the items arrive, the court may permit the parties and their attorneys to inspect all or part of them.

(2) Quashing or Modifying the Subpoena. — On motion made promptly, the court may quash or modify the subpoena if compliance would be unreasonable or oppressive.

(3) Subpoena for Personal or Confidential Information About a Victim. After a complaint, indictment, or information if filed, a subpoena requiring the production of personal or confidential information about a victim may be served on a third party only by court order. Before entering the order and unless there are exceptional circum-

stances, the court must require giving notice to the victim so that the victim can move to quash or modify the subpoena or otherwise object.

(d) *Service.* — A marshal, a deputy marshal, or any nonparty who is at least 18 years old may serve a subpoena. The server must deliver a copy of the subpoena to the witness and must tender to the witness one day's witness-attendance fee and the legal mileage allowance. The server need not tender the attendance fee or mileage allowance when the United States, a federal officer, or a federal agency has requested the subpoena.

(e) *Place of Service.* — (1) In the United States. — A subpoena requiring a witness to attend a hearing or trial may be served at any place within the United States.

(2) In a Foreign Country. — If the witness is in a foreign country, 28 U.S.C. § 1783 governs the subpoena's service.

(f) *Issuing a Deposition Subpoena.* — (1) Issuance. — A court order to take a deposition authorizes the clerk in the district where the deposition is to be taken to issue a subpoena for any witness named or described in the order.

(2) Place. — After considering the convenience of the witness and the parties, the court may order — and the subpoena may require — the witness to appear anywhere the court designates.

(g) *Contempt.* — The court (other than a magistrate judge) may hold in contempt a witness who, without adequate excuse, disobeys a subpoena issued by a federal court in that district. A magistrate judge may hold in contempt a witness who, without adequate excuse, disobeys a subpoena issued by that magistrate judge as provided in 28 U.S.C. § 636(e).

(h) *Information Not Subject to a Subpoena.* — No party may subpoena a statement of a witness or of a prospective witness under this rule. Rule 26.2 governs the production of the statement. (Amended by order adopted December 27, 1948, effective October 20, 1949, by order adopted February 28, 1966, effective July 1, 1966, by order adopted April 24, 1972, effective October 1, 1972, by order adopted April 22, 1974, effective December 1, 1975, by order adopted July 31, 1975, effective December 1, 1975, by order adopted April 30, 1979, effective December 1, 1980, by order adopted March 9, 1987, effective August 1, 1987, by order adopted April 22, 1993, effective December 1, 1993, by order adopted April 29, 2002, effective December 1, 2002, and by order adopted April 23, 2008, effective December 1, 2008.)

CASE NOTES

This rule is not a discovery device. United States v. Schembari, 484 F.2d 931 (4th Cir. 1973).

"John and Jane Doe" subpoenas duces tecum not authorized under subdivision (b). — Requests for "John and Jane Doe" subpoenas duces tecum cannot be squared with the language of subdivision (b) of this rule, which limits the discretion of the trial court to issue subpoenas "on ... named witness[es]." United States v. Schembari, 484 F.2d 931 (4th Cir. 1973).

Materials admissible as evidence are subject to subpoena under subdivision (c). — Under subdivision (c) of this rule, any documents or other materials, admissible as evidence, obtained by the government by solicitation or voluntarily from third persons are subject to subpoena. United States v. Brockington, 21 F.R.D. 104 (E.D. Va. 1957).

Discretion of court as to findings under subdivision (c). — A district court judge normally has considerable discretion in making findings under subdivision (c), at least outside the First Amendment context. It is equally obvious that such discretion must be exercised carefully. United States v. Doe 819, 829 F.2d 1291 (4th Cir. 1987), reh'g denied, 844 F.2d 202 (4th Cir. 1988), cert. denied, 496 U.S. 925, 110 S. Ct. 2618, 110 L. Ed. 2d 639 (1990).

Subpoenas duces tecum are not insulated from review merely because they are issued in connection with a sitting grand jury. They are issued pro forma with no prior court approval. As such they are instrumentalities of the United States Attorney's office although issued under the district court's name and for the grand jury. United States v. Doe 819, 829 F.2d 1291 (4th Cir. 1987), reh'g denied, 844 F.2d 202 (4th Cir. 1988), cert. denied, 496 U.S. 925, 110 S. Ct. 2618, 110 L. Ed. 2d 639 (1990).

Subpoena of material presumptively protected by First Amendment. — When the government seeks to subpoena material that is presumptively protected by the First Amendment, it should do so in the least intrusive manner possible, which means, at a minimum, by identifying the requested material in a way that allows the recipient of the subpoena to know immediately whether an item is to be produced or not. And in reviewing motions to quash such subpoenas duces tecum, district courts should balance the First and Fourth Amendment interests at stake against the marginal gain to the issue of the subpoena in describing the materials by means other than the title of the work. United States v. Doe 819, 829 F.2d 1291 (4th Cir. 1987), reh'g denied, 844 F.2d 202 (4th Cir. 1988), cert. denied, 496 U.S. 925, 110 S. Ct. 2618, 110 L. Ed. 2d 639 (1990).

A court, in deciding to enforce or to quash a subpoena duces tecum that broadly seeks material presumptively protected by the First Amendment, must balance these concerns: on the one hand, the interest of the public and the government in ferreting out crime, on the other, the interest of the subpoena's target in conducting a business or any other personal affairs. The critical inquiry, assuming that the hurdle of relevancy has been cleared, is whether there is too much indefiniteness or breadth in the things required to be produced by the subpoena. United States v. Doe 819, 829 F.2d 1291 (4th Cir. 1987), reh'g denied, 844 F.2d 202 (4th Cir. 1988), cert. denied, 496 U.S. 925, 110 S. Ct. 2618, 110 L. Ed. 2d 639 (1990).

Right of defendant to require production of government's file on case. — See United States v. Brockington, 21 F.R.D. 104 (E.D. Va. 1957).

Court did not abuse its discretion in denying application for subpoenas duces tecum. — In prosecution for conversion and unauthorized conveyance of governmental information and mail fraud, court did not abuse its discretion in denying application for subpoenas duces tecum under subdivision (c) since most of the information defendant sought to subpoena was introduced in testimony of defendant's co-conspirators; furthermore, defendant failed to show material he sought met requirements of relevancy, admissibility and specificity, and the application was little more than a duplication of his discovery motion. United States v. Fowler, 932 F.2d 306 (4th Cir. 1991).

Rule 17.1. Pretrial Conference.

On its own, or on a party's motion, the court may hold one or more pre-trial conferences to promote a fair and expeditious trial. When a conference ends, the court must prepare and file a memorandum of any matters agreed to during the conference. The government may not use any statement made during the conference by the defendant or the defendant's attorney unless it is in writing and is signed by the defendant and the defendant's attorney. (Added by order adopted February 28, 1966, effective July 1, 1966, and amended by order adopted March 9, 1987, effective August 1, 1987, and by order adopted April 29, 2002, effective December 1, 2002.)

V. VENUE.

Rule 18. Place of Prosecution and Trial.

Unless a statute or these rules permit otherwise, the government must prosecute an offense in a district where the offense was committed. The court must set the place of trial within the district with due regard for the convenience of the defendant, any victim, and the witnesses, and the prompt administration of justice. (Amended by order adopted February 28, 1966, effective July 1, 1966, by order adopted April 30, 1979, effective August 1, 1979, by order adopted April 29, 2002, effective December 1, 2002, and by order adopted April 23, 2008, effective December 1, 2008.)

Law Review. — For an article "For the Criminal Practitioner: A review of all 1995 criminal cases decided by the Fourth Circuit," see 53 Wash. & Lee L. Rev. 465 (1996).

CASE NOTES

Venue in a federal criminal case is an issue of constitutional dimension. — U.S. Const., Art. III guarantees a federal defendant a trial "in the State where the said Crimes shall have been committed" and U.S. Const., Amend. 6 provides him with a "jury of the State and district wherein the crime shall have been committed." These fundamental guarantees have been implemented by this rule. United States v. Billups, 692 F.2d 320 (4th Cir. 1982), cert. denied, 464 U.S. 820, 104 S. Ct. 84, 78 L. Ed. 2d 93 (1983).

Locus delicti is determined from nature and location of crime. — Where congress is not explicit, the locus delicti must be determined from the nature of the crime alleged and the location of the acts or acts constituting it. United States v. Cofield, 11 F.3d 413 (4th Cir. 1993), cert. denied, 510 U.S. 1140, 114 S. Ct. 1125, 127 L. Ed. 2d 433 (1994).

Entrapment rules have no applicability to venue. — There is no such thing as "manufactured venue" or "venue entrapment." While it is true that the government may not manipulate events to create federal jurisdiction over a case, this is not the same thing as choice of venue. While it is also true that there are limits on the government's ability to "entrap" persons into crimes, entrapment rules have no applicability to venue. United States v. Al-Talib, 55 F.3d 923 (4th Cir. 1995).

Plea of guilty instead of motion for transfer waives defect in venue. — Where a defendant, being tried in the eastern district of Virginia for unlawfully transporting fireworks, after having been furnished with a bill of particulars which named Stephens City, Virginia, as the terminal point of the shipment charged to be illegal, did not move under Rule 21(b) to transfer his case to the western district of Virginia, but instead entered a plea of guilty to the offense charged, under Rule 12(b) (2), his actions constituted a waiver of any defect in venue which existed. United States v. Semel, 347 F.2d 228 (4th Cir.), cert. denied, 382 U.S. 840, 86 S. Ct. 90, 15 L. Ed. 2d 82, reh'g denied, 382 U.S. 933, 86 S. Ct. 312, 15 L. Ed. 2d 346 (1965).

In a conspiracy case, a prosecution may be brought in any district in which any act in furtherance of the conspiracy was committed.

United States v. Al-Talib, 55 F.3d 923 (4th Cir. 1995).

Venue of prosecution for assaulting employee of District of Columbia institution. — A prosecution under a statute punishing an assault upon an employee of a correctional institution of the District of Columbia whether the institution is "located in the District of Columbia or elsewhere" was properly brought in the eastern district of Virginia where the crime was committed. United States v. Smith, 398 F.2d 595 (4th Cir. 1968). See United States v. Perez, 488 F.2d 1057 (4th Cir. 1974).

Requiring agreement to trial within eastern district of Virginia as condition for fixing location other than in Alexandria. — A defendant urged that it was error for the trial judge to require the defendants to agree on a trial location within the eastern district of Virginia as a condition for fixing the place of trial somewhere within the district other than Alexandria under this rule. But a motion for change of venue under Rule 21(a) had already been denied; the condition was merely an attempt by the trial court to accommodate the defendants in keeping with the rule's mandate that the place of trial is to be fixed within the district "with due regard to the convenience of the defendant and the witnesses." United States v. Wechsler, 392 F.2d 344 (4th Cir.), cert. denied, 392 U.S. 932, 88 S. Ct. 2283, 20 L. Ed. 2d 1389 (1968), reh'g denied, 408 F.2d 1184 (4th Cir.), cert. denied, 395 U.S. 978, 89 S. Ct. 2131, 32 L. Ed. 2d 766, reh'g denied, 396 U.S. 870, 90 S. Ct. 40, 24 L. Ed. 2d 126 (1969).

The prosecution of the offense of endeavoring to obstruct justice as outlined in the federal statute where the indictment charged that in the Middle District of North Carolina, the defendant corruptly endeavored to influence, intimidate and impede a witness in the discharge of her duty as a witness in a federal criminal case then pending in the United States District Court for the Western District of Virginia was in the Western District of Virginia because that was the district where the administration of justice was intended to be obstructed. United States v. Elliott, 446 F. Supp. 209 (W.D. Va. 1978). See 18 U.S.C. § 1503.

Applied in United States v. Newton, 68 F. Supp. 952 (W.D. Va. 1946); United States v. Lember, 319 F. Supp. 249 (E.D. Va. 1970).

Rule 19. [Reserved.]

Rule 20. Transfer for Plea and Sentence.

(a) *Consent to Transfer.* — A prosecution may be transferred from the district where the indictment or information is pending, or from which a warrant on a complaint has been issued, to the district where the defendant is arrested, held, or present if:

(1) the defendant states in writing a wish to plead guilty or nolo contendere and to waive trial in the district where the indictment, information, or complaint is pending, consents in writing to the court's disposing of the case in the transferee district, and files the statement in the transferee district; and

(2) the United States attorneys in both districts approve the transfer in writing.

(b) *Clerk's Duties.* — After receiving the defendant's statement and the required approvals, the clerk where the indictment, information, or complaint is pending must send the file, or a certified copy, to the clerk in the transferee district.

(c) *Effect of a Not Guilty Plea.* — If the defendant pleads not guilty after the case has been transferred under Rule 20(a), the clerk must return the papers to the court where the prosecution began, and that court must restore the proceeding to its docket. The defendant's statement that the defendant wished to plead guilty or nolo contendere is not, in any civil or criminal proceeding, admissible against the defendant.

(d) *Juveniles.* — (1) Consent to Transfer. — A juvenile, as defined in 18 U.S.C. § 5031, may be proceeded against as a juvenile delinquent in the district where the juvenile is arrested, held, or present if:

(A) the alleged offense that occurred in the other district is not punishable by death or life imprisonment;

(B) an attorney has advised the juvenile;

(C) the court has informed the juvenile of the juvenile's rights — including the right to be returned to the district where the offense allegedly occurred — and the consequences of waiving those rights;

(D) the juvenile, after receiving the court's information about rights, consents in writing to be proceeded against in the transferee district, and files the consent in the transferee district;

(E) the United States attorneys for both districts approve the transfer in writing; and

(F) the transferee court approves the transfer.

(2) Clerk's Duties. — After receiving the juvenile's written consent and the required approvals, the clerk where the indictment, information, or complaint is pending or where the alleged offense occurred must send the file, or a certified copy, to the clerk in the transferee district. (Amended by order adopted February 28, 1966, effective July

1, 1966, by order adopted April 22, 1974, effective December 1, 1975, by order adopted July 31, 1975, effective December 1, 1975, by order adopted April 28, 1982, effective August 1, 1982, by order adopted March 9, 1987, effective August 1, 1987, and by order adopted April 29, 2002, effective December 1, 2002.)

CASE NOTES

Applied in Rakes v. United States, 231 F. Supp. 812 (W.D. Va. 1964).

Rule 21. Transfer for Trial.

(a) *For Prejudice.* — Upon the defendant's motion, the court must transfer the proceeding against that defendant to another district if the court is satisfied that so great a prejudice against the defendant exists in the transferring district that the defendant cannot obtain a fair and impartial trial there.

(b) *For Convenience.* — Upon the defendant's motion, the court may transfer the proceeding, or one or more counts, against that defendant to another district for the convenience of the parties, any victim, and the witnesses, and in the interest of justice.

(c) *Proceedings on Transfer.* — When the court orders a transfer, the clerk must send to the transferee district the file, or a certified copy, and any bail taken. The prosecution will then continue in the transferee district.

(d) *Time to File a Motion to Transfer.* — A motion to transfer may be made at or before arraignment or at any other time the court or these rules prescribe. (Amended by order adopted February 28, 1966, effective July 1, 1966, by order adopted March 9, 1987, effective August 1, 1987, by order adopted April 29, 2002, effective December 1, 2002, and by order adopted April 28, 2010, effective December 1, 2010.)

CASE NOTES

Analysis factors in multiple transaction cases. — The following factors are appropriate in determining whether to transfer criminal actions involving multiple transactions in different districts; first, the court should consider the locus of criminal activity charged in the count the defendant seeks to transfer and the significance of any criminal acts committed in the various districts where venue exists. Where venue is proper as to certain counts, but not others, the court should consider the potential for unfairness to the defendant that might be cause by successive prosecutions of related criminal actions, as well as the potential for excessive delay and expense that might be created by failing to grant the motion to transfer. United States v. Donato, 866 F. Supp. 288 (W.D. Va. 1994).

Pleas of guilty instead of motion for transfer waives defect in venue. — Where a defendant, being tried in the eastern district of Virginia for unlawfully transporting fireworks, after having been furnished with a bill of particulars which named Stephens City, Virginia, as the terminal point of the shipments charged to be illegal, did not move under subdivision (b) to transfer his case to the western district of Virginia, but instead entered a plea of guilty to the offense charged, under Rule 12(b) (2), his actions constituted a waiver of any defect in venue which existed. United States v. Semel, 347 F.2d 228 (4th Cir.), cert. denied, 382 U.S. 840, 86 S. Ct. 90, 15 L. Ed. 2d 82, reh'g denied, 382 U.S. 933, 86 S. Ct. 312, 15 L. Ed. 2d 346 (1965).'.

Requiring agreement to trial within eastern district of Virginia as condition for fixing location other than in Alexandria. — A defendant urged that it was error for the trial judge to require the defendants to agree on a trial location within the eastern district of Virginia as a condition for fixing the place of trial somewhere within the district other than Alexandria under Rule 18. But a motion for change of venue under subdivision (a) of this rule had already been denied; the condition was merely an attempt by the trial court to accommodate the defendants in keeping with the rule's mandate that the place of trial is to be fixed within the district "with due regard to the convenience of the defendant and the witnesses." United States v. Wechsler, 392 F.2d 344 (4th Cir.), cert. denied, 392 U.S. 932, 88 S. Ct. 2283, 20 L. Ed. 2d 1389 (1968), reh'g denied, 408 F.2d 1184 (4th Cir.), cert. denied, 395 U.S. 978, 89 S. Ct. 2131, 32 L. Ed. 2d 766, reh'g denied, 396 U.S. 870, 90 S. Ct. 40, 24 L. Ed. 2d 126 (1969).

Publicity must have been recent, widespread and highly damaging to the defendants, in order to warrant a change of venue under this rule. Wansley v. Slayton, 487 F.2d 90 (4th Cir.), rev'g Wansley v. Miller, 353 F. Supp. 42 (E.D. Va. 1973), cert. denied, 416 U.S. 994, 94 S. Ct. 2408, 40 L. Ed. 2d 773 (1974).

Defendant has neither absolute statutory right nor constitutional right to change of venue. — See United States v. Snow, 537 F.2d 1166 (4th Cir. 1976).

Original venue properly laid. — Where the defendant in a federal prosecution was a Virginia resident, the crime charged allegedly occurred at his home in Virginia and he was brought before a federal magistrate in Virginia after his arrest, and in addition, there had been no showing that the requested transfer would have substantially served the convenience of the parties or the witnesses, it is clear that original venue was properly laid in the eastern district of Virginia. United States v. Snow, 537 F.2d 1166 (4th Cir. 1976).

Applied in Loomis v. Peyton, 323 F. Supp. 246 (W.D. Va. 1971); United States v. Escamilla, 467 F.2d 341 (4th Cir. 1972).

Rule 22. [Transferred.]

VI. TRIAL.

Rule 23. Jury or Nonjury Trial.

(a) *Jury Trial.* — If the defendant is entitled to a jury trial, the trial must be by jury unless:

(1) the defendant waives a jury trial in writing;

(2) the government consents; and

(3) the court approves.

(b) *Jury Size.* — (1) In General. — A jury consists of 12 persons unless this rule provides otherwise.

(2) Stipulation for a Smaller Jury. — At any time before the verdict, the parties may, with the court's approval, stipulate in writing that:

(A) the jury may consist of fewer than 12 persons; or

(B) a jury of fewer than 12 persons may return a verdict if the court finds it necessary to excuse a juror for good cause af-ter the trial begins.

(3) Court Order for a Jury of 11. — After the jury has retired to deliberate, the court may permit a jury of 11 persons to return a verdict, even without a stipulation by the parties, if the court finds good cause to excuse a juror.

(c) *Nonjury Trial.* — In a case tried without a jury, the court must find the defendant guilty or not guilty. If a party requests before the finding of guilty or not guilty, the court must state its specific findings of fact in open court or in a written decision or opinion. (Amended by order adopted February 28, 1966, effective July 1, 1966, by order adopted July 30, 1977, effective October 1, 1977, by order adopted April 28, 1983, effective August 1, 1983, and by order adopted April 29, 2002, effective December 1, 2002.)

Law Review. — For article, "Reconceptualizing Competence: An Appeal," see 66 Wash. & Lee L. Rev. 259 (2009).

CASE NOTES

Jury must number twelve unless parties stipulate smaller number in writing. — Subdivision (b) makes it unmistakably clear that a jury shall be of 12 except that the number may be less in the event the parties so stipulate in writing. United States v. Virginia Erection Corp., 335 F.2d 868 (4th Cir. 1964).

The rule's requirement of a written stipulation has been deemed procedural, and courts have found oral stipulations valid where the defendant personally gave knowing and intelligent consent in open court. United States v. Fisher, 912 F.2d 728 (4th Cir. 1990), cert. denied, 500 U.S. 919, 111 S. Ct. 2019, 114 L. Ed. 2d 106 (1991).

Oral consent given in chambers sufficient to waive right. — Defendant's oral consent given in chambers is sufficient under this rule to waive the right to a 12 member jury. United States v. Fisher, 912 F.2d 728 (4th Cir. 1990), cert. denied, 500 U.S. 919, 111 S. Ct. 2019, 114 L. Ed. 2d 106 (1991).

No rule makes provision for jury of more than twelve. — See United States v. Virginia Erection Corp., 335 F.2d 868 (4th Cir. 1964).

Judge under no duty to reconfirm waiver. — Under this rule, when no direct challenge to the prior approval nor request to withdraw the waiver is made, so that no duty to exercise discretion has been imposed on the judge by party action, any judge acting after the waiver must be entitled to presume its continued regularity. He is thus under no duty to reconfirm the validity of the waiver save possibly under circumstances actually known to him that make reconfirmation clearly necessary to correct or prevent manifest injustice. Wyatt v. United States, 591 F.2d 260 (4th Cir. 1979).

Rule 23(a) jury waivers given, as they frequently are, in advance of the trial date do not require that they be reconfirmed by interrogation undertaken sua sponte by the judge presiding at trial to ensure that the waiver earlier given and not sought to be withdrawn remained voluntarily and intelligently given in the face of any personal predilections or special knowledge of the trial judge that might conceivably have influenced the waiver decision had these been known to the defendant at waiver time. Wyatt v. United States, 591 F.2d 260 (4th Cir. 1979).

Presumption of regularity of jury waiver supported by related constitutional doctrine and necessity. — Both the general rule of presumed regularity of the advance jury waiver and its special application to circumstances personal to the bench trial judge are amply supported in related constitutional doctrine and by reason and practical necessity. So far as the general presumption is concerned, a comparable presumption, though not typically so described, exists in the closely related area of guilty pleas and their subsequent withdrawals. There, after a guilty plea has been entered in accordance with Rule 11, Fed. R. Crim. P., it may only be withdrawn in the discretion of the district court, and after the imposition of sentence, "only to correct manifest injustice." To employ a similar presumption in respect of jury waivers, where the defendant's interests surely cannot be thought to be more significant, seems clearly justified. Wyatt v. United States, 591 F.2d 260 (4th Cir. 1979).

Presumption not easily overcome. — In the post-waiver of a jury trial setting under this rule the judge confronts not an original proffer of waiver previously unexamined, but one already given and formally approved by a judge of co-equal authority. That prior approval is entitled to the general presumption of regularity that must attend all judicial acts, whether in the form of interlocutory orders or final judgments, until they are overturned by direct or collateral attack. This is a presumption not easily overcome even in the face of a direct challenge or request to withdraw the waiver, for in such cases the decision to permit withdrawal is committed to the discretion of the district judge to whom the request is made. Wyatt v. United States, 591 F.2d 260 (4th Cir. 1979).

Wisdom of some questioning by judge. — Subdivision (a) of this rule speaks only to approval by the judge considering the formal proffer of the written waiver, and does not in its terms require any interrogation by him as a condition to giving effective approval. However, the wisdom of some questioning by that judge to ensure that proffered waivers will in fact be voluntarily and intelligently given has been urged by the Fourth Circuit Court of Appeals. Wyatt v. United States, 591 F.2d 260 (4th Cir. 1979).

Court not required to make specific findings in absence of request. — Where the testimony of three witnesses was objected to by the defendant as not being connected to the defendant and was admitted by the court subject to objection, it being understood the court would not consider the evidence if not connected up, since no request was made for specific findings of fact by the court in accordance with this rule, the district court was not under obligation to make specific findings as to which evidence it considered connected up and which it did not. United States v. Bolles, 528 F.2d 1190 (4th Cir. 1975).

Mistrial not only remedy when juror biased. — Alternatives less drastic than a mistrial are available to the court. A biased juror can be dismissed and replaced with an alternate juror under Rule 24(c). Another alternative is for the parties to stipulate to a jury of less than 12 persons under subdivision (b) of this rule. United States v. Thompson, 744 F.2d 1065 (4th Cir. 1984).

Applied in United States v. Arnold, 358 F.2d 633 (4th Cir. 1966); United States v. Robinson, 495 F.2d 30 (4th Cir. 1974); Vines v. Muncy, 553 F.2d 342 (4th Cir. 1977).

Rule 24. Trial Jurors.

(a) *Examination.* — (1) In General. — The court may examine prospective jurors or may permit the attorneys for the parties to do so.

(2) Court Examination. — If the court examines the jurors, it must permit the attorneys for the parties to:

(A) ask further questions that the court considers proper; or

(B) submit further questions that the court may ask if it consid-ers them proper.

(b) *Peremptory Challenges.* — Each side is entitled to the number of peremptory challenges to prospective jurors specified below. The court may allow additional peremptory challenges to multiple defendants, and may allow the defendants to exercise those challenges separately or jointly.

(1) Capital Case. — Each side has 20 peremptory challenges when the government seeks the death penalty.

(2) Other Felony Case. — The government has 6 peremptory challenges and the defendant or defendants jointly have 10 peremptory challenges when the defendant is charged with a crime punishable by imprisonment of more than one year.

(3) Misdemeanor Case. — Each side has 3 peremptory challenges when the defendant is charged with a crime punishable by fine, imprisonment of one year or less, or both.

(c) *Alternate Jurors.* — (1) In General. — The court may impanel up to 6 alternate jurors to replace any jurors who are unable to perform or who are disqualified from performing their duties.

(2) Procedure. — (A) Alternate jurors must have the same qualifications and be selected and sworn in the same manner as any other juror.

(B) Alternate jurors replace jurors in the same sequence in which the alternates were selected. An alternate juror who replaces a juror has the same authority as the other jurors.

(3) Retaining Alternate Jurors. — The court may retain alternate jurors after the jury retires to deliberate. The court must ensure that a retained alternate does not discuss the case with anyone until that alternate replaces a juror or is discharged. If an alternate replaces a juror after deliberations have begun, the court must instruct the jury to begin its deliberations anew.

(4) Peremptory Challenges. — Each side is entitled to the number of additional peremptory challenges to prospective alternate jurors specified below. These additional challenges may be used only to remove alternate jurors.

(A) One or Two Alternates. One additional peremptory challenge is permitted when one or two alternates are impaneled.

(B) Three or Four Alternates. Two additional peremptory challenges are permitted when three or four alternates are impaneled.

(C) Five or Six Alternates. Three additional peremptory challenges are permitted when five or six alternates are impaneled. (Amended by order adopted February 28, 1966, effective July 1, 1966, by order adopted March 9, 1987, effective August 1, 1987, by order adopted April 26, 1999, effective December 1, 1999, and by order adopted April 29, 2002, effective December 1, 2002.)

CASE NOTES

Purpose of subdivision (c). — The obvious purpose of subdivision (c) is to make adequate advance provision for meeting a situation where a regular juror becomes incapacitated or disqualified and the defendant relies upon his constitutional right to a jury of 12. The delay and expense necessarily arising as consequences of a mistrial and starting afresh with a new jury are thus avoided. United States v. Virginia Erection Corp., 335 F.2d 868 (4th Cir. 1964).

No provision is made for replacing juror after jury retires. — Subdivision (c) patently makes no provision for the replacement of a juror who becomes disabled after the jury retires to deliberate. United States v. Virginia Erection Corp., 335 F.2d 868 (4th Cir. 1964).

And presence of alternate juror in jury room violates secrecy of jury's deliberations. — The presence of an alternate juror in the jury room violates the cardinal principle that the deliberations of the jury shall remain private and secret in every case. United States v. Virginia Erection Corp., 335 F.2d 868 (4th Cir. 1964).

Alternate juror is disqualified unless he replaces regular juror before jury retires. — Subdivision (c) is explicit in defining the function of an alternate juror and the time when his replacement of a disqualified regular juror begins, that is, prior to the time when the jury retires to consider its verdict. It further provides that an alternate juror who does not so replace a regular juror shall be discharged after the jury retires to consider its verdict. United States v. Virginia Erection Corp., 335 F.2d 868 (4th Cir. 1964).

Mistrial not only remedy when juror biased. — Alternatives less drastic than a mistrial are available to the court. A biased juror can be dismissed and replaced with an alternate juror under subdivision (c) of this rule. Another alternative is for the parties to stipulate to a jury of less than 12 persons under Rule 23(b). United States v. Thompson, 744 F.2d 1065 (4th Cir. 1984).

Questioning jurors as to racial prejudice. — Although it is clearly error to refuse a request to ask the jurors about racial prejudice the trial judge has broad discretion under subsection (a) of this rule as to the verbiage and extent of the inquiry. He need not ask every question on the subject which the ingenuity of counsel can devise. A general query whether any juror is unable to judge the case fairly because of race, creed or color of the defendant should suffice. United States v. Johnson, 527 F.2d 1104 (4th Cir. 1975).

Trial court did not err in not allowing defendant to backstrike potential juror. — Where district court followed its established local practice in using the jury box system and was under no obligation to inform defendant's counsel of the intricacies of that system before the jury was empaneled, particularly given that defendant's Florida counsel had associated local counsel, who presumably was familiar with the district's customs, did not err in refusing to allow him to "backstrike" potential juror after his attorney struck that juror. United States v. Williams, 986 F.2d 86 (4th Cir.), cert. denied, 509 U.S. 911, 113 S. Ct. 3013, 125 L. Ed. 2d 703 (1993).

Applied in United States v. Poitras, 339 F.2d 428 (4th Cir. 1964); United States v. Potts, 420 F.2d 964 (4th Cir. 1970); United States v. Watson, 496 F.2d 1125 (4th Cir. 1973); Childress v. Commonwealth, No. 1890-98-4 (Ct. of Appeals Feb. 15, 2000).

Rule 25. Judge's Disability.

(a) *During Trial.* — Any judge regularly sitting in or assigned to the court may complete a jury trial if:

(1) the judge before whom the trial began cannot proceed because of death, sickness, or other disability; and

(2) the judge completing the trial certifies familiarity with the trial record.

(b) *After a Verdict or Finding of Guilt.* — (1) In General. — After a verdict or finding of guilty, any judge regularly sitting in or assigned to a court may complete the court's duties if the judge who presided at trial cannot perform those duties because of absence, death, sickness, or other disability.

(2) Granting a New Trial. — The successor judge may grant a new trial if satisfied that:

(A) a judge other than the one who presided at the trial cannot perform the post-trial duties; or

(B) a new trial is necessary for some other reason. (Amended by order adopted February 28, 1966, effective July 1, 1966, by order adopted March 9, 1987, effective August 1, 1987, and by order adopted April 29, 2002, effective December 1, 2002.)

CASE NOTES

Subdivision (b) of this rule permits sentencing by a judge who did not try the case. United States v. Bowser, 497 F.2d 1017 (4th Cir.), cert. denied, 419 U.S. 857, 95 S. Ct. 105, 42 L. Ed. 2d 91 (1974), 423 U.S. 997, 96 S. Ct. 427, 46 L. Ed. 2d 372 (1975).

Where the sentencing judge is not the trial judge and has no special knowledge of the case, and where such a judge imposes the maximum sentence despite no aggravating circumstances, the question arises whether there has been an actual exercise of discretion. Under such circumstances a statement of reasons for the sentencing decision would seem to be highly appropriate. United States v. Bowser, 497 F.2d 1017 (4th Cir.), cert. denied, 419 U.S. 857, 95 S. Ct. 105, 42 L. Ed. 2d 91 (1974), 423 U.S. 997, 96 S. Ct. 427, 46 L. Ed. 2d 372 (1975).

However, the better practice is for the judge who presided at trial to impose sentence. United States v. Bowser, 497 F.2d 1017 (4th Cir.), cert. denied, 419 U.S. 857, 95 S. Ct. 105, 42 L. Ed. 2d 91 (1974), 423 U.S. 997, 96 S. Ct. 427, 46 L. Ed. 2d 372 (1975).

Rule 26. Taking Testimony.

In every trial the testimony of witnesses must be taken in open court, unless otherwise provided by a statute or by rules adopted under 28 U.S.C. §§ 2072-2077. (Amended by order adopted November 20, 1972, effective July 1, 1975, and by order adopted April 29, 2002, effective December 1, 2002.)

Rule 26.1. Foreign Law Determination.

A party intending to raise an issue of foreign law must provide the court and all parties with reasonable written notice. Issues of foreign law are questions of law, but in deciding such issues a court may consider any relevant material or source — including testimony — without regard to the Federal Rules of Evidence. (Added by order adopted February 28, 1966, effective July 1, 1966, amended by order adopted November 20, 1972, effective July 1, 1975, and by order adopted April 29, 2002, effective December 1, 2002.)

Rule 26.2. Producting a Witness's Statement.

(a) *Motion to Produce.* — After a witness other than the defendant has testified on direct examination, the court, on motion of a party who did not call the witness, must order an attorney for the government or the defendant and the defendant's attorney to produce, for the examination and use of the moving party, any statement of the witness that is in their possession and that relates to the subject matter of the witness's testimony.

(b) *Producting the Entire Statement.* — If the entire statement relates to the subject matter of the witness's testimony, the court must order that the statement be delivered to the moving party.

(c) *Producting a Redacted Statement.* — If the party who called the witness claims that the statement contains information that is privileged or does not relate to the subject matter of the witness's testimony, the court must inspect the statement in camera. After excising any privileged or unrelated portions, the court must order delivery of the redacted statement to the moving party. If the defendant objects to an excision, the court must preserve the entire statement with the excised portion indicated, under seal, as part of the record.

(d) *Recess to Examine a Statement.* — The court may recess the proceedings to allow time for a party to examine the statement and prepare for its use.

(e) *Sanction for Failure to Produce or Deliver a Statement.* — If the party who called the witness disobeys an order to produce or deliver a statement, the court must strike the witness's testimony from the record. If an attorney for the government disobeys the order, the court must declare a mistrial if justice so requires.

(f) *"Statement" Defined.* — As used in this rule, a witness's "statement" means:

(1) a written statement that the witness makes and signs, or otherwise adopts or approves;

(2) a substantially verbatim, contemporaneously recorded recital of the witness's oral statement that is contained in any recording or any transcription of a recording; or

(3) the witness's statement to a grand jury, however taken or recorded, or a transcription of such a statement.

(g) *Scope.* — This rule applies at trial, at a suppression hearing under Rule 12, and to the extent specified in the following rules:

(1) Rule 5.1(h) (preliminary hearing);

(2) Rule 32(i)(2) (sentencing);

(3) Rule 32.1(e) (hearing to revoke or modify probation or supervised release);

(4) Rule 46(j) (detention hearing); and

(5) Rule 8 of the Rules Governing Proceedings under 28 U.S.C. § 2255. (Amended by order adopted April 30, 1979, effective December 1, 1980, by order adopted March 9, 1987, effective August 1, 1987, by order adopted April 22, 1993, effective December 1, 1993, by order adopted April 24, 1998, effective December 1, 1998, and by order adopted April 29, 2002, effective December 1, 2002.)

CASE NOTES

Exculpatory portions of testimony must be disclosed upon demand. — Any exculpatory portions of grand jury testimony of government witnesses that could potentially require investigation by the defense must be disclosed promptly upon demand. United States v. Shifflett, 798 F. Supp. 354 (W.D. Va. 1992), aff'd in part and rev'd in part on other grounds, 50 F.3d 9 (4th Cir. 1995), cert. denied, 516 U.S. 821, 116 S. Ct. 82, 133 L. Ed. 40 (1995).

Applied in United States v. Breit, 767 F.2d 1084 (4th Cir. 1985).

Rule 26.3. Mistrial.

Before ordering a mistrial, the court must give each defendant and the government an opportunity to comment on the propriety of the order, to state whether that party consents or objects, and to suggest alternatives. (Added by order adopted April 22, 1993, effective December 1, 1993, amended by order adopted April 29, 2002, effective December 1, 2002.)

Rule 27. Proving an Official Record.

A party may prove an official record, an entry in such a record, or the lack of a record or entry in the same manner as in a civil action. (Amended by order adopted April 29, 2002, effective December 1, 2002.)

Rule 28. Interpreters.

The court may select, appoint, and set the reasonable compensation for an interpreter. The compensation must be paid from funds provided by law or by the government, as the court may direct. (Amended by order adopted February 28, 1966, effective July 1, 1966, by order adopted November 20, 1972, effective July 1, 1975, and by order adopted April 29, 2002, effective December 1, 2002.)

Rule 29. Motion for a Judgment of Acquittal.

(a) *Before Submission to the Jury.* — After the government closes its evidence or after the close of all the evidence, the court on the defendant's motion must enter a judgment of acquittal of any offense for which the evidence is insufficient to sustain a conviction. The court may on its own consider whether the evidence is insufficient to sustain a conviction. If the court denies a motion for a judgment of acquittal at the close of the government's evidence, the defendant may offer evidence without having reserved the right to do so.

(b) *Reserving Decision.* — The court may reserve decision on the motion, proceed with the trial (where the motion is made before the close of all the evidence), submit the case to the jury, and decide the motion either before the jury returns a verdict or after it returns a verdict of guilty or is discharged without having returned a verdict. If the court reserves decision, it must decide the motion on the basis of the evidence at the time the ruling was reserved.

(c) *After Jury Verdict or Discharge.* — (1) Time for a Motion. — A defendant may move for a judgment of acquittal, or renew such a motion, within 14 days after a guilty verdict or after the court discharges the jury, whichever is later.

(2) Ruling on the Motion. — If the jury has returned a guilty verdict, the court may set aside the verdict and enter an acquittal. If the jury has failed to return a verdict, the court may enter a judgment of acquittal.

(3) No Prior Motion Required. — A defendant is not required to move for a judgment of acquittal before the court submits the case to the jury as a prerequisite for making such a motion after jury discharge.

(d) *Conditional Ruling on a Motion for a New Trial.* — (1) Motion for a New Trial. — If the court enters a judgment of acquittal after a guilty verdict, the court must also conditionally determine whether any motion for a new trial should be granted if the judgment of acquittal is later vacated or reversed. The court must specify the reasons for that determination.

(2) Finality. — The court's order conditionally granting a motion for a new trial does not affect the finality of the judgment of acquittal.

(3) Appeal. — (A) Grant of a Motion for a New Trial. — If the court conditionally grants a motion for a new trial and an appellate court later reverses the judgment of acquittal, the trial court must proceed with the new trial unless the appellate court orders otherwise.

(B) Denial of a Motion for a New Trial. — If the court conditionally denies a motion for a new trial, an appellee may assert that the denial was erroneous. If the appellate court later reverses the judgment of acquittal, the trial court must proceed as the appellate court directs. (Amended by order adopted February 28, 1966, effective July 1, 1966, by P.L. 99-646, § 54, adopted November 10, 1986, effective December 10, 1986, by order adopted April 29, 1994, effective December 1, 1994, by order adopted April 29, 2002, effective December 1, 2002, by order adopted April 25, 2005, effective December 1, 2005, and by order adopted March 26, 2009, effective December 1, 2009.)

CASE NOTES

Appeal from post-verdict judgment of acquittal. — Because no retrial would be required as a result of allowing an appeal from a post-verdict judgment of acquittal based upon insufficiency of evidence, the Fourth Circuit Court of Appeals had jurisdiction to entertain it, notwithstanding the resulting anomaly that a judgment of acquittal on this ground remains nonappealable if entered at any time before jury verdict but will be appealable if entered on a reserved basis after verdict. United States v. Steed, 646 F.2d 136 (4th Cir. 1981), rev'd on other grounds, 674 F.2d 284 (4th Cir.), cert. denied, 459 U.S. 829, 103 S. Ct. 67, 74 L. Ed. 2d 68 (1982).

Applied in United States v. Brown, 328 F. Supp. 196 (E.D. Va. 1971); United States v. Lee, 485 F.2d 41 (4th Cir. 1973); United States v. Marable, 657 F.2d 75 (4th Cir. 1981); United States v. Arrington, 757 F.2d 1484 (4th Cir. 1985); United States v. Coleman, 11 F. Supp. 2d 689 (W.D. Va. 1998).

Rule 29.1. Closing Argument.

Closing arguments proceed in the following order:

(a) the government argues;

(b) the defense argues; and

(c) the government rebuts. (Added by order adopted April 22, 1974, effective December 1, 1975, and amended by order adopted April 29, 2002, effective December 1, 2002.)

Rule 30. Jury Instructions.

(a) *In General.* — Any party may request in writing that the court instruct the jury on the law as specified in the request. The request must be made at the close of the evidence or at any earlier time that the court reasonably sets. When the request is made, the requesting party must furnish a copy to every other party.

(b) *Ruling on a Request.* — The court must inform the parties before closing arguments how it intends to rule on the requested instructions.

(c) *Time for Giving Instructions.* — The court may instruct the jury before or after the arguments are completed, or at both times.

(d) *Objections to Instructions.* — A party who objects to any portion of the instructions or to a failure to give a requested instruction must inform the court of the specific objection and the grounds for the objection before the jury retires to deliberate. An opportunity must be given to object out of the jury's hearing and, on request, out of the jury's presence. Failure to object in accordance with this rule precludes appellate review, except as permitted under Rule 52(b). (Amended by order adopted February 28, 1966, effective July 1, 1966, by order adopted March 9, 1987, effective August 1, 1987, by order adopted April 25, 1988, effective August 1, 1988, and by order adopted April 29, 2002, effective December 1, 2002.)

CASE NOTES

Trial court must instruct on elements of offense, whether requested or not. — The Fourth Circuit Court of Appeals has said that it cannot and will not affirm a conviction by a jury unless the district court instructed as to the elements of the offense charged in the information or indictment, whether requested or not. The trial court cannot adopt by reference the exposition of the law as argued to the jury by counsel and escape its duty to instruct under this rule. The most important and essential part of instruction as to the law which the jury is to apply in a case is the essential elements of the crime charged. There can be no substitute for such an instruction to the jury by the judge in the presence of counsel and the defendant. United States v. Hutchison, 338 F.2d 991 (4th Cir. 1964).

Objection must be made before jury retires. — Under this rule, error may not be assigned to any portion of the charge or for any "omission therefrom" unless objection is made before the jury retires. United States v. Quinn, 315 F.2d 425 (4th Cir. 1963).

Defects are waived by failure to object or except. United States v. Carrier, 344 F.2d 42 (4th Cir. 1965).

But an appellate court may notice plain error affecting substantial rights. United States v. Carrier, 344 F.2d 42 (4th Cir. 1965) (defects not serious enough to apply exception).

Denial of request to object to charge out of presence of jury. — Rule 30, Fed.R.Crim.P. provides that at his request, a party should be given an opportunity to object to the charge out of the presence of the jury. Although the Supreme Court has indicated that a defendant's request should be granted, it has held that denial, in the absence of prejudice, does not constitute reversible error. United States v. Heyman, 562 F.2d 316 (4th Cir. 1977).

Applied in United States v. Wilkins, 385 F.2d 465 (4th Cir. 1967); United States v. Safley, 408 F.2d 603 (4th Cir. 1969); United States v. Johnson, 497 F.2d 548 (4th Cir. 1974); Coppola v. Warden of Va. State Penitentiary, 222 Va. 369, 282 S.E.2d 10 (1981); United States v. Burgess, 691 F.2d 1146 (4th Cir. 1982).

Rule 31. Jury Verdict.

(a) *Return.* — The jury must return its verdict to a judge in open court. The verdict must be unanimous.

(b) *Partial Verdicts, Mistrial, and Retrial.* — (1) Multiple Defendants. — If there are multiple defendants, the jury may return a verdict at any time during its deliberations as to any defendant about whom it has agreed.

(2) Multiple Counts. — If the jury cannot agree on all counts as to any defendant, the jury may return a verdict on those counts on which it has agreed.

(3) Mistrial and Retrial. — If the jury cannot agree on a verdict on one or more counts, the court may declare a mistrial on those counts. The government may retry any defendant on any count on which the jury could not agree.

(c) *Lesser Offense or Attempt.* — A defendant may be found guilty of any of the following:

(1) an offense necessarily included in the offense charged;

(2) an attempt to commit the offense charged; or

(3) an attempt to commit an offense necessarily included in the offense charged, if the attempt is an offense in its own right.

(d) *Jury Poll.* — After a verdict is returned but before the jury is discharged, the court must on a party's request, or may on its own, poll the jurors individually. If the poll reveals a lack of unanimity, the court may direct the jury to deliberate further or may declare a mistrial and discharge the jury. (Amended by order adopted April 24, 1972, effective October 1, 1972, by order adopted April 24, 1998, effective December 1, 1998, by order adopted April 17, 2000, effective December 1, 2000. and by order adopted April 29, 2002, effective December 1, 2002.)

CASE NOTES

Application and standard of proof. — Subdivision (e) of this rule and Rule 7(c)(2) of the Federal rules of Criminal Procedure indicate that criminal procedures apply to forfeiture an proof beyond a reasonable doubt is a fundamental element of criminal trials. United States v. Real Property Located at 1808 Diamond Springs Rd., 816 F. Supp. 1077 (E.D. Va. 1993).

In bank robbery prosecution failure to give instruction on bank larceny was error. — See United States v. Carter, 540 F.2d 753 (4th Cir. 1976).

Applied in United States v. Blackwell, 515 F.2d 125 (4th Cir. 1975).

VII. POST-CONVICTION PROCEDURES.

Rule 32. Sentencing and Judgment.

(a) [Reserved.]

(b) *Time of Sentencing.* — (1) In General. — The court must impose sentence without unnecessary delay.

(2) Changing Time Limits. — The court may, for good cause, change any time limits prescribed in this rule.

(c) *Presentence Investigation.* — (1) Required Investigation. — (A) In General. — The probation officer must conduct a presentence investigation and submit a report to the court before it imposes sentence unless:

(i) 18 U.S.C. § 3593(c) or another statute requires otherwise; or

(ii) the court finds that the information in the record enables it to meaningfully exercise its sentencing authority under 18 U.S.C. § 3553, and the court explains its finding on the record.

(B) Restitution. — If the law permits restitution, the probation officer must conduct an investigation and submit a report that contains sufficient information for the court to order restitution.

(2) Interviewing the Defendant. — The probation officer who interviews a defendant as part of a presentence investigation must, on request, give the defendant's attorney notice and a reasonable opportunity to attend the interview.

(d) *Presentence Report.* — (1) Applying the Advisory Sentencing Guidelines. — The presentence report must:

(A) identify all applicable guidelines and policy statements of the Sentencing Commission;

(B) calculate the defendant's offense level and criminal history category;

(C) state the resulting sentencing range and kinds of sentences available;

(D) identify any factor relevant to:

(i) the appropriate kind of sentence, or

(ii) the appropriate sentence within the applicable sentencing range; and

(E) identify any basis for departing from the applicable sentencing range.

(2) Additional Information. — The presentence report must also contain the following:

(A) the defendant's history and characteristics, including:

(i) any prior criminal record;

(ii) the defendant's financial condition; and

(iii) any circumstances affecting the defendant's behavior that may be helpful in imposing sentence or in correctional treatment;

(B) information that assesses any financial, social, psychological, and medical impact on any victim;

(C) when appropriate, the nature and extent of nonprison programs and resources available to the defendant;

(D) when the law provides for restitution, information sufficient for a restitution order;

(E) if the court orders a study under 18 U.S.C. § 3552(b), any resulting report and recommendation;

(F) a statement of whether the government seeks forfeiture under Rule 32.2 and any other law; and

(G) any other information that the court requires, including information relevant to the factors under 18 U.S.C. § 3553(a).

(3) Exclusions. — The presentence report must exclude the following:

(A) any diagnoses that, if disclosed, might seriously disrupt a rehabilitation program;

(B) any sources of information obtained upon a promise of confidentiality; and

(C) any other information that, if disclosed, might result in physical or other harm to the defendant or others.

(e) *Disclosing the Report and Recommendation.* — (1) Time to Disclose. — Unless the defendant has consented in writing, the probation officer must not submit a presentence report to the court or disclose its contents to anyone until the defendant has pleaded guilty or nolo contendere, or has been found guilty.

(2) Minimum Required Notice. — The probation officer must give the presentence report to the defendant, the defendant's attorney, and an attorney for the government at least 35 days before sentencing unless the defendant waives this minimum period.

(3) Sentence Recommendation. — By local rule or by order in a case, the court may direct the probation officer not to disclose to anyone other than the court the officer's recommendation on the sentence.

(f) *Objecting to the Report.* — (1) Time to Object. — Within 14 days after receiving the presentence report, the parties must state in writing any objections, including objections to material information, sentencing guideline ranges, and policy statements contained in or omitted from the report.

(2) Serving Objections. — An objecting party must provide a copy of its objections to the opposing party and to the probation officer.

(3) Action on Objections. — After receiving objections, the probation officer may meet with the parties to discuss the objections. The probation officer may then investigate further and revise the presentence report as appropriate.

(g) *Submitting the Report.* — At least 7 days before sentencing, the probation officer must submit to the court and to the parties the presentence report and an addendum containing any unresolved objections, the grounds for those objections, and the probation officer's comments on them.

(h) *Notice of Possible Departure from Sentencing Guidelines.* — Before the court may depart from the applicable sentencing range on a ground not identified for departure either in the presentence report or in a party's prehearing submission, the court must give the parties reasonable notice that it is contemplating such a departure. The notice must specify any ground on which the court is contemplating a departure.

(i) *Sentencing.* — (1) In General. — At sentencing, the court:

(A) must verify that the defendant and the defendant's attorney have read and discussed the presentence report and any addendum to the report;

(B) must give to the defendant and an attorney for the government a written summary of — or summarize in camera — any information excluded from the presentence report under Rule 32(d)(3) on which the court will rely in sentencing, and give them a reasonable opportunity to comment on that information;

(C) must allow the parties' attorneys to comment on the probation officer's determinations and other matters relating to an appropriate sentence; and

(D) may, for good cause, allow a party to make a new objection at any time before sentence is imposed.

(2) Introducing Evidence; Producing a Statement. — The court may permit the parties to introduce evidence on the objections. If a witness testifies at sentencing, Rule 26.2(a)-(d) and (f) applies. If a party fails to comply with a Rule 26.2 order to produce a witness's statement, the court must not consider that witness's testimony.

(3) Court Determinations. — At sentencing, the court:

(A) may accept any undisputed portion of the presentence report as a finding of fact;

(B) must — for any disputed portion of the presentence report or other controverted matter — rule on the dispute or determine that a ruling is unnecessary either because the matter will not affect sentencing, or because the court will not consider the matter in sentencing; and

(C) must append a copy of the court's determinations under this rule to any copy of the presentence report made available to the Bureau of Prisons.

(4) Opportunity to Speak. — (A) By a Party. — Before imposing sentence, the court must:

(i) provide the defendant's attorney an opportunity to speak on the defendant's behalf;

(ii) address the defendant personally in order to permit the defendant to speak or present any information to mitigate the sentence; and

(iii) provide an attorney for the government an opportunity to speak equivalent to that of the defendant's attorney.

(B) By a Victim. — Before imposing sentence, the court must address any victim of the crime who is present at sentencing and must permit the victim to be reasonably heard.

(C) In Camera Proceedings. — Upon a party's motion and for good cause, the court may hear in camera any statement made under Rule 32(i)(4).

(j) *Defendant's Right to Appeal.* — (1) Advicc of a Right to Appeal. — (A) Appealing a Conviction. — If the defendant pleaded not guilty and was convicted, after sentencing the court must advise the defendant of the right to appeal the conviction.

(B) Appealing a Sentence. — After sentencing — regardless of the defendant's plea — the court must advise the defendant of any right to appeal the sentence.

(C) Appeal Costs. — The court must advise a defendant who is unable to pay appeal costs of the right to ask for permission to appeal in forma pauperis.

(2) Clerk's Filing of Notice. — If the defendant so requests, the clerk must immediately prepare and file a notice of appeal on the defendant's behalf.

(k) *Judgment.* — (1) In General. — In the judgment of conviction, the court must set forth the plea, the jury verdict or the court's findings, the adjudication, and the sentence. If the defendant is found not guilty or is otherwise entitled to be discharged, the court must so order. The judge must sign the judgment, and the clerk must enter it.

(2) Criminal Forfeiture. — Forfeiture procedures are governed by Rule 32.2. (Amended by order adopted February 28, 1966, effective July 1, 1966, by order adopted April 24, 1972, effective October 1, 1972, by order adopted April 22, 1974, effective December 1, 1975, by order adopted July 31, 1975, effective December 1, 1975, by order adopted April 30, 1979, effective August 1, 1979, and December 1, 1980, by order adopted October 12, 1982, by order adopted April 28, 1983, effective August 1, 1983, by order adopted October 12, 1984, effective November 1, 1987, by order adopted March 9, 1987, effective August 1, 1987, by order adopted April 25, 1989, effective December 1, 1989, by order adopted April 30, 1991, effective December 1, 1991, by order adopted April 22, 1993, effective December 1, 1993, by order adopted April 29, 1994, effective December 1, 1994, by P.L.103-222, approved September 13, 1994, effective December 1, 1994, by order adopted April 23, 1996, effective December 1, 1996, by order adopted April 24, 1996, by order adopted April 17, 2000, effective December 1, 2000, by order adopted April 29, 2002, effective December 1, 2002, by order adopted April 12, 2006, effective December 1, 2006, by order adopted April 30, 2007, effective December 1, 2007, by order adopted April 23, 2008, effective December 1, 2008, by order adopted March 26, 2009, effective December 1, 2009, and by order adopted April 26, 2011, effective December 1, 2011.)

Law Review. — For an article "For the Criminal Practitioner: A review of all 1995 criminal cases decided by the Fourth Circuit," see 53 Wash. & Lee L. Rev. 465 (1996). For article, "Reconceptualizing Competence: An Appeal," see 66 Wash. & Lee L. Rev. 259 (2009).

CASE NOTES

Rule 25(b) permits sentencing by a judge who did not try the case. United States v. Bowser, 497 F.2d 1017 (4th Cir.), cert. denied, 419 U.S. 857, 95 S. Ct. 105, 42 L. Ed. 2d 91 (1974), 423 U.S. 997, 96 S. Ct. 427, 46 L. Ed. 2d 372 (1975).

However, the better practice is for the judge who presided at trial to impose sentence. United States v. Bowser, 497 F.2d 1017 (4th Cir.), cert. denied, 419 U.S. 857, 95 S. Ct. 105, 42 L. Ed. 2d 91 (1974), 423 U.S. 997, 96 S. Ct. 427, 46 L. Ed. 2d 372 (1975).

Where the sentencing judge is not the trial judge and has no special knowledge of the case, and where such a judge imposes the maximum sentence despite no aggravating circumstances, the question arises whether there has been an actual exercise of discretion. Under such circumstances a statement of reasons for the sentencing decision would seem to be highly appropriate. United States v. Bowser, 497 F.2d 1017 (4th Cir.), cert. denied, 419 U.S. 857, 95 S. Ct. 105, 42 L. Ed. 2d 91 (1974), 423 U.S. 997, 96 S. Ct. 427, 46 L. Ed. 2d 372 (1975).

Defendant sentenced in absentia. — A defendant has the right under Rules 32(a) and 43 of the Federal Rules of Criminal Procedure not to be sentenced for a felony in absentia. The fact that the district court amended a prisoner's sentence by imposing only a required three-year special parole term did not satisfy the pertinent requirement of Rule 43 that the defendant be present. The imposition of a special parole term is not merely a ministerial act because if the district court had been aware at the time of sentencing that the special parole term must be imposed, it may well be that a shorter prison term would have been awarded. Hazelwood v. Arnold, 539 F.2d 1031 (4th Cir. 1976).

Defendant should not have been sentenced under career offender provision. — Since judgment of conviction includes the plea, the verdict or findings, the adjudication, and the sentence, where defendant was sentenced for his second felony after committing an offense during a riot, he should not have been sentenced under the career offender provision which required at least two felony convictions prior to the prison riot offense. United States v. Bassil, 932 F.2d 342 (4th Cir. 1991).

Insufficient information to sentence defendant. — Where defendant pled guilty to reentry of deported alien, the court did not have sufficient information before it to sentence defendant without receiving the presentence report even though the court had the report prepared by federal authorities in preparation for defendant's bond trial, the summary of defendant's prior criminal record in possession of U.S. attorney, and the stipulation of facts entered in record with plea agreement; the court did not have before it defendant's complete criminal history, information regarding defendant's immigration status, or information on defendant's ability to pay any fine that might have been assessed. United States v. Turner, 810 F. Supp. 1102 (E.D. Va. 1993).

Failure to give attorney for government opportunity to speak. — Rule 32(a)(1), Fed.R.Crim.P. after providing a right of allocution to a defendant and his attorney, states: "The attorney for the government shall have an equivalent opportunity to speak to the court." Where the record showed that after the defendant had entered his plea, and after the probation officer had made his presentence report, the attorney for the defendant made an appropriate statement and the defendant was given an opportunity to speak, but it did not appear that the attorney for the government was offered such an opportunity, in favor of a plea bargain which the prosecution and defense had agreed on if such a request had been made and refused, it might be necessary to strike the sentence and remand the case for the imposition of sentence after the attorney for the government had been afforded an opportunity to speak to the court. However, since it did not appear that either the attorney for the government or the attorney for the defendant requested that the attorney for the government be asked if he had anything to say, under these circumstances, the judgment, including the sentence, had to be affirmed. United States v. Jackson, 563 F.2d 1145 (4th Cir. 1977).

When withdrawal of plea of guilty should be permitted. — Under Rule 32(d), Fed.R.Crim.P., a trial court may allow withdrawal of a plea of guilty for any fair and just reason. Withdrawal should be permitted if the plea has been unfairly obtained or given through ignorance, fear or inadvertence. United States v. Strauss, 563 F.2d 127 (4th Cir. 1977).

Withdrawal before sentencing normally should be allowed. — This policy is justified because of the public interest in protecting an accused's right to a jury trial. United States v. Strauss, 563 F.2d 127 (4th Cir. 1977).

Unless prosecution substantially prejudiced by reliance upon plea. — The sounder view, supported both by the language of the rule and by the reasons for it, would be to allow withdrawal of the plea prior to sentencing unless the prosecution has been substantially prejudiced by reliance upon the defendant's plea. When the government has been prejudiced, the trial court must weigh the accused's reasons for changing his plea against the prejudice the government will suffer. United States v. Strauss, 563 F.2d 127 (4th Cir. 1977).

The most common form of prejudice is the difficulty the government would encounter in reassembling far-flung witnesses in a complex case, but prejudice also occurs where a defendant's guilty plea removed him from an on-going trial of codefendants, who were then found guilty. United States v. Strauss, 563 F.2d 127 (4th Cir. 1977).

Denial of motion to withdraw plea of guilty sustained unless trial court abused discretion. — See United States v. Strauss, 563 F.2d 127 (4th Cir. 1977).

An appropriately conducted Rule 11 proceeding raises a strong presumption that the plea is final and binding. United States v. Puckett, 61 F.3d 1092 (4th Cir. 1995).

A presentence report cannot be used to prove an essential element of the crime. Russell v. United States, 507 F.2d 1029 (4th Cir. 1974).

Nor can it be used to supply proof of guilt. Russell v. United States, 507 F.2d 1029 (4th Cir. 1974).

A violation of subdivision (c)(1) gives rise to a presumption of prejudice. Webster v. United States, 330 F. Supp. 1080 (E.D. Va. 1971).

A presumption of prejudice did not arise where the judge who was to try defendant on one charge had seen the presentence report when he sentenced defendant on another charge. Webster v. United States, 330 F. Supp. 1080 (E.D. Va. 1971).

Mere knowledge of background information as to a criminal defendant is not sufficient to require that the judge step aside. Webster v. United States, 330 F. Supp. 1080 (E.D. Va. 1971).

Presentence report may include information about crimes for which defendant was indicted but not convicted. United States v. Legrano, 659 F.2d 17 (4th Cir. 1981).

The court is not required to divulge the contents of the probation officer's sentencing recommendation. United States v. Howard-Arias, 679 F.2d 363 (4th Cir.), cert. denied, 459 U.S. 874, 103 S. Ct. 165, 74 L. Ed. 2d 136 (1982).

Defendant should be invited personally to speak on his own behalf. — Trial judges before sentencing should, as a matter of good judicial administration, unambiguously address themselves to the defendant. Judges should leave no room for doubt that the defendant has been issued a personal invitation to speak prior to sentencing. United States v. Murphy, 530 F.2d 1 (4th Cir. 1976).

Examining the defendant about why he bought contraband and what he meant to do with it does not comply with the rule giving the defendant a right of allocution. United States v. Murphy, 530 F.2d 1 (4th Cir. 1976).

Simply affording defense counsel the right to speak does not satisfy defendant's right of allocution because the most persuasive counsel may not be able to speak for a defendant as the defendant might, with halting eloquence, speak for himself. United States v. Murphy, 530 F.2d 1 (4th Cir. 1976).

But he is not entitled to present testimony regarding accuracy of presentence report. — The trial judge is not required under subdivision (c)(3)(A) of this rule to allow the defendant to present testimony regarding the accuracy of contested portions of the report. United States v. Howard-Arias, 679 F.2d 363 (4th Cir.), cert. denied, 459 U.S. 874, 103 S. Ct. 165, 74 L. Ed. 2d 136 (1982).

Effect of findings as to allegations of inaccuracies in presentence report. — The last sentence of subdivision (c)(3)(D) shows that the effect of any such findings are intended to apply beyond sentencing, specifically, they are to be considered by the Bureau of Prisons and by the Parole Commission. United States v. Williams, 618 F. Supp. 1419 (E.D. Va. 1985), aff'd, 785 F.2d 306 (4th Cir. 1986).

Alleged inaccuracies in presentence report to be resolved before sentence imposed. — Subdivision (c)(3)(D) of this rule is intended to require findings from the bench prior to sentencing. Subdivision (ii) thereof clearly indicates that contentions with respect to inaccuracies in the presentence report are to be dealt with and disposed of before the court imposes sentence. This requirement serves the double purpose of requiring the judge to resolve the dispute in his own mind before he imposes sentence and of requiring the judge to resolve the dispute while the matter is still fresh in mind. United States v. Williams, 618 F. Supp. 1419 (E.D. Va. 1985), aff'd, 785 F.2d 306 (4th Cir. 1986).

Prisoner who later discovers matter which is subject to dispute in his presentence report would want to correct the record, but subdivision (c)(3)(D) does not give him that vehicle. United States v. Williams, 618 F. Supp. 1419 (E.D. Va. 1985), aff'd, 785 F.2d 306 (4th Cir. 1986).

Failure to contest inaccuracies in presentence report. — Disarray at the time of sentencing, which was brought about by a decision of the defendants to fire their lawyers on the eve of sentencing, did not excuse failure to call any inaccuracies in the presentence report to the court's attention. The state of confusion was an excuse for which the defendants derived whatever benefit they sought; they were required also to suffer whatever detriment resulted. United States v. Williams, 618 F. Supp. 1419 (E.D. Va. 1985), aff'd, 785 F.2d 306 (4th Cir. 1986).

A motion to withdraw a plea of guilty may ordinarily be made only before sentence is imposed or while imposition of sentence is suspended. United States v. Roland, 318 F.2d 406 (4th Cir. 1963).

At which time it is allowed with great liberality. United States v. Roland, 318 F.2d 406 (4th Cir. 1963).

But may be granted after sentencing only to correct manifest injustice. — After judgment and the imposition of the sentence, this rule gives the court the power to grant a motion to withdraw a plea of guilty if such action appears to be necessary "to correct manifest injustice." United States v. Roland, 318 F.2d 406 (4th Cir. 1963).

By the provisions of subdivision (d) the withdrawal of a guilty plea after the imposition of sentence is permissible when, in the discretion of the trial judge, such a withdrawal is necessary "to correct manifest injustice." It is to be expected, however, that such a procedure will be appropriate only in extraordinary cases. United States v. Semel, 347 F.2d 228 (4th Cir.), cert. denied, 382 U.S. 840, 86 S. Ct. 90, 15 L. Ed. 2d 82, reh'g denied, 382 U.S. 933, 86 S. Ct. 312, 15 L. Ed. 2d 346 (1965).'.

Discretion in refusing motion after sentence only reversible to prevent injustice. — A motion to withdraw a plea, which should be allowable as of course, or almost so, before judgment and the imposition of sentence, is allowable after sentence has been imposed only in extraordinary cases, and then the district judge has a substantial discretion in making a determination of the requirements of justice. On appeal, the court of appeals can reverse the refusal of such a motion only if it can say that manifest injustice obviously would otherwise be done. United States v. Roland, 318 F.2d 406 (4th Cir. 1963).

But concept of "manifest injustice" is broader than "due process." — While there may be a considerable overlap, the concept of "manifest injustice" under subdivision (d) permits the judge a greater latitude than the requirements of constitutional "due process." The facts disclosed in a hearing might not be sufficient for the court to conclude that the guilty plea was involuntary and violative of due process, yet the court may be of the opinion that clear injustice was done. Pilkington v. United States, 315 F.2d 204 (4th Cir. 1963), rev'g 204 F. Supp. 165 (E.D. Va. 1962).

Factors considered in meeting burden under subdivision (d). — The court is to consider the following factors in determining whether the defendant has met her burden under subdivision (d) of showing a fair and just reason for the withdrawal of the guilty plea: 1) whether the defendant has offered credible evidence that his plea was not knowing or voluntary; 2) whether the defendant has credibly asserted his legal innocence' 3) whether there has been a delay between the entering of the plea and the filing of the motion; 4) whether the defendant has had close assistance of competent counsel; 5) whether withdrawal will cause prejudice to the government; 6) and whether it will inconvenience the court and waste judicial resources. United States v. Puckett, 61 F.3d 1092 (4th Cir. 1995).

Manifest injustice entitling defendant to withdraw plea of nolo contendere not shown. — See United States v. Vidaver, 73 F. Supp. 382 (E.D. Va. 1947); United States v. Howard, 431 F.2d 244 (4th Cir. 1970).

A fair and just reason for withdrawing a guilty plea is one that essentially challenges the fairness of the Rule 11 proceeding. United States v. Puckett, 61 F.3d 1092 (4th Cir. 1995).

Withdrawal of plea not permitted where facts of "defense" known when plea entered. — The district court did not abuse its discretion in refusing to allow defendant to withdraw his guilty plea, where the facts of his proffered "defense" were, as the district court noted, known to him at the time he entered his plea and, additionally, that defense did not negative any element of the false statements charge. United States v. Haley, 784 F.2d 1218 (4th Cir. 1986).

Withdrawal of guilty pleas not permitted where reassembling witnesses was difficult and expensive. — Defendants could not withdraw their guilty pleas because of prejudice to the government, where it was manifest that the government would require a number of witnesses to prove its case. Assembling far-flung witnesses who were not government employees would have been a task of some proportions. Permitting them to scatter and then being required to reassemble them would have added substantially to the problem — and to the expense of the United States. United States v. Namkoong, 616 F. Supp. 579 (E.D. Va. 1985).

Denial of leave to withdraw plea after sentencing held proper. — See United States v. Roland, 318 F.2d 406 (4th Cir. 1963).

Where the record revealed a guilty plea, voluntarily made with the assistance of retained counsel seven months after the defendant had been arraigned and where at a sentencing hearing three months after the plea had been accepted, the defendant candidly admitted all the essential elements of the crime with which he had been charged, the district judge clearly did not abuse his discretion in denying the defendant's motion to withdraw his plea filed after sentencing. United States v. Semel, 347 F.2d 228 (4th Cir.), cert. denied, 382 U.S. 840, 86 S. Ct. 90, 15 L. Ed. 2d 82, reh'g denied, 382 U.S.

933, 86 S. Ct. 312, 15 L. Ed. 2d 346 (1965).'.

Where a defendant, who had been found competent to stand trial, pleaded guilty in the expectation that he would be returned to a mental hospital for psychiatric treatment and not sent to the penitentiary, the district court's denial of defendant's motion under subdivision (d) to set aside his conviction and withdraw his guilty plea was proper, as no "manifest injustice" was shown. The place of imprisonment is determined not by the court, but by the Attorney General of the United States, and if a defendant is in need of mental treatment the Attorney General is authorized to provide such treatment. United States v. Isaacs, 349 F.2d 361 (4th Cir. 1965).

Applied in Wilson v. United States, 215 F. Supp. 661 (W.D. Va. 1963); Hartman v. United States, 228 F. Supp. 402 (W.D. Va. 1964); Rakes v. United States, 231 F. Supp. 812 (W.D. Va. 1964); Rich v. United States, 330 F. Supp. 949 (E.D. Va. 1967); Taylor v. Cox, 315 F. Supp. 1316 (E.D. Va. 1970); Forehand v. United States, 321 F. Supp. 271 (W.D. Va. 1970); Webster v. United States, 330 F. Supp. 1080 (E.D. Va. 1971); Paige v. United States, 443 F.2d 781 (4th Cir. 1971); United States v. Knupp, 448 F.2d 412 (4th Cir. 1971); United States v. Powell, 487 F.2d 325 (4th Cir. 1973); United States v. Johnson, 495 F.2d 377 (4th Cir. 1974); Russell v. United States, 507 F.2d 1029 (4th Cir. 1974); United States v. Lambey, 949 F.2d 133 (4th Cir. 1991); Nesbitt v. United States, 773 F. Supp. 795 (E.D. Va. 1991); United States v. Jones, 916 F. Supp. 558 (E.D. Va. 1996); United States v. Daniels, 996 F. Supp. 563 (W.D. Va. 1998).

Rule 32.1. Revoking or Modifying Probation or Supervised Release.

(a) *Initial Appearance.* — (1) Person in Custody. — A person held in custody for violating probation or supervised release must be taken without unnecessary delay before a magistrate judge.

(A) If the person is held in custody in the district where an alleged violation occurred, the initial appearance must be in that district.

(B) If the person is held in custody in a district other than where an alleged violation occurred, the initial appearance must be in that district, or in an adjacent district if the appearance can occur more promptly there.

(2) Upon a Summons. — When a person appears in response to a summons for violating probation or supervised release, a magistrate judge must proceed under this rule.

(3) Advice. — The judge must inform the person of the following:

(A) the alleged violation of probation or supervised release;

(B) the person's right to retain counsel or to request that counsel be appointed if the person cannot obtain counsel; and

(C) the person's right, if held in custody, to a preliminary hearing under Rule 32.1(b)(1).

(4) Appearance in the District With Jurisdiction. — If the person is arrested or appears in the district that has jurisdiction to conduct a revocation hearing — either originally or by transfer of jurisdiction — the court must proceed under Rule 32.1(b)-(e).

(5) Appearance in a District Lacking Jurisdiction. If the person is arrested or appears in a district that does not have jurisdiction to conduct a revocation hearing, the magistrate judge must:

(A) if the alleged violation occurred in the district of arrest, conduct a preliminary hearing under Rule 32.1(b) and either:

(i) transfer the person to the district that has jurisdiction, if the judge finds probable cause to believe that a violation occurred; or

(ii) dismiss the proceedings and so notify the court that has jurisdiction, if the judge finds no probable cause to believe that a violation occurred; or

(B) if the alleged violation did not occur in the district of arrest, transfer the person to the district that has jurisdiction if:

(i) the government produces certified copies of the judgment, warrant, and warrant application, or produces copies of those certified documents by reliable electronic means; and

(ii) the judge finds that the person is the same person named in the warrant.

(6) Release or Detention. — The magistrate judge may release or detain the person under 18 U.S.C. § 3143(a)(1) pending further proceedings. The burden of establishing by clear and convincing evidence that the person will not flee or pose a danger to any other person or to the community rests with the person.

(b) *Revocation.* — (1) Preliminary Hearing. — (A) In General. — If a person is in custody for violating a condition of probation or supervised release, a magistrate judge must promptly conduct a hearing to determine whether there is probable cause to believe that a violation occurred. The person may waive the hearing.

(B) Requirements. — The hearing must be recorded by a court reporter or by a suitable recording device. The judge must give the person:

(i) notice of the hearing and its purpose, the alleged violation, and the person's right to retain counsel or to request that counsel be appointed if the person cannot obtain counsel;

(ii) an opportunity to appear at the hearing and present evidence; and

(iii) upon request, an opportunity to question any adverse witness, unless the judge determines that the interest of justice does not require the witness to appear.

(C) Referral. — If the judge finds probable cause, the judge must conduct a revocation hearing. If the judge does not find probable cause, the judge must dismiss the proceeding.

(2) Revocation Hearing. — Unless waived by the person, the court must hold the revocation hearing within a reasonable time in the district having jurisdiction. The person is entitled to:

(A) written notice of the alleged violation;

(B) disclosure of the evidence against the person;

(C) an opportunity to appear, present evidence, and question any adverse witness unless the court determines that the interest of justice does not require the witness to appear;

(D) notice of the person's right to retain counsel or to request that counsel be appointed if the person cannot obtain counsel; and

(E) an opportunity to make a statement and present any information in mitigation.

(c) *Modification.* — (1) In General. — Before modifying the conditions of probation or supervised release, the court must hold a hearing, at which the person has the right to counsel and an opportunity to make a statement and present any information in mitigation.

(2) Exceptions. — A hearing is not required if:

(A) the person waives the hearing; or

(B) the relief sought is favorable to the person and does not extend the term of probation or of supervised release; and

(C) an attorney for the government has received notice of the relief sought, has had a reasonable opportunity to object, and has not done so.

(d) *Disposition of the Case.* — The court's disposition of the case is governed by 18 U.S.C. § 3563 and § 3565 (probation) and § 3583 (supervised release).

(e) *Producing a Statement.* — Rule 26.2(a)-(d) and (f) applies at a hearing under this rule. If a party fails to comply with a Rule 26.2 order to produce a witness's statement, the court must not consider that witness's testimony. (Amended by order adopted April 30, 1979, effective December 1, 1980, by P.L. 99-646, § 12(b), (c), adopted November 10, 1986, effective December 10, 1986, by order adopted March 9, 1987, effective August 1, 1987, by order adopted April 25, 1989, effective December 1, 1989, by order adopted April 30, 1991, effective December 1, 1991, by order adopted April 22, 1993, effective December 1, 1993, by order adopted April 29, 2002, effective December 1, 2002, by order adopted April 25, 2005, effective December 1, 2005, by order adopted April 12, 2006, effective December 1, 2006, and by order adopted April 28, 2010, effective December 1, 2010.)

CASE NOTES

Usual rules of evidence do not apply in revocation hearing. — Since a formal trial is not required by this rule in a probation revocation hearing, the usual rules of evidence need not be applied, and the court may consider documentary evidence including letters that would not be admissible in a criminal trial. United States v. McCallum, 677 F.2d 1024 (4th Cir.), cert. denied, 459 U.S. 1010, 103 S. Ct. 365, 74 L. Ed. 2d 400 (1982).

Rule 32.2. Criminal Forfeiture.

(a) *Notice to the Defendant.* — A court must not enter a judgment of forfeiture in a criminal proceeding unless the indictment or information contains notice to the defendant that the government will seek the forfeiture of property as part of any sentence in accordance with the applicable statute. The notice should not be designated as a count of the indictment or information. The indictment or information need not identify the property subject to forfeiture or specify the amount of any forfeiture money judgment that the government seeks.

(b) *Entering a Preliminary Order of Forfeiture.* — (1) Forfeiture Phase of the Trial. (A) Forfeiture Determinations. As soon as practical after a verdict or finding of guilty, or after a plea of guilty or nolo contendere is accepted, on any count in an indictment or information regarding which criminal forfeiture is sought, the court must determine what property is subject to forfeiture under the applicable statute. If the government seeks forfeiture of specific property, the court must determine whether the government has established the requisite nexus between the property and the offense. If the government seeks a personal money judgment, the court must determine the amount of money that the defendant will be ordered to pay.

(B) Evidence and Hearing. The court's determination may be based on evidence already in the record, including any written plea agreement, and on any additional evidence or information submitted by the parties and accepted by the court as relevant and reliable. If the forfeiture is contested, on either party's request the court must conduct a hearing after the verdict or finding of guilty.

(2) Preliminary Order. (A) Contents of a Specific Order. If the court finds that property is subject to forfeiture, it must promptly enter a preliminary order of forfeiture setting forth the amount of any money judgment, directing the forfeiture of specific property, and directing the forfeiture of any substitute property if the government has met the statutory criteria. The court must enter the order without regard to any third party's interest in the property. Determining whether a third party has such an interest must be deferred until any third party files a claim in an ancillary proceeding under Rule 32.2(c).

(B) Timing. Unless doing so is impractical, the court must enter the preliminary order sufficiently in advance of sentencing to allow the parties to suggest revisions or modifications before the order becomes final as to the defendant under Rule 32.2(b)(4).

(C) General Order. If, before sentencing, the court cannot identify all the specific property subject to forfeiture or calculate the total amount of the money judgment, the court may enter a forfeiture order that:

(i) lists any identified property;

(ii) describes other property in general terms; and

(iii) states that the order will be amended under Rule 32.2(e)(1) when additional specific property is identified or the amount of the money judgment has been calculated.

(3) Seizing Property. The entry of a preliminary order of forfeiture authorizes the Attorney General (or a designee) to seize the specific property subject to forfeiture; to conduct any discovery the court considers proper in identifying, locating, or disposing of the property; and to commence proceedings that comply with any statutes governing third-party rights. The court may include in the order of forfeiture conditions reasonably necessary to preserve the property's value pending any appeal.

(4) Sentence and Judgment. (A) When Final. At sentencing — or at any time before sentencing if the defendant consents — the preliminary forfeiture order becomes final as to the defendant. If the order directs the defendant to forfeit specific property, it remains preliminary as to third parties until the ancillary proceeding is concluded under Rule 32.2(c).

(B) Notice and Inclusion in the Judgment. The court must include the forfeiture when orally announcing the sentence or must otherwise ensure that the defendant knows of the forfeiture at sentencing. The court must also include the forfeiture order, directly or by reference, in the judgment, but the court's failure to do so may be corrected at any time under Rule 36.

(C) Time to Appeal. The time for the defendant or the government to file an appeal from the forfeiture order, or from the court's failure to enter an order, begins to run when judgment is entered. If the court later amends or declines to amend a forfeiture order to include additional property under Rule 32.2(e), the defendant or the government may file an appeal regarding that property under Federal Rule of Appellate Procedure 4(b). The time for that appeal runs from the date when the order granting or denying the amendment becomes final.

(5) Jury Determination. (A) Retaining the Jury. In any case tried before a jury, if the indictment or information states that the government is seeking forfeiture, the court must determine before the jury begins deliberating whether either party requests that the jury be retained to determine the forfeitability of specific property if it returns a guilty verdict.

(B) Special Verdict Form. If a party timely requests to have the jury determine forfeiture, the government must submit a proposed Special Verdict Form listing each property subject to forfeiture and asking the jury to determine whether the government has established the requisite nexus between the property and the offense committed by the defendant.

(6) Notice of the Forfeiture Order. (A) Publishing and Sending Notice. If the court orders the forfeiture of specific property, the government must publish notice of the order and send notice to any person who reasonably appears to be a potential claimant with standing to contest the forfeiture in the ancillary proceeding.

(B) Content of the Notice. The notice must describe the forfeited property, state the times under the applicable statute when a petition contesting the forfeiture must be filed, and state the name and contact information for the government attorney to be served with the petition.

(C) Means of Publication; Exceptions to Publication Requirement. Publication must take place as described in Supplemental Rule G(4)(a)(iii) of the Federal Rules of Civil Procedure, and may be by any means described in Supplemental Rule G(4)(a)(iv). Publication is unnecessary if any exception in Supplemental Rule G(4)(a)(i) applies.

(D) Means of Sending the Notice. The notice may be sent in accordance with Supplemental Rules G(4)(b)(iii)-(v) of the Federal Rules of Civil Procedure.

(7) Interlocutory Sale. At any time before entry of a final forfeiture order, the court, in accordance with Supplemental Rule G(7) of the Federal Rules of Civil Procedure, may order the interlocutory sale of property alleged to be forfeitable.

(c) *Ancillary Proceeding; Entering a Final Order of Forfeiture.* — (1) In General. — If, as prescribed by statute, a third party files a petition asserting an interest in the property to be forfeited, the court must conduct an ancillary proceeding, but no ancillary proceeding is required to the extent that the forfeiture consists of a money judgment.

(A) In the ancillary proceeding, the court may, on motion, dismiss the petition for lack of standing, for failure to state a claim, or for any other lawful reason. For purposes of the motion, the facts set forth in the petition are assumed to be true.

(B) After disposing of any motion filed under Rule 32.2(c)(1)(A) and before conducting a hearing on the petition, the court may permit the parties to conduct discovery in accordance with the Federal Rules of Civil Procedure if the court determines that discovery is necessary or desirable to resolve factual issues. When discovery ends, a party may move for summary judgment under Federal Rule of Civil Procedure 56.

(2) Entering a Final Order. — When the ancillary proceeding ends, the court must enter a final order of forfeiture by amending the preliminary order as necessary to account for any third-party rights. If no third party files a timely petition, the preliminary order becomes the final order of forfeiture if the court finds that the defendant (or any combination of defendants convicted in the case) had an interest in the property that is forfeitable under the applicable statute. The defendant may not object to the entry of the final order on the ground that the property belongs, in whole or in part, to a codefendant or third party; nor may a third party object to the final order on the ground that the third party had an interest in the property.

(3) Multiple Petitions. — If multiple third-party petitions are filed in the same case, an order dismissing or granting one petition is not appealable until rulings are made on all the petitions, unless the court determines that there is no just reason for delay.

(4) Ancillary Proceeding Not Part of Sentencing. — An ancillary proceeding is not part of sentencing.

(d) *Stay Pending Appeal.* — If a defendant appeals from a conviction or an order of forfeiture, the court may stay the order of forfeiture on terms appropriate to ensure that the property remains available pending appellate review. A stay does not delay the ancillary proceeding or the determination of a third party's rights or interests. If the court rules in favor of any third party while an appeal is pending, the court may amend the order of forfeiture but must not transfer any property interest to a third party until the decision on appeal becomes final, unless the defendant consents in writing or on the record.

(e) *Subsequently Located Property; Substitute Property.* — (1) In General. — On the government's motion, the court may at any time enter an order of forfeiture or amend an existing order of forfeiture to include property that:

(A) is subject to forfeiture under an existing order of forfeiture but was located and identified after that order was entered; or

(B) is substitute property that qualifies for forfeiture under an applicable statute.

(2) Procedure. — If the government shows that the property is subject to forfeiture under Rule 32.2(e)(1), the court must:

(A) enter an order forfeiting that property, or amend an existing preliminary or final order to include it; and

(B) if a third party files a petition claiming an interest in the property, conduct an ancillary proceeding under Rule 32.2(c).

(3) Jury Trial Limited. — There is no right to a jury trial under Rule 32.2(e). (Adopted April 17, 2000, effective December 1, 2000, amended by order adopted April 29, 2002, effective December 1, 2002, and by order adopted March 26, 2009, effective December 1, 2009.)

Rule 33. New Trial.

(a) *Defendant's Motion.* — Upon the defendant's motion, the court may vacate any judgment and grant a new trial if the interest of justice so requires. If the case was tried without a jury, the court may take additional testimony and enter a new judgment.

(b) *Time to File.* — (1) Newly Discovered Evidence. — Any motion for a new trial grounded on newly discovered evidence must be filed within 3 years after the verdict or finding of guilty. If an appeal is pending, the court may not grant a motion for a new trial until the appellate court remands the case.

(2) Other Grounds. — Any motion for a new trial grounded on any reason other than newly discovered evidence must be filed within 14 days after the verdict or finding of guilty. (Amended by order adopted February 28, 1966, effective July 1, 1966, by order adopted March 9, 1987, effective August 1, 1987, by order adopted April 24, 1998, effective December 1, 1998, by order adopted April 29, 2002, effective December 1, 2002, by order adopted April 25, 2005, effective December 1, 2005, and by order adopted March 26, 2009, effective December 1, 2009.)

CASE NOTES

Trial court's discretion should be exercised sparingly, and a new trial should be granted only when the evidence weighs heavily against the verdict. United States v. Arrington, 757 F.2d 1484 (4th Cir. 1985).

Courts should see that motion on newly discovered evidence is not abused. — While a defendant in a criminal case should be afforded the full benefit of a motion for a new trial on the ground of newly discovered evidence, courts should be on the alert to see that the privilege of its use is not abused. United States v. Williams, 415 F.2d 232 (4th Cir. 1969).

Court's authority when motion attacks weight of evidence. — When the motion attacks the weight of the evidence, the court's authority is much broader than when it is deciding a motion to acquit on the ground of insufficient evidence. United States v. Arrington, 757 F.2d 1484 (4th Cir. 1985).

Judge's disagreement with the jury's verdict does not mandate a new trial. United States v. Arrington, 757 F.2d 1484 (4th Cir. 1985).

Court may evaluate credibility of witnesses. — In deciding a motion for a new trial, the district court is not constrained by the requirement that it view the evidence in the light most favorable to the government; thus, it may evaluate the credibility of the witnesses. United States v. Arrington, 757 F.2d 1484 (4th Cir. 1985).

Requirements of motion on newly discovered evidence. — The requirements of a motion for new trial based on the ground of newly discovered evidence are: (1) It must appear from the motion that the evidence relied on is, in fact, newly discovered, i.e., discovered after the trial; (2) the motion must allege facts from which the court may infer diligence on the part of the movant; (3) the evidence relied on must not be merely cumulative or impeaching; (4) must be material to the issues involved; and (5) must be such as, on a new trial, would probably produce an acquittal. United States v. Williams, 415 F.2d 232 (4th Cir. 1969).

Evidence going to credibility of witness is insufficient. — Newly discovered evidence going only to the question of the credibility of a witness is not sufficient to justify the granting of a new trial. United States v. Williams, 415 F.2d 232 (4th Cir. 1969).

But evidence going directly to interest of prosecution witness may be sufficient. — Generally, evidence which is only impeaching, though newly discovered, does not suffice to obtain a new trial; however, newly discovered evidence may go so directly to the interest of the prosecution witness that, if his testimony was essential to the prosecution, a new trial should be awarded in which the interest of the witness may be shown. United States v. McCoy, 478 F.2d 846 (4th Cir. 1973).

Motion for new trial based on newly-discovered evidence while appeal pending. — This rule provides that a motion for a new trial based on newly-discovered evidence filed while an appeal is pending may be granted by the trial court only on remand of the case. The appeal may render the motion for a new trial moot. If after remand defendant still wants to pursue his motion for a new trial, court would then be permitted under this rule to consider it on its merits. United States v. Williams, 618 F. Supp. 1419 (E.D. Va. 1985), aff'd, 785 F.2d 306 (4th Cir. 1986).

Subsequent recantation of testimony by material witness sufficient to change disposition of criminal trial may be a ground for a new trial pursuant to this rule. United States v. Dworkin, 116 F.R.D. 29 (E.D. Va. 1987).

Elements for granting new trial based on recantation of material witness are: (a) The court must be reasonably well satisfied that the testimony given by a material witness was false; (b) that without it the jury might have reached a different conclusion; and (c) that the party seeking the new trial was taken by surprise when the false testimony was given or did not know of its falsity until after the trial. United States v. Dworkin, 116 F.R.D. 29 (E.D. Va. 1987).

Defendant's motion for new criminal trial based on recantation of his own testimony was denied where the defendant knew very well that he was testifying falsely before the end of the trial. United States v. Dworkin, 116 F.R.D. 29 (E.D. Va. 1987).

Motion for new trial no longer moot after acquittal reversed. — Where motion for a new trial was timely filed but was rendered moot when the district court granted judgment of acquittal, after reversal, the motion was no longer moot, and on remand the judge could properly rule on it. United States v. Arrington, 757 F.2d 1484 (4th Cir. 1985).

District court's denial of a new trial was not inconsistent with its earlier ruling granting motion for acquittal that was overturned on appeal, as court may reach an apparently inconsistent result without committing error, and even the grant of a new trial may be reconsidered before retrial and denied. United States v. Arrington, 757 F.2d 1484 (4th Cir. 1985).

Standard of appellate review. — The denial of a motion for new trial will not be overturned unless the court has abused its discretion. United States v. Arrington, 757 F.2d 1484 (4th Cir. 1985).

Allowing hearing but not decision on motion in case of appeal is expeditious. — The purpose of the provisions of this rule, which permit the hearing, but not the granting of the motion, in a case in which an appeal has been taken, is to expedite proceedings. Rakes v. United States, 163 F.2d 771 (4th Cir. 1947), cert. denied, 335 U.S. 826, 69 S. Ct. 51, 93 L. Ed. 380 (1948).

And court of appeals should remand if district court finds motion should be granted. — Where the district judge has heard the motion and found that it should be granted, the orderly course is for the court of appeals to remand the cause in order that the motion may be granted unless the court of appeals is prepared to say that there was no reasonable basis for the motion and that the district judge abused his discretion in the action taken by him. In this situation it is not the province of the court of appeals to decide whether the motion should have been granted. Rakes v. United States, 163 F.2d 771 (4th Cir. 1947), cert. denied, 335 U.S. 826, 69 S. Ct. 51, 93 L. Ed. 380 (1948).

Applied in United States v. White, 237 F. Supp. 644 (E.D. Va. 1964); Turner v. United States, 423 F. Supp. 581 (E.D. Va. 1976); United States v. Bales, 813 F.2d 1289 (4th Cir. 1987); United States v. Coleman, 11 F. Supp. 2d 689 (W.D. Va. 1998).

Rule 34. Arresting Judgment.

(a) *In General.* — Upon the defendant's motion or on its own, the court must arrest judgment if:

(1) the indictment or information does not charge an offense; or

(2) the court does not have jurisdiction of the charged offense.

(b) *Time to File.* — The defendant must move to arrest judgment within 14 days after the court accepts a verdict or finding of guilty, or after a plea of guilty or nolo contendere. (Amended by order adopted February 28, 1966, effective July 1, 1966, by order adopted April 29, 2002, effective December 1, 2002, by order adopted April 25, 2005, effective December 1, 2005, and by order adopted March 26, 2009, effective December 1, 2009.)

CASE NOTES

Applied in United States v. White, 237 F. Supp. 644 (E.D. Va. 1964); United States v. Pomponio, 511 F.2d 953 (4th Cir. 1975).

Rule 35. Correcting or Reducing a Sentence.

(a) *Correcting Clear Error.* — Within 14 days after sentencing, the court may correct a sentence that resulted from arithmetical, technical, or other clear error.

(b) *Reducing a Sentence for Substantial Assistance.* — (1) In General. — Upon the government's motion made within one year of sentencing, the court may reduce a sentence if the defendant, after sentencing, provided substantial assistance in investigating or prosecuting another person.

(2) Later Motion. — Upon the government's motion made more than one year after sentencing, the court may reduce a sentence if the defendant's substantial assistance involved:

(A) information not known to the defendant until one year or more after sentencing;

(B) information provided by the defendant to the government within one year of sentencing, but which did not become useful to the government until more than one year after sentencing; or

(C) information the usefulness of which could not reasonably have been anticipated by the defendant until more than one year after sentencing and which was promptly provided to the government after its usefulness was reasonably apparent to the defendant.

(3) Evaluating Substantial Assistance. — In evaluating whether the defendant has provided substantial assistance, the court may consider the defendant's presentence assistance.

(4) Below Statutory Minimum. — When acting under Rule 35(b), the court may reduce the sentence to a level below the minimum sentence established by statute.

(c) *"Sentencing" Defined.* — As used in this rule, "sentencing" means the oral announcement of the sentence. (Amended by order adopted February 28, 1966, effective July 1, 1966, by order adopted April 30, 1979, effective August 1, 1979, by order adopted April 28, 1983, effective August 1, 1983, by order adopted October 12, 1984, effective November 1, 1987, by order adopted April 29, 1985, effective August 1, 1985, by order effective October 27, 1986, by P.L. 98-473, Title II, § 215(b), effective November 1, 1987, by P.L. 99-570, § 1009, effective November 1, 1987, by order adopted April 30, 1991, effective December 1, 1991, by order adopted April 24, 1998, effective December 1, 1998, by order adopted April 29, 2002, effective December 1, 2002, by order dated April 26, 2004, effective December 1, 2004, by order adopted April 30, 2007, effective December 1, 2007, and by order adopted March 26, 2009, effective December 1, 2009.)

Editor's note. — Section 22 of P.L. 100-182 provided that the amendment to subdivision (b) of this rule by the order of the Supreme Court adopted April 29, 1985, would apply with respect to all offenses committed before the taking effect of § 215(b) of the Comprehensive Crime Control Act of 1984.

CASE NOTES

Federal sentences are not generally reviewable, and the sentencing judge may draw on varied sources for information that will assist him in determining appropriate punishment. United States v. Powell, 487 F.2d 325 (4th Cir. 1973).

Basis for motion. — Some, but not all, species of surrogate assistance will trigger subdivision (b) and § 5K1.1. Specifically, subdivision (b) and § 5K1.1 motions may be based on assistance rendered by a defendant's surrogate when: (1) the defendant plays some role in instigating, requesting, providing, or directing the assistance; (2) the government would not have received the assistance but for the defendant's participation; (3) the assistance is rendered gratuitously; and (4) the court finds that no other circumstances weigh against rewarding the assistance. United States v. Doe, 870 F. Supp. 702 (E.D. Va. 1994).

But sentence cannot stand if based upon misinformation of constitutional magnitude. — While not every type of misinformation will justify relief, a sentence cannot stand if it is based on assumptions concerning the defendant's criminal record that are materially false, or if it is founded in part upon misinformation of constitutional magnitude. United States v. Powell, 487 F.2d 325 (4th Cir. 1973).

Rule provides only method by which prosecution can have sentence altered. — Where the court indisputably had jurisdiction to pass sentence and it was within the authorized limits of punishment, it is not alterable by the prosecution save to reduce or correct it as illegal under this rule, for the government cannot appeal or by any other process augment it. United States v. Walker, 346 F.2d 428 (4th Cir. 1965).

When deferral motion for sentencing reduction under federal guidelines barred. — If at the time of sentencing, the government deems the defendant's assistance substantial, the government cannot defer its decision to make a U.S.S.G. § 5K1.1 motion on the ground that it will make a Fed. R. Crim. P. 35(b) motion after sentencing. Instead, the government at that time must determine—yes or no—whether it will make a U.S.S.G. § 5K1.1 motion. If the government defers making a U.S.S.G. § 5K1.1 motion on the premise that it will make a Fed. R. Crim. P. 35(b) motion after sentencing, the sentence that follows deprives a defendant of due process, and is therefore in violation of law. United States v. Martin, 25 F.3d 211 (4th Cir. 1994).

120-day period cannot be enlarged. — The broad scope at sentencing is subject to post-sentencing restrictions on the sentencing court's power. It must be borne in mind that the language of subdivision (b) of this rule limits a court's jurisdiction to act on a motion to correct or reduce a sentence to the 120-day period following sentencing. Rule 45(b) circumscribes yet more the limited language of subdivision (b) of this rule by permitting no enlargement of the 120-day period. United States v. Hemby, 583 F. Supp. 58 (E.D. Va. 1983), aff'd, 753 F.2d 30 (4th Cir.), cert. denied, 471 U.S. 1068, 105 S. Ct. 2147, 85 L. Ed. 2d 503 (1985).

Enlargement of the period for taking action under this rule is prohibited by Rule 45(b). United States v. Koneski, 323 F.2d 862 (4th Cir. 1963).

Ruling on motion to reduce sentence cannot be delayed past this period. — Where defendant filed two motions under subdivision (b) of this rule within the 120-day time limit, the second motion requesting a delay in ruling on the first motion in order to consider events that might arise after expiration of that period, the court was without jurisdiction to consider the motion after expiration of the 120-day period. United States v. Breit, 575 F. Supp. 238 (E.D. Va. 1983), modified, 754 F.2d 526 (4th Cir. 1985).

A motion for reduction of sentence is addressed to the sound discretion of the district court. United States v. Stumpf, 476 F.2d 945 (4th Cir. 1973).

When prisoner's presence required on motion under this rule. — On a motion under this rule and 28 U.S.C. § 2255, the production of the prisoner should be ordered only where the court is of the opinion that his presence would aid in arriving at the truth of the matter involved. United States v. Nelms, 190 F. Supp. 677 (W.D. Va. 1960), aff'd, 291 F.2d 390 (4th Cir. 1961).

Motion for modification or reduction of sentence held not timely made. — See United States v. Koneski, 323 F.2d 862 (4th Cir. 1963).

No authority to alter sentence where sentence was not product of error. — When district court unequivocally states a sentence and then imposes it, and the sentence is not the product of error, the district court has no authority to alter that sentence. United States v. Fraley, 988 F.2d 4 (4th Cir. 1993).

District judge could not change sentence under this rule once it was pronounced, and thus "imposed," at sentencing hearing. United States v. Layman, 116 F.3d 105 (4th Cir. 1997), cert. denied, 522 U.S. 1107, 118 S. Ct. 1034, 140 L. Ed. 2d 101 (1998).

Court "may correct an illegal sentence at any time." Although a sentence imposed in a criminal case which does not conform to the applicable penalty statute is illegal, Rule 35 of the Federal Rules of Criminal Procedure provides that the district court "may correct an illegal sentence at any time." Since the trial court had both the authority and the duty to correct its failure to impose a special three-year parole term required by statute and added the special parole term when the requirement to do so became apparent, a prisoner is not entitled to have his sentence vacated on the ground that his original sentence was illegal. Hazelwood v. Arnold, 539 F.2d 1031 (4th Cir. 1976).

Motion for reduction of sentence may not be considered pending appeal. — A district court does not have jurisdiction to consider a motion for reduction of sentence under subdivision (b) pending appeal. United States v. Reilly, 624 F. Supp. 344 (E.D. Va. 1985), aff'd, 785 F.2d 306 (4th Cir. 1986).

Primary responsibility for filing motion to reduce sentence stems from defendant. — See Turner v. United States, 423 F. Supp. 581 (E.D. Va. 1976).

And failure to file motion does not render trial counsel ineffective. — It imposes too great a burden to brand trial counsel as ineffective merely because no motion in reduction of sentence is timely filed, even in situations where the court inferentially invites such action. Turner v. United States, 423 F. Supp. 581 (E.D. Va. 1976).

A judge may not use the commitment order to override the unambiguous sentence orally imposed. — To the extent of any conflict between the written commitment order and the oral sentence, the latter is controlling. The proper remedy is for the District Court to correct the written judgment so that it conforms with the sentencing court's oral pronouncements. United States v. Bussey, 543 F. Supp. 981 (E.D. Va. 1982).

Presumption that sentences will run concurrently. — Although the variance between sentence pronounced from the bench and the sentence set forth in the commitment order might, on its face, be considered to create an ambiguity, absent clear language to the contrary there is a presumption that sentences imposed on more than one offense at the same time, or at different times, will run concurrently. United States v. Bussey, 543 F. Supp. 981 (E.D. Va. 1982).

Remedy for discrepancy between oral pronouncement to written judgment. — The courts are in some disagreement as to whether this rule or Rule 36 is the appropriate means to remedy a discrepancy between oral pronouncement of sentence and the written judgment and commitment order. Rule 36 is the appropriate remedy to make the judgment and commitment papers conform to the sentence pronounced orally, although some courts have spoken of this rule as the applicable rule, but it does not matter which rule is used. United States v. Bussey, 543 F. Supp. 981 (E.D. Va. 1982).

Case sent back to lower court to conform written to oral sentences. — Where the written judgments differed from the oral judgments with respect to which sentences were to be served consecutively and which concurrently, but the total number of years to be served was the same, the sentences to be served were those pronounced in the defendant's presence in open court and not those set out in the written judgments of the court. The court of appeals would not on this account declare the sentences void, but the case would be sent back to the district court in order that the written judgments might be corrected to conform with the oral pronouncements, pursuant to this rule. Rakes v. United States, 309 F.2d 686 (4th Cir. 1962), rev'g 202 F. Supp. 15 (W.D. Va. 1961), cert. denied, 373 U.S. 939, 83 S. Ct. 1543, 10 L. Ed. 2d 694 (1963).

Conversion of sentence under Youth Corrections Act. — A federal Court of Appeals has the authority as the second sentencing court to consider a motion by the United States (or by a defendant) that a defendant sentenced under the Youth Corrections Act, 18 U.S.C. § 5005 et seq., will receive no further benefit from the act. If the court concurs then the remainder of the Youth Corrections Act sentence may be converted to an adult sentence after lapse of the 120-day period in subdivision (b) of this rule. United States v. Hemby, 583 F. Supp. 58 (E.D. Va. 1983), aff'd, 753 F.2d 30 (4th Cir.), cert. denied, 471 U.S. 1068, 105 S. Ct. 2147, 85 L. Ed. 2d 503 (1985).

Applied in Rakes v. United States, 231 F. Supp. 812 (W.D. Va. 1964); Rowe v. Peyton, 383 F.2d 709 (4th Cir. 1967); United States v. Flanagan, 305 F. Supp. 325 (E.D. Va. 1969); United States v. Eubanks, 435 F.2d 1261 (4th Cir. 1971); Tolliver v. United States, 563 F.2d 1117 (4th Cir. 1977); United States v. Burton, 629 F.2d 975 (4th Cir. 1980); United States v. Vaughn, 636 F.2d 921 (4th Cir. 1980); United States v. Breit, 754 F.2d 526 (4th Cir. 1985); United States v. Bourbonnais, 602 F. Supp. 664 (E.D. Va. 1985); United States v. Jackson, 802 F.2d 712 (4th Cir. 1986); In re Phillips, Beckwith & Hall, 806 F. Supp. 553 (E.D. Va. 1995); United States v. Goossens, 84 F.3d 697 (4th Cir. 1996);

Spriggs v. United States, 962 F. Supp. 68 (E.D. Va. 1997); United States v. Astacio, 14 F. Supp. 2d 816 (E.D. Va. 1998); United States v. Whitney, No. 99-4842, 2000 U.S. App. LEXIS 12275 (4th Cir. June 5, 2000).

Rule 36. Clerical Error.

After giving any notice it considers appropriate, the court may at any time correct a clerical error in a judgment, order, or other part of the record, or correct an error in the record arising from oversight or omission. (Amended by order adopted April 29, 2002, effective December 1, 2002.)

CASE NOTES

Remedy for discrepancy between oral pronouncement and written judgment. — The courts are in some disagreement as to whether Rule 35 or this rule is the appropriate means to remedy a discrepancy between oral pronouncement of sentence and the written judgment and commitment order. This rule is the appropriate remedy to make the judgment and commitment papers conform to the sentence pronounced orally, although some courts have spoken of Rule 35 as the applicable rule, but it does not matter which rule is used. United States v. Bussey, 543 F. Supp. 981 (E.D. Va. 1982).

Clerical error not present. — Where there was no evidence whatsoever that district court, at sentencing hearing, intended to impose anything but a sentence of 10 months of imprisonment, there was no clerical error, and this rule which provided district court with authority to correct errors in the sentence was not applicable. United States v. Fraley, 988 F.2d 4 (4th Cir. 1993).

Applied in United States v. Blackwell, 515 F.2d 125 (4th Cir. 1975).

Rule 37. (See Editor's note) Indicative Ruling on a Motion for Relief That Is Barred by a Pending Appeal.

(a) *Relief Pending Appeal.* — If a timely motion is made for relief that the court lacks authority to grant because of an appeal that has been docketed and is pending, the court may:

(1) defer considering the motion;

(2) deny the motion; or

(3) state either that it would grant the motion if the court of appeals remands for that purpose or that the motion raises a substantial issue.

(b) *Notice to the Court of Appeals.* — The movant must promptly notify the circuit clerk under Federal Rule of Appellate Procedure 12.1 if the district court states that it would grant the motion or that the motion raises a substantial issue.

(c) *Remand.* — The district court may decide the motion if the court of appeals remands for that purpose. (Adopted by order dated April 24, 2012, effective December 1, 2012.)

Editor's note. — The Chief Justice signed the letters and orders on April 23, 2012, and the amendments were transmitted to Congress on April 24, 2012. The amendments will take effect on December 1, 2012, unless Congress takes action to reject, modify, or defer them.

Rule 38. Staying a Sentence or a Disability.

(a) *Death Sentence.* — The court must stay a death sentence if the defendant appeals the conviction or sentence.

(b) *Imprisonment.* — (1) Stay Granted. — If the defendant is released pending appeal, the court must stay a sentence of imprisonment.

(2) Stay Denied; Place of Confinement. — If the defendant is not released pending appeal, the court may recommend to the Attorney General that the defendant be confined near the place of the trial or appeal for a period reasonably necessary to permit the defendant to assist in preparing the appeal.

(c) *Fine.* — If the defendant appeals, the district court, or the court of appeals under Federal Rule of Appellate Procedure 8, may stay a sentence to pay a fine or a fine and costs. The court may stay the sentence on any terms considered appropriate and may require the defendant to:

(1) deposit all or part of the fine and costs into the district court's registry pending appeal;

(2) post a bond to pay the fine and costs; or

(3) submit to an examination concerning the defendant's assets and, if appropriate, order the defendant to refrain from dissipating assets.

(d) *Probation.* — If the defendant appeals, the court may stay a sentence of probation. The court must set the terms of any stay.

(e) *Restitution and Notice to Victims.* — (1) In General. — If the defendant appeals, the district court, or the court of appeals under Federal Rule of Appellate Procedure 8, may stay — on any terms considered appropriate — any sentence providing for restitution under 18 U.S.C. § 3556 or notice under 18 U.S.C. § 3555.

(2) Ensuring Compliance. — The court may issue any order reasonably necessary to ensure compliance with a restitution order or a notice order after disposition of an appeal, including:

(A) a restraining order;

(B) an injunction;

(C) an order requiring the defendant to deposit all or part of any monetary restitution into the district court's registry; or

(D) an order requiring the defendant to post a bond.

(f) *Forfeiture.* — A stay of a forfeiture order is governed by Rule 32.2(d).

(g) *Disability.* — If the defendant's conviction or sentence creates a civil or employment disability under federal law, the district court, or the court of appeals under Federal Rule of Appellate Procedure 8, may stay the disability pending appeal on any terms considered appropriate. The court may issue any order reasonably necessary to protect the interest represented by the disability pending appeal, including a restraining order or an injunction. (Amended by order adopted December 27, 1948, effective January 1, 1949, by order adopted February 28, 1966, effective July 1, 1966, by order adopted December 4, 1967, effective July 1, 1968, by order adopted April 24, 1972, effective October 1, 1972, by order adopted October 12, 1984, effective November 1, 1987, by order adopted March 9, 1987, effective August 1, 1987, by P.L. 98-473, Title II, § 215(c), effective November 1, 1987, by order adopted April 17, 2000, effective December 1, 2000, and by order adopted April 29, 2002, effective December 1, 2002.)

Cross references. — As to procedure in appeals to United States courts of appeals generally, see Federal Rules of Appellate Procedure, *infra.* See also local rules of the Court of Appeals for the Fourth Circuit.

CASE NOTES

Former procedure for election not to commence service of sentence. — See Bolden v. Clemmer, 235 F. Supp. 832 (E.D. Va. 1964).

Rule 39. [Reserved].

Cross references. — As to procedure in appeals to United States courts of appeals generally, see Federal Rules of Appellate Procedure, *infra.* See also local rules of the Court of Appeals for the Fourth Circuit, *infra.*

VIII. SUPPLEMENTARY AND SPECIAL PROCEEDINGS.

Rule 40. Arrest for Failing to Appear in Another District or for Violating Conditions of Release Set in Another District.

(a) *In General.* — In General. — A person must be taken without unnecessary delay before a magistrate judge in the district of arrest if the person has been arrested under a warrant issued in another district for:

(i) failing to appear as required by the terms of that person's release under 18 U.S.C. §§ 3141-3156 or by a subpoena; or

(ii) violating conditions of release set in another district.

(b) *Proceedings.* — The judge must proceed under Rule 5(c)(3) as applicable.

(c) *Release or Detention Order.* — The judge may modify any previous release or detention order issued in another district, but must state in writing the reasons for doing so.

(d) *Video Teleconferencing.* — Video teleconferencing may be used to conduct an appearance under this rule if the defendant consents. (Amended by order adopted February 28, 1966, effective July 1, 1966, by order adopted April 24, 1972, effective

October 1, 1972, by order adopted April 30, 1979, effective August 1, 1979, by order adopted April 28, 1982, effective August 1, 1982, by P.L. 98-473, Title II, §§ 209(c), approved October 12, 1984, effective October 12, 1984 and November 1, 1987, by order adopted March 9, 1987, effective August 1, 1987, by P.L. 98-473, Title II, § 215(d), effective November 1, 1987, by order adopted April 25, 1989, effective December 1, 1989, by order adopted April 22, 1993, effective December 1, 1993, by order adopted April 29, 1994, effective December 1, 1994, by order adopted April 27, 1995, effective December 1, 1995, by order adopted April 29, 2002, effective December 1, 2002, by order adopted April 12, 2006, effective December 1, 2006, and by order adopted April 26, 2011, effective December 1, 2011.)

CASE NOTES

The provisions of this rule may not be availed of by a prisoner in escape status. United States v. Mensik, 440 F.2d 1232 (4th Cir. 1971) (decided prior to 1979 amendment).

Parole violator removed without hearing held not entitled to further relief. — Where a parole violator, who was returned after serving a state sentence in another district, asserted that he was removed while he had pending in that district a petition for a writ of habeas corpus and that he was arrested and removed without the hearing called for in this rule, it was held that since the issue in the habeas corpus proceeding referred to was decided against him in the present proceeding and the facts clearly entitled the parole board to issue the parole violator warrant for his arrest, even though at his board hearing later the evidence might conceivably show that he was not subject to recommitment, it was unnecessary that he be afforded further relief for any improper conduct by which he was returned to custody for violating his conditional release. Fuller v. Weakley, 349 F.2d 90 (4th Cir. 1965) (decided prior to 1979 amendment).

Rule 41. Search and Seizure.

(a) *Scope and Definitions.* — (1) Scope. — This rule does not modify any statute regulating search or seizure, or the issuance and execution of a search warrant in special circumstances.

(2) Definitions. — The following definitions apply under this rule:

(A) "Property" includes documents, books, papers, any other tangible objects, and information.

(B) "Daytime" means the hours between 6:00 a.m. and 10:00 p.m. according to local time.

(C) "Federal law enforcement officer" means a government agent (other than an attorney for the government) who is engaged in enforcing the criminal laws and is within any category of officers authorized by the Attorney General to request a search warrant.

(D) "Domestic terrorism" and "international terrorism" have the meanings set out in 18 U.S.C. § 2331.

(E) "Tracking device" has the meaning set out in 18 U.S.C. § 3117(b).

(b) *Authority to Issue a Warrant.* — At the request of a federal law enforcement officer or an attorney for the government:

(1) a magistrate judge with authority in the district — or if none is reasonably available, a judge of a state court of record in the district — has authority to issue a warrant to search for and seize a person or property located within the district;

(2) a magistrate judge with authority in the district has authority to issue a warrant for a person or property outside the district if the person or property is located within the district when the warrant is issued but might move or be moved outside the district before the warrant is executed;

(3) a magistrate judge — in an investigation of domestic terrorism or international terrorism — with authority in any district in which activities related to the terrorism may have occurred has authority to issue a warrant for a person or property within or outside that district;

(4) a magistrate judge with authority in the district has authority to issue a warrant to install within the district a tracking device; the warrant may authorize use of the device to track the movement of a person or property located within the district, outside the district, or both; and

(5) a magistrate judge having authority in any district where activities related to the crime may have occurred, or in the District of Columbia, may issue a warrant for property that is located outside the jurisdiction of any state or district, but within any of the following:

(A) a United States territory, possession, or commonwealth;
(B) the premises — no matter who owns them — of a United States diplomatic or consular mission in a foreign state, including any appurtenant building, part of a building, or land used for the mission's purposes; or
(C) a residence and any appurtenant land owned or leased by the United States and used by United States personnel assigned to a United States diplomatic or consular mission in a foreign state.

(c) *Persons or Property Subject to Search or Seizure.* — A warrant may be issued for any of the following:
(1) evidence of a crime;
(2) contraband, fruits of crime, or other items illegally possessed;
(3) property designed for use, intended for use, or used in committing a crime; or
(4) a person to be arrested or a person who is unlawfully restrained.

(d) *Obtaining a Warrant.* — (1) In General. — After receiving an affidavit or other information, a magistrate judge — or if authorized by Rule 41(b), a judge of a state court of record — must issue the warrant if there is probable cause to search for and seize a person or property or to install and use a tracking device.

(2) Requesting a Warrant in the Presence of a Judge. — (A) Warrant on an Affidavit. — When a federal law enforcement officer or an attorney for the government presents an affidavit in support of a warrant, the judge may require the affiant to appear personally and may examine under oath the affiant and any witness the affiant produces.

(B) Warrant on Sworn Testimony. — The judge may wholly or partially dispense with a written affidavit and base a warrant on sworn testimony if doing so is reasonable under the circumstances.

(C) Recording Testimony. — Testimony taken in support of a warrant must be recorded by a court reporter or by a suitable recording device, and the judge must file the transcript or recording with the clerk, along with any affidavit.

(3) Requesting a Warrant by Telephonic or Other Reliable Electronic Means. — In accordance with Rule 4.1, a magistrate judge may issue a warrant based on information communicated by telephone or other reliable electronic means.

(e) *Issuing the Warrant.* — (1) In General. — The magistrate judge or a judge of a state court of record must issue the warrant to an officer authorized to execute it.

(2) Contents of the Warrant. (A) Warrant to Search for and Seize a Person or Property. Except for a tracking-device warrant, the warrant must identify the person or property to be searched, identify any person or property to be seized, and designate the magistrate judge to whom it must be returned. The warrant must command the officer to:
(i) execute the warrant within a specified time no longer than 14 days;
(ii) execute the warrant during the daytime, unless the judge for good cause expressly authorizes execution at another time; and
(iii) return the warrant to the magistrate judge designated in the warrant.

(B) Warrant Seeking Electronically Stored Information. A warrant under Rule 41(e)(2)(A) may authorize the seizure of electronic storage media or the seizure or copying of electronically stored information. Unless otherwise specified, the warrant authorizes a later review of the media or information consistent with the warrant. The time for executing the warrant in Rule 41(e)(2)(A) and (f)(1)(A) refers to the seizure or on-site copying of the media or information, and not to any later off-site copying or review.

(C) Warrant for a Tracking Device. A tracking-device warrant must identify the person or property to be tracked, designate the magistrate judge to whom it must be returned, and specify a reasonable length of time that the device may be used. The time must not exceed 45 days from the date the warrant was issued. The court may, for good cause, grant one or more extensions for a reasonable period not to exceed 45 days each. The warrant must command the officer to:
(i) complete any installation authorized by the warrant within a specified time no longer than 10 calendar days;
(ii) perform any installation authorized by the warrant during the daytime, unless the judge for good cause expressly authorizes installation at another time; and
(iii) return the warrant to the judge designated in the warrant.

(f) *Executing and Returning the Warrant.* — (1) Warrant to Search for and Seize a Person or Property. (A) Noting the Time. The officer executing the warrant must enter on it the exact date and time it was executed.

(B) Inventory. An officer present during the execution of the warrant must prepare and verify an inventory of any property seized. The officer must do so in the presence of another officer and the person from whom, or from whose premises, the property was taken. If either one is not present, the officer must prepare and verify the inventory in the presence of at least one other credible person. In a case involving the seizure of electronic storage media or the seizure or copying of electronically stored information, the inventory may be limited to describing the physical storage media that were seized or copied. The officer may retain a copy of the electronically stored information that was seized or copied.

(C) Receipt. — The officer executing the warrant must give a copy of the warrant and a receipt for the property taken to the person from whom, or from whose premises, the property was taken or leave a copy of the warrant and receipt at the place where the officer took the property.

(D) Return. — The officer executing the warrant must promptly return it — together with a copy of the inventory — to the magistrate judge designated on the warrant. The officer may do so by reliable electronic means. The judge must, on request, give a copy of the inventory to the person from whom, or from whose premises, the property was taken and to the applicant for the warrant.

(2) Warrant for a Tracking Device. (A) Noting the Time. The officer executing a tracking-device warrant must enter on it the exact date and time the device was installed and the period during which it was used.

(B) Return. Within 10 calendar days after the use of the tracking device has ended, the officer executing the warrant must return it to the judge designated in the warrant. The officer may do so by reliable electronic means.

(C) Service. Within 10 calendar days after the use of the tracking device has ended, the officer executing a tracking-device warrant must serve a copy of the warrant on the person who was tracked or whose property was tracked. Service may be accomplished by delivering a copy to the person who, or whose property, was tracked; or by leaving a copy at the person's residence or usual place of abode with an individual of suitable age and discretion who resides at that location and by mailing a copy to the person's last known address. Upon request of the government, the judge may delay notice as provided in Rule 41(f)(3).

(3) Delayed Notice. Upon the government's request, a magistrate judge — or if authorized by Rule 41(b), a judge of a state court of record — may delay any notice required by this rule if the delay is authorized by statute.

(g) *Motion to Return Property.* — A person aggrieved by an unlawful search and seizure of property or by the deprivation of property may move for the property's return. The motion must be filed in the district where the property was seized. The court must receive evidence on any factual issue necessary to decide the motion. If it grants the motion, the court must return the property to the movant, but may impose reasonable conditions to protect access to the property and its use in later proceedings.

(h) *Motion to Suppress.* — A defendant may move to suppress evidence in the court where the trial will occur, as Rule 12 provides.

(i) *Forwarding Papers to the Clerk.* — The magistrate judge to whom the warrant is returned must attach to the warrant a copy of the return, of the inventory, and of all other related papers and must deliver them to the clerk in the district where the property was seized. (Amended by order adopted December 27, 1948, effective October 20, 1949, by order adopted April 9, 1956, effective July 8, 1956, by order adopted April 24, 1972, effective October 1, 1972, by order adopted March 18, 1974, effective July 1, 1974, by order adopted April 26, 1976 and July 8, 1976, effective August 1, 1976, by order adopted July 30, 1977, effective October 1, 1977, by order adopted April 30, 1979, effective August 1, 1979, by order adopted March 9, 1987, effective August 1, 1987, by order adopted April 25, 1989, effective December 1, 1989, by order adopted May 1, 1990, effective December 1, 1990, by order adopted April 22, 1993, effective December 1, 1993, by order adopted April 29, 2002, effective December 1, 2002, by order adopted April 12, 2006, effective December 1, 2006, by order adopted April 23, 2008, effective December 1, 2008, by order adopted March 26, 2009, effective December 1, 2009, and by order adopted April 26, 2011, effective December 1, 2011.)

Law Review. — As to problems arising from the implementation of the Inspector General's investigative authority, see 12 G.M.U. L. Rev. 227 (1990). For an article, "Wake Up and Smell the Contraband: Why Courts That do Not Find Probable Cause Based On Odor Are Wrong," see 42 Wm. & Mary L. Rev. 289 (2000). For an article "For the Criminal Practitioner: A review of all 1995 criminal cases decided by the Fourth Circuit," see 53 Wash. & Lee L. Rev. 465 (1996).

CASE NOTES

Obligation to make claim of constitutional privacy before trial. — Where the codefendants knew from the outset, and particularly at the pretrial suppression hearing, that a codefendant had given them permission to be in the codefendants' mother's residence, and they could have testified at the suppression hearing to the circumstances under which they were present in the home without in any way compromising their rights to remain silent at trial and without any fear that their testimony would be used against them, under these circumstances, it was their obligation under subsection (e) of this rule to make their derivative claim of constitutional privacy before trial. Having been afforded a full opportunity at their own request to present any and all grounds which might have arguably justified the suppression of the questioned evidence, the district court had it chosen to do so would have been acting well within its discretion in refusing to entertain their belated claims during the course of the trial. United States v. Peterson, 524 F.2d 167 (4th Cir. 1975), cert. denied, 423 U.S. 1088, 96 S. Ct. 881, 47 L. Ed. 2d 99, 424 U.S. 925, 96 S. Ct. 1136, 47 L. Ed. 2d 334 (1976).

De novo review. — This rule's scope is a question of law subject to de novo review. Marex Titanic, Inc. v. Wrecked & Abandoned Vessel, 2 F.3d 544 (4th Cir. 1993).

Foreign intelligence gathering exception to warrant clause. — See United States v. Humphrey, 456 F. Supp. 51 (E.D. Va. 1978), aff'd, 629 F.2d 908 (4th Cir. 1981).

Defense of sovereign immunity inapplicable to proceeding for return of illegally seized property. In re J.W. Schonfeld, Ltd., 460 F. Supp. 332 (E.D. Va. 1978).

Rule ordinarily inapplicable in civil action. In re J.W. Schonfeld, Ltd., 460 F. Supp. 332 (E.D. Va. 1978).

This rule did not apply to a situation where defendant sought to have the government return to defendant money defendant voluntarily paid to government officials as a gratuity in violation of 18 U.S.C. § 201(c)(1). United States v. Kim, 738 F. Supp. 1002 (E.D. Va. 1990).

Standing threshold not met. — The plaintiff did not meet the standing threshold presented by this rule. He failed to allege satisfactory evidence of his personal ownership and any legally cognizable interest in the car, the items in the car, or the U.S. currency seized and forfeited from the car. This rule demands evidence of sufficient interest in any claimed property before the case or controversy prong of Article III may be satisfied. Mere proximity and personal relationship to the owner do not satisfy the standing requirement necessary to bring an action regarding the property in federal court. Matthews v. United States, 917 F. Supp. 1090 (E.D. Va. 1996).

Denial of motion for return of property seized held nonappealable. — Denial of a corporation's motion pursuant to subdivision (e) of this rule for the return of property seized from its offices under a search warrant executed by postal inspectors and for an injunction to restrain the government from using the seized evidence at any future hearing or trial is interlocutory and nonappealable. United States v. North Am. Coal Exch., 676 F.2d 99 (4th Cir. 1982).

Records of credit card expenditures. — This rule in tandem with Rule 57(b) assuredly permits seizure of property such as the record of credit card expenditures evidencing defendant's continued criminal activity, viz., remaining a fugitive. There is, in short, a jurisdictional basis under the Federal Rules of Criminal Procedure for an order that such records be seized. United States v. Hall, 583 F. Supp. 717 (E.D. Va. 1984).

Warrant's probable cause had not become stale nor was there unreasonable delay in execution. — Where search warrant was executed within the time periods prescribed by subdivision (c)(1) and § 19.2-56, and where based on surveillance and drug purchases, the law enforcement officers had good reason to believe that defendants were engaged in an ongoing pattern of drug distribution and had no reason to believe that the situation at the apartment had changed in intervening nine days, warrant's probable cause had not become stale, nor was there any unreasonable delay in its execution. United States v. Byars, 762 F. Supp. 1235 (E.D. Va. 1991).

District court abused discretion by allowing intervenor after notice of dismissal filed. — When plaintiff filed its notice of dismissal, the district court had no discretion to allow second party to intervene in the defunct action filed by plaintiff. Marex Titanic, Inc. v. Wrecked & Abandoned Vessel, 2 F.3d 544 (4th Cir. 1993).

Adult bookstore manager entitled to return of magazines. — For a case discussing whether, and for how long, the government could retain magazines seized in connection with obscenity prosecution, see Eckstein v. Cullen, 803 F. Supp. 1107 (E.D. Va. 1992), aff'd sub nom. Eckstein v. Nelson, 18 F.3d 1181 (4th Cir. 1994).

Applied in United States v. Milanovich, 303 F.2d 626 (4th Cir. 1962); United States v. Gearhart, 326 F.2d 412 (4th Cir. 1964); United States v. White, 237 F. Supp. 644 (E.D. Va. 1964); Parrish v. United States, 256 F. Supp. 793 (E.D. Va. 1966); United States v. Mensik, 440 F.2d 1232 (4th Cir. 1971); United States v. Belcher, 577 F. Supp. 1241 (E.D. Va. 1983); United States v. Bunn, 215 F.3d 430, 2000 U.S. App. LEXIS 13975 (4th Cir. W. Va. 2000); United States v. Holland, 214 F.3d 523, 2000 U.S. App. LEXIS 13976 (4th Cir. 2000).

Rule 42. Criminal Contempt.

(a) *Disposition After Notice.* — Any person who commits criminal contempt may be punished for that contempt after prosecution on notice.

(1) Notice. — The court must give the person notice in open court, in an order to show cause, or in an arrest order. The notice must:

(A) state the time and place of the trial;

(B) allow the defendant a reasonable time to prepare a defense; and

(C) state the essential facts constituting the charged criminal contempt and describe it as such.

(2) Appointing a Prosecutor. — The court must request that the contempt be prosecuted by an attorney for the government, unless the interest of justice requires the appointment of another attorney. If the government declines the request, the court must appoint another attorney to prosecute the contempt.

(3) Trial and Disposition. — A person being prosecuted for criminal contempt is entitled to a jury trial in any case in which federal law so provides and must be released or detained as Rule 46 provides. If the criminal contempt involves disrespect toward or criticism of a judge, that judge is disqualified from presiding at the contempt trial or hearing unless the defendant consents. Upon a finding or verdict of guilty, the court must impose the punishment.

(b) *Summary Disposition.* — Notwithstanding any other provision of these rules, the court (other than a magistrate judge) may summarily punish a person who commits criminal contempt in its presence if the judge saw or heard the contemptuous conduct and so certifies; a magistrate judge may summarily punish a person as provided in 28 U.S.C. § 636(e). The contempt order must recite the facts, be signed by the judge, and be filed with the clerk. (Amended by order adopted March 9, 1987, effective August 1, 1987, and by order adopted April 29, 2002, effective December 1, 2002.)

Law Review. — For note, "The Modern Status of the Rules Permitting a Judge to Punish Direct Contempt Summarily," see 28 Wm. & Mary L. Rev. 553 (1987).

CASE NOTES

Summary contempt power is regarded with disfavor. Such procedure should be used only to fill the need for immediate penal vindication of the dignity of the court. United States v. Willett, 432 F.2d 202 (4th Cir. 1970).

Scope of power to summarily punish for contempt. — This rule allows the trial judge, upon the occurrence in his presence of a contempt, immediately and summarily to punish it, if, in his opinion, delay will prejudice the trial. On the other hand, if he believes the exigencies of the trial require that he defer judgment until its completion he may do so without extinguishing his power. Greene v. Tucker, 375 F. Supp. 892 (E.D. Va. 1974) (construing Virginia statute providing for summary contempt proceedings).

"Summary," as used in this rule, does not refer to the timing of the action with reference to the offense but refers to a procedure which dispenses with the formality, delay and digression that would result from the issuance of process, service of complaint and answer, holding hearings, taking evidence, listening to arguments, awaiting briefs, submission of findings, and all that goes with a conventional court trial. The purpose of that procedure is to inform the court of events not within its own knowledge. Greene v. Tucker, 375 F. Supp. 892 (E.D. Va. 1974) (construing Virginia statute providing for summary contempt proceedings).

The exception to the general requirement of a full fact-finding hearing in cases of contempt committed "directly under the eye or within the view of the court" is not grounded solely in the need for immediate vindication of the court's integrity, but is also supported by the fact that there is no need of evidence or assistance of counsel before punishment, because the court has seen the offense. In such a case the court may proceed upon its own knowledge of the facts, and punish the offender, without further proof, and without issue or trial in any form. Greene v. Tucker, 375 F. Supp. 892 (E.D. Va. 1974) (construing Virginia statute providing for summary contempt proceedings).

This rule is no innovation but simply makes more explicit the long-settled usages of law governing the procedure to be followed in contempt proceedings. United States v. Willett, 432 F.2d 202 (4th Cir. 1970).

The distinction between subdivisions (a) and (b) of this rule is that between a "direct" contempt committed "in the actual presence of the court," which may be punished summarily and an "indirect" contempt, which can be prosecuted only upon notice and hearing. United States v. Willett, 432 F.2d 202 (4th Cir. 1970).

Subdivision (a) of this rule is substantially a restatement of existing law. United States v. Willett, 432 F.2d 202 (4th Cir. 1970).

Although indictment is not necessary for a prosecution for criminal contempt, it is permissible so long as the notice requirements of subdivision (b) are satisfied. United States v. Mensik, 440 F.2d 1232 (4th Cir. 1971).

The notice requirements of subdivision (b) of this rule were fully complied with, where the indictment set forth the essential facts of the criminal contempt, describing it as "criminal contempt," and the indictment was read or described to defendant in court on three separate occasions and he was informed of the trial date. United States v. Mensik, 440 F.2d 1232 (4th Cir. 1971).

The failure of an attorney to appear as scheduled for a hearing, if contumacious, has been held not an act committed in the actual presence of the court, and therefore not punishable summarily under subdivision (a) of this rule. United States v. Willett, 432 F.2d 202 (4th Cir. 1970).

Right to jury trial for "serious" contempt. — Where a person is charged with criminal contempt and where the penalty actually imposed would elevate the contempt from "petty" to "serious," in addition to and independent of congressional enactments giving that person the right to demand a jury trial when charged with criminal contempt, he has a right to a jury trial based upon constitutional principles upon demand. "Serious contempt" occurs where the imprisonments exceed or can exceed six months or, generally, where the fine exceeds 500 dollars. Richmond Black Police Officers Ass'n v. City of Richmond, 548 F.2d 123 (4th Cir. 1977).

Notice requirements of rule not followed. — See Richmond Black Police Officers Ass'n v. City of Richmond, 548 F.2d 123 (4th Cir. 1977).

Failure to specify criminal contempt in show cause order not plain error. — Although the show cause order did not specify that an attorney was charged with criminal conduct, it informed him that he was charged with contempt for failure to appear at his client's trial, and he should have realized that the proceedings were not designed to serve the remedial purposes that characterize civil contempt because the nature of the charges could be readily ascertained from the notice. Failure to specify criminal contempt was not plain error and did not violate Rule 42. United States v. Marx, 553 F.2d 874 (4th Cir. 1977).

Trial judge not required to disqualify himself. — Where an attorney who failed to appear at his client's trial was charged with criminal contempt by the trial judge, at the attorney's contempt hearing the judge was not required to disqualify himself because the attorney's absence was not a personal affront which would constitute "disrespect to or criticism of a judge" within the meaning of subdivision (b) of the rule. United States v. Marx, 553 F.2d 874 (4th Cir. 1977).

Applied in United States v. O'Day, 667 F.2d 430 (4th Cir. 1981).

IX. GENERAL PROVISIONS.

Rule 43. Defendant's Presence.

(a) *When Required.* — Unless this rule, Rule 5, or Rule 10 provides otherwise, the defendant must be present at:

(1) the initial appearance, the initial arraignment, and the plea;

(2) every trial stage, including jury impanelment and the return of the verdict; and

(3) sentencing.

(b) *When Not Required.* — A defendant need not be present under any of the following circumstances:

(1) Organizational Defendant. — The defendant is an organization represented by counsel who is present.

(2) Misdemeanor Offense. — The offense is punishable by fine or by imprisonment for not more than one year, or both, and with the defendant's written consent, the court permits arraignment, plea, trial, and sentencing to occur by video teleconferencing or in the defendant's absence.

(3) Conference or Hearing on a Legal Question. — The proceeding involves only a conference or hearing on a question of law.

(4) Sentence Correction. — The proceeding involves the correction or reduction of sentence under Rule 35 or 18 U.S.C. § 3582(c).

(c) *Waiving Continued Presence.* — (1) In General. — A defendant who was initially present at trial, or who had pleaded guilty or nolo contendere, waives the right to be present under the following circumstances:

(A) when the defendant is voluntarily absent after the trial has begun, regardless of whether the court informed the defendant of an obligation to remain during trial;

(B) in a noncapital case, when the defendant is voluntarily absent during sentencing; or

(C) when the court warns the defendant that it will remove the defendant from the courtroom for disruptive behavior, but the defendant persists in conduct that justifies removal from the courtroom.

(2) Waiver's Effect. — If the defendant waives the right to be present, the trial may proceed to completion, including the verdict's return and sentencing, during the defendant's absence. (Amended by order adopted April 22, 1974, effective December 1, 1975, by order adopted July 31, 1975, effective December 1, 1975, by order adopted March 9, 1987, effective August 1, 1987, by order adopted April 27, 1995, effective December 1, 1995, by order adopted April 24, 1998, effective December 1, 1998, by order adopted April 29, 2002, effective December 1, 2002, and by order adopted April 26, 2011, effective December 1, 2011.)

Law Review. — For article, "Reconceptualizing Competence: An Appeal," see 66 Wash. & Lee L. Rev. 259 (2009).

CASE NOTES

Right to be present is constitutional right. — A defendant has a constitutional right to be present at every stage of the trial, including the impaneling of the jury. United States v. White, 237 F. Supp. 644 (E.D. Va. 1964), aff'd, 342 F.2d 379 (4th Cir.), cert. denied, 382 U.S. 871, 86 S. Ct. 148, 15 L. Ed. 2d 109 (1965).

Protective scope of rule is broader than constitutional right alone. — This rule has traditionally been understood to codify both a defendant's constitutional right and his common law right to presence; accordingly, its "protective scope" is broader than the constitutional right alone. United States v. Camacho, 955 F.2d 950 (4th Cir. 1992), cert. denied, 510 U.S. 1000, 114 S. Ct. 571, 126 L. Ed. 2d 470 (1993).

Construction of rule. — Since this rule is but a restatement of existing law, the language of the rule must be construed in light of the prior law upon which the rule was founded and the evolving meanings and purposes of the common-law right to presence. United States v. Peterson, 524 F.2d 167 (4th Cir. 1975), cert. denied, 423 U.S. 1088, 96 S. Ct. 881, 47 L. Ed. 2d 99, 424 U.S. 925, 96 S. Ct. 1136, 47 L. Ed. 2d 334 (1976).

Defendant's presence at commencement of trial not indispensable. — This rule does not establish the defendant's presence at the commencement of his trial as an indispensable prerequisite to the proceedings. United States v. Peterson, 524 F.2d 167 (4th Cir. 1975), cert. denied, 423 U.S. 1088, 96 S. Ct. 881, 47 L. Ed. 2d 99, 424 U.S. 925, 96 S. Ct. 1136, 47 L. Ed. 2d 334 (1976).

Right to be present at trial and sentencing compared. — This rule distinguishes between the waiver of the right to be present at trial and waiver of the right to be present at sentencing. With regard to the right to be present at trial, the rule provides the same degree of protection as does the Constitution. However, with regard to the defendant's right to be present at sentencing, the rule affords a defendant a greater degree of protection than the Constitution provides. Head v. Commonwealth, 3 Va. App. 163, 348 S.E.2d 423 (1986), overruled on other grounds, Cruz v. Commonwealth, 24 Va. App. 454, 482 S.E.2d 880 (1997).

Sentences to be served are those pronounced in the defendant's presence in open court and not those set out in the written judgments of the court. White v. United States, 6 F. Supp. 2d 553 (W.D. Va. 1998).

A defendant may waive his right to be present at the commencement of his trial just as effectively as he can waive his right to be present at later stages of the proceedings. United States v. Peterson, 524 F.2d 167 (4th Cir. 1975), cert. denied, 423 U.S. 1088, 96 S. Ct. 881, 47 L. Ed. 2d 99, 424 U.S. 925, 96 S. Ct. 1136, 47 L. Ed. 2d 334 (1976); United States v. Muzevsky, 760 F.2d 83 (4th Cir. 1985).

A defendant may waive his constitutional right to be present at his own trial. United States v. Camacho, 955 F.2d 950 (4th Cir. 1992), cert. denied, 510 U.S. 1000, 114 S. Ct. 571, 126 L. Ed. 2d 470 (1993).

Waiver must be knowing and voluntary. — A waiver of the right to be present under this rule must be knowing and voluntary. United States v. Peterson, 524 F.2d 167 (4th Cir. 1975), cert. denied, 423 U.S. 1088, 96 S. Ct. 881, 47 L. Ed. 2d 99, 424 U.S. 925, 96 S. Ct. 1136, 47 L. Ed. 2d 334 (1976).

A defendant's voluntary absence at the commencement of his trial acts as a waiver of his right to be present. United States v. Peterson, 524 F.2d 167 (4th Cir. 1975), cert. denied, 423 U.S. 1088, 96 S. Ct. 881, 47 L. Ed. 2d 99, 424 U.S. 925, 96 S. Ct. 1136, 47 L. Ed. 2d 334 (1976).

The right at issue is the right to be present, not the right to have the trial proceed only in the defendant's presence. Thus, if a defendant is aware of the processes occurring and of his right and obligation to be present, his voluntary absence without compelling justification establishes an effective waiver. United States v. Peterson, 524 F.2d 167 (4th Cir. 1975), cert. denied, 423 U.S. 1088, 96 S. Ct. 881, 47 L. Ed. 2d 99, 424 U.S. 925, 96 S. Ct. 1136, 47 L. Ed. 2d 334 (1976).

A defendant's voluntary absence without compelling justification constitutes a waiver of the right to be present. United States v. Camacho, 955 F.2d 950 (4th Cir. 1992), cert. denied, 510 U.S. 1000, 114 S. Ct. 571, 126 L. Ed. 2d 470 (1993).

Determination whether to proceed to trial in absentia. — Not every case involving a defendant's voluntary absence at the commencement of the trial is a proper one in which to proceed to trial in absentia. Instead, each case turns upon a complex of issues, including the likelihood that the trial could soon take place with the defendant present; the difficulty of rescheduling, particularly in multiple-defendant trials; and the burden on the government in having to undertake two trials, again particularly in multiple-defendant trials where the evidence against the defendants is often overlapping and more than one trial might keep the government's witnesses in substantial jeopardy. Thus the decision whether to proceed to trial is vested in the sound discretion of the trial judge. United States v. Peterson, 524 F.2d 167 (4th Cir. 1975), cert. denied, 423 U.S. 1088, 96 S. Ct. 881, 47 L. Ed. 2d 99, 424 U.S. 925, 96 S. Ct. 1136, 47 L. Ed. 2d 334 (1976).

The decision whether to proceed in the accused's absence is vested in the sound discretion of the trial court. United States v. Muzevsky, 760 F.2d 83 (4th Cir. 1985).

If the court knows the reasons for the defendant's absence, the analysis required by United States v. Peterson, 524 F.2d 167 (4th Cir. 1975) should be undertaken at the time the defendant fails to appear; in the proper circumstances, a short postponement of the trial might prevent the need to try an absent defendant. However, when the court does not know the reasons for the defendant's absence and has no basis to believe that the trial can be rescheduled within a reasonable time, consideration of the government's difficulty in reassembling its proof may dictate an immediate trial. United States v. Muzevsky, 760 F.2d 83 (4th Cir. 1985).

Judge did not abuse discretion in electing to proceed with trial in defendant's absence. — See United States v. Peterson, 524 F.2d 167 (4th Cir. 1975), cert. denied, 423 U.S. 1088, 96 S. Ct. 881, 47 L. Ed. 2d 99, 424 U.S. 925, 96 S. Ct. 1136, 47 L. Ed. 2d 334 (1976).

When a continuance is not granted, a court should withhold decision on the motion for a new trial and sentencing until it can learn whether the defendant voluntarily waived his right to be present. United States v. Muzevsky, 760 F.2d 83 (4th Cir. 1985).

Right includes presence at voir dire and impanelling of jurors. — This rule confers upon a defendant the right to be present at every stage of the trial; included is the right to be present at the voir dire and impaneling of jurors. United States v. Tipton, 90 F.3d 861 (4th Cir. 1996), cert. denied, 520 U.S. 1253, 117 S. Ct. 2414, 138 L. Ed. 2d 179 (1997).

Response to jury question in defendant's absence held harmless error. — Although the district court committed a technical violation of subdivision (a) when it responded to a question posed by the jury during its deliberations at a time when the defendant was not in the courtroom, in light of the fact that defendant's counsel was present and that prompt remedial measures were taken by the district court, beyond any reasonable doubt the error was harmless. United States v. Harris, 814 F.2d 155 (4th Cir. 1987).

In-chambers conference concerning the dismissal of a juror, while a stage of the trial within the meaning of subdivision (a) of this rule and not excluded by subdivision (b) or (c), is not a stage of the trial when the absence of the defendant would frustrate the fairness of the trial, so long as counsel for the defendant is present. United States v. Boone, 759 F.2d 345 (4th Cir.), cert. denied, 474 U.S. 861, 106 S. Ct. 176, 88 L. Ed. 2d 146 (1985).

Defendants could not contend that the district court committed reversible error by not including them in in-chambers conference with counsel in which the district court decided to substitute an alternate juror for a juror who had slept through much of the trial, where not only was defense counsel present, but he actually requested that the juror be removed. United States v. Boone, 759 F.2d 345 (4th Cir.), cert. denied, 474 U.S. 861, 106 S. Ct. 176, 88 L. Ed. 2d 146 (1985).

Necessity of defendant's presence for in-chamber counsel discussions. — It is error to conduct, without the presence of the defendant, an in-chambers discussion with counsel for the government and the defendant about a substantive question with respect to its instructions sent out by a deliberating jury. United States v. Rhodes, 32 F.3d 867 (4th Cir. 1994), cert. denied, 513 U.S. 1164, 115 S. Ct. 1130, 130 L. Ed. 2d 1092 (1995).

Defendant's absence harmless error. — Where the answer that the district court gave to the jury's question was so patently legally correct that it was beyond argument, and it also was the answer which defendant's counsel urged the district court to use, it was obvious that defendant's absence from the in-chambers discussion did not affect his substantial rights and it was therefore harmless beyond a reasonable doubt. United States v. Rhodes, 32 F.3d 867 (4th Cir. 1994), cert. denied, 513 U.S. 1164, 115 S. Ct. 1130, 130 L. Ed. 2d 1092 (1995).

Although right to personal presence is "fundamental", errors in conducting proceedings out of the presence of defendant may be found harmless; reversible error is limited to those circumstances where a defendant's presence has a relation, reasonably substantial, to the fullness of his opportunity to defend himself. The right is thus by definition limited to those circumstances in which absence has a "prejudicial impact' on a defendant's opportunity to effectively assist in his defense; the absences here were of the intermittent sort, not approaching the total denial of any effective participation in critical phases of the voir dire the might warrant the presumption of prejudice. United States v. Tipton, 90 F.3d 861 (4th Cir. 1996), cert. denied, 520 U.S. 1253, 117 S. Ct. 2414, 138 L. Ed. 2d 179 (1997).

Defendant sentenced in absentia. — A defendant has the right under Rules 32(a) and 43 of the Federal Rules of Criminal Procedure not to be sentenced for a felony in absentia. The fact that the district court amended a prisoner's sentence by imposing only a required three year special parole term did not satisfy the pertinent requirement of Rule 43 that the defendant be present. The imposition of a special parole term is not merely a ministerial act because if the district court had been aware at the time of sentencing that the special parole term must be imposed, it may well be that a shorter prison term would have been awarded. Hazelwood v. Arnold, 539 F.2d 1031 (4th Cir. 1976).

State's request to hold trial through video conferencing was permitted. — See Edwards v. Logan, 38 F. Supp. 2d 463 (W.D. Va. 1999).

An exchange of communications between judge and jury does not violate this rule where the contents of the notes, even if not the precise wording, were revealed to counsel, and, more importantly, because the notes dealt not with substantive questions or supplemental jury instructions but rather only informed the judge and jury regarding the state of deliberations. United States v. Head, 697 F.2d 1200 (4th Cir. 1982), cert. denied, 462 U.S. 1132, 103 S. Ct. 3113, 77 L. Ed. 2d 1367 (1983).

Standard of review on appeal. — The Court of Appeals reviews a decision of the district court to proceed with a trial when the defendant is absent under an abuse of discretion standard, and the district court's factual findings will not be disturbed unless clearly erroneous. United States v. Camacho, 955 F.2d 950 (4th Cir. 1992), cert. denied, 510 U.S. 1000, 114 S. Ct. 571, 126 L. Ed. 2d 470 (1993).

The Court of Appeals reviews whether the district court properly exercised its discretion in finding that the defendant knowingly and voluntarily waived the right to be present. If the court properly found the right to be waived, the reviewing court must next consider whether the district court abused its discretion in concluding that there was on balance a controlling public interest to continue the trial in the defendant's absence (typically, these factors will favor proceeding without the defendant in multi defendant trials only). If the district court was in error in finding voluntary waiver or in continuing the trial in defendant's absence, the court must ask whether that error was harmless. United States v. Camacho, 955 F.2d 950 (4th Cir. 1992), cert. denied, 510 U.S. 1000, 114 S. Ct. 571, 126 L. Ed. 2d 470 (1993).

Applied in United States v. Martinez, 923 F. Supp. 861 (E.D. Va. 1996).

Rule 44. Right to and Appointment of Counsel.

(a) *Right to Appointed Counsel.* — A defendant who is unable to obtain counsel is entitled to have counsel appointed to represent the defendant at every stage of the proceeding from initial appearance through appeal, unless the defendant waives this right.

(b) *Appointment Procedure.* — Federal law and local court rules govern the procedure for implementing the right to counsel.

(c) *Inquiry Into Joint Representation.* — (1) Joint Representation. — Joint representation occurs when:

(A) two or more defendants have been charged jointly under Rule 8(b) or have been joined for trial under Rule 13; and

(B) the defendants are represented by the same counsel, or counsel who are associated in law practice.

(2) Court's Responsibilities in Cases of Joint Representation. — The court must promptly inquire about the propriety of joint representation and must personally advise each defendant of the right to the effective assistance of counsel, including separate representation. Unless there is good cause to believe that no conflict of interest is likely to arise, the court must take appropriate measures to protect each defendant's right to counsel. (Amended by order adopted February 28, 1966, effective July 1, 1966, by order adopted April 24, 1972, effective October 1, 1972, by order adopted April 30, 1979, effective December 1, 1980, by order adopted March 9, 1987, effective August 1, 1987, by order adopted April 22, 1993, effective December 1, 1993, and by order adopted April 29, 2002, effective December 1, 2002.)

Law Review. — For article, "Legal Ethics in the Bid Rigging Cases," see 19 U. Rich. L. Rev. 513 (1985).

CASE NOTES

Applied in Jones v. Rivers, 338 F.2d 862 (4th Cir. 1964); United States v. Young, 644 F.2d 1008 (4th Cir. 1981).

Rule 45. Computing and Extending Time.

(a) *Computing Time.* — The following rules apply in computing any time period specified in these rules, in any local rule or court order, or in any statute that does not specify a method of computing time.

(1) Period Stated in Days or a Longer Unit. When the period is stated in days or a longer unit of time:

(A) exclude the day of the event that triggers the period;

(B) count every day, including intermediate Saturdays, Sundays, and legal holidays; and

(C) include the last day of the period, but if the last day is a Saturday, Sunday, or legal holiday, the period continues to run until the end of the next day that is not a Saturday, Sunday, or legal holiday.

(2) Period Stated in Hours. When the period is stated in hours:

(A) begin counting immediately on the occurrence of the event that triggers the period;

(B) count every hour, including hours during intermediate Saturdays, Sundays, and legal holidays; and

(C) if the period would end on a Saturday, Sunday, or legal holiday, the period continues to run until the same time on the next day that is not a Saturday, Sunday, or legal holiday.

(3) Inaccessibility of the Clerk's Office. Unless the court orders otherwise, if the clerk's office is inaccessible:

(A) on the last day for filing under Rule 45(a)(1), then the time for filing is extended to the first accessible day that is not a Saturday, Sunday, or legal holiday; or

(B) during the last hour for filing under Rule 45(a)(2), then the time for filing is extended to the same time on the first accessible day that is not a Saturday, Sunday, or legal holiday.

(4) "Last Day" Defined. Unless a different time is set by a statute, local rule, or court order, the last day ends:

(A) for electronic filing, at midnight in the court's time zone; and

(B) for filing by other means, when the clerk's office is scheduled to close.

(5) "Next Day" Defined. The "next day" is determined by continuing to count forward when the period is measured after an event and backward when measured before an event.

(6) "Legal Holiday" Defined. "Legal holiday" means:

(A) the day set aside by statute for observing New Year's Day, Martin Luther King Jr.'s Birthday, Washington's Birthday, Memorial Day, Independence Day, Labor Day, Columbus Day, Veterans' Day, Thanksgiving Day, or Christmas Day;

(B) any day declared a holiday by the President or Congress; and

(C) for periods that are measured after an event, any other day declared a holiday by the state where the district court is located.

(b) *Extending Time.* — (1) In General. — When an act must or may be done within a specified period, the court on its own may extend the time, or for good cause may do so on a party's motion made:

(A) before the originally prescribed or previously extended time expires; or

(B) after the time expires if the party failed to act because of excusable neglect.

(2) Exception. — The court may not extend the time to take any action under Rule 35, except as stated in that rule.

(c) *Additional Time After Certain Kinds of Service.* — Whenever a party must or may act within a specified period after service and service is made in the manner provided under Federal Rule of Civil Procedure 5(b)(2)(C), (D), (E), or (F), 3 days are added after the period would otherwise expire under subdivision (a). (Amended by order adopted February 28, 1966, effective July 1, 1966, by order adopted December 4, 1967, effective July 1, 1968, by order adopted March 1, 1971, effective July 1, 1971, by order adopted April 28, 1982, effective August 1, 1982, and by order adopted April 29, 1985, effective August 1, 1985, by order adopted March 9, 1987, effective August 1, 1987, by order adopted April 29, 2002, effective December 1, 2002, by order adopted April 25, 2005, effective December 1, 2005, by order adopted April 30, 2007, effective December 1, 2007, by order adopted April 23, 2008, effective December 1, 2008, and by order adopted March 26, 2009, effective December 1, 2009.)

CASE NOTES

120-day period in Rule 35(b) cannot be enlarged. — The broad scope at sentencing is subject to post sentencing restrictions on the sentencing court's power. It must be borne in mind that the language of Rule 35(b) limits a court's jurisdiction to act on a motion to correct or reduce a sentence to the 120-day period following sentencing. Subdivision (b) of this rule circumscribes yet more the limited language of Rule 35(b) by permitting no enlargement of the 120-day period. United States v. Hemby, 583 F. Supp. 58 (E.D. Va. 1983), aff'd, 753 F.2d 30 (4th Cir.), cert. denied, 471 U.S. 1068, 105 S. Ct. 2147, 85 L. Ed. 2d 503 (1985).

Ruling on motion to reduce sentence cannot be delayed past this period. — Where defendant filed two motions under Rule 35(b) within the 120-day time limit, the second motion requesting a delay in ruling on the first motion in order to consider events that might arise after expiration of that period, the court was without jurisdiction to consider the motion after expiration of the 120-day period. United States v. Breit, 575 F. Supp. 238 (E.D. Va. 1983), modified, 754 F.2d 526 (4th Cir. 1985).

Applied in United States v. Koneski, 323 F.2d 862 (4th Cir. 1963); United States v. O'Day, 667 F.2d 430 (4th Cir. 1981); United States v. Breit, 754 F.2d 526 (4th Cir. 1985); United States v. Jackson, 802 F.2d 712 (4th Cir. 1986).

Rule 46. Release from Custody; Supervising Detention.

(a) *Before Trial.* — The provisions of 18 U.S.C. §§ 3142 and 3144 govern pretrial release.

(b) *During Trial.* — A person released before trial continues on release during trial under the same terms and conditions. But the court may order different terms and conditions or terminate the release if necessary to ensure that the person will be present during trial or that the person's conduct will not obstruct the orderly and expeditious progress of the trial.

(c) *Pending Sentence or Appeal.* — The provisions of 18 U.S.C. § 3143 govern release pending sentencing or appeal. The burden of establishing that the defendant will not flee or pose a danger to any other person or to the community rests with the defendant.

(d) *Pending Hearing on a Violation of Probation or Supervised Release.* — Rule 32.1(a)(6) governs release pending a hearing on a violation of probation or supervised release.

(e) *Surety.* — The court must not approve a bond unless any surety appears to be qualified. Every surety, except a legally approved corporate surety, must demonstrate by affidavit that its assets are adequate. The court may require the affidavit to describe the following:

(1) the property that the surety proposes to use as security;

(2) any encumbrance on that property;

(3) the number and amount of any other undischarged bonds and bail undertakings the surety has issued; and

(4) any other liability of the surety.

(f) *Bail Forfeiture.* — (1) Declaration. — The court must declare the bail forfeited if a condition of the bond is breached.

(2) Setting Aside. — The court may set aside in whole or in part a bail forfeiture upon any condition the court may impose if:

(A) the surety later surrenders into custody the person released on the surety's appearance bond; or

(B) it appears that justice does not require bail forfeiture.

(3) Enforcement. — (A) Default Judgment and Execution. — If it does not set aside a bail forfeiture, the court must, upon the government's motion, enter a default judgment.

(B) Jurisdiction and Service. — By entering into a bond, each surety submits to the district court's jurisdiction and irrevocably appoints the district clerk as its agent to receive service of any filings affecting its liability.

(C) Motion to Enforce. — The court may, upon the government's motion, enforce the surety's liability without an independent action. The government must serve any motion, and notice as the court prescribes, on the district clerk. If so served, the clerk must promptly mail a copy to the surety at its last known address.

(4) Remission. — After entering a judgment under Rule 46(f)(3), the court may remit in whole or in part the judgment under the same conditions specified in Rule 46(f)(2).

(g) *Exoneration.* — The court must exonerate the surety and release any bail when a bond condition has been satisfied or when the court has set aside or remitted the forfeiture. The court must exonerate a surety who deposits cash in the amount of the bond or timely surrenders the defendant into custody.

(h) *Supervising Detention Pending Trial.* — (1) In General. — To eliminate unnecessary detention, the court must supervise the detention within the district of any defendants awaiting trial and of any persons held as material witnesses.

(2) Reports. — An attorney for the government must report biweekly to the court, listing each material witness held in custody for more than 10 days pending indictment, arraignment, or trial. For each material witness listed in the report, an attorney for the government must state why the witness should not be released with or without a deposition being taken under Rule 15(a).

(i) *Forfeiture of Property.* — The court may dispose of a charged offense by ordering the forfeiture of 18 U.S.C. § 3142(c)(1)(B)(xi) property under 18 U.S.C. § 3146(d), if a fine in the amount of the property's value would be an appropriate sentence for the charged offense.

(j) *Producing a Statement.* — (1) In General. — Rule 26.2(a)-(d) and (f) applies at a detention hearing under 18 U.S.C. § 3142, unless the court for good cause rules otherwise.

(2) Sanctions for Not Producing a Statement. — If a party disobeys a Rule 26.2 order to produce a witness's statement, the court must not consider that witness's testimony at the detention hearing. (Amended by order adopted April 9, 1956, effective July 8, 1956, by order adopted February 28, 1966, effective July 1, 1966, by order adopted April 24, 1972, effective October 1, 1972, by P.L. 98-473, Title II, §§ 209(d)(1), 209(d)(2), 209(d)(3), 209(d)(4), approved October 12, 1984, and by order adopted March

9, 1987, effective August 1, 1987, by order adopted April 30, 1991, effective December 1, 1991, by order adopted April 22, 1993, effective December 1, 1993, amended by P.L. 103-322 approved September 13, 1994, effective December 1, 1994, and by order adopted April 29, 2002, effective December 1, 2002.)

CASE NOTES

Applied in Sellers v. Roper, 554 F. Supp. 202 (E.D. Va. 1982).

Rule 47. Motions and Supporting Affidavits.

(a) *In General.* — A party applying to the court for an order must do so by motion.

(b) *Form and Content of a Motion.* — A motion — except when made during a trial or hearing — must be in writing, unless the court permits the party to make the motion by other means. A motion must state the grounds on which it is based and the relief or order sought. A motion may be supported by affidavit.

(c) *Timing of a Motion.* — A party must serve a written motion — other than one that the court may hear ex parte — and any hearing notice at least 7 days before the hearing date, unless a rule or court order sets a different period. For good cause, the court may set a different period upon ex parte application.

(d) *Affidavit Supporting a Motion.* — The moving party must serve any supporting affidavit with the motion. A responding party must serve any opposing affidavit at least one day before the hearing, unless the court permits later service. (Amended by order adopted April 29, 2002, effective December 1, 2002, and by order adopted March 26, 2009, effective December 1, 2009.)

Rule 48. Dismissal.

(a) *By the Government.* — The government may, with leave of court, dismiss an indictment, information, or complaint. The government may not dismiss the prosecution during trial without the defendant's consent.

(b) *By the Court.* — The court may dismiss an indictment, information, or complaint if unnecessary delay occurs in:

(1) presenting a charge to a grand jury;

(2) filing an information against a defendant; or

(3) bringing a defendant to trial. (Amended by order adopted April 29, 2002, effective December 1, 2002.)

CASE NOTES

A dismissal without prejudice pursuant to subsection (a) is not immediately reviewable. United States v. Edelman, 809 F. Supp. 431 (E.D. Va. 1992).

Dismissal by prosecutor before trial is without prejudice. — It is true that subdivision (a) states that a United States attorney may, by leave of court, file a dismissal of an indictment "and the prosecution shall thereupon terminate," but the authorities are replete that such a dismissal is without prejudice. According to the rule, it is only when a trial has begun and jeopardy has attached that a dismissal may not be filed without a defendant's consent. United States v. Chase, 372 F.2d 453 (4th Cir. 1967).

Authority of district court to dismiss for unnecessary delay. — Under subdivision (b) of this rule the district court is vested with authority to dismiss an indictment if there is unnecessary delay in presenting a charge to a grand jury, or in bringing a defendant to trial. This authority supplements the district court's obligation to dismiss indictments in order to protect a defendant's constitutional rights, and it is broader in compass. United States v. Balochi, 527 F.2d 562 (4th Cir. 1976).

District court's discretion not exceeded in dismissing indictment. — Where the government's motion to dismiss the second count of a two-count indictment against the defendant was granted before the jury was impaneled because the case was weak and the government represented that it had no intention of bringing up the charge again, but nine months later the government reindicted the defendant on the second count, the district court did not exceed its discretion in dismissing the indictment with prejudice on both grounds authorized by this rule. United States v. Balochi, 527 F.2d 562 (4th Cir. 1976).

Defendant lacks standing to appeal dismissal. — A defendant would lack standing to appeal dismissal because he would not be legally aggrieved absent subsequent proceedings against him. United States v. Edelman, 809 F. Supp. 431 (E.D. Va. 1992).

Subdivision (b) is limited to post-arrest situations. United States v. Sample, 565 F. Supp. 1166 (E.D. Va. 1983).

Period when a prison inmate was no longer in segregative confinement could not, under any circumstances, be considered in resolving the defendant's claim under either subdivision (b) of this rule or the speedy trial constitutional provisions. United States v. Daniels, 698 F.2d 221 (4th Cir. 1983).

Segregative confinement of a prison inmate is not the equivalent of an arrest for purposes either of the rule or of the constitutional provisions. United States v. Daniels, 698 F.2d 221 (4th Cir. 1983).

Rule 49. Service and Filing Papers.

(a) *When Required.* — A party must serve on every other party any written motion (other than one to be heard ex parte), written notice, designation of the record on appeal, or similar paper.

(b) *How Made.* — Service must be made in the manner provided for a civil action. When these rules or a court order requires or permits service on a party represented by an attorney, service must be made on the attorney instead of the party, unless the court orders otherwise.

(c) *Notice of a Court Order.* — When the court issues an order on any post-arraignment motion, the clerk must provide notice in a manner provided for in a civil action. Except as Federal Rule of Appellate Procedure 4(b) provides otherwise, the clerk's failure to give notice does not affect the time to appeal, or relieve — or authorize the court to relieve — a party's failure to appeal within the allowed time.

(d) *Filing.* — A party must file with the court a copy of any paper the party is required to serve. A paper must be filed in a manner provided for in a civil action.

(e) *Electronic Service and Filing.* — A court may, by local rule, allow papers to be filed, signed, or verified by electronic means that are consistent with any technical standards established by the Judicial Conference of the United States. A local rule may require electronic filing only if reasonable exceptions are allowed. A paper filed electronically in compliance with a local rule is written or in writing under these rules.

(Amended by order adopted February 28, 1966, effective July 1, 1966, by order adopted December 4, 1967, effective July 1, 1968, by order adopted April 29, 1985, effective August 1, 1985, by order adopted March 9, 1987, effective August 1, 1987, by order adopted April 22, 1993, effective December 1, 1993, by order adopted April 27, 1995, effective December 1, 1995, by order adopted April 29, 2002, effective December 1, 2002, and by order adopted April 26, 2011, effective December 1, 2011.)

CASE NOTES

Effect on jurisdiction of failure to give notice. — The rule requiring the clerk to give notice of the entry of orders is generally interpreted to make the failure of notice irrelevant to application of the jurisdictional rule. United States v. Schuchardt, 685 F.2d 901 (4th Cir. 1982).

Rule 49.1. Privacy Protection for Filings Made with the Court.

(a) *Redacted Filings.* — Unless the court orders otherwise, in an electronic or paper filing with the court that contains an individual's social-security number, taxpayer-identification number, or birth date, the name of an individual known to be a minor, a financial-account number, or the home address of an individual, a party or nonparty making the filing may include only:

(1) the last four digits of the social-security number and taxpayer-identification number;

(2) the year of the individual's birth;

(3) the minor's initials;

(4) the last four digits of the financial-account number; and

(5) the city and state of the home address.

(b) *Exemptions from the Redaction Requirement.* — The redaction requirement does not apply to the following:

(1) a financial-account number or real property address that identifies the property allegedly subject to forfeiture in a forfeiture proceeding;

(2) the record of an administrative or agency proceeding;

(3) the official record of a state-court proceeding;

(4) the record of a court or tribunal, if that record was not subject to the redaction requirement when originally filed;

(5) a filing covered by Rule 49.1(d);

(6) a pro se filing in an action brought under 28 U.S.C. §§ 2241, 2254, or 2255;

(7) a court filing that is related to a criminal matter or investigation and that is prepared before the filing of a criminal charge or is not filed as part of any docketed criminal case;

(8) an arrest or search warrant; and

(9) a charging document and an affidavit filed in support of any charging document.

(c) *Immigration Cases.* — A filing in an action brought under 28 U.S.C. § 2241 that relates to the petitioner's immigration rights is governed by Federal Rule of Civil Procedure 5.2.

(d) *Filings Made Under Seal.* — The court may order that a filing be made under seal without redaction. The court may later unseal the filing or order the person who made the filing to file a redacted version for the public record.

(e) *Protective Orders.* — For good cause, the court may by order in a case:

(1) require redaction of additional information; or

(2) limit or prohibit a nonparty's remote electronic access to a document filed with the court.

(f) *Option for Additional Unredacted Filing Under Seal.* — A person making a redacted filing may also file an unredacted copy under seal. The court must retain the unredacted copy as part of the record.

(g) *Option for Filing a Reference List.* — A filing that contains redacted information may be filed together with a reference list that identifies each item of redacted information and specifies an appropriate identifier that uniquely corresponds to each item listed. The list must be filed under seal and may be amended as of right. Any reference in the case to a listed identifier will be construed to refer to the corresponding item of information.

(h) *Waiver of Protection of Identifiers.* — A person waives the protection of Rule 49.1(a) as to the person's own information by filing it without redaction and not under seal. (Adopted by order adopted April 30, 2007, effective December 1, 2007.)

Rule 50. Prompt Disposition.

Scheduling preference must be given to criminal proceedings as far as practicable. (Amended by order adopted April 24, 1972, effective October 1, 1972, by order adopted March 18, 1974, effective July 1, 1974, by order adopted April 26, 1976 and July 8, 1976, effective August 1, 1976, by order adopted April 22, 1993, effective December 1, 1993, and by order adopted April 29, 2002, effective December 1, 2002.)

CASE NOTES

Judges are empowered to insist that counsel be prepared so that trials may be held as scheduled. United States v. Fisher, 477 F.2d 300 (4th Cir. 1973).

And trial courts do not lack authority to censure attorneys for dilatory tactics. United States v. Fisher, 477 F.2d 300 (4th Cir. 1973).

But conviction without effective legal representation is a misplaced sanction for the shortcomings of a defendant's attorneys. United States v. Fisher, 477 F.2d 300 (4th Cir. 1973) (case remanded for denial of effective representation).

The purpose of subdivision (b) is to provide defendants with a speedy trial. United States v. Inman, 483 F.2d 738 (4th Cir. 1973), cert. denied, 416 U.S. 988, 94 S. Ct. 2394, 40 L. Ed. 2d 766 (1974).

The matter of continuance is traditionally within the discretion of the trial judge, and it is not every denial of a request for more time that violates due process even if the party fails to offer evidence or is compelled to defend without counsel. United States v. Inman, 483 F.2d 738 (4th Cir. 1973), cert. denied, 416 U.S. 988, 94 S. Ct. 2394, 40 L. Ed. 2d 766 (1974).

A court has the right to control its own docket to require that cases proceed in an orderly and timely fashion, and to that end to deny motions for continuances. United States v. Inman, 483 F.2d 738 (4th Cir. 1973), cert. denied, 416 U.S. 988, 94 S. Ct. 2394, 40 L. Ed. 2d 766 (1974).

Although this rule does not freely countenance pleas for delay, it permits the trial judge to retain sufficient flexibility over his docket to assure proper disposition of justifiable motions for continuance. Consequently, the rule does not deprive the judge of the discretion that he has traditionally exercised in considering a request for a continuance. United States v. Bragan, 499 F.2d 1376 (4th Cir. 1974).

Discretion of court tempered by consideration of defendant's Sixth Amendment rights. — The trial judge's discretion in denying defendant's motion for continuance in order to obtain other counsel with experience in the law pertaining to wiretaps was tempered by proper consideration of defendant's Sixth Amendment rights. United States v. Bragan, 499 F.2d 1376 (4th Cir. 1974).

The policy embodied in subdivision (b) is a factor to be considered in the exercise of discretion as to whether to grant a continuance in a criminal case. But, it is at once obvious that the policy is neither inflexible nor is it the sole consideration if there are present other factors indicating the necessity for a continuance. United States v. Inman, 483 F.2d 738 (4th Cir. 1973), cert. denied, 416 U.S. 988, 94 S. Ct. 2394, 40 L. Ed. 2d 766 (1974).

Effect of recent emphasis on quickening pace of criminal proceedings. — The recent emphasis on quickening the pace of criminal proceedings, exemplified by subdivision (b) of this rule, has created tension between the rule's policy of eliminating undue delay and the occasional attempts of both prosecutors and defendants to seek additional time between arraignment and trial. United States v. Bragan, 499 F.2d 1376 (4th Cir. 1974).

Disclosure of reasons for seeking continuance. — The district court's right to control its own docket and to exact adherence to a reasonable schedule which it prescribed imposes upon a party, or his counsel, who would disrupt it an obligation to make a full disclosure of the reasons why a continuance is sought. United States v. Inman, 483 F.2d 738 (4th Cir. 1973), cert. denied, 416 U.S. 988, 94 S. Ct. 2394, 40 L. Ed. 2d 766 (1974).

Rule 51. Preserving Claimed Error.

(a) *Exceptions Unnecessary.* — Exceptions to rulings or orders of the court are unnecessary.

(b) *Preserving a Claim of Error.* — A party may preserve a claim of error by informing the court — when the court ruling or order is made or sought — of the action the party wishes the court to take, or the party's objection to the court's action and the grounds for that objection. If a party does not have an opportunity to object to a ruling or order, the absence of an objection does not later prejudice that party. A ruling or order that admits or excludes evidence is governed by Federal Rule of Evidence 103. (Amended by order adopted March 9, 1987, effective August 1, 1987, and by order adopted April 29, 2002, effective December 1, 2002.)

Rule 52. Harmless and Plain Error.

(a) *Harmless Error.* — Any error, defect, irregularity, or variance that does not affect substantial rights must be disregarded.

(b) *Plain Error.* — A plain error that affects substantial rights may be considered even though it was not brought to the court's attention. (Amended by order adopted April 29, 2002, effective December 1, 2002.)

CASE NOTES

The decisive factors in applying the standard to determine if error is harmless are the closeness of the case, the centrality of the issue affected by the error, and the steps taken to mitigate the effects of the error. United States v. Nyman, 649 F.2d 208 (4th Cir. 1980).

Purpose of rule. — Both the purposes of the contemporaneous objection rule and considerations of sound judicial administration counsel in favor of plain error review where an objection at trial would have been indefensible because of existing law, but a supervening decision prior to appeal reverses well-settled law, rendering defendant's claim clearly meritorious. United States v. David, 83 F.3d 638 (4th Cir. 1996).

In the realm of nonconstitutional error, the appropriate test of harmlessness is whether the court can say with fair assurance, after pondering all that happened without stripping the erroneous action from the whole, that the judgment was not substantially swayed by the error. The court must believe it highly probable that the error did not affect the judgment. United States v. Nyman, 649 F.2d 208 (4th Cir. 1980).

Defendant's burden of proof. — Defendant bears the burden of demonstrating that the government's remarks affected his substantial rights. United States v. Moore, 11 F.3d 475 (4th Cir. 1993), cert. denied, 511 U.S. 1096, 114 S. Ct. 1864, 128 L. Ed. 2d 486 (1994).

Admission of testimony of psychiatrist as to statements by accused held not "plain error." — A federal statute, 18 U.S.C. § 4244 (1964), provides: "No statement made by the accused in the course of any examination into his sanity or mental competency provided for by this section, whether the examination shall be with or without the consent of the accused, shall be admitted in evidence against the accused on the issue of guilt in any criminal proceeding." Assuming that the testimony of a psychiatrist amounts to the revelation of a "statement made by an accused," the reception of such testimony, in the context of a case in which the only real issue was mental condition, does not amount to "plain error" that should be noticed despite the failure to object. Hall v. United States, 410 F.2d 653 (4th Cir.), cert. denied, 396 U.S. 970, 90 S. Ct. 455, 24 L. Ed. 2d 434 (1969).

Admission of officer's testimony including opinion on the intent of defendant, was not plain error. United States v. Gastiaburo, 16 F.3d 582 (4th Cir.), cert. denied, 513 U.S. 829, 115 S. Ct. 102, 130 L. Ed. 2d 50 (1994).

Error in charge not affecting substantial rights need not be noticed. — In this trial the absence of any enlargement upon "reasonable doubt," not brought to the attention of the trial court, did not affect the substantial rights of the accused so as to require notice of it by the court of appeals non obstante under subdivision (b) of this rule. United States v. Quinn, 315 F.2d 425 (4th Cir. 1963).

Context in which abstract instruction given rendered error "harmless." See United States v. Lemus, 542 F.2d 222 (4th Cir. 1976), cert. denied, 430 U.S. 947, 97 S. Ct. 1584, 51 L. Ed. 2d 794 (1977).

Failure to specify criminal contempt in show cause order held not plain error. — Although the show cause order did not specify that an attorney was charged with criminal conduct, it informed him that he was charged with contempt for failure to appear at his client's trial, and he should have realized that the proceedings were not designed to serve the remedial purposes that characterize civil contempt because the nature of the charges could be readily ascertained from the notice, failure to specify criminal contempt was not plain error and did not violate Rule 42. United States v. Marx, 553 F.2d 874 (4th Cir. 1977).

Closing argument deprived defendant of fair trial. — Where prosecution's closing argument improperly emphasized defendant's brother's conviction for participating in the same conspiracy and arguing that the jury should discredit defendant's brother's testimony because defendant's brother's jury had disbelieved him at his trial, these statements deprived the defendant of a fair trial for it urged the jury to convict the defendant because his brother had been convicted of participating in the same conspiracy. United States v. Mitchell, 1 F.3d 235 (4th Cir. 1993).

Appellate review is foreclosed whenever the error is unclear at the time of appeal, regardless of whether the error was clear at the time of trial. United States v. David, 83 F.3d 638 (4th Cir. 1996).

Authority of reviewing court. — A court of appeals is authorized to invoke its powers under this rule to review an error when the error was plain at trial and was also plain on appeal. United States v. David, 83 F.3d 638 (4th Cir. 1996).

Before an appellate court can correct an error not raised at trial, this rule requires that the error must be plain and affect substantial rights. United States v. David, 83 F.3d 638 (4th Cir. 1996).

Under this rule a court of appeals has authority to correct forfeited error only if it is "plain" and affects substantial rights, and even then is not required to do so unless the error is one that causes the convicting or sentencing of an actually innocent defendant or otherwise seriously affects the fairness, integrity or public reputation of criminal proceedings. United States v. Tipton, 90 F.3d 861 (4th Cir. 1996), cert. denied, 520 U.S. 1253, 117 S. Ct. 2414, 138 L. Ed. 2d 179 (1997).

To reverse for plain error, Court of Appeals must: (1) Identify an error; (2) which is plain; (3) which affects substantial rights; and (4) which seriously affects the fairness, integrity of public reputation of judicial proceedings. United States v. Moore, 11 F.3d 475 (4th Cir. 1993), cert. denied, 511 U.S. 1096, 114 S. Ct. 1864, 128 L. Ed. 2d 486 (1994).

Applied in Gormley v. United States, 167 F.2d 454 (4th Cir. 1948); Hicks v. United States, 173 F.2d 570 (4th Cir. 1949); United States v. Chase, 372 F.2d 453 (4th Cir. 1967); United States v. Brown, 383 F.2d 781 (4th Cir. 1967); United States v. Wilkins, 385 F.2d 465 (4th Cir. 1967); United States v. Goodwin, 405 F.2d 178 (4th Cir. 1968); United States v. Bryant, 417 F.2d 636 (4th Cir. 1969); United States v. King, 420 F.2d 946 (4th Cir. 1970); United States v. Gore, 435 F.2d 1110 (4th Cir. 1970); United States v. Stanley, 455 F.2d 644 (4th Cir. 1972); United States v. Miller, 468 F.2d 1041 (4th Cir. 1972); United States v. Johnson, 497 F.2d 548 (4th Cir. 1974); United States v. Basic Constr. Co., 711 F.2d 570 (4th Cir. 1983); United States v. Malloy, 758 F.2d 979 (4th Cir. 1985); United States v. Fowler, 932 F.2d 306 (4th Cir. 1991); United States v. Hernandez, 975 F.2d 1035 (4th Cir. 1992); United States v. Ince, 21 F.3d 576 (4th Cir. 1994); United States v. Childress, 26 F.3d 498 (4th Cir. 1994); United States v. Rhodes, 32 F.3d 867 (4th Cir. 1994); United States v. Loayza, 107 F.3d 257 (4th Cir. 1997); United States v. Ellis, 121 F.3d 908 (W.D. Va. 1997).

Rule 53. Courtroom Photographing and Broadcasting Prohibited.

Except as otherwise provided by a statute or these rules, the court must not permit the taking of photographs in the courtroom during judicial proceedings or the broadcasting of judicial proceedings from the courtroom. (Amended by order adopted April 29, 2002, effective December 1, 2002.)

Rule 54. [Transferred].

Rule 55. Records.

The clerk of the district court must keep records of criminal proceedings in the form prescribed by the Director of the Administrative Office of the United States Courts. The clerk must enter in the records every court order or judgment and the date of entry. (Amended by order adopted December 27, 1948, effective October 20, 1949, by order adopted February 28, 1966, effective July 1, 1966, by order adopted April 24, 1972, effective October 1, 1972, by order adopted April 28, 1983, effective August 1, 1983, by order adopted April 22, 1993, effective December 1, 1993, and by order adopted April 29, 2002, effective December 1, 2002.)

Rule 56. When Court Is Open.

(a) *In General.* — A district court is considered always open for any filing, and for issuing and returning process, making a motion, or entering an order.

(b) *Office Hours.* — The clerk's office — with the clerk or a deputy in attendance — must be open during business hours on all days except Saturdays, Sundays, and legal holidays.

(c) *Special Hours.* — A court may provide by local rule or order that its clerk's office will be open for specified hours on Saturdays or legal holidays other than than those set aside by statute for observing New Year's Day, Martin Luther King, Jr.'s Birthday, Washington's Birthday, Memorial Day, Independence Day, Labor Day, Columbus Day,

Veterans' Day, Thanksgiving Day, and Christmas Day. (Amended by order adopted December 27, 1948, effective October 20, 1949, by order adopted February 28, 1966, effective July 1, 1966, by order adopted December 4, 1967, effective July 1, 1968, by order adopted March 1, 1971, effective July 1, 1971, by order adopted April 25, 1988, effective August 1, 1988, and by order adopted April 29, 2002, effective December 1, 2002.)

Rule 57. District Court Rules.

(a) *In General.* — (1) Adopting Local Rules. — Each district court acting by a majority of its district judges may, after giving appropriate public notice and an opportunity to comment, make and amend rules governing its practice. A local rule must be consistent with — but not duplicative of — federal statutes and rules adopted under 28 U.S.C. § 2072 and must conform to any uniform numbering system prescribed by the Judicial Conference of the United States.

(2) Limiting Enforcement. — A local rule imposing a requirement of form must not be en-forced in a manner that causes a party to lose rights because of an unintentional failure to comply with the requirement.

(b) *Procedure When There Is No Controlling Law.* — A judge may regulate practice in any manner consistent with federal law, these rules, and the local rules of the district. No sanction or other disadvantage may be imposed for noncompliance with any requirement not in federal law, federal rules, or the local district rules unless the alleged violator was furnished with actual notice of the requirement before the noncompliance.

(c) *Effective Date and Notice.* — A local rule adopted under this rule takes effect on the date specified by the district court and remains in effect unless amended by the district court or abrogated by the judicial council of the circuit in which the district is located. Copies of local rules and their amendments, when promulgated, must be furnished to the judicial council and the Administrative Office of the United States Courts and must be made available to the public. (Amended by order adopted December 27, 1948, effective October 20, 1949, by order adopted December 4, 1967, effective July 1, 1968, by order adopted April 29, 1985, effective August 1, 1985, by order adopted April 22, 1993, effective December 1, 1993, by order adopted April 27, 1995, effective December 1, 1995, and by order adopted April 29, 2002, effective December 1, 2002.)

CASE NOTES

Court may make rules of practice but not rules of law. — The grant of authority found in 28 U.S.C. § 2071 allows courts to make "rules of practice," but not "rules of law." In re Grand Jury Proceedings, 558 F. Supp. 532 (W.D. Va. 1983).

Seizure of records of credit card expenditures. — Rule 41 in tandem with subdivision (b) of this rule assuredly permits seizure of property such as the record of credit card expenditures evidencing defendant's continued criminal activity, viz., remaining a fugitive. There is, in short, a jurisdictional basis under the Federal Rules of Criminal Procedure for an order that such records be seized. United States v. Hall, 583 F. Supp. 717 (E.D. Va. 1984).

Rule 58. Petty Offenses and Other Misdemeanors.

(a) *Scope.* — (1) In General. — These rules apply in petty offense and other misdemeanor cases and on appeal to a district judge in a case tried by a magistrate judge, unless this rule provides otherwise.

(2) Petty Offense Case Without Imprisonment. — In a case involving a petty offense for which no sentence of imprisonment will be imposed, the court may follow any provision of these rules that is not inconsistent with this rule and that the court considers appropriate.

(3) Definition. — As used in this rule, the term "petty offense for which no sentence of imprisonment will be imposed" means a petty offense for which the court determines that, in the event of conviction, no sentence of imprisonment will be imposed.

(b) *Pretrial Procedure.* — (1) Charging Document. — The trial of a misdemeanor may proceed on an indictment, information, or complaint. The trial of a petty offense may also proceed on a citation or violation notice.

(2) Initial Appearance. — At the defendant's initial appearance on a petty offense or other misdemeanor charge, the magistrate judge must inform the defendant of the following:

(A) the charge, and the minimum and maximum penalties, including imprisonment, fines, any special assessment under 18 U.S.C. § 3013, and restitution under 18 U.S.C. § 3556;

(B) the right to retain counsel;

(C) the right to request the appointment of counsel if the defendant is unable to retain counsel — unless the charge is a petty offense for which the appointment of counsel is not required;

(D) the defendant's right not to make a statement, and that any statement made may be used against the defendant;

(E) the right to trial, judgment, and sentencing before a district judge — unless:

(i) the charge is a petty offense; or

(ii) the defendant consents to trial, judgment, and sentencing before a magistrate judge;

(F) the right to a jury trial before either a magistrate judge or a district judge — unless the charge is a petty offense; and

(G) any right to a preliminary hearing under Rule 5.1, and the general circumstances, if any, under which the defendant may secure pretrial release.

(3) Arraignment. — (A) Plea Before a Magistrate Judge. — A magistrate judge may take the defendant's plea in a petty offense case. In every other misdemeanor case, a magistrate judge may take the plea only if the defendant consents either in writing or on the record to be tried before a magistrate judge and specifically waives trial before a district judge. The defendant may plead not guilty, guilty, or (with the consent of the magistrate judge) nolo contendere.

(B) Failure to Consent. — Except in a petty offense case, the magistrate judge must order a defendant who does not consent to trial before a magistrate judge to appear before a district judge for further proceedings.

(c) *Additional Procedures in Certain Petty Offense Cases.* — The following procedures also apply in a case involving a petty offense for which no sentence of imprisonment will be imposed:

(1) Guilty or Nolo Contendere Plea. — The court must not accept a guilty or nolo contendere plea unless satisfied that the defendant understands the nature of the charge and the maximum possible penalty.

(2) Waiving Venue. — (A) Conditions of Waiving Venue. — If a defendant is arrested, held, or present in a district different from the one where the indictment, information, complaint, citation, or violation notice is pending, the defendant may state in writing a desire to plead guilty or nolo contendere; to waive venue and trial in the district where the proceeding is pending; and to consent to the court's disposing of the case in the district where the defendant was arrested, is held, or is present.

(B) Effect of Waiving Venue. — Unless the defendant later pleads not guilty, the prosecution will proceed in the district where the defendant was arrested, is held, or is present. The district clerk must notify the clerk in the original district of the defendant's waiver of venue. The defendant's statement of a desire to plead guilty or nolo contendere is not admissible against the defendant.

(3) Sentencing. — The court must give the defendant an opportunity to be heard in mitigation and then proceed immediately to sentencing. The court may, however, postpone sentencing to allow the probation service to investigate or to permit either party to submit additional information.

(4) Notice of a Right to Appeal. — After imposing sentence in a case tried on a not-guilty plea, the court must advise the defendant of a right to appeal the conviction and of any right to appeal the sentence. If the defendant was convicted on a plea of guilty or nolo contendere, the court must advise the defendant of any right to appeal the sentence.

(d) *Paying a Fixed Sum in Lieu of Appearance.* — (1) In General. — If the court has a local rule governing forfeiture of collateral, the court may accept a fixed-sum payment in lieu of the defendant's appearance and end the case, but the fixed sum may not exceed the maximum fine allowed by law.

(2) Notice to Appear. — If the defendant fails to pay a fixed sum, request a hearing, or appear in response to a citation or violation notice, the district clerk or a magistrate judge may issue a notice for the defendant to appear before the court on a date certain. The notice may give the defendant an additional opportunity to pay a fixed sum in lieu of appearance. The district clerk must serve the notice on the defendant by mailing a copy to the defendant's last known address.

(3) Summons or Warrant. — Upon an indictment, or upon a showing by one of the other charging documents specified in Rule 58(b)(1) of probable cause to believe that an offense has been committed and that the defendant has committed it, the court may issue an arrest warrant or, if no warrant is requested by an attorney for the government, a summons. The showing of probable cause must be made under oath or under penalty of perjury, but the affiant need not appear before the court. If the defendant fails to appear before the court in response to a summons, the court may summarily issue a warrant for the defendant's arrest.

(e) *Recording the Proceedings.* — The court must record any proceedings under this rule by using a court reporter or a suitable recording device.

(f) *New Trial.* — Rule 33 applies to a motion for a new trial.

(g) *Appeal.* — (1) From a District Judge's Order or Judgment. — The Federal Rules of Appellate Procedure govern an appeal from a district judge's order or a judgment of conviction or sentence.

(2) From a Magistrate Judge's Order or Judgment. — (A) Interlocutory Appeal. — Either party may appeal an order of a magistrate judge to a district judge within 14 days of its entry if a district judge's order could similarly be appealed. The party appealing must file a notice with the clerk specifying the order being appealed and must serve a copy on the adverse party.

(B) Appeal from a Conviction or Sentence. — A defendant may appeal a magistrate judge's judgment of conviction or sentence to a district judge within 14 days of its entry. To appeal, the defendant must file a notice with the clerk specifying the judgment being appealed and must serve a copy on an attorney for the government.

(C) Record. — The record consists of the original papers and exhibits in the case; any transcript, tape, or other recording of the proceedings; and a certified copy of the docket entries. For purposes of the appeal, a copy of the record of the proceedings must be made available to a defendant who establishes by affidavit an inability to pay or give security for the record. The Director of the Administrative Office of the United States Courts must pay for those copies.

(D) Scope of Appeal. — The defendant is not entitled to a trial de novo by a district judge. The scope of the appeal is the same as in an appeal to the court of appeals from a judgment entered by a district judge.

(3) Stay of Execution and Release Pending Appeal. — Rule 38 applies to a stay of a judgment of conviction or sentence. The court may release the defendant pending appeal under the law relating to release pending appeal from a district court to a court of appeals. (Added by order adopted May 1, 1990, effective December 1, 1990, amended by order adopted April 30, 1991, effective December 1, 1991, by order adopted April 22, 1993, effective December 1, 1993, by order adopted April 11, 1997, effective December 1, 1997, by order adopted April 29, 2002, effective December 1, 2002, by order adopted April 12, 2006, effective December 1, 2006, and by order adopted March 26, 2009, effective December 1, 2009.)

CASE NOTES

Editor's note. — The annotations appearing below were decided under former Rules of Procedure for the Trial of Misdemeanors Before United States Magistrates, which were abrogated, effective December 1, 1990.

Federal Rules of Appellate Procedure do not control appeals to the district court of a misdemeanor conviction before a magistrate. United States v. Burgess, 602 F. Supp. 1329 (E.D. Va. 1985).

It is the function of the district court to determine on appeal whether the magistrate's decision is supported by adequate evidence and is not clearly erroneous. United States v. Jerge, 738 F. Supp. 181 (E.D. Va. 1990).

Strict adherence to subdivisions (b) and (c) of former Rule 2 was required because the magistrate's trial of a minor offender who is ignorant of his right to be tried by a jury prevents him from asserting his constitutionally protected demand for a jury. United States v. Miller, 468 F.2d 1041 (4th Cir. 1972), cert. denied, 410 U.S. 935, 93 S. Ct. 1389, 35 L. Ed. 2d 599 (1973).

Before a magistrate embarks upon the trial of a person charged with a minor offense, he must explain to the defendant that he has a right to a trial before a judge of the district court and a jury. Only after this has been done may the magistrate accept the defendant's consent to be tried. United States v. Miller, 468 F.2d 1041 (4th Cir. 1972), cert. denied, 410 U.S. 935, 93 S. Ct. 1389, 35 L. Ed. 2d 599 (1973).

Where the defendant had been convicted by the same magistrate several months earlier for a substantially identical act, and where he seized the waiver forms voluntarily, he could not be said to be unfamiliar with all the advice required by the rule, and his conviction would stand. United States v. Kabat, 586 F.2d 325 (4th Cir. 1978).

Statement of potential penalties on entire set of cases held adequate. — Since the purpose of advice regarding maximum penalties is to inform defendants of the possible penalties to which they are exposed in order to assist them in deciding whether to submit to proceedings before the magistrate, and in deciding what plea they wish to enter, a statement alerting defendants to the potential penalties for the entire set of cases to be heard was adequate, even if the statement was not as clearly expressed as might have been desirable. United States v. Doe, 743 F.2d 1033 (4th Cir. 1984).

Defendant not prejudiced by testimony as to second incident not charged before pleading. — Failure to adequately explain the factual basis of the charge on which defendant was convicted did not prejudice defendant despite the insertion of a second incident, which was not presented as part of the factual basis for the charge before pleading, into the officer's testimony and the magistrate's findings. It was not a necessary element of defendant's conviction, and did not materially alter the outcome of the trial, where a finding that defendant had committed either act would have been adequate to convict him of the offense charged, defendant would have been found guilty had the incident never entered into the matter. United States v. Doe, 743 F.2d 1033 (4th Cir. 1984).

Right to counsel in petty cases. — In petty cases, all that is required is that the defendant be made aware that he can have an attorney if he wants to retain one and that the court will make necessary arrangements to allow defendant to take such a step. United States v. Doe, 743 F.2d 1033 (4th Cir. 1984).

Failure to advise defendant as to use of his statements against him. — The magistrate's statement was adequate to advise the defendant that he could remain silent and put the government to its proof, although there was nothing in the statement that advised the defendant that anything he said could be used against him, where there was no indication that defendant would have proceeded differently before the court had he had this information. United States v. Doe, 743 F.2d 1033 (4th Cir. 1984).

This rule contemplates the entry of a formal order by the district court specifying the conviction in the magistrate's court from which the appeal is taken and reflecting the disposition of the appeal by the district judge. United States v. Robinson, 495 F.2d 30 (4th Cir. 1974).

Appellate court has power to pass on question of law. — In an action for a violation of the regulations prohibiting carrying firearms onto an airplane, the district court was found to have misinterpreted the term "willfully" in the statute, and on appeal the conviction would stand if the accused intended voluntarily to carry the firearm in the briefcase. United States v. Moore, 586 F.2d 1029 (4th Cir. 1978).

Rule 59. Matters Before a Magistrate Judge.

(a) *Nondispositive Matters.* — A district judge may refer to a magistrate judge for determination any matter that does not dispose of a charge or defense. The magistrate judge must promptly conduct the required proceedings and, when appropriate, enter on the record an oral or written order stating the determination. A party may serve and file objections to the order within 14 days after being served with a copy of a written order or after the oral order is stated on the record, or at some other time the court sets. The district judge must consider timely objections and modify or set aside any part of the order that is contrary to law or clearly erroneous. Failure to object in accordance with this rule waives a party's right to review.

(b) *Dispositive Matters.* — (1) Referral to Magistrate Judge. A district judge may refer to a magistrate judge for recommendation a defendant's motion to dismiss or quash an indictment or information, a motion to suppress evidence, or any matter that may dispose of a charge or defense. The magistrate judge must promptly conduct the required proceedings. A record must be made of any evidentiary proceeding and of any other proceeding if the magistrate judge considers it necessary. The magistrate judge must enter on the record a recommendation for disposing of the matter, including any proposed findings of fact. The clerk must immediately serve copies on all parties.

(2) Objections to Findings and Recommendations. Within 14 days after being served with a copy of the recommended disposition, or at some other time the court sets, a party may serve and file specific written objections to the proposed findings and recommendations. Unless the district judge directs otherwise, the objecting party must promptly arrange for transcribing the record, or whatever portions of it the parties agree to or the magistrate judge considers sufficient. Failure to object in accordance with this rule waives a party's right to review.

(3) De Novo Review of Recommendations. The district judge must consider de novo any objection to the magistrate judge's recommendation. The district judge may accept, reject, or modify the recommendation, receive further evidence, or resubmit the matter to the magistrate judge with instructions. (Adopted by order April 25, 2005, effective December 1, 2005; amended by order adopted March 26, 2009, effective December 1, 2009.)

Rule 60. Victim's Rights.

(a) *In General.* — (1) Notice of a Proceeding. The government must use its best efforts to give the victim reasonable, accurate, and timely notice of any public court proceeding involving the crime.

(2) Attending the Proceeding. The court must not exclude a victim from a public court proceeding involving the crime, unless the court determines by clear and convincing evidence that the victim's testimony would be materially altered if the victim heard other testimony at that proceeding. In determining whether to exclude a victim, the court must make every effort to permit the fullest attendance possible by the victim and must consider reasonable alternatives to exclusion. The reasons for any exclusion must be clearly stated on the record.

(3) Right to Be Heard on Release, a Plea, or Sentencing. The court must permit a victim to be reasonably heard at any public proceeding in the district court concerning release, plea, or sentencing involving the crime.

(b) *Enforcement and Limitations.* — (1) Time for Deciding a Motion. The court must promptly decide any motion asserting a victim's rights described in these rules.

(2) Who May Assert the Rights. A victim's rights described in these rules may be asserted by the victim, the victim's lawful representative, the attorney for the government, or any other person as authorized by 18 U.S.C. § 3771(d) and (e).

(3) Multiple Victims. If the court finds that the number of victims makes it impracticable to accord all of them their rights described in these rules, the court must fashion a reasonable procedure that gives effect to these rights without unduly complicating or prolonging the proceedings.

(4) Where Rights May Be Asserted. A victim's rights described in these rules must be asserted in the district where a defendant is being prosecuted for the crime.

(5) Limitations on Relief. A victim may move to reopen a plea or sentence only if:

(A) the victim asked to be heard before or during the proceeding at issue, and the request was denied;

(B) the victim petitions the court of appeals for a writ of mandamus within 10 days after the denial, and the writ is granted; and

(C) in the case of plea, the accused has not pleaded to the highest offense charged.

(6) No New Trial. A failure to afford a victim any right described in these rules is not grounds for a new trial. (Added by order adopted April 23, 2008, effective December 1, 2008.)

Rule 61. Title.

These rules may be known and cited as the Federal Rules of Criminal Procedure. (Amended by order adopted April 29, 2002, effective December 1, 2002 and by order adopted April 23, 2008, effective December 1, 2008.)

Index to Federal Rules of Criminal Procedure

A

ACQUITTAL.
Motion for judgment of acquittal, FRCrP 29.

ADDRESSES.
Victims of criminal activity.
Disclosure and protection, FRCrP 12.1.
Witnesses.
Disclosure and protection, FRCrP 12.3.

ALIBI.
Notice of alibi defense, FRCrP 12.1.

ALTERNATE JURORS, FRCrP 24.

APPEALS.
Arrest of judgment, FRCrP 34.
Conviction or sentence.
Advising defendant of right, clerk's filing of notice, FRCrP 32.
Error.
Harmless and plain error, FRCrP 52.
Preserving claim of error, FRCrP 51.
Exceptions to rulings or orders of court unnecessary, FRCrP 51.
Forfeiture, stay pending appeal, FRCrP 32.2.
Misdemeanor or petty offense, FRCrP 58.
Notice of right, FRCrP 58.
Motion for judgment of acquittal, FRCrP 29.
Motion for relief that is barred by pending appeal.
Indicative rulings, FRCrP 37.
Preclusion of review.
Failure to object to instructions, FRCrP 30.
Preserving claim of error, FRCrP 51.
Release from custody pending appeal, FRCrP 46.
Stay of execution, FRCrP 38.

APPEARANCE.
Arraignment.
Waiver of appearance, FRCrP 10.
Failure to appear.
Arrest in another district, FRCrP 40.
Initial appearance upon arrest or in response to summons, FRCrP 5.
Presence of defendant, FRCrP 43.
Misdemeanor or petty offense, FRCrP 58.
Paying fixed sum in lieu of, FRCrP 58.
Probation or supervised release.
Revocation or modification, FRCrP 32.1.
Telecommunications.
Appearance by video teleconferencing, FRCrP 40.

APPOINTMENT OF COUNSEL, FRCrP 44.

ARRAIGNMENT, FRCrP 10.
Misdemeanor or petty offense, FRCrP 58.
Presence of defendant, FRCrP 43.

ARREST.
Failure to appear.
Arrest in another district, FRCrP 40.
Initial appearance upon, FRCrP 5.

ARRESTING JUDGMENT, FRCrP 34.

ARREST WARRANT.
Electronic communications.
Warrant by telephone or other reliable electronic means, FRCrP 4(d).
Issuance, form, execution or service, return.
Issued on complaint, FRCrP 4.
Issued on indictment or information, FRCrP 9.
Misdemeanor or petty offense, FRCrP 58.
Preparing.
Complaint, warrant or summons by telephone or other reliable electronic means, FRCrP 4.1(b).
Telecommunications.
Complaint, warrant or summons by telephone or other reliable electronic means, FRCrP 4.1.
Warrant by telephone or other reliable electronic means, FRCrP 4(d), 9(d).

ASSISTANCE IN INVESTIGATING AND PROSECUTING ANOTHER.
Reduction of sentence, FRCrP 35.

ATTEMPT.
Jury verdict, FRCrP 31.

ATTORNEYS AT LAW.
Assignment of counsel, FRCrP 44.
Joint representation of codefendants, FRCrP 44.
Right of defendant to counsel, FRCrP 44.

B

BAIL.
Release from custody, FRCrP 46.

BAIL FORFEITURE, FRCrP 46.

BILL OF PARTICULARS, FRCrP 7.

BOND.
Release from custody, FRCrP 46.

BROADCASTING PROCEEDINGS, FRCrP 53.

C

CITATION.
Petty offense, proceeding on, FRCrP 58.

CITATION OF RULES, FRCrP 61.

CIVIL DISABILITY CREATED BY CONVICTION OR SENTENCE.
Stay pending appeal, FRCrP 38.

CLERK.
Judgment.
Clerical mistakes, FRCrP 36.
Office hours, FRCrP 56.

CLOSING ARGUMENTS, FRCrP 29.1.

COMPETENCY EXAMINATION.
Authority of court to order, FRCrP 12.2.

COMPLAINT.
Arrest warrant or summons on complaint, FRCrP 4.
Generally, FRCrP 3.
Misdemeanor, proceeding on, FRCrP 58.
Telecommunications.
Complaint, warrant or summons by telephone or other reliable electronic means, FRCrP 4.1.

COMPUTATION OF TIME, FRCrP 45.

CONDITIONAL PLEA, FRCrP 11.

CONSTRUCTION OF RULES, FRCrP 2.

CONTEMPT.
Criminal contempt, FRCrP 42.
Failure to obey subpoena, FRCrP 17.

CORPORATIONS.
Disclosure statement, FRCrP 12.4.

CORRECTION OF SENTENCE.
Clear error, FRCrP 35.

COURT ALWAYS OPEN, FRCrP 56.

COURT APPOINTED COUNSEL, FRCrP 44.

COURT ORDERS.
Court considered always open for entering, FRCrP 56.
Notice, FRCrP 49.

CRIMINAL CONTEMPT, FRCrP 42.

CRIMINAL FORFEITURE, FRCrP 32.2.

D

DEATH SENTENCE.
Stay pending appeal, FRCrP 38.

DEFENDANT'S PRESENCE.
Deposition, FRCrP 15.
When required, not required, exceptions, FRCrP 43.

DEFENSES.
Alibi defense.
Notice of, FRCrP 12.1.
Insanity defense.
Notice of intent to assert, mental examination, FRCrP 12.2.
Notice of defense and disclosure of witnesses, FRCrP 12.3.
Public authority defense.
Notice, FRCrP 12.3.

DEFINITIONS.
Attorney for the government, FRCrP 1.
Court, FRCrP 1.
Daytime, FRCrP 41.
Domestic terrorism, FRCrP 41.
Federal judge, FRCrP 1.
Federal law enforcement officer, FRCrP 41.
International terrorism, FRCrP 41.
Judge, FRCrP 1.
Last day, FRCrP 45.
Legal holiday, FRCrP 45.
Magistrate judge, FRCrP 1.
Next day, FRCrP 45.
Oath, FRCrP 1.
Organization, FRCrP 1.
Petty offenses, FRCrP 1, 58.
Property, FRCrP 41.

DEFINITIONS —Cont'd
State, FRCrP 1.
Statement, FRCrP 26.2.
State or local judicial officer, FRCrP 1.
Telephone, FRCrP 1.
Tracking device, FRCrP 41.
Victim, FRCrP 1.

DEPOSITIONS.
Generally, FRCrP 15.
Subpoena to make, FRCrP 17.

DISABILITY CREATED BY CONVICTION OR SENTENCE.
Stay pending appeal, FRCrP 38.

DISABILITY OF JUDGE, FRCrP 25.

DISCHARGING DEFENDANT.
Preliminary hearing, no probable cause, FRCrP 5.1.

DISCLOSURE STATEMENTS.
Corporations.
Identification of parent and publicly held corporate interest, time for filing, FRCrP 12.4.
Organization victim of criminal activity.
Government statement identifying, FRCrP 12.4.

DISCOVERY, FRCrP 16.
Alibi witnesses, FRCrP 12.1, 16.
Depositions, FRCrP 15.

DISMISSAL.
By attorney for government, FRCrP 48.
By court, FRCrP 48.
Objection to grand jury, motion, FRCrP 6.
Preliminary hearing, no probable cause, FRCrP 5.1.
Removed proceeding.
State law governs, FRCrP 1.
Unnecessary delay, FRCrP 48.

DISTRICT COURT RULES, FRCrP 57.

DNA PROFILE.
Indictment based on DNA profile, not named individual, FRCrP 7.

DUPLICATES OF ORIGINAL, PREPARING.
Complaint, warrant or summons by telephone or other reliable electronic means, FRCrP 4.1(b).

E

ELECTRONIC SERVICE AND FILING, FRCrP 49(e).
Privacy protection for filings made with court, FRCrP 49.1.
Service by mail, leaving with clerk, etc.
Additional time, FRCrP 45(c).
Warrant for arrest.
Execution of warrant by telephone or other reliable electronic means, FRCrP 4, 4.1, 9.

EMPLOYMENT DISABILITY CREATED BY CONVICTION OR SENTENCE.
Stay pending appeal, FRCrP 38.

ERROR.
Harmless and plain error, FRCrP 52.
Preserving claim of error, FRCrP 51.

EVIDENCE.
Alibi defense.
Withdrawal of intention to rely on, FRCrP 12.1.

EVIDENCE —Cont'd
Depositions, FRCrP 15.
Mental disease or defect.
Notice of intent to introduce expert evidence, FRCrP 12.2.
Mental examination ordered by court.
Defendant's statements during, inadmissibility, FRCrP 12.2.
Notice of government's intent to use specified evidence, FRCrP 12.
Official record, proving, FRCrP 27.
Plea, plea discussions and related statements, FRCrP 11.
Preliminary hearing, FRCrP 5.1.
Producing witness's statement, FRCrP 26.2.
Public authority defenses.
Withdrawal in intent to rely on, FRCrP 12.3.
Subpoenas, FRCrP 17.
Suppression, FRCrP 41.
Taking testimony at trial, FRCrP 26.
Video presentation of testimony, FRCrP 26.

EXCEPTIONS TO RULINGS OR ORDERS OF COURT UNNECESSARY, FRCrP 51.

EXECUTION OF ARREST WARRANT.
Issued on complaint, FRCrP 4.
Issued on indictment or information, FRCrP 9.
Telephone or other electronic means, FRCrP 9.

EXECUTION OF SEARCH WARRANT, FRCrP 41.

EXPERT EVIDENCE.
Discovery of expert witnesses, FRCrP 16.
Mental disease or defect.
Notice of intent to introduce evidence relating to mental disease or defect, FRCrP 12.2.

EXTENSION OF TIME, FRCrP 45.
Preliminary hearing, holding, FRCrP 5.1.

F

FAILURE TO APPEAR.
Arrest in another district, FRCrP 40.

FAILURE TO OBJECT TO INSTRUCTIONS.
Appellate review precluded, FRCrP 30.

FELONIES.
Indictment.
Required to be prosecuted by, FRCrP 7.
Initial appearance, procedure upon, FRCrP 5.

FILING PAPERS.
Court considered always open for, FRCrP 56.
Electronic service and filing, FRCrP 49(e).
Privacy protection for filings made with court, FRCrP 49.1.
Service by mail, leaving with clerk, etc.
Additional time, FRCrP 45(c).
Warrant for arrest.
Warrant by telephone or other reliable electronic means, FRCrP 4, 4.1, 9.
Generally, FRCrP 49.
Privacy protection, FRCrP 49.1.

FINES.
Stay pending appeal, FRCrP 38.

FIXED SUM PAYMENT IN LIEU OF APPEARANCE, FRCrP 58.

FOREIGN COUNTRY.
Witnesses outside of United States.
Taking depositions without the defendant's presence, FRCrP 15.

FOREIGN LANGUAGE.
Interpreters at trial, FRCrP 28.

FOREIGN LAW.
Determination of foreign law at trial, FRCrP 26.1.

FORFEITURE OF PROPERTY, FRCrP 32.2.
Bail forfeiture, FRCrP 46.
Notice in indictment.
Defendant's property subject to, FRCrP 7.
Release from custody not to prevent court from disposing of forfeited property, FRCrP 46.

G

GRAND JURY, FRCrP 6.
Alternates, FRCrP 6.
Challenge to, FRCrP 6.
Discharging, FRCrP 6.
Excusal of juror, FRCrP 6.
Foreperson, deputy, FRCrP 6.
Number, FRCrP 6.
Objections, FRCrP 6.
Recording proceedings, FRCrP 6.
Sealed records, FRCrP 6.
Secrecy, exceptions, FRCrP 6.
Summoning, FRCrP 6.

GUILTY PLEA.
Considering and accepting, FRCrP 11.
Petty offense case, FRCrP 58.

H

HARMLESS ERROR, FRCrP 52.
Pleas, variance from requirements, FRCrP 11.

HEARINGS.
Preliminary hearing, FRCrP 5.1.
Revocation hearing.
Probation or supervised release, FRCrP 32.1.

HOLIDAYS.
Computing or extending time, legal holidays, FRCrP 45.
Special office hours.
Saturdays and legal holidays, local rule, FRCrP 56.

I

IDENTIFYING INFORMATION.
Privacy protection for filings made with court, FRCrP 49.1.

INDICTMENT AND INFORMATION, FRCrP 7.
Amending, FRCrP 7.
Arrest warrant or summons issued on, FRCrP 9.
Bill of particulars, FRCrP 7.
Citation error or omission.
Not grounds for dismissal, FRCrP 7.
Dismissal, FRCrP 48.
Objection to grand jury, motion, FRCrP 6.

INDICTMENT AND INFORMATION —Cont'd
DNA profile.
Indictment based on DNA profile, not named individual, FRCrP 7.
Forfeiture of property.
Notice of government intention to seek, FRCrP 32.2.
Notice that defendant's interest in property subject to, FRCrP 7.
Grand jury, FRCrP 6.
Joinder of offenses and defendants, FRCrP 8.
Misdemeanor, proceeding on, FRCrP 58.
Nature and contents, FRCrP 7.
Sealing, FRCrP 6.
Surplusage, FRCrP 7.
Telephone or other reliable electronic means.
Issuance, FRCrP 9(d).
Summons, FRCrP 9(d).
Warrant for arrest, FRCrP 9(d).
Waiver of indictment, FRCrP 7.
When used, FRCrP 7.

INSANITY DEFENSE.
Notice of intent to assert, mental examination, FRCrP 12.2.

INSPECTION.
Discovery and inspection, FRCrP 16.

INTERPRETATION OF RULES, FRCrP 2.

J

JOINDER OF OFFENSES AND DEFENDANTS.
Attorneys at law.
Joint representation of codefendants, FRCrP 44.
Indictment and information, FRCrP 8.
Joint trial of separate cases, FRCrP 13.
Prejudicial joinder.
Relief, FRCrP 14.

JUDGES.
Disability, FRCrP 25.
Magistrate judges.
Referral of matters to magistrate judges, FRCrP 59.

JUDGMENT.
Arrest of judgment pending appeal, FRCrP 34.
Clerical mistakes, FRCrP 36.
Forfeiture, FRCrP 32.2.
Generally, FRCrP 32.
Stay of execution, FRCrP 38.

JUDGMENT OF ACQUITTAL.
Motion, FRCrP 29.

JURY.
Alternate jurors, FRCrP 24.
Examination and challenge of jurors, FRCrP 24.
Instructions, FRCrP 30.
Peremptory challenges, FRCrP 24.
Trial by jury, FRCrP 23.
Verdict, FRCrP 31.

JURY INSTRUCTIONS, FRCrP 30.

JUVENILE DELINQUENTS.
Proceeded against in district arrested, held or present, FRCrP 20.

L

LESSER OFFENSE.
Jury verdict, FRCrP 31.

LOCAL RULES, FRCrP 57.

M

MAGISTRATE JUDGES.
Initial appearance before, FRCrP 5.
Preliminary hearing, FRCrP 5.1.
Referral of matters to magistrate judges, FRCrP 59.
Search warrants.
Authority to issue, FRCrP 41.
Telecommunications.
Complaint, warrant or summons by telephone or other reliable electronic means, FRCrP 4.1(a).

MENTAL CONDITION.
Notice of expert evidence relating to, FRCrP 12.2.

MENTAL EXAMINATION.
Authority to order competency examination, FRCrP 12.2.

MIRANDA RIGHTS.
Initial appearance in felony case.
Advising defendant of rights, FRCrP 5.

MISDEMEANORS.
Appearances.
Presence of defendant by video teleconferencing, when allowed, FRCrP 43.
Indictment.
May be prosecuted by, FRCrP 7.
Initial appearance, FRCrP 5.
Procedures, FRCrP 58.

MISTRIAL, FRCrP 26.3.
Jury unable to agree, FRCrP 31.

MOTIONS, FRCrP 47.
Affidavit supporting, FRCrP 47.
Appeals.
Motion for relief that is barred by pending appeal.
Indicative rulings, FRCrP 37.
Arresting judgment, FRCrP 34.
Court considered always open for filing, FRCrP 56.
Defenses and objections, FRCrP 12.
Form and content, FRCrP 47.
Judgment of acquittal, FRCrP 29.
New trial, FRCrP 33.
Pretrial motions, FRCrP 12.
Producing witness's statement, FRCrP 26.2.
Production of statements at suppression hearing, FRCrP 12.
Service, time for, FRCrP 47.
Suppression of evidence, FRCrP 41.
Production of statements at suppression hearing, FRCrP 12.
Time for motions generally, FRCrP 45.
Time of motion to transfer, FRCrP 21.
Transfer for trial, time for filing, FRCrP 21.

N

NEWLY DISCOVERED EVIDENCE.
New trial, FRCrP 33.

NEW TRIAL, FRCrP 33.
Misdemeanor or petty offense, FRCrP 58.
Motion for judgment of acquittal.
Conditional determination, FRCrP 29.

NOLO CONTENDRE PLEA, FRCrP 11.
Petty offense case, FRCrP 58.

NOTICE.
Alibi defense, FRCrP 12.1.
Court orders, FRCrP 49.
Criminal contempt, FRCrP 42.
Defenses, FRCrP 12.3.
Deposition, FRCrP 15.
Forfeiture of property.
Indictment or information to contain notice, FRCrP 32.2.
Government's intent to use specified evidencc, FRCrP 12.
Insanity defense, intent to assert, FRCrP 12.2.
Mental disease or defect.
Intent to introduce expert evidence, FRCrP 12.2.
Public authority defense.
Notice of intent to assert, FRCrP 12.3.
Sentencing guidelines, departure, FRCrP 32.
Victims of criminal activity.
Rights of victim, notice of proceedings, FRCrP 60.
Violation notice.
Petty offense, proceeding on, FRCrP 58.

O

OATHS AND AFFIRMATIONS.
Complaint.
Complaint, warrant or summons by telephone or other reliable electronic means, FRCrP 4.1(b).

OBJECTIONS, PRESERVING ERROR, FRCrP 51.

OBJECTIONS TO INSTRUCTIONS, FRCrP 30.

OFFICE HOURS, FRCrP 56.

ORDERS.
Court considered always open for entering, FRCrP 56.
Notice, FRCrP 49.

ORGANIZATION VICTIM OF CRIMINAL ACTIVITY.
Disclosure statement by government identifying, FRCrP 12.4.

P

PEREMPTORY CHALLENGES, FRCrP 24.

PETTY OFFENSES.
Procedures, FRCrP 58.

PHOTOGRAPHING PROCEEDINGS, FRCrP 53.

PLACE OF INITIAL APPEARANCE, FRCrP 5.

PLAIN ERROR, FRCrP 52.

PLEA AGREEMENTS.
Procedure, disclosing, accepting or rejecting, FRCrP 11.

PLEADINGS.
Generally, FRCrP 12.

PLEAS, FRCrP 11.
Petty offense case, FRCrP 58.
Transfer for plea and sentence, FRCrP 20.

POLL OF JURY, FRCrP 31.

POST-VERDICT HEARING.
Forfeiture of property, FRCrP 32.2.

PRELIMINARY HEARING, FRCrP 5.1.
Probation or supervised release.
Revocation or modification, FRCrP 32.1.

PRELIMINARY ORDER OF FORFEITURE, FRCrP 32.2.

PRESENCE OF DEFENDANT.
Deposition, FRCrP 15.
When required, not required, exceptions, FRCrP 43.

PRESENTENCE INVESTIGATION AND REPORT, FRCrP 32.

PRESERVATION OF TESTIMONY.
Pretrial deposition, FRCrP 15.

PRESERVING CLAIM OF ERROR, FRCrP 51.

PRETRIAL CONFERENCE, FRCrP 17.1.

PRETRIAL MOTIONS, FRCrP 12.

PRETRIAL RELEASE, FRCrP 46.

PRIVACY.
Filings made with the court, protection, FRCrP 49.1.
Witnesses, disclosure contact information, protection, FRCrP 12.3.

PROBABLE CAUSE.
Preliminary hearing, FRCrP 5.1.
Search warrant, FRCrP 41.

PROBATION.
Revocation or modification, FRCrP 32.1.
Stay pending appeal, FRCrP 38.

PRODUCING WITNESS'S STATEMENT, FRCrP 26.2.

PRODUCTION OF BOOKS, PAPERS AND OTHER DOCUMENTS.
Discovery and inspection, FRCrP 16.
Subpoena for production, FRCrP 17.

PRODUCTION OF STATEMENTS.
Preliminary hearing, FRCrP 5.1.

PROMPT DISPOSITION GIVEN CRIMINAL PROCEEDING, FRCrP 50.

PUBLIC AUTHORITY DEFENSE.
Notice of intent to assert, FRCrP 12.3.

R

RECORDING PROCEEDINGS.
Preliminary hearing, FRCrP 5.1.

RECORDS.
Clerical mistakes, FRCrP 36.

RECORDS —Cont'd
Complaint, warrant or summons by telephone or other reliable electronic means.
Creating record of testimony, FRCrP 4.1(b).
Generally, FRCrP 55.
Proof of official record at trial, FRCrP 27.
Telephones.
Taking testimony by telephone or other electronic means, FRCrP 4.1.

REDACTED FILINGS.
Privacy protection for filings made with court, FRCrP 49.1.

REDUCTION OF SENTENCE.
Assisting investigation and prosecution of another, FRCrP 35.

REHEARING.
New trial, FRCrP 33.

RELEASE FROM CUSTODY, FRCrP 46.
Forfeiture of property, FRCrP 46.

REQUEST FOR INSTRUCTIONS, FRCrP 30.

RESTITUTION.
Stay pending appeal, FRCrP 38.

RETRIAL.
Jury unable to agree, FRCrP 31.

RETURN.
Arrest warrant or summons.
Issued on complaint, FRCrP 4.
Issued on indictment or information, FRCrP 9.
Court considered always open for, FRCrP 56.
Search warrant, FRCrP 41.

REVOCATION HEARING.
Probation or supervised release, FRCrP 32.1.

RIGHTS OF DEFENDANT.
Initial appearance in felony case.
Advising defendant, FRCrP 5.

RIGHT TO APPOINTED COUNSEL, FRCrP 44.

RULES BY DISTRICT COURT, FRCrP 57.

S

SCOPE OF RULES, FRCrP 1.

SEALED RECORDS.
Grand jury proceedings, FRCrP 6.

SEARCH AND SEIZURE, FRCrP 41.

SEARCH WARRANTS, FRCrP 41.
Taking testimony by telephone or other electronic means, FRCrP 4.1.

SENTENCE.
Advisory sentencing guidelines, applying, FRCrP 32.
Changing time limits, FRCrP 32.
Correction of sentence, FRCrP 35.
Departure from guidelines, notice, FRCrP 32.
Generally, FRCrP 32.
Imposition without delay, FRCrP 32.
Opportunity to speak, FRCrP 32.
Petty offense case, FRCrP 58.
Presence of defendant, FRCrP 43.
Presentence investigation and report, FRCrP 32.

SENTENCE —Cont'd
Reduction for assisting in investigation or prosecution of another, FRCrP 35.
Release from custody pending sentence, FRCrP 46.
Transfer for plea and sentence, FRCrP 20.

SERVICE OF PROCESS, FRCrP 49.
Additional time after service, FRCrP 45.
Motions.
Time for serving on party, FRCrP 47.
Subpoenas, FRCrP 17.
Summons.
Issued on complaint, FRCrP 4.
Issued on indictment or information, FRCrP 9.
Telecommunications.
Electronic service and filing, FRCrP 49(e).

SPECIAL OFFICE HOURS.
Saturdays and legal holidays, local rule, FRCrP 56.

STATE LAW GOVERNS.
Dismissal of removed proceeding, FRCrP 1.

STATEMENTS OF DEFENDANT.
Competency examination ordered by court.
Inadmissibility of defendant's statements, FRCrP 12.2.

STATEMENTS OF WITNESSES.
Production, FRCrP 26.2.
Preliminary hearing, FRCrP 5.1.

STAY PENDING APPEAL.
Forfeiture, FRCrP 32.2.
Sentence or disability, FRCrP 38.

SUBPOENAS, FRCrP 17.

SUMMONS.
Initial appearance upon, FRCrP 5.
Issuance, form, execution or service, return.
Issued on complaint, FRCrP 4.
Issued on indictment or information, FRCrP 9.
Misdemeanor or petty offense, FRCrP 58.
Telephone or other reliable electronic means, FRCrP 9(d).
Complaint, warrant or summons by, FRCrP 4.1.
Preparing, FRCrP 4.1(b).
Taking testimony by, FRCrP 4.1.

SUPERVISED RELEASE.
Revocation or modification, FRCrP 32.1.

SUPPRESSION OF EVIDENCE, FRCrP 41.
Complaint, warrant or summons by telephone or other reliable electronic means.
Limitation of suppression, FRCrP 4.1(c).

SURETY.
Release from custody, FRCrP 46.

T

TELECOMMUNICATIONS.
Appearance by video teleconferencing, FRCrP 40(d).
Arrest for failure to appear in another district.
Video teleconferencing for appearance, FRCrP 40.
Complaint, warrant or summons.
Execution by telephone or other electronic means, FRCrP 9.

TELECOMMUNICATIONS —Cont'd
Complaint, warrant or summons —Cont'd
Taking testimony by telephone or other electronic means, FRCrP 4.1.
Complaint, warrant or summons by telephone or other reliable electronic means, FRCrP 4.1.
Defined, FRCrP 1.
Indictment or information.
Issuance, telephone or other reliable electronic means, FRCrP 9(d).
Misdemeanors.
Presence of defendant by video teleconferencing, when allowed, FRCrP 43.
Search warrant by telephone, FRCrP 41.
Service.
Electronic service and filing, FRCrP 49(e).
Telephone defined, FRCrP 1(b).
Warrant for arrest.
Warrant by telephone or other reliable electronic means, FRCrP 4(d).

TELEPHONE NUMBERS.
Victims of criminal activity.
Disclosure and protection, FRCrP 12.1.
Witnesses.
Disclosure and protection, FRCrP 12.3.

TERRITORIAL COURTS.
Applicability of rules in, FRCrP 1.

TERRORISM.
Domestic terrorism defined, FRCrP 41.
International terrorism defined, FRCrP 41.

TIME.
Alibi defense.
Defendant's response to notice request, disclosing government witness, FRCrP 12.1.
Arresting judgment, motion, FRCrP 34.
Computation of time, FRCrP 45.
Disclosure statements.
Corporations or organizational victims, filing, FRCrP 12.4.
Dismissal for unnecessary delay, FRCrP 48.
Extension of time, FRCrP 45.
Preliminary hearing, holding, FRCrP 5.1.
Jury instructions, requesting, giving, FRCrP 30.
Motion for judgment of acquittal.
After jury verdict or discharge, FRCrP 29.
Motion for new trial, FRCrP 33.
Motions, service, FRCrP 47.
Office hours, FRCrP 56.
Preliminary hearing, holding, FRCrP 5.1.
Prompt disposition of criminal cases, FRCrP 50.
Public authority defense.
Response to notice, disclosing government witness, FRCrP 12.3.
Transfer for trial, filing motion, FRCrP 21.

TITLE.
Short title, FRCrP 61.

TRACKING DEVICES.
Defined, FRCrP 41.
Warrants to install, FRCrP 41.

TRIAL.
By the court, FRCrP 23.
Closing argument, FRCrP 29.1.
Exception unnecessary, FRCrP 51.

TRIAL —Cont'd
Foreign law.
Determination, FRCrP 26.1.
Instructions to jury, FRCrP 30.
Interpreters, FRCrP 28.
Joint trial of separate cases, FRCrP 13.
Judge.
Disability during trial, FRCrP 25.
Jury trial, FRCrP 23.
Examination and challenge of jurors, FRCrP 24.
Mistrial, FRCrP 26.3.
Motion for judgment of acquittal, FRCrP 29.
New trial, FRCrP 33.
Objections, preserving error, FRCrP 51.
Place of prosecution and trial, FRCrP 18.
Presence of defendant, FRCrP 43.
Preserving claim of error, FRCrP 51.
Pretrial conference, FRCrP 17.1.
Proof of official record, FRCrP 27.
Taking of testimony, FRCrP 26.
Transfer from the district for trial, FRCrP 21.
Venue.
See VENUE.
Without a jury, FRCrP 23.

V

VENUE.
Initial appearance upon arrest, FRCrP 5.
Motion to transfer.
Time of motion, FRCrP 21.
Petty offense case.
Waiving, FRCrP 58.
Place of prosecution and trial, FRCrP 18.
Time of motion to transfer, FRCrP 21.
Transfer from the district for plea and sentence, FRCrP 20.
Transfer from the district for trial, FRCrP 21.

VERDICT.
Generally, FRCrP 31.
Presence of defendant, FRCrP 43.

VICTIMS OF CRIMINAL ACTIVITY.
Address and telephone number.
Disclosure and protection, FRCrP 12.1.
Initial appearance upon arrest or in response to summons.
Detention or release, interest of victim, FRCrP 5.
Notice of proceedings.
Rights of victim, FRCrP 60.
Notice of public authority defense.
Disclosing government witnesses.
Address and telephone number of victim witness, FRCrP 12.3.
Opportunity to speak, FRCrP 32.
Organizational victim.
Disclosure statement by government identifying, FRCrP 12.4.
Rights of victim, FRCrP 60.
Subpoenas.
Personal or confidential information about victim, FRCrP 17.
Victim defined, FRCrP 1.

VIDEO PRESENTATION OF TESTIMONY, FRCrP 26.

VIDEO TELECONFERENCING.
Arraignment, FRCrP 10.

VIDEO TELECONFERENCING —Cont'd
Initial appearance conducted by, FRCrP 5.

VIOLATION NOTICE.
Petty offense, proceeding on, FRCrP 58.

W

WAIVER OF APPEARANCE.
Arraignment, FRCrP 10.

WAIVER OF DEFENDANT'S CONTINUED PRESENCE, FRCrP 43.

WAIVER OF INDICTMENT, FRCrP 7.

WITHDRAWAL OF PLEA, FRCrP 11.

WITNESSES.
Alibi.
Disclosure of alibi witness, FRCrP 12.1, 16.

WITNESSES —Cont'd
Disclosure of witnesses, FRCrP 12.3.
Outside of United States.
Taking depositions without the defendant's presence, FRCrP 15.
Pretrial deposition to preserve testimony, FRCrP 15.
Public authority defense.
Disclosure of witnesses, FRCrP 12.3.
Statement of witnesses.
Production, FRCrP 26.2.
Subpoena.
Attendance of witnesses, FRCrP 17.
Subpoenas, FRCrP 17.
Taking testimony at trial, FRCrP 26.
Telephones.
Taking testimony by telephone or other electronic means, FRCrP 4.1.
Video presentation of testimony, FRCrP 26.

RULES GOVERNING SECTION 2254 CASES IN THE UNITED STATES DISTRICT COURTS

Effective February 1, 1977, as amended to February 1, 2010.

Rule

1. Scope.
2. The Petition.
3. Filing the Petition; Inmate Filing.
4. Preliminary Review; Serving the Petition and Order.
5. The Answer and the Reply.
6. Discovery.
7. Expanding the Record.
8. Evidentiary Hearing.
9. Second or Successive Petitions.

Rule

10. Powers of a Magistrate Judge.
11. Certificate of Appealability; Time to Appeal.
12. Applicability of the Federal Rules of Civil Procedure.

Appendix of Forms.

Petition Under 28 U.S.C. § 2254 for a Writ of Habeas Corpus.

Index.

Rule 1. Scope.

(a) *Cases Involving a Petition under 28 U.S.C. § 2254.* — These rules govern a petition for a writ of habeas corpus filed in a United States district court under 28 U.S.C. § 2254 by:

(1) a person in custody under a state-court judgment who seeks a determination that the custody violates the Constitution, laws, or treaties of the United States; and

(2) a person in custody under a state-court or federal-court judgment who seeks a determination that future custody under a state-court judgment would violate the Constitution, laws, or treaties of the United States.

(b) *Other Cases.* — The district court may apply any or all of these rules to a habeas corpus petition not covered by Rule 1(a). (Amended by order adopted April 26, 2004, effective December 1, 2004.)

Editor's note. — The Rules Governing Section 2254 Cases in the United States District Courts, Rules 1 through 11, and the official forms accompanying the section 2254 rules, were amended by court order dated April 26, 2004, effective December 1, 2004.

Rule 2. The Petition.

(a) *Current Custody; Naming the Respondent.* — If the petitioner is currently in custody under a state-court judgment, the petition must name as respondent the state officer who has custody.

(b) *Future Custody; Naming the Respondents and Specifying the Judgment.* — If the petitioner is not yet in custody — but may be subject to future custody — under the state-court judgment being contested, the petition must name as respondents both the officer who has current custody and the attorney general of the state where the judgment was entered. The petition must ask for relief from the state-court judgment being contested.

(c) *Form.* — The petition must:

(1) specify all the grounds for relief available to the petitioner;

(2) state the facts supporting each ground;

(3) state the relief requested;

(4) be printed, typewritten, or legibly handwritten; and

(5) be signed under penalty of perjury by the petitioner or by a person authorized to sign it for the petitioner under 28 U.S.C. § 2242.

(d) *Standard Form.* — The petition must substantially follow either the form appended to these rules or a form prescribed by a local district-court rule. The clerk must make forms available to petitioners without charge.

(e) *Separate Petitions for Judgments of Separate Courts.* — A petitioner who seeks relief from judgments of more than one state court must file a separate petition covering the judgment or judgments of each court. (Amended effective August 1, 1982, by order adopted April 29, 2002, effective December 1, 2002, by order adopted April 26, 2004, effective December 1, 2004.)

CASE NOTES

Appropriate respondent in a habeas corpus petition is petitioner's immediate custodian, the warden or superintendent of the facility in which the petitioner is incarcerated. Scott v. United States, 586 F. Supp. 66 (E.D. Va. 1984).

Custodian persons in military justice system. — Just as the state itself, its Attorney General, and its director of corrections are not considered custodians of state prisoners for habeas corpus purposes, neither are the Secretary of the Navy and the Commandant of the Marine Corps considered custodians of individuals convicted of crimes by the military justice system. Instead, the warden or superintendent of the Disciplinary Barracks in which the military prisoner is incarcerated is the legal custodian under federal habeas corpus principles. Scott v. United States, 586 F. Supp. 66 (E.D. Va. 1984).

Attorney General for the Commonwealth of Virginia is empowered to represent guards or custodians of prisoners only if the prisoner is in the custody of or subject to the future custody of the Virginia Department of Corrections. Where the petitioner is not in the custody or subject to the future custody of the Department of Corrections, the Attorney General is not an appropriate party respondent. Van Sant v. Gondles, 596 F. Supp. 484 (E.D. Va. 1983), aff'd, 742 F.2d 1450 (4th Cir. 1984).

Compelled submission to surgery for removal of bullet to be used as evidence. — Where the state seeks to compel removal of a bullet from petitioner's chest for use as evidence in a criminal prosecution, the custody complained of (the compelled surgical removal being sought) would be carried out under the state's auspices, since its action would subject petitioner to custody in the operating room. Accordingly, whether the restraint on the petitioner is viewed as present custody or as future custody of the type referred to in subdivision (b) of this rule, such a petitioner is "in custody" for purposes of 28 U.S.C. § 2241. Lee v. Winston, 551 F. Supp. 247 (E.D. Va. 1982), aff'd in part and vacated in part, 717 F.2d 888 (4th Cir. 1983), aff'd, 470 U.S. 753, 105 S. Ct. 1611, 84 L. Ed. 2d 662 (1985).

Rule 3. Filing the Petition; Inmate Filing.

(a) *Where to File; Copies; Filing Fee.* — An original and two copies of the petition must be filed with the clerk and must be accompanied by:

(1) the applicable filing fee, or

(2) a motion for leave to proceed in forma pauperis, the affidavit required by 28 U.S.C. § 1915, and a certificate from the warden or other appropriate officer of the place of confinement showing the amount of money or securities that the petitioner has in any account in the institution.

(b) *Filing.* — The clerk must file the petition and enter it on the docket.

(c) *Time to File.* — The time for filing a petition is governed by 28 U.S.C. § 2244(d).

(d) *Inmate Filing.* — A paper filed by an inmate confined in an institution is timely if deposited in the institution's internal mailing system on or before the last day for filing. If an institution has a system designed for legal mail, the inmate must use that system to receive the benefit of this rule. Timely filing may be shown by a declaration in compliance with 28 U.S.C. § 1746 or by a notarized statement, either of which must set forth the date of deposit and state that first-class postage has been prepaid. (Amended by order adopted April 29, 2002, effective December 1, 2002, and by order adopted April 26, 2004, effective December 1, 2004.)

Rule 4. Preliminary Review; Serving the Petition and Order.

The clerk must promptly forward the petition to a judge under the court's assignment procedure, and the judge must promptly examine it. If it plainly appears from the petition and any attached exhibits that the petitioner is not entitled to relief in the district court, the judge must dismiss the petition and direct the clerk to notify the petitioner. If the petition is not dismissed, the judge must order the respondent to file an answer, motion, or other response within a fixed time, or to take other action the judge may order. In every case, the clerk must serve a copy of the petition and any order on the respondent and on the attorney general or other appropriate officer of the state involved. (Amended by order adopted April 26, 2004, effective December 1, 2004.)

Rule 5. The Answer and the Reply.

(a) *When Required.* — The respondent is not required to answer the petition unless a judge so orders.

(b) *Contents: Addressing the Allegations; Stating a Bar.* — The answer must address the allegations in the petition. In addition, it must state whether any claim in the petition is barred by a failure to exhaust state remedies, a procedural bar, non-retroactivity, or a statute of limitations.

(c) *Contents: Transcripts.* — The answer must also indicate what transcripts (of pretrial, trial, sentencing, or post-conviction proceedings) are available, when they can be furnished, and what proceedings have been recorded but not transcribed. The respondent must attach to the answer parts of the transcript that the respondent considers relevant. The judge may order that the respondent furnish other parts of existing transcripts or that parts of untranscribed recordings be transcribed and furnished. If a transcript cannot be obtained, the respondent may submit a narrative summary of the evidence.

(d) *Contents: Briefs on Appeal and Opinions.* — The respondent must also file with the answer a copy of:

(1) any brief that the petitioner submitted in an appellate court contesting the conviction or sentence, or contesting an adverse judgment or order in a post-conviction proceeding;

(2) any brief that the prosecution submitted in an appellate court relating to the conviction or sentence; and

(3) the opinions and dispositive orders of the appellate court relating to the conviction or the sentence.

(e) *Reply.* — The petitioner may submit a reply to the respondent's answer or other pleading within a time fixed by the judge. (Amended by order adopted April 26, 2004, effective December 1, 2004.)

Rule 6. Discovery.

(a) *Leave of Court Required.* — A judge may, for good cause, authorize a party to conduct discovery under the Federal Rules of Civil Procedure and may limit the extent of discovery. If necessary for effective discovery, the judge must appoint an attorney for a petitioner who qualifies to have counsel appointed under 18 U.S.C. § 3006A.

(b) *Requesting Discovery.* — A party requesting discovery must provide reasons for the request. The request must also include any proposed interrogatories and requests for admission, and must specify any requested documents.

(c) *Deposition Expenses.* — If the respondent is granted leave to take a deposition, the judge may require the respondent to pay the travel expenses, subsistence expenses, and fees of the petitioner's attorney to attend the deposition. (Amended by order adopted April 29, 2002, effective December 1, 2002, and by order adopted April 26, 2004, effective December 1, 2004.)

Rule 7. Expanding the Record.

(a) *In General.* — If the petition is not dismissed, the judge may direct the parties to expand the record by submitting additional materials relating to the petition. The judge may require that these materials be authenticated.

(b) *Types of Materials.* — The materials that may be required include letters predating the filing of the petition, documents, exhibits, and answers under oath to written interrogatories propounded by the judge. Affidavits may also be submitted and considered as part of the record.

(c) *Review by the Opposing Party.* — The judge must give the party against whom the additional materials are offered an opportunity to admit or deny their correctness. (Amended by order adopted April 26, 2004, effective December 1, 2004.)

Rule 8. Evidentiary Hearing.

(a) *Determining Whether to Hold a Hearing.* — If the petition is not dismissed, the judge must review the answer, any transcripts and records of state-court proceedings, and any materials submitted under Rule 7 to determine whether an evidentiary hearing is warranted.

(b) *Reference to a Magistrate Judge.* — A judge may, under 28 U.S.C. § 636(b), refer the petition to a magistrate judge to conduct hearings and to file proposed findings of fact and recommendations for disposition. When they are filed, the clerk must promptly serve copies of the proposed findings and recommendations on all parties. Within 14 days after being served, a party may file objections as provided by local court rule. The judge must determine de novo any proposed finding or recommendation to which objection is made. The judge may accept, reject, or modify any proposed finding or recommendation.

(c) *Appointing Counsel; Time of Hearing.* — If an evidentiary hearing is warranted, the judge must appoint an attorney to represent a petitioner who qualifies to have counsel appointed under 18 U.S.C.§ 3006A. The judge must conduct the hearing as soon as practicable after giving the attorneys adequate time to investigate and prepare. These rules do not limit the appointment of counsel under Sec. 3006A at any stage of the proceeding. (Amended by order adopted April 29, 2002, effective December 1, 2002, by order adopted April 26, 2004, effective December 1, 2004, and by order adopted March 26, 2009, effective December 1, 2009.)

Rule 9. Second or Successive Petitions.

Before presenting a second or successive petition, the petitioner must obtain an order from the appropriate court of appeals authorizing the district court to consider the petition as required by 28 U.S.C. § 2244(b)(3) and (4). (Amended by order adopted April 29, 2002, effective December 1, 2002, and by order adopted April 26, 2004, effective December 1, 2004.)

CASE NOTES

Petition was dismissed where petitioner's claims fell within statutory list printed on form petitioner used in presenting his previous petition for a writ of habeas corpus to the court. Petitioner's excuse that because of his inexperience and lack of effective assistance of counsel, he was unable to bring these claims in his prior petitions was insufficient. He was fully capable of raising several claims in his prior petition. The court found that his failure to do so constituted inexcusable neglect and an abuse of the writ. Jones v. Garraghty, 582 F. Supp. 1570 (E.D. Va.), cert. of probable cause denied, 735 F.2d 1356 (4th Cir. 1984).

Petitioner's claim was functional equivalent of a "successive petition." — Where substance of petitioner's claim — the constitutionality of Virginia's capital sentencing scheme — had been litigated, evaluated, and affirmed in several different forums, the claim raised no new or colorable issues; as such, it was the functional equivalent of a "successive petition" for habeas corpus within the meaning of subdivision (b) of this rule. Jones v. Murray, 802 F. Supp. 1412 (E.D. Va.), aff'd, 976 F.2d 169 (4th Cir. 1992).

Petitioner bears the burden of showing by a preponderance of the evidence that he has not abused the writ. Briley v. Booker, 594 F. Supp. 1399 (E.D. Va. 1984).

Rule 10. Powers of a Magistrate Judge.

A magistrate judge may perform the duties of a district judge under these rules, as authorized under 28 U.S.C. § 636. (Amended effective August 1, 1979, by order adopted April 29, 2002, effective December 1, 2002, and by order adopted April 26, 2004, effective December 1, 2004.)

Rule 11. Certificate of Appealability; Time to Appeal.

(a) *Certificate of Appealability.* — The district court must issue or deny a certificate of appealability when it enters a final order adverse to the applicant. Before entering the final order, the court may direct the parties to submit arguments on whether a certificate should issue. If the court issues a certificate, the court must state the specific issue or issues that satisfy the showing required by 28 U.S.C. § 2253(c)(2). If the court denies a certificate, the parties may not appeal the denial but may seek a certificate from the court of appeals under Federal Rule of Appellate Procedure 22. A motion to reconsider a denial does not extend the time to appeal.

(b) *Time to Appeal.* — Federal Rule of Appellate Procedure 4(a) governs the time to appeal an order entered under these rules. A timely notice of appeal must be filed even if the district court issues a certificate of appealability. (Adopted by order March 26, 2009, effective December 1, 2009.)

Rule 12. Applicability of the Federal Rules of Civil Procedure.

The Federal Rules of Civil Procedure, to the extent that they are not inconsistent with any statutory provisions or these rules, may be applied to a proceeding under these rules. (Amended by order adopted April 26, 2004, effective December 1, 2004, and renumbered by order adopted March 26, 2009, effective December 1, 2009.)

APPENDIX OF FORMS.

(Amended effective December 1, 2004.)

Petition for Relief From a Conviction or Sentence By a Person in State Custody

(Petition Under 28 U.S.C. § 2254 for a Writ of Habeas Corpus)

Instructions

1. To use this form, you must be a person who is currently serving a sentence under a judgment against you in a state court. You are asking for relief from the conviction or the sentence. This form is your petition for relief.

2. You may also use this form to challenge a state judgment that imposed a sentence to be served in the future, but you must fill in the name of the state where the judgment was entered. If you want to challenge a federal judgment that imposed a sentence to be served in the future, you should file a motion under 28 U.S.C. § 2255 in the federal court that entered the judgment.

3. Make sure the form is typed or neatly written.

4. You must tell the truth and sign the form. If you make a false statement of a material fact, you may be prosecuted for perjury.

5. Answer all the questions. You do not need to cite law. You may submit additional pages if necessary. If you do not fill out the form properly, you will be asked to submit additional or correct information. If you want to submit a brief or arguments, you must submit them in a separate memorandum.

6. You must pay a fee of $5. If the fee is paid, your petition will be filed. If you cannot pay the fee, you may ask to proceed *in forma pauperis* (as a poor person). To do that, you must fill out the last page of this form. Also, you must submit a certificate signed by an officer at the institution where you are confined showing the amount of money that the institution is holding for you. If your account exceeds $ _____, you must pay the filing fee.

7. In this petition, you may challenge the judgment entered by only one court. If you want to challenge a judgment entered by a different court (either in the same state or in different states), you must file a separate petition.

8. When you have completed the form, send the original and two copies to the Clerk of the United States District Court at this address:

   Clerk, United States District Court for ____________________
   Address
   City, State Zip Code

9. **CAUTION: You must include in this petition all the grounds for relief from the conviction or sentence that you challenge. And you must state the facts that support each ground. If you fail to set forth all the grounds in this petition, you may be barred from presenting additional grounds at a later date.**

10. **CAPITAL CASES: If you are under a sentence of death, you are entitled to the assistance of counsel and should request the appointment of counsel.**

PETITION UNDER 28 U.S.C. § 2254 FOR WRIT OF HABEAS CORPUS BY A PERSON IN STATE CUSTODY

United States District Court	District	
Name (under which you were convicted):		Docket or Case No.:
Place of Confinement:		Prisoner No.:
Petitioner (include the name under which you were convicted)	v.	Respondent (authorized person having custody of petitioner)
The Attorney General of the State of		

PETITION

1. (a) Name and location of court that entered the judgment of conviction you are challenging: ____

(b) Criminal docket or case number (if you know): ____

2. (a) Date of the judgment of conviction (if you know): ____

(b) Date of sentencing: ____

3. Length of sentence: ____

4. In this case, were you convicted on more than one count or of more than one crime? Yes ☐ No ☐

5. Identify all crimes of which you were convicted and sentenced in this case: ____

6. (a) What was your plea? (Check one)

(1) Not guilty ☐ (3) Nolo contendere (no contest) ☐

(2) Guilty ☐ (4) Insanity plea ☐

(b) If you entered a guilty plea to one count or charge and a not guilty plea to another count or charge, what did you plead guilty to and what did you plead not guilty to? ____

(c) If you went to trial, what kind of trial did you have? (Check one)

Jury ☐ Judge only ☐

7. Did you testify at a pretrial hearing, trial, or a post-trial hearing?

Yes ☐ No ☐

8. Did you appeal from the judgment of conviction?

Yes ☐ No ☐

9. If you did appeal, answer the following:

(a) Name of court:

(b) Docket or case number (if you know):

(c) Result:

(d) Date of result (if you know):

(e) Citation to the case (if you know):

(f) Grounds raised:

(g) Did you seek further review by a higher state court? Yes ☐ No ☐

If yes, answer the following:

(1) Name of court:

(2) Docket or case number (if you know):

(3) Result:

(4) Date of result (if you know):

(5) Citation to the case (if you know):

(6) Grounds raised:

(h) Did you file a petition for certiorari in the United States Supreme Court? Yes ☐ No ☐

If yes, answer the following:

(1) Docket or case number (if you know):

(2) Result: ____

____

(3) Date of result (if you know): ____

(4) Citation to the case (if you know): ____

10. Other than the direct appeals listed above, have you previously filed any other petitions, applications, or motions concerning this judgment of conviction in any state court?

Yes ☐ No ☐

11. If your answer to Question 10 was "Yes," give the following information:

(a) (1) Name of court: ____

(2) Docket or case number (if you know): ____

(3) Date of filing (if you know): ____

(4) Nature of the proceeding: ____

(5) Grounds raised: ____

____

____

____

____

____

____

____

____

(6) Did you receive a hearing where evidence was given on your petition, application, or motion? Yes ☐ No ☐

(7) Result: ____

(8) Date of result (if you know): ____

(b) If you filed any second petition, application, or motion, give the same information:

(1) Name of court: ____

(2) Docket or case number (if you know): ____

(3) Date of filing (if you know): ____

(4) Nature of the proceeding: ____

(5) Grounds raised: ____

____

____

____

____

(6) Did you receive a hearing where evidence was given on your petition, application, or motion? Yes ☐ No ☐

(7) Result: ___

(8) Date of result (if you know): ___

(c) If you filed any third petition, application, or motion, give the same information:

(1) Name of court: ___

(2) Docket or case number (if you know): ___

(3) Date of filing (if you know): ___

(4) Nature of the proceeding: ___

(5) Grounds raised: ___

(6) Did you receive a hearing where evidence was given on your petition, application, or motion? Yes ☐ No ☐

(7) Result: ___

(8) Date of result (if you know): ___

(d) Did you appeal to the highest state court having jurisdiction over the action taken on your petition, application, or motion?

(1) First petition: Yes ☐ No ☐

(2) Second petition: Yes ☐ No ☐

(3) Third petition: Yes ☐ No ☐

(e) If you did not appeal to the highest state court having jurisdiction, explain why you did not:

___

12. For this petition, state every ground on which you claim that you are being held in violation of the Constitution, laws, or treaties of the United States. Attach additional pages if you have more than four grounds. State the facts supporting each ground.

CAUTION: To proceed in the federal court, you must ordinarily first exhaust (use up) your available state-court remedies on each ground on which you request action by the federal court. Also, if you fail to set forth all the grounds in this petition, you may be barred from presenting additional grounds at a later date.

GROUND ONE: ______________________________

(a) Supporting facts (Do not argue or cite law. Just state the specific facts that support your claim.):

____

(b) If you did not exhaust your state remedies on Ground One, explain why: ______________________________

(c) **Direct Appeal of Ground One:**

(1) If you appealed from the judgment of conviction, did you raise this issue?

Yes ☐ No ☐

(2) If you did not raise this issue in your direct appeal, explain why: ______________________________

(d) **Post-Conviction Proceedings:**

(1) Did you raise this issue through a post-conviction motion or petition for habeas corpus in a state trial court? Yes ☐ No ☐

(2) If your answer to Question (d)(1) is "Yes," state:

Type of motion or petition: ______________________________

Name and location of the court where the motion or petition was filed: ______________________________

Docket or case number (if you know): ______

Date of the court's decision: ______

Result (attach a copy of the court's opinion or order, if available): ______

______

______

(3) Did you receive a hearing on your motion or petition?

Yes ☐ No ☐

(4) Did you appeal from the denial of your motion or petition?

Yes ☐ No ☐

(5) If your answer to Question (d)(4) is "Yes," did you raise this issue in the appeal?

Yes ☐ No ☐

(6) If your answer to Question (d)(4) is "Yes," state:

Name and location of the court where the appeal was filed: ______

______

Docket or case number (if you know): ______

Date of the court's decision: ______

Result (attach a copy of the court's opinion or order, if available): ______

______

______

(7) If your answer to Question (d)(4) or Question (d)(5) is "No," explain why you did not raise this issue: ______

______

______

______

(e) **Other Remedies:** Describe any other procedures (such as habeas corpus, administrative remedies, etc.) that you have used to exhaust your state remedies on Ground One: ______

______

______

GROUND TWO: ______

______

(a) Supporting facts (Do not argue or cite law. Just state the specific facts that support your claim.):

______

______

______

______

____

____

____

(b) If you did not exhaust your state remedies on Ground Two, explain why: _______________

____

____

____

(c) **Direct Appeal of Ground Two:**

(1) If you appealed from the judgment of conviction, did you raise this issue?

Yes ☐ No ☐

(2) If you did not raise this issue in your direct appeal, explain why: _______________

____

____

(d) **Post-Conviction Proceedings:**

(1) Did you raise this issue through a post-conviction motion or petition for habeas corpus in a state trial court?

Yes ☐ No ☐

(2) If your answer to Question (d)(1) is "Yes," state:

Type of motion or petition: _______________

Name and location of the court where the motion or petition was filed: _______________

____

Docket or case number (if you know): _______________

Date of the court's decision: _______________

Result (attach a copy of the court's opinion or order, if available): _______________

____

____

(3) Did you receive a hearing on your motion or petition?

Yes ☐ No ☐

(4) Did you appeal from the denial of your motion or petition?

Yes ☐ No ☐

(5) If your answer to Question (d)(4) is "Yes," did you raise this issue in the appeal?

Yes ☐ No ☐

(6) If your answer to Question (d)(4) is "Yes," state:

Name and location of the court where the appeal was filed: _______________

____

Docket or case number (if you know): ________________

Date of the court's decision: ________________

Result (attach a copy of the court's opinion or order, if available): ________________

____

____

(7) If your answer to Question (d)(4) or Question (d)(5) is "No," explain why you did not raise this issue: ________________

____

____

____

(e) **Other Remedies:** Describe any other procedures (such as habeas corpus, administrative remedies, etc.) that you have used to exhaust your state remedies on Ground Two: ________________

____

____

____

GROUND THREE: ________________

____

(a) Supporting facts (Do not argue or cite law. Just state the specific facts that support your claim.):

____

____

____

____

____

____

(b) If you did not exhaust your state remedies on Ground Three, explain why: ________________

____

____

____

(c) **Direct Appeal of Ground Three:**

(1) If you appealed from the judgment of conviction, did you raise this issue?

Yes ☐ No ☐

(2) If you did <u>not</u> raise this issue in your direct appeal, explain why: ________________

____

____

(d) **Post-Conviction Proceedings:**

(1) Did you raise this issue through a post-conviction motion or petition for habeas corpus in a state trial court? Yes ☐ No ☐

(2) If your answer to Question (d)(1) is "Yes," state:

Type of motion or petition: ____________________

Name and location of the court where the motion or petition was filed: ____________________

____

Docket or case number (if you know): ____________________

Date of the court's decision: ____________________

Result (attach a copy of the court's opinion or order, if available): ____________________

____

____

(3) Did you receive a hearing on your motion or petition?

Yes ☐ No ☐

(4) Did you appeal from the denial of your motion or petition?

Yes ☐ No ☐

(5) If your answer to Question (d)(4) is "Yes," did you raise this issue in the appeal?

Yes ☐ No ☐

(6) If your answer to Question (d)(4) is "Yes," state:

Name and location of the court where the appeal was filed: ____________________

____

Docket or case number (if you know): ____________________

Date of the court's decision: ____________________

Result (attach a copy of the court's opinion or order, if available): ____________________

____

____

(7) If your answer to Question (d)(4) or Question (d)(5) is "No," explain why you did not raise this issue: ____________________

____

____

____

(e) **Other Remedies:** Describe any other procedures (such as habeas corpus, administrative remedies, etc.) that you have used to exhaust your state remedies on Ground Three: ____________________

____

____

GROUND FOUR: ______________________________

____

(a) Supporting facts (Do not argue or cite law. Just state the specific facts that support your claim.): ______________________________

____

____

____

____

____

____

(b) If you did not exhaust your state remedies on Ground Four, explain why: ______________________________

____

____

____

____

(c) **Direct Appeal of Ground Four:**

(1) If you appealed from the judgment of conviction, did you raise this issue?

Yes ☐ No ☐

(2) If you did <u>not</u> raise this issue in your direct appeal, explain why: ______________________________

____

(d) **Post-Conviction Proceedings:**

(1) Did you raise this issue through a post-conviction motion or petition for habeas corpus in a state trial court? Yes ☐ No ☐

(2) If your answer to Question (d)(1) is "Yes," state:

Type of motion or petition: ______________________________

Name and location of the court where the motion or petition was filed: ______________________________

____

Docket or case number (if you know): ______________________________

Date of the court's decision: ______________________________

Result (attach a copy of the court's opinion or order, if available): ______________________________

____

____

(3) Did you receive a hearing on your motion or petition?

Yes ☐ No ☐

(4) Did you appeal from the denial of your motion or petition?

Yes ☐ No ☐

(5) If your answer to Question (d)(4) is "Yes," did you raise this issue in the appeal?

Yes ☐ No ☐

(6) If your answer to Question (d)(4) is "Yes," state:

Name and location of the court where the appeal was filed: ____________________

____

Docket or case number (if you know): ____________________

Date of the court's decision: ____________________

Result (attach a copy of the court's opinion or order, if available): ____________________

____

____

____

(7) If your answer to Question (d)(4) or Question (d)(5) is "No," explain why you did not raise this issue: ____________________

____

____

____

(e) **Other Remedies:** Describe any other procedures (such as habeas corpus, administrative remedies, etc.) that you have used to exhaust your state remedies on Ground Four: ____________________

____

____

____

____

13. Please answer these additional questions about the petition you are filing:

(a) Have all grounds for relief that you have raised in this petition been presented to the highest state court having jurisdiction? Yes ☐ No ☐

If your answer is "No," state which grounds have not been so presented and give your reason(s) for not presenting them: ____________________

____

____

____

(b) Is there any ground in this petition that has not been presented in some state or federal court? If so, which ground or grounds have not been presented, and state your reasons for not presenting them: ____________________

____

____

14. Have you previously filed any type of petition, application, or motion in a federal court regarding the conviction that you challenge in this petition? Yes ☐ No ☐

If "Yes," state the name and location of the court, the docket or case number, the type of proceeding, the issues raised, the date of the court's decision, and the result for each petition, application, or motion filed. Attach a copy of any court opinion or order, if available. ______

15. Do you have any petition or appeal <u>now pending</u> (filed and not decided yet) in any court, either state or federal, for the judgment you are challenging? Yes ☐ No ☐
If "Yes," state the name and location of the court, the docket or case number, the type of proceeding, and the issues raised. ______

16. Give the name and address, if you know, of each attorney who represented you in the following stages of the judgment you are challenging:
(a) At preliminary hearing: ______
(b) At arraignment and plea: ______
(c) At trial: ______
(d) At sentencing: ______
(e) On appeal: ______
(f) In any post-conviction proceeding: ______
(g) On appeal from any ruling against you in a post-conviction proceeding: ______

17. Do you have any future sentence to serve after you complete the sentence for the judgment that you are challenging? Yes ☐ No ☐

(a) If so, give name and location of court that imposed the other sentence you will serve in the future: ______________________________

(b) Give the date the other sentence was imposed: ______________________________

(c) Give the length of the other sentence: ______________________________

(d) Have you filed, or do you plan to file, any petition that challenges the judgment or sentence to be served in the future? Yes ☐ No ☐

18. TIMELINESS OF PETITION: If your judgment of conviction became final over one year ago, you must explain why the one-year statute of limitations as contained in 28 U.S.C. § 2244(d) does not bar your petition.* ______________________________

---

* The Antiterrorism and Effective Death Penalty Act of 1996 ("AEDPA") as contained in 28 U.S.C. § 2244(d) provides in part that:

(1) A one-year period of limitation shall apply to an application for a writ of habeas corpus by a person in custody pursuant to the judgment of a State court. The limitation period shall run from the latest of —

(continued...)

Therefore, petitioner asks that the Court grant the following relief: ______________________________

____

____

or any other relief to which petitioner may be entitled.

____

Signature of Attorney (if any)

I declare (or certify, verify, or state) under penalty of perjury that the foregoing is true and correct and that this Petition for Writ of Habeas Corpus was placed in the prison mailing system on ______________________ (month, date, year).

Executed (signed) on ____________________ (date).

____

Signature of Petitioner

---

*(...continued)

(A) the date on which the judgment became final by the conclusion of direct review or the expiration of the time for seeking such review;

(B) the date on which the impediment to filing an application created by State action in violation of the Constitution or laws of the United States is removed, if the applicant was prevented from filing by such state action;

(C) the date on which the constitutional right asserted was initially recognized by the Supreme Court, if the right has been newly recognized by the Supreme Court and made retroactively applicable to cases on collateral review; or

(D) the date on which the factual predicate of the claim or claims presented could have been discovered through the exercise of due diligence.

(2) The time during which a properly filed application for State post-conviction or other collateral review with respect to the pertinent judgment or claim is pending shall not be counted toward any period of limitation under this subsection.

If the person signing is not petitioner, state relationship to petitioner and explain why petitioner is not signing this petition. ______________________________

____

____

IN FORMA PAUPERIS DECLARATION

____

[Insert appropriate court]

* * * * *

Index to Section 2254 Cases

A

ANSWER, HabCorp 2254 Rule 5.

D

DELAYED PETITIONS, HabCorp 2254 Rule 9.

DISCOVERY, HabCorp 2254 Rule 6.

E

EVIDENTIARY HEARING, HabCorp 2254 Rule 8.

F

FEDERAL RULES OF CIVIL PROCEDURE.
Applicability, HabCorp 2254 Rule 11.

FORMS, HabCorp 2254 Appx.

H

HEARINGS.
Evidentiary hearing, HabCorp 2254 Rule 8.

M

MAGISTRATES.
Powers, HabCorp 2254 Rule 10.

P

PETITION, HabCorp 2254 Rule 2.
Answer, HabCorp 2254 Rule 5.
Delayed or successive petitions, HabCorp 2254 Rule 9.
Filing, HabCorp 2254 Rule 3.
Forms, HabCorp 2254 Appx.
Preliminary consideration by judge, HabCorp 2254 Rule 4.

R

RECORD.
Expansion of record, HabCorp 2254 Rule 7.

S

SCOPE OF RULES, HabCorp 2254 Rule 1.

SUCCESSIVE PETITIONS, HabCorp 2254 Rule 9.

RULES GOVERNING SECTION 2255 PROCEEDINGS FOR THE UNITED STATES DISTRICT COURTS

Effective February 1, 1977, as amended to February 1, 2010.

Rule
1. Scope.
2. The Motion.
3. Filing the Motion; Inmate Filing.
4. Preliminary Review.
5. The Answer and the Reply.
6. Discovery.
7. Expanding the Record.
8. Evidentiary Hearing.
9. Second or Successive Motions.

Rule
10. Powers of a Magistrate Judge.
11. Certificate of Appealability; Time to Appeal.
12. Applicability of the Federal Rules of Civil Procedure and the Federal Rules of Criminal Procedure.

Appendix of Forms.

Motion Under 28 U.S.C. § 2255.
Index.

Rule 1. Scope.

These rules govern a motion filed in a United States district court under 28 U.S.C. § 2255 by:

(a) a person in custody under a judgment of that court who seeks a determination that:

(1) the judgment violates the Constitution or laws of the United States;
(2) the court lacked jurisdiction to enter the judgment;
(3) the sentence exceeded the maximum allowed by law; or
(4) the judgment or sentence is otherwise subject to collateral review; and

(b) a person in custody under a judgment of a state court or another federal court, and subject to future custody under a judgment of the district court, who seeks a determination that:

(1) future custody under a judgment of the district court would violate the Constitution or laws of the United States;
(2) the district court lacked jurisdiction to enter the judgment;
(3) the district court's sentence exceeded the maximum allowed by law; or
(4) the district court's judgment or sentence is otherwise subject to collateral review.

CASE NOTES

Failure to assert grounds of relief listed in model motion. — A petitioner who has his specific attention called to grounds for relief in the (a) through (j) list in the model motion entitled "Motion to Vacate, Set Aside, or Correct Sentence by a Person in Federal Custody" and omits a claim clearly falling within that list may properly be found guilty of inexcusable neglect. United States v. Berryman, 558 F. Supp. 120 (E.D. Va. 1983).

Failure to include claims not listed in model motion. — Absent other bases, a failure to include claims not on that list would generally obviate inexcusable neglect. United States v. Berryman, 558 F. Supp. 120 (E.D. Va. 1983).

Rule 2. The Motion.

(a) *Applying for Relief.* — The application must be in the form of a motion to vacate, set aside, or correct the sentence.

(b) *Form.* — The motion must:

(1) specify all the grounds for relief available to the moving party;
(2) state the facts supporting each ground;
(3) state the relief requested;
(4) be printed, typewritten, or legibly handwritten; and
(5) be signed under penalty of perjury by the movant or by a person authorized to sign it for the movant.

(c) *Standard Form.* — The motion must substantially follow either the form appended to these rules or a form prescribed by a local district-court rule. The clerk must make forms available to moving parties without charge.

(d) *Separate Motions for Separate Judgments.* — A moving party who seeks relief from more than one judgment must file a separate motion covering each judgment. (Amended effective August 1, 1982, by order adopted April 29, 2002, effective December 1, 2002, by order adopted April 26, 2004, effective December 1, 2004.)

Rule 3. Filing the Motion; Inmate Filing.

(a) *Where to File; Copies.* — An original and two copies of the motion must be filed with the clerk.

(b) *Filing and Service.* — The clerk must file the motion and enter it on the criminal docket of the case in which the challenged judgment was entered. The clerk must then deliver or serve a copy of the motion on the United States attorney in that district, together with a notice of its filing.

(c) *Time to File.* — The time for filing a motion is governed by 28 U.S.C. § 2255 para. 6.

(d) *Inmate Filing.* — A paper filed by an inmate confined in an institution is timely if deposited in the institution's internal mailing system on or before the last day for filing. If an institution has a system designed for legal mail, the inmate must use that system to receive the benefit of this rule. Timely filing may be shown by a declaration in compliance with 28 U.S.C. § 1746 or by a notarized statement, either of which must set forth the date of deposit and state that first-class postage has been prepaid. (Amended by order adopted April 29, 2002, effective December 1, 2002, and by order adopted April 26, 2004, effective December 1, 2004.)

Rule 4. Preliminary Review.

(a) *Referral to a Judge.* — The clerk must promptly forward the motion to the judge who conducted the trial and imposed sentence or, if the judge who imposed sentence was not the trial judge, to the judge who conducted the proceedings being challenged. If the appropriate judge is not available, the clerk must forward the motion to a judge under the court's assignment procedure.

(b) *Initial Consideration by the Judge.* — The judge who receives the motion must promptly examine it. If it plainly appears from the motion, any attached exhibits, and the record of prior proceedings that the moving party is not entitled to relief, the judge must dismiss the motion and direct the clerk to notify the moving party. If the motion is not dismissed, the judge must order the United States attorney to file an answer, motion, or other response within a fixed time, or to take other action the judge may order. (Amended by order adopted April 26, 2004, effective December 1, 2004.)

Rule 5. The Answer and the Reply.

(a) *When Required.* — The respondent is not required to answer the motion unless a judge so orders.

(b) *Contents.* — The answer must address the allegations in the motion. In addition, it must state whether the moving party has used any other federal remedies, including any prior post-conviction motions under these rules or any previous rules, and whether the moving party received an evidentiary hearing.

(c) *Records of Prior Proceedings.* — If the answer refers to briefs or transcripts of the prior proceedings that are not available in the court's records, the judge must order the government to furnish them within a reasonable time that will not unduly delay the proceedings.

(d) *Reply.* — The moving party may submit a reply to the respondent's answer or other pleading within a time fixed by the judge. (Amended by order adopted April 26, 2004, effective December 1, 2004.)

Rule 6. Discovery.

(a) *Leave of Court Required.* — A judge may, for good cause, authorize a party to conduct discovery under the Federal Rules of Criminal Procedure or Civil Procedure, or in accordance with the practices and principles of law. If necessary for effective discovery, the judge must appoint an attorney for a moving party who qualifies to have counsel appointed under 18 U.S.C. § 3006A.

(b) *Requesting Discovery.* — A party requesting discovery must provide reasons for the request. The request must also include any proposed interrogatories and requests for admission, and must specify any requested documents.

(c) *Deposition Expenses.* — If the government is granted leave to take a deposition, the judge may require the government to pay the travel expenses, subsistence expenses, and fees of the moving party's attorney to attend the deposition. (Amended by order adopted April 29, 2002, effective December 1, 2002, and by order adopted April 26, 2004, effective December 1, 2004.)

Rule 7. Expanding the Record.

(a) *In General.* — If the motion is not dismissed, the judge may direct the parties to expand the record by submitting additional materials relating to the motion. The judge may require that these materials be authenticated.

(b) *Types of Materials.* — The materials that may be required include letters predating the filing of the motion, documents, exhibits, and answers under oath to written interrogatories propounded by the judge. Affidavits also may be submitted and considered as part of the record.

(c) *Review by the Opposing Party.* — The judge must give the party against whom the additional materials are offered an opportunity to admit or deny their correctness. (Amended by order adopted April 26, 2004, effective December 1, 2004.)

Rule 8. Evidentiary Hearing.

(a) *Determining Whether to Hold a Hearing.* — If the motion is not dismissed, the judge must review the answer, any transcripts and records of prior proceedings, and any materials submitted under Rule 7 to determine whether an evidentiary hearing is warranted.

(b) *Reference to a Magistrate Judge.* — A judge may, under 28 U.S.C. § 636(b), refer the motion to a magistrate judge to conduct hearings and to file proposed findings of fact and recommendations for disposition. When they are filed, the clerk must promptly serve copies of the proposed findings and recommendations on all parties. Within 14 days after being served, a party may file objections as provided by local court rule. The judge must determine de novo any proposed finding or recommendation to which objection is made. The judge may accept, reject, or modify any proposed finding or recommendation.

(c) *Appointing Counsel; Time of Hearing.* — If an evidentiary hearing is warranted, the judge must appoint an attorney to represent a moving party who qualifies to have counsel appointed under 18 U.S.C. § 3006A. The judge must conduct the hearing as soon as practicable after giving the attorneys adequate time to investigate and prepare. These rules do not limit the appointment of counsel under Sec. 3006A at any stage of the proceeding.

(d) *Producing a Statement.* — Federal Rule of Criminal Procedure 26.2(a)-(d) and (f) applies at a hearing under this rule. If a party does not comply with a Rule 26.2(a) order to produce a witness's statement,the court must not consider that witness's testimony. (Amended by order adopted April 22, 1993, effective December 1, 1993, by order adopted April 29, 2002, effective December 1, 2002, by order adopted April 26, 2004, effective December 1, 2004, and by order adopted March 26, 2009, effective December 1, 2009.)

Rule 9. Second or Successive Motions.

Before presenting a second or successive motion, the moving party must obtain an order from the appropriate court of appeals authorizing the district court to consider the motion, as required by 28 U.S.C. § 2255, para. 8. (Amended by order adopted April 29, 2002, effective December 1, 2002, and by order adopted April 26, 2004, effective December 1, 2004.)

Rule 10. Powers of a Magistrate Judge.

A magistrate judge may perform the duties of a district judge under these rules, as authorized by 28 U.S.C. § 636. (Amended effective August 1, 1979, by order adopted April 29, 2002, effective December 1, 2002, and by order adopted April 26, 2004, effective December 1, 2004.)

Rule 11. Certificate of Appealability; Time to Appeal.

(a) *Certificate of Appealability.* — The district court must issue or deny a certificate of appealability when it enters a final order adverse to the applicant. Before entering the final order, the court may direct the parties to submit arguments on whether a certificate should issue. If the court issues a certificate, the court must state the specific issue or issues that satisfy the showing required by 28 U.S.C. § 2253(c)(2). If the court denies a certificate, a party may not appeal the denial but may seek a certificate from the court of appeals under Federal Rule of Appellate Procedure 22. A motion to reconsider a denial does not extend the time to appeal.

(b) *Time to Appeal.* — Federal Rule of Appellate Procedure 4(a) governs the time to appeal an order entered under these rules. A timely notice of appeal must be filed even if the district court issues a certificate of appealability. These rules do not extend the time to appeal the original judgment of conviction. (Amended by order adopted April 26, 2004, effective December 1, 2004, and by order adopted March 26, 2009, effective December 1, 2009.)

Rule 12. Applicability of the Federal Rules of Civil Procedure and the Federal Rules of Criminal Procedure.

The Federal Rules of Civil Procedure and the Federal Rules of Criminal Procedure, to the extent that they are not inconsistent with any statutory provisions or these rules, may be applied to a proceeding under these rules. (Amended by order adopted April 26, 2004, effective December 1, 2004.)

APPENDIX OF FORMS.

(Amended effective December 1, 2004.)

Motion to Vacate, Set Aside, or Correct a Sentence By a Person in Federal Custody

(Motion Under 28 U.S.C. § 2255)

Instructions

1. To use this form, you must be a person who is serving a sentence under a judgment against you in a federal court. You are asking for relief from the conviction or the sentence. This form is your motion for relief.

2. You must file the form in the United States district court that entered the judgment that you are challenging. If you want to challenge a federal judgment that imposed a sentence to be served in the future, you should file the motion in the federal court that entered that judgment.

3. Make sure the form is typed or neatly written.

4. You must tell the truth and sign the form. If you make a false statement of a material fact, you may be prosecuted for perjury.

5. Answer all the questions. You do not need to cite law. You may submit additional pages if necessary. If you do not fill out the form properly, you will be asked to submit additional or correct information. If you want to submit a brief or arguments, you must submit them in a separate memorandum.

6. If you cannot pay for the costs of this motion (such as costs for an attorney or transcripts), you may ask to proceed *in forma pauperis* (as a poor person). To do that, you must fill out the last page of this form. Also, you must submit a certificate signed by an officer at the institution where you are confined showing the amount of money that the institution is holding for you.

7. In this motion, you may challenge the judgment entered by only one court. If you want to challenge a judgment entered by a different judge or division (either in the same district or in a different district), you must file a separate motion.

8. When you have completed the form, send the original and two copies to the Clerk of the United States District Court at this address:

   Clerk, United States District Court for ______________________
   Address
   City, State Zip Code

9. **CAUTION: You must include in this motion all the grounds for relief from the conviction or sentence that you challenge. And you must state the facts that support each ground. If you fail to set forth all the grounds in this motion, you may be barred from presenting additional grounds at a later date.**

10. **CAPITAL CASES: If you are under a sentence of death, you are entitled to the assistance of counsel and should request the appointment of counsel.**

MOTION UNDER 28 U.S.C. § 2255 TO VACATE, SET ASIDE, OR CORRECT SENTENCE BY A PERSON IN FEDERAL CUSTODY

United States District Court	District	
Name (under which you were convicted):		Docket or Case No.:
Place of Confinement:		Prisoner No.:
UNITED STATES OF AMERICA		Movant (include name under which you were convicted)
	v.	

MOTION

1. (a) Name and location of court that entered the judgment of conviction you are challenging: ____

   ____

   ____

   ____

   (b) Criminal docket or case number (if you know): ____

2. (a) Date of the judgment of conviction (if you know): ____

   ____

   (b) Date of sentencing: ____

3. Length of sentence: ____

4. Nature of crime (all counts): ____

   ____

   ____

   ____

   ____

   ____

5. (a) What was your plea? (Check one)

   (1) Not guilty ☐ (2) Guilty ☐ (3) Nolo contendere (no contest) ☐

   (b) If you entered a guilty plea to one count or indictment, and a not guilty plea to another count or indictment, what did you plead guilty to and what did you plead not guilty to? ____

   ____

   ____

   ____

   ____

6. If you went to trial, what kind of trial did you have? (Check one) Jury ☐ Judge only ☐

7. Did you testify at a pretrial hearing, trial, or post-trial hearing? Yes ☐ No ☐

8. Did you appeal from the judgment of conviction? Yes ☐ No ☐

9. If you did appeal, answer the following:

(a) Name of court: ______________________________

(b) Docket or case number (if you know): ______________________________

(c) Result: ______________________________

(d) Date of result (if you know): ______________________________

(e) Citation to the case (if you know): ______________________________

(f) Grounds raised: ______________________________

____

____

____

____

____

____

(g) Did you file a petition for certiorari in the United States Supreme Court? Yes ☐ No ☐

If "Yes," answer the following:

(1) Docket or case number (if you know): ______________________________

(2) Result: ______________________________

____

(3) Date of result (if you know): ______________________________

(4) Citation to the case (if you know): ______________________________

(5) Grounds raised: ______________________________

____

____

____

____

____

____

10. Other than the direct appeals listed above, have you previously filed any other motions, petitions, or applications concerning this judgment of conviction in any court?

Yes ☐ No ☐

11. If your answer to Question 10 was "Yes," give the following information:

(a) (1) Name of court: ______________________________

(2) Docket or case number (if you know): ______________________________

(3) Date of filing (if you know): ______________________________

(4) Nature of the proceeding: ______________________

(5) Grounds raised: ______________________

____

____

____

____

____

____

____

(6) Did you receive a hearing where evidence was given on your motion, petition, or application? Yes ☐ No ☐

(7) Result: ______________________

(8) Date of result (if you know): ______________________

(b) If you filed any second motion, petition, or application, give the same information:

(1) Name of court: ______________________

(2) Docket or case number (if you know): ______________________

(3) Date of filing (if you know): ______________________

(4) Nature of the proceeding: ______________________

(5) Grounds raised: ______________________

____

____

____

____

____

____

____

(6) Did you receive a hearing where evidence was given on your motion, petition, or application? Yes ☐ No ☐

(7) Result: ______________________

(8) Date of result (if you know): ______________________

(c) Did you appeal to a federal appellate court having jurisdiction over the action taken on your motion, petition, or application?

(1) First petition: Yes ☐ No ☐

(2) Second petition: Yes ☐ No ☐

(d) If you did not appeal from the action on any motion, petition, or application, explain briefly why you did not: ______________________________

____

____

12. For this motion, state every ground on which you claim that you are being held in violation of the Constitution, laws, or treaties of the United States. Attach additional pages if you have more than four grounds. State the facts supporting each ground.

GROUND ONE: ______________________________

____

(a) Supporting facts (Do not argue or cite law. Just state the specific facts that support your claim.):

____

____

____

____

____

____

____

____

____

____

____

(b) **Direct Appeal of Ground One:**

(1) If you appealed from the judgment of conviction, did you raise this issue?

Yes ☐ No ☐

(2) If you did not raise this issue in your direct appeal, explain why: ______________________________

____

____

(c) **Post-Conviction Proceedings:**

(1) Did you raise this issue in any post-conviction motion, petition, or application?

Yes ☐ No ☐

(2) If your answer to Question (c)(1) is "Yes," state:

Type of motion or petition: ______________________________

Name and location of the court where the motion or petition was filed: ______________________________

____

Docket or case number (if you know): ______________________

Date of the court's decision: ______________________

Result (attach a copy of the court's opinion or order, if available): ______________________

____

____

(3) Did you receive a hearing on your motion, petition, or application?

Yes ☐ No ☐

(4) Did you appeal from the denial of your motion, petition, or application?

Yes ☐ No ☐

(5) If your answer to Question (c)(4) is "Yes," did you raise this issue in the appeal?

Yes ☐ No ☐

(6) If your answer to Question (c)(4) is "Yes," state:

Name and location of the court where the appeal was filed: ______________________

____

Docket or case number (if you know): ______________________

Date of the court's decision: ______________________

Result (attach a copy of the court's opinion or order, if available): ______________________

____

____

(7) If your answer to Question (c)(4) or Question (c)(5) is "No," explain why you did not appeal or raise this issue: ______________________

____

____

____

____

GROUND TWO: ______________________

____

(a) Supporting facts (Do not argue or cite law. Just state the specific facts that support your claim.):

____

____

____

____

____

____

____

____

____

____

(b) **Direct Appeal of Ground Two:**

(1) If you appealed from the judgment of conviction, did you raise this issue?

Yes ☐ No ☐

(2) If you did not raise this issue in your direct appeal, explain why: ______________

____

____

(c) **Post-Conviction Proceedings:**

(1) Did you raise this issue in any post-conviction motion, petition, or application?

Yes ☐ No ☐

(2) If your answer to Question (c)(1) is "Yes," state:

Type of motion or petition: ______________________________

Name and location of the court where the motion or petition was filed: ______________

____

Docket or case number (if you know): ______________________________

Date of the court's decision: ______________________________

Result (attach a copy of the court's opinion or order, if available): ______________

____

____

(3) Did you receive a hearing on your motion, petition, or application?

Yes ☐ No ☐

(4) Did you appeal from the denial of your motion, petition, or application?

Yes ☐ No ☐

(5) If your answer to Question (c)(4) is "Yes," did you raise this issue in the appeal?

Yes ☐ No ☐

(6) If your answer to Question (c)(4) is "Yes," state:

Name and location of the court where the appeal was filed: ______________

____

Docket or case number (if you know): ______________________________

Date of the court's decision: ______________________________

Result (attach a copy of the court's opinion or order, if available):______________

____

____

(7) If your answer to Question (c)(4) or Question (c)(5) is "No," explain why you did not appeal or raise this issue: ______________________________

GROUND THREE: ______________________________

(a) Supporting facts (Do not argue or cite law. Just state the specific facts that support your claim.):

____

(b) **Direct Appeal of Ground Three:**

(1) If you appealed from the judgment of conviction, did you raise this issue?

Yes ☐ No ☐

(2) If you did not raise this issue in your direct appeal, explain why: ______________________________

(c) **Post-Conviction Proceedings:**

(1) Did you raise this issue in any post-conviction motion, petition, or application?

Yes ☐ No ☐

(2) If your answer to Question (c)(1) is "Yes," state:

Type of motion or petition: ______________________________

Name and location of the court where the motion or petition was filed: ______________________________

Docket or case number (if you know): ______________________________

Date of the court's decision: ______________________________

Result (attach a copy of the court's opinion or order, if available): ____________________

____

____

(3) Did you receive a hearing on your motion, petition, or application?

Yes ☐ No ☐

(4) Did you appeal from the denial of your motion, petition, or application?

Yes ☐ No ☐

(5) If your answer to Question (c)(4) is "Yes," did you raise this issue in the appeal?

Yes ☐ No ☐

(6) If your answer to Question (c)(4) is "Yes," state:

Name and location of the court where the appeal was filed: ____________________

____

Docket or case number (if you know): ____________________

Date of the court's decision: ____________________

Result (attach a copy of the court's opinion or order, if available): ____________________

____

____

(7) If your answer to Question (c)(4) or Question (c)(5) is "No," explain why you did not appeal or raise this issue: ____________________

____

____

____

____

GROUND FOUR: ____________________

____

(a) Supporting facts (Do not argue or cite law. Just state the specific facts that support your claim.):

____

____

____

____

____

____

____

____

____

____

(b) **Direct Appeal of Ground Four:**

(1) If you appealed from the judgment of conviction, did you raise this issue?

Yes ☐ No ☐

(2) If you did not raise this issue in your direct appeal, explain why: ______________

____

____

(c) **Post-Conviction Proceedings:**

(1) Did you raise this issue in any post-conviction motion, petition, or application?

Yes ☐ No ☐

(2) If your answer to Question (c)(1) is "Yes," state:

Type of motion or petition: ______________________________

Name and location of the court where the motion or petition was filed: ______________

____

Docket or case number (if you know): ______________________

Date of the court's decision: ______________________________

Result (attach a copy of the court's opinion or order, if available): ______________

____

____

(3) Did you receive a hearing on your motion, petition, or application?

Yes ☐ No ☐

(4) Did you appeal from the denial of your motion, petition, or application?

Yes ☐ No ☐

(5) If your answer to Question (c)(4) is "Yes," did you raise this issue in the appeal?

Yes ☐ No ☐

(6) If your answer to Question (c)(4) is "Yes," state:

Name and location of the court where the appeal was filed: ______________

____

____

Docket or case number (if you know): ______________________

Date of the court's decision: ______________________________

Result (attach a copy of the court's opinion or order, if available): ______________

____

____

(7) If your answer to Question (c)(4) or Question (c)(5) is "No," explain why you did not appeal or raise this issue: ______________________________

13. Is there any ground in this motion that you have not previously presented in some federal court? If so, which ground or grounds have not been presented, and state your reasons for not presenting them: ______________________________

14. Do you have any motion, petition, or appeal now pending (filed and not decided yet) in any court for the judgment you are challenging? Yes ☐ No ☐
If "Yes," state the name and location of the court, the docket or case number, the type of proceeding, and the issues raised. ______________________________

15. Give the name and address, if known, of each attorney who represented you in the following stages of the judgment you are challenging:
(a) At preliminary hearing: ______________________________
(b) At arraignment and plea: ______________________________
(c) At trial: ______________________________
(d) At sentencing: ______________________________

(e) On appeal: ______________________________

____

(f) In any post-conviction proceeding: ______________________________

____

(g) On appeal from any ruling against you in a post-conviction proceeding: ______________

____

____

16. Were you sentenced on more than one count of an indictment, or on more than one indictment, in the same court and at the same time? Yes ☐ No ☐

17. Do you have any future sentence to serve after you complete the sentence for the judgment that you are challenging? Yes ☐ No ☐

(a) If so, give name and location of court that imposed the other sentence you will serve in the future: ______________________________

____

(b) Give the date the other sentence was imposed: ______________________________

(c) Give the length of the other sentence: ______________________________

(d) Have you filed, or do you plan to file, any motion, petition, or application that challenges the judgment or sentence to be served in the future? Yes ☐ No ☐

18. TIMELINESS OF MOTION: If your judgment of conviction became final over one year ago, you must explain why the one-year statute of limitations as contained in 28 U.S.C. § 2255 does not bar your motion.*______________________________

* The Antiterrorism and Effective Death Penalty Act of 1996 ("AEDPA") as contained in 28 U.S.C. § 2255, paragraph 6, provides in part that:

> A one-year period of limitation shall apply to a motion under this section. The limitation period shall run from the latest of —
>
> (1) the date on which the judgment of conviction became final;
>
> (2) the date on which the impediment to making a motion created by governmental action in violation of the Constitution or laws of the United States is removed, if the movant was prevented from making such a motion by such governmental action;
>
> (3) the date on which the right asserted was initially recognized by the Supreme Court, if that right has been newly recognized by the Supreme Court and made retroactively applicable to cases on collateral review; or
>
> (4) the date on which the facts supporting the claim or claims presented could have been discovered through the exercise of due diligence.

Therefore, movant asks that the Court grant the following relief: ______________________________

____

____

or any other relief to which movant may be entitled.

____

Signature of Attorney (if any)

I declare (or certify, verify, or state) under penalty of perjury that the foregoing is true and correct and that this Motion under 28 U.S.C. § 2255 was placed in the prison mailing system on __________ __________ (month, date, year).

Executed (signed) on ____________________ (date).

____

Signature of Movant

If the person signing is not movant, state relationship to movant and explain why movant is not signing this motion. ____

____

____

IN FORMA PAUPERIS DECLARATION

____

[Insert appropriate court]

* * * * *

Index to Section 2255 Proceedings

A

ANSWER, HabCorp 2255 Rule 5.

APPEALS.
Time for, HabCorp 2255 Rule 11.

D

DELAYED MOTIONS, HabCorp 2255 Rule 9.

DISCOVERY, HabCorp 2255 Rule 6.

E

EVIDENTIARY HEARING, HabCorp 2255 Rule 8.

F

FEDERAL RULES OF CRIMINAL AND CIVIL PROCEDURE.
Applicability, HabCorp 2255 Rule 12.

FORMS, HabCorp 2255 Appx.

H

HEARINGS.
Evidentiary hearing, HabCorp 2255 Rule 8.

M

MAGISTRATES.
Powers, HabCorp 2255 Rule 10.

MOTION, HabCorp 2255 Rule 2.
Answer, HabCorp 2255 Rule 5.
Delayed or successive motions, HabCorp 2255 Rule 9.
Filing, HabCorp 2255 Rule 3.
Forms, HabCorp 2255 Appx.
Preliminary consideration by judge, HabCorp 2255 Rule 4.

R

RECORD.
Expansion of record, HabCorp 2255 Rule 7.

S

SCOPE OF RULES, HabCorp 2255 Rule 1.

SUCCESSIVE MOTIONS, HabCorp 2255 Rule 9.

RULES OF PROCEDURE FOR THE TRIAL OF MISDEMEANORS BEFORE UNITED STATES MAGISTRATES

Editor's note. — The Supreme Court order of May 1, 1990, which amended Rules 5(b), 41(a), 54(b) and 54(c), and added Rule 58, Federal Rules of Criminal Procedure, abrogated the Rules of Procedure for the Trial of Misdemeanors before United States Magistrates, effective December 1, 1990. For case notes construed under former rules, see Rule 58, FRCrim P.

RULES OF EVIDENCE FOR UNITED STATES COURTS AND MAGISTRATE JUDGES

Effective July 1, 1975, as amended December 1, 2013.

I. General Provisions.

Rule
101. Scope; Definitions.
102. Purpose.
103. Rulings on Evidence.
104. Preliminary Questions.
105. Limiting Evidence That Is Not Admissible Against Other Parties or for Other Purposes.
106. Remainder of or Related Writings or Recorded Statements.

II. Judicial Notice.

201. Judicial Notice of Adjudicative Facts.

III. Presumptions in Civil Cases.

301. Presumptions in Civil Cases Generally.
302. Applying State Law to Presumptions in Civil Cases.

IV. Relevancy and Its Limits.

401. Test for Relevant Evidence.
402. General Admissibility of Relevant Evidence.
403. Excluding Relevant Evidence for Prejudice, Confusion, Waste of Time, or Other Reasons.
404. Character Evidence; Crimes or Other Acts.
405. Methods of Proving Character.
406. Habit; Routine Practice.
407. Subsequent Remedial Measures.
408. Compromise Offers and Negotiations.
409. Offers to Pay Medical and Similar Expenses.
410. Pleas, Plea Discussions, and Related Statements.
411. Liability Insurance.
412. Sex-Offense Cases: The Victim's Sexual Behavior or Predisposition.
413. Similar Crimes in Sexual-Assault Cases.
414. Similar Crimes in Child-Molestation Cases.
415. Evidence of Similar Acts in Civil Cases Concerning Sexual Assault or Child Molestation.

V. Privileges.

501. Privilege in General.
502. Attorney-Client Privilege and Work Product; Limitations on Waiver.

VI. Witnesses.

601. Competency to Testify in General.
602. Need for Personal Knowledge.
603. Oath or Affirmation to Testify Truthfully.
604. Interpreter.
605. Judge's Competency as a Witness.

Rule
606. Juror's Competency as a Witness.
607. Who May Impeach a Witness.
608. A Witness's Character for Truthfulness or Untruthfulness.
609. Impeachment by Evidence of Criminal Conviction.
610. Religious Beliefs or Opinions.
611. Mode and Order of Examining Witnesses and Presenting Evidence.
612. Writing Used to Refresh a Witness's Memory.
613. Witness's Prior Statements.
614. Court's Calling or Examining a Witness.
615. Excluding Witnesses.

VII. Opinions and Expert Testimony.

701. Opinion Testimony by Lay Witnesses.
702. Testimony by Expert Witnesses.
703. Bases of an Expert's Opinion Testimony.
704. Opinion on an Ultimate Issue.
705. Disclosure of Facts or Data Underlying an Expert's Opinion.
706. Court Appointed Expert Witnesses.

VIII. Hearsay.

801. Definitions That Apply to This Article; Exclusions from Hearsay.
802. The Rule Against Hearsay.
803. Exceptions to the Rule Against Hearsay — Regardless of Whether the Declarant Is Available as a Witness.
804. Exceptions to the Rule Against Hearsay — When the Declarant Is Unavailable as a Witness.
805. Hearsay Within Hearsay.
806. Attacking and Supporting the Declarant's Credibility.
807. Residual exception.

IX. Authentication and Identification.

901. Authenticating or Identifying Evidence.
902. Evidence That Is Self-Authenticating.
903. Subscribing Witness' Testimony.

X. Contents of Writings, Recordings, and Photographs.

1001. Definitions That Apply to This Article.
1002. Requirement of Original.
1003. Admissibility of Duplicates.
1004. Admissibility of Other Evidence of Content.
1005. Copies of Public Records to Prove Content.
1006. Summaries to Prove Content.
1007. Testimony or Statement of a Party to Prove Content.
1008. Functions of the Court and Jury.

XI. Miscellaneous Rules.

Rule
1101. Applicability of the Rules.
1102. Amendments.
1103. Title.
Index.

Cross references. — See **www.uscourts.gov/rules.**

I. GENERAL PROVISIONS.

Rule 101. Scope; Definitions.

(a) *Scope.* — These rules apply to proceedings in United States courts. The specific courts and proceedings to which the rules apply, along with exceptions, are set out in Rule 1101.

(b) *Definitions.* — In these rules:

(1) "civil case" means a civil action or proceeding;

(2) "criminal case" includes a criminal proceeding;

(3) "public office" includes a public agency;

(4) "record" includes a memorandum, report, or data compilation;

(5) a "rule prescribed by the Supreme Court" means a rule adopted by the Supreme Court under statutory authority; and

(6) a reference to any kind of written material or any other medium includes electronically stored information. (Amended by order adopted March 2, 1987, effective October 1, 1987, by order adopted April 25, 1988, effective November 1, 1988, and by order adopted April 22, 1993, effective December 1, 1993, and by order adopted April 26, 2011, effective December 1, 2011.)

Comment. — The language of Rule 101 has been amended, and definitions have been added, as part of the general restyling of the Evidence Rules to make them more easily understood and to make style and terminology consistent throughout the rules. These changes are intended to be stylistic only. There is no intent to change any result in any ruling on evidence admissibility.

The reference to electronically stored information is intended to track the language of Fed. R. Civ. P. 34.

The Style Project — The Evidence Rules are the fourth set of national procedural rules to be restyled. The restyled Rules of Appellate Procedure took effect in 1998. The restyled Rules of Criminal Procedure took effect in 2002. The restyled Rules of Civil Procedure took effect in 2007. The restyled Rules of Evidence apply the same general drafting guidelines and principles used in restyling the Appellate, Criminal, and Civil Rules.

1. General Guidelines — Guidance in drafting, usage, and style was provided by Bryan Garner, *Guidelines for Drafting and Editing Court Rules*, Administrative Office of the United States Courts (1969) and Bryan Garner, *Dictionary of Modern Legal Usage*(2d ed. 1995). *See also* Joseph Kimble, *Guiding Principles for Restyling the Civil Rules*, in *Preliminary Draft of Proposed Style Revision of the Federal Rules of Civil Procedure*, at page x (Feb. 2005) (available at http://www.uscourts.gov/uscourts/RulesAndPolicies/rules¶relim]draft]proposed]pt1.pdf); Joseph Kimble, *Lessons in Drafting from the New Federal Rules of Civil Procedure*, 12 Scribes J. Legal Writing 25 (2008-2009). For specific commentary on the Evidence restyling project, see Joseph Kimble, *Drafting Examples from the Proposed New Federal Rules of Evidence*, 88 Mich. B.J. 52 (Aug. 2009); 88 Mich. B.J. 46 (Sept. 2009); 88 Mich. B.J. 54 (Oct. 2009); 88 Mich. B.J. 50 (Nov. 2009).

2. Formatting Changes — Many of the changes in the restyled Evidence Rules result from using format to achieve clearer presentations. The rules are broken down into constituent parts, using progressively indented subparagraphs with headings and substituting vertical for horizontal lists. "Hanging indents" are used throughout. These formatting changes make the structure of the rules graphic and make the restyled rules easier to read and understand even when the words are not changed. Rules 103, 404(b), 606(b), and 612 illustrate the benefits of formatting changes.

3. Changes to Reduce Inconsistent, Ambiguous, Redundant, Repetitive, or Archaic Words — The restyled rules reduce the use of inconsistent terms that say the same thing in different ways. Because different words are presumed to have different meanings, such inconsistencies can result in confusion. The restyled rules reduce inconsistencies by using the same words to express the same meaning. For example, consistent expression is achieved by not switching between "accused" and "defendant" or between "party opponent" and "opposing party" or between the various formulations of civil and criminal action/case/proceeding.

The restyled rules minimize the use of inherently ambiguous words. For example, the word "shall" can mean "must," "may," or something else, depending on context. The potential for confusion is exacerbated by the fact the word "shall" is no longer generally used in spoken or clearly written English. The restyled rules replace "shall" with "must," "may," or "should," depending on which one the context and established interpretation make correct in each rule.

The restyled rules minimize the use of redundant "intensifiers." These are expressions that attempt to add emphasis, but instead state the obvious and create negative implications for other rules. The absence of intensifiers in the restyled rules does not change their substantive meaning. See, e.g., Rule 104(c) (omitting "in all cases"); Rule 602 (omitting "but need not"); Rule 611(b) (omitting "in the exercise of discretion").

The restyled rules also remove words and concepts that are outdated or redundant.

4. Rule Numbers — The restyled rules keep the same numbers to minimize the effect on research. Subdivisions have been rearranged within some rules to achieve greater clarity and simplicity.

5. No Substantive Change — The Committee made special efforts to reject any purported style improvement that might result in a substantive change in the application of a rule. The Committee considered a change to be "substantive" if any of the following conditions were met:

a. Under the existing practice in any circuit, the change could lead to a different result on a question of admissibility (e.g., a change that requires a court to provide either a less or more stringent standard in evaluating the admissibility of particular evidence);

b. Under the existing practice in any circuit, it could lead to a change in the procedure by which an admissibility decision is made (e.g., a change in the time in which an objection must be made, or a change in whether a court must hold a hearing on an admissibility question);

c. The change would restructure a rule in a way that would alter the approach that courts and litigants have used to think about, and argue about, questions of admissibility (e.g., merging Rules 104(a) and 104(b) into a single subdivision); or

d. The amendment would change a "sacred phrase" — one that has become so familiar in practice that to alter it would be unduly disruptive to practice and expectations. Examples in the Evidence Rules include "unfair prejudice" and "truth of the matter asserted."

Law Review. — For a casenote, "Abrogating the Exclusionary Rule Outside of the Criminal Trial Context? Pennsylvania Board of Probation & Parole v. Scott: One Step Closer To a Per Se Rule in Fourth Amendment Jurisprudence," see 33 U. Rich. L. Rev. 631 (1999).

Research References. — Ashley Lipson, Art of Advocacy: Demonstrative Evidence (Matthew Bender).

Rule 102. Purpose.

These rules should be construed so as to administer every proceeding fairly, eliminate unjustifiable expense and delay, and promote the development of evidence law, to the end of ascertaining the truth and securing a just determination. (Amended by order adopted April 26, 2011, effective December 1, 2011.)

Comment. — The language of Rule 102 has been amended as part of the restyling of the Evidence Rules to make them more easily understood and to make style and terminology consistent throughout the rules. These changes are intended to be stylistic only. There is no intent to change any result in any ruling on evidence admissibility.

Law Review. — For an article, "Evidence Myopia: The Failure To See the Federal Rules of Evidence As a Codification of the Common Law," see 40 Wm. & Mary L. Rev. 1539 (1999). For an article, "Whether the Federal Rules of Evidence Should Be Conceived As a Perpetual Index Code: Blindness is Worse than Myopia," see 40 Wm. & Mary L. Rev. 1595 (1999). For an article, "The Elusive Identity of the Federal Rules of Evidence," see 40 Wm. & Mary L. Rev. 1613 (1999).

Rule 103. Rulings on Evidence.

(a) *Preserving a Claim of Error.* — A party may claim error in a ruling to admit or exclude evidence only if the error affects a substantial right of the party and:

(1) if the ruling admits evidence, a party, on the record:

(A) timely objects or moves to strike; and

(B) states the specific ground, unless it was apparent from the context; or

(2) if the ruling excludes evidence, a party informs the court of its substance by an offer of proof, unless the substance was apparent from the context.

(b) *Not Needing to Renew an Objection or Offer of Proof.* — Once the court rules definitively on the record — either before or at trial — a party need not renew an objection or offer of proof to preserve a claim of error for appeal.

(c) *Court's Statement About the Ruling; Directing an Offer of Proof.* — The court may make any statement about the character or form of the evidence, the objection made, and the ruling. The court may direct that an offer of proof be made in question-and-answer form.

(d) *Preventing the Jury from Hearing Inadmissible Evidence.* — To the extent practicable, the court must conduct a jury trial so that inadmissible evidence is not suggested to the jury by any means.

(e) *Taking Notice of Plain Error.* — A court may take notice of a plain error affecting a substantial right, even if the claim of error was not properly preserved. (Amended by order adopted April 17, 2000, effective December 1, 2000, and by order adopted April 26, 2011, effective December 1, 2011.)

Comment. — The language of Rule 103 has been amended as part of the restyling of the Evidence Rules to make them more easily understood and to make style and terminology consistent throughout the rules. These changes are intended to be stylistic only. There is no intent to change any result in any ruling on evidence admissibility.

CASE NOTES

Where a party fails to object to the admission of evidence, this rule requires that an appellate court review the admission for plain error. United States v. Chin, 83 F.3d 83 (4th Cir. 1996).

Applied in United States v. Fowler, 932 F.2d 306 (4th Cir. 1991); United States v. Ellis, 121 F.3d 908 (W.D. Va. 1997).

Rule 104. Preliminary Questions.

(a) *In General.* — The court must decide any preliminary question about whether a witness is qualified, a privilege exists, or evidence is admissible. In so deciding, the court is not bound by evidence rules, except those on privilege.

(b) *Relevance That Depends on a Fact.* — When the relevance of evidence depends on whether a fact exists, proof must be introduced sufficient to support a finding that the fact does exist. The court may admit the proposed evidence on the condition that the proof be introduced later.

(c) *Conducting a Hearing So That the Jury Cannot Hear It.* — The court must conduct any hearing on a preliminary question so that the jury cannot hear it if:

(1) the hearing involves the admissibility of a confession;

(2) a defendant in a criminal case is a witness and so requests; or

(3) justice so requires.

(d) *Cross-Examining a Defendant in a Criminal Case.* — By testifying on a preliminary question, a defendant in a criminal case does not become subject to cross-examination on other issues in the case.

(e) *Evidence Relevant to Weight and Credibility.* — This rule does not limit a party's right to introduce before the jury evidence that is relevant to the weight or credibility of other evidence. (Amended by order adopted March 2, 1987, effective October 1, 1987, and by order adopted April 26, 2011, effective December 1, 2011.)

Comment. — The language of Rule 104 has been amended as part of the restyling of the Evidence Rules to make them more easily understood and to make style and terminology consistent throughout the rules. These changes are intended to be stylistic only. There is no intent to change any result in any ruling on evidence admissibility.

Law Review. — For note, "Reducing the Value of Plaintiff's Litigation Option in Federal Court: Daubert v. Merrell Dow Pharmaceuticals, Inc.," see 2 Geo. Mason L. Rev. 159 (Spring 1995).

CASE NOTES

Relevancy dependent upon fulfillment of condition of fact. — Federal Rule of Evidence 901(a) requires authentication "evidence sufficient to support a finding that the matter in question is what its proponent claims." Authenticity is in the category of relevancy dependent upon fulfillment of a condition of fact and is governed by the procedure set forth in Rule 104(b). Rule 104(b) provides that when relevancy depends upon fulfillment of a condition of fact, the court shall admit it upon, or subject to, the introduction of evidence sufficient to support a finding of the fulfillment of the condition. The judge should make "a preliminary determination" whether the foundation evidence is sufficient to support a finding of the fulfillment of the condition. If so, the item is admitted. If after all the evidence is in, pro and con, the jury could reasonably conclude the fulfillment of the condition is not established, the issue is for them. If the evidence is not such as to allow a finding, the judge withdraws the matter from their consideration. In re James E. Long Constr. Co., 557 F.2d 1039 (4th Cir. 1977).

Applied in Benedi v. McNeil-P.P.C., Inc., 66 F.3d 1378 (4th Cir. 1995).

Rule 105. Limiting Evidence That Is Not Admissible Against Other Parties or for Other Purposes.

If the court admits evidence that is admissible against a party or for a purpose — but not against another party or for another purpose — the court, on timely request, must restrict the evidence to its proper scope and instruct the jury accordingly. (Amended by order adopted April 26, 2011, effective December 1, 2011.)

Comment. — The language of Rule 105 has been amended as part of the restyling of the Evidence Rules to make them more easily understood and to make style and terminology consistent throughout the rules. These changes are intended to be stylistic only. There is no intent to change any result in any ruling on evidence admissibility.

Rule 106. Remainder of or Related Writings or Recorded Statements.

If a party introduces all or part of a writing or recorded statement, an adverse party may require the introduction, at that time, of any other part — or any other writing or recorded statement — that in fairness ought to be considered at the same time. (Amended by order adopted March 2, 1987, effective October 1, 1987, and by order adopted April 26, 2011, effective December 1, 2011.)

Comment. The language of Rule 106 has been amended as part of the restyling of the Evidence Rules to make them more easily understood and to make style and terminology consistent throughout the rules. These changes are intended to be stylistic only. There is no intent to change any result in any ruling on evidence admissibility.

CASE NOTES

The purpose of this rule is to permit the contemporaneous introduction of recorded statements that place in context other writings admitted into evidence which, viewed alone, may be misleading. United States v. Jamar, 561 F.2d 1103 (4th Cir. 1977).

The rule is not intended as a vehicle for the introduction of substantive evidence but its role is to permit partially introduced written statements to be placed in context. United States v. Jamar, 561 F.2d 1103 (4th Cir. 1977).

II. JUDICIAL NOTICE.

Rule 201. Judicial Notice of Adjudicative Facts.

(a) *Scope.* — This rule governs judicial notice of an adjudicative fact only, not a legislative fact.

(b) *Kinds of Facts That May Be Judicially Noticed.* — The court may judicially notice a fact that is not subject to reasonable dispute because it:

(1) is generally known within the trial court's territorial jurisdiction; or

(2) can be accurately and readily determined from sources whose accuracy cannot reasonably be questioned.

(c) *Taking Notice.* — The court:

(1) may take judicial notice on its own; or

(2) must take judicial notice if a party requests it and the court is supplied with the necessary information.

(d) *Timing.* — The court may take judicial notice at any stage of the proceeding.

(e) *Opportunity to Be Heard.* — On timely request, a party is entitled to be heard on the propriety of taking judicial notice and the nature of the fact to be noticed. If the court takes judicial notice before notifying a party, the party, on request, is still entitled to be heard.

(f) *Instructing the Jury.* — In a civil case, the court must instruct the jury to accept the noticed fact as conclusive. In a criminal case, the court must instruct the jury that it may or may not accept the noticed fact as conclusive. (Amended by order adopted April 26, 2011, effective December 1, 2011.)

Comment. — The language of Rule 201 has been amended as part of the restyling of the Evidence Rules to make them more easily understood and to make style and terminology consistent throughout the rules. These changes are intended to be stylistic only. There is no intent to change any result in any ruling on evidence admissibility.

CASE NOTES

Rule gives trial court wide discretion regarding judicial notice. Bartl v. Twardy (In re Claxton), 32 Bankr. 219 (Bankr. E.D. Va. 1983); Bartl v. Twardy (In re Claxton), 32 Bankr. 224 (Bankr. E.D. Va. 1983).

Court took judicial notice of bankruptcy schedules filed in a bankruptcy case of which the proceeding in which notice was taken was a part, where the case involved an involuntary petition, eliminating the debtor's interest in proving insolvency, the trustee listed the schedules as part of his pretrial exhibits which was furnished to defendants' counsel in a timely manner, and the schedules themselves were furnished pursuant to the court's pretrial order. Bartl v. Twardy (In re Claxton), 32 Bankr. 224 (Bankr. E.D. Va. 1983).

Applied in Harris v. United States, 431 F. Supp. 1173 (E.D. Va. 1977); Davenport v. City of Alexandria, 710 F.2d 148 (4th Cir. 1983).

III. PRESUMPTIONS IN CIVIL CASES.

Rule 301. Presumptions in Civil Cases Generally.

In a civil case, unless a federal statute or these rules provide otherwise, the party against whom a presumption is directed has the burden of producing evidence to rebut the presumption. But this rule does not shift the burden of persuasion, which remains on the party who had it originally. (Amended by order adopted April 26, 2011, effective December 1, 2011.)

Comment. — The language of Rule 301 has been amended as part of the restyling of the Evidence Rules to make them more easily understood and to make style and terminology consistent throughout the rules. These changes are intended to be stylistic only. There is no intent to change any result in any ruling on evidence admissibility.

CASE NOTES

Applicability to action for assessment of taxes against individuals willfully evading tax. — See United States v. Pomponio, 635 F.2d 293 (4th Cir. 1980).

Rule 302. Applying State Law to Presumptions in Civil Cases.

In a civil case, state law governs the effect of a presumption regarding a claim or defense for which state law supplies the rule of decision. (Amended by order adopted April 26, 2011, effective December 1, 2011.)

Comment. — The language of Rule 302 has been amended as part of the restyling of the Evidence Rules to make them more easily understood and to make style and terminology consistent throughout the rules. These changes are intended to be stylistic only. There is no intent to change any result in any ruling on evidence admissibility.

CASE NOTES

Applied in Hewitt v. Firestone Tire & Rubber Co., 490 F. Supp. 1358 (E.D. Va. 1980).

IV. RELEVANCY AND ITS LIMITS.

Rule 401. Test for Relevant Evidence.

Evidence is relevant if:

(a) it has any tendency to make a fact more or less probable than it would be without the evidence; and

(b) the fact is of consequence in determining the action. (Amended by order adopted April 26, 2011, effective December 1, 2011.)

Comment. — The language of Rule 401 has been amended as part of the restyling of the Evidence Rules to make them more easily understood and to make style and terminology consistent throughout

the rules. These changes are intended to be stylistic only. There is no intent to change any result in any ruling on evidence admissibility.

Law Review. — For note, "Reducing the Value of Plaintiff's Litigation Option in Federal Court: Daubert v. Merrell Dow Pharmaceuticals, Inc.," see 2 Geo. Mason L. Rev. 159 (Spring 1995). For article, "The Epistemology of Prediction: Future Dangerousness Testimony and Intellectual Due Process," see 60 Wash. & Lee L. Rev. 353 (2003). For article, "An Evidentiary Paradox: Defending the Character Evidence Prohibition by Upholding a Non-Character Theory of Logical Relevance, the Doctrine of Chances," see 40 U. Rich. L. Rev. 419 (2006).

CASE NOTES

Expert's testimony as to lifetime earning capacity of infant relevant. — The court was cognizant of the possibility that an expert's testimony as to the lifetime earning capacity of a deceased infant could prove to be prejudicial in the jury assessment of damages but felt that any possible prejudice when weighed against the relevance of the evidence could be cured by the instructions to the jury. Mullins v. Seals, 416 F. Supp. 1098 (W.D. Va. 1976).

Evidence of lost rent in inverse condemnation action. — In an inverse condemnation action, arising out of construction of a mass transit system, evidence of a lessee's refusal to pay rent during the construction period because of interference with lessee's use of the property was properly excluded where the relationship between the parties to the lease was not at arm's length and the owner-lessor had allowed the lessee to fall behind in rent well before construction began. It was doubtful that the rent was relevant evidence as defined by this rule. But even if it had marginal relevance, it was properly excluded under Rule 403 because of the likelihood that it would mislead the jury. Tony Guiffre Distrib. Co. v. Washington Metro. Area Transit Auth., 740 F.2d 295 (4th Cir. 1984).

Exclusion of government reports was not abuse of discretion. — In prosecution for conversion and unauthorized conveyance of governmental information and mail fraud, government reports were not relevant to the issue of defendant's state of mind or his intent and did not assess his actions to show whether he was confused, and the confusion and corruption of others had no tendency to prove whether defendant was confused or corrupt; therefore, government reports did not satisfy the requirement of this rule and their exclusion was not an abuse of the court's discretion. United States v. Fowler, 932 F.2d 306 (4th Cir. 1991).

Gang culture testimony relevant. — Trial court did not abuse its discretion in admitting expert testimony on gang culture in defendant's criminal trial for malicious wounding and use of a firearm during the commission of a felony; the Commonwealth provided a sufficient foundation for the admission of the testimony, the testimony was relevant in that it established a motive for the shooting, and the evidence was not outweighed by prejudice. Hubbard v. Commonwealth, 2006 Va. App. LEXIS 72 (Feb. 28, 2006).

Applied in Environmental Defense Fund, Inc. v. Lamphier, 714 F.2d 331 (4th Cir. 1983); United States v. Samad, 744 F.2d 393 (4th Cir. 1984); 1616 Reminc Ltd. Partnership v. Commonwealth Land Title Ins. Co., 778 F.2d 183 (4th Cir. 1985); Gill v. Rollins Protective Servs. Co., 836 F.2d 194 (4th Cir. 1987); United States v. Hernandez, 975 F.2d 1035 (4th Cir. 1992).

Rule 402. General Admissibility of Relevant Evidence.

Relevant evidence is admissible unless any of the following provides otherwise:

- the United States Constitution;
- a federal statute;
- these rules; or
- other rules prescribed by the Supreme Court.

Irrelevant evidence is not admissible. (Amended by order adopted April 26, 2011, effective December 1, 2011.)

Comment. — The language of Rule 402 has been amended as part of the restyling of the Evidence Rules to make them more easily understood and to make style and terminology consistent throughout the rules. These changes are intended to be stylistic only. There is no intent to change any result in any ruling on evidence admissibility.

Law Review. — For an article, "Evidence Myopia: The Failure To See the Federal Rules of Evidence As a Codification of the Common Law," see 40 Wm. & Mary L. Rev. 1539 (1999). For an article, "Whether the Federal Rules of Evidence Should Be Conceived As a Perpetual Index Code: Blindness is Worse than Myopia," see 40 Wm. & Mary L. Rev. 1595 (1999). For an article, "The Elusive Identity of the Federal Rules of Evidence," see 40 Wm. & Mary L. Rev. 1613 (1999).

CASE NOTES

Admission of photographs of victim's wounds where defense stipulated as to cause of death. — Where defendant stipulated that deceased had been bludgeoned to death with a blunt instrument, but the government sought to introduce photographs of deceased's wounds in order to connect the wounds with one of the government's exhibits, a crescent wrench, admission of the photographs was not an abuse of discretion nor reversible error. United States v. Whitfield, 715 F.2d 145 (4th Cir. 1983).

Admissibility of defendant's knowledge of alleged victim's past sexual behavior. — Where evidence was established that in the week prior to the alleged rape defendant learned that his friend and the alleged victim had recently engaged in consensual sex over a three-day period and where at most, the evidence suggested that defendant's state of mind toward the alleged victim was that she was a woman of easy virtue, such state of mind was neither relevant, nor exculpatory. United States v. Saunders, 736 F. Supp. 698 (E.D. Va. 1990), cert. denied, 502 U.S. 1105, 112 S. Ct. 1199, 117 L. Ed. 2d 439 (1992).

Review of trial court's decision. — In the absence of a clear showing of abuse of discretion, the trial court's decision to admit or reject photographs into evidence should not be disturbed. United States v. Whitfield, 715 F.2d 145 (4th Cir. 1983).

Evidence admissible as to witness's credibility. — Accomplice's testimony that defendant beat and stabbed her was admissible to support the accomplice's credibility and explain her presence at the scene of the offenses; the testimony explained and validated the accomplice's claim of fear and the stabbing illustrated the extent of defendant's abuse and the reality of the accomplice's fear. Hales v. Commonwealth, No. 3226-03-3, 2004 Va. App. LEXIS 636 (Ct. of Appeals Dec. 28, 2004).

Gang evidence improperly excluded. — Defendant's convictions for second-degree murder, use of a firearm during the commission of a felony, and possession of a firearm by a convicted felon were appropriate because at least some of his proffered gang evidence was erroneously excluded. Evidence of gang membership, if credited by the jury, was relevant to the issue of the bias of a witness and whether that witness was biased was material to defendant's theory of the case. Cousins v. Commonwealth, 56 Va. App. 257, 693 S.E.2d 283, 2010 Va. App. LEXIS 214 (2010).

Applied in Wilder Enters., Inc. v. Allied Artists Pictures Corp., 632 F.2d 1135 (4th Cir. 1980); Roberts v. County of Fairfax, 937 F. Supp. 541 (E.D. Va. 1996).

Rule 403. Excluding Relevant Evidence for Prejudice, Confusion, Waste of Time, or Other Reasons.

The court may exclude relevant evidence if its probative value is substantially outweighed by a danger of one or more of the following: unfair prejudice, confusing the issues, misleading the jury, undue delay, wasting time, or needlessly presenting cumulative evidence. (Amended by order adopted April 26, 2011, effective December 1, 2011.)

Comment. — The language of Rule 403 has been amended as part of the restyling of the Evidence Rules to make them more easily understood and to make style and terminology consistent throughout the rules. These changes are intended to be stylistic only. There is no intent to change any result in any ruling on evidence admissibility.

Law Review. — For note, "Impeachment with an Unsworn Prior Inconsistent Statement as Subterfuge," see 28 Wm. & Mary L. Rev. 295 (1987). For casenote, "Clinging to History: The Supreme Court (Mis)interprets Federal Rule of Evidence 801(d)(1)(B) as Containing a Temporal Requirement," see 29 U. Rich. L. Rev. 459 (1995). For article, "The Epistemology of Prediction: Future Dangerousness Testimony and Intellectual Due Process," see 60 Wash. & Lee L. Rev. 353 (2003). For casenote & comment, "No Don't IM Me — Instant Messaging, Authentication, and the Best Evidence Rule," see 13 Geo. Mason L. Rev. 1309 (2006). For article, "An Evidentiary Paradox: Defending the Character Evidence Prohibition by Upholding a Non-Character Theory of Logical Relevance, the Doctrine of Chances," see 40 U. Rich. L. Rev. 419 (2006).

CASE NOTES

Admissibility of defendant's knowledge of alleged victim's past sexual behavior. — Where evidence was established that in the week prior to the alleged rape defendant learned that his friend and the alleged victim had recently engaged in consensual sex over a three-day period and where at most, the evidence suggested that defendant's state of mind toward the alleged victim was that she was a woman of easy virtue, such state of mind was neither relevant, nor exculpatory. United States v. Saunders, 736 F. Supp. 698 (E.D. Va. 1990), cert. denied, 502 U.S. 1105, 112 S. Ct. 1199, 117 L. Ed. 2d 439 (1992).

Discretion of court. — The probativeness-prejudice balance required by this rule is a matter committed to the discretion of the district court. United States v. Whaley, 786 F.2d 1229 (4th Cir. 1986).

The standard for overturning a Rule 403 determination is whether the district court acted in an "arbitrary or irrational" manner. United States v. Penello, 668 F.2d 789 (4th Cir. 1982).

Each situation must be decided on its own facts. — Under this rule, relevant evidence may be excluded if its probative value is substantially outweighed by the danger of unfair prejudice, confusion of the issues or misleading the jury or by considerations of undue delay, waste of time or needless presentation of cumulative evidence. No mechanical test can be set for each situation, thus, each must be decided on its own facts. United States v. Billups, 522 F. Supp. 935 (E.D. Va. 1981), aff'd, 692 F.2d 320 (4th Cir. 1982).

Evidence of prior conduct and crimes. — In a prosecution involving the defendant's participation in a conspiracy to distribute cocaine, evidence of prior conduct and crimes relating to the sale and distribution of cocaine was clearly probative and was not unfairly prejudicial. United States v. Percy, 765 F.2d 1199 (4th Cir. 1985).

Expert testimony as to common knowledge is usually harmless error. — Rule 702 makes inadmissible expert testimony as to a matter which obviously is within the common knowledge of jurors because such testimony, almost by definition, can be of no assistance. At the same time, the admission of such testimony, though technical error, will almost invariably be harmless. Trouble is encountered only when the evaluation of the commonplace by an expert witness might supplant a jury's independent exercise of common sense. This, however, does not seem to be an inquiry under Rule 702, but rather a necessary, independent inquiry under this rule to exclude evidence which is prejudicial. Scott v. Sears, Roebuck & Co., 789 F.2d 1052 (4th Cir. 1986).

Exclusion of alcohol consumption not warranted in bench trial. — Evidence of alcohol consumption by boat operater prior to an accident should not be excluded in a bench trial under this rule on the ground that it was unfairly prejudicial. Schultz v. Butcher, 24 F.3d 626 (4th Cir. 1994).

Expert's testimony as to lifetime earning capacity of infant not prejudicial. — The court was cognizant of the possibility that an expert's testimony as to the lifetime earning capacity of a deceased infant could prove to be prejudicial in the jury's assessment of damages but felt that any possible prejudice when weighed against the relevance of the evidence could be cured by the instructions to the jury. Mullins v. Seals, 416 F. Supp. 1098 (W.D. Va. 1976).

Evidence of assault on process server in assault and battery action. — Evidence concerning an alleged unprovoked assault by defendant on the process server serving the complaint in an action for assault and battery and malicious prosecution was not admissible to show who was the likely aggressor as well as the continuing bias of defendant toward plaintiff. Garrick v. Kelly, 649 F. Supp. 607 (E.D. Va. 1986), aff'd, 842 F.2d 1290 (4th Cir. 1988).

Exclusion should be sparingly used. — Where the evidence sought to be excluded under this rule is probative, a balance should be struck in favor of admissibility, and evidence should be excluded only sparingly. United States v. Aramony, 88 F.3d 1369 (4th Cir. 1996), cert. denied, 520 U.S. 123, 117 S. Ct. 1842, 137 L. Ed. 2d 1046 (1997).

Evidence properly excluded. — Where the government had only the agents' statement that the defendant fishing boat operator admitted to signing a fictitious name on shack fish vouchers, and there was no proof that he actually received any money, the fictitious signature was hardly probative of intent to avoid taxes if he did not even take the money, given the certain prejudice the jury would attach to this testimony, the district court properly excluded the evidence. United States v. Penello, 668 F.2d 789 (4th Cir. 1982).

Under this rule, refusal to exclude certain reports was proper, since the probative value of these reports was not outweighed by the danger of unfair prejudice, because the reports were highly probative on the issue of notice and because defendant was free to, and did, offer testimony rebutting the significance of these reports. Benedi v. McNeil-P.P.C., Inc., 66 F.3d 1378 (4th Cir. 1995).

Improper evidence insufficient for reversal. — While the prosecutors did attempt to introduce improper evidence, in this case, the particularly harmful effect of the government's improper questions was eliminated by the witnesses' answers or was largely remedied by the district court's corrective measures, and the evidence against the appellants was very strong without the prosecution's objectionable tactics; for these reasons, the questions present no ground for reversal. United States v. Lamarr, 75 F.3d 964 (4th Cir. 1996), cert. denied, 519 U.S. 948, 117 S. Ct. 358, 136 L. Ed. 2d 250 (1996).

Probative value outweighed prejudicial effect. — While defendant argued that the prejudicial effect of the phone conversation and the foul language of his letter far outweighed any probative value, the probative value was in fact not minimal, but went directly to establish criminal intent and guilty consciousness; thus the probative value outweighed the prejudicial effect as required. United States v. Hayden, 85 F.3d 153 (4th Cir. 1996).

Evidence that linked defendant to the murder weapon. — When a murder defendant denied possessing the murder weapon at the time of the murder, the trial court properly admitted evidence of an earlier shooting in which the same gun was used and where three witnesses identified defendant as the gunman. Evidence of other crimes was permissible to connect a defendant to a specific murder weapon, and the probative value of the evidence outweighed the prejudicial effect; it was not necessary to limit testimony to one witness. Martin v. Commonwealth, 2006 Va. App. LEXIS 559 (Dec. 12, 2006).

Gang culture testimony not overly prejudicial. — Trial court did not abuse its discretion in admitting expert testimony on gang culture in defendant's criminal trial for malicious wounding and use of a firearm during the commission of a felony; the Commonwealth provided a sufficient foundation for the admission of the testimony, the testimony was relevant in that it established a motive for the shooting, and the evidence was not outweighed by prejudice. Hubbard v. Commonwealth, 2006 Va. App. LEXIS 72 (Feb. 28, 2006).

Evidence of gang membership. — Defendant's convictions for second-degree murder, use of a firearm during the commission of a felony, and possession of a firearm by a convicted felon were appropriate because at least some of his proffered gang evidence was erroneously excluded. Evidence of gang membership, if credited by the jury, was relevant to the issue of the bias of a witness and whether that witness was biased was material to defendant's theory of the case; further, the evidence was more probative than prejudicial. Cousins v. Commonwealth, 56 Va. App. 257, 693 S.E.2d 283, 2010 Va. App. LEXIS 214 (2010).

Drug courier profile inadmissible, while Jamaican citizenship and substantial amount of cash admissible. — In case in which defendant was convicted of unlawfully possessing a firearm and attempting to board an aircraft with a concealed weapon, trial court's admission of testimony concerning drug courier profile and marijuana residue found in one of defendant's jacket pockets was an abuse of discretion, absent any evidence linking defendant to the drug trade. However, evidence of defendant's Jamaican citizenship, about which he lied, and the substantial amount of cash he was carrying at the time of his arrest was properly admitted under this rule, as the money showed that he had the means to purchase a ticket, and his citizenship may have shown a manifestation of his consciousness of guilt when he lied about his true identity. United States v. Simpson, 910 F.2d 154 (4th Cir. 1990).

Evidence of lost rent in inverse condemnation action. — In an inverse condemnation action, arising out of construction of a mass transit system, evidence of a lessee's refusal to pay rent during the construction period because of interference with lessee's use of the property was properly excluded where the relationship between the parties to the lease was not at arm's length and the owner-lessor had allowed the lessee to fall behind in rent well before construction began. It was doubtful that the rent was relevant evidence as defined by Rule 401. But even if it had marginal relevance, it was properly excluded under this rule because of the likelihood that it would mislead the jury. Tony Guiffre Distrib. Co. v. Washington Metro. Area Transit Auth., 740 F.2d 295 (4th Cir. 1984).

Admission of photographs of victim's wounds where defense stipulated as to cause of death. — Where defendant stipulated that deceased had been bludgeoned to death with a blunt instrument, but the government sought to introduce photographs of deceased's wounds in order to connect the wounds with one of the government's exhibits, a crescent wrench, admission of the photographs was not an abuse of discretion nor reversible error. United States v. Whitfield, 715 F.2d 145 (4th Cir. 1983).

Form 10-K properly excluded in securities-fraud action. — District judge did not abuse his discretion by granting computer company's motion in limine to exclude from evidence computer company's Form 10-K annual report for fiscal year 1992. The potential prejudice from introducing the Form 10-K in the securities-fraud class action was clear: jurors likely would view its disclosure of rights of return as proof of culpable conduct, akin to a landlords' fixing a stairway after being sued by an injured tenant. The probative value of the Form 10-K for other purposes was dubious. There was plenty of other evidence at trial to show that some of the distributors could, and did, return unsold units to computer company. Malone v. Microdyne Corp., 26 F.3d 471 (4th Cir. 1994).

Review of trial court's decision. — In the absence of a clear showing of abuse of discretion, the trial court's decision to admit or reject photographs into evidence should not be disturbed. United States v. Whitfield, 715 F.2d 145 (4th Cir. 1983).

Federal court of appeals will defer to a trial court's Rule 403 balancing unless it is an arbitrary or irrational exercise of discretion. And the same standard of review applies to a trial court's rulings under Rule 404(b). Garraghty v. Jordan, 830 F.2d 1295 (4th Cir. 1987).

Although government documents were minimally relevant, exclusion was not abuse of discretion. — In prosecution for conversion and unauthorized conveyance of governmental information, even if governmental reports concerning the processing and management of secret, classified government documents were minimally relevant, their exclusion was not abuse of court's discretion since the probative value of defendant's excerpts from these documents would unfairly prejudice the prosecution and would mislead the jury on the issue of defendant's guilt or innocence. United States v. Fowler, 932 F.2d 306 (4th Cir. 1991).

Applied in Utility Control Corp. v. Prince William Constr. Co., 558 F.2d 716 (4th Cir. 1977); United States v. Black, 692 F.2d 314 (4th Cir. 1982); United States v. Billups, 692 F.2d 320 (4th Cir. 1982); United States v. Portsmouth Paving Corp., 694 F.2d 312 (4th Cir. 1982); Environmental Defense Fund, Inc. v. Lamphier, 714 F.2d 331 (4th Cir. 1983); United States v. Wilson, 721 F.2d 967 (4th Cir. 1983); Ellis v. International Playtex, Inc., 745 F.2d 292 (4th Cir. 1984); El-Meswari v. Washington Gas Light Co., 785 F.2d 483 (4th Cir. 1986); United States v. Larouche, 896 F.2d 815 (4th Cir. 1990); United States v. Hines, 943 F.2d 348 (4th Cir. 1991); United States v. Chin, 83 F.3d 83 (4th Cir. 1996); Roberts v. County of Fairfax, 937 F. Supp. 541 (E.D. Va. 1996); United States v. Dickerson, 166 F.3d 667, 1999 U.S. App. LEXIS 1741 (4th. Cir. 1999); Zeus Enters., Inc. v. Alphin Aircraft, Inc., 190 F.3d 238 (4th Cir. 1999).

Rule 404. Character Evidence; Crimes or Other Acts.

(a) *Character Evidence.* — (1) *Prohibited Uses.* Evidence of a person's character or character trait is not admissible to prove that on a particular occasion the person acted in accordance with the character or trait.

(2) *Exceptions for a Defendant or Victim in a Criminal Case.* The following exceptions apply in a criminal case:

(A) a defendant may offer evidence of the defendant's pertinent trait, and if the evidence is admitted, the prosecutor may offer evidence to rebut it;

(B) subject to the limitations in Rule 412, a defendant may offer evidence of an alleged victim's pertinent trait, and if the evidence is admitted, the prosecutor may:

(i) offer evidence to rebut it; and

(ii) offer evidence of the defendant's same trait; and

(C) in a homicide case, the prosecutor may offer evidence of the alleged victim's trait of peacefulness to rebut evidence that the victim was the first aggressor.

(3) *Exceptions for a Witness.* Evidence of a witness's character may be admitted under Rules 607, 608, and 609.

(b) *Crimes, Wrongs, or Other Acts.* — Evidence of a witness's character may be admitted under Rules 607, 608, and 609.

(1) Prohibited Uses. Evidence of a crime, wrong, or other act is not admissible to prove a person's character in order to show that on a particular occasion the person acted in accordance with the character.

(2) Permitted Uses; Notice in a Criminal Case. This evidence may be admissible for another purpose, such as proving motive, opportunity, intent, preparation, plan, knowledge, identity, absence of mistake, or lack of accident. On request by a defendant in a criminal case, the prosecutor must:

(A) provide reasonable notice of the general nature of any such evidence that the prosecutor intends to offer at trial; and

(B) do so before trial — or during trial if the court, for good cause, excuses lack of pretrial notice. (Amended by order adopted March 2, 1987, effective October 1, 1987, by order adopted April 30, 1991, effective December 1, 1991, by order adopted April 17, 2000, effective December 1, 2000, and by order adopted April 12, 2006, effective December 1, 2006, and by order adopted April 26, 2011, effective December 1, 2011.)

Comment. — The language of Rule 404 has been amended as part of the restyling of the Evidence Rules to make them more easily understood and to make style and terminology consistent throughout the rules. These changes are intended to be stylistic only. There is no intent to change any result in any ruling on evidence admissibility.

Law Review. — For note on admissibility of similar acts, see 40 Wash. & Lee L. Rev. 741 (1983). For article, "An Evidentiary Paradox: Defending the Character Evidence Prohibition by Upholding a Non-Character Theory of Logical Relevance, the Doctrine of Chances," see 40 U. Rich. L. Rev. 419 (2006). For symposium, "The Restyled Federal Rules of Evidence," see 53 Wm and Mary L. Rev. 1435 (2012).

CASE NOTES

Admissibility of evidence of other crimes generally. — This rule, characterized as the "inclusive rule," admits all evidence of other crimes or acts relevant to an issue in a trial except that which tends to prove only criminal disposition. Manifestly, the rule, even though correctly described as "inclusionary," does not permit the automatic admission of any evidence of other "crimes, wrongs or acts." The evidence of other crimes must be relevant for a purpose other than showing the character or disposition of the defendant. Hagy v. Commonwealth, 222 Va. 599, 283 S.E.2d 187 (1981).

The Federal Rules of Evidence eliminate the use of evidence regarding other crimes or bad acts for proving character to show defendant acted in conformity, but allows such evidence to be admitted for other purposes, such as proof of intent, motive, etc., making it clear that the list is only by way of example. The legislative history shows that Congress changed the wording of the version sent by the supreme court to lay greater stress on admissibility. The categories listed in the subdivision (b) of this rule are merely illustrative, not exclusive and the possible circumstances of admissibility may be infinite. The court can admit evidence for one purpose or many, and its admissibility can be upheld if it was proper for any purpose. United States v. Billups, 522 F. Supp. 935 (E.D. Va. 1981), aff'd, 692 F.2d 320 (4th Cir. 1982).

Evidence of other crimes that link defendant to murder weapon. — When a murder defendant denied possessing the murder weapon at the time of the murder, the trial court properly admitted evidence of an earlier shooting in which the same gun was used and where three witnesses identified defendant as the gunman. Evidence of other crimes was permissible to connect a defendant to a specific murder weapon, and the probative value of the evidence outweighed the prejudicial effect; it was not necessary to limit testimony to one witness. Martin v. Commonwealth, 2006 Va. App. LEXIS 559 (Dec. 12, 2006).

Prior acts. — Evidence of prior acts may be admissible if it is relevant in the manner prescribed by this rule, necessary to the government's case, and reliable. In addition, the trial judge must weigh the probative value of the evidence against the risk of undue prejudice to the defendant. The trial judge has wide discretion in balancing possible prejudice. United States v. King, 768 F.2d 586 (4th Cir. 1985).

Under this rule prior bad acts are admissible if they are (1) relevant to an issue other than character; (2) necessary, and (3) reliable. United States v. Hernandez, 975 F.2d 1035 (4th Cir. 1992).

This rule prohibits evidence of other crimes or bad acts to show bad character and propensity to violate the law; however, evidence of other bad acts is admissible for certain purposes unrelated to a defendant's bad character, such as "proof of motive, opportunity, intent, preparation, plan, knowledge, identity, or absence of mistake or accident. United States v. Hayden, 85 F.3d 153 (4th Cir. 1996).

Evidence of prior bad acts is admissible if the acts are relevant to an issue other than character, necessary and reliable. United States v. Aramony, 88 F.3d 1369 (4th Cir. 1996), cert. denied, 520 U.S. 123, 117 S. Ct. 1842, 137 L. Ed. 2d 1046 (1997).

Evidence of other crimes, wrongs, or acts is not admissible to prove the character of a person in order to show action in conformity therewith. United States v. Aramony, 88 F.3d 1369 (4th Cir. 1996), cert. denied, 520 U.S. 123, 117 S. Ct. 1842, 137 L. Ed. 2d 1046 (1997).

Because evidence of prior bruising and scratching that resulted in prior involvement by child protective services, considered together with defendant's inconsistent explanations as to how the injuries occurred, possessed significant probative value as it demonstrated defendant's prior relationship with and feelings toward the child there was no error in its admission. Burnette v. Commonwealth, 60 Va. App. 462, 729 S.E.2d 740, 2012 Va. App. LEXIS 246 (2012).

"Other acts" occurring after events charged in indictment. — The mere fact that the "other acts" at issue occurred after the events charged in the indictment does not render them irrelevant. United States v. Whaley, 786 F.2d 1229 (4th Cir. 1986).

Evidence of ongoing abuse was relevant. — Victim's testimony about ongoing abuse by defendant, not charged in the indictment, was not erroneously admitted because the evidence was relevant to show the conduct or attitude of defendant toward the child, to prove motive or method, and to negate the possibility of mistake. Ortiz v. Commonwealth, 276 Va. 705, 667 S.E.2d 751, 2008 Va. LEXIS 122 (2008).

Witness intimidation admissible. — Evidence of witness intimidation is admissible to prove consciousness of guilt and criminal intent under this rule, if the evidence is related to the offense charged and is reliable, as in this case. United States v. Hayden, 85 F.3d 153 (4th Cir. 1996).

Trial court did not abuse its discretion in permitting the Commonwealth to elicit testimony from a witness concerning an attack on the witness and a threat to kill the witness made by defendant, based on an inference that defendant's motive was to silence or intimidate the witness; when the threat or act of violence against a key witness was done by the defendant himself, the trier of fact could draw a reasonable inference that defendant intended to silence or intimidate the witness. Andrews v. Commonwealth, 280 Va. 231, 699 S.E.2d 237, 2010 Va. LEXIS 239 (2010), cert. denied, 131 S. Ct. 2999, 2011 U.S. LEXIS 4469, 180 L. Ed. 2d 827 (U.S. 2011).

Evidence of two prior worthless checks given by the defendant to the same payee was properly admitted for the purpose of showing both intent and knowledge on the part of the defendant. United States v. Sparks, 560 F.2d 1173 (4th Cir. 1977).

Where testimony is admitted as to acts intrinsic to the crime charged, and is not admitted solely to demonstrate bad character, it is admissible. United States v. Chin, 83 F.3d 83 (4th Cir. 1996).

Rule's list is merely illustrative, not exclusive. — See United States v. Johnson, 634 F.2d 735 (4th Cir. 1980), cert. denied, 451 U.S. 907, 101 S. Ct. 1974, 68 L. Ed. 2d 295 (1981).

Patent litigation. — There can be little doubt that subdivision (b) of this rule is as applicable in patent litigation as in other litigation contexts. Yet, because the inequitable conduct defense is so often frivolously pled, district courts must take care to ensure that assertions of the defense of inequitable conduct plus reliance on Rule 404(b) do not become a license for a fishing expedition into a patentee's files concerning related patents and applications. Semiconductor Energy Lab. Co. v. Samsung Elecs. Co., 4 F. Supp. 2d 477 (E.D. Va. 1998), aff'd, 204 F.3d 1368 (Fed. Cir. 2000).

Discretion of judge. — In exercising discretion granted by the rule, the judge first must determine if the proffered evidence is relevant to an issue other than the accused's character. If so, then the trial judge must balance the evidence's probative value against the dangers of undue prejudice aroused by this form of evidence. United States v. Johnson, 634 F.2d 735 (4th Cir. 1980), cert. denied, 451 U.S. 907, 101 S. Ct. 1974, 68 L. Ed. 2d 295 (1981).

Particularly where a defendant in a criminal case by her own testimony and that of others has deliberately sought as the primary means of defense to depict herself as one whose essential philosophy and habitual conduct in life is completely at odds with the possession of a state of mind requisite to guilt of the offense charged, that defendant may be considered in effect to have forfeited any protection that the first sentence of the rule might otherwise have provided against the type of "other act" evidence here challenged. United States v. Johnson, 634 F.2d 735 (4th Cir. 1980), cert. denied, 451 U.S. 907, 101 S. Ct. 1974, 68 L. Ed. 2d 295 (1981); United States v. Billups, 692 F.2d 320 (4th Cir. 1982), cert. denied, 464 U.S. 820, 104 S. Ct. 84, 78 L. Ed. 2d 93 (1983).

Limiting instructions on evidence. — In this circuit, unlike others, the trial court is not required to make an explicit statement of the purpose for which the evidence is admitted. The use of limiting instructions setting out the purpose for which the evidence is admitted and admonishing the jury against considering it as improper evidence of guilt will do much to alleviate difficulties raised by its admission. United States v. Hernandez, 975 F.2d 1035 (4th Cir. 1992).

Improperly admitted evidence only harmless error on facts. — While the prosecutors did attempt to introduce improper evidence, in this case, the particularly harmful effect of the government's improper questions was eliminated by the witnesses' answers or was largely remedied by the district court's corrective measures, and the evidence against the appellants was very strong without the prosecution's objectionable tactics, for these reasons, the questions present no ground for reversal. United States v. Lamarr, 75 F.3d 964 (4th Cir. 1996), cert. denied, 519 U.S. 948, 117 S. Ct. 358, 136 L. Ed. 2d 250 (1996).

Prior conviction used to show motive may be admitted under this rule. — Rule 609 is concerned solely with the use of evidence of criminal conviction as a means of attacking the credibility of a witness. Where the evidence is proffered primarily to demonstrate motive and only incidentally to attack credibility, the evidence may properly be admitted under Rule 404(b). Roshan v. Fard, 705 F.2d 102 (4th Cir. 1983).

Testimony of a bad act was admissible to rebut the specific "good acts" character testimony of numerous maritime employers that defendant never took bribe money. United States v. Billups, 522 F. Supp. 935 (E.D. Va. 1981), aff'd, 692 F.2d 320 (4th Cir. 1982).

Evidence is necessary if it furnishes part of the context of the crime. United States v. Aramony, 88 F.3d 1369 (4th Cir. 1996), cert. denied, 520 U.S. 123, 117 S. Ct. 1842, 137 L. Ed. 2d 1046 (1997).

Evidence of prior sexual conduct. — Testimony of two male witnesses that the defendant charged with taking indecent liberties with children had made sexual advances to them within three years prior to the offenses charged was admissible to prove intent, knowledge, or absence of mistake, where the defendant was sharply contesting the sufficiency of the government's proof of lascivious intent with respect to the crimes charged. The district court did not err in admitting evidence of other crimes, wrongs or acts, especially since defendant was insisting that under the Virginia statute the burden was on the government to show that defendant's acts were performed with lascivious intent and did not occur by accident, and because intent was a key issue in the case, the threshold requirement that evidence of prior acts be relevant to an issue other than the defendant's character was fully met, and since the probative value of the challenged evidence outweighed its prejudicial effect. United States v. Beahm, 664 F.2d 414 (4th Cir. 1981).

Previous convictions for driving while intoxicated. — In a prosecution for second-degree murder arising out of a fatal automobile accident, defendant's driving record, which showed previous convictions for driving while intoxicated, would not have been admissible to show that defendant had a propensity to drive while drunk. However, the driving record was relevant to establish that defendant had grounds to be aware of the risk his drinking and driving while intoxicated presented to others. United States v. Fleming, 739 F.2d 945 (4th Cir. 1984), cert. denied, 469 U.S. 1193, 105 S. Ct. 970, 83 L. Ed. 2d 973 (1985).

Evidence of assault on process server in assault and battery action. — Evidence concerning an alleged unprovoked assault by defendant on the process server serving the complaint in an action for assault and battery and malicious prosecution was not admissible to show who was the likely aggressor as well as the continuing bias of defendant toward plaintiff. Garrick v. Kelly, 649 F. Supp. 607 (E.D. Va. 1986), aff'd, 842 F.2d 1290 (4th Cir. 1988).

Evidence of later alleged fire not admissible. — Evidence that the defendant's car was burned a year after the burning of a rental vehicle he allegedly used in a kidnapping was not admissible in his trial for kidnapping; because there was no direct or circumstantial evidence that the defendant burned his car or had any motive to burn his car, the probative value of the evidence was slight and it would confuse the issues in the trial. United States v. Young, 65 F. Supp. 2d 370 (E.D. Va. 1999).

In a prosecution for Taft-Hartley violations, the trial court properly admitted evidence of other crimes or wrongdoing where, after balancing the relevance and probative value of the evidence to some issue in the trial against the danger of undue prejudice to defendant, it determined to admit each for certain limited purposes, which were explained to the jury both in limiting instructions at the time of the admission and as part of the charge to the jury, and where the probative value of the evidence on the issues was increased by the similarity of the acts. Except for differences in dates, the earlier and later acts were virtually identical: same parties, same types of problems discussed and resolved, same act of passing money, same types of locales, same modus operandi. United States v. Billups, 522 F. Supp. 935 (E.D. Va. 1981), aff'd, 692 F.2d 320 (4th Cir. 1982).

In an appeal from a conviction for federal income tax evasion, evidence of the doctor's overstated Medicaid billings was not improperly admitted, and government counsel's reference to the doctor's "fraudulent" Medicaid forms did not unduly prejudice the jury in view of the trial court's action where in rebuttal of defendant's portrait of herself as an altruistic healer of the sick, whose concerns lay elsewhere than attending to her financial interests and resulting legal responsibilities, evidence was received showing that defendant reported four times as many services per patient as other Virginia doctors, under rule allowing evidence of other crimes to show motive or knowledge. United States v. Johnson, 634 F.2d 735 (4th Cir. 1980), cert. denied, 451 U.S. 907, 101 S. Ct. 1974, 68 L. Ed. 2d 295 (1981).

Extrinsic acts evidence is inadmissible solely to prove that defendant is a bad character and, therefore, likely to have committed the crime charged. Extrinsic acts evidence, however, may be admissible for other purposes. United States v. Johnson, 634 F.2d 735 (4th Cir. 1980), cert. denied, 451 U.S. 907, 101 S. Ct. 1974, 68 L. Ed. 2d 295 (1981).

In a prosecution involving defendant's participation in a conspiracy to distribute cocaine, evidence of prior conduct and crimes relating to the sale and distribution of cocaine was clearly probative and was not unfairly prejudicial. United States v. Percy, 765 F.2d 1199 (4th Cir. 1985).

Evidence of other crimes showing motive in lying before grand jury. — Evidence relating to other crimes committed by defendant and prosecutorial comments referring to defendant's fear of public corruption charges were not improperly admitted where such evidence and comments showed defendants' motive in lying before the grand jury, the crime for which they were on trial. United States v. Boone, 759 F.2d 345 (4th Cir.), cert.

denied, 474 U.S. 861, 106 S. Ct. 176, 88 L. Ed. 2d 146 (1985).

Testimony concerning defendant's preconspiracy purchase of truck. — Trial court did not abuse its discretion in admitting a co-conspirator's testimony concerning defendant's preconspiracy purchase of a truck, where such evidence was relevant because the truck was used to facilitate the transportation of co-conspirators to and from a cocaine distribution and storage site during the conspiracy. United States v. Campbell, 935 F.2d 39 (4th Cir.), cert. denied, 502 U.S. 929, 112 S. Ct. 348, 116 L. Ed. 2d 287 (1991).

Testimony concerning bad character on cross-examination. — Where appellant had not placed his character or reputation in evidence, the trial judge incorrectly allowed the prosecution in the cross-examination of defense witness to ask, "Is it fair to say that Dr. Tran had a reputation in the community for being an easy source of drugs?". United States v. Tran Trong Cuong, 18 F.3d 1132 (4th Cir. 1994).

Defendant not unduly prejudiced by erroneous admission of evidence. — If any evidence regarding other crimes or bad acts was erroneously admitted against defendant, the court did not act arbitrarily or capriciously in deciding to admit it and the jury's careful and fair treatment of defendant showed that evidence did not unduly prejudice him. United States v. Billups, 522 F. Supp. 935 (E.D. Va. 1981), aff'd, 692 F.2d 320 (4th Cir. 1982).

Government permitted to prove nature of prior convictions despite defendant's offer to stipulate. — Where defendant's prior murder convictions supplied the evidentiary depth needed to tell a continuous story, and where defendant's own statement, that he had "just pulled 20 years for killing two people," made proof of his murder convictions relevant to the case against him, the court did not err when it permitted the government to prove the nature of those convictions despite defendant's offer to stipulate to his status as a convicted felon. Laforce v. United States, 976 F. Supp. 402 (W.D. Va. 1997), appeal dismissed, 139 F.3d 895 (4th Cir. 1998).

Standard of review. — Federal court of appeals will defer to a trial court's Rule 403 balancing unless it is an arbitrary or irrational exercise of discretion. And the same standard of review applies to a trial court's rulings under Rule 404(b). Garraghty v. Jordan, 830 F.2d 1295 (4th Cir. 1987).

Commonwealth's argument supported by substantial evidence. — While there was no evidence during defendant's trial that satisfied the legal definition of "character," namely, reputation evidence, there was unobjected testimony presented during the trial that showed defendant's propensity toward violence. Thus, with or without the instruction on character, the Commonwealth presented a proper argument to the jury that was supported by evidence adduced at trial. Pahno v. Commonwealth, 2008 Va. App. LEXIS 199 (Apr. 22, 2008).

Applied in United States v. Black, 692 F.2d 314 (4th Cir. 1982); United States v. Parker, 699 F.2d 177 (4th Cir. 1983); United States v. Samad, 754 F.2d 1091 (4th Cir. 1984); Leftwich v. Bevilacqua, 635 F. Supp. 238 (W.D. Va. 1986); United States v. Dudley, 941 F.2d 260 (4th Cir. 1991); United States v. Loayza, 107 F.3d 257 (4th Cir. 1997); United States v. Sanchez, 118 F.3d 192 (E.D. Va. 1997).

Rule 405. Methods of Proving Character.

(a) *By Reputation or Opinion.* — When evidence of a person's character or character trait is admissible, it may be proved by testimony about the person's reputation or by testimony in the form of an opinion. On cross-examination of the character witness, the court may allow an inquiry into relevant specific instances of the person's conduct.

(b) *By Specific Instances of Conduct.* — When a person's character or character trait is an essential element of a charge, claim, or defense, the character or trait may also be proved by relevant specific instances of the person's conduct. (Amended by order adopted March 2, 1987, effective October 1, 1987, and by order adopted April 26, 2011, effective December 1, 2011.)

Comment. — The language of Rule 405 has been amended as part of the restyling of the Evidence Rules to make them more easily understood and to make style and terminology consistent throughout the rules. These changes are intended to be stylistic only. There is no intent to change any result in any ruling on evidence admissibility.

Rule 406. Habit; Routine Practice.

Evidence of a person's habit or an organization's routine practice may be admitted to prove that on a particular occasion the person or organization acted in accordance with the habit or routine practice. The court may admit this evidence regardless of whether it is corroborated or whether there was an eyewitness. (Amended by order adopted April 26, 2011, effective December 1, 2011.)

Comment. — The language of Rule 406 has been amended as part of the restyling of the Evidence Rules to make them more easily understood and to make style and terminology consistent throughout the rules. These changes are intended to be stylistic only. There is no intent to change any result in any ruling on evidence admissibility.

Law Review. — For an article, "Evidence Myopia: The Failure To See the Federal Rules of Evidence As a Codification of the Common Law," see 40 Wm. & Mary L. Rev. 1539 (1999). For an article, "Whether the Federal Rules of Evidence Should Be Conceived As a Perpetual Index Code: Blindness is Worse than Myopia," see 40 Wm. & Mary L. Rev. 1595 (1999). For an article, "The Elusive Identity of the Federal Rules of Evidence," see 40 Wm. & Mary L. Rev. 1613 (1999). For symposium, "The Restyled Federal Rules of Evidence," see 53 Wm and Mary L. Rev. 1435 (2012).

CASE NOTES

Habit or pattern of conduct is never to be lightly established, and evidence of examples, for purpose of establishing such habit, is to be carefully scrutinized before admission. The reason for such an attitude toward evidence of habit is the obvious danger of abuse in such evidence resulting from the confusion of issues, collateral inquiry, prejudice and the like, the collateral nature of such proof, the danger that it may afford a basis for improper inferences, the likelihood that it may cause confusion or operate to unfairly prejudice the party against whom it is directed. Wilson v. Volkswagen of Am., Inc., 561 F.2d 494 (4th Cir. 1977), cert. denied, 434 U.S. 1020, 98 S. Ct. 744, 54 L. Ed. 2d 768 (1978).

Proof of something done in a single occasion is hardly proof of a habit. — Particularly is this so when proof is lacking that the occasion on which the habit was supposedly formed and the occasion on which it is claimed that the habit was followed are related or even similar. Utility Control Corp. v. Prince William Constr. Co., 558 F.2d 716 (4th Cir. 1977).

It is only when the examples offered to establish a pattern of conduct or habit are numerous enough to base an inference of systematic conduct and to establish one's regular response to a repeated specific situation or, where they are sufficiently regular or the circumstances sufficiently similar to outweigh the danger, if any, of prejudice and confusion, that they are admissible to establish pattern or habit. Wilson v. Volkswagen of Am., Inc., 561 F.2d 494 (4th Cir. 1977), cert. denied, 434 U.S. 1020, 98 S. Ct. 744, 54 L. Ed. 2d 768 (1978).

Key criteria. — In determining whether the examples are "numerous enough" and "sufficiently regular," the key criteria are "adequacy of sampling and uniformity of response." Wilson v. Volkswagen of Am., Inc., 561 F.2d 494 (4th Cir. 1977), cert. denied, 434 U.S. 1020, 98 S. Ct. 744, 54 L. Ed. 2d 768 (1978).

"Ratio of reactions to situations." — While precise standards for measuring the "extent to which instances must be multiplied and consistency of behavior maintained in order to support an inference of habit and pattern of conduct, cannot be formulated," it is obvious that no finding is supportable under Rule 406, Fed. R. Evid. which fails to examine critically the "ratio of reactions to situations." Wilson v. Volkswagen of Am., Inc., 561 F.2d 494 (4th Cir. 1977), cert. denied, 434 U.S. 1020, 98 S. Ct. 744, 54 L. Ed. 2d 768 (1978).

Rule 407. Subsequent Remedial Measures.

When measures are taken that would have made an earlier injury or harm less likely to occur, evidence of the subsequent measures is not admissible to prove:

- negligence;
- culpable conduct;
- a defect in a product or its design; or
- a need for a warning or instruction.

But the court may admit this evidence for another purpose, such as impeachment or — if disputed — proving ownership, control, or the feasibility of precautionary measures. (Amended by order adopted April 11, 1997, effective December 1, 1997, and by order adopted April 26, 2011, effective December 1, 2011.)

Comment. — The language of Rule 407 has been amended as part of the general restyling of the Evidence Rules to make them more easily understood and to make style and terminology consistent throughout the rules. These changes are intended to be stylistic only. There is no intent to change any result in any ruling on evidence admissibility.

Rule 407 previously provided that evidence was not excluded if offered for a purpose not explicitly prohibited by the Rule. To improve the language of the Rule, it now provides that the court may admit evidence if offered for a permissible purpose. There is no intent to change the process for admitting evidence covered by the Rule. It remains the case that if offered for an impermissible purpose, it must be excluded, and if offered for a purpose not barred by the Rule, its admissibility remains governed by the general principles of Rules 402, 403, 801, etc.

Law Review. — For note, "Subsequent Remedial Measures and Strict Products Liability: A New—Relevant—Answer to an Old Problem," see 81 U. Va. L. Rev. 1141 (1995).

CASE NOTES

This rule does not require the exclusion of evidence of subsequent measures when offered for another purpose, such as proving ownership, control, or feasibility of precautionary measures, if controverted, or impeachment. Benedi v. McNeil-P.P.C., Inc., 66 F.3d 1378 (4th Cir. 1995).

Applied in Allred v. Maersk Line, Ltd., 35 F.3d 139 (4th Cir. 1994).

Rule 408. Compromise Offers and Negotiations.

(a) *Prohibited uses.* — Evidence of the following is not admissible — on behalf of any party — either to prove or disprove the validity or amount of a disputed claim or to impeach by a prior inconsistent statement or a contradiction:

(1) furnishing, promising, or offering — or accepting, promising to accept, or offering to accept — a valuable consideration in compromising or attempting to compromise the claim; and

(2) conduct or a statement made during compromise negotiations about the claim — except when offered in a criminal case and when the negotiations related to a claim by a public office in the exercise of its regulatory, investigative, or enforcement authority.

(b) *Exceptions.* — The court may admit this evidence for another purpose, such as proving a witness's bias or prejudice, negating a contention of undue delay, or proving an effort to obstruct a criminal investigation or prosecution. (Amended by order adopted April 12, 2006, effective December 1, 2006, and by order adopted April 26, 2011, effective December 1, 2011.)

Comment. — The language of Rule 408 has been amended as part of the general restyling of the Evidence Rules to make them more easily understood and to make style and terminology consistent throughout the rules. These changes are intended to be stylistic only. There is no intent to change any result in any ruling on evidence admissibility.

Rule 408 previously provided that evidence was not excluded if offered for a purpose not explicitly prohibited by the Rule. To improve the language of the Rule, it now provides that the court may admit evidence if offered for a permissible purpose. There is no intent to change the process for admitting evidence covered by the Rule. It remains the case that if offered for an impermissible purpose, it must be excluded, and if offered for a purpose not barred by the Rule, its admissibility remains governed by the general principles of Rules 402, 403, 801, etc.

The Committee deleted the reference to "liability" on the ground that the deletion makes the Rule flow better and easier to read, and because "liability" is covered by the broader term "validity." Courts have not made substantive decisions on the basis of any distinction between validity and liability. No change in current practice or in the coverage of the Rule is intended.

CASE NOTES

Applied in 1616 Reminc Ltd. Partnership v. Commonwealth Land Title Ins. Co., 778 F.2d 183 (4th Cir. 1985).

Rule 409. Offers to Pay Medical and Similar Expenses.

Evidence of furnishing, promising to pay, or offering to pay medical, hospital, or similar expenses resulting from an injury is not admissible to prove liability for the injury. (Amended by order adopted April 26, 2011, effective December 1, 2011.)

Comment. — The language of Rule 409 has been amended as part of the restyling of the Evidence Rules to make them more easily understood and to make style and terminology consistent throughout the rules. These changes are intended to be stylistic only. There is no intent to change any result in any ruling on evidence admissibility.

Rule 410. Pleas, Plea Discussions, and Related Statements.

(a) *Prohibited uses.* — In a civil or criminal case, evidence of the following is not admissible against the defendant who made the plea or participated in the plea discussions:

(1) a guilty plea that was later withdrawn;

(2) a nolo contendere plea;

(3) a statement made during a proceeding on either of those pleas under Federal Rule of Criminal Procedure 11 or a comparable state procedure; or

(4) a statement made during plea discussions with an attorney for the prosecuting authority if the discussions did not result in a guilty plea or they resulted in a laterwithdrawn guilty plea.

(b) *Exceptions.* — The court may admit a statement described in Rule 410(a)(3) or (4):

(1) in any proceeding in which another statement made during the same plea or plea discussions has been introduced, if in fairness the statements ought to be considered together; or

(2) in a criminal proceeding for perjury or false statement, if the defendant made the statement under oath, on the record, and with counsel present. (Amended by order adopted December 12, 1975, by order adopted April 30, 1979, effective December 1, 1980, and by order adopted April 26, 2011, effective December 1, 2011.)

Comment. — The language of Rule 410 has been amended as part of the restyling of the Evidence Rules to make them more easily understood and to make style and terminology consistent throughout the rules. These changes are intended to be stylistic only. There is no intent to change any result in any ruling on evidence admissibility.

Rule 411. Liability Insurance.

Evidence that a person was or was not insured against liability is not admissible to prove whether the person acted negligently or otherwise wrongfully. But the court may admit this evidence for another purpose, such as proving a witness's bias or prejudice or proving agency, ownership, or control. (Amended by order adopted March 2, 1987, effective October 1, 1987, and by order adopted April 26, 2011, effective December 1, 2011.)

Comment. — The language of Rule 411 has been amended as part of the general restyling of the Evidence Rules to make them more easily understood and to make style and terminology consistent throughout the rules. These changes are intended to be stylistic only. There is no intent to change any result in any ruling on evidence admissibility.

Rule 411 previously provided that evidence was not excluded if offered for a purpose not explicitly prohibited by the Rule. To improve the language of the Rule, it now provides that the court may admit evidence if offered for a permissible purpose. There is no intent to change the process for admitting evidence covered by the Rule. It remains the case that if offered for an impermissible purpose, it must be excluded, and if offered for a purpose not barred by the Rule, its admissibility remains governed by the general principles of Rules 402, 403, 801, etc.

Rule 412. Sex-Offense Cases: The Victim's Sexual Behavior or Predisposition.

(a) *Prohibited Uses.* — The following evidence is not admissible in a civil or criminal proceeding involving alleged sexual misconduct:

(1) evidence offered to prove that a victim engaged in other sexual behavior; or

(2) evidence offered to prove a victim's sexual predisposition.

(b) *Exceptions.* — (1) Criminal Cases. The court may admit the following evidence in a criminal case:

(A) evidence of specific instances of a victim's sexual behavior, if offered to prove that someone other than the defendant was the source of semen, injury, or other physical evidence;

(B) evidence of specific instances of a victim's sexual behavior with respect to the person accused of the sexual misconduct, if offered by the defendant to prove consent or if offered by the prosecutor; and

(C) evidence whose exclusion would violate the defendant's constitutional rights.

(2) Civil Cases. In a civil case, the court may admit evidence offered to prove a victim's sexual behavior or sexual predisposition if its probative value substantially outweighs the danger of harm to any victim and of unfair prejudice to any party. The court may admit evidence of a victim's reputation only if the victim has placed it in controversy.

(c) *Procedure to Determine Admissibility.* — (1) Motion. If a party intends to offer evidence under Rule 412(b), the party must:

(A) file a motion that specifically describes the evidence and states the purpose for which it is to be offered;

(B) do so at least 14 days before trial unless the court, for good cause, sets a different time;

(C) serve the motion on all parties; and

(D) notify the victim or, when appropriate, the victim's guardian or representative.

(2) Hearing. Before admitting evidence under this rule, the court must conduct an in camera hearing and give the victim and parties a right to attend and be heard. Unless the court orders otherwise, the motion, related materials, and the record of the hearing must be and remain sealed.

(d) *Definition of "Victim."* — In this rule, "victim" includes an alleged victim. (Added by order adopted October 28, 1978, effective November 28, 1978, amended by P.L.100-690, § 7046, signed November 18, 1988, by order adopted April 29, 1994, effective December 1, 1994, by P.L.103-322, approved September 13, 1994, effective December 1, 1994, and by order adopted April 26, 2011, effective December 1, 2011.)

Comment. — The language of Rule 412 has been amended as part of the restyling of the Evidence Rules to make them more easily understood and to make style and terminology consistent throughout the rules. These changes are intended to be stylistic only. There is no intent to change any result in any ruling on evidence admissibility.

CASE NOTES

This rule was amended by the Violent Crime Control and Law Enforcement Act of 1994. P.L. No. 103-322 (1994). The Congressional Conference Report accompanying the Act adopted the Committee Note of the Advisory Committee on Evidence Rules to Rule 412, stating: "The Conferees intend that the Advisory Committee Note on Rule 412, as transmitted by the Judicial Conference of the United States to the Supreme Court on October 25, 1993, applies to Rule 412 as enacted by this section. This section, which modifies Rule 412 of the Federal Rules of Evidence as transmitted to the Congress by the United States Supreme Court, is enacted pursuant to the Rules Enabling Act."

Historical background. — This rule, which is more commonly referred to as the "rape shield law," was enacted in 1978 to protect rape victims from humiliating and excessive cross-examination with regard to their past sexual behavior. Originally limited to criminal rape cases, this rule was later extended to govern all criminal sex offense cases. Sheffield v. Hilltop Sand & Gravel Co., 895 F. Supp. 105 (E.D. Va. 1995).

Applicability broadened. — Effective December 1, 1994, Congress enacted substantial changes to this rule. In essence, this rule was revised so that it applies to all criminal and civil cases involving sexual misconduct, without regard to whether the alleged victim or person accused is a party to the litigation. Sheffield v. Hilltop Sand & Gravel Co., 895 F. Supp. 105 (E.D. Va. 1995).

The Advisory Committee's Note to the 1994 amendments explicitly states that this rule applies "in any civil case in which a person claims to be the victim of sexual misconduct, such as actions for sexual battery or sexual harassment." In addition, the Note explains that a balancing test must be employed in civil cases because "greater flexibility is needed to accommodate evolving causes of action such as claims for sexual harassment. Sheffield v. Hilltop Sand & Gravel Co., 895 F. Supp. 105 (E.D. Va. 1995).

Fundamental to this rule is the notion that the law protects women from forced sexual contact and that this protection extends to all persons even though their past sexual behavior or reputation suggest they are less than virtuous. United States v. Saunders, 736 F. Supp. 698 (E.D. Va. 1990), cert. denied, 502 U.S. 1105, 112 S. Ct. 1199, 117 L. Ed. 2d 439 (1992).

The overarching purpose of this rule, and of the procedures outlined in subdivision (c), is to protect alleged victims against "the invasion of privacy, potential embarrassment, and sexual stereotyping that is associated with public disclosure of intimate sexual details. Sheffield v. Hilltop Sand & Gravel Co., 895 F. Supp. 105 (E.D. Va. 1995).

Meaning of the phrase "constitutionally required." Although the rule provides no guidance as to the meaning of the phrase "constitutionally required," it seems clear that the Constitution requires that a criminal defendant be given the opportunity to present evidence that is relevant, material and favorable to his defense. United States v. Saunders, 736 F. Supp. 698 (E.D. Va. 1990), cert. denied, 502 U.S. 1105, 112 S. Ct. 1199, 117 L. Ed. 2d 439 (1992).

This rule does not mandate the sealing of the record of the pre-trial evidentiary hearing. — This is within the sound discretion of the trial court. Doe v. United States, 666 F.2d 43 (4th Cir. 1981).

Issuance of subpoenas duces tecum for records of pre-trial evidentiary hearing. — The issuance of subpoenas is under this rule within the discretion of the trial court, and its refusal to grant the victim's request to seal the record of the pretrial hearing and deny issuance of subpoenas duces tecum for the records thereof could not be deemed an abuse of discretion, particularly since the defendant had not even sought a subpoena for these items. Doe v. United States, 666 F.2d 43 (4th Cir. 1981).

Temporal element must be taken into account. — Although this rule does not include an explicit timeliness requirement, it seems clear that the temporal element must be taken into account in the weighing process called for in subsection (c)(3). United States v. Saunders, 736 F. Supp. 698 (E.D. Va. 1990), cert. denied, 502 U.S. 1105, 112 S. Ct. 1199, 117 L. Ed. 2d 439 (1992).

Balancing test regarding admissibility. — In civil cases, evidence offered to prove the sexual behavior or predisposition of any alleged victim of sexual misconduct may be admitted if its proponent satisfies the "balancing test" articulated in Rule 412(b)(2). The proponent must demonstrate: (1) that the proffered evidence is otherwise admissible under the Federal Rules of Evidence; and (2) that its probative value "substantially outweighs the danger of harm to the victim and of unfair prejudice to any party." Additionally, the rule specifies that evidence of an alleged victim's reputation is admissible only if it has been placed in controversy by the victim. Sheffield v. Hilltop Sand & Gravel Co., 895 F. Supp. 105 (E.D. Va. 1995).

Admissibility of reputation and opinion evidence to show accused's state of mind. — The legislative history of this rule discloses that reputation and opinion evidence of the past sexual behavior of an alleged victim was excluded because Congress considered that this evidence was not relevant to the issues of the victim's consent or her veracity. There is no indication, however, that this evidence was intended to be excluded when offered solely to show the accused's state of mind. Therefore, its admission is governed by the Federal Rules of Evidence dealing with relevancy in general. Doe v. United States, 666 F.2d 43 (4th Cir. 1981).

Admissibility of past sexual behavior of alleged victim to show accused's state of mind. — This rule is not a bar to evidence of the alleged victim's past sexual behavior where that evidence is offered to show the accused's state of mind; but even in this event, admissibility still hinges on whether the evidence passes muster under this rule. United States v. Saunders, 736 F. Supp. 698 (E.D. Va. 1990), cert. denied, 502 U.S. 1105, 112 S. Ct. 1199, 117 L. Ed. 2d 439 (1992).

Admissibility of prior sexual abuse. — Plaintiff's history of prior sexual abuse was admissible to show that other stressors in her life besides the alleged abuse by the defendant might be responsible for her current psychiatric condition. Delaney v. City of Hampton, 999 F. Supp. 794 (E.D. Va. 1997).

Evidence of victim's past sexual experience with third person inadmissible to corroborate accused's belief victim consented. — Where trial court ruled that evidence of three-day relationship between victim and third person was inadmissible, and where defendant contended that his knowledge that victim was a "skeezer" or prostitute corroborated his belief that she consented, when consent is the issue, however, subdivision (b)(1)(B) permits only evidence of the defendant's past experience with the victim; the rule manifests the policy that it is unreasonable for a defendant to base his belief of consent on the victim's past sexual experiences with third persons, since it is intolerable to suggest that because the victim is a prostitute, she automatically is assumed to have consented with anyone at any time. United States v. Saunders, 943 F.2d 388 (4th Cir. 1991), cert. denied, 502 U.S. 1105, 112 S. Ct. 1199, 117 L. Ed. 2d 439 (1992).

Evidence of conversations the defendant had with other men concerning the alleged promiscuity of the victim and that he had read a love letter she had written to another man, and telephone conversations he had with the victim, all prior to the night of the alleged crime, were admissible as part of the defendant's consent defense as relevant on the issue of the defendant's state of mind and intent. Doe v. United States, 666 F.2d 43 (4th Cir. 1981).

Credibility judgments are for the jury or ultimate fact finder. — Except perhaps in extreme circumstances, courts are not free to make rulings on the basis of credibility judgments; those judgments are for the jury or ultimate fact finder. Instead, courts must consider and resolve issues under this rule without regard to whether a jury or fact finder will ultimately accept or reject all or part of the testimony. United States v. Saunders, 736 F. Supp. 698 (E.D. Va. 1990), cert. denied, 502 U.S. 1105, 112 S. Ct. 1199, 117 L. Ed. 2d 439 (1992).

Inferences permitted by testimony are province of jury. — Courts considering a motion under this rule may not reject inferences reasonably permitted by the testimony or resolve testimonial ambiguities to foreclose such inferences; these are the province of the jury. United States v. Saunders, 736 F. Supp. 698 (E.D. Va. 1990), cert. denied, 502 U.S. 1105, 112 S. Ct. 1199, 117 L. Ed. 2d 439 (1992).

Admissibility of prior sexual relationship between the defendant and alleged victim. — Evidence of a sexual relationship between the defendant and the alleged victim some three years prior to the alleged rape was relevant to consent and, the probative value of this evidence outweighed the danger of its unfair prejudicial effect. United States v. Saunders, 736 F. Supp. 698 (E.D. Va. 1990), cert. denied, 502 U.S. 1105, 112 S. Ct. 1199, 117 L. Ed. 2d 439 (1992).

Rule 413. Similar Crimes in Sexual-Assault Cases.

(a) *Permitted Uses.* — In a criminal case in which a defendant is accused of a sexual assault, the court may admit evidence that the defendant committed any other sexual assault. The evidence may be considered on any matter to which it is relevant.

(b) *Disclosure to the Defendant.* — If the prosecutor intends to offer this evidence, the prosecutor must disclose it to the defendant, including witnesses' statements or a summary of the expected testimony. The prosecutor must do so at least 15 days before trial or at a later time that the court allows for good cause.

(c) *Effect on Other Rules.* — This rule does not limit the admission or consideration of evidence under any other rule.

(d) *Definition of "Sexual Assault."* — In this rule and Rule 415, "sexual assault" means a crime under federal law or under state law (as "state" is defined in 18 U.S.C. § 513) involving:

(1) any conduct prohibited by 18 U.S.C. chapter 109A;

(2) contact, without consent, between any part of the defendant's body — or an object — and another person's genitals or anus;

(3) contact, without consent, between the defendant's genitals or anus and any part of another person's body;

(4) deriving sexual pleasure or gratification from inflicting death, bodily injury, or physical pain on another person; or

(5) an attempt or conspiracy to engage in conduct described in paragraphs (1)-(4).

(Added by P.L. 103-322, approved September 13, 1994, effective July 9, 1995, and by order adopted April 26, 2011, effective December 1, 2011.)

Comment. — The language of Rule 413 has been amended as part of the restyling of the Evidence Rules to make them more easily understood and to make style and terminology consistent throughout the rules. These changes are intended to be stylistic only. There is no intent to change any result in any ruling on evidence admissibility.

Editor's note. — The Judicial Conference of the United States submitted a report to Congress on February 9, 1995 in accordance with section 320935 of the Violent Crime Control and Law Enforcement Act of 1994, Pub. L. No. 103-322 (September 13, 1994). The section adds new Evidence Rules 413, 414, and 415 to the Federal Rules of Evidence.

The Act deferred the effective date of new Evidence Rules 413-415 until February 10, 1995 pending a report from the Judicial Conference. Under the Act the effective date was delayed for an additional 150 days after transmittal of the Conference report, if the Conference made alternative recommendations to the new rules. The recommendations in the report were different from the Act's new rules. Accordingly, Rules 413-415 were to take effect 150 days after the transmittal of this report, unless Congress adopts the alternative recommendations or provides otherwise by law.

Congress took no action on the Report of the Judicial Conference of the United States on the Admission of Character Evidence in Certain Sexual Misconduct Cases, which was transmitted to Congress on February 9, 1995. Accordingly, Evidence Rules 413, 414 and 415, adopted by the Violent Crime Control and Law Enforcement Act of 1994, became effective July 9, 1995.

Law Review. — For article, "An Evidentiary Paradox: Defending the Character Evidence Prohibition by Upholding a Non-Character Theory of Logical Relevance, the Doctrine of Chances," see 40 U. Rich. L. Rev. 419 (2006).

Rule 414. Similar Crimes in Child-Molestation Cases.

(a) *Permitted Uses.* — In a criminal case in which a defendant is accused of child molestation, the court may admit evidence that the defendant committed any other child molestation. The evidence may be considered on any matter to which it is relevant.

(b) *Disclosure to the Defendant.* — If the prosecutor intends to offer this evidence, the prosecutor must disclose it to the defendant, including witnesses' statements or a summary of the expected testimony. The prosecutor must do so at least 15 days before trial or at a later time that the court allows for good cause.

(c) *Effect on Other Rules.* — This rule does not limit the admission or consideration of evidence under any other rule.

(d) *Definition of "Child" and "Child Molestation."* — In this rule and Rule 415:

(1) "child" means a person below the age of 14; and

(2) "child molestation" means a crime under federal law or under state law (as "state" is defined in 18 U.S.C. § 513) involving:

(A) any conduct prohibited by 18 U.S.C. chapter 109A and committed with a child;

(B) any conduct prohibited by 18 U.S.C. chapter 110;

(C) contact between any part of the defendant's body — or an object — and a child's genitals or anus;

(D) contact between the defendant's genitals or anus and any part of a child's body;

(E) deriving sexual pleasure or gratification from the infliction of death, bodily injury, or physical pain on a child; or

(F) an attempt or conspiracy to engage in conduct described in subparagraphs (A)-(E). (Added by P.L. 103-322, approved September 13, 1994, effective July 9, 1995, and amended by order adopted April 26, 2011, effective December 1, 2011.)

Comment. — The language of Rule 414 has been amended as part of the restyling of the Evidence Rules to make them more easily understood and to make style and terminology consistent throughout the rules. These changes are intended to be stylistic only. There is no intent to change any result in any ruling on evidence admissibility.

Editor's note. — The Judicial Conference of the United States submitted a report to Congress on February 9, 1995 in accordance with section 320935 of the Violent Crime Control and Law Enforcement Act of 1994, Pub. L. No. 103-322 (September 13, 1994). The section adds new Evidence Rules 413, 414, and 415 to the Federal Rules of Evidence.

The Act deferred the effective date of new Evidence Rules 413-415 until February 10, 1995 pending a report from the Judicial Conference. Under the Act the effective date was delayed for an additional 150 days after transmittal of the Conference report, if the Conference made alternative recommendations to the new rules. The recommendations in the report were different from the Act's new rules. Accordingly, Rules 413-415 were to take effect 150 days after the transmittal of this report, unless Congress adopts the alternative recommendations or provides otherwise by law.

Congress took no action on the Report of the Judicial Conference of the United States on the Admission of Character Evidence in Certain Sexual Misconduct Cases, which was transmitted to Congress on February 9, 1995. Accordingly, Evidence Rules 413, 414 and 415, adopted by the Violent Crime Control and Law Enforcement Act of 1994, became effective July 9, 1995.

Law Review. — For article, "An Evidentiary Paradox: Defending the Character Evidence Prohibition by Upholding a Non-Character Theory of Logical Relevance, the Doctrine of Chances," see 40 U. Rich. L. Rev. 419 (2006).

Rule 415. Evidence of Similar Acts in Civil Cases Concerning Sexual Assault or Child Molestation.

(a) *Permitted Uses.* — In a civil case involving a claim for relief based on a party's alleged sexual assault or child molestation, the court may admit evidence that the party committed any other sexual assault or child molestation. The evidence may be considered as provided in Rules 413 and 414.

(b) *Disclosure to the Opponent.* — If a party intends to offer this evidence, the party must disclose it to the party against whom it will be offered, including witnesses' statements or a summary of the expected testimony. The party must do so at least 15 days before trial or at a later time that the court allows for good cause.

(c) *Effect on Other Rules.* — This rule does not limit the admission or consideration of evidence under any other rule. (Added by P.L. 103-322, approved September 13, 1994, effective July 9, 1995, and amended by order adopted April 26, 2011, effective December 1, 2011.)

Comment. — The language of Rule 415 has been amended as part of the restyling of the Evidence Rules to make them more easily understood and to make style and terminology consistent throughout the rules. These changes are intended to be stylistic only. There is no intent to change any result in any ruling on evidence admissibility.

Editor's note. — The Judicial Conference of the United States submitted a report to Congress on February 9, 1995 in accordance with section 320935 of the Violent Crime Control and Law Enforcement Act of 1994, Pub. L. No. 103-322 (September 13, 1994). The section adds new Evidence Rules 413, 414, and 415 to the Federal Rules of Evidence.

The Act deferred the effective date of new Evidence Rules 413-415 until February 10, 1995 pending a report from the Judicial Conference. Under the Act the effective date was delayed for an additional 150 days after transmittal of the Conference report, if the Conference made alternative recommendations to the new rules. The recommendations in the report were different from the Act's new rules. Accordingly, Rules 413-415 were to take effect 150 days after the transmittal of this report, unless Congress adopts the alternative recommendations or provides otherwise by law.

Congress took no action on the Report of the Judicial Conference of the United States on the Admission of Character Evidence in Certain Sexual Misconduct Cases, which was transmitted to Congress on February 9, 1995. Accordingly, Evidence Rules 413, 414 and 415, adopted by the Violent Crime Control and Law Enforcement Act of 1994, became effective July 9, 1995.

Law Review. — For article, "An Evidentiary Paradox: Defending the Character Evidence Prohibition by Upholding a Non-Character Theory of Logical Relevance, the Doctrine of Chances," see 40 U. Rich. L. Rev. 419 (2006).

V. PRIVILEGES.

Rule 501. Privilege in General.

The common law — as interpreted by United States courts in the light of reason and experience — governs a claim of privilege unless any of the following provides otherwise:

- the United States Constitution;
- a federal statute; or
- rules prescribed by the Supreme Court.

But in a civil case, state law governs privilege regarding a claim or defense for which state law supplies the rule of decision. (Amended by order adopted April 26, 2011, effective December 1, 2011.)

Comment. — The language of Rule 501 has been amended as part of the restyling of the Evidence Rules to make them more easily understood and to make style and terminology consistent throughout the rules. These changes are intended to be stylistic only. There is no intent to change any result in any ruling on evidence admissibility.

Law Review. — For comment, "Confidential Communication Privileges under Federal and Virginia Law," see 13 U. Rich. L. Rev. 593 (1979). For note, "The Attorney-Client Privilege," see 19 U. Rich. L. Rev. 559 (1985). For article, "The Parent-Child Privileges: Hardly a New or Revolutionary Concept," see 28 Wm. & Mary L. Rev. 583 (1987). For article, "Paging Dr. Google: Personal Health Records and Patient Privacy," see 51 Wm. and Mary L. Rev. 2243 (2010).

CASE NOTES

Greater flexibility for courts. — In enacting this rule, Congress clearly rejected the creation of specific privileges in favor of providing the courts with greater flexibility. Etienne v. Mitre Corp., 146 F.R.D. 145 (E.D. Va. 1993).

Application of privilege. — Since attorney-client privilege "impedes [the] full and free discovery of the truth," and is "in derogation of the public's 'right to every man's evidence,'" it is not "favored" by federal courts. Accordingly, the privilege is to be "strictly confined within the narrowest possible limits consistent with the logic of its principle." Nellis v. Air Line Pilots Ass'n, 144 F.R.D. 68 (E.D. Va. 1992).

Fiduciary-beneficiary exception. — The fiduciary-beneficiary exception is an example of how federal courts have attempted to strictly construe the attorney-client privilege. The exception requires a court to weigh the interests of a fiduciary who opposes production of relevant information by invoking the attorney-client privilege against its own beneficiaries. In weighing these interests, a court should attempt to balance the extent of the beneficiaries' interests in the lawsuit and the likelihood of harm to those interests against the harm to the fiduciary's management flexibility. Nellis v. Air Line Pilots Ass'n, 144 F.R.D. 68 (E.D. Va. 1992).

When substantive decision in a case is governed by state law, the state law also determines the privilege of a witness. Seidman v. Fishburne-Hudgins Educ. Found., Inc., 724 F.2d 413 (4th Cir. 1984).

Exclusionary rules and privileges strictly construed. — Testimonial exclusionary rules and privileges contravene the fundamental principle that the public has a right to every man's evidence. As such, they must be strictly construed and accepted only to the very limited extent that permitting a refusal to testify or excluding relevant evidence has a public good transcending the normally predominant principle of utilizing all rational means for ascertaining truth. United States v. Jones, 683 F.2d 817 (4th Cir. 1982).

Purpose of attorney-client privilege is to promote full and frank communication between attorneys and their clients and to serve the public interest in the administration of justice. Jonathan Corp. v. Prime Computer, Inc., 114 F.R.D. 693 (E.D. Va. 1987); Nellis v. Air Line Pilots Ass'n, 144 F.R.D. 68 (E.D. Va. 1992).

Attorney-client privilege attaches to corporations as well as to individuals. Jonathan Corp. v. Prime Computer, Inc., 114 F.R.D. 693 (E.D. Va. 1987).

Communications between corporation's inhouse counsel and employees of that corporation may be protected by the attorney-client privilege. Jonathan Corp. v. Prime Computer, Inc., 114 F.R.D. 693 (E.D. Va. 1987).

Voluntary disclosure by client to third party waives the attorney-client privilege, not only to that document, but possibly to all communications relating to that subject matter. Jonathan Corp. v. Prime Computer, Inc., 114 F.R.D. 693 (E.D. Va. 1987).

Attorney-client privilege may be lost by inadvertent disclosure of privileged documents where a party did not take reasonable steps to insure and maintain their confidentiality. Jonathan Corp. v. Prime Computer, Inc., 114 F.R.D. 693 (E.D. Va. 1987).

Defendant's failure to indicate on face of memorandum that the document was confidential or contained attorney-client privileged information, although defendant did in fact mark certain documents as confidential, coupled with the fact that the memorandum was distributed to six employees, raised serious doubts as to whether defendant met its burden of demonstrating that the document was intended to be confidential. Jonathan Corp. v. Prime Computer, Inc., 114 F.R.D. 693 (E.D. Va. 1987).

Proponent of attorney-client privilege bears burden of demonstrating its applicability. Under this burden, the proponent must establish not only that an attorney-client relationship existed, but also that the particular communications at issue are privileged and that the privilege has not been waived. Jonathan Corp. v. Prime Computer, Inc., 114 F.R.D. 693 (E.D. Va. 1987).

Intent as to confidentiality. — Where the court examines intent as to confidentiality, inferences regarding intent may be drawn from the circumstances, including steps taken to insure confidentiality. Jonathan Corp. v. Prime Computer, Inc., 114 F.R.D. 693 (E.D. Va. 1987).

Under the common law, executive privilege is defined as the government's privilege to prevent disclosure of certain information whose disclosure would be contrary to the public interest. Castle v. Jallah, 142 F.R.D. 618 (E.D. Va. 1992).

The purpose of executive privilege is to protect the governmental decisionmaking process by shielding from discovery intra-governmental documents reflecting advisory opinions, recommendations and deliberations comprising part of a process by which governmental decisions and policies are formulated. Castle v. Jallah, 142 F.R.D. 618 (E.D. Va. 1992).

Executive privilege does not protect disclosure of purely factual materials. — The executive privilege typically does not protect disclosure of purely factual materials. Accordingly, an agency usually will be required to produce compiled factual material or purely factual material contained in deliberative memoranda and severable from its context. Castle v. Jallah, 142 F.R.D 618 (E.D. Va. 1992).

Party seeking governmental privilege bears burden of justifying application. — The party seeking to invoke a governmental privilege to bar disclosure of certain factual statements bears the burden of justifying its application. Castle v. Jallah, 142 F.R.D 618 (E.D. Va. 1992).

When executive privilege is asserted, the court must balance the public interest in the confidentiality of governmental information against the need of a litigant to obtain data, not otherwise available to him, with which to pursue [his] cause of action. Castle v. Jallah, 142 F.R.D 618 (E.D. Va. 1992).

Factors to be considered in discovery of files in civil rights cases. — The following are 10 factors to be considered in the context of discovery of investigative files in civil rights cases: (1) The extent to which disclosure will thwart governmental processes by discouraging citizens from giving the government information; (2) the impact upon persons who have given information of having their identities disclosed; (3) the degree to which governmental self-evaluation and consequent program improvement will be chilled by disclosure; (4) whether the information sought is factual data or evaluative summary; (5) whether the party seeking the discovery is an actual or potential defendant in any criminal proceeding either pending or reasonably likely to follow from the incident in question; (6) whether the police investigation has been completed; (7) whether any intradepartmental disciplinary proceedings have arisen or may arise from the investigation; (8) whether plaintiff's suit is nonfrivolous and brought in good faith; (9) whether the information sought is available through other discovery or from other sources; and (10) the importance of the information sought to plaintiff's case. Castle v. Jallah, 142 F.R.D 618 (E.D. Va. 1992).

Where institutional security outweighed need for confidential departmental operations procedures. — Where institutional security far outweighed any need plaintiff may have had for the prison's confidential Departmental Operating Procedures, the court denied plaintiff's motion to compel production. Castle v. Jallah, 142 F.R.D 618 (E.D. Va. 1992).

Disclosure of informer's identity. — The trial court is required to balance the public interest in nondisclosure of the identity of persons who furnish information regarding criminal activity to law-enforcement officials against the defendant's right to prepare a defense. A decision on disclosure of such information must depend on the particular circumstances of each case, taking into consideration the crime charged, the possible defenses, the possible significance of the informer's testimony, and other relevant factors. United States v. Smith, 780 F.2d 1102 (4th Cir. 1985).

There is a qualified privilege to withhold the identity of persons who furnish information regarding criminal activity to law-enforcement officials. Such a privilege is designed to protect and foster the interests of law enforcement by encouraging citizens to aid criminal justice without fear of public disclosure. The privilege is a qualified one, however. The privilege ceases once the reasons for it cease, that is, once disclosure occurs to those who would have cause to resent the communication. The privilege must also give way when the informant or the contents of his communication is relevant and helpful to the defense of an accused, or is essential to a fair determination of a cause. United States v. Smith, 780 F.2d 1102 (4th Cir. 1985).

Reversible error to cross-examine wife of accused about wife's invocation of marital privilege. — It is reversible error, subject to a harmless error analysis, for a prosecutor to cross-examine wife of an accused about her invocation of the marital privilege before the grand jury. United States v. Morris, 988 F.2d 1335 (4th Cir. 1993).

Error occurred in allowing prosecutor to cross-examine wife regarding her invocation of marital privilege. — Where wife of defendant was a critical witness, had intimate knowledge of defendant's affairs, was the most important corroborative witness that he had, and that case depended wholly, or almost so, on credibility, harmful error occurred from permitting prosecutor to cross-examine the wife regarding her invocation of the marital privilege, and thus defendant's conviction on various drug charges cannot stand. United States v. Morris, 988 F.2d 1335 (4th Cir. 1993).

There is no judicially or legislatively recognized general "family" privilege. United States v. Jones, 683 F.2d 817 (4th Cir. 1982).

An emancipated, adult child's testimony which only arguably would be adverse to his father, limited to questions unrelated to his familial association with his parent, and involving no communication between father and son is not privileged. United States v. Jones, 683 F.2d 817 (4th Cir. 1982).

Rule 502. Attorney-Client Privilege and Work Product; Limitations on Waiver.

The following provisions apply, in the circumstances set out, to disclosure of a communication or information covered by the attorney-client privilege or work-product protection.

(a) *Disclosure Made in a Federal Proceeding or to a Federal Office or Agency; Scope of a Waiver.* When the disclosure is made in a federal proceeding or to a federal office or agency and waives the attorney-client privilege or workproduct protection, the waiver extends to an undisclosed communication or information in a federal or state proceeding only if:

(1) the waiver is intentional;

(2) the disclosed and undisclosed communications or information concern the same subject matter; and

(3) they ought in fairness to be considered together.

(b) *Inadvertent Disclosure.* When made in a federal proceeding or to a federal office or agency, the disclosure does not operate as a waiver in a federal or state proceeding if:

(1) the disclosure is inadvertent;

(2) the holder of the privilege or protection took reasonable steps to prevent disclosure; and

(3) the holder promptly took reasonable steps to rectify the error, including (if applicable) following Federal Rule of Civil Procedure 26(b)(5)(B).

(c) *Disclosure Made in a State Proceeding.* When the disclosure is made in a state proceeding and is not the subject of a state-court order concerning waiver, the disclosure does not operate as a waiver in a federal proceeding if the disclosure:

(1) would not be a waiver under this rule if it had been made in a federal proceeding; or

(2) is not a waiver under the law of the state where the disclosure occurred.

(d) *Controlling Effect of a Court Order.* A federal court may order that the privilege or protection is not waived by disclosure connected with the litigation pending before the court — in which event the disclosure is also not a waiver in any other federal or state proceeding.

(e) *Controlling Effect of a Party Agreement.* An agreement on the effect of disclosure in a federal proceeding is binding only on the parties to the agreement, unless it is incorporated into a court order.

(f) *Controlling Effect of this Rule.* Notwithstanding Rules 101 and 1101, this rule applies to state proceedings and to federal court-annexed and federal court-mandated arbitration proceedings, in the circumstances set out in the rule. And notwithstanding Rule 501, this rule applies even if state law provides the rule of decision.

(g) *Definitions.* In this rule:

(1) "attorney-client privilege" means the protection that applicable law provides for confidential attorney-client communications; and

(2) "work-product protection" means the protection that applicable law provides for tangible material (or its intangible equivalent) prepared in anticipation of litigation or for trial. (P.L. 110-322, § 1(a), 122 Stat. 3537, effective December 1, 2008, and amended by order adopted April 26, 2011, effective December 1, 2011.)

Comment. — Rule 502 has been amended by changing the initial letter of a few words from uppercase to lowercase as part of the restyling of the Evidence Rules to make style and terminology consistent throughout the rules. There is no intent to change any result in any ruling on evidence admissibility.

VI. WITNESSES.

Rule 601. Competency to Testify in General.

Every person is competent to be a witness unless these rules provide otherwise. But in a civil case, state law governs the witness's competency regarding a claim or defense for which state law supplies the rule of decision. (Amended by order adopted April 26, 2011, effective December 1, 2011.)

Comment. — The language of Rule 601 has been amended as part of the restyling of the Evidence Rules to make them more easily understood and to make style and terminology consistent throughout the rules. These changes are intended to be stylistic only. There is no intent to change any result in any ruling on evidence admissibility.

Law Review. — For a note, "Toward a Level Playing Field: Challenges to Accomplice Testimony in the Wake of United States v. Singleton," see 57 Wash. & Lee L. Rev. 515 (2000).

Research References. — Robert L. Habush, Art of Advocacy: Cross Examination of Non-Medical Experts (Matthew Bender).

Rule 602. Need for Personal Knowledge.

A witness may testify to a matter only if evidence is introduced sufficient to support a finding that the witness has personal knowledge of the matter. Evidence to prove personal knowledge may consist of the witness's own testimony. This rule does not apply to a witness's expert testimony under Rule 703. (Amended by order adopted March 2, 1987, effective October 1, 1987, by order adopted April 25, 1988, effective November 1, 1988, and by order adopted April 26, 2011, effective December 1, 2011.)

Comment. — The language of Rule 602 has been amended as part of the restyling of the Evidence Rules to make them more easily understood and to make style and terminology consistent throughout the rules. These changes are intended to be stylistic only. There is no intent to change any result in any ruling on evidence admissibility.

Rule 603. Oath or Affirmation to Testify Truthfully.

Before testifying, a witness must give an oath or affirmation to testify truthfully. It must be in a form designed to impress that duty on the witness's conscience. (Amended by order adopted March 2, 1987, effective October 1, 1987, and by order adopted April 26, 2011, effective December 1, 2011.)

Comment. — The language of Rule 603 has been amended as part of the restyling of the Evidence Rules to make them more easily understood and to make style and terminology consistent throughout the rules. These changes are intended to be stylistic only. There is no intent to change any result in any ruling on evidence admissibility.

Law Review. — For note, "Religion-Plus-Speech: The Constitutionality of Juror Oaths and Affirmations Under the First Amendment," see 34 Wm. and Mary L. Rev. 287 (1992).

Rule 604. Interpreter.

An interpreter must be qualified and must give an oath or affirmation to make a true translation. (Amended by order adopted March 2, 1987, effective October 1, 1987, and by order adopted April 26, 2011, effective December 1, 2011.)

Comment. — The language of Rule 604 has been amended as part of the restyling of the Evidence Rules to make them more easily understood and to make style and terminology consistent throughout the rules. These changes are intended to be stylistic only. There is no intent to change any result in any ruling on evidence admissibility.

Rule 605. Judge's Competency as a Witness.

The presiding judge may not testify as a witness at the trial. A party need not object to preserve the issue. (Amended by order adopted April 26, 2011, effective December 1, 2011.)

Comment. — The language of Rule 605 has been amended as part of the restyling of the Evidence Rules to make them more easily understood and to make style and terminology consistent throughout the rules. These changes are intended to be stylistic only. There is no intent to change any result in any ruling on evidence admissibility.

Rule 606. Juror's Competency as a Witness.

(a) *At the Trial.* — A juror may not testify as a witness before the other jurors at the trial. If a juror is called to testify, the court must give a party an opportunity to object outside the jury's presence.

(b) *During an Inquiry into the Validity of a Verdict or Indictment.* — (1) *Prohibited Testimony or Other Evidence.* During an inquiry into the validity of a verdict or indictment, a juror may not testify about any statement made or incident that occurred during the jury's deliberations; the effect of anything on that juror's or another juror's vote; or any juror's mental processes concerning the verdict or indictment. The court may not receive a juror's affidavit or evidence of a juror's statement on these matters.

(2) *Exceptions.* A juror may testify about whether:

(A) extraneous prejudicial information was improperly brought to the jury's attention;

(B) an outside influence was improperly brought to bear on any juror; or

(C) a mistake was made in entering the verdict on the verdict form. (Amended by order adopted December 12, 1975, by order adopted March 2, 1987, effective October 1, 1987, by order adopted April 12, 2006, effective December 1, 2006, and by order adopted April 26, 2011, effective December 1, 2011.)

Comment. — The language of Rule 606 has been amended as part of the restyling of the Evidence Rules to make them more easily understood and to make style and terminology consistent throughout

the rules. These changes are intended to be stylistic only. There is no intent to change any result in any ruling on evidence admissibility.

CASE NOTES

If evidence of extraneous prejudicial information or outside influence consists of a juror affidavit, it must be determined whether the affidavit relates solely to the conduct of a nonjuror or extraneous influence upon the juror or jury without reference to any phase of the deliberative process. Herring v. Blankenship, 662 F. Supp. 557 (W.D. Va. 1987).

Rule 607. Who May Impeach a Witness.

Any party, including the party that called the witness, may attack the witness's credibility. (Amended by order adopted March 2, 1987, effective October 1, 1987, and by order adopted April 26, 2011, effective December 1, 2011.)

Comment. — The language of Rule 607 has been amended as part of the restyling of the Evidence Rules to make them more easily understood and to make style and terminology consistent throughout the rules. These changes are intended to be stylistic only. There is no intent to change any result in any ruling on evidence admissibility.

Law Review. — For note, "Impeachment with an Unsworn Prior Inconsistent Statement as Subterfuge," see 28 Wm. & Mary L. Rev. 295 (1987).

CASE NOTES

Party may attack credibility of witness called by him. — Under the Federal Rules of Evidence, the ability of a party to a legal proceeding to attack the credibility of a witness called by him can no longer be questioned. United States v. Osborne, 532 F. Supp. 857 (W.D. Va. 1982).

This rule applies to persons considered to be insane to the same extent that it applies to other persons. United States v. Lightly, 677 F.2d 1027 (4th Cir. 1982).

Admissibility of a guilty plea depends upon the proposed use for which it is offered. United States v. Osborne, 532 F. Supp. 857 (W.D. Va. 1982).

The guilty plea of a codefendant may not be offered by the government as substantive evidence of the guilt of those on trial. United States v. Osborne, 532 F. Supp. 857 (W.D. Va. 1982).

But may be considered in evaluating witness' credibility. — Guilty plea evidence may properly be considered by the jury in evaluating the witness' credibility. United States v. Osborne, 532 F. Supp. 857 (W.D. Va. 1982).

The danger of confusion which arises from the introduction of prior unsworn statements, even where limited to impeachment, necessarily increases the possibility that a defendant may be convicted on the basis of unsworn evidence, for despite proper instructions to the jury, it is often difficult for jurors to distinguish between impeachment and substantive evidence. Thus, the danger of confusion which arises from the introduction of testimony under circumstances such as are presented here is so great as to upset the balance and to warrant continuation of the rule of exclusion. United States v. Ince, 21 F.3d 576 (4th Cir. 1994).

When introduction of guilty plea becomes prejudicial error. — Notwithstanding the legitimate use of guilty plea evidence, the court has the responsibility to insure that the evidence is offered by the prosecutor and used by the jury only for a permissible purpose. Introduction of the plea becomes prejudicial error when, for example, the government suggests that the jury use the plea for a prohibited purpose, when the use of a plea involves "aggravated circumstance," or where the government disproportionately emphasizes or repeats the evidence of the plea before the jury. United States v. Osborne, 532 F. Supp. 857 (W.D. Va. 1982).

Applied in United States v. Karnes, 531 F.2d 214 (4th Cir. 1976); Utility Control Corp. v. Prince William Constr. Co., 558 F.2d 716 (4th Cir. 1977).

Rule 608. A Witness's Character for Truthfulness or Untruthfulness.

(a) *Reputation or Opinion Evidence.* — A witness's credibility may be attacked or supported by testimony about the witness's reputation for having a character for truthfulness or untruthfulness, or by testimony in the form of an opinion about that character. But evidence of truthful character is admissible only after the witness's character for truthfulness has been attacked.

(b) *Specific Instances of Conduct.* — Except for a criminal conviction under Rule 609, extrinsic evidence is not admissible to prove specific instances of a witness's conduct in order to attack or support the witness's character for truthfulness. But the court may, on cross-examination, allow them to be inquired into if they are probative of the character for truthfulness or untruthfulness of:

(1) the witness; or

(2) another witness whose character the witness being cross-examined has testified about.

By testifying on another matter, a witness does not waive any privilege against self-incrimination for testimony that relates only to the witness's character for truthfulness. (Amended by order adopted March 2, 1987, effective October 1, 1987, by order adopted April 25, 1988, effective November 1, 1988, by order adopted March 27, 2003, effective December 1, 2003, and by order adopted April 26, 2011, effective December 1, 2011.)

Comment. — The language of Rule 608 has been amended as part of the general restyling of the Evidence Rules to make them more easily understood and to make style and terminology consistent throughout the rules. These changes are intended to be stylistic only. There is no intent to change any result in any ruling on evidence admissibility.

The Committee is aware that the Rule's limitation of bad-act impeachment to "cross-examination" is trumped by Rule 607, which allows a party to impeach witnesses on direct examination. Courts have not relied on the term "on cross-examination" to limit impeachment that would otherwise be permissible under Rules 607 and 608. The Committee therefore concluded that no change to the language of the Rule was necessary in the context of a restyling project.

Law Review. — For symposium, "The Restyled Federal Rules of Evidence," see 53 Wm. and Mary L. Rev. 1435 (2012).

CASE NOTES

Evidence allowed which had bearing on the truthfulness of defendant as witness. — District court did not err in ruling that government could use evidence of defendant's possession and use of fake identification for impeachment purposes, for such evidence had bearing on the truthfulness of the defendant as a witness. United States v. Williams, 986 F.2d 86 (4th Cir.), cert. denied, 509 U.S. 911, 113 S. Ct. 3013, 125 L. Ed. 2d 703 (1993).

When a witness admits to having performed certain acts, the prohibition against using extrinsic evidence is not applicable. United States v. Zandi, 769 F.2d 229 (4th Cir. 1985).

Plaintiff's character for truthfulness was not attacked where although his recollection of past events was challenged, there was no attempt to portray him as a liar. Mottesheard v. Castern, 256 Va. 11, 500 S.E.2d 512 (1998).

Defendant's cross-examination of witness improperly limited. — Defendant's convictions were reversed as the trial court erred inlimiting defendant's cross-examination of a confidential informant (CI) tocrimes for which he had been convicted where: (1) the CI admitted that he hopedhis work with law enforcement would reduce his sentences for his pendingcharges, (2) defendant sought to show that the CI had an additional biasinducing incentive to seek leniency with respect to misconduct as yetuncharged, but under investigation, (3) although defendant's proposed evidenceinvolved uncharged offenses, it related to a point properly at issue in thecase and was admissible, (4) defendant's proffer alerted the trial court thathe wanted to explore the CI's bias, and (5) evidence impeaching the CI'scredibility was material. Johnson v. Commonwealth, 2006 Va. App. LEXIS 83 (Mar. 7, 2006).

Applied in United States v. Basic Constr. Co., 711 F.2d 570 (4th Cir. 1983).

Rule 609. Impeachment by Evidence of Criminal Conviction.

(a) *In General.* — The following rules apply to attacking a witness's character for truthfulness by evidence of a criminal conviction:

(1) for a crime that, in the convicting jurisdiction, was punishable by death or by imprisonment for more than one year, the evidence:

(A) must be admitted, subject to Rule 403, in a civil case or in a criminal case in which the witness is not a defendant; and

(B) must be admitted in a criminal case in which the witness is a defendant, if the probative value of the evidence outweighs its prejudicial effect to that defendant; and

(2) for any crime regardless of the punishment, the evidence must be admitted if the court can readily determine that establishing the elements of the crime required proving — or the witness's admitting — a dishonest act or false statement.

(b) *Limit on Using the Evidence After 10 Years.* — This subdivision (b) applies if more than 10 years have passed since the witness's conviction or release from confinement for it, whichever is later. Evidence of the conviction is admissible only if:

(1) its probative value, supported by specific facts and circumstances, substantially outweighs its prejudicial effect; and

(2) the proponent gives an adverse party reasonable written notice of the intent to use it so that the party has a fair opportunity to contest its use.

(c) *Effect of a Pardon, Annulment, or Certificate of Rehabilitation.* — Evidence of a conviction is not admissible if:

(1) the conviction has been the subject of a pardon, annulment, certificate of rehabilitation, or other equivalent procedure based on a finding that the person has been rehabilitated, and the person has not been convicted of a later crime punishable by death or by imprisonment for more than one year; or

(2) the conviction has been the subject of a pardon, annulment, or other equivalent procedure based on a finding of innocence.

(d) *Juvenile Adjudications.* — Evidence of a juvenile adjudication is admissible under this rule only if:

(1) it is offered in a criminal case;

(2) the adjudication was of a witness other than the defendant;

(3) an adult's conviction for that offense would be admissible to attack the adult's credibility; and

(4) admitting the evidence is necessary to fairly determine guilt or innocence.

(e) *Pendency of an Appeal.* — A conviction that satisfies this rule is admissible even if an appeal is pending. Evidence of the pendency is also admissible. (Amended by order adopted March 2, 1987, effective October 1, 1987, by order adopted January 26, 1990, effective December 1, 1990, by order adopted April 12, 2006, effective December 1, 2006, and by order adopted April 26, 2011, effective December 1, 2011.)

Comment. — The language of Rule 609 has been amended as part of the restyling of the Evidence Rules to make them more easily understood and to make style and terminology consistent throughout the rules. These changes are intended to be stylistic only. There is no intent to change any result in any ruling on evidence admissibility.

CASE NOTES

The purpose of impeachment is not to show that the defendant is a bad person, but rather to show background facts which bear directly on whether jurors ought to believe him. Bizmark, Inc. v. Kroger Co., 994 F. Supp. 726 (W.D. Va. 1998).

Balancing test of subdivision (a)(1) is to be applied only in situations involving possible prejudice to defendant. Roshan v. Fard, 705 F.2d 102 (4th Cir. 1983).

"Release from confinement" in subdivision (b) means release from actual imprisonment; and therefore, neither parole nor probation constitute confinement under the rule. Bizmark, Inc. v. Kroger Co., 994 F. Supp. 726 (W.D. Va. 1998).

Prior German conviction introduced to impeach defendant. — Although a prior German conviction may have been obtained without a jury trial, it was not error for the trial court to rule that the government could introduce the conviction to impeach the defendant under Rule 609 of the Federal Rules of Evidence. United States v. Wilson, 556 F.2d 1177 (4th Cir.), cert. denied, 434 U.S. 986, 98 S. Ct. 614, 54 L. Ed. 2d 481 (1977).

Prior conviction to show motive is admissible under Rule 404. — This rule is concerned solely with the use of evidence of criminal conviction as a means of attacking the credibility of a witness. Where the evidence is proffered primarily to demonstrate motive and only incidentally to attack credibility, the evidence may properly be admitted under Rule 404(b). Roshan v. Fard, 705 F.2d 102 (4th Cir. 1983).

A prior misdemeanor conviction for willfully failing to provide information for income tax purposes has been held admissible for impeachment purposes as evidence of dishonesty. Zukowski v. Dunton, 650 F.2d 30 (4th Cir. 1981).

Convictions more than ten years old. — A court should only depart from the prohibition against the use for impeachment purposes of convictions more than ten years old very rarely and only in exceptional circumstances. United States v. Beahm, 664 F.2d 414 (4th Cir. 1981).

When the government seeks to use evidence of a conviction more than ten years old for purposes of impeachment, it bears the burden of establishing specific, or articulated, facts and circumstances that support the probative value of the conviction such that it substantially outweighs its prejudicial impact. United States v. Beahm, 664 F.2d 414 (4th Cir. 1981).

In a prosecution for taking indecent liberties with children on a United States military base, where the prosecution sought to have convictions for similar crimes which were eleven years old admitted for impeachment purposes and where the district court not only failed to make any express finding that the probative value substantially outweighed the prejudicial effect of the evidence, but the record was also silent both as to any specific facts supporting the probative value of the conviction for impeachment purposes or showing how its probative value substantially outweighed its prejudicial effect, the district court improperly admitted the evidence even though the conviction was for the same type offense for which the defendant stood accused. United States v. Beahm, 664 F.2d 414 (4th Cir. 1981).

Remote prior offenses. — Where defendant was convicted of conspiracy and of counseling, hiring, procuring and commanding another person to steal, which offenses do not necessarily carry any element of deceit, falsification or untruthfulness, there was nothing which supports a finding that defendant's remote prior offenses would have more than minimal, if any, bearing on the likelihood that he would testify truthfully. Bizmark, Inc. v. Kroger Co., 994 F. Supp. 726 (W.D. Va. 1998).

Applied in United States v. Lamarr, 75 F.3d 964 (4th Cir. 1996); United States v. Coleman, 11 F. Supp. 2d 689 (W.D. Va. 1998); Sulton v. FedEx Ground Package Sys., 80 Va. Cir. 385, 2010 Va. Cir. LEXIS 62 (Fairfax County June 1, 2010).

Rule 610. Religious Beliefs or Opinions.

Evidence of a witness's religious beliefs or opinions is not admissible to attack or support the witness's credibility. (Amended by order adopted March 2, 1987, effective October 1, 1987, and by order adopted April 26, 2011, effective December 1, 2011.)

Comment. — The language of Rule 610 has been amended as part of the restyling of the Evidence Rules to make them more easily understood and to make style and terminology consistent throughout the rules. These changes are intended to be stylistic only. There is no intent to change any result in any ruling on evidence admissibility.

Rule 611. Mode and Order of Examining Witnesses and Presenting Evidence.

(a) *Control by the Court; Purposes.* — The court should exercise reasonable control over the mode and order of examining witnesses and presenting evidence so as to:

(1) make those procedures effective for determining the truth;

(2) avoid wasting time; and

(3) protect witnesses from harassment or undue embarrassment.

(b) *Scope of Cross-Examination.* — Cross-examination should not go beyond the subject matter of the direct examination and matters affecting the witness's credibility. The court may allow inquiry into additional matters as if on direct examination.

(c) *Leading Questions.* — Leading questions should not be used on direct examination except as necessary to develop the witness's testimony. Ordinarily, the court should allow leading questions:

(1) on cross-examination; and

(2) when a party calls a hostile witness, an adverse party, or a witness identified with an adverse party. (Amended by order adopted March 2, 1987, effective October 1, 1987, and by order adopted April 26, 2011, effective December 1, 2011.)

Comment. — The language of Rule 611 has been amended as part of the restyling of the Evidence Rules to make them more easily understood and to make style and terminology consistent throughout the rules. These changes are intended to be stylistic only. There is no intent to change any result in any ruling on evidence admissibility.

CASE NOTES

This rule allows the court reasonable control over the interrogation of witnesses for several reasons, among them, to avoid needless consumption of time. United States v. Billups, 522 F. Supp. 935 (E.D. Va. 1981), aff'd, 692 F.2d 320 (4th Cir. 1982).

Court's action to allow officers to summarize telephone conversations and meetings consistent with rule. — In prosecution for conspiracy to kidnap and exploit a minor in a sexually explicit film where trial court allowed law enforcement officers to summarize their telephone conversations and meetings with the conspirators because the tape and video recordings of these conversations and meetings were lengthy and some contained incomprehensible portions due to overlapping conversations and technical problems, the trial court's action was consistent with this rule. United States v. DePew, 932 F.2d 324 (4th Cir.), cert. denied, 502 U.S. 873, 112 S. Ct. 210, 116 L. Ed. 2d 169 (1991).

Admission of summary chart in federal drug prosecution. — In the ordinary federal drug prosecution, neither a summary witness's testimony nor a chart summarizing testimony of co-conspirators and diagramming drug transactions among members of the conspiracy would be admissible pursuant to Rules 702 or 611(a). United States v. Johnson, 54 F.3d 1150 (4th Cir. 1995), cert. denied, 516 U.S. 903, 116 S. Ct. 266, 133 L. Ed. 2d 188 (1995).

Due to the large number of witnesses and extensive evidence, as well as the curative instructions offered by the district court, the district court acted within its discretion in admitting the summary testimony and summary chart in the instant case. United States v. Johnson, 54 F.3d 1150 (4th Cir. 1995), cert. denied, 516 U.S. 903, 116 S. Ct. 266, 133 L. Ed. 2d 188 (1995).

Manner in which court instructs jury to consider summary chart. — In looking to the policy reasons behind subdivision (a), the concern is not so much with the formal admission as it is with the manner in which the district court instructs the jury to consider the summary chart. Whether or not the chart is technically admitted into evidence, the appellate court is more concerned that the district court ensure the jury is not relying on that chart as independent evidence but rather is taking a close look at the evidence upon which that chart is based. United States v. Johnson, 54 F.3d 1150 (4th Cir. 1995), cert. denied, 516 U.S. 903, 116 S. Ct. 266, 133 L. Ed. 2d 188 (1995).

Applied in United States v. Collier, No. 99-4712, 2000 U.S. App. LEXIS 22639 (4th Cir. Sept. 6, 2000).

Rule 612. Writing Used to Refresh a Witness's Memory.

(a) *Scope.* — This rule gives an adverse party certain options when a witness uses a writing to refresh memory:

(1) while testifying; or

(2) before testifying, if the court decides that justice requires the party to have those options.

(b) *Adverse Party's Options; Deleting Unrelated Matter.* — Unless 18 U.S.C. § 3500 provides otherwise in a criminal case, an adverse party is entitled to have the writing produced at the hearing, to inspect it, to cross-examine the witness about it, and to introduce in evidence any portion that relates to the witness's testimony. If the producing party claims that the writing includes unrelated matter, the court must examine the writing in camera, delete any unrelated portion, and order that the rest be delivered to the adverse party. Any portion deleted over objection must be preserved for the record.

(c) *Failure to Produce or Deliver the Writing.* — If a writing is not produced or is not delivered as ordered, the court may issue any appropriate order. But if the prosecution does not comply in a criminal case, the court must strike the witness's testimony or — if justice so requires — declare a mistrial. (Amended by order adopted March 2, 1987, effective October 1, 1987, and by order adopted April 26, 2011, effective December 1, 2011.)

Comment. — The language of Rule 612 has been amended as part of the restyling of the Evidence Rules to make them more easily understood and to make style and terminology consistent throughout the rules. These changes are intended to be stylistic only. There is no intent to change any result in any ruling on evidence admissibility.

CASE NOTES

Writing can be used as evidence if it meets test of recorded recollection. — It is clear that the witness' recollection must be revived after the writing is presented to him as a stimulus so that his testimony properly constitutes a present recollection. If the writing fails to revive his recollection, the writing may be read into evidence and admitted, but only if it meets the test of recorded recollection set forth in Rule 803(5). "The line between using the writing as an aid to memory and basing one's testimony upon it as a correct record of past memory is sometimes shadowy." United States Elevator Corp. v. 1616 Reminc Ltd. Partnership, 9 Bankr. 679 (Bankr. E.D. Va. 1981).

Rule 613. Witness's Prior Statements.

(a) *Showing or Disclosing the Statement During Examination.* — When examining a witness about the witness's prior statement, a party need not show it or disclose its contents to the witness. But the party must, on request, show it or disclose its contents to an adverse party's attorney.

(b) *Extrinsic Evidence of a Prior Inconsistent Statement.* — Extrinsic evidence of a witness's prior inconsistent statement is admissible only if the witness is given an opportunity to explain or deny the statement and an adverse party is given an opportunity to examine the witness about it, or if justice so requires. This subdivision (b) does not apply to an opposing party's statement under Rule 801(d)(2). (Amended by order adopted March 2, 1987, effective October 1, 1987, by order adopted April 25, 1988, effective November 1, 1988, and by order adopted April 26, 2011, effective December 1, 2011.)

Comment. — The language of Rule 613 has been amended as part of the restyling of the Evidence Rules to make them more easily understood and to make style and terminology consistent throughout the rules. These changes are intended to be stylistic only. There is no intent to change any result in any ruling on evidence admissibility.

CASE NOTES

Prior inconsistent statements. — Trial court did not abuse its discretion in refusing to admit the testimony of a third party to whom two witnesses allegedly made statements regarding the incident because defendant did not lay a proper foundation for the introduction of the third party's testimony and never confronted either witness with his alleged inconsistent statement. Kelly v. Commonwealth, — Va. App. —, — S.E.2d —, 2009 Va. App. LEXIS 33 (Jan. 27, 2009).

Rule 614. Court's Calling or Examining a Witness.

(a) *Calling.* — The court may call a witness on its own or at a party's request. Each party is entitled to cross-examine the witness.

(b) *Examining.* — The court may examine a witness regardless of who calls the witness.

(c) *Objections.* — A party may object to the court's calling or examining a witness either at that time or at the next opportunity when the jury is not present. (Amended by order adopted April 26, 2011, effective December 1, 2011.)

Comment. — The language of Rule 614 has been amended as part of the restyling of the Evidence Rules to make them more easily understood and to make style and terminology consistent throughout the rules. These changes are intended to be stylistic only. There is no intent to change any result in any ruling on evidence admissibility.

CASE NOTES

Powers of trial judge generally. — The trial judge in federal courts retains the common law power to comment on the evidence. He may summarize, discuss and comment on the facts and the evidence, provided he indicates to the jury that they are not bound by his discussion of the evidence. In addition, the Federal Rules of Evidence allow the court to interrogate witnesses. United States v. Billups, 522 F. Supp. 935 (E.D. Va. 1981), aff'd, 692 F.2d 320 (4th Cir. 1982).

Failure to object to court's interrogation of witness. — If a party fails to object to the court's interrogation of a witness at trial, his objection will not be reviewed on appeal. Stillman v. Norfolk & W. Ry., 811 F.2d 834 (4th Cir. 1987).

Waiver of objection to inappropriate remark by judge. — Even if a remark by the court had an inappropriate effect, defendant waived his right to object to it by failing to object at the time the question was put to the witness/defendant or at the first available opportunity, a failure that deprived the court of an opportunity to instruct the jury to disregard the comment. United States v. Billups, 522 F. Supp. 935 (E.D. Va. 1981), aff'd, 692 F.2d 320 (4th Cir. 1982).

Purpose of subdivision (c). — As the Advisory Committee's Notes to subdivision (c) of this rule make clear, the rule is "designed to relieve counsel of the embarrassment attendant upon objecting to questions by the judge in the presence of the jury, while at the same time assuring that objections are made in apt time to afford the opportunity to take possible corrective measures." United States v. Billups, 692 F.2d 320 (4th Cir. 1982), cert. denied, 464 U.S. 820, 104 S. Ct. 84, 78 L. Ed. 2d 93 (1983).

Appeal. — Defendant's failure to object to judge's interrogation of witness during the trial was fatal to his argument on appeal. United States v. Gastiaburo, 16 F.3d 582 (4th Cir.), cert. denied, 513 U.S. 829, 115 S. Ct. 102, 130 L. Ed. 2d 50 (1994).

Applied in United States v. Karnes, 531 F.2d 214 (4th Cir. 1976).

Rule 615. Excluding Witnesses.

At a party's request, the court must order witnesses excluded so that they cannot hear other witnesses' testimony. Or the court may do so on its own. But this rule does not authorize excluding:

(a) a party who is a natural person;

(b) an officer or employee of a party that is not a natural person, after being designated as the party's representative by its attorney;

(c) a person whose presence a party shows to be essential to presenting the party's claim or defense; or

(d) a person authorized by statute to be present. (Amended by order adopted March 2, 1987, effective October 1, 1987, by order adopted April 25, 1988, effective November 1, 1988, by P.L. 100-690, § 7075, effective November 18, 1988, and by order adopted April 24, 1998, effective December 1, 1998, and by order adopted April 26, 2011, effective December 1, 2011.)

Comment. — The language of Rule 615 has been amended as part of the restyling of the Evidence Rules to make them more easily understood and to make style and terminology consistent throughout

the rules. These changes are intended to be stylistic only. There is no intent to change any result in any ruling on evidence admissibility.

CASE NOTES

Strict adherence required where outcome depends on relative credibility. — The sequestration of witnesses effectively discourages and exposes fabrication, inaccuracy, and collusion. Scrupulous adherence to this rule is particularly necessary in those cases in which the outcome depends on the relative credibility of the parties' witnesses. United States v. Farnham, 791 F.2d 331 (4th Cir. 1986).

Exceptions to rule narrowly construed. — This rule reflects an a priori judgment in favor of sequestration, and the exceptions should be construed narrowly in favor of the party requesting sequestration. United States v. Farnham, 791 F.2d 331 (4th Cir. 1986).

Government's chief investigating agent may remain in courtroom. — This rule expressly provides an exception for "an officer or employee of a party which is not a natural person designated as its representative by its attorney." Under this exception, the district court may allow the government's chief investigating agent to remain in the courtroom throughout the proceedings, even if he is expected to testify. United States v. Farnham, 791 F.2d 331 (4th Cir. 1986).

Exclusion of witness's testimony for violation of sequestration order. — District court did not err when it excluded the testimony of defendant's witness for a violation of the court's sequestration order. Although the court of appeals believed that the district court would have been well advised to employ a lesser sanction to punish the violation because to do so would have preserved both the purpose of the sequestration rule and defendant's right to present a defense, given that it was clear that defendant himself was behind this violation in some way, the district court did not abuse its discretion. The court of appeals was particularly unwilling to overturn the district court's judgment on this issue given that the defense did not argue to the court during trial that the exclusion of the witness was excessive or unconstitutional. United States v. Cropp, 127 F.3d 354 (4th Cir. 1997), cert. denied, 522 U.S. 1098, 118 S. Ct. 898, 139 L. Ed. 2d 883 (1998).

Applied in United States v. Burgess, 691 F.2d 1146 (4th Cir. 1982).

VII. OPINIONS AND EXPERT TESTIMONY.

Rule 701. Opinion Testimony by Lay Witnesses.

If a witness is not testifying as an expert, testimony in the form of an opinion is limited to one that is:

(a) rationally based on the witness's perception;

(b) helpful to clearly understanding the witness's testimony or to determining a fact in issue; and

(c) not based on scientific, technical, or other specialized knowledge within the scope of Rule 702. (Amended by order adopted March 2, 1987, effective October 1, 1987, by order adopted April 17, 2000, effective December 1, 2000, and by order adopted April 26, 2011, effective December 1, 2011.)

Comment. — The language of Rule 701 has been amended as part of the general restyling of the Evidence Rules to make them more easily understood and to make style and terminology consistent throughout the rules. These changes are intended to be stylistic only. There is no intent to change any result in any ruling on evidence admissibility.

The Committee deleted all reference to an "inference" on the grounds that the deletion made the Rule flow better and easier to read, and because any "inference" is covered by the broader term "opinion." Courts have not made substantive decisions on the basis of any distinction between an opinion and an inference. No change in current practice is intended.

Law Review. — For a note, "Toward a Level Playing Field: Challenges to Accomplice Testimony in the Wake of United States v. Singleton," see 57 Wash. & Lee L. Rev. 515 (2000).

CASE NOTES

Opinions on basis of relevant historical or narrative facts. — A lay witness in a federal court proceeding is permitted under this rule to offer an opinion on the basis of relevant historical or narrative facts that the witness has perceived. MCI Telecommunications Corp. v. Wanzer, 897 F.2d 703 (4th Cir. 1990).

Bookkeeper testimony based on records kept personally under her control. — District judge erred in refusing to permit a bookkeeper to testify on the basis of records kept by her personally under her control, where her projection of profits under a lease as prepared by her was predicated on her personal knowledge and perception, and as such, she was a lay witness, whose identification as an expert witness under Rules 702 and 703 was not required. MCI Telecommunications Corp. v. Wanzer, 897 F.2d 703 (4th Cir. 1990).

Testimony of officials concerning classified documents and defendant was admissible. — In prosecution for conversion and unauthorized conveyance of governmental information, testimony of officials who expressed their opinions that a person with defendant's experience in the department would know the rules about classified budget documents and that these documents were not available to contractors was admissible under this rule since the witnesses laid an adequate foundation for their testimony, each was familiar with the documents in issue, their secret classification, the reason for their classification, the nature of defendant's work in the department, and the fact that people with defendant's experience knew the department did not authorize contractors to possess the documents; their opinions were helpful to the jury in determining the nature and extent of defendant's knowledge about the documents and whether he acted through negligence, accident, inadvertence, mistake, or confusion. United States v. Fowler, 932 F.2d 306 (4th Cir. 1991).

CIRCUIT COURT OPINIONS

Value of property. — The opinion testimony of the owner of personal property is competent and admissible on the question of the value of such property, regardless of the owner's knowledge of property values; however, ownership of property by a corporation does not automatically qualify a company employee to testify about the value of company property. Where a foundation of knowledge by a witness for a corporation regarding the value of a particular piece of property is established, the witness' lay opinion regarding the value of such property is admissible. Commonwealth Transp. Comm'r v. Pruitt Props., 62 Va. Cir. 95, 2003 Va. Cir. LEXIS 268 (Goochland 2003).

Rule 702. Testimony by Expert Witnesses.

A witness who is qualified as an expert by knowledge, skill, experience, training, or education may testify in the form of an opinion or otherwise if:

(a) the expert's scientific, technical, or other specialized knowledge will help the trier of fact to understand the evidence or to determine a fact in issue;

(b) the testimony is based on sufficient facts or data;

(c) the testimony is the product of reliable principles and methods; and

(d) the expert has reliably applied the principles and methods to the facts of the case. (Amended by order adopted April 17, 2000, effective December 1, 2000, and by order adopted April 26, 2011, effective December 1, 2011.)

Comment. — The language of Rule 702 has been amended as part of the restyling of the Evidence Rules to make them more easily understood and to make style and terminology consistent throughout the rules. These changes are intended to be stylistic only. There is no intent to change any result in any ruling on evidence admissibility.

Law Review. — For article, "Voice Spectrography Evidence: Approaches to Admissibility," see 20 U. Rich. L. Rev. 357 (1986). For article, "Improving Expert Testimony," see 20 U. Rich. L. Rev. 473 (1986). For note, "Reducing the Value of Plaintiff's Litigation Option in Federal Court: Daubert v. Merrell Dow Pharmaceuticals, Inc.," see 2 Geo. Mason L. Rev. 159 (Spring 1995). For article, "The Guardian Ad Litem in Child Custody Cases: The Contours of Our Judicial System Stretched Beyond Recognition," see 6 Geo. Mason L. Rev. 255 (1998). For an ssay, "Sampling Liability," see 85 Va. L. Rev. 329 (1999). For an article, "Evidence Myopia: The Failure To See the Federal Rules of Evidence As a Codification of the Common Law," see 40 Wm. & Mary L. Rev. 1539 (1999). For a casenote, "Kumho Tire v. Carmichael: Stretching Daubert Beyond Recognition," see 8 Geo. Mason L. Rev. 203 (1999). For article, "The Epistemology of Prediction: Future Dangerousness Testimony and Intellectual Due Process," see 60 Wash. & Lee L. Rev. 353 (2003). For comment, "How Antitrust Damages Measure Up with Respect to the Daubert Factors," see 13 Geo. Mason L. Rev. 697 (2005). For article, "Proving Lost Profits after Daubert: Five Questions Every Court Should Ask before Admitting Expert Testimony," see 41 U. Rich. L. Rev. 379 (2007). For symposium, "The Restyled Federal Rules of Evidence," see 53 Wm and Mary L. Rev. 1435 (2012).

Research References. — Marshall Houts, Art of Advocacy: Cross Examination of Medical Experts (Matthew Bender).

CASE NOTES

Diversity actions. — Unlike evidentiary rules concerning burdens of proof or presumptions, the admissibility of expert testimony in a federal court sitting in the diversity jurisdiction is controlled by federal law. State law, whatever it may be, is irrelevant. Scott v. Sears, Roebuck & Co., 789 F.2d 1052 (4th Cir. 1986).

Discretion of court. — This rule does not require the admission of all proffered expert testimony; the trial judge has broad discretion to decide whether such testimony ought to be admitted as helpful to the jury. United States v. Portsmouth Paving Corp., 694 F.2d 312 (4th Cir. 1982).

The trial judge has broad discretion to certify experts. Environmental Defense Fund, Inc. v. Lamphier, 714 F.2d 331 (4th Cir. 1983).

Denial of defendant's motion for the appointment of a defense expert in trace evidence was not an abuse of discretion as defendant received the services defendant requested of a trace evidence expert by cross-examining the Commonwealth's expert. Large v. Commonwealth, 2007 Va. App. LEXIS 399 (Oct. 30, 2007).

Denial of defendant's motion for the appointment of a defense expert in animal behavior was not an abuse of discretion as the Commonwealth never argued pit bulls were inherently dangerous to human beings. Large v. Commonwealth, 2007 Va. App. LEXIS 399 (Oct. 30, 2007).

Admission of summary chart in federal drug prosecution. — In the ordinary federal drug prosecution, neither a summary witness's testimony nor a chart summarizing testimony of co-conspirators and diagramming drug transactions among members of the conspiracy would be admissible pursuant to this rule or Rule 611(a). United States v. Johnson, 54 F.3d 1150 (4th Cir. 1995), cert. denied, 516 U.S. 903, 116 S. Ct. 266, 133 L. Ed. 2d 188 (1995).

Due to the large number of witnesses and extensive evidence, as well as the curative instructions offered by the district court, the district court acted within its discretion in admitting the summary testimony and summary chart in the instant case. United States v. Johnson, 54 F.3d 1150 (4th Cir. 1995), cert. denied, 516 U.S. 903, 116 S. Ct. 266, 133 L. Ed. 2d 188 (1995).

Witness may be qualified by any one of five listed means. — "Or" as used in this rule preceding "education" indicates that a witness may be qualified as an expert by any one of the five listed qualifications. Garrett v. Desa Indus., Inc., 705 F.2d 721 (4th Cir. 1983).

Expert testimony as to common knowledge usually harmless error. — This rule makes inadmissible expert testimony as to a matter which obviously is within the common knowledge of jurors because such testimony, almost by definition, can be of no assistance. At the same time, the admission of such testimony, though technical error, will almost invariably be harmless. Trouble is encountered only when the evaluation of the commonplace by an expert witness might supplant a jury's independent exercise of common sense. This, however, does not seem to be an inquiry under this rule, but rather a necessary, independent inquiry under Rule 403 to exclude evidence which is prejudicial. Scott v. Sears, Roebuck & Co., 789 F.2d 1052 (4th Cir. 1986).

Court may disregard speculation. — A court should disregard expert opinion if it is mere speculation, not supported by facts. Anderson v. National R.R. Passenger Corp., 866 F. Supp. 937 (E.D. Va. 1994), aff'd, 74 F.3d 1230 (4th Cir. 1996).

Officers opinion testimony admissible. — Officers testimony that it is not uncommon for people transporting controlled substances to grant consent to law enforcement officers to search their possessions or their persons and regarding the attributes of persons involved in the distribution of drugs and the "tools of the trade" and regarding addicts' typical levels of crack consumption, typical patterns of addiction, and typical quantities of crack that a user will purchase and hold at any given moment did not violate Rule 702. United States v. Gastiaburo, 16 F.3d 582 (4th Cir.), cert. denied, 513 U.S. 829, 115 S. Ct. 102, 130 L. Ed. 2d 50 (1994).

Expert testimony to show defendant lacked specific intent was inadmissible. — In prosecution for conversion and unauthorized conveyance of governmental information and mail fraud, exclusion of testimony of two expert witnesses whose testimony was to show that defendant lacked specific intent to violate the law, and whose opinions would be based on their perception of confusions, defendant's actions and statements, was proper since the experts' proffered testimony differed little from closing argument of defendant's counsel, and the inquiry was a factual issue that juries regularly decide and need no help from expert witnesses to speculate about defendant's state of mind; moreover, expert witnesses could not testify regarding their opinions that defendant did not have mental state constituting an element of the crime, intent. United States v. Fowler, 932 F.2d 306 (4th Cir. 1991).

Foundation given for gang culture testimony. — Trial court did not abuse its discretion in admitting expert testimony on gang culture in defendant's criminal trial for malicious wounding and use of a firearm during the commission of a felony; the Commonwealth provided a sufficient foundation for the admission of the testimony, the testimony was relevant in that it established a motive for the shooting, and the evidence was not outweighed by prejudice. Hubbard v. Commonwealth, 2006 Va. App. LEXIS 72 (Feb. 28, 2006).

Doctor's testimony as to mother's grief properly excluded in wrongful death action. — In a wrongful death action, the district court's decision to exclude a doctor's expert testimony, concluding that the jury could assess the mother's inner grief without expert guidance, represented a reasonable exercise of the trial judge's broad discretion under this rule to determine that a proposed expert will not significantly assist the arbiter of fact. El-Meswari v. Washington Gas Light Co., 785 F.2d 483 (4th Cir. 1986).

Medical expert opinion properly allowed on the facts. — Under this rule, where plaintiff's treating physicians based their conclusions on the microscopic appearance of his liver, the Tylenol found in his blood upon his admission to the hospital, the history of several days of Tylenol use after regular alcohol consumption, the liver enzyme blood level, and the lack of evidence of a viral or any other cause of the liver failure, and his other experts relied upon a similar methodology: history, examination, lab and pathology data, and study of the peer-reviewed literature, the district court did not abuse its discretion when it determined that the methodology employed by plaintiff's experts was reliable. Benedi v. McNeil-P.P.C., Inc., 66 F.3d 1378 (4th Cir. 1995).

Where biochemist's methodology had not been tested at all, neither his methodology nor his reasoning had been subject to any peer review or publication, and he failed to demonstrate any acceptance within any relevant scientific community, he could not testify for the plaintiff as an expert; although his testimony would be relevant, it would also be wholly unreliable. Ballinger v. Atkins, 947 F. Supp. 925 (E.D. Va. 1996).

Where physician's opinion, as well a his methodology and reasoning, failed to occupy a "significant place" in accepted medicine or science, he could not qualify as an expert with regard to his belief that plaintiff had suffered neurological injuries from ingestion of defendant's artificial sweetener. Ballinger v. Atkins, 947 F. Supp. 925 (E.D. Va. 1996).

The district court correctly concluded that the bases of plaintiffs' doctors' expert opinions were not sufficiently established to warrant their admission into evidence. Cavallo v. Star Enter., 100 F.3d 1150 (4th Cir. 1996), cert. denied, 522 U.S. 1044, 118 S. Ct. 684, 139 L. Ed. 2d 631 (1998).

Opinion needs factual basis. — An expert's opinion is not to be accepted merely because it is articulated, but must instead have a sufficient factual basis. Anderson v. National R.R. Passenger Corp., 866 F. Supp. 937 (E.D. Va. 1994), aff'd, 74 F.3d 1230 (4th Cir. 1996).

Credibility determination for jury. — Even with respect to expert witnesses, the credibility determination is for the jury, not the court. Anderson v. National R.R. Passenger Corp., 866 F. Supp. 937 (E.D. Va. 1994), aff'd, 74 F.3d 1230 (4th Cir. 1996).

Proper backing up procedures for tractor rig. — In a wrongful death action arising from an accident in which the defendant backed over a pedestrian with his tractor rig in a parking lot, the plaintiff's expert testimony about proper backing up procedures was based on sufficient facts and data as it was reasonable for an expert on truck safety and accident reconstruction to look to federal, state, and commercial publications on the subject, and the defendant did not challenge the substance of the manuals or other publications upon which the plaintiff's expert relied and, instead, argued that even if all these materials upon which the expert relied indicated a proper method for backing up a tractor rig, they were still only generalized guidelines and not standards. Hatten v. Sholl, 2002 U.S. Dist. LEXIS 2583 (W.D. Va. Feb. 13, 2002).

Applied in Wilson v. Volkswagen of Am., Inc., 561 F.2d 494 (4th Cir. 1977); Wilder Enters., Inc. v. Allied Artists Pictures Corp., 632 F.2d 1135 (4th Cir. 1980); United States v. Barsanti, 943 F.2d 428 (4th Cir. 1991); Commonwealth v. Duncan, 267 Va. 377, 593 S.E.2d 210, 2004 Va. LEXIS 38 (2004).

Rule 703. Bases of an Expert's Opinion Testimony.

An expert may base an opinion on facts or data in the case that the expert has been made aware of or personally observed. If experts in the particular field would reasonably rely on those kinds of facts or data in forming an opinion on the subject, they need not be admissible for the opinion to be admitted. But if the facts or data would otherwise be inadmissible, the proponent of the opinion may disclose them to the jury only if their probative value in helping the jury evaluate the opinion substantially outweighs their prejudicial effect. (Amended by order adopted March 2, 1987, effective October 1, 1987, by order adopted April 17, 2000, effective December 1, 2000, and by order adopted April 26, 2011, effective December 1, 2011.)

Comment. — The language of Rule 703 has been amended as part of the general restyling of the Evidence Rules to make them more easily understood and to make style and terminology consistent throughout the rules. These changes are intended to be stylistic only. There is no intent to change any result in any ruling on evidence admissibility.

The Committee deleted all reference to an "inference" on the grounds that the deletion made the Rule flow better and easier to read, and because any "inference" is covered by the broader term "opinion." Courts have not made substantive decisions on the basis of any distinction between an opinion and an inference. No change in current practice is intended.

Law Review. — For note, "Reducing the Value of Plaintiff's Litigation Option in Federal Court: Daubert v. Merrell Dow Pharmaceuticals, Inc.," see 2 Geo. Mason L. Rev. 159 (Spring 1995). For a casenote, "Kumho Tire v. Carmichael: Stretching Daubert Beyond Recognition," see 8 Geo. Mason L. Rev. 203 (1999). For article, "Proving Lost Profits after Daubert: Five Questions Every Court Should Ask before Admitting Expert Testimony," see 41 U. Rich. L. Rev. 379 (2007).

CASE NOTES

Expert opinion limited to material facts supported by evidence. — Limitation of expert opinion to material facts supported by or consistent with the evidence has long been the law in the Fourth Circuit, and remains a requirement under the liberal standard of this rule. Cunningham v. Rendezvous, Inc., 699 F.2d 676 (4th Cir. 1983).

Foundation lacking. — Metallurgic engineer called by plaintiff lacked foundation for his expert testimony as to burglar deterrent quality of defendant's safe, where expert had not manufactured or designed safes, was not personally familiar with industry standards, and had not analyzed safes before. Redman v. John D. Brush & Co., 111 F.3d 1174 (W.D. Va. 1997).

Applied in Wilder Enters., Inc. v. Allied Artists Pictures Corp., 632 F.2d 1135 (4th Cir. 1980).

Rule 704. Opinion on an Ultimate Issue.

(a) *In General — Not Automatically Objectionable.* — An opinion is not objectionable just because it embraces an ultimate issue.

(b) *Exception.* — In a criminal case, an expert witness must not state an opinion about whether the defendant did or did not have a mental state or condition that constitutes an element of the crime charged or of a defense. Those matters are for the trier of fact alone. (Amended by P.L. 98-473, Title II, § 406, approved October 12, 1984, and by order adopted April 26, 2011, effective December 1, 2011.)

Comment. — The language of Rule 704 has been amended as part of the general restyling of the Evidence Rules to make them more easily understood and to make style and terminology consistent throughout the rules. These changes are intended to be stylistic only. There is no intent to change any result in any ruling on evidence admissibility.

The Committee deleted all reference to an "inference" on the grounds that the deletion made the Rule flow better and easier to read, and because any "inference" is covered by the broader term "opinion." Courts have not made substantive decisions on the basis of any distinction between an opinion and an inference. No change in current practice is intended.

CASE NOTES

Expert testimony to show defendant lacked specific intent was inadmissible. — In prosecution for conversion and unauthorized conveyance of governmental information and mail fraud, exclusion of testimony of two expert witnesses whose testimony was to show that defendant lacked specific intent to violate the law, and whose opinions would be based on their perception of confusions, defendant's actions and statements, was proper since the experts' proffered testimony differed little from closing argument of defendant's counsel, and the inquiry was a factual issue that juries regularly decide and need no help from expert witnesses to speculate about defendant's state of mind; moreover, expert witnesses could not testify regarding their opinions that defendant did not have mental state constituting an element of the crime, intent. United States v. Fowler, 932 F.2d 306 (4th Cir. 1991).

Rule 704(b) was enacted in the wake of the attempted assassination of President Reagan and the murder of John Lennon, and was an attempt to constrain psychiatric testimony on behalf of defendants asserting the insanity defense. United States v. Gastiaburo, 16 F.3d 582 (4th Cir.), cert. denied, 513 U.S. 829, 115 S. Ct. 102, 130 L. Ed. 2d 50 (1994).

Applied in Garrett v. Desa Indus., Inc., 705 F.2d 721 (4th Cir. 1983).

Rule 705. Disclosure of Facts or Data Underlying an Expert's Opinion.

Unless the court orders otherwise, an expert may state an opinion — and give the reasons for it — without first testifying to the underlying facts or data. But the expert may be required to disclose those facts or data on cross-examination. (Amended by order adopted March 2, 1987, effective October 1, 1987, by order adopted April 22, 1993, effective December 1, 1993, and by order adopted April 26, 2011, effective December 1, 2011.)

Comment. — The language of Rule 705 has been amended as part of the general restyling of the Evidence Rules to make them more easily understood and to make style and terminology consistent throughout the rules. These changes are intended to be stylistic only. There is no intent to change any result in any ruling on evidence admissibility.

The Committee deleted all reference to an "inference" on the grounds that the deletion made the Rule flow better and easier to read, and because any "inference" is covered by the broader term "opinion." Courts have not made substantive decisions on the basis of any distinction between an opinion and an inference. No change in current practice is intended.

Rule 706. Court-Appointed Expert Witnesses.

(a) *Appointment Process.* — On a party's motion or on its own, the court may order the parties to show cause why expert witnesses should not be appointed and may ask the parties to submit nominations. The court may appoint any expert that the parties agree on and any of its own choosing. But the court may only appoint someone who consents to act.

(b) *Expert's Role.* — The court must inform the expert of the expert's duties. The court may do so in writing and have a copy filed with the clerk or may do so orally at a conference in which the parties have an opportunity to participate. The expert:

(1) must advise the parties of any findings the expert makes;

(2) may be deposed by any party;

(3) may be called to testify by the court or any party; and

(4) may be cross-examined by any party, including the party that called the expert.

(c) *Compensation.* — The expert is entitled to a reasonable compensation, as set by the court. The compensation is payable as follows:

(1) in a criminal case or in a civil case involving just compensation under the Fifth Amendment, from any funds that are provided by law; and

(2) in any other civil case, by the parties in the proportion and at the time that the court directs — and the compensation is then charged like other costs.

(d) *Disclosing the Appointment to the Jury.* — The court may authorize disclosure to the jury that the court appointed the expert.

(e) *Parties' Choice of Their Own Experts.* — This rule does not limit a party in calling its own experts. (Amended by order adopted March 2, 1987, effective October 1, 1987, and by order adopted April 26, 2011, effective December 1, 2011.)

Comment. — The language of Rule 706 has been amended as part of the restyling of the Evidence Rules to make them more easily understood and to make style and terminology consistent throughout the rules. These changes are intended to be stylistic only. There is no intent to change any result in any ruling on evidence admissibility.

Law Review. — For article, "The Guardian Ad Litem in Child Custody Cases: The Contours of Our Judicial System Stretched Beyond Recognition," see 6 Geo. Mason L. Rev. 255 (1998). For article, "Proving Lost Profits after Daubert: Five Questions Every Court Should Ask before Admitting Expert Testimony," see 41 U. Rich. L. Rev. 379 (2007).

VIII. HEARSAY.

Rule 801. Definitions That Apply to This Article; Exclusions from Hearsay.

(a) *Statement.* — "Statement" means a person's oral assertion, written assertion, or nonverbal conduct, if the person intended it as an assertion.

(b) *Declarant.* — "Declarant" means the person who made the statement.

(c) *Hearsay.* — "Hearsay" means a statement that:

(1) the declarant does not make while testifying at the current trial or hearing; and

(2) a party offers in evidence to prove the truth of the matter asserted in the statement.

(d) *Statements That Are Not Hearsay.* — A statement that meets the following conditions is not hearsay:

(1) *A Declarant-Witness's Prior Statement.* The declarant testifies and is subject to cross-examination about a prior statement, and the statement:

(A) is inconsistent with the declarant's testimony and was given under penalty of perjury at a trial, hearing, or other proceeding or in a deposition;

(B) is consistent with the declarant's testimony and is offered to rebut an express or implied charge that the declarant recently fabricated it or acted from a recent improper influence or motive in so testifying; or

(C) identifies a person as someone the declarant perceived earlier.

(2) *An Opposing Party's Statement.* The statement is offered against an opposing party and:

(A) was made by the party in an individual or representative capacity;

(B) is one the party manifested that it adopted or believed to be true;

(C) was made by a person whom the party authorized to make a statement on the subject;

(D) was made by the party's agent or employee on a matter within the scope of that relationship and while it existed; or

(E) was made by the party's coconspirator during and in furtherance of the conspiracy.

The statement must be considered but does not by itself establish the declarant's authority under (C); the existence or scope of the relationship under (D); or the existence of the conspiracy or participation in it under (E). (Amended by order adopted October 16, 1975, effective October 31, 1975, and by order adopted March 2, 1987, effective October 1, 1987, by order adopted April 11, 1997, effective December 1, 1997, and by order adopted April 26, 2011, effective December 1, 2011.)

Comment. — The language of Rule 801 has been amended as part of the general restyling of the Evidence Rules to make them more easily understood and to make style and terminology consistent throughout the rules. These changes are intended to be stylistic only. There is no intent to change any result in any ruling on evidence admissibility.

Statements falling under the hearsay exclusion provided by Rule 801(d)(2) are no longer referred to as "admissions" in the title to the subdivision. The term "admissions" is confusing because not all statements covered by the exclusion are admissions in the colloquial sense — a statement can be within the exclusion even if it "admitted" nothing and was not against the party's interest when made. The term "admissions" also raises confusion in comparison with the Rule 804(b)(3) exception for declarations against interest. No change in application of the exclusion is intended.

Law Review. — For note, "Impeachment with an Unsworn Prior Inconsistent Statement as Subterfuge," see 28 Wm. & Mary L. Rev. 295 (1987). For note, "Impeachment with an Unsworn Prior Inconsistent Statement as Subterfuge," see 28 Wm. & Mary L. Rev. 295 (1987). For casenote, "Clinging to History: The Supreme Court (Mis)interprets Federal Rule of Evidence 801(d)(1)(B) as Containing a Temporal Requirement," see 29 U. Rich. L. Rev. 459 (1995). For an article, "Evidence Myopia: The Failure To See the Federal Rules of Evidence As a Codification of the Common Law," see 40 Wm. & Mary L. Rev. 1539 (1999). For a review of criminal law in Virginia for year 1999, see 33 U. Rich. L. Rev. 857 (1999). For a note, "Toward a Level Playing Field: Challenges to Accomplice Testimony in the Wake of United States v. Singleton," see 57 Wash. & Lee L. Rev. 515 (2000).

CASE NOTES

Grand jury proceeding is an "other proceeding" within subdivision (d)(1)(A). United States v. Murphy, 696 F.2d 282 (4th Cir. 1982), cert. denied, 461 U.S. 945, 103 S. Ct. 2123, 2124, 77 L. Ed. 2d 1303 (1983).

Admissibility of employees' statements. — Where employees could only have acquired certain knowledge in the scope of their employment and that, therefore, their statements might, upon establishment of a sufficient foundation by plaintiff, be admissible under this rule as admissions by a party-opponent. Tucker v. Norfolk & W. Ry., 849 F. Supp. 1096 (E.D. Va. 1994).

Employee's admission may bind employer. — As long as the statement concerns a matter within the scope of the employee's agency or employment, virtually any employee may conceivably make admissions binding on his or her employer. Tucker v. Norfolk & W. Ry., 849 F. Supp. 1096 (E.D. Va. 1994).

Independent evidence establishing the existence of the agency must be adduced, but specific authorization to speak need not be shown, in order to establish an admission under subdivision (d)(2). United States v. Portsmouth Paving Corp., 694 F.2d 312 (4th Cir. 1982).

Standard of proof of conspiracy under subdivision (d)(2)(E). — The hearsay "exception" in subdivision (d)(2)(E) applies only if a fair preponderance of independent evidence establishes the existence of and the defendants' participation in the conspiracy. United States v. Portsmouth Paving Corp., 694 F.2d 312 (4th Cir. 1982).

There must be independent evidence of the accused's participation in and the conspiracy itself to permit admission into evidence against him of declarations made by coconspirators. Without independent evidence, the conspiracy exception of Rule 801(d)(2)(E) Fed.R.Evid. is not applicable. United States v. McCormick, 565 F.2d 286 (4th Cir. 1977), cert. denied, 434 U.S. 1021, 98 S. Ct. 747, 54 L. Ed. 2d 769 (1978).

There need not be a conspiracy count in the indictment to make co-conspirator's statements admissible pursuant to subdivision (d)(2)(E). The admissibility of such statements, however, turns on the existence of substantial evidence of the conspiracy other than the statements themselves. United States v. Zandi, 769 F.2d 229 (4th Cir. 1985).

Statements of coconspirators prior to proof of conspiracy admitted in court's discretion. — A district court may, in its discretion, admit the statements of coconspirators prior to proof of the conspiracy, since the judge may, in his discretion, permit the introduction of evidence as to things said and done by an alleged coconspirator subject to being connected up and followed by evidence of the existence of the conspiracy. United States v. McCormick, 565 F.2d 286 (4th Cir. 1977), cert. denied, 434 U.S. 1021, 98 S. Ct. 747, 54 L. Ed. 2d 769 (1978).

Deposition taken in previous trial covering same subject matter held admissible. — Where in a proceeding concerning dischargeability of debt, the defendant's deposition taken in the course of pretrial discovery in a previous trial covering the same subject matter was admitted into evidence, although the deposition was hearsay, it was relevant to the case and admissible under subsection (d)(1) and (d)(2)(a) of this rule. Telstad v. Kelley, 442 F. Supp. 525 (E.D. Va. 1978).

Witness' testimony, not merely statements of out-of-court declarant, provided evidence of the conspiracy. — See United States v. Truong Dinh Hung, 629 F.2d 908 (4th Cir. 1980), cert. denied, 454 U.S. 1144, 102 S. Ct. 1004, 71 L. Ed. 2d 296 (1982).

Communication with defendant's employees. — Plaintiff's counsel is prohibited from engaging in ex parte communication with defendant's current employees once the action has commenced. Tucker v. Norfolk & W. Ry., 849 F. Supp. 1096 (E.D. Va. 1994).

Although counsel may elicit no new information ex parte, he will be permitted to meet with those employees interviewed before the instant action was filed for the limited purpose of clarifying their prior statements and ascertaining their accuracy. Tucker v. Norfolk & W. Ry., 849 F. Supp. 1096 (E.D. Va. 1994).

Hearsay improperly allowed. — Trial court erred in allowing a detective's hearsay statements concerning a stolen or missing automatic pistol, as the evidence was not offered merely to show how the content of a crime database furthered the investigation of the crime, but was offered, at least in part, to establish that defendant had access to the automatic pistol. Andrews v. Commonwealth, 280 Va. 231, 699 S.E.2d 237, 2010 Va. LEXIS 239 (2010), cert. denied, 131 S. Ct. 2999, 2011 U.S. LEXIS 4469, 180 L. Ed. 2d 827 (U.S. 2011).

Statements held hearsay. — Trial court erred in admitting a police officer's testimony as to the locations a confidential informant (CI) transmitted over an audio transmitter for purposes of establishing that the locations of defendant's drug transactions were within 1,000 feet of a school as the statements were out-of-court statements made by the CI to prove the truth of the CI's assertions as to the locations of the drug transactions; the statements were not excited utterances as the statements were not spontaneous, but were reasoned compliance with prior arrangements between the CI and the police. Johnson v. Commonwealth, 2006 Va. App. LEXIS 83 (Mar. 7, 2006).

Statements not hearsay. — The statements "Get the money, get the drugs" and "Oops, we're in the wrong house" were admissible as non hearsay because they were not offered to prove the truth of the matters asserted but rather to exemplify their purpose, i.e., robbery. Paxton v. Commonwealth, No. 3063-01-2, 2002 Va. App. LEXIS 785 (Ct. of Appeals Dec. 31, 2002).

Trial court misapplied the hearsay rule in a way that prevented a mother from demonstrating, through the statement of a third party, that her actions were reasonable reactions to what other people told her because the mother was not offering a doctor's statement for the truth of the matter asserted by the doctor but was offering the statement as evidence that the doctor made a statement that prompted the mother's actions, i.e., to explain why the mother did what she did; thus, the doctor's statement was not hearsay and should have been allowed into evidence. Anonymous C v. Anonymous B, No. 2232-09-2, 2011 Va. App. LEXIS 14 (Ct. of Appeals Jan. 11, 2011).

Limiting instructions on hearsay held insufficient. — With the government setting up the background, through hearsay that the defendant stole certain merchandise and only thereafter calling witnesses whose testimony tended to show that the defendant in fact stole the merchandise, the limiting instructions of the trial court were insufficient to dispel the resulting prejudice from the initial introduction of needless hearsay evidence on four separate occasions to prove that the defendant stole the merchandise. United States v. Brown, 767 F.2d 1078 (4th Cir. 1985).

Evidence properly admitted as relevant. — Note found in defendant's jail cell was properly admitted as both material and relevant to whether he was faking symptoms of insanity. Pahno v. Commonwealth, 2008 Va. App. LEXIS 199 (Apr. 22, 2008).

Applied in United States v. Murphy, 696 F.2d 282 (4th Cir. 1982); United States v. Basic Constr. Co., 711 F.2d 570 (4th Cir. 1983); United States v. Arrington, 719 F.2d 701 (4th Cir. 1983); United States v. Lisotto, 722 F.2d 85 (4th Cir. 1983); United States v. Smith, 592 F. Supp. 424 (E.D. Va. 1984); Corrigan v. United States, 609 F. Supp. 720 (E.D. Va. 1985); Yohay v. City of Alexandria Employees Credit Union, Inc., 827 F.2d 967 (4th Cir. 1987); United States v. Stapleton, 730 F. Supp. 1375 (W.D. Va. 1990); EEOC v. Watergate at Landmark Condominium, 24 F.3d 635 (4th Cir. 1994); United States v. Ellis, 121 F.3d 908 (W.D. Va. 1997).

Rule 802. The Rule Against Hearsay.

Hearsay is not admissible unless any of the following provides otherwise:

- a federal statute;
- these rules; or
- other rules prescribed by the Supreme Court. (Amended by order adopted April 26, 2011, effective December 1, 2011.)

Comment. — The language of Rule 802 has been amended as part of the restyling of the Evidence Rules to make them more easily understood and to make style and terminology consistent throughout the rules. These changes are intended to be stylistic only. There is no intent to change any result in any ruling on evidence admissibility.

Law Review. — For essay, "Constitutional Hearsay: Requiring Foundation Testing and Corroboration Under the Confrontation Clause," see 81 Va. L. Rev. 149 (1995).

CASE NOTES

Applied in Environmental Defense Fund, Inc. v. Lamphier, 714 F.2d 331 (4th Cir. 1983); United States v. Brown, 767 F.2d 1078 (4th Cir. 1985); United States v. Hall, 989 F.2d 711 (4th Cir. 1993).

Rule 803. Exceptions to the Rule Against Hearsay — Regardless of Whether the Declarant Is Available as a Witness.

The following are not excluded by the rule against hearsay, regardless of whether the declarant is available as a witness:

(1) Present Sense Impression. — A statement describing or explaining an event or condition, made while or immediately after the declarant perceived it.

(2) Excited Utterance. — A statement relating to a startling event or condition, made while the declarant was under the stress of excitement that it caused.

(3) Then-Existing Mental, Emotional, or Physical Condition. — A statement of the declarant's then-existing state of mind (such as motive, intent, or plan) or emotional, sensory, or physical condition (such as mental feeling, pain, or bodily health), but not including a statement of memory or belief to prove the fact remembered or believed unless it relates to the validity or terms of the declarant's will.

(4) Statement Made for Medical Diagnosis or Treatment. — A statement that:

(A) is made for — and is reasonably pertinent to — medical diagnosis or treatment; and

(B) describes medical history; past or present symptoms or sensations; their inception; or their general cause.

(5) Recorded Recollection. — A record that:

(A) is on a matter the witness once knew about but now cannot recall well enough to testify fully and accurately;

(B) was made or adopted by the witness when the matter was fresh in the witness's memory; and

(C) accurately reflects the witness's knowledge.

If admitted, the record may be read into evidence but may be received as an exhibit only if offered by an adverse party.

(6) Records of a Regularly Conducted Activity. — A record of an act, event, condition, opinion, or diagnosis if:

(A) the record was made at or near the time by — or from information transmitted by — someone with knowledge;

(B) the record was kept in the course of a regularly conducted activity of a business, organization, occupation, or calling, whether or not for profit;

(C) making the record was a regular practice of that activity;

(D) all these conditions are shown by the testimony of the custodian or another qualified witness, or by a certification that complies with Rule 902(11) or (12) or with a statute permitting certification; and

(E) neither the source of information nor the method or circumstances of preparation indicate a lack of trustworthiness.

(7) Absence of a Record of a Regularly Conducted Activity. — Evidence that a matter is not included in a record described in paragraph (6) if:

(A) the evidence is admitted to prove that the matter did not occur or exist;

(B) a record was regularly kept for a matter of that kind; and

(C) neither the possible source of the information nor other circumstances indicate a lack of trustworthiness.

(8) Public Records. — A record or statement of a public office if:

(A) it sets out:

(i) the office's activities;

(ii) a matter observed while under a legal duty to report, but not including, in a criminal case, a matter observed by lawenforcement personnel; or

(iii) in a civil case or against the government in a criminal case, factual findings from a legally authorized investigation; and

(B) neither the source of information nor other circumstances indicate a lack of trustworthiness.

(9) Public Records of Vital Statistics. — A record of a birth, death, or marriage, if reported to a public office in accordance with a legal duty.

(10) Absence of a Public Record. — Testimony — or a certification under Rule 902 — that a diligent search failed to disclose a public record or statement if:

(A) the testimony or certification is admitted to prove that

(i) the record or statement does not exist; or

(ii) a matter did not occur or exist, if a public office regularly kept a record or statement for a matter of that kind; and

(B) in a criminal case, a prosecutor who intends to offer a certification provides written notice of that intent at least 14 days before trial, and the defendant does not object in writing within 7 days of receiving the notice — unless the court sets a different time for the notice or the objection.

(11) Records of Religious Organizations Concerning Personal or Family History. — A statement of birth, legitimacy, ancestry, marriage, divorce, death, relationship by blood or marriage, or similar facts of personal or family history, contained in a regularly kept record of a religious organization.

(12) Certificates of Marriage, Baptism, and Similar Ceremonies. — A statement of fact contained in a certificate:

(A) made by a person who is authorized by a religious organization or by law to perform the act certified;

(B) attesting that the person performed a marriage or similar ceremony or administered a sacrament; and

(C) purporting to have been issued at the time of the act or within a reasonable time after it.

(13) Family Records. — A statement of fact about personal or family history contained in a family record, such as a Bible, genealogy, chart, engraving on a ring, inscription on a portrait, or engraving on an urn or burial marker.

(14) Records of Documents That Affect an Interest in Property. — The record of a document that purports to establish or affect an interest in property if:

(A) the record is admitted to prove the content of the original recorded document, along with its signing and its delivery by each person who purports to have signed it;

(B) the record is kept in a public office; and

(C) a statute authorizes recording documents of that kind in that office.

(15) Statements in Documents That Affect an Interest in Property. — A statement contained in a document that purports to establish or affect an interest in property if the matter stated was relevant to the document's purpose — unless later dealings with the property are inconsistent with the truth of the statement or the purport of the document.

(16) Statements in Ancient Documents. — A statement in a document that is at least 20 years old and whose authenticity is established.

(17) Market Reports and Similar Commercial Publications. — Market quotations, lists, directories, or other compilations that are generally relied on by the public or by persons in particular occupations.

(18) Statements in Learned Treatises, Periodicals, or Pamphlets. — A statement contained in a treatise, periodical, or pamphlet if:

(A) the statement is called to the attention of an expert witness on cross-examination or relied on by the expert on direct examination; and

(B) the publication is established as a reliable authority by the expert's admission or testimony, by another expert's testimony, or by judicial notice.

If admitted, the statement may be read into evidence but not received as an exhibit.

(19) Reputation Concerning Personal or Family History. — A reputation among a person's family by blood, adoption, or marriage — or among a person's associates or in the community — concerning the person's birth, adoption, legitimacy, ancestry, marriage, divorce, death, relationship by blood, adoption, or marriage, or similar facts of personal or family history.

(20) Reputation Concerning Boundaries or General History. — A reputation in a community — arising before the controversy — concerning boundaries of land in the community or customs that affect the land, or concerning general historical events important to that community, state, or nation.

(21) Reputation Concerning Character. — A reputation among a person's associates or in the community concerning the person's character.

(22) Judgment of a Previous Conviction. — Evidence of a final judgment of conviction if:

(A) the judgment was entered after a trial or guilty plea, but not a nolo contendere plea;

(B) the conviction was for a crime punishable by death or by imprisonment for more than a year;

(C) the evidence is admitted to prove any fact essential to the judgment; and

(D) when offered by the prosecutor in a criminal case for a purpose other than impeachment, the judgment was against the defendant.

The pendency of an appeal may be shown but does not affect admissibility.

(23) Judgments Involving Personal, Family, or General History, or a Boundary. — A judgment that is admitted to prove a matter of personal, family, or general history, or boundaries, if the matter:

(A) was essential to the judgment; and
(B) could be proved by evidence of reputation.
(24) [Other Exceptions]. — [Transferred to Rule 807.] (Amended by order adopted December 12, 1975, by order adopted March 2, 1987, effective October 1, 1987, by order adopted April 11, 1997, effective December 1, 1997, by order adopted April 17, 2000, effective December 1, 2000, by order adopted April 26, 2011, effective December 1, 2011, and by order adopted April 16, 2013, effective December 1, 2013.)

Comment. — The language of Rule 803 has been amended as part of the restyling of the Evidence Rules to make them more easily understood and to make style and terminology consistent throughout the rules. These changes are intended to be stylistic only. There is no intent to change any result in any ruling on evidence admissibility.

Law Review. — For essay, "Constitutional Hearsay: Requiring Foundation Testing and Corroboration Under the Confrontation Clause," see 81 Va. L. Rev. 149 (1995). For symposium, "The Restyled Federal Rules of Evidence," see 53 Wm and Mary L. Rev. 1435 (2012).

CASE NOTES

"Excited utterance." — Admission of the mother's testimony regarding statements that the seven-year-old victim made immediately after the aggravated sexual battery occurred was proper, because the trustworthiness of statements stemmed from their proximity to the startling event and the victim's age; that the mother had to calm the victim down for two or three minutes to understand the victim did not negate the applicability of the excited utterance exception to the hearsay rule. Gaytan v. Commonwealth, 2009 Va. App. LEXIS 255 (June 9, 2009).

911 call. — Admission of a 911 tape recording violated defendant's rights under U.S. Const., Amend. VI, because the tape recording of the 911 call was testimonial within the meaning of the Confrontation Clause as the speaker was not facing an ongoing emergency, but was instead merely providing a narrative report of a larceny in progress. Wilder v. Commonwealth, 55 Va. App. 579, 687 S.E.2d 542, 2010 Va. App. LEXIS 24 (2010).

Although it was true that no witnesses were called to prove that a psychiatric patient had killed a young girl, the parties stipulated that he had been convicted of the murder, and his confession was admitted into evidence without objection. In accordance with the modern view, the court was free to assign this evidence the weight it saw fit. Semler v. Psychiatric Inst., 538 F.2d 121 (4th Cir.), cert. denied, 429 U.S. 827, 97 S. Ct. 83, 50 L. Ed. 2d 90 (1976).

State of mind exception. — Statement made by the testifying witness that the declarant was going to buy marijuana from defendant was not hearsay because it was not offered to prove the truth of the matter asserted. The statement explained why the witness and the declarant went to defendant's residence, which was the scene of the shooting. If the declarant's statement was offered to prove that he intended to buy marijuana from defendant, it was hearsay, but admissible under the state of mind exception. Conaway v. Commonwealth, 2005 Va. App. LEXIS 46 (Feb. 1, 2005).

Victim's statement to a cousin was not admissible under the state-of-mind exception; the Commonwealth's contention that it could be inferred that defendant knew of the victim's intent to testify against defendant was speculative and thus, insufficient to show motive. Hodges v. Commonwealth, 272 Va. 418, 634 S.E.2d 680, 2006 Va. LEXIS 82 (2006).

Based on the overwhelming evidence of defendant's guilt, including testimony from an expert, a police detective, and defendant himself, the latter of which demonstrated a motive and intent to kill, the trial court's admission of alleged hearsay testimony under the "state of mind" exception to the hearsay rule was harmless error. West v. Commonwealth, 2008 Va. App. LEXIS 193 (Apr. 22, 2008).

A memorandum may be used as evidence only if the witness either made or adopted the memorandum with the knowledge that the facts contained therein are accurate. It has been held error to admit a statement pursuant to subdivision (5) where there had been no showing of the witness' insufficient recollection. United States Elevator Corp. v. 1616 Reminc Ltd. Partnership, 9 Bankr. 679 (Bankr. E.D. Va. 1981).

Rule 612 governs the manner in which writings may be used to refresh the recollection of a witness while he is giving testimony. It is clear that the witness' recollection must be revived after the writing is presented to him as a stimulus so that his testimony properly constitutes a present recollection. If the writing fails to revive his recollection, the writing may be read into evidence and admitted, but only if it meets the test of recorded recollection set forth in subdivision (5) of this rule. "The line between using the writing as an aid to memory and basing one's testimony upon it as a correct record of past memory is sometimes shadowy." United States Elevator Corp. v. 1616 Reminc Ltd. Partnership, 9 Bankr. 679 (Bankr. E.D. Va. 1981).

Factors that may be used to determine admissibility of a report under subdivision (8)(C) include: (1) The timeliness of the investigation; (2) the special skill or experience of the official; and (3) possible motivation problems. Ellis v. International Playtex, Inc., 745 F.2d 292 (4th Cir. 1984).

Burden is on party opposing admission of a report under subdivision (8)(C) to demonstrate that the report is not reliable. Ellis v. International Playtex, Inc., 745 F.2d 292 (4th Cir. 1984).

Scientific reports should not be treated any differently from other public findings of fact under a subdivision (8)(C) analysis. Ellis v. International Playtex, Inc., 745 F.2d 292 (4th Cir. 1984).

Under subdivision (8)(C), data need not be published to be admitted. — The rule refers to findings "in any form." Ellis v. International Playtex, Inc., 745 F.2d 292 (4th Cir. 1984).

Availability to testify as to methodology of report not alone grounds to exclude it. — Whether the declarant or the investigator was available to testify about the methodology of a report sought to be admitted under subdivision (8)(C) or whether the report stated its methodology, are not by themselves, reasons to exclude the study. Ellis v. International Playtex, Inc., 745 F.2d 292 (4th Cir. 1984).

Admissibility of "evaluative" reports. — Although there has been some disagreement over whether "evaluative" public records or reports were intended by Congress to be considered "factual findings" for the purposes of subdivision (8)(C), it is well established that the phrase should be interpreted broadly. Thus, the fact that studies contain tentative conclusions as well as statistical findings does not affect the applicability of the rule. Ellis v. International Playtex, Inc., 745 F.2d 292 (4th Cir. 1984).

Methodology affects weight, not admissibility. — Concern about the methodology of scientific studies should have been addressed to the relative weight accorded the evidence and not its admissibility. This position is consistent with the rationale behind the subdivision (8)(C) exception. Although the rule is designed to assume the admissibility of a report in the absence of affirmative indicia of untrustworthiness, there is no indication that Congress intended for the reports to escape searching examination. Allowing the jury to evaluate the reports after careful cross-examination and the presentation of expert testimony, therefore, serves both of these functions well; it permits admission without sacrificing scrutiny. Ellis v. International Playtex, Inc., 745 F.2d 292 (4th Cir. 1984).

Evidence under subdivision (8)(C) presumed to reflect accepted methodology. — Until recently, most courts followed the rule in Frye v. United States, 293 F. 1019 (D.C. Cir. 1923), which required the trial judge to determine the admissibility of scientific data based on whether the techniques used were generally accepted by the relevant scientific community. In recent years, however, the Frye rule has come under increasing attack because of the importance it places on the judge's subjective ability to "count heads" among experts in the scientific community. Evidence that falls within the subdivision (8)(C) exception, however, has already met the Frye standard and may be presumed to reflect methodologies accepted by the scientific community. Application of the federal rule, therefore, avoids the need to "count heads" and encourages increased examination of evidence by the jury in a manner not inconsistent with the rationale behind Frye. Ellis v. International Playtex, Inc., 745 F.2d 292 (4th Cir. 1984).

Proceeding before administrative law judge qualified as an investigation under subsection (8) of this rule. Zeus Enters., Inc. v. Alphin Aircraft, Inc., 190 F.3d 238 (4th Cir. 1999).

"Open" and "blind" inspection reports prepared by companies who conducted them held admissible. — See American Int'l Pictures, Inc. v. Price Enters., Inc., 636 F.2d 933 (4th Cir. 1980), cert. denied, 451 U.S. 1010, 101 S. Ct. 2347, 68 L. Ed. 2d 863 (1981).

Accident reports of National Transportation Safety Board. — While subdivision (8) of this rule suggests that, as a general matter, public reports, including evaluative sections, are admissible evidence, 49 U.S.C., § 1441(e) explicitly states that no part of any accident report of the National Transportation Safety Board shall be admitted as evidence in any action for damages, so that at the least, § 1441(e) forbids the use of conclusory sections of NTSB reports. Travelers Ins. Co. v. Riggs, 671 F.2d 810 (4th Cir. 1982).

Bank records. — Bank manager was a proper custodian for purposes of introducing bank records into evidence under the business records exception to the hearsay rule. Her testimony revealed that she had personal knowledge concerning how the bank's records were created, stored, and maintained as a regular course of business; in addition, the manager was familiar with the records, having reviewed them before testifying. Neofotis v. Commonwealth, 2006 Va. App. LEXIS 406 (Aug. 29, 2006).

Summary of records by federal reserve bank assistant at request of customs agent. — Summary of records prepared by a federal reserve bank staff assistant at the request of a customs agent was prepared pursuant to a legal duty and was admissible in a criminal prosecution for perjury. United States v. Dudley, 941 F.2d 260 (4th Cir. 1991), cert. denied, 502 U.S. 1046, 112 S. Ct. 908, 116 L. Ed. 2d 809 (1992).

Letters admissible under business records exception. — In an action determining rights in certain real property between an LLC and the decedent's alleged widow, five letters exchanged between the decedent and the holder of the deed of trust on the property were admissible under the business records exception to the hearsay rule, as testimony from the decedent's attorney in fact, who was also his daughter, established sufficient foundation for the admission of same because: (1) she had been the custodian of her father's business records since his stroke; and (2) she had worked in her father's office for several years when he was alive, helped maintain the records there, and was familiar with the manner in which her father conducted his various businesses. 1924 Leonard Rd., L.L.C. v. Van Roekel, 272 Va. 543, 636 S.E.2d 378, 2006 Va. LEXIS 114 (2006).

Evidence properly excluded as hearsay. — Trial court properly excluded defendant's conversation he had with police on the way to the police station, despite defendant's claim that such should have been admitted to show his state of mind at the time of the murder, as such was inadmissible hearsay. Moreover, the trial court allowed the expert witnesses to testify about the statement, so any error that may have occurred was harmless. Pahno v. Commonwealth, 2008 Va. App. LEXIS 199 (Apr. 22, 2008).

Applied in United States v. Portsmouth Paving Corp., 694 F.2d 312 (4th Cir. 1982); United States v. Smith, 592 F. Supp. 424 (E.D. Va. 1984); United

States v. Farmer, 820 F. Supp. 259 (W.D. Va. 1993); United States Dep't of HUD v. Cost Control Mktg. & Sales Mgt. of Va., Inc., 64 F.3d 920 (4th Cir. 1995); Maksimuk v. Dalkon Shield Claimants Trust (In re A.H. Robins Co.), 223 Bankr. 492 (Bankr. E.D. Va. 1998).

Rule 804. Exceptions to the Rule Against Hearsay — When the Declarant Is Unavailable as a Witness.

(a) *Criteria for Being Unavailable.* — A declarant is considered to be unavailable as a witness if the declarant:

(1) is exempted from testifying about the subject matter of the declarant's statement because the court rules that a privilege applies;

(2) refuses to testify about the subject matter despite a court order to do so;

(3) testifies to not remembering the subject matter;

(4) cannot be present or testify at the trial or hearing because of death or a then-existing infirmity, physical illness, or mental illness; or

(5) is absent from the trial or hearing and the statement's proponent has not been able, by process or other reasonable means, to procure:

(A) the declarant's attendance, in the case of a hearsay exception under Rule 804(b)(1) or (6); or

(B) the declarant's attendance or testimony, in the case of a hearsay exception under Rule 804(b)(2), (3), or (4).

But this subdivision (a) does not apply if the statement's proponent procured or wrongfully caused the declarant's unavailability as a witness in order to prevent the declarant from attending or testifying.

(b) *The Exceptions.* — The following are not excluded by the rule against hearsay if the declarant is unavailable as a witness:

(1) Former Testimony. — Testimony that:

(A) was given as a witness at a trial, hearing, or lawful deposition, whether given during the current proceeding or a different one; and

(B) is now offered against a party who had — or, in a civil case, whose predecessor in interest had — an opportunity and similar motive to develop it by direct, cross-, or redirect examination.

(2) Statement Under the Belief of Imminent Death. — In a prosecution for homicide or in a civil case, a statement that the declarant, while believing the declarant's death to be imminent, made about its cause or circumstances.

(3) Statement Against Interest. — A statement that:

(A) a reasonable person in the declarant's position would have made only if the person believed it to be true because, when made, it was so contrary to the declarant's proprietary or pecuniary interest or had so great a tendency to invalidate the declarant's claim against someone else or to expose the declarant to civil or criminal liability; and

(B) is supported by corroborating circumstances that clearly indicate its trustworthiness, if it is offered in a criminal case as one that tends to expose the declarant to criminal liability.

(4) Statement of Personal or Family History. — A statement about:

(A) the declarant's own birth, adoption, legitimacy, ancestry, marriage, divorce, relationship by blood, adoption, or marriage, or similar facts of personal or family history, even though the declarant had no way of acquiring personal knowledge about that fact; or

(B) another person concerning any of these facts, as well as death, if the declarant was related to the person by blood, adoption, or marriage or was so intimately associated with the person's family that the declarant's information is likely to be accurate.

(5) [Other Exceptions.] [Transferred to Rule 807.] —

(6) Statement Offered Against a Party That Wrongfully Caused the Declarant's Unavailability. — A statement offered against a party that wrongfully caused — or acquiesced in wrongfully causing — the declarant's unavailability as a witness, and did so intending that result. (Amended by order adopted December 12, 1975, by order adopted March 2, 1987, effective October 1, 1987, by P.L. 100-690, § 7075, effective November 18, 1988, by order adopted April 11, 1997, effective December 1, 1997, by order adopted April 28, 2010, effective December 1, 2010, and by order adopted April 26, 2011, effective December 1, 2011.)

Comment. — The language of Rule 804 has been amended as part of the general restyling of the Evidence Rules to make them more easily understood and to make style and terminology consistent throughout the rules. These changes are intended to be stylistic only. There is no intent to change any result in any ruling on evidence admissibility.

No style changes were made to Rule 804(b)(3), because it was already restyled in conjunction with a substantive amendment, effective December 1, 2010.

Editor's note. — While the following cases were not decided in Virginia, they may prove useful in interpreting this rule: United States v. Brainard, 690 F.2d 1117 (4th Cir. 1982), cert. denied, 471 U.S. 1099, 105 S. Ct. 2320, 85 L. Ed. 2d 839 (1985); United States v. McDonald, 688 F.2d 224 (4th Cir. 1982), cert. denied, 459 U.S. 1103, 103 S. Ct. 726, 74 L. Ed. 2d 951 (1983); United States v. Evans, 635 F.2d 1124 (4th Cir. 1980), cert. denied, 452 U.S. 943, 101 S. Ct. 3090, 69 L. Ed. 2d 958 (1981); Lowery v. Maryland, 401 F. Supp. 604 (D. Md. 1975), aff'd, 532 F.2d 750 (4th Cir.), cert. denied, 429 U.S. 919, 97 S. Ct. 312, 50 L. Ed. 2d 285 (1976).

Law Review. — For essay, "Constitutional Hearsay: Requiring Foundation Testing and Corroboration Under the Confrontation Clause," see 81 Va. L. Rev. 149 (1995). For a note, "Toward a Level Playing Field: Challenges to Accomplice Testimony in the Wake of United States v. Singleton," see 57 Wash. & Lee L. Rev. 515 (2000). For symposium, "The Restyled Federal Rules of Evidence," see 53 Wm and Mary L. Rev. 1435 (2012).

CASE NOTES

Under subdivision (b)(1), either the party against whom the testimony is offered or a predecessor in interest must have had the opportunity and similar motive to develop the testimony by direct or cross-examination. Hewitt v. Hutter, 432 F. Supp. 795 (W.D. Va. 1977), aff'd, 568 F.2d 773 (4th Cir.), 574 F.2d 182 (4th Cir. 1978).

Under subdivision (b)(3) there are three prerequisites to admission of a hearsay statement: (1) the declarant must be unavailable; (2) from the perspective of the average, reasonable person, the statement must be truly adverse to the declarant's penal interest; and (3) corroborating circumstances must clearly establish the trustworthiness of the statement. United States v. Carvalho, 742 F.2d 146 (4th Cir. 1984).

Unavailability not shown. — The government could not introduce hearsay statements of absent declarants pursuant to subsection (b)(3) since the declarants could not be said to be unavailable where the state investigator who heard the statements made no effort to obtain the declarants' names or contact information. United States v. Wrenn, 170 F. Supp. 2d 604, 2001 U.S. Dist. LEXIS 18353 (E.D. Va. 2001).

Nonself-inculpatory statements. — The Supreme Court of Virginia's rationale in Chandler v. Commonwealth, 249 Va. 270, 455 S.E.2d 219 (1995), does not permit the Virginia Court of Appeals to apply in Virginia the rule announced in Williamson v. United States, — U.S. —, 114 S. Ct. 2431 (1994), that nonself-inculpatory statements are unreliable and should not be treated any differently from other hearsay statements that are generally excluded. Fries v. Commonwealth, No. 0837-94-4, (Ct. of Appeals June 6, 1995).

Adoptive admission. — There was no error in admitting a statement by defendant's accomplice, which implicated the two of them in a crime, under the adoptive admission exception to the hearsay rule. Defendant, who was outside the house when the accomplice began to tell a third party what they had done, came into the house and up the stairs, asking why the accomplice had told the other person what they had done; defendant obviously had heard enough of the statement to have understood it, and his conduct and his own question demonstrated that the statement of the accomplice was properly admitted against defendant. Lynch v. Commonwealth, 272 Va. 204, 630 S.E.2d 482, 2006 Va. LEXIS 68 (2006).

It was not error to allow the Commonwealth of Virginia to introduce into evidence the statement that defendant's accomplice made, which implicated them in a crime; the statement was properly admitted as an adoptive admission exception under the proper burden of proof. The Commonwealth satisfied its burden of proof, which was by a preponderance of the evidence, in order to show that the exception applied; the Commonwealth showed by a preponderance of the evidence, rather than by clear and convincing evidence, that the hearsay exemption applied. Lynch v. Commonwealth, 272 Va. 204, 630 S.E.2d 482, 2006 Va. LEXIS 68 (2006).

Penal interest. — Even when an accomplice incriminates himself, statements that shift or spread blame to a criminal defendant are not within a "firmly rooted exception" to the hearsay rule as that concept has been defined in Sixth Amendment jurisprudence. Lilly v. Virginia, 527 U.S. 116, 119 S. Ct. 1887, 144 L. Ed. 2d 117 (1999).

Statement of reasons for entering marriage. — While undoubtedly it is correct that for some purposes a statement regarding one's reasons for entering a marriage might well be a "statement concerning" one's marriage, it is also clear that evidence as to motive or purpose, highly debatable or controversial matters, is simply not within the scope of subdivision (b)(4). United States v. Carvalho, 742 F.2d 146 (4th Cir. 1984).

Applied in United States v. Murphy, 696 F.2d 282 (4th Cir. 1982); Corrigan v. United States, 609 F. Supp. 720 (E.D. Va. 1985); Maksimuk v. Dalkon Shield Claimants Trust (In re A.H. Robins Co.), 223 Bankr. 492 (Bankr. E.D. Va. 1998).

Rule 805. Hearsay Within Hearsay.

Hearsay within hearsay is not excluded by the rule against hearsay if each part of the combined statements conforms with an exception to the rule. (Amended by order adopted April 26, 2011, effective December 1, 2011.)

Comment. — The language of Rule 805 has been amended as part of the restyling of the Evidence Rules to make them more easily understood and to make style and terminology consistent throughout the rules. These changes are intended to be stylistic only. There is no intent to change any result in any ruling on evidence admissibility.

CASE NOTES

Applied in Yohay v. City of Alexandria Employees Credit Union, Inc., 827 F.2d 967 (4th Cir. 1987).

Rule 806. Attacking and Supporting the Declarant's Credibility.

When a hearsay statement — or a statement described in Rule 801(d)(2)(C), (D), or (E) — has been admitted in evidence, the declarant's credibility may be attacked, and then supported, by any evidence that would be admissible for those purposes if the declarant had testified as a witness. The court may admit evidence of the declarant's inconsistent statement or conduct, regardless of when it occurred or whether the declarant had an opportunity to explain or deny it. If the party against whom the statement was admitted calls the declarant as a witness, the party may examine the declarant on the statement as if on cross-examination. (Amended by order adopted March 2, 1987, effective October 1, 1987; by order adopted April 11, 1997, effective December 1, 1997, and by order adopted April 26, 2011, effective December 1, 2011.)

Comment. — The language of Rule 806 has been amended as part of the restyling of the Evidence Rules to make them more easily understood and to make style and terminology consistent throughout the rules. These changes are intended to be stylistic only. There is no intent to change any result in any ruling on evidence admissibility.

Law Review. — For symposium, "The Restyled Federal Rules of Evidence," see 53 Wm and Mary L. Rev. 1435 (2012).

Rule 807. Residual exception.

(a) *In General.* — Under the following circumstances, a hearsay statement is not excluded by the rule against hearsay even if the statement is not specifically covered by a hearsay exception in Rule 803 or 804:

(1) the statement has equivalent circumstantial guarantees of trustworthiness;

(2) it is offered as evidence of a material fact;

(3) it is more probative on the point for which it is offered than any other evidence that the proponent can obtain through reasonable efforts; and

(4) admitting it will best serve the purposes of these rules and the interests of justice.

(b) *Notice.* — The statement is admissible only if, before the trial or hearing, the proponent gives an adverse party reasonable notice of the intent to offer the statement and its particulars, including the declarant's name and address, so that the party has a fair opportunity to meet it. (Added April 11, 1997, effective December 1, 1997, and amended by order adopted April 26, 2011, effective December 1, 2011.)

Comment. — The language of Rule 807 has been amended as part of the restyling of the Evidence Rules to make them more easily understood and to make style and terminology consistent throughout the rules. These changes are intended to be stylistic only. There is no intent to change any result in any ruling on evidence admissibility.

CASE NOTES

Applied in Maksimuk v. Dalkon Shield Claimants Trust (In re A.H. Robins Co.), 223 Bankr. 492 (Bankr. E.D. Va. 1998).

IX. AUTHENTICATION AND IDENTIFICATION.

Rule 901. Authenticating or Identifying Evidence.

(a) *In General.* — To satisfy the requirement of authenticating or identifying an item of evidence, the proponent must produce evidence sufficient to support a finding that the item is what the proponent claims it is.

(b) *Examples.* — The following are examples only — not a complete list — of evidence that satisfies the requirement:

(1) *Testimony of a Witness With Knowledge.* Testimony that an item is what it is claimed to be.

(2) *Nonexpert Opinion About Handwriting.* A nonexpert's opinion that handwriting is genuine, based on a familiarity with it that was not acquired for the current litigation.

(3) *Comparison by an Expert Witness or the Trier of Fact.* A comparison with an authenticated specimen by an expert witness or the trier of fact.

(4) *Distinctive Characteristics and the Like.* The appearance, contents, substance, internal patterns, or other distinctive characteristics of the item, taken together with all the circumstances.

(5) *Opinion About a Voice.* An opinion identifying a person's voice — whether heard firsthand or through mechanical or electronic transmission or recording — based on hearing the voice at any time under circumstances that connect it with the alleged speaker.

(6) *Evidence About a Telephone Conversation.* For a telephone conversation, evidence that a call was made to the number assigned at the time to:

(A) a particular person, if circumstances, including self-identification, show that the person answering was the one called; or

(B) a particular business, if the call was made to a business and the call related to business reasonably transacted over the telephone.

(7) *Evidence About Public Records.* Evidence that:

(A) a document was recorded or filed in a public office as authorized by law; or

(B) a purported public record or statement is from the office where items of this kind are kept.

(8) *Evidence About Ancient Documents or Data Compilations.* For a document or data compilation, evidence that it:

(A) is in a condition that creates no suspicion about its authenticity;

(B) was in a place where, if authentic, it would likely be; and

(C) is at least 20 years old when offered.

(9) *Evidence About a Process or System.* Evidence describing a process or system and showing that it produces an accurate result.

(10) *Methods Provided by a Statute or Rule.* Any method of authentication or identification allowed by a federal statute or a rule prescribed by the Supreme Court.

(Amended by order adopted April 26, 2011, effective December 1, 2011.)

Comment. — The language of Rule 901 has been amended as part of the restyling of the Evidence Rules to make them more easily understood and to make style and terminology consistent throughout the rules. These changes are intended to be stylistic only. There is no intent to change any result in any ruling on evidence admissibility.

Law Review. — For article, "Voice Spectrography Evidence: Approaches to Admissibility," see 20 U. Rich. L. Rev. 357 (1986). For casenote & comment, "No Don't IM Me — Instant Messaging, Authentication, and the Best Evidence Rule," see 13 Geo. Mason L. Rev. 1309 (2006).

CASE NOTES

The "chain of custody" rule is but a variation of the principle that real evidence must be authenticated prior to its admission into evidence. The purpose of this threshold requirement is to establish that the item to be introduced is what it purports to be. United States v. Howard-Arias, 679 F.2d 363 (4th Cir.), cert. denied, 459 U.S. 874, 103 S. Ct. 165, 74 L. Ed. 2d 136 (1982).

The authentication requirement of this rule requires only that a party introducing evidence demonstrate that the evidence is in fact what its proponents claims, and the "chain of custody" rule is simply a variation of this principle; thus it requires that a prosecutor seeking to introduce seized evidence must establish a chain of custody from the time the items were taken to show that they are in "substantially the same condition as when they were seized." United States v. Turpin, 65 F.3d 1207 (4th Cir. 1995), cert. denied, 517 U.S. 1106, 116 S. Ct. 1324, 134 L. Ed. 2d 476 (1996).

The chain of custody is not an iron-clad requirement, and the fact of a missing link does not prevent the admission of real evidence, so long as there is sufficient proof that the evidence is what it purports to be and has not been altered in any material respect. United States v. Ricco, 52 F.3d 58 (4th Cir. 1995), cert. denied, 516 U.S. 898, 116 S. Ct. 254, 133 L. Ed. 2d 179 (1995).

The ultimate question is whether the authentication testimony was sufficiently complete so as to convince the court that it is improbable that the original item had been exchanged with another or otherwise tampered with. United States v. Howard-Arias, 679 F.2d 363 (4th Cir.), cert. denied, 459 U.S. 874, 103 S. Ct. 165, 74 L. Ed. 2d 136 (1982).

Precision in developing the "chain of custody" is not an iron-clad requirement, and the fact of a missing link does not prevent the admission of real evidence, so long as there is sufficient proof that the evidence is what it purports to be and has not been altered in any material aspect. Resolution of this question rests with the sound discretion of the trial judge, and the court cannot say that he abused that discretion in this case. United States v. Howard-Arias, 679 F.2d 363 (4th Cir.), cert. denied, 459 U.S. 874, 103 S. Ct. 165, 74 L. Ed. 2d 136 (1982).

Effect of Rule 902. — Rule 902 recognizes that the possibility of fraud, forgery and misattribution of certain documents is so slight that the general requirement of authentication by extrinsic evidence, provided by this rule, is dispensed with. United States v. Howard-Arias, 679 F.2d 363 (4th Cir.), cert. denied, 459 U.S. 874, 103 S. Ct. 165, 74 L. Ed. 2d 136 (1982).

Authenticity category of relevancy dependent upon fulfillment of condition of fact. — Federal Rule of Evidence 901 (a) requires for authentication "evidence sufficient to support a finding that the matter in question is what its proponent claims." Authenticity is in the category of relevancy dependent upon fulfillment of a condition of fact and is governed by the procedure set forth in Rule 104(b). Rule 104(b) provides that when relevancy depends upon fulfillment of a condition of fact, the court shall admit it upon, or subject to, the introduction of evidence sufficient to support a finding of the fulfillment of the condition. The judge should make "a preliminary determination" whether the foundation evidence is sufficient to support a finding of the fulfillment of the condition. If so, the item is admitted. If after all the evidence is in, pro and con, the jury could reasonably conclude the fulfillment of the condition is not established, the issue is for them. If the evidence is not such as to allow a finding, the judge withdraws the matter from their consideration. Trustees of C.I. Mtg. Group v. Cantrell, 557 F.2d 1039 (4th Cir. 1977).

Applied in United States v. Portsmouth Paving Corp., 694 F.2d 312 (4th Cir. 1982); Pasquotank Action Council, Inc. v. City of Va. Beach, 909 F. Supp. 376 (E.D. Va. 1995).

Rule 902. Evidence That Is Self-Authenticating.

The following items of evidence are self-authenticating; they require no extrinsic evidence of authenticity in order to be admitted:

(1) *Domestic Public Documents That Are Sealed and Signed.* A document that bears:

(A) a seal purporting to be that of the United States; any state, district, commonwealth, territory, or insular possession of the United States; the former Panama Canal Zone; the Trust Territory of the Pacific Islands; a political subdivision of any of these entities; or a department, agency, or officer of any entity named above; and

(B) a signature purporting to be an execution or attestation.

(2) *Domestic Public Documents That Are Not Sealed but Are Signed and Certified.* A document that bears no seal if:

(A) it bears the signature of an officer or employee of an entity named in Rule 902(1)(A); and

(B) another public officer who has a seal and official duties within that same entity certifies under seal — or its equivalent — that the signer has the official capacity and that the signature is genuine.

(3) *Foreign Public Documents.* A document that purports to be signed or attested by a person who is authorized by a foreign country's law to do so. The document must be accompanied by a final certification that certifies the genuineness of the signature and official position of the signer or attester — or of any foreign official whose certificate of genuineness relates to the signature or attestation or is in a chain of certificates of genuineness relating to the signature or attestation. The certification may be made by

a secretary of a United States embassy or legation; by a consul general, vice consul, or consular agent of the United States; or by a diplomatic or consular official of the foreign country assigned or accredited to the United States. If all parties have been given a reasonable opportunity to investigate the document's authenticity and accuracy, the court may, for good cause, either:

(A) order that it be treated as presumptively authentic without final certification; or

(B) allow it to be evidenced by an attested summary with or without final certification.

(4) *Certified Copies of Public Records.* A copy of an official record — or a copy of a document that was recorded or filed in a public office as authorized by law — if the copy is certified as correct by:

(A) the custodian or another person authorized to make the certification; or

(B) a certificate that complies with Rule 902(1), (2), or (3), a federal statute, or a rule prescribed by the Supreme Court.

(5) *Official Publications.* A book, pamphlet, or other publication purporting to be issued by a public authority.

(6) *Newspapers and Periodicals.* Printed material purporting to be a newspaper or periodical.

(7) *Trade Inscriptions and the Like.* An inscription, sign, tag, or label purporting to have been affixed in the course of business and indicating origin, ownership, or control.

(8) *Acknowledged Documents.* A document accompanied by a certificate of acknowledgment that is lawfully executed by a notary public or another officer who is authorized to take acknowledgments.

(9) *Commercial Paper and Related Documents.* Commercial paper, a signature on it, and related documents, to the extent allowed by general commercial law.

(10) *Presumptions Under a Federal Statute.* A signature, document, or anything else that a federal statute declares to be presumptively or prima facie genuine or authentic.

(11) *Certified Domestic Records of a Regularly Conducted Activity.* The original or a copy of a domestic record that meets the requirements of Rule 803(6)(A)-(C), as shown by a certification of the custodian or another qualified person that complies with a federal statute or a rule prescribed by the Supreme Court. Before the trial or hearing, the proponent must give an adverse party reasonable written notice of the intent to offer the record — and must make the record and certification available for inspection — so that the party has a fair opportunity to challenge them.

(12) *Certified Foreign Records of a Regularly Conducted Activity.* In a civil case, the original or a copy of a foreign record that meets the requirements of Rule 902(11), modified as follows: the certification, rather than complying with a federal statute or Supreme Court rule, must be signed in a manner that, if falsely made, would subject the maker to a criminal penalty in the country where the certification is signed. The proponent must also meet the notice requirements of Rule 902(11). (Amended by order adopted March 2, 1987, effective October 1, 1987, by order adopted April 25, 1988, effective November 1, 1988, by order adopted April 17, 2000, effective December 1, 2000, and by order adopted April 26, 2011, effective December 1, 2011.)

Comment. — The language of Rule 902 has been amended as part of the restyling of the Evidence Rules to make them more easily understood and to make style and terminology consistent throughout the rules. These changes are intended to be stylistic only. There is no intent to change any result in any ruling on evidence admissibility.

Law Review. — For casenote & comment, "No Don't IM Me — Instant Messaging, Authentication, and the Best Evidence Rule," see 13 Geo. Mason L. Rev. 1309 (2006).

CASE NOTES

Rule dispenses with requirements of Rule 901 in certain cases. — This rule recognizes that the possibility of fraud, forgery and misattribution of certain documents is so slight that the general requirement of authentication by extrinsic evidence, under Rule 901, is dispensed with. United States v. Howard-Arias, 679 F.2d 363 (4th Cir.), cert. denied, 459 U.S. 874, 103 S. Ct. 165, 74 L. Ed. 2d 136 (1982).

Subdivision (3) of this rule does not embody the formalistic requirement that nothing less than a statement by the affiant that he is the official designated to make such certifications under the foreign country's law can satisfy the requirements of this rule. United States v. Howard-Arias, 679 F.2d 363 (4th Cir.), cert. denied, 459 U.S. 874, 103 S. Ct. 165, 74 L. Ed. 2d 136 (1982).

Diplomatic note demonstrating Panama's grant of permission to United States officials to board fishing vessel of Panamanian registry, which was found to be carrying marijuana, was properly admitted under subdivision (3). United States v. Pena-Jessie, 763 F.2d 618 (4th Cir. 1985).

Rule 903. Subscribing Witness' Testimony.

A subscribing witness's testimony is necessary to authenticate a writing only if required by the law of the jurisdiction that governs its validity. (Amended by order adopted April 26, 2011, effective December 1, 2011.)

Comment. — The language of Rule 903 has been amended as part of the restyling of the Evidence Rules to make them more easily understood and to make style and terminology consistent throughout the rules. These changes are intended to be stylistic only. There is no intent to change any result in any ruling on evidence admissibility.

X. CONTENTS OF WRITINGS, RECORDINGS, AND PHOTOGRAPHS.

Rule 1001. Definitions That Apply to This Article.

In this article:

(a) A "writing" consists of letters, words, numbers, or their equivalent set down in any form.

(b) A "recording" consists of letters, words, numbers, or their equivalent recorded in any manner.

(c) A "photograph" means a photographic image or its equivalent stored in any form.

(d) An "original" of a writing or recording means the writing or recording itself or any counterpart intended to have the same effect by the person who executed or issued it. For electronically stored information, "original" means any printout — or other output readable by sight — if it accurately reflects the information. An "original" of a photograph includes the negative or a print from it.

(e) A "duplicate" means a counterpart produced by a mechanical, photographic, chemical, electronic, or other equivalent process or technique that accurately reproduces the original. (Amended by order adopted April 26, 2011, effective December 1, 2011.)

Comment. — The language of Rule 1001 has been amended as part of the restyling of the Evidence Rules to make them more easily understood and to make style and terminology consistent throughout the rules. These changes are intended to be stylistic only. There is no intent to change any result in any ruling on evidence admissibility.

Research References. — Ashley S. Lipson, Art of Advocay: Documentary Evidence (Matthew Bender).

Law Review. — For casenote & comment, "No Don't IM Me — Instant Messaging, Authentication, and the Best Evidence Rule," see 13 Geo. Mason L. Rev. 1309 (2006).

Rule 1002. Requirement of Original.

An original writing, recording, or photograph is required in order to prove its content unless these rules or a federal statute provides otherwise. (Amended by order adopted April 26, 2011, effective December 1, 2011.)

Comment. — The language of Rule 1002 has been amended as part of the restyling of the Evidence Rules to make them more easily understood and to make style and terminology consistent throughout the rules. These changes are intended to be stylistic only. There is no intent to change any result in any ruling on evidence admissibility.

Law Review. — For casenote & comment, "No Don't IM Me — Instant Messaging, Authentication, and the Best Evidence Rule," see 13 Geo. Mason L. Rev. 1309 (2006).

Rule 1003. Admissibility of Duplicates.

A duplicate is admissible to the same extent as the original unless a genuine question is raised about the original's authenticity or the circumstances make it unfair to admit the duplicate. (Amended by order adopted April 26, 2011, effective December 1, 2011.)

Comment. — The language of Rule 1003 has been amended as part of the restyling of the Evidence Rules to make them more easily understood and to make style and terminology consistent throughout the rules. These changes are intended to be stylistic only. There is no intent to change any result in any ruling on evidence admissibility.

Law Review. — For casenote & comment, "No Don't IM Me — Instant Messaging, Authentication, and the Best Evidence Rule," see 13 Geo. Mason L. Rev. 1309 (2006).

Rule 1004. Admissibility of Other Evidence of Content.

An original is not required and other evidence of the content of a writing, recording, or photograph is admissible if:

(a) all the originals are lost or destroyed, and not by the proponent acting in bad faith;

(b) an original cannot be obtained by any available judicial process;

(c) the party against whom the original would be offered had control of the original; was at that time put on notice, by pleadings or otherwise, that the original would be a subject of proof at the trial or hearing; and fails to produce it at the trial or hearing; or

(d) the writing, recording, or photograph is not closely related to a controlling issue. (Amended by order adopted March 2, 1987, effective October 1, 1987, and by order adopted April 26, 2011, effective December 1, 2011.)

Comment. — The language of Rule 1004 has been amended as part of the restyling of the Evidence Rules to make them more easily understood and to make style and terminology consistent throughout the rules. These changes are intended to be stylistic only. There is no intent to change any result in any ruling on evidence admissibility.

Law Review. — For casenote & comment, "No Don't IM Me — Instant Messaging, Authentication, and the Best Evidence Rule," see 13 Geo. Mason L. Rev. 1309 (2006).

CASE NOTES

Summary of records prepared by a federal reserve bank staff assistant was properly admitted as the "best evidence" of destroyed records, where no ground was raised for contesting the accuracy or trustworthiness of the information contained in the summary. United States v. Dudley, 941 F.2d 260 (4th Cir. 1991), cert. denied, 502 U.S. 1046, 112 S. Ct. 908, 116 L. Ed. 2d 809 (1992).

Rule 1005. Copies of Public Records to Prove Content.

The proponent may use a copy to prove the content of an official record — or of a document that was recorded or filed in a public office as authorized by law — if these conditions are met: the record or document is otherwise admissible; and the copy is certified as correct in accordance with Rule 902(4) or is testified to be correct by a witness who has compared it with the original. If no such copy can be obtained by reasonable diligence, then the proponent may use other evidence to prove the content. (Amended by order adopted April 26, 2011, effective December 1, 2011.)

Comment. — The language of Rule 1005 has been amended as part of the restyling of the Evidence Rules to make them more easily understood and to make style and terminology consistent throughout the rules. These changes are intended to be stylistic only. There is no intent to change any result in any ruling on evidence admissibility.

Rule 1006. Summaries to Prove Content.

The proponent may use a summary, chart, or calculation to prove the content of voluminous writings, recordings, or photographs that cannot be conveniently examined in court. The proponent must make the originals or duplicates available for examination or copying, or both, by other parties at a reasonable time and place. And the court may order the proponent to produce them in court. (Amended by order adopted April 26, 2011, effective December 1, 2011.)

Comment. — The language of Rule 1006 has been amended as part of the restyling of the Evidence Rules to make them more easily understood and to make style and terminology consistent throughout the rules. These changes are intended to be stylistic only. There is no intent to change any result in any ruling on evidence admissibility.

CASE NOTES

Applied in Bristol Steel & Iron Works, Inc. v. Bethlehem Steel Corp., 41 F.3d 182 (4th Cir. 1994).

Rule 1007. Testimony or Statement of a Party to Prove Content.

The proponent may prove the content of a writing, recording, or photograph by the testimony, deposition, or written statement of the party against whom the evidence is offered. The proponent need not account for the original. (Amended by order adopted March 2, 1987, effective October 1, 1987, and by order adopted April 26, 2011, effective December 1, 2011.)

Comment. — The language of Rule 1007 has been amended as part of the restyling of the Evidence Rules to make them more easily understood and to make style and terminology consistent throughout the rules. These changes are intended to be stylistic only. There is no intent to change any result in any ruling on evidence admissibility.

Rule 1008. Functions of the Court and Jury.

Ordinarily, the court determines whether the proponent has fulfilled the factual conditions for admitting other evidence of the content of a writing, recording, or photograph under Rule 1004 or 1005. But in a jury trial, the jury determines — in accordance with Rule 104(b) — any issue about whether:

(a) an asserted writing, recording, or photograph ever existed;

(b) another one produced at the trial or hearing is the original; or

(c) other evidence of content accurately reflects the content. (Amended by order adopted April 26, 2011, effective December 1, 2011.)

Comment. — The language of Rule 1008 has been amended as part of the restyling of the Evidence Rules to make them more easily understood and to make style and terminology consistent throughout the rules. These changes are intended to be stylistic only. There is no intent to change any result in any ruling on evidence admissibility.

XI. MISCELLANEOUS RULES.

Rule 1101. Applicability of the Rules.

(a) *To Courts and Judges.* — These rules apply to proceedings before:

- United States district courts;
- United States bankruptcy and magistrate judges;
- United States courts of appeals;
- the United States Court of Federal Claims; and
- the district courts of Guam, the Virgin Islands, and the Northern Mariana Islands.

(b) *To Cases and Proceedings.* — These rules apply in:

- civil cases and proceedings, including bankruptcy, admiralty, and maritime cases;
- criminal cases and proceedings; and
- contempt proceedings, except those in which the court may act summarily.

(c) *Rules on Privilege.* — The rules on privilege apply to all stages of a case or proceeding.

(d) *Exceptions.* — These rules — except for those on privilege — do not apply to the following:

(1) the court's determination, under Rule 104(a), on a preliminary question of fact governing admissibility;

(2) grand-jury proceedings; and

(3) miscellaneous proceedings such as:

- extradition or rendition;
- issuing an arrest warrant, criminal summons, or search warrant;
- a preliminary examination in a criminal case;

- sentencing;
- granting or revoking probation or supervised release; and
- considering whether to release on bail or otherwise.

(e) *Other Statutes and Rules.* — A federal statute or a rule prescribed by the Supreme Court may provide for admitting or excluding evidence independently from these rules. (Amended by order adopted December 12, 1975, by P.L. 95-598, title II, § 251(b), adopted November 6, 1978, effective October 1, 1979, by P.L. 97-164, adopted April 2, 1982, effective October 1, 1982, by order adopted March 2, 1987, effective October 1, 1987, by order adopted April 25, 1988, effective November 1, 1988, by P.L. 100-690, § 7075, signed November 18, 1988, by order adopted April 22, 1993, effective December 1, 1993, and by order adopted April 26, 2011, effective December 1, 2011.)

Comment. — The language of Rule 1101 has been amended as part of the restyling of the Evidence Rules to make them more easily understood and to make style and terminology consistent throughout the rules. These changes are intended to be stylistic only. There is no intent to change any result in any ruling on evidence admissibility.

CASE NOTES

The federal rules of evidence pertaining to hearsay do not apply to probation revocation hearings. United States v. McCallum, 677 F.2d 1024 (4th Cir.), cert. denied, 459 U.S. 1010, 103 S. Ct. 365, 74 L. Ed. 2d 400 (1982).

Applied in Plaster v. United States, 720 F.2d 340 (4th Cir. 1983).

Rule 1102. Amendments.

These rules may be amended as provided in 28 U.S.C. § 2072. (Amended by order adopted April 30, 1991, effective December 1, 1991, and by order adopted April 26, 2011, effective December 1, 2011.)

Comment. — The language of Rule 1102 has been amended as part of the restyling of the Evidence Rules to make them more easily understood and to make style and terminology consistent throughout the rules. These changes are intended to be stylistic only. There is no intent to change any result in any ruling on evidence admissibility.

Rule 1103. Title.

These rules may be cited as the Federal Rules of Evidence. (Amended by order adopted April 26, 2011, effective December 1, 2011.)

Comment. — The language of Rule 1103 has been amended as part of the restyling of the Evidence Rules to make them more easily understood and to make style and terminology consistent throughout the rules. These changes are intended to be stylistic only. There is no intent to change any result in any ruling on evidence admissibility.

Index to Federal Rules of Evidence

A

ABSENCE OF ENTRIES AS HEARSAY EXCEPTIONS.
Public records, FRE 803.
Regularly conducted activity, records of, FRE 803.

ACCUSED.
Character of accused, admissibility of evidence of, FRE 404.
Preliminary questions, effect of testimony by accused in connection with, FRE 104.

ACKNOWLEDGED DOCUMENTS.
Self-authenticating evidence, FRE 902.

ACTS OF CONGRESS.
Hearsay, exceptions from rule of exclusion of, FRE 802.
Methods of authentication or identification provided by, FRE 901.
Presumed authenticity or genuineness based on declarations in, FRE 902.

ADJUDICATIVE FACTS.
Judicial notice, FRE 201.

ADMISSIBILITY.
Character evidence, FRE 404.
Methods of proving, FRE 405.
Compromise and offers to compromise, FRE 408.
Confusion.
Exclusion of relevant evidence, FRE 403.
Crimes, wrongs or other acts, FRE 404.
Duplicates, FRE 1003.
Exclusion of relevant evidence, FRE 403.
Habit, FRE 406.
Inadmissible evidence.
Preventing jury from hearing, FRE 103.
Irrelevant evidence, FRE 402.
Liability insurance.
Proof of negligence, FRE 411.
Limited admissibility, FRE 105.
Medical and similar expenses, offers to pay, FRE 409.
Misleading the jury.
Exclusion of relevant evidence, FRE 403.
Needlessly cumulative evidence.
Exclusion of relevant evidence, FRE 403.
Negotiations, FRE 408.
Plea discussions and related statements, FRE 410.
Prejudice.
Exclusion of relevant evidence, FRE 403.
Preliminary questions, FRE 104.
Prior statements of witnesses, FRE 613.
Relevant evidence, FRE 402.
Exclusion of relevant evidence, FRE 403.
Test for relevance, FRE 401.
Religious beliefs or opinions of witnesses, FRE 610.
Remedial measures, FRE 407.
Routine practice, FRE 406.

ADMISSIBILITY —Cont'd
Sexual offenses.
Child molestation, evidence of similar crimes, FRE 414.
Relevance of victim's past behavior, FRE 412.
Similar acts.
Civil cases, FRE 415.
Similar crimes, FRE 413.
Subsequent remedial measures, FRE 407.
Undue delay.
Exclusion of relevant evidence, FRE 403.
Wasting time.
Exclusion of relevant evidence, FRE 403.
Writings.
Duplicates, FRE 1003.
Writings, recordings or photographs.
Other evidence of contents, admissibility, FRE 1004.

ADOPTION.
Hearsay exceptions.
Reputation concerning personal or family history, FRE 803.
Unavailability of declarant, statement of personal or family history in case of, FRE 804.

AFFIRMATION, FRE 603.

AGENTS.
Evidence of insurance against liability in connection with proof of, FRE 411.
Hearsay, statement by agent or servant of party against whom offered as, FRE 801.

AMENDMENTS TO RULES, FRE 1102.

ANCIENT DOCUMENTS.
Authenticating or identifying evidence, FRE 901.
Hearsay exceptions, availability of declarant immaterial, FRE 803.

APPEALS.
Hearsay exception, pendency of appeal as affecting admissibility of judgment of previous conviction under, FRE 803.
Impeachment of witness by evidence of conviction for crime as affected by pendency of appeal, FRE 609.
Writing used to refresh memory of witness, preservation for appeal of withheld portions of, FRE 612.

APPLICABILITY OF RULES, FRE 1101.

ATTORNEYS AT LAW.
Attorney-client privilege, FRE 501, 502.
Work product protection, FRE 502.

AUTHENTICATING EVIDENCE, FRE 901.

B

BAPTISM CERTIFICATES.
Hearsay exceptions, availability of declarant immaterial, FRE 803.

BELIEFS OR OPINIONS.
Impending death, hearsay rule as affecting statement under belief of, FRE 804.
Religious beliefs or opinions as admissible for purpose of impairing or enhancing credibility of witness, FRE 610.
Ultimate issue for trier of facts, testimony in form of opinion, FRE 704.

BEST EVIDENCE RULE.
Contents of writings, recordings, and photographs, Evid 1001 to 1008.

BIAS.
Compromise and offers to compromise, relevancy of evidence of, FRE 408.

BIRTH CERTIFICATES.
Hearsay exceptions, availability of declarant immaterial, FRE 803.

BOUNDARIES.
Reputation concerning.
Hearsay exceptions, availability of declarant immaterial, FRE 803.

C

CALCULATIONS.
Proving content of writings, FRE 1006.

CAUSE OF WITNESS'S UNAVAILABILITY.
Statement offered against a party that wrongfully caused the declarant's unavailability.
Hearsay exceptions, declarant unavailable, FRE 804.

CERTIFIED COPIES.
Contents of public records, proof of, FRE 1005.
Self-authenticating evidence, FRE 902.

CHARACTER EVIDENCE.
Generally, FRE 404.
Methods of proving character, FRE 405.
Not admissible to prove conduct, FRE 404.
Rape victim's sexual history, admissibility, FRE 412.
Reputation.
Hearsay exceptions, availability of declarant immaterial, FRE 803.
Witnesses.
Evidence of character of witness, FRE 608.

CHARTS.
Summaries to prove content of writings, FRE 1006.

CHILD MOLESTATION.
Similar acts.
Civil cases, FRE 415.
Similar crimes, FRE 414.

CITATION OF RULES, FRE 1103.

CIVIL CASES.
Defined, FRE 101.
Presumptions, FRE 301.
Sex offense cases.
Victim's sexual behavior or predisposition, FRE 412.
State law, applicability in civil actions and proceedings, FRE 302.

COMMERCIAL PUBLICATIONS.
Hearsay exceptions, availability of declarant immaterial, FRE 803.
Self-authenticating evidence, FRE 902.

COMPETENCY.
General rule, FRE 601.
Judges, FRE 605.
Jurors, FRE 606.

COMPROMISE, FRE 408.

CONDUCT.
Absence of record of regularly conducted activity.
Hearsay exceptions, availability of declarant immaterial, FRE 803.
Records of regularly conducted activities.
Hearsay exceptions, availability of declarant immaterial, FRE 803.
Self-authenticating evidence, FRE 902.
Specific instances.
Character evidence, methods of proving character, FRE 405.

CONFUSION.
Exclusion of relevant evidence on grounds of confusion, FRE 403.

CONSTITUTION OF THE UNITED STATES.
Privileges, exceptions, FRE 501.
Relevant evidence, exclusion by US Constitution, federal statute or rule of the Supreme Court, FRE 402.

CONSTRUCTION OF RULES, FRE 102.

CONVICTIONS.
Impeachment by evidence of conviction of crime, FRE 609.

COURTS.
Judicial notice of adjudicative facts, FRE 201.
Presumptions, FRE 301.

CREDIBILITY OF DECLARANT.
Hearsay, attacking and supporting credibility, FRE 806.

CREDIBILITY OF EVIDENCE.
Preliminary questions, FRE 104.

CRIMINAL CASES.
Character evidence, exceptions, FRE 404.
Child molestation, evidence of similar crimes, FRE 414.
Defined, FRE 101.
Judicial notice of adjudicative facts, FRE 201.
Obstruction of criminal investigation.
Compromise and offers to compromise, relevancy of evidence of, FRE 408.
Other crimes, wrongs or other acts, admissibility, FRE 404.
Hearsay exceptions, availability of declarant immaterial, FRE 803.
Plea discussions and related statements, admissibility, FRE 410.
Preliminary questions.
Defendant not subject to cross-examination, FRE 104.
Sex offense cases.
Child molestation, evidence of similar crimes, FRE 414.
Similar crimes, FRE 413.
Victim's sexual behavior or predisposition, FRE 412.

CRIMINAL LAW.
Judicial notice of adjudicative facts, FRE 201.

CROSS-EXAMINATION.
Scope, FRE 611.

CUMULATIVE EVIDENCE.
Needlessly cumulative evidence.
Exclusion of relevant evidence on grounds of prejudice, confusion, etc, FRE 403.

D

DAMAGES.
Judicial notice of adjudicative facts, FRE 201.

DATA COMPILATION.
Authenticating or identifying evidence, FRE 901.

DATES.
Judicial notice of adjudicative facts, FRE 201.

DEATH.
Statement under belief of imminent death.
Hearsay exceptions, declarant unavailable, FRE 804.

DEFENDANTS.
Character evidence, exceptions, FRE 404.

DEFINED TERMS.
Attorney-client privilege, FRE 502.
Child.
Child molestation, evidence of similar crimes, FRE 414.
Child molestation.
Evidence of similar crimes, FRE 414.
Civil case, FRE 101.
Criminal case, FRE 101.
Declarant.
Hearsay, FRE 801.
Duplicate.
Writings, recordings and photographs, FRE 1001.
Hearsay, FRE 801.
Original.
Writings, recordings and photographs, FRE 1001.
Photograph, FRE 1001.
Public office, FRE 101.
Record, FRE 101.
Recording, FRE 1001.
Rule prescribed by the Supreme Court, FRE 101.
Sexual assault, FRE 413.
Statement.
Hearsay, FRE 801.
Victim, FRE 412.
Work-product protection, FRE 502.
Writing, FRE 1001.

DELAY.
Compromise and offers to compromise, relevancy of evidence of, FRE 408.
Undue delay.
Exclusion of relevant evidence on grounds of prejudice, confusion, etc, FRE 403.

DISTINCTIVE CHARACTERISTICS.
Authenticating or identifying evidence, FRE 901.

DOCUMENTS.
Ancient documents.
Authenticating or identifying evidence, FRE 901.

DOCUMENTS —Cont'd
Authentication.
Authenticating or identifying evidence, FRE 901.
Self-authentication, FRE 902.
Contents.
Other evidence of contents, admissibility, FRE 1004.
Duplicates.
Admissibility, FRE 1003.
Original.
Requirement of original, FRE 1002.
Self-authentication, FRE 902.
Subscribing witnesses' testimony unnecessary, FRE 903.

DUPLICATES.
Writings, recordings and photographs.
Admissibility, FRE 1003.

E

ECONOMICS.
Judicial notice of adjudicative facts, FRE 201.

ELECTIONS.
Judicial notice of adjudicative facts, FRE 201.

ELECTRONIC RECORDS.
References to any kind of written material includes electronically stored information, FRE 101.

EMINENT DOMAIN.
Judicial notice of adjudicative facts, FRE 201.

EMOTIONAL CONDITION.
Then-existing mental, emotional or physical condition.
Hearsay exceptions, availability of declarant immaterial, FRE 803.

ERRORS.
Judicial notice of plain error, FRE 103.
Preserving claim of error, FRE 103.

EXCITED UTTERANCES.
Hearsay exceptions, availability of declarant immaterial, FRE 803.

EXPERTS.
Authenticating or identifying evidence, FRE 901.
Court-appointed experts, FRE 706.
Opinion testimony, FRE 702.
Bases of opinion testimony by experts, FRE 703.
Court-appointed experts, FRE 706.
Disclosure of facts or data underlying expert opinion, FRE 705.
Ultimate issue, FRE 704.
Testimony by experts, FRE 702.

F

FALSE STATEMENTS.
Plea discussions and related statements.
Admissible for proving, FRE 410.

FAMILY RECORDS.
Hearsay exceptions, availability of declarant immaterial, FRE 803.

FEDERAL STATUTES.
Privileges, exceptions, FRE 501.

FEDERAL STATUTES —Cont'd
Relevant evidence, exclusion by US Constitution, federal statute or rule of the Supreme Court, FRE 402.
Self-authenticating evidence, FRE 902.

FORMER TESTIMONY.
Unavailable witness.
Hearsay exceptions, declarant unavailable, FRE 804.

G

GEOGRAPHY.
Judicial notice of adjudicative facts, FRE 201.

GOVERNMENT.
Judicial notice of adjudicative facts, FRE 201.

GUILTY PLEA.
Offer to plead guilty, FRE 410.
Withdrawn plea of guilty, FRE 410.

H

HABIT, FRE 406.
Absence of record of regularly conducted activity.
Hearsay exceptions, availability of declarant immaterial, FRE 803.
Records of regularly conducted activities.
Hearsay exceptions, availability of declarant immaterial, FRE 803.
Self-authenticating evidence, FRE 902.

HANDWRITING.
Authenticating or identifying evidence, FRE 901.
Contents of writings, records, and photographs, definitions in connection with evidence of, FRE 1001.

HEALTH.
Meaning of unavailability of declarant in connection with hearsay exceptions, FRE 804.
Statement as to contemporaneous mental, emotional, or physical condition of declarant as, FRE 803.

HEARSAY.
Credibility of declarant.
Attacking and supporting credibility, FRE 806.
Declarant-witness's prior statements.
Statements that are not hearsay, FRE 801.
Definitions, FRE 801.
Exceptions.
Availability of declarant immaterial, FRE 803.
Declarant unavailable, FRE 804.
Residual exception, FRE 807.
Generally, FRE 802.
Hearsay within hearsay, FRE 805.
Opposing party's statements.
Statements that are not hearsay, FRE 801.
Rule, FRE 802.
Statements that are not hearsay, FRE 801.

HISTORY.
Religious organizations.
Records, personal or family history.
Hearsay exceptions, availability of declarant immaterial, FRE 803.

HISTORY —Cont'd
Reputation, personal or family history.
Hearsay exceptions, availability of declarant immaterial, FRE 803.
Statements of personal or family history.
Hearsay exceptions, declarant unavailable, FRE 804.

HUSBAND AND WIFE.
Privilege, FRE 501.

I

IDENTIFICATION.
Authenticating or identifying evidence, FRE 901.

IMMINENT DEATH.
Statement under belief of imminent death.
Hearsay exceptions, declarant unavailable, FRE 804.

IMPEACHMENT.
By evidence of conviction of crime, FRE 609.
Character evidence and conduct of witness, FRE 608.
Guilty plea or nolo contendere plea, evidence of, FRE 410.
Hearsay statement, attacking credibility of declarant making, FRE 806.
Prior statements of witnesses, FRE 613.
Religious beliefs or opinions to impeach witness, FRE 610.
Subsequent remedial measures, admissibility of evidence of, FRE 407.
Who may impeach, FRE 607.

INFANTS.
Judicial notice of adjudicative facts, FRE 201.

INFORMERS.
Identity of informer.
Privilege, FRE 501.

INNS AND INNKEEPERS.
Judicial notice of adjudicative facts, FRE 201.

INSTRUCTIONS TO JURY.
Judicial notice, FRE 201.
Limited admissibility of evidence, FRE 105.

INSURANCE.
Judicial notice of adjudicative facts, FRE 201.
Liability insurance, admissibility, FRE 411.

INTERPRETATION OF RULES, FRE 102.

INTERPRETERS, FRE 604.

IRRELEVANT EVIDENCE.
Not admissible, FRE 402.

J

JUDGES.
Competency as witnesses, FRE 605.
Writings, photographs and recordings.
Functions of judge, FRE 1008.

JUDICIAL NOTICE.
Adjudicative facts, FRE 201.
Plain error, FRE 103.

JURY.
Competency of juror as witness, FRE 606.

JURY —Cont'd
Hearings excluding jury.
Preliminary questions, FRE 104.
Instructions.
Judicial notice of adjudicative facts, instruction to accept fact as conclusive, FRE 201.
Judicial notice of adjudicative facts, FRE 201.
Misleading the jury.
Exclusion of relevant evidence on grounds of prejudice, confusion, etc, FRE 403.
Writings, recordings or photographs.
Functions of jury, FRE 1008.

K

KNOWLEDGE OF WITNESS.
Authenticating or identifying evidence, FRE 901.

L

LABELS.
Self-authenticating evidence, FRE 902.

LEADING QUESTIONS, FRE 611.

LEARNED TREATISES.
Hearsay exceptions, availability of declarant immaterial, FRE 803.

LIMITED ADMISSIBILITY, FRE 105.

M

MARKET REPORTS.
Hearsay exceptions, availability of declarant immaterial, FRE 803.

MARRIAGE CERTIFICATES.
Hearsay exceptions, availability of declarant immaterial, FRE 803.

MEDICAL AND SIMILAR EXPENSES.
Payment, FRE 409.

MEDICAL DIAGNOSIS OR TREATMENT.
Statements made for.
Hearsay exceptions, availability of declarant immaterial, FRE 803.

MENTAL CONDITION.
Then-existing mental, emotional or physical condition.
Hearsay exceptions, availability of declarant immaterial, FRE 803.

MISLEADING THE JURY.
Exclusion of relevant evidence on grounds of prejudice, confusion, etc, FRE 403.

N

NEEDLESSLY CUMULATIVE EVIDENCE.
Exclusion of relevant evidence on grounds of prejudice, confusion, etc, FRE 403.

NEGLIGENCE.
Liability insurance, admissibility, FRE 411.
Subsequent remedial measures, FRE 407.

NEGOTIABLE INSTRUMENTS.
Compromise and offers to compromise, relevancy of evidence of, FRE 408.

NEWSPAPERS.
Self-authenticating evidence, FRE 902.

NOLO CONTENDERE.
Offer to plea, FRE 410.

O

OATHS, FRE 603.

OBJECTIONS.
No need to renew objection or offer proof to preserve claim, FRE 103.

OBSTRUCTION OF CRIMINAL INVESTIGATION.
Compromise and offers to compromise, relevancy of evidence of, FRE 408.

OFFERS OF PROOF.
Court requirements, FRE 103.

OFFERS TO PAY MEDICAL AND SIMILAR EXPENSES.
Admissibility to prove liability, FRE 409.

OFFICIAL PUBLICATIONS.
Self-authenticating evidence, FRE 902.

OPINION TESTIMONY.
Character evidence, methods of proving character, FRE 405.
Experts, FRE 702.
Bases of opinion testimony by experts, FRE 703.
Court-appointed experts, FRE 706.
Disclosure of facts or data underlying expert opinions, FRE 705.
Opinion on ultimate issue, FRE 704.
Lay witnesses, FRE 701.

P

PAMPHLETS.
Hearsay exceptions, availability of declarant immaterial, FRE 803.

PARTIAL STATEMENTS.
Adverse party may require remainder of statement, FRE 106.

PERIODICALS.
Hearsay exceptions, availability of declarant immaterial, FRE 803.
Self-authenticating evidence, FRE 902.

PERJURY.
Hearsay, prior statement by witness under oath and subject to penalty of perjury as, FRE 801.
Impeachment by evidence of conviction of crime, FRE 609.
Plea discussions and related statements.
Admissible for proving, FRE 410.

PERSONAL KNOWLEDGE.
Lack of personal knowledge, FRE 602.

PHOTOGRAPHS.
Contents, FRE 1001.
Other evidence of contents, admissibility, FRE 1004.
Summaries to prove content, FRE 1006.
Testimony or written admission of party, FRE 1007.

PHOTOGRAPHS —Cont'd
Duplicates.
Admissibility, FRE 1003.
Functions of court and jury, FRE 1008.
Original.
Requirement of original, FRE 1002.

PHYSICAL CONDITION.
Then-existing mental, emotional or physical condition.
Hearsay exceptions, availability of declarant immaterial, FRE 803.

PHYSICIANS AND SURGEONS.
Physician-patient privilege, FRE 501.

PLEAS.
Inadmissibility of plea discussions and related statements, FRE 410.

PREJUDICE.
Compromise and offers to compromise, relevancy of evidence of, FRE 408.
Exclusion of relevant evidence on grounds of prejudice, FRE 403.
Insurance against liability, introduction to show proof of bias or prejudice of witness, FRE 411.
Juror as competent witness in inquiry into validity of verdict or indictment, FRE 606.

PRELIMINARY QUESTIONS, FRE 104.

PRESENT SENSE IMPRESSIONS.
Hearsay exceptions, availability of declarant immaterial, FRE 803.

PRESUMPTIONS.
Generally, FRE 301.
State law, applicability in civil actions and proceedings, FRE 302.

PRIOR CONVICTIONS.
Hearsay exceptions, availability of declarant immaterial, FRE 803.
Other crimes, wrongs or other acts, admissibility, FRE 404.

PRIOR STATEMENTS.
Declarant-witness's prior statements.
Statements that are not hearsay, FRE 801.
Former testimony.
Hearsay exceptions, declarant unavailable, FRE 804.
Witnesses, admissibility, FRE 613.

PRIVILEGES.
Attorney-client privilege and work product, FRE 502.
Existence, preliminary questions, FRE 104.
Generally, FRE 501.

PROCESSES OR SYSTEMS.
Authenticating or identifying evidence, FRE 901.

PRODUCTS LIABILITY.
Subsequent remedial measures, FRE 407.

PUBLIC OFFICERS.
Public office defined, FRE 101.

PUBLIC RECORDS.
Absence of public record.
Hearsay exceptions, availability of declarant immaterial, FRE 803.

PUBLIC RECORDS —Cont'd
Authenticating or identifying evidence, FRE 901.
Copies to prove contents, FRE 1005.
Hearsay exceptions, availability of declarant immaterial, FRE 803.
Self-authenticating evidence, FRE 902.

PURPOSE OF RULES, FRE 102.

R

RAPE CASES.
Child molestation, evidence of similar crimes, FRE 414.
Relevance of victim's past behavior, FRE 412.
Similar acts.
Civil cases, FRE 415.
Similar crimes, FRE 413.

REAL PROPERTY.
Boundaries.
Hearsay exceptions, availability of declarant immaterial, FRE 803.
Records of documents that affect an interest in property.
Hearsay exceptions, availability of declarant immaterial, FRE 803.

REBUTTING PRESUMPTIONS, FRE 301.

RECORDED STATEMENTS.
Absence of record of regularly conducted activity.
Hearsay exceptions, availability of declarant immaterial, FRE 803.
Recorded recollections.
Hearsay exceptions, availability of declarant immaterial, FRE 803.
Records of regularly conducted activities.
Hearsay exceptions, availability of declarant immaterial, FRE 803.
Self-authenticating evidence, FRE 902.
Religious organizations.
Records, personal or family history.
Hearsay exceptions, availability of declarant immaterial, FRE 803.
Remainder of or related recorded statements, FRE 106.

RECORDINGS.
Contents, FRE 1001.
Other evidence of contents, admissibility, FRE 1004.
Summaries to prove content, FRE 1006.
Testimony or written admission of party, FRE 1007.
Duplicates.
Admissibility, FRE 1003.
Functions of court and jury, FRE 1008.
Original.
Requirement of original, FRE 1002.

RECORDS.
Content.
Testimony or written admission of party, FRE 1007.
Court records and proceedings.
Judicial notice of adjudicative facts, FRE 201.
Defined, FRE 101.
Electronic records.
References to any kind of written material includes electronically stored information, FRE 101.

RECORDS —Cont'd
Functions of court and jury, FRE 1008.
Public records.
Copies to prove contents, FRE 1005.
Summaries, FRE 1000.

RELEVANT EVIDENCE.
Child molestation, evidence of similar crimes, FRE 414.
Dependent on fact.
Preliminary questions, existence of fact, conditional admission, FRE 104.
Exclusion by US Constitution, federal statute or rule of the Supreme Court, FRE 402.
Exclusion on grounds of prejudice, confusion or waste of time, FRE 403.
General admissibility, FRE 402.
Sexual offenses.
Child molestation, evidence of similar crimes, FRE 414.
Relevance of victim's past behavior, FRE 412.
Similar acts.
Civil cases, FRE 415.
Similar crimes, FRE 413.
Test for relevant evidence, FRE 401.

RELIGIOUS BELIEFS OR OPINIONS.
Witnesses, admissibility, FRE 610.

RELIGIOUS ORGANIZATIONS.
Records, personal or family history.
Hearsay exceptions, availability of declarant immaterial, FRE 803.

REPAIRS.
Subsequent remedial measures, FRE 407.

REPUTATION.
Character evidence, methods of proving character, FRE 405.
Hearsay exceptions, availability of declarant immaterial, FRE 803.
Personal or family history.
Hearsay exceptions, availability of declarant immaterial, FRE 803.

RESTRICTING EVIDENCE.
Limited admissibility, FRE 105.

ROUTINE PRACTICE, FRE 406.
Absence of record of regularly conducted activity.
Hearsay exceptions, availability of declarant immaterial, FRE 803.
Records of regularly conducted activities.
Hearsay exceptions, availability of declarant immaterial, FRE 803.
Self-authenticating evidence, FRE 902.

RULES OF THE SUPREME COURT.
Privileges, exceptions, FRE 501.
Relevant evidence, exclusion by US Constitution, federal statute or rule of the Supreme Court, FRE 402.

RULINGS ON EVIDENCE, FRE 103.

S

SCOPE OF RULES, FRE 101.

SELF-AUTHENTICATING EVIDENCE, FRE 902.

SELF-INCRIMINATION.
Privilege against self-incrimination, FRE 501.

SEXUAL ASSAULT.
Similar acts.
Civil cases, FRE 415.
Similar crimes, FRE 413.

SEXUAL OFFENSES.
Child molestation, evidence of similar crimes, FRE 414.
Relevance of victim's past behavior, FRE 412.
Similar acts.
Civil cases, FRE 415.
Similar crimes, FRE 413.

SIGNATURES.
Self-authenticating evidence, FRE 902.

STATE LAW.
Applicability in civil actions and proceedings, FRE 302.
Privileges.
Applicability of state law, FRE 501.

STATEMENT AGAINST INTEREST.
Hearsay exceptions, declarant unavailable, FRE 804.

STATUTES.
Authenticating or identifying evidence.
Methods provided by statute or rule, FRE 901.
Exclusion by US Constitution, federal statute or rule of the Supreme Court, FRE 402.
Privileges, exceptions, FRE 501.

SUBSEQUENT REMEDIAL MEASURES, FRE 407.

SYSTEMS.
Authenticating or identifying evidence, FRE 901.

T

TECHNICAL OR SPECIALIZED KNOWLEDGE.
Experts, FRE 702.

TELEPHONE CONVERSATION.
Authenticating or identifying evidence, FRE 901.

TEST FOR RELEVANT EVIDENCE, FRE 401.

THEN-EXISTING MENTAL, EMOTIONAL OR PHYSICAL CONDITION.
Hearsay exceptions, availability of declarant immaterial, FRE 803.

TITLE, FRE 1103.

TRADE INSCRIPTIONS.
Self-authenticating evidence, FRE 902.

TRADE SECRETS.
Privileges, FRE 501.

U

UNAVAILABLE WITNESS.
Hearsay exceptions, declarant unavailable, FRE 804.

UNDUE DELAY.
Compromise and offers to compromise, relevancy of evidence of, FRE 408.

UNDUE DELAY —Cont'd
Exclusion of relevant evidence on grounds of prejudice, confusion, etc, FRE 403.

V

VICTIMS.
Character evidence, exceptions, FRE 404.
Child molestation, evidence of similar crimes, FRE 414.
Defined, FRE 412.
Sex offense cases.
Child molestation, evidence of similar crimes, FRE 414.
Similar acts.
Civil cases, FRE 415.
Similar crimes, FRE 413.
Victim's sexual behavior or predisposition, FRE 412.

VITAL STATISTICS.
Hearsay exceptions, availability of declarant immaterial, FRE 803.

VOICE RECOGNITION.
Authenticating or identifying evidence, FRE 901.

W

WASTE OF TIME.
Exclusion of relevant evidence on grounds of prejudice, confusion, etc, FRE 403.

WEIGHT OF EVIDENCE.
Preliminary questions, FRE 104.

WITNESSES.
Calling by court, FRE 614.
Character.
Evidence of character, FRE 404, 608.
Competency.
See COMPETENCY.
Compromise and offers to compromise, relevancy of evidence of, FRE 408.
Conduct.
Evidence of conduct, FRE 608.
Cross-examination.
Scope of cross-examination, FRE 611.
Exclusion, FRE 615.

WITNESSES —Cont'd
Experts.
See EXPERTS.
Impeachment.
By evidence of conviction of crime, FRE 609.
Prior statements of witnesses, FRE 613.
Who may impeach, FRE 607.
Interpreters, FRE 604.
Interrogation.
By court, FRE 614.
Mode and order of interrogation, FRE 611.
Leading questions, FRE 611.
Oaths or affirmation, FRE 603.
Opinion testimony.
Experts.
See EXPERTS.
Lay witnesses, FRE 701.
Personal knowledge.
Lack of personal knowledge, FRE 602.
Presentation.
Mode and order of presentation, FRE 611.
Prior statement, FRE 613.
Qualifications.
Preliminary questions, FRE 104.
Religious beliefs or opinions, FRE 610.
Unavailable witness.
Hearsay exceptions, declarant unavailable, FRE 804.
Writing.
Used to refresh memory, FRE 612.

WORK PRODUCT PROTECTION.
Attorneys at law, FRE 502.

WRITINGS.
Contents, FRE 1001.
Other evidence of contents, admissibility, FRE 1004.
Summaries to prove content, FRE 1006.
Testimony or written admission of parties, FRE 1007.
Duplicate.
Admissibility, FRE 1003.
Functions of court and jury, FRE 1008.
Original.
Requirement of original, FRE 1002.
Remainder of or related writing, FRE 106.
Remainder of related writings.
Introduction, FRE 1006.
Summaries, FRE 1006.
Witnesses.
Writing used to refresh memory, FRE 612.

RULES OF THE UNITED STATES DISTRICT COURT FOR THE EASTERN DISTRICT OF VIRGINIA

Revision effective March 8, 2004; as amended through November 19, 2010.

Local Civil Rules.

Rule
1. Scope of Rules.
3. Area and Divisions.
4. Service and Return of Summons — Abatement.
5. Designation and Handling of Documents Under Seal.
7. Pleadings — Motions — Continuances — Orders.
7.1. Financial Disclosure.
7.1.
16. Pretrial Conference.
26. Discovery and Disclosure.
30. Depositions — Expenses — Summaries — Reviewing Depositions.
33. Interrogatories [Deleted.]
37. Motions to Compel and Sanctions.
38. Demand for Jury Trial.
45. Subpoenas.
47. Jurors.
51. Proposed Jury Instructions and Voir Dire.
54. Costs — Notice of Appeal — Jury Costs.
56. Summary Judgment.
62. Appeal Bond — Exemption From.
65. Sureties — Security — Bondsman.
67. Deposits into Court.
71A. Land Condemnation Actions.
72. United States Magistrate Judges — Duties.
79. Exhibits.
80. Transcripts — Record on Appeal.
83.1. Attorneys and *Pro Se* Parties
83.1.
83.2. Sales and Distribution of Proceeds of Sales.
83.3. Photographing, Broadcasting, and Televising in Courtroom and Environs.
83.4. Habeas Corpus and Proceedings *In Forma Pauperis*.
83.6. Settlement and Alternative Dispute Resolution.

Rule

Local Criminal Rules.
1. Scope of Rules.
5. United States Magistrate Judges — Duties.
6. Grand Jury.
12. Criminal Cases — Motions.
12.4. Financial Disclosure.
17. Subpoenas.
18. Area and Divisions.
24. Trial Jurors.
30. Proposed Jury Instructions and Voir Dire.
32.2. Sales and Distribution of Proceeds of Sales.
46. Sureties — Security — Bondsman.
47. Pleadings — Motions — Continuances — Orders.
49. Designation and Handling of Documents Under Seal.
53. Photographing, Broadcasting, and Televising in Courtroom and Environs.
55. Exhibits.
57.1. Free Press — Fair Trial Directives.
57.2. Payment of Fees.
57.3. Official Court Reporters Transcripts — Hearing on Transcripts — Record on Appeal.
57.4. Attorneys and *Pro Se* Parties.
58. Collateral Payments.

Local Admiralty Rules.

(a) Authority and Scope.
(b) In Personam Actions: Attachment and Garnishment.
(c) Actions *In Rem:* Special Provisions.
(d) Possessory, Petitory and Partition Actions.
(e) Actions *In Rem* and Quasi *In Rem:* General Provisions.
(f) Limitation of Liability.
Appendix A: Plan for Third Year Practice Rule.
Appendix B: Federal Rules of Disciplinary Enforcement.
Index.

Editor's note. — As required by the Judicial Conference of the United States, this edition of the Local Rules renumbers the local rules so that each local rule bears the same number as the *Federal Rules of Civil Procedure* or the *Federal Rules of Criminal Procedure* to which the local rule most closely corresponds. This edition contains no change in the substance of the Local Rules as they were published on February 1, 1996, except that former Local Rules 27(B)(4) and (C) have been deleted because they were in conflict with the *Prisoner Litigation Reform Act of 1995.*

LOCAL CIVIL RULES.

Rule 1. Scope of Rules.

(A) **Application:** These Local Rules, made pursuant to the authority granted by Fed. R. Civ. P. 83 for the United States District Courts, as prescribed by the Supreme Court of the United States, so far as not inconsistent therewith, shall apply in all civil actions and civil proceedings in the United States District Court for the Eastern District of Virginia.

Effective March 26, 2007, all documents filed with the Court must be filed through the Electronic Case Filing System, except as provided otherwise in the Court's *Electronic Case Filing Policies and Procedures* manual ("manual") which is promulgated and revised by the Clerk. The manual governs if there is a conflict between it and these Local Rules as to the technicalities of electronic case filing. These Local Rules govern where the manual provides for filing paper documents, and in all other matters not involving electronic case filing.

(B) **Statutory Rules:** 1 U.S.C. §§ 1-5, inclusive, shall, as far as applicable, govern the construction of these Local Rules.

(C) **Effective Date of Amendments:** Amendments to these Local Rules shall take effect on the date of entry of the order authorizing the amendments and shall govern all proceedings thereafter commenced and, insofar as just and practicable, all then pending proceedings.

Rule 3. Area and Divisions.

(A) **Area:** The Eastern District of Virginia consists of the counties, cities, and towns specified in 28 U.S.C. § 127, and the places for holding Court within the district are prescribed as Alexandria, Newport News, Norfolk, and Richmond.

(B) **Divisions:** This district shall be divided into four divisions to be designated as the Alexandria, Newport News, Norfolk, and Richmond Divisions; the place for holding Court for each of said divisions shall be the city whose name the division bears, and the territory comprising, and embraced in, each of the said divisions shall be as follows:

(1) The Alexandria Division shall consist of the City of Alexandria and the Counties of Loudoun, Fairfax, Fauquier, Arlington, Prince William, and Stafford and any other city or town geographically within the exterior boundaries of said counties.

(2) The Newport News Division shall consist of the Cities of Newport News, Hampton and Williamsburg, and the Counties of York, James City, Gloucester, Mathews, and any other city or town geographically within the exterior boundaries of said counties.

(3) The Norfolk Division shall consist of the Cities of Norfolk, Portsmouth, Suffolk, Franklin, Virginia Beach, Chesapeake, and Cape Charles, and the Counties of Accomack, Northampton, Isle of Wight, Southampton, and any other city or town geographically within the exterior boundaries of said counties.

(4) The Richmond Division shall consist of the Cities of Richmond, Petersburg, Hopewell, Colonial Heights, and Fredericksburg, and the Counties of Amelia, Brunswick, Caroline, Charles City, Chesterfield, Dinwiddie, Essex, Goochland, Greensville, Hanover, Henrico, King and Queen, King George, King William, Lancaster, Lunenburg, Mecklenburg, Middlesex, New Kent, Northumberland, Nottoway, Powhatan, Prince Edward, Prince George, Richmond, Spotsylvania, Surry, Sussex, Westmoreland, and any other city or town geographically within the exterior boundaries of said counties.

(5) All of the waters, and the lands under such waters, adjacent and opposite to any city, county, or town shall be a part of the division of which said city, county, or town is a part, and wherever there are any waters between any city, county, or town which are in different divisions, then such waters and land under them shall be considered to be in both divisions.

(6) In the event of any annexation or merger of any cities and/or counties the land lying within the merged or annexed area shall be deemed within the exterior boundaries of the original city or county to the same intent and purpose as if the annexation or merger had not occurred, unless otherwise modified by Local Rule.

(C) **Division in Which Suits are to Be Instituted:** Civil actions for which venue is proper in this district shall be brought in the proper division, as well. The venue rules stated in 28 U.S.C. § 1391 et seq. also shall apply to determine the proper division in which an action shall be filed. For the purpose of determining the proper division in which to lay venue, the venue rules stated in 28 U.S.C. § 1391 et seq. shall be construed as if the terms "judicial district" and "district" were replaced with the term "division." However, the Clerk's Office in any division shall accept for filing new complaints which, venue excepted, are in proper form. Such complaints shall be filed on the day submitted, stamped as having been "filed," deemed "filed" for all purposes, and forwarded to the division where venue lies for further proceedings.

Editor's note. — By order adopted January 30, 1992, entered nunc pro tunc to December 10, 1991, the counties of Culpeper, Louisa and Orange are included in the Charlottesville division of the United States District Court for the Western District of Virginia.

CASE NOTES

Venue was improper. — Motion to transfer an action concerning a home financing transaction pursuant to E.D. Va. R. 3(C) was granted because venue in the Richmond Division was improper because (1) even if one of the defendants, five corporations and one individual, resided in the Richmond Division, venue was not proper under 28 U.S.C.S. § 1391(b)(1) because not all of the defendants resided in the same state; (2) venue was improper under § 1391(b)(2) because the activities giving rise to the claim occurred in the Norfolk Division, not the Richmond Division, and the property that was the subject of the action was located in the Norfolk Division; and (3) venue was improper under § 1391(b)(3) because the action could have been brought in the Norfolk Division because the parties agreed that a substantial amount of the activities giving rise to the action occurred there. Williams v. Equity Holding Corp., 2007 U.S. Dist. LEXIS 29795 (E.D. Va. Feb. 9, 2007).

Because venue was improper in the Richmond Division of the Eastern District of Virginia (personal jurisdiction over a corporation was not proper in the state merely because the corporation was incorporated in the state, and a substantial part of the events or omissions giving rise to the claim did not occur within that division), the motion to transfer to the Norfolk Division was granted. Polygroup Ltd. v. General Foam Plastics Corp., 2012 U.S. Dist. LEXIS 90223 (E.D. Va. June 27, 2012).

Applied in Scott v. United States, 586 F. Supp. 66 (E.D. Va. 1984).

Rule 4. Service and Return of Summons — Abatement.

(A) **Service and Abatement:** If service of a summons and complaint is sought other than under Fed. R. Civ. P. 4(d) but is not effected, the Marshal or other person responsible for effecting service shall return the summons and complaint to the Clerk with an endorsement thereon stating the reasons for failure to effect service.

All waivers of service obtained under Fed. R. Civ. P. 4(d) shall be filed within five (5) days after they are returned to plaintiff. Unless, within one hundred and twenty (120) days after the complaint is filed, a defendant has been served, or has appeared or has waived service, the Clerk shall abate the action and dismiss it without prejudice as to such defendant(s) after having given, but received no response to, the notice required by Fed. R. Civ. P. 4(m).

Where the United States, its officers, corporations, or agencies are served by mail pursuant to Fed. R. Civ. P. 4(i)(1)(A), service shall be effective on the date of the postmark or on the date received if there is no postmark or it is illegible. The United States Attorney shall file a certificate reporting the postmark and receipt dates.

(B) **Withholding Service:** Requests by a party to withhold the service of a summons and complaint, or a third-party summons and complaint upon parties as to whom waiver of service provisions are inapplicable shall not be granted by the Clerk without leave of Court first obtained; provided, however, that a party may request the Clerk to withhold the issuance and service of an *in rem* process upon advising the Clerk that the property subject to arrest or attachment is not within the jurisdiction or that arrangements have been made for the acceptance of service.

(C) **Civil Cover Sheet:** The Clerk shall require a complete and executed AO Form JS 44(a), Civil Cover Sheet, to accompany each civil action filed except as to actions filed by prisoners and other litigants proceeding *pro se*.

Rule 5. Designation and Handling of Documents Under Seal.

(A) Unless otherwise provided by law or Court rule, no document may be filed under seal without an order entered by the Court.

(B) A party submitting a document or portion of a document (e.g., exhibit[s]) for filing under seal pursuant to a governing statute, rule, or order shall note on the face of the document that it or a portion of it is filed under seal pursuant to that statute, rule, or order. The Clerk shall provide public notice by stating on the docket that the document contains sealed material.

(C) Any motion for a protective order providing prospectively for filing of documents under seal shall be accompanied by a non-confidential supporting memorandum, a notice that identifies the motion as a sealing motion, and a proposed order. A confidential memorandum for in camera review may also be submitted. The non-confidential memorandum and the proposed order shall include:

(1) A non-confidential description of what is to be sealed;

(2) A statement as to why sealing is necessary, and why another procedure will not suffice;

(3) References to governing case law; and

(4) Unless permanent sealing is sought, a statement as to the period of time the party seeks to have the matter maintained under seal and as to how the matter is to be handled upon unsealing.

The proposed order shall recite the findings required by governing case law to support the proposed sealing.

The Clerk shall provide public notice by docketing the motion in a way that discloses its nature as a motion to seal, with its hearing date (if any). Other parties and non-parties may submit memoranda in support of or opposition to the motion, and may designate all or part of such memoranda as confidential. Any confidential memoranda will be treated as sealed pending the outcome of the ruling on the motion.

(D) Any document not covered by section (B) and filed with the intention of being sealed shall be accompanied by a motion to seal that complies with the requirements of section (C). The Clerk shall provide public notice by docketing the motion in a way that discloses its nature as a motion to seal, with its hearing date (if any). Other parties and non-parties may submit memoranda in support of or in opposition to the motion, and may designate all or part of such memoranda as confidential. The document and any confidential memoranda will be treated as sealed pending the outcome of the ruling on the motion. Failure to file a motion to seal will result in the document being treated as a public record.

(E) Each document that is the subject of an existing sealing order, or the subject of a motion for such an order, shall be submitted to the Clerk's Office securely sealed, with the container clearly labeled "UNDER SEAL." The case number, case caption, a reference to any statute, rule, or order permitting the item to be sealed and a non-confidential descriptive title of the document shall also be noted on the container.

(F) A motion to have an entire case kept under seal shall be subject to the requirements and procedures of sections (C) and (E).

(G) Nothing in this Local Civil Rule limits the ability of the parties, by agreement, to restrict access to documents which are not filed with the Court.

(H) Trial exhibits, including documents previously filed under seal, and trial transcripts will not be filed under seal except upon a showing of necessity demonstrated to the trial judge.

Rule 7. Pleadings — Motions — Continuances — Orders.

(A) **Grounds and Relief to be Stated:** All motions shall state with particularity the grounds therefor and shall set forth the relief or order sought.

(B) **Address and Telephone Number of Attorney and *Pro Se* Litigants:** All pleadings and motions shall include the attorney's office address and telephone number. All pleadings filed by non-prisoner litigants proceeding *pro se* shall contain an address where notice can be served on such person and a telephone number where such person can be reached or a message left. All pleadings filed by prisoners proceeding *pro se* shall contain an address where notice can be served on such person.

(C) **Personal Identifiers:**

(1) Redaction of personal identifiers is governed by Fed.R.Civ.P. 5.2 unless the Court directs otherwise. In all actions for benefits under the Social Security Act, the government shall file the administrative record under seal in paper form, the Court having found that such administrative records are by nature confidential and that applicants' privacy interests outweigh any public interest in disclosure; but this provision does not preclude a motion to unseal in any such action.

(2) The responsibility for redacting personal identifiers rests solely with counsel and the parties. The Clerk will not review each pleading for compliance with this Local Rule. Counsel and the parties are cautioned that failure to redact these personal identifiers may subject them to sanctions.

(D) Abrogated.

(E) **Return Date:** Except as otherwise provided by an order of the Court or by these Local Rules, all motions shall be made returnable to the time obtained from and scheduled by the Court for a hearing thereon. The moving party shall be responsible to set the motion for hearing or to arrange with opposing counsel for submission of the motion without oral argument. Unless otherwise ordered, a motion shall be deemed withdrawn if the movant does not set it for hearing (or arrange to submit it without a hearing) within thirty (30) days after the date on which the motion is filed. The non-moving party also may arrange for a hearing. Before endeavoring to secure an appointment for a hearing on any motion, it shall be incumbent upon the counsel desiring such hearing to meet and confer in person or by telephone with his or her opposing counsel in a good-faith effort to narrow the area of disagreement. In the absence of any agreement, such conference shall be held in the office of the attorney nearest the Court in the division in which the action is pending. In any division that has a regularly scheduled motions day, the motion should be noticed for the first permissible motions day. The hearing date of motions for summary judgment is also governed by Local Civil Rule 56.

(F) **Briefs Required:**

(1) All motions, unless otherwise directed by the Court and except as noted hereinbelow in subsection 7(F)(2), shall be accompanied by a written brief setting forth a concise statement of the facts and supporting reasons, along with a citation of the authorities upon which the movant relies. Unless otherwise directed by the Court, the opposing party shall file a responsive brief and such supporting documents as are appropriate, within eleven (11) days after service and the moving party may file a rebuttal brief within three (3) days after the service of the opposing party's reply brief. No further briefs or written communications may be filed without first obtaining leave of Court.

(2) Unless the court directs otherwise, briefs need not accompany motions for: (a) a more definite statement; (b) an extension of time to respond to pleadings, unless the time has already expired; and (c) a default judgment.

(3) All briefs, including footnotes, shall be written in 12 point Roman style or 10 pitch Courier style with one inch margins. Except for good cause shown in advance of filing, opening and responsive briefs, exclusive of affidavits and supporting documentation, shall not exceed thirty (30) 8-1/2 inch x 11 inch pages double-spaced and rebuttal briefs shall not exceed twenty (20) such pages.

(G) **Continuances:** Motions for continuances of a trial or hearing date shall not be granted by the mere agreement of counsel. No continuance will be granted other than for good cause and upon such terms as the Court may impose.

(H) **Filing of Pleadings:** After the filing of the complaint, all pleadings, motions, briefs, and filings of any kind must be timely filed with the Clerk's Office of the division in which the case is pending.

(I) **Extensions:** Any requests for an extension of time relating to motions must be in writing and, in general, will be looked upon with disfavor.

(J) **Determination of Motions Without Oral Hearing:** In accordance with Fed. R. Civ. P. 78, the Court may rule upon motions without an oral hearing.

(K) **Motions Against *Pro Se* Parties:** It shall be the obligation of counsel for any party who files any dispositive or partially dispositive motion addressed to a party who is appearing in the action without counsel to attach to or include at the foot of the motion a warning consistent with the requirements of *Roseboro v. Garrison,* 528 F.2d 309 (4th Cir. 1975). The warning shall state that:

(1) The *pro se* party is entitled to file a response opposing the motion and that any such response must be filed within twenty-one (21) days of the date on which the dispositive or partially dispositive motion is filed; and

(2) The Court could dismiss the action on the basis of the moving party's papers if the *pro se* party does not file a response; and

(3) The *pro se* party must identify all facts stated by the moving party with which the *pro se* party disagrees and must set forth the *pro se* party's version of the facts by offering affidavits (written statements signed before a notary public and under oath) or by filing sworn statements (bearing a certificate that it is signed under penalty of perjury); and

(4) The *pro se* party is also entitled to file a legal brief in opposition to the one filed by the moving party.

(L) **Court Orders — Objections Noted:** Whenever counsel shall endorse an order and note with such endorsement any objection to the order, unless the grounds of such objection have been previously stated in the record, or unless the grounds are set forth in writing at the time and as a part of the endorsement, or a request made to the Court for a hearing, it will be assumed the objection is without effect and waived. (Amended by order adopted Oct. 25, 2004, effective Feb. 15, 2005; by order adopted October 2008, effective Nov. 25, 2008; and by order effective Nov. 19, 2010.)

Law Review. — For note, "Attorney Fees, Freedom of Information, and Pro Se Litigants: Per Se Prohibitions Frustrate Policies," see 26 Wm. & Mary L. Rev. 349 (1985).

CASE NOTES

The application of the local rules is within the discretion of the court. The purpose of requiring the list of undisputed facts in subdivision (F)(2) is to aid the court and the parties. The parties provided the court with sufficient information in their motions, briefs, and oral argument. Such a list was unnecessary in this case, and it would have belabored the process to require it at this late juncture. Michael v. Sentara Health Sys., 939 F. Supp. 1220 (E.D. Va. 1996).

Counsel violated subdivision (E) and devastated client's legal position by failing to submit opposing brief, memorandum or any other manner or form of filing, thereby causing client to lose her opportunity to meet her rebuttal burden and hampering the ability of the court to engage in thoughtful, informed reflection. In re Fisherman's Wharf Fillet, Inc., 83 F. Supp. 2d 651 (E.D. Va. 1999).

Extension of time to file brief for bankruptcy court appeal. — Debtor/appellant's motion for a third extension of time to file a brief for her appeal of a bankruptcy court decision was dismissed pursuant to Fed. R. Bankr. P. 8001. Appellant's allegations of disability were insufficient to support a finding that good cause existed for further delay, because appellant appeared capable of presenting her arguments to the court when she chose to do so, the court looked upon extensions of time relating to motions with disfavor, as required by E.D. Va. R. 7(I), and even if the appeal was dismissed, appellant would still be entitled to recover nearly half of her losses from appellee. Morris v. Marrin, 2010 U.S. Dist. LEXIS 144885 (E.D. Va. Apr. 29, 2010).

Untimely rebuttal brief. — Where defendants' rebuttal brief was filed 16 days after it was due and defendants made no request for extension or enlargement, and offered no reason for their untimely submission, the rebuttal brief was not considered by the court. Littlejohn v. Moody, 381 F. Supp. 2d 507, 2005 U.S. Dist. LEXIS 16708 (E.D. Va. 2005).

Untimely opposition. — Defendants timely filed their motions for summary judgment on March 16, 2009, and the student's opposition briefs were due by March 30, 2009; in violation of E.D. Va. R. 7(F)(1) and 7(H), the student failed to file any opposition brief in a timely fashion, instead, the student did not file his motion to enlarge his time to respond until three days after the deadline had elapsed. Such motions were looked upon with disfavor even when timely filed and such disfavor could only increase when such a motion was itself not timely filed; the student's motion also violated E.D. Va. R. 7(F)(2)'s requirement that motions be accompanied by a separate brief, and did not attach the untimely opposition brief for which the student sought leave to file; the student notably failed even to meet the extended deadline that he himself requested as his opposition brief and exhibits were not filed until one day after the deadline he sought. Key v. Robertson, 626 F. Supp. 2d 566, 2009 U.S. Dist. LEXIS 51092 (E.D. Va. 2009).

Brief exceeded page limit. — Companies' motion to strike the relators' response to the companies factual allegations, including counter statement of material fact had to be stricken in its entirety because the relators ignored E.D. Va. R. 7(F)(3), which explicitly limited responsive briefs to 30 pages, when they filed two briefs that totaled 45 pages to attempt an end-run around the rules. United States ex rel. DRC, Inc. v. Custer Battles, LLC, 472 F. Supp. 2d 787, 2007 U.S. Dist. LEXIS 8473 (E.D. Va. 2007), aff'd, 2009 U.S. App. LEXIS 7674 (4th Cir. Va. 2009).

Although plaintiffs contended that the district court erred in refusing to strike the memorandum that defendants submitted in support of their summary judgment motion, the district court exercised its discretion by striking the last two pages of defendants' memorandum, and plaintiffs failed to show how the district court abused its discretion in that respect. Iota Xi Chapter of Sigma Chi Fraternity v. Patterson, 566 F.3d 138, 2009 U.S. App. LEXIS 10184 (4th Cir. 2009).

Failure to renew motion to dismiss for improper venue, after initial motion to dismiss was denied without prejudice because motion did not comply with subdivision (F), resulted in waiver regarding venue. Alderman v. Chrysler Corp., 480 F. Supp. 600 (E.D. Va. 1979).

Motion to amend complaint denied pending compliance with subdivisions (A) and (F). — Where after plaintiff's original motion was denied, plaintiff submitted a copy of the proposed amended complaint, but did not renew his motion for leave to amend, nor did he file a supporting brief in accordance with local Rule 11(A) and (F), under such circumstances, the motion would be denied pending plaintiff's compliance with the local rules. Williams v. Wilkerson, 90 F.R.D. 168 (E.D. Va. 1981).

Since defendants' motion was filed as a motion to dismiss pursuant to FRCP Rule 12 (b)(6), and was subsequently converted to a motion for summary judgment by the court, defendants' motion to dismiss was not defective under subdivision (F)(2) for its failure to include a list of undisputed facts. Michael v. Sentara Health Sys., 939 F. Supp. 1220 (E.D. Va. 1996).

Motion for fees. — School board incorrectly claimed defendants' motion for fees was withdrawn in light of E.D. Va. R. 7(E). As the Fourth Circuit's opinion did not expressly lift the stay in the matter, and the court's opinion and order of May 23, 2005, did not provide for any circumstances whereby the stay would be automatically lifted, the court concluded the stay was still in effect so as to render defendants' setting of hearing for its motion for attorneys' fees and costs as proper under the local rule. County Sch. Bd. v. A.L., 2007 U.S. Dist. LEXIS 16395 (E.D. Va. Mar. 6, 2007).

Where affidavits supporting plaintiffs' prayer for attorneys' fees were not detailed and it could not be determined from the affidavit nor from the brief in support of the motion, what a reasonable attorney fee would be, plaintiffs were instructed to submit a detailed brief and proofs as required by subdivisions (F) and (L). Music City Music v. Alfa Foods, Ltd., 616 F. Supp. 1001 (E.D. Va. 1985).

Where plaintiff's third motion sought "declaratory judgment" regarding "the date of the FOIA request to which the defendant should respond, and the types or description of the documents that the defendant should produce pursuant to 5 USC 552," plaintiff's maneuvering was little more than an ineffective attempt to circumvent the local rules of this court that limit parties in the briefing of motions brought before the court. Pully v. IRS, 939 F. Supp. 429 (E.D. Va. 1996).

Application of rule. — After default was set aside in a suit alleging violations of various federal securities laws, common law fraud, breach of contract, breach of fiduciary duty, conversion, and negligence, a pro se litigant was reminded that she was subject to the same rules as counsel, particularly E.D. Va. Civ. R. 7 governing filings, and that her claims could be dismissed should she fail to comply with future deadlines. Vick v. Wong, 263 F.R.D. 325, 2009 U.S. Dist. LEXIS 95597 (E.D. Va. 2009).

Applied in Clark v. Louisa County Sch. Bd., 472 F. Supp. 323 (E.D. Va. 1979); Crawford v. Loving, 84 F.R.D. 80 (E.D. Va. 1979); Bernstein v. Menard, 557 F. Supp. 90 (E.D. Va. 1982); Clarke v. United States, 553 F. Supp. 382 (E.D. Va. 1983); Bernstein v. Menard, 557 F. Supp. 92 (E.D. Va. 1983); Croatan Books, Inc. v. Virginia, 574 F. Supp. 880 (E.D. Va. 1983); Wood v. Kling, 98 F.R.D. 319 (E.D. Va. 1983); Clarke v. United States, 587 F. Supp. 674 (E.D. Va. 1984); Pedigo v. Reynolds Metals Co., 618 F. Supp. 60 (E.D. Va. 1985); Sweeney Co. v. Engineers-Constructors, Inc., 109 F.R.D. 358 (E.D. Va. 1986); Ross v. Keelings, 2 F. Supp. 2d 810 (E.D. Va. 1998); Carter v. Bear Island Paper Co., 2004 U.S. Dist. LEXIS 28109 (E.D. Va. May 25, 2004); CareFirst of Md., Inc. v. First Care, P.C., 422 F. Supp. 2d 592, 2006 U.S. Dist. LEXIS 11423 (E.D. Va. 2006).

Rule 7.1. Financial Disclosure.

(A) **Required Disclosure.** A nongovernmental corporation, partnership, trust, or other similar entity that is a party to, or that appears in, an action or proceeding in this Court shall:

(1) file two (2) copies of a statement that:

a. identifies all its parent, subsidiary, or affiliate entities (corporate or otherwise) that have issued stock or debt securities to the public and also identifies any publicly held entity (corporate or otherwise) that owns 10% or more of its stock, and

b. identifies all parties in the partnerships, general or limited, or owners or members of non-publicly traded entities such as LLCs or other closely held entities, or

c. states that there is nothing to report under Local Civil Rule 7.1(A)(1)(a) and (b); and

(2) file a supplemental statement containing such additional information as may be from time to time required by the Judicial Conference of the United States or this Court.

(B) **Time for Filing.** A statement or form required by Local Civil Rule 7.1(A) shall be filed upon the party's first appearance, pleading, petition, motion, response, or other request addressed to the Court. A supplemental statement or form shall be filed promptly upon any change in the circumstances that Local Civil Rule 7.1(A) requires the party to identify.

(C) **Statement Delivered to Judge.** The Clerk shall deliver a copy of the Local Civil Rule 7.1(A) disclosure to each judge acting in the action or proceeding.

Rule 7.1.

IN THE UNITED STATES DISTRICT COURT
FOR THE EASTERN DISTRICT OF VIRGINIA

____

vs. Civil/Criminal Action No __________

____

FINANCIAL INTEREST DISCLOSURE STATEMENT

Pursuant to Local Rule 7.1 of the Eastern District of Virginia and to enable Judges and Magistrate Judges to evaluate possible disqualification or recusal, the undersigned counsel for

____

in the above captioned action, certifies that the following are parents, trusts, subsidiaries and/or affiliates of said party that have issued shares or debt securities to the public or own more than ten percent of the stock of the following:

____

____

Or

Pursuant to Local Rule 7.1 of the Eastern District of Virginia and to enable Judges and Magistrate Judges to evaluate possible disqualifications or recusal, the undersigned counsel for

____

in the above captioned action, certifies that there are no parents, trusts, subsidiaries and/or affiliates of said party that have issued shares or debt securities to the public.

__________________________ ______________________________________

Date Signature of Attorney or Litigant
Counsel for ____________________

Note: Under L.R. 7.1(A)(1), this form is to be filled in duplicate with the Clerk of Court.

Rev.8/31/00

Rule 16. Pretrial Conference.

(A) **Applicability of Rule 16:** Proceedings upon a defendant's default and matters involving habeas corpus petitions, other *pro se* prisoner petitions, bankruptcy proceedings, condemnation cases, forfeitures, and reviews from administrative agencies, are not subject to the provisions of this Local Rule, but the judge to whom any such case is assigned may, in his or her discretion, follow the procedure outlined herein in whole or in part in any case. (See Fed. R. Civ. P. 16(b).)

(B) **Initial Pretrial Conference and Order and Scheduling Order:** In all other civil actions, as promptly as possible after a complaint or notice of removal has been filed, the Court shall schedule an initial pretrial conference to be conducted in accordance with Fed. R. Civ. P. 16(b). In addition thereto, or in lieu thereof, not later than ninety (90) days from first appearance or one hundred and twenty (120) days after service of the complaint, the Court shall enter an order fixing the cut-off dates for the respective parties to complete the processes of discovery, the date for a final pretrial conference and, whenever practicable, the trial date, and providing for any other administrative or management matters permitted by Fed. R. Civ. P. 16 or by law generally.

The parties and their counsel are bound by the dates specified in any such orders and no extensions or continuances thereof shall be granted in the absence of a showing of good cause. Mere failure on the part of counsel to proceed promptly with the normal processes of discovery shall not constitute good cause for an extension or continuance.

Rule 26. Discovery and Disclosure.

(A) **Discovery:**

(1) In this district, pursuant to Fed. R. Civ. P. 26(f), hereinafter Rule 26(f), it may be required by order that:

(a) the scheduling and planning conference outlined in Fed. R. Civ. P. 16(b) be held fewer than twenty-one (21) days after the conference required by Rule 26(f); and

(b) the written report outlining the discovery plan due under Rule 26(f) be filed fewer than fourteen (14) days after the conference between the parties or the parties be excused from submitting a written report and be permitted to report orally on their discovery plan at the conference required by Fed. R. Civ. P. 16(b).

(2) In this district, magistrate judges are authorized to conduct the scheduling and planning conference and issue the scheduling order for which provision is made in Fed. R. Civ. P. 16(b).

(3) A deposition taken without leave of Court pursuant to a notice under Fed. R. Civ. P. 30(a)(1) before the time required by Fed. R. Civ. P. 12 for filing an answer or responsive pleading shall not be used against a party who demonstrates that, when served with the notice, it was unable through the exercise of diligence to obtain counsel to represent it at the taking of the deposition.

(B) **Requirement of Writing:** All objections to interrogatories, depositions, requests, or applications under Fed. R. Civ. P. 26 through 37, as well as all motions and replies thereto concerning discovery matters, shall be in writing. If time does not permit the filing of a written motion, the Court may, in its discretion, waive this requirement.

(C) **Objections to Discovery Process:** Unless otherwise ordered by the Court, an objection to any interrogatory, request, or application under Fed. R. Civ. P. 26 through 37, shall be served within fifteen (15) days after the service of the interrogatories, request, or application; or, in a case removed or transferred to this Court after discovery was served, within fifteen (15) days after the date of removal or transfer. The Court may allow a shorter or longer time. Any such objection shall be specifically stated. Any such objection shall not extend the time within which the objecting party must otherwise answer or respond to any discovery matter to which no specific objection has been made.

(D) **Expert Disclosures:**

(1) *Agreement Upon Disclosure:* Counsel are encouraged to agree upon the sequence and timing of the expert disclosures required by Fed. R. Civ. P. 26(a)(2). All such agreements must be in the form of a consent order entered by the Court.

(2) *Timing of Mandatory Disclosure:* Absent such a consent order or unless ordered otherwise, the disclosures required by Fed. R. Civ. P. 26(a)(2) shall be made first by the plaintiff not later than sixty (60) days before the earlier of the date set for completion of discovery or for the final pretrial conference, if any, then by the defendant thirty (30) days thereafter. Plaintiff shall disclose fifteen (15) days thereafter any evidence that is solely contradictory or rebuttal evidence to the defendant's disclosure.

(3) *Completion of Disclosure:* Whether accomplished by agreement pursuant to Local Civil Rule 26(D)(1) or pursuant to the schedule set by Local Civil Rule 26(D)(2), all parties shall complete all forms of expert disclosure and discovery not later than thirty (30) days after the date upon which plaintiff is, or would be, required by Fed. R. Civ. P. 26(a)(2)(C) to disclose contradictory or rebuttal evidence.

(4) *General Provisions:* For purposes of this Local Rule, counter-claim plaintiffs, cross-claimants and third-party plaintiffs shall be plaintiffs as to all elements of the counter-claim, cross-claim, or third-party claim. Answers to interrogatories directed at clarification of the written reports of expert witnesses disclosed pursuant to Fed. R. Civ. P. 26(a)(2) shall be due fifteen (15) days after service. (Amended by order adopted Oct. 25, 2004, effective Feb. 15, 2005; and by order effective Nov. 19, 2010.)

CASE NOTES

Rationale for adopting discovery limitations. — See Lykins v. Attorney Gen. of United States, 86 F.R.D. 318 (E.D. Va. 1980).

Good cause requirement of subdivision (A) upheld. — See Lykins v. Attorney Gen. of United States, 86 F.R.D. 318 (E.D. Va. 1980).

Limit on number of interrogatories held exceeded. — See Goodell v. Rehrig Int'l, Inc., 683 F. Supp. 1051 (E.D. Va. 1988), aff'd, 865 F.2d 1257 (E.D. Va. 1989).

Subsection (F) of rule waived by court. — See Hirschkop v. Virginia State Bar Ass'n, 406 F. Supp. 721 (E.D. Va. 1975).

Rule 30. Depositions — Expenses — Summaries — Reviewing Depositions.

(A) **Discovery:** Any party, or representative of a party (e.g., officer, director, or managing agent), filing a civil action in the proper division of this Court must ordinarily be required, upon request, to submit to a deposition at a place designated within the division. Exceptions to this general rule may be made on order of the Court when the party, or representative of a party, is of such age or physical condition, or special circumstances exist, as may reasonably interfere with the orderly taking of a deposition at a place within the division. A defendant, who becomes a counterclaimant, cross-claimant, or third-party plaintiff, shall be considered as having filed an action in this Court for the purpose of this Local Rule. This subsection shall not apply to an involuntary plaintiff or an interpleader plaintiff.

(B) **Recording and Transcribing Transcript of Discovery Deposition:** The expense of recording a deposition shall be paid by the party seeking to take same. The expense of transcribing the deposition shall be paid by any party ordering the preparation of the original. Any other party desiring a copy of said deposition shall pay for same at the copy rate. Parties may, by agreement, equally share the costs of attendance and transcribing, including such copies as desired.

(C) **Attorneys' Fees:** Unless the services of associate counsel are retained, in lieu of travel expense, it is not the policy of the Court to make an allowance of counsel fees in attending any deposition, except to the extent provided by statute and otherwise in this Local Rule, but the Court reserves the right to make a reasonable allowance where the circumstances of the case may justify same.

(D) **Security for Travel Expense:** Any party desiring to take the deposition of a witness (not a party or representative of a party) for discovery or use at trial or a party or representative of a party as ordered by the Court under Local Civil Rule 30(A), beyond a division of the Court in which the action is pending, shall, if such testimony cannot be readily procured in another manner, prepay or secure the reasonable cost of travel of not more than one opposing counsel to the place of taking the deposition and return therefrom, but in no event shall the reasonable costs of travel exceed an amount which would reasonably be required to be paid to associate counsel in the area in which the deposition is being taken unless insufficient time is allowed in giving the notice to take depositions.

(E) **Travel Expense:** The costs of travel as provided in this Local Rule shall consist of the reasonable costs of travel by air or other public transportation, or an allowance for travel by private automobile at the prevailing rate per mile as may be provided for federal government employees on official business, or whichever means of transportation is reasonably selected and used, including the cost of transportation from the office or residence to the terminal of the public transportation and from the destination terminal to the place of the taking of the deposition, and reasonable overnight accommodations, if deemed reasonably necessary, and return. The Court may, in its discretion, make a reasonable allowance for food.

The cost of travel, as herein defined, shall apply to any witness (not a party or the representative of a party) required to attend the taking of a deposition. As to any witness attending a trial or hearing in a civil action, pursuant to Fed. R. Civ. P. 45(b)(2), the expense of such cost of travel shall be taxed as costs if said witness testifies or if it is reasonably necessary for the witness to appear, but said costs of travel shall be limited to what would have been expended if said witness resided within one hundred (100) miles from the place of the trial or hearing, together with such reasonable allowance, if required for the purpose of the witness testifying, for overnight accommodations and food. If the witness resided within one hundred (100) miles of the place of trial or hearing, the cost of travel shall be limited to the mileage and attendance fees as provided by law.

(F) **Reviewing Depositions:** Whenever depositions are expected to be presented in evidence, counsel shall, before the final pretrial conference or if same are not then available before the day of trial, review such depositions and (1) extract therefrom a short statement of the qualifications of any expert witness to read to the jury, (2) eliminate unnecessary and/or irrelevant matters, and (3) eliminate all objections and statements of counsel to avoid reading same to a jury. In the event counsel are unable to agree on what shall be eliminated, they shall submit to the Court for a ruling thereon before the date of trial. Failure to do so will constitute a waiver of objections.

(G) **Summaries of Depositions:** In all nonjury cases, counsel shall attach to any deposition a summary of the examination of the testimony of each witness, thereby pointing out the salient points to be noted by the Court.

(H) **Reasonable Notice:** As a general rule, eleven (11) days in advance of the contemplated taking of a deposition shall constitute reasonable notice of the taking of a deposition in the continental United States, but this will vary according to the complexity of the contemplated testimony and the urgency of taking the deposition of a party or witness at a particular time and place.

CASE NOTES

Applied in Said v. Virginia Commonwealth University/Medical College, 130 F.R.D. 60 (E.D. Va. 1990).

Rule 33. Interrogatories.

Deleted.

Rule 37. Motions to Compel and Sanctions.

(A) **Motions to Compel:** After a discovery request is objected to, or not complied with, within time, and if not otherwise resolved, it is the responsibility of the party initiating discovery to place the matter before the Court by a proper motion pursuant to Fed. R. Civ. P. 37, to compel an answer, production, designation, or inspection. Such motion must be accompanied by a brief as required by Local Civil Rule 37(B).

(B) **Briefing of Discovery Motions:** Unless otherwise ordered, the scheduling and page limitation provisions of Local Civil Rule 7(E) shall apply to all discovery motions; provided that the Court may elect to decide discovery motions without briefing.

(C) **Compliance with Discovery Orders:** After the Court has ruled on a discovery motion, any answer, production, designation, inspection, or examination required by the Court shall be completed within eleven (11) days after the entry of the order on the motion, unless otherwise ordered by the Court.

(D) **Failure to Comply with Order:** A party objecting to the failure of another party to comply with an order on a discovery motion shall be responsible for bringing the non-compliance before the Court by a proper motion for supplementary relief pursuant to Fed. R. Civ. P. 37.

(E) **Consultation Among Counsel:** Counsel shall confer to decrease, in every way possible the filing of unnecessary discovery motions. No motion concerning discovery matters may be filed until counsel shall have conferred in person or by telephone to explore with opposing counsel the possibility of resolving the discovery matters in controversy. The Court will not consider any motion concerning discovery matters unless the motion is accompanied by a statement of counsel that a good faith effort has been made between counsel to resolve the discovery matters at issue.

(F) **Extensions:** Depending upon the facts of the particular case, the Court in its discretion may, upon appropriate written motion by a party, allow an extension of time in excess of the time provided by the Federal Rules of Civil Procedure, these Local Rules, or previous Court order, within which to respond to or complete discovery or to reply to discovery motions. Any agreement between counsel relating to any extension of time is of no force or effect; only the Court, after appropriate motion directed thereto, may grant leave for any extension of time. Unless otherwise specifically provided, such extension will be upon the specific condition that, regardless of what may be divulged by such discovery, it will not in any manner alter the schedule of dates and procedure previously adopted by the Court in the particular case.

(G) **Unnecessary Discovery Motions or Objections:** The presentation to the Court of unnecessary discovery motions, the presentation to another party or non-party of unnecessary discovery requests of any kind, as well as any unwarranted opposition to proper discovery proceedings, will subject such party to appropriate remedies and sanctions, including the imposition of costs and counsel fees.

(H) **Sanctions:** Should any party or attorney fail to comply with any of the provisions of this Local Rule 37 or otherwise fail or refuse to meet and confer in good faith in an effort to narrow the areas of disagreement concerning discovery, sanctions provided by Fed. R. Civ. P. 37 may be imposed.

(I) The provisions of Local Civil Rule 37(A) through (H) above also apply to disputes over the disclosures required by Fed. R. Civ. P. 26(a)(1).

Rule 38. Demand for Jury Trial.

Any demand for jury in a civil action must be in writing and filed strictly in accordance with Fed. R. Civ. P. 38. Removal actions shall be governed by Fed. R. Civ. P. 81(C). In the event another party is added, the additional party may demand trial by jury at any time within twenty-one (21) days after such party is served with process or summons. (Amended by order effective Nov. 19, 2010.)

CASE NOTES

Applied in Vanguard Military Equip. Corp. v. David B. Finestone Co., 6 F. Supp. 2d 488 (E.D. Va. 1997).

Rule 45. Subpoenas.

(A) **Issuance of Subpoenas:** Attorneys of record in an action, or associates in firms of record, as officers of the Court, shall issue all subpoenas in the action as authorized by Fed. R. Civ. P. 45(a)(3).

Parties appearing *pro se* may apply for subpoenas in their own behalf. All such requests by such party must be accompanied by a memorandum setting forth the names and addresses of witnesses or the documents requested and why and for what purpose or purposes. All such requests by *pro se* parties shall be referred to a judge or magistrate judge of this Court who shall first determine whether the requested subpoena shall issue; provided, however, that such determination shall not preclude any witness or person summoned or other interested party from later contesting the subpoena.

(B) **Return Date of Subpoenas:** All subpoenas shall be made returnable to the place, date, and time of trial or hearing, unless otherwise ordered by the Court.

(C) **Proof of Service of Subpoenas:** In civil actions, the party issuing a subpoena for a trial, a hearing, or contempt proceedings, or when it is otherwise necessary to file proof of service, shall file proof of service in the form required by Fed. R. Civ. P. 45(b)(3). Any such proof of service shall be filed promptly and, in any event, within the time during which the person served must respond to the subpoena. Lawyers and parties proceeding *pro se* shall file with the proof of service in civil actions a certificate that all required witness fees and expenses were served with the subpoena requiring the attendance of the witness.

(D) **Subpoenas to Officials:** Without first obtaining permission of the Court, no subpoena shall issue for the attendance at any hearing, trial, or deposition of: (1) the Governor, Lieutenant Governor, or Attorney General of any State; (2) a judge of any court; (3) the President or Vice-President of the United States; (4) any member of the President's Cabinet; (5) any Ambassador or Consul; or (6) any military officer holding the rank of Admiral or General.

(E) **Timely Service of Subpoenas for Trial or Hearings:** Except as otherwise ordered by the Court for good cause shown, subpoenas for attendance of witnesses at hearings or trials in civil actions shall be served not later than fourteen (14) days before the date of the hearing or trial.

(F) **Deposition Subpoenas:** Proof of service of a notice to take depositions as provided in Fed. R. Civ. P. 30(b) and 31(b) constitutes sufficient authorization for the issuance of a subpoena by the Clerk for the district in which the deposition is to be taken for the attendance of persons named or described therein. Except as otherwise ordered by the Court for good cause shown, subpoenas compelling attendance at a deposition shall be served not later than eleven (11) days before the date of the deposition. No subpoena for the taking of depositions shall be issued by the Clerk unless there be exhibited to the Clerk a copy of the notice to take deposition together with a statement of the date and manner of service and of the names of the persons served, certified by the person who made service.

(G) **Civil Actions — Place of Taking Deposition:** Except with respect to a witness in a foreign country (See 28 U.S.C. § 1783), the Clerk shall, upon request, issue a subpoena for taking a deposition requiring the appearance of any party or witness at any place within the district or 100 miles from the place where that person resides, is employed, or transacts business in person, or is served, or at such other convenient place as is fixed by an order of court.

(H) **Subpoenas in Blank:** Whenever there is a question as to whether or not a subpoena in blank should be issued by the Clerk, the applicant shall be referred to a judge of this Court for a final determination. Before issuing a subpoena in blank, the Clerk shall determine the actual pendency of the action and the date and time set for hearing or trial. Except for good cause shown, a blank subpoena returnable in one division will not be issued out of another division. Blank subpoenas shall recite the title and number of the case and shall be completed in every detail except for the name and address of the witness. Returns of service shall be made promptly and filed with the Clerk. Service of subpoenas in blank shall be subject to the requirements of these Local Rules.

Rule 47. Jurors.

(A) **Jury Lists:**

(1) The entire list of names drawn to serve a division of the Court for a particular period and for a particular action or case, together with the questionnaires prepared by the jurors, may be disclosed to counsel for the parties, or to any party acting *pro se*, unless the Court directs otherwise. However, no juror shall be approached, either directly or through any member of his or her immediate family, in an effort to secure information concerning such juror.

(2) When the jurors report for duty at a session of Court, the Clerk shall, upon request, make available to counsel for the parties, or to any party acting *pro se,* a list of such jurors.

(B) **Peremptory Challenges:** In civil actions where there are several plaintiffs and/or several defendants, the Court may allow each or both sides more than the usual number of peremptory challenges permitted by law upon motion made at least twenty-one (21) days before the date set for commencement of trial. Untimely motions will not be entertained.

(C) **Communication with Jurors:** No attorney or party litigant shall personally, or through any investigator or any other person acting for the attorney or party litigant, interview, examine, or question any juror or alternate juror with respect to the verdict or deliberations of the jury in any civil action except on leave of Court granted upon good cause shown and upon such conditions as the Court shall fix.

Rule 51. Proposed Jury Instructions and Voir Dire.

Except as provided otherwise in a pretrial or scheduling order, in all cases tried to a jury the parties shall submit proposed instructions and voir dire questions to the Court in duplicate, with a copy to opposing counsel, at least five (5) business days before the scheduled trial date. Each instruction shall be set forth on a separate page and shall be numbered and identified appropriately by the party submitting it. The original shall bear at its foot a citation of the authority in support of the instruction. Instructions shall be filed as a group together with a cover sheet in pleading form and a certificate of service. Instructions filed with the Court must be proffered to the Court during the instruction conference and ruled upon by the judge to become a part of the official record for appeal.

CASE NOTES

Proposed instruction untimely. — District court's refusal to give a mixed-motive instruction that an employee proposed with respect to a retaliation claim she filed against her employer was not an abuse of discretion because the proposed instruction, which was filed three business days before trial, was untimely under E.D. Va. R. 51. Perez-Tatem v. England, 2007 U.S. App. LEXIS 24832 (4th Cir. Oct. 11, 2007).

Rule 54. Costs — Notice of Appeal — Jury Costs.

(A) **Payment in Advance:** All fees and costs due the Clerk shall be paid in advance except as otherwise provided by law.

(B) **Stipulation for Costs for Certain Admiralty and Maritime Claims:** No stipulation for costs for complaints, petitions, counterclaims, and cross-claims, and the filing of an answer, appearance, or claim shall be required, unless specifically ordered by the Court, except where now or hereafter required by statute, the Federal Rules of Civil Procedure, or the Supplementary Rules for Certain Admiralty and Maritime Claims heretofore or hereafter adopted by Congress or through the rule making process.

(C) **Bond Premiums:** If costs are awarded by the Court, the reasonable premiums or expense paid on any bond or other security given by the prevailing party shall be taxed as part of the costs.

(D) **Taxable Costs And Procedure For Taxing Costs:**

(1) *Bill of Costs.* The party entitled to costs shall file a bill of costs as provided in 28 U.S.C. §§ 1920 and 1924 within eleven (11) days from the entry of judgment, unless such time is extended by order of the Court.

Such bill of costs shall distinctly set forth each item thereof so that the nature of the charge can be readily understood. An itemization and documentation for requested costs in all categories shall be attached to the cost bill. Costs will be disallowed if proper documentation is not provided.

(2) *Objection to the Bill of Costs.* A party from whom costs are sought may serve an opposition to the bill of costs within eleven (11) days after service of the bill of costs. The opposition shall identify each item objected to and the grounds for the objection. Within five (5) days thereafter, the prevailing party may serve responses to the objections.

If no objections are filed, the Clerk shall promptly proceed to tax the costs and shall allow such items specified in the bill of costs as are properly chargeable as costs. The

Clerk shall give notice of such action to the parties or their counsel. The Court shall promptly review the action of the Clerk upon timely motion under Fed. R. Civ. P. 54(d). In the absence of a timely motion the action of the Clerk is final.

If objections are filed and the Clerk is unable to determine all or some of the properly chargeable costs, the application for such costs shall be referred to the judge who presided over the trial or, at the discretion of that judge, to a magistrate judge for report and recommendation under 28 U.S.C. § 636(b)(1)(B).

(E) **Excessive and Unnecessary Costs:** Any party applying for costs which are not recoverable or which are excessive shall be subject to sanction under Fed. R. Civ. P. 11.

(F) **Notice of Appeal — Fees:**

(1) Where there are multiple parties seeking to appeal jointly (e.g., where cases are consolidated or tried together or decided by a single judgment or order) and a joint notice of appeal is filed, the Clerk shall collect only one fee and only one cost bond, if required. Where separate notices of appeal are filed, the Clerk shall collect separate fees and require separate bonds.

(2) Separate notices of appeal, separate fees, and separate bonds are required of a party who exercises a right of appeal under Fed. R. App. P. 4(a)(3), within fourteen (14) days of the date on which the first notice of appeal was filed.

(G) **Jury Costs:** Whenever any civil action scheduled for jury trial is settled, or otherwise disposed of in advance of the actual trial, then, except for good cause shown, juror costs, including service fees, mileage, and per diem, shall be assessed equally against the parties and their counsel or otherwise assessed as directed by the Court, unless the Clerk is notified at least one (1) full business day prior to the day on which the action is scheduled for trial in time to advise the jurors that it will not be necessary for them to attend.

Likewise, when any civil action, proceeding as a jury trial, is settled at trial in advance of the verdict, then, except for good cause shown, all jury costs, service fees, mileage, and per diem shall be assessed equally against the parties and their counsel, or otherwise assessed as directed by the Court. (Amended by order effective Nov. 19, 2010.)

CASE NOTES

Filing fee must accompany complaint. — In the Eastern District of Virginia, the complaint must be accompanied by the filing fee to achieve filed status, with the exceptions noted in subdivision (B). Keith v. Heckler, 603 F. Supp. 150 (E.D. Va. 1985).

Clearly, this rule requires the advance payment of district court filing fees; hence, the clerk properly refused to record the complaint as filed without the payment of the fee. Keith v. Heckler, 603 F. Supp. 150 (E.D. Va. 1985).

Subdivision (C) is valid. White v. Raymark Indus., Inc., 783 F.2d 1175 (4th Cir. 1986).

Subdivision (C) is not inconsistent with and not preempted by federal statutes and uniform federal rules. White v. Raymark Indus., Inc., 783 F.2d 1175 (4th Cir. 1986).

Judgment as a predicate to awarding costs. — Although the language in U.S. Dist. Ct., E.D. Va., Civ. R. 54(D) does not state that a judgment is required in order to tax a party for costs, it does at least contemplate a judgment as a predicate to awarding costs. Bryant v. MV Transportation, Inc., 231 F.R.D. 480, 2005 U.S. Dist. LEXIS 27139 (E.D. Va. 2005).

Presumptive award of costs to prevailing party not overcome where plaintiff only objects generally to costs. — Where the EEOC sued an employer, alleging that it created a racially hostile work environment, but the EEOC voluntarily withdrew its lawsuit after the complaining employee retracted his story at deposition, the employer was entitled to recovery of its costs where (1) it was the prevailing party in the lawsuit, (2) the EEOC objected generally to the award of costs, but it failed to comply with subdivision (D)(2) by specifying the costs that it found objectionable, and (3) the EEOC did not put forth any argument or evidence to overcome the presumptive award of costs to the prevailing party. EEOC v. Greenbriar Pontiac-Oldsmobile-GMC Trucks-KIA, Inc., 314 F. Supp. 2d 581, 2004 U.S. Dist. LEXIS 6555 (E.D. Va. 2004).

Juror costs assessed against defendant where defendant's actions prevented settlement. — Where despite plaintiffs' vigorous attempts to reach a settlement with defendant during the week prior to trial, defendant would not negotiate, defendant's insurance carrier being "unavailable" to authorize a final settlement agreement, and as a result of the insurance carrier's improper conduct, settlement became impossible during the critical period preceding the trial date, under such circumstances, the district court did not abuse its discretion in assessing juror costs pursuant to subdivision (C) against defendant. White v. Raymark Indus., Inc., 783 F.2d 1175 (4th Cir. 1986).

Copy of answer mailed to one of plaintiff's two attorneys triggered 10-day time limit. — Copy of defendant's answer, which was mailed to, and received by, one of plaintiff's two attorneys of record, was properly delivered for purposes of triggering the 10-day time limit provided in Rule 38 of

any quarterly report, or the applicant have more bonds outstanding than can be adequately covered, in the Court's opinion, by the net worth shown, or the applicant fail to file on time any quarterly report, or if for any reason the Court should deem the security offered by the applicant to be inadequate or outstanding bonds not adequately secured, the Court may terminate the right of the applicant to act as surety on any bond, without notice.

Rule 67. Deposits into Court.

Deposit Into Court Procedure: When the Court is requested to enter an order involving the payment of funds into Court for deposit for the benefit of any party, the parties shall submit a draft order, endorsed by counsel for all parties, that specifies (a) the desired depository (which must have sufficient collateral in the Federal Reserve Bank as required by 31 C.F.R. §§ 202 [Circular 176]); (b) whether the Clerk should place the funds into an interest bearing account until the Court orders distribution thereof; and (c) the specific proposed investment instrument with the rate of interest expected. Any party receiving a share of the deposited funds will also receive a proportional share of any interest earned on the funds, minus the court registry assessment fee prescribed by the Judicial Conference of the United States, which fee shall be paid to the Clerk, by check payable to "Clerk of the United States District Court." If the draft order does not specify that the deposited funds will be placed in an interest bearing account, the parties on whose behalf the draft order is submitted shall be deemed to have consented to deposit of the funds into the Court's United States Treasury account, and to have agreed that no interest will accrue. A draft order submitted on behalf of any party under a legal disability shall be endorsed by the party's guardian *ad litem.* A party requesting any disbursement of the deposited funds shall provide to the Clerk in writing the Social Security or tax identification number of any proposed recipient.

Rule 71A. Land Condemnation Actions.

The guidelines for filing, docketing, recording, and reporting land condemnation proceedings approved by the Judicial Conference of the United States at its March 1975 session are approved for use in this jurisdiction and are hereby adopted. The Clerk is directed to implement these guidelines and is authorized, where the United States files separate condemnation actions and a single declaration of taking relating to those separate actions, to establish a master file in which the declaration of taking may be filed. The filing of the declaration of taking therein shall constitute a filing of the same in each of the actions to which it relates.

Rule 72. United States Magistrate Judges — Duties.

Magistrate judges of this district serve as judicial officers of the Court and are authorized and specially designated to perform all duties authorized or allowed to be performed by United States magistrate judges by the United States Code and any rule governing proceedings in this Court.

Duties and cases may be assigned or referred to a magistrate judge by an order entered in the action or on the instructions of a district judge.

CASE NOTES

Mailing of forfeited collateral constitutes guilty plea. — A collateral forfeiture for a misdemeanor offense constitutes a conviction for purposes of the special assessment provision of the Victims of Crime Act of 1984. It is beyond question that the mailing of the collateral is a guilty plea, which is later certified as a conviction pursuant to subdivision (H)(3) of this rule. Scharf v. United States, 606 F. Supp. 379 (E.D. Va. 1985).

Forfeiture of collateral constitutes a guilty plea despite the lack of notice on the ticket to its legal effect. It is persuasive that subdivision (H)(3) of this rule characterizes collateral forfeiture as "tantamount to a finding of guilt." Similarly, the court's local rule impowers the United States Magistrate to "certify the record of any such conviction. . . ." Scharf v. United States, 606 F. Supp. 379 (E.D. Va. 1985).

Application to "Prisoner Cases." — See Coleman v. Hutto, 500 F. Supp. 586 (E.D. Va. 1980).

Applied in Cooper v. Sielaff, 640 F. Supp. 345 (E.D. Va. 1985).

Rule 79. Exhibits.

(A) **Submission of Trial Exhibits:** In all civil actions, unless otherwise ordered by the Court, the party intending to offer exhibits at trial shall place them in a binder, properly tabbed, numbered, and indexed, and the original and two (2) copies shall be delivered to the Clerk, with copies in the same form to the opposing party, one (1) business day before the trial. The submitting party may substitute photographs for demonstrative or sensitive exhibits.

(B) **Custody and Removal of Exhibits During and After Trial:**

(1) *Custody:* After being marked for identification, exhibits offered or admitted in evidence in any action tried in this Court shall be placed in the custody of the Clerk, unless otherwise ordered by the Court. All other exhibits, models, and material not offered and admitted in evidence shall be retained in custody of the attorney or party producing same at trial, unless otherwise directed by the Court.

(2) *Removal:* Whenever any models, diagrams, exhibits, depositions, transcripts, briefs, tables, charts, paper writings, articles, other items, material, or things have been placed in the custody of the Clerk for introduction into evidence or otherwise, and same are not admitted or marked for identification, or otherwise used, they shall be removed by the party who delivered or filed or lodged them with the Clerk immediately following the conclusion of the trial or other disposition of the action, unless otherwise directed by the Court. If such items are not withdrawn within ten (10) days after the right to withdraw them exists, the Clerk may forward them to counsel or the party entitled to them, or destroy or make other disposition of them as the Clerk may deem appropriate.

(3) *Substitutions:* Unless otherwise ordered by the Court, at the conclusion of the trial of a civil action, photographs will be substituted for bulky exhibits and the exhibits shall be returned to the tendering party. The tendering party is responsible for furnishing the photographs, which shall accurately and fully depict the exhibits for which they are substituted.

(C) **Final Disposition of Exhibits:** All exhibits, models, diagrams, depositions, transcripts, briefs, tables, charts, paper writings, articles, other items, material, or things introduced, tendered, lodged, or marked in the trial of a civil action or lodged, filed, or delivered to the Clerk in anticipation of their introduction into evidence or for use at trial, shall be withdrawn by the parties to the litigation or their counsel upon the expiration of thirty (30) days after the judgment has become final and the time for appeal or application for a rehearing or further hearing shall have passed. If such items, material, or things are not so removed within the time aforesaid, the Clerk may forward them to counsel or the party entitled thereto or shall destroy or make such other disposition or use of them as the Clerk may deem appropriate. The Court may at any time direct or order one or more counsel to be the custodian of the exhibits and depositions rather than the Clerk.

Note. — Items which may be subject to forfeiture or confiscation can be claimed by the United States or action taken for their forfeiture, whether pursuant to 18 U.S.C. §§ 492, 545, 924, 969, 1955, 1963, 3611, 3615, 3617, 3618, 3619, or 26 U.S.C. § 5872, or any other statute or law.

CASE NOTES

Amendment creating defense without notice not admissible. — Where the defendant's exhibit list, appended to the Final Pretrial Order, did not contain the policy amendment at issue and admitting defendant's policy amendment into evidence would have significantly altered the issues in this case by establishing a defense which plaintiffs' counsel had no prior notice of, the Court found that defendant's policy amendment was not admissible evidence. Hawks v. City of Newport News, 707 F. Supp. 212 (E.D. Va. 1988).

Applied in Harris v. United States, 431 F. Supp. 1173 (E.D. Va. 1977).

Rule 80. Transcripts — Record on Appeal.

(A) **Court Reporter Management Plan:** In accordance with the provisions of 28 U.S.C. § 753 and the requirements of a resolution adopted by the Judicial Conference of the United States at its March 1982 session, all district courts have been required to file a Court Reporter Management Plan, which is available for inspection and copying in the Clerk's Office. This plan provides information about the supervision, duties and assignments, including the work hours, of court reporters and notes the fee schedule for transcripts. The transcript rates charged by reporters are governed by rates recommended by the Judicial Conference of the United States, if adopted by this Court. The schedule of maximum fees which may be charged is posted in the Clerk's Office.

(B) **Release of Transcript:** The filing, viewing, and purchasing of transcripts of proceedings is governed by the Court's *Electronic Case Filing Policies and Procedures* manual.

(C) **Obligation to Pay Court Reporter:** The obligation to pay the reporter for any and all transcripts shall be the joint and several personal obligation of the attorney, and the party for whose benefit the transcript was obtained, when the order is placed, to the extent so ordered. Any charges for a transcript shall be payable upon the completion of the transcript or any segment thereof, when a proper bill for same has been submitted by the court reporter. If proper charges for transcripts are not paid within a reasonable time after submission, the court reporter may refer the matter to a district judge for such action as may be deemed appropriate.

(D) **Record on Appeal:** Unless otherwise directed by the Court, the record on appeal in civil cases shall not include the examination of the jury on voir dire, counsel's opening statements, arguments of counsel, including arguments of counsel on motions, and the Court's charge to the jury unless there were exceptions to the charge.

(E) **Daily or Expedited Copy:** All requests for daily or expedited transcripts must be made in writing to the court reporter, if known, and, if not, to the Clerk, with copies to opposing counsel, not later than five (5) days before the hearing or trial to be transcribed. (Amended May 12, 2009; and by order effective Nov. 19, 2010.)

Rule 83.1. Attorneys and *Pro Se* Parties.

(A) **Eligibility:** Any person who is an Active Member of the Virginia State Bar in good standing is eligible to practice before this Court upon admission.

(B) **Initial Appearance:** Any person who meets the requirements of the foregoing paragraph and who maintains a law office outside of Virginia shall set forth his or her Virginia State Bar I.D. Number on any initial pleading filed by such person.

(C) **Procedure for Admission:** Every person desiring admission to practice in this Court shall file with the Clerk written application therefor accompanied by an endorsement by two (2) qualified members of the bar of this Court stating that the applicant is of good moral character and professional reputation. The form for such application may be obtained from the Clerk's Office.

As a part of the application, the applicant shall certify that applicant has within ninety (90) days prior to submission of the application read or reread (a) the Federal Rules of Civil Procedure, (b) the Federal Rules of Evidence, and (c) the Local Rules of the United States District Court for the Eastern District of Virginia.

The applicant shall thereafter be presented by a qualified practitioner of the Court who shall in open Court by oral motion, and upon giving assurance to the Court that the practitioner has examined the credentials of the applicant and is satisfied the applicant possesses the necessary qualifications, move the applicant's admission to practice.

The applicant shall in open Court take the oath required for admission, subscribe the roll of the Court, and pay to the Clerk the required fee. For such payment, the applicant shall be issued a certificate of qualification by the Clerk. For good cause shown, the Court may waive payment of the fee.

Federal government attorneys, whether they are Department of Justice attorneys, or assistant United States attorneys, or employed by any other federal agency, are not required to pay the admission fee if they are appearing on behalf of the United States.

(D) **Foreign Attorneys:**

(1) Upon written motion by a member of this Court, a practitioner qualified to practice in the United States District Court of another state or the District of Columbia may appear and conduct specific cases *pro hac vice* before this Court including oral arguments of motions and trial, provided that:

(a) The rules of the United States District Court of the district in which the practitioner maintains an office extend a similar privilege to members of the bar of this Court; and

(b) That such practitioners from another state or the District of Columbia shall be accompanied by a member of the bar of this Court in all appearances before this Court.

For purposes of this Local Civil Rule, a member of the bar of this Court shall be a person admitted to practice under Local Civil Rule 83.1(C).

(2) All practitioners admitted before this Court for the purpose of participating in a particular proceeding *pro hac vice* shall be subject to the Local Rules of the United States District Court for the Eastern District of Virginia and the Federal Rules of Disciplinary Enforcement (Appendix B). Applicants for *pro hac vice* admission shall complete a written application certifying that they have read the Local Rules and shall pay the required fee to the Clerk. Federal government attorneys, whether they are United States Department of Justice attorneys, or assistant United States attorneys, or employed by any other federal agency, are not required to pay the admission fee if they are appearing on behalf of the United States. If the Court finds the application otherwise appropriate, upon payment of the required fee, the Court may order the *pro hac vice* admission of the applicant. Revenues from *pro hac vice* admission fees shall be deposited in the Court's non-appropriated funds account and disbursed by order of the chief judge of the district for such improvements to the Court's administration of justice as the chief judge finds appropriate.

(3) Except where a party conducts his or her own case, no pleading or notice required to be signed by counsel shall be filed unless signed by counsel who shall have been admitted to practice in this Court under subparagraphs (A), (B) and (C) of this Local Rule, with the office address where notice can be served upon said attorney, and who shall have such authority that the Court can deal with the attorney alone in all matters connected with the case. Such appearance shall not be withdrawn without leave of the Court. Service of notice or other proceedings on such an attorney shall be equivalent to service on the parties for whom the attorney appeared.

(4) Federal government attorneys appearing pursuant to the authority of the United States Attorney's Office for the Eastern District of Virginia are not required to secure private local counsel. All other federal government attorneys representing the interests of the United States, including the United States Department of Justice, shall secure local counsel by working with an assistant United States attorney assigned to the Eastern District of Virginia or secure local counsel in accordance with Local Civil Rule 83.1(D)(3).

(E) **Western District of Virginia:** Any attorney admitted to practice in the Western District of Virginia who is an Active Member of the Virginia State Bar in good standing shall be permitted to practice in the Eastern District of Virginia upon the filing of a certificate from the Clerk of the Western District of Virginia showing that such attorney has been duly admitted to practice in that district.

(F) **Attorneys Filing Pleadings:** Any counsel presenting papers, suits, or pleadings for filing, or making an appearance, must be members of the bar of this Court, or must have counsel who are members of the bar of this Court to join in the pleading by endorsement. Any counsel who joins in a pleading, motion, or other paper filed with the Court will be held accountable for the case by the Court. At least one person admitted to practice under subsection (C) of this Local Rule must personally be present at all hearings, pretrials, and trials. This obligation may not be avoided or delegated without leave of Court.

(G) **Withdrawal of Appearance:** No attorney who has entered an appearance in any civil action shall withdraw such appearance, or have it stricken from the record, except on order of the Court and after reasonable notice to the party on whose behalf said attorney has appeared.

(H) **Practicing Before Admission or While Disbarred or Suspended:** Any person who, before admission to the bar of this Court or during any disbarment or suspension, exercises any of the privileges of a member of the bar of this Court, or who pretends to be entitled so to do, shall be guilty of contempt of court and subject to appropriate punishment therefor.

(I) **Professional Ethics:** The ethical standards relating to the practice of law in civil cases in this Court shall be Section II of Part Six of the Rules of the Virginia Supreme Court as it may be amended or superseded from time to time.

(J) **Courtroom Decorum:** Counsel shall at all times conduct and demean themselves with dignity and propriety. When addressing the Court, counsel shall rise unless excused therefrom by the Court. All statements and communications to the Court shall be clearly and audibly made from a standing position at the counsel table or, if the Court is equipped with an attorney's lectern, from a standing position behind the lectern, facing the Court or the witness. Counsel shall not approach the bench unless requested to do so by the Court or unless permission is granted upon the request of counsel.

Examination of witnesses shall be conducted by counsel standing behind the lectern or, if none, behind the counsel table. Counsel shall not approach the witness except for the purpose of presenting, inquiring about, or examining the witness with respect to an exhibit, unless otherwise permitted by the Court. Only one attorney for each party may participate in the examination or cross-examination of a witness.

(K) **Third-Year Law Student:** An eligible law student qualifying pursuant to Paragraph II of the Plan for Third-Year Practice filed in each division of this Court is herewith given leave to participate in any civil case pursuant to said plan and as said plan may, from time to time, be amended. The Plan for Third-Year Practice is Appendix A to these Local Rules.

(L) **Federal Rules of Disciplinary Enforcement:** All counsel admitted to practice before this Court or admitted for the purpose of a particular proceeding *pro hac vice* shall be admitted subject to the rules, conditions and provisions set forth in full as Appendix B to these Local Rules. (Amended by order effective Nov. 19, 2010.)

CASE NOTES

Rule rationally related to court's interest in having knowledgeable attorneys before it. — This rule is rationally related to the court's valid interest in having attorneys before it who are both knowledgeable about Virginia law and local rules of practice and readily subject to the court's discipline and authority. Northern Va. Law Sch., Inc. v. City of Alexandria, 680 F. Supp. 222 (E.D. Va. 1988).

Local attorney held not indispensable party. — Rule 7 (D), requiring foreign attorneys to be associated with local counsel in order to appear and conduct cases in the Eastern District of Virginia, did not make the local counsel, who might have been a joint obligor or joint tort feasor with the foreign attorney, an indispensable party to the plaintiff's action against the foreign attorney for breach of contract and malpractice. The purpose of this rule is to give the court effective control of court business by assuring that attorneys involved in litigation will be available and subject to the court's authority. Such a rule cannot make an otherwise dispensable party indispensable. Willis v. Semmes, Bowen & Semmes, 441 F. Supp. 1235 (E.D. Va. 1977).

Where various pleadings were signed only by plaintiff's New York counsel at the time they were presented initially to the clerk of court, but all the pleadings were signed subsequently by local counsel, the plaintiff technically complied with this rule. Womble v. Dixon, 585 F. Supp. 728 (E.D. Va. 1983), modified, 752 F.2d 80 (4th Cir. 1984).

Copy of answer mailed to one of plaintiff's two attorneys triggered 10-day time limit. — Copy of defendant's answer, which was mailed to, and received by, one of plaintiff's two attorneys of record, was properly delivered for purposes of triggering the 10-day time limit provided in Rule 38 of the Federal Rules of Civil Procedure, even though plaintiff claimed the other attorney who did not receive a copy was his "lead" counsel. Frederick v. Koziol, 130 F.R.D. 620 (E.D. Va. 1990).

Jurisdiction over disbarment. — District court had jurisdiction to consider the motion of the United States for the disbarment of the attorney and, in so doing, to consider not only the attorney's conduct since becoming a member of the bar, but also that part of such conduct which could have occurred during the time his license to practice law was suspended. The district court did not abuse its discretion when it declined to open up a contempt proceeding. In re Morrissey, 305 F.3d 211, 2002 U.S. App. LEXIS 18650 (4th Cir. 2002).

Sanctions. — In an employment discrimination case, where plaintiffs' counsel attempted to skirt U.S. Dist. Ct., E.D. Va., R. 83.1(D)(3), the court took defendants' motion for sanctions under advisement. Chaplin v. Du Pont Advance Fiber Sys., 293 F. Supp. 2d 622, 2003 U.S. Dist. LEXIS 21396 (E.D. Va. 2003).

Although it was improper for an attorney who was having difficulty in securing local counsel to file pleadings on behalf of his clients and to label them pro se, the court, having found no evidence of intentional or malicious wrongdoing on the attorney's part, held that the public reprimand of the attorney was sufficient to serve as a future deterrent and did not impose additional sanctions. Chaplin v. Du Pont Advance Fiber Sys., 303 F. Supp. 2d 766, 2004 U.S. Dist. LEXIS 2535 (E.D. Va. 2004).

Applied in In re Asbestos Cases, 514 F. Supp. 914 (E.D. Va. 1981); Burston v. Virginia, 595 F. Supp. 644 (E.D. Va. 1984).

Rule 83.1.

IN THE UNITED STATES DISTRICT COURT
FOR THE EASTERN DISTRICT OF VIRGINIA

APPLICATION TO QUALIFY AS A FOREIGN ATTORNEY UNDER LOCAL RULE 83.1(D) In Case Number ______, Case Name ____________

To: The Honorable Judges of the United States District Court for the Eastern District of Virginia

PERSONAL STATEMENT

FULL NAME (no initials, please) ____________________
Bar Identification Number ____________ State ____________
Firm Name ____________________
Firm Phone # __________ Direct Dial # __________ FAX # __________
E-Mail Address ____________________
Office Mailing Address ____________________

Name(s) of federal court(s) in which I have been admitted ____________

I certify that the rules of the federal court(s) in which I have been admitted and have my office extend a similar *pro hac vice* admission privilege to members of the bar of the Eastern District of Virginia.

I have not been reprimanded in any court nor has there been any action in any court pertaining to my conduct or fitness as a member of the bar.

I hereby certify that within ninety (90) days prior to the submission of this application I have read (a) The Federal Rules of Civil Procedure, (b) The Federal Rules of Criminal Procedure, (c) The Local Rules of this Court and (d) The Federal Rules of Evidence.

I am ____ am not ____ a full-time employee of the United States of America, and if so, request exemption from the admission fee.

____
(Applicant's Signature)

I, the undersigned, do certify that I am a member of the bar of this Court, not related to the applicant; that I know the applicant personally, that the said applicant possesses all of the qualifications required for admission to the bar of this Court; that I have examined the applicant's personal statement. I affirm that his/her personal and professional character and standing are good, and petition the court to admit the applicant *pro hac vice*.

____________________ Date ____________
(Signature)

____
(Typed or Printed Name)

Court Use Only:

Clerk's $25.00 Fee Paid ____ *or* Exemtion Granted ____

The motion for admission is GRANTED ____ *or* DENIED ____

(Judge's Signature) ____________________ Date ____________

(Rev. 8/31/00)

Rule 83.2. Sales and Distribution of Proceeds of Sales.

(A) **General:** All sales shall be made by the United States Marshal or an authorized Deputy United States Marshal in the name of the Marshal and the provisions of Local Admiralty Rule (e)(15) subparagraphs (b) through (e) shall apply except as may be modified in this Local Rule.

(B) **Confirmation by Court:** All sales shall be subject to confirmation by the Court. The Marshal shall file with the Clerk on the day of sale a report thereof. An interested person may object to the sale by filing written objections with the Clerk within two (2) business days following the sale in conformity with Local Admiralty Rule (e)(15)(c). If no objections are filed, the sale shall stand confirmed unless the Court orders otherwise within said time. If objections are filed within the said two (2) days, the Clerk shall forthwith submit the report and objections to the Court for prompt disposition.

(C) **Marshal's Discretion in Certain Instances:** The Marshal may decline to knock down a vessel or other property to the highest bidder when the highest bid, in his or her opinion, is grossly inadequate.

(D) **Deposit of Sale Proceeds:** The proceeds of all sales by the Marshal shall be forthwith paid into the registry of the Court to be disposed of according to law.

(E) **Distributions:** All distributions of the proceeds of any sale shall be by order of Court.

(F) **Certain Maritime Liens:** Maritime liens filed before sale, including liens filed by leave of Court at anytime prior to sale, shall be paid first. Maritime liens filed after sale shall be paid last. Liens in each of the foregoing two classes shall preserve their respective rank as among themselves, except in the case of maritime liens of the first class, the order of priority between such liens shall be that those which have accrued within one year prior to the filing of the complaint shall be paid first, and claims which have accrued theretofore shall be paid in the inverse order of the years in which they accrued.

Rule 83.3. Photographing, Broadcasting, and Televising in Courtroom and Environs.

(A) **General:** The taking of photographs and operation of tape recorders in a courtroom or its environs, and radio or television broadcasting from a courtroom or its environs during the progress of or in connection with judicial proceedings, including proceedings before a magistrate judge or bankruptcy judge, whether or not Court is actually in session, is prohibited. A judge may, however, permit (1) the use of electronic or photographic means for the presentation of evidence or the perpetuation of a record; and (2) the broadcasting, televising, recording, or photographing of investitive, ceremonial, or naturalization proceedings. Environs, as used in this Local Rule, shall include any floor on which any courtroom or hearing room is located, including all hallways, stairways, windows, and elevators immediately adjacent to any such floor.

(B) **Exception:** With permission of the party or parties to be photographed, pictures may be taken by any permanent occupant of any office within the environs aforesaid when the Court is not in session.

Rule 83.4. Habeas Corpus and Proceedings *In Forma Pauperis*.

(A) **Standard Forms:** All *pro se* petitions for writs of habeas corpora must be filed on a set of standardized forms to be supplied, upon request, by the Clerk without cost to the petitioner. Counsel filing a petition for writ of habeas corpus need not use a standardized form, but any petition shall contain essentially the same information as set forth on said form.

(B) **Filing of Cases by Prisoners *In Forma Pauperis*:** If a party desires to file a proceeding *in forma pauperis* under 28 U.S.C. §§ 1915(a), and if the party desiring to file such proceeding is then confined to a state or federal penal institution, the party shall, within thirty (30) days of the receipt of any order, accomplish one of the following:

(1) Remit the required filing fee to the Clerk, or

(2) Request an extension of time within which to pay the required fee and thereafter pay same, or

(3) Cause to be filed a statement of the prison account of the party showing (a) the amount on deposit in the prison account at the period beginning six months immediately preceding the submission of the complaint or petition herein, and (b) the deposits to that prison account within the six-month period, including the source of said funds so deposited in said account and the reasons for any withdrawal therefrom.

(C) **Effect of Permitting Partial Payment; Reconsideration of Status:** Permission to proceed *in forma pauperis* by making a partial payment shall not be construed as authorizing the order of successive later payments after the order has been entered authorizing the party to proceed *in forma pauperis*. Whenever it appears that there may have been a change in the party's financial condition, the Court may reconsider whether the party may continue to proceed *in forma pauperis*.

(D) **Site of Evidentiary Hearings — Prisoner Cases:** At its discretion, the Court may conduct evidentiary hearings in prisoner cases at any penal institution in Virginia.

Rule 83.6. Settlement and Alternative Dispute Resolution.

(A) The Court encourages the parties to meet and consult with each other to achieve settlement. Pursuant to 28 U.S.C. §§ 651, 652, and 653, as amended by the Alternative Dispute Resolution Act of 1998, the use of mediation as an alternative dispute resolution process in all civil actions, including adversary proceedings in bankruptcy, is authorized. Before the initial pretrial conference or in the scheduling order, litigants in all civil cases shall be advised of the availability of mediation and may request it. The continued utilization of settlement conferences as a form of mediation is also authorized.

(B) The parties by consent may select and compensate any mutually acceptable non-judicial mediator or neutral. No mediator or neutral may be compensated by contingent fee. After mediation ends, the parties and the mediator or neutral shall file ulnder seal a report stating (1) the name and address of the mediator or neutral; (2) his or her compensation and who paid it; and (3) the result of the mediation.

(C) All district judges, magistrate judges, and bankruptcy judges are authorized (a) to act as mediators or neutrals; and (b) to appoint as mediators or neutrals any appropriately trained non-judicial person, in which event the appointing order shall establish the compensation to be paid for the services of such non-judicial person and shall schedule a time for completion of mediation. Any participant or potential participant in ADR who is able to establish an inability to pay a pro rata share of the neutral's proposed compensation, may petition the Court for the appointment of a judicial neutral.

(D) The appointment of a mediator or neutral shall not operate to postpone or stay the scheduling of any case or controversy nor shall such appointment be grounds for the continuance of a previously scheduled trial date or the extension of any deadlines previously scheduled by the Court.

(E) The substance of communication in the mediation process shall not be disclosed to any person other than participants in the mediation process; provided, however, that nothing herein shall modify the application of Federal Rule of Evidence 408 nor shall use in the mediation process of an otherwise admissible document, object, or statement preclude its use at trial.

(F) The chief judge of the district court shall appoint an ADR Administrator for the district. Duties of the Administrator shall include the following: implementing, administering, overseeing and evaluating the Court's ADR programs; providing rules for the qualification of mediators and neutrals; and consulting with the chief judge of the district court, members of the bar, and the United States Attorney relative to exempting specific cases or categories of cases from ADR.

(G) Disqualification of neutrals: Neutrals shall be disqualified from participation in any case in which the individual, his or her law firm, group, or organization may be personally affected by the outcome of the mediation or their impartiality may be called into question. Accordingly, the provisions of 28 U.S.C. § 455 apply to neutrals by application of this Local Rule. Neutrals shall also refrain from activity that may call into question their impartiality, for example, acceptance of gifts or favors of any kind from a party.

(H) By order, a district judge, or a magistrate judge to whom a case has been referred on consent or for settlement conference, may provide that counsel and/or a party representative with full settlement authority shall attend a settlement conference at any time the judge considers appropriate.

LOCAL CRIMINAL RULES.

Rule 1. Scope of Rules.

(A) **Application:** These Local Rules, made pursuant to the authority granted by Fed. R. Crim. P. 57 for the United States District Courts, as prescribed by the Supreme Court of the United States, so far as not inconsistent therewith, shall apply in all criminal cases and criminal proceedings in the United States District Court for the Eastern District of Virginia.

Effective March 26, 2007, all documents filed with the Court must be filed through the Electronic Case Filing System, except as provided otherwise in the Court's *Electronic Case Filing Policies and Procedures* manual ("manual") which is promulgated and revised by the Clerk. The manual governs if there is a conflict between it and these Local Rules as to the technicalities of electronic case filing. These Local Rules govern where the manual provides for filing paper documents, and in all other matters not involving electronic case filing.

(B) **Statutory Rules:** 1 U.S.C. §§ 1-5, inclusive, shall, as far as applicable, govern the construction of these Local Rules.

(C) **Effective Date of Amendments:** Amendments to these Local Rules shall take effect on the date of entry of the order authorizing the amendments and shall govern all proceedings thereafter commenced and, insofar as just and practicable, all then pending proceedings.

Rule 5. United States Magistrate Judges — Duties.

Magistrate judges of this district serve as judicial officers of the Court and are authorized and specially designated to perform all duties authorized or allowed to be performed by United States magistrate judges by the United States Code and any rule governing proceedings in this Court.

Duties and cases may be assigned or referred to a magistrate judge by an order entered in the action or on the instructions of a district judge.

Rule 6. Grand Jury.

(A) When a new grand jury is first convened, the Court shall deliver its charge but, if recessed and later reconvened, the Court shall not be required again to charge the grand jury, but may do so if deemed appropriate.

(B) The grand jury shall be convened on a regular schedule to be set by the Court in each division.

(C) Grand jurors for each division shall be selected in accordance with the Jury Selection and Service Act and the Court's Plan for the Random Selection of Grand and Petit Jurors.

Rule 12. Criminal Cases — Motions.

(A) **General:** Within eleven (11) days from the date of arraignment, or such other time as may be fixed by the Court, the parties shall file all desired motions (1) challenging the sufficiency of the indictment, information, warrant, or violation notice, (2) raising any issues of venue or jurisdiction, (3) for discovery or production, (4) to suppress evidence, (5) for any mental examination, (6) objecting to use by the opposing party of any particular evidence known by a party which may be subject to pretrial ruling, and (7) raising any other matter capable of being raised by a pretrial motion. All motions, unless otherwise directed by the Court, shall be accompanied by a written brief setting forth a concise statement of the facts and supporting reasons, along with a citation of the authorities upon which the movant relied. A response to any motion shall be filed within eleven (11) days after the filing of the motion or such other time as may be fixed by the Court.

(B) **Style of Motions:** All motions and the responses in criminal cases shall bear a caption which identifies the moving party and describes the general nature and the purpose of the motion. A defendant may adopt a motion filed by another defendant only by filing a separate pleading for each motion that the defendant wishes to adopt. This separate pleading must bear the same caption as the original pleading that the defendant wishes to adopt. A single motion to adopt more than one pleading of another defendant is not permitted.

CASE NOTES

Applied in United States v. Sheppard, 559 F. Supp. 571 (E.D. Va. 1983).

Rule 12.4. Financial Disclosure.

(A) **Required Disclosure:** A nongovernmental corporation, partnership, trust, other similar entity that is a party to, or that appears in, an action or proceeding in this Court shall:

(1) file two (2) copies of a statement that

a. identifies all its parent, subsidiary or affiliate entities (corporate or otherwise) that have issued stock or debt securities to the public and also identifies any publicly held entity (corporate or otherwise) that owns 10% or more of its stock, and

b. identifies all parties in the partnerships, general or limited, or owners or members of non-publicly traded entities such as LLCs or other closely held entities, or

c. states that there is nothing to report under Local Criminal Rule 12.4(A)(1)(a) and (b); and

(2) file a supplemental statement containing such additional information as may be from time to time required by the Judicial Conference of the United States or this Court.

(B) **Time for Filing.** A statement or form required by Local Criminal Rule 12.4(A) shall be filed upon the party's first appearance, pleading, petition, motion, response, or other request addressed to the Court. A supplemental statement or form shall be filed promptly upon any change in the circumstances that Local Criminal Rule 12.4(A) requires the party to identify.

(C) **Statement Delivered to Judge.** The Clerk shall deliver a copy of the Local Criminal Rule 12.4(A) disclosure to each judge acting in the action or proceeding.

Rule 17. Subpoenas.

(A) **Issuance of Subpoenas to Pro Se Parties:** Parties appearing *pro se* may apply for subpoenas in their own behalf. All such requests by such party must be accompanied by a memorandum setting forth the names and addresses of witnesses or the documents requested and why and for what purpose or purposes. All such requests by *pro se* parties shall be referred to a district judge or magistrate judge of this Court who shall first determine whether the requested subpoena shall issue; provided, however, that such determination shall not preclude any witness or person summoned or other interested party from later contesting the subpoena.

(B) **Return Date of Subpoenas:** All subpoenas shall be made returnable to the place, date, and time of trial or hearing, unless otherwise ordered by the Court.

(C) **Proof of Service of Subpoenas:** Lawyers and parties proceeding *pro se* shall file, before a witness is required to testify in criminal cases, a certificate that all required witness fees and expenses were served with the subpoena requiring the attendance of the witness.

(D) **Subpoenas to Officials:** Without first obtaining permission of the Court, no subpoena shall issue for the attendance at any hearing, trial, or deposition of (1) the Governor, Lieutenant Governor, or Attorney General of any State; (2) a judge of any Court; (3) the President or Vice-President of the United States; (4) any member of the President's Cabinet; (5) any Ambassador or Consul; or (6) any military officer holding the rank of Admiral or General.

(E) **Subpoenas in Blank:** Whenever there is a question as to whether or not a subpoena in blank should be issued by the Clerk, the applicant shall be referred to a judge of this Court for a final determination. Before issuing a subpoena in blank, the Clerk shall determine the actual pendency of the action and the date and time set for hearing or trial. Except for good cause shown, a blank subpoena returnable in one division will not be issued out of another division. Blank subpoenas shall recite the title and number of the case and shall be completed in every detail except for the name and address of the witness. Returns of service shall be made promptly and filed with the Clerk. Service of subpoenas in blank shall be subject to the requirements of these Local Rules.

Rule 18. Area and Divisions.

(A) **Area:** The Eastern District of Virginia consists of the counties, cities, and towns specified in 28 U.S.C. § 127, and the places for holding Court within the district are prescribed as Alexandria, Newport News, Norfolk, and Richmond.

(B) **Divisions:** This district shall be divided into four divisions to be designated as the Alexandria, Newport News, Norfolk, and Richmond Divisions; the place for holding Court for each of said divisions shall be the city whose name the division bears, and the territory comprising, and embraced in, each of the said divisions shall be as follows:

(1) The Alexandria Division shall consist of the City of Alexandria and the Counties of Loudoun, Fairfax, Fauquier, Arlington, Prince William, and Stafford and any other city or town geographically within the exterior boundaries of said counties.

(2) The Newport News Division shall consist of the Cities of Newport News, Hampton and Williamsburg, and the Counties of York, James City, Gloucester, Mathews, and any other city or town geographically within the exterior boundaries of said counties.

(3) The Norfolk Division shall consist of the Cities of Norfolk, Portsmouth, Suffolk, Franklin, Virginia Beach, Chesapeake, and Cape Charles, and the Counties of Accomack, Northampton, Isle of Wight, Southampton, and any other city or town geographically within the exterior boundaries of said counties.

(4) The Richmond Division shall consist of the Cities of Richmond, Petersburg, Hopewell, Colonial Heights, and Fredericksburg, and the Counties of Amelia, Brunswick, Caroline, Charles City, Chesterfield, Dinwiddie, Essex, Goochland, Greensville, Hanover, Henrico, King and Queen, King George, King William, Lancaster, Lunenburg, Mecklenburg, Middlesex, New Kent, Northumberland, Nottoway, Powhatan, Prince Edward, Prince George, Richmond, Spotsylvania, Surry, Sussex, Westmoreland, and any other city or town geographically within the exterior boundaries of said counties.

(5) All of the waters, and the land under such waters, adjacent and opposite to any city, county or town shall be a part of the division of which said city, county, or town is a part, and wherever there are any waters between any city, county, or town which are in different divisions, then such waters and land under them shall be considered to be in both divisions.

(6) In the event of any annexation or merger of any cities and/or counties, the land lying within the merged or annexed area shall be deemed within the exterior boundaries of the original city or county to the same intent and purpose as if the annexation or merger had not occurred, unless otherwise modified by Local Rule.

Rule 24. Trial Jurors.

(A) **Jury Lists:**

(1) The entire list of names drawn to serve a division of the Court for a particular period and for a particular action or case, together with the questionnaires prepared by the jurors, may be disclosed to counsel for the parties, or to any party acting *pro se*, unless the Court directs otherwise. However, no juror shall be approached, either directly or through any member of his or her immediate family, in an effort to secure information concerning such juror.

(2) When the jurors report for duty at a session of Court, the Clerk shall, upon request, make available to counsel for the parties, or to any party acting *pro se*, a list of such jurors.

(B) **Peremptory Challenges:** In a criminal case where there is more than one defendant, the Court may allow each or both sides more than the usual number of peremptory challenges permitted by law upon motion made at least twenty-one (21) days before the date set for commencement of trial. Untimely motions will not be entertained.

(C) **Communication With Jurors:** No attorney or party litigant shall personally, or through any investigator or any other person acting for the attorney or party litigant, interview, examine, or question any juror or alternate juror with respect to the verdict or deliberations of the jury in any criminal action except on leave of Court granted upon good cause shown and upon such conditions as the Court shall fix.

Rule 30. Proposed Jury Instructions and Voir Dire.

Except as provided otherwise in a pretrial or scheduling order, in all cases tried to a jury, the parties shall submit proposed instructions and voir dire questions to the

Court in duplicate, with a copy to opposing counsel, at least five (5) business days before the scheduled trial date. Each instruction shall be set forth on a separate page and shall be numbered and identified appropriately by the party submitting it. The original shall bear at its foot a citation of the authority in support of the instruction. Instructions shall be filed as a group together with a cover sheet in pleading form and a certificate of service. Instructions filed with the Court must be proffered to the Court during the instruction conference and ruled upon by the judge to become a part of the official record for appeal.

Rule 32.2. Sales and Distribution of Proceeds of Sales.

(A) **General:** All sales shall be made by the United States Marshal or an authorized Deputy United States Marshal in the name of the Marshal.

(B) **Confirmation by Court:** All sales shall be subject to confirmation by the Court. The Marshal shall file with the Clerk on the day of sale a report thereof.

(C) **Marshal's Discretion in Certain Instances:** The Marshal may decline to knock down a vessel or other property to the highest bidder when the highest bid, in his or her opinion, is grossly inadequate.

(D) **Deposit of Sale Proceeds:** The proceeds of all sales by the Marshal shall be forthwith paid into the registry of the Court to be disposed of according to law.

(E) **Distributions:** All distributions of the proceeds of any sale shall be by order of the Court.

Rule 46. Sureties — Security — Bondsman.

(A) **Security:** Except as otherwise provided by law, every bond, undertaking, or stipulation must be secured by (1) the deposit of cash or negotiable government bonds, undertaking, or stipulation; (2) the undertaking or guaranty of a corporate surety doing business in Virginia and holding a certificate of authority from the Secretary of the Treasury; or (3) the undertaking or guaranty of sufficient solvent sureties, residents of Virginia, who own real or personal property within the State of Virginia worth double the amount of the bond, undertaking, or stipulation over all debts and liabilities, and over all obligations assumed on other bonds, undertakings, or stipulations, and exclusive of all legal exemptions. A husband and wife may act as surety on a bond, but they shall be considered as only one surety. If a bond, undertaking, or stipulation is executed by individual sureties, each surety shall execute an affidavit of justification, giving the full name, occupation, residence and business address, showing that he or she is qualified as an individual surety under the provisions of this Local Rule. Provided that, in criminal cases, this Local Rule shall not in any way modify, alter, or change any of the provisions of the Bail Reform Act or any successor statute.

(B) **Prohibited Sureties:** Members of the bar, administrative officers or employees of this Court, the United States Marshal, his deputies or assistants, shall not act as a surety in any criminal case. A member of the bar may execute a bond as attorney-in-fact upon presenting a properly executed power of attorney.

(C) **Powers of Clerk:** To approve security, the Clerk is authorized to approve all recognizances, stipulations, bonds, guaranties, or undertakings, in the penal sum prescribed by statute or order of the Court, whether the security be property or personal or corporate surety. If the bond is offered by a professional bondsman or a person qualifying under (A)(3) above, approval of the Court, magistrate judge, or bankruptcy judge shall be obtained for penal sums in excess of $25,000.00.

(D) **Professional Bondsman:** Any person desiring to become surety for compensation (professional bondsman) on any bond required to be given in any matter before the Court or any of its magistrate judges or bankruptcy judges, or in any other matter under the jurisdiction of this Court, shall, before attempting to act, obtain approval of the Court. Application for such approval shall be by petition, duly sworn to, setting forth:

(1) That the applicant is of good moral character, is a citizen of the Commonwealth of Virginia, and residing within the boundaries of the Eastern District of Virginia.

(2) His or her full name, business and home address, marital status, and the nature of any business conducted by such person.

(3) Whether he or she is licensed in Virginia and/or any of the cities or counties of Virginia to act as a professional bondsman and, if so, where and whether such person has qualified in any of the Courts of Virginia to so act.

(4) Statement (signed by the owners) of assets (including both real estate and personal estate) and liabilities, and as to real estate, its description, location, how titled, and any encumbrances thereon. If a partnership is involved, a statement of the assets of both the partnership and the individual parties must be included, signed by owners of the assets. Assets owned by third parties or jointly with parties who are not partners will not be considered.

(5) A list of any and all bonds on which such person is the surety, the nature of the bond, and where lodged.

(6) That such person will quarter-annually file with the Court a list of all bonds upon which he or she is surety, whether any bonds are in default, whether any action on such bond has been instituted, and whether there are any unpaid judgments against such person.

(7) A certificate from a court of record, or the Chief of Police of the home city or town, or of two other responsible citizens, that such person is of good moral character.

(8) A list of any and all criminal convictions, except traffic violations, and whether there are any pending indictments or warrants against such person.

(9) If the information provided under paragraph (4) above reveals a total net worth of at least $200,000.00, and the applicant is otherwise satisfactory, an order may be entered permitting the applicant to act until further order of the Court. Should at any time the total net worth stated in paragraph (4) fall below $200,000.00 as shown on any quarterly report, or the applicant have more bonds outstanding than can be adequately covered, in the Court's opinion, by the net worth shown, or the applicant fail to file on time any quarterly report, or if for any reason the Court should deem the security offered by the applicant to be inadequate or outstanding bonds not adequately secured, the Court may terminate the right of the applicant to act as surety on any bond, without notice.

Rule 47. Pleadings — Motions — Continuances — Orders.

(A) **Grounds and Relief to be Stated:** All motions shall state with particularity the grounds therefor and shall set forth the relief or order sought.

(B) **Address and Telephone Number of Attorney And *Pro Se* Litigants:** All pleadings and motions shall include the attorney's office address and telephone number. All pleadings filed by non-prisoner litigants proceeding *pro se* shall contain an address where notice can be served on such person and a telephone number where such person can be reached or a message left. All pleadings filed by prisoners proceeding *pro se* shall contain an address where notice can be served on such person.

(C) **Personal Identifiers:**

(1) Redaction of personal identifiers is governed by Fed.R.Crim.P. 49.1 unless the Court directs otherwise.

(2) The responsibility for redacting personal identifiers rests solely with counsel and the parties. The Clerk will not review each pleading for compliance with this Local Rule. Counsel and the parties are cautioned that failure to redact these personal identifiers may subject them to sanctions.

(D) **Use of Forms:** Motions and interrogatories on printed forms, multigraphed, mimeographed, or in any manner reproduced by machine process, other than a typewriter, computer, or word processor, shall not be permitted unless the attorney filing same has deleted all extraneous matter and certifies that he or she has carefully reviewed the remaining portions and in good faith believes that the contents are pertinent to the case.

(E) **Return Date:** Except as otherwise provided by an order of the Court or by these Local Rules, all motions shall be made returnable to the time obtained from and scheduled by the Court for a hearing thereon. The moving party shall be responsible to set the motion for hearing or to arrange with opposing counsel for submission of the motion without oral argument. Unless otherwise ordered, a motion shall be deemed withdrawn if the movant does not set it for hearing (or arrange to submit it without a hearing) within thirty (30) days after the date on which the motion is filed. The non-moving party also may arrange for a hearing. Before endeavoring to secure an appointment for a hearing on any motion, it shall be incumbent upon the counsel desiring such hearing to meet and confer in person or by telephone with his or her opposing counsel in a good-faith effort to narrow the area of disagreement. In the absence of any agreement, such conference shall be held in the office of the attorney nearest the Court in the division in which the action is pending. In any division which has a regularly scheduled motions day, the motion should be noticed for the first permissible motions day.

(F) **Briefs Required:**

(1) All motions, unless otherwise directed by the Court and except as noted hereinbelow in Local Criminal Rule 47(E)(2), shall be accompanied by a written brief setting forth a concise statement of the facts and supporting reasons, along with a citation of the authorities upon which the movant relies. Unless otherwise directed by the Court, the opposing party shall file a responsive brief and such supporting documents as are appropriate, within eleven (11) days after service and the moving party may file a rebuttal brief within three (3) days after the service of the opposing party's reply brief. No further briefs or written communications may be filed without first obtaining leave of Court.

(2) A motion for an extension of time to respond to pleadings need not be accompanied by a brief, unless the time has already expired.

(3) All briefs, including footnotes, shall be written in 12 point Roman style or 10 pitch Courier style with one inch margins. Except for good cause shown in advance of filing, opening and responsive briefs, exclusive of affidavits and supporting documentation, shall not exceed thirty (30) 8-½ inch x 11 inch pages double-spaced and rebuttal briefs shall not exceed twenty (20) such pages.

(G) **Continuances:** Motions for continuances of a trial or hearing date shall not be granted by the mere agreement of counsel. No continuance will be granted other than for good cause and upon such terms as the Court may impose.

(H) **Filing of Pleadings:** All pleadings, motions, briefs, and filings of any kind must be timely filed with the Clerk's Office of the division in which the case is pending.

(I) **Extensions:** Any requests for an extension of time relating to motions must be in writing and, in general, will be looked upon with disfavor.

(J) **Determination of Motions Without Oral Hearing:** The Court may rule upon motions without an oral hearing. (Amended by order adopted Oct. 25, 2004, effective Feb. 15, 2005; by order adopted October 2008, effective Nov. 25, 2008.)

Rule 49. Designation and Handling of Documents Under Seal.

(A) Unless otherwise provided by law or Court rule, no document may be filed under seal without an order entered by the Court.

(B) A government motion to seal a warrant, complaint, supporting affidavit, or indictment shall include:

(1) A statement as to why sealing is necessary, and why another procedure will not suffice;

(2) References to governing case law; and

(3) A statement as to the period of time the government seeks to have the matter maintained under seal and as to how the matter is to be handled upon unsealing.

The motion shall be accompanied by a proposed order that includes findings supporting sealing, and, if appropriate, provisions for unsealing upon the occurrence of specified event(s). The Clerk shall docket the motion in a way that discloses its nature as a motion to seal. No hearing is required on motions covered by this section. No separate motion to seal is necessary in investigative proceedings made confidential by law.

Until an executed search warrant is returned, search warrants and related papers are not filed with the Clerk. No separate motion to seal is necessary to seal a search warrant from the time of issuance to the time the executed warrant is returned.

The Clerk shall provide a copy of any document filed under seal to the party (or attorney for the party) that filed the document upon the request of that party or the party's attorney without an order from the Court.

When any document covered by this section contains one or more personal identifiers within the meaning of the E-Government Act of 2002, and the government would otherwise move to unseal it, the government shall file a redacted version instead.

(C) In all post-arrest proceedings, a party submitting a document or portion of a document (e.g., exhibit[s]) for filing under seal pursuant to a governing statute, rule, or order shall note on the face of the document that it or a portion of it is filed under seal pursuant to that statute, rule, or order. The Clerk shall provide public notice by stating on the docket that the document contains sealed material.

(D) Any post-arrest motion for a protective order providing prospectively for filing of documents under seal shall be accompanied by a non-confidential supporting memorandum, a notice that identifies the motion as a sealing motion, and a proposed order. A confidential memorandum for *in camera* review may also be submitted. The non-confidential memorandum and the proposed order shall include:

(1) A non-confidential description of what is to be sealed;

(2) A statement as to why sealing is necessary, and why another procedure will not suffice;

(3) References to governing case law; and

(4) Unless permanent sealing is sought, a statement as to the period of time the party seeks to have the matter maintained under seal and as to how the matter is to be handled upon unsealing.

The proposed order shall recite the findings required by governing case law to support the proposed sealing.

The Clerk shall provide public notice by docketing the motion in a way that discloses its nature as a motion to seal, with its hearing date (if any). Other parties and non-parties may submit memoranda in support of or opposition to the motion, and may designate all or part of such memoranda as confidential. Any confidential memoranda will be treated as sealed pending the outcome of the ruling on the motion.

(E) Any document not covered by section (C) and filed with the intention of being sealed shall be accompanied by a motion to seal that complies with the requirements of section (D). The Clerk shall provide public notice by docketing the motion in a way that discloses its nature as a motion to seal, with its hearing date (if any). Other parties and non-parties may submit memoranda in support of or in opposition to the motion, and may designate all or part of such memoranda as confidential. The document and any confidential memoranda will be treated as sealed pending the outcome of the ruling on the motion. Failure to file a motion to seal will result in the document being treated as a public record.

(F) Each document that is the subject of an existing sealing order, or the subject of a motion for such an order, shall be submitted to the Clerk's Office securely sealed, with the container clearly labeled "UNDER SEAL." The case number, case caption, a reference to any statute, rule, or order permitting the item to be sealed, and a non-confidential descriptive title of the document shall also be noted on the container.

(G) A motion to have an entire case kept under seal shall be subject to the requirements and procedures of sections (D) and (F).

(H) Nothing in this Local Rule limits the ability of the parties, by agreement, to restrict access to documents that are not filed with the Court.

(I) Trial exhibits, including documents previously filed under seal, and trial transcripts shall not be filed under seal except upon a showing of necessity demonstrated to the trial judge.

(J) The Court having found that all motions for downward departure filed by the government under 18 U.S.C. § 3553(e), United States Sentencing Guidelines § 5.K.1.1, or Fed. R. Crim. P. 35 satisfy, by their nature, the requirements for sealing, such motions and responses thereto may be filed under seal without filing a motion to seal by placing the words "UNDER SEAL" on the face sheet of the motion and by informing the Clerk of the need to file the document under seal. (Amended by order adopted Oct. 25, 2004, effective Feb. 15, 2005.)

Rule 53. Photographing, Broadcasting, and Televising in Courtroom and Environs.

(A) **General:** The taking of photographs and operation of tape recorders in the courtroom or its environs, and radio or television broadcasting from the courtroom or its environs during the progress of or in connection with judicial proceedings, including proceedings before a magistrate judge or bankruptcy judge, whether or not Court is actually in session, is prohibited. A judge may, however, permit (1) the use of electronic or photographic means for the presentation of evidence or the perpetuation of a record; and (2) the broadcasting, televising, recording, or photographing of investitive, ceremonial, or naturalization proceedings. Environs, as used in this Local Rule, shall include any floor on which any courtroom or hearing room is located, including all hallways, stairways, windows, and elevators immediately adjacent to any such floor.

(B) **Exception:** With permission of the party or parties to be photographed, pictures may be taken by any permanent occupant of any office within the environs aforesaid when the Court is not in session.

Rule 55. Exhibits.

(A) **Submission of Trial Exhibits:** All exhibits, models, or diagrams, documentary or physical, introduced in the trial of a criminal case or otherwise lodged in anticipation of their introduction into evidence in the trial of a criminal case, shall be retained by the Clerk to be disposed of at the time and in the manner provided herein or directed by the Court.

(B) **Custody and Removal of Exhibits During Trial:** Unless otherwise ordered by the Court, the courtroom deputy shall maintain custody of all exhibits offered or received in evidence when the Court is in session. During all recesses, the appropriate law enforcement representative or the attorney for the party producing sensitive exhibits shall maintain custody of such exhibits. Sensitive exhibits include, but are not limited to, drugs, weapons, currency, any object capable of being used as a weapon, any hazardous substance, or item of great monetary value.

(C) **Custody and Disposition of Exhibits After Trial:**

(1) Unless otherwise ordered by the Court, at the conclusion of the trial of any criminal case, photographs of all sensitive exhibits will be substituted for the exhibits and the exhibits will be returned to the tendering party. The tendering party is responsible for furnishing the photographs, which shall fully and accurately depict the exhibits for which they are substituted.

(2) Biological evidence (e.g., blood, saliva, or other body fluids or tissue, clothing or objects containing body fluids, rape perk kits, etc.) from which DNA or other forensic tests may be performed shall not be returned to the parties except by leave of Court.

(3) Final Disposition of Exhibits: Forty-five (45) days after the date on which the judgment becomes final by the conclusion of direct review or the expiration of the time for seeking such review, and no party having applied for the return of exhibits, the Clerk may, unless otherwise directed by the Court, deliver to the United States Attorney any exhibit or other physical evidence submitted by any party, and not covered by Local Criminal Rule 55(C)(2), for use by any government agency interested therein, or for destruction or confiscation.

Rule 57.1. Free Press — Fair Trial Directives.

(A) **Potential or Imminent Criminal Litigation:** In connection with pending or imminent criminal litigation with which a lawyer or a law firm is associated, it is the duty of that lawyer or firm not to release or authorize the release of information or opinion (1) if a reasonable person would expect such information or opinion to be further disseminated by any means of public communication, and (2) if there is a reasonable likelihood that such dissemination would interfere with a fair trial or otherwise prejudice the due administration of justice.

(B) **Grand Jury Proceedings:** With respect to a grand jury or other pending investigation of any criminal matter, a lawyer participating in or associated with the investigation shall refrain from making any extrajudicial statement which a reasonable person would expect to be disseminated, by any means of public communication, that goes beyond the public record or that is not necessary to inform the public that the investigation is underway, to describe the general scope of the investigation, to obtain assistance in the apprehension of a suspect, to warn the public of any dangers, or otherwise to aid in the investigation.

(C) **Pending Criminal Proceedings — Specific Topics:** From the time of arrest, issuance of an arrest warrant, or the filing of a complaint, information, or indictment in any criminal matter until the termination of trial or disposition without trial, a lawyer, law firm, or law enforcement personnel associated with the prosecution or defense shall not release or authorize the release of any extrajudicial statement which a reasonable person would expect to be further disseminated by any means of public communication, if such statement concerns:

(1) The prior criminal record (including arrests, indictments, or other charges of crime), or the character or reputation of the accused, except that the lawyer or law firm may make a factual statement of the accused's name, age, residence, occupation, and family status and, if the accused has not been apprehended, a lawyer associated with the prosecution may release any information necessary to aid in his or her apprehension or to warn the public of any dangers such person may present;

(2) The existence or contents of any confession, admission, or statement given by the accused, or the refusal or failure of the accused to make any statement;

(3) The performance of any examinations or tests or the accused's refusal or failure to submit to an examination or test;

(4) The identity, testimony, or credibility of prospective witnesses, except that the lawyer or law firm may announce the identity of the victim if the announcement is not otherwise prohibited by law;

(5) The possibility of a plea of guilty to the offense charged or a lesser offense;

(6) Any opinion as to the accused's guilt or innocence or as to the merits of the case or the evidence in the case.

The foregoing shall not be construed to preclude the lawyer or law firm during this period, in the proper discharge of the official or professional obligations imposed, from announcing the fact and circumstances of arrest (including time and place of arrest, resistance, pursuit, and use of weapons), the identity of the investigating and arresting officer or agency, and the length of the investigation; from making an announcement, at the time of seizure of any physical evidence other than a confession, admission or statement, which is limited to a description of the evidence seized; from disclosing the nature, substance, or text of the charge, including a brief description of the offense charged; from quoting or referring without comment to public records of the Court in the case; from announcing the scheduling or result of any stage in the judicial process; from requesting assistance in obtaining evidence; or from announcing without further comment that the accused denies the charges made against such person.

(D) **Pending Criminal Proceedings — General:** During a jury trial of any criminal matter, including the period of selection of the jury, no lawyer or law firm associated with the prosecution or defense shall give or authorize any extrajudicial statement or interview relating to the trial or the parties or issues in the trial, which a reasonable person would expect to be disseminated by means of public communication, if there is a reasonable likelihood that such dissemination will interfere with a fair trial, except that the lawyer or law firm may quote from or refer without comment to public records of the Court in the case.

(E) **Provisos:** Nothing in this Local Rule is intended to preclude the formulation or application of more restrictive rules relating to the release of information about juvenile or other offenders, to preclude the holding of hearings or the lawful issuance of reports by legislative, administrative, or investigative bodies, or to preclude any lawyer from replying to charges of misconduct that are publicly made against such lawyer.

(F) **Court Personnel:** All Court personnel, including, among others, the U.S. Marshal, deputy Marshals, Clerk's Office staff, court security officers, court reporters, and employees or subcontractors retained by the Court as contract court reporters, are prohibited from disclosing to any person without authorization by the Court, information relating to a pending grand jury proceeding or criminal case that is not part of the public records of the Court. The divulgence of information concerning grand jury proceedings, in camera arguments, and hearings held in chambers or otherwise outside the presence of the public is likewise forbidden.

(G) **Motions:** In a widely publicized or sensational criminal case, the Court, on motion of either party or on its own motion, may issue a special order governing such matters as extrajudicial statements by parties and witnesses likely to interfere with the rights of the accused to a fair trial by an impartial jury, the seating and conduct in the courtroom of spectators and news media representatives, the management and sequestration of jurors and witnesses, and any other matters which the Court may deem appropriate for inclusion in such an order.

(H) **Open Court:** Unless otherwise provided by law, all preliminary criminal proceedings, including preliminary examinations and hearings on pretrial motions, shall be held in open Court and shall be available for attendance and observation by the public; provided that, upon motion made or agreed to by the defense, the Court, in the exercise of its discretion, may order a pretrial proceeding be closed to the public, in whole or in part, on the grounds:

(1) that there is a substantial probability that the dissemination of information disclosed at such proceeding would impair the defendant's right to a fair trial; and

(2) that reasonable alternatives to closure will not adequately protect defendant's right to a fair trial.

If the Court so orders, it shall state for the record its specific findings concerning the need for closure.

CASE NOTES

Rule 57 (C) is constitutional adequate restraint on lawyer speech. — Although in 1991, the United States Supreme Court held that the "substantial likelihood of material prejudice" standard constitutes a constitutionally permissible balance between the First Amendment rights of attorneys in pending cases and the State's interest in fair trials, it does not follow, that it is the only constitutionally acceptable standard. Rather, it appears that the "reasonable likelihood" standard in Rule 57 remains a constitutionally adequate restriction of lawyer speech in pending criminal cases. In re Morrissey, 996 F. Supp. 530 (E.D. Va. 1998), aff'd, 168 F.3d 134 (4th Cir. 1999).

Rule 57 (C) is constitutional as it imposes restraints on lawyer speech that are narrowly tailored to achieve precisely the objectives to which restrictions properly may be directed. Moreover, Rule 57 (C) explicitly prohibits extrajudicial statements which have long been recognized as presenting the greatest risk of prejudice in an adjudicative proceeding, and only sanctions those statements which are reasonably likely to have that effect. In re Morrissey, 996 F. Supp. 530 (E.D. Va. 1998), aff'd, 168 F.3d 134 (4th Cir. 1999).

Agreement to abide by Rule 57 (C) when admitted to practice did not constitute a waiver of lawyer's right to challenge the constitutionality of the rule. In re Morrissey, 996 F. Supp. 530 (E.D. Va. 1998), aff'd, 168 F.3d 134 (4th Cir. 1999).

Rule 57 is aimed at securing the right to a fair trial by an impartial jury and avoiding conduct that imposes unnecessary costs on the judicial system. The language of the rule accomplishes these objectives by imposing a constitutionally permissible restriction on lawyer speech. In re Morrissey, 168 F.3d 134 (4th Cir. 1999), cert. denied, 527 U.S. 1036, 119 S. Ct. 2349, 144 L. Ed. 2d 794 (1999).

Rule 57.2. Payment of Fees.

All fees due the Clerk shall be paid in advance except as otherwise provided by law.

Rule 57.3. Official Court Reporters Transcripts — Hearing on Transcripts — Record on Appeal.

(A) **Court Reporter Management Plan:** In accordance with the provisions of 28 U.S.C. § 753 and the requirements of a resolution adopted by the Judicial Conference of the United States at its March 1982 session, all district courts are required to file a Court Reporter Management Plan, which is available for inspection and copying in the Clerk's Office. This plan provides information about the supervision, duties and assignments, including the work hours, of court reporters and notes the fees for transcripts. The transcript rates charged by court reporters are governed by rates recommended by the Judicial Conference of the United States, if adopted by this Court. The schedule of maximum fees which may be charged is posted in the Clerk's Office.

(B) **Release of Transcript:** The filing, viewing, and purchasing of transcripts of proceedings is governed by the Court's *Electronic Case Filing Policies and Procedures* manual.

(C) **Obligation to Pay Court Reporter:** The obligation to pay the court reporter for any and all transcripts shall be the joint and several personal obligation of the attorney, and the party for whose benefit the transcript was obtained, when the order is placed, to the extent so ordered. Any charges for a transcript shall be payable upon the completion of the transcript or any segment thereof, when a proper bill for same has been submitted by the court reporter. If proper charges for transcripts are not paid within a reasonable time after submission, the court reporter may refer the matter to a district judge for such action as may be deemed appropriate.

(D) **Record on Appeal:** Unless otherwise directed by the Court, the record on appeal in criminal cases shall not include the examination of the jury on voir dire, counsel's opening statements, arguments of counsel, including arguments of counsel on motions, and the Court's charge to the jury unless there were exceptions to the charge.

Unless the parties file a written stipulation with the Clerk within twenty-one (21) days after notice of appeal is filed designating the papers which shall constitute the record on appeal, the Clerk shall certify and forward to the Court of Appeals all of the original pleadings and orders in the file jacket dealing with the action or proceeding in which the appeal is taken, unless otherwise instructed by the Court of Appeals.

(E) **Daily or Expedited Copy:** All requests for daily or expedited transcripts must be made in writing to the court reporter, if known, and, if not, to the Clerk, with copies to opposing counsel, not later than five (5) business days before the hearing or trial to be transcribed. (Amended May 12, 2009; and by order effective Nov. 19, 2010.)

Rule 57.4. Attorneys and Pro Se Parties.

(A) **Eligibility:** Any person who is an Active Member of the Virginia State Bar in good standing is eligible to practice before this Court upon admission.

(B) **Initial Appearance:** Any person who meets the requirements of the foregoing paragraph and who maintains a law office outside of Virginia shall set forth his or her Virginia State Bar I.D. Number on any initial pleading filed by such person.

(C) **Procedure for Admission:** Every person desiring admission to practice in this Court shall file with the Clerk written application therefor accompanied by an endorsement by two (2) qualified members of the bar of this Court stating that the applicant is of good moral character and professional reputation. The form for such application may be obtained from the Clerk's Office.

As a part of the application, the applicant shall certify that applicant has within ninety (90) days prior to submission of the application read or reread (a) the Federal Rules of Criminal Procedure, (b) the Federal Rules of Evidence, and (c) the Local Rules of the United States District Court for the Eastern District of Virginia.

The applicant shall thereafter be presented by a qualified practitioner of the Court who shall in open Court by oral motion, and upon giving assurance to the Court that the practitioner has examined the credentials of the applicant and is satisfied the applicant possesses the necessary qualifications, move the applicant's admission to practice.

The applicant shall in open Court take the oath required for admission, subscribe the roll of the Court, and pay to the Clerk the required fee. For such payment, the applicant shall be issued a certificate of qualification by the Clerk. For good cause shown, the Court may waive payment of the fee.

Federal government attorneys, whether they are Department of Justice attorneys, or assistant United States attorneys, or employed by any other federal agency, are not required to pay the admission fee if they are appearing on behalf of the United States.

(D) **Foreign Attorneys:**

(1) Upon written motion by a member of this Court, a practitioner qualified to practice in the United States District Court of another state or the District of Columbia may appear and conduct specific cases *pro hac vice* before this Court including oral arguments of motions and trial, provided that:

(a) The rules of the United States District Court of the district in which the practitioner maintains an office extend a similar privilege to members of the bar of this Court; and

(b) That such practitioners from another state or the District of Columbia shall be accompanied by a member of the bar of this Court in all appearances before this Court.

For purposes of this Local Rule, a member of the bar of this Court shall be a person admitted to practice under Local Criminal Rule 57.4(C).

(2) All practitioners admitted before this Court for the purpose of participating in a particular proceeding *pro hac vice* shall be subject to the Local Rules of the United States District Court for the Eastern District of Virginia and the Federal Rules of Disciplinary Enforcement (Appendix B). Applicants for *pro hac vice* admission shall complete a written application certifying that they have read the Local Rules and shall pay the required fee to the Clerk. Federal government attorneys, whether they are United States Department of Justice attorneys, or assistant United States attorneys, or employed by any other federal agency, are not required to pay the admission fee if they are appearing on behalf of the United States. If the Court finds the application otherwise appropriate, upon payment of the required fee, the Court may order the *pro hac vice* admission of the applicant. Revenues from *pro hac vice* admission fees shall be deposited in the Court's non-appropriated funds account and disbursed by order of the chief judge of the district for such improvements to the Court's administration of justice as the chief judge finds appropriate.

(3) Except where a party conducts his or her own case, no pleading or notice required to be signed by counsel shall be filed unless signed by counsel who shall have been admitted to practice in this Court under subparagraphs (A), (B) and (C) of this Local Rule, with the office address where notice can be served upon said attorney, and who shall have such authority that the Court can deal with the attorney alone in all matters connected with the case. Such appearance shall not be withdrawn without leave of the Court. Service of notice or other proceedings on such an attorney shall be equivalent to service on the parties for whom the attorney appeared.

Federal government attorneys appearing pursuant to the authority of the United States Attorney's Office for the Eastern District of Virginia are not required to secure private local counsel. All other federal government attorneys representing the interests of the United States, including the United States Department of Justice, shall secure local counsel by working with an assistant United States attorney assigned to the Eastern District of Virginia.

(E) **Western District of Virginia:** Any attorney admitted to practice in the Western District of Virginia who is an Active Member of the Virginia State Bar in good standing shall be permitted to practice in the Eastern District of Virginia upon the filing of a certificate from the Clerk of the Western District of Virginia showing that such attorney has been duly admitted to practice in that district.

(F) **Attorneys Filing Pleadings:** Any counsel presenting papers, suits, or pleadings for filing, or making an appearance, must be members of the bar of this Court, or must have counsel who are members of the bar of this Court to join in the pleading by endorsement. Any counsel who joins in a pleading, motion, or other paper filed with the Court will be held accountable for the case by the Court. At least one person admitted to practice under subsection (C) of this Local Rule must personally be present at all hearings, pretrials, and trials. This obligation may not be avoided or delegated without leave of Court.

(G) **Withdrawal of Appearance:** No attorney who has entered an appearance in any criminal action shall withdraw such appearance, or have it stricken from the record, except on order of the Court and after reasonable notice to the party on whose behalf said attorney has appeared.

(H) **Practicing Before Admission or While Disbarred or Suspended:** Any person who, before admission to the bar of this Court or during any disbarment or suspension, exercises any of the privileges of a member of the bar of this Court, or who pretends to be entitled so to do, shall be guilty of contempt of court and subject to appropriate punishment therefor.

(I) **Professional Ethics:** With the exception of Virginia Rule of Professional Conduct 3.6 (the subject of which is covered by Local Criminal Rule 57.1), the ethical standards relating to the practice of law in criminal cases in this Court shall be Section II of Part Six of the Rules of the Virginia Supreme Court as it may be amended or superseded from time to time.

(J) **Courtroom Decorum:** Counsel shall at all times conduct and demean themselves with dignity and propriety. When addressing the Court, counsel shall rise unless excused therefrom by the Court. All statements and communications to the Court shall be clearly and audibly made from a standing position at the counsel table or, if the Court is equipped with an attorney's lectern, from a standing position behind the lectern, facing the Court or the witness. Counsel shall not approach the bench unless requested to do so by the Court or unless permission is granted upon the request of counsel.

Examination of witnesses shall be conducted by counsel standing behind the lectern or, if none, behind the counsel table. Counsel shall not approach the witness except for the purpose of presenting, inquiring about, or examining the witness with respect to an exhibit, unless otherwise permitted by the Court. Only one attorney for each party may participate in the examination or cross-examination of a witness.

(K) **Third-Year Law Student:** An eligible law student qualifying pursuant to Paragraph II of the Plan for Third-Year Practice filed in each division of this Court is herewith given leave to participate in any criminal case pursuant to said plan and as said plan may, from time to time, be amended. The Plan for Third-Year Practice is Appendix A to these Local Rules.

(L) **Federal Rules of Disciplinary Enforcement:** All counsel admitted to practice before this Court or admitted for the purpose of a particular proceeding *pro hac vice* shall be admitted subject to the rules, conditions and provisions set forth in full as Appendix B to these Local Rules. (Amended by order effective Nov. 19, 2010.)

Rule 58. Collateral Payments.

In accordance with Fed. R. Crim. P. 58(d)(1), payment of a fixed sum may be accepted in suitable types of misdemeanor cases in lieu of appearance and as authorizing the termination of the proceedings. Such fixed sums may be increased or decreased from time to time by the Court, provided such fixed sums shall not exceed the maximum fine which could be imposed upon conviction.

LOCAL ADMIRALTY RULES.

Local Admiralty Rule (a). Authority and Scope.

(1) **Authority.** The Local Admiralty Rules of the United States District Court for the Eastern District of Virginia are promulgated by a majority of the judges as authorized by and subject to the limitations of Fed. R. Civ. P. 83. Any reference to Federal Rule or Federal Rules shall be to the Federal Rules of Civil Procedure.

(2) **Scope.** The Local Admiralty Rules apply only to civil actions that are governed by Supplemental Rule A of the Supplemental Rules for Certain Admiralty and Maritime Claims. All other local rules are applicable in these cases, but to the extent that another local rule is inconsistent with the applicable Local Admiralty Rules, the Local Admiralty Rules shall govern in admiralty cases.

Effective March 26, 2007, all documents filed with the Court must be filed through the Electronic Case Filing System, except as provided otherwise in the Court's *Electronic Case Filing Policies and Procedures* manual ("manual") which is promulgated and revised by the Clerk. The manual governs if there is a conflict between it and these Local Rules as to the technicalities of electronic case filing. These Local Rules govern where the manual provides for filing paper documents, and in all other matters not involving electronic case filing.

(3) **Citation.** The Local Admiralty Rules may be cited by the letters "LAR" and the lower case letters and numbers in parentheses that appear at the beginning of each section. The lower case letter is intended to associate the Local Admiralty Rule with the Supplemental Rule that bears the same capital letter.

(4) **Officers of Court.** As used in the Local Admiralty Rules, "judicial officer" means a United States District Judge or a United States Magistrate Judge; "Clerk" or "Clerk of Court" means the Clerk of the District Court and includes deputy Clerks of Court; and "Marshal" means the United States Marshal and includes deputy Marshals.

Local Admiralty Rule (b). In Personam Actions: Attachment and Garnishment.

(1) **"Not Found Within the District" Defined.** A defendant is considered to be "not found within the district" if, in an action in personam, service upon the defendant cannot be effected in person or upon an authorized officer or agent within the Commonwealth or if the only effective service is through the Clerk of the State Corporation Commission, the Secretary of the Commonwealth, or under the Virginia Long Arm Statute.

(2) **Affidavit That Defendant is Not Found Within the District.** The affidavit required by Supplemental Rule (B)(2) to accompany the complaint shall list every effort made by and on behalf of plaintiff to find and serve the defendant within the district.

(3) **Ownership of Property.** In an action where the debts, credits, or effects named in the process of maritime attachment or garnishment are not delivered up to the process server by the defendant or the garnishee, or are asserted by the possessor not to be the property of the defendant, the process shall be served sufficiently by leaving a copy of the process with the defendant, garnishee and possessor, at his or her residence or usual place of business. When the return of service shows that process was so served, and when the plaintiff shows to the satisfaction of the Court that the property does belong to the defendant or the garnishee, the Court may proceed to hear and decide the case.

(4) **Use of State Procedures.** When the plaintiff invokes a state procedure in order to attach or garnish property under Fed. R. Civ. P. (4)(n)(2), the process of attachment or garnishment shall so state.

Local Admiralty Rule (c). Actions *In Rem:* Special Provisions.

(1) **Undertaking in Lieu of Arrest.** If, before or after commencement of an action by arrest, all parties accept a written undertaking to respond on behalf of the vessel or other property in return for foregoing the arrest, or stipulating to the release of the vessel or other property, the undertaking shall be filed, shall become the party in place of the vessel or other property, and shall be deemed the subject referred to when a pleading, motion, order, or judgment in the action refers to the vessel or property.

(2) **Intangible Property.** The summons issued pursuant to Supplemental Rule C(3) shall direct the person having control of the specified funds or other intangible

property to show cause no later than 10 days after service why the funds or other property should not be delivered to the Marshal to abide the judgment. A judicial officer for good cause shown may lengthen or shorten the time. Service of the summons has the effect of an arrest of the property and brings it within the control of the Court. The person who is served may deliver or pay over to the Marshal (or other person or organization having a warrant for the arrest of the property) the property or funds proceeded against to the extent sufficient to satisfy the plaintiff's claim. If such delivery or payment is made, the person served is excused from the duty to show cause. A claimant of the property may show cause why the property should not be delivered or should be returned by serving and filing a claim as provided in Supplemental Rule C(6) within the time allowed to show cause and by serving and filing an answer to the complaint within twenty-one (21) days thereafter. If a claim is not filed within the time stated in the summons, or an answer is not filed within the time allowed under this rule, the person who was served shall deliver or pay to the Marshal the property or funds proceeded against, or a part thereof sufficient to satisfy plaintiff's claim.

(3) **Publication of Notice of Action and Arrest.** The notice required by Supplemental Rule C(4) shall be published once in a newspaper of general circulation within the Division where arrest is to occur, and plaintiff's attorney shall file a copy of the notice as it was published with the Clerk. The notice shall contain:

(a) the Court, title, and number of the action;

(b) the date of the arrest;

(c) the identity of the property arrested;

(d) the name, address and telephone number of the attorney for plaintiff;

(e)(i) a statement that a person who asserts an interest in or right against the property that is the subject of the civil forfeiture must file a verified statement identifying the interest or right, in compliance with Admiralty Rule C(6)(a), within twenty-one (21) days of the earlier of (1) receiving actual notice of execution of process, or (2) publication of the notice; or

(ii) a statement that a person who asserts a right of possession or any ownership interest in the property that is the subject of the Maritime Arrest or Other Proceeding must file a verified statement of right or interest, in compliance with Admiralty Rule C(6)(b), within 10 days of the earlier of (1) execution of process, or (2) publication of the notice.

(f) a statement that a person who files a statement of interest in or right against the property subject to the civil forfeiture or a person who asserts a right of possession or any ownership interest in the property subject to Maritime Arrest and Other Proceedings must file an answer within twenty-one (21) days of filing the verified statement under LAR (c)(3)(e)(i) or (ii).

(g) a statement that applications for intervention under Federal Rule 24 by persons claiming maritime liens or other interests shall be filed within the 10 days allowed for claims for possession; and

(h) the name, address and telephone number of the Marshal or deputy Marshal.

(4) **Default in Action In Rem.**

(a) Notice Required. A party seeking a default judgment in an action *in rem* must satisfy the judicial officer that due notice of the action and arrest of the property has been given (1) by publication in a newspaper of general circulation within the Division where arrest occurred, (2) by service under Fed. R. Civ. P. 5(a) upon the master or other person having custody of the property, and (3) by service under Fed. R. Civ. P. 5(b) upon every other person who has not appeared in the action and is known to have an interest in the property.

(b) Persons With Recorded Interests. (1) If the defendant property is a vessel documented under the laws of the United States, plaintiff must obtain a current Certificate of Ownership or General Index or Abstract of Title from the United States Coast Guard and give notice to the persons named therein claiming a current interest in or lien against the defendant vessel.

(2) If the defendant property is a vessel numbered as provided in the Federal Boat Safety Act, plaintiff must obtain information from the issuing authority and give notice to the persons named in the records of such authority.

(3) If the defendant property is of such character that there exists a registry of recorded property interests and/or security interests in the property (whether governmental or private), the party must obtain information from each such registry and give notice to the persons named in the records of each such registry.

(5) **Entry of Default and Default Judgment.** After the time for filing an answer has expired, the plaintiff may move for entry of default under Fed. R. Civ. P. 55(a), unless there be an understanding between the parties or counsel to the contrary. Default will be entered upon showing that:

(a) notice has been given as required in LAR (c)(4);

(b) the time for answer has expired; and

(c) no one has filed an appearance to claim the property.

The plaintiff may move for the entry of default judgment under Fed. R. Civ. P. 55(b)(2) at any time after default has been entered. Default judgment may be entered under Fed. R. Civ. P. 55(b)(1) in admiralty proceedings only after the Clerk shall have consulted with the Court. (Amended by order effective Nov. 19, 2010.)

Local Admiralty Rule (d). Possessory, Petitory and Partition Actions.

There is no Local Admiralty Rule (d).

Local Admiralty Rule (e). Actions *In Rem* and Quasi *In Rem:* General Provisions.

(1) **Itemized Demand for Judgment.** The demand for judgment in every complaint filed under Supplemental Rule B or C shall allege the dollar amount of the debt or damages for which the action was commenced; and the demand for judgment shall also allege the dollar amount of every claim for interest, costs, attorneys' fees, and other items of damage. The amount of the special bond posted under Supplemental Rule E(5) may be based upon these allegations.

(2) **Salvage Actions Complaints.** In an action for a salvage reward, the complaint shall allege the dollar value of the vessel, cargo, freight, and other property salved, and the dollar amount of the reward claimed.

(3) **Verification of Pleadings.** Every complaint in Supplemental Rule B, C and D actions shall be verified on oath or solemn affirmation by a party or by an authorized officer of a corporate party. If no party or authorized corporate officer is available, verification of a complaint may be made by an agent, attorney-in-fact, or attorney of record, who shall state the sources of the knowledge, information, and belief contained in the complaint; declare that the document verified is true to the best of that knowledge, information, and belief; state why verification is not made by the party or an authorized corporate officer; and state that the affiant is authorized so to verify. Such a verification will be deemed to have been made by the party to whom a document might apply as if verified personally. Any interested party may move the Court, with or without requesting a stay, for the personal oath of a party or of all parties, or the oath of an authorized corporate officer. If required by the Court, such verification shall be procured by commission or as otherwise ordered.

(4) **Review by Judicial Officer.** Unless otherwise required by a judicial officer, the review of complaints and papers called for by Supplemental Rules B(1) and C(3) does not require the affiant party or attorney to be present. The applicant for review shall include a form of order from the Clerk to the Marshal or other person or organization which, upon signature by the judicial officer, will set in motion the arrest, attachment or garnishment sought by the applicant.

(5)(A) **Service of Warrants and Process of Attachment.** Warrants for the arrest of a vessel, or cargo aboard a vessel, and process to attach a vessel or property aboard a vessel, shall be served only by the Marshal. If other property, tangible or intangible is the subject of the action, the warrant shall be delivered by the Clerk to a person or organization authorized to enforce it, who may be a Marshal, a person or organization contracted with by the United States, a person specially appointed by the Court for that purpose, or, if the action is brought by the United States, any officer or employee of the United States.

(B) If the tangible property to be attached or arrested is a vessel, the Marshal shall affix a copy of the process on the forward bulkhead of the wheelhouse, and at the head of one accommodation where it is visible to people embarking or disembarking the vessel at the ladder. In addition, if the vessel is moored at a shoreside facility, the Marshal shall notify the owner or manager of the facility of the fact of the arrest or attachment.

(6) **Marshal's Forms.** The party who requests a warrant of arrest or process of attachment or garnishment shall provide instructions to the Marshal or other process server on forms supplied by the Marshal and available from the Marshal's Office.

(7) **Property in Possession of United States Officer.** When the property to be attached or arrested is in the custody of an employee or officer of the United States, the Marshal will deliver a copy of the complaint and warrant of arrest or summons and process of attachment or garnishment to that officer or employee if present, and otherwise to the custodian of the property. The Marshal will instruct the officer or employee or custodian to retain custody of the property until ordered to do otherwise by the Court.

(8) **Security for Costs.** In an action under Supplemental Rule E, a party may file and serve upon an adverse party a notice to post security for costs. Unless otherwise ordered by the Court, the amount of security shall be $500.00. The party notified shall post security within five days after service. A party who fails to post security when due may not participate further in the proceedings, except for the purpose of seeking relief from the order.

(9) **Increased Security for Costs.** A party may apply to the Court for an order increasing the amount of security for costs. The Marshal shall notify the Court if a party fails to advance sums as requested, after property has been arrested, attached or garnished, and the Marshal may apply to the Court for directions if a question arises concerning the obligation of a party to advance moneys required under this rule.

(10) **Marshal's Fees and Expenses.** The party who first seeks arrest or attachment of property in an action under Supplemental Rule E or Fed. R. Civ. P. 4(n) shall deposit a sum of money with the Marshal to cover fees, expenses of arrest, and safekeeping charges for ten days. The Marshal is not required to execute process until the deposit is made. The sum of $5,000.00 shall suffice in any case, subject to increase or to reduction following execution, and the party shall advance additional sums from time to time as requested to cover the Marshal's estimated fees and expenses until the property is released or disposed of as provided in Supplemental Rule E.

(11) **Appraisal.** An order for appraisal of property so that security may be given or altered will be entered by the Clerk at the request of any interested party. If the parties do not agree in writing upon an appraiser, a judicial officer will appoint the appraiser. The appraiser shall be sworn to the faithful and impartial discharge of the appraiser's duties before any federal or state officer authorized by law to administer oaths. The appraiser shall give one day's notice of the time and place of making the appraisal to counsel of record. The appraiser shall promptly file the appraisal with the Clerk and serve it upon counsel of record. The appraiser's fee normally will be paid by the moving party, but it is a taxable cost of the action.

(12) **Adversary Hearing.** The adversary hearing following arrest or attachment and garnishment that is called for in Supplemental Rule E(4)(f) shall be conducted by a judicial officer.

(13) **Intervenor's Claims.**

(a) When a vessel or other property has been arrested, attached, or garnished and is in the hands of the Marshal or custodian substituted therefore, anyone having a claim against the vessel or property is required to present the claim by filing an intervening complaint, and not by filing an original complaint, unless otherwise ordered by a judicial officer. Upon the filing of an intervening complaint, the Clerk shall forthwith deliver a conformed copy to the Marshal, who shall deliver the copy to the vessel or custodian of the property, but the Marshal need not re-arrest or re-attach the vessel or property. Intervenors shall thereafter be subject to the rights and obligations of parties.

(b) No party may intervene without first obtaining leave of Court if intervention is sought within 15 days prior to the date for which a sale of the vessel or property has been set by the Court.

(c) An intervenor shall share the deposit for Marshal's fees and expenses in the proportion that its claim bears to the sum of all the claims.

(14) **Custody of Property.**

(a) Safekeeping of Property. When a vessel or other property is brought into the Marshal's custody by arrest or attachment, the Marshal shall arrange for adequate safekeeping, which may include the placing of keepers on or near the vessel, or the appointment of a facility or person as custodian of the property in place of the Marshal.

(b) Cargo Handling, Repairs, and Movement of the Vessel. Following arrest or attachment of a vessel, no cargo handling, repairs, or movement may be made without an order of Court. The applicant for such an order shall give notice to the Marshal and to all parties of record. Upon proof of adequate insurance coverage of the applicant to indemnify the Marshal for his liability, the Court may direct the Marshal to permit cargo handling, repairs, movement of the vessel, or other operations.

(c) Motion for Change in Arrangements. Before or after the Marshal has taken custody of a vessel, cargo, or other property, any party of record may move for an order to dispense with keepers or to remove or place the vessel, cargo or other property at a specified facility, to designate a substitute custodian, or for similar relief. Notice of the motion shall be given to the Marshal and to all parties of record. The judicial officer will require that adequate insurance on the property will be maintained by the successor to the Marshal, before issuing the order to change arrangements.

(d) Insurance. The Marshal may order insurance to protect the Marshal, his deputies, keepers, and substitute custodians, from liabilities assumed in arresting and holding the vessel, cargo, or other property, and in performing whatever services may be undertaken to protect the vessel, cargo, or other property, and to maintain the Court's custody. The party who applies for arrest or attachment of the vessel, cargo, or other property shall reimburse the Marshal for premiums paid for the insurance. The party who applies for removal of the vessel, cargo, or other property to another location, for designation of a substitute custodian, or for other relief that will require an additional premium, shall reimburse the Marshal therefor. The premiums charged for the liability insurance are taxable as administrative costs while the vessel, cargo, or other property is in custody of the Court.

(e) Claims by Suppliers for Payment of Charges. A person who furnishes supplies or services to a vessel, cargo, or other property in custody of the Court who has not been paid and claims the right to payment as an expense of administration shall submit an invoice to the Court for approval in the form of a verified claim at any time before the vessel, cargo, or other property is released or sold. The supplier must serve copies of the claim on the Marshal, substitute custodian (if one has been appointed), and all parties of record. The Court may consider the claims individually or schedule a single hearing for all claims.

(15) **Sale of Property Not Subject to Admiralty — Rule E (9)(b) Interlocutory Sales.**

(a) Notice. Unless otherwise ordered upon good cause shown or as provided by law, a notice of sale of property in an action *in rem,* including the terms of sale, shall be published daily for a period of six days prior to the day of sale in a newspaper of general circulation in the Division where arrest occurred and sale is to take place.

(b) Sale and Report. All sales shall be made by the United States Marshal or his authorized deputy Marshal in the name of the Marshal or by other person or organization authorized to execute the warrant or by any other person assigned by the Court. All sales are subject to confirmation by the Court. The Marshal may, without leave of Court, decline to knock down a vessel or other property to the highest bidder when the highest bid is, in his or her opinion, grossly inadequate. On the day of the sale, the Marshal shall file his report with the Clerk giving all pertinent information, including the fact of the sale, the date, the price obtained and how paid or to be paid, and the name and address of the successful bidder.

(c) Objection to Sale. An interested person may object to the sale by filing a written objection with the Clerk within two Court days following the sale, serving the objection on all parties of record, the successful bidder, and the Marshal. The Marshal is authorized to demand and receive from the objecting party a sum sufficient to pay the expense of keeping the property for at least seven days. The written objection must be endorsed by the Marshal prior to filing with the Clerk, as evidence of the acknowledgment of receipt of the deposit of the required expense funds.

(d) Confirmation of the Sale Without Motion. A sale shall stand confirmed as of course without any action by the Court unless (1) written objection is filed with the Court within the time allowed under these rules, or (2) the purchaser is in default for failure to pay the balance due to the Marshal. The purchaser in a sale so confirmed as of course shall present a form of order reflecting the confirmation of the sale for entry by the Clerk on the fourth Court day following the sale or after the balance of sale funds have been paid, whichever last occurs. The Marshal shall transfer title to the purchaser upon presentation of such order signed by the Clerk.

(e) Confirmation of the Sale Upon Motion. If an objection has been filed or if the successful bidder is in default, the Marshal, the objector, the successful bidder, or a party, may move the Court for relief. The motion will be heard summarily by a judicial officer. The person seeking the hearing on such a motion shall apply to the Court for an order fixing the date and time of the hearing and directing the manner of giving notice and shall give written notice of the motion to the Marshal, all parties, the successful bidder, and the objector. The Court may confirm the sale, order a new sale, or grant such other relief as justice requires. Notice of any hearing on such motion may be informal and, if approved by the Court, by telephone. The parties are expected to be prepared to go forward with any hearing so ordered.

(f) Disposition of Deposits.

(1) Objection Sustained. If an objection is sustained, sums deposited by the successful bidder will be returned to the bidder forthwith. The sum deposited by the objector will be applied to pay the fees and expenses incurred by the Marshal in keeping the property until it is resold, and any balance remaining shall be returned to the objector. The objector will be reimbursed for the expense of keeping the property from the proceeds of a subsequent sale.

(2) Objection Overruled. If the objection is overruled, the sum deposited by the objector will be applied to pay the expense of keeping the property from the day the objection was filed until the day the sale is confirmed, and any balance remaining will be returned to the objector forthwith.

Local Admiralty Rule (f). Limitation of Liability.

(1) **Security for Costs.** The amount of security for costs under Supplemental Rule F(1) shall be $1,000.00, and it may be combined with the security for value and interest, unless otherwise ordered.

(2) **Order of Proof at Trial.** Where the vessel interests seeking statutory limitation of liability have raised the statutory defense by way of answer or complaint, the plaintiff in the former or the damage claimant in the latter, shall proceed with its proof first, as is normal at civil trials.

(3) **Compliance With Supplemental Rule F(4).** The owner shall file within seven (7) days after the date named in the notice proof of compliance with the notice requirement of Supplemental Rule F(4).

APPENDIX A
PLAN FOR THIRD YEAR PRACTICE RULE

I. Activities

A. An eligible law student may appear before the judges, magistrate judges, and bankruptcy judges in this Court on behalf of any person if the person on whose behalf he or she is appearing has indicated in writing consent to that appearance and the supervising lawyer, who must be counsel of record for the person on whose behalf the law student is appearing, has also indicated in writing approval of that appearance, in the following matters:

1. Any civil or criminal matter.
2. Any bankruptcy matter.

B. Any eligible law student may appear in any criminal or civil matter on behalf of the Government with the written approval of the United States Attorney or his authorized representative as the supervising lawyer.

C. In all matters before the judges, magistrate judges or bankruptcy judges, the supervising lawyer must be personally present unless permission to the contra is granted by the Court.

II. Requirements and Limitations

In order to make an appearance pursuant to this rule, the law student must:

A. Be duly enrolled in a law school approved by the American Bar Association or Virginia Board of Bar Examiners.

B. Have completed legal studies amounting to at least four (4) semesters, or the equivalent if the school is on some basis other than a semester basis.

C. Be certified by the dean of his law school as being of good character and competent legal ability, and as being adequately trained to perform as a legal intern.

D. Be introduced to the Court in which he or she is appearing by an attorney admitted to practice in same.

E. Neither ask for nor receive any compensation or remuneration of any kind for services from the person on whose behalf he or she renders services, but this shall not prevent a lawyer, legal aid bureau, law school, public defender agency, or the State, or federal government, from paying compensation to the eligible law student, nor shall it prevent any agency from making such charges for its services as it may otherwise properly require.

F. Certify in writing that he or she has read and is familiar with the Virginia Code of Professional Responsibility.

III. Certification

The certification of a student by the law school dean:

A. Shall be filed with the Clerk of this Court and, unless it is sooner withdrawn, it shall remain in effect until the expiration of eighteen (18) months after it is filed, or until the announcement of the results of the first bar examination following the student's graduation, whichever is earlier. For any student who passes that examination or who is admitted to the bar without taking an examination, the certification shall continue in effect until the date he or she is admitted to the bar.

B. May be withdrawn by the dean at any time by mailing a notice to that effect to the Clerk of this Court. It is not necessary that the notice state the cause for withdrawal.

C. May be terminated by this Court at any time without notice or hearing and without any showing of cause.

IV. Other Activities

A. In addition, an eligible law student may engage in other activities, under the general supervision of a member of the bar of this Court, but outside the personal presence of that lawyer, including:

1. Preparation of pleadings and other documents to be filed in any matter in which the student is eligible to appear, but such pleadings or documents must be signed by the supervising lawyer.

2. Preparation of briefs, abstracts and other documents to be filed, but such documents must be signed by the supervising lawyer.

3. Except when the assignment of counsel in the matter is required by any constitutional provision, statute or rule of this Court, assistance to indigent inmates of correctional institutions or other persons who request such assistance in preparing applications for and supporting documents for post-conviction relief. If there is an attorney of record in the matter, all such assistance must be supervised by the attorney

of record, and all documents submitted to the Court on behalf of such a client must be signed by the attorney of record.

4. Each document or pleading must contain the name of the eligible law student who has participated in drafting it. If he participated in drafting only a portion of it, that fact may be mentioned.

B. Nothing contained herein shall be construed to permit the law student to participate in the taking of depositions in the absence of his supervising attorney.

V. Supervision

The member of the bar under whose supervision an eligible law student does any of the things permitted by this rule shall:

A. Be a lawyer whose service as a supervising lawyer for this program is approved by a judge of this Court. Such approval may be given upon application of any attorney who is a member of the bar of the Court. Such approval may be given by a judge of this Court by formally or informally advising the Clerk of such approval. No approval shall be granted, however, unless and until approval by the dean of the law school in which the law student is enrolled is also obtained.

B. Assume personal professional responsibility for the student's guidance in any work undertaken and for supervising the quality of the student's work.

C. Assist the student in his or her preparation to the extent the supervising lawyer considers it necessary.

D. Agree to notify the dean of the appropriate law school of any alleged failure on the part of the student to abide by the letter and spirit of this order.

E. The Clerk of the Court shall maintain a roll of approved law students and supervising attorneys.

VI. Miscellaneous

Nothing contained in this rule shall affect the right of any person who is not admitted to practice law to do anything he or she might lawfully do prior to the adoption of this Rule.

APPENDIX B
FEDERAL RULES OF DISCIPLINARY ENFORCEMENT

FRDE RULE I

Attorneys Convicted of Crimes

A. Upon the filing with this Court of a certified copy of a judgment of conviction demonstrating that any attorney admitted to practice before the Court has been convicted in any Court of the United States, or the District of Columbia, or of any state, territory, commonwealth or possession of the United States of a serious crime as hereinafter defined, the Court shall enter an order immediately suspending that attorney, whether the conviction resulted from a plea of guilty, or nolo contendere or from a verdict after trial or otherwise, and regardless of the pendency of any appeal, until final disposition of a disciplinary proceeding to be commenced upon such conviction. A copy of such order shall immediately be served upon the attorney. Upon good cause shown, the Court may set aside such order when it appears in the interest of justice to do so.

B. The term "serious crime" shall include any felony and any lesser crime a necessary element of which, as determined by the statutory or common law definition of such crime in the jurisdiction where the judgment was entered, involves false swearing, misrepresentation, fraud, willful failure to file income tax returns, deceit, bribery, extortion, misappropriation, theft, or an attempt or a conspiracy or solicitation of any other to commit a "serious crime."

C. A certified copy of a judgment of conviction of an attorney for any crime shall be conclusive evidence of the commission of that crime in any disciplinary proceeding instituted against that attorney based upon the conviction.

D. Upon the filing of a certified copy of a judgment of conviction of an attorney for a serious crime, the Court shall, in addition to suspending that attorney in accordance with the provisions of this Rule, also refer the matter to counsel for the institution of a disciplinary proceeding before the Court in which the sole issue to be determined shall be the extent of the final discipline to be imposed as a result of the conduct resulting in the conviction, provided that a disciplinary proceeding so instituted will not be brought to final hearing until all appeals from the conviction are concluded. This Rule shall not be applicable if the attorney has surrendered his license to practice law and has submitted a letter to the Clerk withdrawing his or her name from the Roll of Attorneys.

E. Upon the filing of a certified copy of a judgment of conviction of an attorney for a crime not constituting a "serious crime," the Court may refer the matter to counsel for whatever action counsel may deem warranted, including the institution of a disciplinary proceeding before the Court; provided, however, that the Court may in its discretion make no references with respect to convictions for minor offenses.

F. An attorney suspended under the provisions of this Rule will be reinstated immediately upon the filing of a certificate demonstrating that the underlying conviction of a serious crime has been reversed but the reinstatement will not terminate any disciplinary proceeding then pending against the attorney, the disposition of which shall be determined by the Court on the basis of all available evidence pertaining to both guilt and the extent of discipline to be imposed.

FRDE RULE II

Discipline Imposed By Other Courts

A. Any attorney admitted to practice before this Court shall, upon being subjected to public discipline by any other court of the United States or the District of Columbia, or by a Court of any state, territory, commonwealth or possession of the United States, promptly inform the Clerk of this Court of such action.

B. Upon the filing of a certified or exemplified copy of a judgment or order demonstrating that an attorney admitted to practice before this Court has been disciplined by another Court, this Court shall forthwith issue a notice directed to the attorney containing:

1. A copy of the judgment or order from the other Court; and

2. An order to show cause directing that the attorney inform this Court within 30 days after service of that order upon the attorney, personally or by mail, of any claim by the attorney predicated upon the grounds set forth in (D) hereof that the imposition of the identical discipline by the Court would be unwarranted and the reasons therefor.

C. In the event the discipline imposed in the other jurisdiction has been stayed there, any reciprocal discipline imposed in this Court shall be deferred until such stay expires.

D. Upon the expiration of 30 days from service of the notice issued pursuant to the provisions of (B) above, this Court shall impose the identical discipline unless the respondent-attorney demonstrates, or this Court finds, that upon the face of the record upon which the discipline in another jurisdiction is predicated it clearly appears:

1. That the procedure was so lacking in notice or opportunity to be heard as to constitute a deprivation of due process; or

2. That there was such an infirmity of proof establishing the misconduct as to give rise to the clear conviction that this Court could not, consistent with its duty, accept as final the conclusion on that subject; or

3. That the imposition of the same discipline by this Court would result in grave injustice; or

4. That the misconduct established is deemed by this Court to warrant substantially different discipline.

Where this Court determines that any of said elements exist, it shall enter such other order as it deems appropriate.

E. In all other respects, a final adjudication in another Court that an attorney has been guilty of misconduct shall establish conclusively the misconduct for purposes of a disciplinary proceeding in the Court of the United States.

F. This Court may at any stage appoint counsel to prosecute the disciplinary proceedings.

FRDE RULE III

Disbarment on Consent or Resignation in Other Courts

A. Any attorney admitted to practice before this Court who shall be disbarred on consent or resign from the bar of any other Court of the United States or the District of Columbia, or from the Bar of any state, territory, commonwealth or possession of the United States while an investigation into allegations of misconduct is pending, shall, upon the filing with this Court of a certified or exemplified copy of the judgment or order accepting such disbarment on consent or resignation, cease to be permitted to practice before this Court and be stricken from the roll of attorneys admitted to practice before this Court.

B. Any attorney admitted to practice before this Court shall, upon being disbarred on consent or resigning from the bar of any other Court of the United States or the District of Columbia, or from the Bar of any state, territory, commonwealth or possession of the United States while an investigation into allegations of misconduct is pending, promptly inform the Clerk of this Court of such disbarment on consent or resignation.

FRDE RULE IV

Standards of Professional Conduct

A. For misconduct defined in these Rules, and for good cause shown, and after notice and opportunity to be heard, any attorney admitted to practice before this Court may be disbarred, suspended from practice before this Court, reprimanded or subjected to other disciplinary action as the circumstances may warrant.

B. Acts or omissions by an attorney admitted to practice before this Court, individually or in concert with any other person or persons, which violate the Virginia Rules of Professional Conduct adopted by this Court shall constitute misconduct and shall be grounds for discipline, whether or not the act or omission occurred in the course of any attorney-client relationship. The Rules of Professional Conduct adopted by this Court are the Rules of Professional Conduct adopted by the highest Court of the state in which this Court sits, as amended from time to time by that state Court, except as otherwise provided by specific Rule of this Court after consideration of comments by representatives of bar associations within the state.

FRDE RULE V

Disciplinary Proceedings

A. When misconduct or allegations of misconduct which, as substantiated, would warrant discipline on the part of an attorney admitted to practice before this Court shall come to the attention of a judge of this Court, whether by complaint or otherwise, and the applicable procedure is not otherwise mandated by these Rules, the judge shall refer the matter to counsel for investigation and the prosecution of a formal disciplinary proceeding or the formulation of such other recommendation as may be appropriate.

B. Should counsel conclude after investigation and review that a formal disciplinary proceeding should not be initiated against the respondent-attorney because sufficient evidence is not present, or because there is pending another proceeding against the respondent-attorney, the disposition of which in the judgment of the counsel should be awaited before further action by this Court is considered, or for any other valid reason, counsel shall file with the Court a recommendation for disposition of the matter, whether by dismissal, admonition, deferral, or otherwise setting forth the reasons therefor.

C. To initiate formal disciplinary proceedings, counsel shall obtain an order of this Court upon a showing of probable cause requiring the respondent-attorney to show cause within 30 days after service of that order upon that attorney, personally or by mail, why the attorney should not be disciplined.

D. Upon the respondent-attorney's answer to the order to show cause, if any issue of fact is raised or the respondent-attorney wishes to be heard in mitigation, this Court shall set the matter for prompt hearing before one or more judges of this Court, provided however that if the disciplinary proceeding is predicated upon the complaint of a Judge of this Court the hearing shall be conducted before a panel of three other judges of this Court appointed by the chief judge, or, if there are less than three judges eligible to serve or the chief judge is the complainant, by the Chief Judge of the Court of Appeals for this Circuit.

FRDE RULE VI

Disbarment on Consent While Under Disciplinary Investigation or Prosecution

A. Any attorney admitted to practice before this Court who is the subject of an investigation into, or a pending proceeding involving, allegations of misconduct may consent to disbarment, but only by delivering to this Court an affidavit stating that the attorney desires to consent to disbarment and that:

1. the attorney's consent is freely and voluntarily rendered; the attorney is not being subjected to coercion or duress; the attorney is fully aware of the implications of so consenting;

2. the attorney is aware that there is a presently pending investigation or proceeding involving allegations that there exist grounds for the attorney's discipline, the nature of which the attorney shall specifically set forth;

3. the attorney acknowledges that the material facts so alleged are true; and

4. the attorney so consents because the attorney knows that if charges were predicated upon the matters under investigation, or if the proceeding were prosecuted, the attorney could not successfully defend himself or herself.

B. Upon receipt of the required affidavit, this Court shall enter an order disbarring the attorney.

C. The order disbarring the attorney on consent shall be a matter of public record. However, the affidavit required under the provisions of this Rule shall not be publicly disclosed or made available for use in any other proceeding except upon order of this Court.

FRDE RULE VII

Reinstatement

A. **After Disbarment or Suspension.** An attorney suspended for three months or less shall be automatically reinstated at the end of the period of suspension upon the filing with the Court of an affidavit of compliance with the provisions of the order. An attorney suspended for more than three months or disbarred may not resume practice until reinstated by order of this Court.

B. **Time of Application Following Disbarment.** A person who has been disbarred after hearing or by consent may not apply for reinstatement until the expiration of at least five years from the effective date of the disbarment.

C. **Hearing on Application.** Petitions for reinstatement by a disbarred or suspended attorney under this Rule shall be filed with the chief judge of this Court. Upon receipt of the petition, the chief judge shall promptly refer the petition to counsel and shall assign the matter for prompt hearing before one or more judges of this Court, provided however that if the disciplinary proceeding was predicated upon the complaint of a judge of this Court the hearing shall be conducted before a panel of three other judges of this Court appointed by the chief judge, or, if there are less than three judges eligible to serve or the chief judge was the complainant, by the chief judge of the Court of Appeals for this Circuit. The judge or judges assigned to the matter shall within 30 days after referral schedule a hearing at which the petitioner shall have the burden of demonstrating by clear and convincing evidence that he has the moral qualifications, competency and learning in the law required for admission to practice law before this Court and that his resumption of the practice of law will not be detrimental to the integrity and standing of the bar or to the administration of justice, or subversive of the public interest.

D. **Duty of Counsel.** In all proceedings upon a petition for reinstatement, cross-examination of the witnesses of the respondent-attorney and the submission of evidence, if any, in opposition to the petition shall be conducted by counsel.

E. **Deposit for Costs of Proceeding.** Petitions for reinstatement under this Rule shall be accompanied by an advance cost deposit in an amount to be set from time to time by the Court to cover anticipated costs of the reinstatement proceeding.

F. **Conditions of Reinstatement.** If the petitioner is found unfit to resume the practice of law, the petition shall be dismissed. If the petitioner is found fit to resume the practice of law, the judgment shall reinstate him, provided that the judgment may make reinstatement conditional upon the payment of all or part of the costs of the proceedings, and upon the making of partial or complete restitution to parties harmed by the petitioner whose conduct led to the suspension or disbarment. Provided further, that if the petitioner has been suspended or disbarred for five years or more, reinstatement may be conditioned, in the discretion of the judge or judges before whom the matter is heard, upon the furnishing of proof of competency and learning in the law, which proof may include certification by the bar examiners of a state or other jurisdiction of the attorney's successful completion of an examination for admission to practice subsequent to the date of suspension or disbarment.

G. **Successive Petitions.** No petition for reinstatement under this Rule shall be filed within one year following an adverse judgment upon a petition for reinstatement filed by or on behalf of the same person.

FRDE RULE VIII

Attorneys Specially Admitted

Whenever an attorney applies to be admitted or is admitted to this Court for purposes of a particular proceeding (pro hac vice), the attorney shall be deemed thereby to have conferred disciplinary jurisdiction upon this Court for any alleged misconduct of that attorney arising in the course of or in the preparation for such proceeding.

FRDE RULE IX

Service of Papers and Other Notices

Service of an order to show cause instituting a formal disciplinary proceeding shall be made by personal service or by registered or certified mail addressed to the respondent-attorney at the last address of record. Service of any other papers or notices required by these Rules shall be deemed to have been made if such paper or notice is addressed to the respondent-attorney at the last address of record; or to counsel or the respondent's attorney at the address indicated in the most recent pleading or other document filed by them in the course of any proceeding.

FRDE RULE X

Appointment of Counsel

Whenever counsel is to be appointed pursuant to these Rules to investigate allegations of misconduct or prosecute disciplinary proceedings or in conjunction with a reinstatement petition filed by a disciplinary agency of the highest Court of the state wherein the Court sits, or the attorney maintains his or her principal office in the case of the Courts of appeal, or other disciplinary agency having jurisdiction, this Court shall appoint as counsel one or more members of the Bar of this Court to investigate allegations of misconduct or to prosecute disciplinary proceedings under these rules, provided, however, that the respondent-attorney may move to disqualify an attorney so appointed who is or has been engaged as an adversary of the respondent-attorney in any matter. Counsel, once appointed, may not resign unless permission to do so is given by this Court.

FRDE RULE XI

Duties of the Clerk

A. Upon being informed that an attorney admitted to practice before this Court has been convicted of any crime, the Clerk of this Court shall determine whether the Clerk of the Court in which such conviction occurred has forwarded a certificate of such conviction to this Court. If a certificate has not been so forwarded, the Clerk of this Court shall promptly obtain a certificate and file it with this Court.

B. Upon being informed that an attorney admitted to practice before this Court has been subjected to discipline by another Court, the Clerk of this Court shall determine whether a certified or exemplified copy of the disciplinary judgment or order has been filed with this Court, and, if not, the Clerk shall promptly obtain a certified copy or exemplified copy of the disciplinary judgment or order and file it with this Court.

C. Whenever it appears that any person convicted of any crime or disbarred or suspended or censured or disbarred on consent by this Court is admitted to practice law in any other jurisdiction or before any other Court, the Clerk of this Court shall, within ten days of that conviction, disbarment, suspension, censure, or disbarment on consent, transmit to the disciplinary authority in such other jurisdiction, or for such other Court, a certificate of the conviction or a certified or exemplified copy of the judgment or order of disbarment, suspension, censure, or disbarment on consent, as well as the last known office and residence addresses of the defendant or respondent.

D. The Clerk of this Court shall, likewise, promptly notify the National Discipline Data Bank operated by the American Bar Association of any order imposing public discipline upon any attorney admitted to practice before this Court.

FRDE RULE XII

Jurisdiction

Nothing contained in these Rules shall be construed to deny to this Court such powers as are necessary for the Court to maintain control over proceedings conducted before it, such as proceedings for contempt under Title 18 of the United States code or under Rule 42 of the Federal Rules of Criminal Procedure.

FRDE RULE XIII

Effective Date

Any amendments to these disciplinary enforcement rules shall become effective immediately upon the entry and filing of any Order, provided that any formal disciplinary proceedings then pending before this Court shall be concluded under the procedure existing prior to the effective date of these amendments.

Index to U.S. District Court Rules of the Eastern District of Virginia

A

ADDRESS ON PLEADINGS, USDistCt-ED Practice Rule 7.
Criminal proceedings, USDistCt-ED Criminal Rule 47.

ADMIRALTY.
Attachment and garnishment, USDistCt-ED Admiralty Rule (b).
Authority and scope of rules, USDistCt-ED Admiralty Rule (a).
Citation of rules, USDistCt-ED Admiralty Rule (a).
Definition of officers of court, USDistCt-ED Admiralty Rule (a).
Filing of documents.
Electronic case filing system, USDistCt-ED Admiralty Rule (a).
In rem actions, USDistCt-ED Admiralty Rules (c), (e).
Limitation of liability, USDistCt-ED Admiralty Rule (f).
Not found within this district, defined, USDistCt-ED Admiralty Rule (b).
Quasi in rem actions, USDistCt-ED Admiralty Rule (e).
Sales and distribution of proceeds of sales, USDistCt-ED Practice Rule 83.2.

ALTERNATIVE DISPUTE RESOLUTION, USDistCt-ED Practice Rule 83.6.

AMENDMENTS TO RULES.
Effective date of amendments, USDistCt-ED Criminal Rule 1, USDistCt-ED Practice Rule 1.

APPEALS.
Fees and costs bonds, USDistCt-ED Practice Rules 54, 62.
Record on appeal, USDistCt-ED Criminal Rule 57.3, USDistCt-ED Practice Rule 80.

APPLICABILITY OF RULES, USDistCt-ED Criminal Rule 1, USDistCt-ED Practice Rule 1.

AREA ENCOMPASSED BY EASTERN DISTRICT, USDistCt-ED Criminal Rule 18, USDistCt-ED Practice Rule 3.

ATTACHMENTS.
Maritime attachment, USDistCt-ED Admiralty Rule (b).

ATTORNEYS AT LAW, USDistCt-ED Criminal Rule 57.4, USDistCt-ED Practice Rule 83.1.
Federal rules of disciplinary enforcement, USDistCt-ED Appx B.
Plan for third year practice rule, USDistCt-ED Appx A.
Release of information, USDistCt-ED Criminal Rule 57.1.

ATTORNEYS' FEES.
Depositions, USDistCt-ED Practice Rule 30.

B

BAR IDENTIFICATION NUMBER ON PLEADINGS, USDistCt-ED Practice Rule 83.1.

BILL OF COSTS, USDistCt-ED Practice Rule 54.

BLANK SUBPOENAS, USDistCt-ED Practice Rule 45.

BONDS, SURETY, USDistCt-ED Practice Rule 65.
Appeals, USDistCt-ED Practice Rules 54, 62.
Costs of litigation, USDistCt-ED Practice Rule 54.
Maritime attachment and garnishment, USDistCt-ED Admiralty Rule (e).

BRIEFS WITH MOTIONS, USDistCt-ED Practice Rule 7.
Criminal proceedings, USDistCt-ED Criminal Rule 47.
Discovery motions, USDistCt-ED Practice Rule 37.
Summary judgment motions, USDistCt-ED Practice Rule 56.

BROADCASTING COURTROOM PROCEEDINGS, USDistCt-ED Criminal Rule 53, USDistCt-ED Practice Rule 83.3.

C

CAMERAS IN THE COURTROOM, USDistCt-ED Practice Rule 83.3.

CONDEMNATION GUIDELINES, USDistCt-ED Practice Rule 71A.

CONTINUANCES, USDistCt-ED Criminal Rule 47, USDistCt-ED Practice Rule 7.

COSTS.
Generally, USDistCt-ED Practice Rule 54.
Transcript fees, USDistCt-ED Practice Rule 80.

COURT REPORTERS, USDistCt-ED Criminal Rule 57.3, USDistCt-ED Practice Rule 80.
Release of information, USDistCt-ED Criminal Rule 57.1.

CRIMINAL RULES.
Area encompassed by Eastern district, USDistCt-ED Criminal Rule 18.
Attorneys at law, USDistCt-ED Criminal Rule 57.4.
Broadcasting courtroom proceedings, USDistCt-ED Criminal Rule 53.
Continuances, USDistCt-ED Criminal Rule 47.
Court reporters, USDistCt-ED Criminal Rule 57.3.

CRIMINAL RULES —Cont'd
Divisions within Eastern district, USDistCt-ED Criminal Rule 18.
Electronic case filing system, USDistCt-ED Criminal Rule 1.
Exhibits at trial, USDistCt-ED Criminal Rule 55.
Fair trial directives, USDistCt-ED Criminal Rule 57.1.
Fees, USDistCt-ED Criminal Rule 57.2.
Filing of documents.
Electronic case filing system, USDistCt-ED Criminal Rule 1.
Financial interest disclosure statement, USDistCt-ED Criminal Rule 12.4.
Fixed sum in lieu of appearance, USDistCt-ED Criminal Rule 58.
Gag orders, USDistCt-ED Criminal Rule 57.1.
Grand juries, USDistCt-ED Criminal Rule 6.
Identification.
Exclusion of personal identifiers on pleadings, motions and orders, USDistCt-ED Criminal Rule 47.
Instructions to jury, USDistCt-ED Criminal Rule 30.
Jury trials, USDistCt-ED Criminal Rules 24, 30.
Jurors generally, USDistCt-ED Criminal Rule 24.
Voir dire, USDistCt-ED Criminal Rule 30.
Magistrate judges, USDistCt-ED Criminal Rule 5.
Motions, USDistCt-ED Criminal Rules 12, 47.
Photographing in courtroom, USDistCt-ED Criminal Rule 53.
Pro se litigants.
Appearances, USDistCt-ED Criminal Rule 57.4.
Release of information, USDistCt-ED Criminal Rule 57.1.
Sales and distribution of proceeds of sales, USDistCt-ED Criminal Rule 32.2.
Scope of rules, USDistCt-ED Criminal Rule 1.
Sealed instruments.
Designation and handling of documents under seal, USDistCt-ED Criminal Rule 49.
Personal identifiers, excluding, USDistCt-ED Criminal Rule 49.
Televising courtroom proceedings, USDistCt-ED Criminal Rule 53.

D

DECORUM IN THE COURTROOM, USDistCt-ED Practice Rule 83.1.

DEPOSITIONS, USDistCt-ED Practice Rule 30.
Discovery generally, USDistCt-ED Practice Rules 26, 37.
Subpoena for attendance at deposition, USDistCt-ED Practice Rule 45.

DEPOSITS INTO COURT, USDistCt-ED Practice Rule 67.

DISCOVERY, USDistCt-ED Practice Rule 26.
Compelling discovery, USDistCt-ED Practice Rule 37.
Depositions, USDistCt-ED Practice Rule 30.
Subpoena for attendance at deposition, USDistCt-ED Practice Rule 45.
Interrogatories.
Use of forms, USDistCt-ED Practice Rule 7.

DISCOVERY —Cont'd
Sanctions, USDistCt-ED Practice Rule 37.

DIVISIONS WITHIN EASTERN DISTRICT, USDistCt-ED Criminal Rule 18, USDistCt-ED Practice Rule 3.

E

ELECTRONIC CASE FILING SYSTEM, USDistCt-ED Admiralty Rule (a), USDistCt-ED Criminal Rule 1, USDistCt-ED Practice Rule 1.
Transcripts.
Filing, viewing, purchasing.
Civil cases, USDistCt-ED Practice Rule 80.
Criminal cases, USDistCt-ED Criminal Rule 57.3.

EMINENT DOMAIN.
Land condemnation guidelines, USDistCt-ED Practice Rule 71A.

EXHIBITS AT TRIAL, USDistCt-ED Criminal Rule 55, USDistCt-ED Practice Rule 79.

EXPERT DISCLOSURES, USDistCt-ED Practice Rule 26.

F

FAIR TRIAL DIRECTIVES, USDistCt-ED Criminal Rule 57.1.

FEES, USDistCt-ED Criminal Rule 57.2.

FILING OF DOCUMENTS.
Electronic case filing system, USDistCt-ED Admiralty Rule (a), USDistCt-ED Criminal Rule 1, USDistCt-ED Practice Rule 1.
Pleadings, USDistCt-ED Practice Rule 7.
Criminal proceedings, USDistCt-ED Criminal Rule 47.

FINANCIAL INTEREST DISCLOSURE STATEMENT, USDistCt-ED Criminal Rule 12.4, USDistCt-ED Practice Rule 7.1.

FOREIGN ATTORNEYS.
Appearing and conducting specific cases, USDistCt-ED Criminal Rule 57.4, USDistCt-ED Practice Rule 83.1.

FORMS.
Motions and interrogatories, USDistCt-ED Practice Rule 7.
Criminal proceedings, USDistCt-ED Criminal Rule 47.

FREE PRESS, USDistCt-ED Criminal Rule 57.1.

G

GAG ORDERS, USDistCt-ED Criminal Rule 57.1.

GARNISHMENT.
Maritime garnishment, USDistCt-ED Admiralty Rule (b).

GRAND JURY, USDistCt-ED Criminal Rule 6.
Release of information, USDistCt-ED Criminal Rule 57.1.

H

HABEAS CORPUS, USDistCt-ED Practice Rule 83.4.

I

IDENTIFICATION.
Exclusion of personal identifiers on pleadings, motions and orders, USDistCt-ED Criminal Rule 47, USDistCt-ED Practice Rule 7.
Sealed instruments.
Personal identifiers, excluding, USDistCt-ED Criminal Rule 49.

IN FORMA PAUPERIS, USDistCt-ED Practice Rule 83.4.

IN REM ACTIONS.
Maritime cases, USDistCt-ED Admiralty Rules (c), (e).

INSTRUCTIONS TO JURY, USDistCt-ED Criminal Rule 30, USDistCt-ED Practice Rule 51.

INTERROGATORIES.
Discovery generally, USDistCt-ED Practice Rules 26, 37.
Use of forms, USDistCt-ED Practice Rule 7.

J

JURY TRIALS.
Communication with jurors, USDistCt-ED Criminal Rule 24, USDistCt-ED Practice Rule 47.
Costs, USDistCt-ED Practice Rule 54.
Criminal rules, USDistCt-ED Criminal Rules 24, 30.
Demand for jury trial, USDistCt-ED Practice Rule 38.
Instructions to jury, USDistCt-ED Criminal Rule 30, USDistCt-ED Practice Rule 51.
Jury lists, USDistCt-ED Criminal Rule 24, USDistCt-ED Practice Rule 47.
Length of jury service, USDistCt-ED Practice Rule 47.
Peremptory challenges, USDistCt-ED Criminal Rule 24, USDistCt-ED Practice Rule 47.
Voir dire, USDistCt-ED Criminal Rule 30, USDistCt-ED Practice Rule 51.

L

LAW STUDENTS.
Third-year practice, USDistCt-ED Appx A, USDistCt-ED Criminal Rule 57.4, USDistCt-ED Practice Rule 83.1.

LIENS.
Maritime liens.
Distribution of proceeds of sales, USDistCt-ED Practice Rule 83.2.

M

MAGISTRATE JUDGES, USDistCt-ED Criminal Rule 5, USDistCt-ED Practice Rule 72.

MEDIA COVERAGE OF PROCEEDINGS.
Open proceedings, USDistCt-ED Criminal Rule 57.1.
Photographing, broadcasting and televising in courtroom, USDistCt-ED Practice Rule 83.3.
Release of information, USDistCt-ED Criminal Rule 57.1.

MEDIATION.
Alternative dispute resolution, USDistCt-ED Practice Rule 83.6.

MISDEMEANORS.
Fixed sum in lieu of appearance, USDistCt-ED Criminal Rule 58.

MOTIONS, USDistCt-ED Practice Rule 7.
Criminal cases, USDistCt-ED Criminal Rules 12, 47.
Discovery motions, USDistCt-ED Practice Rule 37.
Gag orders, USDistCt-ED Criminal Rule 57.1.
Summary judgment, USDistCt-ED Practice Rule 56.

O

OBJECTIONS TO DISCOVERY PROCESS, USDistCt-ED Criminal Rule 26.

OBJECTIONS TO ORDERS, USDistCt-ED Practice Rule 7.

ORDERS OF COURT.
Objections noted, USDistCt-ED Practice Rule 7.
Scheduling orders, USDistCt-ED Practice Rule 16.

P

PEREMPTORY CHALLENGES, USDistCt-ED Practice Rule 47.

PHOTOGRAPHING IN COURTROOM, USDistCt-ED Criminal Rule 53, USDistCt-ED Practice Rule 83.3.

PLEADINGS.
Address and telephone number of attorney or pro se litigant, USDistCt-ED Practice Rule 7.
Bar identification number on initial pleadings, USDistCt-ED Practice Rule 83.1.
Filing, USDistCt-ED Practice Rule 7.
Criminal proceedings, USDistCt-ED Criminal Rule 47.
Redacted pleadings excluding personal identifiers on motions, pleadings and orders, USDistCt-ED Criminal Rule 47, USDistCt-ED Practice Rule 7.
Verification of pleadings, USDistCt-ED Admiralty Rule (e).

PRETRIAL CONFERENCES, USDistCt-ED Practice Rule 16.
Motions, USDistCt-ED Practice Rule 7.

PRISONERS.
Filing of cases in forma pauperis, USDistCt-ED Practice Rule 83.4,

PRO HAC VICE ADMISSION, USDistCt-ED Practice Rule 83.1.

PRO SE LITIGANTS.
Appearances, USDistCt-ED Criminal Rule 57.4.
Habeas corpus procedures, USDistCt-ED Practice Rule 83.4.
Pleadings to contain address, USDistCt-ED Practice Rule 7.
Subpoenas, USDistCt-ED Practice Rule 45.
Transcript of proceedings, USDistCt-ED Practice Rule 80.
Warnings on motions, USDistCt-ED Practice Rule 7.

Q

QUASI IN REM ACTIONS.
Maritime cases, USDistCt-ED Admiralty Rule (e).

R

RECORDING COURTROOM PROCEEDINGS, USDistCt-ED Practice Rule 83.3.

S

SALES AND DISTRIBUTION OF PROCEEDS OF SALES, USDistCt-ED Criminal Rule 32.2, USDistCt-ED Practice Rule 83.2.
Maritime attachment and garnishment, USDistCt-ED Admiralty Rule (e).

SCHEDULING ORDERS, USDistCt-ED Practice Rule 16.

SCOPE OF RULES, USDistCt-ED Criminal Rule 1, USDistCt-ED Practice Rule 1.
Admiralty rules, USDistCt-ED Admiralty Rule (a).

SEALED INSTRUMENTS.
Designation and handling of documents under seal, USDistCt-ED Criminal Rule 49, USDistCt-ED Practice Rule 5.
Personal identifiers, excluding, USDistCt-ED Criminal Rule 49.

SERVICE OF PROCESS.
Maritime attachment and garnishment, USDistCt-ED Admiralty Rules (b), (e).
Proof of service, USDistCt-ED Practice Rule 7.
Subpoenas, USDistCt-ED Practice Rule 45.
Subpoenas, USDistCt-ED Practice Rule 45.
Summons, USDistCt-ED Practice Rule 4.

SETTLEMENT.
Alternative dispute resolution, USDistCt-ED Practice Rule 83.6.

STIPULATION FOR COSTS, USDistCt-ED Practice Rule 54.
Appeals, USDistCt-ED Practice Rule 62.

SUBPOENAS, USDistCt-ED Criminal Rule 17, USDistCt-ED Practice Rule 45.

SUMMARY JUDGMENT, USDistCt-ED Practice Rule 56.

SURETIES, USDistCt-ED Criminal Rule 46, USDistCt-ED Practice Rule 65.

T

TELEPHONE NUMBER ON PLEADINGS, USDistCt-ED Practice Rule 7.
Criminal proceedings, USDistCt-ED Criminal Rule 47.

TELEVISING COURTROOM PROCEEDINGS, USDistCt-ED Criminal Rule 53, USDistCt-ED Practice Rule 83.3.

TRANSCRIPTS, USDistCt-ED Criminal Rule 57.3, USDistCt-ED Practice Rule 80.

V

VENUE.
Division in which suits to be instituted, USDistCt-ED Practice Rule 3.

VOIR DIRE, USDistCt-ED Practice Rule 51.

LOCAL RULES OF PRACTICE OF THE UNITED STATES BANKRUPTCY COURT FOR THE EASTERN DISTRICT OF VIRGINIA

Revision effective March 1, 2001; amended through September 3, 2013.

Rule
1001-1. Scope of Rules.
1002-1. Petitions — Copies [Repealed].
1002-2. Notice to Individual Debtors of Chapters Available Under Bankruptcy Code [Repealed].
1006-1. Fees: Installment Payments [Repealed].
1006-1. Fees: Installment Payments, Waiver, Refunds.
1006-2. Fees: Electronic Refunds [Repealed].
1006-3. Payment of Filing Fees; Remedies for Nonpayment [Repealed].
1007-1. Lists, Schedules and Statements.
1007-3. Statement of Intention.
1009-1. Amendments to Lists & Schedules.
1014-2. Declaration of Divisional Venue [Repealed].
1015-1. Joint Administration of Estates.
1017-1. Conversion.
1017-2. Dismissal for Substantial Abuse of Chapter 7 [Repealed].
1017-3. Suspension of Automatic Dismissal.
1020-1. Small Business Chapter 11 Reorganization Cases [Repealed].
1071-1. Divisions.
1074-1. Corporations, Limited Liability Companies or Partnerships.
2002-1. Notice to Creditors & Other Interested Parties.
2003-1. Meeting of Creditors & Equity Security Holders.
2004-1. Examination.
2014-1. Service of Motion for an Order Authorizing Employment in a Chapter 11 Case.
2015-(a)-1. Required Reports of Debtors in Possession and Trustees.
2016-1. Compensation of Professionals.
2090-1. Attorneys — Right to Practice Before the Court.
2090-1.
3003-1. Claims in Chapter 11 Cases.
3007-1. Objections to Claims.
3011-1. Unclaimed Funds.
3015-1. Chapter 12 Plan Requirements.
3015-2. Chapter 13 Plan Requirements.
3016-1. Chapter 11 Plan Requirements.
3017-1. Approval of Disclosure Statement [Repealed].
3070-1. Payments in Chapter 12 and Chapter 13 Cases.
4001(a)-1. Relief from Automatic Stay.
4002-1. Duties of the Debtor.
4003-2. Lien Avoidance.

Rule
4008-1. Reaffirmation.
4008-2. Chapter 13 Discharge and Certification of Compliance; Duty of Debtor to Cooperate with Chapter 13 Trustee.
5005-1. Filing of Petitions, Pleadings and Other Papers.
5005-2. Filing of Petitions, Pleadings and Other Papers by Electronic Means.
5010-1. Reopening Cases.
5011-1. Withdrawal of Reference.
5073-1. Photography, Recording Devices, and Broadcasting.
5077-1. Transcripts.
6004-1. Sale of Estate Property.
6004-2. Use, Sale or Lease of Property.
6004-3. Sale or Refinance of Property By Chapter 13 Debtor After Confirmation.
6004-4. Mortgage Loan Modification by Chapter 13 Debtor After Confirmation.
6007-1. Abandonment.
6008-1. Redemption.
7003-1. Adversary Proceeding Cover Sheet.
7004-2. Summons.
7007-1. Financial Disclosure [Repealed].
7013-1. Counterclaims [Repealed].
7016-1. Pretrial Procedures.
7026-1. Discovery.
7030-1. Depositions.
7041-1. Dismissal of Adversary Proceedings.
7054-1. Costs.
7056-1. Summary Judgment.
7067-1. Deposit and Disbursement of Court Registry Funds.
8005-1. Appeal Bond.
8006-1. Record on Appeal.
9010-1. Representation and Apearances; Powers of Attorney.
9013-1. Motions Practice.
9014-1. Whether Hearing is Evidentiary or Preliminary.
9016-1. Subpoenas.
9017-1. Evidence.
9019-1. Settlement and Alternative Dispute Resolution.
9022-1. Court Orders.
9070-1. Exhibits.

Exhibits.

1. Chapter 13 Plan and Related Motions.
2. Special Notice to Secured Creditor.
3. Order Adopting CM/ECF Procedures [Rescinded].

4. Administrative Procedures for CM/ECF Cases [Rescinded].
5. Instructions for Creditor Matrix Diskette.
6. Financial Interest Disclosure Statement.
7. Motions Day Procedure for Alexandria Division.
8. Order Adopting Revision to Interim Rule 1007-I.
Index.

Rule 1001-1. Scope of Rules.

The Supreme Court of the United States has, pursuant to 28 U.S.C. §2075, prescribed rules of procedure in bankruptcy cases. Federal Rule of Bankruptcy Procedure 9029 provides that courts may adopt local rules that are not inconsistent with the Federal Rules of Bankruptcy Procedure.

These Local Rules of the United States Bankruptcy Court for the Eastern District of Virginia are hereby prescribed and promulgated as Local Rules governing practice and procedure before the Court. They are to be cited as the "Local Bankruptcy Rules" except that individual rules may be cited in the following form: "Local Bankruptcy Rule ________", or "LBR________".

COMMENT

The prior set of Local Bankruptcy Rules contained several references that were inconsistent with this rule. Therefore, all incorrect references have been edited so that they are now in compliance.

Rule 1002-1. Petitions — Copies.

[Repealed.]

COMMENT

Changes have been made to allow for the filing of documents by electronic means provided under FRBP 5005(a)(2). For more detail on how this has been implemented on a pilot basis in the Alexandria Division see the "Order Adopting Electronic Case Filing Procedures" attached as Exhibit 3 and the "Administrative Procedures for Electronically Filed Cases" attached as Exhibit 4. It is planned that the ability to file electronically will expand to the other divisions during 1999.

1002-1 The rule is repealed in light of Local Bankruptcy Rule 5005-2, which mandates electronic case filings in the Court's Case Management/Electronic Case Files (CM/ECF) System and authorizes the Clerk to promulgate and revise the Court's Electronic Case Files (CM/ECF) Policy. [Repeal effective 12/01/09.]

Rule 1002-2. Notice to Individual Debtors of Chapters Available Under Bankruptcy Code.

[Repealed.]

COMMENT

1002-2 The contents of the rule are substantially set forth in 11 U.S.C. § 342(b). The rule is repealed for this reason and, further, is repealed in light of Local Bankruptcy Rule 5005-2, which mandates electronic case filings in the Court's Case Management/Electronic Case Files (CM/ECF) System and authorizes the Clerk to promulgate and revise the Court's Electronic Case Files (CM/ECF) Policy. [Repeal effective 12/01/09.]

Rule 1006-1. Fees: Installment Payments.

[Repealed.]

COMMENT

1006-1(B) This revision is due to changes made by the Judicial Conference at its September 1997 session to the Bankruptcy Court Miscellaneous Fee Schedule. The changes were effective January 1, 1998.

1006-1(B) This revision is due to changes made under Public Law No. 106-113, which increased the statutory filing fee for cases commenced under Chapter 7 and Chapter 13 by $25. These changes were effective December 29, 1999.

This change [to (D)(2)] is necessary because of the addition of LBR 1006-1 to LBR 1017-3. [Change effective 3/1/01.]

1006-1(B) This revision is due to changes made

by the Judicial Conference at its September 2003 session to the Bankruptcy Court Miscellaneous Fee Schedule. [Change effective 12/1/03.]

1006-1(D)(2) This subparagraph is amended to clarify that a petition filing accompanied by an Application to Pay the Filing Fee in Installments must also be accompanied by the proper first installment payment. [Change effective 2/1/04.]

1006-1(B) The revision to the "1 Month After Filing" column at the Chapter 11 line from $400 to $409 effects a technical change only. [Change effective 7/1/04.]

1006-1 LBR 1006-1(D) is repealed in light of new LBR 1006-3. [Change effective 9/1/06.]

1006-1 LBR 1006-1 is repealed and a new LBR 1006-1 has been promulgated, which consolidates selected provisions of LBRs 1006-1, 1006-2 and 1006-3 into that LBR. [Repeal effective 12/01/09.]

Rule 1006-1. Fees: Installment Payments, Waiver, Refunds.

(A) *Installment Payments:* Any individual debtor desiring to pay the filing fee in installments must file an application with the Clerk that substantially conforms to that local form entitled "APPLICATION TO PAY FILING FEE IN INSTALLMENTS - EASTERN DISTRICT OF VIRGINIA." The application form is available from the Clerk. If the application meets all the requirements of that local form, the Clerk shall enter an order approving the same. The Clerk is to give notice of the dismissal provisions, as set forth in the application, to the debtor and debtor's counsel.

(B) *Waiver:* Any individual debtor that files a voluntary chapter 7 petition may request a waiver of the filing fee by filing an application that substantially conforms to that local form entitled "APPLICATION FOR WAIVER OF THE CHAPTER 7 FILING FEE FOR INDIVIDUALS WHO CANNOT PAY THE FILING FEE IN FULL OR IN INSTALLMENTS." The application form is available from the Clerk.

(C) *Nonpayment:* If a petition, complaint or other document is not accompanied by the proper filing fee or, if applicable, an application as set forth in paragraph (A) or (B) of this Local Bankruptcy Rule, the Clerk shall give notice to cure the filing fee deficiency. The Clerk may provide such notice personally, electronically, telephonically or by mail. The notice period shall commence for personal, electronic, and telephonic notice when the notice is given and shall commence for mailed notices 3 days after the notice is mailed. Unless the fee is paid or the party requests a hearing on the matter by the close of business on the next day after the notice to cure is given, the Clerk shall dismiss the petition or complaint or strike the pleading or other document without further notice. The Clerk shall reject any partial payment of any fee.

(D)(1) *Request for Refunds:* An attorney or trustee may file a motion for refund of a filing fee paid in a case or proceeding in which payment was made by credit card when:

(a) a fee was paid for filing a duplicate document, bankruptcy petition or adversary proceeding;

(b) a fee was paid for filing a document in the wrong case or proceeding;

(c) the movant is entitled to an exemption from the filing fee paid; or

(d) a trustee or debtor in possession is eligible for deferral of the filing fee in a case in which no funds from the estate exist for payment of the filing fee.

(2) *Motion Required:* The request shall be made promptly after the payment error is discovered by filing a motion for refund. The motion must contain a complete explanation as to why the payment should be refunded. The motion need not contain a supporting memorandum or be noticed for a hearing.

(3) *Motion Required for Disposition of Document:* A separate motion to dispose of a document filed in error, as identified in subparagraphs (D)(1)(a) and (b) of this Local Bankruptcy Rule, is also required.

(4) *Clerk-Authorized Action:* Upon verification of the grounds set forth in the motion the Clerk is authorized to enter an order dismissing or striking the document. The Clerk is also authorized to enter a separate order refunding the filing fee if the refund can be processed as a credit to the credit card account that was used to pay the filing fee.

(5) *Clerk's Referral to the Court:* The Clerk may refer a motion set forth in paragraph (D)(2) of this Local Bankruptcy Rule to the judge assigned to the case or proceeding for such further determination and action as the judge may find appropriate.

(6) *Request for Clearance:* A movant may request clearance of the "filing fee due" status in a case or proceeding in which the fee has not yet been paid by contacting a deputy clerk in the appropriate division of the Clerk's Office.

COMMENT

1006-1 This expanded rule selectively incorporates the fee-related procedures set forth in current Local Bankruptcy Rules 1006-1, 1006-2 and 1006-3. As set forth in paragraph (D)(3), a separate motion is required to dispose of a document filed in error. The amendment to paragraph (D)(4) recognizes that in certain situations, a credit card issued to a cardholder other than one issued to an attorney or trustee, may have been used to pay the filing fee. In addition, time-computation adjustments have been made, as needed, to conform to a revision to the Federal Rules of Bankruptcy Procedure that takes effect December 1, 2009. [Changes effective 12/01/09.]

Rule 1006-2. Fees: Electronic Refunds.

[Repealed.]

COMMENT

1006-2 This new rule adopts a procedure by which filing fees paid over the Internet with a credit card may be administered when errors in electronic payments are made. The rule is consistent with guidance approved, in principle, by the Judicial Conference of the United States. The rule establishes an additional Judicial Conference-authorized narrow exception to the longstanding Judicial Conference policy prohibiting the refund of fees. [New Rule effective 10/17/05.]

1006-2 LBR 1006-2 is repealed and a new LBR 1006-1 has been promulgated, which consolidates selected provisions of LBRs 1006-1, 1006-2 and 1006-3 into that LBR. [Repeal effective 12/01/09.]

Rule 1006-3. Payment of Filing Fees; Remedies for Nonpayment.

[Repealed.]

COMMENT

1006-3 This rule establishes a single rule for payment of filing fees and the procedure the Clerk will follow in the event of nonpayment of a required filing fee. It supersedes LBR 1006-1(D) and LBR 5005-1(F). [New Rule effective 9/1/06.]

1006-3 LBR 1006-3 is repealed and a new LBR 1006-1 has been promulgated, which consolidates selected provisions of LBRs 1006-1, 1006-2 and 1006-3 into that LBR. [Repeal effective 12/01/09.]

Rule 1007-1. Lists, Schedules and Statements.

(A) *Dismissal of Case:* Except as provided in LBR 1017-3, in any case in which lists, schedules and statements are not filed at the time of the filing of a voluntary petition, the Clerk shall enter an order of dismissal unless the same are filed within 14 days after the filing of the petition, or a motion to extend time for filing lists, schedules and statements has been filed prior to the expiration of the 14-day period.

(B) *Motion to Extend Time:* Such motion to extend time for filing shall be accompanied by a proof of service evidencing notice to the United States trustee, any appointed trustee, any official committee appointed in the case and all creditors. If there are more than 30 creditors in the case, the debtor need only provide notice of the motion to extend time to the 10 largest secured creditors, the 20 largest unsecured creditors and any official committee appointed in the case. The motion to extend time shall give notice that parties objecting to the extension of time shall file written objections with the Court within 7 days after service of the motion by the debtor.

(C) *Order Extending Time:* If no objection to the motion to extend the time for filing is timely filed with the Court, the Clerk shall enter an order extending time for filing to not later than the seventh day prior to the scheduled meeting of creditors. If the lists, schedules, statements and other documents are not filed by said date, the Clerk shall enter an order dismissing the case.

(D) *Objections — Determination:* If an objection is filed to the motion for extension of time, the Clerk shall submit the motion and objections to the Court for determination of the motion.

(E) *Hearing on Further Extension:* Any debtor requesting an extension of time to file lists, schedules, statements and other documents to a date less than 7 days prior to the scheduled meeting of creditors must request a hearing date and give notice to parties as set forth in paragraph (B) of this Local Bankruptcy Rule and file a proof of service with the motion to extend time.

(F) *Notice of Possible Dismissal:* The Clerk shall give notice of this Local Bankruptcy Rule to a debtor or debtor's counsel who files a petition not accompanied by all required lists, schedules and statements. The Clerk shall also give notice of this Local Bankruptcy Rule in the meeting of creditors notice.

(G) *List of Creditors Holding 20 Largest Unsecured Claims:* To assist the United States Trustee in appointing a creditors' committee, the list required by FRBP 1007(d) shall include the amount owed, by amount of debt ranging from the largest creditor to the smallest creditor. The list shall also include the name and telephone number of a contact person or representative of the unsecured creditor. If a minor child is one of the creditors holding the 20 largest unsecured claims, indicate that by stating "a minor child" and do not disclose the child's name.

(H) *List of Creditors, Statement of Social Security Number and Payment Advices or Other Evidence of Payment*

(1) *Filing:* The debtor shall file with the petition a list containing the name and address of each creditor which shall serve as a mailing matrix. If not filed via the Electronic Case Files System, the mailing matrix shall be submitted on a computer diskette in the format specified by the Clerk. The mailing matrix shall suffice for the list of creditors referred to in FRBP 1007(a). As required under FRBP 1007(f), the debtor shall submit a verified statement that sets out the debtor's social security number (statement of social security number), or states that the debtor does not have a social security number. If not filed via the Electronic Case Files System, the debtor shall submit the statement with the petition.

(2) *Dismissal of Case:* (a) In any case in which the list of creditors is not filed at the time of the filing of the voluntary petition, the Clerk shall enter an order of dismissal unless the same is filed in the required format not later than 3 days after the filing of the petition.

(b) In any case in which the statement of social security number in a voluntary case is not submitted at the time of the filing of the voluntary petition, the Clerk shall enter an order of dismissal unless the same statement is submitted in the required format not later than 3 days after the filing of the petition.

(3) *Waiver:* An exception to the requirement of submission of creditors on computer diskette will be considered by the court only upon submission of a waiver request filed with the petition. The form shall be provided by the Clerk upon request. In addition to the waiver request, the debtor shall file the list of creditors in the scannable format specified by the Clerk. If the court denies the request, the debtor or the attorney for the debtor shall submit the list of creditors on computer diskette not later than 3 days after the Clerk's notification that the request has been denied.

(4) *Payment Advices or Other Evidence of Payment:* Copies of all payment advices or other evidence of payment received within 60 days before the date of the filing of the petition by the debtor from an employer of the debtor shall:

(a) not be filed with the Court unless otherwise ordered and

(b) be provided to the trustee, and any creditor (who timely requests copies of the payment advices or other evidence of payment) at least 7 days before the date of the meeting of creditors conducted pursuant to 11 U.S.C. §341.

(I) *Individual Debtor's Statement of Compliance with Credit Counseling Requirement*

(1) *Filing:* A debtor who is an individual shall file with the voluntary petition a properly completed statement of compliance, together with attached documents as specified therein, substantially conforming to that local form entitled "EXHIBIT D — INDIVIDUAL DEBTOR'S STATEMENT OF COMPLIANCE WITH CREDIT COUNSELING REQUIREMENT —EASTERN DISTRICT OF VIRGINIA".

(2) *Dismissal of Case; Notice:* In any case in which a properly completed statement of compliance referenced in paragraph (I)(1) of this Local Bankruptcy Rule, together with attached documents as specified therein, is not filed at the time of the filing of the voluntary petition, the Clerk shall enter an order of dismissal unless the same is filed not later than 3 days after the filing of the petition. Unless the Court orders otherwise, if the debtor has filed a statement under FRBP 1007(b)(3)(B), but does not file the documents required by FRBP 1007(b)(3)(A) within 14 days of the order for relief, the Clerk shall enter an order of dismissal. The Clerk shall give notice of this Local Bankruptcy Rule to the debtor or debtor's counsel who files a petition not accompanied by the required statement of compliance with credit counseling requirement referenced in paragraph (I)(1) of this Local Bankruptcy Rule.

(J) *Chapter 13 Debtor's Statement of Completion of Instructional Course Concerning Personal Financial Management:* Pursuant to FRBP 9006(c), and as governed by

FRBP 1007(c), the time to file the chapter 13 debtor(s) statement of completion of a course concerning personal financial management shall be deemed enlarged, and the chapter 13 debtor(s) shall file the statement of completion of a course concerning personal financial management within the time specified in LBR 4008-2(A) for filing the Debtor(s) Certification of Compliance with 11 U.S.C. §1328.

COMMENT

1007-1(A) This change is necessary because of the addition of LBR 1017-3. [Change effective 2/1/00.]

1007-1 (I) This new rule is to implement the procedure approved by the Judges at their November 1997 meeting requiring the submission of the List of Creditors by diskette beginning January 1, 1999. This speeds up the case opening process and reduces overall creditor related errors. For more information on the required procedure, refer to the attached Exhibits 5, 6, and 7. Exhibits 6 (Creditor Matrix Diskette — Cover Sheet for List of Creditors) and 7 (Request for Waiver to File Conventionally) were deleted as exhibits. These forms are available at the Court's Internet web site http://www.vaeb.uscourts.gov and can be accessed by clicking the "Bankruptcy Forms" button on the Court's Internet home page. The former Exhibits 6 and 7 are in Adobe Acrobat format. [Change effective 3/1/01.]

1007-1(I)(2)-(3) The rule provisions have been changed to clarify the time within which the petition filer has to cure a deficiency in the list of creditors. [Change effective 4/1/03.]

1007-1(I) This change is necessary because of the amendment to FRBP 1007, which creates a new subdivision (f) effective December 1, 2003. [Change effective 12/1/03.]

1007-1 Selected text from former Interim Procedure 1007-1(A), (C), (E) and (F) have been incorporated into LBR 1007-1(A), (C), (E) and (F). LBR 1007-1(G) is repealed. Selected text from Interim Procedure 1007-1 (H) is incorporated into new LBR 1007-1(G). Interim Procedure 1007-1(I) is incorporated into new LBR 1007-1(I). The term "time" has been deleted and the term "date" inserted in lieu thereof into LBR 1007-1(H)(4)(b). Selected text from Interim Procedure 1007-1(J)(1) and (4) has been incorporated into LBR 1007-1(I)(1) and (2), respectively. In addition, time-computation adjustments have been made, as needed, to conform to a revision to the Federal Rules of Bankruptcy Procedure that takes effect December 1, 2009. Stylistic changes have been made to the text of the LBR as well. [Changes effective 12/01/09.]

1007-1(J) Paragraph (J) is new and makes the time to to file the Chapter 13 Debtor's Statement of Completion of Instructional Course Concerning Personal Financial Management the same as that specified in LBR 4008-2(A). [New paragraph (J) effective 09/03/13.]

CASE NOTES

The use of local bankruptcy rules for purposes of delay may not only constitute grounds for dismissal of cases with prejudice but also may subject attorneys who engage in this type of practice to appropriate sanctions. Owings v. Doniff, 133 Bankr. 351 (Bankr. E.D. Va. 1991).

For case discussing the abusive manipulation of local bankruptcy rules, Owings v. Doniff, 133 Bankr. 351 (Bankr. E.D. Va. 1991).

Rule 1007-3. Statement of Intention.

(A) *Dismissal of Case:* Except as provided in LBR 1017-3 and 11 U.S.C. § 521(a)(2)(A), the Clerk shall monitor the filing of a Statement of Intention and enter an order of dismissal in any applicable chapter 7 case in which neither the Statement of Intention nor a motion to extend the time for filing the same has been filed within 30 days after the date of the filing of the petition, or on or before the date of the meeting of creditors, whichever is earlier.

(B) *Motion to Extend Time:* A motion to extend time for filing a Statement of Intention shall be accompanied by proof of service evidencing service on the United States trustee, any appointed trustee, and all affected secured creditors. The motion to extend time shall state that any party objecting to the extension of time must file a written objection with the Clerk within 7 days after service of the motion.

(C) *Order Extending Time:* Where no objections to the aforesaid motion are timely filed, the Clerk shall enter an order extending time for filing to 14 days after the scheduled meeting of creditors. If the Statement of Intention is not filed by the fourteenth day after the scheduled meeting of creditors, the Clerk shall enter an order dismissing the case.

(D) *Hearing on Further Extension:* Any debtor requesting an extension of time to file the Statement of Intention more than 14 days after the scheduled meeting of creditors must request a hearing date and give notice to parties as set out in 11 U.S.C. § 521(a)(2)(A) and file proof of service with the motion to extend time.

(E) *Notice of Possible Dismissal:* The Clerk shall give notice of this Local Bankruptcy Rule to a debtor or debtor's counsel who files a petition unaccompanied by the Statement of Intention.

COMMENT

1007-3 (C) This change is necessary because of the addition of LBR 1017-3. [Change effective 2/1/00.]

1007-3 LBR 1007-3(A), (B) and (F) are repealed. LBR 1007-3(C), (D), (E), (G) and (H) are re-designated LBR 1007-3(A), (B), (C), (D) and (E), respectively. The LBR citation at new (D) is deleted and the citation to the noted title 11 provision is inserted. In addition, time-computation adjustments have been made, as needed, to conform to a revision to the Federal Rules of Bankruptcy Procedure that takes effect December 1, 2009. Stylistic changes have been made to the LBR text as well. [Repeals and changes effective 12/01/09.]

Rule 1009-1. Amendments to Lists & Schedules.

(A) *Filing of Amendment with Clerk:* Each amendment shall be accompanied by a properly completed Amendment Cover Sheet. When an amendment adds creditors to a bankruptcy case, the amendment shall be accompanied by a list of the creditors so added. The list shall be in the format specified by the Clerk. An Amendment Cover Sheet form and instructions for preparing the list of creditors added are available from the Clerk upon request.

(B) *Notice to Affected Parties:* If the debtor adds creditors to the case by supplementing either the schedules or the list of creditors previously filed, the debtor shall serve upon each newly-listed creditor a copy of the following:

(1) the amendment;
(2) the meeting of creditors notice;
(3) the order granting discharge (if any);
(4) any other filed document affecting the rights of said creditor; and
(5) the notice required by LBR 3003-1(B).

(C) *Adding Creditors in a Closed Case:* [Repealed]

COMMENT

1009-1 The text at LBR 1009-1(A) and (B) have been removed and substitute text has been adopted for both paragraphs. LBR 1009-1(C) remains unchanged. Paragraph (C) has been removed as it no longer conforms to applicable case law on this subject. Stylistic changes have been made to the LBR as well. [Changes effective 12/01/09.]

Rule 1014-2. Declaration of Divisional Venue.

[Repealed.]

COMMENT

1014-2 In light of changes made to Official Form 1, Voluntary Petition, the Declaration of Venue form no longer is required and this LBR is repealed for that reason. [Repeal effective 12/01/09.]

Rule 1015-1. Joint Administration of Estates.

In all joint petitions filed with the Court, the case will be administered through joint administration of the estates unless the trustee or other interested party files an objection to joint administration within 14 days after the meeting of creditors and gives notice of a hearing date on such objection.

COMMENT

1015-1 A time-computation adjustment has been made to conform to a revision to the Federal Rules of Bankruptcy Procedure that takes effect December 1, 2009. [Change effective 12/01/09.]

Rule 1017-1. Conversion.

(A) *Schedule of Unpaid Debts:* Within 14 days after conversion of a case, the debtor shall file either:

(1) a schedule of unpaid debts incurred after commencement of the original bankruptcy case, and a list of creditors in the format required by the Clerk or

(2) a certification that no unpaid debts have been incurred since the commencement of the case.

(B) *Filing of Schedule of Unpaid Debts:* If the debtor fails to file the schedule and list referred to in paragraph (A)(1) of this Local Bankruptcy Rule on the date of conversion of the case, any such subsequent filing shall be treated as an amendment under LBR 1009-1 and the debtor shall give all required notices.

(C) *Filing of Official Form B22A, B22B or B22C Upon Conversion of Case:* Unless otherwise ordered by the Court, in a case converted from chapter 11, 12 or 13 to chapter 7, the debtor shall file Official Form B22A, "CHAPTER 7 STATEMENT OF CURRENT MONTHLY INCOME AND MEANS-TEST CALCULATION FOR USE IN CHAPTER 7", within 14 days after conversion. In a case of an individual debtor converted to chapter 11, the debtor shall file Official Form B22B, "STATEMENT OF CURRENT MONTHLY INCOME" within 14 days after entry of the conversion order. In a case of an individual debtor converted to chapter 13, the debtor shall file Official Form B22C, "CHAPTER 13 STATEMENT OF CURRENT MONTHLY INCOME AND CALCULATION OF COMMITMENT PERIOD AND DISPOSABLE INCOME", within 14 days after entry of the conversion order.

(D) *Report of the Debtor in Possession or Trustee:* Upon the failure of the debtor in possession or trustee in a superseded case to file the report required under FRBP 1019(5), the United States trustee shall certify the matter to the Court for appropriate action.

COMMENT

1017-1(A) Wording added for clarification and reference to the number of copies required upon conversion and the filing of the Schedule of Unpaid Debts.

1017-1(B) Change of wording necessary so that anything filed after the conversion date is to be treated as an amendment and the debtor is responsible for the noticing.

1017-1(D) It was felt that the responsibility for monitoring the filing of these reports was with the U.S. Trustee since FRBP 1019(5) requires the report go to the U.S. Trustee in the first place.

1017-1 LBR 1017-1 is amended. Reserved (C) is removed and a new paragraph (C) from former Interim Procedure 1017-1(C) is inserted. Paragraph (D) has been amended. In addition, time-computation adjustments have been made, as needed, to conform to a revision to the Federal Rules of Bankruptcy Procedure that takes effect December 1, 2009. Stylistic changes have been made to the text of the LBR as well. [Changes effective 12/01/09.]

Rule 1017-2. Dismissal for Substantial Abuse of Chapter 7.

[Repealed.]

COMMENT

1017-2 Although the Clerk will continue to provide notice, under FRBP 1017(e), doing so need no longer be established by Local Bankruptcy Rule. [Repeal effective 12/01/09.]

Rule 1017-3. Suspension of Automatic Dismissal.

Rule to Show Cause in Lieu of Dismissal in Certain Cases: Nothwithstanding the provisions of LBR 1006-1, 1007-1(A), 1007-3(C), 2003-1(B), 3015-1(G), 3015-2(H) and 3070-1(C), the Clerk shall not enter an order dismissing the debtor's case if the case was previously converted from any other chapter of title 11 or if the debtor was a debtor in another case pending at any time within 12 months preceding the filing of the present case. In such a case, the Clerk shall, in lieu of dismissal, issue a rule to show cause to the debtor and set the matter for a hearing.

COMMENT

1017-3 LBR 3015-2 has been amended. The revision to LBR 1017-3 conforms to that amendment. [Change effective 9/1/06.]

1017-3 A stylistic change has been made to the text of the LBR. [Change effective 12/01/09.]

CASE NOTES

Because the debtor had filed a bankruptcy case in the preceding 12 months, the bankruptcy court suspended automatic dismissal of the instant Chapter 13 case, and in lieu of automatic dismissal, a notice to show cause was issued requiring the debtor to appear and show cause why the case should not be dismissed. In re Harvey, No. 03-32997, 2003 Bankr. LEXIS 1554 (Bankr. E.D. Va. Aug. 20, 2003).

Rule 1020-1. Small Business Chapter 11 Reorganization Cases.

[Repealed.]

COMMENT

1020-1(A) Change from forty-five days to sixty days required due to the amendments to the FRBP that became effective December 1, 1997.

1020-1 This Rule is repealed in light of changes made under the Bankruptcy Abuse Prevention and Consumer Protection Act of 2005 and earlier repeal of Interim Procedure 1020-1. [Repeal effective 12/01/09.]

Rule 1071-1. Divisions.

(A) *District:* The Eastern District of Virginia consists of the counties, cities and towns as set forth in 28 U.S.C. §127, and the places for holding court are therein prescribed as Alexandria, Newport News, Norfolk, and Richmond.

(B) *Divisions:* This district shall be divided into four divisions, to be designated as the Alexandria, Newport News, Norfolk and Richmond Divisions. The place for holding court for each of said divisions shall be the city whose name the division bears, and the territory comprising, and embraced in, each of the said divisions shall be as follows:

(1) The Alexandria Division shall consist of the cities of Alexandria, Fairfax, Falls Church, Manassas and Manassas Park, and the counties of Arlington, Fairfax, Fauquier, Loudoun, Prince William and Stafford, and any other city or town geographically within the exterior boundaries of said counties.

(2) The Newport News Division shall consist of the cities of Hampton, Newport News, Poquoson and Williamsburg, and the counties of Gloucester, James City, Mathews and York, and any other city or town geographically within the exterior boundaries of said counties.

(3) The Norfolk Division shall consist of the cities of Cape Charles, Chesapeake, Franklin, Norfolk, Portsmouth, Suffolk and Virginia Beach, and the counties of Accomack, Isle of Wight, Northampton and Southampton, and any other city or town geographically within the exterior boundaries of said counties.

(4) The Richmond Division shall consist of the cities of Colonial Heights, Emporia, Fredericksburg, Hopewell, Richmond and Petersburg, and the counties of Amelia, Brunswick, Caroline, Charles City, Chesterfield, Dinwiddie, Essex, Goochland, Greensville, Hanover, Henrico, King and Queen, King George, King William, Lancaster, Lunenburg, Mecklenburg, Middlesex, New Kent, Northumberland, Nottoway, Powhatan, Prince Edward, Prince George, Richmond, Spotsylvania, Surry, Sussex and Westmoreland, and any other city or town geographically within the exterior boundaries of said counties.

(5) All of the waters, and the lands under such waters, adjacent and opposite to any city, county or town shall be a part of the division of which said city, county or town is a part, and wherever there are any waters between any city, county or town which are in different divisions, then such waters and land under them shall be considered to be in both divisions.

(6) In the event of any annexation or merger of any cities and/or counties, the land lying within the merged or annexed area shall be deemed within the exterior boundaries of the original city or county to the same intent and purpose as if the annexation or merger had not occurred, unless otherwise modified by local bankruptcy rule.

COMMENT

1071-1 Stylistic changes have been made to the text of the LBR. [Changes effective 12/01/09.]

Rule 1074-1. Corporations, Limited Liability Companies or Partnerships.

A voluntary petition or consent to an involuntary petition filed by a corporation, limited liability company, general partnership, limited liability partnership or limited partnership, shall be signed by an attorney and accompanied by a copy of the corporate resolution or other appropriate authorization, duly attested to, authorizing such filing.

COMMENT

1074-1 In addition to a corporation, a limited liability company, general partnership, limited liability partnership, or limited partnership must meet the requirements set forth in the Rule. [Amendment effective 12/01/09.]

Rule 2002-1. Notice to Creditors & Other Interested Parties.

(A) *Proponent to Give Notice*

Except as stated elsewhere in the Bankruptcy Code, the Federal Rules of Bankruptcy Procedure, these Local Bankruptcy Rules, or by order of the Court, the proponent of any action shall give notice to all parties affected thereby.

(B) *Notice by Publication*

(1) Place of Publication: All notices requiring advertisement shall be published at least once unless otherwise required by rule or statute, and such notice shall be published in newspapers of general circulation as follows:

(a) In proceedings at Alexandria, in the *Washington Post*.

(b) In proceedings at Newport News, in the *Daily Press*.

(c) In proceedings at Norfolk, in *The Virginian-Pilot*.

(d) In proceedings at Richmond, in the *Times-Dispatch*.

(2) Time of Publication: All notices shall be published at least 7 days prior to requiring any action, and a longer notice shall be given when required by rule or statute or where deemed proper by the Court.

(C) *Service on United States Trustee*

Service on the United States trustee shall be made electronically to the following e-mailbox addresses:

Alexandria Division: USTPRegion04.AX.ECF@usdoj.gov
Richmond Division: USTPRegion04.RH.ECF@usdoj.gov
Norfolk and Newport News Divisions: USTPRegion04.NO.ECF@usdoj.gov

(D) *Inspection of List of Creditors:* When any person orders and receives a list of creditors from the Clerk, it shall be the responsibility of that person to inspect the list to ensure that all parties required to receive notice are included thereon.

(E) *Notices to Equity Security Holders:* Unless otherwise ordered by the Court, the debtor is responsible for sending notice of the filing of the bankruptcy to equity security holders except when either:

(1) the list of equity security holders is filed with the petition or

(2) the equity security holders are included on the list of creditors filed with the petition.

(F) *Requirement of Proof of Service:* At the end of each pleading, motion or other document required to be served upon a party, the proof of service shall be signed by counsel (or the *pro se* party) conforming to LBR 5005-1(C)(8).

COMMENT

2002-1(D) This is a result of a suggestion from the bar to clarify and expand on service requirements on the U.S. Trustee. Whereas the Bankruptcy Code and FRBP require service of certain pleadings on the U.S. Trustee, there are many gray areas. This revision clarifies what documents not specifically required under the Bankruptcy Code and FRBP need to be served on the U.S. Trustee and what documents need to be filed with the Clerk of Court for transmittal by the Clerk to the U.S. Trustee. The prior rule only related to documents and pleadings in Chapter 11 cases, whereas this revision covers all chapters.

2002-1(E) Reference to the mailing labels has been deleted to reflect elimination of Item 15 of the Miscellaneous Fee Schedule to Bankruptcy Courts for mailing labels. If a party requests addresses or mailing labels and does not have access to PACER, the Court will provide a list of creditors in lieu of mailing labels.

2002-1 (G) This change simplifies the proof of service language to note that it just needs to conform to LBR 5005-1(C)(8). [Change effective 2/1/00.]

2002-1(D)(3) This addition will allow parties the option to provide service to the United States Trustee's offices by electronic mail to a central office location. [New rule effective 4/1/03.]

2002-1 LBR 2002-1(C)(1)(a) has been amended to substitute the *Washington Examiner* for the *Alexandria Journal*. The *Alexandria Journal* no longer is being published and its place has been taken by the *Washington Examiner*. [Change effective 9/1/06.]

2002-1 Paragraph (A)(2) is deleted as is the

heading to paragraph (A)(1). Paragraph (B) is deleted. Paragraphs (C), (D), (E), (F), (G) and (H) become paragraphs (B), (C), (D), (E), (F) and (G), respectively. New subparagraph (B)(1)(a) is amended. New paragraph (C) is amended by retitling the header, striking paragraph (C)(1) and (C)(2), deleting the header at paragraph (C)(3) and modifying the text by deleting all text through the word "means"and making other noted changes; and deleting the word "paper" at paragraph (F) and inserting in lieu thereof the word "document." Stylistic changes have been made to the text as well. LBR 2002-1(H) is derived from former Interim Procedure 2002-1(I). In addition, time-computation adjustments have been made, as needed, to conform to a revision to the Federal Rules of Bankruptcy Procedure that takes effect December 1, 2009. [Changes effective 12/01/09.]

Rule 2003-1. Meeting of Creditors & Equity Security Holders.

(A) *Policy:* [Repealed.]

(B) *Dismissal for Failure to Appear*

(1) *Notice of Possible Dismissal:* Notice of possible dismissal for failure to attend the meeting of creditors shall be provided in the notice of § 341 meeting.

(2) *Chapter 12 and 13 Cases; No Asset Chapter 7 and 11 Cases*

(a) Except as provided in LBR 1017-3, upon certification by the United States trustee that either debtor or debtor's counsel has not appeared at a meeting of creditors in a chapter 12 or 13 case, the Clerk shall issue an order dismissing the case.

(b) Except as provided in LBR 1017-3, upon certification by the United States trustee that either debtor or debtor's counsel has not appeared at a meeting of creditors in a chapter 7 or 11 case, and it further appears, based upon information in the debtor's schedules or other reports filed by the debtor or debtor's counsel, that there will be no assets available for distribution to creditors, the Clerk shall issue an order dismissing the case.

(3) *Asset Chapter 7 and 11 Cases:* In a chapter 7 or 11 case, upon certification by the United States trustee that either debtor or debtor's counsel has not appeared at a meeting of creditors and that it appears that there may be assets available for distribution to creditors, the Clerk shall issue a rule to show cause to the debtor or counsel, as the case may be, and set the rule for a hearing.

(4) *Rescheduled Meeting of Creditors; Notice:* If the order dismissing the case is subsequently vacated by the Court, then the attorney for the debtor(s), or the debtor(s), if *pro se*, shall forthwith obtain from the judge assigned to the case or the Clerk a new date and time for a rescheduled meeting of creditors. Within 7 days of obtaining a new date and time for a rescheduled meeting of creditors, the attorney for the debtor(s), or the debtor(s), if *pro se*, shall serve written notice to all creditors and other parties in interest and file proof of service with the Clerk. Notice shall be given in a form approved by the Clerk.

(C) *Rescheduled Meeting of Creditors; Notice:* If the United States trustee agrees before a meeting of creditors to reschedule the meeting at the request of the attorney for the debtor(s), or the debtor(s), if *pro se*, then the attorney for the debtor(s), or the debtor(s), if *pro se*, shall forthwith obtain from the United States trustee, a new date and time for a rescheduled meeting of creditors. Within 7 days of obtaining a new date and time for a rescheduled meeting of creditors, the attorney for the debtor(s) or the debtor(s), if *pro se*, shall serve written notice of the rescheduled meeting of creditors to all creditors and other parties in interest and file proof of service with the Clerk. Notice shall be given in a form approved by the Clerk.

COMMENT

2003-1(B) Suggestion made by the Norfolk U.S. Trustee and Chapter 13 Trustee to require the debtor to provide the proper notice of the rescheduled meeting.

2003-1(B) This change retains the automatic dismissal provisions of the Local Bankruptcy Rules, which have proved effective, but now encourages the prompt prosecution and administration of the case. At the same time, the change limits the ability for a quick exit not subject to the review of the trustee, creditors or the court in those circumstances where abuse is likely to occur. [Change effective 2/1/00.]

2003-1(C) This change deletes the requirement that the notice of the rescheduled meeting note the automatic extension of the deadline to file objections to discharge and complaints to determine dischargeability to 60 days after the new date set forth for the meeting. Exhibit 8 has been modified to conform to this change. [Change effective 7/1/00.]

2003-1(C) Suggestion made by the Norfolk U.S. Trustee and Chapter 13 Trustee to require the debtor to provide the proper notice of the rescheduled meeting. In addition, this rule now requires that the notice of the rescheduled meeting note the automatic extension of the deadline to file objections to discharge to 60 days after the new date set for the meeting. Please refer to Exhibit 8 for a copy of the approved form notice.

Exhibit 8 (Hearings/Meetings — Notice of Rescheduled Meeting of Creditors) was deleted as an exhibit. This form is available at the Court's Internet web site http://www.vaeb.uscourts.gov and can be accessed by clicking the "Bankruptcy Forms" button on the Court's internet home page. The former exhibit 8 is in Adobe Acrobat format. [Change effective 3/1/01.]

2003-1(B)(2) This change is intended to clarify the application of the rule to Chapter 7, 11, 12 and 13 cases. [Change effective 4/1/03.]

2003-1(B)(3) This change clarifies that the United States Trustee's certification for the Clerk's issuance of a rule to show cause is applicable only to Chapter 7 and 11 asset cases. [Change effective 4/1/03.]

2003-1(B)(4) While the United States Trustee is responsible for administering meetings of creditors, new meeting dates under the rule best can be provided by the Judge or by the Clerk's Office. [Change effective 4/1/03.]

2003-1(B)(4) This rule clarifies the period of time in which the attorney for the debtor(s), or the debtor(s), if *pro se*, must serve notice of a rescheduled meeting of creditors on all creditors and other parties in interest. [Change effective 8/1/03.]

2003-1(C) The first sentence of the rule has been deleted as being inconsistent with the statutory responsibilities of the Untied States Trustee. The rule also clarifies that only the United States Trustee may permit the rescheduling of a meeting of creditors. [Change effective 8/1/03.]

The rule also has been amended to conform to the service of notice change made in Rule 2003-1(B)(4). [Change effective 8/1/03.]

2003-1(A) This rule has been repealed to conform the Court's practice to that of the other courts in United States Trustee Region 4. [Change effective 8/1/03.]

2003-1 Time-computation adjustments have been made, as needed, to conform to a revision to the Federal Rules of Bankruptcy Procedure that takes effect December 1, 2009. Stylistic changes have been made to the text of the LBR as well. [Changes effective 12/01/09.]

2003-1(B) The phrase "or has appeared not ready to proceed" has been removed where it appears in paragraph (B). [Change effective 09/03/13.]

CASE NOTES

The use of local bankruptcy rules for purposes of delay may not only constitute grounds for dismissal of cases with prejudice but also may subject attorneys who engage in this type of practice to appropriate sanctions. Owings v. Doniff, 133 Bankr. 351 (Bankr. E.D. Va. 1991).

For case discussing the abusive manipulation of local bankruptcy rules, Owings v. Doniff, 133 Bankr. 351 (Bankr. E.D. Va. 1991).

Dismissal. — Because a debtor's incarceration was not within the meaning of "disability" under 11 U.S.C.S. § 109(h)(4) and the United States Trustee had not made a determination regarding the district in which the debtor resided, pursuant to 11 U.S.C.S. § 109(h)(2)(A), the debtor was not entitled to a permanent waiver of the credit counseling requirement of 11 U.S.C.S. § 109(h)(1); however, the incarceration warranted a waiver of Bankr. E.D. Va. R. 2003-1(B)(2)(b), requiring dismissal of the debtor's case for failure to attend the 11 U.S.C.S. § 341 meeting of creditors. In re Michael John Star, 341 B.R. 830, 2006 Bankr. LEXIS 934 (Bankr. E.D. Va. 2006).

Rule 2004-1. Examination.

(A) *Service:* Motions requesting examination under FRBP 2004 shall be served on the debtor, debtor's counsel, the deponent, deponent's counsel (if known), the standing trustee, and the United States trustee and filed with the Clerk.

(B) *Objections:* Parties shall have 7 days from the date of service to object to the motion.

(1) If an objection is filed, the movant shall request from the Court a hearing date, transmit the notice of hearing to all parties in interest, and file the notice and proof of service with the Clerk.

(2) If no objection is filed, the movant shall include in the proposed order either a certification that the date set has been agreed to by the deponent and deponent's counsel (if known) or that a good faith effort has been made to set a date without success.

COMMENT

This new rule notes the requirements for examination motions and objections to them.

2004-1 (B)(2) Because the current portion of this rule may place an undue burden on a movant in obtaining the agreement of the deponent and the deponent's counsel for a date to conduct the examination, this change has been made to add language noting that a good faith effort was made to set a date without success. [Change effective 2/1/00.]

2004-1 A time-computation adjustment has been to conform to a revision to the Federal Rules of Bankruptcy Procedure that takes effect December 1, 2009. A stylistic change has been made to the text of the LBR as well. [Changes effective 12/01/09.]

Rule 2014-1. Service of Motion for an Order Authorizing Employment in a Chapter 11 Case.

The motion, declaration and any proposed order shall be served on the parties listed below. Any party moving for an order authorizing employment in a proceeding under chapter 11 of the Bankruptcy Code shall, in plain language, inform all such parties of the filing of the motion, disclosing in full and complete detail any actual or potentional conflicts of interest, and shall specify the method for objecting to the proposed order. Any objections to the proposed employment shall be made in writing, filed with the Court, with a copy served on the movant and the parties listed below, within 14 days from the date of service of the motion.

The motion, declaration and proposed order shall be served on:

1. the United States trustee;
2. any trustee appointed under 11 U.S.C. § 1104;
3. any committee of unsecured creditors appointed pursuant to 11 U.S.C. § 1102 or, if no committee is appointed, the creditors included on the list filed under FRBP 1007(d);
4. all secured creditors; and
5. any other entity as the Court may direct.

COMMENT

2014-1 In several divisions, employment orders in Chapter 11 cases have been submitted for entry without notice to any other parties except for the United States Trustee, who usually endorses such orders prior to submission to a judge for entry. On several occasions, after entry of such an order, other parties have learned of the retention and moved to reconsider and vacate. This typically results in a hearing substantially after the entry of the original order with the accompanying concerns as to what happens to fees accrued in the gap period, etc., if the employment is denied. This rule requires a motion to retain a professional person be served upon the trustee, the creditors' committee, and the creditors included on the Rule 1007(d) list. [New rule effective 2/1/00.]

2014-1 A time-computation adjustment has been made to conform to a revision to the Federal Rules of Bankruptcy Procedure that takes effect December 1, 2009. Stylistic changes have been made to the text of the LBR as well. [Changes effective 12/01/09.]

Rule 2015-(a)-1. Required Reports of Debtors in Possession and Trustees.

(A) *Operating Business Reports:* When the business of the debtor is authorized to be operated, the trustee in a chapter 7 or 11 case, the debtor in possession in a chapter 11 or 12 case or the debtor in a chapter 13 case in which the debtor is engaged in business, shall file with the United States trustee, with the Court and with appropriate governmental units such reports and summaries as are required under 11 U.S.C. § 704(a)(8). Debtors in possession or trustees in chapter 11 cases shall continue to file operating reports with the Court and the United States trustee, on at least a calendar quarterly basis, until the case is converted, dismissed or a final decree has been entered by the Court.

(B) *Chapter 7 Liquidation Reports:* The trustee in a chapter 7 business case in which the business is not being operated shall file semi-annual liquidation reports with the United States trustee and with the Court.

(C) *Chapter 11 Final or Interim Report:* Chapter 11 cases with confirmed plans shall follow the District Chapter 11 Closing Procedure to prepare and file the final report and motion for final decree. The final report, or an interim report setting forth the status of the case and the reason why the case cannot be closed, shall be filed with the Court and a copy served on the United States trustee within 6 months after entry of the confirmation order.

(D) *Clerk to Give Notice:* When the United States trustee seeks to bring matters of case administration or estate administration before the Court, the Clerk shall give appropriate notice.

COMMENT

2015-(a)-1 Stylistic changes have been made to the text of the LBR as well. [Changes effective 12/01/09.]

2015-(a)-1 A technical change has been made to the referenced title 11, United States Code provision. [Change effective 09/01/11.]

Rule 2016-1. Compensation of Professionals.

(A) *Interim Compensation:* The party seeking interim compensation or reimbursement for services under FRBP 2016 shall obtain a hearing date from the Court and shall give notice as required in FRBP 2002(a)(6) and 2002(c)(2). The party shall file with the Court proof of service evidencing proper notice of the scheduled hearing.

(B) *Attorney's Disclosure Statement:* Pursuant to 11 U.S.C. § 329 and FRBP 2016, each attorney representing a debtor under any chapter of the Bankruptcy Code shall file an Attorney's Disclosure Statement, irrespective of the amount of fees received or requested. The Disclosure Statement, if not filed with the petition, shall be filed not later than 14 days after the later of the filing of the petition or the date that counsel is engaged. If the representation by counsel is not in a case assigned to the Electronic Case Files System, the Statement shall be filed in original only, with a certificate evidencing service upon the United States trustee and the case trustee, if any. Otherwise, the Statement shall be filed consistent with the Electronic Case Files System requirements approved by the Court.

(C) *For Debtor's Attorney in Chapter 13 Case:* [Repealed]

COMMENT

2016-1(B) This change clarifies how compensation should be paid or disclosed when new counsel is substituted. [Change effective 2/1/00.]

2016-1(C) This paragraph is repealed. Its provisions will be governed by standing order of the Court. [Repeal effective 3/17/08.]

2016-1 A time-computation adjustment has been made at paragraph (B) to conform to a revision to the Federal Rules of Bankruptcy Procedure that takes effect December 1, 2009. Stylistic changes have been made to the text of the LBR as well. [Changes effective 12/01/09.]

CASE NOTES

Case to be remanded to ensure compliance with this rule. — Bankruptcy court erred in overruling creditors' objections of its argument that they had not receive notice, required under local bankruptcy rule, of proposed payment to debtors' attorney of over $1,000 (now $1,250) in fees and expenses and of the ten-day time limit for filing objections to such payment, and thus, case was to be remanded to ensure compliance with the local bankruptcy rule. Tillman v. Lombard, 156 Bankr. 156 (E.D. Va. 1993).

Application contents. — Supplemental attorney's fee applications of the debtors' law firm were denied because they presented hours and charges as estimates and averages in a typical Chapter 13 case and not as actual expenses required by 11 U.S.C.S. § 330(a)(1)(A), Fed. R. Bankr. P. 2016(a), and Bankr. E.D. Va. R. 2016-1(C)(6). In re Keatts, 2005 Bankr. LEXIS 2917 (Bankr. E.D. Va. Mar. 31, 2005).

Court was particularly concerned with an attorney's affirmative representation in his application for supplemental compensation under Bankr. W.D. Va. R. 2016-1(c)(1) that the plan contained sufficient provisions to pay the requested fees without prejudice to the creditors. This representation was clearly false and was nothing more than a rote recitation of boiler-plate language. In re Robinson, 368 B.R. 492, 2007 Bankr. LEXIS 1770 (Bankr. E.D. Va. 2007).

Applications for compensation. — In a Chapter 13 action, counsel's application for compensation should be approved in the amount of $1,242.50 for fees and in the amount of $467.63 for reimbursement of costs incurred, for a total award of $1,710.13 where (1) counsel provided time records as requested, and the court was satisfied that the time records supplied were indeed contemporaneous time records; (2) the fees sought by counsel for his additional services rendered in the debtors' case were reasonable given the context of the instant case; and (3) counsel's fees must be reduced for tasks for which the court was unable to locate entries on the time records that corresponded to the entries on the documents. In re Larson, 346 B.R. 693, 2006 Bankr. LEXIS 1529 (Bankr. E.D. Va. 2006).

Fees requested in excess of $1,250. — Debtor's counsel's multi-step attorney fee applications that would have permitted him to bill greater amounts than subdivision (C)(2) of this section permitted and to bypass established procedures for measuring Chapter 13 attorney fees were disallowed in excess of the maximum $1,250 allowed pursuant to subdivision (C)(2), which requires that supplemental fee applications must include time records that substantiate both original and supplemental fees charged. In re Carter, 2003 Bankr. LEXIS 2257 (Bankr. E.D. Va. Mar. 31, 2003).

In excess of $1,500. — Request of a Chapter 13 debtor's counsel for $2,114 in supplemental legal fees was excessive under 11 U.S.C.S. § 330(a)(3) and (a)(4)(B) and E.D. Va. R. 2016-1(C)(5) and, thus, the award was reduced to $1,000 because the request was not justified by the narrative statement and attorneys typically charged $500 to $600 for relief from stay and even less for plan modification. In re Binns, 2006 Bankr. LEXIS 1662 (Bankr. E.D. Va. Apr. 28, 2006).

Rule 2090-1. Attorneys — Right to Practice Before the Court.

(A) *Bar of the Court:* Those attorneys who are admitted to practice before this Court shall comprise the Bar of the United States Bankruptcy Court for the Eastern District of Virginia.

(B) *Qualifications for Admission and the Right to Practice Before the Court:* An attorney, to qualify for admission and to maintain the right to practice before this Court, shall be administered the oath of admission upon the filing of an acceptable application to practice before the Court and shall be and at all times must remain a member in good standing of the Bar of the Commonwealth of Virginia.

(C) *Application and Procedure for Admission:* Every attorney desiring admission to practice before this Court shall file with the Clerk written application therefor accompanied by an endorsement by two qualified members of the Bar of this Court stating that the applicant is of good moral character and professional reputation and is qualified to practice bankruptcy law. The Clerk of this Court shall supply such application upon request. As a part of the application, the applicant shall certify that the said applicant has within 90 days prior to the application read or reread (1) the Federal Rules of Civil Procedure (FRCP), (2) the Federal Rules of Evidence, (3) the Federal Rules of Bankruptcy Procedure (FRBP) and (4) the Local Bankruptcy Rules of this Court.

(D) *Presentation:* A qualified member of the Bar of this Court who has examined the credentials of the applicant and, if found sufficient, may present the applicant to the Court for admission. If admitted, the applicant shall take the oath required for admission, sign the roll of the Bar of this Court and, thereafter, be issued a certificate of qualification by the Clerk.

(E) *Other Attorneys:*

(1) Western District of Virginia: Any attorney who is a member in good standing of the Bar of the United States Bankruptcy Court for the Western District of Virginia shall be permitted to practice in the courts of the Eastern District of Virginia upon filing with the Clerk of this Court:

(a) a certificate of the Clerk of the United States Bankruptcy Court for the Western District of Virginia stating that said attorney is a member in good standing of the Bar of that District and

(b) a certification from the applicant stating that said attorney has, within the preceding 90 days, read the Local Bankruptcy Rules of this Court.

(2) *Foreign Attorneys:*

(a) Application: An attorney from another state, the District of Columbia or a territory of the United States may appear and practice in cases *pro hac vice* before this Court upon motion of a member of the Bar of this Court, provided that in all appearances said attorney shall be accompanied by a member of this Bar. Applicants for *pro hac vice* admission shall complete a written application, which shall be appended to and incorporated by reference in the aforesaid motion. As a part of the application, the applicant shall certify that the said applicant has within 90 days prior to the application read or reread (1) the Federal Rules of Civil Procedure (FRCP), (2) the Federal Rules of Evidence, (3) the Federal Rules of Bankruptcy Procedure (FRBP), and (4) the Local Bankruptcy Rules of this Court. If the Court finds the application otherwise appropriate, the Court may order the *pro hac vice* admission of the applicant. Except where a party is not represented by counsel, any pleading or notice required to be signed by counsel must be signed by counsel who is a member of the Bar of this Court, who shall have entered an appearance of record in the case, with the office address in the state where notice can be served, and who shall have such authority that the Court can deal with that attorney alone in all matters connected with the case. Such appearance shall not be withdrawn without leave of the Court. Service of notice or other proceedings on the attorney shall be equivalent to service on the client. Where a party is not represented by counsel, the party shall include on each pleading an address within the district where notice can be served.

(b) Adversary Proceedings: An attorney intending to appear in an Adversary Proceeding shall file the motion only in the case in which an Adversary Proceeding is pending. Admission shall apply to the case and all related Adversary Proceedings.

(c) Reopened Cases: A foreign attorney wishing to appear in a reopened case shall file a separate motion to appear in the case notwithstanding entry of any order in the case granting admission.

(3) Attorneys for the United States and any State: The following may appear and practice in this Court in the performance of their official duties: The Attorney General

of the United States, any Deputy or Assistant Attorney General, any United States attorney, Assistant United States attorney or attorney employed by a department or agency of the United States Government and authorized by that department or agency to represent it in court; and the Attorney General, any Deputy or Assistant Attorney General, any Commonwealth Attorney and any Assistant Commonwealth Attorney of any state.

(F) *Attorneys Filing Pleadings:* All counsel making an appearance or presenting papers, suits or pleadings for filing other than a request for notices under FRBP 2002(g), must be members in good standing of the Bar of this Court and members in good standing of the Bar of the Commonwealth of Virginia or the state in which he or she is admitted. Attorneys who are not members of the Bar of this Court must have counsel who is a member in good standing of the Bar of this Court join in the pleading by endorsement. Any counsel who is a member in good standing of the Bar of this Court as defined above and who joins in a pleading will be held accountable for the case by the Court.

(G) *Withdrawal of Appearance:* No attorney who has entered an appearance in any case or proceeding shall withdraw as counsel except for cause, on order of the Court after reasonable notice to the party on whose behalf the attorney has appeared.

(H) *Appearance at All Proceedings:*

(1) Appearance by Counsel for the Debtor: Any attorney who is counsel of record for a debtor, or debtors, in a bankruptcy case must be present and appear at all Court proceedings involved in the case unless excused or given permission to withdraw, or unless counsel has filed a pleading stating that the debtor has no objection to, or does not oppose, the relief requested, or counsel has endorsed without objection an order resolving the motion, objection or application.

(2) Appearance by Other Counsel of Record: Any attorney who has filed a pleading in a bankruptcy case must be present and appear at all Court proceedings involving that pleading unless Counsel:

(a) has been excused by the Court;

(b) has been given permission to withdraw by order of the Court;

(c) has provided a notification of settlement in accordance with LBR 9013-1(O); or

(d) has provided opposing or another counsel appearing at the initial pretrial conference with available dates so that a trial date can be established.

(I) *Professional Ethics:* The ethical standards relating to the practice of law in this Court shall be the Virginia Rules of Professional Conduct now in force and as hereafter modified or supplemented.

(J) *Courtroom Decorum:* Counsel shall at all times conduct and demean themselves with dignity and propriety. When addressing the Court, counsel shall rise unless excused therefrom by the Court. All statements and communications to the Court shall be clearly and audibly made from a standing position at the attorneys' lectern facing the Court or the witness. Counsel shall not approach the bench unless requested to do so by the Court or unless permission is granted upon the request of counsel.

Examination of witnesses shall be conducted by counsel standing behind the lectern. Counsel shall not approach the witness except for the purpose of presenting, inquiring about, or examining the witness with respect to an exhibit. Only one attorney for each party may participate in the examination or cross-examination of a witness.

(K) *Third-Year Law Student Practice Plan:* If the United States District Court for the Eastern District of Virginia has in effect any plan for third-year law student practice, the provisions of said plan apply equally to practice before this Court.

(L) *Previous Practice Clause:* All members in good standing of the Bar of the United States District Court for the Eastern District of Virginia as of September 30, 1979, shall be deemed to be members of the Bar of the United States Bankruptcy Court for the Eastern District of Virginia.

COMMENT

2091-1(B) Revision required to conform with requested change to LBR 2090-1(D).

2091-1(D) Change to reflect the decision made by the Judges that attorney admissions do not have to occur in open court.

Paragraph (E)(3) is added to authorize Federal and State Attorney Generals and their assistants to appear and practice in this court in the performance of their official duties. [Changes effective 1/1/97.]

2090-1(H) This changes requires presence of counsel for both debtors and creditors at Court proceedings. [Change effective 2/1/00.]

2090(I) A reference to the Virginia Rules of Professional Conduct, which became effective January 1, 2000, has been substituted for the reference to the American Bar Association Canons of Professional Ethics and Virginia State Bar canons. [Change effective 3/1/01.]

2090-1 Paragraphs (B) and (F) of this Local Bankruptcy Rule have been amended to explicitly provide that an attorney must be and remain a member in good standing of the Bar of the Commonwealth of Virginia or the state in which the attorney is admitted. [Change effective 9/1/06].

2090-1 Stylistic changes have been made to the text of the LBR. [Changes effective 12/01/09.]

CASE NOTES

Counsel's failure to appear. — Though the imposition of sanctions were not warranted given the circumstances, counsel's failure to attend a hearing on a Chapter 7 debtor's motion, filed pro se, for an extension of time to retain new counsel violated Bankr. E.D. Va. R. 2090-1(H)(1) despite the fact that a copy of the motion had not been mailed to him because the notice sent to his email address via the court's CM/ECF system constituted equivalent notice per Bankr. E.D. Va. R. 5005-2. In re Jahed, 2011 Bankr. LEXIS 866 (Bankr. E.D. Va. Mar. 7, 2011).

Withdrawal not permitted. — Counsel was not allowed to withdraw from a Chapter 11 bankruptcy case under Bankr. E.D. Va. R. 2090-1(G) and Va. Sup. Ct. R. pt. 6, § II, R. 1.16. The debtors had to quickly sell their real property or face relief from stay, and it would severely prejudice them and interfere with the administration of justice to release counsel at this stage of the case. In re Schley, 2012 Bankr. LEXIS 2135 (Bankr. E.D. Va. May 9, 2012).

Rule 2090-1.

UNITED STATES BANKRUPTCY COURT
EASTERN DISTRICT OF VIRGINIA

APPLICATION TO QUALIFY AS A FOREIGN ATTORNEY UNDER LOCAL BANKRUPTCY RULE 2090-1(E)(2)

In Case No. __________, * Case Name ____________________

PERSONAL STATEMENT

FULL NAME (no initials, please) ________________________
Bar Identification Number ____________ State ____________
Firm Name ____________________________________
Firm Phone # __________ Direct Dial # __________ FAX # ________
E-Mail Address ________________________________
Office **Mailing** Address ____________________________
Name(s) of federal court(s) in which I have been admitted ____________

I certify that the rules of the federal court in the district in which I maintain my office extend a similar pro hac vice admission privilege to members of the bar of the Eastern District of Virginia.

I have not been reprimanded in any court nor has there been any action in any court pertaining to my conduct or fitness as a member of the bar.

I hereby certify that, within 90 days before the submission of this application, I have read the Local Rules of this Court and that my knowledge of the Federal Rules of Civil Procedure, the Federal Rules of Bankruptcy Procedure, and the Federal Rules of Evidence is current.

____
(Applicant's Signature)

I, the undersigned, do certify that I am a member of the bar of this Court, not related to the applicant; that I know the applicant personally, that the said applicant possesses all of the qualifications required for admission to the bar of this Court; that I have examined the applicant's personal statement. I affirm that his/her personal and professional character and standing are good, and petition the court to admit the applicant *pro hac vice*.

________________________ ____________
(Signature) (Date)

____
(Typed or Printed Name)

____
Pro hac vice admission in a case shall include an adversary proceeding(s) in the case.

Court Use Only:

The motion for admission is GRANTED ________ *or* DENIED ______________

______________________________ ________________
(Judge's Signature) (Date)

Ver. 11/05/09 [effective 12/01/09]

Rule 3003-1. Claims in Chapter 11 Cases.

(A) *Claims Bar Date:* The last date for the filing of claims, other than a claim of a governmental unit, in a chapter 11 case shall be 90 days after the date first scheduled for the meeting of creditors. The last date for a governmental unit to file a proof of claim shall be 180 days after the petition is filed in a voluntary chapter 11 case or an order for relief is entered in an involuntary chapter 11 case. The Clerk shall give notice of the date in a separate notice of bar date mailed with the notice for the meeting of creditors.

(B) *Claims Scheduled as Disputed, Contingent or Unliquidated:* The debtor in a chapter 11 case shall serve creditors whose claims are listed on the schedules as disputed, contingent or unliquidated with a notice of the fact within 14 days after the later of:

(1) the conversion of the case to chapter 11;

(2) the filing of the schedules of liabilities; or

(3) the filing of an amendment to the schedules of liabilities adding such creditors.

The debtor shall file with the Court a certification that service of the notice was made on the affected creditors within 7 days after the notice is served.

COMMENT

The Clerk is directed to provide a separate notice of the claims bar date in chapter 11 cases. Paragraph (B) is new. [Changes effective 1/1/97.]

3003-1 Time-computation adjustments have been made, as needed, to conform to a revision to the Federal Rules of Bankruptcy Procedure that takes effect December 1, 2009. Stylistic changes have been made to the text of the LBR as well. [Changes effective 12/01/09.]

Rule 3007-1. Objections to Claims.

(A) *Contents of Objection:* All objections to claims shall state with particularity the grounds therefore and shall set forth the relief or order sought.

(B) *How Objection Heard:* An objection to a proof of claim may be noticed for a hearing date obtained from the Clerk or may be accompanied by a notice providing opportunity for the creditor to request a hearing. If the notice of opportunity to request a hearing procedure is used, and the creditor serves and files a timely request for a hearing, *it is the responsibility of the objecting party to obtain a hearing date from the clerk and give notice to the creditor of the hearing date.* In any Division which has a regular motions day practice, the objection may be made returnable to a motions day in compliance with the motions day practice in that Division.

(C) [Repealed.]

(D) *Requirement of Written Response:* A creditor served with an objection to claim shall file and serve on the objecting party, a response thereto within 30 days of service if a notice of opportunity to request a hearing is given, or 7 days prior to the hearing if the objection is accompanied by a notice of hearing. If no response is filed, the court may treat the objection as conceded, and may enter an order without holding a hearing disallowing the claim in whole or part as set forth in the objection to claim.

(E) *Notice:* Each objection to claim, whether set to request a hearing or accompanied by notice of opportunity for hearing, shall contain or be accompanied by the following notice substantially in accordance with Official Form 20B, "NOTICE OF OBJECTION TO CLAIM", and also providing notice to the creditor in substantially the following form:

NOTICE

Under Local Bankruptcy Rule 3007-1, unless a written response and a request for hearing on this objection are filed with the Clerk of the Court and served on the objecting party and the trustee within 30 days of the service of this objection, the Court may deem any opposition waived, treat the objection as conceded, and enter an order granting the requested relief without a hearing.

COMMENT

The addition of this rule was made to clarify the procedures with regard to objections to claims. Given that FRBP 3007 expressly deals with objections to claims, the decision was made to add this rule and amend LBR 9013-1 as required. In addition, it notes the use of the Official Form 20B that was approved by the Judicial Conference at its September 1997 meeting with the mandatory implementation date of March 1, 1998.

3007-1 Paragraph (C) is repealed in light of Local Bankruptcy Rule 5005-2, which mandates electronic case filings in the Court's Case Management/ Electronic Case Files (CM/ECF) System and authorizes the Clerk to promulgate and revise the Court's Electronic Case Files (CM/ECF) Policy. In addition, time-computation adjustments have been made, as needed, to conform to a revision to the Federal Rules of Bankruptcy Procedure that takes effect December 1, 2009. Stylistic changes have been made to the text of the LBR as well. [Repeal and changes effective 12/01/09.]

CASE NOTES

Failure to respond. — In a Chapter 13 case, claims filed by entities that allegedly purchased debts from credit card companies were disallowed under subsection (D) of Bankr. E.D. Va. R. 3007-1 because the entities that filed the claims failed to respond to the debtors' objection by providing proof of ownership. Thus, the court treated the lack of response as conceding the objection. In re King, 2009 Bankr. LEXIS 2722 (Bankr. E.D. Va. Apr. 7, 2009).

Rule 3011-1. Unclaimed Funds.

(A) *Deposit of Unclaimed Funds:* All unclaimed funds collected by the Court shall be immediately deposited into the United States Treasury and not into the registry of the Court.

(B) *Disposition of Unclaimed Funds*

(1) Requirements for *Pro Se* Creditor/Claimant — Self Representation — A request for return of an unclaimed dividend must be in writing and in the form of a motion and filed with the Court. A Form W-9, Request for Taxpaper Identification Number and Certification, also must be completed, signed and filed with the motion. The exempt payee box should be checked on the Form W-9. The form and accompanying instructions are accessible at the Bankruptcy Forms page on the Court's Internet web site. Creditor/claimant must sign a certificate of mailing reflecting that the motion was served on the United States attorney for the Eastern District of Virginia, pursuant to 28 U.S.C. § 2042, and on the United States trustee. The motion must state:

(a) the name, address, telephone number and a brief history of the creditor from the filing of the claim to present (to reflect possible reasons for the funds not being deliverable at the time of original distribution);

(b) whether the claim has been assigned to the creditor, and, if so, copies of all documents evidencing assignment must be appended to the motion; and

(c) whether or not the creditor/claimant believes that any other party may be entitled to the funds.

The motion must contain a certificate of a notary public, which bears the seal of the notary, that such notary has examined the motion and documents presented by the creditor/claimant establishing identity.

If the creditor/claimant is a corporation, it must be represented by a member of the bar of this Court. In addition, if the creditor/claimant is a successor corporation, creditor/claimant shall provide documents establishing the chain of ownership of the original corporate claimant as proof of entitlement to the claim. The motion must state whether or not the moving party believes that any other party may be entitled to the funds.

As provided for in LBR 9013-1(M)(1), notice of the motion shall be in substantial compliance with official Form 20A, allowing 21 days' notice for written responses objecting to the relief requested and must contain the "NOTICE" language substantially in the form set forth therein. Movant must sign a certificate of mailing reflecting that the motion was served on the United States attorney for the Eastern District of Virginia and on the United States trustee.

(2) Requirements for the Representative of the Estate of a Deceased Claimant: The representative must comply with all requirements in paragraph (B)(1) of this Local Bankruptcy Rule. Certified copies of all probate documents to substantiate the representative's right to act on behalf of the decedent's estate must be provided as proof of entitlement.

(3) Requirements for any other individual representing the interest of creditor/claimant: The representative must be an attorney admitted to practice in accordance with these Local Bankruptcy Rules. The attorney must file a motion with the Court for an order authorizing return of an unclaimed dividend pursuant to FRBP 9013. A Form W-9, request for Taxpayer Identification Number and Certification, also must be completed, signed and separately submitted, via email or mail, to the Finance Department (Form W-9 and accompanying instructions are accessible on the Court's Internet web site's Bankruptcy Forms page). The exempt payee box should be checked on Form W-9. The motion must contain the name, address, telephone number and brief history of the creditor from the filing of the claim to present (to reflect possible reasons for the funds not being deliverable at the time of original distribution). If applicable, proof of any sale of the company, new and prior owners, and a copy of the terms of any purchase agreement or stipulation by prior and new owners of right of ownership to the unclaimed funds must be provided. If the claim has been assigned to the claimant, copies of all documents evidencing assignment must be appended to the motion.

The motion must state whether or not the moving party believes that any other party may be entitled to the funds.

As provided for in LBR 9013-1(M)(1), notice of the motion shall be in substantial compliance with Official Form 20A, allowing 21 days' notice for written responses objecting to the relief requested and must contain the "NOTICE" language substantially in the form set forth therein. Movant must sign a certificate of mailing reflecting that the motion was served on the United States attorney for the Eastern District of Virginia and on the United States trustee.

An original power of attorney from the creditor/claimant authorizing the attorney to represent the interest of the creditor/claimant must be attached to the motion.

(4) Action on Motion: Twenty-one days following receipt of the above documentation, and if no objections have been filed, the Clerk shall prepare and submit the appropriate order to the Court. Any payment made to a claimant represented by an attorney will be issued jointly to claimant and the attorney and will be mailed to the attorney.

(5) All creditors/claimants: Pursuant to the Vendor Administration and 1099 Issuance Procedures promulgated by the Administrative Office of the United States Courts, the Court requires that each creditor/claimant (the rightful owner of record) complete a Form W-9, Request for Taxpayer Identification Number and Certification, to facilitate the accurate preparation of Court-generated Forms 1099-MISC, Miscellaneous Income, and 1099-INT, Interest Income, as required by the United States Internal Revenue Code. Failure to complete, sign and return a Form W-9 may result in non-payment.

COMMENT

3011-1(B) Inclusion in subparagraph (B)(1)(c) of those items that may be presented to a notary to establish the movant's identity has resulted in some movants appending copies of forms of identification to their motions. This may have the effect of unnecessarily placing personal identifiers into the public record. The listed forms of identification have been removed for this reason. [Change effective 12/1/03.]

3011-1 The third paragraph to LBR 3011-1(B)(3) is amended to make explicit that the procedures set forth in LBR 9013(M)(1) must be followed to meet the requirements set forth in LBR 3011-1(B)(3). [Change effective 9/1/06.]

3011-1 Time-computation adjustments have been made, as needed, to conform to a revision to the Federal Rules of Bankruptcy Procedure that takes effect December 1, 2009. Stylistic changes have been made to the text of the LBR as well. [Changes effective 12/01/09.]

3011-1 Paragraph (B)(1) and (3) are amended to conform to the Vendor Administration and 1099 Issuance Procedures promulgated by the Administrative Office of United States Courts. Paragraph B(5) is new. [Changes effective 09/03/13.]

3011-1 The last sentence of the third paragraph in paragraph (B)(1) is new. The fourth paragraph in paragraph (B)(1) is new and makes explicit that the procedures set forth in LBR 9013-1 (M)(1) must be followed to meet the requirements set forth in LBR 3011-1(B)(1). [Changes effective 09/03/13.]

Rule 3015-1. Chapter 12 Plan Requirements.

(A) *Time for Filing:* The debtor may file a chapter 12 plan with the petition. If a plan is not filed with the petition, it shall be filed within 90 days thereafter unless the Court, pursuant to 11 U.S.C. § 1221, extends the time for filing. Any motion for extension of time to file a plan shall be filed prior to the expiration of the deadline for which the debtor seeks an extension.

(B) *Objections:* Objections to confirmation of the plan shall be filed with the Court and served on the debtor, the debtor's attorney, the trustee, and on any other entity designated by the Court, not less than 7 days prior to the scheduled confirmation hearing.

(C) *Hearing:* After notice as provided in paragraph (D) of this Local Rule, the Court shall conduct a hearing within the time prescribed by 11 U.S.C. § 1224 and rule on confirmation of the plan. If no objection is timely filed, the Court may determine that the plan has been proposed in good faith and not by any means forbidden by law without receiving evidence on those issues.

(D) *Notice:* The debtor shall send notice of the hearing on confirmation to all creditors, the chapter 12 trustee and equity security holders. The notice shall include the time fixed for filing objections to the proposed plan. Unless the Court fixes a different period, notice of the hearing shall be given not less than 28 days before the hearing. A copy of the plan shall accompany the notice. Forthwith upon the giving of such notice, the debtor shall file proof of service with the Clerk.

(E) *Order of Confirmation:* The debtor shall prepare a proposed Order of Confirmation which recites the Court's findings under 11 U.S.C. § 1225. Notice of entry thereof shall be mailed promptly by the Clerk, or some other person as the Court may direct, to the debtor, the trustee, all creditors, all equity security holders, and other parties in interest.

(F) *Retained Power:* Notwithstanding the entry of the Order of Confirmation, the Court may enter all orders necessary to administer the estate.

(G) *Dismissal:* Except as provided in LBR 1017-3, the Clerk is to monitor the filing of chapter 12 plans. If the debtor does not, within 90 days after filing the chapter 12 petition, file either a plan or a motion to extend the time to file a plan, the Clerk shall enter an order dismissing the chapter 12 case.

(H) *Notice of Dismissal Provision:* The Clerk is directed to give notice of the dismissal provision of this Local Rule to the debtor or debtor's attorney not filing a plan with the petition. The Clerk shall also give notice of this Local Rule in the meeting of creditors notice.

COMMENT

3015(G) This change is necessary because of the addition of LBR 1017-3. [Change effective 2/1/00.]

3015-1 Time-computation adjustments have been made, as needed, to conform to a revision to the Federal Rules of Bankruptcy Procedure that takes effect December 1, 2009. Stylistic changes have been made to the text of the LBR as well. [Changes effective 12/01/09.]

LBR 3015-1(D) provides that notice of the confirmation hearing should be sent at least 21 days prior to the hearing. FRBP 2002(a)(8), however, requires 21 days notice of both the confirmation hearing and the objection deadline. Under LBR 3015-1(B), the objection deadline is 7 days prior to the confirmation hearing. To give the needed notice requires 21 days plus 7 days for a total of 28 days. [Change effective 09/01/11.]

Rule 3015-2. Chapter 13 Plan Requirements.

(A) *Form of Plan; Inclusion of Related Motions:* The only acceptable form for a chapter 13 plan shall be that form approved by the Court (Exhibit 1 to these Local Bankruptcy Rules) and available from the Clerk upon request or from the court's Internet web site, www.vaeb.uscourts.gov. Counsel are encouraged, however, to delete the text of inapplicable sections from the plan provided that the section numbering and section headings are retained, followed by an appropriate notation such as "None" or "Not Applicable". If applicable, and without prejudice to a debtor's right to file a stand-alone motion seeking the same relief, the plan shall include the following related motions:

(1) *Motion for Determination of Value Pursuant to 11 U.S.C. § 506(a).*

(2) *Motion for Lien Avoidance Pursuant to 11 U.S.C. § 522(f):* (Lien avoidance under any other provision of the Bankruptcy Code must be by separate adversary proceeding and requires service of a summons and complaint.)

(3) *Motion for Assumption or Rejection of Executory Contracts Pursuant to 11 U.S.C. § 365.*

(B) *Special Notice to Secured Creditors Whose Collateral is to be Valued or Lien Avoided:* Unless a stand-alone motion and appropriate notice is served on the affected creditor at the same time as the plan is filed with the Clerk and transmitted to creditors, the debtor shall serve on each creditor who is the subject of an included motion for valuation under 11 U.S.C. §506(a) or an included motion for lien avoidance under 11 U.S.C. §522(f) a copy of the plan to which is attached a notice in the form approved by the Court (Exhibit 2 to these Local Bankruptcy Rules). Service of the plan and special notice must be made in the manner provided for in FRBP 7004.

(C) *Filing of Original Chapter 13 Plan and Related Motions*

(1) *Requirement:* The Chapter 13 Plan and Related Motions and any special notice to secured creditors required by this rule shall be filed with the Clerk not later than 14 days after the commencement of the case if the case was originally filed under chapter 13 or 14 days after the order converting the case to chapter 13 from some other chapter.

(2) *Proof of Service to include names and addresses of all parties served:* The Chapter 13 Plan and Related Motions must contain a proof of service setting forth the date and manner of service and the names and addresses of all parties to whom the plan was mailed or transmitted.

(3) *Extension of Time to File Chapter 13 Plan and Related Motions*

(a) A motion to extend the time to file a Chapter 13 Plan and Related Motions may be granted by the Clerk for an additional 14 days, if

(i) the motion for extension has been filed before the initial due date has expired and

(ii) notice of the motion has been given by the debtor to the trustee and all creditors.

(b) Any motion that is filed after the due date or that seeks an extension of time beyond the dates specified in subparagraph (C)(3)(a) of this Local Bankruptcy Rule shall be noticed for a hearing before the judge assigned to the case.

(D) *Distribution of Chapter 13 Plan and Related Motions:* The debtor shall distribute a copy of the original Chapter 13 Plan and Related Motions to all creditors, the standing trustee, and other parties in interest at or prior to the time it is filed with the court. Upon receipt of the confirmation date, time and location, the debtor shall serve on affected creditors the special notice required by paragraph (B) of this Local Bankruptcy Rule.

(E) *Objections to Confirmation of Original Chapter 13 Plan or to Related Motions*

(1) *Deadline for Filing:* Any objection to confirmation of the Chapter 13 Plan or to the granting of any included Motion for Determination of Value, Motion for Lien Avoidance, or the Motion to Assume or Reject Executory Contract or Unexpired Lease shall be filed not later than 7 days prior to the date set for the confirmation hearing. Any extension of the original objection period must be requested by motion.

(2) *Service of Objection:* The objecting party shall file an original objection with the Court and serve copies on the standing trustee, the debtor, and the debtor's attorney. The objection shall be accompanied by proof of service evidencing compliance with this requirement.

(3) *Hearings on Objections:* All timely filed objections shall be heard at the confirmation hearing as set forth in the notice of meeting of creditors.

(F) *Modified Chapter 13 Plan and Related Motions*

(1) *Procedure where no plan has been confirmed*

(a) Time for Filing: Unless confirmation of a prior plan has been denied, a modified plan may be filed at any time prior to confirmation. If confirmation of a prior plan has been denied, a modified plan must be filed within the period stated in paragraph (H)(3) of this Local Bankruptcy Rule unless the order denying confirmation states some other period.

(b) Distribution of Modified Chapter 13 Plan and Related Motions: The modified Chapter 13 Plan and Related Motions, and any special notice required by paragraph (B) of this Local Bankruptcy Rule, must be distributed and served in the same manner as the original plan. The special notice required by paragraph (B) of this Local Bankruptcy Rule need not be given, however, if an order has previously been entered granting the relief sought and the modified plan does not contain any provision inconsistent with the order previously entered.

(c) Objections to Confirmation of Modified Chapter 13 Plan and Related Motions: If a modified Chapter 13 Plan and Related Motions is filed, any objections must be filed not later than 7 days prior to the date set for the confirmation hearing. The debtor must obtain a new confirmation hearing date from the Clerk and must include the new date, time and location on the first page of the form of Chapter 13 Plan and Related Motions. The new confirmation hearing date shall not be earlier than the date originally set for the confirmation of the original plan filed in the case and must allow at least 35 days' notice. The debtor shall give notice of the date, time and place of the confirmation hearing by serving a copy of the modified plan on the trustee and all creditors.

(d) Effect on a Hearing Scheduled on Objection(s) to any Previously Filed Unconfirmed Plan

(i) Once a modified plan and related motions has been filed by the debtor, all previously filed unconfirmed plans and related motions are deemed withdrawn.

(ii) Norfolk and Newport News Divisions. In the Norfolk and Newport News Divisions, the filing of a modified plan and related motions does not remove a previously-scheduled hearing on objection to confirmation from the court calendar. Removal of any such hearing must be requested by the objecting party and agreed to by the Court.

(iii) Richmond and Alexandria Divisions. In the Richmond and Alexandria Divisions, the filing of a modified plan and related motions will remove a previously-scheduled hearing on objection to confirmation from the court calendar without further order of the Court, but without prejudice to any party's right to object to the modified plan.

(2) *Procedure when a plan has been confirmed.*

(a) When modification is requested by the trustee or a creditor: If modification of a confirmed plan is sought by the trustee or by a creditor, the modification must be requested by motion. A hearing date shall be obtained from the Clerk, and at least 21 days' notice of the hearing shall be given to the debtor, debtor's counsel, the trustee (if the trustee is not the movant) and all creditors. The time for filing any response is governed by LBR 9013(H)(3).

(b) When modification is requested by the debtor: If modification of a confirmed plan is sought by the debtor, modification must be requested by filing and distributing a modified Chapter 13 Plan and Related Motions and by giving special notice required by paragraph (B) of this Local Bankruptcy Rule. The special notice required by paragraph (B) of this Local Bankruptcy Rule need not be given, however, if a Chapter 13 Plan and Related Motions has previously been confirmed providing the identical treatment of the secured creditor's claim. The debtor must obtain a new confirmation hearing date from the Clerk. The new confirmation hearing date must allow at least 35 days' notice. The debtor shall give notice of the date, time and place of the confirmation hearing as set forth on the first page of the form of Chapter 13 Plan and Related Motions by serving a copy of the modified plan on the trustee and all creditors. Any objection to the modified plan must be filed not later than 7 days prior to the date set for the confirmation hearing.

(G) *Confirmation of Plan and Granting of Related Motions Without a Hearing:* After the time for filing objections has passed and if no objection has been timely filed, the Court may enter an order confirming the plan and granting the relief sought in the related motions without holding a hearing, or the Court may direct that a hearing be held.

(H) *Dismissal of Case for Failure to Timely File or Distribute Plan and Notice, Except as Provided in LBR 1017-3*

(1) *Clerk to Issue:* Except as provided in LBR 1017-3, the Clerk shall issue an order of dismissal in any chapter 13 case not meeting the timeliness of filing requirements of paragraphs B, C or D of this Local Bankruptcy Rule.

(2) *Notice of Possible Dismissal:* The Clerk shall give notice of this Local Bankruptcy Rule to the debtor or debtor's counsel at the time the petition is filed. The Clerk shall also give notice of this Local Bankruptcy Rule in the notice of meeting of creditors.

(3) *Dismissal of Case upon Denial of Confirmation:* Except as provided in LBR 1017-3, if the Court denies confirmation of the debtor's original or subsequently modified Chapter 13 Plan and Related Motions, unless the Court has entered an order previously confirming a plan, the Clerk is directed to issue an order dismissing the chapter 13 case unless, within 21 days after denial of confirmation:

(a) the debtor files a new Modified Chapter 13 Plan and Related Motions;

(b) the debtor converts or moves to convert the case to another chapter of the Bankruptcy Code;

(c) the debtor files a motion for reconsideration or appeals the denial of confirmation; or

(d) the Court otherwise orders.

An order previously entered by the Court confirming a chapter 13 plan shall remain in full force and effect if a subsequently modified Chapter 13 Plan and Related Motions is denied confirmation by the Court.

(I) *Reconversion of Case:* [Repealed.]

COMMENT

Rule 3015-2 Revised Chapter 13 Form Plan:

Since February 15, 1988, the Eastern District of Virginia has required that chapter 13 plans follow a prescribed format. *See In re Walat,* 87 B.R. 408 (Bankr.E.D. Va 1988) (*en banc*), *aff'd* 89 B.R. 11 (E.D. Va. 1988). Following the Fourth Circuit's decisions in *Piedmont Trust Bank v. Linkous (In re Linkous)*, 990 F.2d 160 (4th Cir. 1993) and *Cen-Pen Corp. v. Hanson*, 58 F.3d 89 (4th Cir. 1995), the form plan was expanded to include "related" motions to value collateral and avoid liens, and a separate "Notice of Chapter 13 Plan and related Motions" was adopted for service on creditors in addition to the plan itself.

In 2003, the National Association of Chapter 13 Trustees recommended a model form of chapter 13 plan which had been drafted at an Advanced Practice Institute by a group of debtors' counsel, trustees, creditors' representatives, attorneys and others. After the chapter 13 trustees in the Western District of Virginia proposed a variant of this model plan for adoption in that district, a working group of one judge and one chapter 13 trustee from each district proposed further modifications that would allow the same form of plan to be used in each district. After a period of public comment and a trial use of the model plan at a Virginia CLE Advanced Consumer Bankruptcy Seminar, a redrafted proposal was prepared by the chapter 13 trustees of both districts. This proposal, with some minor changes agreed to by the judges of both districts at two joint meetings, resulted in the current plan.

Adoption of a uniform plan is expected to benefit state-wide and national creditors (who would have only one form of plan from Virginia to decipher) as well as attorneys who practice in both districts and would no longer have to separately configure their form preparation software for each district. Because it is shorter than the existing Eastern District of Virginia plan, it should also be significantly easier for *pro se* parties (many of whom struggle with the current form of plan) to fill out.

The revised plan, like the previous plan, incorporates "related" motions to value collateral and avoid liens. To satisfy the due-process concerns in *Linkous* and *Cen-Pen*, a separate "special" notice must be attached to the copy of the plan mailed to the creditors that are the subject of those motions. [Rule effective 10/17/05.]

3015-2 Subparagraphs (F)(1)(c) and F(2)(b) have been amended to include the date, time, and place of the confirmation hearing when a modified plan is being filed. The first page of the uniform Chapter 13 Form of Plan and Related Motions has been revised to include this change. [Changes effective 9/1/06.]

3015-2(I) This paragraph is new. It provides that a Chapter 13 Plan approved by the Court in the original Chapter 13 case, if any, is deemed reinstated with full force and effect when that case reconverts back to Chapter 13. [New rule effective 3/17/08.]

3015-2 Time-computation adjustments have been made, as needed, to conform to a revision to the Federal Rules of Bankruptcy Procedure that takes effect December 1, 2009. Stylistic changes have been made to the text of the LBR as well. [Changes effective 12/01/09.]

3015-2(E)(1), (F)(1)(c) and (F)(2)(b) The notice required for a new confirmation hearing date conforms to the time-computation changes made to paragraphs (E)(1), (F)(1)(c) and (F)(2)(b). [Changes effective 12/09/09.]

3015-2 (I) The text at paragraph (I) has been removed as no longer being required. [Repeal effective 12/01/09.]

CASE NOTES

Rule is constitutional. — This rule is not inconsistent with Article I, § 8, Clause 4 of the Constitution. In re Walat, 87 Bankr. 408 (Bankr. E.D. Va.), aff'd, 89 Bankr. 11 (Bankr. E.D. Va. 1988).

This rule is a valid rule promulgated under this court's delegated authority under Federal Rule of Bankruptcy Procedure 9029. This rule properly regulates procedure in chapter 13 cases, and it is not a substantive measure that abridges, enlarges or modifies any substantive right provided under title 11 of the United States Code. In re Walat, 87 Bankr. 408 (Bankr. E.D. Va.), aff'd, 89 Bankr. 11 (Bankr. E.D. Va. 1988).

Due process. — The Court must ensure that the local bankruptcy rules do not adversely impact a party's right to due process. Chevy Chase Bank v. Locke, 227 Bankr. 68 (E.D. Va. 1998).

So long as creditors are given notice, reasonably calculated under all the circumstances, to apprise them of the pendency of the action and afford them an opportunity to present their objections, there is no due process concern. Chevy Chase Bank v. Locke, 227 Bankr. 68 (E.D. Va. 1998).

Timing of mailing of notice. — In the U.S. Bankruptcy Court for the Eastern District of Virginia, Alexandria Division and as a practical matter, E.D. Va. R. 3015-2 and Fed. R. Bankr. P. 2002(b)(2) combine to require, in a Chapter 13 bankruptcy case, that any special notice be mailed no less than 35 days prior to the confirmation hearing. In re McIntyre, 2009 Bankr. LEXIS 859 (Bankr. E.D. Va. Mar. 13, 2009).

Special notice requirement in Bankr. E.D. Va. R. 3015-2(B) satisfies the requirement that, in Chapter 13 cases, due process in connection with the bifurcation of a secured creditor's claim under 11 U.S.C.S. § 506 requires more than disclosure in the plan; the creditor must be notified that a hearing is going to be held and that the interest of the creditor may be affected. In re McIntyre, 2009 Bankr. LEXIS 859 (Bankr. E.D. Va. Mar. 13, 2009).

Local rules may not rise higher than the bankruptcy court's derivative power. — Therefore, this rule cannot (1) abridge, enlarge or modify any substantive right established by the Constitution or the Bankruptcy Code, (2) be classified as anything other than practice or procedure, nor (3) be inconsistent with the Federal Rules of Bankruptcy Procedures. In re Walat, 87 Bankr. 408 (Bankr. E.D. Va.), aff'd, 89 Bankr. 11 (Bankr. E.D. Va. 1988).

This rule is procedural in nature. — The rule does not affect any parties' substantive rights under title 11 but merely dictates the procedure by which the bankruptcy court will consider the contents and confirmation of a debtor's chapter 13 plan. In re Walat, 87 Bankr. 408 (Bankr. E.D. Va.), aff'd, 89 Bankr. 11 (Bankr. E.D. Va. 1988).

Purpose. — The purpose of this rule is to require a complete and fair disclosure so that all interested parties may be fully informed of the contents of the plan being proposed as well as the ability of the debtor to comply with the plan. The broad disclosure requirement will not only facilitate the chapter 13 process but by alerting creditors will aid the court in determining whether the plan is proposed in good faith. In re Walat, 87 Bankr. 408 (Bankr. E.D. Va.), aff'd, 89 Bankr. 11 (Bankr. E.D. Va. 1988).

The court adopted this new rule to facilitate the processing of a great volume of chapter 13 cases and plan confirmations, as well as to advance the efficient use of court time given the ever growing demands on the court. The form chapter 13 plan incorporated by this rule is a key to the proper operation of this new rule. In re Walat, 87 Bankr. 408 (Bankr. E.D. Va.), aff'd, 89 Bankr. 11 (Bankr. E.D. Va. 1988).

Former subdivision (D)(1) does not unduly restrict secured creditor's right to seek relief from the automatic stay. If a secured creditor fails to object to a proposed plan, he may not raise that claim in a later motion. However, after confirmation of the plan if circumstances then develop in which a secured creditor will not be adequately protected, then that creditor may make a motion seeking relief from the automatic stay. Chevy Chase Bank v. Locke, 227 Bankr. 68 (E.D. Va. 1998).

Form plan. — An examination of the form plan under this rule demonstrates that the plan is not an inflexible mandate to the debtor. The form plan presents the debtor with many options in compiling a plan. These options give the debtor and the debtor's attorney a wide range of possibilities for choosing the actual contents of the plan. In re Walat, 87 Bankr. 408 (Bankr. E.D. Va.), aff'd, 89 Bankr. 11 (Bankr. E.D. Va. 1988).

Requirement of a form plan does not abridge debtor's right to file a plan since the debtor is still the entity that compiles and files a plan under the rule. The rule merely dictates the form and organization that the plan must take. In re Walat, 87 Bankr. 408 (Bankr. E.D. Va.), aff'd, 89 Bankr. 11 (Bankr. E.D. Va. 1988).

The use of local bankruptcy rules for purposes of delay may not only constitute grounds for dismissal of cases with prejudice but also may subject attorneys who engage in this type of practice to appropriate sanctions. Owings v. Doniff, 133 Bankr. 351 (Bankr. E.D. Va. 1991).

Good faith is determined by judge sua sponte. — Under subsection (E) of this rule, the bankruptcy judge ordinarily will see only those chapter 13 plans that come up for hearing on objection to confirmation. The result is that in most instances, although the parties to the confirmation have not raised the issue, the chapter 13 trustee must determine whether a plan has been proposed in good faith. In re Webster, 165 Bankr. 173 (Bankr. E.D. Va. 1994).

Discriminatory plan was not made in good faith. — Where debtor proposes to pay nothing to her unsecured creditors, but instead wanted to pay for a $20,000.00 asset which would be considered investment property, the plan was thus discriminatory of debtor's creditors and could not be considered as filed in good faith. In re Webster, 165 Bankr. 173 (Bankr. E.D. Va. 1994).

For case discussing the abusive manipulation of local bankruptcy rules, Owings v. Doniff, 133 Bankr. 351 (Bankr. E.D. Va. 1991).

Conditional confirmation despite noncompliance. — Modified Chapter 13 plan was conditionally confirmed despite the debtor's failure to give the creditor holding the sole secured claim the special notice required by Bankr. E.D. Va. R. 3015-2(B) relative to the valuation of the collateral at issue because the trustee could not commence payments to the unsecured creditors, as to which there were no disputes, until the plan was confirmed pursuant to 11 U.S.C.S. § 1326(a)(2). In re McIntyre, 2009 Bankr. LEXIS 859 (Bankr. E.D. Va. Mar. 13, 2009).

Tax refund addendum not required. — Above-median income Chapter 13 debtor, whose plan did not pay unsecured creditors in full, could not be required, as a condition of confirmation, to endorse an addendum to a confirmation order agreeing to turn over income tax refunds during the term of the plan because under the Chapter 13 means test as applicable to above-median income debtors, 11 U.S.C.S. §§ 1325(b)(3), 707(b)(2)(A)(i)-(iv), tax refunds did not figure into the disposable income calculation. While the court overruled the trustee's objection, it noted that with or without the addendum, the trustee could require the debtor to furnish copies of federal and state income tax returns during the term of the plan under 11 U.S.C.S. § 521(f)(1), and to the extent that a tax return disclosed a substantial and unanticipated change in the debtor's financial situation, the trustee could seek modification of the plan to increase payments to unsecured creditors under 11 U.S.C.S. § 1329(a)(1). In re Grunauer, 2010 Bankr. LEXIS 1716 (Bankr. E.D. Va. June 8, 2010).

Rule 3016-1. Chapter 11 Plan Requirements.

(A) *Transmission of Notice of Hearing on Disclosure Statement:* The proponent seeking approval of the disclosure statement shall transmit notice of the hearing on the disclosure statement and other materials as required by FRBP 2002(b) and 3017(a). The court-approved notices, other materials and proof of service shall be filed with the Court.

(B) *Objections to Disclosure Statement:* Objections to the disclosure statement shall be filed with the Court not later than 7 days prior to the date set for hearing on the disclosure statement.

(C) *Transmission and Notice to Creditors and Equity Security Holders:* Upon approval of the disclosure statement, the proponent of the plan shall transmit to all required parties such notices and materials as required by FRBP 2002(b) and FRBP 3017(d) and shall file with the Court the court-approved notices, other materials transmitted and proof of service.

(D) *Summary of Ballots:* Any proponent of a plan in a reorganization case shall file a summary of ballots (acceptances and rejections) with the Clerk prior to the hearing on confirmation in the form approved by the Court. The ballots are not to be filed with the Clerk unless the Court so orders.

(E) *Objection to Confirmation:* Any objection to confirmation of the plan shall be filed with the Court not later than 7 days prior to the date set for the initial hearing on confirmation. The objecting party shall serve a copy of the objection on the United States trustee and the parties designated in FRBP 3020(b)(1).

COMMENT

3016(E) This change clarifies that an objection to confirmation must be filed not later than five (5) business days before the initial hearing on confirmation. Absent leave of Court, an objection that is filed later than five (5) business days before the initial hearing on confirmation is not timely and shall not be considered by the Court. [Change effecitve 7/1/02.]

3016-1 Time-computation adjustments have been made, as needed, to conform to a revision to the Federal Rules of Bankruptcy Procedure that takes effect December 1, 2009. Stylistic changes have been made to the text of the LBR as well. [Changes effective 12/01/09.]

Rule 3017-1. Approval of Disclosure Statement.

[Repealed.]

COMMENT

3017-1 FRBP 3017.1 obviates the need for this Local Bankruptcy Rule. [Repeal effective 12/01/09.]

Rule 3070-1. Payments in Chapter 12 and Chapter 13 Cases.

(A) *Payments to Creditors by Trustee:* In chapter 12 and chapter 13 cases, no payment in an amount less than $25 shall be distributed by the trustee to any creditor. Funds not distributed because of this Local Bankruptcy Rule shall be paid whenever the accumulation totals at least $25. Any funds remaining shall be distributed with the final payment.

(B) *Distribution of Estate Funds Upon Dismissal of Case Prior to Confirmation of Plan:*

(1) Noticing Fees Payable to Clerk of Court: The trustee shall pay all noticing fees due the Clerk out of estate funds before returning any funds to the debtor. If, pending dismissal, the funds on hand are not sufficient to pay all administrative expenses, the trustee shall pay to the Clerk the pro rata portion of the fees due.

(2) Notice of Proposed Distribution: The trustee may file a notice of proposed distribution of estate assets on hand, with copies to the debtor and debtor's counsel. The proposed distribution may include payment to the trustee for compensation as allowed by law and reimbursement of the trustee's out-of-pocket expenses incurred in the case. The notice shall state that if no objection to the proposed distribution is filed within 14 days, the trustee is authorized to proceed with distribution.

(C) *Debtor's Failure to Commence Payments in Chapter 13 Case:* Except as provided in LBR 1017-3, each chapter 13 debtor shall commence payments proposed by the plan not later than 30 days after the date of the filing of the plan or the order for relief, whichever is earlier, unless the Court has set some different time. If payments are not received as required, the trustee shall certify the same to the Clerk. Upon receipt of such a certification, the Clerk shall enter an order dismissing the case.

(D) *Chapter 13 Pre-Confirmation Payments of Personal Property Leases:* Pre-confirmation payments of personal property leases governed by 11 U.S.C. §1326(a)(1)(B) shall be made by the debtor to the chapter 13 trustee as part of the total payment to the trustee, and the trustee shall pay the lessor, both before and after confirmation, unless the debtor's plan provides that lease payments will be made directly by the debtor or no plan provision addresses payment of the debtor's lease obligation, in which event the debtor shall make the pre-confirmation payments directly to the lessor and furnish proof of such payments to the trustee.

(E) *Chapter 13 Pre-Confirmation Adequate Protection Payments:* Pre-confirmation adequate protection payments governed by 11 U.S.C. §1326(a)(1)(C) shall be made by the debtor to the chapter 13 trustee as part of the total payment to the trustee, and the trustee shall pay the amount provided for by the plan to the secured creditor both before and after confirmation, unless the debtor's plan provides that such payments will be made directly by the debtor or no plan provision addresses payment of the secured claim, in which event the debtor shall make the pre-confirmation payments directly to the secured creditor and furnish proof of such payments to the trustee.

COMMENT

3070-1(C) This change is necessary because of the addition of LBR 1017-3. [Change effective 2/1/00.]

3070-1 The amendments to paragraph (C) and new paragraphs (D) and (E) are derived from former Interim Procedure 3070-1(C), (D) and (E). Stylistic changes have been made to the text of the LBR as well. [Changes effective 12/01/09.]

CASE NOTES

Failure to make initial payment. — Chapter 13 was not dismissed for non-payment under 11 U.S.C.S. §§ 1307(c)(4) and 1326(a)(1), where the trustee had not certified noncompliance under E.D. Va., Bankr. R. 3070-1(C), the debtor sought prompt confirmation of his plan, his constructive trust argument appeared to be in good faith, and if established, the creditor would receive a profit from the sale of the house allegedly held by the creditor in constructive trust for the debtor. In re Buividas, 2005 Bankr. LEXIS 280 (Bankr. E.D. Va. Jan. 21, 2005).

Rule 4001(a)-1. Relief from Automatic Stay.

(A) *Applicability of Contested Matter Rules:* All motions for relief from stay, except those under paragraph (G) herein, are contested matters and are governed by FRBP 9014, 11 U.S.C. § 362(c), (d), (e), (h), (l) and (m) and these Local Bankruptcy Rules.

(B) *Caption:* The motion for relief from stay, and any pleading or other paper (excepting exhibits) filed pursuant to such a motion, shall include the same caption as an adversary proceeding except that the caption shall not include an adversary proceeding (AP) number.

(C) *Response Period:* A separate notice of motion (Official Form 20A) is not required, however, unless provided otherwise by the Bankruptcy Code, the Federal Rules of Bankruptcy Procedure or order of the Court. The motion for relief from stay shall clearly state and conspicuously provide the following notice:

NOTICE

Your rights may be affected. You should read these papers carefully and discuss them with your attorney, if you have one in this bankruptcy case. (If you do not have an attorney, you may wish to consult one).

If you do not wish the Court to grant the relief sought in the motion, or if you want the court to consider your views on the motion, then within 14 days from the date of service of this motion, you must file a written response explaining your position with the Court and serve a copy on the movant. Unless a written response is filed and served within this 14-day period, the Court may deem opposition waived, treat the motion as conceded, and issue an order granting the requested relief without further notice or hearing.

If you mail your response to the Court for filing, you must mail it early enough so the Court will receive it on or before the expiration of the 14-day period.

You will be notified separately of the hearing date on the motion.

(D) *Contents of Motion for Relief from Stay:* The following material, when applicable, must be included in a motion for relief from stay:

(1) a detailed statement of the debt owed to the movant;

(2) if periodic payments are in arrears, the amount of arrears accrued prepetition and the amount of arrears accrued post-petition;

(3) a description of the property encumbered;

(4) A description of the security interest and its perfection;

(5) astatement of the basis for the relief claimed, such as, a lack of adequate protection or the absence of equity and that the property is not necessary for an effective reorganization. The specific facts constituting cause shall be set forth if a motion is brought for cause;

(6) if the movant asserts a valuation of the subject property, the motion shall state the amount of the valuation, the date, and the basis therefore (appraisal, bluebook, etc.); and

(7) the specific nature of the relief from stay that is requested.

(E) *Filing Requirements:* With the original motion for relief from stay, the proponent shall also file:

(1) the proper filing fee and

(2) [Repealed]

(3) a properly completed proof of service indicating that the movant served the motion for relief from stay upon each party required to receive notice under paragraph (F)(1) of this Local Bankruptcy Rule.

(4) [Repealed]

(F) *Service:*

(1) Of Motion: The movant shall serve a copy of the motion upon the debtor, and if applicable, upon:

(a) the debtor's attorney;

(b) the trustee;

(c) each official committee appointed in the case or its authorized representatives;

(d) if a Chapter 11 case, any additional creditors if required by FRBP 4001(a)(1); and

(e) any other party as directed by the Court.

The movant shall file, with the motion, proof of service certifying proper service of the motion.

(2) Of Notice of Hearing: The Clerk shall, within 7 days after the date the motion was filed, assign a hearing date and serve notice of such hearing upon the parties indicated in the proof of service filed pursuant to paragraph (E)(3) of this Local Bankruptcy Rule. For Alexandria and Richmond division cases only, the movant must select a preliminary hearing date and time from the schedule provided by the Clerk.

(G) *Requests for Additional Relief:* If a motion filed pursuant to FRBP 4001(a) requests relief beyond the termination, modification or conditioning of the automatic stay, and such additional relief is within the scope of FRBP 7001, it is deemed an adversary proceeding and it shall be accompanied by:

(1) an adversary proceeding filing fee and

(2) a properly completed Adversary Proceeding Cover Sheet as provided in LBR 7003-1.

If a party seeks an expedited hearing under 11 U.S.C. § 362(e), only the specific issue of the automatic stay shall be considered at such hearing, unless the Court otherwise directs.

(H) *Relief from Codebtor Stay in Chapter 13 Cases:* Motions for relief from a stay of action against a codebtor in a chapter 13 case are contested matters and are governed by FRBP 9014, 11 U.S.C. § 1301 and these Local Bankruptcy Rules. The motion shall clearly state in the caption of the motion the subsection of 11 U.S.C. § 1301 under which the party is proceeding.

(1) Caption: The caption for a motion for relief from codebtor stay, and any pleading or other paper (excepting exhibits) filed pursuant to such a motion, shall include the caption described in paragraph (B) of this Local Bankruptcy Rule.

(2) Service and Time for Response: Service shall be as set forth in paragraph (F)(1) of this Local Bankruptcy Rule. The time for response is 21 days from the date of service of the motion. The notice served upon the codebtor in any relief action shall include notice of the response period. In addition, in a relief action under 11 U.S.C. §1301(c)(2) the notice shall include the following language: "If you do not file a written response by

the deadline shown, the law provides that the stay protecting you from further legal action against you by this creditor will automatically terminate [see 11 U.S.C. §1301(d)].”

(I) *Rent Deposit and Transmittal Procedure Under 11 U.S.C. §362(l):* Any deposit of rent made by or on behalf of the debtor, pursuant to §362(l)(1)(B), shall be made in the form of a certified check or money order payable to the order of the lessor, and delivered to the Clerk upon the filing of the petition. The Clerk is directed to promptly transmit the rent deposit to the lessor, by certified mail, return receipt requested, to the address listed on the petition.

COMMENT

4001(a)-1(C) The notice conforms substantially with Official Form 20A so that movant is not required to serve a separate “notice of motion.” The subsection of 11 U.S.C. §1301 under which a party is proceeding must now be clearly stated in the caption of the motion for relief of codebtor stay. [Changes effective 1/1/97.]

4001(a)-1(G)(2) This adjustment was made to note the proper 20 days for response instead of 15, in line with 11 U.S.C. § 1301(d). [Change effective 2/1/00.]

4001(a)-1(D) This rule is new. The rule requires the inclusion of relevant information so that interested parties can formulate a position on the motion prior to the preliminary hearing. The requirements of Local Bankruptcy Rule 9022-1, regarding court orders, apply with respect to motions for relief from the automatic stay. [New Rule effective 8/1/03.]

4001(a)-1 Paragraph (B) of the rule has been amended to effect a technical change in that contested matter (CM) numbers no longer are required. [Change effective 7/1/04.] [Stylistic change effective 1/1/07.]

4001(a)-1 Paragraph (C), at the fourth and final paragraph of the “NOTICE”, is amended by deleting the phrase “by the CLERK” to conform to the procedures to be used in those divisions where available dates may be obtained on-line. Subparagraphs (E)(2) and (E)(4) are repealed in light of the amendments to the Court’s CM/ECF Administrative Procedures at new subparagraph IC7, effective December 1, 2006. Subparagraph (F)(2) is amended by adding a bracketed statement regarding action that a movant must take in Alexandria and Richmond division cases only. [Changes effective 1/15/07.]

4001(a)-1 Former Interim Procedure 4001(a)-1(A) is incorporated, as modified, into LBR 4001(a)-1. Former Interim Procedure 4001(a)-1 is incorporated as new paragraph (I). Paragraphs (E) and (F) are amended. Stylistic changes have been made to the text of the LBR as well. [Amendments effective 12/01/09.]

4001(a)-1 A technical change has been made at paragraph (G)(2). Time-computation adjustments have been made, as needed, to conform to a revision to the Federal Rules of Bankruptcy Procedure that takes effect December 1, 2009. Stylistic changes have been made to the text of the LBR as well. [Changes effective 12/01/09.]

Rule 4002-1. Duties of the Debtor.

(A) *Tax Information Under 11 U.S.C. §521*

(1) Pre-petition Tax Information Dismissal of Debtor’s Case: Pursuant to 11 U.S.C. §521(e)(2)(B), if the debtor fails to comply with either §521(e)(2)(A)(i) or (ii), unless the debtor demonstrates that the failure to so comply is due to circumstances beyond the control of the debtor, the Court shall dismiss the debtor’s case upon either:

(a) certification by the trustee wherein the Clerk shall issue a rule to show cause to the debtor and the debtor’s attorney, if any, and set the matter for a hearing; or

(b) motion by a creditor and after service of the motion by the creditor on the debtor and debtor’s attorney, if any and a hearing. Any motion to dismiss filed by a creditor must state with particularity that the creditor timely requested a copy of the tax return under FRBP 4002(b)(4).

(2) Procedure for Requesting Debtor to File Post-petition Tax Information with the Court:

(a) Motion by Requestor for Court Order Directing Debtor to File Tax Information or Statement: If the debtor does not file the requested tax information or statement with the Court required by 11 U.S.C. §521(f), the movant may file a motion requesting that the Court enter an order directing the debtor to file the requested tax information or statement with the Court. The motion shall be set for hearing in accordance with LBR 9013-1. The Court may determine the motion without oral hearing in accordance with LBR 9013-1(L).

(b) Motion Requesting Access to Tax Information or Statement: The movant may file a motion with the Court requesting access to tax information or statement filed by the debtor. The motion shall be served on the debtor and the debtor’s attorney, if any. The motion shall include:

(i) a description of the movant's status in the case, to allow the Court to ascertain whether the movant may properly be given access to the requested tax information or statement;
(ii) a description of the specific tax information or statement sought;
(iii) a statement indicating that the information or statement cannot be obtained by the movant from any other source; and
(iv) a statement showing a demonstrated need for the tax information or statement.
The motion shall be set for hearing in accordance with LBR 9013-1. The Court may determine the motion without an oral hearing in accordance with LBR 9013-1(L).

(c) Safeguarding the Confidentiality of Tax Information or Statement: If the Court grants the motion filed by the movant pursuant to subparagraph (A)(2)(b) of this Local Bankruptcy Rule, the tax information or statement shall be confidential and shall not be disseminated or disclosed to any person or entity or used for any purpose other than in connection with the case. Sanctions may be imposed for improper use, disclosure or dissemination.

(d) Discovery: Paragraph (A) of this Local Bankruptcy Rule shall have no effect on discovery proceedings under FRBP 2004, 7026, or 7028-7037.

(B) *Dismissal for Failure to Provide Payment Advices or Other Evidence of Payment:* Upon certification by the trustee that the debtor failed to provide the trustee with all payment advices or other evidence of payment, as required by LBR 1007-1(I), the Clerk shall issue a rule to show cause to the debtor and the debtor's attorney, if any, and set the matter for a hearing.

COMMENT

4002-1 This rule is new. It is derived from former Interim Procedure 4002-1. [New Rule effective 12/01/09.

4002-1 A technical change has been made at subparagraph (A)(2)(c). A caption has been added to subparagraph (A)(2)(d). Stylistic changes have been made to the text of the LBR as well. [Changes effective 12/01/09.]

Rule 4003-2. Lien Avoidance.

All motions filed under FRBP 4003(d) are contested matters and are governed by 11 U.S.C. § 522(f), FRBP 9014, and these Local Bankruptcy Rules. Except as provided in LBR 3015-2 governing Chapter 13 Plan Requirements, if no response to a motion for lien avoidance is filed within 21 days after service of the motion, relief may be granted without a hearing.

COMMENT

Revision required to conform with the changes to LBR 3015-2.

4003-1 A time-computation adjustment has been made to conform to a revision to the Federal Rules of Bankruptcy Procedure that takes effect December 1, 2009. [Changes effective 12/01/09.]

Rule 4008-1. Reaffirmation.

(A) *Notice of Rights Under 11 U.S.C. § 524(d):* The Clerk shall, within 14 days after the discharge has been granted, give written notice to each discharged debtor of the debtor's rights under 11 U.S.C. § 524(d).

(B) *Reaffirmation Agreements:* Any debtor or creditor seeking to reaffirm a debt of the kind specified in 11 U.S.C. § 524(c) shall file with the Clerk a properly completed reaffirmation agreement in substantial compliance with the applicable form promulgated by the Administrative Office of the United States Courts and Official Form B27, "REAFFIRMATION AGREEMENT COVER SHEET." The Clerk is directed to provide such forms to the public upon request.

COMMENT

4008-1(B) The current LBR requires the debtor to file summary of reaffirmation agreement. This change allows either the debtor or creditor to do so. [Change effective 2/1/00.]

4008-1(D) This new rule allows reaffirmation agreements to be one of the items that can be filed and docketed in a closed case.

4008-1 The amendments to LBR 4008-1(A) and (B) are derived from former Interim Procedure 4008-1. Paragraph (B) is repealed as no longer being necessary. Paragraph (D) is repealed in light of the recent amendment made to FRBP 4008(a) and 4004(c)(1)(J). [Amendments effective 12/01/09.]

4008-1 The new reaffirmation agreement cover

sheet, effective December 1, 2009, has been added to paragraph (B). A time-computation adjustment has been made to paragraph (A) to conform to a revision to the Federal Rules of Bankruptcy Procedure that takes effect December 1, 2009. [Changes effective 12/01/09.]

Rule 4008-2. Chapter 13 Discharge and Certification of Compliance; Duty of Debtor to Cooperate with Chapter 13 Trustee.

(A) *Certification of Compliance with 11 U.S.C. § 1328.* The debtor(s) shall file the form of Debtor's(s') Certification of Compliance with 11 U.S.C. § 1328 within 45 days of the mailing of the Notice to Debtor(s) and Creditor Concerning Issuance of Discharge. The failure to timely file this certification may result in the case being closed without the entry of a discharge order.

(B) *Debtor's Duty to Cooperate with Chapter 13 Trustee Upon Completion of Plan Payments:* Upon completion of chapter 13 plan payments, the debtor shall comply within 14 days with any requirement of the chapter 13 trustee for information needed to provide the notices required by 11 U.S.C. § 1302(d). Further, if the trustee determines that the debtor has failed to timely provide the trustee with such information, the trustee shall within 30 days of completion of chapter 13 plan payments, file a certification of non-compliance wherein the Clerk shall issue a show cause order to the debtor and the debtor's attorney, if any, why sanctions, including dismissal of the case without a grant of discharge, should not be imposed. The Clerk shall set the show cause order for a hearing.

COMMENT

4008-2 This rule is new and is applicble in all Chapter 13 cases filed on or after October 17, 2005. [New Rule effective 10/15/07.]

4008-2 A time-computation adjustment has been made paragraph (B) to conform to a revision to the Federal Rules of Bankruptcy Procedure that take effect December 1, 2009. A stylistic change has been made to paragraph (A). [Changes effective 12/01/09.]

CASE NOTES

Waiver. — Waiver of the certification required by Bankr. E.D. Va. R. 4008-2(A) was warranted since bankruptcy debtors completed all the requirements for a discharge, including completion of all plan payments and a course in personal financial management, and the death of the debtors rendered the debtors unable to certify their completion of the requirements for discharge. In re Runfola, 2011 Bankr. LEXIS 5072 (Bankr. E.D. Va. Dec. 21, 2011).

Rule 5005-1. Filing of Petitions, Pleadings and Other Papers.

(A) *Filing in Proper Division:*

(1) Petitions: A petition seeking relief under the Bankruptcy Code shall be filed in the division in which the debtor's domicile, residence, principal place of business or principal assets were located for the greater part of the 180 days immediately preceding the filing of the petition.

(2) All Other Documents: All motions, pleadings, complaints and other documents relating to a bankruptcy case or proceeding shall be filed in the divisional office of the court in which the bankruptcy case is pending.

(B) *Proponent to be Member of Bar:* Any attorney offering a petition, pleading or other document other than a request for notices under FRBP 2002(g), for filing on behalf of a client, must be a member in good standing of the bar of this Court.

(C) *Requirements of Form:* All petitions, pleadings and other documents offered for filing shall meet the following requirements of form unless submitted as provided for by an electronic means established by the Court:

(1) Legibility: Documents shall be plainly and legibly typewritten, printed or reproduced on one side of the paper only.

(2) Caption, Official Forms: The caption and form shall be in substantial compliance with the Federal Rules of Bankruptcy Procedure, Official Forms and Local Bankruptcy Rules. Each document filed, except the petition, shall bear the debtor's name, the case number, chapter and adversary proceeding number, if applicable.

(3) Size, Margins, etc.: Documents, including attachments and exhibits, shall be of standard weight and letter size (8 1/2 by 11 inches), photo-reduced if necessary, with a top margin of not less than 1 1/2 inches. All multi-page pleadings and documents shall be fastened into sets at the top.

(4) Signature Required: All petitions, motions, pleadings and other documents shall be signed by counsel of record, or another attorney in the same firm, who shall have been admitted to practice before this Court. *Pro se* individuals shall sign on their own behalf. All documents submitted on behalf of corporations, other than proofs of claim, shall be signed by counsel.

(5) Identification of Attorney: On the first page of each pleading or other document filed with the Court, the attorney filing the same shall be identified by name, State Bar number, complete mailing address, telephone number and the name of the party whom the attorney represents.

(6) Filing of Faxed Petitions, Pleadings and Other Documents: Petitions, pleadings and other papers which have been transmitted by facsimile equipment may be filed with the Court except for the List of Creditors which must be in the format specified by the Clerk as required under LBR 1007-1(I). Once filed, the faxed document constitutes the original and no other copy bearing an original signature should later be filed. All applicable filing requirements must be met, including the payment of any filing fee due.

(7) Acknowledgment Copy: To receive acknowledgment of filing of a petition, pleading or other document, an extra copy must be submitted. If the acknowledgment copy is to be returned by mail, a self-addressed, stamped envelope, large enough to accommodate the copy being returned, must be included with the filing. Failure to submit the additional copy and/or the stamped, self-addressed envelope will result in the acknowledgment copy not being returned.

(8) Proof of Service: Proof of service must be made by declaration of the person accomplishing the service. That declaration shall include the following information:

(a) The day of service;

(b) The specific persons and or entities served:

(c) The method of service employed (e.g., personal, mail, substituted, etc.);

(d) Identification of the documents served;

(e) The exact address at which service was made; and

(f) The capacity in which the person was served.

The full names and addresses should be listed for each person or entity served, including when service is made upon the list of the 20 largest unsecured creditors and insured depository institutions as required under FRBP 7004(h). Service copies shall contain a complete certificate of service, including names and addresses of parties served, if the number of persons and parties served is 25 or fewer. When service is made on more than 25 persons or parties, the certificate of service attached to the service copies need not contain the complete list of names and addresses, but may reference a service list attached to the original filed with the court.

(D) *Additional Requirements:* The following requirements are in addition to those set out in paragraphs (A) through (C) of this Local Bankruptcy Rule unless provided for by an electronic means established by the Court:

(1) Voluntary Petitions: Each petition filed must include an unsworn declaration with the signature of all debtors and must be verified by the signature of the debtor's attorney, if any. More than one entity cannot be listed as the debtor, except that husband and wife may file a joint petition. Each petition filed must be accompanied by:

(a) a List of Creditors, in the format specified by the Clerk, as required by LBR 1007-1(H);

(b) a verification by signature of the attorney for the debtor and an unsworn declaration with the signature of all debtors;

(c) if the debtor is a corporation, the petition must be signed by an attorney and be accompanied by a copy of the corporate resolution authorizing the filing as required by LBR 1074-1; and

(d) if a chapter 11 petition, the List of Creditors Holding 20 Largest Unsecured Claims, as required by LBR 1007-1(G).

(2) Complaints: Each complaint commencing an adversary proceeding must be accompanied by:

(a) the proper filing fee and

(b) a properly completed Adversary Proceeding Cover Sheet as provided in LBR 7003-1.

(3) Motions for Relief from Stay: Each motion for relief from stay must be accompanied by:

(a) the proper filing fee and

(b) proof of service indicating service of the motion upon the parties required to be served pursuant to LBR 4001(a)-1(F).

(4) Claims: Each proof of claim presented for filing must specify the name of the debtor and the applicable bankruptcy case number and must be properly signed by the claimant or the claimant's authorized agent.

(5) Amendments: Each amendment filed shall be accompanied by a properly completed Amendment Cover Sheet, as required by LBR 1009-1(A).

(6) Chapter 13 Plan: As required by LBR 3015-2, each Chapter 13 Plan and Related Motions presented for filing shall be accompanied by a properly completed proof of service.

(7) [Repealed.]

(E) *Notice of Deficient Filing:* The Clerk shall review each filing for compliance with the requirements of these Local Bankruptcy Rules. Those pleadings or other documents not meeting the requirements of these Local Bankruptcy Rules will receive a Notice of Deficient Filing allowing for 14 days to correct the deficiency or to file a request for a hearing on the matter. Failure to cure the deficiency, or to request a hearing within the time allowed, may result in the pleading or other document being stricken without further notice.

(F) *Rejection of Petitions, Pleadings and Other Papers:* [Repealed]

(G) *Judicial Conference Policy Regarding Public Access to Electronic Case Files:* [Repealed]

COMMENT

5005-1(C) Changes have been made to allow for the filing of documents by electronic means provided under FRBP 5005(a)(2). For more detail on how this has been implemented on a pilot basis in the Alexandria Division see the "Order Adopting Electronic Case Filing Procedures" attached as Exhibit 3 and the "Administrative Procedures for Electronically Filed Cases" attached as Exhibit 4. It is planned that the ability to file electronically will expand to the other divisions during 1999.

5005-1(C)(3) Additional language noting the requirement that certain filings be pre-punched with two holes at the top as prescribed by the Judicial Conference. Sufficient top margin should be allowed so that neither the caption nor text is destroyed or obscured.

5005-1(C)(6) This revision is due to the problems encountered while trying to scan a faxed list of creditors and the addition of LBR 1007-1(I) which requires the list to be filed on diskette. The Instructions for Preparing Lists of Creditors has been updated to reflect this change.

5005-1(C)(7) The purpose of this addition is to clearly set forth the need for an extra copy of the item filed as well as a self-addressed, stamped envelope in order for an acknowledgment copy to be sent.

5005-1(C)(8) This addition deals with the concern in bankruptcy cases involving the adequacy of notice. In many instances, the question of proper notice could not be determined by review of the movant's certificate of service. Instead of specifically naming the intended recipients of the pleading, the certificate of service often merely indicated that service was made upon "all parties in interest" or "all necessary parties." In addition, movants often did not attach a copy of the certificate of service to the service copies of the document. It is then impossible for the Court and other affected parties to determine who was served with the document in question.

5005-1(D) This is one of the changes made to allow for the filing of documents by electronic means provided under FRBP 5005(a)(2). For more detail on how this has been implemented on a pilot basis in the Alexandria Division see the "Order Adopting Electronic Case Filing Procedures" attached as Exhibit 3 and the "Administrative Procedures for Electronically Filed Cases" attached as Exhibit 4. It is planned that the ability to file electronically will expand to the other divisions during 1999.

5005-1(D)(4) Revision providing information on the number of copies required when a claim is filed.

5005-1(D)(6) Revision required to conform with the changes to LBR 3015-2.

5005-1(F) Addition based on a decision by the Judges to clearly state that filings not accompanied by the proper filing fee will be rejected by the Clerk's Office.

Paragraph (C)(4) is amended to clarify who may sign pleadings on behalf of counsel of record. [Change effective 1/1/97.]

Paragraph (C)(6) is new. Although the court does not accept fax filings directly to its own fax machines, it will, with the adoption of this local rule, accept for filing papers that originated from a fax machine. Since the faxed petition, pleading or other paper constitutes an original, no other "original" should later be filed. Papers intended for filing with the court could be sent to a fax machine at the court's onsite copy service, some other copy or courier service, a law firm, or other third party. As before, the actual filing takes place when the paper is received by the Clerk's Office. [Change effective 1/1/97.]

5005-1(C)(8) The current LBR requires names and addresses in all circumstances with regard to the proof of service. While this is not a burden in small cases, it is in larger cases. Therefore, this change notes that if there are more than 25 names, service copies need only refer to the service list filed with the original. [Change effective 2/1/00.]

5005-1(G) This paragraph is new. It addresses

the privacy policy promulgated by the Judicial Conference of the United States regarding public access to electronic case files. [New rule effective 01/01/04.]

5005-1(B) A stylistic change has been made to conform this rule provision. [Change effective 10/17/05.]

5005-1 The amendment to subparagraph (D)(1)(a)(ii) is technical in nature and clarifies the type of application referenced. [Change effective 9/1/06.]

5005-1 Paragraph (F) is repealed in light of new LBR 1006-3. [Change effective 9/1/06.]

5005-1 Subparagraphs (D)(1)(a), (b), (c) and (f) are repealed. Subparagraphs (D)(1)(d), (e), (g) and (h) are re-designated as subparagraphs (D)(1)(a), (b), (c) and (d), respectively. Subparagraphs (D)(3)(b) and (d) are repealed. Subparagraph (D)(1)(c) is re-designated as subparagraph (D)(1)(b). Paragraph (D)(7) is repealed. Paragraph (D)(4) is amended. Paragraph (G) is repealed. A technical change has been made at subparagraph (D)(2)(b). In addition, a time-computation adjustment has been made to paragraph (E) to conform to a revision to the Federal Rules of Bankruptcy Procedure that takes effect December 1, 2009. Stylistic changes have been made to the text of the LBR as well. [Repeals and changes effective 12/01/09.]

CASE NOTES

Review of lodged rejected proposal filing is limited. — The court's review of a lodged rejected proposal filing is a very limited review; although some attorneys have attempted to use the lodging/judicial review procedure to extend bankruptcy filing deadlines, or bring other matters before the court, the lodging procedure exists only for the court to review the clerk's actions in rejecting a proposed filing. Crestar Bank v. Silverstein, 110 Bankr. 219 (Bankr. E.D. Va. 1989).

Use of lodging judicial review procedure to extend filing deadlines. — The Bankruptcy Court rejects the use of the lodging judicial review procedure as a backdoor approach to extend filing deadlines in bankruptcy cases and proceedings; procedures exist through which creditors or other parties-in-interest could seek to extend the filing deadlines established by the National and Local Rules of Bankruptcy Procedure. Crestar Bank v. Silverstein, 110 Bankr. 219 (Bankr. E.D. Va. 1989).

Attorney's conduct of electronically filing a bankruptcy petition containing the electronic signatures of the debtor and the attorney, when in fact the attorney did not have the debtor's physical signature on a hard copy of the petition, violated the dictates for electronic filing in Fed. R. Bankr. P. 5005(a)(2), and E.D. Va. Bankr. R. 5005-1, violated the attorney's obligation in Va. Sup. Ct. R. pt. 6, § II, R. 3.1, 3.3 to bring only non-frivolous matters before the court, amounted to fraud on the court in violation of Fed. R. Bankr. P. 9011, and was sanctionable under the equitable powers granted to the court under 11 U.S.C.S. § 105. In re Wenk, 296 Bankr. 719, 2002 Bankr. LEXIS 1733 (Bankr. E.D. Va. 2002).

Defects created sufficient basis for clerk to reject proposed filing. — Where the clerk rejected the proposed dischargeability complaint because the proposed complaint was not accompanied by (1) a properly completed, signed Adversary Proceeding Cover Sheet, A.O. Form B-104, as required under former Local Rule 401 (see now Local Rule 7003-1), nor (2) a properly completed summons and notice, as required under subdivision (D)(2)(b) and former subdivision (D)(2)(c), these defects created a sufficient basis for the clerk to reject the proposed filing. Crestar Bank v. Silverstein, 110 Bankr. 219 (Bankr. E.D. Va. 1989).

Failure to pay filing fee. — Debtor's argument that a creditor's nondischargeability complaint should be dismissed because the creditor failed to pay the filing fee along with its complaint was without merit where the procedure in subsection E of Bankr. E.D. Va. R. 5005-1 was followed and the creditor immediately cured the deficiencies. Highgrove, LC v. Holcombe (In re Holcombe), 2006 Bankr. LEXIS 2540 (Bankr. E.D. Va. May 18, 2006).

Proof of service. — Although the failure to make a proof of service did not affect the validity of the service, the bankruptcy court could not proceed where the debtors failed to show that service was in fact effected. In re King, 2003 Bankr. LEXIS 1159 (Bankr. E.D. Va. July 25, 2003).

Sanctions for violations of the rule. — Where a nonattorney filed a motion to withdraw two proofs of claim filed on behalf of a creditor, and no certificates of service were attached to the withdrawal documents, sanctions were not warranted because there did not appear to be any harm incurred by either the debtors or the court by reason of the violations of Bankr. E.D. Va. R. 5005-1(C)(4) and 5005-1(C)(8). In re Varona, 388 B.R. 705, 2008 Bankr. LEXIS 1544 (Bankr. E.D. Va. 2008).

Applied in In re Smith, 115 Bankr. 84 (Bankr. E.D. Va. 1990).

Rule 5005-2. Filing of Petitions, Pleadings and Other Papers by Electronic Means.

All petitions, motions, memoranda of law, or other pleadings, documents and papers filed with the Court shall be filed through the Case Management/Electronic Case Files System (CM/ECF), except as otherwise provided for in the Court's Electronic Case Files Policy (CM/ECF Policy), which shall be promulgated and revised as specified by the Clerk. The CM/ECF Policy governs if there is a conflict between that Policy and these Local Bankruptcy Rules as to the technicalities of electronic case filing.

COMMENT

This rule mandates electronic case filings in the Court's Case Management/Electronic Case Files (CM/ECF) System and authorizes the Clerk to promulgate and revise the Court's Electronic Case Files (CM/ECF) Policy. [New rule effective 3/17/08.]

CASE NOTES

Electronically-transmitted notice to registered attorney through CM/ECF equivalent to mailed notice. — Though the imposition of sanctions were not warranted given the circumstances, counsel's failure to attend a hearing on a Chapter 7 debtor's motion, filed pro se, for an extension of time to retain new counsel violated Bankr. E.D. Va. R. 2090-1(H)(1) despite the fact that a copy of the motion had not been mailed to him because the notice sent to his email address via the court's CM/ECF system constituted equivalent notice per Bankr. E.D. Va. R. 5005-2. In re Jahed, 2011 Bankr. LEXIS 866 (Bankr. E.D. Va. Mar. 7, 2011).

Rule 5010-1. Reopening Cases.

A party seeking to reopen a case for purposes not related to the debtor's discharge, shall file a motion with the Court and shall give 21 days' notice to all parties in interest. The motion shall be served upon the United States trustee, the previously appointed trustee, and any party being added, if any, as a creditor or party in interest in the case. The motion shall be accompanied by the appropriate fee to reopen the case, a notice containing the hearing date as obtained from the Court and proof of service. The motion shall also state that any objections to the reopening of the case must be filed at least 7 days prior to the hearing.

COMMENT

The appropriate fee to reopen a case must be paid when the motion is filed. [Change effective 1/1/97.]

5010-1 Time-computation adjustments have been made, as needed, to conform to a revision to the Federal Rules of Bankruptcy Procedure that take effect December 1, 2009. Stylistic changes have been made to the text of the LBR as well. [Changes effective 12/01/09.]

Rule 5011-1. Withdrawal of Reference.

(A) *Form of Request; Place for Filing:* A request for withdrawal, in whole or in part, of the reference of a case or proceeding referred to the Bankruptcy Court, other than a *sua sponte* request by a bankruptcy judge, shall be by motion filed with the Clerk of the Bankruptcy Court. All such motions shall conform to LBR 9013-1 and shall be accompanied by the proper filing fee. In addition, all such motions shall clearly and conspicuously state that "RELIEF IS SOUGHT FROM A UNITED STATES DISTRICT COURT JUDGE."

(B) *Stay.* The filing of a motion to withdraw the reference does not stay proceedings in the Bankruptcy Court. The procedures relating to stay shall be those set forth in FRBP 5011.

(C) *Designation of Record:* The moving party shall serve on all interested parties and file with the Clerk of the Bankruptcy Court, together with the motion to withdraw the reference, a designation of those portions of the record of the case or proceeding in the Bankruptcy Court that the moving party believes will reasonably be necessary or pertinent to the District Court's consideration of the motion. Within 14 days after service of such designation of record, any other party may serve and file a designation of additional portions of the record. If the record designated by any party includes a transcript of any hearing or trial, or a part thereof, that party shall immediately after filing the designation, deliver to the court reporter and file with the Clerk of the Bankruptcy Court a written request for the transcript and make satisfactory arrangements for payment of its cost. All parties shall take any action necessary to enable the Clerk to assemble and transmit the record.

(D) *Responses to Motions to Withdraw the Reference; Reply:* Opposing parties shall file with the Clerk of the Bankruptcy Court, and serve on all parties to the matter for which withdrawal of the reference has been requested, their written responses to the motion to withdraw the reference, within 14 days after being served with a copy of the motion. The moving party may serve and file a reply within 14 days after service of a response.

(E) *Transmittal to and Proceedings in District Court:* When the record is complete for purposes of transmittal, but without awaiting the filing of any transcripts, the

Clerk of the Bankruptcy Court shall promptly transmit to the Clerk of the District Court the motion and the portions of the record designated. After the opening of a docket in the District Court, documents pertaining to the matter under review by the District Court shall be filed with the Clerk of the District Court, but all documents relating to other matters in the bankruptcy case or adversary proceeding or contested matter shall continue to be filed with the Clerk of the Bankruptcy Court.

COMMENT

While this does not get raised that often within the District, this addition clarifies where the motion should be filed and puts the responsibility on parties to designate the record to go to the U.S. District Court.

5011-1 Time-computation adjustments have been made, as needed, to conform to a revision to the Federal Rules of Bankruptcy Procedure that takes effect December 1, 2009. [Changes effective 12/01/09.]

CASE NOTES

Procedure. — Although withdrawal of reference is a matter solely within the jurisdiction of the district court, U.S. Bankr. E.D. Va. R. 5011-1 requires that motions to withdraw be filed initially in the bankruptcy court in order to allow the bankruptcy court's clerk's office to assemble the file required by the district court for consideration of the motion. In re US Airways Group, Inc., 296 B.R. 673, 2003 U.S. Dist. LEXIS 14142 (E.D. Va. 2003).

Rule 5073-1. Photography, Recording Devices, and Broadcasting.

(A) *Photographs and Electronic Recordings:* Except with the express written permission of the Court, photography, electronic recording, videotaping and broadcasting are not permitted in the courtroom and its environs during the progress of or in connection with judicial proceedings, whether or not court is actually in session.

(B) *Definition of "Environs":* "Environs", as used in this Local Bankruptcy Rule, shall include any floor on which any courtroom or hearing room is located, including all hallways, stairways, windows and elevators immediately adjacent to any such floor.

(C) *Exception:* With the written permission of the Court and of the party or parties to be photographed, pictures may be taken of any permanent occupant of any office within the environs aforesaid when court is not in session.

Rule 5077-1. Transcripts.

(A) *Certification of Record by Reporter:* [Repealed.]

(B) *Copies of Transcripts Available to Public:* The Clerk shall provide copies of any filed transcript to the public upon request and the payment of prescribed copy fees, unless the Court orders that copies of the transcript not be made or that the transcript be sealed.

(C) *Use of Transcripts by Multiple Parties:* [Repealed.]

(D) *Perfecting Record on Appeal:* [Repealed.]

(E) *Payment for Transcripts:* The obligation to pay the reporter or transcriber for any and all transcripts shall be the joint and several personal obligation of the attorney and the party for whose benefit the transcript was obtained to the extent so ordered. Any charges for a transcript shall be payable upon the completion of the transcript or any segment thereof when a proper bill for same has been submitted by the reporter or transcriber.

(F) *Clerk's Duty to Make Transcripts Remotely Available Electronically; Redaction* [Repealed.]

COMMENT

5077-1(C)-(D) The Administrative Office of the U.S. Courts has provided guidance to the courts on the statutory and policy requirements for copying official court transcripts of court proceedings filed with the clerk of court. Accordingly, paragraphs (C) and (D) of LBR 5077-1 are repealed. [Change effective 4/1/03.]

5007-1 Former Local Bankruptcy Rule 5077-1 is re-designated as Local Bankruptcy Rule 5007-1. Paragraph (A) is repealed. The first sentence of FRBP 5007(a) adequately addresses the requirement set forth in the first deleted sentence and the second deleted sentence is addressed by different means with the reporter. Paragraphs (B) through (E) remain unchanged. Paragraph (F) is new. This paragraph balances the promotion of remote electronic access by the public to transcripts filed with the Clerk with the need to protect personal privacy concerns and other legitimate interests. The procedure set forth therein provides a means by which personal data identifiers and other information may be redacted from a transcript before the transcript is made remotely available electronically to the public. [Re-designated Rule 5007-1, repealed Paragraph (A) and new Paragraph (F) effective 1/15/07.]

5007-1 Former Local Bankruptcy Rule 5007-1 is re-designated as Local Bankruptcy Rule 5077-1. [Re-designated Rule 5077-1 effective 03/16/09.]

5007-1(B) Paragraph (B) is amended to conform to requirements established by the Judicial Conference that limit electronic access to transcripts. [Amendment effective 03/16/09.]

5007-1(E) Paragraph (E) is amended to include the obligation to pay a transcriber for an ordered transcript. [Amendment effective 03/16/09.]

5007-1(F) Paragraph (F) is repealed and a standing order has been entered in view of a new policy of the Judicial Conference of the United States to make electronic transcripts of court proceedings available to the public. [Change effective 03/16/09.]

Rule 6004-1. Sale of Estate Property.

All motions or complaints for sale of real property or any interest therein shall contain the legal description of said real property sufficient to effect a proper conveyance thereof. Orders approving the sale of property of the estate or any interest therein shall comply with LBR 9022-1(D).

COMMENT

6004-1 The cross-reference to LBR 9022-1 (D) has been added to remind the practitioner of the requirement that orders approving the sale of real estate or any interest therein, like all orders, must stand alone without reference to external documents, e.g., the order should not purport to approve the sale of the real estate or any interest therein "in accordance with the terms of the contract attached to the motion" but should state the essential terms of the sale, e.g., "to John and Joanna Doe for the price of $173,000." [Change effective 3/1/01.]

Rule 6004-2. Use, Sale or Lease of Property.

(A) *Notice:* Notice of a proposed use, sale or lease of property other than in the ordinary course of business, shall be given by the proponent of the notice, and the original notice and proof of service shall be filed with the Court. The notice shall comply with FRBP 2002(a)(2) and FRBP 2002(c)(1).

(B) *Objection to Proposed Use, Sale or Lease:* An objection to a proposed use, sale or lease, other than in the ordinary course of business, shall be filed with the Court and served upon the proponent of the action not less than 7 days before the date set for the proposed action. The party objecting shall obtain from the Court a hearing date on the objection and shall serve a notice of hearing. Proof of service shall be filed with the objection and notice.

(C) *Sale of Property When Value of Estate Does Not Exceed $2,500:* The trustee or debtor in possession may give general notice of intent to sell property when all of the non-exempt property of the estate has an aggregate gross value of less than $2,500. Such notice may be given at the meeting of creditors, and the Clerk is to provide notice in the meeting of creditors notice that this procedure may be followed. An objection to such sale must be filed by a party in interest and served upon the proponent of the sale not later than 14 days after the meeting of creditors. The party objecting shall obtain from the Court a hearing date on the objection and shall serve a notice of hearing. Proof of service shall be filed with the objection and notice.

(D) *Report of Sale:* The trustee or debtor in possession shall file with the Court a report of any sale of estate property outside the ordinary course of business. The report shall be filed within 30 days after the sale with service on the United States trustee.

COMMENT

6004-2 Time-computation adjustments have been made, as needed, to conform to a revision to the Federal Rules of Bankruptcy Procedure that takes effect December 1, 2009. Stylistic changes have been made to the text of the LBR as well. [Changes effective 12/01/09.]

Rule 6004-3. Sale or Refinance of Property By Chapter 13 Debtor After Confirmation.

(A) A debtor seeking approval for the sale or refinance of real property following confirmation of a plan that revests such property in the debtor shall provide the chapter 13 trustee and all creditors and parties in interest at least 21 days notice of the motion seeking such approval unless the notice period has been shortened by the Court for cause shown.

(B) In addition to setting forth the information required by FRBP 2002(c)(1) the notice shall state:

(1) the total proposed sale price or maximum amount to be secured by the refinancing, as the case may be, and, in the case of refinancing, the amount of existing secured debt to be paid thereby;

(2) the amount of the sale or loan proceeds to be applied to the debtor's obligations under the confirmed plan;

(3) whether such payment will result in full payment of all allowed claims; and

(4) if all allowed claims will not be paid in full, the amount of the sale or loan proceeds that will be paid to the debtor.

(C) If no objection is filed within the objection period, the court, in its discretion, may enter an order endorsed by the chapter 13 trustee approving the sale or refinance without holding a hearing.

COMMENT

6004-3 [New Rule effective 10/17/05.]

6004-3 Stylistic changes have been made to the text of the Rule. [Changes effective 12/01/09.]

Rule 6004-4. Mortgage Loan Modification by Chapter 13 Debtor After Confirmation.

(A) Unless provided in a Consent Order resolving a Motion for Relief from Stay, a debtor(s) seeking approval for the modification of a mortgage on real property following confirmation of a plan that revests such property in the debtor(s) shall provide the chapter 13 trustee and any creditor who has filed a request for all notices in the case at least 21 days' notice of the motion seeking such approval unless the notice period has been shortened by the Court for cause shown.

(B) The notice shall state:

(1) All terms of the modification including the term, principal, interest rate, and any future payment changes or balloon payments that will occur during the term of the chapter 13 plan;

(2) The current mortgage payment and the new payment after the loan modification;

(3) If the modification results in a higher monthly payment, the source of the funds to be used to make that payment; and

(4) If the modification results in a lower monthly payment, whether the debtor intends to increase the amount of his plan payment.

(C) If no objection is filed within the objection period, the court, in its discretion, may enter an order endorsed by the chapter 13 trustee approving the loan modification.

COMMENT

6004-4 This rule is new and provides a procedure, including the manner in which notice shall be given and the contents of the notice, for a chapter 13 debtor to request court approval to modify a real property mortgage loan following confirmation of the debtor's Plan. [New Rule effective 12/01/09.]

Rule 6007-1. Abandonment.

(A) *Notice of Abandonment:* The Clerk shall give notice in the meeting of creditors notice that the trustee may, at the meeting of creditors, give notice of intention to abandon property of the estate that is burdensome or of inconsequential value to the estate. The Clerk shall give notice that parties in interest who object to such abandonment may state their oral objections at the meeting of creditors, obtain a hearing date from the Court, transmit notice of a hearing on their objection and file such notice with proof of service with the Court, within 14 days after the meeting of creditors.

(B) *Order of Court Directing Abandonment:* Any party in interest requesting the Court to order the trustee to abandon any property of the estate shall obtain a hearing date from the Court, transmit copies of the motion and notice containing the hearing date to all parties in interest and file with the Clerk the motion, notice and proof of service.

(C) *Order of Court for Approval of Abandonment:* Orders for approval of abandonment of property of the estate shall comply with LBR 9022-1(D).

COMMENT

6007-1(C) This new provision conforms to the amendment to LBR 9022-1(D). [Change effective 3/1/01.]

6007-1 A time-computation adjustment has been made at paragraph (A) to conform to a revision to the Federal Rules of Bankruptcy Procedure that takes effect December 1, 2009. [Change effective 12/01/09.]

Rule 6008-1. Redemption.

A party seeking redemption of property from a lien or sale shall request from the Court a hearing date, transmit the motion and notice of hearing to all parties in interest, and file the motion, notice and proof of service with the Clerk. Provided, however, that if the redemption is uncontested the Court may direct that no hearing be held.

COMMENT

Change to note that the Court may direct that no hearing is required if the initial request is uncontested.

Rule 7003-1. Adversary Proceeding Cover Sheet.

At the time of filing an adversary proceeding, counsel, or a *pro se* litigant, shall file with the complaint a properly completed adversary proceeding cover sheet in substantial compliance with the applicable form promulgated by the Administrative Office of the United States Courts. The Clerk is directed to provide such forms to the public upon request.

COMMENT

7003-1 The reference to the adversary proceeding cover sheet form number has been deleted should the form reference change. [Change effective 12/01/09.]

CASE NOTES

Defects created sufficient basis for clerk to reject filing. — Where the clerk rejected the proposed dischargeability complaint because the proposed complaint was not accompanied by (1) a properly completed, signed Adversary Proceeding Cover Sheet, A.O. Form B-104, as required under this rule, nor (2) a properly completed summons and notice, as required under former Local Rule 107 (see now Local Rule 5005-1), subdivision (D)(2)(b) and former subdivision (D)(2)(c), these defects created a sufficient basis for the clerk to reject the proposed filing. Crestar Bank v. Silverstein, 110 Bankr. 219 (Bankr. E.D. Va. 1989).

Rule 7004-2. Summons.

(A) *Issuance:* The Clerk shall issue to the plaintiff for service a summons for each party as listed on the adversary cover sheet.

(B) *Time Limit for Service:* If a summons is not timely delivered or mailed within 14 days following issuance of the summons, the party responsible for the original service shall bear the responsibility for issuance of further process.

COMMENT

7004-2 A time-computation adjustment has been made at paragraph (B) to conform to a revision to the Federal Rules of Bankruptcy Procedure that takes effect December 1, 2009. [Change effective 12/01/09.]

Rule 7007-1. Financial Disclosure.

[Repealed].

COMMENT

The Committee on Codes of Conduct of the Judicial Conference of the United States is undertaking to develop a national rule requiring parties in district and bankruptcy courts to disclose their corporate parents. Pending completion of a national rule that addresses this issue, LBR 7007-1 has been promulgated for the purpose of establishing the required interim financial disclosure. The statement referenced in LBR 7007-1, Financial Interest Disclosure Statement form, is attached as new Exhibit 6. [New Rule effective 3/1/01.]

7007-1 This rule was promulgated as an interim measure pending creation of FRBP 7007.1, which governs the filing of financial disclosure statements. Accordingly, with the exception of the number of statement copies to be filed using the form attached as Exhibit 6, this rule no longer is needed. [Change effective 12/01/03.]

7007-1 The remainder of the rule is repealed in light of Local Bankruptcy Rule 5005-2, which mandates electronic case filings in the Court's Case Management/Electronic Case Files (CM/ECF) System and authorizes the Clerk to promulgate and revise the Court's Electronic Case Files (CM/ECF) Policy. [Repeal effective 12/01/09.]

Rule 7013-1. Counterclaims.

[Repealed]

COMMENT

7013-1 This rule is repealed upon a finding that it is no longer needed. [Repeal effective 10/17/05.]

Rule 7016-1. Pretrial Procedures.

(A) *In Default Cases:* Where the defendant is in default and there has been no appearance on the defendant's behalf, the procedure outlined herein shall not be applicable, but the Court may direct the party not in default to appear for the purpose of noting a default, the entry of a default judgment and for scheduling a date for trial on the issue of damages if required by law. If the party not in default fails to take action to prosecute its claim after reasonable notice to appear or take such action, the Court may dismiss the proceeding for failure to prosecute.

(B) *In All Other Cases:* In all other adversary proceedings, as promptly as possible after suit has been filed, the Court may schedule an initial pretrial conference at which trial counsel shall be present. At such pretrial conference, the Court may issue an order fixing dates for:

(1) the amendment of pleadings and joinder of additional parties;
(2) the completion of discovery;
(3) the filing and hearing of motions; and
(4) a final pretrial conference and/or trial.

(C) *Optional Items in Scheduling Order:* The Court may include in such order, or any supplemental order, such other provisions as are appropriate to assist in expediting the trial or other disposition of the case and may specify the requirements of any final pretrial conference order which shall be presented to the Judge for entry at the time of the final pretrial conference. While the primary obligation of preparing the final pretrial conference order rests upon counsel for plaintiff, all counsel are requested to meet at least 7 days in advance of the conference with the Court in order to discuss and prepare such order, and the Court may require such meeting of counsel by its order.

(D) *Continuance of Dates Set in Scheduling Order:* The parties and their counsel are bound by the dates specified in said order and no extensions or continuances thereof shall be granted in the absence of a showing of good cause. Mere failure on the part of counsel to proceed promptly with the normal processes of discovery shall not constitute good cause for an extension or continuance.

COMMENT

7016-1 Stylistic changes have been made in the text of the Rule. [Changes effective 12/01/09.]

Rule 7026-1. Discovery.

(A) *Objections to be in Writing:* All objections to interrogatories, depositions, requests or applications under FRBP 7026 through FRBP 7037, as well as all motions and replies thereto concerning discovery matters, shall be in writing. If time does not permit the filing of a written motion, the Court may waive this requirement.

(B) *Objections to Discovery Process:* An objection to any interrogatory, deposition, request or application under FRBP 7026 through FRBP 7037, shall be served within 14 days after service of the interrogatory, deposition, request or application, unless otherwise ordered by the Court. Any such objection shall be specific and the reasons for the objection shall be stated. Any such objection shall not extend the time within which the objecting party must otherwise answer or respond to any discovery matter not specifically objected to.

(C) *Motions to Compel:* After a discovery request is objected to or not timely complied with, and if not otherwise resolved, it is the responsibility of the party initiating discovery to place the matter before the Court by a proper motion pursuant to FRBP 7037, to compel an answer, production, designation or inspection. Such motion must be accompanied by a memorandum as required by LBR 9013-1(G).

(D) *Other Discovery Motions:* A motion for a protective order pursuant to FRBP 7026 or a motion for an order compelling disclosure or discovery pursuant to FRBP 7037, or a motion to compel physical or mental examination pursuant to FRBP 7035, shall be accompanied by a memorandum as required by LBR 9013-1(G).

(E) *Replies to Discovery Motions:* Replies to discovery motions mentioned in paragraphs (C), (D) and (I) of this Local Bankruptcy Rule shall be filed within 14 days after service of the motion and memorandum unless otherwise ordered by the Court. Responses, if any, to all other discovery motions also shall be filed within 14 days.

(F) *Compliance with Discovery Orders:* After the Court has ruled on a discovery motion, any answer, production, designation, inspection or examination required by the Court shall be completed within 14 days after the entry of the order of the Court, unless otherwise ordered by the Court.

(G) *Failure to Comply with Order:* Should a party fail to comply with an order of the Court concerning discovery motions, it is the responsibility of the party objecting to such failure to comply to place the matter before the Court by a proper motion for supplementary relief pursuant to FRBP 7037. Such motion must be accompanied by a written memorandum as required by LBR 9013-1(G).

(H) *Consultation Among Counsel:* Counsel are encouraged to participate in pretrial discovery conferences in order to decrease, in every way possible, the filing of unnecessary discovery motions. No motion concerning discovery matters may be filed until counsel shall have explored with opposing counsel the possibility of resolving the discovery matters in controversy. The Court will not consider any motion concerning discovery matters unless the motion is accompanied by a statement of counsel that a good-faith effort has been made between counsel to resolve the discovery matters at issue.

(I) *Extensions:* Depending upon the facts of the particular case, the Court in its discretion may, upon appropriate written motion by a party, allow an extension of time in excess of the time provided by the Federal Rules of Civil Procedure, these Local Bankruptcy Rules, or previous court order, within which to respond to or complete discovery or to reply to discovery motions. Any agreement between counsel relating to any extension of time is of no force or effect; only the Court, after appropriate motion directed thereto, may grant an extension of time. Unless otherwise specifically provided, such extension will be upon the specific condition that, regardless of what may be divulged by such discovery, it will not in any manner alter the schedule of dates and procedure previously adopted by the Court in the particular case.

(J) *Sanctions:* Should any party or the party's attorney fail to comply with any of the provisions of this Local Bankruptcy Rule, or otherwise fail or refuse to meet and confer in good faith in an effort to narrow the areas of disagreement concerning discovery, sanctions provided by FRBP 7037 may be imposed.

(K) *Applicability to Contested Matters:* See LBR 9014-1.

(L) *Expert Disclosure*

(1) Agreement upon Disclosure: Counsel are encouraged to agree upon the sequence and timing of the expert disclosures required by FRBP 7026. All such agreements must be in the form of a consent order entered by the Court.

(2) Timing of Mandatory Disclosure: Absent such a consent order, or unless otherwise ordered, the disclosures required by FRBP 7026 shall be made as follows:

(a) Adversary Proceedings: In adversary proceedings, the disclosures required by FRBP 7026 shall first be made by the plaintiff not later than 60 days before the date set for completion of discovery; then by the defendant 30 days before the date set for completion of discovery. Within 14 days after defendant's disclosure, plaintiff shall disclose any evidence that is solely contradictory or rebuttal evidence to the defendant's disclosure.

(b) Contested Matters Except Relief from Stay: LBR 9014-1 generally excludes the application of FRBP 7026 in contested matters. Pursuant to LBR 9014-1, however, exceptions to this general rule may be made on order of the Court. When so ordered, the disclosures required by FRBP 7026 shall be made by the movant or applicant, as the case may be, within 30 days prior to the hearing date; then by the respondent or objecting party, on the later of 14 days after the movant or applicant presents the required disclosures, or on the date that a response to the motion or application is due.

(c) Relief from Stay: LBR 9014-1 generally excludes the application of FRBP 7026 in relief from stay matters. Pursuant to LBR 9014-1, however, exceptions to this general rule may be made on order of the Court. When so ordered, the disclosures required by FRBP 7026 shall be made by the parties within 14 days prior to the date set for final hearing on the motion. The parties shall disclose 7 days after disclosure any evidence that is solely contradictory or rebuttal evidence to each other's disclosure.

(3) Failure to Comply: Any party who fails to comply with these mandatory disclosure requirements may, at the court's discretion, be prohibited from using the undisclosed expert testimony at trial.

(4) General Provisions: For purposes of this Local Bankruptcy Rule, counterclaim-plaintiffs, cross-plaintiffs and third-party plaintiffs shall be plaintiffs as to all elements of the counterclaim, cross-claim and third-party claim. Answers to interrogatories directed at clarification of the written reports of expert witnesses disclosed pursuant to FRBP 7026 shall be due 14 days after service, unless otherwise ordered.

(M) *Filing With Court:* Unless otherwise permitted by the Court, on its own initiative or for good cause shown by motion, discovery materials, depositions upon oral examination and upon written questions, interrogatories, requests for documents, requests for admission and answers and responses or objections to such discovery requests shall not be filed with the pleadings or papers in any case or proceeding. When specific discovery material appropriately may support or oppose a motion, the specific discovery material in question shall be appended as an exhibit to the motion, or in response thereto, without having been previously filed. Discovery material otherwise permitted to be used at trial may be properly so used, if otherwise admissible, without having been previously filed.

COMMENT

The purpose of this change is to resolve the apparent conflict between 7026-1(D) and 7026-1(P) by noting that the objection is to be served rather than filed within fifteen days after the initial discovery request. If approved, it would bring the rule into compliance with the corresponding local rule for the U.S. District Court.

Paragraph (O) is new and incorporates herein the same rule as in the U.S. District Court for the Eastern District of Virginia. [Changes effective 1/1/97.]

The original language of Paragraphs (A), (B) and (N) opting out of certain provisions of the Federal Rules of Bankruptcy Procedure have been eliminated since such opt out no longer is permitted under the national rules. Rules 26(a)(1), (3) and (4), (b)(1)-(2), (d) and (f), 5(d), 30(d) and 37(c) of the Federal Rules of Civil Procedure were amended effective December 1, 2000. Original Paragraphs (A) and (B) have been repealed. Original Paragraphs (C) through (K) have been redesignated Paragraphs (A) through (I). Original Paragraph (L) (dealing with unnecessary discovery motions or objections), which was repealed effective February 1, 2000, has been eliminated. Original Paragraphs (M) through (P) have been redesignated Paragraphs (J) through (M). The heading and text to original Paragraph (N) (dealing with opt-out provisions) have been eliminated and a new Paragraph (K), which references new LBR 9014-1, has been substituted to conform to F.R.Civ.P. 26. [Change effective 12/1/00.]

7026-1(L) This paragraph is repealed since it was felt that the paragraph no longer is needed. [Change effective 2/1/00.]

7026-1(L)(2)(b) Under the current rule provision, the respondent or objecting party may not have had an affirmative duty to make the required disclosures if the movant or applicant did not make any such disclosures. The amended rule provision makes clear that the expert disclosure requirement of a respondent or objecting party is independent of the requirement imposed on a movant or applicant. [Change effective 3/1/01.]

7026-1(L)(2)(b) and (c) These changes result from an amendment to LBR 9014-1, which added FRBP 7026(a)(2) to those subdivisions of Rule 7026 that are excluded generally from application in contested matters and in relief from stay matters. [Change effective 7/1/02.]

7026-1 Time-computation adjustments have been made, as needed, to conform to a revision to the Federal Rules of Bankruptcy Procedure that take effect December 1, 2009. A technical change has been made at paragraph (E). Stylistic changes have been made to the text of the LBR as well. [Changes effective 12/01/09.]

Rule 7030-1. Depositions.

(A) *Deposition of Party:* Any party or representative (officer, director or managing agent) of a party filing an adversary proceeding in the proper division of this Court ordinarily may be required to submit to a discovery deposition at a place designated within the division. Exceptions to this general rule may be made on order of the Court when the party, or representative of a party, is of such age or physical condition, or special circumstances exist, as reasonably may interfere with the orderly taking of a deposition at a place within the division. A defendant, who becomes a counter-claimant, cross-claimant or third-party plaintiff, shall be considered as having filed an action in this Court for the purpose of this Local Bankruptcy Rule. This subdivision shall not apply to an involuntary plaintiff or an interpleader plaintiff.

(B) *Recording and Transcribing of Discovery Deposition:* The expense of recording a deposition shall be paid by the party seeking to take same. The expense of transcribing the deposition shall be paid by any party ordering the preparation of the original. Any other party desiring a copy of said deposition shall pay for same at the copy rate. Parties may, by agreement, equally share the costs of attendance and transcribing, including such copies as desired. The costs of the original transcript shall be included in the taxable costs, but only if the prevailing party has made use of the deposition during the trial, unless the parties otherwise agree.

(C) *Attorneys' Fees:* Unless the services of associate counsel are retained in lieu of travel expense, it is not the policy of the Court to make an allowance of counsel fees in attending any deposition, except to the extent provided by statute and otherwise in this Local Bankruptcy Rule, but the Court reserves the right to make a reasonable allowance where the circumstances of the case may justify the same.

(D) *Travel Expense:* As provided in this Local Bankruptcy Rule, the "costs of travel" shall consist of the actual cost of travel by air or other public transportation, or an allowance for travel by private automobile at mileage rates as set forth in 28 U.S.C. §1821, whichever means of transportation is actually used, including the cost of transportation from the office or residence to the terminal of the public transportation and from the destination terminal to the place of the taking of the deposition and/or overnight accommodations, if deemed necessary, and return. The Court may, in its discretion, make an appropriate allowance for food and lodging.

The "costs of travel" as herein defined shall apply to any witness other than a party, or representative of a party, required to attend the taking of a deposition. As to any witness attending a trial or hearing pursuant to FRCP 45(b)(1) the expense of such costs of travel shall be taxed as costs if said witness testifies or if it is reasonably necessary for the witness to appear, but said costs of travel shall be limited to what would have been expended if said witness resided 100 miles or more from the place of the trial or hearing, together with such reasonable allowance, if required for the purpose of the witness testifying, for overnight accommodations and food. If the witness resides within 100 miles of the place of trial or hearing, the costs of travel shall be limited to the mileage and attendance fees as provided by law.

(E) *Reviewing Depositions Prior to Jury Trials:* Whenever depositions are expected to be presented in evidence, counsel shall, prior to the final pretrial conference or, if same are not then available, prior to the day of jury trial, review such depositions and:

(1) extract therefrom a short statement of the qualifications of any expert witness to be read to the jury;

(2) eliminate unnecessary and/or irrelevant matters; and

(3) eliminate all objections and statements of counsel to avoid reading same to a jury.

In the event counsel are unable to agree on what shall be eliminated, they shall submit same to the Court for a ruling thereon before the date of trial. Failure to do so will constitute a waiver of objections.

(F) *Summaries of Depositions:* [Repealed.]

(G) *Reasonable Notice:* As a general rule, 7 days in advance of the contemplated taking of a deposition shall constitute reasonable notice of the taking of a deposition in the continental United States, but this will vary according to the complexity of the contemplated testimony and the urgency of taking the deposition of a party or witness at a particular time and place.

COMMENT

7030-1 This rule was changed from 7027-1 to 7030-1; FRBP 7027 refers to depositions taken before the filing of an adversary proceeding in order to preserve the testimony; rule 7030 is the general rule concerning depositions. [Change effective 2/1/00.]

Rule 7030-1 A technical modification referencing FRCP 45 is made in the text to Paragraph (D) of the rule. [Change effective 3/17/08.]

Rule 7030-1(F) is repealed as no longer being needed. [Change effective 3/17/08.]

7030-1 A technical change has been made in the second paragraph to paragraph (D). A time-computation adjustment has been made at paragraph (G) to conform to a revision to the Federal Rules of Bankruptcy Procedure that takes effect December 1, 2009. Stylistic changes have been made to the text of the LBR as well. [Changes effective 12/01/09.]

Rule 7041-1. Dismissal of Adversary Proceedings.

At least 14 days' written notice of a hearing on the proposed voluntary dismissal of a complaint (or count within a complaint) objecting to the debtor's discharge shall be given to the United States trustee, the trustee, any creditor or party in interest who has filed a request for notices, and, in an individual chapter 11 case, the members of the creditors' committee, or, if no creditors committee has been appointed, the creditors on the list of 20 largest unsecured creditors. The notice shall fully and clearly state any consideration paid or promised to be paid by the debtor to the plaintiff in connection with such dismissal. Whether an actual hearing will be required if no objections are filed is within the discretion of the judge.

COMMENT

7041-1 FRBP 7041 provides that "a complaint objecting to the debtor's discharge shall not be dismissed at the plaintiff's instance without notice to the trustee, the United States trustee, *and such other persons as the court may direct. . . .*" This leads to something of a cumbersome situation where a plaintiff does seek to dismiss such a complaint (or count within a complaint). Literally, it seems that the plaintiff would first have to advise the court of such intent and obtain an order directing to whom the notice should be given, then appear again to have the actual order of dismissal considered and entered. This new rule is intended to clarify matters as to who had to be given notice. [New rule effective 2/1/00.]

7041-1 A time-computation adjustment has been made at paragraph (G) to conform to a revision to the Federal Rules of Bankruptcy Procedure that takes effect December 1, 2009. Stylistic changes have been made to the text of the LBR as well. [Changs effective 12/01/09.]

Rule 7054-1. Costs.

(A) *Taxation Generally:* Costs shall be taxed as provided by law in all actions in this Court and, if not otherwise provided by law, in accordance with these Local Bankruptcy Rules.

(B) *Payment in Advance:* All fees and costs due the Clerk in adversary proceedings shall be paid in advance except:

(1) in actions brought on behalf of seamen;

(2) where a party has been authorized to proceed *in forma pauperis;* or

(3) where a party is otherwise exempt by law, such as the debtor (other than a debtor in possession) in a chapter 7, 11, 12 or 13 case, the United States, or in a proceeding where the United States trustee, acting as trustee, or a trustee in a case under title 11 is the plaintiff, the filing fee shall be payable only from the estate and to the extent there are funds in the estate.

(C) *RESERVED*

(D) *Bonds and Security for Costs:* No bond or security for costs shall be required of parties instituting adversary proceedings, unless otherwise ordered by the Court.

(E) *Clerk to Tax:* The Clerk may tax costs in an adversary proceeding as provided by FRBP 7054(b).

COMMENT

7054-1 Stylistic changes have been made to the text of the Rule. [Changes effective 12/01/09.]

Rule 7056-1. Summary Judgment.

Motions for summary judgment are governed by LBR 9013-1. Where the non-moving party is *pro se*, the notice of hearing on the motion shall comply with LBR 9013-1(M)(3).

COMMENT

LBR 7056-1 is new and provides a cross-reference to LBR 9013-1(M)(3), which also is new. [New Rule effective 3/1/01.]

Rule 7067-1. Deposit and Disbursement of Court Registry Funds.

(A) *Order Required:* The Clerk shall deposit into the registry of the Court any sum so directed by order.

(B) *District Registry Procedure and Form of Order:* The order proponent shall follow the District Registry Procedure. In addition to an appropriate caption and attorney identification, a proposed Order Directing Deposit shall include the following elements:

(1) the name, address and telephone number of the person or other entity paying the money into the registry of the Court;

(2) the name and address of the person or other entity for whom the money is being held; and

(3) the sum of money and date to be paid into the Court.

(C) *Order of Deposit:* An order satisfying the requirements of this Local Bankruptcy Rule is available on the Court's website.

(D) *Deposit:* The Clerk shall deposit the funds in accordance with the procedures and guidelines set out by the Administrative Office of the United States Courts.

(E) *Provision for Payment:* In addition to an appropriate caption and attorney identification, a proposed Order Directing Disbursement shall include the following elements:

(1) the sum of money to be paid to the person or other entity receiving the money, and

(2) the name and address of the person or other entity receiving the money.

(F) *Order Directing Disbursement:* An order satisfying the requirements of this Local Bankruptcy Rule is available on the Court's website.

COMMENT

7067-1 Paragraph (B) and subparagraph (B)(2) are amended to bring the rule in line with the Judicial Conference policy on privacy and public access to electronic case files and with conforming amendments to the Federal Rules of Bankruptcy Procedure. The District Registry Procedure makes provision for any required submission of the order proponent's social security number. [Change effective 12/1/03.]

7067-1 Paragraph (B) amends the elements of the Order Directing Deposit. Paragraph (C) is amended to advise that the order is available on the Court's website (at "Bankruptcy Forms"). Paragraphs (D) and (E) are new. Paragraph (F) is new. The form referenced at (F) also is available on the Court's website (at "Bankruptcy Forms"). [Change effective 9/1/06.]

7067-1 Stylistic changes have been made to the text of the Rule. [Changes effective 12/01/09.]

7067-1 Paragraph (D) is amended to remove the requirement that Registry funds be deposited by the Clerk in an interest bearing account and further is amended to add that the deposit of such funds shall be in "accordance with the procedures and guidelines set out by the Administrative Office of the United States Courts." Paragraph (E)(1) is amended to remove the reference to interest accrued on any such sum of money along with the reference to the Judicial Conference of the United States' authorized Court's fee. [Changes effective 09/03/13.]

Rule 8005-1. Appeal Bond.

(A) *Exemption From Appeal Bond:* The Commonwealth of Virginia, or any political subdivision or any office or agent thereof, shall not be required, unless otherwise ordered by the Court, to post a supersedeas bond or other undertaking which includes security for the payment of costs on appeal.

(B) *Failure to Post Appeal Bond:* In any case in which a monetary judgment is entered, and in such other cases as the Court may order, any party desiring to appeal from the adverse effect of such judgment shall be required, unless otherwise ordered by the Court, to post a supersedeas bond with sufficient security to respond to the judgment of the Court in the event of affirmance on appeal. In the event of failure to give such bond with security, the prevailing party may enforce such judgment as provided by law without regard to the pendency of said appeal.

(C) *Stipulation of Parties:* In lieu of any supersedeas bond, the parties may stipulate with respect to any agreement or undertaking. In lieu of any cost bond, the parties may stipulate with respect to any agreement or undertaking conditioned that the moneys and properties of the Court are fully protected or prepaid.

Rule 8006-1. Record on Appeal.

(A) *Record on Appeal — Exclusions:* Unless otherwise directed by the Court, the record on appeal in any matter shall not include counsel's opening statements or arguments of counsel, including arguments of counsel on motions.

(B) *Designating Record on Appeal:* Unless the parties file a timely written designation of record with the Clerk pursuant to FRBP 8006 designating the papers which shall constitute the record on appeal, the Clerk shall forward to the proper appellate court a certification that no designation of record was filed.

(C) *Copies of Record:* The party filing a designation of items to be included in the record on appeal shall file with the designation a complete and correct copy of all designated exhibits that were not filed electronically.

COMMENT

8006-1 A technical change has been made at paragraph (C)(2). [Change effective 12/01/09.]

8006-1 Changes have been made at paragraph (C) and (1)-(2) therein to conform to an internal procedure for administering the record on appeal between the Bankruptcy and District Clerk's Offices. [Changes effective 09/01/11.]

Rule 9010-1. Representation and Apearances; Powers of Attorney.

Requirement for Counsel: Except for filing or withdrawing a proof of claim, notice of mortgage payment change, notice of postpetition mortgage fees, expenses, and charges, response to a notice of final cure payment, request for notices or notice/service, notice of appearance, reaffirmation agreement, creditor change of address, transfer of claim or a transcript of court proceedings, no party or entity other than a natural person acting in his or her own behalf or, to the extent permitted by §304(g) of Pub.L. 103-394, a child support enforcement agency, may appear in a bankruptcy case or proceeding, sign pleadings, or perform any act constituting the practice of law except by counsel permitted to appear under LBR 2090-1. This Local Bankruptcy Rule applies to corporations, partnerships, limited liability companies, associations, and trusts, as well as to individuals acting in a representative capacity (such as under a power of attorney) for another. Any petition, pleading or paper, other than those set forth in this Local Bankruptcy Rule, filed on behalf of an entity that is not a natural person acting in his or her own behalf and not signed by counsel permitted to appear under LBR 2090-1 shall be stricken by the Clerk, or in the case of a petition, dismissed, unless the deficiency is cured within 14 days of the mailing or delivery of a notice of deficiency.

COMMENT

Rule 9010-1. [New rule effective 2/1/00.]

9010-1 This rule adds several new items to the list of items that may be filed with the court without legal representation. [Change effective 10/17/05.]

9010-1 Modifications are made to the list of items that may be filed with the court without legal representation. The rule conforms to Interim Procedure 9010-1, which is repealed. [Change effective 3/17/08.]

9010-1 A time-computation adjustment has been made at paragraph (G) to conform to a revision to the Federal Rules of Bankruptcy Procedure that takes effect December 1, 2009. Stylistic changes have been made to the text of the LBR as well. [Changes effective 12/01/09.]

9010-1 This amendment adds three items to the list of items that may be filed with the Court without legal representation. [Changes effective 09/03/13.]

CASE NOTES

Representation by guardian/conservator. — Guardian of the debtor's person and conservator of his estate, a non-attorney, could not represent the debtor pro se in the bankruptcy case. The bankruptcy court also declined to appoint counsel where the court determined that the guardian/conservator's claims lacked merit. In re Mattern, 2006 Bankr. LEXIS 355 (Bankr. E.D. Va. Jan. 31, 2006).

Illustrative cases. — Bankruptcy court used its powers under 11 U.S.C.S. § 105 to deny an individual's motion for an order that allowed the individual to substitute himself as the defendant in an adversary proceeding a corporate debtor filed against another corporation, which challenged the validity of a claim the other corporation filed against the debtor's Chapter 11 bankruptcy estate. The individual had repeatedly violated the requirement imposed by Bankr. E.D. Va. R. 9010-1 that corporations be represented only by licensed attorneys, and his attempt to substitute himself for the corporation as the defendant in the debtor's adversary proceeding was an unjust attempt to pursue collection on behalf of the corporation without complying with Rule 9010-1; evidence the individual presented did not support his claim that he purchased a promissory note the debtor executed in favor of the corporation and was entitled under Conn. Gen. Stat. § 42a-3-301 to enforce the note. Commonwealth Biotechnologies, Inc. v. Fornova Pharmworld, Inc. (In re Commonwealth Biotechnologies, Inc.), 2013 Bankr. LEXIS 799 (Bankr. E.D. Va. Mar. 4, 2013).

Rule 9013-1. Motions Practice.

(A) *Definition of Motion:* For the purposes of this Local Rule, "motion" shall include any motion, application, other request for relief from the Court, or proposed action to be taken under the Bankruptcy Code, Federal Rules of Bankruptcy Procedure, or Local Bankruptcy Rules but shall not include:

(1) any petition commencing a case under the Bankruptcy Code;

(2) any complaint commencing an adversary proceeding under the Federal Rules of Bankruptcy Procedure;

(3) any motion for relief from the automatic stay;

(4) any proposed order; or

(5) objection to claim [see LBR 3007-1].

(B) *Requirement of Written Motion:* In all cases or proceedings, all motions shall be in writing unless made during a hearing or trial. If time does not permit the filing of a written motion, the Court may, in its discretion, waive this requirement.

(C) *Grounds for, relief sought and whether a hearing has been requested to be stated:* All motions, responses, objections, applications (other than for compensation) and similar requests shall state with particularity the grounds therefor and shall set forth the relief or order sought. If a hearing on the motion has been set or requested by the movant, the motion shall so state.

(D) *Number of Copies:* [Repealed]

(E) *Use of Forms:* Forms, including motions and interrogatories, may be used only if all inapplicable references have been deleted and the proponent so certifies.

(F) *Return Date, Conference of Counsel:* Except as otherwise provided by an order of the Court or by the rules, all motions shall be made returnable to the time obtained from and scheduled by the Court for a hearing thereon. In any Division that has a regular motions day practice, the objection may be made returnable to a motions day in compliance with the motions day practice in that Division. Before requesting a hearing date on any motion, the proponent shall confer with opposing counsel, in person or by telephone, in a good-faith effort to narrow the area of disagreement.

(G) *Memorandum of Points and Authorities*

(1) Unless the Court directs otherwise and except as noted below, all motions shall be accompanied by a written memorandum setting forth a concise statement of the facts and supporting reasons, along with a citation of the authorities upon which the movant relies. The memorandum and the motion or response thereto, may be combined in a single pleading.

(2) A memorandum need not accompany a motion or response thereto:

(a) for a more definite statement;

(b) for an extension of time to respond to pleadings, unless the time has already expired;

(c) for a default judgment;

(d) solely related to discovery matters, except as set forth in LBR 7026-1(C), (D) and (I);

(e) for a continuance;

(f) (i) for a voluntary dismissal or conversion under chapters 7, 11, 12 or 13 of title 11, United States Code, or

(ii) that is stipulated to by all parties in interest; or

(g) to avoid a lien pursuant to § 522(f).

(H) *Responses to Motions*

(1) Requirement of written response: Except as otherwise provided by the Bankruptcy Code, the Federal Rules of Bankruptcy Procedure, these Local Bankruptcy Rules, or by order of the Court, responses in opposition to motions must be in writing, state with particularity the grounds therefor, be filed with the Court and served upon all parties affected thereby and the United States trustee.

(2) Requirement of memorandum: Unless otherwise directed by the Court, except as herein above noted, the party filing a response in opposition to a motion shall file therewith a memorandum of points and authorities setting forth a concise statement of the facts and supporting reasons, along with a citation of the authorities upon which the party relies. The memorandum and the motion or response thereto, may be combined in a single pleading.

(3) Time for filing response and memorandum

(a) When no hearing has been set or requested, the opposing party may file a response, with a supporting memorandum, within 14 days, but not thereafter without leave of the Court unless the motion relates to a matter for which a 21-day notice is required under FRBP 2002(a), in which event a response may be filed within 21 days. The movant may file a rebuttal memorandum within 7 days after the filing of the opposing party memorandum. For good cause, a party may be given additional time or may be required to file a response, memorandum and supporting documents within such shorter period of time as the Court may specify.

(b) When a hearing has been set on at least 21 days' notice, the opposing party may file a response, with a supporting memorandum, not later than 7 days before the date of the hearing.

(c) When a hearing has been set on less than 21 days' notice, unless the Court directs otherwise, the opposing party may file a response, with a supporting memorandum, not later than 3 days before the date of the hearing.

(d) When an objection to a claim is filed, the opposing party may file a response, with supporting memorandum, within 30 days of the filing of the objection. If no response is filed, the Court may enter an order without a hearing.

(4) Effect of not timely filing an objection with a supporting memorandum: If a response with a supporting memorandum is not timely filed and served, the Court may deem the opposition waived, treat the motion, application, pleading, or proposed action as conceded, and enter an appropriate order granting the requested relief. If no objection with supporting memorandum is timely filed, the movant shall, within 14 days thereafter, file and serve a proposed order which satisfies the requirements of LBR 9022-1.

(I) *Summary Judgment — Time of Filing:* A party desiring to file a motion for summary judgment must act with reasonable dispatch. No motion for summary judgment will be considered unless filed within a reasonable time prior to the date of trial, thus permitting time for the Court to hear arguments and consider the merits after completion of the schedule specified in this Local Bankruptcy Rule.

(J) *Continuances:* A motion for continuance of a hearing or trial date shall not be granted by mere agreement of counsel. Any such motion will be considered by the Court only in the presence of all counsel, and no continuance will be granted other than for good cause and upon such terms as the Court may impose.

(K) *Extensions:* Any request for an extension of time relating to motions must be in writing and, in general, will be looked upon with disfavor.

(L) *Determination of Motions Without Oral Hearing:* In accordance with FRCP 78, the Court may rule upon motions without an oral hearing, unless otherwise required by the Bankruptcy Code, the Federal Rules of Bankruptcy Procedure, or these Local Bankruptcy Rules.

(M) *Giving Notice of a Motion or Hearing*

(1) When no hearing is requested or required: The notice of any motion where no hearing is required or requested (i.e., a notice of opportunity for a hearing, where a hearing is set only if a response is filed objecting to the requested relief or requesting a hearing), shall contain language substantially in accordance with Official Form 20A, "NOTICE OF MOTION" and setting forth the requirement of a response under subparagraph (H)(3)(a) of this Local Bankruptcy Rule in substantially the following form:

NOTICE

Under Local Bankruptcy Rule 9013-1, unless a written response to this motion and supporting memorandum are filed with the Clerk of Court and served on the moving party within 14 [or 21] days of the service of this notice objecting to the relief requested, the Court may deem any opposition waived, treat the motion [*or application or proposed action*] as conceded, and issue an order granting the requested relief without further notice or hearing.

(2) When a hearing is required or requested: The notice of any motion where a hearing is required or requested shall contain language substantially in accordance with Official Form 20A and setting forth the requirement of a response under subparagraph (H)(3)(b) or (H)(3)(c) in substantially the following form:

NOTICE

Under Local Bankruptcy Rule 9013-1, unless a written response to this motion and supporting memorandum are filed with the Clerk of Court and served on the moving party at least 7 [or 3] days before the scheduled hearing date, the Court may deem any opposition waived, treat the motion [*or application or proposed action*] as conceded, and issue an order granting the requested relief without further notice or hearing.

(3) When a summary judgment is requested against pro se party: The notice of any motion seeking summary judgment in which the non-moving party is *pro se* shall conform substantially to Official Form 20A and, in addition, shall set forth the requirement for a response in substantially the following form:

NOTICE

A motion for summary judgment is a request that one or more issues in a case be decided without holding a trial. Motions for summary judgment are governed by Rule 56, Federal Rules of Civil Procedure. Summary judgment may be granted if (a) the material facts are not genuinely disputed and (b) based on those facts, the party asking for summary judgment is entitled to judgment as a matter of law. If you wish to oppose the motion, you must file with the court and serve on the other party, a written response at least 3 [or 7] days prior to the hearing. **If you fail to file a timely written response to the motion, the court may assume you do not oppose the motion and may grant the motion without holding a hearing.** If you disagree with any of the facts stated by the other party, you must include with your response sworn statements from yourself or other knowlegeable witnesses supporting your version of the facts. A sworn statement may take the form either of an affidavit or a declaration signed under penalty of perjury. Any documents you want the court to consider should be identified in, and attached to, the sworn statements. If you are unable to obtain sworn statements supporting your position, you must file a sworn statement stating why you are unable to obtain such statements at this time.

(N) *Request for Expedited Hearing:* A motion requesting an expedited hearing shall be accompanied by a certification verifying that the proponent:

(1) has carefully examined the matter and concluded that there is a true need for an expedited hearing;

(2) has not created the emergency through any lack of due diligence; and

(3) has made a *bona fide* effort to resolve the matter without hearing.

(O) *Cancellation of Scheduled Hearings:* It is the responsibility of counsel for the plaintiff/movant to advise the Court of any settlement or any other valid reason that a Court scheduled pretrial conference, hearing or trial need not be conducted. Counsel are advised to provide the Court with such notification as far in advance of any such conference, hearing or trial as is practical under the circumstances. Failure of such counsel to properly and timely notify the Court may result in the imposition of sanctions.

COMMENT

9013-1(A) Revision required to conform with the addition of LBR 3007-1.

9013-1(D) Change recommended to add written memorandum to the list of items requiring an additional copy at the time of filing.

9013-1(F) Change recommended to note the procedure to be used in those Divisions where a regular motions day practice is in place.

9013-1(J) Change recommended to the make the provisions for continuances applicable also to hearings.

9013-1(M) These changes note the use of Official Form 20A approved by the Judicial Conference at its September 1997 meeting with the mandatory implementation date of March 1, 1998.

New paragraph (H)(3)(d) sets the time period for filing a response to the filing of an objection to a claim. Paragraph (M) is rewritten to include the language for the notice of opportunity to respond. Paragraph (N) is amended to emphasize the need for a Priority Handling Cover Sheet for requests for expedited hearing. Paragraph (O) is new and includes rules for cancelling scheduled hearings. [Changes effective 1/1/97.]

9013-1(M)(2) The amendment to paragraph (M)(2) is intended to clarify that the written response, as set forth in the Rule's Notice language, must be filed prior to "7 [or 3] days before the scheduled hearing date." [Change effective 07/01/10.]

9013-1(M)(3) The additional requirements with respect to summary judgment motions against *pro se* parties are included to comply with *Roseboro v. Garrison*, 528 F.2d 309 (4th Cir. 1975), and to conform with changes in the Local Rules of Practice of the United States District Court for the Eastern District of Virginia. [Change effective 3/1/01.]

9013-1 Paragraph (N) is amended by removing the reference to a Priority Handling Cover Sheet. The word "emergency" is deleted at paragraph (N)(1) and the word "expedited" is substituted in lieu thereof. [Change effective 12/01/09.]

9013-1 A technical change has been made in paragraph (G)(2). In addition, time-computation adjustments have been made at paragraph (G) to conform to a revision to the Federal Rules of Bankruptcy Procedure that takes effect December 1, 2009. Stylistic changes have been made to the text of the LBR as well. [Changes effective 12/01/09.]

CASE NOTES

Application. — Chapter 13 debtor's motion for an expedited hearing on the debtor's motion for continuation of an automatic stay was denied because counsel for the debtor had not established that the need for the expedited hearing was not caused by a lack of counsel's own due diligence. Counsel for the debtor waited almost three weeks to file the motion for continuation of the stay, even though the stay was set to expire 30 days after the bankruptcy petition was filed, under 11 U.S.C.S. § 362, and if counsel had filed the motion for a continuation when he had filed the petition, the need for an expedited hearing would not have been required. In re Giragosian, 2007 Bankr. LEXIS 4271 (Bankr. E.D. Va. Dec. 14, 2007).

Lender's request that a hearing be set within five days, instead of the minimum 10 days required by Bankr. E.D. Va. R. 9013-1(H)(3)(a), would normally require the motion to be re-noticed, but the court would hear the motion without a re-notice because the debtor had filed a response and the debtor was not prejudiced by shortened notice. In re Atari, 406 B.R. 715, 2008 Bankr. LEXIS 3999 (Bankr. E.D. Va. 2008).

Written response and supporting memorandum required. — By local rule, the U.S. Bankruptcy Court for the Eastern District of Virginia requires a written response with supporting memorandum in order to oppose any motion, Bankr. E.D. Va. R. 9013-1(H)(1), (2), and, in the absence of a timely response and supporting memorandum, the court may deem the opposition waived, treat the motion as conceded, and enter an order granted the requested relief, Bankr. E.D. Va. R. 9013-1(H)(4). The response, therefore, corresponds to an "answer" for the purpose of applying Fed. R. Civ. P. 41 to a contested matter. In re Rowe Furniture, Inc., 2007 Bankr. LEXIS 2959 (Bankr. E.D. Va. Aug. 28, 2007).

Default for failure to file written response not warranted where notice was accidental and not intended by debtors. — Where debtors filed a motion pursuant to 11 U.S.C.S. § 350(b) to reopen their closed case in order to file an amended schedule of assets listing a legal malpractice claim against their former attorneys, and the former attorneys received notice of the motion because they were listed on the docket sheet as counsel for the debtors, the court refused to default them solely because they did not file a written response to the motion as required by Bankr. E.D. Va. R. 9013-1(H), as they were not included on the certificate of service. Further, the former attorneys had standing to object to the motion because they had a concrete stake in the outcome of the motion, the goal of which was to to revive a cause of action against them which currently stood dismissed with prejudice. In re Brooks, 2010 Bankr. LEXIS 1473 (Bankr. E.D. Va. Apr. 27, 2010).

Opposition waived due to failure to file response. — Court declined to enter into the issue of whether debtors could deduct from their current monthly income under 11 U.S.C.S. § 707(b)(2)(A)(iii) contractual payments on debt secured by collateral they intended to surrender. The debtors failed to respond to the trustee's motion to dismiss for abuse of chapter 7, and the court deemed the opposition waived under Bankr. E.D. Va. R. 9013-1(H)(4). In re Louis, 2008 Bankr. LEXIS 1297 (Bankr. E.D. Va. Apr. 16, 2008).

Waiver of requirement. — Form and manner of notice of the commencement of a Chapter 11 bankruptcy case and the meeting of creditors pursuant to 11 U.S.C.S. § 341 was approved because the requested relief was in the best interest of the debtor's estate, its creditors, and other parties in interest. A requirement to file a memorandum of law under Bankr. E.D. Va. R. 9013-1(G) was waived, the terms and conditions of the order were immediately effective and enforceable, and the court retained jurisdiction with respect to all matters arising from or related to the interpretation or implementation of this order. In re Bear Island Paper Co., L.L.C., 2010 Bankr. LEXIS 5777 (Bankr. E.D. Va. Feb. 26, 2010).

Rule 9014-1. Whether Hearing is Evidentiary or Preliminary.

(A) *Discovery in Contested Matters and Relief from Stay Matters:* [Repealed]

(B) *Whether Hearing is Evidentiary or Preliminary:*

(1) Except as provided for in the Bankruptcy Code, the Federal Rules of Bankruptcy Procedure, these Local Bankruptcy Rules or as otherwise ordered by the Court on its own motion or on motion of a party, all parties shall be prepared to present evidence and testimony at any scheduled hearing where the hearing has been set on at least 30 days notice unless the parties agree or the Court orders that evidence and testimony will be presented at any scheduled hearing that is set on less than 30 days' notice.

(2) Notwithstanding paragraph (B)(1), a preliminary hearing on a contested motion for relief from stay shall be non-evidentiary unless the Court orders that evidence and testimony will be presented at any such scheduled preliminary hearing.

COMMENT

This new Local Bankruptcy Rule clarifies how the requirements of F.R.Civ.P. 26, as incorporated by reference in FRBP 7026, apply to contested matters. [New rule effective 12/1/00.]

9014-1 This change reflects the addition of FRBP 7026(a)(2) to LBR 9014-1. [Change effective 7/1/02.]

9014-1(B) This new provision is intended to conform the Court's practice to new FRBP 9014(e) regarding whether a hearing will be evidentiary or preliminary so as to avoid unnecessary expense and inconvenience. [New rule effective 8/1/03.]

9014-1 With the amendment to FRBP 9014(c) that became effective December 1, 2004, paragraph (A) is repealed. [Change effective 10/17/05.]

9014-1 A technical change has been made to the caption at paragraph (A). Stylistic changes have been made to the text of the LBR. [Changes effective 12/01/09.]

9014-1 Paragraph (B) is reorganized with new paragraphs (B)(1) and (B)(2). Paragraph (B)(2) provides that a preliminary hearing on a motion for relief from stay shall be non-evidentiary unless an exception set forth therein otherwise occurs. [Changes effective 09/01/11.]

Rule 9016-1. Subpoenas.

(A) *Request for Subpoena:* Requests for subpoenas shall be in writing and, except as provided in paragraph (G) with respect to a subpoena for a deposition to be taken in a proceeding pending in another jurisdiction, signed by counsel qualified to practice in this Court and noted of record in the action in which the subpoenas are to issue. Attorneys admitted to practice in this Court may also issue and sign a subpoena on behalf of:

(1) a court in which the attorney is authorized to practice or

(2) a court for a district in which a deposition or production is compelled by the subpoena, if the deposition or production pertains to an action pending in a court in which the attorney is authorized to practice.

Individuals appearing *pro se* may apply for subpoenas in their own behalf.

Each request for subpoena shall be accompanied by a subpoena which has been completed except for issuance by the Clerk.

(B) *Return Date of Subpoenas:* All subpoenas shall be made returnable to the place, date and time of trial or hearing unless otherwise ordered by the Court.

(C) *Service of Subpoenas:* Unless the party requesting same is:

(1) authorized to proceed *in forma pauperis* pursuant to 28 U.S.C. § 1915, or is a seaman authorized to proceed under 28 U.S.C. § 1916,

(2) the United States or an officer or agency of the United States or

(3) otherwise ordered by the Court,

all subpoenas shall be served by a person who is not a party or otherwise interested in the proceeding and is not less than 18 years of age. Proof of service by such person shall be made as provided for proof of service for summons and complaint in FRBP 7004(a). The person serving the subpoena shall make proof of service thereof to the Court promptly and in any event within the time during which the person served must respond to the subpoena. Service of a subpoena upon a person named therein shall be made by delivering a copy thereof to such person and by tendering to the party summoned the fee for one day's attendance and the mileage allowed by law. When the subpoena is issued on behalf of the United States or an officer or agency thereof, fees and mileage need not be tendered. Attorneys and individuals appearing *pro se* shall file a proof of service with a certificate that all required witness fees and expenses were tendered with the subpoena requiring the attendance of the witness. Mileage shall be computed and tendered even though the witness to be subpoenaed lives within the city limits. The United States marshal, deputy United States marshal, or any other person serving subpoenas shall do so only in strict compliance with this Local Bankruptcy Rule.

(D) *Subpoenas to Officials:* Without permission of the Court first obtained, no subpoena shall be issued for the attendance at any hearing, trial or deposition of (1) the Governor, Lieutenant Governor, or Attorney General of any State; (2) the Judge of any court; (3) the President or Vice President of the United States; (4) any member of the President's Cabinet; (5) any Ambassador or Consul; (6) any member of the United States Congress; or (7) any military officer holding the rank of Admiral or General.

(E) *Subpoena Duces Tecum:* Whenever a subpoena *duces tecum* has been directed to any person to produce any books, papers, documents or tangible things to any court and to attend and give testimony at the time scheduled for the trial, taking of depositions or other hearing, the person requested therein to produce, or whenever all parties agree, an alternate, shall produce such items to the Clerk on or before 9:00 a.m. on the day designated, unless the Court orders otherwise, to enable counsel to review the same prior to commencement of the trial or the hearing. Provided, however, if a party has good reason not to produce and surrender custody of same to the Clerk, that party shall so advise the Court in writing promptly upon receipt of the subpoena to enable the Court to rule on the objection. Counsel are required to promptly inspect said items so as to enable the trial to proceed promptly.

The provisions hereof are not intended in any way to change or modify the provisions of FRBP 7026 or FRBP 9016 or any other applicable Federal Rule of Bankruptcy Procedure or Federal Rule of Civil Procedure, but to supplement the provisions of FRBP 9016.

(F) *Timely Requests for Subpoenas:* All requests for the issuance of subpoenas for the attendance of witnesses at hearings or trials shall be filed with the Clerk not later than 14 days before the date upon which the witness will be directed to appear. If the request is made within 14 days prior to the date of the trial or hearing, it may be issued by the Clerk but no continuance will be granted if said witness fails to appear even though served.

(G) *Deposition Subpoenas:* Proof of service of a notice to take depositions as provided in FRCP 30(a) and FRCP 31(a) constitutes sufficient authorization for the issuance of a subpoena by the Clerk for the district in which the deposition is to be taken for the attendance of persons named or described therein. The subpoena may command the person to whom it is directed to produce designated books, papers, documents or tangible things which constitute or contain evidence relating to any of the matters within the scope of the examination permitted by FRCP 26(b), but in that event the subpoena will be subject to the provisions FRCP 30(b) and FRCP 45(b). No subpoena for the taking of depositions shall be issued by the Clerk unless there be exhibited to the Clerk a copy of the notice to take deposition together with a statement of the date and manner of service and of the names of the persons served, certified by the person who made service. FRCP 45(d)(1).

(H) *Place of Taking Depositions:* The Clerk shall issue a subpoena upon request, or an attorney may issue a subpoena in accordance with paragraph (A) of this Local Bankruptcy Rule for FRBP 2004 examinations or for taking a deposition requiring the appearance of any party or witness in any city or county within the division of the district wherein the party or witness resides or is employed or transacts business, or in any city contiguous to any such county or city, without prior order of the Court; provided, however, that no such subpoena shall direct any party or witness who may reside in either Accomack or Northampton Counties to appear in any other city or county, nor may any party or witness residing in any other county or city be required to appear in Accomack or Northampton Counties, unless said party or witness is employed or transacts business in the city or county wherein the deposition is to be taken, or unless otherwise ordered by the Court. Contiguous cities or counties shall be considered as such even though separated by water but only when located within the particular division of the district. The right is reserved to any party or witness directed to attend a deposition in any contiguous city to insist that said deposition be taken within the city (or county) provided by the Federal Rules of Civil Procedure upon a showing of inconvenience of travel, or infirmities of body, or age.

(I) *Subpoenas in Blank:* Whenever there is a question as to whether or not a subpoena in blank should be issued by the Clerk, the request shall be referred to a Judge of this Court for a final determination. Before the Clerk may issue a subpoena in blank, the Clerk shall determine the actual pendency of the action and the date and time set for hearing or trial. Except for good cause shown, a subpoena returnable in one division will not be issued out of another division. Blank subpoenas shall recite the title and number of the case and shall be complete in every detail except the name and address of the witness. Returns of service shall be made promptly and filed with the Clerk. All service shall be made strictly in accordance with these Local Bankruptcy Rules.

COMMENT

9016-1 Stylistic changes have been made to the text of the LBR. [Changes effective 12/01/09.]

9016-1 Paragraph (A) is amended to remove the requirement that a check for witness and mileage fees accompanies a request for subpoena. In lieu thereof, a certificate now must accompany the filed proof of service stating that any such required fees had been served with the subpoena. [Change effective 09/03/13.]

9016-1 Paragraph (C) is amended by deleting the provision that exempted a party proceeding *in forma pauperis* from tendering witness and mileage fees. [Change effective 09/03/13.]

Rule 9017-1. Evidence.

(A) *Presence of Witnesses:* Any counsel desiring to ascertain the presence of witnesses summoned for any particular case shall, before the opening of Court, furnish the Clerk with a list of the names of such witnesses.

(B) *Qualifications of Experts:* Unless the qualifications of an expert witness, including any party litigant, are admitted, a duplicate written statement of such qualifications will be submitted on the morning of trial. As to experts who are expected to appear frequently, a statement of their qualifications may be filed with the Clerk in each of the divisions of the Court for use at trial. When so filed, the Clerk will maintain the statement in a file kept for that purpose. Counsel desiring to make use of the statement will be responsible for obtaining the same from the Clerk.

(C) *Hypothetical Questions:* [Repealed]

(D) *Physical Examination of Litigant:* No doctor or other expert will be permitted to testify as to the nature and extent of the injuries to any litigant unless said expert has previously examined or interviewed such person, or unless such testimony is to be based on hypothetical questions. This Local Bankruptcy Rule is not intended to limit an expert, having previously examined the party, from properly demonstrating any of the injuries of a party.

COMMENT

9017(C) This paragraph of LBR 9017-1 is repealed since it was felt that the paragraph no longer is needed. [Change effective 2/1/00.]

9017-1 A stylistic change has been made to paragraph (B) of the LBR. [Change effective 12/01/09.]

Rule 9019-1. Settlement and Alternative Dispute Resolution.

Rule 83.6, Settlement and Alternative Dispute Resolution, Local Rules of Practice of the United States District Court for the Eastern District of Virginia, applies in adversary proceedings before the Court. For purposes of the Settlement and Alternative Dispute Resolution provisions set out at Rule 83.6, references to: the "court" are to the bankruptcy court; "judge" are to bankruptcy judges assigned to the case; and "Chief Judge" are to the Chief Judge of the District Court.

COMMENT

LBR 9019-1 cross references Rule 83.6 of the Local Rules of Practice of the United States District Court for the Eastern District of Virginia, which makes that rule applicable to adversary proceedings in cases before the Court. [New rule effective 3/1/01.]

Rule 9022-1. Court Orders.

(A) *Identification of Attorney Filing Proposed Order:* On the first page of each proposed order filed with the Court, the attorney filing the same shall be identified by name, State Bar number, complete mailing address, telephone number and the name of the party whom the attorney represents.

(B) *Service List:* With each proposed order:

(1) when submitted, as provided for by an electronic means established by the Court, the order proponent shall file a list of parties, with mailing addresses indicated, who are to receive notice of entry of the same and shall comply with all other requirements set forth therein; or

(2) except as the presiding judge in a case otherwise may direct, when submitted by conventional means, the order proponent shall file a list of parties, with mailing addresses indicated, who are to receive notice of entry of the same.

(C) *Endorsement:* With all proposed orders, the proponent shall file either:

(1) Certification of Endorsement by All Parties: A certification that the proposed order or proposed consent order has been endorsed by all necessary parties or

(2) Proof of Service: A certification that the proposed order has been served upon all necessary parties, and indicating upon whom served and the date and manner of such service.

(D) *Form and Content:* Any proposed order shall be sufficient in description to stand alone without reference to any motion, pleading or other document (except for exhibits attached to the order itself). Orders authorizing the sale of real estate or otherwise affecting title to real estate (e.g., abandonments, avoidance of transfers, avoidance or imposition of liens, or adjudication of lien property) shall contain a legal description sufficient to pass title. Orders for sale of property of the estate or any interest therein shall state the identity of the purchaser and the price to be paid unless sale is to be at public auction, in which event the order shall state the date, time, and place of the auction.

(E) *Consent Orders:* All proposed consent orders shall meet the requirements in paragraphs (A), (B), (C) and (D) of this Local Bankruptcy Rule.

(F) *Order After Trial, Hearing or Other Disposition of the Matter:* Unless the Court specifies otherwise, the prevailing party shall, in addition to the requirements in paragraphs (A), (B), (C) and (D) of this Local Bankruptcy Rule, prepare a proposed order and file the same with the Court within 14 days after the conclusion of the trial, hearing, or other disposition of the matter at issue. If no order is filed within the required period, the Clerk may issue a Notice of Failure to Prosecute. If an order is still not filed in response to that notice, the Clerk may dismiss the original pleading or other paper without further notice.

COMMENT

9022-1(C)(1) & 9022-1(E) Minor changes have been made to include new language concerning consent orders.

9022-1(F) This language is added to clearly state the interest in seeing that supposedly resolved items are properly closed out.

Parties need to submit a stamped envelope for panel trustees. [Change effective 1/1/97.]

9022-1(D) Since the need for an order affecting title to real estate to contain a proper legal description is not limited to orders approving sale of real estate or any interest therein, the requirement has been placed at LBR 9022-1. A cross-reference has been added to LBR 6004-1 as well to remind the practitioner of the requirement that orders approving the sale of real estate or any interest therein, like all orders, must stand alone without reference to external documents, e.g., the order should not purport to approve the sale of the real estate or any interest therein "in accordance with the terms of the contract attached to the motion" but should state the essential terms of the sale, e.g., "to John and Joanna Doe for the price of $173,000." [Changes effective 3/1/01.]

9022-1(B) These technical changes are necessary to conform this subdivision of the LBR to the process of filing proposed orders as provided for by an electronic means established by the Court. [Change effective 7/1/02.]

9022-1 Subparagraphs (B)(2)(a) and (b) are repealed in light of Local Bankruptcy Rule 5005-2, which mandates electronic case filings in the Court's Case Management/Electronic Case Files (CM/ECF) System and authorizes the Clerk to promulgate and revise the Court's Electronic Case Files (CM/ECF) Policy. The caption to paragraph (B) is amended for this reason as well. In addition, a time-computation adjustment has been made at paragraph (F) to conform to a revision to the Federal Rules of Bankruptcy Procedure that takes effect December 1, 2009. Stylistic changes have been made to the text of the LBR as well. [Repeal and changes effective 12/01/09.]

Rule 9070-1. Exhibits.

(A) *Numerous Exhibits:* Whenever the exhibits in any case, to be presented by either party, exceed 5, the party intending to offer such exhibits shall place them in a binder, properly tabbed, numbered and indexed, unless otherwise ordered by the Court.

(B) *Listing and Marking Exhibits:* All exhibits, except such as are prepared in open court or by expert witnesses, must be listed in the final pretrial order in any adversary proceeding and shall be marked by the proponent thereof, in the manner specified by the Clerk, prior to the commencement of the trial unless the Court otherwise directs. Such exhibits, unless too large, shall be seen by opposing counsel at or before the final pretrial conference. At any final pretrial conference, the Court may rule upon the admissibility of any exhibit or reserve ruling thereon. Exhibits agreed upon shall be admitted in evidence; all others shall be considered as numbered and marked for identification.

(C) *Number of Copies:* An original and two copies of both the exhibits and the Exhibit List should be filed with the Court by the date set forth in the pretrial order. Sufficient copies should be made available for each opposing counsel.

(D) *Custody and Disposition of Models and Exhibits:*

(1) Custody: After being marked for identification, exhibits of a documentary nature offered or admitted into evidence in any cause pending or tried in this Court shall be placed in the custody of the Clerk unless otherwise ordered by the Court. All other exhibits, model and material not offered and admitted into evidence shall be retained in custody of the attorney or party producing same at trial, unless otherwise directed by the Court.

(2) Removal: Whenever any models, diagrams, exhibits or material have been placed in custody of the Clerk for introduction into evidence, and same are not admitted or marked for identification, such articles shall be removed by the party who filed them with the Clerk, unless otherwise directed by the Court, immediately following the conclusion of the trial or settlement of the case.

(E) *Disposition of Exhibits:* All exhibits, models, diagrams, depositions, transcripts, briefs, tables, charts or other items or material or things, introduced, tendered or marked in the trial of a matter or filed with or delivered to the Clerk in anticipation of their introduction into evidence or for use at trial, shall be withdrawn by the parties to the litigation or their counsel within 30 days after the judgment and the time for appeal or motion for a rehearing or further hearing shall have passed. If such items, material or things are not so removed within the time stated, the Clerk may forward them to counsel or the party entitled thereto, or shall destroy or make such other disposition or use of them as the Clerk may deem appropriate.

COMMENT

9070-1(A) The threshold number of exhibits for binding was reduced from fifteen to five.

9070-1(C) Change to note information already included in the Instructions for Preparing Exhibit List and Pre-Marking Exhibits.

9070-1 Stylistic changes have been made to the text of the LBR. [Changes effective 12/01/09.]

EXHIBITS.

COMMENT

The bankruptcy forms included in the following exhibits are available at the Court's Internet web site http://www.vaeb.uscourts.gov and can be accessed by clicking the "Bankruptcy Forms" button on the Court's Internet home page. The forms are in Adobe Acrobat format.

Exhibit 1. Chapter 13 Plan and Related Motions.

EXHIBIT 1

UNITED STATES BANKRUPTCY COURT
_____________ DISTRICT OF VIRGINIA
_________________ Division

CHAPTER 13 PLAN
AND RELATED MOTIONS

Name of Debtor(s): Case No:

This Plan, dated ____________________, is:

☐ the *first* Chapter 13 Plan filed in this case.

☐ a modified Plan that replaces the

☐ confirmed or ☐ unconfirmed Plan dated __________________

Date and Time of Modified Plan Confirmation Hearing:
____

Place of Modified Plan Confirmation Hearing:
____

The Plan provisions modified by this filing are:

Creditors affected by this modification are:

NOTICE: YOUR RIGHTS WILL BE AFFECTED. You should read these papers carefully. If you oppose any provision of this Plan, or if you oppose any included motions to (i) value collateral, (ii) avoid liens, or (iii) assume or reject unexpired leases or executory contracts, you MUST file a timely written objection.

This Plan may be confirmed and become binding, <u>and the included motions in paragraphs 3, 6, and 7 to value collateral, avoid liens, and assume or reject unexpired leases or executory contracts may be granted</u>, without further notice or hearing unless a written objection is filed not later than seven (7) days prior to the date set for the confirmation hearing and the objecting party appears at the confirmation hearing.

EXHIBIT 1

The debtor(s)' schedules list assets and liabilities as follows:

Total Assets:
Total Non-Priority Unsecured Debt:
Total Priority Debt:
Total Secured Debt:

1. **Funding of Plan.** The debtor(s) propose to pay the Trustee the sum of $____________ per __________ for ____ months. Other payments to the Trustee are as follows: ____. The total amount to be paid into the Plan is $________________.

2. **Priority Creditors.** The Trustee shall pay allowed priority claims in full unless the creditor agrees otherwise.

   A. **Administrative Claims under 11 U.S.C. § 1326.**

      1. The Trustee will be paid the percentage fee fixed under 28 U.S.C. § 586(e), not to exceed 10%, of all sums disbursed except for funds returned to the debtor(s).
      2. Debtor(s)' attorney will be paid $______________ balance due of the total fee of $______________ concurrently with or prior to the payments to remaining creditors.

   B. **Claims under 11 U.S.C. § 507.**

   The following priority creditors will be paid by deferred cash payments pro rata with other priority creditors or in monthly installments as below, except that allowed claims pursuant to 11 U.S.C. § 507(a)(1) will be paid prior to other priority creditors but concurrently with administrative claims above:

Creditor	Type of Priority	Estimated Claim	Payment and Term

3. **Secured Creditors: Motions to Value Collateral ("cramdown"), Collateral being Surrendered, Adequate Protection Payments, and Payment of certain Secured Claims.**

   A. **Motions to Value Collateral (other than claims protected from "cramdown" by 11 U.S.C. § 1322(b)(2) or by the final paragraph of 11 U.S.C. § 1325(a)). Unless a written objection is timely filed with the Court, the Court may grant the debtor(s)' motion to value collateral as set forth herein.**

This section deals with valuation of certain claims secured by real and/or personal property, other than claims protected from "cramdown" by 11 U.S.C. § 1322(b)(2) [real estate which is debtor(s)' principal residence] or by the final paragraph of 11 U.S.C. § 1325(a) [motor vehicles purchased within 910 days or any other thing of value purchased within 1 year before filing bankruptcy], in which the replacement value is asserted to be less than the amount owing on the debt. **Such debts will be treated as secured claims only to the extent of the replacement value of the collateral. That value will be paid with interest as provided in sub-section D of this section. You must refer to section 3(D) below to determine the interest rate, monthly payment and estimated term of repayment of any "crammed down" loan. The deficiency balance owed on such a loan will be treated as an unsecured claim to be paid only to the extent provided in section 4 of the Plan.** The following secured claims are to be "crammed down" to the following values:

EXHIBIT 1

Creditor	Collateral	Purchase Date	Est. Debt Bal.	Replacement Value

B. Real or Personal Property to be Surrendered.

Upon confirmation of the Plan, or before, the debtor(s) will surrender his/her/their interest in the collateral securing the claims of the following creditors in satisfaction of the secured portion of such creditors' allowed claims. To the extent that the collateral does not satisfy the claim, any timely filed deficiency claim to which the creditor is entitled may be paid as a non-priority unsecured claim. Confirmation of the Plan shall terminate the automatic stay as to the interest of the debtor(s) and the estate in the collateral.

Creditor	Collateral Description	Estimated Value	Estimated Total Claim

C. Adequate Protection Payments.

The debtor(s) propose to make adequate protection payments required by 11 U.S.C. § 1326(a) or otherwise upon claims secured by personal property, until the commencement of payments provided for in sections 3(D) and/or 6(B) of the Plan, as follows:

Creditor	Collateral	Adeq. Protection Monthly Payment	To Be Paid By

Any adequate protection payment upon an unexpired lease of personal property assumed by the debtor(s) pursuant to section 6(B) of the Plan shall be made by the debtor(s) as required by 11 U.S.C. § 1326(a)(1)(B) (payments coming due after the order for relief).

D. Payment of Secured Claims on Property Being Retained (except only those loans provided for in section 5 of the Plan):

This section deals with payment of debts secured by real and/or personal property [including short term obligations, judgments, tax liens and other secured debts]. After confirmation of the Plan, the Trustee will pay to the holder of each allowed secured claim, which will be either the balance owed on the indebtedness or, where applicable, the collateral's replacement value as specified in sub-section A of this section, **whichever is less,** with interest at the rate provided below, the monthly payment specified below until the amount of the secured claim has been paid in full. **Upon confirmation of the Plan, the valuation and interest rate shown below will be binding unless a timely written objection to confirmation is filed with and sustained by the Court.**

Creditor	Collateral	Approx. Bal. of Debt or "Crammed Down" Value	Interest Rate	Monthly Payment & Est. Term

EXHIBIT 1

E. Other Debts.

Debts which are (i) mortgage loans secured by real estate which is the debtor(s)' primary residence, or (ii) other long term obligations, whether secured or unsecured, to be continued upon the existing contract terms with any existing default in payments to be cured pursuant to 11 U.S.C. § 1322(b)(5), are provided for in section 5 of the Plan.

4. Unsecured Claims.

A. Not separately classified. Allowed non-priority unsecured claims shall be paid pro rata from any distribution remaining after disbursement to allowed secured and priority claims. Estimated distribution is approximately _____ %. The dividend percentage may vary depending on actual claims filed. If this case were liquidated under Chapter 7, the debtor(s) estimate that unsecured creditors would receive a dividend of approximately _____ %.

B. Separately classified unsecured claims.

Creditor	Basis for Classification	Treatment

5. Mortgage Loans Secured by Real Property Constituting the Debtor(s)' Primary Residence; Other Long Term Payment Obligations, whether secured or unsecured, to be continued upon existing contract terms; Curing of any existing default under 11 U.S.C. § 1322(b)(5).

A. Debtor(s) to make regular contract payments; arrears, if any, to be paid by Trustee. The creditors listed below will be paid by the debtor(s) pursuant to the contract without modification, except that arrearages, if any, will be paid by the Trustee either pro rata with other secured claims or on a fixed monthly basis as indicated below, without interest unless an interest rate is designated below for interest to be paid on the arrearage claim and such interest is provided for in the loan agreement.

Creditor	Collateral	Regular Contract Payment	Estimated Arrearage	Arrearage Interest Rate	Estimated Cure Period	Monthly Arrearage Payment

B. Trustee to make contract payments and cure arrears, if any. The Trustee shall pay the creditors listed below the regular contract monthly payments that come due during the period of this Plan, and pre-petition arrearages on such debts shall be cured by the Trustee either pro rata with other secured claims or with monthly payments as set forth below.

Creditor	Collateral	Regular Contract Payment	Estimated Arrearage	Interest Rate on Arrearage	Monthly Payment on Arrearage & Est. Term

EXHIBIT 1

C. **Restructured Mortgage Loans to be paid fully during term of Plan**. Any mortgage loan against real estate constituting the debtor(s)' principal residence upon which the last scheduled contract payment is due before the final payment under the Plan is due shall be paid by the Trustee during the term of the Plan as permitted by 11 U.S.C. § 1322(c)(2) with interest at the rate specified below as follows:

Creditor	Collateral	Interest Rate	Estimated Claim	Monthly Payment & Term

6. **Unexpired Leases and Executory Contracts.** The debtor(s) move for assumption or rejection of the executory contracts and leases listed below.

A. **Executory contracts and unexpired leases to be rejected.** The debtor(s) reject the following executory contracts:

Creditor	Type of Contract

B. **Executory contracts and unexpired leases to be assumed.** The debtor(s) assume the following executory contracts. The debtor(s) agree to abide by all terms of the agreement. The Trustee will pay the pre-petition arrearages, if any, through payments made pro rata with other priority claims or on a fixed monthly basis as indicated below.

Creditor	Type of Contract	Arrearage	Monthly Payment for Arrears	Estimated Cure Period

7. **Liens Which Debtor(s) Seek to Avoid.**

A. **The debtor(s) move to avoid liens pursuant to 11 U.S.C. § 522(f).** The debtor(s) move to avoid the following judicial liens and non-possessory, non-purchase money liens that impair the debtor(s)' exemptions. **Unless a written objection is timely filed with the Court, the Court may grant the debtor(s)' motion and cancel the creditor's lien.** If an objection is filed, the Court will hear evidence and rule on the motion at the confirmation hearing.

Creditor	Collateral	Exemption Basis	Exemption Amount	Value of Collateral

B. **Avoidance of security interests or liens on grounds other than 11 U.S.C. § 522(f).** The debtor(s) have filed or will file and serve separate pleadings to avoid the following liens or security interests. The creditor should review the notice or summons

Exhibit 2. Special Notice to Secured Creditor.

UNITED STATES BANKRUPTCY COURT
__________________ DISTRICT OF VIRGINIA
__________________ Division

In re:

Case No. __________________

Chapter 13

Debtor(s)

SPECIAL NOTICE TO SECURED CREDITOR

To: ______________________________, Attn: ______________
Name of creditor

____
Description of collateral

1. The attached chapter 13 plan filed by the debtor(s) proposes (*check one)*:

[ ] To value your collateral. ***See Section 3 of the plan.*** Your lien will be limited to the value of the collateral, and any amount you are owed above the value of the collateral will be treated as an unsecured claim.

[ ] To cancel or reduce a judgment lien or a non-purchase money, non-possessory security interest you hold. ***See Section 7 of the plan.*** All or a portion of the amount you are owed will be treated as an unsecured claim.

2. ***You should read the attached plan carefully for the details of how your claim is treated.*** The plan may be confirmed, and the proposed relief granted, unless you file and serve a written objection by the date specified and appear at the confirmation hearing. A copy of the objection must be served on the debtor(s), their attorney, and the chapter 13 trustee.

Date objection due: __________________
Date and time of confirmation hearing: __________________
Place of confirmation hearing: __________________

____
Name(s) of debtor(s)

By: __________________
Signature

[ ] Debtor(s)' Attorney
[ ] Pro se debtor

____
Name of attorney for debtor(s)

____
Address of attorney [or pro se debtor]

____

Tel. # ______________________

Fax # ______________________

CERTIFICATE OF SERVICE

I hereby certify that true copies of the foregoing Notice and attached Chapter 13 Plan and Related Motions were served upon the creditor noted above by

(   ) first class mail in conformity with the requirements of Rule 7004(b), Fed.R.Bankr.P; or

(   ) certified mail in conformity with the requirements of Rule 7004(h), Fed.R.Bankr.P

on this ______day of _______________, 200_.

____
Signature of attorney for debtor(s)

Ver. 06/17/05

Exhibit 3. Order Adopting CM/ECF Procedures.

[Rescinded effective March 17, 2008.]

Exhibit 4. Administrative Procedures for CM/ECF Cases.

[Rescinded effective March 17, 2008.]

Exhibit 5. Instructions for Creditor Matrix Diskette.

Last Revised: December 1, 2009

The following instructions are applicable to all word processing software and third-party bankruptcy software packages:

1. Open your word processing software and enter the creditor information, making sure of the following:

a. Creditors are listed in a single column.

b. There are two blank spaces separating each creditor.

c. The second line of each creditor listed must be either a street address or a P.O. Box, with the periods included (e.g., 200 South Main Street or P.O. Box 241).

d. The last line of each creditor must be in the format of City, State (two-letter abbreviation), Zip (e.g., Alexandria, VA 22314).

e. No Account numbers may be included within the creditor information.

2. Choose the 'Save As' function in your word processing software. In earlier versions of WordPerfect, this is known as 'Text In/Out'. In most software packages, there will be a box that will indicate the format of the document (e.g. Word 5.0 format, WordPerfect 5.1). This box usually is located just below where the name of the file is entered. The format for all diskettes should be one of the following (depending on your software): ASCII DOS Text, Plain DOS Text or Text Only. These are the only formats that will be accepted. When you have selected the correct format, save the file.

Exhibit 6. Financial Interest Disclosure Statement.

UNITED STATES BANKRUPTCY COURT
EASTERN DISTRICT OF VIRGINIA
__________________ Division

In re:

Debtor(s) Case No.

Plaintiff(s) Chapter

v.

Defendant(s) Adversary No.

FINANCIAL INTEREST DISCLOSURE STATEMENT

Pursuant to Federal Rule of Bankruptcy Procedure 7007.1 and to enable the Judges to evaluate possible disqualification or recusal, the undersigned counsel for

____

____

in the above captioned action, certifies that the following is a (are) corporation(s), other than the debtor or a governmental unit, that directly or indirectly own(s) 10% or more of any class of the corporation's(s') equity interests, or states that there are no entities to report under FRBP 7007.1:

____

____

☐ None [Check if applicable]

____

Date

____

Signature of Attorney or Litigant
Counsel for __________________

Exhibit 7. Motions Day Procedure for Alexandria Division.

Note: The following procedure is applicable only in the Alexandria Division of the United States Bankruptcy Court for the Eastern District of Virginia, and only with respect to motions, other than relief from stay motions, that can be heard in 30 minutes or less. In the Norfolk, Newport News, and Richmond Divisions, hearing dates for motions must in all instances be obtained from the Court in accordance with Local Bankruptcy Rule 9013-1(F).

MOTIONS DATES

* Motions dates for each judge will be posted in the Clerk's office up to 3 months in advance but should be verified by counsel or an unrepresented party prior to sending out notice in order to ensure that the date remains available. ***A judge may require that specified types of matters be returnable to a specified time on a motions day, and counsel or parties setting matters for hearing are responsible for making the motion returnable to the correct time.*** The motion must be set on the motions day for the judge assigned to the case and may not be set on the calendar of another judge except with the express authorization of the assigned judge. If for any reason a problem arises with a hearing date after the date has been posted, the Clerk will notify counsel with a new date, and the attorney or party filing the motion will be responsible for re-noticing the matter

* Motions dates may be used for motions, objections and applications that will take less than one-half hour to hear. There will be at least 1 such day a month. The following matters may **not** be set on a motions day unless specifically authorized by the Court: matters that will take over one-half hour, motions for relief from the automatic stay, confirmation hearings, pretrial conferences and expedited or emergency hearings.

* ***If a judge has a separate Chapter 13 docket, all motions, objections, and applications arising in a Chapter 13 case must be set on that docket and not on the general motions docket.*** Objections to confirmation of the **original** plan filed in a Chapter 13 case **must** be noticed for the date and time of the confirmation hearing as set forth in the 341 notice or separate notice of confirmation hearing given by the Clerk. Objections to confirmation of a modified Chapter 13 plan may be set on any Chapter 13 motions day that provides proper notice.

* The notice of hearing, motion, objection or application must be filed with the Court, ***in an original and one copy,*** together with an orange motions day cover sheet no later than **14 days** prior to the hearing date. The notice of hearing and the motion, objection or application must be served upon all parties entitled to notice in accordance with the Federal Rules of Bankruptcy Procedure and the Local Bankruptcy Rules. If such rules do not specify a time period for service, then service must be made no later than 14 days prior to the hearing. There will be **no** exceptions unless shorter notice has been specifically authorized by the judge to whom the matter is assigned. Any matter not timely noticed will **not** be set on the calendar but will be reassigned by the Clerk to the next available date that complies with the applicable notice requirement, and the counsel or party bringing the matter will be responsible for re-noticing it.

* Motions to be heard on a motions day must be filed, together with a notice of hearing, in an original and one copy. The copy must be attached to an orange notice of hearing cover sheet (available from the Clerk's office). The copy attached to the orange cover sheet need not contain supporting memoranda or exhibits. ***The orange cover sheet is not a substitute for any required notice of hearing.*** The orange cover sheet will alert the intake deputy to deliver the motion and notice of hearing to the courtroom deputy. ***If a copy of the motion and notice is not filed with an orange cover sheet, the matter will not be placed on the motions docket and will have to be reset.***

MOTIONS REQUIRING MORE THAN ONE-HALF HOUR

* For those matters that will take over one-half hour, the counsel or party bringing the motion, objection or application must request a hearing date from the Clerk and must certify to the Court the moving party's estimate of the time required to hear the matter. A certification of time estimate cover sheet is obtainable from the Clerk's office and is the preferred form for requesting a hearing date.

* If a matter is set for a motions day on the good faith belief that it will take less than one-half hour, but it subsequently becomes apparent that the matter will take more than one-half hour, counsel may request a date and time from the Clerk for hearing the matter, provided notice of the rescheduled hearing can be and is given to all affected parties at least **14 days** prior to the scheduled hearing. Otherwise, the moving party or counsel will be required to appear in Court to schedule the matter for final hearing.

CONSENT ORDERS

* A courtroom deputy will be available to take all **fully-endorsed** consent orders and stipulations, including consent orders for a continuance to another scheduled motions day, between 8:45 and 9:15 a.m. on the day that the hearing is scheduled. An order will **not** be treated as a "consent" order merely because no opposition has been filed to the motion, objection, or application.

* **If counsel or an unrepresented party, in lieu of personally presenting a consent order to the courtroom deputy, transmits the order by messenger or mail, or presents it at the intake counter, the counsel or party tendering the order is responsible for verifying with the courtroom deputy that she or he has received it.** Any consent order submitted within 2 days of a hearing **must** be accompanied by a yellow expedited handling cover sheet. Failure to comply with these requirements with respect to an order not personally presented to the courtroom deputy on the morning of the hearing may, in the Court's discretion, result in the motion, objection, or application being dismissed for failure to prosecute.

* Any consent order continuing a relief from stay hearing must contain language continuing the automatic stay in full force and effect pending a ruling by the Court at such continued hearing. Additionally, if a consent order in a relief from stay motion grants relief from the stay, and such order has not been noticed under Bankruptcy Rule 4001(d), a certification must be attached stating either that the order provides no greater or different relief than requested in the motion or that Bankruptcy Rule 4001(d) does not require notice.

COUNSEL HAVING MATTERS BEFORE MORE THAN ONE JUDGE

* Counsel or an unrepresented party having matters before more than one judge on a motions day **must advise the courtroom deputy that the counsel or party is in another courtroom and must provide an estimated time when such counsel or party will be available.** If counsel or a party is in another courtroom when a particular matter is called, and has **not** checked in, the Court may summarily dismiss or dispose of the matter or may hold the offending counsel or party in contempt.

Exhibit 8. Order Adopting Revision to Interim Rule 1007-I.

UNITED STATES BANKRUPTCY COURT
EASTERN DISTRICT OF VIRGINIA

In re	)	
	)	
Adoption of Revision	)	Standing Order No. 11-5
to Interim Rule 1007-I	)	
	)	

ORDER ADOPTING REVISION TO INTERIM RULE 1007-I

On October 20, 2008, the National Guard and Reservists Debt Relief Act of 2008 (2008 Act) was enacted into law; and

The provisions of the Act became effective December 19, 2008; and

The Advisory Committee on Bankruptcy Rules prepared a new Interim Rule 1007-I, Lists, Schedules, and Other Documents; Time Limits; Expiration of Temporary Means Testing Exclusion in addition to an amendment to Official Form 22A, Statement of Current Monthly Income and Means Test Calculation creating a then new Part 1C therein.

The Committee on Rules of Practice and Procedure of the Judicial Conference of the United States approved the new Interim Rule and form amendment and recommended the adoption of both by the Judicial Conference of the United States to provide for uniform procedures and means by which to implement the Act; and

The Judicial Conference of the United States, which had approved both recommendations, transmitted the Interim Rule to the courts for adoption by standing order, effective December 19, 2008; and

The Court adopted Interim Rule 1007-I, in its entirety without change, effective December 19, 2008.

Interim Rule 1007-I previously was revised, effective December 1, 2009, to conform to time deadline changes in Federal Rule of Bankruptcy Procedure 1007 (Rule 1007), as follows: the 10-day period in Rule 1007(h) and the 15-day periods in subdivisions (a)(2), (a)(3), (c), (f) of the rule all became 14-day periods, as part of a comprehensive package of changes to time periods in all federal rules of practice and procedure; and

Interim Rule 1007-I further was revised, effective December 1, 2010, to conform to a deadline change in Rule 1007(c), as follows: the time for the individual debtor to file the statement of completion of a course in personal financial management in a chapter 7 case is extended from within 45 days after the first date set for the meeting of creditors to within 60 days after the first date set for the meeting of creditors.

It is necessary to make further revision to Interim Rule 1007-I, effective December 19, 2011, to conform to an amendment effected by the National Guard and Reservist Debt Relief Extension Act of 2011 (2011 Act), which extends the 2008 Act's original three-year period to a seven-year period commencing December 19, 2008.

NOW, THEREFORE, IT IS ORDERED that:

Pursuant to 28 U.S.C. section 2071, Rule 83 of the Federal Rules of Civil Procedure and Rule 9029 of the Federal Rules of Bankruptcy Procedure, the attached revised Interim Rule 1007-I is adopted by the chief judge of the Court, effective December 19, 2011, conforming to the 2008 Act and 2011 Act. For cases and proceedings not governed by the 2008 Act, as amended by the 2011 Act, the Federal Rules of Bankruptcy Procedure and the Local Rules of this Court, other than Interim Rule 1007-I, as further revised, shall apply. The 2008 Act, as amended by the 2011 Act, applies only to cases commenced in the seven-year period beginning on the effective date of the 2008 Act, December 19, 2008. Interim Rule 1007-I, as further revised, shall remain in effect until further order of the Court.

Dated: December 19, 2011

FOR THE COURT:

DOUGLAS O. TICE JR.
Chief United States Bankruptcy Judge

EXHIBIT 8

Interim Rule 1007-I[1]. Lists, Schedules, Statements, and Other Documents; Time Limits; Expiration of Temporary Means Testing Exclusion[2]

* * * * *

(b) SCHEDULES, STATEMENTS, AND OTHER DOCUMENTS REQUIRED.

* * * * *

(4) Unless either: (A) § 707(b)(2)(D)(i) applies, or (B) § 707(b)(2)(D)(ii) applies and the exclusion from means testing granted therein extends beyond the period specified by Rule 1017(e),

an individual debtor in a chapter 7 case shall file a statement of current monthly income prepared as prescribed by the appropriate Official Form, and, if the current monthly income exceeds the median family income for the applicable state and household size, the information, including calculations, required by § 707(b), prepared as prescribed by the appropriate Official Form.

* * * * *

(c) TIME LIMITS. In a voluntary case, the schedules, statements, and other documents required by subdivision (b)(1), (4), (5), and (6) shall be filed with the petition or within 14 days thereafter, except as otherwise provided in subdivisions (d), (e), (f), (h), and (n) of this rule. In an involuntary case, the list in subdivision

---

[1] Interim Rule 1007-I was adopted by the bankruptcy courts to implement the National Guard and Reservists Debt Relief Act of 2008, Public Law No: 110-438~~.~~, as amended by the National Guard and Reservist Debt Relief Extension Act of 2011, Public Law No. 112-64. The Act, as amended, ~~which~~ provides a temporary exclusion from the application of the means test for certain members of the National Guard and reserve components of the Armed Forces~~,~~. It applies to bankruptcy cases commenced in the ~~three~~ seven-year period beginning December 19, 2008.

[2] Incorporates (1) time amendments to Rule 1007 which took effect on December 1, 2009, and (2) an amendment, effective December 1, 2010, which extended the time to file the statement of completion of a course in personal financial management in a chapter 7 case filed by an individual debtor.

(a)(2), and the schedules, statements, and other documents required by subdivision (b)(1) shall be filed by the debtor within 14 days of the entry of the order for relief. In a voluntary case, the documents required by paragraphs (A), (C), and (D) of subdivision (b)(3) shall be filed with the petition. Unless the court orders otherwise, a debtor who has filed a statement under subdivision (b)(3)(B), shall file the documents required by subdivision (b)(3)(A) within 14 days of the order for relief. In a chapter 7 case, the debtor shall file the statement required by subdivision (b)(7) within 60 days after the first date set for the meeting of creditors under § 341 of the Code, and in a chapter 11 or 13 case no later than the date when the last payment was made by the debtor as required by the plan or the filing of a motion for a discharge under § 1141(d)(5)(B) or § 1328(b) of the Code. The court may, at any time and in its discretion, enlarge the time to file the statement required by subdivision (b)(7). The debtor shall file the statement required by subdivision (b)(8) no earlier than the date of the last payment made under the plan or the date of the filing of motion for a discharge under §§ 1141(d)(5)(B), 1228(b), or 1328(b) of the Code. Lists, schedules, statements, and other documents filed prior to the conversion of a case to another chapter shall be deemed filed in the converted case unless the court directs otherwise. Except as provided in § 1116(3), any extension of time to file schedules, statements, and other documents required under this rule may be granted only on motion for cause shown and on notice to the United States trustee, any committee elected under § 705 or appointed under § 1102 of the Code, trustee, examiner, or other party as the court may direct. Notice of an extension shall be given to the United States trustee and to any committee, trustee, or other party as the

EXHIBIT 8

court may direct.

* * * * *

(n) TIME LIMITS FOR, AND NOTICE TO, DEBTORS TEMPORARILY EXCLUDED FROM MEANS TESTING.

(1) An individual debtor who is temporarily excluded from means testing pursuant to § 707(b)(2)(D)(ii) of the Code shall file any statement and calculations required by subdivision (b)(4) no later than 14 days after the expiration of the temporary exclusion if the expiration occurs within the time specified by Rule 1017(e) for filing a motion pursuant to § 707(b)(2).

(2) If the temporary exclusion from means testing under § 707(b)(2)(D)(ii) terminates due to the circumstances specified in subdivision (n)(1), and if the debtor has not previously filed a statement and calculations required by subdivision (b)(4), the clerk shall promptly notify the debtor that the required statement and calculations must be filed within the time specified by subdivision (n)(1).

Index to U.S. Bankruptcy Court Rules of the Eastern District of Virginia

A

ABANDONMENT OF PROPERTY.
Notice, USBank-ED Rule 6007-1.
Orders.
Order of court directing abandonment, USBank-ED Rule 6007-1.

ADVERSARY PROCEEDING COVER SHEET, USBank-ED Rule 7003-1.

ADVERTISEMENTS.
Newspapers.
Notices requiring advertisements, USBank-ED Rule 2002-1.

ALEXANDRIA DIVISION.
Motions day procedures, USBank-ED Exhibit 7.

ALTERNATIVE DISPUTE RESOLUTION, USBank-ED Rule 9019-1.

AMENDMENTS.
Petitions.
Voluntary petition.
Amendments by debtor, USBank-ED Rule 1009-1.

APPEALS.
Bonds, surety, USBank-ED Rule 8005-1.
Clerk of court.
Rejection of filing by clerk.
Judicial review, USBank-ED Rule 5005-1.

ATTORNEYS AT LAW.
Admission to practice before court.
Application, USBank-ED Rule 2090-1.
Presentation in court, USBank-ED Rule 2090-1.
Procedure, USBank-ED Rule 2090-1.
Qualifications, USBank-ED Rule 2090-1.
Bar of court, USBank-ED Rule 2090-1.
Conflicts of interest.
Authorization of employment, USBank-ED Rule 2014-1.
Consultation among counsel, USBank-ED Rule 7026-1.
Courtroom decorum, USBank-ED Rule 2090-1.
Ethics, USBank-ED Rule 2090-1.
Fees, USBank-ED Rule 2016-1.
Law students.
Third-year practice, USBank-ED Rule 2090-1.
Motions.
Certification of attorney, USBank-ED Rule 9013-1.
Conflicts of interest, motion authorizing employment, USBank-ED Rule 2014-1.
Practice before court, USBank-ED Rule 2090-1.
Law students.
Third-year law students, USBank-ED Rule 2090-1.
Previous practice clause, USBank-ED Rule 2090-1.
Representation and appearances, USBank-ED Rule 9010-1.

ATTORNEYS IN FACT.
Representation and appearances, USBank-ED Rule 9010-1.

B

BAR OF COURT, USBank-ED Rule 2090-1.
Previous practice clause, USBank-ED Rule 2090-1.

BONDS, SURETY.
Appeal bond, USBank-ED Rule 8005-1.
Costs, USBank-ED Rule 7054-1.

BROADCASTING.
Courtrooms and environs, USBank-ED Rule 5073-1.

C

CASE MANAGEMENT/ELECTRONIC FILING PROCEDURES.
Administrative procedures, USBank-ED Exhibit 4.
Order adopting, USBank-ED Exhibit 3.

CHAPTER 7 CASES.
Conversion of case from Chapter 7 to Chapter 13.
Notice and motion, USBank-ED Rule 1017-3.
Statement of individual Chapter 7 debtor with consumer debts secured by property of estate.
Dismissal of actions.
Statement not timely filed, USBank-ED Rule 1007-3.
Reconsideration of dismissal, USBank-ED Rule 1007-3.
Motions.
Extension of time for filing, USBank-ED Rule 1007-3.
Notice.
Dismissal if statement not timely filed.
Notice of possible dismissal, USBank-ED Rule 1007-3.
Orders.
Extension of time for filing, USBank-ED Rule 1007-3.
Time for filing.
Dismissal if statement not timely filed, USBank-ED Rule 1007-3.
Extension of time, USBank-ED Rule 1007-3.

CHAPTER 11 CASES.
Plan.
Objections to confirmation, USBank-ED Rule 3016-1.

CHAPTER 12 CASES.
Dismissal of case.
Plan not timely filed, USBank-ED Rule 3015-1.
Payment to creditors by trustee, USBank-ED Rule 3070-1.

CHAPTER 12 CASES —Cont'd
Plan.
Filing, USBank-ED Rule 3015-1.
Time.
Plan.
Filing, USBank-ED Rule 3015-1.

CHAPTER 13 CASES.
Certification of compliance, USBank-ED Rule 4008-2.
Conversion of case from Chapter 7 to Chapter 13.
Notice and motion, USBank-ED Rule 1017-3.
Discharge and certification of compliance, USBank-ED Rule 4008-2.
Dismissal of case.
Plan not timely filed, USBank-ED Rule 3015-2.
Notice of possible dismissal, USBank-ED Rule 3015-2.
Reconsideration of dismissal, USBank-ED Rule 3015-2.
Mortgage loan modification after confirmation, USBank-ED Rule 6004-4.
Motions.
Plan, USBank-ED Exhibit 1.
Extension of time for filing, USBank-ED Rule 3015-2.
Inclusion of related motions, USBank-ED Rule 3015-2.
Notice.
Dismissal of case.
Plan not timely filed.
Notice of possible dismissal, USBank-ED Rule 3015-2.
Secured creditors whose collateral is to be valued or lien avoided, USBank-ED Rule 3015-2.
Objections to original plan, USBank-ED Rule 3015-2.
Orders.
Plan.
Extension of time for filing, USBank-ED Rule 3015-2.
Payments to creditors by trustee, USBank-ED Rule 3070-1.
Payments to trustee by debtor, USBank-ED Rule 3070-1.
Personal financial management, instructional course.
Debtor's statement of completion.
Filing, USBank-ED Rule 1007-1.
Plan.
Certification of compliance, USBank-ED Rule 4008-2.
Confirmation, USBank-ED Rule 3015-2.
Objections, USBank-ED Rule 3016-1.
Debtor's duty to cooperate with trustee upon completion of plan, USBank-ED Rule 4008-2.
Dismissal of case for defects in, USBank-ED Rule 3015-2.
Distribution, USBank-ED Rule 3015-2.
Filing, USBank-ED Rule 3015-2.
Form, USBank-ED Exhibit 1, USBank-ED Rule 3015-2.
Modified plan and related motions, USBank-ED Rule 3015-2.
Notice, USBank-ED Exhibit 2, USBank-ED Rule 3015-2.

CHAPTER 13 CASES —Cont'd
Plan —Cont'd
Objections to confirmation, USBank-ED Rule 3016-1.
Service, USBank-ED Rule 3015-2.
Reconversion of case, USBank-ED Rule 3015-2.
Sale or refinance of property after confirmation, USBank-ED Rule 6004-3.
Time.
Plan.
Filing, USBank-ED Rule 3015-2.

CLERK OF COURT.
Actions of clerk authorized by court, USBank-ED Rule 5005-1.
Motions.
Rejection of motions by clerk, USBank-ED Rule 5005-1.
Notice of deficient filing, USBank-ED Rule 5005-1.
Petitions.
Rejection by clerk, USBank-ED Rule 5005-1.
Rejection of filings by clerk, USBank-ED Rule 5005-1.

CM/ECF.
Administrative procedures, USBank-ED Exhibit 4.
Order adopting, USBank-ED Exhibit 3.

CONFLICTS OF INTEREST.
Attorneys at law, authorization of employment, USBank-ED Rule 2014-1.

COPIES.
Exhibits.
Number of copies, USBank-ED Rule 9070-1.
Objections to claims.
Number of copies, USBank-ED Rule 3007-1.
United States trustee.
Alternative service of documents by electronic means, USBank-ED Rule 2002-1.
Filing of copies of documents for transmittal to, USBank-ED Rule 2002-1.

COSTS.
Advance payment, USBank-ED Rule 7054-1.
Bonds, surety, USBank-ED Rule 7054-1.
Depositions, USBank-ED Rule 7030-1.
Taxation of costs, USBank-ED Rule 7054-1.

CREDITORS.
List of creditors, USBank-ED Rule 1007-1.
Creditor matrix diskette, instructions, USBank-ED Exhibit 5.
Inspection, USBank-ED Rule 2002-1.

D

DEPOSITIONS.
Costs, USBank-ED Rule 7030-1.
Limits on depositions, USBank-ED Rule 7026-1.
Notice, USBank-ED Rule 7030-1.
Place of taking depositions, USBank-ED Rules 7030-1, 9016-1.
Reviewing depositions, USBank-ED Rule 7030-1.
Subpoenas, USBank-ED Rule 9016-1.

DEPOSITS INTO COURT.
General provisions, USBank-ED Rule 7067-1.
Standing order 13-1, order adopting amendment pending promulgation of final rule, USBank-ED Exhibit 10.

DEPOSITS INTO TREASURY.
Unclaimed funds, USBank-ED Rule 3011-1.

DISCHARGE HEARING.
Chapter 13 cases.
Certification of compliance, USBank-ED Rule 4008-2.
Reaffirmation agreements, USBank-ED Rule 4008-1.

DISCLOSURE STATEMENTS.
Financial interest disclosure statement, USBank-ED Exhibit 6.
Hearings.
Notice of hearing on disclosure statement, USBank-ED Rule 3016-1.
Notice.
Creditors and equity security holders.
Transmission of notice to, USBank-ED Rule 3016-1.
Hearing on disclosure statement, USBank-ED Rule 3016-1.
Objections to, USBank-ED Rule 3016-1.
Time.
Filing, USBank-ED Rule 2016-1.

DISCOVERY.
Depositions.
See DEPOSITIONS.
Interrogatories.
Forms.
Use of forms, USBank-ED Rule 9013-1.
Limits on interrogatories, USBank-ED Rule 7026-1.
Motions, USBank-ED Rule 7026-1.
Motion to compel discovery, USBank-ED Rule 7026-1.
Replies to discovery motions, USBank-ED Rule 7026-1.
Unnecessary motions or objections, USBank-ED Rule 7026-1.
Objections to discovery, USBank-ED Rule 7026-1.
Written objections required, USBank-ED Rule 7026-1.
Orders.
Compliance with discovery orders, USBank-ED Rule 7026-1.
Failure to comply, USBank-ED Rule 7026-1.
Pretrial conferences.
Attorney participation in pretrial discovery conferences, USBank-ED Rule 7026-1.
Sanctions.
Failure to comply with provisions, USBank-ED Rule 7026-1.
Time.
Extensions of time, USBank-ED Rule 7026-1.
Writing.
Requirement of writing, USBank-ED Rule 7026-1.

DISMISSAL OF ACTIONS.
Chapter 12 cases.
Plan not timely filed, USBank-ED Rule 3015-1.
Chapter 13 cases.
Plan not timely filed, USBank-ED Rule 3015-2.
Notice of possible dismissal, USBank-ED Rule 3015-2.
Reconsideration of dismissal, USBank-ED Rule 3015-2.
Meetings of creditors.
Nonappearance by debtors or debtors' counsel, USBank-ED Rule 2003-1.

DISMISSAL OF ACTIONS —Cont'd
Objections to claims.
Notice of hearing on proposed voluntary dismissal, USBank-ED Rule 7041-1.
Orders.
Meeting of creditors.
Nonappearance by debtors or debtors' counsel, USBank-ED Rule 2003-1.
Petitions.
Lists, schedules and statements.
Dismissal if not timely filed, USBank-ED Rule 1007-1.
Social security number.
Dismissal if not timely filed with petition, USBank-ED Rule 1007-1.
Statement of individual Chapter 7 debtor with consumer debts secured by property of estate.
Statement not timely filed, USBank-ED Rule 1007-3.
Reconsideration of dismissal, USBank-ED Rule 1007-3.

DIVISIONS OF DISTRICT, USBank-ED Rule 1071-1.

E

EASTERN DISTRICT OF VIRGINIA.
Composition, USBank-ED Rule 1071-1.
Divisions, USBank-ED Rule 1071-1.

ELECTRONIC FILING, USBank-ED Rule 5005-2.
Administrative procedures for case management/electronic filing, USBank-ED Exhibit 4.
Order adopting case management/electronic filing procedures, USBank-ED Exhibit 3.
Privacy.
Judicial conference policy regarding public access to electronic case files, USBank-ED Rule 5005-1.

ETHICS.
Attorneys at law, USBank-ED Rule 2090-1.

EVIDENCE.
Hearings.
Parties to be prepared to present at scheduled hearings, USBank-ED Rule 9014-1.
Payments, duties of debtor, USBank-ED Rule 4002-1.

EXAMINATIONS.
Motions requiring, USBank-ED Rule 2004-1.

EXHIBITS, USBank-ED Rule 9070-1.

F

FEES.
Attorneys, USBank-ED Rule 2016-1.
Filing fees.
Nonpayment, remedies, USBank-ED Rule 1006-1.
Payment in installments, USBank-ED Rule 1006-1.
Refunds, USBank-ED Rule 1006-1
Waiver, USBank-ED Rule 1006-1.
Refunds, USBank-ED Rule 1006-1.

FINANCIAL INTEREST DISCLOSURE STATEMENT, USBank-ED Exhibit 6.

FOREIGN COURTS.
Communications with foreign courts, USBank-ED Exhibit 9.

FOREIGN REPRESENTATIVES.
Communications with foreign representatives, USBank-ED Exhibit 9.

FORMS.
Chapter 13 cases.
Discharge and certification of compliance, USBank-ED Rule 4008-2.
Interrogatories.
Use of forms, USBank-ED Rule 9013-1.
Motions.
Use of forms, USBank-ED Rule 9013-1.

H

HEARINGS.
Discharge hearing.
Reaffirmation agreements, USBank-ED Rule 4008-1.
Disclosure statements.
Notice of hearing on disclosure statement, USBank-ED Rule 3016-1.
Evidence.
Parties to be prepared to present at scheduled hearings, USBank-ED Rule 9014-1.
Notice, USBank-ED Rule 9013-1.

I

INTERIM COMPENSATION.
Notice.
Party seeking, USBank-ED Rule 2016-1.

INTERROGATORIES.
Forms.
Use of forms, USBank-ED Rule 9013-1.
Limits on interrogatories, USBank-ED Rule 7026-1.

J

JOINT ADMINISTRATION OF JOINT PETITION CASES, USBank-ED Rule 1015-1.

JUDICIAL CONFERENCE.
Privacy.
Judicial conference policy regarding public access to electronic case files, USBank-ED Rule 5005-1.

L

LAW STUDENTS.
Third-year practice, USBank-ED Rule 2090-1.

LEASE OF PROPERTY.
Notice, USBank-ED Rule 6004-2.
Objection to proposed lease, USBank-ED Rule 6004-2.

LIENS.
Avoidance by debtor, USBank-ED Rule 4003-2.

LIENS —Cont'd
Redemption of property from lien, USBank-ED Rule 6008-1.

LIST OF CREDITORS, USBank-ED Rule 1007-1.
Creditor matrix diskette, instructions, USBank-ED Exhibit 5.
Inspection, USBank-ED Rule 2002-1.
Time for filing, USBank-ED Exhibit 8.

M

MEETINGS OF CREDITORS, USBank-ED Rule 2003-1.
Dismissal of case.
Nonappearance by debtors or debtors' counsel, USBank-ED Rule 2003-1.
Rescheduling, USBank-ED Rule 2003-1.

MOTIONS.
Alexandria division, motions day procedures, USBank-ED Exhibit 7.
Attorneys at law.
Certification of attorney, USBank-ED Rule 9013-1.
Bringing motions to attention of court, USBank-ED Rule 9013-1.
Chapter 7 cases.
Conversion of case from Chapter 7 to Chapter 13.
Notice and motion, USBank-ED Rule 1017-3.
Statement of individual Chapter 7 debtor with consumer debts secured by property of estate.
Extension of time for filing, USBank-ED Rule 1007-3.
Chapter 13 cases.
Conversion of case from Chapter 7 to Chapter 13.
Notice and motion, USBank-ED Rule 1017-3.
Plan, USBank-ED Exhibit 1.
Extension of time for filing, USBank-ED Rule 3015-2.
Inclusion of related motions, USBank-ED Rule 3015-2.
Clerk of court.
Rejection of motions by clerk, USBank-ED Rule 5005-1.
Continuances, USBank-ED Rule 9013-1.
Discovery, USBank-ED Rule 7026-1.
Motion to compel discovery, USBank-ED Rule 7026-1.
Replies to discovery motions, USBank-ED Rule 7026-1.
Unnecessary motions or objections, USBank-ED Rule 7026-1.
Examination motions, USBank-ED Rule 2004-1.
Forms.
Use of forms, USBank-ED Rule 9013-1.
Memorandum of points and authorities, USBank-ED Rule 9013-1.
Notice, USBank-ED Rule 9013-1.
Reopening of cases, USBank-ED Rule 5010-1.
Particularity.
Grounds and relief to be stated, USBank-ED Rule 9013-1.
Petitions.
Lists, schedules and statements.
Time for filing.
Extension of time, USBank-ED Rule 1007-1.

MOTIONS —Cont'd
Reopening of cases, USBank-ED Rule 5010-1.
Notice, USBank-ED Rule 5010-1.
Return date, USBank-ED Rule 9013-1.
Ruling upon motions without oral hearing, USBank-ED Rule 9013-1.
Stays.
Relief from automatic stay, USBank-ED Rule 4001(a)-1.
Summary judgment, USBank-ED Rule 7056-1.
Time for filing motion for, USBank-ED Rule 9013-1.
Time.
Extension of time relating to motions.
Request for, USBank-ED Rule 9013-1.
Withdrawal of reference of case to bankruptcy court, USBank-ED Rule 5011-1.
Written motions.
Required, USBank-ED Rule 9013-1.

MOTIONS DAY.
Alexandria division, motions day procedures, USBank-ED Exhibit 7.

N

NEWS MEDIA.
Broadcasting, photographing and televising.
Courtroom and environs, USBank-ED Rule 5073-1.

NEWSPAPERS.
Advertisements.
Notices requiring advertisements, USBank-ED Rule 2002-1.
Notices, USBank-ED Rule 2002-1.

NOTICE.
Abandonment of property, USBank-ED Rule 6007-1.
Chapter 7 cases.
Conversion of case from Chapter 7 to Chapter 13.
Notice and motion, USBank-ED Rule 1017-3.
Statement of individual Chapter 7 debtor with consumer debts secured by property of estate.
Dismissal if statement not timely filed.
Notice of possible dismissal, USBank-ED Rule 1007-3.
Chapter 12 cases, USBank-ED Rule 3015-1.
Chapter 13 cases.
Conversion of case from Chapter 7 to Chapter 13.
Notice and motion, USBank-ED Rule 1017-3.
Dismissal of case.
Plan not timely filed.
Notice of possible dismissal, USBank-ED Rule 3015-2.
Plan.
Extension of time for filing, USBank-ED Exhibit 2, USBank-ED Rule 3015-2.
Secured creditors whose collateral is to be valued or lien avoided, USBank-ED Rule 3015-2.
Chapter 13 plan, USBank-ED Rule 3015-2.
Depositions, USBank-ED Rule 7030-1.
Disclosure statements.
Creditors and equity security holders.
Transmission of notice to, USBank ED Rule 3016-1.

NOTICE —Cont'd
Disclosure statements —Cont'd
Hearing on disclosure statement, USBank-ED Rule 3016-1.
Dismissal of proceedings.
Notice of hearing on proposed voluntary dismissal, USBank-ED Rule 7041-1.
Foreign courts and representatives.
Communications with, time limits, USBank-ED Exhibit 9.
Hearings, USBank-ED Rule 9013-1.
Interested parties.
Notice to, USBank-ED Rule 2002-1.
Interim compensation.
Party seeking, USBank-ED Rule 2016-1.
Lease of property, USBank-ED Rule 6004-2.
Meetings of creditors.
Dismissal for failure to attend, USBank-ED Rule 2003-1.
Rescheduling, USBank-ED Rule 2003-1.
Motions, USBank-ED Rule 9013-1.
Reopening of cases, USBank-ED Rule 5010-1.
Newspapers, USBank-ED Rule 2002-1.
Objections to claims, USBank-ED Rule 3007-1.
Notice of hearing on proposed voluntary dismissal, USBank-ED Rule 7041-1.
Petitions.
Lists, schedules and statements.
Dismissal of case if not timely filed.
Notice of possible dismissal, USBank-ED Rule 1007-1.
Reopening of cases.
Motion to reopen case, USBank-ED Rule 5010-1.
Sale of property, USBank-ED Rule 6004-2.
Chapter 13 cases, sale after confirmation, USBank-ED Rule 6004-3.
Stays.
Automatic stay.
Relief from, USBank-ED Rule 4001(a)-1.
United States trustee.
Alternative service of documents by electronic means, USBank-ED Rule 2002-1.
Copies for, USBank-ED Rule 2002-1.
Use of property.
Proposed use, USBank-ED Rule 6004-2.

O

OBJECTIONS TO CLAIMS, USBank-ED Rule 3007-1.
Chapter 13 cases.
Objections to original plan, USBank-ED Rule 3015-2.
Dismissal of actions.
Notice of hearing on proposed voluntary dismissal, USBank-ED Rule 7041-1.

ORDERS.
Abandonment of property.
Order of court directing abandonment, USBank-ED Rule 6007-1.
After hearing or trial, USBank-ED Rule 9022-1.
Chapter 7 cases.
Statement of individual Chapter 7 debtor with consumer debts secured by property of estate.
Extension of time for filing, USBank-ED Rule 1007-3.

ORDERS —Cont'd
Chapter 13 cases.
Plan.
Extension of time for filing, USBank-ED Rule 3015-2.
Consent orders, USBank-ED Rule 9022-1.
Discovery.
Compliance with discovery orders, USBank-ED Rule 7016-1.
Failure to comply, USBank-ED Rule 7016-1.
Dismissal of actions.
Meeting of creditors.
Nonappearance by debtor or debtors' counsel, USBank-ED Rule 2003-1.
Filing.
Identification of attorney filing proposed order, USBank-ED Rule 9022-1.
Petitions.
Lists, schedules and statements.
Time for filing.
Extension of time, USBank-ED Rule 1007-1.
Pretrial conferences, USBank-ED Rule 7016-1.

P

PAYMENTS.
Costs, advance payment, USBank-ED Rule 7054-1.
Creditors, payments by trustee, USBank-ED Rule 3070-1.
Duties of debtor, USBank-ED Rule 4002-1.
Filing fees, USBank-ED Rule 1006-1.

PERSONAL FINANCIAL MANAGEMENT, INSTRUCTIONAL COURSE.
Chapter 13 cases.
Debtor's statement of completion.
Filing, USBank-ED Rule 1007-1.

PETITIONS.
Amendments.
Voluntary petition.
Amendments by debtor, USBank-ED Rule 1009-1.
Appeals.
Rejection of filings by clerk.
Judicial review, USBank-ED Rule 5005-1.
Clerk of court.
Rejection by clerk, USBank-ED Rule 5005-1.
Conversion to or from chapters.
Lists, inventories, schedules and statements.
Filing, USBank-ED Rule 1017-1.
Post-petition claims, USBank-ED Rule 1017-1.
Report of debtor in possession or trustee, USBank-ED Rule 1017-1.
Corporate resolution.
Filing with petition, USBank-ED Rule 1074-1.
Dismissal of actions.
Lists, schedules and statements.
Dismissal if not timely filed, USBank-ED Rule 1007-1.
Filing.
Electronic filing, USBank-ED Rule 5005-2.
Form, USBank-ED Rule 5005-1.
Joint petitions.
Administration through joint administration of estates, USBank-ED Rule 1015-1.
Lists, schedules and statements.
Conversion.
Filing, USBank-ED Rule 1017-1.

PETITIONS —Cont'd
Lists, schedules and statements —Cont'd
Copies.
Number of copies to be filed, USBank-ED Rule 1007-1.
Time for filing, USBank-ED Rule 1007-1.
Conversion, USBank-ED Rule 1017-1.
Dismissal of case if not timely filed, USBank-ED Rule 1007-1.
Notice of possible dismissal, USBank-ED Rule 1007-1.
Reconsideration of dismissal, USBank-ED Rule 1007-1.
Extension of time, USBank-ED Rule 1007-1.
Waiver request, filing creditors on computer diskette, USBank-ED Rule 1007-1.
Motions.
Lists, schedules and statements.
Time for filing.
Extension of time, USBank-ED Rule 1007-1.
Notice.
Lists, schedules and statements.
Dismissal of case if not timely filed.
Notice of possible dismissal, USBank-ED Rule 1007-1.
Orders.
Lists, schedules and statements.
Time for filing.
Extension of time, USBank-ED Rule 1007-1.
Size of paper, USBank-ED Rule 5005-1.
Social security number statement.
Time for filing, USBank-ED Rule 1007-1.

PHOTOGRAPHY.
Courtrooms and environs, USBank-ED Rule 5073-1.

PHYSICAL EXAMINATION OF LITIGANT, USBank-ED Rule 9017-1.

POWERS OF ATTORNEY.
Representation and appearances, USBank-ED Rule 9010-1.

PRETRIAL CONFERENCES, USBank-ED Rule 7016-1.
Discovery.
Attorney participation in pretrial discovery conferences, USBank-ED Rule 7026-1.
Orders, USBank-ED Rule 7016-1.

PRIVACY.
Judicial conference policy regarding public access to electronic case files, USBank-ED Rule 5005-1.

PROCEEDING COVER SHEET.
Adversary proceeding cover sheet, USBank-ED Rule 7003-1.

PROPERTY UNDER $2,500.
Sale of property, USBank-ED Rule 6004-2.

PRO SE APPEARANCES, USBank-ED Rule 9010-1.

R

REAFFIRMATION AGREEMENTS.
Closed cases.
Filing of summary reaffirmation agreements in, USBank-ED Rule 4008-1.
Court consideration, USBank-ED Rule 4008-1.

REAFFIRMATION AGREEMENTS —Cont'd
Notice of rights, USBank-ED Rule 4008-1.

REAL PROPERTY.
Chapter 13 cases.
Mortgage loan modification after confirmation, USBank-ED Rule 6004-4.
Description, USBank-ED Rule 6004-1.

REFERRAL OF CASE TO BANKRUPTCY COURT.
Withdrawal of reference, USBank-ED Rule 5011-1.

REFINANCING.
Chapter 13 cases.
Mortgage loan modification after confirmation, USBank-ED Rule 6004-4.
Refinancing after confirmation, USBank-ED Rule 6004-3.

REFUNDS.
Filing fees, USBank-ED Rule 1006-1.

REOPENING OF CASES.
Motions, USBank-ED Rule 5010-1.
Notice, USBank-ED Rule 5010-1.
Notice.
Motion to reopen case, USBank-ED Rule 5010-1.

REORGANIZATION CASE CLAIMS.
Ballots.
Summary of ballots.
Filing, USBank-ED Rule 3016-1.
Time.
Filing, USBank-ED Rule 3003-1.

REPORTS.
Debtors in possession and trustees.
Chapter 7 liquidation reports, USBank-ED Rule 2015(a)-1.
Conversion, USBank-ED Rule 1017-1.
Inventory reports, USBank-ED Rule 2015(a)-1.
Operating business reports, USBank-ED Rule 2015(a)-1.
Post-confirmation reports, USBank-ED Rule 2015(a)-1.
Post-consummation application for decree, USBank-ED Rule 2015(a)-1.
Review of reports, USBank-ED Rule 2015(a)-1.

S

SALE OF PROPERTY.
Chapter 13 cases.
Sale after confirmation, USBank-ED Rule 6004-3.
Notice, USBank-ED Rule 6004-2.
Objection to proposed sale, USBank-ED Rule 6004-2.
Property under $2,500, USBank-ED Rule 6004-2.
Redemption of property, USBank-ED Rule 6004-2.

SCHEDULES.
Form, USBank-ED Rule 5005-1.
Size of paper, USBank-ED Rule 5005-1.
Time for filing, USBank-ED Exhibit 8.

SCOPE OF RULES, USBank-ED Rule 1001-1.

SERVICE OF PROCESS.
Chapter 13 plan, USBank-ED Rule 3015-2.

SERVICE OF PROCESS —Cont'd
Proof of service, USBank-ED Rule 5005-1.
Subpoenas, USBank-ED Rule 9016-1.
Summons.
Issuance, USBank-ED Rule 7004-2.
Time for service, USBank-ED Rule 7004-2.
United States trustee.
Alternative service by electronic means, USBank-ED Rule 2002-1.
Service of papers upon, USBank-ED Rule 2002-1.

SETTLEMENT AND ALTERNATIVE DISPUTE RESOLUTION, USBank-ED Rule 9019-1.

SHOW CAUSE ORDER.
Failure to attend meeting of creditors, USBank-ED Rule 2003-1.

SOCIAL SECURITY NUMBER.
Filing with petition, USBank-ED Rule 1007-1.

STAYS.
Automatic stay.
Relief from, USBank-ED Rule 4001(a)-1.
Withdrawal of reference of case to bankruptcy court, USBank-ED Rule 5011-1.

SUBPOENAS.
Application for subpoena, USBank-ED Rule 9016-1.
Timely applications, USBank-ED Rule 9016-1.
Depositions, USBank-ED Rule 9016-1.
Generally, USBank-ED Rule 9016-1.
Return date, USBank-ED Rule 9016-1.
Service, USBank-ED Rule 9016-1.
Subpoena duces tecum, USBank-ED Rule 9016-1.
Subpoenas in blank, USBank-ED Rule 9016-1.
Time.
Application for subpoena, USBank-ED Rule 9016-1.

SUMMARY JUDGMENT.
Motions, USBank-ED Rule 7056-1.
Time for filing motion for, USBank-ED Rule 9013-1.

SUMMONS.
Issuance, USBank-ED Rule 7004-2.
Time.
Service, USBank-ED Rule 7004-2.

T

TAX INFORMATION.
Duties of debtor, USBank-ED Rule 4002-1.

TELEVISION.
Televising in courtrooms and environs, USBank-ED Rule 5073-1.

TIME.
Chapter 7 cases.
Statement of individual Chapter 7 debtor with consumer debts secured by property of estate.
Dismissal if not timely filed, USBank-ED Rule 1007-3.
Extension of time for filing, USBank-ED Rule 1007-3.
Chapter 12 cases.
Plan.
Filing, USBank-ED Rule 3015-1.

TIME —Cont'd
Chapter 13 cases.
Plan.
Filing, USBank-ED Rule 3015-2.
Extension of time, USBank-ED Rule 3015-2.
Disclosure statements.
Filing, USBank-ED Rule 2016-1.
Discovery.
Extensions of time, USBank-ED Rule 7026-1.
Foreign courts and representatives.
Communications with, time limits, USBank-ED Exhibit 9.
Motions.
Extension of time relating to motions.
Request for, USBank-ED Rule 9013-1.
Petitions.
Lists, schedules and statements.
Filing, USBank-ED Exhibit 8, USBank-ED Rule 1007-1.
Reorganization case claims.
Filing, USBank-ED Rule 3003-1.
Subpoenas.
Application for subpoena, USBank-ED Rule 9016-1.
Summons.
Service, USBank-ED Rule 7004-2.

TRANSCRIPTS, USBank-ED Rules 5077-1, 8006-1.

TRIAL.
Exhibits, USBank-ED Rule 9070-1.
Photographing, recording, broadcasting and televising, USBank-ED Rule 5073-1.
Pretrial conferences, USBank-ED Rule 7016-1.
Transcript, USBank-ED Rules 5077-1, 8006-1.
Witnesses.
See WITNESSES.

TRUSTS AND TRUSTEES.
Chapter 12 cases.
Payment to creditors by trustee, USBank-ED Rule 3070-1.
Chapter 13 cases.
Payments to creditors by trustee, USBank-ED Rule 3070-1.
Payments to trustee by debtor, USBank-ED Rule 3070-1.

U

UNCLAIMED FUNDS.
Deposit, USBank-ED Rule 3011-1.

USE OF PROPERTY.
Notice.
Proposed use, USBank-ED Rule 6004-2.
Objection to proposed use, USBank-ED Rule 6004-2.

W

WITHDRAWAL OF REFERENCE OF CASE TO BANKRUPTCY COURT, USBank-ED Rule 5011-1.

WITNESSES.
Expert witnesses.
Qualifications, USBank-ED Rule 9017-1.
Hypothetical questions, USBank-ED Rule 9017-1.
List of witnesses.
Furnishing to clerk, USBank-ED Rule 9017-1.
Subpoenas, USBank-ED Rule 9016-1.

UNITED STATES DISTRICT COURT FOR THE WESTERN DISTRICT OF VIRGINIA LOCAL RULES

Adopted March 9, 2010, effective April 8, 2010; amended effective May 19, 2011; amended March 8, 2012; amended January 30, 2013; and amended August 1, 2013.

TITLE I - GENERAL.

Rule
1. Scope and Purpose of Rules.
2. Divisions of the Western District.
3. Bankruptcy Referrals and Jury Trials.
4. Social Security Cases.
5. Prejudicial Influences.
6. Attorneys.
7. Service and Filing of Pleadings and Other Papers.
8. Redaction of Personal Data Identifiers from Pleadings.
9. Sealed Documents.
10. Communication with Jurors.
11. Imposition of Jury Costs.
12. Trial Exhibits.

TITLE II - CIVIL RULES.

3. Commencing an Action.

Rule
11. Pleadings and Motions.
16. Scheduling Orders.
26. Expert Disclosure.
40. Scheduling of Cases for Trial.
51. Proposed Instructions.
54. Fees and Costs.
56. Summary Judgment — Time of Filing.
67. Deposits Into Court.
73. Magistrate Judges.
83. Alternative Dispute Resolution Program.

TITLE III - CRIMINAL RULES.

12. Style of Motions.
32. Local Procedure for Guideline Sentencing.
58. Collateral Payments.
59. Appeals From Conviction or Sentence by Magistrate Judge.

Index.

Editor's note. — These Local Rules of the United States District Court for the Western District of Virginia were adopted by Standing Order No. 2010-2 on March 9, 2010. The order stated: "The Local Rules shall become effective thirty (30) days following the date of this Standing Order [April 8, 2010]."

TITLE I - GENERAL.

Rule 1. Scope and Purpose of Rules.

(a) **Application.** These rules apply in all civil and criminal cases and other proceedings in the United States District Court for the Western District of Virginia.

(b) **Definitions.** So far as applicable, 1 U.S.C. §§ 1 through 5 govern the construction of these rules. "This Court" refers to the United States District Court for the Western District of Virginia. The words "the Court" or "judge" as used in these rules includes any judicial officer sitting in this Court. "Clerk" as used in these rules means the Clerk of this Court or any authorized deputy thereof. Persons appearing pro se are bound by these rules, and any reference to "attorney" or "counsel" applies to pro se parties unless the context requires otherwise.

(c) **Amendment.** These rules may be amended at any time by this Court, after giving public notice and an opportunity for comment.

(d) **Citation.** These rules may be cited as W.D. Va. Gen. R., W.D. Va. Civ. R., or W.D. Va. Crim. R., as the case may be.

(e) **Effective Date.** These rules and amendments thereto take effect as provided in the order of adoption and govern all proceedings thereafter commenced and, insofar as just and practicable, all then pending proceedings.

Rule 2. Divisions of the Western District.

(a) **Divisions.** The divisions of this Court are as follows.

(1) **Abingdon Division.** The Abingdon Division embraces the counties of Smyth, Tazewell, Russell, Washington, Buchanan and the city of Bristol;

(2) **Big Stone Gap Division.** The Big Stone Gap Division embraces the counties of Dickenson, Wise, Scott, Lee and the city of Norton;

(3) **Charlottesville Division.** The Charlottesville Division embraces the counties of Albemarle, Fluvanna, Madison, Greene, Nelson, Rappahannock, Culpeper, Louisa, Orange, and the city of Charlottesville;

(4) **Danville Division.** The Danville Division embraces the counties of Patrick, Henry, Pittsylvania, Halifax, Charlotte and the cities of Danville, Martinsville and South Boston;

(5) **Harrisonburg Division.** The Harrisonburg Division embraces the counties of Frederick, Clarke, Warren, Shenandoah, Page, Rockingham, Augusta, Highland, Bath and the cities of Harrisonburg, Staunton, Waynesboro and Winchester;

(6) **Lynchburg Division.** The Lynchburg Division embraces the counties of Rockbridge, Amherst, Bedford, Campbell, Appomattox, Buckingham, Cumberland and the cities of Bedford, Buena Vista, Lexington and Lynchburg;

(7) **Roanoke Division.** The Roanoke Division embraces the counties of Alleghany, Botetourt, Craig, Giles, Pulaski, Montgomery, Roanoke, Floyd, Franklin, Carroll, Grayson, Bland, Wythe and the cities of Clifton Forge, Covington, Radford, Roanoke, Salem and Galax.

(b) **Venue in Civil Cases.** Civil actions for which venue is proper in this district must be brought in the proper division as well. The venue rules for United States district courts contained in the United States Code also apply in determining the proper division in which an action must be filed, so that such venue rules are construed as if the terms "judicial district" and "district" were replaced with the word "division."

(c) **Venue in Criminal Cases.** Upon the return of an indictment by any grand jury, it shall be filed in the division in which the crime charged is alleged to have occurred and assigned to the judge next in rotation for that division. Where the indictment charges a crime or crimes that are alleged to have occurred in more than one division, the indictment shall be filed in the division in which it is alleged that a crime occurred that is the residence of a defendant, or if there are more than two defendants, and a majority of the defendants reside in one division, in that division. If the appropriate division cannot be determined using the rules set forth herein, the Clerk shall consult with the chief judge of the district, or in the chief judge's absence, with the next available active district judge in seniority, for direction as to the proper division for filing. Superseding indictments in any case shall be filed in the division in which the existing indictment is filed. Nothing in this rule shall affect the discretion of the presiding judge in any case in determining the proper place of trial.

(d) **Assignment of Cases.** Cases are assigned among the district judges pursuant to Standing Order, as amended from time to time. If a judge to whom a case is assigned is disqualified from the case by statute or by the Code of Conduct for United States Judges, the case must be reassigned by the Clerk to the judge who is next in rotation pursuant to the Standing Order, and if there is no other available judge, then the chief judge must reassign the case, and if the chief judge is so disqualified or is unavailable, then the next available active district judge in seniority must reassign the case.

(e) **Continuous Session.** All of the divisions of this Court shall be deemed in continuous session for transaction of judicial business on all business days throughout the year.

Rule 3. Bankruptcy Referrals and Jury Trials.

(a) **Assignments.** In accordance with the provisions of 28 U.S.C. § 157, all cases under Title 11 of the United States Code and all proceedings arising under Title 11, or arising in or relating to a case under Title 11, are referred to the bankruptcy judges for this district, to be assigned in accordance with their assignment rules.

(b) **Jury Trials.** In accordance with the provisions of 28 U.S.C. § 157(e), bankruptcy judges of this district are hereby specifically designated to conduct jury trials when all parties have expressly consented thereto.

Rule 4. Social Security Cases.

(a) **Applications to Proceed without Prepayment of Funds in Disability Insurance and Supplemental Security Income Appeals.** Pursuant to the provisions of 28 U.S.C. § 636(b)(l)(B) and Federal Rule of Civil Procedure 72(b), all applications to proceed without prepayment of funds in Social Security disability insurance or supplemental security income appeals may be referred to a United States magistrate judge for consideration. Pursuant to Federal Rule of Civil Procedure 72(b), the petitioner may object to any order entered by the magistrate judge denying in forma pauperis status and may seek review by the district judge to whom the case would be assigned by filing a written objection to the order with the court within 14 days of notice thereof.

(b) **Social Security Disability Filings.** Pursuant to the provisions of 42 U.S.C. § 405(g) on judicial review of decisions by the Commissioner of Social Security, the following rules apply:

(1) The parties may use the form Social Security Complaint and Social Security Answer which are hyperlinked here and also available on the Court's website under the "Forms" tab.

(2) The Commissioner must respond to Social Security disability complaints within 120 days after service of the complaint on the United States Attorney;

(3) In all cases in which the Court has entered a judgment affirming, modifying, or reversing the decision of the Commissioner and remands the cause for a rehearing, the order of remand shall be deemed a final order for all purposes, including a petition for approval of attorneys' fees, and the claimant must file a new complaint pursuant to the terms of 42 U.S.C. § 405(g) to obtain further judicial review, and in such cases, the Court shall waive prepayment of any statutory filing fee;

(4) The Court shall retain jurisdiction in all cases in which the Court remands the case to the Commissioner for consideration of new evidence which is material and for which good cause is shown for failure to incorporate the evidence in prior proceedings. Claimants dissatisfied with the Commissioner's decision upon remand may petition the Court to reinstate the case on the active docket for review of the decision; if all parties are satisfied with the decision upon remand, the prevailing party shall petition the Court for entry of a final order adopting and ratifying the decision; and

(c) **Briefing of Social Security Cases.** In all cases seeking judicial review of decisions by the Commissioner of Social Security pursuant to 42 U.S.C. § 405(g), the following procedures are applicable, unless changed by the presiding judge:

(1) The plaintiff must file, within 30 days of service of a copy of the administrative record, a brief addressing why the Commissioner's decision is not supported by substantial evidence or why the decision otherwise should be reversed or the case remanded;

(2) If the plaintiff desires oral argument, it must be requested in writing at the time the plaintiff's brief is filed. Whether to allow oral argument is at the discretion of the Court. If oral argument is allowed, a party may participate either telephonically or in person;

(3) If the Commissioner desires to file a brief in response, such brief must be filed within 30 days after service of the plaintiff's brief. No further briefs by the parties will be submitted unless requested by the Court; and

(4) In the event that the Commissioner files a motion to remand the case to the Commissioner for further proceedings, the motion must set forth whether or not the plaintiff consents to such remand. If no such consent is indicated, the plaintiff must file the grounds of any objection to remand within 14 days of service of the motion to remand, or it will be assumed that plaintiff consents to remand. (Amended effective August 1, 2013.)

Editor's note. — The forms mentioned in (b)(1) as being hyperlinked are at the following locations: Social Security Complaint http://www.vawd.uscourts.gov/forms/ComplaintSocialSecurity.pdf and Social Security Answer http://www.vawd.uscourts.gov/forms/AnswerSocialSecurity.pdf .

Rule 5. Prejudicial Influences.

The conduct of a trial will be insulated by all court personnel, lawyers and litigants from all prejudicial influences. Except for naturalization and ceremonial proceedings, photography during a session of court, as well as sound and video broadcasting or recording, is prohibited in the courtroom, its environs, and the offices of this Court.

Rule 6. Attorneys.

(a) **Eligibility to Practice.** Any person who is an active or emeritus member of the Virginia State Bar in good standing is eligible to practice before this Court upon admission.

(b) **Procedure.** Admission to practice is upon motion in open court any day during which this Court is in session. An attorney desiring to be admitted, not less than 2 weeks before the day on which the motion is to be submitted, must file in the clerk's office at the place where such motion is to be made, an application for admission to practice, which application must be made in writing, stating the qualifications hereinbefore prescribed and, in addition thereto, the name and office address of the applicant; and such application must be accompanied by the certificates of at least 2 members of the bar of this Court, that they are acquainted with the applicant and that the applicant is of good character and ethical conduct. Upon the filing of the application for admission to practice by an attorney, the Clerk must ascertain from the Virginia State Bar that the applicant is an active or emeritus member in good standing. The Court may, in its discretion, hear motions for admission to practice at times other than a day in which court is in session. Persons who are associate, retired, or disabled members of the Virginia State Bar and who do not engage in the practice of law may, in the discretion of the Court, be admitted as members of the bar of this Court upon following the procedures set forth herein, but may not practice before this Court.

(c) **Eastern District Attorneys.** Any attorney admitted to practice in the United States District Court for the Eastern District of Virginia is permitted to practice in this Court upon the filing of a certificate of good standing from the Clerk of the Eastern District of Virginia showing that the attorney has been duly admitted to practice in that district.

(d) **Pro Hac Vice Admission.** Attorneys who are not qualified and licensed to practice under the laws of Virginia, but who are qualified and licensed to the practice before the Supreme Court of the United States, or before the highest court of any state in the United States, or before the courts of the District of Columbia, may not become members of the bar of this Court, but may appear only in association with a member of the bar of this Court, upon motion of such member, and only for the conduct of a case in which he or she is associated and then pending before this Court. In any case removed or transferred to this Court in which a party is represented by an attorney who is not a member of the bar of this Court, such attorney must, within 30 days of such removal or transfer (or such other time as directed by the presiding judge), be admitted to practice before this Court or be permitted to appear in association with a member of the bar of this Court. Pro hac vice admitted attorneys must promptly qualify for electronic case filing. Pro hac vice admitted attorneys may be permitted to appear at hearings or trials in the absence of an associated member of the bar of this Court in the discretion of the presiding judge.

(e) **Signing of Pleadings.** No pleading, notice, or other paper required to be signed by counsel shall be accepted for filing by the Clerk unless signed by a member of the bar of this Court, who shall have entered an appearance of record in the case, with the address where notice can be served upon the attorney, and which attorney is deemed to have such authority that the Court can deal with the attorney alone in all matters affecting the disposition of the case. Such appearance must not be withdrawn without the leave of the Court. Service of notice, process, or any other paper upon the attorney is equivalent to such service on the parties for whom the attorney has appeared. Provided, however, that the foregoing provisions shall not apply to a party who conducts his or her own case. A party who conducts his or her own case shall file with the pleadings a memorandum of an address where notice can be served upon the party.

(f) **Government Attorneys.** Notwithstanding any provision of this rule, any attorney representing the United States government, or any agency thereof, or representing any federal employee sued in the course of employment, or any attorney employed by the Federal Public Defender's Office, may appear and file pleadings in an official capacity without admission to practice in this Court, so long as such attorney is qualified and licensed to the practice before the Supreme Court of the United States, or before the highest court of any state in the United States, or before the courts of the District of Columbia.

(g) **Law Students.** An eligible law student who has qualified under this Court's Plan for Third-Year Practice may participate in any civil or criminal case in accordance with the Plan.

(h) **Discipline.** All attorneys admitted to practice before this Court or admitted for the purpose of a particular proceeding are admitted subject to the disciplinary rules, conditions, and procedures set forth in this Court's Rules of Disciplinary Enforcement.

(i) **Entry and Withdrawal by Attorney.** Any attorney entering a cause, at any time after its inception, must promptly give written notice thereof to the Clerk, requesting to be entered as an attorney of record. No attorney of record shall withdraw from any cause pending in this Court, except with the consent of the Court for good cause shown.

(j) **Surety.** No attorney appearing as counsel in any case shall become bail or surety in any cause or proceeding, civil or criminal, in this Court or to be returned thereto.

Rule 7. Service and Filing of Pleadings and Other Papers.

Pursuant to the authority granted by Federal Rules of Civil Procedure 5(d)(3) and 83, and Federal Rule of Criminal Procedure 57, the following practices and procedures apply to filing, signing, and verifying documents by electronic means:

(a) **Implementation of Procedures by Clerk.** The Clerk is authorized to implement and publish *Administrative Procedures for Filing, Signing, and Verifying Pleadings and Papers by Electronic Means* ("electronic filing procedures"), as amended from time to time, including the procedure for registration of attorneys and for distribution of user login identifications and passwords to permit electronic filing and notice of pleadings and other papers.

(b) **Case Management/Electronic Case Files.** The official court record in all cases shall be the electronic file maintained in the Court's Case Management/Electronic Case Files ("CM/ECF") servers together with any paper attachments and exhibits filed in accordance with the electronic procedures.

(c) **Signatures.** The electronic filing of a petition, pleading, motion, or other paper by an attorney who is a registered participant in this Court's CM/ECF system shall constitute the signature of that attorney under Federal Rule of Civil Procedure 11 and for all other purposes.

(d) **Use of Passwords.** No attorney shall knowingly permit or cause to permit the attorney's password to be utilized by anyone other than an authorized employee of the attorney or the attorney's law firm. No person shall knowingly utilize or cause another person to utilize the password of a registered attorney unless such person is an authorized employee of that attorney's law firm.

(e) **Entry of Pleadings and Other Papers on the Docket.** The electronic filing of a pleading or other paper in accordance with the electronic filing procedures shall constitute entry of that pleading or other paper on the docket kept by the Clerk under Federal Rule of Civil Procedure 79 and Federal Rule of Criminal Procedure 55.

(f) **Entry of Orders and Other Proceedings on the Docket.** The Clerk or chambers staff at the direction of the judge to whom a case is assigned shall enter all orders, decrees, judgments, and proceedings of the Court in accordance with the electronic filing procedures, which shall constitute entry of the order, decree, judgment, or proceeding on the docket kept by the Clerk under Federal Rule of Civil Procedure 58 and Federal Rule of Criminal Procedure 55.

(g) **Service.**

(1) **Notice of Electronic Filing.** Whenever a pleading or other paper is filed electronically in accordance with the electronic filing procedures, the Court's CM/ECF system shall serve the filing party with a "Notice of Electronic Filing" by electronic means at the time of docketing.

(2) **Persons Entitled to Service.** The filing party shall serve the pleading or other paper upon all persons entitled to notice or service in accordance with the applicable rules, or, if service by first class mail is permitted under the rules, the filing party may make service on registered participants in the Court's CM/ECF system in accordance with sub-paragraph three below.

(3) **Service to Registered Participants of CM/ECF.** If the recipient of notice or service is a registered participant in the Court's CM/ECF system, service by electronic means of the "Notice of Electronic Filing" with a hyperlink to the

document shall be the equivalent of service of the pleadings or other paper by first class mail, postage prepaid.

(4) **Service Complete on Transmission.** Service by electronic means is complete on transmission.

(5) **Ineffective Electronic Service.** Service by electronic means is not effective if the party making service learns that the attempted service did not reach the person to be served.

(h) **Consent to Service and Notice by Electronic Means.** Participation in this Court's CM/ECF system by receipt of a user login identification and password from the Court shall constitute a request for and consent to service and notice electronically pursuant to Federal Rule of Civil Procedure 5(b)(2)(E) and Federal Rule of Criminal Procedure 49. Participants in the CM/ECF system, by receiving a user login identification and password from this Court, agree to receive service by electronic means.

(i) **Electronic Filing Required.** All attorneys must file all documents electronically, unless otherwise authorized by the presiding judge in a particular case or the applicable electronic filing procedures.

(j) **Three-day Mailing Rule.** The three-day mailing rule of the Federal Rules of Criminal Procedure 45 and Federal Rules of Civil Procedure 6(d) for service by mail also applies to service by electronic means. (Amended effective August 1, 2013.)

Rule 8. Redaction of Personal Data Identifiers from Pleadings.

The responsibility for redacting personal identifiers as required by the federal rules of procedure rests solely with counsel or with the pro se party. The Clerk will not review each pleading for compliance.

Rule 9. Sealed Documents.

The following procedures govern documents under seal in criminal and civil cases in this Court.

(a) **General.** A "sealed document" is a document in the form of a pleading, exhibit or other paper access to which is prohibited or restricted other than by the Court or its authorized personnel. Portions of a document cannot be filed or placed under seal—only the entire document may be sealed. No sealed document may be disclosed except upon order of the Court.

(b) **Procedures for Filing a Sealed Document.**

(1) **Format.** Any sealed document must be tendered to the Clerk and conspicuously labeled "SEALED."

(2) **Motion to Seal.** To obtain a sealing order a party must file an unsealed written motion containing:

a. a generic, non-confidential identification of the document to be sealed;

b. the bases upon which the party seeks the order, including the reasons why alternatives to sealing are inadequate; and

c. the duration for which sealing is requested.

The moving party also must file with the motion a proposed unsealed order granting the motion and setting forth the bases for the Court's action. If it already has not been tendered, the moving party also must tender to the court, *in camera*, the document proposed to be sealed. The document will be kept under seal by the Clerk pending a decision by the Court on the motion. If the motion to seal is denied, the document will be returned by the Clerk to the party tendering it, unless the Court orders otherwise.

(3) **Public Notice of Motion to Seal or Sealing Order.** A motion to seal and any order to seal must be docketed according to the administrative procedures of the Court.

(4) **Objection to Sealing.** Any person or entity, whether a party or not, may object to a motion to seal a document or may file a motion to unseal a document previously sealed.

(5) **Agreement by Parties.** These provisions do not limit the ability of the parties by agreement to restrict access to documents that are not filed with the Court. Any agreement calling for the sealing of any document to be filed with the Court will be deemed to have incorporated the provisions of this rule.

(6) **Extension of Sealing.** No order to seal will be extended except upon a subsequent order of the Court obtained in accordance with this rule.

(7) **Sealed case.** No case may be sealed in its entirety except by order of the Court for cause shown, obtained in accordance with this rule.

(c) **Exceptions.**

(1) No motion or order is required to file the following under seal:

a. An unredacted version of a pleading, paper, exhibit, a reference list or other document containing personal data identifiers, in compliance with these rules, the federal rules of procedure, or the E-Government Act;

b. An ex parte motion or application where sealing is permitted or required by law;

c. Presentence investigation reports, pretrial services reports, psychiatric or psychological evaluations in criminal cases, including documents incorporating the content of the foregoing documents;

d. Affidavits submitted in support of a motion for in forma pauperis status;

e. Motions, orders, notices, and other matters occurring before the grand jury, subject to the provisions of Fed. R. Cr. P. 6;

f. Applications and orders for the disclosure of tax information (26 U.S.C. § 6103);

g. Motions and orders involving the Classified Information Procedures Act (18 U.S.C. app 3 §§ 1 - 16) or Foreign Intelligence Surveillance Act (50 U.S.C. § 1801);

h. Pleadings and documents involving the Juvenile Delinquency Act;

i. Requests and orders for authorization of investigative, expert, or other services pursuant to the Criminal Justice Act;

j. Other documents required by law to be filed under seal.

(2) No publicly filed motion and order under this rule is required for sealing the following:

a. Motion by the United States for a downward departure or reduction of sentence in a criminal case, with leave of court upon a showing of particular need in an individual case to prevent serious harm;

b. Search, seizure and arrest warrants and affidavits;

(3) A publicly filed motion and order citing only the statutory authority for sealing is required for the following:

a. Applications and orders for pen/trap devices (18 U.S.C. § 2703)

b. Applications and orders for wire, oral, or electronic communication interception (18 U.S.C. § 2516).

(d) **Unsealing.** Unless the Court orders otherwise, the Clerk will unseal the following sealed documents when indicated:

(1) **Search Warrant.** After the search is executed and the warrant is returned to the Clerk;

(2) **Arrest Warrant, and In a Violation Case, Any Violation Report.** After the arrest is made;

(3) **Indictment.** Upon the arrest or appearance of a single defendant. In multi-defendant cases, and unless the court orders otherwise, upon the earliest of any of the following:

a. 10 days following the arrest of any defendant;

b. 30 days after return of the indictment; or

c. when all defendants have been arrested or summoned.

In criminal cases, each defendant must be provided with a copy of the charges against that defendant (with other portions redacted, if necessary), even if the indictment or complaint is otherwise sealed. In multi-defendant cases in which the indictment is to remain sealed, the government is responsible for submitting to the magistrate judge for approval, reasonably in advance of the initial appearance, an appropriately redacted indictment for disclosure to the defendant and to the public.

(4) **Criminal Complaint.** 30 days after issuance or when all defendants named are in custody or have been summoned, whichever is the earliest.

(5) As for any other sealed documents, the documents will be unsealed 120 days from the date of entry of the sealing order, unless the sealing order provides otherwise.
(Amended effective March 8, 2012; amended effective August 1. 2013.)

COMMENT

This rule describes the procedures in criminal and civil cases relating to sealed documents, including pleadings, motions, exhibits, and other material. Case law protects generally the right of public access to documents filed in court, both under the First Amendment and the common law. *See, e.g., Va. Dep't of State Police v. Washington Post,* 386 F.3d 567, 575 (4th Cir. 2004).

Questions relating to sealed documents are presented in varying circumstances. For example, a party to a case may desire to file an exhibit to a brief containing confidential business information that has been disclosed to the opposing party under an agreement of confidentiality, but which the parties do not wish the public to see. The procedure to be followed is to file a motion not under seal that describes in a non-confidential way the document that the party desires to file under seal (in this hypothetical example, the exhibit). The motion must also state, in a generic , non-confidential way, the reasons why sealing is requested (in this case, the fact that the exhibit contains confidential trade secrets whose disclosure would be harmful to the business of the party) and why alternatives to sealing are inadequate. Finally, the motion must also state the length of time that the party desires the document to be sealed. The motion must be accompanied by the document desired to be sealed (the exhibit, in this example) for review by the presiding judge, as well as a proposed unsealed order allowing the document to be sealed, which order recites the necessary findings.

Often the parties to a case will enter into a confidentiality agreement that provides that certain information exchanged between them in the course of discovery will remain confidential. The procedures described in this rule do not affect the ability of the parties to enter into such an agreement. However, the parties cannot agree to the sealing of documents filed in court without following the mandatory procedures set forth in this rule.

In other words, the parties cannot seal documents filed in court merely by agreement or by labeling them "sealed."

There are certain exceptions to the rule that any document to be sealed must be accompanied by an unsealed motion. Where the sealed document is an unredacted version of a document required to be redacted by these rules, the federal rules of procedure, or the E-Government Act, or a reference list of personal data identifiers, then no motion or order is required. Like all sealed documents, however, the unredacted version or the reference list must be clearly labeled "SEALED."

The government, a defendant or other party may have a basis for a confidential communication to the court that is permitted or required by law. There is no need for an unsealed motion or order in those circumstances, but the motion must be clearly labeled "EX PARTE AND SEALED."

This rule provides that unless the Court orders otherwise, all documents in a case will be unsealed at the conclusion of the case. The rule does not flatly prohibit the continued sealing of a document, but leaves that decision to the presiding judge. As an alternative, the judge may order a sealed document in paper form returned to the party submitting it at the conclusion of the case. If a document is ordered sealed for a particular period of time, the period may be extended by a later order, obtained by following the procedures set forth.

Rule 10. Communication with Jurors.

No attorney or party litigant shall personally, or through any investigator or any other person acting for the attorney or party litigant, interview, examine or question any juror or alternate juror during the juror's term of service as a potential juror with respect to the verdict or deliberations of the jury in any action, civil or criminal, except by leave of Court upon good cause shown and upon such conditions as the Court in the particular case may fix.

Rule 11. Imposition of Jury Costs.

The Court may in its discretion impose the costs of a jury where a case is settled or otherwise disposed of after it is too late to reasonably notify the jury not to appear.

Rule 12. Trial Exhibits.

Upon jury verdict or decision by the Court, the Clerk shall retain documentary exhibits. Documents of unusual bulk or weight and physical exhibits, other than documents, shall remain in the custody of the attorney producing them. The attorney shall permit inspection of the same by any party for the purpose of preparing the record on appeal. The attorney also shall be charged with the responsibility for the safekeeping of said exhibits and, if requested, transportation of the exhibits to the appellate court.

In all cases where money, firearms, narcotics, controlled substances or any manner of contraband is introduced into evidence, such evidence shall be returned by the Clerk to the attorney producing them for safekeeping immediately after the return of the jury verdict or, in a nonjury case, at the close of all the evidence. The attorney who introduces an exhibit into evidence in a case will be responsible for its custody.

All documentary exhibits filed in a proceeding must be physically removed by the parties who filed them. In the event no appeal is perfected, the exhibits must be removed within 60 days in civil cases and within 30 days of criminal cases, from the date of final disposition of the case by this Court. In the event an appeal is perfected and thereafter disposed of by the court of appeals, the exhibits must be removed within 30 days after receipt of the judgment, other process or certificate disclosing disposition of the case by that court. In the event that a case is appealed to the Supreme Court, the exhibits must be removed within 30 days after receipt of judgment, other process or certificate disclosing disposition of the case by that court.

In the event that exhibits are not removed from the custody of the Clerk within the required time, the Clerk, after sending a form notice to respective counsel for the parties to remove the exhibits, shall, after 30 days have expired from the time of mailing of such notice, cause the same to be destroyed or otherwise disposed of.

TITLE II - CIVIL RULES.

Rule 3. Commencing an Action.

(a) Pursuant to Federal Rule of Civil Procedure 3, a civil action is commenced by filing a complaint. In any civil case in this Court, the complaint is deemed filed the day the clerk receives it together with payment of the required filing fee. If the filing fee is paid on a later day, the complaint will be deemed filed the day the complaint was received by the Clerk if the presiding judge in the case determines that the late payment of the filing fee was due to good cause.

(b) In the event that a civil complaint is submitted together with an application to proceed without the payment of the required filing fee, the complaint is deemed filed on the day it was received if (a) the application is granted or (b) the application is denied and the filing fee is thereafter paid within a reasonable time.

(c) In the event a fee is erroneously paid by way of credit card through the Court's electronic filing system, no refund may be made except upon the order of the presiding judge in the case. In the event that a user of the system has made repeated mistakes or good cause otherwise exists, the judge may decline to order a refund.

Rule 11. Pleadings and Motions.

(a) **Address and Telephone Number.** All pleadings and motions must include the attorney's office address, telephone number, e-mail address, and the attorney's bar identification number. All pleadings and motions filed by a non-prisoner litigant proceeding pro se must contain an address where notice can be served on such person and a telephone number where such person can be reached or a message left. All pleadings and motions filed by a prisoner proceeding pro se must contain an address where notice can be served on such person.

(b) **Determination of Motions.** The moving party is responsible either to set a motion for hearing or to advise the Court that all parties agree to submission of the motion without a hearing. The non-moving party also may arrange for a hearing. All hearings are to be at a date and time obtained from and scheduled by the Court. Unless otherwise ordered, a motion is deemed withdrawn if the movant does not set it for hearing (or arrange to submit it without a hearing) within 60 days after the date on which the motion is filed. In accordance with Federal Rule of Civil Procedure 78(b), the Court may determine a motion without an oral hearing.

(c) **Briefs Required.**

(1) All motions, unless otherwise directed by the Court and except as noted hereinbelow, must be accompanied by a written brief setting forth a concise statement of the facts and supporting reasons, along with a citation of the authorities upon which the movant relies. Unless otherwise directed by the Court, the opposing party must file a responsive brief and such supporting documents as are appropriate within 14 days after service, and the moving party may file a rebuttal brief within 7 days after the service of the opposing party's reply brief. No further briefs (including letter briefs) are to be submitted without first obtaining leave of court.

(2) Briefs need not accompany motions: (a) for a more definite statement; (b) for an extension of time to respond to or file pleadings, unless the time has already expired; (c) for a default judgment; (d) for continuances; and (e) to amend pleadings or add or substitute parties. These motions, while not requiring a brief, must state good cause justifying the relief requested. In addition, a separate brief is not required where a motion itself contains the legal and factual argument necessary to support the motion.

(3) Procedural motions, including motions for enlargement of time, whether or not opposed, may be acted upon at any time by the Court, without awaiting a response, and any party adversely affected by such action may request reconsideration, vacation, or modification of such action.

Rule 16. Scheduling Orders.

Scheduling orders shall be issued in all cases except pro se prisoner, Social Security, and habeas cases or other cases exempted by the presiding judge and may be issued by a magistrate judge. The scheduling order shall govern any deadline fixed or procedure ordered that is in conflict with that contained in these rules.

Rule 26. Expert Disclosure.

(a) **Agreement Upon Disclosure.** Counsel are encouraged to agree in a discovery plan or otherwise upon the sequence and timing of the expert disclosures required by Federal Rule of Civil Procedure 26(a)(2).

(b) **Objections to Expert Testimony.** Unless otherwise fixed by the Court, or unless good cause is shown, any objections to the admissibility of expert testimony or opinions must be by motion filed and set for hearing or submitted without hearing within a reasonable time before the date of trial, thus permitting an adequate time for the Court to consider the motion.

Rule 40. Scheduling of Cases for Trial.

Cases shall be scheduled for trial in the manner directed by the presiding judge.

Rule 51. Proposed Instructions.

Except as otherwise directed by the Court, in all cases tried to a jury, any proposed instructions must be filed at least 7 days before the scheduled trial date. Each instruction must be set forth on a separate page, numbered and identified appropriately by the party submitting it, bearing at its foot a citation of the authority in support of the instruction. Instructions must be filed as a group together with a cover sheet in pleading form and a certificate of service.

Rule 54. Fees and Costs.

(a) Attorneys' Fees.

(1) Time for Filing. Unless otherwise provided by statute, or in Social Security cases, or as otherwise ordered by the Court, any motion requesting the award of attorneys' fees must be filed no later than 21 days after the entry of judgment. Any opposition must be filed within 21 days of service of the motion.

(2) Contents. Any motion requesting the award of attorneys' fees must be supported by a memorandum setting forth the nature of the case, the claims as to which the party prevailed, the claims as to which the party did not prevail, a detailed description of the work performed broken down by hours or fractions thereof expended on each task, the attorney's customary fee for such like work, the customary fee for like work prevailing in the attorney's community, a listing of any expenditures for which reimbursement is sought, any additional factors which are required by the case law, and any additional factors that the attorney wishes to bring to the Court's attention. (Amended effective August 1, 2013.)

Rule 56. Summary Judgment — Time of Filing.

(a) Except for good cause shown, no motion for summary judgment or other dispositive motion will be considered unless it is filed and set for hearing, or submitted without hearing, within the time fixed by the Court, or if no time is fixed by the Court, within a reasonable time before the date of trial, thus permitting adequate time for the Court to consider the motion.

(b) Any motion for summary judgment or any other dispositive motion must contain a separately captioned section setting forth with specificity the material facts claimed to be undisputed together with specific record citations in support thereof. (Amended effective August 1, 2013.)

Rule 67. Deposits Into Court.

(a) **Receipt of Funds.**

(1) No money shall be sent to the Court or its officers for deposit in the Court's registry without a court order signed by the presiding judge in the case or proceeding.

(2) Unless provided for elsewhere in this Order, all monies ordered to be paid to the Court or received by its officers in any case pending or adjudicated shall be deposited

with the Treasurer of the United States in the name and to the credit of this Court pursuant to 28 U.S.C. § 2041 through depositories designated by the Treasury to accept such deposit on its behalf.

(3) The party making the deposit or transferring funds to the Court's registry shall serve the order permitting the deposit or transfer on the Clerk of Court.

(b) **Investment of Registry Funds.**

(1) Where, by order of the Court, funds on deposit with the Court are to be placed in some form of interest-bearing account, CRIS, administered by the Administrative Office of the United States Courts, shall be the only investment mechanism authorized.

(2) Money from each case deposited in CRIS shall be "pooled" together with those on deposit with Treasury to the credit of other courts in CRIS and used to purchase Government Account Series securities through the Bureau of Public Debt, which will be held at Treasury, in an account in the name and to the credit of the Director of Administrative Office of the United States Courts, hereby designated as custodian for CRIS.

(3) An account for each case will be established in CRIS titled in the name of the case giving rise to the investment in the fund. Income generated from fund investments will be distributed to each case based on the ratio each account's principal and earnings has to the aggregate principal and income total in the fund. Reports showing the interest earned and the principal amounts contributed in each case will be prepared and distributed to each court participating in CRIS and made available to litigants and/or their counsel.

(c) **Deductions of Fees.**

(1) The custodian is authorized and directed by this Order to deduct the registry fee for maintaining accounts in CRIS and the investment services fee for the management of investments. The proper registry fee is to be determined on the basis of the rates published by the Director of the Administrative Office of United States Courts as approved by the Judicial Conference. The investment services fee is assessed from interest earning according to the Court's Miscellaneous Fee Schedule.

(2) If registry fees were assessed against the case under the old 45-day requirement prior to deposit in CRIS, no additional registry fee will be assessed.

(d) **Unclaimed Funds.** Funds paid into this court which have remained unclaimed for five years and for which the right to withdraw has either been adjudicated or is not in dispute shall be deposited in the Treasury in the name and to the credit of the United States and any claimant with full proof of the right to withdraw may petition the court, with notice to the United States Attorney, and obtain an order authorizing payment.

(e) **Criminal Bond Forfeitures.** Upon proper motion, any funds deposited by or on behalf of a criminal defendant for bail bond purposes, with the exception of funds deposited by a third party surety, may be held and paid over to the United States Attorney for payment of any assessment, fine, restitution, or penalty imposed upon the criminal defendant. (Amended effective May 19, 2011.)

Rule 73. Magistrate Judges.

Pursuant to the provisions of 28 U.S.C. § 636 and Federal Rule of Civil Procedure 73, the full time magistrate judges of this Court are designated to conduct any or all proceedings in a jury or nonjury civil matter and order entry of judgment in the case, upon the consent of the parties, and upon entry of an order of reference in the particular civil matter by a district judge of this court, which order specifically transfers, assigns or refers the matter to a magistrate judge for all proceedings and for the entry of dispositive orders or judgment.

Rule 83. Alternative Dispute Resolution Program.

(a) **Availability.** This Court shall offer alternative dispute resolution to all parties in every civil case. Mediation shall be the common and preferred means of alternative dispute resolution. Other means of alternative dispute resolution shall be made available by this Court upon request of all parties, except in those cases in which the alternative form may be prohibited by statute.

(b) **Requests for Referrals.** Alternative dispute resolution shall not be automatically required in every case. Upon joint motion of all parties, the Court shall refer the case for alternative dispute resolution in the form requested by the parties, unless that form is prohibited by statute. If one party makes a unilateral request for referral, the Court may refer the case for alternative dispute resolution in any nonbinding form deemed appropriate by the presiding judge. In any other case, the presiding judge may require the parties to participate in alternative dispute resolution in any nonbinding form permitted by statute and deemed appropriate by this Court.

(c) **Neutrals.** Upon joint motion of all parties, the Court shall refer the case to an alternative dispute resolution resource outside the Court. In all other cases, a United States district judge or magistrate judge shall serve as the neutral when the matter is designated by the presiding judge for alternative dispute resolution.

(d) **Training and Disqualification of Neutrals.** As the primary alternative dispute resolution resource persons for the Court, the magistrate judges shall receive appropriate training as may be offered by the Federal Judicial Center, Administrative Office, or other approved agency. In requesting referral to an outside alternative dispute resolution resource, the parties shall provide to the Court satisfactory documentation as to the qualifications of the designated neutral. Complaints concerning the performance of any neutral, including a magistrate judge, shall be addressed to the chief United States district judge. This Court may disqualify from further service any person, including a magistrate judge, who is deemed unqualified to serve as a neutral in a particular case, or in all cases.

(e) **Confidentiality.** If requested by the applicant, any unilateral request for alternative dispute resolution referral shall be maintained in the strictest confidence by all officers of this Court. Once entered, however, all orders of referral shall be matters of public record. Communications and/or information provided during any alternative dispute resolution process shall be kept confidential by all parties and by the neutral. Any information or document which is otherwise produced through a legitimate discovery process is exempted from this confidentiality requirement. Any party may seek entry of a protective order to prevent or limit discovery of any information or document which has become known to the opposing party only because of participation in an alternative dispute resolution process. Any party who participates in alternative dispute resolution with a magistrate judge of this Court shall be deemed to have consented to any party's ex parte communication with the magistrate judge made in the course of attempted resolution of the dispute.

(f) **Scheduling.** Alternative dispute resolution sessions may be scheduled at the discretion of the parties and the neutral. Alternative dispute resolution shall proceed independently of all other pretrial development in the case. Referral of a case for alternative dispute resolution shall not operate so as to modify or stay any scheduling provisions of any pretrial order. Parties engaged in alternative dispute resolution may apply to the Court for such modifications or stays upon demonstration of exceptional cause.

(g) **Enforceability.** The Court will not assist in the enforcement of any agreement, settlement, or fee arrangement from any alternative dispute resolution process which is not annexed by the Court. In all other situations, the parties may invoke any of the Court's traditional enforcement mechanisms.

(h) **Coordinator.** This Court shall designate an employee or a judicial officer who is knowledgeable in alternative dispute resolution practices and processes to implement, administer, oversee, and evaluate the Court's alternative dispute resolution program.

TITLE III - CRIMINAL RULES.

Rule 12. Style of Motions.

All motions and the responses in criminal cases must bear a caption which identifies the moving party and describes the general nature and the purpose of the motion. A defendant may adopt a motion filed by another defendant only by filing a separate pleading for each motion that the defendant wishes to adopt. This separate pleading must bear the same caption as the original pleading that the defendant wishes to adopt. A single motion to adopt more than one pleading of another defendant is not permitted.

Rule 32. Local Procedure for Guideline Sentencing.

(a) **Disclosure of Recommended Sentence.** Pursuant to Federal Rule of Criminal Procedure 32(e)(3), the probation officer shall not disclose, without court order, the probation officer's recommendation, if any, on the sentence.

(b) **Motion for Substantial Assistance.** The attorney for the Government must file its 18 U.S.C. § 3553(e) motion for substantial assistance, if any, at the same time the attorney for the Government makes objections under Federal Rule of Criminal Procedure 32(f).

(c) **Disclosure of Presentence Report.** Nothing in this rule will require the disclosure of information in the presentence report not disclosable under Federal Rule of Criminal Procedure 32. The presentence report will be deemed to have been disclosed when a copy of the report is physically delivered, 1 day after verbal announcement that the report is available for inspection or 3 days after a copy of the report or notice of its availability is mailed.

Rule 58. Collateral Payments.

In accordance with Federal Rule of Criminal Procedure 58(d)(1), payment of a fixed sum may be accepted in suitable types of petty offense cases in lieu of appearance and as authorizing the termination of the proceedings. Such fixed sums may be increased or decreased from time to time by this Court by standing order, provided such fixed sums shall not exceed the maximum fine which could be imposed upon conviction.

Rule 59. Appeals From Conviction or Sentence by Magistrate Judge.

(a) **Record on Appeal.** Within 14 days, or such other period of time as the district judge may direct, after filing a notice of appeal from a conviction or sentence by a magistrate judge as permitted by Federal Rule of Criminal Procedure 58(g)(2), the appellant must file a statement of the grounds for the appeal and a supporting memorandum of law. If the appellant has ordered a transcript of the trial or other proceedings before the magistrate judge, the appellant must so inform the district judge and the appellee. In such event, the appellant must file a supporting memorandum of law within 14 days, or such other period of time as the district judge may direct, of the filing of the transcript.

(b) **Submission of Appeal.** The appellee has 21 days, or such other period of time as the district judge may direct, from the date of filing of appellant's memorandum of law or the filing of the transcript of proceedings before the magistrate judge, whichever is later, in which to file a responsive memorandum. The appellant has 14 days, or such other period of time as the district judge directs, in which to file a reply. The matter is thereafter deemed submitted for decision, provided that oral argument may be granted in the Court's discretion.

Index to U.S. District Court Rules of the Western District of Virginia

A

ABINGDON DIVISION.
Divisions in Western District, USDistCt-WD I Rule 2.

AGREEMENT BY PARTIES.
Expert witnesses.
Civil cases, USDistCt-WD II Rule 26.
Sealing of documents, USDistCt-WD I Rule 9.

ALTERNATIVE DISPUTE RESOLUTION.
Civil cases, procedure, USDistCt-WD II Rule 83.

AMENDMENT OF RULES, USDistCt-WD I Rule 1.

APPEARANCES IN THE COURT.
Attorneys at law, USDistCt-WD I Rule 6.
Criminal cases.
Collateral payments, USDistCt-WD III Rule 58.

ARREST WARRANT.
Unsealing of documents, USDistCt-WD I Rule 9.

ASSIGNMENT OF CASES, USDistCt-WD I Rule 2.
Bankruptcy cases, USDistCt-WD I Rule 3.

ATTORNEYS AT LAW, USDistCt-WD I Rule 6.
Jury trials.
Communication with jurors, USDistCt-WD I Rule 10.

ATTORNEYS' FEES.
Civil cases, USDistCt-WD II Rule 54.

B

BANKRUPTCY CASES.
Assignment and jury trials, USDistCt-WD I Rule 3.

BIG STONE GAP DIVISION.
Divisions in Western District, USDistCt-WD I Rule 2.

BONDS, SURETY.
Attorneys at law, USDistCt-WD I Rule 6.

BRIEFS.
Civil cases, USDistCt-WD II Rule 11.
Social Security cases, USDistCt-WD I Rule 4.

C

CASE MANAGEMENT/ELECTRONIC CASE FILES (CM/ECF).
Service of process and papers, USDistCt-WD I Rule 7.

CHARLOTTESVILLE DIVISION.
Divisions in Western District, USDistCt-WD I Rule 2.

CITATION OF RULES, USDistCt-WD I Rule 1.

CIVIL CASES.
Alternative dispute resolution, procedure, USDistCt-WD II Rule 83.
Attorneys' fees, USDistCt-WD II Rule 54.
Briefs, USDistCt-WD II Rule 11.
Commencement of action, USDistCt-WD II Rule 3.
Costs, USDistCt-WD II Rule 54.
Deposits into court, USDistCt-WD II Rule 67.
Expert witnesses.
Disclosures, USDistCt-WD II Rule 26.
Jury instructions.
Proposed instructions, USDistCt-WD II Rule 51.
Magistrate judges authorized to conduct proceedings, USDistCt-WD II Rule 73.
Motions, USDistCt-WD II Rule 11.
Pleadings, USDistCt-WD II Rule 11.
Scheduling cases for trial, USDistCt-WD II Rule 40.
Scheduling orders, USDistCt-WD II Rule 16.
Summary judgment, USDistCt-WD II Rule 56.
Venue, USDistCt-WD I Rule 2.

CLERK OF COURT.
Civil cases.
Deposits into court, USDistCt-WD II Rule 67.
Deposits into court.
Civil cases, USDistCt-WD II Rule 67.
Service of process and papers, USDistCt-WD I Rule 7.

COMPLAINTS.
Civil action, commencement, USDistCt-WD II Rule 3.

CONFIDENTIAL RECORDS.
Alternative dispute resolution.
Civil cases, procedure, USDistCt-WD II Rule 83.

COSTS.
Civil cases, USDistCt-WD II Rule 54.
Imposition of jury costs, USDistCt-WD I Rule 11.

CRIMINAL CASES.
Appeals from conviction or sentence, USDistCt-WD III Rule 59.
Collateral payments, USDistCt-WD III Rule 58.
Complaint.
Unsealing of documents, USDistCt-WD I Rule 9.
Motions.
Style of motions, USDistCt-WD III Rule 12.
Sentencing.
Guideline sentencing, USDistCt-WD III Rule 32.
Venue, USDistCt-WD I Rule 2.

D

DANVILLE DIVISION.
Divisions in Western District, USDistCt-WD I Rule 2.

DEFINED TERMS, USDistCt-WD I Rule 1.

DEPOSITS INTO COURT.
Civil cases, USDistCt-WD II Rule 67.

DISABILITY CASES.
Social Security cases, USDistCt-WD I Rule 4.

DISCRIMINATION.
Prejudicial influences, USDistCt-WD I Rule 5.

DIVISIONS IN WESTERN DISTRICT, USDistCt-WD I Rule 2.

DOCKET.
Entry of pleadings, USDistCt-WD I Rule 7.

E

EFFECTIVE DATE OF RULES, USDistCt-WD I Rule 1.

ELECTRONIC CASE FILING, USDistCt-WD I Rule 7.

EXHIBITS.
Trial exhibits, USDistCt-WD I Rule 12.

EXPERT WITNESSES.
Civil cases.
Disclosures, USDistCt-WD II Rule 26.

H

HARRISONBURG DIVISION.
Divisions in Western District, USDistCt-WD I Rule 2.

I

IDENTIFICATION.
Redaction of personal data identifiers from all pleadings, USDistCt-WD I Rule 8.

J

JURY INSTRUCTIONS.
Civil cases.
Proposed instructions, USDistCt-WD II Rule 51.

JURY TRIALS.
Bankruptcy cases, USDistCt-WD I Rule 3.
Communication with jurors, USDistCt-WD I Rule 10.
Imposition of jury costs, USDistCt-WD I Rule 11.

L

LYNCHBURG DIVISION.
Divisions in Western District, USDistCt-WD I Rule 2.

M

MAGISTRATES.
Appeals from conviction or sentence, USDistCt-WD III Rule 59.
Civil cases, USDistCt-WD II Rule 73.

MOTIONS.
Civil cases, USDistCt-WD II Rule 11.
Attorneys' fees and costs, USDistCt-WD II Rule 54.
Summary judgment, USDistCt-WD II Rule 56.
Criminal cases.
Guideline sentencing, motion for substantial assistance, USDistCt-WD III Rule 32.
Style of motions, USDistCt-WD III Rule 12.
Sealing of documents, USDistCt-WD I Rule 9.

N

NOTICE.
Sealing of documents, USDistCt-WD I Rule 9.

O

OBJECTIONS.
Expert witnesses.
Civil cases, USDistCt-WD II Rule 26.
Sealing of documents, USDistCt-WD I Rule 9.

ORDERS.
Civil cases.
Scheduling orders, USDistCt-WD II Rule 16.

P

PASSWORDS.
CM/ECF, protecting, USDistCt-WD I Rule 7.

PHOTOGRAPHY IN THE COURTROOM, USDistCt-WD I Rule 5.

PLEADINGS.
Civil cases, USDistCt-WD II Rule 11.
Entry on docket, USDistCt-WD I Rule 7.
Personal information, redaction, USDistCt-WD I Rule 8.
Signing.
Attorneys at law, effect, USDistCt-WD I Rule 6.

PREJUDICIAL INFLUENCES, USDistCt-WD I Rule 5.

PURPOSE OF RULES, USDistCt-WD I Rule 1.

R

RECORDINGS IN THE COURTROOM, USDistCt-WD I Rule 5.

ROANOKE DIVISION.
Divisions in Western District, USDistCt-WD I Rule 2.

S

SCHEDULING CASES FOR TRIAL.
Civil cases, USDistCt-WD II Rule 40.

SCHEDULING ORDERS.
Civil cases, USDistCt-WD II Rule 16.

SCOPE OF RULES, USDistCt-WD I Rule 1.

SEALING OF DOCUMENTS, USDistCt-WD I Rule 9.

SEARCH WARRANTS.
Unsealing of documents, USDistCt-WD I Rule 9.

SENTENCING.
Appeals from conviction or sentence, USDistCt-WD III Rule 59.
Guideline sentencing, USDistCt-WD III Rule 32.

SERVICE OF PROCESS AND PAPERS, USDistCt-WD I Rule 7.

SESSIONS OF COURT.
Continuous sessions authorized, USDistCt-WD I Rule 2.

SIGNING OF PLEADINGS, USDistCt-WD I Rule 7.
Attorneys at law, effect, USDistCt-WD I Rule 6.

SOCIAL SECURITY CASES, USDistCt-WD I Rule 4.

SUMMARY JUDGMENT.
Civil cases, USDistCt-WD II Rule 56.

SUPPLEMENTAL SECURITY INCOME APPEALS.
Social Security cases, USDistCt-WD I Rule 4.

U

UNSEALING OF DOCUMENTS, USDistCt-WD I Rule 9.

V

VENUE, USDistCt-WD I Rule 2.

VIDEO BROADCASTS, USDistCt-WD I Rule 5.

W

WITHDRAWAL OF APPEARANCE.
Attorneys at law, USDistCt-WD I Rule 6.

WITNESSES.
Expert witnesses.
Civil cases.
Disclosures, USDistCt-WD II Rule 26.

LOCAL RULES OF PRACTICE OF THE UNITED STATES BANKRUPTCY COURT FOR THE WESTERN DISTRICT OF VIRGINIA

Effective June 1, 1989.
As amended through April 1, 2013.

Rule

Local Rule 1001-1. Scope of Rules.
Local Rule 1002-1. Petition — General.
Local Rule 1006-1. Extension of Time to Pay Filing Fees.
Local Rule 1007-1. Filing of Schedules and Statements.
Local Rule 1007-2. Mailing Matrix.
Local Rule 1009-1. Amendments to Petition, Lists, or Schedules.
Local Rule 1015-1. Consolidation of Cases.
Local Rule 1017-1. Post-Discharge Conversions from Chapter 7 to Another Chapter.
Local Rule 1017-2. Dismissal or Suspension — Contemporaneous Petitions.
Local Rule 1017-3. Conversions from Chapter 7 to Chapter 13 at the Request of the Debtor.
Local Rule 1071-1. Divisions of the Western District of Virginia.
Local Rule 1072-1. Places of Holding Court.
Local Rule 1074-1. Corporations, Partnerships, & Limited Liability Companies.
Local Rule 2002-1. Notice to Creditors and Other Interested Parties.
Local Rule 2002-2. Notice to the United States or Federal Agency.
Local Rule 2002-3. United States as a Creditor or Party.
Local Rule 2014-1. Employment of Professionals.
Local Rule 2015-2. Debtor in Possession Duties — Post Confirmation Requirements.
Local Rule 2016-1. Compensation of Professionals in Chapter 7 Cases.
Local Rule 2016-2. Expense Guidelines for Fee Applications.
Local Rule 2090-1. Admission to Practice.
Local Rule 2091-1. Withdrawal of Appearance.
Local Rule 3001-1. Claims and Equity Security Interest — General.
Local Rule 3012-1. Valuation of Securities.
Local Rule 3015-1. Chapter 13 — Plan.
Local Rule 3015-2. Chapter 13 — Amendments to Plan.
Local Rule 3015-3. Chapter 13 — Confirmation Requirements.
Local Rule 3015-4. Chapter 13 — Objections to Confirmation.
Local Rule 3017-2. Conditional Approval of Disclosure Statements in Small Business Cases.
Local Rule 3022-1. Final Report/Decree — Substantial Consummation in Chapter 11 Cases.
Local Rule 4001-2. Pre-Confirmation Adequate Protection and Lease Payments in Chapter 13 Cases.
Local Rule 4002-1. Filing of Payment Advices.
Local Rule 4002-2. Change of Address.
Local Rule 4002-3. Automatic Stay - Rental Deposits.
Local Rule 4004-1. Discharge in Chapter 13 Cases filed after October 16, 2005.
Local Rule 4004-2. Discharge in Chapter 11 Individual Cases Filed After October 16, 2005.
Local Rule 4006-1. Notice of Waiver of Discharge.
Local Rule 5003-1. Records Kept by the Clerk.
Local Rule 5005-3. Filing Papers — Requirements of Form.
Local Rule 5005-4. Electronic Filing of Petitions, Pleadings, Orders and Other Documents.
Local Rule 5071-1. Continuances.
Local Rule 5072-1. Courtroom Decorum.
Local Rule 5073-1. Photographing, Recording, Broadcasting, and Televising in the Courtroom and Environs.
Local Rule 5075-1. Clerk — Delegated Functions.
Local Rule 5080-1. Filing Fees — General.
Local Rule 5081-1. Fees — Form of Payment.
Local Rule 6004-3. Sale or Refinance of Property by Chapter 13 Debtor After Confirmation.
Local Rule 6007-1. Abandonment of Property at Meeting of Creditors.
Local Rule 7001-1. Adversary Proceedings — General Requirements for Allowed Paper Filings.
Local Rule 7003-1. [Deleted.]
Local Rule 7026-1. Discovery.
Local Rule 7067-1. Registry Fund — Deposit in Court.
Local Rule 8006-1. Designation of Record — Appeal.
Local Rule 8007-1. Completion of Record — Appeal.
Local Rule 9001-1. Definitions and Rules of Construction.
Local Rule 9011-1. Attorneys — Duties.
Local Rule 9013-1. Motions Practice.
Local Rule 9015-1. Jury Trials.
Local Rule 9018-1. Sealed Documents.
Local Rule 9070-1. Exhibits.
Local Rule 9072-1. Court Orders.

Appendix of Forms.

Form

1017-3A. Notice and Motion to Convert From Chapter 7 to Chapter 13.

Form
2090-1A. Admission of Attorney to Practice.
2090-1B. Certification of Member in Good Standing.
3012-1A. Motion for Valuation Hearing.
3012-1B. Notice of Valuation Hearing.
3015-1B. Chapter 13 Plan.
3015-1C. Special Notice to Secured Creditors.

Form
3015-3A. Affidavit of Debtor(s) Requesting Confirmation of Plan.
4004-1A. Debtor's Certification of Compliance with 11 U.S.C. § 1328.
4004-2A. Debtor(s)' Certification of Completion of Plan Payments.
Index.

Local Rule 1001-1. Scope of Rules.

The Supreme Court of the United States has prescribed rules of procedure in bankruptcy cases pursuant to 28 U.S.C. § 2075.

Bankruptcy Rule 9029 gives the authority to the United States District Court to promulgate rules for the Bankruptcy Court. Pursuant to Order dated July 18, 1988, by the Honorable James C. Turk, Chief Judge of the United States District Court for the Western District of Virginia, the function of promulgating rules governing practice and procedure in the United States Bankruptcy Court has been granted to the Judges of the United States Bankruptcy Court.

These local rules are to govern practice and procedure solely in the United States Bankruptcy Court for the Western District of Virginia and are designed to clarify and assist in practices and procedures within the United States Bankruptcy Court in the Western District of Virginia in a way that is not inconsistent with any provision of federal law, Federal Rules of Civil Procedure, or the Bankruptcy Rules.

Local Rule 1002-1. Petition — General.

A. *Filing in Proper Division*: A petition seeking relief under the Bankruptcy Code shall be filed in the divisional office in which the debtor's domicile, residence, principal place of business or principal assets were located for the greater part of the 180 days immediately preceding the filing of the petition, unless an extreme hardship would result or justifiable cause can be shown.

B. *Representation by Counsel*: Any entity, as defined in 11 U.S.C. § 101(15), other than a person, must be represented at all times by an attorney who is a member in good standing of the Bar of this Court.

C. *Additional Requirements*:

1. *Original Signature*: The original petition must include an unsworn declaration with the original signature of all debtors and the original signature of the debtor's attorney, if any.

2. *Number of Debtors*: More than one entity cannot be listed as the debtor, except that husband and wife may file a joint petition.

3. *Additional Documents to be filed*:

(a) a schedule of assets and liabilities on the approved bankruptcy form or a Chapter 13 statement, if applicable.

(b) if the debtor is a corporation, partnership, or limited liability company, a copy of the corporate resolution or other appropriate authorization, as specified in Local Rule 1074-1.

(c) if a Chapter 11 petition, a list of 20 largest unsecured creditors (pursuant to Bankruptcy Rule 1007(d)).

(d) a mailing matrix properly formatted and uploaded pursuant to Local Rule 1007-2.

D. *Electronic Filing*: Requirements applicable to petitions filed with the Court in electronic format are governed by Local Rule 5005-4 and the Administrative Procedures authorized by the "Order Adopting Case Management/Electronic Case Filing" in the United States Bankruptcy Court for the Western District of Virginia, which may be modified from time to time and posted on the Court's Internet website. (Amended effective June 28, 2012.)

Local Rule 1006-1. Extension of Time to Pay Filing Fees.

A. *Application for Extension of Time to Pay Filing Fee*: An application to pay a filing fee in installments shall be deemed an application for an extension of time to pay the filing fee. The application shall state that the applicant is unable to pay the filing fee at the time of the filing of the petition and that the applicant has paid no money and transferred no property to his/her attorney for services in connection with the case.

B. *Action on Application*: Prior to the meeting of creditors and unless written objection thereto is made, the Court may enter an Order extending the time within which the filing fee is to be paid to a date no later than the date set for the discharge or confirmation hearing. For cause shown, however, the Court may extend the time for payment to a date not later than six (6) months after the date of filing the petition.

C. *Responsibility for Accumulating Fees*: The attorney for the debtor(s) shall be responsible for accumulating any installment payments made by the debtor toward the payment of the filing fee and shall remit to the Clerk one payment of the filing fee in full within such time as prescribed by the Court.

Note. — 28 U.S.C. § 1930 specifies the filing fees to be paid for petitions under Chapters 7, 9, 11, 12 and 13 of Title 11 U.S.C.

Local Rule 1007-1. Filing of Schedules and Statements.

In the event that schedules and statements are not filed with the petition in a voluntary case, they shall be filed within fourteen (14) days thereafter, unless a motion to extend the time for filing is received prior to the expiration of the fourteen (14) days.

Failure to comply with the provisions of this rule may result in the dismissal of the case without further notice or hearing. (Amended effective December 1, 2009.)

Local Rule 1007-2. Mailing Matrix.

A. *Controlling as List of Creditors*: The mailing matrix is to be a complete list of creditors of the case, and should any discrepancies appear between the matrix and the list of creditors filed within the official form required, the matrix shall be controlling. The filing of a mailing matrix is certification that it is a complete and correct list of all creditors of the debtor(s).

B. *Requirements for Mailing Matrix*:

1. A creditor mailing matrix must be uploaded into the case management/electronic filing system (CM/ECF) for each bankruptcy petition filed.
2. The mailing matrix shall include the names and addresses of all creditors, in alphabetical order.
3. Items are to be typed in proper case.
4. The list is to be in a single vertical column with no grid lines.
5. There must be at least 2 blank lines above and below each creditor name and address combination.
6. Each entry should consist of up to 5 lines and a maximum of 50 characters each. (If the creditor name is more than 50 characters, it will be shortened by the Clerk's office.)
7. Leave at least one single space between the city and state and zip code. A comma between them is unnecessary: Roanoke VA 24010.
8. Use the official United States Postal Service state abbreviations.
9. Addresses shall include zip codes.
10. Individuals must be listed as last name (comma) (space) first name with no periods.

EXAMPLES:

Whoever, John, Jr.
5932 Lovers Lane
Roanoke VA 24019

XYZ Sales & Service
PO Box 92900
Charlotte NC 38902

C. *Incomplete Addresses*: An address containing only a name, or name and incomplete address will **not be mailed**.

D. *Adding Creditors*: When an addition of five or more creditors is made to the mailing matrix, the entire mailing matrix is **not** to be filed. A supplemental mailing matrix, containing only the newly added names and addresses of those creditors added, shall be filed.

E. *Change of Address*: The attorney of record or *pro se* debtor(s) shall notify the Clerk in a separate letter of a change of mailing address for the debtor(s) or debtor's counsel.

F. *Format for Filing*: All non-electronic filings made with the Court must include a compact disk (CD) containing an alphabetical listing of all creditors with their complete mailing address, including zip code, saved in a generic ASCII format (.txt) and attached to the petition.

1. *Compact Disk (CD) Format*: Only compact disk (CD) or such other format that may be permitted in the Administrative Procedures authorized by the "Order Adopting Case Management/Electronic Case Filing" in the United States Bankruptcy Court for the Western District of Virginia shall be accepted. A separate CD must be submitted for each case. The file containing the matrix information shall be saved in a generic ASCII format only, unless otherwise authorized in the previously referenced Administrative Procedures.

2. *Exceptions*: Pro-se debtors, if unable to comply with this requirement, shall file the list of creditors as provided above on paper in scannable format and having the following specifications: white bond or standard copy paper, 8 1/2″ by 11″ in size, margins of at least 1″ top, bottom and left, and typed or printed with a Roman font no smaller than 12 point in size. For other than pro-se debtors, a proper format for the mailing matrix will be considered by the Court only upon submission of a written motion for waiver, proposed order, and list of creditors complying with the provisions of this paragraph.

G. *Returned or Undeliverable Mail*: It is the responsibility of the debtor(s) to provide complete and correct addresses. All undelivered mail will be returned to the debtor(s) (or debtor's counsel), and it shall be the duty of the debtor(s) to forward copies of all notices to the proper parties and notify the Court of the correct address.

Local Rule 1009-1. Amendments to Petition, Lists, or Schedules.

A. *Amending a Petition, List, Schedule or Statement*: Where the debtor(s) files any amendment to the petition, lists, schedules or statements previously filed, the debtor(s) shall send notice of the same to the United States Trustee, any trustee appointed, and to any and all entities affected by the amendment.

B. *Adding Creditors*: Where the debtor(s) adds creditors to the case by supplementing either the schedules or the list of creditors previously filed, the debtor(s) shall serve upon each newly-listed creditor a copy of the following:

1. the amendment, **on the form designated by the Court**;
2. the meeting of creditors notice;
3. the order granting discharge (if any); and
4. any other filed document affecting the rights of said creditor.

C. *Proof of Service*: All amendments of the kind specified in this rule shall be accompanied by the debtor's proof of service evidencing that the required notice was given.

Local Rule 1015-1. Consolidation of Cases.

A party desiring to have bankruptcy cases consolidated procedurally, substantively, or for some other purpose must file a written motion requesting consolidation. Subsections A and B are applicable only after consolidation is granted by the Court.

A. *Procedural Consolidation*:

Cases that are procedurally consolidated are consolidated for noticing purposes only (they will share a joint mailing matrix). The party seeking procedural consolidation shall file a consolidated mailing matrix for each case included in the consolidation within fourteen (14) days from the date of the order granting consolidation.

A pleading, order, or notice which concerns a matter in only one of the procedurally consolidated cases shall be docketed and filed in that case only, but shall reflect the consolidation by stating, in parentheses below the style of the case, "(Procedurally consolidated with Case No.(s) ________)".

A pleading, order, or notice which concerns a matter in all of the procedurally consolidated cases shall contain the style of the cases and shall reflect the consolidation by stating, in parentheses below the style of the cases, "(Procedurally consolidated)".

B. *Substantive Consolidation*:

Cases are substantively consolidated when the assets and liabilities of the debtors are consolidated. When a case is substantively consolidated, the movant shall file within fourteen (14) days from the date of the order granting consolidation a mailing matrix for the combined cases. All further pleadings, orders, and notices shall contain the style of the consolidated cases and the style shall reflect the consolidation by stating, in parentheses below the style of the cases, "(Substantively consolidated)".

C. *Modification of Procedure*:

The Court may, by administrative order, *sua sponte* or upon a motion of a party, modify the rules and procedures applicable to procedural or substantive consolidation. *Authority: Bankruptcy Rule 1015 and 11 U.S.C. §302* (Amended effective December 1, 2009.)

Local Rule 1017-1. Post-Discharge Conversions from Chapter 7 to Another Chapter.

Any debtor(s) who has received a Chapter 7 discharge and files a motion with this Court pursuant to 11 U.S.C. § 706 requesting his/her case be converted to another chapter will be required to either:

A. Set forth in the motion that the debtor(s) waives the benefit of the previously granted Chapter 7 discharge, pursuant to 11 U.S.C. § 727(a)(10) and notices same pursuant to Local Rule 4006-1; or

B. Schedule a hearing on the motion, with notice to all creditors, and demonstrate to the Court good cause to retain the benefits of the Chapter 7 discharge while continuing the case under the new chapter.

Local Rule 1017-2. Dismissal or Suspension — Contemporaneous Petitions.

No debtor as defined by 11 U.S.C. § 109 or § 101(13) may maintain more than one petition under any chapter or chapters of the United States Bankruptcy Code at the same time.

The second petition filed may be dismissed by the Court *sua sponte* or pursuant to motion of the United States Trustee or any interested party.

Local Rule 1017-3. Conversions from Chapter 7 to Chapter 13 at the Request of the Debtor.

Any debtor(s) who desire(s) to convert a case from Chapter 7 to Chapter 13 shall:

A. File a Notice and Motion to Convert to Chapter 13 in substantial compliance with the format attached to these local rules as "Form 1017-3A" and shall serve said Notice and Motion upon all creditors, the U.S. Trustee and the Chapter 7 trustee.

B. If the case was previously converted from one chapter to another chapter under the Bankruptcy Code, the debtor shall set the motion for hearing and shall serve said Notice and Motion pursuant to Bankruptcy Rule 2002(a) upon all creditors, the U.S. Trustee and the Chapter 7 trustee.

C. If the case was not previously converted from one chapter to another chapter under the Bankruptcy Code:

1. Any objection to the Notice and Motion to Convert shall be filed within twenty-one (21) days of the date of the debtor's filing of the Notice and Motion to Convert and the objecting party shall obtain a hearing date for the objection and shall serve the objection and notice of hearing on the debtor(s), debtor's attorney, the U.S. Trustee and the Chapter 7 trustee according to Local Rule 9013-1H.

2. No hearing shall be held on the Notice and Motion to Convert in a previously unconverted case unless a timely objection is filed and the Court, upon the expiration of the twenty-one (21) day period set forth in Paragraph C(1) above, shall enter the standard form order of conversion to Chapter 13.

D. If the case is converted, said conversion will be effective the date of docketing of the Order of Conversion. (Amended effective December 1, 2009.)

Local Rule 1071-1. Divisions of the Western District of Virginia.

A. *Divisional Offices:*

The Western District of Virginia consists of those counties, cities and towns as set forth in 28 U.S.C. § 127. There are three (3) divisional Clerk's offices wherein all petitions, motions, schedules, statements and other documents to be filed with the Court are to be sent. The divisions are as follows:

1. *Roanoke Divisional Office*: Commonwealth of Virginia Building, 210 Church Avenue, Room 200, Roanoke, VA 24011, (540-857-2391) which consists of the counties of Bland, Botetourt, Buchanan, Carroll, Craig, Dickenson, Floyd, Franklin, Giles, Grayson, Lee, Montgomery, Pulaski, Roanoke, Russell, Scott, Smyth, Tazewell, Washington, Wise, Wythe, and the cities of Bristol, Galax, Norton, Radford, Roanoke, and Salem.

2. *Lynchburg Divisional Office*: U. S. Courthouse & Federal Building, 1101 Court Street, Room 166, Lynchburg, VA 24504, (434-845-0317) which consists of the counties of Albemarle, Amherst, Appomattox, Bedford, Buckingham, Campbell, Charlotte, Culpeper, Cumberland, Fluvanna, Greene, Halifax, Henry, Louisa, Madison, Nelson, Orange, Patrick, Pittsylvania, and the cities of Charlottesville, Bedford, Lynchburg, Danville, Martinsville, and South Boston.

3. *Harrisonburg Divisional Office*: U.S. Courthouse and Post Office, 116 N. Main Street, Room 223, Harrisonburg, VA 22802, (540-434-8327) which consists of the counties of Alleghany, Augusta, Bath, Clarke, Frederick, Highland, Page, Rappahannock, Rockbridge, Rockingham, Shenandoah, Warren, and the cities of Harrisonburg, Staunton, Waynesboro, Winchester, Buena Vista, Lexington, Clifton Forge, and Covington.

B. *Judges' Chambers*: There are three Bankruptcy Judges currently sitting in the Western District of Virginia. They are as follows:

The Honorable Ross W. Krumm, Chief Judge
116 N. Main Street
Room 319
Harrisonburg, VA 22802
(540) 434-6747

The Honorable William F. Stone, Jr., Judge
210 Church Avenue SW
Room 210
Roanoke, VA 24011
(540) 857-2394

The Honorable William E. Anderson, Judge
1101 Court Street
Room 246
Lynchburg, VA 24504
(434) 846-3118 (Amended effective June 28, 2012.)

Local Rule 1072-1. Places of Holding Court.

The Bankruptcy Court for the Western District of Virginia sits in eight (8) locations as mandated by 28 U.S.C. § 127 as well as additional locations in the discretion of the United States Judicial Conference. The locations within the Western District of Virginia are:

Abingdon (U.S. Courthouse & Federal Building, Abingdon, VA 24210),
Big Stone Gap (U.S. Courthouse & Post Office, Big Stone Gap, VA 24219),
Charlottesville (U.S. Courthouse & Federal Building, Charlottesville, VA 22901),
Danville (U.S. Courthouse & Post Office, Danville, VA 24541),
Harrisonburg (U.S. Courthouse & Post Office, Harrisonburg, VA 22802),
Lynchburg (U.S. Courthouse & Federal Building, Lynchburg, VA 24504),
Staunton (Staunton Courthouse, 113 East Beverley Street, Staunton, VA 24401), and
Roanoke (Commonwealth of Virginia Building, Roanoke, VA 24011). (Amended effective June 28, 2012.)

Local Rule 1074-1. Corporations, Partnerships, & Limited Liability Companies.

A. *Corporate Resolution:* A voluntary petition filed by, or consent to an involuntary petition filed on behalf of, a corporation shall be accompanied by a duly attested copy of the corporate resolution or other appropriate written authorization.

B. *Partnership Statement:* A voluntary petition filed by, or consent to an involuntary petition filed on behalf of, a partnership shall be accompanied by a duly attested statement that all partners whose consent is required for the filing have consented.

C. *Limited Liability Company Statement:* A voluntary petition filed by, or consent to an involuntary petition filed on behalf of, a limited liability company shall be accompanied by a duly attested statement that all members whose consent is required for the filing have consented.

D. *Representation of Corporations:* Any corporation which maintains an action in this Court under any chapter of the Bankruptcy Code or appears before the Court in any manner must be represented at all times by counsel.

Local Rule 2002-1. Notice to Creditors and Other Interested Parties.

A. *Proponent to Give Notice*:

1. *Generally*: The proponent of any post petition action shall give notice to all parties affected thereby, unless there is a specific prohibition or exception set forth in the Bankruptcy Code, Bankruptcy Rules, Federal Rules of Civil Procedure, or these Local Rules. A certification of such notice is to be promptly filed with the Clerk of Court.

2. *In Reorganization Cases*: All proponents of plans in reorganization cases shall give the notice required under Bankruptcy Rule 2002(b), in a form approved by the Clerk of Court, and shall file proof of service with the Court.

B. *Authority for Agreements to Give Notice*: The Clerk is authorized to enter into agreements with debtors wherein they will provide all required notices to interested parties in cases where the interest of justice and efficiency are served thereby. The Clerk shall approve the form of all such notices, and proof of service shall be filed with the Court.

C. *Notice by Publication*:

1. *Place of Publication*: All notices requiring publication shall be published at least once unless otherwise required by order, rule or statute, and such notice shall be published in newspapers of general circulation as the Court may order.

2. *Time of Publication*: All notices shall be published at least seven (7) days prior to any action to be taken pursuant to the notice, and a longer notice shall be given when required by rule or statute or where deemed proper by the Court.

D. *Notice and Service by Electronic Transmission*:

1. *Automatic Notice of Electronic Filing*: Whenever a pleading or other paper is filed electronically, a Notice of Electronic Filing will be automatically generated by the Electronic Case Filing system at the time of filing, and sent electronically to the party filing the pleading or other paper, as well as to all parties in the case who are registered participants in the Electronic Case Filing system or have otherwise consented to electronic notice.

2. *Required Email Address*: All registered participants shall maintain a current and active e-mail address to receive notification in CM/ECF.

3. *Equivalent to Service by Conventional Mail*: Service by electronic means is complete on transmission unless a party learns that attempted service did not reach the person to be served, and electronic service is treated the same as service by mail for the purpose of giving parties an additional three (3) days to respond.

4. *Electronic Service Required*: The filing party, who is a registered CM/ECF participant, shall serve the pleading or other paper electronically upon all persons entitled to notice or service in accordance with the Federal Rules of Bankruptcy Procedure and this Court's Local Rules.

5. *Registered Participants Consent to Electronic Service*: Pursuant to FRBP 7005, a registered CM/ECF participant consents to receive notice and service by electronic means, which shall constitute proper service. If the recipient of notice or service is a registered CM/ECF participant, service of the "Notice of Electronic Filing" shall be the equivalent of service of the filing by first class mail, postage pre-paid.

EXCEPTIONS:

(a) service of the original complaint and summons for an adversary proceeding pursuant to FRBP 7001;

(b) a motion commencing a contested matter pursuant to FRBP 9014 until such time as FRBP 7004 may be amended to permit electronic service of such a complaint or motion;

(c) service required to be made otherwise pursuant to FRBP 7004(h) (service on an insured depository institution).

6. *Service on Non-Registrants*: Service of any pleading or other document may be made upon non-registrants by any means expressly authorized by the Federal Rules of Bankruptcy Procedure.

7. *Service of Non-Electronically Filed Documents*: Pleadings or other documents which are not filed electronically shall be served in accordance with the Federal Rules of Bankruptcy Procedure and these Local Rules, except as otherwise provided by order of the Court.

F. *Agreements to Use Preferred Addresses*:

1. Scope and Authority: Pursuant 11 U.S.C. §342(e) & (f) an entity and a notice provider may agree that when the notice provider is directed by the Court to give a notice to that entity, the notice provider shall give the notice to the entity in the manner agreed to and at the address or addresses the entity supplies to the notice provider. That address is conclusively presumed to be a proper address for the notice. The notice provider's failure to use the supplied address does not invalidate any notice that is otherwise effective under applicable law.

2. Filing of Notice: The filing of a notice of preferred address pursuant to 11 U.S.C. §342(f) by a creditor directly with the agency or agencies that provide noticing services for the Bankruptcy Court will constitute the filing of such a notice with the Court.

3. Registration: Registration with the National Creditor Registration Service must be accomplished through the agency that provides noticing services for the Bankruptcy Court. Forms and registration information are available at www.ncrsuscourts.com. (Amended effective December 1, 2009.)

Local Rule 2002-2. Notice to the United States or Federal Agency.

A. *Notices to United States Trustee in Chapter 11 Cases*: Unless otherwise specifically directed by the Court or the United States Trustee, a party in interest in a case commenced under Chapter 11 of the Bankruptcy Code shall serve upon the United States Trustee copies of all papers filed with the Court except proofs of claim.

Local Rule 2002-3. United States as a Creditor or Party.

Except as otherwise specified in these rules or applicable statutes, all federal agencies or entities of the United States shall receive notice of all proceedings before this Court as specified in Local Rule 2002-1.

Local Rule 2014-1. Employment of Professionals.

A. *Certified to United States Trustee*: Any and all applications for employment of professional persons pursuant to Bankruptcy Rule 2014 must certify that a copy has been filed with the United States Trustee.

B. *Disclosure of Connections*: All applications for employment shall either: affirmatively aver that the applicant has no connection with the debtor(s), creditors, any other party in interest, their respective attorneys and accountants, the United States Trustee, or any person employed by the Office of the United States Trustee; or make a full disclosure of said connections in the application.

C. *Expedited Entry of Order*: Absent objections within fourteen (14) days of filing with the Court by a party in interest, the Court may approve said application(s) without further notice or hearing. (Amended effective December 1, 2009.)

Local Rule 2015-2. Debtor in Possession Duties — Post Confirmation Requirements.

Once a Chapter 11 plan is confirmed by the Court, the debtor will be required to file a quarterly operating report with the Office of the United States Trustee, on a form prescribed by that office, until the case is closed. A duplicate of this report is to be filed with the Court to satisfy the requirements of Bankruptcy Rule 2015.

Local Rule 2016-1. Compensation of Professionals in Chapter 7 Cases.

Any application pursuant to Bankruptcy Rule 2016 for the payment of professional fees in a case under Chapter 7 of the Bankruptcy Code must be filed no later than seven (7) days before the entry of the order approving the trustee's final distribution in the case. Any applications filed after that time shall be deemed not timely filed and will not be considered by the Court. (Amended effective December 1, 2009.)

Local Rule 2016-2. Expense Guidelines for Fee Applications.

A. *Scope of Rule:* These guidelines apply to all professionals seeking compensation pursuant to 11 U.S.C. §§ 327, 328, 330, and 331.

B. *Allowable Expense Guidelines:*

1. *Photocopies:* Fifteen cents (15¢) per page.

2. *Facsimile Transmissions:* Twenty five cents (25¢) per page plus any actual long distance charges.

C. *Expenses in Excess of Allowed Amounts:* Applications for compensation that vary from the amounts set forth in this local rule will require documented proof of the actual cost incurred.

CASE NOTES

Copying expenses. — Debtor's attorney in a Chapter 13 case did not state how many pages were photocopied so the court was unable to verify that he charged the court-mandated 15¢ per page rate; furthermore, the attorney had not justified the necessity of copy costs. Because the attorney failed to meet his burden of justifying the expenses, his photocopying expenses were not subject to reimbursement at this time. In re Goodbar, 456 B.R. 644, 2011 Bankr. LEXIS 2926 (Bankr. W.D. Va. June 29, 2011).

Local Rule 2090-1. Admission to Practice.

A. *Bar of the Court*: Those attorneys who are admitted to practice before this Court shall comprise the Bar of the United States Bankruptcy Court for the Western District of Virginia.

B. *Qualifications to Practice*: To practice before this Court, an attorney shall at all times be a member in good standing of the Bar of the State of Virginia and have been administered the oath of admission by the Court upon the filing of an acceptable application or as otherwise authorized in this rule.

C. *Application and Procedure for Admission*: Every attorney desiring admission to practice before this Court shall file with the Clerk written application thereof accompanied by an endorsement by one qualified member of the Bar of this Court stating that the applicant is of good moral character and professional reputation and is qualified to practice bankruptcy law. The Clerk of this Court shall supply such application upon request (See Form 2090-1A). As a part of the application, the applicant shall certify that the said applicant has read the Rules of Bankruptcy Procedure and the Local Rules of this Court and is familiar with the Federal Rules of Civil Procedure and the Federal Rules of Evidence.

D. *Presentation in Court*: The endorser of the applicant shall, after approval of the application by the Court, present himself/herself in open Court and by oral motion move for his/her admission to practice. If admitted, the applicant shall, in open Court, take the oath required for admission and sign the roll of the Bar of this Court. Presentation may take place in chambers with leave of the Court.

E. *Other Attorneys*:

1. *Eastern District of Virginia*: Any attorney who is a member in good standing of the Virginia State Bar and the Bar of the United States Bankruptcy Court for the Eastern District of Virginia shall be permitted to practice in the Bankruptcy Court for the Western District of Virginia upon filing with the Clerk of this Court:

(a) a certificate of the Clerk of the United States Bankruptcy Court for the Eastern District of Virginia stating that said attorney is a member in good standing of the Bar of that District, and

(b) a certification from the applicant stating that said attorney has, within the preceding sixty (60) days, read the Local Rules of this Court (Form 2090-1B).

2. *Foreign Attorneys*: Attorneys who are not qualified and licensed to practice under the laws of Virginia, but who are qualified and licensed to practice before the Supreme Court of the United States, or before the highest Court of any state in the United States, or before the Courts of the District of Columbia, may not become members of the Bar of this Court, but may appear on a *pro hac vice* basis only in association with a member of the Bar of this Court, upon motion of such member, and only for the conduct of a case in which associated and then pending before the Court. If said motion is granted, the member of the Bar of this Court that made said motion, will be required to sign all pleadings and appear at all hearings and proceedings before this Court, unless these provisions are waived by the presiding Judge. Such appearance shall not be withdrawn without leave of the Court. Service of notice, process, or any other paper upon the foreign attorney shall be equivalent to such service on the parties for whom appearance has been noted, provided that the foregoing provisions shall not apply to

a *pro se* party. A *pro se* party shall file a memorandum showing an address where notice can be served.

3. *Governmental Attorneys*: Any attorney authorized to represent the interest of the United States pursuant to 28 U.S.C. § 517 is authorized to appear in this Court. In addition, any attorney: (i) licensed to practice and in good standing before the highest court of any State in the United States or before the Courts of the District of Columbia, and (ii) who is regularly employed by the United States or any agency or department thereof or of any State or any political subdivision thereof or any agency or department of any of them as an attorney therefore, may file pleadings and appear in this Court on behalf of that governmental unit, agency or department by which he or she is employed without regard to the requirements contained in section E.2 of this rule.

F. *Student Practice*: To the extent the United States District Court for the Western District of Virginia has in effect a rule authorizing third-year law student practice, the provisions of said rule apply equally to such practice before this Court.

G. *Previous Practice Clause*: All members in good standing of the United States Bankruptcy Court for the Western District of Virginia prior to February 28, 1988, shall be deemed to be members of the Bar of the United States Bankruptcy Court for the Western District of Virginia.

H. *Activities Not Requiring Admission*: The following activities shall not require admission to the bar of this Court:

1. Filing a notice of appearance with a request to be served with pleadings filed in the case.
2. Filing a proof of claim on behalf of a client or an employer.
3. Filing a response on behalf of a client or an employer to any objection to claim or to any pre-hearing order issued by the Court with respect to any objection or motion filed in a case affecting such client's or employer's interest, but not including an appearance in Court in any hearing resulting therefrom except in compliance with section B of this Rule.
4. Such other activities as the Court from time to time for cause shown may authorize. (Amended effective June 28, 2012.)

Local Rule 2091-1. Withdrawal of Appearance.

No attorney of record shall withdraw from any matter pending in this Court, except with the consent of his client stated in writing and by order of the Court or for good cause shown after notice to the client. Any withdrawing attorney shall forthwith give written notice thereof to the Clerk of the Court at such place as said matter is pending. Any attorney entering an action at any time after its inception shall promptly give written notice thereof to the Clerk requesting to be entered as attorney of record.

Local Rule 3001-1. Claims and Equity Security Interest — General.

A. *Case Number*: Each proof of claim presented for filing must specify the case number of the applicable bankruptcy case.

B. *Original Signature*: Each proof of claim presented for filing must be signed by the claimant or the claimant's authorized agent, pursuant to Bankruptcy Rule 3001(b).

C. *Evidence of Debt*: Each proof of claim presented for filing must have attached any applicable security interest or other appropriate documentation evidencing the debt.

D. *Electronic Filing of Proofs of Claim*: In all cases, proofs of claim may be filed electronically with the clerk according to the procedures established and published from time to time by the clerk. Those procedures are available from the clerk's office and are maintained on the court's website at: www.vawb.uscourts.gov.

1. When filing proofs of claim electronically, the claimant shall comply with the requirements of Bankruptcy Rule 3001(c) and (d) regarding the attachment of documentation in electronic format sufficient to establish the validity and status of the claim.
2. The filing of a proof of claim electronically with the clerk shall constitute the filing claimant's approved signature by law and the provisions of 18 U.S.C. §152 shall apply to such filing.
3. The filing of a proof of claim electronically in accordance with the clerk's procedures shall constitute entry of the proof of claim in the claims register maintained by the clerk pursuant to Bankruptcy Rule 5003.

Local Rule 3012-1. Valuation of Securities.

A. *Motion for Valuation*: Any party requesting a determination by the Court on the value of a claim secured by a lien on property in which the estate has an interest must file a motion and notice of hearing using the form and format set forth in Form 3012-1A (Motion for Valuation Hearing) and Form 3012-1B (Notice of Valuation Hearing).

B. *Objections*: Written objections are to be filed with the Court and copies mailed to counsel for the debtor(s) and to the trustee within thirty (30) days from the date of the Notice of Valuation Hearing. Failure to file timely objections may result in an order being entered approving the Motion for Valuation without further notice or hearing.

C. *Entry of Order*: The Trustee shall set forth the Court's ruling(s) on any valuation motions filed in the Order of Confirmation, unless counsel requests entry of a specific order and tenders same to the Court for entry.

Local Rule 3015-1. Chapter 13 — Plan.

A. *Filing of Plan*:

1. *Requirement*: The debtor(s) shall file a Chapter 13 plan not later than fourteen (14) days after the commencement of the Chapter 13 case. The plan shall be accompanied by proof of service.

2. *Required Form Plan*: The Court has supplied a form plan (3015-1B) that is required to be used by Chapter 13 debtors.

3. *Notice to Secured Creditors*: The debtor must also properly serve on each creditor whose collateral is to be valued or whose lien is to be partially or entirely avoided the Special Notice to Secured Creditors attached to these local rules as form 3015-1C.

4. *Extension of Time to File Plan*:

(a) *General Policy*: Motions to extend the time for filing of a Chapter 13 plan must be in writing.

(b) *Motion to Extend Time for Filing Plan*: A motion to extend time for the filing of a plan shall not be considered by the Court unless the same is filed within fourteen (14) days after the date of commencement of the Chapter 13 case, or the failure to file falls under the provisions of Rule 60 of the Federal Rules of Civil Procedure.

(c) *Notice of Extension of Time to File Plan*: If the Court grants the debtor's motion to extend time to file a Chapter 13 plan, the debtor(s) shall forthwith notify the trustee and all creditors of the new deadline set for filing the plan and of the new objection period.

B. *Distribution of Plan*: The debtor(s) shall distribute a copy of the plan to all creditors, the standing trustee, and other interested parties and provide the court with proof of service of the same.

Local Rule 3015-2. Chapter 13 — Amendments to Plan.

A. *Pre-Confirmation Amendments:* — 1. Filed with the court thirty-five (35) or more days prior to confirmation: If an amended plan is filed with the court thirty-five (35) days or more prior to the date first set for a confirmation hearing, the debtor shall file with said amended plan proof of service as set forth in section "D" of this rule. The debtor shall also file a copy of the notice served with such plan advising all creditors and other parties in interest of the date for the confirmation hearing upon such plan and that any objection to its confirmation must be filed in writing at least fourteen (14) days in advance of such hearing in order to be heard.

2. Filed with the court **less** than thirty-five (35) days prior to confirmation: If an amended plan is filed with the court less than thirty-five (35) days prior to the date first set for a confirmation hearing, the debtor(s) is required to file the amended plan with the court to allow the entry of an order setting a new date for the confirmation hearing. The debtor(s) will then be required to serve a copy of said order, along with the proposed plan as set forth in section "C" of this rule.

B. *Post-Confirmation Amendments:* — If an amended plan is filed after confirmation, the debtor(s) is required to file the amended plan with the court to allow the entry of an order setting a date for hearing on the proposed modifications. The debtor(s) will then be required to serve a copy of said order, along with the proposed plan, as set forth in section "C" of this rule.

C. *Distribution of Amended Plan:* — The debtor(s) shall serve any amended plan on:

1. the standing trustee, and

2. all creditors and interested parties on the mailing matrix unless otherwise ordered by the court.

D. *Proof of Service:* — Contemporaneous with the distribution of an amended plan, the debtor(s) shall file a proof of service certification with the court evidencing service on the standing trustee and all creditors on the debtor's mailing matrix unless otherwise ordered by the court. (Amended effective December 1, 2009.)

Local Rule 3015-3. Chapter 13 — Confirmation Requirements.

The Court has determined that it is in the best interest of debtors in Chapter 13 proceedings to receive instructions as to their legal responsibilities. To that end, the Court has prepared a video presentation and written instructions to be reviewed by all Chapter 13 debtors prior to their confirmation hearings.

A. *Duties of Debtors Counsel*:

1. *Video Presentation*: Counsel for Chapter 13 debtor(s) shall have the Chapter 13 debtor(s) view the video Chapter 13 instructions prepared by the Court.

2. *Written Instructions*: Prior to the confirmation hearing, counsel for the Chapter 13 debtor(s) shall deliver the Court's written instructions to the Chapter 13 debtor(s), insure that they are read by or to the Chapter 13 debtor(s), then review them with the Chapter 13 debtor(s), and provide the Chapter 13 debtor(s) an opportunity to ask questions about the instructions of the Court.

B. *Pro Se Debtors*: If the debtor(s) are pro se, the Chapter 13 Trustee will provide said debtor(s) the written instructions at the conclusion of the debtor(s) section 341 meeting and guidance on obtaining both the DVD of the court's instructions and the "Affidavit of Debtor(s) Requesting Confirmation of Plan" (Form 3015-3A).

C. *Certification to the Court*: Prior to a debtor(s)' confirmation hearing, counsel to Chapter 13 debtor(s) and all debtor(s) shall sign the "Affidavit of Debtor(s) Requesting Confirmation of Plan" (Form 3015-3A) to certify compliance with this rule and shall file it with the Clerk of Court and shall deliver a copy to the Chapter 13 Trustee.

Local Rule 3015-4. Chapter 13 — Objections to Confirmation.

A. *Deadline for Original Plan and Related Motions*: Any objection to confirmation of the original Chapter 13 Plan, the Motion for Determination of Value, the Motion for Lien Avoidance or the Motion to Assume or Reject an Executory Contract or Unexpired Lease shall be filed not later than seven (7) days prior to the date set for the confirmation hearing. Any extension of the original objection period must be requested by motion.

B. *Deadline for Modified Plans*: Any objection to a modified Chapter 13 Plan shall be filed at least fourteen (14) days in advance of the confirmation hearing for such Plan, except that an objection may be filed within twenty-eight (28) days after the date of service of such Plan and accompanying notice, if later.

C. *Service of Objection*: The objecting party shall file the original objection to confirmation with the Court and serve copies on the standing trustee, the debtor(s), and the debtor's attorney. The objection shall be accompanied by proof of service evidencing compliance with this requirement. (Amended effective December 1, 2009.)

Local Rule 3017-2. Conditional Approval of Disclosure Statements in Small Business Cases.

A. *Preliminary Review by the United States Trustee*: If a Small Business Debtor as defined in 11 U.S.C. § 101(51D) ("the Debtor") wishes to obtain conditional approval of a disclosure statement, the Debtor shall submit the proposed plan and disclosure statement to the Office of the U.S. Trustee for the Western District of Virginia no fewer than seven (7) days before the proposed plan and disclosure statement are filed with the Court. The U.S. Trustee shall then provide comments to the Debtor within seven (7) days thereafter.

B. *Filing with the Court*: The Debtor shall file with the Court the proposed plan and disclosure statement together with a motion for conditional approval of the proposed disclosure statement certifying compliance with this Rule and containing a statement as to whether the disclosure statement as filed addresses any concerns expressed by the U. S. Trustee. In addition, the Debtor shall attach to the Motion an affidavit attesting to the truthfulness of the contents of said disclosure statement and that all known material facts germane to the financial condition of the Debtor have been disclosed. The affidavit shall be signed by the Debtor(s), or if the Debtor is a legal entity, by such entity's chief officer. Such motion and proposed plan and disclosure statement shall be served upon the Office of the U. S. Trustee, counsel for any appointed creditors' committee, upon any attorney who has filed a notice of appearance or otherwise appeared in the case, and upon any party that has either actually appeared in the case or has filed a request to receive notice.

C. *Response by United States Trustee*: Within seven (7) days after the filing of the plan, disclosure statement and motion for conditional approval, the U.S. Trustee shall file a statement with the Court indicating either that the filed disclosure statement is satisfactory to the Office of the United States Trustee, or if not, in what respects it is considered to be deficient. Any other party in interest may file a similar statement within such period. The Court will consider any such statements filed before ruling on the motion.

D. *Action by the Court*: The Court may either grant or deny the motion for conditional approval without a hearing or may schedule the same for an expedited hearing.

E. *Additional Considerations*:

1. The procedure for conditional approval described herein shall not extend any deadline for filing a plan and disclosure statement previously set by the Court.

2. The Debtor shall bear the burden of obtaining final approval of the disclosure statement in accord with the requirements of 11 U.S.C. § 1125.

3. Conditional approval of the disclosure statement shall not prohibit any party from making timely objection to final approval of such disclosure statement. (Added effective April 1, 2013.)

Local Rule 3022-1. Final Report/Decree — Substantial Consummation in Chapter 11 Cases.

A. *Scope of this Rule*: This rule applies in all Chapter 11 Cases except when the debtors are individuals and the original filing date of the case was on or after October 17, 2005.

B. *Requirement to Apply*: All chapter 11 debtors who are not individuals shall apply for a final decree and file, as an exhibit, a final report evidencing compliance to date with the terms of the plan twelve (12) months after confirmation of said plan.

C. *Notice of Application and Hearing*: Copies of the application and final report shall be mailed to the Office of the United States Trustee and the creditors' committee, if in existence at confirmation, or to the twenty (20) largest unsecured creditors. Debtor's counsel shall also give twenty-eight (28) days notice to all creditors and the United States Trustee of a hearing on the application for final decree and shall certify in writing to the Court compliance with all noticing requirements.

D. *Objections*: Written objections to entry of a final decree and request for hearing thereon must be filed not later than seven (7) days prior to the hearing date with copies to be served on the debtor(s) and debtor's counsel. (Amended effective December 1, 2009.)

Local Rule 4001-2. Pre-Confirmation Adequate Protection and Lease Payments in Chapter 13 Cases.

A. *Payments due under personal property leases governed by 11 U.S.C. § 1326(a)(1)(b)*: All such payments shall be made directly by the debtor to the lessor and the debtor shall furnish proof of such payments to the chapter 13 trustee, unless the debtor's plan expressly provides that such preconfirmation payments will be made to the trustee, in which event the trustee shall pay the lessor, both before and after confirmation, or unless the Court, after motion, notice and opportunity for a hearing, orders otherwise.

B. *Pre-confirmation adequate protection payments governed by 11 U.S.C. § 1326(a)(1)(c)*: If the debtor's proposed plan so provides, pre-confirmation adequate protection payments governed by 11 U.S.C. § 1326(a)(1)(c) shall be made by the debtor to the chapter 13 trustee as part of the total payment to the trustee, who shall pay the amount provided for by the plan as pre-confirmation adequate protection payments to the secured party promptly prior to confirmation, unless and until the Court, after motion, notice and opportunity for a hearing, orders otherwise. In the event the proposed plan makes no provision for the making of such payments or provides that such payments shall be made directly, such payments shall be made by the debtor directly to the creditor(s) entitled to receive them and the debtor shall provide proof and an accounting thereof to the trustee prior to the confirmation hearing. In the event the amount of the proposed pre-confirmation adequate protection payment is less than the regular contractual payment due the secured creditor, the debtor, within seven (7) days after the filing of the original plan or the filing of any amended plan which would make any change in adequate protection payments affecting a secured creditor, shall serve upon such secured creditor, in a manner complying with Bankruptcy Rule 7004 (b), (c), or (h), as may be applicable, a notice stating the proposed amount, method and timing of payment of such pre-confirmation adequate protection payments, which notice shall provide an opportunity for a hearing upon objection being made thereto within fourteen (14) days of the date of service of such notice. In the event no timely objection is made, the parties will be deemed to have stipulated their agreement to the payments provided in such notice. (Amended effective December 1, 2009.)

Local Rule 4002-1. Filing of Payment Advices.

A. *Filing Requirement*: Copies of all payment advices or other evidence of payment, received within 60 days before the date of the filing of the petition by the debtor(s) from any employer of the debtor, shall not be filed with the court, unless otherwise ordered, but with the case trustee.

B. *Interested Creditors*: The debtor(s) shall also provide copies of payment advices to any creditor who timely requests copies of the payment advices or other evidence of payment, at least seven (7) days prior to the meeting of creditors conducted pursuant to 11 U.S.C. § 341. To be considered timely, a creditor's request must be received at least fourteen (14) [days] before the first date set for the meeting of creditors or any adjourned or continued meeting of creditors.

C. *Noncompliance*: The case trustee's certification of non-compliance by the debtor(s) with this rule will be sufficient for dismissal of the case pursuant to 11 U.S.C. § 521(i). (Amended effective December 1, 2009.)

Editor's note. — The bracketed word in subdivision B was added by the publisher.

Local Rule 4002-2. Change of Address.

The attorney of record or *pro se* debtor(s) shall notify the Clerk in writing of a change of mailing address or registered email address for the debtor(s) or debtor's counsel.

Local Rule 4002-3. Automatic Stay - Rental Deposits.

A. *Form of Payment*: Any deposit of rent made by or on behalf of a debtor, pursuant to 11 U.S.C. § 362(l)(1)(B), must be in the form of a certified check or money order payable to the order of the lessor, and delivered to the Clerk of Court with the filing of the petition and certification made pursuant to 11 U.S.C. § 362(l)(1)(A), along with a copy of the Writ of Possession or similar proceeding against a debtor.

B. *Duties of the Clerk*: Upon receipt of a certified check or money order payable to the lessor, the clerk shall log the check or money order and send notice to the lessor setting forth his options to consent to receive the payment or object to the debtor's certification.

C. *Duties of the Lessor*: Within fourteen (14) days of the date of the clerk's notice the lessor must either consent to receive the payment tendered by the debtor(s) or object to the debtor's certification. Failure to respond timely will signify acceptance of the debtor's certification and the clerk is to forward tendered payment to the lessor. (Amended effective December 1, 2009.)

Local Rule 4004-1. Discharge in Chapter 13 Cases filed after October 16, 2005.

A. *Certification of Compliance with § 1328*: The debtor(s) shall file the "Debtor's Certification of Compliance with 11 U.S.C. § 1328" (Local Form 4004-1A) within sixty (60) days of the date the Chapter 13 trustee files the notice of completion of plan payments. The failure to timely file this certification may result in the case being closed without the entry of a discharge order.

B. *Discharge Hearing*: As soon as practicable after the filing of the debtor's certification, the court will send a notice to all creditors and other parties in interest giving them thirty (30) days to dispute the Chapter 13 trustee's report of completion of plan payments or the debtor's Certification of Compliance and request a hearing on the same. The notice shall include the date, time and place of hearing for any timely request for a hearing on the issuance of the discharge. If no request for a hearing is received within the aforementioned time limit, a discharge may be granted without further notice or hearing. (Amended effective December 1, 2009; and April 1, 2013.)

Local Rule 4004-2. Discharge in Chapter 11 Individual Cases Filed After October 16, 2005.

A. *Certification of Compliance with § 1141*: A discharge will not be granted unless the debtor(s) timely file "Debtor's Certification of Compliance with 11 U.S.C. § 1141" (Local Form 4004-2A) upon completion of all payments under their plan.

B. *Discharge Hearing*: As soon as practicable after the filing of the debtor(s)' certification the court will set a discharge hearing pursuant to §1141(5)(C) and the Clerk will send notice to the debtor(s),debtor(s)' attorney, and the United States Trustee.

Local Rule 4006-1. Notice of Waiver of Discharge.

Any debtor(s) who receives an order of the Court approving a waiver of discharge pursuant to 11 U.S.C. § 727(a)(10) will be required to give prompt notice to all creditors, equity security holders, the case trustee, and the United States Trustee.

Local Rule 5003-1. Records Kept by the Clerk.

A. *Authorization to Accept Electronic Filings*: Effective upon the entry of the "Order Adopting Case Management/Electronic Case Filing" in the United States Bankruptcy Court for the Western District of Virginia, the Clerk of Court will accept documents filed electronically pursuant to Local Rule 5005-4. Effecting an electronic filing of a petition, pleading, order, decree, judgment or other document shall constitute entry of that filing on the docket maintained by the Clerk of Court.

B. *Cases Assigned To Electronic Filing System After Opening*: In any case assigned to the Electronic Filing System after such case has been opened, any authorized User who has previously filed documents in paper form shall provide the Clerk, upon request and if reasonably available to the user, electronic copies of all such documents and shall file all subsequent documents in electronic format.

C. *Non-Electronically Filed Documents*: Effective upon the entry of the "Order Adopting Case Management/Electronic Case Filing" in the United States Bankruptcy Court for the Western District of Virginia, any petition, pleading or other document which is filed in paper format shall be required to be filed with the Clerk in scannable format. The Clerk shall scan each such petition, pleading, or other document so filed and convert the same into electronic format. The originals may be shredded or otherwise appropriately discarded by the Clerk after a period of ninety (90) days has elapsed from the date of their filing unless:

(i) at the time of filing, the filing party requests in writing that such petition, pleading or other document be returned and provides to the Clerk a self-addressed envelope bearing the necessary postage;

(ii) within such ninety (90) day period a duly authorized representative of the Office of the United States Trustee or the United States Attorney for this District requests that such petition, pleading or other document be turned over in which case the Clerk shall do so unless the item in question has already been returned to the filing party pursuant to (i) above; or

(iii) the Court orders otherwise.

Local Rule 5005-3. Filing Papers — Requirements of Form.

All pleadings and other papers offered for filing shall meet the following requirements of form:

A. *Legibility*: Papers shall be plainly and legibly type-written, printed, or reproduced on one side of the paper only.

B. *Caption, Official Forms*: The caption and form of all papers filed shall be in compliance with the Bankruptcy Rules, Official Forms, and Local Rules. Each paper or set of papers filed shall bear the case number of the case to which it pertains.

C. *Size, Margins, etc.*: Papers, including attachments and exhibits, shall be of standard weight and letter (8 ½ by 11 inches) size, photo-reduced if necessary, with a top margin of not less than 1 ½ inches. All multi-page pleadings and documents shall be fastened into sets at the top. All papers presented for filing at the same time shall be arranged in case number order.

Local Rule 5005-4. Electronic Filing of Petitions, Pleadings, Orders and Other Documents.

A. *Authorization*: Pursuant to FRBP 5005(a)(2), effective upon the entry of the "Order Adopting Case Management/Electronic Case Filing" in the United States Bankruptcy Court for the Western District of Virginia, petitions, pleadings, orders, and other documents may be filed, signed, or verified by electronic means which (1) are consistent with any technical standard which may be established or modified from time to time by the Judicial Conference of the United States, and (2) are permitted by and are in compliance with the Administrative Procedures authorized by the "Order Adopting Case Management/Electronic Case Filing" in the United States Bankruptcy Court for the Western District of Virginia, as amended from time to time and posted on the Court's Internet website. Any attorney or other person using the Electronic Filing System pursuant to this authorization shall be referred to as a User.

B. *Responsibility and Effect*: The electronic filing of a document by or on behalf of a User of the Electronic Case Filing System shall constitute the signature of such User for all purposes under the Bankruptcy Code and Rules, including specifically FRBP 9011. A User is responsible for any document filed by anyone authorized by such User to effect electronic filings by means of such user's designated password. Such a filing shall further constitute such User's representation to the Court that the User is in possession of the paper original of such document duly signed (and, if applicable, under penalty of perjury) by all necessary parties prior to electronic filing of any document required under the Bankruptcy Code or Rules or this Court's Local Rules to bear the signature(s) of the party(ies) on whose behalf the document is filed, including specifically, the bankruptcy petition, schedules and statement of affairs. The User shall produce the duly signed paper originals of any such documents filed electronically within fourteen (14) days after the making of any written request thereof by the case Trustee or the Office of the United States Trustee or as may be otherwise directed by the Court.

C. *Retention of Originals*: The User shall retain the duly signed paper original of any document required under the preceding paragraph for a period of no less than three (3) years following such case's dismissal or closing, unless otherwise ordered by the Court.

D. *Chapter 11 Cases*: For Chapter 11 cases filed electronically, it will be the responsibility of the Debtor's attorney to mail copies of all notices required to be sent to all creditors under the provisions of FRBP 2002(j).

E. *Payment of Applicable Fees*: Payment of any fee applicable to the filing of any document filed electronically and payment of any fees applicable to the use of the court's electronic filing system, which are authorized or required by the Judicial Conference of the United States, shall be paid in such manner as may be provided for in the Administrative Procedures authorized by the "Order Adopting Case Management/Electronic Case Filing" in the United States Bankruptcy Court for the Western District of Virginia, as the same may be amended from time to time and posted on this Court's Internet website.

F. *Tender of Orders by Counsel*: Proposed orders tendered to the Court by counsel may be done electronically in such manner as may be authorized from time to time by the Administrative Procedures authorized by the "Order Adopting Case Management/Electronic Case Filing" in the United States Bankruptcy Court for the Western District of Virginia, as the same may be amended from time to time and posted on the Court's Internet website.

G. *Electronic Entry of Orders*: The electronic entry of orders by the Court is provided for in Local Rule 9072-1.

H. *Electronic Notice and Service*: Electronic notice and service of petitions, pleadings and other documents are provided for in Local Rule 2002-1(D).

I. *Exhibits*: The electronic filing of exhibits is provided for in the Administrative Procedures authorized by the "Order Adopting Case Management/Electronic Case Filing" in the United States Bankruptcy Court for the Western District of Virginia.

J. *Privacy Protection*: Any limitations on public access to documents filed electronically with this Court shall be provided for in the Administrative Procedures authorized by the "Order Adopting Case Management/Electronic Case Filing" in the United States Bankruptcy Court for the Western District of Virginia, as modified from time to time and posted on the Court's Internet website, which order shall be subject to and in conformity with applicable provisions of statutory law and the Federal Rules of Bankruptcy Procedure.

K. *Disposition of Non-Electronically Filed Documents*: The retention, return and destruction of petitions, pleadings or other documents filed physically with the Clerk are provided for in Local Rule 5003-1.

L. *Hyperlinks*: Hyperlinks or other embedded links to commercial or personal internet sites will not be allowed in any electronic documents filed with the court. (Amended effective December 1, 2009.)

Local Rule 5071-1. Continuances.

Motions for continuance of a hearing date shall not be granted by the mere agreement of counsel. Any such motion must be approved by the Court and after notice to all counsel. No continuance will be granted other than for good cause shown and upon such terms as the Court may impose.

Local Rule 5072-1. Courtroom Decorum.

Counsel shall at all times conduct and demean themselves with dignity and propriety. When addressing the Court, counsel shall rise unless excused therefrom by the Court. All statements and communications to the Court shall be clearly and audibly made from a standing position at the attorney's lectern facing the Court or the witness. Counsel shall not approach the bench unless requested to do so by the Court or unless permission is granted upon the request of counsel.

Local Rule 5073-1. Photographing, Recording, Broadcasting, and Televising in the Courtroom and Environs.

In accordance with the Rules of the Judicial Conference of the United States, photography, electronic recording, video taping, and broadcasting are not permitted in the courtroom and its environs during the progress of, or in connection with judicial proceedings, whether or not Court is actually in session, unless by express permission of the Court.

Local Rule 5075-1. Clerk — Delegated Functions.

The Clerk of the Bankruptcy Court is hereby authorized and directed to grant and enter the following orders without further direction by the Court, subject to suspension, alteration or rescission:

A. *Order and Notice for Meeting of Creditors*: All orders and notices for meetings of creditors may be signed and executed by the Clerk of the United States Bankruptcy Court or his designee, pursuant to Bankruptcy Rule 2002(a).

B. *Authority for Agreements to Give Notice*: The Clerk is authorized to enter into agreements with debtors wherein they will provide all required notices to interested parties in cases where the interest of justice and efficiency are served thereby. The Clerk shall approve the form of all such notices, and proof of service shall be filed with the Court.

C. *Revocation of Privilege to Tender Payments by Cheque*: For justifiable cause, the Clerk of Court may suspend the privilege of any attorney to tender a cheque drawn on his/her law firm for payment of fees to the Court.

D. *Other Orders Grantable by Clerk*: The Clerk may also enter any and all other orders authorized by the Federal Rules of Bankruptcy Procedure, the Federal Rules of Civil Procedure, any Federal statute, these Local Rules, or by direction of the Court. (Amended effective June 28, 2012.)

Local Rule 5080-1. Filing Fees — General.

Except as otherwise provided in Local Rule 1006-1, every petition shall be accompanied by the prescribed filing fees as set forth in 28 U.S.C. § 1930 and the fee schedule approved by the Judicial Conference of the United States.

Cross references. — See Fee Schedule following Local Rule 9072-1.

Local Rule 5081-1. Fees — Form of Payment.

A. *Tender of Payment*: Payment of filing fees will only be accepted by the Clerk if it is tendered through the approved government electronic payment application or by cash, certified or cashier's check, money order, check drawn on the firm of an attorney who is in good standing as a member of this Court's bar. Not withstanding the foregoing, any payment by a registered participant in CM/ECF will be governed by the provisions of Local Rule 5005-4(E).

B. *Revocation of Check or Credit Privilege*: For good cause, the Clerk may suspend the cheque writing or credit privilege(s) of any attorney or other person or entity otherwise entitled to enjoy the same.

Local Rule 6004-3. Sale or Refinance of Property by Chapter 13 Debtor After Confirmation.

A. A debtor seeking approval for the sale or refinance of real property following confirmation of a plan that revests such property in the debtor shall provide the chapter 13 trustee and all creditors and parties in interest at least twenty-one (21) days notice of the motion seeking such approval unless the notice period has been shortened by the court for cause shown.

B. In addition to setting forth the information required by FRBP 2002(c)(1), the notice shall state (i) the total proposed sale price or maximum amount to be secured by the refinancing, as the case may be, and, in the case of a refinancing, the amount of the secured debt to be paid thereby; (ii) the amount of the sale or loan proceeds to be applied to the debtor's obligations under the confirmed plan; (iii) whether such payment will result in full payment of all allowed claims, and (iv) if all allowed claims will not be paid in full, the amount of the sale or loan proceeds that will be paid to the debtor.

C. If no objection (and, if the motion has not already been set for hearing, a request for hearing) is filed within the objection period, the court, in its discretion, may enter an order endorsed by the chapter 13 trustee approving the sale or refinance without holding a hearing. (Amended effective December 1, 2009.)

Local Rule 6007-1. Abandonment of Property at Meeting of Creditors.

Property may be abandoned at a meeting of creditors in any case in which a trustee has been appointed and in which notice that estate property may be abandoned at the meeting has been given in the "Notice of Meeting of Creditors".

To effect abandonment in this manner, the trustee must announce the abandonment at the meeting of creditors and hear no objections. The trustee must then clearly identify the property abandoned, noting that no objections were made, on the courts electronic filing system.

Local Rule 7001-1. Adversary Proceedings — General Requirements for Allowed Paper Filings.

A. *Venue*: All complaints shall be filed in the divisional office of the Court in which the bankruptcy case is pending.

B. *Representation by Counsel*: Any entity, as defined in 11 U.S.C. § 101(15), other than a person, must be represented at all times by an attorney who is a member in good standing of the Bar of this Court.

C. *Requirements of Form*: All papers offered for filing shall meet the following requirements of form:

1. *Legibility*: Papers shall be plainly and legibly type-written, printed, or reproduced.

2. *Caption, Official Forms*: The caption and form of all pleadings, schedules, and other papers shall be in compliance with the Bankruptcy Rules, Official Forms, and Local Rules. Each paper or set of papers filed shall bear the case number of the case to which it pertains.

3. *Size, Margins, etc.*: Papers, including attachments and exhibits, shall be of standard weight and letter (8 ½ by 11 inches) size, photo-reduced if necessary, with a top margin of not less than ½ inches. All multi-page pleadings and documents shall be fastened into sets at the top. All papers presented for filing at the same time shall be arranged in case number order.

4. *Address and, Telephone Number, and Email Address of Attorney*: The lower left-hand portion of the signature page of the pleading shall include the name, address, telephone number, and email address, if any, of the attorney or *pro se* party filing the same.

D. *Additional Requirements*: Each complaint commencing an adversary proceeding must be accompanied by:

1. *Filing Fees*: the proper filing fee, as prescribed by the Judicial Conference pursuant to 28 U.S.C. 1930(b).

2. *Original Signature*: a properly completed and originally signed Adversary Proceeding Cover Sheet (A.O. Form B-104). (Upon request, this form will be provided by the Clerk's Office.) (Amended effective April 1, 2013.)

Local Rule 7003-1.

Deleted.

Editor's note. — Local Rule 7003-1 was eliminated effective June 17, 2007.

Local Rule 7026-1. Discovery.

Unless otherwise permitted by the Court, on its own initiative or for good cause shown by motion, discovery materials, depositions upon oral examination and upon written questions, interrogatories, requests for documents, requests for admission, and answers and responses or objections to such discovery requests shall not be filed with the pleadings or papers in any case or proceeding. Where specific discovery material may appropriately support or oppose a motion, the specific discovery material in question shall be appended as an exhibit to the motion, or in response thereto, without having been previously filed. Discovery material otherwise permitted to be used at trial may be properly so used, if otherwise admissible, without having been previously filed.

Local Rule 7067-1. Registry Fund — Deposit in Court.

A. *Order for Deposit — Interest Bearing Account*: Whenever a party seeks a Court order, or the Judge directs, that money be deposited by the Clerk in an interest-bearing account, the party shall personally deliver the order to the Clerk or financial deputy who will inspect the proposed order for proper form and content and compliance with the Rule prior to signature by the Judge for whom the order is prepared.

B. *Orders Directing Investment of Funds by Clerk*: Any order tendered by a party or parties in an action that directs the Clerk to invest in an interest-bearing account or instrument funds deposited in the registry of the Court pursuant to 28 U.S.C. § 2041 shall include the following:

1. The amount to be invested;

2. The name of the depository approved by the Treasurer of the United States as a depository in which funds may be deposited;

3. A designation of the type of account or instrument in which the funds shall be invested; and,

4. Wording which directs the Clerk to deduct from the income earned on the investment a fee, not exceeding that authorized by the Judicial Conference of the United States and set by the Director of the Administrative Office at 10 percent (10%) of the income earned on the investment, whenever such income becomes available for deduction in the investment so held and without further order of the Court.

Local Rule 8006-1. Designation of Record — Appeal.

A party designating items not previously filed using the courts electronic filing system as part of the record on appeal shall provide copies of the items so designated to the Clerk of the Court. If a party fails to provide copies to the Clerk within fourteen (14) days after the filing of the designation of the record, the Clerk shall prepare copies at the party's expense pursuant to Bankruptcy Rule 8006. The charge assessed will be pursuant to the provisions of 28 U.S.C. § 1930(b). (Amended effective December 1, 2009.)

Local Rule 8007-1. Completion of Record — Appeal.

A. *Transcripts*: A party who files a designation which includes a transcript of any proceeding is required to forthwith deliver to the court reporter and file with the Clerk of the Court, a written request for the transcript and make satisfactory arrangements with the court reporter for payment of the cost involved.

B. *Transmittal of Record to District Court*: It is incumbent on all parties to an appeal to file all required documents with the Clerk of the Court in a timely fashion. If for any reason said record is not complete and ready for transmittal to the District Court forty-five (45) days after the filing of the notice of appeal, the Clerk shall certify to the District Court that said record is incomplete,and further specify all deficiencies so that the District Court may take whatever action it deems necessary to facilitate compliance with the Bankruptcy Rules.

Local Rule 9001-1. Definitions and Rules of Construction.

The definitions of words and phrases in §§ 101, 902 and 1101 of the United States Code and Federal Rules of Bankruptcy Procedure 9001 and the rules of construction in § 102 of the United States Code and Federal Rules of Bankruptcy Procedure 9001 govern their use in these local rules. In addition, the following words and phrases used in these local rules have the meanings indicated unless the context clearly requires otherwise.

A. *Definitions*:

1. **"Appellate Court"** shall mean the United States District Court for the Western District of Virginia exercising its appellate jurisdiction pursuant to 28 U.S.C. § 158.

2. **"Application."** See "Motion". Documents should be captioned "applications" only when the Federal Rules of Bankruptcy Procedure expressly provide that a request for judicial action shall be made by "application."

3. **"Bankruptcy Code"** or **"Code"** means the United States Bankruptcy Code Title 11 U.S.C., as amended.

4. **"Bankruptcy Court"** means the United States Bankruptcy Court for the Western District of Virginia.

5. **"Bankruptcy Rules"** means the Federal Rules of Bankruptcy Procedure.

6. **"Case"** means a bankruptcy case commenced by the filing of a petition pursuant to 11 U.S.C. §§ 301, 302, 303 or 304.

7. **"Clerk"** or **"Bankruptcy Clerk"** or **"Clerk of Court"** means the Clerk of the United States Bankruptcy Court for the Western District of Virginia. When the reference is to a different clerk, it will be specified in the text.

8. **"CM/ECF"** means the Case Management/Electronic Filing System that is in use in the United States Bankruptcy Court for the Western District of Virginia.

9. **"Conventional Filing(s)"** means documents filed with the Clerk of Court by the traditional means that were in effect in the United States Bankruptcy Court for the Western District of Virginia prior to the implementation of CM/ECF.

10. **"Court"** or **"Judge"** means the judicial officer before whom a case or proceeding is pending.

11. **"Defendant"** means any party against whom a claim for relief is made by complaint, counterclaim or cross-claim in an adversary proceeding.

12. **"Deputy Clerk"** means an employee of the United States Bankruptcy Court for the Western District of Virginia appointed by the Clerk.

13. **"District Court"** means the United States District Court for the Western District of Virginia.

14. **"Documents"** means all petitions, pleadings, motions, affidavits, declarations, briefs, points and authorities, and all other papers presented for filing or submission but shall exclude exhibits submitted during a hearing or trial.

15. **"FBR"** or **"FRBP."** means the Federal Rules of Bankruptcy Procedure.

16. **"F.R.C.P."** means the Federal Rules of Civil Procedure.

17. **"File"** includes variations of the word, such as filing, and means the delivery to, and acceptance of a document to be entered on the docket by the Clerk, a deputy clerk, the Court, or other persons authorized by the Court.

18. **"Local Rule"** or **"LBR"** means the Local Bankruptcy Rules of the United States Bankruptcy Court for the Western District of Virginia.

19. **"Plaintiff"** means any party claiming affirmative relief by complaint, counterclaim or cross-claim in an adversary proceeding.

20. **"Proceeding"** includes motions, adversary proceedings, contested matters and other matters presented to the court. It does not include the "Case" as defined above.

21. **"Trustee"** means one to whom the administration of the bankruptcy estate is delegated and to whom the property of the estate is vested in trust for the creditors. It includes a debtor in possession in a chapter 11 case.

22. **"United States Trustee"** means the United States Trustee for Region 4 and includes the Assistant United States Trustee and any designee of the United States Trustee.

B. *Rules of Construction.*

1. *Gender; Plural.* Whenever applicable, each gender does include the other gender and the singular includes the plural.

2. *Terms Not Otherwise Defined.* Terms used in the Local Bankruptcy Rules that are not herein defined will have the meanings provided in the Bankruptcy Code and the Federal Rules of Bankruptcy Procedure. Similarly, the Rules of Construction contained in 11 U.S.C. § 102 also apply.

3. *References to Rules and Statutes.* Any reference in the local rules to a statute or a rule shall include any amendments or successors thereto. (Amended effective December 1, 2009.)

Local Rule 9011-1. Attorneys — Duties.

A. *Appearance at All Hearings*: Counsel of record who files a petition under any chapter in this Court for a debtor, or debtors, must appear at all Court hearings unless excused or given permission to withdraw by the Court.

Local Rule 9013-1. Motions Practice.

A. *Requirement of Written Motion*: In all cases or proceedings, all non CM/ECF motions shall be in writing and be originally signed by the movant or movant's counsel unless made during a hearing or trial.

B. *Grounds and Relief to be Stated*: All motions shall state with particularity the grounds therefor and shall set forth the relief or order sought.

C. *Address, Telephone Number, and Email Address of Attorney*: The lower left-hand portion of the signature page of the pleading shall include the name, address, telephone number, and email address, if any, of the attorney or *pro se* party filing the same.

D. *Return Date, Conference of Counsel*: Except as otherwise provided by an order of the Court or by these Local Rules, all motions shall be made returnable to the time obtained from and scheduled by the Court for a hearing thereon. Before requesting a hearing date on any motion, the proponent shall confer with opposing counsel, in person or by telephone, in a good-faith effort to narrow the area of disagreement.

E. *Requirement of Proof of Service*: At the end of each pleading, motion and other paper required to be served upon a party, there shall be a proof of service signed by counsel (or the *pro se* party) certifying that copies were served and detailing the date, manner of service, and the names and addresses of those served.

F. *Extensions*: Any request for an extension of time relating to motions must be in writing and approved by the Court.

G. *Determination of Motions Without Oral Hearing*: In accordance with Rule 78 of the Federal Rules of Civil Procedure, the Court may rule upon motions without an oral hearing, unless otherwise required by the Bankruptcy Code, the Bankruptcy Rules, or these Local Rules.

H. *Giving Notice of Motion or Hearing*: The party filing a motion, response, or other pleading requiring or requesting a hearing on same, shall make a good-faith effort to contact opposing counsel for dates and then obtain a hearing date from the Court and shall give notice of that hearing date to all parties required to receive notice by the Bankruptcy Rules, these Local Rules, or by order of the Court. The original motion, response, or other pleading, the notice of hearing, and certification that notice of the hearing date has been given must be filed with the Clerk within seven (7) days after the Court has given the hearing date. Failure to file such a certification and notice within the seven (7) days may result in the Court's reassignment, without notice, of the hearing date to other matters.

I. *Caption; Names of Parties:* Every motion initiating a contested matter pursuant to Bankruptcy Rule 9014 shall contain a caption which conforms with Official Form 16B and an additional caption setting forth the debtor's name as shown on the petition, the assigned motion number, and a designation showing the parties as "Movant", "Respondent" and "Trustee" (when applicable). The following is an example:

UNITED STATES BANKRUPTCY COURT
FOR THE WESTERN DISTRICT OF VIRGINIA
____________________ DIVISION

IN RE
JOHN B. DOE
Debtor

Chapter __________

Case No. __________

U. R. BANK
Movant
v.

Motion No. ________

JOHN B. DOE
Respondent
and

I. B. MONEY, TRUSTEE
Respondent

J. *Paragraphs; Separate Statements:* All averments of claim or defense shall be made in numbered paragraphs, the contents of each of which shall be limited as far as practicable to a statement of a single set of circumstances; and a paragraph may be referred to by number in all succeeding pleadings. Each claim founded upon a separate transaction or occurrence and each defense other than denials shall be stated in a separate count or defense whenever a separation facilitates the clear presentation of the matters set forth.

K. *Adoption by Reference; Exhibits:* Statements in a pleading may be adopted by reference in a different part of the same pleading or in another pleading or in any motion. A copy of any written instrument which is an exhibit to a pleading is a part thereof for all purposes.

L. *Electronic Filings:* Service of any pleading filed electronically, other than a complaint and summons initiating an adversary proceeding pursuant to FRBP 7001 or a motion initiating a contested matter pursuant to FRBP 9014, both of which require service pursuant to FRBP 7004, may be made electronically, pursuant to Local Rules 2002-1(D) and 5005-4, upon any attorney or non-represented party who in either case is a registered User of the Electronic Filing System. Service upon others shall be made in accordance with the other provisions of this Rule.

M. *When Written Response Required:* When any party in interest opposes the relief sought in any motion (other than a motion to dismiss the case filed by the standing chapter 12/13 trustee or the chapter 7 case trustee) filed pursuant to Bankruptcy Rule 9014 which has initiated a contested matter, [1] such party shall file a written response to such motion, in the nature of an answer to a complaint in an adversary proceeding, which shall put the party having filed such motion on fair notice of any factual dispute with respect to the allegations contained in such motion and of any affirmative defenses and/or other legal contentions in opposition to such motion which such opposing party intends to present at any hearing thereon. Unless a different time is prescribed by any statute, Bankruptcy Rule or pre-hearing or other order entered by the Court with respect to such motion, such response shall be filed with the Court and served upon the proponent of such motion, or if the motion has been filed by counsel, upon such counsel, at least seven (7) days prior to the date of the noticed hearing, or if that is not practicable due to shortness of notice or other cause shown, as soon in advance of the hearing as may be practicable under the circumstances presented. Failure to file such a response will be cause for the Court to treat the motion as uncontested, to continue the hearing upon the motion, or to take such other action as may be appropriate to further the ends of justice.

(Amended effective December 1, 2009, April 4, 2011, and April 1, 2013.)

Local Rule 9015-1. Jury Trials.

A. *Applicability of Certain Federal Rules of Civil Procedure*: Rules 38, 39, and 47-51 of the Federal Rules of Civil Procedure are hereby adopted for use in jury trials in Bankruptcy Court.

[1] See Advisory Committee Note (1983) to Bankruptcy Rule 9014 for information as to what constitutes a contested matter. See also 10 Collier on Bankruptcy ¶ 9014.01.

B. *Consent*: Not later than twenty-one (21) days after the demand for a jury trial, the demanding party shall file with the Court a consent of all parties for trial by jury in this Court. In the event that the requisite consent is not filed, the demanding party shall have an additional fourteen (14) days to file a motion with the United States District Court to withdraw the reference in order to have the jury trial conducted in District Court. (Amended effective December 1, 2009.)

Local Rule 9018-1. Sealed Documents.

A. *Requesting a Document be Sealed*: A motion to file documents under seal shall contain allegations that show the basis for the necessity of a sealing order. A proposed order granting the motion shall accompany the motion to seal and both the motion and order shall be filed electronically unless permission is granted by the Court for conventional filing.

B. *Procedures*: Documents ordered to be placed under seal must be filed conventionally in a manner prescribed by the Administrative Procedures authorized by the "Order Adopting Case Management/Electronic Case Filing" in the United States Bankruptcy Court for the Western District of Virginia, unless specifically ordered by the Court.

Local Rule 9070-1. Exhibits.

A. *Number to be Filed*: The original and two (2) copies of any exhibit, which is capable of being photocopied, shall be filed with the Court.

B. *Disposition of Exhibits*: All copies of exhibits, models, diagrams, depositions, transcripts, briefs, tables, charts, or other items or things introduced, tendered or marked in the trial of a matter or filed with or delivered to the Clerk, in anticipation of their introduction into evidence, or for use at trial, shall be withdrawn by the parties to the litigation or their counsel, within thirty (30) days after the judgment and the time for appeal or motion for a rehearing or further hearing shall have passed. If such items, materials, or things are not so removed within the time stated, the Clerk may forward them to counsel or the party entitled thereto, or shall destroy or make such other disposition or use of them as the Clerk may deem appropriate.

C. *Electronic Format*: The submission of exhibits in electronic format, including the circumstances under which such submission may be required by the Court, shall be governed by the provisions of the Administrative Procedures authorized by the "Order Adopting Case Management/Electronic Case Filing" in the United States Bankruptcy Court for the Western District of Virginia, as the same may be modified from time to time and posted on the Court's Internet website.

Local Rule 9072-1. Court Orders.

A. *Time for Filing*: When the Court instructs a party to prepare a proposed order, the same shall be filed with the Court within ten (10) days after the conclusion of the trial, hearing, or other disposition of the matter at issue.

B. *Form of Filing*:

1. *Electronic Format*: Effective upon the entry of the "Order Adopting Case Management/Electronic Case Filing" in the United States Bankruptcy Court for the Western District of Virginia, counsel tendering any proposed order to the Court shall do so in electronic format in such manner as may be provided in the Administrative Procedures authorized by the "Order Adopting Case Management/Electronic Case Filing" in the United States Bankruptcy Court for the Western District of Virginia, as the same may be modified from time to time and posted on the Court's internet website.

2. *Paper Format*: Parties appearing *pro se* may submit proposed orders in paper format, provided that they are typed and in scannable form. In addition, the Court may permit or require any proposed order to be submitted in paper format and bearing original signatures of all counsel or parties endorsing the same. Unless otherwise ordered by the Court, the disposition of such order after scanning shall be governed by Local Rule 5003-1(C).

C. *Endorsement*: Endorsement of the order by all parties to the action is encouraged but not required. Difficulty in obtaining endorsements will not excuse the party required to file a proposed order from doing so within the time prescribed by A. of this Rule. An order tendered by counsel in electronic format shall contain the attorney's typed name as follows: /s/ John Doe. An agreed order shall contain in similar manner the signed names of all attorneys or parties whose endorsement is necessary. Counsel's tender of an order containing the typed signatures of other counsel shall constitute proponent counsel's representation that each counsel has reviewed the identical version of the order being tendered and consented thereto, or has objected thereto, in which case the fact of such counsel's objection shall be noted immediately above such counsel's typed name.

D. *Objections Noted*: Whenever counsel shall endorse an order and note with such endorsement any objection to the same, unless the grounds for the objection have been previously stated in the record, or unless the grounds are set forth in writing at the time and as a part of the endorsement, or a request made to the Court for a hearing, the objection will be deemed to be waived.

E. *Notice*: Upon entry of any proposed order, the Clerk shall forthwith send a copy of same to the proponent's counsel, who shall in turn promptly mail copies thereof to all parties directed by the Court and certify same to the Clerk. It will not be necessary to mail copies of orders to parties who have received electronic notice of same from the Court.

F. *Pro Se Debtors*: Upon entry of any proposed order submitted by a *pro se* debtor, the Clerk shall promptly mail copies thereof to all parties directed by the Court. (Amended effective December 1, 2009.)

APPENDIX OF FORMS.

Form 1017-3A.

U. S. BANKRUPTCY COURT
WESTERN DISTRICT OF VIRGINIA
FORM 1017-3A

UNITED STATES BANKRUPTCY COURT
FOR THE WESTERN DISTRICT OF VIRGINIA

In re	**CASE NO.**
Debtor(s)	**CHAPTER 7**

NOTICE AND MOTION TO CONVERT FROM CHAPTER 7 TO CHAPTER 13

Comes now the above-named debtor(s), by counsel, and moves this honorable court to convert this case from chapter 7 to chapter 13.

In support of said motion the debtor(s) further state that the reason the debtor(s) wish to convert their case is: ***(SUMMARY OF REASONS FOR CONVERSION)*** .

The debtor(s) further state that ***(STATE WHETHER CASE WAS PREVIOUSLY CONVERTED OR NOT)***.

A copy of this motion is being served on the case trustee, the U. S. Trustee's Office, and all creditors.

DATED:

____
Attorney for the Debtor(s)

IF THIS CASE HAS <u>NOT</u> PREVIOUSLY BEEN CONVERTED:

The conversion of this case will be effective on the 21st day following the date of the filing of this motion without necessity of a hearing unless timely objection to this motion is filed with the court and the objecting party schedules and notices a hearing pursuant to Local Rule 1017-3.

Form 2090-1A.

UNITED STATES BANKRUPTCY COURT
FOR THE WESTERN DISTRICT OF VIRGINIA

RE: ADMISSION OF ATTORNEY TO PRACTICE

TO THE HONORABLE JUDGE OF SAID COURT:
I, ______________________________, apply for admission to practice before this Court and certify that I am a citizen of the United States, born at ______________; that **I have read the Rules of Bankruptcy Procedure and the Local Rules of this Court**; that I am familiar with the Federal Rules of Civil Procedure and the Federal Rules of Evidence, and that I am qualified and licensed to practice law in the Commonwealth of Virginia.

My Social Security Number is:______________.

Mailing address: Respectfully submitted,

____
Signed: Applicant

....

The undersigned, ______________, a practicing attorney at the Bar of the United States Bankruptcy Court for the Western District of Virginia, certifies that I am acquainted with the applicant who is of good moral character and professional reputation and who meets the qualifications for admission in accordance with the Rules of Court.

Dated: ______________

____
Signed: Member of the Bar

....

VERIFICATION OF LICENSE TO PRACTICE LAW

The validity of the above-named applicant's license to practice law in the Commonwealth of Virginia was verified at the offices of the Virginia State Bar, with ______________ on this the ______ day of __________, 20____.

By: ______________________________
Deputy Clerk

....

ORDER OF ADMISSION

The above applicant having presented himself before the Court in accordance with the Rules of this Court, and having taken the required oath, is ORDERED admitted.

ENTER: ______________

____
JUDGE

Form 2090-1B.

UNITED STATES BANKRUPTCY COURT
FOR THE WESTERN DISTRICT OF VIRGINIA

RE: CERTIFICATION OF MEMBER IN GOOD STANDING

I, ______________________________, a member in good standing of the United States Bankruptcy Court for the Eastern District of Virginia, pursuant to the attached certificate of the Clerk of said Court, do hereby certify that I have, within the preceding sixty (60) days, read the Local Rules of this Court.

My Bar Identification Number is:____________.

Respectfully submitted,

Dated: ______________ ______________________
Member of the Bar

Form 3012-1A.

UNITED STATES BANKRUPTCY COURT
FOR THE WESTERN DISTRICT OF VIRGINIA

IN RE: CHAPTER 13

Debtor CASE NO.

RE:

Creditor

MOTION FOR VALUATION HEARING

Collateral:____
____
Total Debt owed to Creditor: $______________________________
Value of Collateral by Debtor $_____________________________
Special Provisions of Payment of Debt:_______________________
____

Comes now the debtor(s), by counsel, who asks that a valuation hearing be held to determine the value of the collateral upon which the above-named creditor has a lien. The debtor(s) claims the collateral has a fair market value as stated above. If the Court agrees with the debtor(s) that the aforesaid secured fair market value is as shown above then the secured creditor will be paid the fair market value in accordance with the filed Chapter 13 Plan and the remaining debt after the fair market value is deducted will be treated as a general unsecured non-priority debt under the Chapter 13 Plan.

ANY CREDITOR OR PARTY IN INTEREST OBJECTING TO THIS MOTION SHALL FILE WITH THE COURT, THE TRUSTEE AND COUNSEL FOR THE DEBTOR(S) ITS WRITTEN OBJECTION NOT LATER THAN THIRTY (30) DAYS FROM THE DATE BELOW.

Date Mailed:________________

By: ______________________________
Counsel

Counsel for Debtor(s)

____
____
____

Form 3012-1B.

UNITED STATES BANKRUPTCY COURT
FOR THE WESTERN DISTRICT OF VIRGINIA

IN RE: CHAPTER 13

Debtor

CASE NO.

RE:

Creditor

NOTICE OF VALUATION HEARING

The debtor(s) has filed the attached motion asking that a valuation hearing be held to determine the value of the secured collateral of the above-named creditors. The U.S. Bankruptcy Court has set a time period of thirty (30) days from the date below for the above-named creditor to object in writing to the valuation of the collateral listed on the attached motion. If the above-named creditor files an objection to the valuation within the time period specified in this notice, then the Bankruptcy Court has set the date of ________________, 200__ at ________o'clock in the U.S. Bankruptcy Court, located at ________________, ____________, Virginia, for the hearing on the said motion.

IF THE ABOVE-NAMED CREDITOR DOES NOT OBJECT TO THE VALUATION OF THE COLLATERAL WITHIN THE THIRTY(30) DAY TIME PERIOD, AN ORDER APPROVING THE VALUATION WILL BE ENTERED WITHOUT FURTHER NOTICE AND HEARING AND THE ABOVE-NAMED CREDITOR WILL BE BARRED FROM OBJECTING TO SUCH VALUATION OF THE COLLATERAL.

Date Mailed:________________

By: ________________________
Counsel

Counsel for Debtor(s)
____
____
____

CERTIFICATION

I hereby certify that a true copy of this foregoing Notice of Hearing was mailed by U.S. first class mail, postage prepaid this ______ day of ____________, 200__ to the debtor(s), the chapter 13 Trustee, and to the creditor at their address listed above.

____

Form 3015-1B.

U. S. BANKRUPTCY COURT
WESTERN DISTRICT OF VIRGINIA
FORM 3015-1B

UNITED STATES BANKRUPTCY COURT
WESTERN DISTRICT OF VIRGINIA

CHAPTER 13 PLAN
AND RELATED MOTIONS

Name of Debtor(s): **Case No:**

This Plan, dated _________________________, is:

☐ **the *first* Chapter 13 Plan filed in this case.**

☐ **a modified Plan that replaces the**
☐ **confirmed or** ☐ **unconfirmed Plan dated**
____

Date and Time of Modified Plan Confirmation Hearing:
____

Place of Modified Plan Confirmation Hearing:
____

The Plan provisions modified by this filing are:

Creditors affected by this modification are:

NOTICE: YOUR RIGHTS WILL BE AFFECTED. You should read these papers carefully. If you oppose any provision of this Plan, or if you oppose any included motions to (i) value collateral, (ii) avoid liens, or (iii) assume or reject unexpired leases or executory contracts, you MUST file a timely written objection.

This Plan may be confirmed and become binding, <u>and the included motions in paragraphs 3, 6, and 7 to value collateral, avoid liens, and assume or reject unexpired leases or executory contracts may be granted</u>, without further notice or hearing unless a written objection is filed not later than seven (7) days prior to the date set for the confirmation hearing and the objecting party appears at the confirmation hearing.

The debtor(s)' schedules list assets and liabilities as follows:
Total Assets:
Total Non-Priority Unsecured Debt:
Total Priority Debt:
Total Secured Debt:

1. Funding of Plan. The debtor(s) propose to pay the Trustee the sum of $____________ per ___________ for ____ months. Other payments to the Trustee are as follows: ____. The total amount to be paid into the Plan is $__________________.

2. Priority Creditors. The Trustee shall pay allowed priority claims in full unless the creditor agrees otherwise.

A. Administrative Claims under 11 U.S.C. § 1326.

1. The Trustee will be paid the percentage fee fixed under 28 U.S.C. § 586(e), not to exceed 10%, of all sums disbursed except for funds returned to the debtor(s).

2. Debtor(s)' attorney will be paid $______________ balance due of the total fee of $______________ concurrently with or prior to the payments to remaining creditors.

B. Claims under 11 U.S.C. § 507.

The following priority creditors will be paid by deferred cash payments pro rata with other priority creditors or in monthly installments as below, except that allowed claims pursuant to 11 U.S.C. § 507(a)(1) will be paid prior to other priority creditors but concurrently with administrative claims above:

Creditor	**Type of Priority**	**Estimated Claim**	**Payment and Term**

3. Secured Creditors: Motions to Value Collateral ("Cramdown"), Collateral being Surrendered, Adequate Protection Payments, and Payment of certain Secured Claims.

A. Motions to Value Collateral (other than claims protected from "cramdown" by 11 U.S.C. § 1322(b)(2) or by the final paragraph of 11 U.S.C. § 1325(a)). Unless a written objection is timely filed with the Court, the Court may grant the debtor(s)' motion to value collateral as set forth herein.

This section deals with valuation of certain claims secured by real and/or personal property, other than claims protected from "cramdown" by 11 U.S.C. § 1322(b)(2) [real estate which is debtor(s)' principal residence] or by the final paragraph of 11 U.S.C. § 1325(a) [motor vehicles purchased within 910 days or any other thing of value purchased within 1 year before filing bankruptcy], in which the replacement value is asserted to be less than the amount owing on the debt. Such debts will be treated as secured claims only to the extent of the replacement value of the collateral. That value will be paid with interest as provided in sub-section D of this section. You must refer to section 3(D) below to determine the interest rate, monthly payment and estimated term of repayment of any "crammed down" loan. The deficiency balance owed on such a loan will be treated as an unsecured claim to be paid only to the extent provided in section 4 of the Plan. The following secured claims are to be "crammed down" to the following values:

Creditor	**Collateral**	**Purchase Date**	**Est. Debt Bal.**	**Replacement Value**

B. Real or Personal Property to be Surrendered.

Upon confirmation of the Plan, or before, the debtor(s) will surrender his/her/their interest in the collateral securing the claims of the following creditors in satisfaction of the secured portion of such creditors' allowed claims. To the extent that the collateral does not satisfy the claim, any timely filed deficiency claim to which the creditor is entitled may be paid as a non-priority unsecured claim. Confirmation of the Plan shall terminate the automatic stay as to the interest of the debtor(s) and the estate in the collateral.

Creditor	Collateral Description	Estimated Value	Estimated Total Claim

C. Adequate Protection Payments.

The debtor(s) propose to make adequate protection payments required by 11 U.S.C. § 1326(a) or otherwise upon claims secured by personal property, until the commencement of payments provided for in sections 3(D) and/or 6(B) of the Plan, as follows:

Creditor	Collateral	Adeq. Protection Monthly Payment	To Be Paid By

Any adequate protection payment upon an unexpired lease of personal property assumed by the debtor(s) pursuant to section 6(B) of the Plan shall be made by the debtor(s) as required by 11 U.S.C. § 1326(a)(1)(B) (payments coming due after the order for relief).

D. Payment of Secured Claims on Property Being Retained (except only those loans provided for in section 5 of the Plan):

This section deals with payment of debts secured by real and/or personal property [including short term obligations, judgments, tax liens and other secured debts]. After confirmation of the Plan, the Trustee will pay to the holder of each allowed secured claim, which will be either the balance owed on the indebtedness or, where applicable, the collateral's replacement value as specified in sub-section A of this section, whichever is less, with interest at the rate provided below, the monthly payment specified below until the amount of the secured claim has been paid in full. Upon confirmation of the Plan, the valuation and interest rate shown below will be binding unless a timely written objection to confirmation is filed with and sustained by the Court.

Creditor	Collateral	Approx. Bal. of Debt or "Crammed Down" Value	Interest Rate	Monthly Payment & Est. Term

E. Other Debts.

Debts which are (i) mortgage loans secured by real estate which is the debtor(s)' primary residence, or (ii) other long term obligations, whether secured or unsecured, to be continued upon the existing contract terms with any existing default in payments to be cured pursuant to 11 U.S.C. § 1322(b)(5), are provided for in section 5 of the Plan.

4. Unsecured Claims.

A. Not separately classified. Allowed non-priority unsecured claims shall be paid pro rata from any distribution remaining after disbursement to allowed secured and priority claims. Estimated distribution is approximately _____ %. The dividend percentage may vary depending on actual claims filed. If this case were liquidated under Chapter 7, the debtor(s) estimate that unsecured creditors would receive a dividend of approximately _____ %.

B. Separately classified unsecured claims.

Creditor	Basis for Classification	Treatment

5. Mortgage Loans Secured by Real Property Constituting the Debtor(s)' Primary Residence; Other Long Term Payment Obligations, whether secured or unsecured, to be continued upon existing contract terms; Curing of any existing default under 11 U.S.C. § 1322(b)(5).

A. Debtor(s) to make regular contract payments; arrears, if any, to be paid by Trustee. The creditors listed below will be paid by the debtor(s) pursuant to the contract without modification, except that arrearages, if any, will be paid by the Trustee either pro rata with other secured claims or on a fixed monthly basis as indicated below, without interest unless an interest rate is designated below for interest to be paid on the arrearage claim and such interest is provided for in the loan agreement.

Creditor	Collateral	Regular Contract Payment	Estimated Arrearage	Arrearage Interest Rate	Estimated Cure Period	Monthly Arrearage Payment

B. Trustee to make contract payments and cure arrears, if any. The Trustee shall pay the creditors listed below the regular contract monthly payments that come due during the period of this Plan, and pre-petition arrearages on such debts shall be cured by the Trustee either pro rata with other secured claims or with monthly payments as set forth below.

Creditor	Collateral	Regular Contract Payment	Estimated Arrearage	Interest Rate on Arrearage	Monthly Payment on Arrearage & Est. Term

C. Restructured Mortgage Loans to be paid fully during term of Plan. Any mortgage loan against real estate constituting the debtor(s)' principal residence upon which the last scheduled contract payment is due before the final payment under the Plan is due shall be paid by the Trustee during the term of the Plan as permitted by 11 U.S.C. § 1322(c)(2) with interest at the rate specified below as follows:

Creditor	Collateral	Interest Rate	Estimated Claim	Monthly Payment & Term

6. Unexpired Leases and Executory Contracts. The debtor(s) move for assumption or rejection of the executory contracts and leases listed below.

A. Executory contracts and unexpired leases to be rejected. The debtor(s) reject the following executory contracts:

Creditor	Type of Contract

B. Executory contracts and unexpired leases to be assumed. The debtor(s) assume the following executory contracts. The debtor(s) agree to abide by all terms of the agreement. The Trustee will pay the pre-petition arrearages, if any, through payments made pro rata with other priority claims or on a fixed monthly basis as indicated below.

Creditor	Type of Contract	Arrearage	Monthly Payment for Arrears	Estimated Cure Period

7. Liens Which Debtor(s) Seek to Avoid.

A. The debtor(s) move to avoid liens pursuant to 11 U.S.C. § 522(f). The debtor(s) move to avoid the following judicial liens and non-possessory, non-purchase money liens that impair the debtor(s)' exemptions. Unless a written objection is timely filed with the Court, the Court may grant the debtor(s)' motion and cancel the creditor's lien. If an objection is filed, the Court will hear evidence and rule on the motion at the confirmation hearing.

Creditor	Collateral	Exemption Basis	Exemption Amount	Value of Collateral

B. Avoidance of security interests or liens on grounds other than 11 U.S.C. § 522(f). The debtor(s) have filed or will file and serve separate pleadings to avoid the following liens or security interests. The creditor should review the notice or summons accompanying such pleadings as to the requirements for opposing such relief. The listing here is for information purposes only.

Creditor	Type of Lien	Description of Collateral	Basis for Avoidance

8. Treatment and Payment of Claims.

- **All creditors must timely file a proof of claim to receive any payment from the Trustee.**
- **If a claim is scheduled as unsecured and the creditor files a claim alleging the claim is secured but does not timely object to confirmation of the Plan, the creditor may be treated as unsecured for purposes of distribution under the Plan. This paragraph does not limit the right of the creditor to enforce its lien, to the extent not avoided or provided for in this case, after the debtor(s) receive a discharge.**
- **If a claim is listed in the Plan as secured and the creditor files a proof of claim alleging the claim is unsecured, the creditor will be treated as unsecured for purposes of distribution under the Plan.**
- **The Trustee may adjust the monthly disbursement amount as needed to pay an allowed secured claim in full.**

9. Vesting of Property of the Estate. Property of the estate shall revest in the debtor(s) upon confirmation of the Plan. Notwithstanding such vesting, the debtor(s) may not sell, refinance, encumber real property or enter into a mortgage loan modification without approval of the Court after notice to the Trustee, any creditor who has filed a request for notice and other creditors to the extent required by the Local Rules of this Court.

10. Incurrence of indebtedness. The debtor(s) shall not voluntarily incur additional indebtedness exceeding the cumulative total of $5,000 principal amount during the term of this Plan, either unsecured or secured against personal property, except upon approval of the Court after notice to the Trustee, any creditor who has filed a request for notice, and other creditors to the extent required by the Local Rules of this Court.

11. Other provisions of this Plan:

Signatures:

Dated: ______________________

______________________ ______________________

Debtor **Debtor(s)' Attorney**

____

Joint Debtor

Exhibits: **Copy of Debtor(s)' Budget (Schedules I and J);**
Matrix of Parties Served with Plan

Certificate of Service

I certify that on ______________________, I mailed a copy of the foregoing to the creditors and parties in interest on the attached Service List.

____
Signature

____
Address

____

____
Telephone No.

Ver. 09/17/09 [effective 12/01/09]

Form 3015-1C.

U. S. BANKRUPTCY COURT
WESTERN DISTRICT OF VIRGINIA
FORM 3015-1C

UNITED STATES BANKRUPTCY COURT
FOR THE WESTERN DISTRICT OF VIRGINIA

IN RE:

Case No.____________________

Chapter 13

Debtor(s)

SPECIAL NOTICE TO SECURED CREDITORS

To: ____, Attn: __________________________
Name of creditor

____
Description of collateral

1. The attached chapter 13 plan filed by the debtor(s) proposes (*check one)*:

[ ] To value your collateral. ***See Section 3 of the plan.*** Your lien will be limited to the value of the collateral, and any amount you are owed above the value of the collateral will be treated as an unsecured claim.

[ ] To cancel or reduce a judgment lien or a non-purchase money, non-possessory security interest you hold. ***See Section 7 of the plan.*** All or a portion of the amount you are owed will be treated as an unsecured claim.

2. ***You should read the attached plan carefully for the details of how your claim is treated.*** The plan may be confirmed, and the proposed relief granted, unless you file and serve a written objection by the date specified and appear at the confirmation hearing. A copy of the objection must be served on the debtor(s), their attorney, and the chapter 13 trustee.

Date objection due: ______________________
Date and time of confirmation hearing: ______________________
Place of confirmation hearing: ______________________

____
Name(s) of debtor(s)

By: ______________________________
Signature

[ ] Debtor(s)' Attorney
[ ] Pro se debtor

____
Name of attorney for debtor(s)

____
Address of attorney [or pro se debtor]

____

Tel. # ______________________
Fax # ______________________

CERTIFICATE OF SERVICE

I hereby certify that true copies of the foregoing Notice and attached Chapter 13 Plan and Related Motions were served upon the creditor noted above by

( ) first class mail in conformity with the requirements of Bankruptcy Rule 7004(b); or

( ) certified mail in conformity with the requirements of Bankruptcy Rule 7004(h)

on this ____ day of ________________, 20___.

____
Signature of attorney for debtor(s)

Ver. 06/17/05

Form 3015-3A.

U. S. BANKRUPTCY COURT
WESTERN DISTRICT OF VIRGINIA
FORM 3015-3A

UNITED STATES BANKRUPTCY COURT
FOR THE WESTERN DISTRICT OF VIRGINIA

IN RE:

CHAPTER 13

Case No.____________________

Debtor(s)

AFFIDAVIT OF DEBTOR(S) REQUESTING CONFIRMATION OF PLAN

1. **The undersigned affirm(s) that the statements below are true as of the date hereof and certifies that they will be true as of the date of confirmation of my/our chapter 13 plan and may be relied upon by the court unless notice in writing to the contrary is given to the trustee and the court at or prior to such time.**

2. I/We have made all payments to secured creditors, personal property lessors and taxing authorities which have come due since the date on which this case was filed and which I/we were required to make directly to such creditor, lessor or taxing authority. I/we understand that such payments include all mortgage payments, car payments or other secured debts being paid directly, personal property leases, real estate taxes, personal property taxes, federal income taxes, and state income taxes which have come due since this case was filed.

3. Select either A. or B.:

A. Since the filing of this bankruptcy case, I/we have not been required by a judicial or administrative order, or by statute, to pay any domestic support obligation [as that term is defined in 11 U.S.C. section 101(14A)].

B. I/We have paid all amounts that first became due and payable after the filing of this bankruptcy case which I/we were required to pay under a domestic support obligation [as that term is defined in 11 U.S.C. section 101(14A)] required by a judicial or administrative order or by statute.

4. I/we have filed all federal, state, and local tax returns required by law to be filed for all taxable periods ending during the four year period ending on the date of the filing of this bankruptcy case.

By signing this affidavit requesting confirmation of chapter 13 plan, I/we acknowledge that all of the above statements are true and accurate and that the Court may rely upon the truth of each of these statements in determining whether to confirm my/our Chapter 13 Plan. I/We understand that the Court may revoke confirmation of the Chapter 13 Plan if the statements relied upon are not accurate.

Signed:

/s/______________________________________
Debtor

/s/______________________________________
Debtor

Subscribed and sworn to before me, a Notary Public, by the debtor(s) named in this affidavit this _____ day of ______________________________, 20___.

/s/______________________________________
Notary Public

My commission expires: ______________________________

Attorney's Certification (If debtor(s) represented by an attorney):

I certify that I am counsel of record for the debtor(s) and that I have reviewed this Affidavit requesting confirmation of Chapter 13 plan with the debtor(s). Further, I certify that I have complied with the provisions of Local Rule 3015-3. I am filing a copy of this Affidavit with the Court and with the Chapter 13 Trustee this _______ day of ____________________, 20 ___.

/s/______________________________________
Attorney for debtor(s)

Debtor(s) Certification (If debtor(s) not represented by an Attorney):

Yes No (circle one) I have viewed the DVD of the court's Chapter 13 Instructions.

Yes No (circle one) I have received, read and understand the Court's written Chapter 13 Instructions.

I certify that I am filing via first class mail or via the Court's CM/ECF system a true copy of this Affidavit requesting confirmation of Chapter 13 plan with the Court and with the Chapter 13 Trustee this _______ day of ____________________, 20 ___.

/s/____________________

Debtor

/s/____________________

Debtor

Form 4004-1A.

U. S. BANKRUPTCY COURT
WESTERN DISTRICT OF VIRGINIA
FORM 4004-1A

UNITED STATES BANKRUPTCY COURT
FOR THE WESTERN DISTRICT OF VIRGINIA

In re:	CASE NO. CHAPTER 13

DEBTOR'S CERTIFICATION OF COMPLIANCE WITH 11 U.S.C. §1328

The Chapter 13 Trustee has filed a notice of completion of payments in my case and I am hereby requesting that the court issue a discharge. To that end, I/we certify as follows:

1. **I/We have completed an instructional course concerning personal financial management as described in 11 U.S.C. §111 and filed evidence of completion of the same with the Court.**

2. **I/We have not received a discharge in a Chapter 7, 11, or 12 bankruptcy case that was filed within 4 years prior to the filing of this Chapter 13 Bankruptcy or in another Chapter 13 bankruptcy case that was filed within 2 years prior to the filing of this Chapter 13 bankruptcy.**

3. **I/We did not have, either at the time of filing this bankruptcy or at the present time, equity in excess of the statutory amount (see Page 2 at #2) in the type of property described in 11 U.S.C. §522(p)(1) [generally the debtor's homestead].**

4. **There is not currently pending any proceeding in which I may be found guilty of a felony of the kind described in 11 U.S.C. §522(q)(1)(A) or liable for a debt of the kind described in 11 U.S.C. §522(q)(1)(B).**

5. **I/We ____ have made (or _____ have not made) all payments required under the provisions of my/our confirmed Plan which have accrued as of the date below, including any payments to be made by me/us directly to creditors, subject to any agreed deferral of any such payments otherwise due with the consent of the affected creditor.**

6. **I/We (initial the applicable clause or clauses)**

______ (a) did not have at the time this case was filed or at any time since then any domestic support obligation as defined by 11 U.S.C. §101(14A); OR

______ (b) (i) have been (and/or am now) obliged to pay such a domestic support obligation to ________________________, whose current mailing address, or if that address is not known to me, the address used for legal notice purposes, is ____, and whose attorney or other designated agent for the receipt of legal notice is ___________________________, whose last mailing address known to me is ____; AND

_______ (ii) that all amounts due on that obligation at the time this case was filed have been paid in full and all payments that have accrued since that time upon such obligation have also been paid; OR

_______ (iii) that I am not fully current as to all such obligations.

To the best of my/our information and belief the above certifications are correct.

Debtor:_______________________________________ **Date:**____________________

Debtor:_______________________________________ **Date:**____________________

SEE PAGE 2 FOR APPLICABLE DEFINITIONS

PAGE 2

1. A personal financial management course pursuant to 11 U.S.C. §111 is an instructional course approved by the United States Trustee for this District.

2. Pursuant to 11 U.S.C. § 522(p)(1), the statutory amount referred to in paragraph 3 above is $125,000 if the case was filed before April 1, 2007, $136,875 if the case was filed April 1, 2007 through March 31, 2010, $146,450 if the case was filed April 1, 2010 through March 31, 2013, and $155,675 if the case was filed after April 1, 2013.

3. 11 U.S.C. § 101(14A): The term 'domestic support obligation' means "a debt that accrues before, on, or after the date of the order for relief in a case under this title, including interest that accrues on that debt as provided under applicable nonbankruptcy law notwithstanding any other provision of this title, that is —

(A) owed to or recoverable by--

(i) a spouse, former spouse, or child of the debtor or such child's parent, legal guardian, or responsible relative; or

(ii) a governmental unit;

(B) in the nature of alimony, maintenance, or support (including assistance provided by a governmental unit) of such spouse, former spouse, or child of the debtor or such child's parent, without regard to whether such debt is expressly so designated;

(C) established or subject to establishment before, on, or after the date of the order for relief in a case under this title, by reason of applicable provisions of--

(i) a separation agreement, divorce decree, or property settlement agreement;

(ii) an order of a court of record; or

(iii) a determination made in accordance with applicable nonbankruptcy law by a governmental unit; and

(D) not assigned to a nongovernmental entity, unless that obligation is assigned voluntarily by the spouse, former spouse, child of the debtor, or such child's parent, legal guardian, or responsible relative for the purpose of collecting the debt."

4. The type property referred to in 11 U.S.C. §522(p)(1) includes "(A) real or personal property that the debtor or a dependent of the debtor uses as a residence; (B) a cooperative that owns property that the debtor or a dependent of the debtor uses as a residence; (C) a burial plot for the debtor or a dependent of the debtor; or (D) real or personal property that the debtor or a dependent of the debtor claims as a homestead."

5. 11 U.S.C. §522(q)(1)(A) refers to "a felony(as defined in section 3156 of title 18), which under the circumstances, demonstrates that the filing of the case was an abuse of the provisions of this title."

18 U.S.C. § 3156 defines "felony" as "an offense punishable by a maximum term of imprisonment of more than one year."

6. 11 U.S.C. §522(q)(1)(B) refers to any "debt arising from –

(i) any violation of the Federal securities laws (as defined in section 3(a)(47) of the Securities Exchange Act of 1934), any State securities laws, or any regulation or order issued under Federal securities laws or State securities laws;

(ii) fraud, deceit, or manipulation in a fiduciary capacity or in connection with the purchase or sale of any security registered under section 12 or 15(d) of the Securities Exchange Act of 1934 or under section 6 of the Securities Act of 1933;

(iii) any civil remedy under section 1964 of title 18; or

(iv) any criminal act, intentional tort, or willful or reckless misconduct that caused serious physical injury to death to another individual in the preceding 5 years."

Form 4004-2A.

U. S. BANKRUPTCY COURT
WESTERN DISTRICT OF VIRGINIA
FORM 4004-2A

UNITED STATES BANKRUPTCY COURT
FOR THE WESTERN DISTRICT OF VIRGINIA

In Re:	Case No.
	Chapter
Debtor(s)	

DEBTOR'S CERTIFICATION OF COMPLIANCE WITH 11 U.S.C. §1141

The notice of completion of plan payments has been filed in my case and I am hereby requesting that the court issue a discharge.

1. **I/We have completed an instructional course concerning personal financial management as described in 11 U.S.C. §111.**

2. **I/We have not received a discharge in a Chapter 7, 11 or 12 bankruptcy case that was filed within 4 years prior to the filing of this Chapter 11 Bankruptcy.**

3. **There is not currently pending any proceeding in which I may be found guilty of a felony of the kind described in 11 U.S.C. §522(q)(1)(A) or liable for a debt of the kind described in U.S.C. §522(q)(1)(B).**

4. **If applicable, that as of the date of this certification that I/we have paid all amounts due under any domestic support obligation [as that term is defined in 11 U.S.C. §101(14A)] required by a judicial or administrative order, or by statute, including amounts due either (I) before this bankruptcy case was filed and provided for in the Plan, or (ii) due at any time after the filing of this bankruptcy case.**

I/We swear or affirm, under penalty of perjury, that the foregoing is true and correct.

Debtor:_____________________________ **Date:**______________

Debtor:_____________________________ **Date:**______________

Index to U.S. Bankruptcy Court Rules of the Western District of Virginia

A

ABANDONMENT OF PROPERTY AT MEETING OF CREDITORS, USBank-WD Rule 6007-1.

ADVERSARY PROCEEDINGS, USBank-WD Rule 7001-1.

APPEALS.
Completion of record, USBank-WD Rule 8007-1.
Designation of record, USBank-WD Rule 8006-1.

APPELLATE COURT.
Defined, USBank-WD Rule 9001-1.

APPLICABILITY OF RULES, USBank-WD Rule 1001-1.

APPLICATION.
Defined, USBank-WD Rule 9001-1.

ATTORNEYS AT LAW.
Admission to practice, USBank-WD Form 2090-1A, USBank-WD Rule 2090-1.
Change of address, USBank-WD Rule 4002-2.
Chapter 13 cases.
Confirmation requirements, USBank-WD Rule 3015-3.
Affidavit of debtor requesting confirmation of plan, USBank-WD Form 3015-3A.
Duties, USBank-WD Rule 9011-1.
Entities.
Representation by counsel, USBank-WD Rule 1002-1.
Member in good standing, USBank-WD Form 2090-1B.
Withdrawal of appearance, USBank-WD Rule 2091-1.

B

BANKRUPTCY CODE.
Defined, USBank-WD Rule 9001-1.

BANKRUPTCY COURT.
Defined, USBank-WD Rule 9001-1.

BANKRUPTCY RULES.
Defined, USBank-WD Rule 9001-1.

BROADCASTING AND TELEVISING IN COURTROOM, USBank-WD Rule 5073-1.

C

CASE.
Defined, USBank-WD Rule 9001-1.

CHANGE OF ADDRESS, USBank-WD Rule 4002-2.

CHAPTER 7.
Compensation of professionals, USBank-WD Rule 2016-1.

CHAPTER 7 —Cont'd
Conversion to another chapter.
Conversion from Chapter 7 to Chapter 13 at the request of the debtor, USBank-WD Rule 1017-3.
Notice and motion to convert, USBank-WD Form 1017-3A.
Post-discharge conversion, USBank-WD Rule 1017-1.

CHAPTER 11.
Discharge and certification of compliance.
Cases filed after October 16, 2005, USBank-WD Form 4004-2A, USBank-WD Rule 4004-2.
Final decree or report, USBank-WD Rule 3022-1.

CHAPTER 13.
Confirmation requirements, USBank-WD Rule 3015-3.
Affidavit of debtor requesting confirmation of plan, USBank-WD Form 3015-3A.
Sale or refinance of real property by debtor after confirmation, USBank-WD Rule 6004-3.
Conversion to or from another chapter.
Conversion from Chapter 7 to Chapter 13 at the request of the debtor, USBank-WD Rule 1017-3.
Notice and motion to convert, USBank-WD Form 1017-3A.
Discharge and certification of compliance.
Cases filed after October 16, 2005, USBank-WD Form 4004-1A, USBank-WD Rule 4004-1.
Leases.
Pre-confirmation adequate protection and lease payments, USBank-WD Rule 4001-2.
Notice to secured creditors, collateral valued or lien voided, USBank-WD Form 3015-1C, USBank-WD Rule 3015-1.
Objections to confirmation, USBank-WD Rule 3015-4.
Plans, USBank-WD Form 3015-1B, USBank-WD Rule 3015-1.
Amendments, USBank-WD Rule 3015-2.
Sale or refinance of real property by debtor after confirmation, USBank-WD Rule 6004-3.

CLAIMS.
Proof of claims, USBank-WD Rule 3001-1.

CLERK.
Defined, USBank-WD Rule 9001-1.
Deputy clerk, defined, USBank-WD Rule 9001-1.
Duties, USBank-WD Rule 5075-1.

CM/ECF.
Defined, USBank-WD Rule 9001-1.

CODE.
Defined, USBank-WD Rule 9001-1.

CONSOLIDATION OF CASES, USBank-WD Rule 1015-1.

CONSTRUCTION AND INTERPRETATION, USBank-WD Rule 9001-1.

CONTINUANCES, USBank-WD Rule 5071-1.

CORPORATIONS.
Corporate resolution, USBank-WD Rule 1074-1.
Representation, USBank-WD Rule 1074-1.

COURT.
Defined, USBank-WD Rule 9001-1.

COURT ORDERS, USBank-WD Rule 9072-1.

COURTROOM DECORUM, USBank-WD Rule 5072-1.

D

DEBTOR IN POSSESSION.
Duties, USBank-WD Rule 2015-2.

DEFENDANT.
Defined, USBank-WD Rule 9001-1.

DEFINITIONS, USBank-WD Rule 9001-1.

DISCHARGE.
Conversion after discharge to chapter other than 7, USBank-WD Rule 1017-1.
Waiver.
Notice to debtors, USBank-WD Rule 4006-1.

DISCOVERY, USBank-WD Rule 7026-1.

DISTRICT COURT.
Defined, USBank-WD Rule 9001-1.

DIVISIONS OF WESTERN DISTRICT, USBank-WD Rule 1071-1.

DOCUMENTS.
Defined, USBank-WD Rule 9001-1.

E

ELECTRONIC FILING.
CM/ECF, defined, USBank-WD Rule 9001-1.
Conventional filing, defined, USBank-WD Rule 9001-1.
Generally, USBank-WD Rule 5005-4.
Petitions, USBank-WD Rule 1002-1.
Proof of claims, USBank-WD Rule 3001-1.

EQUITY SECURITY INTEREST.
Proof of claims, USBank-WD Rule 3001-1.

EXHIBITS, USBank-WD Rule 9070-1.
Adoption by reference, USBank-WD Rule 9070-1.

EXPENSES.
Fee applications.
Expense guidelines, USBank-WD Rule 2016-2.

F

FACSIMILE TRANSMISSIONS.
Expense guidelines, USBank-WD Rule 2016-2.

FEES.
Applications for fees.
Expense guidelines, USBank-WD Rule 2016-2.

FEES —Cont'd
Filing fees.
Extension of time to pay, USBank-WD Rule 1006-1.
Petitions, USBank-WD Rule 5080-1.
Form of payment, USBank-WD Rule 5081-1.
Revocation of check or credit privileges, USBank-WD Rule 5081-1.

FILE.
Defined, USBank-WD Rule 9001-1.

FILING OF PAPERS.
Adversary proceedings, USBank-WD Rule 7001-1.
Form, USBank-WD Rule 5005-3.

FILING OF PETITIONS, USBank-WD Rule 1002-1.
Electronic filing, USBank-WD Rule 5005-4.
Fees, USBank-WD Rule 5080-1.
Extension of time to pay, USBank-WD Rule 1006-1.

FILING OF SCHEDULES AND STATEMENTS, USBank-WD Rule 1007-1.
Electronic filing, USBank-WD Rule 5005-4.
Payment advices or evidence of payment, USBank-WD Rule 4002-1.

FINAL DECREE.
Chapter 11.
Application, USBank-WD Rule 3022-1.

FINAL REPORT.
Chapter 11, USBank-WD Rule 3022-1.

J

JUDGE.
Defined, USBank-WD Rule 9001-1.

JURY TRIALS, USBank-WD Rule 9015-1.

L

LEASES.
Automatic stays.
Rental deposits, USBank-WD Rule 4002-3.
Chapter 13.
Pre-confirmation adequate protection and lease payments, USBank-WD Rule 4001-2.

LIMITED LIABILITY COMPANY.
Statements, USBank-WD Rule 1074-1.

LIST OF CREDITORS.
Mailing matrix, USBank-WD Rule 1007-2.

LISTS.
Amendments, USBank-WD Rule 1009-1.

M

MAILING MATRIX, USBank-WD Rule 1007-2.

MOTIONS PRACTICE, USBank-WD Rule 9013-1.
Sealed documents, motion to seal, USBank-WD Rule 9018-1.

N

NOTICE.
Chapter 13 plans.
Notice to secured creditors, collateral valued or lien voided, USBank-WD Form 3015-1C, USBank-WD Rule 3015-1.
Creditors and other interested parties, USBank-WD Rule 2002-1.
United States or federal agency, USBank-WD Rule 2002-2.

O

ORDERS.
Court orders, USBank-WD Rule 9072-1.

P

PARTNERSHIPS.
Statements, USBank-WD Rule 1074-1.

PAYMENT ADVICES OR EVIDENCE OF PAYMENT.
Automatic stays.
Rental deposits, USBank-WD Rule 4002-3.
Filing, USBank-WD Rule 4002-1.

PETITIONS.
Amendments, USBank-WD Rule 1009-1.
Dismissal.
Contemporaneous petitions, USBank-WD Rule 1017-2.
Filing, USBank-WD Rule 1002-1.
Electronic filing, USBank-WD Rule 5005-4.
Fees, USBank-WD Rule 5080-1.
Extension of time to pay, USBank-WD Rule 1006-1.
Form, USBank-WD Rule 5005-3.

PHOTOCOPIES.
Expense guidelines, USBank-WD Rule 2016-2.

PHOTOGRAPHS.
Courtroom and environs, USBank-WD Rule 5073-1.

PLACES OF HOLDING COURT, USBank-WD Rule 1072-1.

PLAINTIFF.
Defined, USBank-WD Rule 9001-1.

PLANS.
Chapter 13, USBank-WD Form 3015-1B, USBank-WD Rule 3015-1.
Amendments, USBank-WD Rule 3015-2.

PLEADINGS.
General requirements, USBank-WD Rule 7001-1.

PROCEEDING.
Defined, USBank-WD Rule 9001-1.

PROFESSIONALS.
Compensation.
Chapter 7 cases, USBank-WD Rule 2016-1.

PROFESSIONALS —Cont'd
Employment, USBank-WD Rule 2014-1.

PROPERTY ABANDONMENT AT MEETING OF CREDITORS, USBank-WD Rule 6007-1.

R

REAL PROPERTY.
Chapter 13.
Sale or refinance of real property by debtor after confirmation, USBank-WD Rule 6004-3.

REGISTRY FUND.
Deposit in court, USBank-WD Rule 7067-1.

S

SCHEDULES.
Amendments, USBank-WD Rule 1009-1.
Filing, USBank-WD Rule 1007-1.

SCOPE OF RULES, USBank-WD Rule 1001-1.

SEALED DOCUMENTS, USBank-WD Rule 9018-1.

SECURITIES.
Valuation of securities.
Motion for valuation, USBank-WD Rule 3012-1.
Form, USBank-WD Form 3012-1A.
Notice of valuation hearing, USBank-WD Form 3012-1B.
Objection to valuation, USBank-WD Rule 3012-1.

STATEMENTS.
Filing, USBank-WD Rule 1007-1.

STAYS.
Automatic stays.
Rental deposits, USBank-WD Rule 4002-3.

T

TRUSTEE.
Defined, USBank-WD Rule 9001-1.

U

UNITED STATES.
Creditor or party, USBank-WD Rule 2002-3.

V

VALUATION OF SECURITIES.
Motion for valuation, USBank-WD Rule 3012-1.
Form, USBank-WD Form 3012-1A.
Notice of valuation hearing, USBank-WD Form 3012-1B.
Objection to valuation, USBank-WD Rule 3012-1.

FEDERAL RULES OF APPELLATE PROCEDURE FOR UNITED STATES COURTS OF APPEALS, LOCAL RULES AND INTERNAL OPERATING PROCEDURES FOR THE FOURTH CIRCUIT

Federal Rules of Appellate Procedure as amended through December 1, 2013.

Local Rules and Internal Operating Procedures for the Fourth Circuit as amended through June 1, 2013.

Title I. Applicability of Rules.

Rule
1. Scope of Rules; Definition; Title.
2. Suspension of Rules.

Title II. Appeal From a Judgment or Order of a District Court.

3. Appeal as of Right — How Taken.

Rule
Local Rule 3(a). Filing and Docket Fees.
Local Rule 3(b). Docketing Statement.
IOP 3.1. Transmission of District Court Order.
3.1. (Abrogated.)
4. Appeal as of Right — When Taken.
5. Appeal by Permission.
Local Rule 5. Interlocutory Orders.
5.1. (Abrogated.)
6. Appeal in a Bankruptcy Case from a Final Judgment, Order, or Decree of a District Court or Bankruptcy Appellate Panel.
IOP 6.1. Bankruptcy Appeals.
7. Bond for Costs on Appeal in a Civil Case.
8. Stay or Injunction Pending Appeal.
Local Rule 8. Stay or Injunction Pending Appeal.
9. Release in a Criminal Case.
Local Rule 9(a). Release Prior to Judgment of Conviction.
Local Rule 9(b). Release After Conviction and Notice of Appeal.
Local Rule 9(c). Recalcitrant Witnesses.
10. The Record on Appeal.
Local Rule 10(a). Retention of the Record on Appeal in the District Court.
Local Rule 10(b). Records on Appeal.
Local Rule 10(c). Transcripts.
Local Rule 10(d). Supplemental Records, Modification or Correction.
11. Forwarding the Record.
Local Rule 11(a). Transcript Acknowledgments.
Local Rule 11(b). Time Limits for Filing Transcripts.
Local Rule 11(c). Exhibits.

Rule
Local Rule 11(d). Access of Counsel to Original Record.
IOP 11.1. Sanctions for Court Reporter's Failure to File a Timely Transcript.
12. Docketing the Appeal; Filing a Representation Statement; Filing the Record.
12.1. Remand After an Indicative Ruling by the District Court on a Motion for Relief That Is Barred by a Pending Appeal.
Local Rule 12(a). Appeals by Aggrieved Non-parties in the Lower Court.
Local Rule 12(b). Joint Appeals/Cross-appeals and Consolidations.
Local Rule 12(c). Expedition of Appeals.
Local Rule 12(d). Abeyance.
Local Rule 12(e). Intervention.

Title III. Appeals from the United States Tax Court.

13. Appeals from the Tax Court.
14. Applicability of Other Rules to Appeals from the Tax Court.

Title IV. Review or Enforcement of an Order of an Administrative Agency, Board, Commission, or Officer.

15. Review or Enforcement of an Agency Order — How Obtained; Intervention.
Local Rule 15(a). Docketing Fee.
Local Rule 15(b). Petitions for Review.
15.1. Briefs and Oral Argument in a National Labor Relations Board Proceeding.
16. The Record on Review or Enforcement.
17. Filing the Record.
18. Stay Pending Review.
Local Rule 18. Procedures.
19. Settlement of a Judgment Enforcing an Agency Order in Part.
20. Applicability of Rules to Review or Enforcement of an Agency Order.

Title V. Extraordinary Writs.

21. Writs of Mandamus and Prohibition, and Other Extraordinary Writs.

Rule
Local Rule 21(a). Case Captions for Extraordinary Writs.
Local Rule 21(b). Petitions for Mandamus or Prohibition.
Local Rule 21(c). Fees and Costs for Prisoner Petitions for Mandamus, Prohibition, or other Extraordinary Relief.
Local Rule 21(d). Petitions for Writ of Mandamus Pursuant to 18 U.S.C. § 3771, Crime Victims' Rights.

Title VI. Habeas Corpus; Proceedings In Forma Pauperis.

22. Habeas Corpus and Section 2255 Proceedings.
Local Rule 22(a). Certificates of Appealability.
Local Rule 22(b). Death Penalty Cases and Motions for Stay of Execution.
Local Rule 22(c). Petitions for Rehearing in Death Penalty Cases.
Local Rule 22(d). Motions for Authorization.
IOP 22.1. Death Penalty Cases.
23. Custody or Release of a Prisoner in a Habeas Corpus Proceeding.
24. Proceedings in Forma Pauperis.
Local Rule 24. Prisoner Appeals.

Title VII. General Provisions.

25. Filing and Service.
Local Rule 25(a). Electronic Case Filing System.
Local Rule 25(b). Use of Facsimile Equipment, Service, Certificate of Service.
Local Rule 25(c). Confidential and Sealed Materials.
26. Computing and Extending Time.
Local Rule 26. State Holidays and Inclement Weather.
26.1. Corporate Disclosure Statement.
Local Rule 26.1. Disclosure of Corporate Affiliations and Other Entities with a Direct Financial Interest in Litigation.
27. Motions.
Local Rule 27(a). Content of Motions, Notification and Consent.
Local Rule 27(b). Procedural Orders Acted on by Clerk; Reconsideration Thereof.
Local Rule 27(c). Form of Motions.
Local Rule 27(d). Responses; Replies.
Local Rule 27(e). Panel Assignments and Emergency Motions.
Local Rule 27(f). Motions for Summary Disposition.
28. Briefs.
Local Rule 28(a). Consolidated Cases and Briefs.
Local Rule 28(b). Addenda and Attachments to Briefs.
Local Rule 28(c). Responsibilities of Counsel Listed on a Brief.
Local Rule 28(d). Joint Appeals and Consolidations.
Local Rule 28(e). Citation of Additional Authorities.
Local Rule 28(f). Statement of Facts.
28.1. Cross-Appeals.
29. Brief of an Amicus Curiae.
30. Appendix to the Briefs.
Local Rule 30(a). Attorney Sanctions for Unnecessary Appendix Designations.

Rule
Local Rule 30(b). Appendix Contents; Number of Copies.
Local Rule 30(c). Responsibility of Parties.
Local Rule 30(d). Dispensing with Appendix.
31. Serving and Filing Briefs.
Local Rule 31(a). Shortened Time for Service and Filing of Briefs in Criminal Cases.
Local Rule 31(b). Briefing Orders.
Local Rule 31(c). Briefing Extensions.
Local Rule 31(d). Number of Copies.
32. Form of Briefs, Appendices, and Other Papers.
Local Rule 32(a). Reproduction of Appendices.
Local Rule 32(b). Length of Briefs.
Local Rule 32(c). Correction of Briefs and Appendices.
32.1. Citing Judicial Dispositions.
Local Rule 32.1. Citation of Unpublished Dispositions.
33. Appeal Conferences.
Local Rule 33. Circuit Mediation Conferences.
34. Oral Argument.
Local Rule 34(a). Oral Argument; Pre-argument Review and Summary Disposition of Appeals; Statement Regarding the Need for Oral Argument.
Local Rule 34(b). Informal Briefs.
Local Rule 34(c). Court Sessions and Notification to Counsel.
Local Rule 34(d). Argument Time.
Local Rule 34(e). Motion to Submit on Briefs.
IOP 34.1. Calendar Assignments and Panel Composition.
IOP 34.2. Disposition Without Oral Argument.
IOP 34.3. Audio Files of Oral Argument.
35. En Banc Determination.
Local Rule 35. En Banc Proceedings.
36. Entry of Judgment; Notice.
Local Rule 36(a). Publication of Decisions.
Local Rule 36(b). Unpublished Dispositions; Opinion Distribution.
IOP 36.1. Opinion Preparation Assignments.
IOP 36.2. Circulation of Opinions in Argued Cases.
IOP 36.3. Summary Opinions.
37. Interest on Judgment.
38. Frivolous Appeal — Damages and Costs.
39. Costs.
Local Rule 39(a). Reproduction Costs.
Local Rule 39(b). Bill of Costs.
Local Rule 39(c). Recovery of Costs in the District Court.
40. Petition for Panel Rehearing.
Local Rule 40(a). Filing of Petition.
Local Rule 40(b). Statement of Purpose.
Local Rule 40(c). Time Limits for Filing Petitions.
Local Rule 40(d). Papers Filed After Denial of a Petition for Rehearing.
IOP 40.1. Submission of Petitions for Rehearing to the Court.
IOP 40.2. Panel Rehearing.
41. Mandate: Contents; Issuance and Effective Date; Stay.
Local Rule 41. Motion for Stay of the Mandate.
IOP 41.1. Issuance of the Mandate.
IOP 41.2. Petitions for Writs of Certiorari.
42. Voluntary Dismissal.
Local Rule 42. Voluntary Dismissals.
43. Substitution of Parties.
44. Case Involving a Constitutional Question

Rule
When the United States or the Relevant State Is Not a Party.
45. Clerk's Duties.
Local Rule 45. Dismissals for Failure to Prosecute.
IOP 45.1. Clerk's Office.
IOP 45.2. Public Information.
46. Attorneys.
Local Rule 46(a). Legal Assistance to Indigents by Law Students.
Local Rule 46(b). Admission to Practice.
Local Rule 46(c). Appearance of Counsel; Withdrawal; Substitutions.
Local Rule 46(d). Appointment of Counsel.
Local Rule 46(e). Attorney's Fees and Expenses.
Local Rule 46(f). Proceeding Pro Se.
Local Rule 46(g). Rules of Disciplinary Enforcement.
47. Local Rules by Courts of Appeals.
Local Rule 47(a). Procedures for Adoption of Local Rules and Internal Operating Procedures.
Local Rule 47(b). Advisory Committee on Rules and Procedures.
IOP 47.1. Judicial Conference.
IOP 47.2. Membership in the Judicial Conference of the Circuit.
48. Masters.

Appendices.

Appendix A: Plan of the United States Court of Appeals for the Fourth Circuit in Implementation of the Criminal Justice Act.
Appendix B: Death Penalty Representation in the Fourth Circuit.
Rule
Appendix C: Guidelines for Preparation of Appellate Transcripts in the Fourth Circuit.
Appendix D: Case Management/Electronic Case Filing System.
Appendix E: Panel for the Composition and Administration of the CJA Appellate and Capital Appellate Panels.

Forms.

Form
1. Notice of Appeal to a Court of Appeals From a Judgment or Order of a District Court.
2. Notice of Appeal to a Court of Appeals From a Decision of the Tax Court.
3. Petition for Review of Order of an Agency, Board, Commission or Officer.
4. Affidavit Accompanying Motion for Permission to Appeal In Forma Pauperis.
5. Notice of Appeal to a Court of Appeals From a Judgment or Order of a District Court or a Bankruptcy Appellate Panel.
6. Certificate of Compliance With Rule 32(a).
A. Disclosure of Corporate Affiliations and Other Entities with a Direct Financial Interest in Litigation.
B. Appearance of Counsel.
C. Certificate of Death Penalty Case — Fourth Circuit Local Rule 22(b).
D. United States Court of Appeals for the Fourth Circuit Application for Admission to the Bar
E. Docketing Statement — Tax Court.
F. Docketing Statement — Agency.
G. Docketing Statement — Civil or Criminal.
Index.

TITLE I. APPLICABILITY OF RULES.

Rule 1. Scope of Rules; Definition; Title.

(a) *Scope of Rules.* — (1) These rules govern procedure in the United States courts of appeals.

(2) When these rules provide for filing a motion or other document in the district court, the procedure must comply with the practice of the district court.

(b) *Definition.* — In these rules, "state" includes the District of Columbia and any United States commonwealth or territory.

(c) *Title.* — These rules are to be known as the Federal Rules of Appellate Procedure. (Amended by order adopted April 30, 1979, effective August 1, 1979, by order April 25, 1989, effective December 1, 1989, by order adopted by order April 29, 1994, effective December 1, 1994, by order adopted April 24, 1998, effective December 1, 1998, by order adopted April 29, 2002, effective December 1, 2002, and by order adopted April 28, 2010, effective December 1, 2010.)

Editor's note. — Subdivision (c) of this rule was formerly codified as FRAP 48.

Research References. — Houts and Rogosheske, Art of Advocacy: Appeals (Matthew Bender).

Lawrence J. Smith, Art of Advocacy: Summation (Matthew Bender).

CASE NOTES

Federal Rules of Appellate Procedure do not control appeals to the district court of a misdemeanor conviction before a magistrate. United States v. Burgess, 602 F. Supp. 1329 (E.D. Va. 1985).

Rule 2. Suspension of Rules.

On its own or a party's motion, a court of appeals may — to expedite its decision or for other good cause — suspend any provision of these rules in a particular case and order proceedings as it directs, except as otherwise provided in Rule 26(b). (Amended by order adopted April 24, 1998, effective December 1, 1998.)

CASE NOTES

Court may not waive jurisdictional requirements if they are not met. — Although a court may construe the rules liberally in determining whether they have been complied with, it may not waive the jurisdictional requirements of FRAP Rules 3 and 4, even for "good cause shown" under this rule, if it finds that they have not been met. Torres v. Oakland Scavenger Co., 487 U.S. 312, 108 S. Ct. 2405, 101 L. Ed. 2d 285 (1988), superseded by statute as stated in Retail Flooring Dealers of Am. Inc., v. Beaulieu of Am., LLC, 339 F.3d 1146 (9th Cir. Cal. 2003).

TITLE II. APPEAL FROM A JUDGMENT OR ORDER OF A DISTRICT COURT.

Rule 3. Appeal as of Right — How Taken.

(a) *Filing the Notice of Appeal.* — (1) An appeal permitted by law as of right from a district court to a court of appeals may be taken only by filing a notice of appeal with the district clerk within the time allowed by Rule 4. At the time of filing, the appellant must furnish the clerk with enough copies of the notice to enable the clerk to comply with Rule 3(d).

(2) An appellant's failure to take any step other than the timely filing of a notice of appeal does not affect the validity of the appeal, but is ground only for the court of appeals to act as it considers appropriate, including dismissing the appeal.

(3) An appeal from a judgment by a magistrate judge in a civil case is taken in the same way as an appeal from any other district court judgment.

(4) An appeal by permission under 28 U.S.C. § 1292(b) or an appeal in a bankruptcy case may be taken only in the manner prescribed by Rules 5 and 6, respectively.

(b) *Joint or Consolidated Appeals.* — (1) When two or more parties are entitled to appeal from a district-court judgment or order, and their interests make joinder practicable, they may file a joint notice of appeal. They may then proceed on appeal as a single appellant.

(2) When the parties have filed separate timely notices of appeal, the appeals may be joined or consolidated by the court of appeals.

(c) *Contents of the Notice of Appeal.* — (1) The notice of appeal must:

(A) specify the party or parties taking the appeal by naming each one in the caption or body of the notice, but an attorney representing more than one party may describe those parties with such terms as "all plaintiffs," "the defendants," "the plaintiffs A, B, et al.," or "all defendants except X";

(B) designate the judgment, order, or part thereof being appealed; and

(C) name the court to which the appeal is taken.

(2) A pro se notice of appeal is considered filed on behalf of the signer and the signer's spouse and minor children (if they are parties), unless the notice clearly indicates otherwise.

(3) In a class action, whether or not the class has been certified, the notice of appeal is sufficient if it names one person qualified to bring the appeal as representative of the class.

(4) An appeal must not be dismissed for informality of form or title of the notice of appeal, or for failure to name a party whose intent to appeal is otherwise clear from the notice.

(5) Form 1 in the Appendix of Forms is a suggested form of a notice of appeal.

(d) *Serving the Notice of Appeal.* — (1) The district clerk must serve notice of the filing of a notice of appeal by mailing a copy to each party's counsel of record — excluding the appellant's — or, if a party is proceeding pro se, to the party's last known address. When a defendant in a criminal case appeals, the clerk must also serve a copy of the notice of appeal on the defendant, either by personal service or by mail addressed to the defendant. The clerk must promptly send a copy of the notice of appeal and of the docket entries — and any later docket entries — to the clerk of the court of appeals named in the notice. The district clerk must note, on each copy, the date when the notice of appeal was filed.

(2) If an inmate confined in an institution files a notice of appeal in the manner provided by Rule 4(c), the district clerk must also note the date when the clerk docketed the notice.

(3) The district clerk's failure to serve notice does not affect the validity of the appeal. The clerk must note on the docket the names of the parties to whom the clerk mails copies, with the date of mailing. Service is sufficient despite the death of a party or the party's counsel.

(e) *Payment of Fees.* — Upon filing a notice of appeal, the appellant must pay the district clerk all required fees. The district clerk receives the appellate docket fee on behalf of the court of appeals. (Amended by order adopted April 30, 1979, effective August 1, 1979, by order adopted March 10, 1986, effective July 1, 1986, by order adopted April 25, 1989, effective December 1, 1989, by order adopted April 22, 1993, effective December 1, 1993, by order adopted April 29, 1994, effective December 1, 1994, and by order adopted April 24, 1998, effective December 1, 1998.)

CASE NOTES

Court may not waive jurisdictional requirements if they are not met. — Although a court may construe the rules liberally in determining whether they have been complied with, it may not waive the jurisdictional requirements of this rule and FRAP Rule 4, even for "good cause shown" under FRAP Rule 2, if it finds that they have not been met. Torres v. Oakland Scavenger Co., 487 U.S. 312, 108 S. Ct. 2405, 101 L. Ed. 2d 285 (1988), superseded by statute as stated in Retail Flooring Dealers of Am. Inc., v. Beaulieu of Am., LLC, 339 F.3d 1146 (9th Cir. Cal. 2003).

Committee view that requirements were jurisdictional was of weight in rule construction. — Supreme Court's conclusion that the Advisory Committee viewed the requirements of this rule as jurisdictional in nature, although not determinative, was "of weight" in the Supreme Court's construction of the rule. Torres v. Oakland Scavenger Co., 487 U.S. 312, 108 S. Ct. 2405, 101 L. Ed. 2d 285 (1988).

Litigant has complied with rule if action functional equivalent. — If a litigant files papers in a fashion that is technically at variance with the letter of a procedural rule, a court may nonetheless find that the litigant has complied with the rule if the litigant's action is the functional equivalent of what the rule requires. Torres v. Oakland Scavenger Co., 487 U.S. 312, 108 S. Ct. 2405, 101 L. Ed. 2d 285 (1988).

The specificity requirement of this rule is met only by some designation that gives fair notice of the specific individual or entity seeking to appeal. Torres v. Oakland Scavenger Co., 487 U.S. 312, 108 S. Ct. 2405, 101 L. Ed. 2d 285 (1988), superseded by statute as stated in Garcia v. Wash, 20 F.3d 608 (5th Cir. Tex. 1994).

Use of "et al." was not sufficient to indicate intention to appeal. — Where notice of appeal omitted petitioner's name, the use of "et al." in the notice of appeal was not sufficient to indicate his intention to appeal; the purpose of the specificity requirement of this rule is to provide notice both to the opposition and to the court of the identity of the appellant or appellants; and the use of the phrase "et al.," which literally means "and others," utterly failed to provide such notice to either intended recipient. Torres v. Oakland Scavenger Co., 487 U.S. 312, 108 S. Ct. 2405, 101 L. Ed. 2d 285 (1988), superseded by statute as stated in Garcia v. Wash, 20 F.3d 608 (5th Cir. Tex. 1994).

Court had no jurisdiction over party omitted in notice of appeal. — Where notice of appeal omitted petitioner's name, petitioner failed to comply with the specificity requirement of this rule, even liberally construed; petitioner did not file the functional equivalent of a notice of appeal, he was never named or otherwise designated, however inartfully, in the notice of appeal filed by the fifteen other intervenors, and Nor did petitioner seek leave to amend the notice of appeal within the time limits set by FRAP Rule 4, thus, the Supreme Court was correct that it never had jurisdiction over petitioner's appeal. Torres v. Oakland Scavenger Co., 487 U.S. 312, 108 S. Ct. 2405, 101 L. Ed. 2d 285 (1988), superseded by statute as stated in Garcia v. Wash, 20 F.3d 608 (5th Cir. Tex. 1994).

"Harmless error" analysis not applicable to notice of appeal defects. — Where petitioner argued that courts of appeals should have applied "harmless error" analysis to defects in a notice of appeal, this argument misunderstood the nature of a jurisdictional requirement: litigant's failure to clear a jurisdictional hurdle can never be "harmless" or waived by a court. Torres v. Oakland Scavenger Co., 487 U.S. 312, 108 S. Ct. 2405, 101 L. Ed. 2d 285 (1988).

Local Rule 3(a). Filing and Docket Fees.

Upon filing a notice of appeal, appellant shall pay the clerk of the district court a fee of $455, which includes a $5 filing fee for the notice of appeal and a $250 fee for docketing the appeal in this Court. (Amended by order effective November 1, 2003, and by order effective April 27, 2006.)

Local Rule 3(b). Docketing Statement.

To assist counsel in giving prompt attention to the substance of an appeal, to help reduce the ordering of unnecessary transcripts, to provide the Clerk of the Court of Appeals at the commencement of an appeal with the information needed for effective case management, and to provide necessary information for any mediation conference conducted under Local Rule 33, counsel filing a notice of appeal, petition for review, or application for enforcement for any direct or cross-appeal must complete a docketing statement (form available at www.ca4.uscourts.gov) and file it with the Clerk of the Court of Appeals within 14 days of docketing of the appeal. A copy of the docketing statement must be served on the opposing party or parties.

The docketing statement shall have attached to it any transcript order.

Although a party will not be precluded from raising additional issues, counsel should make every effort to include in the docketing statement all of the issues that will be presented to the Court. Failure to file the docketing statement within the time set forth above will cause the Court to initiate the process for dismissing a case under Local Rule 45.

If an opposing party concludes that the docketing statement is in any way inaccurate, incomplete, or misleading, the Clerk's Office should be informed in writing of any errors and any proposed additions or corrections within 10 days of service of the docketing statement, with copies to all other parties. (Amended effective March 4, 1998, effective April 1, 2008, and effective December 1, 2009.)

IOP 3.1. Transmission of District Court Order.

The clerk of the district court shall transmit to the Clerk of the Court of Appeals a copy of the order appealed from, along with copies of the materials required by FRAP 3(d)(1). (Amended by order effective December 1, 1998.)

Rule 3.1. Appeal from a Judgment Entered by a Magistrate Judge in a Civil Case.

(Abrogated by order adopted April 24, 1998, effective December 1, 1998.)

Rule 4. Appeal as of Right — When Taken.

(a) *Appeal in a Civil Case.* — (1) Time for Filing a Notice of Appeal. — (A) In a civil case, except as provided in Rules 4(a)(1)(B), 4(a)(4), and 4(c), the notice of appeal required by Rule 3 must be filed with the district clerk within 30 days after entry of the judgment or order appealed from.

(B) The notice of appeal may be filed by any party within 60 days after entry of the judgment or order appealed from if one of the parties is:

(i) the United States;

(ii) a United States agency;

(iii) a United States officer or employee sued in an official capacity; or

(iv) a current or former United States officer or employee sued in an individual capacity for an act or omission occurring in connection with duties performed on the United States' behalf — including all instances in which the United States represents that person when the judgment or order is entered or files the appeal for that person.

(C) An appeal from an order granting or denying an application for a writ of error *coram nobis* is an appeal in a civil case for purposes of Rule 4(a).

(2) Filing Before Entry of Judgment. — A notice of appeal filed after the court announces a decision or order — but before the entry of the judgment or order — is treated as filed on the date of and after the entry.

(3) Multiple Appeals. — If one party timely files a notice of appeal, any other party may file a notice of appeal within 14 days after the date when the first notice was filed, or within the time otherwise prescribed by this Rule 4(a), whichever period ends later.

(4) Effect of a Motion on a Notice of Appeal. — (A) If a party timely files in the district court any of the following motions under the Federal Rules of Civil Procedure, the time to file an appeal runs for all parties from the entry of the order disposing of the last such remaining motion:

(i) for judgment under Rule 50(b);

(ii) to amend or make additional factual findings under Rule 52(b), whether or not granting the motion would alter the judgment;

(iii) for attorney's fees under Rule 54 if the district court extends the time to appeal under Rule 58;

(iv) to alter or amend the judgment under Rule 59;

(v) for a new trial under Rule 59; or

(vi) for relief under Rule 60 if the motion is filed no later than 28 days after the judgment is entered.

(B)(i) If a party files a notice of appeal after the court announces or enters a judgment — but before it disposes of any motion listed in Rule 4(a)(4)(A) — the notice becomes effective to appeal a judgment or order, in whole or in part, when the order disposing of the last such remaining motion is entered.

(ii) A party intending to challenge an order disposing of any motion listed in Rule 4(a)(4)(A), or a judgment's alteration or amendment upon such a motion, must file a notice of appeal, or an amended notice of appeal — in compliance with Rule 3(c) — within the time prescribed by this Rule measured from the entry of the order disposing of the last such remaining motion.

(5) Motion for Extension of Time. — (A) The district court may extend the time to file a notice of appeal if:

(i) a party so moves no later than 30 days after the time prescribed by this Rule 4(a) expires; and

(ii) regardless of whether its motion is filed before or during the 30 days after the time prescribed by this Rule 4(a) expires, that party shows excusable neglect or good cause.

(B) A motion filed before the expiration of the time prescribed in Rule 4(a)(1) or (3) may be ex parte unless the court requires otherwise. If the motion is filed after the expiration of the prescribed time, notice must be given to the other parties in accordance with local rules.

(C) No extension under this Rule 4(a)(5) may exceed 30 days after the prescribed time or 14 days after the date when the order granting the motion is entered, whichever is later.

(6) Reopening the Time to File an Appeal. The district court may reopen the time to file an appeal for a period of 14 days after the date when its order to reopen is entered, but only if all the following conditions are satisfied:

(A) the court finds that the moving party did not receive notice under Federal Rule of Civil Procedure 77(d) of the entry of the judgment or order sought to be appealed within 21 days after entry;

(B) the motion is filed within 180 days after the judgment or order is entered or within 14 days after the moving party receives notice under Federal Rule of Civil Procedure 77(d) of the entry, whichever is earlier; and

(C) the court finds that no party would be prejudiced.

(7) Entry Defined. — (A) A judgment or order is entered for purposes of this Rule 4(a):

(i) if Federal Rule of Civil Procedure 58(a) does not require a separate document, when the judgment or order is entered in the civil docket under Federal Rule of Civil Procedure 79(a); or

(ii) if Federal Rule of Civil Procedure 58(a) requires a separate document, when the judgment or order is entered in the civil docket under Federal Rule of Civil Procedure 79(a) and when the earlier of these events occurs:

- the judgment or order is set forth on a separate document, or
- 150 days have run from entry of the judgment or order in the civil docket under Federal Rule of Civil Procedure 79(a).

(B) A failure to set forth a judgment or order on a separate document when required by Federal Rule of Civil Procedure 58(a) does not affect the validity of an appeal from that judgment or order.

(b) *Appeal in a Criminal Case.* — (1) Time for Filing a Notice of Appeal. — (A) In a criminal case, a defendant's notice of appeal must be filed in the district court within 14 days after the later of:

(i) the entry of either the judgment or the order being appealed; or

(ii) the filing of the government's notice of appeal.

(B) When the government is entitled to appeal, its notice of appeal must be filed in the district court within 30 days after the later of:

(i) the entry of the judgment or order being appealed; or

(ii) the filing of a notice of appeal by any defendant.

(2) Filing Before Entry of Judgment. — A notice of appeal filed after the court announces a decision, sentence, or order — but before the entry of the judgment or order — is treated as filed on the date of and after the entry.

(3) Effect of a Motion on a Notice of Appeal. — (A) If a defendant timely makes any of the following motions under the Federal Rules of Criminal Procedure, the notice of appeal from a judgment of conviction must be filed within 14 days after the entry of the

order disposing of the last such remaining motion, or within 14 days after the entry of the judgment of conviction, whichever period ends later. This provision applies to a timely motion:

(i) for judgment of acquittal under Rule 29;

(ii) for a new trial under Rule 33, but if based on newly discovered evidence, only if the motion is made no later than 14 days after the entry of the judgment; or

(iii) for arrest of judgment under Rule 34.

(B) A notice of appeal filed after the court announces a decision, sentence, or order — but before it disposes of any of the motions referred to in Rule 4(b)(3)(A) — becomes effective upon the later of the following:

(i) the entry of the order disposing of the last such remaining motion; or

(ii) the entry of the judgment of conviction.

(C) A valid notice of appeal is effective — without amendment — to appeal from an order disposing of any of the motions referred to in Rule 4(b)(3)(A).

(4) Motion for Extension of Time. — Upon a finding of excusable neglect or good cause, the district court may — before or after the time has expired, with or without motion and notice — extend the time to file a notice of appeal for a period not to exceed 30 days from the expiration of the time otherwise prescribed by this Rule 4(b).

(5) Jurisdiction. — The filing of a notice of appeal under this Rule 4(b) does not divest a district court of jurisdiction to correct a sentence under Federal Rule of Criminal Procedure 35(a), nor does the filing of a motion under 35(a) affect the validity of a notice of appeal filed before entry of the order disposing of the motion. The filing of a motion under Federal Rule of Criminal Procedure 35(a) does not suspend the time for filing a notice of appeal from a judgment of conviction.

(6) Entry Defined. — A judgment or order is entered for purposes of this Rule 4(b) when it is entered on the criminal docket.

(c) *Appeal by an Inmate Confined in an Institution.* — (1) If an inmate confined in an institution files a notice of appeal in either a civil case or a criminal case, the notice is timely if it is deposited in the institution's internal mail system on or before the last day for filing. If an institution has a system designed for legal mail, the inmate must use that system to receive the benefit of this rule. Timely filing may be shown by a declaration in compliance with 28 U.S.C. § 1746 or by a notarized statement, either of which must set forth the date of deposit and state that first-class postage has been prepaid.

(2) If an inmate files the first notice of appeal in a civil case under this Rule 4(c), the 14-day period provided in Rule 4(a)(3) for another party to file a notice of appeal runs from the date when the district court dockets the first notice.

(3) When a defendant in a criminal case files a notice of appeal under this Rule 4(c), the 30-day period for the government to file its notice of appeal runs from the entry of the judgment or order appealed from or from the district court's docketing of the defendant's notice of appeal, whichever is later.

(d) *Mistaken Filing in the Court of Appeals.* — If a notice of appeal in either a civil or a criminal case is mistakenly filed in the court of appeals, the clerk of that court must note on the notice the date when it was received and send it to the district clerk. The notice is then considered filed in the district court on the date so noted. (Amended by order adopted April 30, 1979, effective August 1, 1979, by P.L. 100-690, § 7111, signed November 18, 1988, by order adopted April 30, 1991, effective December 1, 1991, by order adopted April 22, 1993, effective December 1, 1993, by order adopted April 27, 1995, effective December 1, 1995, by order adopted April 24, 1998, effective December 1, 1998, by order adopted April 29, 2002, effective December 1, 2002, by order adopted April 25, 2005, effective December 1, 2005, by order adopted March 26, 2009, effective December 1, 2009, by order adopted April 28, 2010, effective December 1, 2010; and by order adopted April 26, 2011, effective December 1, 2011.)

CASE NOTES

Broad construction favored. — In general, courts have construed Rule 4(a)(1) broadly. Buonocore v. Harris, 65 F.3d 347 (4th Cir. 1995).

Subdivision (b) considered mandatory and jurisdictional. — In the absence of extraordinary circumstances, subdivision (b) of this rule is considered mandatory and jurisdictional. Morin v. United States, 522 F.2d 8 (4th Cir. 1975).

Compliance with subdivision (b) is mandatory and jurisdictional. United States v. Schuchardt, 685 F.2d 901 (4th Cir. 1982).

Notice of appeal in a civil suit must be filed within thirty days of the entry of judgment. This limitation is mandatory and jurisdictional. Thompson v. E.I. DuPont de Nemours & Co., 76 F.3d 530 (4th Cir. 1996).

Court may not waive jurisdictional requirements if they are not met. — Although a court may construe the rules liberally in determining whether they have been complied with, it may not waive the jurisdictional requirements of FRAP Rule 3 and this rule, even for "good cause shown" under FRAP Rule 2, if it finds that they have not been met. Torres v. Oakland Scavenger Co., 487 U.S. 312, 108 S. Ct. 2405, 101 L. Ed. 2d 285 (1988), superseded by statute as stated in Retail Flooring Dealers of Am., Inc. v. Beaulieu of Am., LLC, 339 F.3d 1146 (9th Cir. Cal. 2003).

Where the United States is a "party," the 60-day period in which to appeal applies to all parties to the case, not just the United States. Buonocore v. Harris, 65 F.3d 347 (4th Cir. 1995).

Order granting motion to quash subpoenas was criminal proceeding. — In an appeal where the district court granted movant's motion to quash subpoenas issued by two grand juries with respect to certain papers in its possession, and where the effect of the district court's order was that movant's subsidiary had to turn over all of the papers in its possession to the grand jury, proceeding was criminal rather than civil so that subdivision (b) applied to the proceeding rather than subdivision (a). United States v. Under Seal, 902 F.2d 244 (4th Cir. 1990).

Entry of judgment for purposes of notice of appeal. — A notice of appeal must be filed within thirty days of entry of judgment. Entry of judgment consists of two steps: Creation of a document setting out the judgment and a notation of the document on the docket sheet. The thirty-day period does not begin to run until after the document is entered on the docket sheet. Wilson v. Murray, 806 F.2d 1232 (4th Cir. 1986), cert. denied, 484 U.S. 870, 108 S. Ct. 197, 98 L. Ed. 2d 149 (1987).

Pro se prisoners' notices of appeal are deemed filed with the district court when delivered to prison authorities for forwarding and filing. Wilder v. Chairman of Cent. Classification Bd., 926 F.2d 367 (4th Cir.), cert. denied, 926 U.S. 367, 112 S. Ct. 109, 116 L. Ed. 2d 78 (1991).

A bare notice of appeal cannot be construed as a motion for extension of time under subdivision (a)(5). Wilder v. Chairman of Cent. Classification Bd., 926 F.2d 367 (4th Cir.), cert. denied, 926 U.S. 367, 112 S. Ct. 109, 116 L. Ed. 2d 78 (1991).

Extension of filing period under subdivisions (a) and (b) compared. — Unlike subdivision (a), the language of subdivision (b) empowers the district court to extend the filing period with or without motion. United States v. Reyes, 759 F.2d 351 (4th Cir.), cert. denied, 474 U.S. 857, 106 S. Ct. 164, 88 L. Ed. 2d 136 (1985).

Opportunity to show excusable neglect for late filing. — A criminal defendant who has filed his notice of appeal beyond the time specified in subdivision (b), but within the thirty-day permissible extension period, should have the opportunity to seek relief by showing excusable neglect. United States v. Reyes, 759 F.2d 351 (4th Cir.), cert. denied, 474 U.S. 857, 106 S. Ct. 164, 88 L. Ed. 2d 136 (1985).

Move to vacate temporary restraining order qualifies as motion "to alter or amend judgment." — The plaintiff's contention that the notice of appeal, filed February 14, 1975, was filed more than thirty days after entry of the temporary restraining order (TRO) on December 31, 1974, overlooked the fact that defendants moved to vacate the TRO on January 6, 1975, which qualifies as a motion "to alter or amend judgment" within the meaning of Rule 59, Federal Rules of Civil Procedure. By the terms of Rule 4(a), Federal Rules of Appellate Procedure, the "full time for appeal (thirty days) ... commences to run and is to be computed from the entry of (the) ... (order) granting or denying a motion under Rule 59 to alter or amend the judgment ...." January 20, 1975, was thus the date that the appeal period of thirty days began to run, and February 14, 1975, was within the period. Virginia v. Tenneco, Inc., 538 F.2d 1026 (4th Cir. 1976).

Court of appeals lacks jurisdiction where notice not given in time. — By virtue of subdivision (b) a court of appeals does not have jurisdiction to treat the issues sought to be raised on appeal where notice of appeal was not given within ten days after entry of the judgment, the time was not otherwise extended by order of the district court, and the subsequent motion for a new trial based on newly discovered evidence was not made before or within ten days after entry of the judgment. United States v. Williams, 415 F.2d 232 (4th Cir. 1969).

But belated appeal may be allowed where defendant is prevented from complying. — The original ten-day appeal period prescribed by the federal rules of court as to filing the notice of appeal in criminal cases is jurisdictional. But if a defendant attempted to exercise his right to appeal within the ten-day period specified by the rules and, without fault on his part, was prevented from effective communication with the clerk or the district judge, the defendant may be allowed a belated appeal. United States v. Meyers, 406 F.2d 1015 (4th Cir. 1969) (construing former Fed. R. Crim. P. 37(a).

And court may extend ten-day period on showing of "excusable neglect." — Subdivision (b) permits a district court upon a showing of "excusable neglect" before or after the expiration of the ten-day appeal time to extend the time for filing a notice of appeal for an additional thirty days. United States v. Meyers, 406 F.2d 1015 (4th Cir. 1969).

A non-prisoner litigant who entrusts his filing with the postal processes, without taking further steps to ensure that the notice of appeal is timely filed with the district court, cannot establish excusable neglect. Thompson v. E.I. DuPont de Nemours & Co., 76 F.3d 530 (4th Cir. 1996).

The good cause standard is only applicable to motions for enlargement of time filed within thirty days of entry of judgment. Thompson v. E.I. DuPont de Nemours & Co., 76 F.3d 530 (4th Cir. 1996).

The rule requires that the conduct of the appellant only be looked to and that only if excusable neglect be shown on appellant's part should an extension be granted. Excusable neglect is to be found when appellant receives no notice of the entry of judgment or when other extraordinary or unique circumstances subsumed within the rubric of excusable neglect occur. United States v. Virginia, 508 F. Supp. 187 (E.D. Va. 1981).

Where the mistakes in the case were the solicitor general's indecisiveness, United States attorney's failure to check on a critical procedure when he knew that local counsel was on vacation, and local counsel's failure to personally see to it that another lawyer or his secretary personally accepted responsibility for the filing of the notice in a timely manner, the federal district court could not say that they acted in a timely manner, and that the failure to file was through no fault of theirs. United States v. Virginia, 508 F. Supp. 187 (E.D. Va. 1981).

Notice to pro se litigant of right to extension. — When a pro se litigant files a notice of appeal that is untimely but within the period during which an extension of time might be granted pursuant to this rule, the litigant must be informed of the rule and provided an opportunity to establish excusable neglect. Shah v. Hutto, 704 F.2d 717 (4th Cir. 1983), cert. denied, 466 U.S. 975, 104 S. Ct. 2354, 80 L. Ed. 2d 827 (1984).

District court has no jurisdiction to reconsider and vacate an order of that court which has become final in a criminal case because of the expiration of the time to appeal. United States v. Breit, 754 F.2d 526 (4th Cir. 1985).

Correction of error as to matter not dealt with below. — Without filing a cross-appeal, an appellee may not attack the decree with a view either to enlarging his own rights thereunder or of lessening the rights of his adversary, where what he seeks is to correct an error or to supplement the decree with respect to a matter not dealt with below. Thurston v. United States, 810 F.2d 438 (4th Cir. 1987).

Applied in In re Capshaw, 423 F. Supp. 1388 (E.D. Va. 1977); United States v. Bodden, 736 F.2d 142 (4th Cir. 1984); In re Green, 133 Bankr. 185 (E.D. Va. 1991); United States v. Bunn, 215 F.3d 430, 2000 U.S. App. LEXIS 13975 (4th Cir. W. Va. 2000); Jones v. Angelone, No. 00-6499, 2000 U.S. App. LEXIS 14540 (4th Cir. June 23, 2000).

Rule 5. Appeal by Permission.

(a) *Petition for Permission to Appeal.* — (1) To request permission to appeal when an appeal is within the court of appeals' discretion, a party must file a petition for permission to appeal. The petition must be filed with the circuit clerk with proof of service on all other parties to the district-court action.

(2) The petition must be filed within the time specified by the statute or rule authorizing the appeal or, if no such time is specified, within the time provided by Rule 4(a) for filing a notice of appeal.

(3) If a party cannot petition for appeal unless the district court first enters an order granting permission to do so or stating that the necessary conditions are met, the district court may amend its order, either on its own or in response to a party's motion, to include the required permission or statement. In that event, the time to petition runs from entry of the amended order.

(b) *Contents of the Petition; Answer or Cross-Petition; Oral Argument.* — (1) The petition must include the following:

(A) the facts necessary to understand the question presented;

(B) the question itself;

(C) the relief sought;

(D) the reasons why the appeal should be allowed and is authorized by a statute or rule; and

(E) an attached copy of:

(i) the order, decree, or judgment complained of and any related opinion or memorandum, and

(ii) any order stating the district court's permission to appeal or finding that the necessary conditions are met.

(2) A party may file an answer in opposition or a cross-petition within 10 days after the petition is served.

(3) The petition and answer will be submitted without oral argument unless the court of appeals orders otherwise.

(c) *Form of Papers; Number of Copies.* — All papers must conform to Rule 32(c)(2). Except by the court's permission, a paper must not exceed 20 pages, exclusive of the disclosure statement, the proof of service, and the accompanying documents required by Rule 5(b)(1)(E). An original and 3 copies must be filed unless the court requires a different number by local rule or by order in a particular case.

(d) *Grant of Permission; Fees; Cost Bond; Filing the Record.* — (1) Within 14 days after the entry of the order granting permission to appeal, the appellant must:

(A) pay the district clerk all required fees; and

(B) file a cost bond if required under Rule 7.

(2) A notice of appeal need not be filed. The date when the order granting permission to appeal is entered serves as the date of the notice of appeal for calculating time under these rules.

(3) The district clerk must notify the circuit clerk once the petitioner has paid the fees. Upon receiving this notice, the circuit clerk must enter the appeal on the docket.

The record must be forwarded and filed in accordance with Rules 11 and 12(c). (Amended by order adopted April 30, 1979, effective August 1, 1979, by order adopted April 29, 1994, effective December 1, 1994, by order adopted April 24, 1998, effective December 1, 1998, by order adopted April 29, 2002, effective December 1, 2002, and by order adopted March 26, 2009, effective December 1, 2009.)

CASE NOTES

Applied in Peanut Corp. of Am. v. Hollywood Brands, Inc., 696 F.2d 311 (4th Cir. 1982); City of Va. Beach v. Roanoke River Basin Ass'n, 776 F.2d 484 (4th Cir. 1985).

Local Rule 5. Interlocutory Orders.

The Court of Appeals will initially enter a petition for permission to appeal upon the miscellaneous docket; a docket fee shall not be required unless the petition is granted. A Disclosure of Corporate Affiliations statement must be filed with the petition and answer. See FRAP 26.1 and Local Rule 26.1. Upon granting the petition, the Court of Appeals will notify the district court by copy of the order and transfer the case to the regular docket. (Amended effective December 1, 2009.)

Rule 5.1. Appeals by Permission Under 28 U.S.C. § 636(c)(5).

(Abrogated by order adopted April 24, 1998, effective December 1, 1998.)

Rule 6. Appeal in a Bankruptcy Case from a Final Judgment, Order, or Decree of a District Court or Bankruptcy Appellate Panel.

(a) *Appeal from a Judgment, Order, or Decree of a District Court Exercising Original Jurisdiction in a Bankruptcy Case.* — An appeal to a court of appeals from a final judgment, order or decree of a district court exercising jurisdiction pursuant to 28 U.S.C. § 1334 is taken as any other civil appeal under these rules.

(b) *Appeal from a Judgment, Order, or Decree of a District Court or Bankruptcy Appellate Panel Exercising Appellate Jurisdiction in a Bankruptcy Case.* — (1) Applicability of Other Rules. — These rules apply to an appeal to a court of appeals pursuant to 28 U.S.C. § 158(d) from a final judgment, order or decree of a district court or bankruptcy appellate panel exercising appellate jurisdiction under 28 U.S.C. § 158(a) or (b). But there are 3 exceptions:

(A) Rules 4(a)(4), 4(b), 9, 10, 11, 12(b), 13-20, 22-23, and 24(b) do not apply;

(B) the reference in Rule 3(c) to "Form 1 in the Appendix of Forms" must be read as a reference to Form 5; and

(C) when the appeal is from a bankruptcy appellate panel, the term "district court," as used in any applicable rule, means "appellate panel."

(2) Additional Rules. — In addition to the rules made applicable by Rule 6(b)(1), the following rules apply:

(A) Motion for rehearing. (i) If a timely motion for rehearing under Bankruptcy Rule 8015 is filed, the time to appeal for all parties runs from the entry of the order disposing of the motion. A notice of appeal filed after the district court or bankruptcy appellate panel announces or enters a judgment, order, or decree — but before disposition of the motion for rehearing — becomes effective when the order disposing of the motion for rehearing is entered.

(ii) Appellate review of the order disposing of the motion requires the party, in compliance with Rules 3(c) and 6(b)(1)(B), to amend a previously filed notice of appeal. A party intending to challenge an altered or amended judgment, order, or decree must file a notice of appeal or amended notice of appeal within the time prescribed by Rule 4 — excluding Rules 4(a)(4) and 4(b) — measured from the entry of the order disposing of the motion.

(iii) No additional fee is required to file an amended notice.

(B) The record on appeal. (i) Within 14 days after filing the notice of appeal, the appellant must file with the clerk possessing the record assembled in accordance with Bankruptcy Rule 8006 — and serve on the appellee — a statement of the issues to be presented on appeal and a designation of the record to be certified and sent to the circuit clerk.

(ii) An appellee who believes that other parts of the record are necessary must, within 14 days after being served with the appellant's designation, file with the clerk and serve on the appellant a designation of additional parts to be included.

(iii) The record on appeal consists of:
- the redesignated record as provided above;
- the proceedings in the district court or bankruptcy appellate panel; and
- a certified copy of the docket entries prepared by the clerk under Rule 3(d).

(C) Forwarding the record. (i) When the record is complete, the district clerk or bankruptcy appellate panel clerk must number the documents constituting the record and send them promptly to the circuit clerk together with a list of the documents correspondingly numbered and reasonably identified. Unless directed to do so by a party or the circuit clerk, the clerk will not send to the court of appeals documents of unusual bulk or weight, physical exhibits other than documents, or other parts of the record designated for omission by local rule of the court of appeals. If the exhibits are unusually bulky or heavy, a party must arrange with the clerks in advance for their transportation and receipt.

(ii) All parties must do whatever else is necessary to enable the clerk to assemble and forward the record. The court of appeals may provide by rule or order that a certified copy of the docket entries be sent in place of the redesignated record, but any party may request at any time during the pendency of the appeal that the redesignated record be sent.

(D) Filing the record. Upon receiving the record — or a certified copy of the docket entries sent in place of the redesignated record — the circuit clerk must file it and immediately notify all parties of the filing date. (Amended by order adopted April 30, 1979, effective August 1, 1979, by order adopted April 25, 1989, effective December 1, 1989, by order adopted April 30, 1991, effective December 1, 1991, by order adopted April 22, 1993, effective December 1, 1993, by order adopted April 24, 1998, effective December 1, 1998, and by order adopted March 26, 2009, effective December 1, 2009.)

CASE NOTES

Applied in In re Green, 133 Bankr. 185 (E.D. Va. 1991).

IOP 6.1. Bankruptcy Appeals.

The Fourth Circuit has not established panels of three bankruptcy judges to hear appeals from bankruptcy courts pursuant to 28 U.S.C. § 158.

Rule 7. Bond for Costs on Appeal in a Civil Case.

In a civil case, the district court may require an appellant to file a bond or provide other security in any form and amount necessary to ensure payment of costs on appeal. Rule 8(b) applies to a surety on a bond given under this rule. (Amended by order adopted April 30, 1979, effective August 1, 1979, and by order adopted April 24, 1998, effective December 1, 1998.)

Rule 8. Stay or Injunction Pending Appeal.

(a) *Motion for Stay.* — (1) Initial Motion in the District Court. — A party must ordinarily move first in the district court for the following relief:

(A) a stay of the judgment or order of a district court pending appeal;

(B) approval of a supersedeas bond; or

(C) an order suspending, modifying, restoring, or granting an injunction while an appeal is pending.

(2) Motion in the Court of Appeals; Conditions on Relief. — A motion for the relief mentioned in Rule 8(a)(1) may be made to the court of appeals or to one of its judges.

(A) The motion must:

(i) show that moving first in the district court would be impracticable; or

(ii) state that, a motion having been made, the district court denied the motion or failed to afford the relief requested and state any reasons given by the district court for its action.

(B) The motion must also include:

(i) the reasons for granting the relief requested and the facts relied on;

(ii) originals or copies of affidavits or other sworn statements supporting facts subject to dispute; and

(iii) relevant parts of the record.

(C) The moving party must give reasonable notice of the motion to all parties.

(D) A motion under this Rule 8(a)(2) must be filed with the circuit clerk and normally will be considered by a panel of the court. But in an exceptional case in which time requirements make that procedure impracticable, the motion may be made to and considered by a single judge.

(E) The court may condition relief on a party's filing a bond or other appropriate security in the district court.

(b) *Proceeding Against a Surety.* — If a party gives security in the form of a bond or stipulation or other undertaking with one or more sureties, each surety submits to the jurisdiction of the district court and irrevocably appoints the district clerk as the surety's agent on whom any papers affecting the surety's liability on the bond or undertaking may be served. On motion, a surety's liability may be enforced in the district court without the necessity of an independent action. The motion and any notice that the district court prescribes may be served on the district clerk, who must promptly mail a copy to each surety whose address is known.

(c) *Stay in a Criminal Case.* — Rule 38 of the Federal Rules of Criminal Procedure governs a stay in a criminal case. (Amended by order adopted March 10, 1986, effective July 1, 1986, by order adopted April 27, 1995, effective December 1, 1995, and by order adopted April 24, 1998, effective December 1, 1998.)

CASE NOTES

Law of the case doctrine. — It is clear that the law of the case doctrine is ill-suited for application to a stay order issued pursuant to this rule — even one left in place by a panel on a motion to vacate. Decisions rendered by panels on motions, especially on jurisdictional issues, are tentative rulings only and are not the law of the case. Richmond Med. Ctr. for Women v. Gilmore, 183 F.3d 303 (4th Cir. 1999).

Applied in Elwood v. Lehman, 525 F. Supp. 1148 (E.D. Va. 1981); City of Alexandria v. Helms, 719 F.2d 699 (4th Cir. 1983); Morris v. City of Danville, 744 F.2d 1041 (4th Cir. 1984); Kennedy v. Block, 784 F.2d 1220 (4th Cir. 1986).

Local Rule 8. Stay or Injunction Pending Appeal.

Filing a notice of appeal does not automatically stay the operation of the judgment, order or decision for which review is sought. If an application to the district court for temporary relief pending appeal is not practicable, counsel must make a specific showing of the reasons the application was not made to the district court in the first instance. Any motion to the Court of Appeals should include copies of all previous applications for relief and their outcome and any relevant parts of the record. A Disclosure of Corporate Affiliations statement must accompany the motion and any response unless the parties have previously filed disclosure statements with the Court in the case. See FRAP 26.1 and Local Rule 26.1. Filing and assignment of emergency motions for stay or injunction pending appeal are governed by Local Rule 27(e). An order granting a stay or injunction pending appeal remains in effect until issuance of the mandate or further order of the Court and may be conditioned upon the filing of a supersedeas bond in the district court. (Amended effective December 1, 1995, effective February 1, 2001, and effective December 1, 2009.)

Rule 9. Release in a Criminal Case.

(a) *Release Before Judgment of Conviction.* — (1) The district court must state in writing, or orally on the record, the reasons for an order regarding the release or detention of a defendant in a criminal case. A party appealing from the order, must file with the court of appeals a copy of the district court's order and the court's statement of reasons as soon as practicable after filing the notice of appeal. An appellant who questions the factual basis for the district court's order must file a transcript of the release proceedings or an explanation of why a transcript was not obtained.

(2) After reasonable notice to the appellee, the court of appeals must promptly determine the appeal on the basis of the papers, affidavits, and parts of the record that the parties present or the court requires. Unless the court so orders, briefs need not be filed.

(3) The court of appeals or one of its judges may order the defendant's release pending the disposition of the appeal.

(b) *Release After Judgment of Conviction.* — A party entitled to do so may obtain review of a district-court order regarding release after a judgment of conviction by filing a notice of appeal from that order in the district court, or by filing a motion in the court of appeals if the party has already filed a notice of appeal from the judgment of conviction. Both the order and the review are subject to Rule 9(a). The papers filed by the party seeking review must include a copy of the judgment of conviction.

(c) *Criteria for Release.* — The court must make its decision regarding release in accordance with the applicable provisions of 18 U.S.C. §§ 3142, 3143, and 3145(c). (Amended by order adopted April 24, 1972, effective October 1, 1972, by P.L. 98-473, Title II, § 210, approved October 12, 1984, by order adopted April 29, 1994, effective December 1, 1994, and by order adopted April 24, 1998, effective December 1, 1998.)

CASE NOTES

Applied in United States v. Baum, 785 F. Supp. 570 (E.D. Va. 1992).

Local Rule 9(a). Release Prior to Judgment of Conviction.

A criminal defendant may be released in accordance with the conditions set by the district court prior to judgment of conviction. If the district court refuses to release the prisoner, or sets conditions for release that cannot be met, the order is appealable as a matter of right and will be given prompt consideration by the Court of Appeals. Counsel should submit memoranda in support of their position on appeal and, in cases involving corporate defendants, Disclosure of Corporate Affiliations statements required by FRAP 26.1 and Local Rule 26.1. The appeal is usually decided without oral argument upon the materials presented by the parties. A motion for release pending determination of the appeal may be filed and will be assigned as provided in Local Rule 27(e). (Amended effective February 1, 2001 and December 1, 2009.)

Local Rule 9(b). Release After Conviction and Notice of Appeal.

After the district court has ruled on a motion for bail or reduction of bail pending appeal, the appellant may renew the motion for release, or for a modification of the conditions of release, before the Court of Appeals without noting an additional appeal. A copy of the district court statement of reasons should accompany the motion. The motion will be submitted to a three-judge panel for decision.

Local Rule 9(c). Recalcitrant Witnesses.

When an appeal arises from the incarceration of a witness who refuses to testify or produce evidence in any court or grand jury proceeding, the Court of Appeals is required by statute, 28 U.S.C. § 1826, to decide the appeal within 30 days of the filing of the notice of appeal. Therefore, counsel should immediately contact the Clerk's Office regarding all such witness contempt matters so that the appeal may be expedited for resolution within the statutory guidelines.

Rule 10. The Record on Appeal.

(a) *Composition of the Record on Appeal.* — The following items constitute the record on appeal:

(1) the original papers and exhibits filed in the district court;

(2) the transcript of proceedings, if any; and

(3) a certified copy of the docket entries prepared by the district clerk.

(b) *The Transcript of Proceedings.* — (1) Appellant's Duty to Order. — Within 14 days after filing the notice of appeal or entry of an order disposing of the last timely remaining motion of a type specified in Rule 4(a)(4)(A), whichever is later, the appellant must do either of the following:

(A) order from the reporter a transcript of such parts of the proceedings not already on file as the appellant considers necessary, subject to a local rule of the court of appeals and with the following qualifications:

(i) the order must be in writing;

(ii) if the cost of the transcript is to be paid by the United States under the Criminal Justice Act, the order must so state; and

(iii) the appellant must, within the same period, file a copy of the order with the district clerk; or

(B) file a certificate stating that no transcript will be ordered.

(2) Unsupported Finding or Conclusion. — If the appellant intends to urge on appeal that a finding or conclusion is unsupported by the evidence or is contrary to the

evidence, the appellant must include in the record a transcript of all evidence relevant to that finding or conclusion.

(3) Partial Transcript. — Unless the entire transcript is ordered:

(A) the appellant must — within the 14 days provided in Rule 10(b)(1) — file a statement of the issues that the appellant intends to present on the appeal and must serve on the appellee a copy of both the order or certificate and the statement;

(B) if the appellee considers it necessary to have a transcript of other parts of the proceedings, the appellee must, within 14 days after the service of the order or certificate and the statement of the issues, file and serve on the appellant a designation of additional parts to be ordered; and

(C) unless within 14 days after service of that designation the appellant has ordered all such parts, and has so notified the appellee, the appellee may within the following 14 days either order the parts or move in the district court for an order requiring the appellant to do so.

(4) Payment. — At the time of ordering, a party must make satisfactory arrangements with the reporter for paying the cost of the transcript.

(c) *Statement of the Evidence When the Proceedings Were Not Recorded or When a Transcript Is Unavailable.* — If the transcript of a hearing or trial is unavailable, the appellant may prepare a statement of the evidence or proceedings from the best available means, including the appellant's recollection. The statement must be served on the appellee, who may serve objections or proposed amendments within 14 days after being served. The statement and any objections or proposed amendments must then be submitted to the district court for settlement and approval. As settled and approved, the statement must be included by the district clerk in the record on appeal.

(d) *Agreed Statement as the Record on Appeal.* — In place of the record on appeal as defined in Rule 10(a), the parties may prepare, sign, and submit to the district court a statement of the case showing how the issues presented by the appeal arose and were decided in the district court. The statement must set forth only those facts averred and proved or sought to be proved that are essential to the court's resolution of the issues. If the statement is truthful, it — together with any additions that the district court may consider necessary to a full presentation of the issues on appeal — must be approved by the district court and must then be certified to the court of appeals as the record on appeal. The district clerk must then send it to the circuit clerk within the time provided by Rule 11. A copy of the agreed statement may be filed in place of the appendix required by Rule 30.

(e) *Correction or Modification of the Record.* — (1) If any difference arises about whether the record truly discloses what occurred in the district court, the difference must be submitted to and settled by that court and the record conformed accordingly.

(2) If anything material to either party is omitted from or misstated in the record by error or accident, the omission or misstatement may be corrected and a supplemental record may be certified and forwarded:

(A) on stipulation of the parties;

(B) by the district court before or after the record has been forwarded; or

(C) by the court of appeals.

(3) All other questions as to the form and content of the record must be presented to the court of appeals. (Amended by order adopted April 30, 1979, effective August 1, 1979, by order adopted March 10, 1986, effective July 1, 1986, by order adopted April 30, 1991, effective December 1, 1991, by order adopted April 22, 1993, effective December 1, 1993, by order adopted April 27, 1995, effective December 1, 1995, by order adopted April 24, 1998, effective December 1, 1998, and by order adopted March 26, 2009, effective December 1, 2009.)

CASE NOTES

The term "original papers" refers to all papers presented to the district court and filed in the record and to all papers filed by the district court itself. Himler v. Comprehensive Care Corp., 790 F. Supp. 114 (E.D. Va. 1992).

The "record" includes all pleadings, process and proof of service, motions, supporting papers, and orders in response thereto, instructions to a jury, and in an action tried without a jury, the master's report, if any, the verdict or the findings of fact and conclusions of law with any direction for entry of judgment, the opinion, the judgment and notice of appeal. Himler v. Comprehensive Care Corp., 790 F. Supp. 114 (E.D. Va. 1992).

Subdivision (e) of this rule vests authority in the district court to conform the record to what occurred in the district court either by supplying what has been omitted or correcting what has been erroneously transcribed. This power exists before or after the record is transmitted to the court of appeals, and the court of appeals on its own initiative may direct, inter alia, that any omission from the record be supplied. United States v. Greenwell, 418 F.2d 845 (4th Cir. 1969).

District court not to add matters which did not occur at trial. — It is well-settled that the purpose of Rule 10(e) is not to allow a district court to add to the record on appeal matters that did not occur there in the course of the proceedings leading to the judgment under review. In re Robbins Maritime, Inc., 162 F.R.D. 502 (E.D. Va. 1995).

Supplementation denied. — Where letters only reflected the initial tentative concerns of the court and did not state the court's final conclusions about the propriety of originally denying class action status to the case or denying the attempts to settle by a class action, and where the court's final conclusions and reasoning were contained exclusively in its two orders which were a part of the record, the record therefore accurately reflected what occurred before the court and did not need to be supplemented by the letters in question. Himler v. Comprehensive Care Corp., 790 F. Supp. 114 (E.D. Va. 1992).

To include the information contained in the omitted material now would make the meaning of the "error or accident" be that a litigant can put in part of its case at the trial level and then, if he loses, reconsider his strategy and put in the rest on appeal. In re Robbins Maritime, Inc., 162 F.R.D. 502 (E.D. Va. 1995).

District judge directed to certify statement regarding security measures used at criminal trial. — See United States v. Greenwell, 418 F.2d 845 (4th Cir. 1969).

Applied in Mullins Coal Co. v. Clark, 759 F.2d 1142 (4th Cir. 1985).

Local Rule 10(a). Retention of the Record on Appeal in the District Court.

In cases in which all parties are represented by counsel on appeal, the district court clerk will transmit with the notice of appeal sent to the Court of Appeals a certificate that the record of docket entries is available upon request. The district court clerk will notify the Court of Appeals of the subsequent filing of any transcript in the case. The district court will then retain the record on appeal until and unless a judge of this Court asks the Clerk of this Court to obtain it. Upon receipt of a request from the Clerk of the Court of Appeals, the clerk of the district court will assemble and transmit the record on appeal within 48 hours. (Amended by order effective April 1, 2008.)

Local Rule 10(b). Records on Appeal.

The preparation and transmittal of the record on appeal is the obligation of the clerk of the lower court, board or agency, and any questions concerning form or content should be addressed to the trial forum in the first instance. Parties should check with the clerk of the lower court, board or agency to determine whether everything relevant to the issues on appeal will be included initially in the record on appeal in order to obviate motions to supplement the record. The record is transmitted to the appellate court as soon as it is complete, except as provided in Local Rule 10(a). Local Rule 10(a) does not apply to records in cases in which one or more parties are proceeding without counsel on appeal. (Amended effective December 1, 1995, effective December 1, 1998, and effective December 1, 2009.)

Local Rule 10(c). Transcripts.

(1) *Responsibilities and designation.* — The appellant has the duty of ordering transcript of all parts of the proceedings material to the issues to be raised on appeal whether favorable or unfavorable to appellant's position. Appellant should complete the transcript order (form available at www.ca4.uscourts.gov) and distribute the form to the Clerk of the Court of Appeals, the court reporter, the clerk of the district court, and the appellee.

Before the transcript order is distributed, appellant must make appropriate financial arrangements with the court reporter for either immediate payment in full or in other form acceptable to the court reporter, payment pursuant to the Criminal Justice Act, or at government expense pursuant to 28 U.S.C. § 753(f).

In cross-appeals each party must order those parts of the transcript pertinent to the issues of such appeals. The parties are encouraged to agree upon those parts of the transcript jointly needed and to apportion the cost, with additional portions being ordered and paid for by the party considering them essential to that party's appeal.

If the entire transcript of proceedings is not to be prepared, the appellant's docketing statement filed pursuant to Local Rule 3(b) may constitute the statement of issues required by FRAP 10(b)(3)(A).

(2) *Monitoring and receipt by clerk.* — Failure to order timely a transcript, failure to make satisfactory financial arrangements with the court reporter, or failure to specify in adequate detail those proceedings to be transcribed will subject the appeal to

dismissal by the clerk for want of prosecution pursuant to Local Rule 45. The Clerk's Office is charged with monitoring the status of transcripts pending with court reporters.

(3) *Statement in lieu of transcript.* — The parties may prepare and sign a statement of the case in lieu of the transcript or the entire record on appeal. The use of a statement in lieu of a transcript of a hearing substantially accelerates the appellate process. The statement should contain a description of the essential facts averred and proved or sought to be proved and a summary of pertinent testimony.

(4) *Guidelines for Preparation of Appellate Transcripts in the Fourth Circuit.* — The Fourth Circuit Judicial Council has adopted guidelines to define the obligations of appellants, appellees, clerks of the district court, court reporters and the Clerk of the Court of Appeals in the ordering, preparation, and filing of transcripts completed pursuant to these rules. (Amended effective December 1, 1998 and December 1, 2009.)

Editor's note. — For the Guidelines for Preparation of Appellate Transcripts in the Fourth Circuit, see Appendix D to the Internal Operating Procedures.

Local Rule 10(d). Supplemental Records, Modification or Correction.

Disputes concerning the accuracy or composition of the record on appeal should be resolved in the trial court in the first instance, although the Court of Appeals has the power, either on motion or of its own accord, to require that the record be corrected or supplemented. It is unnecessary to seek permission of the Court of Appeals to supplement the record and the record may be supplemented by the parties by stipulation or by order of the district court at any time during the appellate process.

Rule 11. Forwarding the Record.

(a) *Appellant's Duty.* — An appellant filing a notice of appeal must comply with Rule 10(b) and must do whatever else is necessary to enable the clerk to assemble and forward the record. If there are multiple appeals from a judgment or order, the clerk must forward a single record.

(b) *Duties of Reporter and District Clerk.* — (1) Reporter's Duty to Prepare and File a Transcript. — The reporter must prepare and file a transcript as follows:

(A) Upon receiving an order for a transcript, the reporter must enter at the foot of the order the date of its receipt and the expected completion date and send a copy, so endorsed, to the circuit clerk.

(B) If the transcript cannot be completed within 30 days of the reporter's receipt of the order, the reporter may request the circuit clerk to grant additional time to complete it. The clerk must note on the docket the action taken and notify the parties.

(C) When a transcript is complete, the reporter must file it with the district clerk and notify the circuit clerk of the filing.

(D) If the reporter fails to file the transcript on time, the circuit clerk must notify the district judge and do whatever else the court of appeals directs.

(2) District Clerk's Duty to Forward. — When the record is complete, the district clerk must number the documents constituting the record and send them promptly to the circuit clerk together with a list of the documents correspondingly numbered and reasonably identified. Unless directed to do so by a party or the circuit clerk, the district clerk will not send to the court of appeals documents of unusual bulk or weight, physical exhibits other than documents, or other parts of the record designated for omission by local rule of the court of appeals. If the exhibits are unusually bulky or heavy, a party must arrange with the clerks in advance for their transportation and receipt.

(c) *Retaining the Record Temporarily in the District Court for Use in Preparing the Appeal.* — The parties may stipulate, or the district court on motion may order, that the district clerk retain the record temporarily for the parties to use in preparing the papers on appeal. In that event the district clerk must certify to the circuit clerk that the record on appeal is complete. Upon receipt of the appellee's brief, or earlier if the court orders or the parties agree, the appellant must request the district clerk to forward the record.

(d) *(Abrogated.)*

(e) *Retaining the Record by Court Order.* — (1) The court of appeals may, by order or local rule, provide that a certified copy of the docket entries be forwarded instead of the entire record. But a party may at any time during the appeal request that designated parts of the record be forwarded.

(2) The district court may order the record or some part of it retained if the court needs it while the appeal is pending, subject, however, to call by the court of appeals.

(3) If part or all of the record is ordered retained, the district clerk must send to the court of appeals a copy of the order and the docket entries together with the parts of the original record allowed by the district court and copies of any parts of the record designated by the parties.

(f) *Retaining Parts of the Record in the District Court by Stipulation of the Parties.* — The parties may agree by written stipulation filed in the district court that designated parts of the record be retained in the district court subject to call by the court of appeals or requst by a party. The parts of the record so designated remain a part of the record on appeal.

(g) *Record for a Preliminary Motion in the Court of Appeals.* — If, before the record is forwarded, a party makes any of the following motions in the court of appeals:

- for dismissal;
- for release;
- for a stay pending appeal;
- for additional security on the bond on appeal or on a supersedeas bond; or
- for any other intermediate order —

the district clerk must send the court of appeals any parts of the record designated by any party. (Amended by order adopted April 30, 1979, effective August 1, 1979, by order adopted March 10, 1986, effective July 1, 1986, and by order adopted April 24, 1998, effective December 1, 1998.)

CASE NOTES

Introduction of evidence into record on appeal. — Where the issue of the value of the property was squarely before the district court, failure to have the actual document of appraisal before the district court was an omission and would be a continuing omission in the court of appeals; therefore, subdivision (e) of this section allowed the inclusion of the actual appraisals to be introduced into the record on appeal to the Court of Appeals. Marjec, Inc. v. Estate of Miller, 75 Bankr. 58 (W.D. Va. 1987).

Local Rule 11(a). Transcript Acknowledgments.

Upon receipt of an order for a transcript, the Clerk of the Court of Appeals will prepare for the reporter a transcript order acknowledgment which will set forth the date the transcript order was received in the Clerk's Office and the transcript due date, computed from the order receipt date in accordance with the time limits set forth in the applicable district court reporter management plan. If the transcript order is correct in all respects, except for an order date error in the reporter's favor, no response will be required from the reporter. If the reporter believes that there is a problem with the transcript order, he or she must complete a copy of the acknowledgment form noting the problem and return it to the Court of Appeals within 7 days of receipt of the form by the reporter, or within such further time as the Court of Appeals allows. The time for completion of the transcript will automatically cease to run until the problem has been remedied. The Clerk of the Court of Appeals will send a new transcript order acknowledgment setting forth new transcript order and filing dates taking into account the delay caused by resolving the problem with the original transcript order.

Local Rule 11(b). Time Limits for Filing Transcripts.

Although FRAP 11(b)(1)(B) requires that transcripts be completed within 30 days from the purchase order date, this Court routinely uses instead the time limits set forth in the district court reporter management plans. All of the plans establish a 60-day period for preparation of transcripts, with the following exceptions:

(1) Special provisions adopted by the Fourth Circuit Judicial Council for appeals by incarcerated criminal defendants.

(a) Transcripts of 1000 pages or less shall be filed within 30 days of transcript order and completion of satisfactory financial arrangements.

(b) Transcripts of more than 1000 pages shall be filed within the time ordered by the clerk of the court of appeals.

(2) Special circumstances, such as

(a) Bail appeals,

(b) Death penalty cases, or

(c) Other expedited procedures in which the transcript shall be filed within the time ordered by the Clerk of the Court of Appeals. (Amended by order effective December 1, 1995, and by order effective December 1, 1998.)

Local Rule 11(c). Exhibits.

Counsel should be aware that certain portions of the record will not be transmitted to the Court of Appeals as part of the record. If bulky documents and physical exhibits are required by a party for oral argument, the party must make advance arrangements with the clerks of both courts for their transportation and receipt. Such arrangements are best made after the completion of the briefing schedule on appeal and receipt of notice of oral argument.

Local Rule 11(d). Access of Counsel to Original Record.

Counsel desiring to use the record on appeal in preparing their case should make arrangements with the clerk of the district court for access to the record. Under Local Rule 10(a), records in cases in which all parties are represented by counsel are retained by the district court clerk during appeal unless a judge of the Court of Appeals requests that they be obtained. If the record is transmitted to the Court of Appeals, the record may be withdrawn upon proper application and returned to the trial court or the nearest district court clerk's office for counsel's review. Law professors representing indigents by Court appointment may request that the record be sent to the law school for their review. (Amended by order effective December 1, 1995.)

IOP 11.1. Sanctions for Court Reporter's Failure to File a Timely Transcript.

The Fourth Circuit Judicial Council has implemented a resolution of the Judicial Conference of the United States which mandates sanctions for the late delivery of transcripts. For transcripts not delivered within the time limits set forth in Local Rule 11(b), the reporter may charge only 90 percent of the prescribed fee; for a transcript not delivered within 30 days after that time the reporter may charge only 80 percent of the prescribed fee. The time period in criminal proceedings for the preparation of transcripts that are ordered before sentencing shall not begin to run until after entry of the judgment and commitment order. (Amended by order effective December 1, 1995, and by order effective December 1, 2002.)

Rule 12. Docketing the Appeal; Filing a Representation Statement; Filing the Record.

(a) *Docketing the Appeal.* — Upon receiving the copy of the notice of appeal and the docket entries, from the district clerk under Rule 3(d), the circuit clerk must docket the appeal under the title of the district-court action and must identify the appellant, adding the appellant's name if necessary.

(b) *Filing a Representation Statement.* — Unless the court of appeals designates another time, the attorney who filed the notice of appeal must, within 14 days after filing the notice, file a statement with the circuit clerk naming the parties that the attorney represents on appeal.

(c) *Filing the Record, Partial Record, or Certificate.* — Upon receiving the record, partial record, or district clerk's certificate as provided in Rule 11, the circuit clerk must file it and immediately notify all parties of the filing date. (Amended by order adopted April 1, 1979, effective August 1, 1979, by order adopted March 10, 1986, effective July 1, 1986, by order adopted April 22, 1993, effective December 1, 1993, by order adopted April 24, 1998, effective December 1, 1998, and by order adopted March 26, 2009, effective December 1, 2009.)

Rule 12.1. Remand After an Indicative Ruling by the District Court on a Motion for Relief That Is Barred by a Pending Appeal.

(a) *Notice to the Court of Appeals.* — If a timely motion is made in the district court for relief that it lacks authority to grant because of an appeal that has been docketed and is pending, the movant must promptly notify the circuit clerk if the district court states either that it would grant the motion or that the motion raises a substantial issue.

(b) *Remand After an Indicative Ruling.* — If the district court states that it would grant the motion or that the motion raises a substantial issue, the court of appeals may remand for further proceedings but retains jurisdiction unless it expressly dismisses the appeal. If the court of appeals remands but retains jurisdiction, the parties must promptly notify the circuit clerk when the district court has decided the motion on remand. (Adopted by order March 26, 2009, effective December 1, 2009.)

Local Rule 12(a). Appeals by Aggrieved Non-parties in the Lower Court.
If the appellant was not a party to the lower court proceeding, the appeal shall be styled "In re ____________, Appellant," and the title of the action in the district court shall also be given.

Local Rule 12(b). Joint Appeals/Cross-appeals and Consolidations.
For the purpose of identifying consolidated appeals and cross-appeals, the earliest docketed appeal will be designated the lead case and identified by an "L" following its docket number. The parties should designate lead counsel for each side and communicate lead counsel's identity in writing to the clerk within 14 days of the consolidation order. Although most consolidations will be on the Court's own motion, a party is not precluded from filing a request. (Amended effective December 1, 2009.)

Local Rule 12(c). Expedition of Appeals.
The Court on its own motion or on motion of the parties may expedite an appeal for briefing and oral argument. Any motion to expedite should state clearly the reasons supporting expedition, the ability of the parties to present the appeal on the existing record, and the need for oral argument. (Amended by order effective December 1, 1998.)

Local Rule 12(d). Abeyance.
In the interest of docket control the Court may, either on its own motion or upon request, place a case in abeyance pending disposition of matters before this Court or other courts which may affect the ultimate resolution of an appeal. During the period of time a case is held in abeyance the appeal remains on the docket but nothing is done to advance the case to maturity and resolution. If a case is held in abeyance for cases other than a Fourth Circuit case, the parties will be required to make periodic status reports.

Local Rule 12(e). Intervention.
A party who appeared as an intervenor in a lower court proceeding shall be considered a party to the appeal upon filing a notice of appearance. Otherwise, a motion for leave to intervene must be filed with the Court of Appeals. Any notice of appearance or motion to intervene should indicate the side upon which the movant proposes to intervene. The provisions of FRAP 15(d) govern intervention in appeals from administrative agencies. Intervenors are required to join in the brief for the side which they support unless leave to file a separate brief is granted by the Court.

TITLE III. APPEALS FROM THE UNITED STATES TAX COURT.

Rule 13. Appeals from the Tax Court.
(a) *Appeal as of Right.* — (1) How Obtained; Time for Filing a Notice of Appeal. (A) An appeal as of right from the United States Tax Court is commenced by filing a notice of appeal with the Tax Court clerk within 90 days after the entry of the Tax Court's decision. At the time of filing, the appellant must furnish the clerk with enough copies of the notice to enable the clerk to comply with Rule 3(d). If one party files a timely notice of appeal, any other party may file a notice of appeal within 120 days after the Tax Court's decision is entered.

(B) If, under Tax Court rules, a party makes a timely motion to vacate or revise the Tax Court's decision, the time to file a notice of appeal runs from the entry of the order disposing of the motion or from the entry of a new decision, whichever is later.

(2) Notice of Appeal; How Filed. The notice of appeal may be filed either at the Tax Court clerk's office in the District of Columbia or by mail addressed to the clerk. If sent by mail the notice is considered filed on the postmark date, subject to § 7502 of the Internal Revenue Code, as amended, and the applicable regulations.

(3) Contents of the Notice of Appeal; Service; Effect of Filing and Service. Rule 3 prescribes the contents of a notice of appeal, the manner of service, and the effect of its filing and service. Form 2 in the Appendix of Forms is a suggested form of a notice of appeal.

(4) The Record on Appeal; Forwarding; Filing. (A) Except as otherwise provided under Tax Court rules for the transcripts of proceedings, the appeal is governed by the parts of Rules 10, 11, and 12 regarding the record on appeal from a district court, the time and manner of forwarding and filing, and the docketing in the court of appeals.

(B) If an appeal is taken to more than one court of appeals, the original record must be sent to the court named in the first notice of appeal filed. In an appeal to any other court of appeals, the appellant must apply to that other court to make provision for the record.

(b) Appeal by Permission. An appeal by permission is governed by Rule 5. (Amended by order adopted April 1, 1979, effective August 1, 1979, by order adopted April 29, 1994, effective December 1, 1994, by order adopted April 24, 1998, effective December 1, 1998, and by order adopted April 16, 2013, effective December 1, 2013.)

Rule 14. Applicability of Other Rules to Appeals from the Tax Court.

All provisions of these rules, except Rules 4, 6-9, 15-20, and 22-23, apply to appeals from the Tax Court. References in any applicable rule (other than Rule 24(a)) to the district court and district clerk are to be read as referring to the Tax Court and its clerk. (Amended by order adopted April 24, 1998, effective December 1, 1998, and amended by order adopted April 16, 2013, effective December 1, 2013.)

TITLE IV. REVIEW OR ENFORCEMENT OF AN ORDER OF AN ADMINISTRATIVE AGENCY, BOARD, COMMISSION, OR OFFICER.

Rule 15. Review or Enforcement of an Agency Order — How Obtained; Intervention.

(a) *Petition for Review; Joint Petition.* — (1) Review of an agency order is commenced by filing, within the time prescribed by law, a petition for review with the clerk of a court of appeals authorized to review the agency order. If their interests make joinder practicable, two or more persons may join in a petition to the same court to review the same order.

(2) The petition must:

(A) name each party seeking review either in the caption or the body of the petition — using such terms as "et al.," "petitioners," or "respondents" does not effectively name the parties;

(B) name the agency as a respondent (even though not named in the petition, the United States is a respondent if required by statute); and

(C) specify the order or part thereof to be reviewed.

(3) Form 3 in the Appendix of Forms is a suggested form of a petition for review.

(4) In this rule "agency" includes an agency, board, commission, or officer; "petition for review" includes a petition to enjoin, suspend, modify, or otherwise review, or a notice of appeal, whichever form is indicated by the applicable statute.

(b) *Application or Cross-Application to Enforce an Order; Answer; Default.* — (1) An application to enforce an agency order must be filed with the clerk of a court of appeals authorized to enforce the order. If a petition is filed to review an agency order that the court may enforce, a party opposing the petition may file a cross-application for enforcement.

(2) Within 21 days after the application for enforcement is filed, the respondent must serve on the applicant an answer to the application and file it with the clerk. If the respondent fails to answer in time, the court will enter judgment for the relief requested.

(3) The application must contain a concise statement of the proceedings in which the order was entered, the facts upon which venue is based, and the relief requested.

(c) *Service of the Petition or Application.* — The circuit clerk must serve a copy of the petition for review, or an application or cross-application to enforce an agency order, on each respondent as prescribed by Rule 3(d), unless a different manner of service is prescribed by statute. At the time of filing, the petitioner must:

(1) serve, or have served, a copy on each party admitted to participate in the agency proceedings, except for the respondents;

(2) file with the clerk a list of those so served; and

(3) give the clerk enough copies of the petition or application to serve each respondent.

(d) *Intervention.* — Unless a statute provides another method, a person who wants to intervene in a proceeding under this rule must file a motion for leave to intervene with the circuit clerk and serve a copy on all parties. The motion — or other notice of intervention authorized by statute — must be filed within 30 days after the petition for review is filed and must contain a concise statement of the interest of the moving party and the grounds for intervention.

(e) *Payment of Fees.* — When filing any separate or joint petition for review in a court of appeals, the petitioner must pay the circuit clerk all required fees. (Amended by order adopted April 22, 1993, effective December 1, 1993, by order adopted April 24, 1998, effective December 1, 1998, and by order adopted March 26, 2009, effective December 1, 2009.)

Local Rule 15(a). Docketing Fee.

Upon filing a petition for review of an agency order, petitioner shall pay the prescribed docketing fee of $450, payable to the Clerk, U.S. Court of Appeals, or submit a properly executed application for leave to proceed in forma pauperis. (Added by order effective September 28, 1994; amended by order effective November 1, 2003, and by order effective April 27, 2006.)

Local Rule 15(b). Petitions for Review.

Whenever filing a petition for review or an application or cross-application for enforcement, the party shall attach to the petition, application or cross-application a copy of the agency order for which review or enforcement is sought. The petition, application or cross-application shall also be accompanied by a list of respondents specifically identifying the respondents' names and the addresses where respondents may be served with copies of the petition, application or cross-application. (Added by order effective December 4, 1996.)

Rule 15.1. Briefs and Oral Argument in a National Labor Relations Board Proceeding.

In either an enforcement or a review proceeding, a party adverse to the National Labor Relations Board proceeds first on briefing and at oral argument, unless the court orders otherwise. (Added March 10, 1986, effective July 1, 1986, and amended by order adopted April 24, 1998, effective December 1, 1998.)

Rule 16. The Record on Review or Enforcement.

(a) *Composition of the Record.* — The record on review or enforcement of an agency order consists of:

(1) the order involved;

(2) any findings or report on which it is based; and

(3) the pleadings, evidence, and other parts of the proceedings before the agency.

(b) *Omissions From or Misstatements in the Record.* — The parties may at any time, by stipulation, supply any omission from the record or correct a misstatement, or the court may so direct. If necessary, the court may direct that a supplemental record be prepared and filed. (Amended by order adopted April 24, 1998, effective December 1, 1998.)

Rule 17. Filing the Record.

(a) *Agency to File; Time for Filing; Notice of Filing.* — The agency must file the record with the circuit clerk within 40 days after being served with a petition for review, unless the statute authorizing review provides otherwise, or within 40 days after it files an application for enforcement unless the respondent fails to answer or the court orders otherwise. The court may shorten or extend the time to file the record. The clerk must notify all parties of the date when the record is filed.

(b) *Filing — What Constitutes.* — (1) The agency must file:

(A) the original or a certified copy of the entire record or parts designated by the parties; or

(B) a certified list adequately describing all documents, transcripts of testimony, exhibits, and other material constituting the record, or describing those parts designated by the parties.

(2) The parties may stipulate in writing that no record or certified list be filed. The date when the stipulation is filed with the circuit clerk is treated as the date when the record is filed.

(3) The agency must retain any portion of the record not filed with the clerk. All parts of the record retained by the agency are a part of the record on review for all purposes and, if the court or a party so requests, must be sent to the court regardless of any prior stipulation. (Amended by order adopted April 24, 1998, effective December 1, 1998.)

Rule 18. Stay Pending Review.

(a) *Motion for a Stay.* — (1) Initial Motion Before the Agency. — A petitioner must ordinarily move first before the agency for a stay pending review of its decision or order.

(2) Motion in the Court of Appeals. — A motion for a stay may be made to the court of appeals or one of its judges.

(A) The motion must:

(i) show that moving first before the agency would be impracticable; or

(ii) state that, a motion having been made, the agency denied the motion or failed to afford the relief requested and state any reasons given by the agency for its action.

(B) The motion must also include:

(i) the reasons for granting the relief requested and the facts relied on;

(ii) originals or copies of affidavits or other sworn statements supporting facts subject to dispute; and

(iii) relevant parts of the record.

(C) The moving party must give reasonable notice of the motion to all parties.

(D) The motion must be filed with the circuit clerk and normally will be considered by a panel of the court. But in an exceptional case in which time requirements make that procedure impracticable, the motion may be made to and considered by a single judge.

(b) *Bond.* — The court may condition relief on the filing of a bond or other appropriate security. (Amended by order adopted April 24, 1998, effective December 1, 1998.)

Local Rule 18. Procedures.

This Court's local rules accompanying FRAP 8 and 27 apply also to applications for stays under FRAP 18. (Amended by order effective December 1, 1995.)

Rule 19. Settlement of a Judgment Enforcing an Agency Order in Part.

When the court files an opinion directing entry of judgment enforcing the agency's order in part, the agency must within 14 days file with the clerk and serve on each other party a proposed judgment conforming to the opinion. A party who disagrees with the agency's proposed judgment must within 10 days file with the clerk and serve the agency with a proposed judgment that the party believes conforms to the opinion. The court will settle the judgment and direct entry without further hearing or argument. (Amended by order adopted March 10, 1986, effective July 1, 1986; by order adopted April 24, 1998, effective December 1, 1998; and by order adopted March 26, 2009, effective December 1, 2009.)

Rule 20. Applicability of Rules to Review or Enforcement of an Agency Order.

All provisions of these rules, except Rules 3-14 and 22-23, apply to the review or enforcement of an agency order. In these rules, "appellant" includes a petitioner or applicant, and "appellee" includes a respondent. (Amended by order adopted April 24, 1998, effective December 1, 1998.)

TITLE V. EXTRAORDINARY WRITS.

Rule 21. Writs of Mandamus and Prohibition, and Other Extraordinary Writs.

(a) *Mandamus or Prohibition to a Court: Petition, Filing, Service, and Docketing.* — (1) A party petitioning for a writ of madamus or prohibition directed to a court must file a petition with the circuit clerk with proof of service on all parties to the proceeding in the trial court. The party must also provide a copy to the trial-court judge. All parties to the proceeding in the trial court other than the petitioner are respondents for all purposes.

(2)(A) The petition must be titled "In re [name of petitioner]."

(B) The petition must state:

(i) the relief sought;

(ii) the issues presented;

(iii) the facts necessary to understand the issue presented by the petition; and

(iv) the reasons why the writ should issue.

(C) The petition must include a copy of any order or opinion or parts of the record that may be essential to understand the matters set forth in the petition.

(3) Upon receiving the prescribed docket fee, the clerk must docket the petition and submit it to the court.

(b) *Denial; Order Directing Answer; Briefs; Precedence.* — (1) The court may deny the petition without an answer. Otherwise, it must order the respondent, if any, to answer within a fixed time.

(2) The clerk must serve the order to respond on all persons directed to respond.

(3) Two or more respondents may answer jointly.

(4) The court of appeals may invite or order the trial-court judge to address the petition or may invite an amicus curiae to do so. The trial-court judge may request permission to address the petition but may not do so unless invited or ordered to do so by the court of appeals.

(5) If briefing or oral argument is required, the clerk must advise the parties, and when appropriate, the trial-court judge or amicus curiae.

(6) The proceeding must be given preference over ordinary civil cases.

(7) The circuit clerk must send a copy of the final disposition to the trial-court judge.

(c) *Other Extraordinary Writs.* — An application for an extraordinary writ other than one provided for in Rule 21(a) must be made by filing a petition with the circuit clerk with proof of service on the respondents. Proceedings on the application must conform, so far as is practicable, to the procedures prescribed in Rule 21(a) and (b).

(d) *Form of Papers; Number of Copies.* — All papers must conform to Rule 32(c)(2). Except by the court's permission, a paper must not exceed 30 pages, exclusive of the disclosure statement, the proof of service, and the accompanying documents required by Rule 21(a)(2)(C). An original and 3 copies must be filed unless the court requires the filing of a different number by local rule or by order in a particular case. (Amended by order adopted April 29, 1994, effective December 1, 1994, by order adopted April 23, 1996, effective December 1, 1996, by order adopted April 24, 1998, effective December 1, 1998, and by order adopted April 29, 2002, effective December 1, 2002.)

CASE NOTES

Mandamus is preferred method of review for orders restricting press activity related to criminal proceedings, but an appeal would be treated as a petition for mandamus if the party seeking review has standing and has substantially complied with the requirements of subdivision (a) of this rule concerning mandamus. United States v. Soussoudis, 807 F.2d 383 (4th Cir. 1986).

Local Rule 21(a). Case Captions for Extraordinary Writs.

A petition for a writ of mandamus or writ of prohibition shall not bear the name of the district judge, but shall be entitled simply "In re ______________, Petitioner." To the extent that relief is requested of a particular judge, unless otherwise ordered, the judge shall be represented pro forma by counsel for the party opposing the relief, who shall appear in the name of the party and not that of the judge. (Amended by order effective December 1, 1995.)

Local Rule 21(b). Petitions for Mandamus or Prohibition.

Strict compliance with the requirements of FRAP 21 is required of all petitioners, even pro se litigants. Petitioner must pay the prescribed docket fee of $450, payable to the Clerk, U.S. Court of Appeals; submit the forms required by Local Rule 21(c)(1) for cases subject to that Local Rule; or submit a properly executed application for leave to proceed in forma pauperis. The parties are required to submit Disclosure of Corporate Affiliations statements with the petition and answer. See FRAP 26.1 and Local Rule 26.1.

After docketing, the clerk shall submit the application to a three-judge panel. A motion for emergency relief pending determination of the petition may be filed and will be assigned in accordance with Local Rule 27(e).

If the Court believes the writ should not be granted, it will deny the petition without requesting an answer. Otherwise the Court will direct the clerk to obtain an answer. After an answer has been filed, the Court ordinarily will decide the merits of the petition on the materials submitted without oral argument. Occasionally, however, briefs may be requested and the matter set for oral argument. (Amended effective September 25, 1996; effective February 1, 2001; effective November 1, 2003; effective April 27, 2006; and effective December 1, 2009.)

Local Rule 21(c). Fees and Costs for Prisoner Petitions for Mandamus, Prohibition, or other Extraordinary Relief.

(1) *Proceedings Arising out of Civil Matters.* — A prisoner filing a petition for writ of mandamus, prohibition, or other extraordinary relief in a matter arising out of a civil case must pay the full $450 docket fee. A prisoner who is unable to prepay this fee may apply to pay the fee in installments by filing with the Court of Appeals (1) an application to proceed without prepayment of fees; (2) a certified copy of the prisoner's trust fund account statement for the six-month period immediately preceding the filing of the notice of appeal, obtained from the appropriate official of each prison at which the prisoner is or was confined; and (3) a form consenting to the collection of fees from the prisoner's trust account.

The Court of Appeals will assess an initial partial filing fee of 20% of the greater of:

(a) the average monthly deposits to the prisoner's account for the six-month period immediately preceding the filing of the petition; or

(b) the average monthly balance in the prisoner's account for the six-month period immediately preceding the filing of the petition.

The Court will direct the agency having custody of the prisoner to collect this initial partial fee from the prisoner's trust account, and to collect the remainder of the $450 fee, as well as any other fees, costs, or sanctions imposed by the Court, in monthly installments of 20% of the preceding month's deposits credited to the prisoner's account. The agency having custody of the prisoner shall forward payments from the prisoner's account to the Clerk, U.S. Court of Appeals, each time the amount in the account exceeds $10 until all fees, costs, and sanctions are paid for the petition.

If a prisoner proceeding under this rule fails to file the forms or make the payments required by the Court, the appeal will be dismissed pursuant to Local Rule 45.

(2) *Effect of Prior Actions and Appeals on Proceedings Arising out of Civil Matters.* — A prisoner who has, on three or more prior occasions, while incarcerated or detained in any facility, brought an action or appeal in a court of the United States that was dismissed on the grounds that it was frivolous, malicious, or failed to state a claim upon which relief could be granted, may not proceed in a matter arising out of a civil case without prepayment of fees unless the prisoner is under imminent danger of serious physical injury.

(3) *Proceedings Arising out of Criminal Matters.* — A prisoner who is unable to prepay the full $450 docket fee for a petition for writ of mandamus, prohibition, or other extraordinary relief arising out of a criminal case may apply to proceed without the prepayment of fees by filing an application for leave to proceed in *forma pauperis*. (Added by order effective September 25, 1996; amended by order effective November 1, 2003, and by order effective April 27, 2006.)

Local Rule 21(d). Petitions for Writ of Mandamus Pursuant to 18 U.S.C. § 3771, Crime Victims' Rights.

A petition for writ of mandamus asserting the rights of a crime victim pursuant to 18 U.S.C. § 3771(d)(3) shall bear the caption "PETITION FOR WRIT OF MANDA-

MUS PURSUANT TO 18 U.S.C. § 3771, CRIME VICTIMS' RIGHTS." Before filing such a petition, the petitioner must notify the Court of Appeals that such a petition will be filed and must arrange for immediate service of the petition on the relevant parties. Such notification must be by telephone call to the Office of the Clerk during normal office hours (804-916-2700).

A failure to comply with these requirements will adversely affect the Court's ability to decide the petition within 72 hours as required by 18 U.S.C. § 3771(d)(3). (Added by order adopted June 1, 2006, effective August 1, 2006.)

TITLE VI. HABEAS CORPUS; PROCEEDINGS IN FORMA PAUPERIS.

Rule 22. Habeas Corpus and Section 2255 Proceedings.

(a) *Application for the Original Writ.* — An application for a writ of habeas corpus must be made to the appropriate district court. If made to a circuit judge, the application must be transferred to the appropriate district court. If a district court denies an application made or transferred to it, renewal of the application before a circuit judge is not permitted. The applicant may, under 28 U.S.C. § 2253, appeal to the court of appeals from the district court's order denying the application.

(b) *Certificate of Appealability.* — (1) In a habeas corpus proceeding in which the detention complained of arises from process issued by a state court, or in a 28 U.S.C. § 2255 proceeding, the applicant cannot take an appeal unless a circuit justice or a circuit or district judge issues a certificate of appealability under 28 U.S.C. § 2253(c). If an applicant files a notice of appeal, the district clerk must send to the court of appeals the certificate (if any) and the statement described in Rule 11(a) of the Rules Governing Proceedings Under 28 U.S.C. § 2254 or § 2255 (if any), along with the notice of appeal and the file of the district-court proceedings. If the district judge has denied the certificate, the applicant may request a circuit judge to issue it.

(2) A request addressed to the court of appeals may be considered by a circuit judge or judges, as the court prescribes. If no express request for a certificate is filed, the notice of appeal constitutes a request addressed to the judges of the court of appeals.

(3) A certificate of appealability is not required when a state or its representative or the United States or its representative appeals. (Amended by order effective April 24, 1996, by order adopted April 24, 1998, effective December 1, 1998, and by order adopted March 26, 2009, effective December 1, 2009.)

CASE NOTES

Among other things, this rule ensures that: (1) An appellant need take no action beyond filing a notice of appeal to obtain a ruling on the certificate; (2) a judge of the Supreme Court must await the initial ruling by the district judge before making his own decisions as to whether to grant or withhold the certificate; and, (3) the appellee is uninvolved at this stage. Brown v. Booker, 622 F. Supp. 993 (E.D. Va. 1985), appeal dismissed, 790 F.2d 83 (4th Cir. 1986).

Rule clarifies requirements of 28 U.S.C. § 2253. — The procedural structure established by this rule clarifies the requirements of 28 U.S.C. § 2253 in a number of important respects. Whereas § 2253 seems to permit the district judge and the judges of the court of appeals to simultaneously and independently make the determination of whether to issue or withhold the certificate, subdivision (b) of this rule establishes an obligatory sequence of interlocking procedural steps that begins with the district judge's initial determination of whether the certificate should issue. Brown v. Booker, 622 F. Supp. 993 (E.D. Va. 1985), appeal dismissed, 790 F.2d 83 (4th Cir. 1986).

Certificate must either issue or be refused in every 28 U.S.C. § 2254 appeal, with the reasons stated if refused. Brown v. Booker, 622 F. Supp. 993 (E.D. Va. 1985), appeal dismissed, 790 F.2d 83 (4th Cir. 1986).

Court of appeals bound by grant of certificate. — If the district judge grants the certificate, the court of appeals is bound by his decision and must consider the appeal on its merits. Brown v. Booker, 622 F. Supp. 993 (E.D. Va. 1985), appeal dismissed, 790 F.2d 83 (4th Cir. 1986).

District judge must determine whether to issue certificate upon filing of notice of appeal. — Even without a formal motion or request for the certificate, a petitioner's notice of appeal from the denial of his petition under 28 U.S.C. § 2254 must be brought to the attention of the district judge. The filing of the notice of appeal itself requires the district judge to make a determination of whether to issue a certificate of probable cause. Brown v. Booker, 622 F. Supp. 993 (E.D. Va. 1985), appeal dismissed, 790 F.2d 83 (4th Cir. 1986).

Statement of reasons for withholding certificate. — The district judge is required to explain his decision to withhold the certificate by more than a mere reference to his opinion. Such an abbreviated expression of the reasons for denial would be of no use to the judges of the court of appeals in exercising their own judgment as to whether or not to grant a certificate of probable cause. The opinion deals with the merits; the certificate only with the propriety of an appeal. Brown v. Booker, 622 F. Supp. 993 (E.D. Va. 1985), appeal dismissed, 790 F.2d 83 (4th Cir. 1986).

Applied in Hargrave v. Landon, 584 F. Supp. 302 (E.D. Va. 1984); Satcher v. Netherland, 944 F. Supp. 1222 (E.D. Va. 1996); Bilodeau v. Angelone, 39 F. Supp. 2d 652 (E.D. Va. 1999).

Local Rule 22(a). Certificates of Appealability.

(1) The following procedures apply in cases in which the district court has not granted a certificate of appealability ("certificate"):

(A) The appellant may submit a request for a certificate with the Court of Appeals specifying the issues on which the appellant seeks authorization to appeal and giving a statement of the reasons why a certificate should be issued. The request shall be submitted either in the form prescribed by Fed. R. App. P. 27 for motions or on a form provided by the clerk. The clerk shall refer the request and other relevant materials to a three-judge panel. If the panel denies a certificate, the appeal will be dismissed. If the panel grants a certificate, the clerk shall enter a briefing order specifying the issues the Court will review.

(B) If no express request for a certificate has been filed pursuant to Subsection (1)(A) of this Rule, the notice of appeal will be treated as a request for a certificate. *See* Fed. R. App. P. 22(b)(2). To assist the Court in resolving this request, the clerk shall enter a Preliminary Briefing Order directing the appellant to file a brief on the merits and, if required by applicable rules, an appendix. The Preliminary Briefing Order shall neither require nor authorize a brief from the appellee, nor shall it make any statement regarding a reply brief by the appellant, but in all other respects it shall be substantially identical to a standard briefing order entered pursuant to Local Rule 31(b) or Local Rule 34(b), as appropriate. The clerk shall refer the appellant's brief and other relevant materials to a three-judge panel for a determination of whether the appellant has made a substantial showing of the denial of a constitutional right as to any claim presented in the brief. If the panel denies a certificate, the appeal will be dismissed. If the panel grants a certificate, the clerk shall enter a Final Briefing Order stating that a certificate has been granted and directing the appellee to file a brief addressing the issue or issues that the Court has accepted for review, and providing for the filing of a reply brief by the appellant.

(2) The following procedures apply in cases in which the district court has granted a certificate of appealability as to at least one issue:

(A) The appellant may submit a request for a certificate as to additional issues, along with a statement of the reasons why the expanded certificate should be issued. The request shall be submitted either in the form prescribed by Fed. R. App. P. 27 for motions or on a form provided by the clerk. The clerk shall refer the request and other relevant materials to a three-judge panel. After the panel has granted or denied such a request, the clerk shall enter a briefing order directing the parties to file briefs addressing the issues the Court will review.

(B) If no express request to expand the certificate has been filed pursuant to Subsection (2)(A) of this Rule, the clerk shall enter a briefing order directing the parties to file briefs addressing the issues certified for review by the district court. If the appellant's brief on the merits addresses issues beyond the scope of the certificate granted by the district court, this court will not review those additional issues unless the appellant files, simultaneously with the brief on the merits, a statement containing the names of the parties, the case number, and a list of the issues that the appellant wishes to add to the certificate. Such statement may also, but need not, present reasons why the certificate should be expanded. Upon receipt of the statement, the clerk shall suspend briefing and refer the brief, the statement, and other relevent materials to a three-judge panel. Once the panel has determined whether to expand the certificate, the clerk shall enter a Final Briefing Order specifying the issue or issues the Court will review.

(3) A request to grant or expand a certificate, including a brief filed pursuant to Subsection (1)(B) of this Rule or a brief and statement filed pursuant to Subsection (2)(B), shall be referred to a panel of three judges. If any judge of the panel is of the opinion that the applicant has made the showing required by 28 U.S.C. § 2253(c), the certificate will issue.

(4) In considering a request to grant or expand a certificate, including a brief filed pursuant to Subsection (1)(B) of this Rule or a brief and statement filed pursuant to Subsection (2)(B), the panel or any judge of the panel may request additional submissions from either party.

(5) Notwithstanding any other statement within this Rule, whenever the Court appoints counsel for a pro se appellant, counsel shall have an opportunity to file a brief on the merits addressing all issues as to which the district court or this Court has granted a certificate, unless the Court directs otherwise. (Amended by order effective December 1, 1995, by order effective June 5, 1996, by order effective December 1, 1998, and by order effective July 8, 2003.)

Local Rule 22(b). Death Penalty Cases and Motions for Stay of Execution.

(1) *Statement Certifying Existence of Sentence of Death.* — Whenever a petition for writ of habeas corpus or motion to vacate a federal sentence in which a sentence of death is involved is filed in the district court or the Court of Appeals, the petitioner shall file with the petition a statement certifying the existence of a sentence of death and the emergency nature of the proceedings and listing any proposed date of execution, any previous cases filed by petitioner in federal court and any cases filed by petitioner pending in any other court. The clerk of the district court shall immediately forward to the Court of Appeals a copy of any such statement filed, and shall immediately notify by telephone the Court of Appeals upon issuance of a final order in that case. If a notice of appeal is filed, the clerk of the district court shall transmit the available record forthwith. The clerk of the Court of Appeals will maintain a special docket for such cases and these cases shall be presented to the Court of Appeals on an expedited basis.

(2) *Lodging of Documents.* — In cases in which an execution date has been set, counsel shall lodge with the clerk of the Court of Appeals all district court documents as they are filed and any pertinent state court materials. If an execution date is imminent, counsel may also lodge proposed appellate papers in anticipation of having to seek emergency appellate relief.

(3) *Motion for Stay of Execution.* — Any motion for stay of execution shall be considered initially in conjunction with any pending application for a certificate of appealability. Should a party file a motion to stay execution or a motion to vacate an order granting a stay of execution, the following documents shall accompany such motion:

(a) The habeas petition or motion to vacate filed in the district court;

(b) Each brief or memorandum of authorities filed by either party in the district court;

(c) Any available transcript of proceedings before the district court;

(d) The memorandum opinion giving the reasons advanced by the district court for denying relief;

(e) The district court judgment denying relief;

(f) The application to the district court for stay;

(g) Any certificate of appealability or order denying a certificate of appealability;

(h) The district court order granting or denying a stay and a statement of reasons for its action; and

(i) A copy of the docket entries of the district court. (Amended by order effective December 1, 1995 and by order effective June 5, 1996.)

Local Rule 22(c). Petitions for Rehearing in Death Penalty Cases.

Once the Court's mandate has issued in a death penalty case, any petition for panel or en banc rehearing should be accompanied by a motion to recall the mandate and motion to stay the execution.

Generally, the Court will not enter a stay of execution solely to allow for additional time for counsel to prepare, or for the Court to consider, a petition for rehearing. Consequently, counsel should take all possible steps to assure that any such petition is filed sufficiently in advance of the scheduled execution date to allow it to be considered by the Court. Counsel should notify the Clerk's Office promptly of their intention to file a petition for rehearing so that arrangements can be made in advance for the most expeditious consideration of the matter by the Court. (Amended by order effective December 1, 1995, amended by order effective December 1, 1998, and by order effective December 1, 2002.)

Local Rule 22(d). Motions for Authorization.

Any individual seeking to file in the district court a second or successive application for relief pursuant to 28 U.S.C. § 2254 or § 2255 shall first file a motion with the Court of Appeals for authorization as required by 28 U.S.C. § 2244, on the form provided by the clerk for such motions. The motion shall be entitled "In re ______________, Movant." The motion must be accompanied by copies of the § 2254 or § 2255 application which movant seeks authorization to file in the district court, as well as all prior § 2254 or § 2255 applications challenging the same conviction and sentence, all court opinions and orders disposing of those applications, and all magistrate judge's reports and recommendations issued on those applications. The movant shall serve a copy of the motion with attachments on the respondent named in the proposed application and shall file the original motion with attachments in the Court of Appeals. Failure to provide the requisite information and attachments may result in denial of the motion for authorization.

If the Court requires a response to the motion, it will direct that the response be received by the clerk for filing within no more than seven days. The Court will enter an order granting or denying authorization within 30 days of filing of the motion, and the clerk will transmit a copy of the order to the district court. If authorization is granted, a copy of the application will be attached to the order for filing in the district court. No motion or request for reconsideration, petition for rehearing, or any other paper seeking review of the granting or denial of authorization will be allowed. (Adopted by order effective June 5, 1996; amended by order effective December 1, 2002; amended effective December 1, 2009; amended effective July 2, 2012.)

Editor's note. — On February 6, 2012, the United States Court of Appeals for the 4th Circuit proposed amendments to Local Rules 22(d), 25(a), 25(b), 25(c), 30(b), 31(c) and 32(b), with the amended local rules superseding Administrative Order 08-01, effective April 16, 2012. However, on April 12, 2012, the 4th Circuit issued a notice stating that the court was "suspend[ing] the April 16, 2012, effective date of its proposed amendments to Local Rules 22(d), 25(a), 25(b), 25(c), 30(b), 31(c) & 32(b), and the superseding of Administrative Order 08-01, pending further review of public comments on the proposed amendments." On May 14, 2012, the original amendments were further amended in light of comments received. They became effective July 2, 2012.

IOP 22.1. Death Penalty Cases.

Once a notice of appeal has been filed in a case involving a sentence of death where an execution date has been set, a panel of three judges will be promptly identified for consideration of all matters related to the case. The position of coordinator of case information in death penalty cases has been established in the Clerk's Office of the Court of Appeals for the purpose of establishing personal liaison with district court personnel and counsel to aid in the expeditious treatment of appeals involving a sentence of death. An expedited briefing schedule will be established when necessary to allow the Court the opportunity to review all issues presented. (Amended by order effective June 1, 1999.)

Rule 23. Custody or Release of a Prisoner in a Habeas Corpus Proceeding.

(a) *Transfer of Custody Pending Review.* — Pending review of a decision in a habeas corpus proceeding commenced before a court, justice or judge of the United States for the release of a prisoner, the person having custody of the prisoner must not transfer custody to another unless a transfer is directed in accordance with this rule. When, upon application, a custodian shows the need for a transfer, the court, justice or judge rendering the decision under review may authorize the transfer and substitute the successor custodian as a party.

(b) *Detention or Release Pending Review of Decision Not to Release.* — While a decision not to release a prisoner is under review, the court or judge rendering the decision, or the court of appeals, or the Supreme Court, or a judge or justice of either court, may order that the prisoner be:

(1) detained in the custody from which release is sought;

(2) detained in other appropriate custody; or

(3) released on personal recognizance, with or without surety.

(c) *Release Pending Review of Decision Ordering Release.* — While a decision ordering the release of a prisoner is under review, the prisoner must — unless the court or judge rendering the decision, or the court of appeals, or the Supreme Court, or a judge or justice of either court orders otherwise — be released on personal recognizance, with or without surety.

(d) *Modification of the Initial Order on Custody.* — An initial order governing the prisoner's custody or release, including any recognizance or surety, continues in effect pending review unless for special reasons shown to the court of appeals or the Supreme Court, or to a judge or justice of either court, the order is modified or an independent order regarding custody, release, or surety is issued. (Amended by order adopted March 10, 1986, effective July 1, 1986, and by order adopted April 24, 1998, effective December 1, 1998.)

Rule 24. Proceedings in Forma Pauperis.

(a) *Leave to Proceed in Forma Pauperis.* — (1) Motion in the District Court. — Except as stated in Rule 24(a)(3), a party to a district-court action who desires to appeal in forma pauperis must file a motion in the district court. The party must attach an affidavit that:

(A) shows in the detail prescribed by Form 4 of the Appendix of Forms, the party's inability to pay or to give security for fees and costs;

(B) claims an entitlement to redress; and

(C) states the issues that the party intends to present on appeal.

(2) Action on the Motion. — If the district court grants the motion, the party may proceed on appeal without prepaying or giving security for fees and costs, unless a statute provides otherwise. If the district court denies the motion, it must state its reasons in writing.

(3) Prior Approval. — A party who was permitted to proceed in forma pauperis in the district-court action, or who was determined to be financially unable to obtain an adequate defense in a criminal case, may proceed on appeal in forma pauperis without further authorization, unless:

(A) the district court — before or after the notice of appeal is filed — certifies that the appeal is not taken in good faith or finds that the party is not otherwise entitled to proceed in forma pauperis and states in writing its reasons for the certification or finding; or

(B) a statute provides otherwise.

(4) Notice of District Court's Denial. — The district clerk must immediately notify the parties and the court of appeals when the district court does any of the following:

(A) denies a motion to proceed on appeal in forma pauperis;

(B) certifies that the appeal is not taken in good faith; or

(C) finds that the party is not otherwise entitled to proceed in forma pauperis.

(5) Motion in the Court of Appeals. — A party may file a motion to proceed on appeal in forma pauperis in the court of appeals within 30 days after service of the notice prescribed in Rule 24(a)(4). The motion must include a copy of the affidavit filed in the district court and the district court's statement of reasons for its action. If no affidavit was filed in the district court, the party must include the affidavit prescribed by Rule 24(a)(1).

(b) *Leave to Proceed in Forma Pauperis on Appeal from the United States Tax Court or on Appeal or Review of an Administrative-Agency Proceeding.* — A party may file in the court of appeals a motion for leave to proceed on appeal in forma pauperis with an affidavit prescribed by Rule 24(a)(1);

(1) in an appeal from a United States Tax Court; and

(2) when an appeal or review of a proceeding before an administrative agency, board, commission, or officer proceeds directly in the court of appeals.

(c) *Leave to Use Original Record.* — A party allowed to proceed on appeal in forma pauperis may request that the appeal be heard on the original record without reproducing any part. (Amended by order adopted April 1, 1979, effective August 1, 1979, by order adopted March 10, 1986, effective July 1, 1986, by order adopted April 24, 1998, effective December 1, 1998, by order adopted April 29, 2002, effective December 1, 2002, and by order adopted April 16, 2013, effective December 1, 2013.)

CASE NOTES

Determining what constitutes "good faith" required by subdivision (a) of this rule and 28 U.S.C. § 1915(a) need not involve a subjective inquiry into the appellant's intent. His "good faith" may be demonstrated by the presentation for appellate review of any issue not frivolous. Brown v. Booker, 622 F. Supp. 993 (E.D. Va. 1985), appeal dismissed, 790 F.2d 83 (4th Cir. 1986).

Right to proceed in forma pauperis. — As subdivision (a) of this rule indicates, absent the appeals court's finding that petitioner's appeal is not taken in "good faith," he is automatically entitled to proceed on appeal in forma pauperis. Therefore, for petitioner to so proceed, it is not necessary for the court to "grant" his motion; his in forma pauperis status will continue if the court simply determines not to retract it. Brown v. Booker, 622 F. Supp. 993 (E.D. Va. 1985), appeal dismissed, 790 F.2d 83 (4th Cir. 1986).

Applied in United States v. Britt, 907 F. Supp. 949 (E.D. Va. 1995).

Local Rule 24. Prisoner Appeals.

(a) *Payment of Fees and Costs Required.* — A prisoner appealing a judgment in a civil action must pay in full the $455 fee required for commencement of the appeal. A prisoner who is unable to prepay this fee may apply to pay the fee in installments by filing with the Court of Appeals (1) an application to proceed without prepayment of fees; (2) a certified copy of the prisoner's trust fund account statement or institutional equivalent for the six-month period immediately preceding the filing of the notice of appeal, obtained from the appropriate official of each prison at which the prisoner is or was confined; and (3) a form consenting to the collection of fees from the prisoner's trust account.

The Court of Appeals will assess an initial partial filing fee of 20% of the greater of:

(1) the average monthly deposits to the prisoner's account for the six-month period immediately preceding the filing of the notice of appeal; or

(2) the average monthly balance in the prisoner's account for the six-month period immediately preceding the filing of the notice of appeal.

Based upon the prisoner's consent, the Court will direct the agency having custody of the prisoner to collect this initial partial fee from the prisoner's trust account, and to collect the remainder of the $455 filing fee, as well as any other fees, costs, or sanctions imposed by the Court of Appeals, in monthly installments of 20% of the preceding month's deposits credited to the prisoner's account. The agency having custody of the prisoner shall forward payments from the prisoner's account to the clerk of the district court each time the amount in the account exceeds $10 until all fees, costs, and sanctions are paid for the appeal.

If a prisoner proceeding under this rule fails to file the forms or make the payments required by the Court, the appeal will be dismissed pursuant to Local Rule 45.

(b) *Effect of Prior Actions and Appeals.* — A prisoner who has, on three or more prior occasions, while incarcerated or detained in any facility, brought an action or appeal in a court of the United States that was dismissed on the grounds that it was frivolous, malicious, or failed to state a claim upon which relief could be granted, may not proceed on appeal without prepayment of fees unless the prisoner is under imminent danger of serious physical injury. (Added by order effective September 25, 1996; amended by order effective November 1, 2003, and by order effective April 27, 2006.)

TITLE VII. GENERAL PROVISIONS.

Rule 25. Filing and Service.

(a) *Filing.* — (1) Filing with the Clerk. — A paper required or permitted to be filed in a court of appeals must be filed with the clerk.

(2) Filing: Method and Timeliness. — (A) In general. Filing may be accomplished by mail addressed to the clerk, but filing is not timely unless the clerk receives the papers within the time fixed for filing.

(B) A brief or appendix. A brief or appendix is timely filed, however, if on or before the last day for filing, it is:

(i) mailed to the clerk by First-Class Mail, or other class of mail that is at least as expeditious, postage prepaid; or

(ii) dispatched to a third-party commercial carrier for delivery to the clerk within 3 days.

(C) Inmate filing. A paper filed by an inmate confined in an institution is timely if deposited in the institution's internal mailing system on or before the last day for filing. If an institution has a system designed for legal mail, the inmate must use that system to receive the benefit of this rule. Timely filing may be shown by a declaration in compliance with 28 U.S.C. § 1746 or by a notarized statement, either of which must set forth the date of deposit and state that first-class postage has been prepaid.

(D) Electronic filing. A court of appeals may by local rule permit or require papers to be filed, signed, or verified by electronic means that are consistent with technical standards, if any, that the Judicial Conference of the United States establishes. A local rule may require filing by electronic means only if reasonable exceptions are allowed.

A paper filed by electronic means in compliance with a local rule constitutes a written paper for the purpose of applying these rules.

(3) Filing a Motion with a Judge. — If a motion requests relief that may be granted by a single judge, the judge may permit the motion to be filed with the judge; the judge must note the filing date on the motion and give it to the clerk.

(4) Clerk's Refusal of Documents. — The clerk must not refuse to accept for filing any paper presented for that purpose solely because it is not presented in proper form as required by these rules or by any local rule or practice.

(5) Privacy Protection. — An appeal in a case that was governed by Federal Rule of Bankruptcy Procedure 9037, Federal Rule of Civil Procedure 5.2, or Federal Rule of Criminal Procedure 49.1 is governed by the same rule on appeal. All other proceedings are governed by Federal Rule of Civil Procedure 5.2, except that Federal Rule of Criminal Procedure 49.1 governs when an extraordinary writ is sought in a criminal case.

(b) *Service of All Papers Required.* — Unless a rule requires service by the clerk, a party must, at or before the time of filing a paper, serve a copy on the other parties to the appeal or review. Service on a party represented by counsel must be made on the party's counsel.

(c) *Manner of Service.* — (1) Service may be any of the following:

(A) personal, including delivery to a responsible person at the office of counsel;

(B) by mail;

(C) by third-party commerical carrier for delivery within 3 days; or

(D) by electronic means, if the party being served consents in writing.

(2) If authorized by local rule, a party may use the court's transmission equipment to make electronic service under Rule 25(c)(1)(D).

(3) When reasonable considering such factors as the immediacy of the relief sought, distance, and cost, service on a party must be by a manner at least as expeditious as the manner used to file the paper with the court.

(4) Service by mail or by commerical carrier is complete on mailing or delivery to the carrier. Service by electronic means is complete on transmission, unless the party making service is notified that the paper was not received by the party served.

(d) *Proof of Service.* — (1) A paper presented for filing must contain either of the following:

(A) an acknowledgment of service by the person served; or

(B) proof of service consisting of a statement by the person who made service certifying:

(i) the date and manner of service;

(ii) the names of the persons served; and

(iii) their mail or electronic addresses, facsimile numbers, or the addresses of the places of delivery, as appropriate for the manner of service.

(2) When a brief or appendix is filed by mailing or dispatch in accordance with Rule 25(a)(2)(B), the proof of service must also state the date and manner by which the document was mailed or dispatched to the clerk.

(3) Proof of service may appear on or be affixed to the papers filed.

(e) *Number of Copies.* — When these rules require the filing or furnishing of a number of copies, a court may require a different number by local rule or by order in a particular case. (Amended by order adopted March 10, 1986, effective July 1, 1986; by order adopted April 30, 1991, effective December 1, 1991; by order adopted April 22, 1993, effective December 1, 1993; by order adopted April 29, 1994, effective December 1, 1994; by order adopted April 23, 1996, effective December 1, 1996; by order adopted April 24, 1998, effective December 1, 1998; by order adopted April 29, 2002, effective December 1, 2002; by order adopted April 12, 2006, effective December 1, 2006; by order adopted April 30, 2007, effective December 1, 2007; and by order adopted March 26, 2009, effective December 1, 2009.)

Local Rule 25(a). Electronic Case Filing System.

With the exception of administrative matters, all cases filed in the Court are assigned to the Court's Case Management/Electronic Case Filing System (CM/ECF).

(1) *Scope of Electronic Filing.* Unless granted an exception for good cause or unless filing only a motion to withdraw from representation, counsel must file all documents in accordance with the requirements of this rule. Pro se litigants are not required to file documents electronically but may be authorized to file electronically in a pending case

upon motion and compliance with the Court's CM/ECF registration requirements. Documents filed electronically must be filed in Portable Document Format (PDF). Text-searchable format is required for briefs and preferred for all documents. Except as provided below or ordered by the Court, paper copies of electronic documents are not required.

(A) *New Cases.* New petitions for review, applications for enforcement, petitions for permission to appeal, petitions for mandamus or prohibition, and motions to authorize successive post-conviction applications must be filed using one of the following options:

(i) Submit New Case through CM/ECF Utilities: File petition in electronic form by selecting "Submit New Case" under CM/ECF Utilities and uploading the petition as a new case. Paper copies are not required, but the petition must be served conventionally, outside the CM/ECF system. The petition is deemed filed as of the date the electronic document was received by the clerk's office.

or

(ii) File in Paper Form: File the original petition in paper form and serve the petition conventionally, outside the CM/ECF system. The petition is filed as of the date the paper document was received in the clerk's office. Additional copies are not required.

(B) *Briefs.* Formal briefs must be filed and served electronically. In addition, counsel must file the paper copies required by Local Rule 31(d). The brief is deemed filed as of the date and time stated on the notice of docket activity for the electronic brief, provided that paper copies are mailed, dispatched to a third-party commercial carrier, or delivered to the clerk's office on the next business day. Service of the paper brief is not required if the brief was served electronically on counsel and on any party not represented by counsel.

(C) *Administrative Records.* The agency filing the administrative record in agency review or enforcement cases and in social security appeals must file the original or one certified copy of the record, either in paper form or through CM/ECF in electronic form.

(i) If the agency files the administrative record in electronic form, counsel filing the opening brief may adopt the administrative record in lieu of filing an appendix under section (D) below, file four additional paper copies of the administrative record, and cite to the AR rather than the JA. The paper copies of the administrative record must be produced using doublesided copying, be securely bound down the left side without obscuring text, and be identified as the administrative record on white covers bound with each copy. In social security appeals, appellant's counsel must also file an appendix under section (D) below that contains any district court documents necessary for appellate review.

(ii) If the agency files the administrative record in paper form, counsel filing the opening brief must file an appendix in accordance with section (D) below.

(D) *Appendices.* Unless electronic and paper copies of the administrative record are filed in an agency reivew or enforcement case under (C) above or no appendix is required because a criminal appeal is proceeding under Anders v. California, electronic filing of either the full appendix or an appendix excerpt is required in accordance with option (i) or (ii) below. In addition, counsel must file the paper copies required by Local Rule 30(b)(4). The appendix is deemed filed as of the date and time stated on the notice of docket activity for the electronic filing of the appendix or appendix excerpt, provided that paper copies of the appendix are mailed, dispatched to a third-party commercial carrier, or delivered to the clerk's office on the next business day. Service of the paper appendix is not required if a full electronic appendix under option (i) was served on counsel and on any party not represented by counsel. Service of the paper appendix is required if an electronic appendix excerpt is used under option (ii).

Option (i): File the full appendix in electronic form, separately filing any sealed documents as a sealed appendix.

Option (ii): File an appendix excerpt in electronic form, that begins with a list of the excerpt contents and that includes the following excerpts from the appendix, with the same pagination and in the same order in which they appear in the paper appendix:

- any sealed documents (file separately as a sealed appendix);
- any documents available only in paper form in the record;
- any documents filed by the parties in a social security case;
- any pertinent opinion, findings, or recommendations of a magistrate judge or bankruptcy court;
- the opinion and order or judgment being appealed; and

• the notice of appeal.

Additionally under option (ii), counsel must cite to both the paper appendix and the docket entry and page number of the electronic record for all record references contained in the brief. For example, material located at page 81 of the joint appendix and at district docket entry 20, page 5, would be cited as JA 81; DE 20 at 5. Counsel using option (ii) may, without motion, exceed the length limitations for opening and response briefs by up to 200 words. If appellant uses option (ii), appellee may use the same option or may file the full electronic appendix under option (i).

(E) *Vouchers.* Criminal Justice Act and other payment vouchers are maintained as financial records separate from the docket. The original must be filed in paper rather than electronic form, and no copies are required.

(2) *Eligibility, Registration, Passwords.* Attorneys who intend to practice in this Court should register as filing users of the Court's CM/ECF system. If permitted by the Court, a party to a pending civil case who is not represented by an attorney may register as a filing user of the Court's CM/ECF system solely for purposes of that case. A pro se party's filing user status will be terminated upon termination of the case or termination of the party's pro se status.

Completion of the Fourth Circuit Electronic Case Filer Application constitutes consent to electronic service of all documents as provided in this rule and the Federal Rules of Appellate Procedure. Filing users agree to protect the security of their passwords and immediately notify the PACER Service Center and the clerk if they learn that their password has been compromised. Filing users may be sanctioned for failure to comply with this provision.

A filing user may withdraw from participation in CM/ECF by providing the clerk with written notice of withdrawal. A filing user's withdrawal from participation in CM/ECF does not alter the requirement that documents be filed in compliance with this rule.

(3) *Consequences of Electronic Filing.* Electronic transmission of a document to CM/ECF consistent with this rule, together with the transmission of a notice of docket activity from the Court, constitutes filing of the document under the Federal Rules of Appellate Procedure and the Court's local rules and constitutes entry of the document on the docket kept by the clerk under FRAP 36 and 45(b).

A document filed electronically is deemed filed at the date and time stated on the notice of docket activity from the Court. Unless otherwise directed by the Court, filing must be completed before midnight Eastern Time, as shown on the notice of docket activity, to be considered timely filed that day.

Before filing a document with the Court, a filing user must verify its legibility and completeness. When a document has been filed electronically, the official record is the electronic document stored by the Court, and the filing party is bound by the document as filed.

If an extension of time or leave of Court is required to file a document, a filing user should file the motion to extend filing time or other appropriate motion using the motion event and the underlying document using the document event. If the Court denies the motion, it will strike the underlying document. If the Court grants the motion, the underlying document will remain on the docket.

(4) *Service of Documents by Electronic Means.* The notice of docket activity that is generated by the Court's electronic filing system constitutes service of the filed document on any registered CM/ECF users. Parties who are not registered for electronic service through CM/ECF must be served conventionally, outside the CM/ECF system, with a copy of any document filed electronically.

If a document (such as a sealed document or a new case) cannot be served electronically, the filer must serve the document conventionally, outside the CM/ECF system.

The notice of docket activity generated by the Court's electronic filing system does not replace the certificate of service required by FRAP 25(d).

(5) *Entry of Court-Issued Documents.* Except as otherwise provided by local rule or Court order, all orders, decrees, opinions, judgments, and proceedings of the Court relating to cases filed and maintained in the CM/ECF system will be filed electronically in accordance with these rules, which will constitute entry on the docket kept by the clerk under FRAP 36 and 45(b).

Any order or other Court-issued document filed electronically without the original signature of a judge or authorized court personnel has the same force and effect as if the judge or clerk had signed a paper copy of the order.

(6) *Attachments and Exhibits to Motions and Original Proceedings.* Unless the Court permits or requires traditional paper filing, filing users must submit in electronic form all documents referenced as exhibits or attachments. Material should be excerpted to include only such portions as are germane to the matter under consideration by the Court. Excerpted material must be clearly and prominently identified as such. The Court may require parties to file additional excerpts or the complete document.

(7) *Sealed Documents.* Sealed material must be filed in accordance with Local Rule 25(c) and served conventionally, outside the CM/ECF system.

(8) *Retention Requirements.* Documents that are electronically filed and require original signatures other than that of the filing user must be maintained in paper form by the filing user for a period of three years after issuance of the Court's final mandate in the case. On request of the Court, the filing user must provide original documents for review.

(9) *Signatures.* The user log-in and password required to submit documents to the CM/ECF system serve as the filing user's signature on all electronic documents filed with the Court. They also serve as a signature for purposes of the Federal Rules of Appellate Procedure, the Court's local rules, and any other purpose for which a signature is required in connection with proceedings before the Court.

The name of the filing user under whose log-in and password the document is submitted must be preceded by an "s/" and typed in the space where the signature would otherwise appear.

No filing user or other person may knowingly permit or cause to permit a filing user's log-in and password to be used by anyone other than an authorized agent of the filing user.

Documents requiring signatures of more than one party must be electronically filed either by: submitting a scanned document containing all necessary signatures; representing the consent of the other parties on the document; identifying on the document the parties whose signatures are required and submitting a notice of endorsement by the other parties no later than three business days after filing; or any other manner approved by the Court.

Electronically represented signatures of all parties and filing users as described above are presumed to be valid signatures. If any party, counsel of record, or filing user objects to the representation of his or her signature on an electronic document as described above, he or she must, within 10 days, file a notice setting forth the basis of the objection.

(10) *Notice of Court Orders and Judgments.* Immediately upon the entry of an order, judgment, or opinion in a case assigned to CM/ECF, the clerk will electronically transmit a notice of docket activity to filing users in the case. Electronic transmission of the notice of docket activity constitutes the notice and service required by FRAP 36(b) and 45(c).

The clerk must give notice in paper form to a person who has not consented to electronic service in accordance with the Federal Rules of Appellate Procedure.

(11) *Technical Failures.* A party or attorney who is adversely affected by a technical failure in connection with filing or receipt of an electronic document may seek appropriate relief from the Court.

(12) *Hyperlinks.* Electronically filed documents may contain hyperlinks to: other portions of the same document or other documents filed on appeal; documents filed in the lower court that are part of the record on appeal; and statutes, rules, regulations, and opinions.

Hyperlinks do not replace citations to the appendix, record, or legal authority and are not considered part of the appellate record. Documents must contain standard citations in support of statements of fact or points of law, in addition to any hyperlink. The Court accepts no responsibility for the availability or functionality of any hyperlink and does not endorse any organization, product, or content at any hyperlinked site. (Amended by order effective December 1, 1995, amended by order effective December 1, 1998, by order effective April 1, 2008, and by order effective July 2, 2012.)

Editor's note. — On February 6, 2012, the United States Court of Appeals for the 4th Circuit proposed amendments to Local Rules 22(d), 25(a), 25(b), 25(c), 30(b), 31(c) and 32(b), with the amended local rules superseding Administrative Order 08-01, effective April 16, 2012. However, on April 12, 2012, the 4th Circuit issued a notice stating that the court was "suspend[ing] the April

16, 2012, effective date of its proposed amendments to Local Rules 22(d), 25(a), 25(b), 25(c), 30(b), 31(c) & 32(b), and the superseding of Administrative Order 08-01, pending further review of public comments on the proposed amendments." On May 14, 2012, the original amendments were further amended in light of comments received. They became effective July 2, 2012.

Local Rule 25(b). Use of Facsimile Equipment, Service, Certificate of Service.

(1) *Use of Facsimile Equipment.* — Documents may be transmitted for filing by use of facsimile transmission equipment only when an emergency situation exists and advance permission has been obtained to use the Clerk's Office facsimile equipment. Several printing services in Richmond will accept documents by facsimile for filing with the Court. Their telephone numbers may be obtained from the Clerk's Office. When a facsimile copy is filed, the original, signed document need not be filed.

(2) *Service.* — Except as otherwise provided by local rule or Court order, service on a party represented by counsel must be on all counsel of record.

(3) *Certificate of Service.* — All documents must be accompanied by a valid certificate of service. The certificate of service of a brief should be bound with the brief as the last, unnumbered page. A certificate of service can be prepared in advance of actual service. If service is not actually accomplished in the manner and on the date stated in the certificate, an amended certificate of service is required. (Amended by order effective December 1, 1995, amended by order effective December 1, 1998, by order effective April 1, 2008, and by order effective July 2, 2012.)

Editor's note. — On February 6, 2012, the United States Court of Appeals for the 4th Circuit proposed amendments to Local Rules 22(d), 25(a), 25(b), 25(c), 30(b), 31(c) and 32(b), with the amended local rules superseding Administrative Order 08-01, effective April 16, 2012. However, on April 12, 2012, the 4th Circuit issued a notice stating that the court was "suspend[ing] the April 16, 2012, effective date of its proposed amendments to Local Rules 22(d), 25(a), 25(b), 25(c), 30(b), 31(c) & 32(b), and the superseding of Administrative Order 08-01, pending further review of public comments on the proposed amendments." On May 14, 2012, the original amendments were further amended in light of comments received. They became effective July 2, 2012.

Local Rule 25(c). Confidential and Sealed Materials.

(1) *Certificates of Confidentiality.* — At the time of filing any appendix, brief, motion, or other document containing or otherwise disclosing materials held under seal by another court or agency, counsel or a pro se party shall file a certificate of confidentiality.

(A) Record material held under seal by another court or agency remains subject to that seal on appeal unless modified or amended by the Court of Appeals.

(B) A certificate of confidentiality must accompany any filing which contains or would otherwise disclose sealed materials. The certificate of confidentiality shall:

(i) identify the sealed material;

(ii) list the dates of the orders sealing the material or, if there is no order, the lower court or agency's general authority to treat the material as sealed;

(iii) specify the terms of the protective order governing the information; and

(iv) identify the appellate document that contains the sealed information.

(2) *Motions to Seal.* — Motions to seal all or any part of the record are presented to and resolved by the lower court or agency in accordance with applicable law during the course of trial, hearing, or other proceedings below.

(A) A motion to seal may be filed with the Court of Appeals when:

(i) a change in circumstances occurs during the pendency of an appeal that warrants reconsideration of a sealing issue decided below;

(ii) the need to seal all or part of the record on appeal arises in the first instance during the pendency of an appeal; or

(iii) additional material filed for the first time on appeal warrants sealing.

(B) Any motion to seal filed with the Court of Appeals shall:

(i) identify with specificity the documents or portions thereof for which sealing is requested;

(ii) state the reasons why sealing is necessary;

(iii) explain why a less drastic alternative to sealing will not afford adequate protection; and

(iv) state the period of time the party seeks to have the material maintained under seal and how the material is to be handled upon unsealing.

(C) A motion to seal filed with the Court of Appeals will be placed on the public docket for at least 5 days before the Court rules on the motion, but the materials subject to a motion to seal will be held under seal pending the Court's disposition of the motion.

(3) *Filing of Confidential and Sealed Material.* — (A) Appendices: When sealed material is included in the appendix, it must be segregated from other portions of the appendix and filed in a separate, sealed volume of the appendix. In criminal cases in which presentence reports are being filed for multiple defendants, each presentence report must be placed in a separate, sealed volume that is served only on counsel for the United States and for the defendant who is the subject of the report.

(B) Briefs, Motions, and Other Documents: When sealed material is included in a brief, motion, or any document other than an appendix, two versions of the document must be filed:

(i) a complete version under seal in which the sealed material has been distinctively marked and

(ii) a redacted version of the same document for the public file.

(C) Personal Data Identifying Information: Personal data identifying information, such as an individual's social security number, an individual's tax identification number, a minor's name, a person's birth date, a financial account number, and (in a criminal case) a person's home address, must be excluded or partially redacted from filings in accordance with FRAP 25(a)(5).

(D) Marking of Sealed and Ex Parte Material: The first page of any appendix, brief, motion, or other document tendered or filed under seal shall be conspicuously marked SEALED and all copies shall be placed in an envelope marked SEALED. If filed ex parte, the first page and the envelope shall also be marked EX PARTE.

(E) Method of Filing:

(i) Appendices: Local Rule 30(b)(4) sets forth the number of paper copies required for public and sealed volumes of the appendix. Sealed volumes are accompanied by a certificate of confidentiality or motion to seal, in both paper and electronic form. Electronic sealed volumes are filed using the entry SEALED APPENDIX, which automatically seals the appendix for Court access only.

(ii) Formal Briefs: Local Rule 31(d) sets forth the number of paper copies required for public and sealed versions of formal briefs. The sealed version is accompanied by a certificate of confidentiality or motion to seal, in both paper and electronic form. The electronic sealed version of the brief is filed using the entry SEALED BRIEF, which automatically seals the brief for Court access only.

(iii) Other Documents: Any other sealed document is filed electronically using the entry SEALED DOCUMENT, which automatically seals the document for Court access only. A certificate of confidentiality or motion to seal is also filed electronically.

(F) Method of Service: All sealed appendices, briefs, and documents must be served in paper form, because only the Court can access the sealed electronic appendix, brief, or document.

(G) Responsibility for Compliance: The responsibility for following the required procedures in filing confidential and sealed material rests solely with counsel and the parties. The clerk will not review each filing for compliance with this rule.

(H) Public Access: Unless filed under seal, case documents are publicly available on the Internet, except that in immigration and social security cases, only the Court's orders and opinions are available to the public on the Internet. Remote electronic access to other documents in immigration and social security cases is available only to persons participating in the case as CM/ECF filing users. Counsel should notify clients regarding the availability of filings on the Internet so that an informed decision may be made on what information is to be included in a public document filed with the Court. (Amended by order effective December 1, 2000; by order effective May 18, 2004; by order effective April 16, 2007; by order effective April 1, 2008; and by order effective July 2, 2012.)

Editor's note. — On February 6, 2012, the United States Court of Appeals for the 4th Circuit proposed amendments to Local Rules 22(d), 25(a), 25(b), 25(c), 30(b), 31(c) and 32(b), with the amended local rules superseding Administrative Order 08-01, effective April 16, 2012. However, on April 12, 2012, the 4th Circuit issued a notice stating that the court was "suspend[ing] the April 16, 2012, effective date of its proposed amendments to Local Rules 22(d), 25(a), 25(b), 25(c), 30(b), 31(c) & 32(b), and the superseding of Administrative Order 08-01, pending further review of public comments on the proposed amendments." On May 14, 2012, the original amendments were further amended in light of comments received. They became effective July 2, 2012.

Rule 26. Computing and Extending Time.

(a) *Computing Time.* — The following rules apply in computing any time period specified in these rules, in any local rule or court order, or in any statute that does not specify a method of computing time.

(1) Period Stated in Days or a Longer Unit. When the period is stated in days or a longer unit of time:

(A) exclude the day of the event that triggers the period;

(B) count every day, including intermediate Saturdays, Sundays, and legal holidays; and

(C) include the last day of the period, but if the last day is a Saturday, Sunday, or legal holiday, the period continues to run until the end of the next day that is not a Saturday, Sunday, or legal holiday.

(2) Period Stated in Hours. When the period is stated in hours:

(A) begin counting immediately on the occurrence of the event that triggers the period;

(B) count every hour, including hours during intermediate Saturdays, Sundays, and legal holidays; and

(C) if the period would end on a Saturday, Sunday, or legal holiday, the period continues to run until the same time on the next day that is not a Saturday, Sunday, or legal holiday.

(3) Inaccessibility of the Clerk's Office. Unless the court orders otherwise, if the clerk's office is inaccessible:

(A) on the last day for filing under Rule 26(a)(1), then the time for filing is extended to the first accessible day that is not a Saturday, Sunday, or legal holiday; or

(B) during the last hour for filing under Rule 26(a)(2), then the time for filing is extended to the same time on the first accessible day that is not a Saturday, Sunday, or legal holiday.

(4) "Last Day" Defined. Unless a different time is set by a statute, local rule, or court order, the last day ends:

(A) for electronic filing in the district court, at midnight in the court's time zone;

(B) for electronic filing in the court of appeals, at midnight in the time zone of the circuit clerk's principal office;

(C) for filing under Rules 4(c)(1), 25(a)(2)(B), and 25(a)(2)(C) — and filing by mail under Rule 13(b) — at the latest time for the method chosen for delivery to the post office, third-party commercial carrier, or prison mailing system; and

(D) for filing by other means, when the clerk's office is scheduled to close.

(5) "Next Day" Defined. The "next day" is determined by continuing to count forward when the period is measured after an event and backward when measured before an event.

(6) "Legal Holiday" Defined. "Legal holiday" means:

(A) the day set aside by statute for observing New Year's Day, Martin Luther King Jr.'s Birthday, Washington's Birthday, Memorial Day, Independence Day, Labor Day, Columbus Day, Veterans' Day, Thanksgiving Day, or Christmas Day;

(B) any day declared a holiday by the President or Congress; and

(C) for periods that are measured after an event, any other day declared a holiday by the state where either of the following is located: the district court that rendered the challenged judgment or order, or the circuit clerk's principal office.

(b) *Extending Time.* — For good cause, the court may extend the time prescribed by these rules or by its order to perform any act, or may permit an act to be done after that time expires. But the court may not extend the time to file:

(1) a notice of appeal (except as authorized in Rule 4) or a petition for permission to appeal; or

(2) a notice of appeal from or a petition to enjoin, set aside, suspend, modify, enforce, or otherwise review an order of an administrative agency, board, commission, or officer of the United States, unless specifically authorized by law.

(c) *Additional Time after Service.* — When a party may or must act within a specified time after service, 3 days are added after the period would otherwise expire under Rule 26(a), unless the paper is delivered on the date of service stated in the proof of service. For purposes of this Rule 26(c), a paper that is served electronically is not treated as delivered on the date of service stated in the proof of service. (Amended by order adopted March 1, 1971, effective July 1, 1971; by order adopted March 10, 1986, effective July 1, 1986; by order adopted April 25, 1989, effective December 1, 1989; by order adopted April 30, 1991, effective December 1, 1991; by order adopted April 23, 1996, effective December 1, 1996; by order adopted April 24, 1998, effective December 1, 1998; by order adopted April 29, 2002, effective December 1, 2002; by order adopted April 25, 2005, effective December 1, 2005; and by order adopted March 26, 2009, effective December 1, 2009.)

CASE NOTES

Extension granted merely to prevent unduly harsh result for failure to comply with Rule 41 FRAP. — See Caperton v. Beatrice Pocahontas Coal Co., 585 F.2d 683 (4th Cir. 1978).

Applied in United States v. Breit, 754 F.2d 526 (4th Cir. 1985).

Local Rule 26. State Holidays and Inclement Weather.

Whenever a party in computing a filing or service date relies upon an extension of time due to the inaccessibility of the Clerk's Office because of inclement weather or other conditions, or due to a state holiday, counsel must certify such reliance in the certificate of service or by separate written declaration.

Rule 26.1. Corporate Disclosure Statement.

(a) *Who Must File.* — Any nongovernmental corporate party to a proceeding in a court of appeals must file a statement that identifies any parent corporation and any publicly held corporation that owns 10% or more of its stock or states that there is no such corporation.

(b) *Time for Filing; Supplemental Filing.* — A party must file the Rule 26.1(a) statement with the principal brief or upon filing a motion, response, petition, or answer in the court of appeals, whichever occurs first, unless a local rule requires earlier filing. Even if the statement has already been filed, the party's principal brief must include the statement before the table of contents. A party must supplement its statement whenever the information that must be disclosed under Rule 26.1(a) changes.

(c) *Number of Copies.* — If the Rule 26.1(a) statement is filed before the principal brief, or if a supplemental statement is filed, the party must file an original and 3 copies unless the court requires a different number by local rule or by order in a particular case. (Added by order adopted April 25, 1989, effective December 1, 1989, amended by order adopted April 30, 1991, effective December 1, 1991, by order adopted April 29, 1994, effective December 1, 1994, by order adopted April 24, 1998, effective December 1, 1998, and by order adopted April 29, 2002, effective December 1, 2002.)

Local Rule 26.1. Disclosure of Corporate Affiliations and Other Entities with a Direct Financial Interest in Litigation.

(a) *Disclosure Requirements Applicable to Parties, Including Intervenors.* — (1) Who Must File. (A) Civil, Agency, Bankruptcy, and Mandamus Cases. A party in a civil, agency, bankruptcy, or mandamus case, other than the United States or a party proceeding in forma pauperis, must file a disclosure statement, except that a state or local government is not required to file a disclosure statement in a case in which the opposing party is proceeding without counsel.

(B) Criminal and Post-Conviction Cases. A corporate party in a criminal or postconviction case must file a disclosure statement.

(2) Information to Be Disclosed by Parties, Including Intervenors. (A) Information Required by FRAP 26.1. A party must identify any parent corporation and any publicly held corporation that owns 10% or more of the party's stock, or state that there is no such corporation.

(B) Information About Other Financial Interests. A party must identify any publicly held corporation, whether or not a party to the present litigation, that has a direct financial interest in the outcome of the litigation by reason of a franchise, lease, other profit sharing agreement, insurance, or indemnity agreement, or state that there is no such corporation.

(C) Information About Other Publicly Held Legal Entities. Whenever required by FRAP 26.1 or this rule to disclose information about a corporation that has issued shares to the public, a party shall also disclose information about similarly situated master limited partnerships, real estate investment trusts, or other legal entities whose shares are publicly held or traded, or state that there are no such entities.

(D) Information About Trade Association Members. A party trade association must identify any publicly held member whose stock or equity value could be affected substantially by the outcome of the proceeding or whose claims the trade association is pursuing in a representative capacity, or state that there is no such member.

(b) *Disclosure Requirements Applicable to Corporate Amicus Curiae.* — (1) Who Must File. If an amicus curiae is a corporation, the amicus curiae brief must include a disclosure statement.

(2) Information to Be Disclosed by Corporate Amicus Curiae. A corporate amicus curiae must disclose the same information that sections (a)(2)(A), (B) & (C) require parties to disclose.

(c) *Form.* — The disclosure statement shall be on a form provided by the clerk. A negative statement is required if a filer has no disclosures to make.

(d) *Time of Filing.* — A party's disclosure statement must be filed within 14 days of docketing of the appeal, unless earlier pleadings are submitted for the Court's consideration, in which case the disclosure statement shall be filed at that time.

(e) *Amendment.* — Filers are required to amend their disclosure statements when necessary to maintain their current accuracy. (Amended by order effective December 1, 1998 and August 11, 2008.)

Rule 27. Motions.

(a) *In General.* — (1) Application for Relief. — An application for an order or other relief is made by motion unless these rules prescribe another form. A motion must be in writing unless the court permits otherwise.

(2) Contents of a Motion. — (A) Grounds and relief sought. A motion must state with particularity the grounds for the motion, the relief sought, and the legal argument necessary to support it.

(B) Accompanying documents. (i) Any affidavit or other paper necessary to support a motion must be served and filed with the motion.

(ii) An affidavit must contain only factual information, not legal argument.

(iii) A motion seeking substantive relief must include a copy of the trial court's opinion or agency's decision as a separate exhibit.

(C) Documents barred or not required. (i) A separate brief supporting or responding to a motion must not be filed.

(ii) A notice of motion is not required.

(iii) A proposed order is not required.

(3) Response. — (A) Time to file. Any party may file a response to a motion; Rule 27(a)(2) governs its contents. The response must be filed within 10 days after service of the motion unless the court shortens or extends the time. A motion authorized by Rules 8, 9, 18, or 41 may be granted before the 10-day period runs only if the court gives reasonable notice to the parties that it intends to act sooner.

(B) Request for affirmative relief. A response may include a motion for affirmative relief. The time to respond to the new motion, and to reply to that response, are governed by Rule 27(a)(3)(A) and (a)(4). The title of the response must alert the court to the request for relief.

(4) Reply to Response. — Any reply to a response must be filed within 7 days after service of the response. A reply must not present matters that do not relate to the response.

(b) *Disposition of a Motion for a Procedural Order.* — The court may act on a motion for a procedural order — including a motion under Rule 26(b) — at any time without awaiting a response, and may, by rule or by order in a particular case, authorize its clerk to act on specified types of procedural motions. A party adversely affected by the court's, or the clerk's, action may file a motion to reconsider, vacate, or modify that action. Timely opposition filed after the motion is granted in whole or in part does not constitute a request to reconsider, vacate, or modify the disposition; a motion requesting that relief must be filed.

(c) *Power of a Single Judge to Entertain a Motion.* — A circuit judge may act alone on any motion, but may not dismiss or otherwise determine an appeal or other proceeding. A court of appeals may provide by rule or by order in a particular case that only the court may act on any motion or class of motions. The court may review the action of a single judge.

(d) *Form of Papers; Page Limits; and Number of Copies.* — (1) Format. — (A) Reproduction. A motion, response, or reply may be reproduced by any process that yields a clear black image on light paper. The paper must be opaque and unglazed. Only one side of the paper may be used.

(B) Cover. A cover is not required, but there must be a caption that includes the case number, the name of the court, the title of the case, and a brief descriptive title indicating the purpose of the motion and identifying the party or parties for whom it is filed. If a cover is used, it must be white.

(C) Binding. The document must be bound in any manner that is secure, does not obscure the text, and permits the document to lie reasonably flat when open.

(D) Paper size, line spacing, and margins. The document must be on 8 ½ by 11 inch paper. The text must be double-spaced, but quotations more than two lines long may be indented and single-spaced. Headings and footnotes may be single-spaced. Margins must be at least one inch on all four sides. Page numbers may be placed in the margins, but no text may appear there.

(E) Typeface and type styles. The document must comply with the typeface requirements of Rule 32(a)(5) and the type-style requirements of Rule 32(a)(6).

(2) Page Limits. A motion or a response to a motion must not exceed 20 pages, exclusive of the corporate disclosure statement and accompanying documents authorized by Rule 27(a)(2)(B), unless the court permits or directs otherwise. A reply to a response must not exceed 10 pages.

(3) Number of Copies. An original and 3 copies must be filed unless the court requires a different number by local rule or by order in a particular case.

(e) *Oral Argument.* — A motion will be decided without oral argument unless the court orders otherwise. (Amended by order adopted April 1, 1979, effective August 1, 1979, by order adopted April 25, 1989, effective December 1, 1989, by order adopted April 29, 1994, effective December 1, 1994, by order adopted April 24, 1998, effective December 1, 1998, by order adopted April 29, 2002, effective December 1, 2002, by order adopted April 25, 2005, effective December 1, 2005, and by order adopted March 26, 2009, effective December 1, 2009.)

Local Rule 27(a). Content of Motions, Notification and Consent.

In cases where all parties are represented by counsel, all motions shall contain a statement by counsel that counsel for the other parties to the appeal have been informed of the intended filing of the motion. The statement shall indicate whether the other parties consent to the granting of the motion, or intend to file responses in opposition. (Amended by order effective December 1, 1998.)

Local Rule 27(b). Procedural Orders Acted on by Clerk; Reconsideration Thereof.

Motions and applications for orders if consented to, or if unopposed after due notice to all interested parties has been given or waived, or if the orders sought are procedural or relate to the preparation or printing of the appendix and briefs on appeal, or are such as are ordinarily granted as of course and without notice or hearing, need not be submitted to the Court, or to a judge thereof. Such orders may be entered for the Court by the clerk, who shall forthwith send copies thereof to the parties.

Any party adversely affected by an order entered by the clerk pursuant to this rule shall be entitled to request reconsideration of the clerk's action by the Court, if within 14 days after entry of the order, such party shall file with the clerk and serve upon the parties to the proceedings a request, in writing, for reconsideration, vacation or modification of the order, stating the grounds for such request. The clerk shall thereupon submit to the Court the request for reconsideration, vacation or modification, the motion or application upon which the order was entered, and any responses by other parties which may have been filed in support or opposition to the request. The Court may thereafter take such action as may be proper. (Amended by order effective December 1, 1998.)

Local Rule 27(c). Form of Motions.

A Disclosure of Corporate Affiliations statement must accompany the motion unless previously filed with the Court. See FRAP 26.1 and Local Rule 26.1. Counsel should always review carefully the specific rule which authorizes relief to ascertain the requirements, and any motion should contain or be accompanied by any supporting documents required by a specific rule. If a motion is supported by attachments, these materials should also be served and filed with the motion. The parties should not make requests for procedural and substantive relief in a single motion, but should make each request in a separate motion. (Amended by order effective December 1, 1998; by order effective April 1, 2008; and amended effective December 1, 2009.)

Local Rule 27(d). Responses; Replies.

(1) *Responses.* — Although any party may file a response to a motion, a party need not respond to a motion until requested to do so by the Court. The three-day mailing period permitted by FRAP 26(c) does not apply to responses requested by the Court or clerk by letter wherein a response date is set forth in the request. A Disclosure of Corporate Affiliations statement must accompany any response to a motion unless previously filed with the Court. See FRAP 26.1 and Local Rule 26. If the Court acts upon a motion without a response, any party adversely affected by such action may by application to the Court request reconsideration, vacation or modification of the Court's action.

(2) *Replies.* — The Court will not ordinarily await the filing of a reply before reviewing a motion and response. If movant intends to file a reply and does not want the Court to actively consider the motion and response until a reply is filed, movant shall notify the clerk in writing of the intended filing of the reply and request that this Court not act on the motion until the reply is received. (Amended by order effective December 1, 1995; amended by order effective December 1, 1998; and amended effective December 1, 2009.)

Local Rule 27(e). Panel Assignments and Emergency Motions.

There is a strong presumption that the Court will act, in all but routine procedural matters, through panels or en banc, as prescribed by 28 U.S.C. § 46(c). Ordinarily, counsel shall present all motions to the clerk for presentation to the Court. Application to a single judge should be made only in exceptional circumstances where action by a panel would be impractical due to the requirements of time. In such exceptional circumstances, counsel shall attempt to notify the clerk's office that application is being made directly to a single judge, and copies of all papers presented to the judge shall be presented to the clerk as soon as practical for filing.

When a single judge determines to act, the matter will be referred to a panel as early in the process as is practical. As soon as a matter has been assigned to a panel, any action in the matter will be decided by the panel.

The selection of motion panels is similar to the process set forth in I.O.P. 34.I for hearing panels. In a case where a request for single judge action is made to the clerk and action by a panel is not feasible, the clerk will assign the matter to a judge selected at random. In cases where a single judge, selected at random, has found it necessary to act, the clerk will fill out the panel with the at-random selection of two additional judges. In cases in which a single judge, selected by counsel, has found it necessary to act, the clerk will assign the matter to a three-judge panel selected at random, which may or may not include the single judge who acted in the case. (Amended by order effective December 1, 1995, amended by order effective December 1, 1998, and by order effective February 1, 2001.)

Local Rule 27(f). Motions for Summary Disposition.

Motions for summary affirmance, reversal or dismissal are reserved for extraordinary cases only and should not be filed routinely. Counsel contemplating filing a motion to dispose summarily of an appeal should carefully consider whether the issues raised on appeal are in fact manifestly unsubstantial and appropriate for disposition by motion. Motions for summary affirmance or reversal are seldom granted.

Motions for summary disposition should be made only after briefs are filed. If such motions are submitted before the completion of the briefing schedule, the Court will defer action on the motion until the case is mature for full consideration.

Motions to dismiss based upon the ground that the appeal is not within the jurisdiction of the Court or for other procedural grounds may be filed at anytime. The Court may also sua sponte summarily dispose of any appeal at any time. (Amended by order effective December 1, 1998.)

Rule 28. Briefs.

(a) *Appellant's Brief.* — The appellant's brief must contain, under appropriate headings and in the order indicated:

(1) a corporate disclosure statement if required by Rule 26.1;

(2) a table of contents, with page references;

(3) a table of authorities — cases (alphabetically arranged), statutes, and other authorities — with references to the pages of the brief where they are cited;

(4) a jurisdictional statement, including:

(A) the basis for the district court's or agency's subject-matter jurisdiction, with citations to applicable statutory provisions and stating relevant facts establishing jurisdiction;

(B) the basis for the court of appeals' jurisdiction, with citations to applicable statutory provisions and stating relevant facts establishing jurisdiction;

(C) the filing dates establishing the timeliness of the appeal or petition for review; and

(D) an assertion that the appeal is from a final order or judgment that disposes of all parties' claims, or information establishing the court of appeals' jurisdiction on some other basis;

(5) a statement of the issues presented for review;

(6) a concise statement of the case setting out the facts relevant to the issues submitted for review, describing the relevant procedural history, and identifying the rulings presented for review, with appropriate references to the record (see Rule 28(e));

(7) summary of the argument, which must contain a succinct, clear, and accurate statement of the arguments made in the body of the brief, and which must not merely repeat the argument headings;

(8) the argument, which must contain:

(A) appellant's contentions and the reasons for them, with citations to the authorities and parts of the record on which the appellant relies; and

(B) for each issue, a concise statement of the applicable standard of review (which may appear in the discussion of the issue or under a separate heading placed before the discussion of the issues);

(9) a short conclusion stating the precise relief sought; and

(10) the certificate of compliance, if required by Rule 32(a)(7).

(b) *Appellee's Brief.* — The appellee's brief must conform to the requirements of Rule 28(a)(1)-(8) and (10), except that none of the following need appear unless the appellee is dissatisfied with the appellant's statement:

(1) the jurisdictional statement;

(2) the statement of the issues;

(3) the statement of the case; and

(4) the statement of the standard of review.

(c) *Reply Brief.* — The appellant may file a brief in reply to the appellee's brief. Unless the court permits, no further briefs may be filed. A reply brief must contain a table of contents, with page references, and a table of authorities — cases (alphabetically arranged), statutes, and other authorities — with references to the pages of the reply brief where they are cited.

(d) *References to Parties.* — In briefs and at oral argument, counsel should minimize use of the terms "appellant" and "appellee". To make briefs clear, counsel should use the parties' actual names or the designations used in the lower court or agency proceeding, or such descriptive terms as "the employee," "the injured person," "the taxpayer," "the ship," "the stevedore."

(e) *References to the Record.* — References to the parts of the record contained in the appendix filed with the appellant's brief must be to the pages of the appendix. If the appendix is prepared after the briefs are filed, a party referring to the record must follow one of the methods detailed in Rule 30(c). If the original record is used under Rule 30(f) and is not consecutively paginated, or if the brief refers to an unreproduced part of the record, any reference must be to the page of the original document. For example:

- Answer p. 7;
- Motion for Judgment p. 2;
- Transcript p. 231.

Only clear abbreviations may be used. A party referring to evidence whose admissibility is in controversy must cite the pages of the appendix or of the transcript at which the evidence was identified, offered, and received or rejected.

(f) *Reproduction of Statutes, Rules, Regulations, etc.* — If the court's determination of the issues presented requires the study of statutes, rules, regulations, etc., the relevant parts must be set out in the brief or in an addendum at the end, or may be supplied to the court in pamphlet form.

(g) *[Reserved]*

(h) *[Reserved]*

(i) *Briefs in a Case Involving Multiple Appellants or Appellees.* — In a case involving more than one appellant or appellee, including consolidated cases, any number of appellants or appellees may join in a brief, and any party may adopt by reference a part of another's brief. Parties may also join in reply briefs.

(j) *Citation of Supplemental Authorities.* — If pertinent and significant authorities come to a party's attention after the party's brief has been filed — or after oral argument but before decision — a party may promptly advise the circuit clerk by letter, with a copy to all other parties, setting forth the citations. The letter must state the reasons for the supplemental citations, referring either to the page of the brief or to a point argued orally. The body of the letter must not exceed 350 words. Any response must be made promptly and must be similarly limited. (Amended by order adopted April 30, 1979, effective August 1, 1979, by order adopted March 10, 1986, effective July 1, 1986, by order adopted April 25, 1989, effective December 1, 1989, by order adopted April 30, 1991, effective December 1, 1991, by order adopted April 22, 1993, effective December 1, 1993, by order adopted April 29, 1994, effective December 1, 1994, by order adopted April 24, 1998, effective December 1, 1998, by order adopted April 29, 2002, effective December 1, 2002, by order adopted April 25, 2005, effective December 1, 2005, and by order adopted April 16, 2013, effective December 1, 2013.)

CASE NOTES

Court will not search through record to find material which parties failed to provide. — United States Court of Appeals will not sift through the record to piece together support for computer corporation's contentions that a computer program developed by one of its competitors, infringed upon the copyrights it held in its "Claims Express" and "EDI Link" computer programs where it had not identified any evidence demonstrating that district court clearly erred in finding that the program developed by competitor was not substantially similar to either Claims Express or EDI Link. Comprehensive Technologies Int'l, Inc. v. Software Artisans, Inc., 3 F.3d 730 (4th Cir. 1993).

Failure to include contentions constitute abandonment of claims. — Where none of the briefs filed by either party contains "contentions" about the application of the Virginia Constitution's Declaration of Rights or the Virginia Act for Religious Freedom to the instant case, or citations to authorities that might illuminate the special rights that state charter and religious-freedom statute are said to guarantee, the parties failed to appeal the district court's grant of summary judgment with respect to these state-law theories of recovery; failure of this nature constitutes abandonment of the claims, and precludes appellate court from considering them further herein. Rosenberger v. Rector & Visitors of UVA, 18 F.3d 269 (4th Cir. 1994), rev'd on other grounds, 515 U.S. 819, 115 S. Ct. 2510, 132 L. Ed. 2d 700 (1995).

Applied in Virginians for Dulles v. Volpe, 541 F.2d 442 (4th Cir. 1976); Columbus-America Discovery Group v. Atlantic Mut. Ins. Co., 56 F.3d 556 (4th Cir. 1995); Satcher v. Netherland, 944 F. Supp. 1222 (E.D. Va. 1996).

Local Rule 28(a). Consolidated Cases and Briefs.

Related appeals or petitions for review will be consolidated in the Office of the Clerk, with notice to all parties, at the time a briefing schedule is established. One brief shall be permitted per side, including parties permitted to intervene, in all cases consolidated by Court order, unless leave to the contrary is granted upon good cause shown. In consolidated cases lead counsel shall be selected by the attorneys on each side and that person's identity made known in writing to the clerk within 14 days of the date of the order of consolidation. In the absence of an agreement by counsel, the clerk shall designate lead counsel. The individual so designated shall be responsible for the coordination, preparation and filing of the briefs and appendix. (Amended effective December 1, 2009.)

Local Rule 28(b). Addenda and Attachments to Briefs.

A party may comply with the requirements of FRAP 28(f) and FRAP 32.1(b) by including material or items designated therein in an addendum at the end of the brief or by supplying them to the Court under separate cover. Should a party wish to supplement the brief with matters other than those designated in FRAP 28(f) or FRAP 32.1(b), the additional material must be presented to the Court under separate cover, accompanied by a motion for leave to file such supplemental material as an attachment to the brief. (Amended by order effective December 1, 1995, by order effective December 1, 1998, by order effective December 1, 2006, and by order effective August 20, 2007.)

Local Rule 28(c). Responsibilities of Counsel Listed on a Brief.

The court will interpret the listing of an attorney on a brief as a representation that he or she is capable of arguing the appeal if lead counsel is unavailable.

Local Rule 28(d). Joint Appeals and Consolidations.

Where multiple parties are directed to file a consolidated brief, counsel on the same side of the case should confer and agree upon a means for assuring that the positions of all parties are addressed within the length limits allowed and that each counsel will have an opportunity to review and approve the consolidated brief before it is filed.

Motions to file separate briefs are not favored by the Court and are granted only upon a particularized showing of good cause, such as, but not limited to, cases in which the interests of the parties are adverse. Generally unacceptable grounds for requests to file separate briefs include representations that the issues presented require a brief in excess of the length limitations established by FRAP 32(a)(7) (appropriately addressed by a motion to exceed length limit), that counsel cannot coordinate their efforts due to different geographical locations, or that the participation of separate counsel in the proceedings below entitles each party to separate briefs on appeal.

If a motion to file separate briefs is granted, the length of such briefs may be limited by the Court. The parties shall continue to share the time allowed for oral argument. (Amended by order effective December 1, 1995, and amended by order effective December 1, 1998.)

Local Rule 28(e). Citation of Additional Authorities.

Counsel may, without leave of Court, present a letter drawing the Court's attention to supplemental authorities under Rule 28(j) and serve a copy on all counsel of record. The Court may grant leave for or direct the filing of additional memoranda, which may include additional argument before, during or after oral argument. (Amended by order effective December 1, 1998, by order effective December 1, 2002, and by order effective April 1, 2008.)

Local Rule 28(f). Statement of Facts.

Every opening brief filed by appellants in this Court shall include a separate section, the title of which is STATEMENT OF FACTS. In this section the attorneys will prepare a narrative statement of all of the facts necessary for the Court to reach the conclusion which the brief desires. The said STATEMENT OF FACTS will include exhibit, record, transcript, or appendix references showing the source of the facts stated. An appellee's brief shall also include a STATEMENT OF FACTS so prepared unless appellee is satisfied with appellant's statement of facts. (Adopted by order effective June 5, 1996, amended by order effective December 4, 1996, and amended by order effective December 1, 1998.)

Rule 28.1. Cross-Appeals.

(a) *Applicability.* — This rule applies to a case in which a cross-appeal is filed. Rules 28(a)-(c), 31(a)(1), 32(a)(2), and 32(a)(7)(A)-(B) do not apply to such a case, except as otherwise provided in this rule.

(b) *Designation of Appellant.* — The party who files a notice of appeal first is the appellant for the purposes of this rule and Rules 30 and 34. If notices are filed on the same day, the plaintiff in the proceeding below is the appellant. These designations may be modified by agreement of the parties or by court order.

(c) *Briefs.* — In a case involving a cross-appeal:

(1) Appellant's Principal Brief. The appellant must file a principal brief in the appeal. That brief must comply with Rule 28(a).

(2) Appellee's Principal and Response Brief. The appellee must file a principal brief in the cross-appeal and must, in the same brief, respond to the principal brief in the appeal. That appellee's brief must comply with Rule 28(a), except that the brief need

not include a statement of the case unless the appellee is dissatisfied with the appellant's statement.

(3) Appellant's Response and Reply Brief. The appellant must file a brief that responds to the principal brief in the cross-appeal and may, in the same brief, reply to the response in the appeal. That brief must comply with Rule 28(a)(2)-(8) and (10), except that none of the following need appear unless the appellant is dissatisfied with the appellee's statement in the cross-appeal:

(A) the jurisdictional statement;

(B) the statement of the issues;

(C) the statement of the case; and

(D) the statement of the standard of review.

(4) Appellee's Reply Brief. The appellee may file a brief in reply to the response in the cross-appeal. That brief must comply with Rule 28(a)(2)-(3) and (10) and must be limited to the issues presented by the cross-appeal.

(5) No Further Briefs. Unless the court permits, no further briefs may be filed in a case involving a cross-appeal.

(d) *Cover.* — Except for filings by unrepresented parties, the cover of the appellant's principal brief must be blue; the appellee's principal and response brief, red; the appellant's response and reply brief, yellow; and the appellee's reply brief, gray. The front cover of a brief must contain the information required by Rule 32(a)(2).

(e) *Length.* — (1) Page Limitation. Unless it complies with Rule 28.1(e)(2) and (3), the appellant's principal brief must not exceed 30 pages; the appellee's principal and response brief, 35 pages; the appellant's response and reply brief, 30 pages; and the appellee's reply brief, 15 pages.

(2) Type-Volume Limitation.

(A) The appellant's principal brief or the appellant's response and reply brief is acceptable if:

(i) it contains no more than 14,000 words; or

(ii) it uses a monospaced face and contains no more than 1,300 lines of text.

(B) The appellee's principal and response brief is acceptable if:

(i) it contains no more than 16,500 words; or

(ii) it uses a monospaced face and contains no more than 1,500 lines of text.

(C) The appellee's reply brief is acceptable if it contains no more than half of the type volume specified in Rule 28.1(e)(2)(A).

(3) Certificate of Compliance. A brief submitted under Rule 28(e)(2) must comply with Rule 32(a)(7)(C).

(f) *Time to Serve and File a Brief.* — Briefs must be served and filed as follows:

(1) the appellant's principal brief, within 40 days after the record is filed;

(2) the appellee's principal and response brief, within 30 days after the appellant's principal brief is served;

(3) the appellant's response and reply brief, within 30 days after the appellee's principal and response brief is served; and

(4) the appellee's reply brief, within 14 days after the appellant's response and reply brief is served, but at least 7 days before argument unless the court, for good cause, allows a later filing. (Adopted by order dated April 25, 2005, effective December 1, 2005, amended by order adopted March 26, 2009, effective December 1, 2009, and amended by order adopted April 16, 2013, effective December 1, 2013.)

Rule 29. Brief of an Amicus Curiae.

(a) *When Permitted.* — The United States or its officer or agency or a state may file an amicus-curiae brief without the consent of the parties or leave of court. Any other amicus curiae may file a brief only by leave of court or if the brief states that all parties have consented to its filing.

(b) *Motion for Leave to File.* — The motion must be accompanied by the proposed brief and state:

(1) the movant's interest; and

(2) the reason why an amicus brief is desirable and why the matters asserted are relevant to the disposition of the case.

(c) *Contents and Form.* — An amicus brief must comply with Rule 32. In addition to the requirements of Rule 32, the cover must identify the party or parties supported and indicate whether the brief supports affirmance or reversal. An amicus brief need not comply with Rule 28, but must include the following:

(1) if the amicus curiae is a corporation, a disclosure statement like that required of parties by Rule 26.1;

(2) a table of contents, with page references;

(3) a table of authorities — cases (alphabetically arranged), statutes, and other authorities — with references to the pages of the brief where they are cited;

(4) a concise statement of the identity of the amicus curiae, its interest in the case, and the source of its authority to file;

(5) unless the amicus curiae is one listed in the first sentence of Rule 29(a), a statement that indicates whether:

(A) a party's counsel authored the brief in whole or in part;

(B) a party or a party's counsel contributed money that was intended to fund preparing or submitting the brief; and

(C) a person — other than the amicus curiae, its members, or its counsel — contributed money that was intended to fund preparing or submitting the brief and, if so, identifies each such person;

(6) an argument, which may be preceded by a summary and which need not include a statement of the applicable standard of review; and

(7) a certificate of compliance, if required by Rule 32(a)(7).

(d) *Length.* — Except by the court's permission, an amicus brief may be no more than one-half the maximum length authorized by these rules for a party's principal brief. If the court grants a party permission to file a longer brief, that extension does not affect the length of an amicus brief.

(e) *Time for Filing.* — An amicus curiae must file its brief, accompanied by a motion for filing when necessary, no later than 7 days after the principal brief of the party being supported is filed. An amicus curiae that does not support either party must file its brief no later than 7 days after the appellant's or petitioner's principal brief is filed. A court may grant leave for later filing, specifying the time within which an opposing party may answer.

(f) *Reply Brief.* — Except by the court's permission, an amicus curiae may not file a reply brief.

(g) *Oral Argument.* — An amicus curiae may participate in oral argument only with the court's permission. (Amended by order adopted April 24, 1998, effective December 1, 1998, and by order adopted April 28, 2010, effective December 1, 2010.)

CASE NOTES

Applied in United States v. Dickerson, 166 F.3d 667, 1999 U.S. App. LEXIS 1741 (4th. Cir. 1999).

Rule 30. Appendix to the Briefs.

(a) *Appellant's Responsibility.* — (1) Contents of the Appendix. — The appellant must prepare and file an appendix to the briefs containing:

(A) the relevant docket entries in the proceeding below;

(B) the relevant portions of the pleadings, charge, findings, or opinion;

(C) the judgment, order, or decision in question; and

(D) other parts of the record to which the parties wish to direct the court's attention.

(2) Excluded Material. — Memoranda of law in the district court should not be included in the appendix unless they have independent relevance. Parts of the record may be relied on by the court or the parties even though not included in the appendix.

(3) Time to File; Number of Copies. — Unless filing is deferred under Rule 30(c), the appellant must file 10 copies of the appendix with the brief and must serve one copy on counsel for each party separately represented. An unrepresented party proceeding in forma pauperis must file 4 legible copies with the clerk, and one copy must be served on counsel for each separately represented party. The court may by local rule or by order in a particular case require the filing or service of a different number.

(b) *All Parties' Responsibilities.* — (1) Determining the Contents of the Appendix. — The parties are encouraged to agree on the contents of the appendix. In the absence of an agreement, the appellant must, within 14 days after the record is filed, serve on the appellee a designation of the parts of the record the appellant intends to include in the appendix and a statement of the issues the appellant intends to present for review. The appellee may, within 14 days after receiving the designation, serve on the appellant a designation of additional parts to which it wishes to direct the court's attention. The appellant must include the designated parts in the appendix. The parties must not engage in unnecessary designation of parts of the record, because the entire record is available to the court. This paragraph applies also to a cross-appellant and a cross-appellee.

(2) Costs of Appendix. — Unless the parties agree otherwise, the appellant must pay the cost of the appendix. If the appellant considers parts of the record designated by the appellee to be unnecessary, the appellant may advise the appellee, who must then advance the cost of including those parts. The cost of the appendix is a taxable cost. But if any party causes unnecessary parts of the record to be included in the appendix, the court may impose the cost of those parts on that party. Each circuit must, by local rule, provide for sanctions against attorneys who unreasonably and vexatiously increase litigation costs by including unnecessary material in the appendix.

(c) *Deferred Appendix.* — (1) Deferral Until After Briefs Are Filed. — The court may provide by rule for classes of cases or by order in a particular case that preparation of the appendix may be deferred until after the briefs have been filed and that the appendix may be filed 21 days after the appellee's brief is served. Even though the filing of the appendix may be deferred, Rule 30(b) applies; except that a party must designate the parts of the record it wants included in the appendix when it serves its brief, and need not include a statement of the issues presented.

(2) References to the Record. — (A) If the deferred appendix is used, the parties may cite in their briefs the pertinent pages of the record. When the appendix is prepared, the record pages cited in the briefs must be indicated by inserting record page numbers, in brackets, at places in the appendix where those pages of the record appear.

(B) A party who wants to refer directly to pages of the appendix may serve and file copies of the brief within the time required by Rule 31(a), containing appropriate references to pertinent pages of the record. In that event, within 14 days after the appendix is filed, the party must serve and file copies of the brief, containing references to the pages of the appendix in place of or in addition to the references to the pertinent pages of the record. Except for the correction of typographical errors, no other changes may be made to the brief.

(d) *Format of the Appendix.* — The appendix must begin with a table of contents identifying the page at which each part begins. The relevant docket entries must follow the table of contents. Other parts of the record must follow chronologically. When pages from the transcript of proceedings are placed in the appendix, the transcript page numbers must be shown in brackets immediately before the included pages. Omissions in the text of papers or of the transcript must be indicated by asterisks. Immaterial formal matters (captions, subscriptions, acknowledgments, etc.) should be omitted.

(e) *Reproduction of Exhibits.* — Exhibits designated for inclusion in the appendix may be reproduced in a separate volume, or volumes, suitably indexed. Four copies must be filed with the appendix, and one copy must be served on counsel for each separately represented party. If a transcript of a proceeding before an administrative agency, board, commission, or officer was used in a district-court action and has been designated for inclusion in the appendix, the transcript must be placed in the appendix as an exhibit.

(f) *Appeal on the Original Record Without an Appendix.* — The court may, either by rule for all cases or classes of cases or by order in a particular case, dispense with the appendix and permit an appeal to proceed on the original record with any copies of the record, or relevant parts, that the court may order the parties to file. (Amended by order adopted March 30, 1970, effective July 1, 1970; by order adopted March 10, 1986, effective July 1, 1986; by order adopted April 30, 1991, effective December 1, 1991; by order adopted April 29, 1994, effective December 1, 1994; by order adopted April 24, 1998, effective December 1, 1998; and by order adopted March 26, 2009, effective December 1, 2009.)

CASE NOTES

The obligation to file an appendix is clearly that of the appellant. United States v. Seaboard Coast Line R.R., 517 F.2d 881 (4th Cir. 1975).

Appeal dismissed where appendix failed to meet minimum requirements. — The government's appeal from an order dismissing a complaint in an action under the Carmack amendment was dismissed, where the brief filed by the government purported to include an appendix, but the appendix failed to meet the minimum requirements of subdivision (a), where the appendix to the government's brief consisted of two pages reproducing only two bills of lading and where the government neither sought nor obtained an order under subdivision (c) which authorizes the filing of a deferred appendix, nor did it seek or obtain an order under subdivision (f) authorizing an appeal to be heard on the original record. United States v. Seaboard Coast Line R.R., 517 F.2d 881 (4th Cir. 1975).

Applied in Sivertsen v. Guardian Life Ins. Co. of Am., 423 F.2d 443 (4th Cir. 1970); Webb v. Hutto, 720 F.2d 375 (4th Cir. 1983).

Local Rule 30(a). Attorney Sanctions for Unnecessary Appendix Designations.

The Court, on its own motion or on motion of any party, may impose sanctions against attorneys who unreasonably and vexatiously increase the costs of litigation through the inclusion of unnecessary material in the appendix. Attorneys shall receive reasonable notice and opportunity to respond before the imposition of any sanction. A party's motion for the imposition of sanctions will be entertained only if filed within 14 days after entry of judgment and only if counsel for the moving party previously objected to the designation of the allegedly unnecessary material in writing to opposing counsel within 14 days of the material's designation. (Amended effective December 1, 2009.)

Local Rule 30(b). Appendix Contents; Number of Copies.

(1) Required Contents: In designating or agreeing upon the contents of the appendix, and in assembling the appendix, the parties should avoid unnecessary duplication of materials. The appellee's designation should only include those additional parts of the record to which it wishes to direct the Court's attention that have not already been designated by the appellant.

The use of a selectively abridged record allows the judges to refer easily to relevant parts of the record and saves the parties the considerable expense of reproducing the entire record. Although there is no limit on the length of the appendix except as provided in Local Rule 32(a), it is unnecessary to include everything in the appendix. The appendix should, however, contain the final order or order appealed from, the complaint or petition, as finally amended (civil appeals) or indictment (criminal appeals), as well as all other parts of the record which are vital to the understanding of the basic issues on appeal. Although the entire record is available to the Court should it believe that additional portions are important to a full understanding of the issues, citations to portions of the record not included in the appendix is not favored.

(2) Table of Contents; Witness Names and Type of Examination: The table of contents to the appendix should be sufficiently detailed to be helpful to the Court. Referring to the transcript of a trial under a single reference to "proceeding" or "trial transcript" is not sufficient. When the testimony of a witness is included in the appendix, the testimony should be clearly identified in the table of contents, beneath the proceeding in which it occurred. The name of the testifying witness and the type of examination (e.g., direct, cross, redirect, or recross) should also be clearly indicated at the top of each page of the appendix where the witness's testimony appears. Exhibits should be listed in the table of contents by number or letter <u>and</u> by name or brief description.

(3) Sentencing Guideline Appeals: In all criminal appeals seeking review of the application of the sentencing guidelines, appellant shall include the sentencing hearing transcript and presentence report in the appendix. The presentence report must be included in a separate sealed volume, stamped "SEALED" on the volume itself and on the envelope containing it, and be accompanied by a certificate stating that the volume contains sealed material. In criminal cases in which presentence reports are being filed for multiple defendants, each presentence report must be placed in a separate, sealed volume that is served only on counsel for the United States and for the defendant who is the subject of the report.

(4) Number of Copies:

(a) Filing: Six paper copies of the appendix and any supplemental appendix must be filed. Appointed counsel may file five copies of an appendix or supplemental appendix, and any party proceeding in forma pauperis who is not represented by Court-appointed counsel may file four copies. In addition, the full appendix or an appendix excerpt must be filed electronically in accordance with Local Rule 25(a)(1)(C).

(b) Service: If the full appendix is filed electronically and served on counsel and on any party not represented by counsel, service of the paper appendix is not required. If an appendix excerpt instead of the full appendix is filed electronically, one paper copy of the appendix must be served on lead counsel for each party separately represented and on any party not represented by counsel.

(c) Sealed Appendix Volumes: For sealed volumes of the appendix, four paper copies must be filed and one paper copy must be served on lead counsel for each party separately represented who is authorized to have access to the sealed volume and on any party not represented by counsel who is authorized to have access to the sealed volume. (Amended by order effective December 1, 1995; by order effective December 1, 1998; by order effective April 16, 2007; by order effective April 1, 2008; and by order effective September 1, 2011.)

Editor's note. — On February 6, 2012, the United States Court of Appeals for the 4th Circuit proposed amendments to Local Rules 22(d), 25(a), 25(b), 25(c), 30(b), 31(c) and 32(b), with the amended local rules superseding Administrative Order 08-01, effective April 16, 2012. However, on April 12, 2012, the 4th Circuit issued a notice stating that the court was "suspend[ing] the April 16, 2012, effective date of its proposed amendments to Local Rules 22(d), 25(a), 25(b), 25(c), 30(b), 31(c) & 32(b), and the superseding of Administrative Order 08-01, pending further review of public comments on the proposed amendments." On May 14, 2012, the original amendments were further amended in light of comments received. They became effective July 2, 2012.

Local Rule 30(c). Responsibility of Parties.

Notwithstanding that FRAP 30 provides that the appellant shall prepare and file the appendix, the Court considers the coordination of preparing the appendix to be the responsibility of both sides. The failure of a side to designate does not absolve the other side from the responsibility.

Except under the most extraordinary circumstances, supplementary appendices will not be accepted. If the appellant omits from the appendix the portions designated by the appellee, the appellant will be required to file a corrected appendix incorporating such material, and to bear the cost regardless of the outcome of the appeal.

If a party files a motion for leave to file a supplemental appendix, the motion must specifically identify the contents of the supplemental appendix, state that the items are matters of record, and set forth good cause why the original appendix should not be returned for insertion of the additional materials.

Local Rule 30(d). Dispensing with Appendix.

Motions to proceed on the original record pursuant to FRAP 30(f) are carefully reviewed in the Fourth Circuit and are not usually granted unless the appellant is proceeding in forma pauperis, the record is short, or the appeal is expedited. Even if the motion is granted, counsel must include an abbreviated appendix consisting of:

i. pertinent district court docket entries,

ii. indictment or complaint,

iii. judgment or order being appealed,

iv. notice of appeal,

v. any crucial portions of the transcript of proceedings referred to in appellant's brief,

vi. a copy of the order granting leave to proceed on the original record.

The requisite number of copies of the abbreviated appendix as set forth in Local Rule 30(b) must be filed with the brief. (Amended by order effective December 1, 1995, and by order effective April 1, 2008.)

Rule 31. Serving and Filing Briefs.

(a) *Time to Serve and File a Brief.* — (1) The appellant must serve and file a brief within 40 days after the record is filed. The appellee must serve and file a brief within 30 days after the appellant's brief is served. The appellant may serve and file a reply brief within 14 days after service of the appellee's brief but a reply brief must be filed at least 7 days before argument, unless the court, for good cause, allows a later filing.

(2) A court of appeals that routinely considers cases on the merits promptly after the briefs are filed may shorten the time to serve and file briefs, either by local rule or by order in a particular case.

(b) *Number of Copies.* — Twenty-five copies of each brief must be filed with the clerk and 2 copies must be served on each unrepresented party and on counsel for each separately represented party. An unrepresented party proceeding in forma pauperis must file 4 legible copies with the clerk, and one copy must be served on each unrepresented party and on counsel for each separately represented party. The court may by local rule or by order in a particular case require the filing or service of a different number.

(c) *Consequence of Failure to File.* — If an appellant fails to file a brief within the time provided by this rule, or within an extended time, an appellee may move to dismiss the appeal. An appellee who fails to file a brief will not be heard at oral argument unless the court grants permission. (Amended by order adopted March 30, 1970, effective July 1, 1970, by order adopted March 10, 1986, effective July 1, 1986, by order adopted April 29, 1994, effective December 1, 1994, by order adopted April 24, 1998, effective December 1, 1998, by order adopted April 29, 2002, effective December 1, 2002, and by order adopted March 26, 2009, effective December 1, 2009.)

Local Rule 31(a). Shortened Time for Service and Filing of Briefs in Criminal Cases.

Pursuant to the authority conferred by FRAP 31(a)(2), the time for serving and filing briefs in criminal appeals is shortened as follows: the appellant shall serve and file appellant's brief and appendix within thirty-five days after the date on which the briefing order is filed; the appellee shall serve and file appellee's brief within twenty-one days after service of the brief of the appellant; the appellant may serve and file a reply brief within ten days after service of the brief of the appellee. (Amended by order effective December 1, 1995; by order effective December 1, 1998; by order effective December 1, 2002; and amended effective December 1, 2009.)

Local Rule 31(b). Briefing Orders.

A formal briefing schedule shall be sent to the parties upon receipt of the record or determination by the Clerk that the record is complete — whichever occurs first. Thus, the time for designating the contents of the joint appendix and the filing of briefs is controlled by the briefing order and not the receipt of the record as provided in FRAP 31(a)(1). (Amended by order effective December 4, 1991; by order effective December 1, 1995; by order effective December 1, 1998; and amended effective December 1, 2009.)

Local Rule 31(c). Briefing Extensions.

Extensions will be granted only when extraordinary circumstances exist. A motion for an extension of time to file a brief must be filed well in advance of the date the brief is due and must set forth the additional time requested and the reasons for the request. The Court discourages these motions and may deny the motion entirely or grant a lesser period of time than the time requested. (Amended by order effective December 4, 1996; by order adopted April 1, 2008; amended effective December 1, 2009; and amended effective July 2, 2012.)

Editor's note. — On February 6, 2012, the United States Court of Appeals for the 4th Circuit proposed amendments to Local Rules 22(d), 25(a), 25(b), 25(c), 30(b), 31(c) and 32(b), with the amended local rules superseding Administrative Order 08-01, effective April 16, 2012. However, on April 12, 2012, the 4th Circuit issued a notice stating that the court was "suspend[ing] the April 16, 2012, effective date of its proposed amendments to Local Rules 22(d), 25(a), 25(b), 25(c), 30(b), 31(c) & 32(b), and the superseding of Administrative Order 08-01, pending further review of public comments on the proposed amendments." On May 14, 2012, the original amendments were further amended in light of comments received. They became effective July 2, 2012.

Local Rule 31(d). Number of Copies.

(1) Filing: In addition to the electronic brief, each party must file eight paper copies of the brief with the clerk, except that appointed counsel may file six copies, and any party proceeding in forma pauperis who is not represented by Court-appointed counsel may file four copies.

(2) Service: Service of paper copies of briefs is not required if the brief was served electronically on counsel and on any party not represented by counsel. If the brief was not served electronically, one paper copy must be served on lead counsel for each party separately represented and on any party not represented by counsel.

(3) Sealed Briefs: For sealed briefs, four paper copies of the sealed version must be filed and one paper copy must be served on lead counsel for each party separately represented who is authorized to have access to the sealed version and on any party

not represented by counsel who is authorized to have access to the sealed version. Filing and service of the public version of the brief are governed by (1) and (2) above.

(4) Page-Proof Briefs: If the Court allows a deferred appendix, the parties are required to file their page-proof briefs in electronic form only. After the deferred appendix is filed, filing and service of final briefs are governed by (1) and (2) above. (Amended by order effective December 4, 1991, by order effective December 1, 1998, and by order effective July 1, 2010, and by order effective September 1, 2011.)

Rule 32. Form of Briefs, Appendices, and Other Papers.

(a) *Form of a Brief.* — (1) Reproduction. — (A) A brief may be reproduced by any process that yields a clear black image on light paper. The paper must be opaque and unglazed. Only one side of the paper may be used.

(B) Text must be reproduced with a clarity that equals or exceeds the output of a laser printer.

(C) Photographs, illustrations, and tables may be reproduced by any method that results in a good copy of the original; a glossy finish is acceptable if the original is glossy.

(2) Cover. — Except for filings by unrepresented parties, the cover of the appellant's brief must be blue; the appellee's, red; an intervenor's or amicus curiae's, green; any reply brief, gray; and any supplemental brief, tan. The front cover of a brief must contain:

(A) the number of the case centered at the top;

(B) the name of the court;

(C) the title of the case (see Rule 12(a));

(D) the nature of the proceeding (e.g., Appeal, Petition for Review) and the name of the court, agency, or board below;

(E) the title of the brief, identifying the party or parties for whom the brief is filed; and

(F) the name, office address, and telephone number of counsel representing the party for whom the brief is filed.

(3) Binding. — The brief must be bound in any manner that is secure, does not obscure the text, and permits the brief to lie reasonably flat when open.

(4) Paper Size, Line Spacing, and Margins. — The brief must be on 8 ½ by 11 inch paper. The text must be double-spaced, but quotations more than two lines long may be indented and single-spaced. Headings and footnotes may be single-spaced. Margins must be at least one inch on all four sides. Page numbers may be placed in the margins, but no text may appear there.

(5) Typeface. — Either a proportionally spaced or a monospaced face may be used.

(A) A proportionally spaced face must include serifs, but sans-serif type may be used in headings and captions. A proportionally spaced face must be 14-point or larger.

(B) A monospaced face may not contain more than 10 ½ characters per inch.

(6) Type Styles. — A brief must be set in a plain, roman style, although italics or boldface may be used for emphasis. Case names must be italicized or underlined.

(7) Length. — (A) Page limitation. A principal brief may not exceed 30 pages, or a reply brief 15 pages, unless it complies with Rule 32(a)(7)(B) and (C).

(B) Type-volume limitation. (i) A principal brief is acceptable if:

- it contains no more than 14,000 words; or
- it uses a monospaced face and contains no more than 1,300 lines of text.

(ii) A reply brief is acceptable if it contains no more than half of the type volume specified in Rule 32(a)(7)(B)(i).

(iii) Headings, footnotes, and quotations count toward the word and line limitations. The corporate disclosure statement, table of contents, table of citations, statement with respect to oral argument, any addendum containing statutes, rules or regulations, and any certificates of counsel do not count toward the limitation.

(C) Certificate of compliance. (i) A brief submitted under Rules 28.1(e)(2) or 32(a)(7)(B) must include a certificate by the attorney, or an unrepresented party, that the brief complies with the type-volume limitation. The person preparing the certificate may rely on the word or line count of the word-processing system used to prepare the brief. The certificate must state either:

- the number of words in the brief; or
- the number of lines of monospaced type in the brief.

(ii) Form 6 in the Appendix of Forms is a suggested form of a certificate of compliance. Use of Form 6 must be regarded as sufficient to meet the requirements of Rules 28.1(e)(3) and 32(a)(7)(C)(i).

(b) *Form of an Appendix.* — An appendix must comply with Rule 32(a)(1), (2), (3), and (4), with the following exceptions:

(1) The cover of a separately bound appendix must be white.

(2) An appendix may include a legible photocopy of any document found in the record or of a printed judicial or agency decision.

(3) When necessary to facilitate inclusion of odd-sized documents such as technical drawings, an appendix may be a size other than 8 ½ by 11 inches, and need not lie reasonably flat when opened.

(c) *Form of Other Papers.* — (1) Motion. — The form of a motion is governed by Rule 27(d).

(2) Other Papers. — Any other paper, including a petition for panel rehearing and a petition for hearing or rehearing en banc, and any response to such a petition, must be reproduced in the manner prescribed by Rule 32(a), with the following exceptions:

(A) A cover is not necessary if the caption and signature page of the paper together contain the information required by Rule 32(a)(2). If a cover is used, it must be white.

(B) Rule 32(a)(7) does not apply.

(d) *Signature.* — Every brief, motion, or other paper filed with the court must be signed by the party filing the paper or, if the party is represented, by one of the party's attorneys.

(e) *Local Variation.* — Every court of appeals must accept documents that comply with the form requirements of this rule. By local rule or order in a particular case a court of appeals may accept documents that do not meet all of the form requirements of this rule. (Amended by order adopted April 24, 1998, effective December 1, 1998, by order adopted April 29, 2002, effective December 1, 2002, and by order adopted April 25, 2005, effective December 1, 2005.)

Local Rule 32(a). Reproduction of Appendices.

Double-sided copying of appendices is preferred in all cases. If an appendix is prepared by a commercial printer in a court-appointed case, the materials contained in the appendix should be reproduced on both sides of a sheet because reimbursement for copying expenses will be limited to 35 cents per double-sided sheet of the joint appendix. No joint appendix in a court-appointed case should exceed 250 sheets without advance permission from the Court; unless such permission is granted, reimbursement of copy expenses will limited to 250 sheets. (Amended by order effective December 1, 1992, by order effective December 1, 1995, by order effective December 1, 1998, and by order effective December 1, 2002.)

Local Rule 32(b). Length of Briefs.

The Fourth Circuit encourages short, concise briefs. An opening or response brief that cites to both the paper appendix and the electronic record may, without motion, exceed the length limitations in FRAP 32(a)(7) and FRAP 28.1(e)(2) by up to 200 words. Briefs may not otherwise exceed the length limitations without the Court's advance permission.

A motion for permission to submit a longer brief must be made to the Court of Appeals at least 10 days prior to the due date of the brief and must be supported by a statement of reasons. These motions are not favored and will be granted only for exceptional reasons. (Amended by order effective January 1, 1994; by order effective December 1, 1995; by order effective December 1, 1998; by order effective December 1, 2002; amended effective December 1, 2009; amended effective July 1, 2012.)

Editor's note. — On February 6, 2012, the United States Court of Appeals for the 4th Circuit proposed amendments to Local Rules 22(d), 25(a), 25(b), 25(c), 30(b), 31(c) and 32(b), with the amended local rules superseding Administrative Order 08-01, effective April 16, 2012. However, on April 12, 2012, the 4th Circuit issued a notice stating that the court was "suspend[ing] the April 16, 2012, effective date of its proposed amendments to Local Rules 22(d), 25(a), 25(b), 25(c), 30(b), 31(c) & 32(b), and the superseding of Administrative Order 08-01, pending further review of public comments on the proposed amendments." On May 14, 2012, the original amendments were further amended in light of comments received. They became effective July 2, 2012.

Local Rule 32(c). Correction of Briefs and Appendices.

If briefs, appendices, or other papers are illegible or are not in the form required by the federal rules or by this Court's local rules or standards when filed, counsel will be required to file corrected copies of the document. If the corrected copies are not submitted within the time allowed by the clerk, they must be accompanied by a motion to file out of time. (Amended by order effective December 1, 1995, and amended by order effective December 1, 1998.)

Rule 32.1. Citing Judicial Dispositions.

(a) *Citation Permitted.* A court may not prohibit or restrict the citation of federal judicial opinions, orders, judgments, or other written dispositions that have been:

(1) designated as "unpublished," "not for publication," "non-precedential," "not precedent," or the like; and

(2) issued on or after January 1, 2007.

(b) *Copies Required.* If a party cites a federal judicial opinion, order, judgment, or other written disposition that is not available in a publicly accessible electronic database, the party must file and serve a copy of that opinion, order, judgment, or disposition with the brief or other paper in which it is cited. (Adopted by order effective December 1, 2006.)

Law Review. — For symposium article, "The Dog That Did Not Bark: No-Citation Rules, Judicial Conference Rulemaking, and Federal Public Defenders," see 62 Wash. & Lee L. Rev. 1491 (2005). For symposium article, "Parade of Horribles, Circles of Hell: Ethical Dimensions of the Publication Controversy," see 62 Wash. & Lee L. Rev. 1653 (2005). For symposium article, "Judicial Triage: Reflections on the Debate over Unpublished Opinions," see 62 Wash. & Lee L. Rev. 1667 (2005). For symposium article, "Unspoken Questions in the Rule 32.1 Debate: Precedent and Psychology in Judging," see 62 Wash. & Lee L. Rev. 1709 (2005). For symposium article, "Much Ado About the Tip of an Iceberg," see 62 Wash. & Lee L. Rev. 1723 (2005). For symposium article, "Fourth Circuit Publication Practices," see 62 Wash. & Lee L. Rev. 1733 (2005).

Local Rule 32.1. Citation of Unpublished Dispositions.

Citation of this Court's unpublished dispositions issued prior to January 1, 2007, in briefs and oral arguments in this Court and in the district courts within this Circuit is disfavored, except for the purpose of establishing res judicata, estoppel, or the law of the case.

If a party believes, nevertheless, that an unpublished disposition of this Court issued prior to January 1, 2007, has precedential value in relation to a material issue in a case and that there is no published opinion that would serve as well, such disposition may be cited if the requirements of FRAP 32.1(b) are met. (Amended by order effective December 1, 1995, and amended by order effective December 1, 1998; renumbered by order effective December 1, 2006.)

Rule 33. Appeal Conferences.

The court may direct the attorneys — and, when appropriate, the parties — to participate in one or more conferences to address any matter that may aid in disposing of the proceedings, including simplifying the issues and discussing settlement. A judge or other person designated by the court may preside over the conference, which may be conducted in person or by telephone. Before a settlement conference, the attorneys must consult with their clients and obtain as much authority as feasible to settle the case. The court may, as a result of the conference, enter an order controlling the course of the proceedings or implementing any settlement agreement. (Amended by order adopted April 29, 1994, effective December 1, 1994, and by order adopted April 24, 1998, effective December 1, 1998.)

Local Rule 33. Circuit Mediation Conferences.

All civil and agency cases in which all parties are represented by counsel on appeal will be reviewed by a circuit mediator after the filing of the docketing statements required by Local Rule 3(b). The circuit mediator will determine whether a mediation conference may assist either the Court or the parties. Counsel for a party may also request a conference if counsel believes it will be of assistance to the Court or the parties. Counsel's participation is required at any scheduled conference. Mediation conferences will generally be conducted by telephone but may be conducted in person in the discretion of a circuit mediator. Mediation conferences may be adjourned from time to time by a circuit mediator. Purposes of the mediation conference include:

(a) Jurisdictional review;

(b) Simplification, clarification, and reduction of issues;

(c) Discussion of settlement; and

(d) Consideration of any other matter relating to the efficient management and disposition of the appeal.

Although the time allowed for filing of briefs is not automatically tolled by proceedings under this local rule, if the parties wish to pursue, or are engaged in, settlement discussions, counsel for any party may move to extend the briefing schedule. The mediator, through the Clerk of the Court, may enter orders which control the course of proceedings and, upon agreement of the parties, dispose of the case.

Statements and comments made during all mediation conferences and papers or electronic information generated during the process, are not included in Court files except to the extent disclosed by orders entered under this local rule. Information disclosed in the mediation process shall be kept confidential and shall not be disclosed to the judges deciding the appeal or to any other person outside the mediation program participants. Confidentiality is required of all participants in the mediation proceedings. All statements, documents, and discussions in such proceedings shall be kept confidential. The mediator, attorneys, and other participants in the mediation shall not disclose such statements, documents, or discussions without prior approval of the Standing Panel on Attorney Discipline. Any alleged violations of this rule shall be referred to the Court's Standing Panel on Attorney Discipline for a determination pursuant to Local Rule 46(g) of whether imposition of discipline is warranted. All proceedings before the Standing Panel on Attorney Discipline involving confidential information under this procedure shall be confidential. (Amended by order effective December 1, 1995, and by order effective March 4, 1998, and by order adopted October 12, 2001, effective December 11, 2001.)

Rule 34. Oral Argument.

(a) *In General.* — (1) Party's Statement. — Any party may file, or a court may require by local rule, a statement explaining why oral argument should, or need not, be permitted.

(2) Standards. — Oral argument must be allowed in every case unless a panel of three judges who have examined the briefs and record unanimously agrees that oral argument is unnecessary for any of the following reasons:

(A) the appeal is frivolous;

(B) the dispositive issue or issues have been authoritatively decided; or

(C) the facts and legal arguments are adequately presented in the briefs and record, and the decisional process would not be significantly aided by oral argument.

(b) *Notice of Argument; Postponement.* — The clerk must advise all parties whether oral argument will be scheduled, and, if so, the date, time, and place for it, and the time allowed for each side. A motion to postpone the argument or to allow longer argument must be filed reasonably in advance of the hearing date.

(c) *Order and Contents of Argument.* — The appellant opens and concludes the argument. Counsel must not read at length from briefs, records, or authorities.

(d) *Cross-Appeals and Separate Appeals.* — If there is a cross-appeal, Rule 28.1(b) determines which party is the appellant and which is the appellee for purposes of oral argument. Unless the court directs otherwise, a cross-appeal or separate appeal must be argued when the initial appeal is argued. Separate parties should avoid duplicative argument.

(e) *Nonappearance of a Party.* — If the appellee fails to appear for argument, the court must hear appellant's argument. If the appellant fails to appear for argument, the court may hear the appellee's argument. If neither party appears, the case will be decided on the briefs, unless the court orders otherwise.

(f) *Submission on Briefs.* — The parties may agree to submit a case for decision on the briefs, but the court may direct that the case be argued.

(g) *Use of Physical Exhibits at Argument; Removal.* — Counsel intending to use physical exhibits other than documents at the argument must arrange to place them in the courtroom on the day of the argument before the court convenes. After the argument, counsel must remove the exhibits from the courtroom, unless the court directs otherwise. The clerk may destroy or dispose of the exhibits if counsel does not reclaim them within a reasonable time after the clerk gives notice to remove them. (Amended by order adopted April 1, 1979, effective August 1, 1979, by order adopted March 10, 1986, effective July 1, 1986, by order adopted April 30, 1991, effective December 1, 1991, by order adopted April 22, 1993, effective December 1, 1993, by order adopted April 24, 1998, effective December 1, 1998, and by order adopted April 25, 2005, effective December 1, 2005.)

CASE NOTES

Applied in Ward v. Virginia, No. 00-6243, 2000 U.S. App. LEXIS 14443 (4th Cir. June 22, 2000); Jung Kwang Kim v. Angelone, No. 00-6411, 2000 U.S. App. LEXIS 14532 (4th Cir. June 23, 2000).

Local Rule 34(a). Oral Argument; Pre-argument Review and Summary Disposition of Appeals; Statement Regarding the Need for Oral Argument.

In the interest of docket control and to expedite the final disposition of pending cases, the chief judge may designate a panel or panels to review any pending case at any time before argument for disposition under this rule.

In reviewing pending cases before argument, the panel will utilize the minimum standards set forth in FRAP 34(a)(2). If all of the judges of the panel to which a pending appeal has been referred conclude that oral argument is not to be allowed, they may make any appropriate disposition without oral argument including, but not limited to, affirmance or reversal.

Because any case may be decided without oral argument, all major arguments should be fully developed in the briefs. In furtherance of the disposition of pending cases under this rule, parties may include in their briefs at the conclusion of the argument a statement setting forth the reasons why, in their opinion, oral argument should be heard. (Amended by order effective December 1, 1995, and amended by order effective December 1, 1998.)

Local Rule 34(b). Informal Briefs.

Whenever the Court determines pursuant to Local Rule 22(a) that briefing is appropriate on an appeal in a non-capital case from the denial of a writ of habeas corpus or of a motion under 28 U.S.C. § 2255, or whenever any pro se appeal is filed from any other type of judgment or order, the clerk shall notify the appellant that appellant shall file, within 21 days after service of such notice, an informal brief, listing the specific issues and supporting facts and arguments raised on appeal. Appellee is permitted, but not required, to file an informal response brief within 14 days after service of appellant's informal brief, and appellant is permitted, but not required, to file an informal reply brief within 10 days after service of appellee's informal response brief. Appellant's informal brief and any informal response and reply briefs filed by the parties shall be considered, together with the record and other relevant documents, by the panel to which the proceeding has been referred. The Court will limit its review to the issues raised in the informal brief.

The informal brief may be submitted on a form provided by the clerk and shall provide the specific information required by the form. The parties need not limit their briefs solely to the form. An additional supporting memorandum may be attached if a party deems it necessary in order to address adequately the issues raised, but the informal brief and any supporting memorandum shall not exceed the length limitations established by FRAP 32(a)(7). It is unnecessary to attach record excerpts since the record is before the Court. It is not necessary to cite cases in an informal brief. Unless additional copies are requested by the Clerk, only the original informal brief must be filed with the Court and copies served on the other parties to the case.

Once an informal briefing schedule has been established the parties may file a formal brief only with the permission of the Court. The Court initially reviews cases that are informally briefed under its procedures set forth in Local Rule 34(a) pertaining to pre-argument review.

If the panel reviewing an informal brief submitted by an indigent pro se litigant determines that further briefing and possible oral argument would be of assistance, counsel will be appointed and directed to file additional formal briefs. In any appeal that has been informally briefed, the Court may direct that additional briefs be filed prior to oral argument. (Amended by order effective December 1, 1995; by order effective June 5, 1996; by order effective September 25, 1996; by order effective December 1, 1998; by order effective October 9, 2003; by order adopted April 1, 2008; and amended effective December 1, 2009.)

Local Rule 34(c). Court Sessions and Notification to Counsel.

The Court sits in Richmond, Virginia, to hear cases during six to eight separate argument weeks scheduled between September and June. The Court also sits at law schools within the Circuit and at other special argument sessions. The Court's oral argument schedule is available on the Court's Internet site, www.ca4.uscourts.gov.

The Court initially hears and decides cases in panels consisting of three judges with the Chief Judge or most senior active judge presiding. Each panel regularly hears oral argument in four cases each day during court week; additional cases are added as required.

Attorneys appearing for oral argument must register with the Clerk's Office on the morning of argument to learn of courtroom assignment, order of appearance, and allocation of oral argument time. Counsel not already a member of the Fourth Circuit bar will be admitted to practice before the Court at that time upon compliance with the provisions of Local Rule 46(b).

The Court convenes at 9:30 a.m., with the exception of Friday, when it convenes at 8:30 a.m.

Preparation for the argument calendar begins in the Clerk's Office at least two months prior to argument. Upon receiving notice that a case has been tentatively assigned to an argument session, counsel must inform the clerk, within the time provided in the notice, of any conflict or other matter that would affect scheduling of the case for that session. After a case has been scheduled for argument, any motion that would affect the argument date must show good cause for the requested relief and that the relief could not have been requested within the period set by the Court for notice of conflicts. Continuance of an established oral argument date is not granted because of a prior professional commitment. Although a case will not be removed from the calendar because of a scheduling conflict by counsel after the notification of oral argument has been issued, the Court may direct another lawyer from the same firm to argue the appeal if counsel of record cannot be present. (Amended by order effective December 1, 1995, and by order effective April 1, 2008.)

Local Rule 34(d). Argument Time.

Briefs for the cases assigned to a hearing panel are distributed by the clerk to the judges on a hearing panel at the time the hearing panel assignments are made. The members of the Court hearing oral argument will have read the briefs before the hearing and therefore will be familiar with the case. In oral argument, counsel should emphasize the dispositive issues.

Since the appellant is allowed to open and close the argument, counsel for appellant should indicate at registration before oral argument how much time counsel wants to reserve for rebuttal. It is recommended that no more than two attorneys argue per side. Each side is normally allowed 20 minutes, even in consolidated cases, but counsel may not need the full time allotted or the Court may shorten or extend the time allotted. In social security disability cases, black lung cases, and labor cases where the primary issue is whether the agency's decision is supported by substantial evidence and in criminal cases where the primary issue involves the application of the sentencing guidelines, each side is limited to 15 minutes. In black lung cases in which the Director, Office of Workers' Compensation Programs, has been granted leave to file a separate brief, the Director will share argument time with whichever side the Director's brief supports.

If counsel believes that more time is needed for oral argument, a written motion setting forth the reasons for additional time and whether the other parties consent must be submitted well in advance of the hearing date. The Court may sua sponte extend the allotted time during the argument or it may terminate the argument whenever in its judgment further argument is unnecessary. (Amended by order effective December 1, 1995, amended by order effective December 1, 1998, and amended by order effective June 1, 1999.)

Local Rule 34(e). Motion to Submit on Briefs.

As soon as possible upon completion of the briefing schedule or within 10 days of tentative notification of oral argument, whichever is earlier, any party may file a motion to submit the case on the briefs without the necessity of oral argument. Such motions are not granted as a matter of course. A motion to submit on briefs should not be used to alleviate a scheduling conflict after the notification of oral argument has been issued. (Amended by order effective December 1, 1998; by order effective December 1, 2002; and amended effective December 1, 2009.)

IOP 34.1. Calendar Assignments and Panel Composition.

The Clerk of Court maintains a list of mature cases available for oral argument and on a monthly basis merges those cases with a list of three-judge panels provided by a computer program designed to achieve total random selection.

The composition of each panel usually changes each day during court week except on those occasions where only one panel is sitting in a given geographical location. Every effort is made to assign cases for oral argument to judges who have had previous involvement with the case on appeal through random assignment to a preargument motion or prior appeal in the matter, but there is no guarantee that any of the judges who have previously been involved with an appeal will be assigned to a hearing panel. The varied assignment of judges to panels and the independent assignment of varied cases to panels is designed, insofar as practicable, to assure the opportunity for each judge to sit with all other judges an equal number of times, and to assure that both the appearance and the fact of presentation of particular types of cases to particular judges is avoided. (Amended by order effective February 1, 2001.)

IOP 34.2. Disposition Without Oral Argument.

A decision against oral argument must be unanimous, and if a case is decided without oral argument the decision on the merits must be unanimous also. Whenever at least one member of the review panel determines that oral argument would be of assistance, the panel notifies the clerk who places the case on the oral argument calendar. (Amended by order effective December 1, 1995.)

IOP 34.3. Audio Files of Oral Argument.

Effective with its May 2011 argument session, the Court will make audio files of oral arguments available on the Court's Internet site, without charge, two days after argument. Counsel are reminded that the following information should not be included in argument to the Court:

(A) Personal data protected by Fed. R. App. P. 25(a)(5):
(1) social security and taxpayer identification numbers;
(2) dates of birth;
(3) names of minor children;
(4) financial account numbers; and
(5) home addresses in criminal cases.

(B) Criminal case information protected by the Judiciary's Privacy Policy for Electronic Case Files:
(1) unexecuted summonses or warrants;
(2) pretrial bail or presentence investigation reports;
(3) statements of reasons in the judgment of conviction;
(4) juvenile records;
(5) identifying information about jurors or potential jurors;
(6) financial affidavits filed under the Criminal Justice Act;
(7) ex parte requests to authorize services under the Criminal Justice Act; and
(8) sealed documents (e.g., motions for downward departure for substantial assistance, plea agreements indicating cooperation, or victim statements).

Any motion to seal argument must be filed on the public docket at least five days before oral argument, in accordance with Local Rule 25(c)(2). Audio files of sealed arguments will not be released absent an order of the Court unsealing the argument. (Adopted by order May 2, 2011, effective May 2, 2011.)

Rule 35. En Banc Determination.

(a) *When Hearing or Rehearing En Banc May Be Ordered.* — A majority of the circuit judges who are in regular active service and who are not disqualified may order that an appeal or other proceeding be heard or reheard by the court of appeals en banc. An en banc hearing or rehearing is not favored and ordinarily will not be ordered unless:

(1) en banc consideration is necessary to secure or maintain uniformity of the court's decisions; or

(2) the proceeding involves a question of exceptional importance.

(b) *Petition for Hearing or Rehearing En Banc.* — A party may petition for a hearing or rehearing en banc.

(1) The petition must begin with a statement that either:

(A) the panel decision conflicts with a decision of the United States Supreme Court or of the court to which the petition is addressed (with citation to the conflicting case or cases) and consideration by the full court is therefore necessary to secure and maintain uniformity of the court's decisions; or

(B) the proceeding involves one or more questions of exceptional importance, each of which must be concisely stated; for example, a petition may assert that a proceeding presents a question of exceptional importance if it involves an issue on which the panel decision conflicts with the authoritative decisions of other United States Courts of Appeals that have addressed the issue.

(2) Except by the court's permission, a petition for an en banc hearing or rehearing must not exceed 15 pages, excluding material not counted under Rule 32.

(3) For purposes of the page limit in Rule 35(b)(2), if a party files both a petition for panel rehearing and a petition for rehearing en banc, they are considered a single document even if they are filed separately, unless separate filing is required by local rule.

(c) *Time for Petition for Hearing or Rehearing En Banc.* — A petition that an appeal be heard initially en banc must be filed by the date when the appellee's brief is due. A petition for a rehearing en banc must be filed within the time prescribed by Rule 40 for filing a petition for rehearing.

(d) *Number of Copies.* — The number of copies to be filed must be prescribed by local rule and may be altered by order in a particular case.

(e) *Response.* — No response may be filed to a petition for an en banc consideration unless the court orders a response.

(f) *Call for a Vote.* — A vote need not be taken to determine whether the case will be heard or reheard en banc unless a judge calls for a vote. (Amended by order adopted April 1, 1979, effective August 1, 1979, by order adopted April 29, 1994, effective December 1, 1994, by order adopted April 24, 1998, effective December 1, 1998, and by order adopted April 25, 2005, effective December 1, 2005.)

Local Rule 35. En Banc Proceedings.

(a) *Petition for Rehearing En Banc.* — A petition for rehearing en banc must be made at the same time, and in the same document, as a petition for rehearing. The request for en banc consideration shall be stated plainly in the title of the petition. Petitions for rehearing en banc will be distributed to all active and senior judges of the Court, and to any visiting judge who may have heard and decided the appeal.

(b) *Decision to Hear or Rehear a Case En Banc.* — A majority of the circuit judges who are in regular active service and who are not disqualified may grant a hearing or rehearing en banc. A poll on whether to rehear a case en banc may be requested, with or without a petition, by an active judge of the Court or by a senior or visiting judge who sat on the panel that decided the case originally. Unless a judge requests that a poll be taken on the petition, none will be taken. If no poll is requested, the panel's order on a petition for rehearing will bear the notation that no member of the Court requested a poll. If a poll is requested and hearing or rehearing en banc is denied, the order will reflect the vote of each participating judge. A judge who joins the Court after a petition has been submitted to the Court, and before an order has been entered, will be eligible to vote on the decision to hear or rehear a case en banc.

(c) *Decision of Cases Heard or Reheard En Banc.* — An en banc hearing will be before all eligible, active and participating judges of the Court. An en banc rehearing will be before all eligible and participating active judges, and any senior judge of the Court who sat on the panel that decided the case originally. An active judge who takes senior status after a case is heard or reheard by an en banc Court will be eligible to participate in the en banc decision. A judge who joins the Court after argument of a case to an en banc Court will not be eligible to participate in the decision of the case.

A judge who joins the Court after submission of a case to an en banc Court without oral argument will participate in the decision of the case. Granting of rehearing en banc vacates the previous panel judgment and opinion; the rehearing is a review of the judgment or decision from which review is sought and not a review of the judgment of the panel. (The circuit takes the position that the change of wording in 28 U.S.C. § 46(c) referring to participation in en banc decisions does not alter the long-standing rule that the en banc court reviews the decision from which review is sought in this Court, not the decision of a panel.)

(d) *Additional Copies of Briefs and Appendix for En Banc Hearing or Rehearing.* — The Court's order granting hearing or rehearing en banc may require the parties to file additional copies of the briefs and appendix. Each party will bear the initial cost of additional copies of its own briefs. The party that requested the hearing or rehearing en banc will bear the initial cost of filing additional copies of the appendix. In the event that cross petitions for hearing or rehearing en banc are granted, the parties will share equally the initial cost of preparing additional copies of the appendix. (Amended by order effective December 1, 1995, by order effective December 4, 1996, by order effective December 1, 1998, by order effective December 1, 2003, and by order effective December 1, 2005.)

Rule 36. Entry of Judgment; Notice.

(a) *Entry.* — A judgment is entered when it is noted on the docket. The clerk must prepare, sign, and enter the judgment:

(1) after receiving the court's opinion — but if settlement of the judgment's form is required, after final settlement; or

(2) if a judgment is rendered without an opinion, as the court instructs.

(b) *Notice.* — On the date when judgment is entered, the clerk must serve on all parties a copy of the opinion — or the judgment, if no opinion was written — and a notice of the date when the judgment was entered. (Amended by order adopted April 24, 1998, effective December 1, 1998, and by order adopted April 29, 2002, effective October 1, 2002.)

Local Rule 36(a). Publication of Decisions.

Opinions delivered by the Court will be published only if the opinion satisfies one or more of the standards for publication:

i. It establishes, alters, modifies, clarifies, or explains a rule of law within this Circuit; or

ii. It involves a legal issue of continuing public interest; or

iii. It criticizes existing law; or

iv. It contains a historical review of a legal rule that is not duplicative; or

v. It resolves a conflict between panels of this Court, or creates a conflict with a decision in another circuit.

The Court will publish opinions only in cases that have been fully briefed and presented at oral argument. Opinions in such cases will be published if the author or a majority of the joining judges believes the opinion satisfies one or more of the standards for publication, and all members of the Court have acknowledged in writing their receipt of the proposed opinion. A judge may file a published opinion without obtaining all acknowledgments only if the opinion has been in circulation for ten days and an inquiry to the non-acknowledging judge's chambers has confirmed that the opinion was received. (Amended by order effective December 1, 2002; and amended effective December 1, 2009.)

Local Rule 36(b). Unpublished Dispositions; Opinion Distribution.

Unpublished opinions give counsel, the parties, and the lower court or agency a statement of the reasons for the decision. They may not recite all of the facts or background of the case and may simply adopt the reasoning of the lower court. Published and unpublished opinions are sent to the trial court or agency in which the case originated, to counsel for all parties in the case, and to litigants in the case not represented by counsel. Published and unpublished opinions are also posted on the Court's Web site each day and distributed in electronic form to subscribers to the Court's daily opinion lists. Published and unpublished opinions issued since January 1, 1996 are available free of charge at www.ca4.uscourts.gov .

Counsel may move for publication of an unpublished opinion, citing reasons. If such motion is granted, the unpublished opinion will be published without change in result. (Amended by order effective January 1, 1994; by order effective December 1, 1995; by order effective December 1, 2002; by order effective October 5, 2004; by order effective January 7, 2005; amended effective December 1, 2009; and by order effective June 1, 2013.)

IOP 36.1. Opinion Preparation Assignments.

The custom of the Fourth Circuit is to reserve judgment at the conclusion of oral argument. A conference of the panel is held promptly after oral argument, usually immediately after the presentation of the case. Although a tentative decision may be reached at this conference, additional conferences are sometimes necessary. Opinion assignments are made by the Chief Judge on the basis of recommendations from the presiding judge of each panel on which the Chief Judge did not sit.

IOP 36.2. Circulation of Opinions in Argued Cases.

Although one judge writes the opinion, every panel member is equally involved in the process of decision. An appeal may be heard and decided by two of the three judges assigned to a panel, when one judge becomes unavailable. If a panel is reduced to two and the two cannot agree, however, the case will be reargued before a new three-judge panel which may or may not include prior panel members.

When a proposed opinion in an argued case is prepared and submitted to other panel members, copies are provided to the non-sitting judges, including the senior judges, and their comments are solicited. The opinion is then finalized. The Clerk's Office never receives advance notice of when a decision will be rendered, so counsel should not call for such information. (Amended by order effective January 1, 1994; by order effective December 1, 1995; and by order adopted April 1, 2008.)

IOP 36.3. Summary Opinions.

If all judges on a panel of the Court agree following oral argument that an opinion in a case would have no precedential value, and that summary disposition is otherwise appropriate, the Court may decide the appeal by summary opinion. A summary opinion identifies the decision appealed from, sets forth the Court's decision and the reason or reasons therefor, and resolves any outstanding motions in the case. It does not discuss the facts or elaborate on the Court's reasoning.

Rule 37. Interest on Judgment.

(a) *When the Court Affirms.* — Unless the law provides otherwise, if a money judgment in a civil case is affirmed, whatever interest is allowed by law is payable from the date when the district court's judgment was entered.

(b) *When the Court Reverses.* — If the court modifies or reverses a judgment with a direction that a money judgment be entered in the district court, the mandate must contain instructions about the allowance of interest. (Amended by order adopted April 24, 1998, effective December 1, 1998)

Rule 38. Frivolous Appeal — Damages and Costs.

If a court of appeals determines that an appeal is frivolous, it may, after a separately filed motion or notice from the court and reasonable opportunity to respond, award just damages and single or double costs to the appellee. (Amended by order adopted April 29, 1994, effective December 1, 1994, and by order adopted April 24, 1998, effective December 1, 1998.)

CASE NOTES

Since inmate's litigation over pancake syrup in the face of pre-filing review and the threat of sanctions was ineffective in deterring such a frivolous suit, the federal circuit court would impose a sanction of $500 on inmate, to be paid prior to the filing of any future civil appeals, absent certification by the district court that subsequent suit had arguable merit. Brock v. Angelone, 105 F.3d 952 (4th Cir. 1997).

Applied in Gaiters v. Lynn, 831 F.2d 51 (4th Cir. 1987); Bast v. Cohen, Dunn & Sinclair, 59 F.3d 492 (4th Cir. 1995).

Rule 39. Costs.

(a) *Against Whom Assessed.* — The following rules apply unless the law provides or the court orders otherwise:

(1) if an appeal is dismissed, costs are taxed against the appellant, unless the parties agree otherwise;

(2) if a judgment is affirmed, costs are taxed against the appellant;

(3) if a judgment is reversed, costs are taxed against the appellee;

(4) if a judgment is affirmed in part, reversed in part, modified, or vacated, costs are taxed only as the court orders.

(b) *Costs For and Against the United States.* — Costs for or against the United States, its agency, or officer will be assessed under Rule 39(a) only if authorized by law.

(c) *Costs of Copies.* — Each court of appeals must, by local rule, fix the maximum rate for taxing the cost of producing necessary copies of a brief or appendix, or copies of records authorized by Rule 30(f). The rate must not exceed that generally charged for such work in the area where the clerk's office is located and should encourage economical methods of copying.

(d) *Bill of Costs: Objections; Insertion in Mandate.* — (1) A party who wants costs taxed must — within 14 days after entry of judgment — file with the circuit clerk, with proof of service, an itemized and verified bill of costs.

(2) Objections must be filed within 14 days after service of the bill of costs, unless the court extends the time.

(3) The clerk must prepare and certify an itemized statement of costs for insertion in the mandate, but issuance of the mandate must not be delayed for taxing costs. If the mandate issues before costs are finally determined, the district clerk must — upon the circuit clerk's request — add the statement of costs, or any amendment of it, to the mandate.

(e) *Costs on Appeal Taxable in the District Court.* — The following costs on appeal are taxable in the district court for the benefit of the party entitled to costs under this rule:

(1) the preparation and transmission of the record;

(2) the reporter's transcript, if needed to determine the appeal;

(3) premiums paid for a supersedeas bond or other bond to preserve rights pending appeal; and

(4) the fee for filing the notice of appeal. (Amended by order adopted April 30, 1979, effective August 1, 1979, and by order adopted March 10, 1986, effective July 1, 1986, by order adopted April 24, 1998, effective December 1, 1998, and by order adopted March 26, 2009, effective December 1, 2009.)

CASE NOTES

Discretion of court. — Under this rule, an appellate court has wide discretion in the taxation of costs. Square Constr. Co. v. Washington Metro. Area Transit Auth., 800 F.2d 1256 (4th Cir. 1986).

Local Rule 39(a). Reproduction Costs.

The cost of producing and binding necessary copies of briefs and appendices in the form required by Fed. R. App. P. 32 shall be taxable as costs at a rate equal to actual cost, but not higher than 15 cents per page for each copy required for filing and service by Local Rules 30(b)(4) and 31(d) or by order of the Court. (Amended by order effective December 1, 1998, and by order effective September 1, 2011.)

Local Rule 39(b). Bill of Costs.

The verified bill of costs may be that of a party or counsel, and should be accompanied by the printer's itemized statement of charges. When costs are sought for or against the United States, counsel should cite the statutory authority relied upon. Taxation of costs will not be delayed by the filing of a petition for rehearing or other postjudgment motion. A late affidavit for costs must be accompanied by a motion for leave to file. The clerk rules on all bills of costs and objections in the first instance. (Amended by order effective December 1, 1995.)

Local Rule 39(c). Recovery of Costs in the District Court.

The only costs generally taxable in the Court of Appeals are:

(1) the docketing fee if the case is reversed; and

(2) the cost of printing or reproducing briefs and appendices, including exhibits.

Although some costs are "taxable" in the Court of Appeals, all costs are recoverable in the district court after issuance of the mandate. If the matter of costs has not been settled before issuance of the mandate, the clerk will send a supplemental "Bill of Costs" to the district court for inclusion in the mandate at a later date.

Various costs incidental to an appeal must be settled at the district court level. Among such items are: (1) the cost of the reporter's transcript; (2) the fee for filing the notice of appeal; (3) the fee for preparing and transmitting the record; and (4) the premiums paid for any required appeal bond.

Application for recovery of these expenses by the successful party on appeal must be made in the district court, and should be made only after issuance of the mandate by the Court of Appeals. These costs, if erroneously applied for in the Court of Appeals, will be disallowed without prejudice to the right to reapply for them in the district court. (Amended by order effective December 1, 1995.)

Rule 40. Petition for Panel Rehearing.

(a) *Time to File; Contents; Answer; Action by the Court if Granted.* — (1) Time.— Unless the time is shortened or extended by order or local rule, a petition for panel rehearing may be filed within 14 days after entry of judgment. But in a civil case, unless an order shortens or extends the time, the petition may be filed by any party within 45 days after entry of judgment if one of the parties is:

(A) the United States;

(B) a United States agency;

(C) a United States officer or employee sued in an official capacity; or

(D) a current or former United States officer or employee sued in an individual capacity for an act or omission occurring in connection with duties performed on the United States' behalf — including all instances in which the United States represents that person when the court of appeals' judgment is entered or files the petition for that person.

(2) Contents.— The petition must state with particularity each point of law or fact that the petitioner believes the court has overlooked or misapprehended and must argue in support of the petition. Oral argument is not permitted.

(3) Answer.— Unless the court requests, no answer to a petition for panel rehearing is permitted. But ordinarily rehearing will not be granted in the absence of such a request.

(4) Action by the Court.— If a petition for panel rehearing is granted, the court may do any of the following:

(A) make a final disposition of the case without reargument;

(B) restore the case to the calendar for reargument or resubmission; or

(C) issue any other appropriate order.

(b) *Form of Petition; Length.* — The petition must comply in form with Rule 32. Copies must be served and filed as Rule 31 prescribes. Unless the court permits or a local rule provides otherwise, a petition for panel rehearing must not exceed 15 pages. (Amended by order adopted April 30, 1979, effective August 1, 1979, by order adopted April 29, 1994, effective December 1, 1994, by order adopted April 24, 1998, effective December 1, 1998, and by order adopted April 26, 2011, effective December 1, 2011.)

Local Rule 40(a). Filing of Petition.

Although petitions for rehearing are filed in a great many cases, few are granted. Filing a petition solely for purposes of delay or in order merely to reargue the case is an abuse of privilege. Whenever a request for a rehearing en banc is contained in a petition, such fact must be stated plainly on the cover of and in the title of the document. Only the original petition for rehearing or rehearing en banc is required unless additional copies are requested by the Clerk. (Amended by order effective December 4, 1991, by order effective December 1, 1998, by order effective October 5, 2004, and by order effective April 1, 2008.)

Local Rule 40(b). Statement of Purpose.

A petition for rehearing must contain an introduction stating that, in counsel's judgment, one or more of the following situations exist:

i. A material factual or legal matter was overlooked in the decision.

ii. A change in the law occurred after the case was submitted and was overlooked by the panel.

iii. The opinion is in conflict with a decision of the United States Supreme Court, this Court or another court of appeals and the conflict is not addressed in the opinion.

iv. The proceeding involves one or more questions of exceptional importance.

A petition should only be made to direct the Court's attention to one or more of the above situations. The points to be raised should be succinctly listed in counsel's statement of purpose. (Amended by order effective December 1, 1998.)

Local Rule 40(c). Time Limits for Filing Petitions.

The Court strictly enforces the time limits for filing petitions for rehearing and petitions for rehearing en banc. The Clerk's Office will deny as untimely any petition received in the Clerk's Office later than 45 days after entry of judgment in any civil case where the United States, or an agency or officer thereof is a party, or 14 days after the entry of judgment in any other case. The only grounds for an extension of time to file a petition, or to accept an untimely petition, are as follows:

i. the death or serious illness of counsel, or of a member of counsel's immediate family (or in the case of a party proceeding without counsel, the death or serious illness of the party or a member of the party's immediate family); or

ii. an extraordinary circumstance wholly beyond the control of counsel or of a party proceeding without counsel.

Petitions for rehearing and petitions for en banc rehearing from incarcerated persons proceeding without the assistance of counsel are deemed filed when they are delivered to prison or jail officials. All other such petitions are deemed filed only when received in the Clerk's Office. (Amended by order effective December 1, 1994, and amended by order effective December 1, 1998.)

Local Rule 40(d). Papers Filed After Denial of a Petition for Rehearing.

Except for timely petitions for rehearing en banc, cost and attorney fee matters, and other matters ancillary to the filing of an application for writ of certiorari with the Supreme Court, the Office of the Clerk shall not receive motions or other papers requesting further relief in a case after the Court has denied a petition for rehearing or the time for filing a petition for rehearing has expired. (Amended by order effective January 1, 1994, and amended by order effective December 1, 1998.)

IOP 40.1. Submission of Petitions for Rehearing to the Court.

The Clerk's Office will hold any petition for rehearing or petition for rehearing en banc until the time for filing all such petitions, or any extension thereof granted in the particular case, has run. Thereafter, all petitions for rehearing in the same case will be distributed to the Court simultaneously. (Amended by order effective December 1, 1998.)

IOP 40.2. Panel Rehearing.

The panel of judges who heard and decided the appeal will rule on the petition for rehearing. Such panel may include a senior circuit judge or a visiting judge sitting in the Fourth Circuit by designation.

If a petition for rehearing is granted, the original judgment and opinion of the Court are vacated and the case will be reheard before the original panel. The Court may direct the filing of additional briefs, or the parties may seek leave of Court to file additional briefs. (Amended by order effective December 1, 1995.)

Rule 41. Mandate: Contents; Issuance and Effective Date; Stay.

(a) *Contents.* — Unless the court directs that a formal mandate issue, the mandate consists of a certified copy of the judgment, a copy of the court's opinion, if any, and any direction about costs.

(b) *When Issued.* — The court's mandate must issue 7 days after the time to file a petition for rehearing expires, or 7 days after entry of an order denying a timely petition for panel rehearing, petition for rehearing en banc, or motion for stay of mandate, whichever is later. The court may shorten or extend the time.

(c) *Effective Date.* — The mandate is effective when issued.

(d) *Staying the Mandate.* — (1) On Petition for Rehearing or Motion. — The timely filing of a petition for panel rehearing, petition for rehearing en banc, or motion for stay of mandate, stays the mandate until disposition of the petition or motion, unless the court orders otherwise.

(2) Pending Petition for Certiorari. — (A) A party may move to stay the mandate pending the filing of a petition for a writ of certiorari in the Supreme Court. The motion must be served on all parties and must show that the certiorari petition would present a substantial question and that there is good cause for a stay.

(B) The stay must not exceed 90 days, unless the period is extended for good cause or unless the party who obtained the stay files a petition for the writ and so notifies the circuit clerk in writing within the period of the stay. In that case, the stay continues until the Supreme Court's final disposition.

(C) The court may require a bond or other security as a condition to granting or continuing a stay of the mandate.

(D) The court of appeals must issue the mandate immediately when a copy of a Supreme Court order denying the petition for writ of certiorari is filed. (Amended by order adopted April 29, 1994, effective December 1, 1994, by order adopted April 24, 1998, effective December 1, 1998, by order adopted April 29, 2002, effective December 1, 2002, and by order adopted March 26, 2009, effective December 1, 2009.)

CASE NOTES

Applied in In re Green, 133 Bankr. 185 (E.D. Va. 1991).

Local Rule 41. Motion for Stay of the Mandate.

A motion for stay of the issuance of the mandate shall not be granted simply upon request. Ordinarily the motion shall be denied unless there is a specific showing that it is not frivolous or filed merely for delay. A motion to stay the mandate pending the filing of a petition for certiorari must show that the certiorari petition would present a substantial question and set forth good cause for a stay. Stay requests are normally acted upon without a request for a response. (Amended by order effective December 1, 1995; by order effective October 1, 2012.)

IOP 41.1. Issuance of the Mandate.

On the date of issuance of the mandate, the Clerk of the Court will issue written notice to the parties and the clerk of the lower court that the judgment of the Court of Appeals takes effect that day. The trial court record will be returned to the clerk of that court once the mandate has issued. (Amended by order effective December 1, 1995.)

IOP 41.2. Petitions for Writs of Certiorari.

A petition for a writ of certiorari must be filed with the Supreme Court within 90 days of the entry of judgment in a criminal case or a civil case. The time for the petition does not run from the issuance of the mandate, but from the date of judgment which is also the opinion date. If a petition for rehearing or a petition for rehearing en banc is timely filed, the time runs from the date of denial of that petition. Counsel should consult the Rules of the Supreme Court for details on how to proceed with the petition.

The Rules of the Supreme Court do not require that the record accompany a petition for certiorari and the record will not be forwarded unless specifically requested by the petitioner or counsel. Requests to certify and transmit the record to the Supreme Court prior to action on the petition for a writ of certiorari are disfavored by the Supreme Court. The Clerk of the Supreme Court will request the record from the Court of Appeals when review of the record is desired by the Supreme Court prior to action on a petition for writ of certiorari or upon granting certiorari if the record has not been transmitted earlier. The same procedures are followed for Supreme Court review by certification pursuant to 28 U.S.C. § 1254(2).

If a case is remanded to the Court of Appeals from the Supreme Court, the case shall be reopened under the original docket number and the Court of Appeals may require additional briefs and oral argument, summarily dispose of the case, or take any other action consistent with the Supreme Court's opinion. (Amended by order effective December 1, 1995, and amended by order effective December 1, 1998.)

Rule 42. Voluntary Dismissal.

(a) *Dismissal in the District Court.* — Before an appeal has been docketed by the circuit clerk, the district court may dismiss the appeal on the filing of a stipulation signed by all parties or on the appellant's motion with notice to all parties.

(b) *Dismissal in the Court of Appeals.* — The circuit clerk may dismiss a docketed appeal if the parties file a signed dismissal agreement specifying how costs are to be paid and pay any fees that are due. But no mandate or other process may issue without a court order. An appeal may be dismissed on the appellant's motion on terms agreed to by the parties or fixed by the court. (Amended by order adopted April 24, 1998, effective December 1, 1998.)

CASE NOTES

Applied in White v. Boyle, 390 F. Supp. 514 (W.D. Va. 1975).

Local Rule 42. Voluntary Dismissals.

In civil cases, the stipulation of dismissal or motion for voluntary dismissal may be signed by counsel. In criminal cases, however, the agreement or motion must be signed or consented to by the individual party appellant personally or counsel must file a statement setting forth the basis for counsel's understanding that the appellant wishes to dismiss the appeal and the efforts made to obtain the appellant's written consent. Counsel must serve a copy of this statement on appellant. (Amended by order effective December 1, 1995.)

Rule 43. Substitution of Parties.

(a) *Death of a Party.* — (1) After Notice of Appeal Is Filed. — If a party dies after a notice of appeal has been filed or while a proceeding is pending in the court of appeals, the decedent's personal representative may be substituted as a party on motion filed with the circuit clerk by the representative or by any party. A party's motion must be served on the representative in accordance with Rule 25. If the decedent has no representative, any party may suggest the death on the record, and the court of appeals may then direct appropriate proceedings.

(2) Before Notice of Appeal Is Filed — Potential Appellant. — If a party entitled to appeal dies before filing a notice of appeal, the decedent's personal representative — or, if there is no personal representative, the decedent's attorney of record — may file a notice of appeal within the time prescribed by these rules. After the notice of appeal is filed, substitution must be in accordance with Rule 43(a)(1).

(3) Before Notice of Appeal Is Filed — Potential Appellee. — If a party against whom an appeal may be taken dies after entry of a judgment or order in the district court, but before a notice of appeal is filed, an appellant may proceed as if the death had not occurred. After the notice of appeal is filed, substitution must be in accordance with Rule 43(a)(1).

(b) *Substitution for a Reason Other Than Death.* — If a party needs to be substituted for any reason other than death, the procedure prescribed in Rule 43(a) applies.

(c) *Public Officer: Identification; Substitution.* — (1) Identification of Party. — A public officer who is a party to an appeal or other proceeding in an official capacity may be described as a party by the public officer's official title rather than by name. But the court may require the public officer's name to be added.

(2) Automatic Substitution of Officeholder. — When a public officer who is a party to an appeal or other proceeding in an official capacity dies, resigns, or otherwise ceases to hold office, the action does not abate. The public officer's successor is automatically substituted as a party. Proceedings following the substitution are to be in the name of the substituted party, but any misnomer that does not affect the substantial rights of the parties may be disregarded. An order of substitution may be entered at any time, but failure to enter an order does not affect the substitution. (Amended by order adopted March 10, 1986, effective July 1, 1986, by order adopted April 24, 1998, effective December 1, 1998.)

CASE NOTES

Applied in City of Va. Beach v. Roanoke River Basin Ass'n, 776 F.2d 484 (4th Cir. 1985).

Rule 44. Case Involving a Constitutional Question When the United States or the Relevant State Is Not a Party.

(a) *Constitutional Challenge to Federal Statute.* — If a party questions the constitutionality of an Act of Congress in a proceeding in which the United States or its agency, officer, or employee is not a party in an official capacity, the questioning party must give written notice to the circuit clerk immediately upon the filing of the record or as soon as the question is raised in the court of appeals. The clerk must then certify that fact to the Attorney General.

(b) *Constitutional Challenge to State Statute.* — If a party questions the constitutionality of a statute of a State in a proceeding in which that State or its agency, officer, or employee is not a party in an official capacity, the questioning party must give written notice to the circuit clerk immediately upon the filing of the record or as soon as the question is raised in the court of appeals. The clerk must then certify that fact to the attorney general of the State. (Amended by order adopted April 24, 1998, effective December 1, 1998, and and by order adopted April 29, 2002, effective December 1, 2002.)

Rule 45. Clerk's Duties.

(a) *General Provisions.* — (1) Qualifications. — The circuit clerk must take the oath and post any bond required by law. Neither the clerk nor any deputy clerk may practice as an attorney or counselor in any court while in office.

(2) When Court Is Open. — The court of appeals is always open for filing any paper, issuing and returning process, making a motion, and entering an order. The clerk's office with the clerk or a deputy in attendance must be open during business hours on all days except Saturdays, Sundays, and legal holidays. A court may provide by local rule or by order that the clerk's office be open for specified hours on Saturdays or on legal holidays other than New Year's Day, Martin Luther King, Jr.'s Birthday, Washington's Birthday, Memorial Day, Independence Day, Labor Day, Columbus Day, Veterans' Day, Thanksgiving Day, and Christmas Day.

(b) *Records.* — (1) The Docket. — The circuit clerk must maintain a docket and an index of all docketed cases in the manner prescribed by the Director of the Administrative Office of the United States Courts. The clerk must record all papers filed with the clerk and all process, orders, and judgments.

(2) Calendar. — Under the court's direction, the clerk must prepare a calendar of cases awaiting argument. In placing cases on the calendar for argument, the clerk must give preference to appeals in criminal cases and to other proceedings and appeals entitled to preference by law.

(3) Other Records. — The clerk must keep other books and records required by the Director of the Administrative Office of the United States Courts, with the approval of the Judicial Conference of the United States, or by the court.

(c) *Notice of an Order or Judgment.* — Upon the entry of an order or judgment, the circuit clerk must immediately serve a notice of entry on each party, with a copy of any opinion, and must note the date of service on the docket. Service on a party represented by counsel must be made on counsel.

(d) *Custody of Records and Papers.* — The circuit clerk has custody of the court's records and papers. Unless the court orders or instructs otherwise, the clerk must not permit an original record or paper to be taken from the clerk's office. Upon disposition of the case, original papers constituting the record on appeal or review must be returned to the court or agency from which they were received. The clerk must preserve a copy of any brief, appendix, or other paper that has been filed. (Amended by order adopted March 1, 1971, effective July 1, 1971, by order adopted March 10, 1986, effective July 1, 1986, by order adopted April 24, 1998, effective December 1, 1998, by order adopted April 29, 2002, effective December 1, 2002, and by order adopted April 15, 2005, effective December 1, 2005.)

Local Rule 45. Dismissals for Failure to Prosecute.

When an appellant in either a docketed or non-docketed appeal fails to comply with the Federal Rules of Appellate Procedure or the rules or directives of this Court, the clerk shall notify the appellant or, if appellant is represented by counsel, appellant's counsel that upon the expiration of 15 days from the date thereof the appeal will be dismissed for want of prosecution, unless prior to that date appellant remedies the default. Should the appellant fail to comply within said 15-day period, the clerk shall then enter an order dismissing said appeal for want of prosecution, and shall issue the mandate. In no case shall the appellant be entitled to reinstate the case and remedy the default after the same shall have been dismissed under this rule, unless by order of this Court for good cause shown. The dismissal of an appeal shall not limit the authority of this Court, in an appropriate case, to take disciplinary action against defaulting counsel. (Amended by order effective December 1, 1995, by order effective December 1, 1998, and by order effective April 1, 2008.)

IOP 45.1. Clerk's Office.

The Clerk's Office is located on the fifth floor of the United States Courthouse Annex in Richmond, Virginia, and is open from 8:30 a.m. to 5:00 p.m. every weekday, except federal holidays. All correspondence concerning cases pending before the Court should be addressed to:

Clerk, United States Court of Appeals
for the Fourth Circuit
1100 East Main Street, Suite 501
Richmond, Virginia 23219-3517
Telephone 804/916-2700
(Amended by order effective March 31, 1993.)

IOP 45.2. Public Information.

The Court's opinions, rules, procedures, forms, and argument calendar are available at **www.ca4.uscourts.gov**. Docket information is also available at **www.ca4.uscourts.gov** to users with a log-in name and password for the Judiciary's PACER system (Public Access to Court Electronic Records). Information concerning the status of appeals and the operation of rules and procedures may be obtained from the Clerk's Office by telephone inquiry. Matters of public record may be reviewed upon request at the Clerk's Office and case documents may be transmitted to the district court for review by counsel upon proper application to the Clerk's Office. (Amended by order effective December 1, 2002.)

Rule 46. Attorneys.

(a) *Admission to the Bar.* — (1) Eligibility. — An attorney is eligible for admission to the bar of a court of appeals if that attorney is of good moral and professional character and is admitted to practice before the Supreme Court of the United States, the highest court of a state, another United States court of appeals, or a United States district court (including the district courts for Guam, the Northern Mariana Islands, and the Virgin Islands).

(2) Application. — An applicant must file an application for admission, on a form approved by the court that contains the applicant's personal statement showing eligibility for membership. The applicant must subscribe to the following oath or affirmation:

"I, ______________________, do solemnly swear [or affirm] that I will conduct myself as an attorney and counselor of this court, uprightly and according to law; and that I will support the Constitution of the United States."

(3) Admission Procedures. — On written or oral motion of a member of the court's bar, the court will act on the application. An applicant may be admitted by oral motion in open court. But, unless the court orders otherwise, an applicant need not appear before the court to be admitted. Upon admission, an applicant must pay the clerk the fee prescribed by local rule or court order.

(b) *Suspension or Disbarment.* — (1) Standard. — A member of the court's bar is subject to suspension or disbarment by the court if the member:

(A) has been suspended or disbarred from practice in any other court; or
(B) is guilty of conduct unbecoming a member of the court's bar.

(2) Procedure. — The member must be given an opportunity to show good cause, within the time prescribed by the court, why the member should not be suspended or disbarred.

(3) Order. — The court must enter an appropriate order after the member responds and a hearing is held, if requested, or after the time prescribed for a response expires, if no response is made.

(c) *Discipline.* — A court of appeals may discipline an attorney who practices before it for conduct unbecoming a member of the bar or for failure to comply with any court rule. First, however, the court must afford the attorney reasonable notice, an opportunity to show cause to the contrary, and, if requested, a hearing. (Amended by order adopted March 10, 1986, effective July 1, 1986, and by order adopted April 24, 1998, effective December 1, 1998.)

Local Rule 46(a). Legal Assistance to Indigents by Law Students.

An eligible law student with the written consent of an indigent and the attorney of record may appear in this Court on behalf of that indigent in any case. An eligible law student with the written consent of the United States Attorney or authorized representative may also appear in this Court on behalf of the United States in any case. An eligible law student with the written consent of the State Attorney General or authorized representative may also appear in this Court on behalf of that state in any case. In each case, the written consent shall be filed with the clerk.

An eligible law student may assist in the preparation of briefs and other documents to be filed in this Court, but such briefs or documents must be signed by the attorney of record. The student may also participate in oral argument with leave of the Court, but only in the presence of the attorney of record. The attorney of record shall assume personal professional responsibility for the law student's work and for supervising the quality of that work. The attorney should be familiar with the case and prepared to supplement or correct any written or oral statement made by the student.

In order to make an appearance pursuant to this rule, the law student must:

1. Be duly enrolled in a law school approved by the American Bar Association;
2. Have completed legal studies amounting to at least four (4) semesters, or the equivalent if the school is on some basis other than a semester basis;
3. Be certified by the dean of the student's law school as being of good character and competent legal ability which certification shall be filed with the clerk. This certification may be withdrawn by the dean at any time by mailing notice to the clerk or by termination by this Court without notice of hearing and without any showing of cause;
4. Be introduced to the Court by an attorney admitted to practice before this Court;
5. Neither ask for nor receive any compensation or remuneration of any kind from the person on whose behalf the student renders services, but this shall not prevent an attorney, legal aid bureau, law school, public defender agency, a State, or the United States from paying compensation to the eligible law student, nor shall it prevent any agency from making such charges for its services as it may otherwise properly require;
6. Certify in writing that he or she has read and is familiar with the Code of Professional Responsibility or Rules of Professional Conduct in force in the state in which the student's law school is located. (Amended by order effective December 1, 1995.)

Local Rule 46(b). Admission to Practice.

Only attorneys admitted to the bar of this Court may practice before the Court. An attorney may be named on a brief filed in this Court without being admitted to the bar of the Fourth Circuit, provided that at least one lawyer admitted to practice in this Court also appears on the brief. Any other document submitted by an attorney who is not a member of the bar of the Fourth Circuit will be accepted for filing conditioned on his or her qualifying for membership within a reasonable time.

Each applicant for admission to the bar of this Court shall file with the clerk an application on the form approved by the Court and furnished by the clerk. Thereafter, upon written or oral motion of a member of the bar of the Court, the Court will act upon the application. A qualified attorney may be admitted upon personal appearance in open court. It is not necessary that an applicant appear in open court for the purpose of being admitted unless the Court shall otherwise order.

The requisite $216 fee must accompany the application, but attorneys appointed by the Court to represent a party in forma pauperis, counsel for the United States and any agency thereof who has a case pending before this Court, and law clerks to the judges of the Court and to the district judges, magistrate judges, and bankruptcy judges within this Circuit shall be admitted to the bar of this Court without the payment of an admission fee. The clerk shall credit $176 of each $216 fee to the Judiciary's fee account and designate the remaining $40 for deposit to a fund maintained by the Court for the benefit of the bench and bar in the administration of justice.

A certificate indicating that an attorney has been admitted to practice before the Fourth Circuit will be sent to counsel by mail after admission. (Amended effective September 30, 2003, February 15, 2005, November 1, 2011, and October 1, 2012.)

Local Rule 46(c). Appearance of Counsel; Withdrawal; Substitutions.

Each attorney of record must file a written appearance with the clerk within 14 days after the appeal is docketed or after being retained or appointed. At the time of docketing, the clerk will send to each counsel or party in the trial court an "appearance of counsel" form. This form should be filled out and returned to the Clerk of the Fourth Circuit within 14 days. Thereafter, the Court will send correspondence, notices of oral argument, and copies of final decisions only to those attorneys who have filed their appearance forms. This form does not affect the attorney information listed on opinions, as that information is drawn from the names listed on the briefs.

Once an appearance in an appeal has been filed, an attorney may not withdraw from representation without notice to the party he or she is representing and consent of the Court. A motion to withdraw should state fully the reason for the request. Substitution of counsel of record can be accomplished by submitting a counsel of record form or written appearance for new counsel along with existing counsel's motion to withdraw or strike appearance. (Amended by order effective December 1, 1995, and by order effective December 1, 2002; and by order effective June 1, 2013.)

Local Rule 46(d). Appointment of Counsel.

In any appeal in which appointment of counsel is mandated by section (a)(1) of the Criminal Justice Act, 18 U.S.C. § 3006A(a)(1), counsel is appointed upon the docketing of the appeal without prior notice to the attorney who represented the indigent in the case below. The duty of counsel appointed under the CJA extends through advising an unsuccessful appellant in writing of the right to seek review in the Supreme Court. If the appellant requests in writing that a petition for a writ of certiorari be filed and in counsel's considered judgment there are grounds for seeking Supreme Court review, counsel shall file such a petition. If appellant requests that a petition for a writ of certiorari be filed but counsel believes that such a petition would be frivolous, counsel may file a motion to withdraw with the Court of Appeals. The motion must reflect that a copy was served on the client and that the client was informed of the right to file a response to the motion within seven days. The Clerk will hold the motion after filing for fifteen days before submitting it to the Court to allow time for appellant's response, if any, to be received.

Assignment of counsel is discretionary in other indigent cases. Therefore, such cases receive a preliminary review before a decision is made regarding appointment of counsel. In assigning counsel, the Court may direct counsel to brief a particular issue, but counsel is free to address any additional issues which appear to be meritorious.

Payment of counsel appointed under the CJA is governed by 18 U.S.C. § 3006A(d) and this Circuit's Plan in Implementation of the Criminal Justice Act. Unless compensation for legal services becomes available to assigned counsel by statute, the Court will pay counsel assigned for appellate representation not covered by the CJA a maximum fee of $750 plus expenses from the Attorney Admission Fund.

To receive payment from the Court, court-appointed or court-assigned counsel in all cases must submit to the Clerk's Office an itemized statement of expenses, with receipts, within sixty days of final disposition of the case. Depending upon the course of the case, this may be sixty days from (1) the date of judgment, (2) dismissal of the appeal, or (3) denial of a petition for rehearing. Before the expiration of the sixty-day time period the Court, for good cause shown, may grant counsel an extension of time to file the application for compensation and reimbursement. If court-appointed counsel files a petition for writ of certiorari with the Supreme Court, the 60-day period for applying for compensation and reimbursement runs from the date of filing the petition for writ of certiorari. (Amended by order effective March 15, 1992; by order effective December 1, 1995; and by order adopted February 1, 2001.)

Local Rule 46(e). Attorney's Fees and Expenses.

The Court may award attorney's fees and expenses whenever authorized by statute. Any application for an award must include a reference to the statutory basis for the request and a detailed itemization of the amounts requested. Court-appointed counsel may apply for an award of fees and expenses, but any award by the Court is in lieu of the regular appointment fees provided by the Court. In certain agency cases, counsel may submit the standard government form for fees and expenses provided by the agency for approval by the Court.

Law Review. — For note, "Attorney Fees, Freedom of Information, and Pro Se Litigants: Per Se Prohibitions Frustrate Policies," see 26 Wm. & Mary L. Rev. 349 (1985).

Local Rule 46(f). Proceeding Pro Se.

An individual may proceed without the aid of counsel, but should so inform the Court at the earliest possible time. In any pro se appeal, the clerk shall notify the parties that they shall file informal briefs as provided by Local Rule 34(b). The Court will limit its review to the issues raised in the informal briefs and will consider the need for the appointment of counsel when reviewing the appeal under Local Rule 34(a). Cases involving pro se litigants are ordinarily not scheduled for oral argument. (Amended by order effective September 25, 1996.)

Local Rule 46(g). Rules of Disciplinary Enforcement.

(1) A member of the bar of this Court may be disciplined by this Court as a result of

(a) Conviction in any court of the United States, the District of Columbia, or any state, territory or commonwealth of the United States, of any felony or of any lesser crime involving false swearing, misrepresentation, fraud, willful failure to file income tax returns, deceit, bribery, extortion, misappropriation, or theft;

(b) Imposition of discipline by any other court of whose bar the attorney is a member, or an attorney's disbarment by consent or resignation from the bar of such court while an investigation into allegations of misconduct is pending;

(c) Conduct with respect to this Court which violates the rules of professional conduct or responsibility in effect in the state or other jurisdiction in which the attorney maintains his or her principal office, the Federal Rules of Appellate Procedure, the local rules of this Court, or orders or other instructions of this Court; or

(d) Any other conduct unbecoming a member of the bar of this Court.

(2) Discipline may consist of disbarment, suspension from practice before this Court, monetary sanction, removal from the roster of attorneys eligible for appointment as Court-appointed counsel, reprimand, or any other sanction that the Court may deem appropriate. Disbarment is the presumed discipline for conviction of a crime specified in paragraph (1)(a) above. The identical discipline imposed by another court is presumed appropriate for discipline taken as a result of that other court's action pursuant to paragraph (1)(b). A monetary sanction imposed on disciplinary grounds is the personal responsibility of the attorney disciplined, and may not be reimbursed by a client.

(3) The clerk reviews reports received from other courts concerning discipline imposed on members of the bar of this Court. He refers to the Court all disbarments, suspensions, resignations during the pendency of misconduct investigations, and other actions sufficient to cast doubt upon the member's continuing qualification to practice before this Court.

(4) The clerk issues a notice to show cause why a member of the bar shall not be disciplined by this Court upon receipt of official notification of an attorney's conviction of a crime specified in paragraph (1)(a) or of the imposition of discipline by another court referred to this Court pursuant to paragraph (3) above, or upon the Court's determination that cause may exist for discipline pursuant to paragraphs (1)(c) or (1)(d). Such notice is sent by certified mail, directs that a response be filed within 30 days of the date of the notice, and directs that the attorney complete and return to the clerk within that time a declaration of the names and addresses of other bars to which he or she is admitted, using the form supplied by the clerk, whether or not the attorney chooses otherwise to respond to the notice. The clerk also appends a copy of Local Rule 46(g).

(5) Upon receiving official notification that a member of the bar has been convicted of a crime specified in paragraph (1)(a), the clerk automatically will issue an order

suspending the attorney's privilege to practice before this Court pending the Court's determination of appropriate discipline.

(6) An attorney to whom a notice to show cause has been sent may consent to disbarment, by filing with the clerk an affidavit stating that the attorney desires to consent to disbarment and that:

(a) The attorney's consent is freely and voluntarily rendered; the attorney is not being subjected to coercion or duress; the attorney is fully aware of the implications of so consenting;

(b) The attorney is aware that there is a presently pending proceeding involving allegations that there exist grounds for the attorney's discipline, the nature of which the attorney shall specifically set forth;

(c) The attorney acknowledges that the material facts so alleged are true; and

(d) The attorney so consents because the attorney knows that he or she cannot successfully defend himself or herself.

The order disbarring the attorney on consent is a matter of public record. However, the affidavit will not be publicly disclosed or made available for use in any other proceeding except upon order of this Court.

(7) If the attorney fails to respond to the notice within 30 days, or such other time as the Court shall allow, the clerk enters an order imposing the presumptive discipline. If no presumptive discipline is specified for the conduct, the clerk notifies the court of the attorney's non-response and the court takes such action as it deems appropriate.

(8) All matters pertaining to discipline of attorneys are submitted to the Court's Standing Panel on Attorney Discipline, which consists of three active circuit judges, each of whom is appointed by the Chief Judge to serve on the Panel for a three-year term. The initial members of the Standing Panel are appointed for terms of one, two, and three years so that the Panel members' terms are staggered for continuity of decisionmaking. If any member of the Standing Panel is unable to hear a particular matter, the clerk randomly designates another active circuit judge to the Panel for the purpose of disposing of that matter.

(9) The Standing Panel considers all materials submitted by an attorney to whom notice to show cause has issued. The Panel may request further information from a court that has previously imposed discipline on the attorney, or from its disciplinary agency. A copy of any such information is made available to the attorney or to his or her counsel. Should an attorney request a hearing on the matter it will be heard by the Standing Panel at a time and place of its choosing.

(10) The Court may at any time appoint counsel to investigate or prosecute a disciplinary matter, or to represent an indigent attorney instructed to show cause. The Court prefers to appoint as prosecuting counsel the disciplinary agency of the highest court of the state in which the attorney maintains his or her principal office. However, if the state disciplinary agency declines appointment, or the Court deems other counsel more appropriate, it may appoint any other member of the bar as prosecuting counsel. Counsel appointed either for prosecution or defense will be compensated for his or her services according to the Court's plan for appointment of counsel in criminal cases, from the attorney admission fund.

(11) The Court's order imposing discipline will set forth the nature of the discipline imposed; if disbarment or suspension from practice before the Court, the terms upon which reinstatement will occur or be considered by the Court; and any instructions to the clerk concerning the notification of the Court's action to be given to other courts or official bodies.

(12) The clerk is responsible for

(a) Automatically initiating show cause proceedings when official notice of an attorney's conviction of a crime specified in paragraph (1)(a) or discipline by another court pursuant to paragraph (3) is brought to his or her attention;

(b) Bringing to the attention of the Standing Panel instances of violations by members of the bar of this Court of the Federal Rules of Appellate Procedure, this Court's local rules, or this Court's orders or other instructions that may warrant discipline;

(c) Obtaining declarations of the names and addresses of other bars of which an attorney possibly subject to discipline by this Court may be a member; and

(d) Unless directed otherwise by the Court, within 10 days of the imposition of discipline upon a member of the bar of this Court, notifying all other courts of those bars the attorney reports that he or she is a member, and the American Bar

Association's National Disciplinary Data Bank, of the Court's action, enclosing a certified copy of the Court's order. (Amended by order effective December 1, 1995.)

Rule 47. Local Rules by Courts of Appeals.

(a) *Local Rules.* — (1) Each court of appeals acting by a majority of its judges in regular active service may, after giving appropriate public notice and opportunity for comment, make and amend rules governing its practice. A generally applicable direction to parties or lawyers regarding practice before a court must be in a local rule rather than an internal operating procedure or standing order. A local rule must be consistent with — but not duplicative of — Acts of Congress and rules adopted under 28 U.S.C. § 2072 and must conform to any uniform numbering system prescribed by the Judicial Conference of the United States. Each circuit clerk must send the Administrative Office of the United States Courts a copy of each local rule and internal operating procedure when it is promulgated or amended.

(2) A local rule imposing a requirement of form must not be enforced in a manner that causes a party to lose rights because of a nonwillful failure to comply with the requirement.

(b) *Procedure When There Is No Controlling Law.* — A court of appeals may regulate practice in a particular case in any manner consistent with federal law, these rules, and local rules of the circuit. No sanction or other disadvantage may be imposed for noncompliance with any requirement not in federal law, federal rules, or the local circuit rules unless the alleged violator has been furnished in the particular case with actual notice of the requirement. (Amended by order adopted April 27, 1995, effective December 1, 1995, and by order adopted April 24, 1998, effective December 1, 1998.)

Local Rule 47(a). Procedures for Adoption of Local Rules and Internal Operating Procedures.

Following tentative approval of an amendment to its local rules or internal operating procedures, and consultation with its Advisory Committee on Rules and Procedures, the Court of Appeals will provide public notice of the proposed amendment and an opportunity for comment.

The Court will set a period for comment for each proposed amendment, based upon the urgency of the matter involved. If the Court determines that there is an immediate need for a rule, the Court may provide that an amendment take immediate effect, and promptly thereafter afford notice and opportunity for comment.

Notice of a proposed amendment will be provided by distribution of the proposed change to all district judges, bankruptcy judges, magistrate judges, district and bankruptcy clerks, United States Attorneys, and state bar associations within the Circuit. Notice will also be sent to all legal newspapers and bar journals within the Circuit. Such notice shall include the text of a proposed amendment, unless it is lengthy. If the amendment is lengthy, the notice will describe the purpose and effect of the proposed amendment, and advise interested parties to obtain copies of the text of the proposed amendment from the clerk. Any person or organization requesting routine notice of proposed amendments to the Court's rules and internal operating procedures may, by letter to the clerk, be placed on the mailing list for such proposed changes.

All comments will be addressed to the Clerk of the Court of Appeals. If comments are received, they will be circulated to all members of the Court prior to the effective date of the proposed amendment, unless the amendment was given immediate effect.

Local Rule 47(b). Advisory Committee on Rules and Procedures.

The Court's Advisory Committee on Rules and Procedures shall consist of five attorneys, one from each of the states constituting the Fourth Circuit.

The members shall be appointed by the Chief Judge of the Circuit for three-year terms. The terms shall be staggered, so that no more than two members' terms expire in any year. No person may serve more than two full three-year terms.

The Chief Judge of the Circuit shall designate one of the members to serve as chair of the Committee. The clerk shall serve as the Court's principal liaison with the Committee.

The Committee shall study the Court's local rules and internal operating procedures, make recommendations concerning them, and advise the Court concerning all proposed changes to them.

IOP 47.1. Judicial Conference.

(A) There shall be held pursuant to 28 U.S.C. § 333 a conference of all the circuit and district judges, all bankruptcy judges and all full-time magistrate judges of the Circuit for the purpose of considering the business of the courts, advising means of improving the administration of justice within the Circuit, and discussion of ideas with respect to the administration of justice. It shall be the duty of every judge of the Circuit in active service and every full-time magistrate judge to attend such conference.

(B) The first day of the conference shall be devoted to a session for the judges alone, in which there shall be discussed matters affecting the state of the dockets and the administration of justice in their respective districts.

(C) Members of the bar to be designated, as hereafter set forth, shall be members of the conference. Such members, except members emeritus, shall participate in the conference's discussions and deliberations on the second and third days.

(D) Members of the conference from the bar shall be as provided in I.O.P. 47.2 as approved by the active circuit judges sitting from time to time in administrative session.

(E) The Circuit Executive of this Court shall be the secretary of the conference, and shall make and preserve an accurate record of its proceedings.

(F) Each member of the bar designated as a member of the conference shall pay a membership fee in an amount fixed by the Court of Appeals, to be applied to the payment of the expenses of the conference as approved by the Chief Judge of the Circuit. The payment of the membership fee shall be a condition to retention of conference membership. The Chief Judge is entitled to excuse payment of such fee in the proper circumstances. (Amended by order effective March 31, 1993; by order effective August 1, 2005; and by order effective December 1, 2008.)

IOP 47.2. Membership in the Judicial Conference of the Circuit.

Commencing with the 2009 conference, there shall be four types of members of the conference: ex officio members, invited members, permanent members, and members emeritus.

(A) Ex officio members.

(1) The Attorney General of the United States, or designee.

(2) The presidents of the state bar associations of the states of the Circuit. When two bar associations in the same state are both recognized under this rule, the president of each shall be entitled to attend, and the maximum number of members of the conference from the bar, from any state, under this provision, shall be limited to two. As long as there is only one state bar association in Maryland, the Bar Association of Baltimore City may be treated as a state bar association under this provision.

(3) One representative of the federal bar association elected to the Federal Bar Council from the Fourth Circuit, each conference year, on a rotational basis.

(4) All United States Attorneys in the Circuit.

(5) All Federal Public Defenders in the Circuit.

(6) All Community Defenders in the Circuit.

(7) All Chief Justices of the courts of last resort of the states comprising this Circuit.

(8) All Attorneys General of the states comprising this Circuit.

(9) The Chief Judge of the United States Court of Appeals for the Armed Forces.

(10) The Chief Judge of the United States Tax Court.

(11) One representative of each accredited law school within the Circuit.

(B) Members designated by judges.

(1) Invited members.

Lawyers who are not permanent members of the conference as set forth under (B)(2) below are invited by the Chief Judge as guests of a scheduled conference upon designation by an active or senior circuit or district judge.

(a) Each active or senior circuit judge or district judge may designate two guests for invitation to the conference.

(b) Each new circuit or district judge attending his or her first two conferences as a judge may designate three guests for invitation to the conference.

(2) Permanent members. (a) By attending two biennial conferences (or, alternatively, one biennial and two annual conferences, or three annual conferences) as an invited member under (B)(1) above, a lawyer shall become a permanent member of the conference, entitled to attend future conferences. In order to retain such permanent member status, a permanent member must have, in a given year, paid the annual

membership fee and, commencing after the 2009 conference, attended the most recent conference or at least one of the two conferences preceding it.

(b) A former or retired circuit or district judge of the Circuit shall be a permanent member of the conference, entitled for life to attend all conferences.

(3) Members emeritus. A permanent member for ten years or more shall become a member emeritus upon either:

(a) Failing to satisfy the requirements for retaining permanent member status under (B)(2) above; or

(b) Electing to assume member emeritus status and properly notifying the conference secretary of such decision.

In order to retain member emeritus status, a member emeritus must have, in a given year, paid the annual membership fee in the amount fixed for emeritus membership. A member emeritus will not be invited to attend future conferences, except as an invited member under (B)(1) above. A member emeritus may be reinstated as a permanent member by designation of the Chief Judge for good cause shown, or by again qualifying for permanent membership under (B)(2) above. (Added by order effective April 30, 1992; amended by order effective March 31, 1993; amended by order effective September 25, 1996; amended by order effective February 1, 2001; amended by order effective August 1, 2005; amended by order effective April 16, 2007; amended by order effective December 1, 2008, and amended by order effective February 1, 2011.)

Rule 48. Masters.

(a) *Appointment; Powers.* — A court of appeals may appoint a special master to hold hearings, if necessary, and to recommend factual findings and disposition in matters ancillary to proceedings in the court. Unless the order referring a matter to a master specifies or limits the master's powers, those powers include, but are not limited to, the following:

(1) regulating all aspects of a hearing;

(2) taking all appropriate action for the efficient performance of the master's duties under the order;

(3) requiring the production of evidence on all matters embraced in the reference; and

(4) administering oaths and examining witnesses and parties.

(b) *Compensation.* — If the master is not a judge or court employee, the court must determine the master's compensation and whether the cost is to be charged to any party. (Added by order adopted April 29, 1994, effective December 1, 1994, and amended by order adopted April 24, 1998, effective December 1, 1998.)

Editor's note. — The provisions of this rule are new. Former FRAP 48 is now codified as subdivision (c) of FRAP 1.

APPENDICES.

Appendix A

Plan of the United States Court of Appeals for the Fourth Circuit In Implementation of The Criminal Justice Act

---

The Judicial Council of the Fourth Circuit adopts the following plan, in implementation of the Criminal Justice Act.

I. RIGHT TO COUNSEL

1. *Direct Appeals:* In every direct appeal involving a person

(a) who is charged with a felony or misdemeanor (other than a petty offense), or with juvenile delinquency as defined in 18 U.S.C. § 5031, or with a violation of probation or supervised release; or who faces modification, reduction, or enlargement of a condition, or extension or revocation of a term of supervised release; or who is under arrest and representation is required by law; or who is subject to a mental condition hearing under Chapter 13 of Title 18; or who is held in custody as a material witness; or who appeals from parole proceedings conducted pursuant to 18 U.S.C. § 4106A; or,

(b) for whom the Sixth Amendment to the Constitution requires the appointment of counsel or for whom, in a case in which he faces the loss of liberty, any federal law requires the appointment of counsel,

whether the appeal be by a defendant from a judgment of conviction or other order, or by the United States from a judgment of acquittal or dismissal, a defendant shall be entitled to be represented by counsel as a matter of right.

If the appeal involves a petty offense for which confinement is authorized, the court may appoint counsel for a financially eligible person upon a determination that the interests of justice so require.

In these cases, unless an application for the appointment of counsel has already been received, or notice of appearance has been filed by retained counsel, the clerk of this court shall promptly notify the defendant of his right to counsel and shall inform him that counsel will be appointed if he is financially unable to obtain adequate representation. Where an attorney had previously been appointed to represent the defendant in district court, that attorney shall be reappointed, without prior notice, upon the docketing of the appeal in this court. If there is no such reappointment, either because defendant appeared pro se or was represented by retained counsel in the district court, the clerk shall appoint the attorney of record in the district court, where appropriate, or select an appointee from a panel of approved attorneys.

In pro se cases in which the appellant exercises his right to represent himself as suggested by *Faretta v. California,* 422 U.S. 806 (1975); 28 U.S.C. § 1654, the court may find it appropriate to appoint standby counsel for the appellant to assist in the appeal to protect the integrity and ensure the continuity of the judicial proceedings. (*McKaskle v. Wiggins,* 465 U.S. 168 (1984); *Faretta, supra*). Accordingly, if a pro se appellant is represented, at least in part, by standby counsel, compensation may be provided under the CJA.

2. *Collateral Proceedings:* In an appeal in a post-conviction proceeding under 28 U.S.C. §§ 2254 or 2255, seeking to vacate or set aside a death sentence, a petitioner who is financially unable to obtain adequate representation shall be entitled to appointment of one or more attorneys. 18 U.S.C. 3599(a)(2). In an appeal in a collateral proceeding brought by the petitioner from any other order denying the relief requested pursuant to 28 U.S.C. §§ 2241, 2254, or 2255, a petitioner shall not be entitled to be represented by counsel as a matter of right. In these cases, counsel will be appointed only after the court has decided to hear the case on the merits, as in the granting of leave to appeal or the issuance of a certificate of appealability. However, in an appeal brought by the United States or a state from an order granting the relief requested, a petitioner shall be entitled to representation as a matter of right.

In any non-capital case brought pursuant to 28 U.S.C. §§ 2241, 2254, or 2255, the court may, on motion of the petitioner or on its own motion, appoint counsel where the court determines that (a) petitioner is financially unable to obtain adequate representation and (b) the interests of justice require legal representation, as when petitioner needs the assistance of counsel to go forward with an apparently meritorious petition. The clerk shall thereupon appoint the attorney of record in the district court, where appropriate, or select an appointee from a panel of approved attorneys.

Where a petitioner is under sentence of death, the clerk shall appoint counsel upon receipt of the notice of appeal.

II. APPOINTMENT OF COUNSEL

1. *Court Order:* Every appointment of counsel pursuant to the Criminal Justice Act and this Plan shall be made by an order of this court. A prerequisite to appointment shall be an affirmative finding by the court that a defendant is financially unable to employ counsel. However, where counsel was appointed in the lower court, this court will presume, until reason to the contrary appears, that the defendant remains financially unable to retain counsel, and no such finding shall be required.

The selection of counsel under the Criminal Justice Act shall be the exclusive responsibility of the court, and no person entitled to court-appointed counsel shall be permitted to select counsel to represent him.

2. *Retroactivity:* An appointment may be made retroactive to include any representation furnished to an indigent by an attorney prior to appointment pursuant to this Plan.

3. *Scope:* A person for whom counsel is appointed shall be represented at every stage of the proceedings, through appeal, including ancillary matters appropriate to the proceedings and including a petition for writ of certiorari to the Supreme Court if non-frivolous grounds exist for filing such a petition.

4. *Substitution of Counsel:* The court may, in the interests of justice, substitute one appointed counsel for another at any stage of the proceedings. The total compensation to be paid both attorneys shall not exceed the statutory maximum for one appointment, unless the case involves extended or complex representation.

5. *One Attorney for Multiple Defendants:* In appeals involving multiple defendants, separate counsel will normally be appointed for each defendant, unless there has been a waiver on the record by the defendants or good cause is shown. If one attorney is appointed to represent more than one defendant, a separate order of appointment shall be entered for each defendant. The attorney may be compensated for his services up to the maximum for each defendant represented; however, time spent in common on one or more defendants must be prorated.

6. *Multiple Appointments for One Defendant:* In capital cases, and in other cases of extreme difficulty where the interests of justice so require, the court may appoint an additional attorney to represent a defendant. Each attorney so appointed shall be eligible to receive the maximum compensation allowed under the Criminal Justice Act. Any defendant indicted for a capital offense is entitled to have two attorneys appointed. 18 U.S.C. § 3005.

7. *Defendant's Objection to Appointed Attorney:* The court shall give consideration to a defendant's expression of dissatisfaction with his counsel only if specific grounds for dissatisfaction are stated. Appointed counsel shall be relieved only when the court, in its discretion, determines that the interests of justice so require.

8. *Withdrawal of Counsel:* An attorney appointed to represent a defendant in the lower court is generally obliged to continue that representation upon appeal unless relieved by this court. *See infra* Part V.1. An attorney who does not desire to continue the representation must file a motion to withdraw with the clerk of this court promptly after filing the notice of appeal.

Counsel's request to be relieved from representation on appeal shall be given due consideration. While the court recognizes there may be benefits to maintaining continuity of counsel, it also recognizes that the skills necessary to proceed as appellate counsel may differ from those required for trial counsel. Substitution of counsel shall not reflect negatively in any way on the conduct of the lawyer involved.

In its discretion, this court may appoint the attorney who represented the eligible person in the district court, a Federal Public Defender's office from the circuit, or a lawyer from the court's Criminal Justice Act panel. *See infra* Part IV.4.

III. DEFENDANT'S FINANCIAL STATUS

1. *Filing Application:* A defendant who, in the district court, was represented by employed counsel, or was unrepresented, or was represented by appointed counsel but has nonetheless been requested to file a new application in this court, may apply to this court for the appointment of counsel. Such application shall be accompanied by an affidavit disclosing the applicant's financial status and any resources available to him to compensate counsel.

2. *Re-examination by Court:* The court, at any time, may re-examine a defendant's financial status as it bears upon the appointment of counsel and, thereupon, (a) appoint counsel to represent the defendant, if the defendant is not already represented or is unable to pay previously retained counsel, (b) terminate the appointment of counsel, or (c) require a partial payment of counsel fees by the defendant. The defendant shall furnish such financial and related information as may be requested during the re-examination, unless he desires to proceed without counsel.

3. *Insufficiency of Funds; Partial Payment:* If a defendant's net financial resources and anticipated income are in excess of the amount needed to provide him and his dependents with the necessities of life and to provide for his release on bond, but are insufficient to pay fully for retained counsel, this court will find the defendant eligible for the appointment of counsel but will direct him to pay the available excess funds to the clerk at the time of appointment. The court may increase or decrease the amount of such payments and impose appropriate conditions, where applicable. All such payments by the defendant shall be received pursuant to the prescriptions of subsection (f) of the Criminal Justice Act.

4. *Family Resources:* Funds and property standing in the name of, or held by, members of a defendant's family will be considered available for the payment of the fees of retained counsel if there is a finding, upon a reasonable basis of fact, that the family has indicated a willingness and a financial ability to pay all or part of the costs of representation. The initial determination of a defendant's eligibility for the appointment of counsel should be made without regard to family resources unless the family plans and is financially able to retain counsel promptly.

5. *Attorney's Information:* If at any time after appointment, counsel obtains information that a client is financially able to make payment, in whole or in part, for legal services in connection with his representation, and the source of the attorney's information is not protected as a privileged communication, counsel shall so advise this court.

IV. PANEL OF ATTORNEYS

1. *CJA Appellate Panel Committee:* A CJA appellate panel committee will be appointed by the court for the purpose of recommending minimum standards of eligibility for the CJA appellate panel, developing legal education and training opportunities for panel members, and otherwise improving CJA appellate representation.

2. *Panel Composition:* The clerk, subject to this court's approval, shall prepare a list of attorneys from which appointments shall be made. Attorneys, to be eligible for appointment, must be admitted to practice before this court under Rule 46 of the Federal Rules of Appellate Procedure, and must meet the minimum standards of eligibility recommended by the CJA appellate panel committee and adopted by the court. In preparing a list, the clerk will review and consider the standards of eligibility adopted by the court and the court's experience with attorneys.

3. *Periodic Revision:* The panel shall be revised periodically to ensure an adequate number of competent attorneys to provide effective representation to all persons entitled to appointed counsel.

4. *Appointments:* Appointments shall be made by the clerk on a rotational basis, subject to this court's discretion. Consideration will be given to the nature of the case, the place of the trial, the residence of the indigent person if on bail, the place of confinement, and other relevant matters. In death penalty cases at least one attorney appointed must have been admitted to practice in the Fourth Circuit Court of Appeals for not less than five years, and must have had not less than three years experience in the handling of appeals in the Fourth Circuit in felony cases. For good cause however, the court may appoint another attorney whose background, knowledge, or experience would otherwise enable him or her to properly represent the petitioner, with due

consideration to the seriousness of the possible penalty and to the unique and complex nature of the litigation. The Court will look to the factors articulated in the American Bar Association's guidelines for selection of appellate counsel in capital cases including the length of bar membership, general experience in criminal defense litigation, and specific experience in death penalty appeals and appeals of murder, aggravated murder or other serious felonies. The Court will also consider whether counsel has attended and successfully completed a recent training or educational program on criminal advocacy which focused on the appeal of cases in which a sentence of death was imposed. Finally, the Court will review the availability of ongoing consultation support to appointed counsel from experienced counsel.

When the court determines that the appointment of an attorney, who is not a member of the CJA panel, is appropriate in the interest of justice, judicial economy, or some other compelling circumstance warranting his or her appointment, the attorney may be admitted to the CJA panel pro hac vice and appointed to represent the appellant. These appointments should be made only in exceptional circumstances, such as the appointment in a death penalty case of an attorney furnished by a state or local public defender organization or legal aid agency where the attorney had represented the appellant during prior state court proceedings. Further, the attorney should possess such qualities as would qualify him or her for admission to the CJA panel in the ordinary course of panel selection.

5. *Removal from the Panel:* An attorney may be removed from the panel by the clerk for twice refusing to accept an appointment or by the court for any good reason.

V. ATTORNEY'S DUTY TO CONTINUE REPRESENTATION

1. *Trial Counsel:* Every attorney, including retained counsel, who represented a defendant in the district court shall continue to represent the client after termination of those proceedings, unless relieved of further responsibility by this court. Where counsel has not been relieved:

If there is a judgment of conviction or an order revoking probation, counsel shall inform the defendant of his right to appeal and of his right to have counsel appointed on appeal. If so requested by the defendant, counsel shall file a timely notice of appeal. Thereafter, unless the defendant otherwise so instructs, counsel shall take appropriate and timely steps to perfect and present the appeal, including, where appropriate, the ordering of such part of the transcript as may be necessary for consideration on appeal.

Similarly, if there is an appeal by the United States from an order or judgment adverse to it, counsel shall continue to represent the client.

In any case brought pursuant to 28 U.S.C. §§ 2241, 2254, or 2255 which results in an order by the district court denying the relief requested, counsel shall inform the petitioner of his right to appeal and of the court's authority to appoint appellate counsel in its discretion. If so requested by the petitioner, counsel shall file a timely notice of appeal and a motion for appointment of appellate counsel, and counsel's duty is thereby ended. On the other hand, if petitioner is granted the relief requested, counsel shall continue to represent the petitioner in the event the respondent appeals the judgment.

2. *Appellate Counsel:* Every attorney, including retained counsel, who represents a defendant in this court shall continue to represent his client after termination of the appeal unless relieved of further responsibility by this court or the Supreme Court. Where counsel has not been relieved:

If the judgment of this court is adverse to the defendant, counsel shall inform the defendant, in writing, of his right to petition the Supreme Court for a writ of certiorari. If the defendant, in writing, so requests and in counsel's considered judgment there are grounds for seeking Supreme Court review, counsel shall prepare and file a timely petition for such a writ and transmit a copy to the defendant. Thereafter, unless otherwise instructed by the Supreme Court or its clerk, or unless any applicable rule, order or plan of the Supreme Court shall otherwise provide, counsel shall take whatever further steps are necessary to protect the rights of the defendant, until the petition is granted or denied.

If the appellant requests that a petition for writ of certiorari be filed but counsel believes that such a petition would be frivolous, counsel may file a motion to withdraw with this court wherein counsel requests to be relieved of the responsibility of filing a petition for writ of certiorari. The motion must reflect that a copy was served on the client.

If the United States seeks a writ of certiorari to review a judgment of this court, counsel shall take all necessary steps to oppose the United States' petition.

Similarly, in any proceeding brought pursuant to 28 U.S.C. §§ 2241, 2254, or 2255 which results in an order by this court, appointed counsel shall take those steps necessary, as set forth above, to protect the rights of the defendant in the Supreme Court.

VI. COMPENSATION AND REIMBURSEMENT OF EXPENSES

1. *Voucher:* Upon the completion of service in this court, appointed counsel shall submit a voucher for compensation and reimbursement on the Criminal Justice Act form currently approved by the Administrative Office of the United States Courts. Vouchers shall be submitted no later than 60 days after the final disposition of the case, unless good cause is shown. The clerk will determine the amount of compensation and reimbursement to be paid. The approved voucher will then be reviewed by the Circuit Executive, signed by the Chief Judge, and forwarded to the Administrative Office for payment or further handling.

2. *Hourly Rates:* Counsel may be compensated at rates authorized by the Judicial Conference pursuant to 18 U.S.C. § 3006A(d)(1) for non-capital cases and pursuant to 18 U.S.C. § 3599(g)(1) for capital cases.

3. *Maximum Compensation Allowable:* Limitations on maximum compensation shall be as prescribed in 18 U.S.C. § 3006A(d)(2) for non-capital cases. In capital cases, maximum compensation limits do not apply, and compensation shall be in such amounts as the court determines to be reasonably necessary.

In all cases where there has been a substitution of counsel, or where multiple defendants have been represented by one attorney or multiple appointments have been made for one defendant, total compensation shall be determined pursuant to Section II, Paragraphs 4, 5, and 6.

Payment in excess of the prescribed limitations may be made to provide fair compensation in a case involving extended or complex representation, upon approval by the Chief Judge of this court or other active circuit judge designated by him. Counsel claiming in excess of the statutory maximum must submit with his voucher a detailed memorandum supporting and justifying counsel's claim that the representation given was in a complex or extended case, and that the excess payment is necessary to provide fair compensation. If the legal or factual issues in a case are unusual, thus requiring the expenditure of more time, skill and effort by the lawyer than would normally be required in an average case, the case is "complex.' If more time is reasonably required for total processing than would normally be required in the average case, the case is "extended." Attorneys seeking compensation have the burden of providing sufficient details to support their claim that the case is more complex or time consuming than the average case. This burden also exists with regard to the reasonableness of hours claimed for representation.

4. *Reimbursable Expenses:* Counsel shall be entitled to reimbursement for reasonably incurred out-of-pocket expenditures. Travel by privately owned automobile should be claimed at the mileage rate currently applicable to federal employee travel, plus parking fees and tolls. Transportation other than by privately owned automobile should be claimed on an actual expense basis. Necessary airline travel will be reimbursed only at coach class rates. Expenditures for meals and lodging, as well as for telephone toll calls, telegrams, and copying are reimbursable. The cost of photocopying or similar copying services is reimbursable, while the cost of printing is not. Where photocopying services are performed in counsel's office, the reimbursement shall be limited to out-of-pocket expenses, not to exceed 15 cents per copy. For photocopying and other services in preparation of briefs and appendices by commercial printers, reimbursement shall not exceed 35 cents per copy. All materials contained in appendices prepared by commercial printers in court-appointed cases will be reproduced on both sides of a sheet. No joint appendix in a court-appointed case shall exceed 250 sheets without advance permission from the Court. Compensation paid to law students for legal research is reimbursable, but expenses incurred by the law student in assisting counsel are not. When necessary for adequate representation in death penalty cases, reasonable employment and compensation of public and private organizations which provide consulting services to counsel are reimbursable to assist in such areas as records completion, identification of potential issues, exhaustion of

state remedies, and review of draft pleadings and briefs. Detailed receipts are required for all travel and lodging expenses, non-office copying services, and any other expense in excess of $50.00. Failure to provide detailed receipts may result in the expense being denied. Any expense in excess of $50.00 must be itemized in a manner which will permit a review of the amount expended.

5. *Representation to the Supreme Court:* Counsel's time and expenses involved in the preparation of a petition for a writ of certiorari to the Supreme Court, and in the protection of the defendant's rights up until the time that Court disposes of a petition, should be included in the voucher for services performed in this court.

6. *Number of Copies:* Appointed counsel is required to file six copies of the brief and five copies of the appendix with the clerk of the court, with service of one copy on counsel for each party separately represented. Appointed counsel shall be entitled to reimbursement for the cost of photocopying required copies.

7. *Non-reimbursable Expenses:* General office overhead, personal items and non-legal personal services for the person represented, filing fees, services of process, and printing are non-reimbursable. (A person represented under the Criminal Justice Act is not required to pay filing fees or costs, or give security therefor, nor must he file the 28 U.S.C. § 1915(a) affidavit, for an appeal.)

8. *Authorized Transcripts:* Authorized transcripts should not be claimed in the voucher by an attorney. The Administrative Office will pay the appropriate court reporter directly.

9. *Interim Payment of Expenses:* This court, in rare cases, will entertain requests for interim reimbursement of extraordinary and substantial expenses.

10. *Direct Payment from Person Represented:* No appointed counsel shall accept a payment or a promise of payment from a defendant for representation in this court without prior authorization from the court on an appropriate Criminal Justice Act form.

11. *Public Defender:* Where a defendant is represented by a federal public defender, the defender shall be compensated solely by his federal salary and shall not submit a Criminal Justice Act form for compensation.

12. *Non-appointed Co-Counsel:* Non-appointed attorneys may not be compensated, but an appointed attorney may claim compensation for services furnished by a partner, associate, or co-counsel, within the maximum compensation allowed to the appointed attorney.

VII. RULES, REGULATIONS, FORMS

1. *Rules and Regulations:* This Plan shall be subject to and held to have been amended pro tanto by any rule or regulation adopted by the Judicial Conference of the United States concerning the operation of plans under the Criminal Justice Act.

The Judicial Council or this court may adopt rules or regulations concerning the operation of this Plan, which, when promulgated, shall have the same force as provisions of this Plan.

2. *Forms:* Forms approved by the Administrative Office of the United States Courts for use in the administration of the Criminal Justice Act shall be used whenever appropriate. Where there are no approved forms, this court may approve and require the use of designated forms or other instruments.

VIII. ADMINISTRATION

Generally; Clerk's Office: Any act to be done by the court may be done by any judge of the court, by the clerk, or by a deputy clerk pursuant to delegated authority.

IX. DEFINITIONS

1. *Supreme Court:* Supreme Court of the United States.
2. *Administrative Office:* Administrative Office of the United States Courts.
3. *This court; the court:* the United States Court of Appeals for the Fourth Circuit.
4. *Criminal Justice Act:* Criminal Justice Act of 1964, 18 U.S.C. § 3006A, as amended.
5. *Defendant; Defendants:* Where appropriate in this Plan, the word "defendant" or "defendants" shall be construed to include petitioner or petitioners in a collateral proceeding.

6. *Judicial Council:* Judicial Council of the Fourth Judicial Circuit of the United States.

X. AMENDMENTS

This Plan may be amended at any time by the Judicial Council effective when a copy of the amendatory resolution is filed with the Administrative Office or at such later date as may be specified in the resolution.

XI. EFFECTIVE DATE

This amended plan is effective October 1, 2008. (Amended by order effective March 31, 1993, by order effective March 30, 1995, by order effective February 26, 1996, by order effective December 19, 2000, by order effective April 1, 2001, by order effective May 1, 2002, by order effective July 14, 2005, by order effective January 1, 2006, by order effective September 17, 2007, and by order effective October 1, 2008.)

APPENDIX B

DEATH PENALTY REPRESENTATION IN THE FOURTH CIRCUIT

I. STATUTORY PROVISIONS PRESENTLY APPLICABLE TO APPOINTMENT OF ATTORNEYS FOR CAPITAL REPRESENTATION

A. APPOINTMENT OF COUNSEL FOR INDIGENT CAPITAL DEFENDANTS IS STATUTORILY GUARANTEED FOR FEDERAL TRIALS, DIRECT APPEAL FROM FEDERAL CONVICTIONS, § 2255 PROCEEDINGS, AND § 2254 PROCEEDINGS.

Congress has enacted special provisions guaranteeing that "in every criminal action in which a defendant is charged with a crime which may be punishable by death" and in "any post conviction proceeding under section 2254 or 2255 of Title 28, seeking to vacate or set aside a death sentence, any defendant who is or becomes financially unable to obtain adequate representation ... shall be entitled to the appointment of one or more attorneys." 18 U.S.C.A. § 3599(a)(1) & (2). Any defendant indicted for a federal capital crime is entitled to have two attorneys appointed. 18 U.S.C.A. § 3005.

B. THE MINIMUM QUALIFICATIONS OF APPOINTED COUNSEL ARE STATUTORILY DEFINED.

The lead attorney appointed to represent one indicted on an offense punishable by death "must have been admitted to practice in the court in which the prosecution is to be tried for not less than five years, and must have had not less than three years experience in the actual trial of felony prosecutions in that court." 18 U.S.C.A. § 3599(b). And, at least one of the attorneys appointed to represent a defendant indicted with a federal capital crime must "be learned in the law applicable to capital cases." 18 U.S.C.A. § 3005.

A lead attorney appointed after conviction to represent a capital defendant on direct appeal, or during § 2255 proceedings, "must have been admitted to practice in the court of appeals for not less than five years, and must have had not less than three years experience in the handling of appeals in that court in felony cases." 18 U.S.C.A. § 3599(c).

A court may, for good cause shown, appoint another attorney who does not meet the requirements set forth in 18 U.S.C.A. § 3599(b)-(c). but whose experience otherwise enables him or her to adequately represent the defendant. 18 U.S.C.A. § 3599(d).

Attorneys that have been appointed typically continue the representation on appeal. See 18 U.S.C.A. § 3599(e) (providing that once appointed attorneys continue representation throughout subsequent proceedings); 18 U.S.C.A. § 3006A(c).

C. COMPENSATION FOR FEES IS PRESENTLY LIMITED ONLY TO A "REASONABLE FEE" IN THE VIEW OF THE DISTRICT COURT.

Attorneys appointed pursuant to § 3599 may be compensated at the rate authorized by the Judicial Conference pursuant to § 3599(g)(1). Counsel is also bound by the limitation of $7,500 for investigative, expert, and other reasonably necessary expenses unless a higher fee is approved by the court. 18 U.S.C.A. § 3599(g)(2).

II. RECOMMENDATIONS

A. SOLICIT QUALIFIED AND INTERESTED COUNSEL AND MAINTAIN LISTS OF ATTORNEYS QUALIFYING FOR APPOINTMENT AS LEAD COUNSEL AND SECOND-CHAIR COUNSEL.

District Court

** **It is recommended that a plan be adopted under which the district court would contact the bar and solicit applications for a panel of attorneys qualified to represent capital defendants.**

Some districts have experienced difficulty in locating qualified and interested counsel to undertake capital representation. But, it is believed that there are many attorneys who would seek the opportunity for appointment if they were made aware of that opportunity. Accordingly, it is recommended that on a district-by-district basis, a program of solicitation of the bar should be implemented in order to increase the number of attorneys seeking appointment.

** **It is recommended that the district courts maintain lists of those attorneys qualified to represent capital defendants as lead counsel and as second-chair counsel and that these attorneys' expertise in trial, appellate, and habeas representation be identified.**

Because the statutory requirements for lead counsel are more stringent than those for second-chair counsel, courts should maintain separate lists of those attorneys who are qualified for each type of appointment. In addition to the statutory qualifications, specialized skills and experience are necessary to represent capital defendants in trial, appellate, and habeas proceedings. Courts may find separate lists of attorneys with trial, appellate, and/or habeas experience useful. Alternatively, courts may conclude that some other method of identifying various types and levels of expertise is preferable.

In ascertaining which attorneys of those expressing an interest in capital representation and seeking appointment are qualified to be placed on lists of those available for appointment as lead and second-chair counsel, the court may wish to consider appointment of an oversight committee composed of district judges, magistrate judges, district court clerks, and the Federal Public Defender, see 18 U.S.C.A. § 3005.

It is envisioned that over time attorneys chosen for appointment from the second-chair counsel list will develop the qualifications to be placed on the lead counsel list, and that appointment of second-chair attorneys is desirable in order to develop a wider range of expertise available for lead counsel appointment. In addition, special consideration should be given to appointment of the attorney who represented a § 2254 petitioner during state collateral proceedings, if interested in appointment and qualified for it. See 18 U.S.C.A. § 3599(d).

Circuit Court

** **It is recommended that the circuit court solicit the bar for applications, maintain lists of those attorneys qualified to represent capital defendants as lead counsel and as second-chair counsel, and identify attorneys' expertise in appellate and habeas representation.**

Although attorneys that have been appointed at the district court level typically continue their representation on appeal, from time to time it is necessary to appoint attorneys pursuant to § 3599 during appellate proceedings. Consequently, it is recommended that a plan to solicit the bar for applications for appointment to capital representation be adopted and that lists of those attorneys qualified and interested in capital representation as lead and second-chair counsel be maintained.

B. USE FEDERAL PUBLIC DEFENDERS FOR REPRESENTATION OF FEDERAL CAPITAL CHARGES AND COLLATERAL ATTACKS ON FEDERAL CAPITAL CONVICTIONS AND SENTENCES; DO NOT UTILIZE FEDERAL PUBLIC DEFENDERS FOR PROSECUTION OF HABEAS PROCEEDINGS FILED BY STATE PRISONERS.

** **It is recommended that Federal Public Defenders be utilized for representation of individuals charged with federal capital crimes and collateral attacks on federal capital convictions.**

Providing representation for defendants charged with federal crimes punishable by the death penalty is within the statutory responsibility of the Federal Public Defender (FPD) to provide representation for all indigents charged with federal crimes. It is contemplated that FPDs will be placed in the pool of attorneys available to represent capital defendants in federal capital trials, on direct appeal, and in § 2255 proceedings. For some period of time, until FPDs develop the qualifications and experience, their appointments may be limited to second-chair positions. See 18 U.S.C.A. § 3599(d). However, such appointments should be encouraged whenever possible in order to permit FPDs to attain expertise in this area.

** **It is recommended that FPDs not be appointed to represent criminal defendants petitioning pursuant to 28 U.S.C.A. § 2254 for relief from a state death sentence.**

The consensus of opinion among FPDs in the circuit is that FPD representation in § 2254 proceedings challenging a state sentence of death is undesirable for a number of reasons. First, the prospect of a federal agency opposing the validity of state convictions creates the appearance of an unacceptable conflict between separate and independent sovereigns. Second, although the FPD is authorized to represent defendants seeking a writ of habeas corpus, encouraging such representation is problematic because litigation of collateral state-court proceedings and issues may be necessary, raising the question of the appropriateness of FPDs appearing in state court and presenting issues outside their traditional area of expertise. Finally, appointing FPDs to represent § 2254 petitioners could be viewed as an attempt to circumvent the will of Congress, given its recent decision to withdraw funding from death penalty resource centers.

C. IMPOSE RESTRAINTS ON TIME FOR DECISION.

** **It is recommended that the limitations on time for decision set forth in 28 U.S.C.A. § 2266 be adopted at the district and circuit court levels and that the Circuit Executive be authorized to inquire into the reasons for any noncompliance with the limitations.**

Under 28 U.S.C.A. § 2266 (enacted by the Antiterrorism and Effective Death Penalty Act of 1996), proceedings brought pursuant to § 2254 that are governed by Chapter 154 of Title 28 and proceedings brought pursuant to § 2255 in which the defendant was sentenced to death must be decided by the district court and the circuit court within specified time limits. The district court is required to render a decision and enter a final judgment (including a resolution of any motion to alter or amend the judgment) within 450 days of the date on which the petition is filed or 60 days after the date on which the case is submitted for decision, whichever is earlier, subject to an extension of up to 30 days if the district court determines that the ends of justice would best be served by the delay. See 28 U.S.C.A. § 2266(a)-(b). The court of appeals is required to render a decision within 120 days of the date on which the reply brief is filed and to rule on any petition for rehearing or rehearing en banc within 30 days of the date the petition is filed or the date a response thereto is filed, whichever is later. See 28 U.S.C.A. § 2266(c). Furthermore, if the petition is granted, any hearing must be conducted and a final decision rendered within 120 days of the entry of the order granting rehearing. Id. And, following a remand by the court of appeals en banc or the Supreme Court for further proceedings, the period for decision runs from the date the remand is ordered. Id.

The time limitations imposed by § 2266 are applicable only in those § 2254 proceedings governed by Chapter 154, (i.e., those challenging a state death sentence where the state has adopted specified procedures for appointment of counsel to represent the defendant in state post-conviction proceedings) and in § 2255 proceedings in which the defendant was sentenced to death. As such, the limitations presently will not apply to the majority of § 2254 petitions challenging a death sentence because of the relatively recent adoption of those mechanisms. See Bennett v. Angelone, No. 95-4004, 1996 WL 469705, at *4 (4th Cir. Aug. 20, 1996) (stating that question of whether Virginia's mechanism for appointment of counsel satisfied requirements for application of Chapter 154 was irrelevant because Chapter 154 would not apply when the mechanism was not in place during the petitioner's state collateral proceedings). Time constraints, however, are sorely needed at present. See, e.g., Correll v. Thompson, 63 F.3d 1279, 1285 n.4 (4th Cir. 1995), cert. denied, 116 S. Ct. 688 (1996) (noting that § 2254 petition was pending in district court for in excess of three years prior to final decision). Consequently, it is recommended that the time limitations for decision imposed by § 2266 be adopted and implemented by rule immediately. It is contemplated that the limitations would apply to cases pending when the rule became effective, but that the limitations would apply prospectively. (For example, an appeal in a § 2255 proceeding challenging a death sentence that had been argued to this court and was pending decision would have to be decided within 120 days of the date the rule becomes effective.)

Additionally, it is recommended that a mechanism be established to track cases to which the time limitations apply, and in the event that cases remain pending after the date on which they were due to be decided, the Circuit Executive be authorized to make appropriate inquiry on behalf of the Judicial Council to seek an explanation of the reasons why the judge or panel of judges failed to comply with the time limitation.

Amended: October 1, 2008.

Appendix C

Guidelines for Preparation of Appellate Transcripts in the Fourth Circuit

---

I. INTRODUCTION

A. Purpose

These guidelines set forth in detail the following:

1. Duties of the district court clerk's office, appellant and appellee in ordering the transcript;
2. Responsibilities of the court reporter for preparing and timely filing the transcript;
3. Duties of the court of appeals for acknowledging transcript orders and monitoring the timeliness of the filing of transcripts;
4. Procedures for court reporters to follow in requesting extensions of time and waivers of fee sanctions;
5. Criteria to be used by the court of appeals in acting on requests for extensions and waivers;
6. Common problems that have been encountered by court reporters and the court of appeals in the ordering, preparation and filing of transcripts; and
7. Provisions for supplementation of these guidelines by local procedures adopted by a district court.

B. Relation to Federal Rules of Appellate Procedure

Although Rule 11(b), Federal Rules of Appellate Procedure, requires transcripts to be filed within 30 days of the purchase order date, the court of appeals will use the time limits set forth in the district court reporter management plans governing the application of fee sanctions as the time periods within which transcripts will be due. All of the plans establish a 60-day period for preparation of transcripts without financial penalty. Exceptions are:

1. Special provisions adopted by the Fourth Circuit Judicial Council for appeals by incarcerated criminal defendants;
2. Special circumstances, such as
   (a) bail appeals,
   (b) death penalty cases,
   (c) expedited sentencing appeals,
   (d) recalcitrant witness appeals, or
   (e) other expedited procedures.

The Table on the next page sets forth the time requirements in detail.

TABLE OF TRANSCRIPT DUE DATES AND APPLICABLE SANCTIONS

NATURE OF CASE	LENGTH OF TRANSCRIPT	TRANSCRIPT DUE	10% FEE SANCTION	20% FEE SANCTION
Direct criminal appeals, appellant incarcerated	1000 pages or less	within 30 days of transcript order or judgment and commitment order, whichever is later	if filed after 30th day	if filed after 60th day
	more than 1000 pages	as ordered by clerk following consultation with reporter and parties	if due date missed	if due date missed by more than 30 days
All other cases, in other than exceptional circumstances	any length	within 60 days of transcript order or judgment and commitment order, whichever is later	if filed after 60th day	if filed after 90th day
Exceptional circumstances (e.g., bail appeals, death penalty cases, expedited sentencing appeals, etc.)	any length	as ordered by clerk following consultation with reporter and parties	*	*

* Twenty percent fee sanction automatically imposed if due date missed. Letter to chief district judge, after consultation with chief circuit judge requiring immediate preparation of the transcript.

C. Effective Date

These guidelines will take effect on June 1, 1986, and will apply to all Fourth Circuit cases subject to F.R.A.P. 11(b) in which the transcript is ordered after that date.

D. Definitions

For purposes of these guidelines, references to appellant-appellee will refer to counsel for appellant-appellee unless appellant-appellee is proceeding pro se, in which case all duties and responsibilities are those of appellant-appellee individually.

II. ORDERING AND ACKNOWLEDGING TRANSCRIPTS

A. Duties of District Court Clerk's Office

1. When a notice of appeal is filed, the district court clerk's office will notify appellant of the availability of appellate forms from the court of appeals, www.ca4.uscourts.gov.

2. Upon entry of an order authorizing preparation of a transcript at government expense pursuant to the Criminal Justice Act or 28 U.S.C. § 753(f), the district court reporter coordinator or appeals deputy will notify the court of appeals of the date on which the order was entered.

3. When substitute reporters or contract reporters are used, the district court reporter coordinator or district court appeals deputy will furnish them with copies of these guidelines and explain the procedures to be followed in preparing appellate transcripts.

4. When the transcript is filed, the district court clerk's office will transmit notice of the filing to the court of appeals through CM/ECF.

B. Duties of Appellant

1. Within 14 days after filing the notice of appeal, the appellant is required by F.R.A.P. 10(b)(1) to order from the court reporter such transcript of the proceedings as the appellant deems necessary. The notice of docketing issued by the court of appeals shall inform the appellant that the docketing statement and transcript order must be filed in the court of appeals within 14 days of the docketing notice.

2. By service of a copy of the docketing statement, appellant will notify appellee(s) that (a) a transcript is not needed for the appeal, (b) a transcript is already on file in the district court, or (c) less than the complete transcript will be ordered. The statement of issues in the docketing statement will satisfy the requirement of F.R.A.P. 10(b)(3).

3. Before a transcript can be ordered, the appellant must obtain from the court reporter an estimate of the length of the transcript and make appropriate financial arrangements with the reporter by immediate payment in full or by another payment arrangement acceptable to the reporter, such as filing a CJA 24 form with the district court for authorization of transcript in a criminal case pursuant to the Criminal Justice Act. [Local Rule 10(c)(1)]. Payment or other financial arrangements satisfactory to the reporter must accompany the court reporter's copy of the transcript order. [F.R.A.P. 10(b)(4)].

4. In criminal cases, counsel may seek authorization from the district court to order transcript after entry of verdict but prior to sentencing. The district court may authorize the early ordering of transcript if it determines that defense counsel has informed the defendant of the right to appeal and the defendant has instructed counsel to appeal regardless of the nature or length of the sentence imposed. The time requirements for the preparation of transcripts that are ordered before sentencing shall not begin to run until after entry of the judgment and commitment order.

5. To order a transcript, the appellant completes the transcript order form (and CJA 24 form as needed) and distributes copies to the court reporter, the district court, the court of appeals (attached to docketing statement), and opposing counsel (attached to docketing statement).

A separate transcript order (and CJA 24 form) must be prepared for each court reporter from whom a transcript is requested.

6. Failure by the appellant to timely order a transcript, failure to make satisfactory financial arrangements with the court reporter, or failure to specify in adequate detail those proceedings to be transcribed will subject the appeal to dismissal by the clerk of the court of appeals for want of prosecution pursuant to Local Rule 45.

7. When supplemental transcripts are requested, appellant must complete another transcript order form, make satisfactory financial arrangements with the reporter, and distribute copies to the same persons to whom the original transcript order was sent.

8. If payment is waived by the reporter at the time of ordering the transcript, the appellant must make full payment upon receipt of the reporter's invoice. If payment is not made within a reasonable period of time, the appeal will be subject to dismissal by the clerk of the court of appeals pursuant to Local Rule 45.

9. Transcripts ordered under the Criminal Justice Act do not include opening and closing statements, voir dire, or jury instructions unless prior special authorization has been received by appellant. CJA 24 forms should be obtained from the district court or from www.ca4.uscourts.gov and submitted to the district court judge for approval. In multi-defendant cases involving CJA defendants, only original transcripts should be ordered from the court reporter(s). Requests for copies will be arranged by the district court or appointed counsel at commercially competitive rates. Contact the district court reporter coordinator or district court clerk's office for further instructions.

10. When an appellant has ordered a transcript, he or she is obligated to pay the reporter for it. If the appeal is dismissed voluntarily, the appellant is nonetheless responsible to the reporter for the cost of transcript prepared prior to the reporter's receipt of notification from the appellant of the appeal's dismissal.

11. Appellant is required to review the transcript upon filing in the district court and provide the court reporter with a statement of the personal data identifiers, including the page number, line number, and text to be redacted, in accordance with the Judicial Conference Policy on Privacy and Public Access to Electronic Case Files.

C. Duties of Appellee

1. If the appellee deems a transcript of other parts of the proceedings to be necessary, he or she is required by F.R.A.P. 10(b)(3), within 14 days after service of the docketing statement by the appellant, to file and serve on the appellant a designation of additional parts to be included. Unless within 14 days after service of such designation the appellant has ordered such parts, and has so notified the appellee, the appellee may within the following 14 days either order the parts or move the district court for an order requiring the appellant to do so.

2. If the appellee wishes to obtain a copy of the transcript which has been ordered by the appellant, he or she may do so by ordering the copy directly from the court reporter. Satisfactory financial arrangements must be completed with the reporter before obtaining the copy. It is not appellant's responsibility to order and pay for a copy of the transcript for appellee.

3. Appellee is required to review the transcript upon filing in the district court and provide the court reporter with a statement of the personal data identifiers, including the page number, line number, and text to be redacted, in accordance with the Judicial Conference Policy on Privacy and Public Access to Electronic Case Files.

D. Duties of the Court Reporter

1. Upon receipt of the transcript order form and completion of satisfactory financial arrangements, the reporter must prepare the required transcript within the time set forth in the applicable district court reporter management plan.

2. The appellant attaches copies of the transcript order (and any CJA 24 form) to the docketing statement filed with the court of appeals. Upon receiving the transcript order, the court of appeals will complete and send to the reporter, and to the court reporter coordinator and the district court, a transcript order acknowledgment form to verify the transcript order. The acknowledgment will include a copy of the transcript order and any CJA 24 form and will show the date by which the transcript must be filed to avoid sanctions. The due date is computed from issuance of the transcript order acknowledgment in accordance with the time specified in the district court reporter management plans. Seven days are added to the applicable time period to permit confirmation of financial arrangements, including approval by the district court of the CJA 24 form. If the transcript order form is complete and accurate and financial arrangements are satisfactory, no response is required from the court reporter to the transcript order form or the transcript acknowledgment form.

3. If there is a problem with financial arrangements (e.g., the CJA 24 form is not approved within 7 days of issuance of the transcript order acknowledgment), with identification of the transcript ordered, with proper designation of the court reporters involved in the case, or with any other aspect of the transcript order, the court reporter must complete and file a transcript order deficiency notice with the court of appeals within 14 days of issuance of the transcript order acknowledgment (time may be extended for vacation, serious illness or other unusual circumstances). The deficiency notice is served on the parties and the district court reporter coordinator through CM/ECF. The court reporter need not inform the court of appeals if he or she in fact received the transcript order early. The court reporter may use any additional time so created for preparation of the transcript without fear of incurring a sanction for late filing. The court of appeals' acknowledgment constitutes an implied fee sanction waiver to the due date set forth on the form.

4. The deadline for completion of the transcript will be rescinded or extended upon filing of the transcript order deficiency notice, indicating a problem with the terms of the order, for whatever reasonable period of time is required for the reporter or district court reporter coordinator to resolve the problem with the appellant. The court of appeals transcript coordinator will be in touch with the reporter or district court reporter coordinator upon receipt of the transcript order deficiency notice to offer assistance, such as notification to the appellant that the appeal will be dismissed if the problem is not remedied promptly.

5. The court of appeals will send a revised transcript order acknowledgment or transcript extension order setting forth a new transcript filing date reflecting the delay caused by the problem with the original transcript order.

6. Unless the court of appeals is notified of a problem with the transcript order, or of some other reason why the information on the transcript order acknowledgment form prepared by the court of appeals is incorrect, the reporter will be held to the schedule set forth therein absent the granting of an extension of time. It is the court reporter's responsibility to notify the court of appeals of any problem.

7. If the transcript is estimated to be more than 1000 pages and is ordered in a criminal appeal in which the appellant is incarcerated, the reporter will receive an acknowledgment form with a due date which will be established by the court of appeals.

8. Transcript provided to counsel for use on appeal shall comply with appellate requirements for full-sized, rather than condensed, transcript and for identification of

the testifying witness and type of testimony (e.g., direct, cross, deposition) at the top of each page of in-court and deposition testimony.

9. When the transcript has been completed and the court copy filed in the district court, notice of the filing must be sent to the court of appeals through CM/ECF. If the transcript was filed late, the court reporter must file a transcript certification form in the court of appeals showing that the proper fee reduction sanction was taken. A copy of the certification is served on the parties and the district court reporter coordinator through CM/ECF.

10. The court reporter must make any requested redactions to the transcript and file a redacted version of the transcript in the district court in accordance with the Judicial Conference Policy on Privacy and Public Access to Electronic Case Files. Notice of filing of the redacted version of the transcript must be sent to the court of appeals through CM/ECF.

11. Unless a written motion is filed by the appellant with the court of appeals, and an extension granted by the clerk of the court of appeals, requests by an appellant that a reporter suspend or delay preparation of a transcript that has been ordered will have no effect on the date the transcript is due, or on the appellant's obligation to pay for it when it is prepared. The only exception is when a motion for voluntary dismissal of the appeal has been granted; in that instance the appellant is responsible for paying only for that portion of the transcript completed prior to the reporter's receipt of notification from the appellant of the appeal's dismissal.

E. Duties of Court of Appeals

1. F.R.A.P. 10(b)(1) requires the appellant to order the transcript within 14 days after filing the notice of appeal. If the completed form is not received by the court of appeals within 14 days of the court's notice of docketing of the appeal, the court of appeals will notify the appellant that no order has been received and that failure to comply with F.R.A.P. 10(b)(1) will subject the appeal to dismissal by the clerk for want of prosecution pursuant to Local Rule 45.

2. When the court of appeals receives the transcript order form, it will be reviewed for any obvious defects (e.g., multiple reporters on one form, or incompleteness as far as nature of proceedings requested or certification of satisfaction of financial requirements). If it appears to be in order, the court of appeals will prepare for the reporter a transcript order acknowledgment which will include the transcript order and any CJA 24 form and will show the due date, computed in accordance with the time limits set forth in the applicable district court reporter management plan. The court of appeals clerk's office will work together with reporters and parties to remedy any deficiencies in the transcript order that are brought to its attention by the reporter. (See Sections D.3 - 8 for full description of procedures.)

III. REPORTS

Reports on outstanding transcripts will be generated monthly and will be distributed to the court reporters involved, as well as to the district court clerks or their court reporter coordinators. If the report shows a transcript outstanding when it has actually been filed, the reporter or district court reporter coordinator should call the court of appeals and report the date of filing. If everything in the report is correct and none of the transcripts are overdue, no response is required from the reporter.

IV. TIME LIMITS FOR FILING TRANSCRIPTS— FEE REDUCTION SANCTIONS

A. Requests for Extensions of Time

As set forth in the district court reporter management plans, all requests for extensions of time for the filing of appellate transcripts (F.R.A.P. 11(b) transcripts) are submitted to the clerk of the court of appeals. They should be in writing, on the designated form. They are served on counsel through CM/ECF. A request for an extension of time will automatically constitute a corresponding request for a waiver of any applicable fee reduction sanction. Requests for extensions must be filed 10 days in advance of the deadline from which relief is sought, unless unforeseen circumstances make later requests necessary, in which case the reasons will be set out by the reporter in the request. When requesting an extension, the information furnished should be very specific. Failure to submit complete information will delay action on the request and lead to additional paperwork for the reporter. After reviewing the request for extension, the court of appeals will issue an order granting, granting in part, or denying the request, which will set forth the resulting time frames for purposes of fee sanction imposition. Counsel, the district court reporter coordinator, and the district court clerk will also receive copies of this order.

B. Grounds for Extensions of Time

1. *Excessive burden of transcript, considering length and complexity of the proceedings ordered within a short period of time.* — District court reporter coordinators are expected to make court reporter assignments within a district so as to anticipate and to avoid to the extent possible the imposition of excessive transcript loads on individual reporters. When these efforts are unsuccessful, reporters may apply for relief from applicable fee sanctions and have the court of appeals assign the relative priority to be given to competing appellate transcript orders. The fact that a reporter has accumulated orders for more than 3000 pages within three months will be presumed to establish the existence of an "excessive burden." The existence of outstanding overdue transcripts may or may not be grounds for extending the time for subsequently ordered transcripts. In computing the amount of transcript for purposes of demonstrating excessive burden, the reporter can include all transcripts ordered within ninety days of the request for extension. The reporter may include transcript obligations for the district court as well as those ordered for appellate purposes. However, the orders must be "firm orders". A "firm order" for an appellate transcript is one for which the court of appeals has received a transcript order from the appellant. For a district court transcript it is an order communicated by a judge or a party; it cannot be a reporter's speculation that an order will be forthcoming.

2. *Vacation.* — A reporter can plan to take reasonable vacations, as authorized by the district court, and obtain extensions of deadlines that would fall within those periods or become impossible to meet in light of them.

3. *Unavoidable, excessive time required for attendance in court.* — It is the responsibility of the district court reporter coordinator to adjust reporter assignments to ensure that the needs of the trial and appellate courts can be met. Occasions may arise, nonetheless, when a court reporter's courtroom obligations, including official travel required to reach the courtroom, prevent his or her meeting transcript obligations. Reasonable extensions of time will be given in such instances.

4. *Incapacitation or serious illness.* — A reporter may certify to the clerk of the court of appeals that he or she has become temporarily incapacitated or seriously ill, and obtain reasonable relief from pending deadlines. This ground does not include common colds or other ailments that would not prevent attendance in court.

5. *Unforeseen emergencies.* — Reporters may seek extensions for any other good cause which makes the completion of a transcript within the allotted time impossible.

V. SANCTIONS

A. Fee Reduction Sanctions

An official court reporter will be required to deduct from his or her charges for a completed transcript not timely filed with the district court the amount of any fee reduction sanction applicable by the terms of a district court reporter management plan.

B. Removal from Courtroom and Request for Substitute Reporter

The chief judge of the court of appeals, following consultation with the chief judge of the district court, may order a reporter to remain out of the courtroom, and pay the costs of a satisfactory substitute reporter, if a transcript is ninety days overdue.

VI. MONITORING OF TRANSCRIPT FILING

The clerk of the court of appeals will monitor the filing of all appellate transcripts and the fees charged by reporters when a transcript is filed untimely. The fee sanction mechanism exists by virtue of the district court reporter management plans which require reporters to take fee reductions if a transcript is not filed on time. Therefore, the court of appeals will not issue a sanction order. It is the reporter's duty to abide by the provisions of his or her district court reporter management plan and to take a fee reduction if one is applicable.

The court of appeals will take no action if the transcript is filed on time or, if not filed on time, the appropriate fee reduction has been taken as shown by the transcript certification form that the reporter submitted to the court of appeals when the transcript was filed. If a fee reduction was applicable and was not taken by the reporter, the court of appeals will send notice to the reporter setting forth the fee reduction that should have been taken. Copies of this notice will be sent to counsel, the district court reporter coordinator (if any) and the judge to whom the reporter reports or the chief district judge. If the certification is not submitted within a reasonable period after the filing of the transcript, the reporter will be requested to submit a copy of his or her invoice.

The court of appeals will also send a letter to the chief district judge when a transcript is sixty days overdue. The letter will identify the particular transcript involved and the date of the order. Copies of the letter will be sent to the judge (if any) to whom the reporter reports, the district court reporter coordinator, the district court clerk, and the reporter. The letter will alert the chief judge of the district court to the possibility that the reporter may be required to remain out of the courtroom, paying for a substitute reporter, until the transcript is completed, if the transcript becomes ninety days overdue.

VII. COMMON PROBLEMS

A. Transcripts Prepared at Government Expense

1. *Criminal Justice Act* [18 U.S.C. § 3006A]. — When the reporter receives the approved CJA form, preparation of the transcript should begin immediately. To allow time for the district court to act on the CJA 24 application, the court of appeals adds 7 days to the transcript deadline set upon receipt of its copy of the transcript order and CJA 24 forms. If the district court does not approve the CJA 24 form within 7 days, the court reporter may request rescission or extension of the deadline using the transcript order deficiency notice.

Pursuant to the Guidelines for the Administration of the Criminal Justice Act, in multi-defendant cases involving CJA defendants, no more than one original transcript should be purchased from the court reporter on behalf of CJA defendants. One of the appointed counsel or the district court should arrange for the duplication, at commercially competitive rates, of enough copies of the transcript(s) for each of the CJA defendants for whom a transcript has been approved.

2. *In Forma Pauperis Litigants* [28 U.S.C. § 753(f)]. — When an order is entered directing preparation of a transcript at government expense pursuant to 28 U.S.C. § 753(f), the transcript order date is the date the reporter receives the court's order authorizing preparation of the transcript.

B. Supplemental Transcripts

Supplemental transcripts are usually ordered after the original transcript has been filed and a briefing schedule established by the court of appeals. Therefore, these transcripts should be expedited. Counsel is under an obligation to notify the court of appeals that a supplemental transcript has been ordered. The court of appeals will then send the transcript order acknowledgment form to the reporter with the request that the reporter prepare these transcripts as quickly as possible.

C. Expedited Proceedings

When a transcript is requested for an expedited proceeding, the due date for filing the transcript is established by the court of appeals. If an expedited transcript is requested and prepared within 7 days after receipt or notification of the order, the court reporter may charge the higher rates for expedited transcripts.

Transcripts for appeals arising from a criminal sentence imposed under 18 U.S.C. § 3742 will only be expedited if a motion for expedited review of criminal sentence is granted by the court of appeals. Only those portions of the transcript pertinent to the appeal must be prepared on an expedited basis. The court reporter will be notified by the court of appeals when a motion to expedite has been granted.

In bail appeals, only the portion of the transcript dealing with the bail issue should be ordered on a rush basis. Even though there may be other portions of the transcript that the appellant has ordered, the portion dealing with the bail issue should be prepared first. In expedited proceedings, a twenty percent fee sanction from the regular transcript rate will be imposed if the due date is missed. At the same time, a letter will be sent to the chief judge of the district court, advising of the delinquency and warning that the chief judge of the court of appeals may order the reporter to remain out of the courtroom, and pay the costs of a satisfactory substitute reporter, if the transcript is not filed immediately. IF THE COURT REPORTER ANTICIPATES A PROBLEM WITH PROMPT PREPARATION OF AN EXPEDITED TRANSCRIPT, THE DISTRICT COURT REPORTER COORDINATOR AND THE COURT OF APPEALS SHOULD BE NOTIFIED IMMEDIATELY.

D. Payment for Transcript

The court of appeals approves of reporters' demanding a substantial deposit or full payment in advance for preparation of a transcript. In those instances where a reporter does not demand full payment in advance, and upon transcript completion has not been paid fully by the appellant, the following procedures should be followed:

1. Timely file the court copy of the transcript with the district court clerk's office.
2. Contact the court of appeals immediately and a letter will be sent to the appellant stating that if full payment is not made to the court reporter within fifteen days of the date of the letter, the appeal will be dismissed for failure to prosecute.

Fee reduction sanctions will be applicable if the court copy of the transcript is not timely filed. Problems with payment for the transcript after its completion will have no effect on the established due date.

E. Substitute Reporters

When an official court reporter hires a substitute, the official reporter still retains responsibility for the timely filing of the transcript. All provisions applicable to an official court reporter will be applicable to the substitute. If there is a problem with the filing of a transcript, the official court reporter will be notified as well as the substitute reporter. All correspondence and orders by the court of appeals will be sent to both reporters. The substitute can request extensions of time and waivers of applicable fee sanctions from the court of appeals. However, all guidelines applicable to the official reporter will be applicable to the substitute reporter and the proper procedures for requesting extensions must be followed.

F. Contract Reporters

Contractual reporting services in district courts are provided as supplements to the services of official staff. Contractual services are used after the district court reporter coordinator has determined that no official court reporter is available. Contract reporters must follow the procedures set out below.

1. All contractors are subject to the terms and conditions of their contacts with the district courts. Standard contract terms for delinquent transcript provide that the contract reporter may charge only 90% of the prescribed fee for transcript not delivered within 30 days of the date ordered (with payment arrangements made) and may charge only 80% of the prescribed fee for transcript not delivered within 60 days of the date ordered (with payment arrangements made).
2. Extensions of time for filing transcripts for F.R.A.P. 11(b) cases may be requested in writing following the procedures set forth in these Guidelines. However, the court of appeals cannot waive the fee sanctions for contract reporters. A waiver of applicable fee reduction sanctions may be requested, in writing, from the contracting officer. A copy of the letter requesting a waiver of fee sanctions should be sent to the court of appeals.

G. Filing of Transcripts with the District Court

When the proceedings that are transcribed have been taken in another division of the district court, the reporter may file the court copy of the transcript in the district in which his or her office is located. That division will file stamp the copy and forward it to the appropriate division for inclusion in the record to be transmitted to the court of appeals.

VIII. ADDITIONAL LOCAL PROCEDURES

Following prior consultation with the clerk of the court of appeals, a district court may institute supplemental local procedures designed to adapt these Guidelines to the structure of court reporting services in place in that district.

REVISED: 12/1/2009

FOURTH CIRCUIT TRANSCRIPT ORDER FORM

Case Style ______________________________

Dist. Ct. No. __________ District ______________________________

Date Notice of Appeal filed __________ Ct. of Appeals No. ______________

Name of Court Reporter/Electronic Rec. (use separate form for each reporter) ______

____

Address of Reporter ______________________________

Appellant must order any necessary transcript, completing a separate transcript order form (and separate CJA 24 Form) for each reporter and submitting the order to the court reporter and the district court within 14 days of noting the appeal. The completed form must show that necessary financial arrangements have been made or that a CJA 24 Form has been submitted to the district judge for approval. Copies of the transcript order form must be attached to the docketing statement filed in the Court of Appeals and served on opposing counsel within 14 days of docketing of the appeal, or the appeal will be subject to dismissal pursuant to Local Rule 45. If appellee finds other parts of the proceedings necessary, appellee must designate the additional parts within 14 days after service of the transcript order. If appellant has not ordered the additional parts within 14 days, appellee may, within the following 14 days, order the additional parts or move in the district court for an order requiring appellant to do so. In sentencing appeals, a transcript of the sentencing hearing must be ordered. In *Anders* appeals, plea (or trial) and sentencing transcript must be ordered. If appellee wishes to obtain a copy of transcript ordered by appellant, appellee must order a copy from the court reporter. In multi-defendant cases involving CJA defendants, only one original trial transcript should be purchased from the court reporter on behalf of CJA defendants, and copies should thereafter be made at commercially competitive rates. Counsel must review transcript and notify the district court of any intention to direct redaction of personal data identifiers within 7 days of filing of the transcript, and thereafter submit a statement of redactions to the court reporter within 21 days of filing of the transcript, as required by the *Judicial Conference Policy on Privacy and Public Access to Electronic Case Files*. Counsel should verify that the witness name and type of examination appear in the top margin of each page of testimony, as required for inclusion in the appendix on appeal. Local Rule 30(b).

A. This constitutes an order of the transcript of the following proceedings. Check appropriate box(es), provide date of hearing, and indicate total number of estimated pages. Failure to specify in adequate detail the proceedings to be transcribed is grounds for dismissal. Specific authorization is required under the CJA for opening and closing statements, voir dire, or jury instructions.

PROCEEDING	HEARING DATE(S)
☐ Voir Dire	______________
☐ Opening Statement (Plaintiff)	______________
☐ Opening Statement (Defendant)	______________
☐ Closing Argument (Plaintiff)	______________
☐ Closing Argument (Defendant)	______________
☐ Opinion of Court	______________
☐ Jury Instructions	______________
☐ Sentencing	______________
☐ Bail Hearing	______________
☐ Pre-Trial Proceedings (specify)	______________
☐ ______________	______________
☐ Testimony (specify)	______________
☐ ______________	______________
☐ Other (specify)	______________
☐ ______________	______________

TOTAL ESTIMATED PAGES ______

B. I certify that I have contacted the court reporter (or coordinator if electronic recording from the District of Maryland) and satisfactory financial arrangements for payment of the transcript have been made.

☐ Private funds. (Deposit of $______ enclosed with court reporter's copy. Check No. ______.)

- ☐ Criminal Justice Act. A CJA 24 Form has been submitted to the district court and a copy is attached.
- ☐ Government expense (civil case — IFP). Motion for transcript at government expense is pending with district judge.
- ☐ Advance payment waived by court reporter. Payment in full is due upon receipt of transcript.
- ☐ Federal Public Defender — no CJA 24 Form necessary.
- ☐ United States appeal — copy of litigation expense form attached, if applicable.

Signature ____________________ Typed Name ______________________________
Address ____
Telephone No. ___________ Date Sent to Reporter ____________________________

INSTRUCTIONS TO APPELLANT FOR ORDERING TRANSCRIPT

You have ten days after filing your notice of appeal to order transcript from the court reporter and file a copy of this form with the clerk of the district court. Within fourteen days of filing the notice of appeal, additional copies of this form must be filed with two copies of the Docketing Statement with the clerk of the court of appeals and served with the Docketing Statement on opposing counsel.

DO NOT SUBMIT THIS FORM UNTIL YOU HAVE MADE SATISFACTORY FINANCIAL ARRANGEMENTS WITH THE COURT REPORTER.

1. Contact each court reporter involved in reporting the proceedings, obtain an estimate of total pages, and make arrangements for payment. If you are unsure of the reporter(s) involved, contact the district court clerk's office for that information. A SEPARATE TRANSCRIPT ORDER MUST BE PREPARED FOR EACH COURT REPORTER FROM WHOM A TRANSCRIPT IS REQUESTED. MAKE COPIES OF BLANK FORM AS NECESSARY.
2. If payment is waived by the reporter until completion of the transcript, the appellant must remit full payment within a reasonable period of time upon receipt of the reporter's invoice.
3. If this was an electronic recording from the District of Maryland, contact the district court reporter coordinator for further instructions.
4. Transcripts ordered under the Criminal Justice Act do not include opening and closing statements, voir dire, or jury instructions unless prior special authorization has been received by the appellant. Request CJA Form 24 from the district court and submit the form(s) to the district court judge for approval. A separate CJA Form 24 must be completed for each court reporter. In multi-defendant cases involving CJA defendants, only original transcripts should be purchased from the court reporter(s). Requests for copies will be arranged by the district court using commercial printers. Contact the district court reporter coordinator or district court clerk's office for further instructions.
5. Complete the Transcript Order in its entirety.
6. Distribute the Transcript Order as follows:

   court reporter — mail original to court reporter within 10 days of filing notice of appeal

   district court — file copy in district court clerk's office within 10 days of filing notice of appeal

   court of appeals — attach copies to both copies of Docketing Statement filed in court of appeals clerk's office within 14 days of filing notice of appeal. For CJA attorneys, a <u>copy</u> of the CJA Form 24 must also be attached.

   opposing counsel — attach copy to Docketing Statement served on opposing counsel within 14 days of filing notice of appeal

IF THE TRANSCRIPT ORDER IS NOT FILED WITHIN THE TIME PERIODS SET FORTH ABOVE, PROCEDURES WILL BE INITIATED TO DISMISS THE APPEAL FOR FAILURE TO PROSECUTE.

If you have further questions, contact the Clerk's Office, U.S. Court of Appeals (804-916-2700).

Appendix D

ADMINSTRATIVE ORDER 08-01
CASE MANAGEMENT/ELECTRONIC CASE FILING SYSTEM

Editor's note. — Administrative Order 08-01, which provided for a Case Management/Electronic Case Filing System, has been superseded, effective July 2, 2012. The Court's electronic case filing provisions have been moved to Local Rule 25(a).

Appendix E

PLAN FOR THE COMPOSITION AND ADMINISTRATION OF THE CJA APPELLATE AND CAPITAL APPELLATE PANELS

I. COMPOSITION OF PANELS

A. PANEL TYPES

The Court shall establish two panels of attorneys who are eligible and willing to accept appellate appointments of the types identified below. The Court shall approve attorneys for membership on the panels after receiving recommendations from the CJA Appellate Panel Committee established pursuant to section II of this Plan. An attorney may be a member of more than one panel.

1. CJA Appellate Panel. Members of the CJA Appellate Panel are appointed in criminal cases when new counsel must be appointed on appeal. To qualify for the CJA Appellate Panel, attorneys must be members in good standing of the Fourth Circuit bar and have demonstrated experience in, and knowledge of, federal criminal law and appellate procedure and the Sentencing Guidelines.

2. Capital Appellate Panel. Members of the Capital Appellate Panel are appointed in capital cases when new counsel must be appointed on direct appeal or on collateral appeal under 28 U.S.C. § 2254 or § 2255. The Capital Appellate Panel is composed of first-chair and second-chair counsel lists. First-chair counsel must have been a Fourth Circuit bar member for at least five years and have at least three years experience in the handling of felony appeals in the Fourth Circuit. See 18 U.S.C. § 3599. Qualification requirements for second-chair counsel are the same as for CJA Appellate Panel members.

B. PANEL SIZE.

The CJA and Capital Appellate Panels shall be large enough to provide a sufficient number of experienced attorneys to handle the caseload, yet small enough so that panel members will receive an adequate number of appointments to maintain their proficiency and thereby provide a high quality of representation.

C. TERMS OF PANEL MEMBERSHIP.

The initial CJA Appellate Panel established pursuant to this Plan will be divided into three groups, equal in number. Members will be assigned to one of the three groups on a random basis. Members of the first group will serve on the panel for a term of one year, members of the second group will serve on the panel for a term of two years, and members of the third group will serve on the panel for a term of three years. Thereafter, attorneys admitted to the panel will each serve for a term of three years. Members of the Capital Appellate Panel will remain on the panel unless removed at their request or at the direction of the Court.

A panel member may be removed from any panel whenever the Court, in its discretion, determines that the member has failed to fulfill satisfactorily the obligations of panel membership, including the duty to afford competent counsel, or has engaged in other conduct that renders inappropriate his or her continued service on the panel.

D. PANEL REAPPOINTMENTS.

Upon expiration of the term of a CJA Appellate Panel member, the panel member must apply for renewal of membership if he or she wishes to continue as a member of the panel.

E. PANEL APPLICATIONS.

The Court will set and publicize an annual application period for panel appointments. Application forms for membership and renewal of membership shall be available on the Court's web site and from the Clerk. Completed applications shall be submitted to the Clerk, who will transmit the applications to the CJA Appellate Panel Committee.

II. CJA APPELLATE PANEL COMMITTEE

A. MEMBERSHIP.

A CJA Appellate Panel Committee shall be established by the Court. The Committee shall consist of the following members appointed by the Chief Circuit Judge: a Circuit

Judge, a Federal Public or Community Defender from within the Circuit, at least one attorney from each District within the Circuit, the Circuit Executive, the Clerk, and the Senior Staff Attorney. The Committee shall be chaired by the Circuit Judge. Attorneys appointed to the Committee shall serve staggered three year terms and may serve two consecutive terms. The Federal Defender representative shall serve a three-year term and may serve two consecutive terms.

B. DUTIES.

The CJA Appellate Panel Committee shall meet at least once a year in person or by teleconference to consider applications for the CJA and Capital Appellate Panels. The Committee shall review the qualifications of applicants for the panels and recommend, for approval by the Court, those applicants best qualified to fill the panels.

At its annual meeting the Committee shall also review the operation and administration of the panels over the preceding year and the legal education and training opportunities provided to panel members and make any recommendations for improvement to the Court.

III. SELECTION FOR APPOINTMENT

A. CJA APPELLATE PANEL

1. Maintenance of List and Distribution of Appointments. The Clerk shall maintain a current list of all attorneys included on the CJA Appellate Panel, with law firm names, current office addresses, and telephone numbers. The Clerk shall also maintain a record of all new appointments made on appeal and statistical data reflecting the proration of new appointments between private attorneys and the Federal Public or Community Defender Offices.

2. Method of Selection. Appointments shall be initially offered to the Federal Public or Community Defender for the district out of which the appeal arises. If the Defender for that district has a conflict of interest, appointments may be made to the Federal Public or Community Defender for another district within the Circuit or to a member of the CJA Appellate Panel. CJA Appellate Panel appointments should be made on a rotational basis to the next panel member from the district in which the appeal arises who is qualified and available for appointment. Exceptions to these guidelines may be made due to the nature and complexity of the case, an attorney's experience or expertise, the defendant's place of confinement or residence if on bail, or the relative unavailability of counsel within the district from which the appeal arises. When such an exception is appropriate, the attorney selected for appointment need not be a member of the CJA Appellate Panel. Any variance in the appointment of attorneys by rotation must be approved in advance by the Chief Judge or the Chief Judge's designee.

B. CAPITAL APPELLATE PANEL

1. Maintenance of List and Distribution of Appointments. The Clerk shall maintain a current list of all first-chair and second-chair attorneys included on the Capital Appellate Panel, with law firm names, current office addresses, and telephone numbers. The Clerk shall also maintain a record of all new appointments made on appeal in capital cases.

2. Method of Selection. Appointments shall be made after appropriate consultation with the Federal Public or Community Defender or the Administrative Office of the United States Courts, in accordance with 18 U.S.C. § 3005 and the Guidelines for Representation in Federal Death Penalty Cases and Federal Habeas Corpus Proceedings, Volume 7, Chapter VI, Guide to Judiciary Policies and Procedures. First-chair counsel must meet the qualification standards of 18 U.S.C. § 3599, as further articulated in the Plan of the United States Court of Appeals for the Fourth Circuit in Implementation of the Criminal Justice Act, ¶ IV, § 4 (Sept. 17, 2007), and in Fourth Circuit Judicial Council Order 113 (Oct. 3, 1996). Second-chair counsel should be appointed after consultation with first-chair counsel.

APPLICATION FOR MEMBERSHIP ON THE CRIMINAL JUSTICE ACT AND/OR CAPITAL APPELLATE PANELS FOR THE UNITED STATES COURT OF APPEALS FOR THE FOURTH CIRCUIT

INSTRUCTIONS

To be considered for membership on the CJA Appellate Panel for the United States Court of Appeals for the Fourth Circuit, an attorney must be a member of the bar of the

Fourth Circuit in good standing and have demonstrated experience in, and knowledge of, federal criminal law and appellate procedure and the Sentencing Guidelines.

To be considered for membership as second-chair counsel on the Fourth Circuit's Capital Appellate Panel, an attorney must satisfy the qualifications for CJA Appellate Panel membership and have an interest in capital representation. To be considered for membership as first-chair counsel on the Fourth Circuit's Capital Appellate Panel, an attorney must have an interest in capital representation and must have been admitted to practice in the Fourth Circuit not less than 5 years and have had not less than 3 years experience in the handling of appeals in the Fourth Circuit in felony cases.

Counsel applying for membership on the CJA Appellate Panel should complete questions 1 through 7. Counsel applying for membership on the Capital Appellate Panel should complete questions 1 through 8.

Please submit:

- the completed questionnaire
- your resume
- an appellate brief you have prepared and a copy of the court opinion, or other writing sample (see question 5.B)

via email to: 4CCA-CJA]Apps@ca4.uscourts.gov

APPLICATION FOR MEMBERSHIP ON (check all that apply)

____ CJA Appellate Panel

____ Capital Appellate Panel

(Attach additional sheets if needed in answering the following questions)

1. **Name** ______________________________
   Firm Name ______________________________
   Office Address ______________________________
   City, State, Zip ______________________________
   Email ______________ Fax No. ______________
   Office Phone No. ______________________________

2. **Education** — Graduated from:
   School of Law ______________________________
   Year ______________________________

3. **Bar Admissions** — List each court with date of admission:
   ____
   ____
   ____

4. **Disciplinary Actions** — Have you ever been disciplined, or are you the subject of any pending disciplinary proceeding, by the bar of any jurisdiction or by any court? ______________ If so, please explain in detail on a separate sheet of paper.

5. **Criminal Actions** — Have you ever been convicted of any criminal offense (misdemeanor or felony)? ______________ If so, please explain in detail on a separate sheet of paper.

6. **Experience**

   A. **Prior CJA Experience** — If you have at any time been a member of a CJA panel, or the member of a comparable state court panel, please list the court(s) and approximate dates of service:
   ____
   ____

   B. **Previous Appellate Experience** — Approximately how many appellate briefs have you prepared? ______________ Of these appeals, approximately how many were federal appeals? ______________ Approximately how many were criminal (state or federal) appeals? ______________ How many appeals have you argued? ______________

Please list up to three criminal or habeas corpus appeals you have handled, preferably federal appeals. If you have not handled any criminal appeals, you may list civil appeals. Please provide a copy of the brief you authored in one of these cases. If the brief is an Anders brief or is not a good example of your writing and advocacy skills, please substitute a brief that better represents your qualifications.

C. **Trial Experience** — Please briefly describe any criminal trial experience, federal or state, relevant to evaluating your competence to serve on this panel:

D. **Other** — Have you ever been employed as a prosecutor, public defender, or law clerk to a judge or justice? ________ If so, please describe the position, the name of your employer, and the approximate dates of employment.

7. **References** — Please list the name, address, and telephone number of two references who can assess your skills relevant to this panel:

8. **Special Qualifications** — Are you fluent in Spanish? ________ Please indicate whether you have any other special qualifications, such as expertise in a specialized area of law or relevant legal experience, which you believe is helpful in evaluating your competence to serve on this panel.

9. **Capital Appellate Panel**

A. **Statement of Interest** — Please state whether you would like to be considered for:

____ First-chair counsel in capital appeals
____ Second-chair counsel in capital appeals

B. **Previous Felony Appeals in this Court** — First-chair counsel must have been admitted to practice in this Court for not less than 5 years and must have had not less than 3 years experience in the handling of appeals in this Court in felony cases. Please list all felony appeals you have handled in this Court:

C. **Other Relevant Experience** — Please identify any background, knowledge, experience, education, training, or other special qualifications that would be helpful in evaluating your competence to provide capital representation:

Date Applicant's Signature

FORMS.

Form 1. Notice of Appeal to a Court of Appeals From a Judgment or Order of a District Court.

United States District Court for ______________________
District of ______________________
File Number ______________________

______________)
v.) Notice of Appeal
______________)

Notice is hereby given that ______________________ (plaintiffs) (defendants) in the above named case,* hereby appeal to the United States Court of Appeals for the __________ Circuit (from the final judgment) (from the order (describing it)) entered in this action on the ___ day of ____________, 20___.

(s) ______________________
Attorney for ______________________
Address ______________________
____

(Amended by order adopted April 22, 1993, effective December 1, 1993, by order adopted March 27, 2003, effective December 1, 2003, and by order effective December 1, 2006.)

Form 2. Notice of Appeal to a Court of Appeals From a Decision of the Tax Court.

UNITED STATES TAX COURT
Washington, D.C.

______________)
v.) Docket No. __________
______________)

Notice of Appeal

Notice is hereby given that ______________________, hereby appeal to the United States Court of Appeals for the ______________ Circuit from (that part of) the decision of this court entered in the above captioned proceeding on the ___ day of ____________, 20___ (relating to ______________________).

(s) ______________________
Counsel for ______________________
Address: ______________________

(Amended by order adopted April 22, 1993, effective December 1, 1993, by order adopted March 27, 2003, effective December 1, 2003, and by order effective December 1, 2006.)

Form 3. Petition for Review of Order of an Agency, Board, Commission or Officer.

United States Court of Appeals for the ________ Circuit

______________)
______________)
v.

* See Rule 3(c) for permissible ways of identifying appellants.

) Petition for Review
)
)

_________________________ hereby petition the court for review of the Order of the __________________ Commission _________________ entered on _______________

____
Attorney for Petitioners
Address: ___________________________

(Amended by order adopted April 22, 1993, effective December 1, 1993, by order adopted March 27, 2003, effective December 1, 2003, and by order effective December 1, 2006.)

Form 4. Affidavit Accompanying Motion for Permission to Appeal In Forma Pauperis.

Motion and Affidavit for Permission to Appeal In Forma Pauperis

v.

Appeal No. ______________
District Court or Agency No. ______________

Affidavit in Support of Motion	**Instructions**
I swear or affirm under penalty of perjury that, because of my poverty, I cannot prepay the docket fees of my appeal or post a bond for them. I believe I am entitled to redress. I swear or affirm under penalty of perjury under United States laws that my answers on this form are true and correct. (28 U.S.C. § 1746; 18 U.S.C. § 1621.)	Complete all questions in this application and then sign it. Do not leave any blanks: if the answer to a question is "0," "none," or "not applicable (N/A)," write in that response. If you need more space to answer a question or to explain your answer, attach a separate sheet of paper identified with your name, your case's docket number, and the question number.
Signed: ______________________________	Date: ______________________________

My issues on appeal are:

1. *For both you and your spouse estimate the average amount of money received from each of the following sources during the past 12 months. Adjust any amount that was received weekly, biweekly, quarterly, semiannually, or annually to show the monthly rate. Use gross amounts, that is, amounts before any deductions for taxes or otherwise.*

Income source	**Average monthly amount during the past 12 months**		**Amount expected next month**	
	You	**Spouse**	**You**	**Spouse**
Employment	$______	$______	$______	$______
Self-employment	$______	$______	$______	$______
Income from real property (such as rental income)	$______	$______	$______	$______
Interest and dividends	$______	$______	$______	$______
Gifts	$______	$______	$______	$______
Alimony	$______	$______	$______	$______

Child support	$_____	$_____	$_____	$_____
Retirement (such as social security, pensions, annuities, insurance	$_____	$_____	$_____	$_____
Disability (such as social security, insurance payments)	$_____	$_____	$_____	$_____
Unemployment payments	$_____	$_____	$_____	$_____
Public-assistance (such as welfare)	$_____	$_____	$_____	$_____
Other (specify):_____	$_____	$_____	$_____	$_____
Total monthly income:	$_____	$_____	$_____	$_____

2. *List your employment history, most recent employer first. (Gross monthly pay is before taxes or other deductions.)*

Employer	**Address**	**Dates of employment**	**Gross monthly pay**
_____	_____	_____	_____
_____	_____	_____	_____
_____	_____	_____	_____

3. *List your spouse's employment history, most recent employer first. (Gross monthly pay is before taxes or other deductions.)*

Employer	**Address**	**Dates of employment**	**Gross monthly pay**
_____	_____	_____	_____
_____	_____	_____	_____
_____	_____	_____	_____

4. *How much cash do you and your spouse have?* $_____

Below, state any money you or your spouse have in bank accounts or in any other financial institution.

Financial institution	**Type of account**	**Amount you have**	**Amount your spouse has**
_____	_____	$_____	$_____
_____	_____	$_____	$_____
_____	_____	$_____	$_____

If you are a prisoner, you must attach a statement certified by the appropriate institutional officer showing all receipts, expenditures, and balances during the last six months in your institutional accounts. If you have multiple accounts, perhaps because you have been in multiple institutions, attach one certified statement of each account.

5. *List the assets, and their values, which you own or your spouse owns. Do not list clothing and ordinary household furnishings.*

Home (Value)	Other real estate (Value)	Motor vehicle #1 (Value)
______________	______________	Make & year: ______________
______________	______________	Model: ______________
______________	______________	Registration #: ______________

Motor vehicle #2 (Value)	Other assets (Value)	Other assets (Value)
Make & year: ______________	______________	______________
Model: ______________	______________	______________
Registration #: ______________	______________	______________

6. *State every person, business, or organization owing you or your spouse money, and the amount owed.*

Person owing you or your spouse money	Amount owed to you	Amount owed to your spouse
______________	______________	______________
______________	______________	______________
______________	______________	______________

7. *State the persons who rely on you or your spouse for support.*

Name	Relationship	Age
______________	______________	______________
______________	______________	______________
______________	______________	______________

8. *Estimate the average monthly expenses of you and your family. Show separately the amounts paid by your spouse. Adjust any payments that are made weekly, biweekly, quarterly, semiannually, or annually to show the monthly rate.*

	You	Your Spouse
Rent or home-mortgage payment (include lot rented for mobile home)	$______	$______
Are real-estate taxes included? ☐ Yes ☐ No		
Is property insurance included? ☐ Yes ☐ No		
Utilities (electricity, heating fuel, water, sewer, and telephone)	$______	$______
Home maintenance (repairs and upkeep)	$______	$______
Food	$______	$______
Clothing	$______	$______
Laundry and dry-cleaning	$______	$______

Medical and dental expenses	$______	$______
Transportation (not including motor vehicle payments)	$______	$______
Recreation, entertainment, newspapers, magazines, etc.	$______	$______
Insurance (not deducted from wages or included in Mortgage payments)	$______	$______
Homeowner's or renter's	$______	$______
Life	$______	$______
Health	$______	$______
Motor Vehicle	$______	$______
Other: ______________	$______	$______
Taxes (not deducted from wages or included in Mortgage payments) (specify): ______________	$______	$______
Installment payments		
Motor Vehicle	$______	$______
Credit card (name): ______________	$______	$______
Department Store (name): ______________	$______	$______
Other: ______________	$______	$______
Alimony, maintenance, and support paid to others	$______	$______
Regular expenses for operation of business, profession, or farm (attach detailed statement)	$______	$______
Other (specify): ______________	$______	$______
Total monthly expenses:	$______	$______

9. Do you expect any major changes to your monthly income or expenses or in your assets or liabilities during the next 12 months?
□ Yes □ No If yes, describe on an attached sheet.

10. Have you paid — or will you be paying — an attorney any money for services in connection with this case, including the completion of this form? □Yes □ No

If yes, how much? $_________

If yes, state the attorney's name, address, and telephone number:

____

____

____

11. Have you paid — or will you be paying — anyone other than an attorney (such as a paralegal or a typist) any money for services in connection with this case, including the completion of this form?
□Yes □ No

If yes, how much? $_________

If yes, state the person's name, address, and telephone number:

____

____

____

12. Provide any other information that will help explain why you cannot pay the docket fees for your appeal.

13. State the address of your legal residence.

____

____

Your daytime phone number: (___) ____________

Your age: ______ Your years of schooling: ______

Your social-security number: _______________

Form 5. Notice of Appeal to a Court of Appeals From a Judgment or Order of a District Court or a Bankruptcy Appellate Panel.

United States District Court for ____________ ________ District of ____________

In re ____________,
Debtor

)
File No. ________
v.)
)

Notice of Appeal to United States Court of Appeals
for the ________ Circuit

____________, the plaintiff [or defendant or other party] appeals to the United States Court of Appeals for the ________ Circuit from the final judgment [or order or decree] of the District Court for ____________, entered in this case on ________, 20____

[here describe the judgment, order, or decree] ____________

The parties to the judgment [or order or decree] appealed from and the names and addresses of their respective attorneys are as follows:

Dated ____________

Signed ____________ ____________

Attorney for Appellant Attorney for Appellant

Address: Address:

(Added by order adopted April 25, 1989, effective December 1, 1989, amended by order adopted March 27, 2003, effective December 1, 2003, and by order effective December 1, 2006.)

Form 6. Certificate of Compliance With Rule 32(a).

Certificate of Compliance With Type-Volume Limitation,
Typeface Requirements, and Type Style Requirements

1. This brief complies with the type-volume limitation of Fed. R. App. P. 32(a)(7)(B) because:

☐ this brief contains [*state the number of*] words, excluding the parts of the brief exempted by Fed. R. App. P. 32(a)(7)(B)(iii); *or*

☐ this brief uses a monospaced typeface and contains [*state the number of*] lines of text, excluding the parts of the brief exempted by Fed. R. App. P. 32(a)(7)(B)(iii).

2. This brief complies with the typeface requirements of Fed. R. App. P. 32(a)(5) and the type style requirements of Fed. R. App. P. 32(a)(6) because:

☐ this brief has been prepared in a proportionally spaced typeface using [*state name and version of word processing program*] in [*state font size and name of type style*], *or*

☐ this brief has been prepared in a monospaced typeface using [*state name and version of word processing program*] with [*state number of characters per inch and name of type style*].

(s) ____________

____

Attorney for ____________

Dated: ____________

(Added by order adopted April 29, 2002, effective December 1, 2002.)

Form A. Disclosure of Corporate Affiliations and Other Entities with a Direct Financial Interest in Litigation.

ONLY ONE FORM NEED BE COMPLETED FOR A PARTY EVEN IF THE PARTY IS REPRESENTED BY MORE THAN ONE ATTORNEY. DISCLOSURES MUST BE FILED ON BEHALF OF INDIVIDUAL PARTIES AS WELL AS CORPORATE PARTIES. DISCLOSURES ARE REQUIRED FROM

AMICUS CURIAE ONLY IF AMICUS IS A CORPORATION. COUNSEL HAS A CONTINUING DUTY TO UPDATE THIS INFORMATION. PLEASE FILE AN ORIGINAL AND THREE COPIES OF THIS FORM.

Pursuant to FRAP 26.1 and Local Rule 26.1,
____________________ who is __________________________________,
(name of party/amicus) (appellant/appellee)
makes the following disclosure:

1. Is party/amicus a publicly held corporation or other publicly held entity?

   ( ) YES ( ) NO

2. Does party/amicus have any parent corporations?

   ( ) YES ( ) NO

   If yes, identify all parent corporations, including grandparent and great-grandparent corporations:

3. Is 10% or more of the stock of a party/amicus owned by a publicly held corporation or other publicly held entity?

   ( ) YES ( ) NO

   If yes, identify all such owners:

4. Is there any other publicly held corporation or other publicly held entity that has a direct financial interest in the outcome of the litigation (Local Rule 26.1(b))?

   ( ) YES ( ) NO

   If yes, identify entity and nature interest:

5. Is party a trade association?

   ( ) YES ( ) NO

   If yes, identify all members of the association, their parent corporations, and any publicly held companies that own 10% or more of a member's stock:

____________________________________ ________________
(Signature) (date)

(Amended June 25, 1993.)

Form B. Appearance of Counsel.
No. __________.

THE CLERK WILL ENTER MY APPEARANCE AS COUNSEL ON BEHALF OF:
____ as the
(party name)

[ ] appellant(s) [ ] appellee(s) [ ] amicus curiae
[ ] petitioner(s) [ ] respondent(s) [ ] intervenor(s)

____
(Signature)

Area Code & Phone No.: __________

[ ] IF YOU WILL NOT BE PARTICIPATING IN THIS CASE, PLEASE CHECK HERE AND RETURN, AND GIVE US THE NAME AND ADDRESS OF ANOTHER ATTORNEY, IF ANY, WHO WILL PROVIDE APPELLATE REPRESENTATION.

____
____

NOTE: Must be signed by an Attorney admitted to practice before the United States Court of Appeals for the Fourth Circuit pursuant to Local Rule 46(b). Individual and

not firm names must be signed.
If your name has changed since you were admitted to the Fourth Circuit Bar PLEASE show the name under which you were admitted.

Form C. Certificate of Death Penalty Case — Fourth Circuit Local Rule 22(b).

CERTIFICATE OF DEATH PENALTY CASE
Fourth Circuit Local Rule 22(b)

U.S. District Court for the	
Case Caption:	
Counsel for Petitioner/Defendant (name, address, phone)	Counsel for Respondent/Plaintiff: (name, address, phone)
Institution of Incarceration:	
Explanation of Emergency Nature of Proceedings	
Has petitioner/defendant previously filed cases in federal court? [ ] No [ ] Yes (give court, caption, number, filing date, disposition and disposition date)	
Does petitioner/defendant have cases pending in other courts? [ ] No [ ] Yes (give court, caption, number, filing date and status)	
I hereby certify under penalty of perjury that the petitioner/defendant is presently under a sentence of death and that the information provided on this form is currently accurate and correct.	
Date	Signature

Note: The Court of Appeals will periodically request case status reports. Counsel is under a continuing affirmative obligation to immediately notify the Fourth Circuit of any changes or additions to the information contained on this form. In cases with a pending execution date, counsel must provide the Court of Appeals with four copies of all documents filed in the U.S. District Court and any pertinent state court materials.

Form D. UNITED STATES COURT OF APPEALS FOR THE FOURTH CIRCUIT APPLICATION FOR ADMISSION TO THE BAR.

UNITED STATES COURT OF APPEALS
FOR THE FOURTH CIRCUIT

APPLICATION FOR ADMISSION TO THE BAR

Instructions: Only attorneys admitted to the bar of the United States Court of Appeals for the Fourth Circuit may practice before the Court. An attorney who has been admitted to practice before the Supreme Court of the United States, the highest court of a state, another United States Court of Appeals, or a United States District Court (including the District Courts for Guam, the Northern Mariana Islands, and the Virgin Islands), and who is of good moral and professional character, may become a member of the bar by:

- providing the information requested below;
- having a member of the bar of the Court move admission by signing the Motion for Admission;
- swearing or affirming the Oath before the clerk, a deputy clerk, a notary public or the Court (admission by personal appearance before the Court is usually reserved for ceremonial occasions);
- paying the admission fee of $20.00 by check made payable to "Clerk, United States Court of Appeals." (The fee is waived for attorneys appointed to represent a party in forma pauperis, law clerks to judges of the Court, and counsel for the United States or any agency thereof who have a case pending before the Court. If a fee waiver is sought, add the Fourth Circuit docket number here: __________); and
- mailing or delivering the completed form and check to the Clerk of the United States Court of Appeals, 1100 E. Main Street, Suite 501, Richmond, VA 23219-3517.

NAME (present practicing name):

Last ______________________________

First ______________________________ Middle ______________________________

Generation (Jr., Sr., II, III, etc.) __________ Title (if applicable) ______________________________

Prefix (Mr., Mrs., Miss, Ms., Professor, etc.) ____________________

STATE OF RESIDENCE (for use on your certificate): ____________________

FIRM: ____

BUSINESS ADDRESS: ____
____
____

City ______________________________

State ________ Zip Code ________-______ Phone (____) ______-______ Ext. ________

Fax (____) ______-______ E-mail ______________________________

DATE OF BIRTH: ____-____-____
Month Day Year

PLEASE COMPLETE PAGE TWO OF THIS FORM

STATE AND FEDERAL COURT ADMISSIONS (attach additional page if more space is needed):

	Status (active, inactive)	Approx. Date Admitted (if available)
1.		
2.		
3.		

AVAILABILITY FOR COURT-APPOINTMENT:

Do you want to be considered for court appointments Yes [ ] No [ ]

If yes, specify case types below:

1. Prisoner civil rights cases [ ]	4. Habeas corpus cases [ ]
2. Capital punishment cases [ ]	5. Indigent civil cases [ ]
3. Federal criminal appeals [ ]	6. All case types [ ]

If yes, state whether you are fluent in a language other than English: Yes [ ] ________________ No [ ]
language(s)

OATH

I, ______________________, do solemnly swear (or affirm) that I will conduct myself as an attorney and counselor of this court, uprightly and according to law; and that I will support the Constitution of the United States.

____
(signature)

Subscribed and sworn to before me this ________ day of ____________, 20____

Notary commission expires:

______________________ (date) ______________________ (signature and title)

MOTION FOR ADMISSION

I, ______________________, a member of the Bar of the United States Court of Appeals for the Fourth Circuit, hereby move the admission of the applicant to the Bar of the Court. I am satisfied that the applicant possesses the qualifications provided by Federal Rule of Appellate Procedure 46(a). [This rule states, in part: "An attorney is eligible for admission to the bar of a court of appeals if that attorney is of good moral and professional character and is admitted to practice before the Supreme Court of the United States, the highest court of a state, or another United States court of appeals, or a United States district court . . . ."]

______________________ (date) ______________________ (signature and title)

FOURTH CIRCUIT E-MAIL NOTICING SYSTEM

Attorneys and pro se parties are encouraged to register for the Fourth Circuit's E-Mail Noticing System (FENS). With FENS, you will receive immediate service of court orders, opinions, notices, and correspondence at your preferred e-mail address, thereby receiving notice of court action several days earlier than you would through U.S. Mail.

FENS works automatically. When an order, opinion, or notice is entered on the docket, the system calls up your previously entered e-mail address. You receive your electronic copy of the document shortly after its entry on the docket.

The e-mail address you provide for FENS will be used to serve you with court documents in all Fourth Circuit cases in which you are counsel of record or in which you are representing yourself. FENS can accommodate only one address per person for service. You must notify the clerk's office immediately of any change in your e-mail address.

Service via e-mail is fast and enables you to save and forward documents in electronic form. To ensure that court documents are pulled and distributed when you are out of the office, you may wish to provide a general office or shared e-mail address. Please ensure that your automation staff has been notified to set filtering software on computers and servers so that it does not block delivery of e-mail from casenotify@ca4.uscourts.gov, the e-mail address used by FENS. Otherwise, e-mail could be discarded as "spam" without notice to either you or the court. If the court does receive notice of a failed e-mail transmission, the deputy who sent the e-mail will call and verify the e-mail address and condition of equipment and ensure that you receive a copy of the document. Documents are sent as e-mail attachments in Adobe Acrobat PDF format only. Therefore, the only software required to open and print documents is a current version of Adobe Acrobat Reader, available as a free download from the Adobe site: http://www.adobe.com/products/acrobat/readstep2.html. Since you will be relying on the internet for notice of court action, it is also essential to have anti-virus software in place that automatically updates your virus definitions on a daily basis.

Generally, electronic service of a court document will be the only service provided. Although most court documents are issued through FENS, occasions may arise when FENS is not used, in which instance the document will be sent outside the FENS system. The clerk's office will provide a paper copy of any document upon request.

I hope you will consider participating in FENS; the system will provide you with earlier notice of action by the court in your cases. Please contact Suzanne Ruble or Beth Walton at 804-916-2708 with any questions about FENS.

Patricia Connor
Clerk, Fourth Circuit Court of Appeals

AGREEMENT TO PARTICIPATE IN ELECTRONIC NOTICING SYSTEM

Do Not Return this Form More than Once. It Applies to All Cases in this Court.
Do Not Return This Form if You Wish to Receive Documents Via U.S. Mail.

To participate in FENS, simply complete this form and provide the e-mail address at which you wish to receive service of documents from the court. A separate form must be completed for each attorney or party participating. By signing the form, you consent to service of court documents by e-mail pursuant to FRAP 25(c)(1)(D) in all cases in which you are counsel of record or are representing yourself, with the understanding that electronic service will be the only form of service you receive. Consent to service of court documents by e-mail does not constitute consent to service of a party's documents by e-mail, though the parties may enter into such an agreement separately.

I consent to electronic service of orders, correspondence, opinions, and other documents issued by the United States Court of Appeals for the Fourth Circuit.

____
Signature

____
Name (printed or typed)

____
Firm Name (if applicable)

____
Address

____
City, State, Zip Code

____
Voice Phone

____
E-mail address (print or type)

Please send the completed form to **Clerk, U.S. Court of Appeals for the Fourth Circuit, 1100 East Main St., Suite 501, Richmond, VA 23219, or via fax to 804-916-2713** (fax number may be used only for FENS registration). We will register you in FENS and ask you to confirm receipt of a test message issued through FENS.

Form E.

DOCKETING STATEMENT — TAX COURT INSTRUCTIONS

1. Counsel for appellant must file two copies of a docketing statement with all attachments for every case appealed or cross-appealed to the court of appeals within fourteen days of the docketing of the appeal. The docketing statement must be received by the clerk's office within the fourteen days allowed to be deemed timely filed. Copies must be served on the opposing party or parties.
2. The attorney filing the notice of appeal is responsible for filing the docketing statement, even if different counsel will handle the appeal. In the case of multiple appellants represented by separate counsel, the parties must confer and decide who will file the docketing statement. Appellants proceeding pro se may file a docketing statement, but are not required to do so.
3. The docketing statement is not a brief and should not contain argument or motions. The nature of proceedings and relief sought should be stated succinctly. The issues should be expressed in terms and circumstances of the case but without unnecessary detail. Conclusory statements such as "the judgment of the tax court is not supported by the law or facts" are unacceptable. Although a party will not be precluded from raising additional issues, counsel should make every effort to include in the docketing statement all of the issues that will be presented to the Court. The docketing statement will be used in any mediation conducted under Fourth Circuit Local Rule 33. If counsel in a case in which all parties are represented by counsel believes a mediation conference would be beneficial, counsel may make a confidential request for mediation by contacting the Office of the Circuit Mediator directly at (843) 521-4022.
4. Counsel's failure to file the docketing statement within the time set forth above will cause the Court to initiate the process for dismissal of the appeal under Fourth Circuit Local Rule 45.
5. If an opposing party concludes that the docketing statement is in any way inaccurate, incomplete, or misleading, that party should file two copies of any additions or corrections to the docketing statement with the clerk's office within seven (7) days of service of the docketing statement, with copies to all other parties.

DOCKETING STATEMENT — TAX COURT

Caption of Case 4CCA Docket No. (IF KNOWN) ______________

Tax Court Docket Number ______________ Judge ______________

Statute or other authority establishing jurisdiction in the:

Tax Court ______________

Court of Appeals ______________

A. Timeliness of Appeal

1. Date of entry of judgment or order appealed from ______________

2. Date this notice of appeal filed ______________ If cross appeal, date first notice of appeal filed ______________

B. Finality of Order or Judgment

1. Is the order or judgment appealed from a final decision on the merits? yes ( ) no ( )

2. If no, Is the order appealed from a collateral or interlocutory order reviewable under any exception to the finality rule? yes ( ) no ( )

If yes, explain

____

C. Has this case previously been appealed? yes ( ) no ( )

If yes, give the case name, docket number, and disposition of each prior appeal on a separate sheet.

D. Are any related cases or cases raising related issues pending in this Court, the Tax Court or the Supreme Court? yes ( ) no ( )

If yes, cite the case and manner in which it is related on a separate sheet. If abeyance, consolidation, or in seriatim argument is warranted, counsel must file a separate motion seeking such relief.

If related case is pending in this Court, has it been accepted for mediation by the Office of the Circuit Mediator? yes ( ) no ( )

E. State the nature of the suit, the relief sought and the outcome below. Attach additional page if necessary.

F. Issues to be raised on appeal. Attach additional page if necessary.

G. Is settlement being discussed? yes ( ) no ( )

H. Is expedited disposition of this case necessary? yes ( ) no ( )

If yes, you must file an appropriate motion.

Is oral argument necessary? yes ( ) no ( )

I. List each adverse party to the appeal. Attach additional sheets if necessary. If no attorney, give address and telephone number of the adverse party.

Adverse party______________

Attorney______________

Address______________

____

Telephone______________

E-mail______________

J. List name(s) and address(es) of appellant(s) who filed this notice of appeal and appellant's counsel. Attach additional page if necessary.

Appellant(s) Name______________

Address______________

____

Telephone______________

E-mail______________

Attorney's Name______________

Firm______________

Address______________

____

Telephone______________

E-mail______________

Will you be handling the appeal? yes ( ) no ( )

FRAP 12(b) provides that each attorney who files a notice of appeal must file with the clerk of the court of appeals a statement naming each party represented on appeal by that attorney. Any counsel, other than the attorney filing this form, who filed a notice of appeal must provide the requisite statement to be attached to this form.

Signature ______________________________
Date ______________________________

ATTACH:

1. ADDITIONAL PAGES, IF ANY, CONTAINING EXTENDED ANSWERS TO QUESTIONS ON THIS FORM.
2. THE NOTICE OF APPEAL.
3. A COPY OF THE ORDER OR JUDGMENT FROM WHICH THE APPEAL IS TAKEN.
4. ANY OPINION OR FINDINGS.
5. A CERTIFICATE OF SERVICE.

Form F.

DOCKETING STATEMENT — AGENCY INSTRUCTIONS

1. Counsel for the petitioner or applicant must file two copies of a docketing statement for any petition for review, cross petition, application for enforcement, or cross application within fourteen days of docketing of the petition or application. The docketing statement must be received by the clerk's office within the fourteen days allowed to be deemed timely filed. Copies must be served on the opposing party or parties. Petitioners proceeding pro se may file a docketing statement but are not required to do so.
2. Only one docketing statement shall be filed for each petition or application. If there are multiple petitioners or applicants, the parties should confer and decide who will file the docketing statement. A list of all names and addresses of parties, their attorneys and attorneys' names and addresses, and a certification that all parties have conferred and concurred in the filing must be attached to the docketing statement.
3. The docketing statement is not a brief and should not contain argument or motions. The nature of proceedings and relief sought should be stated succinctly. The issues should be expressed in terms and circumstances of the case but without unnecessary detail. Conclusory statements such as "the findings of the administrative law judge are not supported by the law or facts" are unacceptable. Although a party will not be precluded from raising additional issues, counsel should make every effort to include in the docketing statement all of the issues that will be presented to the Court. The docketing statement will be used in any mediation conducted under Fourth Circuit Local Rule 33. If counsel in a case in which all parties are represented by counsel believes a mediation conference would be beneficial, counsel may make a confidential request for mediation by contacting the Office of the Circuit Mediator directly at (843) 521-4022.
4. Counsel's failure to file the docketing statement within the time set forth above will cause the Court to initate the process for dismissal under Fourth Circuit Local Rule 45.
5. If an opposing party concludes that the docketing statement is in any way inaccurate, incomplete, or misleading, that party should file two copies of any additions or corrections to the docketing statement with the clerk's office within seven (7) days of service of the docketing statement, with copies to all other parties.

DOCKETING STATEMENT — AGENCY

Caption of Case 4CCA Docket No. (If Known) ____________

Type of Action

____ Application for Enforcement

____ Petition for Review

____ Cross Petition

Name of Agency____________

Administrative Law Judge____________

Agency Number____________

Statute or other authority establishing jurisdiction in the Court of Appeals______

A. Timeliness

1. Date of entry of order____________
2. Time allowed for review or enforcement ____________

   Authority____________

B. Finality

1. Tribunal or board issuing order or regulation____________
2. Is the order or judgment appealed from a final decision on the merits? yes [ ] no [ ]
3. If no, is the order appealed from a collateral or interlocutory order reviewable under any exception to the finality rule? yes [ ] no [ ]

   If yes, explain ____________

C. If INS case, is petitioner subject to deportation while this petition is pending? yes [ ] no [ ]

If yes, do you intend to file a motion to stay deportation? yes [ ] no [ ]

D. Has this case been before the Court previously? yes [ ] no [ ]

If yes, give case name, docket number, and disposition of each prior appeal on a separate sheet.

E. Is there any case now pending or about to be brought before this Court, any other court or administrative agency, or the Supreme Court which either arises from the same case or controversy or involves substantially related issues? yes [ ] no [ ]

If yes, cite the case and manner in which it is related on a separate sheet. If abeyance, consolidation, or in seriatim argument is warranted, counsel must file a separate motion seeking such relief.

If related case is pending in this Court, has it been accepted for mediation by the Office of the Circuit Mediator? yes [ ] no [ ]

F. State the nature of the proceeding, the relief sought, and the outcome below. Attach additional page if necessary.

G. Issues to be raised on petition or application. Attach additional page if necessary.

H. Is settlement being discussed? yes [ ] no [ ]

I. Is expedited disposition of this case necessary? yes [ ] no [ ]

If yes, you must file an appropriate motion.

Is oral argument necessary? yes [ ] no [ ]

J. List each adverse party to this action. Attach additional sheets if necessary. If no attorney, give address and telephone number of the adverse party.

Adverse party____________

Attorney____________

Address____________

Telephone____________

E-mail____________

K. Petitioner's or Applicant's Name____________

Address____________

Telephone____________

E-mail____________

L. Attorney or pro se litigant filing this docketing statement.

Will you be handling the appeal? yes [ ] no [ ]

Name____________

Attorney [ ] Pro Se [ ]

Firm____________

Address____________

Telephone______________________________
E-mail______________________________
If this is a joint statement by multiple petitioners or applicants, add the names and addresses of other petitioners or applicants and their counsel on an additional sheet, accompanied by a certification that all petitioners or applicants concur in this filing.

Signature________________________
Date________________________

EACH COPY OF THE DOCKETING STATEMENT SERVED OR FILED SHALL HAVE ATTACHED TO IT COPIES OF:

(1) THE APPLICATION FOR ENFORCEMENT, OR PETITION FOR REVIEW;

(2) THE DOCKET SHEET OF THE AGENCY FROM WHICH THE APPEAL IS TAKEN;

(3) THE JUDGMENT OR ORDER SOUGHT TO BE REVIEWED AND ANY OPINION OR FINDING;

(4) ANY OPINION, FINDINGS, OR RECOMMENDATION OF AN ADMINISTRATIVE LAW JUDGE UNDERLYING THE ORDER AT ISSUE;

(5) ANY TRANSCRIPT ORDER (WITH ATTACHMENTS, IF ANY); AND

(6) A CERTIFICATE OF SERVICE FOR THIS DOCKETING STATEMENT.

Form G.

DOCKETING STATEMENT INSTRUCTIONS

1. Counsel for appellant must file two copies of a docketing statement with all attachments within fourteen days of filing the notice of appeal for every case appealed or cross-appealed to the court of appeals. The docketing statement must be received by the court of appeals clerk's office within the fourteen days allowed to be deemed timely filed. Copies must be served on the opposing party or parties.
2. The attorney filing the notice of appeal is responsible for filing the docketing statement, even if different counsel will handle the appeal. In the case of multiple appellants represented by separate counsel, the parties must confer and decide who will file the docketing statement. Appellants proceeding pro se may file a docketing statement, but are not required to do so.
3. The docketing statement is not a brief but will be used by the circuit mediator for pre-briefing review of civil cases in which all parties are represented by counsel, and in mediation conducted in such cases under Fourth Circuit Local Rule 33. The nature of proceedings and relief sought should be stated succinctly. The issues should be framed with reference to the specific facts and circumstances of the case. Conclusory statements such as "the judgment of the trial court is not supported by the law or facts" are unacceptable. Although a party will not be precluded from raising additional issues in the brief, counsel should make every effort to include in the docketing statement all of the issues that will be presented to the Court. The docketing statement should not contain motions or other requests for interim relief. If counsel in a civil case believes a mediation conference would be beneficial, counsel may make a confidential request for mediation by contacting the Office of the Circuit Mediator directly at (843) 521-4022.
4. Counsel's failure to file the docketing statement within the time set forth will cause the Court to initiate the process for dismissal of the appeal under Fourth Circuit Local Rule 45.
5. If an opposing party concludes that the docketing statement is in any way inaccurate, incomplete, or misleading, that party should file two copies of any additions or corrections to the docketing statement with the clerk's office within seven days of service of the docketing statement, with copies to all other parties.
6. You must attach to this docketing statement:
   - ADDITIONAL PAGES CONTAINING EXTENDED ANSWERS TO QUESTIONS ON THIS FORM.
   - THE NOTICE OF APPEAL.
   - THE DISTRICT COURT DOCKET SHEET.
   - A COPY OF THE ORDER OR JUDGMENT FROM WHICH THE APPEAL IS TAKEN (in criminal cases, DO NOT attach any confidential sections of the Judgment Order, such as the Statement of Reasons).
   - ANY OPINION OR FINDINGS.
   - ANY OPINION, FINDINGS, OR RECOMMENDATION OF A UNITED STATES MAGISTRATE JUDGE, AN ADMINISTRATIVE LAW JUDGE, A SOCIAL SECURITY APPEALS COUNCIL, OR A BANKRUPTCY COURT.
   - A COPY OF THE TRANSCRIPT ORDER (WITH ATTACHMENTS), IF ANY.
   - A CERTIFICATE OF SERVICE FOR THIS DOCKETING STATEMENT.

UNITED STATES COURT OF APPEALS
FOR THE FOURTH CIRCUIT

United States Courthouse
1100 East Main Street, 5th Floor
Richmond, Virginia 23219-3517
(804) 916-2700

DOCKETING STATEMENT

Caption of Case 4CCA Docket No. (IF KNOWN) ____________
Type of Action

____ Civil
v. ____ Criminal/Prisoner
____ Cross Appeal

District____________________ Judge____________________
District Court Docket Number____________________
Statute or other authority establishing jurisdiction in the:
District Court____________________
Court of Appeals____________________

A. Timeliness of Appeal
1. Date of entry of judgment or order appealed from____________
2. Date this notice of appeal filed____________
If cross appeal, date first notice of appeal filed____________
3. Filing date of any post-judgment motion filed by any party which tolls time under FRAP 4(a)(4) or 4(b)____________
4. Date of entry of order deciding above post-judgment motion____________
5. Filing date of any motion to extend time under FRAP 4(a)(5), 4(a)(6) or 4(b)
____
Time extended to____________

B. Finality of Order or Judgment
1. Is the order or judgment appealed from a final decision on the merits? [ ] Yes [ ] No
2. If no,
a.) Did the district court order entry of judgment as to fewer than all claims or all parties pursuant to FRCP 54(b)? [ ] Yes [ ] No
b.) Is the order appealed from a collateral or interlocutory order reviewable under any exception to the finality rule? [ ] Yes [ ] No
If yes, explain
____

(Criminal only)
3. Has the defendant been convicted? [ ] Yes [ ] No
4. Has a sentence been imposed? [ ] Yes [ ] No Term ____________
5. Is the defendant incarcerated? [ ] Yes [ ] No

C. Has this case previously been appealed? [ ] Yes [ ] No
If yes, give the case name, docket number and disposition of each prior appeal on a separate page.

D. Based on your present knowledge:
Will this appeal involve a question of first impression?
[ ] Yes [ ] No
If yes, please explain briefly on a separate page.

E. Are any related cases or cases raising related issues pending in this Court, any district court of this circuit, or the Supreme Court? [ ] Yes [ ] No
If yes, cite the case and the manner in which it is related on a separate page. If abeyance, consolidation, or in seriatim argument is warranted, counsel must file a separate motion seeking such relief.
If a related case is pending in this Court, has it been accepted for mediation by the Office of the Circuit Mediator? [ ] Yes [ ] No

F. State the nature of the suit, the relief sought, and the outcome below. Attach additional page if necessary.

G. Issues to be raised on appeal. Attach additional page if necessary.

H. Does this appeal challenge the constitutionality of a federal or state statute in a case to which the United States or the affected state is not a party? [ ] Yes [ ] No
If yes, you must given written notice to the circuit clerk for certification of that fact to the United States Attorney General or the state attorney general.

I. Is settlement being discussed? [ ] Yes [ ] No

J. Is expedited disposition of this case necessary? [ ] Yes [ ]
If yes, you must file an appropriate motion.
Is oral argument necessary? [ ] Yes [ ] No

K. Were there any in-court proceedings below? [ ] Yes [ ] No
Is a transcript necessary for this appeal? [ ] Yes [ ] No
If yes, is transcript already on file with district court?
[ ] Yes [ ] No
If transcript is not already on file, attach copy of transcript order.

L. List each adverse party to the appeal. If no attorney, give address and telephone number of the adverse party. Attach additional pages if necessary.

1. Adverse party__________
Attorney__________
Address__________
____
Telephone__________
E-mail__________

2. Adverse party__________
Attorney__________
Address__________
____
Telephone__________
Email__________

M. If this case arises out of a bankruptcy proceeding, attach a copy of the caption of the case in the bankruptcy court showing the parties' status as debtor, creditor, trustee, plaintiff, defendant, etc.

M. List name(s) and address(es) of appellant(s) who filed this notice of appeal and appellant's counsel. Attach additional page if necessary.
Appellant(s) Name__________
Address __________
____
Telephone __________
E-mail __________
Attorney's Name __________
Firm __________
Address __________
____
Telephone __________
E-mail __________

Will you be handling the appeal? (In criminal cases counsel below will handle the appeal unless relieved by this court.)
[ ] Yes [ ] No

FRAP 12(b) provides that each attorney who files a notice of appeal must file with the clerk of the court of appeals a statement naming each party represented on appeal by that attorney. Any counsel, other than the attorney filing this form, who filed a notice of appeal must provide the requisite statement to be attached to this form.

Signature__________
Date__________

ATTACH:

1. ADDITIONAL PAGES CONTAINING EXTENDED ANSWERS TO QUESTIONS ON THIS FORM.
2. THE NOTICE OF APPEAL.
3. THE DISTRICT COURT DOCKET SHEET.
4. A COPY OF THE ORDER OR JUDGMENT FROM WHICH THE APPEAL IS TAKEN.
(DO NOT attach Statement of Reasons or other confidential sections of Criminal Judgment).

5. ANY OPINION OR FINDINGS.
6. ANY OPINION, FINDINGS, OR RECOMMENDATION OF A UNITED STATES MAGISTRATE JUDGE, AN ADMINISTRATIVE LAW JUDGE, A SOCIAL SECURITY APPEALS COUNCIL, OR A BANKRUPTCY COURT.
7. A COPY OF THE TRANSCRIPT ORDER (WITH ATTACHMENTS, IF ANY).
8. A CERTIFICATE OF SERVICE FOR THIS DOCKETING STATEMENT.

Index to Federal Rules of Appellate Procedure for the United States Court of Appeals, Local Rules and Internal Operating Procedures of the Fourth Circuit

A

ABEYANCE.
Holding case in abeyance, 4thCir Rule 12(d).

ACKNOWLEDGMENT OF RECEIPT OF ORDER FOR TRANSCRIPT.
Order acknowledgment, 4thCir Rule 11(a).

ADMINISTRATIVE AGENCIES.
Docketing statement, 4thCir Form F.
In forma pauperis proceedings.
Leave to proceed on appeal or review in forma pauperis in administrative agency proceedings, FRAP 24.
Review and enforcement of orders.
See ORDERS.

ADMISSION OF ATTORNEY TO BAR OF COURT.
Fee schedule, 4thCir Appx IV.

AMICUS CURIAE BRIEFS, FRAP 29.
Disclosure of corporate affiliations, 4thCir Rule 26.1.

ANNOUNCEMENT OF DECISION.
Circulation of opinions in argued cases, 4thCir IOP 36.2.

APPEALABILITY.
Certificates, 4thCir Rule 22(a).

APPEALS BY PRISONERS, 4thCir Rule 24.

APPEALS CONFERENCE, FRAP 33.

APPEALS FROM JUDGMENTS AND ORDERS OF DISTRICT COURTS.
Appeal as of right.
Civil cases, FRAP 4.
Consolidated appeals, FRAP 3.
Criminal cases, FRAP 4.
How taken, FRAP 3.
Joint appeals, FRAP 3.
Notice of appeal.
Content, FRAP 3.
Filing, FRAP 3.
Service, FRAP 3.
When taken, FRAP 4.
Appeals by permission under 28 USCS 1292(b).
Answer, FRAP 5.
Bonds, surety.
Cost bond, FRAP 5.
Copies of papers.
Number of copies, FRAP 5.
Cost bond, FRAP 5.
Form of papers, FRAP 5.
Grant of permission, FRAP 5.
Petition for permission to appeal, FRAP 5.
Content of petition, FRAP 5.
Records.
Filing of record, FRAP 5.

APPEALS FROM JUDGMENTS AND ORDERS OF DISTRICT COURTS —Cont'd
Appeals from orders respecting release entered prior to a judgment of conviction, FRAP 9.
Bankruptcy cases.
Court or bankruptcy panel exercising appellate jurisdiction, FRAP 6.
District court exercising original jurisdiction, FRAP 6.
Bonds, surety.
Appeals by permission under 28 USCS 1292(b).
Cost bond, FRAP 5.
Civil cases.
Bonds for cost on appeal in civil cases, FRAP 7.
Stay pending appeal.
Proceedings against sureties, FRAP 8.
Stay may be conditioned upon giving of bond, FRAP 8.
Civil cases.
Appeal as of right, FRAP 4.
Clerks of court.
Transmission of record.
Duty of clerk, FRAP 11.
Consolidated appeals.
Appeal as of right, FRAP 3.
Designated lead case, designating lead counsel, 4thCir Rule 12(b).
Contempt matters.
Incarceration of witness for refusal to testify or produce evidence.
Expedited appeal for resolution within statutory guidelines, 4thCir Rule 9(c).
Costs.
Appeals by permission under 28 USCS 1292(b).
Cost bond, FRAP 5.
Civil cases.
Bonds for cost on appeal in civil cases, FRAP 7.
Prisoner appeals, 4thCir Rule 24.
Criminal cases.
Appeal as of right, FRAP 4.
Release in criminal cases.
Appeal of order, FRAP 9.
Criteria for release, FRAP 9.
Stay pending appeal, FRAP 8.
Cross appeals.
Designated lead case, designating lead counsel, 4thCir Rule 12(b).
Docketing appeal, FRAP 12.
Docketing statements, filing, FRAP 3.
Injunction pending appeal, FRAP 8.
Stay or injunction pending appeal, 4thCir Rule 8.
Joint appeals.
Appeal as of right, FRAP 3.
Notice of appeal.
Appeal as of right, FRAP 3.
Civil cases, FRAP 4.

APPEALS FROM JUDGMENTS AND ORDERS OF DISTRICT COURTS —Cont'd
Notice of appeal —Cont'd
Appeal as of right —Cont'd
Criminal cases, FRAP 4.
Motions, effect on notice, FRAP 4.
Certificate of appealability, when treated as, 4thCir Rule 22(a).
Form, 4thCir Form 5.
Petition.
Appeals by permission under 28 USCS 1292(b), FRAP 5.
Record.
Appeals by permission under 28 USCS 1292(b).
Filing of record, FRAP 5.
Composition, FRAP 10.
Correction, FRAP 10.
Court of appeals.
Record for preliminary hearing in court of appeals, FRAP 11.
Filing, FRAP 12.
Modification, FRAP 10.
Preliminary hearing.
Record for preliminary hearing in court of appeals, FRAP 11.
Retention in district court.
By order of court, FRAP 11.
Stipulation of parties that parts of record be retained in district court, FRAP 11.
Temporary retention for use in preparing appellate papers, FRAP 11.
Statement of evidence or proceedings.
Agreed statement as the record on appeal, FRAP 10.
When no report made or transcript not available, FRAP 10.
Transcript of proceedings, FRAP 10.
Reporter to prepare and file, FRAP 11.
Transmission of record, FRAP 11.
Duty of clerk to transmit record, FRAP 11.
Reporter to prepare and file transcript, FRAP 11.
Retention in district court.
By order of court, FRAP 11.
Stipulation of parties that parts of record to be retained in district court, FRAP 11.
Temporary retention for use in preparing appellate papers, FRAP 11.
Temporary retention in district court for use in preparing appellate papers, FRAP 11.
Release in criminal cases.
Appeals from orders respecting release, FRAP 9.
Criteria for release, FRAP 9.
Pending appeal from a judgment of conviction, FRAP 9.
Stay pending appeal, 4thCir Rule 8.
Bonds, surety.
Proceedings against sureties, FRAP 8.
Stay may be conditioned upon giving of bond, FRAP 8.
Criminal cases, FRAP 8.
Motion for stay in court of appeals, FRAP 8.
Ordinarily must be sought in first instance in district court, FRAP 8.
Transcript of proceedings.
Duty of appellant to order, FRAP 10.
Generally, FRAP 10.
Partial transcript.
Notice to appellee that partial transcript ordered, FRAP 10.

APPEALS FROM JUDGMENTS AND ORDERS OF DISTRICT COURTS —Cont'd
Transcript of proceedings —Cont'd
Unavailability.
Statement of evidence or proceedings when transcript unavailable, FRAP 10.
Transmission of district court order appealed from, 4thCir IOP 3.1.
Witness incarcerated for refusal to testify or produce evidence.
Expedited appeal for resolution within statutory guidelines, 4thCir Rule 9(c).

APPEARANCE OF COUNSEL, 4thCir Form B, 4thCir Rule 46(c).

APPENDIX.
Arrangement, FRAP 30.
Attorney sanctions for unnecessary appendix designations, 4thCir Rule 30(a).
Certificate of compliance type-volume, typeface and type style requirements, 4thCir Form 6.
Contents, FRAP 30.
Alternative method of designating content, FRAP 30.
Determination of contents, FRAP 30.
Copies.
Number of copies, 4thCir Rule 30(b).
Correction when not in form required, 4thCir Rule 32(c).
Costs, FRAP 30, 39.
Dispensing with appendix, 4thCir Rule 30(d).
Duty of appellant to file, FRAP 30.
En banc hearing.
Additional copies, 4thCir Rule 35.
Exhibits.
Reproduction of exhibit, FRAP 30.
Filing.
Time for filing, FRAP 30.
Forms, FRAP 32.
Illegible or not in form required.
Corrected copies, 4thCir Rule 32(c).
In forma pauperis proceedings.
Form, FRAP 24.
Length of appendix, 4thCir Rule 30(b).
Number of copies, FRAP 30.
Parties.
Responsibilities, 4thCir Rule 30(c).
Preparation.
Duty of appellant to prepare, FRAP 30.
Printing costs taxable as costs, rate, 4thCir Rule 39(a).
Record on appeal, FRAP 30.
Original record.
Hearing of appeal on original record without the necessity of an appendix, FRAP 30.
Reproduction, 4thCir Rule 32(a).
Responsibility of parties, 4thCir Rule 30(c).

APPLICABILITY OF RULES, FRAP 1, 2.

APPOINTMENT OF COUNSEL, 4thCir Rule 46(d).

ARGUMENT.
Counsel listed on brief.
Responsibilities of listed counsel, 4thCir Rule 28(c).
Motions, 4thCir Rule 27(a).
Oral argument, 4thCir Rule 34(a).
See ORAL ARGUMENT.

ARGUMENT —Cont'd
Pre-argument review and summary disposition of appeals, 4thCir Rule 34(a).

ARGUMENT CALENDAR.
Internet availability, 4thCir IOP 45.2.
Preparation, 4thCir Rule 34(c).
Removal of case, 4thCir Rule 34(c).

ATTACHMENTS TO BRIEFS, 4thCir Rule 28(b).

ATTORNEYS AT LAW.
Admission to bar of court of appeals, FRAP 46.
Application for admission, 4thCir Form D.
Admission to practice, 4thCir Rule 46(b).
Application for admission, 4thCir Form D.
Fee schedule, 4thCir Appx IV.
Appearance of counsel, 4thCir Form B, 4thCir Rule 46(c).
Appointment of counsel, 4thCir Rule 46(d).
Death penalty representation, 4thCir Appx VI.
Implementation of criminal justice act plan, FRAP Appx A.
Consolidated appeals.
Selecting lead counsel, 4thCir Rule 28(a).
Consolidated or cross appeals.
Designating lead counsel, 4thCir Rule 12(b).
Death penalty.
Representation standards, 4thCir Appx VI.
Death penalty representation, FRAP Appx B.
Disbarment, FRAP 46.
Disciplinary power of court over attorneys, FRAP 46.
Fees.
Appointed counsel, compensation, 4thCir Rule 46(d).
Expenses and attorneys' fees, 4thCir Rule 46(e).
Lead counsel.
Consolidated cases, selecting, 4thCir Rule 28(a).
Consolidated or cross appeals, designating, 4thCir Rule 12(b).
Pro se proceeding, 4thCir Rule 46(f).
Record on appeal.
Access of counsel to original record, 4thCir Rule 11(d).
Rules of disciplinary enforcement, 4thCir Rule 46(g).
Substitution of counsel, 4thCir Rule 46(c).
Suspension, FRAP 46.
Telephone number of counsel.
Indicated on brief covers, 4thCir Rule 32(c).
Withdrawal of counsel, 4thCir Rule 46(c).

AUDIO RECORDINGS.
Audio files of oral argument, 4thCir IOP 34.3, 4thCir Rule 34.

AUTHORITY.
Citation of additional authority, 4thCir Rule 28(e).

AUTHORIZATION.
Motion for authorization, 4thCir Rule 22(d).

B

BAD WEATHER.
Computing filing or service date, 4thCir Rule 26.

BANKRUPTCY APPEALS.
Manner of taking appeals, 4thCir IOP 6.1.

BILL OF COSTS.
Taxation of costs, 4thCir Rule 39(b).

BOARDS.
Forms.
Petition for review of order of board, 4thCir Form 3.
Review and enforcement of orders.
See ORDERS.

BONDS, SURETY.
Appeals from judgments and orders of district courts.
See APPEALS FROM JUDGMENTS AND ORDERS OF DISTRICT COURTS.

BRIEFING ORDERS.
Civil and criminal cases, 4thCir Rule 31(b).

BRIEFS.
Amicus curiae, FRAP 29.
Appellant brief, FRAP 28.
Appellee's brief, FRAP 28.
Appendices.
See APPENDIX.
Attachments to briefs, 4thCir Rule 28(b).
Certificate of compliance type-volume, typeface and type style requirements, 4thCir Form 6.
Citation of unpublished decisions, FRAP 32.1.
Consolidated brief, 4thCir Rule 28(d).
Consolidated cases and briefs, 4thCir Rule 28(a).
Copies.
Number of copies, 4thCir Rule 31(d).
Correction of brief not in form required, 4thCir Rule 32(c).
Costs, FRAP 39.
Criminal cases.
Shortened time for service and filing of briefs, 4thCir Rule 31(a).
Cross-appeals, FRAP 28.1.
En banc hearing.
Additional copies, 4thCir Rule 35.
Exceeding limits on length of brief.
Motion for permission to submit longer brief, 4thCir Rule 32(b).
Extraordinary writs, FRAP 21.
Filing.
Failure to file.
Consequence of failure to file, FRAP 31.
Number of copies to be filed, FRAP 31.
Time for filing, FRAP 31.
Form, FRAP 32.
Hearing panel.
Argument time, 4thCir Rule 34(d).
Illegible briefs.
Failure to comply with rules or standards, 4thCir Rule 32(c).
Informal briefs, 4thCir Rule 34(b).
In forma pauperis proceedings.
Form of briefs, FRAP 24.
Joint brief, 4thCir Rule 28(d).
Length, FRAP 28.
Short, concise briefs encourage, permission to exceed limits, 4thCir Rule 32(b).
Motion to for permission to submit longer brief, 4thCir Rule 32(b).
Motion to submit on brief, 4thCir Rule 34(e).
National labor relations board proceedings, FRAP 15.1.

BRIEFS —Cont'd
Number of copies, 4thCir Rule 31(d).
Oral argument.
Admission on briefs, FRAP 34.
Disposition without oral argument, 4thCir IOP 34.2.
Parties.
References in briefs to parties, FRAP 28.
Printing costs taxable as costs, rate, 4thCir Rule 39(a).
Record on appeal.
References in briefs to the record, FRAP 28.
Reply briefs, FRAP 28.
Reproduction, 4thCir Rule 32(a).
Retrieval from archives.
Fee schedule, 4thCir Appx IV.
Service.
Number of copies to be served, FRAP 31.
Time for service, FRAP 31.
Signature, requirement, FRAP 32.
Statement of facts, 4thCir Rule 28(f).
Statutes, rules, regulations, etc.
Reproduction, FRAP 28.
Supplemental authorities, FRAP 28.
Unpublished decisions.
Citation, FRAP 32.1.
Unpublished opinions, citing, 4thCir Rule 32.1.

C

CALENDAR, FRAP 45.
Argument calendar.
Assignments, 4thCir IOP 34.1.
Internet availability, 4thCir IOP 45.2.
Preparation, 4thCir Rule 34(c).

CAPITAL APPELLATE PANEL, 4thCir Appx E.

CAPITAL PUNISHMENT.
Certificate of death penalty case.
Form, 4thCir Form C.
Death penalty cases, 4thCir IOP 22.1, 4thCir Rule 22(b).
Forms.
Certificate of death penalty case, 4thCir Form C.
Petition for rehearing, 4thCir Rule 22(c).
Representation of defendants, FRAP Appx B.
Stay of execution.
Motion for stay, 4thCir Rule 22(b).

CARRIER.
Service by commercial carrier, FRAP 25.

CASE MANAGEMENT/ELECTRONIC CASE FILING SYSTEM (CM/ECF), 4thCir Appx V.

CERTIFICATE OF APPEALABILITY, 4thCir Rule 22(a).
Informal brief, 4thCir Rule 34(b).

CERTIFICATE OF CONFIDENTIALITY, 4thCir Rule 25(c).

CERTIFICATE OF SERVICE, 4thCir Rule 25(b).

CERTIFICATES.
Fee schedule, 4thCir Appx IV.

CERTIORARI.
CJA appellate and capital appellate panels.
Certiorari status form, 4thCir Appx VIII.
Petitions for writs, 4thCir IOP 41.2.

CIRCUIT COURT MEDIATION CONFERENCES, 4thCir Rule 33.

CITATION.
Additional authorities, 4thCir Rule 28(e).

CJA APPELLATE AND CAPITAL APPELLATE PANELS.
Certiorari status form, 4thCir Appxs IV, VIII.
Plan for composition and administration, 4thCir Appx VIII.

CLERKS OF COURT.
Calendar, FRAP 45.
Custody of records and papers, FRAP 45.
Docket, FRAP 45.
Duties, FRAP 45.
Noncontroversial orders granted by clerk, 4thCir Rule 27(b).
Notice of orders or judgments, FRAP 45.
Papers.
Custody of papers, FRAP 45.
Procedural orders acted on by clerk, 4thCir Rule 27(b).
Record on appeal.
Responsibility for preparation of record, 4thCir Rule 10.
Records, FRAP 45.

CLERK'S OFFICE.
Address, 4thCir IOP 45.1.
Hours, 4thCir IOP 45.1.
Location, 4thCir IOP 45.1.

CM/ECF SYSTEM, 4thCir Appx V.
Attachments and exhibits to motions, 4thCir Appx V Rule 6.
Consequences of electronic filing, 4thCir Appx V Rule 3.
Eligibility to use system, 4thCir Appx V Rule 2.
Entry of court-issued documents, 4thCir Appx V Rule 5.
Hyperlinks, 4thCir Appx V Rule 13.
Notice of court orders and judgments, 4thCir Appx V Rule 10.
Passwords, 4thCir Appx V Rule 2.
Public access, 4thCir Appx V Rule 12.
Registration, 4thCir Appx V Rule 2.
Retention of documents, requirements, 4thCir Appx V Rule 8.
Scope of electronic filing, 4thCir Appx V Rule 1.
Sealed documents, 4thCir Appx V Rule 7.
Service of documents by electronic means, 4thCir Appx V Rule 4.
Signatures, 4thCir Appx V Rule 9.
Technical failures, effect, 4thCir Appx V Rule 11.

COMMERCIAL CARRIER.
Service by, FRAP 25.

COMMISSIONS.
Forms.
Petition for review of order of commission, 4thCir Form 3.
Prehearing conference, FRAP 33.
Review and enforcement of orders.
See ORDERS.

COMPUTATION OF TIME, FRAP 26.

CONFERENCES.
Judicial conference, 4thCir IOP 47.1.
Mediation conferences, 4thCir Rule 33.
Opinion preparation assignments, 4thCir IOP 36.1.

CONFIDENTIALITY OF INFORMATION.
Certificate of confidentiality, 4thCir Rule 25(c).
Filing of confidential and sealed materials, 4thCir Rule 25(c).
Sealed records.
Motions to seal, 4thCir Rule 25(c).

CONSOLIDATED APPEALS, 4thCir Rule 12(b).
Designating lead case, designating lead counsel, 4thCir Rule 12(b).

CONSOLIDATED CASES AND BRIEFS, 4thCir Rule 28(a).

CONSTITUTIONAL LAW.
Cases involving constitutional questions where United States is not a party, FRAP 44.

CONTEMPT.
Recalcitrant witnesses, 4thCir Rule 9(c).

CONVICTIONS.
Notice of appeal.
Release after conviction and notice of appeal, 4thCir Rule 9(b).
Release prior to judgment of conviction, 4thCir Rule 9(a).

COPIES.
Appendix.
Number of copies, 4thCir Rule 30(b).
Fee schedule, 4thCir Appx IV.
Number of copies.
Appendix, 4thCir Rule 30(b).
Briefs, 4thCir Rule 31(d).
Unpublished opinions cited in briefs, 4thCir Rule 32.1.

CORPORATIONS.
Disclosure statements, FRAP 26.1.
Corporate affiliations, 4thCir Rule 26.1.
Form, 4thCir Form A.

CORRECTED COPIES.
Brief, appendix or other paper illegible or not in form required, 4thCir Rule 32(c).

COSTS.
Appeals from judgments and orders of district courts.
See APPEALS FROM JUDGMENTS AND ORDERS OF DISTRICT COURTS.
Appendices, FRAP 30, 39.
Bill of costs, 4thCir Rule 39(b), FRAP 39.
Briefs, FRAP 39.
Clerk to insert costs in mandate, FRAP 39.
Generally, FRAP 39.
Insertion of costs in mandate, FRAP 39.
Mandate.
Clerk to insert costs in mandate, FRAP 39.
Objections, FRAP 39.
Printing costs, 4thCir Rule 39(a), FRAP 39.
Printing costs of briefs and appendix.
Taxable as costs, rate, 4thCir Rule 39(a).
Prisoner appeals, 4thCir Rule 24.
Prisoner petitions for mandamus, prohibition or other extraordinary relief, 4thCir Rule 21(c).
Record on appeal.
Copies of record, FRAP 39.
Recovery in district court, 4thCir Rule 39(c).
Reproduction costs, 4thCir Rule 39.
Taxable in district courts, FRAP 39.

COSTS —Cont'd
To whom allowed, FRAP 39.
United States.
Costs for and against United States, FRAP 39.

COURT OF APPEALS.
Dismissal.
Voluntary dismissal in court of appeals, FRAP 42.
Rules by courts of appeals, FRAP 47.

COURT REPORTERS.
Sanctions for late delivery of transcripts, 4thCir IOP 11.1.

COURT SESSIONS, 4thCir Rule 34(c).

CRIME VICTIMS' RIGHTS.
Petition for writ of mandamus to enforce, 4thCir Rule 21(d).

CRIMINAL CASES.
Appointment of counsel, 4thCir Rule 46(d).
Briefs.
Shortened time for service and filing of briefs, 4thCir Rule 31(a).
Death penalty cases.
Petition for rehearing, 4thCir Rule 22(c).

CRIMINAL JUSTICE ACT.
CJA appellate and capital appellate panels.
Plan for composition and administration, 4thCir Appx VIII.

CROSS-APPEALS, FRAP 28.1.
Briefs, FRAP 28.1.
Designating lead case, designating lead counsel, 4thCir Rule 12(b).
Docketing statement, 4thCir Rule 3(b).
Identifying cross appeals, 4thCir Rule 12(b).
Oral argument, FRAP 34.

D

DAMAGES.
Frivolous appeal, FRAP 38.

DEATH PENALTY CASES.
Attorneys.
Representation standards, 4thCir Appx VI.
Expedited briefing schedule, 4thCir IOP 22.1.
Forms.
Certificate of death penalty case, 4thCir Form C.
Generally, 4thCir IOP 22.1, 4thCir Rule 22(b).
Petition for rehearing, 4thCir Rule 22(c).
Representation, 4thCir Appx VI.

DECISIONS.
Fee for decisions, 4thCir Appx IV.
Subscription fees, 4thCir Appx IV.

DEFAULT JUDGMENTS.
Review and enforcement of orders of administrative agencies, boards, commissions and officers, FRAP 15.

DETERMINATION OF CAUSES BY THE COURT EN BANC, FRAP 35.

DISCLOSURE STATEMENTS.
Corporations, FRAP 26.1.
Corporate affiliations, 4thCir Rule 26.1.
Form, 4thCir Form A.

DISMISSAL.
Failure to prosecute, 4thCir Rule 45.

DISMISSAL —Cont'd
In forma pauperis.
Leave to proceed on appeal in forma pauperis from district court to court of appeals, FRAP 24.
Voluntary dismissal, 4thCir Rule 42.
Court of appeals, FRAP 42.
District court, FRAP 42.

DISTRICT COURTS.
Appeals from judgments and orders of district courts.
See APPEALS FROM JUDGMENTS AND ORDERS OF DISTRICT COURTS.
Bankruptcy appeals, 4thCir IOP 6.1.
Indicative ruling by district court.
Relief barred by pending appeal, remand, FRAP 12.1.
In forma pauperis proceedings.
Leave to proceed on appeal in forma pauperis from district court to court of appeals, FRAP 24.
Orders.
Transmission of district court order, 4thCir IOP 3.1.

DOCKET, FRAP 45.
Appeals from judgments and orders of district courts.
Docketing appeal, FRAP 12.
Consolidated or cross appeals.
Designating lead case, 4thCir Rule 12(b).
Docketing statement, 4thCir Rule 3(b).
Agencies, 4thCir Form F.
Tax court, 4thCir Form E.
Fees, 4thCir Rule 3(a).
Review of agency order, 4thCir Rule 15(a).
Internet availability, 4thCir IOP 45.2.

DOCKETING STATEMENTS, 4thCir Form G.
Filing on appeal, FRAP 3.

E

E-FILING.
Case management/Electronic case filing system (CM/ECF system), 4thCir Appx V.

ELECTRONIC FILING, FRAP 25.
Case management/Electronic case filing system (CM/ECF), 4thCir Appx V.
Electronic availability case information, notice of, 4thCir Appx VII.
Electronic case filing system, 4thCir Rule 25(a).

ELECTRONIC SIGNATURES, FRAP 25.

EMAIL.
CM/ECF system, 4thCir Appx V.

EN BANC PROCEEDINGS.
Appendix.
Additional copies, 4thCir Rule 35.
Briefs.
Additional copies, 4thCir Rule 35.
Decision of causes heard or reheard en banc, 4thCir Rule 35.
Determination of causes by court en banc, FRAP 35.
Rehearings, 4thCir Rule 35.
Suggestion for rehearing en banc, 4thCir Rule 35.

ENTRY OF JUDGMENT, FRAP 36.

EXECUTION.
Motions for stay of execution, 4thCir Rule 22(b).

EXHIBITS.
Appendices.
Reproduction of exhibits in appendices, FRAP 30.
Documentary exhibits.
Included in record, 4thCir Rule 11(c).
Oral argument.
Removal of exhibits, FRAP 34.
Use of physical exhibits, FRAP 34.

EXPANDED CERTIFICATE OF APPEALABILITY, 4thCir Rule 22(a).

EXPEDITION OF APPEALS, 4thCir Rule 12(c).

EXPENSES.
Attorneys' fees and expenses, 4thCir Rule 46(e).

EXTENSION OF TIME, FRAP 26.
Notice of appeal, motion, FRAP 4.

EXTRAORDINARY WRITS, FRAP 21.
Case captions, 4thCir Rule 21(a).
Habeas corpus.
See HABEAS CORPUS.
Petitions for special writs, 4thCir Rule 21(b).

F

FAILURE TO PROSECUTE.
Dismissal for failure to prosecute, 4thCir Rule 45.

FAX FILING, 4thCir Rule 25(b).

FEDERAL STATUTE.
Constitutional challenge, notice, FRAP 44.

FEES.
Attorneys' fees and expenses, 4thCir Rule 46(e).
Docket fees, 4thCir Rule 3(a).
Review of agency order, 4thCir Rule 15(a).
Filing fees, 4thCir Rule 3(a).
Prisoner appeals, 4thCir Rule 24.
Prisoner petitions for mandamus, prohibition or other extraordinary relief, 4thCir Rule 21(c).
Schedule of fees, 4thCir Appx IV.

FILING.
Appendices.
Time for filing, FRAP 30.
Briefs, FRAP 31.
Briefs in criminal cases.
Shortened time for service and filing of briefs, 4thCir Rule 31(a).
Civil cases, 4thCir Rule 31(c).
CM/ECF system, 4thCir Appx V.
Confidential and sealed materials, 4thCir Rule 25(c).
Criminal cases, 4thCir Rule 31(c).
Documents generally, 4thCir Rule 25(b).
Electronic case filing system, 4thCir Rule 25(a).
Facsimile equipment, use, 4thCir Rule 25(b).
Fees, 4thCir Rule 3(a).
Generally, FRAP 25.
Petition for rehearing, FRAP 40.

FILING —Cont'd
Time.
Effect of holiday or bad weather, 4thCir Rule 26.

FORMS.
Agencies.
Petition for review of order of agency, 4thCir Form 3.
Appeals from judgments and orders of district courts.
Notice of appeal, 4thCir Form 5.
Appearance of counsel, 4thCir Form B.
Attorneys at law.
Application for admission to practice, 4thCir Form D.
Boards.
Petition for review of order of board, 4thCir Form 3.
Briefs.
Certificate of compliance type-volume, typeface and type style requirements, 4thCir Form 6.
Capital punishment.
Certificate of death penalty case, 4thCir Form C.
Commissions.
Petition for review of order of commission, 4thCir Form 3.
Corporations.
Disclosure of corporate affiliations, 4thCir Form A.
Death penalty cases.
Certificate of death penalty case, 4thCir Form C.
Electronic case filing system, 4thCir Rule 25(a).
In forma pauperis.
Affidavit to accompany motion for leave to appeal, 4thCir Form 4.
Briefs, appendices and other papers, FRAP 24.
Internet availability, 4thCir IOP 45.2.
Motions.
Form of papers, FRAP 27.
Notice of appeal.
Decision of United States tax court, 4thCir Form 2.
Judgment or order of bankruptcy appellate panel, 4thCir Form 5.
Judgment or order of district court, 4thCir Forms 1, 5.
Officer.
Petition for review of order of officer, 4thCir Form 3.
Papers generally, FRAP 32.
Petitions, FRAP 24.

FRIVOLOUS APPEALS.
Damages, FRAP 38.

G

GOVERNMENTAL BODIES AND OFFICIALS.
Review and enforcement of orders of administrative agencies.
See ORDERS.

H

HABEAS CORPUS.
Appealable cause.
Necessity of certificate of probable cause for appeal, FRAP 22.
Application for original writ, FRAP 22.

HABEAS CORPUS —Cont'd
Certificates of probable cause, 4thCir Rule 22(a).
Custody of prisoners in habeas corpus proceedings.
Detention or release of prisoner pending review of decision failing to release, FRAP 23.
Modification of initial order respecting custody, FRAP 23.
Release of prisoner pending review of decision ordering release, FRAP 23.
Transfer of custody pending review, FRAP 23.
Death penalty cases, 4thCir Rule 22(b).
Detention or release of prisoner pending review of decision failing to release, FRAP 23.
Informal brief, 4thCir Rule 34(b).
Release of prisoner pending review of decision ordering release, FRAP 23.

HOLIDAYS.
Computing filing or service date, 4thCir Rule 26.

I

ILLEGIBLE BRIEF, APPENDIX OR OTHER PAPER.
Certificate of compliance type-volume, typeface and type style requirements, 4thCir Form 6.
Corrected copies, 4thCir Rule 32(c).

INCLEMENT WEATHER.
Computing filing or service date, 4thCir Rule 26.

INDIGENT PERSONS.
Appointment of counsel, 4thCir Rule 46(d).
Death penalty representation, 4thCir Appx VI.
Law students.
Legal assistance to indigents by law students, 4thCir Rule 46(a).

INFORMAL BRIEF, 4thCir Rule 34(b).

IN FORMA PAUPERIS PROCEEDINGS.
Administrative agency proceedings.
Leave to proceed on appeal or review in forma pauperis in administrative agency proceedings, FRAP 24.
Appendices.
Form, FRAP 24.
Briefs.
Form of briefs, FRAP 24.
District court.
Leave to proceed on appeal in forma pauperis from district court to court of appeals, FRAP 24.
Forms.
Affidavit to accompany motion for leave to appeal, 4thCir Form 4.
Briefs, appendices and other papers, FRAP 24.
Leave to proceed on appeal in forma pauperis from district court to court of appeals, FRAP 24.
Leave to proceed on appeal or review in forma pauperis in administrative agency proceedings, FRAP 24.
Form, FRAP 24.

INJUNCTIONS.
Appeals from judgments and orders of district courts.
Injunction pending appeal, FRAP 8.
Stay or injunction pending appeal, 4thCir Rule 8.

INTEREST ON JUDGMENTS, FRAP 37.

INTERLOCUTORY ORDERS, 4thCir Rule 5.

INTERNAL OPERATING PROCEDURES.
Advisory committee, 4thCir Rule 47(b).
Procedure for adoption, 4thCir Rule 47(a).

INTERNET.
Audio files of oral argument, 4thCir IOP 34.3.
Public information of court available on Internet, 4thCir IOP 45.2.

INTERVENTION.
Motion to intervene, 4thCir Rule 12(e).
Notice of appearance, 4thCir Rule 12(e).
Review and enforcement of orders of administrative agencies, boards, commissions and officers, FRAP 15.

J

JUDGES, FRAP 21.
Single judges.
Applications to a single judge, 4thCir Rule 27(e).
Motions before single judge, 4thCir Rule 27(e).
Three judge panels.
See THREE JUDGE PANELS.

JUDGMENT OF CONVICTION.
Release prior to judgment of conviction, 4thCir Rule 9(a).

JUDGMENTS.
District courts.
Appeals from judgments.
See APPEALS FROM JUDGMENTS AND ORDERS OF DISTRICT COURTS.
Entry of judgment, FRAP 36.
Interest on judgments, FRAP 37.
Notice of judgments, FRAP 45.

JUDICIAL CONFERENCE, 4thCir IOP 47.1.
Membership, types of members, 4thCir IOP 47.2.

L

LAW STUDENTS.
Indigent persons.
Legal assistance to indigents by law students, 4thCir Rule 46(a).

LEAD CASE.
Consolidated or cross appeals, designating, 4thCir Rule 12(b).

LEAD COUNSEL.
Consolidated cases, selecting, 4thCir Rule 28(a).
Consolidated or cross appeals, designating, 4thCir Rule 12(b).
Unavailability.
Counsel listed on brief.
Deemed capable of arguing appeal in lead counsel's absence, 4thCir Rule 28(c).

LEGAL ASSISTANCE TO INDIGENTS BY LAW STUDENTS, 4thCir Rule 46(a).

LOCAL RULES.
Advisory committee, 4thCir Rule 47(b).
Procedure for adoption, 4thCir Rule 47(a).

M

MANDAMUS, FRAP 21.
Case captions, 4thCir Rule 21(a).
Crime victims' rights, 4thCir Rule 21(d).
Petitions for special writs, 4thCir Rule 21(b).

MANDATE.
Costs.
Clerk to insert costs in mandate, FRAP 39.
Motion for stay of the mandate, 4thCir Rule 41.
Stay of mandate.
Pending petition for certiorari, FRAP 41.
Suggestion of a party for hearing or rehearing en banc.
Suggestion does not stay mandate, FRAP 35.
What constitutes the mandate, 4thCir IOP 41.1.

MASTERS, FRAP 48.

MEDIATION CONFERENCES, 4thCir Rule 33.

MOTIONS.
Argument calendar.
Motions that would require rescheduling of hearing, requirements, 4thCir Rule 34(c).
Authorization.
Second or successive application for relief, 4thCir Rule 22(d).
Briefs.
Submitting the case on the brief, 4thCir Rule 34(e).
Content, 4thCir Rule 27(b), FRAP 27.
Determination of motions for procedural orders, FRAP 27.
Electronic case filing system, 4thCir Rule 25(a).
Emergency motions, 4thCir Rule 27(e).
Form, 4thCir Rule 27(c).
Form of papers, FRAP 27.
Generally, FRAP 27.
Number of copies, FRAP 27.
Papers.
Form of papers, FRAP 27.
Number of copies, FRAP 27.
Power of single judge to entertain motions, FRAP 27.
Remand.
Indicative ruling by district court on motion for relief barred by pending appeal, FRAP 12.1.
Reply, FRAP 27.
Court to await filing before reviewing motion, 4thCir Rule 27(d).
Response, 4thCir Rule 27(d), FRAP 27.
Signature, requirement, FRAP 32.
Single judge, 4thCir Rule 27(e).
Summary disposition, 4thCir Rule 27(f).

N

NATIONAL LABOR RELATIONS BOARD.
Briefs and oral arguments, FRAP 15.1.

NON-PARTIES.
Appeals by aggrieved non-parties in lower court, 4thCir Rule 12(a).

NOTICE.
Appeals from judgments and orders of district courts.
Appeal as of right, FRAP 3.
Civil cases, FRAP 4.
Criminal cases, FRAP 4.
Motions, effect on notice, FRAP 4.
Form, 4thCir Form 5.
Appearance as intervenor, 4thCir Rule 12(e).
Case information.
Electronic availability, 4thCir Appx VII.
CM/ECF system.
Notice of court orders and judgments, 4thCir Appx V Rule 10.
Constitutional challenge to federal or state statute, FRAP 44.
Oral argument, FRAP 34.
Orders or judgments, FRAP 45.
Release after conviction and notice of appeal, 4thCir Rule 9(b).

NOTICE OF APPEAL.
Appeals from judgments and orders of district court.
See APPEALS FROM JUDGMENTS AND ORDERS OF DISTRICT COURTS.
Forms.
Decision of United States tax court, 4thCir Form 2.
Judgment or order of bankruptcy appellate panel, 4thCir Form 5.
Judgment or order of district court, 4thCir Forms 1, 5.
Review and enforcement of orders of administrative agencies, boards, commissions and officers, FRAP 15.
Review of decisions of tax court, FRAP 13.

O

OPERATION OF RULES AND PROCEDURES.
Public information, 4thCir IOP 45.2.

OPINIONS.
Assignments, 4thCir IOP 36.1.
Circulation of opinions in argued cases, 4thCir IOP 36.2.
Citing unpublished opinions, 4thCir Rule 32.1.
CM/ECF system.
Notice of court orders and judgments, 4thCir Appx V Rule 10.
Fees for decisions, 4thCir Appx IV.
Internet availability, 4thCir IOP 45.2.
Publication of decisions, 4thCir Rule 36(a).
Public information.
Internet availability, 4thCir IOP 45.2.
Subscription fees, 4thCir Appx IV.
Summary opinions, 4thCir IOP 36.3.
Unpublished opinions, 4thCir Rule 36(b).
Citing, 4thCir Rule 32.1.

ORAL ARGUMENT.
Audio files of oral argument, 4thCir IOP 34.3, 4thCir Rule 34.
Briefs.
Submission on briefs, FRAP 34.
Content, FRAP 34.

ORAL ARGUMENT —Cont'd
Counsel listed on brief.
Deemed capable of arguing appeal in absence of lead counsel, 4thCir Rule 28(c).
Cross-appeals, FRAP 34.
Disposition of case without oral argument, 4thCir IOP 34.2.
Exhibits.
Removal, FRAP 34.
Use of physical exhibits at argument, FRAP 34.
Generally, 4thCir Rule 34(a), FRAP 34.
Local rule, FRAP 34.
National labor relations board proceedings, FRAP 15.1.
Nonappearance of parties, FRAP 34.
Notice of argument, FRAP 34.
Order of argument, FRAP 34.
Parties.
Nonappearance of parties, FRAP 34.
Postponement, FRAP 34.
Separate appeals, FRAP 34.
Statement regarding need for oral argument, 4thCir Rule 34(a).
Submission on briefs, FRAP 34.

ORDER ACKNOWLEDGMENT.
Receipt of order for transcript, 4thCir Rule 11(a).

ORDERS.
Administrative agencies.
Review and enforcement of orders. See within this heading, "Review and enforcement of orders of administrative agencies, boards, commissions and officers."
Boards and commissions.
Review and enforcement of orders. See within this heading, "Review and enforcement of orders of administrative agencies, boards, commissions and officers."
Briefing orders.
Civil and criminal cases, 4thCir Rule 31(b).
CM/ECF system.
Notice of court orders and judgments, 4thCir Appx V Rule 10.
District courts.
Appeals.
See APPEALS FROM JUDGMENTS AND ORDERS OF DISTRICT COURTS.
Transmission of district court order, 4thCir IOP 3.1.
Electronic case filing system, 4thCir Rule 25(a).
Interlocutory orders, 4thCir Rule 5.
Noncontroversial orders granted by clerk, 4thCir Rule 27(b).
Notice of orders, FRAP 45.
Officers.
Review and enforcement of orders. See within this heading, "Review and enforcement of orders of administrative agencies, boards, commissions and officers."
Petitions.
Review and enforcement of orders. See within this heading, "Review and enforcement of orders of administrative agencies, boards, commissions and officers."
Reports.
Review and enforcement of orders. See within this heading, "Review and enforcement of orders of administrative agencies, boards, commissions and officers."

ORDERS —Cont'd
Review and enforcement of orders of administrative agencies, boards, commissions and officers.
Answer, FRAP 15.
Applicability of other rules.
To review or enforcement, FRAP 20.
Application for enforcement, FRAP 15.
Cross-application for enforcement, FRAP 15.
Service, FRAP 15.
Cross-application for enforcement, FRAP 15.
Default, FRAP 15.
Docketing fee, 4thCir Rule 15(a).
How obtained, FRAP 15.
In forma pauperis proceedings.
Leave to proceed on appeal or review in forma pauperis in administrative agency proceedings, FRAP 24.
Intervention, FRAP 15.
Petition, FRAP 15.
Attachments to petition, 4thCir Rule 15(b).
Form, 4thCir Form 3.
Joint petition, FRAP 15.
Service, FRAP 15.
Record.
Admissions from record, FRAP 16.
Composition, FRAP 16.
Filing.
Agency to file, FRAP 17.
Notice of filing, FRAP 17.
Time for filing, FRAP 17.
What constitutes filing, FRAP 17.
Statements in record, FRAP 16.
Settlements of judgments enforcing orders, FRAP 19.
Stay pending review, FRAP 18.
Applicable provisions, 4thCir Rule 18.
Transcript order acknowledgments, 4thCir Rule 11(a).

P

PARTIES.
Aggrieved non-parties.
Appeals from lower from lower court, 4thCir Rule 12(a).
Appendix.
Responsibility of parties, 4thCir Rule 30(c).
Death.
Public officers, FRAP 43.
Substitution of parties, FRAP 43.
Disclosure of corporate affiliations, 4thCir Rule 26.1.
Form, 4thCir Form A.
Multiple parties.
Consolidated or joint brief, 4thCir Rule 28(d).
Oral argument.
Nonappearance of parties, FRAP 34.
References in briefs to parties, FRAP 28.
Substitution of parties.
Death of a party, FRAP 43.
Generally, FRAP 43.
Public officers, FRAP 43.

PETITIONS.
Action by the court if granted, FRAP 40.
Answer, FRAP 40.
Appeals from judgments and orders of district courts.
See APPEALS FROM JUDGMENTS AND ORDERS OF DISTRICT COURTS.

PETITIONS —Cont'd
Content, FRAP 40.
Death penalty cases.
Rehearing in death penalty cases, 4thCir Rule 22(c).
District courts.
Appeals from judgments and orders of district courts.
See APPEALS FROM JUDGMENTS AND ORDERS OF DISTRICT COURTS.
Electronic case filing system, 4thCir Rule 25(a).
Form of petition, FRAP 40.
Length of petition, FRAP 40.
Mandamus or prohibition to a judge or judges, FRAP 21.
Rehearing, 4thCir Rule 40(a).
Death penalty cases, 4thCir Rule 22(c).
En banc, 4thCir Rule 35.
Panel rehearing, 4thCir Rule 40(b).
Statement of purpose, 4thCir Rule 40(b).
Strict enforcement of time limits for filing, 4thCir Rule 40(c).
Time for filing, FRAP 40.
Review and enforcement of orders of administrative agencies, boards, commissions and officers, FRAP 15.
Attachments to petition, 4thCir Rule 15(b).
Docketing fee, 4thCir Rule 15(a).
Extraordinary writs.
Fees and costs for prisoner petitions, 4thCir Rule 21(c).
Mandamus.
Crime victims' rights, 4thCir Rule 21(d).
Fees and costs for prisoner petitions, 4thCir Rule 21(c).
Prohibition, writ of.
Fees and costs for prisoner petitions, 4thCir Rule 21(c).
Special writs, 4thCir Rule 21(b).
Writs of certiorari, 4thCir IOP 41.2.

PRINTING COSTS, FRAP 39.

PRISONER APPEALS.
Payment of fees and costs, 4thCir Rule 24.

PROHIBITION, WRIT OF, FRAP 21.
Case captions, 4thCir Rule 21(a).
Petitions for special writs, 4thCir Rule 21(b).

PROOF OF FILING, FRAP 25.

PROOF OF SERVICE, FRAP 25.

PRO SE PROCEEDINGS, 4thCir Rule 46(f).
Informal brief, 4thCir Rule 34(b).

PUBLIC ACCESS.
CM/ECF system, 4thCir Appx V Rule 12.

PUBLICATION OF DECISIONS, 4thCir Rule 36(a).

PUBLIC INFORMATION, 4thCir IOP 45.2.

PUBLIC OFFICERS.
Parties.
Death or separation from office.
Substitution of parties, FRAP 43.
Review and enforcement of orders.
See ORDERS.

R

RECORDINGS.
Audio files of oral argument, 4thCir IOP 34.3.

RECORD ON APPEAL.
Access of counsel to original record, 4thCir Rule 11(d).
Appeals from judgments and orders of district courts.
See APPEALS FROM JUDGMENTS AND ORDERS OF DISTRICT COURTS.
Appendices, FRAP 30.
Original record.
Hearing of appeal on original record without the necessity of an appendix, FRAP 30.
Attorneys at law.
Access of counsel to original record, 4thCir Rule 11(d).
Briefs.
References in briefs to the record, FRAP 28.
Certificate of completeness, 4thCir Rule 10.
Clerks of court, FRAP 45.
Clerks of lower courts, boards, etc.
Responsibility for preparation, 4thCir Rule 10.
Correction of record, 4thCir Rule 10.
Costs.
Copies of record, FRAP 39.
District courts.
Appeals from judgments and orders of district courts.
See APPEALS FROM JUDGMENTS AND ORDERS OF DISTRICT COURTS.
Modification of record, 4thCir Rule 10.
Original record.
Access of counsel to original record, 4thCir Rule 11(d).
Responsibility for preparation, 4thCir Rule 10.
Retention.
District court to retain record until request, 4thCir Rule 10.
Review and enforcement of orders of administrative agencies, boards, commissions and officers.
See ORDERS.
Sealing records, 4thCir Rule 10.
Statement in lieu of transcript, 4thCir Rule 10.
Supplemental records, 4thCir Rule 10.
Transcript, 4thCir Rule 10.

REHEARING.
En banc, 4thCir Rule 35.
Petition, 4thCir Rule 40(a).
Death penalty case, 4thCir Rule 22(c).
En banc rehearing, 4thCir Rule 35.
Extension of time.
Application from United States, 4thCir IOP 40.1.
Panel rehearing, 4thCir Rule 40(d).
Statement of purpose, 4thCir IOP 40.2.
Strict enforcement of time limits for filing, 4thCir Rule 40(c).

RELEASE.
After conviction and notice of appeal, 4thCir Rule 9(b).
Judgment of conviction.
Prior to judgment of conviction, 4thCir Rule 9(a).

REMANDS.
Indicative ruling by district court.
Relief barred by pending appeal, FRAP 12.1.

REPLY TO RESPONSE TO MOTION, 4thCir Rule 27(d).

REPORTERS.
Sanctions for late delivery of transcripts, 4thCir IOP 11.1.

REPRODUCTION COSTS, 4thCir Rule 39.

RESPONSE TO MOTIONS, 4thCir Rule 27(d).

REVIEW OF DECISIONS OF TAX COURT.
Applicability of other rules to review, FRAP 14.
How obtained, FRAP 13.
Notice of appeal.
Content, FRAP 13.
Form, 4thCir Form 2.
How filed, FRAP 13.
Service, FRAP 13.
Time for filing, FRAP 13.
Record on appeal.
Filing, FRAP 13.
Generally, FRAP 13.
Transmission of record, FRAP 13.

RULES OF DISCIPLINARY ENFORCEMENT, 4thCir Rule 46(g).

S

SCOPE OF RULES, FRAP 1.

SEALED RECORDS.
Filing of confidential and sealed materials, 4thCir Rule 25(c).
Motions to seal, 4thCir Rule 25(c).

SEALED RECORDS ON APPEAL, 4thCir Rule 10.
CM/ECF system, 4thCir Appx V Rule 7.

SERVICE OF PROCESS, FRAP 25.
Additional time if the service by mail, FRAP 26.
Appeals from judgments and orders of district courts.
See APPEALS FROM JUDGMENTS AND ORDERS OF DISTRICT COURTS.
Briefs, FRAP 31.
Briefs in criminal cases.
Shortened time for service and filing of briefs, 4thCir Rule 31(a).
Certificate of service, 4thCir Rule 25(b).
Civil cases, 4thCir Rule 31(c).
CM/ECF system.
Service of documents by electronic means, 4thCir Appx V Rule 4.
Criminal cases, 4thCir Rule 31(c).
Mandamus or prohibition to a judge or judges.
Service of petition for writ, FRAP 21.
Manner of service, FRAP 25.
Proof of service, FRAP 25.
Review and enforcement of orders of administrative agencies, boards, commissions and officers, FRAP 15.
Review of decisions of tax court, FRAP 13.
Time.
Effect of holiday or bad weather, 4thCir Rule 26.

SESSIONS OF COURT, 4thCir Rule 34(c).

SIGNATURES.
Briefs, motions or other papers.
Requirement, FRAP 32.
CM/ECF system, 4thCir Appx V Rule 9.

SIGNATURES —Cont'd
Electronic signatures, FRAP 25.

STATEMENT IN LIEU OF TRANSCRIPT, 4thCir Rule 10.

STATEMENT OF FACTS.
Briefs, 4thCir Rule 28(f).

STATE STATUTE.
Constitutional challenge, notice, FRAP 44.

STATUS OF APPEALS.
Public information, 4thCir IOP 45.2.

STATUTES.
Briefs.
Reproduction of statutes and briefs, FRAP 28.

STAY OR INJUNCTION.
Administrative review.
Stay pending, 4thCir Rule 18.

STAY PENDING APPEAL.
Review and enforcement of orders of administrative agencies, boards, commissions and officers, FRAP 18.

STAYS.
Execution.
Motions for stay of execution, 4thCir Rule 22(b).
Injunction or stay pending appeal, 4thCir Rule 8.
Mandate.
Motion for stay of the mandate, 4thCir Rule 41.
Pending appeal, 4thCir Rule 8.

SUBSCRIPTION RATES.
Fee schedule, 4thCir Appx IV.

SUBSTITUTION OF COUNSEL, 4thCir Rule 46(c).

SUMMARY DISPOSITION.
Motions, 4thCir Rule 27(f).

SUMMARY DISPOSITION OF APPEALS.
Pre-argument review and summary disposition, 4thCir Rule 34(a).

SUMMARY OPINIONS, 4thCir IOP 36.3.

SUSPENSION OF RULES, FRAP 2.

T

TAX COURT.
Docketing statement, 4thCir Form E.
Review of decisions of tax court.
See REVIEW OF DECISIONS OF TAX COURT.

THREE JUDGE PANELS.
Argument time, 4thCir Rule 34(d).
Composition of panel, 4thCir IOP 34.1.

TIME.
Additional time if service by mail, FRAP 26.
Computation of time, FRAP 26.
Disclosure statements.
Corporations, time for filing, FRAP 26.1.
Extension of time, FRAP 26.
Notice of appeal, motion, FRAP 4.
Holidays or bad weather.
Effect on filing and service dates, 4thCir Rule 26.

TIME —Cont'd
Notice of appeal.
Civil cases, FRAP 4.
Criminal cases, FRAP 4.
Transcripts, filing, 4thCir Rule 11(b).

TITLE OF RULES, FRAP 1.

TRANSCRIPTS.
Appeals from judgments and orders of district courts.
Transcript of proceedings, FRAP 10.
Appellate transcripts.
Order form, FRAP Appx C.
Preparation guidelines, FRAP Appx C.
Clerks of court to monitor, 4thCir Rule 10.
Order acknowledgments, 4thCir Rule 11(a).
Responsibility for, 4thCir Rule 10.
Sanctions for court reporter's failure to file.
Timely transcript, 4thCir IOP 11.1.
Statement in lieu of transcript, 4thCir Rule 10.
Time limits for filing, 4thCir Rule 11(b).
Sanctions for failure to file timely transcript, 4thCir IOP 11.1.

U

UNITED STATES.
Costs for and against United States, FRAP 39.

UNPUBLISHED DECISIONS.
Citation, FRAP 32.1.

UNPUBLISHED OPINIONS, 4thCir Rule 36(b).
Citing, 4thCir Rule 32.1.

V

VICTIMS' RIGHTS.
Petition for writ of mandamus to enforce, 4thCir Rule 21(d).

W

WEATHER.
Inclement weather.
Computing filing or service date, 4thCir Rule 26.

WITHDRAWAL OF COUNSEL, 4thCir Rule 46(c).

WITNESSES.
Recalcitrant witnesses, 4thCir Rule 9(c).

WRIT OF CERTIORARI.
Petitions for writs, 4thCir IOP 41.2.

WRIT OF ERROR CORAM NOBIS.
Appeal from order granting or denying.
Notice of appeal, time for filing, FRAP 4.

WRITS.
Extraordinary writs, FRAP 21.
Case captions for extraordinary writs, 4thCir Rule 21(a).
Fees and costs for prisoner petitions, 4thCir Rule 21(c).
Petitions, 4thCir Rule 21(b).
Habeas corpus.
See HABEAS CORPUS.

RULES FOR JUDICIAL-CONDUCT AND JUDICIAL-DISABIITY PROCEEDINGS

As effective April 10, 2008.

Article I. General Provisisons.

Rule
1. Scope.
2. Effect and Construction.
3. Definitions.
4. Covered Judges.

Article II. Initiation of a Complaint.

5. Identification of a Complaint.
6. Filing a Complaint.
7. Where to Initiate Complaints.
8. Action by Clerk.
9. Time for Filing or Identifying a Complaint.
10. Abuse of the Complaint Procedure.

Article III. Review of a Complaint by the Chief Judge.

11. Review by the Chief Judge.

Article IV. Investigation and Report by Special Committee.

12. Composition of Special Committee.
13. Conduct of an Investigation.
14. Conduct of Hearings by Special Committee
15. Rights of Subject Judge.
16. Rights of Complainant in Investigation.

Rule
17. Special-Committee Report.

Article V. Judicial-Council Review.

18. Petitions for Review of Chief Judge Dispositions Under Rule 11(c), (d), or (e).
19. Judicial-Council Disposition of Petitions for Review.
20. Judicial-Council Consideration of Reports and Recommendations of Special Committees.

Article VI. Review by Judicial Conference Committee on Conduct and Disability.

21. Committee on Judicial Conduct and Disability.
22. Procedures for Review.

Article VII. Miscellaneous Rules.

23. Confidentiality.
24. Public Availability of Decisions.
25. Disqualification.
26. Transfer to Another Judicial Council.
27. Withdrawal of Complaints and Petitions for Review.
28. Availability of Rules and Forms.
29. Effective Date.

Appendix
Complaint Form

Index.

Preface

These Rules were promulgated by the Judicial Conference of the United States, after public comment, pursuant to 28 U.S.C. §§ 331 and 358, to establish standards and procedures for addressing complaints filed by complainants or identified by chief judges, under the Judicial and Disability Act, 28 U.S.C. §§ 351-364.

ARTICLE I. GENERAL PROVISISONS.

Rule 1. Scope.

These Rules govern proceedings under the Judicial Conduct and Disability Act, 28 U.S.C. §§ 351-364 (the Act), to determine whether a covered judge has engaged in conduct prejudicial to the effective and expeditious administration of the business of the courts or is unable to discharge the duties of office because of mental or physical disability.

COMMENT

In September 2006, the Judicial Conduct and Disability Act Study Committee, appointed in 2004 by Chief Justice Rehnquist and known as the "Breyer Committee," presented a report, known as the "Breyer Committee Report," 239 F.R.D. 116 (Sept. 2006), to Chief Justice Roberts that evaluated implementation of the Judicial Conduct and Disability Act of 1980, 28 U.S.C. §§ 351-364. The Breyer Committee had been formed in response to criticism from the public and the Congress regarding the effectiveness of the Act's implementation. The Executive Committee of the Judicial Conference directed the Judicial Conference Committee on Judicial Conduct and Disability to consider the recommendations made by the Breyer Committee and to report on their implementation to the Conference.

The Breyer Committee found that it could not evaluate implementation of the Act without establishing interpretive standards, Breyer Committee Report, 239 F.R.D. at 132, and that a major problem faced by chief judges in implementing the Act was the lack of authoritative interpretive standards. *Id.* at 212-15. The Breyer Committee then established standards to guide its evaluation, some of which were new formulations and some of which were taken from the "Illustrative Rules Governing Complaints of Judicial Misconduct and Disability," discussed below. The principal standards used by the Breyer Committee are in Appendix E of its Report. *Id.* at 238.

Based on the findings of the Breyer Committee, the Judicial Conference Committee on Judicial Conduct and Disability concluded that there was a need for the Judicial Conference to exercise its power under Section 358 of the Act to fashion standards guiding the various officers and bodies who must exercise responsibility under the Act. To that end, the Judicial Conference Committee proposed rules that were based largely on Appendix E of the Breyer Committee Report and the Illustrative Rules.

The Illustrative Rules were originally prepared in 1986 by the Special Committee of the Conference of Chief Judges of the United States Courts of Appeals, and were subsequently revised and amended, most recently in 2000, by the predecessor to the Committee on Judicial Conduct and Disability. The Illustrative Rules were adopted, with minor variations, by circuit judicial councils, to govern complaints under the Judicial Conduct and Disability Act.

After being submitted for public comment pursuant to 28 U.S.C. § 358(c), the present Rules were promulgated by the Judicial Conference on March 11, 2008.

Rule 2. Effect and Construction.

(a) *Generally.* — These Rules are mandatory; they supersede any conflicting judicial council rules. Judicial councils may promulgate additional rules to implement the Act as long as those rules do not conflict with these Rules.

(b) *Exception.* — A Rule will not apply if, when performing duties authorized by the Act, a chief judge, a special committee, a judicial council, the Judicial Conference Committee on Judicial Conduct and Disability, or the Judicial Conference of the United States expressly finds that exceptional circumstances render application of that Rule in a particular proceeding manifestly unjust or contrary to the purposes of the Act or these Rules.

COMMENT

Unlike the Illustrative Rules, these Rules provide mandatory and nationally uniform provisions governing the substantive and procedural aspects of misconduct and disability proceedings under the Act. The mandatory nature of these Rules is authorized by 28 U.S.C. § 358(a) and (c). Judicial councils retain the power to promulgate rules consistent with these Rules. For example, a local rule may authorize the electronic distribution of materials pursuant to Rule 8(b).

Rule 2(b) recognizes that unforeseen and exceptional circumstances may call for a different approach in particular cases.

Rule 3. Definitions.

(a) *Chief Judge.* — "Chief judge" means the chief judge of a United States Court of Appeals, of the United States Court of International Trade, or of the United States Court of Federal Claims.

(b) *Circuit Clerk.* — "Circuit clerk" means a clerk of a United States court of appeals, the clerk of the United States Court of International Trade, the clerk of the United States Court of Federal Claims, or the circuit executive of the United States Court of Appeals for the Federal Circuit.

(c) *Complaint.* — A complaint is:

(1) a document that, in accordance with Rule 6, is filed by any person in his or her individual capacity or on behalf of a professional organization; or

(2) information from any source, other than a document described in (c)(1), that gives a chief judge probable cause to believe that a covered judge, as defined in Rule 4, has engaged in misconduct or may have a disability, whether or not the information is framed as or is intended to be an allegation of misconduct or disability.

(d) *Court of Appeals, District Court, and District Judge.* — "Courts of appeals," "district court," and "district judge," where appropriate, include the United States Court of Federal Claims, the United States Court of International Trade, and the judges thereof.

(e) *Disability.* — "Disability" is a temporary or permanent condition rendering a judge unable to discharge the duties of the particular judicial office. Examples of disability include substance abuse, the inability to stay awake during court proceedings, or a severe impairment of cognitive abilities.

(f) *Judicial Council and Circuit.* — "Judicial council" and "circuit," where appropriate, include any courts designated in 28 U.S.C. § 363.

(g) *Magistrate Judge.* — "Magistrate judge," where appropriate, includes a special master appointed by the Court of Federal Claims under 42 U.S.C. § 300aa-12(c).

(h) *Misconduct.* — Cognizable misconduct:

(1) is conduct prejudicial to the effective and expeditious administration of the business of the courts. Misconduct includes, but is not limited to:

(A) using the judge's office to obtain special treatment for friends or relatives;

(B) accepting bribes, gifts, or other personal favors related to the judicial office;

(C) having improper discussions with parties or counsel for one side in a case;

(D) treating litigants or attorneys in a demonstrably egregious and hostile manner;

(E) engaging in partisan political activity or making inappropriately partisan statements;

(F) soliciting funds for organizations; or

(G) violating other specific, mandatory standards of judicial conduct, such as those pertaining to restrictions on outside income and requirements for financial disclosure.

(2) is conduct occurring outside the performance of official duties if the conduct might have a prejudicial effect on the administration of the business of the courts, including a substantial and widespread lowering of public confidence in the courts among reasonable people.

(3) does not include:

(A) an allegation that is directly related to the merits of a decision or procedural ruling. An allegation that calls into question the correctness of a judge's ruling, including a failure to recuse, without more, is merits-related. If the decision or ruling is alleged to be the result of an improper motive, e.g., a bribe, ex parte contact, racial or ethnic bias, or improper conduct in rendering a decision or ruling, such as personally derogatory remarks irrelevant to the issues, the complaint is not cognizable to the extent that it attacks the merits.

(B) an allegation about delay in rendering a decision or ruling, unless the allegation concerns an improper motive in delaying a particular decision or habitual delay in a significant number of unrelated cases.

(i) *Subject Judge.* — "Subject judge" means any judge described in Rule 4 who is the subject of a complaint.

COMMENT

Rule 3 is derived and adapted from the Breyer Committee Report and the Illustrative Rules.

Unless otherwise specified or the context otherwise indicates, the term "complaint" is used in these Rules to refer both to complaints identified by a chief judge under Rule 5 and to complaints filed by complainants under Rule 6.

Under the Act, a "complaint" may be filed by "any person" or "identified" by a chief judge. *See* 28 U.S.C. § 351(a) and (b). Under Rule 3(c)(1), complaints may be submitted by a person, in his or her individual capacity, or by a professional organization. Generally, the word "complaint" brings to mind the commencement of an adversary proceeding in which the contending parties are left to present the evidence and legal arguments, and judges play the role of an essentially passive arbiter. The Act, however, establishes an administrative, inquisitorial process. For example, even absent a complaint under Rule 6, chief judges are expected in some circumstances to trigger the process — "identify a complaint," *see* 28 U.S.C. § 351(b) and Rule 5 — and conduct an investigation without becoming a party. *See* 28 U.S.C. § 352(a); Breyer Committee Report, 239 F.R.D. at 214; Illustrative Rule 2(j). Even when a complaint is filed by someone other than the chief judge, the complainant lacks many rights that a litigant would have, and the chief judge, instead of being limited to the "four corners of the complaint," must, under Rule 11, proceed as though misconduct or disability has been alleged where the complainant reveals information of misconduct or disability but does not claim it as such. *See* Breyer Committee Report, 239 F.R.D. at 183-84.

An allegation of misconduct or disability filed under Rule 6 is a "complaint," and the Rule so provides in subsection (c)(1). However, both the nature of the process and the use of the term "identify" suggest that the word "complaint" covers more than a document formally triggering the process. The process relies on chief judges considering known information and triggering the process when appropriate. "Identifying" a "complaint," therefore, is best understood as the chief judge's concluding that information known to the judge constitutes probable cause to believe that misconduct occurred or a disability exists, whether or not the information is framed as, or intended to be an accusation. This definition is codified in (c)(2).

Rule 3(e) relates to disability and provides only the most general definition, recognizing that a fact-specific approach is the only one available.

The phrase "prejudicial to the effective and expeditious administration of the business of the courts" is not subject to precise definition, and subsection (h)(1) therefore provides some specific examples. Although the Code of Conduct for United States Judges may be informative, its main precepts are highly general; the Code is in many potential applications aspirational rather than a set of disciplinary rules. Ultimately, the responsibility for determining what constitutes misconduct under the statute is the province of the judicial council of the circuit subject to such review and limitations as are ordained by the statute and by these Rules.

Even where specific, mandatory rules exist — for example, governing the receipt of gifts by judges, outside earned income, and financial disclosure obligations — the distinction between the misconduct statute and the specific, mandatory rules must be borne in mind. For example, an inadvertent, minor violation of any one of these Rules, promptly remedied when called to the attention of the judge, might still be a violation but might not rise to the level of misconduct under the statute. By contrast, a pattern of such violations of the Code might well rise to the level of misconduct.

An allegation can meet the statutory standard even though the judge's alleged conduct did not occur in the course of the performance of official duties. The Code of Conduct for United States Judges expressly covers a wide range of extra-official activities, and some of these activities may constitute misconduct. For example, allegations that a judge solicited funds for a charity or participated in a partisan political event are cognizable under the Act.

On the other hand, judges are entitled to some leeway in extra-official activities. For example, misconduct may not include a judge being repeatedly and publicly discourteous to a spouse (not including physical abuse) even though this might cause some reasonable people to have diminished confidence in the courts. Rule 3(h)(2) states that conduct of this sort is covered, for example, when it might lead to a "substantial and widespread" lowering of such confidence.

Rule 3(h)(3)(A) tracks the Act, 28 U.S.C. § 352(b)(1)(A)(ii), in excluding from the definition of misconduct allegations "[d]irectly related to the merits of a decision or procedural ruling." This exclusion preserves the independence of judges in the exercise of judicial power by ensuring that the complaint procedure is not used to collaterally attack the substance of a judge's ruling. Any allegation that calls into question the correctness of an official action of a judge — without more — is merits-related. The phrase "decision or procedural ruling" is not limited to rulings issued in deciding Article III cases or controversies. Thus, a complaint challenging the correctness of a chief judge's determination to dismiss a prior misconduct complaint would be properly dismissed as merits-related — in other words, as challenging the substance of the judge's administrative determination to dismiss the complaint — even though it does not concern the judge's rulings in Article III litigation. Similarly, an allegation that a judge had incorrectly declined to approve a Criminal Justice Act voucher is merits-related under this standard.

Conversely, an allegation — however unsupported — that a judge conspired with a prosecutor to make a particular ruling is not merits-related, even though it "relates" to a ruling in a colloquial sense. Such an allegation attacks the propriety of conspiring with the prosecutor and goes beyond a challenge to the correctness — "the merits" — of the ruling itself. An allegation that a judge ruled against the complainant because the complainant is a member of a particular racial or ethnic group, or because the judge dislikes the complainant personally, is also not merits-related. Such an allegation attacks the propriety of arriving at rulings with an illicit or improper motive. Similarly, an allegation that a judge used an inappropriate term to refer to a class of people is not merits-related even if the judge used it on the bench or in an opinion; the correctness of the judge's rulings is not at stake. An allegation that a judge treated litigants or attorneys in a demonstrably egregious and hostile manner while on the bench is also not merits-related.

The existence of an appellate remedy is usually irrelevant to whether an allegation is merits-related. The merits-related ground for dismissal exists to protect judges' independence in making rulings, not to protect or promote the appellate process. A complaint alleging an incorrect ruling is merits-related even though the complainant has no recourse from that ruling. By the same token, an allegation that is otherwise cognizable under the Act should not be dismissed merely because an appellate remedy appears to exist (for example, vacating a ruling that resulted from an improper *ex parte* communication). However, there may be occasions when appellate and misconduct proceedings overlap, and consideration and disposition of a complaint under these Rules may be properly deferred by a chief judge until the appellate proceedings are concluded in order to avoid, *inter alia*, inconsistent decisions.

Because of the special need to protect judges' independence in deciding what to say in an opinion or ruling, a somewhat different standard applies to determine the merits-relatedness of a non-frivolous allegation that a judge's language in a ruling reflected an improper motive. If the judge's language was relevant to the case at hand — for example a statement that a claim is legally or factually "frivolous" — then the judge's choice of language is presumptively merits-related and excluded, absent evidence apart from the ruling itself suggesting an improper motive. If, on the other hand, the challenged language does not seem relevant on its face, then an additional inquiry under Rule 11 is necessary.

With regard to Rule 3(h)(3)(B), a complaint of delay in a single case is excluded as merits-related. Such an allegation may be said to challenge the correctness of an official action of the judge — in other words, assigning a low priority to deciding the particular case. But, by the same token, an allegation of a habitual pattern of delay in a significant number of unrelated cases, or an allegation of deliberate delay in a single case arising out of an illicit motive, is not merits-related.

The remaining subsections of Rule 3 provide technical definitions clarifying the application of the Rules to the various kinds of courts covered.

Rule 4. Covered Judges.

A complaint under these Rules may concern the actions or capacity only of judges of United States courts of appeals, judges of United States district courts, judges of United States bankruptcy courts, United States magistrate judges, and judges of the courts specified in 28 U.S.C. § 363.

COMMENT

This Rule tracks the Act. Rule 8(c) and (d) contain provisions as to the handling of complaints against persons not covered by the Act, such as other court personnel, or against both covered judges and noncovered persons.

ARTICLE II. INITIATION OF A COMPLAINT.

Rule 5. Identification of a Complaint.

(a) *Identification.* — When a chief judge has information constituting reasonable grounds for inquiry into whether a covered judge has engaged in misconduct or has a disability, the chief judge may conduct an inquiry, as he or she deems appropriate, into the accuracy of the information even if no related complaint has been filed. A chief judge who finds probable cause to believe that misconduct has occurred or that a disability exists may seek an informal resolution that he or she finds satisfactory. If no informal resolution is achieved or is feasible, the chief judge may identify a complaint and, by written order stating the reasons, begin the review provided in Rule 11. If the evidence of misconduct is clear and convincing and no informal resolution is achieved or is feasible, the chief judge must identify a complaint. A chief judge must not decline to identify a complaint merely because the person making the allegation has not filed a complaint under Rule 6. This Rule is subject to Rule 7.

(b) *Noncompliance with Rule 6(d).* — Rule 6 complaints that do not comply with the requirements of Rule 6(d) must be considered under this Rule.

COMMENT

This Rule is adapted from the Breyer Committee Report, 239 F.R.D. at 245-46.

The Act authorizes the chief judge, by written order stating reasons, to identify a complaint and thereby dispense with the filing of a written complaint. *See* 28 U.S.C. § 351(b). Under Rule 5, when a chief judge becomes aware of information constituting reasonable grounds to inquire into possible misconduct or disability on the part of a covered judge, and no formal complaint has been filed, the chief judge has the power in his or her discretion to begin an appropriate inquiry. A chief judge's decision whether to informally seek a resolution and/or to identify a complaint is guided by the results of that inquiry. If the chief judge concludes that there is probable cause to believe that misconduct has occurred or a disability exists, the chief judge may seek an informal resolution, if feasible, and if failing in that, may identify a complaint. Discretion is accorded largely for the reasons police officers and prosecutors have discretion in making arrests or bringing charges. The matter may be trivial and isolated, based on marginal evidence, or otherwise highly unlikely to lead to a misconduct or disability finding. On the other hand, if the inquiry leads the chief judge to conclude that there is clear and convincing evidence of misconduct or a disability, and no satisfactory informal resolution has been achieved or is feasible, the chief judge is required to identify a complaint.

An informal resolution is one agreed to by the subject judge and found satisfactory by the chief judge. Because an informal resolution under Rule 5 reached before a complaint is filed under Rule 6 will generally cause a subsequent Rule 6 complaint alleging the identical matter to be concluded, *see* Rule 11(d), the chief judge must be sure that the resolution is fully appropriate before endorsing it. In doing so, the chief judge must balance the seriousness of the matter against the particular judge's alacrity in addressing the issue. The availability of this procedure should encourage attempts at swift remedial action before a formal complaint is filed.

When a complaint is identified, a written order stating the reasons for the identification must be provided; this begins the process articulated in Rule 11. Rule 11 provides that once the chief judge has identified a complaint, the chief judge, subject to the disqualification provisions of Rule 25, will perform, with respect to that complaint, all functions assigned to the chief judge for the determination of complaints filed by a complainant.

In high-visibility situations, it may be desirable for the chief judge to identify a complaint without first seeking an informal resolution (and then, if the circumstances warrant, dismiss or conclude the identified complaint without appointment of a special committee) in order to assure the public that the allegations have not been ignored.

A chief judge's decision not to identify a complaint under Rule 5 is not appealable and is subject to Rule 3(h)(3)(A), which excludes merits-related complaints from the definition of misconduct.

A chief judge may not decline to identify a complaint solely on the basis that the unfiled allegations could be raised by one or more persons in a filed complaint, but none of these persons has opted to do so.

Subsection (a) concludes by stating that this Rule is "subject to Rule 7." This is intended to establish that only: (i) the chief judge of the home circuit of a potential subject judge, or (ii) the chief judge of a circuit in which misconduct is alleged to have occurred in the course of official business while the potential subject judge was sitting by designation, shall have the power or a duty under this Rule to identify a complaint.

Subsection (b) provides that complaints filed under Rule 6 that do not comply with the requirements of Rule 6(d), must be considered under this Rule. For instance, if a complaint has been filed but the form submitted is unsigned, or the truth of the statements therein are not verified in writing under penalty of perjury, then a chief judge must nevertheless consider the allegations as known information, and proceed to follow the process described in Rule 5(a).

Rule 6. Filing a Complaint.

(a) *Form.* — A complainant may use the form reproduced in the appendix to these Rules or a form designated by the rules of the judicial council in the circuit in which the complaint is filed. A complaint form is also available on each court of appeals' website or may be obtained from the circuit clerk or any district court or bankruptcy court within the circuit. A form is not necessary to file a complaint, but the complaint must be written and must include the information described in (b).

(b) *Brief Statement of Facts.* — A complaint must contain a concise statement that details the specific facts on which the claim of misconduct or disability is based. The statement of facts should include a description of:

(1) what happened;

(2) when and where the relevant events happened;

(3) any information that would help an investigator check the facts; and

(4) for an allegation of disability, any additional facts that form the basis of that allegation.

(c) *Legibility.* — A complaint should be typewritten if possible. If not typewritten, it must be legible. An illegible complaint will be returned to the complainant with a request to resubmit it in legible form. If a resubmitted complaint is still illegible, it will not be accepted for filing.

(d) *Complainant's Address and Signature; Verification.* — The complainant must provide a contact address and sign the complaint. The truth of the statements made in the complaint must be verified in writing under penalty of perjury. If any of these requirements are not met, the complaint will be accepted for filing, but it will be reviewed under only Rule 5(b).

(e) *Number of Copies; Envelope Marking.* — The complainant shall provide the number of copies of the complaint required by local rule. Each copy should be in an envelope marked "Complaint of Misconduct" or "Complaint of Disability." The envelope must not show the name of any subject judge.

COMMENT

The Rule is adapted from the Illustrative Rules and is self-explanatory.

Rule 7. Where to Initiate Complaints.

(a) *Where to File.* — Except as provided in (b),

(1) a complaint against a judge of a United States court of appeals, a United States district court, a United States bankruptcy court, or a United States magistrate judge must be filed with the circuit clerk in the jurisdiction in which the subject judge holds office.

(2) a complaint against a judge of the United States Court of International Trade or the United States Court of Federal Claims must be filed with the respective clerk of that court.

(3) a complaint against a judge of the United States Court of Appeals for the Federal Circuit must be filed with the circuit executive of that court.

(b) *Misconduct in Another Circuit; Transfer.* — If a complaint alleges misconduct in the course of official business while the subject judge was sitting on a court by designation under 28 U.S.C. §§ 291-293 and 294(d), the complaint may be filed or identified with the circuit clerk of that circuit or of the subject judge's home circuit. The proceeding will continue in the circuit of the first-filed or first-identified complaint. The judicial council of the circuit where the complaint was first filed or first identified may transfer the complaint to the subject judge's home circuit or to the circuit where the alleged misconduct occurred, as the case may be.

COMMENT

Title 28 U.S.C. § 351 states that complaints are to be filed with "the clerk of the court of appeals for the circuit." However, in many circuits, this role is filled by circuit executives. Accordingly, the term "circuit clerk," as defined in Rule 3(b) and used throughout these Rules, applies to circuit executives.

Section 351 uses the term "the circuit" in a way that suggests that either the home circuit of the subject judge or the circuit in which misconduct is alleged to have occurred is the proper venue for complaints. With an exception for judges sitting by designation, the Rule requires the identifying or filing of a misconduct or disability complaint in the circuit in which the judge holds office, largely based on the administrative perspective of the Act. Given the Act's emphasis on the future conduct of the business of the courts, the circuit in which the judge holds office is the appropriate forum because that circuit is likely best able to influence a judge's future behavior in constructive ways.

However, when judges sit by designation, the non-home circuit has a strong interest in redressing misconduct in the course of official business, and where allegations also involve a member of the bar — *ex parte* contact between an attorney and a judge, for example — it may often be desirable to have the judicial and bar misconduct proceedings take place in the same venue. Rule 7(b), therefore, allows transfer to, or filing or identification of a complaint in, the non-home circuit. The proceeding may be transferred by the judicial council of the filing or identified circuit to the other circuit.

Rule 8. Action by Clerk.

(a) *Receipt of Complaint.* — Upon receiving a complaint against a judge filed under Rule 5 or 6, the circuit clerk must open a file, assign a docket number according to a uniform numbering scheme promulgated by the Judicial Conference Committee on Judicial Conduct and Disability, and acknowledge the complaint's receipt.

(b) *Distribution of Copies.* — The clerk must promptly send copies of a complaint filed under Rule 6 to the chief judge or the judge authorized to act as chief judge under Rule 25(f), and copies of complaints filed under Rule 5 or 6 to each subject judge. The clerk must retain the original complaint. Any further distribution should be as provided by local rule.

(c) *Complaints Against Noncovered Persons.* — If the clerk receives a complaint about a person not holding an office described in Rule 4, the clerk must not accept the complaint for filing under these Rules.

(d) *Receipt of Complaint about a Judge and Another Noncovered Person.* — If a complaint is received about a judge described in Rule 4 and a person not holding an office described in Rule 4, the clerk must accept the complaint for filing under these Rules only with regard to the judge and must inform the complainant of the limitation.

COMMENT

This Rule is adapted from the Illustrative Rules and is largely self-explanatory.

The uniform docketing scheme described in subsection (a) should take into account potential problems associated with a complaint that names multiple judges. One solution may be to provide separate docket numbers for each subject judge. Separate docket numbers would help avoid difficulties in tracking cases, particularly if a complaint is dismissed with respect to some, but not all of the named judges.

Complaints against noncovered persons are not to be accepted for processing under these Rules but may, of course, be accepted under other circuit rules or procedures for grievances.

Rule 9. Time for Filing or Identifying a Complaint.

A complaint may be filed or identified at any time. If the passage of time has made an accurate and fair investigation of a complaint impractical, the complaint must be dismissed under Rule 11(c)(1)(E).

COMMENT

This Rule is adapted from the Act, 28 U.S.C. §§ 351, 352(b)(1)(A)(iii), and the Illustrative Rules.

Rule 10. Abuse of the Complaint Procedure.

(a) *Abusive Complaints.* — A complainant who has filed repetitive, harassing, or frivolous complaints, or has otherwise abused the complaint procedure, may be restricted from filing further complaints. After giving the complainant an opportunity to show cause in writing why his or her right to file further complaints should not be limited, a judicial council may prohibit, restrict, or impose conditions on the complainant's use of the complaint procedure. Upon written request of the complainant, the judicial council may revise or withdraw any prohibition, restriction, or condition previously imposed.

(b) *Orchestrated Complaints.* — When many essentially identical complaints from different complainants are received and appear to be part of an orchestrated campaign, the chief judge may recommend that the judicial council issue a written order instructing the circuit clerk to accept only a certain number of such complaints for filing and to refuse to accept further ones. The clerk must send a copy of any such order to anyone whose complaint was not accepted.

COMMENT

This Rule is adapted from the Illustrative Rules.

Rule 10(a) provides a mechanism for a judicial council to restrict the filing of further complaints by a single complainant who has abused the complaint procedure. In some instances, however, the complaint procedure may be abused in a manner for which the remedy provided in Rule 10(a) may not be appropriate. For example, some circuits have been inundated with submissions of dozens or hundreds of essentially identical complaints against the same judge or judges, all submitted by different complainants. In many of these instances, persons with grievances against a particular judge or judges used the Internet or other technology to orchestrate mass complaint-filing campaigns against them. If each complaint submitted as part of such a campaign were accepted for filing and processed according to these Rules, there would be a serious drain on court resources without any benefit to the adjudication of the underlying merits.

A judicial council may, therefore, respond to such mass filings under Rule 10(b) by declining to accept repetitive complaints for filing, regardless of the fact that the complaints are nominally submitted by different complainants. When the first complaint or complaints have been dismissed on the merits, and when further, essentially identical submissions follow, the judicial council may issue a second order noting that these are identical or repetitive complaints, directing the circuit clerk not to accept these complaints or any further such complaints for filing, and directing the clerk to send each putative complainant copies of both orders.

ARTICLE III. REVIEW OF A COMPLAINT BY THE CHIEF JUDGE.

Rule 11. Review by the Chief Judge.

(a) *Purpose of Chief Judge's Review.* — When a complaint is identified by the chief judge or is filed, the chief judge must review it unless the chief judge is disqualified under Rule 25. If the complaint contains information constituting evidence of misconduct or disability, but the complainant does not claim it as such, the chief judge must treat the complaint as if it did allege misconduct or disability and give notice to the subject judge. After reviewing the complaint, the chief judge must determine whether it should be:

(1) dismissed;

(2) concluded on the ground that voluntary corrective action has been taken;

(3) concluded because intervening events have made action on the complaint no longer necessary; or

(4) referred to a special committee.

(b) *Inquiry by Chief Judge.* — In determining what action to take under Rule 11(a), the chief judge may conduct a limited inquiry. The chief judge, or a designee, may communicate orally or in writing with the complainant, the subject judge, and any others who may have knowledge of the matter, and may review transcripts or other relevant documents. In conducting the inquiry, the chief judge must not determine any reasonably disputed issue.

(c) *Dismissal.* — (1) Allowable grounds. A complaint must be dismissed in whole or in part to the extent that the chief judge concludes that the complaint:

(A) alleges conduct that, even if true, is not prejudicial to the effective and expeditious administration of the business of the courts and does not indicate a mental or physical disability resulting in inability to discharge the duties of judicial office;

(B) is directly related to the merits of a decision or procedural ruling;

(C) is frivolous;

(D) is based on allegations lacking sufficient evidence to raise an inference that misconduct has occurred or that a disability exists;

(E) is based on allegations which are incapable of being established through investigation;

(F) has been filed in the wrong circuit under Rule 7; or

(G) is otherwise not appropriate for consideration under the Act.

(2) Disallowed grounds. A complaint must not be dismissed solely because it repeats allegations of a previously dismissed complaint if it also contains material information not previously considered and does not constitute harassment of the subject judge.

(d) *Corrective Action.* — The chief judge may conclude the complaint proceeding in whole or in part if:

(1) an informal resolution under Rule 5 satisfactory to the chief judge was reached before the complaint was filed under Rule 6, or

(2) the chief judge determines that the subject judge has taken appropriate voluntary corrective action that acknowledges and remedies the problems raised by the complaint.

(e) *Intervening Events.* — The chief judge may conclude the complaint proceeding in whole or in part upon determining that intervening events render some or all of the allegations moot or make remedial action impossible.

(f) *Appointment of Special Committee.* — If some or all of the complaint is not dismissed or concluded, the chief judge must promptly appoint a special committee to investigate the complaint or any relevant portion of it and to make recommendations to the judicial council. Before appointing a special committee, the chief judge must invite the subject judge to respond to the complaint either orally or in writing if the judge was not given an opportunity during the limited inquiry. In the chief judge's discretion, separate complaints may be joined and assigned to a single special committee. Similarly, a single complaint about more than one judge may be severed and more than one special committee appointed.

(g) *Notice of Chief Judge's Action; Petitions for Review.* — (1) When special committee is appointed. If a special committee is appointed, the chief judge must notify the complainant and the subject judge that the matter has been referred to a special committee and identify the members of the committee. A copy of the order appointing the special committee must be sent to the Judicial Conference Committee on Judicial Conduct and Disability.

(2) When chief judge disposes of complaint without appointing special committee. If the chief judge disposes of the complaint under Rule 11(c), (d), or (e), the chief judge must prepare a supporting memorandum that sets forth the reasons for the disposition. Except as authorized by 28 U.S.C. § 360, the memorandum must not include the name of the complainant or of the subject judge. The order and the supporting memorandum, which may be one document, must be provided to the complainant, the subject judge, and the Judicial Conference Committee on Judicial Conduct and Disability.

(3) Right of petition for review. If the chief judge disposes of a complaint under Rule 11(c), (d), or (e), the complainant and subject judge must be notified of the right to petition the judicial council for review of the disposition, as provided in Rule 18. If a petition for review is filed, the chief judge must promptly transmit all materials obtained in connection with the inquiry under Rule 11(b) to the circuit clerk for transmittal to the judicial council.

(h) *Public Availability of Chief Judge's Decision.* — The chief judge's decision must be made public to the extent, at the time, and in the manner provided in Rule 24.

COMMENT

Subsection (a) lists the actions available to a chief judge in reviewing a complaint. This subsection provides that where a complaint has been filed under Rule 6, the ordinary doctrines of waiver do not apply. A chief judge must identify as a complaint any misconduct or disability issues raised by the factual allegations of the complaint even if the complainant makes no such claim with regard to those issues. For example, an allegation limited to misconduct in fact-finding that mentions periods during a trial when the judge was asleep must be treated as a complaint regarding disability. Some formal order giving notice of the expanded scope of the proceeding must be given to the subject judge.

Subsection (b) describes the nature of the chief judge's inquiry. It is based largely on the Breyer Committee Report, 239 F.R.D. at 243-45. The Act states that dismissal is appropriate "when a limited inquiry ... demonstrates that the allegations in the complaint lack any factual foundation or are conclusively refuted by objective evidence." 28 U.S.C. § 352(b)(1)(B). At the same time, however, Section 352(a) states that "[t]he chief judge shall not undertake to make findings of fact about any matter that is reasonably in dispute." These two statutory standards should be read together, so that a matter is not "reasonably" in dispute if a limited inquiry shows that the allegations do not constitute misconduct or disability, that they lack any reliable factual foundation, or that they are conclusively refuted by objective evidence.

In conducting a limited inquiry under subsection (b), the chief judge must avoid determinations of reasonably disputed issues, including reasonably disputed issues as to whether the facts alleged constitute misconduct or disability, which are ordinarily left to a special committee and the judicial council. An allegation of fact is ordinarily not "refuted" simply because the subject judge denies it. The limited inquiry must reveal something more in the way of refutation before it is appropriate to dismiss a complaint that is otherwise cognizable. If it is the complainant's word against the subject judge's — in other words, there is simply no other significant evidence of what happened or of the complainant's unreliability — then there must be a special-committee investigation. Such a credibility issue is a matter "reasonably in dispute" within the meaning of the Act.

However, dismissal following a limited inquiry may occur when the complaint refers to transcripts or to witnesses and the chief judge determines that the transcripts and witnesses all support the subject judge. Breyer Committee Report, 239 F.R.D. at 243. For example, consider a complaint alleging that the subject judge said X, and the complaint mentions, or it is independently clear, that five people may have heard what the judge said. *Id.* The chief judge is told by the subject judge and one witness that the judge did not say X, and the chief judge dismisses the complaint without questioning the other four possible witnesses. *Id.* In this example, the matter remains reasonably in dispute. If all five witnesses say the judge did not say X, dismissal is appropriate, but if potential witnesses who are reasonably accessible have not been questioned, then the matter remains reasonably in dispute. *Id.*

Similarly, under (c)(1)(A), if it is clear that the conduct or disability alleged, even if true, is not cognizable under these Rules, the complaint should be dismissed. If that issue is reasonably in dispute, however, dismissal under (c)(1)(A) is inappropriate.

Essentially, the standard articulated in subsection (b) is that used to decide motions for summary judgment pursuant to Fed. R. Civ. P. 56. Genuine issues of material fact are not resolved at the summary judgment stage. A material fact is one that "might affect the outcome of the suit under the governing law," and a dispute is "genuine" if "the evidence is such that a reasonable jury could return a verdict for the nonmoving party." *Anderson v. Liberty Lobby,* 477 U.S. 242, 248 (1986). Similarly, the chief judge may not resolve a genuine issue concerning a material fact or the existence of misconduct or a disability when conducting a limited inquiry pursuant to subsection (b).

Subsection (c) describes the grounds on which a complaint may be dismissed. These are adapted from the Act, 28 U.S.C. § 352(b), and the Breyer Committee Report, 239 F.R.D. at 239-45. Subsection (c)(1)(A) permits dismissal of an allegation that, even if true, does not constitute misconduct or disability under the statutory standard. The proper standards are set out in Rule 3 and discussed in the Commentary on that Rule. Subsection (c)(1)(B) permits dismissal of complaints related to the merits of a decision by a subject judge; this standard is also governed by Rule 3 and its accompanying Commentary.

Subsections (c)(1)(C)-(E) implement the statute by allowing dismissal of complaints that are "frivolous, lacking sufficient evidence to raise an inference that misconduct has occurred, or containing allegations which are incapable of being established through investigation." 28 U.S.C. § 352(b)(1)(A)(iii).

Dismissal of a complaint as "frivolous," under Rule 11(c)(1)(C), will generally occur without any inquiry beyond the face of the complaint. For instance, when the allegations are facially incredible or so lacking in indicia of reliability that no further inquiry is warranted, dismissal under this subsection is appropriate.

A complaint warranting dismissal under Rule 11(c)(1)(D) is illustrated by the following example. Consider a complainant who alleges an impropriety and asserts that he knows of it because it was observed and reported to him by a person who is identified. The judge denies that the event occurred. When contacted, the source also denies it. In such a case, the chief judge's proper course of action may turn on whether the source had any role in the allegedly improper conduct. If the complaint was based on a lawyer's statement that he or she had an improper *ex parte* contact with a judge, the lawyer's denial of the impropriety might not be taken as wholly persuasive, and it would be appropriate to conclude that a real factual issue is raised. On the other hand, if the complaint quoted a disinterested third party and that disinterested party denied that the statement had been made, there would be no value in opening a formal investigation. In such a case, it would be appropriate to dismiss the complaint under Rule 11(c)(1)(D).

Rule 11(c)(1)(E) is intended, among other things, to cover situations when no evidence is offered or identified, or when the only identified source is unavailable. Breyer Committee Report, 239 F.R.D. at 243. For example, a complaint alleges that an unnamed attorney told the complainant that the judge did X. *Id.* The subject judge denies it. The chief judge requests that the complainant (who does not purport to have observed the judge do X) identify the unnamed witness, or that the unnamed witness come forward so that the chief judge can learn the unnamed witness's account. *Id.* The complainant responds that he has spoken with the unnamed witness, that the unnamed witness is an attorney who practices in federal court, and that the unnamed witness is unwilling to be identified or to come forward. *Id.* at 243-44. The allegation is then properly dismissed as containing allegations that are incapable of being established through investigation. *Id.*

If, however, the situation involves a reasonable dispute over credibility, the matter should proceed. For example, the complainant alleges an impropriety and alleges that he or she observed it and that there were no other witnesses; the subject judge denies that the event occurred. Unless the complainant's allegations are facially incredible or so lacking indicia of reliability warranting dismissal under Rule 11(c)(1)(C), a special committee must be appointed because there is a material factual question that is reasonably in dispute.

Dismissal is also appropriate when a complaint is

filed so long after an alleged event that memory loss, death, or changes to unknown residences prevent a proper investigation.

Subsection (c)(2) indicates that the investigative nature of the process prevents the application of claim preclusion principles where new and material evidence becomes available. However, it also recognizes that at some point a renewed investigation may constitute harassment of the subject judge and should be foregone, depending of course on the seriousness of the issues and the weight of the new evidence.

Rule 11(d) implements the Act's provision for dismissal if voluntary appropriate corrective action has been taken. It is largely adapted from the Breyer Committee Report, 239 F.R.D. 244-45. The Act authorizes the chief judge to conclude the proceedings if "appropriate corrective action has been taken." 28 U.S.C. § 352(b)(2). Under the Rule, action taken after the complaint is filed is "appropriate" when it acknowledges and remedies the problem raised by the complaint. Breyer Committee Report, 239 F.R.D. at 244. Because the Act deals with the conduct of judges, the emphasis is on correction of the judicial conduct that was the subject of the complaint. *Id.* Terminating a complaint based on corrective action is premised on the implicit understanding that voluntary self-correction or redress of misconduct or a disability is preferable to sanctions. *Id.* The chief judge may facilitate this process by giving the subject judge an objective view of the appearance of the judicial conduct in question and by suggesting appropriate corrective measures. *Id.* Moreover, when corrective action is taken under Rule 5 satisfactory to the chief judge before a complaint is filed, that informal resolution will be sufficient to conclude a subsequent complaint based on the identical conduct.

"Corrective action" must be voluntary action taken by the subject judge. Breyer Committee Report, 239 F.R.D. at 244. A remedial action directed by the chief judge or by an appellate court without the participation of the subject judge in formulating the directive or without the subject judge's subsequent agreement to such action does not constitute the requisite voluntary corrective action. *Id.* Neither the chief judge nor an appellate court has authority under the Act to impose a formal remedy or sanction; only the judicial council can impose a formal remedy or sanction under 28 U.S.C. § 354(a)(2). *Id.* Compliance with a previous council order may serve as corrective action allowing conclusion of a later complaint about the same behavior. *Id.*

Where a judge's conduct has resulted in identifiable, particularized harm to the complainant or another individual, appropriate corrective action should include steps taken by that judge to acknowledge and redress the harm, if possible, such as by an apology, recusal from a case, or a pledge to refrain from similar conduct in the future. *Id.* While the Act is generally forward-looking, any corrective action should, to the extent possible, serve to correct a specific harm to an individual, if such harm can reasonably be remedied. *Id.* In some cases, corrective action may not be "appropriate" to justify conclusion of a complaint unless the complainant or other individual harmed is meaningfully apprised of the nature of the corrective action in the chief judge's order, in a direct communication from the subject judge, or otherwise. *Id.*

Voluntary corrective action should be proportionate to any plausible allegations of misconduct in the complaint. The form of corrective action should also be proportionate to any sanctions that a judicial council might impose under Rule 20(b), such as a private or public reprimand or a change in case assignments. Breyer Committee Report, 239 F.R.D at 244-45. In other words, minor corrective action will not suffice to dispose of a serious matter. *Id.*

Rule 11(e) implements Section 352(b)(2) of the Act, which permits the chief judge to "conclude the proceeding," if "action on the complaint is no longer necessary because of intervening events," such as a resignation from judicial office. Ordinarily, however, stepping down from an administrative post such as chief judge, judicial-council member, or court-committee chair does not constitute an event rendering unnecessary any further action on a complaint alleging judicial misconduct. Breyer Committee Report, 239 F.R.D. at 245. As long as the subject of the complaint performs judicial duties, a complaint alleging judicial misconduct must be addressed. *Id.*

If a complaint is not disposed of pursuant to Rule 11(c), (d), or (e), a special committee must be appointed. Rule 11(f) states that a subject judge must be invited to respond to the complaint before a special committee is appointed, if no earlier response was invited.

Subject judges, of course, receive copies of complaints at the same time that they are referred to the chief judge, and they are free to volunteer responses to them. Under Rule 11(b), the chief judge may request a response if it is thought necessary. However, many complaints are clear candidates for dismissal even if their allegations are accepted as true, and there is no need for the subject judge to devote time to a defense.

The Act requires that the order dismissing a complaint or concluding the proceeding contain a statement of reasons and that a copy of the order be sent to the complainant. 28 U.S.C. § 352(b). Rule 24, dealing with availability of information to the public, contemplates that the order will be made public, usually without disclosing the names of the complainant or the subject judge. If desired for administrative purposes, more identifying information can be included in a non-public version of the order.

When complaints are disposed of by chief judges, the statutory purposes are best served by providing the complainant with a full, particularized, but concise explanation, giving reasons for the conclusions reached. *See also* Commentary on Rule 24, dealing with public availability.

Rule 11(g) provides that the complainant and subject judge must be notified, in the case of a disposition by the chief judge, of the right to petition the judicial council for review. A copy of a chief judge's order and memorandum, which may be one document, disposing of a complaint must be sent by the circuit clerk to the Judicial Conference Committee on Judicial Conduct and Disability.

ARTICLE IV. INVESTIGATION AND REPORT BY SPECIAL COMMITTEE.

Rule 12. Composition of Special Committee.

(a) *Membership.* — Except as provided in (e), a special committee appointed under Rule 11(f) must consist of the chief judge and equal numbers of circuit and district judges. If the complaint is about a district judge, bankruptcy judge, or magistrate judge, then, when possible, the district-judge members of the committee must be from districts other than the district of the subject judge. For the courts named in 28 U.S.C. § 363, the committee must be selected from the judges serving on the subject judge's court.

(b) *Presiding Officer.* — When appointing the committee, the chief judge may serve as the presiding officer or else must designate a committee member as the presiding officer.

(c) *Bankruptcy Judge or Magistrate Judge as Adviser.* — If the subject judge is a bankruptcy judge or magistrate judge, he or she may, within 14 days after being notified of the committee's appointment, ask the chief judge to designate as a committee adviser another bankruptcy judge or magistrate judge, as the case may be. The chief judge must grant such a request but may otherwise use discretion in naming the adviser. Unless the adviser is a Court of Federal Claims special master appointed under 42 U.S.C. § 300aa-12(c), the adviser must be from a district other than the district of the subject bankruptcy judge or subject magistrate judge. The adviser cannot vote but has the other privileges of a committee member.

(d) *Provision of Documents.* — The chief judge must certify to each other member of the committee and to any adviser copies of the complaint and statement of facts in whole or relevant part, and any other relevant documents on file.

(e) *Continuing Qualification of Committee Members.* — A member of a special committee who was qualified to serve when appointed may continue to serve on the committee even though the member relinquishes the position of chief judge, active circuit judge, or active district judge, as the case may be, but only if the member continues to hold office under Article III, Section 1, of the Constitution of the United States, or under 28 U.S.C. § 171.

(f) *Inability of Committee Member to Complete Service.* — If a member of a special committee can no longer serve because of death, disability, disqualification, resignation, retirement from office, or other reason, the chief judge must decide whether to appoint a replacement member, either a circuit or district judge as needed under (a). No special committee appointed under these Rules may function with only a single member, and the votes of a two-member committee must be unanimous.

(g) *Voting.* — All actions by a committee must be by vote of a majority of all members of the committee.

COMMENT

This Rule is adapted from the Act and the Illustrative Rules.

Rule 12 leaves the size of a special committee flexible, to be determined on a case-by-case basis. The question of committee size is one that should be weighed with care in view of the potential for consuming the members' time; a large committee should be appointed only if there is a special reason to do so.

Although the Act requires that the chief judge be a member of each special committee, 28 U.S.C. § 353(a)(1), it does not require that the chief judge preside. Accordingly, Rule 12(b) provides that if the chief judge does not preside, he or she must designate another committee member as the presiding officer.

Rule 12(c) provides that the chief judge must appoint a bankruptcy judge or magistrate judge as an adviser to a special committee at the request of a bankruptcy or magistrate subject judge.

Subsection (c) also provides that the adviser will have all the privileges of a committee member except a vote. The adviser, therefore, may participate in all deliberations of the committee, question witnesses at hearings, and write a separate statement to accompany the special committee's report to the judicial council.

Rule 12(e) provides that a member of a special committee who remains an Article III judge may continue to serve on the committee even though the member's status otherwise changes. Thus, a committee that originally consisted of the chief judge and an equal number of circuit and district judges, as required by the law, may continue to function even though changes of status alter that composition. This provision reflects the belief that stability of membership will contribute to the quality of the work of such committees.

Stability of membership is also the principal concern animating Rule 12(f), which deals with the case in which a special committee loses a member before its work is complete. The Rule permits the chief judge to determine whether a replacement member should be appointed. Generally, appointment of a replacement member is desirable in these situations unless the committee has conducted evidentiary hearings before the vacancy occurs. However, cases may arise in which a committee is in the late stages of its work, and in which it would be difficult for a new member to play a meaningful role. The Rule also preserves the collegial character of the committee process by prohibiting a single surviving member from serving as a committee and by providing that a committee of two surviving members will, in essence, operate under a unanimity rule.

Rule 12(g) provides that actions of a special committee must be by vote of a majority of all the members. All the members of a committee should participate in committee decisions. In that circumstance, it seems reasonable to require that committee decisions be made by a majority of the membership, rather than a majority of some smaller quorum.

Rule 13. Conduct of an Investigation.

(a) *Extent and Methods of Special-Committee Investigation.* — Each special committee must determine the appropriate extent and methods of the investigation in light of the allegations of the complaint. If, in the course of the investigation, the committee has cause to believe that the subject judge may have engaged in misconduct or has a disability that is beyond the scope of the complaint, the committee must refer the new matter to the chief judge for action under Rule 5 or Rule 11.

(b) *Criminal Conduct.* — If the committee's investigation concerns conduct that may be a crime, the committee must consult with the appropriate prosecutorial authorities to the extent permitted by the Act to avoid compromising any criminal investigation. The committee has final authority over the timing and extent of its investigation and the formulation of its recommendations.

(c) *Staff.* — The committee may arrange for staff assistance to conduct the investigation. It may use existing staff of the judicial branch or may hire special staff through the Director of the Administrative Office of the United States Courts.

(d) *Delegation of Subpoena Power; Contempt.* — The chief judge may delegate the authority to exercise the committee's subpoena powers. The judicial council or special committee may institute a contempt proceeding under 28 U.S.C. § 332(d) against anyone who fails to comply with a subpoena.

COMMENT

This Rule is adapted from the Illustrative Rules.

Rule 13, as well as Rules 14, 15, and 16, are concerned with the way in which a special committee carries out its mission. They reflect the view that a special committee has two roles that are separated in ordinary litigation. First, the committee has an investigative role of the kind that is characteristically left to executive branch agencies or discovery by civil litigants. 28 U.S.C. § 353(c). Second, it has a formalized fact-finding and recommendation-of-disposition role that is characteristically left to juries, judges, or arbitrators. *Id.* Rule 13 generally governs the investigative stage. Even though the same body has responsibility for both roles under the Act, it is important to distinguish between them in order to ensure that appropriate rights are afforded at appropriate times to the subject judge.

One of the difficult questions that can arise is the relationship between proceedings under the Act and criminal investigations. Rule 13(b) assigns responsibility for coordination to the special committee in cases in which criminal conduct is suspected, but gives the committee the authority to determine the appropriate pace of its activity in light of any criminal investigation.

Title 28 U.S.C. § 356(a) provides that a special committee will have full subpoena powers as provided in 28 U.S.C. § 332(d). Section 332(d)(1) provides that subpoenas will be issued on behalf of judicial councils by the circuit clerk "at the direction of the chief judge of the circuit or his designee." Rule 13(d) contemplates that, where the chief judge designates someone else as presiding officer of a special committee, the presiding officer also be delegated the authority to direct the circuit clerk to issue subpoenas related to committee proceedings. That is not intended to imply, however, that the decision to use the subpoena power is exercisable by the presiding officer alone. *See* Rule 12(g).

Rule 14. Conduct of Hearings by Special Committee.

(a) *Purpose of Hearings.* — The committee may hold hearings to take testimony and receive other evidence, to hear argument, or both. If the committee is investigating allegations against more than one judge, it may hold joint or separate hearings.

(b) *Committee Evidence.* — Subject to Rule 15, the committee must obtain material, nonredundant evidence in the form it considers appropriate. In the committee's discretion, evidence may be obtained by committee members, staff, or both. Witnesses offering testimonial evidence may include the complainant and the subject judge.

(c) *Counsel for Witnesses.* — The subject judge has the right to counsel. The special committee has discretion to decide whether other witnesses may have counsel present when they testify.

(d) *Witness Fees.* — Witness fees must be paid as provided in 28 U.S.C. § 1821.

(e) *Oath.* — All testimony taken at a hearing must be given under oath or affirmation.

(f) *Rules of Evidence.* — The Federal Rules of Evidence do not apply to special-committee hearings.

(g) *Record and Transcript.* — A record and transcript must be made of all hearings.

COMMENT

This Rule is adapted from Section 353 of the Act and the Illustrative Rules.

Rule 14 is concerned with the conduct of fact-finding hearings. Special-committee hearings will normally be held only after the investigative work has been completed and the committee has concluded that there is sufficient evidence to warrant a formal fact-finding proceeding. Special-committee proceedings are primarily inquisitorial rather than adversarial. Accordingly, the Federal Rules of Evidence do not apply to such hearings. Inevitably, a hearing will have something of an adversary character. Nevertheless, that tendency should be moderated to the extent possible. Even though a proceeding will commonly have investigative and hearing stages, committee members should not regard themselves as prosecutors one day and judges the next. Their duty — and that of their staff — is at all times to be impartial seekers of the truth.

Rule 14(b) contemplates that material evidence will be obtained by the committee and presented in the form of affidavits, live testimony, etc. Staff or others who are organizing the hearings should regard it as their role to present evidence representing the entire picture. With respect to testimonial evidence, the subject judge should normally be called as a committee witness. Cases may arise in which the judge will not testify voluntarily. In such cases, subpoena powers are available, subject to the normal testimonial privileges. Although Rule 15(c) recognizes the subject judge's statutory right to call witnesses on his or her own behalf, exercise of this right should not usually be necessary.

Rule 15. Rights of Subject Judge.

(a) *Notice.* — (1) Generally. The subject judge must receive written notice of:

(A) the appointment of a special committee under Rule 11(f);

(B) the expansion of the scope of an investigation under Rule 13(a);

(C) any hearing under Rule 14, including its purposes, the names of any witnesses the committee intends to call, and the text of any statements that have been taken from those witnesses.

(2) Suggestion of additional witnesses. The subject judge may suggest additional witnesses to the committee.

(b) *Report of the Special Committee.* — The subject judge must be sent a copy of the special committee's report when it is filed with the judicial council.

(c) *Presentation of Evidence.* — At any hearing held under Rule 14, the subject judge has the right to present evidence, to compel the attendance of witnesses, and to compel the production of documents. At the request of the subject judge, the chief judge or the judge's designee must direct the circuit clerk to issue a subpoena to a witness under 28 U.S.C. § 332(d)(1). The subject judge must be given the opportunity to cross-examine committee witnesses, in person or by counsel.

(d) *Presentation of Argument.* — The subject judge may submit written argument to the special committee and must be given a reasonable opportunity to present oral argument at an appropriate stage of the investigation.

(e) *Attendance at Hearings.* — The subject judge has the right to attend any hearing held under Rule 14 and to receive copies of the transcript, of any documents introduced, and of any written arguments submitted by the complainant to the committee.

(f) *Representation by Counsel.* — The subject judge may choose to be represented by counsel in the exercise of any right enumerated in this Rule. As provided in Rule 20(e), the United States may bear the costs of the representation.

COMMENT

This Rule is adapted from the Act and the Illustrative Rules.

The Act states that these Rules must contain provisions requiring that "the judge whose conduct is the subject of a complaint ... be afforded an opportunity to appear (in person or by counsel) at proceedings conducted by the investigating panel, to present oral and documentary evidence, to compel the attendance of witnesses or the production of documents, to cross-examine witnesses, and to present argument orally or in writing." 28 U.S.C. § 358(b)(2). To implement this provision, Rule 15(e) gives the judge the right to attend any hearing held for the purpose of receiving evidence of record or hearing argument under Rule 14.

The Act does not require that the subject judge be permitted to attend all proceedings of the special committee. Accordingly, the Rules do not give a right to attend other proceedings — for example, meetings at which the committee is engaged in investigative activity, such as interviewing persons to learn whether they ought to be called as witnesses or examining for relevance purposes documents delivered pursuant to a subpoena duces tecum, or meetings in which the committee is deliberating on the evidence or its recommendations.

Rule 16. Rights of Complainant in Investigation.

(a) *Notice.* — The complainant must receive written notice of the investigation as provided in Rule 11(g)(1). When the special committee's report to the judicial council is filed, the complainant must be notified of the filing. The judicial council may, in its discretion, provide a copy of the report of a special committee to the complainant.

(b) *Opportunity to Provide Evidence.* — If the committee determines that the complainant may have evidence that does not already exist in writing, a representative of the committee must interview the complainant.

(c) *Presentation of Argument.* — The complainant may submit written argument to the special committee. In its discretion, the special committee may permit the complainant to offer oral argument.

(d) *Representation by Counsel.* — A complainant may submit written argument through counsel and, if permitted to offer oral argument, may do so through counsel.

(e) *Cooperation.* — In exercising its discretion under this Rule, a special committee may take into account the degree of the complainant's cooperation in preserving the confidentiality of the proceedings, including the identity of the subject judge.

COMMENT

This Rule is adapted from the Act and the Illustrative Rules.

In accordance with the view of the process as fundamentally administrative and inquisitorial, these Rules do not give the complainant the rights of a party to litigation, and leave the complainant's role largely to the discretion of the special committee. However, Rule 16(b) provides that, where a special committee has been appointed and it determines that the complainant may have additional evidence, the complainant must be interviewed by a representative of the committee. Such an interview may be in person or by telephone, and the representative of the committee may be either a member or staff.

Rule 16 does not contemplate that the complainant will ordinarily be permitted to attend proceedings of the special committee except when testifying or presenting oral argument. A special committee may exercise its discretion to permit the complainant to be present at its proceedings, or to permit the complainant, individually or through counsel, to participate in the examination or cross-examination of witnesses.

The Act authorizes an exception to the normal confidentiality provisions where the judicial council in its discretion provides a copy of the report of the special committee to the complainant and to the subject judge. 28 U.S.C. § 360(a)(1). However, the Rules do not entitle the complainant to a copy of the special committee's report.

In exercising their discretion regarding the role of the complainant, the special committee and the judicial council should protect the confidentiality of the complaint process. As a consequence, subsection (e) provides that a special committee may consider the degree to which a complainant has cooperated in preserving the confidentiality of the proceedings in determining what role beyond the minimum required by these Rules should be given to that complainant.

Rule 17. Special-Committee Report.

The committee must file with the judicial council a comprehensive report of its investigation, including findings and recommendations for council action. The report must be accompanied by a statement of the vote by which it was adopted, any separate or dissenting statements of committee members, and the record of any hearings held under Rule 14. A copy of the report and accompanying statement must be sent to the Judicial Conference Committee on Judicial Conduct and Disability.

COMMENT

This Rule is adapted from the Illustrative Rules and is self-explanatory. The provision for sending a copy of the special-committee report and accompanying statement to the Judicial Conference Committee is new.

ARTICLE V. JUDICIAL-COUNCIL REVIEW.

Rule 18. Petitions for Review of Chief Judge Dispositions Under Rule 11(c), (d), or (e).

(a) *Petitions for Review.* — After the chief judge issues an order under Rule 11(c), (d), or (e), a complainant or subject judge may petition the judicial council of the circuit to review the order. By rules promulgated under 28 U.S.C. § 358, the judicial council may refer a petition for review filed under this Rule to a panel of no fewer than five members of the council, at least two of whom must be district judges.

(b) *When to File; Form; Where to File.* — A petition for review must be filed in the office of the circuit clerk within 35 days of the date on the clerk's letter informing the parties of the chief judge's order. The petition should be in letter form, addressed to the circuit clerk, and in an envelope marked "Misconduct Petition" or "Disability Petition." The name of the subject judge must not be shown on the envelope. The letter should be typewritten or otherwise legible. It should begin with "I hereby petition the judicial council for review of ..." and state the reasons why the petition should be granted. It must be signed.

(c) *Receipt and Distribution of Petition.* — A circuit clerk who receives a petition for review filed within the time allowed and in proper form must:

(1) acknowledge its receipt and send a copy to the complainant or subject judge, as the case may be;

(2) promptly distribute to each member of the judicial council, or its relevant panel, except for any member disqualified under Rule 25, or make available in the manner provided by local rule, the following materials:

(A) copies of the complaint;

(B) all materials obtained by the chief judge in connection with the inquiry;

(C) the chief judge's order disposing of the complaint;

(D) any memorandum in support of the chief judge's order;

(E) the petition for review; and

(F) an appropriate ballot;

(3) send the petition for review to the Judicial Conference Committee on Judicial Conduct and Disability. Unless the Judicial Conference Committee requests them, the clerk will not send copies of the materials obtained by the chief judge.

(d) *Untimely Petition.* — The clerk must refuse to accept a petition that is received after the deadline in (b).

(e) *Timely Petition Not in Proper Form.* — When the clerk receives a petition filed within the time allowed but in a form that is improper to a degree that would substantially impair its consideration by the judicial council — such as a document that is ambiguous about whether it is intended to be a petition for review — the clerk must acknowledge its receipt, call the filer's attention to the deficiencies, and give the filer the opportunity to correct the deficiencies within 21 days of the date of the clerk's letter about the deficiencies or within the original deadline for filing the petition, whichever is later. If the deficiencies are corrected within the time allowed, the clerk will proceed according to paragraphs (a) and (c) of this Rule. If the deficiencies are not corrected, the clerk must reject the petition.

COMMENT

Rule 18 is adapted largely from the Illustrative Rules.

Subsection (a) permits a subject judge, as well as the complainant, to petition for review of a chief judge's order dismissing a complaint under Rule 11(c), or concluding that appropriate corrective action or intervening events have remedied or mooted the problems raised by the complaint pursuant to Rule 11(d) or (e). Although the subject judge may ostensibly be vindicated by the dismissal or conclusion of a complaint, a chief judge's order may include language disagreeable to the subject judge. For example, an order may dismiss a complaint, but state that the subject judge did in fact engage in misconduct. Accordingly, a subject judge may wish to object to the content of the order and is given the opportunity to petition the judicial council of the circuit for review.

Subsection (b) contains a time limit of thirty-five days to file a petition for review. It is important to establish a time limit on petitions for review of chief judges' dispositions in order to provide finality to the process. If the complaint requires an investigation, the investigation should proceed; if it does not, the subject judge should know that the matter is closed.

The standards for timely filing under the Federal Rules of Appellate Procedure should be applied to petitions for review. *See* Fed. R. App. P. 25(a)(2)(A) and (C).

Rule 18(e) provides for an automatic extension of the time limit imposed under subsection (b) if a person files a petition that is rejected for failure to comply with formal requirements.

Rule 19. Judicial-Council Disposition of Petitions for Review.

(a) *Rights of Subject Judge.* — At any time after a complainant files a petition for review, the subject judge may file a written response with the circuit clerk. The clerk must promptly distribute copies of the response to each member of the judicial council or of the relevant panel, unless that member is disqualified under Rule 25. Copies must also be distributed to the chief judge, to the complainant, and to the Judicial Conference Committee on Judicial Conduct and Disability. The subject judge must not otherwise communicate with individual council members about the matter. The subject judge must be given copies of any communications to the judicial council from the complainant.

(b) *Judicial-Council Action.* — After considering a petition for review and the materials before it, a judicial council may:

(1) affirm the chief judge's disposition by denying the petition;

(2) return the matter to the chief judge with directions to conduct a further inquiry under Rule 11(b) or to identify a complaint under Rule 5;

(3) return the matter to the chief judge with directions to appoint a special committee under Rule 11(f); or

(4) in exceptional circumstances, take other appropriate action.

(c) *Notice of Council Decision.* — Copies of the judicial council's order, together with any accompanying memorandum in support of the order or separate concurring or dissenting statements, must be given to the complainant, the subject judge, and the Judicial Conference Committee on Judicial Conduct and Disability.

(d) *Memorandum of Council Decision.* — If the council's order affirms the chief judge's disposition, a supporting memorandum must be prepared only if the judicial council concludes that there is a need to supplement the chief judge's explanation. A memorandum supporting a council order must not include the name of the complainant or the subject judge.

(e) *Review of Judicial-Council Decision.* — If the judicial council's decision is adverse to the petitioner, and if no member of the council dissented on the ground that a special committee should be appointed under Rule 11(f), the complainant must be notified that he or she has no right to seek review of the decision. If there was a dissent, the petitioner must be informed that he or she can file a petition for review under Rule 21(b) solely on the issue of whether a special committee should be appointed.

(f) *Public Availability of Judicial-Council Decision.* — Materials related to the council's decision must be made public to the extent, at the time, and in the manner set forth in Rule 24.

COMMENT

This Rule is largely adapted from the Act and is self-explanatory.

The council should ordinarily review the decision of the chief judge on the merits, treating the petition for review for all practical purposes as an appeal. The judicial council may respond to a petition by affirming the chief judge's order, remanding the matter, or, in exceptional cases, taking other appropriate action.

Rule 20. Judicial-Council Consideration of Reports and Recommendations of Special Committees.

(a) *Rights of Subject Judge.* — Within 21 days after the filing of the report of a special committee, the subject judge may send a written response to the members of the judicial council. The judge must also be given an opportunity to present argument through counsel, written or oral, as determined by the council. The judge must not otherwise communicate with council members about the matter.

(b) *Judicial-Council Action.* — (1) Discretionary actions. Subject to the judge's rights set forth in subsection (a), the judicial council may:

(A) dismiss the complaint because:

(i) even if the claim is true, the claimed conduct is not conduct prejudicial to the effective and expeditious administration of the business of the courts and does not indicate a mental or physical disability resulting in inability to discharge the duties of office;

(ii) the complaint is directly related to the merits of a decision or procedural ruling;

(iii) the facts on which the complaint is based have not been established; or

(iv) the complaint is otherwise not appropriate for consideration under 28 U.S.C. §§ 351-364.

(B) conclude the proceeding because appropriate corrective action has been taken or intervening events have made the proceeding unnecessary.

(C) refer the complaint to the Judicial Conference of the United States with the council's recommendations for action.

(D) take remedial action to ensure the effective and expeditious administration of the business of the courts, including:

(i) censuring or reprimanding the subject judge, either by private communication or by public announcement;

(ii) ordering that no new cases be assigned to the subject judge for a limited, fixed period;

(iii) in the case of a magistrate judge, ordering the chief judge of the district court to take action specified by the council, including the initiation of removal proceedings under 28 U.S.C. § 631(i) or 42 U.S.C. § 300aa—12(c)(2);

(iv) in the case of a bankruptcy judge, removing the judge from office under 28 U.S.C. § 152(e);

(v) in the case of a circuit or district judge, requesting the judge to retire voluntarily with the provision (if necessary) that ordinary length-of-service requirements will be waived; and

(vi) in the case of a circuit or district judge who is eligible to retire but does not do so, certifying the disability of the judge under 28 U.S.C. § 372(b) so that an additional judge may be appointed.

(E) take any combination of actions described in (b)(1)(A)-(D) of this Rule that is within its power.

(2) Mandatory actions. A judicial council must refer a complaint to the Judicial Conference if the council determines that a circuit judge or district judge may have engaged in conduct that:

(A) might constitute ground for impeachment; or

(B) in the interest of justice, is not amenable to resolution by the judicial council.

(c) *Inadequate Basis for Decision.* — If the judicial council finds that a special committee's report, recommendations, and record provide an inadequate basis for decision, it may return the matter to the committee for further investigation and a new report, or it may conduct further investigation. If the judicial council decides to conduct further investigation, the subject judge must be given adequate prior notice in writing of that decision and of the general scope and purpose of the additional investigation. The judicial council's conduct of the additional investigation must generally accord with the procedures and powers set forth in Rules 13 through 16 for the conduct of an investigation by a special committee.

(d) *Council Vote.* — Council action must be taken by a majority of those members of the council who are not disqualified. A decision to remove a bankruptcy judge from office requires a majority vote of all the members of the council.

(e) *Recommendation for Fee Reimbursement.* — If the complaint has been finally dismissed or concluded under (b)(1)(A) or (B) of this Rule, and if the subject judge so requests, the judicial council may recommend that the Director of the Administrative Office of the United States Courts use funds appropriated to the Judiciary to reimburse the judge for reasonable expenses incurred during the investigation, when those expenses would not have been incurred but for the requirements of the Act and these Rules. Reasonable expenses include attorneys' fees and expenses related to a successful defense or prosecution of a proceeding under Rule 21(a) or (b).

(f) *Council Action.* — Council action must be by written order. Unless the council finds that extraordinary reasons would make it contrary to the interests of justice, the order must be accompanied by a memorandum setting forth the factual determinations on which it is based and the reasons for the council action. The order and the supporting memorandum must be provided to the complainant, the subject judge, and the Judicial Conference Committee on Judicial Conduct and Disability. The complainant and the subject judge must be notified of any right to review of the judicial council's decision as provided in Rule 21(b).

COMMENT

This Rule is largely adapted from the Illustrative Rules.

Rule 20(a) provides that within twenty-one days after the filing of the report of a special committee, the subject judge may address a written response to all of the members of the judicial council. The subject judge must also be given an opportunity to present oral argument to the council, personally or through counsel. The subject judge may not otherwise communicate with council members about the matter.

Rule 20(c) provides that if the judicial council decides to conduct an additional investigation, the subject judge must be given adequate prior notice in writing of that decision and of the general scope and purpose of the additional investigation. The conduct of the investigation will be generally in accordance with the procedures set forth in Rules 13 through 16 for the conduct of an investigation by a special committee. However, if hearings are held, the council may limit testimony or the presentation of evidence to avoid unnecessary repetition of testimony and evidence before the special committee.

Rule 20(d) provides that council action must be taken by a majority of those members of the council who are not disqualified, except that a decision to remove a bankruptcy judge from office requires a majority of all the members of the council as required by 28 U.S.C. § 152(e). However, it is inappropriate to apply a similar rule to the less severe actions that a judicial council may take under the Act. If some members of the council are disqualified in the matter, their disqualification should not be given the effect of a vote against council action.

With regard to Rule 20(e), the judicial council, on the request of the subject judge, may recommend to the Director of the Administrative Office of the United States Courts that the subject judge be reimbursed for reasonable expenses, including attorneys' fees, incurred. The judicial council has the authority to recommend such reimbursement where, after investigation by a special committee, the complaint has been finally dismissed or concluded under subsection (b)(1)(A) or (B) of this Rule. It is contemplated that such reimbursement may be provided for the successful prosecution or defense of a proceeding under Rule 21(a) or (b), in other words, one that results in a Rule 20(b)(1)(A) or (B) dismissal or conclusion.

Rule 20(f) requires that council action normally be supported with a memorandum of factual determinations and reasons and that notice of the action be given to the complainant and the subject judge. Rule 20(f) also requires that the notification to the complainant and the subject judge include notice of any right to petition for review of the council's decision under Rule 21(b).

ARTICLE VI. REVIEW BY JUDICIAL CONFERENCE COMMITTEE ON CONDUCT AND DISABILITY.

Rule 21. Committee on Judicial Conduct and Disability.

(a) *Review by Committee.* — The Committee on Judicial Conduct and Disability, consisting of seven members, considers and disposes of all petitions for review under (b) of this Rule, in conformity with the Committee's jurisdictional statement. Its disposition of petitions for review is ordinarily final. The Judicial Conference of the United States may, in its sole discretion, review any such Committee decision, but a complainant or subject judge does not have a right to this review.

(b) *Reviewable Matters.* — (1) Upon petition. A complainant or subject judge may petition the Committee for review of a judicial-council order entered in accordance with:

(A) Rule 20(b)(1)(A), (B), (D), or (E); or

(B) Rule 19(b)(1) or (4) if one or more members of the judicial council dissented from the order on the ground that a special committee should be appointed under Rule 11(f); in that event, the Committee's review will be limited to the issue of whether a special committee should be appointed.

(2) Upon Committee's initiative. At its initiative and in its sole discretion, the Committee may review any judicial-council order entered under Rule 19(b)(1) or (4), but only to determine whether a special committee should be appointed. Before undertaking the review, the Committee must invite that judicial council to explain why it believes the appointment of a special committee is unnecessary, unless the reasons are clearly stated in the judicial council's order denying the petition for review. If the Committee believes that it would benefit from a submission by the subject judge, it may issue an appropriate request. If the Committee determines that a special committee should be appointed, the Committee must issue a written decision giving its reasons.

(c) *Committee Vote.* — Any member of the Committee from the same circuit as the subject judge is disqualified from considering or voting on a petition for review. Committee decisions under (b) of this Rule must be by majority vote of the qualified Committee members. If only six members are qualified to vote on a petition for review, the decision must be made by a majority of a panel of five members drawn from a randomly selected list that rotates after each decision by a panel drawn from the list. The members who will determine the petition must be selected based on committee membership as of the date on which the petition is received. Those members selected to hear the petition should serve in that capacity until final disposition of the petition, whether or not their term of committee membership has ended. If only four members are qualified to vote, the Chief Justice must appoint, if available, an ex-member of the Committee or, if not, another United States judge to consider the petition.

(d) *Additional Investigation.* — Except in extraordinary circumstances, the Committee will not conduct an additional investigation. The Committee may return the matter to the judicial council with directions to undertake an additional investigation. If the Committee conducts an additional investigation, it will exercise the powers of the Judicial Conference under 28 U.S.C. § 331.

(e) *Oral Argument; Personal Appearance.* — There is ordinarily no oral argument or personal appearance before the Committee. In its discretion, the Committee may permit written submissions from the complainant or subject judge.

(f) *Committee Decisions.* — Committee decisions under this Rule must be transmitted promptly to the Judicial Conference of the United States. Other distribution will be by the Administrative Office at the direction of the Committee chair.

(g) *Finality.* — All orders of the Judicial Conference or of the Committee (when the Conference does not exercise its power of review) are final.

COMMENT

This Rule is largely self-explanatory.

Rule 21(a) is intended to clarify that the delegation of power to the Judicial Conference Committee on Judicial Conduct and Disability to dispose of petitions does not preclude review of such dispositions by the Conference. However, there is no right to such review in any party.

Rules 21(b)(1)(B) and (b)(2) are intended to fill a jurisdictional gap as to review of dismissals or conclusions of complaints under Rule 19(b)(1) or (4). Where one or more members of a judicial council reviewing a petition have dissented on the ground that a special committee should have been appointed, the complainant or subject judge has the right to petition for review by the Committee but only as to that issue. Under Rule 21(b)(2), the Judicial Conference Committee on Judicial Conduct and Disability may review such a dismissal or conclusion in its sole discretion, whether or not such a dissent occurred, and only as to the appointment of a special committee. No party has a right to such review, and such review will be rare.

Rule 21(c) provides for review only by Committee members from circuits other than that of the subject judge. To avoid tie votes, the Committee will decide petitions for review by rotating panels of five when only six members are qualified. If only four members are qualified, the Chief Justice must appoint an additional judge to consider that petition for review.

Under this Rule, all Committee decisions are final in that they are unreviewable unless the Judicial Conference, in its discretion, decides to review a decision. Committee decisions, however, do not necessarily constitute final action on a complaint for purposes of Rule 24.

Rule 22. Procedures for Review.

(a) *Filing a Petition for Review.* — A petition for review of a judicial-council decision may be filed by sending a brief written statement to the Judicial Conference Committee on Judicial Conduct and Disability, addressed to:

Judicial Conference Committee on Judicial Conduct and Disability
Attn: Office of General Counsel
Administrative Office of the United States Courts
One Columbus Circle, NE
Washington, D.C. 20544

The Administrative Office will send a copy of the petition to the complainant or subject judge, as the case may be.

(b) *Form and Contents of Petition for Review.* — No particular form is required. The petition must contain a short statement of the basic facts underlying the complaint, the history of its consideration before the appropriate judicial council, a copy of the judicial council's decision, and the grounds on which the petitioner seeks review. The petition for review must specify the date and docket number of the judicial-council order for which review is sought. The petitioner may attach any documents or correspondence arising in the course of the proceeding before the judicial council or its special committee. A petition should not normally exceed 20 pages plus necessary attachments.

(c) *Time.* — A petition must be submitted within 63 days of the date of the order for which review is sought.

(d) *Copies.* — Seven copies of the petition for review must be submitted, at least one of which must be signed by the petitioner or his or her attorney. If the petitioner submits a signed declaration of inability to pay the expense of duplicating the petition, the Administrative Office must accept the original petition and must reproduce copies at its expense.

(e) *Action on Receipt of Petition for Review.* — The Administrative Office must acknowledge receipt of a petition for review submitted under this Rule, notify the chair of the Judicial Conference Committee on Judicial Conduct and Disability, and distribute the petition to the members of the Committee for their deliberation.

COMMENT

Rule 22 is self-explanatory.

ARTICLE VII. MISCELLANEOUS RULES.

Rule 23. Confidentiality.

(a) *General Rule.* — The consideration of a complaint by the chief judge, a special committee, the judicial council, or the Judicial Conference Committee on Judicial Conduct and Disability is confidential. Information about this consideration must not be disclosed by any judge or employee of the judicial branch or by any person who records or transcribes testimony except as allowed by these Rules. In extraordinary circumstances, a chief judge may disclose the existence of a proceeding under these Rules when necessary to maintain public confidence in the federal judiciary's ability to redress misconduct or disability.

(b) *Files.* — All files related to complaints must be separately maintained with appropriate security precautions to ensure confidentiality.

(c) *Disclosure in Decisions.* — Except as otherwise provided in Rule 24, written decisions of the chief judge, the judicial council, or the Judicial Conference Committee on Judicial Conduct and Disability, and dissenting opinions or separate statements of members of the council or Committee may contain information and exhibits that the authors consider appropriate for inclusion, and the information and exhibits may be made public.

(d) *Availability to Judicial Conference.* — On request of the Judicial Conference or its Committee on Judicial Conduct and Disability, the circuit clerk must furnish any requested records related to a complaint. For auditing purposes, the circuit clerk must provide access to the Committee to records of proceedings under the Act at the site where the records are kept.

(e) *Availability to District Court.* — If the judicial council directs the initiation of proceedings for removal of a magistrate judge under Rule 20(b)(1)(D)(iii), the circuit clerk must provide to the chief judge of the district court copies of the report of the special committee and any other documents and records that were before the judicial council at the time of its decision. On request of the chief judge of the district court, the judicial council may authorize release to that chief judge of any other records relating to the investigation.

(f) *Impeachment Proceedings.* — If the Judicial Conference determines that consideration of impeachment may be warranted, it must transmit the record of all relevant proceedings to the Speaker of the House of Representatives.

(g) *Subject Judge's Consent.* — If both the subject judge and the chief judge consent in writing, any materials from the files may be disclosed to any person. In any such disclosure, the chief judge may require that the identity of the complainant, or of witnesses in an investigation conducted by a chief judge, a special committee, or the judicial council, not be revealed.

(h) *Disclosure in Special Circumstances.* — The Judicial Conference, its Committee on Judicial Conduct and Disability, or a judicial council may authorize disclosure of information about the consideration of a complaint, including the papers, documents, and transcripts relating to the investigation, to the extent that disclosure is justified by special circumstances and is not prohibited by the Act. Disclosure may be made to judicial researchers engaged in the study or evaluation of experience under the Act and related modes of judicial discipline, but only where the study or evaluation has been specifically approved by the Judicial Conference or by the Judicial Conference Committee on Judicial Conduct and Disability. Appropriate steps must be taken to protect the identities of the subject judge, the complainant, and witnesses from public disclosure. Other appropriate safeguards to protect against the dissemination of confidential information may be imposed.

(i) *Disclosure of Identity by Subject Judge.* — Nothing in this Rule precludes the subject judge from acknowledging that he or she is the judge referred to in documents made public under Rule 24.

(j) *Assistance and Consultation.* — Nothing in this Rule precludes the chief judge or judicial council acting on a complaint filed under the Act from seeking the help of qualified staff or from consulting other judges who may be helpful in the disposition of the complaint.

COMMENT

Rule 23 was adapted from the Illustrative Rules.

The Act applies a rule of confidentiality to "papers, documents, and records of proceedings related to investigations conducted under this chapter" and states that they may not be disclosed "by any person in any proceeding," with enumerated exceptions. 28 U.S.C. § 360(a). Three questions arise: Who is bound by the confidentiality rule, what proceedings are subject to the rule, and who is within the circle of people who may have access to information without breaching the rule?

With regard to the first question, Rule 23(a) provides that judges, employees of the judicial branch, and those persons involved in recording proceedings and preparing transcripts are obliged to respect the confidentiality requirement. This of course includes subject judges who do not consent to identification under Rule 23(i).

With regard to the second question, Rule 23(a) applies the rule of confidentiality broadly to consideration of a complaint at any stage.

With regard to the third question, there is no barrier of confidentiality among a chief judge, judicial council, the Judicial Conference, and the Judicial Conference Committee on Judicial Conduct and Disability. Each may have access to any of the confidential records for use in their consideration of a referred matter, a petition for review, or monitoring the administration of the Act. A district court may have similar access if the judicial council orders the district court to initiate proceedings to remove a magistrate judge from office, and Rule 23(e) so provides.

In extraordinary circumstances, a chief judge may disclose the existence of a proceeding under these Rules. The disclosure of such information in high-visibility or controversial cases is to reassure the public that the federal judiciary is capable of redressing judicial misconduct or disability. Moreover, the confidentiality requirement does not prevent the chief judge from "communicat[ing] orally or in writing with ... [persons] who may have knowledge of the matter," as part of a limited inquiry conducted by the chief judge under Rule 11(b).

Rule 23 recognizes that there must be some exceptions to the Act's confidentiality requirement. For example, the Act requires that certain orders and the reasons for them must be made public. 28 U.S.C. § 360(b). Rule 23(c) makes it explicit that memoranda supporting chief judge and council orders, as well as dissenting opinions and separate statements, may contain references to information that would otherwise be confidential and that such information may be made public. However, subsection (c) is subject to Rule 24(a) which provides the general rule regarding the public availability of decisions. For example, the name of a subject judge cannot be made public in a decision if disclosure of the name is prohibited by that Rule.

The Act makes clear that there is a barrier of confidentiality between the judicial branch and the legislative. It provides that material may be disclosed to Congress only if it is believed necessary to an impeachment investigation or trial of a judge. 28 U.S.C. § 360(a)(2). Accordingly, Section 355(b) of the Act requires the Judicial Conference to transmit the record of the proceeding to the House of Representatives if the Conference believes that impeachment of a subject judge may be appropriate. Rule 23(f) implements this requirement.

The Act provides that confidential materials may be disclosed if authorized in writing by the subject judge and by the chief judge. 28 U.S.C. § 360(a)(3). Rule 23(g) implements this requirement. Once the subject judge has consented to the disclosure of confidential materials related to a complaint, the chief judge ordinarily will refuse consent only to the extent necessary to protect the confidentiality interests of the complainant or of witnesses who have testified in investigatory proceedings or who have provided information in response to a limited inquiry undertaken pursuant to Rule 11. It will generally be necessary, therefore, for the chief judge to require that the identities of the complainant or of such witnesses, as well as any identifying information, be shielded in any materials disclosed, except insofar as the chief judge has secured the consent of the complainant or of a particular witness to disclosure, or there is a demonstrated need for disclosure of the information that, in the judgment of the chief judge, outweighs the confidentiality interest of the complainant or of a particular witness (as may be the case where the complainant is delusional or where the complainant or a particular witness has already demonstrated a lack of concern about maintaining the confidentiality of the proceedings).

Rule 23(h) permits disclosure of additional information in circumstances not enumerated. For example, disclosure may be appropriate to permit a prosecution for perjury based on testimony given before a special committee. Another example might involve evidence of criminal conduct by a judge discovered by a special committee.

Subsection (h) also permits the authorization of disclosure of information about the consideration of a complaint, including the papers, documents, and transcripts relating to the investigation, to judicial researchers engaged in the study or evaluation of experience under the Act and related modes of judicial discipline. The Rule envisions disclosure of information from the official record of complaint proceedings to a limited category of persons for appropriately authorized research purposes only, and with appropriate safeguards to protect individual identities in any published research results that ensue. In authorizing disclosure, the judicial council may refuse to release particular materials when such release would be contrary to the interests of justice, or that constitute purely internal communications. The Rule does not envision disclosure of purely internal communications between judges and their colleagues and staff.

Under Rule 23(j), chief judges and judicial councils may seek staff assistance or consult with other judges who may be helpful in the process of complaint disposition; the confidentiality requirement does not preclude this. The chief judge, for example, may properly seek the advice and assistance of another judge who the chief judge deems to be in the best position to communicate with the subject judge in an attempt to bring about corrective action. As another example, a new chief judge may wish to confer with a predecessor to learn how similar complaints have been handled. In consulting with other judges, of course, the chief judge should disclose information regarding the complaint only to the extent the chief judge deems necessary under the circumstances.

Rule 24. Public Availability of Decisions.

(a) *General Rule; Specific Cases.* — When final action has been taken on a complaint and it is no longer subject to review, all orders entered by the chief judge and judicial council, including any supporting memoranda and any dissenting opinions or separate statements by members of the judicial council, must be made public, with the following exceptions:

(1) if the complaint is finally dismissed under Rule 11(c) without the appointment of a special committee, or if it is concluded under Rule 11(d) because of voluntary corrective action, the publicly available materials must not disclose the name of the subject judge without his or her consent.

(2) if the complaint is concluded because of intervening events, or dismissed at any time after a special committee is appointed, the judicial council must determine whether the name of the subject judge should be disclosed.

(3) if the complaint is finally disposed of by a privately communicated censure or reprimand, the publicly available materials must not disclose either the name of the subject judge or the text of the reprimand.

(4) if the complaint is finally disposed of under Rule 20(b)(1)(D) by any action other than private censure or reprimand, the text of the dispositive order must be included in the materials made public, and the name of the subject judge must be disclosed.

(5) the name of the complainant must not be disclosed in materials made public under this Rule unless the chief judge orders disclosure.

(b) *Manner of Making Public.* — The orders described in (a) must be made public by placing them in a publicly accessible file in the office of the circuit clerk or by placing the orders on the court's public website. If the orders appear to have precedential value, the chief judge may cause them to be published. In addition, the Judicial Conference Committee on Judicial Conduct and Disability will make available on the Federal Judiciary's website, www.uscourts.gov, selected illustrative orders described in paragraph (a), appropriately redacted, to provide additional information to the public on how complaints are addressed under the Act.

(c) *Orders of Judicial Conference Committee.* — Orders of this Committee constituting final action in a complaint proceeding arising from a particular circuit will be made available to the public in the office of the clerk of the relevant court of appeals. The Committee will also make such orders available on the Federal Judiciary's website, www.uscourts.gov. When authorized by the Committee, other orders related to complaint proceedings will similarly be made available.

(d) *Complaints Referred to the Judicial Conference of the United States.* — If a complaint is referred to the Judicial Conference under Rule 20(b)(1)(C) or 20(b)(2), materials relating to the complaint will be made public only if ordered by the Judicial Conference.

COMMENT

Rule 24 is adapted from the Illustrative Rules and the recommendations of the Breyer Committee.

The Act requires the circuits to make available only written orders of a judicial council or the Judicial Conference imposing some form of sanction. 28 U.S.C. § 360(b). The Judicial Conference, however, has long recognized the desirability of public availability of a broader range of orders and other materials. In 1994, the Judicial Conference "urge[d] all circuits and courts covered by the Act to submit to the West Publishing Company, for publication in Federal Reporter 3d, and to Lexis all orders issued pursuant to [the Act] that are deemed by the issuing circuit or court to have significant precedential value to other circuits and courts covered by the Act." Report of the Proceedings of the Judicial Conference of the United States, Mar. 1994, at 28. Following this recommendation, the 2000 revision of the Illustrative Rules contained a public availability provision very similar to Rule 24. In 2002, the Judicial Conference again voted to encourage the circuits "to submit non-routine public orders disposing of complaints of judicial misconduct or disability for publication by on-line and print services." Report of the Proceedings of the Judicial Conference of the United States, Sept. 2002, at 58. The Breyer Committee Report further emphasized that "[p]osting such orders on the judicial branch's public website would not only benefit judges directly, it would also encourage scholarly commentary and analysis of the orders." Breyer Committee Report, 239 F.R.D. at 216. With these considerations in mind, Rule 24 provides for public availability of a wide range of materials.

Rule 24 provides for public availability of orders of the chief judge, the judicial council, and the Judicial Conference Committee on Judicial Conduct and Disability and the texts of any memoranda supporting their orders, together with any dissenting opinions or separate statements by members of the judicial council. However, these orders and memoranda are to be made public only when final action on the complaint has been taken and any right of review has been exhausted. The provision that decisions will be made public only after final action has been taken is designed in part to avoid public disclosure of the existence of pending proceedings. Whether the name of the subject judge is disclosed will then depend on the nature of the final action. If the final action is an order predicated on a finding of misconduct or disability (other than a privately communicated censure or reprimand) the name of the judge must be made public. If the final action is dismissal of the complaint, the name of the subject judge must not be disclosed. Rule 24(a)(1) provides that where a proceeding is concluded under Rule 11(d) by the chief judge on the basis of voluntary corrective action, the name of the subject judge must not be disclosed. Shielding the name of the subject judge in this circumstance should encourage informal disposition.

If a complaint is dismissed as moot, or because intervening events have made action on the complaint unnecessary, after appointment of a special committee, Rule 24(a)(2) allows the judicial council to determine whether the subject judge will be identified. In such a case, no final decision has been rendered on the merits, but it may be in the public interest — particularly if a judicial officer resigns in the course of an investigation — to make the identity of the judge known.

Once a special committee has been appointed, and a proceeding is concluded by the full council on the basis of a remedial order of the council, Rule 24(a)(4) provides for disclosure of the name of the subject judge.

Finally, Rule 24(a)(5) provides that the identity of the complainant will be disclosed only if the chief judge so orders. Identifying the complainant when the subject judge is not identified would increase the likelihood that the identity of the subject judge would become publicly known, thus circumventing the policy of nondisclosure. It may not always be practicable to shield the complainant's identity while making public disclosure of the judicial council's order and supporting memoranda; in some circumstances, moreover, the complainant may consent to public identification.

Rule 25. Disqualification.

(a) *General Rule.* — Any judge is disqualified from participating in any proceeding under these Rules if the judge, in his or her discretion, concludes that circumstances warrant disqualification. If the complaint is filed by a judge, that judge is disqualified from participating in any consideration of the complaint except to the extent that these Rules provide for a complainant's participation. A chief judge who has identified a complaint under Rule 5 is not automatically disqualified from considering the complaint.

(b) *Subject Judge.* — A subject judge is disqualified from considering the complaint except to the extent that these Rules provide for participation by a subject judge.

(c) *Chief Judge Not Disqualified from Considering a Petition for Review of a Chief Judge's Order.* — If a petition for review of a chief judge's order entered under Rule 11(c), (d), or (e) is filed with the judicial council in accordance with Rule 18, the chief judge is not disqualified from participating in the council's consideration of the petition.

(d) *Member of Special Committee Not Disqualified.* — A member of the judicial council who serves on a special committee, including the chief judge, is not disqualified from participating in council consideration of the committee's report.

(e) *Subject Judge's Disqualification After Appointment of a Special Committee.* — Upon appointment of a special committee, the subject judge is automatically disqualified from participating in any proceeding arising under the Act or these Rules as a member of any special committee, the judicial council of the circuit, the Judicial Conference of the United States, and the Judicial Conference Committee on Judicial Conduct and Disability. The disqualification continues until all proceedings on the complaint against the subject judge are finally terminated with no further right of review.

(f) *Substitute for Disqualified Chief Judge.* — If the chief judge is disqualified from participating in consideration of the complaint, the duties and responsibilities of the chief judge under these Rules must be assigned to the most-senior active circuit judge not disqualified. If all circuit judges in regular active service are disqualified, the judicial council may determine whether to request a transfer under Rule 26, or, in the interest of sound judicial administration, to permit the chief judge to dispose of the complaint on the merits. Members of the judicial council who are named in the complaint may participate in this determination if necessary to obtain a quorum of the judicial council.

(g) *Judicial-Council Action When Multiple Judges Are Disqualified.* — Notwithstanding any other provision in these Rules to the contrary,

(1) a member of the judicial council who is a subject judge may participate in its disposition if:

(A) participation by one or more subject judges is necessary to obtain a quorum of the judicial council;

(B) the judicial council finds that the lack of a quorum is due to the naming of one or more judges in the complaint for the purpose of disqualifying that judge or judges, or to the naming of one or more judges based on their participation in a decision excluded from the definition of misconduct under Rule 3(h)(3); and

(C) the judicial council votes that it is necessary, appropriate, and in the interest of sound judicial administration that one or more subject judges be eligible to act.

(2) otherwise disqualified members may participate in votes taken under (g)(1)(B) and (g)(1)(C).

(h) *Disqualification of Members of the Judicial Conference Committee.* — No member of the Judicial Conference Committee on Judicial Conduct and Disability is disqualified from participating in any proceeding under the Act or these Rules because of consultations with a chief judge, a member of a special committee, or a member of a judicial council about the interpretation or application of the Act or these Rules, unless the member believes that the consultation would prevent fair-minded participation.

COMMENT

Rule 25 is adapted from the Illustrative Rules.

Subsection (a) provides the general rule for disqualification. Of course, a judge is not disqualified simply because the subject judge is on the same court. However, this subsection recognizes that there may be cases in which an appearance of bias or prejudice is created by circumstances other than an association with the subject judge as a colleague. For example, a judge may have a familial relationship with a complainant or subject judge. When such circumstances exist, a judge may, in his or her discretion, conclude that disqualification is warranted.

Subsection (e) makes it clear that the disqualification of the subject judge relates only to the subject judge's participation in any proceeding arising under the Act or these Rules as a member of a special committee, judicial council, Judicial Conference, or the Judicial Conference Committee. The Illustrative Rule, based on Section 359(a) of the Act, is ambiguous and could be read to disqualify a subject judge from service of any kind on each of the bodies mentioned. This is undoubtedly not the intent of the Act; such a disqualification would be anomalous in light of the Act's allowing a subject judge to continue to decide cases and to continue to exercise the powers of chief circuit or district judge. It would also create a substantial deterrence to the appointment of special committees, particularly where a special committee is needed solely because the chief judge may not decide matters of credibility in his or her review under Rule 11.

While a subject judge is barred by Rule 25(b) from participating in the disposition of the complaint in which he or she is named, Rule 25(e) recognizes that participation in proceedings arising under the Act or these Rules by a judge who is the subject of a special committee investigation may lead to an appearance of self-interest in creating substantive and procedural precedents governing such proceedings; Rule 25(e) bars such participation.

Under the Act, a complaint against the chief judge is to be handled by "that circuit judge in regular active service next senior in date of commission." 28 U.S.C. § 351(c). Rule 25(f) provides that seniority among judges other than the chief judge is to be determined by date of commission, with the result that complaints against the chief judge may be routed to a former chief judge or other judge who was appointed earlier than the chief judge. The Rules do not purport to prescribe who is to preside over meetings of the judicial council. Consequently, where the presiding member of the judicial council is disqualified from participating under these Rules, the order of precedence prescribed by Rule 25(f) for performing "the duties and responsibilities of the chief circuit judge under these Rules" does not apply to determine the acting presiding member of the judicial council. That is a matter left to the internal rules or operating practices of each judicial council. In most cases the most senior active circuit judge who is a member of the judicial council and who is not disqualified will preside.

Sometimes a single complaint is filed against a large group of judges. If the normal disqualification rules are observed in such a case, no court of appeals judge can serve as acting chief judge of the circuit, and the judicial council will be without appellate members. Where the complaint is against all circuit and district judges, under normal rules no member of the judicial council can perform the duties assigned to the council under the statute.

A similar problem is created by successive complaints arising out of the same underlying grievance. For example, a complainant files a complaint against a district judge based on alleged misconduct, and the complaint is dismissed by the chief judge under the statute. The complainant may then file a complaint against the chief judge for dismissing the first complaint, and when that complaint is dismissed by the next senior judge, still a third complaint may be filed. The threat is that the complainant will bump down the seniority ladder until, once again, there is no member of the court of appeals who can serve as acting chief judge for the purpose of the next complaint. Similarly, complaints involving the merits of litigation may involve a series of decisions in which many judges participated or in which a rehearing en banc was denied by the court of appeals, and the complaint may name a majority of the judicial council as subject judges.

In recognition that these multiple-judge complaints are virtually always meritless, the judicial council is given discretion to determine: (1) whether it is necessary, appropriate, and in the interest of sound judicial administration to permit the chief judge to dispose of a complaint where it would otherwise be impossible for any active circuit judge in the circuit to act, and (2) whether it is necessary, appropriate, and in the interest of sound judicial administration, after appropriate findings as to need and justification are made, to permit subject judges of the judicial council to participate in the disposition of a petition for review where it would otherwise be impossible to obtain a quorum.

Applying a rule of necessity in these situations is consistent with the appearance of justice. *See, e.g.*, *In re Complaint of Doe*, 2 F.3d 308 (8th Cir. Jud. Council 1993) (invoking the rule of necessity); *In re Complaint of Judicial Misconduct*, No. 91-80464 (9th Cir. Jud. Council 1992) (same). There is no unfairness in permitting the chief judge to dispose of a patently insubstantial complaint that names all active circuit judges in the circuit.

Similarly, there is no unfairness in permitting subject judges, in these circumstances, to participate in the review of a chief judge's dismissal of an insubstantial complaint. The remaining option is to assign the matter to another body. Among other alternatives, the council may request a transfer of the petition under Rule 26. Given the administrative inconvenience and delay involved in these alternatives, it is desirable to request a transfer only if the judicial council determines that the petition is substantial enough to warrant such action.

In the unlikely event that a quorum of the judicial council cannot be obtained to consider the report of a special committee, it would normally be necessary to request a transfer under Rule 26.

Rule 25(h) recognizes that the jurisdictional statement of the Judicial Conference Committee contemplates consultation between members of the Committee and judicial participants in proceedings under the Act and these Rules. Such consultation should not automatically preclude participation by a member in that proceeding.

Rule 26. Transfer to Another Judicial Council.

In exceptional circumstances, a chief judge or a judicial council may ask the Chief Justice to transfer a proceeding based on a complaint identified under Rule 5 or filed under Rule 6 to the judicial council of another circuit. The request for a transfer may be made at any stage of the proceeding before a reference to the Judicial Conference under Rule 20(b)(1)(C) or 20(b)(2) or a petition for review is filed under Rule 22. Upon receiving such a request, the Chief Justice may refuse the request or select the transferee judicial council, which may then exercise the powers of a judicial council under these Rules.

COMMENT

Rule 26 is new; it implements the Breyer Committee's recommended use of transfers. Breyer Committee Report, 239 F.R.D. at 214-15.

Rule 26 authorizes the transfer of a complaint proceeding to another judicial council selected by the Chief Justice. Such transfers may be appropriate, for example, in the case of a serious complaint where there are multiple disqualifications among the original council, where the issues are highly visible and a local disposition may weaken public confidence in the process, where internal tensions arising in the council as a result of the complaint render disposition by a less involved council appropriate, or where a complaint calls into question policies or governance of the home court of appeals. The power to effect a transfer is lodged in the Chief Justice to avoid disputes in a council over where to transfer a sensitive matter and to ensure that the transferee council accepts the matter.

Upon receipt of a transferred proceeding, the transferee council shall determine the proper stage at which to begin consideration of the complaint — for example, reference to the transferee chief judge, appointment of a special committee, etc.

Rule 27. Withdrawal of Complaints and Petitions for Review.

(a) *Complaint Pending Before Chief Judge.* — With the chief judge's consent, a complainant may withdraw a complaint that is before the chief judge for a decision under Rule 11. The withdrawal of a complaint will not prevent a chief judge from identifying or having to identify a complaint under Rule 5 based on the withdrawn complaint.

(b) *Complaint Pending before Special Committee or Judicial Council.* — After a complaint has been referred to a special committee for investigation and before the committee files its report, the complainant may withdraw the complaint only with the consent of both the subject judge and either the special committee or the judicial council.

(c) *Petition for Review.* — A petition for review addressed to a judicial council under Rule 18, or the Judicial Conference Committee on Judicial Conduct and Disability under Rule 22 may be withdrawn if no action on the petition has been taken.

COMMENT

Rule 27 is adapted from the Illustrative Rules and treats the complaint proceeding, once begun, as a matter of public business rather than as the property of the complainant. Accordingly, the chief judge or the judicial council remains responsible for addressing any complaint under the Act, even a complaint that has been formally withdrawn by the complainant.

Under subsection 27(a), a complaint pending before the chief judge may be withdrawn if the chief judge consents. Where the complaint clearly lacked merit, the chief judge may accordingly be saved the burden of preparing a formal order and supporting memorandum. However, the chief judge may, or be obligated under Rule 5, to identify a complaint based on allegations in a withdrawn complaint.

If the chief judge appoints a special committee, Rule 27(b) provides that the complaint may be withdrawn only with the consent of both the body before which it is pending (the special committee or the judicial council) and the subject judge. Once a complaint has reached the stage of appointment of a special committee, a resolution of the issues may be necessary to preserve public confidence. Moreover, the subject judge is given the right to insist that the matter be resolved on the merits, thereby eliminating any ambiguity that might remain if the proceeding were terminated by withdrawal of the complaint.

With regard to all petitions for review, Rule 27(c) grants the petitioner unrestricted authority to withdraw the petition. It is thought that the public's interest in the proceeding is adequately protected, because there will necessarily have been a decision by the chief judge and often by the judicial council as well in such a case.

Rule 28. Availability of Rules and Forms.

These Rules and copies of the complaint form as provided in Rule 6(a) must be available without charge in the office of the clerk of each court of appeals, district court, bankruptcy court, or other federal court whose judges are subject to the Act. Each court must also make these Rules and the complaint form available on the court's website, or provide an Internet link to the Rules and complaint form that are available on the appropriate court of appeals' website.

Rule 29. Effective Date.

These Rules will become effective 30 days after promulgation by the Judicial Conference of the United States.

APPENDIX

Judicial Council of the ______ Circuit

COMPLAINT OF JUDICIAL MISCONDUCT OR DISABILITY

To begin the complaint process, complete this form and prepare the brief statement of facts described in item 5 (below). The RULES FOR JUDICIAL-CONDUCT AND JUDICIAL-DISABILITY PROCEEDINGS, adopted by the Judicial Conference of the United States, contain information on what to include in a complaint (Rule 6), where to file a complaint (Rule 7), and other important matters. The rules are available in federal court clerks' offices, on individual federal courts' Web sites, and on www.uscourts.gov.

Your complaint (this form and the statement of facts) should be typewritten and must be legible. For the number of copies to file, consult the local rules or clerk's office of the court in which your complaint is required to be filed. Enclose each copy of the complaint in an envelope marked "COMPLAINT OF MISCONDUCT" or "COMPLAINT OF DISABILITY" and submit it to the appropriate clerk of court. **Do not put the name of any judge on the envelope.**

1. Name of Complainant: ______
   Contact Address: ______

   Daytime telephone: (____) ______
2. Name(s) of Judge(s): ______
   Court: ______
3. Does this complaint concern the behavior of the judge(s) in a particular lawsuit or lawsuits?
   [ ] Yes [ ] No
   If "yes," give the following information about each lawsuit:
   Court: ______
   Case Number: ______
   Docket number of any appeal to the ______ Circuit: ______
   Are (were) you a party or lawyer in the lawsuit?
   [ ] Party [ ] Lawyer [ ] Neither
   If you are (were) a party and have (had) a lawyer, give the lawyer's name, address, and telephone number:
   ______
4. Have you filed any lawsuits against the judge?
   [ ] Yes [ ] No
   If "yes," give the following information about each lawsuit:
   Court: ______
   Case number: ______
   Present status of lawsuit: ______
   Name, address, and telephone number of your lawyer for the lawsuit against the judge:
   ______

   Court to which any appeal has been taken in the lawsuit against the judge:
   ______
   Docket number of the appeal: ______
   Present status of the appeal: ______
5. Brief Statement of Facts. Attach a brief statement of the specific facts on which the claim of judicial misconduct or disability is based. Include what happened, when and where it happened, and any information that would help an investigator check the facts. If the complaint alleges judicial disability, also include any additional facts that form the basis of that allegation.

6. Declaration and signature:

I declare under penalty of perjury that the statements made in this complaint are true and correct to the best of my knowledge.

(Signature) ____________________ (Date) ______________________________

Index to Fourth Circuit Judicial Council

A

ABUSIVE COMPLAINTS.
Abuse of complaint procedure, JCJD Rule 10.

APPLICABILITY OF RULES, JCJD Rule 2.

ATTORNEYS AT LAW.
Special committee, right to counsel.
Rights of complainant, JCJD Rule 16.
Rights of subject judges, JCJD Rules 14, 15.

AVAILABILITY OF RULES AND FORMS, JCJD Rule 27.

B

BANKRUPTCY COURTS AND JUDGES.
Covered judges, JCJD Rule 4.
Special committee.
Advisers, JCJD Rule 12.

C

CHIEF JUDGE.
Complaints.
Identification of a complaint, JCJD Rule 5.
Public availability of decisions, JCJD Rule 24.
Review by chief judge, JCJD Rule 11.
Petitions for review of chief judge dispositions, JCJD Rule 18.
Defined, JCJD Rule 3.
Disqualification of judges, JCJD Rule 25.
Transfer to another judicial council, JCJD Rule 26.

CIRCUIT.
Defined, JCJD Rule 3.

CIRCUIT CLERK.
Availability of rules and forms, JCJD Rule 27.
Complaints.
Action by clerk, JCJD Rule 8.
Defined, JCJD Rule 3.

COMMITTEE ON JUDICIAL CONDUCT AND DISABILITY.
Disqualification of judges, JCJD Rule 25.
Public availability of decisions, JCJD Rule 24.
Review of judicial council dispositions, JCJD Rule 21.
Procedures for review, JCJD Rule 22.

COMPLAINTS.
Abuse of complaint procedure, JCJD Rule 10.
Abusive complaints.
Abuse of complaint procedure, JCJD Rule 10.
Chief judge.
Identification of a complaint, JCJD Rule 5.
Review by chief judge, JCJD Rule 11.
Judicial council review of chief judge dispositions, JCJD Rule 18.
Circuit clerk.
Action by clerk, JCJD Rule 8.

COMPLAINTS —Cont'd
Confidentiality of information, JCJD Rule 23.
Copies, JCJD Rule 6.
Distribution, JCJD Rule 8.
Corrective actions.
Review by chief judge, JCJD Rule 11.
Judicial council review of chief judge dispositions, JCJD Rule 18.
Defined, JCJD Rule 3.
Dismissal.
Review by chief judge, JCJD Rule 11.
Judicial council review of chief judge dispositions, JCJD Rule 18.
Disqualification of judges, JCJD Rule 25.
Filing, JCJD Rule 6.
Time for filing, JCJD Rule 9.
Where to file, JCJD Rule 7.
Form, JCJD Rule 6, JCJD Appx.
Identification of a complaint, JCJD Rule 5.
Initiation, JCJD Rules 5 to 10.
Intervening events.
Review by chief judge, JCJD Rule 11.
Judicial council review of chief judge dispositions, JCJD Rule 18.
Misconduct in another circuit.
Where to file, JCJD Rule 7.
Noncovered persons, complaints against.
Actions by circuit clerk, JCJD Rule 8.
Notice.
Review by chief judge, JCJD Rule 11.
Orchestrated complaints.
Abuse of complaint procedure, JCJD Rule 10.
Receipt of complaint.
Action by circuit clerk, JCJD Rule 8.
Review by chief judge, JCJD Rule 11.
Judicial council review of chief judge dispositions, JCJD Rule 18.
Signatures, JCJD Rule 6.
Special committee.
Appointment.
Review by chief judge, JCJD Rule 11.
Investigation and report, JCJD Rules 12 to 17.
Judicial council review, JCJD Rule 20.
Statement of facts, JCJD Rule 6.
Time for filing, JCJD Rule 9.
Transfer to another judicial council, JCJD Rule 26.
Where to file, JCJD Rule 7.
Withdrawal, JCJD Rule 27.

CONFIDENTIALITY OF INFORMATION, JCJD Rule 23.
Public availability of decisions, JCJD Rule 24.

CORRECTIVE ACTIONS.
Complaints.
Review by chief judge, JCJD Rule 11.
Judicial council review of chief judge dispositions, JCJD Rule 18.

COURTS OF APPEALS.
Covered judges, JCJD Rule 4.
Defined, JCJD Rule 3.

COVERED JUDGES, JCJD Rule 4.
Noncovered persons, complaints against.
Actions by circuit clerk, JCJD Rule 8.

D

DEFINED TERMS, JCJD Rule 3.

DISABILITY.
Defined, JCJD Rule 3.

DISMISSAL OF COMPLAINTS.
Review by chief judge, JCJD Rule 11.
Judicial council review of chief judge dispositions, JCJD Rule 18.

DISQUALIFICATION OF JUDGES, JCJD Rule 25.

DISTRICT COURTS AND JUDGES.
Covered judges, JCJD Rule 4.
Defined, JCJD Rule 3.

E

EFFECTIVE DATE OF RULES, JCJD Rule 29.

EFFECT OF RULES, JCJD Rule 2.

EVIDENCE.
Special committee, JCJD Rule 14.
Rights of complainant, JCJD Rule 16.

F

FILING COMPLAINTS, JCJD Rule 6.
Time for filing, JCJD Rule 9.
Where to file, JCJD Rule 7.

FINAL ACTIONS.
Chief judge's review, JCJD Rule 11.
Committee on judicial conduct and disability.
Review of judicial council dispositions, JCJD Rule 21.
Judicial council.
Disposition of petitions for review, JCJD Rule 19.
Review of reports and recommendations of special committee, JCJD Rule 20.
Public availability of decisions, JCJD Rule 24.
Special committee report, JCJD Rule 17.

FORMS.
Availability of rules and forms, JCJD Rule 27.
Complaints, JCJD Rule 6, JCJD Appx.

H

HEARINGS.
Special committee, JCJD Rule 14.

I

INQUIRIES.
Chief judge.
Identification of a complaint, JCJD Rule 5.
Review of complaints by chief judge, JCJD Rule 11.
Judicial council review of chief judge dispositions, JCJD Rule 18.

INTERVENING EVENTS.
Complaints.
Review by chief judge, JCJD Rule 11.
Judicial council review of chief judge dispositions, JCJD Rule 18.

INVESTIGATIONS.
Committee on judicial conduct and disability.
Review of judicial council dispositions, JCJD Rule 21.
Procedures for review, JCJD Rule 22.
Special committee, JCJD Rule 13.

J

JUDICIAL CONFERENCE COMMITTEE ON CONDUCT AND DISABILITY.
Disqualification of judges, JCJD Rule 25.
Public availability of decisions, JCJD Rule 24.
Review of judicial council dispositions, JCJD Rule 21.
Procedures for review, JCJD Rule 22.

JUDICIAL COUNCIL.
Defined, JCJD Rule 3.
Disqualification of judges, JCJD Rule 25.
Petitions for review.
Chief judge dispositions, JCJD Rule 18.
Disposition, JCJD Rule 19.
Review of judicial council decision, JCJD Rule 19.
Public availability of decisions, JCJD Rule 24.
Review, JCJD Rules 18 to 20.
Review of judicial council decision, JCJD Rule 19.
Committee on judicial conduct and disability, JCJD Rule 21.
Procedures for review, JCJD Rule 22.
Special committee.
Review of reports and recommendations, JCJD Rule 20.
Transfer to another judicial council, JCJD Rule 26.

M

MAGISTRATE JUDGES.
Covered judges, JCJD Rule 4.
Defined, JCJD Rule 3.
Special committee.
Advisers, JCJD Rule 12.

MISCONDUCT.
Defined, JCJD Rule 3.

N

NONCOVERED PERSONS.
Complaints against.
Actions by circuit clerk, JCJD Rule 8.

NOTICE.
Complaints, review by chief judge.
Notice of chief judge's actions, JCJD Rule 11.
Judicial council.
Petitions for review, JCJD Rule 19.
Special committee.
Rights of complainant, JCJD Rule 16.

O

ORCHESTRATED COMPLAINTS.
Abuse of complaint procedure, JCJD Rule 10.

P

PETITIONS FOR REVIEW.
Committee on judicial conduct and disability, JCJD Rule 22.
Confidentiality of information, JCJD Rule 23.
Judicial council.
Chief judge dispositions, JCJD Rule 18.
Withdrawal, JCJD Rule 27.

PUBLIC AVAILABILITY OF DECISIONS, JCJD Rule 24.

R

RECORDS.
Confidentiality of information, JCJD Rule 23.
Judicial council.
Petitions for review.
Memorandum of council decision, JCJD Rule 19.
Special committee, JCJD Rule 14.

REPORTS.
Special committee, JCJD Rule 17.
Judicial council review, JCJD Rule 20.

RIGHTS OF COMPLAINANT.
Special committee.
Right to counsel, JCJD Rule 16.

RIGHTS OF SUBJECT JUDGE.
Judicial council.
Petitions for review, JCJD Rule 19.
Special committee.
Review of reports and recommendations, JCJD Rule 20.
Special committee, JCJD Rule 15.
Right to counsel, JCJD Rules 14, 15.

S

SCOPE OF RULES, JCJD Rule 1.
Exception, JCJD Rule 2.

SIGNATURES.
Complaints, JCJD Rule 6.

SPECIAL COMMITTEE, JCJD Rules 12 to 17.
Advisers, JCJD Rule 12.
Appointment.
Complaints, review by chief judge, JCJD Rule 11.

SPECIAL COMMITTEE —Cont'd
Attorneys at law.
Right to counsel, JCJD Rule 14.
Composition, JCJD Rule 12.
Disqualification of judges, JCJD Rule 25.
Evidence, JCJD Rule 14.
Rights of complainant, JCJD Rule 16.
Hearings, JCJD Rule 14.
Investigations, JCJD Rule 13.
Judicial council review.
Reports and recommendations, JCJD Rule 20.
Presiding officer, JCJD Rule 12.
Public availability of decisions, JCJD Rule 24.
Records, JCJD Rule 14.
Report, JCJD Rule 17.
Judicial council review, JCJD Rule 20.
Rights of complainant, JCJD Rule 16.
Rights of subject judge, JCJD Rule 15.
Right to counsel, JCJD Rules 14, 15.
Right to counsel.
Rights of complainant, JCJD Rule 16.
Rights of subject judge, JCJD Rules 14, 15.
Subpoenas.
Investigations, JCJD Rule 13.
Transcripts, JCJD Rule 14.
Voting, JCJD Rule 12.
Witnesses, JCJD Rule 14.

SUBJECT JUDGE.
Confidentiality of information, JCJD Rule 23.
Defined, JCJD Rule 3.
Disqualification of judges, JCJD Rule 25.
Special committee.
Rights, JCJD Rule 15.
Right to counsel, JCJD Rule 14.

SUBPOENAS.
Special committee.
Investigations, JCJD Rule 13.

T

TRANSCRIPTS.
Special committee, JCJD Rule 14.

TRANSFER TO ANOTHER JUDICIAL COUNCIL, JCJD Rule 26.

W

WITHDRAWAL.
Complaints or petitions for review, JCJD Rule 27.

WITNESSES.
Special committee, JCJD Rule 14.

RULES OF THE UNITED STATES SUPREME COURT

As amended through July 1, 2013.

Part I. The Court.

Rule
1. Clerk.
2. Library.
3. Term.
4. Sessions and Quorum.

Part II. Attorneys and Counselors.

5. Admission to the Bar.
6. Argument *Pro Hac Vice*.
7. Prohibition Against Practice.
8. Disbarment and Disciplinary Action.
9. Appearance of Counsel.

Part III. Jurisdiction on Writ of Certiorari.

10. Considerations Governing Review on Certiorari.
11. Certiorari to a United States Court of Appeals Before Judgment.
12. Review on Certiorari: How Sought; Parties.
13. Review on Certiorari: Time for Petitioning.
14. Content of a Petition for a Writ of Certiorari.
15. Briefs in Opposition; Reply Briefs; Supplemental Briefs.
16. Disposition of a Petition for a Writ of Certiorari.

Part IV. Other Jurisdiction.

17. Procedure in an Original Action.
18. Appeal from a United States District Court.
19. Procedure on a Certified Question.
20. Procedure on a Petition for an Extraordinary Writ.

Part V. Motions and Applications.

21. Motions to the Court.
22. Applications to Individual Justices.
23. Stays.

Rule

Part VI. Briefs on the Merits and Oral Argument.

24. Briefs on the Merits: In General.
25. Briefs on the Merits: Number of Copies and Time to File.
26. Joint Appendix.
27. Calendar.
28. Oral Argument.

Part VII. Practice and Procedure.

29. Filing and Service of Documents; Special Notifications; Corporate Listing.
30. Computation and Extension of Time.
31. Translations.
32. Models, Diagrams, Exhibits, and Lodgings.
33. Document Preparation: Booklet Format; 8½- by 11-Inch Paper Format.
34. Document Preparation: General Requirements.
35. Death, Substitution, and Revivor; Public Officers.
36. Custody of Prisoners in Habeas Corpus Proceedings.
37. Brief for an *Amicus Curiae*.
38. Fees.
39. Proceedings *In Forma Pauperis*.
40. Veterans, Seamen, and Military Cases.

Part VIII. Disposition of Cases.

41. Opinions of the Court.
42. Interest and Damages.
43. Costs.
44. Rehearing.
45. Process; Mandates.
46. Dismissing Cases.

Part IX. Definitions and Effective Date.

47. Reference to "State Court" and "State Law."
48. Effective Date of Rules.

Index.

PART I. THE COURT.

Rule 1. Clerk.

1. The Clerk receives documents for filing with the Court and has authority to reject any submitted filing that does not comply with these Rules.

2. The Clerk maintains the Court's records and will not permit any of them to be removed from the Court building except as authorized by the Court. Any document filed with the Clerk and made a part of the Court's records may not thereafter be withdrawn from the official Court files. After the conclusion of proceedings in this Court, original records and documents transmitted to this Court by any other court will be returned to the court from which they were received.

3. Unless the Court or the Chief Justice orders otherwise, the Clerk's office is open from 9 a.m. to 5 p.m., Monday through Friday, except on federal legal holidays listed in 5 U.S.C. § 6103.

Rule 2. Library.

1. The Court's library is available for use by appropriate personnel of this Court, members of the Bar of this Court, Members of Congress and their legal staffs, and attorneys for the United States and for federal departments and agencies.

2. The library's hours are governed by regulations made by the Librarian with the approval of the Chief Justice or the Court.

3. Library books may not be removed from the Court building, except by a Justice or a member of a Justice's staff.

Rule 3. Term.

The Court holds a continuous annual Term commencing on the first Monday in October and ending on the day before the first Monday in October of the following year. See 28 U.S.C. § 2. At the end of each Term, all cases pending on the docket are continued to the next Term.

Rule 4. Sessions and Quorum.

1. Open sessions of the Court are held beginning at 10 a.m. on the first Monday in October of each year, and thereafter as announced by the Court. Unless it orders otherwise, the Court sits to hear arguments from 10 a.m. until noon and from 1 p.m. until 3 p.m.

2. Six Members of the Court constitute a quorum. See 28 U.S.C. § 1. In the absence of a quorum on any day appointed for holding a session of the Court, the Justices attending—or if no Justice is present, the Clerk or a Deputy Clerk—may announce that the Court will not meet until there is a quorum.

3. When appropriate, the Court will direct the Clerk or the Marshal to announce recesses.

PART II. ATTORNEYS AND COUNSELORS.

Rule 5. Admission to the Bar.

1. To qualify for admission to the Bar of this Court, an applicant must have been admitted to practice in the highest court of a State, Commonwealth, Territory or Possession, or the District of Columbia for a period of at least three years immediately before the date of application; must not have been the subject of any adverse disciplinary action pronounced or in effect during that 3-year period; and must appear to the Court to be of good moral and professional character.

2. Each applicant shall file with the Clerk (1) a certificate from the presiding judge, clerk, or other authorized official of that court evidencing the applicant's admission to practice there and the applicant's current good standing, and (2) a completely executed copy of the form approved by this Court and furnished by the Clerk containing (a) the applicant's personal statement, and (b) the statement of two sponsors endorsing the correctness of the applicant's statement, stating that the applicant possesses all the qualifications required for admission, and affirming that the applicant is of good moral and professional character. Both sponsors must be members of the Bar of this Court who personally know, but are not related to, the applicant.

3. If the documents submitted demonstrate that the applicant possesses the necessary qualifications, and if the applicant has signed the oath or affirmation and paid the required fee, the Clerk will notify the applicant of acceptance by the Court as a member of the Bar and issue a certificate of admission. An applicant who so wishes may be admitted in open court on oral motion by a member of the Bar of this Court, provided that all other requirements for admission have been satisfied.

4. Each applicant shall sign the following oath or affirmation:

I, ..., do solemnly swear (or affirm) that as an attorney and as a counselor of this Court, I will conduct myself uprightly and according to law, and that I will support the Constitution of the United States.

5. The fee for admission to the Bar and a certificate bearing the seal of the Court is $200, payable to the United States Supreme Court. The Marshal will deposit such fees in a separate fund to be disbursed by the Marshal at the direction of the Chief Justice for the costs of admissions, for the benefit of the Court and its Bar, and for related purposes.

6. The fee for a duplicate certificate of admission to the Bar bearing the seal of the Court is $15, and the fee for a certificate of good standing is $10, payable to the United

States Supreme Court. The proceeds will be maintained by the Marshal as provided in paragraph 5 of this Rule.

Rule 6. Argument *Pro Hac Vice*.

1. An attorney not admitted to practice in the highest court of a State, Commonwealth, Territory or Possession, or the District of Columbia for the requisite three years, but otherwise eligible for admission to practice in this Court under Rule 5.1, may be permitted to argue *pro hac vice.*

2. An attorney qualified to practice in the courts of a foreign state may be permitted to argue *pro hac vice.*

3. Oral argument *pro hac vice* is allowed only on motion of the counsel of record for the party on whose behalf leave is requested. The motion shall state concisely the qualifications of the attorney who is to argue *pro hac vice.* It shall be filed with the Clerk, in the form required by Rule 21, no later than the date on which the respondent's or appellee's brief on the merits is due to be filed, and it shall be accompanied by proof of service as required by Rule 29.

Rule 7. Prohibition Against Practice.

No employee of this Court shall practice as an attorney or counselor in any court or before any agency of government while employed by the Court; nor shall any person after leaving such employment participate in any professional capacity in any case pending before this Court or in any case being considered for filing in this Court, until two years have elapsed after separation; nor shall a former employee ever participate in any professional capacity in any case that was pending in this Court during the employee's tenure.

Rule 8. Disbarment and Disciplinary Action.

1. Whenever a member of the Bar of this Court has been disbarred or suspended from practice in any court of record, or has engaged in conduct unbecoming a member of the Bar of this Court, the Court will enter an order suspending that member from practice before this Court and affording the member an opportunity to show cause, within 40 days, why a disbarment order should not be entered. Upon response, or if no response is timely filed, the Court will enter an appropriate order.

2. After reasonable notice and an opportunity to show cause why disciplinary action should not be taken, and after a hearing if material facts are in dispute, the Court may take any appropriate disciplinary action against any attorney who is admitted to practice before it for conduct unbecoming a member of the Bar or for failure to comply with these Rules or any Rule or order of the Court.

Rule 9. Appearance of Counsel.

1. An attorney seeking to file a document in this Court in a representative capacity must first be admitted to practice before this Court as provided in Rule 5, except that admission to the Bar of this Court is not required for an attorney appointed under the Criminal Justice Act of 1964, see 18 U.S.C. § 3006A(d)(6), or under any other applicable federal statute. The attorney whose name, address, and telephone number appear on the cover of a document presented for filing is considered counsel of record, and a separate notice of appearance need not be filed. If the name of more than one attorney is shown on the cover of the document, the attorney who is counsel of record shall be clearly identified. See Rule 34.1(f).

2. An attorney representing a party who will not be filing a document shall enter a separate notice of appearance as counsel of record indicating the name of the party represented. A separate notice of appearance shall also be entered whenever an attorney is substituted as counsel of record in a particular case.

PART III. JURISDICTION ON WRIT OF CERTIORARI.

Rule 10. Considerations Governing Review on Certiorari.

Review on a writ of certiorari is not a matter of right, but of judicial discretion. A petition for a writ of certiorari will be granted only for compelling reasons. The following, although neither controlling nor fully measuring the Court's discretion, indicate the character of the reasons the Court considers:

(a) a United States court of appeals has entered a decision in conflict with the decision of another United States court of appeals on the same important matter; has decided an important federal question in a way that conflicts with a decision by a state court of last resort; or has so far departed from the accepted and usual course of judicial proceedings, or sanctioned such a departure by a lower court, as to call for an exercise of this Court's supervisory power;

(b) a state court of last resort has decided an important federal question in a way that conflicts with the decision of another state court of last resort or of a United States court of appeals;

(c) a state court or a United States court of appeals has decided an important question of federal law that has not been, but should be, settled by this Court, or has decided an important federal question in a way that conflicts with relevant decisions of this Court.

A petition for a writ of certiorari is rarely granted when the asserted error consists of erroneous factual findings or the misapplication of a properly stated rule of law.

Rule 11. Certiorari to a United States Court of Appeals Before Judgment.

A petition for a writ of certiorari to review a case pending in a United States court of appeals, before judgment is entered in that court, will be granted only upon a showing that the case is of such imperative public importance as to justify deviation from normal appellate practice and to require immediate determination in this Court. See 28 U.S.C. § 2101(e).

Rule 12. Review on Certiorari: How Sought; Parties.

1. Except as provided in paragraph 2 of this Rule, the petitioner shall file 40 copies of a petition for a writ of certiorari, prepared as required by Rule 33.1, and shall pay the Rule 38(a) docket fee.

2. A petitioner proceeding *in forma pauperis* under Rule 39 shall file an original and 10 copies of a petition for a writ of certiorari prepared as required by Rule 33.2, together with an original and 10 copies of the motion for leave to proceed *in forma pauperis*. A copy of the motion shall precede and be attached to each copy of the petition. An inmate confined in an institution, if proceeding *in forma pauperis* and not represented by counsel, need file only an original petition and motion.

3. Whether prepared under Rule 33.1 or Rule 33.2, the petition shall comply in all respects with Rule 14 and shall be submitted with proof of service as required by Rule 29. The case then will be placed on the docket. It is the petitioner's duty to notify all respondents promptly, on a form supplied by the Clerk, of the date of filing, the date the case was placed on the docket, and the docket number of the case. The notice shall be served as required by Rule 29.

4. Parties interested jointly, severally, or otherwise in a judgment may petition separately for a writ of certiorari; or any two or more may join in a petition. A party not shown on the petition as joined therein at the time the petition is filed may not later join in that petition. When two or more judgments are sought to be reviewed on a writ of certiorari to the same court and involve identical or closely related questions, a single petition for a writ of certiorari covering all the judgments suffices. A petition for a writ of certiorari may not be joined with any other pleading, except that any motion for leave to proceed *in forma pauperis* shall be attached.

5. No more than 30 days after a case has been placed on the docket, a respondent seeking to file a conditional cross-petition (*i.e.*, a cross-petition that otherwise would be untimely) shall file, with proof of service as required by Rule 29, 40 copies of the cross-petition prepared as required by Rule 33.1, except that a cross-petitioner proceeding *in forma pauperis* under Rule 39 shall comply with Rule 12.2. The cross-petition shall comply in all respects with this Rule and Rule 14, except that material already reproduced in the appendix to the opening petition need not be reproduced again. A cross-petitioning respondent shall pay the Rule 38(a) docket fee or submit a motion for leave to proceed *in forma pauperis*. The cover of the cross-petition shall indicate clearly that it is a conditional cross-petition. The cross-petition then will be placed on the docket, subject to the provisions of Rule 13.4. It is the cross-petitioner's duty to notify all cross-respondents promptly, on a form supplied by the Clerk, of the date of filing, the date the cross-petition was placed on the docket, and the docket number of the cross-petition. The notice shall be served as required by Rule 29. A cross-petition for a writ of certiorari may not be joined with any other pleading,

except that any motion for leave to proceed *in forma pauperis* shall be attached. The time to file a conditional cross-petition will not be extended.

6. All parties to the proceeding in the court whose judgment is sought to be reviewed are deemed parties entitled to file documents in this Court, unless the petitioner notifies the Clerk of this Court in writing of the petitioner's belief that one or more of the parties below have no interest in the outcome of the petition. A copy of such notice shall be served as required by Rule 29 on all parties to the proceeding below. A party noted as no longer interested may remain a party by notifying the Clerk promptly, with service on the other parties, of an intention to remain a party. All parties other than the petitioner are considered respondents, but any respondent who supports the position of a petitioner shall meet the petitioner's time schedule for filing documents, with the following exception: A response of a party aligned with petitioner below who supports granting the petition shall be filed within 30 days after the case is placed on the docket, and that time will not be extended. Counsel for such respondent shall ensure that counsel of record for all parties receive notice of its intention to file a brief in support within 20 days after the case is placed on the docket. A respondent not aligned with petitioner below who supports granting the petition, or a respondent aligned with petitioner below who takes the position that the petition should be denied, is not subject to the notice requirement and may file a response within the time otherwise provided by Rule 15.3. Parties who file no document will not qualify for any relief from this Court.

7. The clerk of the court having possession of the record shall keep it until notified by the Clerk of this Court to certify and transmit it. In any document filed with this Court, a party may cite or quote from the record, even if it has not been transmitted to this Court. When requested by the Clerk of this Court to certify and transmit the record, or any part of it, the clerk of the court having possession of the record shall number the documents to be certified and shall transmit therewith a numbered list specifically identifying each document transmitted. If the record, or stipulated portions, have been printed for the use of the court below, that printed record, plus the proceedings in the court below, may be certified as the record unless one of the parties or the Clerk of this Court requests otherwise. The record may consist of certified copies, but if the lower court is of the view that original documents of any kind should be seen by this Court, that court may provide by order for the transport, safekeeping, and return of such originals. (Amended effective July 1 2013.)

Rule 13. Review on Certiorari: Time for Petitioning.

1. Unless otherwise provided by law, a petition for a writ of certiorari to review a judgment in any case, civil or criminal, entered by a state court of last resort or a United States court of appeals (including the United States Court of Appeals for the Armed Forces) is timely when it is filed with the Clerk of this Court within 90 days after entry of the judgment. A petition for a writ of certiorari seeking review of a judgment of a lower state court that is subject to discretionary review by the state court of last resort is timely when it is filed with the Clerk within 90 days after entry of the order denying discretionary review.

2. The Clerk will not file any petition for a writ of certiorari that is jurisdictionally out of time. See, *e.g.*, 28 U.S.C. § 2101(c).

3. The time to file a petition for a writ of certiorari runs from the date of entry of the judgment or order sought to be reviewed, and not from the issuance date of the mandate (or its equivalent under local practice). But if a petition for rehearing is timely filed in the lower court by any party, or if the lower court appropriately entertains an untimely petition for rehearing or sua sponte considers rehearing, the time to file the petition for a writ of certiorari for all parties (whether or not they requested rehearing or joined in the petition for rehearing) runs from the date of the denial of rehearing or, if rehearing is granted, the subsequent entry of judgment.

4. A cross-petition for a writ of certiorari is timely when it is filed with the Clerk as provided in paragraphs 1, 3, and 5 of this Rule, or in Rule 12.5. However, a conditional cross-petition (which except for Rule 12.5 would be untimely) will not be granted unless another party's timely petition for a writ of certiorari is granted.

5. For good cause, a Justice may extend the time to file a petition for a writ of certiorari for a period not exceeding 60 days. An application to extend the time to file shall set out the basis for jurisdiction in this Court, identify the judgment sought to be reviewed, include a copy of the opinion and any order respecting rehearing, and set out

specific reasons why an extension of time is justified. The application must be filed with the Clerk at least 10 days before the date the petition is due, except in extraordinary circumstances. The application must clearly identify each party for whom an extension is being sought, as any extension that might be granted would apply solely to the party or parties named in the application. For the time and manner of presenting the application, see Rules 21, 22, 30, and 33.2. An application to extend the time to file a petition for a writ of certiorari is not favored.

CASE NOTES

Applied in In re Green, 133 Bankr. 185 (E.D. Va. 1991).

Rule 14. Content of a Petition for a Writ of Certiorari.

1. A petition for a writ of certiorari shall contain, in the order indicated:

(a) The questions presented for review, expressed concisely in relation to the circumstances of the case, without unnecessary detail. The questions should be short and should not be argumentative or repetitive. If the petitioner or respondent is under a death sentence that may be affected by the disposition of the petition, the notation "capital case" shall precede the questions presented. The questions shall be set out on the first page following the cover, and no other information may appear on that page. The statement of any question presented is deemed to comprise every subsidiary question fairly included therein. Only the questions set out in the petition, or fairly included therein, will be considered by the Court.

(b) A list of all parties to the proceeding in the court whose judgment is sought to be reviewed (unless the caption of the case contains the names of all the parties), and a corporate disclosure statement as required by Rule 29.6.

(c) If the petition prepared under Rule 33.1 exceeds 1,500 words or exceeds five pages if prepared under Rule 33.2, a table of contents and a table of cited authorities. The table of contents shall include the items contained in the appendix..

(d) Citations of the official and unofficial reports of the opinions and orders entered in the case by courts or administrative agencies.

(e) A concise statement of the basis for jurisdiction in this Court, showing:

(i) the date the judgment or order sought to be reviewed was entered (and, if applicable, a statement that the petition is filed under this Court's Rule 11);

(ii) the date of any order respecting rehearing, and the date and terms of any order granting an extension of time to file the petition for a writ of certiorari;

(iii) express reliance on Rule 12.5, when a cross-petition for a writ of certiorari is filed under that Rule, and the date of docketing of the petition for a writ of certiorari in connection with which the cross-petition is filed;

(iv) the statutory provision believed to confer on this Court jurisdiction to review on a writ of certiorari the judgment or order in question; and

(v) if applicable, a statement that the notifications required by Rule 29.4(b) or (c) have been made.

(f) The constitutional provisions, treaties, statutes, ordinances, and regulations involved in the case, set out verbatim with appropriate citation. If the provisions involved are lengthy, their citation alone suffices at this point, and their pertinent text shall be set out in the appendix referred to in subparagraph 1(i).

(g) A concise statement of the case setting out the facts material to consideration of the questions presented, and also containing the following:

(i) If review of a state-court judgment is sought, specification of the stage in the proceedings, both in the court of first instance and in the appellate courts, when the federal questions sought to be reviewed were raised; the method or manner of raising them and the way in which they were passed on by those courts; and pertinent quotations of specific portions of the record or summary thereof, with specific reference to the places in the record where the matter appears (*e.g.,* court opinion, ruling on exception, portion of court's charge and exception thereto, assignment of error), so as to show that the federal question was timely and properly raised and that this Court has jurisdiction to review the judgment on a writ of certiorari. When the portions of the record relied on under this subparagraph are voluminous, they shall be included in the appendix referred to in subparagraph 1(i).

(ii) If review of a judgment of a United States court of appeals is sought, the basis for federal jurisdiction in the court of first instance.

(h) A direct and concise argument amplifying the reasons relied on for allowance of the writ. See Rule 10.

(i) An appendix containing, in the order indicated:

(i) the opinions, orders, findings of fact, and conclusions of law, whether written or orally given and transcribed, entered in conjunction with the judgment sought to be reviewed;

(ii) any other relevant opinions, orders, findings of fact, and conclusions of law entered in the case by courts or administrative agencies, and, if reference thereto is necessary to ascertain the grounds of the judgment, of those in companion cases (each document shall include the caption showing the name of the issuing court or agency, the title and number of the case, and the date of entry);

(iii) any order on rehearing, including the caption showing the name of the issuing court, the title and number of the case, and the date of entry;

(iv) the judgment sought to be reviewed if the date of its entry is different from the date of the opinion or order required in sub-subparagraph (i) of this subparagraph;

(v) material required by subparagraphs 1(f) or 1(g)(i); and

(vi) any other material the petitioner believes essential to understand the petition.

If the material required by this subparagraph is voluminous, it may be presented in a separate volume or volumes with appropriate covers.

2. All contentions in support of a petition for a writ of certiorari shall be set out in the body of the petition, as provided in subparagraph 1(h) of this Rule. No separate brief in support of a petition for a writ of certiorari may be filed, and the Clerk will not file any petition for a writ of certiorari to which any supporting brief is annexed or appended.

3. A petition for a writ of certiorari should be stated briefly and in plain terms and may not exceed the word or page limitations specified in Rule 33.

4. The failure of a petitioner to present with accuracy, brevity, and clarity whatever is essential to ready and adequate understanding of the points requiring consideration is sufficient reason for the Court to deny a petition.

5. If the Clerk determines that a petition submitted timely and in good faith is in a form that does not comply with this Rule or with Rule 33 or Rule 34, the Clerk will return it with a letter indicating the deficiency. A corrected petition submitted in accordance with Rule 29.2 no more than 60 days after the date of the Clerk's letter will be deemed timely.

Rule 15. Briefs in Opposition; Reply Briefs; Supplemental Briefs.

1. A brief in opposition to a petition for a writ of certiorari may be filed by the respondent in any case, but is not mandatory except in a capital case, see Rule 14.1(a), or when ordered by the Court.

2. A brief in opposition should be stated briefly and in plain terms and may not exceed the word or page limitations specified in Rule 33. In addition to presenting other arguments for denying the petition, the brief in opposition should address any perceived misstatement of fact or law in the petition that bears on what issues properly would be before the Court if certiorari were granted. Counsel are admonished that they have an obligation to the Court to point out in the brief in opposition, and not later, any perceived misstatement made in the petition. Any objection to consideration of a question presented based on what occurred in the proceedings below, if the objection does not go to jurisdiction, may be deemed waived unless called to the Court's attention in the brief in opposition.

3. Any brief in opposition shall be filed within 30 days after the case is placed on the docket, unless the time is extended by the Court or a Justice, or by the Clerk under Rule 30.4. Forty copies shall be filed, except that a respondent proceeding *in forma pauperis* under Rule 39, including an inmate of an institution, shall file the number of copies required for a petition by such a person under Rule 12.2, together with a motion for leave to proceed *in forma pauperis,* a copy of which shall precede and be attached to each copy of the brief in opposition. If the petitioner is proceeding *in forma pauperis,* the respondent shall prepare its brief in opposition, if any, as required by Rule 33.2, and shall file an original and 10 copies of that brief. Whether prepared under Rule 33.1 or Rule 33.2, the brief in opposition shall comply with the requirements of Rule 24 governing a respondent's brief, except that no summary of the argument is required. A brief in opposition may not be joined with any other pleading, except that any motion

for leave to proceed *in forma pauperis* shall be attached. The brief in opposition shall be served as required by Rule 29.

4. No motion by a respondent to dismiss a petition for a writ of certiorari may be filed. Any objections to the jurisdiction of the Court to grant a petition for a writ of certiorari shall be included in the brief in opposition.

5. The Clerk will distribute the petition to the Court for its consideration upon receiving an express waiver of the right to file a brief in opposition, or, if no waiver or brief in opposition is filed, upon the expiration of the time allowed for filing. If a brief in opposition is timely filed, the Clerk will distribute the petition, brief in opposition, and any reply brief to the Court for its consideration no less than 14 days after the brief in opposition is filed, unless the petitioner expressly waives the 14-day waiting period.

6. Any petitioner may file a reply brief addressed to new points raised in the brief in opposition, but distribution and consideration by the Court under paragraph 5 of this Rule will not be deferred pending its receipt. Forty copies shall be filed, except that petitioner proceeding *in forma pauperis* under Rule 39, including an inmate of an institution, shall file the number of copies required for a petition by such a person under Rule 12.2. The reply brief shall be served as required by Rule 29.

7. If a cross-petition for a writ of certiorari has been docketed, distribution of both petitions will be deferred until the cross-petition is due for distribution under this Rule.

8. Any party may file a supplemental brief at any time while a petition for a writ of certiorari is pending, calling attention to new cases, new legislation, or other intervening matter not available at the time of the party's last filing. A supplemental brief shall be restricted to new matter and shall follow, insofar as applicable, the form for a brief in opposition prescribed by this Rule. Forty copies shall be filed, except that a party proceeding *in forma pauperis* under Rule 39, including an inmate of an institution, shall file the number of copies required for a petition by such a person under Rule 12.2. The supplemental brief shall be served as required by Rule 29.

Rule 16. Disposition of a Petition for a Writ of Certiorari.

1. After considering the documents distributed under Rule 15, the Court will enter an appropriate order. The order may be a summary disposition on the merits.

2. Whenever the Court grants a petition for a writ of certiorari, the Clerk will prepare, sign, and enter an order to that effect and will notify forthwith counsel of record and the court whose judgment is to be reviewed. The case then will be scheduled for briefing and oral argument. If the record has not previously been filed in this Court, the Clerk will request the clerk of the court having possession of the record to certify and transmit it. A formal writ will not issue unless specially directed.

3. Whenever the Court denies a petition for a writ of certiorari, the Clerk will prepare, sign, and enter an order to that effect and will notify forthwith counsel of record and the court whose judgment was sought to be reviewed. The order of denial will not be suspended pending disposition of a petition for rehearing except by order of the Court or a Justice.

PART IV. OTHER JURISDICTION.

Rule 17. Procedure in an Original Action.

1. This Rule applies only to an action invoking the Court's original jurisdiction under Article III of the Constitution of the United States. See also 28 U.S.C. § 1251 and U.S. Const., Amdt. 11. A petition for an extraordinary writ in aid of the Court's appellate jurisdiction shall be filed as provided in Rule 20.

2. The form of pleadings and motions prescribed by the Federal Rules of Civil Procedure is followed. In other respects, those Rules and the Federal Rules of Evidence may be taken as guides.

3. The initial pleading shall be preceded by a motion for leave to file, and may be accompanied by a brief in support of the motion. Forty copies of each document shall be filed, with proof of service. Service shall be as required by Rule 29, except that when an adverse party is a State, service shall be made on both the Governor and the Attorney General of that State.

4. The case will be placed on the docket when the motion for leave to file and the initial pleading are filed with the Clerk. The Rule 38(a) docket fee shall be paid at that time.

5. No more than 60 days after receiving the motion for leave to file and the initial pleading, an adverse party shall file 40 copies of any brief in opposition to the motion, with proof of service as required by Rule 29. The Clerk will distribute the filed documents to the Court for its consideration upon receiving an express waiver of the right to file a brief in opposition, or, if no waiver or brief is filed, upon the expiration of the time allowed for filing. If a brief in opposition is timely filed, the Clerk will distribute the filed documents to the Court for its consideration no less than 10 days after the brief in opposition is filed. A reply brief may be filed, but consideration of the case will not be deferred pending its receipt. The Court thereafter may grant or deny the motion, set it for oral argument, direct that additional documents be filed, or require that other proceedings be conducted.

6. A summons issued out of this Court shall be served on the defendant 60 days before the return day specified therein. If the defendant does not respond by the return day, the plaintiff may proceed *ex parte*.

7. Process against a State issued out of this Court shall be served on both the Governor and the Attorney General of that State.

Rule 18. Appeal from a United States District Court.

1. When a direct appeal from a decision of a United States district court is authorized by law, the appeal is commenced by filing a notice of appeal with the clerk of the district court within the time provided by law after entry of the judgment sought to be reviewed. The time to file may not be extended. The notice of appeal shall specify the parties taking the appeal, designate the judgment, or part thereof, appealed from and the date of its entry, and specify the statute or statutes under which the appeal is taken. A copy of the notice of appeal shall be served on all parties to the proceeding as required by Rule 29, and proof of service shall be filed in the district court together with the notice of appeal.

2. All parties to the proceeding in the district court are deemed parties entitled to file documents in this Court, but a party having no interest in the outcome of the appeal may so notify the Clerk of this Court and shall serve a copy of the notice on all other parties. Parties interested jointly, severally, or otherwise in the judgment may appeal separately, or any two or more may join in an appeal. When two or more judgments involving identical or closely related questions are sought to be reviewed on appeal from the same court, a notice of appeal for each judgment shall be filed with the clerk of the district court, but a single jurisdictional statement covering all the judgments suffices. Parties who file no document will not qualify for any relief from this Court.

3. No more than 60 days after filing the notice of appeal in the district court, the appellant shall file 40 copies of a jurisdictional statement and shall pay the Rule 38 docket fee, except that an appellant proceeding *in forma pauperis* under Rule 39, including an inmate of an institution, shall file the number of copies required for a petition by such a person under Rule 12.2, together with a motion for leave to proceed *in forma pauperis,* a copy of which shall precede and be attached to each copy of the jurisdictional statement. The jurisdictional statement shall follow, insofar as applicable, the form for a petition for a writ of certiorari prescribed by Rule 14, and shall be served as required by Rule 29. The case will then be placed on the docket. It is the appellant's duty to notify all appellees promptly, on a form supplied by the Clerk, of the date of filing, the date the case was placed on the docket, and the docket number of the case. The notice shall be served as required by Rule 29. The appendix shall include a copy of the notice of appeal showing the date it was filed in the district court. For good cause, a Justice may extend the time to file a jurisdictional statement for a period not exceeding 60 days. An application to extend the time to file a jurisdictional statement shall set out the basis for jurisdiction in this Court; identify the judgment sought to be reviewed; include a copy of the opinion, any order respecting rehearing, and the notice of appeal; and set out specific reasons why an extension of time is justified. For the time and manner of presenting the application, see Rules 21, 22, and 30. An application to extend the time to file a jurisdictional statement is not favored.

4. No more than 30 days after a case has been placed on the docket, an appellee seeking to file a conditional cross-appeal (*i.e.*, a cross-appeal that otherwise would be untimely) shall file, with proof of service as required by Rule 29, a jurisdictional statement that complies in all respects (including number of copies filed) with paragraph 3 of this Rule, except that material already reproduced in the appendix to

the opening jurisdictional statement need not be reproduced again. A cross-appealing appellee shall pay the Rule 38 docket fee or submit a motion for leave to proceed *in forma pauperis*. The cover of the cross-appeal shall indicate clearly that it is a conditional cross-appeal. The cross-appeal then will be placed on the docket. It is the cross-appellant's duty to notify all cross-appellees promptly, on a form supplied by the Clerk, of the date of filing, the date the cross-appeal was placed on the docket, and the docket number of the cross-appeal. The notice shall be served as required by Rule 29. A cross-appeal may not be joined with any other pleading, except that any motion for leave to proceed *in forma pauperis* shall be attached. The time to file a cross-appeal will not be extended.

5. After a notice of appeal has been filed in the district court, but before the case is placed on this Court's docket, the parties may dismiss the appeal by stipulation filed in the district court, or the district court may dismiss the appeal on the appellant's motion, with notice to all parties. If a notice of appeal has been filed, but the case has not been placed on this Court's docket within the time prescribed for docketing, the district court may dismiss the appeal on the appellee's motion, with notice to all parties, and may make any just order with respect to costs. If the district court has denied the appellee's motion to dismiss the appeal, the appellee may move this Court to docket and dismiss the appeal by filing an original and 10 copies of a motion presented in conformity with Rules 21 and 33.2. The motion shall be accompanied by proof of service as required by Rule 29, and by a certificate from the clerk of the district court, certifying that a notice of appeal was filed and that the appellee's motion to dismiss was denied. The appellant may not thereafter file a jurisdictional statement without special leave of the Court, and the Court may allow costs against the appellant.

6. Within 30 days after the case is placed on this Court's docket, the appellee may file a motion to dismiss, to affirm, or in the alternative to affirm or dismiss. Forty copies of the motion shall be filed, except that an appellee proceeding *in forma pauperis* under Rule 39, including an inmate of an institution, shall file the number of copies required for a petition by such a person under Rule 12.2, together with a motion for leave to proceed *in forma pauperis*, a copy of which shall precede and be attached to each copy of the motion to dismiss, to affirm, or in the alternative to affirm or dismiss. The motion shall follow, insofar as applicable, the form for a brief in opposition prescribed by Rule 15, and shall comply in all respects with Rule 21.

7. The Clerk will distribute the jurisdictional statement to the Court for its consideration upon receiving an express waiver of the right to file amotion to dismiss or to affirm or, if no waiver or motion is filed, upon the expiration of the time allowed for filing. If a motion to dismiss or to affirm is timely filed, the Clerk will distribute the jurisdictional statement, motion, and any brief opposing the motion to the Court for its consideration no less than 14 days after the motion is filed, unless the appellant expressly waives the 14-day waiting period.

8. Any appellant may file a brief opposing a motion to dismiss or to affirm, but distribution and consideration by the Court under paragraph 7 of this Rule will not be deferred pending its receipt. Forty copies shall be filed, except that an appellant proceeding *in forma pauperis* under Rule 39, including an inmate of an institution, shall file the number of copies required for a petition by such a person under Rule 12.2. The brief shall be served as required by Rule 29.

9. If a cross-appeal has been docketed, distribution of both jurisdictional statements will be deferred until the cross-appeal is due for distribution under this Rule.

10. Any party may file a supplemental brief at any time while a jurisdictional statement is pending, calling attention to new cases, new legislation, or other intervening matter not available at the time of the party's last filing. A supplemental brief shall be restricted to new matter and shall follow, insofar as applicable, the form for a brief in opposition prescribed by Rule 15. Forty copies shall be filed, except that a party proceeding *in forma pauperis* under Rule 39, including an inmate of an institution, shall file the number of copies required for a petition by such a person under Rule 12.2. The supplemental brief shall be served as required by Rule 29.

11. The clerk of the district court shall retain possession of the record until notified by the Clerk of this Court to certify and transmit it. See Rule 12.7.

12. After considering the documents distributed under this Rule, the Court may dispose summarily of the appeal on the merits, note probable jurisdiction, or postpone consideration of jurisdiction until a hearing of the case on the merits. If not disposed

of summarily, the case stands for briefing and oral argument on the merits. If consideration of jurisdiction is postponed, counsel, at the outset of their briefs and at oral argument, shall address the question of jurisdiction. If the record has not previously been filed in this Court, the Clerk of this Court will request the clerk of the court in possession of the record to certify and transmit it.

13. If the Clerk determines that a jurisdictional statement submitted timely and in good faith is in a form that does not comply with this Rule or with Rule 33 or Rule 34, the Clerk will return it with a letter indicating the deficiency. If a corrected jurisdictional statement is submitted in accordance with Rule 29.2 no more than 60 days after the date of the Clerk's letter it will be deemed timely.

Rule 19. Procedure on a Certified Question.

1. A United States court of appeals may certify to this Court a question or proposition of law on which it seeks instruction for the proper decision of a case. The certificate shall contain a statement of the nature of the case and the facts on which the question or proposition of law arises. Only questions or propositions of law may be certified, and they shall be stated separately and with precision. The certificate shall be prepared as required by Rule 33.2 and shall be signed by the clerk of the court of appeals.

2. When a question is certified by a United States court of appeals, this Court, on its own motion or that of a party, may consider and decide the entire matter in controversy. See 28 U.S.C. § 1254(2).

3. When a question is certified, the Clerk will notify the parties and docket the case. Counsel shall then enter their appearances. After docketing, the Clerk will submit the certificate to the Court for a preliminary examination to determine whether the case should be briefed, set for argument, or dismissed. No brief may be filed until the preliminary examination of the certificate is completed.

4. If the Court orders the case briefed or set for argument, the parties will be notified and permitted to file briefs. The Clerk of this Court then will request the clerk of the court in possession of the record to certify and transmit it. Any portion of the record to which the parties wish to direct the Court's particular attention should be printed in a joint appendix, prepared in conformity with Rule 26 by the appellant or petitioner in the court of appeals, but the fact that any part of the record has not been printed does not prevent the parties or the Court from relying on it.

5. A brief on the merits in a case involving a certified question shall comply with Rules 24, 25, and 33.1, except that the brief for the party who is the appellant or petitioner below shall be filed within 45 days of the order requiring briefs or setting the case for argument.

Rule 20. Procedure on a Petition for an Extraordinary Writ.

1. Issuance by the Court of an extraordinary writ authorized by 28 U.S.C. § 1651(a) is not a matter of right, but of discretion sparingly exercised. To justify the granting of any such writ, the petition must show that the writ will be in aid of the Court's appellate jurisdiction, that exceptional circumstances warrant the exercise of the Court's discretionary powers, and that adequate relief cannot be obtained in any other form or from any other court.

2. A petition seeking a writ authorized by 28 U.S.C. § 1651(a), § 2241, or § 2254(a) shall be prepared in all respects as required by Rules 33 and 34. The petition shall be captioned "*In re* [name of petitioner]" and shall follow, insofar as applicable, the form of a petition for a writ of certiorari prescribed by Rule 14. All contentions in support of the petition shall be included in the petition. The case will be placed on the docket when 40 copies of the petition are filed with the Clerk and the docket fee is paid, except that a petitioner proceeding *in forma pauperis* under Rule 39, including an inmate of an institution, shall file the number of copies required for a petition by such a person under Rule 12.2, together with a motion for leave to proceed *in forma pauperis*, a copy of which shall precede and be attached to each copy of the petition. The petition shall be served as required by Rule 29 (subject to subparagraph 4(b) of this Rule).

3.(a) A petition seeking a writ of prohibition, a writ of mandamus, or both in the alternative shall state the name and office or function of every person against whom relief is sought and shall set out with particularity why the relief sought is not available in any other court. A copy of the judgment with respect to which the writ is sought, including any related opinion, shall be appended to the petition together with any other document essential to understanding the petition.

(b) The petition shall be served on every party to the proceeding with respect to which relief is sought. Within 30 days after the petition is placed on the docket, a party shall file 40 copies of any brief or briefs in opposition thereto, which shall comply fully with Rule 15. If a party named as a respondent does not wish to respond to the petition, that party may so advise the Clerk and all other parties by letter. All persons served are deemed respondents for all purposes in the proceedings in this Court.

4.(a) A petition seeking a writ of habeas corpus shall comply with the requirements of 28 U.S.C. §§ 2241 and 2242, and in particular with the provision in the last paragraph of § 2242, which requires a statement of the "reasons for not making application to the district court of the district in which the applicant is held." If the relief sought is from the judgment of a state court, the petition shall set out specifically how and where the petitioner has exhausted available remedies in the state courts or otherwise comes within the provisions of 28 U.S.C. § 2254(b). To justify the granting of a writ of habeas corpus, the petitioner must show that exceptional circumstances warrant the exercise of the Court's discretionary powers, and that adequate relief cannot be obtained in any other form or from any other court. This writ is rarely granted.

(b) Habeas corpus proceedings, except in capital cases, are *ex parte*, unless the Court requires the respondent to show cause why the petition for a writ of habeas corpus should not be granted. A response, if ordered, or in a capital case, shall comply fully with Rule 15. Neither the denial of the petition, without more, nor an order of transfer to a district court under the authority of 28 U.S.C. § 2241(b), is an adjudication on the merits, and therefore does not preclude further application to another court for the relief sought.

5. The Clerk will distribute the documents to the Court for its consideration when a brief in opposition under subparagraph 3(b) of this Rule has been filed, when a response under subparagraph 4(b) has been ordered and filed, when the time to file has expired, or when the right to file has been expressly waived.

6. If the Court orders the case set for argument, the Clerk will notify the parties whether additional briefs are required, when they shall be filed, and, if the case involves a petition for a common-law writ of certiorari, that the parties shall prepare a joint appendix in accordance with Rule 26.

PART V. MOTIONS AND APPLICATIONS.

Rule 21. Motions to the Court.

1. Every motion to the Court shall clearly state its purpose and the facts on which it is based and may present legal argument in support thereof. No separate brief may be filed. A motion should be concise and shall comply with any applicable page limits. Non-dispositive motions and applications in cases in which certiorari has been granted, probable jurisdiction noted, or consideration of jurisdiction postponed shall state the position on the disposition of the motion or application of the other party or parties to the case. Rule 22 governs an application addressed to a single Justice.

2.(a) A motion in any action within the Court's original jurisdiction shall comply with Rule 17.3.

(b) A motion to dismiss as moot (or a suggestion of mootness), a motion for leave to file a brief as *amicus curiae*, and any motion the granting of which would dispose of the entire case or would affect the final judgment to be entered (other than a motion to docket and dismiss under Rule 18.5 or a motion for voluntary dismissal under Rule 46) shall be prepared as required by Rule 33.1, and 40 copies shall be filed, except that a movant proceeding *in forma pauperis* under Rule 39, including an inmate of an institution, shall file a motion prepared as required by Rule 33.2, and shall file the number of copies required for a petition by such a person under Rule 12.2. The motion shall be served as required by Rule 29.

(c) Any other motion to the Court shall be prepared as required by Rule 33.2; the moving party shall file an original and 10 copies. The Court subsequently may order the moving party to prepare the motion as required by Rule 33.1; in that event, the party shall file 40 copies.

3. A motion to the Court shall be filed with the Clerk and shall be accompanied by proof of service as required by Rule 29. No motion may be presented in open Court,

other than a motion for admission to the Bar, except when the proceeding to which it refers is being argued. Oral argument on a motion will not be permitted unless the Court so directs.

4. Any response to a motion shall be filed as promptly as possible considering the nature of the relief sought and any asserted need for emergency action, and, in any event, within 10 days of receipt, unless the Court or a Justice, or the Clerk under Rule 30.4, orders otherwise. A response to a motion prepared as required by Rule 33.1, except a response to a motion for leave to file an *amicus curiae* brief (see Rule 37.5), shall be prepared in the same manner if time permits. In an appropriate case, the Court may act on a motion without waiting for a response.

Rule 22. Applications to Individual Justices.

1. An application addressed to an individual Justice shall be filed with the Clerk, who will transmit it promptly to the Justice concerned if an individual Justice has authority to grant the sought relief.

2. The original and two copies of any application addressed to an individual Justice shall be prepared as required by Rule 33.2, and shall be accompanied by proof of service as required by Rule 29.

3. An application shall be addressed to the Justice allotted to the Circuit from which the case arises. An application arising from the United States Court of Appeals for the Armed Forces shall be addressed to the Chief Justice. When the Circuit Justice is unavailable for any reason, the application addressed to that Justice will be distributed to the Justice then available who is next junior to the Circuit Justice; the turn of the Chief Justice follows that of the most junior Justice.

4. A Justice denying an application will note the denial thereon. Thereafter, unless action thereon is restricted by law to the Circuit Justice or is untimely under Rule 30.2, the party making an application, except in the case of an application for an extension of time, may renew it to any other Justice, subject to the provisions of this Rule. Except when the denial is without prejudice, a renewed application is not favored. Renewed application is made by a letter to the Clerk, designating the Justice to whom the application is to be directed, and accompanied by 10 copies of the original application and proof of service as required by Rule 29.

5. A Justice to whom an application for a stay or for bail is submitted may refer it to the Court for determination.

6. The Clerk will advise all parties concerned, by appropriately speedy means, of the disposition made of an application.

Rule 23. Stays.

1. A stay may be granted by a Justice as permitted by law.

2. A party to a judgment sought to be reviewed may present to a Justice an application to stay the enforcement of that judgment. See 28 U.S.C. § 2101(f).

3. An application for a stay shall set out with particularity why the relief sought is not available from any other court or judge. Except in the most extraordinary circumstances, an application for a stay will not be entertained unless the relief requested was first sought in the appropriate court or courts below or from a judge or judges thereof. An application for a stay shall identify the judgment sought to be reviewed and have appended thereto a copy of the order and opinion, if any, and a copy of the order, if any, of the court or judge below denying the relief sought, and shall set out specific reasons why a stay is justified. The form and content of an application for a stay are governed by Rules 22 and 33.2.

4. A judge, court, or Justice granting an application for a stay pending review by this Court may condition the stay on the filing of a supersedeas bond having an approved surety or sureties. The bond will be conditioned on the satisfaction of the judgment in full, together with any costs, interest, and damages for delay that may be awarded. If a part of the judgment sought to be reviewed has already been satisfied, or is otherwise secured, the bond may be conditioned on the satisfaction of the part of the judgment not otherwise secured or satisfied, together with costs, interest, and damages.

CASE NOTES

Applied in In re Green, 133 Bankr. 185 (E.D. Va. 1991).

PART VI. BRIEFS ON THE MERITS AND ORAL ARGUMENT.

Rule 24. Briefs on the Merits: In General.

1. A brief on the merits for a petitioner or an appellant shall comply in all respects with Rules 33.1 and 34 and shall contain in the order here indicated:

(a) The questions presented for review under Rule 14.1(a). The questions shall be set out on the first page following the cover, and no other information may appear on that page. The phrasing of the questions presented need not be identical with that in the petition for a writ of certiorari or the jurisdictional statement, but the brief may not raise additional questions or change the substance of the questions already presented in those documents. At its option, however, the Court may consider a plain error not among the questions presented but evident from the record and otherwise within its jurisdiction to decide.

(b) A list of all parties to the proceeding in the court whose judgment is under review (unless the caption of the case in this Court contains the names of all parties). Any amended corporate disclosure statement as required by Rule 29.6 shall be placed here.

(c) If the brief exceeds 1,500 words, a table of contents and a table of cited authorities.

(d) Citations of the official and unofficial reports of the opinions and orders entered in the case by courts and administrative agencies.

(e) A concise statement of the basis for jurisdiction in this Court, including the statutory provisions and time factors on which jurisdiction rests.

(f) The constitutional provisions, treaties, statutes, ordinances, and regulations involved in the case, set out verbatim with appropriate citation. If the provisions involved are lengthy, their citation alone suffices at this point, and their pertinent text, if not already set out in the petition for a writ of certiorari, jurisdictional statement, or an appendix to either document, shall be set out in an appendix to the brief.

(g) A concise statement of the case, setting out the facts material to the consideration of the questions presented, with appropriate references to the joint appendix, *e.g.*, App. 12, or to the record, *e.g.*, Record 12.

(h) A summary of the argument, suitably paragraphed. The summary should be a clear and concise condensation of the argument made in the body of the brief; mere repetition of the headings under which the argument is arranged is not sufficient.

(i) The argument, exhibiting clearly the points of fact and of law presented and citing the authorities and statutes relied on.

(j) A conclusion specifying with particularity the relief the party seeks.

2. A brief on the merits for a respondent or an appellee shall conform to the foregoing requirements, except that items required by subparagraphs 1(a), (b), (d), (e), (f), and (g) of this Rule need not be included unless the respondent or appellee is dissatisfied with their presentation by the opposing party.

3. A brief on the merits may not exceed the word limitations specified in Rule 33.1(g). An appendix to a brief may include only relevant material, and counsel are cautioned not to include in an appendix arguments or citations that properly belong in the body of the brief.

4. A reply brief shall conform to those portions of this Rule applicable to the brief for a respondent or an appellee, but, if appropriately divided by topical headings, need not contain a summary of the argument.

5. A reference to the joint appendix or to the record set out in any brief shall indicate the appropriate page number. If the reference is to an exhibit, the page numbers at which the exhibit appears, at which it was offered in evidence, and at which it was ruled on by the judge shall be indicated, *e.g.*, Pl. Exh. 14, Record 199, 2134.

6. A brief shall be concise, logically arranged with proper headings, and free of irrelevant, immaterial, or scandalous matter. The Court may disregard or strike a brief that does not comply with this paragraph.

Rule 25. Briefs on the Merits: Number of Copies and Time to File.

1. The petitioner or appellant shall file 40 copies of the brief on the merits within 45 days of the order granting the writ of certiorari, noting probable jurisdiction, or postponing consideration of jurisdiction. Any respondent or appellee who supports the petitioner or appellant shall meet the petitioner's or appellant's time schedule for filing documents.

2. The respondent or appellee shall file 40 copies of the brief on the merits within 30 days after the brief for the petitioner or appellant is filed.

3. The petitioner or appellant shall file 40 copies of the reply brief, if any, within 30 days after the brief for the respondent or appellee is filed, but any reply brief must actually be received by the Clerk not later than 2 p.m. one week before the date of oral argument. Any respondent or appellee supporting the petitioner or appellant may file a reply brief.

4. If cross-petitions or cross-appeals have been consolidated for argument, the Clerk, upon request of the parties, may designate one of the parties to file an initial brief and reply brief as provided in paragraphs 1 and 3 of this Rule (as if the party were petitioner or appellant), and may designate the other party to file an initial brief as provided in paragraph 2 of this Rule and, to the extent appropriate, a supplemental brief following the submission of the reply brief. In such a case, the Clerk may establish the time for the submission of the briefs and alter the otherwise applicable word limits. Except as approved by the Court or a Justice, the total number of words permitted for the briefs of the parties cumulatively shall not exceed the maximum that would have been allowed in the absence of an order under this paragraph.

5. The time periods stated in paragraphs 1, 2, and 3 of this Rule may be extended as provided in Rule 30. An application to extend the time to file a brief on the merits is not favored. If a case is advanced for hearing, the time to file briefs on the merits may be abridged as circumstances require pursuant to an order of the Court on its own motion or that of a party.

6. A party wishing to present late authorities, newly enacted legislation, or other intervening matter that was not available in time to be included in a brief may file 40 copies of a supplemental brief, restricted to such new matter and otherwise presented in conformity with these Rules, up to the time the case is called for oral argument or by leave of the Court thereafter.

7. After a case has been argued or submitted, the Clerk will not file any brief, except that of a party filed by leave of the Court.

8. The Clerk will not file any brief that is not accompanied by proof of service as required by Rule 29.

9. An electronic version of every brief on the merits shall be transmitted to the Clerk of Court and to opposing counsel of record at the time the brief is filed in accordance with guidelines established by the Clerk. The electronic transmission requirement is in addition to the requirement that booklet-format briefs be timely filed.

Rule 26. Joint Appendix.

1. Unless the Clerk has allowed the parties to use the deferred method described in paragraph 4 of this Rule, the petitioner or appellant, within 45 days after entry of the order granting the writ of certiorari, noting probable jurisdiction, or postponing consideration of jurisdiction, shall file 40 copies of a joint appendix, prepared as required by Rule 33.1. The joint appendix shall contain: (1) the relevant docket entries in all the courts below; (2) any relevant pleadings, jury instructions, findings, conclusions, or opinions; (3) the judgment, order, or decision under review; and (4) any other parts of the record that the parties particularly wish to bring to the Court's attention. Any of the foregoing items already reproduced in a petition for a writ of certiorari, jurisdictional statement, brief in opposition to a petition for a writ of certiorari, motion to dismiss or affirm, or any appendix to the foregoing, that was prepared as required by Rule 33.1, need not be reproduced again in the joint appendix. The petitioner or appellant shall serve three copies of the joint appendix on each of the other parties to the proceeding as required by Rule 29.

2. The parties are encouraged to agree on the contents of the joint appendix. In the absence of agreement, the petitioner or appellant, within 10 days after entry of the order granting the writ of certiorari, noting probable jurisdiction, or postponing consideration of jurisdiction, shall serve on the respondent or appellee a designation of parts of the record to be included in the joint appendix. Within 10 days after receiving the designation, a respondent or appellee who considers the parts of the record so designated insufficient shall serve on the petitioner or appellant a designation of additional parts to be included in the joint appendix, and the petitioner or appellant shall include the parts so designated. If the Court has permitted the respondent or appellee to proceed *in forma pauperis*, the petitioner or appellant may seek by motion to be excused from printing portions of the record the petitioner or appellant considers

unnecessary. In making these designations, counsel should include only those materials the Court should examine; unnecessary designations should be avoided. The record is on file with the Clerk and available to the Justices, and counsel may refer in briefs and in oral argument to relevant portions of the record not included in the joint appendix.

3. When the joint appendix is filed, the petitioner or appellant immediately shall file with the Clerk a statement of the cost of printing 50 copies and shall serve a copy of the statement on each of the other parties as required by Rule 29. Unless the parties agree otherwise, the cost of producing the joint appendix shall be paid initially by the petitioner or appellant; but a petitioner or appellant who considers that parts of the record designated by the respondent or appellee are unnecessary for the determination of the issues presented may so advise the respondent or appellee, who then shall advance the cost of printing the additional parts, unless the Court or a Justice otherwise fixes the initial allocation of the costs. The cost of printing the joint appendix is taxed as a cost in the case, but if a party unnecessarily causes matter to be included in the joint appendix or prints excessive copies, the Court may impose these costs on that party.

4. (a) On the parties' request, the Clerk may allow preparation of the joint appendix to be deferred until after the briefs have been filed. In that event, the petitioner or appellant shall file the joint appendix no more than 14 days after receiving the brief for the respondent or appellee. The provisions of paragraphs 1, 2, and 3 of this Rule shall be followed, except that the designations referred to therein shall be made by each party when that party's brief is served. Deferral of the joint appendix is not favored.

(b) If the deferred method is used, the briefs on the merits may refer to the pages of the record. In that event, the joint appendix shall include in brackets on each page thereof the page number of the record where that material may be found. A party wishing to refer directly to the pages of the joint appendix may serve and file copies of its brief prepared as required by Rule 33.2 within the time provided by Rule 25, with appropriate references to the pages of the record. In that event, within 10 days after the joint appendix is filed, copies of the brief prepared as required by Rule 33.1 containing references to the pages of the joint appendix in place of, or in addition to, the initial references to the pages of the record, shall be served and filed. No other change may be made in the brief as initially served and filed, except that typographical errors may be corrected.

5. The joint appendix shall be prefaced by a table of contents showing the parts of the record that it contains, in the order in which the parts are set out, with references to the pages of the joint appendix at which each part begins. The relevant docket entries shall be set out after the table of contents, followed by the other parts of the record in chronological order. When testimony contained in the reporter's transcript of proceedings is set out in the joint appendix, the page of the transcript at which the testimony appears shall be indicated in brackets immediately before the statement that is set out. Omissions in the transcript or in any other document printed in the joint appendix shall be indicated by asterisks. Immaterial formal matters (*e.g.*, captions, subscriptions, acknowledgments) shall be omitted. A question and its answer may be contained in a single paragraph.

6. Two lines must appear at the bottom of the cover of the joint appendix: (1) The first line must indicate the date the petition for the writ of certiorari was filed or the date the appeal was docketed; (2) the second line must indicate the date certiorari was granted or the date jurisdiction of the appeal was noted or postponed.

7. Exhibits designated for inclusion in the joint appendix may be contained in a separate volume or volumes suitably indexed. The transcript of a proceeding before an administrative agency, board, commission, or officer used in an action in a district court or court of appeals is regarded as an exhibit for the purposes of this paragraph.

8. The Court, on its own motion or that of a party, may dispense with the requirement of a joint appendix and may permit a case to be heard on the original record (with such copies of the record, or relevant parts thereof, as the Court may require) or on the appendix used in the court below, if it conforms to the requirements of this Rule.

9. For good cause, the time limits specified in this Rule may be shortened or extended by the Court or a Justice, or by the Clerk under Rule 30.4.

Rule 27. Calendar.

1. From time to time, the Clerk will prepare a calendar of cases ready for argument. A case ordinarily will not be called for argument less than two weeks after the brief on the merits for the respondent or appellee is due.

2. The Clerk will advise counsel when they are required to appear for oral argument and will publish a hearing list in advance of each argument session for the convenience of counsel and the information of the public.

3. The Court, on its own motion or that of a party, may order that two or more cases involving the same or related questions be argued together as one case or on such other terms as the Court may prescribe.

Rule 28. Oral Argument.

1. Oral argument should emphasize and clarify the written arguments in the briefs on the merits. Counsel should assume that all Justices have read the briefs before oral argument. Oral argument read from a prepared text is not favored.

2. The petitioner or appellant shall open and may conclude the argument. A cross-writ of certiorari or cross-appeal will be argued with the initial writ of certiorari or appeal as one case in the time allowed for that one case, and the Court will advise the parties who shall open and close.

3. Unless the Court directs otherwise, each side is allowed one-half hour for argument. Counsel is not required to use all the allotted time. Any request for additional time to argue shall be presented by motion under Rule 21 in time to be considered at a scheduled Conference prior to the date of oral argument and no later than 7 days after the respondent's or appellee's brief on the merits is filed, and shall set out specifically and concisely why the case cannot be presented within the half-hour limitation. Additional time is rarely accorded.

4. Only one attorney will be heard for each side, except by leave of the Court on motion filed in time to be considered at a scheduled Conference prior to the date of oral argument and no later than 7 days after the respondent's or appellee's brief on the merits is filed. Any request for divided argument shall be presented by motion under Rule 21 and shall set out specifically and concisely why more than one attorney should be allowed to argue. Divided argument is not favored.

5. Regardless of the number of counsel participating in oral argument, counsel making the opening argument shall present the case fairly and completely and not reserve points of substance for rebuttal.

6. Oral argument will not be allowed on behalf of any party for whom a brief has not been filed.

7. By leave of the Court, and subject to paragraph 4 of this Rule, counsel for an *amicus curiae* whose brief has been filed as provided in Rule 37 may argue orally on the side of a party, with the consent of that party. In the absence of consent, counsel for an *amicus curiae* may seek leave of the Court to argue orally by a motion setting out specifically and concisely why oral argument would provide assistance to the Court not otherwise available. Such a motion will be granted only in the most extraordinary circumstances.

8. Oral arguments may be presented only by members of the Bar of this Court. Attorneys who are not members of the Bar of this Court may make a motion to argue *pro hac vice* under the provisions of Rule 6.

PART VII. PRACTICE AND PROCEDURE.

Rule 29. Filing and Service of Documents; Special Notifications; Corporate Listing.

1. Any document required or permitted to be presented to the Court or to a Justice shall be filed with the Clerk.

2. A document is timely filed if it is received by the Clerk within the time specified for filing; or if it is sent to the Clerk through the United States Postal Service by first-class mail (including express or priority mail), postage prepaid, and bears a postmark, other than a commercial postage meter label, showing that the document was mailed on or before the last day for filing; or if it is delivered on or before the last day for filing to a third-party commercial carrier for delivery to the Clerk within 3 calendar days. If submitted by an inmate confined in an institution, a document is timely filed if it is deposited in the institution's internal mail system on or before the

last day for filing and is accompanied by a notarized statement or declaration in compliance with 28 U.S.C. § 1746 setting out the date of deposit and stating that first-class postage has been prepaid. If the postmark is missing or not legible, or if the third-party commercial carrier does not provide the date the document was received by the carrier, the Clerk will require the person who sent the document to submit a notarized statement or declaration in compliance with 28 U.S.C. § 1746 setting out the details of the filing and stating that the filing took place on a particular date within the permitted time.

3. Any document required by these Rules to be served may be served personally, by mail, or by third-party commercial carrier for delivery within 3 calendar days on each party to the proceeding at or before the time of filing. If the document has been prepared as required by Rule 33.1, three copies shall be served on each other party separately represented in the proceeding. If the document has been prepared as required by Rule 33.2, service of a single copy on each other separately represented party suffices. If personal service is made, it shall consist of delivery at the office of the counsel of record, either to counsel or to an employee therein. If service is by mail or third-party commercial carrier, it shall consist of depositing the document with the United States Postal Service, with no less than first-class postage prepaid, or delivery to the carrier for delivery within 3 calendar days, addressed to counsel of record at the proper address. When a party is not represented by counsel, service shall be made on the party, personally, by mail, or by commercial carrier. Ordinarily, service on a party must be by a manner at least as expeditious as the manner used to file the document with the Court. An electronic version of the document shall also be transmitted to all other parties at the time of filing or reasonably contemporaneous therewith, unless the party filing the document is proceeding *pro se* and *in forma pauperis* or the electronic service address of the party being served is unknown and not identifiable through reasonable efforts.

4.(a) If the United States or any federal department, office, agency, officer, or employee is a party to be served, service shall be made on the Solicitor General of the United States, Room 5614, Department of Justice, 950 Pennsylvania Ave., N.W., Washington, DC 20530-0001. When an agency of the United States that is a party is authorized by law to appear before this Court on its own behalf, or when an officer or employee of the United States is a party, the agency, officer, or employee shall be served in addition to the Solicitor General.

(b) In any proceeding in this Court in which the constitutionality of an Act of Congress is drawn into question, and neither the United States nor any federal department, office, agency, officer, or employee is a party, the initial document filed in this Court shall recite that 28 U.S.C. § 2403(a) may apply and shall be served on the Solicitor General of the United States, Room 5614, Department of Justice, 950 Pennsylvania Ave., N.W., Washington, DC 20530-0001. In such a proceeding from any court of the United States, as defined by 28 U.S.C. § 451, the initial document also shall state whether that court, pursuant to 28 U.S.C. § 2403(a), certified to the Attorney General the fact that the constitutionality of an Act of Congress was drawn into question. See Rule 14.1(e)(v).

(c) In any proceeding in this Court in which the constitutionality of any statute of a State is drawn into question, and neither the State nor any agency, officer, or employee thereof is a party, the initial document filed in this Court shall recite that 28 U.S.C. § 2403(b) may apply and shall be served on the Attorney General of that State. In such a proceeding from any court of the United States, as defined by 28 U.S.C. § 451, the initial document also shall state whether that court, pursuant to 28 U.S.C. § 2403(b), certified to the State Attorney General the fact that the constitutionality of a statute of that State was drawn into question. See Rule 14.1(e)(v).

5. Proof of service, when required by these Rules, shall accompany the document when it is presented to the Clerk for filing and shall be separate from it. Proof of service shall contain, or be accompanied by, a statement that all parties required to be served have been served, together with a list of the names, addresses, and telephone numbers of counsel indicating the name of the party or parties each counsel represents. It is not necessary that service on each party required to be served be made in the same manner or evidenced by the same proof. Proof of service may consist of any one of the following:

(a) an acknowledgment of service, signed by counsel of record for the party served, and bearing the address and telephone number of such counsel;

Type of Document	Word Limits	Color of Cover
(i) Petition for a Writ of Certiorari (Rule 14); Motion for Leave to File a Bill of Complaint and Brief in Support (Rule 17.3); Jurisdictional Statement (Rule 18.3); Petition for an Extraordinary Writ (Rule 20.2)	9,000	white
(ii) Brief in Opposition (Rule 15.3); Brief in Opposition to Motion for Leave to File an Original Action (Rule 17.5); Motion to Dismiss or Affirm (Rule 18.6); Brief in Opposition to Mandamus or Prohibition (Rule 20.3(b)); Response to a Petition for Habeas Corpus (Rule 20.4): Respondent's Brief in Support of Certiorari (Rule 12.6)	9,000	orange
(iii) Reply to Brief in Opposition (Rules 15.6 and 17.5); Brief Opposing a Motion to Dismiss or Affirm (Rule 18.8)	3,000	tan
(iv) Supplemental Brief (Rules 15.8, 17, 18.10, and 25.5)	3,000	tan
(v) Brief on the Merits for Petitioner or Appellant (Rule 24); Exceptions by Plaintiff to Report of Special Master (Rule 17)	15,000	light blue
(vi) Brief on the Merits for Respondent or Appellee (Rule 24.2); Brief on the Merits for Respondent or Appellee Supporting Petitioner or Appellant (Rule 12.6); Exceptions by Party Other Than Plaintiff to Report of Special Master (Rule 17)	15,000	light red
(vii) Reply Brief on the Merits (Rule 24.4)	6,000	yellow
(viii) Reply to Plaintiff's Exceptions to Report of Special Master (Rule 17)	15,000	orange
(ix) Reply to Exceptions by Party Other Than Plaintiff to Report of Special Master (Rule 17)	15,000	yellow
(x) Brief for an *Amicus Curiae* at the Petition Stage or pertaining to a Motion for Leave to file a Bill of Complaint (Rule 37.2)	6,000	cream
(xi) Brief for an *Amicus Curiae* in Support of the Plaintiff, Petitioner, or Appellant, or in Support of Neither Party, on the Merits or in an Original Action at the Exceptions Stage (Rule 37.3)	9,000	light green
(xii) Brief for an *Amicus Curiae* in Support of the Defendant, Respondent, or Appellee, on the Merits or in an Original Action at the Exceptions Stage (Rule 37.3)	9,000	dark green
(xiii) Petition for Rehearing (Rule 44)	3,000	tan

(h) A document prepared under Rule 33.1 must be accompanied by a certificate signed by the attorney, the unrepresented party, or the preparer of the document stating that the brief complies with the word limitations. The person preparing the certificate may rely on the word count of the word-processing system used to prepare the document. The word-processing system must be set to include footnotes in the word count. The certificate must state the number of words in the document. The certificate shall accompany the document when it is presented to the Clerk for filing and shall be separate from it. If the certificate is signed by a person other than a member of the Bar of this Court, the counsel of record, or the unrepresented party, it must contain a notarized affidavit or declaration in compliance with 28 U. S. C. § 1746.

2. 8½- by 11-Inch Paper Format: (a) The text of every document, including any appendix thereto, expressly permitted by these Rules to be presented to the Court on 8½- by 11-inch paper shall appear double spaced, except for indented quotations, which shall be single spaced, on opaque, unglazed, white paper. The document shall be stapled or bound at the upper left-hand corner. Copies, if required, shall be produced on the same type of paper and shall be legible. The original of any such document (except a motion to dismiss or affirm under Rule 18.6) shall be signed by the party proceeding pro se or by counsel of record who must be a member of the Bar of this Court or an attorney appointed under the Criminal Justice Act of 1964, see 18 U.S.C.

§ 3006A(d)(6), or under any other applicable federal statute. Subparagraph 1(g) of this Rule does not apply to documents prepared under this paragraph.

(b) Page limits for documents presented on 8½- by 11-inch paper are: 40 pages for a petition for a writ of certiorari, jurisdictional statement, petition for an extraordinary writ, brief in opposition, or motion to dismiss or affirm; and 15 pages for a reply to a brief in opposition, brief opposing a motion to dismiss or affirm, supplemental brief, or petition for rehearing. The exclusions specified in subparagraph 1(d) of this Rule apply.

Rule 34. Document Preparation: General Requirements.

Every document, whether prepared under Rule 33.1 or Rule 33.2, shall comply with the following provisions:

1. Each document shall bear on its cover, in the order indicated, from the top of the page:

(a) the docket number of the case or, if there is none, a space for one;

(b) the name of this Court;

(c) the caption of the case as appropriate in this Court;

(d) the nature of the proceeding and the name of the court from which the action is brought (*e.g.*, "On Petition for Writ of Certiorari to the United States Court of Appeals for the Fifth Circuit"; or, for a merits brief, "On Writ of Certiorari to the United States Court of Appeals for the Fifth Circuit");

(e) the title of the document (*e.g.*, "Petition for Writ of Certiorari," "Brief for Respondent," "Joint Appendix");

(f) the name of the attorney who is counsel of record for the party concerned (who must be a member of the Bar of this Court except as provided in Rule 9.1) and on whom service is to be made, with a notation directly thereunder identifying the attorney as counsel of record and setting out counsel's office address, e-mail address, and telephone number. Only one counsel of record may be noted on a single document, except that counsel of record for each party must be listed on the cover of a joint appendix. The names of other members of the Bar of this Court or of the bar of the highest court of State acting as counsel, and, if desired, their addresses, may be added, but counsel of record shall be clearly identified. Names of persons other than attorneys admitted to a state bar may not be listed, unless the party is appearing *pro se*, in which case the party's name, address, and telephone number shall appear.

(g) The foregoing shall be displayed in an appropriate typographical manner and, except for identification of counsel, may not be set in type smaller than standard 11-point, if the document is prepared as required by Rule 33.1.

2. Every document (other than a joint appendix), that exceeds 1,500 words when prepared under Rule 33.1, or that exceeds five pages when prepared under Rule 33.2, shall contain a table of contents and a table of cited authorities (*i. e.,* cases alphabetically arranged, constitutional provisions, statutes, treatises, and other materials) with references to the pages in the document where such authorities are cited.

3. The body of every document shall bear at its close the name of counsel of record and such other counsel, identified on the cover of the document in conformity with subparagraph 1(f) of this Rule, as may be desired.

4. Every appendix to a document must be preceded by a table of contents that provides a description of each document in the appendix.

5. All references to a provision of federal statutory law should ordinarily be cited to the United States Code, if the provision has been codified therein. In the event the provision has not been classified to the United States Code, citation should be to the Statutes at Large. Additional or alternative citations should be provided only if there is a particular reason why those citations are relevant or necessary to the argument.

Rule 35. Death, Substitution, and Revivor; Public Officers.

1. If a party dies after the filing of a petition for a writ of certiorari to this Court, or after the filing of a notice of appeal, the authorized representative of the deceased party may appear and, on motion, be substituted as a party. If the representative does not voluntarily become a party, any other party may suggest the death on the record and, on motion, seek an order requiring the representative to become a party within a designated time. If the representative then fails to become a party, the party so moving, if a respondent or appellee, is entitled to have the petition for a writ of certiorari or the appeal dismissed, and if a petitioner or appellant, is entitled to

proceed as in any other case of nonappearance by a respondent or appellee. If the substitution of a representative of the deceased is not made within six months after the death of the party, the case shall abate.

2. Whenever a case cannot be revived in the court whose judgment is sought to be reviewed, because the deceased party's authorized representative is not subject to that court's jurisdiction, proceedings will be conducted as this Court may direct.

3. When a public officer who is a party to a proceeding in this Court in an official capacity dies, resigns, or otherwise ceases to hold office, the action does not abate and any successor in office is automatically substituted as a party. The parties shall notify the Clerk in writing of any such successions. Proceedings following the substitution shall be in the name of the substituted party, but any misnomer not affecting substantial rights of the parties will be disregarded.

4. A public officer who is a party to a proceeding in this Court in an official capacity may be described as a party by the officer's official title rather than by name, but the Court may require the name to be added.

Rule 36. Custody of Prisoners in Habeas Corpus Proceedings.

1. Pending review in this Court of a decision in a habeas corpus proceeding commenced before a court, Justice, or judge of the United States, the person having custody of the prisoner may not transfer custody to another person unless the transfer is authorized under this Rule.

2. Upon application by a custodian, the court, Justice, or judge who entered the decision under review may authorize transfer and the substitution of a successor custodian as a party.

3.(a) Pending review of a decision failing or refusing to release a prisoner, the prisoner may be detained in the custody from which release is sought or in other appropriate custody or may be enlarged on personal recognizance or bail, as may appear appropriate to the court, Justice, or judge who entered the decision, or to the court of appeals, this Court, or a judge or Justice of either court.

(b) Pending review of a decision ordering release, the prisoner shall be enlarged on personal recognizance or bail, unless the court, Justice, or judge who entered the decision, or the court of appeals, this Court, or a judge or Justice of either court, orders otherwise.

4. An initial order respecting the custody or enlargement of the prisoner, and any recognizance or surety taken, shall continue in effect pending review in the court of appeals and in this Court unless for reasons shown to the court of appeals, this Court, or a judge or Justice of either court, the order is modified or an independent order respecting custody, enlargement, or surety is entered.

Rule 37. Brief for an *Amicus Curiae*.

1. An *amicus curiae* brief that brings to the attention of the Court relevant matter not already brought to its attention by the parties may be of considerable help to the Court. An *amicus curiae* brief that does not serve this purpose burdens the Court, and its filing is not favored. An *amicus curiae* brief may be filed only by an attorney admitted to practice before this Court as provided in Rule 5.

2.(a) An *amicus curiae* brief submitted before the Court's consideration of a petition for a writ of certiorari, motion for leave to file a bill of complaint, jurisdictional statement, or petition for an extraordinary writ may be filed if accompanied by the written consent of all parties, or if the Court grants leave to file under subparagraph 2(b) of this Rule. An *amicus curiae* brief in support of a petitioner or appellant shall be filed within 30 days after the case is placed on the docket or a response is called for by the Court, whichever is later, and that time will not be extended. An *amicus curiae* brief in support of a motion of a plaintiff for leave to file a bill of complaint in an original action shall be filed within 60 days after the case is placed on the docket, and that time will not be extended. An *amicus curiae* brief in support of a respondent, an appellee, or a defendant shall be submitted within the time allowed for filing a brief in opposition or a motion to dismiss or affirm. An *amicus curiae* filing a brief under this subparagraph shall ensure that the counsel of record for all parties receive notice of its intention to file an *amicus curiae* brief at least 10 days prior to the due date for the *amicus curiae* brief, unless the *amicus curiae* brief is filed earlier than 10 days before the due date. Only one signatory to any *amicus curiae* brief filed jointly by more than one *amicus curiae* must timely notify the parties of its intent to file that brief. The *amicus curiae* brief shall indicate that counsel of record received timely notice of the intent to file the brief under this Rule and shall specify whether consent was granted, and its cover shall identify the party supported. Only one signatory to an *amicus curiae* brief filed jointly by more than one *amicus curiae* must obtain consent of the parties to file that brief. A petitioner or respondent may submit to the Clerk a letter granting blanket consent to *amicus curiae* briefs, stating that the party consents to the filing of *amicus curiae* briefs in support of either or of neither party. The Clerk will note all notices of blanket consent on the docket.

(b) When a party to the case has withheld consent, a motion for leave to file an *amicus curiae* brief before the Court's consideration of a petition for a writ of certiorari, motion for leave to file a bill of complaint, jurisdictional statement, or petition for an extraordinary writ may be presented to the Court. The motion, prepared as required by Rule 33.1 and as one document with the brief sought to be filed, shall be submitted within the time allowed for filing an *amicus curiae* brief, and shall indicate the party or parties who have withheld consent and state the nature of the movant's interest. Such a motion is not favored.

3. (a) An *amicus curiae* brief in a case before the Court for oral argument may be filed if accompanied by the written consent of all parties, or if the Court grants leave to file under subparagraph 3(b) of this Rule. The brief shall be submitted within 7 days after the brief for the party supported is filed, or if in support of neither party, within 7 days after the time allowed for filing the petitioner's or appellant's brief. Motions to extend the time for filing an *amicus curiae* brief will not be entertained. The 10-day notice requirement of subparagraph 2(a) of this Rule does not apply to an *amicus curiae* brief in a case before the Court for oral argument. An electronic version of every *amicus curiae* brief in a case before the Court for oral argument shall be transmitted to the Clerk of Court and to counsel for the parties at the time the brief is filed in accordance with guidelines established by the Clerk. The electronic transmission requirement is in addition to the requirement that booklet-format briefs be timely filed. The *amicus curiae* brief shall specify whether consent was granted, and its cover shall identify the party supported or indicate whether it suggests affirmance or reversal. The Clerk will not file a reply brief for an *amicus curiae*, or a brief for an *amicus curiae* in support of, or in opposition to, a petition for rehearing. Only one signatory to an *amicus curiae* brief filed jointly by more than one *amicus curiae* must obtain consent of the parties to file that brief. A petitioner or respondent may submit to the Clerk a letter granting blanket consent to *amicus curiae* briefs, stating that the party consents to the filing of *amicus curiae* briefs in support of either or of neither party. The Clerk will note all notices of blanket consent on the docket.

(b) When a party to a case before the Court for oral argument has withheld consent, a motion for leave to file an *amicus curiae* brief may be presented to the Court. The motion, prepared as required by Rule 33.1 and as one document with the brief sought to be filed, shall be submitted within the time allowed for filing an *amicus curiae* brief, and shall indicate the party or parties who have withheld consent and state the nature of the movant's interest.

4. No motion for leave to file an *amicus curiae* brief is necessary if the brief is presented on behalf of the United States by the Solicitor General; on behalf of any agency of the United States allowed by law to appear before this Court when submitted by the agency's authorized legal representative; on behalf of a State, Commonwealth, Territory, or Possession when submitted by its Attorney General; or on behalf of a city, county, town, or similar entity when submitted by its authorized law officer.

5. A brief or motion filed under this Rule shall be accompanied by proof of service as required by Rule 29, and shall comply with the applicable provisions of Rules 21, 24, and 33.1 (except that it suffices to set out in the brief the interest of the *amicus curiae*, the summary of the argument, the argument, and the conclusion). A motion for leave to file may not exceed 1,500 words. A party served with the motion may file an objection thereto, stating concisely the reasons for withholding consent; the objection shall be prepared as required by Rule 33.2.

6. Except for briefs presented on behalf of *amicus curiae* listed in Rule 37.4, a brief filed under this Rule shall indicate whether counsel for a party authored the brief in whole or in part and whether such counsel or a party made a monetary contribution intended to fund the preparation or submission of the brief, and shall identify every person other than the *amicus curiae*, its members, or its counsel, who made such a monetary contribution. The disclosure shall be made in the first footnote on the first page of text.

Rule 38. Fees.

Under 28 U.S.C. § 1911, the fees charged by the Clerk are:

(a) for docketing a case on a petition for a writ of certiorari or on appeal or for docketing any other proceeding, except a certified question or a motion to docket and dismiss an appeal under Rule 18.5, $300;

(b) for filing a petition for rehearing or a motion for leave to file a petition for rehearing, $200;

(c) for reproducing and certifying any record or paper, $1 per page; and for comparing with the original thereof any photographic reproduction of any record or paper, when furnished by the person requesting its certification, $.50 per page;

(d) for a certificate bearing the seal of the Court, $10; and

(e) for a check paid to the Court, Clerk, or Marshal that is returned for lack of funds, $35.

Rule 39. Proceedings *In Forma Pauperis*.

1. A party seeking to proceed *in forma pauperis* shall file a motion for leave to do so, together with the party's notarized affidavit or declaration (in compliance with 28 U. S. C. § 1746) in the form prescribed by the Federal Rules of Appellate Procedure, Form 4. The motion shall state whether leave to proceed *in forma pauperis* was sought in any other court and, if so, whether leave was granted. If the court below appointed counsel for an indigent party, no affidavit or declaration is required, but the motion shall cite the provision of law under which counsel was appointed, or a copy of the order of appointment shall be appended to the motion.

2. If leave to proceed *in forma pauperis* is sought for the purpose of filing a document, the motion, and an affidavit or declaration if required, shall be filed together with that document and shall comply in every respect with Rule 21. As provided in that Rule, it suffices to file an original and 10 copies, unless the party is an inmate confined in an institution and is not represented by counsel, in which case the original, alone, suffices. A copy of the motion, and affidavit or declaration if required, shall precede and be attached to each copy of the accompanying document.

3. Except when these Rules expressly provide that a document shall be prepared as required by Rule 33.1, every document presented by a party proceeding under this Rule shall be prepared as required by Rule 33.2 (unless such preparation is impossible). Every document shall be legible. While making due allowance for any case presented under this Rule by a person appearing *pro se*, the Clerk will not file any document if it does not comply with the substance of these Rules or is jurisdictionally out of time.

4. When the documents required by paragraphs 1 and 2 of this Rule are presented to the Clerk, accompanied by proof of service as required by Rule 29, they will be placed on the docket without the payment of a docket fee or any other fee.

5. The respondent or appellee in a case filed *in forma pauperis* shall respond in the same manner and within the same time as in any other case of the same nature, except that the filing of an original and 10 copies of a response prepared as required by Rule 33.2, with proof of service as required by Rule 29, suffices. The respondent or appellee may challenge the grounds for the motion for leave to proceed *in forma pauperis* in a separate document or in the response itself.

6. Whenever the Court appoints counsel for an indigent party in a case set for oral argument, the briefs on the merits submitted by that counsel, unless otherwise requested, shall be prepared under the Clerk's supervision. The Clerk also will reimburse appointed counsel for any necessary travel expenses to Washington, D.C., and return in connection with the argument.

7. In a case in which certiorari has been granted, probable jurisdiction noted, or consideration of jurisdiction postponed, this Court may appoint counsel to represent a party financially unable to afford an attorney to the extent authorized by the Criminal Justice Act of 1964, 18 U.S.C. § 3006A, or by any other applicable federal statute.

8. If satisfied that a petition for a writ of certiorari, jurisdictional statement, or petition for an extraordinary writ is frivolous or malicious, the Court may deny leave to proceed *in forma pauperis*.

Rule 40. Veterans, Seamen, and Military Cases.

1. A veteran suing under any provision of law exempting veterans from the payment of fees or court costs, may proceed without prepayment of fees or costs or furnishing

security therefor and may file a motion for leave to proceed on papers prepared as required by Rule 33.2. The motion shall ask leave to proceed as a veteran and be accompanied by an affidavit or declaration setting out the moving party's veteran status. A copy of the motion shall precede and be attached to each copy of the petition for a writ of certiorari or other substantive document filed by the veteran.

2. A seaman suing under 28 U. S. C. § 1916 may proceed without prepayment of fees or costs or furnishing security therefor and may file a motion for leave to proceed on papers prepared as required by Rule 33.2. The motion shall ask leave to proceed as a seaman and be accompanied by an affidavit or declaration setting out the moving party's seaman status. A copy of the motion shall precede and be attached to each copy of the petition for a writ of certiorari or other substantive document filed by the seaman.

3. An accused person petitioning for a writ of certiorari to review a decision of the United States Court of Appeals for the Armed Forces under 28 U.S.C. § 1259 may proceed without prepayment of fees or costs or furnishing security therefor and without filing an affidavit of indigency, but is not entitled to proceed on papers prepared as required by Rule 33.2, except as authorized by the Court on separate motion under Rule 39.

PART VIII. DISPOSITION OF CASES.

Rule 41. Opinions of the Court.

Opinions of the Court will be released by the Clerk immediately upon their announcement from the bench, or as the Court otherwise directs. Thereafter, the Clerk will cause the opinions to be issued in slip form, and the Reporter of Decisions will prepare them for publication in the preliminary prints and bound volumes of the United States Reports.

Rule 42. Interest and Damages.

1. If a judgment for money in a civil case is affirmed, any interest allowed by law is payable from the date the judgment under review was entered. If a judgment is modified or reversed with a direction that a judgment for money be entered below, the courts below may award interest to the extent permitted by law. Interest in cases arising in a state court is allowed at the same rate that similar judgments bear interest in the courts of the State in which judgment is directed to be entered. Interest in cases arising in a court of the United States is allowed at the interest rate authorized by law.

2. When a petition for a writ of certiorari, an appeal, or an application for other relief is frivolous, the Court may award the respondent or appellee just damages, and single or double costs under Rule 43. Damages or costs may be awarded against the petitioner, appellant, or applicant, against the party's counsel, or against both party and counsel.

Rule 43. Costs.

1. If the Court affirms a judgment, the petitioner or appellant shall pay costs unless the Court otherwise orders.

2. If the Court reverses or vacates a judgment, the respondent or appellee shall pay costs unless the Court otherwise orders.

3. The Clerk's fees and the cost of printing the joint appendix are the only taxable items in this Court. The cost of the transcript of the record from the court below is also a taxable item, but shall be taxable in that court as costs in the case. The expenses of printing briefs, motions, petitions, or jurisdictional statements are not taxable.

4. In a case involving a certified question, costs are equally divided unless the Court otherwise orders, except that if the Court decides the whole matter in controversy, as permitted by Rule 19.2, costs are allowed as provided in paragraphs 1 and 2 of this Rule.

5. To the extent permitted by 28 U.S.C. § 2412, costs under this Rule are allowed for or against the United States or an officer or agent thereof, unless expressly waived or unless the Court otherwise orders.

6. When costs are allowed in this Court, the Clerk will insert an itemization of the costs in the body of the mandate or judgment sent to the court below. The prevailing side may not submit a bill of costs.

7. In extraordinary circumstances the Court may adjudge double costs.

Rule 44. Rehearing.

1. Any petition for the rehearing of any judgment or decision of the Court on the merits shall be filed within 25 days after entry of the judgment or decision, unless the Court or a Justice shortens or extends the time. The petitioner shall file 40 copies of the rehearing petition and shall pay the filing fee prescribed by Rule 38(b), except that a petitioner proceeding *in forma pauperis* under Rule 39, including an inmate of an institution, shall file the number of copies required for a petition by such a person under Rule 12.2. The petition shall state its grounds briefly and distinctly and shall be served as required by Rule 29. The petition shall be presented together with certification of counsel (or of a party unrepresented by counsel) that it is presented in good faith and not for delay; one copy of the certificate shall bear the signature of counsel (or of a party unrepresented by counsel). A copy of the certificate shall follow and be attached to each copy of the petition. A petition for rehearing is not subject to oral argument and will not be granted except by a majority of the Court, at the instance of a Justice who concurred in the judgment or decision.

2. Any petition for the rehearing of an order denying a petition for a writ of certiorari or extraordinary writ shall be filed within 25 days after the date of the order of denial and shall comply with all the form and filing requirements of paragraph 1 of this Rule, including the payment of the filing fee if required, but its grounds shall be limited to intervening circumstances of a substantial or controlling effect or to other substantial grounds not previously presented. The time for filing a petition for the rehearing of an order denying a petition for a writ of certiorari or extraordinary writ will not be extended. The petition shall be presented together with certification of counsel (or of a party unrepresented by counsel) that it is restricted to the grounds specified in this paragraph and that it is presented in good faith and not for delay; one copy of the certificate shall bear the signature of counsel (or of a party unrepresented by counsel). The certificate shall be bound with each copy of the petition. The Clerk will not file a petition without a certificate. The petition is not subject to oral argument.

3. The Clerk will not file any response to a petition for rehearing unless the Court requests a response. In the absence of extraordinary circumstances, the Court will not grant a petition for rehearing without first requesting a response.

4. The Clerk will not file consecutive petitions and petitions that are out of time under this Rule.

5. The Clerk will not file any brief for an *amicus curiae* in support of, or in opposition to, a petition for rehearing.

6. If the Clerk determines that a petition for rehearing submitted timely and in good faith is in a form that does not comply with this Rule or with Rule 33 or Rule 34, the Clerk will return it with a letter indicating the deficiency. A corrected petition for rehearing submitted in accordance with Rule 29.2 no more than 15 days after the date of the Clerk's letter will be deemed timely.

Rule 45. Process; Mandates.

1. All process of this Court issues in the name of the President of the United States.

2. In a case on review from a state court, the mandate issues 25 days after entry of the judgment, unless the Court or a Justice shortens or extends the time, or unless the parties stipulate that it issue sooner. The filing of a petition for rehearing stays the mandate until disposition of the petition, unless the Court orders otherwise. If the petition is denied, the mandate issues forthwith.

3. In a case on review from any court of the United States, as defined by 28 U.S.C. § 451, a formal mandate does not issue unless specially directed; instead, the Clerk of this Court will send the clerk of the lower court a copy of the opinion or order of this Court and a certified copy of the judgment. The certified copy of the judgment, prepared and signed by this Court's Clerk, will provide for costs if any are awarded. In all other respects, the provisions of paragraph 2 of this Rule apply.

Rule 46. Dismissing Cases.

1. At any stage of the proceedings, whenever all parties file with the Clerk an agreement in writing that a case be dismissed, specifying the terms for payment of costs, and pay to the Clerk any fees then due, the Clerk, without further reference to the Court, will enter an order of dismissal.

2.(a) A petitioner or appellant may file a motion to dismiss the case, with proof of service as required by Rule 29, tendering to the Clerk any fees due and costs payable. No more than 15 days after service thereof, an adverse party may file an objection, limited to the amount of damages and costs in this Court alleged to be payable or to showing that the moving party does not represent all petitioners or appellants. The Clerk will not file any objection not so limited.

(b) When the objection asserts that the moving party does not represent all the petitioners or appellants, the party moving for dismissal may file a reply within 10 days, after which time the matter will be submitted to the Court for its determination.

(c) If no objection is filed—or if upon objection going only to the amount of damages and costs in this Court, the party moving for dismissal tenders the additional damages and costs in full within 10 days of the demand therefor—the Clerk, without further reference to the Court, will enter an order of dismissal. If, after objection as to the amount of damages and costs in this Court, the moving party does not respond by a tender within 10 days, the Clerk will report the matter to the Court for its determination.

3. No mandate or other process will issue on a dismissal under this Rule without an order of the Court.

PART IX. DEFINITIONS AND EFFECTIVE DATE.

Rule 47. Reference to "State Court" and "State Law."

The term "state court," when used in these Rules, includes the District of Columbia Court of Appeals, the Supreme Court of the Commonwealth of Puerto Rico, the courts of the Northern Mariana Islands, the local courts of Guam, and the Supreme Court of the Virgin Islands. References in these Rules to the statutes of a State include the statutes of the District of Columbia, the Commonwealth of Puerto Rico, the Commonwealth of the Northern Mariana Islands, the Territory of Guam, and the Territory of the Virgin Islands.

Rule 48. Effective Date of Rules.

1. These Rules, adopted January 12, 2010, will be effective February 16, 2010.

2. The Rules govern all proceedings after their effective date except to the extent that, in the opinion of the Court, their application to a pending matter would not be feasible or would work an injustice, in which event the former procedure applies.

3. In any case in which a petitioner or appellant has filed its brief on the merits prior to the effective date of these revised Rules, all remaining briefs in that case may comply with the October 1, 2007, version of the Rules of the Supreme Court of the United States rather than with these revised Rules.

Index to Rules of the United States Supreme Court

A

ABATEMENT AND REVIVOR.
Generally, US SupCt Rule 35.

ADJOURNMENT.
Docket.
Continuance to next term of cases on docket, US SupCt Rule 3.

ADMIRALTY CASES.
Generally, US SupCt Rule 40.

ADMISSION TO BAR.
Certificate of admission, US SupCt Rule 5.
Fees, US SupCt Rules 5, 38.
Oath upon admission to bar, US SupCt Rule 5.
Procedure, US SupCt Rule 5.
Qualifications, US SupCt Rule 5.

AFFIDAVITS.
Service.
Proof of service, US SupCt Rule 29.

AMENDMENTS.
Effective date, US SupCt Rule 48.

AMICUS CURIAE.
Briefs, US SupCt Rule 37.

APPEALS.
Damages.
Award of damages for frivolous appeals, US SupCt Rule 42.
District court, US SupCt Rule 18.
Frivolous appeals.
Award of damages, US SupCt Rule 42.
Records.
Original record and papers returned to court from which received, US SupCt Rule 1.
Time.
Extension of time, US SupCt Rule 30.

APPEARANCE OF COUNSEL, US SupCt Rule 9.

APPENDIX.
Certified cases.
Use of appendix, US SupCt Rule 19.
Certiorari, US SupCt Rule 14.
Joint appendix.
Printing, US SupCt Rule 20.
Costs.
Joint appendix, US SupCt Rules 26, 43.
Form, US SupCt Rule 33.
Joint appendix, US SupCt Rules 26, 43.
Costs, US SupCt Rule 26.
Court may dispense with a requirement of joint appendix, US SupCt Rule 26.
Form, US SupCt Rule 33.
Time.
Extension of time, US SupCt Rule 30.

ARGUMENTS.
Additional time, US SupCt Rule 28.
Amicus curiae, US SupCt Rule 28.
Bar membership required, SupCt Rule 28.

ARGUMENTS —Cont'd
Briefs.
Filing prerequisite to oral argument, US SupCt Rule 28.
Two week interval customary between answering briefs and argument, US SupCt Rule 27.
Certified cases, US SupCt Rule 19.
Cross-appeals and cross-writs of certiorari.
Order of argument, US SupCt Rule 28.
Divided arguments not favored, US SupCt Rule 28.
Generally, US SupCt Rule 28.
Number of counsel who will be heard, US SupCt Rule 28.
Opening, US SupCt Rule 28.
Pro hac vice.
Permitted in particular cases, US SupCt Rule 6.
Pro hac vice appearances, SupCt Rule 28.
Requiring oral argument.
Court may require, US SupCt Rule 28.
Time.
Additional time, US SupCt Rule 28.
Generally, US SupCt Rule 28.
Hearing arguments at open session, US SupCt Rule 4.

ATTORNEYS AT LAW.
Admission to practice before court, US SupCt Rules 5, 6.
Appearance of counsel, US SupCt Rule 9.
Disbarment, US SupCt Rule 8.
Disciplinary action, US SupCt Rule 8.
Employees.
Practice of law prohibited, US SupCt Rule 7.
Foreign attorneys.
Admission for particular case, US SupCt Rule 6.
Oath upon admission to bar, US SupCt Rule 5.
Procedure for admission to bar, US SupCt Rule 5.
Pro hac vice arguments, US SupCt Rule 6.
Qualifications for admission to bar, US SupCt Rule 5.
Requirements for admission to practice, US SupCt Rules 5, 6.
Suspension from practice, US SupCt Rule 8.

B

BONDS, SURETY.
Stays, US SupCt Rule 23.

BRIEFS.
Amicus curiae, US SupCt Rule 37.
Application to exceed word limits, SupCt Rule 33.
Arguments.
Filing prerequisite to oral argument, US SupCt Rule 28.
Two week interval customary between answering briefs and argument, US SupCt Rule 27.

BRIEFS —Cont'd
Briefs on the merits.
Generally, US SupCt Rule 24.
Time for filing, US SupCt Rule 25.
Certified cases, US SupCt Rule 19.
Certiorari.
Opposing or replying to petition for certiorari, US SupCt Rule 15.
See CERTIORARI.
Constitutionality of statutes.
Special rule for service, US SupCt Rule 29.
Contents, US SupCt Rule 24.
Copies.
Number of copies required, US SupCt Rule 25.
Electronic copies of brief, required, US SupCt Rule 25.
Filing, US SupCt Rule 28.
Briefs on the merits, US SupCt Rule 25.
Time for filing, US SupCt Rule 25.
Form, US SupCt Rule 33.
General requirements, US SupCt Rule 29.
Original actions, US SupCt Rule 17.
Reply briefs.
Certiorari, US SupCt Rule 15.
Time for filing, US SupCt Rule 25.
Service, US SupCt Rule 29.
Supplemental briefs, US SupCt Rule 25.
Filing supplemental briefs while writ of certiorari pending, US SupCt Rule 15.
Time.
Extension of time for filing, US SupCt Rule 29.
Filing briefs on the merits, US SupCt Rule 25.
Filing reply briefs, US SupCt Rule 25.
Time for filing.
Briefs on the merits, US SupCt Rule 25.
Word limitations, US SupCt Rule 33.

C

CALENDAR.
Call of calendar, US SupCt Rule 27.
Order of calendar, US SupCt Rule 27.
Two week interval customary between answering brief and argument, US SupCt Rule 27.

CERTIFIED QUESTIONS.
Appendix.
Use of appendix, US SupCt Rule 19.
Arguments.
Setting case for argument, US SupCt Rule 19.
Briefs on merits, US SupCt Rule 19.
Certificate.
Contents, US SupCt Rule 19.
Costs, US SupCt Rule 43.
Court of appeals, US SupCt Rule 19.
Court of claims, US SupCt Rule 19.
Docketing, US SupCt Rule 19.
Preliminary examination, US SupCt Rule 19.
Procedure in certified cases, US SupCt Rule 19.
Record.
Application for direction that entire record be sent up, US SupCt Rule 19.
Requirements for certified questions, US SupCt Rule 19.

CERTIORARI.
Appendix, US SupCt Rule 14.
Joint appendix.
Printing, US SupCt Rule 20.

CERTIORARI —Cont'd
Argument.
Cross-writs of certiorari.
Order of argument, US SupCt Rule 28.
Brief in opposition to petition, US SupCt Rule 15.
Brief in support of petition, US SupCt Rule 14.
Conflicting decisions of courts of appeals, US SupCt Rule 10.
Considerations governing review on certiorari, US SupCt Rule 10.
Court of appeals.
Granting certiorari before judgment, US SupCt Rule 11.
Damages.
Award of damages for frivolous appeals or petitions, US SupCt Rule 42.
Denial of petition.
Denial not suspended by petition for rehearing, US SupCt Rule 16.
Fees, US SupCt Rule 38.
Form of writs, US SupCt Rule 33.
How review on certiorari sought, US SupCt Rule 12.
Notice.
Review on certiorari, US SupCt Rule 12.
Number of petitions, US SupCt Rule 12.
Parties.
Separate or joint petitions, US SupCt Rule 12.
Petitions.
Content, US SupCt Rule 14.
Disposition of petition, US SupCt Rule 16.
Printing, US SupCt Rule 14.
Review on certiorari, US SupCt Rule 12.
Time for petitioning, US SupCt Rule 13.
Records.
Returned to court from which received, US SupCt Rule 1.
Rehearings, US SupCt Rule 44.
Reply or supplemental briefs, US SupCt Rule 15.
Review on certiorari.
Considerations governing review, US SupCt Rule 10.
How sought, US SupCt Rule 12.
Time for petitioning, US SupCt Rule 13.
State court decisions, US SupCt Rules 10, 13.
Consideration governing review, US SupCt Rule 10.
Summary disposition on merits, US SupCt Rule 16.
Supplemental briefs, US SupCt Rule 15.
Time.
Petitioning for writ, US SupCt Rule 13.
Review on certiorari, US SupCt Rule 13.

CHECKS.
Returned check.
Fee, US SupCt Rule 38.

CLERK.
Attorneys at law.
Practice of law prohibited, US SupCt Rule 7.
Fees.
Schedule, US SupCt Rule 38.
Office.
Hours, US SupCt Rule 1.
Opinions of court.
Printing, delivery and filing of opinions, US SupCt Rule 41.

CLERK —Cont'd
Practice of law, US SupCt Rule 7.
Prohibited, US SupCt Rule 7.
Recesses.
Court may direct clerk to announce, US SupCt Rule 4.
Records.
Custody, US SupCt Rule 1.
Restrictions on removal, US SupCt Rule 1.
Returned to court from which received, US SupCt Rule 1.
Time.
Office hours, US SupCt Rule 1.

CONSTITUTIONALITY OF PROVISIONS QUESTIONED.
Service of documents, US SupCt Rule 29.

CONSTRUCTION AND INTERPRETATION.
State courts, US SupCt Rule 47.
State law, US SupCt Rule 47.

CORPORATE DISCLOSURE STATEMENTS.
Documents to be filed to contain, US SupCt Rule 29.

COSTS.
Appendix.
Joint appendix, US SupCt Rules 26, 43.
Assessment and payment of costs, US SupCt Rule 43.
Certified questions, US SupCt Rule 43.
Dismissal, US SupCt Rule 46.
Double costs, US SupCt Rule 43.
Frivolous appeals, petitions, etc., US SupCt Rule 42.
Payment, US SupCt Rule 43.
United States.
Costs for or against United States, US SupCt Rule 43.

COURT OF APPEALS.
Certified questions, US SupCt Rule 19.
Conflicting decisions, US SupCt Rule 10.
Review by appeal.
See APPEALS.
Review on certiorari.
See CERTIORARI.

CROSS-APPEALS.
Argument.
Order of argument, US SupCt Rule 28.

D

DAMAGES.
Appeals.
Award of damages for frivolous appeals, US SupCt Rule 42.
Certiorari.
Award of damages for frivolous appeals or petitions, US SupCt Rule 42.
Generally, US SupCt Rule 42.

DEATH.
Party.
Procedure upon death of party, US SupCt Rule 35.
Public officer.
Procedure upon death, US SupCt Rule 35.
Revivor of cases, US SupCt Rule 35.

DIAGRAMS.
Clerk's custody, US SupCt Rule 32.

DISBARMENT.
Suspension from practice before court, US SupCt Rule 8.

DISMISSAL.
Agreement of parties, US SupCt Rule 46.
Costs, US SupCt Rule 46.
Generally, US SupCt Rule 46.

DISTRICT COURT.
Appeals from district court, US SupCt Rule 18.

DOCKET.
Adjournment.
Continuance to next term of cases on docket, US SupCt Rule 3.
Certified cases, US SupCt Rule 19.
Continuance to next term of cases on docket at end of term, US SupCt Rule 3.
Fees, US SupCt Rule 38.

DOCUMENTS.
Contents.
Inclusions in all documents, US SupCt Rule 34.
Electronic filing, required, SupCt Rule 29.
Form, US SupCt Rule 33.
Preparation, US SupCt Rule 33.
General requirements, US SupCt Rule 34.
Word limitations, US SupCt Rule 33.

DOUBLE COSTS, US SupCt Rule 43.
Frivolous appeals, petitions, etc., US SupCt Rule 42.

E

EFFECTIVE DATE.
Amendments, US SupCt Rule 48.

ELECTRONIC FILING.
Briefs.
Electronic copies of brief, required, US SupCt Rule 25.
Documents, required, SupCt Rule 29.

EVIDENCE.
Custody of evidence by clerk, US SupCt Rule 32.
Models, diagrams and exhibits of material.
Placed in custody of clerk, US SupCt Rule 32.

EXHIBITS.
Custody of evidence by clerk, US SupCt Rule 32.

EXTRAORDINARY WRITS.
Form, US SupCt Rule 33.
Habeas corpus, US SupCt Rule 20.
Issuance.
Considerations governing issuance, US SupCt Rule 20.
Extraordinary writs sparingly issued, US SupCt Rule 20.
Mandamus, US SupCt Rule 20.
Petition for extraordinary writ, US SupCt Rule 20.
Procedure in seeking, US SupCt Rule 20.
Prohibition, US SupCt Rule 20.
Writ of prohibition, US SupCt Rule 20.

F

FEDERAL HOLIDAYS.
Computation and extension of time, US SupCt Rule 30.

FEES.
Admission to bar, US SupCt Rule 5.
Clerks docketing fees, US SupCt Rule 38.
Schedule, US SupCt Rule 38.

FOREIGN LANGUAGES.
Translation of records, US SupCt Rule 31.

FORMS.
Documents, US SupCt Rule 33.
Generally, US SupCt Rule 33.
Motions, US SupCt Rule 21.
Word limitations, US SupCt Rule 33.

FRIVOLOUS APPEALS, PETITIONS, ETC.
Damages and costs, US SupCt Rule 42.

H

HABEAS CORPUS, US SupCt Rule 20.
Custody of prisoners, US SupCt Rule 36.
Extraordinary writs generally.
See EXTRAORDINARY WRITS.

HOLIDAYS.
Computation and extension of time, US SupCt Rule 30.

I

IN FORMA PAUPERIS.
Proceedings in forma pauperis, US SupCt Rule 39.

INTEREST.
Generally, US SupCt Rule 42.

J

JURISDICTIONAL STATEMENT.
Form, US SupCt Rule 33.

JUSTICES.
Applications to individual justices, US SupCt Rule 22.
Motions.
Motion addressed to individual justices, US SupCt Rule 22.
Stays.
When justices may grant stay, US SupCt Rule 23.

L

LAW CLERKS.
Barred from participating in cases pending during service, US SupCt Rule 7.
Practice of law.
Barred before court for two years after separation, US SupCt Rule 7.
Forbidden before any court or agency during service, US SupCt Rule 7.
Prohibition against practice, US SupCt Rule 7.

LIBRARY.
Access, US SupCt Rule 2.
Persons entitled to use, US SupCt Rule 2.

LIBRARY —Cont'd
Regulations generally, US SupCt Rule 2.
Removal of books, US SupCt Rule 2.

LODGINGS WITH CLERK.
Non-record material.
Submitting party or amicus, duties, US SupCt Rule 32.

M

MANDAMUS, US SupCt Rule 20.

MANDATES.
Cases coming from federal courts.
Former mandate issuance, US SupCt Rule 45.
Stays.
Rehearing petition filing will stay the mandate, US SupCt Rule 45.
When mandates issued, US SupCt Rule 45.

MARSHAL.
Court may direct marshal to announce recesses, US SupCt Rule 4.

MILITARY CASES.
Proceedings in veterans, admiralty, and military cases, US SupCt Rule 40.

MODELS.
Clerk's custody, US SupCt Rule 32.

MOTIONS.
Admiralty cases.
Generally, US SupCt Rule 40.
Admissions to practice.
Foreign attorney for particular cases, US SupCt Rule 6.
Application to exceed word limits, SupCt Rule 33.
Argument.
Oral argument on motions discretionary, US SupCt Rule 21.
Constitutionality of statutes.
Special rule for service, US SupCt Rule 29.
Filing, US SupCt Rules 21, 29.
Forms, US SupCt Rules 21, 33.
General requirements, US SupCt Rules 21, 29.
In forma pauperis, US SupCt Rule 39.
Justices.
Motion addressed to individual justices, US SupCt Rule 22.
Object of motion to be clearly stated, US SupCt Rule 21.
Original actions, US SupCt Rule 17.
Printed motions.
When required, US SupCt Rule 21.
Response to motions, US SupCt Rule 21.
Service, US SupCt Rule 29.
Time.
Extension of time for filing, US SupCt Rule 30.

N

NOTICE.
Certiorari.
Review on certiorari, US SupCt Rule 12.
Filing, US SupCt Rule 29.

NSF CHECKS.
Fee, US SupCt Rule 38.

O

OATH.
Attorneys at law.
Oath upon admission to bar, US SupCt Rule 5.

OPINIONS OF THE COURT, US SupCt Rule 41.
Copies to reporter of decisions, US SupCt Rule 41.

ORAL ARGUMENTS.
See ARGUMENTS.

ORIGINAL ACTIONS.
Briefs, US SupCt Rule 17.
Motion, US SupCt Rule 17.
Procedure, US SupCt Rule 17.
Summons, US SupCt Rule 17.
Time.
Service of summons on defendant in an original action, US SupCt Rule 17.

P

PARTIES.
Certiorari.
Separate or joint petitions, US SupCt Rule 12.
Death.
Procedure upon death of party, US SupCt Rule 35.

PETITIONS.
Certiorari.
Content, US SupCt Rule 14.
Disposition of petition, US SupCt Rule 16.
Printing, US SupCt Rule 14.
Review on certiorari, US SupCt Rule 12.
Time for petitioning, US SupCt Rule 13.
Extraordinary writs, US SupCt Rule 20.
Forms, US SupCt Rule 33.
Rehearings, US SupCt Rule 44.

PRISONERS.
Custody in habeas corpus proceedings, US SupCt Rule 36.

PRO HAC VICE ARGUMENTS, US SupCt Rule 6.

PROHIBITION.
Writ of prohibition, US SupCt Rule 20.

PUBLIC OFFICERS.
Death.
Substitution and description, US SupCt Rule 35.

Q

QUORUM.
Absence of quorum, US SupCt Rule 4.
Number constituting, US SupCt Rule 4.

R

RECESSES.
Court may direct clerk or marshal to announce, US SupCt Rule 4.

RECORDS.
Appeals.
Original record and papers returned to court from which received, US SupCt Rule 1.
Certified questions.
Application for direction that entire record be sent up, US SupCt Rule 19.
Clerk.
Custody, US SupCt Rule 1.
Restrictions on removal, US SupCt Rule 1.
Fees for certifying, reproducing, etc., US SupCt Rule 38.
Foreign language.
Translation, US SupCt Rule 31.
Original records and papers transmitted as record on appeal or certiorari.
Return to court, US SupCt Rule 1.
Translations.
Foreign languages, US SupCt Rule 31.

REHEARINGS.
Certiorari, US SupCt Rule 44.
Fees, US SupCt Rule 38.
Generally, US SupCt Rule 44.

REPORTER OF DECISIONS.
Opinions of court.
Duties of reporter, US SupCt Rule 41.

REVIVOR.
Generally, US SupCt Rule 35.

S

SATURDAYS.
Computation and extension of time, US SupCt Rule 30.

SEALS.
Fee for certificate bearing seal of court, US SupCt Rule 38.

SERVICE OF PROCESS.
Affidavits.
Proof of service, US SupCt Rule 29.
Briefs, US SupCt Rule 29.
Constitutionality of statutes.
Special rule for service, US SupCt Rule 29.
Issuance of process, US SupCt Rule 45.
Motions, US SupCt Rule 29.
Names in process, US SupCt Rule 29.
Original actions.
Service of summons on defendant in an original action, US SupCt Rule 17.
Proof of service, US SupCt Rule 29.

SESSIONS.
Open sessions, US SupCt Rule 4.
Time, US SupCt Rule 4.

STATE COURTS.
Certiorari.
Consideration governing review, US SupCt Rule 10.
State court decisions, US SupCt Rules 10, 13.
Construction and interpretation, US SupCt Rule 47.
Guam local courts included in term state court, US SupCt Rule 47.
Northern Mariana Island courts included in term state court, US SupCt Rule 47.
Puerto Rico included in term state court, US SupCt Rule 47.

STAYS.
Bonds, surety, US SupCt Rule 23.
Generally, US SupCt Rule 23.
Justices.
When justices may grant stay, US SupCt Rule 23.
Mandates.
Rehearing petition filing will stay the mandate, US SupCt Rule 45.

SUBSTITUTION.
Generally, US SupCt Rule 35.

SUMMONS.
Original actions, US SupCt Rule 17.

SUNDAYS.
Computation and extension of time, US SupCt Rule 30.

SUPERSEDEAS.
Bond.
Stays, US SupCt Rule 23.

SUSPENSION FROM PRACTICE, US SupCt Rule 8.

T

TERMS.
Generally, US SupCt Rule 3.

TIME.
Appendix.
Extension of time, US SupCt Rule 30.
Argument.
Additional time, US SupCt Rule 28.
Generally, US SupCt Rule 28.
Briefs.
Extension of time for filing, US SupCt Rules 25, 30.
Filing briefs on the merits, US SupCt Rule 25.
Filing reply briefs, US SupCt Rule 25.
Time for filing.
Briefs on the merits, US SupCt Rule 25.

TIME —Cont'd
Certiorari.
Petitioning for writ, US SupCt Rule 13.
Review on certiorari, US SupCt Rule 13.
Clerk.
Office hours, US SupCt Rule 1.
Computation of time, US SupCt Rule 30.
Extension of time.
Generally, US SupCt Rule 30.
Filing of documents, US SupCt Rule 29.
Motions.
Extension of time for filing, US SupCt Rule 30.
Original actions.
Service of summons on defendant in an original action, US SupCt Rule 17.
Service of summons on defendant in an original action, US SupCt Rule 17.
Sessions, US SupCt Rule 4.

TRANSLATIONS.
Records.
Foreign languages, US SupCt Rule 31.

V

VETERANS.
Establishment of reemployment rights, US SupCt Rule 40.
Proceedings, US SupCt Rule 40.

W

WRITS.
Certiorari.
See CERTIORARI.
Extraordinary writs.
See EXTRAORDINARY WRITS.
Habeas corpus, US SupCt Rule 20.
Mandamus, US SupCt Rule 20.
Prohibition, US SupCt Rule 20.